International Handbook of
Behavior Modification
and Therapy

International Handbook of
Behavior Modification and Therapy

Edited by

Alan S. Bellack
Medical College of Pennsylvania at EPPI
Philadelphia, Pennsylvania

Michel Hersen
and
Alan E. Kazdin
Western Psychiatric Institute and Clinic
University of Pittsburgh School of Medicine
Pittsburgh, Pennsylvania

PLENUM PRESS · NEW YORK AND LONDON

Library of Congress Cataloging in Publication Data

Main entry under title:

International handbook of behavior modification and therapy.

Includes bibliographical references and index.
1. Behavior therapy—Handbooks, manuals, etc. 2. Behavior modification—Handbooks, manuals, etc. I. Bellack, Alan S. II. Hersen, Michel. III. Kazdin, Alan E.
RC489.B4I54 1982   616.89′142   82-12371
ISBN 0-306-40777-9

© 1982 Plenum Press, New York
A Division of Plenum Publishing Corporation
233 Spring Street, New York, N.Y. 10013

Printed in the United States of America

Walter and Natalie
Victoria, Gordon, and Helen
Alan, Michael, Daniel, and Steven

Contributors

Russell M. Bauer
Department of Psychology
Pennsylvania State University
University Park, Pennsylvania

Alan S. Bellack
Medical College of Pennsylvania at EPPI
2900 Henry Avenue
Philadelphia, Pennsylvania

T. D. Borkovec
Department of Psychology
Pennsylvania State University
University Park, Pennsylvania

Richard A. Brown
Department of Psychology
University of Oregon
Eugene, Oregon

Jan Bruno
Department of Psychology
University of Alabama Medical School
Birmingham, Alabama

John D. Burchard
Department of Psychology
University of Vermont
Burlington, Vermont

Marjorie H. Charlop
Division of Behavioral Psychology
The Johns Hopkins University School of
    Medicine and the John F. Kennedy
    Institute
707 North Broadway
Baltimore, Maryland

Donald P. Corriveau
Department of Psychology
Brown University Medical School and
    Veterans Administration Medical Center
Providence, Rhode Island

James P. Curran
Department of Psychology
Brown University Medical School and
    Veterans Administration Medical Center
Providence, Rhode Island

Daniel M. Doleys
Department of Psychology
University of Alabama Medical School
Birmingham, Alabama

Andrew L. Egel
Department of Special Education
University of Maryland
College Park, Maryland

Paul M. G. Emmelkamp
Department of Clinical Psychology
Academic Hospital
Oostersingel 59
Groningen, The Netherlands

Seth Ersner-Hershfield
Newton Memorial Hospital
Newton, New Jersey

M. Philip Feldman
Department of Psychology
The University of Birmingham
Birmingham, England

Jerry M. Friedman
Sex Therapy Center
Department of Psychiatry and Behavioral
  Science
State University of New York at Stony
  Brook,
Stony Brook, Long Island, New York

Marvin R. Goldfried
Department of Psychology
State University of New York at Stony
  Brook
Stony Brook, Long Island, New York

Robert J. Goldsworthy
Department of Psychology
Arizona State University
Tempe, Arizona

Anthony M. Graziano
Department of Psychology
State University of New York at Buffalo
Buffalo, New York

Donald P. Hartmann
Department of Psychology
University of Utah
Salt Lake City, Utah

Michel Hersen
Department of Psychiatry
Western Psychiatric Institute and Clinic
University of Pittsburgh School of
  Medicine
Pittsburgh, Pennsylvania

Harry M. Hoberman
Psychology Department
University of Oregon
Eugene, Oregon

Douglas R. Hogan
Sex Therapy Center
Department of Psychiatry and Behavioral
  Science
State University of New York at Stony
  Brook,
Stony Brook, Long Island, New York

James N. Katz
Department of Psychology
State University of New York at Buffalo
Buffalo, New York

Alan E. Kazdin
Department of Psychiatry
Western Psychiatric Institute and Clinic
University of Pittsburgh School of
  Medicine
Pittsburgh, Pennsylvania

Robert L. Koegel
Social Process Research Institute
University of California
Santa Barbara, California

Theodore W. Lane
Department of Psychology
University of Vermont
Burlington, Vermont

Richard I. Lanyon
Department of Psychology
Arizona State University
Tempe, Arizona

Judith M. LeBlanc
Department of Human Development
University of Kansas
Lawrence, Kansas

Donald J. Levis
Department of Psychology
State University of New York at
  Binghamton
Binghamton, New York

Peter M. Lewinsohn
Psychology Department
University of Oregon
Eugene, Oregon

Edward Lichtenstein
Department of Psychology
University of Oregon
Eugene, Oregon

Joseph LoPiccolo
Sex Therapy Center
Department of Psychiatry and Behavioral
  Science
State University of New York at Stony
  Brook,
Stony Brook, Long Island, New York

ix

CONTRIBUTORS

Nathaniel McConaghy
School of Psychiatry
University of New South Wales
Sydney, Australia

Ronald A. Madle
Director of Training and Evaluation
Laurelton Center
Laurelton, Pennsylvania and Division of
    Individual and Family Studies
The Pennsylvania State University
University Park, Pennsylvania

Isaac Marks
Institute of Psychiatry
de Crespigny Park
Denmark Hill
London, England

W. L. Marshall
Department of Psychology
Queen's University
Kingston, Ontario, Canada

Peter M. Monti
Department of Psychology
Brown University Medical School and
    Veterans Administration Medical Center
Providence, Rhode Island

Randall L. Morrison
Clinical Psychology Center
University of Pittsburgh
Pittsburgh, Pennsylvania

John T. Neisworth
Department of Special Education
The Pennsylvania State University
University Park, Pennsylvania

Ted D. Nirenberg
Sea Pines Behavioral Institute
Hilton Head Island, South Carolina

Clifford R. O'Donnell
Department of Psychology
University of Hawaii
Honolulu, Hawaii

Martin J. Pollack
Department of Psychology
Mansfield Training School
Mansfield Depot, Connecticut

Jill Peay
Centre for Criminological Research
12 Bevington Road
Oxford, England

S. J. Rachman
Department of Psychology
University of British Columbia
Vancouver, British Columbia, Canada

Todd R. Risley
Department of Human Development
University of Kansas
Lawrence, Kansas

Ted R. Ruggles
Department of Human Development
University of Kansas
Lawrence, Kansas

Laura Schreibman
Psychology Department
Claremont McKenna College
Claremont, California

Jan Sheldon-Wildgen
Department of Human Development
University of Kansas
Lawrence, Kansas

Linda C. Sobell
Clinical Institute
Addiction Research Foundation and
    University of Toronto
Toronto, Ontario, Canada

Mark B. Sobell
Clinical Institute
Addiction Research Foundation and
    University of Toronto
Toronto, Ontario, Canada

Albert J. Stunkard
Department of Psychiatry
University of Pennsylvania
Philadelphia, Pennsylvania

Beth Sulzer-Azaroff
Department of Psychology
University of Massachusetts
Amherst, Massachusetts

C. Barr Taylor
Department of Psychiatry
Stanford University Medical Center
Stanford, California

Ronald G. Tharp
Department of Psychology
University of Hawaii
Honolulu, Hawaii

Gary B. Weider
Department of Psychology
Straub Hall
University of Oregon
Eugene, Oregon

Stephen J. Weiler
Sex Therapy Center
Department of Psychiatry and Behavioral
    Science
State University of New York at Stony
    Brook,
Stony Brook, Long Island, New York

Robert L. Weiss
Department of Psychology
Straub Hall
University of Oregon
Eugene, Oregon

David D. Wood
Department of Psychology
University of Utah
Salt Lake City, Utah

Preface

The rapid growth of behavior therapy over the past 20 years has been well documented. Yet the geometric expansion of the field has been so great that it deserves to be recounted. We all received our graduate training in the mid to late 1960s. Courses in behavior therapy were then a rarity. Behavioral training was based more on informal tutorials than on systematic programs of study. The behavioral literature was so circumscribed that it could be easily mastered in a few months of study. A mere half-dozen books (by Wolpe, Lazarus, Eysenck, Ullmann, and Krasner) more-or-less comprised the behavioral library in the mid-1960s. Seminal works by Ayllon and Azrin, Bandura, Franks, and Kanfer in 1968 and 1969 made it only slightly more difficult to survey the field. Keeping abreast of new developments was not very difficult, as *Behaviour Research and Therapy* and the *Journal of Applied Behavior Analysis* were the only regular outlets for behavioral articles until the end of the decade, when *Behavior Therapy* and *Behavior Therapy and Experimental Psychiatry* first appeared.

We are too young to be maudlin, but "Oh for the good old days!" One of us did a quick survey of his bookshelves and stopped counting books with *behavior* or *behavioral* in the titles when he reached 100. There were at least half again as many behavioral books without those words in the title. We hesitate to guess how many other behavioral books have been published that he does not own! Another of us subscribes to no less than 10 behavioral journals. A quick count indicated that there are at least 6 others. Moreover, such nonbehavioral publications as *Journal of Consulting and Clinical Psychology, Clinical Psychology Review*, and *Psychological Bulletin* sometimes appear to be more behavioral than anything else.

Needless to say, it is no longer possible to be up-to-date with the entire field. In fact, it is difficult to follow all of the literature in some popular subareas (e.g., behavioral medicine and cognitive behavior therapy). This information overload has a number of undesirable consequences in the research and practice of behavior therapy. It also has a pragmatic implication. Unless one is a prolific book-buyer and journal-subscriber, it is no longer even possible to have a comprehensive behavioral reference library.

Most books currently available fall into one of two classes: elementary surveys (e.g., textbooks) or narrow, highly specialized volumes. Neither type of book meets the need of most professionals for a convenient source of sophisticated reviews. There has been no resource for the person who must get a current but general picture of an area outside of his or her area of specialization. The need for such a resource served as the stimulus for this handbook. Our intention is to provide a basic reference source, in which leaders in the field provide up-to-date reviews of their areas of expertise. Each chapter is intended to give an overview of current knowledge and to identify questions and trends that will be important in the field during the next decade.

In developing the outline for the book, it quickly became apparent that it was impossible to include chapters on every topic studied by behavior therapists. Many readers will find omissions or imbalances in what they regard as vital areas. We have tried to represent major areas of interest and effort. The behavior change chapters, in particular, cover areas that have been subjected to extensive research, rather than areas in which major problems have been solved or exciting new areas with little support as yet. We have also chosen to focus on behavior problems rather than on techniques or models. While many behavior therapists identify with techniques or models (e.g., cognitive behavior therapy), they generally focus on specific problems (e.g., depression and chronic patients). Similarly, the general reader is more likely to be interested in the best treatment for a particular problem than in an overview of a general strategy.

A work of this scope requires the diligent efforts of a great number of people. We would like to thank the contributors for producing a set of uniformly excellent manuscripts. Special appreciation is extended to Mary Newell, Claudia Wolfson, and Lauretta Guerin for their matchless secretarial assistance. Finally, we express our gratitude to our friend and editor, Len Pace, who served a central role in this project from beginning to end.

ALAN S. BELLACK
MICHEL HERSEN
ALAN E. KAZDIN

Contents

PART II ASSESSMENT AND METHODOLOGY

PART III GENERAL ISSUES AND EXTENSIONS

Anthony M. Graziano and James N. Katz

M. Philip Feldman and Jill Peay

Chapter 14 Depression 397

Peter M. Lewinsohn and Harry M. Hoberman

Chapter 15 Treatment of Schizophrenia 433

James P. Curran, Peter M. Monti, and Donald P. Corriveau

Chapter 16 **Adult Medical Disorders** 467

C. Barr Taylor

Chapter 17 **Alcohol and Drug Problems** 501

Mark B. Sobell, Linda C. Sobell, Seth Ersner-Hershfield,
and Ted D. Nirenberg

PART V   INTERVENTION AND BEHAVIOR CHANGE: CHILD

Richard I. Lanyon and Robert J. Goldsworthy

PART I

Foundations of Behavior Modification and Therapy

CHAPTER 1

History of Behavior Modification

Alan E. Kazdin

Introduction

Behavior modification encompasses a variety of conceptual and theoretical positions, methodological approaches, treatment techniques, and historical developments. Because behavior modification is not a monolithic approach, it is important to convey the range of developments that converged over the course of the history of the field. This chapter traces the history of behavior modification as a general movement. Individual conceptual approaches and techniques that comprise behavior modification are obviously important in tracing the history, but they are examined as part of the larger development rather than as ends in their own right. This chapter examines major influences that finally led to the formal develop-

ment of behavior modification and behavior therapy.[1]

Background

The development of behavior modification can be viewed in part as a reaction to the dominant views within psychiatry and clinical psychology on the nature of abnormal behavior and its treatment. Several sources of dissatisfaction arose that made the field more readily amenable to alternative positions regarding disordered behavior and treatment. Hence, to portray the history of behavior modification, it is important to highlight the traditional approach within psychiatry and clinical psychology.

Alan E. Kazdin • Department of Psychiatry, Western Psychiatric Institute and Clinic, University of Pittsburgh School of Medicine, Pittsburgh, Pennsylvania 15213. Preparation of this chapter was facilitated by a grant from the National Institute of Mental Health (MH31047). The material in the chapter is based on a more extensive examination of the history of behavior modification (Kazdin, 1978b) completed under the auspices of the National Academy of Sciences.

[1] For present purposes, the terms *behavior modification* and *behavior therapy* will be used synonymously. Occasionally, behavior modification and behavior therapy have been distinguished based on such criteria as the theoretical approaches, the treatment techniques, the manner in which the techniques are applied, and the countries in which the techniques have emerged (Franzini & Tilker, 1972; Keehn & Webster, 1969; Krasner, 1971; Yates, 1970). However, consistent distinctions have not been adopted, and the terms usually are used interchangeably in contemporary writing.

Prior to highlighting the context out of which behavior modification grew, it is especially interesting to place many techniques in a different historical perspective. As a movement, behavior modification is new in many ways, but several techniques used in the field emerged much earlier. Selected examples illustrate that what is new, important, and perhaps of greatest historical interest in the field are not the ancestors of current practices but the development of the overall approach that characterizes contemporary behavior modification.

Historical Precursors of Behavioral Techniques

Many treatment techniques developed prior to behavior modification bear a striking similarity to techniques in current use. However, behavior modification is not a conglomeration of various techniques; tracing the history of the field in a way that emphasizes individual techniques might misrepresent the overall thrust of the larger movement. Nevertheless, by way of background, it is interesting to mention that many techniques currently popular in behavior therapy are frequently encountered in the history of treatment—under different names, of course—decades before behavior therapy developed. Consider two among the many types of examples that could be provided: systematic desensitization and reinforcement.

Systematic Desensitization. Desensitization is one of the most well researched and practiced treatment techniques in behavior therapy. Briefly, the technique consists of pairing responses that inhibit anxiety (usually muscle relaxation) with events that provoke anxiety. By pairing relaxation with anxiety-provoking stimuli (actual situations or imaginal representations of them) in a graduated fashion, the anxiety and avoidance reaction can be eliminated. The development of desensitization by Joseph Wolpe (1958) was extremely innovative for a variety of reasons, as discussed later in the chapter. Yet, the underlying rationale and procedure in various forms were evident long before its development in the 1950s.

For example, in France in the 1890s, a procedure that resembled contemporary desensitization was used to relieve tics (Brissaud, 1894). Patients were trained to keep their muscles motionless and to perform exercises to maintain a state of relaxation that would compete with the movements of the tic. Variations of the technique involved performing behaviors incompatible with the response rather than merely remaining motionless (Meige & Feindel, 1907). Indeed, deep breathing exercises and relaxation as a method to overcome tics were relatively popular in France (Pitres, 1888; Tissié, 1899).

More recently, relaxation was used in Germany in the form of "autogenic training," a procedure that was developed in the 1920s (Schultz, 1932; Schultz & Luthe, 1959). The procedure grew out of hypnosis and auto-suggestion and was used to train patients to relax themselves through self-suggestion. Self-induced relaxation successfully treated a range of psychological and physical problems in applications that often closely resembled desensitization.

In the late 1920s, Alexander (1928) suggested that disturbing thoughts could be controlled by "direct switching," that is, thinking of something that was incompatible with the thought that came to mind. Others advocated performing incompatible responses as a way to overcome maladaptive habits or thought patterns (Bagby, 1928). In the 1940s, hierarchical presentation of fear-provoking stimuli was used to overcome combat neuroses. Fear-provoking stimuli associated with combat were presented in a graduated fashion (Schwartz, 1945). In other applications, phobic patients engaged in graded steps of fear-provoking behaviors while performing responses that would compete with anxiety (Terhune, 1949).

Other precursors can be readily identified that apparently influenced the final development of desensitization in various ways. The familiar child case of Peter reported by Mary Cover Jones (1924b) used performance of responses incompatible with anxiety (eating) while the feared stimulus (a rabbit) was presented in progressively closer proximity. Similarly, Edmund Jacobson (1938) successfully applied relaxation to reduce the tension associated with a wide range of disorders, including general anxiety, phobias, hypertension, colitis, insomnia, and tics. Finally, in the early 1940s, Herzberg proposed a treatment of "graduated tasks," in which patients performed a series of tasks *in vivo* to overcome their fears and a variety of other problems (Herzberg, 1945). Even though other precursors of desensitization can be identified, they reflect isolated efforts rather than a continuous historical line culminating in contemporary procedures.

Reinforcement. Reinforcement techniques are used extensively in contemporary behavior modification and have been extended to almost every clinical population from young children to geriatric patients and across a host of problems (Kazdin, 1978a). It is not difficult to find historical precursors of contemporary reinforcement techniques. Unlike precursors to desensitization, the incentive systems that preceded those used in behavior modification occasionally achieved widespread application. Although many examples can be provided, one in particular illustrates the extensive use of rewards to alter behavior and bears extremely close resemblance to current practices.

In England in the early 1800s, Joseph Lancaster devised a reinforcement system for use in the classroom (Lancaster, 1805; Salmon, 1904). The system was developed for classrooms that housed hundreds of students in the same room. The system was developed for largely economic reasons and utilized peer monitors in the class, rather than teachers, to provide rewards. The system relied on what currently is referred to as a *token economy*. Tickets were provided for paying attention and for completing academic tasks. The tickets were backed up by other rewards and prizes to encourage progress in basic academic skills.

A comparison of the specific procedures of this program with those in use in contemporary classroom behavior-modification programs reveals marked similarities (Kazdin & Pulaski, 1977). Interestingly, Lancaster's system became popular throughout the British Empire, Europe, Africa, Russia, Asia, South America, Canada, and the United States (Kaestle, 1973). These applications, primarily in the middle and late 1800s, preceded the development of operant conditioning and the explicit recognition of positive reinforcement and its implications.

General Comments. Historical precursors can be readily identified for many existing behavior-modification techniques, such as flooding, modeling, self-instruction training, variations of operant techniques, aversion therapy, and covert conditioning (Kazdin, 1978b). However interesting such precursors may be, they generally fall outside of the historical purview of contemporary behavior modification. The history of behavior modification reflects a larger movement that synthesizes several influences in psychology more generally. This chapter emphasizes these larger themes, which reveal the movements within psychology, clinical psychology, and psychiatry that led to the formal emergence of behavior modification.

Traditional Approaches in Psychiatry and Clinical Psychology

Behavior modification represents an alternative conceptual approach in research and treatment to the prevailing approach within psychiatry and clinical psychology. The dominant approach has often been referred to as a *disease model* because of its emphasis on extrapolations from medicine. The general approach consists of looking for underlying pathological or disease processes to account for disordered behavior. The underlying processes may reflect organic factors, but reservations about the model have arisen primarily when intrapsychic factors are proposed to account for behavior.

Traditional conceptualizations have emphasized disordered psychological processes within the psyche to account for deviant behavior in cases where organic causal agents cannot be identified. The intrapsychic processes are regarded as being the basis for disordered behavior and as requiring psychological treatment. The intrapsychic approach represents an extension of the disease model to abnormal behavior and has dominated the mental health professions for many years. The development of behavior modification can be viewed in part as a reaction to the intrapsychic conceptualization of abnormal behavior and its treatment.

Perhaps within the disease model, the most significant development from the standpoint of subsequent events in behavior modification is the impact of psychoanalysis on conceptualizations of behavior. In his development of psychoanalysis as a theory of personality and a form of treatment, Sigmund Freud provided a detailed conceptual account of the psychological process, personality mechanisms, and drives that allegedly account for normal and abnormal behavior. The development of psychological symptoms was traced to underlying psychodynamic processes. The general disease model represented by psychoanalysis and the specific propositions of the theory had a tremendous impact on psychiatric diagnosis, assessment, and treatment.

Impact of the Intrapsychic Disease Approach. The general disease model has had important implications for psychiatric diagnosis, assessment, and treatment. With regard to psychiatric diagnosis, the disease model has led to attempts to devise a method of identifying specific and distinct disease entities. A psychiatric diagnostic system developed that delineated various disorders, many of which reflect disease underlying psychological processes ("mental illnesses"). Usually, the concern about these disorders is not with the problematic behaviors themselves but in large part with the underlying psychodynamic factors that have been proposed to account for these disorders. Similarly, in psychological assessment, many efforts have focused on identifying the intrapsychic processes regarded as accounting for the behavior. The underlying intrapsychic processes—as, for example, reflected on projective test performance—received considerable attention, often in place of samples of actual behavior.

Perhaps the greatest impact of the intrapsychic disease model can be seen in the practice of therapy. Psychoanalytically oriented therapy has dominated outpatient treatment in psychiatry and clinical psychology. Treatment consists of focusing on underlying unconscious processes, childhood conflicts, sources of resistance, and other aspects of psychodynamic functioning that are tied to current behaviors through an intricate set of assumptions. Many therapy techniques, such as client-centered therapy (Rogers, 1951), developed as alternatives but often adhered to the overall assumptions about the impact of intrapsychic processes on behavior.

Dissatisfaction with the Disease Model

and Psychoanalysis. Although the disease model has dominated psychiatry and clinical psychology, within the last 30 years dissatisfaction has increased in several areas. Psychoanalysis as the major intrapsychic position generated into its own sources of criticism based on the difficulty in testing various assumptions and the lack of support in many areas where hypotheses have been tested relating psychodynamic processes to behavior (Bailey, 1956; Hovey, 1959; Orlansky, 1949; Sears, 1944). Doubts about the theory focused on specific propositions regarded as stemming from orthodox psychoanalytic theory, such as the notion that underlying psychic processes rather than "symptoms" (overt behavior) invariably needed to be treated. The idea that symptomatic treatment led to the appearance of other maladaptive behaviors or *substitute* symptoms had been questioned seriously (M. C. Jones, 1924b; Mowrer & Mowrer, 1938).

Psychiatric diagnosis has also been the center of criticism. The identification of psychiatric disorders has hardly been a straightforward task, and research on the reliability and validity of the system has led to repeated criticism (e.g., Hersen, 1976; Mischel, 1968; Zubin, 1967). Perhaps more importantly, reservations have been expressed about the utility of diagnosis. Psychiatric diagnosis has had few implications for etiology, prognosis, or treatment. Other objections were made to the diagnosis of psychiatric disorders because most disorders consist of deviant behavior defined by social norms rather than by a demonstrable disease process (Ellis, 1967; Ferster, 1965; Laing, 1967; Scheff, 1966; Szasz, 1960).

A major source of dissatisfaction focused on traditional psychotherapy, particularly psychoanalysis and psychoanalytically oriented therapy. The efficacy of psychotherapy has been seriously questioned by many investigators (Denker, 1946; Landis, 1937; Wilder, 1945; Zubin, 1953). The most influential criticism was that of Hans J. Eysenck (1952), who reviewed the literature and concluded that improvement because of treatment was not better than *spontaneous remission*, that is, the improvements clients experience without formal treatment. Although the conclusions have been challenged (Meltzoff & Kornreich, 1970), Eysenck's critical evaluation stimulated concern about the failure of the traditional psychotherapies and the need for vastly improved research. Even so, subsequent evaluations of psychotherapy research noted that little attention has been devoted to outcome research (Parloff & Rubinstein, 1962).

Criticism of treatment is not restricted to psychotherapy. Institutional care for psychiatric patients has also been under attack because of its largely custodial nature. Major breakthroughs have been made in treatment, primarily chemotherapy. Yet, reservations have been expressed about the need to confine individuals, the depersonalization of institutional life, and the deterioration associated with custodial care (Paul, 1969; Sommer & Osmond, 1961; Wanklin, Fleming, Buck, & Hobbs, 1956). In general, the prospect of discharge for many patients has been poor, and the prospect of readmission for many who have been discharged has been high. Many patients become chronic, and custodial treatment becomes a dominant mode of care.

General Comments. Of course, the impact, benefits, and criticism associated with the disease model in the areas of diagnosis, assessment, and treatment are rich topics in their own right and cannot be elaborated here. From the standpoint of the history of behavior modification, it is important merely to acknowledge the several sources of dissatisfaction with the traditional approach in psychiatry and clinical psychology. The dissatisfaction paved the way for a new approach to enter into the field.

As psychology has grown as a science, experimental findings about behavior and its development have had little impact on the dominant position within psychiatry. Specific psychological constructs, as well as the approach of scientific research, have provided viable alternatives that address many of the criticisms of the disease model. Behavior modification represents a psychological account of behavior relatively free from the medical influences evident in the disease model and psychoanalysis. Behavior modification is not merely a conceptual change; rather, the strengths of behavior modification as an alternative paradigm or approach have been expressly in those areas where the intrapsychic approach has been weak, namely, research and treatment.

Foundations of Behavior Modification

The foundations of behavior modification can be traced by examining developments in philosophy, the physical and biological sciences, and medicine, which are no doubt interrelated and also reflect political and social climates. However, rather direct historical lines can be traced to the foundations of behaviorism in psychology and the antecedents of this movement. In the eighteenth century, developments in the biological and physical sciences exerted a marked impact on psychology. For example, biological research began to progress in identifying the basis of selected organic diseases and their treatment. Theory and research in physics supported a basic scientific approach to understanding physical matter. Also, Darwin's development of the theory of evolution had impact not only on the biological sciences but on the social sciences as well. Darwin emphasized the adaptability of organisms to their environment and the continuity of the species, ideas that directly influenced research in psychology.

The development of behaviorism and its antecedents must be viewed in a larger intellectual climate. Many of the tenets and approaches of behaviorism reflect rather than constitute the overall movement toward a greater appreciation of science and a mechanistic and materialistic approach to topics in the physical, biological, and social sciences. Among the many factors that can be identified, three particularly important antecedents to behavior modification include developments in physiology in Russia, the emergence of behaviorism in America, and developments in the psychology of learning.

Conditioning in Russia

Much of the history of behavior modification can be traced to developments in research on physiology in Russia. In the early 1800s, the influence of scientific research and experimentation increased in Europe. The movement extended to Russia, primarily through the neurophysiological work of Ivan M. Sechenov (1829–1905). Sechenov, who received training in Europe, developed a program of research that helped establish him as the father of Russian physiology.

Sechenov was interested in topics relevant to psychology, which at the time was largely an area of subjective inquiry and speculation about states of consciousness. He believed that the study of reflexes represented a point at which psychology and physiology might merge. Sechenov (1865/1965) suggested that behavior could be accounted for by various "reflexes of the brain." Complex reflexes that accounted for behavior, Sechenov maintained, were developed through learning. Various stimuli in the environment became associated with muscle movements; the repeated association of the stimuli with the movements made the acts habitual. Sechenov's general views about behavior reflected positions that were later embraced by such behaviorists as John B. Watson and B. F. Skinner. Behavior was considered a function of environmental events and learning.

Basically, Sechenov provided two interrelated contributions in the history of behavioral research. First, he advocated the study of reflexes as a way of addressing problems of psychology. The study of reflexes, he believed, provided the basis for understanding behavior. Second, he advocated application of the objective methods of physiology to the problems of psychology. He felt that the research methods of physiology would vastly improve on the subjective and introspective methods of psychology. Sechenov's recognition of the importance of reflexes and his strong advocation of objective research methods were very important. Many of his specific views about the reflexes that caused behavior were speculative, as he recognized. Yet, their impact was marked, in part, no doubt, because of the tremendous respect that Sechenov had earned as a rigorous researcher himself. Sechenov's views influenced two younger contemporaries, Ivan P. Pavlov (1849–1936) and Vladimir M. Bechterev (1857–1927).

Pavlov's work is extremely well known, and hence, I need not elaborate on it here, except to acknowledge his pivotal role in the unfolding history of conditioning. Pavlov's research essentially followed directly from Sechenov's views by using physiological research methods to examine neurological functioning. In his work on digestion, Pavlov investigated reflexes involving primarily glandular secretions. In the process of this research, which earned him a Nobel prize, Pavlov (1902) discovered *psychical secretions*. He found that gastric secretions in the dog would often begin prior to presenting the stimulus (e.g., food); the sight of the food or the approaching experimenter could stimulate secretions. The secretions were referred to as psychical because they were not evoked by physical stimulation. But *psychical* referred to subjective states of the organism and hence was given up and replaced with *conditional reflex* (Pavlov, 1903/1955).[2]

Pavlov's research turned to the investigation of conditioned reflexes. His work spanned several years and involved a large number of investigators in his laboratory who methodically elaborated diverse process associated with the development and the elimination of the conditioned reflexes, such as extinction, generalization, and differentiation. Pavlov's main interest in studying reflexes was to elaborate the activity of the brain. Over the years, his interests in reflexes extended to understanding behavior as well as being reflected in topics of language and psychopathology.

Pavlov's contributions to psychology in general are extensive. His main contribution was in objectively investigating conditioned reflexes from the standpoint of a physiologist. He strongly advocated objectivism in research and was critical of subjective lines of psychological inquiry (e.g., Pavlov, 1906). His programmatic work demonstrated the importance of learning in accounting for animal behavior and eventually provided a research paradigm for investigating human behavior as well.

Bechterev, a contemporary of Pavlov who was also influenced by Sechenov, began a program of research that applied the methods of physiology to the study of the functioning of the brain. Most of Bechterev's work focused on reflexes of the motoric system (i.e., the striated muscles) rather than of the glands and the digestive system studied by Pavlov. Bech-

---

[2] Apparently, *conditional reflex* is closer to the meaning of the Russian term that Pavlov used; it became the more familiar *conditioned reflex* through translation (Hilgard & Bower, 1966).

terev also encountered the conditioned reflexes (which he referred to as "associative reflexes") and investigated processes associated with their development. Interestingly, Bechterev's method was more readily applicable to human behavior than was Pavlov's method because he used shock and muscle flexion as the unconditioned stimulus and response, respectively. The special surgery and the assessment of salivation required by Pavlov's early methods were less readily applicable to humans for obvious reasons.

Although Bechterev's work as a neurophysiologist is important in its own right, his significant role in the history of behavior modification stems from his interest in problems of psychiatry and clinical psychology. Bechterev (1913), more than Pavlov and Sechenov, developed the notion that conditioning could account for a variety of human behaviors and provided an objective basis for psychology. Bechterev believed that problems of psychology could be studied by examining reflexes and developed what he considered a separate discipline—which he referred to as "reflexology," devoted to that end (Bechterev, 1932).

Reflexology addressed many problems of psychology including explanations of personality and of normal and deviant behavior. Bechterev attacked psychoanalytic theory from a scientific standpoint and argued the substantive and methodological superiority of reflexology in its place. Bechterev founded and actively headed a variety of institutes for the treatment of clinical populations, including psychiatric patients, alcoholics, epileptics, and the mentally retarded. Bechterev was eager to apply information from basic research on reflexes, which he was conducting at the time, to clinical populations.

In general, Bechterev's interest in reflexes and their applicability to behavior was much broader than that of Pavlov. Bechterev's writings encompassed many of the topics characteristic of more recent developments in behavior modification, including the explanation of personality and abnormal behavior in terms of learning. Indeed, it was Bechterev's views about behavior and its malleability, as a function of conditioning, that Watson initially drew on when the movement of behaviorism crystallized in America.

The development of conditioning in Russia represents an extremely significant set of events in the history of behaviorism. The emergence of conditioning from physiology may be an important fact because the objective methods of physiological research provided an alternative to the subjective, introspective methods of psychology. Also, the role of learning assumed increased importance in accounting for behavior. Sechenov, Pavlov, and Bechterev pointed to the importance of the environment as the source of behavior.

Although the work of Pavlov and Bechterev was similar, they extended Sechenov's original views in different ways. Pavlov established lawful relationships on conditioning and provided years of programmatic research that elaborated many basic processes. Bechterev also conducted basic work on conditioning, but he is more readily distinguished by his interests in applying conditioning as a conceptual basis for behavior—all behavior—and for the treatment of abnormal behavior. To replace psychology Bechterev developed a new discipline, reflexology, which had considerable impact in Russia. Reflexology itself did not have much direct impact on American psychology. However, the movement of behaviorism in America drew heavily on reflexology and provided the radical departure for psychological research that Bechterev had envisioned.

Emergence of Behaviorism

The work on conditioning in Russia was part of a larger movement toward an increased objectivism and materialism within the sciences. In the history of behavior modification, expression of this larger movement took the form of behaviorism in America as espoused by Watson (1878–1958). Watson's early interest was in animal psychology, which had profited from the objective experimental methods characteristic of physiology to a much greater extent than other areas within psychology. As his research continued, Watson became increasingly convinced that animal psychology was an objective science that could function independently of the mentalism characteristic of other areas of psychology. At the time psychology followed the school of functionalism, which analyzed consciousness. Introspection had been used to examine the operations of consciousness by having people "observe" their own mental processes. Watson criticized the study of consciousness through introspection as highly mentalistic and subjective.

Essentially, Watson crystallized a movement toward objectivism that was already well in progress. Indeed, in the early years of the nineteenth century, many psychologists were beginning to define psychology as the science of behavior rather than of consciousness or private events (e.g., McDougall, 1908; Meyer, 1911). The movement toward objective research methods was well underway in comparative and animal psychology, which had expanded considerably by the end of the nineteenth century. Prominent among the many available examples is the work by Edward L. Thorndike (1874–1949), who investigated learning among diverse animal species in the late 1890s. Also, Robert Yerkes (1876–1956) began research on diverse species and helped introduce Pavlov's method of conditioning to American psychology (Yerkes & Morgulis, 1909). Research on animal behavior assumed increasing importance after the emergence of Darwin's influential publications outlining his views of evolution (Darwin, 1859, 1871, 1872). Darwin's views on evolution assumed the continuity of the species, so that investigation of infrahuman species was quite relevant to an understanding of human behavior.

Watson's behavioristic position developed in the early 1900s. Although the view can be traced in early lectures, the clearest and most influential statement came from his widely disseminated article "Psychology as the Behaviorist Views It" (Watson, 1913). The article noted that psychology from the behaviorist perspective was purely objective and experimental and excluded introspection as a method of study and consciousness as the appropriate subject matter. Watson wrote several books that addressed various topics of psychology and at the same time conveyed the appropriate domain and methods of the study of behaviorism (Watson, 1914, 1919, 1924).

Watson had many specific views about a variety of topics of psychology. It was important to show that behaviorism could address diverse topics within psychology, such as thoughts, emotions, and instincts. The substantive views that Watson promulgated can be readily distinguished from the methodological tenets of behaviorism. These methodological tenets, which exerted the more lasting impact on behaviorism, were very similar to those advanced by Sechenov, Pavlov, and Bechterev, who had earlier advocated the replacement of speculative and introspective inquiry into subjective states with the objective study of overt behavior. Watson's own work on conditioning had been stimulated directly by translations of Bechterev's work and, later, the work and methods of Pavlov. Indeed, Bechterev had extended conditioning to a wide range of human behaviors and had provided Watson with a detailed view of the implications of conditioning.

In behaviorism, conditioning was initially a method of study meant to replace introspection (Watson, 1913), but eventually, it became a central concept used to explain the development of behavior (Watson, 1924). As Sechenov and Bechterev before him, Watson regarded behavior as a series of reflexes. The assumption had marked heuristic value because it suggested that complex human behavior could be investigated by studying simple reflexes and their combinations.

Watson made conditioning the cornerstone of his approach to behavior. Although arguments can be made that relatively few of the specific methodological tenets were new (Herrnstein, 1969), Watson actively promulgated behaviorism as a movement in order to overthrow existing views in psychology. Aside from his general influence on psychology, Watson's contributions included specific instances of work that had applied implications directly related to behavior modification, which are discussed here later.

Psychology of Learning

The work on conditioning in both Russia and America emphasized the modifiability of behavior, and indeed, this was consistent with the influential views of Darwin on adaptation to the environment. Watson and Bechterev attempted to develop broad theories of behavior based on the conditioned reflex. Conditioning was advocated as the basis of behavior and firmly established learning as a central topic. Complex behaviors were regarded as combinations of simple responses, but explanations restricted to reflex conditioning became increasingly strained.

In America, the psychology of learning began to receive increased attention and was used to explain how behaviors are acquired. The methodological tenets of behaviorism were generally retained, but the specific research paradigms and breadth of theories of learning increased. For behavior modification, early work on the psychology of learning provided important roots. To begin with, the psychology of learning provided the theoretical positions and laboratory paradigms on which behavior modification later freely drew. In addition, proponents of individual theoretical positions occasionally addressed practical problems that touched on learning or maladaptive behavior.

As noted earlier, prior to the development of behaviorism, Thorndike began programmatic animal research that employed objective research methods. Thorndike's research on learning was distinct from that of Pavlov and Bechterev, although at this stage of research, the distinction was not entirely clear (Hilgard & Marquis, 1940). Thorndike did not study how reflexive behavior came to be elicited by other new stimuli. Rather, he was interested in how animals learned new responses that were not in their repertoire to begin with. Among many careful experiments, the most widely known is his work with cats that learned to escape from a puzzle box to earn food. Through "trial and error," the cats became increasingly skilled in escaping from the puzzle box. On the basis of his extensive research showing the influence of consequences on behavior and repeated practice, Thorndike formulated various "laws of learning." The most influential from the standpoint of current work was the law of effect, which noted that "satisfying consequences" increase the bond between a stimulus and a response and "annoying consequences" weaken the bond (Thorndike, 1931). Although the various laws that Thorndike developed evolved over the course of his work (Thorndike, 1932, 1933), the importance of the positive consequences in strengthening behavior remained and has

had a continued impact on contemporary developments in learning and behavior modification.

Several other learning theorists and positions emerged in the years that followed behaviorism. The range of complexity of positions cannot be treated in detail or even adequately highlighted here. Guthrie, Tolman, Hull, Mowrer, and Skinner provided particularly influential views on developments in the psychology of learning and on aspects of behavior modification. For example, Guthrie (1935) viewed learning as a function of the repeated pairing of stimuli and responses. He believed that a response could be established by repeatedly pairing its occurrence with the desired stimulus conditions. Similarly, to eliminate a response, new responses needed to be performed in the presence of stimuli that had previously evoked other (undesirable) responses. Aside from experimental research, Guthrie advanced practical recommendations to break unwanted habits. For example, to overcome fear, Guthrie recommended gradually introducing the fear-provoking stimuli and pairing responses incompatible with fear with these stimuli. This recommendation bears obvious similarity to the contemporary practice of systematic desensitization. Indeed, Guthrie's strong advocacy of the repeated practice of desired responses and of the pairing of responses with appropriate stimulus conditions can be seen in the practice of many contemporary behavioral techniques.

Similarly, Mowrer (1947, 1960) was concerned about the development and elimination of avoidance behavior and proposed the combination of "two factors" to provide an adequate account. Mowrer reasoned that initially, fear is established through Pavlovian conditioning. Fear develops in the organism and is reduced by escaping from the situation through Thorndikean learning. The development of this two-factor theory was important in the history of behavior modification because it provided an account of an important problem in human behavior, namely, avoidance reactions. Hence, there were immediate implications for extending learning conceptualizations to account for maladaptive avoidance behavior and perhaps to develop treatments based on learning.

Perhaps of all the individuals who can be identified with a specific theory or position on learning, B. F. Skinner has had the greatest direct impact on contemporary behavior modification. The impact is readily apparent because the principles of operant conditioning developed in laboratory research have been widely extrapolated to applied settings. In the first few decades of the nineteenth century, the distinction between Pavlovian and Thorndikean learning was not always clear. Fundamental differences between the research paradigms were obscured because of the different types of responses that were studied and the investigation of combined learning paradigms in which both operant and respondent conditioning were intertwined. Attempts were made to clarify the different types of learning by bringing them under a single theoretical framework or by explaining their interrelationship as theorists such as Hull and Mowrer had done.

Skinner (1935, 1937) brought the distinction between respondent and operant learning into sharp focus and delineated special cases where the distinction seemingly was unclear (i.e., cases where operant responses are a function of antecedent stimuli, and learning is under discriminative control). Although the distinction between these types of learning was not new, the importance and implications of the distinction had not been elaborated.

Skinner (1938) began elaborating operant behavior in a series of experimental studies. In addition to advocating a particular type of learning in accounting for the majority of human and animal behavior, Skinner became associated with a particular approach in conceptualizing the subject matter of psychology and in conducting research. The approach, referred to as the *experimental analysis of behavior*, tended to reject theory, to focus on frequency or rate of responding, and to study individual organisms using special experimental designs that departed from the usual research (Skinner, 1938, 1950, 1953b). Aside from experimental work, Skinner pointed to the clinical and social relevance of operant behavior and, to a greater extent than other learning theorists, pointed to possible applications (Skinner, 1953a).

Developments in the psychology of learning cannot be traced in detail here. It is important to note that the psychology of learning occupied a central role in psychological research after the development of behaviorism. The different views that developed and the research they generated provide the underpinnings for the general approaches and specific techniques in contemporary behavior modification. Indeed, many of contemporary debates in behavioral research often have a rather clear precedent in developments in learning theory. For example, the debate over the need for intervening variables, cognitive factors, and the limitations of stimulus–response accounts of behavior reflects major issues in the history of the psychology of learning (Spence, 1950) and remains a source of controversy in contemporary behavior modification (Kazdin, 1979).

Extensions of Conditioning and Learning

Soon after conditioning research was begun, its concepts were extended well beyond the laboratory paradigms from which it was derived. Extensions were quickly made to human behavior, following the early work of Bechterev. For example, in 1907 in Russia and a few years later in the United States, conditioning as a method of study was applied to infants and normal and retarded children (see Krasnogorski, 1925; Mateer, 1918). Also, various forms of psychopathology were interpreted on the basis of conditioning, and the methods were extended to the diagnosis, study, and treatment of selected clinical populations (see Aldrich, 1928; Bechterev, 1923, 1932; Gantt & Muncie, 1942; Reese, Doss, & Gantt, 1953). The relevance of conditioning to psychopathology, personality, and psychotherapy became increasingly apparent over the years. A few events in particular highlight this development, including selected extensions of laboratory paradigms to the study of disordered behavior, applications of conditioning to clinically relevant behavior, and interpretations and extensions of learning to psychotherapy.

Laboratory Paradigms and Analogues

Experimental Neuroses. A particularly significant extension of conditioning was the investigation of experimental neuroses, which consists of experimentally induced states that are regarded as resembling neurotic behavior found in humans. The reactions of laboratory animals to various methods of inducing "neuroses" vary, depending on the species, but they often include avoidance; withdrawal; accelerated pulse, heart, and respiration rates; irritability; and other reactions that bear some resemblance to human anxiety (see Hunt, 1964).

Initial demonstrations of experimental neuroses developed as part of the research in Pavlov's laboratory on differentiation in conditioning dogs. In separate investigations in 1912 and 1913, investigators in Pavlov's laboratory found that when animals were required to make subtle discriminations in the conditioned stimulus, all previously trained conditioned reactions were lost. Moreover, the animals showed distinct disturbances in behavior and became agitated and aggressive. Pavlov (1927) termed the resulting emotional responses "experimentally induced neuroses" and speculated on the neurological bases for the reaction.

Pavlov turned much of his research effort to these unexpected neurotic reactions. Pavlov viewed these reactions, like the conditioned reflex, as a way of investigating higher neurological processes. Yet, he also recognized the potential connection between his results and psychopathology in human behavior. To that end, he familiarized himself with psychiatric disorders by visiting various clinics, and he speculated about the basis of many symptoms of psychopathology, including apathy, negativism, stereotyped movements, fear, and catalepsy (Pavlov, 1928).

The study of experimental neuroses became an area of research in its own right and was continued in America by such researchers as W. Horsely Gantt and Howard S. Liddell. A particularly important extension of research on experimental neuroses, from the standpoint of the development of treatment, was made by Jules H. Masserman, a psychiatrist at the University of Chicago. Masserman (1943) conducted research on experimentally induced neuroses with animals, primarily cats. His work attempted to integrate conditioning concepts with psychopathology and psychoanalytic theory. Moreover, he developed several procedures to overcome the neurotic reactions of the animals. These procedures included animal analogues of contemporary behavior-modification techniques such as modeling (putting a nonfearful animal in the cage with the fearful animal), exposure (physically forcing the animal to have contact with the fear-provoking stimulus), and self-control (self-administration of food by controlling the delivery device). Masserman's main interest in these procedures was in providing an experimental basis for the psychodynamic processes used in psychotherapy. Concepts from psychodynamic therapy (e.g., working through) were used to explain the mechanisms through which the laboratory procedures had ameliorated anxiety in the animals. Hence, this overall thrust is especially interesting because many later developments in behavior modification proceeded in the opposite direction, namely, utilizing laboratory-based procedures and concepts from learning to generate new therapeutic procedures.

Clinically Relevant Applications

Research on conditioning, with few exceptions, was begun with infrahuman subjects. However, the methods were extended to human behavior in a variety of ways. Among the many extensions that can be cited, a few proved to be especially significant in the history of behavior modification.

Conditioning and Deconditioning of Emotions. Certainly one of the most influential applications of conditioning to human behavior was made by Watson, who studied the emotional reactions of human infants. The study of emotional reactions was especially important because Watson was interested in conditioning emotional reactions, in part to show that behavioral concepts and methods could be used to study feelings and private experience.

Watson and Rosalie Rayner reported an influential case in 1920 that attempted to condition fear in an 11-month-old infant named Albert. Albert was not afraid of a variety of stimuli, including a white rat, a rabbit, a dog, and others presented to him as part of an assessment battery prior to the study. The rat was selected as a neutral stimulus because, like the other stimuli, it did not provoke fear. Pairing the presentation of the rat to Albert with a loud noise, produced by striking a hammer on a steel bar, elicited a startle response. Within a matter of only seven pairings of the conditioned stimulus (rat) and the unconditioned stimulus (noise), presentation of the rat alone evoked crying and withdrawal. Moreover, the fear reaction transferred to other objects, including a rabbit, a dog, a fur coat, and cotton wool, which had not elicited fear prior to the conditioning trials.

The case was extremely significant because it was regarded as providing clear evidence that fears can be conditioned. The implications of such an interpretation were great, suggesting at once that learning might account for fears and avoidance behavior and, by implication, that such behaviors might be overcome by alternative learning experiences. The significance of the case is especially noteworthy because the phenomena that were demonstrated proved difficult to replicate (Bregman, 1934; English, 1929); the original study itself is usually inaccurately cited, so that the actual findings are misrepresented (Harris, 1979); and whether the study demonstrated respondent conditioning as usually conceived can readily be challenged by examining the actual procedures that were used (Kazdin, 1978b).

The original report about Albert was only a first step, and the full significance of the demonstration was accentuated three years later by M. C. Jones, a student working under the advice of Watson. Jones (1924b) reported the case of Peter, a 34-month-old boy who was a natural sequel to Albert. Essentially, Peter was afraid of the diverse stimuli that Albert had been conditioned to fear. The task was to develop ways to overcome Peter's fears. Because a rabbit elicited greater fear than other stimuli in the testing situation, it was used as the feared object during treatment. Several procedures were used to overcome fear, primarily the gradual presentation of the rabbit

to Peter under nonthreatening conditions. While Peter ate, the caged rabbit was gradually brought closer to him without eliciting fear. The purpose was to associate pleasant stimuli (food) and responses (eating) with the feared object. Eventually, Peter did not react adversely when the rabbit was free to move outside of the cage, and indeed, he played with it.

In addition to the successful treatment of Peter, Jones (1924a) published a more extensive report that included several different methods of treating institutionalized children who had a variety of fears (e.g., being left alone, being in a dark room, and being near small animals). Two methods appeared to be particularly successful, namely, direct conditioning, in which a feared object was associated with positive reactions (e.g., as had been done with Peter); and social imitation, in which nonfearful children modeled fearless interaction with the stimulus.

The demonstrations by Watson, Rayner, and Jones that fears could be conditioned and deconditioned were of obvious significance by themselves. In addition, the investigators were explicit in pointing out the implications of the findings for existing conceptions of psychopathology. For example, Watson and Rayner (1920) scoffed at the psychoanalytic interpretations that might be applied to Albert's newly acquired fear, despite the fact that the fear had been conditioned in the laboratory. Thus, the demonstrations of the conditioning and deconditioning of fear were placed in the larger arena of psychopathology and its treatment and were posed as a challenge to existing approaches.

Additional Applications

Many extrapolations of conditioning were made to clinically relevant topics similar to those of Watson and his collaborators. For example, the implications of conditioning for educational psychology and child development were suggested by William H. Burnham, who was the adviser of Florence Mateer and encouraged her basic research on respondent conditioning with children. Burnham (1917, 1924) believed that mental hygiene consisted of developing appropriate conditioned reflexes. His major applications of conditioning were to educational settings. Interestingly, his writings anticipated many different behavior modification practices. For example, he encouraged the use of positive consequences in the classroom and gradually providing these consequences for increasingly complex behaviors. These procedures, of course, form an active part of contemporary applications of operant techniques in the classroom.[3] In addition, Burnham suggested that fear could be overcome by employing fear-inhibiting responses, including thoughts and imagery, and by gradually exposing oneself to those situations that provoked fear. These recommendations anticipated contemporary procedures of overcoming anxiety, including variations of systematic desensitization and flooding.

In general, Burnham suggested the utility of conditioning procedures for altering behavior and improving the child's adjustment at school and in the home. In addition to outlining possible applications of conditioning, Burnham was very explicit in noting that learning-based formulations of behavior were more parsimonious than alternative views, such as psychoanalytic theory. Indeed, in anticipation of behavior modification, Burnham (1924) was critical of psychoanalysis, noting that psychoanalytic interpretations of behavior were merely a form of "psychological astrology" (p. 628). The significance of Burnham's position derives from both advocating learning and juxtaposing conditioning formulations as an alternative to psychoanalytic theory.

A significant advance in applying conditioning was the work of Mowrer and Mowrer (1938). In 1935, they began a program to treat enuretic children using the bell-and-pad method. The apparatus was a pad, which was placed in the child's bed and attached to an alarm. The child's urination completed a circuit that triggered an alarm. Eventually, the child learned either to anticipate urination prior to having an accident or, more commonly, to sleep through the night without an accident.

The procedure the Mowrers used to treat enuresis had been available in isolated applications in Europe and Russia. The primary contribution of the Mowrers was their conceptualization of the procedure. The Mowrers viewed the treatment of enuresis from the standpoint of learning and habit training rather than as a function of altering psychodynamic processes. Specifically, they conceptualized enuresis on the basis of respondent conditioning, where various stimuli (e.g., bladder distension) failed to elicit the desired unconditioned response (waking and sphincter control). The bell-and-pad method proved to be very successful in overcoming enuresis (Mowrer & Mowrer, 1938). The marked success of the treatment not only supported the efficacy of the specific procedure but was considered an important advance in using a learning approach to conceptualize and treat problems in general. Indeed, the Mowrers were explicit about the superiority of a learning-based approach compared with a psychoanalytic approach. They viewed psychoanalytic propositions as unparsimonious. Moreover, they challenged the notion that symptom substitution would result from the direct treatment of problematic behavior. The challenge was more than speculative because the Mowrers argued from their favorable follow-up data in treating enuretics.

In general, conditioning concepts were increasingly applied to clinical purposes. The applications extended to treatment and were proposed as a preferable alternative to the psychoanalytic notions that were in vogue at the time. This general pattern is illustrated by the work of Burnham and the Mowrers. However, these cases merely reflect a larger movement.

Personality and Psychotherapy

Integrative Theories of Behavior. The extensions of conditioning were not isolated applications of Pavlov's findings, as the previous section might imply. Conditioning had a marked impact at many different levels. From the 1930s through 1950s, attempts were made to develop general theories to explain normal and abnormal behavior and therapeutic processes based on learning (e.g., French, 1933; Kubie, 1934; Mowrer, 1950).

---

[3] It is worth noting in passing that Burnham's recommendations for mental hygiene primarily involved the application of what are now recognized as techniques derived from operant conditioning. Burnham, however, viewed his work as the application of respondent conditioning, following the breakthroughs of Pavlov, Watson, and others.

An especially noteworthy integrative theory was proposed in 1950 by John Dollard, a sociologist, and Neal E. Miller, an experimental psychologist, who attempted to provide a comprehensive theory of behavior that united learning, psychopathology, and psychotherapy. The work drew heavily on Pavlov, Thorndike, and Hull. The fundamental view was that psychopathology and psychotherapy could be explained by learning concepts and that both symptom development and symptom elimination could be conceived of as learning. Concepts and processes from psychoanalytic theory (e.g., the pleasure principle, transference, neurotic conflict) were reexplained in learning terms (e.g., reinforcement, stimulus generalization, and acquired drives). Concepts that had not been well based and researched were grounded in learning concepts that were the source of active theory and research at the time Dollard and Miller developed their theory.

Other people than Dollard and Miller developed theories of personality and psychotherapy that incorporated learning theory. For example, Julian B. Rotter drew on the work of learning and experimental psychology in general and from specific theorists (Tolman, Thorndike, Hull, and Kurt Lewin) to develop a general theory of behavior (Rotter, 1954). Therapy was also viewed as a learning process, and concepts from the psychology of learning were applied to explain conventional therapy.

In the history of behavior modification, the conceptual work of Dollard and Miller and Rotter is important because it reflects a move toward developing comprehensive theories of behavior that address psychopathology and psychotherapy. Learning theory and research had achieved prominence, if not dominance, in experimental psychology and were viewed as the best candidate for a sound conceptual basis for understanding psychopathology and psychotherapy. The specific theories of Dollard and Miller and Rotter have had little direct impact on contemporary practices in behavior modification. The theories primarily explained existing treatment in terms of learning. Increasingly, learning principles were looked at as a source of new therapy techniques, which ultimately had the greater impact on current work. However, the conceptualization of existing psychotherapy as a learning process and the serious application of contemporary learning research to personality and psychotherapy were very important first steps.

Verbal Conditioning. Merely reexplaining conventional therapy in learning terms did not greatly stimulate research on psychotherapy. Extrapolations from operant conditioning to the dyadic interaction of therapy, however, generated considerable research that provided an important intermediary step toward applications of learning principles for treatment purposes. Specifically, operant methods were investigated in the context of verbal conditioning. Skinner had extended operant conditioning principles to a variety of behaviors, including verbal behavior, beginning in the 1940s. Skinner proposed that verbal behavior was an operant maintained by the consequences of the listener (Skinner, 1953a, 1957).

Laboratory research began to examine the influence of the experimenter on verbalizations of the subject. The general model of laboratory research in which an animal that responded would receive a reinforcing consequence was adhered to in devising an experimental situation to investigate human verbal behavior. Verbal behavior (e.g., selecting pronouns when constructing sentences) served as the response and was followed by reactions of the experimenter (e.g., statements of "good" or "mmm-hmm"). Several demonstrations showed that specific types of speech and conversation could be influenced by the consequences provided by the listener (Greenspoon, 1962).

Verbal conditioning research initially began in the 1950s and was conducted primarily with college students in an interview type of situation. Within a few years, verbal conditioning was extended to areas of clinical work by applying the methods to various clinical populations and to situations such as diagnostic testing where client behavior could be influenced by the examiner. The major extension of verbal conditioning was to situations resembling psychotherapy. Verbal conditioning research was used in tasks more closely resembling actual client behavior (e.g., speaking freely rather than constructing sentences) while the therapist responded to selected word classes. The word classes increased in clinical focus (e.g., emotional responses, self-acceptance statements, "hallucinatory" statements), and the populations included psychiatric patients rather than college students. Increasing parallels were drawn between verbal conditioning and psychotherapy (Krasner, 1955, 1958, 1962), an analogy later bolstered by findings that therapists actually did respond selectively to client behaviors (Truax, 1966).

Generally, verbal conditioning provided an analogue in which isolated processes of dyadic interaction could be investigated. The fact that verbal behavior could be conditioned suggested the role of learning in concrete ways (i.e., how the client talked about things) that were relevant to client change. Moreover, verbal conditioning supported a general approach toward behavior in the therapy session, namely, that behavior might be partially or perhaps even largely a function of external determinants rather than intrapsychic processes. Although many investigators challenged the similarity to psychotherapy of the situations in which verbal conditioning was conducted (Heller & Marlatt, 1969; Luborsky & Strupp, 1962), the fact that parallels were drawn at all increased the salience of learning in relation to psychotherapeutic processes. Also, demonstrations that verbal behavior could be altered by consequences provided by others led to direct extensions in clinical work to the modification of problematic verbal behavior, such as incoherent or irrational speech among psychotic patients (Ayllon & Michael, 1959; Isaacs, Thomas, & Goldiamond, 1960; Rickard, Dignam, & Horner, 1960).

Emergence of Behavior Modification

The extension of learning paradigms to behavior problems was clearly evident in the work of Watson, Rayner, M. C. Jones, and the Mowrers, to mention particularly salient examples. These investigators not only applied learning principles but placed their work in the larger context of psychopathology and therapy in general. Essentially, they viewed their work as representing a new approach to psychopathology. Hence, this initial work il-

lustrates a movement toward treatment that is difficult to distinguish from later conceptualizations and applications that were explicitly labeled as behavior modification. It is difficult to pinpoint a particular date in history at which behavior modification formally emerged. Developments in several places, primarily South Africa, England, and the United States, eventually merged as a formal movement.

Developments in South Africa

Certainly one of the most significant events in the emergence of behavior modification was the work of Wolpe in South Africa. Wolpe's development of systematic desensitization not only provided an innovative technique but in different ways helped crystallize the larger conceptual shift toward behavior therapy. Wolpe was interested in the psychology of learning as a possible source for understanding neurotic reactions and for developing treatment techniques. He was especially interested in the work of Pavlov and Hull and began research on experimental neuroses, using the work of Masserman (1943) as a point of departure.

Wolpe noted that the neurotic reaction established in cats extended to situations other than those in which the reaction was initially induced. Interestingly, the severity of the neurotic reaction appeared to be a function of the similarity of the cats' surroundings to those in the original situation. The more similar the room in which the cats were placed to the room in which fear had been established, the more severe the symptoms. To establish these neurotic reactions originally, Wolpe associated shock with approach toward food; eventually, the neurotic reaction inhibited feeding. This result suggested that feeding might, under different circumstances, inhibit anxiety; that is, the two reactions might be "reciprocally inhibiting" (see Wolpe, 1952a, 1954).

To overcome neurotic reactions, Wolpe placed the animals in situations that resembled, in varying degrees, the original situation in which the neurotic reactions had been developed, and he provided opportunities and physical guidance to encourage eating. After eating had been established, Wolpe induced feeding in rooms that more closely resembled the original room, and he continued this procedure until the animal could eat freely in the original room without anxiety. When feeding in the original situation was successfully accomplished, fear was eliminated.

Wolpe (1958) accounted for the "cures" on the basis of inhibition of the anxiety reaction and formulated a general principle of reciprocal inhibition: "If a response antagonistic to anxiety can be made to occur in the presence of anxiety-evoking stimuli so that it is accompanied by a complete or partial suppression of the anxiety responses, the bond between these stimuli and the anxiety responses will be weakened (p. 71)." This principle served as the basis for developing treatments to overcome human fear, an exceedingly important step that greatly extended previous work on experimental neuroses. Wolpe developed the idea that humans could be exposed to anxiety-provoking situations in a way similar to the exposure of the cats to rooms associated with fear. Although Wolpe first exposed clients to actual situations in which anxiety was provoked, he explored the use of imagery in which clients imagined a graded series of situations. Also, following the work of the physiologist Edmund Jacobson (1938), who had used relaxation to treat anxiety and other disorders, Wolpe selected muscle relaxation as a response that could inhibit anxiety in the same way that feeding was used as a response incompatible with fear among the animals.

The procedure that Wolpe developed was systematic desensitization, consisting of relaxation, the development of a graded series of anxiety-provoking situations (hierarchy), and the pairing of the imagination of the hierarchy items with relaxation. This variation is the major technique developed from the reciprocal inhibition principle, but it can be practiced in a variety of ways (e.g., using responses other than relaxation as the incompatible response, *in vivo* presentation of the anxiety-provoking situations).

The significance of the development of psychotherapy based on reciprocal inhibition and many steps and influences along the way cannot be easily highlighted here (see Kazdin, 1978b). Briefly, Wolpe can be credited with several accomplishments. First, he developed a set of specific therapy techniques. The techniques were provided in the context that suggested their efficacy and superiority to alternative treatment methods (Wolpe, 1952b, 1958). The actual percentage of "cures" with diverse patients was claimed to be high (80%) relative to reports available from other treatment centers using traditional psychotherapeutic treatments. Others who applied learning concepts to psychotherapy had suggested that learning-based treatments were better than traditional treatments. Wolpe, more than others before him, made this issue salient by directly comparing his case data with reports of outcomes from other facilities. The comparison made explicit a challenge to others to develop and test their techniques against desensitization.

Second, the development and theoretical context of reciprocal inhibition therapies were consistent with the *Zeitgeist*. Wolpe drew on the psychology of learning, including the research of Pavlov, Hull, Mowrer, Miller, Masserman, and others, and on physiology in explaining the mechanisms through which behavior change was accomplished. Thus, the technique was placed on a conceptual foundation with a high degree of respectability in terms of its scientific basis.

Third, and related to each of the above, Wolpe developed *new* techniques. Rather than using learning as a basis to explain existing techniques, Wolpe utilized his findings from laboratory work to generate new approaches in clinical treatment. This important leap distinguishes Wolpe's work since many of the findings in experimental neuroses and even the procedures for overcoming neuroses were evident in the work of others (Masserman, 1943). Using experimental work to generate treatment techniques was innovative.

Finally, Wolpe made very specific and testable claims about therapy. He suggested that certain conditions must be included in treatment (e.g., relaxation, hierarchy construction, and the pairing of relaxation with imagination of the hierarchy items). The specificity of Wolpe's treatment encouraged a plethora of research projects in the ensuing years that helped formalize behavior therapy.

Wolpe's influential book, *Psychotherapy by Reciprocal Inhibition,* was written while he was on leave from South Africa in the United

States. Aside from publication of the book in 1958, the spread of desensitization and other techniques included in the book was facilitated by Stanley Rachman and Arnold A. Lazarus, who worked with Wolpe in South Africa and helped extend desensitization to England and the United States, respectively. Through their extensive writings, Rachman and Lazarus increased research and clinical practice in behavior therapy and contributed uniquely in their own ways to the final development of the field.

Developments in England

The development of behavior therapy in England began independently of Wolpe's work in South Africa but can be traced during the same period, namely, the early 1950s. The major impetus for formal development of behavior therapy can be traced to Eysenck and work done at the Institute of Psychiatry at the Maudsley Hospital in London.

Eysenck was trained as an experimental psychologist and advocated a rigorous scientific approach to psychiatry and clinical psychology. He incisively criticized traditional psychiatric and psychological practices, including psychiatric diagnosis and psychotherapy. A well-known and highly influential critique was published in 1952, entitled "The Effects of Psychotherapy: An Evaluation." This paper essentially noted that no firm evidence was available that psychotherapy was more effective than improvements likely to occur without formal treatment, that is, spontaneous remission. The paper stirred considerable controversy about the accomplishments of psychotherapy and whether traditional practices were worth the effort (see, for example, Eysenck, 1966).

Concurrently with Eysenck's writings, important developments were taking place at Maudsley. Eysenck, who was head of the research section of the psychology department, and M. B. Shapiro, who was head of the clinical teaching section, were dissatisfied with the role of the psychologist in the psychiatric setting. Eysenck believed that the psychologist should serve as a researcher and rely primarily on findings from general psychology for clinical practice (e.g., Eysenck, 1950, 1952a; Paynes, 1953). Shapiro (1957) believed that the role of the psychologist should not be the routine administration of psychological tests. Indeed, he felt that traditional assessment devices lacked diagnostic, etiological, and treatment implications. Shapiro maintained that the psychologist should draw on general psychology for leads on how to evaluate and treat the patient.

Eysenck advocated learning-based formulations in conceptual papers about psychopathology and psychotherapy. Shapiro advanced a similar approach in the concrete applications of treatment to alter the behavior of patients at Maudsley. Early applications of interventions based on the work of Pavlov, Hull, and others were reported from Maudsley to alter such problems as enuresis, fear, and tics (e.g., H. G. Jones, 1956; Meyer, 1957; Yates, 1958).

By the late 1950s and early 1960s, extensions of learning to psychopathology and psychotherapy had increased. Eysenck took the lead in using learning theory to explain various disorders such as anxiety and hysteria (Eysenck, 1957). In 1959, he published a paper that explicitly applied learning theory to therapeutic applications and coined this extension as "behavior therapy."[4] This paper helped crystallize the movement toward behavior therapy by distinguishing behavior therapy from Freudian psychotherapy on several criteria.

Many of the distinctions were made sharply, perhaps to polarize the different positions. For example, Freudian psychotherapy was regarded as drawing on uncontrolled observations and as being based on inconsistent theory, whereas behavior therapy was seen as being derived from experimental studies and as being based on consistent and properly formulated theory. Behavior therapy was posed as scientifically superior and clinically more

---

[4] Interestingly, Lindsley and Skinner were the first to use the term *behavior therapy* (Skinner, Solomon, & Lindsley, 1953; Skinner, Solomon, Lindsley, & Richards, 1954). However, the term remained in unpublished reports that did not receive wide circulation. The term became popular primarily through Eysenck's (1959, 1960) early writings on the topic. Lazarus (1958) had used the term earlier than Eysenck, but his use was not adopted or widely publicized.

effective than traditional forms of psychotherapy. Eysenck (1960b, 1966) revised his classic paper, originally published in 1952, and extended the range of his conclusions. He retained the notion that psychotherapy had not been shown to be effective and further suggested that learning-based therapies provided the most promising leads. In short, in different writings, Eysenck made comparisons between behavior therapy and psychotherapy. The individual claims that Eysenck made about the specific differences between the areas might have been challenged, but the comparison clearly placed behavior therapy in the arena as an alternative to traditional Freudian therapy.

The movement toward the formalization of behavior progressed rather quickly in England. By the early 1960s, behavior therapy had emerged explicitly at Maudsley Hospital, representing a convergence of several activities within the setting. Rachman had come from South Africa and had brought with him Wolpe's method of systematic desensitization. From a different origin, Maudsley Hospital had already tried to apply a method of providing patients with graduated tasks to perform in anxiety-provoking situations to overcome their fear. This method was similar to that of Wolpe but derived from Herzberg (1945), who had suggested the procedure to Eysenck. At Maudsley, a psychiatrist, Michael Gelder, and a psychiatrist in training, Isaac Marks, began to apply desensitization in research with phobic patients. Within a very short time, Rachman, Gelder, and Marks began programmatic work applying and evaluating behavior therapy techniques for clinical patients.

Developments in the United States

The development of behavior modification in the United States was much more diffuse than in South Africa and England. Independent lines of work were evident without a central spokesperson, school of thought, or set of proponents. For example, in their work, Watson, the Mowrers, Burnham, and others were relatively isolated from each other, although they reflected a similar thrust. When additional applications in the United States are considered, the diffuseness of the approaches is even more evident. Selected applications that reflect the movement toward learning-based therapy and eventually behavior modification are illustrated below.

Knight Dunlap and Negative Practice. In the late 1920s and the early 1930s, Knight Dunlap (1875–1949) was interested in the formation and elimination of habits. Dunlap, an experimental psychologist and a colleague of Watson, relied on learning as a basis for changing clinically relevant behavior. He was especially interested in eliminating undesirable habits through repetition, and he developed the procedure referred to as *negative practice* (Dunlap, 1928, 1932). Dunlap believed that habits could be altered by repetition of the undesirable behavior. By repeatedly engaging in the undesired behavior and by expecting improvement, the behavior could be altered. Dunlap reported several case applications where negative practice appeared to be effective in eliminating stuttering, nail biting, daydreaming, tics, thumb sucking, masturbation, and homosexuality.

Dunlap's work is significant in part because he drew on learning to generate treatment. He emphasized the role of repetition, consistent with contiguity views of learning at the time, and believed that clinical treatment in general should draw on the principles of learning (Dunlap, 1932). Later his technique was applied clinically in England and reformulated into Hullian learning theory (Yates, 1958).

Walter L. Voegtlin, Frederick Lemere, and Aversion Therapy for Alcoholics. In the 1930s, aversion therapy began to be applied systematically to the treatment of alcoholism in the United States. Treatment was begun at Shadel Sanatorium in Washington by Walter L. Voegtlin, who was joined by Frederick Lemere a couple of years later. The treatment consisted of pairing nausea with alcohol, consistent with the general paradigm of respondent conditioning. The work can be traced to applications in Russia, primarily that of Kantorovich (1929), who had used electric shock as the unconditioned stimulus and alcohol as the conditioned stimulus to bring about an aversive reaction. Other Russian investigators (e.g., Sluchevski & Friken, 1933) used apomorphine as the unconditioned stimulus with reported success. As a result of these early applications, aversion therapy began to spread throughout Europe and eventually to America.

Voetglin and Lemere began large-scale studies evaluating the effectiveness of aversion therapy (e.g., Lemere & Voegtlin, 1950; Voegtlin, Lemere, & Broz, 1940; Voegtlin, Lemere, Broz, & O'Hollaren, 1942). Follow-up ranged from 1 to 13 years and encompassed over 4,000 patients. The magnitude of the project and its strong commitment to treatment evaluation make the program at Shadel a significant step in the history of behavior modification. Essentially, this work can be considered on a par with many applications of behavior modification that followed in terms of its systematic evaluation, conceptual basis, and therapeutic focus. However, it was reported long before the formal development of behavior modification.

Andrew Salter and Conditioned-Reflex Therapy. A significant development in the history of behavior modification is the work of Andrew Salter, who developed treatments for outpatient psychotherapy. Salter's initial interest was in hypnosis. He was influenced by Hull's (1933) learning-based interpretation of how hypnosis achieves its effects. Hull had suggested that the therapist's speech served as the conditioned stimuli that evoked various reactions on the part of the client.

Salter began to apply hypnosis in private clinical practice and developed techniques of autohypnosis that clients could use effectively as self-control procedures for such problems as stuttering, nail biting, and insomnia (Salter, 1941). However, Salter was interested in expanding his techniques and the conditioning basis of treatment. He drew heavily on the work of Pavlov and Bechterev to provide an explanation for the conditioning that he believed goes on in therapy. Conditioning concepts also were relied on to explain the basis for maladaptive behavior. Salter drew on Pavlov's notions of excitation and inhibition, which had been proposed as neurological processes that accounted for conditioning. Salter suggested that maladjustment comes primarily from excessive inhibition, that is, the inhibition of feelings, thoughts, and behaviors. In 1949, he elaborated his therapeutic procedures based on conditioning notions in his book *Conditioned Reflex Therapy: The Direct Approach*

to the Reconstruction of Personality. Conditioned-reflex therapy conveys the conceptual basis of the technique in terms of respondent conditioning. The *direct* approach conveys the therapeutic tasks that Salter required of his patients.

Salter noted that to overcome their inhibitions, clients had to practice expressing themselves in everyday life. Actual practice of the desired behaviors was advocated as the best way to produce therapeutic change. Several adjunctive procedures were used, such as relaxation training for individuals who were anxious and imagery to induce pleasant or relaxing states; but the main recommendation was to facilitate actual performance in everyday situations.

Salter's work is significant for several reasons. To begin with, he developed a theory of maladaptive behavior and therapeutic change based on concepts and contemporary research on conditioning. His conceptual framework drew on several researchers, including Gantt, Masserman, Mowrer, Maier, Hull, and Guthrie, aside from the basic work of Pavlov and Bechterev, as already mentioned. Both psychopathology and psychotherapy were viewed as based on learning.

Second, Salter was concerned with the larger movement toward learning-based therapy as an alternative to traditional psychoanalytically oriented psychotherapy. He referred to work of others such as Watson and Rayner, Voegtlin and Lemere, and Dunlap as successful learning-based approaches. In addition, Salter actively argued that underlying psychodynamic processes were not important in therapeutic change. The main goal of treatment was to change how a person behaves and acts. Salter (1952) criticized psychoanalytic theory and its assumptions about psychotherapy and hence placed behavior therapy in the larger context of representing an alternative to traditional treatment formulations and procedures.

Finally, Salter reported using several treatment techniques that very closely resembled contemporary practices in assertion training, systematic desensitization, self-control, behavioral rehearsal, and imagery-based treatment. Salter applied his conditioned-reflex therapy to a variety of cases and provided the first hint of the range of clinical problems to which learning-based treatments might be applied.

Extensions of Operant Conditioning. In the 1950s and 1960s, operant conditioning was extended to human behavior along several different fronts. The applications illustrate a systematic progression, beginning primarily with conceptual extensions of operant principles, extensions of operant methods to experimentation with humans, and direct clinical applications. Each part of the progression is elaborate and hence can be illustrated only by reference to selected achievements.

To begin with, the breadth of operant conditioning was suggested in conceptual extensions to diverse areas of human behavior (e.g., Keller & Schoenfeld, 1950; Skinner, 1948). For example, Skinner's book *Science and Human Behavior* (1953a) explained the role of operant conditioning principles in government, law, religion, psychotherapy, economics, and education. Of special interest were his extensions to psychotherapy, which suggested that the reinforcement contingencies of the therapist were primarily responsible for any change that was achieved in the client.

Basic laboratory work was initiated to extend operant methods to human behavior. In 1953, Ogden R. Lindsley and Skinner began to apply operant methods to psychotic patients at the Metropolitan State Hospital in Massachusetts. They studied adult and child patients as well as "normal" persons individually in an experimental chamber in order to evaluate the effects of reinforcement. The chamber permitted the performance of a simple response (plunger pulling) followed by reinforcement (e.g., the delivery of candy or cigarettes). Individual patients' behavior was evaluated daily for extended periods (up to several years for some patients) on the basis of the patient's responsiveness to operant contingencies. Although the purpose of the research was merely to extend operant methods to human behavior, the clinical implications were evident. Symptomatic behavior (e.g., hallucinations) occasionally interfered with operant behavior. Developing responses to the apparatus competed with symptomatic behaviors and hence decreased the symptoms. In general, the significance of this initial extension was the application of scientific methods to an investigation of the behavior of psychotic patients and their responsiveness to various experimental manipulations (Lindsley, 1956, 1960).

In the early 1950s, Sidney W. Bijou began to apply operant methods to a study of the behavior of children (Bijou, 1957). Bijou developed a laboratory situation to study the responsiveness of children to various contingency manipulations that was similar in many ways to what Lindsley and Skinner had done with psychiatric patients. Bijou conducted several experimental investigations at the University of Washington (e.g., Bijou, 1955, 1957, 1958). By the late 1950s and the early 1960s, Bijou had extended operant conditioning beyond the laboratory to mental retardation and developmental psychology in general (Bijou, 1959, 1963).

Another extension of operant methods to human behavior was made by Charles B. Ferster, who had collaborated closely with Skinner on basic operant research. Ferster came to the Indiana School of Medicine in the late 1950s and began to apply operant methods to a study of the behavior of autistic children. A programmatic series of studies elaborated the nature of the operant behavior of autistic children on a variety of tasks and in a variety of contingency conditions (e.g., Ferster & DeMyer, 1961, 1962). The experiments led Ferster to suggest that the deficits found in autistic children might be overcome by developing more complex response repertoires through operant training. Similarly, in the late 1950s, Arthur Staats began a program of research at Arizona State University, applying operant methods to children with learning disabilities. Children performed individually on a laboratory apparatus where academic responses could earn reinforcers. Through a series of studies, Staats demonstrated the utility of operant methods with normal, retarded, culturally deprived, and disturbed children as they performed tasks that developed reading, writing, and arithmetic skills (e.g., Staats, Finley, Minke, & Wolf, 1964; Staats, Minke, Finley, Wolf, & Brooks, 1964; Staats, Staats, Schulz, & Wolf, 1962).

As laboratory extensions of operant conditioning increased, they began to reflect an increasingly applied relevance. The examples proliferated to such an extent that they would be difficult to document fully. For instance, Barrett and Lindsley (1962) applied operant methods to children in work similar to the work with psychotic patients that Lindsley and Skinner had begun earlier. Individual reports appeared suggesting that operant methods represented more than a method of studying human behavior. Early applications demonstrated that simple responses of the retarded could be altered (Fuller, 1949), tics could be reduced (Barrett, 1962), thumb sucking could be decreased (Baer, 1962), stuttering could be altered (Flanagan, Goldiamond, & Azrin, 1958), and so on.

Of all the applied extensions, two research programs provided particular impetus for extensions of operant techniques. First, the work of Teodoro Ayllon, beginning in 1958, was especially important. Ayllon applied operant techniques to the behaviors of psychiatric patients while at Saskatchewan Hospital. Patients' behaviors on the ward, such as interrupting nurses' work, engaging in violent acts and psychotic talk, or hoarding, were shown to be influenced dramatically by operant consequences (e.g., Ayllon & Michael, 1959; Ayllon, 1963; Ayllon & Haughton, 1964). This series of studies demonstrated very clearly that operant techniques could be applied to the behaviors of patients on the ward that were relevant to their everyday functioning and to their symptomatology. Such work encouraged more extensive and larger-scale applications. For example, Ayllon moved to Anna State Hospital and collaborated with Nathan Azrin on the development of a wardwide token-reinforcement system for a large number of patients (Ayllon & Azrin, 1965, 1968).

Another program that exerted considerable impact began at the University of Washington in the early 1960s. As noted earlier, Bijou began applying operant conditioning methods in laboratory studies. However, this work was extended in child clinical and educational settings. In 1962, Montrose M. Wolf began classroom applications of reinforcement to alter the behavior of retarded students at Rainier School in Washington. Wolf had previously worked with Staats in applying token reinforcement to alter children's reading behavior. When Wolf came to the University of Washington,

he collaborated with others to develop a token reinforcement system at Rainier School that included pioneering studies showing the value of operant procedures in educational settings (Bijou, Birnbrauer, Kidder, & Tague, 1966; Birnbrauer, Bijou, Wolf, & Kidder, 1965). Wolf also was involved with the staff at the laboratory preschool of the University of Washington and developed several programs with children to decrease such behaviors as excessive crawling, crying, and social isolation (e.g., Allen, Hart, Buell, Harris, & Wolf, 1964; Harris, Johnston, Kelley, & Wolf, 1964).

Additional applications emerged from the University of Washington, such as the now-classic report of an autistic boy named Dicky who had many behavioral problems, including tantrums, self-destructive behavior, and refusal to wear glasses, that, if not corrected, might have resulted in partial loss of vision. The successful treatment of Dicky (Wolf, Risley, & Mees, 1964) demonstrated that reinforcement and punishment contingencies could indeed be used to alter important behaviors in clinical cases.

Applications of operant techniques were evident at many different institutions in the early and middle 1960s. The work at the University of Washington was especially important because of the range of applications across settings, the number of projects reported, and their dramatic and carefully demonstrated effects on child behavior. From this research in particular, the influence of applied operant research grew.

General Comments. Spanning the period of the 1940s through the early 1960s, several innovative applications of learning-based treatment could be identified in the United States. However, even up to the very early 1960s, there was relatively little unity that conveyed an overall movement or singular conceptual stance similar to what had developed in England and South Africa. The diffuse movements in the United States included applications and extensions of operant methods and independent development of classical conditioning methods. Even in cases where seemingly similar methods might be unified, they remained somewhat independent. For example, both Voegtlin and Salter had independently drawn on classical conditioning to develop treatment methods; both had even chanced on the same name for their treatments: *conditioned-reflex therapy*. However, they applied very different methods in treatment based on their different clientele and treatment settings (inpatient alcoholics vs. outpatient treatment of diverse problems). The applications reflect a definite move toward learning-based treatments but not a clearly unified movement that could be recognized as such in the United States.

Formalization of Behavior Therapy

Although developments in South Africa, England, and the United States began independently, cross-fertilization and integration of the ideas and techniques followed relatively quickly. Persons active in the initial developments of behavior therapy moved across geographic boundaries to spread the movement further and to integrate separate developments. For example, in the late 1950s and early 1960s, Wolpe left South Africa to visit and eventually to settle in the United States, thereby bringing desensitization to the United States. Wolpe had also visited Eysenck in London. Eysenck had already been interested in reciprocal inhibition. Rachman, who had worked with Wolpe, as mentioned earlier, settled in London and introduced Wolpe's therapy procedures at Maudsley Hospital. Lazarus, who had been in South Africa with Wolpe and Rachman, also settled in the United States. In general, there was some early cross-fertilization of techniques and ideas across the geographical boundaries in which initial developments took place.

Behavior therapy became a visible movement in the early 1960s. Although it is difficult to mark the point at which the movement became identifiable, selected publications seem to have crystallized existing developments. Eysenck (1960a) edited the first book including *behavior therapy* in the title, which brought diverse writings applying learning principles to therapeutic problems. The identity of the field was demarcated further in 1963, when Eysenck started the first behavior therapy journal, *Behaviour Research and Therapy*. Within a matter of a few years, several additional publications emerged that brought together therapeutic applications that were based on learning (Eysenck, 1964; Franks, 1964;

Staats, 1964; Wolpe, Salter, & Reyna, 1964) and behavior therapy or that identified the conditioning therapies as a distinct area of research and approach to treatment. Although books proliferated in the middle 1960s, one completed by Ullmann and Krasner (1965) in the United States was particularly noteworthy for bringing together a variety of case applications of behavioral techniques and for providing a historical overview of the development of behavior modification.

Along with the integration of existing behavioral practices into a single movement, attacks against the disease model conceptualization of abnormal behavior, especially psychoanalytic theory, continued (e.g., Eysenck, 1959; Rachman, 1963; Salter, 1952). Criticism of the existing position helped unify proponents of behavior therapy. Many initial attacks on psychoanalytic theory were polemical and served to delineate behavior therapy as a unique area. Apart from attacking the traditional disease model, behavior therapy became increasingly visible by defending itself from criticism as illustrated in an exchange that was widely circulated (Breger & McGaugh, 1965, 1966; Rachman & Eysenck, 1966).

Aside from publications, the formal development of behavior therapy as a distinct area was aided by the formation of various interest groups and societies. The earliest in the United States was the Association for Advancement of Behavior Therapy, which was formed in 1966 as a multidisciplinary interest group. This organization held annual meetings, published a newsletter, and affiliated with other groups, all of which helped to establish behavior therapy formally. Within a few years, additional organizations emerged, such as the Behavior Therapy and Research Society in 1970, to develop a professional group of behavior therapists rather than simply an interest group. By the late 1960s and the early 1970s, journals, conferences, and organizations devoted to behavior therapy proliferated (see Kazdin, 1978b).

Contemporary Behavior Modification

By the early 1960s, behavior therapy had become a formal movement as ideas spread across different conceptual and geographical boundaries. Behavior therapy consisted of several different developments, including varied theoretical approaches and treatment techniques. However, common denominators of the approach were extracted to provide unity to the field.

Characteristics of Behavior Modification

Behavior modification can be characterized by several assumptions about abnormal behavior as well as by an approach toward treatment and its evaluation. A major characteristic of the field is its reliance on findings or techniques that are derived from general psychology. The psychology of learning has served as the major impetus for and the conceptual basis of many techniques. Learning conceptions are relied on to explain the development and the treatment of abnormal behavior.

A second characteristic of the behavioral approach is the view that normal and abnormal behavior are not qualitatively different. Some behaviors are not "sick" and others "healthy" based on characteristics inherent in the behaviors. There is a continuity of behavior, and psychological principles apply to all behaviors whether or not they are identified as normal. Thus, maladaptive behavior can be unlearned and replaced by adaptive behavior.

A third characteristic of behavior therapy is its direct focus on the maladaptive behavior for which the client seeks treatment. Behavior is not viewed as a sign of disordered intrapsychic processes but is of direct interest in its own right. The direct treatment of behavior does not mean that internal states are necessarily rejected. Indeed, behavior therapy often focuses on thoughts or beliefs when these are conceived of as problems in their own right. However, the focus is on the identified problem rather than on the underlying intrapsychic states considered the basis of the problem.

Another characteristic of behavior modification is its emphasis on the assessment of behavior and the experimental evaluation of treatment. An attempt is made to specify the target problem very carefully so that it can be assessed. This specificity extends to treatment, so that the procedures can be carefully evaluated and systematically replicated. Behavior therapy has a strong commitment to the experimental evaluation of treatment, as evident in several journals heavily committed to outcome research.

Several characteristics of behavior modification reflect a departure from traditional approaches to diagnosis, assessment, and treatment. Diagnosis in behavior modification emphasizes specific problematic behaviors and the conditions under which they are performed. Traditional diagnostic categories generally are eschewed for a careful delineation of the precise behaviors in need of treatment and the influences that may contribute to or that may be used to alter these behaviors (e.g., Cautela & Upper, 1973; Kanfer & Saslow, 1969). Behavioral assessment focuses on the target behavior directly. Behavior is often observed in the actual situations in which it is a problem or under simulated conditions, so that the therapist can see the problem behavior directly (see Ciminero, Calhoun, & Adams, 1977; Hersen & Bellack, 1976). Several response modalities are incorporated into behavioral assessment, in addition to samples of overt behavior, to provide a full picture of the target problem.

Treatment in behavior modification is closely tied to the diagnosis and assessment of behavior. Once the specific maladaptive behaviors are identified and assessed, treatment is directed to the problem behavior itself. The treatment strategies vary considerably according to the problem behavior that is studied. The major treatment approaches that are used include systematic desensitization, flooding, modeling, covert conditioning, aversion therapy, reinforcement and punishment techniques, biofeedback, and cognitive behavior therapy. Each of these refers to general techniques that include a large number of specific variations not easily enumerated here.

Diversity within Behavior Modification

Behavior modification is not a uniform or homogeneous position. At the inception of the field, many independent attempts to provide a scientific and learning-based foundation for psychotherapy were unified under the rubrics *behavior therapy* and *behavior modification*. The justification for unifying different developments was the common reaction against the prevailing view in psychiatry and clinical psychology and the adherence to learning theory, broadly conceived. Differences within the areas of behavior modification were minimized or ignored for the purpose of developing a relatively unified movement to oppose the traditional disease model of abnormal behavior and its treatment.

Actually, behavior modification is extremely diverse. The diversity was evident from the inception of the field but has become increasingly apparent in recent years. After behavior therapy emerged, individual approaches within the field developed over the years, and differences among the approaches could be even more readily identifiable. Consider some of the major dimensions along which diversity exists.

Conceptual Approaches. Different conceptual approaches can be readily identified within behavior therapy, including a stimulus–response (S–R) mediational view, applied behavior analysis, and cognitive behavior modification (Kazdin & Wilson, 1978). The S–R mediational view consists primarily of the application of learning concepts and emphasizes stimulus–response pairing, as derived from the contiguity learning views of Pavlov, Guthrie, Mowrer, and others. Intervening variables and hypothetical constructs are relied on to account for behavior. Illustrative of this general theoretical approach are techniques such as systematic desensitization and flooding, which focus on extinguishing the underlying anxiety that accounts for and sustains avoidant behavior. Characteristic of this approach is an attempt to link mediational constructs to antecedent stimuli and responses that can be readily operationalized.

Applied behavior analysis is quite different as an approach within behavior therapy because it draws primarily on the substantive and methodological heritage of operant conditioning and the experimental analysis of behavior. Emphasis is placed on antecedent and consequent events; mediational states, private events, and cognitions are avoided. Treatment focuses on altering antecedents and consequences in order to alter the target behavior. A unique methodological approach also characterizes applied behavior analysis and includes the experimental evaluation of the performance of individuals using intrasubject-

replication designs, usually in place of between-group designs. Applied behavior analysis includes a variety of techniques based on reinforcement, punishment, extinction, stimulus, control, and other principles derived from laboratory research (Catania & Brigham, 1978).

Cognitive behavior therapy is an approach that stresses thoughts, beliefs, and the assumption that people make their own environment. Maladaptive behavior is viewed as resulting from faulty cognitions, and therapy focuses on eliminating these cognitions and replacing them with thoughts and self-statements that will promote more adaptive behavior. Although behavior is viewed as a result of cognitive symbolic processes (e.g., Bandura, 1977), often behavioral methods are used to alter these cognitive processes, such as practicing and receiving reinforcing consequences for making self-statements that promote the desired behaviors (e.g., Mahoney, 1974; Meichenbaum, 1977).

Additional Dimensions. The diversity of behavior therapy can be illustrated by noting several dimensions in passing. For example, behavior therapy techniques vary in the extent to which they draw on psychological theory and laboratory findings. Many techniques derive from theory in the broad sense, such as S–R learning, operant conditioning, and cognitive theories. Other techniques do not rely on theory. Indeed, drawing on resources in theory or basic research has been discouraged by some authors. For example, Lazarus (1971) has suggested that behavior therapy should include techniques useful in treatment whether or not they derive from theory or laboratory research. Finally, other techniques have emerged from a general learning orientation but have developed from actual practice in applied settings (Azrin, 1977). In short, behavior therapy techniques differ markedly on the extent to which they derive from theory or laboratory research paradigms.

As already hinted at, research methods for evaluating clinical interventions vary considerably in behavior therapy. Different experimental design and data evaluation strategies are evident. Applied behavior analysis relies primarily on single-case experimental designs, evaluated with visual inspection, whereas other areas embrace more traditional between-group research and statistical evaluation.

Current Status

The diversity of views and the different types of techniques and approaches make the term *behavior therapy* almost devoid of meaning (see Lazarus, 1977; Wilson, 1978). The definition of *behavior therapy* has evolved over the course of the field's brief history. Early definitions regarded behavior therapy as a conceptualization of behavior and treatment on the basis of the laws and principles of learning (e.g., Eysenck, 1964; Wolpe & Lazarus, 1966). Although learning theory and findings have been especially useful, the domain has expanded, so that *behavior modification* has been defined more generally as treatment based on experimental findings from the psychology and social sciences (e.g., Krasner & Ullmann, 1973; Yates, 1970).

Because of the expanded definition of the field and the development of alternative and often diametrically opposed conceptual interpretations of behavior and therapeutic change, few characteristics of the field can be set forth that encompass all factions. Currently, the distinguishing characteristics of behavior therapy appear to lie in its approach to treatment and its conceptualization rather than in a specific theoretical basis or set of techniques (Agras, Kazdin, & Wilson, 1979). In general, behavior therapy tends to:

1. Focus on current rather than historical determinants of behavior.
2. Emphasize overt behavior change as the major criterion in evaluating treatment.
3. Rely on basic research from psychology to generate hypotheses about treatment and specific techniques.
4. Specify treatment in objective and operational terms so that the procedures can be replicated.
5. Specify very carefully the target behavior and the techniques for measuring outcome.

In addition to these five characteristics, current behavior therapy still rejects the major tenets of the disease approach in general and the intrapsychic approach in particular. However, the major *positive* characteristics that distinguish behavior therapy reflect more of a general scientific approach toward treatment and clinical practice rather than a particular conceptual stance or set of theoretical propositions.

Summary and Conclusions

When behavior therapy first emerged as a formal movement, it encompassed different conceptual positions and treatment techniques. However, the differences at the inception of the movement were deemphasized to promote the important common characteristics, namely, treatment procedures based on learning and a conceptual alternative to the intrapsychic approaches. Early definitions stressed the ties of behavior therapy to learning theory and conditioning principles as a common ingredient. Within the last 25 years, the field has developed considerably. The heterogeneity of approaches has increased. Consequently, the field cannot be characterized accurately by pointing to a particular set of theories or domain of psychology as the basis of treatment.

A major characteristic of contemporary behavior modification is an empirical approach to treatment and its evaluation. Interestingly, this common feature of the approaches within behavior modification reflects the general methodological tenets of behaviorism to which the overall movement can be traced. Within the general methodological approach, diversity within the field is encouraged at both the conceptual and the technical levels. Approaches are welcome as long as they are amenable to empirical evaluation. On the other hand, behavior modification is not a blind empiricism as applied to psychotherapy, since many techniques and procedures draw quite heavily from scientific psychology and learning theories in particular. Further, advancing research techniques often generate their own theoretical approaches, which are subjected to further validation. The present chapter has traced the major developments that led to the emergence of behavior modification as an overall movement and approach toward therapy.

References

Agras, W. S., Kazdin, A. E., & Wilson, G. T. *Behavior therapy: Toward an applied clinical science.* San Francisco: W. H. Freeman, 1979.

Aldrich, C. A. A new test for learning in the new born: The conditioned reflex. *American Journal of Disease of Children,* 1928, *35,* 36–27.

Alexander, J. *Thought-control in everyday life* (5th ed.). New York: Funk & Wagnalls, 1928.

Allen, K. E., Hart, B. M., Buell, J. S., Harris, F. R., & Wolf, M. M. Effects of social reinforcement on isolate behavior of a nursery school child. *Child Development,* 1964, *35,* 511–518.

Ayllon, T. Intensive treatment of psychotic behavior by stimulus satiation and food reinforcement. *Behaviour Research and Therapy,* 1963, *1,* 53–61.

Ayllon, T., & Azrin, N. H. The measurement and reinforcement of behavior of psychotics. *Journal of the Experimental Analysis of Behavior,* 1965, *8,* 356–383.

Ayllon, T., & Azrin, N. H. *The token economy: A motivational system for therapy and rehabilitation.* New York: Appleton-Century-Crofts, 1968.

Ayllon, T., & Haughton, E. Modification of symptomatic verbal behavior of mental patients. *Behaviour Research and Therapy,* 1964, *2,* 87–97.

Ayllon, T., & Michael, J. The psychiatric nurse as a behavioral engineer. *Journal of the Experimental Analysis of Behavior,* 1959, *2,* 323–334.

Azrin, N. H. A strategy for applied research: Learning based but outcome oriented. *American Psychologist,* 1977, *32,* 140–149.

Baer, D. M. Laboratory control of thumbsucking by withdrawal and re-presentation of reinforcement. *Journal of the Experimental Analysis of Behavior,* 1962, *5,* 525–528.

Bagby, E. *The psychology of personality.* New York: Holt, 1928.

Bailey, P. The great psychiatric revolution. *American Journal of Psychiatry,* 1956, *113,* 387–406.

Bandura, A. *Social learning theory.* Englewood Cliffs, N.J.: Prentice-Hall, 1977.

Barrett, B. H. Reduction in rate of multiple tics by free operant conditioning methods. *Journal of Nervous and Mental Disease,* 1962, *135,* 187–195.

Barrett, B. H., & Lindsley, O. R. Deficits in acquisition of operant discrimination in institutionalized retarded children. *American Journal of Mental Deficiency,* 1962, *67,* 424–436.

Bechterev, V. M. *La psychologie objective.* Paris: Alcan, 1913.

Bechterev, V. M. Die Perversitaten und Inversitaten vom Standpunkt der Reflexologie. *Archiv fuer Psychiatrie und Nervenkrankheiten,* 1923, *68,* 100–213.

Bechterev, V. M. *General principles of human reflexology: An introduction to the objective study of personality.* Trans. E. Murphy & W. Murphy. New York: International Publishers, 1932.

Bijou, S. W. A systematic approach to an experimental analysis of young children. *Child Development,* 1955, *26,* 161–168.

Bijou, S. W. Patterns of reinforcement and resistance to extinction in young children. *Child Development,* 1957, *28,* 47–54.

Bijou, S. W. Operant extinction after fixed-interval schedules with young children. *Journal of Experimental Analysis of Behavior,* 1958, *1,* 25–29.

Bijou, S. W. Learning in children. *Monographs of the Society for Research in Child Development,* 1959, *24,* No. 5 (Whole No. 74).

Bijou, S. W. Theory and research in mental (developmental) retardation. *Psychological Record,* 1963, *13,* 95–110.

Bijou, S. W., Birnbrauer, J. S., Kidder, J. D., & Tague, C. Programmed instruction as an approach to the teaching of reading, writing, and arithmetic to retarded children. *Psychological Record,* 1966, *16,* 505–522.

Birnbrauer, J. S., Bijou, S. W., Wolf, M. M., & Kidder, J. D. Programmed instructions in the classroom. In L. P. Ullmann & L. Krasner (Eds.), *Case studies in behavior modification.* New York: Holt, Rinehart, & Winston, 1965.

Breger, L., & McGaugh, J. L. Critique and reformulation of "learning theory" approaches to psychotherapy and neurosis. *Psychological Bulletin,* 1965, *63,* 338–358.

Breger, L., & McGaugh, J. L. Learning theory and behavior therapy: Reply to Rachman and Eysenck. *Psychological Bulletin,* 1966, *65,* 170–175.

Bregman, E. P. An attempt to modify the emotional attitudes of infants by the conditioned response technique. *Journal of Genetic Psychology,* 1934, *45,* 169–198.

Brissaud, E. Tics et spasmes cloniques de la face. *Journal de Médecine et de Chirurgie Pratiques,* 1894, *65,* 49–64.

Burnham, W. H. Mental hygiene and the conditioned reflex. *Journal of Genetic Psychology,* 1917, *24,* 449–488.

Burnham, W. H. *The normal mind.* New York: Appleton, 1924.

Catania, A. C., & Brigham, T. A. (Eds.), *Handbook of applied behavior analysis: Social and instructional processes.* New York: Irvington, 1978.

Cautela, J. R., & Upper, D. *A behavioral coding system.* Paper presented at meeting of the Association for Advancement of Behavior Therapy, Miami, December, 1973.

Ciminero, A. R., Calhoun, J. S., & Adams, H. E. (Eds.), *Handbook of behavioral assessment.* New York: Wiley, 1977.

Darwin, C. *On the origin of species by means of natural selection.* London: Murray, 1859.

Darwin, D. *The descent of man.* New York: Appleton, 1871.

Darwin, C. *The expression of the emotions in man and animals.* London: Murray, 1872.

Denker, P. G. Results of treatment of psychoneuroses by the general practitioner. *New York State Journal of Medicine,* 1946, *46,* 2164–2166.

Dollard, J., & Miller, N. E. *Personality and psychotherapy.* New York: McGraw-Hill, 1950.

Dunlap, K. A. A revision of the fundamental law of habit formation. *Science,* 1928, *67,* 360–362.

Dunlap, K. *Habits: Their making and unmaking.* New York: Liveright, 1932.

Ellis, A. Should some people be labeled mentally ill? *Journal of Consulting Psychology*, 1967, *31*, 435–446.

English, H. B. Three cases of the conditioned fear response. *Journal of Abnormal and Social Psychology*, 1929, *24*, 221–225.

Eysenck, H. J. Function and training of the clinical psychologist. *Journal of Mental Science*, 1950, *96*, 710–725.

Eysenck, H. J. Discussion on the role of the psychologist in psychiatric practice. *Proceedings of the Royal Society of Medicine*, 1952, *45*, 447–449. (a)

Eysenck, H. J. The effects of psychotherapy: An evaluation. *Journal of Consulting Psychology*, 1952, *16*, 319–324. (b)

Eysenck, H. J. *The dynamics of anxiety and hysteria.* London: Routledge and Kegan Paul, 1957.

Eysenck, H. J. Learning theory and behaviour therapy. *Journal of Mental Science*, 1959, *105*, 61–75.

Eysenck, H. J. (Ed.). *Behavior therapy and the neuroses.* New York: Pergamon, 1960. (a)

Eysenck, H. J. The effects of psychotherapy. In H. J. Eysenck (Ed.), *Handbook of abnormal psychology: An experimental approach.* London: Pittman, 1960. (b)

Eysenck, H. J. (Ed.). *Experiments in behaviour therapy.* New York: Macmillan, 1964.

Eysenck, H. J. *The effects of psychotherapy.* New York: International Science Press, 1966.

Ferster, C. B. Classification of behavioral pathology. In L. Krasner & L. P. Ullmann (Eds.), *Research in behavior modification.* New York: Holt, Rinehart & Winston, 1965.

Ferster, C. B., & DeMyer, M. K. The development of performances in autistic children in an automatically controlled environment. *Journal of Chronic Diseases*, 1961, *13*, 312–345.

Ferster, C. B., & DeMyer, M. K. A method for the experimental analysis of the behavior of autistic children. *American Journal of Orthopsychiatry*, 1962, *1*, 87–110.

Flanagan, B., Goldiamond, I., & Azrin, N. H. Operant stuttering: The control of stuttering behavior through response-contingent consequences. *Journal of the Experimental Analysis of Behavior*, 1958, *1*, 173–177.

Franks, C. M. (Ed.). *Conditioning techniques in clinical practice and research.* New York: Springer, 1964.

Franzini, L. R., & Tilker, H. A. On the terminological confusion between behavior therapy and behavior modification. *Behavior Therapy*, 1972, *3*, 279–282.

French, T. M. Interrelations between psychoanalysis and the experimental work of Pavlov. *American Journal of Psychiatry*, 1933, *89*, 1165–1203.

Fuller, P. R. Operant conditioning of a vegetative human organism. *American Journal of Psychology*, 1949, *62*, 587–590.

Gantt, W. H., & Muncie, W. Analysis of the mental defect in chronic Korsakoff's Psychosis by means of the conditional reflex method. *Bulletin of the Johns Hopkins Hospital*, 1942, *70*, 467–487.

Greenspoon, J. Verbal conditioning and clinical psychology. In A. J. Backrach (Ed.), *Experimental foundations of clinical psychology.* New York: Basic Books, 1962.

Guthrie, E. R. *The psychology of human learning.* New York: Harper, 1935.

Harris, B. Whatever happened to Little Albert? *American Psychologist*, 1979, *34*, 151–160.

Harris, F. R., Johnston, M. K., Kelley, C. S., & Wolf, M. M. Effects of positive social reinforcement on regressed crawling on a nursery school child. *Journal of Educational Psychology*, 1964, *55*, 35–41.

Heller, K., & Marlatt, G. A. Verbal conditioning, behavior therapy, and behavior change: Some problems in extrapolation. In C. M. Franks (Ed.), *Behavior therapy: Appraisal and status.* New York: McGraw-Hill, 1969.

Herrnstein, R. J. Behaviorism. In D. L. Krantz, (Ed.), *Schools of psychology.* New York: Appleton-Century-Crofts, 1969.

Hersen, M. Historical perspectives in behavioral assessment. In M. Hersen & A. S. Bellack (Eds.), *Behavioral assessment: A practical handbook.* Oxford: Pergamon, 1976.

Hersen, M., & Bellack, A. S. (Eds.). *Behavioral assessment: A practical handbook.* Oxford: Pergamon, 1976.

Herzberg, A. *Active psychotherapy.* New York: Grune & Stratton, 1945.

Hilgard, E. R., & Bower, G. H. *Theories of learning.* New York: Appleton-Century-Crofts, 1966.

Hilgard, E. R., & Marquis, P. G. *Conditioning and learning.* New York: Appleton-Century, 1940.

Hovey, H. B. The questionable validity of some assumed antecedents of mental illness. *Journal of Clinical Psychology*, 1959, *15*, 270–272.

Hull, C. L. *Hypnosis and suggestibility.* New York: Appleton, 1933.

Hunt, H. F. Problems in the interpretation of "experimental neurosis." *Psychological Reports*, 1964, *15*, 27–35.

Isaacs, W., Thomas, J., & Goldiamond, I. Application of operant conditioning to reinstate verbal behavior in psychotics. *Journal of Speech and Hearing Disorders*, 1960, *25*, 8–12.

Jacobson, E. *Progressive relaxation.* Chicago: University of Chicago Press, 1938.

Jones, H. G. The application of conditioning and learning techniques to the treatment of a psychiatric patient. *Journal of Abnormal and Social Psychology*, 1956, *52*, 414–419.

Jones, M. C. The elimination of children's fears. *Journal of Experimental Psychology*, 1924, *7*, 382–390. (a)

Jones, M. C. A laboratory study of fear: The case of Peter. *Pedagogical Seminary*, 1924, *31*, 308–315. (b)

Kaestle, C. F. (Ed.), *Joseph Lancaster and the monitorial school movement: A documentary history.* New York: Teachers College Press, 1973.

Kanfer, F. H., & Saslow, G. Behavioral diagnosis. In C. M. Franks (Ed.), *Behavior therapy: Appraisal and status.* New York: McGraw-Hill, 1969.

Kantorovich, N. V. An attempt of curing alcoholism by associated reflexes. *Novoye Reflexologii nervnoy i Fiziologii Sistemy*, 1929, *3*, 436–445.

Kazdin, A. E. The application of operant techniques in treatment, rehabilitation, and education. In S. L. Garfield & A. E. Bergin (Eds.), *Handbook of psychotherapy and behavior change* (2nd ed.). New York: Wiley, 1978. (a)

Kazdin, A. E. *History of behavior modification: Experimental foundations of contemporary research.* Baltimore: University Park Press, 1978. (b)

Kazdin, A. E. Fictions, factions, and functions of behavior therapy. *Behavior Therapy*, 1979, *10*, 629–654.

Kazdin, A. E., & Pulaski, J. L. Joseph Lancaster and

behavior modification in education. *Journal of the History of the Behavioral Sciences,* 1977, *13,* 261–266.

Kazdin, A. E., & Wilson, G. T. *Evaluation of behavior therapy: Issues, evidence, and research strategies.* Cambridge, Mass.: Ballinger, 1978.

Keehn, J. D., & Webster, C. D. Behavior therapy and behavior modification. *Canadian Psychologist,* 1969, *10,* 68–73.

Keller, F. S., & Schoenfeld, W. N. *Principles of psychology.* New York: Appleton-Century-Crofts, 1950.

Krasner, L. The use of generalized reinforcers in psychotherapy research. *Psychological Reports,* 1955, *1,* 19–25.

Krasner, L. Studies of the conditioning of verbal behavior. *Psychological Bulletin,* 1958, *55,* 148–170.

Krasner, L. The therapist as a social reinforcement machine. In H. H. Strupp & L. Luborsky (Eds.), *Research in psychotherapy,* Vol. 2. Washington, D.C.: American Psychological Association, 1962.

Krasner, L. Behavior therapy. In P. H. Mussen (Ed.), *Annual review of psychology,* Vol. 22. Palo Alto, Calif.: Annual Reviews, 1971.

Krasner, L., & Ullmann, L. P. *Behavior influence and personality: The social matrix of human action.* New York: Holt, Rinehart & Winston, 1973.

Krasnogorski, N. I. The conditioned reflexes and children's neuroses. *American Journal of Diseases in Children,* 1925, *30,* 753–768.

Kubie, L. S. Relation of the conditioned reflex to psychoanalytic technic. *Archives of Neurology and Psychiatry,* 1934, *32,* 1137–1142.

Laing, R. D. *The politics of experience.* New York: Pantheon, 1967.

Lancaster, J. *Improvements in education, as it respects the industrious classes of the community* (3rd ed.). London: Darton and Harvey, 1805.

Landis, C. A statistical evaluation of psychotherapeutic methods. In L. E. Hinsie (Ed.), *Concepts and problems of psychotherapy.* New York: Columbia University Press, 1937.

Lazarus, A. A. New methods in psychotherapy: A case study. *South African Medical Journal,* 1958, *32,* 660–664.

Lazarus, A. A. *Behavior therapy and beyond.* New York: McGraw-Hill, 1971.

Lazarus, A. A. Has behavior therapy outlived its usefulness? *American Psychologist,* 1977, *32,* 550–554.

Lemere, F., & Voegtlin, W. L. An evaluation of the aversion treatment of alcoholism. *Quarterly Journal of Studies on Alcohol,* 1950, *11,* 199–204.

Lindsley, O. R. Operant conditioning methods applied to research in chronic schizophrenia. *Psychiatric Research Reports,* 1956, *5,* 118–139.

Lindsley, O. R. Characteristics of the behavior of chronic psychotics as revealed by free-operant conditioning methods. *Diseases of the Nervous System (Monograph Supplement),* 1960, *21,* 66–78.

Luborsky, L. & Strupp, H. H. Research problems in psychotherapy: A three-year follow-up. In H. H. Strupp & L. Luborsky (Eds.), *Research in psychotherapy,* Vol. 2. Washington, D.C.: American Psychological Association, 1962.

Mahoney, M. J. *Cognition and behavior modification.* Cambridge, Mass.: Ballinger, 1974.

Masserman, J. H. *Behavior and neurosis.* Chicago: University of Chicago Press, 1943.

Mateer, F. *Child behavior: A critical and experimental study of young children by the method of conditioned reflexes.* Boston: R. G. Badger, 1918.

McDougall, W. *An introduction to social psychology.* Boston: J. W. Luce, 1908.

Meichenbaum, D. H. *Cognitive behavior modification.* New York: Plenum Press, 1977.

Meige, H., & Feindel, E. *Tics and their treatment.* Trans. S. A. K. Wilson. London: Sidney Appleton, 1907.

Meltzoff, J., & Kornreich, M. *Research in psychotherapy.* New York: Atherton, 1970.

Meyer, M. F. *The fundamental laws of human behavior.* Boston: R. G. Badger, 1911.

Meyer, V. The treatment of two phobic patients on the basis of learning principles. *Journal of Abnormal and Social Psychology,* 1957, *55,* 261–266.

Mischel, W. *Personality and assessment.* New York: Wiley, 1968.

Mowrer, O. H. On the dual nature of learning—a reinterpretation of "conditioning" and "problem solving." *Harvard Educational Review,* 1947, *17,* 102–148.

Mowrer, O. H. *Learning theory and personality dynamics.* New York: Ronald Press, 1950.

Mowrer, O. H. *Learning theory and behavior.* New York: Wiley, 1960.

Mowrer, O. H., & Mowrer, W. M. Enuresis: A method for its study and treatment. *American Journal of Orthopsychiatry,* 1938, *8,* 436–459.

Orlansky, H. Infant care and personality. *Psychological Bulletin,* 1949, *46,* 1–49.

Parloff, M. B., & Rubinstein, E. A. Research problems in psychotherapy. In E. A. Rubinstein & M. B. Parloff (Eds.), *Research in psychotherapy, Volume 1.* Washington, D.C.: American Psychological Association, 1962.

Paul, G. L. Chronic mental patient: Current status—future directions. *Psychological Bulletin,* 1969, *71,* 81–94.

Pavlov, I. P. *The work of the digestive glands.* Trans. W. H. Thompson. London: Charles Griffin, 1902.

Pavlov, I. P. Experimental psychology and psychopathology in animals. Speech presented to the International Medical Congress, Madrid, April 1903. (Also reprinted in I. P. Pavlov, *Selected works.* Moscow: Foreign Languages Publishing House, 1955.)

Pavlov, I. P. The scientific investigation of the psychical faculties or processes in the higher animals. *Science,* 1906, *24,* 613–619.

Pavlov, I. P. *Conditioned reflexes: An investigation of the physiological activities of the cerebral cortex.* London: Oxford University Press, 1927.

Pavlov, I. P. *Lectures on conditioned reflexes.* Trans. W. H. Gantt. New York: International Publishers, 1928.

Paynes, R. W. The role of the clinical psychologist at the Institute of Psychiatry. *Revue de Psychologie Appliquée,* 1953, *3,* 150–160.

Pitres, A. Des spasmes rythmiques hysteriques. *Gazette Medicale de Paris,* 1888, *5,* 145–307.

Rachman, S. (Ed.). *Critical essays on psychoanalysis.* New York: Macmillan, 1963.

Rachman, S., & Eysenck, H. J. Reply to a "critique and reformulation" of behavior therapy. *Psychological Bulletin,* 1966, *65,* 165–169.

Reese, W. G., Doss, R., & Gantt, W. H. Autonomic responses in differential diagnosis of organic and psychogenic psychoses. *Archives of Neurology and Psychiatry*, 1953, *70*, 778–793.

Rickard, H. C., Dignam, P. J., & Horner, R. F. Verbal manipulation in a psychotherapeutic relationship. *Journal of Clinical Psychology*, 1960, *16*, 364–367.

Rogers, C. R. *Client-centered therapy*. Boston: Houghton, Mifflin, 1951.

Rotter, J. B. *Social learning and clinical psychology*. New York: Prentice-Hall, 1954.

Salmon, D. *Joseph Lancaster*. London: British and Foreign School Society, 1904.

Salter, A. Three techniques of autohypnosis. *Journal of General Psychology*, 1941, *24*, 423–438.

Salter, A. *Conditioned reflex therapy*. New York: Straus and Young, 1949.

Salter, A. *The case against psychoanalysis*. New York: Holt, 1952.

Scheff, T. J. *Being mentally ill: A sociological theory*. Chicago: Aldine, 1966.

Schultz, J. H. *Das autogene training*. Leipzig: Georg Thieme, 1932.

Schultz, J. H., & Luthe, W. *Autogenic training*. New York: Grune & Stratton, 1959.

Schwartz, L. A. Group psychotherapy in the war neuroses. *American Journal of Psychiatry*, 1945, *101*, 498–500.

Sears, R. R. Experimental analysis of psychoanalytic phenomenon. In J. M. Hunt (Ed.), *Personality and the behavior disorders*. New York: Roland Press, 1944.

Sechenov, I. M. *Reflexes of the brain: An attempt to establish the physiological basis of psychological processes (1865)*. Trans. S. Belsky. Cambridge, Mass.: MIT Press, 1965.

Shapiro, M. B. Experimental method in the psychological description of the individual psychiatric patient. *International Journal of Social Psychiatry*, 1957, *3*, 89–102.

Skinner, B. F. Two types of conditioned reflex and a pseudo type. *Journal of General Psychology*, 1935, *12*, 66–77.

Skinner, B. F. Two types of conditioned reflex: A reply to Konorski and Miller. *Journal of General Psychology*, 1937, *16*, 272–279.

Skinner, B. F. *The behavior of organisms*. New York: Appleton-Century-Crofts, 1938.

Skinner, B. F. *Walden Two*. New York: Macmillan, 1948.

Skinner, B. F. Are theories of learning necessary? *Psychological Review*, 1950, *57*, 193–216.

Skinner, B. F. *Science and human behavior*. New York: Free Press, 1953. (a)

Skinner, B. F. Some contributions of an experimental analysis of behavior to psychology as a whole. *American Psychologist*, 1953, *8*, 69–78. (b)

Skinner, B. F. *Verbal behavior*. New York: Appleton-Century-Crofts, 1957.

Skinner, B. F., Solomon, H. C., & Lindsley, O. R. Studies in behavior therapy. Metropolitan State Hospital, Waltham, Mass., Status Report I, November 1953.

Skinner, B. F., Solomon, H. C., Lindsley, O. R., & Richards, M. E. Studies in behavior therapy. Metropolitan State Hospital, Waltham, Mass., Status Report II, May, 1954.

Sluchevski, I. F., & Friken, A. A. Apomorphine treatment of chronic alcoholism. *Sovetskaya Vrachebnaya Gazeta*, June 1933, 557–561.

Sommer, R., & Osmond, H. Symptoms of institutional care. *Social Problems*, 1961, *8*, 254–263.

Spence, K. W. Cognitive vs. stimulus-response theories of learning. *Psychological Review*, 1950, *57*, 159–172.

Staats, A. W. (Ed.), *Human learning: Studies extending conditioning principles to complex behavior*. New York: Holt, Rinehart & Winston, 1964.

Staats, A. W., Staats, C. K., Schutz, R. E., & Wolf, M. M. The conditioning of textual responses using "extrinsic" reinforcers. *Journal of the Experimental Analysis of Behavior*, 1962, *5*, 33–40.

Staats, A. W., Finley, J. R., Minke, K. A., & Wolf, M. M. Reinforcement variables in the control of unit reading responses. *Journal of the Experimental Analysis of Behavior*, 1964, *7*, 139–149.

Staats, A. W., Minke, K. A., Finley, J. R., Wolf, M., & Brooks, L. O. A reinforcer system and experimental procedure for the laboratory study of reading acquisition. *Child Development*, 1964, *35*, 209–231.

Szasz, T. S. The myth of mental illness. *American Psychologist*, 1960, *15*, 113–118.

Terhune, W. B. Phobic syndrome: Study of 86 patients with phobic reactions. *Archives of Neurology and Psychiatry*, 1949, *62*, 162–172.

Thorndike, E. L. *Human learning*. New York: Century, 1931.

Thorndike, E. L. *The fundamentals of learning*. New York: Teachers College, 1932.

Thorndike, E. L. *An experimental study of rewards*. New York: Teachers College, 1933.

Tissié, P. Tic oculaire et facial droit accompagné de toux spasmodique, traité et guéri par la gymnastique médicale respiratoire. *Journal de Médicine de Bordeaux*, 1899, *29*, 326–330.

Truax, C. B. Reinforcement and non-reinforcement in Rogerian psychotherapy. *Journal of Abnormal Psychology*, 1966, *71*, 1–9.

Ullmann, L. P., & Krasner, L. (Eds.), *Case studies in behavior modification*. New York: Holt, Rinehart & Winston, 1965.

Voegtlin, W. L., Lemere, F., & Broz, W. R. Conditioned reflex therapy of alcoholic addiction. III. An evaluation of the present results in light of previous experiences with this method. *Quarterly Journal of Studies on Alcohol*, 1940, *1*, 501–516.

Voegtlin, W. L., Lemere, F., Broz, W. R., & O'Hollaren, P. Conditioned reflex therapy of chronic alcoholism. IV. A preliminary report on the value of reinforcement. *Quarterly Journal of Studies on Alcohol*, 1942, *2*, 505–511.

Wanklin, J. M., Fleming, D. F., Buck, C., & Hobbs, G. E. Discharge and readmission among mental hospital patients. *Archives of Neurology and Psychiatry*, 1956, *76*, 660–669.

Watson, J. B. Psychology as the behaviorist views it. *Psychological Review*, 1913, *20*, 158–177.

Watson, J. B. *Behavior: An introduction to comparative psychology*. New York: Holt, 1914.

Watson, J. B. *Psychology from the standpoint of a behaviorist*. Philadelphia: Lippincott, 1919.

Watson, J. B. *Behaviorism*. Chicago: University of Chicago Press, 1924.

Watson, J. B., & Rayner, R. Conditioned emotional reactions. *Journal of Experimental Psychology*, 1920, *3*, 1–14.

Wilder, J. Facts and figures on psychotherapy. *Journal of Clinical Psychopathology*, 1945, *7*, 311–347.

Wilson, G. T. On the much discussed nature of behavior therapy. *Behavior Therapy*, 1978, *9*, 89–98.

Wolf, M. M., Risley, T., & Mees, H. Application of operant conditioning procedures to the behavior problems of an autistic child. *Behaviour Research and Therapy*, 1964, *1*, 305–312.

Wolpe, J. Experimental neuroses as learned behavior. *British Journal of Psychology*, 1952, *43*, 243–268. (a)

Wolpe, J. Objective psychotherapy of the neuroses. *South African Medical Journal*, 1952, *26*, 825–829. (b)

Wolpe, J. Reciprocal inhibition as the main basis of psychotherapeutic effects. *Archives of Neurology and Psychiatry*, 1954, *72*, 205–226.

Wolpe, J. *Psychotherapy by reciprocal inhibition*. Stanford, Calif.: Stanford University Press, 1958.

Wolpe, J., & Lazarus, A. A. *Behavior therapy techniques: A guide to the treatment of neurosis*. New York: Pergamon, 1966.

Wolpe, J., Salter, A., & Reyna, L. J. (Eds.). *The conditioning therapies: The challenge in psychotherapy*. New York: Holt, Rinehart & Winston, 1964.

Yates, A. J. The application of learning theory to the treatment of tics. *Journal of Abnormal and Social Psychology*, 1958, *56*, 175–182.

Yates, A. J. *Behavior therapy*. New York: Wiley, 1970.

Yerkes, R., & Morgulis, S. The method of Pavlov in animal psychology. *Psychological Bulletin*, 1909, *6*, 257–273.

Zubin, J. Evaluation of therapeutic outcome in mental disorders. *Journal of Nervous and Mental Disease*, 1953, *117*, 95–111.

Zubin, J. Classification of the behavior disorders. In P. R. Farnsworth, O. McNemar, & Q. McNemar (Eds.), *Annual review of psychology*, Vol. 18. Palo Alto, Calif.: Annual Reviews, 1967.

CHAPTER 2

Experimental and Theoretical Foundations of Behavior Modification

Donald J. Levis

Introduction

The importance of the subject matter of this volume, which deals with issues of the assessment and treatment of human psychological disturbance, cannot be overstressed. A dramatic increase has occurred in the number of individuals requesting solutions to their psychological problems. The cost to society in terms of human suffering, loss of productivity, and dollars is staggering. It was not until World War II that the extent of this problem was recognized. Nearly 5 million men in the United States, almost 1 out of 5, were rejected for military service, and many thousands were discharged following acceptance because of neuropsychiatric problems. The seriousness of the problems was even more clearly demonstrated in the Midtown Manhattan Study conducted by Srole and his co-workers (1962). These investigators reported that fewer than 1 out of 4 persons was judged to be psycho-

logically healthy, and nearly 1 out of 5 persons was considered "incapacitated" by psychological disturbance. Adding to this conclusion is Lemkow and Crocetti's (1958) estimate that between 14 and 20 of every 1,000 children born will be hospitalized in a mental institution within their lifetime. Recent attention has also been focused on the possibility that a large percentage of the presenting physical health problems may be affected by and related to psychological factors.

The mental health field's response to this growing crisis has been slow, inefficient, and ineffectual. Despite an arsenal of over 50 different psychotherapy theories and treatment techniques, many of which are designed to cover a wide variety of psychopathological problems, disenchantment with the status quo exists. Treatment is costly, lengthy, and of dubious effect. Claims of therapeutic efficacy, which not only accompany the introduction of most techniques but are perpetuated in the literature as accepted fact, are almost completely lacking in documentation via controlled research. Furthermore, what research is available for the most part falls short of in-

Donald J. Levis • Department of Psychology, State University of New York at Binghamton, Binghamton, New York 13901.

corporating even a minimal degree of methodological sophistication, a conclusion reached by many and tendentiously and at times cogently championed by Eysenck (1960, 1966). Unfortunately, the obvious possibility that traditional psychotherapy may not be an effective therapeutic tool has only scratched the defense system of a field that apparently has generated a fetish for psychotherapy. Nor can the practitioner turn to nonpsychotherapeutic approaches like chemotherapy for a satisfactory solution. At best, psychopharmacology simply provides a "holding" period, and at worst, it delays or prevents an individual from dealing directly with the issues that prevent corrective behavioral change.

The Case for Behavioral Therapeutic Approaches

As a first step in resolving the existing chaos within the mental health field, a solid experimental and theoretical foundation is needed on which treatment techniques can be developed, assessed, and improved. Unfortunately, the vast majority of psychotherapy movements, such as those reflected in the psychoanalytic, Adlerian, existential, and humanistic approaches, have produced theoretical structures that are difficult to test and treatment techniques that lack operational specificity. These movements have also appealed to individuals who manifest little interest in subjecting their efforts to scientific evaluation.

The presentation of this volume reflects yet another new movement, which has been referred to as *behavior modification* or *therapy*. This approach has been labeled the "fourth psychotherapeutic revolution," following moral therapy, psychoanalysis, and community mental health (Levis, 1970a). Although this movement actually encompasses a variety of different theories and techniques, each is based on the learning and conditioning literature.

It is the thesis of this chapter that the behavior modification approach, which utilizes for its development the empirical and theoretical offering of experimental psychology, represents the kind of foundation needed if inroads are to be made on our mental health

problems. The uniqueness of this approach is reflected in its emphasis on behavior and its measurement, in its isolation of relevant environmental variables, in its attempt to develop precise definitions and specifiable operations, and in its stress on experimental control (Greenspoon, 1965).

The fruits of this approach have already materialized with the development of a variety of new techniques that appear quite promising. Although considerable attention has been given to behavior therapy's treatment success, the importance of this movement is independent of any claims of success. Such claims can be found for other techniques prior to 1900 (Tourney, 1967). Considerably more research is needed on a variety of homogeneous patient populations with long-term follow-ups before any concrete conclusions can be reached about any given technique. However, what may prove to be of critical importance is the potential fruitfulness of the philosophy, orientation, and strategy behind this movement, and the possible impact it will have on the rest of the mental health field. Three of these potential assets particularly stand out and are discussed below.

Assets

Emphasis on Learning and Conditioning Principles. Few clinicians would object to the statement that learning plays an important role in the development of psychopathological behavior. In fact, most nonbehavioral explanations of psychopathology acknowledge the role of conditioning and learning in early childhood, the effects of punishment and withdrawal of love by the parents, and the importance of anxiety and fear in motivating human symptomatology. Yet, prior to the advent of the behavior therapy approach, no systematic attempt was made to draw on the established principles of conditioning and learning to develop treatment approaches.

Perhaps the clinical field's inability to show systematic growth is related to the reluctance of other approaches to utilize the tools and procedures of basic researchers in the field of psychology. The development of related applied sciences can be shown to be a direct function of the applied scientists' ability to draw on the established principles developed by basic researchers in the area. Prior to the development of the behavioral approach to treatment, this strategy was largely ignored by the mental health field. The obliviousness of clinicians to the potentially huge volume of human and subhuman data has markedly reduced communication among psychological areas within the field. As Ford and Urban (1967) suggested: "One index of the viability and growth potential of a particular therapeutic approach may well be the extent to which it exposes itself to influences from, and attempts to utilize knowledge from, other domains. If the psychotherapy community does not adopt the responsibility for 'bridge building,' the therapy subject may be the victim" (p. 338).

This lack of integration will be perpetuated as long as the clinician remains deficient in scientific training and unconcerned about the need for a common language to facilitate this communication. The behavior modification approach to clinical problems is an attempt to break down both of the above barriers and clearly represents one of its major contributions to the field.

The Nature of Theory Construction. The strategy common to most nonbehavioral approaches has been to develop complex, all-encompassing theories that are designed to explain the whole and complete human organism. This objective has been achieved by sacrificing clarity, precision, and predictability. Although these theories are occasionally riddled with creative and potentially fruitful ideas, the meshing and interlacing of so many surplus meaning concepts makes experimental analysis difficult, if not impossible. Unfortunately, these theories provide their followers only with a comforting set of terminology and an illusory sense of understanding.

In contrast, the strategy of a behavioral viewpoint is to start from a descriptive, better-defined, and more controllable account of behavior and then systematically and progressively work to build on this foundation. The objective is to produce clarity in communication and operational specificity of variables, which in turn permit the systematic manipulation of critical variables, predictability, and evaluation.

Commitment to Assessment. The last asset to be discussed is perhaps the most important and the most ignored factor in the development of the mental health field. The concern about evaluation in most therapeutic approaches has rarely moved beyond the case history level. Those studies that have attempted experimental analysis have fallen far short of the rigor required of a discipline striving for scientific respectability. The behavioral modification movement has been the only psychotherapeutic approach that has been committed to objective outcome evaluation from its inception. It is well known that therapeutic techniques frequently are reported to be more effective initially (Tourney, 1967), but their effectiveness diminishes eventually. Although the data suggest that one should be cautious in making therapeutic claims, unsupported enthusiastic claims of success still dominate the field.

The behavioral movement is also not free of making premature claims of success, displaying inadequate methodological sophistication, and committing errors of overgeneralization. However, the commitment of the behavioral field to a scientific analysis has resulted in an open system of checks and balances and of self-criticism that in time should result in the establishment of reliable and valid contributions. The existing crisis in the mental health field can be resolved only by an objective evaluation of treatment approaches.

Basic Experimental Learning Paradigms and Principles

The systematic application of learning principles to applied areas has unfortunately been a relatively slow development, gaining impetus only in the last 20 years. The main factors contributing to this delay have been the tendency of psychologists to separate theory and application, a reluctance to use the clinic as a laboratory, and the acceptance of the traditional psychodynamic methods as the model for psychotherapy (Kalish, 1965). The learning psychologist's retreat to the laboratory during the first half of this century was not without its value, because it was during this period that the groundwork for the development of the principles and theories utilized by behavior theorists was laid and well documented. The literature generated on issues of acquisition, response maintenance, extinction, counter-conditioning, generalization and discrimination learning, schedules of reinforcement, punishment, and social imitation and reinforcement proved extremely helpful in the development of applied techniques. Furthermore, the theoretical contributions of Pavlov, Hull, Guthrie, Mowrer, and Tolman shed additional light on the development and treatment of psychopathology. In order to facilitate a better understanding of the rationale underlying the various strategies adopted by contemporary behavior therapists, a review of some of the basic experimental paradigms will be presented here, followed by an outline of some of the theoretical positions that influenced the field's growth.

Classical Conditioning

Changing behavior can be achieved in the laboratory through the use of one of two distinct conditioning procedures, which are commonly referred to as resulting in the development of classical or instrumental learning. Descriptively, the classical conditioning paradigm differs from the instrumental procedure in that the sequence of events presented is *independent* of the subject's behavior. The typical sequence consists of an unconditioned stimulus (UCS), a stimulus known to evoke a regular and measurable response (UCR), and the conditioned stimulus (CS), a stimulus that at the outset of an experiment does not evoke the UCR. The usual order of the sequence used to produce conditioning is to present the CS followed closely in time by the UCS. The regular and measurable response elicited by the UCS is called an *unconditioned response* (UCR). Conditioning is said to have occurred if the CS presentation follows pairings of the CS–UCS results in the elicitation of a conditioned response, which usually resembles the UCR. Pavlov's (1927) work with the conditioning of salivation of dogs illustrates the procedure used in classical conditioning.

The effects of classical conditioning can be demonstrated at almost all levels of animal life. Furthermore, it is just as easily established in primitive animals as in humans, which suggests that conditioning may involve the same mechanism in all species.

Pavlov and his colleagues were responsible for isolating some of the most basic phenomena of classical conditioning learning. These phenomena include:

1. *Conditioning*—the acquisition of a stimulus–response relationship.
2. *Generalization*—the tendency of the organism to transfer as a function stimulus similarity its acquired response to new stimulus situations.
3. *Conditioned discrimination*—the learning to respond only to a specified stimulus or to respond in two different ways to two different stimuli.
4. *Higher-order conditioning*—a conditioning sequence in which a neutral stimulus is conditioned by being paired with a previously conditioned CS.
5. *Extinction*—the training procedure in which the CS is presented in the absence of the UCS, with the resulting effect being a loss in the strength of the CR.
6. *Inhibition*—a hypothetical process that actively prevents the performance of the CR during extinction.
7. *Spontaneous recovery*—the partial reappearance of an extinguished CR following a lapse of time and without any new conditioning.

Operant or Instrumental Learning

Following the work of Thorndike (1911) and Skinner (1938), learned responses have also been developed by procedures labeled *operant* or *instrumental learning*. With the operant procedure, the UCS or reward presentation is made *dependent*—not independent, as in the classical conditioning procedure—on the subject's behavior. An essential aspect of this procedure is that reward (whether negative or positive) follows the subject's response in some systematic manner. For example, every time a rat presses a bar (CR), a food pellet is dispensed (UCS).

Although the condition of operant responses can refer to the selection of isolated responses, the term usually refers to the conditioning of a class of behavior, which in turn is defined by the requirements for reinforcement set by the experimenter or by the environment in a given situation. Thus, unlike the classical conditioning procedures, which is usually confined to the study of isolated responses, operant conditioning widens the range of behaviors that can be studied, including the majority of human behaviors. Thus, as Kazdin (1978) noted, the principles explaining the development, maintenance, and elimination of operants are likely to have wide generality. Some of the basic principles of operant conditioning are outlined below:

1. *Reinforcement.* Reinforcement of a behavior is determined operationally by noting whether an increase in the frequency of a response occurs following certain consequences that are labeled *reinforcers.* If behavior increases following the presentation of an event after a response, the reinforcing state of affairs is referred to as being *positive.* If a behavioral response increases following the removal of an event, the event is labeled a *negative reinforcement.* For example, if a rats' pressing a bar increases following the presentation of food, the food can be labeled a *positive reinforcement.* If such behavior increases following the cessation of shock, shock can be viewed as a *negative reinforcer.*

2. *Punishment.* Punishment refers to an event that is made contingent on a response that results in a decrease in the probability of the response's occurrence. Stimuli that can be classified as punishers can be divided into two classes: those that result in a decrease in responding following the onset of the stimulus event (e.g., electric shock paired with a barpress response) and those that produce the same result following the withdrawal of an event (e.g., withdrawal of food following a response).

It should be noted that the effects of reward and punishment have important implications for helping us meet the objective of modifying maladaptive human behavior. However, controversy still exists over the effects of punishment on behavior, a source of confusion reflected in Thorndike's early work. His original position was that learning is a reversible process; that reward strengthens behavior and punishment weakens it. Later (1931), he reversed

this position and concluded that although reward does strengthen behavior, punishment does not weaken it. It only results in the suppression of responding. Although recent data provide some support for Thorndike's original position, the issue is far from resolved (Church, 1963; Mowrer, 1960). Such a resolution will have important implications for applied behavior modification.

3. *Extinction.* Extinction, as is the case with classical conditioning procedures, refers simply to a procedural manipulation: the removal of a reinforcer. Although extinction usually results in a decrease or an elimination of responding, it differs from a punishment procedure in that reinforcement is simply discontinued, and its negative effects are not made directly contingent on the occurrence or nonoccurrence of a given response class.

4. *Stimulus control.* Stimulus control is related to the concept of discrimination and to the empirical finding that antecedent events (stimuli) can also control behavior by associating different reinforcement consequences for a particular response class across different stimuli. For example, if Stimulus A is reinforced in one situation and not in another, or if Stimulus A is reinforced in one situation and Stimulus B is not, differential stimulus control over behavior can be established. Thus, *stimulus control* refers to the extent to which antecedent stimuli determine the probability of response occurrence.

5. *Schedules of reinforcement.* It has been established that behavior changes and maintenance can be markedly affected by manipulating the ways in which discriminative or reinforcing stimuli are presented in relation to responses. For example, by varying the frequency and magnitude of reinforcement density, response output can be regulated at high, medium, or low rates of responding. An analysis of certain schedules of reinforcement has resulted in important advances in our understanding of what stimulus reinforcement consequences maintain behavior as well as what changes are needed to alter behavior. The clinical application of such principles has important implications for our quest to alter maladaptive behavior.

6. *Superstitious behaviors.* By the repeated presentation of a reinforcer independent of any

given response class, one can demonstrate that such noncontingent delivery can increase the rate of responding of behavior performed at the time of reinforcement dispensing.

Avoidance Learning: A Combination of Procedures

Bekhterev (1928) provided the reference experiment for the avoidance paradigm by conditioning to a signal the withdrawal response of a hand or foot. In this experiment, which represents the usual form of the avoidance training, the subject could prevent the occurrence of a noxious stimulus such as electric shock by responding to a signal. What makes this paradigm of interest is that it includes both a classical and an operant procedure. The paradigm is designed to present CS–UCS presentations (a classical conditioning procedure) which can be altered if a designated response (operant) is emitted to the CS. If such an operant response is made within the required time period (CS–UCS interval), the UCS is not presented on that trial. Thus, the term *avoidance learning* comes into being.

Most of the laboratory studies of avoidance conditioning use a trial-by-trial procedure in which a discrete warning stimulus is presented. Sidman (1953), however, developed an avoidance procedure within the context of a free-responding situation in which a discrete external signal was not provided. In the Sidman procedure, a noxious stimulus is presented at a fixed interval (e.g., every 20 seconds). If the subject (e.g., rat) makes an appropriate response (e.g., bar press) within the fixed interval, the noxious stimulus is postponed and is therefore avoided for a specified time interval (e.g., 10 seconds). In such a procedure, organisms do learn and develop high rates of responding.

Another procedure closely related to avoidance conditioning and requiring no external warning stimulus is escape training. In this procedure, the subject can turn off (escape) an aversive UCS (e.g., electric shock) by emitting an operant or instrumental response. For example, Mowrer (1940) conditioned a rat to terminate electric shock by pressing a pedal arrangement located at one end of the conditioning chamber.

Implication of Conditioning Principles

The preceding discussion of conditioning procedures and principles represents only a cursory review of the topic. To provide an adequate description of the relevant principles and techniques involved would require a separate volume. A detailed discussion of these topics can be found in Kimble (1961) and Mackintosh (1974).

Until the advent of the behavior therapy movement, the implications of learning principles for the understanding of human maladaptive behavior received only sporadic historical attention. One of the most influential applications of conditioning principles to an understanding of human fear behavior was reported by Watson and Rayner in 1920. These investigators attempted to determine whether they could condition a startle reaction in a child to a previously neutral stimulus. A white rat, which elicited no fear, was paired with a loud, fear-producing noise in the presence of a 11-month-old infant named Albert. After seven such pairings, the presentation of the rat alone elicited avoidance and fearful behavior in the child. This conditioned reaction generalized to other similar stimuli, such as a rabbit, a dog, a fur coat, and cotton. The fear response was not elicited by inanimate objects such as blocks. Extending Watson's work, Mary Cover Jones (1924) attempted to determine whether learning principles could help remove children's fears. Among the techniques employed were principles of extinction, counterconditioning, and social imitation. The impact of the above work is critical in that it suggested the possibility that learning principles may be involved in the development, maintenance, and removal of maladaptive behavior.

Despite the importance of this early work, the systematic application of learning principles has unfortunately developed relatively slowly until recently. However, in recent years, the behavior modification movement has resulted in the use of learning paradigms and principles in the attempt to modify or eliminate maladaptive behavior or to reinforce socially appropriate behavior. Classical conditioning, punishment, escape–avoidance, extinction, and operant paradigms have each been used with apparent success over a wide range of behaviors, including social, sexual, addictive, eating, self-destructive, psychotic, and criminal behaviors. General treatment techniques designed to treat a wide variety of maladaptive behaviors have also emerged based on such learning principles as emotional extinction (implosive and flooding therapy), counterconditioning (systematic desensitization), and higher-order conditioning (covert sensitization procedures).

This initial success in applying laboratory principles to the human situation should strengthen even further the links between experimental and applied psychology. As this relationship becomes stronger, so should there be an increase in the sophistication, applicability, and success of the approach. But for behavioral therapy to remain viable, it must also provide a conceptual framework for understanding, predicting, and eventually preventing maladaptive behaviors. Basic learning theory has already proved helpful in providing an initial conceptual framework from which to start.

Theoretical Foundations

Without question, formal theory construction has played a major and critical role in the development and advancement of the experimental learning field. In the quest to develop a science of behavior, learning theory has kept critical issues at the forefront, has heightened controversy, has resulted in differential predictions, and has stimulated a variety of new research areas. The applied-behavior-therapy movement has also profited from the development of learning theory, since the rationale for a number of its techniques is based directly on classical laboratory theories. However, the direct extrapolation of learning theory to justify applied treatment techniques and to aid us in understanding psychopathology has not proved as successful as the transfer of learning paradigms. Critics (e.g., Breger & McGaugh, 1965) have been correct in their assessment that behavior therapists are working with antiquated models and have yet to establish a direct relationship between theory and treatment techniques.

Part of the above problem stems from the observation that certain clinical phenomena seem to contradict the laboratory findings on which existing learning theory is based. Mowrer (1950) was one of the first theorists to recognize that human "neurotic" behavior appears to represent a paradox in that it is self-punitive, self-defeating, and perhaps self-perpetuated. Patients frequently report being fully aware at a cognitive level that their maladaptive behavior is "irrational" and counterproductive. Such an observation seems contrary to most learning positions, which are essentially hedonistic, stressing what Thorndike (1911) called the "law of effect" and Skinner (1938) the "law of reinforcement." From a learning viewpoint, the symptomatic behavior of the neurotic is functioning in the absence of a UCS. This is in essence why such behavior is labeled irrational, in that failure to exhibit a symptom will not result in any biological harm. Yet, human maladaptive behavior maintains itself over long periods of time in the absence of a biological threat. On the other hand, laboratory data strongly suggest that whether the behavior in question is overt or emotional, unlearning or extinction will follow rather rapidly once the UCS is removed (Mackintosh, 1974).

Classical and modern learning theory has been concerned largely with isolating and explaining general laws of behavior. It has not, as yet, fully addressed the exceptions to these laws reflected in the unusual and puzzling behaviors labeled *psychopathological*. Applied behavior therapists as a group have also not undertaken this task seriously. It is this writer's opinion that this state of affairs exists because behavior therapists have been poorly trained in the areas of theory construction and existing learning theory. It is the further belief of this writer that the existing theories of learning do provide an important starting point from which laws of psychopathology and treatment can be developed and that such a development is critical to the future survival of the behavior therapy movement. Therefore, in this section, the purpose and basic principles of theory construction will be outlined, along with a brief description of those classical and modern learning positions, that may well provide the stepping stones for the development of viable models of psychopathology and treatment.

The Function of Theory

The scientist's task in regard to theory construction has been succinctly stated by Spence (1951):

Briefly, it may be said that the primary aim of the scientist is to develop an understanding or knowledge of a particular realm of events or data. Such scientific understanding consists in formulating relationships between concepts that have reference to the particular event under observation. Thus, beginning with the sense data or events provided by observation, the scientist abstracts out of them certain ones on which he concentrates. To particular descriptive events and pattern of events he assigns, arbitrarily, language symbols (concepts), and then formulates the relationship observed to hold between these events (or concepts) in the form of laws. These observed regularities or laws provide at least partial explanation of the particular event under consideration, for explanation in science basically consists of nothing more than a statement of relations of a particular event to one or more events. (p. 239)

In other words, the function of theory is to provide a systematic expansion of knowledge mediated by specific empirical propositions, statements, hypotheses, and predictions that are subject to empirical tests. It should be noted that it is only the derivations of propositions derived from the theory that are open to emperical test. The theory itself is assumed; acceptance or rejection of it is determined by its utility, not by its truth or falsity (Hall & Lindzey, 1957, p. 13). The utility of a theory lies essentially in its ability to serve as a guide for empirical studies. Unguided experimentation usually results in an unorganized mass of data.

Although the ordering and interpretation of data are important functions of theory, history supports the claim that a viable theory is one that predicts and explains in advance laws or results that were unknown before. Important theories in science have satisfied this test.

Nonbehavioral theories of psychopathology clearly have not met the above boundary conditions for theory construction. However, the argument is made that human behavior is complex and in need of explanation by postulating a variety of constructs. The language of the laboratory is viewed as inadequate and nondescriptive of human interactions. Unfortunately, the model of human behavior generated by the psychoanalytic, humanistic, and existential movements, although adequate in postdiction, lack prediction. Relationships among constructs are not adequately explained, and terms and propositions generated by the theories are unclear and full of surplus meaning. For theory to aid in the advancement of knowledge, definitional precision of terms is essential. As Feigl (1953) suggested, "This obvious standard scientific method requires that the concepts used in the formulation of scientific knowledge-claims be as definitely delimited as possible. On the level of the qualitative-classificatory sciences this amounts to the attempt to reduce all border-zone vagueness to a minimum. On the level of quantitative science the exactitude of the concepts is enormously enhanced through the application of the techniques of measurement" (p. 12). Precision of psychological terms requires that they be capable of operational analysis. As Skinner (1945) warned, "we must explicate an operational definition for every term unless we are willing to adopt the vague usage of the vernacular" (p. 270).

Learning theory attempts to meet the tenets of good theory construction, and herein lie its distinct advantage and potential explanatory and predictive power. The issue, of course, is whether it is feasible to apply existing learning or conditioning laws in our quest to understand human psychopathology. Eysenck (1960) perhaps said it best when he reasoned: "If the laws which have been formulated are not necessarily true, but at least partially correct, then it must follow that we can make the deductions from them to cover the type of behavior represented by neurotic patients, construct a model which will duplicate the important and relevant features of the patient and suggest new and possible helpful methods of treatment along lines laid down by learning theory" (p. 5). The issue is, of course, an empirical one, and fortunately, Eysenck's suggestion has already materialized. Learning theory has been responsible for generating a number of new ideas and treatment procedures.

Skinner's Antitheoretical Position

Skinner, who himself has made important contributions to the advancement of learning theory (Skinner, 1938), changed his position and became one of the most eloquent critics of formal theory construction. For Skinner

(1950), a science of behavior must eventually deal with behavior in its relation to certain manipulable variables. He stated that theories in the field generally deal with the intervening steps in these relationships. Therefore, instead of prompting us to search for and explore more relevant variables, these intervening steps frequently serve only to provide verbal answers in place of the factual data we might find through further study. Such a state, from Skinner's viewpoint, can easily create a false sense of security. Skinner further argued that research designed in relation to theory was likely to be wasteful since considerable energy and skill most likely would be devoted to its defense. This energy, he felt, could be directed toward a more "valuable" area of research.

Skinner's position will not be rebutted here, since his viewpoint was mainly taken as a stance against the movement in the 1940s to provide an all-encompassing general theory of behavior. Today, learning theory is much more specific and problem-oriented. Skinner's own attempt to provide an inductive data base for psychology is reflected in the large volume of empirical data published by Ferster and Skinner (1957). This volume, which reports important findings, reads a little like a phone book and falls far short of Skinner's own expectations. The failure of the purely inductive approach has largely been a failure to provide the organizational and integrative structure that theory offers. Today, this point is well recognized by Skinner's followers in the basic research areas. Operant research has clearly moved from an inductive analysis to a functional theoretical structure.

Skinner's antitheoretical stance has influenced and is still influencing many behavior therapists. These individuals, referred to as *operant behavior modifiers*, are mainly interested in the question of what techniques will shape a patient's behavior to the desired outcome, rather than attempting to understand why and how the techniques operate. This strategy has already resulted in the development of some important and interesting techniques, which have greatly enhanced the behavior modification movement. But as the data base of the field increases, the need exists, as was the case in the basic research areas, for better organizational structure, which perhaps can be best achieved from this orientation by a functional theoretical analysis.

Since formal models of learning also have played a significant role in the development of this new applied field, these implications for the behavior therapy movement are now addressed.

The Impact of Formal Models

The classical theories of learning developed by Pavlov, Hull, Guthrie, and Tolman played a major heuristic role in providing the initial foundations for the development of many of the behavioral modification techniques. It should be understood that these approaches were designed as general theories of behavior and not as models of psychopathology. Today, learning theorists have moved away from such general theories to providing more explicit and detailed models of various empirical findings. However, the influence of the masters can still be felt.

It is the opinion of this reviewer that applied behavioral theorists should also move away from using the classical theories as a foundation for their techniques. Contemporary learning positions may well provide a much stronger base for extrapolating to psychopathology. The need for the applied behavior field to upgrade and sharpen its theoretical foundation is clearly evident. Therefore, only a cursory review of the classical theories is provided here, followed by a description of a couple of contemporary models that may prove of use to the behavior modification field.

Theories of learning can be grouped under a variety of different headings. The subdivisions frequently used are one-factor versus two-factor theories, reinforcement versus nonreinforcement theories, drive versus nondrive theories, and inhibition versus noninhibition theories. It is possible for a given theory to be cross-indexed under more than one heading (e.g., a reinforcement, drive position). For the purposes of this review, the strategy was adopted of grouping theories along the lines of how they conceptualize changing or extinguishing established behaviors. Applied-behavior-therapy techniques are designed to emphasize the principle believed responsible for such changes. Therapeutic techniques have already been developed that emphasize the role of excitation and inhibition, counterconditioning, nonreinforced emotional extinction, and changes in cognitive expectancies. It should be noted, however, that these divisions are neither mutually exclusive nor all-inclusive.

Excitation and Inhibition Models of Behavior Change

Concepts of excitation and inhibition play both a historical and a contemporary role in theory development. Under this heading, only Pavlov's classic theory is discussed here, but it should be noted that Hull's theory can also be labeled an excitation–inhibition model.

Pavlov's Physiological Theory of the Cerebral Cortex. Pavlov's (1927) theory was one of the first major approaches to have an impact on both the learning and the behavior therapy fields. He viewed conditioning as a function of cortical extinction and cortical inhibition. According to this position, when a "neutral" stimulus (for example, a tone) is presented to a subject, the afferent stimulation elicited by the tone produces an excitatory process at some definite point in the cortex. At the point of cortical stimulation, the excitatory process is believed to spread gradually over the entire sensory area. The intensity of the spreading effect or "irradiation" of excitation is hypothesized to decrease as the distance from the point of origin increases. With the onset of the UCS (for example, shock), this process is repeated, but at a different point in the cortex. Because of the differences in intensity, the irradiation is considered greater for the UCS than for the neutral stimulus. Following repeated presentations of the neutral stimulus and the UCS (CS–UCS pairings), the cortical stimulation elicited by the tone is expected to gravitate toward the stronger cortical stimulation of the shock until the locus of the neutral stimulus is of sufficient intensity to elicit a CR.

According to Pavlov, one can reduce the strength of the CS by presenting it in the absence of the UCS (extinction). Under these conditions, the cortical process of excitation is changed to inhibition, which like the pre-

vious excitation irradiates to the surrounding region of the cortex. The assumption is further made that when the elicitation of either cortical excitation or cortical inhibition occurs, the surrounding areas of the cortex concurrently produce the opposite process. Borrowing a term suggested by E. Hering and C. S. Sherrington, Pavlov called the effect "induction." Excitation in one area of the cortex leads to increased inhibition in another area (negative induction), while inhibition is believed to lead to increased excitation (positive induction).

Implications. Pavlov was the first and one of the few classical theorists to extend his model to explain psychopathology. He reasoned that when cortical irradiation of the inhibitory process is extreme, the resultant effect is sleep, while extreme excitation is believed to produce alert, active behavior. A functional breakdown leading to psychopathology can occur with the active clashing of the excitatory and inhibitory processes or with the presentation of intense stimulation. According to this model, such excessive cortical excitation or inhibition can result in symptoms such as hysteria, neurasthenia, depression, mania, and catatonia.

Pavlov's theory inspired a number of applied behavior therapists, most notably Andrew Salter (1949, 1965), who developed his conditioned-reflex therapy. For Salter, the neurotic individual is suffering basically from an excess of inhibition, thus blocking his or her normal output of excitation. Therapy is therefore designed to encourage the patient to express feelings directly. Wolpe's (1958) "assertive" response approach represents a very similar technique and conceptualization.

However, learning theorists long ago abandoned Pavlov's theoretical thinking, partly because of the lack of direct experimental support and partly because neurophysiologists are committed to the concept of synaptic transmission of neural impulses. Nevertheless, the role of the concepts of excitation and inhibition have been incorporated into other more modern theories, such as those proposed by Hull (1943), by Amsel (1958), and more recently by Rescorla (1969), Rescorla and Lo Lordo (1965), and Rescorla and Wagner (1972).

Counterconditioning Models of Behavior Change

Counterconditioning theories of extinction have held both historical and contemporary interest. Under this heading the classical models of Hull and Guthrie are described briefly, along with Denny's more recent extension of Hullian theory.

Hull's Monistic Reinforcement Theory. Hull (1943, 1952) attempted to synthesize the data obtained from Pavlov's classical conditioning procedure and Thorndike's trial-and-error learning into a unitary concept of reinforcement (namely, drive reduction). Briefly, the theory states that whenever any receptor activity (a stimulus) and effector activity (a response) occur in close temporal contiguity, and this temporal contiguity is closely associated with the diminution of a need (drive reduction), there will result an increment in the tendency of that afferent impulse to evoke that reaction on later occasions. These increments of successive reinforcements are believed to summate to yield a combined habit strength ($_sH_R$), which is hypothesized to be a simple positive growth function of the number of reinforcements received. Motivational variables like drive are believed to interact in a multiplicative manner with habit strength to produce performance ($D \times {_sH_R}$).

Concurrently with the development of excitatory behavior, Hull, like Pavlov, drew on inhibition theory. In brief, the assumption is made that every response, whether reinforced or not, results in an increment of reactive inhibition (I_R), which according to Hull is a primary negative drive resembling fatigue. The magnitude of I_R is considered an increasing function of the rate of response elicitation and the effortfulness of the response. In short, as I_R builds up, the strength of the response just preceding it becomes weakened, a function of the direct incompatibility of the two responses. It follows that since I_R (fatigue) is a drive, the reduction of this state is reinforcing and therefore is capable of strengthening any response that precedes it closely in time. Since I_R leads to cessation of activity, a resting response is conditioned—or more appropriately, *counterconditioned*—to the CS. Hull referred to this latter process as conditioned inhibition ($_sI_R$). The total inhibition in the situation results from an additive combination of both I_R and $_sI_R$. Thus, behavior equals $D \times {_sH_R} - (I_R + {_sI_R})$. With the removal of the UCS (reinforcement), inhibition can exceed the strength of excitation resulting in the extinction or the counterconditioning of the previous learned response.

The implications of the Hullian counterconditioning model of extinction for psychotherapy were first noted by Shoben (1949) and Dollard and Miller (1950), who retranslated existing insight therapy into a learning, reinforcement framework. However, the applied importance of Hullian theory was not fully realized until Joseph Wolpe (1958) extrapolated from the model to develop new behavioral techniques that launched the behavior therapy movement.

Wolpe, borrowing theoretical notions from Hull (1943), Sherrington (1947), and Jacobson (1938), developed the counterconditioning approach of systematic desensitization that is designed to reciprocally inhibit anxiety-eliciting stimulus. He also rekindled interest in assertive training, as well as developing conditioning techniques to reduce sexual inhibition.

Hullian theory, however, may not be the best conceptual framework from which to view Wolpe's reciprocal inhibition therapy. Wolpe interpreted symptoms as avoidance behavior motivated by fear-eliciting stimuli. Although Hull's theory is a general theory of behavior, he never directly applied his theory to the area of avoidance and fear conditioning. Miller (1948) finally made the appropriate extrapolations, but a classical Hullian interpretation of avoidance responding has long since lost the interest of researchers in this area. A recent theoretical extension of Hull's theory that does directly address avoidance behavior has been offered by Denny (1971) and may be found by applied behavior modifiers to be more useful and reflective of the process underlying their techniques.

Denny's Elicitation Theory. Denny (1971, 1976) has offered a counterconditioning model of behavior that stresses concepts like relief and relaxation for the explanation of behavior involving aversive stimuli. In his theory, the removal of a UCS in an established behavior sequence also serves as a UCS or eliciting stimulus for a class of response that is typically antagonistic to the responses that were elicited by the original UCS. For example, in situations that involve aversive stimuli, the removal of these stimuli elicit relief and relaxation, which Denny views as being antagonistic to fear and fear-related behavior. The countercondition effect, then, in turn, mediates approach rather than withdrawal behavior. Relief is a construct that is viewed as essentially autonomic and as occurring almost immediately after the termination of an aversive stimulus. Relaxation is a construct that is viewed as essentially musculoskeletal and as reaching a peak of responding about 2½ minutes after aversive stimulation ends. Relief and relaxation, which make a situation positive and safe, become dominant when the situation is no longer aversive and bring about the extinction of fear-related behavior.

A critical aspect of Denny's elicited-relaxation theory is that relief and relaxation automatically occur when the aversive stimulus is removed or remains harmless. From this model, direct methods for producing relaxation, as used in Wolpe's desensitization procedure, would not be required to produce extinction. Of course, such a procedure should facilitate the extinction procedure. Denny has also suggested that his theory may be useful in explaining the effects of flooding or implosive therapy (Stampfl & Levis, 1967).

Guthrie's Contiguous Conditioning Theory. Guthrie's (1935) theory provides a completely different counterconditioning viewpoint of extinction. According to his contiguity position, all that is necessary for learning to occur is the pairing of a stimulus and a response. Unlike in Hull's theory, reinforcement or reward does not strengthen the learned connection. Rewards are important only in that they change the stimuli or the situation so that no new response can be associated with the previous stimulus. In other words, a reward removes the organism from the stimulus to which the response was conditioned, thus ensuring that unlearning will not take place. The best predictor of learning is the response in the situation that last occurred. According to

Guthrie, learning is permanent unless interfered with by new learning. Therefore, from this model, extinction always occurs as associative inhibition (i.e., through the learning of an incompatible response).

To weaken activities (S–R connections) or remove undesirable behavior, Guthrie suggested three approaches. The first technique involves a gradual stimulus–approximation approach, in which one introduces the stimulus that one wishes to have disregarded, but only in such a faint degree that it will not elicit a response. For example, if a person is afraid of a dog, one could introduce furry objects such as stuffed dogs, then pictures of dogs, then a very small dog, etc.

The second method is to repeat the stimulus until the original response is fatigued and then to continue the sequence until new responses to the signal are learned. For example, if one is afraid of tall buildings, she or he should repeatedly climb the stairs to the top of a tall building until fatigue and exhaustion counteract the fear behavior (a point similar to Hull's prediction).

Finally, Guthrie suggested that behavior can be changed by presenting the stimulus that elicits the undesirable response but then inhibiting the response by presenting a stronger stimulus that elicits an incompatible response. For example, one can let an exhibitor expose himself in the stimulus situation that elicits such behavior and then shock him prior to sexual arousal.

The implications of Guthrie's suggestions for applied behavior change are apparent, but his model in this context has unfortunately been neglected. It clearly deserves more attention.

Behavior Change via Emotional Extinction

It should be noted that *all* major learning positions predict that nonreinforced (UCS absence) presentation of the CS will result in extinction or the unlearning of a previous conditioned response. This is true whether the behavior in question be overt-motor or emotional. As has already been seen, differences exist at a theoretical level about whether the underlying extinction process is facilitated by inhibition, counterconditioning, or simple weakening of the previous response. The major position described in this section was proposed by Mowrer (1947, 1960), who emphasized the principle of CS exposure in the unlearning of emotional responses, which in turn leads to the extinction of overt behavior. As will be seen, Mowrer's model and the existing extensions by Eysenck and Stampfl and Levis are believed to have important theoretical implications for our understanding and treatment of psychopathology.

Mowrer's Two-Factor Theory of Avoidance. Although Mowrer (1947) was influenced by Hull, he broke away from a one-factor or monistic reinforcement position because of the awkwardness Hull's theory in handling problems associated with avoidance learning. For Mowrer, avoidance learning involved two types of learning: one based on the procedure of classical conditioning, which incorporates only a contiguity principle, and one based on operant or instrumental learning, which includes both a contiguity and a drive-reduction notion of reinforcement. In the typical discrete-trial avoidance paradigm, a CS (e.g., a tone) is presented, say, for a five-second period and is followed by a UCS (e.g., shock). With repeated CS–UCS pairing, fear or anxiety is believed to become conditioned to the CS and is mediated by the autonomic nervous system. The conditioning of fear is simply a result of the above classical-conditioning pairing, with drive reduction playing no part in this learning. Fear is conceptualized as having activation or drive properties that result in energizing or increasing the organism's activity. These activation properties are also elicited by UCS onset, resulting in the organism's escaping the shock. The escape response involves motor behavior that is viewed as being mediated by the central nervous system and reinforced by pain reduction. As fear becomes conditioned to the CS, it also activates motor behavior, which results in a response prior to UCS onset. This response is labeled an *avoidance response* and is believed to be learned because it results in the termination of the aversive CS and in a subsequent reduction of fear, which strengthens the avoidance behavior. For the avoidance behavior to become unlearned, one need only estinguish the fear stimuli eliciting the avoidance behavior. To achieve this objective, all one must do is present the CS in the absence of the UCS (Pavlovian extinction). Nonreinforced CS exposure will result in weakening the fear behavior. Once fear is sufficiently weakened, it will cease to activate the avoidance behavior.

In 1960, Mowrer revised the above two-factor theory and extended it to explain appetitive (approach) as well as avoidance theory. In his new model, Mowrer concluded that all learning by implication was a result of the classical conditioning of internal states. The new version remains "two-factor" only in terms of whether the form of reinforcement is incremental (punishment) or decremental (reward).

Mowrer's 1947 version of avoidance behavior, however, still seems to be the preferred interpretation (see Rescorla & Solomon, 1967). The basic tenets of the model have received considerable empirical support (Brown & Jacobs, 1949; Brown, Kalish, & Farber, 1951; Miller, 1948). Although not free of criticism (Herrnstein, 1969), two-factor theory has survived the test of time and is still considered a very viable explanatory model for infrahuman and human avoidance behavior.

For theorists who view human psychological symptoms as avoidance behavior, Mowrer's two-factor theory provides an initial theoretical framework that has already proved profitable to build on. Two such extensions, which clearly illustrate this point, are briefly described below.

Eysenck's Extension. Concerned with the issues involved in the "neurotic paradox," Eysenck (1968, 1976, 1979) has modified Mowrer's theory to explain clinical observations that appear to contrast with the laws of classical learning theory. Three major areas are addressed in this reformation.

First, an attempt is made to explain why certain classes of phobic behavior are much more prevalent than others. To do this, Eysenck challenged the doctrine of equipotentiality, which states that stimuli that are equated for sensory input should be of equal conditionability when paired with a UCS. He argued that a notion such as Seligman's (1971) concept of "CS preparedness" is required. Briefly, Seligman suggested that certain CSs are biologically prepared to be connected more readily with anxiety responses than others.

Eysenck's second modification centers on his observation that basic personality differences are believed to affect conditionability. This conclusion helps to explain differences among nosologies.

And third, and perhaps more importantly, Eysenck reasoned that if we are to explain why symptoms persist for so long in the absence of UCS presentation, the laws of extinction have to be amended and the law of incubation or enhancement of fear needs to be added.

According to Eysenck's (1979) reformulation of the law of Pavlovian extinction, two consequences may follow the presentation of the CS in the absence of the UCS. First, presentation of the CS alone may be followed by a decrement or an extinction of the CR, which is the law of Pavlovian extinction. Second, and contrary to the position of Mowrer and others, CS presentation in the absence of the UCS may lead to an enhancement of the CR. The implication of this latter statement with respect to fear conditioning is that somehow, exposure to the CS alone can enhance or add new fear to the situation despite the fact the UCS has been removed. According to Eysenck, incubation of the CS is more probable when conditioning involves a drive (emotions), a strong UCS, and short CS exposure periods when the UCS is removed. Eysenck's theory clearly has important implications for those behavior theorists interested in developing a viable conditioning model of neurosis. However, his position has not been free of serious criticism (see the commentaries following the Eysenck, 1979, article).

Stampfl and Levis's Extension. Stampfl and Levis (1967, 1969, 1976) not only have extended Mowrer's two-factor theory to the area of psychopathology but also have suggested the use of a new treatment technique developed by Stampfl called *implosive* or *flooding therapy*. In agreement with Eysenck, Stampfl and Levis believe that the critical question from a learning position is why human symptoms (avoidance behaviors) resist extinction for such long periods of time in the absence of any real danger. Laboratory examples of extreme resistance to extinction are rare. However, unlike Eysenck, these authors do not believe that two-factor theory has to be so drastically modified by adding such concepts as *preparedness* or *incubation* (see Levis, 1979).

Extrapolating from the laboratory model, Stampfl and Levis see most psychopathology as resulting from past specific experiences of punishment and pain, which confer strong emotional reactions to initially nonpunishing stimuli (classical conditioning). The resulting conditioned stimuli provide the motivational source for developing symptom behavior designed to escape or avoid the source of the conditioned aversive stimulation (instrumental conditioning). Furthermore, the past specific conditioning experiences are believed to be encoded in memory and on recall may function as a conditioned emotional stimulus.

According to Stampfl and Levis, the issue of symptom maintenance is best conceptualized by extending the Solomon and Wynne (1954) conservation-of-anxiety hypothesis to encompass complex sets of conditioned cues, ordered sequentially in terms of their accessibility and aversive loadings. Briefly, Solomon and Wynne postulated that exposing an organism to a long CS exposure results in an increase in fear level because of more CS exposure, and that on subsequent trials, such an increase in fear could recondition the avoidance response, resulting in shorter latency responding. Furthermore, the more short-latency avoidance responding that occurs, the less CS exposure experienced and the greater the conservation of fear to the unexposed segments of the CS interval.

If the CS interval comprises a series of complex stimuli that differ on a stimulus dimension from the preceding set, then such conditions should greatly enhance or maximize the conservation-of-anxiety principle. Therefore, from this analysis, the onset of environmental stimulus-eliciting symptoms for human clients is believed to represent only the initial part (S_1) of a chain of stimuli being avoided (S_2, S_3, S_4). As noted earlier, many of these avoided stimuli are assumed to be encoded in memory and capable of functioning on exposure as higher-order, conditioning stimuli. As S_1 is extinguished, S_2 is released from memory, markedly increasing the level of fear and resulting in the reestablishment of avoidance responding to the S_1 segment. As long as the organism is capable of protecting itself or controlling the amount and duration of CS exposure through avoidance behavior, extinction will be retarded considerably (see Levis & Boyd, 1979; Levis & Hare, 1977).

For human symptoms to extinguish, all that one need do is to extinguish the emotional response by presenting the total CS complex in the absence of the UCS. Since the UCS is believed to be long since removed, all that is required is to present an approximation of the CS. Thus, like Pavlov, Hull, and Mowrer, Stampfl and Levis argued that extinction is a direct function of nonreinforced CS exposure, which is the main principle on which the implosive or flooding technique is based.

Extension to Conflict Theory. Fear theorists are drive theorists and thus are cognizant that more than a single drive may be present in a learning situation. If the drive states elicited result in the simultaneous arousal of competitive tendencies, then conflict is said to exist. Miller (1959) has studied this problem extensively, and Dollard and Miller (1950) have provided numerous examples illustrating the important role that conflict plays in the development and maintenance of psychopathology. Since human learning can be motivated by more than a single drive, it is likely that psychopathology involves conflict-learning paradigms that are more complex than that suggested by the simple avoidance model. Levis and Hare (1977) outlined four possible conflict paradigms that may be directly related to the development of psychopathology.

Interaction of Fear and Hunger Drives. The hunger drive and the strong responses it excites may pave the way under certain circumstances for important learning, especially in childhood developmental patterns. As Dollard and Miller (1950, p. 132) pointed out, if a child is repeatedly left to "cry itself out" when hungry, the child may learn that no matter what it tries, it can do nothing that will alleviate the painful experience of hunger. Such training may lay the basis for apathy or helplessness, the behavior of not trying to avoid when in pain (Seligman, 1975). Furthermore, if an intensive hunger develops, the responses involved can attach fearfulness to situational cues like the bedroom, darkness, quietness, being alone, or the absence of the parents. An approach—avoidance conflict may develop between two primary drives (hunger and externally induced pain) if the child cries when hungry and is subsequently punished for crying or is directly punished for certain eating behaviors that meet with the displeasure of the parents. Thus, by pitting two drives against each other, the desire to eat and the fear of being punished for eating, the resulting conflict can heighten fearfulness and the conditionability of situational cues associated with the stressful situation.

Interaction of Fear and Sex Drives. Probably no other primary drive is so severely inhibited in our society as sex. Research has indicated that the sex drive can produce positive reinforcement effects early in life. For example, Kinsey, Pomeroy, and Martin (1948) concluded that small boys acquire the capacity for orgasm long before they become able to ejaculate. Yet, many parents view such reinforcement as "nasty," "dirty," and "evil." Even in the present "enlightened" age, it is not uncommon for parents to inhibit their childrens' sexual play by directly punishing such behavior or threatening to administer punishment, such as cutting off the penis, if the undesired behavior reoccurs. It is also not uncommon for parents to create an approach—avoidance conflict by directly stimulating their children sexually and then punishing the child's response. It is little wonder that sexual inhibitions play such an important role in the development of many cases of psychopathology. Since sex is a relatively weak primary drive, a frequent learned response is to remove the conflict and guilt associated with the response by the avoidance (repression) of sexual feelings and thoughts. Such conflicts frequently reemerge in adult life, when society partially removes its taboos and places strong pressure on the individual to be active in this area.

Interaction of Fear and Positive Reinforcing Drives Labeled "Affection" or "Love." Stimuli made contingent on positive reinforcement can acquire the capacity to elicit a positive emotional response in the same manner as described for stimuli conditioned to elicit negative affect. To describe an individual as feeling good emotionally, or as having a feeling of well-being and of security, is to say in learning terms that environmental and internal cues previously conditioned to produce positive affect are currently being elicited. A decrease in the positive emotional state experienced is considered a direct function of eliminating or reducing the cues eliciting the positive affect. This is true whether they are labeled *conditioned* or *unconditioned* stimuli. If the loss of positive affect is of sufficient magnitude, the experience generates a negative emotional state resulting in the aversive conditioning of those situational cues correlated with the reduction in stimulation of the positive affective cues. Depending on the individual's previous conditioning history, such a sequence of events can elicit additional cues (thoughts, images, memories) representing similar conditioning sequences. The resulting compounding of negative affective stimuli can generate the strong negative emotional states frequently described by clinicians as representing feelings of guilt, worthlessness, and depression (Stampfl & Levis, 1969).

Thus, goal-directed behavior designed to elicit a positive emotional state may become inhibited because of the presence of previously conditioned stimuli that were associated with a reduction in the positive emotional state (e.g., rejection). The presence of such aversive stimuli may result in the anticipation that such negative consequences may occur again if the positive goal-directed behavior is carried out. This, in turn, should result in an inhibition of such behavior in an attempt to avoid the possible ngative outcome. Whether such behavior is engaged in depends on the conditioning and the motivational strength of the two sets of approach–avoidance stimuli (Miller, 1951). For a fairly typical conditioning sequence depicting the above process and believed to reflect a common childhood occurrence, the reader is referred to an article by Stampfl and Levis (1969).

Interaction of Fear, Anger, and Frustration Drives. As previous models have suggested, the excessive or severe use of punishment as a behavioral controller leads to the conditioning of fear to previously nonfearful stimuli. Punishment can also have the effect of inhibiting ongoing, goal-directed behavior. The blocking of such responses frequently creates a state of frustration, which has been shown experimentally to lead to an increase in drive

(anger) and to behavior labeled as aggression (Amsel, 1958). The affects of the interaction of these two emotions (fear and anger) on the development of psychopathology are well documented in the clinical literature. It is not surprising that Dollard and Miller (1950) concluded, "Lift the veil of repression covering the childhood mental life of a neurotic person and you come upon the smoking responses of anger" (p. 148).

The conflict resulting from the interaction of fear and anger frequently leads, in theory, to behavior best described in the context of a multiprocess approach–avoidance paradigm (see Stampfl & Levis, 1969). The first stage consists of conditioned anxiety's being associated with cues correlated with a desired approach response. This is achieved by pairing the goal-directed response with punishment (pain). Because the goal-directed behavior is thwarted, frustration is elicited, in addition to pain, and may lead to aggressive behavior. Especially in the case of children, such aggressive tendencies are usually followed by more punishment, inhibiting the aggressive responses. With sufficient repetition of the above sequence, aggressive responses will, in turn, become inhibited by conditioned anxiety.

By channeling the aggressive behavior into internal cues involving thoughts, images, or ruminations concerning the punishing agent, a partial discharge of the anger response can occur. However, if the punishing agent is a source of considerable positive primary and secondary reinforcement, such as in the case of a mother who plays a protective, nurturant role, the stage is set for an additional conflict. By the child's harboring aggressive impulses toward such a figure, the strength and positive reinforcement obtained from viewing the mother as a supportive, loving figure is decreased.

The above conflict can be resolved by avoiding (suppressing) the aggressive fantasies and responses associated with the aggressive behavior. Such behavior is engaged in so as to avoid diminishing the positive reinforcement associated with the child's conceptualization of the punishing agent and to reduce additional secondary anxiety (guilt) over expressing the internal aggressive cues. If the avoidance pattern is not completely successful in removing the conflict, defense mechanisms such as displacement, reaction formation, and projection may develop. A depressive reaction is also believed to be a frequent outgrowth of such conditioning sequences.

Depression can play added functional roles in that the self-punitive effects of the reaction may help reduce the secondary anxiety of guilt as well as setting the stage for the attainment of positive responses from the punisher or other individuals (secondary gain). Furthermore, such conditioning experience usually leads to a decrease in assertive behavior in an effort to avoid increasing the probability of additional conditioning trials.

The above four conditioning models are only suggestive of some possible interactions that can occur to produce symptoms. Clearly, the models are speculative in nature and in need of scientific evaluation at the human level of analysis. Yet, such speculation may prove to be useful in determining directions in which therapy might proceed.

Cognitive Models of Behavior Change

Historically, cognitive models of learning have not been popular with those who hold an S–R, behavioristic viewpoint. Issues of contention have largely focused on the lack of theoretical precision and parsimony and on the difficulty of establishing an empirical framework. Nevertheless, cognitive interpretations have become more popular in the recent learning literature and have had a similar impact on the behavior therapy movement. In the following section, Tolman's classic theory is discussed along with some recent contributions.

Tolman's Sign Learning. Tolman (1932) departed from the traditional stimulus–response orientation of conditioning in an attempt to develop a theoretical system that would be applicable to all of psychology. Tolman attempted to integrate into one theory the facts of classical conditioning, trial-and-error learning, and "inventive" or higher learning processes.

According to Tolman, all learning is sign-gestalt learning, or the acquiring of bits of "knowledge" or "cognitions." Sign-gestalts can be conceptualized as consisting of three

parts: a sign, a significate, and a behavior route leading from sign to significate. In Tolman's language a sign-gestalt is equivalent to an expectation by the organism that the sign, if behaved to in such and such a way (the behavior route), will lead to this or that significate.

When signs (certain sets of stimuli) become integrated within the nervous system with certain sign-gestalt expectations, learning occurs. Hypotheses are created and rejected. When one is confirmed, it (the expectation) is learned. Unlearning, or extinction, requires the disconfirmation of a previously learned hypothesis. In Tolman's viewpoint, reinforcement, in the sense of an S–R position, is not essential for learning to occur.

Breger and McGaugh's Informational Analysis. Tolman's theory had little impact on the development of the behavior modification movement, largely because of its cognitive emphasis. Behavior therapy's identity initially resided in its emphasis on changing overt behavior and freeing itself of mentalistic concepts. However, a few earlier attempts were made to introduce cognitive notions into the behavioral movement. Breger and McGaugh (1965), for example, suggested that the problem of neurosis may be better understood by incorporating concepts like information storage and retrieval. From this viewpoint, neurosis is seen as a learned set of central strategies that guide the person's adaptation to his or her environment. Therefore, neurosis is not viewed as symptoms, and therapy is conceived of as involving the learning of a new set of strategies via a new language, that is, a new syntax as well as a new vocabulary.

Rotter's Expectancy-Reinforcement Theory. A cognitive influence can also be found in Rotter's (1954, 1970) "expectancy-reinforcement" theory, which was also designed to provide a different learning framework within which the clinician could operate. Although Rotter was influenced by Hull and others, Tolman's impact is clearly seen in Rotter's position. Behavior for Rotter is goal-directed, and the directional aspect of behavior is inferred from the effect of the reinforcing conditions. An individual's behaviors, needs, and goals are viewed as belonging to a functionally related system. The behavior potential is considered a function of both the individual's expectancy of the goal and the reinforcement value of the external reinforcement. Emphasis is placed on a person's social interactions as opposed to his or her internal feelings as an explanation or criterion for pathology. It is not so much the underlying motivation that needs to be altered or removed according to Rotter as it is the manner in which the patient has learned to gratify needs. The question asked is "What is the patient trying to obtain by a given behavior," rather than "What is being avoided?" Once the answer to this question has been ascertained, the assumption is made that the present mode of responding is viewed by the patient as the best way to obtain the desired goal. In addition, more efficient behaviors for achieving the same goal are either not available in the patient's repertoire or are believed to lead to punishment or the frustration of another need. The task of the therapist then becomes one of manipulating expectancies and reinforcement values in such a way as to bring about new behaviors.

The cognitive viewpoints of Rotter and Breger and McGaugh have provided mainly a framework from which to operate rather than providing alternative behavioral techniques. This point, plus the fact the behavior modification movement initially was in large part a reaction against cognitive, insight-oriented therapies, minimized the influence of any learning-based cognitive positions. However, recently there has been a renewed interest in a cognitive-based behavioral viewpoint that has become a substantial influence within the behavioral therapy movement (Mahoney, 1977). The position that changing cognitions are central to changing overt behavior has led to the development of a variety of new techniques focusing on changing thought processes (e.g., cognitive restructuring, thought stopping, and covert assertion).

S–R-oriented behavior therapists (Levis, 1980; Wolpe, 1978) have been quick to criticize this new development, suggesting that an emphasis on changing cognitions will not only remove the identity of the behavioral movement but result in a return to the less objective, insight-oriented treatment approaches.

Whatever the final outcome of this new debate, cognitive-behavioral modification is here to stay, at least in the immediate future. However, even supporters of this movement should recognize that the theoretical foundations on which cognitive-behavioral modification is based are deplorably weak. What clearly is needed is to update the cognitive-behavioral approach by incorporating the theoretical thinking of modern-day cognitive psychology. An excellent start in this direction has been offered by Bowrer (1978).

Seligman and Johnston's Expectancy Theory. Two other models developed from infrahuman experimentation are worthy of note. Seligman and Johnston (1973) have proposed a cognitive-expectancy model of avoidance conditioning. Avoidance behavior is initially learned via a process of fear conditioning similar to that in the models previously outlined. However, unlike traditional S–R theorists, Seligman and Johnston have argued that once the UCS is removed, fear extinction will be rapid. Yet, they noted that in some cases, avoidance responding is quite resistant to extinction. At the clinical level, this clearly appears to be the normal state of affairs. From their viewpoint, fear has long since extinguished, and what is motivating responding is a cognitive expectancy that if responding is stopped, pain will follow. From this model, extinction results only if the expectancy is changed to one in which absence of responding will not be followed by an aversive consequence. If one extrapolates this model to a therapeutic situation, then the task of therapy is not to extinguish fear-producing cues but to change the expectancies of response-contingent outcomes.

Seligman's Learned-Helplessness Theory. In a related theoretical development, Maier and Seligman (1976) attempted to explain why infrahuman subjects under certain experimental manipulations failed to learn to avoid or escape aversive consequences. This position is referred to as *learned-helplessness theory* and has been extended by Seligman (1975) to explain human depression. Three stages are postulated in the development of learned helplessness. The first stage consists of the organism's receiving information that the probability of the outcome is independent of performing a given response class. The distinction between controllable and uncontrollable reinforcement is central to the theory.

The concepts of controllability are operationally defined within a response-reinforced contingency space. If the conditional probability of that outcome (i.e., reinforcement), given a specific response, does not differ from the conditional probability of that outcome in the absence of that response, then the outcome is independent of responding and, by definition, uncontrollable. On the other hand, if the conditional probability of the outcome, given a specific response, is not equal to the conditional probability of the outcome in the absence of that response, then the outcome is controllable. A person or infrahuman is "helpless" with respect to some outcome when the outcome occurs independently of all voluntary responses.

The critical stage of the theory involves the organism's registering and processing cognitively the information obtained from the contingency exposure in which responding was independent of outcome. This event can be subdivided into two processes for the organism subject to helplessness: (1) learning that a contingency exists concering the independence of responding and outcome, and (2) developing the expectation that responding and outcome will remain independent on future trials. Coinciding with the second stage is a reduction in the motivation (activity) to control the outcome and thus the designation of nonmotivational theory once depression or helplessness is learned. The final stage includes the generalization and transference of the expectation that responding and outcome are independent of new learning situations. The behavioral outcome of this generalization is referred to as the *learned-helplessness effect* or *depression*.

Abramson, Seligman, and Teasdale (1978) have extended Seligman's earlier position to include attribution theory. They have added to the model the response class of self-esteem, which is considered orthogonal to controllability, presumably being dependent on attributional considerations. For these writers, the expectation of response–outcome performance is regarded only as a sufficient condition for depression. Other factors like physiological and hormonal states, postpartum conditions, chemical depletions, and loss of interest in reinforcers may also produce depression in the absence of expectations of uncontrollability.

From the above discussion of theory and its applied implications, it should be recognized that formal theory aids in the scientist's quest to heighten diversified viewpoints, strategies, and predictions. It should also be noted that many important theoretical models have not been presented here that may at some point also contribute in a significant way to the applied-behavior-therapy movement (see Hilgard & Bower, 1966; Mackintosh, 1974). For example, experimental work on modeling and imitation learning at the infrahuman level stimulated Bandura (1962) to develop and research important principles that have resulted in behavior techniques usable at the human level. As was noted in relation to the value of extrapolating learning principles and paradigms, theory also plays an important role in making a workable and profitable marriage between behavioral science and the application of this knowledge.

Methodological Foundations

The behavior modification movement's reliance on the principles and theories of experimental psychology has also resulted in this field's adoption or acceptance of the validity of certain research strategies. For example, many of the established principles that form the foundation of various behavioral techniques are based on infrahuman or human laboratory research. Furthermore, its identification with experimental psychology has also required that the behavioral movement adopt the methodological principles of the behavioral scientist. Although at times a source of controversy, the acceptance of each of the points of heritage has strengthened and clarified the rationale and commitment of this new applied science. The following section attempts to highlight some of the positive fallout of such a strategy.

Infrahuman Analogue Research

Most of the behavior principles and theories just reviewed were initially and sometimes solely developed from research data that utilized laboratory animals, especially the rat, as subject material. Skepticism naturally arises concerning the applicability of these laws to human behavior, since marked differences are apparent between rat behavior and human's social and verbal development. Nevertheless, many of the principles developed at the infrahuman level have been shown to operate at the human level. It may also turn out that data collected from infrahuman species will prove more useful for generalizing than the vast amount of research now being conducted with humans. If, say, maladaptive behavior is tied to the conditioning of emotional or autonomic responses, and if mediated internal cues such as words, thoughts, images, and memories in the human turn out to follow essentially the same conditioning laws as extroceptive stimuli, the argument for the implications of infrahuman research becomes much stronger. Not only does the rat provide a less complex organism, which may be more advantageous for deciphering basic laws, it is also equipped with an autonomic nervous system not unlike that of the human. Further, animals are expendable and can be used in expermentation that for ethical reasons cannot be carried out on humans. They also have the advantage of being less complex than the human, which increases the probability of isolating basic principles of behavior. In fact, if infrahuman experimentation provides a vehicle for illustration and confirmation of suspected hypotheses about the human, the effort is more than worthwhile.

Despite the various arguments pro and con and the obvious need for confirmation at the human level, the value of infrahuman research in developing other sciences like biology, behavioral genetics, and medicine is beyond debate. And as far as behavior therapy is concerned, animal research has been directly responsible for influencing the development of the applied behavioral movement. Both Wolpe and Stampfl's research with animals was instrumental in developing their respective theories, and Skinner's work with animals has had a profound influence on the operant conditioning approach. Justified or not, these infrahuman findings have given impetus to the development of treatment techniques that previously were undeveloped or unhighlighted. This is certainly no small accomplishment (Levis, 1970a).

Human Analogue Research

Human laboratory or analogue research has also become an ingrained part of the methodological arsenal of the applied behavioral movement. These studies, usually carried out in a laboratory setting with college students, mainly involve studying the fears and avoidance behaviors of nonpatient populations. Cooper, Furst, and Bridger (1969) were one of the first teams to criticize this strategy by suggesting that the treatment of nonclinical fears may be irrelevant to an understanding of treating clinical neuroses. Cooper *et al.* were quite correct then, and unfortunately, the criticism still applies today: too much of the analogue research was and is used by behavior therapists to validate their techniques, a major error of overgeneralization. The naiveté of some behavior therapists in attempting to justify the validity of their techniques without documenting them with clinical populations is disconcerting. Even today, reviews frequently fail to discriminate between research performed with analogue and clinical populations.

Human analogue research, however, has been proved of value as a vehicle for obtaining information about various treatment manipulations, for isolating critical principles of behavior change associated with a given technique, for developing and testing ideas or hypotheses in a controlled setting, for clarifying theoretical issues, and for establishing the validity and reliability of previous findings. The laboratory setting using nonpatient populations is useful because it permits the selection of an adequate sample of homogeneous target behaviors, the equation of avoidance tendencies, the operational definition of independent and dependent measures, and the selection of appropriate control conditions. Such experimental precision is exceedingly difficult, if not impossible, when one is using patient populations (Levis, 1970b).

The value of the analogue population is based on essentially the same strategy that led investigators to study the rat so intensively. Studying less complex sets of behaviors under more controlled conditions may well be more advantageous for deciphering basic laws. This strategy has clearly helped the behavioral therapy movement in isolating and developing important principles in the areas of assessment, treatment, and theory (see Bandura, 1978, an excellent article on this subject).

Patient Research

Perhaps the most important aspect of the behavior modification movement is its continual commitment to objective assessment and scientific analysis. Not only have behavior therapists embraced the methodological techniques developed by behaviorism and experimental psychology, but they have also built on these, adding to the arsenal available to applied scientists. However, more advances in this area are badly needed. Experimental precision is exceedingly difficult to achieve when using a clinical population to assess therapeutic techniques. Anyone who has conducted therapy-outcome research is aware of the numerous problems that continually confront the researcher. Difficulty with administrative interference, cooperation of staff, control over patient selection and drug administration, issues of ethics, and sample size are only a few of the frustrations facing the investigators.

The complexity of the therapeutic interaction also necessitates the use of numerous control groups to deal with such issues as the therapist's skill, experience, commitments, and potential extratherapeutic factors, such as the patient's expectations or uncontrolled demand effects. It is precisely because of this lack of experimental control that outcome research has not even begun to consider the questions raised at the analogue level of analysis. In fact, it is because of the control problem that patient research has not had much of an impact on the scientific community. Appropriate design and statistical techniques for evaluation are readily available, but the issue is one of implementation.

In an attempt to resolve the problem of the large sample sizes required by the traditional between-group analysis, a number of behavior therapists have adopted the philosophy developed by Skinner and other operant researchers of using within-group analysis of small samples. In such a design, each subject serves as his or her own control. Such a strategy has already been proved of value in establishing useful behavioral principles at the

infrahuman level of analysis, and it appears to be the only methodological solution with those populations for whom adequate sample size or homogeneous behavioral patterns cannot be obtained.

However, the use of these designs with humans creates new methodological problems that are not a factor when conducting animal research. For one thing, the within-group analysis of a small sample (ABA design) is based on the assumption that large numbers of subjects are not required if environmental variance can be eliminated or controlled. This kind of control may be readily achieved by using the rat or pigeon Skinner box, but it is almost impossible or too costly to maintain within the clinical setting. For another thing, the experimental manipulation (e.g., reinforcement administration) is free of bias at the infrahuman level because it is usually programmed by an apparatus. At the human level, such manipulations are usually made with the aid of other humans or in the presence of an experimenter. Drug research has overwhelmingly documented the methodological point that such manipulations, unless done on a completely blind basis, can result in subtle communications (suggestive and demand effects) to patients, resulting in the alteration of behavior in the absence of any experimental effect (the so-called placebo effect). Such dangers must be considered when evaluating research of this type.

It should be clear from the above comments that new designs are needed at the applied level that reinforce the feasibility of conducting patient research. Ideally, these designs should permit research on small samples while addressing the issue of control. One possibility that may have merit involves the combination of a between-group design with a within-group analysis. One major difficulty in evaluating any therapeutic technique is the lack of control over how effectively the technique is administered. The therapist's skill and expertise, personality interaction, and suggestive effects are currently allowed to vary, greatly increasing error variance. Control groups can be added to the design, but they are costly and imprecise.

One of the key advantages of the behavioral approaches is that the procedural technique used and the principles outlined for creating behavioral change can be operationalized. However, this is rarely done on a subject-by-subject basis or for that matter even on a group basis. For example, systematic desensitization maintains that for therapy to work, the relaxation response must be dominant over the anxiety response. Implosive therapy argues that therapy will be effective if the cues introduced elicit a high level of anxiety and if extinction of this response results from continual repetition. Error variance would be markedly reduced if the boundary condition of the technique used were established on a subject-by-subject basis. That is to say, the technique administration needs to be monitored by an objective dependent measure.

For systematic desensitization, a measure for relaxation (e.g., EMG) and for anxiety (e.g., GSR) would be needed. For implosive therapy, a measure of anxiety is required. Thus, with appropriate monitoring, it can be empirically established whether the boundary conditions for a given technique were met by the subject. When it has been established that they have been met, a direct correspondence should be achieved with symptom reduction. If symptom reduction does not occur, the principle suggested by the therapy is not effective with the population tested. If the boundary conditions are not met and behavior changes occur, such changes must be attributed to a principle other than that suggested by the therapy.

Because of space limitations, all of the implications of the above design cannot be addressed. But it is the writer's conclusion that only two groups would be required: an experimental group and a nontreated, control-baseline group. With adequate replications, such a design would provide a quantitative index for establishing whether a relationship exists between meeting the boundary conditions of the technique and symptom reduction and for determining whether extratherapeutic factors are effectively operating. Whether or not the above ideas are workable requires testing. But the objective of an economical design is correct, and the future of the clinical areas is dependent on reaching an adequate solution. The behavioral therapy movement is committed to achieving this objective and enhancing scientific rigor.

Epilogue

In a relatively short time, the behavior therapy movement has made many important inroads, which have been achieved largely through the strategy of extrapolating from extensive laboratory research and theory dealing with conditioning and learning principles. As Stampfl (1970) observed:

Research of this nature has yielded relatively precise statements of the relationship existing between critical variables (for example, immediacy of reinforcement and schedules of reinforcements) and behavioral variables. The relatively precise statements of the relationship between critical independent variables and behavioral change makes the task of the applied practitioner a vastly simpler one. When confronted with the problem of what might be tried to modify behavior, the applied operant practitioner has a ready set of behavioral principles that furnish guidelines for the initiation of procedures in relation to the behavioral problem considered. One can hardly overemphasize the advantages that result from the knowledge and confidence provided by the basic behavioral principles established through laboratory research. (p. 103)

Additional attractive features of the behavior modification movement are also apparent. For one thing, behavior therapy is based on principles that are readily observed in everyday experience. Behavior certainly appears to be directed and modified in social cultures by rewards and punishments. As Stampfl (1970) noted, such observations give a strong presumptive face validity to the procedures used. Furthermore, the strength of the approach is reflected in the attitude of those involved in the movement. Behavior therapists are willing to tackle almost any behavioral problem on an empirical basis and to relinquish any preconceptions as to which behaviors are susceptible to change. This refusal to accept *a priori* conclusions on clinical dogma is critical for the field's advancement. Without this attitude, important contributions to the treatment of the difficult behavior problems of chronic schizophrenics, autistic children, juvenile delinquents, and other diagnostic populations might never have been attempted or achieved.

Despite the applied behavioral movement's numerous achievements, many of which are reviewed in this volume, the future holds the promise of even more exciting contributions. These dividends will materialize if the foundations on which the movement rests are not ignored and are continually developed.

References

Abramson, L. Y., Seligman, M. E. P., & Teasdale, J. P. Learned helplessness in humans: Critique and reformulation. *Journal of Abnormal Psychology*, 1978, *87*, 49–74.

Amsel, A. The role of frustrative nonreward in noncontinuous reward situations. *Psychological Bulletin*, 1958, *55*, 102–119.

Bandura, A. Social learning through imitation. In M. R. Jones (Ed.), *Nebraska symposium on motivation*. Lincoln: University of Nebraska Press, 1962.

Bandura, A. On paradigms and recycled ideologies. *Cognitive Therapy and Research*, 1978, *2*, 79–103.

Bekhterev, V. M. *General principles of human reflexology*. Trans. E. & W. Murphy. New York: International, 1928.

Breger, L., & McGaugh, J. L. Critique and reformulation of "learning-theory" approaches to psychotherapy and neurosis. *Psychological Bulletin*, 1965, *63*, 338–358.

Brown, J. S., & Jacobs, A. The role of fear in the motivation and acquisition of responses. *Journal of Experimental Psychology*, 1949, *39*, 747–759.

Brown, J. S., Kalish, H. I., & Farber, I. E. Conditioned fear as revealed by magnitude of startle response to an auditory stimulus. *Journal of Experimental Psychology*, 1951, *41*, 317–328.

Church, R. M. The varied effects of punishment on behavior. *Psychological Review*, 1963, *70*, 369–402.

Cooper, A., Furst, J. B., & Bridger, W. H. A brief commentary on the usefulness of studying fears of snakes. *Journal of Abnormal Psychology*, 1969, *74*, 413–414.

Denny, M. R. Relaxation theory and experiments. In F. R. Brush (Ed.), *Aversive conditioning and learning*. New York: Academic Press, 1971.

Denny, M. R. Post-aversive relief and relaxation and their implications for behavior therapy. *Journal of Behavior Therapy and Experimental Psychiatry*, 1976, *7*, 315–322.

Dollard, J., & Miller, N. E. *Personality and psychotherapy*. New York: McGraw-Hill, 1950.

Eysenck, H. J. (Ed.). *Behaviour therapy and the neuroses*. New York: Pergamon, 1960.

Eysenck, H. J. *The effects of psychotherapy*. New York: International Science Press, 1966.

Eysenck, H. J. A theory of the incubation of anxiety fear responses. *Behaviour Research and Therapy*, 1968, *6*, 309–322.

Eysenck, H. J. The learning theory model of neurosis—a new approach. *Behaviour Research and Therapy*, 1976, *14*, 251–267.

Eysenck, H. J. The conditioning model of neurosis. *The Behavioral and Brain Sciences*, 1979, *2*, 155–166.

Feigl, H. The scientific outlook: Naturalism and humanism. In H. Feigl & M. Brodbeck (Eds.), *Readings in the philosophy of science*. New York: Appleton-Century-Crofts, 1953.

Ferster, C. B., & Skinner, B. F. *Schedules of reinforcement*. New York: Appleton-Century-Crofts, 1957.

Ford, D. H., & Urban, H. B. Psychotherapy. *Annual Review of Psychology*, 1967, *17*, 333–372.

Greenspoon, J. Learning theory contributions to psychotherapy. *Psychotherapy: Theory, Research and Practice*, 1965, *2*, 145–146.

Guthrie, E. R. *The psychology of learning*. New York: Harper, 1935.

Hall, C., & Lindzey, G. *Theories of personality*. New York: Wiley & Sons, 1957.

Herrnstein, R. Method and theory in the study of avoidance. *Psychological Review*, 1969, *76*, 49–69.

Hilgard, E. R., & Bower, G. H. *Theories of learning*. New York: Appleton-Century-Crofts, 1966.

Hull, C. L. *Principles of behavior*. New York: Appleton-Century-Crofts, 1943.

Hull, C. L. A behavior system: An introduction to behavior theory concerning the individual organism. New Haven, Conn.: Yale University Press, 1952.

Jacobson, E. *Progressive relaxation*. Chicago: University of Chicago Press, 1938.

Jones, M. C. The elimination of children's fears. *Journal of Experimental Psychology*, 1924, *7*, 383–390.

Kalish, H. I. Behavior therapy. In B. Wolman (Ed.), *Handbook of clinical psychology*. New York: McGraw-Hill, 1965.

Kazdin, A. E. *History of behavior modification: Experimental foundations of contemporary research*. Baltimore: University Park Press, 1978.

Kimble, G. A. *Hilgard and Marquis' conditioning and learning*. New York: Appleton-Century-Crofts, 1961.

Kinsey, A., Pomeroy, W., & Martin, C. *Sexual behavior in the human male*. Philadelphia: W. B. Saunders, 1948.

Levis, D. J. & Boyd, T. L. Symptom maintenance: An infrahuman analysis and extension of the conservation of anxiety principle. *Journal of Abnormal Psychology*, 1979, *88*, 107–120.

Levis, D. J., & Hare, N. A review of the theoretical rationale and empirical support for the extinction approach of implosive (flooding) therapy. In M. Hersen, R. M. Eisler, & P. M. Miller (Eds.), *Progress in behavior modification, Vol. 4*. New York: Academic Press, 1977.

Lemkow, P. V., & Crocetti, G. M. Vital statistics of schizophrenia. In L. Bellak (Ed.), *Schizophrenia: A review of the syndrome*. New York: Grune & Stratton, 1958.

Levis, D. J. Behavioral therapy: The fourth therapeutic revolution? In D. J. Levis (Ed.), *Learning approaches to therapeutic behavior change*. Chicago: Aldine Publishing Company, 1970. (a)

Levis, D. J. The case for performing research on non-patient populations with fears of small animals: A reply to Cooper, Furst, and Bridger. *Journal of Abnormal Psychology*, 1970, *76*, 36–38. (b)

Levis, D. J. A reconsideration of Eysenck's conditioning model of neurosis. *The Behavioral and Brain Sciences*, 1979, *2*, 172–174.

Levis, D. J. Do cognitive constructs enhance or threaten the survival of clinical behaviorism? In W. W. Tryon, C. B. Ferester, C. M. Franks, A. E. Kazdin, D. J. Levis, & G. S. Tryon, On the role of behaviorism in clinical psychology. *Pavlovian Journal of Biological Science*, 1980, *15*, 15–17.

Mackintosh, N. J. *The psychology of animal learning.* New York: Academic Press, 1974.

Mahoney, J. J. Cognitive therapy and research: A question of questions. *Cognitive Therapy and Research,* 1977, *1,* 5–16.

Maier, S. F., & Seligman, M. E. P. Learned helplessness: Theory and evidence. *Journal of Experimental Psychology: General,* 1976, *105,* 3–46.

Miller, N. E. Studies of fear as an aquirable drive. I: Fear as motivation and fear-reduction as reinforcement in the learning of a new response. *Journal of Experimental Psychology,* 1948, *38,* 89–101.

Miller, N. E. Learnable drives and rewards. In S. S. Stevens (Ed.), *Handbook of experimental psychology.* New York: Wiley, 1951.

Miller, N. E. Liberalization of basic S-R concepts: Extensions to conflict behavior, motivation and social learning. In S. Koch (Ed.), *Psychology: A study of a science,* Vol. 2. New York: McGraw-Hill, 1959.

Mowrer, O. H. Anxiety-reduction and learning. *Journal of Experimental Psychology,* 1940, *27,* 497–516.

Mowrer, O. H. On the dual nature of learning—A reinterpretation of "conditioning" and "problem-solving." *Harvard Educational Review,* 1947, *17,* 102–148.

Mowrer, O. H. Pain, punishment, guilt, and anxiety. *Anxiety.* New York: Grune & Stratton, 1950.

Mowrer, O. H. *Learning theory and behavior.* New York: Wiley, 1960.

Pavlov, I. P. *Conditioned reflexes.* London: Oxford University Press, 1927.

Rescorla, R. A. Pavlovian conditioned inhibition. *Psychological Bulletin,* 1969, *72,* 77–94.

Rescorla, R. A., & Lo Lordo, V. M. Inhibition of avoidance behavior. *Journal of Comparative and Physiological Psychology,* 1965, *59,* 406–412.

Rescorla, R. A., & Solomon, R. L. Two-process learning theory: Relationships between Pavlovian conditioning and instrumental learning. *Psychological Review,* 1967, *74,* 151–182.

Rescorla, R. A., & Wagner, R. R. A theory of Pavlovian conditioning variations in the effectiveness of reinforcement and nonreinforcement. In A. H. Black & W. F. Prokasy (Eds.), *Classical conditioning. Vol. 2: Current research and theory.* New York: Appleton-Century-Crofts, 1972.

Rotter, J. B. *Social learning and clinical psychology.* Englewood Cliffs, N.J.: Prentice-Hall, 1954.

Rotter, J. B. Some implications of a social learning theory for the practice of psychotherapy. In D. J. Levis (Eds.), *Learning approaches to therapeutic behavior change.* Chicago: Aldine, 1970.

Salter, A. *Conditioned reflex therapy.* New York: Farrar, Straus, 1949.

Salter, A. The theory and practice of conditioned reflex therapy. In J. Wolpe, A. Salter, L. J. Reyna's (Eds.), *The conditioning therapies.* New York: Holt, Rinehart & Winston, 1965.

Seligman, M. E. P. Phobias and preparedness. *Behavior Therapy,* 1971, *2,* 307–320.

Seligman, M. E. P. *Helplessness: On depression, development and death.* San Francisco: W. H. Freeman, 1975.

Seligman, M. E. P., & Johnston, J. C. A cognitive theory of avoidance learning. In F. J. McGuigan & D. B. Lumsden (Eds.), *Contemporary prospectives in learning and conditioning.* Washington: Scripta Press, 1973.

Sherrington, C. S. *The integrative action of the central nervous system.* Cambridge: Cambridge University Press, 1947.

Shoben, E. J. Psychotherapy as a problem in learning theory. *Psychological Bulletin,* 1949, *46,* 366–392.

Sidman, M. Two temporal parameters of the maintenance of avoidance behavior in the rat. *Journal of Comparative and Physiological Psychology,* 1953, *46,* 253–261.

Skinner, B. F. *The behavior of organisms: An experimental analysis.* New York: Appleton-Century, 1938.

Skinner, B. F. The operational analysis of psychological terms. *Psychological Review,* 1945, *52,* 270–278.

Skinner, B. F. Are theories of learning necessary? *Psychological Review,* 1950, *57,* 193–216.

Solomon, R. L., & Wynne, L. C. Traumatic avoidance learning: The principle of anxiety conservation and partial irreversibility. *Psychological Review,* 1954, *61,* 353–385.

Spence, K. W. Theoretical interpretations of learning. In C. P. Stone (Ed.), *Comparative psychology.* New York: Prentice-Hall, 1951.

Srole, L., Langner, T. S., Michael, S. T., Opler, M. K., & Rennie, T. A. C. *Mental health in the metropolis: Midtown Manhattan Study,* Vol. 1. New York: McGraw-Hill, 1962.

Stampfl, T. G. Comment. In D. J. Levis (Ed.), *Learning approaches to therapeutic behavior change.* Chicago: Aldine, 1970.

Stampfl, T. G., & Levis, D. J. The essentials of implosive therapy: A learning-theory-based psychodynamic behavioral therapy. *Journal of Abnormal Psychology,* 1967, *72,* 496–503.

Stampfl, T. G., & Levis, D. J. Learning theory: An aid to dynamic therapeutic practice. In L. D. Eron & R. Callahan (Eds.), *Relationship of theory to practice in psychotherapy.* Chicago: Aldine, 1969.

Stampfl, T. G., & Levis, D. J. Implosive therapy: A behavioral therapy. In J. T. Spence, R. C. Carson, & J. W. Thibaut (Eds.), *Behavioral approaches to therapy.* Morristown, N.J.: General Learning Press, 1976.

Thorndike, E. S. *Animal intelligence.* New York: Macmillan, 1911.

Throndike, E. L. *Human learning.* New York: Macmillan, 1931.

Tolman, E. C. *Purposive behavior in animals and man.* New York: Macmillan, 1932.

Tourney, G. A history of therapeutic fashions in psychiatry, 1800–1966. *American Journal of Psychiatry,* 1967, *124*(6), 784–796.

Watson, J. B., & Rayner, R. Conditioned emotional reaction. *Journal of Experimental Psychology,* 1920, *3,* 1–4.

Wolpe, J. *Psychotherapy by reciprocal inhibition.* Stanford, Calif.: Stanford University Press, 1958.

Wolpe, J. Cognition and causation in human behavior and its therapy. *American Psychologist,* 1978, *33,* 437–446.

CHAPTER 3

A Model of Dysfunctional Behavior

W. L. Marshall

Introduction

This chapter represents an attempt to provide a framework for the valuable task of generating problem-specific theories of abnormal behavior, as well as providing a guide for clinicians in their endeavor to identify the factors that control a given difficulty in a particular client. In addition to the obvious practical advantages that derive from explicit attempts to delineate theories, there is the less obvious, but nonetheless critical, benefit of thereby building a more complete science of behavior (Franks, 1969; Yates, 1975).

Science versus Technology

The past decade has seen a concentrated research effort that has produced a substantial technology of behavior change, while ignoring, for the most part, attempts at building theories of human dysfunctions. Of course, this has not always involved a deliberate attempt to eschew a science of behavior, nor has it simply been an unstructured series of investigations. There were practical demands of at

least two kinds that produced this technological orientation. In the first place, there was, and continues to be, a demand to get on with the business of modifying behavior, which could not await the slow growth in theory necessary to generate treatment implications. Second, we needed the technological developments, in both measurement and change procedures, in order to have a basis for generating theories. During the first full decade of the widespread deployment of behavior therapy (the 1960s), claims were made (Eysenck, 1964) for strong ties with general theories in basic psychology (particularly learning theories). The historical value of this general position was to give our arguments and our proposals for treatment a cloak of scientific respectability (London, 1972). Such was the success of behavior therapists that during the past decade they no longer needed this cloak, so that it became possible generally to ignore theorizing and to concentrate instead on technological progress. Again, this was valuable within the context of the time, but we are now in a position to call for a change in strategy away from technology toward a science of behavior.

The value of theory in the development of a science of behavior (in our present case, a

W. L. Marshall • Department of Psychology, Queen's University, Kingston, Ontario K7L 3N6 Canada.

science of abnormal behavior) has been contested (e.g., Arthur, 1971, 1972; Lazarus, 1971; London, 1972), and the claim is made, in particular, that approaches to the modification of dysfunctional behavior should follow a "technological" rather than a "scientific" model. This claim seems to mean that we should amass a body of techniques, which we might then apply directly to problems, without bothering ourselves with generating theories. Indeed, from this perspective, theories are irrelevant. One might reasonably ask, "Who, then, will develop this body of techniques?" The answer to this question appears to be that clinicians will, and that they will do so by drawing on their own experience. There appear to be at least two things wrong with this. In the first place, this is just what clinicians were doing for all those years preceding the advent of behavior therapy, and we are all aware of the unproductive nature of those years. Second, practitioners pointing to the serendipitous discoveries made in the history of medicine in nonscientific ways as evidence for their technological view is a misunderstanding of the context of those findings. Those discoveries were not made in a vacuum. They were made against a background of knowledge (carefully gathered by scientists in a scientific manner) that these scientists had obviously integrated into some, perhaps loosely structured, framework. Without this framework, these lucky observations would have gone unnoticed. Thus, such clinicians do generate hypotheses, even if they are not well articulated. All that a scientific perspective would demand is that similar behavioral hypotheses be clearly defined, and that they be consistent with (or guided by) what might be described as higher-order hypotheses (i.e., theories). It is only by the guided, careful, and continued accumulation of knowledge that the behavioral approach will maintain its status as a progressive scientific movement (Lakatos & Musgrave, 1970).

I hope that this chapter will illustrate the value of identifying, within a general theoretical framework, those influences that guide behavior. For evidence of the contribution to our understanding of abnormal behavior of problem-specific theories, which may be seen as more precise examples of the general

model, I refer the reader to the proposals of Lewinsohn (1974) and Seligman (1975) on depression; Rachman (1977) on fears; Solomon (1977) on addiction; and McGuire, Carlisle, and Young (1965) on sexual deviations. The theoretical propositions of these writers have been subjected to critical experimental analyses that have expanded very considerably our understanding and management of these difficult problem behaviors. Finally, in the philosophy of science, Kuhn (1962), in particular, is contemptuous of the nontheoretical approach that he calls "blind empiricism." Only by building testable theories, Kuhn claims, does science continue to advance knowledge over the long run. Momentary benefits may appear to accrue to the technological approach, but this method tends to stifle the creative aspect of the acquisition of knowledge, which is the cornerstone of understanding.

Macro- versus Microtheories

The goal of outlining a model that encompasses all disturbed human behavior is overly ambitious and is probably of little heuristic value except in the sense of drawing attention to those factors that might be included in a more specific theory concerning a particular behavioral problem. In this regard, two levels of theorizing, or model building, might be distinguished. Theories at the macrolevel, which is where the present model is aimed, attempt to explain how abnormal behavior in general is caused and maintained. To attempt a genuine theory at this level is probably fruitless, not only because of the present limits to knowledge, but also because the range of behavior described as "abnormal" is so broad as to require a seemingly endless list of specific modifiers. The description of these specific modifiers would render a general theory impossible, and we only have to look at the history of the psychology of learning to see the ultimate lack of utility inherent in attempting to formulate detailed comprehensive accounts of all behavior (Bolles, 1975; Hilgard & Bower, 1974). Attempts at explaining all learning within one grand theory led to "misdirected experimentation and bootless theorizing" (Skinner, 1938, p. 426), which finally resulted in researchers turning to a microlevel of analysis. The valuable contribution that a model at the macrolevel can make is to identify the general categories of factors that influence the appearance and continuation of behavior.

The second level of theorizing concerns explanations of specific problem behaviors (e.g., phobias, depression, schizophrenic behavior). These microtheories should be the focus of most work, since the greatest advances in knowledge ought to result from the experimental analyses of precise propositions. This is because these theories can be more specific in details and more restrictive in their range of application, making the job of deriving and testing particular hypotheses easier. Indeed, while macrolevel theories have provided the framework within which behavior modifiers have expressed their views, these models have not themselves received much research attention, nor is it the case that any therapeutic strategies appear to have been generated by grand theorizing. The greatest advances in both experimentation and the development of modification procedures have come about as a result of theorizing at the microlevel. This is not to deny, however, that macromodels can provide a guide for developing more specific theories, and this should be seen as the real value of such proposals. Indeed, the aim of this chapter is simply to identify those sources that may play a role in the development and maintenance of any dysfunctional behavior, rather than attempting to define their specific influence on any particular behavior. In this sense, I will offer a framework or model, rather than a precise theory.

General Assumptions

There is no doubt that elaborating perspectives at each level is valuable, but the greatest value will certainly come from the less ambitious theories. In order to elaborate the present model, I will discuss those events that I deem to be important under three separate categories. However, the distinction between these types of events is somewhat arbitrary, since they always stand in such a reciprocally interactive relationship that to describe them as separate events is artificial. Nevertheless, it is convenient, for the purpose of clarity, to distinguish: (1) external stimuli, from both (2) organismic characteristics and (3) the responses of the individual.

It is as well to keep in mind three general assumptions that will guide my proposals. In the first place, in common with other essentially behavioral theorists, I assume that the distinction between "abnormal" and "normal" behavior is arbitrary and prejudicial, and that there is no qualitative difference (although there may be a quantitative one) between these types of behavior. Sidman (1960), for example, pointed out "that maladaptive behavior can result from quantitative and qualitative combinations of processes which are themselves intrinsically orderly, strictly determined, and normal in origin" (p. 61). Thus, he sees no difference between normal and abnormal behavior in terms of the processes governing their etiology, nor does he see any need to equate "abnormal" with "unlawful" or "disorderly." In this respect, the normal–abnormal distinction is quantitative rather than qualitative. After all, each of us is anxious at times, is depressed now and then, is obsessive in some of our thoughts, is compulsive about some routines, occasionally imagine having the symptoms of some dreadful disease, gets overly excited, becomes confused in our thinking, and so on. We should not, therefore, classify people as abnormal. On the other hand, we should not rush to classify behaviors as abnormal either. Since all of the above mentioned behaviors occur in normal individuals, they may be valuable experiences rather than something to be avoided. Indeed, we cannot do without some degree of anxiety if we want to be sufficiently motivated to function effectively (Matarazzo & Phillips, 1955; Spence, Farber, & McFann, 1956). And finally, the experiences of depression, confusion, and so on may just make us better able to understand others, to tolerate a degree of variability in human behavior, and in the long-run to foster a more compassionate society.

Second, I am persuaded that although environmental experiences play by far the most significant role in the emergence of human behaviors, one cannot disregard the influence of constitutional factors. In this regard, I am in agreement with Frank's (1969) declaration that "abnormal behavior is not regarded solely as a matter of faulty learning: genetic and biochemical factors may also need to be taken into consideration'' (p. 3). To ignore the evidence regarding the influence of these constitutional factors in favor of those that sit more easily with our particular, preferred variables would not only be foolhardy, it would open us to accusations of following blind dogma.

The third assumption I wish to make explicit reflects a generally held conviction that the behaviors to be accounted for within any theory may be manifest at the motoric, the physiological, or the cognitive levels. Therefore, functioning within each of these levels needs to be incorporated within any theoretical framework. As a final point, before elaborating the possible sources of influence on the genesis of dysfunctional behavior, I want to make it clear that while the principle of parsimony directs theorists to limit their propositions to only those necessary to explain behavior, it is becoming increasingly clear that it is foolish to expect one single factor to account for any aspect of human behavior. Indeed, the single-minded pursuit of one causal agent for human difficulties has hindered the advancement of knowledge in this area and has certainly led to a limited approach to treatment, from which we are only now beginning to free ourselves (Marshall, 1981).

External Events

Again, for convenience, I will separate physical from social stimuli, although it is clear that the former often arise as a result of the latter (e.g., parents often deliver punishments and rewards in a tangible physical form).

Physical Stimuli

Many early behavioral theories considered aversive physical experiences the basis of the development of dysfunctional behavior in humans (Watson & Rayner, 1920). These aversive experiences might result from stimuli that innately produce distress or painful responses or from stimuli that signal these events. Although most behavioral theories, which emphasize the role of the physical stimulation, have focused on the occurrence of aversive

events, there is no doubt that the absence of positive physical stimulation (e.g., deprivation of food or affection) plays an important part in the development of abnormal behavior. To their study of mother–infant interactions, Ainsworth and Bell (1967) concluded that those babies who cried less had a greater capacity to tolerate frustration. Those whose patterns were more regular and predictable were those who had received consistently gratifying or interesting attention from their mothers. In a similar vein, Harlow (1958; Harlow & Harlow, 1966; Harlow & Zimmerman, 1959) has shown that a failure to obtain early experience with what he calls ''contact comfort'' can produce quite severe disturbances in the organism's capacity to develop appropriate affectional behaviors.

Sometimes, of course, physical punishment and deprivation from positive stimulation go hand-in-hand. For example, in a survey of a prison population, we (Christie, Marshall, & Lanthier, 1979) found evidence of a high incidence of severe childhood discipline experiences among violent sexual aggressors, where the frequent beatings administered by parents appeared to be inconsistently related to the child's behavior. This evidence points to one of the serious dangers in the use of physical punishment, namely, the disruptive effects on the person punished. Indeed, Skinner (1953) considers many forms of aberrant behavior entirely the result of attempts at punitive control. For example, he pointed out that punishment elicits an emotional response that may very well be incompatible not only with the punished response, but also with any similar responses that we may not wish to suppress. Skinner (1953) gave an example of the effects on the later sexual behavior of a punished child: ''One possible outcome, then, is that punishment for (unacceptable) sexual behavior may interfere with similar behavior under socially acceptable circumstances—for example, in marriage'' (p. 187). Furthermore, individuals who are consistently punished learn to deal with problems by behaving aggressively or punitively themselves (Bandura, 1969), and they often learn quite inappropriate alternative behaviors to avoid punishment (Becker, 1971). Finally, punished individuals may learn to resent authority in general and the punishing agent in particular (Meachem & Wiesen, 1969). Of course, these detrimental effects ensue from the improper administration of punishment and may not occur when it is used judiciously.

In the Christie *et al,* (1979) study of sex offenders, individuals were described by probation officers and Children's Aid staff as having been consistently rejected by their parents. Swanson (1968) also noted a history of family conflict in the childhood of adult pedophiles, while Brancale, Ellis, and Doorbar (1952) found that almost half of their groups of sexual offenders had been severely emotionally deprived during childhood. Finally, while McCord and McCord (1958), in their intensive (5-year close examination) and extensive (20-year follow-up) study of 253 boys and their families, found that criminal behavior in the father and an absence of warmth in the mother were the most significant factors predicting later delinquency, these influences could be offset by consistent discipline and love from at least one parent.

While it is clear that the absence of positive experiences can be harmful, it is also true that the occurrence of positive or desired outcomes can, either deliberately or inadvertently, increase the occurrence of inappropriate behavior (Ayllon, Haughton, & Hughes, 1965; Gelfand, Gelfand, & Dobson, 1967; Rosenhan, 1973). Staff in institutions frequently reinforce passivity and dependence, which serve to make their jobs easier but do not help their patients. Similarly, some schoolteachers, and some early behavior modifiers, have presented positive incentives to children to "be still, be quiet, be docile," rather than encouraging them to be creative and to develop their talents and enjoyment of learning (Winnett & Winkler, 1972). Williams (1959) reported that a well-meaning aunt increased a child's tantrum behavior by offering comfort and attention when the disruptive behavior occurred. Nevertheless, as I mentioned, most behavioral theories have emphasized the effects of aversive stimulation on the development of behavioral abnormalities.

In Dollard and Miller's (1950) account of neurotic behaviors, primary noxious drives, such as pain, form the basis of the acquisition of secondary noxious drives, such as fear.

When any of these primary or secondary drives arise, they impel the individual to seek relief, and any response that brings relief is then said to be reinforced by the reduction of the aversive drive state. Within this drive-reduction theory, cues, which were associated with the occurrence of the primary drive (pain), subsequently serve to signal the imminent occurrence of the painful experience, thereby initiating the secondary drive (fear), which triggers an avoidance response. In this way, the individual avoids any contact with the anticipated painful situation, so that even if things change and the cues evoking the secondary drive no longer actually precede pain, the individual, by her or his avoidance of the situation, will never find this out. Thus, Dollard and Miller were able to account for the persistence of neurotic behaviors even though they appear to be self-defeating.

This position, in various forms (e.g., Eysenck & Rachman, 1965; Mowrer, 1947), is called *two-factor theory,* because it posits two processes leading to persistent neurotic behavior. The first process is said to be an instance of classical conditioning, whereby previously neutral stimuli acquire fear-evoking properties. The second process concerns instrumental learning and specifically involves the avoidance of the situation, which is said to be triggered by the conditioned fear-evoking stimuli. To take an example of this type of theorizing, let us consider Wolpe and Rachman's (1960) analysis of Freud's famous case of Little Hans. Hans was brought to Freud's attention because he had developed a fear of riding in streetcars, which were pulled by horses at that time in Vienna. According to Wolpe and Rachman, the single most salient event related to the development of this fear occurred when Little Hans's nurse took him for a ride on a streetcar and the horse bolted. No doubt the short but hectic ride terrified everyone, including Hans. Wolpe and Rachman claimed that subsequently, the previously neutral stimuli (i.e., streetcars and horses) associated with this experience (i.e., terror) evoked strong anticipatory fear in Hans and came to haunt him sufficiently so that he could no longer even think of streetcars without considerable distress. His subsequent refusal to ride the cars meant that he could not relearn that the probability of such an unpleasant experience was extremely low.

The two factors in this account of phobias, then, are (1) the conditioned emotional response (i.e., Little Hans's fearful response to the streetcars) and (2) the avoidance behavior (i.e., his refusal to ride on streetcars). These two factors are said to be interrelated (Eysenck & Rachman, 1965; Miller, 1951; Mowrer, 1939, 1950; Solomon & Wynne, 1954). On the basis of contiguity (classical conditioning), the organism learns that a previously neutral stimulus (e.g., a streetcar) predicts an aversive experience (e.g., terror), and consequently, the individual comes to fear that stimulus (i.e., the streetcar). This fear gives rise to attempts to escape or avoid the stimulus, which, when successful, are reinforced by fear reduction (instrumental learning). This avoidance behavior removes the organism from the possibility of learning that the feared stimulus no longer predicts the occurrence of an aversive event, and so the phobia is "protected" from extinction.

This account of the etiology of Little Hans's neurosis seems sensible and appears to explain the behavior in question. However, it is important to note that not all behaviors appear to be acquired in just this way, and not even all phobics have such experiences (Donelson, 1973). Furthermore, subsequent evidence from animal laboratories appears to have seriously undermined the comprehensive utility of this two-factor theory (Hernnstein, 1969; Rachman, 1976; Rescorla & Solomon, 1967). However, there has been, and continues to be, a determination on the part of some theorists to see conditioned anxiety as the basis for all neuroses (see, for example, Wolpe, 1958, 1969, 1979).

In an attempt to substantiate their claim that all but three innate fears (fear of sudden loud noises, loss of support, and pain) are acquired by a process of classical conditioning, Watson and Rayner (1920) induced a fearful response in a previously fearless infant. Prior to the conditioning phase, the infant showed pleasurable responses to a white rat. At subsequent presentations, the appearance of the white rat immediately preceded the occurrence of a sudden loud noise to which the infant showed a fear response. After seven such pairings, little

Albert, as the infant was known, showed anticipatory fear of the white rat and of some other similar objects.

Although Waston took this study to support his position, it is more accurate to say that it demonstrated that fears can be acquired by conditioning. While some subsequent research has supported the notion that conditioning experiences may induce fears of previously neutral stimuli (Campbell, Sanderson, & Laverty, 1964; Jones, 1931; Keltner & Marshall, 1975; Moss, 1924), other researchers have found it difficult to condition fear to more than a limited range of stimuli (Bregman, 1934; English, 1929). Seligman (1971) has taken this and other evidence to indicate that organisms are biologically predisposed to develop fear reactions to certain stimuli and not to others. While this elaboration by Seligman is essential to the survival of a conditioning theory of fears, such a theory, even in this modified form, still cannot account for the full range of human fearfulness, and even some of its direct predictions have not been upheld (de Silva, Rachman, & Seligman, 1977; Ohmann, Fredrikson, & Hugdahl, 1978; Rachman & Seligman, 1976). Furthermore, this theory—and in particular, Seligman's (1971) and Gray's (1971) interpretations of the early failures to replicate Watson and Rayner's study—have come under attack by Delprato (1980). In this particularly incisive analysis of the evidence, Delprato shows that a learning interpretation may be a more parsimonious account of these findings, and that such an analysis may also apply to the "taste aversion" literature (Garcia, Hankins, & Rusiniak, 1976; Garcia, McGowan, & Green, 1972; Revusky, 1968), which has heretofore been considered clear evidence of the evolutionary basis of aversions.

It is clear that traumatic experiences do occasionally provide the basis for the development of phobias and anxieties, but it is also equally clear that many fears are acquired without a direct frightful experience, and that some occur even in the absence of direct contact with the feared object (Rachman, 1977). Eysenck (1968, 1976) has suggested an important modification of the conditioning argument, allowing for the possibility that exposure to highly arousing stimuli may sometimes result in an acquired emotional response or its exacerbation, while under other circumstances such exposure may lead to the extinction of these responses. These differential effects are said to be the result of the duration of exposure, with brief encounters producing, or enhancing, fear, while prolonged exposures result in the elimination of the unpleasant emotional reaction. However, even in this modified form, a conditioning theory requires firsthand experience with both the feared object and the emotional reaction to it. Bandura (1969) has pointed to the role of vicarious experiences in the acquisition of learned fearfulness, and this leads us directly to a consideration of the role of social stimuli.

Social Experiences

There are two sets of social experiences that directly affect behavior and may therefore be relevant to our understanding of dysfunctional responses: (1) the acquisition of information and (2) social learning that results from exposure to other people.

Information Acquisition. This term refers to any process whereby the individual is exposed to material that may increase his or her store of knowledge or modify his or her present attitudes, beliefs, etc. Whether this process is formal (education, religious instruction, or therapy) or informal (remarks of friends, private reading, exposure to television, etc.) does not seem to matter as much as the manner in which the material is presented, the perceived character of the instructor, and the consequences associated with participation in learning. In any case, inadequate informational learning may result in an individual being unaware of the behavior expected in certain situations, or he or she may have acquired attitudes, beliefs, etc., that stand in the way of behaving appropriately.

It has been found (Rutter, Yule, Tizard, & Graham, 1966), for example, that failure to acquire adequate reading skills is related to a higher incidence of delinquent behavior in young people, and one can readily see that educational deficiencies would reduce the individual's capacity to succeed by legitimate means. Many individuals are said to be deficient in the skills necessary to execute essential overt behaviors (Bellack & Hersen, 1977),

and this is particularly obvious in the case of the demands of social interaction. For instance, it has been consistently found that psychiatric patients lack social competence (Hersen & Bellack, 1976; Phillips & Zigler, 1961; Zigler & Levine, 1973; Zigler & Phillips, 1960), and so do inmates in prisons (Marshall, Keltner, & Marshall, 1981). However, it is sometimes presumed that these individuals know what to do but are prevented from doing it by anxiety or some other response-inhibiting factor (Wolpe, 1958). In our studies of prisoners, we found (Keltner, Marshall, & Marshall, 1979) that, not only were these individuals unable to display appropriate behavior in interpersonal situations, they lacked knowledge concerning what was appropriate. They simply did not know what to do!

Of course, not knowing what to do in a situation reduces one's control over that situation, and Mandler (1968) considers lack of control one of the main sources of anxiety. It is clear that control over noxious stimulation reduces subjects' anxiety in an aversive situation (Glass, Singer, & Friedman, 1969), as does knowledge of its intensity and its temporal occurrence (Staub, Tursky, & Schwartz, 1971). Knowing what to do, of course, is not simply a function of having the skills available. We have to know when it is appropriate to emit certain behaviors. For example, I once had a friend who had good delivery when telling rather rude jokes, but he was not a master at distinguishing when he had, or did not have, a receptive audience. It is probably acceptable to tell such a story to a group of men in the bar of a hotel, but it is certainly not appropriate to tell the same story to a gathering of the "Christian Ladies Society for the Abolition of Pornography," nor, perhaps, even to the same group of men, from the hotel bar, when they are at an annual meeting of the board of directors.

Religious training sometimes inadvertently inculcates attitudes toward normal human functioning that may interfere with a person's peace of mind. I reported the case (Marshall, 1975) of a young man whose attitudes toward masturbation, which he saw as conforming to his religious beliefs, made him feel so guilty that he despised himself whenever he gave in to his normal sexual urges.

There is, of course, abundant evidence (Eron, Huesmann, Lefkowitz & Walder, 1972; Leyens, Camino, Parke, & Berkowitz, 1975; Parke, Berkowitz, Leyens, West, & Sebastian, 1977; Steuer, Applefield, & Smith, 1971) documenting the effects of television programs and movies on the aggressive behavior of youngsters, and no doubt these media convey all manner of other disadvantageous behaviors and attitudes (Mankiewicz & Swerdlow, 1977). For instance, while the depiction of the full range of acceptable sexual behaviors appears to exert little or no disadvantageous influence on the individual (Mann, 1974; Wilson,1970), there are reasons for supposing that the depiction of sexual aggression in movies or on television might instigate aberrant behavior. Sexual researchers (Abel, Barlow, Blanchard, & Guild, 1977; Barbaree, Marshall, & Lanthier, 1979) have found that the responses elicited by mutually consenting sex do not differentiate rapists from normal males, whereas their responses to scenes of sexual aggression do.

In all these instances, I am suggesting that formal and informal information sources may fail to prepare the individual appropriately in terms of either the skills necessary to function effectively or the attitudes that facilitate adequate performance. Rachman (1977) claimed that one of the most common means by which individuals develop fears is via "informational and instructional transmission," and this opinion is supported by evidence concerning training certain responses. For example, instructions have been shown to be an essential element in training programs where the target behaviors are complex or somewhat abstract, or when the required responses are not present in the subject's repertoire. McFall (1976) demonstrated that relationships, principles, rules, response sequences, directions, classifications, and other abstractions are taught most efficiently by verbal communication, while other researchers (Edelstein & Eisler, 1976; Hersen, Eisler, & Miller, 1973; Jaffe & Carlson, 1976) have shown that instructions are either sufficient on their own or enhance the effects of modeling in teaching social skills. So long as the behaviors involved are relatively simple, instructions are sufficient to institute novel responses (McFall & Twentyman, 1973), and although modeling needs to be added for more complex acts, instructions remain an essential element (Voss, Arrick, & Rimm, 1976). A most important informal source of behavior and attitude training concerns the impact of other people in the individual's environment.

Social Learning. I have already noted the effect of physical stimuli on the development of behavior, and I pointed out that some of these physical stimuli might be delivered by other people. In addition to the immediate and long-term effects on behavior of physical punishment or reward delivered by parents, teachers, friends, etc., there is the effect of associating the presentation of such stimuli with praise or condemnation. Subsequently, such remarks come to exercise control over actions in the absence of the physical consequences, and I could write another complete chapter on the role of verbal approval or disapproval in shaping human behavior. However, it is sufficient here to note these influences, and particularly to note the disturbing effects of inconsistent verbal remarks. Trasler (1962) has drawn attention to an extensive literature documenting the unfortunate results of inconsistent discipline and lack of a consistent display of affection on the later behavior of young people. Many of these inconsistencies had to do with the way the parents spoke to their children.

In addition to these effects, humans, along with other animals, learn much of their behavior and attitudes from observing others. I have already noted the influence of vicarious learning via media presentations, so I will focus on the direct influence of exposure to the behavior of others. Bandura and Walters (1963) documented the impact of adult behavior on the subsequent actions of children who observed these adults, and there is evidence that these effects endure (Hicks, 1965). The particular effects that have been highlighted in this research have to do with the imitation of aggressive behavior, and I have noted earlier that violent sexual offenders have aggressive parents. Shaw and McKay (1942) and Glueck and Glueck (1962) observed that most delinquents come from homes where the parents or siblings are delinquent, and Bandura (1973) has demonstrated the immediate effects on children's behavior of observing an aggressive model. In addition to the modeling influences on aggression, however, it appears that other inappropriate behaviors can be similarly acquired. For instance, McConaghy (1959) found that at least one parent of every schizophrenic patient studied showed noticeable signs of disturbed or eccentric thinking, whereas only 6 of 65 parents of nonschizophrenics manifested thinking disorders.

On the other side of the coin, it has also been shown that watching a model cope with a fearful situation can reduce the phobic behavior of an observer (Bandura, Blanchard, & Ritter, 1969). This beneficial use of modeling had been extended to other problem behaviors, such as deficits in assertion (McFall & Lillesand, 1971) and difficulties in public speaking (Marshall, Parker, & Hayes, 1982). Thus, the imitation of others, although sometimes resulting in problem behaviors, may also facilitate the acquisition of positive, constructive action. And finally, although modeling influences are most profound on children, they also affect the behavior of adults (Bandura 1969; Rachman, 1972).

In addition to observational learning, one of the most important social practices affecting behavior concerns the tendency to label behaviors or people. Ullmann and Krasner (1975) elaborated in some detail the various effects of labeling on the behaviors of the person so labeled, and the way in which this labeling changes the behaviors of others toward the labeled person. They pointed out that when a behavior is identified by some expert as deviant, then it is the individual who is labeled rather than the behavior. This labeling influences the expectations that others hold about the individual and, of course, modifies their behavior toward him or her. Ullmann and Krasner gave the example of Thomas Eagleton, who was required to stand down as a vice-presidential candidate because he had, at one time, received psychiatric treatment. Another example, familiar to those who work with sexual deviates, is the hostile response that many people show toward such individuals in the absence of knowing anything more about them except that they once committed a sexual offense.

Not only do others respond according to the label applied to a person, so does the individual himself or herself. Indeed, this self-labeling process (or *attribution*, as it is usually called) has been the focus of considerable research (Bem, 1972), and it is clear that both the individual and others attribute dispositions to the person rather than looking for situational influences on behavior (Ross, 1977). I once saw a young man who had previously been told by an earlier therapist that he was a "latent homosexual." He had never engaged in any homosexual behavior prior to this labeling, nor had he ever even entertained such thoughts. The problem that he sought help for was anxiety evoked by interpersonal contact with females of his own age. In the course of treatment, he told the therapist that his broad-ranging interests included poetry and ballet and excluded physical-contact sports such as football and boxing. These revelations, plus the difficulties with females, apparently persuaded the therapist that his patient was "really" a homosexual. After being told that he was a latent homosexual, this young man, in an attempt to prove to himself that he was *not* a homosexual, attended football and ice hockey games. He found these to be boring and saw this as confirmation of his therapist's opinion. So, one evening after some heavy drinking, he made a bungled effort to approach sexually a man he thought looked "gay." The result was a black eye, a feeling of revulsion, and a conviction that his therapist was a fool. A fortunate outcome, indeed, since it is easy to see how things might have otherwise developed.

Of course, the effect of these social factors, and of all external stimuli, is at least partly a function of how the events are perceived by the individual. Neisser (1967) favors a constructive theory of attention, which suggests that perception is not a function of the passive reception of "stimuli as presented," but an active process that enables the organism to create or distort its input to suit its current internal state. Thus, attentional and perceptual processes—and consequently, the form in which stimuli are actually received—are a function of the internal state of the individual, and it is to these internal states that I now turn.

Organismic Variables

There are many variables within the organism that may affect not only the nature of the input (both directed attention and distorted perception) but also how the input effects the ongoing system and the manner in which the individual evaluates the input. Those factors that affect the input itself, I refer to here as *moderating variables,* while those that have to do with the evaluation of input and the production of responses I describe as *generating variables.* All of these influences determine the way in which the individual reacts to the external world, but again, for convenience' sake, I will consider separately two sets of internal influences on behavior: biological and cognitive factors.

Biological Influences

Genetic endowment sets limits to behavior and provides the organism with certain dispositions that will influence the reaction to external stimulation. For example, a large number of studies, despite the methodological limitations of some of them (Gottesman & Shields, 1976), have nevertheless shown a consistently higher-than-expected concordance for schizophrenic behaviors in the relatives of individuals diagnosed as schizophrenic (Berheim & Lewine, 1979). On the other hand, it cannot be said that there is any satisfactory evidence for a genetic basis to those problems described as *neuroses* or *personality disorders* (Greer & Cawley, 1966), although research points to a heritable factor in depressive behaviors (Fuller & Thompson, 1960; Shields & Slater, 1961; Stern, 1960). Of course, as noted earlier, Seligman (1971) has proposed that biological dispositions, shaped by evolutionary forces, determine which fears and phobias will result from conditioning experiences. Seligman's position would suggest that the typical strategies for evaluating a genetic contribution to fears are mistaken, and his conviction that there is a significant evolutionary

character in these inherited dispositions is shared by Gray (1971).

Given our knowledge of the transmission of heredity and the manifold possible arrangements of constitutional factors, it ought not to surprise anyone that genetic endowment influences behavior. However, even a casual inspection of the available data indicates that a genetic explanation alone cannot account for the incidence of even schizophrenic behavior. Environmental experiences, such as occur pre-, peri-, and postnatally, may also set limits on behavior. For instance, Hirsch and Spinelli (1970) and Blakemore and Cooper (1970) showed that the nature of the environment in which young kittens were raised affected not only their later behaviors but also the brain structures underlying their behavior. Clearly, environmental or other individual factors interact with whatever genetic disposition is passed on to individuals, and these nongenetic variables may very well be the most important influence on behavior. Indeed, even where constitutional disadvantages are clearly present, there is very often little that can be done, given present knowledge, to directly change these aspects of the individual. Direct manipulation of the environment, or training the individual in particular skills that will allow him or her to cope with inherited disadvantages, seems to be the only recourse that therapists have. The successful modification of retarded individuals' behavior (Birnbrauer, Wolf, Kidder, & Tague, 1965; Neuhaus, 1967; Whitman, Mercurio, & Caponigri, 1970) bears witness to both the benefits of the environmentalist approach, even where the causation is biological, and the errors of supposing that because limits are imposed biologically, they are therefore immutable. Ogden Lindsley (1964) has put this latter point quite clearly: "Children are not retarded. Only their behavior in average environments is sometimes retarded. In fact, it is modern science's ability to design suitable environments for these children that is retarded" (p. 62). Finally, the recent successful incursion of behavior therapists into tradiional medical areas adds further evidence of the value of such an approach to problems having a clearly organic basis (Katz & Zlutnick, 1975).

Of course, the evidence testifying to the

benefits gained by manipulating external variables, even where these external factors were not the causal agents, should not lead one to conclude that biological influences are irrelevant and can safely be ignored. This position is all too commonly accepted as the proper stance of the behavior therapist, and yet to do so is to ignore factors that may contribute to the sensible choice of treatment procedures.

One of the preeminent researchers in the area of chronic anxiety, Malmo (1975), has elaborated a theory that implicates various factors in the development and maintenance of anxiety neuroses. Lader (1969) had already established that the physiological regulatory mechanisms are defective in patients suffering from chronic anxiety, and Malmo and his colleagues (Malmo & Shagass, 1949; Malmo, Shagass, & Davis, 1950) showed that these disruptions resulted in exaggerated responses to stimuli. Anxiety neurotics, compared with normal controls, overreacted to stimuli, showing a greater immediate muscle tension response that was also far more prolonged. Indeed, this heightened muscle tension remained above baseline levels for as long as the subject was exposed to the stimulus.

Malmo suggested that prolonged stress produces this chronic loss of regulatory control over muscle tension responses to stimulation, so that any and all stimuli elicit these exaggerated responses. Of course, an equally reasonable argument might be that such overreactivity was an inherited feature of some of these individuals, and Eysenck (1957, 1960) has persistently maintained that constitutional differences in autonomic-nervous-system functioning predispose individuals to neurotic disorders. Eysenck claims that the combination of an inherited overly labile emotional system (which he calls "neuroticism") and an autonomic nervous system that is readily conditionable ("introversion") markedly increases the likelihood that an individual will become neurotic. Environmental stress does, of course, play an important role in Eysenck's theory. The effects of prolonged or traumatic stress interact with these constitutional factors, so that when the inherited disposition is marked, only minimal stress is required to precipitate a breakdown. On the other hand, even in the absence of a biological proclivity, severe or prolonged stress will initiate an anxiety attack that may persist.

Malmo suggested that this prolonged state of muscle tension produces an excess of lactic acid in the blood. It is well known, for instance, that during physical exercise, when muscle fibers contract (as they do in chronic muscle-tension states), large quantities of glycogen are converted to lactic acid, which diffuses into the blood. Malmo reported studies showing that blood lactate is higher among chronic anxiety patients than among normals, and Pitts (1969) has shown that injecting patients with lactate induces the symptoms of chronic anxiety (e.g., heart pounding, breathing difficulties, feelings of apprehension). Of course, this theory is not necessarily correct, just because it seems to fit well with the available evidence. It is, however, a readily testable microtheory and does point to the possible interaction (if we allow an integration with Eysenck's theory) of inherited dispositions and environmental experiences in producing a physiologically based, chronic anxiety. As I noted earlier, theories that posit a single factor (be it external environment, a genetic basis, a biochemical disruption, or whatever) as the cause of any disturbed behavior are likely to be either plain wrong or at best very limited in scope. In this respect, Malmo's theory has obvious advantages.

I could elaborate at length on the role of physiological, biochemical, and other similar organismic variables in the genesis of abnormal behavior, but it is sufficient simply to draw attention to their possible influence, so that any theory that ignores these factors may very well be deficient.

In the search for a clue to the basis of schizophrenic behavior, many biochemical proposals have been advanced (Heath, Krupp, Byers, & Liljekvist, 1967; Mandell, Segal, Kuczenski, & Knapp, 1972), with the "dopamine hypothesis" (Meltzer & Stahl, 1976) representing the best fit with current data. I will not detail this particular proposal, but I will point out that I do not think that behaviorists, in their attempts to account for human functioning, can ignore the possibility that biochemical or physiological disruptions affect behavior. Even the design of appropriate treatment strategies can be more accurately determined given a knowledge of these possible disturbances. For example, Pariser, Jones, Pinta, Young, and Fontana (1979) have recently observed cardiovascular irregularities in patients suffering from panic attacks. Such patients often develop a fear of leaving the security of their homes because they are afraid of being away from help should they have an attack. These individuals are usually called *agoraphobics*, and behavioral therapists have had problems in conceptualizing these difficulties in terms that lead to clearly defined treatment programs (Goldstein & Chambless, 1978). Given Pariser *et al.*'s findings, it is possible that some of these patients experience environmentally independent, periodic cardiovascular disturbances that may frighten them sufficiently to make them housebound. The behaviorists' search for external triggering stimuli would be fruitless in this case, and it is perhaps no surprise that agoraphobics have not responded as well to behavioral interventions as other phobic patients. From a knowledge of Pariser *et al.*'s findings, we might conclude that treatment procedures should aim at reducing the patient's fear of the improbable unfortunate consequences that he or she imagines will follow when these cardiovascular irregularities occur. A very similar proposal, guided by somewhat different observations, has been made by Goldstein and Chambless (1980). The point to be made here is that it is unwise to ignore evidence testifying to the role of biological factors in any dysfunctional behavior.

Cognitive Factors

The biological factors that I have discussed may all be understood as influences that modify, in some way, the input received by the individual from the external environment. Moderating variables also include, perhaps most importantly, those influences that are usually described as *cognitive factors*.

I have already noted the sources of information that impinge on an individual, and I have hinted at the influence of attentional strategies on the reception of this information. Constitutional dispostions and disturbed physiological or biochemical systems can likewise change the "stimulus as presented" into a quite different "stimulus as perceived." In addition, the very thinking processes themselves may be disrupted by constitutional defects, biochemical abnormalities, physical trauma, or overarousal, or as a result of the modeling of inappropriate thinking patterns. Individuals diagnosed as schizophrenic, for example, have been shown to manifest quite disturbed thinking, which has been demonstrated (Marshall, 1973) to be due to faulty decision-making rather than faulty reception processes, as was once thought (McGhie, 1969; Payne, 1960). Similarly, Claridge (1967) found that while dysthymic neurotics (patients who display anxiety, phobias, or obsessional or compulsive behaviors) detected significantly more signals in a vigilance task than did normals, hysterics were quite inferior to both other groups, especially as the duration of the task was extended. This finding was taken to indicate a deficiency in concentration, and it is true that many so-called neurotics complain of an inability to concentrate. Of course, the disruptive effects of anxiety on performance are well known (Maher, 1966) and appear to be primarily the result of interference with concentration on the task at hand (Wine, 1971). Thus, anxiety interferes with attentional strategies and therefore moderates input.

Even allowing for these possible distortions of input, the individual nevertheless receives and stores information of various kinds and then evaluates this input prior to responding. Perhaps one of the most important cognitive functions has to do with this evaluation of input, which leads directly to a decision to act in some way. Such evaluations are a function of the individual's history of previous input and the manner in which it was received and evaluated, as well as her or his ability to encode and retrieve this information. Of course, as I noted earlier with respect to schizophrenics in particular, this very process of evaluation and decision making may be disturbed. Similarly, the most important effects of both aging and brain damage involve the encoding of information and its retrieval from memory (Miller, 1977; Nathan, 1967). Excessive anxiety, by the very fact that it disrupts concentration, interferes with information-gathering and -storing processes, as well as with memory.

The evaluation of input results from a comparison with previously stored information, and in particular with the standards and expectations that experience has generated. Miller, Galanter, and Pribram (1960) offered a model suggesting that plans for implementing behavior are a function of the evaluation of both input and possible responses to that input. They proposed that stimulation received by the individual is tested against a standard, and that the individual then generates a response alternative. This response alternative, or plan for action, is then tested against standards for action, and if this evaluation is satisfactory, the response is executed. Miller *et al.* described this procedure as a "test–operate–test–exit," or TOTE, model, and something like this process obviously goes on in problem solving, where there is a considerable range of individual variability (Goldfried & Goldfried, 1975). For example, D'Zurilla and Goldfried (1971) pointed out the importance of problem-solving abilities for effective daily living and noted that many people lack these skills to a significant degree. Those individuals who lack effective problem-solving skills are impulsive and are not persistent in their attempts to overcome difficulties (Bloom & Broder, 1950). The recent movement toward providing training in "life skills" for those who have not successfully participated in the working world (Conger, 1973) appears to be at least partly based on the assumption that these individuals are poor at solving life's continual problems.

One of the consequences of this evaluation process we have been discussing is that the individual must make a decision on how to react. It is well documented that such decision making produces anxiety, the degree of anxiety being a function of the difficulty of the decision. The difficulty of the decision, of course, relates to many things, for example, the individual's skill in discriminating the elements in the situation, his or her experience with success or failure in making decisions, the attractiveness of the alternative actions, and so on. In his now classic studies of parachute jumpers, Epstein (1967; Epstein & Fenz, 1962) demonstrated a progressive increase in anxiety up to the point where the decision to jump was made. For novice jumpers, anxiety increased during the week before

and continued to rise after they boarded the plane, until the "ready-to-jump" signal was given, after which anxiety decreased. The experienced jumpers, on the other hand, showed increases in anxiety up to the morning of the jump, when they made their decision, after which it decreased.

Bandura (1969, 1971) has drawn attention to the importance of standards in this evaluation process. He pointed out that "when behavior falls short of one's evaluative standards, the person judges himself negatively or holds himself in low self-esteem" (Bandura, 1971, p. 258). In this way, performance possibilities are measured against (1) the levels of performance that the individual has achieved in the past; or (2) the perceived level of performance of others; or (3) some ideal standard of possible performance. It is important to note that this evaluative process often occurs in the absence of actual overt behavior. For instance, we often rehearse what we might say or do in anticipation of contact with someone, and by this means, we eliminate various alternatives. Of course, one alternative might be not to proceed at all; that is, we might decide to avoid the situation altogether because we are convinced that we cannot produce behaviors that will satisfy our standards. On this point, Bandura (1977) distinguished between "efficacy expectations" and "outcome expectations." The former refers to "the conviction (or not) that one can successfully execute the behavior required to produce the outcome" (p. 193), whereas outcome efficacy has to do with judgments about whether or not a given behavior will produce certain outcomes.

To illustrate Bandura's point, let us consider someone who has been invited out for supper. If this person is sorely lacking in self-confidence, he or she may refuse the invitation, judging himself or herself to be incapable of producing the required social-interactive behaviors. Sometimes this judgment is accurate, and a course in social-skills training is called for, but more likely, such people are inaccurate in their estimate of their own capability. This may reflect on their ability to monitor themselves accurately, but most importantly, it suggests that they have inappropriate standards for assessing their likely performance. They may misperceive the behavior of others as being superior to their own, or they may determine that their own capacities are less than ideal.

Although having some ideal as a goal to strive toward may not in itself be harmful, it certainly is when failure to achieve such a standard sets the stage for self-denigration and withdrawal. Similarly, it is probably impossible to avoid comparisons with others. Again, such comparisons become a serious problem only when they lead to misery and seclusive behavior. There can be no doubt that the best standard against which to measure one's potential responses is one's own behavior. Even here, the individual is better off avoiding performance criteria that demand improvement in every instance. Overall gradual improvement or maintenance of functionally satisfactory behavior is likely to be the standard that will result in the most personal satisfaction.

Most of this discussion concerning cognitive variables has centered on how we evaluate our prospective behavior. There is, however, another imaginative factor that guides human behavior. This final cognitive influence concerns the very human tendency to engage in reverie or fantasy.

Abel and Blanchard (1974) have documented the role of fantasy in the etiology, maintenance, and modification of deviant sexuality; it is also apparent that fantasy plays an important role in the very evaluation process I have just been discussing. In order to weigh the various alternatives available to me in an imminent interaction, I find it easiest to play out in imagination the whole behavioral sequence relating to each alternative, and it is clear from the evidence available that others do the same. Beck (1970) and Singer (1972) have amassed evidence indicating that in a broad range of activities, humans characteristically engage in extensive "mental practice" before actually committing themselves to a particular overt behavior. Similarly, both Mahoney (1974) and Suinn (1972) have demonstrated that successful athletes prepare themselves for action by imagining themselves completing a flawless performance. These processes are usually helpful, but at times they are not. For instance, when entering a stressful situation, the individual may visualize himself or herself as failing to cope, which has the effect of exacerbating the difficulty. Such imagining is not useful.

Fantasizing deviant sexual behavior is an obvious example of self-induced arousal that may be dangerous to the individual or others, and there are other clear-cut instances of such disadvantageous thinking. Ruminations regarding guilt, obsessional doubts, and reenactments in imagination of situations that provoked anger that elevate anger to potentially dangerous levels are all instances of nonfunctional fantasizing.

Thus, the internal influences on human behavior that contribute to the emergence of dysfunctional acts involve biological influences as well as those mediating variables that are usually described as *cognitions*. The effect of the biological factors is to modify input and to place limits on output. Cognitive mediators play similar roles, but they also direct and generate output, and it is to this output that I now turn.

Response Factors

The response output of humans may involve any one, or all, of three systems: motoric, cognitive, or physiological. To a large extent I have already dealt with the latter two sets of responding, and all that it is necessary here is to point out that such responses provide feedback that may augment or attenuate ongoing processing and responding. For instance, if after evaluating input a person decides that the situation is one to fear, then she or he may feel apprehensive and think something like "I'm starting to get scared" or "I'm really frightened." Such feelings and self-statements serve to heighten the person's fear, and no doubt his or her heart rate will increase and become variable, as will the respiration rate. The person will also perspire, and in various other ways, his or her physiological arousal will change. The detection of such changes will very likely confirm the individual's assessment that he or she is afraid and further worsen the state.

Of course, all of these experiences increase the likelihood that our subject will attempt some overt behavior that will permit her or him to escape or avoid the situation. I have already noted that many individuals are deficient in the skills necessary to deal with social situations, and it is clear that nonsocial behavioral inadequacies might interfere with effective functioning (Marshall, 1981). When overt behavior fails to resolve the problem effectively, feedback from this failure will further confirm the individual's judgment regarding his or her incapacity to deal with the situation at hand. Thus, the response-generated feedback from any one, or all, of the three systems (cognitive, motoric, or physiological) will serve to augment or attenuate responding.

In addition to these immediate consequences of feedback, there are also the longer-term effects on the future probability of responding that result from response-contingent feedback, which is said to arise from two sources: (1) subject-independent rewards or punishments, which may be tangible or may come in the form of some verbal approval or disapproval; or (2) self-generated reinforcement or punishment, which again may involve tangible rewards or punishments but may also take the form of self-congratulations or self-denigrations.

This distinction between self-generated contingencies and independent sources of reinforcement or punishment is usually made in the literature dealing with self-control (e.g., Goldfried & Merbaum, 1973; Mahoney & Thoresen, 1974; Thoresen & Mahoney, 1974), where the lawful relations between behavior and its consequences are said to be the same whether these consequences are delivered by the individuals themselves or by some other agent. However, the particular use of the term *self-reinforcement* (or *self-punishment*) in this literature has come under attack. Goldiamond (1976), in particular, suggested that *self-reinforcement* contains more than the usual meaning of the term *reinforcement,* over and above the distinction between the sources of control. He drew attention to Skinner's (1953) point that when contingencies are controlled by the individual, it is possible for him or her to cheat. This possibility is markedly reduced when an external agent controls the consequences. Thus, categorizing self-control within an operant analysis suggests that we have explained the observed changes in behavior as resulting from self-reinforcement or self-punishment,

whereas such a description actually diverts attention from the search for the factors that enable the individual to resist temptation. Yet surely, this is the most important aspect of self-control?

As I noted in the section on external stimuli, an important source of learning for humans is their observation of the behavior of others and, in particular, the consequences of other people's behavior. Whether or not we imitate someone else's behavior depends, to a large extent, on whether it is rewarded or punished (Bandura, 1969). Thus, we may learn the functional value of a behavior without having to try it out for ourselves. Of course, the results of these observations are not always profitable. We can just as readily learn to withhold responses that might generally be adaptive, just because we observe a single instance where such behavior was punished. Similarly, we may observe someone being reinforced for inappropriate behavior and try afterward to emulate him or her. The same is true of direct reinforcement or punishment by others. Youthful companions often reward instances of behavior just because they are contrary to adult ideals, despite the disadvantageous nature of the behavior within the broader society (Martin & Fitzpatrick, 1964; Vedder, 1963).

As I noted earlier, phobias sometimes arise because of an inadvertent association between certain stimuli, or responses, and an aversive event. Actually, in such cases, it is more the individual's attribution of a causal connection between the two events, rather than the adventitious contiguity, that forms the basis for learning to be afraid of a neutral stimulus or response. After all, a variety of stimuli and responses are usually contiguously related to the aversive event, and yet we causally associate only one of these with the unpleasant experience. Which events we choose to associate with one another depends on our genetic endowment (Gray, 1971; Seligman, 1971), our accumulated knowledge and experience concerning the events (Buchwald, 1959), and our understanding of the currently operating contingencies. For example, Dulany (1968) showed that unless subjects understood the purpose of a signal, it did not affect their behavior, however carefully the contingencies were arranged. It has also been demonstrated that unless we are aware that certain events are correlated, we will remain relatively unaffected by feedback (Dawson & Furedy, 1976; Grings, 1973). In fact, it is not even the moment-to-moment feedback that controls our behavior; rather, it is the aggregated contingencies over a period of time that provide the basis for changing behavior (Baum, 1973). As a final qualifier to the direct effects of consequences, Davison (1973) has shown that even when subjects are aware of the relationship between behaviors and their consequences, they may defy the influence of these rewards or punishers depending on their view of the situation, the modifier, the incentives, or the behavior of others in the same situation.

In addition to these moderating influences on response-contingent feedback, we must take into account the subject's characteristic attributional disposition. For example, success in a particular situation may be attributed to features of the situation (e.g., "the presence of the therapist made it easy"; "this was a contrived or controlled situation"; "I was lucky today") rather than to oneself (Bem, 1972), and this attribution obviously influences learning. Indeed, the subject's attribution of responsibility for behavioral consequences affects, in very important ways, his or her perception of feedback. Davison, Tsujimoto, and Glaros (1973) gave all of their insomniac patients both an appropriate dosage of a sleep-inducing drug and training in muscle relaxation. After this regimen had improved their sleeping, half the subjects were told that they had received an optimal dosage of the drug, while the other half were told that they had been given a subclinical dosage. When treatment was withdrawn, only those who attributed control over sleeping, during treatment, to their own efforts (i.e., the subclinical-dosage group) maintained their therapeutic gains. Those who believed that the drug produced the treatment benefits (i.e., the optimal-dosage group) returned to their insomniac behavior with the suspension of treatment.

All of the factors I have just mentioned point again to the moderating influence of the individual on her or his environment. Indeed, the effects of reinforcement have been claimed to operate by inducing "anticipations" (Bolles, 1972), and it has become quite common practice to call on "cognitive" mediators to explain these particular research findings (Mahoney, 1974). However, it must be said that at the moment, many of these explanations in cognitive terms are little more than a rephrasing of the evidence. While Neisser (1967) has suggested that a satisfactory reason for studying cognitions is that "they are there," their agreed-upon existence does not automatically render them accessible to scientific analyses, although Neisser and other "cognitive" psychologists (e.g., Broadbent, 1958; Norman, 1969) have brought their focus of interest under experimental control. Despite these advances in other areas, considerable work is still required to refine our currently crude measurement of some of these cognitive mediators (Marshall, 1981) before they can serve as elements in a satisfactory analysis of human behavior. Until these refinements occur, all we can do is point to the obvious mediating role of these processes.

Structure and the Elements of Behavior

I have now completed my outline of the influences that operate to control behavior, and it is clear that difficulties can be encountered at any of the many and varied stages that I have suggested are important. In addition to this obvious possibility, it is also necessary to note that the factors that play a part in the genesis of a behavior may not continue to influence its maintenace. For example, many people start smoking tobacco as adolescents in the expectation of receiving the admiration of others for having attained adulthood or for having rebelled against adult controls. During this initial period, acquisition of the smoking habit is facilitated, despite the distasteful experience, by the self-generated pleasure of feeling either adult or rebellious. By the time the individual actually reaches adulthood, smoking has come under the control of quite different factors, such as anxiety reduction, nicotine effects, and the comfort engendered by a fixed routine or ritual that may be, by itself, intrinsically satisfying. Nothing short of a careful analysis of the presenting behavior, as it occurs in the context of the factors noted in this chapter, will reveal the controlling variables that are now maintaining the problem behavior. This search, however, will be guided by the therapist's sentiments concerning those influences that guide behavior. I hope the present chapter offers some suggestions as to what these influences might be.

What I would now like to do is put the model in perspective by outlining its major elements and the overall structural relationships. Figure 1 describes the elements and their structural relationships, although, as I noted earlier, the distinction between these elements is arbitrary since they overlap considerably. Similarly, the structure is not only metaphorical but also suggests that things proceed in an orderly progression when, in fact, this is rarely the case. Of course, the whole aim of this chapter is simply to identify the general categories of functioning that can be disturbed and that may contribute, in any number of complex interactive ways, to the appearance and maintenance of dysfunctional behavior. Given this goal, I need not apologize for the imposition of a somewhat arbitrary structure, nor for the seemingly whimsical distinction between the elements.

Decisions regarding the importance of the elements in this structure are best left to the consideration of the model's application to particular problem behaviors. The generation of a microtheory concerning any specific dysfunction will reveal the greater or lesser importance of the factors I have distinguished, and their relative importance will vary across problems. Indeed, even within such a seemingly restrictive area as the analysis of "phobias," the relative importance of physiological disturbances may depend on whether or not the disorder is chronic (Malmo, 1975), or whether or not panic attacks are present (Goldstein & Chambless, 1980). Nevertheless, in the modification of dysfunctional human behavior, long-term benefits are likely to occur only when most, if not all, of the factors I have mentioned are considered.

Summary and Conclusions

In summary, then, I have tried to identify the factors that seem to me to be important in the development and maintenance of dysfunctional human behavior. I have also tried to point to some variables that behaviorally oriented writers often neglect or simply ignore. The suggestion here is that any theory that attempts to explain a particular problem behavior needs to take into account the diverse complexity of factors that I presented in the

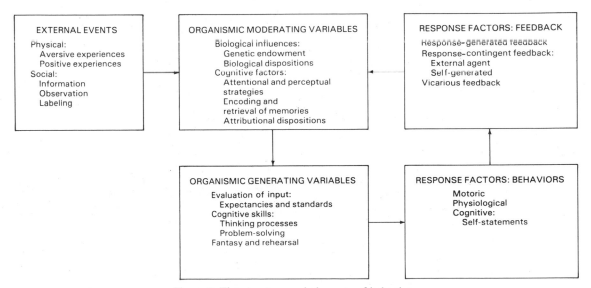

Figure 1. The structure and elements of behavior.

model. I believe that many of the early behavioral theories, although appropriate when
viewed within their historical context, failed
to guide research and treatment effectively
because they claimed that a single agent was
the controlling factor, and that clinicians have
realized for a long time that this was a defective analysis. Finally, I wish to restate my earlier claim that progress in our understanding
and modification of dysfunctional behavior
will be best achieved by careful attempts to
explain specific problem behaviors, rather
than by the elaboration of grand theories that
attempt to put all aberrant behaviors within
the one framework. In particular, the continuing attempts by Rachman and Eysenck
(Eysenck, 1968, 1976, 1977; Eysenck & Rachman, 1965; Rachman, 1974, 1976, 1977, 1978,
1979) to isolate the components that lead to
fear and courage are excellent examples of
what Lakatos and Musgrave (1970) have called
a "progressive scientific program," which in
this case is an endeavor that produces research
and modifies clinical approaches to problems.

ACKNOWLEDGMENTS

I wish to thank Howard Barbaree, Marilyn
Christie, Art Gordon, and Nina Marshall for
their helpful comments on an earlier draft of
this chapter.

References

Abel, G. G., & Blanchard, E. B. The role of fantasy in
the treatment of sexual deviation. *Archives of General
Psychiatry*, 1974, *30*, 467–475.

Abel, G. G., Barlow, D. H., Blanchard, E. B., & Guild,
D. The components of rapist's sexual arousal. *Archives
of General Psychiatry*, 1977, *34*, 895–903.

Ainsworth, M. D. S., & Bell, S. M. Some contemporary
patterns of mother-infant interaction in the feeding situation. In A. Ambrose (Ed.), *Stimulation in early infancy*. New York: Academic Press, 1967.

Arthur, A. Z. Psychology as engineering and technology
of behavior. *Canadian Psychologist*, 1971, *12*, 30–36.

Arthur, A. Z. Theory- and action-oriented research. *Journal of Consulting and Clinical Psychology*, 1972, *38*,
129–133.

Ayllon, T., Haughton, E., & Hughes, H. B. Interpretation
of symptoms: Fact or fiction. *Behaviour Research and
Therapy*, 1965, *3*, 1–7.

Bandura, A. *Principles of behavior modification*. New
York: Holt, Rinehart & Winston, 1969.

Bandura, A. Vicarious- and self-reinforcement processes.

In R. Glaser (Ed.), *The nature of reinforcement*. New
York: Academic Press, 1971.

Bandura, A. *Aggression: A social learning analysis*. Englewood Cliffs, N.J.; Prentice-Hall, 1973.

Bandura, A. Self-efficacy: Toward a unifying theory of
behavioral change. *Psychological Review*, 1977, *84*,
191–215.

Bandura, A., & Walters, R. H. *Social learning and personality development*. New York: Holt, Rinehart &
Winston, 1963.

Bandura, A., Blanchard, E. B., & Ritter, R. The relative
efficacy of desensitization and modeling approaches for
inducing behavioral, affective, and attitudinal changes.
Journal of Personality and Social Psychology, 1969, *13*,
173–199.

Barbaree, H. E., Marshall, W. L., & Lanthier, R. D.
Deviant sexual arousal in rapists. *Behaviour Research
and Therapy*, 1979, *14*, 215–222.

Baum, W. M. The correlation-based law of effect. *Journal
of the Experimental Analysis of Behavior*, 1973, *20*,
137–153.

Beck, A. T. Role of fantasies in psychotherapy and psychopathology. *Journal of Nervous and Mental Disease*,
1970, *150*, 3–17.

Becker, W. C. *Parents are teachers*. Champaign, Ill.:
Research Press, 1971.

Bellack, A. S., & Hersen, M. *Behavior modification: An
introductory text book*. New York: Oxford University
Press, 1977.

Bem, D. J. Self-perception theory. In. L. Berkowitz (Ed.),
Advances in experimental social psychology, Vol. 6.
New York: Academic Press, 1972.

Bernheim, K. F., & Lewine, R. R. J. *Schizophrenia:
Symptoms, causes, treatment*. New York: W. W. Norton, 1979.

Birnbrauer, J. S., Wolf, M. M., Kidder, J. D., & Tague,
C. E. Classroom behavior of retarded pupils with token
reinforcement. *Journal of Experimental Child Psychology*, 1965, *2*, 219–235.

Blakemore, C., & Cooper, G. F. Development of the brain
depends on the visual environment. *Nature*, 1970, *228*,
477–478.

Bloom, B. S., & Broder, L. J. *Problem-solving processes
of college students*. Chicago: University of Chicago
Press, 1950.

Bolles, R. C. Reinforcement, expectancy, and learning.
Psychological Review, 1972, *79*, 394–409.

Bolles, R. C. *Learning theory*. New York: Holt, Rinehart
& Winston, 1975.

Brancale, R., Ellis, A., & Doorbar, R. Psychiatric and
psychological investigations of convicted sex offenders:
A summary report. *American Journal of Psychiatry*,
1952, *109*, 17–21.

Bregman, E. O. An attempt to modify the emotional attitudes of infants by the conditioned response technique. *Journal of Genetic Psychology*, 1934, *45*, 169–198.

Broadbent, D. E. *Perception and communication*. New
York: Pergamon Press, 1958.

Buchwald, A. M. Experimental alterations in the effectiveness of verbal reinforcement combinations. *Journal
of Experimental Psychology*, 1959, *57*, 351–361.

Campbell, D. T., Sanderson, R. E., & Laverty, S. G.
Characteristics of a conditioned response in human subjects during extinction trials following a single traumatic

conditioning trial. *Journal of Abnormal and Social Psychology,* 1964, *68,* 627–639.

Christie, M. M., Marshall, W. L., & Lanthier, R. D. *A descriptive study of incarcerated rapists and pedophiles.* Report to the Solicitor General of Canada, 1979.

Claridge, G. S. *Personality and arousal: A psychophysiological study of psychiatric disorders.* London: Pergamon, 1967.

Conger, D. S. *Life skills coaching manual.* Prince Albert, Saskatchewan: Newstart Inc., 1973.

Davidson, G. C. Counter-control in behavior modification. In L. A. Hamerlynck, L. C. Handy, & E. T. Mash, (Eds.), *Behavior change: Methodology, concepts, and practice.* Champaign, Ill.: Research Press, 1973.

Davison, G. C., Tsujimoto, R. N., & Glaros, A. G. Attribution and the maintenance of behavior change in falling asleep. *Journal of Abnormal Psychology,* 1973, *82,* 124–133.

Dawson, M. E., & Furedy, J. J. The role of awareness in human differential autonomic classical conditioning: The necessary-gate hypothesis. *Psychophysiology,* 1976, *13,* 50–53.

Delprato, D. J. Hereditary determinants of fears and phobias: A critical review. *Behavior Therapy,* 1980, *1,* 79–103.

de Silva, P., Rachman, S., & Seligman, M. E. P. Prepared phobias and obsessions: Therapeutic outcome. *Behaviour Research and Therapy,* 1977, *15,* 65–77.

Dollard, J., & Miller, N. E. *Personality and psychotherapy.* New York: McGraw-Hill, 1950.

Donelson, E. *Personality: A scientific approach.* New York: Appleton-Century-Crofts, 1973.

Dulany, D. E. Awareness, rules, and propositional controls: A confrontation with S-R behavior theory. In T. R. Dixon & D. L. Horton (Eds.), *Verbal behavior and general behavior theory.* Englewood Cliffs, N.J.: Prentice-Hall, 1968.

D'Zurilla, T. J., & Goldfried, M. R. Problem solving and behavior modification. *Journal of Abnormal Psychology,* 1971, *78,* 107–126.

Edelstein, B. A., & Eisler, R. M. Effects of modeling and modeling with instructions and feedback on the behavioral components of social skills. *Behavior Therapy,* 1976, *7,* 382–389.

English, H. B. Three cases of the conditional fear response. *Journal of Abnormal and Social Psychology,* 1929, *29,* 221–225.

Epstein, S. Toward a unified theory of anxiety. In B. A. Maher (Ed.), *Progress in experimental personality research.* New York: Academic Press, 1967.

Epstein, S., & Fenz, W. D. Theory and experiment on the measurement of approach-avoidance conflict. *Journal of Abnormal and Social Psychology,* 1962, *64,* 97–112.

Eron, L. D., Huesmann, L. R., Lefkowitz, M. M., & Walder, L. O. Does television violence cause aggression? *American Psychologist,* 1972, *27,* 253–263.

Eysenck, H. J. *The dynamics of anxiety and hysteria.* London: Routledge & Kegan Paul, 1957.

Eysenck, H. J. *The structure of human personality.* New York: Macmillan, 1960.

Eysenck, H. J. The nature of behavior therapy. In H. J. Eysenck (Ed.), *Experiments in behavior therapy.* London: Pergamon, 1964.

Eysenck, H. J. A theory of the incubation of anxiety/fear responses. *Behaviour Research and Therapy,* 1968, *6,* 309–322.

Eysenck, H. J. The learning model of neurosis: A new approach. *Behaviour Research and Therapy,* 1976, *14,* 251–267.

Eysenck, H. J. *You and neurosis.* London: Temple Smith, 1977.

Eysenck, H. J., & Rachman, S. *The causes and cures of neurosis.* London: Routledge & Kegan Paul, 1965.

Franks, C. M. Introduction: Behavior therapy and its Pavlovian origins: Review and perspectives. In C. M. Franks (Eds.), *Behavior therapy: Appraisal and status.* New York: McGraw-Hill, 1969.

Fuller, J. L., & Thompson, W. R. *Behavior genetics.* New York: Wiley, 1960.

Garcia, J., McGowan, B. K., & Green, K. F. Biological constraints on conditioning. In A. H. Black & W. F. Prokasy (Eds.), *Classical conditioning. II: Current research and theory.* New York: Appleton-Century-Crofts, 1972.

Garcia, J., Hankins, W. G., & Rusiniak, K. W. Flavor aversion studies. *Science,* 1976, *192,* 265–266.

Gelfand, D. M., Gelfand, S., & Dobson, W. R. Unprogrammed reinforcement of patients' behavior in a mental hospital. *Behaviour Research and Therapy,* 1967, *5,* 201–207.

Glass, D. C., Singer, J. E., & Friedman, L. N. Psychic cost of adaptation to an environmental stressor. *Journal of Personality and Social Psychology,* 1969, *12,* 200–210.

Glueck, S., & Glueck, E. T. *Family environment delinquency.* Boston: Houghton, Mifflin, 1962.

Goldfried, M. R., & Goldfried, A. P. Cognitive change methods. In F. H. Kanfer & A. P. Goldstein (Eds.), *Helping people change: A textbook of methods.* New York: Pergamon Press, 1975.

Goldfried, M. R., & Merbaum, M. *Behavior change through self-control.* New York: Holt, Rinehart & Winston, 1973.

Goldiamond, I. Self-reinforcement. *Journal of Applied Behavior Analysis,* 1976, *9,* 509–514.

Goldstein, A. J., & Chambless, D. L. A reanalysis of agoraphobia. *Behavior therapy,* 1978, *9,* 47–59.

Goldstein, A. J., & Chambless, D. L. Agoraphobia. In A. J. Goldstein & E. B. Foa (Eds.), *Handbook of behavioral interventions.* New York: Wiley, 1980.

Gottesman, I., & Shields, J. A critical review of recent adoption, twin and family studies of schizophrenia: Behavioral genetics perspective. *Schizophrenia Bulletin,* 1976, *2,* 360–401.

Gray, J. *The psychology of fear and stress.* London: World University Library, 1971.

Greer, H. S., & Cawley, R. H. Some observations on the natural history of neurotic illness. *Mervyn Archdall Medical Monographs* (No. 3, Australian Medical Association), 1966.

Grings, W. W. The role of consciousness and cognition in autonomic behavior change. In F. J. McGuigan & R. A. Schoonover (Eds.), *The psychophysiology of thinking.* New York: Academic Press, 1973.

Harlow, H. F. The nature of love. *American Psychologist,* 1958, *13,* 673–685.

Harlow, H. F., & Harlow, M. K. Learning to love. *American Scientist,* 1966, *54,* 244–272.

Harlow, H. F., & Zimmerman, R. R. Affectional response in the infant monkey. *Science,* 1959, *130,* 421–432.

Heath, R. G., Krupp, I. M., Byers, L. W., & Liljekvist, J. I. Schizophrenia as an immunologic disorder. 11: Effects of serum protein fractions on brain function. *Archives of General Psychiatry,* 1967, *16,* 10–23.

Herrnstein, R. Method and theory in the study of avoidance. *Psychological Review,* 1969, *76,* 49–69.

Hersen, M., & Bellack, A. S. Social skills training for chronic psychiatric patients: Rationale, research findings, and future directions. *Comprehensive Psychiatry,* 1976, *17,* 559–580.

Hersen, M., Eisler, R. M., & Miller, P. M. Development of assertive responses: Clinical measurement and research considerations. *Behaviour Research and Therapy,* 1973, *11,* 505–521.

Hicks, D. J. Imitation and retention of film-mediated aggressive peer and adult models. *Journal of Personality and Social Psychology,* 1965, *2,* 97–100.

Hilgard, E. R., & Bower, G. H. *Theories of learning* (4th ed.). New York: Appleton, 1974.

Hirsch, H. V. B., & Spinelli, D. N. Visual experience modifies distribution of horizontally and vertically oriented receptive fields in cats. *Science,* 1970, *168,* 869–871.

Jaffe, P. G., & Carlson, P. M. Relative efficacy of modeling and instructions in eliciting social behavior from chronic psychiatric patients. *Journal of Consulting and Clinical Psychology,* 1976, *44,* 200–207.

Jones, H. E. The conditioning of overt emotional responses. *Journal of Education Psychology,* 1931, *22,* 127–130.

Katz, R. C., & Zlutnick, S. *Behavior therapy and health care: Principles and applications.* New York: Pergamon Press, 1975.

Keltner, A., & Marshall, W. L. Single-trial exacerbation of an anxiety habit with second-order conditioning and subsequent desensitization. *Journal of Behavior Therapy and Experimental Psychiatry,* 1975, *6,* 323–324.

Keltner, A., Marshall, P. G., & Marshall, W. L. The description of assertive behavior in a prison population. Report to the Solicitor General of Canada, 1979.

Kuhn, T. S. *The structure of scientific revolutions.* Chicago: University of Chicago Press, 1962.

Lader, M. H. Psychophysiological aspects of anxiety. In M. H. Lader (Ed.), *Studies of anxiety.* Ashford, Kent: Hedley Bros., 1969.

Lakatos, I., & Musgrave, A. *Criticism and the growth of knowledge.* Cambridge: University Press, 1970.

Lazarus, A. A. *Behavior therapy and beyond.* New York: McGraw-Hill, 1971.

Lewinsohn, P. M. The behavioral study and treatment of depression. In M. Hersen, R. M. Eisler, & P. M. Miller, (Eds.), *Progress in behavior modification,* Vol. 1. New York: Academic Press, 1974.

Leyens, J. P., Camino, L., Parke, R. D., & Berkowitz, L. Effects of movie violence on aggression in a field setting as a function of group dominance and cohesion. *Journal of Personality and Social Psychology,* 1975, *32,* 346–360.

Lindsley, O. R. Direct measurement and prothesis of retarded behavior. *Journal of Education,* 1964, *147,* 62–81.

London, P. The end of ideology in behavior modification. *American Psychologist,* 1972, *27,* 913–920.

Maher, B. A. *Principles of psychopathology: An experimental approach.* New York: McGraw-Hill, 1966.

Mahoney, M. J. *Cognition and behavior modification.* Cambridge, Mass.: Ballinger, 1974.

Mahoney, M. J., & Thoresen, C. E. *Self-control: Power to the person.* Monterey, Calif.: Brooks Cole, 1974.

Malmo, R. B. *On emotions, needs, and our archaic brain.* New York: Holt, Rinehart & Winston, 1975.

Malmo, R. B., & Shagass, C. Physiologic studies of reaction to stress in anxiety and early schizophrenia. *Psychosomatic Medicine,* 1949, *11,* 9–24.

Malmo, R. B., Shagass, C., & Davis, J. F. A method for the investigation of somatic response mechanisms in psychoneurosis. *Science,* 1950, *112,* 325–328.

Mandell, A. J., Segal, D. S., Kuczenski, R. T., & Knapp, S. The search for the schizococcus. *Psychology Today,* Oct. 1972, *6,* 68–72.

Mandler, G. Anxiety. In D. L. Sills (Eds.), *International encyclopedia of the social sciences,* Vol. 1. New York: Free Press, 1968.

Mankiewicz, F., & Swerdlow, J. *Remote control.* New York: Quadrangle, 1977.

Mann, J. The effects of erotica. In L. Gross (Ed.), *Sexual behavior: Current issues.* Flushing, N.Y.: Spectrum, 1974.

Marshall, P. G., Keltner, A., & Marshall, W. L. The role of anxiety-reduction, assertive training, and enactment of consequences in the modification of nonassertion and social fear: a comparative treatment study. *Behavior Modification,* 1981, *5,* 85–102.

Marshall, W. L. Cognitive functioning in schizophrenia. *British Journal of Psychiatry,* 1973, *123,* 413–433.

Marshall, W. L. Reducing masturbatory guilt. *Journal of Behavior Therapy and Experimental Psychiatry,* 1975, *6,* 260–261.

Marshall, W. L. Behavioral treatment of phobic and obsessive-disorders. In L. Michelson, M. Hersen, & S. M. Turner (Eds.), *Future perspectives in behavior therapy.* New York: Plenum Press, 1981.

Marshall, W. L., Parker, L., & Hayes, B. Flooding and the elements of skill training in the treatment of public-speaking problems. *Behavior Modification,* 1982.

Martin, J. M., & Fitzpatrick, J. P. *Delinquent behavior: A redefinition of the problem.* New York: Random House, 1964.

Matarazzo, J. D., & Phillips, J. S. Digit symbol performance as a function of increasing levels of anxiety. *Journal of Consulting Psychology,* 1955, *19,* 131–134.

McCord, J., & McCord, W. The effects of parental role model on criminality. *Journal of Social Issues,* 1958, *14,* 66–75.

McFall, R. M. Behavioral training: A skill-acquisition approach to clinical problems. In J. T. Spence, R. C. Carson, & J. W. Thibaut (Eds.), *Behavioral approaches to therapy.* Morristown, N.J.: General Learning Press, 1976.

McFall, R. M., & Lillesand, D. B. Behavior rehearsal with modelling and coaching in assertion training. *Journal of Abnormal Psychology,* 1971, *77,* 313, 323.

McFall, R. M., & Twentyman, C. Four experiments on the relative contribution of rehearsal, modeling and coaching to assertion training. *Journal of Abnormal Psychology*, 1973, *81*, 199–218.

McGhie, A. *Pathology of attention*. Harmondsworth, England: Penguin, 1969.

McConaghy, N. The use of an object sorting test in elucidating the hereditary factor in schizophrenia. *Journal of Neurology, Neurosurgery, and Psychiatry*, 1959, *22*, 243–246.

McGuire, R. J., Carlisle, J. M., & Young, B. G. Sexual deviations as conditioned behavior. *Behaviour Research and Therapy*, 1965, *2*, 185–190.

Meachem, M. L., & Wiesen, A. E. *Changing classroom behavior: A manual for precision teaching*. Scranton, Pa.: International Textbook, 1969.

Meltzer, H., & Stahl, S. The dopamine hypothesis of schizophrenia: A review. *Schizophrenia Bulletin*, 1976, *2*, 19–76.

Miller, E. *Abnormal aging: The psychology of senile and presenile dementia*. London: Wiley, 1977.

Miller, G. A., Galanter, E., & Pribram, K. H. *Plans and the structure of behavior*. New York: Henry Holt, 1960.

Miller, N. E. Learnable drives and rewards. In S. Stevens (Ed.), *Handbook of experimental psychology*. New York: Wiley, 1951.

Moss, E. A. Note on building likes and dislikes in children. *Journal of Experimental Psychology*. 1924, *7*, 475–478.

Mowrer, O. H. A stimulus-response analysis of anxiety and its role as a reinforcing agent. *Psychological Review*, 1939, *46*, 553–565.

Mowrer, O. H. On the dual nature of learning—a reinterpretation of "conditioning" and "problem-solving." *Harvard Educational Review*, 1947, *17*, 102–148.

Mowrer, O. H. *Learning theory and personality dynamics*. New York: Ronald Press, 1950.

Nathan, P. E. *Cues, decisions and diagnoses*. New York: Academic Press, 1967.

Neisser, U. *Cognitive psychology*. New York: Appleton-Century-Crofts, 1967.

Neyhaus, E. C. Training the mentally retarded for competitive employment. *Exceptional Children*, 1967, *33*, 625–628.

Norman, D. A. *Memory and attention*. New York: Wiley, 1969.

Ohmann, A., Fredrikson, M., & Hugdahl, K. Towards an experimental model for simple phobic reactions. *Behavioral Analysis and Modification*, 1978, *2*, 97–114.

Pariser, S. F., Jones, B. A., Pinta, E. R., Young, E. A., & Fontana, M. E. Panic attacks: Diagnostic evaluations of 17 patients. *American Journal of Psychiatry*, 1979, *136*, 105–106.

Parke, R. D., Berkowitz, L., Leyens, J. P., West, S. G., & Sebastian, R. J. Some effects of violent and nonviolent movies on the behavior of juvenile delinquents. In L. Berkowitz (Ed.), *Advances in experimental social psychology*, Vol. 10. New York: Academic Press, 1977.

Payne, R. W. Cognitive abnormalities. In H. J. Eysenck (Ed.), *Handbook of abnormal psychology*. London: Basic Books, 1960.

Phillips, L., & Zigler, E. Social competence: The action-thought parameter and vicariousness in normal and pathological behaviors. *Journal of Abnormal and Social Psychology*, 1961, *63*, 137–146.

Pitts, F. N. The biochemistry of anxiety. *Scientific American*, 1969, *220*, 69–75.

Rachman, S. Clinical applications of observational learning, imitation and modeling. *Behavior Therapy*, 1972, *3*, 379–397.

Rachman, S. *The meanings of fear*. Harmondsworth, Middlesex: Penguin, 1974.

Rachman, S. The passing of the two-stage theory of fear and avoidance: Fresh possibilities. *Behaviour Research and Therapy*, 1976, *14*, 125–131.

Rachman, S. The conditioning theory of fear-acquisition: A critical examination. *Behaviour Research and Therapy*, 1977, *15*, 375–388.

Rachman, S. *Fear and courage*. San Francisco: W. H. Freeman, 1978.

Rachman, S. The return of fear. *Behaviour Research and Therapy*, 1979, *17*, 164–165.

Rachman, S., & Seligman, M. E. P. Unprepared phobias: Be prepared. *Behaviour Research and Therapy*, 1976, *14*, 333–338.

Rescorla, R., & Solomon, R. Two-process learning theory. *Psychological Review*, 1967, *74*, 151–182.

Revusky, S. Aversion to sucrose produced by contingent x-irradiation: Temporal and dosage parameters. *Journal of Comparative and Physiological Psychology*, 1968, *65*, 17–22.

Rosehan, D. L. On being sane in insane places. *Science*, 1973, *179*, 250–258.

Ross, L. The intuitive psychologist and his shortcoming: Distortions in the attribution process. In L. Berkowitz (Ed.), *Advances in experimental social psychology*, Vol. 10. New York: Academic Press, 1977.

Rutter, M., Yule, W., Tizard, J., & Graham, P. Severe reading retardation: Its relationship to maladjustment, epilepsy and neurological disorder. Report to the Proceedings of the International Conference Association for Special Education, London, 1966.

Seligman, M. E. P. Phobias and preparedness. *Behavior Therapy*, 1971, *2*, 307–320.

Seligman, M. E. P. *Helplessness*. San Francisco: W. H. Freeman, 1975.

Shaw, C. R., & McKay, H. D. *Juvenile delinquency and urban areas*. Chicago: University of Chicago Press, 1942.

Shields, J., & Slater, E. Heredity and psychological abnormality. In H. J. Eysenck (Ed.), *Handbook of abnormal psychology*. New York: Basic Books, 1961.

Sidman, M. Normal sources of pathological behavior. *Science*, 1960, *132*, 61–68.

Singer, J. L. Imagery and daydream techniques employed in psychotherapy: Some practical and theoretical implications. In C. D. Spielberger (Ed.), *Current topics in clinical and community psychology*. New York: Academic Press, 1972.

Skinner, B. F. *The behavior of organisms*. New York: Appleton, 1938.

Skinner, B. F. *Science and human behavior*. New York: Macmillan, 1953.

Solomon, R. L. An opponent process theory of motivation: The affective dynamics of drug addiction. In J. D. Maser & M. E. P. Seligman (Eds.), *Psychopathology: Experimental models*. San Francisco: W. H. Freeman, 1977.

Solomon, R. L., & Wynne, L. Traumatic avoidance learning: The principles of anxiety conservation and partial irreversibility. *Psychological Review,* 1954, *61,* 353–385.

Spence, K. W., Farber, I. E., & McFann, H. H. The relation of anxiety (drive) level to performance in competitional and non-competitional paired-associates learning. *Journal of Experimental Psychology,* 1956, *52,* 296–305.

Staub, E., Tursky, B., & Schwartz, G. Self-control and predictability: Their effects on reactions to aversive stimulation. *Journal of Personality and Social Psychology,* 1971, *18,* 157–162.

Stern, C. *Principles of human genetics* (2nd ed.), San Francisco: W. H. Freeman, 1960.

Steuer, F. B., Applefield, J. M., & Smith, R. Televised aggression and the interpersonal aggression of preschool children. *Journal of Experimental Child Psychology,* 1971, *11,* 422–447.

Suinn, R. M. Behavior rehearsal training for ski racers. *Behavior Therapy,* 1972, *3,* 519–520.

Swanson, D. W. Adult sexual abuse of children. *Diseases of the Nervous System,* 1968, *29,* 677–683.

Thoresen, C. E., & Mahoney, M. J. *Behavioral self-control.* New York: Holt, Rinehart & Winston, 1974.

Trasler, G. *The explanation of criminality.* London: Routledge & Kegan Paul, 1962.

Ullmann, L. P., & Krasner, L. *A psychological approach to abnormal behavior* (2nd ed.). Englewood Cliffs, N.J.: Prentice-Hall, 1975.

Vedder, C. B. *Juvenile offenders* Springfield, Ill.: Charles C Thomas, 1963.

Voss, J., Arrick, C., & Rimm, D. C. The role of task difficulty and modeling in assertive training. Unpublished manuscript, Southern Illinois University, 1976.

Watson, J. B., & Rayner, R. Conditioned emotional reactions. *Journal of Experimental Psychology,* 1920, *3,* 1–14.

Whitman, T. L., Mercurio, J. R., & Caponigri, V. Development of social responses in two severely retarded children. *Journal of Applied Behavior Analysis,* 1970, *3,* 133–138.

Williams, C. D. The elimination of tantrum behavior by extinction procedures. *Journal of Abnormal and Social Psychology,* 1959, *59,* 269.

Wilson, W. C. *Presidential reports of the Commission on Obscenity and Pornography.* San Diego, Calif.: Greenleaf Classics, 1970.

Wine, J. Test anxiety and direction of attention. *Psychological Bulletin,* 1971, *76,* 92–104.

Winnett, R. A., & Winkler, R. C. Current behavior modification in the classroom: Be still, be quiet, be docile. *Journal of Applied Behavior Analysis,* 1972, *5,* 499–504.

Wolpe, J. *Psychotherapy by reciprocal inhibition.* Stanford, Calif.: Stanford University Press, 1958.

Wolpe, J. *The practice of behavior therapy.* Oxford: Pergamon, 1969.

Wolpe, J. The experimental model and treatment of neurotic depression. *Behaviour Research and Therapy,* 1979, *17,* 555–565.

Wolpe, J., & Rachman, S. Psychoanalytic "evidence": A critique based on Freud's case of Little Hans. *Journal of Nervous and Mental Diseases,* 1960, *130,* 135–148.

Yates, A. J. *Theory and practice in behavior therapy.* New York: Wiley, 1975.

Zigler, E., & Levine, J. Premorbid adjustment and paranoid-nonparanoid status in schizophrenics. *Journal of Abnormal Psychology,* 1973, *82,* 189–199.

Zigler, E., & Phillips, L. Social effectiveness and symptomatic behaviors. *Journal of Abnormal and Social Psychology,* 1960, *61,* 231–238.

PART II

Assessment and Methodology

CHAPTER 4

Behavioral Assessment

AN OVERVIEW

Marvin R. Goldfried

Introduction

Within the past decade, the field of behavioral assessment has grown dramatically. This growth is reflected by the numerous books on this topic (Barlow, 1980; Ciminero, Adams, & Calhoun, 1977; Cone & Hawkins, 1977; Haynes, 1978; Haynes & Wilson, 1979; Nay, 1980; Hersen & Bellack, 1976, 1981; Keefe, Kopel, & Gordon, 1978; Kendall & Hollon, 1981; Mash & Terdal, 1976, 1980; Merluzzi, Glass, & Genest, 1981; Wiggins, 1973), as well as by two journals devoted to behavioral assessment (*Behavioral Assessment* and *Journal of Behavioral Assessment*). Such increased interest is due to the recognition that effective clinical behavior therapy is only as good as its initial behavioral analysis, and that clinical outcome research on behavior therapy cannot

be undertaken without adequate measures of change.

Despite such interest in behavioral assessment—perhaps even because of it—we face the potential danger of developing measures that are poorly conceived and developed. This was clearly the case in the 1940s, when there was an indiscriminate proliferation of projective techniques (see Rabin, 1968). Although the conceptual underpinnings of behavioral assessment do not parallel those associated with projective techniques, it should not be assumed that we are immune from many of the pitfalls that the field of assessment has experienced in the past. This unfortunate tendency for history to repeat itself may occur with behavioral assessment, as the need for measures outstrips the procedures currently available.

This chapter provides an overview of the field of behavioral assessment; it deals with the underlying theoretical and methodological assumptions associated with such procedures, outlines some of the currently available assessment methods, discusses the relationship between behavior therapy and behavioral assessment, and ends with a note on future perspectives.

Portions of this chapter were adapted from Goldfried and Davison (1976), Goldfried (1976), and Goldfried and Linehan (1977).

Marvin R. Goldfried • Department of Psychology, State University of New York at Stony Brook, Stony Brook, New York 11794. Preparation of this chapter was facilitated by grant MH 24327 from the National Institute of Mental Health.

Basic Assumptions

The distinction between traditional and behavioral approaches to assessment has been discussed at length by Goldfried (1976), Goldfried and Kent (1972), Mischel (1968), and Wiggins (1973). Each of these writers has noted that behavioral assessment is characterized by relatively fewer inferential assumptions, remaining instead closer to observables. This holds true for the behavioral conceptualization of human functioning, as well as the interpretation of the person's response to situations within the assessment setting.

One of the earliest arguments for using operational terms in assessing and changing human behavior can be found in Johnson's *People in Quandaries* (1946):

> To say that Henry is mean implies that he has some sort of inherent trait, but it tells us nothing about what Henry has done. Consequently, it fails to suggest any specific means of improving Henry. If, on the other hand, it is said that Henry snatched Billy's cap and threw it in the bonfire, the situation is rendered somewhat more clear and actually more helpful. You might never eliminate "meanness," but there are fairly definite steps to be taken in order to remove Henry's incentives or opportunities for throwing caps in bonfires. . . .
>
> What the psychiatrist has to do . . . is to get the person to tell him not what he is or what he *has*, but what he *does*, and the conditions under which he does it. When he stops talking about what *type* of person he is, what his outstanding *traits* are, and what type of disorder he *has*—when he stops making these subject–predicate statements, and begins to use actional terms to describe his behavior and its circumstances—both he and the psychiatrist begin to see what specifically may be done in order to change both the behavior and the circumstances. (p. 220)

Within the scope of contemporary behavioral assessment, *personality* is typically construed as an intervening variable that provides a summary of the individual's reactions to a wide variety of life situations. Stated in this way, however, the concept *personality* has little practical utility for behavioral assessment, in that it would be a near-impossible task to obtain systematic samples of all day-to-day situations. In actual practice, behavioral assessment has instead focused on behavior patterns associated with a given class of performance capabilities, such as social skills or fearfulness.

The concept of *behavioral capability* refers to whether or not an individual has given response available in his or her repertoire. The specific focus of assessment is on the determination of which capabilities a person has in any given class of situations. It should be clear that the specification of "capabilities" relates to maladaptive behavioral repertoires as well as to behavioral competencies. Thus, it may be inferred that a person who is observed to berate others is capable of taking on an aggressive role or has aggressive capabilities.

A capabilities conceptualization of personality functioning, when viewed within the broad context of psychometric methodology, relates most directly to *content validity,* where careful item-sampling becomes a most important issue. As described in the *Standards for Educational and Psychological Tests* (American Psychological Association, American Educational Research Association, and National Council on Measurement in Education, 1974), "Evidence of content validity is required when the test user wishes to estimate how an individual performs in the universe of situations the test is intended to represent" (p. 28). Although content validity has long been described as an important aspect of test construction, it has typically been related to achievement tests, not personality assessment.

In their discussion of the behavioral-analytic approach to assessing competence, Goldfried and D'Zurilla (1969) have outlined a procedure for establishing the content validity of behavioral measures. The initial step consists of a *situational analysis,* involving a sampling of typical situations in which a given behavior of interest is likely to occur (e.g., aggressive behavior, heterosexual interaction). The next phase consists of a *response enumeration,* which entails a sampling of typical responses to each of the situations generated during the situational analysis. Both this phase and the previous one may be carried out by means of direct observations, that is, reports from individuals who have occasion to observe the behaviors within a naturalistic setting, as well as self-observations by those for whom the assessment is specifically designed. The final phase of the criterion analysis uses a *response evaluation* to judge each response with regard to capability level. In the measurement of competence, these judgments are carried out by significant others in the environment who typically label behavior patterns as being effective or maladaptive. In other instances, such as the assessment of empathic or fearful behavior, these judgments are made in light of how well they fit the definition of the behavioral capability of interest to the investigator. Each situation may have associated with it an array of different responses, which can be grouped functionally according to their judged capability level. One may then use this three-stage criterion analysis to select the items in one's measuring instrument and also to find the empirically derived criteria for scoring the measure.

The basic assumption underlying this approach to establishing scoring criteria is that there exist common standards or behavioral norms for effectiveness within the particular life setting in question, and that these standards are relatively stable over the period of time during which the assessment is to take place. In light of the rapidly changing value system associated with many aspects of our society, this assumption may at times prove to be faulty. It should be emphasized, however, that failure to confirm empirically the existence of a stable set of behavioral norms would have implications not only for the establishment of scoring criteria, but also for the selection of criterion behaviors against which any validation could take place. However, this problem would be present in any attempt to predict human behavior, whether it be behavioral or traditional.

Although the behavioral-analytic model was originally developed for the study of the effectiveness of college freshmen (Goldfried & D'Zurilla, 1969), it has been applied to a wide variety of different content areas. Thus, the behavioral-analytic model has been used to develop measures of social competence (Levenson & Gottman, 1978; Mullinix & Galassi, 1981), heterosocial skills (Bellack, Hersen, & Lamparski, 1979; Kulich & Conger, 1978; Perri & Richards, 1979), interpersonal skills among retarded adults (Bates, 1980), children's social skills (Edleson & Rose, 1978), skill deficits in delinquent boys (Freedman, Rosenthal, Donahoe, Schlundt, & McFall, 1978), depression (Funabiki & Calhoun, 1979), assertiveness (MacDonald, 1974), guilt over assertion (Klass, 1980), methods of coping with chronic illness (Turk, 1979), occupational skills (Mathews, Whang, & Fawcett, 1980), and managerial effectiveness (Bernstein, 1978).

It should also be emphasized that the behavioral-analytic model for test construction focuses only on sampling and not on methodological issues. Once a criterion analysis is conducted, the assessor must consider the format for measuring the obtained situation–response interactions. Should one observe the individual in a naturalistic setting? Should one somehow contrive situations within the laboratory setting and then observe the person's response? Should the individual sit back and imagine the situation and then verbalize how he or she might react to it if it were actually occurring? Should the measuring procedure take the form of a structured interview? Should it involve a paper-and-pencil test? In deciding on which procedure to employ, various issues of method variance become relevant, such as the reactivity of the measuring procedure and the reliability of the observers or scorers, as well as the comparative validities of the several assessment procedures.

Behavioral Assessment Methods

There are a variety of different approaches that one may employ in sampling an individual's response to certain life situations. Behavioral assessment has made use of (1) direct observation in naturalistic settings; (2) the observation of responses to situations that have been contrived by the assessor; (3) responses that manifest themselves in role-playing situations; and (4) the individual's own self-report of behavior. Each of these different approaches to assessment is discussed below.

Observations in Naturalistic Settings

In attempting to implement the criterion-sampling orientation to behavioral assessment described in the previous section, it follows logically that behavioral assessors would have turned to the use of direct observation in naturalistic settings. Not only can such observation allow one to measure the various dimensions of the behavior of interest (e.g., frequency, strength, pervasiveness), but it can also provide a good opportunity for understanding those variables that may be currently maintaining the behavior.

Naturalistic observation is hardly an invention of behavior therapists. Psychologists, anthropologists, and sociologists have made use of such procedures long before the current behavioral orientation came into being. For example, Barker and Wright emphasized the importance of observing the "stream of behavior" in its appropriate ecological setting. They illustrated this approach to observation dramatically in their book *One Boy's Day* (1951) in which they provided a detailed account of the activities of a 7-year-old boy whom observers literally followed around for an entire day. Any such attempt to observe the natural stream of behavior represents an admirable if not staggering undertaking, as is attested to by the fact that Barker and Wright's observational data for a single day encompass an entire book.

Largely as a function of practical considerations, behaviorally oriented assessors have typically been more goal-oriented in making their observations than were Barker and Wright. Thus, depending on the particular purpose of the assessment, behavioral codes are customarily devised that outline the categories of behavior to be attended to during the observation procedure. Different codes have been devised by investigators for observing behavior as it occurs in various settings, such as schools, homes, and hospitals. These observations are typically carried out at specified periods of time and are tailored to the particular subject population being assessed.

An early attempt to employ behavioral observations within the school setting is described by O'Leary and Becker (1967). The main goal of their observation was to evaluate the effect of a token reinforcement program with a class consisting of disruptive children. Teams of trained observers recorded the incidence of various behavioral categories for specific time periods, typically lasting 1½ hours each. The observers sat toward the rear of the classroom and attempted to be as unobtrusive as possible. Included among the categories within the behavioral code were such

behaviors as making disruptive noises, speaking without raising one's hand, and pushing. Based on extensive research and continual revisions, the code has been refined and updated (O'Leary & O'Leary, 1972) for future applications.

An observation code has also been developed for the assessment of positively reinforcing behaviors (Bersoff & Moyer, 1973). Included among the 10 behavioral categories in this code are positive reactions (e.g., the administration of concrete rewards, verbal or nonverbal praise, attention, and physical contact), behaviors that presumably are neutral with respect to their reinforcement qualities (e.g., asking questions), and responses of an aversive nature (e.g., admonishment and nonverbal disapproval).

The use of behavioral observation codes involving frequency counts of various categories of behavior has provided researchers and clinicians with an invaluable approach for evaluating the effectiveness of various therapeutic intervention programs. Despite the obvious utility of such behavioral codes, one may nonetheless raise questions as to the relevance of data that they may ignore. Of particular importance is the likelihood that an individual behaving in a given way is probably reacting to some antecedent event in her or his environment, and that the behavior being observed may also have certain environmental consequences.

Toward the goal of evaluating the antecedent and/or consequent occurrences that may maintain any particular behavior, Patterson, Ray, Shaw, and Cobb (1969) developed an observational code to evaluate the interaction between an individual and significant others in the environment. The observations specifically focus on predelinquent boys, particularly as they interact with members of their families within the home setting. The code essentially attempts to take the complex stream of behavior and break it down into categories focused on various aspects of the child's behavior (e.g., yelling, talking, teasing, hitting, and crying) and the way in which other members of the family react to him (e.g., positive physical contact, ignoring, and disapproval). The behavioral code is utilized by trained observers who go directly to the home and record the family interactions on a time-sampling basis.

A code for assessing the interaction among adults has been developed by Lewinsohn and Shaffer (1971), who have focused specifically on the observation of depressed individuals. Here, too, observers go directly into the home and time-sample the interaction among family members at mealtime. Although the distinction may be difficult to make at times, Lewinsohn and Shaffer's code attempts to classify an individual's behavior as being either an "action" or a "reaction" to another family member's behavior. Among the class of "actions" are such categories as criticism, information request, statement of personal problem, and complaint. The "reactions," which are presumed to have the potential of maintaining a given behavior, may be either "positive" or "negative." Among the positive categories are approval, laughter, and interest; the negative reactions comprise such responses as disagreement, criticism, punishment, and ignoring.

Within the context of observations in hospital settings, Paul and his associates (Mariotto & Paul, 1974; Paul & Lentz, 1977; Paul, Tobias, & Holly, 1972) developed a time-sample behavioral checklist for use with chronic psychiatric patients. Among the behaviors recorded by trained observers are such categories as verbalized delusions or hallucinations, repetitive and stereotypic movements, grimacing or frowning without apparent stimulus, physical assault, blank staring, and various other forms of inappropriate behavior. Interobserver reliability is high for this checklist, with coefficients typically in the .90s.

Although it might appear at first blush that direct naturalistic observation is the procedure par excellence for carrying out a behavioral assessment, nonetheless, certain methodological problems are associated with this approach. Although there has been a considerable amount of research focusing on method assumptions in naturalistic observations, relatively little attention has been paid to the question of the representativeness of the behaviors sampled. In the case of the time-sample behavioral checklist developed by Paul for use with psychiatric patients, this is not much of an issue, as the observations are carried out

for 2-second intervals during each of the patient's waking hours. Where the issue of sampling assumptions does come into play, however, is with codes in which the observations are made only during certain times and at certain places. The question becomes the legitimacy of generalizing from what is observed to some larger class of behaviors or interactions. As yet, virtually no research efforts have been directed toward this most important issue.

One of the method assumptions associated with naturalistic observations is the extent to which the observers actually interfere with or influence the phenomena they are attempting to assess. This has been labeled the *reactivity* problem within behavioral observation methods. In studying this problem, Purcell and Brady (1966) attempted to determine the extent to which being monitored by a miniature wireless radio transmitter would alter the verbal behavior of a group of adolescents. The subjects were monitored 1 hour per day for a total of 10 successive days, and they seemed to behave more naturally after the first few days. However, the indications that their behavior became more natural were based on somewhat weak criteria, such as the decrease in the number of references made to the transmitter, the amount of talking done, and impressionistic reports of the subjects themselves.

The reactivity issue was followed up by Moos (1968), who studied the effect of wearing a radio transmitter on a group of psychiatric patients observed both when they were wearing the transmitter and when the transmitter was absent. Moos's findings indicated that the effect of being monitored by the radio transmitter was small, and that when it did occur, it occurred in the more disturbed patients. He also found an interaction between individual differences and the setting in which the observation was taking place. One limitation to keep in mind in interpreting these data, however, is that what was really determined was not simply the effect of being observed but the patients' reactions to wearing a transmitter when they knew they were otherwise being observed. In other words, there was no "pure" measure of the patients' behavioral tendencies. The same interpretative limitation applies to the more recent study by Johnson and Bolstad (1975), who found that tape-recorded family interactions were no different when observers were present or absent.

The problem of reactivity is obviously a complex issue, and one that is not easy to study. The nature of the reactivity that may exist probably depends on the subject's knowledge of what aspect of his or her behavior is being observed. There is ample research evidence to indicate that when people are made self-conscious about certain aspects of their behavior by means of self-monitoring, there is a clear effect on the frequency of this behavior (Kazdin, 1974b). However, if individuals are told that they are being observed by someone but are not informed as to what aspects of their behavior are being noted, then the effects are likely to be a more general self-consciousness, and perhaps an attempt to second-guess what the observer is looking for.

With the exception of the ethically questionable procedure of observing individuals without their knowledge, the possibility of reactivity remains a methodological issue to which a behavioral assessor must attend. Thus, observers are usually instructed to remain as unobtrusive as possible (e.g., to "become part of the furniture"). One should also allow for a period of acclimation, to let subjects become accustomed to the presence of observers, and this initial period of observation should not be used as part of the actual baseline against which any behavior change is compared.

Another potential difficulty in satisfying method assumptions has to do with the observers themselves and the extent to which any source of bias may be associated with the observation process. In this regard, unreliability among independent observers may be a function of differential expectancies about what is supposed to be occurring and/or idiosyncratic interpretations of the behavior code.

Researchers in the area of behavioral observation have been concerned about the findings of Rosenthal (1966) and others that an experimenter or observer effect may exist under certain circumstances. The question here is whether any initial hypotheses or expectations regarding what is "supposed to be seen" can influence the observation process

itself. Some data by Kent, O'Leary, Diament, and Dietz (1974) suggest that, to the extent to which one uses a behaviorally anchored observational code, biases resulting from differential expectancy can be kept to a minimum. This study used the code described in O'Leary and O'Leary (1972), and the authors experimentally manipulated observers' expectations regarding the type of change likely to occur. In one condition, the observers were told that the therapeutic treatment procedures being used on the children they were observing were expected to produce a decrease in disruptive behavior. In the second condition, the observers were told that no behavior change was anticipated. In reality, both groups of observers viewed the same videotapes, which in fact showed no change in the frequency of disruptive behavior from baseline to treatment phase. The study did not show any differences in the *use of the behavioral code* as a function of differential expectations; in contrast, the overall, more *impressionistic judgments* of change in the two conditions were significantly influenced by initial expectations. The influence on global impression is particularly striking, especially since these observers had just carried out concrete and detailed observations providing information contrary to their overall impressions.

A follow-up study by O'Leary, Kent, and Kanowitz (1975) showed that it *was* possible to influence the observer so that a biased observation would emerge even with the use of a concrete behavioral code. The observers were informed that the children they would be rating on the videotapes were participating in a token reinforcement program in which two specific disruptive classes of behavior were being modified while two others were not being treated. As was the case in the previous study, the tapes revealed no actual behavior change whatsoever. Each time the observers coded the behavior and turned in their data, the experimenter provided them with differential feedback. If the data submitted were consistent with what was initially stated as an anticipated predicted change, the experimenter offered positive feedback (e.g., "These tokens are really reducing the level of vocalization"). If no change from baseline was manifested in the observation, but one was actually "predicted," the experimenter would say such things as "We really ought to be picking up some decreases in the rate of playing by now." The results of this study revealed that when the observers received this differential feedback, they eventually presented the "expected" results.

In dealing with the expectancy issue, then, every attempt should be made to define the behavioral categories as concretely and operationally as possible. Observers should not be informed of the changes expected, and, if possible, they should be kept "blind" as to the experimental or therapeutic manipulations applied to the individuals being observed. Further, the observational data should not be inspected in any detail while the study is under way, so that any inadvertent reinforcement for what the observer has recorded may be avoided.

A related methodological problem is the extent to which independent observers can reliably utilize a given behavioral code. Although it seems evident that potential sources of unreliability are reduced when one utilizes a coding system focusing on specific behaviors, it should also be pointed out that most behavioral codes nonetheless require a certain amount of interpretation. For example, if one is attempting to observe the incidence with which children in a classroom are engaging in "off-task" behavior (i.e., not doing their work), some problems of interpretation may arise. Such a category represents a large behavior class, under which a wide variety of specific behaviors may fall, and the observer needs to be familiar with the potential specific behaviors that can be scored in this category, and to be able to differentiate them from "on-task" behaviors. There are times, however, when a judgment about a specific behavior may be most difficult to make. What of a child who is supposed to be doing his or her arithmetic assignment in class but spends periods of time toying with his or her pencil? Should this be considered an instance of off-task behavior? Or is this recurrent behavior something the child engages in when he or she pauses to concentrate on a problem? For each particular observational code, the specificity of guidelines for resolving such ambiguities can have substantial bearing on observer reliability.

A typical finding reported for each of the behavioral observational codes described above has been that interobserver reliability is in fact quite good. But what has emerged in looking at this issue more closely is that a kind of reactivity exists when observers realize that *their* behavior is being observed. This effect was dramatically demonstrated in a study by Reid (1970), who trained and examined the performance of observers in the use of a behavioral code and then had them apply the code in observations of behavior they viewed on videotape recordings. Before viewing the videotapes, the observers were led to believe that no reliability check would be made and that they would be the only ones doing the rating. The results indicated that in comparison with a reliability coefficient of .76 when the observers thought their reliability was being evaluated, there was a sharp drop to a coefficient of .51 once the raters felt that they were completely on their own.

Elaborating this phenomena are some findings by Romanczyk, Kent, Diament, and O'Leary (1973), who not only confirmed Reid's finding that interobserver reliability was higher when the observers felt that their accuracy was being evaluated but additionally found that interobserver agreement could be increased further by providing the raters with information as to exactly who was going to be checking their reliability. In other words, it was possible for the observers to modify their interpretation of the code so as to be more consistent with the criteria employed by the specific person doing the reliability check.

Another potential source of unreliability that sometimes goes unnoticed is the "drift" problem (O'Leary & Kent, 1973). A typical procedure in the application of behavioral codes involves the use of terms of observers. Following the observation periods, the teams often have the opportunity to compare their observations more closely and to discuss among themselves any potential sources of unreliability. As a result of working together, various ambiguities in the use of a code are clarified. Although this at first does not seem to be an undesirable practice, a problem arises when each team begins to develop its own idiosyncratic interpretation of the code. This problem is not readily apparent, as the reliability checks made between pairs of observers lead one to conclude that interobserver agreement is good. However, even though teams of observers are in fact reliably applying the behavioral code, they may drift away from each other with regard to what they are actually observing. To the extent that such drift occurs, the different teams of observers are unwittingly utilizing different behavioral codes.

As in the case of the expectancy problem, unreliability among observers may be kept to a minimum by clarifying any ambiguities inherent in the behavioral code. Further, a more extensive training period can be utilized, the reliability of observers can be constantly monitored, and teams of observers can be continually rotated so as to prevent any potential drift.

One final point might be made in this discussion of observations in naturalistic settings. From a practical point of view, it may not always be feasible to have trained observers readily available. In fact, much of what has been described thus far is much more likely to be carried out within the context of a research program than in routine clinical work. The reason should be obvious: the systematic implementation of many of these observation procedures can be very costly. As a practical compromise, behavioral observations have been carried out by individuals typically present in the subject's naturalistic environment, such as friends, spouses, parents, teachers, nurses, and other significant individuals. Although their observations are not likely to be detailed or precise as those of more highly trained observers, there is a definite advantage in obtaining information from individuals who have occasion to view the subject over relatively long periods of time, in a wide variety of situations, and with minimal likelihood of reactivity. Among the various behavior checklists that have been employed are those that utilize the observations of psychiatric nurses (Honigfeld, Gillis, & Klett, 1966), classmates (Wiggins & Winder, 1961), and teachers (Ross, Lacey, & Parton, 1965).

Situation Tests

A basic limitation associated with observations in naturalistic settings is that one typically has little control over the situation to which the subject or client must respond. Although every attempt is made to standardize the setting in which the observation is to take place—such as carrying out home observations during dinnertime—little can be done to control exactly what goes on at this time and place. Thus, depending on what may be said or done to the person being observed, his or her behavior can vary greatly. As a way of circumventing these shortcomings, behavioral assessors have made use of various situation tests.

Although situation tests have been used for assessment purposes in the past (e.g., Office of Strategic Services Assessment Staff, 1948), their use by behavioral assessors has focused specifically on confronting the subject with situations likely to elicit the type of behavior toward which the assessment is specifically directed. Not only is the individual's behavior objectively observed in such situations but, whenever relevant, subjective and physiological measures of anxiety are employed as well.

One frequently employed situation test was devised by Paul (1966) in conjunction with an outcome study on the effectiveness of systematic desensitization in treating speech anxiety. The situation test, which was used as a measure of improvement, required subjects to present a 4-minute speech before a live audience. Immediately before giving the talk, they were administered self-report and physiological measures of anxiety. During the speech itself, trained observers in the audience recorded various overt signs of anxiety, coding such behaviors as extraneous hand movements, hand tremors, pacing, and absence of eye contact. This type of situation test has proved useful in a variety of other clinical outcome studies (e.g., Goldfried & Trier, 1974; Meichenbaum, Gilmore, & Fedoravicious, 1971).

Situation tests have also been employed for the assessment of interpersonal anxiety (e.g., Borkovec, Fleischmann, & Caputo, 1973; Borkovec, Stone, O'Brien, & Kaloupek, 1974; Kanter & Goldfried, 1979). In these assessments, the subject is required to maintain a brief conversation with one or two trained confederates of the experimenter, the interaction is videotaped, and the subject's performance is evaluated in terms of behavioral, subjective report and physiological indexes of anxiety.

Research on this procedure has demonstrated that the interaction situation is capable of eliciting emotional arousal in individuals for whom interpersonal anxiety is a problem.

The interpersonal skills of chronic psychiatric patients have been assessed by means of the Minimal Social Behavior Scale, a procedure originally developed by Farina, Arenberg, and Guskin (1957). The scale is applied within a standardized interview requiring the interviewer to do various things (e.g., drop a pencil on the floor) or to ask various questions (e.g., "How are you today?"). The scale comprises 32 different items, each of which is scored as eliciting either an appropriate or an inappropriate response. The scoring criteria are clearly spelled out, and the interrater reliability is high. Although one may legitimately raise the question whether the behavior observed within the context of the particular interview setting is a representative sample of the patient's behavior in all situations, the scale has nonetheless been shown to be sensitive to behavior change following drug treatment and to discriminate among patients at varying levels of functioning (Farina *et al.*, 1957; Ulmer & Timmons, 1966).

Numerous attempts have been made to assess assertive behavior by means of controlled situation tests (e.g., Kazdin, 1974a; McFall & Lillesand, 1971; McFall & Marston, 1970; McFall & Twentyman, 1973). Subjects were called on the telephone, and some unreasonable request was made of them. This request, which varied from study to study, entailed either purchasing a subscription to several magazines or lending one's lecture notes immediately prior to a final examination. The subject's response was unobtrusively recorded and later evaluated by judges for its assertiveness. In most of these studies, however, the assessment procedure failed to discriminate between individuals who were otherwise found to have changed as a function of assertion training. Although it is certainly possible that the inability to obtain positive results could have resulted from a failure to sample adequately from situations in which the subject actually achieved behavior change, positive results found in one instance by McFall and Twentyman (1973) suggest that the methodology may have been at fault. Instead of making a single unreasonable request during the telephone conversation, they presented the subject with a series of seven increasingly unreasonable requests. The telephone calls were made less than a week before a scheduled final examination and began by simply asking the subject to spend a few minutes discussing the lecture material. The subject was then confronted with a series of more and more outlandish requests, which culminated in a request to lend out his or her lecture notes for two full days prior to the examination. By extending the nature of the interaction in this manner, the assessment procedure was found to be more sensitive in detecting changes resulting from assertion training.

Situation tests have also been employed in observations of the way in which parents interact with their children. This procedure is frequently done behind a one-way mirror, with the situation constructed in such a way as to sample the type of instances in which the child's problematic behaviors typically occur. For example, if the child's primary problem consists of having difficulty in working independently, one might set up a section of the room where he or she is asked to carry out various homework problems while his or her mother is involved in some other task in another section of the room. The behavior of both parent and child can then be observed, providing data useful in a functional analysis of the child's difficulties.

One additional example of a situation test should be discussed, not only because it represents one of the more frequently used behavioral assessment procedures but also because it may serve to illustrate some of the potential methodological problems inherent in situation tests. The assessment procedure is the Behavioral Avoidance Test (BAT), which is used as a means of evaluating the strength of fears and phobias. Although the exact procedures have varied somewhat from study to study (see Bernstein & Nietzel, 1973), the test basically requires that the individual enter a room in which the feared object is present (e.g., a snake in a cage), walk closer to the object, look at it, touch it, and, if possible, hold it. In addition to evaluating how closely the subject is willing to approach the object, subjective, physiological, and overt behavioral indexes of anxiety may be assessed as well. In addition to various small-animal phobias (e.g., snakes, rats, spiders, dogs), more clinically relevant fears have also been assessed by means of the BAT, such as the fear of enclosed places and heights.

For several years, behavioral assessors utilizing the BAT in their research have assumed that the measure provided them with a completely accurate assessment of an individual's phobia. More recent tests of the method assumptions underlying this procedure, however, have revealed that this may not always be the case. When an individual enters an assessment session, whether for research or clinical purposes, there are certain socially defined characteristics of the situation that can influence his or her response. An illustration of such so-called demand characteristics of situations was first demonstrated by Orne (1962), who showed that the mere participation in an experiment was reactive, causing subjects to behave in ways that were perhaps atypical of them. In one experiment, for example, Orne had a group of subjects enter a room and gave them the tedious task of adding up columns of figures on a sheet of paper, after which they were instructed to tear the paper into small pieces, throw them in the air, and begin with a new list of figures. The subjects persisted at this task for long periods of time, simply because it was the thing to do in this situation.

In the case of the BAT, research evidence is accumulating to the effect that here, too, subjects' perception of the demand characteristics of the assessment can greatly influence the extent to which they will approach the feared object or stay in the phobic situation. A study by Miller and Bernstein (1972), for example, divided a group of claustrophobic subjects into two experimental conditions, after which they were individually put in a small, dark chamber. Under a low-demand condition, subjects were told that they could leave the room at any point by simply signaling, whereas under a high-demand condition, they were encouraged to stay in the room regardless of how anxious they might be. Following this experimental procedure, the conditions were reversed, so that the subjects who were initially in the low-demand group were

now in the high-demand group, and vice versa. The findings clearly demonstrated the very powerful effect that the demand-characteristic instructions had on the subjects' behavior, in that the subjects under low-demand instructions behaved more phobically than those under the high-demand condition. This was true when a comparison was made between groups of subjects and also when the instructions were changed for each subject individually. A second finding of some interest was that the experimental instructions, although they had a clear effect on the subjects' behavior, had no impact on their anxiety reactions as measured by either subjective report or physiological measures.

Further investigation of the effect of demand characteristics when the BAT was used to assess small-animal phobias has similarly revealed that changing the subjects' perception of the task requirements can significantly influence their willingness to approach caged rats (Smith, Diener, & Beaman, 1974) and snakes (Bernstein & Neitzel, 1973). The Smith *et al.* study additionally confirmed the finding noted by Miller and Bernstein (1972) that although the demand characteristics of the situation can significantly alter approach behavior, they have relatively little impact on the subjective and physiological indexes of anxiety.

In evaluating the BAT in light of the research findings on demand characteristics, as well as with the hindsight that the early users of this assessment procedure obviously did not have, it is not at all surprising that subjects' approach behavior is influenced by factors unrelated to their actual phobia. All of us are aware of instances in which otherwise fearful individuals have been able to do things ''on a dare,'' or in which people have displayed unusual acts of courage despite the high level of anxiety they might have been experiencing at the time.

The nature of the demand characteristics one chooses to convey in administering the BAT should probably vary as a function of the experimenter's or clinician's purpose for the assessment. If one wishes to screen out all but the most phobic of individuals, then the demand characteristics for approaching the feared objects should be set as high as possible. If, however, one wishes to predict how the individual is likely to respond in a more naturalistic context—such as when one is out in the woods and notices a snake climbing down a tree—then the BAT should be contrived so as to parallel the real-life situation more accurately. The exact way in which this parallel may be implemented and validated constitutes a challenge to the ingenuity of behavioral assessors.

One of the problems associated with the assessment of phobic behavior is that it is comprised of an operant as well as a respondent, the implication of which is that it can at times be influenced by external contingencies. The fact that demand characteristics are not necessarily an issue in all situation tests, however, is clearly illustrated in a study by Borkovec, Stone, O'Brien, and Kaloupek (1974). Borkovec *et al.* found that instructions to behave "in a relaxed, nonanxious manner" had no influence on subjects' performance in a situation test of heterosexual anxiety. In comparison with the assessment of phobic behavior, this situation test focused solely on anxiety, as measured by self-report, behavior signs, and physiological indexes. In all likelihood, the potential influence of demand characteristics on situation tests depends on the extent to which the behavior being measured is under the subject's voluntary control.

In concluding this discussion of situation tests, there is a possible methodological issue inherent in all of them that has yet to be investigated, namely, the *difficulty level* of the task presented to the subject. Take, for example, the use of a situation test for assessing public-speaking anxiety. Although practical limitations obviously limit what can actually be implemented, one can easily think of a wide variety of situations in which to place the speech-anxious individual: audiences may vary in their size and composition, the length of the speech can be short or long, the preparation period can be extensive or minimal, the topic can be familiar or strange, and numerous other variations may be introduced to vary the aversiveness of the situation.

What most users of situation tests have not addressed themselves to is just how difficult the task should be for the subject. To take the extremes, it is obvious that speaking to two individuals for a brief period of time about a topic with which one is familiar is likely to elicit less anxiety than speaking at length to a group of several hundred about an unfamiliar topic. In a situation test used to assess change in clinical outcome studies, there is probably some interaction between the effectiveness of one's treatment procedure and the difficulty level reflected in the test situation. More powerful and extensive therapeutic interventions are likely to have more of an impact on higher levels of anxiety, whereas briefer and less effective therapies will probably reflect changes at lower levels only. Thus, depending on how one constructs the situation test in such research, the experimental findings are likely to vary. What may be called for in the use of the situation tests in the future, then, is to present a series of increasingly difficult tasks to the subject, thereby providing a potentially more sensitive measure of behavior change.

Role Playing

Although there are similarities between certain situation tests as described above and a role-playing approach to assessment, the primary distinction between the two is that the situation test focuses on placing subjects in the real-life situation, whereas role playing requires subjects to react "as if" the event were occurring to them in real life. Although the line between the two may be a fine one at times, it is probably wise to maintain this distinction until it has been demonstrated empirically that the differences between the two procedures are nonfunctional.

The use of role playing for assessment purposes was described several years ago in a report by Rotter and Wickens (1948), whose stated rationale for the procedure is quite consistent with a behavioral orientation to assessment. They suggested that sampling behavioral interactions has considerable potential for providing the assessor with useful information, primarily because of the extent to which it parallels criterion behavior. Rotter and Wickens were interested mainly in demonstrating the feasibility of conducting such an assessment, and consequently, they report no validity data for their procedure. The subjects in their study were required to respond to various simulated situations, and their behavior in these instances was rated by judges according to the degree to which "social aggressiveness" was reflected. This report is important in that it offers an early statement of the potential utility of this procedure.

Another early use of role playing as an assessment device is reported in a study by Stanton and Litwak (1955), who provided validity data of a most encouraging sort. Using foster parents and college students as their subject populations, they attempted to assess "interpersonal competence." The subjects were presented with three situations—meeting a troubled friend, handling an interfering parent, and criticizing an employee—and their responses were rated for competence with the aid of a behavior checklist. Highly significant correlations were found between observers' ratings of the subjects' behavior during role-playing situations and evaluations obtained from individuals who knew the subjects well. For the foster parents, a correlation of .82 was found with social workers' ratings; in the case of students, friends' ratings correlated .93 with the scores obtained from the role-playing assessment. Not unexpected, but nonetheless providing discriminant validity, was the finding that criterion ratings provided by individuals who did not know the subjects well did not correlate nearly as well with the role-playing assessment. Moreover, when the role playing was compared with an assessment based on 12 hours of intensive interviews, the role playing was found to fare considerably better in matching the ratings of well-acquainted individuals.

In more recent years, role playing has gained in popularity among behavioral assessors as a means of evaluating the effectiveness of various therapeutic procedures. One of the initial uses of role playing in this context is described by Rehm and Marston (1968), who developed a procedure for assessing heterosexual anxiety in males. In an attempt to standardize the procedure and to make it otherwise more practically feasible, a series of 10 social situations was presented on audiotape. Each situation begins with a description of the context, after which there is a comment by a female requiring some response on the part of the subject.

For example, one situation starts with the narrator describing a scene in the college cafeteria in which the subject is walking out, when he suddenly is approached by a female. At this point in the tape, a female voice states, "I think you left this book." For each of these situations, the subject is asked to imagine that it is actually occurring to him at the moment and to respond as he would in real life. The response is recorded on a separate tape recorder and evaluated later for such characteristics as anxiety, adequacy of response, length of response, and delay before responding. In comparisons with the scores of subjects not volunteering for a therapy program focusing on heterosexual anxiety, the role-playing scores for those participating in the clinical research were found by Rehm and Marston to be significantly different. Performance on the role-playing assessment was furthermore found to change as a function of the therapeutic intervention.

A role-playing assessment procedure similar to that used by Rehm and Marston was investigated by Arkowitz, Lichtenstein, McGovern, and Hines (1975), who compared the performance of high versus low socially competent males as determined independently on the basis of their frequency of dating and their subjective comfort, social skills, and general satisfaction in their heterosexual behaviors. Two role-playing situations were studied, one conducted *in vivo* with a female confederate and the other involving a role-played telephone conversation. In the face-to-face situation, subjects were asked to imagine that they had just met this female and were attempting to get to know her better. In the telephone conversation, the subject was instructed to ask the female confederate for a date. The primary finding was that the low socially competent individuals displayed a lower rate of verbal activity than the high socially competent subjects in each of these role-played situations.

In a comprehensive program designed to assess and facilitate interpersonal skills among psychiatric inpatients, Goldsmith and McFall (1975) employed the behavioral-analytic model (Goldfried & D'Zurilla, 1969) in developing a role-playing assessment procedure. Twenty-five separate situations were sampled from various aspects of the patients' typical day-today interactions, each of which was then presented to them on audiotape with instructions to respond as they would in a real-life situation. The subjects' responses to each situation were rated on the basis of certain predetermined and reliably applied criteria for interpersonal effectiveness. Goldsmith and McFall found that as a result of a behavior training program designed to facilitate interpersonal skills, the scores of these patients on the role-playing assessment procedures showed significant improvement. No change was found for control subjects who had been assigned to attention-placebo or no-contact conditions.

Another related problem area that has been assessed by means of role-playing procedures is assertive behavior. The initial work in this area was reported by McFall and Marston (1970), who sampled several situations representative of instances in which college students might be required to assert themselves. These included being interrupted by a friend while attempting to study, having one's laundry lost by the cleaners, and being asked to work by an employer at a time that would be inconvenient. Following the methodology originally devised by Rehm and Marston (1968), the situations were presented to subjects on audiotapes, and their responses were recorded on a second tape recorder. In this particular study, the subjects' responses were not scored; instead, independent judges carried out a paired comparison between the subjects' behavior before and after assertion training. These judges' ratings, which were completely blind as to which interaction was obtained before and which after therapy, revealed significant improvement in role-played assertive behavior.

A later report by McFall and Lillesand (1971) indicated that when assertiveness was rated on the basis of a 5-point scale, interrater reliability was in the .90s. McFall and Lillesand also reported some experimentation with a modification of the role-played assessment procedure. Rather than presenting the situation and asking the subject to give his or her typical response, the interaction was extended so as to parallel more closely what might occur in a real-life situation. Specifically, if the subject was successful in refusing the unreasonable request, the taped confederate would press him or her further, for a total of five "pushes." This variation in the assessment procedure also revealed changes reflecting the effects of assertion training.

A series of studies on the role-playing assessment of assertive behavior within a population of psychiatric patients has also been carried out by Eisler and his associates (Eisler, Hersen, & Agras, 1973a,b; Eisler, Hersen & Miller, 1973; Eisler, Miller, & Hersen, 1973; Hersen, Eisler, Miller, Johnson, & Pinkston, 1973). The role-playing assessment procedure consisted of 14 situations in which a male psychiatric patient was required to interact with a female confederate in such standard impositions as having someone cut ahead in line, having one's reserved seat taken at a ball game, having a steak delivered overcooked at a restaurant, and having a service station carry out extensive repairs on one's car without previous approval. Unlike most role-playing measures of assertive training, the Eisler interaction is carried out *in vivo*, and the ratings of assertiveness are based on videotape recordings of the interaction. The reliability of ratings is generally high for both an overall rating of assertiveness and ratings of several behavioral components. Among those components that have been found to improve as a result of assertion training are duration of reply, affective quality of response, loudness of response, and content of assertive reply (Eisler, Hersen, & Miller, 1973).

Although much of the work on the use of role playing as an assessment procedure is promising, relatively little attention has been paid to any potential methodological problems that may serve to attenuate its effectiveness, such as the failure to satisfy both method and sampling assumptions (see Goldfried & Kent, 1972). Among the method assumptions that need to be satisfied is the extent to which the behavior of the confederate can be appropriately standardized. Standardization can be achieved by providing the confederate with detailed guidelines and adequate training, or more simply by presenting a tape-recorded stimulus situation.

Although most users of role-playing assessment report good interrater reliability, virtually no attempt has been made to control for the possible occurrence of a "halo effect."

That a halo effect may be an issue is reflected in the study by Rotter and Wickens (1948). They found that when a given subject's role-played responses to two separate situations were rated by the same judges, the average interrater reliability of the subject's behavior in these two situations was .78. However, when different judges were used to rate the subjects' behavior in the two separate situations, the average correlations were only .55. The erroneously imposed cross-situational consistency may very well have accounted for the spuriously higher correlation obtained originally. As discussed in conjunction with behavioral observation in naturalistic settings, there are numerous potential sources of bias when one sets out to observe and code human behavior. Thus, the issues of observer expectancies, continual monitoring of reliability, and the possibility of drift among pairs of observers need to be attended to in the coding of role-playing interactions as well.

The question of demand characteristics has yet to be a topic of empirical investigation in the use of role-playing assessment. Are subjects truly "in role" during the assessment procedure, or are they somehow responding to some unique aspects of the demand characteristics within the assessment setting? Is it easier or more difficult for subjects to behave as they typically would when the stimulus situation is presented on audiotape as compared with an *in vivo* interaction? Are there any individual differences associated with subjects' abilities to immerse themselves naturally in the role-playing interaction? These are only some of the questions related to method assumptions that need to be answered.

With regard to the question of sampling assumptions, most developers of role-playing assessment procedures have used only a few situations, selected more or less on an *a priori* basis. Among the exceptions have been the procedures outlined by Bates (1980), Bellack, Hersen, and Lamparski (1979), DeLange, Lanham, and Barton (1981), Edleson and Rose (1978), Freedman *et al.* (1978), Goldsmith and McFall (1975), Mathews *et al.* (1980), and Perri and Richards (1979), who conducted an empirically based situational analysis. Unless one assumes cross-situational consistency with whatever variable one is as-

sessing (e.g., social skills or assertiveness), some form of empirical sampling is essential if one wishes to generalize the finding of the assessment.

Self-Report

In using self-report procedures, behavioral assessors have focused on the report of specific behavioral interactions, on subjective reports of emotional response, and on perceptions of environmental settings. Each of these areas of assessment is described below.

Self-Report of Overt Behavior. The behavioral characteristic that has been the focus of most self-report measures of overt behavior is assertiveness. For example, Wolpe and Lazarus (1966) described a series of 30 questions that they recommend be asked of clients in assessing the extent to which they may be inhibited in expressing their opinion in interpersonal situations. More recent questionnaires, based in part on the questions described by Wolpe and Lazarus, have been devised by Rathus (1973), Galassi, DeLo, Galassi, and Bastien (1974), Gambrill and Richey (1975), and Gay, Hollandsworth, and Galassi (1975). Although the formats of these more recent questionnaires are slightly different, the assessment inventories are more similar than they are different. In fact, some of the items are virtually identical. The questionnaires are similarly limited in the sense that they fail to satisfy the sampling assumptions essential in the development of behavioral assessment procedures. For the most part, the items in these inventories were taken from previous questionnaires or were determined on an *a priori* basis. In using these inventories, the general trait of assertiveness is assumed, and no subscales reflecting different aspects of one's interactions (e.g., with friends, strangers, or authority figures) are available.

A more sophisticated approach to the development of a measure of assertiveness may be seen in the work of McFall and Lillesand (1971), whose focus was specifically on the ability of college students to refuse unreasonable requests. Their Conflict Resolution Inventory consists of 35 items, each of which is specific to a particular situation in which some unreasonable request might be made of the subject. For example, one such item is "You are in the thick of studying for exams when a person whom you know only slightly comes into your room and says, 'I'm tired of studying. Mind if I come in and take a break for awhile?'" For each item, subjects are to indicate the likelihood that they would refuse each of the requests and how comfortable they would feel about either refusing or giving in. Unlike the developers of the other assertiveness questionnaires described above, McFall and Lillesand derived their items empirically on the basis of extensive pilot work, in which the sample of college students used in generating the initial item pool was similar to the subject population to whom the assessment measure was later to be applied. The Conflict Resolution Inventory has been found to be useful as a dependent variable in clinical outcome studies (McFall & Lillesand, 1971; McFall & Twentyman, 1973), in which change was found to occur as a function of assertion training.

Self-Report of Emotion. Although the assessment of overt behavior—whether via self-reports of behavior, naturalistic observation, situation tests, or role playing—holds considerable promise, there is more to human functioning than a person's overt behavior can reveal. As noted earlier, several reports indicate that even when demand characteristics influence an individual's performance on a behavioral avoidance test, subjective reports of anxiety remain unaffected (Miller & Bernstein, 1972; Smith, Diener, & Beaman, 1974). Furthermore, there are instances, as in an outcome study on acrophobia reported by Jacks (1972), in which subjective reports of anxiety may be more sensitive to differential change than is approach behavior.

A measure frequently used by behavioral assessors in the self-report of anxiety is the Fear Survey Schedule (Geer, 1965). The schedule consists of a series of 51 potentially anxiety-arousing situations and objects (e.g., snakes, being alone, looking foolish), which subjects are asked to rate for the degree of fear typically elicited in them. The schedule is at best a gross screening device and should probably be viewed as nothing more than that. Although some researchers have attempted to carry out extensive factor analyses of the

schedule to determine the potential dimensions of fear, such research activities are of dubious value, especially as no attempt was originally made to sample representatively the full range of fears and phobias typically present in most individual's lives.

Although several attempts have been made to use the Fear Survey Schedule to predict subjects' reactions to a behavioral avoidance task, the data on its predictive efficiency have been mixed. In viewing these conflicting findings, it is important to keep in mind that these two measures of fear are of a very different form, in the sense that one is primarily verbal and the other more behaviorally observable. Moreover, these two measures appear to focus on different aspects of anxiety. In the case of the Fear Survey Schedule, subjects are asked to state how afraid they would feel when in the presence of certain situations or objects. When subjects are placed in the behavioral avoidance task, the primary measure consists of the extent to which they will approach the feared object. As noted earlier, there are often situations in which the demand characteristics or the task requirements are such that individuals, despite their feelings of fear and trepidation, will approach a feared object or remain in anxiety-producing circumstances.

In the context of research on the way in which demand characteristics affect performance on the behavioral avoidance test, Bernstein (1973) demonstrated that the Fear Survey Schedule could differentially predict approach behavior, depending on the situational context in which the behavioral avoidance test was carried out. When the test was carried out in a clinic context, subjects' initial reports on the Fear Survey Schedule were predictive of their actions. However, the verbal reports of subjects who participated in the avoidance test conducted in a laboratory setting had no relationship to their likelihood of approaching a feared object.

Whatever assets the Fear Survey Schedule may have as a relatively quick and easily administered screening device, there are nonetheless certain limitations that severely restrict its utility. Perhaps the most telling of these is the fact that subjects are required to indicate their degree of fear about situations or objects that are described in only general

and very vague terms (e.g., "being criticized"). The nature of the situation (e.g., who
is doing the criticizing and what the criticism
is about) is left unspecified. Furthermore, the
nature of the person's anxiety response (e.g.,
sweaty palms, increased heart rate, or desire
to run away) is not assessed by the questionnaire.

A commonly used self-report measure of
anxiety that takes into account the nature of
the situation, as well as each of the possible
components of the anxiety response, is described by Endler, Hunt, and Rosenstein
(1962). Their assessment prodecure, called the
S–R Inventory of Anxiousness, consists of a
series of potentially anxiety-arousing situations that are briefly described in writing, after
which there are several rating scales reflecting
varying ways in which a person might become
anxious. For example, one such situation is
"You are about to take an important final examination," for which subjects are asked to
indicate the extent to which their "heart beats
faster," they "get an uneasy feeling," their
"emotions disrupt action," and several other
reactions indicative of anxiety.

The S–R inventory is important for its utility
as a dependent measure and also as a vehicle
for studying the question of cross-situational
behavioral consistency. In keeping with the
behavioral orientation to assessment, which
emphasizes the importance of the situation to
which an individual reacts, research with the
S–R inventory is useful in learning more about
the extent to which individual differences and
consistencies may manifest themselves in various types of situations.

Both the Fear Survey Schedule and the S–R
Inventory of Anxiousness ask subjects to indicate their typical reaction. In a sense, these
self-reports are hypothetical, since they are
based on the subjects' *recollections* of how
they reacted in the past to certain types of
situations. Consistent with the overall philosophy that behavioral assessment should focus
directly on criterion behavior, it seems only
reasonable that behavioral assessors have also
made attempts to elicit self-reports of emotional reactivity during the time the individual
is actually *in* certain situations, rather than
recollecting them. Among the several avail-

able subjective measures of situational state
anxiety are Spielberger, Gorsuch, and Lushene's (1970) State–Trait Anxiety Inventory
and Zuckerman and Lubin's (1965) Multiple
Affect Adjective Checklist. The former measures involve a series of descriptive statements,
such as "I am tense," "I am jittery," and
"I feel calm," which the subject is asked to
rate on a 4-point scale for their accuracy as a
self-descriptive statements. In the case of the
Multiple Affect Adjective Checklist, feelings
of depression and hostility, as well as those of
anxiety, are assessed. For both of these measures, appropriate changes are frequently found
in response to various kinds of experimental
manipulations, such as those intended to elicit
or reduce stress.

In addition to focusing on various negative
emotional states, behavioral assessors have
also developed self-report measures to assess
positive feelings. For example, Cautela and
Kastenbaum (1967) developed a Reinforcement Survey Schedule, which in part parallels
the Fear Survey Schedule. Various objects
and situations are presented in questionnaire
form, and subjects are asked to indicate the
extent to which they prefer each of them. This
measure suffers from numerous problems, not
the least of which is the fact that the items
themselves were not empirically derived from
a pool of potentially reinforcing events or objects.

In contrast, the Pleasant Events Schedule
constructed by MacPhillamy and Lewinsohn
(1972) includes items generated from an actual
situational analysis. College students were
asked to specify "events, experiences, or activities which you find pleasant, rewarding, or
fun," and the net result of this sampling was
a series of 320 items of both a social and a
nonsocial type. In responding to the Pleasant
Events Schedule, subjects are asked to indicate not only how often each of these various
events might have occurred within the past
month but also how pleasant and enjoyable
they were. If for some reason subjects have
not experienced any particular event, they are
simply asked to estimate how enjoyable it
might have been if it had occurred. This more
sophisticated approach to the assessment of
potential reinforcers has been found to be use-

ful in research in the area of depression (Lewinsohn & Graf, 1973; Lewinsohn & Libet, 1972).

Self-Report of Environment. Consistent with the behavioral assessor's interest in the nature of the social environment with which individuals must interact, there is a growing interest in what has been referred to as *social ecology* (Insel & Moos, 1974; Moos, 1973). Moos and his colleagues have been actively involved in developing questionnaires for assessing the social-psychological impact made by various environments, including psychiatric wards, community-oriented psychiatric treatment programs, correctional institutions, military basic-training companies, university student residences, junior and senior high-school classrooms, work environments, and social, therapeutic, and decision-making groups. The questionnaires focus on the individual's perception of various aspects of her or his social environment and include such items as "On this ward everyone knows who's in charge," "Members are expected to take leadership here," and "Members here follow a regular schedule every day."

In assessments of the impact made by varying environmental settings, three dimensions appear to be common across several diverse environmental contexts: the nature and intensity of interpersonal relationships (e.g., peer cohesion and spontaneity); personal development opportunities (e.g., competition and intellectuality); and the stability and responsivity of the social system to change (e.g., order and organization, innovation). In much the same way as the assessment of behavioral characteristics within an individual is relevant to behavioral change, so the various environmental assessment questionnaires have implications for the modification of social environments (Moos, 1974).

Behavioral Assessment and Behavior Therapy

If one interprets behavior therapy in its broadest sense as involving the application of what we know about psychology in general to problems that may manifest themselves within the clinical setting, it follows that the number and variety of behavior therapy procedures available to the clinician are large and forever changing (Goldfried & Davison, 1976). This is clearly a double-edged sword, which provides one with several potentially effective treatment methods, and also with the dilemma of which to use in any given case. With this dilemma in mind, Goldfried and Pomeranz (1968) have argued that "assessment procedures represent a *most crucial and significant* step in the effective application of behavior therapy" (p. 76).

In considering behavioral assessment in the clinical setting, it is useful to make a conceptual distinction between (1) those variables associated with a behavioral analysis of the maladaptive behavior and (2) those that have implications for the selection and implementation of the most relevant therapeutic procedures. In essence, the first set of variables sheds light on *what* has to be manipulated in order to bring about behavior change, while the second set provides information about *how* best to bring about this change.

Variables Associated with Maladaptive Behavior

Viewing the client's maladaptive behavior as a dependent variable, the therapist is required to decide which of many potential independent variables one can best "manipulate" to bring about behavior change. There has been some confusion in the literature about whether behavior therapists actually are manipulating "underlying causes" when attempting to modify problem behaviors. If by *underlying causes* one necessarily means early social learning experiences, then the answer is no. This answer does not imply, however, that the treatment always focuses on the presenting problem. Take, for example, the man whose marriage is foundering because of the frequent arguments he has with his wife. In carrying out a behavioral analysis, it may be revealed that the arguments typically occur when he has been drinking. When does he drink? Whenever he's had a hard day at work. What contributes to the pressure at work? The excessively high standards he imposes on his own performance. Here the therapist would probably focus more on the husband's unrealistic standards of self-evaluation and not on the fighting behavior itself. In other words, the behavioral analysis may "uncover" other relevant variables—not early social learning experiences, but additional concurrent variables within the chain of potential determinants of behavior.

In deciding which variables should be manipulated, the behavior therapist can select from one or more of the following: (1) the antecedent stimulus variables, which may elicit or set the stage for the maladaptive behavior; (2) organismic variables, whether psychological or physiological; (3) the overt maladaptive behavior itself; and (4) the consequent changes in the environmental situation, including the reactions of others to the maladaptive behavior. While the distinction among these four types of variables may at times be arbitrary, it is useful to discuss each separately.

Stimulus Antecedents. Although once highly centralistic, clinicians and personality theorists have begun to recognize the significant role of the environment as an important determinant of behavior. In considering the role of antecedent stimulus events, one may draw a distinction between those that elicit emotional or autonomic responses and those that function as discriminative cues for occurrence of maladaptive instrumental responses.

In dealing with such maladaptive emotional responses as anxiety or depression, the behavior therapist operates under the assumption that some external situation is eliciting the behavior. We must admit, however, that at times it may be no easy task to specify exactly which events in the client's life are determining his or her emotional response. Some individuals report being anxious all of the time or being in very chronic and pervasive states of depression. In such a case, the client's emotional reaction apparently becomes so salient that he or she is unable to pinpoint its functional antecedents. Other clients may be able to indicate general classes of situations to which they are reacting (e.g., heights, enclosed spaces, or social-evaluative situations). Although this general indication clearly simplifies the task of assessment, the need nonetheless exists for greater specification of those situations that have been eliciting the emotional upset.

In the assessment of the discriminative stimuli that set the stage for maladaptive instrumental behaviors that will be reinforced, the therapist must obtain detailed information on the precise nature of the situation, such as time, place, and frequency. Mischel (1968) has argued convincingly that an individual's response, whether it be deviant or nondeviant, is greatly influenced by the specific nature of the situation in which the behavior occurs. We have all had the experience of being surprised when a friend or colleague acts "out of character" in certain situations. Clinically, it is not uncommon to observe a child who presents a behavior problem at home but creates no difficulties in the school. As in the specification of stimuli that elicit maladaptive emotional responses, relevant discriminative stimuli must be described in detail (e.g., What is it about the school setting that differs from the home environment?).

The way individuals interpret events is often important in determining the stimulus antecedents of their behavior. The issue of defining the effective stimulus has prompted those involved in research on perception to focus on the significant role played by the physiological and cognitive states of the individual. We refer to these factors as *organismic variables.*

Organismic Variables. While the increasing recognition of environmental variables as determinants of behavior is a welcome trend, the exclusion of all inferential concepts and the refusal to consider mediating factors can seriously limit the therapist's ability to understand and modify behavior. The completely environmentalistic, noninferential orientation to the study of human functioning, which Murray (1938) has called the *peripheralistic approach,* can limit one's understanding of human behavior as much as an entirely centralistic orientation can. Although an individual's attitudes, beliefs, and expectations may often be modified by changes in overt behavior, there are times when such organismic variables should themselves be the target for direct modification.

One type of mediator consists of the client's

expectations, or set, about certain situations. As suggested by Dollard and Miller (1950), Beck (1967), and Ellis (1962), the way in which people label or categorize events can greatly color their emotional reaction in such situations. In addition to interpreting situations in ways that can create problems, people may also create difficulties by the way they label their own behavior. To the extent that individuals construe their maladaptive behavior as indicative of "going crazy," being out of control, or manifesting a serious physical illness, their problems will be compounded. Another important mediating variable consists of the standards one sets for self-reinforcement. Although clients may be functioning at an appropriate level of proficiency according to societal standards, their primary problem may result from the fact that they construe their behavior as being substandard; in such instances, it would appear that the standard is unrealistic and in need of modification.

In the assessment of organismic variables, one should attend also to any physiological factors that may contribute to the maladaptive behavior. Included here would be the direct and side effects of any psychoactive drugs, the client's general energy level, states of fatigue, and other similar physiological and constitutional factors that might influence his or her behavior. It is not uncommon, for example, for depression to coincide with some women's menstrual periods. It is clear that presenting problems such as headaches, forgetfulness, sexual inadequacy, and other potentially biologically mediated problems require a thorough physical examination.

Response Variables. The primary focus here should be consistent with the general guidelines suggested by Mischel (1968): "In behavioral analysis the emphasis is on what a person *does* in situations rather than on inferences about what attributes he *has* more globally" (p. 10). In other words, the assessment of response variables should focus on situation-specific samples of the maladaptive behavior, including information on duration, frequency, pervasiveness, and intensity.

Although the distinction is at times difficult to make, it is important to differentiate responses that are primarily *respondents* from those that are *operants*. Respondents, where consequences play a relatively minimal role in maintaining the response, typically include such emotional reactions as anxiety, depression, anger, and sexual arousal. Operant or instrumental behavior, on the other hand, includes those responses for which the consequent reinforcement plays a significant role. Examples of maladaptive instrumental behaviors are typically seen in children, particularly where the primary difficulty consists of "behavioral problems." The extensive work done with token economies in schools and institutional settings has similarly focused on instrumental behaviors. Still further examples of operant behavior seen in clinical settings are social skill deficits, such as lack of assertiveness and inappropriate heterosexual behaviors.

There are times when one cannot distinguish between operants and respondents. For example, children who consistently delay going to bed at night because they are "afraid to be alone" may pose assessment problems. The same is true of a multitude of other problems of a primarily avoidant nature, which may be maintained both by an emotional reaction to antecedent stimuli and by consequent changes in the environment following the avoidance response.

Consequent Variables. To a great extent, many of our day-to-day responses, both adaptive and maladaptive, are maintained by their consequences. In determining whether something "pays off," the timing of the consequences can play a significant role. For example, the so-called neurotic paradox (Mowrer, 1950) refers to behaviors having immediate positive consequences, but long-term negative ones, as in the case of alcohol or drug addiction. A frequently existing positive reinforcement may consist of the reactions of significant others. Such reinforcements can include approval and praise, but in some cases, they may simply be attention, as when a parent or teacher becomes angry over a child's refusal to obey a given command. In addition to the delay and content of reinforcement, one should note also the frequency of reinforcement, as in the case of depressed individuals who have few reinforcing events in their life situation.

Variables Associated with the Selection and Implementation of Techniques

In addition to using assessment procedures to determine which variables—whether antecedent, organismic, response, or consequent—need to be modified, the clinician must also make an assessment to find the most appropriate therapeautic technique. Unlike many other clinicians, behavior therapists choose from a wide range of possible procedures. In part, the selection of therapeutic technique is determined by the target in need of modification. For example, if a detailed behavioral analysis done with a test-anxious client reveals that the difficulties arise because this individual does not study, one would obviously not utilize a technique such as desensitization. Or, for a client whose anxiety in social situations is due to an actual behavioral deficit, some sort of skill-training procedure would be more appropriate than desensitization.

At present, we have relatively little empirical data on specific variables associated with the effective implementation of the various behavior therapy procedures. Some findings are just beginning to become available, such as Kanter and Goldfried's (1979) report that cognitive restructuring may be more appropriate than desensitization in cases of social anxiety. However, most of our clinical decisions are based on the intrinsic nature of the procedure itself (e.g., you cannot use systematic desensitization with a client who is unable to conjure up an aversive image) as well as on clinical experience in the use of the various procedures.

There are certain client characteristics that are relevant to the selection and implementation of therapeutic procedures. The client's ability to report specific concrete examples is frequently crucial in the implementation of a number of therapeutic techniques. One clinical observation is that those clients who have the greatest initial difficulty in reporting actual behavioral sample tend to be brighter and more "psychologically sophisticated." Clients who have this difficulty must be trained to be more specific (e.g., via repeated instructions, selective reinforcement, and homework assignments) before anything can be done therapeutically.

A number of the techniques used by behavior therapists include ongoing homework assignments, in which clients must keep a record of various behavioral events between sessions or practice certain skills *in vivo*. If clients tend to be disorganized or to procrastinate, which may or may not be part of the primary target behaviors toward which the therapy is being directed, they will probably be less likely to carry through on the between-session assignments. In such instances, the therapist must decide to rely less on homework or must attempt to persuade or otherwise aid the client to follow through on these tasks.

The therapist should also be attuned to clients' standards for self-reinforcement. Clients with perfectionistic standards may expect too much too fast and consequently may become discouraged with the gradualness of behavior change. It is important to take great care to discuss this potential difficulty with such clients prior to the actual implementation of whatever technique is to be used. One can also dispel potential dissatisfaction by focusing continually on the client's appropriate evaluation of behavior change as it begins to occur. A fuller discussion of this issue can be found in Goldfried and Robins (in press).

In addition to client variables, certain environmental variables may be important in the selection and implementation of therapeautic procedures. Included here are such considerations as the availability of appropriate role models in a client's life or the extent to which certain reinforcers are likely to be available for certain behaviors. In the treatment of sexual problems, for example, the availability of a partner can have obvious implications for the specific therapeutic procedures utilized. Other examples are the various phobias, where the feasibility of *in vivo* desensitization depends on the availability of fear-related situations or objects.

At present, one typically uses clinical intuition and experience as an aid in determining what seems to be the most appropriate behavior-therapy technique for a particular client. Clinical practice involves selecting a few seemingly relevant techniques and then trying each in turn until one proves to be effective. A better strategy would seem to involve the use of a thorough "criterion analysis" of each behavior-therapy procedure, with the goal being the determination of those variables necessary for the selection of the most effective treatment for any given client. In the most comprehensive sense, the relevant research question is "*What* treatment, by *whom*, is most effective for *this* individual with *that* specific problem, and under *which* set of circumstances?" (Paul, 1967, p. 111).

Classification of Behavior Disorders

The Kraepelinian system of classifying deviant behavior has been criticized on a number of counts, not the least of which is its scant relevance to a behavioral approach to the understanding and modification of behavior (Adams, Doster, & Calhoun, 1977; Kanfer & Saslow, 1969). Alternate classification systems that are more behavioral in nature have been described by Adams *et al.* (1977) and Staats (1963). What follows is based on Staats's suggestions, which have been elaborated on by Bandura (1968) and Goldfried and Sprafkin (1974). In outlining various categories of deviant behaviors, this interim approximation attempts to take into account stimulus as well as client variables. Further, it categorizes deviant behaviors according to the variables that are probably maintaining them.

Difficulties in Stimulus Control of Behavior

Within this general category, the distinction is drawn between the failure of environmental stimuli to control maladaptive *instrumental* behavior and the tendency of some stimuli to elicit maladaptive *emotional* reactions.

Defective Stimulus Control. In instances of defective stimulus control, the individual presumably possesses an adequate behavioral repertoire but is unable to respond to socially appropriate discriminative stimuli. An extreme example of defective stimulus control would be an individual who tells jokes at a funeral. Although the jokes may be objectively funny (i.e., the behavioral repertoire is adequate), they are clearly out of place in that particular situation. An example with more clinical relevance is those children so eager to show the teacher they know the correct an-

swer that they continually speak out of turn in class. Assuming the child is capable of maintaining silence at times, he or she must learn to respond to those situational cues that indicate when it is appropriate to speak up. There are numerous clinical examples that show how parents inadvertently train their children to respond to incorrect discriminative stimuli. For example, parents often complain that their children will not obey them when they speak quietly, but only when they shout. The child has probably learned that neither aversive nor positive consequences follow ordinary requests, but that failure to heed an angry parent's request can result in a variety of aversive consequences. Such children are clearly capable of obeying but do not do so when the parents want them to.

Inappropriate Stimulus Control. In this category, one would include intense aversive emotional reactions elicited by objectively innocuous cues. These emotional reactions have presumably been conditioned to these specific stimuli, either by direct or by vicarious social learning experiences. Anxiety, gastrointestinal disturbances, insomnia, and other direct or indirect manifestations of intense emotional reactions would be included in this category. Such problems are frequently complicated by attempts to avoid these emotional states (as in the case of phobias) and also by the symbolic presentation of aversive stimuli, that is, ruminating about fears.

Deficient Behavioral Repertoires

This category includes behavior problems in which individuals lack the skills needed to cope effectively with situational demands. For example, they may never have learned what to say or do in social, academic, or vocational situations. Although the problem may be construed as a skill deficit, the clinical picture is often complicated by such individuals' failure to achieve adequate social reinforcement. They may even experience punishing consequences, such a loss of status, ridicule, and rejection. As a result, clients manifesting behavioral deficits frequently report negative subjective attitudes, including anxiety, depression, lack of self-confidence, and sometimes generalized anger toward others.

Aversive Behavioral Repertoires

The defining characteristic of this category is a maladaptive behavior pattern that is aversive to other individuals surrounding the client. Included here, then, would be persons who manifest antisocial behavior, who are overly aggressive, or who in some other ways are inconsiderate of others. Some writers have characterized these individuals as manifesting a "behavioral excess." In contrast to clients with behavioral deficiencies, individuals with aversive behavioral repertoires know what to say and do in various situations, but they ultimately make life difficult for themselves by being obnoxious or otherwise bothersome to others.

Difficulties with Incentive Systems (Reinforcers)

Included here are deviant behaviors that are functionally tied to reinforcing consequences, either because the incentive system of the individual is deficient or inappropriate, or because the environmental contingencies are creating problems.

Defective Incentive System in the Individual. In these instances, social stimuli that are reinforcing for most people are not capable of controlling the individual's behavior. Thus, attention, approval, and praise may not be positively reinforcing, nor may criticism or disapproval be negatively reinforcing. Two clinical examples are autistic children, whose behavior cannot be readily controlled by conventional social reinforcers (Rimland, 1964), and delinquents, for whom social reinforcers in the larger society have little relevance, as their behavior conforms to the standards of a subculture.

Inappropriate Incentive System in the Individual. This category includes those persons for whom the incentive system itself is maladaptive, that is, those things reinforcing to the individual are harmful and/or culturally disapproved. Excessive involvement with alcohol, drugs, and sexual practices such as pedophilia are some clinical examples.

Absence of Incentives in the Environment. Problems in this category include situations in which reinforcement is lacking in an individual's particular environment. The most clearly delineated example is a state of prolonged depression resulting from the loss of a spouse. More subtle examples are apathy and boredom.

Conflicting Incentives in the Environment. Much maladaptive behavior stems from conflicting environmental consequences. The clearest clinical examples are children whose maladaptive behavior appears to pay off, where there is a contradiction between what has been labeled by the environment as maladaptive and what, in fact, the environment is inadvertently reinforcing. Sometimes certain individuals in the environment positively reinforce a deviant behavior, as with the class clown who attracts the attention of his or her peers, despite the fact that the teacher disapproves of his or her actions. More subtly, parents or teachers may reinforce children for lack of persistence by helping them as soon as they experience some difficulty in handling a situation. Problems associated with conflicting incentives in the environment are not limited to children. As pointed out by Goffman (1961), Rosenhan (1973), and others, institutional settings, including psychiatric hospitals, may inadvertently foster behavior that is then labeled as deviant. On the more interpersonal level, individuals may verbally encourage their spouses to behave in one way but may act otherwise to discourage or even outrightly punish such attempts.

Aversive Self-Reinforcing Systems

Assuming that cognitive processes are capable of maintaining various forms of behavior, it is important to recognize that individuals are capable of reinforcing themselves for adequate behavior. If individuals' standards for "adequacy" are unrealistically high, they are likely to find themselves in few situations where their performance merits self-reinforcement, regardless of how adequate they may be according to external criteria. The consistent lack of self-reinforcement may lead to chronic states of depression and subjective feelings of inadequacy.

Although the system outlined above can be useful in carrying out a behavioral analysis of deviate behavior, it should be viewed as only a first attempt to categorize maladaptive behavior within a social learning context. Obviously, the categories are not mutually exclusive. Any one person may manifest a number of behavioral problems, which can be classified according to several of the headings. Further, certain behavior problems may be so complex as to warrant a multiple classification. Still, the system can serve its purpose by isolating those environmental or client variables that can be manipulated for maximum therapeutic benefit.

Future Perspectives

In concluding this overview of behavioral assessment, I would like to raise some additional considerations yet to be answered by behaviorally oriented researchers and clinicians. These issues are practically and conceptually complex and clearly present a challenge to the ingenuity of behavioral assessors.

Comparative Validity of Behavioral and Traditional Assessment

In light of the growing interest in behavioral assessment procedures, it is somewhat surprising to find that virtually no research has been carried out to compare their validity and predictive efficiency with more traditionally oriented methods. When one recognizes that problems with the validity and reliability of many traditional assessment procedures were, to a large extent, responsible for the rejection of traditional models of human functioning, this lack of comparative research is even more surprising. Although a few isolated studies have tended to support a more behaviorally oriented approach to assessment (Goldfried & Kent, 1972), there are insufficient findings at present to draw any firm conclusions regarding the comparative validity of both orientations. Just as one can view behavior therapy as a broad orientation for approaching the full gamut of clinical problems, so can one construe behavioral assessment as providing clinical psychology with a new paradigm for measuring human functioning. As has been demonstrated with various behavior therapy procedures, the acceptance of a behaviorally oriented approach to assessment by clinical psychology in general is not likely to occur until it can be shown that it does a better job than what is currently available.

Standardization of Procedures

A direction in which we need to move is toward the eventual standardization of the assessment measures used in our outcome research and clinical work. By varying the assessment methodologically from study to study—in ways that are not always very apparent—we make it extremely difficult to compare and synthesize our findings. For example, when role playing has been used as an outcome measure, the procedures have varied by virtue of whether the subject offers a single response or several responses in an extended interaction, whether the procedure entails a live interaction or the situation is presented on audiotape, what is the content of the items used, and what particular scoring criteria are employed.

What we need to do is to work toward achieving an interim consensus on the best few measures currently available for assessing each class of behaviors of interest, and then to encourage comparative research so as to narrow down the pool to only those procedures that have been demonstrated to be most valid. Once we have decided on the best methods for assessing a given variable, the next step may be to use these measures until it can be demonstrated empirically that others may surpass them in validity and discriminability. Until that time occurs, I would even go so far as to suggest that journal editors not consider for publication any studies using measures that have been shown to have inferior validity. This is not to say that we should leave no room for improvement or refinement, but that we avoid the proliferation of procedures that serve only to add confusion, not growth, to the field.

Need for a Theoretical Framework

One of the major problems with behavioral assessment—and with behavior therapy in general—is that we have no "theory" to guide our work. Although we clearly have developed an important technology for assessing and modifying various "behaviors of interest," we need to have clearer direction as to exactly what we should be interested in, as well as the parameters and determinants of such behaviors. In talking about *theory*, I am referring not to any highly conceptual scheme but to a compilation of close-to-observable functional relationships between various behaviors and their determinants. Those of us involved in the clinical application of behavior therapy can offer a rich source of hypotheses about those variables that we need to investigate empirically in order to build up a pool of such functional relationships.

Summary

This chapter has discussed some of the underlying theoretical and methodological assumptions associated with behavioral assessment procedures, contrasting them with more traditional approaches to personality assessment. Consistent with an abilities conceptualization of personality, the relevance of behavioral assessment to proficiency tests and the assessment of competence has been noted. Some of the more frequently used methods of behavioral assessment were discussed, including direct observations in naturalistic settings and the sampling of responses to situations that have been contrived by the assessor, responses that manifest themselves in role-playing situations, and the person's own self-reports of overt behavior, emotions, and perceived environmental settings. Some of the methodological problems associated with each of these procedures were also considered. The relationship between behavioral assessment and behavior therapy was outlined, and those variables associated with clinical behavioral assessment were described. In addition, a system for classifying clinical problems within a behavioral framework was outlined.

The chapter ends by raising some unanswered questions that we need to deal with in order to advance the field, including those surrounding the comparative validity of behavioral and traditional assessment, the need to standardize our procedures, and the need for a low-level theoretical framework within which behavioral assessment can take place.

References

Adams, H. E., Doster, J. A., & Calhoun, K. S. A psychologically based system of response classification. In A. R. Ciminero, K. S. Calhoun, & H. E. Adams (Eds.) *Handbook of Behavioral Assessment*. New York: Wiley-Interscience, 1977.

American Psychological Association, American Educational Research Association, and National Council on Measurement in Education. *Standards for educational and psychological tests*. Washington, D.C.: American Psychological Association, 1974.

Arkowitz, H., Lichtenstein, E., McGovern, K., & Hines, P. The behavioral assessment of social competence in males. *Behavior Therapy*, 1975, *6*, 3–13.

Bandura, A. A social learning interpretation of psychological dysfunctions. In P. London & D. Rosenhan (Eds.), *Foundations of abnormal psychology*. New York: Holt, Rinehart & Winston, 1968, pp. 293–344.

Barker, R. G., & Wright, H. F. *One boy's day*. New York: Harper & Row, 1951.

Barlow, D. H. (Ed.), *Behavioral assessment of adult dysfunctions*. New York: Guilford Press, 1980.

Bates, P. The effectiveness of interpersonal skills training on the social skill acquisition of moderately and mildly retarded adults. *Journal of Applied Behavioral Analysis*, 1980, *13*, 237–248.

Beck, A. T. *Depression: Clinical, experimental, and theoretical aspects*. New York: Harper & Row, 1967.

Bellack, A. S., Hersen, M., & Lamparski, D. Role-play tests for assessing social skills: Are they valid? Are they useful? *Journal of Consulting and Clinical Psychology*, 1979, *47*, 335–342.

Bernstein, D. A., & Nietzel, M. T. Procedural variation in behavioral avoidance tests. *Journal of Consulting and Clinical Psychology*, 1973, *41*, 165–174.

Bernstein, G. S. *Behavior manager effectiveness inventory*. Unpublished manuscript, 1978.

Bersoff, D. N., & Moyer, D. Positive reinforcement observation schedule (PROS): Development and use. Paper presented at the annual meeting of the American Psychological Association, Montreal, August 1973.

Borkovec, T. D., Fleischmann, D. J., & Caputo, J. A. The measurement of anxiety in an analogue social situation. *Journal of Consulting and Clinical Psychology*, 1973, *41*, 157–161.

Borkovec, T. D., Stone, N. M., O'Brien, G. T., & Kaloupek, D. G. Evaluation of a clinically relevant target behavior for analog outcome research. *Behavior Therapy*, 1974, *5*, 503–513.

Cautela, J. R., & Kastenbaum, R. A. A reinforcement survey schedule for use in therapy, training, and research. *Psychological Reports*, 1967, *20*, 1115–1130.

Ciminero, A. R., Adams, H. E., & Calhoun, K. S. *Handbook of Behavioral Assessment*. New York: Wiley-Interscience, 1977.

Cone, J. D., & Hawkins, R. P. (Eds.). *Behavioral assessment: New directions in clinical psychology*. New York: Brunner-Mazel, 1977.

Delange, J. M., Lanham, S. L., & Barton, J. A. Social skills training for juvenile delinquents: Behavioral skill training and cognitive techniques. In D. Upper & S. Ross (Eds.), *Behavioral group therapy*. Champaign, Ill.: Research Press, 1981.

Dollard, J., & Miller, N. E. *Personality and psychotherapy*. New York: McGraw-Hill, 1950.

Edleson, J. L., & Rose, S. D. A behavioral roleplay test for assessing children's social skills. Paper presented at the Twelfth Annual Convention of the Association for the Advancement of Behavior Therapy, Chicago, 1978.

Eisler, R. M., Hersen, M., & Agras, W. S. Effects of videotape and instructional feedback on non-verbal marital interactions: An analogue study. *Behavior Therapy*, 1973, *4*, 551–558. (a)

Eisler, R. M., Hersen, M., & Agras, W. S. Videotape: A method for the controlled observation of non-verbal interpersonal behavior. *Behavior Therapy*, 1973, *4*, 420–425. (b)

Eisler, R. M., Hersen, M., & Miller, P. M. Effects of modeling on components of assertive behavior. *Journal of Behavior Therapy and Experimental Psychiatry*. 1973, *4*, 1–6.

Eisler, R. M., Miller, P. M., & Hersen, M., Components of assertive behavior. *Journal of Clinical Psychology*, 1973, *24*, 295–299.

Ellis, A. *Reason and emotion in psychotherapy*. New York: Lyle Stuart, 1962.

Endler, N. S., Hunt, J. McV., & Rosenstein, A. J. An S-R inventory of anxiousness, *Psychological Monographs*, 1962, *76*, (17, Whole No. 536).

Farina, A., Arenberg, D., & Guskin, S. A scale for measuring minimal social behavior. *Journal of Consulting Psychology*, 1957, *21*, 265–268.

Freedman, B. J., Rosenthal, L., Donahoe, C. P., Jr., Schlundt, D. J., & McFall, R. M. A social-behavioral analysis of skill deficits in delinquent and nondelinquent adolescent boys. *Journal of Consulting and Clinical Psychology*, 1978, *46*, 1448–1462.

Funabiki, D., & Calhoun, J. F. Use of a behavioral-analytic procedure in evaluating two models of depression. *Journal of Consulting and Clinical Psychology*, 1979, *47*, 183–185.

Galassi, J. P., DeLo, J. S., Galassi, M. D., & Bastien, S. The college self-expression scale: A measure of assertiveness. *Behavior Therapy*, 1974, *5*, 165–172.

Gambrill, E. D., & Richey, C. A. An assertion inventory for use in assessment and research. *Behavior Therapy*, 1975, *6*, 550–561.

Gay, M. L., Hollandsworth, J. G., & Galassi, J. P. An assertiveness inventory for adults. *Journal of Counseling Psychology*, 1975, *4*, 340–344.

Geer, J. H. The development of a scale to measure fear. *Behaviour Research and Therapy*, 1965, *13*, 45–53.

Goffman, E. *Asylums*. Garden City, N.Y.: Doubleday, 1961.

Goldfried, M. R. Behavioral assessment. In I. B. Weiner (Ed.), *Clinical methods in psychology*. New York: Wiley-Interscience, 1976.

Goldfried, M. R., & Davison, G. C. *Clinical behavior therapy*. New York: Holt, Rinehart & Winston, 1976.

Goldfried, M. R., & D'Zurilla, T. J. A behavioral-analytic model for assessing competence. In C. D. Spielberger (Ed.), *Current topics in clincal and community psychology*. New York: Academic Press, 1969.

Goldfried, M. R., & Kent, R. N. Traditional versus behavioral personality assessment: A comparison of methodological and theoretical assumptions. *Psychological Bulletin*, 1972, *77*, 409–420.

Goldfried, M. R., & Linehan, M. Basic issues in behavioral assessment. In A. R. Ciminero, H. E. Adams, & K. S. Calhoun, *Handbook of behavioral assessment*. New York: Wiley Interscience, 1977.

Goldfried, M. R., & Pomeranz, D. M. Role of assessment in behavior modification. *Psychological Reports*, 1968, *23*, 75–87.

Goldfried, M. R., & Robins, C. On the facilitation of self-efficacy. *Cognitive Therapy and Research*, in press.

Goldfried, M. R., & Sprafkin, J. N. *Behavioral personality assessment*. Morristown, N.J.: General Learning Press, 1974.

Goldfried, M. R., & Trier, C. S. Effectiveness of relaxation as an active coping skill. *Journal of Abnormal Psychology*, 1974, *83*, 348–355.

Goldsmith, J. B., & McFall, R. M. Development and evaluation of an interpersonal skill-training program for psychiatric inpatients. *Journal of Abnormal Psychology*, 1975, *84*, 51–58.

Haynes, S. N. *Principles of behavioral assessment*. New York: Gardner, 1978.

Haynes, S. N., & Wilson, C. C. *Behavioral assessment*. San Francisco: Jossey-Bass, 1979.

Hersen, M., & Bellack, A. (Eds.). *Behavioral assessment: A practical handbook*. New York: Pergamon, 1976.

Hersen, M., & Bellack, A. (Eds.). *Behavioral assessment: A practical handbook*. New York: Pergamon, 1976.

Hersen, M., & Bellack, A. (Eds.), *Behavioral assessment: A practical handbook*. (2nd Ed.). Elmsford, N.Y.: Pergamon, 1981.

Hersen, M., Eisler, R. M., Miller, P. M., Johnson, M. B., & Pinkston, S. G. Effects of practice instructions and modeling on components of assertive behavior. *Behaviour Research and Therapy*, 1973, *11*, 443–451.

Honigfeld, G., Gillis, R. D., & Klett, C. J. Nosic-30: A treatment-sensitive ward behavior scale. *Psychological Reports*, 1966, *19*, 180–182.

Insel, P. M., & Moos, R. H. Psychological environments: Expanding the scope of human ecology. *American Psychologist*, 1974, *29*, 179–188.

Jacks, R. N. Systematic desensitization versus a self-control technique for the reduction of acrophobia. Unpublished doctoral dissertation. Stanford University, 1972.

Johnson, S. M., & Bolstad, O. D. Reactivity to home observation: A comparison of audio recorded behavior with observers present or absent. *Journal of Applied Behavioral Analysis*, 1975, *8*, 181–185.

Johnson, W. *People in quandaries*. New York: Harper & Row, 1946.

Kanfer, F. H., & Saslow, G. Behavioral diagnosis. In C. M. Franks (Ed.), *Behavior Therapy: Appraisal and status*. New York: McGraw-Hill, 1969.

Kanter, N. J., & Goldfried, M. R. Relative effectiveness of rational restructuring and self-control desensitization in the reduction of interpersonal anxiety. *Behavior Therapy*, 1979, *10*, 472–490.

Kazdin, A. E. Effects of covert modeling and model reinforcement on assertive behavior. *Journal of Abnormal Psychology*, 1974, *83*, 240–252. (a)

Kazdin, A. E. Self-monitoring and behavior change. In M. J. Mahoney & C. E. Thoresen (Eds.). *Self-control:*

Power to the person. Monterey, Calif.: Brooks/Cole, 1974. (b)

Keefe, F. J., Kopel, S. A., & Gordon, S. B. *A practical guide to behavioral assessment.* New York: Springer, 1978.

Kendall, P. C., & Hollon, S. D. (Eds.), *Assessment strategies for cognitive-behavioral interventions.* New York: Academic Press, 1981.

Kent, R. N., O'Leary, K. D., Diament, C., & Dietz, A. Expectation biases in observational evaluation of therapy change. *Journal of Consulting and Clinical Psychology,* 1974, *42,* 774–780.

Klass, E. T. A cognitive-behavioral approach to research on guilt. Paper presented at 25th Anniversary Conference on Rational-Emotive Therapy, June 1980, New York City.

Kulich, R. J., & Conger, J. A step towards a behavior analytic assessment of heterosocial skills. Paper presented at Association for Advancement of Behavior Therapy, Chicago, 1978.

Levenson, R. W., & Gottman, J. M. Toward the assessment of social competence. *Journal of Consulting and Clinical Psychology,* 1978, *46,* 453–462.

Lewinsohn, P. M., & Graf, M. Pleasant activities and depression. *Journal of Consulting and Clinical Psychology,* 1973, *41,* 261–268.

Lewinsohn, P. M., & Libet, J. Pleasant events, activity schedules, and depressions. *Journal of Abnormal Psychology,* 1972, *79,* 291–295.

Lewinsohn, P. M., & Shaffer, M. Use of home observations as an integral part of the treatment of depression: Preliminary report and case studies. *Journal of Consulting and Clinical Psychology,* 1971, *37,* 87–94.

Macdonald, M. *A behavioral assessment methodology applied to the measurement of assertiveness.* Doctoral dissertation, University of Illinois, 1974.

MacPhillamy, D. J., & Lewinsohn, P. M. Measuring reinforcing events. *Proceedings of the 80th Annual Convention, American Psychological Association,* 1972.

Mariotto, M. J., & Paul, G. L. A multimethod validation of the inpatient multidimensional psychiatric scale with chronically institutionalized patients. *Journal of Consulting and Clinical Psychology,* 1974, *42,* 497–508.

Mash, E. J., & Terdal, L. G. (Eds.) *Behavioral therapy assessment.* New York: Springer, 1976.

Mash, E., & Terdal, L. (Eds.), *Behavioral assessment of childhood disorders.* New York: Guilford Press, 1980.

Mathews, R. M., Whang, P. L., & Fawcett, S. B. Development and validation of an occupational skills assessment instrument. *Behavioral Assessment,* 1980, *2,* 71–85.

McFall, R. M., & Lillesand, D. B. Behavior rehearsal with modeling and coaching in assertion training. *Journal of Abnormal Psychology,* 1971, *77,* 313–323.

McFall, R. M., & Marston, A. An experimental investigation of behavior rehearsal in assertive training. *Journal of Abnormal Psychology,* 1970, *6,* 295–303.

McFall, R. M., & Twentyman, C. T. Four experiments in the relative contributions of rehearsal, modeling, and coaching to assertive training. *Journal of Abnormal Psychology,* 1973, *81,* 199–218.

Meichenbaum, D. H., Gilmore, J. B., & Fedoravicious, A. Group insight versus group desensitization in treating speech anxiety. *Journal of Consulting and Clinical Psychology,* 1971, *36,* 410–421.

Merluzzi, T. V., Glass, C. R., & Genest, M. *Cognitive assessment.* New York: Guilford Press, 1981.

Miller, B., & Bernstein, D. Instructional demand in a behavioral avoidance test for claustrophobic fears. *Journal of Abnormal Psychology,* 1972, *80,* 206–210.

Mischel, W. *Personality and assessment.* New York: Wiley, 1968.

Moos, R. H. Behavioral effects of being observed: Reactions to a wireless radio transmitter. *Journal of Consulting and Clinical Psychology,* 1968, *32,* 383–388.

Moos, R. H. Conceptualizations of human environments. *American Psychologist,* 1973, *28,* 652–665.

Moos, R. H. *Evaluating treatment environments: A social ecological approach.* New York: Wiley, 1974.

Mowrer, O. H. *Learning theory and personality dynamics.* New York: Ronald, 1950.

Mullinix, S. D., & Gallasi, J. P. Deriving the content of social skills training with a verbal response components approach. *Behavioral Assessment,* 1981, *3,* 55–66.

Murray, H. A. *Explorations in personality.* New York: Oxford University Press, 1938.

Nay, W. R. *Multimethod clinical assessment.* New York: Gardner, 1979.

Office of Strategic Services Assessment Staff. *Assessment of men.* New York: Rinehart, 1948.

O'Leary, K. D., & Becker, W. C. Behavior modification of an adjustment class: A token reinforcement program. *Exceptional Children,* 1967, *33,* 637–642.

O'Leary, K. D., & Kent, R. Behavior modification for social action: Research tactics and problems. In L. A. Hamerlynck, L. C. Handy, & E. J. Mash (Eds.), *Critical issues in research and practice.* Champaign, Ill.: Research Press, 1973.

O'Leary, K. D., & O'Leary, S. G. (Eds.). *Classroom management.* Elmsford, N.Y.: Pergamon Press, 1972.

O'Leary, K. D., Kent, R. N., & Kanowitz, J. Shaping data collection congruent with experimental hypothesis. *Journal of Applied Behavior Analysis,* 1975, *8,* 43–51.

Orne, M. T. On the social psychology of the psychological experiment: With particular reference to demand characteristics and their implication. *American Psychologist,* 1962, *17,* 776–783.

Patterson, G. R., Ray, R. S., Shaw, D. A., & Cobb, J. Manual for coding of family interactions, 1969. Available from ASIS/NAPS, c/o Microfiche Publications, 305 E. 46th Street, New York, N.Y. 10017. Document #01234.

Paul, G. L. *Insight vs. desensitization in psychotherapy.* Stanford, Calif.: Stanford University Press, 1966.

Paul, G. L. Insight versus desensitization in psychotherapy two years after termination. *Journal of Consulting Psychology,* 1967, *31,* 333–348.

Paul, G. L., & Lentz, R. J. *Psychosocial treatment of chronic mental patients.* Cambridge, Mass.: Harvard University Press, 1977.

Paul, G. L., Tobias, L. L., & Holly, B. L. Maintenance psychotropic drugs in the presence of active treatment programs: A "triple-blind" withdrawal study with long-term mental patients. *Archives of General Psychiatry,* 1972, *27,* 106–115.

Perri, M. G., & Richards, C. S. Assessment of heterosocial skills in male college students: Empirical development of a behavioral role-playing test. *Behavior Modification*, 1979, *3*, 337–354.

Purcell, K., & Brady, K. Adaptation to the invasion of privacy: Monitoring behavior with a miniature radio transmitter. *Merrill-Palmer Quarterly of Behavior and Development*, 1966, *12*, 242–254.

Rabin, A. I. Projective methods: An historical introduction. In A. I. Rabin (Ed.), *Projective techniques in personality assessment*. New York: Springer, 1968.

Rathus, S. A. A 30-item schedule for assessing assertive behavior. *Behavior Therapy*, 1973, *4*, 398–406.

Rehm, L. P., & Marston, A. R. Reduction of social anxiety through modification of self-reinforcement: An instigation therapy technique. *Journal of Consulting and Clinical Psychology*, 1968, *32*, 565–574.

Reid, J. B. Reliability assessment of observation data: A possible methodological problem. *Child development*, 1970, *41*, 1143–1150.

Rimland, B., *Infantile autism*. New York: Appleton-Century Crofts, 1964.

Romanczyk, R. G., Kent, R. N., Diament, C., & O'Leary, K. D. Measuring the reliability of observational data: A reactive process. *Journal of Applied Behavior Analysis*, 1973, *6*, 175–184.

Rosenhan, D. L., On being sane in insane places. *Science*, 1973, *179*, 250–258.

Rosenthal, R. *Experimenter effects in behavioral research*. New York: Appleton-Century-Crofts, 1966.

Ross, A. O., Lacey, H. M., & Parton, D. A. The development of a behavior checklist for boys, *Child Development*, 1965, *36*, 1013–1027.

Rotter, J. B., & Wickens, D. D. The consistency and generality of ratings of "social aggressiveness" made from observations of role playing situations. *Journal of Consulting Psychology*, 1948, *12*, 234–239.

Smith, R. E., Diener, E., & Beaman, A. L. Demand characteristics and the behavioral avoidance measure of fear in behavior therapy analogue research. *Behavior Therapy*, 1974, *5*, 172–182.

Spielberger, C. D., Gorsuch, R. L., & Lushene, R. E. *The state-trait anxiety inventory (STAI) test manual for form X*. Palo Alto, Calif.: Consulting Psychologists Press, 1970.

Staats, A. W. (with contributions by C. K. Staats). *Complex human behavior*. New York: Holt, Rinehart & Winston, 1963.

Stanton, H. R., & Litwak, E. Toward the development of a short form test of interpersonal competence. *American Sociological Review*, 1955, *20*, 668–674.

Turk, D. C. Factors influencing the adaptive process with chronic illness: Implications for intervention. In I. Sarason & C. Spielberger (Eds.), *Stress and anxiety*, Vol. 6. Washington, D.C.: Hemisphere, 1979.

Ulmer, R. A., & Timmons, E. O. An application and modification of the minimal social behavior scale (MSBS): A short objective, empirical, reliable measure of personality functioning. *Journal of Consulting Psychology*, 1966, *30*, 1–7.

Wiggins, J. S. *Personality and prediction: Principles of personality assessment*. Reading, Mass.: Addison-Wesley, 1973.

Wiggins, J. S., & Winder, C. L. The peer nomination inventory: An empirical derived sociometric measure of adjustment in preadolescent boys. *Psychological Reports*, 1961, *9*, 643–677.

Wolpe, J., & Lazarus, A. A. *Behavior therapy techniques*. New York: Pergamon, 1966.

Zuckerman, M., & Lubin, B. *Manual for the multiple affect adjective checklist*. San Diego, Calif.: Educational and Industrial Testing Service, 1965.

CHAPTER 5

Observational Methods

Donald P. Hartmann and David D. Wood

Introduction

Behavior observation has been variously described as the "hallmark" (Ciminero, Calhoun, & Adams, 1977, p. 10) and the "*sine qua non*" (Gelfand & Hartmann, 1975, p. 21) of applied behavior analysis, as well as "the greatest contribution of behavior modification to the treatment of human problems" (Johnson & Bolstad, 1973, p. 7). Although these descriptions may contain some hyperbole, direct observation is an important behavioral assessment technique. Recent surveys indicate that observation procedures are employed in over 70% of the research articles published in major behavioral journals (Bornstein, Bridgwater, Hickey, & Sweeney, 1980; Kelly, 1977). Direct observations are reported to occupy a similarly important role in the clinical practice of behavior therapists (Swan & MacDonald, 1978; Wade, Baker, & Hartmann, 1979). In addition, observational methods of assessment are used frequently by researchers in other fields, including anthropology (e.g., Whiting & Whiting, 1973), child development

(e.g., Cairns, 1979; Lytton, 1971), education (e.g., Boyd & DeVault, 1966), ethology (e.g., Hutt & Hutt, 1970), and social psychology (e.g., Weick, 1968).

Despite the widespread popularity of observation methodologies, their association with behavioral psychology is unique. The work by Watson and his students (e.g., Jones, 1924; Watson & Rayner, 1920) provided an important early stimulus to observational studies, particularly with children (Arrington, 1939). Child behavior researchers subsequently developed observation procedures to a level of technical sophistication only recently equaled by contemporary applied-behavior analysts (see the reviews of early observation studies by Arrington, 1939, 1943). Compared with other assessment methods, direct observation is more consistent with behaviorism's epistemological emphasis on overt behavior, public events, quantification, low levels of inference, and assumptions of environmental causality (e.g., Goldfried & Kent, 1972; Haynes, 1978).

Apart from ideology, direct observation has other strengths that cause it to be preferred to alternative assessment methods. The strengths of behavior observations include (1) their flexibility in providing varied forms of data ranging from narrative descriptions of complex interactions to quantitative summaries of individual behavior; (2) their relative simplicity and

Donald P. Hartmann and David D. Wood • Department of Psychology, University of Utah, Salt Lake City, Utah 84112.
Preparation of this manuscript was supported in part by research grant HDMH 06914 from the National Institute of Mental Health, United States Public Health Service, to Donna M. Gelfand and Donald P. Hartmann.

hence their economy of use by lay or para-professional observers; and (3) their wide range of applicability across populations, behaviors, and settings. Observations can be particularly useful in assessing young children and other verbally deficient or unsophisticated subjects. Direct observation can also provide measures for behaviors that most subjects cannot accurately describe, such as interaction rates, expressive movements, and fleeting responses. Observation may further prove useful in generating measures for events that subjects may be unwilling to report or else may distort as a function of the event's social undesirability or of the effort required for adequate description (e.g., Weick, 1968). Additional advantages of observation procedures are discussed by Fiske (1978), by Mischel (1968), and by Wiggins (1973).

The purpose of all assessment is to aid in decision making, including the selection and classification of individuals, the evaluation of interventions, and the testing of scientific hypotheses (Cronbach, 1960). Hawkins (1979) has grouped the many functions served by behavior assessment data into two broad categories: data that influence treatment decisions and data that influence policy decisions, program evaluation, and scientific knowledge. The specific treatment-related assessment functions served by observational procedures are described by Hawkins (1979), by Haynes (1978), and by Mash and Terdal (1976). These functions include (1) identifying target behaviors and their controlling stimuli; (2) designing interventions; and (3) monitoring treatment progress and outcome. A well-constructed and carefully evaluated observation system is required to serve these purposes effectively.

This chapter focuses on issues relevant to selecting or developing behavior observation systems. Major topics include the factors important in designing an observation system, selecting and training observers, and assessing the reliability and the validity of observation data. Our discussion of these issues focuses on observations conducted in naturalistic settings by independent observers when the descriptions of behavior require little inference and the recordings are made during the time the events occur, or soon after (cf. Jones, 1977). However, much of this material is applicable to other circumstances, such as observations conducted in contrived settings by participant–observers. Because each of the general topics surveyed rightfully deserves its own separate chapter, many of the important details necessary to an adequate understanding of the issues have had to be treated briefly. Readers interested in more extensive discussions of these issues may refer to the technical references we list, many of which are outside of the traditional behavioral literature.

Designing an Observation System

An observation system is a more-or-less formalized set of rules for extracting information from the stream of behavior. These rules specify the target events or behaviors, the observation settings, and the observers; they also specify how the events are sampled, the dimensions of the events that are assessed, and how the data are recorded. Furthermore, observation rules may specify how the resulting data are combined to form scores. Thus, the unique set of rules defining a specific observation system also determines the cost, the detail, and the generality of the resulting information, as well as the questions to which the information is relevant. The alternative rules that may be adopted to define an observation system and the consequences of their adoption are reviewed elsewhere (Altmann, 1974; Boyd & DeVault, 1966; Gellert, 1955; Weick, 1968; Wright, 1960). Our discussion of these issues draws heavily on these sources as well as on more recent contributions to the behavioral assessment literature. Many of these issues are interrelated and deserve consideration at the preliminary stages of an investigation.

Developing Behavioral Categories

The behavioral categories that define the content of an observation system can vary in a number of ways. Category or taxonomic systems differ in the breadth of information they provide. Observation systems that provide information on a broad set of categories—broad-bandwidth (Cronbach, 1960) or extensive (Crano & Brewer, 1973) observation systems—often do so by sacrificing measurement precision or fidelity. Simultaneous breadth and precision of observations are possible in those unusual settings where observers are abundant and subjects are both accessible and tolerant of extensive observation (e.g., Paul & Lentz, 1977). Generally, the use of broad-bandwidth observation categories is restricted to situations such as the preliminary phases of assessment, when hypotheses are either initially formulated or subjected to informal tests (e.g., Bijou, Peterson, & Ault, 1968; Hawkins, 1979). More narrowly focused observation categories are appropriate for formal hypothesis testing, as when one or more target behaviors are monitored for the purpose of establishing the causal effects of a treatment intervention (e.g., Hersen & Barlow, 1976).

Categories in behavioral observation systems may be either molar or molecular. Molar categories are used to code global units of behavior, such as "aggresses" or "plays," that often define functional response classes. Molecular categories are used to code more narrowly defined units of behavior, such as "bites" or "smiles," that are often defined in terms of specific sequences of motor movements (e.g., Hutt & Hutt, 1970). While molar categories typically code events into psychologically meaningful classes, they may be troublesome since they require observers to make inferences about events. In contrast, molecular observation categories may be more difficult to interpret subsequent to data collection, but they are relatively easy for observers to use (e.g., Hollenbeck, 1978). Molecular categories can also be collapsed into molar categories for summary data analyses, but molar categories cannot be broken down into smaller, more molecular units. Thus, the level of data obtained can influence the level of interpretation possible.

Observation categories also differ in exclusiveness and exhaustiveness. Exclusive observation categories are used when only one act or series of acts can be scored for each unit of observation. When behaviors occur simultaneously, a priority coding rule must be developed to determine which behavior is recorded and which behaviors are ignored, or alternatively, the system must be constructed so that a separate coding category is available for each possible combination of jointly occurring behaviors. With exhaustive observation categories, some behavior code must be scored for each observation unit. Sackett (1978) described the advantages of using mutually exclusive and exhaustive behavior categories, particularly when behavioral sequences or social interactions are the focus of interest.

Categories can also vary in other ways that may be relevant to behavior analysts. Categories may be qualitative (e.g., yes/no) or may involve quantitative judgments along some response dimension (e.g., Gelfand & Hartmann, 1975). A single set of categories may be appropriate for all subjects, or different sets of observation categories may be required for different subjects. Separate categories may be required when, for example, the intent is to investigate parental determinants of children's problem behaviors (e.g., Patterson & Cobb, 1971) or to evaluate staff interactions with patients in residential treatment programs (e.g., Paul & Lentz, 1977; Licht, 1979). Ultimately, decisions about properties of behavioral categories depend on the functions that the observations are to serve. Regardless of assessment goals, behavioral taxonomies and classification schemata are central to applied behavior analysis (cf. Adams, Doster, & Calhoun, 1977; Begelman, 1976; Menzel, 1979; Rosenblum, 1978). They often are developed by first conducting pilot observations.

Pilot Observations. Useful paradigms for conducting pilot observations have been described by investigators with ethological perspectives (e.g., Blurton Jones & Woodson, 1979; Hutt & Hutt, 1970). The general procedure is initially to obtain narrative observational accounts of behavior in the assessment setting. Since this may prove demanding (Gellert, 1955), observers should use the simplest descriptive synonyms (with the least number of syllables) possible for accurately describing behavior (e.g., Hutt & Hutt, 1970). These narrative data can then be reviewed with the intent of developing a more restrictive list of potentially important target behaviors. Subsequent field testing and refinement may be conducted as indicated. This procedure represents a refinement from initial, unstructured descriptive data to more structured, evaluative data (e.g., Boyd & DeVault, 1966). When important observation targets have been identified, the investigator can then generate formal operational definitions. These definitions should represent discrimination rules for coding targets, thereby facilitating observer accuracy and consistency.

Operational Definitions. Hawkins and Dobes (1977) suggested that adequate operational definitions should possess at least three characteristics. First, a definition should be objective and should refer to directly observable components of the target. Second, the definition should be clear, unambiguous, and easily understood, so that any experienced observer can accurately paraphrase it. Third, the operational definition should require little or no inference, even when used across a variety of observation settings. Thus, operational definitions should ideally include examples of what events belong in the category as well as examples of what events do not belong. One test for the adequacy of operational definitions is to provide naive observers with a written copy of the definitions. Then, without any formal training, observers should use the definitions to independently observe the same subject(s) for one or more sessions. Provided there are adequate controls for timing errors (Gelfand & Hartmann, 1975), the extent of observer consistency obtained by this method is an index of the relative adequacy of the operational definitions (Hawkins & Dobes, 1977). Related considerations in developing operational definitions and behavior codes have been previously outlined (Arrington, 1939; Gelfand & Hartmann, 1975; Gellert, 1955; Heyns & Lippitt, 1954; Hutt & Hutt, 1970). During the development of operational definitions, it is also helpful to specify response dimensions that can be accurately and easily monitored.

Response Dimensions. The choice of response dimension(s) is ordinarily based on the nature of the response, the availability of suitable measurement devices, and, again, the purpose of the study (e.g., Altmann, 1974; Bakeman, 1978; Sackett, 1978). Duration, or one of its derivatives, such as latency or percentage of time spent in some activity, is assessed when a temporal characteristic of a response is targeted, when behaviors vary in the length of time required to perform them, and

when timing devices are available. Frequency is measured when the incidence of a response is targeted, when behaviors are of constant duration, and when timing devices are unavailable. Novice behavior modifiers sometimes record the wrong response characteristic, as when "attending" is targeted for intervention and frequency rather than duration of eye contact is recorded.

In most investigations, the appropriate response characteristic will be apparent. When it is not, the examination of decision flowcharts provided by Alevizos, Campbell, Callahan, and Berck (1974) and by Gelfand and Hartmann (1975) may be useful. If a qualitative dimension of responding is required, such as the creativity of block constructions (Goetz & Baer, 1973), standard references on the construction of rating scales should be consulted (e.g., Anastasi, 1976; also, see Cone & Foster, 1982). Many investigators may be able to adopt or easily modify behavior observation codes already reported in the literature (see Haynes, 1978, pp. 119–120, for a sample listing; Simon & Boyer, 1974, for an anthology; and topic-area reviews as surveyed in Ciminero, Calhoun, & Adams, 1977; Hersen & Bellack, 1976). While meaningful observation targets and their dimensions (or relevant published observation codes) are selected, the investigator should also determine the context or sampling of settings where the observations will be conducted.

Selecting Observation Settings

The settings used for conducting behavior observations have been limited only by the creativity of investigators and the location of subjects. Although most observations are conducted in homes, schools, clinics, and laboratories, relevant settings may include bars, public restrooms, factories, summer camps, museums, and shopping centers (e.g., Bickman, 1976; Haynes, 1978; Weick, 1968). The number, locale, and correspondence between observation settings and important naturalistic settings require careful consideration by the investigator.

Sampling of Settings. Observations conducted in a single setting are appropriate when problems are limited to a specific environment, such as school problems and discrete phobias, or when the rate of problem behavior is uniform across settings, as may be the case with some forms of seizure activity. Because many behaviors are dependent on specific environmental stimuli, behavior rates may well vary across settings containing different stimuli (e.g., Kazdin, 1979a). More representative data may therefore be obtained by conducting observations in a number of settings (e.g., Ayllon & Skuban, 1973; Hutt & Hutt, 1970). Given the infrequency with which settings are typically sampled (Bornstein *et al.,* 1980), behaviorists must either be assessing targets that do not require the sampling of settings or they are disregarding possible situational specificity in their data. The issue of specificity or generalizability of behavior across settings is especially important when the observation settings differ somehow from important naturalistic settings.

Control of Settings. The correspondence between observation and naturalistic settings varies as a function of similarities in their physical characteristics, in the persons present, and in the control exerted by the observation process (Nay, 1979). Observations may be conducted in contrived settings of minimal naturalistic importance to most clients, or they may be conducted in primary living environments, such as homes or schools. Even if observations are conducted in naturalistic settings, the observations may produce variations in the cues that are normally present in these settings.

Setting cues may vary when structure is imposed on observation settings. Structuring may range from presumably minor restrictions in the movement and activities of family members during home observations to the use of highly contrived situations such as behavioral avoidance tests. Haynes (1978) and others (e.g., McFall, 1977; Nay, 1977, 1979) have provided examples of representative studies that employed various levels and types of structuring in observation settings; they have also described the potential advantages of structuring, including cost-effectiveness and measurement sensitivity.

Cues in observation settings may also be affected by the type of observers used and their relationship to the persons observed. Observers can vary in their level of participation with the observed. At one extreme are nonparticipant (independent) observers whose only role is to gather data. At the other extreme are self-observations conducted by the target subject. Intermediate levels of participant–observation are represented by significant others, such as parents, peers, siblings, teachers, aides, and nurses who are normally present in the setting where the observations take place (e.g., Bickman, 1976). The major advantages of participant–observers result from their presence at times that may otherwise be inconvenient for independent observers and the possibility that their presence may be less obtrusive. On the other hand, they may be less dependable, more subject to biases, and more difficult to train and evaluate than are independent observers (Nay, 1979).

Unless self-observations are employed, ethical issues related to informed consent must be considered as well as the need to verify the level of awareness of the assessment when the subjects are assumed to be naive (Wiggins, Renner, Clore, & Rose, 1971). The specific problems associatd with self-observation are described by Nelson (1977) and by Nay (1979).

When observation settings vary from natural life settings because of either the presence of external observers or the imposition of structure, the ecological validity of the observations is open to question (e.g., Barker & Wright, 1955, Rogers-Warren & Warren, 1977). Kazdin (1979a,b) suggested that threats to ecological validity may require greater use of nonobtrusive measures (e.g., Webb, Campbell, Schwartz, & Sechrest, 1966) or increased reliance on reports from informants who are a natural part of the client's interpersonal environment.

Settings are just one of a number of technical aspects of observations that involve sampling issues. While sampling of observation settings is an important issue, investigators must also determine how best to sample behaviors within these settings. The sampling of behavior is influenced by how observations are scheduled.

Scheduling Observations

Behavior cannot be observed and recorded continuously unless the targets are low-frequency events in captive populations (see, for example, the Clinical Frequency Recording System employed by Paul and Lentz, 1977), or when self-observation procedures are employed (see Nelson, 1977). Otherwise, partial records must suffice, and the time in which observations are conducted must be sampled. If sampling is required, decisions must be made about the number of observation sessions to be scheduled and the basis for scheduling. Haynes (1978) suggested that more samples are required when behavior rates are low, variable, and changing (either increasing or decreasing); when events controlling the target behaviors vary substantially; and when observers are asked to employ complex coding procedures. These suggestions should be taken as tentative, since sampling issues have not attracted the attention of most behavioral researchers (Linehan, 1980). A notable exception and potential model for future investigators is the work by Alevizos, DeRisi, Liberman, Eckman, and Callahan (1978). Alevizos and his colleagues examined sampling issues involving settings, observers, subjects, target behaviors, and observation intervals and sessions.

Observation sessions may be scheduled on the basis of time, events, or both time and events. When complex observation codes are employed, or if the target behavior is a free operant, such as crying or smoking, sessions are often scheduled on a temporal basis. If time is the scheduling basis, the observations may be scheduled at fixed intervals, at random intervals, or on a stratified random basis. For discriminated operants, such as responding to requests, sessions are scheduled on either an event or a combined temporal–event basis (Gelfand & Hartmann, 1975). Finally, observation sessions may occur without regard to scheduling rules. Such *ad lib* scheduling (Altmann, 1974) is probably appropriate only for observations conducted during the formative stages of an investigation.

Once a choice has been made about how frequently and on what basis to schedule sessions, a session duration must be decided on. In general, briefer sessions are necessary to limit observer fatigue when a complex coding system is used, when coded behaviors occur at high rates, and when more than one subject must be observed simultaneously. Ultimately, however, session duration as well as the number of observation sessions should be chosen

to minimize costs and to maximize the representativeness and reliability of the data as well as the output of information per unit of time. For an extended discussion of these issues as they apply to scheduling, see Arrington (1943), Smith (1933), and Olson and Cunningham (1934). If observations are to be conducted on more than one subject, decisions must be made concerning the length of time and the order in which each subject will be observed. Sequential methods, in which subjects are observed for brief periods in a previously randomized, rotating order, are apparently superior to fewer but longer observations or to haphazard sampling (e.g., Thomson, Holmberg, & Baer, 1974).

Selecting Observation Procedures

Decisions about sampling dimensions should also take into account the type of observation procedure best suited to the purposes of the investigation. Altmann (1974) and others (e.g., Wright, 1960; Sackett, 1978, 1979) have described a variety of different observation procedures (traditionally called *sampling procedures*), at least five of which seem particularly relevant to applied behavioral researchers. Selection of one of these procedures will determine which response characteristics are recorded as a function of how the behavioral stream is segregated or divided.

Ad lib sampling, also called *nonsystematic sampling* or *informal observation,* hardly deserves formal recognition because of its nonrigorous nature. This casual method of informal note-taking may be particularly suitable for the preliminary mapping of a behavioral domain, for obtaining a crude estimate of the frequency or duration of the target responses, for identifying potential problems in implementing a more formal recording procedure, and for developing preliminary definitions. Although this method may serve pilot observation functions well, it is not recommended as a method for gathering formal data in the course of a structured investigation.

While the *ad lib* method is the least rigorous observation procedure, *real-time observations* are the most rigorous and powerful. With these latter procedures, both event frequency and duration are recorded on the basis of their occurrence in the noninterrupted, natural (i.e., "real") time flow (Sanson-Fisher, Poole, Small, & Fleming, 1979). Data from real-time recording are the most flexible; they can be used for purposes such as sequential analysis that may not be well served by other methods (Bakeman, 1978). If the observation code used in real-time recording is not mutually exclusive, the initiation and termination time of each behavior category must be noted. When the code is mutually exclusive and exhaustive, only initiations are recorded, since the onset of a new category automatically signals the offset, or end, of the preceding coded event (Sackett, 1978). The real-time method and event recording (the technique we discuss next) are the only two procedures commonly employed to obtain unbiased estimates of response frequency, to determine the rate of responses, and to calculate conditional probabilities.

Event recording, sometimes called *frequency recording,* the *tally method,* or *trial scoring* when it is applied to discrete trial behavior—is used when frequency is the response dimension of interest. With event recording, initiations of the target behavior are scored for each occurrence in an observation session or during brief intervals within a session (Wright, 1960). Event recording is a commonly used method in applied behavior analysis (Kelly, 1977); examples can be found in Gelfand and Hartmann (1975), in Nay (1979), and in most issues of major applied behavioral journals. Because event sampling breaks up the continuity of behavior, it is sometimes supplemented with narrative recording. This may be particularly helpful in the early phases of assessment to assist in identifying antecedent and consequent stimuli that may exert some control over the target behavior. Other advantages and limitations of event recording are described by Nay (1979).

Scan sampling, also referred to as *instantaneous time sampling, momentary time sampling,* and *discontinuous probe-time sampling,* is particularly useful with behaviors for which duration is a more meaningful dimension than frequency. With scan sampling, the observer periodically scans each subject and notes whether or not the behavior is occurring at that instant. An impressive application of scan sampling is described by Paul and his associates (Paul & Lentz, 1977; Power, 1979).

The final procedure, *interval recording*, is also referred to as *time sampling, one-zero recording,* and the *Hansen system.* It is at the same time one of the most popular recording methods (Kelly, 1977) and one of the most troublesome (e.g., Altmann, 1974; Kraemer, 1979). With this technique, an observation session is divided into brief observe–record intervals, and the observation category is scored if the relevant target behavior occurs within any part of the interval. Powell, Martindale, and Kulp (1975) have distinguished between two variants of interval recording: whole-interval recording, in which a behavior is scored only when it occurs during the entire interval, and partial-interval recording, in which a behavior is scored even though it occurs during just part of the interval. While interval-recording procedures have been recommended for their ability to measure both response frequency and response duration, recent research indicates that this method may seriously misrepresent results by providing distorted estimates of both of these response characteristics (Altmann, 1974; Green & Alverson, 1978; Kraemer, 1979; Murphy & Goodall, 1980; Powell *et al.,* 1975; Powell, Martindale, Kulp, Martindale, & Bauman, 1977; Powell & Rockinson, 1978; Repp, Roberts, Slack, Repp, & Berkler, 1976).

As a measure of frequency, the rate of interval-recorded data varies depending on the duration of the observation interval. With long intervals, more than one occurrence of a response may be observed, yet only one response would be scored. With short intervals, a single response may extend beyond an interval and thus would be scored in more than one interval.

As a measure of response duration, interval-recorded data also present problems. For example, duration is overestimated whenever responses are scored yet occur for only a portion of any observation interval. The interval method provides a good estimate of duration only when the observation intervals are very short in comparison with the mean duration of the target behavior. Under these conditions, the interval method becomes procedurally similar to scan sampling. Other limitations of

interval-recording procedures, particularly for
sequential analysis, are described by Sackett
(1979), by Bakeman (1978), and by Sanson-
Fisher *et al.* (1979).

In view of the numerous liabilities of interval
recording, behavior analysts would be well
advised to consider alternative observation
procedures. If real-time sampling is not required or is prohibitively expensive, adequate
measures of response duration and frequency
can be obtained from scan sampling or event
recording. Economical measures of both response frequency and duration can result from
combining the scan- and event-recording techniques. However, data produced by combining these two methods do not have the same
range of applications as data obtained by the
real-time procedure.

Human observers using one of these five
observation procedures will undoubtedly continue to serve as the primary "apparatus" for
obtaining observational data. However, various technologies are available to aid or even
supplant observers in recording behavioral
data. In some instances, the new observation
technologies far exceed the limits of more traditional procedures, consequently allowing
much more sophisticated analyses of highly
complex behavioral phenomena (see Lamb,
Suomi, & Stephenson, 1979).

Selecting Technological Aids

The technologies available to assist in collecting observation data range from simple
pencil-and-paper recording forms to complicated computer-assisted sensing, recording,
and retrieval systems. Selection from among
existing technologies can determine the obtrusiveness and efficiency of data collection, the
representativeness of sampling, the ease of
data management (storage and retrieval), and
the feasibility of conducting various statistical
analyses. These logistical problems are basic
considerations that should be reviewed *before*
commitment to any given technology (Sykes,
1977). Table 1 presents the major classes of
technologies typically used by applied behavior analysts.

Written Records. Pencil-and-paper media
remain popular today because of their general
simplicity and inexpensiveness as well as their
importance in generating a preliminary obser-

**Table 1. Levels of Observation Technology
and Sample References**[a]

Type	Sample references
Written records	
Behavior checklists	Walls, Werner, Bacon, & Zane (1977)
"Countoons"	Kunzelman (1970)
Narrative accounts	Barker & Wright (1955)
Questionnaires	Haynes (1978)
Rating forms	Nay (1979)
Discussions	Nay (1977, 1979)
Electromechanical equipment	
Event recorders	Alban & Nay (1976)
Stenography equipment	Carter, Haythorn, Meirowitz, & Lanzetta (1951); Heimstra & Davis (1962)
Timing devices	Washburn (1936); Wolach, Roccaforte, & Breuning (1975)
Discussions	Rugh & Schwitzgebel (1977); Schwitzgebel & Schwitzgebel (1973)
Audio recording	
Automatic speech processing	Jaffe & Feldstein (1970)
Computer analysis	Cassota, Jaffe, Feldstein, & Moses (1964)
For narrative observation	Hutt & Hutt (1970); Schoggen (1964)
For unobtrusive observation	Bernal, Gibson, William, & Pesses, (1971); Christensen (1979)
From radio transmitters	Purcell & Brady (1965); Soskin & John (1963)
Typescripts from	Powell & Jackson (1964); Thelen (1950)
Voice spectrometer	Hargreaves & Starkweather (1963)
Film and videotape records	
Computer analysis	Futrelle (1973); Ledley (1965)
Time-lapse photography	Delgado (1964); Withall (1956)

Table 1. *Continued*

Type	Sample references
Film and videotape records (*cont.*)	
Discussions	Berger (1978); Collier (1967); Hutt & Hutt (1970)
Computers	
Observer-to-computer links	Sanson-Fisher, Poole, Small, & Fleming (1979); Simpson (1979); Tobach, Schneirla, Aronson, & Laupheimer (1962)
Discussions	Borko (1962); Stephenson (1979)
Direct observations compared to:	
Videotape or film	Boyd & DeVault (1966); Eisler, Hersen, & Agras (1973)
One-way mirror; live video monitor observations	Kent, O'Leary, Dietz, & Diament (1979); also see Knapp (1978)
Audio- or typescript-recorded interactions	Steinzor (1949)

ª Note. For additional material on audio recording, see *ASHA Reports, 5,* 1970; Lass (1976); and recent issues of the *Journal of Speech and Hearing Disorders; Journal of Speech and Hearing Research;* and *Folio Phoniatrica.* Additional observation technology is described in *Behavior Research Methods and Instrumentation,* particularly 9(5), 1979, pp. 403–455; and in the *Journal of Applied Behavior Analysis.*

vation code (see discussions of ethograms and the relevance of ethological perspectives and procedures in Blurton Jones, 1972; Hutt & Hutt, 1970). However, hand-written records may prove cumbersome or ill suited to complex observation methodologies such as sequential analysis (Sidowski, 1977). When pencil-and-paper recording procedures are used, careful attention to the construction of record forms may spare investigators considerable grief during data collection, storage, retrieval, and analyses (Bakeman, 1978; Heyns & Lippitt, 1954; Weick, 1968). In fact, the development of appropriate record forms should coincide with the piloting stages of a behavior observation system; mutual refinements can allow more efficient assessment and increase the subsequent data-management capability. Procedures for engineering effective record forms are described by Gelfand and Hartmann (1975) and by Weick (1968). In general, a record form should be designed for convenience in data collection, storage, and retrieval. Adequate identifying information should be included on the form, such as the date of the observation session, the target subject(s), the observer, and the numbered observation intervals. The record form could also include the observation code or symbols and ample space to write descriptive or narrative comments, which can help clarify the obtained data. Sample record forms are given in a variety of sources (e.g., Arrington, 1939; Haynes, 1978; Nay, 1979; Wright, 1960).

When recording data using written records or keyboards, observers should be protected from mechanical errors by employing a redundant coding procedure (e.g., Sykes, 1977) or other simple methods, such as single-letter abbreviations or a minimum number of writing movements (e.g., Gelfand & Hartmann, 1975). Pictograms are particularly useful since they are unique and easily discriminated shorthand symbols for behavior (e.g., using the letter *V* or *U* for *smile*). Since recording often takes place during brief intervals following a period of observation, some signaling device such as an electronic beeper may be used to signal the beginning and the end of each interval. A tape recorder with previously recorded interval numbers ("interval 1, observe . . . interval 1, record") is a preferable method as it can be used not only to signal the beginning and the end of the observation and recording intervals but also to identify each interval uniquely. By means of this procedure, it is relatively easy to ensure that the data will be recorded in the proper space on a data sheet (Gelfand & Hartmann, 1975).

It is surprising to note that relatively little empirical evaluation has been conducted to evaluate data sheets and record forms. Two investigations (Ellis & Wilson, 1973; Wood, Callahan, Alevizos, & Teigen, 1979) have demonstrated significant gains in reported behavioral data simply by modifying the traditional record formats used in psychiatric settings. These results should remind us that our final data are only as good as our records (Sykes, 1977).

Electromechanical Equipment. Keyboards and event recorders are now commonplace data-collection aids. These devices enable observers to spend a greater proportion of their time observing behavior with less distraction imposed by recording requirements; both the occurrence and the duration of events can be more easily recorded; and the records are time-locked, thus facilitating reliability analysis (e.g., Simpson, 1979). The availability of sophisticated transducers has further allowed behavior analysts precise and continuous access to events such as gradations in noise level that previously were only crudely measured (Rugh & Schwitzgebel, 1977). Useful reviews of electromechanical equipment are provided by the Schwitzgebels and their associates (Rugh & Schwitzgebel, 1977; Schwitzgebel, 1976; Schwitzgebel & Kolb, 1974; Schwitzgebel & Schwitzgebel, 1973).

The major advantages to using electromechanical devices include increased data-collection capabilities, adaptability to automated data analysis, and the possibility of less obtrusive assessment than is typically associated with live observers using clipboards, stopwatches, and awkward signaling devices to identify observation intervals. Major limitations include increased downtime and data loss due to equipment failure, data overload caused by injudiciously adding performance measures, and limited generality within and across studies due to poor standardization of procedures and nomenclature (e.g., Rugh & Schwitzgebel, 1977).

Audio and Visual Recording Devices. Standardization may prove less of a problem with audio and visual recorders, which are often used as an intermediate step in data collection. Auditory and visual stimuli are first recorded on tape and later coded by trained observers. These devices may be useful when the presence of observers would be reactive or when the events to be coded are so complex that the observational stimuli require repeated examination. Nay (1979) cogently reviewed the ethics of using such recording techniques and made recommendations for informed consent and subject-controlled editing of tapes. Clients should be allowed to turn off the re-

cording device and even to "censor" the records (e.g., Christensen, 1979).

Comparisons of audiovisual recording procedures (film and videotape) with live observations reveal few differences in results due to differences in media (Boyd & DeVault, 1966; Eisler, Hersen, & Agras, 1973; Kent, O'Leary, Dietz, & Diament, 1979). However, with film or tape media, there is the temptation to make analyses increasingly detailed and, accordingly, time-consuming. This may result in what has been aptly called *data tyranny* (Bakeman, Cairns, & Appelbaum, 1979). Hutt and Hutt (1970) suggested that film or videotape is preferable when behavioral events of interest occur quickly, are highly complex, and present subtle changes or sequential changes in complex behavior, and when precise measurement is required of brief, complex events. For detailed analyses requiring slow and/or multiple projection, film is more durable and generally superior to videotape; 16-mm film is characterized by better resolution, definition, durability, and higher cost than 8-mm film. Videotape may be preferable to film in settings where obtrusive cameras, lights, and technicians should be avoided. Investigators may also wish to consider the time-sampling observation properties of time-lapse photography (e.g., Delgado, 1964). Finally, videotape or film observations should not be ruled out if there are efficient data-management procedures to cope with the substantial amount of information they provide. Promising initial steps have been made in combining film records with computer technologies (e.g., Duncan & Fiske, 1977; Hutt & Hutt, 1970).

Computers. The accessibility of computers is certainly the most promising (and perhaps to many the most threatening) development in behavior observation technology. Early discussions of this topic were provided by Lang (1969), while more contemporary considerations are presented in Cairns (1979), Lamb *et al.* (1979), and Sackett (1978). Pencil-and-paper observation media have been adapted to computer technology for some time (e.g., Heyns & Lippitt, 1954), and other researchers (e.g., Tobach, Schneirla, Aronson, & Laupheimer, 1962) have anticipated direct observer-to-computer links in behavior assessment (cf. Sanson-Fisher *et al.,* 1979; Simpson, 1979). Despite the considerable merits of computer technologies for behavior observation, the wary consumer might consider the fact that such media require considerable investments in equipment, observer training, and software and programming (e.g., Sykes, 1977). Furthermore, the data management capabilities of computers are not a substitute for the data interpretation capabilities of investigators: the computer can analyze only what it is provided with, however it is programmed. Thus, computer applications are useful only when researchers ask meaningful questions, obtain appropriate data, plan relevant analyses, and interpret their results correctly.

Observers: Errors and Training

Although observers are a critical component of most observation systems, their performance is fallible and may result in seriously flawed data (e.g., Heyns & Lippitt, 1954; Menzel, 1979). The field of applied behavior analysis has typically assumed that most potential observer effects may be overcome or controlled by adequate training. Observer training is therefore usually conducted with the intent to control error by standardizing the observation procedures across raters.

Sources of Observer Effects

Observer effects represent a conglomerate of the systematic or directional errors in behavior observations that may result from using human observers. Our discussion of observer effects highlights the important sources of errors also identified in previous reviews of the literature (e.g., Johnson & Bolstad, 1973; Kent & Foster, 1977; Wildman & Erickson, 1977).

Reactivity. Behavior observation often is an intrusive assessment procedure (e.g., Weick, 1968). The presence of an observer may represent a novel stimulus that can evoke atypical responses from the observed subjects (Haynes, 1978). This reaction to observation is the basis for the term *reactivity* (Lambert, 1960). The outcomes of research conducted on the potential reactive effects of observation have not been uniform; nevertheless, five factors appear to contribute to reactivity (e.g., Arrington, 1939; Goodrich, 1959; Haynes, 1978;

Johnson & Bolstad, 1973; Kazdin, 1977; Wildman & Erickson, 1977). These factors are the valence or social desirability of target behaviors, subject characteristics, conspicuousness of observation, observer attributes, and the rationale for observation.

Valence of the Behavior. Socially desirable or appropriate behaviors may be facilitated while socially undesirable or "private" behaviors may be suppressed when subjects are aware of being observed (e.g., Haynes, 1978). Adults, for example, display higher rates of positive interactions with children during direct observation (e.g., Baum, Forehand, & Zegiob, 1979). If we can assume that accuracy and consistency are positively valenced by observers, then reactivity due to social desirability may also be illustrated when observer performance improves in the presence of a second observer (e.g., Taplin & Reid, 1973; see review by Kazdin, 1977).

Subject Characteristics. Young children under the age of 6 and subjects who are open and confident or perhaps merely insensitive may react less to direct observation than subjects who do not share these characteristics (e.g., Arrington, 1939; Gellert, 1955). While numerous suggestions of observation reactivity are discussed in reference to more socially adept or older subjects, these hypotheses await empirical confirmation (Kent & Foster, 1977; Wildman & Erickson, 1977).

Conspicuousness of Observation. The most extensively researched contributing factor to reactivity is the level of obtrusiveness or conspicuousness of observation. The obtrusiveness of observation can be manipulated by varying the activity level of the participant–observers (e.g., Melbin, 1954); by instructions that alert subjects to the observation conditions (e.g., Bales, 1950); by the observer's proximity to the subjects (O'Leary & O'Leary, 1976); by the presence of observation instrumentation (Roberts & Renzaglia, 1965); and by the length of exposure to observation (Haynes, 1978). The more obtrusive or obvious the assessment procedure, the more likely it is to evoke reactive effects. However, numerous contrary findings have been obtained, and none of these obtrusive factors necessarily guarantees that subjects will react to observations in an atypical manner (e.g., Bernal, Gibson, William, & Pesses, 1971;

Hagen, Craighead, & Paul, 1975; Liberman, DeRisi, King, Eckman, & Wood, 1974).

Observer Attributes. When behavior assessment is conducted by observers in natural settings, sex, activity level or responsiveness, and age appear to be important observer attributes that influence reactivity in children (Connolly & Smith, 1972; Martin, Gelfand, & Hartmann, 1971). Appearance, tact, and public-relations skills can also affect the level of reactivity, as when rather casually attired observers invade an upper-middle-class household (e.g., Haynes, 1978) or when scientific detachment prevents appropriate supervision of aggressive interactions between children (e.g., Spiro, 1958). Other attributes of observers, such as race, socioeconomic class (Rosenthal, 1966), and professional status (Wallace, 1976), may also contribute to reactivity (Johnson & Bolstad, 1973).

Rationale for Observation. Goodrich (1959) has described the role of the observer as "helpless" scapegoat or even one of representing potential danger to subjects. While this description may seem overly dramatic, it followed an investigation where ambiguity about observer roles was met with aggression against observers by delinquent boys (Polansky, Freeman, Horowitz, Irwin, Papanis, Rappaport, & Whaley, 1949). Thus, the manner in which an observer joins a group may be very important (see discussion by Weick, 1968). Johnson and Bolstad (1973) recommended providing a thorough rationale for observation procedures in order to reduce subject concerns and potential reactive effects due to the observation process.

Other methods of reducing reactivity are also available to investigators. Rules for observer dress, etiquette, and other ways to minimize reactivity were discussed by Gelfand and Hartmann (1975), Haynes (1978), and by Weick (1968). It is possible that reactivity represents a problem only with data obtained early in an investigation; subjects may be expected to habituate to observations with repeated assessment (Haynes, 1978). The length of time or the number of observation sessions required for habituation is still an empirical question. Littman, Pierce-Jones, and Stern (cited in Haynes, 1978) recommended a 6-hour adaptation period for home observations, while other researchers have recommended even

less time for observations of young children (e.g., Bijou, Peterson, Harris, Allen, & Johnston, 1969; Werry & Quay, 1969). If none of these options proves satisfactory, investigators may elect to employ covert assessments using concealed recording procedures (Kent & Foster, 1977). For the special case of self-observation and reactivity, Nelson (1977) provided a summary of relevant research.

Observer Bias. Observer bias is a systematic error in assessment usually associated with the observers' expectancies and prejudices as well as their information-processing limitations. Campbell (1958), in a rare *conceptual* review of observer bias, described a number of cognitively based distortions, including a "bias toward central tendency." Thus, observers may impose patterns of regularity and orderliness on otherwise complex and unruly behavioral data (Hollenbeck, 1978; Mash & Makohoniuk, 1975). Methodological solutions to these cognitively based biases were described by Heyns and Lippitt (1954) and by Weick (1968).

Other systematic errors are due to observer expectancies, including explicit or implicit hypotheses about the purposes of an investigation, how subjects should behave, or perhaps even what might constitute "appropriate" data (e.g., Haynes, 1978; Kazdin, 1977; Nay, 1979). The observer may develop an implicit bias during training as a function of serendipitous factors. For example, the characteristics of the behavioral coding schema may prompt the observer to search out specific targets to the exclusion of less salient events (Rosenblum, 1978). Observers may also develop biases on the basis of more overt expectations resulting from a knowledge of experimental hypotheses, subject characteristics, and prejudices conveyed explicitly or implicitly by the investigator.

Several studies have been specifically designed to evaluate the role of observer expectancies in contributing systematic bias to behavioral assessments (e.g., O'Leary, Kent, & Kanowitz, 1975; Redfield & Paul, 1976). The accuracy of quantitative measures was not affected by observer expectancies, especially when *stringent training criteria* were coupled with a *low-inference observation code* (Redfield & Paul, 1976). When observer expectancies were also strengthened by social reinforcement from the investigator, the combination of expectancy and feedback produced obvious bias in the observational data (O'Leary *et al.,* 1975).

Some ways to deal with implicit or explicit biases might include, the use of more "professional"—that is, graduate-student—observers (Rosenthal, 1966); assessment of the nature and extent of observer biases (Johnson & Bolstad, 1973; Hartmann, Roper, & Gelfand, 1977); the use of videotape recording with a subsequent rating of randomly ordered sessions (Kazdin, 1977); and attempts to maintain experimental naiveté among observers who have been cautioned about bias and who are using precise, low-inference operational definitions (Haynes, 1978).

Observer Drift. Another source of error in behavioral investigations is measurement decay in observer performance (Cook & Campbell, 1979). Observer consistency and accuracy may decrease, sometimes precipitously, from the end of training to the beginning of formal data collection (e.g., Taplin & Reid, 1973). Reductions in accuracy have been described as *instrument decay* or *observer drift* (Johnson & Bolstad, 1973; O'Leary & Kent, 1973). When interobserver consistency remains high yet observer accuracy falls, the phenomenon is labeled *consensual observer drift* (Johnson & Bolstad, 1973). Consensual observer drift occurs when a recording-interpretation bias has gradually evolved over time (Arrington, 1939, 1943; Gellert, 1955) or when response definitions or measurement procedures are informally altered to suit novel changes in the topography of some target behavior (Doke, 1976). Reductions in observer consistency (drift) can also result from observer satiation or boredom (Weick, 1968).

Observer drift has been repeatedly demonstrated in the behavior assessment literature (e.g., Kent, O'Leary, Diament, & Dietz, 1974; Romanczyk, Kent, Diament, & O'Leary, 1973; Wildman, Erickson, & Kent, 1975). The results of these studies suggest that reliability estimates may be inflated when based on data obtained either during training sessions or from a long-standing, familiar team of observers during the course of a lengthy investigation.

Drift can be limited by providing continuing training throughout a project, by training and recalibrating all observers at the same time (Johnson & Bolstad, 1973; Kazdin, 1977), by conducting reliability assessment across rotating members of observation teams (Haynes, 1978; Nay, 1974), by using independent reliability assessors (Kent *et al.,* 1974), and by inserting random and covert reliability probes throughout the course of the investigation (Romanczyk *et al.,* 1973; Taplin & Reid, 1973).

Observer Cheating. In all the recent behavioral assessment texts, only the chapter by Kent and Foster (1977) devotes more than passing mention to cheating. Outright observer fabrication of data has been reported by Azrin, Holz, Ulrich, and Goldiamond (1961); observers have also been known to calculate inflated reliability coefficients (Kent *et al.,* 1974). However, these calculation mistakes are not necessarily the result of intentional fabrication (e.g., Rusch, Walker, & Greenwood, 1975), even though unsupervised observers obtain higher reliability when alone than when joined by a supervisor (O'Leary & Kent, 1973). Precautions against observer cheating include making random, unannounced reliability spot-checks, collecting data forms immediately after an observation session ends, restricting data analysis and reliability calculations to individuals who did not collect the data, and providing raters with pens rather than pencils (obvious corrections might then be evaluated as an indirect measure of cheating). In addition, observers might be repeatedly reminded of the canons of science and warned that cheating will bring about dire consequences (e.g., O'Leary & Kent, 1973). Collateral sources, such as nurses in the observation setting, might be asked to report periodically on observer behavior, thereby providing the investigator with both valuable feedback and the confidence of the institutional staff.

Selecting and Training Observers

The preceding discussion considered sources of error in observation data, at least some of which may be partially controlled by adequate observer training. Surprisingly little effort has been devoted to the systematic evaluation of observer characteristics that may help or hinder such training.

Selecting Observers. Certain aptitudes and

perceptual-motor skills of observers may prove directly relevant to training efficiency and to the maintenance of desired levels of observer performance (e.g., Nay, 1979). Skindrud (1973) used testing to screen potential observers on the basis of above-average verbal and clerical skills. Additional observer attributes may also be important, including morale (Guttman, Spector, Sigal, Rakoff, & Epstein, 1971); motivation (Dancer, Braukmann, Schumaker, Kirigin, Willner, & Wolf, 1978); and even socioeconomic status (Alvevizos *et al.,* 1978). Yarrow and Waxler (1979) suggested that good observers have the ability to sustain attention without habituation and to manage high levels of environmental stimulation without confusion; have a compulsive regard for detail and precision and an overriding commitment to scientific detachment; and are "intense," analytical, and introspective. Applied behavior analysts interested in improving observer performance may wish to supplement these hypotheses with others gleaned from the literature on information processing and applied decision-making (e.g., Lachman, Lachman, & Butterfield, 1979; Ostrom, Werner, & Saks, 1978; Weick, 1968).

Observer Training. Unusually thorough models of observer training aimed at reducing timing and interpretation errors have been available for approximately 50 years (Arrington, 1932; Jersild & Markey, 1935; Thomas, Loomis, & Arrington, 1933). Recent reviews of the observer training literature (e.g., Haynes, 1978; Johnson & Bolstad, 1973; Kazdin, 1977; Kent & Foster, 1977; Nay, 1979; Wildman & Erickson, 1977) and our own evaluation of this literature suggest a seven-step general model for observer training.

STEP 1. ORIENTATION

A. *Pilot Observations* (*optional*). Prior to training, observers might be exposed to the observation setting and might attempt to record behaviors without the benefit of formal instruction or the aid of any coding schema. This procedure may be useful in convincing observers of the need for training and the value of a structured observation system (Heyns & Zander, 1953).

B. *Sensitization to Research Issues.* Even if pilot observations are not conducted, some form of preliminary observer orientation should take place. It is important that observers remain naive about the purposes of the investigation and any experimental hypotheses; a suitable rationale and introduction should cover these issues, while emphasizing the continued need for experimentally blind and objective assessment throughout the entire course of the investigation. Observers should be warned against attempts to generate their own hypotheses and instructed to avoid private discussions of coding procedures and problems. Observers should also be familiarized with the *Ethical Principles in the Conduct of Research with Human Participants* (1973); particular emphasis should be placed on confidentiality. Proper observer screening may eliminate some potential trainees, without penalty, at this step.

STEP 2. LEARNING THE OBSERVATION MANUAL

Trainees should learn the operational definitions and scoring procedures of the observation system as presented in a formal observation training-manual (suggestions for observation manuals are discussed by Nay, 1979, p. 237). After pilot observations, trainees might help to develop the code and the related definitions (Heyns & Lippitt, 1954). Observer trainees at this step are required to memorize the operational definitions (see Hawkins & Dobes, 1977, for a discussion of operational definitions) as well as to learn examples and the rules for scoring the target behaviors. Investigators should utilize appropriate instructional principles, such as successive approximations and ample positive reinforcement, in teaching their observer trainees appropriate observation, recording, and interpersonal skills.

STEP 3. FIRST CRITERION CHECK

After studying the observational manual, observers should pass a pencil-and-paper test or score a written protocol presenting sample target events (e.g., Bertucci, Huston, & Perloff, 1974). In this phase, the trainee is required to have a working knowledge of the observation system in order to code the test items accurately.

STEP 4. ANALOGUE OBSERVATIONS

Having passed the written test, observers should next be trained to criterion accuracy and consistency on a series of analogue assessment samples, such as film clips (e.g., Loomis, 1931) or role plays. Training should be based on varied and representative samples of the target behaviors (Nay, 1979). If response topographies can be expected to change over the course of the investigation, then the trainees should be exposed to both earlier and later response variants. Film or videotape is particularly useful in this regard (Arrington, 1939), especially if sample vignettes meet several important requirements. First, vignettes should present rather complex interaction sequences (Kent & Foster, 1977). Second, the sample interaction sequences should be unpredictable and variable in response patterning (Mash & Makohoniuk, 1975; Mash & McElwee, 1974). Third, observers should be *overtrained* on these difficult vignettes in order to minimize decrements in performance from training to *in vivo* observations (Kazdin, 1977; Wildman & Erickson, 1977). Discussion of procedural problems and confusions should be encouraged throughout this training phase, provided all observers are informed of (and, ideally, present during) such discussions and the resulting clarifications. Decisions should be posted in an observer log or noted in the observation manual that each observer carries (Gelfand & Hartmann, 1975).

STEP 5. IN SITU PRACTICE

Observers should next attain some criterion performance accuracy, such as 90% during "live" practice in the observation setting (Conger & McLeod, 1977). Practice in the observation setting can serve the dual purpose of desensitizing observers to fears about the setting (i.e., inpatient psychiatric units) and allowing the subjects to habituate to the observation procedures. The training considerations outlined in Step 4 are also relevant here. In addition, regular accuracy feedback should be provided *throughout* training. House (1980) has described a quick and convenient statis-

tical procedure for monitoring systematic errors in observation data; this procedure may be useful in monitoring observer performance during training and could serve as a useful format to provide feedback to observers. It is important to remember that feedback about accuracy improves accuracy, while feedback about consistency (e.g., interobserver agreements during coding) improves consistent scoring tendencies and not necessarily accuracy (DeMaster, Reid, & Twentyman, 1977). Observer feedback must avoid social reinforcement for ratings consistent with the outcome expectancies of the investigation (O'Leary *et al.*, 1975). Observers should also be informed either that all observation sessions will be checked for reliability or that reliability will be checked covertly at unannounced times. Reliance on periodic overt reliability checks should be avoided (see Kazdin, 1977).

STEP 6. RETRAINING–RECALIBRATION SESSIONS

During the course of the investigation, periodic retraining and recalibration sessions should be conducted with all observers (Johnson & Bolstad, 1973; Kazdin, 1977): recalibration could include spot tests on the observation manual (see Paul & Lentz, 1977) and reviews of sample observation events. Perhaps an alternate set of criterion vignettes on film or videotape might be developed for just these purposes. Nay (1974) suggested that observers attain predetermined criteria for reliability across multiple partners, and Haynes (1978) recommended that observers be rotated to constitute various teams or pairs during the investigation. Another strategy is to train a second, independent observer group to provide reliability cross-checks (Kent *et al.*, 1974).

STEP 7. POSTINVESTIGATION DEBRIEFING

At the end of the investigation, observers should be interviewed to assess any biases or potential mistakes that may have influenced their observations (Hartmann *et al.*, 1977; Johnson & Bolstad, 1973). Following these interviews, observers should be extended the professional courtesy of being informed about the nature and results of the investigation and should receive footnote acknowledgment in technical reports or publications.

In reporting on observers in technical reports, researchers should describe the observers' characteristics, including the selection factors, the length and type of training to attain criterion, and the criterion-level accuracy and consistency that were selected. A method section that omits these details could be considered deficient in describing one of the most significant methods in any observation study.

Reliability

Reliability issues are relevant to scores obtained from any assessment method. Reliability is therefore an important factor in evaluating observations. Dimensions of reliability include measures of scorer consistency (sometimes referred to as *observer agreement*), temporal stability, and internal as well as situational consistency. Poor reliability on any of these dimensions would *not necessarily* rule out the use of an observation system (Nelson, Hay, & Hay, 1977). However, poor reliability in one or more of these respects would indicate limitations in the extent to which the observation scores could be generalized. The explicit relationship between reliability and the generalizability of observations stems from the theory of generalizability proposed by Cronbach and his associates (Cronbach, Gleser, Nanda, & Rajaratnam, 1972).

Generalizability Theory

The theory of generalizability offers a detailed conceptual analysis of the components of a score, methods for analyzing those components, statistics for summarizing the analysis, and an interpretive framework for evaluating the limits of score generalizability. The components of a score are determined by the specific conditions under which the score was obtained, including time, context, scoring system, and observer. The contributions of these conditions of measurement, called *facets* in generalizability theory, are determined by analysis-of-variance procedures. The results of the analysis are summarized in terms of

variance components, intraclass correlation coefficients, and measurement error statistics. Large variance components associated with a facet or an interaction of facets serve as a warning that the generalizability of the observations may be limited along those dimensions. For example, a large variance component associated with the facet of observers may suggest that a replication of similar results is unlikely with a change in observers.

The conceptualization and applied procedures of generalizability theory are readily accessible to assessors who employ direct observations. Nontechnical descriptions of the theory and illustrations of its applicability to observational data are given in Berk (1979), Coates and Thoresen (1978), Cone (1977), Jones (1977), Jones, Reid, and Patterson (1975), Mitchell (1979), and Wiggins (1973). In addition, Jones (1977) has described some of the computational limitations of the generalizability theory approach for individual subject data. Strossen, Coates, and Thoresen (1979) have discussed possible solutions to these problems. Our discussion here focuses on the facet of observation score generalizability that is most often considered by applied behavior analysts: generalizability across observers.

Interobserver Generalizability

Since early discussions of the methodology of behavior analysis (Baer, Wolf, & Risley, 1968; Bijou *et al.*, 1968), applied behavioral researchers have focused on the observer facet of generalizability in observation scores (Kelly, 1977). Despite this attention, assessment of the generalizability of results across observers has been plagued by a number of problems. These problems have included definitions of basic concepts, decisions regarding the level of data at which observer generalizability should be assessed, and methods of summarizing these data (e.g., generalizability formulas). These problems are not new; they have a long and apparently overlooked history dating back in psychology more than 40 years (e.g., Arrington, 1939). Our discussion here focuses primarily on definitions of basic concepts and a consideration of generalizability formulas referred to as *summary statistics*.

Definitions. *Observer agreement, observer*

reliability, and *observer accuracy* are the three terms that have been used with some frequency to describe interobserver generalizability. *Observer agreement* and *observer reliability* are often used interchangeably to describe consistency of ratings among two or more observers who score the same behaviors independently. When the two terms are distinguished, *observer agreement* refers to consistency indexed by an agreement statistic, whereas *observer reliability* refers to consistency indexed by a correlation coefficient (e.g., Tinsley & Weiss, 1975). These indexes should not be considered interchangeable since they assess different properties of the same data. Agreement statistics measure the degree to which observers assign the same score to an event or a person, and correlation coefficients measure the degree to which observers assign the same *standard score* to an event or a person. When observations require dichotomous judgments (occurrence/nonoccurrence), the two approaches tend to merge.

Observer accuracy, sometimes called *criterion-referenced agreement* (Frick & Semmel, 1978), refers to consistency between the ratings of an observer and a criterion rating. The common usage of these observer generalizability terms may be confusing or troublesome because the terms do not clearly distinguish between the standard of comparison (another observer vs. criterion) and the statistic used to summarize the data (agreement vs. correlation statistic). A more accurate lexicon for the discussion of interobserver generalizability would then be based on four distinct categories: (a) observer consistency indexed by agreement statistics; (b) observer consistency indexed by correlation coefficients; (c) observer accuracy indexed by agreement statistics; and (d) observer accuracy indexed by correlation coefficients.

These four categories do not typically produce the same results when applied to the same data. Tinsley and Weiss (1975) demonstrated that observer consistency indexed with agreement statistics can vary independently from observer consistency indexed with correlation coefficients. They also described conditions in which independence between these two statistics might be expected. DeMaster *et al.* (1977) presented data demonstrating that

consistency and accuracy can also vary independently.

As an applied issue, Frick and Semmel (1978) argued for an increased use of accuracy measures, and Nay (1979) provided useful suggestions for the construction of criterion videotapes, which are the common standard used for assessing accuracy. However, the development of criterion ratings may be infeasible in many situations. Even if feasible, criterion ratings may provide unrepresentative estimates of accuracy if observers can discriminate between accuracy assessment trials and more typical observations. In such a case, users of observational systems are left with observer consistency as an indirect measure of accuracy (Hartmann, 1979a). Tinsley and Weiss (1975) argued that both agreement and correlational measures of consistency should be calculated on observational data. In contrast, Hartmann (1977) suggested that the two approaches may be differentially relevant, depending on the purpose of the study and the form of the major data analysis. Some of the various measures that can be calculated are discussed in the next section.

Summary Statistics. Following the choice of method for assessing interobserver generalizability, selection from well over 20 procedures is possible for summarizing the reliability data that are collected. Berk (1979) described 22 different summary statistics, and Tinsley and Weiss (1975) and Frick and Semmel (1978) listed still others. While some of these methods are equivalent under special conditions (e.g., Fleiss, 1975), it is apparent that different summary statistics provide different—sometimes substantially different—results when applied to the same data (e.g., Frick & Semmel, 1978; Hartmann, 1977; Repp, Dietz, Boles, Dietz, & Repp, 1976).

Observation data are typically obtained in one or both of two forms: categorical data such as occur/nonoccur, correct/incorrect, or yes/no that might be observed in brief time intervals or scored in response to discrete trials; and quantitative data such as response frequency, rate, or duration (Gelfand & Hartmann, 1975; Hartmann, 1977). Somewhat different agreement and correlational statistics have been developed for the two kinds of data. The percentage-of-agreement statistic is the most common index for summarizing the interobserver consistency of categorical judgments (Kelly, 1977). The percentage of agreement is the ratio of the number of agreements to the total number of observations (agreements plus disagreements) multiplied by 100. This agreement statistic has been repeatedly criticized, especially since inflated reliability estimates may result when the target behavior occurs at extreme rates (Costello, 1973; Johnson & Bolstad, 1973; Hartmann, 1977; Hopkins & Herman, 1977; Mitchell, 1979). A variety of techniques have been suggested to remedy this problem. Some procedures exclude entries in either the occurrence or the non–occurrence agreement category before calculating an agreement statistic (e.g., Hawkins & Dotson, 1975), while other procedures provide formal correction for chance agreements. These latter statistics are referred to as *kappa-like statistics* because of their similarity to their precursor, Cohen's kappa (Cohen, 1960). Kappa-like statistics have been discussed and illustrated by Hartmann (1977) and Hollenbeck (1978), and a useful technical bibliography on kappa-like statistics is given by Hubert (1977). These statistics may be used for summarizing observer accuracy (Light, 1971), for determining consistency among many raters (Fleiss, 1971), and for evaluating scaled (partial) consistency among observers (Cohen, 1968).

A percentage-of-agreement statistic for quantitative data has also been frequently used in applied behavioral research. This statistic, sometimes called *marginal agreement* (Frick & Semmel, 1978), is the ratio of the smaller value (frequency or duration) to the larger value obtained by two observers multiplied by 100. It too has been criticized for potentially inflating reliability estimates (Hartmann, 1977). Flanders (1967) and Garrett (1972) offered chance-corrected formulas for marginal agreement statistics.

Berk (1979) advocated the use of generalizability coefficients as an alternative to the above-described statistics. He argued that the generalizability approach "produces estimates of the reliability of a single observation and sets of observations, . . . provides data for deciding the number and assignment of observers in the principle experiment, [and]

permits researchers to choose between the inclusion and exclusion of observer bias as part of the error variance term" (p. 464). In all, Berk, listed 11 advantages associated with the generalizability approach to assessing reliability. Some investigators, however, have argued that generalizability and related correlational approaches should be avoided. The reasons for this avoidance include fears that such procedures "cook numbers to provide highly abstract outcomes" (Baer, 1977, p. 117) or that such mathematical approaches may inhibit applied behavior analysis from becoming a "people's science" (Hawkins & Fabry, 1979, p. 546).

Disagreement about procedures for summarizing observer reliability are also related to differing recommendations for "acceptable values" of observer reliability estimates. Given the variety of available statistics—with various statistics based on different metrics and employing different conceptions of error—a common standard for satisfactory reliability seems unlikely. In general, values closer to the maximum value of the statistic (e.g., 100% or 1.0) are preferable to values less close to the maximum, though Frick and Semmel (1978) warned about overly high observer consistency for field observation. Kelly (1977) recommended a minimum value of 90% for percentage of agreement, and Jones *et al.* (1975) suggested 70% agreement as an acceptable level of observer consistency when complex coding schemes are used. Gelfand and Hartmann (1975) recommended 80% agreement and .60 for kappa-like statistics and reliability coefficients. Some investigators (e.g., Birkimer & Brown, 1979a; Yelton, 1979) have suggested that the statistical significance of the reliability summary statistics should be considered the minimally acceptable level of interobserver consistency. This approach has been criticized for the unusual reason that statistical significance is dependent on sample size (Hopkins & Hermann, 1977).

A more serious concern is that significance levels based on traditional inferential tests may be grossly in error when they are applied to serially dependent time-series data (Gardner, Hartmann, & Mitchell, 1982). In general, it is not possible to stipulate an acceptable level of interobserver consistency without additional information concerning such factors as the variability of the data, the magnitude of effect to be detected, and the risk of Type II error (or level of power) that the investigator finds acceptable. A novel graphic approach focusing on disagreement rather than agreement between observers has recently been proposed by Birkimer and Brown (1979b). Unfortunately, this approach fails to consider any of the aforementioned factors, such as variability (Hartmann & Gardner, 1979).

Other Facets of Generalizability

Other facets of generalizability relevant to the reliability of observations include items (subclasses of behaviors), time, and settings (e.g., Cone, 1977; Jones, 1977; Wiggins, 1973). These facets apparently have not engaged the attention of behavioral researchers interested in observation systems. Recent chapters on behavior observation by Kent and Foster (1977) and by Wildman and Erickson (1977) limited their reliability considerations to observer generalizability. Mitchell (1979) reported a similar neglect of other facets of generalizability in her review of observation studies published in *Child Development* and *Developmental Psychology*. Thus, it seems that with few exceptions (e.g., Johnson & Bolstad, 1973; Jones *et al.,* 1975; Paul & Lentz, 1977), the effects of items, time, and settings have not been the subject of *systematic* methodological investigations.

This one-sided treatment of reliability may reflect the belief of some investigators that behavior is highly discriminated across response modes, time, and situations (e.g., Nelson, Hay, & Hay, 1977). While the belief in response specificity seems appropriate for some behaviors (Mischel, 1968), for many other responses the issues of stability and generality remain empirical questions (Wiggins, 1973). Because of the apparent importance of temporal and situational consistency to applied behavioral practices, these generalizability facets deserve more systematic attention.

Behavioral researchers must also be concerned about another aspect of generalizability that is particularly relevant to exploratory or descriptive analyses in which direct observa-

tions provide one source of data (see examples in Paul & Lentz, 1977). In order for these analyses to produce meaningful results, the scores must be based on adequate (reliable) samples of behavior. This demand is analogous to the demand imposed on traditional psychometric assessors to develop tests of adequate length. In the case of scores derived from observations, the samples of behaviors that are observed must be sufficient in both number and duration. Investigators can attempt to meet these sampling requirements by trusting their luck, their intuition, or their prior experience—alternatives associated with some risk—or they may base their decisions on the results of a generalizability analysis. Additional advantages that may accrue to a more extensive investigation of other generalizability facets are described by Cone (1977), by Hartmann, Roper, and Bradford (1979), and by Mitchell (1979).

As behavioral researchers increase their focus on generalizability facets other than observers, they would be well advised to consult the existing literature before engaging in extensive research and development. The alternative approach of reinventing a technology, as has been done with observer reliability (Hartmann, 1979a,b; Peterson & Hartmann, 1975), is substantially less efficient even though it may be temporarily more rewarding.

Recommendations for Reporting Reliability Information

A variety of recommendations have been advanced for reporting reliability information (e.g., Hartmann, 1977; Hawkins & Dotson, 1975; Hopkins & Hermann, 1977; Johnson & Bolstad, 1973; Kratochwill & Wetzel, 1977; Mitchell, 1979; Tinsley & Weiss, 1975). The recommendations range from the suggestion that investigators embellish their primary data with disagreement ranges and chance agreement levels (Birkimer & Brown, 1979b) to advocacy of what appear to be cumbersome tests of statistical significance (Yelton, Wildman, & Erickson, 1977). We suggest a collection of what appear to be the most reasonable recommendations.

The first set of recommendations concerns the type(s) of reliability that should be reported. For most purposes, reliability estimates should be reported on interobserver accuracy and/or consistency as well as on the reliability of the data sample. In the case of interobserver consistency or accuracy assessed with percentage-of-agreement statistics, either a chance-corrected index or the chance level of agreements for the index used should be reported. The reliability of the data sample may be assessed by either internal consistency or test–retest reliability. If a generalizability approach is employed for estimating any design facet, the components that contribute to error should be indicated. If unusual statistics are employed for reliability purposes, a convenient reference should be cited.

The second set of recommendations concerns the sources of the data on which reliability calculations should be based (also see the section on observers). Reliability based on data collected during training or from preliminary trials may not be representative of the data reported in the formal study. Therefore, reliability should be assessed for those data that are reported in the study. Because reliability may vary for different subjects and across experimental conditions, data sampled across these dimensions should contribute accordingly to reliability calculations.

The third set of recommendations specifies the scores for which reliability should be reported. Reliability should be reported for each variable that is the focus of a substantive analysis. Thus, if analyses are conducted on each of five observed behaviors, reliability should be reported for each of the five behaviors. Some investigators violate this principle by reporting a single overall measure of reliability, such as interobserver agreement, for an entire multicategory observation system. This approach can be troublesome, particularly when the overall measure of reliability is not representative of the reliability of each category or behavior in the system. If analyses are conducted on composite variables, such as difference scores (e.g., postscores minus prescores) or sum scores (e.g., total deviant behaviors), reliability analyses should be conducted on the composite variables, and perhaps also on the more elementary component behaviors that make up the composite. While composite variables based on sums of posi-

tively correlated components are typically more reliable than their components (Nunnally, 1978), composite variables based on differences between positively correlated components may be substantially less reliable than their components (McNemar, 1969). This potential discrepancy between composite and component score reliabilities underlies our recommendation for evaluating both indices.

Further consideration of composite scores forms the basis for our final recommendation: reliability assessments should be performed at the data level that is analyzed (e.g., Heyns & Lippitt, 1954). Thus, if weekly behavior rate is the focus of analysis, the reliability of the rate measure should be assessed at the level of data summed over the seven days in a week. Reliability assessed at the level of monthly rate would almost certainly overestimate the reliability of the weekly rate scores, while reliability assessed at the level of daily rate would very likely underestimate their reliability. In some situations, as we previously suggested, reliability assessed at a finer level of data than that at which the analysis is conducted may be useful. For example, reliability assessed at the level of brief intervals within a session may be useful for identifying observer difficulties with a coding schema even if the data are analyzed at the level of daily session totals (e.g., Hartmann, 1977). Interval reliability assessments, however, will almost certainly provide a conservative estimate of the reliability of daily session totals (Hartmann, 1976). In advocating a conservative and thorough analysis of reliability facets, our primary concern is to prompt investigators to describe the characteristics of their data at least as well as they describe the characteristics of the subjects, the target behaviors, the intervention procedures, and the assessment methods.

Validity

Validity, the extent to which a score measures what it is intended to measure, has not received much attention in observation research (e.g., Johnson & Bolstad, 1973; O'Leary, 1979). This relative neglect of validity issues is ironic: behavior analysts have repeatedly criticized traditional assessment methodologies for their limited reliability and validity (Linehan, 1980). In fact, observations have been considered inherently valid insofar as they are based on direct sampling of behavior and require minimal inferences on the part of observers (Goldfried & Linehan, 1977). Observation data have been excused from the requirements of external validation, yet they often serve as *the* criteria for validating other types of assessment data (e.g., Mash & Terdal 1976). This assumption of inherent validity in observations involves a serious epistemological error (Haynes, 1978). The data obtained by human observers may not be veridical descriptions of behavior.

Accuracy of observations can be attenuated by various sources of unreliability and contaminated by reactivity effects and other sources of measurement bias (e.g., Kazdin, 1977, 1979a). The occurrence of such measurement-specific sources of variation provides convincing evidence for the need to validate observation scores (Campbell & Fiske, 1959; Cook & Campbell, 1979). Validation is further indicated when observations are combined to measure some higher-level construct such as "deviant behavior" or when observation scores are used as predictors (e.g., Hartmann *et al.,* 1979; Hawkins, 1979). While the theory of generalizability formulated by Cronbach *et al.* (1972) can accommodate discussion of validity issues relevant to behavior observation (Cone, 1977), our discussion reviews traditional validity categories that are generally better known and similarly applicable. The categories include content, criterion-related (concurrent and predictive), and construct validity.

Content Validity

While each of the traditional types of validity is relevant to observation systems (e.g., Hartmann *et al.,* 1979), content validity is especially important in the initial development of a behavior-coding schema. Content validity is determined by the adequacy with which an observation instrument samples the behavioral domain of interest (Cronbach, 1971). According to Linehan (1980), three requirements must be met to establish content validity. First, the universe of interest (i.e., domain of relevant events) must be completely and un-

ambiguously defined. Depending on the nature and purposes of an observation system, this demand for specification may apply to the behaviors of the target subject, to antecedent and consequent events provided by other persons, or to settings and temporal factors. Next, these relevant factors should be representatively sampled for inclusion in the observation system. Finally, the method for evaluating and combining observations to form scores should be specified.

Most observation systems have generally conformed to the operational requirements of content validity by specifying sampling and analysis procedures. However, less attention has been devoted to definitional requirements, particularly in the case of multipurpose observation systems when definition of the relevant behavior domain or universe assumes particular importance (e.g., Haynes & Kerns, 1979). Thorough enumeration of the stimuli, the responses, and other important elements in the domain (analogous to performing a task analysis) could promote more adequate sampling of the appropriate observation dimensions. This procedure would also clearly specify the limits of applicability of an observation system.

Criterion-Related Validity

The criterion-related validity of observation scores refers to their usefulness or accuracy in predicting some performance criterion (predictive validity) or in substituting for some other established measure (concurrent validity). The two criterion-related validity paradigms are both potentially important for behavior observation (Hawkins, 1979; Kazdin, 1979b); they are central to two currently prominent issues in behavioral assessment.

The first issue is the determination of the validity of observation and other behavior assessment data when they are used to identify problem behaviors and controlling stimuli and to select treatment interventions (e.g., Haynes, 1978; Mash & Terdal, 1974). In this instance, the utility of observations for such classification decisions must be determined by predictive validity studies. Noteworthy work in this direction has been performed by Paul and his associates in the validation of three observation systems used to assess chronically hospitalized psychiatric patients (Paul, in press; Paul & Lentz, 1977; *Journal of Behavioral Assessment,* 1979, *1*[3]).

Predictive validity studies are susceptible to numerous methodological difficulties. Thus, investigators should be sensitive to issues of subject sampling, control of irrelevant variables, and methods of establishing incremental validity when decisions involve extreme base rates. Additional considerations include the seemingly inevitable problems of chance findings and cross-validation which frequently occur in multivariate prediction studies based on small numbers of subjects (see related discussions by Kupke, Calhoun, & Hobbs, 1979; Kupke, Hobbs, & Cheney, 1979). Fortunately, these problems have been identified and specified, and effective solutions have been developed by traditional assessment researchers (Megargee, 1966; Wiggins, 1973; *Journal of Consulting and Clinical Psychology,* 1978, *46*[4]).

A second criterion-related validity issue is the degree to which one source of behavioral assessment data can be substituted for another. This issue is particularly important in evaluating treatment outcomes, as when assessing the effects of social skills training (e.g., Bellack, 1979). Although the literature on the consistency between alternative sources of assessment data is small and inconclusive, there is evidence of poor correspondence between observation data obtained in structured (analogue) settings and naturalistic settings. Poor correspondence has also been shown when contrasting observation data with less reactive assessment data (Kazdin, 1979a,b). These results suggest that behavioral outcome data might have restricted generalizability. Moreover, these results further underscore the desirability of concurrent validity studies when behavioral and alternative data sources are used to assess treatment outcome.

Construct Validity

Construct validity is indexed by the degree to which observations accurately measure some psychological construct. The need for construct validity is most apparent when observation scores are combined to yield a measure of some molar behavior category or construct, such as "deviant behavior." Patterson and his colleagues (e.g., Johnson & Bolstad, 1973; Jones *et al.,* 1975) have exemplified construct validation procedures with their Total Deviancy score, which is derived by combining scores for a number of behaviors included in their Behavioral Coding System (BCS). Separate studies have demonstrated that parents consider behaviors included in the Total Deviancy score more noxious than other behaviors included in the BCS. The Total Deviancy score also is susceptible to fake-bad instructional sets (e.g., Johnson & Bolstad, 1973). Moreover, the Total Deviancy score discriminates between clinical and nonclinical groups of children and is sensitive to the social-learning intervention strategies for which it was initially developed. Thus, the construct validity of this measure subsumes two additional validity categories proposed by Nelson and Hayes (1979): the BCS and its measure of Total Deviancy can be used to promote an experimental analysis (theoretical validity) and to assist in the development of effective treatments (treatment validity). In general, the sensitivity of observations in evaluating treatment outcomes has provided the most impressive evidence for their construct validity (Haynes, 1978).

To conclude, it is important to realize that validity is not a general or absolute property of an assessment instrument (Anastasi, 1976). Observations may have impressive validity for evaluating the effectiveness of behavioral interventions, but they may be only moderately valid or even invalid measures for other assessment purposes. Observations may be used for various assessment functions, and the validity of observation data for each of these functions must be independently verified (e.g., Hartmann *et al.,* 1979; Hawkins, 1979; Kazdin, 1979b; Mash & Terdal, 1974). Behavior analysts, no less than other clinician–investigators, are responsible for establishing the utility of their assessment systems.

Final Observations

Our review of the observation literature prompts five concluding observations on apparent trends.

First, direct behavior observation no longer

appears to have the elevated status it once held. This more realistic evaluation is directly related to behaviorists' increasing sensitivity to the psychometric properties of their assessment procedures (e.g., Cone, 1977; *Behavioral Assessment,* 1979, *1*[1]). While observations continue to be the preferred source of behavioral assessment data, they, like other sources of assessment data, are subject to errors and biases.

A second and somewhat related issue is the apparent independence of the behavior observation literature both from its precursors in behavioral child psychology and from the observation literatures in anthropology, education, ethology, and social psychology (see a related criticism by Boyd & DeVault, 1966). The insular qualities of behavioral psychology in general and of behavior assessment in particular have been previously noted by Krantz (1971) and by Peterson and Hartmann (1975). The consequences of this isolation, including restrictions on methodology and on conceptual models as well as the pursuit of needlessly redundant investigations, hardly seem worth the effort spared by such "scholarly selectivity" (see earlier and similar discussions by Hare, 1962; Withall, 1960).

Our third observation is again reminiscent of "quality-of-science" issues. Most of the observation literature and the reviews of it are limited in their level of conceptual analysis. Notable exceptions are Campbell's (1958) communication system analogy for observation error and Heyns and Lippitt's (1954) solutions to these problems derived from the laws of psychophysics. The conceptual power of information-processing theory and theories of instruction have yet to be consistently applied to problems of observer training; this may be one reason that observer training has not substantially changed over the course of 50 years (see Cochrane & Sobol, 1976, for similar concerns about the entire behavior therapy field).

A fourth issue involves the increasing availability of sophisticated observational technology. Compact keyboard and data storage devices with easy access to computers for data processing and analysis can now be constructed for well under $1,000 (e.g., Sanson-Fisher *et al.,* 1979). While these developments simplify the work of observers and allow more complex and molecular analyses of behavioral phenomena, potential problems with such technologies are just beginning to be realized (e.g., Simpson, 1979; Sykes, 1977). The use of these devices will require caution by investigators to ensure that they do not lose contact with their basic data (see Michael, 1974, for related concerns about the application of statistics to behavioral data).

The fifth and final issue concerns the information available on observation instruments. Behavioral investigators who have developed observation systems frequently fail to represent them with the level of specificity required for critical evaluation. Herbert and Attridge (1975) provided a detailed set of criteria for describing observation instruments: separate categories provide descriptive, psychometric, and practical information for applied use of the observation technique. Thorough reporting practices would enable investigators to select existing observation procedures that could satisfy their research or clinical requirements and might also promote the use of existing observation procedures beyond the laboratories or clinics where they were originally developed (see O'Leary, 1979).

In conclusion, we have attempted to alert behavior analysts interested in observational methods to the numerous decisions involved in constructing or selecting direct behavior-assessment techniques. We have also surveyed the range of alternatives available at each decision point, and we have highlighted some potentially significant consequences associated with these alternatives. Although most of our discussion of issues was admittedly brief, more complete information may be obtained by reference to the array of behavioral and nonbehavioral observation sources we have cited.

ACKNOWLEDGMENTS

Special thanks to Carol Shigetomi for her critical reading of an earlier draft.

References

Adams, H. E., Doster, J. A., & Calhoun, K. S. A psychologically based system of response classification. In A. R. Ciminero, K. S. Calhoun, & H. E. Adams (Eds.),

Handbook of behavioral assessment. New York: Wiley, 1977.

Alban, L. S., & Nay, W. R. Reduction of ritual checking by a relaxation-delay treatment. *Journal of Behavior Therapy and Experimental Psychiatry,* 1976, *7,* 151–154.

Alevizos, P. N., Campbell, M. D., Callahan, E. J., & Berck, P. L. Communication. *Journal of Applied Behavior Analysis,* 1974, *7,* 472.

Alevizos, P., DeRisi, W., Liberman, R., Eckman, T., & Callahan, E. The Behavior Observation Instrument: A method of direct observation for program evaluation. *Journal of Applied Behavior Analysis,* 1978, *11,* 243–257.

Altmann, J. Observational study of behavior: Sampling methods. *Behaviour,* 1974, *49,* 227–267.

Anastasi, A. *Psychological testing* (4th ed.). New York: Macmillan, 1976.

Arrington, R. E. Interrelations in the behavior of young children. *Child Development Monographs,* 1932, No. 8.

Arrington, R. E. Time-sampling studies of child behavior. *Psychological Monographs,* 1939, *51*(2).

Arrington, R. E. Time-sampling in studies of social behavior: A critical review of techniques and results with research suggestions. *Psychological Bulletin,* 1943, *40,* 81–124.

Ayllon, T., & Skuban, W. Accountability in psychotherapy: A test case. *Journal of Behavior Therapy and Experimental Psychiatry,* 1973, *4,* 19–30.

Azrin, N. H., Holz, W., Ulrich, R., & Goldiamond, I. The control of the content of conversation through reinforcement. *Journal of the Experimental Analysis of Behavior,* 1961, *4,* 25–30.

Baer, D. M. Reviewer's comment: Just because it's reliable doesn't mean that you can use it. *Journal of Applied Behavior Analysis,* 1977, *10,* 117–119.

Baer, D. M., Wolf, M. M., & Risley, T. R. Some current dimensions of applied behavior analysis. *Journal of Applied Behavior Analysis,* 1968, *1,* 91–97.

Bakeman, R. Untangling streams of behavior: Sequential analysis of observational data. In G. P. Sackett (Ed.), *Observing behavior.* Vol. 2: *Data collection and analysis methods.* Baltimore: University Park Press, 1978.

Bakeman, R., Cairns, R. B., & Applebaum, M. Note on describing and analyzing interactional data: Some first steps and common pitfalls. In R. B. Cairns (Ed.), *The analysis of social interactions: Methods, issues, and illustrations.* Hillsdale, N.J.: Lawrence Erlbaum, 1979.

Bales, R. F. *Interaction process analysis.* Cambridge, Mass.: Addison-Wesley, 1950.

Barker, R. G., & Wright, H. F. *Midwest and its children: The psychological ecology of an American town.* New York: Harper & Row, 1955.

Baum, C. G., Forehand, R., & Zegiob, L. E. A review of observer reactivity in adult-child interactions. *Journal of Behavioral Assessment,* 1979, *1,* 167–178.

Begelman, D. A. Behavioral classification. In M. Hersen & A. S. Bellack (Eds.), *Behavioral assessment: A practical handbook.* New York: Pergamon Press, 1976.

Bellack, A. S. A critical appraisal of strategies for assessing social skill. *Behavioral Assessment,* 1979, *1,* 157–176.

Berger, M. M. *Videotape techniques in psychiatric training and treatment* (2nd ed.). New York: Brunner-Mazel, 1978.

Berk, R. A. Generalizability of behavioral observations: A clarification of interobserver agreement and interobserver reliability. *American Journal of Mental Deficiency,* 1979, *83,* 460–472.

Bernal, M. E., Gibson, D. M., William, D. E., & Pesses, D. I. A device for automatic audio tape recording. *Journal of Applied Behavior Analysis,* 1971, *4,* 151–156.

Bertucci, M., Huston, M., & Perloff, E. Comparative study of progress notes using problem-oriented and traditional methods of charting. *Nursing Research,* 1974, *23,* 351–354.

Bickman, L. Observational methods. In C. Selltiz, L. S. Wrightsman, & S. W. Cook (Eds.), *Research methods in social relations.* New York: Holt, Rinehart & Winston, 1976.

Bijou, S. W., Peterson, R. F., & Ault, M. H. A method to integrate descriptive and experimental field studies at the level of data and empirical concepts. *Journal of Applied Behavior Analysis,* 1968, *1,* 175–191.

Bijou, S. W., Peterson, R. F., Harris, F. R., Allen, K. E., & Johnston, M. S. Methodology for experimental studies of young children in natural settings. *Psychological Record,* 1969, *19,* 177–210.

Birkimer, J. C., & Brown, J. H. Back to basics: Percentage agreement measures are adequate, but there are easier ways. *Journal of Applied Behavior Analysis,* 1979, *12,* 535–543. (a)

Birkimer, J. C., & Brown, J. H. A graphical judgmental aid which summarizes obtained and chance reliability data and helps assess the believability of experimental effects. *Journal of Applied Behavior Analysis,* 1979, *12,* 523–533. (b)

Blurton Jones, N. (Ed.). *Ethological studies of child behaviour.* Cambridge, England: Cambridge University Press, 1972.

Blurton Jones, N. G., & Woodson, R. H. Describing behavior: The ethologists' perspective. In M. E. Lamb, S. J. Suomi, & G. R. Stephenson (Eds.), *Social interaction analysis: Methodological issues.* Madison: University of Wisconsin Press, 1979.

Borko, H. (Ed.). *Computer applications in the behavioral sciences.* Englewood Cliffs, N.J.: Prentice-Hall, 1962.

Bornstein, P. H., Bridgwater, C. A., Hickey, J. S., & Sweeney, T. M. Characteristics and trends in behavioral assessment: An archival analysis. *Behavioral Assessment,* 1980, *2,* 125–133.

Boyd, R. D., & DeVault, M. V. The observation and recording of behavior. *Review of Educational Research,* 1966, *36,* 529–551.

Cairns, R. B. (Ed.). *The analysis of social interactions: Methods, issues, and illustrations.* Hillsdale, N.J.: Lawrence Erlbaum, 1979.

Campbell, D. T. Systematic error on the part of human links in communication systems. *Information and Control,* 1958, *1,* 334–369.

Campbell, D. T., & Fiske, D. Convergent and discriminant validation by the multi-trait, multi-method matrix. *Psychological Bulletin,* 1959, *56,* 81–105.

Carter, L., Haythorn, W., Meirowitz, B., & Lanzetta, J. A note on a new technique of interaction recording. *Journal of Abnormal and Social Psychology,* 1951, *46,* 258–260.

Cassota, L., Jaffe, J., Feldstein, S., & Moses, R. *Operating manual: Automatic vocal transaction analyzer.*

New York: William Alanson White Institute, 1964. (Research Bulletin No. 1.)

Christensen, A. Naturalistic observation of families: A system for random audio recordings in the home. *Behavior Therapy*, 1979, *10*, 418–422.

Ciminero, A. R., Calhoun, K. S., & Adams, H. E. (Eds.). *Handbook of behavioral assessment*. New York: Wiley, 1977.

Coates, T. J., & Thoresen, C. E. Using generalizability theory in behavioral observation. *Behavior Therapy*, 1978, *9*, 605–613.

Cochrane, R., & Sobol, M. P. Myth and methodology in behaviour therapy research. In M. P. Feldman & A. Broadhurst (Eds.), *Theoretical and experimental bases of the behaviour therapies*. London: Wiley, 1976.

Cohen, J. A coefficient of agreement for nominal scales. *Educational and Psychological Measurement*, 1960, *20*, 37–46.

Cohen, J. Weighted Kappa: Nominal scale agreement with provisions for scale disagreement or partial credit. *Psychological Bulletin*, 1968, *70*, 213–220.

Collier, J. *Visual anthropology: Photography as a research method*. New York: Holt, Rinehart & Winston, 1967.

Cone, J. D. The relevance of reliability and validity for behavior assessment. *Behavior Therapy*, 1977, *8*, 411–426.

Cone, J. D., & Foster, S. L. Direct observation in clinical psychology. In J. N. Butcher & P. C. Kendall (Eds.), *Handbook of research methods in clinical psychology*. New York: Wiley, 1982.

Conger, R. D., & McLeod, D. Describing behavior in small groups with the Datamyte event recorder. *Behavior Research Methods and Instrumentation* 1977, *9*, 418–424.

Connolly, K., & Smith, P. K. Reactions of preschool children to a strange observer. In N. Blurton Jones (Ed.), *Ethological studies of child behaviour*. Cambridge, England: Cambridge University Press, 1972.

Cook, T. D., & Campbell, D. T. *Quasi-Experimentation: Design and analysis issues for field settings*. Chicago: Rand McNally, 1979.

Costello, A. J. The reliability of direct observations. *Bulletin of the British Psychological Society*, 1973, *26*, 105–108.

Crano, W. D., & Brewer, M. B. *Principles of research in social psychology*. New York: McGraw-Hill, 1973.

Cronbach, L. J. *Essentials of psychological testing* (2nd ed.). New York: Harper & Row, 1960.

Cronbach, L. J. Test validation. In R. L. Thorndike (Ed.), *Educational measurement*. Washington: American Council on Education, 1971.

Cronbach, L. J., Gleser, G. C., Nanda, H., & Rajaratnam, N. *The dependability of behavioral measurements*. New York: Wiley, 1972.

Dancer, D. D., Braukmann, C. J., Schumaker, J. B., Kirigin, K. A., Willner, A. G., & Wolf, M. M. The training and validation of behavior observation and description skills. *Behavior Modification*, 1978, *2*, 113–134.

Delgado, J. M. R. Free behaviour and brain stimulation. In C. C. Pfeiffer & J. R. Smythies (Eds.), *International review of neurobiology*, Vol. 6. New York: Academic Press, 1964.

DeMaster, B., Reid, J., & Twentyman, C. The effects of different amounts of feedback on observer's reliability. *Behavior Therapy*, 1977, *8*, 317–329.

Doke, L. A. Assessment of children's behavioral deficits. In M. Hersen & A. S. Bellack (Eds.), *Behavioral assessment: A practical handbook*. New York: Pergamon Press, 1976.

Duncan, S., Jr., & Fiske, D. W. *Face-to-face interaction: Research, methods, and theory*. New York: Lawrence Erlbaum, 1977.

Eisler, R. M., Hersen, M., & Agras, W. S. Videotape: A method for the controlled observation of non-verbal interpersonal behavior. *Behavior Therapy*, 1973, *4*, 420–425.

Ellis, R. H., & Wilson, N. C. Z. Evaluating treatment effectiveness using a goal-oriented automated progress note. *Evaluation*, 1973, *1*, 6–11.

Ethical principles in the conduct of research with human participants. Washington, D.C.: American Psychological Association, 1973.

Fiske, D. W. *Strategies for personality research: The observation versus interpretation of behavior*. San Francisco: Jossey-Bass, 1978.

Flanders, N. A. Estimating reliability. In E. J. Amidon & J. B. Hough (Eds.), *Interaction analysis: Theory, research, and application*. Reading, Mass.: Addison-Wesley, 1967.

Fleiss, J. L. Measuring nominal scale agreement among many raters. *Psychological Bulletin*, 1971, *76*, 378–382.

Fleiss, J. L. Measuring agreement between two judges on the presence or absence of a trait. *Biometrics*, 1975, *31*, 651–659.

Frick, T., & Semmel, M. I. Observer agreement and reliabilities of classroom observational measures. *Review of Educational Research*, 1978, *48*, 157–184.

Futrelle, R. P. GALATEA, A proposed system for computer-aided analysis of movie films and videotape. *The University of Chicago Institute for Computer Research Quarterly Report*, 1973, No. 37, I-F.

Gardner, W., Hartmann, D. P., & Mitchell, C. The effect of serial dependency on the use of χ^2 for analyzing sequential data. *Behavioral Assessment*, 1982, *4*, 75–82.

Garrett, C. S. *Modification of the Scott coefficient as an observer agreement estimate for marginal form observation scale data*. Occasional Paper #6. Bloomington: Center for Innovation in Teaching the Handicapped, Indiana University, 1972. (Cited in Frick, T., & Semmel, M. I., Observer agreement and reliabilities of classroom observational measures. *Review of Educational Research*, 1978, *48*, 157–184.)

Gelfand, D. M., & Hartmann, D. P. *Child behavior analysis and therapy*. New York: Pergamon Press, 1975.

Gellert, E. Systematic observation: A method in child study. *Harvard Educational Review*, 1955, *25*, 179–195.

Goetz, E. M., & Baer, D. M. Social control of form diversity and the emergence of new forms in children's blockbuilding. *Journal of Applied Behavior Analysis*, 1973, *6*, 209–217.

Goldfried, M. R., & Kent, R. N. Traditional versus behavioral personality assessment: A comparison of methodological and theoretical assumptions. *Psychological Bulletin*, 1972, *77*, 409–420.

Goldfried, M. R., & Linehan, M. M. Basic issues in behavioral assessment. In A. R. Ciminero, K. S. Calhoun,

& H. E. Adams (Eds.), *Handbook of behavioral assessment*. New York: Wiley, 1977.

Goodrich, D. W. The choice of situation for observational studies of children. *American Journal of Orthopsychiatry*, 1959, *29*, 227–234.

Green, S. B., & Alverson, L. G. A comparison of indirect measures for long-duration behaviors. *Journal of Applied Behavior Analysis*, 1978, *11*, 530.

Guilford, J. P. *Psychometric methods* (2nd ed.). New York: McGraw-Hill, 1954.

Guttman, H. A., Spector, R. M., Sigal, J. J., Rakoff, V., & Epstein, W. B. Reliability of coding affective communications in family therapy sessions: Problems of measurement and interpretation. *Journal of Consulting and Clinical Psychology*, 1971, *37*, 397–402.

Hagen, R. L., Craighead, W. E., & Paul, G. L. Staff reactivity to evaluative behavioral observations. *Behavior Therapy*, 1975, *6*, 201–205.

Hare, A. P. *Handbook of small group research*. New York: Free Press of Glencoe, 1962.

Hargreaves, W. A., & Starkweather, J. A. Recognition of speaker identity. *Language and Speech*, 1963, *6*, 63–67.

Hartmann, D. P. Some restrictions in the application of the Spearman-Brown prophesy formula to observational data. *Educational and Psychological Measurement*, 1976, *36*, 843–845.

Hartmann, D. P. Considerations in the choice of interobserver reliability estimates. *Journal of Applied Behavior Analysis*, 1977, *10*, 103–116.

Hartmann, D. P. Inter- and intra-observer agreement as a function of explicit behavior definitions in direct observation: A critique. *Behaviour Analysis and Modification*, 1979, *3*, 229–233. (a)

Hartmann, D. P. A note on reliability: Old wine in a new bottle. *Journal of Applied Behavior Analysis*, 1979, *12*, 298. (b)

Hartmann, D. P., & Gardner, W. On the not so recent invention of interobserver reliability statistics: A commentary on two articles by Birkimer and Brown. *Journal of Applied Behavior Analysis*, 1979, *12*, 559–560.

Hartmann, D. P., Roper, B. L., & Gelfand, D. M. Evaluation of alternative modes of child psychotherapy. In B. B. Lahey & A. E. Kazdin (Eds.), *Advances in clinical child psychology*, Vol. 1. New York: Plenum Press, 1977.

Hartmann, D. P., Roper, B. L., & Bradford, D. C. Some relationships between behavioral and traditional assessment. *Journal of Behavioral Assessment*, 1979, *1*, 3–21.

Hawkins, R. P. The functions of assessment: Implications for selection and development of devices for assessing repertoires in clinical, educational, and other settings. *Journal of Beahvioral Assessment*, 1979, *12*, 501–516.

Hawkins, R. P., & Dobes, R. W. Behavioral definitions in applied behavior analysis: Explicit or implicit. In B. C. Etzel, J. M. LeBlanc, & D. M. Baer (Eds.), *New developments in behavioral research: Theory, method and application. In honor of Sidney W. Bijou*. Hillsdale, N.J.: Lawrence Erlbaum, 1977.

Hawkins, R. P., & Dotson, V. A. Reliability scores that delude: An Alice in Wonderland Trip through the misleading characteristics of interobserver agreement scores in interval recording. In E. Ramp & G. Semb (Eds.),

Behavior analysis: Areas of research and application. Englewood Cliffs, N.J.: Prentice-Hall, 1975.

Hawkins, R. P., & Fabry, B. D. Applied behavior analysis and interobserver reliability: A commentary on two articles by Birkimer and Brown. *Journal of Applied Behavior Analysis*, 1979, *12*, 545–552.

Haynes, S. N. *Principles of behavioral assessment*. New York: Gardner Press, 1978.

Haynes, S. N., & Kerns, R. D. Validation of a behavioral observation system. *Journal of Consulting and Clinical Psychology*, 1979, *47*, 397–400.

Heimstra, N. W., & Davis, R. T. A simple recording system for the direct observation technique. *Animal Behavior*, 1962, *10*, 208–210.

Herbert, J., & Attridge, C. A guide for developers and users of observation systems and manuals. *American Educational Research Journal*, 1975, *12*, 1–20.

Hersen, M., & Barlow, D. H. *Single-case experimental designs: Strategies for studying behavior change*. Oxford: Pergamon Press, 1976.

Hersen, M., & Bellack, A. S. (Eds.). *Behavioral assessment: A practical handbook*. New York: Pergamon Press, 1976.

Heyns, R. W., & Lippitt, R. Systematic observational techniques. In G. Lindzey (Ed.), *Handbook of social psychology*, Vol. 1. Reading, Mass.: Addison-Wesley, 1954.

Heyns, R. W., & Zander, A. F. Observation of group behavior. In L. Festinger & D. Katz (Eds.), *Research methods in the behavioral sciences*. New York: Dryden, 1953.

Hollenbeck, A. R. Problems of reliability in observational research. In G. P. Sackett (Ed.), *Observing behavior*. Vol. 2: *Data collection and analysis methods*. Baltimore: University Park Press, 1978.

Hopkins, B. L., & Hermann, J. A. Evaluating interobserver reliability of interval data. *Journal of Applied Behavior Analysis*, 1977, *10*, 121–126.

House, A. E. Detecting bias in observational data. *Behavioral Assessment*, 1980, *2*, 29–31.

Hubert, L. Kappa revisited. *Psychological Bulletin*, 1977, *84*, 289–297.

Hutt, S. J., & Hutt, C. *Direct observation and measurement of behavior*. Springfield, Ill.: Charles C Thomas, 1970.

Jaffe, J., & Feldstein, S. *Rhythms of dialogue*. New York: Academic Press, 1970.

Jersild, A. T., & Markey, F.V. Conflicts between preschool children. *Child Development Monographs*, 1935, No. 21.

Johnson, S. M., & Bolstad, O. D. Methodological issues in naturalistic observation: Some problems and solutions for field research. In L. A. Hamerlynck, L. C. Handy, & E. J. Mash (Eds.), *Behavior change: Methodology, concepts, and practice*. Champaign, Ill.: Research Press, 1973.

Jones, M. C. The elimination of children's fears. *Journal of Experimental Psychology*, 1924, *7*, 383–390.

Jones, R. R. Conceptual vs. analytic uses of generalizability theory in behavioral assessment. In J. D. Cone & R. P. Hawkins (Eds.), *Behavioral assessment: New directions in clinical psychology*. New York: Brunner/Mazel, 1977.

Jones, R. R., Reid, J. B., & Patterson, G. R. Naturalistic

observation in clinical assessment. In P. McReynolds (Ed.), *Advances in psychological assessment,* Vol. 3. San Francisco: Jossey-Bass, 1975.

Kazdin, A. E. Artifact, bias, and complexity of assessment: The ABCs of reliability. *Journal of Applied Behavior Analysis,* 1977, *10,* 141–150.

Kazdin, A. E. Situational specificity: The two-edged sword of behavioral assessment. *Behavioral Assessment,* 1979, *1,* 57–75. (a)

Kazdin, A. E. Unobtrusive measures in behavioral assessment. *Journal of Applied Behavior Analysis,* 1979, *12,* 713–724. (b)

Kelly, M. B. A review of the observational data-collection and reliability procedures reported in *The Journal of Applied Behavior Analysis. Journal of Applied Behavior Analysis,* 1977, *10,* 97–101.

Kent, R. N., & Foster, S. L. Direct observational procedures: Methodological issues in naturalistic settings. In A. R. Ciminero, K. S. Calhoun, & H. E. Adams (Eds.), *Handbook of behavioral assessment.* New York: Wiley, 1977.

Kent, R. N., O'Leary, K. D., Diament, C., & Dietz, A. Expectation biases in observational evaluation of therapeutic change. *Journal of Consulting and Clinical Psychology,* 1974, *42,* 774–780.

Kent, R. N., O'Leary, K. D., Dietz, A., & Diament, C. Comparison of observational recordings *in vivo, via* mirror, and *via* television. *Journal of Applied Behavior Analysis,* 1979, *12,* 517–522.

Knapp, C. W. Communication: A portable one-way observation screen. *Journal of Applied Behavior Analysis,* 1978, *11,* 284.

Kraemer, H. One-zero sampling in the study of primate behavior. *Primates,* 1979, *20,* 237–244.

Krantz, D. L. The separate worlds of operant and nonoperant psychology. *Journal of Applied Behavior Analysis,* 1971, *4,* 61–70.

Kratochwill, T. R., & Wetzel, R. J. Observer agreement, credibility, and judgment: Some considerations in presenting observer agreement data. *Journal of Applied Behavior Analysis,* 1977, *10,* 133–139.

Kunzelman, H. D. (Ed.). *Precision teaching.* Seattle: Special Child Publications, 1970.

Kupke, T. E., Calhoun, K. S., & Hobbs, S. A. Selection of heterosocial skills. II. Experimental validity. *Behavior Therapy,* 1979, *10,* 336–346.

Kupke, T. E., Hobbs, S. A., & Cheney, T. H. Selection of heterosocial skills. I. Criterion-related validity. *Behavior Therapy,* 1979, *10,* 327–335.

Lachman, R., Lachman, J. L., & Butterfield, E. C. *Cognitive psychology and information processing: An introduction.* Hillsdale, N.J.: Lawrence Erlbaum, 1979.

Lamb, M. E., Suomi, S. J., & Stephenson, G. R. (Eds.). *Social interaction analysis: Methodological issues.* Madison: University of Wisconsin Press, 1979.

Lambert, W. W. Interpersonal behavior. In P. H. Mussen (Ed.), *Handbook of research methods in child development.* New York: Wiley, 1960.

Lang, P. J. The on-line computer in behavior therapy research. *American Psychologist,* 1969, *24,* 236–239.

Lass, N. J. (Ed.). *Contemporary issues in experimental phonetics.* New York: Academic Press, 1976.

Ledley, R. S. *Use of computers in biology and medicine.* New York: McGraw-Hill, 1965.

Liberman, R. P., DeRisi, W. J., King, L. W., Eckman, T. A., & Wood, D. D. Behavioral measurement in a community mental health center. In P. O. Davidson, F. W. Clark, & L. A. Hamerlynck (Eds.), *Evaluation of behavioral programs in community, residential, and school settings.* Champaign, Ill.: Research Press, 1974.

Licht, M. H. The Staff-Resident Interaction Chronograph: Observational assessment of staff performance. *Journal of Behavioral Assessment,* 1979, *1,* 185–197.

Light, R. J. Measures of response agreement for qualitative data, some generalizations and alternatives. *Psychological Bulletin,* 1971, *76,* 365–377.

Linehan, M. M. Content validity: Its relevance to behavioral assessment. *Behavioral Assessment,* 1980, *2,* 147–159.

Loomis, A. M. A technique for observing the social behavior of nursery school children. *Child Development Monographs,* 1931, No. 5.

Lytton, H. Observation studies of parent-child interaction: A methodological review. *Child Development,* 1971, *42,* 651–684.

Martin, M. F., Gelfand, D. M., & Hartmann, D. P. Effects of adult and peer observers on boys' and girls' responses to an aggressive model. *Child Development,* 1971, *42,* 1271–1275.

Mash, E. J., & Makohoniuk, G. The effects of prior information and behavioral predictability on observer accuracy. *Child Development,* 1975, *46,* 513–519.

Mash, E. J., & McElwee, J. D. Situational effects on observer accuracy: Behavioral predictability, prior experience, and complexity of coding categories. *Child Development,* 1974, *45,* 367–377.

Mash, E. J., & Terdal, L. G. Behavior therapy assessment: Diagnosis, design, and evaluation. *Psychological Reports,* 1974, *35,* 587–601.

Mash, E. J., & Terdal, L. G. *Behavior therapy assessment: Diagnosis, design, and evaluation.* New York: Springer, 1976.

McFall, R. M. Analogue methods in behavioral assessment: Issues and prospects. In J. D. Cone & R. H. Hawkins (Eds.), *Behavioral assessment: New directions in clinical psychology.* New York: Brunner/Mazel, 1977.

McNemar, Q. *Psychological statistics* (4th ed.). New York: Wiley, 1969.

Megargee, E. I. *Research in clinical assessment.* New York: Harper & Row, 1966.

Melbin, M. An interaction recording device for participant observers. *Human Organization,* 1954, *13,* 29–33.

Menzel, E. W. General discussion of the methodological problems involved in the study of social interaction. In M. E. Lamb, S. J. Suomi, & G. R. Stephenson (Eds.), *Social interaction analysis: Methodological issues.* Madison: University of Wisconsin Press, 1979.

Michael, J. Statistical inference for individual organism research: Mixed blessing or curse? *Journal of Applied Behavior Analysis,* 1974, *7,* 647–653.

Mischel, W. *Personality and assessment.* New York: Wiley, 1968.

Mitchell, S. K. Interobserver agreement, reliability, and generalizability of data collected in observational studies. *Psychological Bulletin,* 1979, *86,* 376–390.

Murphy, G., & Goodall, E. Measurement error in direct observations: A comparison of common recording methods. *Behaviour Research and Therapy,* 1980, *18,* 147–150.

Nay, W. Comprehensive behavioral treatment in a training school for delinquents. In K. Calhoun, H. Adams, & K. Mitchell (Eds.), *Innovative treatment methods in psychopathology.* New York: Wiley, 1974.

Nay, W. R. Analogue measures. In A. R. Ciminero, K. S. Calhoun, & H. E. Adams (Eds.), *Handbook of behavioral assessment.* New York: Wiley, 1977.

Nay, W. R. *Multimethod clinical assessment.* New York: Gardner Press, 1979.

Nelson, R. O. Methodological issues in assessment via self-monitoring. In J. D. Cone & R. P. Hawkins (Eds.), *Behavioral assessment: New directions in clinical psychology.* New York: Brunner/Mazel, 1977.

Nelson, R. O., & Hayes, S. C. Some current dimensions of behavioral assessment. *Behavioral Assessment,* 1979, *1,* 1–16.

Nelson, R. O., Hay, L. R., & Hay, W. M. Comments on Cone's "The relevance of reliability and validity for behavioral assessment." *Behavior Therapy,* 1977, *8,* 427–430.

Nunnally, J. *Psychometric theory* (2nd ed.). New York: McGraw-Hill, 1978.

O'Leary, K. D. Behavioral assessment. *Behavioral Assessment,* 1979, *1,* 31–36.

O'Leary, K. D., & Kent, R. N. Behavior modification for social action: Research tactics and problems. In L. A. Hamerlynck, P. O. Davidson, & L. E. Acker (Eds.), *Critical issues in research and practice.* Champaign, Ill.: Research Press, 1973.

O'Leary, S. G., & O'Leary, K. D. Behavior modification in the school. In H. Leitenberg (Ed.), *Handbook of behavior modification and behavior therapy.* Englewood Cliffs, N.J.: Prentice-Hall, 1976.

O'Leary, K. D., Kent, R. N., & Kanowitz, J. Shaping data collection congruent with experimental hypotheses. *Journal of Applied Behavior Analysis,* 1975, *8,* 43–51.

Olson, W. C., & Cunningham, E. M. Time-sampling techniques. *Child Development,* 1934, *5,* 41–58.

Ostrom, T. M., Werner, C., & Saks, M. J. An integration theory analysis of jurors' presumptions of guilt or innocence. *Journal of Personality and Social Psychology,* 1978, *36,* 436–450.

Patterson, G. R., & Cobb, J. A. A dyadic analysis of aggressive behaviors: An additional step toward a theory of aggression. In J. P. Hill (Ed.), *Minnesota symposium on child psychology,* Vol. 5. Minneapolis: University of Minnesota Press, 1971.

Paul, G. L. (Ed.). *Observational assessment instrumentation for institutional research and treatment.* Cambridge, Mass.: Harvard University Press, in press.

Paul, G. L., & Lentz, R. J. *Psychological treatment of chronic mental patients: Milieu versus social-learning programs.* Cambridge, Mass.: Harvard University Press, 1977.

Peterson, L., & Hartmann, D. P. A neglected literature and an aphorism. *Journal of Applied Behavior Analysis,* 1975, *8,* 331–332.

Polansky, N., Freeman, W., Horowitz, M., Irwin, L., Papanis, N., Rappaport, D., & Whaley, F. Problems of interpersonal relations in research on groups. *Human Relations,* 1949, *2,* 281–291.

Powell, J., & Rockinson, R. On the instability of interval time sampling to reflect frequency of occurrence data. *Journal of Applied Behavior Analysis,* 1978, *11,* 531–532.

Powell, J., Martindale, A., & Kulp, S. An evaluation of time-sample measures of behavior. *Journal of Applied Behavior Analysis,* 1975, *8,* 463–469.

Powell, J., Martindale, B., Kulp, S., Martindale, A., & Bauman, R. Taking a closer look: Time sampling and measurement error. *Journal of Applied Behavior Analysis,* 1977, *10,* 325–332.

Powell, J. P., & Jackson, P. A note on a simplified technique for recording group interaction. *Human Relations,* 1964, *17,* 289–291.

Power, C. T. The Time-Sample Behavioral Checklist: Observational assessment of patient functioning. *Journal of Behavioral Assessment,* 1979, *1,* 199–210.

Purcell, K., & Brady, K. Adaptation to the invasion of privacy: Monitoring behavior with a miniature radio transmitter. *Merrill-Palmer Quarterly,* 1965, *12,* 242–254.

Redfield, J. P., & Paul, G. L. Bias in behavioral observation as a function of observer familiarity with subjects and typicality of behavior. *Journal of Consulting and Clinical Psychology,* 1976, *44,* 156.

Repp, A. C., Dietz, D. E. D., Boles, S. M., Dietz, S. M., & Repp, C. F. Differences among common methods for calculating interobserver agreement. *Journal of Applied Behavior Analysis,* 1976, *9,* 109–113.

Repp, A. C., Roberts, D. M., Slack, D. L., Repp, C. F., & Berkler, M. S. A comparison of frequency, interval, and time-sampling methods of data collection. *Journal of Applied Behavior Analysis,* 1976, *9,* 501–508.

Roberts, R., & Renzaglia, G. The influence of tape recording on counseling. *Journal of Counseling Psychology,* 1965, *12,* 10–16.

Rogers-Warren, A., & Warren, S. F. *Ecological perspectives in behavior analysis.* Baltimore: University Park Press, 1977.

Romanczyk, R. G., Kent, R. N., Diament, C., & O'Leary, K. D. Measuring the reliability of observational data: A reactive process. *Journal of Applied Behavior Analysis,* 1973, *6,* 175–184.

Rosenblum, L. A. The creation of a behavioral taxonomy. In G. P. Sackett (Ed.), *Observing behavior.* Vol. 2: *Data collection and analysis methods.* Baltimore: University Park Press, 1978.

Rosenthal, R. *Experimenter effects in behavior research.* New York: Appleton-Century-Crofts, 1966.

Rugh, J. D., & Schwitzgebel, R. L. Instrumentation for behavioral assessment. In A. R. Ciminero, K. S. Calhoun, & H. E. Adams (Eds.), *Handbook of behavioral assessment.* New York: Wiley, 1977.

Rusch, F. R., Walker, H. M., & Greenwood, C. R. Experimenter calculation errors: A potential factor affecting interpretation of results. *Journal of Applied Behavior Analysis,* 1975, *8,* 460.

Sackett, G. P. Measurement in observational research. In G. P. Sackett (Ed.), *Observing behavior.* Vol. 2: *Data collection and analysis methods.* Baltimore: University Park Press, 1978.

Sackett, G. P. The lag sequential analysis of contingency and cyclicity in behavioral interaction research. In J. D. Osofsky (Ed.), *The handbook of infant development.* New York: Wiley, 1979.

Sanson-Fisher, R. W., Poole, A. D., Small, G. A., &

Fleming, I. R. Data acquisition in real time—An improved system for naturalistic observations. *Behavior Therapy*, 1979, *10*, 543–554.

Schoggen, P. Mechanical aids for making specimen records of behavior. *Child Development*, 1964, *35*, 985–988.

Schwitzgebel, R. K., & Kolb, D. A. *Changing human behavior: Principles of planned intervention*. New York: McGraw-Hill, 1974.

Schwitzgebel, R. L. Behavioral technology. In H. Leitenberg (Ed.), *Handbook of behavior modification and behavior therapy*. Englewood Cliffs, N.J.: Prentice-Hall, 1976.

Schwitzgebel, R. L., & Schwitzgebel, R. K. (Eds.). *Psychotechnology: Electronic control of mind and behavior*. New York: Holt, Rinehart & Winston, 1973.

Sidowski, J. B. Observational research: Some instrumental systems for scoring and storing behavioral data. *Behavior Research Methods and Instrumentation*, 1977, *9*, 403–404.

Simon, A., & Boyer, E. G. *Mirrors for behavior. III: An anthology of observation instruments*. Wyncote, Pa.: Communication Materials Center, 1974.

Simpson, M. J. A. Problems of recording behavioral data by keyboard. In M. E. Lamb, S. J. Suomi, & G. R. Stephenson (Eds.), *Social interaction analysis: Methodological issues*. Madison: University of Wisconsin Press, 1979.

Skindrud, K. Field evaluation of observer bias under overt and covert monitoring. In L. A. Hamerlynck, L. C. Handy, & E. J. Mash (Eds.), *Behavior change: Methodology, concepts, and practice*. Champaign, Ill.: Research Press, 1973.

Smith, M. A method of analyzing the interaction of children. *Journal of Juvenile Research*, 1933, *17*, 78–88.

Soskin, W., & John, V. The study of spontaneous talk. In R. G. Barker (Ed.), *The stream of behavior*. New York: Appleton-Century-Crofts, 1963.

Spiro, M. E. *Children of the kibbutz*. Cambridge, Mass.: Harvard University Press, 1958.

Steinzor, B. The development and evaluation of a measure of social interaction. *Human Relations*, 1949, *2*, 103–122.

Stephenson, G. R. PLEXYN: A computer-compatible grammar for coding complex social interactions. In M. E. Lamb, S. J. Suomi, & G. R. Stephenson (Eds.), *Social interaction analysis: Methodological issues*. Madison: University of Wisconsin Press, 1979.

Strossen, R. J., Coates, T. J., & Thoresen, C. E. Extending generalizability theory to single-subject designs. *Behavior Therapy*, 1979, *10*, 606–614.

Swan, G. E., & MacDonald, M. L. Behavior therapy in practice: A national survey of behavior therapists. *Behavior Therapy*, 1978, *9*, 799–807.

Sykes, R. E. Techniques of data collection and reduction in systematic field observation. *Behavior Research Methods and Instrumentation*, 1977, *9*, 404–417.

Taplin, P. S., & Reid, J. B. Effects of instructional set and experimental influences on observer reliability. *Child Development*, 1973, *44*, 547–554.

Thelen, H. Techniques for collecting data on interaction. *Journal of Social Issues*, 1950, *6*, 77–93.

Thomas, D. S., Loomis, A. M., & Arrington, R. E. *Observational studies of social behavior*. New Haven, Conn.: Institute of Human Relations, Yale University, 1933.

Thomson, C., Holmberg, M., & Baer, D. M. A brief report on a comparison of time-sampling procedures. *Journal of Applied Behavior Analysis*, 1974, *7*, 623–626.

Tinsley, H. E. A., & Weiss, D. J. Interrater reliability and agreement of subjective judgments. *Journal of Counseling Psychology*, 1975, *22*, 358–376.

Tobach, E., Schneirla, T. C., Aronson, L. R., & Laupheimer, R. The ATSL: An observer-to-computer system for a multivariate approach to behavioural study. *Nature*, 1962, *194*, 257–258.

Wade, T. C., Baker, T. B., & Hartmann, D. P. Behavior therapists' self-reported views and practices. *Behavior Therapist*, 1979, *2*, 3–6.

Wallace, C. J. Assessment of psychotic behavior. In M. Hersen & A. S. Bellack (Eds.), *Behavioral assessment: A practical handbook*. New York: Pergamon Press, 1976.

Walls, R. T., Werner, T. J., Bacon, A., & Zane, T. Behavior checklists. In J. D. Cone and R. P. Hawkins (Eds.), *Behavioral assessment: New directions in clinical psychology*. New York: Brunner/Mazel, 1977.

Washburn, R. W. A simultaneous observation-and-recording method with specimen records of activity patterns in young children. *Psychological Monographs*, 1936, *47*, 74–82.

Watson, J. B., & Rayner, R. Conditioned emotional reactions. *Journal of Experimental Psychology*, 1920, *3*, 1–12.

Webb, E. J., Campbell, D. T., Schwartz, R. D., & Sechrest, L. *Unobtrusive measures. Nonreactive research in the social sciences*. Chicago: Rand McNally, 1966.

Weick, K. E. Systematic observational methods. In G. Lindzey & E. Aronson (Eds.), *The handbook of social psychology*, Vol. 2 (2nd ed.). Menlo Park, Calif.: Addison-Wesley, 1968.

Werry, J. S., & Quay, H. C. Observing the classroom behavior of elementary school children. *Exceptional Children*, 1969, *35*, 461–470.

Whiting, B. B., & Whiting, J. W. M. Methods for observing and recording behavior. In R. Naroll & R. Cohen (Eds.), *Handbook of methods in cultural anthropology*. New York: Columbia University Press, 1973.

Wiggins, J. S. *Personality and prediction: Principles of personality assessment*. Reading, Mass.: Addison-Wesley, 1973.

Wiggins, J. S., Renner, K. E., Clore, G. L., & Rose, R. J. *The psychology of personality*. Menlo Park, Calif.: Addison-Wesley, 1971.

Wildman, B. G., & Erickson, M. T. Methodological problems in behavioral observation. In J. D. Cone & R. P. Hawkins (Eds.), *Behavioral assessment: New directions in clinical psychology*. New York: Brunner/Mazel, 1977.

Wildman, B. G., Erickson, M. T., & Kent, R. N. The effect of two training procedures on observer agreement and variability of behavior ratings. *Child Development*, 1975, *46*, 520–524.

Withall, J. An objective measurement of a teacher's classroom interactions. *Journal of Educational Psychology*, 1956, *47*, 203–212.

Withall, J. Observing and recording behavior. *Review of Educational Research*, 1960, *30*, 496–512.

Wolach, A. H., Roccaforte, P., & Breuning, S. E. Converting an electronic calculator into a counter. *Behavior Research Methods and Instrumentation*, 1975, *7*, 365–367.

Wood, D. D., Callahan, E. J., Alevizos, P. N., & Teigen, J. R. Inpatient behavioral assessment with a problem-oriented psychiatric logbook. *Journal of Behavior Therapy and Experimental Psychiatry*, 1979, *10*, 229–235.

Wright, H. F. Observational child study. In P. Mussen (Ed.), *Handbook of research methods in child development*. New York: Wiley, 1960.

Yarrow, M. R., & Waxler, C. Z. Observing interaction: A confrontation with methodology. In R. B. Cairns (Ed.), *The analysis of social interactions: Methods, issues, and illustrations*. Hillsdale, N.J.: Lawrence Erlbaum, 1979.

Yelton, A. R. Reliability in the context of the experiment: A commentary on two articles by Birkimer and Brown. *Journal of Applied Behavior Analysis*, 1979, *12*, 565–569.

Yelton, A. R., Wildman, B. G., & Erickson, M. T. A probability-based formula for calculating interobserver agreement. *Journal of Applied Behavior Analysis*, 1977, *10*, 127–131.

CHAPTER 6

Experimental Design in Group Outcome Research

T. D. Borkovec and Russell M. Bauer

Introduction

One of the primary goals of experimental research in behavior therapy is to discover, describe, and apply systematic cause–effect relationships involving therapeutic interventions, on the one hand, and clinical behavior change, on the other (cf. Underwood, 1957). Achieving this goal has both pragmatic and theoretical importance. The pragmatic interest resides primarily in devising more efficient and helpful behavior–change strategies. The theoretical interest derives from an accumulated ability to induce general behavioral laws from individual research findings. Despite differing interests, the fundamental design goal is the same for both endeavors: unambiguous demonstration of a cause-and-effect relationship.

The elements that make up effective therapeutic interventions comprise the bulk of what we call *independent variables* in this research area. In the recent history of therapy research, it has become customary to search for the "active ingredients" responsible for mediating changes in clinically relevant target behaviors. One of the primary foci of research to date has been the construction of designs that are capable of clearly demonstrating specific cause–effect relationships by ruling out likely artifacts or rival hypotheses that could reasonably account for observed outcomes (cf. Campbell & Stanley, 1963; Barber, 1976; Kazdin & Wilson, 1978b). The search for active ingredients in therapy interventions is an exceedingly complex activity because formulations of potent therapeutic mechanisms must take place within the broader context of extant theoretical models regarding environmental, motivational, cognitive-affective, and socio-cultural influences on behavior. Such theoretical models are currently in an embryonic stage within scientific psychology. The major problem resulting from this exceedingly complex picture is that the specification of relevant independent variables for study in therapeutic contexts is usually far from obvious. Advances in research on therapy mechanisms often occur haphazardly, through hindsight, or through reinterpretations of data necessitated by conflicting findings.

On the dependent-variable side, therapy researchers have emphasized the overt or covert changes that directly or indirectly result from therapy. The specification of such outcome

T. D. Borkovec and Russell M. Bauer • Department of Psychology, Pennsylvania State University, University Park, Pennsylvania 16802.

criteria is, by itself, a crucial aspect of therapy research because (1) by these criteria, the success (or failure) of therapy will be assessed; and (2) these criteria tie therapeutic changes to the available theories of behavior change mechanisms. As with the specification of independent variables, the predominant historical trend in criterion specification has been to shift away from global statements concerning psychological adjustment before and after therapy, and to move toward greater operational specificity and objectifiability (cf. Bergin, 1966; Bergin & Lambert, 1978; Kazdin & Wilson, 1978b; Paul, 1969). Assessment and measurement issues abound here; lively debate continues to be generated over issues concerning who will assess therapeutic change (Strupp & Hadley, 1977), how change will be assessed, when assessments will be conducted, what the appropriate measurement units are, and so on.

In part, the purpose of this chapter is to provide suggestions concerning the future conduct of psychotherapy outcome research in light of some of the issues alluded to above. At a basic level, we need to begin asking why progress in therapy outcome research has been so slow, and why, at every turn of the road, we seem to uncover two or three important, but unexpected, conceptual or methodological issues that cast doubt on prior progress. We feel that, although significant advances continue to be realized in the discovery of methodological errors and in the construction of powerful experimental-design approaches to important therapy questions (cf. Gottman & Markman, 1978; Orlinski & Howard, 1978; Kazdin & Wilson, 1978a,b; O'Leary & Borkovec, 1978; Waskow & Parloff, 1975), basic difficulties continue to exist in the very approach we take to the business of determining therapy–outcome relationships. We agree with Meehl's (1978) observations that progress within scientific psychology lacks the cumulative quality apparent in other scientific disciplines. Why is this the case? Much of the problem is due to a lasting reliance on confirmatory inferential strategies (Mahoney, 1976; Popper, 1959), rewarding in the short run, but inefficient, logically invalid, and often downright misleading when applied to the long-range task of determining the truth value of

some of our basic therapy–outcome hypotheses.

A chapter on experimental design in group outcome research can easily evolve into a list of potent designs capable of fulfilling some of our basic goals. While we will provide some of these, we propose to emphasize the context rather than the content of therapy outcome research for two reasons. First, such design alternatives have been effectively presented elsewhere (Campbell & Stanley, 1963; Chassan, 1967; Gottman & Markman, 1978; Hersen & Barlow, 1976; Kiesler, 1971; Mahoney, 1978). Second, we feel that our purposes are more directly served by an emphasis on the empirical game plan within which such design alternatives are employed. The reasons for slow progress in therapy–outcome research and other areas of soft psychology (Meehl, 1978) reside not only in difficulties inherent in the selection of appropriate means of achieving our goals (e.g., the selection of designs) but also, and perhaps more basically, in the way the research questions themselves are approached.

After we describe a strong-inference model for therapy outcome research, we will explore the ways in which this model might be applied to independent-variable specification. In this context, we explore potent design alternatives that lend themselves to the empirical approach suggested by the strong inference model. After this, we will briefly attempt to show how strong inference applies as well to the thoughtful specification of dependent variables and/or change criteria.

The Logic of Strong Inference

The basic principles behind the use of inductive inference are familiar to everyone who has completed even a beginning course in experimental methodology. One normally constructs a hypothesis that is scientifically testable (cf. Popper, 1959), designs an experiment capable of furnishing data that bear on the truth value of the hypothesis, controls for rival hypotheses extraneous to the experimental hypothesis that would be capable of producing the observed results, performs the experiment according to plan (cf. Barber, 1976), and conducts logical or statistical analyses designed to assign a formal or informal probability value describing the data, given the possible occurrence of a set of alternative states of the world. Our basic purpose here is to make an appeal for a systematic reevaluation of our use of these principles in the context of therapy outcome research. To some, this may seem unnecessary, but in light of the slow progress currently being made toward the resolution of many meaningful therapy–outcome issues, we feel justified in questioning our efficiency in performing the basic sequential steps of scientific induction. We do not agree with those who attribute slow progress within scientific psychology exclusively to the inherent complexity of the subject matter (see, however, Meehl, 1978, for a humbling view of some of the complicating factors). Instead, we attribute it in large part to the rather unsystematic application of the basic inductive principles outlined above.

We are especially attracted to a model of inductive inference outlined by Platt (1964), which abounds in the physical sciences, particularly molecular biology and high-energy physics. Platt called his approach "strong inference" because its systematic application seems to be related to efficient scientific behavior and the rapid scientific advance in the fields that utilize its strengths. It is based primarily on disconfirmatory logic (Mahoney, 1976; Popper, 1959) and consists of the sequential evaluation of hypotheses that survive disconfirmation in experimental test. Strong inference consists of the formal application of the following sequence to every scientific problem:

1. Devising alternative hypotheses
2. Devising a "crucial experiment," with alternative possible outcomes, each of which will exclude one of the alternative hypotheses
3. Carrying out the experiment so as to get a clean result
4. Recycling the procedure, this time concentrating on the hypotheses that survive disconfirmation (Platt, 1964)

At this point, the reader may ask, "So what?" The constituent steps are just the elements of good old inductive inference, which psychologists have been using for as long as anyone can remember. The difference, however, lies in the systematic, formal application of all of these steps to every scientific question that arises. To determine whether you have been using strong inference all along, ask yourself, when is the last time you devised alternative possible outcomes, based on different and perhaps contrasting theoretical models, then proceeded to design and carry out an experiment that eliminated some of these possibilities, and followed up by recycling the remaining alternatives? When applied in its entirety, this approach to inductive inference has tremendous power for efficient scientific progress. It may be helpful if we consider each step separately in order to specify the resulting implications for therapy outcome research.

Devising Alternative Hypotheses. It is customary in behavioral research to contrast one's experimental hypothesis with the null hypothesis, which, as it turns out, is often a euphemism for the anything-else hypothesis. The unidimensional null-hypothesis test has become so indigenous to scientific methodology in psychology that we often forget that there are alternative, perhaps better, ways of going about the business of scientific induction. The null hypothesis test, of course, has been the subject of increasingly heated debate in recent years on a number of statistical and logical grounds. One of the basic arguments is that the null is always false. Because of the multitude of uncontrolled factors extraneous to the specific experiment, it is highly unlikely that two treatment groups will be exactly equal. It is common knowledge, for example, that simply by increasing sample size and taking advantage of error variance, one can cause a rejection of the null hypothesis even in situations where the experimental variable is totally impotent.

Another antinull argument centers on whether acceptance or rejection of the null hypothesis allows for the subsequent inference of higher-order principles. In its most basic form, the null-hypothesis test pits a difference hypothesis (e.g., $x > y, x \neq y$) against a hypothesis that postulates that $x = y$. Any outcome that does not corroborate the experimental hypothesis is interpreted as a failure to reject the null hypothesis. Such findings are inconclusive. When we look more closely at the information inherent in the null hypothesis, we see that it is an "anything-else" hypothesis; it represents an amalgam of the other possible relationships between x and y not in line with the experimental prediction. Lumping all these other possibilities into a null hypothesis (in this sense, it really is not a null hypothesis at all) results in a tremendous loss of important information.

What, instead, if we devoted more explicit attention to the different specific outcomes that could result from each of our experimental designs, so that each and every possible outcome would carry with it unique information concerning the status of a set of alternative hypotheses? The answer is clear: Based on the observed pattern of results, we could immediately determine which of the alternative hypotheses remained viable and which did not. The phrasing of our hypotheses is essential: If X exists, then A, B, and C will obtain; however, if D occurs, then something must be wrong with X.

Suppose, as an example, we are interested in developing efficient biofeedback–relaxation programs designed to help patients cope with chronic pain. Based on one of several rationales for the use of biofeedback in this context (Blanchard, 1979), we might hypothesize that the treatment exerts its effects through learned control of autonomic response mechanisms. However, other possibilities exist: Biofeedback might exert its effects simply by enabling clients to achieve deep states of relaxation that could also be achieved by other methods (e.g., progressive relaxation or pharmacotherapy); or biofeedback may be effective because of unanticipated demand or expectancy effects primarily affecting pain reports, while having little effect on pain experience. These possibilities may be contrasted by setting up alternative hypotheses and observing subsequent outcomes. Assuming adequate control of extraneous or nonspecific factors, if biofeedback simply involves technical training in relaxation, then clinical change resulting from this procedure and from progressive relaxation should be comparable; if sympathetic quieting is all that is involved, then any treatment procedure designed to reduce sympathetic activation should produce clinical change in proportion to the amount of quieting achieved.

However, if there is an attention-focusing component to biofeedback that is effective only in the presence of muscular relaxation, then treatment combinations incorporating both biofeedback and progressive relaxation will show up as the most effective clinical tools. Other possibilities, of course, could be specified, but by now, the main point should be clear. Each and every one of these alternative specified outcomes carries with it important information concerning a set of alternative hypotheses about the relative efficacy of treatment components, treatment combinations, etc. And, of course, outcome patterns, if thoughtfully explored, have eventual implications for possible mechanisms of change.

The specification of such alternative outcomes needs to proceed on a more *a priori* basis, along with a specification of the theoretical context from which those outcomes derive. Alternative outcomes must be anticipated, prior to executing the experiment, not explained *post hoc*. This process necessarily increases efficiency, because the logical derivations underlying surviving hypotheses can then be directly applied in the subsequent recycling of the strong-inference procedure.

Devising Crucial Experiments. In Platt's (1964) terms, a crucial experiment is one that provides unconfounded data relevant to the retention or rejection of a subset of the alternative hypotheses. The emphasis here is on disconfirming one or more of the alternatives and turning subsequent attention to the survivors. Thus, the process of strong inference at this point involves devising experiments that are powerful enough (in a logical as well as a statistical sense) to exclude some alternative hypotheses.

The shift to disconfirmation as an inferential strategy is one that has been repeatedly suggested by psychologists and philosophers of science. Despite these invitations, confirmatory inference, whereby predicated results in line with theory are interpreted as furnishing support for or confirmation of the theory, remains the method of choice. The unfortunate part is that no empirical hypothesis can ever be confirmed (Mahoney, 1978; Weimer, 1979). Disconfirmatory strategies are superior in that only false conclusions can bear conclusively on a premise. Most empirical hypotheses in psychology are of the form "If X, then Y" (in most cases, "If my theory is true, then *Y* will result"). However, simply observing *Y* has no logical bearing on the truth value of the theory; there are many other ways to obtain *Y*. However, if *Y* does not occur, then we have something: this tells us something definitive about the truth value of our theory. As a model, strong inference is attractive because it specifies ways in which we can set up such disconfirmatory trials.

In practice, creating crucial experiments of this type is a complex, multidimensional activity that involves (1) techniques designed to control for extraneous causative factors (Campbell & Stanley, 1963); (2) the selection of appropriate target populations (Borkovec, Stone, O'Brien, & Kaloupek, 1974); (3) the construction of viable therapy packages (cf. Kazdin & Wilson, 1978b; McNamara & MacDonough, 1972); and (4) the specification of change criteria that adequately assess the extent, the desirability, and the durability of the observed change (Bergin & Lambert, 1978; Kazdin & Wilson, 1978a; Strupp & Hadley, 1977). The selection of these latter criteria must be explicitly and formally tied to the nature of the presenting problem(s) and to the kinds of changes expected, given a consideration of the theoretical mechanism. For example, research designs for studying fear-reduction therapies must employ outcome criteria that simultaneously tap the important responses about which anxious clients complain and the specific responses that the therapy in question seeks to modify. This two-stage process of dependent-variable specification, expanded in a later section of this chapter, is perhaps the aspect of therapy research that most clearly indicates the essential link between pragmatic-efficacy questions and the-oretical-mechanism questions. Crucial experiments are never just pragmatically or theoretically oriented; they are simultaneously related to efficacy and mechanism, outcome and process.

Performing Experiments Cleanly. This stage is so basic to inductive inference that it requires little elaboration. Designing clean experiments is not enough; they must be performed cleanly as well. The reader may, at this point, wish to consult one of the available sources on experimental design (Campbell & Stanley, 1963) and experimental conduct (Bar-

ber, 1976). Of primary importance in performing clean experiments is the provision of careful experimental control over rival hypotheses that might reasonably account for therapeutic change. Depending on the specific issues under study, one may need to control for such factors as general therapeutic contact independent of therapy content (Frank, 1961), individual differences in the expectation of therapeutic success (Wilkins, 1973), the relative credibility of the treatment package (Borkovec & Nau, 1972), or the demand characteristics for improvement (Orne, 1969), which might spuriously favor one treatment over another. These issues have been eloquently presented elsewhere (Kazdin & Wilson, 1978b), and some will be discussed more fully later in this chapter.

The incorporation of design elements capable of controlling these factors is, however, only part of the solution. Attempts should always be made to ensure that such factors will indeed be controlled in any given study. For example, a pretreatment evaluation of the credibility of different therapy rationales on an analogue population does not ensure that such therapies will be equally credible when administered to clinical populations. Also, it is always judicious to provide independent-variable checks to confirm that the treatment manipulations have operated as intended. Failure to demonstrate differences in outcome attributable to different therapies is meaningless, for example, unless it can be shown that the therapies were, indeed, discriminable in their important dimensions.

Recycling the Procedure. This is the hallmark of the strong-inference approach. The steps outlined so far are familiar enough to have achieved reasonable approximation in experimental practice, but the systematic recycling of the inferential process with surviving hypotheses is relatively new. The purpose of recycling hypotheses is similar in many respects to that of its ecological counterpart in returning glass bottles or aluminum cans: It is performed primarily to clean up what is left. One recycles the strong-inference procedure with surviving hypotheses for the purpose of providing additional crucial tests of increasingly specific cause–effect relationships that remain as viable explanations of the observed therapeutic effects. The general approach is thus programmatic, involving sequential experiments on the same clinical problem, the same population, or the same set of techniques. We can think of no greater practical implication of the strong-inference approach than its clear suggestion of the necessity of programmatic research in furthering knowledge about relationships between therapy interventions (and their component elements) and changes in clinically relevant target behaviors.

We are not the first to suggest programmatic research as a viable future trend. In their chapter on research design, Gottman and Markman (1978) advocated an approach to therapy outcome research that also favored programmatic research. Their Program Development Model (PDM) had, as its outstanding feature, a recycling phase in which experimental results from early developmental phases fed back to influence the further functioning of the model. The process of following a therapeutic strategy or a clinical problem through successive phases of development, specification, and refinement seems to us a crucial advancement in therapy outcome research. Kiesler (1971) and Gottman and Markman (1978) recommended strategies, entirely consistent with our approach, that successively isolate increasingly homogeneous patient subgroups (e.g., failures, successes, dropouts) and attempt to determine the pertinent factors and organismic variables responsible for patients' membership in these homogeneous groupings. We wish to make a similar point: Group outcome research is not—indeed, should not be—performed on a one-shot basis. As with a good wine, an appreciation of the efficacy of procedures, the presumed mechanisms underlying these procedures, and the individual and interactional characteristics that predict the extent, the quality, and the durability of clinical behavior change can come only with age.

Questions of Efficacy and the Scientific Approach

Everyone now believes that the question "Is this therapy technique effective?" is unanswerable and requires greater specificity, for example, "What therapist behaviors produce what kinds of change in which types of clients with what problems under which circumstances and how does the change come about?" (Paul, 1969). Thus, the outcome questions involve an increasing specification of independent and dependent variables and the processes by which they are related. We will first consider a strong-inference approach to address independent-variable specification, that is, identifying what precisely is causing the change.

A scientific approach to this question necessarily involves systematic attempts to reject the assertion that Technique A causes changes in Behavior B. Furthermore, each attempt is made in the context of numerous known and unknown factors having to do with the characteristics of the therapist, the client, the measurement, and the setting. The ideal is to hold all known variables constant and to assess unambiguously the causative effect of A on B. We feel confident in corroborating such an effect if our design allows us to reject the numerous other rival hypotheses that might explain a demonstrated empirical relationship between A and B. Keep in mind that we are able to rule out only those rival interpretations of which we are aware and that other rival factors will be identified as our knowledge of the phenomenon increases.

Assume that a client or, for that matter, 40 clients present themselves to a therapist with the common complaint of social anxiety. Assume also that the therapist administers a variety of anxiety questionnaires and sends each client to a bar where several assistants observe and record overt signs of anxiety, the quality of interactions initiated by the client, the number of friendships made in the course of the evening, the number of unreasonable requests staged by other assistants and denied or accepted by the client, etc., while heart rate and skin conductance are continuously monitored telemetrically. The therapist administers a variety of techniques (desensitization, assertion training, and social and heterosexual social-skill training) to each client during the succeeding four months and repeats the assessment procedure at termination. The data show that the mean subjective behavioral and physiological indicants of anxiety for the group as a whole have declined 80%, while the denial of unreasonable requests increased from 0% to 90% and the number of friendships made increased from 0 to 5. All of these changes are statistically significant and appear to be clinically significant as well.

The primary outcome question is whether or not therapy *caused* the change. If no change had occurred, we would reject the causative claim. In fact, each clinical case that fails to respond to a particular therapeutic package is indeed excellent falsifying evidence for that package with that therapist and that client with those characteristics in that setting; but of course we do not know which one or which combination of factors rendered the package ineffective. When significant change is found, we unfortunately have evidence that not only corroborates the hypothesis that therapy caused the change but corroborates several rival hypotheses to an equal degree, and we have no way of falsifying any of them.

Specification of the Independent Variable

Treatment versus No-Treatment Design

The most common rival hypotheses for this one-group pretest–posttest design are well known and are discussed in detail in Campbell and Stanley's (1963) monograph on experimental and quasi-experimental designs. Significant reductions in "social anxiety" may have been due to:

1. Other historical events occurring during the four months of treatment (meeting new friends, reading books on social interaction, talking with ministers or bartenders, repeated exposure to people, etc.).
2. Maturational factors (of unknown influence on anxiety but clearly of importance in other problems, for example, enuresis).
3. Effects of repeated testing (the second bar test is less novel; performance improves on practice).
4. Instrumentation (polygraphs drift; observers change their scoring procedures, especially if they know that the assessment is a posttest after treatment).

5. Statistical regression (since our measurement instruments do not possess perfect reliability, subjects selected because of their extreme scores will show regression toward the overall mean on repeated tests).

In group research, if we are to provide rejection of these hypotheses and leave the causative role of treatment unrejected, a no-treatment comparison group is required. This comparison group is assumed to be equally likely to be influenced by the above five factors but is not administered the therapy package. While no-contact control groups have been employed, wherein the subjects do not realize that they are in a comparison condition (e.g., Paul, 1966), the most commonly used condition is that of a waiting-list no-treatment group. Typically, all prospective subjects are assessed prior to treatment; half are subsequently assigned to therapy, and the remaining half are told that therapy will begin later.

Random assignment is an essential requirement in the formation of the treatment and control conditions. With random assignment, we can assume that if the rival factors are operative, they have an equal probability of influencing both groups. Thus, changes due to those factors will be equally represented, and we can look for differential change to reflect the presence or absence of the treatment effect. Without random assignment, three additional rival hypotheses become viable:

6. Selection (the two groups may differ initially on known or unknown variables, and these differences, often related to the earlier rival hypotheses, may account for the differential change).
7. Attrition (if lost data are differential, the groups may no longer be equivalent and therefore no longer equally influenced by rival factors; random assignment at least maximizes the probability of equivalent attrition from both groups, although this is not guaranteed).
8. Selection–maturation interaction, etc. (interactions of the first five factors with the selection factor).

It is important to note that random assignment allows us to assume that the above rival influences are equally distributed over the conditions of the study *in the long run,* not necessarily in this particular study. That is, if we conduct a particular study 100 times, most of the time the groups will be more-or-less equivalently influenced by these various factors, whereas some of the time they will be differentially affected. In the latter case, our outcome comparisons are confounded. A few steps can be taken to assess which case holds for a particular study and to minimize the likelihood of the latter case. For example, reviewers and readers of the literature expect to see pretest analyses demonstrating initial equivalence on the primary dependent measures, especially those related to age, sex, the severity of the target problem, and any other variable potentially related to outcome change. Often, subjects are blocked on initial pretest severity and randomly assigned to conditions so that the likelihood of pretest equivalence on that crucial variable will be maximized. The attrition rate of subjects between conditions can be compared for equivalence on whatever measures were obtained. Reliability checks on instruments and observers can reduce measurement drift; observers can be kept "blind" to the pretest–posttest and treatment status of the subjects observed. Finally, and most importantly, the whole nature of random assignment in group research and the probabilistic nature of our equivalence claims demand that we recognize the necessity of replication. A single study never confirms or supports a hypothesis (Mahoney, 1978). A single study may allow a tentative rejection of rival hypotheses, but only after replications of the study continue to falsify those hypotheses do we feel any confidence in those rejections.

The above pretest–posttest control-group design provides our first opportunity to say that a differential outcome corroborates the hypothesis that treatment caused improvement. That is, controlling for (holding constant) several other factors that relate to change still resulted in differential change; since the groups differed only in terms of one variable (presence or absence of treatment), the main hypothesis as yet unrejected by the data was the causative effect of the treatment factor.

There may, of course, be several other rival hypotheses that remain equally corroborated by the above outcome. Progress in outcome research may be seen in terms of increasing the specificity of the rival factors that are rejected, leaving an increasingly specific treatment–effect hypothesis yet to be rejected. Thus, as in other scientific fields, the design goal over time is to specify the independent variable with more and more precision.

Placebo Control Design

The most obvious progress in this regard was the incorporation of placebo controls, producing what Paul (1969) regarded as the *sine qua non* of outcome methodology. "Therapy," as the unrejected hypothesis remaining after the treatment–no-treatment design, must be further broken down into its hypothetical components. Because most therapeutic techniques share a variety of extratherapeutic ingredients (attention to the problem, presence of an interacting therapist, presumed generation of expected improvement, faith, hope, and sometimes charity), researchers recognized the necessity of including a comparison condition that is theoretically inert but includes all of these potential outcome-influencing factors in amounts equivalent to the treatment condition. Thus, subjects are randomly assigned to no-treatment, placebo, and treatment conditions. The placebo group provides a control for all of the eight rival hypotheses and, in addition, holds constant the nonspecific factors. Differential change showing treatment superiority allows rejection of the eight rival factors (present in two independent control groups) and rejection of the nonspecific factor (present in the placebo control condition). The increasingly specific hypothesis escaping falsification is that some ingredients specific to this particular treatment caused the improvement.

Types of Placebo Conditions. All placebo conditions are presumably theoretically inert. A procedure that is theoretically inert to one investigator may, however, be theoretically active to another. Depending on one's perspective and the target problem, commonly used placebos in the behavior therapy literature, such as relaxation or recall of early childhood memories, may be considered potentially efficacious to some extent. Investigators have created rather ingenious rationales to convince their subjects that the sometimes truly bizarre placebo condition is indeed effective and based on very reasonable assumptions. What if the made-up assumptions turn out to be correct?

At any rate, scanning the types of placebo commonly used in the literature, one might classify them along a dimension of theoretical relevance to the compared treatment condition. Most placebos seem to be the result of the imagination of the investigator and nothing more. Indeed, the more bizarre the procedure, the more confident the investigator feels that the procedure is inert. Two issues are associated with this state of affairs. First, differential credibility, discussed below, is often a function of the degree of procedural dissimilarity between the treatment and the placebo conditions (Borkovec & Nau, 1972). Second, since theoretical inertness depends on one's theoretical perspective, a wiser course of action may be to create a placebo procedure that is specifically inert from the theoretical perspective of the therapy procedure to which it will be compared. This can be accomplished in one of two ways. The procedural elements of both conditions can be matched as closely as possible except for some theoretically crucial aspect. For example, a procedure that involves hierarchy scene presentations during the first half of the session followed by relaxation training during the second half would match systematic desensitization procedures exactly on procedural elements, but the theoretically critical contiguity of the elements is absent. Second, a placebo can be created in terms of what specific conditions are predicted by the theory of the therapy procedure to have no effect on the problem. For example, imagining avoidance responses to phobic scenes is simply an imaginal analogue of what desensitization, implosive, or flooding theories suggest happens in real life to prevent anxiety reduction.

Issues in Placebo Control. Recently, further rival hypotheses have been developed with regard to the placebo condition. Although we may have been able to hold the therapist's contact time and attention to the problem con-

stant with our theoretically inert placebo, some researcher suggested a few years ago that maybe the placebo treatments were not very effective in generating expectancy equivalent to the active treatment conditions. In fact, empirical studies showed that commonly used placebos were not rated as being as credible as commonly used treatments. As a consequence, more than a decade of very rigorous research on systematic desensitization has been called into question (Kazdin & Wilcoxon, 1976). We could no longer assume that expectation of improvement had been held constant in those scores of studies.

The expectancy–credibility issue has stimulated three developments. First, various methods of equating and assessing credibility and expectancy have been discussed along with numerous methodological problems associated with that endeavor (see Jacobson & Baucom, 1977; Kazdin & Wilcoxon, 1976). Second, researchers have become increasingly concerned about matching treatment and control conditions on all known variables. The approach seems reasonable, since the experimental method mandates holding all else constant while only one variable is allowed to vary. Jacobson and Baucom (1977), for example, suggested that placebo and treatment conditions be matched on several stylistic variables previously ignored in the outcome literature: therapist activity level, therapist directiveness, and client activity level. (As we sit here arguing for increasing specificity and control, it is difficult to decide whether we are strengthening our methodology so as to accelerate the accumulation of scientific knowledge, or we are stimulating a *reductio ad absurdum* that will paralyze the scientific approach to therapy outcome research.) Third, the very concept of expectancy, its relevance, and our ability to research its presumed influence have been questioned (see, for example, Wilkins, 1973). Obviously, many unresolved problems remain.

Furthermore, it is now clear that *non-specific, placebo,* and *theoretically inert* are all misnomers (Kazdin & Wilcoxon, 1976). If a placebo group displays greater improvement than a no-treatment comparison group, as often happens (otherwise we would not be so interested in controlling for placebo effects), then the placebo effect would remain a viable hypothesis, suggesting that increasingly specific research could isolate its active ingredients. If the placebo effect can be dramatic in both medicine and clinical psychology, as Shapiro and Morris (1978) suggested, then some very specific mechanism is responsible for the effect and warrants systematic attention. Negative emotional experiences have long been the focus of clinical psychology, but the time appears to be ripe for greater attention to positive emotions. Rachman's (1978) discussions of fear and courage exemplify a recent conception that considers antithetical processes in emotion, while Eysenck's (1979) latest theory places the notion of anxiety in the context of antithetical extinction and incubation principles. Perhaps the study of processes that underlie faith healing and placebo effects in general (e.g., Frank, 1961) is a prerequisite to a complete understanding of emotional disturbance. Faith, hope, positive expectancy—indeed, love—may form the antitheses to what clinical researchers typically address and may represent essential points on a continuum of psychological experience. Dialectics have been helpful in other areas of knowledge; they may be useful in behavior therapy.

Placebo effects, then, appear to involve fundamentally important though as-yet-undiscovered principles of behavior change, whereas ruling out such effects in our efforts to elucidate the ingredients of active treatment conditions remains an as-yet-unresolved requirement by current outcome research standards. Recently, some writers (e.g., O'Leary & Borkovec, 1978) have raised questions about the advisability of considering the placebo comparison design the ideal outcome approach. Conceptually, placebo effects cannot be due to inert factors. Methodologically, the creation of a placebo condition that matches a therapy condition on all factors except the active ingredients of the therapy is very difficult. Finally, clear ethical problems remain unsettled, especially in studies involving clinical subjects who have sought help from the profession. Because of these problems, the time has come to develop and evaluate alternative approaches for ruling out rival hypotheses re-

lated to the placebo effect. O'Leary and Borkovec (1978) recommended several possibilities:

1. *The "best available" control group:* A treatment procedure is compared with whatever other procedure appears most promising for a particular target behavior. The problems in this approach are similar to those involved in comparative treatment research of any type (see Kazdin & Wilson, 1978b).

2. *A component control group:* A treatment procedure is compared with one or more of its own components; component research will be discussed at greater length below.

3. *Neutral expectancy:* All treatments are conducted without reference to being treatments; rather, they are presented as experimental manipulations. A type of deception (the converse of the deception inherent in placebo administration) remains, however, and the use of neutral expectancy over an extended clinical trial or with serious clinical problems would be inappropriate.

4. *Counterdemand:* Treatments are administered for n sessions, but subjects are told that no improvement is expected to occur until $n - 1$ sessions. This manipulation attempts to control for demand and expectancy without recourse to a placebo condition. Its problems include difficulty in knowing how many sessions are necessary to produce improvement, the unlikelihood that expectancy will remain neutral over extended trials, and the inability to rule out therapist contact and attention to the problem.

5. *Informed consent:* A placebo group is employed, but the subjects consent to participate in an experiment in which they may receive a placebo procedure. Ethical problems are circumvented, but problems of creating a good placebo procedure remain, and over time, the subjects' awareness of the placebo possibility may influence their expectation of improvement.

Obviously, none of these alternatives is totally satisfactory, but they represent an initial effort to solve the clear problems associated with placebo methodology. There appear, then, to be two crucial issues regarding placebo that will no doubt gain wide attention in the future: the active mechanisms of what appear to be powerful therapeutic effects involved in placebo conditions and alternative methods of controlling for those effects in order to identify what else contributes to change.

Component Control Design

The reader may have anticipated that our suggestions about types of placebo groups result in control conditions that are not very different from treatment component designs. There is method to our madness. We suggest that if an investigator wishes to control for nonspecific effects via a placebo control group, that control group may as well do double duty for both that purpose and the purpose of addressing some other theoretical question regarding the therapy technique being investigated. The use of a component design or a design approximating component comparisons aids in the development of a useful placebo group for evaluating efficacy, as argued above, and creates in an experiment the opportunity to rule out hypotheses regarding effective ingredients and/or the underlying theoretical mechanisms responsible for change.

Our basic design question has been whether Treatment A causes change in Behavior B. As in any scientific endeavor, our primary interest is in ruling out as many rival explanations of observed relationships between *A* and *B* as possible, leaving unrejected increasingly specific hypotheses about the relationship. The addition of a no-treatment group allows the rejection of several of the most common rival contributors to change, while the inclusion of a placebo condition or alternative methods of controlling for placebo effects allows rejection of the change factors common to most therapy techniques. With a demonstration of the latter type, we retain the more specific hypothesis that the therapy technique contains some active ingredient(s) specific to its procedures and that these ingredients cause the change. Progress toward further specificity can continue by the same methods of strong inference: the generation of rival hypotheses regarding the procedural elements of the effective technique, and the creation of comparison conditions that rule out one or more of the rival factors.

Therapy procedures, of course, vary in their complexity, and some are more readily susceptible to a component analysis than others. Conceptually, however, any technique should be so well defined operationally that a listing of its components is possible. Virtually every writer in the recent outcome literature has emphasized the need for greater operational specificity of the independent variable (e.g., Bergin & Lambert, 1978; Kiesler, 1971; Kazdin & Wilson, 1978b), and as yet, no convincing argument has been offered against this proposition. While the call for operational precision is primarily motivated by a desire to promote replicability and to provide demonstrations of specific efficacy, the additional by-product is a capability of asking and answering highly specific theoretical and pragmatic questions about therapy intervention.

Once the specification of procedural ingredients is made, a single design or a sequential series of designs can evaluate the relative effects of each of the ingredients and their possible combinations. Those elements or combinations found to be equivalent to no-treatment and placebo controls can be rejected as inactive factors, while those showing greater contributions prevent falsification. The process continues: Remaining ingredients are separated either into increasingly specific aspects of the elements, or alternate theories are generated about why each remaining element is active. Experiments are then designed to further rule out rival elements or theories.

On each successful falsification, the causative relationship between *A* and *B* becomes increasingly specific: "This specific aspect of *A* causes change in *B*," or "This specific aspect of *A* causes change in *B* for this specific reason."

The component–analysis approach can go a long way in answering the specific efficacy question and at the same time provides information on the theoretical basis of a technique's efficacy, that is, "How does that change come about?" (Paul, 1969). Kiesler (1971) has argued that the efficacy question is unanswerable in its general form until the criterion problem is solved and greater specificity in therapist behavior, client characteristics, and measurements is achieved. His ideal is to pursue what he considers the most heuristic outcome question, "What is the evidence for your theory of behavior modification?" (p. 44), a question that is never answered but progressively evolves. If we view outcome research in terms of strong inference (the elimination of rival hypotheses regarding causes of change), no fundamental difference exists between questions of efficacy and questions of underlying theoretical mechanisms. The apparent difference has to do with points along a continuum of specificity of relationship between independent and dependent variables and/or the general or specific nature of the theory relating those variables. Gottmann and Markman (1978) argued that the Kiesler approach perhaps unduly emphasizes differences between the artisan and the scientist, and they offer a Program Development Model to reduce the distinction. There is much to be said for their approach. The differences between Kiesler and Gottmann and Markman actually are not very great, however. Moreover, if efficacy and theoretical research can be viewed as not fundamentally different, then there would seem to be little reason to justify a dichotomous view of researchers.

Let us exemplify the use of component analysis at this point, in terms of a strong inference approach to independent-variable specification. Randomly selecting a treatment procedure and a problem out of the subject index of a behavior therapy text, we came up with progressive relaxation and insomnia. What good fortune! We could begin by comparing the effects of relaxation on insomnia (by whatever measurement definition) to the effects of a procedurally similar placebo condition and no treatment. The placebo we choose might be hierarchically arranged bedtime scenes presented in a pseudodesensitization fashion with varied, neutral imagery interspersed between scenes. Such a placebo is theoretically inert on the basis of the hypothesis that insomnia involves physiological overactivation and that relaxation reduces physiological activity. (Notice, however, that from Bootzin's, 1973, stimulus control theory of insomnia, there may be some reason to believe that repeated exposure to bed-related stimuli may lead to extinction of the sleep-incompatible behavior conditioned to those stimuli, although our placebo would not create these

processes in an ideal fashion from the point of view of Wolpe's, 1958, desensitization theory.) Perhaps because a believable rationale could be developed and because the placebo shares many of the procedural characteristics inherent in relaxation training (e.g., reclined position, darkened room, inward attention-focusing), credibility ratings between the two conditions turn out to be equivalent. We throw in a counterdemand manipulation to reduce further the likelihood of demand and expectancy effects. Our outcome indicates that relaxation is superior to placebo and no treatment at the end of the counterdemand period. We have some basis for ruling out history, maturation, etc., as well as demand, expectancy, and other nonspecific factors as causative factors. We are left with something specific in progressive relaxation that accounts for the change.

We can now dismantle relaxation and assess its components. The technique involves at least two major manipulations: the tension–release of muscle groups and instructions to focus on the resulting physiological sensations. The 2×2 table defining the presence and absence of each component gives us the conditions necessary for isolating the critical ingredient(s). Instead of physiological attention-focusing, we substitute pleasant imagery in two of the cells. One study comparing all four cells (with a pure placebo defined by the absence of both ingredients) or a succession of studies involving replication and extension to the next cell could serve our purpose equally well. However, because of subject availability and, more importantly, the importance of replication, we choose the latter course. Ultimately, we find that the presence of muscle tension–release is crucial to generating subjective improvement, but it does not matter whether attention is instructionally focused on physiological sensations or pleasant imagery. Our more specific hypothesis now reads, "Muscle tension–release with attention focused on physiological sensations or pleasant imagery causes change in subjective insomnia."

Once again, we can attempt to further dissect the active ingredient. We have not yet ruled out attention focusing *per se*. Thus, we conduct a study comparing progressive relaxation (tension–release plus physiological attention-focusing) with a condition involving muscle tension–release with no attentional instructions at all. Let us assume that we find an equivalence between these two conditions. We would now conclude that muscle tension–release is the crucial ingredient. This conclusion has some practical implications, as do the outcomes of most component investigations: Therapists need not bother with procedural elements that are of no use.

However, even if we have reduced the technique to its last irreducible state, we can continue to generate rival hypotheses regarding theoretical mechanism. For example, anticipating our discussion of dependent-variable specification, we can maintain that muscle tension–release in and of itself reduces physiological overactivation and thereby produces a decrease in insomnia. Alternately, as Underwood (1957) suggested, we can place our problem in the context of some other theoretical area from which to draw predictions. We know that variable–interval stimulation is soporific, that is, engages active sleep mechanisms (Bohlin, 1971), and that greater soporific effects occur as the intertone interval decreases. We could then compare various tension–release conditions that vary in intertensing interval. We also know that instructing subjects to attend to such stimulation results in more rapid sleep onset than instructing them to ignore the stimulation (Nau, 1977). Consequently, we can conduct a crucial experiment in which two tension–release conditions are administered, in which one of the groups is instructed to attend to the tension–release cycles and the other group is instructed to ignore the cycles. If decreasing intertensing intervals and attending to the cycles produces greater facilitation of sleep onset without differential effects on physiological activity, then the monotonous-stimulation hypothesis is corroborated and the physiological overactivation hypothesis is rejected. Further isolation of the monotonous-stimulation effect would then proceed. Notice that the increasing-specificity approach has necessarily led us to place the discovered relationship in a broader theoretical context from another domain, outside our initial theorizing. Increasing specificity can result in increasing breadth.

Parametric Design

With either a theoretical or a pragmatic question in mind, an investigation may make use of parametric manipulations to evaluate a therapy technique. Every therapy technique involves a particular set of procedures that represent points on a series of dimensions that distinguish it from all other procedures. Variations along each of those dimensions may be introduced in order to identify the most efficacious and/or efficient level of the parameter. Alternately, there may be specific predictions from the technique's alternative theories with regard to the function of change due to parameter values.

For example, the duration of conditioned-stimulus (CS) exposure represents a parameter of crucial importance to Eysenck's (1979) incubation theory. The theory predicts that brief exposures to phobic stimuli may enhance fear relative to the extinguishing effects of prolonged exposure. Subjects can be randomly assigned to differing exposure times (e.g., Miller & Levis, 1971), and the degree of posttest fear can be plotted against the CS–exposure parameter. Once the incubation effect is reliably demonstrated, subsequent research can focus on crucial experiments designed to rule out rival hypotheses explaining the phenomenon. At least two sets of rival factors can be delineated. Eysenck's theory is currently vague with regard to the conditions under which brief CS exposure produces the paradoxical enhancement of fear. The parameters of the setting, subject characteristics, diagnosis, etc., can be manipulated to identify the restricted conditions under which incubation occurs. Second, theories differ in terms of the account they would provide for the phenomenon when it does occur. Eysenck (1979) has suggested that factors such as the intensity of the original unconditioned stimulus (UCS) and personality dimensions contribute to increasing the likelihood of incubation, while implosive theorists discuss the role of fear–cue redintegration (Miller & Levis, 1971), and cognitive theorists (e.g., Mahoney, 1974) might argue for the role of self-statements in facilitating anxiety or preventing extinction. A factorial design involving the intensity of the UCS, introversion–extraversion, and in-

structed self-statements during the conditioning and extinction of a laboratory-induced fear
would provide information allowing the rejection of some of these theoretical deductions.
Notice the reciprocal relationship between the
above two parametric approaches. Identifying
the restricted conditions of a phenomenon establishes increasingly specific cause-and-effect relationships, to be ultimately explained
theoretically. Theory (e.g., implosive theory,
learning theory, or cognitive theory), on the
other hand, can suggest what conditions may
maximize or minimize the effect and thus contribute to the choice of dimensions and the
specific values of the parameters.

Constructive and Comparative Designs

Two other designs have become popular in
recent years. The constructive design (e.g.,
McFall & Twentyman, 1973) involves adding
components to a basic treatment strategy in
order to increase its effectiveness. Comparative studies typically contrast the efficacious-
ness of two dissimilar techniques (e.g., Sloane,
Staples, Cristol, Yorkston, & Whipple, 1975).

Constructive designs can make significant
contributions to both the applied and the theoretical arenas, as long as the usual dictates
of consensus methodology are adopted. Combining separately effective techniques seems
to be a heuristic move for identifying increasingly efficacious treatments for applied purposes. Once such a combination of components is found to be superior to either element
alone, the major theoretical question remaining is whether the components are simply separate but additive in effect or a significant interaction exists (i.e., one serves as a catalyst
for the maximal effects of the other). In the
latter case, subsequent strong inference can
be applied to rule out rival hypotheses regarding the interactive effects of the components.
For example, although the issue of relaxation's
contribution to desensitization remains debatable, some theoretical (e.g., Mathews, 1971)
and empirical (e.g., Borkovec & Sides, 1979)
perspectives suggest that imagery vividness,
autonomic reactivity, and autonomic habituation are augmented by its presence. Elaboration of independent- and dependent-variable
specification and the processes relating the

two domains would bear on rather fundamental principles of imagery, phobic disorders,
and their reduction via imaginal treatment
(another example of specificity leading to
broader theoretical implications).

Comparative studies appear to be another
matter. They do not fit easily into a strong-
inference approach; indeed, in many ways,
they represent a diametrically opposed stance
to specification of major variables. As other
authors have indicated (Gottman & Markman,
1978; Kazdin & Wilson, 1978b), the question
of whose therapy is more effective simply doubles the problems inherent in the original outcome question, "Is therapy effective?" Consequently, we will not discuss comparative
research further.

Concluding Comments on Independent-Variable Specification

Strong inference suggests branching a research program contingent on the rejection of
rival hypotheses at each stage of analysis.
Therapy outcome researchers, when concerned with the efficacy and mechanisms of
a therapy technique, as most of us are, involve
themselves in branches that increasingly isolate that aspect of the therapy procedure that
causes the change. At each step, comparison
conditions are created that incorporate some
hypothetically contributory factors and not
others, with differential outcomes leading us
to pursue the analysis of noncommon factors
in the effective procedure. This branching
strategy is exemplified in general form in Figure 1, with the top branches representing an
example of strong inference applied to therapy. Notice that the exemplified branching is
based on primary procedural elements, and
that theoretical rivals can be introduced at any
point with regard to the mechanism by which
specific elements relate to change.

Figure 1 also shows that strong inference
can be applied to any issue raised in the context of outcome research. Two examples are
provided: the isolation of spontaneous remission and placebo effects. The events and processes that contribute to spontaneous remission become the domain of studies on
nontreated populations. Strong inference applied to that domain might start with assessing

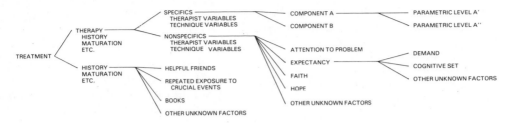

Figure 1. The strong-inference approach to independent-variable specification.

the therapeutic influence of history, maturation, etc., the very rival variables that needed to be ruled out relative to therapy! Each factor left unrejected can be further broken down in branching pathways of rival elements or theories. Notice that identifying the active ingredients in the effectiveness of historical and other factors can contribute to the development of both more efficacious, more formalized treatment strategies and increasingly valid theories of behavioral change.

The same outcomes can emerge from similar attacks on the placebo effect. Some headway has already been made in isolating some of the contributory factors. More rapid progress may occur if we continue to think in terms of strong inference.

Specification of the Dependent Variable

Thus far, the application of strong inference has revolved around an increasing specification of the independent variable (i.e., the therapy technique) by generating rival factors that may account for an observed relationship between treatment and outcome, by conducting experiments that rule out some of those factors, and by continuing that process on what remains. If we apply the same approach to the dependent-variable side of the cause–effect relationship, we can achieve an elegant methodological symmetry. Symmetry is nice in and of itself, but in addition, this approach offers us two advantages. First, applying a strong-inference method to both sides of the cause–effect equation will allow us a slightly different way of conceptualizing a variety of traditional outcome-research concerns (e.g.,

transfer of behavioral change, maintenance of change, types of outcome measures, process measures, external validity). These issues ordinarily appear to be heterogeneous, but there may be some advantage to looking at them in terms of sets of rival hypotheses. Second, and more importantly, strong inference applied to dependent variables will result in increasing specification of what is actually being changed and the process by which that change takes place.

We will regard dependent-variable specification via strong inference as revolving around two basic sets of issues: outcome content and outcome context. Our task within each domain is to generate rival hypotheses with regard to the elements in each domain and to empirically rule out the various elements. In a more traditional way, we are interested in *reducing* the generality of our conclusions with regard to the dependent variable, thus producing highly specific conclusions about the nature of the change induced.

Outcome Content

Exactly what is being changed by therapy is a crucial question for both applied and theoretical concerns. We will discuss three subheadings here. The first involves the outcome criterion problem itself. The second focuses on peripheral outcome measures that may not have apparent importance to our criteria for improvement but that may be crucial in the elucidation of the mechanisms by which such improvement occurs. Finally, we will include the eminently important but frequently ignored variable of subject characteristics, since the role of individual differences empirically emerges via the specification of the content of the dependent variable.

The Outcome Criterion Problem. Kiesler (1971) indicated several years ago that the criterion efficacy question ("Is therapy as the clinician conducts therapy effective?") will remain unanswerable until the outcome criterion problem is resolved. That is, mental health practitioners and researchers need to arrive at some consensus on how to measure improvement before we can document the efficacy of therapy. What defines improvement is, of course, heavily influenced by the theoretical framework of the investigator. Thus, the dynamic theorist places importance on intrapsychic change and its measurement, while the behavioral theorist holds changes in overt actions in higher regard. In fact, clinical criteria vary according to any relevant perspective with an interest in the definition of improvement. Such perspectives encompass not only the differing approaches to the psychology of human behavior (e.g., psychoanalysis, client-centered therapy, behavior therapy) but also the views of the clients themselves and those segments of society with an investment in the welfare of those clients. Consequently, as both Kiesler (1971) and Strupp and Hadley (1977) have argued, the criterion problem is filled with issues of value—values represented by specific psychological theories, values held by the clients with regard to their definition of adjustment and well-being, values ascribed to by the society *vis-à-vis* social order. Kiesler rightly indicated, then, that there is no criterion problem; rather, there are many criteria for therapeutic outcome. Which is most important is a matter of perspective and of the values inherent in that perspective.

Perhaps we should carry this argument even further, to suggest that values also come into play in making decisions about other aspects of the measurement of improvement. Pretest–posttest outcome designs focusing primarily on behavioral criteria have certainly been the most prevalent approach in outcome research, yet both theoretical and social perspectives on client change have begun to stress the importance of numerous other criteria for evaluating either the efficacy of a treatment and/or its theoretical basis.

For example, Kazdin and Wilson (1978a) distinguished the following aspects of change that require evaluation, among others, depending on one's perspective:

1. Clinical (as opposed to statistical) significance of the change (e.g., comparison of outcome with the typical behavior of individuals who do not have the target problem)
2. Proportion of patients who improve
3. Breadth of the changes (e.g., influence on social, marital, or occupational adjustment)
4. Durability of the change
5. Efficiency in terms of therapy duration
6. Efficiency in terms of the manner of therapy administration
7. Cost in terms of the professional expertise of the therapists
8. Cost to the client (both financial and emotional)
9. Cost relative to the effectiveness of the therapy
10. Acceptability of the therapy to the population served

Scientific method is blind to the issue of value judgments; scientists must not be. However, it may be useful to distinguish between the scientific methods applied for the purpose of the establishment of cause-and-effect relationships between therapy and chosen outcome criteria and the value-based choosing of criteria by the investigator. As researchers, we will benefit as a group if we pursue each criterion and specify its functional relationships to our therapeutic interventions. As professionals, and as individuals, we will benefit from careful consideration of our values and their relationship to the various outcome criteria. Strong inference as a scientific approach is potentially relevant to the former, but not the latter. In the spirit of this chapter, then, we suggest the application of the strong-inference approach as before. Each criterion for change may be viewed as a rival hypothesis regarding the nature of the effects of the therapeutic technique. Research programs can be conducted to rule out some criteria while leaving others unrejected. Our cause-and-effect conclusions thus become increasingly specific in terms of what kinds of changes under what conditions can be expected from this technique. Notice that some of Kazdin and Wilson's (1978a) criteria seem to refer almost exclusively to values (e.g., cost). However, even these criteria can be entered into an empirical scheme by investigations that compare variations of a technique in terms of both cost and associated efficacy as defined by other outcome criteria, and empirical data can allow rejection of some of those variations.

Thus, the issue of efficacy raises numerous outcome-criteria possibilities, all of which relate to values. Scientific assessment can provide answers about functional relationships between treatment and any of the specific criteria, but in the final analysis, judgments about the relevance of these relationships to the client, the therapist, and society will be based on such values.

While realizing the value judgments involved and taking steps to provide whatever outcome measures he or she can for determining the effects of treatment in terms of these numerous criteria, the investigator will still be required to specify the *content* of the problem behavior in some operational way. This is true whether the value perspective adopted involves the client's view, the therapist's theoretical view, society's view, etc. In the typical outcome study, assessments of the severity of the problem defined by some set of measurements are administered before and after therapy. Behavioral researchers have for several years called for multimodal assessment of the target behavior. To some extent, this recommendation has been based on a desire to provide convergent validation for our operational definitions of target problems. Furthermore, many problems (like anxiety) have been regarded by investigators as involving functionally an interaction of the cognitive, behavioral, and physiological response systems (Lang, 1969). Past and current research has not been influenced very much by these positions. Commonly low correlations among response systems have been described as reflecting poor measurement procedure. Furthermore, although lip service has been dutifully paid to the multiple response-system approach, we at times still ignore the "soft"

self-report measures, understandably fail to obtain expensive physiological indexes, and insist on the primary importance of overt behavioral change. This picture may be changing, as there appears to be a growing awareness of the necessity of considering the multiple aspects of the suffering human being (Kazdin & Wilson, 1978a). Furthermore, it must be kept in mind that low correlations among response systems do not imply that response systems are not related within an individual organism. All systems are perfectly related, even though individuals differ in terms of the functional relationships that exist.

Thus, how the person feels, what he or she is thinking about, what overt behaviors are occurring, what autonomic events are taking place, etc., are all ultimately necessary and interactive components in a full description of a particular problem. The basic measurement issue is to provide valid and reliable assessment of these essential components; the basic outcome question is identifying what changes in what response systems among what kinds of individuals can be elicited most efficiently by what procedures; and the basic theoretical issue revolves around the mechanisms interrelating the various response systems to each other and to therapeutic independent variables. Such a view has several implications for outcome research:

1. Because various response systems represent somewhat arbitrary classifications of interacting processes within a unified organism, a technique that focuses on one response system may also affect other response systems directly or indirectly through the interactive influence of the former on the latter. Thus, change may be measurable by means of several instruments or may be seen sequentially over time in different response systems.

2. The initial goal of outcome research is to identify as specifically as possible what response systems are being influenced and how they interact for different individuals.

3. A strong-inference approach to the dependent variable requires making multiple assessments, identifying what changes are in a cause-and-effect relationship with the independent variable, breaking up the dependent variable into increasingly specific response

components, and ruling out rival components with crucial experiments.

4. As research progresses in this way, we will eventually isolate very specific cause-and-effect relationships between independent-variable ingredients and response processes. Such identification will contribute to our understanding of the mechanisms that maintain the disorder and that mediate change in the disorder.

Thus, the notion of separate but interacting response systems in the anxiety literature has taught us two lessons. One is to work for convergent validation of our measures. The other, however, is that when measures of what is presumably the same construct fail to share much variance, then we have separate but possibly interacting responses, each of which may be essential to a full understanding of the original global construct. There has recently been in behavior therapy a growing awareness of the necessity of breaking down our operational definitions of a problem behavior into its components (just as we do with the independent variable in component research) and of studying the functional relationships between, and thus establishing separate laws governing, environmental manipulations and component response systems. Two obvious examples in anxiety research—one historically old, the other more recent—are provided below.

Early desensitization researchers very quickly discovered that many anxiety problems (e.g., social, test, sexual) involve conditioned anxiety, reactive anxiety, or some combination of the two. While global anxiety reports were elicited from many prospective subjects, it was clear that individuals differed in terms of the functional dynamics of their fear (past histories of aversive associations with the target situation vs. skill deficits), that different theoretics might explain any given case (classical vs. operant conditioning), and therefore that different therapeutic regimes were appropriate (exposure procedures vs. skill training). The heterosexual anxiety area now is about to confront its own component breakdown. Researchers have variously selected subjects on the basis of reported anxiety in social situations and frequency of dating experiences. It now appears that these two criteria are not wholly related and that sepa-

ration will occur in selection, theory, and, undoubtedly, treatment. The point of this discussion is to indicate that the history of research on a given problem has always involved an increasing specification of the components contained in the original global construct. The reason is rarely a deliberate choice of the strong-inference approach to the dependent variable. Rather, empirical research simply demonstrates a general lack of interrelationships among construct measures, and therefore a general lack of conclusiveness about independent–dependent-variable relationships and a growing awareness of the heterogeneity of the subject population. The end result, discussed more fully later, is the specification of subject characteristics relevant to the original problem.

Auxiliary Outcome Measures. In addition to whatever central measures are chosen to reflect improvement, the investigator may also include pre- posttest measures of other responses thought to relate to the improvement. Identifying a cause-and-effect relationship between a therapy procedure and outcome improvement in the targeted behavior is only one descriptive way of looking at the situation. The therapy technique was originally chosen on the basis of some implicit or explicit theory relating the technique to the problem behavior. That theory, then, contains assumptions about the mechanisms responsible for the relationship. This involves, from the point of view of the therapy, the processes presumably elicited by the procedures and, with respect to the client, the site of the effect of those procedures. In the test of a single theory, the researcher may choose a set of measures that hypothetically reflects those processes, or two or more contrasting theories may be compared by administering sets of auxiliary measures reflecting those theories. In either case, we are interested in observing whether the auxiliary measures show outcome changes that parallel those of the central outcome assessments. Thus, if treatment leads to significant improvement in the targeted behavior without influencing the auxiliary measure in the direction specified by the theory, we can tentatively rule out the process underlying that measure as a potential mediator or mechanism by which the cause-and-effect relationship between treatment and improvement is established. Conversely, parallel change in the auxiliary measure provides evidence of the possible role played by that process. Since the nature of the design allows only correlational conclusions, subsequent research will need to directly manipulate the hypothetical process to more firmly establish its mediational position. However, the simple addition of auxiliary measures to an outcome design is a good beginning.

For an oversimplified example, assume that we apply a cognitive-behavioral approach to the treatment of depression. In addition to measures of the target problem, we also include posttest assessments of the nature and frequency of various self-statements and of the beliefs held by the client. If treatment leads to significant reductions in our depression measures and significant increases in the use of positive self-statements but has no effects on belief assessments, whereas control conditions result in no change in any of these measures, we have correlational evidence for the mediational role of self-statements. Notice that this evidence concurrently corroborates the hypothesis that self-statement change is the mechanism by which the technique produces improvement in depression and the hypothesis that depression (as operationally defined) is maintained by an absence of positive self-statements. Neither of these hypotheses is proved, obviously; but the data continue to point us in a particular direction to be pursued by further strong-inference steps.

Subject Characteristics. The process of dependent-variable specification via strong inference with either targeted outcome criteria or the auxiliary measures leads quite obviously to a recognition of the interactive role of subject characteristics. That is, increasing specification of the response components within our original definition of the problem and specification of various auxiliary processes force us to recognize the heterogeneity of the persons having that global problem. Not only do we see that heterogeneity, but we have also identified some of the individual-difference dimensions that produce the heterogeneity. With that knowledge, we can proceed with strong inference aimed at organismic variables: homogenizing subgroups along relevant subject dimensions and ruling out rival hypotheses with regard to treatment components, response components, and underlying process components for each of the subgroups.

We will now attempt to provide an example of dependent-variable specification via the strong-inference approach applied to outcome content, auxiliary measures, and subject characteristics. Outcome research on a problem usually begins with a rather general definition of the problem, although clinical lore and earlier research may already have provided some descriptive classifications. *Insomnia*, for example, refers to disturbed sleep reflected in retardation of sleep onset latency, frequent awakening, inability to fall back to sleep on awakening, or some combination of these. Choosing sleep onset insomnia (already an example of homogenization), we may operationally define the problem in terms of the number of minutes from retiring to the onset of sleep. How to measure sleep onset seems to be a fairly straightforward question. EEG measures represent one of psychophysiology's best examples of a strong relationship between the physiological and the behavioral definitions of a construct. But we confront a problem immediately. There are enormous individual differences in sleep behavior. Some people require 10 hours of sleep, whereas others sleep only 2–4 hours. Some individuals report taking over an hour to fall asleep but claim that this does not represent a problem for them, whereas others say that the 20 minutes spent in bed tossing and turning before sleep onset is a major source of concern. Thus, a strictly physiological definition of insomnia would be unsatisfactory. We decide initially to define insomnia operationally in terms of a reported latency to sleep onset of 60 minutes or more among individuals who consider such a latency a problem.

Reported latency to sleep onset is a very gross measure of our construct, but in the beginning attempts to study a problem behavior, a global definition may be useful in establishing whether any change at all has occurred as a function of treatment (Gottman & Markman, 1978). With some reliable relationship established, research can proceed toward an increasing specification of the dependent variable, allowing an increasing isolation of the response system being changed. Notice the analogy to independent-variable specification, wherein one begins with a treatment package and pursues an analysis of its components.

If reported sleep-onset is our global choice, the measurement problem is to provide an assessment methodology that maximizes the validity of that measure. Thus, as with any subjective data, we become concerned with the hypothesis that reported sleep parameters do indeed reflect the subjective experience, or phenomenology, of sleep for the individual. Taking a strong inference approach, we wish to rule out the most reasonable rival hypotheses that might account for the subjective report. Demand characteristics are recognized as the most likely factors influencing the measure and reducing the likelihood that the reports reflect the phenomenology of the subject. Various methods could be used to rule out this rival, but Steinmark (Steinmark & Borkovec, 1974) chose counterdemand instructions. He demonstrated that insomniacs receiving relaxation training reported significant reductions in sleep onset even though experimental demand was in opposition to reports of improvement, while placebo subjects reported no change during the same period. Thus, the reports appeared to be based on the actual subjective experience of the insomniac, at least insofar as we were able to rule out the most likely alternative explanation.

Assuming the establishment of a reliable phenomenon, we can proceed to isolate more specifically what is contributing to the subjective experience of the subjects. Phenomenological sleep may be based on cortical states reflected in EEG measures, peripheral physiological activity, cognitive activity, or some combination. Consequently, multiple assessment must occur at some time in order to (1) delineate all of the apparent effects of the independent variable and (2) identify the basis for a previously observed relationship between treatment and our more global measure of the problem.

Replication and extension, therefore, proceed along the dependent-variable domain as they do along the treatment factor domain. All-night EEG measures and peripheral physiological measures are obtained. Furthermore, we add measures of the frequency of nighttime cognitive intrusion and the level of bodily tension experienced. After several studies, the following effects emerge and are replicated:

1. Treatment effects on sleep disturbance are unrelated to changes in physiological activity.
2. Reports of cognitive intrusions show changes paralleling those of sleep-onset latency, whereas bodily tension reports are unchanged.
3. EEG-defined sleep-onset shows the same improvement effects evidenced in self-report as a function of relaxation components.

These data allow us tentatively to rule out peripheral physiology as a major mediating factor in the phenomenology of sleep and its therapeutic change. The same is true of experienced tension. We are left with cognitive activity and EEG as the possible bases for reported improvement. Strong inference then suggests a further isolation of the EEG and cognitive variables.

Over the past 10 years, several subtypes of insomnia have already been delineated. Taking a heterogeneous group globally reporting "insomnia," we find that numerous and qualitatively different causative agents may elicit such reports: sleep apnea, drug dependency, circadian rhythm shifts, and nocturnal myoclonus. All of these causative factors were identified because investigators obtained multiple measures, for example, respiration during sleep, drug history, body temperature, and leg EMG. Isolating different subtypes through dependent-variable specification led to the positing of different causes and subsequently to the identification of the most specific and efficacious treatment for each cause. Research to find highly specific treatments was vastly accelerated for each subtype once identified, since more homogeneous populations could be employed, and a more limited number of likely, rival interventions were suggested by the nature of the response systems involved.

When all of these factors are ruled out, a group of primary insomnias remains with unknown cause. As was true of anxiety studies, insomnia researchers found that reported and EEG-defined sleep-onset did not correlate well. Unlike in the anxiety area, where we continue to search, perhaps in vain, for highly correlated measures of the anxiety construct, the discrepancy was somewhat astonishing in its extreme form. Dement (1972) reported that half of his insomniacs claimed requiring a long time to fall asleep, yet the EEG records indicated rapid sleep onset. Perhaps a more dramatic demonstration occurred in Slama's study (cf. Borkovec, 1979), in which 80% of her insomniacs, when directly awakened from five minutes of continuous Stage 2 sleep, reported being awake the entire time. There thus appear to be two major subtypes of primary insomnia, experiential and objective. Whether these two subtypes involve wholly different principles of causation and mechanisms of remediation remains to be established, but the route to be followed will simply be a strong-inference approach on each type.

With regard to cognitive intrusions, we have recently attempted to specify further the components of those intrusions. A factor analysis of a sleep questionnaire emphasizing the quantity and mood quality of cognitive events at night and during the day revealed two factors that significantly differentiated insomniacs from good sleepers. The first factor involved affectively laden dreams, presleep cognitions, and daydreams, along with a general mood of anxiety, depression, and worrying. The second factor included no negative affect or mood but a high frequency of uncontrollable thoughts and vivid dreams. Thus, the cognitive intrusions reported by insomniacs as a whole may reflect two subtypes, again a function of possibly different mechanisms and perhaps related to the experiential and objective insomnia subtyping.

Dependent-variable specification on outcome content thus involves the isolation of what is being changed in terms of specific response processes. Further specification of change can be achieved by a similar consideration of the spatial and temporal context of the change, a topic to which we turn now.

Outcome Context and Generalization

In the traditional sense, a generalization involves the issue of external validity: Can we generalize our cause-and-effect relationships beyond the specific conditions of our study?

In its broadest form, this question bears on all dimensions of the outcome investigation: types of therapists, types of procedural variations, types of subjects, types of measurements, etc. Notice that we could have recast our discussion of outcome measures, auxiliary measures, and subject characteristics in terms of such generalizability. In fact, we could view science in terms of two sides of the same question coin: (1) What is the generality of our relationship? and (2) What are the restrictions of our relationship? Independent- and dependent-variable specification are simply methods of establishing the former through identifying the latter. Ultimately, from the strong-inference approach to both variables, the discovery of highly specific, restricted relationships will lead empirically to the collapsing across various dimensions en route to the discovery of more global laws of behavior.

But if one wishes to look at the world from the generality side, two things are apparent. First, as all writers have argued, the generality of a finding is always an empirical question. We must test our phenomenon under the conditions to which we wish to generalize if we are to have any confidence in our generalization. Second, certain conditions minimize or maximize the likelihood of finding generalization on empirical test. For example, the use of multiple therapists, the Solomon four-group designs for evaluating pretest sensitization, and the random selection of clients from targeted populations are all attempts to maximize this likelihood.

Two aspects of generalization are of particular concern to the outcome researcher: generality over situations and generality over time. The former refers to the transfer of change outside the therapy setting, whereas the latter includes issues regarding both the maintenance of improvement and the therapeutic process.

Transfer. Strictly speaking, we cannot conclude that our observed posttest improvement will generalize outside our assessment situation. This represents a serious problem, since our clinical goal is always to ameliorate the targeted problem in its setting of occurrence. On the other hand, we need to obtain the most reliable and valid assessments of improvement that we can get. Obviously, there is a trade-off between highly standardized laboratory assessment and the more difficult assessment of the client's behavior in his or her naturalistic setting. Remedies to this situation do not appear to be immediately forthcoming, but two things are clear: We must increase the ecological validity of our laboratory assessments, and we must continue to develop more valid and reliable means of assessing the client's change in his or her environment.

Two additional considerations are worth noting here. First, the current state of affairs suggests that we include, whenever possible, measures from both laboratory and naturalistic settings to facilitate our identification of specific cause-and-effect relationships, on the one hand, and to obtain preliminary information on the generality of treatment effects, on the other. Second, it is probably inappropriate to assume that techniques effective in producing some improvement will necessarily result in generalized effects. That is, we must develop methods within the technique or adjunctive to the technique that will maximize situational generalization. For example, if situational generalization is to occur in imaginal desensitization, graduated *in vivo* exposure is usually required as a homework assignment. (See Kanfer and Goldstein, 1979, for other examples.) Thus, ultimately, we will be faced with issues involving not only the primary technique but also transfer techniques and the functional relationships between the nature and the process of change in both procedures.

Maintenance. The same discussion is relevant to the temporal aspects of assessment. The cry for long-term follow-up data remains somewhat desperate. Our clinical goal is obviously to produce lasting improvement, yet our research has rarely assessed maintenance. Various authors (e.g., Kazdin & Wilson, 1978a) have stressed that it is important to obtain such information and that the assessments should be as thorough in nature and condition as the posttest assessments. Second, as with situational generalization, we can view the maintenance issue in terms of the targeted treatment, the adjunctive procedures designed to maximize maintenance, and the interaction of the processes involved in both.

Finally, transfer and maintenance can be seen as continua along which strong inference can place a particular technique. Rivals with regard to situational generalization, for example, might involve laboratory measures, structured assessments in the natural environment, unstructured (*ad lib*) assessments in the client's environment, etc. Rejection and failure to reject hypotheses of change in any of these settings help to define the restricted conditions of a cause-and-effect relationship and point the direction for further development. If the relationship occurs only in the laboratory, we can still pursue that relationship in order to learn about some aspect of human behavior. The same is true if change occurs only outside the laboratory. Either functional relationship provides an opportunity for expanding our knowledge of human behavior. Our value judgments with regard to clinical efficacy, however, will also force us to deal with maximizing the generalization of technique effectiveness. Subsequent work in this direction can focus pragmatically on methods of increasing the ecological usefulness of the change or theoretically on the processes relating laboratory change to improvement in the naturalistic setting.

Process. Distinctions between the terms *process* and *outcome* may not be substantive (Kiesler, 1971), and both relate closely to transfer and maintenance. Descriptively, client improvement subsequent to therapy is generally regarded as outcome, while client and/or therapist behavior and their interaction during the treatment period are seen as reflecting the process of change. However, if one views the time and the place of measurement as dimensions of evaluation rather than as qualitatively different aspects of change, then the issues raised by these constructs become rather indistinguishable. There is a tendency to view transfer, maintenance, and outcome as having primarily applied implications, while process data are seen as having theoretical significance. Our preference is to regard all four issues, because of their interrelatedness, as bearing on both applied and conceptual problems, depending on one's perspective, and to pursue the establishment of the functional relations between treatment and each aspect of change reflected by these terms.

Measures taken during the treatment period can be viewed as interim outcome measures

(Kazdin & Wilson, 1978b; Kiesler, 1971). The choice of the process measures may be determined by theoretical or pragmatic issues. For example, physiological data collected during desensitization treatment can directly test counterconditioning, extinction, and other assumptions related to the conceptual underpinnings of the technique (e.g., Van Egeren, 1971). The same data may be used to predict posttreatment outcome (e.g., Lang, Melamed, & Hart, 1970), for either applied or theoretical reasons. A hypothetical case is helpful here. If an investigator finds that heart rate reaction to phobic scenes habituates more rapidly under relaxed than under nonrelaxed conditions, further research into desensitization mechanisms would be directed toward counterconditioning or more complex extinction notions. Furthermore, if significant correlations are found between rate of habituation and posttherapy outcome, support is provided for the theoretical and/or applied significance of this process measure.

Process measures need not refer only to during-therapy activities. The frequency of the daily practice of technique-related skills or other homework assignments, for example, should relate significantly to the outcome. If no such relationship exists, then we would question whether our assumptions were correct about the skills and the learning required for the technique to be effective, and we would look elsewhere to identify its mechanisms.

Part of the process–outcome issue can be translated into generalization terms. In relating behavior during therapy to behavior after therapy, we are interested in the degree to which the process change generalizes to outcome. We must assume that there are measurable processes put into motion by treatment that lay the foundation for ultimate improvement, and that this foundation exists both for immediate gains and long-term gains, and under various laboratory and naturalistic settings. Other variables may contribute to the likelihood of generalization to those times and setting, but some process in therapy is a necessary prerequisite.

A strong-inference approach, then, would attempt to rule out numerous processes of theoretical or applied relevance, as was the case with auxiliary outcome measures, and to pursue the increasingly specific relationships between unrejected processes and the change reflected in both short- and long-term behavior in the laboratory and in the client's natural environment.

Strong Inference and Programmatic Research

The application of strong inference to both independent and dependent variables is a powerful scientific approach. Highly specific cause-and-effect relationships are the end result. There is nothing really new about what we are suggesting. The strong-inference approach is implicit in the writings of Paul (1969) on the ultimate therapy question; of Kiesler (1971) in his grid model of therapist behavior, client characteristics, and measurement variable interactions; and of Gottman and Markman (1978) in their program development model. For two reasons, we feel compelled to repeat their urgings and place these urgings explicitly within the formal logic of strong inference. First, research in behavior therapy has apparently been uninfluenced by the suggestions of these authors. Despite the proliferation of journals and hundreds of published studies, it is hard to get a sense of accumulated scientific knowledge. Old issues that were once the heuristic springs for lively debate and ingenious research have been abandoned, not because the theoretical issues were settled but because people lost interest in the topic or became interested in some new topic. For example, we probably have a great debt of gratitude to pay to the systematic desensitization issue. The question of the active mechanism of the technique has been left unresolved, and few researchers remain interested. There is some very important principle of human behavior yet to be elucidated in that old question. Whatever accumulation of knowledge occurred has become relatively useless and no longer forms a basis from which to continue isolating that principle. Instead, a more effective technique is discovered (e.g., participant modeling), and research interest shifts. We are hardly arguing that new techniques should not be pursued, only that a strong-inference approach is a desirable way to accumulate knowledge and to build a steadily expanding science of behavioral change regardless of what technique is used as the initial independent variable. Perhaps knowledge accrues more meaningfully to the extent that we go deeply into the problem we have chosen.

Second, while urgings to answer highly specific questions through factorial designs are appropriate, a modus operandi is required. We feel that an explicit application of strong inference is a particularly useful method of providing guidance in the research enterprise. The approach is best observed in hard-science areas, where strong, testable theory is already present and where highly exact measurement systems are already available. Clinical psychology has neither. However, our argument is that strong inference is equally applicable to independent and dependent variables as a first step. Once highly specific, lawful relationships are established through this system of ruling out rival factors, then reasonable theory construction can proceed, and the contrasting of rival theories can be accomplished through crucial experiments, the essential urging of Platt's (1964) paper. As we argued by example earlier, specificity leads to breadth, but only if the investigator is committed to the full spirit of strong inference.

If one accepts these arguments, it is difficult to see research in any way other than as programmatic. The clear commitment is to replication and extension following a systematic branching approach, regardless of the applied or basic setting of the enterprise. Eysenck (1976) has nicely portrayed the importance of such research programs in science. While the programmatic possibilities are obvious for the single investigator, we need also to keep in mind that the same programmatic notion is equally applicable to the interacting scientific community as a whole. From our point of view, the future of our field and its accumulation of knowledge will be to some extent dependent on the degree to which individuals and groups of individuals together commit themselves to this enterprise. What if all of us interested in a particular problem jointly embarked on a strong-inference program (replicating and extending one another's procedures and branches), entertaining the same, shared

multiple hypotheses (Platt, 1964) and exchanging information on recently ruled-out hypotheses?

Science and Strong Inference in Perspective

We have just outlined the little bit we know about outcome design and methodology and have attempted to place it in the strong-inference context because, of the various approaches, this one seems to make the most sense for building a cumulative basis of knowledge in our field. Thus, from our view, perhaps this is the best scientific approach we can take in the long run. There should be a cautionary note here. The approach implies the development of important laws of behavior on the basis of increasingly specific cause-and-effect relationships. Such a development is a promissory note, although we did try to exemplify how this can come about. When we consider Kiesler's (1971) grid model, or our own specification procedures, we can easily feel the enormity and complexity of the task we are suggesting. Each outcome study contributes to one, very small intersection of a host of therapist, therapy, time, setting, and measurement dimensions. How many such identified intersections will be required before general laws can emerge is unknown. We may enjoy making our living asking questions and obtaining interesting bits of functional-relationship information, but our overall task of understanding human nature and experience or of developing meaningful ways of helping suffering people may never be accomplished solely through scientific method. This is, incidentally, no more and no less of a general problem in any other approach to human behavior.

There may be another problem here as well. As scientists, regardless of the approach within science we choose, we are committed to objective measurement and the testing of hypotheses, using observable treatment variables and observable improvement indexes. Even when we allow for intervening variables (e.g., anxiety), we must operationally define them with behavioral referents. As others (e.g., Mahoney, 1976; Weimer, 1979) in psychology have pointed out, there is no way to study a scientific problem without studying the psychology of the scientist. Thus, for example, the notion of *objective observation* is a myth at certain levels of analysis. Our observations of facts are heavily determined by our theories, not only of human behavior but of life itself. Thus, the "facts" are dependent on our way of perceiving things. If we share the critical components of a perspective, we can achieve interrater reliability, but that reliability may reflect less about the nature of the observed phenomenon than about the similarity of perspectives of the two observers. This may be fine for scientists as a community interested in similar methods of obtaining knowledge. That knowledge may even be useful, in the sense that it can sometimes be translated into effective therapy procedures. However, we must keep in mind that ours is only one way of looking at things, and that there may be no way of knowing whether that way is most true or most useful, or of knowing whether it is least true or least useful. We do not know what we do not know. Once we adopt a particular way of perceiving things, it is difficult to see anything that exists outside that view. Consequently, it is important to view our methods within the broadest of contexts to reduce our necessary myopia as much as possible. Such a perspective would both show the usefulness of those methods for understanding certain aspects of human behavior and, at the same time, identify their relative position. Thus, our final comments will hopefully place the strong-inference approach to the scientific study of human behavior in this broader context.

Strong inference applied to independent and dependent measures in behavior therapy research is, by its very nature, reductionistic. We have suggested the potential power of the approach for leading to a broadening of theoretical perspective, yet we must also recognize its relative (restricted) properties. Both points seem to be exemplified by the following metaphor, suggested by a "children's story" by L'Engle (1973).

Imagine the Earth as rotating on its axis every 24 hours and circling the sun every 365 days. Think of the Milky Way as rotating once every 200 billion years. Imagine the atomic activity of one of your living cells and the speed with which electrons race around the nucleus. All of this activity derives from a common source of energy. One of your atoms is as small to you as you are to your galaxy. Push your imagination further upward toward the infinite universe and downward to subatomic levels as yet undiscovered. The sheer enormity is incomprehensible; the harmonious similarities across such an expanse are equally overwhelming. There seems to be something absolute running through this relativity. Whether one deeply studies the atom or the galaxies, identical knowledge of long-lasting value may emerge.

This chapter reviewed what many of us, as a scientific-consensus community in psychology, currently *believe* to be the necessary and sufficient experimental conditions for demonstrating cause-and-effect relationships in behavior therapy. As is obvious from the various issues that were raised, our specific beliefs are constantly changing as we learn about the influence of previously ignored variables. Outcome methodology in behavior therapy is thus temporally relative. It is also conceptually relative to more general scientific perspectives (we chose, for example, a strong-inference approach), and those perspectives undergo continuous revisions within each area of scientific inquiry and in response to developments in the philosophy of science. Finally, science itself is only one perspective among many from which to discover knowledge about human nature, human experience, and human behavior. Its greatest contribution is, as Schumacher (1977) pointed out, to the elucidation of the factors influencing the *external* aspects of *other* human beings. Strong inference appears to be a very useful method in the pursuit of this type of knowledge. Its increasing specificity can lead to theoretical generality. We imagine that one could develop a more molar approach to human behavior, and that its ultimate outcome would be specificity. Perhaps beyond the universe and below the atomic level, there is a connection. Perhaps that connection can be found at any level in between, if one explores that level of inquiry deeply enough, and as long as one realizes the larger context of that effort.

References

Barber, T. X. *Pitfalls in human research: Ten pivotal points.* Elmsford, N.Y.: Pergamon Press, 1976.

Bergin, A. E. Some implications of psychotherapy research for therapeutic practice. *Journal of Abnormal Psychology,* 1966, *77,* 235–246.

Bergin, A. E., & Lambert, M. J. The evaluation of therapeutic outcome. In S. Garfield & A. E. Bergin (Eds.), *Handbook of psychotherapy and behavior change* (2nd ed.). New York: Wiley, 1978.

Blanchard, E. B. The use of temperature biofeedback in the treatment of chronic pain due to causalgia. *Biofeedback and Self-Regulation,* 1979, *4,* 183–188.

Bohlin, G. Monotonous stimulation, sleep onset, and habituation of the orienting reaction. *Electroencephalography and Clinical Neurophysiology,* 1971, *31,* 593–601.

Bootzin, R. R. Stimulus control and insomnia. Paper presented at the annual meeting of the American Psychological Association, Montreal, August 1973.

Borkovec, T. D. Pseudo (experiental)-insomnia and idiopathic (objective) insomnia: Theoretical and therapeutic issues. *Advances in Behaviour Research and Therapy,* 1979, *2,* 27–55.

Borkovec, T. D., & Nau, S. D. Credibility of analogue therapy rationales. *Journal of Behavior Therapy and Experimental Psychiatry,* 1972, *3,* 257–260.

Borkovec, T. D., & Sides, J. K. The contribution of relaxation and expectancy to fear reduction via graded, imaginal exposure to feared stimuli. *Behaviour Research and Therapy,* 1979, *17,* 529–540.

Borkovec, T. D., Stone, N. M., O'Brien, G. T., & Kaloupek, D. G. Evaluation of a clinically relevant target behavior for analogue outcome research. *Behavior Therapy,* 1974, *5,* 503–573.

Campbell, D. T., & Stanley, J. C. *Experimental and quasi-experimental designs for research.* Chicago: Rand-McNally, 1963.

Chassan, J. B. *Research design in clinical psychology and psychiatry.* New York: Appleton-Century-Crofts, 1967.

Dement, W. C. *Some must watch, while some must sleep.* Stanford, Calif.: Stanford Alumni Association, 1972.

Eysenck, H. J. Behaviour therapy: Dogma or applied science? In M. P. Feldman & A. Broadhurst (Eds.), *Theoretical and experimental bases of the behaviour therapies.* New York: Wiley, 1976.

Eysenck, H. J. A conditioning model of neurosis. *The Behavioral and Brain Sciences,* 1979, *2,* 155–199.

Frank, J. D. *Persuasion and healing.* Baltimore: Johns Hopkins University Press, 1961.

Gottman, J. M., & Markman, H. J. Experimental designs in psychotherapy research. In S. Garfield & A. E. Bergin (Eds.), *Handbook of psychotherapy and behavior change* (2nd ed.). New York: Wiley, 1978.

Hersen, M., & Barlow, D. H. *Single-case experimental designs: Strategies for studying behavior change.* New York: Pergamon Press, 1976.

Jacobson, N. S., & Baucom, D. H. Design and assessment of nonspecific control groups in behavior modification research. *Behavior Therapy,* 1977, *8,* 709–719.

Kanfer, F. H., & Goldstein, A. P. *Maximizing treatment gains: Transfer enhancement in psychotherapy.* New York: Academic Press, 1979.

Kazdin, A. E., & Wilcoxon, L. A. Systematic desensitization and nonspecific treatment effects: A methodological evaluation. *Psychological Bulletin,* 1976, *83,* 729–758.

Kazdin, A. E., & Wilson, G. T. Criteria for evaluating psychotherapy. *Archives of General Psychiatry,* 1978, *35,* 407–416. (a)

Kazdin, A. E., & Wilson, G. T. *Evaluation of behavior therapy: Issues, evidence, and research strategies.* Cambridge, Mass.: Ballinger, 1978. (b)

Kiesler, D. J. Experimental designs in psychotherapy research. In A. E. Bergin & S. Garfield (Eds.), *Handbook of psychotherapy and behavior change.* New York: Wiley, 1971.

Lang, P. J. The mechanics of desensitization and the laboratory study of fear. In C. M. Franks (Ed.), *Behavior therapy: Appraisal and status.* New York: McGraw-Hill, 1969.

Lang, P. J., Melamed, B. G., & Hart, J. A psychophysiological analysis of fear modification using an automated desensitization procedure. *Journal of Abnormal Psychology,* 1970, *76,* 220–234.

L'Engle, M. *A wind in the door.* New York: Farrar, Straus, & Giroux, 1973.

Mahoney, M. J. *Scientist as subject: The psychological imperative.* Cambridge, Mass.: Ballinger, 1976.

Mahoney, M. J. Experimental methods and outcome evaluation. *Journal of Consulting and Clinical Psychology,* 1978, *46,* 660–672.

Mathews, A. M. Psychophysiological approaches to the investigation of desensitization and related procedures. *Psychological Bulletin,* 1971, *76,* 73–91.

McFall, R. M., & Twentyman, C. T. Four experiments on the relative contributions of rehearsal, modeling, and coaching to assertion training. *Journal of Abnormal Psychology,* 1973, *81,* 199–218.

McNamara, J. R., & MacDonough, T. S. Some methodological considerations in the design and implementation of behavior therapy research. *Behavior Therapy,* 1972, *3,* 361–378.

Meehl, P. E. Theoretical risks and tabular asterisks: Sir Karl, Sir Ronald, and the slow progress of soft psychology. *Journal of Consulting and Clinical Psychology,* 1978, *46,* 806–834.

Miller, B. V., & Levis, D. J. The effects of varying short visual exposure times to a phobic test stimulus on subsequent avoidance behavior. *Behaviour Research and Therapy,* 1971, *9,* 17–21.

Nau, S. D. *The soporific effect of monotonous stimulation as a function of perceptual set and stimulus intensity.* Unpublished doctoral prospectus, University of Iowa, 1977.

O'Leary, K. D., & Borkovec, T. D. Conceptual, methodological, and ethical problems of placebo groups in psychotherapy research. *American Psychologist,* 1978, *33,* 821–830.

Orlinsky, D. E., & Howard, K. I. The relation of process

to outcome in psychotherapy. In S. Garfield & A. E. Bergin (Eds.), *Handbook of psychotherapy and behavior change* (2nd ed.). New York: Wiley, 1978.

Orne, M. T. Demand characteristics and the concept of quasi-controls. In R. Rosenthal & R. L. Rosnow (Eds.), *Artifact in behavioral research.* New York: Academic Press, 1969.

Paul, G. L. *Insight versus desensitization in psychotherapy.* Stanford: Stanford University Press, 1966.

Paul, G. L. Behavior modification research: Design and tactics. In C. M. Franks (Ed.), *Behavior therapy: Appraisal and status.* New York: McGraw-Hill, 1969.

Platt, J. R. Strong inference. *Science,* 1964, *146,* 347–353.

Popper, K. R. *The logic of scientific discovery.* New York: Harper, 1959.

Rachman, S. J. *Fear and courage.* San Francisco: W. H. Freeman, 1978.

Schumacher, E. F. *A guide for the perplexed.* New York: Harper & Row, 1977.

Shapiro, A. K., & Morris, L. A. Placebo effects in medical and psychological therapies. In S. Garfield & A. E. Bergin (Eds.), *Handbook of psychotherapy and behavior change* (2nd ed.). New York: Wiley, 1978.

Sloane, R. B., Staples, F. R., Cristol, A. H., Yorkston, J. J., & Whipple, K. *Psychotherapy versus behavior therapy.* Cambridge: Harvard University Press, 1975.

Steinmark, S., & Borkovec, T. D. Active and placebo treatment effects on moderate insomnia under counterdemand and positive demand instructions. *Journal of Abnormal Psychology,* 1974, *83,* 157–163.

Strupp, H. H., & Hadley, S. W. A tripartite model of mental health and therapeutic outcomes. *American Psychologist,* 1977, *32,* 187–196.

Underwood, B. J. *Psychological research.* New York: Appleton-Century-Crofts, 1957.

Van Egeren, L. F. Psychophysiological aspects of systematic desensitization: Some outstanding issues. *Behaviour Research and Therapy,* 1971, *9,* 65–78.

Waskow, I., & Parloff, M. (Eds.). *Psychotherapy change measures.* Washington, D.C.: U.S. Government Printing Office, 1975.

Weimer, W. B. *Notes on the methodology of scientific research.* Hillsdale, N.J.: Lawrence Erlbaum, 1979.

Wilkins, W. Expectancy of therapeutic gain: An empirical and conceptual critique. *Journal of Consulting and Clinical Psychology,* 1973, *40,* 69–77.

Wolpe, J. *Psychotherapy by reciprocal inhibition.* Stanford, Calif.: Stanford University Press, 1958.

CHAPTER 7

Single-Case Experimental Designs

Michel Hersen

Introduction

Behavior modification and therapy perhaps are best distinguished from other therapeutic and educational approaches by their dependence on the experimental-empirical methods for solving human problems. Thus, in evaluating the efficacy of emerging therapeutic and educational techniques, a large variety of experimental strategies has been carried out by behavioral researchers. Included, of course, are both group-comparison designs (cf. Kazdin, 1980) and single-case experimental designs (cf. Hersen & Barlow, 1976).

Although group comparison and single-case design strategies are both well within the armamentarium of behavioral researchers, the single-case design approach to evaluating technical efficacy is almost uniquely tied in with the behavioral movement of the last two decades. That is, the single-case research approach has been followed not only in clinical psychology (Leitenberg, 1973), psychiatry (Barlow & Hersen, 1973), and education (Risley & Wolf, 1972; Thoresen, 1972), but also in the practice of social work (Thomas 1978), physical rehabilitation (Martin & Epstein, 1976) and behavioral medicine (Barlow, Blanchard, Hayes, & Epstein, 1977). Thus, the widespread application attests to both its popularity and its utility.

The importance of the single-case experimental study to behavior therapy was best illustrated by Yates (1970). Indeed, he felt compelled to define behavior therapy specifically in relation to single-case methodology. He argued that "Behavior therapy is the attempt to utilize systematically that body of empirical and theoretical knowledge which has resulted from the application of the experimental method in psychology and its closely related disciplines (physiology and neurophysiology) in order to explain the genesis and maintenance of abnormal patterns of behavior; and to apply that knowledge to the treatment or prevention of those abnormalities by means of controlled experimental studies of single cases, both descriptive and remedial" (p. 18). This strong link between behavior therapy and research is reflected in the single-case publications in psychological (e.g., *Journal of Consulting and Clinical Psychology*), psychiatric (*American*

Michel Hersen • Department of Psychiatry, Western Psychiatric Institute and Clinic, University of Pittsburgh School of Medicine, Pittsburgh, Pennsylvania 15261. Preparation of this chapter was facilitated by Grant MH 28279-01A1 from the National Institute of Mental Health.

Journal of Psychiatry, Archives of General Psychiatry), and, of course, the behavioral journals (e.g., *Behavior Modification, Behaviour Research and Therapy, Behavior Therapy, Journal of Applied Behavior Analysis, Journal of Behavior Therapy and Experimental Psychiatry*).

In this chapter, we first briefly trace the history of the single-case approach, particularly as it relates to the problems and limitations of the group comparison method. This is to be followed by a discussion of more general issues involved in research, such as variability, intrasubject averaging, and the generality of findings. Next, we outline the basic procedures followed in single-case evaluations: repeated measurement, choice of a baseline, changing of one variable at a time, length of phases, distinction between reversal and withdrawal, and evaluation of irreversible procedures. Then we discuss and illustrate A-B-A designs and their extensions (e.g., interaction designs, drug evaluations). This is followed by our examination of additional design strategies (e.g., the three types of multiple-baseline designs, the multiple-schedule and simultaneous-treatment designs and the changing criterion design). Next, we tackle the thorny issue of the role of statistical analyses in evaluating treatment efficacy in single case studies. Highlighted are the arguments in support of and against the use of such statistical techniques. Finally, we discuss the importance of replication in single-case research. Three types of replication methods are to be considered: direct, clinical, and systematic.

History

A historical perusal clearly shows that the single-case approach, as currently applied, owes its heritage to many disciplines (cf. Hersen & Barlow, 1976, Chapter 1; Kazdin, 1978). There can be no doubt that the single case study has been important in the development of physiology, medicine, early experimental psychology, and psychoanalysis. In all of these disciplines, many critical findings have emerged from the careful study of individual organisms and subjects.

The tradition of single-case research dates back to the 1830s, as exemplified by the work of Johannes Müller and Claude Bernard in physiology. More important from a historical perspective, however, is the contribution of Paul Broca in 1861. At that time, Broca was treating a patient who had suffered a severe speech loss. However, the patient died while still under his care. Broca subsequently performed an autopsy and discovered a lesion in the man's cerebral cortex (i.e., in the third frontal convolution). He correctly assumed that this part of the brain controlled speech functions. As pointed out by Hersen and Barlow (1976), Broca's clinical method was an extension of prior work done in laboratories in which parts of the brains of experimental animals were systematically excised (i.e., the extirpation of parts). The relationship of such surgical excisions and subsequent behavioral changes in single organisms was meticulously studied, thus providing "an anatomical map of brain functions." The critical point to be underscored here is that findings of wide generality were gleaned on the basis of experimental work with very few research subjects.

It is generally agreed that Fechner's publication in 1860 of *Elemente der Psychophysik* heralded the beginning of experimental psychology. In this treatise, Fechner described studies he had conducted, using individual subjects, to determine sensory thresholds and just-noticeable differences in a variety of sense modalities. Although he did apply some statistical methods in evaluating his work, such statistics were employed to ascertain variability within a given subject. Following Fechner's studies in psychophysics, Wundt and his colleagues evaluated sensation and perception, while Ebbinghaus assessed the processes of learning, developing a new tool for conducting such research: the nonsense syllable. Both of these giants in the history of psychology accomplished their goals by studying individual subjects. Later, in the early part of the twentieth century, Pavlov's classical experiments in physiology, learning, and conditioning were all conducted with single organisms.

With the emergence of the group comparison methods, bolstered by the statistical genius of R. A. Fisher in the 1930s (i.e., inferential statistics), interest in the single-case approach during the middle part of this century waned considerably. Of course, the psychoanalysts did (and continue to) publish their descriptions of protracted treatments of individual patients. Probably the first was Breuer and Freud's case history published in 1895 (1957), describing the systematic treatment of Anna O's hysterical symptoms. (Parenthetically, we might note that Hersen and Barlow [1976, Chapter 1] have likened Breuer and Freud's approach to the multiple-baseline design across behaviors.) Nonetheless, these reports, albeit of tremendous therapeutic import, generally had subjective interpretations of results in that usually, no hard data were presented. However, the psychoanalytic case study certainly may be considered one of the antecedents to the single-case experimental tactic.

In the 1920s and 1930s, there were some sporadic descriptions of the behavioral treatment of individual cases of unusual interest (cf. Max, 1935; Watson & Rayner, 1920). But these single-case descriptions appear to have had little impact on therapeutic attitudes of the day and on subsequent strategies developed to assess therapeutic efficacy.

There are several other historical antecedents that warrant our attention. Most outstanding, of course, is the operant work of B. F. Skinner and his students in the 1940s and 1950s. Skinner (1966) has stated his philosophy of research in very succinct form: "instead of studying a thousand rats for one hour each, or a hundred rats for ten hours each, the investigator is likely to study one rat for a thousand hours" (p. 21). The specific experimental strategies used in the experimental analysis of behavior (with special emphasis on research with animals) were compiled and elucidated in Sidman's (1960) now-classic tome entitled *Tactics of Scientific Research*. However, this book was written prior to the plethora of behavior therapy studies that appeared in the 1960s, the 1970s, and now in the 1980s. (For a more comprehensive description of the use of single-case strategies as applied to humans in therapeutic endeavors, the reader is referred to Hersen and Barlow, 1976.)

In the more clinical realm, the contribution of Shapiro (1966) and Chassan (1967) must not be overlooked. Both were committed to the intensive study of the single case in a methodologically rigorous manner. Although neither of the two used the current nomenclature (e.g., A-B-A) for describing their single-case strategies, a number of the reported cases (e.g., Shapiro & Ravenette, 1959) bear a striking similarity to the prototypical A-B-A design. However, for the most part, the work of Shapiro and Chassan may be described as correlational. That is, the experimental control of therapeutic variables over dependent measures is not as clearly specified as in the reports of today's behavior analysts (cf. Hersen & Barlow, 1976; Kazdin, 1975; Leitenberg, 1973).

Group Comparison Designs

It was in the late 1940s and 1950s that the effects of psychotherapy began to be evaluated in large-scale group-comparison designs (see Rubenstein & Parloff, 1959, for a review of the issues). However, very quickly some of the major shortcomings were pointed out in both the therapeutic techniques themselves (cf. Eysenck, 1952) and the design strategies carried out by clinical researchers (cf. Bergin, 1966). Eysenck (1952) compared the improvement rates of treated patients and "spontaneous remission" rates (evaluated from insurance company records) and concluded that the effects of psychotherapy (as then practiced) were negligible at best. This finding, of course, sparked a tremendous controversy in the psychological world, which still rages at times. Bergin (1966) reevaluated the disappointing results of psychotherapy when contrasted with control group procedures and discovered that some patients improved as a function of treatment, whereas others actually worsened. Indeed, the statistical averaging of results (employing the group comparison method) led to a canceling of treatment effects for a fairly substantial number of patients.

Bergin's (1966) work in particular clearly indicated some of the limitations of the group comparison approach to studying the efficacy of psychotherapy. As noted by Hersen and Barlow (1976), "These difficulties or objections, which tend to limit the usefulness of a group comparison approach in applied research, can be classified under five headings: (1) ethical objectives, (2) practical problems in collecting large numbers of patients, (3) averaging of results over the group, (4) generality

of findings, and (5) inter-subject variability''
(p. 14).

We briefly comment here on each of these
limitations in turn. *First*, with regard to ethical
concerns, the primary one is that in the group
comparison strategy, the control group subjects do not receive treatment and, of consequence, are denied potential benefits. This
objection, naturally, is predicated on the notion (albeit erroneous at times) that the treatment being evaluated is efficacious in the first
place (cf. Eysenck, 1952). *Second*, the practical problems in identifying and matching subjects in large-scale group-comparison studies,
in addition to selecting and remunerating suitable therapists, are overwhelming. Moreover,
this approach to research is time-consuming
and usually requires large federal allocations.
It is not at all uncommon for a three- to four-
year outcome study in psychotherapy to cost
the National Institute of Mental Health up-
wards of $500,000. *Third*, already discussed,
are the pitfalls involved in the statistical averaging of patients who improve or worsen as
a function of treatment. Such problems led
Paul (1967) to conclude that psychotherapy
researchers should identify the patient who
would profit from a specific therapy under
very specific circumstances. *Fourth* is the
issue of generality of findings. Inasmuch as
group averaging may ''wash out'' the individual effects of particular treatments, the practicing clinician in the community cannot ascertain which specific patient characteristics
may be correlated with improvement. Nonetheless, if a study of this kind is planned pro-
spectively (usually a factorial design), such
information may be teased out statistically.
Fifth is the concern with intersubject variability. Although ideally in the group comparison study a frequent objective is to contrast
homogeneous groups of patients, in practice
this often is neither feasible nor practicable.
(It is obviously impossible to control for the
individual learning histories of patients, irrespective of whether the presenting symptoms
are identical.) Thus, again, the unique response of the individual patient to treatment
is lost. Also, in most group comparison studies, the effects of treatment are indicated on
a pre–post basis. As a result, the vicissitudes
of therapeutic response throughout the full
course of treatment are not clarified. This certainly is one area of marked import to every
practicing clinician, who knows through experience about the ''ups and downs'' of responsivity to treatment, regardless of the theoretical approach cherished.

Experimental Analysis of Behavior

In addition to the problems inherent in evaluating the effects of psychotherapy in group
comparison designs, some other factors contributed to the growing importance of the single-case approach in the late 1960s and through
the 1980s. First was the then-prevalent scientist–practitioner split. That is, many clinical
psychologists pursued esoteric research interests that had little or no bearing on the work
they conducted with their patients. Indeed,
often the research carried out by such clinicians was only of academic import. As late as
1972, Matarazzo pointed out that ''Even after
15 years, few of my research findings affect
my practice. Psychological science *per se*
doesn't guide me one bit. I still read avidly but
this is of little direct practical help. My clinical
experience is the only thing that has helped
me in my practice to date'' (Bergin & Strupp,
1972, p. 340). As argued by Hersen and Barlow
(1976), ''Since this view prevailed among
prominent clinicians who were well acquainted with research methodology, it follows that clinicians without research training
or expertise were largely unaffected by the
promise or substance of scientific evaluation
of behavior change procedures'' (p. 22).

With the advent of behavior therapy and the
emergence of a new journal devoted to the
experimental study of the individual in depth
(*Journal of Applied Behavior Analysis*), much
of the scientist–practitioner split was bridged.
Although initially the great majority of the
work was operant in nature, more recently
other types of therapeutic strategies (e.g., systematic desensitization) have also been assessed by means of single-case methodology
(see Van Hasselt, Hersen, Bellack, Rosenblum, & Lamparski, 1979). Generally, single-
case research as now practiced is referred to
as the *experimental analysis of behavior*.

General Issues

Intrasubject Variability

To determine the sources of variability in the subject is probably the most important task of the single-case researcher. The assessment of variability, of course, is facilitated by observing the individual over time under highly standardized conditions (i.e., repeated measurement). In the quest to determine the causes of variability, the greater the control over the subject's environment (external and internal), the greater the likelihood of accurately identifying such variability. As noted by Hersen and Barlow (1976), the task is made easier by studying lower organisms (e.g., the white rat):

In response to this, many scientists choose to work with lower life forms in the hope that laws of behavior will emerge more rapidly and be generalizable to the infinitely more complex area of human behavior. Applied researchers do not have this luxury. The task of the investigator in the area of human behavior disorders is to discover functional relations among treatments and specific behavior disorders over and above the welter of environmental and biological variables impinging on the patient at any given time. Given these complexities, it is small wonder that most treatments, when tested, produce small effects. (p. 35)

In identifying sources of variability at the human level, the researcher needs to consider biological, cognitive, and environmental variables. Although these three systems are obviously interconnected, each has some unique contributions to the problem. Biological or cyclical variability in humans (and animals, for that matter) is best represented by the female's estrus cycle. As is well known clinically and is equally well documented empirically (see Hersen & Barlow, 1976, Chapter 4), the dramatic hormonal changes that occur in women throughout the entire cycle (be it 24, 28, or 30 days) often yield equally dramatic changes in mood, affect, and behavior. Applied behavioral researchers evaluating effects of therapeutic interventions, particularly in female subjects whose menstrual changes in behavior are extreme, need to consider this factor when deriving conclusions from their data. Thus, it is quite conceivable that a behavioral intervention may coincide with a given part of the cycle, yielding changes in behavior (either improvement or worsening) and thus confounding the possible controlling effects of the specific behavioral technique. Indeed, what behavioral change does take place simply may be due to biological (internal) mechanisms. Certainly in the case of the woman whose postmenses mood typically improves, improved mood after the introduction of a behavioral treatment for depression may have nothing to do with the behavioral intervention. To the contrary, improved mood most likely is the progression of natural biological events rather than therapeutic efficacy.

Although of somewhat more recent interest to applied behavioral researchers (cf. Bellack & Schwartz, 1976; Hersen, 1979; Meichenbaum, 1976), the importance of the subject's cognitions can be neither ignored nor discounted. The strict operant interpretation of behavior, albeit more parsimonious, probably fails to reflect completely what truly distinguishes humans from the lower species. Thus, when repeated measurements are conducted, the subject's emotional-cognitive state requires attention, both as to how he or she feels and thinks over time (a dependent measure) and also as to how such thinking and feeling themselves can be causative agents for altering overt behavior.

Finally, but hardly least of all, we must consider the contribution of the external environment (i.e., the contingencies of reinforcement) on specific behavioral manifestations. To date, most of the work in single-case methodology has been devoted to elucidating the environmental variables that control directly observable motor responses (cf. Kazdin, 1975). For example, in a case of conversion reaction where the patient presented himself as unable to walk, Kallman, Hersen, and O'Toole (1975) clearly documented how the family's reactions to the symptoms resulted directly in the patient's continued symptomatology. That is, the family tended to reinforce the patient's verbalizations about symptoms (as well as serving him meals in bed and absolving him from all household responsibilities) while concurrently ignoring any of the few positive verbal and motoric initiatives he did take. It was only when the family was instructed and taught to reverse the contingencies (i.e., to ignore symptomatic presentation and to reinforce positive verbal and motor behaviors) that there was a marked change in the patient's behavior that maintained itself through a lengthy post-treatment follow-up period.

Intersubject Variability

To this point, we have focused our discussion on the attempt to ascertain the sources of variability within the individual subject. However, another type of variability that concerns the single-case researcher involves the differences between and among subjects in reaction to a therapeutic or educational procedure. Small and large differences in responding between and among subjects is termed *intersubject variability*. We have already touched on this issue when discussing the limitations and problems of the group comparison approach to research. There we pointed out how some patients may improve as a function of treatment, while others may worsen. But when the entire treatment group's data are averaged and contrasted with the control condition, no statistically significant differences emerge. From the aforementioned, it is clear that intersubject variability poses an enormous problem for the group comparison researcher, even if homogeneous groups are to be contrasted. For the single-case researcher who is conducting replications of treatments in a series of patients (presumably homogeneous with regard to a particular disorder), intersubject variability is also a problem but may result in subsequent refinements of procedures. In addition, with extensive intersubject variability, the power of a particular procedure may be determined in addition to an evaluation of its possible limitations.

More specifically, a behavioral treatment for depression may prove efficacious for both males and females who have had no prior episodes of the disorder. On the other hand, for those patients who have suffered several prior depressive episodes, the same technique may be only partially effective. Under these circumstances, the single-case researcher may alter some aspect of the treatment strategy in the hope of getting improved results. As stated by Hersen and Barlow (1976), "The task confronting the applied researcher at this point is

to devise experimental designs to isolate the cause of change, or lack of change. One advantage of single case experimental designs is that the investigator can begin an immediate search for the cause of an experimental behavior trend by altering his experimental designs on the spot. This feature, when properly employed, can provide immediate information on hypothesized sources of variability" (p. 40).

On the other hand, the same behavioral treatment applied to depressives who have had prior episodes may yield absolutely no change if the patients in addition are severely obsessive. At this point, the upper limits of the behavioral strategy may have been discovered, and it behooves the single-case researcher to consider either a different behavioral strategy or the combined (synergistic) effects of the behavioral-pharmacological approach (cf. Hersen, 1979).

Magnitude of Change

In the section on statistical analysis, we consider in some detail the advantages and disadvantages of the statistical versus the visual evaluation of data trends. However, here it is important to consider the magnitude of change brought about by a particular intervention. Because of the frequently exploratory nature of single-case work, it is especially important to document the power of the technique under consideration. For example, in the treatment of a depressed individual, one may be able to document a statistically significant change if the Beck Depression Inventory (BDI) score decreases, say, from 20 at baseline to about 15 following treatment. However, the question to be raised at this juncture is: How meaningful (clinically and socially) is this 5-point diminution? Certainly, a score of 15 on the BDI still represents a considerable residue of depression. Thus, although potentially of statistical significance, the therapeutic technique would have to yield a much greater change if it is to be considered of value to the practicing clinician. In his incisive review of this issue, Kazdin (1977) has argued about the importance of providing social validation. That is, to be given clinical credence, a therapeutic technique should be able to bring about sufficient change so that the treated individual approaches the *social norm*. Thus, in the case of our depressive, the change brought about should lead to a posttreatment score of 0–5 on the BDI. Otherwise, the norm for the non-pathological population will not have been closely enough approached.

Generality of Findings

As will be apparent in the following sections of this chapter, the main objective of the experimental analysis-of-behavior model (i.e., the single-case design) is to demonstrate the functions of the therapeutic or educational strategy that control the target behavior of interest. However, single-case researchers are intent on demonstrating this functional relationship not only in the individual case but also for other individuals who bear similar characteristics. This, then, is referred to as *subject generality*. That is, the same therapeutic strategy should prove effective over a number of patients with homogeneous features. Such features may relate to sex of the patients, their age, their diagnosis, their premorbid personality structure, or the family history of the disorder under investigation.

A second kind of generality concerns the *behavior change agent* (i.e., the therapist or educator). Given the same type of patient and the identical therapeutic strategy, do the unique characteristics of the therapist affect the outcome? More specifically, is the male therapist who carries out assertion training with an unassertive female client as effective as the female therapist doing the same treatment who is also highly committed to the goals of the woman's movement? This naturally is an empirical question whose answer can be determined only via careful replication across different therapists (see the sections on direct, clinical, and systematic replication).

A third type of generality deals with the *setting* in which the therapeutic or educational technique is being applied. That is, will a given intervention work as well in one type of setting as in another? For example, if the flooding treatment of an agoraphobic in a rural setting appears to work, will the same therapy for an agoraphobic living in an urban center prove as efficacious?

The three types of generality discussed above are problems for the single-case researcher. Indeed, critics of the single-case approach most often point to generality of findings as one of the weaker features of this research strategy:

> The most obvious limitation of studying a single case is that one does not know if the results from this case would be relevant to other cases. Even if one isolates the active therapeutic variable in a given client through a rigorous single case experimental design, critics . . . note that there is little basis for inferring that this therapeutic procedure would be equally effective when applied to clients with similar behavior disorders (client generality) or that different therapists using this technique would achieve the same results (therapist generality). Finally, one does not know if the technique would work in a different setting (setting generality). This issue, more than any other, has retarded the development of single case methodology in applied research and has caused many authorities on research to deny the utility of studying a single case for any other purpose than the generation of hypotheses. . . . Conversely, in the search for generality of applied research findings, the group comparison approach appeared to be the logical answer. (Hersen & Barlow, 1976, p. 53)

However, as the old adage goes, "Appearances can be misleading." A careful scrutiny of the group comparison strategy reveals that there are limitations here, too, on establishing generality of findings. These have been discussed in considerable detail in Hersen and Barlow (1976, Chapter 2), and the interested reader is referred to that source. However, for purposes of exposition at this point, there are two problems that warrant our attention. The *first* is that one cannot automatically infer that the results from a homogeneous group of subjects are necessarily representative of the population of such subjects. *Second*, and probably of paramount importance, it is difficult to take the average response of a group of subjects and generalize to the individual case. In the section on replication (direct, clinical, and systematic), we examine how single-case researchers have attempted to document the general applicability of their findings.

Variability as Related to Generality

On the surface, one would think that variability and generality are unrelated. However, on closer inspection it is clear that by identifying as many sources of variability as possible, single-case researchers are able to improve and refine their techniques so that overall treatments have greater applicability to a wider range of subjects. Sidman (1960) contended that

Tracking down sources of variability is then a primary technique for establishing generality. Generality and variability are basically antithetical concepts. If there are major undiscovered sources of variability in a given set of data, any attempt to achieve subject or principle generality is likely to fail. Every time we discover control of a factor that contributes to variability, we increase the likelihood that our data will be reproducible with new subjects and in different situations. Experience has taught us that precision of control leads to more extensive generalization of data. (pp. 50–51)

Of course, Sidman was referring primarily to work with infrahuman species. Although the same principles hold in clinical and educational investigation with human subjects, the methods for achieving control and ferreting out sources of variability are both more difficult and more time-consuming. It is highly unlikely that the kind of environmental control that one is capable of obtaining in the animal laboratory will ever be possible in the clinical situation, because of the multiplicity of variables impinging on humans as well as because of the more obvious ethical considerations.

General Procedures

Repeated Measurement

The hallmark of the single-case experimental design is that dependent measures are repeatedly taken during baseline and treatment phases. Such measures may involve the observation of motoric behavior (e.g., the number of social interactions per half hour of free play in a socially isolated child), the assessment of physiological functioning (e.g., the heart rate of a phobic patient on presentation of the feared stimulus), or the evaluation of the cognitive-attitudinal state of the subject (e.g., the score on a self-report anxiety or depression scale).

Irrespective of the measurement system under consideration, "the operations involved in obtaining such measurements . . . must be clearly specified, observable, public, and replicable in all respects. . . . Secondly, measurements taken repeatedly, especially over ex-

tended periods of time must be done under exacting and totally standardized conditions with respect to measurement devices used, personnel involved, time or times of day; . . . instructions to the subject, and the specific environmental conditions (e.g., location) where the measurement session occurs" (Hersen & Barlow, 1976, p. 71).

Each of the measurement systems poses some unique challenges to the single-case researcher. When motoric measures are taken and human observers are used, independent reliability checks are required. These reliability checks can be expressed either as a percentage of agreement for interval data (with 80% considered minimally acceptable) or as a correlation for continuous data (with $r = .80$ considered minimally acceptable). (For a more comprehensive survey of behavioral assessment strategies, see Chapter 4.)

When physiological measures are repeatedly taken, this too must be done under totally standardized conditions. Here, investigators must be concerned not only with the functioning of the electronic devices but with the subject's adaptation to the equipment. In addition, concern for fatigability is of some importance, particularly if intertrial time periods are not sufficiently long. In cases where sexual responding in males is being repeatedly evaluated, assessment sessions should be programmed to guarantee maximum possible responding. Thus, the fatigue factor, if not properly attended to in this instance, might lead to a confounding of conclusions. This could occur if decreased deviant sexual responding to stimuli is erroneously attributed to treatment but is, in fact, simply a function of fatigue.

A major problem in using repeated self-reports of subjects in single-case evaluations of treatments involves the external validity of such data. As noted by Hersen and Barlow (1976), "When using this type of assessment technique, the possibility always exists, even in clinical subjects, that the subject's natural responsivity will not be tapped, but that data in conformity to experimental demand are being recorded" (p. 73). That is, the subject verbally responds to what he or she perceives as the therapist's expectation at that point in the treatment. Of course, the use of alternate forms of the scale and the establishment of external validity by correlating self-report with motoric and physiological indexes are two methods for avoiding some of the pitfalls of attitudinal measures. However, there is ample evidence in the behavioral literature that de-synchrony exists among the three response systems (i.e., motoric, physiological, and cognitive) (Hersen, 1973, 1978). Indeed, there is the suggestion that clinical subjects' self-reports of how they feel should be given credence, irrespective of how motoric and physiological data change during the course of treatment (cf. Hersen, 1978). It is assumed that if sufficient improvements do not take place in motoric and physiological areas, but the cognitive-attitudinal system remains unmodified, treatment should be considered only partially successful.

A specific issue faced by the single-case researcher who works in the psychiatric setting (Hersen & Bellack, 1978) that obviously can affect the standardization of data is the different composition of the staff at various times. Not only may variable levels of staff cooperation yield a differing quality in the data collected within a stated time period (e.g., the morning), but the marked staff differences in number and attitude during day, evening, and weekend shifts are variables that may lead to confounded data. Thus, when conducting single-case research in the psychiatric setting, standardization of data collection times and data collectors (e.g., nursing personnel) assumes even greater importance.

Choosing a Baseline

With the exception of the B-A-B design, where treatment precedes baseline assessment, in most single-case experimental designs the initial period of observation involves the natural frequency of occurrence of the behavior of interest. This initial phase is referred to as *baseline* and is labeled *A*. Baseline serves as the standard by which subsequent treatment phases are contrasted.

In the ideal case, the assessment of baseline functioning yields a stable pattern of data, thus facilitating the interpretation of treatment effects in the B phase. However, more often than not, such stability of data is not to be

found. This is less of a problem for the basic animal researcher, who is in a position to program the subject's responding through the application of a variety of interval- and ratio-scheduling methodologies. It is understandable, then, why Sidman's (1960) definition of stability is a 5% range of variability. If variability exceeds that range, it is recommended that the experimenter evaluate sources of variability systematically.

In evaluating human subjects, the experimenter's flexibility in creating and choosing a baseline is much more constricted. Generally, the applied researcher does not have the luxury of "creating" ideal baseline conditions and is compelled to accept the baseline pattern as a given. Furthermore, the applied researcher is usually under time constraints; hence there is less opportunity to search for the manifold causes of variability. However, sometimes adjustment in the measurement scale being used may reduce extensive variability. That is, at times, the measurement interval may not be appropriate for the behavior under study and therefore leads to extraneous variability.

In the following discussion, we illustrate some of the baseline patterns typically encountered when conducting applied research with human subjects. Problems inherent in each of the patterns and methods for dealing with them are outlined.

Hersen and Barlow (1976) have identified and illustrated eight specific baseline patterns (see Table 1). These, of course, are the most representative, but many other possibilities, combinations, and permutations exist. Each of the baseline patterns illustrated contains six data points. In single-case research, an oft-raised question is: "How many points do I

Table 1. Baseline Patterns

1. Stable baseline
2. Increasing baseline (target behavior worsening)
3. Decreasing baseline (target behavior improving)
4. Variable baseline
5. Variable–stable baseline
6. Increasing–decreasing baseline
7. Decreasing–increasing baseline
8. Unstable baseline

need for an appropriate baseline assessment?" Although this is a straightforward question, the answer to it is a bit complex. The first issue, of course, is how many data points are required in order to ascertain some trend in the data. Barlow and Hersen (1973) argued that, "A minimum of three separate observation points, plotted on the graph, during this baseline phase are required to establish a trend in the data" (p. 320). Sometimes more data points are needed if the baseline is initially variable or unstable. But, of course, the exigencies of a treatment situation may, at time, demand that the investigator forego experimental purity and institute treatment as rapidly as possible.

An upward trend in the data is represented by three successively increasing points. Conversely, a decreasing trend in the data is represented by three successively decreasing points. However, the power of the trend is dictated by the slope of the curve, with steeper slopes indicating greater power. The statistical methods for assessing slopes and trends in single-case research have been reviewed by Kazdin (1976). However, to date, despite considerable controversy in the field (cf. Baer, 1977; Michael, 1974a; Jones *et al.*, 1977; Thoresen & Elashoff, 1974), most applied behavioral researchers rely on a visual analysis of the data.

The stable baseline is depicted in Figure 1. As is quite apparent, there is some minor variability in tic frequency, but this variability is

minimal, with the data essentially representing a straight line (i.e., no upward or downward trend). The application of treatment following such a baseline would permit an unambiguous interpretation of its effect (no change, improvement, or worsening).

As indicated in Table 1, the second pattern is the increasing baseline, where the target behavior is worsening. This, of course, is an acceptable pattern that could lead to a meaningful interpretation if subsequent treatment were to reverse the trend. However, if treatment were ineffective, then no difference in the slope of the curve might be noted. On the other hand, if treatment were detrimental to the patient, it would be difficult to determine whether the data in the intervention phase simply represent a continuation of the trend begun in baseline or whether they indicate further deterioration due to the treatment itself. However, a marked change in the slope of the curve could be interpreted as a deterioration effect due to treatment.

The third pattern is one where the baseline is decreasing and the target behavior is improving. This pattern is problematic inasmuch as subsequent treatment application might just result in a continuation of the trend begun in baseline. If there were a marked change in the slope of the curve, the improvement might be attributed to treatment, but this would be difficult to evaluate via visual inspection. Generally, in this instance, treatment would have to be withdrawn and reinstituted if its controlling effects are to be established. If treatment were to lead to a worsening of the patient's condition, then a reversed trend in the data would be apparent.

The fourth pattern, portrayed in Figure 2, is the variable baseline. We should note that this is a pattern frequently encountered in applied clinical research. The figure shows a tic frequency ranging from 24 to 255; no clear trend is apparent in the data. Nonetheless, there is a clear pattern of alternating low and high data points. Some investigators who obtain this pattern block the data by averaging tic frequency over a two-day period. This would lead to an apparently stable pattern, at least visually. However, this is an artificial manner of dealing with variability that is "cosmetic" but does not alter the basic pattern. In

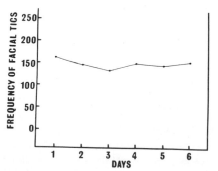

Figure 1. The stable baseline. Hypothetical data for mean numbers of facial tics averaged over three daily 15-minute videotaped sessions. (From Fig. 3-1 in *Single Case Experimental Designs* by Michel Hersen and David H. Barlow. Copyright 1976 by Pergamon Press, New York. Reprinted by permission.)

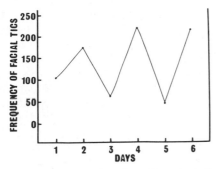

Figure 2. The variable baseline. Hypothetical data for mean number of facial tics averaged over three 15-minute videotaped sessions. (From Fig. 3-4 in *Single Case Experimental Designs* by Michel Hersen and David H. Barlow. Copyright 1976 by Pergamon Press, New York. Reprinted by permission.)

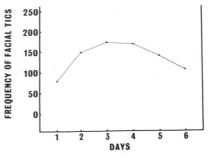

Figure 3. The increasing–decreasing baseline. Hypothetical data for mean number of facial tics averaged over three daily 15-minute videotaped sessions. (From Fig. 3-6 in *Single Case Experimental Designs* by Michel Hersen and David H. Barlow. Copyright 1976 by Pergamon Press, New York. Reprinted by permission.)

light of the extreme variability seen in this pattern, subsequent interpretations of a treatment effect could be quite difficult unless the treatment itself were successful in reducing both variability and tic frequency. As recommended by Sidman (1960), if time permits, the researcher should attempt to identify the source(s) of variability. But in the clinical situation, this usually is not the case.

As can be seen in Table 1, the fifth pattern is the variable–stable baseline. Here, despite initial variability, the investigator extends the baseline observation until the data are less variable. Indeed, this is one of the methods for dealing with the fourth pattern: the variable baseline. After stability is achieved, the institution of a given treatment should once again lead to an unambiguous interpretation of the resulting data. The only problem here is that extensive baseline observation may not be possible or ethical in certain clinical situations (e.g., severe head-banging or severe depression where suicidal ideation is present).

The sixth pattern (increasing–decreasing baseline), presented in Figure 3, is one where after an initial period of deterioration, improvement is quite apparent in the subject's condition. But as in the case of the decreasing baseline, the subsequent treatment application might only result in the continuation of the trend in the second part of baseline (i.e., continued improvement). Therefore, here, as in the case of the decreasing baseline, withdrawal and reinstatement of treatment are

needed to document the effects controlling the intervention strategy.

The seventh pattern (decreasing–increasing baseline) is the converse of the sixth: improvement followed by deterioration. In this instance, application of treatment that results in a reversal of data trends permits a clear interpretation of the effect. However, in the event that treatment is detrimental to the patient, visual inspection should prove extremely difficult unless there is a marked change in the slope of the curve.

The final pattern, the unstable baseline, is graphically portrayed in Figure 4. In this example, we have an extended baseline assessment that fails to reveal any particular pattern in the data. Thus, even the cosmetics of block-

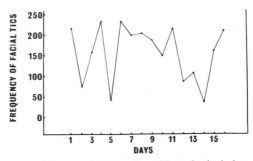

Figure 4. The unstable baseline. Hypothetical data for mean number of facial tics averaged over three daily 15-minute videotaped sessions. (From Fig. 3-8 in *Single Case Experimental Designs* by Michel Hersen and David H. Barlow. Copyright 1976 by Pergamon Press, New York. Reprinted by permission.)

ing would fail to yield visual improvement as to stability. As noted by Hersen and Barlow (1976), "To date, no completely satisfactory strategy for dealing with this type of baseline has appeared; at best, the kinds of strategies for dealing with variable baseline are also recommended here" (p. 82).

Changing One Variable at a Time

One of the basic tenets of the single-case approach is that only one variable is altered at a time when proceeding from one phase to the next (Barlow & Hersen, 1973; Hersen & Barlow, 1976). It should be noted that if two variables are manipulated simultaneously from one phase to another, then it is impossible to determine which of the two was responsible for or contributed most to behavioral change. This one-variable structure holds irrespective of whether the beginning, the middle, or the end phase is being evaluated.

Let us examine this basic tenet in greater detail. In the A-B-A-B design, for example, only one variable is changed from one adjacent phase to the next. Baseline is followed by treatment, which is succeeded by baseline and then treatment again. If treatment consists of a single therapeutic strategy—say, social reinforcement—then only one variable is altered from A to B. However, many treatments (e.g., social skills training) consist of a mélange of techniques (i.e., instructions, feedback, modeling, and social reinforcement). Thus, in an A-B-A-B design involving the application of such treatment, B represents the full combination of techniques. In this analysis, it is not possible to evaluate the separate contribution of each technique. However, in an A-B-A-B-BC-B design, where A is baseline, B is feedback, and C is social reinforcement, the separate contributions of feedback and social reinforcement to the overall treatment effect can be determined.

Although the one-variable rule is generally adhered to by behavioral researchers, examples in the literature may be found where incorrect applications have been carried out and published. Two prime examples are the A-B-A-C design, where the investigator erroneously assumes that the differential effects of A and C can be determined, and the A-B-A-BC design, where the investigator assumes that the combined effects of BC may be contrasted with the original B phase. Not only is this idea erroneous in terms of the one-variable tenet, but the investigator has failed to consider the additional factor of the sequencing of possible treatment effects and the time lapses between treatment applications. With respect to these two examples, it should be pointed out that the experimental error is most frequently committed toward the latter part of the experimental analysis.

We might also note that in drug evaluations, the one-variable rule also holds but has some additional implications. Instead of progressing from a baseline phase (where no treatment is being administered) to a treatment phase (active drug), an additional step (i.e., placebo) is needed to control for the mere fact that the subject is ingesting a substance. Thus, a typical drug evaluation accomplished in the experimental single-case design might involve the following sequence: (1) no drug; (2) placebo; (3) active drug; (4) placebo; and (5) active drug. This design, labeled A-A′-B-A′-B, allows for evaluation of the contribution of the placebo over baseline and the drug over and above placebo alone.

Length of Phases

A number of factors need to be considered when determining length of baseline and treatment phases in single-case research. Included are time limitations, staff reactions, the relative length of adjacent phases, and ethical considerations. Johnston (1972) argued that "It is necessary that each phase be sufficiently long to demonstrate stability (lack of trend and constant range of variability) and to dispel any doubts of the reader that the data shown are sensitive to and representative of what was happening under the described conditions" (p. 1036).

In the ideal case, of course, the investigator attempts to secure a relatively equal number of data points per phase. This is especially important in the A-B-A-B design; otherwise, if, for example, a treatment phase were substantially longer than the preceding baseline, effects could be attributed to the extended time factor rather than to the treatment *per se* (see Hersen & Barlow, 1976, p. 101).

An excellent example of an A-B-A-B design with equal phases (with the exception of the last B phase) was presented by Miller (1973). In this study, the effects of retention control training were evaluated in a secondary enuretic child, with two targets (number of enuretic episodes and frequency of daily urination) selected as dependent measures (see Figure 5). The reader will note the relative stability in the baseline, the initial effects of the treatment, the return to baseline stability, and the renewed effects of the treatment during the second B phase. However, the second B phase was extended to 7 data points (instead of 3) to ensure the permanence of the treatment effects. This is a procedure commonly carried out in the last phase of the A-B-A-B design, and it has clinical implications, but the importance of the equality of the data points in the A-B-A phase of the study is clear.

Sometimes, when the targeted behavior is potentially injurious to the subject under study (e.g., head banging) and/or the staff in the institution are eager to get the behavior under control very quickly because it is annoying, the initial baselines and the subsequent withdrawals of treatment (second and third A phases) may be very brief as contrasted with the intervention phases. Here, it is quite clear that ethical considerations have precedence over experimental rigor.

Still another factor related to length of phase is the carry-over effects of treatment to baseline. In the A-B-A-B design evaluating a behavioral strategy, this occurs in the second A phase, where the experimenter is unable to recover the initial baseline level that appeared in the first A phase. This is one of the primary reasons that Bijou, Peterson, Harris, Allen, and Johnston (1969) stated that "In studies involving stimuli with reinforcing properties, relatively short experimental periods are advocated, since long ones might allow enough time for the establishment of new conditioned reinforcers" (p. 202).

A special problem concerning carry-over effects involves evaluations of pharmacological treatments in single-case designs. Whereas with a behavioral intervention it is possible to terminate treatment (hopefully with minimal carry-over effects from treatment to baseline), in pharmacological applications the biological effects of the drug may actually persist into the placebo and baseline phases. Thus, it generally is not feasible to evaluate the long-term effects of drugs in single-case studies without the use of additional phases ("washout" phases, where there is no intervention) interposed between treatment and placebo. However, for the short-term evaluation of drugs, where they are rapidly introduced and removed, the single-case strategy is quite satisfactory (see Liberman & Davis, 1975).

Reversal and Withdrawal

In the behavioral literature (e.g., Baer, Wolf, & Risley, 1968; Barlow & Hersen, 1973; Kazdin, 1973), the A-B-A-B design is considered prototypical of the reversal strategy: "When speaking of a reversal, one typically refers to the removal (withdrawal) of the treatment variable that is applied after baseline measurement has been concluded. In practice, the reversal involves a withdrawal of the B

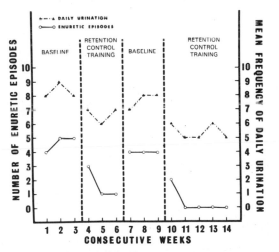

Figure 5. Number of enuretic episodes per week and mean number of daily urinations per week for Subject 1. (From "An Experimental Analysis of Retention Control Training in the Treatment of Nocturnal Enuresis in Two Institutionalized Adolescents" by Peter M. Miller, *Behavior Therapy*, 1973, *4*, 288–294, Fig. 1. Copyright 1973 by *Behavior Therapy*. Reprinted by permission.)

phase (in the A-B-A design) after behavioral change has been successfully demonstrated. If the treatment (B phase) indeed exerts control over the targeted behavior under study, a decreased or increased trend (depending on which direction indicates deterioration) in the data should follow its removal'' (Hersen & Barlow, 1976, p. 92).

However, although the word *reversal* is used to describe the A-B-A-B design and the removal of treatment in the second A phase, Leitenberg (1973) and, more recently, Hersen and Barlow (1976) argued that the term *withdrawal* better describes the technical operation carried out by the applied behavioral researcher. Also, Leitenberg (1973) and Hersen and Barlow (1976) contended that there is a specific experimental strategy that is to be labeled the *reversal design*. An illustration of this design appears in Figure 6. Allen, Hart, Buell, Harris, and Wolf (1964) evaluated the effects of social reinforcement in a 4½-year-old withdrawn girl attending a preschool nursery. The target behaviors selected for study were the percentage of interaction with adults and the percentage of interaction with children. As can be seen in Figure 6, during baseline, a greater percentage of social interaction took place with adults than with children. In the second phase, the teacher was instructed to reinforce the child socially when she was interacting with other children and to ignore her when she was interacting with adults. In the next phase, the teacher was instructed to *reverse* the contingencies (i.e., to reinforce interaction with adults and to ignore interactions with children). Again, interaction with adults increased while interaction with children decreased. According to Leitenberg (1973), this is a *true* reversal (of differential attention) and is vastly different from simple withdrawal of treatment in the second A phase of the A-B-A-B design. In the fourth phase of the Allen *et al.* (1964) study, the contingencies were once more reversed, this reversal leading to increased interaction with children and decreased interaction with adults.

We should note parenthetically, however, that despite this distinction drawn between withdrawal and reversal, most applied behavioral researchers persist in referring to the A-B-A-B design as a reversal strategy. In short, the distinction made has not been reinforced by journal editors.

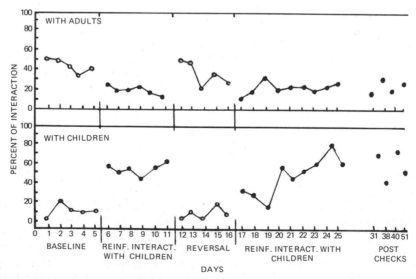

Figure 6. Daily percentages of time spent in social interaction with adults and with children during approximately 2 hours of each morning session. (From "Effects of Social Reinforcement on Isolate Behavior of a Nursery School Child" by K. E. Allen *et al.*, *Child Development*, 1964, *35*, 511–518, Fig. 2. Copyright 1964 by The Society for Research in Child Development, Inc. Reprinted by permission.)

Evaluating Irreversible Procedures

In single-case research, variables such as feedback, social reinforcement, and a variety of punishment techniques can be readily introduced and withdrawn in a number of designs (withdrawal and reversal). However, one variable, instructions, cannot be withdrawn in the technical sense. That is, once an instructional set has been given to the subject a number of times, simply ceasing to remind him or her of the instructions cannot be equated with cessation of feedback or reinforcement. Indeed, there is an analogy here to the physical discontinuation of a drug whose biological effect in the body may persist through the placebo and baseline phases of experimentation. Nonetheless, it is possible to study the very short-term effects of an instructional set that is periodically introduced and removed (Eisler, Hersen, & Agras, 1973) and the effects of changing the instructional set from a positive to a negative expectation (Barlow, Agras, Leitenberg, Callahan, & Moore, 1972). But usually, instructions tend to be maintained as a constant across the various phases of treatment, so that only one therapeutic variable is changed at a time (cf. Kallman *et al.*, 1975). When this is not possible, alternative experimental strategies, such as the multiple-baseline design, may be used to evaluate specific instructional effects on targeted behaviors (e.g., Hersen & Bellack, 1976).

Basic A-B-A Designs

A-B Design

The A-B design is the simplest of the single-case strategies, with the exception of the so-called B design, where measures are repeatedly taken throughout the course of treatment (i.e., in an uncontrolled case study with repeated measures). On the other hand, in the A-B design, the natural frequency of the behavior under study is first assessed in baseline (A). Then, in the B phase, treatment is instituted.

Of the single-case strategies, the A-B design is one of the weakest in terms of inferring causality. Indeed, the design is often referred to as correlational in that the effects of treatment that control the dependent measures are not completely documented unless treatment is withdrawn subsequent to B (i.e., the A-B-A design). Thus, in the A-B design, it is possible that changes in B are not the direct result of treatment *per se* but perhaps of some other factor, such as passage of time, that is correlated with the treatment.

Nonetheless, the A-B design does have its use and certainly represents a vast improvement over the uncontrolled case study. Also, for therapeutic or educational problems that have long proved recalcitrant, if intervention in B yields behavioral improvement, then with *some* degree of confidence one may attribute the effects to the specific intervention. However, only by demonstrating such change in a withdrawal or reversal design will dispel the remaining doubts of the more "hard-headed" operant researcher.

An example of an A-B design that also includes follow-up was presented by Epstein and Hersen (1974). The subject was a 26-year-old psychiatric inpatient who had suffered from gagging episodes for about two years in spite of numerous medical interventions. However, the problem appeared to have no direct medical etiology; hence the patient was admitted to the psychiatric service of a Veterans Administration hospital. During baseline (A), the patient was asked to record on an index card the specific time and frequency of each gagging episode. During treatment (B), the patient was given $2 in canteen books (exchangeable at the hospital commissary) for an $n - 1$ decrease in his gagging rate from the previous day. In treatment, the emphasis was on the patient's managing his disorder himself, with canteen booklets serving as the incentive. During the 12-week follow-up, the patient continued recording his gagging rate at home, with self-reports corroborated by his wife.

Figure 7 baseline data reveal a gagging frequency of 8–17 instances per day. The institution of treatment led to a marked decrease, to 0 on Day 14. However, renewed symptomatology was evidenced on Day 15, and treatment was continued, with the criterion for Day 15 reset to that originally used for Day 13. Improvements were noted between Days 15 and 18, and treatment was continued an additional six days.

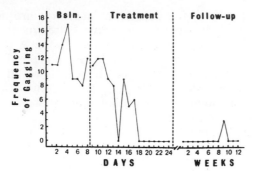

Figure 7. Frequency of gagging during baseline treatment and follow-up. (From "Behavioral Control of Hysterical Gagging" by L. H. Epstein and M. Hersen, *Journal of Clinical Psychology*, 1974, *30*, 102–104, Fig. 1. Copyright 1974 by the American Psychological Association. Reprinted by permission.)

From a design perspective, the reader should note the initial variability in baseline, which then stabilized to some degree. Further, the length of the treatment phase was double that of the baseline; it was extended for obvious clinical considerations (i.e., renewed symptomatology on Day 15).

Although the treatment appeared to be efficacious, it is possible that some unidentified variable, correlated with reinforcement procedures, led to behavioral change. But as previously noted, the A-B design does not allow for a completely unambiguous interpretation of causality. However, given the longevity of this patient's disorder and the repeated failure of medical interventions, there is a good likelihood that the treatment *per se* caused the improvement.

A-B-A Design

The A-B-A design corrects for one of the major shortcomings of the A-B design: lack of experimental control. Removal of treatment in the second A phase is used to confirm experimental control over the dependent measure initially suggested when improvement occurs in B. However, the A-B-A design is not completely adequate either, as it terminates in a no-treatment phase. For very obvious clinical and ethical reasons, this is problematic; at times, the experimenter may have intended to follow the more complete A-B-A-B strategy, but for any number of reasons, the subject

terminates the treatment prematurely. Even under these circumstances, data from A-B-A designs are of value.

Let us consider an example of an A-B-A design published by Hersen *et al.* (1973) some years ago. In this study, the investigators evaluated the effects of a token economy on neurotic depression in a married, white, 52-year-old farmer who had become depressed following the sale of his farm. The two dependent measures selected for study were the number of points earned and the behavioral ratings of depression (talking, smiling, and motor activity), with higher ratings indicating less depression. During baseline (A), the patient was able to earn points, but they had no exchange value. In B (token economy), the patient had to purchase privileges on the ward with points earned. Then, in the third phase (A), baseline procedures were reinstated.

The results of this experimental analysis are presented graphically in Figure 8. Inspection of baseline shows that the number of points earned was increasing, whereas decreased behavioral ratings of depression indicated a slight worsening of the patient's condition. It is quite clear that with the introduction of

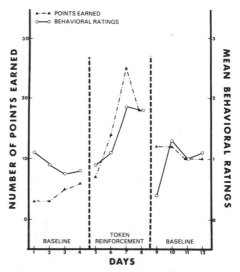

Figure 8. Number of points earned and mean behavioral ratings for Subject 1. (From "Effects of Token Economy on Neurotic Depression: An Experimental Analysis" by Michel Hersen *et al.*, *Behavior Therapy*, 1973, *4*, 392–397, Fig. 1. Copyright 1973 by *Behavior Therapy*. Reprinted by permission.)

token reinforcement in the B phase, there was a sharp increase both in the number of points earned and in the behavioral ratings, suggesting the efficacy of the intervention. Removal of treatment in the second A phase led to a marked diminution of points earned; decreased behavioral ratings also confirmed the controlling effects of the treatment.

From a design perspective, the fact that the number of points earned in baseline was on the increase makes it a bit more difficult to interpret the greater number of points earned during token reinforcement. However, the marked change in the slope of the curve during the token economy phase is highly suggestive. Moreover, data in the second A phase (showing a marked decrease in the number of points earned) confirmed the initial impression of the token economy's controlling effects. The data for behavioral ratings, because of the specific trends obtained, are definitely less ambiguous to interpret and clearly indicate the controlling effects of the token economy.

A-B-A-B Design

The A-B-A-B design, as previously noted, controls for deficiencies inherent in the A-B-A strategy, and elsewhere it has been termed the "equivalent time-samples design" (Campbell & Stanley, 1966). Not only does this design end on a treatment phase (B), but it provides two opportunities for showing the controlling effects of treatment over the dependent measure (B to A and A to B).

Let us now examine a recent example of the successful use of an A-B-A-B single-case design. Lombardo and Turner (1979) evaluated the effects of thought stopping in a 26-year-old male psychiatric inpatient who was severely obsessive. Obsessions focused on "imaginal relationships" he had had with other patients on the ward during previous hospitalizations. Although the patient attempted to control obsessive ruminations through distraction, this approach failed to reduce the disorder's full intensity.

In all phases of the experimental analysis, the patient was instructed to note the beginning and ending times of each obsessive episode, thus allowing a determination of both the rate of ruminations and the total time per day. Baseline (A) consisted of six days of observation. Treatment (thought stopping) began on Day 7 and consisted of the patient raising his right index finger whenever he had obtained a vivid obsessive image. At that point, the therapist shouted, "Stop," and the patient lowered his finger: "Fading of 'STOP' intensity and transfer of control from therapist to patient in all training was accomplished as follows. Initially, the therapist provided the 'STOP,' first shouting, then saying it loudly, then using a normal speaking voice, then saying it softly, and finally whispering 'STOP.' The patient then verbalized 'STOP' in the same manner with an additional final step of saying 'STOP' covertly. Depending upon how rapidly the patient gained control, four to six repetitions of stopping were used at each voice intensity" (Lombardo & Turner, 1979, p. 269). Treatment was discontinued on Day 18 and recommenced on Day 28. In addition, a six-week follow-up was carried out.

The results of this study appear in Figure 9. Following a period of baseline stability (the modal response was 40 minutes), thought stopping led to a marked decrease of obsessions to a 0 level. When treatment was then withdrawn in the second A phase (baseline), obsessions increased considerably, well over baseline levels, albeit in a very unstable fashion. However, reintroduction of the treatment led to renewed improvement to a 0 level, maintained through Days 33–40. Furthermore, improvement continued throughout the six-week follow-up period.

Although the functional effects of treatment appeared to be documented, "this conclusion must be tempered by the fact that controls were not provided for the possible therapeutic effects of instructions and therapist as well as patient expectancies" (Lombardo & Turner, 1979, p. 270). This kind of problem is definitely more prevalent when self-report data are used as opposed to motoric and physiological measures. As earlier noted, motoric and physiological measures are less susceptible to such confounding.

B-A-B Design

The B-A-B design, although not as complete an experimental analysis as the A-B-A-B de-

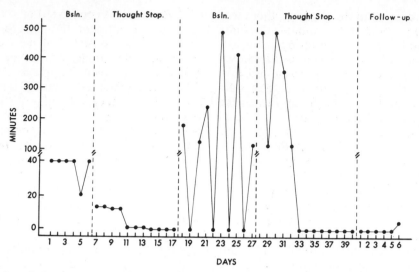

Figure 9. Duration of obsessive ruminations during baseline, treatment, and six-week follow-up. (From "Thought-Stopping in the Control of Obsessive Ruminations" by T. W. Lombardo and S. M. Turner, *Behavior Modification*, 1979, *3*, 267–272, Fig. 1. Copyright by Sage Publications. Reprinted by permission.)

sign, is superior to the A-B-A strategy, as it ends in a treatment phase. Since the experimental analysis begins in a treatment phase in the B-A-B design, the natural frequency (i.e., rate) of the behavior under investigation is not initially obtained. On the other hand, the B-A-B design may be useful for experimentation in institutional settings, particularly if the staff are eager to get some disruptive or unpleasant behavior under quick control. In such instances, the staff will undoubtedly require persuasion with regard to withdrawal of the treatment in the second phase (i.e., in A).

Let us consider an example of a B-A-B design in which the effects of token economic procedures on work performance were evaluated for 44 chronic schizophrenic patients (Ayllon & Azrin, 1965). In the first phase (B), the patients were awarded tokens contingently for engaging in a variety of hospital-ward work activities. Tokens, of course, were exchangeable for a large menu of "backup" reinforcers. In the second phase (A), the patients were given tokens noncontingently, based on the individual rates obtained in B. In the third phase (B), treatment was reinstated.

The results of this study are depicted in Figure 10. During the first B phase, the group of patients averaged a total of 45 work hours per day. When the contingency was removed in

A, the work level dropped to 1 hour by Day 36. The reinstatement of the treatment in the second B phase led to a marked increase of work output similar to that in the first phase. The data in the second B phase clearly document the controlling effects of the token economy on the work performance of these chronic schizophrenic patients.

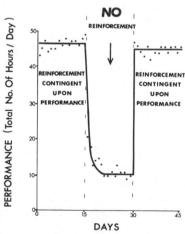

Figure 10. The total number of hours of the on-ward performance by a group of 44 patients. (From "The Measurement and Reinforcement of Behavior of Psychotics" by T. Ayllon and N. H. Azrin, *Behaviour Research and Therapy*, 1965, *8*, 357–383, Fig. 4. Copyright 1965 by Pergamon Press, Ltd. Reprinted by permission.)

Inasmuch as group data were averaged in this experimental analysis, Ayllon and Azrin (1965) also presented individual data, indicating that 36 of the 44 patients were affected by the contingency in force; 8 of the patients did not respond to token economic procedures. As argued by Hersen and Barlow (1976), when group data are presented graphically, the investigator should also display data for selected subjects: "Individual data presented for selected subjects can be quite useful, particularly if data trends differ. Otherwise, difficulties inherent in the traditional group comparison approach (e.g., averaging out of effects, effects due to a small minority while the majority remains unaffected by treatment) will be carried over to the experimental analysis procedure" (Hersen & Barlow, 1976, p. 190).

Extensions of the A-B-A Design

Extensions of the basic A-B-A design have appeared in numerous behavioral publications. In this section, we will consider three categories of such extensions.

The first involves a more extended replication of the basic A-B pattern (e.g., A-B-A-B-A-B: Mann, 1972) or the A-B-A-C-A design, where the controlling effects of B and C on A are examined in one study (e.g., Wincze et al., 1972). However, in the A-B-A-C-A design, it is not possible to make a comparison of the relative effects of B and C, since these two interventions are confounded by a third factor: time.

The second category we will look at involves the additive or interactive effects of two therapeutic variables (e.g., A-B-A-B-BC-B design). Here, given the appropriate data trends, it is possible to evaluate the contribution of C above and beyond that of B.

Finally, the third category is concerned with the assessment of pharmacological treatments. As already noted, there are some unique problems in evaluating the effects of drugs in single-case designs (e.g., the need for placebo phases and the carry-over effects). Also, it should be noted that at this juncture the use of single-case analyses for pharmacological interventions is not widespread. Thus,

in our discussion, we will highlight possibilities for the future.

A-B-A-B-A-B and A-B-A-C-A-C' Designs

Mann (1972) repeatedly evaluated the effects of contingency contracting (A-B-A-B-A-B design) in his efforts to treat an overweight subject. At the beginning of the study, the subject surrendered a number of prize possessions (i.e., variables) to the investigator, which could be regained (one at a time), contingent on a 2-pound weight loss over a previous low within a designated time period. By contrast, a 2-pound weight gain led to the subject's permanent loss of the valuable, to be disposed of by the investigator in equitable fashion. That is, he did not profit in any way from the subject's loss.

As can be seen in Figure 11, the institution of the treatment (contingency contracting) led to marked decreases in weight, with interposed baseline data evincing a plateauing effect or an upward trend. In short, the controlling effects of the contingency contract on weight loss were firmly demonstrated several times in this experimental analysis.

Wincze et al. (1972) evaluated the effects of feedback and token reinforcement on the verbal behavior of a delusional psychiatric inpatient using an A-B-A-C-A-C'-A design. During each of the phases of study, the patient was asked daily to respond to 15 questions selected at random from a pool of 105. The proportion of the responses containing delusional material was recorded for the individual sessions, as was the percentage of delusional talk on the ward monitored by nurses 20 times a day.

During A (baseline), no contingencies were in effect, and the patient received "free" tokens. Feedback (B) involved the patient's being corrected whenever he responded delusionally. Tokens were still given to him noncontingently in this phase. In A, baseline procedures were reinstituted. In the fourth phase (C), tokens were earned *contingently* for nondelusional talk. This was followed by a return to baseline conditions. In C', tokens were awarded contingently for nondelusional talk that exceeded a given criterion (nondelusional talk more than 90%). Finally, in the last phase

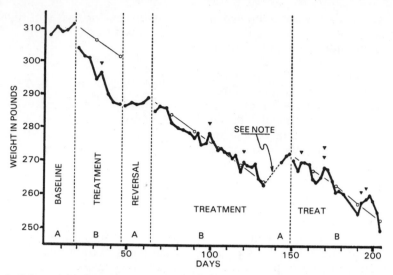

Figure 11. A record of the weight of Subject 1 during all conditions. Each open circle (connected by the thin solid line) represents a 2-week minimum-weight-loss requirement. Each of the solid dots (connected by the thick solid line) represents the subject's weight on each of the days he was measured. Each triangle indicates the point at which the subject was penalized by a loss of valuables, either for gaining weight or for not meeting the 2-week minimum-weight-loss requirement. *Note*: The subject was ordered by his physician to consume at least 2,500 calories per day for 10 days, in preparation for medical tests. (From "The Behavior Therapeutic Use of Contingency Contracting to Control on Adult Behavior Problem: Weight Control" by R. A. Mann, *Journal of Applied Behavior Analysis*, 1972, *5*, 99–109, Fig. 1. Copyright 1972 by the Society for the Experimental Analysis of Behavior, Inc. Reprinted by permission.)

(A), baseline procedures were reinstated for the fourth time.

The results of this study appear in Figure 12. These data indicate that none of the treatment variables applied effected any change in delusional talk on the ward. Similarly, feedback (B) yielded no effects on delusional talk in individual sessions. But token sessions (Phase 4) and token bonus (Phase 6) procedures led to decreased delusional talk in individual sessions, thus demonstrating the controlling power of these treatments over the dependent measure. However, as has already been underscored, this design does not permit

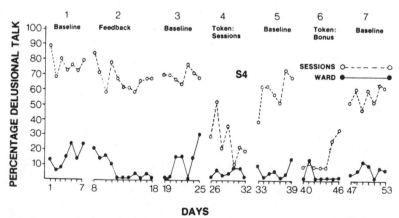

Figure 12. Percentage of delusional talk of Subject 4 during therapist sessions and on the ward for each experimental day. (From "The Effects of Token Reinforcement and Feedback on the Delusional Verbal Behavior of Chronic Paranoid Schizophrenics" by J. P. Wincze *et al.*, *Journal of Applied Behavior Analysis*, 1972, *5*, 247–262, Fig. 4. Copyright 1972 by the Society for the Experimental Analysis of Behavior, Inc. Reprinted by permission.)

an analysis of the relative effects of token sessions and the token bonus treatment.

Interaction Designs

As previously pointed out in Hersen and Barlow (1976), "Most treatments contain a number of therapeutic components. One task of the clinical researcher is to experimentally analyze these components to determine which are effective and which can be discarded, resulting in a more efficient treatment. Analyzing the separate effects of single therapeutic variables is a necessary way to begin to build therapeutic programs, but it is obvious that these variables may have different effects when interacting with other treatment variables. In advanced states of the construction of complex treatments it becomes necessary to determine the nature of these interactions" (p. 213).

As clearly noted in an earlier section, the importance of the one-variable rule (i.e., changing one variable across phases) holds in particular in interaction designs. In some instances, the introduction of one therapeutic variable will lead to some behavioral change, but the addition of a second variable will lead to still further increases, as marked by a significant change in the slope of the curve (see Hersen & Barlow, 1976, p. 217). In other instances, the first variable may lead to a min-

imal effect, while the second suggests considerable additional effects. Let us consider one such example.

Kallman *et al.* (1975) evaluated the effects of reinforcing standing and walking on the mean distance in yards walked per instruction in a white, 42-year-old married, patient suffering from a conversion reaction (i.e., an inability to walk). Figure 13 shows that in the first phase, when standing was reinforced with verbal praise, only minimal efforts were made to walk. In the second phase, when walking and standing were both reinforced, a marked linear increase in walking was noted. In the third phase, standing alone was reinforced; the result was a plateauing effect. However, when reinforcement for standing and walking was reinstituted in the fourth phase, further improvements in walking appeared. In the next two phases, reinforcement for standing and walking were maintained, but with the addition of a walker in the fifth phase and its removal in the sixth. The nomenclature for the first six phases of this study is as follows: (1) B; (2) BC; (3) B; (4) BC; (5) BCD; and (6) BC. An evaluation of the analysis clearly indicates the controlling effects of C (reinforcing walking) over B (reinforcing standing), but it does not reveal the controlling effects of the walker (BCD) over no walker (BC), inasmuch as improvements in walking continued after the walker was removed.

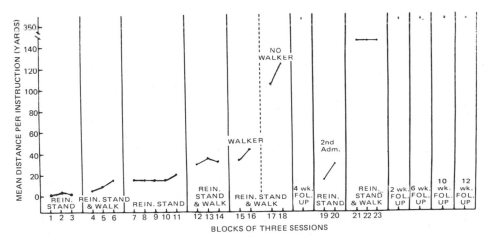

Figure 13. Mean distances walked during all phases of treatment and follow-up. (From "The Use of Social Reinforcement in a Case of Conversion Reaction" by W. M. Kallman *et al.*, *Behavior Therapy*, 1975, 6, 411–413, Fig. 1. Copyright 1975 by *Behavior Therapy*. Reprinted by permission.)

Let us consider still another example of the interaction design, an evaluation of the effects of feedback and reinforcement on the eating behavior of an anorexia nervosa patient (Agras *et al.,* 1974). This study was done in an A-B-BC-B-BC design, with A as baseline, B as reinforcement, and C as feedback. Throughout the study, the patient was provided four meals daily, each consisting of 1,500 calories. Reinforcement consisted of granting the patient privileges, contingent on weight gain. Feedback, on the other hand, involved giving the patient specific information as to weight, caloric intake, and actual mouthfuls consumed.

The data presented in Figure 14 show a slight increase in weight during baseline but decreased caloric intake. The introduction of reinforcement led to decreased weight and a continued decrease in caloric intake. When feedback was added to reinforcement in the third phase, a marked increase in weight and

caloric intake was noted. This leveled off when feedback was removed in Phase 4 but increased when feedback once again was added to reinforcement in the final phase. In summary, this study failed to document the controlling effects of reinforcement on weight gain and caloric intake, but it definitely reflects the controlling effects of feedback on these two dependent measures.

Drug Evaluations

So far in this chapter, we have touched on some of the issues related to the evaluation of pharmacological agents in single-case designs (namely, the placebo phase and the carry-over effects from adjacent phases). A third important issue in drug research, of course, is the use of double-blind assessments; that is, neither the patient nor the assessor is aware of whether a placebo or an active drug is being

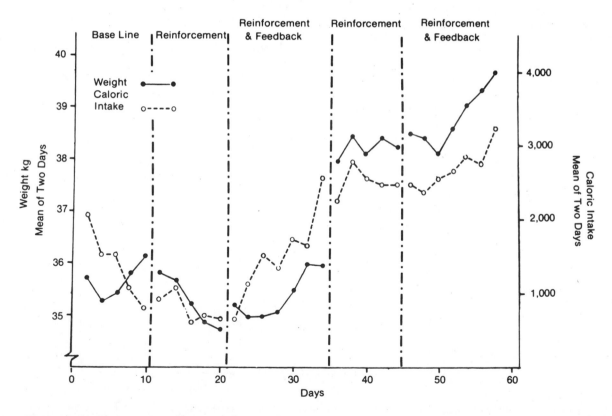

Figure 14. Data from an experiment examining the effect of feedback on the eating behavior of a patient with anorexia nervosa. (From "Behavior Modification of Anorexia Nervosa" by W. S. Agras *et al., Archives of General Psychiatry,* 1974, *30,* 279–286, Fig. 4. Copyright 1974, American Medical Association. Reprinted by permission.)

administered. In the single-blind assessment, only the patient typically is unaware of whether he or she is receiving a drug or a placebo.

Hersen and Barlow (1976) have pointed out the difficulties inherent in conducting the double-blind assessment in single-case analysis:

A major difficulty in obtaining a "true" double-blind trial in single case research is related to the experimental monitoring of data (i.e., making decisions as to when baseline observation is to be concluded and when various phases are to be introduced and withdrawn) throughout the course of investigation. It is possible to program phase lengths on an *a priori* basis, but then one of the major advantages of the single case strategy (i.e., its flexibility) is lost. However, even though the experimenter is fully aware of treatment changes, the spirit of the double-blind trial can be maintained by keeping the observer . . . unaware of drug and placebo changes. . . . We might note here additionally that despite the use of the double-blind procedure, the side effects of drugs in some cases . . . and the marked changes in behavior resulting from removal of active drug therapy in other cases often betray to nursing personnel whether a placebo or drug condition is currently in operation. (p. 206)

In spite of the aforementioned difficulties, which equally plague the group comparison researcher, there are some good examples of single-case work using drugs. In some, the drug is a constant across phases while behavioral strategies are evaluated (cf. Wells, Turner, Bellack, & Hersen, 1978); in others, the addition of a drug to a behavioral intervention

is assessed (Turner, Hersen, & Alford, 1974; Turner, Hersen, Bellack, & Wells, 1979); in still others (Liberman *et al.*, 1973; Williamson, Calpin, DiLorenzo, Garris, & Petti, 1981), the primary effects of the drug are evaluated.

Listed in Table 2 are some of the possible design strategies for assessing drugs. Designs 4–15 are all experimental in that the controlling effects of the drug on targeted behaviors may be ascertained. Also indicated is whether a single- or double-blind procedure is possible. Let us consider a published example of one of the designs (Number 13).

Liberman *et al.* (1973) assessed the effects of placebo and Stelazine on the social interaction of a 21-year-old chronic schizophrenic patient who was quite withdrawn. Social interaction was evaluated by noting the patient's willingness to engage in 18 daily half-minute chats with nursing personnel on the ward. Refusals to engage in such chats were labeled asocial responses. In the first phase (A), the patient was withdrawn from all medication. In the next phase (A'), he was administered a placebo, followed by 60 mg per day of Stelazine (Phase B). Next, he was withdrawn from Stelazine (Phase A'), and then Stelazine was reinstated (Phase B).

As can be seen in Figure 15, removal of the drugs in the first phase led to increased asocial behavior. With the introduction of placebo,

Table 2. Single-Case Experimental Drug Strategies[a]

No.	Design[b]	Type	Blind possible
1.	A-A_1	Quasi-experimental	None
2.	A-B	Quasi-experimental	None
3.	A_1-B	Quasi-experimental	Single or double
4.	A-A_1-A	Experimental	None
5.	A-B-A	Experimental	None
6.	A_1-B-A_1	Experimental	Single or double
7.	A_1-A-A_1	Experimental	Single or double
8.	B-A-B	Experimental	None
9.	B-A_1-B	Experimental	Single or double
10.	A-A_1-A-A_1	Experimental	Single or double
11.	A-B-A-B	Experimental	None
12.	A_1-B-A_1-B	Experimental	Single or double
13.	A-A_1-B-A_1-B	Experimental	Single or double
14.	A-A_1-A-A_1-BA_1-B	Experimental	Single or double
15.	A_1-B-A_1-C-A_1-C	Experimental	Single or double

[a] *From* Hersen and Barlow (1976), Table 6.1.
[b] A = no drug; A_1 = placebo; B = drug 1; C = drug 2.

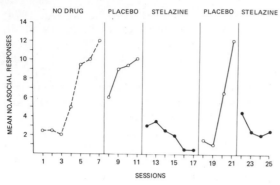

Figure 15. Average number of refusals to engage in a brief conversation. (From "Research Design for Analyzing Drug-Environment-Behavior Interactions" by R. P. Liberman *et al.*, *Journal of Nervous and Mental Disease*, 1973, *156*, 432–439, Fig. 2. Copyright © 1973 The Williams & Wilkins Co. Reprinted by permission.)

there was initial improvement and then a return of asocial behavior. The introduction of Stelazine in the third phase led to a marked improvement, followed by deterioration when Stelazine was removed in the fourth phase. The reinstitution of Stelazine in the fifth phase clearly documents the controlling effects of the drug on improved social responding.

Additional Designs

Although the basic A-B-A design and its numerous extensions have been used extensively and successfully by applied behavioral researchers to evaluate many therapeutic and educational problems, at times some of these designs simply are not appropriate. Inappropriateness may be due to practical, ethical, or design considerations. For example, if a given therapeutic procedure cannot be reversed or withdrawn (e.g., therapeutic instructions), then a different design (such as the multiple-baseline design across behaviors) could be employed to document the controlling effects of instructions on independent target behaviors. On the other hand, if an investigator is intent on showing the effects of some kind of shaping procedure where behavior is to be accelerated or decelerated, then the changing-criterion design would be more suitable. Finally, if the relative efficacy of two treatment strategies is to be contrasted in a single subject, then

the simultaneous treatment design (sometimes referred to as the *multielement* or *alternating-treatment design*) is the design strategy of choice.

Let us now consider each of these designs in turn, beginning with the three varieties of the multiple-baseline strategy.

Multiple Baseline

Baer *et al.* (1968) first described the multiple-baseline design as follows: "In the multiple-baseline technique, a number of responses are identified and measured over time to provide baselines against which changes can be evaluated. With these baselines established, the experimenter then applies an experimental variable to one of the behaviors, produces a change in it, and perhaps notes little or no change in the other baselines" (p. 94). The investigator then applies treatment to succeeding behaviors until some criterion point has been achieved. Generally, the treatment is then withheld until baseline stability has been achieved.

The strategy described above is referred to as the *multiple-baseline design across behaviors*. An assumption, of course, is that the targeted behaviors are independent of one another. Otherwise, treatment for one may lead to covariation in a second, thus obfuscating the controlling effects of the treatment. In essence, the multiple-baseline design across behaviors is a series of A-B designs, with every succeeding A phase applied to one targeted behavior until treatment has finally been applied to each. Treatment effects are inferred from the untreated baselines. That is, the controlling effects of treatment on dependent measures are documented if, and only if, change occurs when treatment is directly applied. In this respect, the design certainly is weaker than that in the A-B-A-B design, where the effects of controlling variables are directly shown.

Let us consider an example of the multiple-baseline design across behaviors. Bornstein *et al.* (1977) assessed the effects of social skills training on the role-played performance of an unassertive 8-year-old female third-grader (Jane). During baseline, specific behaviors were assessed (ratio of eye contact to speech duration, loudness of speech, number of requests, and overall assertiveness) in role-played scenarios requiring assertive responding. As can be seen in Figure 16, the baseline levels of responding for target behaviors were low. Treatment applied to each baseline under time-lagged and cumulative conditions led to marked increases in responding. The reader should note that only when social skills treatment was directly applied to each of the first three targeted behaviors did changes take place. There was no evidence that the targeted behaviors were correlated, nor did concurrent change take place in untreated target measures. In short, the controlling effects of social skills treatment were demonstrated. It also should be noted that although overall assertiveness was not directly treated, independent ratings of overall assertiveness reflected improvement throughout the course of treat-

ment, with all treatment gains generally maintained in follow-up.

Unless there is a specific theoretical rationale or the investigator has had prior experience working with a given set of target behaviors, there is no accurate way to predict whether the three or more targeted behaviors selected for treatment truly are independent of one another. Following the initial logic of the multiple-baseline design across behaviors, if change in target behaviors 1 and 2 occur as a result of treatment application to only the first, then the controlling effects of the treatment will not have been demonstrated. The baselines are correlated, but that does not necessarily imply that the treatment in general is ineffective. Kazdin and Kopel (1975) have offered a solution to this dilemma sometimes encountered in applied clinical research. They argue that

In case of ambiguity with the effects of a multiple-baseline design, it often is possible to include a partial reversal in the design for one of the behaviors. The reversal phase, or return to baseline, need not be employed for all of the behaviors (i.e., baselines) for which data are collected. Indeed, one of the reasons for using a multiple-baseline design is to avoid the ABAB design and its temporary removal of treatment. However, when the specific effect of the intervention is not evident in a multiple-baseline design, one may have to resort to a temporary withdrawal of the intervention for one of the baselines to determine the effect of the intervention. (p. 607)

A problem with the Kazdin and Kopel solution is that in the case of instructions, a *true* reversal or withdrawal is not possible. Thus, their recommendations apply best to the assessment of such techniques as feedback, reinforcement, and modeling.

A second type of multiple-baseline strategy is the one across settings. That is, a given treatment is applied to one subject (or group of subjects) across several different settings (e.g., different classroom periods). The logic of the design, however, remains the same. Baselines for separate settings increase in length, with treatment applied under time-lagged and cumulative conditions. Generally, only one behavior is targeted for time-lagged treatment. But there is no reason that concurrent changes in other behaviors should not be monitored.

An example of a multiple-baseline design across settings was presented by Allen (1973).

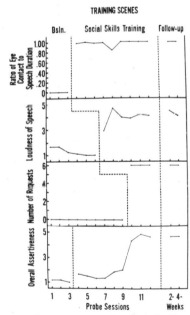

Figure 16. Probe sessions during baseline, social skills treatment, and follow-up for training scenes for Jane. A multiple-baseline analysis of ratio to speech duration of eye contact while speaking, loudness of speech, number of requests, and overall assertiveness. (From "Social-Skills Training for Unassertive Children: A Multiple-Baseline Analysis" by M. R. Bornstein *et al.*, 1977, *10*, 183–195, Fig. 1. Copyright 1977 by the Society for the Experimental Analysis of Behavior, Inc. Reprinted by permission.)

In his study, the subject was an 8-year-old boy with minimal brain damage who was attending a special summer camp. The target selected for modification was the child's high rate of bizarre verbalizations in four separate camp settings: walking on a trail, in the dining hall, in the cabin, and during education sessions. Treatment simply involved instructing the camp counselors to systematically ignore such bizarre verbalizations. (Previously, these verbalizations had attracted considerable social reinforcement from the counselors.)

The results of this experimental analysis appear in Figure 17. Following seven days of baseline, treatment was implemented for walking on the trail, with a resultant decrease in bizarre talk. However, no concurrent changes

were noted in the dining hall. Only when treatment was specifically applied to the dining hall did bizarre talk decrease. Note, however, that when treatment was applied in the dining hall, there were some concurrent decreases in bizarre talk in the cabin. Similarly, when treatment was applied in the cabin, there were some concurrent decreases noted during education sessions. Thus, the last two baselines were not totally independent. Indeed, this was an instance in which Kazdin and Kopel's (1975) recommendation of a partial reversal (withdrawal) for Baselines 3 and 4 would have added confirmatory evidence to the treatment's effectiveness.

A third type of multiple-baseline design strategy is the one across subjects. Although not strictly a *single case* study, the general principles of the multiple-baseline strategy apply. As described by Hersen and Barlow (1976), "a particular treatment is applied in sequence across *matched* subjects presumably exposed to 'identical' environmental conditions. Thus, as the same treatment variable is applied to succeeding subjects, the baseline for each subject increases in length. In contrast to the multiple baseline design across behaviors (the within-subject multiple baseline design), in the multiple baseline across subjects a single targeted behavior serves as the primary focus of inquiry. However, there is no experimental contraindication to monitoring concurrent . . . behaviors as well" (p. 228).

A recent example of the multiple-baseline design across subjects appeared in a paper by Ortega (1978). In this study, Ortega evaluated the effects of relaxation training on the spasticity level of four cerebral palsied adults. The dependent measures involved two timed trials of the Placing Test and the Turning Test from the Minnesota Rate of Manipulation Tests, which test the speed and dexterity of finger, hand, and arm movements.

Figure 18 shows that all four subjects' performance on the two tests was slow, but that slight improvements generally occurred throughout baseline as a function of repeated trials. However, only when progressive relaxation exercises were practiced by each subject did marked changes in speed take place. Moreover, follow-up data indicate that performance improvement was maintained for at least three

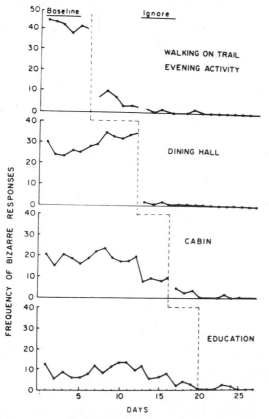

Figure 17. Daily number of bizarre verbalizations in specific camp settings. (From "Case Study: Implimentation of Behavior Modification Techniques in Summer Camp Setting" by G. J. Allen, *Behavior Therapy*, 1973, *4*, 570–575, Fig. 1. Copyright 1973 by *Behavior Therapy*. Reprinted by permission.)

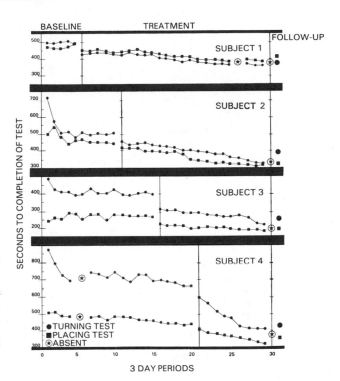

Figure 18. The time required to complete two trials of both the Placing Test and the Turning Text, from the Minnesota Rate of Manipulation Tests, during baseline, treatment, and follow-up phases of research. Testing sessions, which measured the amount of time required to complete various manual manipulations involving pegs and pegboard, were conducted every third working day throughout the experiment. During the treatment condition, relaxation exercises were performed every working day. Subject 1 was absent throughout Test Period 26 because of illness. Subject 4 was vacationing during Periods 5 and 6. Severe cold weather and heavy snows forced the closure of both sheltered workshop-facilities for eight working days, so Test Period 30 was canceled. (From "Relaxation Exercise with Cerebral Palsied Adults Showing Spasticity" by D. F. Ortega, *Journal of Applied Behavior Analysis*, 1978, *11*, 447–451, Fig. 1. Copyright 1978 by the Society for the Experimental Analysis of Behavior, Inc. Reprinted by permission.)

weeks. Performance improvement from baseline to treatment (averaged over the four subjects) was 28% on the Turning Test and 21% on the Placing Test.

Changing-Criterion Design

The changing-criterion design (cf. Hartmann & Hall, 1976) appears to be ideal for assessing shaping programs to accelerate or decelerate behaviors (e.g., increasing activity in overweight individuals; decreasing alcohol consumption in heavy drinkers). As a strategy, it bears characteristics similar to those of the A-B design and has some features of the multiple-baseline strategy. Following initial baseline observation, treatment is applied until a given criterion is achieved and stability at that level appears. Then, a more rigorous criterion is selected, and treatment is applied until the performance level is met. Changes in criterion level as a result of the second treatment are contrasted with the lower criterion in Treatment 1. Treatment is thereby continued in this stepwise fashion until the final criterion is met. "Thus, each phase of the design provides a

baseline for the following phase. When the rate of the target behavior changes with each stepwise change in the criterion, therapeutic change is replicated and experimental control is demonstrated" (Hartmann & Hall, 1976, p. 527).

An excellent example of the changing-criterion design was provided by Hartmann and Hall (1976) in their evaluation of a smoking-deceleration program. The baseline smoking level is graphically depicted in Panel A of Figure 19. In B (treatment), the criterion rate was established as 95% of baseline (i.e., 45 cigarettes per day). An escalating-response cost of $1 was set for smoking Cigarette 47, $2 for Cigarette 48, etc. If the subject smoked fewer than the criterion number of cigarettes, an escalating bonus of 10 cents per cigarette was established. Subsequent treatment in C through G involved the same contingencies, with the criterion for each succeeding phase set at 94% of the previous one.

The experimental analysis clearly shows the efficacy of the contingencies established in reducing cigarette smoking by 6% or more from the preceding phase. In addition, within the individual analysis, there were six clear

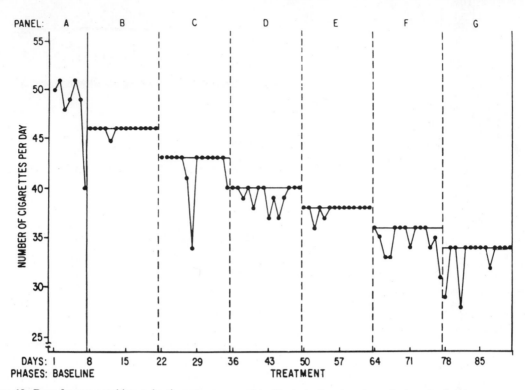

Figure 19. Data from a smoking-reduction program used to illustrate the stepwise criterion-change design. The solid horizontal lines indicate the criterion for each treatment phase. (From "The Changing Criterion Design" by D. P. Hartmann and R. V. Hall, *Journal of Applied Behavior Analysis*, 1976, *9*, 527–532, Fig. 2. Copyright 1976 by the Society for the Experimental Analysis of Behavior, Inc. Reprinted by permission.)

replications of the treatment's effect. In short, we agree with Hartmann and Hall (1976) that "the changing criterion design is capable of providing convincing demonstrations of experimental control, seems applicable to a wide range of problematic behaviors, and should be a useful addition to applied individual subject methodology" (p. 532).

Simultaneous Treatment Design

In the simultaneous treatment design (cf. Kazdin & Geesey, 1977; Kazdin & Hartmann, 1978), there is the opportunity to compare two or more treatments within a single subject. This, of course, is in marked contrast to the other strategies we have discussed to this point, wherein design limitations *do not* allow for such comparisons.

As with all single-case designs, there are particular circumstances under which the simultaneous treatment design may be imple-

mented. Thus, there must be the opportunity to evaluate at least two stimulus dimensions (e.g., different times of day, locations, or treatment agents). In a classroom study, different time periods may be the stimulus dimension (morning versus afternoon). During the baseline phase, the targeted behavior is evaluated in each of the stimulus dimensions. Then two (or possibly more) interventions (e.g., individual versus group contingencies) are applied concurrently in each of the stimulus dimensions. In order to avoid a possible treatment–stimulus dimension confound, each of the two interventions is counterbalanced across dimensions. For example, on the first day, Treatment A is administered in the morning; Treatment B is administered in the afternoon. On the second day, Treatment B is administered in the morning; Treatment A is administered in the afternoon, etc. The results of the two treatments are plotted and visually examined. (It is possible to evaluate the effects of counterbalanced treatment with statistical analyses similar to those employed in the analysis of a Latin square design; see Benjamin, 1965.) In the third phase of the study, the most efficacious treatment is applied across each of the stimulus conditions.

Let us look at an example of this design in a study carried out by Kazdin and Geesey (1977). In this investigation of classroom behavior, the effects of token reinforcement for the subject alone versus token reinforcement for the subject and the rest of his class were evaluated, with percentage of attentive behavior as the dependent measure. This study was done in counterbalanced fashion for two separate classroom periods. Figure 20 (bottom part) reveals that the percentage of attentive behavior during baseline ranged from 40% to 60%. Implementation of the token program for the subject alone (i.e., self) led to an average percentage of attentive behavior of 72.5%. By contrast, the token program for the subject and the rest of the class (i.e., class: backup reinforcers were earned for himself and the entire class) led to 91% attentive behavior. Thus, in the third phase, the superior procedure was continued across both class periods, with a mean percentage of attentive behavior of 91.2% attained.

In further considering the simultaneous treatment design, Kazdin and Hartmann (1978) pointed out that the behaviors selected for study must be those that can rapidly shift and that *do not* evince carry-over effects after termination. By necessity, this would preclude the evaluation of certain drugs in this kind of design. Also, because of the counterbalancing requirement, relatively few behaviors can be evaluated (probably not more than three). Finally, "The client must make at least two sorts of discriminations. First, the client must discriminate that the treatment agents and time periods are not associated with a particular intervention because the interventions vary across each of the dimensions. Second, the client must be able to distinguish the separate interventions. One would expect that the greater the discrimination made by the client the more likely there will be clear effects or discrepancies between (among) treatments" (Kazdin & Hartmann, 1978, p. 919).

Statistical Analysis

There has probably been no aspect of single-case research in recent times more fraught with controversy than that involving statistical analysis (cf. Baer, 1977; Hartmann, 1974; Jones *et al.*, 1977; Kazdin, 1976; Keselman & Leventhal, 1974; Kratchowill, Alden, Demuth, Dawson, Panicucci, Arntson, McMurray, Hempstead, & Levin, 1974; Michael 1974a,b; Thoresen & Elashoff, 1974). The crit-

Figure 20. Attentive behavior of Max across experimental conditions. Baseline (base): no experimental intervention. Token reinforcement (token rft): implementation of the token program, in which tokens earned could purchase events for himself (self) or the entire class (class). Second phase of token reinforcement (token rft₂): implementation of the class exchange intervention across both time periods. The upper panel presents the overall data collapsed across time periods and interventions. The lower panel presents the data according to the time periods across which the interventions were balanced, although the interventions were presented only in the last two phases. (From "Simultaneous-Treatment Design Comparisons of the Effects of Earning Reinforcers for One's Peers versus for Oneself" by A. E. Kazdin and S. Geesey, *Behavior Therapy*, 1977, 8, 682–693, Fig. 2. Copyright 1977 by *Behavior Therapy*. Reprinted by permission.)

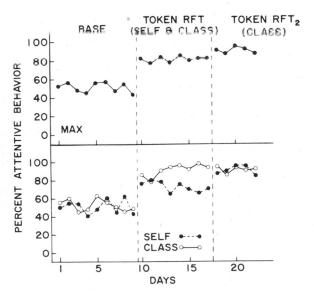

ics and the advocates of the use of statistics are equally intense about attempting to persuade colleagues and students to their respective positions. In this section, it is not our purpose to attempt to resolve the controversy. Rather, it is our explicit intention to look at the arguments and to ferret out the data in relation to these arguments. In so doing, we will briefly examine the opposing positions while considering some of the recommended statistical procedures.

The Case Against

The basic argument against the use of statistics in single-case research involves the distinction between *clinical* and *statistical* significance. Indeed, one of the specific arguments against the group comparison method is that statistics do not give the experimenter a "true" picture of the individual pattern of results. That is, positive and negative treatment effects cancel out; in addition, statistics may possibly yield significance from very weak overall treatment strategies. Thus, if the effect of treatment is not sufficiently substantial to be detected by visual inspection (i.e., considerable overlap of data between baseline and treatment phases), then the treatment applied is not clinically potent and its controlling effects have not been clearly documented. On the other hand, if treatment is of sufficient potency to yield considerable clinical change, then there is the expectation that such change may approach the social norm (i.e., social rather than statistical validation) (see Kazdin, 1977). This being the case, statistical analysis should prove superfluous.

Kazdin (1976) has summarized the case against statistical analysis in single-subject research as follows: "Individuals who advocate non-statistical criteria for evaluation caution against 'teasing out' subtle effects because these effects are least likely to be replicable. Moreover, involving statistical significance as the only criterion for evaluation does not encourage the investigator to obtain clear unequivocal experimental control over behavior. Finally, many investigators believe that in clinical work statistical evaluation is simply not relevant for assessing therapeutic change" (p. 272).

The Case For

The advocates of statistical analyses for single-case research recommend them for several reasons. The most persuasive argument has been presented by Jones *et al.* (1977). In contrasting the statistical approach with visual analysis for a number of studies published in the *Journal of Applied Behavior Analysis,* it was found that in some instances, time-series analyses (cf. Glass, Willson, & Gottman, 1975) confirmed the experimenters' conclusions based on visual inspection. In other instances, time-series analyses did not confirm the experimenters' conclusions. In still other cases, time-series analyses indicated the presence of statistically significant findings not identified by the experimenters. Consequently, Jones *et al.* (1977) concluded that "All three kinds of supplementary information provided by time-series analysis are useful. It is rewarding to have one's visual impressions supported by statistical analysis. It is humbling and/or educational to have other impressions not supported. And it is clearly beneficial to have unseen changes in the data detected by a supplementary method of analysis. It is difficult to see how operant researchers can lose in the application of time-series analysis to their data" (p. 166).

Statistical analysis may prove helpful when baseline stability is difficult to establish and considerably overlap exists between the baseline and the treatment phases. As pointed out by Kazdin (1976), "Whereas visual inspection of the data often entails noting distinct changes in trends across phases, statistical analysis can scrutinize continuous shifts across phases where there is no change in trend" (p. 270).

A third use advocated for statistical analysis is for investigations in so-called new areas of research. Presumably, in these newer areas, therapeutic techniques are unlikely to be fully refined and developed; hence, there is a lesser likelihood that marked clinical differences will appear on visual inspection. Thus, in the early stages of research, it is argued that statistics may reveal small but important differences with clinical implications.

A fourth reason offered for the use of statistical analyses (cf. Kazdin, 1976) is the increased intrasubject variability in uncontrolled research settings (e.g., in the natural environment). Again, the argument put forth is that the statistical approach may detect changes that could eventually have some clinical impact when the specific therapeutic or educational strategy is later refined.

T Test and ANOVA

A number of *t*-test and analysis-of-variance (ANOVA) techniques have been adapted for use in single-case research across the different phases of a given study (cf. Gentile, Roden, & Klein, 1972; Shine & Bower, 1971). If we compare the ANOVA in single-case research and group comparison designs, the treatment factor in the single-case study is analogous to the between-group factor. Similarly, the number of observations within a phase is comparable to the within-group factor. In developing their ANOVA technique, Gentile *et al.* (1972) assumed that the performance of a response within a phase is independent of each other response. However, it should be noted that they were aware of "the high autocorrelation of adjacent observations" (Kazdin, 1976, p. 276). To control for this factor, Gentile *et al.* suggested combining nonadjacent phases in the A-B-A-B design (i.e., $A_1 + A_2$; $B_1 + B_2$) in computing the statistical analysis.

Despite the correction factor suggested by Gentile *et al.*, there are two basic problems in using the ANOVA model. First and foremost is the issue of dependency. As argued by Kazdin (1976), "combining phases does not at all affect the problem of non-independent data points and the decreased variability among observations *within* phases, two factors that can positively bias *F* tests" (p. 277). The second is that the ANOVA essentially contrasts the means of each phase. Thus, the statistical model proposed fails to take into account data trends as represented by the slope of the curve. In short, it would appear that the criticisms of applications of traditional group statistics to the single-case study are warranted (see Hartmann, 1974; Keselman & Leventhal, 1974).

Time-Series Analysis

Time-series analysis controls for the problems alluded to above in that the statistical strategy takes into account change in the level, change in the slope of the curve, and the presence or absence of drift or slope in the curve (see Jones *et al.*, 1977). Indeed, Figure 21 depicts six illustrative treatment effects that may be ascertained through the use of time-series analyses. As noted by Jones *et al.*, in some instances the mere visual analysis of such data might yield erroneous conclusions.

Despite the obvious utility of the time-series approach, it is not without its limitations. First, to meet the requirements of the analysis, a fairly large number of observations may be required (i.e., 50–100). Although feasible in some investigations, this number would preclude the use of statistics in many others where short-term treatment effects are being evaluated. Second, and equally important at this time, time series analysis requires computerized programs and the ready availability of the requisite facilities. Although in time we would expect them to proliferate, these facilities are now relatively scarce.

Additional Comments

There can be no doubt that statistical analysis for single-case research has its merits and should proliferate in the future. Also, the reader should keep in mind that many other statistical strategies (not discussed in this chapter) have appeared and undoubtedly will continue to appear in the press. (For a more comprehensive coverage of the area, the reader is referred to Kazdin, 1976; Kratchowill, 1978.)

Replication

In the previous section, we looked at some of the statistical techniques that might serve to confirm (or even to supplant) the experimenter's visual analysis of his or her data. The objective in using a statistical technique is to guarantee that the visual inspection of trends indicating controlling effects of treatment variables on dependent measures is indeed valid. Assuming a high concordance between a visual and a statistical analysis of the data (thus confirming the treatment's efficacy for the one subject), the question, of course, remains

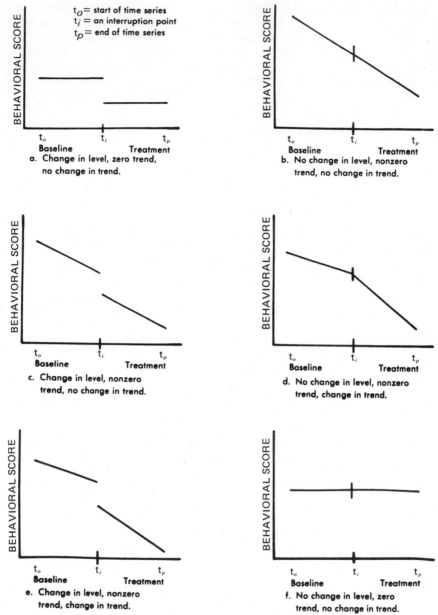

Figure 21. Six illustrative treatment effects: combinations of level and trend changes detectable by time-series analysis. (From "Time-Series Analysis in Operant Research" by R. R. Jones *et al.*, *Journal of Applied Behavior Analysis*, 1973, 6, 517–531, Fig. 1. Copyright 1973 by the Society for the Experimental Analysis of Behavior, Inc. Reprinted by permission.)

whether the same effect can be repeated in a different subject. Thus, replication is concerned with the reliability and the generality of findings.

Elsewhere, Hersen and Barlow (1976) noted that "Replication is at the heart of any science. In all science, replication serves at least two purposes: First, to establish the reliability of previous findings and, second, to determine the generality of these findings under differing conditions. These goals, of course, are intrinsically interrelated. Each time that certain results are replicated under different conditions, this not only establishes generality of findings, but also increases confidence in the reliability of these findings" (p. 317).

The importance of replication in single-case research should be quite obvious from a strictly scientific standpoint. Also, however, critics of the single-case research approach have chastised applied behavioral researchers for reporting chance findings in single cases, despite the apparent demonstration of experimental control in each. Thus, as in the use of statistics in the experimental analysis of behavior, replication (or its absence) is a controversial point.

In this section, we are concerned with the description of three types of replication strategies referred to in Hersen and Barlow (1976): (1) direct; (2) clinical; and (3) systematic. For each type of replication series, the specific issues and guidelines are considered.

Direct Replication

Sidman (1960) has defined direct replication as "repetition of a given experiment by the same investigator" (p. 72). This could involve replication of a procedure within the same subject or across several similar subjects. As argued by Hersen and Barlow (1976), "While repetition on the same subject increases confidence in the reliability of findings and is used occasionally in applied research, generality of findings across clients can be ascertained only by replication on different subjects" (p. 310). Generally, the same investigator (or research team) repeats the study in the same setting (e.g., school, hospital, or clinic) with a set of clients who present with a similar educational or psychological disorder (e.g., unipolar nonpsychotic depression). Although such clients may differ to some extent on demographic variables such as age, education, and sex, it is better for a direct replication series if these are closely matched. This is of special importance for instances where failure to replicate occurs. In such cases, failure, then, should not be attributed to differences in demographic variables. Of paramount concern is that the identical procedure be applied

across the different subjects. Otherwise, possible failures or unusual successes may occur, with attribution to subject characteristics erroneously assumed.

Hersen and Barlow (1976) have described several series where direct replications have been undertaken. In one, the initial experiment was successful followed by two replications in the treatment of agoraphobia (Agras, Leitenberg, & Barlow, 1968). (The same held true for a study reported by Hersen et al., 1973 on token economy and neurotic depression.) In a second example (Mills, Agras, Barlow, & Mills, 1973), there were four successful replications with design modifications during replications. In still another series (Wincze, Leitenberg, & Agras, 1972), there were mixed results in nine replications.

When mixed results occur, the investigator should search for the causes of failure and refine the treatment procedures. According to Hersen and Barlow (1976), if one successful experiment is followed by three successful replications, then it is useful to begin a systematic replication series, in which different behaviors in the same setting or similar behavior in different settings are treated by different therapists. If, on the other hand, one successful treatment is followed by two failures to replicate, the investigator should carefully study the variables that account for the failure. This can be as important as a successful attempt at direct replication, inasmuch as new hypotheses may be generated, leading to vastly improved treatments.

Clinical Replication

Hersen and Barlow (1976) have defined "*clinical replication* as the "administration of a treatment package containing two or more distinct treatment procedures by the same investigator or group of investigators. These procedures would be administered in a specific setting to a series of clients presenting similar combinations of multiple behavioral and emotional problems, which cluster together" (p. 336). Examples might be schizophrenia or childhood autism (e.g., Lovaas, Koegel, Simmons, & Long, 1973).

"The usefulness of this effort also depends to some extent on the consistency or reliability of the diagnostic category. If the clustering of the target behaviors is inconsistent, then the patients within the series would be so heterogeneous that the same treatment package could not be applied to successive patients. For this reason, and because of the advanced nature of the research effort, clinical replications are presently not common in the literature'' (Hersen & Barlow, 1976, p. 336).

Guidelines for clinical replication are essentially the same as for direct replication. However, interclient characteristics are, by definition, likely to be more heterogeneous, thus necessitating a longer replication series than in the case of direct replication. Also, successful clinical replication should lead to a systematic replication series.

Systematic Replication

Systematic replication is defined ''as any attempt to replicate findings from a direct replication series, varying settings, behavior change agents, behavior disorders, or any combination thereof. It would appear that any successful systematic replication series in which one or more of the above-mentioned factors is varied also provides further information on generality of findings across clients since new clients are usually included in these efforts'' (Hersen & Barlow, 1976, p. 339).

As for specific guidelines, systematic replication ideally begins after one successful initial experiment and three direct replications have been carried out. However, although the word *systematic* is included, usually such a series is carried out by researchers, either concurrently or in succession, in a number of settings. Some researchers may be in direct communication with one another, but more frequently, it turns out that they are simply working on similar problems, hence the possibility (albeit not really systematic) of replications with variation. Probably the largest such series in the behavioral literature is the one involving dozens of single-case studies showing the efficacy of differential procedures for adults and children (cf. Hersen & Barlow, 1976, pp. 344–352).

In examining a systematic replication series, it is important to note differences in therapists, treatment settings, and clients. In that sense,

the objective of a systematic replication series is to determine exceptions to the rule (i.e., those instances in which a given treatment strategy will not work for a given client or for a particular therapist). This certainly was the case when Wahler (1969) found that differential attention *was not* an effective treatment for dealing with oppositional children. Thus, the limits of applicability of differential attention were ascertained.

Since a systematic replication series involves decentralized research (i.e., in several research settings) and since the search for exceptions to the rule is inevitable in any scientific endeavor, there really can be no finite ending to a systematic replication series. As more data are adduced, however, clinicians applying a given technique should have a greater sense of its likelihood of being effective and successful. This, then, should decrease the trial-and-error approach followed by many practitioners of therapeutic and educational strategies.

Summary and Conclusions

Of the research stragegies employed by behavioral researchers, the single-case approach has been the one uniquely tied in with the behavioral tradition. As a research strategy, the single-case approach has had a long and interesting history. In this chapter, we first examined the historical roots of the current experimental analysis-of-behavior model. Then, we considered general issues, such as intrasubject variability, intersubject variability, generality of findings, and variability as related to generality. We next looked at some of the general procedures that characterize most single-case research (repeated measurement, choice of a baseline, the changing of one variable at a time, length of phases, reversal and withdrawal, and evaluation of irreversible procedures). This was followed by a discussion of basic A-B-A designs, their extensions, and the additional designs required when conditions for the A-B-A strategies cannot be met. We briefly looked at the thorny issue of statistical analysis in single-case research and ended with a discussion of direct, clinical, and systematic replication.

In conclusion, we should point out that the field is not static and that newer design and statistical techniques will undoubtedly emerge over the course of the next few years. This, of course, is a healthy phenomenon that we can only applaud. Moreover, we should acknowledge that there are some inherent limitations in all design strategies, including single-case analysis, that all researchers need to recognize. Thus, we see nothing inherently wrong in, at times, using the single-case approach to generate treatment hypotheses that subsequently may be refined and then pitted against one another in larger-scaled group-comparison studies.

References

Agras, W. S., Leitenberg, H., & Barlow, D. H. Social reinforcement in the modification of agoraphobia. *Archives of General Psychiatry*, 1968, *19*, 423–427.

Agras, W. S., Barlow, D. H., Chapin, H. N., Abel, G. G., & Leitenberg, H., Behavior modification of anorexia nervosa. *Archives of General Psychiatry*, 1974, *30*, 279–286.

Allen, G. J. Case study: Implimentation of behavior modification techniques in summer camp setting. *Behavior Therapy*, 1973, *4*, 570–575.

Allen, K. E., Hart, B. M., Buell, J. S., Harris, F. R., & Wolf, M. M. Effects of social reinforcement on isolate behavior of a nursery school child. *Child Development*, 1964, *35*, 511–518.

Ayllon, T., & Azrin, N. H. The measurement and reinforcement of behavior of psychotics. *Behaviour Research and Therapy*, 1965, *8*, 357–383.

Baer, D. M. Perhaps it would be better not to know everything. *Journal of Applied Behavior Analysis*, 1977, *10*, 167–172.

Baer, D. M., Wolf, M. M., & Risley, T. R. Some current dimensions of applied behavior analysis. *Journal of Applied Behavior Analysis*, 1968, *1*, 91–97.

Barlow, D. H., & Hersen, M. Single case experimental designs: Uses in applied clinical research. *Archives of General Psychiatry*, 1973, *29*, 319–325.

Barlow, D. H., Agras, W. S., Leitenberg, H., Callahan, E. J., & Moore, R. C. The contribution of therapeutic instruction to covert sensitization. *Behaviour Research and Therapy*, 1972, *10*, 411–415.

Barlow, D. H., Blanchard, D. B., Hayes, S. C., & Epstein, L. H. Single case designs and clinical biofeedback experimentation. *Biofeedback and Self-Regulation*, 1977, *2*, 221–236.

Bellack, A. S., & Schwartz, J. S. Assessment for self-control programs. In M. Hersen & A. S. Bellack (Eds.), *Behavioral assessment: A practical handbook*. New York: Pergamon Press, 1976.

Benjamin, L. S. A special latin squre for the use of each subject "as his own control." *Psychometrika*, 1965, *30*, 499–513.

Bergin, A. E. Some implications of psychotherapy research for therapeutic practice. *Journal of Abnormal Psychology*, 1966, *71*, 235–246.

Bergin, A. E., & Strupp, H. H. *Changing frontiers in the science of psychotherapy*. New York: Aldine-Atherton, 1972.

Bijou, S. W., Peterson, R. F., Harris, F. R., Allen, K. E., & Johnston, M. S. Methodology for experimental studies of young children in natural settings. *Psychological Record*, 1969, *19*, 177–210.

Bornstein, M. R., Bellack, A. S., & Hersen, M. Social-skills training for unassertive children: A multiple-baseline analysis. *Journal of Applied Behavior Analysis*, 1977, *10*, 183–195.

Breuer, J., & Freud, S. *Studies on hysteria*. New York: Basic Books, 1957.

Campbell, D. T., & Stanley, J. C. Experimental and quasi-experimental designs for research and teaching. Chicago: Rand-McNally, 1966.

Chassan, J. B. *Research design in clinical psychology and psychiatry*. New York: Appleton-Century-Crofts, 1967.

Eisler, R. M., Hersen, M., & Agras, W. S, Effects of videotape and instructional feedback on nonverbal marital interaction: An analog study. *Behavior Therapy*, 1973, *4*, 551–558.

Epstein, L. H., & Hersen, M. Behavioral control of hysterical gagging. *Journal of Clinical Psychology*, 1974, *30*, 102–104.

Eysenck, H. J. The effects of psychotherapy: An evaluation. *Journal of Consulting Psychology*, 1952, *16*, 319–324.

Fisher, R. A. On the mathematical foundations of the theory of statistics. In *Theory of statistical estimation* (Proceeding of the Cambridge Philosophical Society), 1925.

Gentile, J. R., Roden, A. H., & Klein, R. D. An analysis of variance model for the intrasubject replication design. *Journal of Applied Behavior Analysis*, 1972, *5*, 193–198.

Glass, G. V., Willson, V. L., & Gottman, J. M. *Design and analysis of time-series experiments*. Boulder: Colorado Associated University Press, 1974.

Hartmann, D. P. Forcing square pegs into roundholes: Some comments on "an analysis-of-variance model for the intrasubject replication design." *Journal of Applied Behavior Analysis*, 1974, *7*, 635–638.

Hartmann, D. P., & Hall, R. V. The changing criterion design. *Journal of Applied Behavior Analysis*, 1976, *9*, 527–532.

Hersen, M. Self-assessment of fear. *Behavior Therapy*, 1973, *4*, 241–257.

Hersen, M. Do behavior therapists use self-reports as the major criteria? *Behavioural Analysis and Modification*, 1978, *2*, 328–334.

Hersen, M. Limitations and problems in the clinical application of behavioral techniques in psychiatric settings. *Behavior Therapy*, 1979, *10*, 65–80.

Hersen, M., & Barlow, D. H. *Single case experimental designs: Strategies for studying behavior change*. New York: Pergamon Press, 1976.

Hersen, M., & Bellack, A. S. (Eds.). *Behavioral assessment: A practical handbook*. New York: Pergamon Press, 1976.

Hersen, M., & Bellack, A. S. (Eds.). *Behavior therapy*

in the psychiatric setting. Baltimore: Williams & Wilkins, 1978.

Hersen, M., Eisler, R. M., Alford, G. S., & Agras, W. S. Effects of token economy on neurotic depression: An experimental analysis. *Behavior Therapy*, 1973, *4*, 392–397.

Johnston, J. M. Punishment of human behavior. *American Psychologist*, 1972, *27*, 1033–1054.

Jones, R. R., Vaught, R. S., & Weinrott, M. Time-series analysis in operant research. *Journal of Applied Behavior Analysis*, 1977, *10*, 151–166.

Kallman, W. M., Hersen, M., & O'Toole, D. H. The use of social reinforcement in a case of conversion reaction. *Behavior Therapy*, 1975, *6*, 411–413.

Kazdin, A. E. Methodological and assessment considerations in evaluating reinforcement programs in applied settings. *Journal of Applied Behavior Analysis*, 1973, *6*, 517–531.

Kazdin, A. E. *Behavior modification in applied settings.* Homewood, Ill.: Dorsey Press, 1975.

Kazdin, A. E. Statistical analysis for single-case experimental designs. In M. Hersen & D. H. Barlow (Eds.), *Single case experimental designs: Strategies for studying behavior change.* New York: Pergamon Press, 1976.

Kazdin, A. E. Assessing the clinical or applied importance of behavior change through social validation. *Behavior Modification*, 1977, *1*, 427–451.

Kazdin, A. E. *History of behavior modification.* Baltimore: University Park Press, 1978.

Kazdin, A. E. *Research design in clinical psychology.* New York: Harper & Row, 1980.

Kazdin, A. E., & Geesey, S. Simultaneous-treatment design comparisons of the effects of earning reinforcers for one's peers versus for oneself. *Behavior Therapy*, 1977, *8*, 682–693.

Kazdin, A. E., & Hartmann, D. P. The simultaneous-treatment design. *Behavior Therapy*, 1978, *9*, 912–922.

Kazdin, A. E., & Kopel, S. A. On resolving ambiguities of the multiple-baseline design: Problems and recommendations. *Behavior Therapy*, 1975, *6*, 601–608.

Keselman, H. J., & Leventhal, L. Concerning the statistical procedures enumerated by Gentile *et al.*: Another perspective. *Journal of Applied Behavior Analysis*, 1974, *7*, 643–645.

Kratochwill, T. R. (Ed.). *Single subject research: Strategies for evaluating change.* New York: Academic Press, 1978.

Kratochwill, T., Alden, K., Demuth, D., Dawson, D., Panicucci, C., Arntson, P., McMurray, N., Hempstead, J., & Levin, J. A further consideration in the application of an analysis-of-variance model for the intrasubject replication design. *Journal of Applied Behavior Analysis*, 1974, *7*, 629–633.

Leitenberg, H. The use of single-case methodology in psychotherapy research. *Journal of Abnormal Psychology*, 1973, *82*, 87–101.

Liberman, R. P., & Davis, J. Drugs and behavior analysis. In M. Hersen, R. M. Eisler, & P. M. Miller (Eds.), *Progress in behavior modification*, Vol. 1. New York: Academic Press, 1975.

Liberman, R. P., Davis, J., Moon, W., & Moore, J. Research design for analyzing drug-environment-behavior interactions. *Journal of Nervous and Mental Disease*, 1973, *156*, 432–439.

Lombardo, T. W., & Turner, S. M. Thought-stopping in the control of obsessive ruminations. *Behavior Modification*, 1979, *3*, 267–272.

Lovaas, O. I., Koegel, R., Simmons, J. Q., & Long, J. D. Some generalization and follow-up measures on autistic children in behavior therapy. *Journal of Applied Behavior Analysis*, 1973, *5*, 131–166.

Mann, R. A. The behavior-therapeutic use of contingency contracting to control an adult behavior problem: Weight control. *Journal of Applied Behavior Analysis*, 1972, *5*, 99–109.

Martin, J. E., & Epstein, L. H. Evaluating treatment effectiveness in cerebral palsy: Single subject designs. *Physical Therapy*, 1976, *56*, 285–294.

Max, L. W. Breaking up a homosexual fixation by the conditioned reaction technique: A case study. *Psychological Bulletin*, 1935, *32*, 734 (abstract).

Meichenbaum, D. A cognitive-behavior modification approach to assessment. In M. Hersen & A. S. Bellack (Eds.), *Behavioral assessment: A practical handbook.* New York: Pergamon Press, 1976.

Michael, J. Statistical inference for individual organism research: Mixed blessing or curse? *Journal of Applied Behavior Analysis*, 1974, *7*, 647–653. (a)

Michael, J. Statistical inference for individual organism research: Some reactions to a suggestion by Gentile, Roden, & Klein. *Journal of Applied Behavior Analysis*, 1974, *7*, 627–628. (b)

Miller, P. M. An experimental analysis of retention control training in the treatment of nocturnal enuresis in two institutionalized adolescents. *Behavior Therapy*, 1973, *4*, 288–294.

Mills, H. L., Agras, W. S., Barlow, D. H., & Mills, J. R. Compulsive rituals treated by response prevention: An experimental analysis. *Archives of General Psychiatry*, 1973, *28*, 524–529.

Ortega, D. F. Relaxation exercise with cerebral palsied adults showing spasticity. *Journal of Applied Behavior Analysis*, 1978, *11*, 447–451.

Paul, G. L. Strategy of outcome research in psychotherapy. *Journal of Consulting Psychology*, 1967, *31*, 104–118.

Risley, T. R., & Wolf, M. M. Strategies for analysing behavioral change over time. In J. Nesselroade & H. Reese (Eds.), *Life-span developmental psychology: Methodological issues.* New York: Academic Press, 1972.

Rubenstein, E. A., & Parloff, M. B. Research problems in psychotherapy. In E. A. Rubenstein & M. B. Parloff (Eds.), *Research in psychotherapy*, Vol. 1. Washington, D.C.: American Psychological Association, 1959.

Shapiro, M. B. The single case in clinical-psychological research. *Journal of General Psychology*, 1966, *74*, 3–23.

Shapiro, M. B., & Ravenette, A. T. A preliminary experiment of paranoid delusions. *Journal of Mental Science*, 1959, *105*, 295–312.

Shine, L. C., & Bower, S. M. A one-way analysis of variance for single subject designs. *Educational and Psychological Measurement*, 1971, *31*, 105–113.

Sidman, M. *Tactics of scientific research: Evaluating experimental data in psychology.* New York: Basic Books, 1960.

Skinner, B. F. Operant behavior. In W. K. Konig (Ed.),

Operant behavior: Areas of research and application. New York: Appleton-Century-Crofts, 1966.

Thomas, E. J. Research and service in single-case experimentation: Conflicts and choices. *Social Work Research and Abstracts,* 1978, *14,* 20–31.

Thoresen, C. E. The intensive design: An intimate approach to counseling research. Paper read at American Educational Research Association, Chicago, April 1972.

Thoresen, C. E., & Elashoff, J. D. "An analysis-of-variance model for intrasubject replication design": Some additional comments. *Journal of Applied Behavior Analysis,* 1974, *7,* 639–641.

Turner, S. M., Hersen, M., & Alford, H. Case histories and shorter communications. *Behaviour Research and Therapy,* 1974, *12,* 259–260.

Turner, S. M., Hersen, M., Bellack, A. S., & Wells, K. C. Behavioral treatment of obsessive-compulsive neurosis. *Behaviour Research and Therapy,* 1979, *17,* 95–106.

Van Hasselt, V. B., Hersen, M., Bellack, A. S., Rosenblum, N., & Lamparski, D. Tripartite assessment of the effects of systematic desensitization in a multiphobic child: An experimental analysis. *Journal of Behavior Therapy and Experimental Psychiatry,* 1979, *10,* 51–56.

Wahler, R. G. Oppositional children: A quest for parental reinforcement control. *Journal of Applied Behavior Analysis,* 1969, *2,* 159–170.

Watson, J. B., & Rayner, R. Conditioned emotional reactions. *Journal of Experimental Psychology,* 1920, *3,* 1–14.

Wells, K. C., Turner, S. M., Bellack, A. S., & Hersen, M. Effects of cue-controlled relaxation on psychomotor seizures: An experimental analysis. *Behaviour Research and Therapy,* 1978, *16,* 51–53.

Williamson, D. A., Calpin, J. P., DiLorenzo, T. M., Garris, R. P., & Petti, T. A. Combining dexedrine (dextro-amphetamine) and activity feedback for the treatment of hyperactivity. *Behavior Modification,* 1981, *5,* 399–416.

Wincze, J. P., Leitenberg, H., & Agras, W. S. The effects of token reinforcement and feedback on the delusional verbal behavior of chronic paranoid schizophrenics. *Journal of Applied Behavior Analysis,* 1972, *5,* 247–262.

Yates, A. J. *Behavior Therapy.* New York: Wiley, 1970.

PART III

General Issues and Extensions

CHAPTER 8

Training Paraprofessionals

Anthony M. Graziano and James N. Katz

Introduction

The paraprofessional movement in mental health has shown remarkable growth in size and diversity since World War II. As summarized by Alley and Blanton (1978), over a thousand articles, books, and unpublished papers concerned with paraprofessionals appeared from 1966 to 1977. Several junior colleges began offering curricula for mental-health paraprofessional training (Gershon & Biller, 1977; Young, True, & Packard, 1974). Sobey (1970) found 10,415 paraprofessionals employed in the 185 mental health projects she studied in the late 1960s. These new mental-health workers had been recruited from among poverty groups, high school dropouts, and college and junior college students and graduates, and they filled positions from ward aides to intake interviewers and psychotherapists. Levenson and Reff (1970) estimated that 40% of all positions in the mental health field would eventually be filled by paraprofessionals. Cohen (1976) estimated there were up to 2 million paraprofessionals employed in all human service areas, including mental health.

The rationale for the use of paraprofessionals is centered on the notion that minimally trained personnel can have a positive impact on an overly professionalized field; that is, they might affect the cost-efficiency of the delivery of services and the creation and implementation of new services with their presumably fresh, unprofessionalized input. It is further assumed that if they are indigenous to the client population, the paraprofessionals are better able than professionals to establish rapport, trust, and cooperation with the clients. In addition, the indigenous workers might themselves benefit from being in the "helper" role, as suggested by Reissman's (1965) "helper-therapy" principle.

However, the primary rationale, which has been stated repeatedly, is that paraprofessionals offer great potential to relieve the personnel shortage in mental health services. The importance of this rationale is evident from the many books and articles in which this issue is cited either in the titles or in the opening sentence (e.g., Gardner, 1975; Sobey, 1970).

In this paper, we briefly review the historical development of the paraprofessional field and examine its major research and a sample of its training programs. Because of the behavioral emphasis of this book and the large number of papers that make up the field, we will limit our critical evaluation of specific training programs primarily to those utilizing

Anthony M. Graziano and James N. Katz • Department of Psychology, State University of New York at Buffalo, Buffalo, New York 14226.

some form of social learning model and emphasizing behavioral approaches.

Historical Changes in Staffing Patterns

Although used earlier, the designation *paraprofessional* was not applied to any significant portion of mental health staff until the early 1960s, when a paraprofessional "revolution" seemed suddenly to have appeared. The revolution of course, was only apparently sudden. Its components had developed for more than a hundred years, were given great impetus by the human services demands of World War II, and, finally, grew large enough to have flowed together and become apparent in the 1960s recognition of the pervasive severity of social problems in the United States.

The factors that led to paraprofessionalism included those specific to mental-health staffing practices, as well as conceptual, professional, and historical changes of a more general nature since World War II. Those later, more general factors are discussed in the next section. In this section, we identify and briefly discuss four of the staffing changes, those that we believe were particularly important in the development of paraprofessionalism. They are (1) the tradition of amateurs and volunteers in mental health services; (2) the development of the ward aide's position in mental hospitals; (3) the paraprofessional precedents set in other professional areas; and (4) the professionals' shift, in the 1950s and 1960s, from an almost totally intraindividual focus to a more interindividual and social-cultural focus in mental health.

Amateurs and Volunteers

Assistance given to the mentally disturbed by neighbors, family, and friends, generally well-meaning but untrained people, is a historical fact long predating the paraprofessional "revolution" of the 1960s. Having little systematic understanding of behavior, these nonprofessionals may have caused as much upset as alleviation of distress—but so may the "professionals" for much of human history. There are notable exceptions, such as moral treatment from about 1800 to 1850. According

to Bockhaven's (1963) research into historical records, small living units run by untrained, well-meaning, idealistic people achieved considerable success with "disturbed" residents. E. L. Witmer, in his work, beginning just before 1900, that led to the development of clinical psychology, emphasized the systematic work with naturally occurring helpers, such as teachers, for children with psychological problems (Brotemarckle, 1931). In the pre–World War I settlement houses, untrained people carried out apparently effective community and personal services with many people in real distress (Levine & Levine, 1970).

In the 1800s America's severe social problems, including the broken human wastes of used-up and crippled labor, could no longer be ignored. At that time, when Spencer's distorted Darwinism served as an apologia for unrestrained capitalism (Hofstadter, 1955), some concerned people tried to alleviate the human distress caused by industry's predations by developing privately sponsored charities. These were the efforts of well-meaning and often successful amateurs, who tried to provide social, psychological, economic, and medical services to the poor. There could be little systematic study of the social issues, given the massiveness and the immediacy of the distress, and the small groups of amateurs labored to do what seemed "right," "useful," and "necessary." They worked to help, not their neighbors—for they were surely from vastly different social classes—but their "less fortunate" compatriots.

In the early twentieth century, medicine, psychiatry, and nursing became increasingly professionalized. By the mid-1920s, psychology and social work had emerged as applied professions. As the twentieth-century professionalism continued to develop and to assume dominance in mental health and related fields, the amateurs were gradually displaced. The nature of mental health services was changing, from the crisis-stimulated direct-activism of the commonsense amateurs, to the highly abstracted and increasingly specialized focus of professionals. The amateurs gradually acceded to the inevitable growth of the professional domains. They accepted their own status as secondary and, at best, ancillary to the highly educated, trained, and increasingly specialized professonals.

The Ward Aide

In the traditional hospital psychiatry that developed in the late nineteenth and early twentieth centuries, nonmedical ward staff regularly carried out those everyday duties that were necessary to care for the growing numbers of patients, who were housed in increasingly crowded wards. The medical professionals had little treatment to offer. Instead, they performed autopsies on schizophrenics and examined slides of brain tissues, seeking biological clues to the cause and cure of schizophrenia (Ullmann & Krasner, 1965). The position of the hospital orderly, aide, or ward attendant evolved into the unambiguous role of carrying out routine tasks and maintaining order on the wards. As late as the 1960s, an NIMH survey (1964) of 282 state and county mental hospitals revealed that 90% of the duties of the 96,200 ward aides who were employed were "menial and routine involving little which could be called therapeutic" (Sobey, 1970, p. 97).

The psychiatric aide was not a professional by education, training, or employment status, and that fact was so clearly apparent to everyone that clarifying labels, such as *nonprofessionals*, were not needed. The aides, viewed as anonymous and interchangeable, performed the tasks that the professionals were not willing to do themselves.

While the ward physicians continued to believe in the effectiveness of their monthly therapy sessions and their electroconvulsive treatments, the aides and other ward staff began to realize that they, in fact, held considerable controlling power over the patients' behavior. Without the aides, the wards could not operate. The all-important details of daily interactions—interpreting rules to the patients and giving instructions, rewards, corrections, and punishments—were all administered by the ward staff. As with any group of people who perform basic, necessary duties that no one else wants to perform, the ward staff became increasingly important in fact, if not in status, in the operation of the hospital.

Until the 1950s, the ward physician, who supposedly knew something of human functioning, paid virtually no attention to the details of daily living on the wards and did not recognize any therapeutic potential in the everyday living situation. The nonprofessional staff had the immediate responsibility for ward management but were given little practical guidance or professional supervision. Consequently, the ward staff had to guide themselves.

It is important to note, though little recognized or discussed, that as the staff structured their growing control over the wards, they had no guiding conceptual models of human behavior, psychological disorder, or treatment. Rather, they evolved their procedures largely through trial and error based on what seemed most expedient in everyday functions; essentially, they did what they had gradually discovered to be least demanding for themselves. In effect, they created an environment in which the patients learned sufficient docility to pose few management problems. The ward staff's gradual structuring of the ward environments was a creation around day-by-day needs, and it was inherently devoid of conceptualizing intermediate or long-range goals for the patients. Without such future orientation, the reality of patients' lives seems to have become structured as a single day, repeated endlessly, with no expectations of significant change toward future goals. The management of uniformity, even across time, seems to have become the aides' major assurance of efficiency.

As Ullmann and Krasner (1969, 1975) have suggested, an aide or ward culture evolved, complete with its own history and traditions, entrance requirements, appropriate socialization experiences, behavioral rules, criteria for success and status hierarchies. By the 1950s, when postwar professionals began to recognize the importance of the ward environment in treatment programs, they found that their "discovery" had long been preempted by the staff; the social structure of the hospital ward had already concretized through the evolving aide culture of some 50 years' traditions. In suggesting the new potential of the ward staff as important paraprofessionals, professionals were, to a large extent, belatedly recognizing the effective ward control that the staff had already achieved.

The direct treatment of hospitalized, adult schizophrenics—treatment that we have euphemistically termed *tertiary prevention*—came to be the real province of the minimally trained, admittedly nonprofessional staff without whom the wards could not operate. Given that reality, we should not have been surprised at the evolution of the aides' and nonprofessionals' recognition of their own importance, a recognition that led to conflicts with the reigning professionals. Some pointedly assertive moves occurred, such as the 1968 Topeka State Hospital takeover by 60 aides, who proceeded to run eight wards, complete with wall placards reading, "This is a union-administered ward," to demonstrate to the professionals how wards ought to be managed (Efthin, 1968). The power of unionized nonprofessionals has become well known to executive directors and to naive young professionals, who periodically try to establish new programs in old wards without first recognizing in whose hands the effective social power lies, that is, without, as Sarason (1972) pointed out, becoming familiar with that agency's history and traditions. In a 1974 report, the Group for the Advancement of Psychiatry stated,

Community workers are not content with non-professional status, but are seeking to professionalize their status. This effort is particularly noticeable in a setting where professional status is equivalent to "first class" and non-professional status equaivalent to "second class" or lower . . . the resulting struggles between professionals and nonprofessionals are so severe in some medical-psychiatric community centers that patient care does suffer tremendously. In fact the struggles attain such magnitude that patients are lost in the battle. (p. 83)

The evolving ward culture had supported the institutionalization of the power of amateurs, of staff who had no guiding, future-oriented (i.e., predictive) conceptual model of human behavior but instead had developed their procedures to maintain uniformity, orderliness, and ease of management.

Paraprofessional Precedents

Following World War II, professionals in all disciplines became increasingly specialized. Gradually a growing disparity occurred within the mental health field, between the professionals' abstract pursuits and the patients' immediate and real needs for more basic, personal services. The field then found itself in interesting metamorphoses at both ends, that is, the simultaneous processes of becoming more professionalized at the upper end and

more "basic" and deprofessionalized at the other. During and following the war, the ostensible reason for the latter process was the personnel shortage. But even before that, several professions had systematically expanded their lower ranks by training technicians. This occurs when any field develops its procedures to the point of reliable and readily taught technology, and it occurred in nursing, radiology, medicine, and dentistry with their respective development of nurses' aides and X-ray, medical laboratory, and dental technicians. But the technology of mental health is, of course, far more tenuous than that of cleaning teeth, making chemical tests, or taking X-ray pictures, and the question must be raised whether the mental health profession has even yet reached the requisite level of technology to make such technicians feasible.

Under the personnel demands of the war, that question was not seriously raised. Rather, the mental health profession took its cue from the successes of the others and began developing its own lower-level staff. There were paramedics, nurse's aides, teachers' aides, and psychiatric aides. Psychologists were not yet an important part of the clinical field and thus had no aides of their own. In fact, in those early postwar years, psychologists were themselves sometimes cast in the role of "parapsychiatrist" and were just beginning to find openings in the medically dominated field.

World War II thus spurred, under the banner of "personnel shortages," the expansion of the professional base through the addition of ancillary staff in several applied disciplines. They were clearly adjuncts to professionals, lower in education, training, responsibility, and status. These ancillary personnel were soon given more duties that had formerly been carried out by professionals, and they became in many ways indistinguishable from professionals. A clear label was then needed to mark the differences, a label that gave some recognition to their new status but still carefully denied their equivalence with full professionals, and they became *paraprofessionals*.

Shift from an Individual to a Social Focus

The late 1950s and the 1960s brought a growing awareness of social problems in the United States and increased attention to poor and oth-

211

erwise disadvantaged people. The recognition that so many were in need of human services was at least partly due to the large numbers of psychiatric draft rejections and casualties during the war. This led to recognition of the problem on a national level, as evidenced by congressional passage of the Mental Health Study Act in 1955, which established the Joint Commission on Mental Health and Illness. The report of the Joint Commission in 1961, *Action for Mental Health*, contained Albee's (1959) discussion of the personnel shortage in mental health and advocated the expansion of the definition of those who could engage in the delivery of mental health services to include persons with varied levels and types of knowledge and training. This expansion set the stage for more active recruitment and utilization of paraprofessionals as human service caregivers.

Concern about the many social problems and the great need for human services, coupled with the recognition of the association of mental illness with poverty (Levine, Tulkin, Intagliatta, Perry, & Whitson, 1979), led to the establishment of more social service and welfare programs, which created an even greater need for personnel for the delivery of services. Many of the programs used paraprofessionals to fulfill the personnel needs, but at first, these workers were not from the local community. Soon, however, programs created through the passage of federal legislative acts, such as the Juvenile and Youth Offenders Control Act of 1961 (Gartner, 1971), began to involve some use of workers taken from among the population being served. In 1963, the President's Committee on Juvenile Delinquency and Youth Crime funded major programs that made extensive use of indigenous paraprofessionals, most notably, as Gartner (1971) pointed out, the Mobilization for Youth program in New York City. With the enactment of the Economic Opportunity Act in 1964, which called for the "maximum feasible participation" of the poor in the programs and services provided in their community as part of the antipoverty employment efforts, the use of indigenous paraprofessionals was greatly increased. Several legislative acts have since been passed to make possible programs for the training and employment of paraprofessionals, the most important of which was the Scheuer Amendment to the Economic Opportunity Act, called the Career Opportunity Act of 1966 (Gartner, 1971). This legislation established the New Careers program under the Department of Labor as part of the antipoverty program, and it provided for career training and development in the human services and education fields.

Thus, with the recognition of social needs and the passage of important legislation added to the other influences discussed above, all was set for the apparently sudden paraprofessional "revolution" in the 1960s.

Changes in the Mental Health Field

Paraprofessionalism is related to many significant changes that have occurred in the mental health field since the early 1940s. At that time, the major mental-health models were those of organic psychiatry and Freudian psychoanalysis. The professional believed to have the requisite skills and knowledge was the psychiatrist. The certainties of the day were not challenged, and all perceived weaknesses were attributed to lack of general social support for psychiatry. This view is well expressed in this summary statement by Alexander and Selesnick (1966): "the challenge will continue because today only a relatively small number of men, women and children who need psychiatric help can obtain it. Lack of money, lack of facilities and lack of enlightened public policy still conspire with man's ancient prejudices to keep the emotionally disturbed in chains of neglect and misery. Not until all people, whatever their wealth, race, creed, locale or status, can find the help psychiatry can offer will the great psychiatric tradition truly come into its own" (p. 404).

But the demands of the war shook those certainties and pointed up some of the inadequacies, such as the inability of psychiatry to deal adequately with the number and complexities of wartime psychiatric casualties. The wartime task, of course, was well beyond the abilities of any treatment model. In their first attempts to assess and explain their failures, the professionals questioned the adequacy of their numbers but not of their psychodynamic and somatic concepts and approaches. To ease the perceived personnel shortages, the professional base was enlarged by admitting other professionals, primarily psychologists, as well as by increasing the duties and responsibilities of nonprofessional aides.

The admission of the new professionals and the paraprofessionals was initially viewed as a temporary, emergency expedient to help relieve wartime personnel problems. The new personnel had clearly limited roles and remained "ancillary" to the supervising psychiatrists. Little objective criticism of the field occurred, and the new personnel adopted the still-unquestioned traditional mental-health concepts and approaches. "More of the same" was occurring; they were not expected to— and at first did not—change much the "way things were done."

In time, however, change did occur. Psychologists brought with them training and education different from that of psychiatrists and began to define their roles beyond the limitations that had originally been imposed. Most notably, psychologists introduced their focus on behavioral facts and empirical research methods. In the 1960s, this focus ultimately helped to bring about the reemergence of behavior modification (Graziano, 1975), which has evolved into a major emphasis in the contemporary field. The most important conceptual change associated with behavior modification was the emphasis on environmental events as factors in maladaptive behavior and its treatment. The behavioral view clearly pulled the field away from the internal focus of both organic and psychodynamic psychiatry. The development of behavior modification, the growing emphasis on child mental-health problems and treatment, and the community-mental-health movement are largely due to the growing influence of psychologists in the mental health field.

A related change was the new interest in group dynamics or social factors, in addition to traditional individual psychodynamics. Hospital wards began to be viewed as small communities within which individual patients interacted, and a flurry of group and milieu therapy approaches occurred.

Not only were small group influences being considered but also, largely influenced by the public health point of view in medicine, interest in the mental health issues of entire communities gained momentum. The community-mental-health field emerged, emphasizing the epidemiology of mental disorders and large-scale interventions that incorporate as much of the natural social environment as possible.

The developments of behavior modification, small-group dynamics, and community mental health, although ostensibly separate, were variations of a common, emerging theme, perhaps the most important theme to emerge into prominence since the late 1940s. This theme is the assumption of the critical importance of the external physical and social environment in creating, maintaining, and treating psychological problems on a large or a small scale. The emotional disorders seen by individually oriented psychodynamic and organic psychiatrists were gradually undergoing redefinition toward a greater focus on external and social processes.

Still another important concept emerged from the public health influence: the *prevention* of mental disorders. Prior to the 1950s, virtually all of the concepts and approaches were treatment-oriented, after-the-fact attempts to correct what had already gone awry. Although a prevention emphasis is implicit, and is becoming explicit, in behavior modification's focus on teaching skills to people for managing their own lives, it is primarily and fundamentally a part of the community-mental-health ideology. The focus on prevention, opposed to postonset amelioration of mental disorders, in community mental health efforts is viewed as one means of circumventing the problems of lack of personnel, ineffective treatment methods, and difficulty in reaching the large numbers of people in need of mental health care (Rappaport, 1977).

The concepts of prevention currently in use derive from Caplan's (1964) discussion of three types of prevention: primary, secondary, and tertiary. Caplan suggested that mental health interventions can avert the onset of disorders, as well as treat those already existing.

Primary prevention focuses on the reduction or elimination of harmful influences so that they will not lead to the occurrence of disorders. The incidence of mental disturbances in the population should thus be lowered. Primary prevention efforts do not concentrate on specific individuals; rather, they strive to reduce the risk for an entire community and promote the general health of the population.

Secondary prevention aims to reduce the prevalence of mental disorders by either altering the incipient influences or reducing the duration and severity of existing cases of disturbance through early identification and intervention in the initial stages of the development of the disorder.

Tertiary prevention addresses itself to the reduction of mental disorders in a community through the rehabilitation of persons suffering fully developed disturbances. Although tertiary prevention is usually directed at limiting the degree and duration of impairment for disturbed persons, its intent is to reduce the prevalence of mental disability in the community.

Prevention is still primarily a theoretical concept, an abstraction in today's mental-health system. Despite our growing acceptance of the idea, virtually nothing of any practical, large-scale value has been done to prevent mental disorders. Few primary and secondary prevention programs exist, and tertiary prevention, as currently practiced, is only a euphemism for therapeutic treatment or residential care. The importance of the prevention concept in mental health lies in its potential and not in any as-yet-established value.

Finally, it should be pointed out that these major changes in the mental health field were part of a widespread increase in the use of paraprofessionals and new technicians across all human service areas: corrections, education, legal services, mental health, medicine and public health, rehabilitation, and various antipoverty programs. A Ford Foundation report in 1970 (cited by D. Cohen, 1977) estimated that human service fields then employed some 400,000 paraprofessionals. Later reports summarized by R. Cohen (1976) estimated a total of some 2 million paraprofessionals in the human services. Many of those positions, particularly in the medical areas and those such as hospital aides, had existed prior to World War II and thus cannot be attributed to the postwar paraprofessional movement. But the point made here is that by the mid-1970s, a very large number of paraprofessionals were employed in the various human services, and mental health paraprofessionalism was but one example of a far larger movement.

In summary, the emergence of paraprofessionals in mental health occurred in the context of significant general changes in the field: the admission of psychologists in large numbers and the resulting greater emphasis on behavioral facts in the mental health professions; the growing emphasis on the social and physical environments as critical variables in human behavior and in the treatment of functional disorders; the influence of the public health view and its traditional focus on the prevention of disorders; and the general development, across all human-service areas, of enlarging the professional base by increasing the number and functions of paraprofessionals.

Evaluating Paraprofessionals

As we have noted, the emergence of mental health paraprofessionals over the past 35–40 years is part of a general development across all of the human services. Furthermore, within the mental health field, it is one of several significant trends that have occurred since the end of World War II. There is little doubt that the paraprofessional movement has contributed considerable personnel to mental health efforts, clearly fulfilling its original major rationale, and would appear to have had a large impact on the mental health field. However, a question crucial to determining the impact of paraprofessionalism has not been dealt with: have these additional personnel, growing for so many years, appreciably improved mental health services or appreciably helped to reduce the overall mental-health problems of the nation as a whole? As Arnhoff (1972) asked in his discussion of the field's continuing demands for more personnel, the question is "manpower for what?"

Nonetheless, it is a contemporary reality that there are a large number of paraprofessionals occupying a variety of positions and carrying out diverse functions in which they are in direct contact with many thousands of clients, apparently contributing information and even making decisions that affect the daily care, the diagnoses, and the treatment of those clients. What began as a move by professionals in World War II to gain some assistants has evolved into a large force of workers who perform many tasks that were once limited to the domain of the professional. These workers, though minimally trained in general, even claim that they have adequately demonstrated their skills and can therefore rightly challenge professionals in demanding professional status for themselves. In essence, the "democratizing" moves to deprofessionalize seem to have resulted in a new growth on the professional tree, albeit, of course, a lower branch.

In addition to altering the professional structure of the mental health field, the large influx of minimally trained workers into the field implies further changes to the very nature of mental health services. The dimensions of the impact of this influx of workers, actual and potential, have not yet been assessed, nor has much attention even been paid to this issue. As pointed out by Graziano and Fink (1973), any full evaluation of treatment impact must be sensitive to possible negative effects as well as any positive effects. If, indeed, some 40% of the staff in mental health services is or will soon be composed of paraprofessionals (Levenson & Reff, 1970), the concern about possible negative effects should reasonably be of paramount importance. However, sensitivity to such possible negative effects does not seem to have developed.

The increase in paraprofessional personnel attests to the feasibility of locating and recruiting relatively untrained persons for mental health positions. Summarizing recruitment procedures in a behavioral treatment program for autistic children operated in the early 1960s, and employing high school and college students, housewives, and other adults as "nontraditional" staff, Graziano (1974) concluded,

There is no doubt that an abundance of interested persons did exist and there were many more applicants than positions available. . . . locating applicants for positions in mental health programs is a relatively simple task posing no problems beyond the careful investment of time in reaching beyond traditional sources. . . . potentially effective child psychotherapists exist in abundance in any city and can readily be identified and trained." (p. 49)

Summarizing the conclusions of a decade of studies made across the entire human-services

area, Cohen (1976), stated, "Taken collectively these projects provide very strong evidence that paraprofessional workers are capable of making a significant contribution to the delivery of human services" (p. 70). Many other writers concur in this positive assessment of the effectiveness of paraprofessionals. They are impressed by the variety of studies from different human-service areas and by the different professional approaches, the varying theoretical models, and the profusion of backgrounds and characteristics of the paraprofessionals themselves. The large amount of varied work in diverse settings has led to a generalized, positive impression of paraprofessionals. Such quantity and diversity are certainly impressive but provide no more than an impression of a general, nonspecific sense of great activity and good results. But nonspecific impressions do not constitute validation, and we must not let ourselves be too readily convinced by such vague—albeit massive and varied—evidence.

Many investigators have tried to evaluate the effectiveness of paraprofessionals more systematically, but the task is difficult. The main problem is that the variations within the field make it impossible to arrive at any general assessment, just as we cannot easily evaluate professionals, or psychotherapy, in general. The term *paraprofessional* applies to such divergent people, tasks, theoretical positions, skills, duties, clinical settings, clients, and treatment goals that no overall assessment is now possible. The very complexity that stimulates some to optimistic overviews of the field's dynamism and apparent success should also caution us that a meaningful assessment of effectiveness is going to be a difficult and lengthy affair.

A note seems in order on the use of the term *paraprofessional* in mental health. The defining characteristics of a *para* anything are that it possesses resemblance and relationship to but not identity with some definable referent. Clearly, the paraprofessional is an aide or assistant to a professional and functions in some subsidiary capacity. That meaning seems to have been the intent of the mental health professionals who helped spur the paraprofessional movement. But when the paraprofessional idea was adopted by the mental health field, its original, rather straightforward meaning seems to have exploded into many directly conflicting suggestions: that paraprofessionals are not as qualified as trained professionals; that they are better qualified than trained professionals; that they have necessary qualities that have been trained out of professionals; that they *are* trained professionals; that they are trained nonprofessionals; that they are untrained nonprofessionals; and, perhaps most perplexing of all, that they are nontrained professionals. The confusing elaborations have been so remarkable that they are reflected in the title of a book by Staub and Kent (1973), *The Paraprofessional in the Treatment of Alcoholism: A New Profession.* At least according to this title, our new mental-health workers may be making a profession out of not being professional. In light of such confusion, it may be wise for us to dispense with the term *paraprofessional* entirely and, instead, use terms more descriptive of actual functions, such as *psychiatric ward attendant* or *child group worker.*

Gartner (1971) suggested that at least some of the confusing variation within the field can be reduced by conceptualizing paraprofessionals in terms of their "origins." He suggests that three groups of paraprofessionals have developed across many human-service areas. The "old paraprofessionals," who comprise that traditional group of hospital-based workers such as psychiatric aides, typically perform relatively routine patient-care duties. They do not hold college degrees and are not recruited from the groups they serve.

The "indigenous paraprofessionals" have been recruited from the target population—from the poor, former drug addicts and legal offenders, mental patients, and so on. The indigenous paraprofessionals do not hold college degrees, often have not even completed high school, and are usually employed in community-mental-health centers. Their particular strength is supposedly in their identification with the group to be served, and they purportedly possess skills, independently of any training, for good interaction with clients from that particular target population.

The "new middle-class paraprofessionals" include fairly well-educated middle-class people, particularly women. These paraprofessionals often hold college degrees, may be changing their employment status (e.g., from housewife to mental health paraprofessional), and in their socioeconomic backgrounds, their values, beliefs, and behavior, are very similar to the professionals with whom they will work. College students and associate-degree graduates are included in this group.

To Gartner's three groups, we add a fourth: parents as mental health paraprofessionals. Their own children are their clients, and the parents bear special, prior relationship to them. The parents form a distinctively different group of mental health workers, and this group is further discussed in the following section, "Behavioral Paraprofessionals."

A profusion of books and articles has described paraprofessional training programs and discussed the paraprofessionals' experiences, their problems in various settings, their conflicts with professionals, their role uncertainties, and so on. Many have reported qualitative evaluations of paraprofessionals, and there is general, even enthusiastic agreement that, overall, the paraprofessional services are effective and useful. Karlsruher (1974) concluded that nonprofessionals have empirically demonstrated that they can help adult, psychotic, inpatients to improve. Durlak (1979) reviewed 42 empirical research studies comparing professional with paraprofessional workers. Durlak reported that paraprofessionals "generally" achieve clinical outcomes equal to or, in a small number of studies, "significantly better" than those obtained by professionals.

Those findings clearly support paraprofessionals but cannot properly be generalized across all paraprofessionals, clients, or settings. The data are limited to the training and utilization of the "new" middle-class paraprofessionals and college students, particularly in the treatment of hospitalized adult psychotics and college students.

Few, if any, studies of the "old" or the "indigenous" paraprofessionals provide valid and reliable evidence that those groups are effective. At this point, after some 20 years of work with indigenous paraprofessionals, it is yet to be established that they do, indeed, contribute to therapeutic improvement in clients. The indigenous and "old" paraprofessionals may very well make other important contributions to the mental health endeavors of many agencies, but they are not yet validated as effective mental-health counselors, and certainly not as substitutes for professional therapists.

As noted, the evaluative research with the "new," middle-class, and college-student paraprofessionals is considerably more positive. The "classical" research in this area—such as that by Rioch, Elkes, and Flint (1965), who provided a year's full-time training to 16 housewives, and the evaluation of college-student paraprofessionals utilized in schools (Cowen, Zax, & Laird, 1966; Goodman, 1972); in children's mental hospitals and clinics (Kreitzer, 1969; Stollak, 1969); more recent reviews (Durlak, 1979; Gruver, 1971; Karlsruher, 1974; Zax & Specter, 1974)—underscore such positive interpretations. Heller and Monahan (1977) suggested that the apparent success of college students with hospitalized psychotics might have been due in part to the college students' youth and enthusiasm, which might have helped to change the generally low-stimulation hospital environment for the "hopeless" patients.

The limitations, however, must be kept in mind: middle-class and college-student paraprofessionals, with training, can carry out some limited therapeutic functions as well as professionals, with a limited array of adult clients. It may be instructive to note that in recent years, as the field has continued to develop, there appears to have been a shift in emphasis from the indigenous to the new, middle-class, and college-student paraprofessional (Cohen, 1976). This shift may reflect the field's implicit recognition of the latter's greater success and relative ease of training, compared with the indigenous group.

To answer the question, "How effective are paraprofessionals?" a good deal more specific definition is needed. The major variables of concern are (1) the paraprofessionals themselves, their backgrounds and personal skill and motivational characteristics; (2) the training process, including the type, duration, complexity, and "completeness" of training; the theoretical models used; the operational skills taught; and the nature of the trainers themselves; (3) the clients to be served, and their

characteristics and particular problems; (4) the goals and procedures of the interventions to be used; and (5) the nature of the service delivery systems in which the paraprofessional is to work, including the type and amount of supervision, the nature and training of the supervisors, the type of setting (e.g., inpatient, outpatient), and even the political and social issues operating between professionals and paraprofessionals. Thus, instead of the general question of the effectiveness of paraprofessionals, the more meaningful questions will be posed to assess *what* paraprofessionals, and *what* kinds of training, carrying out *what* specific functions, are effective with *what* kinds of clients and problems and in *what* settings?

Each of those different and interacting variables contributes to the overall function of paraprofessionals and poses complex problems of evaluation. Taken together, they present a formidable task, in view of which the overall impressions so far formed in the field are of little value.

In summary, we have few data to support the value of the "old" and "indigenous" paraprofessionals in assuming parts of the professionals' therapeutic functions. These paraprofessionals may very well provide other useful services within the mental health system, but neither group has been shown to function effectively in carrying out parts of professional roles. The "new" middle-class and college-student paraprofessional group appears much more promising. Good data support their effectiveness with particular groups of adult clients. The "new" paraprofessionals appear to have held up over the years as potentially useful contributors to the mental health field. A "professionalization" process within this group may be occurring too, as we see a greater emphasis in recent years on the use of the new paraprofessional group (Cohen, 1976) and the growth and refinement of more specialized, didactic associate-degree, junior-college programs for mental health workers (Becker, 1978; Young *et al.*, 1974).

Behavioral Paraprofessionals

Paraprofessionals have been employed in a great variety of mental health and related areas. They have brought diverse backgrounds to the field, worked in different settings, carried out varied duties, treated a range of clients and problems, and received training in different types of programs. Paraprofessionals have been trained in—or at least been introduced to—a number of theoretical models. The models have varied from minimal, near-zero conceptual rigor, such as those that assume that the paraprofessionals enter the field with sufficient "natural" skills and thus do not require any teaching or training, through some associate-degree programs that include fairly lengthy didactic and applied training. The theoretical models, to whatever degree they might be directly taught to the paraprofessionals, include psychodynamic models, medical or somatic treatment models, and educational, custodial, and social learning or behavioral treatment models. It should be pointed out that there has been virtually no research on the comparative effectiveness of professionals trained in the various models.

The training of paraprofessionals in behavior modification has been a very large part of the behavior modification field since its "reemergence" (Graziano, 1975) in the late 1950s. Those early behavior modifiers trained and employed teachers, parents, college students, and other adults. The overall impression from the early work was very positive. It seemed that many "nontraditional" personnel or, as the group will be labeled here, *behavioral paraprofessionals*, could, with little difficulty, be taught behavioral skills for working with clients. However, the limitations of poor generalizability apply to the behavioral paraprofessionals just as they apply to paraprofessionals in general.

Teachers and Teachers' Aides

Before briefly discussing some of this work, we wish to point out that while teachers' aides are clearly paraprofessionals and can be drawn from the "indigenous" and "new" paraprofessionals, teachers themselves are not paraprofessionals. The frequent reference to training teachers as paraprofessionals in mental health is, we believe, in error. When teachers are trained in behavior modification and they carry out therapeutic as opposed to more traditional educational functions, they bring all the values, goals, ethics, and skills of their own profession: education. They are not paraprofessionals at all; rather, they are professionals who are being taught some of the technology of a related profession. It would be more accurate to label them as professionals who are learning a greater degree of specialization than to label them as paraprofessionals. To claim that success in training teachers as paraprofessionals adds credence to the notion of creating successful assistants from groups of nonprofessionals is misleading.

Teachers and teachers' aides have been trained in the use of behavior modification approaches with children in classrooms. The bulk of training has been focused on the normal educational goals of improving academic performance, increasing attentive behavior, and decreasing classroom disruption (Ayllon & Roberts, 1974; O'Leary & Drabman, 1971). In most teacher and teachers' aide training, the goals are educational rather than oriented to mental health treatment, and the teachers and aides operate well within their professional framework of education. Thus, most of the behavioral training of teachers and aides appears not to have been in mental health issues, but in the service of their own profession.

As reviewed by O'Leary and O'Leary (1976), a rapidly growing literature indicates that teachers and teachers' aides have been trained in carrying out functional behavioral analyses of creative behavior (Goetz & Baer, 1973; Maloney & Hopkins, 1973); self-control (Broden, Hall, & Mitts, 1971; Bolstad & Johnson, 1972; Schneider, 1974); and the therapeutic use of peers in classrooms (Graubard, Rosenberg, & Miller, 1971; Solomon & Wahler, 1973).

In some studies, teachers have been trained to function briefly in what are more clearly "treatment" capacities. For example, Barabasz (1975) successfully trained teachers in a special school to carry out group desensitization of students' test anxiety. Other "clinical" applications include training teachers to work with autistic children (e.g., Koegel, Russo, & Rincover, 1977).

Those who do attempt teachers' training find that bringing about lasting change in teachers' behavior, such as sharpening their differential reinforcement of desirable academic behavior, is a demanding task. Although such changes can be brought about in cooperative teachers, the new, contingent behavior of the teachers frequently decays, and they interact with their pupils much as they had before. Perhaps this apparently inevitable decay occurs because the traditional school setting is so powerfully controlling that any new, "incompatible" behavior by teachers is not long supported. Direct instructions regarding target behavior, contingent attention, and providing informational feedback to teachers at the end of the day do not seem to be effective training procedures (O'Leary & O'Leary, 1976). What does appear effective in changing teachers' behavior is very frequent feedback (as often as every 10 minutes) concerning their success (Cooper, Thomson, & Baer, 1970). Rule (1972) found that praising the teachers every 5 minutes was effective. O'Leary and O'Leary (1976) concluded, "praise or frequent feedback appears to be the most useful teacher-training procedure" (p. 502).

Although teachers and teachers' aides have been trained in the application of behavioral methods for children, their role as mental health paraprofessionals has not been developed. Rather, their new psychological training, it is hoped, will help them to be more effective in their own traditional educational goals and, perhaps, in a mental-health preventive capacity. The latter, however, has yet to be adequately developed.

Training Parents as Behavior Therapists

As discussed in earlier reviews by Berkowitz and Graziano (1972), Graziano (1977), and Johnson and Katz (1972), many parents have been trained in the use of behavior therapy procedures with their own children. Although these parents carry out psychological work, they are not generally considered true paraprofessionals. Rather, they are thought of more as clients, as are their children. But these parents are somewhat between clients receiving service and paraprofessionals receiving training. Unlike others labeled as paraprofessionals, these parents do not seek training to enhance their occupational skills or status, and they typically do not set out to apply their own skills to help people with whom they have no prior or close personal commitment.

But the training provided for many of these parents is sometimes quite detailed and well supervised. Some of the parents might, in fact, receive far better training than many of the paraprofessionals! In a very real sense, these parents may contribute to the major rationale of paraprofessional development, helping to ease the personnel shortage, to the degree that they perform parts of professional-level functions. Further, some parents, after being trained, have expressed interest in using their new skills and seeking volunteer or employment positions in mental health agencies or schools.

But the major potential value of training parents in therapeutic and educational skills for working with their own children is in their potential contribution to fulfilling a true community-mental-health role. That is, the (hopefully) knowledgeable and trained parent may be an important embodiment of the concept of both treatment and prevention in the child's natural environment. Thus, parent training reflects paraprofessionalism in a truly community-mental-health context.

Parents have been trained to modify behaviors that virtually cover the range of problems presented to child clinics. This literature has been reviewed elsewhere (Graziano, 1977) and is only briefly summarized in the following few pages.

Problems grouped in complex syndromes, such as mental retardation, schizophrenia, and autism, constitute categories of complex, severely disturbed, or deficient and highly generalized behavior. The diagnostic labels imply some common characteristics that are supposedly shared by all members of each class. Most of the behavioral treatment of these children has occurred over the past 15 years and is almost always carried out in institutional settings, including outpatient units and special schools. Parent training as a component of treatment has been used, probably starting with workers in the mental retardation field, prior to the "reemergence" of behavior modification in the late 1950s. Parents have been successfully trained to carry out home programs with retarded children (e.g., Tavormina, 1975) and autistic children (e.g., Graziano, 1974; Lovaas, Koegel, Simmons, & Long, 1973).

A number of writers (e.g., Clancy & McBride, 1969) have urged the treatment of psychotic children within the context of the family system, thus requiring parental training, and a large number of case studies and some controlled research have been reported. Despite the enthusiasm of investigators and the potential of such training, there is doubt as to the real effectiveness in helping these children. When one recognizes that the effectiveness of even the most sophisticated professional programs (e.g., Browning, 1971; Graziano, 1974; Lovaas *et al.*, 1973) is questionable, it seems clear that the demanding aspects of working with these children are certainly no less for the trained parent. It may be that the parents' strong personal commitment to their children helps to sustain their considerable efforts, but the effectivenss of training parents in significantly helping their children is yet to be demonstrated. Perhaps parent training will prove most useful in home "management" or maintenance programs rather than in generating therapeutic or educational gains. If limited even to that, which is yet to be demonstrated, the training of parents of psychotic children might potentially be an important part of the mental-health treatment endeavor.

Childhood psychophysiological disorders include obesity, chronic stomach aches, tics, nail biting, thumb sucking, a variety of skin disorders, enuresis and encopresis, chronic constipation, bronchial asthma, ulcerative colitis, and anorexia nervosa (Verville, 1967). These disorders have traditionally been treated medically, or with a combination of medical and psychoanalytic approaches. Recent research has explored operant and respondent conditioning approaches to the psychological aspects of these conditions. Among these research studies are reports of home programs, carried out by trained parents. Children's problems so treated have included bronchial asthma (Neisworth & Moore, 1972), self-injurious behavior (Allen & Harris, 1966), seizures (Gardner, 1967), and eating problems (Bernal, 1973). Enuresis and encopresis have been treated through parent training and re-

ported in a vast number of studies. Overall, reasonably good results have been reported in this area.

Negativistic, noncompliant, oppositional, and aggressive behavior is a common complaint, and a large part of the behavior-modification parent training has focused on the reduction of this group of behaviors. They include high rates of surplus behaviors that are disruptive, aversive, and demandingly intense in the lives of parents. Among papers focusing on parent training to reduce children's noncompliant behavior are those by Forehand and associates (e.g., Forehand, King, Peed, & Yoder, 1975; Flanagan, Adams, & Forehand, 1979).

Patterson and associates (e.g., Patterson, Cobb, & Ray, 1972) have trained parents to work with children's aggressive behavior. Others, such as Alexander and Parsons (1973), have trained parents to help improve the prosocial behavior of delinquent children and adolescents.

Reducing children's fears has not been well researched despite the vast literature on adults' fear reduction (Graziano, 1975). Children's fears, like childhood obesity, seem particularly well suited to parent-administered treatment at home. However, with the single exception of school phobias (reviewed by Hersen, 1971), very few researchers have been concerned with reducing the severe fears of childhood. A series of recent papers (Graziano, DeGiovanni, & Garcia, 1979; Graziano, Mooney, Huber, & Ignasiuk, 1979; Graziano & Mooney, 1980) discuss the potential use of parents as behavior modifiers for their children's fears. The latter two papers describe two fear-reduction programs in which parents and children were trained to eliminate the severe, highly disruptive, and long-standing nighttime fears of the children. Those studies strongly support the continued investigation of parent and child behavioral training to reduce children's severe fears at home.

Language and speech disorders have not generated many papers describing the training of parents to work with children who have speech and language problems. Like fears and obesity, this seems to be a problem area that may be particularly well suited to parental home intervention.

Several single-case studies involving parents in some aspects of speech training have been reported with autistic children (e.g., Hewitt, 1965), with a "disturbed" and illiterate child (Mathis, 1971); and with cases of elective mutism (e.g., Wulbert, Nyman, Snow, & Owen, 1973). At this point, the most reasonable involvement of parents with regard to language development is as ancillary support, in cases of speech problems where there is no other serious, grossly interfering dysfunction.

Common behavior problems at home have been the focus of numerous single-case studies in which parents were trained to cope with less traditionally clinical or pathological problems at home. Hall, Axelrod, Tyler, Grief, Jones, and Robertson (1972) trained four parents in baseline assessment and contingent reinforcement to get the child to wear dental braces, to keep his or her bedroom clean, to stop whining and shouting, and, in one case, to reduce the child's average dressing time in the morning from over 3 hours to a more normal 20 minutes. Knight and McKenzie (1974) helped parents eliminate their children's thumb sucking. To whatever degree these relatively simple and straightforward applications of behavioral parent training can reduce the often sharp conflicts that occur in virtually all homes, they are of social value, particularly in terms of primary and secondary prevention goals.

Parent training has been virtually limited to mothers only. A few exceptions that included fathers, at least minimally, have been summarized by Graziano (1977). Training procedures have ranged from one-to-one clinical interviews, through systematic, detailed, didactic, and practical training in laboratorylike settings, as well as in the more natural environment of the home. A particularly interesting series of investigations has been carried out by Forehand and associates (e.g., Forehand, Wells, & Sturgis, 1978) and by Reisinger and Ora (1977). Parents have been trained individually and in groups. Earlier group projects used unstructured group discussions, and more recent projects have included structured and more comprehensive classes. In individual or group settings, "consultation," or structured learning environments, a variety of training methods are employed. Parents may be observed and coached by the trainer as they work with their children. Radio communications, light and buzzer signals, videotaping for later review and discussion, lectures, films, programmed texts, home assignments, and case discussions have all been used. Whatever the settings, specific techniques, and complexity or sophistication of the training package, therapists have attempted to teach parents to specify target behaviors, control environmental conditions, use contingency management, and monitor and evaluate results.

Parent behavior training as an approach to mental health treatment and prevention appears to be a highly promising area, and perhaps one of the most important recent developments in the child mental-health field. It has been adequately demonstrated that selected mothers can be trained to bring about improvement in their children and/or improve their interactions with their children. Little is known yet, however, concerning the characteristics of successful compared with unsuccessful mother trainees, the generalizability or the permanence of the observed behavioral changes, and the "personal" or "clinical" value of the changes to the parents and children. Much more research is needed, but at this point, it seems that training parents as behavioral paraprofessionals to work with their own children is a highly promising approach with many important implications for community mental health.

Behavioral Aides

The role of the ward attendant has been recognized as important in the treatment and rehabilitation of institutionalized patients, if only because of the extensive contact that occurs between the patients and aides (Sobey, 1970). With the increased adoption of behavior modification programs and procedures in various mental-health-care institutions, the role of the paraprofessional attendant has often become that of a behavioral technician.

Behavior modification techniques have been carried out by paraprofessional aides predominantly in such settings as institutions for the mentally retarded (Christian, Holloman, & Lanier, 1973; Gardner & Giampa, 1971; Mansdorf, Bucich, & Judd, 1977; Shane, 1974); hospitals for psychiatric patients (Buel & Born, 1977; Flowers & Goldman, 1976; Lee, 1969; Lee & Znachko, 1968); and agencies for the treatment of drug and alcohol abuse (Cheek, Tomarchio, Burtle, Moss, & McConnell, 1975). A variety of behavior modification techniques have been used in these settings, including time out (Christian *et al.*, 1973); rewards, specific reinforcements, or contingency management programs (Hollander & Plutchik, 1972; Lee & Znachko, 1968; Pomerleau, Bobrove, & Smith, 1973); and assertive training (Cheek *et al.*, 1975; Flowers & Goldman, 1976). In all cases, these techniques are claimed to be effective, but the empirical evidence for effectiveness is either not provided or is based on outcome measures that reflect factors other than patient behavior change, such as worker attitudes.

The training of behavioral aides has taken several forms. Much of the training has involved the use of instructions (Cheek, *et al.*, 1975; Christian *et al.*, 1973; Patterson, Griffin, & Panyan, 1976; Shane, 1974); modeling (Christian *et al.*, 1973; Cook, Kunce, & Sleater, 1974); or role plays and videotaped feedback (Lee & Znachko, 1968). Much of the discussion about training of behavioral aides in the literature has centered on comparisons of the effectiveness of these different training methods. Comparisons of the methods of modeling, feedback, and instructions or lectures revealed that modeling was the most effective means of training (Cook *et al.*, 1974; Panyan & Patterson, 1974). However, the studies are open to interpretation because the measures of effectiveness were more reflective of the attendants' attitudes than their actual behaviors (Cook *et al.*, 1974), and the number of subjects studied was quite small (Panyan & Patterson, 1974). In other comparative studies, it was found that the measure of the effectiveness of the training method was influenced by the form of evaluation. In one study (Gardner, 1972), lectures and role plays were compared, and in another study (Paul, McInnis, & Mariotto, 1973), training by means of brief instructions integrated with on-ward observations was compared with extensive instructions without clinical observations as the training method. In both studies, evaluations were obtained by two means: written tests of knowledge of the principles of behavior modification and on-ward demonstrations of the application of the behavior modification skills learned. Those aides who were trained by role plays in the Gardner (1972) study or by receiving brief instructions with observations in the Paul *et al.* (1973) study performed better on evaluations of on-ward applications of skills than on the written tests, whereas those aides who received training by lectures in one study or by instructions alone in the other study performed better on the written tests.

These differential evaluation results indicate that different methods used in behavioral training programs may lead to different gains, either in the knowledge of the principles of behavior modification or in the ability to apply behavioral skills. This finding is important, not only because it contrasts with Gardner's (1972) claim that there is a relationship between the knowledge of behavioral principles and the ability to apply behavior modification techniques, but because it suggests that the form of training of behavioral aides should be chosen and instituted with some regard for the type of improvements desired.

In addition to training behavioral aides, there has been much attention to maintaining the aides' behavior-modification skills through reinforcement of their behavior. In one study (Buel & Born, 1977), monetary bonuses given to untrained aides contingent on the improvement of patients' behavior did lead to increased interactions between the aides and the patients. However, significant improvement in the patients' behaviors was not achieved until after the aides were given training in specific behavioral treatment plans in addition to receiving the contingent rewards. Pomerleau, Bobrove, and Smith (1973) showed that the reinforcement of trained aides' interactions with patients contingent on the improvement of the patients' behaviors, as opposed to noncontingent rewards, did result in patient improvement. Other studies revealed that the reward of monetary (Patterson *et al.*, 1976) or trading-stamp (Hollander & Plutchik, 1972) reinforcements to trained aides contingent on the aides' application of behavior modification techniques to patients resulted in an increased number of therapeutic contacts between the aides and the patients over the number that occurred after training alone. Although no evidence was reported of the effect of increased patient–aide interaction on patient improvement, one implication of these findings is that merely instituting an aide-training program may not be a sufficient measure for utilizing institutional aides to their fullest advantage as a source of paraprofessional therapy.

Another issue that is addressed in relation to the training of behavioral aides is whether the attendants' behavior is actually different as a result of the behavioral training. In a study of the behavior of ward attendants who had received training in behavior modification skills compared with attendants who had not received such training, the behaviorally trained attendants were found to engage in less custodial behavior and more teaching, training, and management behavior with patients (Gardner & Giampa, 1971). Although no measures were made of the effectiveness of the behaviorally trained aides compared with the other aides on improving patient behavior, it was concluded that the behavioral aides focused more on behavior that was considered likely to produce adaptive patient behavior. In an investigation of the behavior modification skills put in practice by untrained aides, it was found that of a total of 10 behavioral skills considered necessary in any behavioral treatment plan, only two were predominantly engaged in with great frequency: use of verbal prompts and physical guidance. All 10 behavioral skills were engaged in to some (albeit a small) degree, but the weakest skills were those reflecting the methods of behavior analysis necessary in the preparation and implementation of a behavioral treatment plan. These findings have implications for the development of training programs for behavioral aides that take into account those skills the aides already possess versus the targeting of their weakest skills.

It is difficult to come to any general conclusions about the training and use of behavioral aides based on the available literature. The studies are plagued by such methodological inadequacies as poor research designs, lack of control groups, and very small sample sizes. Few studies report data on measures of effectiveness, and most of those that do used measures that are not directly related to patients' behavior changes.

In spite of these reservations, it is possible to recognize the great potential of institutional attendants as paraprofessional behavioral-change agents. Given the proper training, which emphasizes both practical skills in the application of behavior modification techniques and conceptual skills based on an adequate knowledge of behavioral principles, with reinforcement for the use of these skills, behavioral aides have the potential to exercise potent therapeutic effects through their large contribution to the treatment of institutionalized patients.

College Students as Behavioral Paraprofessionals

The use of undergraduate college students has been cited in studies of paraprofessionals as one possible means of relieving the personnel shortage in mental health care (Gruver, 1971). College students have been focused on in particular because they are believed to have personal qualities and unique characteristics that enable them to work with persons in need of mental health services, and because the student population represents a large pool of personnel resources.

College students have been used in a variety of settings in several capacities. Much of the use of students has been in psychiatric hospitals, where they have functioned as companions to patients and have engaged them in general social interactions, as leaders of individual and group activities, and as case-aide workers involved in one-to-one relationships with patients under professional supervision (Gruver, 1971). Students have also been used in more behaviorally oriented capacities to operate token economy programs (Johnson, Katz, & Gelfand, 1972), to conduct incentive reward programs (Bergman, 1976), or to carry out other types of social learning and operant behavior-modification programs on the hospital ward (Poetter, Alvarez, Van Den Abell, & Krop, 1974).

Another major area of involvement of students is in working with children. Programs for modifying the behavior of severely handicapped children have utilized both college students (Graziano, 1974; Guralnick, 1972) and high school students (Rouse & Farb, 1974). Undergraduates have also worked with children in schools and homes, both as behavior modifiers and as consultants to teachers and parents in the development and implementation of behavior modification programs for child management problems (Keeley, Shemberg, & Ferber, 1973; Suinn, 1974) and child phobias (Pomerantz, Peterson, Marholin, & Stern, 1977). In addition, students have worked with children in hospitals (Kreitzer, 1969) and with adults at home (King & Turner, 1975). College students have also been used to a large extent in student or peer counseling (Gruver, 1971; Wasserman, McCarthy, & Ferree, 1975).

The training of undergraduate paraprofessionals has involved a variety of procedures, spanning a range of methods from informal discussions with agency staff psychologists and psychiatrists (Johnson et al., 1972) to an extensive series of well-planned sessions involving both didactic and practical instruction in specific methods (Suinn, 1974). Some of the programs have used students who were in or had just completed behaviorally oriented courses in college at the time, and these courses were regarded as serving as the bulk of the students' training (Bergman, 1976; Guralnick, 1972; King & Turner, 1975; Pomerantz et al., 1977). Other programs used a special instructional workshop (Powell, 1975) or specially developed didactic sessions (Rouse & Farb, 1974) for training students. Some training methods made great use of reading assignments in behavior modification textbooks and journal articles to provide a background in behavioral principles and modification techniques (Guralnick, 1972; Johnson et al., 1972; King & Turner, 1975; Rouse & Farb, 1974). Several of the training procedures relied heavily on the use of such techniques as videotaped or live modeling, behavior rehearsal, and role playing (Keeley et al., 1973; King & Turner, 1975; Poetter et al., 1974; Powell, 1975; Rouse & Farb, 1974; Suinn, 1974; Wasserman et al., 1975). The student paraprofessionals were generally trained and supervised by professional psychologists or psychiatrists, either exclusively (Poetter, Alvarez, Van Den Abell, & Krop, 1974; Suinn, 1974a) or in conjunction with graduate-student psychology interns (Johnson et al., 1972; Pomerantz et al., 1977). However, in some cases, much of the training and supervision of student paraprofessionals was carried out by other students (King & Turner, 1975; Wasserman et al., 1975).

It is difficult to evaluate the effectiveness of students as paraprofessionals based on the present literature. Few studies have been concerned with the effect of the student paraprofessionals on the clientele they worked with; rather, they have focused more on the positive developmental influences that the students' efforts as mental health workers have had on their personalities (Gruver, 1971). Of those studies that have looked at the effectiveness of students as behavior modifiers, none are methodologically adequate enough to offer any definite conclusions. These design inadequacies include a lack of proper control groups, the use of pretests and posttests, appropriate multiple-baseline designs, and adequate objective measures. Some studies claimed successful results but did not report any data or the measures used, except for subjective impressions in case reports (Keeley et al., 1973; Rouse & Farb, 1974). Powell (1975) reported results of 80–90% improvement of clients who were treated in a variety of field placement settings, but no clear outcome criteria were reported. In most cases, the outcome criteria of improvement involved progression through the established hierarchies for the attainment of specified target behaviors, although not necessarily completion and attainment of that behavior (Guralnick, 1972; King & Turner, 1975; Pomerantz et al., 1977; Suinn, 1974), and in some of these cases, no baseline was initially established. Of particular interest for the evaluation of the effectiveness of student paraprofessionals would be studies comparing students' work with that of professionals; there is a noticeable lack of such studies in the behavioral literature. In fact, the only comparative study of student paraprofessionals is that by Bergman (1976), which involves a comparison of two programs: a behavior modification program and a case-aide program, both carried out by student paraprofessionals; however, comparisons are not actually possible because comparable measures of behavioral change were not used for the two groups.

In light of the inadequacies of the research on the effectiveness of students as behavioral paraprofessionals and the lack of empirical substantiation, it is interesting to note the continued persistence in viewing college students as being as good as if not better than professionals in developing effectively beneficial working relationships with patients. It is asserted that students have this ability because of their natural personality characteristics, such as warmth, humaneness, altruism, and enthusiasm or sense of conviction in performing a worthwhile task (Gruver, 1971). However, the possession of such qualities should not be implicitly assumed as applying to all students, for when the traits of college students were investigated in efforts to select those most effective in therapeutic programs, it was found that some students had characteristics that were less conducive to being effective therapeutic agents (Suinn, 1974).

Other cautions should be kept in mind before engaging in an unrestrained use of college students as paraprofessional therapeutic agents. In most of the programs involving undergraduates, the students worked in the agency setting part time or on a temporary basis. When the student comes into an agency for a brief time, she or he is unlikely to be well aware of the general operating procedures or "culture" of the institution and may inadvertently create antagonism on the part of the permanent staff through trying to implement new procedures. The permanent staff may regard the student as an intruder and may resist or at least fail to reinforce the inclusion of the paraprofessional's efforts into the agency operation procedure. The student paraprofessional, being a transitory member of the agency organization, is in a weak position, with little power or authority to effect and carry through changes in the organization (Heller & Monahan, 1977). The college student's transitory involvement as a therapeutic agent also suggests that students may be little more than a temporary solution to the personnel shortage in mental health care. The costs of repeatedly training new student workers, because of the higher

turnover, must be weighed against the other benefits of recruiting students as paraprofessional mental-health personnel.

Despite these problems, college students do represent a promising source of paraprofessional personnel. Although not all students may be qualified or suitable for being paraprofessional behavioral aides, many are keenly interested and strongly committed to doing work in mental health care. It should be possible, with further careful research and the continuing development of programs, to effectively take advantage of the large numbers of well-educated and behaviorally trained students.

Summary and Conclusions

Paraprofessionalism in many disciplines has shown its major growth since about 1945, spurred by the continuing demands of World War II. In the mental health field, paraprofessionalism began as a means of easing the personnel shortage but has since expanded its rationale to include improving existing services, creating new services, and even helping to reduce poverty. However, easing personnel problems still remains the field's most often voiced and major rationale.

The mental-health paraprofessional movement occurred in the context of significant general changes in the field, including the admission of psychologists in large numbers to the clinical field and the resulting emphasis on behavioral concepts; the growing emphasis on the social environments as a critical variable in human behavior and in the treatment of functional disorders; and the influence of the public health view and its traditional emphasis on the prevention of disorders.

Paraprofessionals now occupy thousands of positions in the mental health field and carry out functions that include previously professional duties such as intake interviewing and individual psychotherapy, as well as more traditionally ancillary tasks such as those of the ward aide. The paraprofessionals' diverse functions bring them into direct contact with thousands of clients, and they contribute information and even help make decisions that affect the daily care, diagnoses, and treatment of these clients.

Evaluating the impact of the paraprofessionals on the mental health field has been a difficult task that is still far from completed. While earlier, impressionistic reports seemed enthusiastic and highly positive, the empirical data on paraprofessionals has been meager, has been generated in poorly controlled studies, and, at best, has been mixed. One of the difficulties has been the confusing diversity of people, roles, tasks, and interactions with many groups of clients in various types of settings, which leaves the term *paraprofessional* without specific or clear meaning. The great variability has made it impossible to arrive at any assessment of the value of paraprofessionals as a whole.

As a start toward evaluation, four major groups have been identified: (1) the "old" paraprofessionals (e.g., traditional ward aides); (2) the "indigenous" paraprofessionals; (3) the "new, middle-class" paraprofessionals; and (4) parents as paraprofessionals.

When the evaluative literature is examined for each group, we find that the old paraprofessionals continue to function as ancillary staff and contribute little beyond routine caretaking duties. There are virtually no data to support the effectiveness of the indigenous paraprofessional group, and we must conclude that this group has been of little demonstrable value.

The new, middle-class paraprofessionals, people who are sociologically similar to middle-class professionals, appear to have fared somewhat better under evaluation. Housewives (many with college degrees), college students, and other people with middle-class backgrounds have been shown in many studies to provide effective mental-health services comparable to those provided by professionals. The data are largely limited to their work with hospitalized adult psychotics and with groups very similar to themselves, such as college students. Those limitations must be kept in mind; that is, some middle-class and college-student paraprofessionals, with training, can carry out limited therapeutic functions as effectively as professionals, with limited groups of clients. In recent years, perhaps in recognition of the apparent differential effec-tiveness of these groups, there appears to have been a shift toward support for the more middle-class paraprofessionals and decreased interest in the indigenous group.

Parents as paraprofessionals have also held up well under evaluation. Trained almost exclusively in behavior modification methods, mothers have been highly successful in working with the psychological problems of their own children. A great deal of research is yet needed to determine which parents will be effective with what problems. Parent behavioral training is not ordinarily thought of in terms of paraprofessionalism, but we have suggested that this is a potentially important community-mental-health development.

Paraprofessionals have been trained in, or introduced to, various models of intervention, ranging from "common sense" through "organic," intrapsychic, behavioral, and social models. Few researchers have investigated the differential effectiveness of training in the various models.

To answer the question of paraprofessionals' effectiveness, a great deal of research is yet needed regarding major variables such as (1) the paraprofessionals' backgrounds and personal skills and characteristics; (2) the training processes; (3) the characteristics of the clients to be served; (4) the characteristics of the paraprofessional skills taught; and (5) the nature of the service settings in which the paraprofessionals will work. The research task is to assess which paraprofessionals, with what types of training, are effective with what problems, of which clients, and in what settings.

Much of the training and subsequent work of the new middle-class paraprofessionals has involved behavioral models and approaches, and a subgroup, whom we have labeled *behavioral paraprofessionals*, can be distinguished. This group includes parents, teachers' aides, and behavioral aides, such as those in hospital wards and in special education or treatment programs for children.

Based on this brief review of so large a literature we conclude that the emergence of paraprofessionals in mental health has been a major development, but sufficient research has not yet been carried out to adequately test paraprofessional effectiveness with clients and their impact on the field. Although a large proportion of mental health personnel are now involved in paraprofessional activities and there has been a great deal of enthusiasm expressed in the literature, the paraprofessional movement appears to have fallen short of any of its goals beyond that of adding personnel. There is little evidence that the movement as a whole has met the early, highly optimistic expectations.

Some paraprofessionals in specific settings and with limited treatment roles have been highly effective when compared with professionals.

The new, middle-class paraprofessionals and the parents as paraprofessionals appear to be the most promising groups. Much of the training of these groups has been based on behavioral models.

It is important to recognize that the influx of so large a number of minimally trained personnel into the mental health field may have a potentially drastic and negative impact on the nature of the profession. This possibility, however remote, does not appear to have been seriously investigated.

Finally, the term *paraprofessional* has so many diverse, conflicting, nonspecific and surplus meanings that it should be dropped, and more specific, task-descriptive labels should be developed and used.

References

Albee, G. *Mental health manpower trends.* New York: Basic Books, 1959.

Alexander, F. G., & Selesnick, S. T. *The history of psychiatry.* New York: Harper & Row, 1966.

Alexander, J. F., & Parsons, B. V. Short term behavioral intervention with delinquent families: Impact on family process and recidivism. *Journal of Abnormal Psychology*, 1973, *81*, 219–225.

Allen, K. S., & Harris, F. R. Elimination of a child's excessive scratching by training the mother in reinforcement procedures. *Behaviour Research and Therapy*, 1966, *4*, 79–84.

Alley, S., & Blanton, J. *Paraprofessionals in mental health.* Berkeley, Calif.: Social Action Research Center, 1978.

Arnhoff, F. N. Manpower needs, resources and innovations. In H. H. Barten & L. Bellack (Eds.), *Progress in community mental health*, Vol. 2. New York: Grune & Stratton, 1972.

Ayllon, T., & Roberts, M. D. Eliminating discipline problems by strengthening academic performance. *Journal of Applied Behavior Analysis*, 1974, *7*, 71–76.

Barbasz, A. F. Classroom teachers as paraprofessional therapists in group systematic desensitization of test anxiety. *Psychiatry*, 1975, *38*, 388–392.

Becker, H. J. Curricula of associate degree mental health/human services training programs. *Community Mental Health Journal*, 1978, *14*, 133–146.

Bergman, J. S. Effectiveness of college students in an incentive community program for chronic hospitalized patients. *Community Mental Health Journal*, 1976, *12*, 192–202.

Berkowitz, B. P., & Graziano, A. M. Training parents as behavior therapists: A review. *Behaviour Research and Therapy*, 1972, *10*, 297–317.

Bernal, M. E. *Preliminary report of a preventative intervention project.* Paper read at the Rocky Mountain Psychological Association, Las Vegas, Nevada, May 1973.

Bockhoven, J. *Moral treatment in American psychiatry.* New York: Springer, 1963.

Bolstad, O. D., & Johnson, S. M. Self-regulation in the modification of disruptive behavior in the classroom. *Journal of Applied Behavior Analysis*, 1972, *5*, 433–454.

Broden, M., Hall, R., & Mitts, B. The effect of self-recording on the classroom behaviors of two eighth-grade students. *Journal of Applied Behavior Analysis*, 1971, *4*, 191–199.

Brotemarckle, R. A. (Ed.). *Clinical psychology: Studies in honor of Lightner Witmer.* Philadelphia: University of Pennsylvania Press, 1931.

Browning, R. M. Treatment effects of a total behavior modification program with five autistic children. *Behaviour, Research and Therapy*, 1971, *9*, 319–327.

Buel, C. L., & Born, D. G. Indirect modification of patient behavior with instructors, bonus contingencies and training programs applied to nursing aides. *Psychological Record*, 1977, *27*, 743–751.

Caplan, G. *Principles of preventative psychiatry*, New York: Basic Books, 1964.

Cheek, F. E., Tomarchio, T., Burtle, V., Moss, H., & McConnell, D. A behavior modification training program for staff working with drug addicts. *International Journal of the Addictions*, 1975, *10*, 1073–1101.

Christian, W. P., Holloman, S. W., & Lanier, C. L. An attendant operated feeding program for severely and profoundly retarded females. *Mental Retardation*, 1973, *11*, 35–37.

Clancy, H., & McBride, G. The autistic process and its treatment. *Journal of Child Psychology and Psychiatry*, 1969, *10*, 233–244.

Cohen, D. *Psychologists on psychology: Modern innovators talk about their work.* New York: Taplinger, 1977.

Cohen, R. *New careers grow older: A perspective on the paraprofessionals experience, 1965–1975.* Baltimore: Johns Hopkins University Press, 1976.

Cook, D. W., Kunce, J. T., & Sleater, S. M. Vicarious behavior induction and training psychiatric aides. *Journal of Community Psychology*, 1974, *2*, 293–297.

Cooper, M. L., Thomson, C. L., & Baer, D. M. The experimental modification of teacher attending behavior. *Journal of Applied Behavior Analysis*, 1970, *3*, 153–157.

Cowen, E. L., Zax, M., & Laird, J. D. A college student volunteers program in the elementary school setting. *Community Mental Health Journal*, 1966, *2* 319–328.

Durlak, J. S. Comparative effectiveness of paraprofessional and professional helpers. *Psychological Bulletin*, 1979, *86*, 80–92.

Efthin, A. The non-professional revolt. *The Nation*, Aug. 5, 1968.

Flanagan, S., Adams, H. E., & Forehand, R. A comparison of four instructional techniques for teaching parents to use time-out. *Behavior Therapy*, 1979, *10*, 94–102.

Flowers, J. V., & Goldman, R. D. Assertion training for mental health paraprofessionals. *Journal of Counseling Psychology*, 1976, *23*, 147–150.

Forehand, R., King, H. E., Peed, S., & Yoder, P. Mother-child interactions: Comparison of a non-complaint clinic group and non-clinic group. *Behaviour Research and Therapy*, 1975, *13*, 79–84.

Forehand, R., Wells, K. C., & Sturgis, E. T. Predictors of child noncompliant behaviors in the home. *Journal of Consulting and Clinical Psychology*, 1978, *46*, 1979.

Gardner, J. E. *Paraprofessional work with troubled children*. New York: Gardner Press, 1975.

Gardner, J. M. Selection of nonprofessionals for behavior modification programs. *American Journal of Mental Deficiency*, 1972, *76*, 680–685.

Gardner, J. M., & Giampa, F. L. The attendant behavior checklist: Measuring on-the-ward behavior of institutional attendants. *American Journal of Mental Deficiency*, 1971, *75*, 617–622.

Gardner, W. I. Behavior therapy treatment approach to a psychogenic seizure case. *Journal of Consulting Psychology*, 1967, *3*, 209–212.

Gartner, A. *Paraprofessionals and their performance: A survey of education, health, and social service programs*. New York: Praeger, 1971.

Gershon, M., & Biller, H. B. *The other helpers: Paraprofessionals and nonprofessionals in mental health*. Lexington, Mass.: Lexington Books, 1977.

Goetz, E. M., & Baer, D. M. Social control of form diversity and the emergence of new forms in children's block building. *Journal of Applied Behavior Analysis*, 1973, *6*, 209–217.

Goodman, G. *Companionship therapy: Studies in structured intimacy*. San Francisco: Jossey-Bass, 1972.

Graubard, P. S., Rosenberg, H., & Miller, M. B. Student applications of behavior modification to teachers and environments as ecological approaches to social deviancy. In E. A. Ramp & B. L. Hopkins (Eds.) *A new direction for education: Behavior analysis, 1971*, Vol. I. Lawrence: University of Kansas, Support and Developmental Center for Follow-Through, 1971.

Graziano, A. M. *Child without tomorrow*. Elmsford, N.Y.: Pergamon Press, 1974.

Graziano, A. M. *Behavior therapy with children*, Vol. 2. New York: Aldine, 1975.

Graziano, A. M. Parents as behavior therapists. In M. Hersen, R. M. Eisler, & P. M. Miller (Eds.), *Progress in behavior modification*, Vol. 14. New York: Academic Press, 1977, pp. 251–298.

Graziano, A. M., & Fink, R. S. Second order effects in mental health treatment. *Journal of Clinical and Consulting Psychology*, 1973, *40*, 356–364.

Graziano, A. M., & Mooney, K. C. Family self-control instruction for children's nighttime fear reduction. *Journal of Consulting and Clinical Psychology*, 1980, *48*, 206–213.

Graziano, A. M., DeGiovanni, T. S., & Garcia, K. A. Behavioral treatment of children's fears: A review. *Psychological Bulletin*, 1979, *86*, 804–830.

Graziano, A. M., Mooney, K. C., Huber, C., & Ignasiak, D. Self control instruction for children's fear reduction. *Journal of Behavior Therapy and Experimental Psychiatry*, 1979, *10* 221–227.

Group for the Advancement of Psychiatry. *Current and future issues: Professional-nonprofessional struggles*. In *The community worker: A response to human need*. New York: GAP, Committee on Therapeutic Care, 1974.

Gruver, C. College students as therapeutic agents. *Psychological Bulletin*, 1971, *76*, 111–127.

Guralnick, M. J. A language development program for severely handicapped children. *Exceptional Children*, 1972, *39*, 45–49.

Hall, R. V., Axelrod, S., Tyler, L., Grief, E., Jones, F. C., & Robertson, R. Modification of behavior problems in the home with a parent as observer and experimenter. *Journal of Applied Behavior Analysis*, 1972, *5*, 53–64.

Heller, K., & Monahan, J. *Psychology and community change*. Homewood, Ill.: Dorsey press, 1977.

Hersen, M. The behavioral treatment of school phobias. *Journal of Nervous and Mental Disease*, 1971, *153*, 99–107.

Hewitt, F. M. Teaching speech to autistic children through operant conditioning. *American Journal of Orthopsychiatry*, 1965, *35*, 927–936.

Hofstadter, R. *Social Darwinism in American thought*. Boston: Beacon Press, 1955.

Hollander, M. A., & Plutchik, R. A reinforcement program for psychiatric attendants. *Journal of Behavior Therapy and Experimental Psychiatry*, 1972, *3*, 297–300.

Johnson, C. A., & Katz, C. Using parents as change agents for their children: A review. *Journal of Child Psychology and Psychiatry*, 1972, *14*, 181–200.

Johnson, C. A., Katz, R. C., & Gelfand, S. Undergraduates as behavioral technicians on an adult token economy word. *Behavior Therapy*, 1972, *3*, 589–592.

Karlsruher, A. E. The nonprofessional as a psychotherapeutic agent: A review of the empirical evidence pertaining to his effectiveness. *American Journal of Community Psychology*, 1974, *2*, 61–77.

Keeley, S. M., Shemberg, K. M., & Ferber, H. The training and use of undergraduates as behavior analysts in the consultative process. *Professional Psychology*, 1973, *4*, 59–63.

King, L. W., & Turner, R. D. Teaching a profoundly retarded adult at home by non-professionals. *Journal of Behavior Therapy and Experimental Psychiatry*, 1975, *6*, 117–121.

Knight, M. F., & McKenzie, H. S. Elimination of bedtime thumbsucking in home settings through contingent reading. *Journal of Applied Behavior Analysis*, 1974, *7*, 33–38.

Koegel, R. L., Russo, D. C., & Rincover, A. Assessing and training teachers in the generalized use of behavior modification with autistic children. *Journal of Applied Behavior Analysis*, 1977, *10*, 197–205.

Kreitzer, S. F. College students in a behavior therapy program with hospitalized emotionally disturbed children. In B. Guerney, Jr. (Ed.), *Psychotherapeutic agents: New roles for nonprofessionals, parents and teachers*. New York: Holt, Rinehart, & Winston, 1969, pp. 226–230.

Lee, D. An adjunct to training psychiatric aides in behavioral modification techniques. *Journal of Psychiatric Nursing and Mental Health Services*, 1969, *7*, 169–171.

Lee, D., & Znachko, G. Training psychiatric aides in behavioral modification techniques. *Journal of Psychiatric Nursing and Mental Health Services*, 1968, *6*, 7–11.

Levenson, A. J., & Reff, S. R. Community mental health center staffing patterns. *Community Mental Health Journal*, 1970, *6*, 118–125.

Levine, M., & Levine, A. *A social history of helping services*. New York: Appleton-Century-Crofts, 1970.

Levine, M., Tulkin, S., Intagliatta, J., Perry, J., & Whitson, E. *The paraprofessional: A brief social history.* Unpublished paper, SUNY Buffalo, 1979.

Lovaas, O. I., Koegel, R., Simmons, J. Q., & Long, J. S. Some generalizations and follow-up measures on autistic children in behavior therapy. *Journal of Applied Behavior Analysis*, 1973, *6*, 131–166.

Maloney, K. B., & Hopkins, B. L. The modification of sentence structure and its relationship to subjective judgement of creativity in writing. *Journal of Applied Behavior Analysis*, 1973, *6*, 425–433.

Mansdorf, I. J., Bucich, D. A., & Judd, L. C. Behavioral treatment strategies of institutional ward staff. *Mental Retardation*, 1977, *15*, 22–24.

Mathis, M. I. Training of a disturbed boy using the mother as a therapist: A case study. *Behavior Therapy*, 1971, *2*, 233–239.

Neisworth, J. T., & Moore, F. Operant treatment of asthmatic responding with the parent as therapist. *Behavior Therapy*, 1972, *3*, 95–99.

O'Leary, K. D., & Drabman, R. S. Token reinforcement programs in the classroom: A review. *Psychological Bulletin*, 1971, *75*, 379–398.

O'Leary, S. G., & O'Leary, K. D. Behavior modification in the schools. In H. Leitenberg (Ed.), *Handbook of behavior modification and behavior therapy*. Englewood Cliffs, N.J.: Prentice-Hall, 1976.

Panyan, M. C., & Patterson, E. T. Teaching attendants the applied aspects of behavior modification. *Mental Retardation*, 1974, *12*, 30–32.

Patterson, G. R., Cobb, J. A., & Ray, R. S. A social engineering technology for retraining aggressive boys. In H. Adams & L. Unikel (Eds.), *Georgia sympsoium in experimental clinical psychology*, Vol. 2. Oxford: Pergamon Press, 1972, pp. 139–210.

Patterson, E. T., Griffin, J. C., & Panyan, M. C. Incentive maintenance of self-help skill training programs for nonprofessional personnel. *Journal of Behavior Therapy and Experimental Psychiatry*, 1976, *7*, 249–253.

Paul, G. L., McInnis, T. L., & Mariotto, M. J. Objective performance outcomes associated with two approaches to training mental health technicians in milieu and social-learning programs. *Journal of Abnormal Psychology*, 1973, *82*, 523–532.

Poetter, R., Alvarez, C., Van Den Abell, T., & Krop, H. Using college students as paraprofessionals. *Hospital and Community Psychiatry*, 1974, *25*, 305–307.

Pomerantz, P. B., Peterson, N. T., Marholin, D., & Stern, S. The *in vivo* elimination of a child's water phobia by a paraprofessional at home. *Journal of Behavior Therapy and Experimental Psychiatry*, 1977, *8*, 417–422.

Pomerleau, O. F., Bobrove, P. H., & Smith, R. H. Rewarding psychiatric aides for the behavioral improvement of assigned patients. *Journal of Applied Behavior Analysis*, 1973, 6, 383–390.

Powell, D. R. Behavior modification: Students as paraprofessionals. *Journal of Biological Psychology*, 1975, 17, 19–25.

Rappaport, J. *Community Psychology: Values, research and action.* New York: Holt, Rinehart, & Winston, 1977.

Reisinger, J. J., & Ora, J. P. Parent-child clinic and home interaction during toddler/management training. *Behavior Therapy*, 1977, *8*, 771–786.

Rioch, M. J., Elkes, C., & Flint, A. A. NIMH pilot projects in training mental health counselors. US Department of HEW, RHS Service, publication #1254, 1965.

Rouse, B. M., & Farb, J. Training adolescents to use behavior modification with the severely handicapped. *Exceptional Children*, 1974, *40*, 268–288.

Rule, S. A comparison of three different types of feedback on teacher's performance. In G. Semb (Ed.), *Behavior analysis and education—1972*. Lawrence: University of Kansas, Support and Development Center for Follow Through, 1972.

Sarason, S. B. *The creation of settings and the future societies.* San Francisco: Jossey-Bass, 1972.

Schneider, M. Turtle technique in the classroom. *Teaching Exceptional Children*, 1974, *7*, 22–24.

Shane, H. Command performance: A behavior modification technique in a game format. *Mental Retardation*, 1974, *12*, 118–120.

Sobey, F. *The non-professional revolution in mental health.* New York: Columbia University Press, 1970.

Solomon R. W., & Wahler, R. G. Peer reinforcement control of classroom problem behavior. *Journal of Applied Behavior Analysis*, 1973, *6*, 49–56.

Staub, G. E., & Kent, L. M. (Eds.). *The paraprofessionals in the treatment of alcoholism: A new profession.* Springfield, Ill.: Charles C Thomas, 1973.

Stollak, G. E. The experimental effects of training college students as play therapists. In B. Guerney, Jr. (Ed.), *Psychotherapeutic agents: New roles for paraprofessionals, parents, and teachers.* New York: Holt, Rinehart, & Winston, 1969, pp. 510–518.

Suinn, R. M. Traits for selection of paraprofessionals for behavior-modification consultation training. *Community Mental Health Journal*, 1974, *10*, 441–449.

Tavormina, J. B. Relative effectiveness of behavioral and reflective group counseling with parents of mentally retarded children. *Journal of Consulting and Clinical Psychology*, 1975, *43*, 22–31.

Ullmann, L. & Krasner, L. *Case studies in behavior modification.* New York: Holt, Rinehart, & Winston, 1965.

Ullmann, L., & Krasner, L. *A psychological approach to abnormal behavior.* Englewood Cliffs, N.J.: Prentice-Hall, 1969.

Ullmann, L., & Krasner, L. *A psychological approach to abnormal behavior* (2nd ed.). Englewood Cliffs, N.J.: Prentice-Hall, 1975.

Verville, E. *Behavior problems of children*. Philadelphia: W. B. Saunders, 1967.

Wasserman, C. W., McCarthy, B. W., & Ferree, E. H. Training and use of student paraprofessionals as behavior change agents. *Professional Psychology*, 1975, 6, 217–223.

Wulbert, M., Nyman, B. A., Snow, D., & Owen, Y. The efficacy of stimulus fading and contingency management in the treatment of elective mutism: A case study. *Journal of Applied Behavior Analysis*, 1973, 6, 434–441.

Young, C. E., True, J. E., & Packard, M. E. A national survey of associate degree mental health programs. *Community Mental Health Journal*, 1974, 10, 466–474.

Zax, M., & Specter, G. A. *An introduction to community psychology*. New York: Wiley, 1974.

CHAPTER 9

Ethical and Legal Issues

M. Philip Feldman and Jill Peay

Introduction

In this chapter we shall discuss, first, ways in which behavior therapists might order their own professional conduct toward their clients and, second, the relationships between external legal agencies and therapists. In attempting to derive ethical principles to guide professional conduct, behavior therapists have been concerned with both "voluntary" and "involuntary" clients. The former, very broadly, are those with a range of nonpsychotic problems, ranging from specific phobias to sexual difficulties. The latter are characterized by being in a relatively helpless or dependent relationship with therapists and include children, the mentally handicapped, and those in institutions of varying types (e.g., prisons and long-stay psychiatric hospitals). The courts have tended to be much more concerned with the involuntary group, although most of the key issues that give cause for concern apply to both groups. In the longer run, it is possible that legally derived principles may provide a systematic framework for professionally self-monitored sets of guidelines. We conclude by speculating as to the consequences of such a dialogue between behavior therapists and lawyers.

Ethical Issues

Therapists who fall short of what is desirable in their goals, their methods, or both damage both their clients and the good name of the profession. Damage to the latter may further reduce the effectiveness of ethical therapists in helping individual clients or of researchers in forwarding knowledge, which may assist clients in general.

Ethics, Society, and Behaviorism

There appear to be two major reasons for public disquiet about behavior therapy. The first concerns the apparently massive power of behavior therapy procedures to control and radically change human behaviors to an extent not before possible. This belief in the omnipotence of the behavior therapies is widespread. It has been fed by an assumed association between behavior therapy and such feared psychological procedures as brainwashing and thought control and by the images of a bleak future portrayed in George Orwell's *1984*.

A number of writers in popular journals

M. Philip Feldman • Department of Psychology, The University of Birmingham, Birmingham B15 2TT England. Jill Peay • Centre for Criminological Research, 12 Bevington Road, Oxford, England.

have used *behavior modification* as a catch-all phrase to include all methods of controlling and manipulating behavior, from contingency management programs to psychosurgery. For example, an article in the magazine *Harper's* included the following: "The most blatant behavior modification procedures . . . involve direct physical or chemical intervention into central nervous system functions. . . . While conditioning is a less dramatic form of behavior modification than, for example, psychosurgery, it should concern us no less, especially when the federal government is preparing programs along Skinnerian lines" (Gaylon, 1973, p. 48, cited by Krasner, 1976).

Some psychologists have contributed to this picture of an all-powerful psychology. For example, McConnell (1970) asserted, "I foresee the day when we could convert the criminal into a decent, respectable citizen in a matter of a few months" (p. 74). A less crass example, but one easily misconstrued, has been pointed out by Krasner (1976): "Skinner's use of the phrase 'Beyond Freedom and Dignity' as a book title, has had aversive impact, both among professionals and the general public. People have reacted to the title in many instances without having read the book and have cited the title as an illustration of the anti-humanism of the behavior modifiers, particularly those influenced by Skinner" (p. 640). Krasner himself (1976) noted the reaction to the title of a paper he presented at the Second Conference on Research in Psychotherapy (Krasner, 1962). In order to dramatize the difference of behavior therapy from traditional psychotherapy, he entitled his paper "The Therapist as a Social Reinforcement Machine." Despite his careful qualification of the word *machine*, subsequent critiques cited the title as illustrating "the mechanical nature and inhumanity of the behavioral position" (Krasner, 1976, p. 640). He commented ruefully, "in retrospect, a title such as 'The Therapist as a Warm, Humane and Loving Social Reinforcer' would have been preferable and no less inaccurate than the original title" (Krasner, 1976, p. 640).

The second source of public concern has come from something more substantial and serious than verbal association, exaggerated assertions, or language capable of wilful misinterpretation, namely, several widely publi-

cized examples of behavior modification programs that represented flagrant abuses of those exposed to them. The first example comes from a study carried out in the chronic wards of a Vietnamese hospital, mainly comprising schizophrenic patients. On the basis of a limited knowledge of operant conditioning, Cotter (1967), who was trained as a psychiatrist, devised a program aimed at getting patients to work in order to demonstrate their capability to live outside the hospital. Out of 30 who had indicated their desire to live outside, 20 had refused to work. The refusers were each given 120 treatments of unmodified electro-convulsive therapy (ECT) three times a week. As a result, most began to work. The "program" then proceeded to job finding outside the institution, the eventual workplace being U.S. Army advanced bases, where the ex-patients grew crops (this was during the Vietnam war). Krasner (1976) identified a number of issues raised by this program: "the lack of appropriate training for the planner of the program, the use of aversive and denigrating procedures, ignoring the 'rights' of patients to basic subsistence, and most important of all, the 'bad' social consequences of the changed behaviors" (p. 639).

The Cotter study exemplified those approaches that make the receipt of basic positive reinforcers contingent on certain behaviors, rather than regarding them as rights. Severe criticism has also been expressed of the explicit use of aversive stimuli in the application of punishment paradigms to modification procedures. *Time* (1974) gave a graphic description: "The convicted child molester in the Connecticut State Prison at Somers reclines on a treatment table with an electrode wired to his upper thigh. Whenever pictures of naked children are flashed on a screen, he gets stinging shocks in his groin." As a further example of the use of aversive stimuli, *Time* reported, "At the Iowa Security Medical Faculty inmates who commit infractions like lying or swearing are given a shot of apomorphine, which brings on violent vomiting for 15 minutes or more" (p. 42). Here, attention is focused on methods rather than on goals, and we are reminded that ethical debates include both components.

Clearly, there is a considerable need for behavior therapists to protect both their clients and the good name of their discipline from abuses of behavioral methods and their applications toward undesirable ends. But how do we define *abuses* and *undesirable*? In answering such questions, there is no escape from two important conclusions. First, the ethical framework of a discussion of the relationship between behavior therapy and society is personal to the writer. Second, this framework is not susceptible to one of the crucial features of the scientific method, namely, falsifiability by empirical test and its appeal, and is therefore *persuasive* and *emotional* (i.e., subjective rather than objective). Those who have both a common learning history and the same current group membership will be more likely to find the framework acceptable than those who have only one or neither. To some extent, the degree of acceptance of the ways in which the framework is applied to particular problems will depend on the vigor and the logical consistency of that application, but the axioms of the framework, the central summary statements from which actions flow, will be accepted or rejected according to whether or not they agree with the existing beliefs of the audience. Insofar as behavior therapy is the application of methods and findings arrived at by the use of the scientific method, it seems logical to expect behavior therapists to accept as given "goods" the desirability of grounding their clinical practice largely in empirical evidence concerning the efficacy and the efficiency of competing methods of treatment. However, as behavior therapists are not immune from influences of other sets of values, it would be no surprise if their clinical behaviors were not, in part, influenced by such extrascientific considerations as avoiding therapeutic failures (Feldman, 1976b) and the social and political acceptability of methods, objectives, and consequences (Feldman, 1976a). *The American Heritage Dictionary* (Morris, 1969) defines *ethics* as "the study of the nature of morals and of the specific moral choices to be made by the individual in relation with others . . . the rules or standards governing the conduct of the profession" (p. 450). This definition is particularly apt to a discussion concerning the desirable means and ends of behavior therapy, as is one of the definitions of

value given by the same source: "A principle, standard, or quality considered worthwhile or desirable" (p. 1415). The problem, of course, is that what is "good" to one person may be "bad" to another, and the heart of the question, as we shall see, is: Who is empowered (and by whom), first, to decide what is good and, second, to act so as to achieve it?

Krasner and Ullman (1973) believe that there is wide agreement about what are "desirable behaviours to design into an ongoing society" (p. 488), citing as examples altruism, generosity, and co-operation, and that such behaviors can be deliberately enhanced by the appropriate training procedures. The latter part of their assertion may be much more correct than the former. For example, the acquisition, maintenance, and performance of altruistic (helping) behaviors have been shown to be responsive to the same environmental causes and consequences that govern behaviors in general (Feldman, 1977a). However, there are obvious wide disagreements, both within and between societies, concerning *which* behaviors are desirable. In Western society, some support the ownership of industry by the State and others oppose it, in both cases on ideological (i.e., value-laden) grounds, partially irrespective of the factual merits of the case. Citizens of the liberal democracies, exposed to one set of training experiences, tend to place the goals of the individual before those of the State; the reverse is true of the Communist countries. If we move from the political to the personal, prohibitionists regard laws limiting access to alcohol as desirable, social drinkers as undesirable; similar differences of opinion concerning what is "good" can be found in the areas of gambling, sexual behavior, drug taking, educational methods (e.g. "progressive" versus "formal"), and in many other contexts.

We agree with Krasner (1976) that there is no finished and ultimate set of specific ethical principles, and that a code developed in one decade may be seriously inadequate, perhaps because of new technical developments, for a later decade. Instead, we set out a broad framework within which the ethical debate can be carried on, raising along the way a number of questions, and enunciating a very few broad guidelines to deal with such questions, finally applying them to some currently contentious areas in order to indicate our view of the desirable guiding principles for behavior therapists in the early 1980s.

The Parties and the Issues

The Interested Parties

Therapists. There are inevitably wide variations between therapists, in both their professional and their nonprofessional experiences, that influence their general views concerning desirable therapeutic methods, aims, and consequences. For example, following an initial training that included many discussions on ethical guidelines, Therapist A might have worked in an institution in which she found that patients were systematically deprived of basic rights in order to promote the overall smooth working of the institution. Following complaints from professionals of greater standing than she, a consequent public inquiry might result in the dismissal of most of the senior staff and a total revision of the program. This outcome would strengthen her already sharp awareness of ethical considerations. In contrast, Therapist B has had an entirely pragmatic training, concentrating on means rather than ends. He then takes up a post in a similar institution to that in which Therapist A works, marked by the same practices, but in this case, no one complains, and he rapidly comes to share the general view of the senior staff that the regime is thoroughly desirable in all respects. The outcome for his future clients is likely to be a considerably less sensitive awareness of ethical issues than is the case for Therapist A.

Clients. Clients vary even more than therapists, in sex, occupation, age, religious and political affiliations, and so on. Their problems range in nature over the full gamut of human behaviors and in severity from the trivial to the totally incapacitating. Attitudes toward therapists vary from total belief to nearly complete skepticism, depending on previous direct or vicarious experiences with therapists and the outcome of those experiences.

The Family and Other Persons Significant to the Client. The extent to which family, friends, etc., are interested in the client depends on the age of the client, the degree to which he or she is "legally responsible," and the nature of the problem. A particularly salient example is the young child whose behavior is complained of by his or her parents. The therapist is then the agent of the parents in bringing about changes in the behavior of the child—although in order to do so the therapist may have to change the behavior of the parents. In this case, the parents are very much interested parties, as are the partners of persons complaining of sexual dysfunction, the families of those carrying out obsessional rituals in which other family members participate, and the families of alcoholics. It is difficult to suggest examples of problems experienced by those living in family settings that have absolutely no effect on the other members of the family, so the family members are usually interested parties in the cases of all those who live with other persons. At the other extreme are persons who live alone, interacting, at best, only with uncaring acquaintances.

The Institution. The *raisons d'être* of institutions vary from custodial care of patients—at best, training them in skills relevant to a continued life within the institution—to the goal of effective preparation for a full life outside the institution. It follows that the requirements imposed on therapists and the expectations held out to inmates and their families also vary. The reputation of institutions becomes known and partially determines which therapists seek employment in a particular setting: those who are treatment-oriented may either avoid a "custodial" institution or see a challenge in trying to change the orientation of such an institution.

The Legal System. The courts and other legal agencies are interested parties in several contexts. For example, decisions as to the disposal of an offender may be based partially on psychological evidence and on the appropriateness and availability of treatment. Such a course of treatment may be made a condition of a probation order or part of a custodial sentence. The legal machinery is involved in the commitment to institutions of persons deemed in need of such care. Whether or not psychologists become parties to legal requirements for the treatment of offenders and others referred by society is a key ethical question, as is that of the extent to which civil rights considerations mesh or conflict with considerations of therapeutic efficacy and efficiency.

On the other hand, the courts might be appealed to by inmates of institutions to protect their rights (e.g., not to be exposed to a particular treatment or, conversely, to be given access to a treatment that might lead to their discharge). Finally, the courts may place constraints both on the goals of treatment and on the methods used.

Professional Organizations. It is a feature of professional organizations that they produce sets of guidelines for their members. The extent to which these have a real influence on the conduct of the profession depends on the power of an administering committee to withhold approval—for example, of a grant for research into treatment or of permission to proceed with a novel procedure—and even to apply sanctions for specific examples of misconduct. The latter power usually depends on whether the profession concerned is legally registered, so that removal from the register may mean an end to one's livelihood. For a sanction to be invoked, the potential complainants must know which behaviors are considered professionally abhorrent, and the method by which a complaint may be made, and they must enjoy the usual protection the law affords to those making formal complaints of misconduct (for examples, protection against subsequent victimization by the profession).

Political and Other Pressure Groups. A number of groups have as their major purpose the protection of the interests of clients in general. Some seek to protect the civil rights of prisoners and others who have been committed to institutions for custody, treatment, or care.

The above list of interested parties is not exhaustive. For example, therapists are influenced by informal social pressures from their own friends and family, the views of the client's family and friends, and the views of professional colleagues; by the possibility of publication in professional journals of the particular case or cases; and by their current status in the profession and their job security, as well as by all the other factors listed above. Similarly, clients are influenced by their prob-

lem (its nature and severity), by their previous experience with therapists and those in allied professions, by their expectations as to the outcome of therapy modeled by significant others, by their family and friends, sometimes by legal constraints or pressure groups, and in all cases, by their perception of the current therapist as determined by both the verbal and the nonverbal behavior of the therapist. Further, the other interested parties are influenced by specific therapists and by clients, and all concerned are subject to changes due to broad social movements. For example, it is difficult to envisage that in the 1930s the use of sexual surrogates could have been contemplated, let alone discussed, as a serious possibility. The key point is that the interested parties are numerous, the content of their influence is shifting, and their lines of influence are reciprocal and interacting.

The Issues

The Problem. Behavior therapists tend to assume that most clients are capable of reporting their problems accurately. They are likely to accept the presenting complaint at face value, at least as a starting point, and then to ask detailed questions concerning the relevant situational variables as well as (possibly) carrying out actual observations.

So far, there are no implications of an ethical nature. However, the wise therapist might first ask herself or himself: Is there a problem, and if so, who has it? The answer to both questions is often affected by considerations of an ethical, or value-laden, nature. A particularly salient contemporary example is that of homosexual behavior. Is the therapist to accept the client's statement that he or she is homosexual and would rather be heterosexual and proceed to assist this change to occur? Alternatively, is the therapist to suggest to the client that his or her "problem" is of society's making? In the latter event, the client is encouraged to believe that if there is a problem, it is one of learning how to adapt, without anxiety, to his or her homosexual preference. Implicit in this example is an assertion that if there is indeed a problem, it is that of society in general, so that if the therapist has a role of any kind, it is to apply his or her professional knowledge to help to change social attitudes rather than the behavior of his or her clients. We return to this issue below.

Another example of the question "*Who* has the problem?" is that of the parent or teacher who complains of the behavior of a child, with the clear implication that the "problem" resides in the child, and that he or she should be "treated." On careful examination, however, it might become apparent that the "problem" concerns the behaviors of the adult, and that it is these that require modifying to effect a change in the behavior of the child. In this case, the question concerns the *locus* of the problem, in the individual complained of or in significant others. In other instances, the choice may be between the individual and his or her total life situation. In severely socially deprived areas, the only behaviors available to achieve valued reinforcers may be those classified as illegal. Should a change agent focus on the individual or on the situation in which she or he lives? We will return to this issue.

In general, the answers to such questions as "Is there a problem?" and "If so, has it to do with the individual, with particular others, or with her or his total life situation?" depend on who asks the questions, of whom, and what weight is assigned to the sources of the answers.

The Goal. Having decided that there is a problem and having described its salient features, the therapist then has to make a number of decisions about how to proceed. The first of these concerns an appraisal of the existing behavioral repertoire of the client: which behaviors are to be maintained at their present level, which are to be enhanced, which are to be diminished, and which are absent, but desirable, so that new behaviors have to be added. The subjective question here concerns what attributes result in the behavior's being labeled worthy of maintenance, of change, or of incorporation. That is, what attributes label a current or an alternative behavior as "bad" or "good"? For some problem areas, there may be only one alternative to present behaviors or, if there are several, one that stands out as clearly preferable. An example is that of a client who avoids situations in which she has a clear view of a steep drop. Unfortunately, the client's job as a managing clerk of

a London firm of lawyers takes her daily into such situations. London law courts contain many steep stairwells, and it is very difficult, if not impossible, to avoid looking down. Her distress is such that some action has to be taken. The alternatives open are to change the nature of her work within the firm, to seek other employment, or to overcome the problem of avoidance of a specific situation. As the first two alternatives involve both loss of income and the acquisition of new skills, they are clearly less attractive than the third, provided that the goal of substituting approach for avoidance behavior is technically attainable (i.e., if an effective method is available). Below, we discuss the criteria, including those of efficacy and efficiency, relevant to methods of treatment.

But the question is a good deal less straightforward when a current behavior labeled as worthy of change might be replaced by a number of apparently equally preferable alternatives. For a male client whose current sexual preference is for preadolescent boys, with whom he carries out overt sexual activities, and who is in danger of suffering legal penalties, a number of alternatives are open:

1. To maintain his present sexual preference, practicing overtly with the same partners, with the same degree of risk.
2. To maintain it, but to select his partners so as to minimize the risk of legal sanctions as much as possible.
3. To maintain it, but to restrict his overt sexual activities to self-masturbation (it is assumed that some sexual outlet is necessary).
4. To change his preference to males of legal age (currently, over 21).
5. To change his preferences to females of legal age (currently, over 16).

(The remaining choice—to change his preference to females under 16—while logically conceivable, is hardly likely to be considered seriously. The legal restrictions remain, so that there are no compensatory benefits to outweigh the difficulties of changing his sexual preference.) It is likely that each of the above possibilities will be attractive to some clients and some therapists (although the first seems *a priori* not to commend itself to therapists with a preference for a mode of intervention more active than simple support).

The most difficult case of all arises when the client has a pervading feeling of unhappiness, even hopelessness, but only the vaguest sense of which goals are desirable, let alone possible. Such clients tend to be described as having "problems in living," or even an "existential neurosis." The individual behavior therapist may have a clear notion as to what is the "good life," basing this on his or her own satisfying experiences as a committed adherent of a religious, political, social, or occupational group. Should the therapist seek to draw on his or her own life in order to satisfy the client's search for "happiness"? An example is that of a female client whose activities centered on her family, home, and immediate neighbors and who complained of being depressed. It was "evident" to the therapist that her problem arose from her social role as an "unliberated housewife," and he resolved to guide the client toward a very different way of life, in which she would get a job and share the economic burden of maintaining the home. In his turn, her husband would share the domestic chores. Is it desirable for therapists to take on the role of leading clients in directions that go well beyond the problem they present and that have considerable effects on others, such as immediate family members? In this instance, the client was not actually asking for answers to a "good life" question, but in other instances, clients may well do so.

Questions of "purpose" have been central to a number of schools of therapy, particularly the Jungians and those therapists influenced by Abraham Maslow. Behavior therapists have tended to concentrate on enhancing the skills of their clients so as to extend the range of options open to them. As Goldiamond (1974) put it, "the focus is on the production of desirables through means which directly increase available options or extend social repertoires" (p. 14). Krasner (1968) suggested that an important goal is for "an individual to be enabled to make choices in his life. If he has more than one behavior in his repertoire, an individual is obviously freer than if he has no alternative" (p. 170).

However, social repertoires can be extended in numerous ways. We are still left with the problem of who is empowered to select the additional skills and what criteria ought to guide their choice. This question relates to the vital issue of "informed consent." We take this topic up later in this section of the chapter and again in the legal section.

For the moment, let us assume that our client has formulated his or her goals clearly. It is unlikely that all therapists will find equally desirable or possible all goals sought by all clients. There are at least seven constraints possible on such an inclusive acceptance. First, therapists are unlikely to work for goals that may have unfavorable legal consequences, whether criminal or civil, for themselves. Second, they may be equally reluctant to pursue objectives that contravene the formal ethical code of their profession. Third, therapists, like people in general, are likely to have formed personal evaluations of the various possible goals of therapy and may be inclined to persuade clients of the merits of goals that they themselves value highly, and vice versa.

Fourth among the influences on the therapist are those exerted by political and other pressure groups. For example, Alcoholics Anonymous asserts that the only desirable goal of treatment for an alcoholic is complete abstinence and vehemently opposes a conceivable alternative, namely, controlled "social" drinking. Fifth, therapists employed by an institution or other organization are potentially under the constraint of their employing institution, for reasons either of wider (e.g., national) policy or because their activities, whether general or specific, are perceived by other (and powerful) professional groups in the same institution as threatening. Thus, it is possible to be too successful. (See Serber, 1972, for a cautionary tale of the reaction of entrenched opinion in one institution to attempts at innovation: the replacement of therapeutic for custodial goals.) Sixth, constraint is provided by the families and friends of clients. A goal attractive to the client may produce consequences perceived as undesirable by significant others. Finally, some goals may be quite unattainable, either in the present state of knowledge or within the constraints of the available finance. It would be a distortion of the situation to suggest that one or more of the above constraints operate in every case, but they are likely to do so with sufficient frequency to make their analysis a useful part of the "case history."

The Method. Having established whether or not there is a problem and, if so, its nature and the goals of treatment, the therapist next has to consider how to achieve these goals. Typically, several methods are conceivable. What considerations and which interested parties will influence the selection of the method actually used?

1. Efficacy: The argument that demonstrated efficacy is a key factor in the selection of method is at first sight a scientific one, but it is, in fact, an ethical consideration (i.e., relating to what is held to be "good"). Our own assertion is that persons seeking help are as much entitled to the most effective available help as those buying any product are entitled to honesty in the results claimed for it (e.g., that a particular baby food does, indeed, contain "all the food value necessary for normal growth"). An alternative view is that efficacy is not measurable and that therapeutic experiences are simply experiences, valuable in and of themselves.

2. Efficiency: Although it is obvious that methods of behavior change differ in the time taken to proceed from entry into treatment to a specified outcome, the importance of this variable appears to be discussed rather rarely. Yet, it is of major consequence. If, for example, Method A achieves a given outcome in 10 hours of the therapist's time, while Method B achieves it in 100 hours, it follows that 10 patients can be helped by Method A, and to the same extent, in the time taken by Method B to help 1 patient. If keeping psychologists in gainful employment is the major criterion for selecting a treatment method, then Method B will be preferred; if it is helping the maximum number of clients per unit of economic cost, then A will be preferred. There are other considerations, also, principally the fact that the demands on public and on private purses typically exceed the depth of both. Other personal care services, as well as alternative forms of personal expenditure, are in constant competition. There is an increasing tendency for cost–benefit analyses to be applied to many areas of public and private life, from "best buys" in public housing to "best buys" in can openers and margarines. In our view, this kind of analysis is wholly desirable.

3. The client: Bandura (1969) has suggested a division of priority in the primacy of therapist and client: the latter selects the goals of treatment, and the former uses her or his greater technical expertise to select the most appropriate method for achieving that goal. Many therapists would agree with such a division. But just as there is a case, as argued earlier, for allowing therapists to decline to assist a client to achieve a goal that is personally distasteful to the therapist (or that is legally or professionally proscribed), so there is a case for allowing clients to reject a particular method, even if it is both more effective and more efficient than an available alternative. The point, once again, is that both parties (client and therapist) should *agree* about the problem, the goals, and the methods. If they disagree, discussion should continue until either a mutually satisfactory resolution is reached or the client withdraws and seeks another therapist. This apparently simple statement conceals considerable difficulties, as we shall see when we consider the concept of informed consent.

4. The therapist: Just as certain goals may be evaluated unfavorably by therapists, so also may certain methods, even if they are both the most effective and the most efficient available. An example is the employment of an aversive stimulus, such as electrical stimulation, to influence behavior (we discuss the legal aspects below); another is the use of surrogates to assist in the treatment of sexual dysfunction.

5. Other interested parties: Legal authorities, political groups, families, and friends may all seek to proscribe or prescribe particular methods—or would do so given the opportunity. As we shall see, legal authorities in the United States have acted to impose limitations on the token economy as a method of rehabilitating institutional patients. Interested pressure groups have urged that certain penal methods, such as imprisonment, should be replaced by noninstitutional approaches. Conversely, it is not unknown for families or

friends to urge that a client be treated as an inpatient because of their own inability to maintain her or him in the home environment.

There will be complex interactions between two or more of the above influences on the method used. Other factors being equal, when one method is both more effective and more efficient than another, it is preferred. If the two are equally effective, the more efficient is preferred; or if both are equally efficient, the more effective is the method of choice. But what is the outcome when one is more efficient, the other more effective? Perhaps the most pertinent question of all is do therapists indeed seek the cost–benefit information relevant to such decisions, even if it exists at all? Some would urge that not only does the information not exist but that it is not obtainable and that it is good that this should be so. Our own contentions are (1) that the relevant information is often measurable, and (2) that to attempt such a measurement is not only desirable but should be mandatory on all who attempt to relieve the distress of others, irrespective of whether they are paid for doing so or, if paid, are in the public or the private sector of the health industry.

Certain therapists may find particular goals emotionally unacceptable. We suggest that they resolve their dilemma by referring the client to a therapist known to be prepared to seek those goals. The same course of action is desirable for a therapist who finds a particular method emotionally unacceptable, whatever the evidence on effectiveness and efficiency. Similar negative evaluations affecting efficient and effective methods may be held by other interested parties. It is urged that the overriding consideration be the right of the client to seek his or her preferred goal, by the most effective and efficient available method that he or she finds acceptable.

Therapists are likely to be deterred by legal and professional constraints that promise damage to themselves for a particular course of therapeutic action. They may be sensitive enough to be deterred by public criticism leveled by a particular pressure group. Would they also be deterred from a method that, though beneficial to the client, would be deleterious to a third party, namely, family and/or friends? The issues of who benefits and who loses are central to the ethical problems surrounding therapies and therapists, and we shall discuss them in more detail later. At the moment, it is asserted that the interests of the client should be paramount over those of pressure groups opposed to a method acceptable both to the client and to the therapist. Whether they are put into practice depends on the political weight of the pressure group concerned, the outcomes of the therapist's previous experiences of such attempts at influence, and the extent to which the particular goal is attainable by alternative methods that are reasonably near to the proscribed one in efficacy and efficiency.

What is a therapist to do if no currently available method is more effective than no treatment at all? On the efficiency criterion, he or she ought to prefer not to offer any treatment. However, his or her response to the particular client will take several forms, depending on such factors as his or her subjective perception of the client's distress. For example, an extremely distressed client may be given nonspecific "support" rather than be turned away. A succession of such experiences may result in the therapist's carrying out research to find a method that promises to be more effective. Alternatively, he or she may assist in a system of custodial care that does no more than keep the problem from the public attention: "Out of sight, out of mind."

Informed Consent. We postpone until the legal section our major discussion of this issue, which underlies the other issues of goals and methods. Briefly, for the present, the term has two components: information and consent. It is obvious that the therapist has vastly more information than the client about the explanation of problems and about goals and methods. Next, the therapist has control over what information she or he presents to clients and how she or he presents it, with obvious results. According to Stahlman, a professor of pediatrics: 'I can persuade 99 per cent of amy patients to my way of thinking if I really work at it, even if I am 100 per cent wrong . . . I think informed consent is an absolute farce legalistically, morally, ethically—any point of view you want to talk about. The information is what I want it to be" (p. 66, cited by Goldiamond, 1974, p. 13). The last sentence in the above quotation is crucial. It highlights the key issue. Decisions about goals and methods are based on the sum total of available factual information and on the components of persuasive communication (see McGuire, 1969). The greater the proportion of significant information conveyed by the particular clinician and the more effectively she or he manipulates the relevant components of persuasion, the more she or he is likely to move a client to the position she or he, the clinician, holds. There has been no obvious violation of "informed consent," simply the presentation of information by a skilled and authoritative communicator. Manifestly, not only is consent manipulable, but such manipulation may be followed by a statement by the client that he or she has arrived at the decision voluntarily and without coercion. What counts is who is empowered to present the information, what information is presented, and how it is presented.

The second component is that of consent. It is clear this means very little if it is based on incomplete or biased information, so that one key issue is how to give clients access to the same level of information as that available to therapists. To achieve this, clients and their guardians should have available to them an agency that would supply accurate factual information concerning such variables as efficacy, efficiency, and the nature of the events that constitute psychological treatment. Essentially, what is proposed is an extension to the context of psychological problems of "consumerism," the movement that has led in Britain (there are parallel development in the United States) to such organizations as the Consumers' Association, the publishers of *Which?*, a journal offering "best buys" in terms of *explicit criteria*. The overriding criterion in consumerism is the consumer's "right to know," and to know with accuracy. Such accurate information is more likely to come from disinterested than from interested parties. Thus, the particular therapist may well be biased; so may his or her professional organization. At the present time, such an independent agency does not exist. It is desirable that it be set up and staffed by those whose statutory responsibility is accuracy of information. Experts in therapy must obviously be involved, but they would be disqualified in particular instances involving their own work.

A further question concerns *who* is empowered to consent. As Goldiamond (1974) puts it: "Who is the client of the change agent?" He asserted that the clients are the change agent and the party subject to change. For example, if parents are concerned about their child, "the contract is with them to change *their* repertoires to they can improve relations with their child" (p. 44). Goldiamond continued, "I do not contract with them to change their child's behaviour. If we do see the child, we contract with him separately" (p. 44). Similarly, "if an institution is concerned about its inmates, the contract should concern change in *institutional* behaviour" (p. 44, Goldiamond's italics in each case). In both instances, the change agent contracts, in addition, with the child or with the inmates.

Two points are left unanswered. The first arises when it is not necessary to see the child/inmate for the change in the parental/institutional repertoire to occur. No "consent" is needed, so none is sought. Nevertheless, there may be consequences for the child/inmate. In our view, the consent of the person affected by a change in the behavior of another is relevant, whether or not her or his presence is actually required in order to bring about that change. The second point arises if it *is* necessary to see the child/inmate and it becomes clear that the changes in his or her behavior that would result from a change in the repertoire of the parents/institutions are unwelcome to them, and consent is withheld. Should the change agent then decline to act? Goldiamond (1974) glossed over the problem with the phrase "so they can improve their relations with their child." The perceptions of parents/institutions about what is "good" for children/inmates may well differ from those of the children/inmates.

Some Tentative Principles

As a first step, we require some general statement as to what is "desirable" (i.e., what are the "goods" and what the "ills" in the social context in which therapy occurs). It has to be said immediately that total agreement is unlikely within any one society, let alone between societies. Instead of specifying the content of goods and ills, we might restrict ourselves to the following assertion, which allows individuals and groups to supply their own content. Therapists should act so as (1) to increase the access of their clients to those consequences defined as positive by the client and (2) to remove consequences defined by the clients as aversive. Ideally, both (1) and (2) should be goals for therapists, but if one is not possible, the other should still be sought. This statement means that it is the *client* who usually has the primacy of place in decisions concerning key issues. He/she requires accurate and unbiased information relevant to the issues. It is the goods and ills as he/she conceives of them that represent the behavioral repertoires to be added, maintained, or removed.

The question then emerges: *Who* is the client? One way to answer this is to seek the answer to another question: Who is currently suffering directly through the receipt of aversive consequences or (at least indirectly) through the absence of positive ones? The answer to the question names the potential client, who becomes the actual client when she/he approaches the therapist for assistance. The next questions are: What has to happen in order to deliver positive consequences to or remove negative ones from the client? and Who else is affected by what has to happen? If any other person is involved, that person automatically becomes an interested party, with the same right to unbiased information as the client who makes the initial contact with the therapist. We can call the latter the initial and the former the consequential client. The "other person" may be involved to the extent that the initial client's "goods" can be met only by a change in the behavior of the "other person." In this case, the latter is *actively* involved. If the change in behavior has to occur in the repertoire of the initial client, but this change has an effect on the life of the other person, then the latter is *passively* involved. The fact that the other person *is* involved is more important than whether the involvement is active or passive.

Then we have to ask: Are the same consequences considered positive and aversive by both clients? In a more homely form: Do they agree on what is meat and what is poison? If they do, then the therapist should be in little doubt as to what is desired. But suppose the clients differ. Who then has the primacy?

It is probably not possible to lay down a universal principle. Some guidance is provided by the general principles set out earlier, which might be characterized briefly as *maximum benefit* and *least harm,* with pride of place going to those interested parties whose lives are most negatively affected by the problem behavior concerned and who would most benefit from absence of the problem. A secondary criterion is *least consequential harm.* For example, if there are two competing therapeutic strategies, equal in every way in their effects on the recipients of therapy but with different consequential negative effects for other persons, then select the one that has the least negative effects.

How do we decide when an interested party can speak for her/himself and when her/his interests need to be represented by others? In extreme cases there is no problem. It is obvious that a university-educated adult, suffering from neither organic brain disease nor a functional psychosis can represent her own interests, whereas a deaf, blind, intellectually impaired child who mutilates himself, unless restrained, cannot do so. But what of the intelligent child of 14 who is described by parents or teachers as "behaving badly" or as "rather shy"? It is desirable that therapists be alert for such instances and that they seek the views of the consequential, as well as of the initial, client. Further, it is essential that therapists, the clients, and the other interested parties have available an independent arbitration body to which reference may be made by any of those concerned and whose decisions are binding. We discuss arbitration machinery in much more detail in the last section of this chapter.

Some Problem Areas

Children. The interested parties in parent–teacher–child problems are the therapist, the initial client (parent–teachers), and the consequential clients (the children). The last named include those actively involved (e.g., the "problem child") and those passively involved (siblings–classmates). Behavior therapists have been very active in modifying the behaviors of children both at home and in school. Winett and Winkler (1972) characterized many of their activities as inducing children to "be still, be quiet, be docile" (i.e., to produce child behaviors that are beneficial to parents and teachers, and possibly to other children, but that may or may not be desired by the child concerned). This conclusion has been criticized by O'Leary (1972), who questioned the desirability of "informal" (i.e., "progressive") methods for children with social or academic problems. The nub of the question however is: who decides what is "good" for a child, the child or the child's parents–teachers? The answer depends on what are the agreed-upon goals of parenthood–teaching. While people will disagree as to their precise content, they are likely to agree that the goals are to produce positive consequences for children and to avoid aversive ones for them. Note that the locus of consequences is the *child,* not the *parent–teacher.* The therapist should ask her/himself if the objective of parent–teachers is to make life better for themselves, for the child, or both. In the latter two instances, the therapist's involvement is desirable, in the former less so, and not at all if the consequence would be better for the parent but might actually be worse for the child. However, the rights of other children must also be taken into account. For example, even if a particular child would gain little or nothing from a change of procedure, if his current behavior produces negative consequences for his siblings–classmates, then treatment may be desirable. This may sound harsh, but the utilitarian principle "the greatest good of the greatest number" is well established in our society. However, this principle must be sharply restricted so as to apply only to behaviors that are unusually damaging to others or to the individual concerned.

Inmates of Institutions. We referred earlier to the very justifiable criticism of the program established by Cotter (1967). Wexler (1973) pointed out that less attention had been paid to positive control programs, such as token economies, to modify the behavior of long-stay institutional patients. The key feature of token economies is that they involve the receipt of reinforcers for designated approved behaviors. However, the judgment handed down in the American legal case of *Wyatt* v. *Stickney* (1972, see next section) has made it clear that American law will not tolerate the use of forced patient labor devoid of demonstrable therapeutic purpose. The decision in *Wyatt* v. *Stickney,* widely used in America as a precedent, barred privileges or release from hospital being conditional on the performance of labor involving hospital maintenance. This means that the receipt of basic reinforcers cannot be made contingent on appropriate behaviors. The consequences from the viewpoint of behavior modification "is that the items and activities that are emerging as absolute rights are the very same items and activities that behavioural psychologists would employ as reinforcers—that is as 'contingent rights'" (Wexler, 1973, pp. 11–12). The force of the above statement derives from the *Wyatt* definition of minimum rights in terms of specific physical and recreational facilities. Thus, "the major problem faced by the token economy is the current trend towards an *expansion* of the category of protected inmate interests" (Wexler, 1973, p. 17).

Wexler went on to point out that token economy programs, while effective in promoting socially desired behaviors within hospitals, have been less effective in transferring generalized coping behaviors to the outside world after discharge. Treatment programs are desirable that not only stress positive training and involve no deprivation of basic rights but, in addition, successfully overcome the transfer problem. The client is then removed from the dependent setting into one in which he/she is relatively independent and, in principle, able to establish and work towards his/her own goals. The onus is on the interested parties first to define the goals of therapy. We can characterize these as building repertoires beneficial to clients because they are both relevant to life outside the institution and transferable to that external life, and next, to consider how best to achieve this end, without deprivation of those reinforcers reasonably deemed by the courts to be minimal and not to be made contingent on particular behaviors. Once again, the issue turns on what is good for the client (the inmate) and not on what is good for the institution.

Offenders. Whereas it is becoming a common practice for therapists to ask voluntary clients what they would like to achieve, this approach appears to be unheard of in the world of care for offenders, whether community- or institution-based. There is little evidence that the recipients of care share the aims of those providing it, other than a common desire of many offenders and custodial agents for a quiet and well-run institution, with neither side causing difficulties for the other.

The question of common aims occurs with particular force in the context of psychologically based programs for offenders. Such programs are derived from methods developed for those who have sought help for problems from which they lose much and benefit little, either materially or in terms of social approval. Most importantly, the sufferer has often sought help voluntarily and is usually pleased when his/her problems cease or ease. In direct contrast, the performance of criminal behaviors is damaging to those carrying them out only when they are caught and convicted. Do offenders, in fact, seek to avoid a repetition of their acts or merely to avoid reconviction?

Those involved in psychologically based programs, both psychotherapeutic and behavioral, give equal weight, sometimes pride of place, to other indexes (e.g., the relatively concrete, such as educational and occupational skills and various aspects of social skill, as well as less easily defined variables such as "maturity" and "ego strength"). However, we do not yet know whether enhancing social, occupational, and educational attainments helps to reduce reoffending.

One of us has suggested elsewhere (Feldman, 1977a) that when working in the penal system, both psychotherapists and behavior therapists concentrate on the "problems" of the offenders, rather than on the problems caused by offenders to others. The former emphasis enables therapists to retain their traditional role as agents of the client. Psychologists are likely to continue to be reluctant to apply behavioral principles directly to the behaviors involved in criminal acts, even if the change program also includes the provision of alternative behaviors. It might be possible to reconcile the requirements of society to be protected and of offenders not to have inflicted on them involuntary change programs by separating behavioral programs from the formal penal system and applying them solely to two groups of clients: those who have already discharged whatever legal penalty has been imposed on them (or have very nearly finished doing so), and those who feel in danger of committing an offense in the immediate future. Would volunteers be forthcoming?

Experience at Birmingham Prison, England (Perkins, 1978), suggests that a significant proportion of sex offenders near the end of their sentence voluntarily participate in a program of behavior therapy. The Shape program, again in Birmingham, is concerned with voluntary participants who have served sentences in institutions for juveniles, usually following property offenses (Reid, Feldman, & Ostapiuk, 1980). Residents in the Shape program contract to undertake a stepwise program in self-help and social and occupational skills to provide comprehensive alternatives to offending behaviors.

Aversive Procedures. The issue of acceptability to the general public, irrespective of efficacy and efficiency, is particularly pertinent to aversive procedures such as response–cost and the use of painful stimuli. To some extent, advances in knowledge have enabled a shift from such procedures' being used as a method of first resort to their use as a method of last resort. For example, early studies on minority sexual practices concentrated on reducing the unwanted behavior, with more recent ones on training or enhancing alternative behavior with no direct attack being made on the existing one. However, as Krasner (1976) pointed out, "there are situations in certain areas, particularly in institutions for retardates, in which procedures involving positive, educational techniques do not work . . . in which retardates are so dangerous to themselves in terms of self-mutilation or aggressiveness to others, that they are usually kept under heavy sedation, in physical restraint, and in isolated unlocked rooms" (p. 645). He cited a suggested set of guidelines produced by Risley and Twardosz (1974) for such procedures. They include the "establishment of a department and treatment unit within an institution for its administration . . . the department should be closely monitored by a public committee heavily composed of representatives of community organisations and parents of the retarded, who would consult on the admission of residents for treatment, and who would periodically observe the procedures and be able to interpret them to the concerned public'' (p. 6). In line with our general emphasis on accountability to the public, we regard this proviso as particularly important. In addition, such programs should be only the first phase in a wider attempt to supply a repertoire of positive skills, with the eventual target, if possible, of independent life outside the institution.

Sexual Concerns. The first example comes from the largest group of clients seeking help for a sexual difficulty: heterosexual couples or individuals. Therapists might proceed as follows:

1. *Is there a problem?* It might be that brief questioning will establish that the clients' pattern of sexual activity is entirely within normal limits for that age group and that it is generally pleasurable. There is no problem in any important sense.

2. *What is the problem?* Conversely, the extent of the clients' distress, and the dislocation caused to their daily lives, makes it clear that there is indeed a problem, but in what area? And what should be the focus of the attempt to help? In the case of sexual response of couples, the emphasis of many therapists, following the general view of Masters and Johnson (1970), has been that it is the sexual relationship that has broken down or has never been established effectively. Therefore, this should be the focus of attention. It is asserted that if an improvement can be brought about in the sexual area, the same improvement is very likely to follow in the nonsexual area.

3. *Who is to be helped?* This is a question that arises whenever the problem affects more than one person, whether directly or indirectly. In the sexual context, it is very often a member of a well-established partnership who seeks help, but unattached individuals also consult therapists. In that case, the question of whether help should be offered and, if

so, how this is to be accomplished are very relevant. As indicated earlier, the possible use of surrogate therapists is becoming an important ethical issue for sex therapists. In the case of a couple seeking help, the apparent focus of help may be the male or the female, depending on the apparent problem (e.g. ''impotence'' or ''orgasmic difficulties''), but more often it is the couple itself that is the true focus.

The second example is from the much smaller group: homosexual clients. But the issues raised are very important ones and apply widely.

A symposium published in the *Journal of Homosexuality* explored the ethical issue very fully. On the one hand, Silverstein (1977) asserted, ''under no circumstances should a therapist attempt to change the sexual orientation of a patient, including those circumstances where the patient requests such a change. Opposition is based on ethical and moral issues that transcend the argument of the efficacy of various treatment modes, i.e., not whether we can change the sexual orientation, but whether we *should* change it'' (Feldman, 1977b, p. 241). In the same symposium, Davison (1977) agreed, arguing that participation in therapy aimed at change condones current societal prejudices. Essentially, what Davison and Silverstein were saying is that the homosexual client who seeks greater ease should be helped. The one who seeks a change of preference should not. This rejection of clients' stated goals should extend to withholding the names of therapists who might be prepared to help toward reorientation.

Silverstein illustrated his view with the case of an English clergyman seeking change from a homosexual to a heterosexual orientation. The client had been successively refused help in England, Sweden, and Canada before coming to New York. He telephoned Silverstein, who also refused not only to give the help requested but also to make a referral to someone who might. ''I do not believe that it is my responsibility to meet any demand on the part of the person seeking therapy that conflicts with my own principles and values'' (Silverstein, 1977, p. 206). In contrast, Feldman (1977b) asserted the following general view of desirable therapist behavior toward the homosexual who approaches the therapist for *any* kind of help: (1) explore the client's social context and social possibilities and the range of information, both accurate and inaccurate, currently available to him/her as to the homosexual and heterosexual preferences and settings; (2) fill in the gaps in information or place the client in contact with those best able to do so, such as the gay organizations; (3) offer a *range* of alternatives, including reorientation to the heterosexual preference, greater ease with the homosexual preference, and an increase in heterosexual behavior, coexisting with continued homosexual behavior; (4) find out the client's current goals and help him/her attempt to achieve them.

Some therapists find it personally, or professionally, difficult to offer help in attaining the particular goal sought by the particular client. In that case, the remedy is simple: refer the client to another therapist known to offer the form of help sought.

We share the concern of Silverstein and Davison with the social distress of homosexuals and their desire that this be alleviated. But we do not think that the pursuit of this wholly proper aspiration should override the rights of homosexual clients to be responded to by therapists in the manner we have outlined as desirable for clients in general. It may or may not be the case that the existence of therapists prepared to help homosexuals reorient their sexual behavior increases the social disabilities of homosexuals in general. Even if this were so, we would still have to think very carefully indeed before sacrificing the aspirations of individual clients to the long-term success of the general cause.

Research into Behavior Therapy

As indicated earlier, Stolz (1975) reviewed a sample of behavior-therapy grant applications submitted to the National Institute of Mental Health (NIMH). As laid down by the U.S. Department of Health, Education, and Welfare (DHEW) the guiding policy for all concerned in submitting and evaluating grant applications is that they should

Determine that the rights and welfare of the subjects involved are adequately protected, that the risks to an individual are outweighed by the potential benefits to him, or by the importance of the knowledge to be gained, and

that informed consent is to be obtained by methods that are adequate and appropriate . . . an individual is considered to be "at risk" if he may be exposed to the possibility of harm—physical, psychological, sociological, or other—as a consequence of any activity which goes beyond the application of those established and accepted methods necessary to meet his needs. (Department of Health, Education and Welfare, 1971, pp. 1–2)

Stolz pointed out,

Quantification of risk and benefit is not now possible. Instead, various segments of society often have different views about the risks and benefits involved in a behavioral research project because each segment sees the practice in a different context. Thus peer reviewers and behavioral researchers may find a technique acceptable because it produces rapid improvement in seriously maladaptive behavior, while civil libertarians might object to that same technique because it violates the client's right or restricts his freedom, however briefly, and regardless of ensuing benefits. (p. 240)

A number of key issues were raised by NIMH reviewers. The first is the *definition of deviance*: Who decides that a particular behavior should be modified and in what direction? This is probably the most basic decision made by the behavioral researcher. Unless the knowledge exists as to *how* to modify a particular behavior, the clinician is unable to respond to a client's complaint of the behavior concerned, irrespective of how strongly therapist and client agree as to goals and methods. Stolz pointed out the conflict between those who would see the individual as requiring adjustment and those who urge instead changes in her/his social environment. There is a further conflict Stolz does not discuss: Should restrictions be placed on the right of scientists to advance knowledge as they see fit, irrespective of where their explorations lead, or should certain questions be declared "off limits", and if so, by whom? Examples of this conflict have come recently from the biological sciences (e.g., genetic engineering), which seems to hold immense possibilities both for social benefits and for social damage. As Krasner (1976) pointed out, "the usage of any set of procedures . . . in the ultimate control of our society (even for our own 'good') is still a thing of the indefinite future" (p. 628).

Whether or not a behavior therapy researcher (1) seeks to answer a particular question and (2) obtains funds to do so will depend on the balance perceived by the review committee between the readily visible social and/or personal distress caused by the behavior concerned, the eminence of the researcher seeking funds, and the relative political weights of those supporting and opposing the research's being carried out. Not all researchers seek public funds, and a private-enterprise effort is possible. But there seems to be an increasing tendency for individual researchers to submit their projects to local committees of professional colleagues—not for financial support, but for peer evaluation of their ethical merit—and for institutions to require such submissions by their employees.

A related issue is the *justification of the intervention*: Who will benefit from the control that results from the intervention, as against the harm that might result? The clearest case in favor of a project is provided when the research subjects are also clients in distress who have sought help urgently, when existing methods are ineffective, when the risks of the procedure to anyone are minimal, and when the potential gain is considerable, both to the clients and to significant others.

DHEW policy on *informed consent* is clear and explicit. As applied to research into behavior therapy, it means "that the clients or their representatives should be told that the clients will be getting therapy; what the therapeutic procedures will involve; what problems might arise, if any; what the goal of the therapy is; and that the client should feel free to drop out of the study at any time" (Stolz, 1975, p. 247). Stolz added that it is essential "whenever possible that the client should cooperate with the therapist in specifying the way in which he wishes to be changed" (p. 247).

We have already pointed out, in the treatment context, that the key issue is who provides the information, and hence the need for a disinterested agency to do so. The same applies to the research context, the consumer being the potential research subject.

An associated issue is the use of *unobtrusive measures* that are cheap and that avoid the interpretive problems of direct observation but raise complex ethical difficulties. Stolz (1975) concluded "the risk-to-benefit ratio needs to be considered. There is no list of prescribed

or unethical procedures; rather, procedures have to be evaluated in the context of the entire study and its potential benefits to the subjects involved and to society. While in general it is best to obtain fully informed consent, in some cases the benefits from not doing so are considerable, and the risks are minimal" (p. 249).

Several other issues discussed by Stolz have in common the risks to which experimental or controlled subjects may be exposed. They include reversal designs (e.g., whether the reversal is reversible), control group designs (e.g., whether it is justifiable to leave one group untreated) and the use of new therapeutic procedures that are of unknown risks or that carry risks if inadequately monitored. Essentially, the desirable course of action is indicated by the general rubric of "maximum possible benefit and minimum possible loss to the subject involved." It is very tempting for researchers fascinated by a particular problem to play down the risk to subjects from their procedures, so that committee review is an essential protection against risks to potential subjects.

Finally, we would agree with Stolz's view (1975) of aversive procedures used in behavior therapy research, when applied to the elimination of self-injurious behavior to children: "In such cases the risk to the child is serious, alternative treatments appear to be ineffective, and potential benefits to the child from the treatment are great. This is the kind of situation in which the risk from the treatment itself, unexpected side-effects and temporary discomfort, appear to be more than outweighed by the benefits . . . by contrast, it is hard to be sympathetic with a proposal to use severe shocks as a way of facilitating the learning of nonsense syllables, a highly dubious benefit, when the risk looms large in comparison" (p. 254).

Legal Issues

Experience should teach us to be most on our guard to protect liberty when the Government's purposes are beneficent. Men born to freedom are naturally alert to repel invasion of their liberty by evil-minded rulers. The greatest danger to liberty lurks in insidious encroachments by men of zeal, well-meaning, but without understanding. (Mr. Justice Brandeis in *Olmstead* v. *United States,* 1927)

It would be possible to complete this chapter concerning the ethical and legal issues raised by the behavior therapies with a general discussion of the ethical justifiability of laws that permit or limit the technologies of behavioral control. However, since legal intervention into therapeutic practices is a relatively recent phenomenon (and this chapter is being written with practitioners rather than theoreticians in mind), it would seem more profitable to limit the discussion of legal issues. Accordingly, this section of the chapter outlines the recognition of the desirability of a legal framework for professional practice and its development via the courts and recent legislation. Much of the legislation reviewed does not specifically refer to cases involving behavior therapy, but the emerging legal principles are discussed with reference to their likely effect when applied in the field of behavior therapy. Finally, strategies for legal intervention in therapy are reviewed, and a framework is developed that we feel to be capable of encompassing many of the ethical and legal issues raised in this chapter. We feel that the quotation given above, although dating from 1927, is as relevant to our current discussion as it was then.

The Arguments for and against Legal Intervention

The Traditional Assumptions. Historically, there has been little legal intervention in and regulation of therapeutic practices. This lack of intervention has been based on the assumption that patients benefit by allowing the helping professions freedom of action, since treatment can then be individually designed with the patients' best interests served, and that protection of the patient from abuse will result from the high professional standards of the therapists. It has generally been felt that the intervention of the law in such an area of specialist knowledge can only handicap the therapeutic intentions and efforts of that profession.

Variations of this traditional approach are proposed by therapists who recognize the need for regulation but advocate a form of self-regulation (Halleck, 1974). Similarly, other therapists (Rappaport, 1974) have justified enforced treatment—in this case, at Patuxent Institution—on the basis that it is more humane than an alternative such as indefinite detention. The recommendations of the Royal College of Psychiatrists with reference to treatment without consent in the United Kingdom (HMSO, 1976) also derive from the approach of the noninterventionists. The Royal College proposed a "code of practice," which would permit the imposition of treatment without consent on patients who were either unwilling or unable to give consent, provided the next of kin had been consulted and a second opinion had been obtained in writing from an independent consultant. It should be stressed that the code of practice did not require that these alternative opinions concur with the proposed course of action.

The traditional predominance of the noninterventionist approach in the helping professions has limited legal control largely to the area of malpractice. In the field of mental disorder, the law has been similarly confined. Involvement has been limited to commitment proceedings, and there has been no intervention in treatment practices. The assumption has been made that legal involvement in the committal stages permitted only those individuals to be confined involuntarily who were a danger either to themselves or to others or who were mentally impaired to a degree that necessitated treatment.

Libertarian philosophers who have propounded the case for limiting coercive intervention to only a narrow category of individuals—those likely to be a danger to others (Beauchamp, 1977)—have often quoted in support of their argument John Stuart Mill's *Essay on Liberty* (1859). However, it has recently been suggested (Monahan, 1977) that Mill's treatise actually excludes the mentally disordered—thus limiting the scope of such libertarian philosophy. In practice, therapeutic interventions *have* included those individuals considered likely to benefit from treatment. The application of such extensive paternalistic principles (Feinberg, 1978), combined with the discretion permitted where benevolent therapeutic intentions are practiced, has been legally controversial.

The special nature of mental disorder, the criteria adopted for involuntary commitment, and a reliance on therapeutic discretion have combined to result in an application of the law on a far wider basis than may initially have been intended. The inherent elasticity of therapeutic legal rules (Bean, 1975) and the problem associated with the identification, treatment, and prognosis of both mental disorder and dangerousness have resulted in some individuals' being confined on the basis of welfare considerations. Similarly, in what Kittrie (1971) has termed "the divestment of criminal justice," individuals have been detained for treatment on the basis of nonconforming rather than of disordered behaviors. Once confined, both the length of that confinement and the conditions that existed during it were largely dependent on the discretion of those designated as professional caretakers. Complaints of the infringement of constitutional rights have often been regarded as symptoms of mental disorder. Periodic reformist zeal had drawn attention to the institutional environment but had little long term effect on conditions (examples of such continuing scandals in U.K. institutions are St. Augustines, 1968; Whittingham, 1972).

The Growing Concern. It is only during the last two decades that the courts have become increasingly willing to investigate and intervene in matters from which they have traditionally been excluded. The courts have begun to demand adequate institutional performance in exchange for an individual's loss of liberty. The public concern about the potential of the new behavioral technologies for almost unlimited social control, combined with therapists' own demands for assessment and experimental control of the new therapies, has resulted in increasing legal involvement in the therapeutic process.

The areas that initially and justifiably attracted such attention were those therapies of an intrusive or irreversible nature. The behavior therapies, with their emphasis on positive reinforcement, were a less immediate target (Wexler, 1975). However, as has become apparent, the behavior therapies require legal intervention and regulation for a number of reasons. First, being more widely accessible and applicable than organic therapies, the behavior therapies are more open to abuse and misuse. An incomplete understanding of the theoretical bases of the behavior therapies or an inadequate application of the principles can result in conditions that most individuals would regard as intolerable in a humane society. Hoffman (1977) reported, for instance, a lack of consistency in shaping inmate behavior and a lack of visibility as to which behaviors were the object of reinforcement at Patuxent Institution. Second, not all of the behavior therapies involve only positive control: token economies have involved the deprivation of basic rights. At the abandoned federal START program, the tier system utilized involved initial isolation states. Similarly, conditions at Patuxent have been less than ideal: participation in psychotherapy, although technically voluntary, has been vital to obtain release, since a "refusal to participate in therapy results in no promotion beyond lower tiers" (Contract Research Corporation, 1977). Finally, the necessity of regulating goals as well as means (Wexler, 1975) requires legal regulation because the relative desirability of the behaviors to be achieved involve judgments of a social rather than a therapeutic nature.

Perhaps the most contentious uses of the behavior therapies have been their application to the rehabilitation of individuals who suffer from no definable disorder but whose behavior is considered socially deviant. Legal recognition of the desirability of a therapeutic approach to social deviance came in *Robinson* v. *California* (1962), when the court held it to be a violation of the cruel and unusual punishment clause in the U.S. Constitution criminally to punish a person for the illness of addiction. However, in a dictum, the court stated that it was constitutionally proper to confine addicts involuntarily for treatment. The legitimization of social deviance as a sanctioned area for therapeutic effort resulted, as Rothman (1971) has pointed out, in techniques' being enthusiastically utilized in pursuit of rehabilitation that society had been reluctant to adopt in the name of retribution or deterrence. It was not until *In re Gault* (1967) that the courts recognized that "unbridled discretion, however benevolently motivated, is frequently a poor substitute for principle and procedure." Legal restraint on the therapeutic model was to follow.

The Justification of Therapeutic Inter-

vention by the State: Parens patriae Powers. The assumption of guardianship over those individuals whom the state has found incapable of controlling their own lives has been known as its *parens patriae* powers. However, the extension of these powers as a justification for therapeutic intervention has raised a number of problems. First, the invocation of those powers with respect to individuals categorized on the basis of social deviance rather than personal inadequacy has caused problems of unjustifiable invocation for borderline individuals. This problem is particularly active in the absence of effective therapy for many of those individuals deemed to be in need of treatment. Second, even where it is possible to identify the relevant groups and their best interests, the provision–enforcement of those interests is not always attainable. There has been growing support for the view that the state has become more concerned with the exercise of its powers of restraint than with the provision of adequate care.

The invocation of the states *parens patriae* powers often conflict with an individual's right to due process. It has now been recognized that this right should not be neglected as a result of an understandable wish to help the individual concerned. In his *In re Ballay* opinion (1973), Judge Tamm noted that beneficent guardianship can result in both an avoidance of rigorous procedures *and* a lack of dedication to meaningful care and treatment. Even in cases of apparent medical need, the civil commitment of an individual represents such a gross infringement of civil liberties that it should not be undertaken without an additional social–legal judgment of its necessity. Mental disorder cannot be assumed always to impair judgment to a degree that justifies the use of *parens patriae* powers.

However, it would be dangerous to assume that the provision of due process safeguards at committal will result in the detention only of individuals for whom the state's action is justified, or that all committed patients continue to fulfill those criteria. In the light of the lack of evidence of specifiable differences between committed and voluntary patients, judicial intervention and protection must extend beyond commitment.

In fact, the state's *parens patriae* powers

have been questioned as to their fulfillment with respect to conditions after commitment. Some court cases (e.g., *Wyatt* v. *Stickney*) have been based on the premise that the state has not adequately fulfilled its duties and have resulted in the specification of minimum standards for adequate care.

The Judicial Regulation of Therapy. Although the arguments in favor of judicial intervention in therapy are considerable, problems remain as to the form and extent of that regulation. The notions of personal autonomy and privacy outlined in *Roe* v. *Wade* (1973) have as many implications for the provision of and access to therapy as for its prohibition. As a general rule, therapists may do well to limit compulsory therapeutic intervention to cases where the state has demonstrated a "compelling justification" for the denial of an individual's right to be free from intervention, on the basis of existing, relevant, intolerable behavior. Similarly, as Wald (1976) has suggested, intervention and deprivation of liberty should be justified on an individual basis and not on the basis of membership in any particular group (e.g., the "mentally retarded"). If society considers it desirable to restrict basic personal rights, they should be restricted for all persons; any rights denied on an individual basis should be justified with a judicial determination that their exercise will almost certainly result in serious harm.

The Existing Legal Framework

The initial impetus for the courts' involvement in therapeutic practices resulted largely from concern about intrusive, hazardous, or irreversible procedures. However, these earlier decisions do have implications for the practitioners of behavior therapy, and decisions have been made concerning behavior therapists directly. Although more widely applicable and thus more vulnerable to charges of unjustifiable intervention, the behavior therapies were not initially considered as great a threat to civil liberties as the organic therapies. However, the courts have been concerned with the use, by behavior therapists, of basic reinforcers, the aversive therapies (particularly those involving drugs, e.g., anective therapy involving succinylcholine, which paralyzes respiratory muscles), and the use of token economies in closed institutions. As a profession, behavior therapists have been involved in efforts to limit their own procedures by legal constraints. There appear to be two contributory reasons. First, the emphasis in behavior therapy has always been on the client's preferred view of his/her problem and its solutions. Therefore, clients have always been active in their own therapies, without therapists' imposing solutions that necessitate legal intervention. Second, of all the behavior control technologies, behavior therapy is the most amenable to tailoring its procedures to legal requirements and to fulfilling requirements that may prove impossible for other therapies.

This chapter does not attempt to detail the development of the constitutional and procedural limitations on therapy as they have emerged from court decisions, since this subject has been more than adequately reviewed elsewhere (Martin, 1975; Perlin, 1976). Instead, the emphasis is on discussion of the implications of these decisions for behavior therapy and on possible solutions.

The Doctrine of the "Least Restrictive Alternative." The initial development of the constitutional doctrine of the "least restrictive alternative" came in *Shelton* v. *Tucker* (1960), where it was affirmed that even where the government's purpose was both legitimate and beneficial, the means adopted to achieve that purpose must be those that least restrict individual rights. In *Lake* v. *Cameron* (1966), the court endorsed the principle of "least drastic means" and placed on the government the burden of providing treatment in the "least restrictive setting." In *Covington* v. *Harris* (1969), the principle was further extended to the type of treatment adopted. As a result of these decisions, therapists are required to utilize the least intrusive form of therapy for which a positive outcome can reasonably be expected. Behavior therapists are in an advantageous position with regard to this ruling because of their reliance on natural reinforcers as agents of behavior change and maintenance.

The assumption in the *Lake* case that the gains of care had to be balanced against the principle of infringement of liberty in the adversary process was extended in *Lessard* v. *Schmidt* (1972). In this case, it was stated that the Constitution required an affirmative demonstration "beyond reasonable doubt" that there was no suitable, less restrictive alternative to involuntary hospitalization.

It has been suggested (Hawkins & Sullivan, 1974) that such a strict criterion proves impossible to demonstrate in the area of civil commitment, where vague concepts appear unavoidable in practice; Hawkins and Sullivan advocated a "preponderance" standard of evidence as a compromise between the involvement of the adversary process and a complete identification of civil commitment procedures with the area of criminal law.

However, there is one further important application of the principle of the "least restrictive alternative." Golann (1976) has highlighted the danger that stringent due-process safeguards and a centering of legal interests on institutional rights may contribute to the legitimization of institutional care as a solution for the problems of the mentally disordered. He suggests that institutions, particularly for the mentally retarded, are likely to be antithetical to adequate care because long-term care in an institutional environment may permit physical and mental deterioration. Any legal framework must recognize the need to develop a full range of alternative community-based facilities. We would endorse his view that the fulfillment of institutional standards should not be achieved at the expense of alternative facilities. Otherwise, the demonstration that institutional care represents the most satisfactory, "least restrictive alternative" will become meaningless.

The "Right to Treatment." Although many of the court-ordered reforms are beneficial, some of the emerging standards limit the use of demonstrably effective techniques (Budd & Baer, 1976) and may result in either the delay or the prohibition of important therapeutic intervention for some individuals. The problem of controlling the behavior control technologies without jeopardizing attempts to cure or alleviate mental disorders is highlighted by the effects of the right-to-treatment litigation. Although one of the effects has been to establish the right of access of institutionalized patients to effective treatment, it has, in addition, guaranteed certain basic minimal rights as absolute. As Wexler (1975) pointed out, the prevention of the use of contingent reinforcers may deny some chronic patients access to a proven effective therapy. Szasz (1977) maintained that there is a third effect: the legitimization of the right of psychiatry to treat. However, in the light of the recent "right-to-refuse-treatment" decisions, this position would appear less tenable.

The impetus for the eventual recognition of a due-process constitutional right to receive adequate treatment came from *Rouse* v. *Cameron* (1966). Although in this particular case Judge Bazelon could have concentrated his decision on the constitutional right to an adequate hearing before confinement, he preferred to raise issues concerning treatment. He noted that the failure to provide individualized treatment presented constitutional questions of due process, equal protection, and cruel and unusual punishment. Since it was recognized that hospitals could guarantee neither cure nor effective treatment, the court decision limited the hospitals' legal obligations to a demonstrable *bona fide* effort to provide treatment in the light of existing knowledge. However, inadequate staffing would not be legally acceptable as a justification of the failure to provide treatment.

The eventual establishment of a constitutional right to treatment was to encounter a number of problems: how to create standards, how to enforce standards, and, not least, how to ensure that the establishment and enforcement of a constitutional right to treatment would not have the effect of perpetuating the system of institutional care.

The first federal court decision unequivocally to establish the constitutional right to treatment and right to habilitation came in the *Wyatt* v. *Stickney* case (1972) concerning Alabama's mentally disordered involuntarily institutionalized. The court developed a number of standards that were to affect the kinds of treatment that could be given. Specific standards were established that were considered necessary to provide a humane psychological and physical environment, and numerical and qualification standards were established for "adequate staffing." (For details and a discussion of the standards see Budd & Baer,

1976.) The standards developed represented the first real attempt by the courts to limit medical discretion in mental health. This ruling established a precedent of rights that the courts had specifically affirmed for inmates in noncriminal institutions. Having established standards that could be objectively measured, the courts were expected to become further involved in enforcement.

The Relevance of the Right-to-Treatment Decisions for Behavior Therapy. Several specific standards have relevance for behavior therapists. First, certain privileges previously used by therapists as contingent reinforcers were to become available on an unrestricted basis. Wexler (1975) has suggested that for those chronic patients for whom sleeping and eating had been thought to be the only effective reinforcers, therapy may no longer be available. However, since most therapists would maintain that it is the timing of the deprivation that is important, it may prove possible to achieve some compromise between legal standards and the practicalities of offering treatment. Other therapists have suggested that the use of reinforcer sampling combined with generalization to natural reinforcers may fulfill the legal requirements and help chronic patients. The legal requirement for individual treatment programs can only assist in the search for individually effective reinforcers. Access to those reinforcers via tokens, used as secondary reinforcers, may prove to be a legally satisfactory compromise.

Second, the *Wyatt* ruling prohibited the use of therapy either to extinguish socially appropriate behavior or to develop new behavior patterns that serve only institutional convenience. Neither prohibition would appear to be controversial. However, some therapists may feel that problems will be caused by the ruling that no resident is to be required to perform institution-maintaining labor. Often this kind of activity has been used as a basis for assessing readiness for discharge. However, in a period of economic recession, such skills would seem to be of questionable value in relation to other more personally relevant skills that residents might acquire. The discussion may be terminated by the application of minimum-wage laws (*Souder* v. *Brennan,* 1973) to the mentally disordered in an attempt to prevent institutional peonage (Halpern, 1976). This may have the effect of preventing residents from performing institutional tasks on even a voluntary basis. If so, it would be an unfortunate development. The intention of the ruling would appear to be to adopt realistic reinforcers at a realistic level, not to prevent the performance of the tasks as such. This kind of legal effect, although unintended and requiring careful organization to ensure compliance, is, however, preferable to large-scale, nonindividualized deprivations justified on the basis of administrative convenience.

The use of aversive therapies was also severely curtailed by the *Wyatt* decision: physical restraint, not often employed by behavior therapists because it involves giving attention to undesirable behaviors, is to be used only to prevent injury and then only after less restrictive alternatives have been explored. This ruling highlights one of the problems for therapists posed by the "least-restrictive-alternative" approach to be discussed later. In the absence of established hierarchies of alternative treatments, the therapist may be forced to choose between a less intrusive and possibly less effective therapy and a therapy that may provide immediate relief but may be highly intrusive. The former choice may actually prolong the client's suffering. Similar arguments apply to *Wyatt*'s restriction of electric shock therapy to cases of severe self-mutilation, and only after the failure of alternative treatments.

For other serious conditions, *Wyatt* limits the use of aversive therapy to cases where the patient gives informed consent and the proposed course of treatment has been approved by a human rights committee—all time-consuming activities. Although *Wyatt* restricts the use of seclusion, it would appear unlikely to affect behavior therapists' use of seclusion techniques or "time out" (Budd & Baer, 1976). However, the *Wyatt* requirement of the presence of professional staff with reference to the use of aversive therapies may cause some problems. The increasing reliance in behavior therapy on staff trained in appropriate techniques but without professional qualifications is not reflected in *Wyatt*'s criteria.

Friedman (1974) and Halpern (1976) have both stressed that *Wyatt*'s concentration on objective standards is no guarantee of effective treatment. Although behavior therapists are adept at outlining treatment in terms of goals as well as methods, it would seem an impossible task for the courts to specify in advance which goals are appropriate or to evaluate their outcome, particularly in the light of concentration on the desirability of individualized treatment plans. This is obviously a task that can be better undertaken at a local level.

As a sequel to the *Wyatt* case, in *Donaldson v. O'Connor* (1973) the court recognized a constitutional right to receive such individual treatment as will give an individual a realistic opportunity to have her/his condition improved. The court decided that the establishment of the provision of such treatment was within their powers. Damages were subsequently awarded against the state hospital. The loss of due process had to be balanced by the reality of benefit from treatment, and the court demonstrated its willingness to impose penalties where court decisions were not observed.

The Right to Refuse Treatment. The judicial establishment of the right to refuse treatment has been seen as a natural corollary of the right to receive treatment. It is generally assumed that the constitutional protection of autonomy has been derived from two common-law standards: the right to self-determination and the right to bodily integrity. The former standard was developed in *Griswold v. Connecticut* (1962) and amplified in *Roe v. Wade* (1973). In the latter case, the court recognized that although the Constitution does not explicitly mention any right of privacy, grounds do exist to support a right of personal privacy. The common-law standard of the right to inviolability of the person was developed in *Pratt v. Davies* (1906), and it is from this standard that the doctrine of informed consent is derived. In nonemergency situations, it is necessary for an individual to obtain the informed consent of another before touching can take place. Treatment without consent violates this standard and, in addition, violates personal autonomy since it may both impose values and interfere with existing values (Schwartz, 1975). This type of action by the state can be justified only after determination of a compelling state interest.

The right to refuse treatment on religious grounds, even in cases of involuntary detainment, has long been recognized (e.g., *Winters* v. *Miller*, 1971). However, in both *Knecht* v. *Gillman* (1973) and *Mackey* v. *Procunier* (1973), the courts stated that the nonconsensual administration of certain drugs violated the Eighth Amendment (cruel and unusual punishment) when used during aversive behavior therapy. The court, in the *Knecht* case, outlined four standards that in the future would be required before administration of these drugs. These standards included written consent, the opportunity to revoke consent at any time during the therapy, and being given the drug only by a professional staff member who has witnessed the behavior for which the drug is being administered. It is the opportunity to revoke consent during therapy that is apt to cause problems, particularly in the use of aversive procedures.

Traditionally, the operation of Eighth Amendment protections has been excluded in cases where the purpose of confinement had been "rehabilitation." However, with the distinctions between retribution and treatment having been discarded (e.g., *In re Gault,* 1967; *Inmates of Boys' Training Schools* v. *Affleck,* 1972), protections against enforced treatment would appear to operate regardless of the resident's status. As was stated in *Hamilton* v. *Love* (1971), "any deprivation of liberty is in reality a form of punishment." Further support for the proposition that committed status would no longer be considered a corollary of a right to impose treatment came in *Lessard* v. *Schmidt* (1972). In this case, the traditional state justification for involuntary commitment was narrowed to include only those considered a danger to themselves or to others. Medical need for treatment was no longer a sufficient justification. In reaching this decision, the courts recognized such factors as the uncertainty of diagnosis and prognosis, the summary nature of commitment, and the antitherapeutic environment existing in many hospitals. However, the debate concerning consent and status continues, with Malmquist (1979) proposing that a patient with a deter-

mination of mental illness and dangerousness should not have the right to refuse chemotherapy, regardless of the individual's competence to make that decision.

The Implications of the Kaimowitz Case for Treatment. Although the case of *Kaimowitz* v. *Michigan Department of Mental Health* (1973) concerned a patient who underwent experimental psychosurgery, the court's reasoning does have implications for practitioners of behavior therapy. Essentially, the court found that an involuntarily committed patient could not give consent to undergo experimental psychosurgery, thus running counter to the progressive trend of refuting legal incompetence based solely on the patient's status.

The court reasoned that since "mentation" was a logically prior antecedent of any communication, the First Amendment protection of communication extended to mentation: "A person's mental processes, the communication of ideas and the generation of ideas, come within the ambit of the First Amendment. To the extent that the First Amendment protects the dissemination of ideas and expression of thoughts, it equally must protect the individual's right to generate ideas." Although in the case concerned, the patient had given his consent to the procedure and the project had been approved by a human rights committee, the court reasoned that the patient's consent could be neither informed nor voluntary. Therefore, the state had no right to abridge the individual's First Amendment rights. Since the proposed procedure was experimental, with a high cost–benefit ratio, the patient could not comply with the "informed" criterion. Further, since the patient was in an institution involuntarily, he was subject to an inherently coercive atmosphere and his ability to make independent or voluntary decisions was questionable.

A critical account of the case and its implications had already been undertaken (Shuman, 1977). The assumption by the court of an interaction between the status of the procedure as experimental and the status of the patient as involuntarily confined has similarly been questioned (O'Callaghan & Carroll, 1982). The preferred emphasis to be adopted later in this chapter with reference to consent will be the alternative of treatment status. However, the case does raise several points of relevance to behavior therapy. First, the increasing recognition by therapists of the importance of cognitive processes both as maintainers of behavioral problems and as relevant variables in therapy suggests that behavior therapy does come within the domain of First Amendment protections. Behavior therapists can no longer be safeguarded by their claim to being modifiers solely of overt behavior. Second, as Wexler (1975) has pointed out, it is very difficult to make any hard-and-fast distinctions between an experimental therapy and an established one. Undergoing therapy usually involves some degree of risk. Third, since any behavioral program that attempts to change a person against his/her will had already come within the ambit of the protection of personal autonomy, the *Kaimowitz* decision further discriminated against involuntary patients since it outlaws certain kinds of therapy that would have remained available to voluntary patients.

However, Shapiro (1974) has suggested that qualitative differences between the behavior therapies and organic therapies may permit the continued use of the former with confined populations. Shapiro maintained that the behavior therapies are largely nonintrusive, reversible, and gradual in effect and that the client's goal is self-maintenance rather than maintenance by intrusive elements (e.g., antidepressive drugs). Since therapy and change are considered largely resistible, the client's ongoing, active consent is required throughout treatment. Successful behavioral change depends on the client's continued cooperation. Revocation can usually be achieved by noncooperation. These factors do not apply to the aversive therapies, but aversive therapies have other legal safeguards, already outlined.

Shapiro maintained that to remove an individual's right to consent to a therapy on the basis of his/her status, also abridges his/her First Amendment rights. Removal of that right requires the state to demonstrate a compelling state interest. This may well be true, but the logical extension of that argument would appear to be that a patient should have a right of access to any therapy available, whether performed in his/her institution or not. This obviously is a complex issue still to be re-

solved. The only comment that seems appropriate is that in the field of mental disorder, almost any en masse solution, laudable in origin or not, will have pitfalls avoidable on the basis of individualized solutions. Prevention of treatment as well as access to treatment should be individually based.

The Mentally Retarded. The legal position of the mentally retarded (Halpern, 1976) is largely similar to that of the mentally ill; that is, the *Wyatt* case established for them an "inviolable constitutional right to habilitation." It had already been established in *Jackson* v. *Indiana* (1972) that due process requires that the nature and duration of commitment bear some reasonable relation to the purpose for which the individual is committed. The U.S. Supreme Court established, on the basis of equal protection, that if a classification is made—say, of mental retardation—there first have to be substantial and compelling reasons for that classification and also evidence of a justification for that classification in terms of the relevance of the classification. In mental retardation, the reason was found to be adequate habilitation.

In addition, the assumption in *Martarella* v. *Kelley* (1972) that civil commitment of nondelinquent children under primitive conditions without rehabilitative treatment violates due process also holds true for the mentally retarded adult: "effective treatment must be the *quid quo pro* for society's right to exercise its *parens patriae* controls." Further, in *Robinson* v. *California* (1962), the court disputed the appropriateness of punishment for involuntary behavior and decided that involuntary confinement of the mentally retarded without adequate habilitation violated the criterion of cruel and unusual punishment.

The *Wyatt* case reaffirmed the fundamental habilitation purposes of such institutions. Custodial care could no longer be regarded as constitutionally sufficient. In addition, if the normalization principle were to become a reality, the need to develop adequate community alternatives was fundamental to the prevention of institutionalization. Behavior therapy, as a demonstrably effective habilitative therapy, had its particular approach legally ratified.

Although *Wyatt* had established a constitutional right to treatment, the *Willowbrook* case (*New York State Association for Retarded Children* v. *Rockefeller* [*Willowbrook*], 1973) recognized only the more limited rights of residents to be protected from harm. The court did not define "protection from harm," but nonetheless justified it on the criteria of due process, equal protection, and cruel and unusual punishment. However, the aspect of this case that was important was the court's decision that those constitutional protections found in *Willowbrook* were to apply to voluntary as well as involuntary patients. The court stated that all institutionalized retarded persons should be regarded as involuntarily confined, since even voluntary patients were "for the most part confined without the possibility of meaningful waiver of their right to freedom." The court, in addition, granted preliminary relief and specified staffing standards. In our view, therapists would do well to follow this judicial lead and make no arbitrary distinctions on the basis of a client's status (instead, controlling procedures when the procedure merits control).

The Mentally Abnormal Offender. The legal rights of the mentally abnormal offender are less clear than those of the nonoffender. However, their position with regard to psychosurgery and conditioning techniques has been reviewed by Gobert (1975), who stated that if rehabilitative programs are to be adopted, then the courts must recognize that such programs constitute part of the offender's sentence and should be subject to judicial scrutiny and not left within the discretion of officials. That behavior therapy programs, whether through overenthusiastic application or through ignorance, can result in intolerable conditions has been well documented. The prison environment is particularly liable to this type of abuse (e.g., the abandoned federal START program). In addition, some programs aimed at preventing both criminal activity and thoughts about criminal activity may raise constitutional questions as regards the First Amendment. The selection for participation in such programs may also raise questions of equal protection: in *Clonce* v. *Richardson* (1974), the court implied that when a prisoner's status within an institution is altered to his/her detriment, due process must be provided. The doubtful scientific validity of some of the procedures may also raise due process questions as regards the legitimacy of the state's purpose. The nature of the treatment adopted also raises constitutional questions: in the case of *Weems* v. *United States* (1910), a test was developed by which the nature of treatment must be related to the gravity of the offense. In cases where an ingrained, though relatively innocuous, form of behavior is treated by means of, say, an aversive therapy, this procedure may violate the criterion of cruel and unusual punishment.

The limited value of therapy in a coerced situation, possibilities of sham cooperation, and problems regarding the prediction of individual recidivism should make therapists cautious of offering treatment in a prison environment. The growing trend within penal reform, away from the disappointing effects of applied rehabilitative ideals and toward a system of "just deserts" (Von Hirsch, 1976) or circumscribed consequences following specified prescribed actions, is one for which therapists should be prepared.

The Problem of Consent. Questions have thus been raised about the constitutionality of many procedures, particularly those involving aversive techniques or negative reinforcement. The fact that any constitutional right can be waived, provided that the waiver is a voluntary, informed, intelligent act undertaken with a good awareness of the relevant circumstances and the likely consequences, has made consent an important concept. The issue of what constitutes adequate consent has thus been assumed to be fundamental to a discussion of the legal issues raised by the behavior therapies (e.g., Friedman 1973). This assumption will be questioned.

First, although consent is considered fundamental, no widely acceptable standards for consent have been developed as yet. Before outlining those elements of consent that have acquired some standing, one proviso will be made regarding therapists' attitudes toward obtaining consent. Therapists should not regard obtaining consent simply as a means of protecting themselves from malpractice suits: consent given willingly is an indication of the future involvement of the client in the therapeutic process and in the decision to undergo therapy. As a general rule, therapy should not proceed without *active* consent, regardless of legal requirements, since consent represents an element desirable in therapy.

Certainly, doctors do have a legal duty to fulfill with regard to obtaining consent. Patients should be given sufficient information to enable them to reach an *informed decision*. This involves patients' being able to understand the nature of the treatment, its purpose, those aspects of the treatment that are experimental, the likely risks as well as benefits of the treatment, the probability of success, and the alternative treatments that may be available. Malpractice case-law abounds with instances of doctors' failing to disclose information or to communicate that information adequately. Patients are, of course, in the particularly vulnerable position of usually having no access to alternative sources of information. Doctors, naturally enough, believe that patients will benefit from the proposed course of treatment and may become overzealous in obtaining consent by abusing the doctor–patient relationship in the patient's best interests. As had already been outlined, the manipulability of consent is openly admitted. Individual freedom, as has often been pointed out (Annas, 1974), can be guaranteed only if it includes the freedom to make wrong decisions.

A number of issues are raised by the requirement that consent be informed. There are problems concerning experimental therapies. How can consent be informed when the relative cost–benefit ratio is unknown? How, for instance, can therapies achieve nonexperimental status without controlled trials, and how can the problems of obtaining consent in a double-blind study be resolved? How can physicians be expected to demonstrate an adequate exploration of alternative treatments when their own views may be partial? Engineering consent to an unproven but possibly more effective technique transgresses "least restrictive alternatives" but may result in genuinely more effective therapies. Certainly, the *Knecht* (1973) guideline of written notification of one's opportunity to revoke consent during experimental–aversive procedures (see p. 253) could be extended to include all therapies—possibly by means of some form of treatment contract. The institutionalized abuse of consent has also been common (e.g., the practice of consent by default). Under the Cal-

ifornia Welfare and Institute Code, consent is deemed to have been given if a patient raises no objections to therapy within 30 days of written notification of treatment.

A second element in consent concerns competency or rationality. The assumption of incompetency as a consequence of involuntary status has already been explored. Incompetency should be decided on an individual basis on evidence of observable behavior. Competency may also be affected by the length of an individual's confinement (i.e., by his/her degree of institutionalization and by the therapy that he/she may be undergoing, as well as by his/her problem). Methods of behavior control can deprive an individual of both the ability and the inclination to exercise the right to self-determination.

The usual course of action where an individual is deemed unable to make a rational decision is to revert to proxy consent. That third-party consent has usually been obtained from one of the patient's relatives. However, the desirability of seeking consent from a relative is questionable, when that relative could be neither rational, independent, nor maximally sensitive. Transferring actions from the involuntary to the voluntary region by means of relative consent has the additional drawback of not including any of the obligatory safeguards such as demonstrating the least restrictive alternative, that result when the state intervenes. Ideally, proxy consent requires a decision with no conflict of interest, where the desirability of the treatment can be separated from the question of the capacity of the person to consent.

The issue of whether consent has been voluntarily given has also caused problems. The *Kaimowitz* decision questioned the ability of an *involuntary* patient to give consent to an experimental procedure. For consent to be voluntary, the patient or inmate has to be free from coercion. There must be no promise, either real or imagined, of early discharge or change of status, and no threat of punitive measures. The institutional environment may not only impair decision-making capacities but may *also* bias decisions toward a given outcome. Concepts of voluntariness may also be affected by the nature of the choice. At Patuxent, where treatment is supposedly voluntary, under the new guidelines the choice for some offenders is between treatment and a 25-year sentence (Zenoff & Courtless, 1977).

However, it is not clear at what point coercion vitiates consent. To prohibit consent on the basis that a decision may be rational but coerced would seem further to infringe the civil liberties of individuals already in a deprived situation. Institutions that are coercive may be coercive with both voluntary and involuntary patients (cf. *Willowbrook*). Certainly the coercive nature of any physician–client relationship applies equally to any patient, regardless of status.

With these kinds of question being pursued about the value of consent, perhaps an alternative approach should be adopted by concentrating on the nature of the treatment rather than on the patient's status. In the United Kingdom, the recent white paper on Mental Health Legislation (DHSS) has adopted this approach. Treatments that are hazardous, irreversible, or not fully established would be permissible only on certain conditions, including eliciting an independent second opinion, even where the patient gives consent or is a voluntary patient. For nonconsenting patients, treatment would be permissible only to save life or to prevent violence. Patients not capable of giving consent would be allowed to undergo therapy only to alleviate or cure their condition, but again the therapy could not be hazardous, irreversible, or not fully established. All the areas of uncertainty, such as consent, competency, and which treatments fall into which categories, would be referred to a multidisciplinary panel. The white paper, however, gives no guidance as to whether behavior therapy would be considered a treatment deserving of special regulation. However, the white paper's hierarchical approach to treatment can be paralleled by a hierarchical approach to safeguards—other than a blanket prohibition or a reliance on informed voluntary consent.

There are some exceptions to the general rule that all patients should have the same standards for access and consent to treatment. The state does not appear to have a compelling enough interest to justify the rehabilitation of offenders by means of intrusive behavioral procedures over competent objection. The possibility of not making therapy available has to be considered in the light of the lack of any proven effective therapeutic techniques. Further, the problem of generalizing results of experimental therapy on volunteers to coerced "volunteers" or nonvolunteers may prohibit therapy's being made available.

Methods of Legal Control: The Alternatives

The Incentive Approach. Two forms of legal device have thus been explored as methods of limiting the excesses of behavior therapists. These two approaches have been characterized by Burton (1974) as the incentive approach and the specific prohibition and directives approach. Both, however, have drawbacks. The least rigid form of intervention, the incentive approach, relies on the limitation of the exercise of discretion by the therapist, by means of informed consent and the threat of malpractice suits. However, this traditional form of regulation can work effectively only where the two parties have equal bargaining power. Institutionalized patients, possibly being unaware of their legal rights and having no access to the courts or other means of making responsible and independent decisions, are not adequately protected by this form of regulation. Even voluntary patients are in an unequal and unfavorable position as an inevitable result of the nature of the client–therapist relationship.

The Directive and Prohibition Approach. The alternative approach of limiting certain kinds of actions presupposes agreement about which kinds of actions should be limited. In addition, it relies on stability of agreement over time once it is achieved. The behavior therapies are still evolving as treatments; it would be difficult to achieve such rigid prohibitions without their quickly becoming outdated or limiting the development of more effective therapies. Any prohibitive legislation would also have the drawback of being open to circumvention by individuals not sympathetic to the aims of the legislation. The therapeutic relationship is ultimately of a private nature and open to private abuse. Any law that is regularly abused in this manner will be only unevenly enforced, with a resulting weak deterrent effect.

Court-Based Review. Both of these alternatives also have the disadvantage of relying ultimately on court-based justice. Although Bazelon (1974) has stated, "For monitoring the performance of a profession there is no substitute in the end, for the adversary process,'' one might question whether this process is best founded on court-based reviews. The history of the involvement of the courts in mental health has not been outstandingly successful, particularly with reference to commitment. The assumption (still prevalent among some members of the legal profession) that treatment is in the patients' best interests has often resulted in perfunctory reviews by the courts in the light of definitive medical evidence. Even when exposed to a variety of expert testimony, the ability to reach a correct decision may be limited when the adjudicator has no personal knowledge in the field and her/his access to information is limited to those giving evidence. Second, court-based decisions are much less flexible when applied to individual cases. Administrative discretion at least allowed the possibility of individual review and action, even if at the expense of constitutional rights! Third, court-based decisions can never be self-enforcing and require either further litigation (e.g., for damages) or are dependent on other factors within society to effect meaningful change. Litigation can do little more than cause inconvenience. The maintenance of standards requires constant vigilance at a local level. Legal, court-based reform can provide only a framework; other forms of control will be necessary to maintain standards.

Peer Review. One of the forms of compromise normally recommended in these circumstances is *peer review.* This recommendation is predicated on the assumption that only those blessed with the same expertise can assess the activities of professional therapists. However, as was explored earlier, although highly desirable, self-regulation by professionals has been disappointing.

Role Definition Approach: The Recommended Alternative. The form of intervention required is one that combines the individual flexibility of administrative discretion with the controls and standards of judicial intervention. The role definition approach, Burton's (1974) third approach, depends on the definition of social roles through the law and can hopefully both accommodate therapeutic goals and protect human autonomy. It is this form of control that is recommended here.

Review should be undertaken by an independent, multidisciplinary panel of informed individuals, separate from, but with equivalent status to, the proponents of therapy. This panel would be guided by an established legal framework and would have access to information of an independently assessed nature concerning the merits of relative therapies. Such a panel would be expected to reach decisions (in an adversary setting if thought desirable), and patients would also have access to independent sources of information (see above) and be legally represented. The panel could decide many of the issues raised in this chapter with reference to individual cases. Questions regarding experimental ethics and design, as well as the evaluation and improvement of therapies, could come within the panel's domain. Although administratively costly, this form of control, given unambiguous guidelines and access to pertinent, up-to-date information, may prove to be the most effective.

It should be mandatory for anyone offering behavior therapy services to be a member of a professional group, monitored by a reviewing body that would consider the general and specific desirability of both goals and methods and would lay down boundary criteria adapted as appropriate to changing social circumstances. Through the publication of referred cases, the professions concerned would be made constantly aware of the need to inform their professional decisions with ethical criteria of a kind acceptable to both professionals and consumers. For serious infractions of these criteria, the review body would have such powers as removing the names of individuals from the relevant professional register. As several professional groups supply behavior therapy services, each might have its own review body, and a central interdisciplinary liaison committee would be necessary to enable formal contact and thus harmonize standards. In contrast to the ''closed shop'' that currently operates in the older professions, such as medicine and the law, the membership of review bodies, including the interdisciplinary review bodies, should not be restricted to the professions supplying behavior therapy services but should include representatives of other relevant professions, such as the law, and of the major employing agencies.

It should also be a requirement for anyone

offering psychological services of any kind, including behavior therapy, to have received a training approved by a standing committee of the profession.

The last recommendation is, of course, particularly difficult, as there is a constant proliferation of "new" therapies for psychological problems. But at the very least, the major professions concerned (psychiatry, psychology, social work, and so on) should set up the necessary machinery for their own members and other representatives, as indicated above, and should ensure that it is appropriately publicized to clients and potential clients. The functions of the information agency outlined above might include supplying the names of locally available members of professions offering proper safeguards, together with information on the arbitration body.

Summary

Obviously, this form of control has drawbacks. Individuals on the type of panel suggested tend to reach internally consistent decisions without adequate feedback about decisions, established principles for action, and open, contested discussions (wherever possible). The need for regular judicial review of those guidelines must also be stressed; otherwise, this kind of decision-making body can easily reach decisions not in keeping with the spirit of the legislation in laudable attempts to achieve the best results in any given case. The ease with which the law can be evaded and reinterpreted in such situations is demonstrated by the operation of the Mental Health Review Tribunal (MHRT) system in England and Wales. These independent panels, comprising legal, psychiatric, and lay representatives, make decisions about the discharge of detained patients in cases where discharge is opposed by the patient's consulting psychiatrist. Research undertaken by one of the authors (1981) has demonstrated that such decisions are taken in most cases on the basis of the panel's individual understanding of the law's intentions rather than on the basis of the defined legal criteria. It is nevertheless believed that these multidisciplinary panels do offer the greatest potential for accommodating the competing interests of society, its individual members, and therapeutic concerns. To assume that this kind of committee would not be welcomed by practitioners would be to disregard further evidence from the operation of the MHRT system, where difficult discharge decisions are avoided by individual physicians and the responsibility is left to an independent panel. Review need not always be critical of individual actions. Although the diagnosis and treatment of psychological problems should remain an expert area, the determination to compel treatment, or to give a particular treatment, or to treat within a particular environment remain areas that concern society in general. Deviance alone can never justify state intervention. Behavior therapy can fulfill a valuable role of service to society and its members, without being an unquestioning tool of the central power of the state.

One further word of warning needs articulation. Although behavior therapists are currently in the position of being able to claim complacently that the worst excesses of the behavior control technologies have not emanated from schools of behavior therapy, they should guard against the abuse of their knowledge and, as a profession, should be active in that protection. Behavior therapy is exploitable, the more so because the therapies rarely involve sophisticated equipment (or techniques). Therapists should first question the direction of their experimental work and the uses to which it may be put: there may often be arguments in favor of not undertaking certain kinds of exploratory therapy. Second, reliance on legal regulation is insufficient. Behavior therapists as a professional body should not have to look to the law for guides to therapeutic standards. The law cannot become a fail-safe mechanism for any specific case: the ultimate control has to come from the therapists and from the nature of the techniques available to them. "Search for the 'Manchurian Candidate'" (Marks, 1979), which highlights the work of the CIA in the field of behavior control, includes details of the work of a past president of both the American Psychiatric Association and the World Psychiatric Association. This research, undertaken on psychiatric inpatients, involved the use of sensory deprivation, electroshock, and drug techniques of no proven therapeutic value to those individuals. The book should serve as a timely reminder to all those who work in the field of behavior control that ethical and legal abuses are matters of concern to all members of the profession.

In conclusion, one of the great current hopes of behavior therapists is that we will move toward a preventive and educational role in order to equip the public at large with the skills to modify their own lives and environments in directions that they consider appropriate, with psychologists taking on the role of program advisers and consultants, rather than of omnipotent experts to whom the problem is handed over. Such a development would be the best of all safeguards against ethical abuse for the relatively independent majority of the population.

References

Annas, G. The hospital: A human rights wasteland. *Civil Liberties Review*, 1974, *3*, 9–29.

Bandura, A. *Principles of Behavior Modification*. New York: Holt, Rinehart & Winston, 1969.

Bazelon, D. Psychiatrists and the adversary process. *Scientific American*, 1974, *230*, 18–23.

Bean, P. The Mental Health Act 1959—Some issues concerning rule enforcement. *Law and Society*, 1975, *2*, 2.

Beauchamp, T. Paternalism and bio-behavioral control. *The Monist*, 1977, *60*, 1.

Budd, K., & Baer, D. Behavior modification and the law: Implications of recent judicial decisions. *Journal of Psychiatry and Law*, 1976, *4*, 171–244.

Burton, S. J. The new biotechnology and the role of legal intervention. *American Journal of Orthopsychiatry*, 1974, *44*, 688–696.

Clonce v. *Richardson*, 379. F.Supp. 338 (1974).

Contract Research Corporation. *The evaluation of Patuxent Institution: Final Report*, 1977, *83*, 84.

Cotter, L. H. Operant conditioning in a Vietnamese mental hospital. *American Journal of Psychiatry*, 1967, *124*, 23–28.

Covington v. *Harris*, 419. F.2d. 617, 623 (D.C. Cir. 1969).

Davison, G. C. Homosexuality, the ethical challenge. *Journal of Homosexuality*, 1977, *2*, 195–204.

Department of Health, Education and Welfare. *The institutional guide to DHEW policy on protection of human subjects*. Department of Health, Education and Welfare Publication No. (N.I.H.) 72-102, December 1, 1971.

DHSS, Welsh Office, Lord Chancellor's Dept., 1978, *Review of the 1959 Mental Health Act*. London: cmnd. 7320.

Donaldson v. *O'Connor*, Civ. Action No. 1693, ND Fla. (1973).

Feinberg, J. Liberty-limiting principles. In T. Beauchamp & J. Walters (Eds.), *Contemporary issues in bioethics*. Encino, Calif.: Dickenson Publishing Co. 1978.

Feldman, M. P. The behavior therapies and society. In M. P. Feldman & A. Broadhurst (Eds.), *Experimental bases of the behavior therapies*. London: Wiley, 1976. (a)

Feldman, M. P. Social psychology and the behavior therapies. In M. P. Feldman & A. Broadhurst (Eds.), *Experimental bases of the behavior therapies*. London: Wiley, 1976. (b)

Feldman, M. P. *Criminal behavior: A psychological analysis*. London: Wiley, 1977. (a)

Feldman, M. P. Helping homosexuals with problems. *Journal of Homosexuality*, 1977, *2*, 241–249. (b)

Friedman, P. Legal regulation of applied behavior analysis in mental institutions and prisons. *Arizona Law Review*, 1973, *17*, 39.

Friedman, P. Mentally handicapped citizen and institutional labor. *Harvard Law Review*, 1974, *87*, 567–587.

Gaylon, W. Skinner redux. *Harper's Magazine*, Oct. 1973, pp. 48–56.

Gobert, J. Psychosurgery, conditioning and the prisoners right to refuse rehabilitation. *Virginia Law Review*, 1975, *61*, 155–196.

Golann, S. The core problem controversy. In President's Committee on Mental Retardation, *The mentally retarded citizen and the law*. New York: Free Press, 1976.

Goldiamond, I. Towards a constructional approach to social problems. *Behaviorism*, 1974, *2*, 1–85.

Griswold v. *Connecticut*, 381. U.S. 479 (1962).

Halleck, S. Legal and ethical aspects of behavior control. *American Journal of Psychiatry*, 1974, *131*, 381–385.

Halpern, C. The right to habilitation. In President's Committee on Mental Retardation, *The mentally retarded citizen and the law*. New York: Free Press, 1976.

Hamilton v. *Love*, 328, F. Supp. 1182 (Ed. Ark. 1971).

Hawkins, H., & Sullivan, P. Due process and the development of "criminal" safeguards in civil commitment adjudications. *Fordham Law Review*, 1974, *42*, 611–625.

HMSO (Her Majesty's Stationers' Office). *A review of the Mental Health Act 1959—A consultative document*. London: Department of Health and Social Security, 1976.

Hoffman, P. B. Patuxent Institution from a psychiatric perspective circa 1977. *Bulletin of the American Academy of Psychiatry and Law*, 1977, *5*, 171–199.

Inmates of Boys Training Schools v. *Affleck*, 346, F. Supp. 1354 (D.R.I. 1972).

In re Ballay, 482, F.2d, 648 (1973).

In re Gault, 387, U.S. 1 at 18 (1967).

Jackson v. *Indiana*, 406 U.S. 715 (1972).

Kaimowitz v. *Michigan Department of Mental Health*, 42, U.S.L.W. 2063 (1973), and Civ. No. 73-19434, Civ. Ct. Wayne County, Michigan, (1973).

Kittrie, N. *The right to be different: Deviance and enforced therapy*. Baltimore: Johns Hopkins Press, 1971.

Knecht v. *Gillman*, 488, F2d, 1136 (8th Cir. 1973).

Krasner, L. The therapist as a social reinforcement machine. In H. H. Strupp & L. Luborsky (Eds.), *Research in psychotherapy*, Vol. 2. Washington, D.C.: American Psychological Association, 1962.

Krasner, L. Assessment of token economy programmes in psychiatric hospitals. In R. Porter (Ed.), *Learning theory and psychotherapy*. London: Churchill, 1968.

Krasner, L. Behavioral modification: Ethical issues and

future trends. In H. Leitenberg (Ed.), *Handbook of behavior modification and behavior therapy.* Englewood Cliffs, N.J.: Prentice-Hall, 1976.

Krasner, L., & Ullmann, L. P. *Behavior influence and personality: The social matrix of human action.* New York: Holt, Rinehart & Winston, 1973.

Lake v. *Cameron*, 364, F2d, 657 (1966).

Lessard v. *Schmidt*, 349, F. Supp. 1078, 1084–87 (1972).

Mackey v. *Procunier*, 477, F2d, 877 (9th Cir. 1973).

Malmquist, C. Can the committed patient refuse chemotherapy? *Archives of General Psychiatry,* 1979, *36,* 351–354.

Marks, J. *The search for the "Manchurian Candidate."* London: Allen Lane, 1979.

Martarella v. *Kelley*, 349, F.Supp. 575 (1972).

Martin, R. *Legal challenges to behavior modification: Trends in schools, corrections and mental health.* Champaign, Ill.: Research Press, 1975.

Masters, W. H., & Johnson, V. E. *Human sexual inadequacy.* Boston: Little, Brown, 1970.

McConnell, J. V. Stimulus/response. Criminals can be brainwashed—now. *Psychology Today,* 1970, *3,* 14–18.

McGuire, W. J. The nature of attitudes and attitude change. In G. Lindzey & E. Aronson (Eds.), *Handbook of social psychology,* Vol. 3. Reading, Mass.: Addison-Wesley, 1969.

Mill, J. S. *Essay on liberty* (2nd ed.). London: Parker, 1859.

Monahan, J. John Stuart Mill on the liberty of the mentally ill—A historical note. *American Journal of Psychiatry,* 1977, *134,* 1428–1429.

Morris, W. (Ed.). *The American Heritage Dictionary.* New York: American Heritage Publishing Company, 1969.

New York State Association for Retarded Children v. *Rockefeller (Willowbrook),* 357, F.Supp. 752. (E.D.N.Y. 1973).

O'Callaghan, M., & Carroll, D. *Psychosurgery: A Scientific analysis.* Springfield, Ill.: Charles C Thomas, 1982.

O'Leary, K. D. Behavior modification in the classroom: A rejoinder to Winett. *Journal of Applied Behavior Analysis,* 1972, *5,* 505–511.

Olmstead v. *United States,* 227, U.S. 438, 479 (1927).

Peay, J. Mental health tribunals—just or efficacious safeguards? *Law and Human Behaviour,* in press.

Perkins, D. E. Personal communications. D. E. Perkins, Senior Psychologist, Birmingham Prison, 1978.

Perlin, M. Legal implications of behavior modification programs. *Bulletin of the American Academy of Psychiatry and Law,* 1976, *4,* 175–183.

Pratt v. *Davies*, 118, Ill. App. 161, aff'd 224, Ill. 30, 79, N.E. 562 (1906).

Rappaport, J. Enforced treatment—Is it treatment? *Bulletin of the American Academy of Psychiatry and Law,* 1974, *2,* 148–158.

Reid, I. D., Feldman, M. P., & Ostapiuk, E. The Shape Project for young offenders. *Journal of Offender Rehabilitation,* 1980, *4,* 233–246.

Risley, T. R., & Twardosz, S. Suggested guidelines for the humane management of the behavior problems of the retarded. Unpublished manuscript, Johnny Cake Child Study Center, January 1974.

Robinson v. *California,* 370 U.S. 660 (1962).

Roe v. *Wade*, 410, U.S. 113, 153 (1973).

Rothman, D. *The discovery of the asylum: Social order and disorder in the new Republic.* Boston: Little, Brown, 1971.

Rouse v. *Cameron*, 373, F.2d, 451 (1966).

Schwartz, B. In the name of treatment: Autonomy, civil commitment and right to refuse treatment. *Notre Dame Lawyer,* 1975, *50,* 808–842.

Serber, M. A word of warning to behavior modifiers working in a restricted ward setting. *Behavior Therapy,* 1972, *3,* 517–519.

Shapiro, M. H. Legislating the control of behavior control: Autonomy and coercive use of organic therapies. *Southern California Law Review,* 1974, *47,* 237–353.

Shelton v. *Tucker*, 364, U.S. 479, 488 (1960).

Shuman, S. I. *Psychosurgery and the medical control of violence.* Detroit: Wayne State University Press, 1977.

Silverstein, G. Homosexuality and the ethics of behavioral interventions. *Journal of Homosexuality,* 1977, *2,* 205–211.

Souder v. *Brennan.* Civ. Ac. No. 482-72 (D.D.C.), (1973).

Stahlman, M. Ethical dilemmas in current obstetric and newborn care. In T. D. Moore (Ed.), *Report of the 65th Ross Conference on Paediatric Research.* Columbia, Ohio: Ross Laboratories, 1973.

Stolz, S. B. Ethical issues in research on behavior therapy. In W. S. Wood (Ed.), *Issues in evaluating behavior modification.* Champaign, Ill.: Research Press, 1975.

Szasz, T. S. *Psychiatric slavery.* New York: Free Press, 1977.

Time. "Behavior modification" behind the walls. March 11, 1974, pp. 42–43.

Von Hirsch, A. *Doing justice—the choice of punishments.* Report of the Committee for the Study of Incarceration. New York: Hill & Wang, 1976.

Wald, P. Basic personal and civil rights. In President's Committee on Mental Retardation, *The mentally retarded citizen and the law.* New York: Free Press, 1976.

Weems v. *United States.* 217, U.S. 349 (1910).

Wexler, D. B. Token and taboo: Behavior modification, token economies and the law. *California Law Review,* 1973, *61,* 81–109.

Wexler, D. B. Behavior modification and other behavior change procedures: The emerging law and the proposed Florida guidelines. *Criminal Law Bulletin,* 1975, *11,* 600–616.

Winett, R. A., & Winkler, R. C. Current behavior modification in the classroom: Be still, be quiet, be docile. *Journal of Applied Behavior Analysis,* 1972, *5,* 499–506.

Winters v. *Miller.* 446, F.2d, 65 (1971).

Wyatt v. *Stickney.* 344, F. Supp. 373 and 344, F. Supp. 387 (M.D. Aba) (1972).

Zenoff, E., & Courtless, T. Autopsy of an experiment: The Patuxent experience. *Journal of Psychiatry and Law,* 1977, *5,* 531–550.

CHAPTER 10

Balancing Clients' Rights

THE ESTABLISHMENT OF HUMAN-RIGHTS AND PEER-REVIEW COMMITTEES

Jan Sheldon-Wildgen and Todd R. Risley

Introduction

In the last two decades, society has witnessed a dramatic increase in the amount of litigation concerning incarcerated mentally ill and developmentally disabled persons. These lawsuits reflect a heightened concern with the conditions and practices to which these people have been exposed. Of prime importance in many of those cases have been alleged harmful practices, including such things as physical and mental abuse, unsanitary living conditions, and exposure to aversive treatment procedures such as electric shock, psychosurgery, physical restraints, and seclusion (*Halderman and the United States* v. *Pennhurst*, 1977; *Kaimowitz* v. *Department of Mental Health*, 1973; *New York State Association for Retarded Children and Parisi* v. *Carey*, 1975; *Wyatt* v. *Stickney*, 1972). Evidence from the cases indicated that individuals in residential programs could also be exposed to harmful conditions because of an absence of appropriate treatment; without appropriate treatment, many individuals can regress or deteriorate in their functioning (Walker & Peabody, 1979). A number of important conclusions have resulted from these lawsuits. Two of the most important are: (1) the right of residential clients to be free from abusive and harmful procedures and conditions and (2) the right of clients to receive treatment appropriate to their needs.

These two rights are not always compatible and often may present problems to behavior therapists and treatment providers (Begelman, 1975, 1978; Friedman, 1975; Wexler, 1978). For some severely debilitated residents, providing effective treatment may expose the person to some risk or potential harm because less intrusive treatment procedures have not accomplished the desired goals (Budd & Baer, 1976; Wexler, 1973, 1974; Wildgen, 1976). The purpose of this chapter is to describe human-rights and peer–review committees, mechanisms by which these two rights, the right to effective treatment and the right to be free from harm, may be balanced and protected. To understand these protective mechanisms and their importance, it will be helpful to trace briefly the development and current state of the two potentially conflicting rights.

Jan Sheldon-Wildgen and Todd R. Risley • Department of Human Development, University of Kansas, Lawrence, Kansas 66045.

Right to Treatment

There is no specific constitutional right to treatment; rather, the "right to treatment" has been found to exist because of the involuntary incarceration of mentally ill and developmentally disabled individuals. Relying on the constitutional guarantees of due process and equal protection and the prohibition on cruel and unusual punishment, courts have held that there must be a justification for allowing the government to involuntarily confine a person who has not committed a crime (Friedman & Halpern, 1974). This justification, or *quid pro quo*, for the deprivation of liberty is the fact that the government will provide the individual with treatment.

The first judicial decision to recognize specifically a right to treatment for mental patients was *Rouse* v. *Cameron* (1966). The court, relying on a District of Columbia statute, held that a right to treatment existed by stating: "The purpose of involuntary hospitalization is treatment, not punishment. . . . Absent treatment, the hospital is 'transform[ed] . . . into a penitentiary where one could be held indefinitely for no convicted offence'" (pp. 452–453). Many subsequent cases have recognized a right to treatment based on either statutory or constitutional grounds (e.g., *Covington* v. *Harris*, 1969; *Davis* v. *Watkins*, 1974; *Millard* v. *Cameron*, 1966; *Nason* v. *Superintendent of Bridgewater State Hospital*, 1968; *Sinohar* v. *Parry*, 1979; *Tribby* v. *Cameron*, 1967; *Welsch* v. *Likins*, 1974; *Wuori* v. *Zitnay*, 1978; *Wyatt* v. *Stickney*, 1971, 1972; *Wyatt* v. *Aderholt*, 1974; *Wyatt* v. *Ireland*, 1979). In recognizing this right, the courts have also referred to "adequate," "appropriate," "effective," "proper," "suitable," "necessary," and "optimal" treatment, and "a realistic opportunity to be cured or to improve his or her mental condition" (e.g., *Cook* v. *Ciccone*, 1970; *Clatterbuck* v. *Harris*, 1968; *Eckerhart* v. *Hensley*, 1979; *In re Jones*, 1972; *Millard* v. *Cameron*, 1966; *Nason* v. *Superintendent of Bridgewater State Hospital*, 1968; *Rouse* v. *Cameron*, 1966; *Welsch* v. *Likins*, 1974; *Wyatt* v. *Stickney*, 1972).

Although the courts used terms such as *appropriate* and *optimal* treatment, judges have been reluctant to define exactly what they meant by these terms (Schwitzgebel, 1973). After all, there often appeared to be little agreement among mental health professionals as to what constituted appropriate treatment. It was therefore not unusual that judges, with little or no psychological training, did not feel competent to specify what must take place in order for treatment to have occurred. In the last few years, however, the courts have been much more willing to specify what goals must be attained and what changes must take place in order to demonstrate that treatment has been provided. It is debatable whether this change reflects a new respect for the mental health profession in acknowledging that professionals can determine when "appropriate treatment" has occurred, or whether it reflects a strong dissatisfaction because, after a decade of having mandated that treatment take place, little has occurred in terms of actually providing residents with much-needed skills. Whatever the reason, courts now often require specific changes in behavior. Recently, for example, a court ruled that a client in a facility had a right to a habilitation program that would maximize the client's human abilities, enhance the client's ability to cope with the environment, and create a reasonable expectation of progress toward the goal of independent community living (*Wyatt* v. *Ireland*, 1979). Thus, the courts recognize that procedures must be employed to produce appropriate changes in the individual's behavior. The type of treatment used to accomplish these changes, however, has been left, within certain guidelines, to the discretion of the mental health profession (Schwitzgebel, 1973).

Right to Be Free from Harm

While recognizing a right to treatment for incarcerated mentally ill and developmentally disabled individuals, the courts simultaneously addressed the issue of the harmful or potentially dangerous conditions that existed in institutions and the aversive procedures that were being employed as treatment. The courts found that because of the lack of community, professional, or judicial scrutiny, many institutional residents had been subjected to conditions and procedures that raised questions of cruel and unusual punishment, which is prohibited by the Eighth Amendment to the Constitution (Wildgen, 1976).

Many procedures have been critically examined and either have been absolutely forbidden or have been prohibited unless the resident (or someone acting in the resident's best interest when the resident is incompetent) has given expressed, uncoerced, and informed consent. Obviously, most courts have banned the use of corporal punishment and physical abuse (*Morales* v. *Turman*, 1973; *New York State Association for Retarded Children* v. *Rockefeller*, 1973). Procedures involving physical abuse such as slapping, kicking, and tying a resident to a bed for lengthy periods have been held to degrade human dignity, to serve no necessary purpose, and to be so severe as to be unacceptable to society (*Wheeler* v. *Glass*, 1973). Other institutional conditions that the courts have banned as violating the Eighth Amendment include inadequate nutrition or medical services and unsanitary living conditions, such as inadequate plumbing and ventilation or insect infestations (Walker & Peabody, 1979).

The conditions mentioned above have no justification either as treatment procedures or as part of a humane living environment. Where these conditions have existed, it seems clear that the residents have not been protected from harm, let alone provided with appropriate treatment. More difficult discriminations are involved when the courts have had to address the use of techniques that are accepted as therapeutic but that expose the resident to potential harm or detriment. Clearly, some procedures (e.g., lobotomies and electroconvulsive shock treatment) seem much more intrusive and damaging than others (e.g., psychotropic drugs or seclusion). All, however, present the problem of being open to inappropriate use or misuse, sometimes to the permanent detriment of the resident. The courts have required that these procedures be used only for legitimate therapeutic purposes and only if less restrictive procedures have failed. For example, one court ruled that electric shock could be used only in extraordinary circumstances to prevent self-mutilation that might result in permanent damage (*Wyatt* v. *Stickney*, 1972). Similarly, physical restraints have been closely examined, and restrictions

have been placed on their use (e.g., *Inmates of Boys' Training School* v. *Affleck*, 1972; *Welsch* v. *Likins*, 1974; *Wheeler* v. *Glass*, 1973; *Wyatt* v. *Stickney*, 1972). One court stated that restraints should be applied "only if alternative techniques have failed and only if such restraint imposes the least possible restriction consistent with its purpose" and only when absolutely necessary to prevent a client from seriously injuring her/himself or others (*Wyatt* v. *Stickney*, 1972).

The use of seclusion has been condemned by some courts, which have either totally prohibited its use or strictly limited the situations under which it can be employed (*Inmates of Boys' Training School* v. *Affleck*, 1972; *Morales* v. *Turman*, 1973; *New York State Association for Retarded Children* v. *Rockefeller*, 1973; *Wyatt* v. *Stickney*, 1972). Many courts (e.g., *Wyatt* v. *Stickney*, 1972), however, have made a distinction between the use of seclusion (often defined as locking a resident in a barren room, unsupervised, for long periods of time) and the use of "therapeutic time-out" which normally involves placing a person in a room alone or off to the side of ongoing activities for a short period of time immediately following the occurrence of an inappropriate behavior. Therapeutic time-out requires constant supervision by the staff to ensure that the patient does not harm him/herself while being confined (Budd & Baer, 1976).

Additionally, the use of chemical restraints in the form of medication has received widespread attention (e.g., *Horacek* v. *Exon*, 1975; *Wyatt* v. *Stickney*, 1972). Psychotropic drugs, many of which have potentially dangerous side effects, often cannot be used unless the patient gives informed consent or unless the patient presents a clear danger to him/herself or others. Recent cases have held that a client who is nondangerous has a right to refuse treatment that consists of the use of psychotropic drugs (*Rennie* v. *Klein*, 1978; *Rogers* v. *Okin*, 1979).

Aversive techniques, which have some potentially therapeutic value, present a major problem for courts as well as the mental health profession (Kazdin, 1980). It is necessary to determine when these techniques are being employed as part of a comprehensive treatment program designed to enable the person to move to the least restrictive type of environment, as opposed to when they are used for retribution, for the convenience of the staff, as a substitute for less intrusive treatment, or simply to accommodate the individual to the existing environment. Protective devices must be developed to ensure that when these techniques are advocated by the staff, they are reasonably appropriate and are carefully and professionally administered so that patients, especially the severely debilitated, receive effective, yet humane, treatment.

Establishing Protective Mechanisms

Developing an effective, legally justified, and ethically sound program is a difficult task, especially when a program's clientele are severely debilitated and difficult to treat. To meet both present legal mandates and professional requirements, therapists must provide appropriate and individualized treatment suitable to each client's particular needs and at the same time make sure that the treatment is ethical and humane. There are two basic problems that a therapist must address: choosing appropriate goals and designing and implementing treatment techniques that will allow those goals to be obtained in the most effective, efficient, and professionally appropriate manner possible. Additionally, a third consideration, involving the public's perspective of what is ethical and humane, must be examined.

Selecting Appropriate Goals

Several authors have addressed the problem of selecting appropriate goals (e.g., Davison & Stuart, 1975; Hawkins, 1975; Martin, 1975; Wexler, 1978). Clearly, the goals chosen should reflect individual needs and should be relevant and useful to a particular client. For example, a person should not be subjected to a group training program that is teaching skills that the client already possesses or that are of little value to the client. The goals should be developed after a comprehensive, but not overly intrusive, assessment has been made. Then,

after considering all aspects of the client's life, the objectives should be prioritized and arranged in terms of short- and long-term goals. They should be organized together to make an integrated program plan for the individual, with the overall objective of teaching the individual the skills needed to allow removal of restrictions on activities and opportunities. Examining whether this type of progression has taken place is one of the best ways to evaluate whether appropriate goals have been established. Obviously, these kinds of goals may require more work for programs that, in the past, have been primarily custodial in nature. With some planning and organization, however, programs should be able to develop and prioritize goals and treatment plans for the clients served.

For severely debilitated individuals, the task of selecting goals may present some problems. One of the primary issues in developing appropriate goals is to assure that the goal is established because it will benefit the client in some way rather than being beneficial for only the staff or others in the client's environment. Often, the severely debilitated individuals in a treatment program engage in behaviors that the staff or others find particularly disruptive, aggressive, or inappropriate. The staff may wish to eliminate all behaviors that they find aversive or that cause them more work. Thus, the treatment may benefit the staff more than it does the client. Clients must be protected against this potential problem in addition to being assured of an appropriate evaluation, with relevant goals having been established.

Establishing Effective Treatment Techniques. Effective treatment usually implies that the techniques used are sufficient to give the client an increased latitude in what she/he is able to do. In deciding what techniques should be used and which will produce the highest probability of being effective, treatment providers should rely on the relevant published literature for justifying the techniques and conditions of use (Risley, 1975). This approach may require considerable training of staff and supervisors before the procedures are implemented. With proper goals and proper implementation of treatment techniques, effective treatment that will allow a client to progress to less restrictive environments and activities should occur.

For many programs, establishing effective treatment techniques should present few problems, other than being creative. Wexler (1973), for example, proposed that instead of depriving people of their "basic rights" (e.g., food, clothes, bed, closet, outdoor activity, or access to a telephone) in order to use these "rights" as reinforcers to motivate the person, the therapist should find idiosyncratic or more individualized reinforcers (i.e., something that is very special to that particular person). Thus, items out of a mail-order catalog, special trips to favorite places, or the right to engage in activities for extended periods of time might be used to reward a person for engaging in appropriate behaviors or to help teach a needed skill. Therapists can no longer rely on the easiest-to-think-of and most convenient variables, but providing legally sanctioned treatment techniques should not present an overwhelming ethical, legal, or professional decision for the majority of clients.

With the "hard-to-treat" or the severely debilitated clients, however, problems may arise for a therapist. For example, many of the most debilitated clients have a limited range of items or activities that are reinforcing to them. Perhaps because of their limited exposure to other reinforcers, only the most basic items (e.g., food) may appear to motivate them. Often, therapists are presented with the problem that if the use of food or meals as a reinforcer is limited, it is difficult to teach or train many clients. Another example is clients who are so extremely aggressive, disruptive, or self-abusive that a limitation on the use of aversive or unpleasant treatment techniques may mean that the clients will be harmed either physically (because of their self-destructive behavior) or by the lack of treatment (because of the inability of the therapist to initiate a constructive form of treatment while the aggressive or disruptive behavior is being emitted or anticipated) (Baer, 1970; Stolz, 1975). The therapist is therefore placed in a dilemma. For this type of hard-to-treat client, should treatment programs be implemented that may potentially deprive the clients of basic rights or expose them to unpleasant techniques in an attempt to accomplish effective treatment and, thus, move them to less restrictive environments and conditions of living? Or, rather, should these clients be placed in a pleasant environment where noncontroversial treatment techniques are used, even though the techniques have a low probability of success in accomplishing effective treatment that will allow the client more freedom?

Providing Ethical and Human Safeguards. "Effective" treatment can be defined as the selection of goals and treatment techniques that allow a client to progress to less restrictive living conditions. Providing effective treatment is normally the concern of the professionals in charge of the treatment program. To provide effective treatment, however, may involve procedures or techniques that, because of their intrusive, controversial, aversive, or restrictive nature, are not viewed as acceptable to the general public or (to borrow a phrase used by the U.S. Supreme Court in criminal law cases, e.g., *Rochin* v. *California*, 1952) that "shock the conscience" of the public. Thus, there must be a balance between accomplishing effective treatment and protecting human rights (Kazdin, 1980). Allowing efficient and effective treatment procedures to exist without a consideration of how humane and appropriate they are could encourage abuse and misuse of the procedures that might result in detriment to both the clients and the treatment program.

The Need for Protective Mechanisms

Who should make the decisions about whether goals and treatment techniques are effective and appropriate? The most convenient method is to allow the program staff to make these decisions. This approach, however, may not be the most desirable if client and staff protection are to be provided. The staff, including the therapist, often have a vested interest in having the program operate smoothly and efficiently. One could argue, therefore, that the goals chosen and the techniques used benefit the staff more than the clients and, perhaps, could even potentially harm the clients. Protective mechanisms need to be developed to ensure that goals and treatment procedures are developed for the benefit of the clients and are ethical and humane. Additionally, some method is needed to determine whether the staff are using the most up-to-date and professionally appropriate techniques. It would be problematic, for example, if new treatment procedures were developed especially for use with the severely debilitated client, and the staff were not implementing those procedures. The treatment staff may not be in the best position to make a decision about the professional justification of certain procedures because of the possibility of personal bias or potential conflict of interests.

Independent review and protection mechanisms need to be developed to assure that the legal, ethical, and professional decisions being made are in the best interest of the clients (Griffith, 1980; May, Risley, Twardosz, Friedman, Bijou, Wexler *et al.*, 1976). This procedure would be advantageous to the clients because their interests would be considered and protected. There would also be a higher probability that appropriate treatment would be provided. Independent review mechanisms would also serve to help the staff by providing outside professional expertise that could be extremely useful. Additionally, if the mechanisms included some procedures for addressing legal and ethical questions, the staff would have assistance in determining whether their procedures will withstand public or judicial scrutiny.

The protective mechanisms developed need to address three issues: the development and specification of appropriate goals; the implementation of effective treatment techniques; and the consideration of whether the goals and treatment procedure are ethical and humane. The first two issues involve the judgments of professionals in the field. The third issue involves judgments of people who represent the viewpoints of society. Thus, two separate review committees are proposed: a peer review committee to address professional considerations and a human rights committee to address the ethical and humane considerations of society.

Employing these two types of review mechanisms can strongly benefit all types of treatment programs, but especially those serving the severely debilitated, where professional, legal, and ethical questions could constantly be raised as a result of the type of treatment programs developed. As pointed out by May *et al.* (1976), these committees can accomplish the following:

1. Protect the rights and welfare of . . . clients;
2. Maximize the quality and extent of services provided to clients;
3. Allow conscientious and well-trained persons to administer appropriate treatment procedures with a sense of security, and
4. Enable institutions to comply as economically and practically as possible, with both the form and spirit of protective requirements set forth in recent legislation and court decisions. (p. 35)

Most importantly, these review and protection mechanisms can ensure that the clients' best interests are served. Specifically, this means that appropriate and humane goals and treatment procedures can be implemented in order to accomplish *effective* and *appropriate treatment*. Thus, each case can be examined individually and treatment plans developed accordingly. This procedure is especially relevant for the "hard-to-treat" client, who is an easy target for mistreatment and nontreatment. This type of client, who once was the subject of much abuse, has recently been left untreated because only controversial procedures appeared effective. With review and protection mechanisms, one can determine whether the controversial techniques are professionally justified, and if they are, protective procedures can be implemented to ensure that they are humanely administered. The right to effective treatment can therefore be provided simultaneously to protecting the client from unnecessary or unjustified exposure to harm. The following sections describe in detail how to establish peer-review and human-rights committees, what their functions should be, and how they might most efficiently and effectively operate.

The Human Rights Committee

Wyatt v. *Stickney* (1972) was one of the first judicial decisions to require the establishment of a human rights committee. The court specified that the human rights committee "review . . . all research proposals and all habilitation programs to ensure that the dignity and human rights of residents are preserved." Additionally, the committee was to guarantee that residents would be afforded the legal rights and habilitation that had been judicially ordered. Thus, the committee was to advise and assist those residents who felt they had been denied appropriate treatment or who felt that their legal rights had been violated. Unfortunately, the court did not state how the committee was to be formed or exactly how it was to operate (Mahan, Maples, Murphy, & Tubb, 1975). Nonetheless, the consequences of the mandate to form a human rights committee were far-reaching. Human rights committees are very common now, and most institutional and residential programs have one. The problem is that it is still not clear who should be on the human rights committee or, more importantly, what the function of the committee should be beyond ensuring that clients receive humane treatment, and finally, how it should operate (Repp & Deitz, 1978); only a few authors have addressed the requirements in detail (e.g., Mahan *et al.*, 1975; Risley & Sheldon-Wildgen, 1980). Described below are several considerations that should be addressed when developing a human rights committee that will operate most effectively to protect clients while ensuring that they receive appropriate treatment.

Composition

A human rights committee is normally composed of a group of dedicated and concerned people who are willing to give freely of their time and energy to make sure that the clients of a particular program are treated humanely. While some authors (e.g., Griffith, 1980; Mahan *et al.*, 1975; May *et al.*, 1976) advocate that a behavioral scientist and an attorney should be members of this committee, it is not clear that this is necessary. Although it may be nice to have a behavioral scientist on the committee, the input that that member would make

may be obtained from the peer review committee. Likewise, although it may be desirable to have an attorney (especially one knowledgeable in the law relating to handicapped people or civil liberties) on the committee, most treatment programs have an attorney on retainer who can give advise on liability and legal issues. It is most critical that the members of this committee be genuinely concerned about the clients and willing to devote considerable time and energy to investigating and deliberating about individualized treatment plans as well as treatment techniques.

Many advocate that consumers of the treatment program be on this committee. Thus, one may want a client representative and a relative of a similarly situated client. Depending on the particular person, it may be undesirable to have parents, guardians, or relatives of *actual* clients on the committee, since they may be too intimately involved with the client to make unbiased decisions.

Normally, the human rights committee is composed of laypersons who represent the sentiments of the community, much as a jury is composed. To aid in making the committee a credible protective mechanism, the majority of members should have *no* affiliation with the treatment program. It is not necessary that the members of this committee have any professional expertise; rather, the critical qualities that members should possess are being interested enough to be willing to dedicate time to examine the functioning of the treatment program and staff, and being able to make independent decisions about whether the treatment procedures are humanely justified. The credibility of the committee can be improved by addressing the issues listed below.

Purpose

The primary purposes of a human rights committee are to provide sufficient and adequate safeguards for the clients of a treatment program to ensure against inhumane or improper treatment and, at the same time, to ensure that appropriate treatment will be accomplished with the greatest speed possible in the least restrictive manner. The importance of a human rights committee is most readily recognized in those programs that employ controversial procedures. With severely debilitated clients, procedures are often implemented that the general public may find objectionable, if considered out of context. For example, one may read of a treatment program that shocks small children or that squirts lemon juice into their mouths. The general public, reading only that, may be appalled. The duty of the human rights committee is to determine if the procedures are, indeed, objectionable if considered in the totality of the circumstances. Thus, the committee may not find it objectionable to shock small children who are engaging in such serious self-destructive behavior that it threatens their health and welfare. The committee must consider all the surrounding circumstances to decide if the treatment is appropriate. They must also determine if the same effect could be obtained by treatment that is less intrusive or aversive. A balance must always be considered: the client's right to be free from aversive and intrusive procedures against the right to obtain effective treatment when all reasonable and less intensive treatment techniques have been considered.

One common trap that human rights committees fall into is an overpreoccupation with protection from aversive or intrusive techniques. Equally important, however, is the need to make steady and rapid progress in the treatment. For example, consider severely debilitated clients who live with many restrictions. The restrictions may be determined by the fact that the clients have few behaviors in their repertoire or by the fact that their destructive behavior may require the staff to impose restrictive forms of treatment in order to protect them or other clients adequately. Human rights committees often address only the intrusiveness or restrictiveness of a treatment plan without recognizing that every day the person goes without effective treatment, the person remains untreated and, thus, in an inherently restricted state. This statement is not to imply that human rights committees should not be concerned with aversive techniques; they definitely should. They also must be concerned with observing the corollary right to effective treatment in order to remove the restrictions with which the client lives. This treatment should be provided in the quickest, most effective, and least restrictive way possible.

The human rights committee can function much as a jury does in obtaining and evaluating evidence to protect those who cannot adequately protect themselves. Also, like a jury, the human rights committee can evaluate whether due process is followed when implementing a treatment program. Thus, the committee members will need to develop (or make sure that the treatment staff develops) and implement a fair, independent, and unbiased procedure that examines each client's treatment plan to determine if it appears justified and humane. For example, if the committee observed a client who could feed, dress, bathe, and look after him/herself fairly well, the committee might feel that the goal of learning how to dress him/herself is unjustified because the client already knows and demonstrates that skill. Likewise, if none of the self-care skills were in a client's repertoire, it may appear unjustified to attempt to teach the client to read and write since the self-care skills are more fundamental. The committee would also examine the treatment techniques to determine if they are justified and humane. Thus, the committee members may prohibit, for example, the use of shock to teach social skills because they feel the procedure is inhumane with respect to the behavior being targeted; they may, on the other hand, allow the use of shock to decrease serious self-destructive behavior. The critical element is that the human rights committee follow a fair procedure that attempts to protect the clients' rights; that is the key to due process. (A suggested procedure will be described later.)

Members of the human rights committee often do not have the expertise to propose or professionally evaluate procedures. However, they may seek independent professional input as to the guidelines to be followed in addition to obtaining information on the effectiveness of certain procedures as compared with their intrusiveness. The members should remember that their function is not to make professional decisions but to make decisions, representing the community, relating to the justification for selecting goals and treatment procedures and to the humane and ethical nature of any treatment plan developed.

The human rights committee should write a *statement of purpose* that will allow the committee to state their overall objective and to outline their goals. Such a statement makes clear the duties of all the members of the committee. More importantly, however, it provides a concrete statement that can be used as a source of information for others by detailing exactly what objectives the committee is designed to address and the procedures the committee follows in making any recommendation. Thus, others will be encouraged to bring relevant topics, questions, or grievances to the Committee that could potentially benefit both the client and staff.

Education

To fulfill their duties adequately, members of the human rights committee should know what predominant issues they should be considering. As mentioned previously, it is not necessary for committee members to possess professional expertise. If the committee as a whole, or any member, has any question involving a particular professional issue concerning the program, the committee should contact outside experts (perhaps someone from the peer review committee) and advocates in this area. It is *necessary*, however, that the members have some knowledge of the types of issues they should be addressing. For example, they should know about the judicial limitations and the expressed public opinions concerning the use of electroconvulsive shock, the denial of basic rights, the use of psychotropic drugs, or the use of seclusion. They should know that there may be some instances in which an unpleasant or an aversive technique may be necessary, but they need to know enough to inquire about less restrictive alternatives and about whether the techniques are being used legitimately as a treatment procedure or, rather, to adapt the individual to the existing environment. A committee member cannot be effective if the member does not fully comprehend what are the duties of the job and what issues must be addressed. Therefore, the members of the human rights committee should read and acquaint themselves with the guidelines and standards promulgated by relevant advocacy groups, including the National Society for Autistic Children's *White Paper on Behavior Modification with Autistic Children* (1975), the National Association for Retarded Citizens' *Guidelines for the Use of Behavioral Procedures on State Programs for Retarded Persons* (May *et al.*, 1976), the Joint Commission on Accreditation of Hospitals' *Standards for Services for Developmentally Disabled Individuals* (1978), and the National Teaching-Family Association's *Standards of Ethical Conduct* (1979). Additionally, the members should read descriptions in books and chapters of the ethical and legal issues in treatment programs (e.g., Berkler, Bible, Boles, Deitz, & Repp, 1978; Budd & Baer, 1976; Martin, 1974, 1975; Roos, 1974). Being more knowledgeable about the key issues will make the members' job easier and their decisions more credible.

The Formal Review Process: The Use of Aversive Procedures

In any treatment program, the use of aversive or unpleasant procedures should be minimized as much as possible. At times, however, in an attempt to accomplish *effective* treatment, it may be necessary to use some form of aversive technique. Obviously, since the procedure is unpleasant, it easily draws the attention of the human rights committee, which must consider whether it is necessary and whether it is humane. Although protecting clients from the indiscriminate and inhumane application of aversive procedure is one of the committee's main charges, it is not the only task the members have to accomplish. Additionally, it is important to be able to provide effective treatment as quickly as possible (Repp & Deitz, 1978). Therefore, it is useful for the committee to have a formalized review process that will enable it to address, systematically and efficiently, the different types of aversive techniques that the staff may employ. Having a standard procedure to follow will inform the staff about which procedures may and may not be used without prior approval of the human rights committee.

All clients should be protected, since the techniques and the procedures to be followed with each technique will be explicitly spelled out in advance, and staff ignorance of these procedures would not act as a defense to any liability or sanctions that may be imposed. Aversive procedures can be categorized into three basic groups (May *et al.*, 1976), which are outlined below along with the type of review process best suited to the technique. (Although examples of procedures are provided for the first two groups, these are only examples, and each human rights committee should make its own decision about which procedures are included in each of the three categories.)

1. Some forms of aversive procedures are mild and fairly nonintrusive. These procedures might include such techniques as the use of some expression of social disapproval, for example, the word *no* (other than shouting or demeaning, threatening, or abusive comments); extinction or ignoring an inappropriate behavior that is not self-destructive or injurious to others; and contingent observation and positive-practice overcorrection (when implemented by trained personnel and only for limited amounts of time). These procedures should be applied only contingent on inappropriate behaviors (e.g., self-mutilation, inappropriate self-stimulation, aggressive, or disruptive behavior). Unless it is observed or reported that these procedures are being abused, they might be approved for use without specific approval of the human rights committee before, during, or after their use. It is good practice, however, to reevaluate the use of these procedures at least once each year to determine that they are not being applied inappropriately.

2. There are some procedures that might be allowed *without* the *prior* approval of the human rights committee but that require *post hoc* review. These procedures might include such techniques as therapeutic time-out, fines or response–cost techniques, and differential reinforcement of low rates of behavior, all of which should be applied only contingent on inappropriate behaviors. Additionally, there may be some qualifications imposed on their use. For example, the committee might decide that the use of differential reinforcement of other behavior or reinforcement of incompatible behaviors may be used to eliminate an inappropriate behavior only while concurrently reinforcing an appropriate substitute

behavior. Or minimeals (without food deprivation) may be allowed to be used not as a procedure to decrease behavior but rather as a technique to teach appropriate behaviors. The procedures delineated in this section could be implemented by the treatment staff when they felt such procedures were justified, but their continued use for each client would require review by the human rights committee and approval at the next meeting of the human rights committee. After approval has been obtained, reports of the use of the procedure and its effectiveness with a particular client should be presented at each subsequent meeting of the human rights committee for the duration of the use of the procedure.

3. Aversive techniques not specified above in (1) or (2) might require prior approval before they could be prescribed for any problem or client. As May *et al.* (1976) pointed out, there are certain issues that should be considered before allowing the use of any of these techniques. It should be demonstrated that the client, if competent to do so, has given informed consent (or a parent or guardian when the client is unable to do so); that the peer review committee has approved this technique as professionally justified; and that the staff has demonstrated that all reasonable, less intensive treatment modalities have been tried or would clearly be ineffective. Finally, if the technique or procedure has serious side effects that would be more damaging to the client than the benefits that the client would receive, the technique should not be approved. It should be noted that although the human rights committee may have previously approved the use of a procedure described in this section with one client, prior approval should be obtained before the procedure may be used with another client or with another problem of the same client. Once the procedure has been approved for use with a particular client's problem, the human righs committee should review the effect of the procedure on a regular basis.

The Formal Review Process: Determining Individualized Treatment

Human rights committees can become so involved in protecting clients from aversive treatment techniques and from being deprived of basic privileges that they forget to make sure that clients are provided with appropriate and effective treatment. Additionally, the clients with the most controversial problems and treatment techniques are the ones who normally receive the committee's attention. Equally important as protecting clients from aversive treatment procedures is evaluating and assessing the treatment and progress of each individual client (including those receiving noncontroversial treatment) to determine if appropriate treatment is being provided. A formal review process should be developed that *regularly* assesses the treatment of all clients. Although staff input should be requested in this process, this review and evaluation should also be conducted independently. In other words, the committee should investigate on its own and make an independent determination of whether appropriate treatment is being provided. The following paragraphs describe a procedure that might be used to address this issue:

This review process is very similar to a judicial hearing: at least two opposing sides are considered, a specific procedure is followed, evidence is presented, and the burden of proving that a particular type of treatment is justified rests with the treatment staff. For this review process to function appropriately, it is best if one member of the human rights committee is individually assigned to present several clients' cases at a committee meeting (each case would be presented individually). In doing this, the committee member would assume the role of a client advocate. Being a client advocate includes the following: (1) reviewing the client's records; (2) observing the treatment that the client is receiving; and (3) spending time talking with the client (if possible) to understand how the client feels about the treatment that he/she is receiving and about the living environment. Thus, the committee member who is representing or acting as advocate for a client should know generally what skill deficits the client has, what the client needs to learn, what behaviors should be decreased, and what treatment program is already in effect for the client. Having this firsthand information means that the human rights committee need not rely only on the information given to them by the treatment staff.

At each meeting of the human rights committee, a specified number of client cases should be reviewed. Committee members who have been assigned as representatives or advocates for those clients are responsible for presenting the information they have obtained through records and observations. The treatment staff or a representative of the staff should also attend this meeting. The staff member is responsible for presenting the staff's perspective of the client's case. During this discussion of each client's case, the human rights committee, as a whole, must weigh and evaluate the evidence to determine whether the overall goals established for the client are appropriate, whether the goals are being reached, and whether the least restrictive or intrusive form of treatment is being utilized.

So that the committee can make an intelligent and fair decision, it is useful that someone present a point of view opposing the desires of the treatment staff. That "someone" should be the member of the human rights committee who is representing the client. If the committee member assumes a position advocating a type of treatment opposite that which the staff is suggesting, then both sides of the case or issue can be heard. Although the treatment staff may have the best intentions when presenting information about clients, they have a vested interest in the treatment program as it currently exists. Additionally, the treatment staff may become so involved in a particular client's program that they can see no alternatives other than what is currently being done. By requiring that an opposite, or at least an alternative, view be considered, other options are made available. The treatment staff would then have the "burden of proof" of convincing the human rights committee that the staff's present or proposed treatment is the best for the client.

The procedure might work as follows: If the treatment staff wanted to institute an aversive or intrusive procedure for a particular client, they would need to present their reasons for desiring this type of treatment. The designated member of the human rights committee, after having reviewed the case, observed the present treatment, and talked with the client, would advocate a less restrictive type of treatment procedure. This opposition would then require the treatment staff to justify their recommendations to the committee. If, on the other hand, the treatment staff suggested no changes in a client's program, the designated committee member could advocate a more intense program with the rationale of producing more rapid change, or if progress was adequate, the member would advocate a reduction in intrusiveness. In this case, the staff would have to provide clear rationales and justifications for advocating no changes.

The main objective in the procedure is to consider several alternatives for goals and treatment for each client. These different options should be weighed, and the human rights committee, acting much like a jury, should decide on the best treatment for a client as justified by the evidence presented. This is another protection against the human rights committee's acting merely as a "rubber stamp" for the treatment staff. This procedure also requires that the committee periodically review the program for *each* client, rather than reviewing the programs only for clients who are receiving aversive techniques. Additionally, the committee should address and evaluate the ultimate treatment goals every time it reviews a client's program to ensure that the skills being taught are relevant to the reason that the client is receiving treatment. The human rights committee may find that they need to refer to the results of standardized assessment procedures to aid in evaluating each client's progress. Records, however, should not be relied on solely; actual observation and interaction with the client is necessary.

Operating Independently of the Treatment Staff

To function appropriately in a protection and advocacy role and to be viewed as a *credible* protective mechanism, the human rights committee must be able to meet and deliberate as an independent body. Thus, the committee needs to set its own meeting dates and periodically meet without the treatment staff present. The committee, obviously, can ask any staff member to be present at the meetings whenever necessary. Additionally, the committee members must have independent access to the treatment program and the records and should maintain independent contact with each client. Only in this way can the committee retain its autonomy and resist undue influence from the treatment staff. Human rights committees should not become so intertwined with the treatment staff that they lose an independent perspective and are no longer adequately able to represent and protect the clients. The human rights committee should not operate in opposition to the treatment staff, but it is necessary that the two remain very separate entities.

Public Dissemination of Purpose and Procedures

The human rights committee should disseminate its statement of purpose together with a description of its review process. These should be made public so that any person with questions concerning the ethical or humane treatment or care of clients can contact the human rights committee. Letters should be sent to all parents, guardians, or the nearest relatives of the clients informing them of the existence of the human rights committee and stating that parents, guardians, or concerned relatives are welcome to attend the meetings when the client they are interested in is being discussed. Additionally, they, along with any other people in the community (including treatment staff personnel), should be able to present, confidentially, any questions or criticisms of the program to the human rights committee at any time. To enable more people to know about the human rights committee and perhaps to utilize it, pictures of the committee members along with names, addresses and phone numbers underneath the pictures should be displayed at the treatment facility along with the statement of purpose.

Making the human rights committee visible helps in the protection of the clients. Often, it is the relatives of the client who are most concerned about the client's welfare and who have the most contact with the client, besides the treatment staff. Thus, the relatives may be the ones who are in the best position to know if abuse has taken place or if the client is making any progress. In cases of abuse or lack of progress, the relatives or concerned citizens know where to direct questions and can be assured of a specified procedure that will be followed in dealing with questions or complaints.

Written Records and Checklists

Appendixes 1 and 2 contain checklists that the human rights committee can use to provide a written record of the committee's action. Appendix 1 is the "Human Rights Committee 'Due Process' Summary Report." This report should be filled out during, or directly after, each committee meeting. The main purpose of this report is to have a written record of the procedures that the committee follows, to determine whether the committee acts as a credible, independent review and protection mechanism, and to indicate whether it consistently follows the prescribed procedures.

The first point listed in Appendix 1 asks the committee to note those instances where the committee refused or delayed consent of a treatment procedure and sought additional information concerning less intrusive procedures. Although it is not expected that this will occur at each meeting, it would be noteworthy if it *never* occurred, thus appearing that the committee accepted all the treatment procedures presented to them by the staff without question. The second point is concerned with outside advice and opinion sought by the committee. It is not necessary to have such advice reported at every meeting. Again, though, it would be noteworthy if outside advice were never sought. The third and fourth points attempt to determine if the human rights committee functions independently of the treatment staff or whether it is so directly tied to the staff by member selection and presence of treatment staff at each meeting that the committee is not a separate and independent entity. The issue of notifying the public of the committee's existence is addressed in the fifth point.

The actual "due process" procedure of presenting a client's case and advocating alternative forms of treatment to that proposed by the treatment staff is directly addressed in point 6. Point 7 examines the number of actual on-site visits made by the committee members. Finally, points 8, 9, and 10 involve the review process, described above, to be used with aversive or intrusive procedures.

In filling out this checklist, when "instances" are asked for, the human rights committee should briefly note what evidence, if any, there is to show that the objective has been partially or fully accomplished. If nothing has occurred since the last meeting, "none" should be recorded. As mentioned previously, it is not expected that each item can or should be filled in at each meeting. The credibility of the human rights committee in providing due-process protection for clients, however, is strengthened with each entry.

The second checklist (Appendix 2), the "Summary of Human Rights Committee Review of Client Individual Habilitation Plan," should be completed for each client whose program is formally reviewed by the committee. Since it is desirable that all clients' cases be periodically reviewed by the committee, it is likely that this checklist will be completed at least once a year for each client. This checklist is primarily concerned with identifying treatment goals and techniques and determining how appropriate these goals or treatment techniques are. Several issues are considered, and the questions have been taken directly from the Association for Advancement of Behavior Therapy's *Ethical Issues for Human Services* (1977). As the title might imply, the topics address the ethical concerns involved in treatment, including (1) the *goals*, the method in which they have been determined, and the benefit to the client in having these goals; (2) the choice of *treatment procedures*, whether the procedure has been documented as professionally, legally, and ethically justified, and the consideration of other treatment methods; (3) the client's *voluntary participation* in the treatment program and whether a range of treatment techniques were offered; (4) the assurance that the *client's best interests* are still addressed even when the client is incompetent to make treatment decisions; (5) the *evaluation* of the treatment procedure in general and with the client in question; (6) the *confidentiality* of the treatment; (7) the *referral* of the client to other therapists if the therapy is unsuccessful or if the client is unhappy with the therapy; and (8) the *qualifications* of the therapist who is to provide the therapy.

Whereas the first checklist is primarily concerned with the *procedures* that the human rights committee follows in reviewing aversive or intrusive treatment techniques as well as in developing treatment plans, this second checklist addresses the *specific* issues in developing and implementing all treatment programs. Both checklists are necessary. It is important to know that the general procedure the human rights committee follows is a fair and complete one, independent of staff coercion. Additionally, it is important to determine that when evaluating a particular client's treatment program, the committee addresses the critical issues that will protect that client. By consistently following a standard and fair procedure that addresses critical issues, clients' rights should be protected.

Adapting the Committee to the Size of the Program

Depending on the size of the program, what is normally thought of as the human rights committee may need to vary. For instance, some large metropolitan areas have decided to institute a human rights committee for all developmentally disabled clients in that area. Sometimes, the number of clients covered reaches into the thousands. It would be impossible for a group of 10–15 citizens on a human rights committee to protect the interests of all those persons. Therefore, it has been recommended that the large area be divided into smaller regions or catchments and that each area have its own human rights committee. Another committee with jurisdiction over the entire area could serve to make general policy decisions and act as an appellate hearing body in cases of disputes between staff and clients or between the staff and the regional human rights committee. In any event, a human rights committee should probably not be required to serve more than 100 clients. Any larger number makes it impossible to protect the *individual* needs of each client and to make sure that they are receiving appropriate and humane treatment.

The opposite type of situation may also occur. Many small residential programs in the community serve only 8–10 clients, or at the most, 20–30. Most of these not-for-profit programs have a board of directors consisting of interested persons from the community. Rather than attempting to assemble another group of community persons, the board of directors, reflecting the values of the community, can serve as the human rights committee and provide the protective function. This procedure is most useful if the program is not a controversial one. If, on the other hand, the program serves severely debilitated clients and employs controversial techniques, it may be wise to have a separate human rights committee. In either case, the board or the committee should still address the issues outlined in the checklist to be sure that appropriate treatment is being provided.

Ensuring Staff Compliance

The human rights committee is an advisory group to the treatment staff. Should the treatment staff be required to follow all recommendations of the human rights committee? This is a difficult question, and the answer will be influenced by a number of considerations. In some situations, a human rights committee may be mandated by law or by acceptance of funds from certain sources. It may still not be clear, however, that all of the recommendations of this committee need to be followed. In other cases, institutional policy may require compliance with the recommendations of the human rights committee. In most cases, whether or not the recommendations of the human rights committee are followed will be up to the treatment staff. Thus, discussion, negotiation, and compromise between the human rights committee and the treatment staff may be necessary. Where systematic and pervasive noncompliance with recommendations of the human rights committee exists, however, it would seem that the appropriate action of the committee members should be to resign. Continued membership, after pervasive noncompliance with recommendations, would indicate that the committee believes the program is operating properly. Thus, the primary sanction the human rights committee can impose is resignation. The resignation of all members would be a public indication of a definite problem with the program, and in some instances, the program would be unable to comply with the legal mandate of having a human rights committee.

Compensation

Most members of a human rights committee serve because of their strong commitment to improving conditions for clients in the program. Such service, however, requires considerable effort and time. Whether or not to compensate committee members is a difficult issue to resolve. Obviously, it is necessary to pay any travel or lodging expenses that a member might incur. The payment of any additional amount, however, has advantages and disadvantages. On one hand, if the program pays committee members, it is possible that they may not seriously evaluate treatment staff decisions because they fear being asked to resign from the committee and, thereby, losing the money being paid to them. Further, the public credibility of the committee's decisions may be weakened by the fact that the members are paid by the program. On the other hand, it may be unrealistic to expect people to devote the amount of time and energy that are involved in serving on this committee without some compensation for their time and efforts, and thus, some guidelines specify that members should indeed be compensated (e.g., May *et al.*, 1976).

Probably the most critical issue to consider is protecting the independence of committee members from undue influence by the treatment staff. It appears that members could be compensated and at the same time be able to maintain a protected, independent status separate from the treatment program. This might be done by appointing members for a specified term (e.g., two or three years), which could be terminated only by the member's resigning from the committee or by failure to fulfill the responsibilities determined by the committee (not the treatment staff). No member could serve consecutive appointments, and at least one or two years should elapse before reappointment to the committee. Finally, the compensation received by each committee member should be reasonable in view of the time spent and the prevailing standards of compensation in that location. Following procedures similar to these should allow members to be adequately compensated, at the same time allow their tenure on the committee to be protected so that they can operate independently of treatment staff influence, and, additionally, maintain the public credibility of the committee.

Benefits to the Program

Program staff may view the human rights committee as a burden that they must bear in order to be able to continue their program. The committee, however, can serve two critically important functions that ultimately benefit both the clients and the staff. First and foremost, the committee should exist for the protection and advocacy of all of the program's clients. It should be an independent evaluative mechanism that attempts not only to protect clients from unnecessary aversive techniques but that also ensure that effective treatment is being provided for each client. Second, it serves to reassure others about the treatment program. Any person or organization questioning whether the treatment being provided is humane and appropriate may speak directly with the human rights committee. As an independent evaluator, this committee can speak without bias about the treatment being provided. Thus, the treatment staff, if they comply with the committee's procedures and recommendations, have an advocate that protects their public image.

The Peer Review Committee

While the human rights committee acts as a representative of society to be sure that clients are treated humanely and ethically, in addition to determining that each client is actually receiving treatment, the peer review committee's primary function is to consider the professional justification of the procedures being used. The systematic and critical review of treatment programs by competent professionals has been emphasized as a much needed, but often neglected, process to determine the appropriateness, adequacy, and necessity of treatment programs, especially those that involve unpleasant or aversive procedures (Serber, Hiller, Keith, & Taylor, 1975).

Unfortunately, peer review has not been an easy process to establish for a variety of reasons. Many treatment providers have been reluctant to allow outside professionals to evaluate their programs, often because they feel that outside evaluators do not know enough about the operation of the program or about the clients to make intelligent and reasonable recommendations. In some instances, treatment providers have been evaluated by professionals with very different theoretical perspectives, who have made broad, sweeping recommendations to change whole treatment programs, based on theoretical differences rather than on a consideration of the effectiveness of the procedures being used. Obviously, treatment providers who have experienced this type of peer review have little respect for the system. Likewise, professionals, in general, have been reluctant to begin a process of evaluating one another's programs because of the camaraderie that exists among those in the same discipline and their reluctance to say anything derogatory about a fellow therapist or treatment provider (Hare-Mustin, Maracek, Kaplan, & Liss-Levinson, 1979).

The need for peer review, however, cannot be easily dismissed (Bailey, 1978; Claiborn, 1978; May *et al.*, 1976; Risley & Sheldon-Wildgen, 1982). If competent professionals are unwilling or are not allowed to review treatment programs, especially controversial ones, it is unlikely that anyone will be able to determine whether certain procedures are professionally justified. Once we have recognized the need, there are several ways that peer review can be accomplished, depending on the type of program being provided and the procedures being utilized (Risley & Sheldon-Wildgen, 1982). These often range from informal review to systematic full-scale evaluations. Thus, there may be situations in which a therapist is presented with a unique situation and desires to discuss this case with another professional who has had experience working with the particular type of client or problem in question. This discussion, although informal, provides a type of peer review, since the therapist receives professional input from others and does not have to rely solely on his/her own judgment.

Another form of peer review may involve having relevant and competent professionals review the written materials that describe a particular program and its operation. This type of review could be accomplished in much the same way that journal articles are reviewed for publication. This procedure is most useful for programs employing noncontroversial techniques. Additionally, other programs involving noncontroverial techniques may find it useful, as well as educational, to periodically ask a group of peers to make an on-site evaluation of their programs. Doing this may be a fresh, innovative method of evaluating problems, in addition to making sure that the most effective and efficient procedures are being utilized.

Finally, there are those programs that employ aversive, or otherwise controversial, procedures. A more systematic, organized, and intensive peer review seems required for them. The remainder of this section of the chapter is devoted to describing this type of peer review mechanism, how it can be established, and how it can best function to safeguard both the client and the program's interests, in addition to making sure that the best treatment procedures available are being provided.

Composition

To be a credible protective mechanism, a peer review committee should consist of independent professionals who have expertise in using procedures that are of the same theoretical (e.g., behavioral) orientation as those being utilized by the treatment staff or who have a demonstrated competency in working with the type of client being served by the program. It is necessary that the committee have a representation of both these competencies in order to protect the clientele adequately and to protect the program. Ideally, it would be advantageous to have some members who both subscribe to the same basic treatment views and who also work with the same clientele, but this is not always feasible. Thus, the members, in combination, should be intimately familiar with the current literature, programs, and disorders that are relevant to the procedures used and the clients served in the program. In instances where aversive or controversial treatment procedures are being utilized, one may not be able to recruit members for the committee who use exactly the same treatment techniques. Nonetheless, the committee should be comprised of individuals who have either the current credentials and involvement with similar clients or expertise in using techniques that are derived from the same theoretical basis as the aversive or controversial procedure.

An issue pertaining to the composition of the peer review committee that program personnel may want to consider is whether professionals from different theoretical perspectives should serve on this committee (Bailey, 1978). Each program must decide individually if this is desirable, but programs should be aware of the type of input that these professionals can give to the program. *Overall program* improvement can often be enhanced by having people from other perspectives on the peer review committee. These people can address general considerations in addition to comparing this program with other programs serving similar clients. These professionals, however, would not be the best individuals to address the issue of *procedure improvement* because they do not work with, nor are they acquainted with the literature on, the procedures in question. To obtain the best input regarding the appropriateness of the procedures being utilized by the treatment staff, it is advisable to have people who either have used those procedures or are of the theoretical background from which those procedures were derived.

Peer review committees can consist of members chosen both at the national level and from the local area (if available). There are advantages to having both types of members. Those at the local level have greater opportunities to visit the program in operation, while those at the national level can normally provide a broader perspective of the program since they do not have as frequent contact. It is critical that all members be independent of the treatment program and not under any monetary, professional, or political obligations to the program or staff. Members of the peer review committee must feel free to make whatever recommendations they feel are necessary

without fear of reprisal. Thus, independence, as well as competence, is a critical characteristic of the committee members.

Purpose

The peer review committee can serve a twofold purpose. First, the committee can provide independent and explicit advice and consultation to the administrative and treatment staff of the program and also to the human rights committee, if that committee so desires. Second, where appropriate, the peer review committee can provide implicit consent and endorsement of the treatment program, thus reassuring those outside of the program that the treatment procedures are justified and that the clients are protected.

The primary purpose, as mentioned above, is to help make sure that the procedures used by the treatment program are in accord with the treatment standards found in the current relevant literature. Thus, the committee members must attend to discrepancies or concordance between the program practices and the professional literature. Two considerations are extremely important in fulfilling this function. The members must examine all aversive and controversial procedures to determine if these techniques are professionally justified; normally benign procedures need little, if any, justification (the human rights committee, however, should examine even benign procedures to determine if treatment was accomplished by using them). *Professionally justified* means that they have support in the professional literature, that is, that they have been experimentally evaluated and have been shown to be effective as evidenced by published data in reputable journals. The committee must also determine if the procedures are justified by *current* professional literature. Thus, a controversial procedure at one time may have been justified, but perhaps more effective and less controversial procedures have been developed and evaluated since then. In light of the evidence of the effectiveness of the new techniques, the controversial procedure would no longer be professionally warranted. Committee members, therefore, must be familiar with the treatment program as well as with the most current professional literature that is relevant to the techniques used and the clients served in the program.

Once the peer review committee has examined the program, the members may provide an educational service to the treatment program personnel by providing a broader knowledge and perspective of the professional literature and practices. Thus, those involved in making treatment decisions can be advised of the most current procedures in use with a particular clientele. The educational purpose of the peer review committee cannot be overemphasized. It should provide current, as well as new, ways to address problems if it finds that the procedures in use are not justified by the professional literature.

The second function of the peer review committee is to answer publicly any questions about the professional justification of the procedures used by the treatment staff. Often, controversial programs need to respond to questions and criticism from the public and governmental officials who are in charge of licensing or regulating the programs. Questioning from outside sources can be good, since it indicates that people are concerned about the welfare of the clients. Unfortunately, however, what normally happens is that the treatment staff and the program administrators spend an inordinate amount of time defending the program. This can be an emotional and time-consuming battle between the "critics" of the program and the staff. Usually, nothing is resolved because the staff is viewed as being biased and as merely defending their own actions. The peer review committee can alleviate some of the problems caused by the public questioning. The committee should be available to respond knowledgeably, authoritatively, and independently to private or public questions or criticism concerning the appropriateness and effectiveness of the treatment program. The committee will be viewed as a much more credible source of answers to questions or responses to criticism than the treatment staff, who have a vested interest in the program. The peer review committee is an independent group, knowledgeable about both the program and the current professionally justifiable procedures, with no reason to promote or support unjustifiable practices. Thus, the committee members are viewed as being better able to assess accurately if the treatment is professionally sound.

The Formal Review Process

Because of the use of aversive, or otherwise controversial, techniques, it is necessary that the peer review committee make on-site visits and meet together to deliberate about the appropriateness of the general program policy and the individual habilitation programs. The more controversial the procedures are, the more visits there should be to the program. Here the local peer review members are most useful. They are more readily available and are able to make more frequent visits to the program. Additionally, because of their closeness, they can make unannounced visits to the program. Each peer review committee must determine whether they want to make unannounced visits. When visits are announced, one can argue that the treatment staff will prepare for the visit and, in essence, act in an unrepresentative fashion for the benefit of the committee. There are certain things that the staff can prepare for and engage in when the peer review committee is visiting that would not be characteristic of what normally occurs in the program. Other things, however, such as lack of staff training (so that the staff does not know how to implement the treatment procedures properly) or lack of client progress, cannot be easily hidden even with advance warning. In some cases, the committee may feel that certain procedures should not be used or should be implemented only in a certain manner with certain safeguards. Unannounced visits by both the peer-review and the human-rights committees would help make sure that the procedures are carried out as prescribed on a day-to-day basis.

In reviewing the program and the procedures used, the committee should engage in a two-step process whereby members examine written treatment plans in addition to actually observing how the treatment techniques are being implemented. When examining written treatment plans, the committee members can assess whether the techniques advocated by the staff are justified by the current professional literature. If they are not, recommendations should be made that more professionally justifiable techniques be used. If the treatment plans are justified by the current professional literature, the committee must then determine if the plans are actually being implemented with the precision, consistency, and supervision called for by the professional literature. Obviously, the implementation of the procedures is extremely critical, since many aversive techniques are justifiable only if they are properly implemented.

Since implementation is critical, it may be desirable to place in the program persons who have direct links with members of the peer review committee, to work on a day-to-day basis. This procedure would serve a function similar to that of having unannounced visit, except that it is more desirable, since the persons would be in the program daily. This type of procedure can be most easily utilized when the members of the peer review committee have faculty positions at universities and have students who would like to work as interns or assistants or who would like to carry out research in the treatment program. These students ultimately report and answer to the peer review committee member who is their faculty adviser, and thus, they are independent of the treatment staff. The treatment staff should be aware who the students are so that there are no "undercover" operations going on to make the staff feel as if people are spying on them. They will know that the students can observe what they are doing and are presumed to be reporting to the peer review committee. Thus, the treatment staff are likely to conform their daily behavior to the standards set by the peer review committee. If they do not, it will be readily seen. This procedure can therefore provide one of the most credible assurances about the implementation of the treatment plans.

Operating Independently of the Treatment Staff

To be a *credible* protective mechanism, the peer review committee, like the human rights committee, must be able to meet and deliberate as an independent entity. It is usually easier for a peer review committee to maintain its independent status, since this committee is comprised of professionals who are just as knowledgeable about appropriate treatment procedures as is the treatment staff and may be even more knowledgeable. Although the peer review committee will undoubtedly have considerable contact with the program staff, it is important that they retain their independent status by meeting without the staff present, so that they can openly and honestly discuss treatment procedures and program policy.

Public Responsiveness

Like the human rights committee, the peer review committee should publicly make known its existence by disseminating the committee's statement of purpose together with a description of the review process. Parents, guardians, and the nearest relatives of the clients specifically should be made aware of the existence of the peer review committee. They, along with any individual in the community, should be encouraged to ask the committee, either publicly or confidentially, any questions relating to the program's procedures or the implementation of treatment techniques and the professional justification of them.

After making themselves visible, the peer review committee should take an active role in speaking publicly about the treatment program and in publicly answering questions or addressing any criticisms. As mentioned previously, this committee can be much more credible in addressing issues raised by the public than can the treatment staff, who have a vested interest in the treatment program. Depending on how independently the committee functions and how knowledgeable the members are about using similar procedures, about working with a similar population, or about operating similar programs, the peer review committee can provide the needed assurances to allow a controversial, yet professionally appropriate, program to remain in operation to serve a difficult-to-treat clientele.

Written Records and Checklists

The peer review committee may want to keep extensive records or minutes of their meetings. This is an acceptable practice and often greatly aids committee members who live at great distances and are not in frequent actual contact with the program. Detailed minutes can easily refresh a member's memory of what the critical considerations of the program are. Often these minutes, however, are not appropriate for external distribution. Thus, the peer review committee, in addition to keeping minutes for their own use, should have a summary report that would be acceptable for public dissemination. Appendix 3 contains a sample "Peer Review Committee Summary Report" that might be used.

The first question on the "Peer Review Committee Summary Report" asks the committee to note which program policies were considered and what recommendations were made at the current meeting, in addition to noting whether previously recommended policies had been satisfactorily implemented. This question provides the public with information about whether the committee is considering critical policy decisions as well as whether the staff has complied with the recommendations that have been made.

The second topic may be of importance to much of the public, since it addresses the use of specific treatment procedures and provides a public record of which procedures were considered and what recommendations were made for the use of these procedures. It is usually wise to include a short statement of the rationale for any recommendation so that the public can understand the justification for the decision. Additionally, it is critical to document whether previous recommendations were satisfactorily implemented.

The peer review committee should take responsibility not only for reviewing treatment procedures but also for reviewing clients' individual treatment plans. Most procedures are normally not evaluated in a vacuum; rather, they are considered according to their appropriateness with an individual client. Although this committee is not necessarily concerned with either the ethical or the humane considerations of the procedures, the members must consider whether a particular procedure is professionally justified with an individual client. If other procedures appeared to be more professionally warranted because they are either more effective or less intrusive than those the program is currently using, then the committee should recommend them. Items 3

and 4 address these issues and provide a permanent record of the decisions made.

It should be noted that following each of the first three points, there is a question asking whether the treatment staff has implemented the peer review committee's previous recommendations. If the staff has not, "No" should be marked, with an explanation given in the "Comments" section. Normally, a "No" would indicate that the staff is in noncompliance with the committee's recommendation, but, in some instances, this noncompliance may be justified. Any justification could be written in the "Comments" section. If, on the other hand, the staff routinely disregards the committee's recommendations, a problem would be indicated and should be addressed.

Items 5–10 help document the credibility of the peer review mechanism. Whenever literature or references are recommended, the peer review committee is providing an educational service to the treatment staff. Direct observation of the program (which is covered in topic 6) is essential, and the more that it occurs, the more effective and credible the committee will be. As previously mentioned, the human rights committee should feel free (and should even be encouraged) to consult with the peer review committee. Often, for the human rights committee to make intelligent and wise decisions, they need information about the professional justification of a particular procedure. They may find that the most appropriate source of this information is the peer review committee. Keep in mind, however, that although the peer review committee may state that a procedure is professionally justified, the human rights committee may decide that the procedure should not be used, for ethical or humane reasons. They cannot make this decision wisely, though, without the necessary information from the peer review committee, and this is the essence of item 7.

The peer review committee should always record any instances in which a member, or the committee, has publicly interpreted or answered questions concerning the treatment program. In recording such instances, the members should note what the action specifically concerned; to whom it was addressed; when it occurred; what, in general, the member said; and what the public's response was. Finally, the committee should note what students or interns are working in the program and when the committee meets privately, in the absence of the treatment staff. By consistently filling out this checklist, an ongoing record of the peer review committee's activities will be available to substantiate further that the committee is a credible protective mechanism.

Adapting the Committee to the Size of the Program

As with the human rights committee, it may be necessary to vary the structure of the peer review committee. Since this committee does not have the ultimate responsibility of reviewing each client's individual habilitation plan and progress (that responsibility rests with the human rights committee), the peer review committee is normally able to review a large program that serves many clients. Many programs, however, are small or use controversial techniques with only a small number of clients. For those programs it may not be feasible to have a large peer review committee. It may be more practical to use consultants to advise them on any problems that arise as well as on the appropriate use of controversial procedures.

If individual consultants are being used by a treatment program in a peer review role, it is necessary to demonstrate that these individuals are, indeed, independent of the staff and able to make whatever recommendations they feel are appropriate. Thus, although the consultant may be compensated with per diem and travel costs in addition to a consultant's fee, the money earned from this service should be minimal and supplementary to the consultant's normal earnings. In other words, if the consultant were no longer to consult with the program, it should not financially hurt him/her. The consultant should have no personal or professional ties to the program and should not be under any professional, political, or financial obligations to the program.

Ensuring Staff Compliance

Like the human rights committee, the peer review committee is only an advisory group

to the treatment staff. The committee can make recommendations to the staff as well as provide educational information. The treatment staff, however, can choose to comply or not. If the staff chooses not to comply, the only sanction the members of the peer review committee can impose is to withdraw from the committee. When they withdraw, they can state the reason for doing so and thus indicate public disapproval of the program's procedures. Additionally, they will no longer be available to respond to public inquiries about the program.

Obviously, a treatment program may not incorporate all recommendations made for it by the peer review committee. Each member of the committee, as well as the entire committee, must decide which noncompliances are acceptable and which are not. When a point is reached when a member can no longer endorse the treatment program, it is time for this member to resign from the committee. Thus, while on the committee, each member should be willing not only to respond to public inquiries but also to generally endorse the program and the procedures being used.

Compensation

The compensation of peer review committee members raises the same issues as the compensation of members of the human rights committee and can be handled in much the same way. Since many of these members may live at a distance from the treatment program, it is necessary that the members receive travel and per diem expenses. If necessary, compensation for their services can also be provided at much the same rate one would pay any consultant. The same protections to ensure independence from the treatment staff as were described for the human rights committee might be in effect: Members should receive a specified term of appointment that only they can terminate or that the committee can terminate for failure to fulfill duties, and consecutive terms of appointment should not be allowed.

Benefits to the Program

Normally, the treatment staff and administrators view the peer review committee as a beneficial source of ideas for solving problems and presenting alternative perspectives. The committee's educational function can be useful to both the treatment staff and the human rights committee. In addition to providing invaluable information, the peer review committee can serve as an assurance that the goals developed and the techniques implemented are professionally justified. Once the committee is satisfied that the treatment provided by the program is professionally sound, the members can provide a service to the program that no one else is able to: they can act as public spokespersons for the professional aspects of the program, assuring the public that the procedures in use are professionally warranted. This independent endorsement, by people knowledgeable in the area of interest, can often mean the difference between a program that is allowed to continue to operate and one that is forced to close.

Conclusion

Providing appropriate treatment for the severely debilitated client will always present a challenge to treatment providers. The challenge, however, must be met. Courts, legislatures, and consumer groups have mandated the right of these people to receive treatment appropriate to their needs. Providing this treatment, in methods acceptable to the public, often requires creative thinking. In the past, many programs, whose goals for treating the difficult-to-treat were admirable, have received considerable criticism because of the procedures employed. Some programs have even been terminated. Although it is clear that no one should be exposed to treatment techniques that can be labeled as cruel and unusual punishment, it is also clear that many techniques that at first blush appear to be cruel are professionally justified for use with certain individuals. To propose a blanket disapproval of them would mean that many severely debilitated individuals would never receive the treatment appropriate to their needs.

The critical issue is determining what is appropriate and effective treatment and making sure that it is provided. Since it is impossible to specify treatment goals and techniques that would be appropriate and effective for all in-

dividuals, it is necessary to develop mechanisms to ensure that humane and effective treatment will be provided. Human-rights and peer-review committees have been developed to address the issue of providing *professionally justified* and *ethically appropriate* treatment, especially for the difficult-to-treat. These committees represent both the professional and the general community view of what type of treatment should be provided. These committees act to ensure that treatment will be provided that is appropriate to each individual's needs, professionally warranted, and ethically humane.

In addition to monitoring the client's interests, these committees can also provide protection for treatment programs. Acting as independent spokespersons for these programs, the committee members can provide public assurance that the goals developed and used are both effective and appropriate. These committees are credible, however, only if they consistently follow appropriate procedures for evaluating treatment goals and techniques and protecting client rights. Additionally, they must be independent from the treatment staff.

Establishing credible human-rights and peer-review committees often means that individuals who in the past may not have been treated can receive appropriate treatment, and that programs that might have been closed because of public disapproval of their treatment techniques may be allowed to remain open to serve those who most desperately need them. Finally, the public can be assured that safeguards are continually in effect to protect those individuals not capable of protecting themselves.

ACKNOWLEDGMENT

The authors wish to express their sincere appreciation to Dr. James A. Sherman for his invaluable editorial assistance and his support and contributions given throughout the preparation of this chapter.

Appendixes

The three checklists presented here for use by the human-rights and peer-review committees were developed by the Professional Consultation and Peer Review Committee of the Association for Advancement of Behavior Therapy (AABT). These checklists are reprinted with the permission of that committee.

Appendix 1: Human Rights Committee "Due Process" Summary Report

Persons attending meeting: Date:

1. Instances in which the human rights committee has refused or delayed consent for the initiation of a treatment procedure and has requested additional information, opinions, or the use of less intrusive procedures.

2. Instances in which the human rights committee has sought outside opinions and advice. (Note who, when, and topic of concern. Note whether this advice was sought from the peer review committee; from other outside, independent professionals; from the professional literature; or from a client advocacy group.)

3. Instances of the human rights committee's deliberations in the absence of program personnel (i.e., executive sessions). (Note dates and who attended.)

4. Instances of independence in selecting new members of the human rights committee, such as the human rights committee's providing a list of potential new members and the program director's choosing from that list. (Characterize how the selection was done.)

5. Instances of public display and public awareness of the human rights committee, its members, and its activities. (Note displays and any approaches to members of the human rights committee by staff, outside persons, or agencies.)

6. Instances of the appointment of (and the subsequent presentations made by) one member of the human rights committee for each client or case considered, who acts as an advocate for that client and whose role is to suggest a treatment that is the opposite of the treatment the staff is proposing. (Note the members' names and the clients' initials or iden-

tifying numbers; note also the dates when the appointments were made and the dates when the presentations were made.)

7. Instances of on-site visits made by members of the human rights committee to observe program implementation. (Note the names and dates.)

8. Instances of any revisions of a statement of approval for *generally used procedures*. Also provide any corollary statements of the conditions of use, monitoring, and reporting that were approved.

9. a. Instances of any revisions of a statement of approval for procedures that can be implemented on an *interim basis* but that require the human rights committee's review and approval for continuation at the next meeting of the human rights committee.

   b. Instances of subsequent review and approval or disapproval of procedures in this category.

10. Instances of the human rights committee's *prior* review and approval or disapproval of other procedures.

Signatures of human rights committee members participating:

Appendix 2: Summary of Human Rights Committee Review of Client Individual Habilitation Plan

Client's initials or   Admission date:
identification code: Date of this review:

Name of designated
client advocate:

Long-range habilitative goal(s) with target date for each:

Current program goals (one year or less):

Treatment procedures currently in effect:

   In reviewing this client's habilitation plan, the human rights committee has addressed each of the following questions and indicates by a "Yes" those questions that have been answered to the committee's satisfaction. (These questions have been taken directly from the Association for Advancement of Behavior Therapy's *Ethical Issues for Human Services*. Please note that wherever the term *client* is used with an asterisk, *each* of the following should also be considered a "client": the person in the program; the person's parent or guardian; the person or agency providing funds for the treatment.)

A. Have the goals of treatment been adequately considered? _____

  1. To be sure that the goals are explicit, are they written? _____
  2. Has the client's* understanding of the goals been assured by having the client* restate them orally or in writing? _____
  3. Have the therapist and the client* agreed on the goals of therapy? _____
  4. Will serving the client's* interests be contrary to the interests of other persons? _____
  5. Will serving the client's* immediate interests be contrary to the client's* long-term interest? _____

B. Has the choice of treatment methods been adequately considered? _____

  1. Does the published literature show the procedure to be the best one available for that problem? _____
  2. If no literature exists regarding the treatment method, is the method consistent with federally accepted practice? _____
  3. Has the client* been told of alternative procedures that might be preferred by the client* on the basis of significant differences in discomfort, treatment time, cost, or degree of demonstrated effectiveness? _____
  4. If a treatment procedure is publicly, legally, or professionally controversial, has formal professional consultation been obtained, has the reaction of the affected segment of the public been adequately considered, and have the alternative treatment methods been more closely reexamined and reconsidered? _____

C. Is the client's* participation voluntary? _____

  1. Have possible sources of coercion of the client's* participation been considered? _____
  2. If treatment is legally mandated, has the available range of treatments and therapists been offered? _____
  3. Can the client* withdraw from treatment without a penalty or financial loss that exceeds actual clinical costs? _____

D. When another person or an agency is empowered to arrange for therapy, have the interests of the subordinated client been sufficiently considered? _____

  1. Has the subordinated client been informed of the treatment objectives and participated in the choice of treatment procedures? _____
  2. Where the subordinated client's competence to decide is limited, has the client as well as the guardian participated in the treatment discussions to the extent that the client's abilities permit? _____
  3. If the interests of the subordinated person and the superordinate persons or agency conflict, have attempts been made to reduce the conflict by dealing with both interests? _____

E. Has the adequacy of treatment been evaluated? _____

  1. Have quantitative measures of the problem and its progress been obtained? _____
  2. Have the measures of the problem and its progress been made available to the client* during treatment? _____

F. Has the confidentiality of the
    treatment relationship been
    protected?   _____

    1. Has the client* been told who has
        access to the records?   _____
    2. Are records available only to
        authorized persons?   _____

G. Does the therapist refer the clients*
    to other therapists when necessary?   _____

    1. If treatment is unsuccessful, is the
        client* referred to other therapists?   _____
    2. Has the client* been told that if
        dissatisfied with the treatment,
        referral will be made?   _____

H. Is the therapist qualified to provide
    treatment?   _____

    1. Has the therapist had training or
        experience in treating problems
        like the client's?   _____
    2. If deficits exist in the therapist's
        qualifications, has the client* been
        informed?   _____
    3. If the therapist is not adequately
        qualified, is the client* referred to
        other therapists, or has supervision
        by a qualified therapist been
        provided? Is the client* informed
        of the supervisory relation?   _____
    4. If the treatment is administered by
        mediators, have the mediators
        been adequately supervised by a
        qualified therapist?   _____

Comments on the above questions:

Outside persons who have been consulted by
staff or the human rights committee in determining
recommended treatment (names and dates):

Based on this review, are any changes indicated
in long- or short-term goals or treatment procedures? (Characterize.)

Signatures of participating members of the human
rights committee:

_____

_____

Appendix 3: Peer Review Committee Summary Report

Persons attending meeting: Date

1. Policies considered and recommendations
    made:

    Have previous policy recom-
    mendations been implemented to
    the committee's satisfaction?   No*   Yes

2. Procedures considered and recommenda-
    tions made:

    Have previous recommenda-
    tions concerning procedures been
    implemented to the committee's
    satisfaction?   No*   Yes

3. Clients discussed (initials or identifying num-
    bers only) and recommendations made:

    Have previous recommenda-
    tions concerning clients' pro-
    grams been implemented to the
    committee's satisfaction?   No*   Yes

4. Clients receiving complete review of their
    individual habilitation plan (initials or iden-
    tifying numbers only):

    *Actions by members of the peer review com-
    mittee subsequent to the last committee
    meeting (including actions during present
    meeting):*

5. Literature or references supplied or recom-
    mended by the peer review committee:

6. Direct observation of program (names of
    committee members and dates):

7. Consultation with members of the human
    rights committee (names of members of peer
    review committee and human rights com-
    mittee, dates).

8. Actions taken by members of peer review
    committee supporting or interpreting the pro-
    gram to others (characterize):

9. Peer-review-committee members' students,
    interns, etc., recently working in program

(name, starting and ending date, the name of the peer-review-committee member–sponsor):

10. Peer-review-committee executive session (discussions in the absence of staff or administrators; persons attending, date):

* Comments:

Signatures of participating members of the peer review committee:

References

Association for Advancement of Behavior Therapy. *Ethical issues for human services.* New York: AABT, 1977.

Baer, D. A case for the selective reinforcement of punishment. In C. Neuringer & J. S. Michael (Eds.), *Behavior modification in clinical psychology.* New York: Appleton-Century-Crofts, 1970.

Bailey, B. *Peer review manual for human service programs.* Nacogdoches, Texas: PCEA, Inc., 1978.

Begelman, D. A. Ethical and legal issues of behavior modification. In M. Hersen, R. M. Eisler, & P. M. Miller (Eds.), *Progress in behavior modification,* Vol. 1. New York: Academic Press, 1975.

Begelman, D. A. Ethical issues for the developmentally disabled. In M. Berkler, G. Bible, S. Boles, D. Deitz, & A. Repp (Eds.), *Current trends for the developmentally disabled.* Baltimore: University Park Press, 1978.

Berkler, M. S., Bible, G. H., Boles, S. M., Deitz, D. E., & Repp, A. C. (Eds.). *Current trends for the developmentally disabled.* Baltimore: University Park Press, 1978.

Budd, K. S., & Barer, D. M. Behavior modification and the law: Implications of recent judicial decisions. *The Journal of Psychiatry and Law,* 1976, *Summer,* 171–244.

Claiborn, W. (Chair). *APA/CHAMPUS outpatient psychological peer review manual.* Washington: APA, 1978.

Clatterbuck v. *Harris,* 295 F. Supp. 84 (D.D.C. 1968).

Cook v. *Ciccone,* 312 F. Supp. 822 (W.D. Mo. 1970).

Covington v. *Harris,* 419 F.2d 617 (D.C. Cir. 1969).

Davis v. *Watkins,* 384 F. Supp. 1196 (N.D. Ohio 1974).

Davison, G. C., & Stuart, R. B. Behavior therapy and civil liberties. *American Psychologist,* 1975, *30,* 755–763.

Eckerhart v. *Hensley,* 475 F. Supp. 908 (W.D. Mo. 1979).

Friedman, P. R. Legal regulations of applied analysis in mental institutions and prisons. *Arizona Law Review,* 1975, *17,* 39–104.

Friedman, P., & Halpern, C. The right to treatment. In B. Ennis & P. Friedman (Eds.), *Legal rights of the mentally handicapped,* Vol. 1. New York: Practicing Law Institute, 1974.

Griffith, R. An administrative perspective on guidelines for behavior modification: The creation of a legally safe environment. *Behavior Therapist,* 1980, *3,* 5–7.

Halderman and the United States v. *Pennhurst,* 446 F. Supp. 1295 (E.D. Pa. 1977).

Hare-Mustin, R., Maracek, J., Kaplan, A., & Liss-Levinson, N. Rights of clients, responsibilities of therapists. *American Psychologist,* 1979, *34,* 3–16.

Hawkins, R. P. Who decided that was the problem? Two stages of responsibility for applied behavior analysts. In W. S. Wood (Ed.), *Issues in evaluating behavior modification.* Champaign, Ill.: Research Press, 1975.

Horacek v. *Exon,* Civ. No. 72-L-299 (D. Neb., Aug. 6, 1975) (consent decree).

Inmates of Boys' Training School v. *Affleck,* 346 F. Supp. 1354 (D.R.I. 1972).

In re Jones, 338 F. Supp. 428 (D.D.C. 1972).

Joint Commission on Accreditation of Hospitals. *Standards for services for developmentally disabled individuals.* Chicago, Ill.: JCAH, 1978.

Kaimowitz v. *Department of Mental Health,* Civ. No. 73-19434-AW (Mich. Cir. Ct., Wayne County, 1973).

Kazdin, A. E. Acceptability of alternative treatments for deviant child behavior. *Journal of Applied Behavior Analysis,* 1980, *13,* 259–273.

Mahan, S., Maples, S., Murphy, S., & Tubb, G. A mechanism for enforcing the right to treatment: The Human Rights Committee. *Law & Psychology Review,* 1975, *Spring,* 131–149.

Martin, R. *Behavior modification: Human rights and legal responsibilities.* Champaign, Ill.: Research Press, 1974.

Martin, R. *Legal challenges to behavior modification.* Champaign, Ill.: Research Press, 1975.

May, J. G., Risley, T. R., Twardosz, S., Friedman, P., Bijou, S. W., Wexler, D., *et al. Guidelines for the use of behavioral procedures in state programs for retarded persons.* Arlington, Texas: NARC, 1976.

Millard v. *Cameron,* 373 F.2d 468 (D.C. Cir. 1966).

Morales v. *Turman,* 364 F. Supp. 166 (E.D. Texas 1973), *aff'd* 383 F. Supp. 53 (E.D. Texas 1974). *rev'd* 535 F.2d 864 (5th Cir. 1976), *reinstated* 430 U.S. 322 (1977).

Nason v. *Superintendent of Bridgewater State Hospital,* 353 Mass. 604, 233 N.E.2d 908 (1968).

National Society for Autistic Children. *White paper on behavior modification with autistic children.* Washington, D.C.: NSAC, 1975.

National Teaching-Family Association. *Standards of ethical conduct.* Boys Town, Neb.: NaTFA, 1979.

New York State Association for Retarded Children v. *Rockefeller,* 357 F. Supp. 752 (E.D.N.Y. 1973).

New York State Association for Retarded Children and Parisi v. *Carey,* 393 F. Supp. 715 (E.D.N.Y. 1975).

Rennie v. *Klein,* 462 F. Supp. 1131 (D.N.J. 1978), *aff'd on rehearing,* 476 F. Supp. 1294 (D.N.J. 1979), *aff'd on rehearing,* 481 F. Supp. 552 (D.N.J. 1979), *modified,* 653 F. 2d 836 (3d. Cir. 1981).

Repp, A., & Deitz, D. Ethical responsibilities in reductive programs for the retarded. In M. Berkler, G. Bible, S. Boles, D. Deitz, & A. Repp (Eds.), *Current trends for the developmentally disabled.* Baltimore: University Park Press, 1978.

Risley, T. R. Certify procedures not people. In W. S. Wood (Ed.), *Issues in evaluating behavior modification.* Champaign, Ill.: Research Press, 1975.

Risley, T. R., & Sheldon-Wildgen, J. Suggested procedures for Human Rights Committees of potentially controversial treatment programs. *Behavior Therapist,* 1980, *3*, 9–10.

Risley, T. R., & Sheldon-Wildgen, J. Invited peer review: The AABT experience. *Professional Psychology,* 1982, *13*, 125–131.

Rochin v. *California,* 342 U.S. 165 (1952).

Rogers v. *Okin,* 478 F. Supp. 1342 (D. Mass. 1979), *aff'd in part, rev'd in part,* 634 F. 2d 650 (1st Cir. 1980), *cert. granted,* 68 L. Ed. 2d 293 (1981).

Roos, P. Human rights and behavior modification. *Mental Retardation,* 1974, *12,* 3–6.

Rouse v. *Cameron,* 373 F.2d 451 (D.C. Cir. 1966).

Schwitzgebel, R. K. Right to treatment for the mentally disabled: The need for realistic standards and objective criteria. *Harvard Civil Rights-Civil Liberties Law Review,* 1973, *8,* 513–535.

Serber, M., Hiller, C., Keith, C., & Taylor, J. Behavior modification in maximum security settings: One hospital's experience. *The American Criminal Law Review,* 1975, *13,* 85–99.

Sinohar v. *Parry,* No. 14138/77 (N.Y. Sup. Ct. Jan. 16, 1979).

Stolz, S. Ethical issues in research on behavior therapy. In W. S. Wood (Ed.), *Issues in evaluating behavior modification.* Champaign, Ill.: Research Press, 1975.

Tribby v. *Cameron,* 379 F.2d 104 (D.C. Cir. 1967).

Walker, L., & Peabody, A. The right of the mentally disabled to protection from harm and to services in institutions and in the community. In P. Friedman (Chairman), *Legal rights of mentally disabled persons,* Vol. 1. New York: Practicing Law Institute, 1979.

Welsch v. *Likins,* 373 F. Supp. 487 (M.D. Minn. 1974).

Wexler, D. Token and taboo: Behavior modification, token economies, and the law. *California Law Review,* 1973, *61,* 81–109.

Wexler, D. Of rights and reinforcers. *San Diego Law Review,* 1974, *11,* 957–971.

Wexler, D. The emerging law and the proposed Florida guidelines. In M. Berkler, G. Bible, S. Boles, D. Deitz, & A. Repp (Eds.), *Current trends for the developmentally disabled.* Baltimore: University Park Press, 1978.

Wheeler v. *Glass,* 473 F.2d 983 (7th Cir. 1973).

Wildgen, J. S. Rights of institutionalized mental patients: Issues, implications, and proposed guideline. *Kansas Law Review,* 1976, *25,* 63–85.

Wuori v. *Zitnay,* No. 75-80-SD (D. Maine July 14, 1978).

Wyatt v. *Ireland,* Civ. No. 3195-N (M.D. Ala. Oct. 25, 1979).

Wyatt v. *Stickney,* 325 F. Supp. 781, *aff'd on rehearing,* 334 F. Supp. 1341 (M.D. Ala. 1971), *aff'd on rehearing,* 344 F. Supp. 373, *aff'd in separate decision,* 344 F. Supp. 387 (M.D. Ala. 1972), *aff'd sub nom, Wyatt* v. *Adherholt,* 503 F.2d 1305 (5th Cir. 1974).

CHAPTER 11

Community Intervention and the Use of Multidisciplinary Knowledge

Clifford R. O'Donnell and Roland G. Tharp

Introduction

The modern history of community approaches to human problems began in the 1890s, with the origins of settlement houses, juvenile courts, and child guidance clinics (Levine & Levine, 1970). Since the 1960s, community approaches have also been an important part of the behavioral literature (Nietzel, Winett, MacDonald, & Davidson, 1977; O'Donnell, 1977). Despite this lengthy history and extensive current use, there is little consensus on a definition of a community orientation and on how it differs from an individual one. Indeed, Goodstein and Sandler (1978) cited the lack of a definition as the most critical problem for the field of community psychology. In this amorphic condition, so many services have been called community services that the development of a viable model to guide applications has been hindered.

A definition that has been useful for us is that in the community approach, human problems are addressed through the environmental context in which the problems occur. In contrast, in an individual orientation, the focus is on the specific people who manifest the problems. This definition has several implications for community services. First, intervention occurs in natural settings such as homes and schools, rather than in facilities that have been specifically designed to treat people with behavior problems, such as hospitals and therapists' offices. Second, because of this focus on natural settings, a multidisciplinary knowledge base is necessary. Assessment of the variables that influence problems within various settings is likely to benefit from the theories and methods of many fields. Third, professional services are indirect, that is, mediated through the setting and the people who usually participate in the setting, such as parents, teachers, and paraprofessionals. Finally, greater emphasis is placed on the prevention of human problems. After all, if problems are influenced by the environmental context in which they occur, then it might be possible to design settings to prevent these problems.

Clifford R. O'Donnell and Roland G. Tharp • Department of Psychology, University of Hawaii, Honolulu, Hawaii 96822.

With this emphasis on intervention in the natural environment, multidisciplinary knowledge, indirect services, and especially prevention, it is hoped that eventually more human problems can be reduced, with greater economy and efficiency, than is possible through the direct treatment of people who seek help. It should be noted, however, that the community and individual approaches supplement, rather than oppose, each other. For the foreseeable future, many people will seek direct professional help for behavior problems that are unlikely to be prevented or alleviated through community methods. Both approaches have their advantages, and neither has located the sole source of human problems. The persons-versus-situations debate (e.g., Bem & Funder, 1978; Bowers, 1973; Endler & Magnusson, 1976; Mischel, 1968) has made the interactionist position a truism. While the community and individual orientations have focused on different aspects of this interaction, both are required in the understanding of human behavior.

The purpose of this chapter is to suggest a redirection in the community applications of behavior modification. In the second section, an overview of current community applications to a variety of problems is presented with a brief discussion of issues that warrant further research. This is followed by a discussion of the limitations of the behavioral approach in community settings. It is argued that these limitations and the complexity of natural-world phenomena require the use of ideas and methods developed within other disciplines. Accordingly, in the third section, examples are provided of some of these ideas and methods. Finally, the implications of this presentation are discussed in the fourth sction, with an emphasis on linking the knowledge gained through the full array of scientific methods to the behavioral methods and thereby extending the achievements of community programs.

Community Settings

If human problems are to be addressed through their environmental context, then knowledge about the functioning of many community settings is required. Obviously, problems can occur in any of the everyday activities of people, whether at home, school, work, or play. To date, most of the behavioral applications have taken place in homes and schools or within programs developed for general community problems such as crime, the reintegration of people discharged from institutional care, unemployment, energy conservation, and litter control. An overview of these applications, followed by a discussion of their limitations, is presented in this section.

Home

Intervention programs in the home have focused on the modification of children's behavior. Parents have been trained to intervene in both routine and complex problems, including behavior during shopping trips (Barnard, Christophersen, & Wolf, 1977), weight control (Aragona, Cassady, & Drabman, 1975), asthmatic responding (Neisworth & Moore, 1972), seizures (Zlutnick, Mayville, & Moffat, 1975), and autism (Lovaas, Koegel, Simmons, & Long, 1973).

The effectiveness of parental intervention has been comprehensively reviewed by Graziano (1977). He concluded that it has been most successful with somatic problems such as enuresis and encopresis, is highly promising with phobias, and has potential with asthma. However, he pointed out that with severe behavior problems such as autism, a maximum effort is required in order to achieve even limited effectiveness, and that our current knowledge is not sufficient for the use of parental intervention with severe speech disorders. As Graziano noted, with the exception of enuresis, most studies have involved the use of contingency management for aggressive behavior.

It is in this area that family intervention studies have encountered many difficulties. These have included high rates of families dropping out of the program, questions about the reliability of the behavioral observation codes, possible reactivity to the intrusiveness of behavior observation in the home, lack of control groups, mixed behavioral-observation results (especially during follow-up), and validity questions about the interpretation of parental reports (O'Donnell, 1977, pp. 81–91). These problems suggest that the effectiveness of current programs is limited and that both variations and alternatives to this approach are likely to be increasingly explored.

One of these possible variations is a greater emphasis on sibling interaction. For example, Patterson and Cobb (1973) examined stimuli that preceded both high and low rates of targeted behavior. Their data indicated that sibling rather than parental behaviors were the important stimuli in the control of socially aggressive behavior. Younger siblings in particular have been seen to initiate and maintain social aggression (Patterson, 1977). This finding indicates that siblings might be useful as behavior change agents. Several case studies support this view: Tharp and Wetzel (1969) reported two uses of sibling-as-reinforcing-mediator; Colletti and Harris (1977) reported the improved behavior of a neurologically impaired brother and an autistic sister. The behavior of siblings has also been shown to improve when they are used as change agents (Lavigueur, 1976). An alternative possibility is to develop family support systems. These may help to reduce some of the daily pressures of multiproblem families, while providing settings outside of the home for children to acquire appropriate social behavior. An excellent example of such a support system has been developed by Risley, Clark, and Cataldo (1976). It includes infant day care, toddler and preschool care, recreational programs for older children, and a center that gives advice to families on specific problems. The success of this approach might also serve to increase the effectiveness of parents in coping with their children's behavior problems in the home.

School

The classroom has been one of the major settings for behavioral intervention. Many studies have demonstrated the effectiveness of reward and punishment in modifying both academic and social behaviors. Teacher attention, praise, special activities, and material goods have been used as rewards in both individual contingency and token economy programs. Response–cost and time-out procedures have been the most effective uses of punishment, while the use of reprimands has shown mixed results (see Drabman, 1976, pp. 228–239, and O'Leary & O'Leary, 1976, pp. 480–490, for detailed reviews).

A potentially important finding in this research is the evidence that improving academic performance reduces inappropriate social behavior (e.g., Ayllon & Roberts, 1974; Winett, Battersby, & Edwards, 1975; Winett & Roach, 1973). This finding suggests that the emphasis on the contingent management of inappropriate behavior may be misplaced. The emphasis might be better placed on academic performance; if academic behavior is improved, more appropriate social behavior will very likely occur. This approach may well require that behavioral planners develop different skills. As suggested by Nietzel *et al.* (1977), knowledge of curriculum development may be most useful in the design of more effective behavioral interventions.

Another important finding is the pervasive influence of the peer group. Peers have been effective as tutors (Cloward, 1967; Dineen, Clark, & Risley, 1977; Gartner, Kohler, & Riessman, 1971; Harris & Sherman, 1973; Johnson & Bailey, 1974; Schwartz, 1977); as models (Keller & Carlson, 1974; O'Connor, 1969, 1972); as behavioral managers (Greenwood, Sloane, & Baskin, 1974; Solomon & Wahler, 1973; Surratt, Ulrich, & Hawkins, 1969); and as participants in group contingency programs (reviewed by Hayes, 1976).

Although effective while the programs were in operation, the behavioral procedures in all of these studies were intrusive in the sense that they were implemented in addition to the regular program because of the problems of a few children. It would be preferable, of course, if the setting could be designed to minimize the need for special procedures. A review of the preschool literature by Risley and Twardosz (1976) suggests that this may be possible. Especially noteworthy is their emphasis on the design of the physical environment and the everyday activities to prevent and remediate behavior problems. For example, the careful scheduling of quiet and active activities was reported as helping to maintain attention and prevent disruptions. Individual intervention was needed only as a supplement. In addition, once again, the importance of the peer group was noted, this time in the normal development of social, verbal, and motor skills. It was pointed out that intervention might be needed to introduce some children into the group and to be sure that they have the level of skill necessary for acceptable interaction, but that peers can, in effect, teach the components of social play. The authors suggested that even with language and academic deficiencies, incidental teaching during free play may be more effective than a teacher-structured learning situation.

If we are to make greater use of the everyday activities of peer groups, much more knowledge of their behavior is needed. This knowledge cannot be based on data only from referred children or from special programs that alter the everyday interactions among peers. Instead, it must be based on the behavior of all of the participants in the setting as they engage in their normal routine.

One means of obtaining this information is to develop behavioral norms. For example, Melahn and O'Donnell (1978) developed norms for 32 behaviors in Head Start classrooms, with comparisons for age, sex, exceptional status, referral status, and semester reported. These norms were based on a random sample of all of the children in the program, in addition to those who were referred for behavior problems. This approach could be used to provide data on the formation of peer groups, on the interaction of their members, on the skills needed for group acceptance, on how skills are learned within the group, and on comparisons between classrooms differing in physical environment and activity schedules. Such information would be useful in designing classrooms to minimize behavior problems and in using the influence of peer groups in the remediation of those problems. In this way, behavioral intervention would be less intrusive, would be interrelated with the everyday activities of the setting, and might alleviate the problem, associated with the use of special procedures, of how to maintain improved behavior. As will be argued below, it may well be necessary to observe peers in settings other than that of the target institution, which may itself be suppressing desirable portions of the available peer repertoire.

General Community Problems

General community problems are those that occur outside a specific type of setting, such as homes or schools. Behaviorists have con-

centrated their work on two of these problems: crime and the reintegration of people discharged from institutional care. In addition, some recent work has addressed such miscellaneous problems as energy conservation, litter control, and unemployment. An overview of community applications with these problems is presented in this section.

Crime. Most of the behavioral applications in the correctional field have focused on juveniles. These problems may be classified as either residential or nonresidential. The nonresidential programs are more community-oriented since they do not remove the youngsters from their natural environment; therefore, these are the programs discussed here.

One of the major nonresidential applications has been to improve academic performance. The relationship between poor achievement in school and delinquency is often cited as the rationale for these programs. The assumption is that if these youngsters do better academically, delinquent behavior will be less likely. Therefore, programs have been offered to those not doing well in school and to those who have dropped out. A good example of a comprehensive school program has been developed by Filipczak, Friedman, and Reese (1979). The components of this program included the use of self-instructional materials, contingency management, social skills training for the students, and behavior management training for parents and teachers. Significant differences, favoring those in the program compared with control youths, were reported on a variety of academic and social measures.

Other programs have been independent of the public school system. In one example, athletic participation was used to reward academic achievement (O'Donnell, Chambers, & Ling, 1973). Youngsters from 10 to 15 years of age came to a neighborhood settlement house after school to participate in a programmed learning center. The points that they earned for completing their academic work, with at least 90% accuracy, were used to play on the settlement house's football and basketball teams. Average academic gains on standardized achievement tests ranged from .5 to 1.2 grade levels during the 10-week athletic seasons. Finally, some programs have provided an opportunity for teenagers who have dropped out of high school to obtain a high-school-equivalency degree. In an example of this type of program (O'Donnell & Stanley, 1973), participants earned up to $50 for approximately 25 hours of academic activities each week. Average achievement test scores improved .8 to 8.3 grade levels within three to nine months of participation in the program. Of the 11 youths who entered this demonstration project, 5 received their high-school-equivalency degrees and were accepted into community colleges.

Programs such as these have shown that it is possible to improve the academic performance of youths considered higher risks for delinquency. However, the question is whether doing so reduces the likelihood of delinquent behavior. Although many studies have reported that police contacts and arrests are higher for youths who are not doing well in school (e.g., Elliott & Voss, 1974; Wolfgang, Figlio, & Sellin, 1972), this finding does not mean that improving academic achievement will prevent delinquency (cf. Feldman, 1977, pp. 264–265). To date, no study has presented such evidence.

Indeed, the results of two studies suggest that the relationship between academic achievement and delinquency is more complex than is typically thought. In a longitudinal study of 2,617 ninth-graders, Elliott and Voss (1974) found limited academic achievement and association with delinquent classmates to be two of the most powerful predictors of male delinquency. One of their most important findings, however, was that dropping out of high school led to a *decrease* in delinquency because school problems and contact with delinquent friends in school decreased. They concluded that "school is the critical social context for the generation of delinquent behavior" (p. 204). The other study (Jensen, 1976) involved a reanalysis of delinquency data based on approximately 10,000 boys of a birth cohort (Wolfgang *et al.,* 1972). These data showed little variation in delinquency among those with low to average achievement levels (Jensen, 1976). Delinquency rates became markedly lower only when achievement levels varied from average to high. This finding suggests that achievement-based delinquency-prevention programs may have to raise achievement

to at least average, and possibly to above-average, levels to be effective.

Taken together, these two studies indicate that academic programs designed to prevent dropping out of school can actually help to maintain delinquent behavior. This could happen if such programs were effective enough to keep youths in school, and thus in contact with delinquent classmates, but not enough to raise achievement levels sufficiently to reduce school-related problems and affect the social network of lower-achieving students. These findings, and the lack of evidence that improving academic performance affects delinquent behavior, suggest that a reconsideration of the academically based approach is warranted. At the very least, data on delinquency and friendship patterns need to be obtained in these programs.

The other major approach has been behavioral contracting. Most of the studies in this area have concentrated on contracting within the families of delinquents. These studies have encountered all of the difficulties of working with multiproblem families, and in general, the results have been disappointing (O'Donnell, 1977, pp. 78–80). Perhaps family contracting will still be useful, however, as part of a more comprehensive approach. An example is the use of contracting in the Learning House Project (Thoresen, Thoresen, Klein, Wilbur, Becker-Haven, & Haven, 1979). In this program, elementary-school-age children live in a group home that stresses the development of self-control. When they return home, a consultant develops an individual plan with each family that includes weekly contracts for all family members. In this way, the child is not singled out. Although outcome data are not yet available on this project, some support for the contracting procedure within a more comprehensive approach was reported by Alexander and Parsons (1973). They used contracting as part of a behavioral family treatment package and found an effect on status, but not on criminal offenses.

Other programs, which were independent of the family, have shown an effect on criminal offenses. One trained university students in child advocacy and behavior contracting to work with youths referred by the police (Seidman, Rappaport, & Davidson, 1976). Intervention was individually established for each youngster and was carried out for six to eight hours per week over three to five months. A two-year follow-up showed that these youths had fewer police and court contacts than those randomly assigned to the control group.

The results of a similar program have implications for increasing the effectiveness of delinquency projects. Based on the triadic model of Tharp and Wetzel (1969), indigenous nonprofessionals were employed as "buddies" of youngsters referred for behavior and academic problems. Individual intervention plans were developed for each youth. The behavioral procedures were evaluated by comparing those randomly assigned to either contingency management, a noncontingent relationship, or a no-treatment control group (Fo & O'Donnell, 1974). School attendance and other behaviors, except school grades, improved during the contingency conditions. The degree of improvement was shown to be partly a function of the relative locus of control of buddy–youth pairs: more improvement occurred for pairs in which the youth scored higher in externality than the buddy (O'Donnell & Fo, 1976).

The main purpose of the buddy system, however, was the prevention and remediation of delinquent behaviors. A recent study reported its effect on arrests for major criminal offenses over a three-year period for 335 project and 218 control youngsters (O'Donnell, Lydgate, & Fo, 1979). These data showed that the project was effective for those who had been arrested for a major offense in the prior year. Arrest rates were lower for project (56.0%) than for control (78.3%) youths. The reverse, however, was true for those without an arrest in the prior year. Here, youngsters in the buddy system had a significantly higher arrest rate (22.5%) than did those in the control condition (16.4%). In addition, this negative effect occurred largely with those who were in the project for more than one year. This finding lends support to the speculation that the effect was a result of friendship, established in the project, between those with and without offenses in the prior year.

These results suggest caution in the development of programs for those who have not been recently arrested for a major criminal offense. The need for caution was further underscored by data on the base rate of arrests for these youths, provided by the control condition. These data showed that only about 10% of the females and 20% of the males were arrested for a major offense in the next three years. Therefore, any intervention program would have to be highly effective to be successful with these youths. Overall, effectiveness might be increased by concentrating on juveniles *with* a recent major offense and separating them from those with no or less serious offenses.

Contracting programs have also been developed for older teenagers and young adults, with employment as the major concern. In one of the few programs for adults, those placed on probation for the use of dangerous drugs received time off probation for employment, nondrug activity, improving living accommodations, etc. (Polakow & Doctor, 1974). Those randomly assigned to the contracting group had fewer probation violations and arrests and were employed for more months than those who received traditional probation services. In a more comprehensive approach, Mills and Walter (1977) trained delinquents with felony convictions in basic job skills and their employers in the use of reinforcement. Behavior contracts were then developed directly between the employers and the delinquents. One year after the initial interview, 91% of the participants and only 30% of those in a comparison group were arrest-free.

To summarize, behavioral correction programs have focused on improving academic achievement and contracting. Although many programs have been successful in raising achievement levels, none has presented data showing that higher achievement levels reduce delinquency. The results of family-contracting with delinquents have been disappointing, but this approach still has promise if it is used as part of a more comprehensive program for multiproblem families. The only programs reporting an effect on criminal offenses have intervened outside the family. These studies indicate that programs are more likely to be effective with youths who have been recently arrested for a major offense and that caution should be used in developing programs for other youngsters. For older teenagers and young adults, a focus on employment has been most successful so far.

Aftercare. Many hospital programs have demonstrated an improvement in patient behavior (Erickson, 1975) and have increased their patients' chances of being discharged (e.g., O'Donnell, 1972). The work of Paul and Lentz (1977) is especially impressive. Their data indicate that social-learning programs can improve the behavior of some of the most severely dehabilitated patients, to the extent that they can be released to aftercare facilities. The improved prospects for the discharge of inpatients and the desire to prevent the hospitalization of outpatients have led to the need for effective community-based programs.

The focus of these programs has been on the coordination of a supportive environment rather than on producing a cure (Liberman, King, & DeRisi, 1976, pp. 595–598). The importance of a supportive environment is indicated in studies showing that a lack of family and residential instability were the variables most strongly related to first-admission rates to psychiatric facilities (Stack, 1975), and that financial and employment variables were the best predictors of hospital recidivism (Miller & Willer, 1976).

Some of the most comprehensive supportive systems have been developed in halfway-house programs. These programs frequently provide a place to live, employment opportunities, social activities, and, sometimes, continued help with behavior problems. Results have shown that these programs can be operated at a lower cost than hospitalization and that they also reduce the rate of unemployment and recidivism, as long as the participants remain in the program (e.g., Fairweather, Sanders, Cressler, & Maynard, 1969).

Another approach to providing support services is the day treatment center. Spiegler and Agigian (1977) have developed an exemplary program based on an educational-behavioral-social systems model. The educational-behavioral components included operating the center as a school, with classes on the skills needed to function independently in everyday life, and the use of a token economy and behavioral contracting. By these means patients developed skills in such areas as interpersonal relations, problem solving, community survival (e.g., money management, cooking, and driving), health care, and academic subjects. An innovative feature was the linking of these components to the systematic use of social systems to help maintain improved behavior. This included the use of social clubs, community educational programs, crisis intervention, advocates, volunteers, and employment services.

Spiegler and Agigian also discussed how this model may be used in prevention programs for the general population. Such services would be especially valuable if they were effective in the prevention of behavior problems. The development of these services might be facilitated by a focus on the needs of higher-risk groups. Illustrative programs have been developed for the alcoholic (Azrin, 1976), the unemployed (Azrin, Flores, & Kaplan, 1975), and the aged (Nietzel *et al.,* 1977, pp. 287–292). Outreach services could also be incorporated to encourage the use of these services. For example, Beard, Malamud, and Rossman (1978) reported a doubling in the use of their aftercare program through the use of home visits, telephone follow-ups, and letters. At the present time, it is likely that the greatest progress on the problems of community aftercare will come from preventing hospitalization by providing support services for outpatients and members of higher-risk groups.

Miscellaneous. Behavioral procedures have been applied to a variety of miscellaneous community concerns, including litter control (e.g., Clark, Burgess, & Hendee, 1972; Powers, Osborne, & Anderson, 1973); energy conservation (e.g., Foxx & Hake, 1977; Hayes & Cone, 1977; Kohlenberg, Phillips, & Proctor, 1976; Palmer, Lloyd, & Lloyd, 1977); unemployment (e.g., Jones & Azrin, 1973); getting parents to seek dental care for their children (Reiss, Piotrowski, & Bailey, 1976); reducing cash shortages in business (Marholin & Gray, 1976); reducing the use of telephone directory assistance (McSweeny, 1978); locating cases of smallpox (Fawcett, 1977); lowering noise levels (Meyers, Artz, & Craighead, 1976); and improving the packaging of refuse (Stokes & Fawcett, 1977). The use of behavioral procedures with these problems is relatively recent, and therefore, any conclusions about their success with any one of these problems would be premature. Overall, however, prompting has shown mixed results (Geller, 1973; Geller, Farris, & Post, 1973; Witmer & Geller, 1976), with greater success when multiple prompts were used (Palmer *et al.*, 1977; Reiss *et al.*, 1976). Generally, contingent conditions have been more effective, whether incentives have been offered (e.g., Foxx & Hake, 1977; Hayes & Cone, 1977; Kohlenberg *et al.*, 1976; Winett & Nietzel, 1975; Witmer & Geller, 1976) or response–cost has been imposed (Marholin & Gray, 1976; McSweeny, 1978).

Two of the difficulties in the problems of litter control and energy conservation have been to make the procedures cost-effective and to increase the participation of the general population (O'Donnell, 1977, pp. 91–93). The most promising resolution of these difficulties has occurred in the efforts to reduce household electricity consumption through the use of feedback. When families were given frequent feedback on the rate of their consumption, their use of electricity declined (Hayes & Cone, 1977; Kohlenberg, *et al.*, 1976; Palmer *et al.*, 1977). Since it is possible to install devices in the home that provide immediate feedback (e.g., Kohlenberg, *et al.*, 1976), this procedure might become cost-effective and reach a sizable proportion of the general population.

Overall, studies in this area have demonstrated the potential of behavioral procedures for a broad range of community problems beyond the traditional concerns of crime and aftercare.

Limitations

There are two related limitations on the community applications of behavior modification that, in our opinion, will require a fundamental shift in direction. These are the familiar lack of generalization and maintenance of behavior and the, not as often recognized, lack of knowledge about natural settings. It is contended that a general resolution of these limitations is not likely within a behavioral approach and will require the ideas and methods developed within other disciplines.

The lack of generalization has been noted in many different types of problems, for example, fear (Lick & Unger, 1977); speech (Miller & Sloane, 1976); assertion (Hersen,

Eisler, & Miller, 1974); social skills (Hersen & Bellack, 1976; Shepherd, 1977); and academic performance (Cloward, 1967; O'Donnell, 1974). In addition, Keeley, Shemberg, and Carbonell (1976), in reviewing all types of problems, reported that very few studies presented follow-up data. Of those that did, with the exception of self-reports, most showed that the behavior was not maintained. Others have reported similiar conclusions in reviews of desensitization and aversion therapy (Gruber, 1971); delinquency (Davidson & Seidman, 1974); and obesity (Brightwell & Sloan, 1977). A review of studies in community settings also showed an almost complete lack of generalization and maintenance (O'Donnell, 1977).

A number of people have addressed the generalization and maintenance issue and have discussed potential strategies (see, e.g., Conway & Bucher, 1976; Kazdin, 1975; Marholin, Siegel, & Phillips, 1976; Stokes & Baer, 1977). It is clear, however, that the success of these strategies will vary with the type of problem, client, and setting. Overall, the success has been limited, and it appears that none will achieve a general resolution.

Most of these strategies can be categorized as those that (1) develop a special procedure in the nonintervention setting; (2) build resistance to extinction; (3) train significant others; or (4) use cognitions. The first typically uses some variation of the intervention and attempts to extend it into the nonintervention setting. This is not really generalization or maintenance, since some form of intervention is still being used. Its usefulness is limited to those situations in which there is some control over the nonintervention setting and where it is practical to, in effect, continue a modified form of intervention. In the second, the use of different conditions of training, fading, and partial reinforcement or delay of reinforcement cannot succeed unless the nonintervention setting eventually supports the behavior (cf. Marholin *et al.*, 1976). The training of significant others can be useful in those cases where there is a strong incentive for them to follow the training procedures. An example is where parents are trained to care for children with severe behavior disorders such as asthma (Neisworth & Moore, 1972) or autism (Lovaas *et al.*, 1973). In most cases, however, the procedure begs the question, because it is not clear how the behavior of the significant others is to be maintained. Finally, studies using cognitive strategies have also experienced problems with the generalization and maintenance of behavior (e.g., Conway & Bucher, 1976, pp. 144–151; Franks & Wilson, 1978, pp. 512–513; Harris, 1975).

An alternative is to view behavior not as generalizing from one setting to another but as a part of the setting in which it is assessed (cf. O'Donnell, 1977, p. 96). As the setting variables differ, the behavior would be expected to differ also. Different settings and times could then be compared by means of the procedures of generalizability theory (Cone, 1977; Cronbach, Gleser, Nanda, & Rajaratnam, 1972; Mitchell, 1979) to assess the likelihood of similar behavior.

The exploration of this alternative will require much more attention to natural (i.e., nonintervention) settings. In addition to addressing the generalization–maintenance issue from a different perspective, the knowledge gained might also help to resolve other limitations of behavior therapy as discussed by Kazdin and Wilson (1978, pp. 35–43): the lack of a conceptual basis of behavior, the lack of information on the development of behavior disorders, and the clinical relevance of treatment effects. Further, such knowledge may help us to design settings to prevent behavior problems.

The first step is to recognize that we know little about how settings function in the absence of our procedures and restricted observational methods. Most of our knowledge comes from studies based on intervention. If that is our strength, it is also our weakness. We might do well, then, to look at how investigators from other disciplines have proceeded. Their methods and concepts might be useful in our shift in direction. Examples of how these may be helpful are presented in the following section.

Suggested Extensions: The State of the Art

Earlier we suggested that the community approach is distinguished by addressing problems through the environmental context in which the problems occur. Accordingly, community intervention may take the form of developing new programs within the existing structure of natural settings, creating alternative structures, or modifying the existing structure of the setting itself. Typically, intervention has taken the form of using the existing apparatus of social settings to organize influences on the target behaviors of problem individuals or groups (training parents and teachers to reinforce more rationally); or, as an alternate form of address, creating special procedures, *ad hoc,* to do the same thing for specific problem populations (the buddy system; halfway houses). As a rule, the alternate strategy of a radical attack on the structure of the settings themselves has been left to that brand of "community psychology" that uses political means and paradigms. And no community interventionist lacks experience of the intransigence of institutional structures. It is difficult enough to change one child, let alone an entire state's school system.

However, we suggest another reason for the relative neglect of the strategy of seeking a radical change in settings, a reason that lies in the history and the continuing assumptions of most behavioral community psychologists. Most of us have been trained as clinicians. The field has grown gradually from the roots of behavior modification in the careful shaping of desirable behaviors in institutionalized children, and though we have "moved out into the community," we have taken along with us one limiting assumption and process. Typically, we look at the target person or group in the environment where the problem is located. We find an absence of desirable behavior, or an excess of undesirable behavior. We design programs to create the desirable behavior, and if we are community-sophisticated, we urge the social environment to become a more rational influence on that process of creation. If we have inventiveness and power, we may even develop structures to create the behavior.

In this process, we carry the assumption that the flaw, lack, or problem lies in the individual, and that the behavioral task is to create desirable behavior. The alternative view occurs to us too seldom: perhaps the problem lies in the existing environmental context. If the desirable behavior is indeed missing from the individual's repertoire, we might ask why the natural setting hasn't created it. Why should special procedures be necessary to create it? Instead of implementing special procedures so that the individual or group may acquire the behavior (e.g., token systems), why not assess the environmental context to see if the flaw or lack might lie there?

In doing so, we may find that in many cases, the desirable behaviors do in fact exist within the repertoire of the target individual or group, but that the existing environmental context does not allow its occurrence and improvement. For such conditions, the intervention strategy would be quite different. The context would become the target, and the goal would be to *allow* the repertoire rather than to create it.

We do not suggest that this is a universal condition, nor that all contexts are tractable to reform. But we will risk some overstatement to call attention to this possibility, because where it is so, appropriate intervention will differ radically from standard practice.

Before proceeding to examples, let us take the argument one step further and, for that purpose, assume that a target group may well have buried deep within its repertoire such qualities as cooperativeness, compliance, cognitive flexibility, self-care skills, or whatever behavior's nonappearance in a given setting constitutes the consultation problem. Why would we not discover these elements? First, we too often confine assessment to the environment that reports the deficiency. If the school complains, we watch the child in the classroom; if the family complains, we send observers to the home; but we rarely assess the total environment by including sibling, peer, playground, or street culture. That inadequacy of assessment can be corrected by greater diligence and more resources, but we suggest that a second cause for nondiscovery of a desirable repertoire is more potent and, again, lies deep in the common processes of our profession. *Conventional behavioristic methods and constructs themselves are inadequate for comprehensive assessment and conceptualization.* That may be the root problem.

In the first example, we present several knotty community-intervention problems, the solution of which required the use of assessment procedures developed by some sister disciplines: anthropology, linguistics, sociolinguistics, and discourse analysis. The use of these methods allowed the *discovery* of the repertoires of concern. That discovery altered the consultation task, which then became institutional modification, modification that would *allow* the desired behavior to occur. In the second example, the concept of social networks, developed within social anthropology and sociology, is presented. Evidence that social networks influence a wide range of behavioral problems is briefly reviewed. It is then suggested that this development has implications for conceptualizing the environmental context of behavior—for all forms of community intervention, whether within existing settings or in their modification—and for resolving the limitations of a behavioral approach. Following these examples, we discuss the issue of the expansion of the behavioral assessment and conceptual armamentarium, and we conclude that this expansion does not threaten the integrity of behaviorism; we argue that such expansion will increase our knowledge of natural settings, contribute toward a resolution of the generalization–maintenance problem, and indeed is necessary to fulfill the deepest promise of behavioral empiricism.

Example One: The Kamehameha Early Education Program

The Kamehameha Early Education Program (KEEP) is a remarkably successful research-and-development enterprise, which has produced consistent national-norm-level educational achievement for ethnic minority children, both in its own laboratory school and in its export operations in the public schools of the State of Hawaii. Like other minority children, those of Polynesian-Hawaiian ancestry do not ordinarily prosper in the public schools. A case can be made that Hawaiian children experience the lowest level of academic achievement among ethnic minorities in the United States: by the fourth grade, statewide testing on Stanford achievement tests in reading has placed the means of schools with predominantly Hawaiian populations in the lowest stanine of national norms.

Polynesian-Hawaiian adults, though there are notable exceptions, are underrepresented in middle-class and leadership groups and are overrepresented in the registers of distress: welfare rolls, prison populations, and unemployment. The KEEP program, designed to produce educational competence in the earliest years of school, and thus to interrupt the compounding effects of poor reading ability (school failure, dropout, delinquency, poor earnings, social disorganization), may be seen in community mental-health terms as a primary prevention program. KEEP operates a laboratory and demonstration school in Honolulu, enrolling primarily Hawaiian and part-Hawaiian urban, poor children in kindergarten through the third grade. KEEP is a multidisciplinary program, involving anthropologists, linguists, and educators, but is under the immediate control of behavioral psychologists. Its purpose is to design, demonstrate, and export an effective school program for Hawaiian children. A fuller description of the research-and-development strategy may be found in Tharp and Gallimore (1979); of culture-and-education issues, in Jordan and Tharp (1979); and of evaluation results, in Gallimore, Tharp, Sloat, and Klein (1980).

When in the ordinary school setting, Hawaiian children are most often described as "lazy, disinterested, disorderly, disruptive," and lacking basic cognitive and linguistic skills requisite for school learning (Tharp & Gallimore, 1976). In the first four years of the KEEP operation, the basic strategy was to create, by a rich diet of positive reinforcement, a repertoire of attentiveness, industriousness, and orderliness. This effort was successful: an average on-task rate of 90% was achieved; positive reinforcement rates double those of control groups were emitted by KEEP teachers; and the children and their parents were happy with the school environment (Tharp & Gallimore, 1976).

During this phase, the same strategy was employed in the training of cognitive skills. A careful task analysis was drawn from the reading-skills literature, and the cognitive strategies of word attack, decoding, vocabulary memorization, and the like were carefully programmed, assessed, and reinforced. Creation of a cognitive skill repertoire was undertaken

by sophisticated behavior-modification procedures. The result of all this hard work by children, teachers, and researchers was nil, for so long as this strategy of repertoire creation *ex nihilo* was employed, the KEEP children did no better on standardized test results than did control children in public schools. A typical result was a mean 27th percentile on the Gates-MacGinitie Tests of Reading Achievement (Gallimore *et al.*, 1980). Of particular interest here is the experience of this behavioral community program, which required drastic revision of behavioral strategy in order to solve this minority-education problem, which it has apparently now done. The program authors attribute this success to an altered strategy of (1) discovering, rather than creating, the desired repertoire (2) by the use of methods of sister disciplines and then (3) modifying the school institution, rather than the children, so that the desirable behaviors are allowed to occur (Tharp, 1979). Three illustrations of this altered strategy will now be adduced.

Illustration #1: Ethnography. The first is the use of the basic "assessment" method of anthropology: ethnography. Elements of the revised KEEP program have drawn heavily from a five-year ethnographic study of Hawaiian culture (Gallimore, Boggs, & Jordan, 1974; Howard, 1973) and a continuing ethnographic process within the school itself (Jordan, 1977, 1978).

Ethnography is the careful observation, by a sensitive individual, of the regular life of a society, and the writing down of these observations, together with conclusions about their regularities. The observations are not quantified: interobserver reliability is not an issue. The observer is the "measuring" instrument, and the role of the observer, as participant–observer, is sharply different from the detached, objective role assumed by the behavioristic observer. The ethnographer lives with the people, participates in the life of the culture, and tries, insofar as possible, to understand the meanings and interweavings of the acts and values seen.

When Hawaiian children are seen in their home environments, the ethnographic descriptions are utterly different from a repertoire catalog as exhibited in the classroom environment, where they are typically (and not inaccurately) described as "lazy, disinterested, uninvolved, and irresponsible." Ethnography has revealed to KEEP that the Hawaiian children are unusually responsible; from their earliest years, they participate in the life of the family: cooking, cleaning, laundry, caring for their younger brothers and sisters, and, most importantly, taking responsibility for organizing these tasks themselves. Most often it is not the parent who assigns tasks and directly supervises, but the oldest child, which means that, in fact, any supervision is minimal, and initiative and good performance rest with the individual 5- and 6-year-old. When there is a task to be done, some child up and does it. The parent is often unaware of which child does what; but in Hawaiian culture, that is not important. The work is a family need, and the group of siblings is the unit that gets it done (Tharp, Jordan, Baird, & Loganbeel, 1980; Gallimore *et al.*, 1974). From an ethnographic perspective, then, it is possible to see that this repertoire, so desired by the school, is present in the children; the school institution itself prevents its occurrence. The task of the behavioral interventionist is to modify the school to allow initiative, responsibility, and effort. On a community or institutional level, the task is not to create and shape a new repertoire; it is to modify the school so that it more nearly approximates the cue functions, which in family life elicit that responsibility-and-effort performance. Again, the ethnographic description provided the information needed; the KEEP solution was as follows.

In the morning, before school, the teacher (typically) is at his/her desk, organizing the morning's work. Outside, the children are on the playground, playing tag or marbles as they wait for the first bell, which signals them to line up at the door of the classroom. In an ordered way, they enter the classroom and sit in a specified pattern, and the teacher conducts the first business of the day. Typically, "monitors" or "captains" may be appointed for various duties: leading the Pledge of Allegiance, changing the calendar, taking attendance, etc. And on the teacher's instruction, instructional activities begin.

As a response to the ethnographic data, the KEEP teacher adopted a different strategy:

First, she opened the door to the classroom a half hour or so before the bell and then went about her business of setting up the classroom chairs, taping newspaper to the top of the art table, counting out assignment sheets for various children's morning work, and the like. *She gave no assignments and did not ask that any children join her.*

She merely allowed the children to observe the necessary work and allowed them to observe her in its performance. This was a sufficient cue to trigger their high-probability response, which was to join in, take over, and organize the execution of the tasks for themselves. Within a matter of days, a dependable group of about eight children appeared regularly each morning to participate in this morning work. Within a matter of weeks, the activity was so institutionalized that virtually every member of the class participated in some degree, on some days, as the spirit moved them. Although the individual roster of participants was somewhat different from day to day, and thus the exact tasks performed by each child varied, all the work of setting up the classroom was done by the children. By the end of the school year, the academic tasks themselves were being organized by children; that is, they would look at the daily schedule of learning centers, and then they would count out appropriate work sheets, textbooks, and art supplies and distribute them around the room and into the storage boxes. (This task contained more academic learning opportunity, perhaps, than did the eventual exercises themselves.) This system of child responsibility extended to the cleanup phase of the school day. The teacher merely indicated that the children should also see that the classroom was restored to order, at the end of each day, and the phenomenon was repeated: On an entirely volunteer, informal, and child-organized basis, the learning centers were disassembled, files were restored, chairs were stacked on tables, and sweeping or mopping was done as necessary. As a matter of experimental test, the teacher (in this pilot classroom) *gave no instructions whatsoever* and no assignments *to individual children*. In fact, this absence of specific instruction was the cue that elicited, from these children, the very behavior wanted.

The side effects of this program alteration

were considerable, though difficult to specify in behavioral terms. Observers of the classroom repeatedly commented on the sense of involvement, ownership, and pride exhibited by the children. The form of the classroom radically altered; the necessity for monitors disappeared; and the rigid, hard-edged boundaries between one activity and another gave way to a softer, more impressionistic flow. Visitors commented that it was difficult to see any exact moment when "school" actually began. KEEP's ethnographer reported that the classroom took on the major organizational and emotional features of Hawaiian cultural life. The phenomenon is apparently a stable one; a similar strategy has now been used by KEEP in four other classrooms, with virtually identical processes and effects. A detailed presentation of this program is available in both 16-mm film and videotape formats (Tharp et al., 1980).

Illustration #2: Sociolinguistics and Cognitive Skill. The first illustration focused on *social* behaviors. In the next, we focus on intellectual behaviors. And we will see the same principles illustrated: the contributions of a sister discipline toward the discovery of the needed child behaviors—in this instance, those cognitive and linguistic repertoires upon which learning to read rests.

Sociolinguistics is the study of the social parameters that affect language use. In education, it is necessary to fully engage the linguistic and cognitive capacities of children. It is reasonable to assume that when Hawaiian children perform poorly in conventional education, their linguistic and cognitive capabilities have not been engaged.

Observation of conventional Hawaiian classrooms confirm it: When teachers call on individual children to recite or answer questions, in a formal context typical of classrooms, the children's answers are minimal, stilted, and embarrassed (in contrast to their speech among themselves, which is lively). The classroom stereotype of Hawaiian children is of language deficiency. As we shall see, an alternative formulation is possible: the typical classroom is deficient in those setting events that produce linguistic richness of repertoire in these children. Stephen Boggs, Richard Day, and Karen Watson-Gegeo conducted extensive sociolinguistic explorations with Hawaiian children in order to discover those social settings in which children display maximal linguistic and cognitive complexity. They obtained speech samples of Hawaiian children in varied ways: planting tape recorders at the dinner tables of families; conducting experiments of standard interviews with children, with different numbers of other children and adults present; creating little dollhouse and doll-store settings; and simply by talking with children in every available setting and circumstance (Day, 1975a,b).

Perhaps the richest of these settings is that called *talk-story* or a subtype of talk-story, called *storytelling* (Watson-Gegeo & Boggs, 1977). Among the features present in such settings are a small group of children, a sympathetic and receptive adult, informality, turn taking, overlapping speech, and co-narration. The image is of a group of children under a tree with a friendly adult, all enthusiastically creating or recalling a story together. Under such circumstances, verbal sequences of great richness and complexity are produced by quite young Hawaiian children. This is an image quite different from the listless, disinterested, or resistant Hawaiian child often seen in the school setting.

The KEEP program evolved an element that duplicates many features of the talk-story–storytelling format. During the daily small-group, direct-instruction reading lessons, about five children are seated in a semicircle before the teacher. Typically, there is a text for each person, and often a brief period of silent reading occurs. Then the teacher begins to ask questions about the story at hand. Details, main ideas, alternative outcomes, speculations about the characters' motives or feelings, and related personal experiences of the children—all are interwoven into a group discussion that is experienced by the teacher as planned instruction *but is experienced by the child as storytelling* (Au & Jordon, 1978). That is, the teacher's behaviors are the children's storytelling linguistic repertoire. Many of the features described by Watson-Gegeo and Boggs are present: co-narration, overlapping speech, and enthusiastic engagement. There are differences. The teacher does enforce roughly equal opportunities for each child to speak, over a period of days—apparently the self-regulating, equal-time principle, characteristic of the fully developed adult form of Hawaiin "talk-story" activity, does not develop until about age 12 (Boggs, 1972). The teachers do not, however, enforce a rigid turn-taking system, nor do they demand responses from a child who is not ready to participate, thus preserving the child-experienced informality of the enterprise, which is vital to the child's continued engagement (Jordan & Tharp, 1979, pp. 281–282).

Illustration #3: Linguistics, Dialect, and Discourse Analysis. Most Hawaiian children speak pidgin, more properly known as Hawaiian creole. This speech code has developed over many decades from a true pidgin, composed of Hawaiian language, English, Chinese, etc., but is now a widely used creole, characteristic of most Hawaiian and thousands of Oriental and Caucasian residents of Hawaii. Technically, this code is undergoing "decreolization"; that is, it is becoming a dialect of English, comparable to the other many dialects of English: Appalachian, black, Texican. Like other dialects, the code is considered low-status both by its speakers and by non-speakers. Pidgin-speaking parents generally want their children to learn standard American English, in addition to pidgin, for the advantages in employment and status that standard speech brings. Most children in Hawaii are, in fact, bidialectal; even those who speak almost entirely in pidgin can also understand, and to some extent produce, standard speech.

Should there be, in the public schools, specific instruction in the speaking of standard English? Both citizens and professionals are sharply divided on this issue. The KEEP research, however, indicates that learning to read—even learning to read standard English—is facilitated if children are allowed to discuss the text in their own dialect, because in the child's own dialect are found the greatest complexity and richness of expression. In the child's own dialect are found the tools for the cognitive operations necessary to comprehend the meaning of written material.

Within their own dialects, the children produce thought and language equal in equality to anyone's. How can this judgment of quality be made? The methods of *discourse analysis*

offer an analytic tool of great value to behaviorists. We can only allude here to those methods. They are, in fact, not highly structured, and basically, they involve making a typescript transcription of all the speech that occurs in a conversation and the making of a painstaking study of that transcript, using the concepts of *themes*, *routines*, or any number of other qualities. Natural speech goes by so quickly that often, we cannot analyze it for quality. But when careful study is made of storytelling sessions, or of the talk-story reading lesson, we find the linguistic competences of syntactic complexity, flexible use of vocabulary, the ability to generate new and alternate forms of construction—all those tools of language that are the tools of thought—to be present in dialect speech, more than in the standard speech of these bidialectal children. That is, the KEEP linguistic research, using discourse analysis, has *found* a sufficient linguistic repertoire. The intervention task is to persuade the school to allow it.

During school instruction, the KEEP teacher always accepts the children's pidgin speech. He/she may restate a child's remark, into standard English, especially if it contains a grammatical structure crucial to deciphering the text's meaning. But even such restatements are done in such a way as to emphasize that standard English is what the teacher speaks, not in such a way as to be punitive to the child's speech.

There is a stage in reading instruction when even the text used is in pidgin. Many poor children do not have much experience with written language. Many of the homes in the KEEP sample altogether lack text—no newspapers, magazines, or books. Many have to learn in school that text is another form of spoken language, that it contains images, memories, and meaning. The earliest KEEP texts are those dictated by the children themselves. They tell stories, in pidgin, and the teacher writes them down, in pidgin. The result becomes the text for study, and the children can learn that the marks on the page somehow store the words they spoke. Their own words form the earliest of written vocabulary. They learn to read their own stories back to themselves and to talk about them. This method is known as *language experience*, in education circles. KEEP did not invent it, although KEEP has perhaps adopted it more radically than is typical.

In ordinary pacing, this self-created text method ends in early first grade, and instruction moves to standard text material. From kindergarten through the third grade, however, the teachers accept the children's speech in the code in which it is preferred. As fluency in standard English increases, so does the proportion of standard English, but there is great individual variation, and the instructional strategy remains constant: to allow the children to use their own developing linguistic repertoire.

The KEEP reports emphasize that there are also elements, deemed necessary to children's learning, that have not been discovered in the children's existing repertoires and that must be shaped in more conventional ways (Gallimore, 1978; Jordan & Tharp, 1979). Neither they nor we argue that every target population has all necessary behaviors. The point here is that if the community psychologist looks for preexistent repertoires, they are more likely to be found. And if they are found, the intervention strategy appropriate is easier to implement, more elegant in conception, and of greater potential effectiveness. The KEEP program, for example, over a period of four years, three sites, and four grades, has produced class averages of about the 50th percentile on standardized tests of reading achievement, compared with control groups averaging about the 35th percentile (Gallimore *et al.*, 1980).

Example Two: Social Networks

Social networks are the structure of social relations among units, typically individuals, groups, or institutions. Diagramatically, the units are represented by points and the relations among them are represented by lines. Networks are important sources of information, emotional support, and access to desired resources for their members. Each individual's network consists of all of those people with whom he/she has contact. Many of the formal characteristics of networks have been identified and discussed (Barnes, 1972; Boissevain, 1974; Craven & Wellman, 1973; Mitch-

ell, 1969). Among the more important dimensions are the size of a network; the density or interconnectedness among units (see Niemeijer, 1973, for useful computation formulas); the number and type of clusters within a network (e.g., an individual's network may consist of clusters of co-workers, neighbors, relatives, and various friendship groups); and whether the relations are uniplex or multiplex (i.e., involve one or more roles). A mathematical topology useful for the analysis of the structural features of networks is graph theory (Harary, Norman, & Cartwright, 1965). The emphasis of this example, however, is not on the structure of networks but on the influence of networks on behavior and on how this influence can be used in behavioral intervention.

Our purpose is to show that the study of social networks can contribute to the conceptualization of the environmental context of behavior and to the resolution of the limitations of the lack of knowledge of natural settings and the generalization–maintenance problem. To show this, we first briefly review the influence of networks on academic performance, attitudes toward school, choice of field of study, delinquency, employment, and the assistance of network members with personal problems. We also review the effect of the lack of supportive networks, the disruption of networks, and the network differences of those with psychotic behavior problems. This influence is discussed in terms of the network's providing a context for behavior, in which a number of variables have reciprocal, rather than causal, relationships. Second, we discuss network intervention both within existing settings and in their modification, which includes the development of new programs, the creation of alternative structures, and the use of social and physical design to modify the existing structure itself.

Network Influence. Several studies have shown the influence of student networks on academic performance, attitudes toward school, and choice of field of study. As would be expected, members of cliques are similar in academic performance and in attitudes toward school (Bradley, 1977; Damico, 1976). That this relationship is at least partly due to the influence of the cliques, rather than the result of similar people forming friendships, is in-

dicated by the greater correspondence between achievement and intelligence found
among the most popular clique members
(Bradley, 1977), suggesting that the level of
academic performance of clique members is
influenced in the direction of its most popular
members. Similarly, in a study in which high-
ability college students were randomly assigned to residence halls with other high-abil-
ity students, they did better academically and
reported that this was so because of the influence of their fellow residents (De Coster,
1966). Holland (1963) also found that students
who attended a college dominated by those
with similar majors achieved more than did
those who attended college where their fields
of study were in the minority. The latter also
tended to change their majors to those of the
majority. That the change in majors was very
likely influenced by contact with students in
other fields was clearly demonstrated in a
study by Brown (1968). He assigned science
majors to floors in a residence hall dominated
by humanity majors and humanity majors to
floors dominated by science majors. More of
those whose majors were in the minority
changed their majors to those of the majority
or become less certain of their choice.

Other studies have indicated the importance
of social networks in delinquency. Boys who
associate with delinquent friends are more involved in delinquent activities (Voss, 1969).
Indeed, in a longitudinal study, delinquency
was found to result from the friendships made
among lower-achieving students in school
(Elliott & Voss, 1974). In another study,
friendships that youths formed with their delinquent peers in a delinquency prevention
project were thought to be responsible for their
subsequent higher arrest rate (O'Donnell *et
al.*, 1979).

In addition, the network concept has been
useful in understanding how employment is
located and maintained. Granovetter (1973)
has suggested that finding out about job openings is related to the number of different people
with whom one has contact. Therefore, the
greater the variety of people the unemployed
are in contact with, the greater would be their
chances of employment. This suggestion is
supported by the finding that those who have
the most difficulty in becoming employed tend
to associate with people who are also unemployed (Goodman, Salipante, & Paransky,
1973). Furthermore, in a study of 478 of the
hard-core unemployed, social support received from supervisors and peers was the
only factor that influenced job retention. Factors typically thought to have an effect (attitudes toward work, demographic characteristics, and job training) made no difference
(Friedlander & Greenberg, 1971).

One of the most common functions of networks is to provide assistance to people with
personal problems. Typically, such people
seek help from members of their social network (Gourash, 1978). The assistance can be
provided directly or can result in referral to
professionals (Gottlieb, 1976; Hamburg & Killilea, 1979). For health problems, there is some
indication that family members are more likely
to provide direct assistance, while friends
serve as a source of referrals (Salloway &
Dillion, 1973).

One of the most important forms of assistance that network members can provide is social support during a time of stress. Social support has been associated with fewer job-related
reports of psychological problems (Pinneau,
1976); lower cholesterol levels and fewer reports of illness following job loss (Gore, 1978);
a lower rate of depression among women
(Brown & Harris, 1978); better mental-health
reports among older women returning to college (Hirsh, 1980); a lower rate of angina pectoris among men (Medalie & Goldbourt, 1976);
and a faster recovery and a lower death rate
from myocardial infarction (Bruhn, Chandler,
Miller, Wolf, & Lynn, 1966; Finlayson, 1976).
It is important to note that in these studies,
support was provided by various network
members, including family, an intimate other,
friends, neighbors, and supervisors at work.
Different types of support are needed at different times. For example, a close relationship
seemed to be helpful for the women at higher
risk for depression, while less intimate ties
were useful for the women returning to college.

Many, however, do not have supportive networks. For example, in a sample of working-
class adults, 40% reported a lack of everyday
support and 19% did not have anyone to turn
to in an emergency (Wellman, Craven, Whi-

taker, Stevens, Shorter, Du Toit, & Bakker 1973).

Just as support from others has been shown to be helpful, lack of support has been related to negative effects. Those whose demographic characteristics put them in a minority in their communities (by ethnic group, age, marital status, place of birth, and occupation) and who are therefore less likely to receive support have higher rates of psychiatric hospitalization than do those in the majority (Mintz & Schwartz 1964; Wechsler & Pugh, 1967). People who live alone or tend to be socially isolated have higher rates of psychological problems (Eaton, 1978; Ludwig & Collette, 1970; Miller & Ingham, 1976) and illness (Fanning, 1967) and use more drugs to alleviate stress (Webb & Collette, 1975). In one of the most extensive studies of this type, Berkman and Syme (1979) conducted a nine-year mortality study of 6,928 randomly sampled adults from Alameda County, California. The age-adjusted mortality rates for people who had fewer social ties averaged out to be over twice as high for men and almost three times as high for women. This result was independent of health status, socioeconomic class, health-related habits, and year of death. Finally, children living with a more socially isolated parent are subject to higher rates of abuse (Garbarino, 1976; Giovannoni & Billingsley, 1970) and accidents (Brown & Harris, 1978).

Another way to assess the influence of networks is to investigate the effects when networks are disrupted. Bloom, Asher, and White (1978) have reviewed the effects of marital disruption and found it to be associated with higher rates of behavior problems, illness, motor vehicle accidents, alcoholism, suicide, and homicide. Moreover, mortality rates are higher for the elderly when their networks are disrupted through relocation or the death of a significant other (Rowland, 1977). Nor is this effect limited to the elderly. Kraus and Lilienfeld (1959) reported much higher mortality rates for those under the age of 35 who were widowed, especially males. Suicide rates have also been found to increase markedly in the two years following the death of a parent or a spouse (Bunch, 1972). This was especially true for those who received less social support from other relatives or were left living alone.

Finally, studies of social networks have contributed to our understanding of psychotic behavior. The networks of people with psychotic behavior problems are smaller in size, typically composed of 10–12 people instead of the 20–30 of most people (Cohen & Sokolovsky, 1978; Pattison, 1977; Pattison, Llamas, & Hurd, 1979; Westermeyer & Pattison, 1979). Furthermore, most network members are family members, rather than the usual balance of family members, friends, neighbors, work associates, etc. (Cohen & Sokolovsky, 1978; Henderson, Duncan-Jones, McAuley, & Ritchie, 1978; Pattison, 1977; Tolsdorf, 1976; Westermeyer & Pattison, 1979). Thus, these networks are more dense (i.e., more network members also have social contact with each other). Although denser networks provide more social support (Hirsch, 1979; Wellman et al., 1973), they are also instrumental in social control and the enforcement of group norms (Epstein, 1961; Laumann, 1973). Thus, the elderly report a higher morale when they have contact with friends (Arling, 1976; Wood & Robertson, 1978) and confidants (Lowenthal & Haven, 1968; Moriwaki, 1973) than they do when they have contact with family members. College students also have reported denser networks to be less satisfying emotionally, even when they are providing more support (Hirsch, 1979). Therefore, the less satisfying relationships psychotics report with their network members (Henderson et al., 1978; Pattison, 1977; Tolsdorf, 1976; Westermeyer & Pattison, 1979) may be related to the density of their networks.

These network characteristics of smaller size, family domination, and greater density result in restricted social contacts and activities. Another feature is that the networks are asymmetrical (i.e., network members provide social support to the psychotic and get little support in return). Restricted social contact and asymmetrical networks have been associated with higher rehospitalization rates (Cohen & Sokolovsky, 1978; Strauss & Carpenter, 1977).

All of these studies suggest the pervasive influence of networks on behavior. How this influence occurs, however, has received much less attention, most of which has been focused on social support as a buffer against the stresses of life (e.g., Cassel, 1976; Cobb, 1976), sometimes emphasizing the importance of this social support to particular subgroups, such as schizophrenics (Hammer, Makiesky-Barrow, & Gutwirth, 1978; Marsella & Snyder, 1979) or lower-social-class members (Liem & Liem, 1978).

The influence of networks, however, appears to be much more general than the buffer-against-stress hypothesis would suggest. As we have seen, networks may also influence many other aspects of life, including academic choices and performance, employment status, and delinquent activities. The influence may be negative as well as positive. Also network members may be a source of problems and stress at times, rather than always providing support. Moreover, the methodology of many of these studies allows for alternative interpretations (cf. Dean & Lin, 1977; Heller, 1979). For example, some have noted the additional importance of social competence (e.g., Cowen, 1977; Dohrenwend, 1978). In this view, more competent individuals are better able to establish social support relationships as well as, perhaps independently, to cope effectively with the stresses of life.

In our view, social networks provide an important context for behavior. Social support is just one of the resources that networks can provide, and social competence is acquired through interactions with network members. The relationships among these variables is reciprocal: interactions with others increases social competence; social competence helps establish and maintain relationships with others; others can be a source of stress as well as support; networks influence behavior and, therefore, psychological problems, and these problems can affect the size and structure of networks. In these reciprocal relationships, no one variable is causal; therefore, effects may be supported by either correlational or experimental studies. The question of causality is set aside until a general theory of human social behavior is developed and accepted.

Network Intervention. In the meantime, experimental studies can be used to assess the practical consequences of network intervention. As a form of community intervention, this may involve, as noted earlier, the development of new programs within the existing

structure, the creation of alternative structures, or the modification of the existing structure of the setting itself. In all of these forms, social networks provide the conceptual rationale for intervention.

Programs within existing institutions have provided new roles for network members. Most have attempted to use the influence of the network to achieve the desired goals. The use of peers in school programs as tutors, models, behavior managers, and teachers is an example of the effective use of an influential network. In other cases, where peers are influential in developing antisocial behavior, it may be necessary to disrupt the network. The finding of Elliott and Voss (1974), that two of the most important factors in male delinquency were limited academic achievement and association with delinquent classmates, suggests that delinquency prevention programs should attempt to encourage more association between lower- and higher-achieving students. This might be more easily accomplished through nonacademic activities such as athletics, music, mechanics, and drama. Certainly, the present policy of bringing academically marginal students together in one program should be reevaluated, as participation in these programs may be leading to a peer network more likely to support antisocial activities.

Most of the *alternative structures* developed to date have focused on providing support to higher-risk groups. The unemployed are one such group. Unemployment has been associated with stressful life events and related emotional problems (Catalano & Dooley, 1977; Dooley & Catalano, 1979); alcoholism (Brenner, 1975); heart disease (Brenner, 1971); infant mortality (Brenner, 1973a); and mental hospital admission (Brenner, 1973b). To provide a supportive network for this group, Azrin *et al.* (1975) formed a job-finding club. A network of social contacts was established to provide assistance with job leads, résumés, interview skills, transportation, vocational choices, time planning, and support from family and club members. In comparison to a randomly assigned control group, club members found more jobs, in less time, and at higher salaries. Similar networks have been organized for alcoholics (Hunt & Azrin, 1973), with successful results reported through a two-year follow-up period (Azrin, 1976). Programs are also being developed for others with higher risks, such as new widows (Walker, Mac-Bride, & Vachon, 1977).

Alternative support structures also have often achieved lower rehospitalization rates for psychiatric patients. This has been true for home-visit programs (Davis, Dinitz, & Pasamanick, 1974), as well as for those providing more extensive living, working, and social arrangements (Fairweather et al., 1969). What has been discouraging, however, is that the rehospitalization rates typically increase markedly when the programs are terminated. Network studies have added to our understanding of why this may occur. First, patients have a greater need for support on leaving a hospital because they are likely to experience more undesirable events than comparable individuals who have remained in the community (Schwartz & Myers, 1977). Second, as noted above, they have less extensive support networks, and these are dominated by family members. These studies suggest that the need is for aftercare programs that can provide supplementary support services on a continual rather than a transitional basis. Such services would also help to reduce the demands on the family that the care of psychiatric patients entails.

Indeed, even families without psychiatric patients frequently need assistance with everyday marital and child-care problems. But often those with the greatest need are less likely to seek traditional professional help (e.g., depressed women with children, as in Brown & Harris, 1978) and more likely to drop out of treatment (see O'Donnell, 1977, pp. 83–84). Therefore, it is encouraging to note the beginnings of a more comprehensive family support system, such as the one mentioned earlier, which included infant day care, toddler and preschool care, recreational programs for older children, and a center that gives advice to families on specific problems (Risley et al., 1976). It would be useful to assess these systems for impact on the problems associated with the disruption of families.

The remaining form of intervention, *the modification of the existing structure of settings*, is more difficult to achieve, but it has considerable potential for the prevention of psychological problems. One of the difficulties has been to determine the appropriate variables for modification. Some have been suggested in a recent review (O'Donnell, 1980), which concluded that the design of a setting affects the frequency and type of social contact among people, thereby influencing the development of social networks and related behavior.

One of the most important of the variables suggested is the manning level of a setting (Barker, 1960, 1968). *Manning level* refers to the ratio of the number of people to the number of roles. Settings with relatively few people for the number of roles are considered undermanned. In these, the demands to participate placed on people are greater, and the standards for participation are lower. Since people are needed, those with marginal abilities are more likely to be accepted. In overmanned settings, the reverse is true. Standards for participation are higher, withdrawal is encouraged, and those with marginal abilities are less likely to be accepted.

These effects were noted in a large number of the studies and settings reviewed. When there are fewer people, those present participate in activities and interact with each other more. This reaction has been found in high schools, churches, mental hospitals, emergency helping situations, industry, and college dormitories and during children's play. People also report a greater sense of obligation and responsibility to others in settings with fewer people. *In this way, undermanned settings facilitate the development of social networks.*

It is important to note that manning levels typically affect people whose abilities are considered marginal for the setting. These people, of course, are usually at higher risk for behavior problems and are often the objects of intervention efforts. They, in particular, would benefit from interventions that lower manning levels and thereby lead to their increased participation, interaction with others, and development of networks. These interventions involve altering the setting to permit the existing competency of these people to receive support and the means for continued development.

One way to lower manning levels is by decentralization. For example, large housing projects could be designed into units with separate facilities (e.g., recreation, parking, and laundry areas) for a small number of households. The smaller number of people using these facilities might increase social contact and the development of neighborhood networks. Also, since social support from supervisors and peers is the major factor in job retention among the hard-core unemployed, tax incentives for decentralization could be offered to industries that employ them.

In instances where the relevant population declines, institutions naturally become more decentralized, unless their facilities are consolidated. With the lowered birthrate of the 1970s, we are likely to witness an effect opposite that of the famed post–World War II baby boom. There should be relatively fewer people entering our schools and, eventually, employment and housing markets, thus lowering manning levels.

In other cases, manning levels could be lowered by increasing the number of activities and roles for people in the setting. Schools, for example, might increase student participation in athletics, plays, clubs, etc., by sponsoring events for students of all ability levels, rather than only for those able to compete for the typically limited number of openings. Likewise, parents might increase their children's participation in family activities and their sense of family responsibility by making sure there are roles for them, as in the care of pets or a garden and in household tasks.

Variables related to the physical design and activities of a setting were also found to influence the development of social networks (O'Donnell, 1980). For example, the studies reviewed showed that the availability of toys influenced social interactions among young children. Puzzles and games did the same among residents in nursing homes, and seat location among most students. One of the most important variables for social interaction in larger settings was proximity, which was influenced by the physical design of a setting. Thus, greater interaction occurred among people within enclosed space, friendships varied inversely with the functional distance between people in housing units, and social contact occurred less frequently among people living in multiple-family housing.

These studies suggest that the development of social networks could be facilitated by providing activities to attract people and designing the setting to promote social interaction. Specific suggestions for accomplishing this in the public areas of housing projects and neighborhoods have been offered by several investigators (Brower & Williamson, 1974; Freedman, 1975, Chapter 10; Holahan, 1976; Sanoff & Coates, 1971).

The activities and design of a setting can also affect the development of crime-related networks. Since crime rates are higher in low-surveillance areas (Ley & Cybriwsky, 1974; Newman, 1973), settings that support the development of neighborhood networks help to control crime by providing surveillance in the course of everyday activities. Alternatively, certain settings may attract people who are more likely to commit crimes. O'Donnell and Lydgate (1980) developed a land-use classification code and counted the number and type of businesses, services, and residences in Honolulu. They found several crime patterns that varied with the classification categories. For example, areas with a high concentration of businesses that offered retail goods, food and alcohol for consumption on the premises, entertainment, and sex-related goods and services had the highest rate of violent crimes. Moreover, the rate was lower in areas with a high concentration of only some of these types of businesses. Therefore, it appeared that this adult entertainment setting was attracting people and promoting activities that increased the likelihood of violence. It was suggested that the crime rate might be reduced by zoning ordinances that disrupt this pattern by dispersing the high concentration of these businesses (e.g., by segregating sex-related businesses in other locations, such as a light manufacturing district).

In general, settings can facilitate the development of social networks by promoting social contact and providing activities that foster feelings of obligation and responsibility among people. The activities and physical design of a setting can attract people and increase social contact. Feelings of obligation and responsibility are fostered among people engaged in common tasks in relatively undermanned environments. Thus, in institutional settings, such as schools and places of work, the physical design, the number of people, the number of roles available, and the type and quantity of activities affect the development of social networks. The same variables operate in neighborhood settings: physical design influences social contact, and the number and type of businesses, services, and residences strongly affect the number and type of people in the neighborhood, the times they are there, the activities they are likely to engage in, and the roles available for people. These variables determine the manning levels within the neighborhood settings. Just as administrators might use these variables to affect behavior through social networks, zoning and land-use regulations can be used to affect neighborhood behavior patterns.

Earlier, we contended that the resolution of the related limitations, lack of knowledge about natural settings and the generalization–maintenance problem, will require the ideas and methods of other disciplines. The study of social networks is offered as an example that could contribute to this process. Social networks are not only an important influence on behavior in natural settings, their development is also partly a function of how we structure the physical and social design of settings. Therefore, social networks offer an opportunity for the systematic study and conceptualization of the natural environment.

The results of such study would provide information useful in avoiding the problems of the generalization and maintenance of treatment effects. It is suggested that since behavior is largely acquired and maintained through everyday social interactions, intervention that affects this natural system would not require generalization. Moreover, rather than simply being maintained, behavior would continue to develop as a function of the social system of which it is a part. For example, while efforts to generalize and maintain effects are important in most programs used to modify inappropriate behavior in school, they would not be relevant to an intervention that lowered manning levels in school settings. If effective, such an intervention would increase the social commitment and the participation of marginal students and, indirectly, would lower their rate of inappropriate behavior. These changes

should also affect the networks of these students and, therefore, influence the continued development of their behavior. Finally, generalization–maintenance problems can be avoided by interventions, such as those suggested, that *prevent* behavior problems. This is both a goal of the community approach and a promise of the study of social networks.

Summary

As one possible extension of behavioral-community intervention activities, we have suggested that behaviorists open themselves more freely to the methods and concepts of their sister disciplines in the social sciences. As examples, we have offered methods and concepts developed by anthropology, sociology, linguistics, and sociolinguistics. Of course we do not suggest that behaviorists *become* anthropologists, sociologists, or linguists, in the sense of abandoning those attitudes and methods by which behaviorism has distinguished itself. As a benign critic of the KEEP operation has observed, ethnography and linguistic analysis have been around for decades, but one has not known what to *do* with their findings (I. M. Evans, personal communication, 1979). This is clearly so, but the behavior-analytic framework of repertoires, setting events, environmental control, and situational specificity can be linked with the conceptual and methodological contributions of other disciplines to provide the basis by which various social-scientific observations can be brought to the task of changing settings.

A conception of the use of such material might be as follows. The target population of a community intervention should be assessed as thoroughly as possible, particularly with regard to the presence, in an alternate environment, of those behaviors of concern in the target setting. In many instances, methods of assessment not now routine for behaviorism are the methods of choice. In those instances, when the repertorial elements are indeed discovered, the further task becomes to identify the cue functions by which the environment elicits those desirable behaviors. One intervention strategy will be thereby revealed: the modification of the target setting so that those cues will be present and so that the desired repertoire will be allowed to occur.

The effectiveness of this strategy is most clearly illustrated by the KEEP example. It is important to note, however, that the strategy is a general one, and that the relevant cues need not be cultural. In Hawaiian culture, the social network strongly supports cooperative activities. By its emphasis on individual performance, the school structure prevented the occurrence of initiative and responsibility in social behaviors and of demonstrations of linguistic and cognitive capacity. When these behaviors were found in the course of cooperative activities in the home, the school setting was altered to allow the network to function in a similar manner at school. This approach could be implemented in many other settings as well: assess the setting where the desired behaviors are found, determine their role in the functioning of the network, and then use this information to decide on the changes needed in the setting in which the behaviors are desired. In KEEP, the structure of the activities was altered so that the children's behavior could assume the cooperative role in the school network that it did in the home network.

In other settings, a somewhat different problem may occur. Perhaps the existing network does not support the desired behaviors of some of its members. In this case, the strategy of choice might be to lower the manning levels of the specific activities in which it is desired that the behaviors occur, *to permit* the development of a network to support them.

In all cases in which the desired behavior is not occurring in the setting, we should assess the setting to see if the problem might be located there. If the behavior has been acquired, we need to change the setting to allow it. If the network is not supporting the behavior, we need to alter the physical or social design (e.g., manning levels) of the setting to permit a supporting network to develop. We suggest that these strategies be considered before considering a program of creation *ex nihilo* by shaping and differential reinforcement, although the latter may in many instances be necessary.

It is perhaps necessary to discuss further the assertion that methods of assessment not now

typical of behaviorism may be the methods of choice for many complex assessment tasks. In the first place, we do not suggest that such methods are appropriate for all stages of the scientific or intervention process. The argument has been presented elsewhere (Tharp & Gallimore, 1979) that informal observation—of which ethnography is the most refined example—is highly appropriate to the stage of hypothesis generation and in the task of forming the best concepts or categories. We also resist the movement toward the use of ethnography as a tool for evaluation outcome, arguing that informal observation can never replace the fixed-effect experiment as an outcome measure (Tharp & Gallimore, 1979). What we do here suggest is that the methods of sister disciplines offer a rich resource both for *assessment*, prior to and during interventions, and for the *conceptualization* of the environmental context of behavior.

The behavioristic tools of reliable, objective, nonreactive measurement come into play only after the formation of the categories of behavior to be observed. Certainly, during the formative stages of the establishment of reliabilities, category definitions are reaffected, and the process is interactive, but the original notions of categories must come from elsewhere. This "elsewhere" would best be the experience of those sciences whose domain is at issue. For example, for linguistic phenomena, it would be absurd and wasteful not to avail ourselves of the concepts and categories that a century of research has developed, and, further, to avail ourselves of those methods of observation that have been tailored to the concepts. Ethnography, linguistics, and network analysis have been involved here, but other methods and categories, such as architecture, sociology, criminology, literary criticism, and economics, are also ready for the using. If we behaviorists insist on reinventing each disciplines wheel, it will turn out not to be round.

This call for a broadening of the base of behaviorism in no way implies an abandonment of that stance peculiarly and proudly ours. Behavioristic methods have provided detailed knowledge of how behaviors may be acquired and altered. What is needed is a conceptual basis for this knowledge. An important contribution in developing this basis, we have argued, can come from the methods and concepts of sister disciplines. They have a history of studying and conceptualizing natural settings. Just as their methods might be linked to behavioral assessment, so, too, their concepts of the environmental context for behavior may be linked with the knowledge provided by behavioral methods. These links may well help us to understand the development of behavioral problems, to acquire new strategies of intervention and prevention, and to discover the means by which behaviors are maintained in natural settings. As we have suggested that target populations may well have desired repertoires already in their possession, so, too, may sister disciplines. Therefore, we make our suggestion to ourselves as well: find the repertoire, and allow it.

References

Alexander, J. F., & Parsons, B. V. Short-term behavioral intervention with delinquent families: Impact on family process and recidivism. *Journal of Abnormal Psychology*, 1973, *81*, 219–225.

Aragona, J., Cassady, J., & Drabman, R. S. Treating overweight children through parental training and contingency contracting. *Journal of Applied Behavior Analysis*, 1975, *8*, 269–278.

Arling, G. The elderly widow and her family, neighbors and friends. *Journal of Marriage and the Family*, 1976, *38*, 757–768.

Au, K. H., & Jordan, C. Teaching reading to Hawaiian children: Finding a culturally appropriate solution. In C. Jordan, T. Weisner, R. G. Tharp, R. Gallimore, & K. H. Au (Eds.), *A multidisciplinary approach to research in education: The Kamehameha Early Education Program* (Tech. Rep. No. 81). Honolulu, Hawaii: The Kamehameha Schools. The Kamehameha Early Education Program, 1978.

Ayllon, T., & Roberts, M. Eliminating discipline problems by strengthening academic performance. *Journal of Applied Behavior Analysis*, 1974, *7*, 71–76.

Azrin, N. H. Improvements in the community-reinforcement approach to alcoholism. *Behaviour Research and Therapy*, 1976, *14*, 339–348.

Azrin, N. H., Flores, T., & Kaplan, S. J. Job-finding club: A group-assisted program for obtaining employment. *Behaviour Research and Therapy*, 1975, *13*, 17–27.

Barker, R. G. Ecology and motivation. In M. R. Jones (Ed.), *Nebraska symposium on motivation*. Lincoln: University of Nebraska Press, 1960.

Barker, R. G. *Ecological psychology*. Stanford, Calif.: Stanford University Press, 1968.

Barnard, J. D., Christophersen, E. R., & Wolf, M. M. *Journal of Applied Behavior Analysis*, 1977, *10*, 49–59.

Barnes, J. A. Social networks. *Addison-Wesley Modular Publications*, Module 26, 1972, 1–29.

Beard, J. H., Malamud, T. J., & Rossman, E. Psychiatric rehabilitation and long-term rehospitalization rates: The findings of two research studies. *Schizophrenia Bulletin*, 1978, *4*, 622–635.

Bem, D. J., & Funder, D. C. Predicting more of the people more of the time: Assessing the personality of situations. *Psychological Review*, 1978, *85*, 485–501.

Berkman, L. F., & Syme, S. L. Social networks, host resistance, and mortality: A nine-year follow-up study of Alameda County residents. *American Journal of Epidemiology*, 1979, *109*, 186–204.

Bloom, B. L., Asher, S. J., & White, S. W. Marital disruption as a stressor: A review and analysis. *Psychological Bulletin*, 1978, *85*, 867–894.

Boggs, S. T. The meaning of questions and narratives to Hawaiian children. In C. B. Cazden, V. P. John, & D. Hymes (Eds.), *Functions of language in the classroom*. New York: Teachers College Press, 1972.

Boissevain, J. *Friends of friends: Networks, manipulators and coalitions*. New York: St. Martin's Press, 1974.

Bowers, K. S. Situationism in psychology: An analysis and a critique. *Psychological Review*, 1973, *80*, 307–336.

Bradley, J. Clique membership and academic achievement. *Research in Education*, 1977, *18*, 1–8.

Brenner, M. H. Economic changes and heart disease mortality. *American Journal of Public Health*, 1971, *61*, 606–611.

Brenner, M. H. Fetal, infant, and maternal mortality during periods of economic instability. *International Journal of Health Services*, 1973, *3*, 145–159. (a)

Brenner, M. H. *Mental illness and the economy*. Cambridge: Harvard University Press, 1973. (b)

Brenner, M. H. Trends in alcohol consumption and associated illness: Some effects of economic changes. *American Journal of Public Health*, 1975, *65*, 1279–1292.

Brightwell, D. R., & Sloan, C. L. Long-term results of behavior therapy for obesity. *Behavior Therapy*, 1977, *8*, 898–905.

Brower, S. N., & Williamson, P. Outdoors recreation as a function of the urban housing environment. *Environment and Behavior*, 1974, *6*, 295–345.

Brown, G. W., & Harris, T. *Social origins of depression: A study of psychiatric disorder in women*. New York: Free Press, 1978.

Brown, R. Manipulation of the environmental press in a college residence hall. *Personnel and Guidance Journal*, 1968, *46*, 555–560.

Bruhn, J. G., Chandler, B., Miller, M. C., Wolf, S., & Lynn, T. N. Social aspects of coronary heart disease in two adjacent, ethnically different communities. *American Journal of Public Health*, 1966, *56*, 1493–1506.

Bunch, J. Recent bereavement in relation to suicide. *Journal of Psychosomatic Research*, 1972, *16*, 361–366.

Cassel, J. The contribution of the social environment to host resistance. *American Journal of Epidemiology*, 1976, *106*, 107–123.

Catalano, R., & Dooley, C. D. Economic predictors of depressed mood and stressful life events in a metropolitan community. *Journal of Health and Social Behavior*, 1977, *18*, 292–307.

Clark, R. N., Burgess, R. L., & Hendee, J. C. The development of anti-litter behavior in a forest campground. *Journal of Behavior Analysis*, 1972, *5*, 1–5.

Cloward, R. D. Studies in tutoring. *Journal of Experimental Education*, 1967, *36*, 14–25.

Cobb, S. Social support as a moderator of life stress. *Psychosomatic Medicine*, 1976, *38*, 300–315.

Cohen, C. I., & Sokolovsky, J. Schizophrenia and social networks: Ex-patients in the inner city. *Schizophrenia Bulletin*, 1978, *4*, 546–560.

Colletti, G., & Harris, S. L. Behavior modification in the home: Siblings as behavior modifiers, parents as observers. *Journal of Abnormal Child Psychology*, 1977, *5*, 21–30.

Cone, J. D. The relevance of reliability and validity for behavioral assessment. *Behavior Therapy*, 1977, *8*, 411–426.

Conway, J. B., & Bucher, B. D. Transfer and maintenance of behavior change in children: A review and suggestions. In E. J. Mash, L. A. Hamerlynck, & L. C. Handy (Eds.), *Behavior modification and families*. New York: Brunner/Mazel, 1976.

Cowen, E. L. Baby-steps toward primary prevention. *American Journal of Community Psychology*, 1977, *5*, 1–22.

Craven, P., & Wellman, B. The network city. *Sociological Inquiry*, 1973, *43*, 57–88.

Cronbach, L. J., Gleser, G. C., Nanda, H., & Rajaratnam, N. *The dependability of behavioral measurements: Theory of generalizability for scores and profiles*. New York: Wiley, 1972.

Damico, S. B. Clique membership and its relationship to academic achievement and attitude toward school. *Journal of Research and Development in Education*, 1976, *9*, 29–35.

Davidson, W. S., II, & Seidman, E. Studies of behavior modification and juvenile delinquency: A review, methodological critique, and social perspective. *Psychological Bulletin*, 1974, *81*, 998–1011.

Davis, A. E., Dinitz, S., & Pasamanick, B. *Schizophrenics in the new custodial community: Five years after the experiment*. Columbus: Ohio State University Press, 1974.

Day, R. *The acquisition of plurality and tense by pidgin-speaking children* (Tech. Rep. No. 30). Honolulu, Hawaii: The Kamehameha Schools. The Kamehameha Early Education Program, 1975. (a)

Day R. *The teaching of English to Hawaiian Creole-speaking children* (Tech. Rep. No. 29). Honolulu, Hawaii: The Kamehameha Schools. The Kamehameha Early Education Program, 1975. (b)

Dean, A., & Lin, N. The stress-buffering role of social support. *Journal of Nervous and Mental Disease*, 1977, *165*, 403–417.

De Coster, D. Housing assignments for high ability students. *Journal of College Student Personnel*, 1966, *7*, 10–22.

Dineen, J. P., Clark, H. B., & Risley, T. R. Peer tutoring in elementary students: Educational benefits to the tutor. *Journal of Applied Behavior Analysis*, 1977, *10*, 231–238.

Dohrenwend, B. S. Social stress and community psychology. *American Journal of Community Psychology*, 1978, *6*, 1–14.

Dooley, D., & Catalano, R. Economic, life, and disorder changes: Time-series analyses. *American Journal of Community Psychology*, 1979, *7*, 381–396.

Drabman, R. S. Behavior modification in the classroom. In W. E. Craighead, A. E. Kazdin, & M. J. Mahoney (Eds.), *Behavior modification: Principles, issues, and applications*. Boston: Houghton Mifflin, 1976.

Eaton, W. W. Life events, social supports, and psychiatric symptoms: A re-analysis of the New Haven data. *Journal of Health and Social Behavior*, 1978, *19*, 230–234.

Elliott, D. S., & Voss, H. L. *Delinquency and dropout*. Lexington, Mass.: D. C. Heath, 1974.

Endler, N. S., & Magnusson, D. *Interactional psychology and personality*. Washington, D.C.: Hemisphere, 1976.

Epstein, A. L. The network and urban social organization. *Rhodes-Livingstone Institute Journal*, 1961, *29*, 29–61.

Erickson, R. C. Outcome studies in mental hospitals: A review. *Psychological Bulletin*, 1975, *82*, 519–540.

Fairweather, G. W., Sanders, D. H., Cressler, D. L., & Maynard, H. *Community life for the mentally ill: An alternative to institutional care*. Chicago: Aldine, 1969.

Fanning, D. M. Families in flats. *British Medical Journal*, 1967, *4*, 382–386.

Fawcett, S. B. Behavioral technology and smallpox eradication. *Journal of Applied Behavior Analysis*, 1977, *10*, 558.

Feldman, M. P. *Criminal behavior: A psychological analysis*. New York: Wiley, 1977.

Filipczak, J., Friedman, R. M., & Reese, S. C. PREP: Educational programming to prevent juvenile problems. In J. S. Stumphauzer (Ed.), *Progress in behavior therapy with delinquents*. Springfield, Ill.: Charles C Thomas, 1979.

Finlayson, A. Social networks as coping resources. *Social Science and Medicine*, 1976, *10*, 97–103.

Fo, W. S. O., & O'Donnell, C. R. The buddy system: Relationship and contingency conditions in a community intervention program for youth with nonprofessionals as behavior change agents. *Journal of Consulting and Clinical Psychology*, 1974, *42*, 163–169.

Foxx, R. M., & Hake, D. F. Gasoline conservation: A procedure for measuring and reducing the driving of college students. *Journal of Applied Behavior Analysis*, 1977, *10*, 61–74.

Franks, C. M., & Wilson, G. T. *Annual review of behavior therapy theory and practice*, Vol. 6. New York: Brunner/Mazel, 1978.

Freedman, J. L. *Crowding and behavior*. New York: Viking Press, 1975.

Friedlander, F., & Greenberg, S. Effect of job attitudes, training, and organization climate on performance of the hard-core unemployed. *Journal of Applied Psychology*, 1971, *55*, 287–295.

Gallimore, R. The role of dialect and general verbal/cognitive abilities in school performance of Hawaiian Creole speakers. In C. Jordan, R. G. Tharp, K. H. Au, T. S. Weisner, & R. Gallimore (Eds.), *A multidisciplinary approach to research in education: The Kamehameha Early Education Program* (Tech. Rep. No. 81). Honolulu, Hawaii: The Kamehameha Schools. The Kamehameha Early Education Program, 1978.

Gallimore, R., Boggs, J. W., & Jordan, C. *Culture, behavior, and education: A study of Hawaiian-Americans*. Beverly Hills, Calif.: Sage Publications, 1974.

Gallimore R., Tharp, R. G., Sloat, K. C. M., & Klein, T. *The Kamehameha Early Education Program: Results 1972–1979* (Tech. Rep. No. 95). Honolulu, Hawaii: The

Kamehameha Schools. The Kamehameha Early Education Program, 1980.

Garbarino, J. A preliminary study of some ecological correlates of child abuse: The impact of socioeconomic stress on mothers. *Child Development*, 1976, *47*, 178–185.

Gartner, A., Kohler, M., & Reissman, F. *Children teach children: Learning by teaching.* New York: Harper & Row, 1971.

Geller, E. S. Prompting antilitter behaviors. *Proceeding, 81st Annual Convention, American Psychological Association*, 1973, *8*, 901–902. (Summary.)

Geller, E. S., Farris, J. C., & Post, D. S. Prompting a consumer behavior for pollution control. *Journal of Applied Behavior Analysis*, 1973, *6*, 367–376.

Giovannoni, J. M., & Billingsley, A. Child neglect among the poor: A study of parental adequacy in families of three ethnic groups. *Child Welfare*, 1970, *49*, 196–204.

Goodman, P. S., Salipante, P., & Paransky, H. Hiring, training, and retaining the hard-core unemployed: A selected review. *Journal of Applied Psychology*, 1973, *58*, 22–33.

Goodstein, L. D., & Sandler, I. Using psychology to promote human welfare: A conceptual analysis of the role of community psychology. *American Psychologist*, 1978, *33*, 882–892.

Gore, S. The effect of social support in moderating the health consequences of unemployment. *Journal of Health and Social Behavior*, 1978, *19*, 157–165.

Gottlieb, B. H. Lay influences on the utilization and provision of health services: A review. *Canadian Psychological Review*, 1976, *17*, 126–136.

Gourash, N. Help-seeking: A review of the literature. *American Journal of Community Psychology*, 1978, *6*, 413–423.

Granovetter, M. S. The strength of weak ties. *American Journal of Sociology*, 1973, *78*, 1360–1380.

Graziano, A. M. Parents as behavior therapists. In M. Hersen, R. M. Eisler, & P. M. Miller (Eds.), *Progress in behavior modification*, Vol. 4. New York: Academic Press, 1977.

Greenwood, C. R., Sloane, H. N., & Baskin, A. Training elementary aged peer-behavior managers to control small group programmed mathematics. *Journal of Applied Behavior Analysis*, 1974, *7*, 103–114.

Gruber, R. P. Behavior therapy: Problems in generalization. *Behavior therapy*, 1971, *2*, 361–368.

Hamburg, B. A., & Killilea, M. Relation of social support, stress, illness, and use of health services. In The Surgeon General's Report on Health and Disease Prevention Background Papers, *Healthy People*. Washington, D.C.: U.S. Government Printing, 1979.

Hammer, M., Makiesky-Barrow, S., & Gutwirth, L. Social networks and schizophrenia. *Schizophrenia Bulletin*, 1978, *4*, 522–545.

Harary, F., Norman, R. Z., & Cartwright, D. *Structural models: An introduction to the theory of directed graphs*. New York: Wiley, 1965.

Harris, S. L. Teaching language to nonverbal children—with emphasis on problems of generalization. *Psychological Bulletin*, 1975, *82*, 565–580.

Harris, V. W., & Sherman, J. A. Effects of peer tutoring and consequences on the math performance of elementary classroom students. *Journal of Applied Behavior Analysis*, 1973, *6*, 587–598.

Hayes, L. A. The use of group contingencies for behavioral control: A review. *Psychological Bulletin*, 1976, *83*, 628–648.

Hayes, S. C., & Cone, J. D. Reducing residential electrical energy use: Payments, information, and feedback. *Journal of Applied Behavior Analysis*, 1977, *10*, 425–435.

Heller, K. The effects of social support: Prevention and treatment implications. In A. P. Goldstein & F. H. Kanfer (Eds.), *Maximizing treatment gains: Transfer enhancement in psychotherapy*. New York: Academic Press, 1979.

Henderson, S., Duncan-Jones, P., McAuley, H., & Ritchie, K. The patient's primary group. *British Journal of Psychiatry*, 1978, *132*, 74–86.

Hersen, M., & Bellack, A. S. Social skills training for chronic psychiatric patients: Rationale, research findings, and future directions. *Comprehensive Psychiatry*, 1976, *17*, 559–580.

Hersen, M., Eisler, R. M., & Miller, P. M. An experimental analysis of generalization in assertive training. *Behaviour Research and Therapy*, 1974, *12*, 295–310.

Hirsch, B. J. Psychological dimensions of social networks: A multimethod analysis. *American Journal of Community Psychology*, 1979, *7*, 263–277.

Hirsch, B. J. Natural support systems and coping with major life changes. *American Journal of Community Psychology*, 1980, *8*, 159–172.

Holahan, C. J. Environmental effects on outdoor social behavior in a low-income urban neighborhood: A naturalistic investigation. *Journal of Applied Social Psychology*, 1976, *6*, 48–63.

Holland, J. Explorations of a theory of vocational choice and achievement. II. A four-year predictive study. *Psychological Reports*, 1963, *12*, 547–594.

Howard, A. Education in Aina Pumehana. In S. T. Kimball & J. H. Burnett (Eds.), *Learning and culture*. Seattle: American Ethnological Society, 1973.

Hunt, G. M., & Azrin, N. H. A community-reinforcement approach to alcoholism. *Behaviour Research and Therapy*, 1973, *11*, 91–104.

Jensen, G. F. Race, achievement, and delinquency: A further look at delinquency in a birth cohort. *American Journal of Sociology*, 1976, *82*, 379–387.

Johnson, M., & Bailey, J. S. Cross-age tutoring: Fifth graders as arithmetic tutors for kindergarten children. *Journal of Applied Behavior Analysis*, 1974, *7*, 223–232.

Jones, R. J., & Azrin, N. H. An experimental application of a social reinforcement approach to the problem of job-finding. *Journal of Applied Behavior Analysis*, 1973, *6*, 345–353.

Jordan, C., *Maternal teaching, peer teaching and school adaption in an urban Hawaiian population* (Tech. Rep. No. 67). Honolulu, Hawaii: The Kamehameha Schools. The Kamehameha Early Education Program, 1977.

Jordan, C., *Peer relationships among Hawaiian children and their educational implications*. Paper read at the meeting of The American Anthropological Association, Los Angeles, December 1978.

Jordan, C., & Tharp, R. G. Culture and education. In A. Marsella, R. G. Tharp, & T. Ciborowski (Eds.), *Perspectives in cross-cultural psychology*. New York: Academic Press, 1979.

Kazdin, A. E. Recent advances in token economy research. In M. Hersen, R. M. Eisler, & P. M. Miller

(Eds.), *Progress in behavior modification*, Vol. 1. New York: Academic Press, 1975.

Kazdin, A. E., & Wilson, G. T. *Evaluation of behavior therapy: Issues, evidence, and research strategies.* Cambridge, Mass.: Ballinger, 1978.

Keeley, S. M., Shemberg, K. M., & Carbonell, J. Operant clinical intervention: Behavior management or beyond? Where are the data? *Behavior Therapy*, 1976, *7*, 292–305.

Keller, M. F., & Carlson, P. M. The use of symbolic modeling to promote social skills in preschool children with low levels of social responsiveness. *Child Development*, 1974, *45*, 912–919.

Kohlenberg, R., Phillips, T., & Proctor, W. *Journal of Applied Behavior Analysis*, 1976, *9*, 13–18.

Kraus, A. S., & Lilienfeld, A. M. Some epidemiologic aspects of the high mortality rate in the young widowed group. *Journal of Chronic Disease*, 1959, *10*, 207–217.

Laumann, E. O. *Bonds of pluralism: The form and substance of urban society.* New York: Wiley, 1973.

Lavigueur, H. The use of siblings as an adjunct to the behavioral treatment of children in the home with parents as therapists. *Behavior Therapy*, 1976, *7*, 602–613.

Levine, M., & Levine, A. *A social history of helping services: Clinic, court, school and community.* New York: Appleton, 1970.

Ley, D., & Cybriwsky, R. The spatial ecology of stripped cars. *Environment and Behavior*, 1974, *6*, 53–68.

Liberman, R. P., King, L. W., & De Risi, W. J. Behavior analysis and therapy in community mental health. In H. Leitenberg (Ed.), *Handbook of behavior modification and behavior therapy.* Englewood Cliffs, N.J.: Prentice-Hall, 1976.

Lick, J. R., & Unger, T. E. The external validity of behavioral fear assessment: The problem of generalizing from the laboratory to the natural environment. *Behavior Modification*, 1977, *1*, 283–306.

Liem, R., & Liem, J. Social class and mental illness reconsidered: The role of economic stress and social support. *Journal of Health and Social Behavior*, 1978, *19*, 139–156.

Lovaas, O. I., Koegel, R., Simmons, J. Q., & Long, J. S. Some generalizations and follow-up measures on autistic children in behavior therapy. *Journal of Applied Behavior Analysis*, 1973, *6*, 131–166.

Lowenthal, M. F., & Haven, C. Interaction and adaptation: Intimacy as a critical variable. *American Sociological Review*, 1968, *33*, 20–30.

Ludwig, E. G., & Collette, J. Dependency, social isolation and mental health in a disabled population. *Social Psychiatry*, 1970, *5*, 92–95.

Marholin II, D., & Gray, D. Effects of group response-cost procedures on cash shortages in a small business. *Journal of Applied Behavior Analysis*, 1976, *9*, 25–30.

Marholin II, D., Siegel, L. J., & Phillips, D. Treatment and transfer: A search for empirical procedures. In M. Hersen, R. M. Eisler, & P. M. Miller (Eds.), *Progress in behavior modification*, Vol. 3. New York: Academic Press, 1976.

Marsella, A. J., & Snyder, K. L. *Stress, social supports, and schizophrenic disorders: Toward an interactional model.* Paper presented at the Conference on Stress, Social Supports and Schizophrenia, Burlington, Vt., September 1979.

McSweeny, A. J. Effects of response cost on the behavior of a million persons: Charging for directory assistance in Cincinnati. *Journal of Applied Behavior Analysis*, 1978, *11*, 47–51.

Medalie, J. A., & Goldbourt, U. Angina pectoris among 10,000 men. II. Psychosocial and other risk factors as evidenced by a multivariate analysis of a five year incidence study. *American Journal of Medicine*, 1976, *60*, 910–921.

Melahn, C. L., & O'Donnell, C. R. Norm-based behavioral consulting. *Behavior Modification*, 1978, *2*, 309–338.

Meyers, A. W., Artz, L. M., & Craighead, W. E. The effects of instructions, incentive, and feedback on a community problem: Dormitory noise. *Journal of Applied Behavior Analysis*, 1976, *9*, 445–457.

Miller, G. H., & Willer, B. Predictors of return to a psychiatric hospital. *Journal of Consulting and Clinical Psychology*, 1976, *44*, 898–900.

Miller, P. M., & Ingham, J. G. Friends, confidants and symptoms. *Social Psychiatry*, 1976, *11*, 51–58.

Miller, S. J., & Sloane, H. N. The generalization effects of parent training across stimulus settings. *Journal of Applied Behavior Analysis*, 1976, *9*, 355–370.

Mills, C. M., & Walter, T. L. A behavioral employment intervention program for reducing juvenile delinquency. *Behavior Therapy*, 1977, *8*, 270–272.

Mintz, N. L., & Schwartz, D. T. Urban ecology and psychosis: Community factors in the incidence of schizophrenia and manic-depression among Italians in greater Boston. *International Journal of Social Psychiatry*, 1964, *10*, 101–118.

Mischel, W. *Personality and assessment.* New York: Wiley, 1968.

Mitchell, J. C. The concept and use of social networks. In J. C. Mitchell (Ed.), *Social networks in urban situations.* Manchester: Manchester University Press, 1969.

Mitchell, S. K. Interobserver agreement, reliability, and generalizability of data collected in observational studies. *Psychological Bulletin*, 1979, *86*, 376–390.

Moriwaki, S. Y. Self-disclosure, significant others and psychological well-being in old age. *Journal of Health and Social Behavior*, 1973, *14*, 226–232.

Neisworth, J. T., & Moore, F. Operant treatment of asthmatic responding with the parent as therapist. *Behavior Therapy*, 1972, *3*, 95–99.

Newman, O. *Defensible space: Crime prevention through urban design.* New York: Collier, 1973.

Niemeijer, R. Some applications of the notion of density. In J. Boissevain & J. C. Mitchell (Eds.), *Network analysis: Studies in human interaction.* Paris: Mouton, 1973.

Nietzel, M. T., Winett, R. A., MacDonald, M. L., & Davidson, W. S. *Behavioral approaches to community psychology.* New York: Pergamon Press, 1977.

O'Connor, R. D. Modification of social withdrawal through symbolic modeling. *Journal of Applied Behavior Analysis*, 1969, *2*, 15–22.

O'Connor, R. D. Relative efficacy of modeling, shaping, and the combined procedures for modification of social withdrawal. *Journal of Abnormal Psychology*, 1972, *79*, 327–334.

O'Donnell, B. *The effect of Palama Settlement's academic-athletic program on future school performance.* Unpublished master's thesis, University of Hawaii, 1974.

O'Donnell, C. R. Group behavior modification with

chronic inpatients: A case study. *Psychotherapy: Theory, Research and Practice*, 1972, *9*, 120–122.

O'Donnell, C. R. Behavior modification in community settings. In M. Hersen, R. M. Eisler, & P. M. Miller (Eds.), *Progress in behavior modification*, Vol. 4. New York: Academic Press, 1977.

O'Donnell, C. R. Environmental design and the prevention of psychological problems. In P. Feldman & J. Orford (Eds.), *Psychological problems: The social context*. New York: Wiley, 1980.

O'Donnell, C. R., & Fo, W. S. O. The buddy system: Mediator-target locus of control and behavior outcome. *American Journal of Community Psychology*, 1976, *4*, 161–166.

O'Donnell, C. R., & Lydgate, T. The assessment of physical resources and their relationship to crimes. *Environment and Behavior*, 1980, *12*, 207–230.

O'Donnell, C. R., & Stanley, K. Paying students for academic performance: A demonstration project. *Journal of Community Psychology*, 1973, *1*, 215–216.

O'Donnell, C. R., Chambers, E., & Ling, K. Athletics as reinforcement in a community program for academic achievement. *Journal of Community Psychology*, 1973, *1*, 212–214.

O'Donnell, C. R., Lydgate, T., & Fo, W. S. O. The buddy system: Review and follow-up. *Child Behavior Therapy*, 1979, *1*, 161–169.

O'Leary, S. G., & O'Leary, K. D. Behavior modification in the school. In H. Leitenberg (Ed.), *Handbook of behavior modification and behavior therapy*. Englewood Cliffs, N.J.: Prentice-Hall, 1976.

Palmer, M. H., Lloyd, M. E., & Lloyd, K. E. An experimental analysis of electricity conservation procedures. *Journal of Applied Behavior Analysis*, 1977, *10*, 665–671.

Patterson, G. R. Accelerating stimuli for two classes of coercive behaviors. *Journal of Abnormal Child Psychology*, 1977, *5*, 335–350.

Patterson, G. R., & Cobb, J. A. Stimulus control for classes of noxious behaviors. In J. F. Knutson (Ed.), *The control of aggression*. Chicago: Aldine, 1973.

Pattison, E. M. A theoretical-empirical base for social system therapy. In E. F. Foulks, R. M. Wintrob, J. Westermeyer, & A. R. Favazzo (Eds.), *Current perspectives in cultural psychiatry*. New York: Spectrum, 1977.

Pattison, E. M., Llamas, R., & Hurd, G. Social network mediation of anxiety. *Psychiatric Annals*, 1979, *9*, 56–67.

Paul, G. L., & Lentz, R. J. *Psychosocial treatment of chronic mental patients: Milieu versus social-learning programs*. Cambridge: Harvard University Press, 1977.

Pinneau, S. R. Effects of social support on psychological and physiological strains. *Dissertation Abstracts*, 1976, *36*, 5359B–5360B.

Polakow, R. L., & Doctor, R. M. A behavioral modification program for adult drug offenders. *Journal of Research in Crime and Delinquency*, 1974, *11*, 63–69.

Powers, R. B., Osborne, J. G., & Anderson, E. G. Positive reinforcement of litter removal in the natural environment. *Journal of Applied Behavior Analysis*, 1973, *6*, 579–586.

Reiss, M. L., Piotrowski, W. D., & Bailey, J. S. Behavioral community psychology: Encouraging low-income patients to seek dental care for their children. *Journal of Applied Behavioral Analysis*, 1976, *9*, 387–398.

Risley, T. R., & Twardosz, S. The preschool as a setting for behavioral intervention. In H. Leitenberg (Ed.), *Handbook of behavior modification and behavior therapy*. Englewood Cliffs, N.J.: Prentice-Hall, 1976.

Risley, T. R., Clark, H. B., & Cataldo, M. F. Behavioral technology for the normal middle-class family. In E. J. Mash, L. A. Hamerlynck, & L. C. Handy (Eds.), *Behavior modification and families*. New York: Brunner/Mazel, 1976.

Rowland, K. F. Environmental events predicting death for the elderly. *Psychological Bulletin*, 1977, *84*, 349–372.

Salloway, J. C., & Dillon, P. B. A comparison of family networks and friend networks in health care utilization. *Journal of Comparative Family Studies*, 1973, *4*, 131–142.

Sanoff, H., & Coates, G. Behavioral mapping: An ecological analysis of activities in a residential setting. *International Journal of Environmental Studies*, 1971, *2*, 227–235.

Schwartz, C. C., & Meyers, J. K. Life events and schizophrenia. I. Comparison of schizophrenics with a community sample. *Archives of General Psychiatry*, 1977, *34*, 1238–1241.

Schwartz, G. J. College students as contingency managers for adolescents in a program to develop reading skills. *Journal of Applied Behavior Analysis*, 1977, *10*, 645–655.

Seidman, E., Rappaport, J., & Davidson III, W. S. *Adolescents in legal jeopardy: Initial success and replication of an alternative to the criminal justice system*. Paper presented at the meeting of the American Psychological Association, Washington, D.C., September 1976.

Shepherd, G. Social skills training: The generalization problem. *Behavior Therapy*, 1977, *8*, 1008–1009.

Solomon, R. W., & Wahler, R. G. Peer reinforcement control of classroom problem behavior. *Journal of Applied Behavior Analysis*, 1973, *6*, 49–56.

Spiegler, M. D., & Agigian, H. *The community training center: An educational-behavioral-social systems model for rehabilitating psychiatric patients*. New York: Brunner/Mazel, 1977.

Stack, L. C. Ecological factors related to first psychiatric admissions. *Journal of Community Psychology*, 1975, *3*, 215–223.

Stokes, T. F., & Baer, D. M. An implicit technology of generalization. *Journal of Applied Behavior Analysis*, 1977, *10*, 349–367.

Stokes, T. F., & Fawcett, S. B. Evaluating municipal policy: An analysis of a refuse-packaging program. *Journal of Applied Behavior Analysis*, 1977, *10*, 391–398.

Strauss, J. S., & Carpenter, W. T. Prediction of outcome in schizophrenia. III. Five-year outcome and its predictors. *Archives of General Psychiatry*, 1977, *34*, 159–163.

Suratt, P. P., Ulrich, R. E., & Hawkins, R. P. An elementary student as a behavioral engineer. *Journal of Applied Behavior Analysis*, 1969, *2*, 85–92.

Tharp, R. G. *The education of minority children*. Paper presented at the meeting of the Southern California Conference on Behavior Modification, Los Angeles, October 1979.

Tharp, R. G., & Gallimore R. *The uses and limits of social reinforcement and industriousness for learning to read*

(Tech. Rep. No. 60). Honolulu, Hawaii: The Kamehameha Schools. The Kamehameha Early Education Program, 1976.

Tharp, R. G., & Gallimore R. The ecology of program research and development: A model of evaluation succession. In L. Sechrist and associates (Eds.), *Evaluation studies review annual*, Vol. 4. Beverly Hills, Calif.: Sage, 1979.

Tharp, R. G., & Wetzel, B. J. *Behavior modification in the natural environment*. New York: Academic Press, 1969.

Tharp, R. G., Jordan, C., Baird, L., & Loganbeel, L. *Coming home to school*, 16-mm film; 16 min. Honolulu, Hawaii: The Kamehameha Schools. The Kamehameha Early Education Program, 1980.

Thoresen, K. E., Thoresen, C. E., Klein, S. B., Wilbur, C. S., Becker-Haven, J. F., & Haven, W. G. Learning house: Helping troubled children and their parents change themselves. In J. S. Stumphauzer (Ed:), *Progress in behavior therapy with delinquents*. Springfield, Ill.: Charles C Thomas, 1979.

Tolsdorf, C. C. Social networks, support, and coping: An exploratory study. *Family Process*, 1976, *15*, 407–417.

Voss, H. L. Differential association and containment theory: A theoretical convergence. *Social Forces*, 1969, *47*, 381–391.

Walker, K. N., MacBride, A., & Vachon, M. L. S. Social support networks and the crisis of bereavement. *Social Science and Medicine*, 1977, *11*, 35–41.

Watson-Gegeo, K. A., & Boggs, S. T. From verbal play to talk-story: The role of routines in speech events among Hawaiian children. In S. Ervin-Tripp & C. Mitchell-Kernan (Eds.), *Child discourse*. New York: Academic Press, 1977.

Webb, S. D., & Collette, J. Urban ecological and household correlates of stress-alleviative drug use. *American Behavioral Scientist*, 1975, *18*, 750–770.

Wechsler, H., & Pugh, T. F. Fit of individual and community characteristics and rate of psychiatric hospitalization. *American Journal of Sociology*, 1967, *73*, 331–338.

Wellman, B., Craven, P., Whitaker, M., Stevens, H., Shorter, A., Du Toit, S., & Bakker, H. Community ties and support systems: From intimacy to support. In L. S. Bourne, R. D. MacKinnon, & J. N. Simmons (Eds.), *The form of cities in central Canada*. Toronto: University of Toronto Press, 1973.

Westermeyer, J., & Pattison, E. M. *Social networks and psychosis in a peasant society*. Paper presented at the meeting of the American Psychiatric Association, Chicago, 1979.

Winett, R. A., & Nietzel, M. T. Behavioral ecology: Contingency management of consumer energy use. *American Journal of Community Psychology*, 1975, *3*, 123–133.

Winett, R. A., & Roach, A. M. The effects of reinforcing academic behavior on social behavior. *The Psychological Record*, 1973, *23*, 391–396.

Winett, R. A., Battersby, C., & Edwards, S. M. The effects of architectural change, individualized instruction and group contingencies on the behavior and academic production of sixth graders. *Journal of School Psychology*, 1975, *13*, 28–40.

Witmer, J. F., & Geller, E. S. Facilitating paper recycling: Prompting versus reinforcement effects. *Journal of Applied Behavior Analysis*, 1976, *9*, 315–322.

Wolfgang, M. E., Figlio, R. M., & Sellin, T. *Delinquency in a birth cohort*. Chicago: University of Chicago Press, 1972.

Wood, V., & Robertson, J. F. Friendship and kinship interaction: Differential effect on the morale of the elderly. *Journal of Marriage and the Family*, 1978, *40*, 367–375.

Zlutnick, S., Mayville, W. J., & Moffat, S. Modification of seizure disorders: The intervention of behavioral chains. *Journal of Applied Behavior Analysis*, 1975, *8*, 1–12.

CHAPTER 12

Drugs Combined with Behavioral Psychotherapy

Isaac Marks

Introduction

Pharmacological agents have been used in psychiatric disorder since time immemorial. Less old is their combination with psychological treatments, and only recently has there been systematic study of the interaction between psychotropic drugs and psychotherapeutic techniques. The main principles of interaction are still unknown.

The joint use of behavioral treatments and drugs has mainly been in syndromes in which anxiety or depression is prominent. The commonest psychological techniques employed have been of the exposure genre, such as desensitization, flooding, or other exposure in fantasy and *in vivo*. Although most reports in this area are uncontrolled, an increasing number have adopted double-blind procedures, and these form the substance of this chapter.

In reviewing this field, issues to be borne in mind were well summarized by Paykel (1979). The effects of any two treatments given together might be (1) *addition*, where they simply summate arithmetically; (2) *potentiation*,

where they are synergistic beyond mere simple addition; (3) *inhibition*, where together they have a smaller action than separately; or (4) *reciprocation*, where together their action is no greater than separately. Other considerations include the magnitude of the effect, its universality, its generality across symptoms and situations, its acceptability to patient and therapist, the stability of the effect over time, and last but not least, the safety of the treatment.

Abreaction

Abreaction is one of the oldest procedures to deliberately combine drugs and psychotherapy. The drugs concerned include those that are inhaled (chloroform, ether, or nitrous oxide) or given intravenously (barbiturates such as hexobarbitone, pentobarbitone, or amylobarbitone, and nonbarbiturates like methamphetamine or diazepam). There is no evidence that drugs are essential for abreaction (Bond, 1952). Abreaction, or catharsis, can occur spontaneously or be triggered by sudden noises, alcohol, or discussion about combat, or in psychotherapy. It can be in-

Isaac Marks • Institute of Psychiatry, de Crespigny Park, Denmark Hill, London, SE5 8AF England.

duced by hypnosis, psychodrama, films, or simple suggestion. The clinical features and consequences of abreaction appear similar regardless of the way in which the emotion has been induced. As yet, we do not know which events decide whether abreaction is sensitizing, habituating, or simply ineffective.

Intravenous and Inhaled Agents

There is little doubt that several classes of drugs can reduce anxiety or depression, at least temporarily (cf. Lader, 1980). From time to time, it becomes fashionable to administer these classes of drugs intravenously, though there is little evidence that intravenous is any better than oral administration beyond instilling a sense of potency in the doctor. Intravenous drugs carry two disadvantages. They can be dangerous and usually require the presence of a doctor at the patient's side during treatment. Oral drugs do not require a medical presence beyond the act of prescribing and require a minimum of monitoring thereafter. This is an important consideration at a time when therapy is being given increasingly by nonmedical personnel. Convincing controlled data are mandatory to justify the routine use of intravenous agents. Such data are sadly lacking.

King and Little (1959) contrasted intravenous thiopental with placebo injections and with psychotherapy. Although the thiopental group showed more improvement than controls during a follow-up of up to three months, the controls included patients who had not had an injection and the report gave too few details to allow adequate assessment.

Intravenous thiopental was also studied by Husain (1971), who contrasted its effects with that of a saline infusion in patients with agoraphobia or social phobias. Patients had either flooding or desensitization in fantasy assisted either by thiopental or saline intravenously. Thiopental facilitated flooding but made no difference to desensitization in fantasy. The design involved crossover of treatments, which precludes conclusions about persistence of effects during follow-up.

Another intravenous barbiturate, methoh-

exitone, is often recommended as an adjunct to desensitization in fantasy. Four studies have examined this approach with some kind of control, but none have yet included the crucial control for the effect of an injection alone. Yorkston, Sergeant, and Rachman (1968) found discouraging results in severe agoraphobics. In less severe phobics, Mawson (1970) noted that intravenous methohexitone significantly enhanced the value of desensitization compared with that of muscular relaxation without an injection. This was a crossover design, which did not allow assessment of follow-up beyond a few days, nor did it include a saline control for the effect of the injection. In another study of severe agoraphobia, Lipsedge, Hajioff, Huggings, Napier, Pearce, Pike, and Rich (1973) reported that methohexitone desensitization in fantasy reduced phobias more than did desensitization with simple muscular relaxation, but again, there was no saline injection control.

A fourth investigation of methohexitone (Chambless, Foa, Groves, & Goldstein, 1979) treated 27 agoraphobic outpatients in eight sessions of flooding in fantasy either with intravenous methohexitone or without it, while a third group served as a control. By the end of treatment, methohexitone was found to slightly retard the effectiveness of flooding.

Another sedative, propanidid, has been used intravenously during exposure *in vivo* of agoraphobics (Hudson, Tobin, & Gaind, 1972), and the tricylic clomipramine has been used intravenously in obsessives (Capstick, 1971; Rack, 1971). All these studies were uncontrolled.

In brief, the value of intravenous drugs used in combination with psychological treatment has yet to be substantiated from experimental evidence. Furthermore, this combination carries distinct disadvantages compared with the use of oral drugs of the same class.

Inhalations of carbon dioxide have occasionally been tried for the reduction of anxiety in neurotic patients. Slater and Leavy (1966) administered these to 12 anxious inpatients who served as their own controls for three treatments: (1) a carbon dioxide–oxygen mixture; (2) hyperventilation; and (3) full inhalation of air. Ten minutes after treatment, a carbon dioxide mixture resulted in a significantly greater reduction in anxiety on self-ratings, but this change was not significant after 24 hours. Haslam (1971) gave lactate infusions to 16 patients with anxiety states. Of the 10 who developed anxiety with this procedure, 9 were said to be calmed by subsequent carbon dioxide inhalation. Of the 6 who showed no anxiety with lactate infusion, only one improved with carbon dioxide inhalation. Ratings were obtained immediately after the inhalations.

In 15 specific phobics, Orwin, LeBoeuf, Dovey, and James (1975) compared the effect of adding inhalation of a mixture of carbon dioxide and oxygen to a "respiratory relief" procedure that included brief trials of exposure *in vivo*. There were up to eight exposure trials per session, each lasting up to 15 seconds. Exposure trials coincided with the restarting of breathing after prolonged holding the the breath. No superiority was claimed for the CO_2 procedure over "respiratory relief" without it. Both "respiratory relief" procedures were said to be better than brief exposure immediately after treatment. However, the ratings were not blind; there were only 5 patients per condition; there was no control of homework exposure instructions; and during follow-up, exposure-only patients were crossed over into "respiratory relief" conditions, so that no long-term follow-up was possible. This study cannot be regarded as demonstrating the value of respiratory relief with or without the addition of inhalations of CO_2/O_2. Evidence for the persistent value of carbon dioxide inhalation is still negligible, and longer-term studies are desirable.

Orally Administered Drugs

In contrast, evidence for the value of *oral* drugs with psychological treatment is of a firmer kind, and the rest of this chapter reviews controlled studies of oral drugs. Most investigations have concerned phobic-obsessive syndromes, a few have dealt with "neurotic" forms of depression, and two have concerned sexual dysfunction. Table 1 summarizes controlled work with phobias.

Phobic-Obsessive Syndromes

Anxiolytics

Beta Blockers. These have not been found to be of impressively lasting value where tested, and sometimes they are counterproductive. A systematic combination of alprenelol with exposure *in vivo* of agoraphobics was made by Ullrich, Ullrich, Crombach, and Peikert (1972) in a double-blind trial. Patients received 2 hr of exposure *in vivo* daily for 14 days after they signed a contract not to escape from the situation. During exposure, they received either alprenelol or placebo. Two other groups either had exposure *in vivo* without placebo or were put on a waiting list. Exposure with alprenelol produced a superior reduction in autonomic anxiety, which became apparent by the second week. Alprenelol did not enhance decrease in avoidance. This greater reduction in anxiety than in avoidance parallels the findings of Lipsedge et al. (1973) with iproniazid.

In a small study of oxprenolol (Gaind, 1976), 6 specific phobics were treated in a crossover design; 160 mg daily of oxprenolol over 8 days was contrasted with the same dosage of placebo. One hour of exposure *in vivo* was given on Days 7 and 8. At the end of treatment, fear and avoidance actually improved *less* after oxprenolol than after placebo.

The use of propranolol with exposure *in vivo* was studied in 20 chronic agoraphobics who completed treatment and 3-month follow-up (Hafner & Milton, 1977). Patients were treated in groups of 4–6 in half-hour-long sessions 3 times weekly. They took 40 mg of propranolol 15 min before starting each session of exposure. During group exposure, panic and heart-rate were significantly decreased in propranolol patients compared with controls. However, the propranolol patients did not do significantly better at the end of treatment, and at 3-month follow-up, they were actually slightly worse than placebo patients with respect to phobic and other neurotic symptoms.

A study of bupranolol by Butollo, Burkhardt, Himmler, and Muller (1978) found that during drug-assisted exposure *in vivo*, patients with cardiac neurosis experienced less anxiety

Table 1. Controlled Studies of Drugs and Exposure Treatments for Phobias

Drug	Population[a]	Author	Type of exposure[b]	Comments
Sedatives				
Inhalation of CO_2	Anxious IP	Slater & Leavy, 1966	—	Outcome measured immediately posttreatmet
" "	" "	Haslam, 1971	—	" " " "
	Specific phobic OP	Orwin et al., 1975	E	" " " "
Intravenous barbiturates				
Thiopental	Anxious phobics	King & Little, 1959	—	50% of control subjects had no injection; scanty detail
"	" "	Husain, 1971	df & ff	
Methohexitone	Agoraphobic IP	Yorkston et al., 1968	df	No injection control
"	" OP	Lipsedge et al., 1973	hp, df	" " "
"	Mixed phobic "	Mawson, 1970	df	" " "
"	Agoraphobic "	Chambless et al., 1978	ff	" " " methohexitone patients did worse
Benzodiazepines				
Diazepam	Specific phobic OP	Marks et al., 1972	E	Crossover design; outcome measured 2 days posttreatment
"	Agoraphobic IP	Johnston & Gath, 1973	ff & E	Crossover design; outcome measured 1 day posttreatment (n = 4 only)
"	" OP	Hafner & Marks, 1976	E & hp	Group exposure; parallel design
Beta blockers	" "			
Alprenolol	" "	Ullrich et al., 1972	E & hp	Alprenolol helped anxiety, not avoidance
Oxyprenelol	Specific "	Gaind, 1976	E	Oxprenelol patients did worse
Propranolol	Agoraphobic "	Hafner & Milton, 1977	E & hp	Group exposure; propranolol patients did worse at 3-month follow-up
Bupramolol	Agora, social phobics	Butollo et al., 1978	E	Bupramolol did not aid exposure effect
Tolamolol	Specific OP	Bernhardt et al., 1980	E	Alprenolol did not help anxiety
Antidepressants				
Tricyclics				
Imipramine	Agoraphobics	Klein, 1964	hp	
"	School phobic OP	Gittelman-Klein & Klein, 1971	hp	Delay before improvement
"	Agoraphobics	Sheehan et al., 1977	—	Imipramine > placebo; no follow-up
"	Agoraphobics OP	Zitrin et al., 1978, 1979	df	

[a] IP = inpatients; OP = outpatients.
[b] df = desensitization in fantasy; ff = floating in fantasy; hp = homework practice of exposure *in vivo*; E = exposure *in vivo*, therapist aided.

than did agoraphobics and social phobics; in the latter categories, bupranolol even led to more anxiety during exposure in comparison with placebo. However, neither for patients with cardiac neurosis nor for agoraphobics or social phobics did the addition of bupranolol to exposure prove to be superior to exposure *in vivo* alone at the end of treatment.

Tolamolol was involved in an analogue investigation of specific phobics (Bernardt, Singleton, & Silverstone, 1980). Subjects were not patients, having only mild fears of snakes and spiders: those who were too frightened were excluded from the trial. In a double-blind crossover design, subjects were given either 200 mg of tolamolol, 10 mg of diazepam, or placebo 1½ hr before a *10-min* exposure session. There were only three sessions, one week apart. Findings were that tolamolol abolished the stress-induced tachycardia during

exposure but had no effect on the behavioral avoidance test or the subjective anxiety during it. In contrast, diazepam reduced avoidance but not tachycardia. The problems with this study are that it employed volunteers, exposure was very brief, and there was no follow-up or measure in the drug-free state.

Benzodiazepines. Like the beta blockers, these drugs have proved to be little more than palliatives without durable effect on behavior change.

Three controlled studies examined the combination of *diazepam* with exposure *in vivo* in phobics. In four agoraphobic inpatients, Johnston and Gath (1973) contrasted the effect of 20 mg of oral diazepam with placebo and with the presence of a dummy syrup to which the patients attributed drug effects. Treatment was given on three consecutive days of each of four weeks, a total of 12 sessions in an incomplete Latin-square design. Exposure consisted of 45 min of flooding in imagination followed by 60 min *in vivo* practice of hierarchy items. Exposure treatment was more effective when given together with diazepam. Improvement was unaffected by the patient's attribution of effects to a dummy syrup. The outcome was measured the day after each treatment block, and the crossover design did not allow an assessment of follow-up effects.

This result was in accord with that of an similar study done earlier at the Maudsley Hospital on 12 specific phobics. This and a subsequent larger study will be discussed in detail to highlight a few of the problems that beset the researcher in this area. The designs tried to get over the hypothesized presence of drug dissociation and aimed to make exposure treatment more pleasant. In clinical practice, phobics often become able to enter their phobic situation under the influence of sedatives, but as the drug effect wears off, they begin to escape from the situation once more. This might be a form of state-dependent or drug-dissociative behavior. In animal experiments, behavior learned in a sedative-drug state often fails to transfer to the undrugged state (Miller, 1964). It seems probable that this effect might be more pronounced during the phase of peak drug effect and less when the drug effect is

wearing off. In rats, exposure to the phobic situation during slow withdrawal of sedative drugs has been effective in extinguishing conditioned avoidance responses (Sherman, 1967). Whether this result is true for humans was tested in the studies. A "waning" experimental condition involved exposure *in vivo* during the transitional phase from drug to nondrug state while drug effects were presumed to be declining. A "peak" group was exposed while psychotropic effects were presumed to be at their highest. A third group was exposed with placebo.

In the first study of diazepam, a crossover design, Marks, Viswanathan, and Lipsedge (1972) treated 18 outpatients with chronic specific phobias. The patients were allocated at random to individual exposure for 2 hr to the real phobic situation in one or two out of three possible treatment conditions. Exposure began either (1) 4 hr after oral diazepam .1 mg/kg ("waning" group); (2) 1 hr after oral diazepam .5 mg/kg ("peak" group); or (3) 4 hr or 1 hr after oral placebo. Each patient had two treatment sessions in a balanced sequence. Assessment was blind for the patient, the therapist, and an independent rater. The design of the first study is detailed in Figure 1. The average dose was 7.5 mg. The dose of diazepam was sufficiently small so that it did not produce

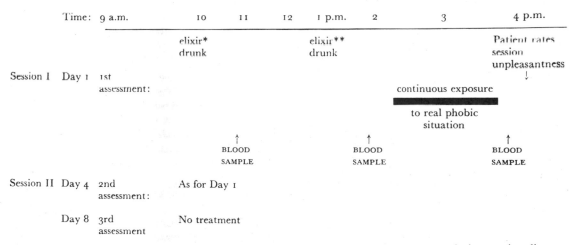

Figure 1. The experimental design of the study: (*) contained diazepam if exposure was during waning diazepam, otherwise contained placebo; (**) contained diazepam if exposure was during peak diazepam, otherwise contained placebo. (From "Enhanced Extinction of Fear by Flooding during Waning Diazepam Effect" by I. M. Marks *et al., British Journal of Psychiatry*, 1972, *121*, 493–505, Fig. 1. Copyright 1972 by the British Journal of Psychiatry. Reprinted by permission.)

obviously visible sleepiness, and the patients were not asked about the effect of their elixir so as to avoid clues being given to the therapist about their treatment condition. The outcome was measured 2–3 days after the end of treatment.

Exposure *in vivo* under all three conditions produced significant improvement. However, the waning group was significantly superior to the placebo group, and the peak group was in between. The trend of superiority was consistent for clinical, attitudinal, and physiological ratings. The trend was already present significantly after the first treatment session, before crossover (Figure 2).

There was no evidence of drug dissociation at the moderate dosage employed, since the peak group, if anything, did slightly better than the placebo group. The absence of drug dissociation was interesting. Perhaps dissociation might have occurred had exposure been for only a few minutes rather than for 2 hr. A third possibility might be that the psychotropic effect, like the serum level, was waning even between 1 and 3 hr after ingestion, so that the so-called peak group was actually a partially waning group, which might account for its slight superiority to the placebo group. No measure of psychotropic effect was made that

was independent of the phobia. Theoretically, one might speculate that the rate of degradation or excretion of diazepam is affected by an individual's activity. Perhaps, during great anxiety, the rate is accelerated, thus obscuring differences in serum level in the two diazepam groups, which might otherwise have been apparent. Conversely, anxiety might equally retard the rate of breakdown of diazepam.

The serum level of diazepam fluctuated so widely among individuals that it was of little value in studying differences between groups. Nevertheless, individual patients had reliably similar serum levels when they took the drug in successive sessions. Serum levels of diazepam bore no obvious relation to the drug's psychotropic effect as measured by subjective anxiety. Present technology does not allow us to measure levels of drugs or active metabolites in those parts of the brain that might reflect psychotropic activity.

The outcome of this study suggested that phobics might be treated better by exposure *in vivo* that begins several hours, not immediately, after oral sedation and continues for several hours while psychotropic effects are declining. A partial replication of this idea was tried by Hafner and Marks (1976), but variations in the experimental design affected the

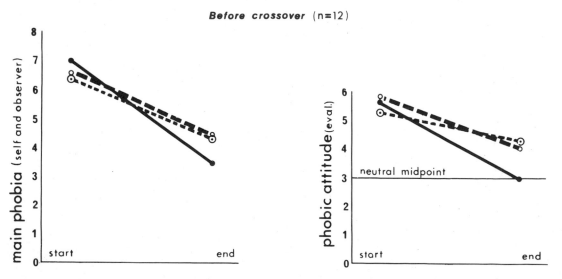

Figure 2. Outcome of the study: (⊙--⊙) exposure during placebo; (●—●) exposure during waning diazepam; (○--○) exposure during peak diazepam. (From "Enhanced Extinction of Fear by Flooding during Waning Diazepam Effect" by I. M. Marks *et al.*, *British Journal of Psychiatry*, 1972, *121*, 493–505, Fig. 3. Copyright 1972 by the British Journal of Psychiatry. Reprinted by permission.)

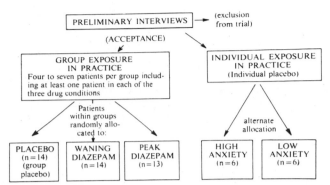

Figure 3. The experimental design of the study. (From "Exposure in Vivo of Agoraphobics: The Contributions of Diazepam, Group Exposure and Anxiety Evocation" by J. Hafner and I. M. Marks, Psychological Medicine, 1976, *6*, 71–88, Fig. 1. Copyright 1976 by the Cambridge University Press. Reprinted by permission.)

conclusions that can be drawn (Figure 3). In four sessions over two weeks, they assigned 42 agoraphobic outpatients randomly to treatment in one of three conditions of exposure *in vivo*. Each session of exposure was $3\frac{1}{2}$ hr long and began $\frac{1}{2}$ hr after .1 mg/kg of oral diazepam in the "peak" condition, $3\frac{1}{2}$ hr after in the "waning" condition, or after similar time intervals following placebo in a third condition. Assessment was blind with respect to drug and psychological treatments. The controlled parallel design allowed comparative evaluation of each treatment to six-month follow-up.

An important difference from the previous study was that exposure *in vivo* was given in groups of six patients at a time, not individually as in the first experiment. Every group of six contained two patients in each of the three drug or placebo conditions. A fourth randomly assigned condition ($n = 12$) consisted of individual exposure *in vivo* with placebo. Another difference from the previous study was that this was a parallel design without

crossover, so that follow-up effects could be studied; each patient was treated in only one exposure condition. A final difference was that the patients here were agoraphobics, not specific phobics.

The patients in all treatment conditions improved significantly in phobias and in related life areas (Figure 4). The results of group exposure to phobias and on other measures were similar in all three drug conditions (placebo, waning diazepam, and peak diazepam), and there were no significant differences between them.

Outcome two days after treatment showed a slight but nonsignificant trend toward superiority in phobia reduction in the waning-diazepam group, and this difference disappeared totally at one-, three-, and six-month follow-ups. Diazepam patients had significantly less discomfort than placebo patients during group-exposure treatment. Diazepam turned out to be a mild palliative during group exposure that did not facilitate results of the treatment. An attempt was made to measure

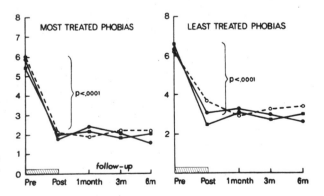

Figure 4. Outcome of group exposure *in vivo*. Combined ratings by patient and assessor: (●—●) waning diazepam; (■—■) peak diazepam; (○--○) placebo. (From "Exposure in Vivo of Agoraphobics: The Contributions of Diazepam, Group Exposure and Anxiety Evocation" by J. Hafner and I. M. Marks, Psychological Medicine, 1976, *6*, 71–88, Fig. 4. Copyright 1976 by the Cambridge University Press. Reprinted by permission.)

the psychotropic effects of diazepam by measuring critical flicker-fusion thresholds. These did not discriminate in any way between drug and placebo conditions. Serum drug levels were not measured.

Group-exposure patients improved slightly but significantly more than individual-exposure patients on nonphobic measures. Group exposure was accompanied by more panics during treatment yet was easier to run by the therapist. This group effect might have washed out any differences due to the drug because the pace of exposure *in vivo* was set by the groups as a whole, and every group contained patients in waning-diazepam, in peak-diazepam, and in placebo conditions. Thus, the pace of exposure in this experiment was not tailored to any one person, unlike the individual exposure in the preceding study by Marks *et al.* (1972). If diazepam works at all, it might be by allowing a more rapid pace of exposure to the phobic situation. Future studies would need to measure this pace of exposure more carefully. The results from this and the previous study might also have differed because diazepam could conceivably affect specific phobics and agoraphobics differently, but this is speculation. Because of the contrast in designs, this investigation cannot be regarded as a total failure of replication of the preceding one. However, it seriously questions whether there is any point in prescribing sedatives to facilitate benefit from exposure treatments.

Antidepressants

Antidepressants appear to have more value for phobic-obsessive syndromes than do anxiolytic sedative drugs, though the effect of antidepressants may be mainly in those patients whose depressed mood complicates their phobias or rituals.

Monoamine Oxidase Inhibitors. Monoamine oxidase inhibitors (MAOIs) are frequently prescribed outside the United States. There have been four controlled studies. At the Maudsley, phenelzine was studied by Tyrer, Candy, and Kelly (1973) in chronic agoraphobics and social phobics. The patients entered a double-blind trial of phenelzine versus placebo in a flexible dosage for two

months. Throughout the trial all patients were advised to expose themselves gradually to phobic situations so that the effect of the tablets could be evaluated. Of the 40 patients who entered the trial, 32 completed it, among whom there were 14 matched pairs. The phenelzine patients improved significantly more on overall assessment, secondary phobias, and work. There was no correlation between dose and response in the phenelzine group. The average dose was 45 mg daily. As in the study by Gittelman-Klein and Klein (1971) with imipramine, the superiority of phenelzine took time to emerge; though it began at the four-week rating, it was significant only by the eight-week rating. Nevertheless, initial depression did not correlate with outcome.

During the one-year follow-up of 26 of these patients (13 phenelzine, 13 placebo), additional treatment was given, especially to placebo patients. Many of the phenelzine patients relapsed on withdrawal of their drug, and at one-year follow-up, there was no significant difference between phenelzine and placebo controls (Tyrer & Steinberg, 1975). In this study, the effect on phobias was measured on the scale described by Gelder and Marks (1966). The degree of improvement at the end of treatment was very similar to that obtained with desensitization in fantasy in a comparable population (Gelder, Mark, & Wolff, 1966). Desensitization in fantasy is a weak form of exposure compared with exposure *in vivo*. Thus, the effect of phenelzine, though initially significant, was not large, and relapse was common on withdrawal. A necessary future study would be a comparison of phenelzine plus exposure *in vivo* rather than in fantasy, with prolonged follow-up after drug withdrawal.

A double-blind study (Solyom *et al.*, 1981) of 40 agoraphobics and social phobics compared the effects of phenelzine with placebo. The dose was 45 mg for 8 weeks, after which it was slowly withdrawn over 6 weeks, with final assessment at 16 weeks, two weeks after the final dose had been given. Patients were instructed to face their phobic situations a set number of times, but there was no therapist-aided exposure. There was no significant effect of phenelzine at the end of treatment. In this study the phobics began with only moderate depressed mood; the initial mean score on the Zung self-rated Depression Scale was only 45(SD9) (Solyom, personal communication), compared with 63 (SD10) for the sample of Sheehan *et al.* (1980, see below), a difference that is highly significant. Sheehan found a significant phenelzine effect, Solyom *et al.* did not.

A comparison of 45 mg phenelzine with 150 mg imipramine and with placebo was carried out by Sheehan, Ballenger, and Jacobson (1977) in 57 anxious agoraphobics who were seen supportively every 2 weeks. Only vague encouragement to carry out exposure homework was given. At the end of 12 weeks, phenelzine and imipramine patients improved significantly more than placebo patients, with a tendency for phenelzine to be superior to imipramine. No drug-free follow-up stage was reported.

The tendency to relapse on stopping monoamine oxidase inhibitors was noted by Lipsedge *et al.* (1973) with iproniazid in severe agoraphobics. Sixty outpatients were assigned at random to one of six groups in a 2 × 3 factorial design. The main comparison relevant here is that of iproniazid with placebo. During treatment, all patients were encouraged to carry out a daily home program of graded exposure and to keep a daily diary of these activities, and they were praised for improvement. The dosage of iproniazid was up to 150 mg daily over 8 weeks. While still on medication at the end of treatment, iproniazid patients showed significantly more improvement than placebo patients on anxiety but not on avoidance. The withdrawal of iproniazid was followed by frequent relapse. Interestingly, on the Gelder–Marks phobia scales, the effect of iproniazid plus home exposure *in vivo* was greater than that of placebo with the same program but was not improved by the addition of desensitization in fantasy.

In brief, controlled studies of monoamine oxidase inhibitors agree that this class of drug has a significant if limited effect in reducing agoraphobia and social phobia and that there is a high relapse rate following drug withdrawal. The way these drugs interact with systematic exposure treatment is still obscure.

Tricyclics

Imipramine for Phobias. Imipramine has been the subject of six double-blind controlled studies. In school phobics (Gittelman-Klein & Klein, 1971), more imipramine children than children in a placebo group returned to school and improved on ratings of global help, depression, physical complaints, and school phobias. These differences were not present at 3 weeks and developed only after 6 weeks. This outcome might have been related to dose rather than time, as the mean medication at 3 weeks was 107 mg a day, compared with 152 mg at 6 weeks. Patients and families had been seen weekly; case workers instructed the families to maintain a firm attitude toward school attendance and acted as a liaison with the school. The authors suggested that the presence of the case workers played an essential part in producing the greater improvement seen in children treated with imipramine. The authors thought that imipramine alone, without insistence on a return to school, would have led to the children's being happier while staying at home, without returning to school. Feeling better did not automatically lead to school return. Of the children on imipramine who felt better, not all went back to school. Imipramine was seen as instrumental in reducing general anxiety, which then facilitated the effect of parental pressure on the child to expose her/himself to the feared school situation.

In agoraphobics, Klein (1964) suggested that imipramine reduced panic more than did a placebo, thus helping patients to enter phobic situations. Systematic exposure was not part of this study. Zitrin *et al.* (1978) explored the contribution of imipramine to desensitization in fantasy of chronic agoraphobics, mixed phobics, and specific phobics. One hundred and eleven patients had 26 weekly sessions 45 min long with either (1) imipramine in a mean dose of 180 mg daily plus desensitization in fantasy, (2) imipramine with support only, or (3) placebo plus desensitization in fantasy. At the end of treatment, imipramine showed a clear superiority over placebo in agoraphobics and in mixed phobics, but not in simple phobics. The most improvement occurred between Sessions

13 and 26. At follow-up one year after treatment ended, there were more relapses among imipramine than among placebo patients.

Several issues limit the conclusions that can be drawn from the design. Although the authors suggested that imipramine selectively reduced free-floating panic attacks, no measures of change in panic attacks were made to support this contention. Another problem is that the authors reported results only in terms of "improvement" and did not note the pretreatment scores or the absolute amount of change that occurred in treatment. A final difficulty is that the drug was combined with the weak behavioral treatment of desensitization in fantasy, which is no longer of particular interest for agoraphobics.

The fourth controlled study of imipramine, by Sheehan, Ballenger, and Jacobsen (1980), was described in the section above on MAOIs, with superiority being found over placebo, but no drug-free follow-up was made.

In a fifth study (Marks, Grey, Cohen, Hill, Mawson, Ramm, & Stern, 1982), 45 chronic agoraphobic outpatients were randomly assigned to treatment by placebo or by imipramine up to 200 mg daily for 28 weeks. Every patient had six 1-hr treatment sessions over 10 weeks. All patients had systematic self-exposure homework, including an instruction manual. In addition, half of each drug group had therapist-aided exposure and half had therapist-aided relaxation, each to a total of 3 hr.

Patients improved substantially on nearly all measures, maintaining their gains to one-year follow-up. There was no significant therapeutic effect of imipramine on any measure of outcome despite plasma levels which are usually considered therapeutic for depression and despite significant drug side effects. Patients had low initial scores on the Hamilton Depression Scale, which probably accounts for the absence of a drug effect. There was a significant, though limited, effect of brief therapist-aided exposure on phobias and on panics.

A sixth study, of 26 volunteer agoraphobics (McNair & Kahn, 1981), involved 8 weeks of imipramine or chlordiazepoxide. Imipramine was significantly superior to the benzodiazepine not only for panics but also on two or three measures of depression (SCL90 and POMS), and had no significant effect on either

of the two measures of phobias. The imipramine was thus clearly antidepressant as well as antipanic, despite the fact that the antipanic effect was independent of the level of depression.

Table 2 summarizes evidence that antidepressant drug studies with negative outcomes have included patients with lower levels of initial dysphoric mood than in studies with positive outcomes. Wherever comparable data of initial mood level is available, the starting level was significantly lower in the negative compared with the positive study.

Clomipramine and Exposure for Obsessive-Compulsive Rituals. Despite claims to the contrary, it has yet to be established that clomipramine has specific antiobsessive properties in addition to the antidepressant action that it shares with other tricyclics (Symes, 1967; Rack, 1973). There are some pharmacological differences between clomipramine and these related compounds. Clomipramine is a specific inhibitor of serotonin uptake, but only a weak inhibitor of noradrenaline uptake, though its metabolite desmethylclomipramine is antinoradrenergic (Horn, 1976). Unlike amitriptyline, clomipramine elevates plasma prolactin (Francis, Williams, Williams, Link, Zole, & Hughes, 1976), and in this respect, it resembles chlorpromazine, to which it is structurally similar. Finally, clomipramine is the most potent depressor of REM (rapid eye movement) sleep among the tricyclic group (Oswald, 1973).

Early suggestions that clomipramine might be valuable in treating obsessive-compulsive

Table 2. Initial Depressed Mood Is Higher in Studies Finding Drug Effects

Initial scores	Drug effect	
	Present	Absent
"Extremely blue, depressed"	32%[a] *	13%[b]
Zung depression (mean)	63[a] *	45[c]
Hamilton depression (mean)	15[d] *	8[b]

* Depression scores significantly different for all three paired comparisons.
[a] Sheehan *et al.* (1980), Tables 2 and 3, agora- and social phobics (imipramine).
[b] Marks *et al.* (1982) agoraphobics (imipramine).
[c] Solyom *et al.* (1981) agora- and social phobics (phenelzine).
[d] Marks *et al.* (1980) compulsive rituals (clomipramine).

disorders were based on uncontrolled and/or short-term studies over a few weeks (e.g., Fernandez & Lopez-Ibor, 1967; Beaumont, 1973; Capstick, 1975; Ananth, Pecknold, Van den Steen, & Engelsmann, 1978). Controlled studies were therefore indicated, of which there have been two so far.

A double-blind Swedish trial (Thoren, Asberg, Cronholm, Jornestedt, & Traskman, 1980) compared the effects of up to 150 mg of clomipramine or of nortriptyline, or placebo, in inpatients with chronic compulsive rituals of a median of 10 years' duration. Drugs were given for 5 weeks, and thereafter all patients were offered clomipramine up to 225 mg daily so that no drug-free comparison could be made at follow-up. Until Week 5, exposure consisted of only mild encouragement to resist compulsions. Thereafter, more systematic exposure *in vivo* was given.

By Week 5, clomipramine became significantly superior to placebo in reducing rituals and depression, while the effects of nortriptyline were in between. Patients who then went on to an open clomipramine phase improved. Of the 16 responders to clomipramine, 15 were followed up for a year or more and remained better—except for 6, who relapsed a few weeks after reducing or stopping their clomipramine. Poorer clinical results were predicted by a low level of the serotonin metabolite 5-hydroxyindoleacetic acid (5HIAA) in the cerebrospinal fluid *before* treatment began.

The authors kindly supplied their data to this author for a more detailed analysis, which showed that clomipramine seemed to act more as an antidepressant than as a directly anticompulsive agent, just as it had in a previously uncontrolled study (Capstick & Seldrup, 1973), where a better outcome had been noted with clomipramine in depressed obsessives than in "true" obsessives. In the study of Thoren *et al.* (1980), their Table 1 indicates that of their eight obsessives who began with clomipramine, the three who scored highest on the depression scale before their treatment began improved three times more in obsessions than did the remaining five patients in that group. The items making up the depression scale are sadness, inattention, inability to feel, thoughts, suicidal thoughts, lassitude, concentration difficulties, reduced appetite, and reduced sleep. Figure 5 shows the greater improvement in patients who had a higher depressed mood before the treatment began.

It could perhaps be argued that "depression" scales of the kind used by Thoren *et al.* and in the next study to be discussed (Marks, Stern, Mawson, Cobb, & McDonald, 1980) measure something different from what has been diagnosed as depressive illness by psychiatrists (e.g., general distress). It is true that higher "depression-scale" scores predicted greater overall incapacity in the patients of Marks *et al.* (1980). However, the idea that scores on depression *scales* reflect something different from the *diagnosis* of depression is not useful unless we can specify what that difference is. For practical purposes, high scores

CPRS SCALES

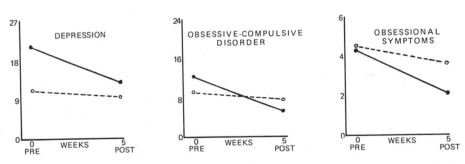

Figure 5. Effect of depression on outcome with clomipramine: $n = 4$ (●—●) depressed (score 18$^+$ on Clinical Psychopathological Rating Scale [CPRS] depression before treatment); $n = 4$ (O--O) not depressed (score 17$^-$ on CPRS depression before treatment).

on depression scales in the study of Thoren *et al.* and of Marks *et al.* predicted a better outcome with the use of clomipramine, and in patients with low scores on such scales, clomipramine was of no demonstrable value.

The larger investigation of Marks *et al.* (1980) included a two-year follow-up phase and will be described in detail. It examined the short- and long-term effects of clomipramine with and without exposure *in vivo* and also measured plasma levels of clomipramine. The study was triple-blind in that neither patient, therapist, nor assessor knew the drug condition and the rater did not know the psychological treatment condition.

The study consisted of a 2 × 2 factorial design examining the effects of clomipramine as opposed to placebo and exposure as opposed to relaxation. Forty patients were randomly allocated to either the clomipramine or the placebo condition. Four weeks on drugs were followed by six weeks of inpatient psychological treatment given every weekday for 45 min. The clomipramine (C) and placebo (P) groups were subdivided into exposure (E) or relaxation (R) groups from Weeks 4 to 7, thus giving four groups of 10 patients each (CE, CR, PE, and PR; see Figure 6, Weeks 4 to 7). The design was balanced for treatment conditions up to Week 7. At this point, the two relaxation groups were switched to exposure, so that all patients had exposure from Weeks 7 to 10. Patients were assessed on eight occasions up to two-year follow-up (Figure 6).

Forty patients were selected who had chronic handicapping obsessive-compulsive rituals of at least one year's duration. Other selection criteria were age range 18–59, no history of psychosis, agreement to involve relatives in treatment if necessary, and no previous adequate behavioral treatment. In addition, patients had to agree to inpatient therapy for six weeks and to stop all previous medication at least two weeks before starting the trial. Of the 40 patients selected, 30 were referred by psychiatrists and 10 by general practitioners. The sample consisted of 11 men and 29 women, with a mean age of 35 and a mean problem duration of 12 years. The four treatment groups were of comparable composition regarding age, sex, problem duration, and previous treatment.

All patients attended weekly as outpatients in the first four weeks. Oral clomipramine or placebo was given in a single nightly dose, starting at 10 mg and rising to 225 mg *nocte* within 2 weeks except in cases of excessive side effects; the patients continued at the 225-

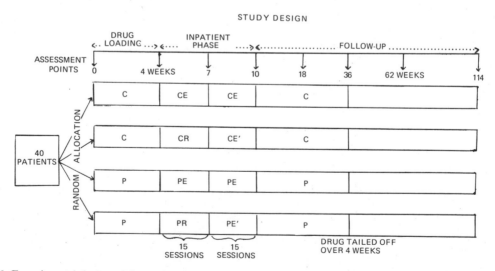

Figure 6. Experimental design of the study: C = clomipramine; P = placebo; E = exposure; R = relaxation; ↓ = assessment points. (From "Clomipramine and Exposure for Obsessive-Compulsive Rituals, I and II" by I. M. Marks *et al.*, *British Journal of Psychiatry*, 1980, *136*, 1–24, Fig. 1. Copyright 1980 by the British Journal of Psychiatry. Reprinted by permission.)

mg level for the next 8 months. The mean dose was 183 mg daily for Weeks 4 to 10 and 145 mg daily at Week 18.

After 4 weeks, the patients were admitted to the hospital, where they were assigned to one of three trained therapists. Psychological treatment, either relaxation or exposure *in vivo*, began on the day after admission, following a detailed interview. The sessions lasted 45 min and took place each weekday morning. After 15 sessions of treatment, those patients who had had relaxation treatment were switched to exposure treatment, and all patients continued with exposure for 15 more sessions. After 6 weeks as inpatients (30 sessions), the patients were discharged from the hospital unless their clinical condition made further treatment desirable. From Week 36, medication was tapered off over 4 weeks, so that the patients were off all capsules by Week 40.

The psychological treatments were similar to those reported by Rachman, Hodgson and Marks (1971), Rachman, Marks, and Hodgson (1973), Hodgson, Rachman, and Marks (1972), and Marks, Rachman, and Hodgson (1975). Exposure was carried out *in vivo*, with modelling and self-imposed response prevention. Patients were asked to practice relaxation or exposure exercises between sessions according to their group of assignment. Before and after discharge, some patients had treatment at home for problems concerning rituals (a mean of 2.5 sessions per patient for the whole group). Where relatives had been involved in the patients' rituals, they were seen with the patient for advice about helping him/her to continue self-exposure and to refrain from carrying out rituals. Relatives were asked to desist from helping the patient to complete rituals. Of the 40 patients, 12 brought their families to a weekly therapeutic group for a mean of 4 sessions. The design afforded a comparison between exposure and relaxation of Week 7 only and between clomipramine and placebo at every measurement point. Two-way analyses of variance tested the effects of the behavioral treatment and of the drug and of their interaction at Week 7; the pretreatment scores at Week 0 were covaried out.

Compared with relaxation at Week 7 exposure *in vivo* produced significantly more im-

provement in the performance and discomfort ratings on the behavioral avoidance test as well as the assessor-rated compulsion checklist and the time involved in the target rituals. Exposure had no significant effect on mood or social adjustment at this stage, though it did later. Although the exposure effect on rituals was significant when the clomipramine and the placebo groups were pooled for analysis, it was less obvious in the clomipramine groups CE versus CR (Figure 7) than in the placebo groups PE versus PR (Figure 8). In the former, the clomipramine effect partly obscured the exposure effect.

Compared with placebo (Figures 9 and 10), clomipramine produced significantly more improvement on the two depression measures (Wakefield and Hamilton) as well as on anxiety ratings; assessor-rated compulsion checklists; and leisure, family, and social adjustment.

At Week 7, on analysis of variance there was no significant interaction of clomipramine with exposure. The improvement obtained from Weeks 4–7 is seen in Figure 11. There was consistently more improvement in rituals among patients who had both clomipramine and exposure (CE) rather than either alone (PE or CR). In the absence of statistical *interaction*, this trend reflects an additive influence of two effective treatments given together rather than of one potentiating the other. The trend was not seen on measures of mood or social adjustment.

From Weeks 4 to 7, there was a consistent tendency for exposure to improve rituals more than did clomipramine (Figure 11), but this superiority attained significance on only two measures: pooled targets (self–time) and compulsion checklist (self) (groups PE versus CR in Figure 11). At Week 7, clomipramine and exposure improved rituals significantly more than the control treatments on 3 and 4 out of 8 measures, respectively. In addition, at Week 7 clomipramine improved mood and social adjustment significantly more than did placebo, while exposure relative to relaxation had no significant effect on these areas of function at that stage.

Results at Weeks 4, 10, 18, 36, and 62 could be obtained only for clomipramine versus placebo. On an analysis of mean level, patients

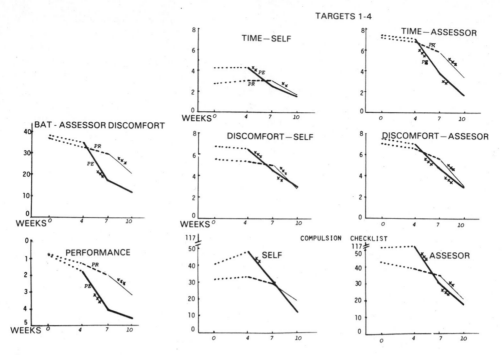

Figure 7. Outcome of two placebo groups: PE = exposure (n = 10) versus PR = relaxation (n = 10; (····) drug-loading phase; (---) relaxation; (—) exposure; ** p < .01, *** p < .001 (significance of change over three weeks). (From "Clomipramine and Exposure for Obsessive-Compulsive Rituals, I and II" by I. M. Marks *et al.*, *British Journal of Psychiatry*, 1980, *136*, 1–24, Fig. 2A. Copyright 1980 by the British Journal of Psychiatry. Reprinted by permission.)

on clomipramine improved more than the placebo group on rituals, mood, and social adjustment, the difference being significant on all but two measures. Significant linear effects were obtained on ratings of target rituals for discomfort, on the Wakefield and on leisure; thus, from Weeks 4 to 18, the clomipramine patients continued to improve in these measures relative to placebo patients (Figures 9 and 10).

The superiority of clomipramine over exposure was beginning to be apparent by Week 4, before exposure began, and was maximum between Weeks 10 and 18, after which it began to taper off. By Week 36 (six-month followup), the point when medication was tapered off, the drug effect was less marked, and at one-year follow-up (Week 62), it was significant on only one measure, though a trend remained for clomipramine to be superior.

Within-group effects are seen in Figures 7 and 8, and from Weeks 7 to 10 the two exposure groups (CE and PE) showed further significant improvement on all measures of

rituals except for discomfort ratings on the behavioral avoidance test. This finding suggested that the full effect of exposure had not yet been obvious at Week 7.

In the two "relaxation" groups (CR and PR), little change had been evident from Weeks 4 to 7. In contrast, when these groups had exposure from Weeks 7 to 10, the means of all but one measure of rituals improved highly significantly.

At Weeks 18 and 36, the two placebo groups, both of which had had exposure by then, showed a significant improvement of mood, family, leisure, and social adjustment, which might reflect generalization of the earlier improvement seen in rituals (Figure 10).

Is clomipramine anticompulsive or antidepressant? From a total of 40 patients, two subsamples of 10 patients each were extracted, half of whom were on the drug and the other half on placebo. One subsample consisted of the 10 least depressed patients, and the other the 10 most depressed patients. (According to the clinical cutoff point of 14 on the Wakefield,

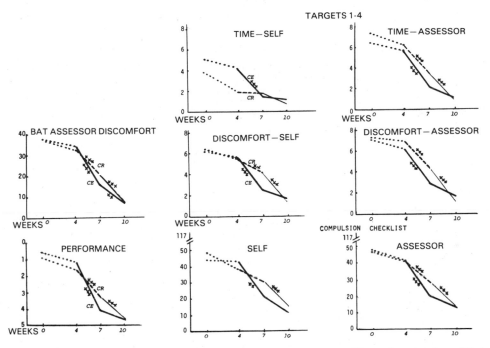

Figure 8. Outcome of two clomipramine groups: CE = exposure ($n = 10$) versus CR = relaxation ($n = 10$); (····) drug-loading phase; (---) relaxation; (—) exposure; ** $p < .01$, *** $p < .001$ (significance of change over three weeks). (From ''Clomipramine and Exposure for Obsessive-Compulsive Rituals, I and II'' by I. M. Marks *et al., British Journal of Psychiatry,* 1980, *136,* 1–24, Fig. 2B. Copyright 1980 by the British Journal of Psychiatry. Reprinted by permission.)

only 2 of the 40 patients were not depressed, the mean for the total sample being 24.) The least depressed patients were selected if their score on the Wakefield was within the lower quartile and on the Hamilton was at least below the median, or vice versa. Similarly, the most depressed subsample was selected according to the patients' scores in the upper quartile of the Wakefield and above the median of the Hamilton.

The two subsamples differed significantly before treatment on all three measures of mood. However, the two subsamples were also found to differ significantly on the pretreatment means of four of eight measures of rituals, so the two subsamples were analyzed separately for Weeks 4, 10, and 18 (orthogonal polynomial analysis, covarying out scores at Week 0).

In the least depressed patients, clomipramine conferred no advantage over placebo despite similar starting levels (Figure 12); a significant drug effect was found on only one measure: target rituals (time, self-assessed).

In contrast, the most depressed subsample improved significantly more with clomipramine than with placebo on the Wakefield and Hamilton measures of depression, on target rituals (self-rated time and discomfort and assessor-rated discomfort), and in leisure and family adjustment (Figure 5).

In short, there was no substantive evidence of a direct anticompulsive effect of clomipramine, but there was a clear antidepressant effect.

Compliance of Patients. The presence of substantial plasma levels of clomipramine in the patients from the clomipramine group allowed the inference that they took the drug, though not necessarily in the dose prescribed. Similarly, placebo patients had no clomipramine in their plasma.

Most patients were compliant with psychological treatment. There were no differences between ratings of compliance during exposure and during relaxation, although exposure is generally considered a more difficult treatment for the patient.

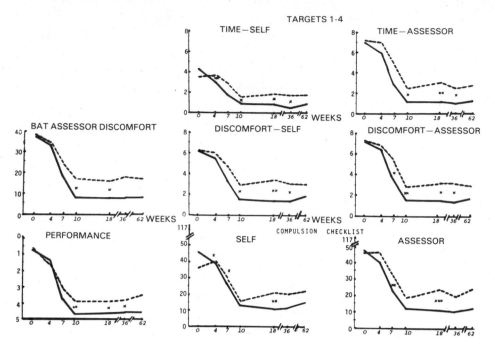

Figure 9. Outcome on rituals: clomipramine (——; *n* = 20) versus placebo (---; *n* = 20); * *p* < .05, ** *p* < .01, ***
p < .001 (between groups at times shown). (From "Clomipramine and Exposure for Obsessive-Compulsive Rituals,
I and II" by I. M. Marks *et al., British Journal of Psychiatry,* 1980, *136,* 1–24, Fig. 3A. Copyright 1980 by the British
Journal of Psychiatry. Reprinted by permission.)

Compliance with treatment during sessions
correlated highly with compliance in carrying
out homework instructions between sessions
(*r* = .59, *p* < .01 for relaxation, *r* = .67, *p*
< .001 for exposure). Compliance during and
between exposure sessions in the first three
inpatient weeks also correlated highly with
compliance during and between exposure sessions in the second three inpatient weeks (*r*
= .70, *p* < .001). There was little evidence of
a general compliance factor across psychological treatments; compliance with relaxation
and with exposure correlated positively together but failed to reach significance (*r* = .36).

Patients who received clomipramine had
higher compliance ratings than those receiving
placebo, both during relaxation and during
exposure. The difference was significant on
three of the four measurement occasions of
compliance, both between and during sessions, from Weeks 4 to 10. On the four ratings
combined, clomipramine patients were significantly more compliant than were placebo patients (*p* < .002).

Drug Side Effects. At Week 0, *before* taking
any tablets, the patients already had many
physical complaints (e.g., dry mouth, sweating, drowsiness). Over the subsequent weeks,
these complaints increased significantly in
clomipramine patients, peaking at Week 4. By
Week 10, however, most of the complaints had
diminished substantially, except for sweating.

Plasma Levels of Clomipramine (see Stern,
Marks, Mawson, & Luscombe, 1980). The
mean plasma concentrations for clomipramine
and its metabolite *N*-desmethylclomipramine
steadily increased over the first four weeks of
treatment, after which they remained relatively steady. At Week 4, concentrations were
160 and 430 ng/ml, respectively, and subsequently, they were 150 and 360 ng/ml, concentrations that were well above the minimum
level said to be therapeutic in depressives
(Jones & Luscombe, 1976). No clomipramine
or its metabolite was found in the two plasma
samples analyzed from the seven taken from
each placebo patient.

The plasma levels correlated significantly

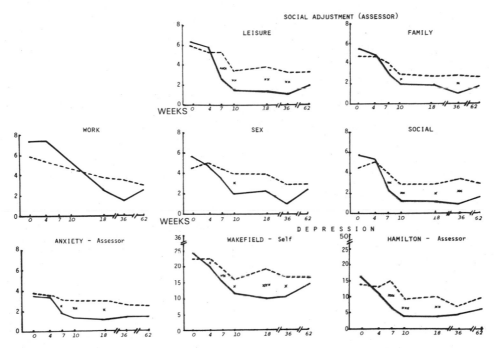

Figure 10. Outcome on mood and social adjustment; clomipramine (——; $n = 20$) versus placebo (---; $n = 20$); * p < .05, ** p < .01, *** p < .001 (between groups at time shown). (From "Clomipramine and Exposure for Obsessive-Compulsive Rituals, I and II" by I. M. Marks *et al., British Journal of Psychiatry*, 1980, *136*, 1–24, Fig. 3B. Copyright 1980 by the British Journal of Psychiatry. Reprinted by permission.)

with dose but not with side effects, and side effects were not related to outcome, although plasma concentrations were. Patients with plasma clomipramine levels in the range 100–250 ng/ml and plasma *N*-desmethylclomipramine levels between 230 and 550 ng/ml were found to improve significantly more than patients with levels outside these ranges, thus suggesting a "therapeutic window" for clomipramine and its primary metabolite.

Tricyclic Medication. During follow-up, clomipramine and placebo patients had comparable amounts of further treatment by exposure and support. Tricyclic drugs were given to nearly half the sample and were started earlier and continued for longer periods in the placebo patients. Repeated measures were available from five clomipramine patients, whose depression and rituals increased again after clomipramine was stopped at Week 36. One patient relapsed a month later at Week 40; the other 4 patients relapsed nine months later at Week 72. All five patients improved again on restarting the clomipramine.

Figure 13 shows the course of these five patients, plotting the results of the patient who relapsed early to appear at Week 72 instead of Week 40. It is noteworthy that depression relapsed totally, returning to its pretreatment score, whereas the relapse of rituals was only partial (see Week 72), some gains in rituals being retained at this stage.

Discussion of Study of Marks *et al.* (1980). Clomipramine-treated patients improved significantly more than placebo-treated patients on nearly all measures of rituals, mood, and social adjustment. This superiority became apparent by Week 4 and maximum by Weeks 10 and 18, after which it diminished. By Week 62 (one-year follow-up), when the patients had been off drugs for four months, the overall superiority of clomipramine to placebo continued on mean scores, but this superiority was no longer significant.

The effect of clomipramine could be demonstrated only in those patients who had high depression scores at the start, and it was absent in undepressed patients. For the latter,

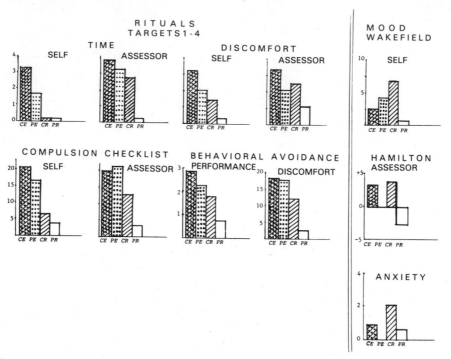

Figure 11. Change from Weeks 4 to 7 (higher scores = more improvement): CE = clomipramine + exposure; PE = placebo + exposure; CR = clomipramine + relaxation; PR = placebo + relaxation. (From "Clomipramine and Exposure for Obsessive-Compulsive Rituals, I and II" by I. M. Marks *et al., British Journal of Psychiatry,* 1980, *136,* 1–24, Fig. 4. Copyright 1980 by the British Journal of Psychiatry. Reprinted by permission.)

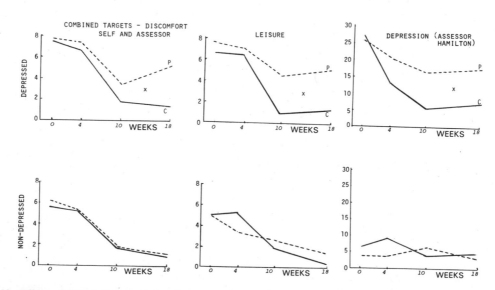

Figure 12. Effect of initial depressed mood on outcome: clomipramine (——; *n* = 5) versus placebo (---; *n* = 5) depressed and nondepressed subsamples; * *p* < .05. (From "Clomipramine and Exposure for Obsessive-Compulsive Rituals, I and II" by I. M. Marks *et al., British Journal of Psychiatry,* 1980, *136,* 1–24, Fig. 5. Copyright 1980 by the British Journal of Psychiatry. Reprinted by permission.)

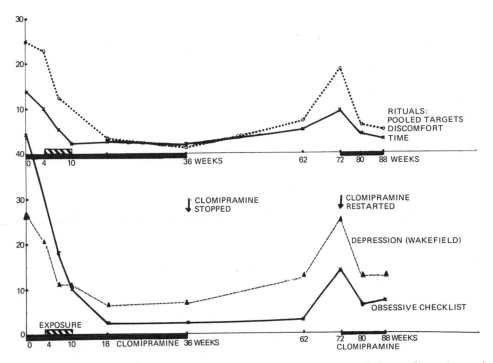

Figure 13. Relapse on stopping clomipramine and improvement on restarting it. Relapse affects depression (▲---▲) more than rituals (○---○, ×—×) (*n* = 5). Self-ratings (lower scores = improvement). (From "Clomipramine and Exposure for Obsessive-Compulsive Rituals, I and II" by I. M. Marks *et al.*, *British Journal of Psychiatry*, 1980, *136*, 1–24, Fig. 7. Copyright 1980 by the British Journal of Psychiatry. Reprinted by permission.)

exposure *in vivo* remains the treatment of choice. Furthermore, we do not yet know the outcome of obsessive-compulsive patients in the long run with clomipramine *in the absence of exposure*. All the patients had had exposure by Week 10, and their rituals may well have shown less improvement without it. There were already signs by Week 36, the point where patients came off the drugs, that the effect of clomipramine was beginning to wane. Clinically, one meets occasional patients who responded initially to clomipramine, but not when it was given subsequently. Perhaps the results of clomipramine medication depend on the presence of depression associated with the rituals, or, independently, some patients may eventually become refractory to clomipramine.

No study has yet examined the long-term controlled effect of clomipramine without any exposure at all, and such an investigation is now necessary and ethical. Studies to date have been uncontrolled, controlled over only one or two months, or controlled for longer with exposure treatment as a confounding variable.

The effect of clomipramine took surprisingly long to reach a maximum, reaching a peak after 10 weeks rather than the 4 weeks said to obtain in depressives. This slow response accords with the finding of Thoren, Asberg, Cronholm, Jornestedt, & Traskman (1980) that the improvement of obsessive-compulsive patients with clomipramine only reached significance at 5 weeks. It also agrees with Ananth *et al.* (1978), Karatanow (1977), and Singh, Saxena, and Gent (1977), who found that improvement in obsessive-compulsive features continued to increase after 4 weeks of clomipramine. In phobics, too, the same slow response has been noted to phenelzine (Tyrer *et al.*, 1973; Solyom *et al.*, 1974) and to imipramine (Zitrin, Klein, & Woerner, 1978). Whether this delayed response to antidepressants of obsessives and of phobics compared with depressives indicates some biochemical difference between them remains to be seen.

The Role of Depression. Clomipramine seemed to act more as an antidepressant than as a directly anticompulsive agent in the study of Marks *et al.* (1980), as it did in the study of Thoren *et al.* (1979).

Though the study of Marks *et al.* excluded patients with severe primary depression, as judged by psychiatrists at interview, nevertheless, before treatment began, the sample as a whole was moderately depressed on the Wakefield and Hamilton scales, the women being significantly more depressed than the men. Similar measures of depression have not generally been used systematically on such patients. It is unlikely that the inpatient sample of Marks *et al.* (1980) was atypical of obsessive-compulsive inpatients. Blind ratings of the clinical protocols of Marks *et al.*'s patients and those of Thoren *et al.* in the Karolinska Institute in Stockholm agreed well on which patients were suitable for treatment in the research designs, suggesting that the two samples were clinically comparable, even though they were not measured on the same instruments. Both samples were mainly female, which was also true of the samples of Marks *et al.* (1975) and Foa and Goldstein (1978).

It is probable that obsessives are more likely to seek treatment—and even more likely to agree to admission—when they are depressed than at other times. Kringlen (1965) noted that depressive symptoms had been present in only 19% of his phobic and obsessive inpatients at the onset of their problem, but in 46% at the time of their hospital admission. Similarly, more of the patients of Marks *et al.* had been at least moderately depressed at the time they entered the trial than they said they had been when their obsessions had begun years before (55% versus 37%). If this is generally true, inpatient samples might be more depressed than obsessives as a whole, and clomipramine might be less effective in a less depressed group of obsessives in outpatient clinics or in general practice.

Relationship between Depression and Obsessive-Compulsive Problems. Links between depression and obsessions have been noted by many workers. First, among depressive illnesses, obsessive traits and symptoms are common, being present in one-third of depressed inpatients (Lewis, 1934; Gittleson, 1966). Depressed patients had scores on the Leyton Obsessional Inventory midway between those for obsessive-compulsive neurosis and normals (Kendell & DiScipio, 1970). Among depressed patients, compulsive rituals and obsessive thoughts are associated more with features of "neurotic" depression (anxiety, hypochondriasis, depersonalization) that with "psychotic" depression and retardation (Vaughan, 1976; Videbech, 1975). Gittleson (1966) examined the case notes of 398 inpatient depressives. Of these, 13% showed obsessions before the onset of depression, and their depression began at a younger age than in the remaining depressives. A quarter of the 13% *lost* their obsessions during subsequent depression, and the same proportion developed them; samples of obsessive-compulsives in treatment trials obviously exclude the former type of patient and include the latter and may thus overemphasize the association of depression with obsessions.

Next, among obsessive-compulsive patients, there is a slightly increased prevalence of depression and manic-depressive psychosis in their relatives (Black, 1974). Nearly one-third of obsessive-compulsive inpatients had depression as a complication (Marks, 1965; Rosenberg, 1968). Goodwin, Guze, and Robins (1969) noted that depression is probably the most common complication in obsessive-compulsive disorders. The sample of Marks *et al.* (1980) was moderately depressed on entering the study, with a mean Wakefield score of 24 (cutoff point from normals is 14/15) and a mean Hamilton score of 15 (median for moderate depression is 13 and for severe depression 24; Knesevitch, Biggs, Clayton, & Zeigler, 1977). In their 40 patients, 8 had a family history of treated obsessions and 9 of treated depression, but these two subsamples did not overlap at all; that is, none had a family history of both, which is the opposite one might expect where there is a genetic link.

In the patients of Marks *et al.* (1980), the scores for depression and for rituals correlated highly significantly before and after treatment. However, important differences between depression and rituals became apparent on closer inspection. In the five patients for whom measures were available at the time that their depression increased during follow-up, relapse was complete for depression but only partial for rituals, indicating some dissociation then between depression and rituals. This dissociation is concordant with that found by Marks et al. (1975) and by Foa and Goldstein (1978), whose patients' rituals remained improved up to two years following exposure in vivo, even though their depression had changed little from its original level. Similarly, in the placebo patients of Marks et al. (1980), all of whom had also had exposure treatment by follow-up, mood change was unimpressive, in contrast to the substantial and persistent improvement in ritual and in social adjustment. Perhaps exposure treatment partially dissociates the link between rituals and depression by teaching patients how to deal with reemerging rituals, so that during subsequent depressive episodes, fewer rituals return than might otherwise have been the case.

Depressive Tendencies Persist despite Treatment. In contrast to the continuing improvement in rituals and social adjustment for years after exposure (Marks et al., 1975, 1980; Foa & Goldstein, 1978; Meyer, Levy, & Schnurer, 1974; Boulougouris, 1977), neither exposure treatment nor eight months on clomipramine seems to affect the tendency for obsessives (and phobics) to continue to have occasional depressive episodes over the next two years. The patients of Marks et al. (1980) had their medication stopped after eight months, but during their subsequent follow-up to two years, they had a strong tendency to have depressive episodes, leading their doctors to prescribe antidepressants during this period to nearly half the sample.

These antidepressants were prescribed later in the follow-up phase, and for shorter periods, in patients who had previously been in the clomipramine rather than the placebo group. Had clomipramine patients developed dependency on their drug, then the opposite should have been the case. If anything, eight months of clomipramine had slightly reduced the need for subsequent tricyclics, though the underlying disturbance in mood usually continued. The need that many ritualizers seem to have for continued tricyclics over long periods is

consonant with the findings noted earlier of Thoren et al. (1980). A high relapse rate on stopping antidepressants has similarly been noted in other conditions, for example, in phobics after iproniazid (Lipsedge, 1973), phenelzine (Tyrer & Steinberg, 1975; Solyom et al., 1974), and imipramine (Zitrin et al., 1978), and in depression after amitriptyline (Weissman, Kasl, & Klerman, 1975).

The anxious, "neurotic" type of depression associated with obsessive-compulsives is similar to that often seen in phobics, and it is possible that phobics and obsessives are especially likely to seek treatment during depressive episodes. Results indicate that at such times, antidepressant medication is worthwhile, but it is disheartening that patients may need to take it for years, and that as yet we have no way of modifying the trend toward recurrent affective problems, even though the rituals usually remain improved for years with no or minimal further exposure treatment.

Cost-Effectiveness Considerations. In the short run, clomipramine is a relatively acceptable and inexpensive treatment. It could thus be argued that in depressed patients with rituals, clomipramine is cheaper in the short run than exposure treatment. However, clomipramine has drawbacks that are not present in exposure; for example, it can have toxic cardiovascular effects (Jefferson, 1976), and there are occasional fatalities from even a single small dose when given together with or within four weeks of MAOIs (Lader, 1980). In one of the patients of Marks et al. (1980), the development of hypomania forced the discontinuation of clomipramine.

Role of Relaxation and Therapist Contact. These variables had a minimal effect in the patients of Marks et al. (1980), as shown by the trivial improvement in the PR group until exposure was introduced at Week 7 (Figure 7). This result confirmed the findings of two previous studies (Hodgson et al., 1972; Roper, Rachman, & Marks, 1975).

Role of Exposure. In the patients of Marks et al. (1980) at the only point where exposure could be compared directly with its control treatment of relaxation (Weeks 4 to 7), exposure had a significant effect in reducing rituals, but it did not affect mood, while relaxation affected neither. Thereafter, when "relaxation'' patients switched from relaxation to exposure, improvement began in rituals. Exposure and clomipramine produced a slightly greater improvement in rituals when given together than when given separately, but they did not potentiate one another. The effect on rituals of exposure alone was marginally greater than that of clomipramine alone.

The results at Week 7 underestimated the extent of the improvements eventually achieved by exposure, for two reasons. First, exposure was given for suboptimal session durations (45 min instead of 2 hr; Rabavilas, Boulougouris, & Stefanis, 1976), because the study was controlling for the amount of therapist time across relaxation and exposure conditions, and 2-hr relaxation sessions did not seem feasible. The effect of exposure, particularly at Week 7, might thus be weaker than in routine clinical conditions that are not subject to the constraints of such a design (e.g., Marks, Hallam, Philpott, & Connolly, 1977; Marks, Bird, & Lindley, 1978). Second, at Week 7, no patients had yet completed all their exposure treatment, and further significant improvement in rituals occurred thereafter. Ethical constraints at the time the study was planned dictated a switch from relaxation to exposure at Week 7, so that all patients had had exposure by Week 10, thus precluding a comparison of relaxation and exposure from that point onward. It is relevant that during follow-up, the placebo groups, who all had exposure eventually as well, not only maintained their improvement in rituals but had also showed substantial gains by then in social adjustment and a slight improvement in mood. This finding suggested that the improvement produced by exposure was fairly stable for the group as a whole.

The significant effects of exposure are consistent with earlier research on the subject, reviewed by Marks (1978), Rachman and Hodgson (1979), and Foa and Steketee (1979). Exposure treatment improved rituals earlier and more than it did mood and social adjustment, though both, especially the latter, improved significantly at follow-up, as shown in the placebo groups. The findings of Marks *et al.* (1980) are in keeping with those of previous workers that exposure improves rituals more than it does mood (Marks *et al.*, 1975; Foa & Goldstein, 1978). Improvement in mood

was just significant at follow-up in the placebo patients, as was also found by Boersma, Den Hengst, Dekker, and Emmelkamp (1976). It is fitting that treatment that focuses on the direct modification of particular behavior should produce more alterations in that behavior than in other aspects of the person's problems. Such relative specificity and the lack of response to relaxation training discourages explanations in terms of nonspecific factors, such as the therapist–patient relationship. Improvements in rituals anticipated improvement in mood, arguing against the latter as the prime mechanism of change.

In contrast to exposure, clomipramine had its greatest effect on mood, though it also significantly reduced rituals and improved social adjustment. The mood-relieving effects of the drug seemed to be primary, and the improvements observed in obsessive-compulsive problems seemed secondary.

It is possible that the failure to find synergistic interaction between exposure and clomipramine arose from the type of experimental design adopted. As mentioned earlier, the major comparison took place at Week 7, and at this stage, neither exposure nor clomipramine had achieved their full effects. Perhaps with different timing, an interaction between the two treatments might have become evident.

Role of Compliance. The patients of Marks *et al.* (1980) were usually compliant in both relaxation and exposure treatments. Clomipramine significantly enhanced compliance in both psychological treatments, possibly by improving mood. This greater compliance might have contributed to the superiority of clomipramine over placebo. Perhaps clomipramine acts by reducing patients' discomfort in the presence of stimuli that evoke rituals, thus enabling them to come into contact with such stimuli and so to habituate. It is also possible that clomipramine directly increases the rate of habituation to noxious stimuli. These last two possibilities are less likely, as there was no evidence that clomipramine has a direct anticompulsive effect.

Conclusions from Controlled Studies of Clomipramine. Depressed mood is common among obsessive-compulsives who come for treatment, and clomipramine seems to act more as an antidepressant than as an anticompulsive agent. When depression is minimal, clomipramine has no demonstrable value, and exposure *in vivo* remains the treatment of choice. Relaxation training is little better than a placebo. Clomipramine affects mood more than rituals, whereas exposure affects rituals more than mood. The effect of clomipramine takes up to 10 weeks to reach a maximum and shows some signs of waning by 8 months. On stopping clomipramine, depression tends to return to its original level, and rituals less so, but lasting improvement in rituals might be more dependent on exposure treatment. The obsessive-compulsive inpatients seemed to have two interacting, but partially independent, sets of psychopathology. First, many had a disturbance of mood, which responded more to a tricyclic than to exposure, though depression often recurred when the drug was stopped. Second, compulsive rituals responded to exposure treatment on a more lasting basis. In the study of Marks *et al.*, the effects of clomipramine and of exposure were not synergistic but additive.

Neurotic Depression

We have seen that the evidence to date for the value of drugs in behavioral treatment of anxiety syndromes supports their use in the presence of a depressive mood, and that their value is still debatable when such a depressive mood is absent. In neurotic depression where phobias or obsessions have not dominated the clinical picture, there have been three controlled studies in which drugs combined with psychotherapy have been examined. Although these studies did not use behavioral methods, their results have some bearing on behavioral thinking and will therefore be included here. The three studies have been ably reviewed by Weissman (1978).

The first investigation was that of Weissman *et al.* (1975). One hundred and fifty depressed women entered remission after treatment by amitriptyline and were thereafter followed up for one year. The first eight months of this followup were either on amitriptyline or on placebo and either on casework psychotherapy or support. The antidepressant effect of amitriptyline was clear, as more patients on placebo experienced a return of the depression, but amitriptyline did not improve social functioning. In contrast, the "psychotherapy" did not improve the depression, though it did improve the women's social adjustment.

The second controlled study (Covi, Lipman, Derogatis, Smith, & Pattison, 1974) involved 200 female outpatients with chronic neurotic depression who, over 18 months, had imipramine or diazepam or placebo and either group psychotherapy or minimal support. Once again, imipramine protected against relapse in depression, and this time also improved interpersonal perceptions. Four months of group psychotherapy, in contrast, had no effect on depression but did improve empathic understanding and interpersonal sensitivities.

In the third controlled study, 196 patients had amitriptyline or placebo combined with marital therapy (Friedman, 1975). Amitriptyline was found to decrease depression at one-month follow-up, and this trend continued at the three-month follow-up, but with no effect on the marriage. The reverse was true for marital therapy that improved family participation and function but improved "symptoms" less than did amitriptyline.

Taken together, these outcomes indicate that there are differential effects of tricyclic drugs and of the problem-solving type of psychotherapy, the drugs reducing depression, the problem-solving approach improving the personal relationships and other difficulties in patients' lives. It could be that the active ingredient of "cognitive behavior therapy" for depression, which is so fashionable, is enhancement of general skills in coping with life's difficulties.

Like the tricyclics, the monoaminoxidase inhibitors, too, may have their effect on neurotic anxiety–depression rather than on other functions. In an uncontrolled report, Paykel (1978) noted that prognosis with phenelzine was better in patients who had mixed anxiety and other neurotic symptoms.

Sexual Dysfunction

Only two controlled studies are available of drugs plus psychological treatment in this area

(Carney, Bancroft, & Mathews, 1978; Mathews, 1982). As an adjuvant to sexual counseling, sublingual testosterone before lovemaking was found to be of significantly more effect than diazepam on behavioral and attitudinal measures after three months and also at follow-up six months after the hormone had been withdrawn. This apparent benefit was not replicated in a second study by Mathews (1982), in which testostorone conferred no advantage over placebo. Mathews concluded that in his previous study diazepam had probably reduced the benefits of directed practice, thus producing an apparent superiority for testostorone, and that the hormone did not specially aid the effects of directed sexual practice.

Perspectives and Conclusions

This review has dealt only with work with adults and has omitted relevant work with children. Systematic investigation of drugs used together with behavioral treatments has begun only recently, and few conclusions can be drawn from most of the studies done to date. For definitive appraisal, minimal requirements for designs in this area are (1) ratings that are blind with respect both to the drugs and to the behavioral treatments that are being manipulated; (2) the control of both factors and their interaction (i.e., the drug versus placebo and the behavioral technique in question versus the control technique appropriate to the hypothesis being tested; and (3) follow-up of at least a year after the drug is withdrawn.

Ideally, there should also be good measures of the psychotropic effects of the drugs being used. Most physiological measures are too far removed from the relevant subjective state to be of value. Also generally unavailable at present are methods for measuring the levels of most drugs or their active metabolites in the cerebrospinal fluid or brain, as the techniques needed are usually too invasive. Serum levels are of some value in indicating drug metabolism, but they are too far from the operative psychological events to be of predictive value. Dosage is also obviously important.

An important issue is the type of behavioral treatment being given. It makes a difference in phobic-obsessive problems whether the exposure used is in fantasy or *in vivo*, how soon after drug administration it begins, how long it continues afterward, and with what speed the patient is brought into contact with the evoking stimuli in all its frightening aspects. It is also important to know how much anxiety or unpleasantness occurs during exposure treatment. Though benzodiazepine drugs are traditionally regarded as anxiolytics, their decrease of discomfort during exposure is not especially great.

Another theoretical and practical problem is whether and when drug dissociation exists. That is, when does learning fail to transfer from the drug to the nondrug state or vice versa? The evidence in humans is inconclusive. If drug dissociation does exist, it is likely to vary with many circumstances.

The use of cumbersome procedures like the inhalation of carbon dioxide or the intravenous injection of barbiturates has little to commend it. Oral drugs are preferable for easy and economy of administration, as well as for greater safety. Several trials of beta blockers have shown that while these reduce heart rate during exposure treatments, at follow-up there is either no significant enhancement of improvement from exposure or a tendency for patients on beta blockers actually to do slightly worse. The use of small doses of diazepam neither helps nor hinders exposure treatment.

Antidepressants seem more worthwhile for some patients with phobic-obsessive problems, though there is no clear-cut evidence yet that such drugs potentiate behavioral treatments, or that they directly reduce phobias and obsessions rather than acting indirectly by improving mood. Several controlled studies have found the tricyclics, imipramine, and monoamine oxidase inhibitors (phenelzine and iproniazid) to be significantly better than placebo in agoraphobics, social phobics, and school phobics, as long as the drug is given. The same applies to clomipramine for compulsive rituals. There is general agreement that these antidepressants take from 5 to 10 weeks to have their maximum effect, and there is a strong tendency to relapse on stopping these drugs even after they have been given from 8 to 12 months continuously in adequate dosage.

Most studies have not sufficiently examined

the effect of depressed mood on the utility of antidepressants. It may be that phobics and obsessives who are treated at hospitals have more depression than their untreated peers, that this depression is a partly independent problem, and that antidepressants are indicated only for depressed mood, while exposure alone is indicated for phobic-obsessive difficulties. Where this issue has been looked at carefully, in two independent studies of compulsive ritualizers, the clomipramine was of value only where a depressed mood was present at the start, and the drugs had little effect in the absence of such a depressive mood. For ritualizers without depression, exposure *in vivo* remains the treatment of choice. The same trend is emerging for phobics. Antidepressants given for phobic-obsessive problems appear useful mainly when concurrent depressive mood is present, and apart from this do not act synergistically with exposure treatment.

The same might be true of neurotic depression uncomplicated by phobias or rituals. Three studies agree on the value of imipramine and of amitriptyline for depression, and of brief psychotherapy for interpersonal relationships. So far, directive behavioral treatments have not been studied together with drugs for neurotic depression.

In sexual dysfunction two controlled studies found methyltestosterone to be superior to diazepam but not to placebo as an adjuvant to sex counseling.

References

Ananth, J., Pecknold, J. C., Van den Steen, & Engelsmann, F. Double blind comparative study of clomipramine in obsessive neurosis. Paper given at meeting of Congress International of Neuropharmacology, Vienna, July 1978.

Beaumont, G. Clomipramine (Anafranil) in the treatment of obsessive-compulsive disorders—A review of the work of Dr. G. H. Collins. *Journal of International Medical Research*, 1973, *1*, 423–424.

Bernardt, M. W., Singleton, W., & Silverstone, T. Behavioural and subjective effects of beta-adrenergic blockade in phobic subjects. *British Journal of Psychiatry*, 1980, *137*, 452–457.

Black, A. The natural history of obsessional neurosis. In H. R. Beech (Ed.), *Obsessional states*. London: Methuen, 1974.

Boersma, K., Den Hengst, S., Dekker, J., & Emmelkamp,

P. M. G. Exposure and response prevention in the natural environment: A comparison with obsessive-compulsive patients. *Behaviour Research and Therapy*, 1976, *14*, 19–24.

Bond, D. D. *The love and fear of flying.* New York: International Universities Press, 1952.

Boulougouris, J. C. Variables affecting the behaviour of obsessive-compulsive patients treated by flooding. In J. C. Boulougouris & A. Rabavilas (Eds.), *Studies in phobic and obsessive-compulsive disorders.* New York: Pergamon, 1977.

Butollo, W., Burkhardt, P., Himmler, C., & Muller, M. Mehrdimensionale Verhaltenstherapie und Beta-Blocker bei functionellen Dysrytmien und chronischen korperbezogenen Angstreaktionen. Paper presented at Die Tagung der Deutschen Konferenz fur Psychosomatische Medizin, Köln, 1978.

Capstick, N. Anafranil in obsessional states—A followup study. Paper given at Fifth World Congress of Psychiatry, Mexico, 1971.

Capstick, N. Clomipramine in the treatment of the true obsessional state—A report on four patients. *Psychosomatics*, 1975, *16*(1), 21–25.

Capstick, N., & Seldrup, J. Phenomenological aspects of obsessional patients treated with clomipramine. *British Journal of Psychiatry*, 1973, *122*, 719–720.

Carney, A., Bancroft, J., & Mathews, A. Combination of hormonal and psychological treatment for female sexual unresponsiveness. *British Journal of Psychiatry*, 1978, *132*, 339–346.

Chambless, D. L., Foa, E. B., Groves, G., & Goldstein, A. J. Flooding with Brevital in the treatment of agoraphobia, countereffective? *Behavior Research and Therapy*, 1979, *17*, 243–251.

Covi, L., Lipman, R. S., & Guzman, R. A. Drug psychotherapy interactions in depression. Paper 97 in *Proceedings and Summary of the APA Annual Meeting*, Anaheim, Calif., 1975, pp. 89–90.

Fernandez, J., & Lopez-Ibor, J. J. Monochlorimipramine in the treatment of psychiatric patients resistant to other therapies. *Actas Luso-Espanolas de Neurologia*, 1967, *26*, 119–147.

Foa, E. D., & Goldstein, A. Continuous exposure and complete response prevention treatment of obsessive-compulsive neurosis. *Behavior Therapy*, 1978, *9*, 821–829.

Foa, E. B., & Steketee, G. Obsessive-compulsive disorders and their treatment. In R. M. Hersen, R. M. Eisler, & E. P. M. Miller (Eds.), *Progress in Behavior Modification*. New York: Academic Press, 1979.

Francis, A. D., Williams, P., Williams, R., Link, G., Zole, E. N., & Hughes, D. The effect of clomipramine on prolactin levels—Pilot studies. *Postgraduate Medical Journal*, Supplement 3, 1976, *52*, 87–92.

Friedman, A. S. Interaction of drug therapy with marital therapy in depressive patients. *Archives of General Psychiatry*, 1975, *32*, 619–637.

Gaind, R. The role of beta blockers as an adjunct in behaviour therapy. Paper presented to European Association of Behavior Therapy, Greece, Sept. 1976.

Gelder, M. G., Marks, I. M., & Wolff, H. Desensitisation and psychotherapy in phobic states: A controlled enquiry. *British Journal of Psychiatry*, 1967, *113*, 53–73.

Gelder, M. G., & Marks, I. M. Severe agoraphobia: A

controlled prospective trial of behaviour therapy. *British Journal of Psychiatry*, 1966, *112*, 309–319.

Gittelman-Klein, R., & Klein, D. F. Controlled imipramine treatment of school phobia. *Archives of General Psychiatry*, 1971, *25*, 204–207.

Gittleson, N. L. The effect of obsessions on depressive psychosis. *British Journal of Psychiatry*, 1966, *112*, 253–259.

Goodwin, D. W., Guze, S. B., & Robins, E. Followup studies in obsessional neurosis. *Archives of General Psychiatry*, 1969, *20*, 182–187.

Hafner, J., & Marks, I. M. Exposure in vivo of agoraphobics: The contributions of diazepam, group exposure and anxiety evocation. *Psychological Medicine*, 1976, *6*, 71–88.

Hafner, J., & Milton, F. The influence of propanolol on the exposure in vivo of agoraphobics. *Psychological Medicine*, 1977, *7*, 419–425.

Haslam, M. T. The relationship between the effect of lactate infusion on anxiety states, and their amelioration by carbon dioxide inhalation. Paper presented to Fifth World Congress of Psychiatry, Mexico, 1971.

Hodgson, R., Rachman, S., & Marks, I. M. The treatment of obsessive-compulsive neurosis: Followup and further findings. *Behaviour Research and Therapy*, 1972, *10*, 181–189.

Horn, A. S. The interaction of tricyclic antidepressants with the biogenic amine uptake systems in the central nervous system. *Postgraduate Medical Journal Supplement*, 1976, *52*, 25–31.

Hudson, B. L., Tobin, J. C., & Gaind, R. Followup of a group of agoraphobic patients. Paper presented to Second Annual Conference of the European Association of Behaviour Therapy, Wexford, Eire, 1972.

Husain, M. Z. Desensitisation and flooding (implosion) in the treatment of phobias. *American Journal of Psychiatry*, 1971, *127*, 1509–1514.

Jefferson, J. W. A review of the cardiovascular effects and toxicity of tricyclic antidepressants. *Psychosomatic Medicine*, 1976, *37*, 160–179.

Johnston, D., & Gath, D. Arousal levels and attribution effects in diazepam assisted flooding. *British Journal of Psychiatry*, 1973, *122*, 463.

Jones, R. B., & Luscombe, D. K. Plasma levels of clomipramine and its *N*-desmethylmetabolite following oral administration of clomipramine in man. *British Journal of Pharmacology*, 1976, *57*, 4308.

Karatanow, O. Double blind controlled study in phobias and obsessions complicated by depression. *International Journal of Medical Research*, 1977, *5* (Suppl. 5), 42–48.

Kendell, R. E., & DiScipio, W. J. Obsessional symptoms and obsessional personality traits in patients with depressive illnesses. *Psychological Medicine*, 1970, *1*, 65–72.

King, A., & Little, J. C. Thiopentone treatment of the phobic-anxiety-depersonalization syndrome. *Proceedings of the Royal Society of Medicine*, 1959, *52*, 595–596.

Kringlen, E. Obsessional neurotics: A long term followup. *British Journal of Psychiatry*, 1965, *111*, 709–722.

Klein, D. F. Delineation of two drug-responsive anxiety syndromes. *Psychopharmacologia*, 1964, *5*, 397.

Knesevitch, J. W., Biggs, J. T., Clayton, P. J., & Zeigler, V. E. Validity of the Hamilton rating scale for depression. *British Journal of Psychiatry*, 1977, *131*, 49–52.

Lader, M. Clinical anxiety and its drug treatment. In G. C. Palmer (Ed.), *Neuropharmacology of Central and Behavioral Disorders*. New York: Academic Press, 1980.

Lewis, A. J. Melancholia: A clinical survey of depressive states. *Journal of Mental Science*, 1934, *80*, 277–378.

Lipsedge, M., Hajioff, J., Huggings, P., Napier, L., Pearce, J., Pike, D. J., & Rich, M. The management of severe agoraphobia: A comparison of iproniazid and systematic desensitisation. *Psychopharmacologia*, 1973, *32*, 67.

Marks, I. M. Patterns of meaning in psychiatric patients. *Maudsley Monograph* No. 13. Oxford: Oxford University Press, 1965.

Marks, I. M. *Living with fear*. New York: McGraw-Hill, 1978.

Marks, I. M., Viswanathan, R., & Lipsedge, M. S. Enhanced extinction of fear by flooding during waning diazepam effect. *British Journal of Psychiatry*, 1972, *121*, 493–505.

Marks, I. M., Rachman, S., & Hodgson, R. Treatment of chronic obsessive-compulsive neurosis by in vivo exposure: A two-year followup and issues in treatment. *British Journal of Psychiatry*, 1975, *7*, 349–364.

Marks, I. M., Hallam, R. S., Philpott, R., & Connolly, J. *Nursing in behavioural psychotherapy*. Research Series of Royal College of Nursing, Cavendish Square, Henrietta Street, London WC1, 1977.

Marks, I. M., Bird, J., & Lindley, P. Psychiatric nurse therapy—Developments and implications. *Behavioural Psychotherapy*, 1978, *6*, 25–36.

Marks, I. M., Stern, R. S., Mawson, D., Cobb, J., & McDonald, R. Clomipramine and exposure for obsessive-compulsive rituals, I & II. *British Journal of Psychiatry*, 1980, *136*, 1–24.

Marks, I. M., Grey, S., Cohen, S. D., Hill, R., Mawson, D., Ramm, L., & Stern, R. S. Imipramine and brief therapist-aided exposure in agoraphobics having self-exposure homework: A controlled trial. *Archives of General Psychiatry*, in press.

Mathews, A. N. Treatment of female sexual dysfunction. In J. C. Boulougouris (Ed.), *Learning theories approaches to psychiatry*. New York: Wiley, 1982.

Mawson, A. N. Methohexitone-assisted desensitisation in the treatment of phobias. *Lancet*, 1970, *1*, 1084–1086.

McNair, D. M., & Kahn, R. J. Imipramine compared with a benzodiazepine for agoraphobia. In D. F. Klein & J. Rabkin (Eds.) *Anxiety: New research and changing concepts*. New York: Raven Press, 1981.

Meyer, V., Levy, R., & Schnurer, A. The behavioural treatment of obsessive-compulsive disorders. In H. R. Beech (Ed.), *Obsessional states*. London: Methuen, 1974.

Miller, N. E. In H. Steinberg (Ed.), *Animal behaviour and drug action*. London: Churchill, 1964.

Orwin, A., Le Boeuf, A., Dovey, J., & James, S. A comparative trial of exposure and respiratory relief therapies. *Behaviour Research and Therapy*, 1975, *13*, 205–214.

Oswald, I. Sleep studies with clomipramine and related

drugs. *Journal of International Medical Research*, 1973, *1*, 296–298.

Paykel, E. S. Prediction of outcome on phenelzine. *Abstracts C.I.M.P.* Vienna, July 1978.

Paykel, E. S. Continuous exposure and complete response prevention of obsessive compulsive neurosis. Paper presented to Society for Psychotherapy Research, Oxford, July 1979.

Rabavilas, A. D., Boulougouris, J. C., & Stefanis, D. Duration of flooding session in the treatment of obsessive-compulsive patients. *Behaviour Research and Therapy*, 1976, *14*, 349–355.

Rachman, S., & Hodgson, R. *Obsessions and Compulsions*. Englewood Cliffs, N.J.: Prentice-Hall, 1979.

Rachman, S., Hodgson, R., & Marks, I. M. Treatment of chronic obsessive-compulsive neurosis. *Behaviour Research and Therapy*, 1971, *9*, 237–247.

Rachman, S., Marks, I. M., & Hodgson, R. The treatment of obsessive-compulsive neurotics by modelling and flooding in vivo. *Behaviour Research and Therapy*, 1973, *11*, 463.

Rack, P. H. Intravenous anafranil and obsessional states. Paper presented at the Fifth World Congress of Psychiatry, Mexico, 1971.

Rack, P. H. Clomipramine in the treatment of obsessional states with special reference to the Leyton Obsessional Inventory. *Journal of International Medical Research*, 1973, *1*, 332, 397–402.

Roper, G., Rachman, S., & Marks, I. M. Passive and participant modelling in exposure treatment of obsessive compulsive neurotics. *Behaviour Research and Therapy*, 1975, *13*, 271–279.

Rosenberg, C. M. Complications of obsessional neurosis. *British Journal of Psychiatry*, 1968, *114*, 477–478.

Sheehan, D., Ballenger, J., & Jacobsen, G. Drug treatment of endogenous anxiety with phobic symptoms. Abstract 328 in *Proceedings of World Psychiatric Association Meeting*, Honolulu, Sept. 1977.

Sheehan, D. V., Ballenger, J., & Jacobsen, G. Treatment of endogenous anxiety with phobic, hysterical and hypochondriacal symptoms. *Archives of General Psychiatry*, 1980, *37*(1), 51–59.

Sherman, A. R. Therapy of maladaptive fear-motivated behaviour in the rat by the systematic gradual withdrawal of a fear-reducing drug. *Behaviour Research and Therapy*, 1967, *5*, 121–129.

Singh, A. N., Saxena, B., & Gent, M. Clomipramine in depressive patients with obsessive neurosis. *International Journal of Medical Research: Supplement 5*, 1977, 25–32.

Slater, S. L., & Leavy, A. The effects of inhaling a 35% CO_2-65% O_2 mixture upon anxiety level in neurotic patients. *Behaviour Research and Therapy*, 1966, *4*, 309–316.

Solyom, L., Heseltine, G. F. O., McClure, D. J., Solyom, C., Ledwidge, B., & Steinberg, G. In agoraphobics MAOIs are significantly better than placebo. *Canadian Psychological Association Journal*, 1973, *18*, 25–32.

Solyom, L., Lapierre, Y. D., Solyom, C., & Smyth, D. The interaction of phenelzine and exposure to the phobic situation in the treatment of phobias. Paper presented to Meeting of Canadian Psychiatric Association, Ottawa, 1974.

Solyom, C., Solyom, L., Lapierre, Y., Pecknold, J., & Morton, L. Phenelzine and exposure in the treatment of phobias. *Biological Psychiatry*, 1981, *16*, 239–248.

Stern, R. S., Marks, I. M., Mawson, D., & Luscombe, D. K. Clomipramine and exposure for compulsive rituals. II: Plasma levels, side effects and outcome. *British Journal of Psychiatry*, 1980, *136*, 161–166.

Symes, M. H. Monochlorimipramine: A controlled trial of a new antidepressant. *British Journal of Psychiatry*, 1967, *113*, 671–675.

Thoren, P., Asberg, M., Cronholm, B., Jornestedt, L., & Traskman, L. Clomipramine treatment of obsessive-compulsive disorder. I: A controlled clinical trial. *Archives of General Psychiatry*, 1980, *37*, 1281–1288.

Tyrer, P., & Steinberg, D. Symptomatic treatment of agoraphobics and social phobics: A followup study. *British Journal of Psychiatry*, 1975, *127*, 163–168.

Tyrer, P. J., Candy, J., & Kelly, D. H. W. Phenelzine in phobic anxiety: A controlled trial. *Psychological Medicine*, 1973, *3*, 120.

Ullrich, R., Ullrich, R., Crombach, G., & Peikert, V. Three flooding procedures in the treatment of agoraphobics. Paper presented at the Second European Conference on Behaviour Modification, Wexford, Ireland, 1972.

Vaughan, M. Relationships between obsessional personality, obsessions in depression and symptoms of depression. *British Journal of Psychiatry*, 1976, *129*, 36–39.

Videbech, T. The psychopathology of endogenous depression. *Acta Psychiatrica Scandinavica*, 1975, *52*, 336–373.

Weissman, M. H. Psychotherapy and its relevance to the pharmacotherapy of affective disorders: From ideology to evidence. In M. A. Lipton *et al.* (Eds.), *Psychopharmacology: A generation of progress*. New York: Raven Press, 1978.

Weissman, M. M., Kasl, S. V. & Klerman, G. L. Depressed women one year after maintenance therapy. Paper 97 in *Proceedings Summary, American Psychiatric Association Meeting*, Anaheim, Calif., 1975, pp. 88–89.

Yorkston, N., Sergeant, H., & Rachman, S. Methohexitone relaxation for desensitising agoraphobic patients. *Lancet*, 1968, *2*, 651–653.

Zitrin, C. M., Klein, D. F. & Woerner, M. G. Behaviour therapy, supportive psychotherapy, imipramine and phobias. *Archives of General Psychiatry*, 1978, *35*, 307–316.

PART IV

Intervention and Behavior Change

ADULT

CHAPTER 13

Anxiety and Fear

Paul M. G. Emmelkamp

Introduction

Most behavioral research in the area of anxiety and fear has been of the analogue type. Researchers have typically employed volunteers, usually students, with small animal phobias (e.g., snake phobia) or social anxiety (e.g., speech anxiety, dating anxiety) as subjects. While some researchers have selected only highly fearful subjects, others have used mildly fearful subjects or those with low fear. For instance, in a study by De Moor (1970), about one-third of the sample of "snake phobics" could touch the snake at the pretest; Melnick (1973) employed subjects with "dating anxiety" who dated less than twice a week. Analogue researchers have usually excluded subjects from participation who have real psychological problems. To give just a few examples, subjects who were undergoing or had undergone any form of psychiatric treatment (e.g., Mathews & Rezin, 1977; Mealiea & Nawas, 1971) or who manifested emotional disorder or psychological difficulties (e.g., Barrett, 1969; Beiman, Israel, & Johnson, 1978; De Moor, 1970) have been excluded. However, it should be noted that subjects with

psychological difficulties may be more similar to phobic patients than subjects without such problems.

Analogue studies are often not internally valid. Several studies have demonstrated that demand characteristics can influence behavioral assessment in such studies. For instance, in a study of Emmelkamp and Boeke-Slinkers (1977a) using snake phobics as subjects, the level of demand for approach behavior in a behavioral avoidance test was varied. Both high-demand and low-demand subjects were regarded as phobic if they could not touch the snake with a gloved hand. On the basis of the results of the low-demand test, 16.9% of the subjects would have been classified as phobic and would have qualified for treatment, whereas on the basis of the high-demand test, the percentage would have been only 6.8%. Thus, behavioral avoidance tests used in analogue studies are easily influenced by demand characteristics. Other studies clearly indicate the influence of situational and instructional effects on behavioral assessment procedures (e.g., Barrios, 1978; Bernstein, 1974; Bernstein & Nietzel, 1973, 1974; Smith, Diener, & Beaman, 1974).

There are several important differences between clinical and analogue populations. Phobic patients differ from controls and phobic students on various measures of psychopath-

Paul M. G. Emmelkamp • Department of Clinical Psychology, Academic Hospital, Oostersingel 59, Groningen, The Netherlands.

ology (Emmelkamp, 1979a). In addition, subjects in analogue and clinical studies may differ markedly with respect to approach contingencies (Hayes, 1976). Even though both types of subjects may show substantial avoidance behavior, phobic patients may experience much stronger approach contingencies than subjects in laboratory studies. Furthermore, the kind of phobias treated in clinical and analogue studies differ widely. While analogue researchers have typically employed students with small-animal phobias or social anxiety as subjects, agoraphobia forms the greatest category of phobias seen in clinical settings. Because of the differences between clinical and analogue populations, the clinical value of such studies has been questioned (e.g., Cooper, Furst, & Bridger, 1969; Emmelkamp, 1980a).

The difficulty in generalizing results from analogue studies to clinical patients is illustrated by the differential effectiveness of treatment with analogue populations, on the one hand, and with clinical populations, on the other. For many years, the behavioral treatment of phobias was dominated by systematic desensitization. In contrast with analogue studies, where this procedure has consistently been found to be effective in improving minor fears, a recent review (Emmelkamp, 1979a) suggests that this procedure has only small effects on socially anxious and agoraphobic patients. Branham and Katahn (1974) compared desensitization and no treatment, with both volunteer students and patients as subjects. Volunteers improved significantly more than patients. In their volunteer sample, desensitization was significantly superior to the control condition, whereas in their patient sample, desensitization was no more effective than no treatment. With cognitive modification procedures, the same picture arises. Cognitive modification procedures have been found to be quite effective with analogue populations. However, recent studies at out department show that these procedures have clinically insignificant effects with agoraphobic (Emmeikamp, Kuipers, & Eggeraat, 1978) and obsessive-compulsive patients (Emmelkamp, Van de Helm, Van Zanten, & Plochg, 1980). Other studies have found differential effectiveness with biofeedback (Shepherd & Watts,

1974) and relaxation (Borkovec & Sides, 1979) for patients and for volunteers.

It is not my purpose to dismiss the findings of analogue studies entirely. Whether analogue research is relevant or not depends on the question that one wants to investigate. Since several recent papers (Bandura, 1978; Borkovec & Rachman, 1979; Kazdin, 1978) deal with this issue, I will not discuss it further. However, while analogue studies may be of some value for certain research questions, the clinical effectiveness of treatments can be studied only with clinical patients as subjects.

In this chapter, I first briefly discuss the current status of behavioral theories concerning the functioning of phobic behavior; then, the effectiveness of nonbehavioral treatments (i.e., psychopharmaca and psychotherapy) is discussed. The bulk of the chapter is devoted to a critical analysis of behavioral treatments. In a separate section, the *clinical* effectiveness of behavioral procedures with socially anxious and agoraphobic patients is reviewed. In the last section, some future trends are discussed.

Historical Perspective

Current Status of the Process Learning Theory of Fear Acquisition

In the early days of behavior therapy, therapists held that phobic reactions could be adequately explained in terms of conditioning. Until several years ago, Mowrer's (1950) theory of fear acquisition was widely accepted by behavior therapists as a model for the development of clinical phobias. In Mowrer's view, classically conditioned fear motivates avoidance behavior, which leads to a reduction of fear and a strengthening of the avoidance behavior (negative reinforcement). According to this theory, anxiety and avoidance are causally linked, and avoidance behavior should be reduced as soon as anxiety is eliminated.

The two-stage theory of learning is disputed by several lines of evidence (Emmelkamp, 1979a; Eysenck, 1976; Rachman, 1976, 1977). First, a traumatic experience relating to the genesis of phobias often cannot be found. For instance, both phobic volunteers (Fazio, 1972;

Murray & Foote, 1979; Rimm, Janda, Lancaster, Nahl & Dittmar, 1977) and phobic patients (Buglass, Clarke, Henderson, Kreitman, & Presley, 1977; Goldstein & Chambless, 1978; Goorney & O'Connor, 1971; Lazarus, 1971; Liddell & Lyons, 1978; Solyom, Beck, Solyom, & Hugel, 1974) are often unable to recall any traumatic experience in the setting in which they were subsequently phobic. Second, repeated failures to condition phobias are an even greater problem for the conditioning theory. Several studies have failed to replicate the famous "Little Albert" experiment of Watson and Rayner (1920), who conditioned a phobia in a 1-year-old child. And finally, the conditioning paradigm is inadequate (1) in explaining the gradual development of phobias as sometimes seen in phobic patients and (2) in explaining the preponderance of phobias such as agoraphobia or snake phobia as compared with the infrequency of phobias for hammers and electrical appliances.

Several modifications and alternative theories have been proposed, but to date, evidence based on research with clinical patients is lacking (Emmelkamp, 1979a). For instance, some have argued that clinical phobias can develop through *vicarious learning* (e.g., Bandura, 1977) or that fear can be acquired through the *transmission of information and instruction* (e.g., Rachman, 1977). Although there is some evidence that children often share their parents' fears, which may be explained in terms of observational and instructional learning, other explanations are equally plausible (e.g., genetic influences or similar traumatic experiences). As far as retrospective reports of phobic subjects are concerned, the data are inconclusive. Few of the subjects in the Fazio (1972) and Rimm *et al.* (1977) studies reported vicarious learning experiences, while Murray and Foote (1979) found that fear was often acquired through observational and instructional experiences that communicate negative information.

According to Seligman (1971), phobias are instances of highly *prepared* learning; in his view, the human species has been preprogrammed through evolution to acquire phobias easily for potentially dangerous situations. Öhman and his colleagues have conducted a

series of ingenious experiments to test the preparedness theory experimentally (for review, see Öhman, 1979). The results of their experiments, conducted with normal volunteer subjects, indicate that conditioned electrodermal responses to fear-relevant stimuli (e.g., pictures of spiders or snakes) showed much higher resistance to extinction than responses conditioned to neutral stimuli (e.g., pictures of flowers or mushrooms). However, the effect of the stimulus content variable was less clear-cut during the acquisition phase. Thus, the experiments partially supported the preparedness theory.

Despite the bulk of evidence in favor of preparedness provided by this series of experiments, the results of these studies need to be qualified in several ways. In passing, it should be noted that all experiments have been conducted by only one research group. Cross-validation of this theory in a different center would be valuable. Moreover, the laboratory model of fear acquisition seems to be of questionable relevance to clinical phobias (Emmelkamp, 1979a). Finally, the preparedness theory does not seem to have any implication for the treatment of phobias.

Another influential theory concerning phobic behavior has been proposed by cognitive-behavior therapists. In their view, anxiety reactions are mediated by faulty *cognitions* or anxiety-inducing self-instructions. Several studies have been conducted to test this theory. Two types of faulty thinking have been investigated: (1) negative self statements and (2) irrational beliefs.

Studies investigating the influence of self-instructions on anxiety indicated that negative self-statements may enhance arousal (May & Johnson, 1973; Rimm & Litvak, 1969; Rogers & Craighead, 1977; Russell & Brandsma, 1974). However, in a study with phobic subjects, Rimm *et al.* (1977) found that only half of the subjects reported *in vivo* thoughts preceding fear in the phobic situation. According to the cognitive theory, the thoughts always should precede the fear.

Irrational thinking is identified with Ellis's (1962) theory, suggesting that phobics have a tendency to think irrationally and that these irrational beliefs produce their anxiety reactions. Several studies indicate that irrational beliefs are related to phobic anxiety (Goldfried & Sobocinsky, 1975; Rimm *et al.,* 1977). While the results of these studies might indicate that such irrational beliefs are causally linked to anxiety evocation, it is equally plausible that increased emotional arousal in certain situations may sensitize individuals to certain irrational expectancies (Goldfried & Sobocinski, 1975). The studies reviewed so far are of questionable relevance to clinical phobias, because of none of these studies investigated the thoughts of phobic patients.

Recently, Sutton-Simon and Goldfried (1979) reported a study involving patients, although not necessarily phobic, who requested psychotherapy at a community clinic. In this study, the relationship between two types of faulty thinking (irrational beliefs vs. negative self-statements) on the one hand and type of phobia (social anxiety vs. acrophobia) on the other was investigated. The results showed that social anxiety was correlated only with irrational thinking, while acrophobia was correlated with both types of faulty thinking.

In my opinion (Emmelkamp, 1980a), behavioral interpretations of phobic behavior have been rather naive and simple and can offer at best only a partial explanation. In addition to conditioning and cognitive factors, we have to search for other factors as well. One suggestion is that a more comprehensive theory of phobia development should take into account the role of *interpersonal conflicts.* Although the evidence on this point is less than satisfactory (Emmelkamp, 1979a), comprising mainly anecdotes, clinical observations do suggest the importance of clients' interpersonal relationships in the development of clinical phobias, especially in the case of agoraphobia. Moreover, a really comprehensive theory of fear acquisition should also take into account the role that the client's system plays in the functioning of the phobic behavior. It is not sufficient merely to point out that family members "reinforce" the phobic behavior of the identified patient; their motives to do so and the reason that the patient lets them do so deserve special attention. Conceptualizing interpersonal conflicts solely in terms of conditioning may seriously hinder progress in this area.

Another point that deserves more attention is the role of individual differences in phobia acquisition. Although far from conclusive, there is some evidence (Emmelkamp, 1979a) that level of emotional arousal, hormonal processes, and premorbid dependency may significantly contribute to the development of phobias.

Obviously, several factors interact in determining phobic behavior. In my opinion, laboratory studies using either animals or volunteer students as subjects are not useful in developing and evaluating a more comprehensive theory of phobia development.

Nonbehavioral Treatments

Until Wolpe's (1958) introduction of systematic desensitization for the treatment of phobias, treatment for this condition consisted of psychopharmacological or insight-oriented psychotherapy. In this section, research with respect to the effectiveness of psychopharmacology and psychotherapy is reviewed.

Psychopharmaca. Both monoamine oxidase inhibitors (MAOIs) and tricyclic antidepressants have been reported to be beneficial in the treatment of anxiety neurosis and phobic states. However, most of these studies have severe methodological flaws (e.g., no adequate controls, retrospective assessment of results, lack of independent assessments, and no homogeneous population).

Monoamine Oxidase Inhibitors. More recently, several controlled researches into the effectiveness of MAOIs have been conducted. Tyrer, Candy and Kelly (1973) found phenelzine more effective as compared with placebo after eight weeks, but the clinical improvement was not very impressive. Solyom, Heseltine, McClure, Solyom, Ledwidge, and Steinberg (1973) compared phenelzine with various behavioral treatments (systematic desensitization, aversion relief, and flooding, all in imagination). Although the effect of phenelzine was the most rapid, two weeks after the termination of treatment all 6 (out of 10) patients who had stopped taking the drug had relapsed, as compared with only 10% of the patients who had been treated by behavior therapy.

Lipsedge, Hajioff, Huggins, Napier, Pearce,

Pike, and Rich (1973) compared iproniazid with systematic desensitization (in imagination) and placebo. While both treatments proved to be more effective than placebo, no significant differences between systematic desensitization and iproniazid were found. Finally, Solyom, Solyom, La Pierre, Pecknold, and Morton (1981) compared phenelzine and placebo and could not find any difference between them.

Thus, there is some evidence that MAOIs may have beneficial effects on phobic cases, but the effects found were rather small. This conclusion needs to be qualified in several ways. First, most studies instructed patients to expose themselves *in vivo* between treatment sessions. Thus, the effects of MAOIs have not been assessed independently of the effects of exposure *in vivo*. In the only study that attempted to separate these effects (Solyom *et al.*, 1981), phenelzine proved to be no more effective than placebo. Second, discontinuation of medication generally leads to relapse (Lipsedge *et al.*, 1973; Solyom *et al.*, 1973; Tyrer *et al.*, 1973). Third, side effects have often been reported with the use of this class of drugs, including difficulty with micturition, inhibition of ejaculation and anorgasmia, fatigue, dry mouth, blurred vision, edema, and insomnia (e.g., Kelly, Guirguis, Frommer, Mitchell-Heggs, & Sargant, 1970; Mountjoy, Roth, Garside, & Leitch, 1977; Solyom *et al.*, 1973; Tyrer *et al.*, 1973). Fourth, severe interaction with some foods containing a high concentration of amines (Blackwell, 1963) and other drugs (Sjöqvist, 1965) and hepatoxicity (Pare, 1964) have been reported. Finally, as far as comparisons with behavioral treatments are concerned, only "weak" forms of behavioral treatment have been involved. No study has directly compared MAOIs with prolonged exposure *in vivo*, which is far more effective than systematic desensitization, especially with agoraphobics. Briefly, MAOIs have little to recommend them in the treatment of phobias and anxiety states.

Imipramine. Zitrin, Klein, and Woerners (1978) compared the relative effectiveness of imipramine and behavior therapy. Behavior therapy consisted of systematic desensitization in imagination and assertive training. In order to have treatment time equivalent to behavior therapy, patients who received imipramine were also given supportive psychotherapy. Three conditions were compared: (1) behavior therapy plus imipramine; (2) behavior therapy plus placebo; and (3) supportive psychotherapy plus imipramine. The treatment consisted of 26 weekly sessions. The preliminary results indicate that imipramine had beneficial effects for patients who experienced spontaneous panic attacks (including agoraphobics). Imipramine had no therapeutic effects on simple phobics. Rather, it led to a high dropout rate due to medication side effects.

Psychotherapy. Reports of psychoanalysts concerning the treatment of phobias have involved theoretical essays on the dynamics of the patients; the effectiveness of treatment is rarely discussed (Emmelkamp, 1979a). However, Friedman (1950) reported that "after the dynamics of the case were worked through, many patients failed to recover" (p. 274). Other psychoanalysts have also reported unsatisfactory results. Both Freud and Fenichel used exposure *in vivo* in the treatment of phobic cases, which seems to have been forgotton by their followers. Freud wrote (1959), "One can hardly ever master a phobia if one waits till the patient lets the analysis influence him to give it up. . . . one succeeds only when one can induce them through the influence of the analysis . . . to go about alone and struggle with the anxiety while they make the attempt" (Freud, 1959, p. 399). Fenichel (1963) stated the same point, perhaps even more clearly: "The analyst must actively intervene in order to induce the patient to make his first effort to overcome the phobia; he must induce the patient to expose himself to the feared experiences" (p. 215). One can only wonder why the suggestion of these authorities have not been taken seriously by their followers.

Several authors have reported on the treatment of anxiety neurosis and phobias with psychotherapy (Errera & Coleman, 1963; Miles, Barrabee, & Finesinger, 1951; Robert, 1964; Terhune, 1949). These studies have serious methodological flaws, such as no control groups, retrospective assessment of results, no independent assessment of results, and no homogeneous population. In addition, more often than not the results are confounded by additional medication, electroconvulsive therapy (ECT), or unsystematic exposure *in vivo,* which preclude the drawing of any conclusion with respect to the effectiveness of psychotherapy.

Several studies have compared the effectiveness of psychotherapy and behavioral treatments. Only prospective studies involving real clinical phobic patients are discussed here. Gelder and Marks (1966) were the first to conduct such a study. In their study, systematic desensitization and psychotherapy were compared with severe agoraphobic inpatients. After 60–70 sessions, no significant differences were found between the treatments. Overall improvement was small. In a subsequent study involving mixed phobic patients as subjects (Gelder, Marks, & Wolff, 1967), systematic desensitization proved to be more effective than individual or group psychotherapy at the posttest, despite the fact that the desensitization patients had received less treatment than the psychotherapy patients. In a following study in this series (Gelder & Marks, 1968), seven patients who were unimproved after group psychotherapy were treated with desensitization. The patients improved three times as much after four months of desensitization as after two years of group psychotherapy. Finally, Dormaar and Dijkstra (1975) and Gillan and Rachman (1974) also found systematic desensitization to be superior to psychotherapy, although in the Dormaar and Dijkstra study, the between-group difference was not statistically significant.

In summary, systematic desensitization has been found to be more effective than psychotherapy where mixed phobic patients or socially anxious patients (Dormaar & Dijkstra, 1975) were concerned. With agoraphobics, systematic desensitization was no more effective than psychotherapy.

Current Empirical Status

In this section, the current empirical status of behavioral procedures is reviewed. This section is divided in two parts. The first part evaluates the theoretical underpinnings of various treatments and presents an integrated treatment model. The second part is devoted to an evaluation of the clinical effectiveness of treatments, especially with socially anxious and agoraphobic patients.

Behavioral Procedures

Systematic Desensitization. In desensitization, clients are first trained in muscular relaxation; then, they move gradually up a hierarchy of anxiety-arousing situations, while remaining relaxed. Systematic desensitization may be applied either in imagination or *in vivo,* but most studies involved the imaginal variant.

Although numerous studies have demonstrated the effectiveness of systematic desensitization in reducing circumscribed phobias in analogue populations, the theoretical underpinnings of this procedure are still vague. Several theoretical explanations have been put forward, including reciprocal inhibition (Wolpe, 1958), counterconditioning (Davison, 1968), cognitive processes (Emmelkamp, 1975a), and psychoanalytic interpretations (Silverman, Frank, & Dachinger, 1974). Since a detailed review of the research in this area could fill a whole volume, only the major research findings are presented in this section.

Reciprocal Inhibition and Counterconditioning. Both the reciprocal inhibition and the counterconditioning interpretations hold that a graded hierarchy and an incompatible response (relaxation) are essential for the successful desensitization of fear. However, desensitization with relaxation has been found to be as effective as desensitization without relaxation (graded exposure). Marks (1975) reviewed research in this area and found no evidence that relaxation enhanced the effectiveness of imaginal exposure to the phobic stimuli. More recent studies have also demonstrated that desensitization with relaxation is no more effective than graded exposure to the hierarchy items (e.g., Goldfried & Goldfried, 1977; Ladouceur, 1978). Even more importantly, studies with clinical phobics have also found negative results with respect to relaxation in a systematic desensitization context (Agras, Leitenberg, Barlow, Curtis, Edwards, & Wright, 1971; Benjamin, Marks, & Huson, 1972; Gillan & Rachman, 1974). Briefly, there is no evidence that the effects of systematic desensitization should be interpreted in terms of counterconditioning or reciprocal inhibition.

Cognitive Factors. There has been a continuous debate over the influence of cognitive factors, particularly the expectancy of therapeutic gain on systematic desensitization (Davison & Wilson, 1973; Emmelkamp, 1975a,b; Wilson & Davison, 1975; Wilkins, 1979). One strategy of evaluating the influence of cognitive (i.e., expectancy) factors on systematic desensitization is to compare desensitization with placebo conditions. However, most studies that have followed this strategy do not permit the drawing of any conclusions with respect to expectancy factors, because the credibility of the placebo controls has not been adequately assessed. Several studies (e.g., Borkovec & Nau, 1972; McGlynn & McDonell, 1974; Nau, Caputo, & Borkovec, 1974) have demonstrated that the "expectancy of improvement" produced by a placebo therapy must be assessed rather than assumed. In many cases, placebo rationales have not been as credible as the rationale of systematic desensitization. Nevertheless, it is noteworthy that several studies could not find any difference in effectiveness between systematic desensitization and placebo conditions (e.g., Holroyd, 1976; Kirsch & Henry, 1977; Lick, 1975; Marcia, Rubin, & Efran, 1969; McGlynn, 1971; McGlynn, Gaynor, & Puhr, 1972; McGlynn, Reynolds, & Linder, 1971; McReynolds, Barnes, Brooks, & Rehagen, 1973; Tori & Worell, 1973).

A different approach to the study of the influence of expectancy on treatment outcome is to vary instructional sets. Two strategies can be distinguished (Emmelkamp, 1975a). First, subjects who are given a therapeutically oriented instructional set are compared with subjects who are led to believe that they are participating in experimental procedures concerned with physiological reactions. Studies that have followed this strategy have generally found a clear expectancy effect. Second, all subjects are informed that they are to receive therapy, but the instructions concerning the anticipated outcome are varied (positive, neutral, or negative). Studies following this paradigm have produced conflicting results. However, as noted earlier (Emmelkamp, 1975a), "it is inappropriate to conclude that expect-

ancy does not play an important part in the systematic desensitization procedure, because all subjects had received a therapeutic instruction" (p. 5). These therapeutic instructions may lead to expectations of improvement regardless of what the subject is subsequently told. In addition, regardless of instructions given by the experimenter, systematic desensitization may be experienced at face value as a treatment.

Several alternative explanations have been proposed to explain the expectancy effects, particularly experimenter bias (Wilkins, 1973) and demand characteristics (Borkovec, 1973). In his review of expectancy studies, Wilkins (1973) concluded that the studies reporting an expectancy effect involved therapists who were not blind to the experimental manipulations, whereas in studies failing to demonstrate an expectancy effect, the therapists were blind. However, several studies have found expectancy effects with experimenters who were unaware of the expectancy manipulations applied to the subjects (Emmelkamp & Straatman, 1976; Emmelkamp & Walta, 1978; Rosen, 1974; Sullivan & Denney, 1977). Thus, experimenter bias does not adequately explain the differences found in expectancy studies.

Borkovec (1973) proposed that the subjects' characteristics could explain the contradictory results among expectancy studies. In a retrospective analysis of expectancy studies, he suggested that the studies failing to find an expectancy effect employed fearful subjects, whereas studies demonstrating expectancy effects employed low-fear subjects. The post hoc classification of fearful–low-fear subjects, as used by Borkovec (1973) has been criticized by Emmelkamp (1975b); his reanalysis of the studies reviewed by Borkovec indicates that several studies that did find expectancy effects involved highly fearful subjects. More recently, several studies found expectancy effects regardless of the phobic level of the subjects (Emmelkamp & Boeke-Slinkers, 1977b; Sullivan & Denney, 1977). Thus, contrary to Borkovec's (1973) hypothesis, highly fearful subjects were no less susceptible to expectancy effects than were low-fear subjects.

Finally, assessment in most expectancy studies has been limited to self-report and behavioral tests. Thus, it could be argued that expectancy might influence the subjective and behavioral components of fear, but not the physiological component. Indeed, Borkovec (1972) and Rappaport (1972) failed to obtain expectancy effects on physiological indexes of anxiety. However, Beiman (1976) and Kirsch and Henry (1977) demonstrated expectancy effects on physiological measures. Thus, expectancy influences have been demonstrated on subjective, behavioral, and psychophysiological indexes of anxiety.

In summary, expectancy factors appear to play an important role in systematic desensitization. It is still questionable whether systematic desensitization is not merely a highly effective placebo procedure. In order to investigate to what extent desensitization produces an effect independent of expectancy factors, the procedure should be compared with pseudotherapies with the same credibility and face validity (Emmelkamp, 1975a).

Psychoanalytic Interpretation. Silverman, Frank, and Dachinger (1974) hypothesized that part of the effectiveness of systematic desensitization resides in the fact that it activates an unconscious fantasy of merging with the therapist as mother substitute, an activation that is made particularly likely by the use of the muscle relaxation procedure. To test this hypothesis, these authors compared two variants of systematic desensitization with insect-phobic subjects. Instead of using relaxation as an incompatible response, the subjects were given subliminal exposures of either a symbiosis gratification stimulus (*Mommy and I are one*) or a neutral stimulus (*People walking*). The group that received subliminal exposure to the symbiotic gratification stimulus manifested more improvement than the group with the neutral stimulus, thus supporting the authors' hypothesis that the effectiveness of systematic desensitization resides in its activation of unconscious merging fantasies.

Emmelkamp and Straatman (1976) replicated the study by Silverman *et al.* (1974) with special reference to demand characteristics, using snake-phobic volunteers as subjects. In this experiment, *Mommy and I are one* was used as the symbiotic gratification stimulus and *Snake and I are one* as the neutral stimulus; it was assumed that to subjects with a snake phobia, this stimulus would be more rel-

evant than the stimulus *People walking*. The results indicated that sytematic desensitization with a symbiotic gratification stimulus was not more effective than desensitization with a neutral stimulus. Rather, it was shown that subjects receiving the neutral stimulus improved more on the behavioral avoidance test. The difference in outcome from the Silverman *et al.* (1974) study may be explained by the fact that the neutral stimulus *Snake and I are one* was experienced as more relevant than the simulus *Mommy and I are one*. Thus, there seems to be no support for a psychoanalytic reinterpretation of the effectiveness of systematic desensitization.

Systematic Desensitization as Self-Control. Instead of a passive conditioning conceptualization, Goldfried (1971) argued that systematic desensitzation should be viewed as a self-control procedure, in which clients are taught to exert voluntary control over their feelings of anxiety. Several modifications of the standard systematic-desensitization procedure were recommended by Goldfried: first, relaxation is conceptualized as a coping skill; second, different fears are placed within a single multidimensional hierarchy; third, the clients are instructed to stay in the imaginal situation, when anxiety occurs, and to cope with anxiety by relaxing it away; and finally, the clients have to apply relaxation skills in real-life anxiety-provoking situations.

Since self-control desensitization focuses on applying relaxation coping skills whenever proprioceptive cues of anxiety or tension are perceived, the effects of this procedure should transfer across anxiety-arousing situations. As far as targeted anxieties are concerned, self-control desensitization has been found to be as effective as traditional desensitization (Deffenbacher & Parks, 1979; Spiegler, Cooley, Marshall, Prince, Puckett, & Skenazy, 1976; Zemore, 1975) or more effective (Denney & Rupert, 1977). The studies that have compared traditional and self-control desensitization on generalization measures have provided conflicting results. Several studies (Deffenbacher & Parks, 1979; Zemore, 1975) did find a transfer of treatment effects across anxiety-arousing situations, whereas others did not (Denney & Rupert, 1977; Spiegler *et al.*, 1976). More importantly, however, in neither study was self-control desensitization found to be superior to standard desensitization with respect to nontargeted anxiety reduction.

Goldfried and Goldfried (1977) compared two self-control desensitization procedures with speech-anxious subjects: one with a hierarchy relevant to speech anxiety and the second involving a hierarchy totally unrelated to public-speaking situations. No differential effectiveness was found between the two self-control desensitization conditions, an outcome that suggests that the learning of an active coping skill is an important factor in self-control desensitization.

Several other self-management procedures have been developed in which clients are trained in relaxation as a coping skill: clients are trained to recognize the physiological cues of tension and to apply relaxation whenever tension is perceived (e.g., applied relaxation, Deffenbacher, 1976, and anxiety management, Suinn & Richardson, 1971; Suinn, 1976). In contrast to self-control desensitization, no hierarchy of anxiety-arousing situations is used. In anxiety management training, the client imagines a single highly anxiety-arousing situation and actively attempts to relax away anxiety feelings. In applied relaxation, clients have to apply relaxation to stressful and anxiety-provoking situations in real life.

Several studies indicate that relaxation presented as a coping skill is more effective than standard relaxation exercises (Chang-Liang & Denney, 1976; Goldfried & Trier, 1974). Other studies have found relaxation to be as effective as desensitization, provided that both are presented as self-management procedures (Deffenbacher, Mathis, & Michaels, 1979; Deffenbacher & Payne, 1977; Snyder & Deffenbacher, 1977). Finally, Deffenbacher and Shelton (1978) found anxiety management to be more effective than standard systematic desensitization, at least at follow-up. However, the positive results of self-management relaxation procedures may be attributed to expectancy factors. McGlynn, Kinjo, and Doherty (1978) compared cue-controlled relaxation with an equally credible placebo treatment and could not find any difference in effectiveness.

Imaginal versus in vivo Exposure. Wolpe's (1963) statement that "there is almost invariably a one to one relationship between what the patient can imagine without anxiety and what he can experience in reality without anxiety" (p. 1063) receives little support. A transfer gap between what a client can imagine without feeling anxiety and what the client can deal with *in vivo* without feeling tension has been reported a number of times (e.g., Agras, 1967; Barlow, Leitenberg, Agras, & Wincze, 1969; Hain, Butcher, & Stevenson, 1966; Meyer & Crisp, 1966; Sherman, 1972). Clients who had been successfully desensitized in imagination nevertheless proved to react with anxiety when they were confronted with the phobic stimuli *in vivo*.

Several studies have directly compared systematic desensitization in imagination and *in vivo*. The results indicated that *in vivo* exposure is far more effective (Dyckman & Cowan, 1978; Barlow *et al.*, 1969; Litvak, 1969; Sherman, 1972). It is noteworthy that much effort has gone into studying imaginal desensitization; few studies have been conducted with respect to systematic desensitization in real life. Presumably, the consensual notion that imaginal desensitization is equivalent to *in vivo* desensitization originated in the conceptualization of desensitization in conditioning terms and has been reinforced for years by the lack of tests with real clinical patients.

Flooding. Flooding therapies are derived from the work of Stampfl (Stampfl & Levis, 1967, 1968) on implosive therapy. The implosive procedure used by Stampfl and his associates has been claimed to be based on the principle of extinction. During treatment, the therapist presents a *complex* of conditioned stimuli to the patient without primary reinforcement and without allowing an avoidance response. The therapist tries to maximize anxiety throughout the treatment, which eventually leads to "extinction." Sessions are continued until a significant reduction in anxiety is achieved. It is essential to the implosive approach not only that the "symptom-contingent" cues are presented, but also that the patient is exposed to the aversive stimuli assumed to be underlying the patient's problems ("hypothesized-sequential cues"). Hypothesized cues are defined as "those which are not directly correlated with symptom onset but which represent 'guesses' as to the remaining

components of the avoided CS complex"
(Levis & Hare, 1977, p. 321). These hypothesized cues may concern such dynamic themes
as aggression, guilt, punishment, rejection,
loss of control, and oral, anal or sexual material. For a detailed excursion into implosive
theory, the reader is referred to Levis and
Hare (1977).

Apart from the psychodynamic cues, the implosive therapy for phobias has got wide attention from behavior therapists. So far, only
one study has compared implosive therapy
with psychodynamic cues and implosive therapy without such cues (Prochaska, 1971). Both
procedures were found to be about equally
effective. Almost all controlled studies (both
with analogue and with clinical populations)
have conducted implosive therapy without
such psychodynamic cues. Since the therapeutic procedures used differ considerably
from the implosive therapy as originally developed by Stampfl, the term *flooding* will be
used throughout this chapter.

Duration of Exposure. One of the most important variables in determining the effectiveness of flooding seems to be the duration of
exposure to the stimulus variable within each
session. Too early termination of flooding sessions may lead to an exacerbation instead of
a reduction of fear. In fact, the patient is then
allowed to escape the fearful situation (either
in imagination or *in vivo*), and the escape may
lead to an immediate anxiety reduction (negative reinforcement). It is noteworthy that in
most studies with clinical patients, much longer
exposure duration has been used than has typically been carried out in analogue research.
In the analogue studies, flooding sessions last
from 20 to 60 min. In contrast, however, in
clinical studies where flooding has been found
to be effective, it lasts up to several hours.

The process of anxiety reduction during
flooding-in-imagination sessions has been examined in several studies. Only a few clinical
studies have assessed physiological changes
continuously during flooding sessions. In an
uncontrolled study (Watson, Gaind, & Marks,
1972) (10 patients with specific phobias), heart
rate tended to return to resting levels in time.
However, considerable variation was observed between patients. Most patients showed

their greatest anxiety early in the sessions,
others showed the greatest anxiety only to
particular themes, and a few patients showed
no significant change in heart rate during
flooding in imagination. In the Stern and
Marks (1973) study, there was little tachycardia or skin conductance activity throughout
flooding in imagination. It should be noted that
in both the Watson *et al.* (1972) and the Stern
and Marks (1973) study, patients listened to
tape-recorded flooding themes. Clinical studies are lacking that have assessed arousal during flooding in imagination conducted by a live
therapist.

Foa and Chambless (1978) assessed *subjective* anxiety throughout flooding in imagination
with agoraphobic and obsessive-compulsive
patients. Patients were instructed to imagine
the scenes described by the therapist as vividly
as possible. Flooding sessions lasted 90 min.
Patients had to indicate their anxiety every 10
min on a scale of 0–100. Figure 1 shows the
mean SUDS of the agoraphobics during second and last (eight) treatment sessions. The
results of this study showed that habituation
of subjective anxiety occurs within sessions.
Most often, it follows a curvilinear pattern. In
addition, evidence was provided for habituation across sessions. It is interesting to see that
in the Foa and Chambless study, subjective
anxiety started to decline only after 50 min,
whereas in most analogue studies, the duration
of exposure during flooding is often much
shorter.

One clinical study (Stern & Marks, 1973)
compared short (20-min) and long (80-min)
fantasy sessions. No significant differences
were found. However, as already noted, the
treatment was given with a tape recorder and
did not lead to significant changes in arousal.

Let us now turn our attention to analogue
studies. In a study with spider phobics, Mathews and Shaw (1973) found habituation
within sessions on both heart rate and skin
conductance measures but not on subjective
anxiety. However, the subjects had to listen
to tape-recorded material, and the exposure
duration was only 48 min. Moreover, the experimenters may have provided the possibility
of escape to their subjects, since their subjects
had to open their eyes and then rate their anx

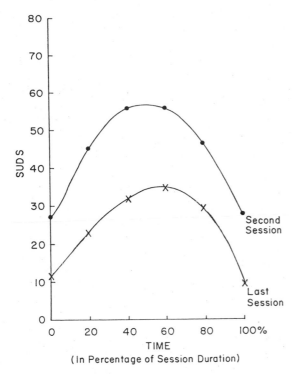

Figure 1. Mean SUDS during second and last treatment sessions with agoraphobics ($N = 6$). (From "Habituation of Subjective Anxiety during Flooding in Imagery" by E. B. Foa and D. L. Chambless, *Behavior Research and Therapy*, 1978, *16*, 391–399, Fig. 3. Copyright 1978 by Pergamon Press. Reprinted by permission.)

iety every 8 min. The results of the Mc-Cutcheon and Adams (1975) study shed further light on the habituation of physiological arousal during flooding in imagination: A 20-min tape-recorded flooding session (imagery of witnessing a surgical operation) did not lead to habituation. In fact, there appeared to be an increase in arousal as measured by the non-specific fluctuation of the galvanic skin response (GSR). In a second study, flooding lasted 60 min. After an intial increase in arousal, as in their first experiment, arousal finally decreased, thus showing a curvilinear habituation curve. A similar pattern of habituation during flooding was found by Orenstein and Carr (1975), as measured by heart rate.

Let us turn now to habituation during *flooding in vivo*. In the study by Watson *et al.* (1972), heart rate was monitored during pro-longed exposure *in vivo*. In general, the heart rate tended to return to resting levels. Similar results were found by Nunes and Marks (1975).

In the Watson *et al.* (1972) study, flooding in fantasy evoked less tachycardia than exposure *in vivo*. Even after habituation to imaginal stimuli had occurred, the patients responded with much tachycardia when exposed to the phobic stimuli *in vivo*. During the *in vivo* sessions, both habituation within and across sessions was found.

In the study by Stern and Marks (1973), heart rate was monitored during exposure *in vivo* with agoraphobics. They compared short (four half-hour) sessions with long (two-hour) sessions. Prolonged *in vivo* sessions were clearly superior to shorter ones. There was little decrement in heart rate and subjective anxiety during the first hour. During the second hour, improvement was significantly greater. Findings with agoraphobics contradict those of specific phobics. In the latter category, heart rate was found to decrease much earlier (Watson *et al.*, 1972). Finally, in a study by Rabavilas, Boulougouris, and Stefanis (1976) with 12 obsessive-compulsive patients, prolonged exposure *in vivo* (80 min) was found to be superior to short exposure *in vivo* (10 min). In fact, short exposure had a deteriorating effect on the patients' affective state.

To summarize the results of clinical and analogue studies, there is evidence that habituation of physiological arousal and subjective anxiety occurs when the duration of exposure lasts long enough. The duration of exposure and the anxiety reduction as its result are the boundary conditions for treatment to be called *flooding*. Obviously, it is important to continue flooding until anxiety has declined. However, which criterion should be used for the termination of sessions is as yet far from clear: Should anxiety be reduced on psychophysiological, subjective, or behavioral measures, or should anxiety reduction occur across all these systems?

Only one analogue study (Gauthier & Marshall, 1977) has been reported that addresses itself to this question. The investigators compared variants of termination of flooding sessions with snake-phobic volunteers. The treatment consisted of three sessions of imaginal exposure. The criterion for session termination in the "subjective" group was the subject's report of not feeling any anxiety. In the "autonomic group," the criterion was the reduction of the heart rate to the resting rate. In the "behavioral" condition, session termination was determined by agreement between two observers that anxiety had declined. Finally, in the last group, all criteria (i.e., autonomic, subjective, and behavioral) had to be met before the session was terminated. The results of this study revealed that session termination determined by the observers led to the greatest reduction in anxiety as measured behaviorally and by self-reports. The "autonomic" group, in which session termination was determined by heart-rate reduction, did not do much better than the control groups. There was almost no difference between the "subjective" and the "behavioral" groups. The group in which all criteria were used to determine session termination did no better than the controls. The results of this study indicate that behavioral and subjective anxiety reduction may be more important criteria for session termination than heart-rate reduction. Research into this question with clinical patients is lacking.

Horrific Cues. Another continuing debate in the flooding literature concerns the stimulus content during flooding. Some therapists have used actual depictions of the feared situations, whereas others have employed depictions of horrifying scenes, often including adverse consequences to the patient. For example, during flooding, one can have a car-phobic patient imagine that he is driving a car on a busy motorway or have him imagine that he is involved in a terrible car accident. Although Bandura (1969) has suggested the use of the term *flooding* for realistic scenes and the term *implosion* for horrifying scenes with adverse consequences, this distinction is confusing, since the use of horrifying themes is only one detailed aspect of implosion therapy as originally developed by Stampfl. For present purposes, I shall distinguish flooding without adverse consequences and flooding with adverse consequences, even though such a distinction is rather artificial. Even if adverse consequences to the subject are excluded, the content of

flooding scenes may differ considerably. For instance, flooding scenes can contain either coping statements or helplessness statements (Mathews & Rezin, 1977). In some studies (e.g., De Moor, 1970), even reassuring statements have been used with snake-phobic subjects: "You really never looked at a snake. Now, look at it. A long body getting thinner at the ends. One end is the tail, it's a pointed one. The other end is the head, a very little head with two piercing eyes, a little mouth and a very little forked tongue flicking in and out. Look at it. *That's what a snake is all about*" (p. 49). Unfortunately, in most studies, the details of the flooding procedures used are not reported. Therefore, cross-study comparisons are virtually impossible.

Several studies have compared flooding with and without horrifying scenes. The results of a study by Foa, Blau, Prout, and Latimer (1977) with rat-phobic students are equivocal. After four 40-min sessions, flooding with and flooding without horrifying cues were about equally effective with regard to the subject's willingness to approach a live rat, in addition to subjective ratings of anxiety. However, the independent evaluator found that the subjects who had been treated by flooding with horrifying cues improved significantly more with respect to interference of their fear in everyday life as compared with pleasant flooding and no-treatment control subjects.

Marshall, Gauthier, Christie, Currie, and Gordon (1977) also compared flooding without horrific images with flooding with a horrifying content, using spider-phobic volunteers as subjects. The treatment consisted of three 45-min sessions of taped stimulus material. The pleasant flooding condition was found to be more effective.

Finally, the work by Mathews and his colleagues is relevant with respect to this issue. Mathews and Shaw (1973) compared flooding with pleasant scenes and flooding with horrifying scenes using spider-phobic volunteers as subjects. Treatment consisted of one session only. Flooding with pleasant scenes was found to be the most effective.

Stimulus content with flooding in the studies so far reviewed may have been confounded by the degree of helplessness depicted in the scenes. In the studies by Foa *et al.* (1977),

Marshall *et al.* (1977), and Mathews and Shaw (1973), during flooding with horrifying themes subjects were depicted as helpless. For instance, in the scenes used by Mathews and Shaw (1973), the subjects are described as being covered by spider webs and powerless to escape. Mathews and Rezin (1977) compared horrifying with pleasant and coping with no-coping rehearsal in a 2 × 2 factorial design. The subjects were dental-phobic volunteers, who referred themselves for treatment following announcements in a local paper. The treatment in each condition consisted of four sessions of 50-min duration. The scenes were presented by tape. Coping rehearsal had no effect on anxiety. However, pleasant themes led to more anxiety reduction than horrifying themes. Moreover, an interaction effect was found with respect to dental attendance. Coping rehearsal had most effect when combined with horrifying themes; pleasant themes did not reduce avoidance.

To summarize the analogue studies reviewed so far, it may be concluded that the inclusion of horrifying stimuli during flooding in imagination does not enhance effectiveness. Rather, it seems that flooding with pleasant scenes is more effective. In addition, coping statements may increase the effectiveness of flooding, at least when horrifying stimuli are used. However, these conclusions must be qualified in several ways. In the first place, all studies were of the analogue type. Thus, generalization of the results to the population of clinical patients seems unwarranted. Second, Mathews and Rezin (1977), Mathews and Shaw (1973), and Marshall *et al.* (1977) used taped stimulus material. It is quite possible that during taped flooding scenes, cognitive avoidance on the part of the subject is more likely when horrifying cues are presented than when pleasant scenes are offered. If cognitive escape and avoidance occur during flooding, habituation of the anxiety may be prevented; and theoretically, this state may even lead to an exacerbation of the fear. Unfortunately, the studies did not investigate this particular issue.

It seems to me that flooding should always use realistic themes: Patients should be able to imagine themselves in the depicted situations. The point at issue here is that for some patients horrifying cues may be quite realistic, whereas for others these cues may be quite unrealistic and therefore can be easily avoided by internal statements like "That isn't real; that will not happen to me." If we agree that flooding themes should be realistic in order to prevent cognitive avoidance, it follows that flooding treatment should be tailor-made. Let me illustrate my point with a clinical example. In our flooding treatment with agoraphobic patients, we have included such "horrifying scenes" as feeling dizzy, getting a panic attack, and fainting; people looking at the patient and making comments about him/her while he/she is lying down; and being taken to a mental hospital. However, only those horrifying cues were used of which the patient was really afraid. For example, patients who feared going insane were flooded on this theme, whereas flooding for patients who feared being observed in public consisted of such scenes. Thus, even within a relatively homogeneous population of phobic patients, the situations the patients are really afraid of might differ from patient to patient. Therefore, flooding scenes should be adapted to the individual fears.

Now, let us turn back to the analogue studies. The horrifying themes used seem to have been quite unrealistic for most of the spider-phobic or rat-phobic subjects. For instance, as already mentioned, the spider phobics in the Mathews and Shaw (1973) study had to imagine that they were covered by webs and had no possibility of escape. I wonder how many spider phobics are really afraid of having this happen. In fact, Mathews and Shaw (1973) found no difference between horrifying cues and realistic cues in terms of self-reported anxiety *during* flooding, a finding that seems to emphasize my point.

Before meaningful conclusions can be drawn with respect to the contribution of horrific cues to flooding in imagination, studies are needed in which *realistic* flooding themes with and without horrific cues are compared with each other: The content of these scenes must be based on the patients' fears. In addition, treatment has to be given by a life therapist to prevent any possible cognitive avoidance-behavior on the parts of the subject.

Several studies have investigated the effects of anxiety evocation during exposure *in vivo*.

In the early days of exposure *in vivo*, guidelines for conducting treatments were derived from implosion and flooding theory; it was thought to be essential to maximize anxiety during exposure *in vivo* before extinction or habituation could occur. In the first controlled study that included flooding *in vivo* with phobic patients (Marks *et al.*, 1971), therapists tried to evoke anxiety deliberately during exposure *in vivo*. Hafner and Marks (1976) allocated 12 agoraphobics randomly across high-anxiety and low-anxiety conditions. In the high-anxiety condition, the patients were encouraged to confront their symptoms during exposure *in vivo*; the therapists' reassurance was minimized. Instead, throughout the exposure *in vivo* procedure, the therapist tried to induce anxiety by statements such as "Imagine yourself feeling worse and worse, giddy, sweaty, nauseated, as if you are about to vomit any moment. . . . you fall to the floor half conscious, people gather round you, someone calls for an ambulance" (p. 77). In the low-anxiety condition, the patients were allowed to distract themselves, and they were even encouraged to do relaxation exercises. No anxiety-inducing statements were made by the therapists. The patients in the high-anxiety condition experienced more anxiety and panic attacks than the patients in the low-anxiety condition. However, *no* differences in improvement were found between both conditions; thus, deliberately inducing anxiety during exposure *in vivo* did not enhance improvement.

In an analogue study by Kirsch, Wolpin, and Knutson (1975), speech-anxious college students were treated with several variants of exposure *in vivo*. The results of this study revealed that delivering a speech without anxiety provocation was more effective than when anxiety was deliberately provoked by a "booing" audience. However, the treatment consisted of five sessions of 4 min only; this rather short exposure time precludes drawing any conclusions.

Imaginal Exposure versus In Vivo Exposure. Several clinical studies have been conducted comparing flooding in imagination with flooding *in vivo* (Emmelkamp & Wessels, 1975; Mathews, Johnston, Lancashire, Munby,

Shaw, & Gelder, 1976; Stern & Marks, 1973; Watson, Mullett, & Pillay, 1973). All of these studies involved the treatment of agoraphobics.

Watson *et al.* (1973) compared both treatments in a crossover design. The treatment was conducted in groups. Flooding *in vivo* was found to be more effective than imaginal flooding. However, flooding was applied by means of a tape recorder. Another methodological flaw concerns the differences in treatment time. Patients received six *in vivo* sessions as compared with three fantasy sessions.

In the study by Stern and Marks (1973), flooding *in vivo* was also found to be superior. However, delay or carry-over effects may partly explain the superior results of flooding *in vivo*, since flooding in imagination always preceded flooding *in vivo*. In addition, imaginal treatment was tape-recorded.

Two studies in which (1) imaginal flooding, (2) flooding *in vivo*, and (3) a combined procedure were compared in a between-group design produced conflicting results. In the study by Emmelkamp and Wessels (1975), four sessions of exposure *in vivo* were found to be superior to imaginal exposure; the effects of the combined procedure were between those of the imaginal and *in vivo* conditions. However, after 16 sessions, Mathews *et al.* (1976) found no differences among these three procedures. The following differences between both studies might explain the conflicting results (Emmelkamp, 1977). First of all, the procedures actually used may have been quite different. The procedures of Emmelkamp and Wessels resembled flooding, whereas for the Mathews *et al.* procedures, the term *gradual exposure* seems more appropriate. More important is the mixing of exposure *in vivo* and in imagination in the imaginal condition in the study by Mathews *et al.* Their patients were instructed to practice at home between treatment sessions. Since they treated their patients once a week, there was ample opportunity for the practice at home. In fact, a check of the diaries completed by the patients revealed that on the average, they went out once a day throughout the treatment. In the Emmelkamp and Wessels study, the patients were not instructed to practice between treatment sessions, and since the treatment was conducted three times weekly, there was little room for self-practice between treatment sessions.

Johnston, Lancashire, Mathews, Munby, Shaw, and Gelder (1976) reported the results of measures taken during the treatment in the Mathews *et al.* study. On measures of the immediate effects of treatment, exposure *in vivo* had consistent positive effects, whereas imaginal flooding had little or no effect. These results suggest that the long-term effects after imaginal flooding were indeed due to the exposure *in vivo* between treatment sessions.

In conclusion, flooding *in vivo* has been found to be far more effective than flooding in imagination, when agoraphobics are the subjects. Finally, one study (Rabavilas *et al.*, 1976) compared flooding in imagination and flooding *in vivo* with obsessive-compulsive patients. Here, flooding *in vivo* was also found to be superior to imaginal flooding.

Flooding versus Desensitization. Numerous studies have been carried out comparing systematic desensitization with flooding. However, these studies have yielded equivocal results. Several studies (Boudewyns & Wilson, 1972; Marks *et al.*, 1971; Hussain, 1971; Marshall *et al.*, 1977) found flooding to be more effective; others found systematic desensitization superior to flooding (Hekmat, 1973; Mealiea & Nawas, 1971; Smith & Nye, 1973; Suarez, Adams, & McCutcheon, 1976; Willis & Edwards, 1969). Still others found them to be about equally effective (Barrett, 1969; Borkovec, 1972; Calef & MacLean, 1970; Cornish & Dilley, 1973; Crowe, Marks, Agras, & Leitenberg, 1972; De Moor, 1970; Gelder *et al.,*, 1973; Horne & Matson, 1977; Mylar & Clement, 1972; Shaw, 1976; Solyom *et al.*, 1973). Research in this area is encumbered by the vague theoretical notions and terminological confusion concerning flooding. Therefore, straightforward comparisons across studies are rather difficult.

Table 1 summarizes the main features of the studies that compared systematic desensitization and flooding. It should be noted that apart from the studies by Boudewyns and Wilson (1972), Boulougouris *et al.* (1971), Crowe *et al.* (1972), Gelder *et al.* (1973), Hus-

sain (1971), Shaw (1976), and Solyom *et al.* (1973), all other comparisons have involved analogue populations (most often small-animal phobias).

1. *Clinical studies.* The study by Boudewyns and Wilson (1972) involved a heterogeneous sample of psychiatric patients. The outcome was assessed by means of the Minnesota Multiphasic Personality Inventory (MMPI) and the Mooney Problem Checklist. Although flooding was found to be somewhat more effective than a modified desensitization procedure, the results are difficult to evaluate because of the heterogeneous sample and the unsatisfactory measures.

Two studies of clinical phobics found flooding to be superior to desensitization. Hussain (1971) compared both treatments (in imagination) in a crossover design. Half of the patients received thiopental as the first treatment, and the other half received saline. The thiopental–flooding condition proved to be more effective than the other treatments. However, because of several methodological flaws (all patients treated by the same therapist, inadequate statistical analysis, and no "blind" observer), the conclusions are not definitive. Another study in which flooding was found to be more effective than systematic desensitization on clinical as well as physiological measures of fear was reported by Marks *et al.* (1971). In this study, both treatments involved six sessions of imaginal exposure followed by two sessions of exposure *in vivo*. The superiority of flooding was most pronounced in the agoraphobics.

In the study by Gelder *et al.* (1973), both treatments also were carried out in imagination and *in vivo*. Their treatments involved three information sessions and eight imaginal sessions followed by four *in vivo* sessions. In contrast with the Marks *et al.* (1971) study, no differences were found between flooding and desensitization. As the imaginal part of the treatment used in both studies was similar, differences in outcome are probably due to the differences in exposure *in vivo* that the patients received. First, Gelder *et al.* (1973) made no attempt to differentiate both treatments in the exposure *in vivo* phase, whereas in the Marks *et al.* (1971) study, exposure *in*

Table 1. Flooding versus Systematic Desensitization

Study	Population	Treatment	Sessions (minutes)	Mode of treatment presentation	Results
A. Phobic patients					
Crowe, Marks, Agras, & Leitenberg (1972)	Mixed (n = 14)	Flooding / SD[a] / Reinforced practice (block design)	4 × 50	L[d]	3 > 2[b] (behavioral measure)
Gelder, Bancroft, Gath, Johnston, Mathews, & Shaw (1973)	18 Agoraphobics / 18 Other phobics	Flooding / SD / Nonspecific control	15 × 45 – 60	L	1 = 2[c] / 1 & 2 > 3 (agoraphobics)
Hussain (1971)	Agoraphobics or social phobics (n = 40)	Flooding-thiopental / Flooding saline / SD-thiopental / SD-saline (crossover)	6 × 45	L	1 > 2, 3, & 4
Marks, Boulougouris, & Marset (1971)	9 Agoraphobics / 7 Specific	Flooding / SD (crossover)	8 × 50 – 70	L	1 > 2
Shaw (1976)	Social phobics (n = 30)	Flooding / SD / Social skills	10 × 60 / 10 × 60 / 10 × 75	L	1 = 2 = 3
Solyom, Heseltine, McClure, Solyom, Ledwidge, & Steinberg (1973)	39 Agoraphobics and social phobics / 11 Other phobics	Flooding / SD / Aversion relief / Phenelzine / Placebo	12 × 60 / 12 × 60 / 24 × 30 / 6 × 60 / 6 × 60	L	1 > 2 (FSS only) / 3 > 1, 2, 4, & 5 (psychiatric rating) / 4 > 5 (psychiatric rating)
B. Analogue studies					
Barrett (1969)	Snake phobia	Flooding / SD / No treatment	± 2 / ± 12	L	1 = 2 / 1 & 2 > 3 / 1 more efficient
Borkovec (1972)	Snake phobia	Flooding / SD / Placebo / No treatment	4 × 50	L	1 = 2

Study	Type	Treatments	Sessions		Results
Calef & MacLean (1970)	Speech anxiety	Flooding SD No treatment	5 × 60	L	1 = 2 1 & 2 > 3
Cornish & Dilley (1973)	Test anxiety	Flooding SD Counseling No treatment	4 × 40	T[e]	1 = 2 1 & 2 > 4
De Moor (1970)	Snake phobia	Flooding SD No treatment	5 × 20	L	1 = 2 1 & 2 > 3
Hekmat (1973)	Rat phobia	Flooding SD Semantic desensitization Pseudodesensitization	2 × 40 5 × 40	L	2 & 3 > 1 4 > 1 (behavioral measure) 2 & 3 > 4
Horne & Matson (1977)	Test anxiety	Flooding SD Modeling Study skills No treatment	10 × 60	L	1, 2 & 3 > 4 & 5 (test anxiety) 3 > 2 > 1 (test anxiety) 2, 3 & 4 > 1 & 5 (grade point average)
Marshall, Gauthier, Christie, Currie, & Gordon (1977)	Snake phobia	Flooding SD Placebo No treatment	3 × 40	L	1 > 2 1 & 2 > 3 & 4 3 = 4
Mealiea & Nawas (1971)	Snake phobia	Flooding Implosive desensitization SD Placebo No treatment	5 × 30	T	3 > all others (behavioral measure) 1 = 5 (behavioral measure) 2 & 4 > 5 (behavioral measure) 1 = 2 = 3 = 4 = 5 (self-report)
Mylar & Clement (1972)	Speech anxiety	Flooding SD No treatment	5 × 60	T	1 = 2 1 & 2 > 3
Smith & Nye (1973)	Test anxiety	Flooding SD No treatment	7 × 45	L	1 = 2 (test anxiety) 2 > 1 (other measures)

(Continued)

Table 1. Flooding versus Systematic Desensitization (*Continued*)

Study	Population	Treatment	Sessions (minutes)	Mode of treatment presentation	Results
Suarez, Adams, & McCutcheon (1976)	Surgical operation	Flooding SD No treatment	3 × 30	?	1 = 2 (behavioral measure) 2 > 1 (self-report)
Willis & Edwards (1969)	Mouse phobia	Flooding SD Placebo	± 4 × ?	L	2 > 1 & 3 1 = 3

[a] SD = systematic desensitization.
[b] a > b = Treatment a superior to treatment b.
[c] a = b = Treatment a about as effective as Treatment b.
[d] L = treatment presented by live therapist.
[e] T = treatment presented by tape.

vivo was relaxed during desensitization and forceful during flooding (Marks, 1975). Second, the different results might be explained by different amounts of self-exposure *in vivo* between treatment sessions. Since Marks *et al.* treated patients three times a week rather than once a week (as in the Gelder *et al.* study), there was in the former study less time between sessions for an effect to develop from self-exposure *in vivo*. That self-exposure *in vivo* may have beneficial effects on its own was recently demonstrated by McDonald, Sartory, Grey, Cobb, Stern, and Marks (1979).

In the studies by Crowe *et al.* (1972), Shaw (1976), and Solyom *et al.* (1973), systematic desensitization and flooding were carried out in imagination. Both procedures were found to be about equally effective.

To summarize the studies of phobic patients, it can be concluded that desensitization in imagination and flooding in imagination are about equally effective. Moreover, the way in which exposure *in vivo* is carried out might be crucial.

2. *Analogue studies.* In most studies that found systematic desensitization (SD) to be superior to flooding, the flooding was not correctly carried out. First, in the studies by Horne and Matson (1977), Hekmat (1973), Mealica and Nawas, (1971), and Willis and Edwards (1969), a hierarchy was used. If we assume that one essential characteristic of flooding is anxiety evocation, the use of a hierarchy seems not to be the optimal procedure to achieve this. Second, often insufficient time was provided for anxiety to dissipate. For instance, flooding in the study by Hekmat (1973) consisted of one session only in which five different scenes had to be visualized in 40 min. In the study by Mealiea and Nawas (1971), each flooding session lasted only 30 min, which is much too short a time for anxiety reduction to occur in most subjects. In fact, anxiety reduction within sessions was prevented in several subjects in the study by Willis and Edwards (1969), since they stated, "treatment may have been terminated somewhat prematurely because it was felt that the S. had reached the upper level of her tolerance" (p. 393). Finally, Mealiea and Nawas (1971) used taped flooding material.

Since procedural descriptions in the Suarez *et al.* (1976) study are lacking, the results are difficult to evaluate. To date, only one study, in which flooding was carried out within the boundary conditions, shows SD on some measures to be more effective than flooding (Smith & Nye, 1973). Smith and Nye compared SD, flooding, and a no-treatment control with test-anxious subjects. The treatment consisted of seven 45-min sessions. During flooding, the subjects were exposed (five-sessions) to anxiety-inducing stimuli until they exhibited behavioral evidence of reduced anxiety. Both treatments led to significant improvements on the Test Anxiety Scale. However, on the A-state questionnaire and increase in grade-point averages, SD was found to be superior. It should be noted that the flooding group had a higher pretreatment mean grade-point average than the SD subjects. A ceiling effect might be responsible for their lack of change, as Smith and Nye (1973) have pointed out.

The studies that found both procedures to be about equally effective are also marred by several procedural and methodological flaws. Cornish and Dilley (1973) and Mylar and Clement (1972) used taped stimulus material, which might have led to cognitive avoidance on the part of the subjects. In addition, Borkovec (1972), Calef and MacLean (1970), and Mylar and Clement (1972) used a graded approach (hierarchy) during flooding. In the Borkovec (1972) study, each scene was presented only twice, and in the Calef and MacLean (1970) study, the treatment was conducted in groups. Thus, the progress with new material during flooding was not determined by anxiety reduction but predetermined by the experimenter. Finally, in the study by De Moor (1970), flooding sessions lasted only 20 min. Since the boundary conditions of flooding were not met, definitive conclusions from these studies seem unwarranted.

In the study by Barrett (1969), flooding was carried out according to the rules: scenes were presented until they ceased to elicit anxiety. Although flooding was found to be about as effective as SD, the treatment time with SD subjects was much longer. Therefore, Barrett concluded that flooding was more efficient. However, both treatments were conducted by the same therapist, a condition that might have confounded results.

Finally, one analogue study (Marshall *et al.*, 1977) found flooding to be more effective than SD with snake-phobic subjects. Both treatments were carried out with tapes. The subjects had to imagine the most intense scene of the fear hierarchy (picking up the snake); these instructions were accompanied by slides showing snakes. Immediately after each session, the subjects had to participate in a behavioral avoidance test, which required them to approach the snake. Thus, the treatment consisted of a combination of imaginal rehearsal and *in vivo* exposure. Flooding produced greater behavioral changes than desensitization.

In summary, any conclusions are premature. There is no evidence that SD is superior to flooding or vice versa. The methodological and procedural flaws are so grave and the procedures used are so far removed from clinical practice that most of the efforts that have gone into this enterprise seem to have been a waste of time.

Successive Approximation and Self-Controlled Exposure. While in systematic desensitization it is assumed that anxiety must first be inhibited before avoidance behavior can be reduced, in successive approximation the avoidance behavior is changed directly, a process that may eventually lead to a decrease in anxiety (Leitenberg, Agras, Butz, & Wincze, 1971). Working within an operant-conditioning paradigm, Leitenberg and his colleagues demonstrated that graded exposure *in vivo* in an anxiety-arousing situation, plus contingent reinforcement by means of verbal praise for approach behavior, was successful in the treatment of a variety of clinical phobic cases (Agras, Leitenberg, & Barlow, 1968; Agras, Leitenberg, Barlow, & Thomson, 1969; Agras, Leitenberg, Wincze, Butz, & Callahan, 1970) and in the treatment of such common fears as fear of heights, fear of snakes, fear of painful electric shock, and (in young children) fear of darkness (Leitenberg & Callahan, 1973). This treatment procedure has been called *successive approximation, reinforced practice,* or *shaping.*

Several studies have compared successive approximation with other behavioral treatments. Successive approximation proved to be more effective than systematic desensitization

in imagination with phobic volunteers (Barlow, Agras, Leitenberg, & Wincze, 1970; McReynolds & Grizzard, 1971) and with phobic patients (Crowe *et al.*, 1972). Successive approximation and flooding were found to be about equally effective with phobic patients, including agoraphobics (Crowe *et al.*, 1972; Everaerd, Rijken, & Emmelkamp, 1973).

Reinforcement versus Feedback. In successive approximation, reinforcement and feedback have been confounded, since patients are given both social reinforcement and contingent feedback for time spent in the phobic situation. In order to investigate the relative contribution of feedback and reinforcement, Emmelkamp and Ultee (1974) compared successive approximation and self-observation using agoraphobics as subjects. With both procedures, the patient had to walk a course leading in a straight line from the patient's home, with instructions to turn back on experiencing undue anxiety. With successive approximation, the patient was informed by the therapist about the time he/she had stayed away after each trial; in addition, the patient was reinforced whenever there was an increase in the time spent outside. The differences between successive approximation and self-observation are that during the latter procedure, the patient observes his/her progress by recording the time he/she is able to spend outside (feedback) and that he/she is never reinforced by the therapist. The patient had to record the duration of each trial in a notebook. No difference in effect was found between successive approximation and self-observation: Thus, verbal praise contingent on achievement did not enhance the effects of graduated exposure plus feedback. The effectiveness of graduated exposure plus feedback has further been demonstrated in analogue (Becker & Costello, 1975) and clinical studies (Emmelkamp, 1974, 1980; Emmelkamp & Emmelkamp-Benner, 1975; Emmelkamp & Wessels, 1975; Leitenberg, Agras, Allen, Butz, & Edwards, 1975).

Whether feedback enhanced the effectiveness of graduated exposure was studied by Rutner (1973) in an analogue study involving rat-fearful female volunteers as subjects. The treatment consisted of self-controlled exposure to a live rat. Each subject was instructed to look into a box containing a rat and to keep viewing the rat for as long as she could before releasing a handle that terminated the trial. *In toto*, 35 experimental trials were conducted. Four experimental conditions were created: (1) exposure only; (2) exposure plus self-monitored feedback; (3) exposure plus therapeutically oriented instruction; and (4) exposure plus therapeutically oriented instruction with feedback. The results indicated that feedback enhanced the effectiveness of self-controlled exposure, while no significant effects were found for either the therapeutically oriented instruction or the interaction factor. Thus, the results of this study showed the importance of precise trial-by-trial feedback in self-controlled exposure *in vivo*.

Self-Control of Exposure Time. With both successive approximation and self-observation procedures, the exposure time is controlled by the patient. Whether such self-control enhances the effects of graduated exposure *in vivo* was studied by Hepner and Cauthen (1975), using snake-phobic volunteers as subjects. Graduated exposure under subject control with feedback was compared with graduated exposure under therapist control with feedback. Self-control of exposure time proved to be superior to therapist control in reducing avoidance behavior. Presumably, the cognitive process of enhancement of the self-attribution of personal competence is associated with self-controlled exposure *in vivo*.

In summary, self-controlled exposure *in vivo* has been found to be quite effective in clinical trials. There is little evidence that reinforcement enhances the effectiveness of this procedure. The results of analogue studies indicate that both feedback and self-control of exposure time are important factors that both enhance the effectiveness of graduated exposure *in vivo*.

Covert Reinforcement. The procedure of covert positive reinforcement, originally developed by Cautela (1970), has been applied to phobic cases. The procedure involves a positive stimulus presented in imagination after the subject imagines approach behavior in a phobic situation. The procedure is conceptualized in operant terms. Apart from a few clinical case studies, all controlled studies concern analogue populations.

Several studies found covert positive rein-

forcement more effective than no treatment control groups (Bajtelsmit & Gershman, 1976; Finger & Galassi, 1977; Guidry & Randolph, 1974; Hurley, 1976; Kostka & Galassi, 1974; Ladouceur, 1974, 1977, 1978; Marshall, Boutilier, & Minnes, 1974) and attention–placebo groups (Flannery, 1972; Guidry & Randolph, 1974; Ladouceur, 1977, 1978; Marshall *et al.*, 1974). However, in the Bajtelsmit and Gershman (1976) study, covert positive reinforcement was found to be no more effective than placebo. Comparative evaluations of covert positive reinforcement and systematic desensitization have found both procedures to be about equally effective (Kostka & Galassi, 1974; Ladouceur, 1978; Marshall *et al.*, 1974).

The theoretical rationale of the procedure has been seriously questioned. The results of several studies indicate that covert reinforcement is not a crucial element of this procedure, since omitting the reinforcer or noncontiguous presentation of the reinforcer led to similar outcome (Bajtelsmit & Gershman, 1976; Hurley, 1976; Ladouceur, 1974, 1977, 1978; Marshall *et al.*, 1974). The results of these studies cast doubt on the operant model underlying this procedure. The rationale of covert positive reinforcement was most seriously challenged by the findings of Bajtelsmit and Gershman (1976): Covert reinforcement following anxious behavior was as effective as when it followed the desired behavior. According to the operant model, reinforcement of anxiety should have led to an increase instead of a reduction of anxiety.

The most parsimonious explanation for the effects of covert positive reinforcement appears to be exposure to the phobic stimuli. Only one study (Flannery, 1972) tested the relative effectiveness of covert reinforcement presented either after imaginal or after *in vivo* exposure; *in vivo* exposure was found to be the most effective. Controlled clinical studies using this technique are lacking.

Cognitive Therapy. Behavior therapy is "going cognitive," as demonstrated by the vast increase of articles dealing with cognitive behavior modification in the behavioral journals (Ledwidge, 1978). Most of the cognitive-behavior-modification studies have involved phobic or anxiety-related problems. Now, at least 30 controlled studies in this area have been reported, but we are still far from a definitive evaluation of the usefulness of the cognitive approach for anxiety-related problems. First, almost all the controlled studies involved analogue populations, most often students, who were treated for relatively mild problems. Second, the category of cognitive behavior modification contains such diverse treatment procedures as rational emotive therapy, systematic rational restructuring, self-instructional training, stress inoculation, attentional training, and stimulus reappraisal. The evaluation of these various procedures and cross-study comparisons is often complicated by inadequate reports of the treatment procedures actually used. Third, almost two-thirds of these studies deal with social evaluative anxiety or unassertiveness. It is interesting to note that only two studies deal with snake phobias (Meichenbaum, 1971; Odom, Nelson, & Wein, 1978). The interested reader may take a look at Table 1, which summarizes the studies comparing systematic desensitization and flooding, and may be surprised by the fact that seven studies involve small-animal phobias, while only two studies involve social anxiety. The preponderance of social evaluative anxiety as a target behavior in the cognitive modification studies might indicate that cognitive procedures are more useful with this type of anxiety than with small-animal phobias.

The cognitive-behavior-modification procedures can be divided roughly into two categories: (1) procedures that focus on insight into irrational beliefs and on challenging these beliefs, for example, rational emotive therapy (Ellis, 1962) and systematic rational restructuring (Goldfried, Decenteceo, & Weinberg, 1974); and (2) procedures that focus on the modification of the client's internal dialogue, for example, self-instructional training (Meichenbaum, 1975). In the latter procedure, productive or coping self-statements are rehearsed. It should be noted, however, that in self-instructional training, "insight" into negative or unproductive self-statements is often an integral part of the treatment procedure. Research on social evaluative anxiety, test anxiety, and specific phobias as target behaviors are discussed here separately.

Social Evaluative Anxiety. In this section, studies are discussed that deal with speech anxiety, communication apprehension, interpersonal anxiety, dating anxiety, and unassertiveness. Even though there are some technical differences in both procedures, for present purposes no differentiation will be made between rational emotive therapy and systematic rational restructuring, since both procedures appear to be very similar.

Several studies have compared rational emotive therapy with *systematic desensitization* and have provided conflicting results. In the study by Di Loreto (1971), systematic desensitization was found to be more effective than rational emotive therapy. In contrast with the results of this study, rational emotive therapy proved to be more effective than self-control desensitization in the study by Kanter and Goldfried (1979). Further, it was found that a combined treatment approach (rational emotive therapy plus self-control desensitization) was more effective than self-control desensitization, but *less* effective than rational restructuring alone.

Both Meichenbaum (1971) and Thorpe (1975) found self-instructional training to be superior to systematic desensitization with unassertive subjects. Weissberg (1977) compared (1) desensitization; (2) desensitization with coping imagery; and (3) self-instructional training plus desensitization. No consistent differences among the three treatments were found.

Cognitive therapy has been compared with other treatment approaches, too. Although Di Loreto (1971) found no significant differences between rational therapy and client-centered therapy, an interesting interaction effect was found: Rational emotive therapy was more effective with introvert clients, while client-centered therapy was more effective with extravert clients.

Karst and Trexler (1970) compared (1) rational emotive therapy, (2) *fixed-role therapy* (Kelly, 1955), and (3) a no-treatment control. Both therapies were superior to no treatment; fixed-role therapy proved to be more effective than rational therapy on some measures.

Several studies have investigated the issue of whether unassertiveness should be considered the result of social skills deficits or the result of unproductive self-statements or ir-rational beliefs. Some studies involving a comparison of social skills training and cognitive modification found no significant differences between the two procedures (Alden, Safran, & Weideman, 1978; Fremouw & Zitter 1978; Thorpe, 1975). One study (Linehan, Goldfried, & Powers-Goldfried, 1979) found social skills training to be more effective than a cognitive modification procedure. Finally, Glass, Gottman, and Shmurak (1976) found cognitive restructuring more effective than skills training with respect to transfer of training to nontraining situations. However, the results indicated that skills training was the most effective treatment for the training situations and the total situations on a role-play test.

Several studies found a combined cognitive–social skills treatment to be no more effective than either social skills treatment alone (Carmody, 1978; Glass et al., 1976) or cognitive therapy alone (Glass et al., 1976). In contrast to these studies, the results of other studies indicate that a combined cognitive–social skills approach might be superior. For instance, using as subjects unassertive women in an outpatient clinical setting, Wolfe and Fodor (1977) compared (1) social skills training; (2) social skills training plus rational therapy; (3) a consciousness-raising group; and (4) a waiting-list control group. Both skills training and the combined procedure were superior to the consciousness-raising group and the waiting-list control group on the behavioral measure. Only the patients who had received rational therapy showed anxiety reduction. Derry and Stone (1979) also found a combined procedure to be more effective than social skills training alone. However, the treatment in both the Wolfe and Fodor (1977) and Derry and Stone (1979) study involved two sessions only, so that only limited conclusions can be drawn.

In a well-executed study, Linehan et al. (1979) compared (1) social skills training; (2) rational therapy; (3) a combined approach, and (4) pseudotherapy and a waiting list. The results of this study indicated that the combined cognitive–social skills treatment was superior to all other conditions.

In summary, studies comparing the effect of cognitive restructuring and skills training have produced conflicting results. However, several studies indicate that cognitive modification might enhance the effectiveness of social skills training.

Test Anxiety. The effectiveness of various cognitive-restructuring procedures has been investigated with test-anxious subjects. Cognitive restructuring has been found to be superior to systematic desensitization (Holroyd, 1976; Meichenbaum, 1972) and to prolonged exposure in imagination (Goldfried, Linehan, & Smith, 1978). In Holroyd's (1976) study, the effects of a combined procedure (cognitive restructuring plus desensitization) were not found to be consistently different from desensitization and a pseudotherapy.

According to Liebert and Morris (1967), a distinction should be made between the cognitive ("worry") and the emotional (affective and physiological responses) components of test anxiety. Little and Jackson (1974) investigated whether a treatment approach aimed at both the cognitive and the emotional component of test anxiety was more effective than treatments that focused on one component only. Therefore, they compared the following conditions: (1) attention training (cognitive component); (2) relaxation training (emotional component); (3) attention training plus relaxation; (4) placebo; and (5) no treatment as a control. The results indicated that the combined procedure was more effective than relaxation and attentional training by themselves.

More recently, Finger and Galassi (1977) also compared (1) attentional training; (2) relaxation; (3) attentional training plus relaxation; and (4) no treatment. While all the treatments resulted in beneficial effects, the treatments did not differentially affect the cognitive component and the emotional component of test anxiety. The findings obtained with the two major self-report measures, "emotionality" and "worry," indicated that improvement resulted from each treatment, regardless of whether the treatment focused on the cognitive or the emotional component.

There is some evidence that focusing on the emotional component only, as is typically done in systematic desensitization and relaxation training, is not appropriate in the case of test anxiety. The results of laboratory studies (Hollandsworth, Glazeski, Kirkland, Jones, & Van Norman, 1979; Holroyd, Westbrook, Wolf, & Bradhorn, 1978) indicate that low and high test-anxious subjects exhibit almost similar arousal levels during testing. Although the level of arousal during test taking does not adequately discriminate effective and ineffective test-takers, the use of negative self-verbalizations may do so. Hollandsworth *et al.* (1979) found that low-anxious subjects labeled their arousal as facilitative, while high-anxious subjects viewed their arousal as debilitative. Hollandsworth *et al.* (1979) suggested that it may be more productive to train test-anxious subjects to relabel arousal as facilitative, rather than attempting to reduce it by means of relaxation.

Specific Phobias. Two studies have been conducted using snake-phobic volunteers as subjects. Meichenbaum (1971) compared variants of videotaped modeling: (1) mastery model; (2) mastery model plus self-statements; (3) coping model; and (4) coping model plus self-statements. A coping model was found to be more effective than a mastery model. Self-statements did not enhance the effectiveness of the mastery model. With the coping models, the addition of self-statements yielded more positive results on the difficult tasks of the behavioral avoidance test only.

Odom *et al.* (1978) compared (1) exposure *in vivo* (guided participation); (2) systematic desensitization; (3) cognitive restructuring; (4) verbal extinction; (5) placebo; and (6) no treatment. On the behavioral measure and fear thermometer, exposure *in vivo* was found to be superior to all other conditions. Cognitive restructuring was found to be more effective on the psychophysiological modality (heart rate) only.

Cognitive restructuring was found to be as effective as prolonged exposure in imagination in a study by D'Zurilla, Wilson, and Nelson (1973) involving volunteers who were afraid of dead rats. The results of this study further indicated that systematic desensitization was no more effective than no treatment as a control.

Finally, a study by Girodo and Roehl (1978) should be mentioned. Using volunteers with a fear of flying, they compared (1) information giving; (2) self-instructional training; and (3) a combined procedure. The anxiety ratings that were obtained during a normal flight indicated that self-instructional training was no more effective than prior information-giving.

Rational Therapy versus Self-Instructional Training. As already noted, cognitive restructuring procedures differ in their emphasis on insight into irrational beliefs and the training of incompatible positive self-statements. Several studies have been conducted to investigate which component of cognitive restructuring is the most productive. In a study of speech-anxious teenagers, Thorpe, Amatu, Blakey, and Burns (1976) compared (1) general insight (discussion of Ellis's irrational beliefs; (2) specific insight (discussion of irrational ideas relevant to public speaking); (3) self-instructional training; and (4) a combination of specific insight and self-instructional training. The results indicated that insight (general and specific) contributes more to cognitive restructuring than self-instructional training or a combination of insight and self-instructional training. However, the reverse was found by Glogower, Fremouw, and McKroskey (1978). Here, self-instructional training was found to be superior to specific insight into negative self-statements. In addition, it was found that a procedure that combined specific insight and self-instructional training was consistently more effective than any single procedure, although this difference did not reach significance. Finally, Carmody (1978) compared the effectiveness of two variants of assertion training. The results of this study indicated that assertiveness training plus rational therapy along the lines of Ellis was as effective as assertiveness training plus self-instructional training.

In summary, studies comparing various components (i.e., insight vs. self-instructional training) have produced conflicting results. A related issue is whether during self-instructional training coping statements of a specific nature are more productive than more generalized coping statements. The relative contribution of specific coping statements and generalized coping statements was investigated by Hussian and Lawrence (1978), who used test-anxious volunteers as subjects. Generalized coping statements included statements such as

"When fear comes, just pause." Specific coping statements referred to test taking and preparation, such as "I know I'm well prepared for this test, so just relax"; or "The test is a challenge, nothing to get worked up over." The results of this study indicated that the test-specific statements were more productive than the generalized coping statements.

Sutton-Simon and Goldfried (1979) investigated the differential involvement of two forms of faulty thinking (irrational thinking and negative self-statements) in two types of anxiety (social anxiety and fear of heights). In contrast to social anxiety, which was significantly correlated with only irrational thinking, acrophobia was correlated with both irrational thinking and negative self-statements. The results of this study suggest that it might be more productive to match cognitive treatment procedures with types of faulty thinking rather than treating all anxiety-related problems with an identical cognitive treatment package.

Concluding Remarks. Almost all studies in the cognitive area have involved analogue populations. It is remarkable that the journal *Cognitive Therapy and Research,* which is devoted entirely to the cognitive approach, has not yet published one study involving real clinical phobic patients. So far, only a few studies have involved real clinical patients, and the picture that arises on the basis of these studies is far less optimistic with respect to the cognitive approach. Only one study (Wolfe & Fodor, 1977) in the area of social evaluative anxiety involved real patients, but the external validity of this study is presumably small. Patients were selected who had a score not more than one and-one-half standard deviations above or below the mean of the Rathus Assertiveness Schedule. The use of this criterion might have excluded patients with social anxiety and unassertiveness as the major problem. Other studies with clinical patients, involving agoraphobics (Emmelkamp, Kuipers, & Eggeraat, 1978; Emmelkamp & Mersch, 1982) and obsessive-compulsives (Emmelkamp *et al.,* 1980), have produced inconclusive results.

Although cognitive modification procedures have yielded beneficial effects, it is far from clear whether the effects can be attributed to a modification of cognitive processes. Only a few studies found a change in irrational beliefs after cognitive restructuring. In addition, it is questionable if these changes in cognitions are specific for the cognitive procedures. For instance, Alden *et al.* (1978) found an even greater reduction of irrational beliefs after assertion training than after cognitive restructuring.

Biofeedback. Biofeedback procedures are often applied in the treatment of anxiety or phobic states. In this section, an overview is given of the research that has been conducted in this area. Most of the research has concerned electromyographic feedback and heart-rate feedback.

Electromyographic Feedback. A number of researchers have investigated whether electromyographic (EMG) biofeedback results in a reduction of anxiety symptoms. Studies involving normal volunteers as subjects have produced equivocal results. Several studies (Coursey, 1975; Haynes, Moseley, & McGowan, 1975; Reinking & Kohl, 1975) found EMG feedback superior to relaxation instructions as far as changes in EMG level were concerned; no differences were found on other measures. However, other studies found EMG feedback no more effective (Schandler & Grings, 1976) or even less effective than relaxation procedures (Beiman *et al.,* 1978).

Several controlled studies have been conducted with anxious patients as subjects. Both Canter, Kondo, and Knott (1975) and Townsend, House, and Addario (1975) found EMG feedback superior to control conditions, when EMG was taken as the primary dependent variable. As far as anxiety symptoms were concerned, *no* significant differences were reported between EMG and relaxation (Canter *et al.,* 1975) and between EMG and group psychotherapy (Townsend *et al.,* 1975). Finally, it is noteworthy that Jessup and Neufeld (1977) could not demonstrate a significant change on the EMG measure in a study involving psychiatric patients. Perhaps even more significantly, noncontingent tone presentation (control condition) led to significant changes in heart rate and anxiety measures, while EMG feedback (contingent tone) did not.

Counts, Hollandsworth, and Alcorn (1978) sought to determine whether biofeedback could enhance the effectiveness of cue-controlled relaxation in the treatment of test anxiety. The results of this study indicated that biofeedback did not contribute to the effectiveness of cue-controlled relaxation.

In summary, there is no evidence that EMG feedback has something to offer that other treatments (e.g., relaxation) do not. The few differences that have been found in favor of EMG feedback all concerned EMG level as the dependent variable. Although it has generally been assumed that high levels of frontal EMG are related to anxiety, a study by Burish and Horn (1979) indicates that this is not the case. While several arousal-producing situations were successful in increasing arousal as measured by self-report and physiological measures, these situations had *no* effect on EMG levels.

Heart-Rate Feedback. Gatchel and his colleagues have investigated whether heart-rate biofeedback can be used in the treatment of speech anxiety. In the first study of this series (Gatchel & Proctor, 1976), heart-rate control was found to be more effective than a condition of no heart-rate control on physiological indexes, self-report, and observers' rating. There was also a near-significant expectancy effect, indicating that improvement was at least partially due to expectancy factors. In a subsequent study (Gatchel, Hatch, Watson, Smith, & Gaas, 1977), the relative effectiveness of heart-rate feedback and muscle relaxation was assessed. Therefore, the effects of (1) heart-rate feedback, (2) relaxation, (3) relaxation plus heart-rate feedback, and (4) false heart-rate feedback (placebo) were compared in a between-group design. The results indicated that all treatments (including placebo) improved on self-report measures, with no differences among the groups. Only on physiological indexes during the posttest speech situation did the placebo group differ from the active treatment groups. Moreover, the combined procedure was found to be the most effective on this measure. Finally, the last study of this series (Gatchel, Hatch, Maynard, Turns, & Taunton-Blackwood, 1979) replicated the placebo effect found in the Gatchel *et al.* (1977) study. The results of this study demonstrated that false heart-rate feedback was as effective as true heart-rate feedback and systematic desensitization on self-report indexes and overt motor components of anxiety. Only on heart-rate level, was heart-rate feedback found to be more effective relative to desensitization and placebo. No significant group differences were found for skin conductance and EMG indexes. Moreover, the results indicated that the placebo effect was not short-lived, since identical results were obtained at one-month follow-up.

Nunes and Marks (1975, 1976) investigated whether true heart-rate feedback enhanced the effectiveness of exposure *in vivo*. In contrast to the studies by Gatchel and his colleagues, this study involved real patients with specific phobias. Although it was found that heart-rate feedback substantially reduced heart rate, this effect did not generalize to skin conductance or to subjective anxiety. In addition to the studies by Nunes and Marks, some case reports have been published demonstrating the effectiveness of heart-rate feedback with phobic patients (e.g., Blanchard & Abel, 1976; Wickramasekera, 1974; Gatchel, 1977). However, these studies have typically confounded exposure and biofeedback and thus prevent the drawing of any conclusion.

Finally, the results of several studies indicate that heart-rate feedback is more effective with low-anxious subjects than with high-anxious subjects (Blankstein, 1975; Shepherd & Watts, 1974). The results of the Shepherd and Watts study are the most interesting, since they compared student volunteers with agoraphobic patients. It was found that agoraphobic patients did significantly worse than phobic students in decreasing their heart rate.

In summary, while heart-rate feedback may lead to some control over heart rate, this control does not lead to a greater reduction of subjective anxiety relative to control conditions. Thus, feedback of heart rate seems to have little to offer in the treatment of anxiety. Furthermore, it should be noted that heart rate feedback during exposure to a phobic stimulus may even inhibit approach behavior, as was found in two analogue studies with snake-phobic volunteers (Carver & Blaney, 1977a,b).

In 1974, Engel had already questioned the usefulness of heart-rate feedback in the treatment of anxiety: "it may not be feasible to treat anxiety by teaching subjects to slow their heart rates since heart rate is merely one peripheral manifestation of anxiety and not the illness itself. If one taught an anxious patient to slow his heart, the end results could be an anxious patient whose heart beats slower'' (p. 303). The present review suggests that this is indeed the case.

Concluding Remark. Despite claims made by the proponents of biofeedback, there is no substantial evidence that biofeedback is of any value in the treatment of anxiety-related disorders. The application of biofeedback in this area seems to have been more beneficial to the industry than to anxious and phobic patients.

Modeling. Modeling procedures have been successfully applied in the treatment of phobias. However, it should be noted that almost all studies in this area have dealt with analogue populations (most often animal phobics). Thus, the utility of modeling procedures with clinical phobic cases remains to be demonstrated.

Modeling procedures vary in several aspects: The model may be presented live (*overt modeling*), displayed on film (*symbolic modeling*), or imagined covertly (*covert modeling*). In addition, guided participation *in vivo* after observing the therapist's approach behavior is referred to as *participant modeling*.

No meaningful modeling procedure can be applied devoid of exposure to the phobic stimulus. Thus, it is questionable whether the effects of modeling should be ascribed to vicarious learning processes. Rather, an explanation in terms of exposure is equally plausible. Several studies have sought to test whether modeling was more effective than mere exposure to the phobic stimuli. These studies have provided conflicting results. Rankin (1976) found modeling more effective than mere exposure after anxiety was reduced through prior exposure to the phobic stimulus; modeling was no more effective than exposure when both were presented as the first treatment.

The results of other studies comparing modeling and exposure procedures (including systematic desensitization) are difficult to evaluate since modeling is often mixed with relaxation and narratives. Denney and Sullivan (1976) attempted to separate the effects of modeling and relaxation: Several variants of exposure and modeling were compared. Modeling alone was more effective than mere exposure to the phobic object. However, when both exposure and modeling were combined with relaxation and narratives, modeling was no more effective than exposure. In my opinion, the results of this study might be interpreted in terms of treatment-generated "expectancies." It is quite possible that the modeling subjects believed they were receiving a valid treatment, whereas the exposure-only subjects did not. On the other hand, when exposure was made equally credible as a treatment procedure by adding relaxation and narratives, the effects of modeling did not surpass the effects of exposure. Unfortunately, expectancy ratings are lacking. The above hypothesis suggests that the effects of modeling may be ascribed to placebo factors rather than to vicarious learning. Current research efforts do not yet provide sufficient evidence to rule out an interpretation of modeling effects in terms of a cognitive expectancy model.

During *covert modeling*, clients imagine rather than watch models approach and handle fearful stimuli. The covert modeling studies have been reviewed by Kazdin and Smith (1979) and are not repeated here. Briefly, while several studies found covert modeling effective in comparison with control conditions, in other studies control conditions were found to be equally effective.

Participant modeling involves two stages: The therapist initially models approach behavior to the phobic stimulus, followed by the therapist's guiding the subject's participation through progressively more demanding tasks. Participant modeling has been found to be far more effective than modeling alone (Bandura, Adams, & Beyer, 1977; Blanchard, 1970; Lewis, 1974; Ritter, 1969) and than covert modeling (Thase & Moss, 1976). The participant-modeling approach consists of two components: (1) modeling and (2) gradual exposure *in vivo*. To date, there is no evidence that the modeling component is an esssential feature of this approach; modeling does not enhance the effectiveness of gradual exposure *in vivo* with obsessive-compulsive patients (Emmelkamp, in press).

Several recent studies have contributed to further clarification of the role of exposure *in vivo* in participant modeling. The results of these studies (Bandura, Jeffery, & Gajdos, 1975; Smith & Coleman, 1977) indicate that self-directed practice enhances the effectiveness of participant modeling. In the Smith and Coleman (1977) study, rat-phobic volunteers were assigned to one of three groups. After treatment by means of participant modeling, the subjects received either self-directed practice (subject without therapist) with the treatment rat or self-directed treatment with varied rats, or they continued with participant modeling. Both self-directed practice conditions led to greater fear reduction to generalization stimuli than did the participant-modeling condition. The results of this study indicate that successful performance in real-life situations might be more important than modeling.

In summary, whether modeling potentiates the effects of exposure procedures is still a question for further studies. Moreover, the relative contribution of modeling may depend on the target behavior under study. While modeling is presumably of limited value with agoraphobics, it might be more important in the treatment of socially anxious patients who lack adequate social skills. Further, the need for additional work with clinical patients is underscored. Modeling therapies applied to clinical phobic patients are currently based on extrapolations from laboratory data and require further examination in clinical cases.

A Cognitive Expectancy Model. It is clear that all procedures reviewed so far have beneficial effects in the treatment of fear and anxiety, at least in analogue populations. The mechanisms by which these procedures achieve their results are, however, far from being understood. While it is obvious that almost all procedures contain elements of exposure to phobic stimuli, this fact does not elucidate the therapeutic processes involved. Exposure is merely a description of what is going on during treatment and not an explanation of its process.

In my opinion, the conditioning explanation presumed to underly the various treatment techniques seems no longer tenable. Rather, cognitive processes appear to be more important. Elsewhere (Emmelkamp, 1975a), I have presented a cognitive expectancy model to explain the effects of various behavioral treatments on anxiety and fear. This model emphasizes *self-observation of improvement* and *expectancy of therapeutic gain*. All imaginally

based treatments consist of exposure to the phobic stimuli. However, it is not exposure *per se* but self-observation of improvement that seems to be the crucial factor. Through continuous exposure to the phobic stimuli, habituation may occur. Eventually, the patient observes that the imagining of fearful situations no longer arouses anxiety. However, this discovery does not mean that the real-life phobic situation no longer arouses anxiety (e.g., Agras, 1967; Barlow *et al.*, 1969). There is a transfer gap between what patients can imagine without feeling anxiety and what they can perform in real life without anxiety. In my opinion, the self-observation that imagined phobic stimuli no longer arouse anxiety—combined with the therapeutic suggestion of improvement—prompts reality testing *in vivo*. Through successful performance in the real-life situations, habituation *in vivo* is eventually effected. Briefly, while exposure plays a role in the "first" and "second" stages of the treatment process, other important variables seem to be the patient's self-observation of improvement and the expectancy of therapeutic gain. Thus, the effect of exposure depends on the attitude and the set of the patient.

Such other procedures as "self-control relaxation" and cognitive restructuring may work through a similar mechanism. Having learned a coping skill, patients are instructed to venture into the phobic situations *in vivo*. The self-observation of successful performance *in vivo* may lead to further cognitive changes and may motivate further coping efforts.

There is now sufficient evidence that imaginal treatments are often redundant. Treatment may start directly with exposure *in vivo*. The routine use of imaginal procedures with phobic patients seems unwarranted. However, I do not mean to say that all imaginal treatments should be abandoned. Imaginal procedures are still the treatment of choice when real-life exposure is difficult to arrange (e.g., thunderstorm phobias) or when habituation in imagination is the primary aim of treatment (e.g., obsessional ruminations, Emmelkamp & Kwee, 1977).

Self-directed treatments may have several advantages as compared with therapist-directed treatments. In the latter treatments, patients may attribute their improvement to their therapist rather than to their own efforts. Therefore, it seems therapeutically wise to fade out the role of the therapist as soon as possible. The few comparative clinical studies (with agoraphobics and obsessive-compulsives) indicate that self-directed treatment *in vivo* is at least as effective as therapist-directed treatment (Emmelkamp, 1974; Emmelkamp & Kraanen, 1977; Emmelkamp & Wessels, 1975). Moreover, there is some evidence that therapist-directed treatment followed by self-directed practice is more effective than either approach alone (Emmelkamp, 1974).

Finally, the results of analogue studies comparing therapist-directed treatment (participant modeling) and self-directed treatment indicate the superiority of the self-directed approach (Bandura *et al.,* 1975; Smith & Coleman, 1977). Compared with subjects who received therapist-directed treatment, subjects who had the benefit of independent-mastery experiences displayed greater fear reduction.

Clinical Outcome Studies

In this section, research with clinical patients is reviewed. This review is limited to the behavioral treatment of social anxiety and agoraphobia, because of the preponderance of these conditions in clinical settings. A more detailed review of the clinical effectiveness of behavioral treatments is provided elsewhere (Emmelkamp, 1979a).

Social Anxiety. In contrast with the numerous analogue studies that deal with social anxiety, speech anxiety, dating anxiety, unassertiveness, etc. (reviewed by Arkowitz, 1977; Curran, 1977), relatively few studies in the area of social anxiety have used real patients. Studies using patients who are socially inadequates or unassertive are included in the present review, since most patients with social interaction difficulties experience anxiety in social situations (Hall & Goldberg, 1977).

Generally, three behavioral theories concerning the functioning of social anxiety can be distinguished: (1) skills-deficit theory; (2) conditioned-anxiety theory; and (3) cognitive theory. These theories are associated with different therapeutic strategies. If anxiety experienced in social situations is the result of an inadequate handling of these situations due to a lack of interpersonal skills, anxiety may be overcome through social skills training. On the other hand, if patients do have adequate skills but are inhibited in social situations by conditioned anxiety, then treatments that deal directly with this anxiety may be effective. Finally, if anxiety is mediated by faulty thinking, cognitive restructuring may be the treatment of choice.

Systematic Desensitization. Several studies have investigated the effectiveness of systematic desensitization with socially anxious patients (Hall & Goldberg, 1977; Marzillier, Lambert & Kellett, 1976; Shaw, 1976; Trower, Yardley, Bryant, & Shaw, 1978; Van Son, 1978). In general, limited clinical improvements were achieved. In only three studies was systematic desensitization compared with no-treatment conditions, and in neither study did desensitization subjects improve significantly more than controls. In addition, Dormaar and Dijkstra (1975) found no significant between-group differences between psychotherapy and desensitization. Finally, Kanter and Goldfried (1979), using socially anxious community residents as subjects, found systematic desensitization as self-control more effective than a waiting-list control; however, overall improvement was small.

Briefly, systematic desensitization is of limited value with socially anxious patients. The results of studies dealing with real patients contrast with those of studies using analogue populations. In the latter studies, desensitization has consistently been found to be effective in the treatment of social anxiety.

Social Skills Training. Social skills training seems to be of more value in the treatment of social anxiety. However, the evidence in favor of this approach is far from conclusive. Although several studies could not find consistent differences between systematic desensitization and social skills training (Hall & Goldberg, 1977; Shaw, 1976; Trower *et al.,* 1978, social phobics; Van Son, 1978) social inadequates, the results of other studies indicate that social skills training may be superior (Marzillier *et al.,* 1976; Trower *et al.,* 1978, social inadequates; Van Son, 1978, erythophobics).

The skills-deficit model assumes that social

anxiety is caused by a lack of adequate social skills. Thus, the effectiveness of skills training may be interpreted as support for this hypothesis. Alternatively, the effects of this treatment may be due not to skills training *per se* but to exposure *in vivo* to anxiety-arousing situations. During the treatment sessions, the patients are exposed to anxiety-arousing situations and have to give up their avoidance behavior, which may lead eventually to anxiety reduction. Furthermore, the homework patients usually have to carry out between treatment sessions results in a further exposure to real-life situations.

Cognitive Approach. Relatively few studies have examined the effectiveness of cognitive therapy with clinically relevant populations. In the Kanter and Goldfried (1979) study referred to earlier, the following treatment conditions were compared: (1) cognitive restructuring; (2) self-control desensitization; (3) cognitive restructuring plus self-control desensitization; and (4) waiting-list control. Cognitive restructuring proved to be superior to the desensitization and control groups. It is noteworthy that the combined treatment (cognitive restructuring plus desensitization) was *less* effective than cognitive restructuring alone.

Further evidence for the effectiveness of cognitive restructuring was provided by Wolfe and Fodor (1977). The results of their study indicated that both skills training and cognitive restructuring yielded improvements on the behavioral measure; cognitive restructuring, however, was the only condition that led to anxiety reduction.

Concluding Remarks. Both skills training and cognitive restructuring seem to be promising treatments for socially anxious patients, although further studies are certainly needed before more definitive conclusions can be drawn. The effectiveness of systematic and prolonged exposure *in vivo* has not been studied, presumably because such an exposure is difficult to arrange in real life situations. It is well to remember that both cognitive restructuring and social skills training contain elements of exposure *in vivo*. For instance, *in vivo* homework assignments are an integral part of Ellis's rational emotive therapy: "For unless phobic individuals act against their irrational beliefs that they must not approach fearsome objects or situations and that it is horrible if they do, can they ever really be said to have overcome such beliefs?" (Ellis, 1979, p. 162).

Most research in this area has been plagued by the uniformity myth that all socially anxious patients are similar. Generally, researchers do not distinguish among various categories of socially anxious patients: A functional analysis is not made, but patients are randomly assigned to treatment conditions. It is too easy, however, to conceptualize social anxiety in terms of a single theory. Cognitive restructuring, social skills training, and exposure procedures surely can be critical elements in treatment, but no method is so powerful that it can be applied universally across socially anxious patients. For patients who lack adequate social skills, the training of such skills seems essential. On the other hand, for those patients who do have the necessary social skills but whose anxiety is mediated by faulty thinking, cognitive therapy combined with exposure *in vivo* to test the newly acquired cognitions may be the treatment of choice.

Agoraphobia. Systematic desensitization seems to have little to offer in the treatment of agoraphobia (Cooper, Gelder, & Marks, 1965; Evans & Kellam, 1973; Gelder & Marks, 1966; Gelder *et al.*, 1967; Marks *et al.*, 1971; Marks & Gelder, 1965; Yorkston, Sergeant, & Rachman, 1968). Studies that involved both agoraphobics and specific phobics generally found that systematic desensitization was more effective for specific phobics than with agoraphobics. In contrast to the above-cited researchers, Gelder *et al.* (1973) found no differential effectiveness of desensitization for agoraphobics and for other phobics. However, most of the improvements found may be attributed to exposure *in vivo*: Most changes seemed to have occurred *after* systematic desensitization during four sessions of exposure *in vivo*.

Aversion relief is also of little value in the treatment of agoraphobia. Solyom, McClure, Heseltine, Ledwidge, and Solyom (1972) investigated the effects of this treatment on agoraphobics. Overall improvement was rather small: Patients rated their main phobia as unimproved.

As already discussed, flooding in imagination is less effective than flooding or prolonged exposure *in vivo*. There is no evidence that flooding in imagination is more effective than systematic desensitization in imagination. Most studies that found favorable results for flooding in imagination have confounded imagination and *in vivo* exposure (e.g., Mathews *et al.*, 1976). Briefly, the rather small effects of systematic desensitization, aversion relief, and flooding in imagination do not warrant widespread clinical application. In the last few years, research on agoraphobics has been concentrated on the development of exposure *in vivo* programs, which will be discussed in some detail.

Prolonged Exposure In Vivo. Although prolonged exposure *in vivo* may be applied in individual cases (e.g., Emmelkamp & Wessels, 1975), group exposure *in vivo* seems to offer several advantages. Besides the aspect of saving the therapist time, groups may provide the patient with coping models and may lead to fewer dropouts. It should be noted, however, that both Emmelkamp and Emmelkamp-Benner (1975) and Hand, Lamontagne, and Marks (1974) reported cases of negative modeling during group exposure *in vivo*. For instance, one group treated by Emmelkamp and Emmelkamp-Benner (1975) was dominated by a patient who repeatedly simulated heart attacks. Studies comparing individual and group exposure *in vivo* found no clear differences in effectiveness (Emmelkamp & Emmelkamp-Benner, 1975; Hafner & Marks, 1976).

To illustrate this treatment approach, the prolonged exposure treatment conducted by Emmelkamp *et al.* (1978) is described in some detail. During the first half hour of the first session, the patients exchanged information about the onset and the development of their phobias, and the therapists gave the treatment rationale. The role played by avoidance behavior in maintaining phobias was emphasized, and the patients were instructed to remain in the phobic situations until they had experienced anxiety reduction. Then, the patients and the therapists took a short walk to the center of the town, the place where the patients would have to walk more on their own in the future. After 90 min of prolonged exposure *in vivo*, the patient's experiences were assessed in a brief group discussion at the hospital. During prolonged exposure *in vivo*, the patients were exposed to anxiety-provoking situations, at first in groups of two or three patients but, as the treatment progressed, more and more on their own. Difficult situations were, for example, walking in busy streets, shopping in department stores and supermarkets, and riding in buses. The therapists consciously faded from the groups and, after a few sessions, were present only at the discussions preceding and following the exposure periods.

Various investigators in three different centers have found prolonged exposure *in vivo* conducted in groups to be a very effective treatment for agoraphobics (Emmelkamp *et al.*, 1978; Emmelkamp & Mersch, 1982; Emmelkamp, 1979b; Hafner & Marks, 1976; Hand *et al.*, 1974; Teasdale, Walsh, Lancashire, & Mathews, 1977). Often, dramatic improvements with respect to anxiety and avoidance are achieved even in a few days, but generally, a lack of continuing improvement has been found when treatment ends (e.g., Emmelkamp & Mersch, 1982; Emmelkamp, 1979b; Hafner & Marks, 1976; Teasdale *et al.*, 1977).

Self-Management Programs. In Andrews's (1966) view, the phobic patient is characterized by dependency relationships with others and by an avoidance of activity that involves the independent handling of difficult and fear-arousing situations. This lack of independency constitutes a fairly broad pattern of responses and not just a response to the phobic stimulus itself. In agoraphobics, Emmelkamp and Cohen-Kettenis (1975) found a significant correlation between external locus of control and phobic anxiety. This finding suggests that an agoraphobic can be characterized as someone who avoids anxiety-arousing situations because of a lack of internal control. In light of this consideration, acquiring self-control may be an important therapeutic goal for agoraphobics. If this reasoning is correct, then treatment for agoraphobics should focus on teaching generalizable coping skills.

Problems with respect to a lack of continuing improvement when formal treatment ends may be prevented by self-management programs in the patient's natural environment. An additional advantage of this approach is that the most severe agoraphobics, who are unable to visit a therapist, can be treated. To date, two treatment programs, have been developed that can be managed by patients in their own environment.

The first self-management program was developed by Emmelkamp (1974). The treatment consisted of self-controlled exposure plus feedback (self-observation). After an instructional phase in the presence of the therapist, the patient had to carry on alone. The procedure involved a graduated approach by the patient to the actual feared situation. Right from the first session, the client had to enter the phobic situation. The client had to walk alone a route through the city with instructions to turn back on experiencing undue anxiety. The client had to record the duration of each trial and to write it down in a notebook. Then she/he had to enter the phobic situation in the same way. This procedure was repeated until the 90-min. session was over. At the end of each session, the patient had to send the results to the therapist.

In a study by Emmelkamp (1974), the effects of the following treatments were compared: (1) self-observation; (2) flooding; (3) flooding followed by self-observation; and (4) no-treatment control. Each flooding session consisted of 45 min of flooding in imagination, immediately followed by 45 min of flooding *in vivo*. During self-observation, the therapist was present only at the first few sessions. At the following sessions, the patients had to practice alone. All treatments proved to be superior to no treatment. No significant differences were found between flooding and self-observation, despite the fact that the therapist's involvement was at least twice as much during flooding. In addition, flooding plus self-observation proved to be the most effective. The effectiveness of self-observation as a self-management procedure was further demonstrated in the studies by Emmelkamp (1980b), Emmelkamp and Emmelkamp-Benner (1975), Emmelkamp and Wessels (1975), and Emmelkamp and Kuipers (1979). In conrast to the results found with prolonged exposure *in vivo*, with this self-management program most patients went on to make further gains during follow-up. (Emmelkamp, 1974, 1980b; Emmelkamp & Kuipers, 1979).

More recently, Mathews, Teasdale, Munby,

Johnston, and Shaw (1977) developed another self-management program for agoraphobics. Their program differs from our program in that their patients' spouses were actively involved in planning and encouraging practice attempts. Furthermore, their patients had to remain in the phobic situation long enough for anxiety to decline, rather than to return on experiencing undue anxiety, as in self-observation. Mathews, Jannoun and Gelder (1979) reported the results of two controlled studies, demonstrating the effectiveness of this program. As in our self-observation program, there was a trend toward continuing improvement between posttest and follow-up.

The role of the partner in the Mathews *et al.* program is questionable. By using the partner as a cotherapist, the therapist may inadvertently reinforce the dependent relationship between patient and partner. One study (Mathews *et al.*, 1979) compared home practice with the partner with home practice alone. While the partner condition was more effective at the posttest, it is interesting to see that only the condition of home practice alone showed continuing improvement between posttest and follow-up. Moreover, it should be remembered that the self-management program developed by Emmelkamp produced at least equivalent change without the help of the patient's partner.

Spaced versus Massed. Until recently, there was little evidence of whether massed practice of exposure *in vivo* was superior to spaced practice or vice versa. Foa and Turner (1979) compared 10 sessions of massed practice with 10 sessions of spaced practice in a crossover design. In the massed-practice condition, the treatment was conducted on consecutive days, whereas in the spaced condition, the sessions were held only once a week. The results indicated that massed practice was more effective than spaced practice. Foa and Turner (1979) suggested that the massed condition may be superior because massed practice provides less opportunity for accidental exposure between treatment sessions and for the reinforcement of avoidance or escape behavior.

Follow-Up. Follow-up in the various studies into exposure *in vivo* ranges from a few weeks to one year. Thus, there is little evidence of termination persistence effects. Recently, we conducted a follow-up study (Emmelkamp & Kuipers, 1979) with 70 agoraphobics who were treated at an average of four years ago in the trials of Emmelkamp (1974), Emmelkamp and Ultee (1974), Emmelkamp and Wessels (1975), and Emmelkamp and Emmelkamp-Benner (1975). Although the treatment procedures varied from study to study (including self-controlled exposure *in vivo*, flooding or prolonged exposure *in vivo*, and flooding in imagination), all patients had been treated by exposure *in vivo*. After the clinical trial, a number of patients were further treated individually. The number of treatment sessions averaged around 18 (clinical trial plus further treatment).

The results on the anxiety and avoidance scales at pretest, postest, and follow-up are shown in Figure 2. The improvements that were achieved during the treatment were maintained and partly continued during follow-up. Hafner (1976) found the emergence of fresh symptoms one year after exposure *in vivo* treatment with a number of his agoraphobics. However, in the present study, the patient did not report the emergence of other problems than agoraphobia. Moreover, it should be noted that results at follow-up revealed even further continuing improvement in depression.

As can be seen in Figure 2, the treatment led to clinically significant improvements at

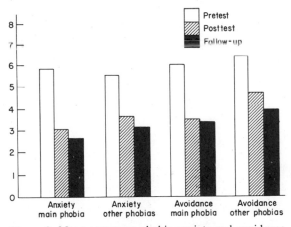

Figure 2. Mean scores on phobic anxiety and avoidance scales. (From "Agoraphobia: A Follow-Up Study Four Years after Treatment" by P. M. G. Emmelkamp and A. Kuipers, *British Journal of Psychiatry*, 1979, *134*, 352–355, Fig. 1. Copyright 1979 by the British Journal of Psychiatry. Reprinted by permission.)

four-year follow-up. However, there was a great variance in the results of the treatment. Some patients were symptom-free, some were moderately improved, and a few patients did not benefit at all. Obviously, while exposure *in vivo* procedures may be quite effective for a number of agoraphobics, it is not the panacea for the treatment of agoraphobia.

There are several factors that may complicate treatment by exposure procedures. For present purposes, I will limit the discussion to (1) anxiety-inducing cognitions and (2) interpersonal problems. Of course, I do not mean to say that these are the only factors that may complicate treatment by exposure *in vivo*.

Cognitive Approach. Agoraphobics often complain of anxiety-inducing thoughts. With a number of patients these "negative" cognitions change "spontaneously" as a result of treatment by exposure *in vivo*. For example, during exposure *in vivo*, patients may notice that the awful things that they fear, such as fainting, getting a heart-attack or "going crazy," do not take place. However, while we have found these cognitive changes in a number of patients, clearly not *all* patients do change their cognitions during treatment, and in some patients, these cognitive changes are only short-lived.

Another point also deserves attention. Although the patients are exposed to the phobic situation *in vivo*, real exposure may still be avoided by the patients through thoughts, as, for example, "there is a hospital; if something goes wrong, there will be help." Similarly, *after* treatment sessions, some patients "reassure" themselves with such statements as "Well, this time nothing did go wrong because I had a good day, but tomorrow I can get a real attack." Thus, the patients may use private speech that interferes with real exposure to the anxiety-inducing situations. Although as yet no research has been conducted into the effects of such negative private speech, it is tempting to assume that such cognitive avoidance militates against the effects of *in vivo* exposure.

In the last few years, we have directed some research into cognitive change methods for agoraphobics and obsessive-compulsives. In our first study (Emmelkamp *et al.*, 1978), cognitive restructuring was compared with prolonged exposure *in vivo* in a crossover design. Both prolonged exposure *in vivo* and cognitive restructuring were conducted in groups. Each procedure consisted of five sessions. Exposure *in vivo* was found to be far more effective than cognitive restructuring on the behavioral measure, on phobic anxiety, and on avoidance scales. However, treatment was conducted in a relatively short time period (one week), which might be too short to result in significant cognitive changes. Moreover, the use of the crossover design precluded conclusions about the long-term effectiveness of our cognitive package.

In a following study (Emmelkamp & Mersch, 1982), three treatments were compared in a between-group design: (1) cognitive restructuring; (2) prolonged exposure *in vivo*; and (3) a combination of cognitive restructuring and prolonged exposure *in vivo*. Each session lasted 2 hr, and each treatment consisted of eight sessions. During cognitive restructuring, more emphasis was placed on insight into unproductive thinking than in the cognitive procedure used by Emmelkamp *et al.* (1978). In each session, the patient had to analyze their own feelings in terms of Ellis's ABC theory. In the combined procedure, half of the time was spent on self-instructional training, the other half on prolonged exposure *in vivo*. During the latter phase of the combined treatment,

the patients were instructed to use their positive self-statements during their *in vivo* exercises. The results of the patients' ratings on the phobic anxiety and avoidance scales (Watson & Marks, 1971) are presented in Figure 3. At the posttest, prolonged exposure *in vivo* and the combined procedure were clearly superior to cognitive restructuring. At the one-month follow-up, however, the differences between the treatments partly disappeared because of a continuing improvement in the cognitive modification group and a slight relapse in the exposure *in vivo* condition. Thus, although the short-term effects were similar to the results of the Emmelkamp *et al.* (1978) study, in the long run, cognitive modification was about equally effective. Unfortunately, self-instructional training did not enhance the effects of exposure *in vivo*. At follow-up, the results of the combined procedure were comparable with the results of the exposure and cognitive procedures.

Similar results were found in a study with obsessive-compulsive patients (Emmelkamp *et al.*, 1980), in which 10 sessions of exposure *in vivo* were compared with 10 sessions of a combined procedure, which consisted of self-instructional training and exposure *in vivo*. Each session lasted 2 hr. The results on the anxiety and avoidance scales are presented in Figure 4. Self-instructional training did not

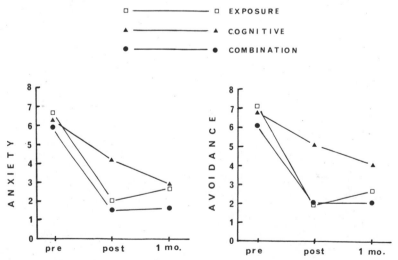

Figure 3. Mean scores on phobic anxiety and avoidance scales. (From ''Cognition and Exposure *in Vivo* in the Treatment of Agoraphobia: Short Term and Delayed Effects'' by P. M. G. Emmelkamp and P. Mersch, *Cognitive Therapy and Research,* 1982, 6, 77–88. Fig. 1. Copyright 1982 by Plenum Press. Reprinted by permission.)

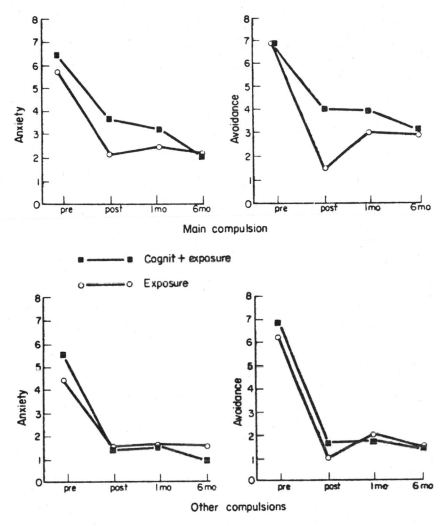

Figure 4. Contributions of self-instructional training. (From "Treatment of Obsessive-Compulsive Patients: The Contribution of Self-Instructional Training to the Effectiveness of Exposure," by P. M. G. Emmelkamp *et al.*, *Behaviour Research and Therapy*, 1980, *18*, 61–66, Fig. 2. Copyright 1980 by Pergamon Press. Reprinted by permission.)

enhance treatment effectiveness, either at the posttest or at the one- or six-month follow-ups.

The results of our studies with clinical populations using cognitive procedures have not yet given an answer for the usefulness of the cognitive approach for clinical patients. However, these results have stressed the necessity of conducting outcome research with real patients instead of with students in need of some credit points for their course requirements.

Although as yet no definitive conclusions can be drawn with respect to the usefulness

of the cognitive approach for clinical phobics, a comparison of our studies leads to a few suggestions about effective parameters: (1) Cognitive therapy conducted over a longer time interval might prove to be more effective than when conducted over a short period; and (2) Insight into unproductive thinking might prove to be more relevant than self-instructional training.

Interpersonal Problems. The interpersonal problems of phobic patients might also complicate treatment by exposure *in vivo*. Both psychotherapists (e.g., Fry, 1962; Goodstein

& Swift, 1977) and behavior therapists (Goldstein-Fodor, 1974; Goldstein, 1973; Goldstein & Chambless, 1978; Wolpe, 1973) have stressed the importance of the client's interpersonal relationships in the development of agoraphobia. According to Goldstein and Wolpe, female agoraphobics wish to flee the marriage but cannot because of their fears of being alone. Goldstein-Fodor holds that agoraphobia in women develops because the patients in infancy were reinforced for stereotypical female behavior like helplessness and dependency. In her view, interpersonal trappedness, particularly the feeling of being dominated with no outlet for assertion, might enhance the tendency to develop agoraphobia. However, experimental studies to test these notions are sparse and are not discussed here (see review by Emmelkamp, 1979a).

More important to our present discussion is whether such interpersonal factors interfere with treatment by exposure *in vivo*. Therefore, in a recent study by Emmelkamp (1980b), two types of interpersonal problems were distinguished: (1) problems with the significant partner and (2) unassertiveness. Agoraphobics were divided for low and high marital satisfaction and for low and high assertiveness on the basis of their scores on questionnaires. After four treatment sessions with self-controlled exposure *in vivo*, it appeared that low-assertive patients improved as much as high-assertive patients. Moreover, patients with low marital satisfaction improved as much as patients with high marital satisfaction. The effects of the treatment were not influenced by the interpersonal problems of agoraphobics either at the posttest or at the one-month follow-up. However, one should interpret these results cautiously. First, only short-term effects were assessed, since the treatment involved four sessions only. Second, the assignment to conditions was based on self-report questionnaires. Thus, patients may have faked their responses on the questionnaires, although we have no evidence that this was the case. Finally, this study should not be seen as proof or disproof of the system-theoretic hypothesis. A true test of the system-theoretic hypothesis concerning agoraphobia would require a demonstration that improvement in the agoraphobic patient was uninfluenced by family factors.

If lack of assertion is at the root of agoraphobia, as some have suggested, then agoraphobics may profit from assertiveness training. Emmelkamp (1979b) reported a study in which assertiveness training was compared with prolonged exposure *in vivo*. Only low-assertive agoraphobics were accepted in this experiment. The preliminary data of this study indicate that assertiveness training is less effective than exposure *in vivo*. Nevertheless, assertion training did lead to clinically significant improvements in some agoraphobics. In addition, it should be noted that assertion training may teach patients a more adequate handling of interpersonal stress situations, which might prevent relapse in the future.

Although a number of agoraphobics have problems with their partners, they often want treatment for their phobias instead of for these problems. In our experience, few agoraphobics accept help for marital difficulties. Recently, Cobb, McDonald, Marks and Stern (1979) compared marital treatment with exposure *in vivo*; the subjects were both agoraphobics and obsessive-compulsives who also manifested marital discord. The results indicated that exposure *in vivo* led to improvements with respect to both the compulsive and phobic problems and the marital relationship, while marital therapy improved only the marital interaction. Further studies in this area are surely needed.

Future Perspectives

This section delineates some issues for further investigation, though these suggestions are by no means exhaustive.

Behavioral Analysis

One of the major issues for further research relates to a differential diagnosis and treatment tailored to the individual needs of patients. Most studies have used a between-groups design: Subjects are randomly assigned to different treatments. It would be advisable for researchers to put a larger emphasis on making a functional analysis of the problem behavior, rather than neglecting individual differences by assigning patients randomly to groups.

So far, research on phobic patients has focused narrowly on the removal of phobias. It should be noted that clinical phobias are often complicated by other problems. Obviously, complex problems deserve complex treatments. Studies of agoraphobics (Emmelkamp, 1979b) and of obsessional patients (Emmelkamp & Van der Heyden, 1980) indicate that for some patients, assertiveness training might be at least as effective as treatments that focus on the phobias and obsessions directly.

For clinical purposes, the effects of proper combinations of various treatments need to be evaluated. To give just one example, for some agoraphobics exposure *in vivo* may suffice as treatment, whereas for others this approach needs to be supplemented by assertiveness training, cognitive restructuring, or marital therapy. Such clinical decisions are often based on intuition and need to be supplemented by hard data.

Prevention

Another issue for future research concerns the prevention of anxiety and fear. Several studies have evaluated the effectiveness of immunization programs (including systematic desensitization, modeling, and cognitive rehearsal) in preventing snake phobias (Jaremko & Wenrich, 1973); fears of dental treatment (Melamed, 1979); and speech anxiety (Cradock, Cotler, & Jason, 1978; Jaremko & Wenrich, 1973). Generally, the results of these studies demonstrate the utility of immunization programs in preventing anxiety. However, Cradock *et al.* (1978) could not find any difference in the behavioral manifestations of anxiety for systematic desensitization and cognitive rehearsal relative to their control group.

The studies cited above can be criticized along several lines. First, only short-term effects were assessed. Thus, whether immunization programs are effective in preventing phobias in later life is still questionable. Further, some of these studies (e.g., Jaremko & Wenrich, 1973) may have included subjects who were already phobic prior to the inter-

vention program. In that case, the term *treatment* is more appropriate than the term *prevention*.

In my opinion, meaningful prevention programs can be applied only when we have a better understanding of the etiology of phobic disorders. It is well to remember that attempts to explain the acquisition of fears have created the widest conceptual disagreements among behavior therapists. The various speculations put forth by behavior therapists clearly suggest the many variables that require examination as critical determinants of the development of phobic behavior. This view implies that a great deal of research has yet to be done before meaningful prevention programs can be developed.

Drug-Assisted Exposure

Several recent studies have investigated whether drugs enhance the effectiveness of exposure *in vivo*. Neither beta blockers (Butollo, Burkhardt, Himmler, & Müller, 1978; Hafner & Milton, 1977; Ullrich, Ullrich, Cromback, & Peikert, 1972) nor MAOIs (Solyom *et al.*, 1981) seem to enhance the effects of exposure *in vivo*. Only diazepam has been found to have some effects, particularly with specific phobics (Hafner & Marks, 1976; Johnston & Gath, 1973; Marks, Viswanathan, Lipsedge, & Gardner, 1972). In addition, there is some evidence suggesting that diazepam might influence anxiety experienced *during* exposure sessions. For those few patients for whom exposure *in vivo* is too terrifying, diazepam-assisted exposure might offer a solution.

Whether imipramine might potentiate the effects of exposure *in vivo* has not been studied. However, data from the study by Zitrin *et al.* (1978) indicate that imipramine has beneficial effects in patients who experience spontaneous panic attacks. Studies investigating whether imipramine facilitates exposure *in vivo* are surely needed.

Therapeutic Relationship

Nonbehavioral psychotherapists presume the therapeutic relationship to be of paramount importance in the process of therapy. The relationship between therapist and patient has been neglected in the behavioral literature (De Voge & Beck, 1978).

As far as behavior therapy for phobias is concerned, the role of the therapist is largely ignored. There are, however, a few studies that shed some light on this issue. For example, analogue studies by Morris and Suckerman (1974a,b) demonstrated that a warm therapeutic voice produced significantly better results than a cold voice. Thus, even with desensitization in an analogue context, therapist variables appear to be of importance.

Let us now turn our attention to clinical studies. In several studies, a significant therapist interaction was found (e.g., Mathews *et al.* 1976, 1979). The "therapist effect" found in these studies indicates that the improvements achieved cannot be ascribed solely to technical procedures.

A study by Rabavilas and Boulougouris (1979) contributes to an understanding of the role of the therapist during behavioral treatment. Phobic and obsessive-compulsive patients who had been treated with exposure *in vivo* had to rate their therapists' qualities at follow-up. The results indicated that therapists' respect, understanding, and interest was positively related to outcome. However, gratification of patients' dependency needs was negatively related to outcome.

Subsequent studies pertaining to relationship factors should use direct observational measures of therapist–patient interactions in addition to ratings of therapists' qualities. Another research strategy that might prove to be fruitful is to vary therapeutic styles experimentally. The therapeutic relationship, then, is an important target for further research.

Summary

Phobics are typically considered a homogeneous group. This uniformity myth has plagued behavioral research: Generally, outcome research has been technique- rather than problem-oriented. As we have seen, a good deal of effort has been directed toward evaluating various techniques. But it is essential to note that there are important differences among various categories of phobic behavior. Therefore, conclusions cannot be generalized from one population (e.g., social anxiety) to another population (e.g., agoraphobia).

In the early days, behavioral treatments for anxiety and fear were defined as the application of "established laws of learning" or were viewed as being based on "modern learning theories." The claim that these procedures are exclusively based on learning paradigms seems no longer tenable nowadays. The present review suggests that additional factors, such as the therapeutic relationship, the expectancy of therapeutic gain, and the self-observation of improvements, play an important role. The preceding review indicates that *in vivo* procedures are more powerful than imaginal ones. Taken together, these data lead to the clinical emphasis on *in vivo* treatments and self-attributed success experiences to enhance therapeutic changes.

The clinical utility of most behavioral procedures is questionable. To give just one example, although systematic desensitization has been found to be effective in improving specific phobias, the benefits of this treatment for social phobics and agoraphobics are doubtful. Generalizing results from analogue populations to clinical populations, as has typically been done in the past, ignores crucial differences between these populations. The time may be ripe for taking a fresh look at the value of analogue studies. In my opinion, the hard job, but the only one that will lead to meaningful conclusions, is to develop and evaluate treatments using real clinical patients as subjects.

References

Agras, W. S. Transfer during systematic desensitization therapy. *Behaviour Research and Therapy*, 1967, *5*, 193–199.

Agras, W. S., Leitenberg, H., & Barlow, D. H. Social reinforcement in the modification of agoraphobia. *Archives of General Psychiatry*, 1968, *19*, 423–427.

Agras, W. S., Leitenberg, H., Barlow, D. H., & Thomson, L. E. Instructions and reinforcements in the modification of neurotic behavior. *American Journal of Psychiatry*, 1969, *125*, 1435–1439.

Agras, W. S., Leitenberg, H., Wincze, J. P., Butz, R. A., & Callahan, E. J. Comparison of the effects of instructions and reinforcement in the treatment of a neurotic avoidance response: A single case experiment. *Journal of Behavior Therapy and Experimental Psychiatry*, 1970, *1*, 53–58.

Agras, W. S., Leitenberg, H., Barlow, D. H., Curtis, N. A., Edwards, J., & Wright, D. Relaxation in systematic desensitization. *Archives of General Psychiatry*, 1971, *25*, 511–514.

Alden, L., Safran, J., & Weideman, R. A comparison of cognitive and skills training strategies in the treatment of unassertive clients. *Behavior Therapy*, 1978, *8*, 843–846.

Andrews, J. D. W. Psychotherapy of phobias. *Psychological Bulletin*, 1966, *66*, 455–480.

Arkowitz, H. Measurement and modification of minimal dating behavior. In M. Hersen, R. M. Eisler, & P. M. Miller (Eds.), *Progress in behavior modification*, Vol. 5. New York: Academic Press, 1977.

Bajtelsmit, J. W., & Gershman, L. Covert positive reinforcement: Efficacy and conceptualization. *Journal of Behavior Therapy and Experimental Psychiatry*, 1976, *7*, 207–212.

Bandura, A. *Principles of behavior modification*. New York: Holt, Rinehart & Winston, 1969.

Bandura, A. *Social learning theory*. Englewood Cliffs, N.J.: Prentice-Hall, 1977.

Bandura, A. On paradigms and recycled ideologies. *Cognitive Therapy and Research*, 1978, *2*, 79–103.

Bandura, A., Jeffery, R. W., & Gajdos, E. Generalizing change through participant modeling with self-directed mastery. *Behaviour Research and Therapy*, 1975, *13*, 141–152.

Bandura, A., Adams, N. E., & Beyer, J. Cognitive processes mediating behavioral change. *Journal of Personality and Social Psychology*, 1977, *35*, 125–139.

Barlow, D. H., Leitenberg, H., Agras, W. S., & Wincze, J. P. The transfer gap in systematic desensitization: An analogue study. *Behaviour Research and Therapy*, 1969, *7*, 191–196.

Barlow, D. H., Agras, W. S., Leitenberg, H., & Wincze, J. P. An experimental analysis of the effectiveness of "shaping" in reducing maladaptive avoidance behavior: an analogue study. *Behaviour Research and Therapy*, 1970, *8*, 165–173.

Barrett, C. L. Systematic desensitization versus implosive therapy. *Journal of Abnormal Psychology*, 1969, *74*, 587–592.

Barrios, B. A. Note on demand characteristics in analogue research on small animal phobias. *Psychological Reports*, 1978, *42*, 1264–1266.

Becker, H. G., & Costello, C. G. Effects of graduated exposure with feedback of exposure times of snake phobias. *Journal of Consulting and Clinical Psychology*, 1975, *43*, 478–484.

Beiman, I. The effects of instructional set on physiological response to stressful imagery. *Behaviour Research and Therapy*, 1976, *14*, 175–180.

Beiman, I., Israel, E., & Johnson, S. During training and posttraining effects of live and taped extended progressive relaxation, self-relaxation, and electromyogram feedback. *Journal of Consulting and Clinical Psychology*, 1978, *46*, 314–321.

Benjamin, S., Marks, I. M., & Huson, J. Active muscular relaxation in desensitization of phobic patients. *Psychological Medicine*, 1972, *2*, 381–390.

Bernstein, D. A. Manipulation of avoidance behavior as a function of increased or decreased demand on repeated behavioral tests. *Journal of Consulting and Clinical Psychology*, 1974, *42*, 896–900.

Bernstein, D. A., & Nietzel, M. T. Procedural variations in behavioral avoidance tests. *Journal of Consulting and Clinical Psychology*, 1973, *41*, 165–174.

Bernstein, D. A., & Nietzel, M. T. Behavioral avoidance tests: The effects of demand characteristics and repeated measures on two types of subjects. *Behavior Therapy*, 1974, *5*, 183–192.

Blackwell, B. Hypertensive crisis due to mono-amine oxidase inhibitors. *Lancet*, 1963, *2*, 849–851.

Blanchard, E. B. The relative contributions of modeling, informational influences, and physical contact in the extinction of phobic behavior. *Journal of Abnormal Psychology*, 1970, *76*, 55–61.

Blanchard, E. B., & Abel, G. G. An experimental case study of the biofeedback treatment of a rape-induced psychophysiological cardiovascular disorder. *Behavior Therapy*, 1976, *7*, 113–119.

Blankstein, K. R. Heart rate control, general anxiety, and subjective tenseness. *Behavior Therapy*, 1975, *6*, 699–700.

Borkovec, T. D. Effects of expectancy on the outcome of systematic desensitization and implosive treatments for analogue anxiety. *Behavior Therapy*, 1972, *3*, 29–40.

Borkovec, T. D. The role of expectancy and physiological feedback in fear research: A review with special reference to subject characteristics. *Behavior Therapy*, 1973, *4*, 491–505.

Borkovec, T. D., & Nau, S. D. Credibility of analogue therapy rationales. *Journal of Behavior Therapy and Experimental Psychiatry*, 1972, *3*, 257–260.

Borkovec, T. D., & Rachman, S. The utility of analogue research. *Behaviour Research and Therapy*, 1979, *17*, 253–261.

Borkovec, T. D., & Sides, J. K. Critical procedural variables related to the physiological effects of progressive relaxation: A review. *Behaviour Research and Therapy*, 1979, *17*, 119–125.

Boudewyns, P. A., & Wilson, A. E. Implosive therapy and desensitization therapy using free association in treatment of inpatients. *Journal of Abnormal Psychology*, 1972, *79*, 252–268.

Boulougouris, J. C., Marks, I. M., & Marset, P. Superiority of flooding (implosion) to desensitization for reducing pathological fear. *Behaviour Research and Therapy*, 1971, *9*, 7–16.

Branham, L., & Katahn, M. Effectiveness of automated desensitization with normal volunteers and phobic patients. *Canadian Journal of Behavioral Sciences*, 1974, *6*, 234–245.

Buglass, D., Clarke, J., Henderson, N., Kreitman, N., & Presley, A. S. A study of agoraphobic housewives. *Psychological Medicine*, 1977, *7*, 73–86.

Burish, T. G., & Horn, P. W. An evaluation of frontal EMG as an index of general arousal. *Behavior Therapy*, 1979, *10*, 137–147.

Butollo, W., Burkhardt, P., Himmler, C., & Müller, M.

Mehrdimensionale Verhaltenstherapie und Beta-Blocker bei functionellen Dysrytmien und chronischen körperbezogenen Angstreaktionen. Paper read at the meeting of the German Society of Psychosomatic Medicine, Cologne, 1978.

Calef, R. A., & MacLean, G. D. A comparison of reciprocal inhibition and reactive inhibition therapies in the treatment of speech anxiety. *Behavior Therapy,* 1970, *1,* 51–58.

Canter, A., Kondo, C. Y., & Knott, J. R. A comparison of EMG feedback and progressive muscle relaxation training in anxiety neurosis. *British Journal of Psychiatry,* 1975, *127,* 470–477.

Carmody, T. P. Rational-emotive, self-instructional, and behavioral assertion: Facilitating maintenance. *Cognitive Therapy and Research,* 1978, *2,* 241–253.

Carver, C. S., & Blaney, P. H. Avoidance behavior and perceived arousal. *Motivation and Emotion,* 1977, *1,* 61–73. (a)

Carver, C. S., & Blaney, P. H. Perceived arousal, focus of attention, and avoidance behavior. *Journal of Abnormal Psychology,* 1977, *86,* 154–162. (b)

Cautela, J. R. Covert reinforcement. *Behavior Therapy,* 1970, *2,* 192–200.

Chang-Liang, R., & Denney, D. R. Applied relaxation as training in self-control. *Journal of Counseling Psychology,* 1976, *23,* 183–189.

Cobb, J. P., McDonald, R., Marks, I. M., & Stern, R. S. *Marital versus exposure treatment for marital plus phobic-obsessive problems.* Unpublished manuscript, 1979.

Cooper, A., Furst, J. B., & Bridger, W. H. A brief commentary on the usefulness of studying fear of snakes. *Journal of Abnormal Psychology,* 1969, *74,* 413–414.

Cooper, J. E., Gelder, M. G., & Marks, I. M. Results of behaviour therapy in 77 psychiatric patients. *British Medical Journal,* 1965, *1,* 1222–1225.

Cornish, R. D., & Dilley, J. S. Comparison of three methods of reducing test anxiety: Systematic desensitization, implosive therapy, and study counseling. *Journal of Counseling Psychology,* 1973, *20,* 499–503.

Counts, D. K., Hollandsworth, J. G., & Alcorn, J. D. Use of electromyographic biofeedback and cue-controlled relaxation in the treatment of test anxiety. *Journal of Consulting and Clinical Psychology,* 1978, *46,* 990–996.

Coursey, R. D. Electromyograph feedback as a relaxation technique. *Journal of Consulting and Clinical Psychology,* 1975, *43,* 825–834.

Cradock, C., Cotler, S., & Jason, L. A. Primary prevention: Immunization of children for speech anxiety. *Cognitive Therapy and Research,* 1978, *2,* 389–396.

Crowe, M. J., Marks, I. M., Agras, W. S., & Leitenberg, H. Time-limited desensitization implosion and shaping for phobic patients: A cross-over study. *Behaviour Research and Therapy,* 1972, *10,* 319–328.

Curran, J. P. Skills training as an approach to the treatment of heterosexual-social anxiety: A review. *Psychological Bulletin,* 1977, *84,* 140–157.

Davison, G. C. Systematic desensitization as a counter-conditioning process. *Journal of Abnormal Psychology,* 1968, *73,* 91–99.

Davison, G. C., & Wilson, G. T. Processes of fear-reduction in systematic desensitization: Cognitive and social reinforcement factors in humans. *Behavior Therapy,* 1973, *4,* 1–21.

Deffenbacher, J. L. Relaxation in vivo in the treatment of test anxiety. *Journal of Behavior Therapy and Experimental Psychiatry,* 1976, *7,* 289–292.

Deffenbacher, J. L., & Parks, D. H. A comparison of traditional and self-control desensitization. *Journal of Counseling Psychology,* 1979, *26,* 93–97.

Deffenbacher, J. L., & Payne, D. M. J. Two procedures for relaxation as self-control in the treatment of communication apprehension. *Journal of Counseling Psychology,* 1977, *24,* 255–258.

Deffenbacher, J. L., & Shelton, J. L. Comparison of anxiety management training and desensitization in reducing test and other anxieties. *Journal of Counseling Psychology,* 1978, *25,* 277–282.

Deffenbacher, J. L., Mathis, H., & Michaels, A. C. Two self-control procedures in the reduction of targeted and nontargeted anxieties. *Journal of Counseling Psychology,* 1979, *26,* 120–127.

De Moor, W. Systematic desensitization versus prolonged high intensity stimulation (flooding). *Journal of Behavior Therapy and Experimental Psychiatry,* 1970, *1,* 45–52.

Denney, D. R., & Rupert, P. A. Desensitization and self-control in the treatment of test anxiety. *Journal of Counseling Psychology,* 1977, *24,* 272–280.

Denney, D. R., & Sullivan, B. J. Desensitization and modeling treatments of spider fear using two types of scenes. *Journal of Consulting and Clinical Psychology,* 1976, *44,* 573–579.

Derry, P. A., & Stone, G. L. Effects of cognitive-adjunct treatments on assertiveness. *Cognitive Therapy and Research,* 1979, *3,* 213–223.

De Voge, J. T., & Beck, S. The therapist-client relationship in behavior therapy. In M. Hersen, R. M. Eisler, & P. M. Miller (Eds.), *Progress in Behavior Modification,* Vol. 6. New York: Academic Press, 1978.

Di Loreto, A. O. *Comparative psychotherapy: An experimental analysis.* Chicago: Aldine, 1971.

Dormaar, M., & Dijkstra, W. Systematic desensitization in social anxiety. Paper read at the Conference of the European Association of Behaviour Therapy, 1975.

Dyckman, J. M., & Cowan, P. A. Imagining vividness and the outcome of in vivo and imagined scene desensitization. *Journal of Consulting and Clinical Psychology,* 1978, *48,* 1155–1156.

D'Zurilla, T. J., Wilson, G. T., & Nelson, R. A preliminary study of the effectiveness of graduated prolonged exposure in the treatment of irrational fear. *Behavior Therapy,* 1973, *4,* 672–685.

Ellis, A. *Reason and emotion in psychotherapy.* New York: Lyle-Stuart, 1962.

Ellis, A. A note on the treatment of agoraphobics with cognitive modification with prolonged exposure *in vivo. Behaviour Research and Therapy,* 1979, *17,* 162–164.

Emmelkamp, P. M. G. Self-observation versus flooding in the treatment of agoraphobia. *Behaviour Research and Therapy.* 1974, *12,* 229–237.

Emmelkamp, P. M. G. Effects of expectancy on systematic desensitization and flooding. *European Journal of Behavioral Analysis and Modification,* 1975, *1,* 1–11. (a).

Emmelkamp, P. M. G. Face-validity and behaviour therapy. *European Journal of Behavioral Analysis and Modification*, 1975, *1*, 15–19. (b)

Emmelkamp, P. M. G. Phobias: Theoretical and behavioural treatment considerations. In J. C. Boulougouris & A. D. Rabavilas (Eds.), *The treatment of phobic and obsessive compulsive disorders*. New York: Pergamon, 1977.

Emmelkamp, P. M. G. The behavioral study of clinical phobias. In M. Hersen, R. M. Eisler, & P. M. Miller (Eds.), *Progress in Behavior Modification*, Vol. 8. New York: Academic Press, 1979. (a)

Emmelkamp, P. M. G. Recent advances in the treatment of clinical phobias. Paper presented at the Ninth Conference of the European Association of Behaviour Therapy, Paris, September 1979. (b)

Emmelkamp, P. M. G. Relationship between theory and practice in behavior therapy. In W. De Moor, & H. Wijngaarden (Eds.), *Psychotherapy*. Amsterdam: Elsevier, 1980. (a)

Emmelkamp, P. M. G. Agoraphobics' interpersonal problems: Their role in the effects of exposure *in vivo* therapy. *Archives of General Psychiatry*, 1980, *37*, 1303–1306. (b)

Emmelkamp, P. M. G. Obsessive-compulsive disorders: A clinical-research approach. In I. Hand (Ed.), *Obsessions and compulsions—Recent advances in behavioral analysis and modification*. New York: Springer, in press.

Emmelkamp, P. M. G., & Boeke-Slinkers, I. Demand characteristics in behavioral assessment. *Psychological Reports*, 1977, *41*, 1030. (a)

Emmelkamp, P. M. G., & Boeke-Slinkers, I. *The contribution of therapeutic instruction to systematic desensitization with low-fearful and high-fearful subjects.* Unpublished manuscript. University of Groningen, 1977. (b)

Emmelkamp, P. M. G., & Cohen-Kettenis, P. Relationship of locus of control to phobic anxiety and depression. *Psychological Reports*, 1975, *36*, 390.

Emmelkamp, P. M. G., & Emmelkamp-Benner, A. Effects of historically portrayed modeling and group treatment on self-observation: A comparison with agoraphobics. *Behaviour Research and Therapy*, 1975, *13*, 135–139.

Emmelkamp, P. M. G., & Kraanen, J. Therapist controlled exposure *in vivo* versus self-controlled exposure *in vivo*: A comparison with obsessive-compulsive patients. *Behaviour Research and Therapy*, 1977, *15*, 491–495.

Emmelkamp, P. M. G., & Kuipers, A. Agoraphobia: A follow-up study four years after treatment. *British Journal of Psychiatry*, 1979, *134*, 352–355.

Emmelkamp, P. M. G., & Kwee, K. G. Obsessional ruminations: A comparison between thought-stopping and prolonged exposure in imagination. *Behaviour Research and Therapy*, 1977, *15*, 441–444.

Emmelkamp, P. M. G., & Mersch, P. Cognition and exposure in vivo in the treatment of agoraphobia: Short term and delayed effects. *Cognitive Therapy and Research*, 1982, *6*, 77–88.

Emmelkamp, P. M. G., & Straatman, H. A psychoanalytic reinterpretation of the effectiveness of systematic desensitization: Fact or fiction? *Behaviour Research and Therapy*, 1976, *14*, 245–249.

Emmelkamp, P. M. G., & Ultee, K. A. A comparison of successive approximation and self-observation in the treatment of agoraphobia. *Behavior Therapy*, 1974, *5*, 605–613.

Emmelkamp, P. M. G., & Van der Heyden, H. The treatment of harming obsessions. *Behavioural Analysis and Modification*, 1980, *4*, 28–35.

Emmelkamp, P. M. G., & Walta, C. The effects of therapy-set on electrical aversion therapy and covert sensitization. *Behavior Therapy*, 1978, *9*, 185–188.

Emmelkamp, P. M. G., & Wessels, H. Flooding in imagination vs flooding *in vivo*: A comparison with agoraphobics. *Behaviour Research and Therapy*, 1975, *13*, 7–16.

Emmelkamp, P. M. G., Kuipers, A., & Eggeraat, J. Cognitive modification versus prolonged exposure *in vivo*: A comparison with agoraphobics. *Behaviour Research and Therapy*, 1978, *16*, 33–41.

Emmelkamp, P. M. G., Van der Helm, M., Van Zanten, B., & Plochg, I. Treatment of obsessive-compulsive patients: The contribution of self-instructional training to the effectiveness of exposure. *Behaviour Research and Therapy*, 1980, *18*, 61–66.

Engel, B. T. Operant conditioning of cardiac function: Some implications for psychosomatic medicine. *Behavior Therapy*, 1974, *5*, 302–303.

Errera, P., & Coleman, J. V. A long-term follow-up study of neurotic phobic patients in a psychiatric clinic. *Journal of Nervous and Mental Disease*, 1963, *136*, 267–271.

Evans, P. D., & Kellam, A. M. P. Semi-automated desensitization: A controlled clinical trial. *Behaviour Research and Therapy*, 1973, *11*, 641–646.

Everaerd, W. T. A. M., Rijken, H. M., & Emmelkamp, P. M. G. A comparison of "flooding" and "successive approximation" in the treatment of agoraphobia. *Behaviour Research and Therapy*, 1973, *11*, 105–117.

Eysenck, H. J. The learning model of neurosis. *Behaviour Research and Therapy*, 1976, *14*, 251–267.

Fazio, A. F. Implosive therapy with semiclinical phobias. *Journal of Abnormal Psychology*, 1972, *80*, 183–188.

Fenichel, O. *Psychoanalytic theory of neurosis*. New York: Norton, 1963.

Finger, R., & Galassi, J. P. Effects of modifying cognitive versus emotiality responses in the treatment of test anxiety. *Journal of Consulting and Clinical Psychology*, 1977, *45*, 280–287.

Flannery, R. B. A laboratory analogue of two covert reinforcement procedures. *Journal of Behavior Therapy and Experimental Psychiatry*, 1972, *3*, 171–177.

Foa, E. B., & Chambless, D. L. Habituation of subjective anxiety during flooding in imagery. *Behaviour Research and Therapy*, 1978, *16*, 391–399.

Foa, E. B., & Turner, R. M. Massed vs. spaced exposure sessions in the treatment of agoraphobia. Paper presented at the 9th European Conference of Behavior Modification, Paris, Sept. 1979.

Foa, E. B., Blau, J. S., Prout, M., & Latimer, P. Is horror a necessary component of flooding (implosion)? *Behaviour Research and Therapy*, 1977, *15*, 397–402.

Fremouw, W. J., & Zitter, R. E. A comparison of skills training and cognitive restructuring—Relaxation for the treatment of speech anxiety. *Behavior Therapy*, 1978, *9*, 248–259.

Freud, S. Turnings in the world of psycho-analytic therapy. In *Collected papers*, Vol. 2. New York: Basic Books, 1959, pp. 392–402.

Friedman, J. H. Short-term psychotherapy of "phobia of travel." *American Journal of Psychotherapy*, 1950, *4*, 259–278.

Fry, W. F. The marital context of an anxiety syndrome. *Family Process*, 1962, *1*, 245–252.

Gatchel, R. J. Therapeutic effectiveness of voluntary heart rate control in reducing anxiety. *Journal of Consulting and Clinical Psychology*, 1977, *45*, 689–691.

Gatchel, R. J., & Proctor, J. D. Effectiveness of voluntary heart rate control in reducing speech anxiety. *Journal of Consulting and Clinical Psychology*, 1976, *44*, 381–389.

Gatchel, R. J., Hatch, J. P., Watson, P. J., Smith, D., & Gaas, E. Comparative effectiveness of voluntary heart rate control and muscular relaxation as active coping skills for reducing speech anxiety. *Journal of Consulting and Clinical Psychology*, 1977, *45*, 1093–1100.

Gatchel, R. J., Hatch, J. P., Maynard, A., Turns, R., & Taunton-Blackwood, A. Comparison of heart rate biofeedback, and systematic desensitization in reducing speech anxiety: Short- and Long-term effectiveness. *Journal of Consulting and Clinical Psychology*, 1979, *47*, 620–622.

Gauthier, J., & Marshall, W. L. The determination of optimal exposure to phobic stimuli in flooding therapy. *Behaviour Research and Therapy*, 1977, *15*, 403–410.

Gelder, M. G., & Marks, I. M. Severe agoraphobia: A controlled prospective trial of behaviour therapy. *British Journal of Psychiatry*, 1966, *112*, 309–319.

Gelder, M. G., & Marks, I. M. Desensitization and phobias: A crossover study. *British Journal of Psychiatry*, 1968, *114*, 323–328.

Gelder, M. G., and Marks, I. M., & Wolff, H. H. Desensitization and psychotherapy in the treatment of phobic states: A controlled enquiry. *British Journal of Psychiatry*, 1967, *113*, 53–73.

Gelder, M. G., Bancroft, J. H. J., Gath, D. H., Johnston, D. W., Mathews, A. M., & Shaw, P. M. Specific and non-specific factors in behaviour therapy. *British Journal of Psychiatry*, 1973, *123*, 445–462.

Gillan, P., & Rachman, S. An experimental investigation of desensitization in phobic patients. *British Journal of Psychiatry*, 1974, *124*, 392–401.

Girodo, M., & Roehl, J. Cognitive preparation and coping self-talk: Anxiety management during the stress of flying. *Journal of Consulting and Clinical Psychology*, 1978, *46*, 978–989.

Glass, C. R., Gottman, J. M., & Shmurak, S. H. Response acquisition and cognitive self-statement modification approaches to dating-skills training. *Journal of Counseling Psychology*, 1976, *23*, 520–526.

Glogower, F. D., Fremouw, W. J., & McCroskey, J. C. A component analysis of cognitive restructuring. *Cognitive Therapy and Research*, 1978, *2*, 209–223.

Goldfried, M. R. Systematic desensitization as training in self-control. *Journal of Consulting and Clinical Psychology*, 1971, *37*, 228–234.

Goldfried, M. R., & Goldfried, A. P. Importance of hi-

erarchy content in the self-control of anxiety. *Journal of Consulting and Clinical Psychology*, 1977, *45*, 124–134.

Goldfried, M. R., & Sobocinski, D. The effect of irrational beliefs on emotional arousal. *Journal of Consulting and Clinical Psychology*, 1975, *43*, 504–510.

Goldfried, M. R., & Trier, C. S. Effectiveness of relaxation as an active coping skill. *Journal of Abnormal Psychology*, 1974, *83*, 348–355.

Goldfried, M. R., Decenteceo, E. T., & Weinberg, L. Systematic rational restructuring as a self-control technique. *Behavior Therapy*, 1974, *5*, 247–254.

Goldfried, M. R., Linehan, M. M., & Smith, J. L. The reduction of test anxiety through rational restructuring. *Journal of Consulting and Clinical Psychology*, 1978, *37*, 228–234.

Goldstein, A. J. Learning theory insufficiency in understanding agoraphobia: A plea for empiricism. *Proceedings of the European Association for Behaviour Therapy*. München: Urban & Schwarzenberg, 1973.

Goldstein, A. J., & Chambless, D. L. A reanalysis of agoraphobia. *Behavior Therapy*, 1978, *9*, 47–59.

Goldstein-Fodor, I. G. The phobic syndrome in women. In V. Franks & V. Burtle (Eds.), *Women in therapy*. New York: Brunner/Mazel, 1974.

Goodstein, R. K., & Swift, K. Psychotherapy with phobic patients: The marriage relationship as the source of symptoms and focus of treatment. *American Journal of Psychotherapy*, 1977, *31*, 284–293.

Goorney, A. B., & O'Connor, P. J. Anxiety associated with flying. *British Journal of Psychiatry*, 1971, *119*, 159–166.

Guidry, L. S., & Randolph, D. L. Covert reinforcement in the treatment of test anxiety. *Journal of Counseling Psychology*, 1974, *21*, 260–264.

Hafner, R. J. Fresh symptom emergence after intensive behaviour therapy. *British Journal of Psychiatry*, 1976, *129*, 378–383.

Hafner, R. J., & Marks, I. M. Exposure *in vivo* of agoraphobics: Contributions of diazepam, group exposure, and anxiety evocation. *Psychological Medicine*, 1976, *6*, 71–88.

Hafner, R. J., & Milton, F. The influence of propranolol on the exposure *in vivo* of agoraphobics. *Psychological Medicine*, 1977, *7*, 419–425.

Hain, J. D., Butcher, H. C., & Stevenson, I. Systematic desensitization therapy: An analysis of results in twenty-seven patients. *British Journal of Psychiatry*, 1966, *112*, 295–307.

Hall, R., & Goldberg, D. The role of social anxiety in social interaction difficulties. *British Journal of Psychiatry*, 1977, *131*, 610–615.

Hand, I., Lamontagne, Y., & Marks, I. M. Group exposure (flooding) *in vivo* for agoraphobics. *British Journal of Psychiatry*, 1974, *124*, 588–602.

Hayes, S. C. The role of approach contingencies in phobic behavior. *Behavior Therapy*, 1976, *7*, 28–36.

Haynes, S. N., Moseley, D., & McGowan, W. T. Relaxation training and biofeedback in the reduction of frontalis muscle tension. *Psychophysiology*, 1975, *12*, 547–552.

Hekmat, H. Systematic versus semantic desensitization and implosive therapy: A comparative study. *Journal of Consulting and Clinical Psychology*, 1973, *40*, 202–209.

Hepner, A., & Cauthen, N. R. Effect of subject control and graduated exposure on snake phobias. *Journal of Consulting and Clinical Psychology*, 1975, *43*, 297–304.

Hollandsworth, J. G., Glazeski, R. C., Kirkland, K., Jones, G. E., & Van Norman, L. R. An analysis of the nature and effects of test anxiety: Cognitive, behavioral, and physiological components. *Cognitive Therapy and Research*, 1979, *3*, 165–180.

Holroyd, K. A. Cognition and desensitization in the group treatment of test anxiety. *Journal of Consulting and Clinical Psychology*, 1976, *44*, 991–1001.

Holroyd, K. A., Westbrook, T., Wolf, M., & Bradhorn, E. Performance, cognition, and physiological responding in test anxiety. *Journal of Abnormal Psychology*, 1978, *87*, 442–451.

Horne, A. M., & Matson, J. L. A comparison of modeling, desensitization, flooding, study skills, and control groups for reducing test anxiety. *Behavior Therapy*, 1977, *8*, 1–8.

Hurley, A. D. Covert reinforcement: The contribution of the reinforcing stimulus to treatment outcome. *Behavior Therapy*, 1976, *7*, 374–378.

Hussain, M. Z. Desensitization and flooding (implosion) in treatment of phobias. *American Journal of Psychiatry*, 1971, *127*, 1509–1514.

Hussian, R. A., & Lawrence, P. S. The reduction of test, state, and trait anxiety by test-specific and generalized stress inoculation training. *Cognitive Therapy and Research*, 1978, *2*, 25–37.

Jaremko, M., & Wenrich, W. A prophylactic usage of systematic desensitization. *Journal of Behavior Therapy and Experimental Psychiatry*, 1973, *4*, 103–108.

Jessup, B. A., & Neufeld, R. W. J. Effects of biofeedback and "autogenic relaxation" techniques on physiological and subjective responses in psychiatric patients: A preliminary analysis. *Behavior Therapy*, 1977, *8*, 160–167.

Johnston, D. W., & Gath, D. Arousal levels and attribution effects in diazepam-assisted flooding. *British Journal of Psychiatry*, 1973, *123*, 463–466.

Johnston, D. W., Lancashire, M., Mathews, A. M., Munby, M., Shaw, P. M., & Gelder, M. G. Imaginal flooding and exposure to real phobic situations: Changes during treatment. *British Journal of Psychiatry*, 1976, *129*, 372–377.

Kanter, N. J., & Goldfried, M. R. Relative effectiveness of rational restructuring and self-control desensitization in the reduction of interpersonal anxiety. *Behavior Therapy*, 1979, *10*, 472–490.

Karst, T. O., & Trexler, L. D. Initial study using fixed-role and rational-emotive therapy in treating public speaking anxiety. *Journal of Consulting and Clinical Psychology*, 1970, *34*, 360–366.

Kazdin, A. E. Evaluating the generality of findings in analogue research. *Journal of Consulting and Clinical Psychology*, 1978, *46*, 673–686.

Kazdin, A. E., & Smith, G. A. Covert conditioning: A review and evaluation. *Advances in Behaviour Research and Therapy*, 1979, *2*, 57–98.

Kelly, D., Guirguis, W., Frommer, E., Mitchell-Heggs, N., & Sargant, W. Treatment of phobic states with antidepressants, a retrospective study of 246 patients. *British Journal of Psychiatry*, 1970, *116*, 387–398.

Kelly, G. A. *The psychology of personal constructs.* New York: Norton, 1955.

Kirsch, I., & Henry, D. Extinction versus credibility in the desensitization of speech anxiety. *Journal of Consulting and Clinical Psychology*, 1977, *45*, 1052–1059.

Kirsch, I., & Henry, D. *Self-desensitization and meditation in the reduction of public speaking anxiety.* Unpublished manuscript, 1979.

Kirsch, I., Wolpin, M., & Knutson, J. L. A comparison of in vivo methods for rapid reduction of "stage fright" in the college classroom: A field experiment. *Behavior Therapy*, 1975, *6*, 165–171.

Kostka, M. P., & Galassi, J. P. Group systematic desensitization versus covert positive reinforcement in the reduction of test anxiety. *Journal of Counseling Psychology*, 1974, *21*, 464–468.

Ladouceur, R. An experimental test of the learning paradigm of covert positive reinforcement in deconditioning anxiety. *Journal of Behavior Therapy and Experimental Psychiatry*, 1974, *5*, 3–6.

Ladouceur, R. Rationale of covert positive reinforcement: Additional evidence. *Psychological Reports*, 1977, *41*, 547–550.

Ladouceur, R. Rationale of systematic desensitization and covert positive reinforcement. *Behaviour Research and Therapy*, 1978, *16*, 411–420.

Lazarus, A. A. *Behavior therapy and beyond.* New York: McGraw-Hill, 1971.

Ledwidge, B. Cognitive behavior modification: A step in the wrong direction? *Psychological Bulletin*, 1978, *85*, 353–375.

Leitenberg, H., & Callahan, E. J. Reinforced practice and reduction of different kinds of fear in adults and children. *Behaviour Research and Therapy*, 1973, *11*, 19–30.

Leitenberg, H., Agras, S., Butz, R., & Wincze, J. Relationship between heart rate and behavioral change during the treatment of phobias. *Journal of Abnormal Psychology*, 1971, *78*, 59–68.

Leitenberg, H., Agras, W. S., Allen, R., Butz, R., & Edwards, J. Feedback and therapist praise during treatment of phobia. *Journal of Consulting and Clinical Psychology*, 1975, *43*, 396–404.

Levis, D. J., & Hare, N. A review of the theoretical rationale and empirical support for the extinction approach of implosive (flooding) therapy. In M. Hersen, R. M. Eisler, & P. M. Miller (Eds.), *Progress in behavior modification*, Vol. 4. New York: Academic Press, 1977.

Lewis, S. A. A comparison of behavior therapy techniques in the reduction of fearful avoidance behavior. *Behavior Therapy*, 1974, *5*, 648–655.

Lick, J. Expectancy, false galvanic skin response feedback, and systematic desensitization in the modification of phobic behavior. *Journal of Consulting and Clinical Psychology*, 1975, *43*, 557–567.

Liddell, A., & Lyons, M. Thunderstorm phobias. *Behaviour Research and Therapy*, 1978, *16*, 306–308.

Liebert, R. M., & Morris, L. W. Cognitive and emotional components of test anxiety: A distinction and some initial data. *Psychological Reports*, 1967, *20*, 975–978.

Linehan, M. M., Goldfried, M. R., & Powers-Goldfried,

A. Assertion therapy: Skills training or cognitive restructuring. *Behavior Therapy*, 1979, *10*, 372–388.

Lipsedge, M. S., Hajioff, J., Huggins, P., Napier, L., Pearce, J., Pike, D. J., & Rich, M. The management of severe agoraphobia: A comparison of iproniazid and systematic desensitization. *Psychopharmacologia*, 1973, *32*, 67–88.

Little, S., & Jackson, B. The treatment of test anxiety through attentional and relaxation training. *Psychotherapy: Theory, Research and Practice*, 1974, *11*, 175–178.

Litvak, S. B. A comparison of two brief group behavior therapy techniques on the reduction of avoidance behavior. *Psychological Record*, 1969, *19*, 329–334.

Marcia, J. E., Rubin, B. M., & Efran, J. S. Systematic desensitization: Expectancy change or counter-conditioning? *Journal of Abnormal Psychology*, 1969, *74*, 382–387.

Marks, I. M. Behavioural treatments of phobic and obsessive-compulsive disorders: A critical appraisal. In M. Hersen, R. M. Eisler, & P. M. Miller (Eds.), *Progress in behavior modification*, Vol. 1. New York: Academic Press, 1975.

Marks, I. M., Boulougouris, J., & Marset, P. Flooding versus desensitization in the treatment of phobic patients: A cross-over study. *British Journal of Psychiatry*, 1971, *119*, 353–375.

Marks, I. M., Viswanathan, R., Lipsedge, M. S., & Gardner, R. Enhanced relief of phobias by flooding during waning diazepam effect. *British Journal of Psychiatry*, 1972, *121*, 493–506.

Marshall, W. L., Boutilier, J., & Minnes, P. The modification of phobic behavior by covert reinforcement. *Behavior Therapy*, 1974, *5*, 469–480.

Marshall, W. L., Gauthier, J., Christie, M. M., Currie, D. W., & Gordon, A. Flooding therapy: Effectiveness, stimulus characteristics, and the value of brief in vivo exposure. *Behaviour Research and Therapy*, 1977, *15*, 79–87.

Marzillier, J. S., Lambert, C., & Kellett, J. A controlled evaluation of systematic desensitization and social skills training for social inadequate psychiatric patients. *Behaviour Research and Therapy*, 1976, *14*, 225–228.

Mathews, A. M., & Rezin, V. Treatment of dental fears by imaginal flooding and rehearsal of coping behaviour. *Behaviour Research and Therapy*, 1977, *15*, 321–328.

Mathews, A. M., & Shaw, P. M. Emotional arousal and persuasion effects in flooding. *Behaviour Research and Therapy*, 1973, *11*, 587–598.

Mathews, A. M., Johnston, D. W., Lancashire, M., Munby, M., Shaw, P. M., & Gelder, M. G. Imaginal flooding and exposure to real phobic situations: Treatment outcome with agoraphobic patients. *British Journal of Psychiatry*, 1976, *129*, 362–371.

Mathews, A. M., Teasdale, J. D., Munby, M., Johnston, D. W., & Shaw, P. M. A home-base treatment program for agoraphobia. *Behavior Therapy*, 1977, *8*, 915–924.

Mathews, A., Jannoun, L., & Gelder, M. Self-help methods in agoraphobia. Paper presented at the Conference of the European Association of Behavior Therapy, Paris, Sept. 1979.

May, J. R., & Johnson, J. Physiological activity to internally elicited arousal and inhibitory thoughts. *Journal of Abnormal Psychology*, 1973, *82*, 239–245.

McCutcheon, B. A., & Adams, H. E. The physiological basis of implosive therapy. *Behaviour Research and Therapy*, 1975, *13*, 93–100.

McDonald, R., Sartory, G., Grey, S. J., Cobb, J., Stern, R., & Marks, I. M. The effects of self-exposure instruction on agoraphobic outpatients. *Behaviour Research and Therapy*, 1979, *17*, 83–86.

McGlynn, F. D., & McDonell, R. M. Subjective ratings of credibility following brief exposures to desensitization and pseudotherapy. *Behaviour Research and Therapy*, 1974, *12*, 141–146.

McGlynn, F. D., Reynolds, E. J., & Linder, L. H. Experimental desensitization following therapeutically oriented and physiologically oriented instructions. *Journal of Behavior Therapy and Experimental Psychiatry*, 1971, *2*, 13–18.

McGlynn, F. D., Gaynor, R., & Puhr, J. Experimental desensitization of snake-advoidance after an instructional manipulation. *Journal of Clinical Psychology*, 1972, *28*, 224–227.

McGlynn, F. D., Kinjo, K., Doherty, G. Effects of cue-controlled relaxation, a placebo treatment, and no-treatment on changes in self-reported test anxiety among college students. *Journal of Clinical Psychology*, 1978, *34*, 707–714.

McReynolds, W. T., & Grizzard, R. H. A comparison of three fear reduction procedures. *Psychotherapy: Theory, Research and Practice*, 1971, *8*, 264–268.

McReynolds, W. T., Barnes, A. R., Brooks, S., & Rehagen, N. J. The role of attention-placebo influences in the efficacy of systematic desensitization. *Journal Consulting and Clinical Psychology*, 1973, *41*, 86–92.

Mealiea, W. L., & Nawas, M. M. The comparative effectiveness of systematic desensitization and implosive therapy in the treatment of snake phobia. *Journal of Behavior Therapy and Experimental Psychiatry*, 1971, *2*, 185–194.

Meichenbaum, D. H. Examination of model characteristics in reducing avoidance behavior. *Journal of Personality and Social Psychology*, 1971, *17*, 298–307.

Meichenbaum, D. H. Cognitive modification of test anxious college students. *Journal of Consulting and Clinical Psychology*, 1972, *39*, 370–380.

Meichenbaum, D. H. Self instructional methods. In F. H. Kanfer & A. P. Goldstein (Eds.), *Helping people change*. New York: Pergamon, 1975.

Melamed, B. G. Behavioral approaches to fear in dental settings. In M. Hersen, R. M. Eisler, & P. M. Miller (Eds.), *Progress in behavior modification*, Vol. 7. New York: Academic Press, 1979.

Melnick, J. A. A comparison of replication techniques in the modification of minimal dating behavior. *Journal of Abnormal Psychology*, 1973, *81*, 51–59.

Meyer, V., & Crisp, A. H. Some problems in behavior therapy. *British Journal of Psychiatry*, 1966, *112*, 367–381.

Miles, H., Barrabee, E., & Finesinger, J. Evaluation of psychotherapy: With a follow-up study of 62 cases of anxiety neurosis. *Psychosomatic Medicine*, 1951, *13*, 83–106.

Morris, R. J., & Suckerman, K. R. The importance of the

therapeutic relationship in systematic desensitization. *Journal of Consulting and Clinical Psychology*, 1974, *42*, 147. (a)

Morris, R. J., & Suckerman, K. R. Therapist warmth as a factor in automated systematic systematic desensitization. *Journal of Consulting and Clinical Psychology*, 1974, *42*, 244–250. (b)

Mountjoy, C. Q., Roth, M., Garside, R. F. & Leitch, I. M. A clinical trial of phenelzine in anxiety depressive and phobic neuroses. *British Journal of Psychiatry*, 1977, *131*, 486–492.

Mowrer, O. H. *Learning theory and personality dynamics.* New York: Arnold Press, 1950.

Murray, E. J., & Foote, F. The origins of fear of snakes. *Behaviour Research and Therapy*, 1979, *17*, 489–493.

Mylar, J. L., & Clement, P. W. Prediction and comparison of outcome in systematic desensitization and implosion. *Behaviour Research and Therapy*, 1972, *10*, 235–246.

Nau, S. D., Caputo, J. A., & Borkovec, T. D. The relationship between therapy credibility and simulated therapy response. *Journal of Behavior Therapy and Experimental Psychiatry*, 1974, *5*, 129–134.

Nunes, J. S., & Marks, I. M. Feedback of true heart rate during exposure *in vivo*. *Archives of General Psychiatry*, 1975, *32*, 933–936.

Nunes, J. S., & Marks, I. M. Feedback of true heart rate during exposure *in vivo*: Partial replication with methodological improvement. *Archives of General Psychiatry*, 1976, *33*, 1346–1350.

Odom, J. V., Nelson, R. O., & Wein, K. S. The differential effectiveness of five treatment procedures on three response systems in a snake phobia analog study. *Behavior Therapy*, 1978, *9*, 936–942.

Ohman, A. Fear relevance, autonomic conditioning, and phobias: A laboratory model. In S. Bates, W. S. Dockens, K. Götestam, I. Melin, & P. O. Sjöden (Eds.), *Trends in behavior therapy.* New York: Academic Press, 1979.

Orenstein, H., & Carr, J. Implosion therapy by tape-recording. *Behaviour Research and Therapy*, 1975, *13*, 177–182.

Pare, C. M. B. Side-effects and toxic effects of antidepressants. *Proceedings of Royal Society of Medicine*, 1964, *57*, 757–758.

Prochaska, J. O. Symptom and dynamic cues in the implosive treatment of test anxiety. *Journal of Abnormal Psychology*, 1971, *77*, 133–142.

Rabavilas, A. D., & Boulougouris, J. C. Therapeutic relationship and long term outcome with flooding treatment. Paper presented at the Ninth Conference of the European Association of Behaviour Therapy, Paris, Sept. 1979.

Rabavilas, A. D., Boulougouris, J. C., & Stefanis, C. Duration of flooding sessions in the treatment of obsessive-compulsive patients. *Behaviour Research and Therapy*, 1976, *14*, 349–355.

Rachman, S. The passing of the two-stage theory of fear and avoidance: Fresh possibilities. *Behaviour Research and Therapy*, 1976, *14*, 125–134.

Rachman, S. The conditioning theory of fear-acquisition: A critical examination. *Behaviour Research and Therapy*, 1977, *15*, 375–387.

Rankin, H. Are models necessary? *Behaviour Research and Therapy*, 1976, *14*, 181–183.

Rappaport, H. Modification of avoidance behavior: Expectancy, autonomic reactivity, and verbal report. *Journal of Consulting and Clinical Psychology*, 1972, *39*, 404–414.

Reinking, R. H., & Kohl, M. L. Effects of various forms of relaxation training on physiological and self-report measures of relaxation. *Journal of Consulting and Clinical Psychology*, 1975, *43*, 595–600.

Rimm, D., & Litvak, S. Self-verbalization and emotion arousal. *Journal of Abnormal Psychology*, 1969, *74*, 181–187.

Rimm, D. C., Janda, L. H., Lancaster, D. W., Nahl, M., & Dittmar, K. An exploratory investigation of the origin and maintenance of phobias. *Behaviour Research and Therapy*, 1977, *15*, 231–238.

Ritter, B. The use of contact desensitization, demonstration-plus-participation and demonstration alone in the treatment of acrophobia. *Behaviour Research and Therapy*, 1969, *7*, 157–164.

Robert, A. H. House-bound housewives: A follow-up study of a phobic anxiety state. *British Journal of Psychiatry*, 1964, *110*, 191–197.

Rogers, T., & Craighead, W. E. Physiological responses to self-statements: The effects of statement valence and discrepancy. *Cognitive Therapy and Research*, 1977, *1*, 99–119.

Rosen, G. M. Therapy set: Its effect on subjects' involvement in systematic desensitization and treatment outcome. *Journal of Abnormal Psychology*, 1974, *83*, 291–300.

Russell, P. L., & Brandsma, J. M. A theoretical and empirical integration of the rational emotive and classical conditioning theories. *Journal of Consulting and Clinical Psychology*, 1974, *42*, 389–397.

Rutner, I. T. The effects of feedback and instructions on phobic behavior. *Behavior Therapy*, 1973, *4*, 338–348.

Schandler, S. L., & Grings, W. W. An examination of methods for producing relaxation during short-term laboratory sessions. *Behaviour Research and Therapy*, 1976, *14*, 419–426.

Seligman, M. E. P. Phobias and preparedness. *Behavior Therapy*, 1971, *2*, 307–320.

Shaw, P. M. A comparison of three behaviour therapies in the treatment of social phobia. Paper read at the British Association for Behavioral Psychotherapy, Exeter, 1976.

Shepherd, G. W., & Watts, F. N. Heart rate control in psychiatric patients. *Behavior Therapy*, 1974, *5*, 153–154.

Sherman, A. R. Real-life exposure as a primary therapeutic factor in the desensitization treatment of fear. *Journal of Abnormal Psychology*, 1972, *79*, 19–28.

Silverman, L. H., Frank, S. G., & Dachinger, P. A. A psychoanalytic reinterpretation of the effectiveness of systematic desensitization: Experimental data bearing on the role of merging fantasies. *Journal of Abnormal Psychology*, 1974, *83*, 313–318.

Sjöqvist, F. Interaction between mono-amine oxidase inhibitors and other substances. *Proceedings of the Royal Society of Medicine*, 1963, *58*, 967–978.

Smith, G. P., & Coleman, R. E. Processes underlying

generalization through participant modeling with self-directed practice. *Behaviour Research and Therapy*, 1977, *15*, 204–206.

Smith, R. E., & Nye, S. L. A comparison of implosive therapy and systematic desensitization in the treatment of test anxiety. *Journal of Consulting and Clinical Psychology*, 1973, *44*, 37–42.

Smith, R. E., Diener, E., & Beaman, A Demand characteristics and the behavioral avoidance measures of fear in behavior therapy analogue research. *Behavior Therapy*, 1974, *5*, 172–182.

Snyder, A. L., & Deffenbacher, J. L. Comparison of relaxation as self-control and systematic desensitization in the treatment of test anxiety. *Journal of Consulting and Clinical Psychology*, 1977, *45*, 1202–1203.

Solyom, L., McClure, D. J., Heseltine, G. F. D., Ledwidge, B., & Solyom, C. Variables in the aversion relief therapy of phobics. *Behavior Therapy*, 1972, *3*, 21–28.

Solyom, L., Heseltine, G. F. D., McClure, D. J., Solyom, C., Ledwidge, B., & Steinberg, L. Behaviour therapy versus drug therapy in the treatment of phobic neurosis. *Canadian Psychiatric Association Journal*, 1973, *18*, 25–31.

Solyom, L., Beck, P., Solyom, C., & Hugel, R. Some etiological factors in phobic neurosis. *Canadian Psychiatric Association Journal*, 1974, *19*, 69–78.

Solyom, C., Solyom, L., La Pierre, Y., Pecknold, J. C., & Morton, L. Phenelzine and exposure in the treatment of phobias. *Journal of Biological Psychiatry*, 1981, *16*, 239–248.

Spiegler, M. D., Cooley, E. J., Marshall, G. J., Prince, H. T., Puckett, S. P., & Skenazy, J. A. A self-control versus a counterconditioning paradigm for systematic desensitization: An experimental comparison. *Journal of Counseling Psychology*, 1976, *23*, 83–86.

Stampfl, T. G., & Levis, D. J. Essentials of implosive therapy: A learning-theory-based psychodynamic behavioral therapy. *Journal of Abnormal Psychology*, 1967, *72*, 496–503.

Stampfl, T. G., & Levis, D. J. Implosive therapy: A behavioral therapy? *Behaviour Research and Therapy*, 1968, *6*, 31–36.

Stern, R., & Marks, I. M. Brief and prolonged flooding: A comparison in agoraphobic patients. *Archives of General Psychiatry*, 1973, *28*, 270–276.

Suarez, Y., Adams, H. E., & McCutcheon, B. A. Flooding and systematic desensitization: Efficacy in subclinical phobics as a function of arousal. *Journal of Consulting and Clinical Psychology*, 1976, *44*, 872.

Suinn, R. M. Anxiety management training to control general anxiety. In J. D. Krumboltz & C. E. Thoresen (Eds.), *Counseling Methods*. New York: Holt, Rinehart, & Winston, 1976.

Suinn, R. M., & Richardson, F. Anxiety management training: A non-specific behavior therapy program for anxiety control. *Behavior Therapy*, 1971, *2*, 498–511.

Sullivan, B. J., & Denney, D. R. Expectancy and phobic level: Effects on desensitization. *Journal of Consulting and Clinical Psychology*, 1977, *45*, 763–771.

Sutton-Simon, K., & Goldfried, M. R. Faulty thinking patterns in two types of anxiety. *Cognitive Therapy and Research*, 1979, *3*, 193–203.

Teasdale, J. D., Walsh, P. A., Lancashire, M., & Mathews, A. M. Group exposure for agoraphobics: A replication study. *British Journal of Psychiatry*, 1977, *130*, 186–193.

Terhune, W. The phobic syndrome. *Archives of Neurology and Psychiatry*, 1949, *62*, 162–172.

Thase, M. E., & Moss, M. K. The relative efficacy of covert modeling procedures and guided participant modeling in the reduction of avoidance behavior. *Journal of Behavior Therapy and Experimental Psychiatry*, 1976, *7*, 7–12.

Thorpe, G. L. Desensitization, behavior rehearsal, self-instructional training and placebo effects on assertive-refusal behavior. *European Journal of Behavioural Analysis and Modification*, 1975, *1*, 30–44.

Thorpe, G. L., Amatu, H. I., Blakey, R. S., & Burns, L. E. Contributions of overt instructional rehearsal and "specific insight" to the effectiveness of self-instructional training: A preliminary study. *Behavior Therapy*, 1976, *7*, 504–511.

Tori, C., & Worell, L. Reduction of human avoidant behavior: A comparison of counterconditioning, expectancy and cognitive information approaches. *Journal of Consulting and Clinical Psychology*, 1973, *41*, 269–278.

Townsend, R. E., House, J. F., & Addario, D. A comparison of biofeedback mediated relaxation and group therapy in the treatment of chronic anxiety. *American Journal of Psychiatry*, 1975, *32*, 598–601.

Trower, P., Yardley, K., Bryant, B. M., & Shaw, P. The treatment of social failure: A comparison of anxiety-reduction and skills-acquisition procedures on two social problems. *Behavior Modification*, 1978, *2*, 41–60.

Tyrer, P., Candy, J., & Kelly, D. A study of the clinical effects of phenelzine and placebo in the treatment of phobic anxiety. *Psychopharmacologica*, 1973, *32*, 237–254.

Ullrich, R., Ullrich, R., Crombach, G., & Peikert, V. *Three flooding procedures in the treatment of agoraphobics*. Paper read at the European Conference on Behaviour Modification, Wexford, Ireland, 1972.

Van Son, M. J. M. *Sociale vaardigheidstherapie*. Amsterdam: Swets and Zeitlinger, 1978.

Watson, J. P., & Marks, I. M. Relevant and irrelevant fear in flooding—A crossover study of phobic patients. *Behavior Therapy*, 1971, *2*, 275–293.

Watson, J., & Rayner, R. Conditioned emotional reactions. *Journal of Experimental Psychology*, 1920, *3*, 1–22.

Watson, J. P., Gaind, R., & Marks, I. M. Physiological habituation to continuous phobic stimulation. *Behaviour Research and Therapy*, 1972, *10*, 269–278.

Watson, J. P., Mullett, G. E., & Pillay, H. The effects of prolonged exposure to phobic situations upon agoraphobic patients treated in groups. *Behaviour Research and Therapy*, 1973, *11*, 531–546.

Weissberg, M. A comparison of direct and vicarious treatments of speech anxiety: Desensitization, desensitization with coping imagery, and cognitive modification. *Behavior Therapy*, 1977, *8*, 606–620.

Wickramasekera, I. Heart rate feedback and the management of cardiac neurosis. *Journal of Abnormal Psychology*, 1974, *83*, 578–580.

Wilkins, W. Expectancy of therapeutic gain: An empirical and conceptual critique. *Journal of Consulting and Clinical Psychology*, 1973, *40*, 69–77.

Wilkins, W. Expectancies and therapy effectiveness: Emmelkamp versus Davison and Wilson. *Behavioural Analysis and Modification*, 1979, *3*, 109–116.

Willis, R. W., & Edwards, J. A. A study of the comparative effectiveness of systematic desensitization and implosive therapy. *Behaviour Research and Therapy*, 1969, *7*, 387–395.

Wilson, G. T., & Davison, G. C. "Effects of expectancy on systematic desensitization and flooding." A critical analysis. *European Journal of Behavioural Analysis and Modification*, 1975, *1*, 12–14.

Wolfe, J. L., & Fodor, I. G. Modifying assertive behavior in women: A comparison of three approaches. *Behavior Therapy*, 1977, *8*, 567–574.

Wolpe, J. *Psychotherapy and reciprocal inhibition*. Stanford, Calif.: Standford University Press, 1958.

Wolpe, J. Quantitative relationships in the systematic desensitization of phobias. *American Journal of Psychiatry*, 1963, *119*, 1062–1068.

Wolpe, J. *The practice of behavior therapy*. New York: Pergamon, 1973.

Yorkston, N. J., Sergeant, H. G. S., & Rachman, S. Methohexitone relaxation for desensitizing agoraphobic patients. *Lancet*, 1968, *2*, 651–653.

Zemore, R. Systematic desensitization as a method of teaching a general anxiety-reducing skill. *Journal of Consulting and Clinical Psychology*, 1975, *43*, 157–161.

Zitrin, C. M., Klein, D. F., & Woerner, M. G. Behavior therapy, supportive psychotherapy, imipramine and phobias. *Archives of General Psychiatry*, 1978, *35*, 307–316.

Depression

Peter M. Lewinsohn and Harry M. Hoberman

Introduction

The behavioral study of depression has reached its adolescence. As recently as 5 years ago, Becker (1974) observed that the behaviorists had relatively little to say about depression. The first behaviorally oriented single-case studies began to appear in the literature only some 10 years ago (e.g., Burgess, 1969; Johansson, Lewinsohn, & Flippo, 1969; Lazarus, 1968). It was not until 1973 that the first group-design studies appeared in the literature (McLean, Ogston, & Grauer, 1973; Shipley & Fazio, 1973). Thus, the systematic investigation of depression within a behavioral framework is a very recent phenomenon. Since 1973, at least 42 outcome studies of behavioral treatments of depression have been reported, and several major reviews have appeared (e.g., Blaney, 1979; Craighead, 1979; Hollon, 1979; Parloff, Wolfe, Hadley, & Waskow, 1978; Rehm & Kornblith, 1979; Rush & Beck, 1978). In a short period of time, both the scope and the number of behavioral studies of depression have increased dramatically. Stimulated by the increasing evidence that a variety of structured behavioral and cognitive therapies are effective in ameliorating depression, this prolific activity has resulted in an increased acceptance of such approaches among clinicians.

Overview

The purpose of this chapter is to review the steadily accumulating literature on behavioral and cognitive theories of and interventions for depression in adults. The intention of the authors is to be "illuminatory"; we seek to clarify the assumptions and implications of the major behavioral theories and therapies for a subset of affective disorders, what is referred to as *unipolar depression*. Bipolar and psychotic depression are not discussed. To the end of clarification, the chapter begins with a review of the historical development of behavioral approaches to depression. Epidemiological considerations relevant to depression are then noted. Next, the major theories or models of depression are discussed, including experimental findings on the mechanisms hypothesized to be significant in the onset and maintenance of depressive behavior. Following this discussion, the assessment of depression level and of behaviors functionally related to depression is considered. Subsequently, theory-based treatment strategies, as well as

Peter M. Lewinsohn and Harry M. Hoberman • Psychology Department, University of Oregon, Eugene, Oregon 97403.

more eclectic intervention procedures, are examined; relevant outcome studies of cognitive and/or behavioral therapies are evaluated. Finally, in light of the preceding review of significant research findings, new directions in the behavioral study and treatment of depressive behavior are discussed.

Historical Perspective

Psychoanalytic formulations (e.g., Abraham, 1960; Bibring, 1953; Freud, 1917/1957; Jacobson, 1971) dominated the psychological study of depression for many years. The psychoanalytic position compares depression with grief reactions, suggesting that depression may occur following the loss of a real or a fantasied love object in conjunction with certain intrapsychic processes, such as a loss of self-esteem and internalized hostility. However, this conceptualization has not been productive in generating empirical research or in developing treatment procedures specific to depression.

Despite this void, behavioral researchers, as was indicated, have only recently begun to study the phenomena of depression. Several reasons have been suggested to explain why behavior modification was late in attacking the problem of depressive disorders (Craighead, 1979; Lewinsohn, Weinstein, & Shaw, 1969):

1. The early proponents of behavior modification focused on circumscribed problems that were amenable to study in the experimental-clinical laboratory.
2. A major symptom of depression refers to a subjective state; depression had traditionally not been defined in terms of *specific* somatic-motor behaviors, which until the 1970s were the focus of behavioral assessment and intervention.
3. It was difficult to fit depression within the "learning theory" formulation espoused during the early years of behavior modification. As the theoretical underpinnings of behavior modification were broadened (e.g., Bandura, 1977; Mahoney, 1974) and the diagnostic description of depression improved, the behavioral treatment of depression began moving into the mainstream of behavior modification.

Two significant developments or trends can be seen as contributing to the advance of behavioral research on depression. The first trend concerns the empirical delineation of depressive behaviors. As a result of many historical influences, depression emerged as a ubiquitous and elusive phenomenon. A number of weakly defined diagnostic entities (neurotic, psychotic, involutional melancholic, etc.) were said to represent different kinds of affective disorders. In conducting the first descriptive study of clinically depressed individuals, Grinker, Miller, Sabshin, Nunn, and Nunnally (1961) utilized behavior and symptom checklists to investigate the components of the depression syndrome. Through factor analysis, they identified several patterns of feelings and of behavior that delineated the phenomena of depression (dysphoria, self-depreciation, guilt, material burden, social isolation, somatic complaints, and a reduced rate of behavior). In so doing, Grinker *et al.* (1961) made it possible to define depression operationally in terms of several distinct symptom clusters.

The second trend developed as several behavioral theorists attempted to link depression to principles of learning and, in particular, to the concept of reinforcement. The first attempt at a behavioral analysis of depression is contained in Skinner's *Science and Human Behavior* (1953), in which depression is described as a weakening of behavior due to the interruption of established sequences of behavior that have been positively reinforced by the social environment. This conceptualization of depression as an extinction phenomenon, and as a reduced frequency of emission of positively reinforced behavior, has been central to all behavioral positions. Ferster (1965, 1966) provided more detail by suggesting that such diverse factors as sudden environmental changes, punishment and aversive control, and shifts in reinforcement contingencies can give rise to depression (e.g., to a reduced rate of behavior).

Lazarus (1968) also hypothesized depression to be due to insufficient or inadequate

CHAPTER 14 • DEPRESSION   **399**

reinforcement. In his view, the antecedent for depression is a reaction to an actual or anticipated reduction of great magnitude in positive reinforcers. Depressive behavior is maintained by lack of ability, opportunity, or capacity to recognize or utilize available reinforcers. Wolpe (1971) hypothesized depression to be a protective, inhibitory type of behavior in response to prolonged, intense anxiety. Costello (1972) argued that depression results not from the loss of reinforcers *per se* but instead from the loss of reinforcer effectiveness.

Lewinsohn and his associates (Lewinsohn & Shaw, 1969, 1975b, 1976) have also maintained that a low rate of response-contingent positive reinforcement constitutes a sufficient explanation for parts of the depressive syndrome, such as the low rate of behavior. The Lewinsohn group amplified the "behavioral" position through several additional hypotheses:

1. A causal relationship between the low rate of response-contingent positive reinforcement and the feeling of dysphoria.
2. An emphasis on the maintenance of depressive behaviors by the social environment through the provision of contingencies in the form of sympathy, interest, and concern.
3. An emphasis on deficiencies in social skill as an important antecedent to the low rate of positive reinforcement.

The therapeutic implications of these conceptualizations were relatively straightforward. Since the onset of depression was assumed to be preceded by a reduction in response-contingent positive reinforcement, improvement should follow from an increase in positive reinforcement. Hence, the principal goal of treatment should be to restore an adequate schedule of positive reinforcement for the patient by altering the level, the quality, and the range of his/her activities and interpersonal interactions.

Working within a cognitive framework, Beck (1963, 1964, 1967, 1970, 1976; and Beck, Rush, Shaw, & Emery, 1978, 1979) developed both a theory and a therapy for depression that has paralleled and, in a number of important ways, interacted with the development of behavioral approaches to depression. Beck assigned the primary causal role in depression to negative cognitions. Such distorted or unrealistic cognitions were postulated as producing misinterpretations of experiences that lead to the affective reactions and the other behaviors associated with depression.

Currently, the most influential theoretical formulations and clinical approaches may be roughly divided into those that emphasize "reinforcement" and those that emphasize "cognitions" in the etiology of depression. While these two conceptualizations differ fundamentally in where they place the locus of causation, it is important to recognize their similarities: both assume that the depressed patient has *acquired* maladaptive reaction patterns that can be *unlearned*, and the treatments in both are aimed at the modification of relatively specific behaviors and cognitions rather than at a general reorganization of the patient's personality.

Major Theories of Depression

Despite a variety of problems (Eastman, 1976; Blaney, 1977), a number of behavioral formulations have been proposed to explain the phenomena of depression. As noted, contemporary theories of depression fall into two general categories: reinforcement and cognitive (which includes self-control) theories. All of these concern themselves with tracing the course of depression, including its genesis and maintenance, and they have direct implications for treatment. Each formulation assumes one central mechanism to be causal in depression and only secondarily takes account of other symptoms and problem behaviors. Some empirical support has been provided for each of the theories. Two kinds of data are typically presented to justify theoretical formulations: treatment outcome studies and correlational studies using depressed individuals. In the first approach, theorists test their models by way of treatment comparisons. If a theory-based treatment is successful in reducing depression level, the model is said to have been supported. Studies of the second kind present evidence demonstrating covariation between depression level and other variables. As is well known, correlation does not prove causation, and from the available literature, it is impossible to know whether the distinguishing characteristics of depressives that have been identified in correlational studies are of etiological significance or result from the disorder.

Reinforcement Theories[1]

The behavioral or social learning theory of depression, initially proposed by Lewinsohn, Weinstein, and Shaw (1969), has been responsible for generating a substantial amount of empirical research on the phenomena of depression. On the basis of the results of a number of correlational studies on aspects of depressed persons' behavior, as well as from treatment outcome studies (Brown & Lewinsohn, 1982; Lewinsohn, Youngren, & Grosscup, 1980; Sanchez, Lewinsohn, & Larson, 1980; Zeiss, Lewinsohn, & Muñoz, 1979), a model of depression centered on the construct of reinforcement has been progressively refined (Lewinsohn & Amenson, 1978; Lewinsohn & Graf, 1973; Lewinsohn & Talkington, 1979; Lewinsohn, Youngren, & Grosscup, 1980; MacPhillamy & Lewinsohn, 1974).

In contrast to more strictly cognitive theories, Lewinsohn has suggested that the feeling of dysphoria is the central phenomenon of depression. Cognitive symptoms (e.g., low self-esteem, pessimism, feelings of guilt) are viewed as depressives' efforts to explain to themselves, and to others, why they feel bad. The large number of available labeling alternatives (e.g., "I'm sick"; "I'm inadequate") may account for the variety of the specific cognitive symptoms shown by different individuals. Lewinsohn's theory suggests that dysphoria is a direct result of a reduction in the rate of response-contingent reinforcement.

Thus, the relative presence or absence of reinforcing events is postulated as playing the major role in the development and maintenance of depression.

As defined by Glazer (1971), a reinforcer is "any event, stimulus, or state of affairs that changes subsequent behavior when it temporally follows an instance of that behavior" (p. 1). Throughout the various theoretical interpretations of reinforcement mechanisms, this description of reinforcing situations has remained relatively constant. Some consequences increase the probability of the behavior they follow (positive reinforcers); others reduce the probability of the behavior they follow (aversive events). Whether an event has positive or negative reinforcing properties is inferred from its empirical effect on the behavior. As used by Lewinsohn, Youngren, & Grosscup (1980), *reinforcement* is defined by the rate and the quality of a person's interactions with his/her environment. Research has shown that the rate of occurrence of positively reinforcing and of aversive events are independent of one another (e.g., Lewinsohn & Amenson, 1978). Dysphoria is assumed to result when there is either too little positive reinforcement or too much punishment. A low rate of response-contingent positive reinforcement might occur in three ways. First, events contingent on behavior may not be reinforcing, perhaps, as Costello (1972) has suggested, because of a loss of reinforcer effectiveness. Second, events that are reinforcing may become unavailable. For example, an incapacitating injury may prevent an individual from engaging in sports or social activities that have previously been significant in maintaining his/her behavior. Third, reinforcers may be available, but because the individual lacks the necessary repertoire (e.g., social skill), the individual is unable to elicit them. These possibilities are, of course, not mutually exclusive.

Conversely, aversive events or punishment is assumed to play a role in depression when aversive events occur at a high rate; when the individual has a heightened sensitivity to aversive events; and lastly, if the individual lacks the necessary coping skills to terminate aversive events. Finally, Lewinsohn *et al.* (1969) have suggested a feedback loop for the maintenance of depressive behaviors as operants.

[1] Considerable variation exists in the definition of depression employed in the different research studies. Consequently, in order to allow meaningful comparisons across studies, a distinction is made here between depression as defined by rigorous criteria (e.g., diagnostic criteria) and depression as defined by weak criteria (e.g., a high Beck Depression Inventory [BDI] score). Individuals in the former classification are referred to as *patients*, while those in the latter classification are termed *subjects*.

Initially, depressive behaviors (dysphoria and associated symptoms and the low rate of behavior) are elicited or caused by the low rate of reinforcement. Very often, however, the social environment provides social reinforcements in the form of sympathy, interest, and concern, which strengthen and maintain depressive behaviors. These reinforcements are typically provided by a small segment of the depressed person's social environment (e.g., the immediate family). However, since most people in the depressed person's environment (and eventually even his/her family) find these depressive behaviors aversive (Coyne, 1976), they will avoid him/her as much as possible, thus further decreasing the person's rate of receiving positive reinforcement and further accentuating the depression.

As the relationship between reinforcement and depression is central to Lewinsohn's conceptualization, a great deal of the research generated by this group has focused on (1) developing methods of identifying reinforcing and punishing events; (2) comparing the rates of positive reinforcement and of the occurrence of aversive events in depressed and nondepressed groups; and (3) trying to identify specific reinforcement events of special importance in depression.

Lewinsohn and his associates have developed several psychometric instruments: the Pleasant Events Schedule (PES) (MacPhillamy & Lewinsohn, 1971); the Unpleasant Events Schedule (UES) (Lewinsohn, 1975b); and the Interpersonal Events Schedule (IES) (Youngren, Zeiss, & Lewinsohn, 1975). Each of these instruments attempts to measure events assumed to have reinforcing properties. Frequency ratings are obtained for the rate of occurrence of particular behaviors (events) during the preceding month. Additionally, subjective impact scores are obtained; these are assumed to reflect the potential reinforcing value of the events in question. Finally, a multiplicative function of frequency and impact ratings is derived for each event. The sum of these cross-product scores is assumed to be an approximate measure of response-contingent reinforcement obtained over a specific period of time.

Studies using these instruments have consistently shown the depressed to have lower rates of positive reinforcement and higher rates of negative reinforcement and have also shown that predicted changes occur as a function of clinical improvement. Lewinsohn and Graf (1973) found that depressed persons had significantly lower mean numbers of pleasant activities averaged over 30 days. MacPhillamy and Lewinsohn (1974) administered the PES to 120 paid volunteer subjects; the results indicated that the depressed group evidenced significantly lower positive reinforcement because of lower levels of engagement in pleasant activities, decreased enjoyability of the events, and a restricted range of activities. Finally, Lewinsohn, Youngren, and Grosscup (1980) demonstrated that after treatment, depressives who evinced a decrease in depression level showed a corresponding increase in PES cross-product scores and consistent improvement in enjoyability ratings.

An early experiment by Lewinsohn, Lobitz, and Wilson (1973) presented data consistent with the hypothesis that depressives are more sensitive to aversive stimuli (e.g., mild electric shock) when compared with psychiatric and normal control groups. More recently, Lewinsohn, and Amenson (1978) and Lewinsohn and Talkington (1979) found that compared with controls, depressed persons did not report significant differences in the frequency of moderately unpleasant events. While the total amount of experienced aversiveness was substantially higher for depressives than for controls, this difference was the result of depressed persons generally rating events as more aversive.

Youngren and Lewinsohn (1980) attempted to distinguish interpersonal behaviors and events that especially raise difficulties for depressed persons. The results showed that depressed persons reported significantly lower rates of engagement and higher rates of experienced discomfort in social activity and in giving and receiving positive responses. Consequently, it appears that they derive less positive social reinforcement from these interpersonal behaviors and events. Assertion was also found to be a problem for depressives. Additionally, it was found that depressed individuals uniquely reported more discomfort as a result of negative cognitions concerning personal interactions. After treatment, depressed individuals demonstrated significant increases in the frequency and amount of reinforcement obtained from social activity and giving and receiving positive interpersonal responses. Significant decreases in the degree of discomfort associated with negative cognitions regarding interpersonal interactions were also found for the depressed as compared with the controls.

A related, but somewhat different, strategy for identifying events with potential reinforcing or punishing properties has been to ask people to monitor the occurrence of specified events and to complete mood ratings on a daily basis for periods of 30 days or more. By studying the correlations between the occurrence of events and mood level, it has been possible to show a statistically significant ($p < .01$) covariation between feeling good and the occurrence of pleasant events and between feeling bad and the occurrence of aversive events. Specific event–mood correlations for an individual are assumed to identify particular events that have reinforcing or punishing impact for that person. Events that are correlated with mood for a substantial (10% or more) proportion of the population (mood-related events) are assumed to represent events that have reinforcing or punishing properties in the population at large. Hence, mood-related events are assumed to bear a critical relationship to the occurrence of depression; and they are assumed to be the major types of events that act as reinforcement for people. Data consistent with these hypotheses are discussed by Lewinsohn and Amenson (1978).

A significant association between mood and number and kind of pleasant activities engaged in was demonstrated by Lewinsohn and Libet (1972) and Lewinsohn and Graf (1973). Similarly, Lewinsohn, Youngren, and Grosscup (1980) reported significant covariations between feeling good and the frequency of pleasant events. A study by Graf (1977) indicated that depressed persons who increased mood-related pleasant events improved more than depressed persons who increased non-mood-related pleasant events.

Significant covariations have also been found between feeling bad and the occurrence of aversive events (Lewinsohn, Youngren, & Grosscup, 1980). The rate of occurrence of mood-related unpleasant events was shown to be uniquely elevated in depressives by Lewinsohn and Amenson (1978). This study found the mood-related items, for both the UES and the PES, to be especially discriminating between the depressed and the nondepressed.

Lewinsohn and his associates have also been interested in the social behavior of depressed individuals because the lack of social skill could be one of the antecedent conditions producing a low rate of positive reinforcement and a high rate of punishment. Social skill is defined as the ability to emit behaviors that are positively reinforced by others and that terminate negative reactions from others. An individual may be considered skillful to the extent that he/she elicits positive and avoids negative consequences from the social environment. On the basis of an extensive analysis of social interactional data obtained by observing depressed and nondepressed individuals in group therapy interactions and in their home environment (e.g., Lewinsohn, Weinstein, & Alper, 1970; Lewinsohn and Shaffer, 1971; Libet & Lewinsohn, 1973), the depressed as a group were found to be less socially skilled than the nondepressed control groups. Coyne (1976) also found that in phone conversations with normal individuals, depressed persons (as compared with nondepressed persons) induced more negative affects and elicited greater feelings of rejection from others, suggesting that depressed individuals relate to others in a fashion that reduces the likelihood that they will be reinforced.

In another study, Youngren and Lewinsohn (1980) contrasted the verbal and nonverbal behavior and interpersonal style of depressed patients with that of nondepressed controls in group and dyadic laboratory interactions. Differences on the verbal and nonverbal measures, while generally in the predicted direction, were often small and not uniquely related to depression. In the group situation, but not in dyadic interactions, the depressed were rated by others as less socially skilled. On ratings of interpersonal style scales (e.g., friendly, speaks fluently), the depressed rated themselves more negatively and received more negative ratings from others compared with controls. After treatment, the depressed improved on all ratings of interpersonal style.

Prkachin, Craig, Papageorgis, and Reith (1977) studied the receptive and expressive skills of depressed, psychiatric control, and normal control subjects within a nonverbal communication paradigm. The results indicated that the facial expressions of depressed subjects were the most difficult to judge correctly, while no differences were apparent between the other two groups. Prkachin *et al.* interpreted their findings as suggesting that depressed individuals exhibit a deficit in nonverbal communicative behavior (e.g., their expressive behavior is both ambiguous and nonresponsive) and as supporting Lewinsohn's hypothesis that a lack of social skill represents a major antecedent condition for the occurrence of depression.

While many studies can thus be cited that, in general, are consistent with the hypothesis that depressed individuals are less socially skillful and that they obtain less reinforcement in social interaction, the specific nature of the behavioral (overt) deficits associated with depression have, as yet, not been clearly delineated. Further research is needed that is aimed at the identification of discriminating behaviors through empirical analysis (Jacobson, 1979). The results may be situation-specific, or they may be influenced by the duration of the interaction and its demands for intimacy. Also, the sex of the individual acts as a moderator variable (Hammen & Peters, 1977).

Cognitive Theories

Cognitive theorists such as Beck (1967), Ellis and Harper (1961), Rehm (1977), and Seligman (1974, 1975) have advanced hypotheses that attribute a causal role to cognitions in the etiology of depression. But they differ in regard to the specific nature of the cognitions that are assumed to lead to depression.

Beck. Beck and his associates (1967, 1976; and Beck, Rush, Shaw, & Emery, 1978, 1979) conceive of depression as a disorder of thinking. The signs and symptoms of the depressive syndrome are a *consequence* of the activation of negative cognitive patterns. Affect, according to Beck, is intimately linked with cognition. Between an event and an individual's emotional reaction to that event, a cognition or an automatic thought intervenes that determines the resulting affect. When the cognitions represent an inaccurate or distorted appraisal of the event, the subsequent affect will be inappropriate or extreme. Beck (1976) believes that the dysphoria or sadness associated with depression derives from an individual's tendency to interpret her/his experiences in terms of being deprived, deficient, or defeated.

Several specific cognitive structures are postulated as being central in the development of depression: the cognitive triad, schemata and cognitive errors (Beck, Rush, Shaw, & Emery, 1979). The cognitive triad consists of three cognitive patterns asserted to dominate depressive ideation: a negative view of oneself (depressed individuals perceive themselves as inadequate, defective, and lacking the attributes necessary to obtain happiness); a negative view of the world (depressed individuals believe that the world presents unreasonable demands and/or obstacles to reaching important life goals); and a negative view of the future (depressed individuals believe that their current difficulties will continue indefinitely).

Beck has also postulated the existence of superordinate schemata that lead to the systematic filtering or distortion of the stimuli that confront the individual. These schemata represent stable cognitive patterns of the individual that mold raw data (sensory inputs) in the direction of making them accord with these prepotent schemata (Beck *et al.*, 1979). The existence of such schemata, asserts Beck, explains why depressed persons cling to painful attitudes ("I am unlovable") despite objective evidence to the contrary. As a result of the increased domination of dysfunctional schemata, systematic errors in the logic of depressives' thinking are said to occur. Such errors are automatic and involuntary and include arbitrary inference (drawing conclusions without evidence or despite contrary evidence); selective abstraction (ignoring the context of an event by fixating on a detailed aspect of a situation while ignoring more salient features); overgeneralization (drawing a general conclusion on the basis of limited detail or limited occurrences of an event); magnification and minimization (undue exaggerating or limiting of the significance of the information); personalization (attaching subjective significance to external events when no basis exists for making such a connection); and absolutistic thinking (placing all experiences in one or two opposite categories) (Beck *et al.*, 1979).

Several different kinds of studies were initially conducted by Beck and his associates (summarized in Beck, 1967) to test these hypotheses. Early studies focused on the content of various types of ideational productions, involving dreams, early memories, storytelling, and responses to picture cards. The productions of depressed patients were found to show a greater frequency of themes of failure and fewer successes and to focus on personal defects and rejection, and their responses to verbal tests involving self-concept tended to be more negative.

In recent years, a considerable amount of experimental literature has accumulated relating to the variety of predictions implied by Beck's theory. This research, conducted by Beck and his co-workers, as well as a number of other investigators, has focused on the effects of success and failure, perceptual distortion, memory distortion, negative expectancies, and other cognitive deficits in depressed individuals.

Effects of Success and Failure. A number of studies focused on the differential effects of success and failure experiences on self-esteem, mood, and expectation of future success on the task-and-performance evaluation in depressed and in nondepressed groups. Critical to Beck's theory is the prediction that following a failure experience, the depressed, compared with the nondepressed, will become *more negative* (in their self-esteem, mood, expectancies, and performance evaluation) and *less* positive following a success experience. On the basis of the cognitive mechanisms postulated by Beck, it would be expected that the depressed should be particularly responsive to negative information about themselves and unresponsive to positive information.

The experimental procedure for testing the effects of success and failure has typically been similar to one developed by Diggory and Loeb (1962), in which "success" and "failure" were experimentally produced either by manipulating the time allowed for completing the task or by manipulating the length of the task. This and similar tests have consistently been shown to produce systematic change in self-esteem (e.g., Flippo & Lewinsohn, 1971).

One of the earliest studies was done by Rosenzweig (1960), who hypothesized that following a failure or success experience, the self-concept of depressed persons changes on the evaluative dimension more than does the self-concept of nonpsychiatric control subjects. Rosenzweig found depressed patients to be less consistent, but not more negative, in their self-concept ratings following either a success or a failure experience. Loeb, Feshback, Beck, and Wolf (1964) compared depressed and nondepressed male psychiatric patients prior to and immediately following experimentally induced "superior" and "inferior" performance conditions. Prior to and immediately following the experimental task, the subjects rated their mood; after the task, they were also assessed for self-confidence and expectation of future performance. Trends were found for depressed patients to show more negative mood and lower expectancies after inferior performances. However, a number of findings were obtained contrary to what Beck's theory would predict: depressives were more optimistic and had higher expectancies following superior performances.

In another experiment, Loeb, Beck, Diggory, and Tuthill (1967) manipulated success and failure on a card-sorting task. Inspection of the means suggests a comparable change in probability-of-future-success estimates following success and following failure in individuals with high and low depression. Using anagrams as the experimental task and self-esteem ratings as the dependent variable, Flippo and Lewinsohn (1971) found that the magnitude of change from before to after three different failure–success conditions did not differ between depressed and nondepressed subjects. Alloy and Abramson (1979) found greater *positive* change in depressed than in nondepressed subjects on mood ratings following "win" or "lose" tasks.

Klein and Seligman (1976) and Miller and Seligman (1973, 1975, 1976)—and learned helplessness studies in general—have found depressed students to exhibit *smaller* expectancy changes following success and failure on a skill task than nondepressed students. In addition, Abramson, Garber, Edwards, and Seligman (1978) reported that relative to hospitalized control subjects and schizophrenics, unipolar depressives showed small expectancy changes in a skill task.

The results of laboratory studies relevant to the prediction of differential effects of success and failure from Beck's theory have thus provided little support for the theory.

Perceptual Distortion. Studies have also been directed at Beck's hypothesis that the depressed person screens out or fails to integrate "successful experiences that contradict his negative view of himself" (Beck, 1976, p. 119). From this hypothesis, it may be predicted that depressed individuals will distort their perception of environmental feedback in a negative direction. DeMonbreun and Craighead (1977) and Craighead, Hickey, and DeMonbreun (1979) failed to find differences between depressed and nondepressed subjects in immediate perception of positive, negative, and ambiguous feedback information, which was provided after each response on the experimental task.

Alloy and Abramson (1979) studied the ability of depressed and nondepressed subjects to detect the degree of contingency between responding and outcomes in a series of problems that varied in the actual degree of objective contingency between the performance responses and outcomes obtained. No differences between more and less depressed subjects were found in their ability to detect the degree of contingency between their responses and environmental outcomes on three contingency problems. In problem situations lacking contingency, the nondepressed subjects showed an illusion of control in the high-density but not in the low-density problem, while the depressed were relatively accurate in both problems. In a third experiment, the nondepressed judged that they had more control (erroneously) in a "win" situation than in a "lose" situation, while the depressed subjects accurately reported that responding and not responding were equally effective regardless of whether they were winning or losing money.

Judgments of contingency of the depressed individuals were remarkably accurate. The nondepressed subjects, by contrast, tended to overestimate the degree of contingency for frequent and/or desired outcomes and to underestimate the degree of contingency between their responses and their outcomes when the contingent outcomes were undesired.

Another experiment (Lewinsohn, Mischel, Chaplin, & Barton, 1980a) also found *less* perceptual distortion in depressed than in nondepressed individuals. The findings indicated that nondepressed persons perceived themselves more positively than others saw them, while the depressed saw themselves as they were seen. If social reality is defined by the extent of agreement with objective observers, the depressed were the most realistic in their self-perceptions, while the controls were engaged in self-enhancing distortions.

Thus, laboratory studies have not provided support for the perceptual distortion hypothesis. If anything, nondepressed persons distort their perceptions, while the depressed are quite accurate in theirs.

Memory Distortion. Studies have also been conducted to investigate the presence of selective memory effects in depressed individuals. From Beck's theory, more forgetting of hedonically positive (pleasant) and less selective forgetting of hedonically negative (unpleasant) information would be expected. The results have generally supported these predictions. Wener and Rehm (1975) found that at the end of a series of trials, depressed subjects reported that they were correct less often than nondepressed subjects. Buchwald (1977) asked subjects to estimate the percentage of "right" responses and found a significant negative correlation between a measure of depression and estimates of "right" for female but not for male subjects. Nelson and Craighead (1977) reported that compared with the control group, depressed subjects underestimated the number of "bad" responses. DeMonbreun and Craighead (1977), also introducing their memory probe at the end of the experiment, found that the depressed "recalled" having received less positive feedback than did the controls. It is possible that the obtained differences reflect differences in incidental learning rather than in memory formation, retention, and retrieval (i.e., of hedonically toned information through intentional learning). It is also impossible to determine whether the hedonic selectivity of depressed individuals, which is suggested by the studies, constitutes an enduring characteristic of depressed individuals that predisposes them to become depressed (as required by Beck's hypothesis) or whether the hedonic selectivity is secondary to being in a depressed state.

Relevant to this last question are a series of studies that very strongly suggest that the state of depression increases the accessibility of memories of unpleasant events relative to the accessibility of memories of pleasant events. Lloyd and Lishman (1975) asked depressed patients, in response to a standard set of stimulus words, to retrieve from memory pleasant or unpleasant experiences from their past life. With increasing depression, subjects retrieved unpleasant experiences faster than pleasant experiences, a reversal of the pattern shown by nondepressed subjects. Lloyd and Lishman (1975) suggested that depression exerts its effects mainly by speeding up the recall of unpleasant memories. In a well-designed study, Teasdale and Fogarty (1979) extended these findings by showing that a mood induction procedure, in which student subjects were made happy on one occasion and depressed on another, exerted a significant effect on the time taken to retrieve pleasant memories relative to the time taken to retrieve unpleasant memories. In contrast to the findings of Lloyd and Lishman (1975), Teasdale and Fogarty's (1979) results indicate that depression exerts its effect by increasing the latency of pleasant memories.

Negative Expectancies. Beck's construct of negative expectancies has also been the subject of several investigations. Weintraub, Segal, and Beck (1974) devised a test consisting of incomplete stories involving a principal character with whom the subject was asked to identify. The expected relationship between negative expectancies and depression level was found. Another study (Beck, Weissman, Lester, & Trexler, 1974) made use of the Hopelessness Scale which consists of 20 true–false items. This scale was found to correlate well with clinical ratings of hopelessness

and was sensitive to change in patients' state of depression over time.

A related study was conducted specifically to test Beck's cognitive triad (Lewinsohn, Larson, & Muñoz, 1978; Muñoz, 1977). To incorporate the distinctions between self and the world, and present and future, a test (the Subjective Probability Questionnaire: Muñoz & Lewinsohn, 1976c) was constructed along three dichotomous and crossed dimensions: self versus world, present versus future, and positive versus negative. Depressives had higher expectancies about negative, and lower expectancies for positive, events pertaining to the self (in the present and in the future) but not about the "world."

Other Cognitive Deficits. Studies have also been aimed at other cognitive distortions hypothesized by Beck to be characteristic of depressed individuals. Using the Dysfunctional Attitude Scale (Weissman & Beck, 1978) to probe respondents' degree of agreement with beliefs hypothesized by Beck to characterize depressed patients, Weissman and Beck (1978) found a substantial, and statistically significant, correlation between the Dysfunctional Attitude Scale and the Beck Depression Inventory (Beck, 1976) and the Depression Scale of the Profile of Mood States (McNair, Lorr, & Droppleman, 1971). Substantial correlation was also found between the Dysfunctional Attitude Scale and a measure of cognitive distortion developed by Hammen and Krantz (1976). In this study depressed individuals were found to select a greater number of depression-distorted responses.

Ellis. Ellis (e.g., Ellis & Harper, 1961) attaches primary importance to irrational beliefs in the development of depression. Depression in this view occurs when a particular situation triggers an "irrational belief." It is this belief that is hypothesized to cause the person to overreact emotionally to the situation. For example, the person may become depressed after being rejected because he/she believes that "if one is not loved by everyone, one is unlovable."

The prediction that depressives subscribe more to irrational beliefs in general was tested and supported by Muñoz (1977) and by Nelson (1977). In these studies, the subjects were asked to indicate their degree of agreement or disagreement with absolute statements of various kinds (e.g., ''The main goal and purpose of life is achievement and success''). Attempting to delineate the specific nature of the irrational beliefs associated with depression, Lewinsohn, Larson, and Muñoz (1978) identified beliefs that in their, and in Nelson's, study had been found to be discriminating (at a high level of statistical significance) between depressed and nondepressed persons. Factors obtained from a factor analysis of the most discriminating items were then contrasted with factors derived from a factor analysis of a set of nondiscriminating beliefs. A particular set of ''irrational'' beliefs was identified to which depressed individuals subscribed more than nondepressed individuals.

Rehm. Rehm (1977) has developed a self-control theory of depression in which negative self-evaluations, as well as low rates of self-reinforcement and high rates of self-punishment, are seen as leading to the low rate of behavior that characterizes depressed individuals. Rehm's theory builds on Kanfer's (1971) notion of behavioral self-control. Three processes are postulated to be important: self-monitoring, self-evaluation, and self-reinforcement. Self-monitoring is the observation of one's own behavior. Rehm suggested that depressed persons self-monitor in two characteristic ways: they attend selectively to negative events and they attend selectively to the immediate versus the delayed outcomes of their behavior. Self-evaluation involves assessing one's performance against an internal standard. Two forms of maladaptive self-evaluation are said to characterize depressives: they often fail to make accurate internal attributions of causality (for success experiences), and they tend to set stringent criteria for self-evaluation (i.e., they have high thresholds for positive self-evaluation and low thresholds for negative self-evaluation). Self-reinforcement is the self-administration of overt or covert contingent reward or punishment. In controlling behavior, self-reinforcement is theorized to supplement external reinforcement; it functions to maintain behavior, especially where long-term goals are involved, when external reinforcement is delayed.

The self-control model thus accounts for the diverse symptoms of depression by a variety of cognitive deficits. Self-monitoring of negative events is assumed to result in a negative view of the self, the world, and the future. Strict evaluatory criteria are asserted to produce lowered self-esteem and feelings of helplessness. Finally, a lack of self-reward is postulated to be associated with retarded activity levels and lack of initiative, while excessive self-punishment is said to be reflected in negative self-statements and other forms of self-directed hostility.

Several studies have been conducted to test Rehm's hypotheses about the role of self-reinforcement and self-punishment in depression. The rates that subjects self-reinforce or self-punish in these experiments is assumed to be an analogue measure of the person's tendency to self-reinforce and to self-punish in other settings, but no evidence for the validity of this assumption has been provided.

An early self-reinforcement study was conducted by Rozensky, Rehm, Pry, and Roth (1977), using hospitalized medical patients who had been divided into high- and low-depression groups. The high-depression group were found to give themselves fewer self-rewards and more self-punishment than the low-depression group. This was true despite the lack of differences in the number of correct responses.

Other studies have yielded less consistent results. Roth, Rehm, and Rozensky (1975) found that the depressed gave themselves significantly more self-punishments but did not differ from the control group on the number of self-rewards administered. Nelson and Craighead (1977) found no differences between depressed and nondepressed subjects in regard to self-punishment. The nondepressed reinforced more than the depressed (and then justified this by their objective accuracy scores) after low-density but not high-density reinforcement.

Ciminero and Steingarten (1978) found no differences in performance, self-evaluation, and self-reinforcement between depressed and nondepressed groups on a task involving the Digit Symbol subtest of the Wechsler Adult Intelligence Scale (Wechsler, 1955). When subjects were assigned to low- or high-standard conditions and repeated the task, the results suggested that differential rates of self-reinforcement exist only when standards are available regarding performance. Using a similar procedure, Garber, Hollon, and Silverman (1979) found that female depressed subjects gave themselves fewer rewards following substandard performance than nondepressed females. Depressed male subjects, however, did not show such a pattern.

Lobitz and Post (1979) used a word association task, the Digit Symbol Test, and a Ward Assistance Task to test hypotheses about self-reinforcement. Two groups of hospitalized psychiatric patients (clinically depressed and clinically nondepressed) were used. The dependent measures included a scale of level of self-expectation (obtained prior to each task) and a self-reward measure (tokens), which was obtained following self-evaluation. The depressed group was significantly lower on all three measures. However, the intercorrelations among the three dependent measures were substantial. When level of self-expectation was used as the covariate, no significant differences between groups in level of self-reward were obtained. In other words, the differences between the depressed and the nondepressed on a self-reward measure were completely predictable from the level-of-expectation scores, which, of course, were obtained prior to the subject's engagement in the experimental task. Lobitz and Post suggested that the deficits in self-reinforcement found in their study and in previous studies (e.g., Nelson & Craighead, 1977) may be accounted for by the cognitive set (low self-expectations) that the subjects brought to the tasks and that a more global factor, such as low self-esteem, could be underlying all variables.

A very different approach to testing aspects of Rehm's hypothesis is represented in another study (Lewinsohn, Larson, & Muñoz, 1978; Muñoz, 1977). Starting with the assumption that the hedonic content of thoughts (positive vs. negative) constitutes a measure of covert reinforcement, a psychometric instrument, the Cognitive Events Schedule (Muñoz & Lewinsohn, 1976a), was constructed. On the basis of Rehm's hypotheses, depressed patients were expected, and found, to be characterized by a greater number of negative and a fewer number of positive thoughts about the self. In addition, the interaction between diagnostic groups and hedonic quality (positive vs. negative) was highly significant because in the depressed group, the excess of negative thoughts was much greater than the deficit of positive thoughts. Rehm and Plakosh (1975) found that depressed compared with nondepressed subjects expressed a greater preference for immediate as opposed to delayed rewards.

In short, then, mixed experimental support exists for the self-control theory of depression. Some findings provide evidence for certain predictions of the theory, while others do not. The results of Lobitz and Post suggest an important qualification to the research in this area.

Seligman. Working from an experimental paradigm developed initially with dogs and other animals, Seligman (1974, 1975) has proposed a theory of human depression, the central tenet of which concerns the effect of the independence of behavior and outcomes (noncontingency). The critical issue is uncontrollability; consequently, the distinction between controllable and uncontrollable events is critical to Seligman's position. With repeated instances of uncontrollability, the organism learns that responding is independent of reinforcement. This fact is *transformed* into a cognitive representation, called an *expectation,* that responding and outcomes are independent. This expectation is the causal condition for the motivational (reduced responding), cognitive (interference with later instrumental learning), and emotional (first fear, and then depression) debilitation that accompanies helplessness.

The term *learned helplessness* was first used to describe interference with avoidance responding in dogs produced by inescapable shock. Indeed, the debilitating consequences of exposure to situations in which responses and outcomes are unrelated have been observed across a wide variety of experimental situations and within a large number of species (Seligman, 1975). The main psychological phenomena of learned helplessness are (1) passivity; (2) retarded learning; (3) lack of aggressiveness and competitiveness; and (4) weight loss and undereating. The critical antecedent for learned helplessness is not trauma *per se,* but not having control over trauma. A key assumption of Seligman's theory of depression is that "if the symptoms of learned helplessness and depression are equivalent then what we have learned experimentally about the cause, cure, and prevention of learned helplessness can be applied to depression" (1973, p. 43). Depressed individuals are presumed to have been, or to be, in situations in which responding and reinforcement are independent. As a result, the depressed person believes that he/she is helpless. Recovery of belief that responding produces reinforcement is the critical attitudinal change for the cure of depression.

The learned-helplessness theory has stimulated much research, and one issue of the *Journal of Abnormal Psychology* (February 1978) was devoted to a review of methodological and conceptual issues and empirical findings on the relationship between learned helplessness and depression.

A number of different experimental paradigms have been used to study predictions from the learned-helplessness theory. Using a triadic design analogous to that employed in animal helplessness studies, Seligman and his associates (e.g., Hiroto, 1974) have compared subjects exposed to three prior conditions: contingent, noncontingent, or no trauma (aversive noise). All groups were subsequently tested in a human shuttle box for escape–avoidance responses to noise. The results were similar to those obtained in other species; students who had received prior exposure to noncontingent noise showed impaired performance on the requisite escape–avoidance response in the shuttle box test, compared with students receiving prior exposure to contingent noise or no noise.

In their studies on the locus-of-control construct, Rotter and his associates (e.g., James, 1957; James & Rotter, 1958) demonstrated that the outcomes of previous trials have a greater effect on expectancies of future success on skill tasks when the person believes that outcomes are dependent on responses (internal) than when the person believes that outcomes are independent of responses (external). Using this logic, Miller and Seligman (1976) and Klein and Seligman (1976) examined verbalized expectancies of success on skill and chance tasks for subjects who were, again, given prior exposure to contingent, noncon-

tingent, or no trauma (an aversive tone). The subjects exposed to prior uncontrollable noises showed less expectancy change in the skill task than the students exposed to prior controllable noises or no noises, although the groups did not differ in a chance task. Furthermore, depth of depression was significantly correlated with small expectancy change in skill tasks but did not correlate with expectancy changes in chance tasks. Similarly to nondepressed subjects who received experience with uncontrollable events, naive depressed students exhibited *smaller* expectancy changes following success (Klein & Seligman, 1976; Miller & Seligman, 1973, 1975) and failure (Klein & Seligman, 1976; Miller & Seligman, 1975, 1976) in a skill task. In addition, Abramson, Garber, Edwards, and Seligman (1978) reported that unipolar depressives also showed small expectancy changes in a skill task relative to hospitalized control subjects and schizophrenics. On the assumption that expectancy changes in chance and skill tasks represent valid indexes of people's beliefs about response–outcome contingencies, these studies have been used to infer that depressives believe less in the relationship between outcomes and responding. This assumption has been questioned by a number of theorists (Buchwald, Coyne & Cole, 1978; Costello, 1978; Huesmann, 1978), who have suggested that the above-mentioned studies do not provide convincing evidence for the specific cognitive deficit postulated by learned-helplessness theory.

A more direct method for the assessment of depressed and nondepressed persons' perception of response–outcome contingencies is provided in a recent experiment by Alloy and Abramson (1979). In a series of experiments, depressed and nondepressed students were confronted with problems that varied in the actual degree of objective contingency between the performance responses and the outcomes obtained. Surprisingly, the judgments of contingency of the depressed students were remarkably accurate; if anything, the results suggest that nondepressives have difficulty in assessing response–outcome relationships.

The emotional component of learned helplessness has also come under investigation. The helplessness theory requires that exposure to uncontrollable events result in depressive affect. In some studies (Gatchel, Paulus, & Maples, 1975), nondepressed college students exposed to uncontrollable noise became depressed in comparison with either a group that received controllable noises or a group that received no noise. But in other studies (Miller & Seligman, 1975), the different treatments with noise did not produce significantly different effects on depressive mood. When the helplessness manipulation does affect depression ratings, it also typically affects anxiety as well as ratings of hostility (Alloy & Abramson, 1979; Gatchel *et al.*, 1975). The fact that research indicates that the helplessness induction results in anxiety and hostility as well as depression raises the question of whether such helplessness bears a unique relation to depression or whether there is a sequence of emotional reactions to the experience of noncontrol (Klinger, 1975; Wortman & Brehm, 1975) and the discrepancies between studies result because various subjects had arrived at various points in the sequence when the dependent measures were collected.

An interesting "paradox" has been discussed by Abramson and Sackheim (1977), who noted that despite viewing events (as in the learned-helplessness theory) as uncontrollable and themselves as helpless, depressives blame themselves for those events; that is, depressive individuals assume the responsibility for events that they believe they neither cause nor control. A recent study by Peterson (1979) provides empirical support for this so-called paradox in depression.

In response to these and other criticisms, Seligman (Abramson, Seligman, & Teasdale, 1978) has recently proposed a reformulation of the learned-helplessness theory by incorporating extensions from attribution theory (Weiner, Frieze, Kukla, Reed, Rest, & Rosenbaum, 1971; Weiner, Nierenberg, & Goldstein, 1976). The reformulated theory suggests that the attributions the individual makes for the perceived noncontingency between his/her acts and outcomes (personal helplessness) are the source of subsequent expectations of future noncontingency (expected uncontrollability). The dimensions of attributions said to be particularly relevant to learned helplessness and depression include internality–externality, globality–specificity, and stability–instability. The depressive attributional style is hypothesized to (1) consist in a tendency to make internal attributions for failure but external attributions for success; (2) make stable attributions for failure but unstable attributions for success; and (3) make global attributions for failure but specific attributions for success. The person is more likely to be depressed, it is hypothesized, if his/her attributions for failure and lack of control are internal ("It is my fault"), global ("I am incompetent"), and stable ("I will always be like that"), while his/her attributions for successes are external ("I was lucky"), specific ("in this particular situation"), and unstable ("just this time").

The low self-esteem associated with depression is hypothesized to result from internal attributions for personal helplessness, while the affect (depression) results from the expectation that bad outcomes will result in the future. The severity of the motivational and cognitive deficits of depression is postulated as depending jointly on the strength (or the certainty) of the expectation of aversive outcomes *and* the strength of the uncontrollability. The severity of the affective and self-esteem deficits is said to be governed by the importance of uncontrollable outcomes.

Recently, Seligman, Abramson, Semmel, and Von Baeyer (1979) have presented evidence for the reformulated theory. Using a new Attributional Style Scale (Semmel, Abramson, Seligman, & Van Baeyer, 1978) with a sample of college students, they computed correlations between the Beck Depression Inventory and the Attributional Style Scale scores. For bad outcomes, the depression measure correlated with internality, stability, and globality; for good outcomes, the depression measure correlated with externality and instability, but not significantly with specificity. In a prospective pilot study, the same students who had completed the Attributional Style Scale, and who were faced with an exam, rated what grade they would consider a failure before they took the exam. It was found that students who actually attained what they considered a grade low enough to be a failure were more likely to *become* depressed (i.e., it was found that students, who, eight weeks before, had made stable and global attributions for failure on the Attributional Style Scale, were more likely to be depressed after attaining a low grade on the exam).

In conclusion, limited experimental evidence exists in support of the original learned-helplessness theory of depression. A reformulation of that model based on attributional theory has been proposed; a preliminary study suggests that the association between degree of depression and attributional style is in the direction predicted by the revised theory of learned helplessness.

Epidemiological Considerations in Depression

A number of research findings of an epidemiological nature are relevant to an understanding of depression. The prevalence (number of cases of diagnosable episodes of depression at any point in time) has typically been estimated at between 3% and 4% (Lehman, 1971). The National Institute of Mental Health (1970) estimated that in any given year, 15% of all adults experience a clinically significant depressive episode. The commonness of depression is further illustrated by the finding (Amenson & Lewinsohn, 1979) that more than half (62% of the women and 49% of the men) of the subjects in two general community samples were diagnosed, by the Research Diagnostic Criteria (RDC) (Spitzer, Endicott, & Robins, 1978) criteria, as having experienced a diagnosable episode of depression at some time during their lives. The oft-quoted metaphor that depression is the common cold of mental health (e.g., Seligman, 1975) seems most appropriate.

Perhaps the most consistent epidemiological finding concerning depression is the substantial sex difference in prevalence: a female preponderance (often 2:1) is almost always reported (Weissman & Klerman, 1977). In their extensive study on the sex difference in prevalence of unipolar depression, Amenson and Lewinsohn (1979) found that the incidences of depression (i.e., the number of persons without a history of previous depression who became depressed during the course of the study) in men and women were quite comparable

(6.9% vs. 7.1%). Women did not have longer-lasting episodes; nor were there any differences in age at first onset. The major difference between the sexes was observed in persons with a history of previous depression. Women with a history of previous depression were much more likely to become depressed again (21.8%) than men with a history of previous depression (12.9%). Thus, it is clear that persons with a previous history of depression, and especially females, are at very high risk, and treatment and *prevention* programs should be aimed at them.

The relationship between age and depression is less clear. On the basis of the studies reviewed by Gurland (1976), it appears that when psychiatric diagnosis is used as the criterion, high rates of depressive disorders occur between the ages of 25 and 65 years, with a decline in younger and older groups. However, these data are probably distorted by the demonstrated underutilization of mental health services on the part of elderly people and by the tendency on the part of clinicians to underdiagnose depression among elderly people (Ernst, Badash, Beran, Kosovsky, & Kleinhauz, 1977). There is confusion among practitioners and researchers alike about how to distinguish between complaints due to "normal aging" and those that are due to real depressive disorder (Gurland, 1976; Raskin & Jarvik, 1979).

Another important epidemiological fact about depression is its time-limited and episodic nature (e.g., Beck, 1967; Weissman & Paykel, 1974). The mean length of episodes is reported as seven months by Robins and Guze (1969), and the median as 22 weeks by Amenson and Lewinsohn (1979). With and without treatment, most depressed patients improve. However, there is a small minority of patients (approximately 15%) who remain chronic, or in partial remission, and this subgroup needs to be studied more carefully (Weissman & Klerman, 1977).

Although exact suicide rates among depressed persons are difficult to pinpoint, the probability of self-injurious and suicidal behavior is significantly elevated in depressed populations. The suicide rate of depressed individuals exceeds that of people with any other psychological disorder (Becker, 1974). Lehman (1971) estimated that 1 out of 200 depressed persons commit suicide. The death rate, from all causes, for depressed females is twice, and for males triple, the normal rate. Any clinician involved in the diagnosis and treatment of depressed individuals needs to be able to assess the risk of suicide and to take appropriate preventive steps. Several studies (e.g., Burglass & Horton, 1974) indicate that on the basis of relatively simple information, it is possible to make quantitative predictions about the probability of serious suicidal behavior on the part of the patient.

Assessment of Depression

A major difficulty with the term *depression* is that it is commonly used both as a construct and as a designation of specific behavioral events. In the former usage, the term *depression* is used in a diverse set of circumstances, and the nature of these circumstances is frequently neither well defined nor consistent from one clinician to another. Used as a construct, *depression* implies the existence of a distinct and consistent set of internal events and behaviors that is characteristic of all "depressed" individuals.

Inadequacies in the use of the construct of *depression* have led some behavior therapists to reject such a diagnostic label because of its lack of precise behavioral referents. This position denies the existence of a unique syndrome (or symptom cluster) for which a specific term (*depression*) is needed. Rather, they concern themselves with the occurrence of specific behaviors in individual depressed patients, such as the low rate of social behavior, sadness, and verbal expressions of guilt and personal inadequacy.

While there can be no question of the legitimacy of this position, which focuses attention on the details of the individual patient's behaviors, certain evidence suggests that this may not be the most adequate conceptualization of depression. Analyses of the behaviors that are commonly exhibited by persons who have been diagnosed as depressed (e.g., "bootstrap" approaches, such as that of Grinker et al., 1961) indicate substantial agreement as to the constituents of the depression syndrome that extends across studies.

That is, good agreement exists as to the behaviors and symptoms that characterize "depressed" individuals.

The fact that considerable agreement can be found on the behavioral components of the depression syndrome has been used to postulate the existence of a syndrome that may be labeled as *depression,* even though some specific behavioral manifestations of depression differ from one individual to the next. While not denying the importance of schedules of reinforcement or of the operant characteristics of depressive behaviors, this position views depression as a *psychopathological condition* or syndrome whose existence can be defined in terms of the occurrence (frequency and intensity) of certain kinds of behaviors and symptoms. This syndrome includes verbal statements of dysphoria, self-depreciation, guilt, material burden, social isolation, somatic symptoms, and a reduced rate of behavior.

Given this conceptualization, the assessment of depressed patients has several related goals:

1. *Differential diagnosis.* Assessment must first determine whether or not depression is *the,* or at least *a,* problem for the individual.
2. *Functional diagnosis and identification of targets for intervention.* Assessment should also identify events and behavior patterns that are functionally related to the person's depression.
3. *Evaluation.* Evaluation involves periodic assessment not only of changes in depression level but also of concomitant changes in the events presumed to be related to the patient's depression. This two-pronged approach to assessment allows the therapist (researcher) to evaluate the effectiveness of treatment in changing the targeted behavior patterns and also to determine whether these are accompanied by changes in depression level.

Differential Diagnosis

The diagnosis of depression is rendered difficult because the term *depression* does not have a single, generally accepted set of referents. Consequently, individuals who are labeled depressed are quite heterogeneous. Given this heterogeneity it is especially important that one explicitly define the criteria that are used to diagnose patients as depressed.

The differential diagnosis of depression can be accomplished by four different, but complementary, methods: (1) psychiatric diagnosis; (2) symptom ratings; (3) self-report depression scales; and (4) observations of overt behavior.

Psychiatric Diagnosis. Even though behaviorally oriented clinicians, and many others, have questioned the adequacy of psychiatric diagnosis, it is by far the most commonly used diagnostic procedure. Furthermore, there is evidence that with the use of recently developed interview schedules, such as the Schedule for Affective Disorders and Schizophrenia (Endicott & Spitzer, 1978), and diagnostic systems, such as the Research Diagnostic Criteria (RDC) (Spitzer *et al.,* 1978), very good interrater reliability, can be achieved.

The RDC provides operational definitions for many of the subtypes of depression that have at one time or another been thought to be important; these subtypes are treated as not being mutually exclusive. Thus, the RDC is the most elaborate and probably the best currently available diagnostic system for the affective disorders. Its use in research studies is recommended, so that patient samples can be compared across studies. The other major diagnostic systems are the Diagnostic and Statistical Manual of mental disorders, second edition (DSM II; 1968), now replaced by the DSM III (1980).

The DSM II allowed for four "psychotic" depressions (schizoaffective, involutional melancholia, manic-depressive, and psychotic depressive reaction) and for one "neurotic" depression (depressive neurosis). Involutional melancholia has been eliminated from the newer schemata because there is little rational basis for using a separate diagnostic category simply on the basis of the age of onset of the disorder (Beck, 1967; Rosenthal, 1968). The neurotic versus psychotic depression *dichotomy,* which implied that these were qualitatively different types of disorders, has also been eliminated.

Patients with manic, and those with a history of both manic and depressive, episodes

have always been recognized as a separate diagnostic group. In the DSM III, a manic episode is defined by the presence of at least one distinct period of elevated, expansive, or irritable mood, associated with a specified number of manic symptoms. Whether or not the patient is also psychotic (defined by the presence of delusions or hallucinations) is indicated by a "level-of-severity" rating. A diagnosis of bipolar affective disorder is given to a patient who is currently depressed and who also has a history of one or more manic episodes, or vice versa. The general distinction between unipolar and bipolar depressions is becoming increasingly recognized as important to therapy outcome. There is evidence that these two subgroups differ in response to pharmacological intervention (Morris & Beck, 1974) and that they may have different genetic and/or biochemical bases (Becker, 1977; Cadoret & Tanna, 1977).

The DSM III uses one major category ("Affective Disorders") within which three subgroups are distinguished. The first group is termed "Episodic Affective Disorders." The term *episodic* is used to indicate that there is a period of disorder that is clearly distinguishable from previous functioning. The second group is referred to as "Chronic Affective Disorders." The term *chronic* is used to indicate a long-standing (lasting at least two years) disorder that usually does not have a clear onset. The disturbance in mood and related symptoms may be sustained throughout the period or may be intermittent. The third group, "Atypical Affective Disorders," is a residual category for individuals with a mood disturbance that cannot be classified as either episodic or chronic. Within each of the three groups, distinctions are made between manic (hypomanic), major depressive (unipolar), and bipolar (cyclothymic) disorders, based on whether both manic and depressive episodes are involved or only one of them is involved.

Symptom Ratings. Another way of measuring the presence and severity of the manifestations of depression is through ratings on items presumed to represent the symptoms of depression. Such items, and their broader dimensions, have been identified in descriptive studies of depressed individuals (e.g., Grinker *et al.,* 1961). On the basis of such studies, there is considerable agreement as to the constituents of the depression syndrome. The symptoms of depression may be grouped into six general categories: dysphoria, reduced rate of behavior, social-interactional problems, guilt, material burden, and somatic symptoms. Depressed patients manifest different combinations of these.

The task of assessing the presence and severity of the phenomena of depression is facilitated by the use of one of several available interviewer rating-scales. Among the better-known scales are the Feelings and Concerns Checklist (Grinker *et al.*, 1961), the Hamilton Rating Scale for Depression (Hamilton, 1960, 1967), and the more global ratings of the Raskin Depression Scales (Raskin, Schulterbrandt, Reatig, Crook, & Odle, 1974). Other similar rating scales are the Psychiatric Judgment of Depression Scale (Overall, 1962) and the Depression Rating Scale (Wechsler, Grosser, & Busfield, 1963). When used by well-trained raters, these scales possess high interrater reliability. They differentiate significantly between depressed and nondepressed patients, and between depressed patients differing with respect to intensity of depression.

Levitt and Lubin (1975) list 23 self-administered depression scales. Only the more popular ones are mentioned here. All of them have been shown to correlate significantly with each other (e.g., Lubin, 1967; Zung, Richards, & Short, 1965) and to correlate substantially with interview ratings. They differ from each other in terms of the number of items, the types of symptoms represented by the items, and the time frame for which ratings are made. Since elderly individuals tend to acknowledge more somatic symptoms (Gaitz, 1977) and to check fewer socially undesirable items (Harnatz & Shader, 1975), there is a significant question about whether the self-report depression scales are in fact measuring the same phenomena in the elderly as they do in younger persons (Gallagher, McGarvey, Zelinksi, & Thompson, 1978). With the exception of the Minnesota Multiphasic Personality Inventory (MMPI)—D Scale (Dahlstrom, Welsh, & Dahlstrom, 1972) and the Depression Adjective Checklist (Lubin, 1967), available measuring instruments have not been standardized on elderly samples.

The best known of the self-report measures for depression is the D Scale of the MMPI. It has been used widely for the measurement of depression for clinical and research purposes. For example, Lewinsohn and his colleagues (e.g., Lewinsohn & Libet, 1972) have used multiple MMPI criteria to define depressed populations for research.

By far the most popular brief self-report depression inventory is the Beck Depression Inventory (BDI; Beck, Ward, Mendelson, Mock, & Erbaugh, 1961) consisting of 21 items. Beck and Beck (1972) developed a shorter version of the BDI that has only 13 items, which correlated .96 with the original BDI. Another useful test is the Self-Rating Depression Scale (SDS; Zung *et al.*, 1965; Zung, 1973), which consists of 20 statements.

The Center for Epidemiologic Studies—Depression Scale (CES-D; Radloff, 1977) is a 20-item self-report scale selected from previously validated scales (e.g., the MMPI-D Scale, the Zung SDS, and the BDI). The wording of the items is simple. The time frame for rating is clearly specified in the directions and refers to the *past week*.

The Depression Adjective Check List (DACL) was developed by Lubin (1965, 1967, 1977) and consists of seven parallel lists of adjectives designed to provide a measure of what has been called *state depression* (i.e., the individual's mood at a particular moment in time). The subject is asked to "Check the words which describe *How you feel now—today*." The availability of alternate forms and their brevity make the DACL especially useful for repeated measurement research. The DACL differs from the previously described self-report depression scales in sampling a much more limited range of depression behavior (i.e., depressed affect), in contrast to the BDI and the SDS, which include items involving overt-motor, physiological, and other cognitive manifestations. The DACL is somewhat less valuable for pre- and posttreatment assessment because of the large day-to-day intrasubject variability of DACL scores.

An even simpler method of assessing depressed affect is to have patients rate their mood on a line that is defined as representing a continuum from "best mood" to "worst mood."

Assessment of Overt Behavior. The construct of depression includes a variety of relatively specific overt behaviors, and a number of methods have been developed to measure them. A Ward Behavior Checklist for use with hospitalized patients has been described by Williams, Barlow, and Agras (1972). The presence or absence of simple, observable behavior is rated by aides using a time-sampling procedure (e.g., once per hour). Excellent interrater reliability (96%) was reported for this scale.

There have been other attempts to count specific behaviors in depressed patients. Reisinger (1972) used a time-sampling method to count the frequency of crying and smiling behavior. Interrater reliability exceeded 90% for observation periods of up to two hours. Johansson, Lewinsohn, and Flippo (1969) and Robinson and Lewinsohn (1973) used a coding system developed by Lewinsohn (1974) to partition verbal behavior into discrete response categories. McLean, Ogston, and Grauer (1973) described a simplified method of measuring verbal behavior based on Lewinsohn's coding system. Patients were required to make half-hour tape recordings of a problem discussion with their spouse at home. These recordings were separated into 30-sec intervals and coded for positive and negative initiations and reactions. Interrater agreement was high.

Fuchs and Rehm (1977) videotaped 10-min segments of interaction among groups of depressed subjects. The number of statements spoken in 10 min was counted. Interrater agreement ranged from 83% to 100% with a mean of 87%.

Kupfer, Weiss, Detre, Foster, Delgado, and McPartland (1974) described an apparatus that records activity in inpatient settings. A miniature transmitter, with a range of 100 feet, is worn on a leather wristband. Receivers transform data into pulses, which are read out digitally as the number of counts per minute. This measure of psychomotor activity was shown to possess high reliability (e.g., between wrist and ankle transmitters). It has also been shown to be correlated with various sleep parameters, such as EEG movement, minutes awake, time asleep, REM (rapid-eye-movement) time, and REM activity.

Functional Diagnosis and Identification of Targets for Intervention

Functional diagnosis involves pinpointing specific person–environment interactions and events related to depression. This part of the diagnostic process is needed to guide the formulation of a treatment plan designed to change the events contributing to depression. Behavior patterns may be postulated as being functionally related to depression on the basis of three criteria: (1) if the pattern occurs with increased, or decreased frequency in depressed vis-à-vis appropriate control groups; (2) if the behavior–environment interaction is present when the person is depressed but is absent, or attenuated, when the person is not depressed; and (3) if the occurrence of the person–environment interaction covaries with fluctuations in daily mood.

The following areas may be listed as functionally related to depression: social-interactional problems, depressive cognitions, a low rate of engagement in pleasant activities, and a high rate of occurrence of unpleasant events.

Social Behavior: Significance and Assessment. There now appears to be a general consensus that depressed persons, as a group, manifest social-interactional problems (e.g., Lewinsohn, Biglan, & Zeiss, 1976; Weissman & Paykel, 1974; Youngren & Lewinsohn, 1980). Complaints about various inadequacies in social relationships are frequently among the problems that are identified by the patient.

An instrument designed to assess aspects of social behavior by self-report is the Interpersonal Events Schedule (IES; Youngren, Zeiss, & Lewinsohn, 1975). The IES consists of a list of 160 items, all of which involve interpersonal activities or cognitions concerning such interactions. The item pool was drawn largely from a variety of preexisting instruments. Subjects complete ratings of the frequency and the subjective comfort and discomfort of events. A cross-product score of these ratings is assumed to provide an approximate measure of the response-contingent positive social reinforcement obtained, or of the interpersonal aversiveness experienced.

At the level of self-report, the following have been found to be associated with depression: (1) infrequent engagement, discomfort, and low levels of obtained pleasure in social activity (Youngren & Lewinsohn, 1980; (2) discomfort in being assertive (Langone, 1979; Sanchez, 1977; Youngren & Lewinsohn, 1980); and (3) discomfort experienced in conjunction with negative cognitions concerning personal interactions (Youngren & Lewinsohn, 1980). Depressed persons tend to feel that they are boring, worry about appearing foolish, feel themselves to be inferior and socially incompetent, and have conflicted interactions with their spouse or partner (Lewinsohn & Talkington, 1979; Weissman & Paykel, 1974).

It is essential to be specific in describing and delineating particular social skill problems if manifested by a given depressed individual and to focus interventions on the modification of the behaviors relevant to these problems. Several reviews of the literature relevant to the assessment of social behavior have appeared in the last few years (e.g., Arkowitz, Lichtenstein, McGovern, & Hines, 1975; Curran, 1977; Lewinsohn & Lee, 1981; Sundberg, Snowden, & Reynolds, 1978), and hence no systematic review is attempted here.

Cognitions: Significance and Assessment. There is no doubt that the phenomena of depression include cognitive manifestations, and a number of relevant assessment devices have been developed.

Negative Expectancies. The relevance of negative expectations to depression has been stressed by Beck (1967), and a number of different tests have been developed to measure expectancies. Weintraub *et al.* (1974) devised a test consisting of incomplete stories involving a principal character with whom the subject was asked to identify; the subject was asked to select alternative story completions. The expected relationship between negative expectancies and depression level was found. Another instrument designed to assess a respondent's negative expectancies is the Hopelessness Scale (Beck *et al.* 1974), which consists of 20 true–false items. The scale was found to have a high degree of internal consistency, showed good correlation with clinical ratings of hopelessness, and was sensitive to changes in the patient's state of depression over time.

The Subjective Probability Questionnaire (SPQ) is yet another attempt to operationalize Beck's cognitive triad (Muñoz & Lewinsohn, 1976c). The SPQ consists of 80 statements constructed along three dichotomous and crossed dimensions: self versus world, present versus future, and positive versus negative. Respondents indicate on an 11-point scale (0

= 0% probability; 10 = 100% probability) "What you think the chances are that the statement is true or that it will become true." The SPQ has been shown to possess a good test–retest reliability and to discriminate well between depressed and nondepressed samples (Muñoz, 1977).

Cognitive Distortion. A number of different conceptual distortions have been hypothesized by Beck (1963) as being uniquely associated with depression. A measure of cognitive distortion in depression has been developed by Hammen and Krantz (1976; Krantz & Hammen 1978). The Hammen and Krantz procedure assesses an individual's interpretations of events depicted in brief stories, and it measures the presence of a tendency to select the most depressed and distorted response options. Depressed individuals have consistently been found to select a greater number of depressed and distorted responses.

Irrational Beliefs and Dysfunctional Attitudes. A number of scales have been developed to measure the degree to which respondents hold various irrational beliefs (Murphy & Ellis, 1976). Nelson (1977) found a significant correlation between scores on the Irrational Beliefs Test (Jones, 1968) and the Beck Depression Inventory. The Personal Belief Inventory (PBI; Muñoz & Lewinsohn, 1976b) consists of 30 statements representing irrational beliefs hypothesized to be important in the occurrence of depression. The PBI was found to discriminate well between depressed and nondepressed control groups. A methodologically similar instrument is represented by the Dysfunctional Attitudes Scale (Weissman & Beck, 1978), which consists of 40 Likert-type items and has two alternate forms. The Dysfunctional Attitude Scale also probes the respondent's degree of agreement with beliefs hypothesized by Beck as characterizing depressed patients.

Negative Thoughts. The Cognitive Events Schedule (CES; Muñoz & Lewinsohn, 1976a) was intended to probe for the content of thoughts by asking the respondent to report the frequency of occurrence, and the emotional impact, of each of 160 thoughts during the past 30 days. The frequency of occurrence of each specific thought is rated on a 3-point scale, and its impact is rated on a 5-point scale.

Paralleling the SPQ, CES items were constructed along three dichotomous and crossed dimensions: self versus world, present versus future, and positive versus negative. Depressed individuals have been shown to report a much larger number of negative and a smaller number of positive thoughts than nondepressed controls (Lewinsohn, Larson, & Munoz, 1978).

Attributions of Causality. The causation of outcomes is central to learned-helplessness theory. Locus of control is assumed to be a cognitive set within this framework, and it has been typically measured with the Locus of Control Scale (Rotter, 1966, 1975). Dimensions of behavioral attributions can be assessed with the Multidimensional Multiattributional Causality Scale (Lefcourt, 1978). Seligman *et al.* (1979) reported on the use of their Attributional Style Scale; the results were in accord with the reformulated learned-helplessness theory.

Engagement in Pleasant Activities: Significance and Assessment. It is well established that depressed individuals as a group engage in relatively few activities, and in even fewer activities that they consider pleasant or rewarding.

The patient's rate of engagement in pleasant activities can be assessed in several ways:

1. The patient may fill out the Pleasant Events Schedule (PES; MacPhillamy & Lewinsohn, 1971). The PES contains 320 events generated by exhaustively sampling events that were reported to be sources of pleasure by highly diverse samples of people. The person is asked to rate both the frequency and the subjective enjoyability of each event; a multiplicative cross-product of these ratings is assumed to provide an approximate measure of response-contingent positive reinforcement. Extensive normative data and results consistent with the construct validity of the scale have been presented elsewhere (Lewinsohn & Amenson, 1978; MacPhillamy & Lewinsohn, 1975).
2. The subject may monitor his/her daily rate of engagement in pleasant activities over a period of time through the use of "activity schedules" (Lewinsohn, 1976).

An activity schedule consists of the items judged by the patient to be most pleasant, and patients are asked to indicate at the end of each day which of the activities he/she performed. Fuchs and Rehm (1977) employed an activity schedule procedure in a self-control–oriented therapy program.

3. Harmon, Nelson, and Hayes (1978) described the use of a portable timer that is carried by the patient and that is used to cue self-monitoring on a variable-interval schedule of one hour. The person is provided with a list of the variable intervals used to set the timer and is asked to set the timer for the first interval on awakening in the morning and to reset it for the next interval immediately after being cued. When cued, the person is instructed to record a description of her/his activity, in addition to a numerical rating of pleasantness from 1 to 5. In contrast to the procedure used by the Lewinsohn group, which is not reactive (Lewinsohn, 1976), the Harmon *et al.* procedure apparently was quite reactive, resulting in substantial increases in engagement in pleasant activities.

Aversive Events: Significance and Assessment. Aversive events have been shown to be related to depression in the following ways:

1. Aversive events have been found to precede the occurrence of clinical depression (e.g., Brown, Bhrolchain, & Harris, 1975; Paykel, Myers, Dienelt, Klerman, Lindenthal, & Pepper, 1969).
2. Depressed persons have been found to be particularly sensitive to aversive events (e.g., Lewinsohn, Lobitz, & Wilson, 1973; Lewinsohn & Talkington, 1979).
3. The rate of occurrence of aversive events covaries with dysphoria (Lewinsohn & Talkington, 1979; Rehm, 1978).

The most frequently used assessment device for the occurrence of life events has been the Social Readjustment Rating Scale (SRRS; Holmes & Rahe, 1967). It consists of 43 items intended to represent fairly common events arising from family, personal, occupational, and financial situations that require, or signify, changes in ongoing adjustment. The occurrence of the events during the preceding six months is established during an interview. Weights are assigned to each item based on ratings made by a sample of judges (Holmes & Rahe, 1967). However, there are many serious methodological and conceptual problems that limit the potential usefulness and the theoretical interpretation of results obtained with the SRRS (Rabkin & Struening, 1976). Instruments that incorporate refinements suggested by criticisms of the SRRS are the PERI (Psychiatric Epidemiology Research Interview) developed by Dohrenwend, Krasnoff, Askenasy, and Dohrenwend (1978), the LES (Life Experiences Survey) developed by Sarason, Johnson, and Siegel (1977), and the UES (Unpleasant Events Schedule) developed by Lewinsohn and Talkington (1979).

Events for the PERI were selected from a population of events generated by asking respondents, "What was the last major event in your life that, for better or worse, interrupted or changed your usual activities?" The 102 events obtained were then rated on the dimension of "change" by a probability-randomized sample from New York City (Dohrenwend, 1978).

The LES is a 57-item self-report measure that asks respondents to indicate the events that they have experienced during the past year. The respondents are then asked to indicate (1) whether they viewed the event as positive or negative at the time and (2) to rate the impact of the particular event on their lives. The LES thus approaches the individualized approach to the measurement of life events advocated by Brown (e.g., Brown, 1974).

The UES consists of 320 events generated on the basis of an extensive search of events considered unpleasant, distressing, and aversive by many people. As with the PES, individuals are asked to rate both the frequency and the subjective aversiveness of an event; a multiplicative cross-product is derived from these ratings. Data on the psychometric properties of the UES—including test–retest reliability, aspects of validity and internal consistency, and relationships with depression—are provided in Lewinsohn and Talkington (1979) and Lewinsohn, Tursky, and Arconad (1979).

Therapeutic Programs for Depression

While the number of fundamental empirical studies of the etiology and the behavior of depression has grown "arithmetically" in recent years, the number of behavioral treatment-outcome studies of depression has grown "exponentially." Treatment strategies and methods reflect the diversity of models of depression. While different therapies posit specific strategies for alleviating depression, commonalities among the various approaches have been noted (Blaney, 1979; Rehm & Kornblith, 1979). There seems little doubt that a variety of structured behavioral and cognitive therapies are, in fact, efficacious in ameliorating depression (Rehm & Kornblith, 1979). In particular, two studies—Rush, Beck, Kovacs, and Hollon (1977) and McLean and Hakstian (1979)—have demonstrated the superiority of cognitive and/or behavioral treatments over chemotherapy.

Decreasing Unpleasant Events and Increasing Pleasant Activities

A treatment approach has evolved out of Lewinsohn's research and theory emphasizing the role of reinforcement in the etiology and maintenance of depression (Lewinsohn, Biglan, & Zeiss, 1976; Lewinsohn, Youngren, & Grosscup 1980). Being depressed is regarded as resulting from few person–environment interactions with positive outcomes and/or an excess of such interactions with aversive or punishing outcomes. Consequently, this approach aims to change the quality and the quantity of the depressed patient's interactions in the direction of increasing positive and decreasing negative events. The treatment is time-limited (12 sessions) and highly structured, and a therapist's manual is available (Lewinsohn & Grosscup, 1978). During the diagnostic phase, which precedes treatment, extensive use is made of the Pleasant Events Schedule (MacPhillamy & Lewinsohn, 1971) and of the Unpleasant Events Schedule (Lewinsohn, 1975b) to begin to pinpoint specific person–environment interactions related to the patient's depression. An Activity Schedule (Lewinsohn, 1976), consisting of 80 items rated by the patient as most pleasant and frequent and 80 items rated by the patient as most unpleasant and frequent, is constructed. Then, patients begin daily monitoring of the occurrence of pleasant and unpleasant activities and of their mood. The covariation of certain pleasant and unpleasant events with changes in mood is used to pinpoint specific person–environment interactions influencing the patient's dysphoria. Subsequently, the treatment provides assistance to the patient in decreasing the frequency and the subjective aversiveness of unpleasant events in his/her life and then concentrates on increasing pleasant ones.

The general goal of the treatment is to *teach* depressed persons skills that they can use to change problem patterns of interaction with the environment, as well as the skills needed to maintain these changes after the termination of therapy. To accomplish the goals of treatment, the therapist makes use of a wide range of cognitive-behavioral interventions, such as assertion, relaxation training, daily-planning and time-management training, and cognitive procedures intended to allow the person to deal more adaptively with aversive situations. A more detailed description and case illustrations are presented in Lewinsohn, Sullivan, and Grosscup (1980).

Lewinsohn, Youngren, and Grosscup (1980) examined the relationship between reinforcement and depression across four samples of depressives as a result of treatment. They found that the rate of positive reinforcement increased as a function of improvement in clinical depression level. Similarly, the rate of experienced aversiveness diminished as clinical depression decreased. In Lewinsohn, Sullivan, and Grosscup (1980), a program of increasing pleasant events was tested across two samples of depressed individuals, while another sample of patients received therapy emphasizing both decreasing unpleasant events and increasing pleasant events. All three samples demonstrated highly significant amounts of clinical improvement.

Interpersonal Therapy

The interpersonal disturbance model of depression postulated by McLean (McLean, Ogston, & Grauer, 1973; McLean, 1976) regards the depressed person's interaction with his/her social environment as the basis of the development and the reversal of depression. As McLean views it, depression results when individuals lose the ability to control their interpersonal environment. When ineffective coping techniques are utilized to remedy situational life problems, the consequence may be depression.

From this interpersonal conception of the etiology and the maintenance of depression, McLean (McLean, 1976; McLean & Hakstian, 1979) has developed a treatment program that incorporates techniques of both a behavioral and a cognitive nature, and that has several distinctive features. The unique aspects of McLean's therapy include an emphasis on decision making regarding appropriate intervention components and the incorporation of procedures for involving relevant social-network members (e.g., the spouse) in treatment.

Like most behaviorally oriented treatments, interpersonal therapy is highly structured and is time-limited to approximately 12 weeks. Six specific therapeutic components are suggested by McLean: communication training, behavioral productivity, social interactions, assertiveness, decision making and problem solving, and cognitive self-control.

Communication training attempts to correct two problems: (1) aversive marital interactions producing spouse avoidance-behavior and (2) a constricted quantity and range of interaction sources. Therapy involves a structured type of communication training. It aims to provide an opportunity for positive feedback and enhanced self-esteem and to facilitate other forms of social interaction.

The primary treatment block, especially important in the early stages of therapy, is called *behavioral productivity*. As McLean has noted, successful performance or mastery experiences are the most powerful antidepressant. Tasks are explicitly graduated, with attention focused on the task and what has been accomplished. Reinforcement, preferably of a social nature from significant others, is made contingent on the successful performance of behavioral tasks.

Social interaction, by acting as a reinforcer and by providing an incompatible response to withdrawal, is used to moderate the experience of depression. Graduated performance assignments are employed to promote social engagement and are prompted by rehearsal and by resource-person accompaniment.

Assertiveness training, decision-making, and problem-solving skills, and *cognitive self-control techniques* are implemented as required by the particular individual's condition.

McLean *et al.* (1973) conducted a study to compare the therapeutic efficacy of an earlier version of McLean's therapeutic program to a varied comparison group. Twenty patients, referred by physicians, were randomly assigned to one of two treatment conditions. The experimental group received training in social learning principles, communication skills, and behavioral contracts. Treatment for the comparison group varied as a function of the treatment agency that they were initially referred from but usually involved either medication, group therapy, individual psychotherapy, or some combination of these. The results showed that the experimental condition produced a significant decrease in problem behaviors, as well as improvements in verbal communication style. The experimental group was also less depressed than the control group at the end of treatment. At a three-month follow-up, the treatment effects were maintained.

More recently, McLean and Hakstian (1979) conducted a large-scale treatment outcome study. One hundred and seventy-eight moderately clinically depressed patients were selected on interview screening and psychometric criteria. The subjects were randomly assigned to one of four treatment conditions: behavior therapy as described in McLean (1976), short-term psychotherapy, relaxation training, and drug treatment (amitriptyline). The therapists were selected on the basis of their preferred treatment modality. The patients encouraged their spouses or significant others to participate in the treatment sessions; the treatment took place over 10 weeks of weekly sessions.

The results demonstrated the unequivocal superiority of the behavioral intervention. Behavior therapy was best on 9 of 10 outcome measures immediately after treatment and marginally superior at follow-up (best on 7 of 10 outcome measures). Additionally, behavior therapy showed a significantly lower attrition rate (5%) than the other conditions, which had dropout rates of 26–36%. The psychotherapy treatment proved to be least effective in the post-treatment and follow-up evaluation periods. Generally it fared worse than the control condition (relaxation training).

Cognitive Therapy

Beck's model of depression assigns the primary causal significance in depression to automatic negative cognitions. Such distorted or unrealistic cognitions are thought to produce misinterpretations of experiences, which lead to affective reactions and other behaviors associated with depression. As one would expect, cognitive therapy aims to assist the client in identifying certain assumptions and themes that are supporting recurrent patterns of stereotypical negative thinking and in pointing out the specific stylistic errors in thinking. Detailed treatment protocols are presented in Rush and Beck (1978) and in Beck, Rush, Shaw, and Emery (1978, 1979).

Cognitive therapy is conceived of as a short-term, time-limited intervention. While both behavioral and cognitive techniques are seen as important in alleviating depression in cognitive therapy, Beck has argued that the former should precede the latter in treatment. In his view, often depressives are initially unable to engage directly in cognitive tasks. At the same time, he considers it a priority to restore a patient's behavioral functioning quickly to counteract withdrawal and to induce involvement in constructive activities. Consequently, behavioral assignments are given to increase environmental input. Additionally, these series of "experiments" enable the patient to test the validity of his/her ideas about him/herself.

To these ends, a number of behavioral techniques are utilized. Graduated task assignments in conjunction with cognitive rehearsal are employed so that patients can test their beliefs about their competence. Activity schedules (e.g., hourly assignments) are also assigned, and patients may be asked to place mastery and pleasure ratings on their scheduled activities. Finally, assertiveness training and role playing may be implemented.

As a patient begins to change his/her negative estimations of his/her capabilities as a result of behavioral exercises, the therapist focuses more directly on the assumed core of depression, namely, cognitions. The therapist teaches the close relationship between feelings, behavior, and thoughts by presenting evidence that the negative way of thinking contributes to depression. The patient learns that there are many ways of interpreting any situation and that a particular interpretation is related to specific feelings. Thus, the therapist assists the patient in searching for alternative interpretations and solutions to problem events. Among the cognitive techniques utilized to ameliorate depression, the triple-column exercise is of particular importance. Patients are asked to identify upsetting events, the nature of the feelings those events elicit, and the automatic negative cognitions associated with dysphoria, and to examine and test the validity of such cognitions on the basis of concrete evidence.

Considerable evidence exists that cognitive therapy is an effective treatment for depression. Rush, Khatami, and Beck (1975) reported that the cognitive and behavioral techniques used in their study produced effective and lasting results with three severely depressed persons with a history of recurrent relapses who had responded poorly to antidepressant medication. Using an A-B-A design, Schmickley (1976) employed cognitive therapy to treat 11 outpatients selected on the basis of MMPI and BDI scores and clinical interview data. While the self-report and observation measures showed improvement during treatment, during the withdrawal phase the improvement lessened. The treatment was not reinstituted and no follow-up was reported.

Gioe (1975) selected 40 college students on the basis of BDI scores. Comparisons were made among a cognitive modification condition, cognitive modification in combination with a "positive group experience," a treatment condition consisting of the "positive group experience" alone, and a waiting-list control. All treatments were given in a group modality, and the results, measured by the BDI, showed that the combined treatment was significantly better than the other conditions. No follow-up was reported.

Taylor and Marshall (1977) compared cognitive therapy with a behavioral approach based on treatment strategies suggested by Ferster (1965), Lazarus (1968), and Lewinsohn (1975a). The subjects were 28 college students selected on the basis of their BDI scores, who were randomly assigned to one of four treatment conditions: cognitive therapy, behavior therapy, a combined cognitive-behavioral treatment, and a waiting-list control. The treatment consisted of six individual sessions. While both the cognitive and the behavioral treatments were more effective than being in the control group according to self-report measures, the combined treatment was more effective than either treatment alone. At a one-month follow-up, however, no significant differences between the cognitive and the behavioral groups could be identified, though the depression scores were generally lower for the cognitive treatment group.

Kovacs and Rush (1976) compared "cognitive-behavioral psychotherapy" with tricyclic antidepressant medication in treating 33 outpatients selected on the basis of scores on the BDI, the Hamilton Scale, and therapists' ratings of symptoms. All subjects were seen individually. Both treatment conditions were found to produce similar decreases in symptoms, although more chemotherapy subjects dropped out of treatment. At six-month follow-up, gains were maintained for both conditions.

Finally, Rush *et al.* (1977) replicated Kovacs and Rush's study with a sample of 41 outpatients carefully selected by means of BDI, Hamilton Scale, and MMPI scores, as well as clinical criteria. The subjects were randomly assigned to treatments and received a mean of 11 weeks of active treatment. Again, the results showed that a higher percentage of chemotherapy patients dropped out of treatment. In contrast to the earlier study, cognitive therapy led to significantly greater improvement on the dependent measures. At three- and six-month follow-ups, this trend continued but was statistically significant only at the three-month period. An important finding was that while only 16% of those treated with cognitive therapy reentered therapy during the follow-up period, 68% in the chemotherapy sample did so.

Self-Control Therapy

As already noted, Rehm (1977) has proposed a model of depression that emphasizes cognitive distortion processes and the importance of self-administered contingent reward and punishment. Three processes—self-monitoring, self-evaluation, and self-reinforcement—are hypothesized to interact in a feedback loop. Depression, according to Rehm, can be accounted for by a number of deficits in self-control behavior.

A self-control behavior therapy for depression has been described by Fuchs and Rehm (1977). This six-week cumulative, sequential program consists of three phases, during which emphasis is placed on training self-monitoring, self-evaluating, and then self-reinforcing skills. Each phase consists of two therapy sessions. Primarily didactic, the first session of each phase involves a presentation and discussion of self-control principles relevant to the assumed deficits of depression, plus a behavioral homework assignment. In the second of these sessions, the patients review their preceding week's assignment. The principles of self-control are reiterated by the therapist, and appropriate use of these concepts by patients is reinforced.

The self-monitoring phase of treatment involves the use of logs to record positive activities; daily average mood is also noted. In the self-evaluation phase, patients are instructed in setting subgoals for desirable positive activities associated with good mood and to rate their accomplished behaviors toward those goals. Finally, during the self-reinforcement phase, the patients are presented with the general principles of reinforcement and taught to self-reinforce, overtly and covertly.

Fuchs and Rehm (1977) compared a group behavior-therapy program based on self-control principles to a non-specific group-therapy condition and to a waiting-list control-group conditions. The subjects were volunteers who were selected on the basis of MMPI scores and interview criteria. After a six-week treatment period, those in the self-control condition showed clear improvement, which was superior to the control conditions. At a six-week follow-up, the treatment effects were maintained, although differences between conditions had dissipated somewhat.

Rehm, Fuchs, Roth, Kornblith, and Romano (1979) compared 24 volunteer subjects with moderate depression on two treatment conditions: self-control therapy and a social skills treatment (essentially, assertion training). The results indicated that the social skills subjects improved more in social skills, while the self-control subjects improved more on self-control dependent measures. At six-week follow-up, the treatment effects were maintained.

A Psychoeducational Approach

The most recent experimental development in the behavioral and cognitive treatment of depression has been the use of an explicit educational experience (i.e., a course entitled "Coping with Depression") as the vehicle for treatment (Lewinsohn & Brown, 1979). The course consists of 12 two-hour class sessions spaced out over eight weeks. The typical number of participants has been eight. The course utilizes a textbook *Control Your Depression* (Lewinsohn, Muñoz, Youngren, & Zeiss, 1978) and represents a multicomponent approach emphasizing general self-help skills (two sessions), self-control techniques relevant to thoughts (two sessions), pleasant activities (two sessions), relaxation (two sessions), interpersonal interaction (two sessions), and maintenance (two sessions). The efficacy of the course was evaluated in an initial study (Brown & Lewinsohn, in press; Lewinsohn & Brown, 1979), which was designed to compare three different modes of teaching the course (class, individual tutoring, and minimal phone contact) with a waiting-list control condition. Large and statistically significant clinical improvement was shown in all of the active conditions, which together were significantly superior to the waiting control condition. Improvement shown at the termination of the course was maintained at the one-month and at the six-month follow-up.

An important feature of the "Coping With Depression" courses is that the participants are able to meet in groups to assist each other in overcoming their depression. With relatively few exceptions (e.g., Barerra, 1979; Fuchs & Rehm, 1977), previous cognitive-behavioral treatments have been offered within an individual therapy mode. This is not surprising, since most authorities in the area of group therapy (e.g., Yalom, 1975) advise against homogeneous groups of depressed patients. Our results indicate that within the structure presented by the course, depressives work together very effectively. Another feature of the course is that it represents a community-oriented outreach approach to impact on the great majority of depressives who never avail themselves of the services of clinics and mental health professionals. The educational focus reduces the stigma involved in seeking "psychiatric" or "psychological" treatment, which is especially important to the elderly depressed.

"Eclectic" Tactics in Treating Depression

Several investigators have explored therapy programs whose elements are not commonly associated with the treatment of depression. Perhaps the most distinctive of these are the comparisons between running or jogging and individual psychotherapy in two studies conducted and reported by Greist, Klein, Eischens, Faris, Gurman, and Morgan (1979). In their pilot study, 28 patients were randomly assigned to running or either time-limited or time-unlimited psychotherapy. The subjects were selected on the basis of scores on the Depression Symptom Checklist-90 (Derogatis, Lipman, & Covi, 1973). Also, they had to meet RDC criteria for minor depression. The results of two studies indicated that the running treatment was as effective in alleviating depressive symptomatology and target complaints as either of the psychotherapy treatments.

Assertion training has also been used with depressed individuals. It was first reported in case studies by Wolpe and Lazarus (1966). Lazarus (1968) trained a depressed outpatient to make assertive statements and requests of significant others with whom she was experiencing frequent conflict. As a result of these skills, her depressive symptoms were reportedly alleviated, although no data were presented. Following the application of assertiveness training in the treatment of one of his patients, Seitz (1971) reported a significant decrease in the level of depression.

Sanchez, Lewinsohn, and Larson (1980) reported the results of a treatment outcome study in which subassertive depressed outpatients were randomly assigned either to an assertion-training group or to a "traditional" (i.e., insight-oriented) therapy group. The results indicated that assertion training was effective in increasing self-reported assertiveness and in alleviating depression. Additionally, it was more effective than the traditional psychotherapy that lasted for a comparable period of time.

Because marital relationships are often a problem for depressed individuals (Coleman & Miller, 1975; Weiss & Aved, 1978; Weissman & Paykel, 1974), treatment approaches focusing on the marital relationship have also been described (e.g., Lewinsohn & Shaw, 1969; McLean, Ogston, & Grauer, 1973; Stuart, 1967).

Final Comments

It is clear that cognitive-behavioral approaches and conceptualizations are characterized by great diversity but that empirical support for the therapeutic efficacy of each has been provided. Since all are theoretically derived (i.e., they are specifically designed to modify *the* specific cognitions and/or behaviors assumed by the theory to be a critical antecedent of depression), a question needs to be raised: How could they all be effective? Our own thinking has been greatly influenced by the results of a particular treatment outcome (Zeiss *et al.*, 1979). In this study, three treatments (cognitive, pleasant activities, and social skill training) were compared. The results indicated that while all three treatments were equally effective in reducing depression level, the changes on the intervening dependent measures were not specific to the treatment (i.e., the thinking of the social skill treatment patients changed as much as the thinking of those in the cognitive treatment and vice versa). The major finding of this study (i.e., that the treatments did not selectively impact the relevant target behaviors) was completely unexpected, and we feel that it has theoretical and clinical implications.

On the basis of these results, we have tried to hypothesize what the "critical components" might be for successful short-term cognitive-behavioral therapy for depression (Zeiss, Lewinsohn, & Muñoz, 1979), to wit:

1. Therapy should begin with an elaborated, well-planned rationale.

2. Therapy should provide training in skills that the patient can utilize to feel more effective in handling his/her daily life.
3. Therapy should emphasize the independent use of these skills by the patient outside the therapy context and must provide enough structure so that the attainment of independent skill is possible for the patient.
4. Therapy should encourage the patient to believe that improvement in mood is caused by the patient's increased skillfulness, not by the therapist's skillfulness.

Similarly, McLean and Hakstian (1979) noted that high structure, a social learning rationale, a goal attainment focus, and increasing social interaction were significant elements in the behavioral treatment of depression.

Conclusions and Recommendations

It is clear that the past 10 years have been a period of very busy and exciting progress in the psychological treatment of depression and in depression theory. Great strides have been made in the differential diagnosis of depressive disorders. Existing assessment procedures have the capacity to generate reliable and replicable data on patients' depression in terms of specific symptoms, manifestations, severity level, and perhaps even subtypes. Investigators should be expected to define their populations in much more rigorous terms than has been the case in the past. It is no longer defensible for researchers (or clinicians) to base their diagnosis of depression entirely on arbitrary cutoff scores on self-report inventories like the Beck Depression Inventory (Beck, 1967). Self-report depression measures like the Center for Epidemiologic Studies–Depression Scale (Radloff, 1977) are very useful as screening devices but need to be followed by a clinical interview.

An area of weakness is the differential diagnosis and treatment of depression among the elderly. Differential diagnosis in the elderly is complicated both by the increase in the incidence of physical illness and of somatic symptoms with age and by the difficulty in distinguishing the symptoms of depression from those of senile dementia (Epstein, 1976). More work needs to be done to develop instruments appropriate to elderly populations and to standardize existing instruments across the total age range. Existing treatment programs will need to be modified and then tested with elderly persons (e.g., Gallagher, in press).

Depression in childhood and early adolescence is becoming an area of increasing importance and interest. Promising new developments are being reported, particularly in the area of assessment. A self-report rating of childhood depression, the Children's Depression Inventory (CDI), has been developed by Kovacs and Beck (1977). A Peer Nomination Inventory of Depression (PNID) has been found to possess good psychometric properties and has been used to identify depression in normal populations of children (Lefkowitz & Tesiny, 1980).

At the level of depression theory, there has been a shift from global (and obviously too simple) single-sentence theoretical statements ("Depression is due to . . .") to more sophisticated conceptualizations that begin to recognize the complexity and the diversity of the phenomena of depression. The general outline of the end point of depression theorizing may have been anticipated by Akiskal and McKinney (1973) and by Becker (1974) in their attempts to provide "unified" hypotheses to integrate the many relevant clinical, experimental, genetic, biochemical, and neurophysiological findings.

At the level of empirical research, it is important that studies include a carefully defined and matched nondepressed "psychiatric control" group (i.e., persons who show psychological deviations *other* than depression). The inclusion of a psychiatric control group permits the attribution of observed group differences to depression rather than to psychological deviation. Research is also needed to assess the *etiological* significance of the various variables that have been shown to be uniquely associated with depression. On the basis of existing research findings, it is impossible to determine whether the factors that have been shown to be correlated with depression constitute antecedent conditions for the occurrence of depression, or whether they are secondary to depression. Support for the etiological significance of the problem behaviors that have been found to be associated with depression can come only from longitudinal studies of the sequence of events leading to depression.

At a recent conference convened by the National Institute of Mental Health (Rehm, 1979), it was concluded that there is promising evidence of the efficacy of behavior therapies in the treatment of depression. At the same time, a number of serious limitations to this conclusion were noted. Among other things, the treatments that have been developed differ in certain specific components, although they also overlap to a considerable degree. Yet, the *effective* ingredients of behavior therapy programs for depression are essentially unknown. The *relative* contribution of specific components, and of so-called nonspecific effects, clearly needs to be investigated, and the results of such studies will be important theoretically.

Not all therapeutic elements are appropriate for every depressed individual. Hence, research efforts need to be concerned with matching patients to treatments. Additionally, attention needs to be focused on developing and testing maintenance programs for depressives treated by behavioral and cognitive treatments. More needs to be known, as well, about the distinguishing characteristics of patients who do not respond to behavioral and cognitive treatments. Finally, as research produces evidence of antecedent conditions and/or predispositional variables in the etiology of depression, prevention programs directed at high-risk populations should be tested and employed.

References

Abraham, K. Notes on the psychoanalytic investigation and treatment of manic-depressive insanity and allied conditions. *Selected Papers on Psychoanalysis.* New York: Basic Books, 1960.

Abramson, L. Y., & Sackheim, H. A. A paradox in depression: Uncontrollability and self-blame. *Psychological Bulletin,* 1977, *84,* 838–851.

Abramson, L. Y., Garber, J., Edwards, N. B., & Seligman, M. E. P. Expectancy changes in depression and schizophrenia. *Journal of Abnormal Psychology,* 1978, *87,* 102–109.

Abramson, L. Y., Seligman, M. E. P., & Teasdale, J. D. Learned helplessness in humans: Critique and reformulation. *Journal of Abnormal Psychology,* 1978, *87,* 49–74.

Akiskal, H. S., & McKinney, W. T., Jr. Depressive disorders: Toward a unified hypothesis. *Science,* 1973, *182,* 20–29.

Alloy, L. B., & Abramson, L. Y. Judgment of contingency in depressed students: Sadder but wiser? *Journal of Experimental Psychology: General,* 1979, *108,* 441–485.

Amenson, C. S., & Lewinsohn, P. M. An investigation into the observed sex differences in prevalence of unipolar depression. *Journal of Abnormal Psychology,* 1981, *90,* 1–13.

Arkowitz, H., Lichtenstein, E., McGovern, K., & Hines, P. The behavioral assessment of social competence in males. *Behavior Therapy,* 1975, *6,* 3–13.

Bandura, A. *Social learning theory.* Englewood Cliffs, N.J.: Prentice-Hall, 1977.

Barrera, M. An evaluation of a brief group therapy for depression. *Journal of Consulting and Clinical Psychology,* 1979, *47,* 413–415.

Beck, A. T. Thinking and depression: Idiosyncratic content and cognitive distortions. *Archives of General Psychiatry,* 1963, *9,* 324–333.

Beck, A. T. Thinking and depression. II: Theory and therapy. *Archives of General Psychiatry,* 1964, *10,* 561–571.

Beck, A. T. *Depression: Clinical, experimental and theoretical aspects.* New York: Harper & Row, 1967.

Beck, A. T. Cognitive therapy: Nature and relation to behavior therapy. *Behavior Therapy,* 1970, *1,* 184–200.

Beck, A. T. *Cognitive therapy and the emotional disorders.* New York: International Universities Press, 1976.

Beck, A. T., & Beck, R. W. Screening depressed patients in family practice—A rapid technique. *Postgraduate Medicine,* 1972, *52,* 81–85.

Beck, A. T., Ward, C. H., Mendelson, M., Mock, J., & Erbaugh, J. An inventory for measuring depression. *Archives of General Psychiatry,* 1961, *4,* 561–571.

Beck, A. T., Weissman, A., Lester, D., & Traxler, L. The measurement of pessimism: The hopelessness scale. *Journal of Consulting and Clinical Psychology,* 1974, *42,* 861–865.

Beck, A. T., Rush, A. J., Shaw, B. F., & Emery, G. *Cognitive therapy of depression: A treatment manual.* Unpublished manuscript, University of Pennsylvania, 1978.

Beck, A. T., Rush, A. J., Shaw, B. F., & Emery, G. *Cognitive therapy of depression.* New York: Guilford Press, 1979.

Becker, J. *Depression: Theory and research.* New York: V. H. Winston & Sons, 1974.

Becker, J. *Affective disorders.* Morristown, N.J.: General Learning Press, 1977.

Bibring, E. The mechanism of depression. In P. Greenacre (Ed.), *Affective disorders.* New York: International Universities Press, 1953.

Blaney, P. H. Contemporary theories of depression: Critique and comparison. *Journal of Abnormal Psychology*, 1977, *86*, 203–223.

Blaney, P. H. The effectiveness of cognitive and behavior therapies. In L. P. Rehm (Ed.), *Behavior therapy for depression: Present status and future directions*. New York: Academic Press, 1981.

Brown, G. W. Meaning, measurement and stress of life-events. In B. S. Dohrenwend & B. P. Dohrenwend (Eds.), *Stressful life events: Their nature and effects*. New York: Wiley, 1974.

Brown, G. W., Bhrolchain, M. N., & Harris, T. Social class and psychiatric disturbance among women in an urban population. *Sociology*, 1975, *9*, 225–254.

Brown, R. A., & Lewinsohn, P. M. *A psychoeducational approach to the treatment of depression: Comparison of group, individual and minimal contact procedures*, in preparation.

Buchwald, A. M. Depressive mood and estimates of reinforcement frequency. *Journal of Abnormal Psychology*, 1977, *86*, 443–446.

Buchwald, A. M., Coyne, J. C., & Cole, C. S. A critical evaluation of the learned helplessness model of depression. *Journal of Abnormal Psychology*, 1978, *87*, 180–193.

Burgess, E. The modification of depressive behaviors. In R. Rubin & C. M. Franks (Eds.), *Advances in behavior therapy, 1968*. New York: Academic Press, 1969.

Burglass, D., & Horton, J. A scale for predicting subsequent suicidal behavior. *British Journal of Psychiatry*, 1974, *124*, 573–578.

Cadoret, R. J., & Tanna, V. L. Genetics of affective disorders. In G. Usdin (Ed.), *Depression: Clinical, biological and psychological perspectives*. New York: Brunner/Mazel, 1977.

Ciminero, A. R., & Steingarten, K. A. The effects of performance standards on self-evaluation and self-reinforcement on depressed and nondepressed individuals. *Cognitive Therapy and Research*, 1978, *2*, 179–182.

Coleman, R. E., & Miller, A. G. The relationship between depression and marital adjustment in a clinic population: A multitrait-multimethod study. *Journal of Consulting and Clinical Psychology*, 1975, *43*, 647–651.

Costello, C. G. Depression: Loss of reinforcers or loss of reinforcer effectiveness. *Behavior Therapy*, 1972, *3*, 240–247.

Costello, C. G. A critical review of Seligman's laboratory experiments of learned helplessness and depression in humans. *Journal of Abnormal Psychology*, 1978, *87*, 21–31.

Coyne, J. C. Depression and the response of others. *Journal of Abnormal Psychology*, 1976, *85*, 186–193.

Craighead, W. E. Issues resulting from treatment studies. In L. P. Rehm (Ed.), *Behavior therapy for depression: Present status and future directions*. New York: Academic Press, 1981.

Craighead, W. E., Hickey, K. S., & DeMonbreun, B. G. Distortion of perception and recall of neutral feedback in depression. *Cognitive Therapy and Research*, 1979, *3*, 291–298.

Curran, J. P. Skills training as an approach to the treatment of heterosexual-social anxiety: A review. *Psychological Bulletin*, 1977, *84*, 140–157.

Dahlstrom, W. G., Welsh, G. S., & Dahlstrom, L. E. *An MMPI handbook*. Minneapolis: University of Minnesota Press, 1972.

DeMonbreun, W., & Craighead, W. E. Distortion of perception and recall of positive and neutral feedback in depression. *Cognitive Therapy and Research*, 1977, *1*, 311–329.

Derogatis, L. R., Lipman, R. S., & Covi, L. SCL-90: An outpatient psychiatric rating scale—Preliminary report. *Psychopharmacology Bulletin*, 1973, *9*, 13–27.

Diagnostic and statistical manual of mental disorders, Second edition. Washington, D.C.: American Psychiatric Association, 1968.

Diagnostic and statistical manual of mental disorders, Third edition. Washington, D.C.: American Psychiatric Association, 1980.

Diggory, J. C., & Loeb, A. Motivation of chronic schizophrenics by information about their abilities in a group situation. *Journal of Abnormal and Social Psychology*, 1962, *65*, 48–52.

Dohrenwend, B. S., Krasnoff, L., Askenasy, A. R., & Dohrenwend, B. P. Exemplification of a method for scaling life events: The Peri life events scale. *Journal of Health and Social Behavior*, 1978, *19*, 205–229.

Eastman, C. Behavioral formulations of depression. *Psychological Review*, 1976, *83*, 277–291.

Ellis, A., & Harper, R. A. *A guide to rational living*. Hollywood, Calif.: Wilshire, 1961.

Endicott, J., & Spitzer, R. L. A diagnostic interview, the schedule for affective disorders and schizophrenia. *Archives of General Psychiatry*, 1978, *35*, 837–844.

Epstein, S. Anxiety, arousal, and the self-concept. In I. G. Sarason & C. D. Spielberger (Eds.), *Stress and anxiety*, Vol. 3. Washington, D.C.: Hemisphere, 1976.

Ernst, P., Badash, D., Beran, B., Kosovsky, R., & Kleinhauz, M. Incidence of mental illness in the aged: Unmasking the effect of a diagnosis of chronic brain syndrome. *Journal of the American Geriatrics Society*, 1977, *25*, 371–375.

Ferster, C. B. Classification of behavior pathology. In L. Krasner & L. P. Ullmann (Eds.), *Research in behavior modification*. New York: Holt, Rinehart & Winston, 1965.

Ferster, C. B. Animal behavior and mental illness. *Psychological Record*, 1966, *16*, 345–356.

Flippo, J. R., & Lewinsohn, P. M. Effects of failure on the self-esteem of depressed and nondepressed subjects. *Journal of Consulting and Clinical Psychology*, 1971, *36*, 151.

Freud, S. Mourning and melancholia. In *The complete works of Sigmund Freud, Vol. XIV*. London, Hogarth Press, 1957. (Originally published, 1917.)

Fuchs, C. Z., & Rehm, L. P. A self-control behavior therapy program for depression. *Journal of Consulting and Clinical Psychology*, 1977, *45*, 206–215.

Gaitz, C. M. Depression in the elderly. In W. Fann, I. Karacan, A. Pokorny, & R. Williams (Eds.), *Phenomenology and treatment of depression*. New York: Spectrum, 1977.

Gallagher, D. Behavioral group therapy with elderly depressions: An experimental study. In D. Upper & S. Ross (Eds.), *Behavioral group therapy*. Champaign, Ill.: Research Press, 1981.

Gallagher, D., McGarvey, W., Zelinski, E., & Thompson, C. W. Age and factor structure of the Zung depression scale. Unpublished mimeo, 1978.

Garber, J., Hollon, S. D., & Silverman, V. *Evaluation and reward of self vs. others in depression.* Paper presented at the Annual Meeting of Association for Advancement of Behavior Therapy, San Francisco, 1979.

Gatchel, R. J., Paulus, P. B., & Maples, C. W. Learned helplessness and self-reported affect. *Journal of Abnormal Psychology,* 1975, *84,* 589–620.

Gioe, V. J. *Cognitive modification and positive group experience as a treatment for depression.* Paper presented at the Association for Advancement of Behavior Therapy, San Francisco, 1975.

Glazer, R. (Ed.). *The nature of reinforcement.* New York: Academic Press, 1971.

Graf, M. G. *A mood-related activities schedule for the treatment of depression.* Unpublished doctoral dissertation, Arizona State University, 1977.

Greist, J. H., Klein, M. H., Eischens, R. R., Faris, J., Gurman, A. J., & Morgan, W. P. Running as treatment for depression. *Comprehensive Psychiatry,* 1979, *20,* 41–54.

Grinker, R. R., Miller, J., Sabshin, M., Nunn, R., & Nunnally, J. C. *The phenomena of depressions.* New York: Paul B. Hoeber, 1961.

Gurland, B. J. The comparative frequency of depression in various adult age groups. *Journal of Gerontology,* 1976, *31,* 283–292.

Hamilton, D. A rating scale for depression. *Journal of Neurology, Neurosurgery, and Psychiatry,* 1960, *23,* 56–61.

Hamilton, D. Development of a rating scale for primary depressive illness. *Journal of Clinical and Social Psychology,* 1967, *6,* 278–296.

Hammen, C. L., & Krantz, S. *The story completion test.* Unpublished mimeo, University of California at Los Angeles, 1976.

Hammen, C. L., & Peters, S. D. Differential responses to male and female depressive reactions. *Journal of Consulting and Clinical Psychology,* 1977, *45,* 994–1001.

Harnatz, J., & Shader, R. Psychopharmacologic investigations in healthy elderly volunteers: MMPI depression scale. *Journal of American Geriatrics Society,* 1975, *23,* 350–354.

Harmon, T. H., Nelson, R. O., & Hayes, S. C. *Self-monitoring of mood vs. activity by depressed clients.* Paper presented at the Association for Advancement of Behavior Therapy, Chicago, 1978.

Hiroto, D. S. Locus of control and learned helplessness. *Journal of Experimental Psychology,* 1974, *102,* 187–193.

Hollon, S. D. Comparisons and combinations with alternative approaches. In L. P. Rehm (Ed.), *Behavior therapy for depression: Present status and future directions.* New York: Academic Press, 1981.

Holmes, T. H., & Rahe, R. H. The social readjustment rating scale. *Journal of Psychosomatic Research,* 1967, *11,* 213–218.

Huesmann, L. R. Cognitive processes and models of depression. *Journal of Abnormal Psychology,* 1978, *87,* 194–198.

Jacobson, E. *Depression—Comparative studies of normal, neurotic, and psychotic conditions.* New York: International Universities Press, 1971.

Jacobson, N. S. The assessment of overt behavior. In L. P. Rehm (Ed.), *Behavior therapy for depression: Present status and future directions.* New York: Academic Press, 1981.

James, W. H. *Internal versus external control of reinforcement as a basic variable in learning theory.* Unpublished doctoral dissertation, Ohio State University, 1957.

James, W. H., & Rotter, J. B. Partial and one hundred percent reinforcement under chance and skill conditions. *Journal of Experimental Psychology,* 1958, *55,* 397–403.

Johansson, S. L., Lewinsohn, P. M., & Flippo, J. F. *An application of the Premack principle to the verbal behavior of depressed subjects.* Paper presented at the meeting of the Association for Advancement of Behavior Therapy, Washington, D.C., 1969.

Jones, R. G. *A factored measure of Ellis' irrational beliefs system.* Wichita, Kansas: Wichita Test Systems, Inc., 1968.

Kanfer, F. H. The maintenance of behavior by self-generated stimuli and reinforcement. In A. Jacobs & L. B. Sachs (Eds.), *The psychology of private events: Perspectives on covert response systems.* New York: Academic Press, 1971.

Klein, D. C., & Seligman, M. E. P. Reversal of performance deficits in learned helplessness and depression. *Journal of Abnormal Psychology,* 1976, *85,* 11–26.

Klinger, E. Consequences of commitment to and disengagement from incentives. *Psychological Review,* 1975, *82,* 1–25.

Kovacs, M., & Beck, A. T. An empirical-clinical approach toward a definition of childhood depression. In J. G. Schulterbrandt & A. Raskin (Eds.), *Depression in childhood: Diagnosis, treatment, and conceptual models.* New York: Raven Press, 1977.

Kovacs, M., & Rush, A. J. *Cognitive psychotherapy versus anti-depressant medication in the treatment of depression.* Paper presented at Eastern Psychological Association, New York, April 1976.

Krantz, S., & Hammen, C. *The assessment of cognitive bias in depression.* Unpublished mimeo, University of California at Los Angeles, 1978.

Kupfer, D. J., Weiss, B. G. F., Detre, T. P., Foster, F. G., Delgado, J., & MacPartland, R. Psychomotor activity in affective states. *Archives of General Psychiatry,* 1974, *30,* 765–768.

Langone, M. Assertiveness and Lewinsohn's theory of depression: An empirical test. *The Behavior Therapist,* 1979, *2,* 21.

Lazarus, A. A. Learning theory and the treatment of depression. *Behaviour Research and Therapy,* 1968, *6,* 83–89.

Lefcourt, H. M. Locus of control for specific goals. In L. C. Perlmuter & R. A. Monty (Eds.), *Choice and perceived control.* Hillside, N.J.: Lawrence Erlbaum, 1978.

Lefkowitz, M. M., & Tesiny, E. P. Assessment of childhood depression. *Journal of Consulting and Clinical Psychology,* 1980, *48,* 43–50.

Lehman, H. E. Epidemiology of depressive disorders. In

R. R. Fieve (Ed.), *Depression in the 70's: Modern theory and research.* Princeton, N.J.: Excerpta Medica, 1971.

Levitt, E. E., & Lubin, B. *Depression.* New York: Springer, 1975.

Lewinsohn, P. M. Manual of instructions for the behavior ratings used for the observations of interpersonal behavior. In E. J. Mash & L. G. Terdal (Eds.), *Behavior therapy assessment: Diagnosis design, and evaluation.* New York: Springer, 1974.

Lewinsohn, P. M. The behavioral study and treatment of depression. In M. Hersen, R. M. Eisler, & P. M. Miller (Eds.), *Progress in behavior modification,* Vol. 1. New York: Academic Press, 1975. (a)

Lewinsohn, P. M. The unpleasant events schedule: A scale for the measurement of aversive events. Unpublished mimeo, University of Oregon, 1975. (b)

Lewinsohn, P. M. Activity schedules in the treatment of depression. In C. E. Thoresen & J. D. Krumboltz (Eds.), *Counseling methods.* New York: Holt, Rinehart & Winston, 1976.

Lewinsohn, P. M., & Amenson, C. S. Some relations between pleasant and unpleasant mood-related events and depression. *Journal of Abnormal Psychology,* 1978, *87,* 655–654.

Lewinsohn, P. M., & Brown, R. A. *Learning how to control one's depression: An educational approach.* Paper presented at the meeting of the American Psychological Association, New York, 1979.

Lewinsohn, P. M., & Graf, M. Pleasant Activities and depression. *Journal of Consulting and Clinical Psychology,* 1973, *41,* 261–268.

Lewinsohn, P. M., & Grosscup, S. J. *Decreasing unpleasant events and increasing pleasant events: A treatment manual for depression.* Unpublished manuscript, University of Oregon, 1978.

Lewinsohn, P. M., & Lee, W. M. L. Assessment of affective disorders. In D. H. Barlow (Ed.), *Behavioral assessment of adult disorders.* New York: Guilford Press, 1981.

Lewinsohn, P. M., & Libet, J. Pleasant events, activity schedules, and depressions. *Journal of Abnormal Psychology,* 1972, *79,* 291–295.

Lewinsohn, P. M., & Shaffer, M. Use of home observations as an integral part of the treatment of depression: Preliminary report and case studies. *Journal of Consulting and Clinical Psychology,* 1971, *37,* 87–94.

Lewinsohn, P. M., & Shaw, D. Feedback about interpersonal behavior as an agent of behavior change: A case study in the treatment of depression. *Psychotherapy and Psychosomatics,* 1969, *17,* 82–88.

Lewinsohn, P. M., & Talkington, J. Studies on the measurement of unpleasant events and relations with depression. *Applied Psychological Measurement,* 1979, *3,* 83–101.

Lewinsohn, P. M., Weinstein, M., & Shaw, D. Depression: A clinical-research approach. In R. D. Rubin & C. M. Frank (Eds.), *Advances in behavior therapy,* 1968. New York: Academic Press, 1969.

Lewinsohn, P. M., Weinstein, M., & Alper, T. A behavioral approach to the group treatment of depressed persons: A methodological contribution. *Journal of Clinical Psychology,* 1970, *26,* 525–532.

Lewinsohn, P. M., Lobitz, W. C., & Wilson, S. "Sensitivity" of depressed individuals to aversive stimuli. *Journal of Abnormal Psychology,* 1973, *81,* 259–263.

Lewinsohn, P. M., Biglan, A., & Zeiss, A. M. Behavioral treatment of depression. In P. O. Davidson (Ed.), *The behavioral management of anxiety, depression and pain.* New York: Brunner/Mazel, 1976.

Lewinsohn, P. M., Larson, D. W., & Muñoz, R. F. *The measurement of expectancies and other cognitions in depressed individuals.* Paper presented at the Association for Advancement of Behavior Therapy, Chicago, 1978.

Lewinsohn, P. M., Muñoz, R. F., Youngren, M. A., & Zeiss, A. M. *Control your depression.* Englewood Cliffs, N.J.: Prentice-Hall, 1978.

Lewinsohn, P. M., Tursky, S. P., & Arconad, M. *The relationship between age and the frequency of occurrence, and the subjective impact, of aversive events.* Unpublished mimeo, University of Oregon, 1979.

Lewinsohn, P. M., Mischel, W., Chaplin, W., & Barton, R. Social competence and depression: The role of illusory self-perception? *Journal of Abnormal Psychology,* 1980, *89,* 203–212.

Lewinsohn, P. M., Sullivan, M. J., & Grosscup, S. J. Changing reinforcing events: An approach to the treatment of depression. In *Psychotherapy: Theory, Research and Practice,* 1980, *17,* 322–334.

Lewinsohn, P. M., Youngren, M. A., & Grosscup, S. L. Reinforcement and depression. In R. A. Depue (Ed.), *The psychobiology of the depressive disorders: Implications for the effects of stress.* New York: Academic Press, 1980.

Libet, J., & Lewinsohn, P. M. The concept of social skill with special reference to the behavior of depression persons. *Journal of Consulting and Clinical Psychology,* 1973, *40,* 304–312.

Lloyd, G. G., & Lishman, W. A. Effect of depression on the speed of recall of pleasant and unpleasant experiences. *Psychological Medicine,* 1975, *5,* 173–180.

Lobitz, W. C., & Post, R. D. Parameters of self-reinforcement and depression. *Journal of Abnormal Psychology,* 1979, *88,* 33–41.

Loeb, A., Feshbach, S., Beck, A. T., & Wolfe, A. Some effects of reward upon the social perception and motivation of psychiatric patients varying in depression. *Journal of Abnormal and Social Psychology,* 1964, *68,* 609–611.

Loeb, A., Beck, A. T., Diggory, J. C., & Tuthill, R. Expectancy, level of aspiration, performance, and self-evaluation in depression. *Proceedings of the 75th Annual Convention of the American Psychological Association, 1967,* pp. 193–194.

Lubin, B. Adjective check lists for measurement of depression. *Archives of General Psychiatry,* 1965, *12,* 57–62.

Lubin, B. *Manual for the depression adjective check lists.* San Diego: Educational and Industrial Testing Service, 1967.

Lubin, B. *Bibliography for the depression adjective check lists: 1966–1977.* San Diego, Calif.: Educational and Industrial Testing Service, 1977.

MacPhillamy, D. J., & Lewinsohn, P. M. *A scale for the*

measurement of positive reinforcement. Unpublished mimeo, University of Oregon, 1971.

MacPhillamy, D. J., & Lewinsohn, P. M. Depression as a function of levels of desired and obtained pleasure. *Journal of Abnormal Psychology,* 1974, *83,* 651–657.

MacPhillamy, D., & Lewinsohn, P. M. *Manual for the Pleasant Events Schedule.* Unpublished mimeograph, University of Oregon, 1975.

Mahoney, M. J. *Cognition and behavior modification.* Cambridge, Mass.: Ballinger, 1974.

McLean, P. Therapeutic decision making in the behavioral treatment of depression. In P. O. Davidson (Ed.), *The behavioral management of anxiety, depression, and pain.* New York: Brunner/Mazel, 1976.

McLean, P. D., & Hakstian, A. R. Clinical depression: Comparative efficacy of outpatient treatments. *Journal of Consulting and Clinical Psychology,* 1979, *47,* 818–836.

McLean, P. D., Ogston, K., & Grauer, L. A behavioral approach to the treatment of depression. *Journal of Behavior Therapy and Experimental Psychiatry,* 1973, *4,* 323–330.

McNair, D., Lorr, M., & Droppleman, L. *EITS manual for the profile of mood states.* San Diego, Calif.: Educational and Industrial Testing Service, 1971.

Miller, W. R., & Seligman, M. E. P. Depression and the perception of reinforcement. *Journal of Abnormal Psychology,* 1973, *82,* 62–73.

Miller, W. R., & Seligman, M. E. P. Depression and learned helplessness in man. *Journal of Abnormal Psychology,* 1975, *84,* 228–238.

Miller, W. R., & Seligman, M. E. P. Learned helplessness, depression, and the perception of reinforcement. *Behaviour Research and Therapy,* 1976, *14,* 7–17.

Morris, J. B., & Beck, A. T. The efficacy of anti-depressant drugs: A review of research, 1958–1972. *Archives of General Psychiatry,* 1974, *30,* 667–674.

Muñoz, R. F. A cognitive approach to the assessment and treatment of depression. *Dissertation Abstracts International, 1977, 38,* 2873B (University Microfilms No. 77-26, 505, 154.)

Muñoz, R. F., & Lewinsohn, P. M. *The Cognitive Events Schedule.* Unpublished mimeo, University of Oregon, 1976. (a)

Muñoz, R. B., & Lewinsohn, P. M. *The Personal Belief Inventory,* Unpublished mimeo, University of Oregon, 1976. (b)

Muñoz, R. F., & Lewinsohn, P. M. *The Subjective Probability Questionnaire.* Unpublished mimeo, University of Oregon, 1976. (c)

Murphy, R., & Ellis, A. *Rationality scales: A bibliography.* New York: Institute for Rational Living, 1976.

National Institute of Mental Health. *Special report: The depressive illnesses.* 1970.

Nelson, R. E. Irrational beliefs in depression. *Journal of Consulting and Clinical Psychology,* 1977, *45,* 1190–1191.

Nelson, R. E., & Craighead, W. E. Selective recall of positive and negative feedback, self-control behaviors, and depression. *Journal of Abnormal Psychology,* 1977, *86,* 379–388.

Overall, J. E. Dimensions of manifest depression. *Journal of Psychiatric Research,* 1962, *1,* 239–245.

Parloff, M. B., Wolfe, B., Hadley, S., & Waskow, I. *Assessment of psychosocial treatment of mental disorders:*

Current status and prospects. Unpublished mimeo, 1978.

Paykel, E. S., Myers, J. K., Dienelt, M. N., Klerman, G. L., Lindenthal, J. J., & Pepper, M. P. Life events and depression: A controlled study. *Archives of General Psychiatry,* 1969, *21,* 753–760.

Peterson, C. Uncontrollability and self-blame in depression: Investigation of the paradox in a college population. *Journal of Abnormal Psychology,* 1979, *88,* 620–624.

Prkachin, K., Craig, K., Papageorgis, D., & Reith, G. Nonverbal communication deficits in response to performance feedback in depression. *Journal of Abnormal Psychology,* 1977, *86,* 224–234.

Rabkin, J. G., & Struening, E. L. Life events, stress, and illness. *Science,* 1976, *194,* 1013–1020.

Radloff, L. The CES-D Scale: A self-report depression scale for research in the general population. *Applied Psychosocial Measurement,* 1977, *1,* 385–401.

Raskin, A., & Jarvik, L. F. (Eds.), *Psychiatric symptoms and cognitive loss in the elderly.* Washington, D.C.: Hemisphere Publications, 1979.

Raskin, A., Schulterbrandt, J. G., Reatig, N., Crook, T. H., & Odle, D. Depression subtypes and response to phenelzine, diazepam, and a placebo. *Archives of General Psychiatry,* 1974, *30,* 66–75.

Rehm, L. P. A self-control model of depression. *Behavior Therapy,* 1977, *8,* 787–804.

Rehm, L. P. Mood, pleasant events, and unpleasant events: Two pilot studies. *Journal of Consulting and Clinical Psychology,* 1978, *46,* 854–859.

Rehm, L. P. (Ed.). *Behavior therapy for depression: Present status and future directions.* New York: Academic Press, 1981.

Rehm, L. P., & Kornblith, S. J. Behavior therapy for depression: A review of recent developments. In M. Hersen, R. M. Eisler, & P. M. Miller (Eds.), *Progress in behavior modification,* Vol. 7. New York: Academic Press, 1979.

Rehm, L. P., & Plakosh, P. Preference for immediate reinforcement in depression. *Journal of Behavior Therapy and Experimental Psychiatry,* 1975, *6,* 101–103.

Rehm, L. P., Fuchs, C. Z., Roth, D. M., Kornblith, S. J., & Romano, J. M. A comparison of self-control and social skills treatments of depression. *Behavior Therapy,* 1979, *10,* 429–442.

Reisinger, J. J. The treatment of "anxiety depression" via positive reinforcement and response cost. *Journal of Applied Behavior Analysis,* 1972, *5,* 125–130.

Robins, E., & Guze, S. B. Classification of affective disorders: The primary-secondary, the endogenous-reactive, and the neurotic-psychotic concepts. In T. A. Williams *et al.* (Eds.), *Recent advances in the psychobiology of the depressive illnesses.* Chevy Chase, Md.: U.S. Department of Health, Education, and Welfare, 1969, pp. 283–295.

Robinson, J. C., & Lewinsohn, P. M. An experimental analysis of a technique based on the Premack principle for changing the verbal behavior of depressed individuals. *Psychological Reports,* 1973, *32,* 199–210.

Rosenthal, S. H. The involutional depressive syndrome. *American Journal of Psychiatry,* 1968, *124,* May Supplement.

Rosenzweig, S. The effects of failure and success on evaluation of self and others: A study of depressed patients and normals. *Dissertation Abstracts*, 1960, *21*, 675.

Roth, D., Rehm, L. P., Rosensky, R. A. *Self-reward, self-punishment, and depression.* Unpublished mimeo, University of Pittsburgh, 1975.

Rotter, J. B. Generalized expectancies of internal vs. external control of reinforcement. *Psychological Monographs*, 1966, *80* (Whole No. 609), 1.

Rotter, J. B. Some problems and misconceptions related to the construct of internal vs. external locus of control. *Journal of Consulting and Clinical Psychology*, 1975, *43*, 56–67.

Rozensky, R. H., Rehm, L. P., Pry, G., & Roth, D. Depression and self-reinforcement behavior in hospitalized patients. *Journal of Behavior Therapy and Experimental Psychiatry*, 1977, *8*, 35–38.

Rush, A. J., & Beck, A. T. Behavior therapy in adults with affective disorders. In M. Hersen & A. S. Bellack (Eds.), *Behavior therapy in the psychiatric setting*. Baltimore: Williams & Wilkins, 1978.

Rush, A. J., Khatami, M., & Beck, A. T. Cognitive and behavioral therapy in chronic depression. *Behavior Therapy*, 1975, *6*, 398–404.

Rush, A. J., Beck, A. T., Kovacs, M., and Hollon, S. Comparative efficacy of cognitive therapy and imipramine in the treatment of depressed outpatients. *Cognitive Therapy and Research*, 1977, *1*, 17–37.

Sanchez, V. *A comparison of depressed, psychiatric control, and normal subjects on two measures of assertiveness.* Unpublished master's thesis, University of Oregon, 1977.

Sanchez, V., & Lewinsohn, P. M. Assertive behavior and depression. *Journal of Consulting and Clinical Psychology*, 1980, *48*, 119–120.

Sanchez, V. C., Lewinsohn, P. M., & Larson, D. W. *Assertion training: Effectiveness in the treatment of depression.* Unpublished manuscript, University of Oregon, 1979.

Sarason, I. G., Johnson, J. H., & Siegel, J. M. *Assessing the impact of life change: Development of the life experience survey.* Unpublished mimeo, University of Washington, 1977.

Schmickley, V. G. The effects of cognitive behavior modification upon depressed outpatients. Dissertation Abstracts International, 1976, 37, 987B-988B. (University Microfilms No. 76-18, 675.)

Seitz, F. A behavior modification approach to depression: A case study. *Psychology*, 1971, *8*, 58–63.

Seligman, M. E. P. Fall into helplessness. *Psychology Today*, 1973, *7*, 43–48.

Seligman, M. E. P. Depression and learned helplessness. In R. J. Friedman, & M. M. Katz (Eds.), *The Psychology of depression: Contemporary theory and research*. New York: Wiley, 1974.

Seligman, M. E. P. *Helplessness: On depression, development, and death.* San Francisco: Freedman, 1975.

Seligman, M. E. P., Abramson, L. Y., Semmel, A., & Von Baeyer, C. Depressive attributional style. *Journal of Abnormal Psychology*, 1979, *88*, 242–247.

Semmel, A., Abramson, L. Y., Seligman, M. E. P., & Von Baeyer, C. A. *Scale for measuring attributional style.* Manuscript in preparation, University of Pennsylvania, 1978.

Shipley, C. R., & Fazio, A. F., Pilot study of a treatment for psychological depression. *Journal of Abnormal Psychology*, 1973, *82*, 372–376.

Skinner, B. F. *Science and human behavior.* New York: Free Press, 1953.

Spitzer, R. L., Endicott, J., & Robins, E. Research diagnostic criteria. *Archives of General Psychiatry*, 1978, *35*, 773–782.

Stuart, R. B. Operant-interpersonal treatment of marital discord. *Journal of Consulting and Clinical Psychology*, 1967, *33*, 675–682.

Sundberg, N. D., Snowden, L. R., & Reynolds, W. M. Toward assessment of personal competence and incompetence in life situations. *Annual Review of Psychology*, 1978, *29*, 179–221.

Taylor, F. G., & Marshall, W. L. Experimental analysis of a cognitive-behavioral therapy for depression. *Cognitive Therapy and Research*, 1977, *1*, 59–72.

Teasdale, J. D., & Fogarty, S. J. Differential effects of induced mood on retrieval of pleasant and unpleasant events from episodic memory. *Journal of Abnormal Psychology*, 1979, *88*, 248–257.

Wechsler, D. *Wechsler adult intelligence scale.* New York: The Psychological Corporation, 1955.

Wechsler, H., Grosser, F., & Busfield, B. The depression rating scale: A quantitative approach to the assessment of depressive symptomatology. *Archives of General Psychiatry*, 1963, *9*, 334–343.

Weiner, B., Frieze, I., Kukla, A., Reed, L., Rest, S., & Rosenbaum, R. M. *Perceiving the causes of successes and failure.* Morristown, N.J.: General Learning Press, 1971.

Weiner, B., Nierenberg, R. & Goldstein, M. Social learning (locus of control) versus attributional (causal stability) interpretations of expectancy of success. *Journal of Personality*, 1976, *44*, 52–68.

Weintraub, M., Segal, R. M., & Beck, A. T. An investigation of cognition and affect in the depressive experience of normal men. *Journal of Consulting and Clinical Psychology*, 1974, *42*, 911.

Weiss, R. L., & Aved, B. M. Marital satisfaction and depression as predictors of physical health status. *Journal of Consulting and Clinical Psychology*, 1978, *56*, 1379–1384.

Weissman, A., & Beck, A. T. *A preliminary investigation of the relationship between dysfunctional attitudes and depression.* Unpublished manuscript, University of Pennsylvania, 1978.

Weissman, M., & Klerman, G. L. Sex differences and the epidemiology of depression. *Archives of General Psychiatry*, 1977, *34*, 98–111.

Weissman, M., & Paykel, E. G. *The depressed woman: A study of social relationships.* Chicago: University of Chicago Press, 1974.

Wener, A. E., & Rehm, L. P. Depressive affect: A test of behavioral hypotheses. *Journal of Abnormal Psychology*, 1975, *84*, 221–227.

Williams, J. G., Barlow, D. H., & Agras, W. S. Behavioral measurement of severe depression. *Archives of General Psychiatry*, 1972, *27*, 330–337.

Wolpe, J. Neurotic depression: An experimental analog, clinical syndromes, and treatment. *American Journal of Psychotherapy*, 1971, *25*, 362–368.

Wolpe, J., & Lazarus, A. A. *Behavior therapy techniques.* New York: Pergamon Press, 1966.

Wortman, C. B., & Brehm, J. W. Responses to uncontrollable outcomes: An integration of reactance theory and the learned helplessness model. In L. Berkowitz (Ed.), *Advances in experimental social psychology.* Academic Press, 1975.

Yalom, I. D. *The theory and practice of group psychotherapy* (2nd ed.). New York: Basic Books, 1975.

Youngren, M. A., & Lewinsohn, P. M. The functional relationship between depression and problematic interpersonal behavior. *Journal of Abnormal Psychology,* 1980, *89,* 333–341.

Youngren, M. A., Zeiss, A., & Lewinsohn, P. M. *Interpersonal events schedule.* Unpublished mimeo, University of Oregon, 1975.

Zeiss, A. M., Lewinsohn, P. M., & Muñoz, R. F. Nonspecific improvement effects in depression using interpersonal skills training, pleasant activity schedules, or cognitive training. *Journal of Consulting and Clinical Psychology,* 1979, *47,* 427–439.

Zung, W. W. K. From art to science: The diagnosis and treatment of depression. *Archives of General Psychiatry,* 1973, *29,* 328–337.

Zung, W. W. K., Richards, C. B., & Short, M. J. Self-rating depression scale in an outpatient clinic. *Archives of General Psychiatry,* 1965, *13,* 508–516.

CHAPTER 15

Treatment of Schizophrenia

James P. Curran, Peter M. Monti, and Donald P. Corriveau

Introduction

Although some theorists, such as Szasz (1961, 1976), charge that schizophrenia is a myth and does not exist, the vast majority of mental health workers would quite adamantly maintain that schizophrenia is an extremely pervasive disorder. Definitional problems notwithstanding, the behavioral disturbances that generally characterize this construct appear throughout the world irrespective of culture, race, language, or time. Furthermore, there is no solid evidence that the incidence has changed in the last 150 years. Out of the U.S. population, 2–3% are estimated to be included in this classification (Keith, Gunderson, Reifman, Buchsbaum & Mosher, 1976). According to the National Institute of Mental Health, about 25% of all patients admitted to state mental hospitals are diagnosed as schizophrenic, and 50% of the inpatient populations in state mental hospitals bear the same diagnosis. Schizophrenics clearly comprise the vast majority of psychiatric patients residing in long-term custodial facilities. The chronicity

of this disorder is reflected in a 50% readmission rate within only 2 years after discharge (Mosher, Govera, & Menn, 1972). The expected length of stay within an institution increases with subsequent readmission (Kraft, Binner, & Dickey, 1967). Once a schizophrenic patient has spent two years in a mental hospital, the probability of release is only 6% (Ullmann, 1967). The prognosis for rehabilitation is alarmingly poor. A staggering 65–85% of discharged patients with the schizophrenic diagnosis are unable to function more than minimally in the community. Gunderson and Mosher (1975) also estimate that beyond the $2–$4 billion directly spent on treatment costs, the loss of productivity attributable to this disorder is beyond $10 billion.

Despite years of research devoted to both studying the etiology of schizophrenia and developing viable remedial interventions, the overall progress in this area of research is, at best, only modest. Several authors have cited the failures of traditional treatment methods, especially individual psychotherapy, with schizophrenics (May, 1968; Stahl & Leitenberg, 1976). While chemotherapy has shown some success in alleviating some of the symptoms associated with this disorder, the prognosis of rehabilitation into the community remains notoriously poor, and recivivism rates

James P. Curran, Peter M. Monti, and Donald P. Corriveau • Department of Psychology, Brown University Medical School and Veterans Administration Medical Center, Providence, Rhode Island 02912.

remain uncomfortably high (Coleman, 1976; Hersen, 1979). While relatively new to this research area, behavioral principles of treatment have been systematically applied to schizophrenic populations for approximately 30 years. The major thrust of this chapter is to examine critically behavior therapy's contribution to this major health problem.

In this chapter, we separately review published studies in three broad areas of behaviorally oriented treatment procedures. We begin by examining those studies that appear to share as a common denominator a central focus on specific, well-delineated behavioral objectives. Although the major impetus for these treatments comes mainly from operant paradigms, this behavioral technology has been gradually influenced by social learning theory and other branches of psychology. The second area of treatment that we review includes treatments that fit under the general label of *token economies*. The major influence behind the development of this behavioral area appears to be pragmatic concerns with ward management, which has led to the application of contingency management procedures to target variables much wider in scope and more practical in implication. The third and last major area to be reviewed is the general area currently referred to as *social skills training*. As a whole, this relatively new research area has addressed the frequently reported interpersonal deficits in schizophrenic populations. Treatment efforts have specifically focused on training interpersonal competencies. Since the target behaviors examined and trained by social skill investigators appear crucial in posttreatment adjustment to the community, the social skills research area has, at the very least, great potential in establishing viable treatment procedures for schizophrenic patients.

Before examining the behavioral literature, a few important issues need to be addressed. Definitional problems are perhaps the most salient issues beleaguering the general area of schizophrenia research. To adequately understand the controversies and theoretical nuances within this general area, it is first important to note that as with other disorders subsumed under current nosological systems, the concept of schizophrenia was developed primarily within what is now called the *medical model* or the *disease model*. In its simplest form, the medical model is an orientation in which an analysis of symptomatology leads to a diagnosis of the underlying disease. Even today, the issue of whether schizophrenia should be considered a unitary or a multimodal disease entity continues to be debated in the literature (cf. Rieder, 1974; Tuma, 1968). An interesting observation is that about two decades before Kraepelin laid down psychiatry's first comprehensive system of classification, much debate revolved around the value of "disease entities." In his own formulations, Kraepelin adopted a disease model and has always been credited for grouping a variety of abnormal behaviors under one heading, *dementia praecox*. Unfortunately, Kraepelin's descriptions of this disorder contain concurrent conceptualizations of both behavioral observations and theoretical inferences. His descriptions of symptoms include hallucinations, delusions, thought disorders, attentional problems, and a dissociation between thought and affect. Beyond these descriptions, however, Kraepelin strongly emphasized that the deterioration of psychological processes (dementia) usually began early in life (hence, the word *praecox*) and was always in part irreversible. Aligning himself with other medical contemporaries, Kraepelin assumed that he had discovered a "disease entity," but recent theorists charge that he had simply invented a concept (Kendell, 1978; Szasz, 1978). Therefore, his formulations have received much criticism and revision.

Eugen Bleuler, who coined the word *schizophrenia*, rejected deterioration as an essential criterion of schizophrenia, yet accepted Kraepelin's inference of an underlying cerebral defect. Bleuler placed particular emphasis on four categories of fundamental symptoms: altered affectivity, altered associations, ambivalence, and autism (often called *Bleuler's four As*). Bleuler emphasized these symptoms above all others, including delusions and hallucinations.

Historically, attempts to define, let alone understand, the concept of schizophrenia have always generated a cloud of confusion, producing nearly as many definitions as diagnosticians. In the 1920s, each large teaching center employed its own system of classification, developed to meet its own esoteric needs. Zubin (1967) detailed how the original nosological system construed by the American Psychiatric Association was compiled by majority voting because of the vast disagreement among its members. Despite these valiant efforts to operationalize definitional criteria, reliability across diagnosticians has often been alarmingly poor (Zubin, 1967). In a series of classic articles, Zigler and Phillips (1961a,b) implied that the then-current nosological system focused much of its efforts on etiology and therefore fostered an inferential instead of an empirical approach. Despite the truism that diagnoses were based on symptoms, these researchers found that few symptoms could be predicted based on diagnosis.

The last decade, however, has witnessed numerous concerted efforts to operationalize major psychiatric syndromes. The first major comprehensive set appears to be the St. Louis Criteria (Feighner, Robins, Guze, Woodruff, Winokur, & Muñoz, 1972). Since then, several rival operational definitions have appeared in the field, including the New Haven Criteria (Astrachan, Harrow, Adler *et al.*, 1972); Carpenter's Flexible Criteria (Carpenter, Strauss, & Bartko, 1973); the Research Diagnostic Criteria of Spitzer, Endicott, and Robins (1975); and Schneider's first-rank symptoms (see Kendell, Brockington, & Leff, 1979). Two international studies have helped clarify the way *schizophrenic* is used in different parts of the world. Both the US–UK Diagnostic project (Cooper, Kendell, Gurland, Sharpe, Copeland, & Simon, 1972) and the International Pilot Study of Schizophrenia (WHO, 1973) relied extensively on the Present State Examination (PSE), a standard interviewing procedure that appears highly reliable. A computer program called CATEGO has been developed to profile these symptoms (Wing, Cooper, & Sartorius, 1974). Most recently, the American Psychiatric Association has published a major revision of its Diagnostic and Statistical Manual of Mental Disorders (American Psychiatric Association, 1980). Although it would be premature to evaluate its strengths and limitations, the task force, headed by Robert L. Spitzer, that developed this revision should be commended for its increased reliance on em-

pirical development and verification. The classificatory system contained in this manual is supported by an abundance of operational definitions and has clear potential for significantly improved diagnostic reliability.

Behavior therapists, in their haste to reject the basic tenets of the medical model, have often shunned the use of diagnostic labels. Instead of persevering with symptomatology and its theoretical relation to diagnosis, etiology, and disease process and treatment, behavior therapists have traditionally narrowed their interests to specific problem behaviors. Concepts such as diagnosis and treatment have been reformulated into the generation of hypotheses and verification of functional relationships between environment and behaviors. By separating itself from conventional nosological systems, behavior therapists' selection of target variables is mostly arbitrary and these variables are selected, at times, solely for the convenience of the experimenter. Regrettably, this approach has fostered several unfortunate consequences.

First, behavior therapists' selective choice of target behaviors has done little to assure congruence between the criteria used for diagnosis or admission and the variables targeted for treatment. Behavior therapists may, in fact, become overly specific in their identification of target behaviors.

Second, although behavior therapists' emphasis on target behaviors to some extent circumvents issues of diagnosis in individual case studies, greater attention must be given to identifying a subject population for group designs. Unless these criteria are delineated more precisely, comparisons across group studies become meaningless. A review of the literature on behavioral interventions with schizophrenics shows that the diagnostic criteria are not even specified in the vast majority of these studies. Case studies, which sometimes report successes and sometimes report treatment failures, become quite difficult to evaluate when diagnostic criteria are not specified.

Third, the relative contribution of any group study may be jeopardized by the potential heterogeneity within its subject population. For example, several treatment studies simultaneously select subjects from vastly different major classificatory groupings (personality disorders, neurotics, and psychotics), who are then treated identically. Before we can systematically examine which behavioral treatments are more efficacious for particular groups of patients, we must be able to identify these patient groups reliably. While current nosological systems are not without problems, it would behoove behavioral researchers to include some of the more objective diagnostic schemes discussed above (cf. Endicott, Foreman, & Spitzer, 1979).

Definitional issues notwithstanding, our present intention is to examine the general applicability of behavioral interventions to a schizophrenic population. Although a complete and thorough review of the behavioral literature is beyond the scope of this chapter, our initial goal is to reflect on behavior therapists' successes and failures with a wide variety of target behaviors, most notably those commonly employed as diagnostic criteria for the classification of schizophrenia. At the risk of appearing unduly critical, we place particular emphasis on delineating the major weaknesses of our current technology. By bringing attention to these weaknesses, we hope to generate future renewed interest in the development and research of improved treatment strategies.

Operant Paradigms

The systematic application of behavioral principles to a schizophrenic population is best traced to the work of Lindsley and Skinner, beginning in 1954. Essentially, these investigators extended their operant technology developed from research with animals lower on the phylogenetic scale to a series of experiments with schizophrenics. Following the same initiative for experimental control, they used a small experimental room with very little furniture or other distracting stimuli. A review of this early experimental work is particularly interesting (see Inglis, 1966; Lindsley, 1956, 1960). Lindsley experimented with a variety of reinforcers and measured a variety of responses. Furthermore, since he recorded the patients' behavior regularly over long periods of time (in some cases, years), Lindsley had

several opportunities to observe the cyclical nature of such phenomena as psychotic episodes. In essence, Lindsley's work helped to provide the framework for an operant orientation often referred to as *behavior modification*. This orientation provided two major contributions to the treatment of schizophrenics. The first represents the development of behavioral principles whose main target variables were specific symptomatologies. The second contribution is in the area of ward management or, more specifically, "token economies." In a later section of this chapter, we devote considerable attention to both the potential benefits and the limitations of token economies. First, let us examine the application of operant principles to the target behaviors that characterize schizophrenic symptomatology.

In the treatment literature, several operant-oriented treatments have been applied to the modification of delusional speech. The majority of these studies share a general emphasis on increasing appropriate speech with positive reinforcement. In one of the first studies to modify delusional verbal behavior, Rickard and his colleagues (Rickard, Digman, & Horner, 1960; Rickard & Dinoff, 1962) used a verbal reinforcement procedure and reported a dramatic decrease in the delusional talk of a 60-year-old male who had been hospitalized for 20 years. These investigators simply expressed interest and approval whenever this patient's verbalizations were found to be appropriate. Whenever the speech became delusional, the therapist simply turned away from the patient. Although the results were very suggestive, the investigators unfortunately used an A-B design, which precluded strong conclusions.

In another study, Ayllon and Haughton (1964) also used a single-case design and reported more impressive results in light of their reversal design. In this study, nurses recorded a series of verbal interactions with each of three patients. Verbal interactions were limited to a maximum of three minutes, and these were recorded for 15–20 days before any experimental manipulation. Each interaction was classified as either psychotic or neutral. Contingent reinforcement, which was successively applied to each class of verbal behavior, consisted of listening and showing interest to the patient and intermittently providing candy or cigarettes. The extinction procedures entailed withholding both social attention and tangible reinforcers. The results showed that when contingent reinforcement was applied to neutral verbalizations, that response class increased in frequency. Conversely, when that procedure was applied to psychotic verbalization, the frequency of that response class increased. When the extinction procedure was applied to either response class, the frequency of that response class decreased below that of baseline levels. In addition to the small number of subjects, however, one limitation of this study was the absence of reliability checks on the nurses' recordings.

Wincze, Leitenberg, and Agras (1972) incorporated a more sophisticated design and compared the effects of both feedback and reinforcement procedures in reducing the delusional talk of 10 paranoid schizophrenics. Recordings of delusional talk were made both within therapeutic sessions and on the ward. Reliability checks of these recordings were always high (usually above 90% agreement). Additionally, a psychiatric resident naive to the design of the study supplied general "improvement" ratings at the beginning and end of each experimental phase. The results of this study indicate that the feedback procedure showed some success in reducing the percentage of delusional speech for about half the subjects, but it also produced adverse reactions in at least three subjects. The reinforcement procedure appeared to be more consistent, reducing delusional talk in seven of the nine subjects who completed this phase of the program. The results of the psychiatric interviews showed either no change at all in some of the patients or gradual improvement over the course of the experiment regardless of the experimental contingencies (e.g., feedback, baseline, or reinforcement).

These results are important in two ways. First, they indicate the potential limitations of feedback procedures with a psychotic population, an issue less salient with normal or neurotic populations (e.g., Leitenberg, Agras, Thompson, & Wright, 1968). Second, the data are important in highlighting the crucial problem of generalization. The effects of both treatment procedures were clearly specific to the therapeutic environment. The reductions of delusional speech during therapeutic sessions were far greater than those observed on the ward.

Major difficulties in obtaining generalization of treatment effects are also illustrated in a study by Liberman, Teigen, Patterson, and Baker (1973), who attempted to reduce the delusional speech of four chronic patients by providing "evening chats" with the therapists of their choice. The length of this interaction covaried directly with the amount of rational speech observed in an interview occurring earlier in the day, and the "chat" was terminated whenever the patient emitted irrational speech. These authors found an appreciable reduction of delusional speech in both the daily interview and the evening chat, but no generalization to ward surroundings was found. In fact, one of the four patients actually increased his delusional talk on the ward. In a subsequent study, Patterson and Teigen (1973) gave specific ward training to one of these four original patients, who subsequently showed improvement on the ward and was later discharged.

Difficulty in obtaining generalization effects is a problem shared by the majority of individual behavioral programs involving schizophrenics. Another potential limitation of this research area is the lack of strong empirical evidence documenting the maintenance of treatment effects. Although early behavioral studies should be commended for their groundbreaking attempts at developing their behavioral interventions, relatively few early studies reported adequate follow-up data. Although some studies suggest that decreases in delusional speech *per se* may continue after discharge, these effects appear to be maximized when family members are programmed to reinforce rational speech and to ignore irrational speech (cf. Nydegger, 1972). While addressing the maintenance issue, Liberman, Wallace, Teigen, and Davis (1974) have specifically called for the use of simultaneous procedures to decrease delusional speech and reinforce rational conversation. The suggestion that punishment procedures be used to reduce delusional speech, however, is not without risk, since treatment effects are often temporary and erratic. Davis, Wallace, Liberman, and Finch (1976) used a time-out procedure to reduce delusional statements and found only temporary and specific effects. Delusional references were reduced only in the observational samples where contingencies were applied. Moreover, the authors observed that when the time-out procedure was applied, the patient often placed a hand over the mouth and mumbled what were presumably delusional statements.

Problems in obtaining adequate generalization of treatment effects are well known to investigators who have attempted to reinstate speech in mute schizophrenic patients. Isaacs, Thomas, and Goldiamond (1960) attempted to reinstate speech in two patients who had been mute for 14 and 19 years. In a clever shaping procedure, one patient was initially reinforced with a stick of gum for simply looking at the gum. Once this response was established, the patient was additionally required to make a vocalization. Finally, the patient was required to say, "Gum, please." Eventually, the patient answered direct questions presented in group sessions. The specificity of these treatment effects, however, soon became apparent. Although the patient spoke to the experimenter on the ward, his verbal behavior failed to generalize to other ward personnel. To increase the generalization of reinstated verbal behavior to people other than the experimenters, the investigators were required to bring a nurse into the therapeutic room and to reinstate the shaping procedure. Thus, although the generalization was extremely poor, the results did demonstrate the conditionability of verbal behavior.

An even more convincing demonstration of the effect of positive reinforcement on verbal behavior is found in a study by Sherman (1965). He employed both imitation and fading procedures with three schizophrenic patients who had been hospitalized for 20–45 years and had a history of mutism ranging from 16 to 43 years. After speech had been reinstated with these procedures, Sherman used a reversal procedure to rule out alternative explanations. In this experimental phase of the study, the subjects were reinforced for not replying to the experimenter for 30 seconds. Under these reverse contingencies, the subjects did not speak.

An additional problem in this research area has been noted by investigators who have experimented with various modes of reinforcement. While the use of tangible reinforcers such as cigarettes or candy with mute or near-mute schizophrenics has consistently been shown to be effective (Thomson, Fraser, & McDougall, 1974; Wilson & Walters, 1966), procedures that rely on vicarious learning have questionable effectiveness with this patient population. Wilson and Walters (1966), for example, found that modeling without reinforcement was much less effective than modeling with reinforcement.

Other Behavioral Procedures

One area of clinical research that has incorporated a wider range of behavioral treatments is represented by those studies aimed at reducing hallucinatory behavior. Rutner and Bugle (1969) applied a self-monitoring procedure to a long-term female patient who experienced hallucinations of a controlling nature. For the first 3 days of their program, the patient privately recorded the following frequencies of hallucinations: 181, 80, and 11. Following these private recordings, the patient's chart was placed on public display, and she received praise and social reinforcement from both staff and other patients whenever a reduction in hallucinatory behavior was evident. During the course of this case study, the patient reported that hallucinations decreased to 0 within 13 days and remained completely suppressed at a six-month follow-up.

Bucher and Fabricatore (1970) treated a schizophrenic patient who complained of disturbing hallucinations by providing him with a portable shock device and instructing him to deliver a shock to himself whenever he experienced a hallucination. After several days, the patient reported that he was no longer hallucinating and was subsequently discharged. Unfortunately, the general applicability of this procedure appears to be greatly restricted. The authors warned that very few chronic patients could be persuaded to follow this procedure. These restrictions were also reported by Anderson and Alpert (1974), who, after a two-week unsuccessful attempt with the shock device and procedure used by Bucher and Fabricatore, were prompted to develop an alternative procedure. Their particular patient apparently exhibited ritualistic hand and face movements, which reportedly accompanied hallucinations. Since these ritualistic behaviors were very disruptive of his normally routine activities, such as eating meals, he was positively reinforced for reducing the time it took to eat meals. One experimentally blind observer independently recorded the frequencies of these behaviors. The results of this new procedure showed a dramatic reduction in these behaviors when the contingencies were applied, and a reversal procedure witnessed a rapid return to baseline.

The effectiveness of self-administered shock procedures in reducing hallucinations was examined in a group-design study by Weingaertner (1971) with 45 schizophrenic inpatients. Weingaertner compared a self-shock condition to a self-administered "placebo" condition (subjects wore the same shock apparatus on their belts, which ostensibly delivered subliminal shock) and to an untreated control condition. His results showed that all three groups reported fewer hallucinations and improved as well on other symptomatology ratings following the two-week treatment. However, no significant differences were found between the groups. Weingaertner concluded that the major change agent was patient expectations. In viewing these results, the issue of self-administration itself must be considered. In a case report, Alford and Turner (1976) found positive results in reducing hallucinations when shock was administered by the experimenter. Again, further research is needed to examine this issue.

Following a somewhat different paradigm, Haynes and Geddy (1973) used a "time-out" procedure with a female patient hospitalized for over 20 years. Since the subject had difficulty describing her subjective experiences, let alone monitoring them, these investigators operationally defined a hallucination as observations that the patient was mumbling to herself or yelling loudly without any visible provocation. Their time-out procedure consisted of removing the patient from the ward and isolating her in an unfurnished time-out room for 10 minutes. Although time-out procedures, like other punishment procedures, appear generally more effective when applied continuously, every time the behavior is emitted, these authors applied the procedure in only some instances, about four times a day. Nonetheless, the procedure proved effective in reducing the frequency of baseline observations from 80% to 30% after 35 days. No further reduction beyond this rate was achieved.

Another separate group of investigations, following Davison's (1969) general suggestion to examine antecedent conditions, speculated that the hallucinatory behavior of schizophrenics may be related to anxiety. Although phobic or anxiety-motivated behavior is not typically included in any conceptualization of the primary-rank symptoms of schizophrenics, some patients diagnosed as schizophrenic nonetheless emit behavior that would fit the research criteria for phobic behavior. Not surprisingly, systematic desensitization has been tried in both single-case and group research with this population. Unfortunately, the general efficacy of this procedure with a psychiatric population appears equivocal. A review of single-case reports reveals a proportionate rate of success and failure. Slade (1972), for example, attempted a functional analysis of the hallucinations and situational antecedents of a 19-year-old schizophrenic. It appeared that the patient experienced tension before hallucinating episodes, which subsided thereafter. Slade also reported that mood states deteriorated during episodes of hallucinations. In his systematic desensitization procedure, Slade included an *in vitro* hierarchy of tension-provoking stimuli and reported that hallucinations significantly reduced in frequency, especially at follow-up. Unfortunately, the patient was later rehospitalized with depression, albeit free of hallucinations. In a later controlled study, however, Slade (1973) was unable to replicate his earlier success. In another study, Lambley (1973) attempted to desensitize distressing thoughts, but his patient was again reporting hallucinations and uncomfortable thoughts at a 6-month follow-up. In another study, Alumbaugh (1971) reported success in reducing anxiety associated with cigarette smoking. Unfortunately, his results are seriously confounded because of the introduction of a concurrent procedure that reduced cigarette-smoking behavior itself.

Two case studies that do report success include as a common denominator the incorporation of an *in vivo* hierarchy. Cowden and Ford (1962) reported the success of a systematic desensitization procedure with a patient diagnosed as paranoid schizophrenic who was extremely panicky and frightened when he talked with other people. Other forms of treatment with this patient were all unsuccessful. Following the desensitization procedure, the patient was reported as more talkative, more relaxed, and more productive in his work, and he was then able to leave the hospital grounds at the conclusion of treatment. Similarly, Weidner (1970) successfully applied an *in vivo* hierarchy to a paranoid patient who would not leave the hospital grounds for fear of assassination by the CIA. Following treatment, this patient was reportedly able to leave the hospital grounds on a pass.

Although these case reports suggest that systematic desensitization may indeed be effective with some patients, the results of published group studies are extremely difficult to evaluate. One well-controlled study examining the effects of systematic desensitization in reducing anxiety in a schizophrenic population is that of Zeisset (1968). This study specifically examined "interview anxiety" recorded by experimentally blind observers. Although Zeisset found moderate success with systematic desensitization, the results are tempered by the fact that the subjects included both neurotic and psychotic patients selected principally because they could converse *without* overt delusional or hallucinatory behavior. Two other group studies, which at first glance appear to demonstrate the ineffectiveness of this procedure with schizophrenic patients, may not provide a fair examination. In the first of these (Serber & Nelson, 1971), a nonstandard procedure was employed. In the second study, Weinman, Gelbart, Wallace, and Post (1972) compared desensitization with socioenvironmental therapy or relaxation alone in increasing assertive behavior. Unfortunately, this study failed to provide any convincing evidence that the target behavior (interpersonal assertion) was related in any way to anxiety. In fact, the authors noted that if their patients could not describe an anxiety-related situation, one was provided for them from six "standardized" situations.

At best, the demonstrated efficacy of desensitization with schizophrenics is equivocal. It is interesting to note that Wolpe (1958, 1961), who first introduced this technique, cautioned against the application of this procedure to psychotic patients. For different theoretical reasons, Wilkins (1971) has suggested that systematic desensitization is effective in large part because of increased expectancy of therapeutic outcome or increased cognitive or attentional control. Given the cognitive and communicative deficiencies found in schizophrenic populations (Lang & Buss, 1965; Payne, 1966), it is not surprising that several authors have noted the difficulties involved in implementing systematic desensitization procedures with schizophrenics. Cowden and Ford (1962) reported that schizophrenic patients have difficulty in selecting anxiety-related stimuli. Their patients appeared inattentive and lacked concentration during the experimental sessions, and they infrequently practiced relaxation exercises. Both Weinmann *et al.* (1972) and Serber and Nelson (1971) reported that their subjects had considerable difficulty in completing hierarchies and had limited imagery abilities. Zeisset (1968) suggested, "perhaps pessimistically," that the relaxation exercises themselves may be the only component helpful to this population. In summary, these results are not very encouraging. Besides the need for better-controlled research, two directives should be noted. First, future research should pay closer attention to specifically delineating a functional relationship between anxiety-related stimuli and apparently anxiety-motivated behavior. Second, more effort should be directed toward incorporating *in vivo* hierarchies into the procedure, obviating some of the cognitive components necessarily involved in imagery procedures.

Although very few behavioral interventions have been applied to other major "symptoms" associated with the diagnosis of schizophrenia, a few other interesting procedures have been directed at specific behavior problems of schizophrenic patients. One of these procedures, stimulus satiation, calls for the repeated presentation of a reinforcing stimulus. Presumably, the patient will become satiated and the reinforcing stimulus or reinforcing activity will become neutral or aversive. Although only a few reports of this procedure have appeared in the literature, most have appeared to be successful. Using this procedure, Ayllon (1963) successfully treated a patient who hoarded towels in her room, and Ayllon and Michael (1959) treated a patient who carried so much trash on his person that he eventually suffered skin rashes. Wolff (1971) also successfully applied this procedure to the delusional behavior of a patient by requiring her to voice her delusions for one hour a day. Liberman *et al.* (1974), however, had less success in reducing visual hallucinations using this technique.

Other researchers have combined elements of aversive conditioning with covert processes. Agras (1967) successfully eliminated glass breaking in a chronic patient by administering faradic shock whenever the patient reported "visualizing" this behavioral sequence. Royer, Flynn, and Osadca (1971) also reported success in treating a patient's persistent fire setting by having him light pieces of paper and throw them into a pail of water, simultaneously shocking the patient when he did so.

While these studies reflect the creative application of behavioral interventions in problem behaviors, future research is needed to systematically examine the application of these procedures to the symptomatology of schizophrenia.

Cognitive-Behavior Therapy

In recent years, cognitive-behavioral interventions have been successfully applied to a large variety of problem behaviors (Kendall & Hollon, 1979; Mahoney, 1974). The general popularity of these techniques has been prompted, in part, by an increased effort to obtain adequate generalization of treatment effects and also, in part, by the pragmatic intention of behavior therapists of providing their patients with methods of controlling their own behavior. Conceptually, cognitive interventions are founded on two independent assumptions. The first is that cognitive processes serve an important mediating role in controlling human behavior. The second major assumption is that these covert processes are subject to the same basic principles of learning (both classical and instrumental) that explain overt behavior. Although most behaviorally oriented researchers were initially hesitant to include nonobservable events in their behavioral paradigms, interest in these clinical procedures has grown geometrically in the last 10 years.

Meichenbaum (1969) reported one of the first attempts to utilize these cognitive procedures with a schizophrenic population. In a well-controlled design, Meichenbaum compared both token and reinforcement procedures in their ability to increase the relevant and logical use of proverbs in an interview setting. Ultimately, these procedures were designed to promote "healthy talk." The results revealed that both treatment groups showed significantly more improvement than control groups. The token reinforcement procedure was more effective than social reinforcement. Meichenbaum also reported that the treatment effects were maintained at a follow-up interview and were generalized to other verbal skills. Unfortunately, his follow-up interval was only one week after posttest.

In attempting to better understand the processes of generalization, Meichenbaum rather serendipitously observed some of the patients talking aloud to themselves, apparently giving themselves instructions such as "Be logical" or "Be coherent." He reasoned that these self-statements or self-instructions provided the patient with a useful aid in ignoring distractions (especially self-generated ones) and in increasng task-oriented attention.

To further examine the effects of what Meichenbaum coined as "self-instructional training," he and Cameron (Meichenbaum & Cameron, 1973) specifically tried to train subjects to think to themselves in this fashion. By means of procedures such as modeling and social approval, patients were eventually shaped to internalize their thinking. Lastly, the subjects were trained to become more perceptive of this ordered speech in others. The results of two experiments showed that the patients receiving this cognitive training improved more in problem-solving skill and reduced their disordered speech more than yoked-practice control subjects who received similar reinforcement for correct performance but without self-instructional training.

Although Meichenbaum's procedure appears especially robust with respect to these target variables, little research has examined the general applicability of this technique to other schizophrenic symptomatology. In a case study, Meyers, Mercatoris, and Sirota (1976) applied a self-instructional procedure to reduce a chronic schizophrenic's psychotic speech. The results of their treatment showed a marked reduction of inappropriate verbalization. The results also showed good generalization of treatment effects as well as continued reduction of these inappropriate verbalizations at a six-month follow-up.

While these studies point to the potential benefits of cognitive interventions in general and self-instructional training in particular, at least one attempt to replicate Meichenbaum and Cameron's research has been unsuccessful. Margolis and Shemberg (1976) assigned a group of process schizophrenics and a group of reactive schizophrenics to either a self-instructional training procedure or a yoked-practice control group. Although these authors employed two half-hour sessions instead of a single one-hour session, both the treatment and the assessment procedures were modeled after Meichenbaum and Cameron's study. Although Margolis and Shemberg's study would appear to have greater statistical power (e.g., eight subjects per group as compared with only five subjects per group in the Meichenbaum study), they were hard-pressed to explain the absence of any significant treatment or interaction effects. In attempting to explain these findings, the authors noted that their subjects often described the treatment as "silly" or "babyish." Second, they found that most subjects had forgotten their training during posttesting. Third, the authors suggested that self-instructional training may be highly task-specific, detrimental, in fact, in those tasks with a speed component (e.g., digit symbol). In any case, the brief duration of treatment in both studies suggests a need for further research examining a more comprehensive and thorough training procedure.

Another applied research area using cognitive principles includes methods of increasing subjects' problem-solving ability. The major impetus in this area is D'Zurilla and Goldfried's (1971) premise that the basis for most abnormal behaviors is the person's inability to solve situational problems. When problems remain unresolved, they subsequently lead to both cognitive and behavioral deficits. The ultimate goal of problem-solving training is to initially delineate the problem, to develop alternative strategies, and to monitor the effectiveness of the chosen alternative. Although these techniques are particularly attractive at the theoretical or conceptual level, surprisingly little data exist to support their effectiveness in modifying schizophrenic behavior. Those studies that have specifically examined problem-solving procedures (Coche & Douglas, 1977; Coche & Flick, 1975; Siegel & Spivack, 1976) report positive changes on self-report data. Unfortunately, they fail to include behavioral measures.

As will be noted later in this chapter, several ambitious projects are currently under way that include an intensive "social-skill-training" approach to the treatment of schizophrenia (Brown, 1982; Liberman, 1982; Wallace, 1982). To say the least, these investigators have employed an extremely comprehensive treatment package, including components of problem-solving training. Although the preliminary data clearly pointed to a particularly promising treatment of schizophrenia (e.g., in reducing recidivism), further component research is needed to isolate the respective contribution of problem-solving processes *per se*.

In summary, the contribution of individual behavioral programs in the treatment of schizophrenia is extremely difficult to evaluate. Although early researchers should be commended for their ingenuity in applying behavioral principles to the treatment of schizophrenic symptomatology, attempts to assess *both* the maintenance (durability) and the generalization of treatment have appeared in only relatively recent literature. Moreover, investigators are often hard-pressed to demonstrate any generalization. Further research is especially needed to isolate those factors responsible for the promotion of generalization. Although common sense would dictate the potential utility and benefits of cognitive interventions (especially in promoting generalization), extremely few controlled studies have appeared in the literature. Research is needed to further examine these potentially viable procedures.

Token Economies

Establishment of a Token Economy: Problems and Suggestions

This section of the chapter is based largely upon the first author's experience as an intern on a research project directed by Gordon L. Paul (Paul & Lentz, 1977) and later consulting work with various institutionalized populations. The problems and issues addressed as well as the suggestions made are not meant to be comprehensive but merely illustrative of the complexities involved in establishing a token economy. Any and all the problems discussed, if not addressed, can severely diminish the effectiveness of such a program. The management of such a program requires a continual monitoring of all aspects of the program and a dedicated and knowledgeable staff.

Selecting and Defining Criterion Behaviors. Before establishing a token economy program, it is obviously imperative that one decide which criterion behaviors and their components are to be reinforced within the system. It is useful to view these criterion behaviors in a hierarchical fashion. For example, one major grouping of behaviors may be self-care (such as bathing, shaving, dressing, and feeding); occupational (good work habits such as promptness and staying on task); educational (basic rudiments of reading, writing, and arithmetic), and social (such as initiating conversations and participating in games and social activities). Deviant or crazy behavior is another category of behavior that must be attended to, but since these are behaviors we are wishing to eliminate rather than to reinforce, we will discuss them in a later section.

Under each of these four major headings one further has to stipulate an exhaustive list of those behaviors that are to be reinforced. For example, under self-care behaviors, one could include such things as appropriate eating, bathing, feeding, and dressing. Each of these behaviors must then be operationalized. For example, on Paul's (Paul & Lentz, 1977) research project, appearance checks were made in order to reinforce appropriate dressing patterns. The 11 subcomponents of appropriate appearance used were (1) proper use of makeup; (2) clean fingernails; (3) hair combed; (4) teeth brushed; (5) all appropriate clothing on; (6) clothing buttoned, zipped, and tucked in; (7) clothing clean and neat; (8) body clean; (9) no odor; (10) shaven; and (11) hair cut appropriately (Paul & Lentz, 1977). Each of these subcomponents was further operationalized (e.g., "teeth brushed" was defined as no food on teeth, no grit on teeth, breath that allowed one to stand within a few feet, nicotine stains acceptable, and dentures in).

It is extremely important to have each of the criterion behaviors well defined in order to prevent inconsistencies among those individuals responsible for dispensing the tokens. If the token dispensers are inconsistent, then the token program will appear arbitrary to the patients and produce resentment. It is also important when operationalizing these criterion behaviors that the capabilities of the residents (i.e., the individuals residing within the token economy) be given some consideration. For example, if residents are to receive tokens for engaging in recreational activities such as volleyball, some consideration must be given to their athletic talent. One would not expect a 50-year-old chronically institutionalized psychiatric patient to play volleyball as well as a well-coordinated college athlete. Hence, playing volleyball may be defined as standing mostly in one's assigned zone, attempting to hit the ball over the net, not kicking the ball or catching it and throwing it at another patient, etc.

One must always remain extremely vigilant so that the operationalized definitions of the criterion behaviors are consistent with the goals of the program. For example, when Paul's project was first started, residents received tokens for "on-task" behavior in a classroom. It became apparent after a short while that some residents were extremely ingenious at "looking as if they were busy" and doing classroom work, when in reality, they were producing only little work, which was of inferior quality given their capabilities. Consequently, a production criterion was built into the system whereby the teachers, based on their knowledge of the residents' capabilities, judged whether the person had performed acceptable work. One may also find that the operational definition of these criterion behaviors may have to be changed over a period of time because of numerous factors. For example, the absolute hair length of young male patients that was judged acceptable changed when long hair on males became fashionable in the late 1960s. A constant reevaluation of the criterion behaviors and their components is critical. If any changes are made, some means must be established by which these changes can be communicated to the staff. In addition, in all likelihood, new behaviors will have to be added because it is difficult if not impossible to conceive of all of the criterion behaviors that will prove useful to the resident after discharge. For example, it may not occur to one when first establishing a program that patients need to know how to write checks, use credit cards, etc., in order to facilitate their functioning in the natural environment.

Elicitation of Criterion Behaviors. As anyone knows who has worked with schizophrenic patients, it is highly inefficient to wait for a patient to exhibit the total criterion behaviors before reinforcing them. Chronic patients may never have exhibited these behaviors or may no longer be exhibiting them because of institutionalization, psychopathology, etc. Various activities must be arranged in which these behaviors are to be expected, and teaching devices must be employed in order to elicit and develop the criterion behaviors. For example, self-help classes can be arranged in which residents are shown how to shave, make their beds, bathe, wash their clothes, iron their clothes, etc. Other classes can be arranged wherein residents are taught how to make change, write checks, use a telephone, etc. Activities can be planned in which residents are expected to interact both with other residents and with treatment staff members. Residents can be taught how to initiate a social interaction, how to terminate one, how to make small talk, etc. Numerous learning techniques may be used to teach these target behaviors, including instruction, mod-

eling, verbal and physical prompts, fading procedures, response chaining, and response shaping.

Any and all of these techniques may be used to teach a skill, although some procedures may work best for a particular skill or for a given resident. For example, in teaching highly regressed residents to shave, we found the following procedures useful: modeling criterion behaviors; providing verbal prompts such as "Pick up the razor" and "Hold it up to your face"; using physical prompts such as holding the patient's wrist and pulling down on his wrist when the razor was adjacent to his face; fading these prompts with time; shaping better and better approximations to removing all whiskers; and chaining a series of behaviors such as washing the face and applying the shaving cream. Another example of the use of these procedures can be found in our attempts to get many of the mute residents to speak. Modeling and prompting procedures were first used to get the patient to imitate nonverbal behaviors. Physical prompts such as holding the patient's mouth in such a way as to make a particular sound were utilized. Chaining procedures were used to get residents to emit several sounds in sequence that corresponded to words, etc.

Shaping was the most common procedure utilized. Shaping was generally employed on either a time dimension or by reinforcing subcomponents of the criterion behaviors. As already mentioned, many criterion behaviors were broken down into subcomponents (e.g., appropriate appearance had 11 subcomponents). At each appearance check, a resident would have to maintain his/her previous gains (e.g., 3 out of 11 subcomponents) plus 1 additional subcomponent in order to receive a token. A set number of failures on the new criterion would result in a drop back to the previous criterion. Other criterion behaviors, such as participation in recreational activities, were shaped on a time dimension. For some residents, this meant 30 sec of participation and for other residents participation during the whole time period (e.g., 50 min). Careful recording of each resident's attainment of the various criteria set out for him/her that day is necessary in order to adequately shape criterion behaviors.

Promoting Transfer of Attained Skills to the Natural Environment. Skills are developed and behavior is shaped in a token economy in a much more systematic and direct fashion than is usually the case in the natural environment. Unless residents are gradually introduced back into the natural environment and extramural support systems are established, there is some likelihood that the skills developed within the token economy may deteriorate. A useful procedure for promoting transfer back into the natural environment is a concept of step levels within the token system. As a resident progresses through the step levels, he/she is "weaned" from the token system, and more time is spent in the natural environment. In the initial steps, reinforcement is immediate (e.g., a resident is given a token immediately after the appearance check), while on the more advanced step levels, residents may receive the tokens that they have earned only at the end of the week, much like a check. In the most advanced steps, a resident may essentially be given a credit card. He/she may also be working eight hours a day in the community and just sleeping in the residential unit at night. To advance to the upper step levels, a resident's behavior must become more and more appropriate. That is, a resident must meet more and more of the criterion behaviors established within the program. At the earliest step levels, a resident earns only enough tokens to purchase minimal and necessary reinforcers. As a resident progresses through the steps, more individualization of the treatment program can also occur. At more advanced levels, a resident can join a prerelease group, the goal of which is to prepare the resident for self-supporting functioning in the community. The leader of the prerelease group can serve as the liaison person for the resident between the community and the treatment staff within the residential treatment center. The leader of the prerelease group assists the resident in securing employment and a place to live. Previous research (Paul, 1969) would seem to indicate that an important factor in preventing recidivism is for a released resident to have established a good relationship with a "significant other" individual. A significant other may be a relative; however, great care must be exercised in choosing this significant other.

The research of Brown, Monck, Carstairs, and Wing (1962) demonstrated that residents returning to a home where relatives show a high degree of emotional involvement are more likely to relapse than those who do not return to such homes (Vaughn & Leff, 1976).

Several other methods may be employed to introduce residents to the community gradually. Once or several times a week, a community trip may be planned for those residents who meet individualized criteria. Trips to restaurants, bowling alleys, etc., may be arranged so that residents can gain valuable exposure to community facilities. The taking of day, night, and weekend passes should be encouraged. In fact, in order to maintain status at the upper step levels, residents may be required to take passes of various durations. Another means by which to give residents exposure to the community is to bring the community to them. For example, in the Paul program (Paul & Lentz, 1977), an off-unit evening activity program was run, mainly with volunteers from the community. These individuals generally volunteered for one night a week and engaged in various types of activities, such as teaching the residents to use makeup, serving as lifeguards at a swimming pool, and showing the residents how to bake a cake. These volunteers need to be extensively trained in the principles of a token economy system so that their interactions are consistent with the overall program. These volunteers often serve as valuable liaison persons in the community after a resident has been discharged.

Token Distribution. Individual staff members must be assigned specified times to distribute tokens and should be held responsible for their distribution. For example, one staff member may be assigned to room inspection from 6:30 A.M. to 7:00 A.M. and to appearance check at 7:00 A.M., while another staff member may be assigned to distribute tokens for appropriate eating behavior at breakfast, and so on. When the staff member distributes the token, verbal praise should be given, and the behavior that is being reinforced should be specified. In addition, staff individuals should also specify the criteria that the resident will have to meet in the next check. For example, the staff individual might say, "Here's your token, John, for working ten minutes during class today. You did a super job, and I'm really proud of you. Tomorrow, in order to earn your token, you'll have to be working twenty minutes.'' The staff member will then record that the resident has been given a token and specify the criterion for the next activity of a similar kind. When working with extremely low-functioning residents, it is important for them to receive direct, immediate, and constant reinforcement. Often, these residents need to be reinforced every 5 min or for even briefer periods of time. For logistical purposes, it is often useful to have what is called a *shaping chip* to distribute to these low-functioning residents. A shaping chip is similar in form to a token except that it has a different color. These chips may be distributed at frequent intervals during an activity and may be exchanged for a token at the end of the activity if the resident has met the criterion. For example, one resident might have to earn 10 shaping chips during an activity in order to receive 1 token, while another resident may have to earn only 4 chips.

Backup Reinforcers. In order to motivate low-functioning residents to earn tokens, it is essential to have control over their access to reinforcers. This control may have to include basic reinforcers such as cigarettes, clothing, and meals. It is important to have many and varied reinforcers available as backups to the token system. Though it may not be physically possible to have all these backups located in the residential treatment center, they can still be made available. For instance, catalogs from various department stores and other outlets may be available to the residents. Exchange rates can be established (i.e., x tokens equal y dollars), so that a patient may earn tokens for merchandise illustrated in these catalogs. Civic organizations such as Lions Clubs, Kiwanis, and Knights of Columbus are often willing to donate reinforcers if other funds are lacking.

It is important to determine what is reinforcing for any particular resident. Very often, quite idiosyncratic reinforcers are found, and determining these idiosyncratic reinforcers may make all the difference in the world. Numerous methods are available to determine what a resident may find reinforcing, including asking them and asking relatives, friends, etc.

It has been our experience that very often, many of these residents have been isolated for such long periods of time it is actually necessary to expose them to a wide variety of reinforcers and have them sample them in order to make a determination of what they find reinforcing.

A Balanced Economy. There is a very thin line between having a depressed or an inflated economy. Both depression and inflation must be avoided, or the functioning of the token economy may be jeopardized. Therefore, tokens should be dispersed only at scheduled times, by designated members of the staff, and only for specific behaviors. Minimal functioning should result in minimal token earnings and minimal reinforcement. As a resident passes through the various step levels, earning power should increase, and more and varied reinforcers should be made available. As in any community, individual residents may attempt to live outside the monetary system by such behaviors as stealing, black-marketeering, and counterfeiting. One manner of handling disruptions to the economy such as stealing would be to place an individual offender on a different-color token, so that stolen tokens become valueless because they cannot be spent.

Inappropriate and Intolerable Behaviors. A token economy is basically a rewarding system that reinforces individuals for appropriate behaviors. Residents are not forced to do anything; rather, they are free to choose within the token system to work for reinforcers. Inappropriate behaviors, such as "crazy talk," are handled by a complete absence of reinforcement; that is, engagement in inappropriate behavior is often incompatible with earning tokens, and the staff are trained to ignore and not to socially reinforce inappropriate behaviors. Intolerable behaviors, such as striking another resident or a staff member, can be handled in a number of ways, including a response cost, time-out, restitution procedures, and demotion to a lower step level. However, it is important to note again that a token economy should be a rewarding system and should not be seen as a means of punishment.

Data Collection. Some form of data collection is absolutely necessary in order to maintain a token economy system. One needs to know how many tokens were dispensed and to what residents, how many tokens each resident spent, and on what reinforcers. The staff needs to know what the criterion is for any particular resident for any particular activity during the day. Summary recordings for each individual resident indicating their level of functioning with respect to the criterion behaviors must be recorded in order to determine the residents' status with respect to the various step levels. The amount of a fine for an intolerable behavior must be recorded because the fined residents then have to pay back the fine. Without these types of recordings, a token system could not operate. Forms may be developed to make these recordings extremely efficient, so that they require only a few seconds of staff time after each scheduled activity (Paul & Lentz, 1977). In addition to these necessary data recordings, other forms of data collection are desirable. Incidences of inappropriate behaviors can be recorded in order to determine the effectiveness of a token system in reducing inappropriate behavior. Staff behavior can also be periodically monitored in order to determine whether they are behaving in a fashion consistent with the program. If a staff member is behaving unprogrammatically, then direct and immediate feedback should be given.

Staff Training, Communications, and Morale. In order to establish an effective token economy, it is essential that the staff be thoroughly trained in its procedures so that their behavior is consistent with the goals of the program. There are numerous skills that the treatment staff must master. The staff must be able to judge reliably whether any resident has met a criterion behavior and all its subcomponents. They must learn to complete daily recording sheets accurately and efficiently. They need to learn how to administer verbal and nonverbal prompts, how to chain behavior, and how to shape it. Extensive training needs to be undertaken before a staff member should be allowed to operate as a member of the treatment team. Training can include reading instructional material, viewing videotapes emphasizing criterion behavior, and on-the-unit training with an experienced staff member.

The morale in any unit dealing with low-functioning chronic psychiatric patients can be a problem. Teaching low-functioning residents more appropriate behaviors is an extremely slow, painstaking process. Staff members need to be constantly informed of the patient's progress from the beginning to the end of the program. It helps to have members of the senior staff working on the "front lines" with junior staff members for morale purposes. In addition, senior members of the staff are more likely to voice opinions regarding the appropriateness of specific procedures for a particular resident. It is also important to have a representative from each treatment shift attend a weekly meeting to discuss potential problems and changes in the program.

Good communication among all staff members is extremely important in a token economy. All staff members need to know the present status of each resident with respect to step levels, whether anyone has been fined, changes in medication, who has been caught stealing, who has been promoted, which residents are working and what hours, and so on. This type of communication should be recorded in a log book, which is read by the incoming staff "out loud" in the presence of the outgoing staff so that all individuals may be informed and any difficulties cleared up. Because there will often be changes in how the token economy operates during the course of several months, it is important that all staff members be made aware of these changes via memos, etc., and periodically tested on the rules and regulations of the program.

Conclusions. It is the contention of the authors that all the above issues need to be addressed in some fashion in order to establish an efficient and effective token economy. Suggestions regarding each of these issues were largely based on the first author's experience in the use of token economies with severely psychotic, chronic mental patients. Token-economy treatment programs dealing with less debilitated patients may not require some of the features suggested. For example, programs focusing on less debilitated patients may not require such elaborate procedures for teaching patients various instrumental skills because these skills already exist in the patients' repertoire, and the contingency system alone will serve to attain the desired performance. Likewise, in working with less debilitated patients, it may not be necessary to depend on primary reinforcers as "backups" to the token system. However, although elaborate procedures may not be necessary to overcome each of these problems, they still need to be addressed in some sort of systematic fashion if the token economy is to be successful.

Problems in Evaluation

It is difficult to draw a firm conclusion regarding the outcomes of most of the token economy studies reported in the literature because they contain numerous flaws in experimental design (e.g., failure to equate subjects and failure to equate treatment staffs). It is even more difficult to compare results across studies because of differences in the patient populations used, differences in the dependent measures, and major differences in program components within the token economies. Some studies include severely debilitated patients, while others concern mildly debilitated patients or a mixture of mildly and severely debilitated patients. Even in those studies in which an attempt has been made to use a relatively homogeneous (with respect to one or several dimensions) group of residents, other patient characteristics may interact with treatment effectiveness. For example, Kowalski, Daley, and Gripp (1976) suggested that paranoid schizophrenic patients seem to improve more than other types of schizophrenics in a token economy.

The types of dependent variables used as outcome measures have varied greatly in the literature. In some studies, the focus is on measuring decreases in psychotic behaviors, such as delusions or bizarre repetitive motoric behaviors, while in other studies, the dependent measures focus on measuring increases in behavior such as socialization, and attendance at unit activities. Some studies employ discharge into the community as a major dependent variable, although discharge is more often a function of an administrative decision than a reflection of improved functioning on the part of the resident. Comparisons across studies are also made difficult by the lack of

specification of the details of the treatment program and/or the lack of attention paid to the components addressed in the previous section. As Paul and Lentz (1977) stated:

> Reports of so-called token economy programs that do not articulate, let alone monitor, the specific classes of patient behavior of focus, the criterion for disbursing or withholding tokens and other sociable and tangible consequences, the range and control of backups, the nature of staff patient interaction, etc., may be no more related to other token economy programs than the action of heroin is related to that of penicillin, even though both are administered by injection. (p. 434)

The first author once had the experience of serving as a consultant to an already-established "token-economy" program in a state hospital. He was flabbergasted to discover that although tokens were dispensed, there were no backup reinforcers supplied within this system. Amusingly enough, the administrators were puzzled over the lack of success of their "token" program. While none of the reviewed studies contain such a glaring omission of a component of a token program, many of them do not appear to have paid sufficient detailed attention to all of the components addressed above. A brief review of token economy studies is contained in the next section. Single-case studies are not reviewed here because the use of operant procedures in a single-case format have been discussed elsewhere in this chapter.

Treatment

The pioneer research on token economies was conducted by Ayllon and Azrin (1968). Their research was directed at developing and testing operant procedures rather than evaluating the overall effectiveness of a token economy. Nevertheless, their findings, which indicated that an operant system could change certain types of psychotic behavior in a controlled setting, stimulated interest in the use of token economies for the treatment of chronic psychiatric patients.

Schaefer and Martin (1966) compared the relative effect of a contingent and a noncontingent token system on severely regressed psychiatric patients. The same treatment staff administered the contingent and noncontingent tokens, therefore controlling for staff attention and ward atmosphere. The results indicated significant decreases in apathy and increases in responsibility and general activity in the patients receiving contingent tokens when compared with the patients who were receiving noncontingent tokens. Baker, Hall, and Hutchinson (1974) also compared the effects of the use of contingent tokens. A group of seven schizophrenic patients were exposed to differential aspects of a token economy system in a sequential manner. The patients were first transferred to a smaller ward with a better standard of care. After 6 weeks of just ward exposure, a stimulating activity program was initiated. After the activity program had been in operation for 3 weeks, noncontingent tokens were disbursed for a 7-week period, followed by a contingent token program of 14 weeks. The patients improved in several areas; however, most of this improvement occurred before the application of contingent tokens. The authors concluded that token reinforcement components did not emerge as the critical therapeutic agent. In another study, Baker, Hall, Hutchinson, and Bridge (1977) compared patients in a contingent token program with patients in a noncontingent milieu-type program. The results suggested that the patients in the milieu noncontingent program improved more than the patients in the token program. However, in both of the Baker studies, there appeared to be little attempt within the token programs to teach and shape instrumental behaviors.

A number of investigators (Ellsworth, 1969; Foreyt, Rockwood, Davis, Desvousges, & Hollingsworth, 1975; Liberman, 1971) have reported higher discharge rates and lower readmission rates after token systems have been introduced for chronic patients who had been previously unaffected by other treatments. Heap, Boblitt, Moore, and Hord (1970) studied the effects on discharge of a treatment program that combined features of both a token economy and a milieu treatment. Significantly more patients treated in the combined token economy and milieu program were discharged from the hospital than patients in a control ward. Lower readmission rates were reported by Hollingsworth and Foreyt (1975) for patients who had been exposed to a token economy program in comparison with a hospital control group. However, there

were few differences between the discharged token-economy patients and the discharged control patients with respect to community functioning. Although, as mentioned previously, discharge is often the result of an administrative decision rather than improvement in a patient's behavior, the consistency of results obtained across different investigators is encouraging.

Token economies have been reported to affect many different types of behavior. Gorham, Green, Caldwell, and Bartlett (1970) found an initial increase in psychotic symptoms after a token economy had been introduced, but improved functioning after a short period of time. Gripp and Magaro (1971) compared the effects of a token economy program on chronic female patients with patients in three other units. The authors reported significantly more improvement for the residents of the token economy unit with respect to symptomatic behaviors (e.g., agitated depression, social withdrawal, and thought disorders). Residents on the token program were also seen as improving more with respect to social competence and self-care maintenance. Presly, Black, Gray, Hartie, and Seymour (1976) reported increases in social interaction among chronic male patients after the introduction of the token economy system, but no major changes in bizarre psychotic behavior. Neither the Presly et al. (1976) study nor the Gripp and Magaro (1971) study adequately equated patients in their treatment and control groups, and therefore, caution should be used in interpreting the results. Two studies, one of male psychiatric patients (Shean & Zeidberg, 1971) and one of female psychiatric patients (Maley, Feldman, & Ruskin, 1973), reported significant increases on measures of cooperation, communication, and social contact in patients in the token economy program when compared with control groups. Olson and Greenberg (1972) found that group contingencies resulted in increased attendance at activities by mildly disabled patients when compared with patients in control groups. Although each of these studies possesses some methodological flaws, the consistency of results would seem to suggest that token economies can modify a wide variety of behaviors.

In one of the better controlled studies in the

literature, Stoffelmayr, Faulkner, and Mitchell (1973) studied the differential effectiveness of four treatment programs with severely chronic male psychiatric patients over a one-year period. The patients were assigned to one of four groups: a hospital control, a token system group, and two different milieu groups, one of which was more structured and had more meetings than the other group. The residents in the token economy program, when compared with the hospital control group, evidenced significantly greater improvement in all areas of functioning measured. When compared with the residents in either of the milieu treatment programs, the residents in the token program demonstrated significantly more improvement in self-care skills, overall increases in activity, and decreases in apathy. The residents in either of the milieu programs demonstrated initial improvement over the hospital controls but these improvements were not maintained over time.

In what is recognized (by Gomes-Schwartz, 1979) as the most comprehensive and best-controlled study in the literature, Paul and Lentz (1977) compared the relative effectiveness of a token economy to an enriched milieu treatment and a hospital control treatment. This study evaluated the effects of four years of treatment on severely regressed, chronic schizophrenics. A multitude of assessment instruments were used to evaluate the relative effectiveness of these programs. In general, the results clearly indicate the superiority of the token economy system over either the milieu treatment program or the hospital control program. At the end of treatment, 89.3% of the token economy patients were significantly improved, in contrast with 46.4% of the milieu patients. Unfortunately, this program was prematurely ended after a four-year period (Paul & Lentz, 1977). At the termination of the program, all the residents capable of functioning in the community were placed in the community. Some of these residents were placed with their families, others in extended-care facilities, and others achieved independent functioning. After termination of the program, a six-month follow-up was conducted. The percentages of residents who had achieved a release and had evidenced a continuous community stay were 92.5% for the token economy unit, 71% for the milieu treatment unit, and 48.4% for the hospital comparison unit. Of the patients on the token economy unit, 10% were able to live independently and be self-supporting. Clearly, the results of this well-controlled study are both the dramatic and encouraging.

Conclusions

Although many of the studies reviewed have severe methodological flaws, the mostly consistent positive results seem to support the contention that token economies can be effective in treating chronic schizophrenics. Given the fact that many of the token programs reviewed "shortchanged" some of the components listed in the previous section (e.g., did little to develop the target behaviors or paid little attention to posthospital care), one would expect even more dramatic results if all these issues were clearly faced and effectively resolved.

It is our contention that the major advantage of a token economy is that it provides a structure and a motivational system wherein patients learn new skills and coping strategies through various therapeutic interventions. We agree with D'Zurilla and Goldfried's (1971) suggestion that abnormal behavior may be viewed as an inability (for whatever reason) on the part of the individual to resolve situational problems. Subsequently, the individual's ineffective attempts to resolve the problems results in an increase in or a maintenance of emotional, cognitive, and behavioral pathologies. Since schizophrenics do not possess adequate coping skills to handle the stresses in their lives effectively, it is essential in treating schizophrenics to teach them adequate coping strategies and instrumental skills.

It is interesting to note that in the Paul program (Paul & Lentz, 1977), there was little focus on psychopathology *per se*. Psychotic behaviors were ignored except when they presented a danger to either the residents or the treatment staff. The major focus was on training patients in instrumental behaviors. As the residents developed more instrumental behaviors, decreases in psychotic behaviors occurred (Paul & Lentz, 1977).

In the next section of this chapter, we review studies in which systematic attempts have been made to teach psychiatric patients social skills in order to increase their overall social functioning. Although previous research (Zigler & Phillips, 1961c,1962) has demonstrated the important role that patients' social skill level plays with respect to hospitalization, posthospital functioning, recidivism rate, etc., it has been only in the last decade that investigators have systematically attempted to increase the social functioning of psychiatric patients.

Social Skills Training

The many studies cited earlier in this chapter demonstrate that operant technology can be and has been successfully employed in modifying specific maladaptive behaviors of individuals who are labeled schizophrenic. The limitations of this technology have been discussed with regard to the issues of maintenance of behavior change and generalization of treatment effects. Durability and generalization of treatment effects have been especially poor in the treatment of deficit interpersonal behaviors (Paul, 1969). One reason may be that most operant approaches merely reinforce behaviors that exist in the patient's repertoire and do not teach patients how to cope with problems in interpersonal interactions. The problem is that many schizophrenic patients do not have appropriate social behaviors in their interpersonal repertoires that can be strengthened through reinforcement. Since interpersonal problem behaviors are especially severe among many schizophrenic patients, a more comprehensive intervention strategy is warranted.

Although recognition of the relationships between social competence and psychiatric disorder date as far back as 20 years ago (Strauss & Carpenter, 1974, Zigler & Phillips, 1960, 1961a,b), relatively few treatment strategies have been developed that systematically address the problem of social inadequacy among psychiatric patients. The significance of socially relevant treatment strategies for schizophrenics is reflected in a recent summary report of research on the psychosocial treatment of schizophrenia submitted to the Institute of Medicine, National Academy of Sciences. It concludes, "it is noteworthy that the positive findings from controlled studies are most consistent for those treatments that involve extensive attention to the individual patient's social environment" (Mosher & Keith, 1979, p. 629). No treatment has more directly or systematically attempted to influence patients' social environments than social skills training.

Definition and Patient Population

Social skills training consists of a comprehensive treatment package that usually includes the following components: behavior rehearsal, modeling, reinforcement, prompts, homework assignments, feedback, and instructions (Goldstein, 1973; Hersen & Bellack, 1976b). Although several conceptual definitions of social skills training have been offered, each having slightly different theoretical and treatment implications, we have found Goldsmith and McFall's (1975) description concise and useful:

A general therapy approach aimed at increasing performance competence in critical life situations. In contrast to therapies aimed primarily at the elimination of maladaptive behaviors, skill training emphasizes the positive, educational aspects of treatment. It assumes that each individual always does the best he can, given his physical limitations and unique learning history, to respond as effectively as possible in every situation. Thus, when an individual's "best effort" behavior is judged to be maladaptive, this indicates the presence of a situation-specific skill deficit in that individual's repertoire. . . . Whatever the origins of this deficit (e.g., lack of experience, faulty learning, biological dysfunction) it often may be overcome or partially compensated for through appropriate training in more skillful response alternatives. (p. 51)

Although social skills training has been implemented with many psychiatric disorders (Hersen, 1979), our comments in this section are based on studies of patients who fall under the diagnostic category of schizophrenia. Before commenting on these studies, a major methodological-strategic problem regarding diagnosis deserves attention. Given the behavior therapist's general philosophy concerning diagnosis, it is not surprising to find that in most cases, little effort has been expended in securing reliably diagnosed schizophrenics. Indeed, it is questionable whether most patients labeled schizophrenic in social skills studies would fit the DSM III criteria for schizophrenia. This is unfortunate, since unreliable diagnoses make comparability across studies very difficult and make it almost impossible to explain contradictory findings (Wallace, Nelson, Liberman, Aitchison, Lukoff, Elder, & Ferris, 1980). Nevertheless, the studies that have been considered for the present section are those that have used the labels *schizophrenic* or *psychotic* to describe at least some of their patient population. Though such a pooling procedure makes interpretation difficult, consideration of only those reports describing their patient populations as *schizophrenic* would include only a small fraction of the studies available, and we feel that little information would be gained from such a review. Studies that have clearly excluded patient groups labeled *schizophrenic* or *psychotic* have not been drawn upon.

Social skills training for schizophrenic patients is based on the notion that poor social performance may be due to one or several of the following factors: (1) the individual may never have learned the appropriate social behavior; (2) if appropriate social behavior has been learned, it may not now be available because of disuse resulting from a lengthy psychiatric illness; (3) the individual may have a faulty cognitive-evaluative appraisal of the contingencies and consequences of a particular social interaction; and (4) the individual may have a high level of anxiety, which interferes with what otherwise might be adequate performance. It should be noted that the skills training approach is primarily focused on performance, not on hypotheses about why the deficits may or may not exist.

Treatment Protocols

A consideration of some of the major features of various social skills treatment protocols reveals that although many of the training packages utilize many of the same essential procedures, there is little precise consistency in protocols across treatment studies (Curran, 1979). This situation is similar to that mentioned earlier in relation to token economy programs. For example, although nearly all social-skills training protocols include the

components of rehearsal, modeling, reinforcement, feedback, and instructions, some researchers (e.g., Hersen & Bellack, 1976a) employ these specifically to increase or decrease certain circumscribed target behaviors (e.g., eye contact or speech latency), whereas other researchers (e.g., Monti, Fink, Norman, Curran, Hayes, & Caldwell, 1979) apply the same treatment components to a much more global target (e.g., giving criticism). Another example may be found in the more recent interest in patients' "internal states." Once again, the level of emphasis has varied for different treatment protocols. For example, Bellack and Hersen (1978) have included components such as listening, identifying emotions, and getting clarification. Along similar lines, Trower, Bryant, and Argyle's (1978) protocol emphasizes training observational skills, meshing skills (timing and relevance), listening skills, and problem-solving skills. An even more cognitively oriented program is provided by the work being done by Wallace, Liberman, and their colleagues (Wallace, 1978; Wallace, Nelson, Lukoff, Webster, Rappe, & Ferris, 1978). These investigators reason that a skillful response is the result of an integrated chain of behaviors. This chain begins with the accurate "reception" of social stimuli, progresses to the "processing" of these stimuli, and results in the "sending" of an appropriate response. Wallace and his colleagues have identified sets of variables that are important for each of these behaviors. The assessment and treatment of schizophrenic patients is focused on each of these variables. Another significant aspect of this approach that differentiates it from others is the intensity of the treatment protocol. Liberman, Nuechterlein, and Wallace (1982) have suggested that a minimum of six months of intensive treatment may be necessary to establish clinically significant changes in schizophrenic patients.

Since space limitations preclude a detailed presentation of each of the treatment protocols that have been developed for schizophrenic patients, we present here a summary of the social-skills treatment protocol that we use in our treatment groups at the Behavior Training Clinic of the Providence Veterans Administration Medical Center. The reader is referred to Monti, Corriveau, and Curran (1982) for a more detailed presentation of this treatment package.

Treatment sessions led by co-therapists are usually conducted during the week on a daily basis for 60 min over a 4-week period (a total of 20 sessions). Groups usually consist of 7–10 patients. The treatment sessions are based on a 10-chapter treatment manual, which consists of the following topics: starting conversations, nonverbal behavior, giving and receiving compliments, self-instructional training, giving criticism, receiving criticism, feeling talk and listening skills, being assertive in business situations, close relationships, and intimate relationships. Each chapter is the focus of two sessions. The first session of a particular chapter is largely concerned with teaching the content of that chapter. A good deal of role playing and modeling is done by the co-therapists, who model appropriate behavior utilizing material in the text. Patients in the group are asked about their personal experiences as they might relate to examples mentioned in the text. Through this procedure, role-play situations are modified and developed, and the material is made more relevant to the specific needs of the members of any particular group. Patients are encouraged to rehearse and role-play material in the text during this session. This gives the co-therapists a sense of the group's baseline level of functioning regarding a particular area. The second session on a chapter is used for additional teaching and rehearsal. During this session, patients role-play their responses with each other as well as with the co-therapists. A good deal of coaching and instruction is provided by the co-therapists. Feedback and reinforcement are provided by both therapists and patients following each rehearsal. Videotape feedback is often used to provide more specific feedback. Care is taken not to emphasize the negative aspects of the patients' behavior. Rather, positive aspects are emphasized, and through gradual shaping procedures, appropriate behavior replaces inappropriate behavior. If after role playing, information, and feedback, members of the group are still deficient in certain behaviors, the cycle is repeated as time allows.

Homework assignments accompany both sessions of each chapter. Homework consists of having the patient practice outside of the group the behaviors discussed and learned during a particular session. For example, a homework assignment for the chapter on starting conversations might include instructions directing the patient to start a conversation with someone he/she knows and then to start a conversation with a stranger. Patients are given homework forms and are encouraged to write down the specifics of the situation (e.g., who the conversation was with and the difficulties encountered). Homework assignments are collected and discussed at the beginning of each session. The completion of homework assignments may be publicly charted, depending on the particular group. Patients are encouraged to bring problems they had in the homework into the group, where they can role-play the homework assignment and receive feedback from the group. Homework assignments are specifically used to promote extrasession generalization.

Generalization is also promoted through the use of adjunct role-players. These are staff members or trained students, usually unknown to the patients, who attend a group on occasion and serve as additional role-players. This procedure provides patients with opportunities to practice their new response repertoires with "strangers," in the context of support and encouragement from other group members.

Evidence of Treatment Effectiveness

It is not our purpose to provide an exhaustive review of the literature, since excellent recent reviews of the experimental evidence on social skills training with schizophrenic patients are available (Hersen, 1979; Wallace et al., 1980). Rather, consistent with the theme of this chapter, we shall summarize the social-skills-treatment literature giving special emphasis to the maintenance and generalization of treatment effects. Since the experimental literature can be clearly divided, on methodological grounds, into single-case experimental design and group-design studies (Wallace et al., 1980), a prototypical example of each study design is provided, accompanied by a summary of the most consistent findings obtained by each method. Next, the evidence for the generalization and durability of behavior change is reviewed. Finally, suggestions are made regarding possible ways of promoting or enhancing the effects of social skills training for schizophrenics.

Single-Case Experimental Design Studies. Single-case experimental methodology, usually employing multiple baselines across behaviors, patients, and/or situations, have contributed a great deal to our understanding of the effects of social skills training on the behavior of schizophrenics. Indeed, almost all of the studies reported to date that have carefully identified schizophrenic patients have been conducted in the single-case experimental design fashion. Most of these studies have employed laboratory-type procedures, such as the Behavioral Assertiveness Test (BAT; Eisler, Miller, & Hersen, 1973), to do both training and assessment. Nearly all single-case experimental design studies report positive treatment effects.

A good example of a single-case study that is particularly relevant to the present chapter is the Hersen, Turner, Edelstein, and Pinkston (1975) study. This investigation is especially pertinent since it considers a schizophrenic patient who, prior to social skills training, was on a general token-economy program as well as a combination of medications. After several weeks, it was clear that the general token economy was not therapeutic for this patient. At this point, an individualized token-economy program was designed and implemented, and within two days "remarkable improvement in the patient's appearance was noted" (p. 589). Next, a behavioral analysis of the patient's social interactions was conducted, and it revealed certain social skills deficits (e.g., poor eye contact and response latency). The BAT scenes served as both the training and the assessment instrument.

Training in this study consisted of instructions, behavioral rehearsal, feedback, and *in vivo* modeling of four of the eight BAT scenes. The remaining four scenes served as a measure of generalization. A multiple-baseline design was employed. Eye contact, response latency, and requests for new behavior were targeted and monitored, while the patient's verbal initiations during group therapy were unobtrusively monitored as an additional measure of generalization. A baseline and each of four

experimental phases lasted approximately one week each. The results suggested that sequential treatment for eye contact, latency, and requests for new behavior showed improvement over baseline. Three other behaviors (overall assertiveness, voice trials, and speech disruptions), although not treated, improved, as did verbal initiations in group therapy sessions. Follow-up interviews, conducted at 4-week intervals to 22 weeks postdischarge, indicated that the patient's progress had been maintained.

This single-case study emphasizes several important aspects of treating schizophrenic patients. First, medication was and should be regulated prior to experimental intervention (Hersen, 1979). This regulation is especially important when dealing with schizophrenics, since cognitive functions can be significantly affected by changes in psychotropic medications and, in turn, can interact with the effectiveness of social skills training. Second, the patient's participation in a token economy program as well as the social skills training program points to another important aspect of dealing with this patient population, namely, that often a response acquisition approach is needed in addition to a simple token-economy approach because the appropriate behavior may not exist in the patient's repertoire and may actually have to be taught.

The results of the Hersen *et al.* study have been replicated in other similarly designed studies conducted by Hersen, Bellack, and their colleagues (Eisler, Hersen, & Miller, 1974; Hersen & Bellack, 1976a; Williams, Turner, Watts, Bellack, & Hersen, 1977) as well as by other researchers (e.g., Matson & Stephens, 1978; Wood, Barrios, & Cohn, 1979). In general, the results of these studies indicate a definite improvement in specific behavioral components of social skill, such as eye contact, voice volume and tone, latency and duration of speech, and posture. Clearly, the short-term effects of social skills training on specific behavioral components of social skills are well documented in single-case experimental design studies.

Group-Design Studies. Studies that have examined the effect of social skills training on schizophrenics by means of group-comparison designs are particularly difficult to summarize since there is a great deal of variance in patient characteristics (e.g., rigor of diagnoses and severity of skills deficits) and assessment methodologies, both across and sometimes within studies. In addition, treatment methods vary considerably across studies (Wallace *et al.*, 1980). Nevertheless, group-design studies can be generally characterized as offering relatively few group treatment sessions and yet showing positive treatment effects. Such effects are typically measured by laboratory-based pre- and postassessment instruments (e.g., the BAT), which are given to both experimental group and control group patients.

A study conducted by Finch and Wallace (1977) is used here as an illustration of a group-comparison design study. This study compared the effectiveness of a social skills training program to an assessment only control condition. The subjects in the study were 16 nonassertive male schizophrenic inpatients. The treatment, which was conducted in a group format, included 12 sessions of interpersonal skills training designed to "increase assertive behavior both in and out of the group and to decrease anxiety in interpersonal situations" (p. 887). The treatment effects were assessed by comparing pre–post differences on three role-playing and four spontaneously enacted interpersonal encounters, which were audiotaped. The role-play situations were initiating a conversation, offering an apology, and extending a social invitation. The spontaneous situations were expressing an opinion, receiving a compliment, refusing an unreasonable request, and accepting thanks. All situations were rated on loudness and fluency of speech, affect, latency, and content. All but latency, which was timed, were rated on 5-point scales. In addition, quality of eye contact was judged by the confederate. Compared with the control group, the skills training group significantly improved on all measures. The improvements were apparent across both role-played and spontaneously enacted situations and across trained and untrained situations. Finch and Wallace did not report any evidence of generalization outside their assessment situations, nor did they report any follow-up data.

The findings of Finch and Wallace (1977), that specific behavioral components of social skills do improve as a function of treatment when tested in situations similar to treatment situations, are consistent with those of almost all of the group-design studies reported in the literature (Field & Test, 1975; Goldsmith & McFall, 1975; Goldstein, Martens, Hubben, van Belle, Schaaf, Wiersma, & Goedhart, 1973). Other consistent findings in the group-design literature are that more global measures of social skill (e.g., overall social skill) improve as a function of treatment (Monti *et al.*, 1979; Monti, Curran, Corriveau, DeLancey, & Hagerman, 1980), as do self-report measures of social skill and social anxiety (Goldsmith & McFall, 1975; Monti *et al.*, 1980). Thus, there is good consistency across both single-case designs and group-design studies, suggesting that social skills training can change posttest performance on either specific behavioral components or more global measures of social skill when tested in laboratory-based situations similar in kind to the treatment situations. Clearly, at this level of analysis, social skills training does seem to be effective in modifying the social behavior of schizophrenic patients. We now turn to an examination of more clinically relevant issues, namely, the generalization and maintenance of behavior change resulting from social skills training.

Evidence of Generalization of Behavior Change

Although consistently positive treatment effects have been reported for nearly all single-case and group-design studies that utilize assessment instruments similar to training instruments (e.g., Finch & Wallace, 1977; Hersen *et al.*, 1975; Monti *et al.*, 1979), much less consistency is found when testing scenes or situations that are not similar to those presented in training (Wallace *et al.*, 1980). Several studies (Bellack, Hersen, & Turner, 1976; Frederiksen, Jenkins, Foy, & Eisler, 1976; Williams *et al.*, 1977) have shown little or no improvement on scenes dissimilar to those presented in training, whereas other studies (Finch & Wallace, 1977; Monti *et al.*, 1979) do show improved performance on untrained scenes as well as trained scenes. Finally, the results of both single-case and group-comparison studies typically show poor generalization of improvement as measured by assessment situations clearly different (i.e., non-laboratory-based) from those trained. For example, Gutride, Goldstein, and Hunter (1973) found only limited improvement in ward behavior, and Jaffe and Carlson (1976) found no improvement in ward behavior. Hence, treatment results typically form a kind of gradient of generalization, and treatment effects are more consistently demonstrated on measures that are similar to training situations and less consistently demonstrated on measures dissimilar to training situations.

In contrast to the general trend of poor generalization to situations dissimilar to training situations, Goldsmith and McFall (1975) demonstrated clear improvement in a situation different from situations presented in treatment. Goldsmith and McFall's study involved both the development and the evaluation of a social skills training program for schizophrenic inpatients. Perhaps the most significant feature of this study is that a behavioral-analytic approach was used to identify the problem behaviors of the patient population. Based on this analysis, a social skills training program was designed and compared with both a pseudotherapy control group and an assessment-only control group. The social skills training program involved training in initiating and terminating conversations, dealing with rejection, being more assertive and self-disclosing, etc. The results of this study indicated that the social skills training group proved superior to both the pseudotherapy control group and the assessment-only control group in producing significant pre–post therapeutic changes as measured by both self-report and behavioral instruments. Behavioral changes were obtained on both laboratory measures as well as on the Simulated Real-Life Behavior Test, which was based on a five-minute social interaction. The results were, for the most part, maintained at follow-up.

In another study where good generalization was obtained, Monti et al. (1979) compared the effectiveness of a systematic social skills group-training program with both a bibliotherapy program group and an assessment-only control group. In this study, 30 patients were randomly assigned to one of the three treatment conditions. The social skills treatment included modeling, role playing, coaching, rehearsal, and written homework assignments, which accompanied each session and which were thoroughly discussed both before and after they were completed. The results on a pre–post behavioral test (role-play performance on eight simulated social interactions) suggested that the patients in the social skills training group were more skillful after treatment than the control-group patients. Two unique aspects of this study are that follow-up data were collected across treatments at the longest interval (10 months) recorded in the group-design literature, and that measures of generalization were given at follow-up. The follow-up data suggested that the treatment effects were maintained and that the generalization effects were demonstrated in an analysis of trained versus untrained scenes, as well as on the Clinical Outcome Criteria Scale (Strauss & Carpenter, 1972) based on a clinical interview. The interview was conducted by a psychiatrist who was blind to the treatment conditions. Items on the scale reflected aspects of the patients' posthospital adjustment, such as job status and number of acquaintances seen. The findings on this measure showed that the patients who received social skills training were significantly improved as compared with the control-group patients.

Evidence of Durability of Behavior Change

Evidence of the durability of behavior change as a result of social skills training has been rather inconsistent. That is, some studies report the maintenance of treatment effects, while others report no treatment effects at follow-up. In addition, in many studies, no follow-up data are reported at all, and in others, only very short-term follow-up data are reported.

Let us first consider the status of follow-up data among the single-case experimental design studies. Most studies in this category that report positive treatment effects also report some follow-up data. These are usually for relatively brief, three- to five-month follow-up periods (e.g., Bellack et al., 1976; Hersen & Bellack, 1976a; Hersen et al., 1975). Although these follow-up results are usually positive, the follow-up data are sometimes merely impressions from a follow-up clinical interview.

The one single-case experimental design study in the literature (Liberman, Lillie, Falloon, Vaughn, Harpin, Leff, Hutchinson, Ryan, & Stoute, 1978) that reported a more extended one-year follow-up is perhaps the most ambitious study of social skills training and schizophrenia reported to date. This study treated three chronic schizophrenics who were at high risk for relapse with 300 hours of intensive skills training. A multiple-baseline design across areas of homework assignments (interactions with nursing staff, parents, and community agents) was utilized to demonstrate improvements in the patients' performance as a function of treatment. Improvements were measured by the number of homework assignments completed as reported by the patients and a validating staff member, parent, or community agent. One of the many significant features of this study was that the patients were diagnosed by means of the Present State Examination (Wing, Cooper, & Sartorius, 1974), one of the most reliable measures of schizophrenia available. Social skills training was judged to be effective as measured by completed homework assignments changing only when appropriate training was applied to each respective setting. Unfortunately, the one-year follow-up data indicated that the patients' levels of social competence returned to baseline after they had been discharged from treatment.

Relevant data on the maintenance of behavior change as a result of skills training are less available for group design studies than they are for single-case studies, as evidenced by the fact that only one-third of the group-design studies reviewed include any follow-up assessment whatsoever. Among those few group-design studies that do report follow-up data, nearly all report maintenance of treatment effects (e.g., Field & Test, 1975; Goldsmith & McFall, 1975; Monti et al., 1979, 1980). However, some of these studies report incomplete follow-up data and/or no follow-up data for control subjects. For example, Field and Test (1975) reported follow-up data for four experimental patients, all of whom maintained their gains in three role-play test situations. Control-group patients were not tested at follow-up, since many had received treatment during the follow-up interval. The absence of appropriate control-group follow-up data makes the interpretation of experimental data very difficult. Two studies (Monti et al., 1979, 1980) reported follow-up data on appropriate control patients. Although both of these studies suggest relatively long-term treatment effects, neither study looked at schizophrenic patients exclusively. The need for more long-term follow-up data with schizophrenic patients is obvious.

Promoting Generalization and Maintenance of Behavior Change

Given the paucity of evidence for the generalization and maintenance of behavior change resulting from social skills training with schizophrenics, it is clear that we need more work directed at these problem areas. In this section, we consider possible avenues through which generalization and maintenance might be enhanced, in the hopes that such a discussion will prompt further thought on and empirical testing of some of these ideas. One treatment variable that might benefit from closer examination is the nature of the behaviors that are taught in social skills training protocols. Many of the single-case studies and some of the group-design studies have focused on circumscribed target behaviors (e.g., eye contact and speech latency). It is possible that such emphasis on specific components may be too simplistic, since it may omit other important aspects of social skill, such as timing, monitoring, sequencing, and other "process skills" (Trower, 1980). Experimental evidence provided by Fischetti, Curran, and Wessberg (1977) has pointed to the importance of some of these process variables in discriminating between groups of skilled and unskilled individuals. Since it is unlikely that we have identified all of the relevant variables involved in skillful responding, training on more global dimensions (so as to include both component and process variables) may be more profitable, given our present level of understanding of social skill.

A related variable that may be important and deserving of further empirical attention is the nature of the situations employed in training protocols. Most social skills training programs have selected their training material on the basis of clinicians' experience and intuition. Since most protocols have not employed much care in identifying those situations that are especially difficult for their patients, it may well be that we are using training situations that are not as relevant to patients as we assume they are. One notable exception is the painstaking, empirically based behavioral-analytic approach that Goldsmith and McFall (1975) employed in identifying the problem areas of their patients prior to treatment. Since Goldsmith and McFall's treatment results do seem to have generalized, it is possible that their empirically based treatment content was, in part, responsible for the generalization obtained. It is quite plausible that greater relevancy will facilitate learning and thereby influence the generalization and maintenance of behavior change. We are in agreement with Goldsmith and McFall's position that "content of a skill-training program is at least as critical to its ultimate success as the training methods it employs" (p. 51). We feel that more empirical work needs to be done in identifying relevant training material prior to embarking on treatment.

Yet another approach to facilitating learning and generalization might involve expanding on potential target areas for training. The recent interest on "internal states" (e.g., cognitive and emotional processes) is a step in this direction. An example of such an expended approach to the problems of social skills training and schizophrenia is provided by the work of Wallace (1978), which was discussed earlier. Wallace's approach emphasizes the receiving and processing as well as the sending components of social skill. The model proposed by Wallace and his colleagues is clearly more "cognitive" than many proposed to date. Given the well-documented cognitive deficits apparent in schizophrenia, Wallace's approach would seem to have particular promise for this patient population. Although no data were available at the time this chapter was written, Wallace and his colleagues are currently testing the adequacy of their model. Hopefully, the results of their innovative treatment work will show improvement in the durability and generalization of social-skills treatment effects with schizophrenic patients.

Another source for improving social skills training, generalization, and durability may be the existing literature on schizophrenia. As Liberman *et al.* (1982) have suggested, "It's as though the behavior therapists using social skills training and the experimentalists and psychopathologists studying the nature of schizophrenia live in two separate worlds" (p. 6). We feel that more integrated work is needed in studying the social skills training process and how it might interact with the known characteristics and deficits of schizophrenics. A study reported by Eisler, Blanchard, Fitts, and Williams (1978) provides an illustration of how a more integrated approach to the study of skills training and schizophrenia may prove useful. These authors reasoned that since schizophrenic patients suffer from increased thought and speech disturbances and more withdrawal than nonpsychotic patients, different training strategies might be necessary to teach these two different patient groups most effectively. In a 3 × 2 design, 24 schizophrenic and 24 nonpsychotic patients, all of whom had been preselected on the basis of their poor skill performance on the Behavioral Assertiveness Test-Revised (BAT-R), were randomly assigned to one of three experimental conditions: social skills training without modeling, social skills training with modeling, and a practice control (*n* = 8 per group). The treatment for each condition consisted of six 30-min rehearsal sessions, during which the patients role-played BAT-R training scenes. The patients in the social-skills training group without modeling received coaching, feedback, and practice on problem behaviors. The patients in the program of social skills training plus modeling received all of the above plus, prior to coaching, a videotape of a highly skilled model responding to a confederate. The results of pre–post BAT-R analyses and additional data obtained from a semistructured interpersonal conversation suggested that both social-skills training programs had positive effects. Tests of specific interaction effects suggested that modeling was essential in improving the performance of schizophrenics and "seemingly detrimental to non-psychotic individuals" (p. 167).

In this study, attention to the psychopathology of schizophrenia led to a different evaluation of training strategies for different patient groups. The obtained results emphasize the potential benefits of integrating knowledge from other areas of study on schizophrenia with our treatment approaches. We agree with the conclusion of Eisler *et al.* that "More effort is needed to design more specific training strategies for groups who share characteristic skill deficits and who are amenable to different sorts of learning experiences" (p. 170). In the absence of such specification, we may be inhibiting learning, and thus generalization and maintenance, by "turning off" our schizophrenic patients to our treatment because of deficiencies in our training procedures.

A factor that may influence the generalization and the durability of social skills training with schizophrenics is medication. Although many single-case studies have taken this possibility into some consideration (Hersen, Bellack, and their colleagues usually report that medication is regulated prior to beginning training), most group-design studies do not even mention medication, let alone control for its effects. Since psychotropic medications are apt to influence thought processes and behavior, it is likely that their effects influence treatment results and therefore should be carefully considered. An additional possible complication emerges when considering the literature on state-dependent learning in psychopharmacology. This literature suggests that learning under certain drugs may not readily transfer to drug-free states. Consequently, the issues of maintenance and generalization may be somewhat contingent on whether or not the schizophrenic patient continues on the same or similar medication (Paul, Tobias, & Holly, 1972). Experimental data that specifically examine the independent and interaction effects of social skills training and psychotropic medication, with well-diagnosed schizophrenics, are needed in order to address this important area adequately. Medication maintenance issues are especially important since a review of the literature outside the boundaries of social skills training suggests that in the long run, the most effective treatment for this patient population includes a combination of both pharmacological control and socioenvironmental interventions (Wing, 1978).

Another possible way to promote generalization and to maximize the long-term effects of our skills training programs may simply be to do more training. It is quite surprising to find that several group-design studies done on schizophrenics (e.g., Goldstein *et al.*, 1973; Goldsmith & McFall, 1975) have employed as few as 1, 3, or 4 sessions of social skills training. The studies reporting relatively good maintenance of behavior change have employed 10 or 20 intensive sessions (Monti *et al.*, 1979, 1980). Since these studies include relatively few schizophrenics, it is likely that much more training would be required when dealing exclusively with schizophrenics. Support for this argument may be found in the work of Shepherd (1978), who has recently demonstrated that increased frequency and duration of training have improved the generalization of behavior change with schizophrenics. Indeed, as mentioned previously, Liberman *et al.* (1982) suggested that at least 6 months and perhaps as much as two to four years of treatment are necessary for clinically significant and durable results with chronically and severely impaired schizophrenics. In addition to more extensive training, the inclusion of periodic "booster sessions" that extend well into follow-up periods may also enhance treatment effects. Since social skills training, like other therapeutic treatments, is rather expensive in terms of staff time and energy, we need research directed toward identifying what the optimal number of treatment and "booster sessions" might be for enhancing treatment effects.

Another factor that may contribute to generalization and maintenance is the attention given to the accurate completion and review of homework assignments during which the newly learned skills are practiced. This component was emphasized in the Monti *et al.* (1979) study, which produced relatively long-lasting and generalized treatment effects. Although Monti *et al.*'s use of extrasession homework assignments is not unique, few studies report as much emphasis on this component. Although the homework component was not formally tested in this study, it did provide patients with many opportunities to practice newly learned behaviors in different settings, and such procedures have been shown to promote generalization (Stokes & Bear, 1977).

At a different level of intervention, several recent innovative skills-training programs have utilized *in vivo* social skills training (Brown, 1982; Stein & Test, 1978) to further promote the generalization of treatment effects. Such *in vivo* treatment differs from typical homework assignments in that the therapist actually accompanies the patient into the real world and does "on-site" training. Several *in vivo* programs have placed schizophrenic patients in community-based living environments among ordinary people. On a rotating basis, trained staff provide *in vivo* treatment, which consists of performing day-to-day activities, such as cooking, shopping, and job hunting, along with the patient. The emphasis of such programs is on modeling, prompting, and shaping. Although too few relevant data are available regarding the generality of the effects of such comprehensive *in vivo* treatment approaches, it is probable that generalization will be maximized when it is so clearly programmed. As Brown (1982) suggested, it may well be time to pack up our cameras and begin to make the real world our training ground.

Summary

Although the relationship between social competence and psychiatric disorder has been known for quite some time, researchers have only recently begun to study the effect of social skills training on schizophrenic patients. In general, the studies that have been done have clearly demonstrated, on laboratory-based assessment tasks, the effectiveness of social skills procedures in improving specific behavioral components of social skill as well as more global measures of social skill.

When measuring the durability and generalization of behavior change, the results have been mixed. Most studies do not demonstrate a long-term maintenance of behavior change, nor have most studies adequately demonstrated the generalization of treatment effects. Several suggestions were offered for enhancing the generalization and/or the durability of behavior change. These include the development of a more empirically based training content; a possible expansion of the behaviors to be taught; movement toward a theoretically and practically more integrative approach; the control of medication; more extensive train-

ing; more systematic use of homework assignments; and more *in vivo* skills training.

Although the treatment results obtained to date have been promising, the poor generalization of treatment effects and the absence of long-term follow-up data reflect the state of an area that is still in its infancy. We need to identify and integrate more of the relevant theoretical and practical variables before we embark on future treatment-outcome work. Indeed, only then can we expect clinically meaningful results that can be predictably obtained with this most challenging group of patients.

General Summary and Conclusions

In the introduction to this chapter, the gravity of the problem of schizophrenia was stressed. A brief review of the definitional problems revolving around schizophrenia led to a plea for the use of more objective criteria in defining schizophrenia, such as those endorsed by DSM III. The treatment section of this chapter is divided into three general sections. Two of these sections, the ones on token economies and on social skills training, involve attempts to make major, multiple, and comprehensive changes in the functioning of a schizophrenic patient. The first treatment section is in reality a "catchall" treatment section. Most of the procedures reviewed in this section are operant, although other behavioral procedures, such as desensitization and more cognitive-behavioral approaches, are also reviewed. In most cases, these treatment interventions are aimed at a rather circumscribed aspect of the schizophrenic's functioning. In general, these studies indicate that these procedures can be successfully employed in modifying specific maladaptive behaviors of schizophrenics. These studies are important because they demonstrate that schizophrenic symptomatology can be modified. However, in most cases, there are few data to support treatment maintenance and generalization and whether the treatment results in major changes in the clinical status of the individuals treated.

The section on token economies involves a discussion of some of the problems in establishing a token economy and presents some suggestions for the resolution of these problems. Some of the problems discussed were selecting, defining, and eliciting criterion behavior; developing procedures to handle inappropriate and intolerable behavior; establishing methods of token distribution; balancing the economy; and developing potent "backups." The crucial issue of promoting transfer was discussed, along with staff-related issues and the necessity for data collection. In reviewing the treatment outcome studies on token economies, we feel that many of these problems have not been adequately addressed; consequently, the effectiveness of token intervention programs has been limited. Nevertheless, the outcome studies still generally indicate positive, if limited, results. In those studies where these issues were adequately addressed, significant clinical changes appear to have occurred and to have generalized to the natural environment and to have been maintained. We feel that the major advantage of a token economy is that it provides a structure and motivational system wherein patients learn new skills and coping strategies that are instrumental in their functioning in the natural environment.

Social skills training is a systematic attempt to teach patients behaviors that will increase their social functioning. The training procedures generally include behavioral rehearsal, modeling, reinforcement, prompts, homework assignments, feedback, and instructions. Although most social-skills training programs utilize most of these procedures, there are numerous differences in the treatment protocols described in the literature. Consequently, making comparisons across studies is difficult at best. The evidence from both single-case studies and group-design studies indicates positive treatment effects, as measured by laboratory-based assessment procedures. However, the evidence with respect to the generalization of these behaviors to the natural environment and the maintenance of these positive changes over time is much less consistent. Several suggestions for enhancing generalization and maintenance included developing more empirically based training content; extending target behaviors; including more cognitive procedures; giving more extensive

training; and using more systematic homework and more *in vivo* skills training.

Although it is difficult to summarize the results of behavioral interventions with schizophrenics, some general conclusions can still be made. First, it is clearly possible to produce changes in the circumspect aspects of schizophrenic behavior. Unfortunately, these results often do not maintain or generalize very well, and hence, these changes are often of little clinical significance. Clinically significant changes appear to be found only when comprehensive and systematic procedures, such as token economies and social skills training, are applied in such a manner as to produce generalization and maintenance. These procedures involve teaching schizophrenics instrumental behaviors that will assist them in their functioning in the natural environment. The present status of our treatment of schizophrenia, which resembles a "revolving-door" approach (i.e., short stays, rapid turnover, and resulting high readmission rates), is not acceptable. Evaluations of intensive treatment programs are called for to determine whether they result in improved functioning of the schizophrenic patient.

While behavior therapists have made some strides in developing treatment procedures for use with schizophrenics, we have quite simply not met the challenge fully. Our immediate attention should now focus on the criteria we select to evaluate treatment success. While criteria such as "statistically significant reductions of delusional speech" have served a timely purpose in the development of a behavioral technology for schizophrenic patients, we must now attend to more clinically significant criteria, such as reducing the notoriously high readmission rates, promoting successful deinstitutionalization, and assisting schizophrenic patients to return to truly productive lives.

Before further strides can be made in this treatment area, we must first accept the reality that productive research will be difficult. Collectively, the studies reviewed in this chapter point to the need for comprehensive, long-term treatment programs for schizophrenic patients. Admittedly, this is not an easy task. Nonetheless, we are faced with an important challenge: to further develop treatment procedures for schizophrenic patients, a responsibility that must be accepted if we are to continue to point to the utility of behavioral technology with schizophrenics.

References

Agras, W. Behavior therapy in the management of chronic schizophrenia. *American Journal of Psychiatry*, 1967, *124*, 240–243.

Alford, G. S., & Turner, S. M. Stimulus interference and conditioned inhibition of auditory hallucinations. *Journal of Behavior Therapy and Experimental Psychiatry*, 1976, *7*, 155–160.

Alumbaugh, R. V. Use of behavior modification techniques towards reduction of hallucinating behavior: A case study. *The Psychological Record*, 1971, *21*, 415–417.

American Psychiatric Association, *Diagnostic and statistical manual of mental disorders*, III. Washington, D.C.: Author, 1980.

Anderson, L. R., & Alpert, M. Operant analysis of hallucination frequency in a hospitalized schizophrenic. *Journal of Behavior Therapy and Experimental Psychiatry*, 1974, *5*, 13–18.

Astrachan, B. M., Harrow, M., Adler, D., *et al.* A checklist for the diagnosis of schizophrenia. *British Journal of Psychiatry*, 1972, *121*, 529–539.

Ayllon, T. Intensive treatment of psychotic behavior by stimulus satiation and food reinforcement. *Behaviour Research and Therapy*, 1963, *1*, 53–61.

Ayllon, T., & Azrin, N. H. *The token economy.* New York: Appleton-Century-Crofts, 1968.

Ayllon, T., & Haughton, E. Modification of symptomatic verbal behaviour of mental patients. *Behaviour Research and Therapy*, 1964, *2*, 87–97.

Ayllon, T., & Michael, J. The psychiatric nurse as a behavioral engineer. *Journal of Experimental Analysis of Behavior*. 1959, *2*, 323–334.

Baker, R., Hall, J. N., & Hutchinson, K. A token economy project with chronic schizophrenic patients. *British Journal of Psychiatry*, 1974, *124*, 367–384.

Baker, R., Hall, J. N., Hutchinson, K., & Bridge, G. Symptom changes in chronic schizophrenic patients on a token economy: A controlled experiment. *British Journal of Psychiatry*, 1977, *131*, 381–393.

Bellack, A. S., & Hersen, M. Chronic psychiatric patients: Social skills training. In M. Hersen & A. S. Bellack (Eds.), *Behavior therapy in the psychiatric setting.* Baltimore: Williams & Wilkins, 1978.

Bellack, A. S., Hersen, M., & Turner, S. M. Generalization effects of social skills training with chronic schizophrenics: An experimental analysis *Behaviour Research and Therapy*, 1976, *14*, 391–398.

Brown, M. Maintenance and generalization issues in skills training with chronic schizophrenics. In J. P. Curran & P. M. Monti (Eds.), *Social skills training: A practical handbook for assessment and treatment.* New York: Guilford Press, 1982.

Brown, G. W., Monck, E. M., Carstairs, S. M., & Wing, J. K. Influence of family life on the course of schizophrenic illness. *British Journal of Preventive and Social Medicine*, 1962, *16*, 55–68.

Bucher, B., & Fabricatore, J. Use of patient-administered shock to suppress hallucinations. *Behavior Therapy*, 1970, *1*, 382–385.

Carpenter, W. T., Strauss, J. S., & Bartko, J. J. A flexible system for the identification of schizophrenia: A report from the International Pilot Study of Schizophrenia. *Science*, 1973, *182*, 1275–1278.

Coche, E., & Douglas, A. A. Therapeutic effects of problem-solving training and play-reading groups. *Journal of Clinical Psychology*, 1977, *33*, 820–827.

Coche, E., & Flick, A. Problem-solving training groups for hospitalized psychiatric patients. *The Journal of Psychology*, 1975, *91*, 19–29.

Coleman, J. C. *Abnormal psychology and modern life.* Glenview, Ill.: Scott, Foreman, 1976.

Cooper, J. E., Kendell, R. E., Gurland, B. J., Sharpe, L., Copeland, J. R., & Simon. *Psychiatric diagnosis in New York and London.* London: Oxford University Press, 1972.

Cowden, R. C., & Ford, L. Systematic desensitization of phobic schizophrenia. *American Journal of Psychiatry*, 1962, *119*, 241–245.

Curran, J. P. Social skills: Methodological issues and future directions. In A. S. Bellack & M. Hersen (Eds.), *Research and practice in social skills training.* New York: Plenum Press, 1979.

Davis, J. R., Wallace, C. J., Liberman, R. P., & Finch, B. E. The use of brief isolation to suppress delusional and hallucinatory speech. *Journal of Behavior Therapy and Experimental Psychiatry*, 1976, *7*, 269–275.

Davison, G. C. Appraisal of behavior modification techniques with adults in institutional settings. In C. M. Franks (Ed.), *Behavior therapy: Appraisal and status.* New York: McGraw-Hill, 1969.

D'Zurilla, T. J., & Goldfried, M. R. Problem solving and behavior modification. *Journal of Abnormal Psychology*, 1971, *78*, 107–126.

Eisler, R. M., Miller, P. M., & Hersen, M. Components of assertive behavior. *Journal of Clinical Psychology*, 1973, *29*, 295–299.

Eisler, R. M., Hersen, M., & Miller, P. M. Shaping components of assertive behavior with instructions and feedback. *American Journal of Psychiatry*, 1974, *131*, 1344–1347.

Eisler, R. M., Blanchard, E. B., Fitts, H., & Williams, J. G. Social skill training with and without modeling for schizophrenic and non-psychotic hospitalized psychiatric patients. *Behavior Modification*, 1978, *2*, 147–172.

Ellsworth, J. R. Reinforcement therapy with chronic patients. *Hospital and Community Psychiatry*, 1969, *20*, 238–240.

Endicott, J., Forman, J. B., & Spitzer, R. L. *Diagnosis of schizophrenia: Research criteria.* Paper presented at the 132nd Annual Meeting of the American Psychiatric Association, Chicago, 1979.

Feighner, J. P., Robins, E., Guze, S. B., Woodruff, R. A., Winokur, G., & Muñoz, R. Diagnostic criteria for use in psychiatric research. *Archives of General Psychiatry*, 1972, *26*, 57–63.

Field, G. D., & Test, M. A. Group assertive training for severely disturbed patients. *Journal of Behavior Therapy and Experimental Psychiatry*, 1975, *6*, 129–134.

Finch, B. E., & Wallace, C. J. Successful interpersonal skills training with schizophrenic inpatients. *Journal of Consulting and Clinical Psychology*, 1977, *45*, 885–890.

Fischetti, M., Curran, J. P., & Wessberg, H. Sense of timing: A skill deficit in heterosexual-socially anxious males. *Behavior Modification*, 1977, *1*, 179–194.

Foreyt, J. P., Rockwood, C. E., Davis, J. C., Desvousges, W. H., & Hollingsworth, R. Benefit-cost analysis of a token economy program. *Professional Psychology*, 1975, *6*, 26–33.

Frederiksen, L. W., Jenkins, J. O., Foy, D. W., & Eisler, R. M. Social skills training to modify abusive verbal outbursts in adults. *Journal of Applied Behavior Analysis*, 1976, *9*, 117–127.

Goldsmith, J. B., & McFall, R. M. Development and evaluation of an interpersonal skills training program for psychiatric inpatients. *Journal of Abnormal Psychology*, 1975, *84*, 51–58.

Goldstein, A. P. *Structured learning therapy: Toward a psychotherapy for the poor.* New York: Academic Press, 1973.

Goldstein, A. P., Martens, J., Hubben, J., van Belle, H. H., Schaaf, W., Wiersma, H., & Goedhart, H. The use of modeling to increase independent behaviors. *Behaviour Research and Therapy*, 1973, *11*, 31–42.

Gomes-Schwartz, B. The modification of schizophrenic behavior. *Behavior Modification*, 1979, *3*, 439–468.

Gorham, D. R., Green, L. W., Caldwell, L. R., & Bartlett, E. R. Effect of operant conditioning techniques on chronic schizophrenics. *Psychological Reports*, 1970, *27*, 223–224.

Gripp, R. F., & Magaro, P. A. A token economy program evaluation with untreated control ward comparisons. *Behaviour Research and Therapy*, 1971, *9*, 137–149.

Gunderson, J. G., & Mosher, L. R. The cost of schizophrenia. *American Journal of Psychiatry*, 1975, *132*, 1257–1264.

Gutride, M. E., Goldstein, A. P., & Hunter, G. F. The use of modeling and role-playing to increase social interaction among asocial psychiatric patients. *Journal of Consulting and Clinical Psychology*, 1973, *40*, 408–415.

Haynes, S. N., & Geddy, P. Suppression of psychotic hallucinations through time-out. *Behavior Therapy*, 1973, *4*, 123–127.

Heap, R. F., Boblitt, W. E., Moore, C. H., & Hord, J. G. Behavior-milieu therapy with chronic neuropsychiatric patients. *Journal of Abnormal Psychology*, 1970, *76*, 349–354.

Hersen, M. Modification of skill deficits in psychiatric patients. In A. S. Bellack & M. Hersen (Eds.), *Research and practice in social skills training.* New York: Plenum Press, 1979.

Hersen, M., & Bellack, A. S. A multiple-baseline analysis of social skills training in chronic schizophrenics. *Journal of Applied Behavior Analysis*, 1976, *9*, 239–245. (a)

Hersen, M., & Bellack, A. S. Social skills training for chronic psychiatric patients: Rationale, research findings, and future directions. *Comprehensive Psychiatry*, 1976, *17*, 559–580. (b)

Hersen, M., Turner, S. M., Edelstein, B. A., & Pinkston, S. G. Effects of phenothiazines and social skills training in a withdrawn schizophrenic. *Journal of Clinical Psychology*, 1975, *34*, 588–594.

Hollingsworth, R., & Foreyt, J. P. Community adjustment of released token economy patients. *Journal of Behavior Therapy and Experimental Psychiatry*, 1975, *6*, 271–274.

Inglis, J. *The scientific study of abnormal behavior.* New York: Aldine, 1966.

Isaacs, W., Thomas, J., & Goldiamond, I. Application of operant conditioning to reinstate verbal behavior in psychotics. *Journal of Speech and Hearing Disorders*, 1960, *25*, 8–12.

Jaffe, P. G., & Carlson, P. M. Relative efficacy of modeling and instructions in eliciting social behaviors from chronic psychiatric patients. *Journal of Consulting and Clinical Psychology*, 1976, *44*, 200–207.

Keith, S., Gunderson, J., Reifman, A., Buchsbaum, S., & Mosher, L. R. Special report: Schizophrenia 1976. *Schizophrenic Bulletin*, 1976, *2*, 509–565.

Kendall, P. C., & Hollon, S. D. *Cognitive-behavioral interventions.* New York: Harcourt Brace, Jovanovich, 1979.

Kendell, R. E. Schizophrenia—The disease concept defined. *Trends in Neurosciences*, 1978, July, 24–26.

Kendell, R. E., Brockington, I. F., & Leff, J. P. Prognostic implications of sex alternative definitions of schizophrenia. *Archives of General Psychiatry*, 1979, *35*, 25–31.

Kowalski, P. A., Daley, G. D., & Gripp, R. P. Token economy: Who responds how? *Behaviour Research and Therapy*, 1976, *14*, 372–374.

Kraft, A., Binner, P., & Dickey, R. The community mental health program and the longer stay patient. *Archives of General Psychiatry*, 1967, *16*, 64–70.

Lambley, P. Behavior modification techniques and the treatment of psychosis: A critique of Alumbaugh. *The Psychological Record*, 1973, *23*, 93–97.

Lang, P. J., & Buss, A. H. Psychological deficit in schizophrenia. II: Interference and activation. *Journal of Abnormal Psychology*, 1965, *70*, 77–106.

Leitenberg, H., Agras, W. S., Thompson, L. E., & Wright, D. E. Feedback in behavior modification: An experimental analysis of two phobic cases. *Journal of Applied Behavior Analysis*, 1968, *11*, 131–137.

Liberman, R. P. Behavior modification with chronic mental patients. *Journal of Chronic Diseases*, 1971, *23*, 803–812.

Liberman, R. P., Nuechterlein, K., & Wallace, C. J. Social skills training and the nature of schizophrenia. In J. P. Curran & P. M. Monti (Eds.), *Social skills training: A practical handbook for assessment and treatment.* New York: Guilford Press, 1982.

Liberman, R. P., Teigen, J., Patterson, R., & Baker, V. Reducing delusional speech in chronic paranoid schizophrenics. *Journal of Applied Behavior Analysis*, 1973, *6*, 57–64.

Liberman, R. P., Wallace, C. J., Teigen, J., & Davis, J. Interventions with psychotic behaviors. In K. S. Calhoun, H. E. Adams, & K. M. Mitchell (Eds.), *Innovative treatment methods in psychopathology.* New York: Wiley, 1974.

Liberman, R. P., Lillie, F., Falloon, I., Vaughn, C., Harpin, E., Leff, J., Hutchinson, W., Ryan, P., & Stoute, M. *Social skills training for schizophrenic patients and their families.* Unpublished manuscript, Camarillo, Calif., 1978.

Lindsley, O. R. Operant conditioning methods applied to

research in chronic schizophrenia. *Psychiatric Research Reports*, 1956, *5*, 118–139.

Lindsley, O. R. Characteristics of the behavior of chronic psychotics as revealed by free-operant conditioning methods. Diseases of the Nervous System. *Monograph Supplement*, 1960, *21*, 66–78.

Mahoney, M. *Cognition and behavior modification.* Cambridge, Mass.: Ballinger, 1974.

Maley, R. F., Feldman, C. L., & Ruskin, R. S. Evaluation of patient improvement in a token economy treatment program. *Journal of Abnormal Psychology*, 1973, *82*, 141–144.

Margolis, R., & Shemberg, K. Cognitive self-instruction in process and reactive schizophrenics: A failure to replicate. *Behavior Therapy*, 1976, *7*, 668–671.

Matson, J. L., & Stephens, R. M. Increasing appropriate behavior of explosive chronic psychiatric patients with a social skills training package. *Behavior Modification*, 1978, *2*, 61–77.

May, P. R. A. *Treatment of schizophrenia.* New York: Science House, 1968.

Meichenbaum, D. The effects of instructions and reinforcement on thinking and language behavior of schizophrenics. *Behaviour Research and Therapy*, 1969, *7*, 101–114.

Meichenbaum, D. H., & Cameron, R. Training schizophrenics to talk to themselves: A means of developing attentional controls. *Behavior Therapy*, 1973, *4*, 515–534.

Meyers, A., Mercatoris, M., & Sirota, A. Case study: Use of covert self-instruction for the elimination of psychotic speech. *Journal of Consulting and Clinical Psychology*, 1976, *44*, 480–482.

Monti, P. M., Fink, E., Norman, W., Curran, J. P., Hayes, S., & Caldwell, H. Effect of social skills training groups and social skills bibliotherapy with psychiatric patients. *Journal of Consulting and Clinical Psychology*, 1979, *47*, 189–191.

Monti, P. M., Curran, J. P., Corriveau, D. P., DeLancey, A. L., & Hagerman, S. The effects of social skills training groups and social skills bibliotherapy with psychiatric patients. *Journal of Consulting and Clinical Psychology*, 1980, *48*, 241–248.

Monti, P. M., Corriveau, D. P., & Curran, J. P. Social skills training for psychiatric patients: Treatment and outcome. In J. P. Curran & P. M. Monti (Eds.), *Social skills training: A practical handbook for assessment and treatment.* New York: Guilford Press, 1982.

Mosher, L. R., & Keith, S. J. Research on the psychosocial treatment of schizophrenia: A summary report. *The American Journal of Psychiatry*, 1979, *136*, 623–631.

Mosher, L. R., Govera, L., & Menn, A. The treatment of schizophrenia as a developmental crisis. *American Journal of Orthopsychiatry*, 1972, *42*, 320.

Nydegger, R. U. The elimination of hallucinatory and delusional behavior by verbal conditioning and assertive training: A case study. *Journal of Behavior Therapy and Experimental Psychiatry*, 1972, *3*, 225–227.

Olson, R. P., & Greenberg, D. J. Effects of contingency contracting and decision-making groups with chronic mental patients. *Journal of Consulting and Clinical Psychology*, 1972, *38*, 376–383.

Patterson, R. L., & Teigen, J. R. Conditioning and post-hospital generalization of non-delusional responses in a chronic psychotic patient. *Journal of Applied Behavior Analysis*, 1973, *6*, 65–70.

Paul, G. L. Chronic mental patient: Current status-future directions. *Psychological Bulletin*, 1969, *71*, 81–94.

Paul, G. L., & Lentz, R. J. *Psychosocial treatment of chronic mental patients: milieu vs. social learning programs.* Cambridge: Harvard University Press, 1977.

Paul, G. L., Tobias, L. L., & Holly, B. L. Maintenance psychotropic drugs in the presence of active treatment programs: A "triple-blind" withdrawal study with long-term mental patients. *Archives of General Psychiatry*, 1972, *27*, 106–115.

Payne, R. W. The measurement and significance of overinclusive thinking and retardation in schizophrenic patients. In P. H. Hock & J. Zubin (Eds.), *Psychopathology of schizophrenia.* New York: Grune & Stratton, 1966.

Presly, A. S., Black, D., Gray, A., Hartie, A., & Seymour, E. The token economy in the national health service: Possibilities and limitations. *Acta Psychiatrica Scandinavica*, 1976, *53*, 258–270.

Rickard, H. C., & Dinoff, M. A follow-up note on "Verbal manipulation in a psychotherapeutic relationship." *Psychological Reports*, 1962, *11*, 506.

Rickard, H. C., Digman, P. J., & Horner, R. F. Verbal manipulation in a psychotherapeutic relationship. *Journal of Clinical Psychology*, 1960, *16*, 364–367.

Rieder, R. O. The origins of our confusion about schizophrenia. *Psychiatry*, 1974, *37*, 197–208.

Royer, F. L., Flynn, W. F., & Osadca, B. S. Case history: Aversion therapy for fire setting by a deteriorated schizophrenic. *Behavior Therapy*, 1971, *2*, 229–232.

Rutner, I. T., & Bugle, C. An experimental procedure for the modification of psychotic behavior. *Journal of Consulting and Clinical Psychology*, 1969, *33*, 651–653.

Schaefer, H. H., & Martin, P. L. Behavior therapy for apathy of hospitalized schizophrenics. *Psychological Reports*, 1966, *19*, 1147–1158.

Serber, M., & Nelson, P. The ineffectiveness of systematic desensitization and assertive training in hospitalized schizophrenics. *Journal of Behavior Therapy and Experimental Psychiatry*, 1971, *2*, 107–109.

Shean, G. D., & Zeidberg, Z. Token reinforcement therapy: A comparison of matched groups. *Journal of Behavior Therapy and Experimental Psychiatry*, 1971, *2*, 95–105.

Shepherd, G. Social skills training: The generalization problem—Some further data. *Behaviour Research and Therapy*, 1978, *16*, 287–288.

Sherman, J. A. Use of reinforcement and imitation to reinstate verbal behavior in mute psychotics. *Journal of Abnormal Psychology*, 1965, *70*, 155–164.

Siegel, J., & Spivack, G. Problem-solving therapy: The description of a new program for chronic psychiatric patients. *Psychotherapy: Theory, Research, and Practice*, 1976, *10*, 368–373.

Slade, P. D. The effects of systematic desensitization on auditory hallucinations. *Behaviour Research and Therapy*, 1972, *10*, 85–91.

Slade, P. D. The psychological investigation and treatment of auditory hallucinations: A second case report. *British Journal of Medical Psychology*, 1973, *46*, 293–296.

Spitzer, R. L., Endicott, J., & Robins, E. *Research diagnostic criteria (RDC) for a selected group of functional disorders*. New York: Biometric Research, 1978.

Stahl, J. R., & Leitenberg, H. Behavioral treatment of the chronic mental hospital patient. In H. Leitenberg (Ed.), *Handbook of behavior modification and behavior therapy*. Englewood Cliffs, N.J.: Prentice-Hall, 1976.

Stein, L. I., & Test, M. A. *Alternatives to mental hospital treatment*. New York: Plenum Press, 1978.

Stoffelmayr, B. E., Faulkner, G. E., & Mitchell, W. S. *The rehabilitation of chronic hospitalized patients—A comparative study of operant conditioning methods and social therapy techniques*. Edinburgh: Scottish Home and Health Department, 1973.

Stokes, T. F., & Baer, D. M. An implicit technology of generalization. *Journal of Applied Behavior Analysis*, 1977, *10*, 349–367.

Strauss, J. S., & Carpenter, W. T. The prediction of outcome in schizophrenia. I: Characteristics of outcome. *Archives of General Psychiatry*, 1972, *27*, 739–746.

Strauss, J. S., & Carpenter, W. T. The prediction of outcome in schizophrenia. II: The relationship between prediction and outcome variables. *Archives of General Psychiatry*, 1974, *31*, 39–42.

Szasz, T. S. *The myth of mental illness—Foundations of a theory of personal conduct*. New York: Dell, 1961.

Szasz, T. S. *Schizophrenia*. New York: Basic Books, 1976.

Szasz, T. S. Schizophrenia—A category error. *Trends in Neurosciences*, July 1978, 26–28.

Thomson, N., Fraser, D., & McDougall, A. The reinstatement of speech in near-mute chronic schizophrenics by instructions, imitative prompts and reinforcements. *Journal of Behavior Therapy and Experimental Psychiatry*, 1974, *5*, 83–89.

Trower, P. Situational analysis of the components and processes of behavior of socially skilled and unskilled patients. *Journal of Consulting and Clinical Psychology*, 1980, *48*, 327–339.

Trower, P., Bryant, B., & Argyle, M. *Social skills and mental health*. Pittsburgh: University of Pittsburgh Press, 1978.

Tuma, A. H. Treatment of schizophrenia, an historical perspective. In P. R. A. May (Ed.), *Treatment of schizophrenia*. New York: Science House, 1968.

Ullman, L. P. *Institution and outcome: A comparative study of psychiatric hospitals*. New York: Pergamon Press, 1967.

Vaughn, C. E., & Leff, J. P. The influence of family and social factors on the course of psychiatric illness. A comparison of schizophrenic and depressed neurotic patients. *British Journal of Psychiatry*, 1976, *159*, 125–137.

Wallace, C. J. *The assessment of interpersonal problem solving skills with chronic schizophrenics*. Paper presented at the Annual Meeting of the American Psychological Association, New York, Sept. 1978.

Wallace, C. J. The social skills training project of the Mental Health Clinical Research Center for the Study of Schizophrenia. In J. P. Curran & P. M. Monti (Eds.), *Social skills training: A practical handbook for assessment and treatment*. New York: Guilford Press, 1982.

Wallace, C. J., Nelson, C., Lukoff, D., Webster, C.,

Rappe, S., & Ferris, C. *Cognitive skills training*. Paper presented at the Annual Meeting of the Association for the Advancement of Behavior Therapy, Chicago, Nov. 1978.

Wallace, C. J., Nelson, C. J., Liberman, R. P., Aitchison, R. A., Lukoff, D., Elder, J. P., & Ferris, C. A review and critique of social skills training with schizophrenic patients. *Schizophrenia Bulletin*, 1980, *6*, 42–64.

Weidner, F. In vivo desensitization of a paranoid schizophrenic. *Journal of Behavior Therapy and Experimental Psychiatry*, 1970, *1*, 79–81.

Weingaertner, A. H. Self-administered aversive stimulation with hallucinating hospitalized schizophrenics. *Journal of Consulting and Clinical Psychology*, 1971, *36*, 422–429.

Weinman, B., Gelbart, P., Wallace, M., & Post, M. Inducing assertive behavior in chronic schizophrenics: A comparison of socioenvironmental, desensitization, and relaxation therapies. *Journal of Consulting and Clinical Psychology*, 1972, *39*, 246–252.

WHO (World Health Organization). *International Pilot Study Of Schizophrenia*, Vol. 1. Geneva: World Health Organization, 1973.

Wilkins, W. Desensitization: Social and cognitive factors underlying the effectiveness of Wolpe's procedure. *Psychological Bulletin*, 1971, *76*, 311–317.

Williams, M. T., Turner, S. M., Watts, J. G., Bellack, A. S., & Hersen, M. Group social skills training for chronic psychiatric patients. *European Journal of Behavioral Analysis and Modification*, 1977, *1*, 223–229.

Wilson, F. S., & Walters, R. H. Modification of speech output of near mute schizophrenics through social learning procedures. *Behaviour Research and Therapy*, 1966, *4*, 59–67.

Wincze, J. P., Leitenberg, H., & Agras, W. S. The effects of token reinforcement and feedback on the delusional verbal behavior of chronic paranoid schizophrenics. *Journal of Applied Behavior Analysis*, 1972, *5*, 247–262.

Wing, J. K. *Schizophrenia: Towards a new synthesis*. London: Academic Press, 1978.

Wing, J. K., Cooper, J. E., & Sartorius, N. *The description and classification of psychiatric symptoms: An instruction manual for the PSE and CATEGO system*. London: Cambridge University Press, 1974.

Wolff, R. The systematic application of the satiation procedure to delusional verbiage. *Psychological Record*, 1971, *21*, 459–463.

Wolpe, J. *Psychotherapy by reciprocal inhibition*. Johannesburg: Witwatersrand University Press, 1958.

Wolpe, J. The systematic desensitization treatment of neurosis. *Journal of Nervous and Mental Disease*, 1961, *132*, 189–203.

Wood, D. D., Barrios, B. A., & Cohn, N. B. *Generalization effects of a cognitive rule in social skills training with hospitalized chronic schizophrenics*. Paper presented at the Annual Convention of the Association for the Advancement of Behavior Therapy, San Francisco, 1979.

Zeisset, R. M. Desensitization and relaxation in the modification of psychiatric patients' interview behavior. *Journal of Abnormal Psychology*, 1968, *73*, 18–24.

Zigler, E., & Phillips, L. Social effectiveness and symptomatic behaviors. *Journal of Abnormal and Social Psychology*, 1960, *61*, 231–238.

Zigler, E., & Phillips, L. Psychiatric diagnosis: A critique. *Journal of Abnormal and Social Psychology*, 1961, *63*, 607–618. (a)

Zigler, E., & Phillips, L. Psychiatric diagnosis and symptomatology. *Journal of Abnormal and Social Psychology*, 1961, *63*, 69–75. (b)

Zigler, E., & Phillips, L. Social competence and outcome in psychiatric disorders. *Journal of Abnormal and Social Psychology*, 1961, *63*, 264–271. (c)

Zigler, E., & Phillips, L. Social competence and the process-reactive distinction in psychopathology. *Journal of Abnormal and Social Psychology*, 1962, *65*, 215–222.

Zubin, J. Classification of the behavior disorders. *Annual Review of Psychology*, 1967, *18*, 373–406.

CHAPTER 16

Adult Medical Disorders

C. Barr Taylor

Introduction

Identification of Problem or Topic

Behavior, at long last, may be taking its proper place in Western medicine. The study of behavior in medicine has even spawned a new discipline, sometimes called *behavioral medicine*. In the broadest sense, *behavioral medicine* refers to the application of behavioral science knowledge and techniques to the understanding of physical health and illness and to prevention, diagnosis, treatment, and rehabilitation. In this chapter, we discuss behavioral medicine only in terms of the application of behavioral therapy and applied analysis to these same areas. An astonishing number of studies have been published in this area, mostly in the past 10 years, and the numbers are increasing exponentially.

Most of the behavior therapy techniques used in behavioral medicine are the same as those used to treat other problems: progressive muscle relaxation, systematic desensitization, positive reinforcement, and feedback, for example, have all been used extensively to treat medical problems. The methodologies for evaluating such techniques are also similar in behavioral medicine to those in behavior therapy; for example, single-case subject designs, direct measures of behaviors, and reversals have all been applied to medical problems.

But behavioral medicine differs from other areas of behavioral therapy because of its close connection with medicine, borrowing heavily from the knowledge of physiology, biochemistry, pathophysiology, pharmacology, epidemiology, and prevention to determine both the focus and the outcome of interventions. For instance, behavior therapy techniques designed to reduce dietary cholesterol intake do so because of the epidemiological data showing a correlation between serum cholesterol and increased risk for heart disease; biofeedback was derived in part from techniques and instruments developed by physiologists.

Although behavioral medicine relies on medicine, the relationship between them is an interactive one: behavioral techniques, which can be characterized in part by their specificity of measuring behavior, enhance medical methodology, technique, and science. For instance, few pharmacological studies measure a patient's direct drug use; they may monitor drug metabolites appearing in the urine or obtain a self-report of drug use, but both are indirect measures of actual use. A recent behavioral medicine paper described a technique for substantiating a subject's daily drug use, which

C. Barr Taylor • Department of Psychiatry, Stanford University Medical Center, Stanford, CA 94305.

could be used as a direct measure (Epstein & Masek, 1978). Or behavioral research, by examining classes of behavior, may show the important and otherwise unobserved impact of drugs on behavior. For instance, by monitoring a class of behaviors for five retarded adults, both on and off chlorpromazine, Marholin, Touchette, and Malcolm (1979) demonstrated that some desirable behaviors, such as eye contact, time out of bed, and proximity to others, increased when the subjects were taken off medication. Physicians frequently prescribe drugs for one problem and note the side effects on the physiological systems, but rarely note behavioral changes that may be critical, as in the case of the study reported above.

As a final example, behavioral medicine techniques may uncover close connections between behavior and morbidity. For instance, investigators have explored how eating behaviors relate to obesity (Adams, Ferguson, Stunkard, & Agras, 1978) or how Type A behavior relates to atherogenesis (Blumenthal, Williams, Wong, Schanberg, & Thompson, 1978).

Contemporary Importance

The preceding examples of interactions between behavioral medicine and branches of medicine indicate the mutual interaction that has already occurred between these two fields and suggest the clear importance of behavioral medicine to medicine in general. Because of the close connection between behavioral medicine and medicine, it is reasonable to assume that behavioral medicine researchers and practitioners will continue to make broad contributions to medicine. Thus, one important feature of behavioral medicine is that it focuses on the relationship between behavior and the development of health and disease and demands specific measurements to facilitate such discoveries. But behavioral medicine is important in other ways: (1) behavioral medicine has provided specific treatments for certain medical problems; and (2) it has potential for improving general patient care and healthy lifestyles.

Overview of the Chapter

In this chapter, we review the application of various behavior techniques to treat illnesses, to enhance health care, and to reduce disability. We then summarize the usefulness of the two techniques (relaxation and biofeedback) that have been most extensively studied in this literature. Before reviewing the application of behavioral medicine techniques, it is important to review the historical roots of behavioral medicine and to discuss some overall problems that affect the field.

Historical Perspective

Because behavioral medicine is an interface discipline, relating behavioral science to medicine, its history embodies many trends. Three disciplines are particularly important: the history of patient care, psychosomatic medicine, and behavioral approaches to medical problems.

Patient Care

Patient care involves two important aspects: how patients are cared for and who cares for them. As Benjamin Rush, one of the fathers of American medicine, noted, patients can be "cured" through four processes: first, from their own natural recuperative properties; second, from medicines and allied procedures; third, through surgery; and fourth, through nonspecific factors (Binger, 1966). The history of medical "cures" in this century is largely that of the second and third types. The advancement of technology in medicine and surgery has been nothing less than spectacular; many diseases previously fatal are now curable. But how well patients recover because of their own "natural properties" may, if anything, have taken a setback (Illich, 1976), and nonspecific factors continue to be viewed by physicians as a nuisance rather than a benefit (Goodwin, Goodwin, & Vogel, 1979).

Historically, technological medication has placed the care of sick individuals firmly in the hands of physicians. As a result, preventive care for adults has not achieved great importance in the health care system, and preventive practices for adults, except as they are prescribed by physicians, have not achieved widespread use. Physicians have come to expect large changes from their interventions, to recognize illness, and to consider clinical but not statistical significance. These attitudes reflect treatment practice. For instance, few physicians would bother prescribing a medication to reduce blood pressure by 2 mm. For a particular individual, a reduction of 2 mm of blood pressure may not be clinically significant, but for a society, 2 mm may mean a significant reduction in morbidity and mortality. Achieving the 2-mm change in a population requires attention to everybody's habits as they relate to blood pressure. Thus, statistical significance may be more important for the wellness of society than clinical significance, and behavioral approaches may be particularly important in facilitating these changes.

This ownership of who treats disease and the great financial benefits that accrue from it necessarily create conflicts of role and identity and reimbursement between medical and so-called nonmedical practitioners. Many major insurance carriers do not pay for "health education" or even many behavioral medicine procedures (e.g., Medicare will not reimburse for biofeedback). As more nonmedical practitioners enter the medical field, we can expect such conflicts and issues to be heightened.

Psychosomatic Medicine

The second field directly related to behavioral medicine is psychosomatic medicine. In part, psychosomatic medicine has arisen in the last 50 years as an attempt to care for the whole patient, who has been lost in an increasingly mechanistic and technological medical system. As Lipowski noted (1977), developments in psychosomatic medicine since its beginning in the 1920s have followed two major directions: first, attempts to identify specific psychological variables postulated to underlie specific somatic disorders; and second, attempts by experiment or epidemiological study to discover correlations between social stimulus situations, a subject's psychological and physiological responses, and/or changes in health status. The first approach was largely directed by Franz Alexander, a psychoanalyst, who studied asthma, hypertension, peptic ulcer disease, ulcerative colitis, rheumatoid arthritis, hyperthyroidism, and headaches in particular (Alexander, French, & Pollock, 1968). Such disorders were viewed as symptoms of underlying intrapsychic conflicts and as being connected with certain personality types. But, as noted in several recent reviews, attempts to demonstrate that certain personalities correlate with specific disease states or that the procedures generated by these psychosomatic theoreticians and practices are effective in bringing about change has been disappointing (Weiner, 1977). No psychosomatic therapy has been demonstrated as having a specific effect on preventing or improving the outcome of any particular disease in carefully controlled group outcome studies. For instance, while some patients may exhibit reduced blood pressure in the course of psychotherapy, it has not been demonstrated that the psychotherapy *per se* brings about the reductions in blood pressure. Because of this lack of success and probably because psychosomatic theory has tended to be too abstruse for most general practitioners, it has not achieved a widespread impact in changing medical care or in influencing the practice of medicine. Nevertheless, behavioral medicine researchers continue to focus on many of the same diseases identified by early psychosomatic practitioners.

The second trend in psychosomatic medicine focused on the scientific study of the relationships among sociological, social, and biological factors in determining health and disease. Wolff and Goodell (1968) undertook many classic studies relating biological and interpersonal factors, and many of the studies are close in design to those now undertaken by behavioral medicine researchers.

Behavioral Medicine

Behavioral medicine as a discipline has a short history. A few early studies relevant to behavioral medicine can be found scattered throughout the medical literature. For example, Ferster, Nurnberger, & Levitt (1962) outlined many of the eating behaviors that would subsequently become the focus of behavioral interventions aimed at changing eating patterns; Yates (1958) used massed practice to treat tics; Raymond (1964) used aversive conditioning to change smoking behavior in a young boy; Jacobson, in the 1920s, used relaxation to effect change; and the 1960s provided EMG feedback for polio victims to restore muscle strength. The first collection of articles (focusing mostly on biofeedback) appeared only in 1973 (Birk, 1973). In 1975, when Katz and Zlutnick prepared a collection of behavioral medicine articles, they noted that although examples could be found in behavior therapy of interventions applicable to many medical disorders, the literature was neither broad nor deep. Since Katz and Zlutnick's (1975) publication, the field has exploded. Already three journals are devoted to behavioral medicine (*The Journal of Behavioral Medicine* and *Behavioral Medicine Update*), and one is in its second year, *Behavioral Medicine Abstracts*. There are now eight textbooks published or in preparation. Behavioral medicine articles appear throughout the behavioral medicine literature and throughout the medical literature as well. The field even has a society, the Society for Behavioral Medicine, which, in its first year, accepted 800 members, and an Academy of Behavioral Medicine devoted to the more scientific aspects of behavioral medicine. The direction and importance of the behavioral medicine explosion are yet to be determined. Because of the clear usefulness of behavioral approaches to medical practice, it is more curious why this explosion was so slow in coming rather than that it occurred at all.

Possible Adoption and Disillusionment

Unfortunately, behavioral medicine has grown so rapidly that already behavioral techniques have been "oversold" and greater promises made than the procedures can actually accomplish. A model of adaptation of new drugs described by Goodman (1966) is relevant to the practice and dispersal of behavioral techniques. According to Goodman, when a new drug is introduced, it tends to be widely used. As side effects are observed, as some people fail to improve with the medication, or as the drug does not seem to be clearly superior to those already on the market, the drug may then be underutilized relative to its true effect. Eventually, perhaps over a period of years, the drug assumes a position more appropriate to its worth, assuming the usual promotional techniques by drug companies.

Behavioral procedures may follow the same course of early adoption, disillusionment (which has already occurred with weight programs), and then a more appropriate use. Here the analogy ends. Behavioral therapies become popular and are included in practice without the extensive animal and biochemical preparation that often precedes the development of a new drug. Furthermore, federal requirements are such that drugs must not only undergo such early animal and biological testing but must also be demonstrated to be harmless and efficacious in carefully controlled studies. Often, once a drug has been demonstrated to be potent and harmless (relative to the merits of its use), it is then tried on large populations over extensive periods before it becomes generally available to the public. Also, even if a drug is available to the public, it may be withdrawn if these trials fail to show that it is particularly efficacious.

There is no analogous testing of behavioral procedures, although a few techniques have undergone carefully controlled studies to determine their worth. Furthermore, a behavioral technique, unlike a drug, may fail not so much because of its biopotency, but because of insufficient attention to maintenance of the technique or incorrect application of the technique in the first place. Unfortunately, no procedures have been developed to monitor the usefulness of behavioral techniques or to establish any kind of quality control in the realm of practice.

Clinical versus Statistical Significance

The extent of changes in a particular variable achieved by behavioral techniques has been criticized in the medical literature as lacking clinical significance. Such criticism implies that there are clear standards as to when a particular problem needs to be treated.

In fact, in medicine, the decision to treat is often complex, varying from one physician to another and frequently changing. The case of blood pressure illustrates this point. Ten years ago it was not considered appropriate to treat blood pressures under 160/100. However, several large prospective studies proved that even lower blood pressures are associated with reduced morbidity and mortality (e.g., Hypertension Detection and Follow-Up Program Cooperative Group, 1979). Nevertheless, many physicians are reluctant to treat blood pressures below certain levels. Also, physicians are trained to think in a dichotomous fashion (e.g., that blood pressure is either normal or not) rather than in a progressive fashion (e.g., that as blood pressures are distributed on a curve, any reduction may, in fact, be beneficial). This ingrained notion among physicians that biochemical and physiological values are normal or not creates a gap between when and how physicians may use the emerging technology of behavioral medicine. It may be frustrating for nonmedically trained professionals to have treatment techniques that would be clearly useful to patients and not be able to use them because physicians refuse to recommend such treatment.

Side Effects

Behavioral interventions, like medical ones, may have side effects. Although there has been no systematic attempt to determine the side effects of behavioral procedures, the need is indicated by the evidence that some potentially harmful procedures, like rapid smoking, have already achieved extremely wide use. Lichtenstein and Glasgow (1977), for example, estimated that rapid puffing has been practiced by as many as 30,000 smokers. From a conceptual standpoint, the side effects of behavioral procedures, as of pharmacological agents, can occur from the direct effects of a procedure or may simply be associated with the procedure. Direct effects include such things as psychotic episodes occurring during prolonged meditation (which presumably could occur with relaxation) (French, Schmid, & Ingalls, 1976), ST segment changes during rapid puffing (Horan, Hackett, Nicholas, Linberg, Stone, & Lusaki, 1977), conditioning of un-

pleasant feelings about objects other than those intended during aversive conditioning (Raymond, 1964), or the development of undesirable behavior as another behavior is extinguished (Epstein, Doke, Sajwaj, Sorrell, & Rimmer, 1974). Indirect effects are those that occur secondarily to a behavioral procedure. Examples include adverse reactions occurring from an underlying disease or associated treatment of that disease changed by a behavioral approach, for example, relaxation leading to decreased insulin requirements in a diabetic who continues to use the same dosage of insulin; or failure to comply with a medical procedure because the patient prefers a behavioral treatment. For example, a patient stops hypertensive medication because she prefers to practice relaxation (Taylor, 1980). Since behavior techniques have already achieved mass acceptance without frequent problems being reported, we need not be overly alarmed or fearful of their use. However, behavioral researchers and practitioners need to pay more attention to the possible direct and indirect side effects of their procedures.

Current Empirical Status

Cardiovascular Disorders

Behavioral medicine researchers have made significant advances in understanding and treating cardiovascular disorders. Most of the work has focused on hypertension, arrhythmias, Type A behavior, cardiovascular risk reduction, and Raynaud's disease.

Hypertension. Hypertension is a major national health problem, affecting as many as 24 million Americans and leading to increased cardiovascular morbidity and mortality unless controlled (Smith, 1977a). There are many etiologies of hypertension, and some forms can be completely cured by surgery. The mainstay of treatment is, however, pharmacological. Unfortunately, as many as 10% of patients refuse to take medication because of drug intolerance, and many more adhere poorly to medication for this and other reasons (Smith, 1977b). In theory, behavioral techniques would be of value in patients (1) who have essential hypertension but are intolerant to medications or are poorly controlled on medication or (2) who have blood pressure levels not customarily treated by physicians but who might benefit from reduced blood pressure levels. Behavioral techniques might also be useful in all patients as an adjunct to other blood pressure therapies.

Methodological Problems. On the surface, blood pressure would seem to be the perfect measure for a behavioral intervention: easily and noninvasively obtained, it can frequently be sampled with minimal harm to the patient. Unfortunately, blood pressure levels are extremely labile, since they are controlled by a variety of interacting variables like peripheral resistance, blood volume, and cardiac output.

These variables are, in turn, influenced by one another and may in and of themselves be under complex control. For instance, peripheral resistance is controlled by interactions among at least six different hormones! Furthermore, the measurement of blood pressure itself is subject to much error: differences in sphygmomanometer size, the arm radius, the rate of deflation, the hearing acuity of the examiner, the position of the arm, and the stethoscope are all variables that affect the accuracy of a reading. Other noninvasive blood-pressure-measuring devices, like random zero sphygmomanometers (in which the examiner does not know the actual reading of the column until the measurement has been taken) or automatic cuffs that "listen" for the same heart sounds have advantages but are subject to many of the same measurement errors.

Finally, blood pressure levels are subject to a variety of nonspecific influences: instruc-

tions, experimenter demands, placebos, and time of day have all been demonstrated to bring about considerable and sometimes long-lasting effects (Taylor, 1980). Thus, the inter- and intravariations in error in blood pressure measurement make this seemingly perfect measure less so. Furthermore, the extent of change from any treatment is greater the higher the initial blood pressure, so that the results of studies cannot be easily compared unless the initial blood pressures are the same. To overcome the problem, Jacob, Kraemer, and Agras (1977) have calculated a regression line that compares pretreatment systolic pressure with decreases in systolic pressure. An active treatment must produce significantly greater changes than would be predicted by the regression line alone. This procedure allows studies to be compared in terms of pre- and posttreatment (although a similar procedure has not been developed for long-term outcome studies). Kraemer, Jacob, Jeffery, and Agras (1979) have also described the most ideal designs for outcome research on hypertension.

Behavioral Interventions. The vast majority of studies on behavioral approaches to blood pressure have reported the effect of relaxation and related procedures or biofeedback on reducing blood pressure levels. In fact, behavioral approaches besides relaxation and biofeedback are of potential use. In Table 1 we have listed behavioral approaches (on the right), which might affect a physiological event (on the left) that influences blood pressures. For instance, relaxation may reduce peripheral catecholamine level (Davidson, Winchester, Taylor, Alderman, & Ingels, 1979; Stone

Table 1. Possible Mechanisms of Behavioral Intervention Aimed at Blood Pressure Reduction

Blood pressure pathophysiology	Behavioral intervention
Increased cardiac output	Reduced salt intake, pulse-transit time biofeedback, relaxation and related procedures, medication compliance, weight reduction, exercise
Increased fluid volume	Reduced salt intake, medication compliance
Increased vascular reactivity	Relaxation and related techniques
Increased catecholamine excretion and/or elevated renin	Caffeine reduction, relaxation and related techniques

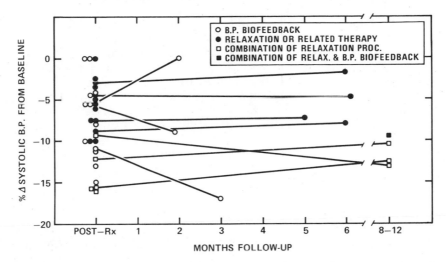

Figure 1. Immediate posttreatment systolic blood pressure changes from baseline in 41 studies using biofeedback, relaxation and related therapy, or combinations of these procedures. The follow-up results are for 11 of these studies. (Adapted from Taylor, 1980.)

& DeLeo, 1976), which may, in turn, reduce blood pressure. Adherence to a low-salt diet reduces blood volume and consequently blood pressure. As a final example, pulse-wave transit time, as measured by the R-wave and a peripheral pulse, may, in fact, reflect changes in cardiac output, which is elevated in some types of hypertension (Obrist, Light, McCubbin, Hutcheson, & Hoffer, 1979). Pulse-wave transit-time feedback may be used to reduce cardiac output. Thus, interventions aimed at increasing compliance with taking blood pressure medication, increasing exercise, and reducing weight and salt intake are relevant to blood pressure control. However, most studies have focused on only a few procedures: relaxation and related techniques, biofeedback, or combinations of these procedures.

Figure 1 shows the percentage of change in systolic blood pressure from baseline for 41 studies in which a behavioral treatment was compared with another treatment (Taylor, 1980). We will discuss each of these treatments independently.

Relaxation and Related Procedures. Many studies have compared relaxation and related procedures in terms of their effects on lowering blood pressure. Relaxation procedures have generally been modeled after Jacobson's (1938) or Wolpe (1958), although Benson's

(1975) relaxation response has also been used. The posttreatment effects of relaxation have generally led to as much as a 10% reduction from baseline in systolic and diastolic blood pressure. Three studies with adequate controls and design have found the initial effects to be maintained at six months. There have been too few studies to make comparisons between procedures; simple relaxation procedures appear as effective as more elaborate ones.

Combination of Relaxation Procedures. Some studies have combined several relaxation procedures to reduce blood pressure. In the first large-scale application of relaxation therapy, Datey, Deshmukh, Dalvi, and Vinekar (1969) used *shavasan,* a yogic exercise in which patients assume a supine position while they practice a slow, rhythmic diaphragmatic breathing to lower blood pressure and at the same time practice relaxing thoughts. This procedure was combined with EMG-assisted biofeedback in the next major study (Patel, 1973). This combination of procedures has brought about the most significant long-term effects and greatest pre–post changes seen in Figure 1. However, these same studies also have the highest mean pretreatment systolic pressure and fall along the same regression line as the studies mentioned in the previous paragraph. Thus, the effects of combinations of procedures are not certain. Such procedures have brought about the greatest and most long-lasting changes, but they have not been compared directly with more simple procedures.

Biofeedback of Blood Pressure. Biofeedback has been used in several imaginative ways to lower blood pressure. Basically, three procedures have been used. The first procedure merely involves measuring the patient's blood pressure with a conventional sphygmomanometer and reporting blood pressure to the subject orally or visually. Unfortunately, this method requires frequent measurement, and the cuff needs to be inflated often and may cause discomfort to the patient. Another approach has been to use a constant cuff. With this procedure, a cuff is inflated to about the subject's average systolic pressure and held constant at that level. Whenever the systolic pressure rises to above the cuff pressure, a Korotkoff's sound is detected on a microphone (Shapiro, Mainardi, & Surwit, 1977). To lower blood pressure, patients are then instructed to eliminate the sounds, which can occur only when the blood pressure is decreased. The third approach is to measure blood pressure indirectly by using blood pressure velocity. Blood pressure velocity can be measured by using two pulses separated in space or by using the ECG R-wave (which represents the presystolic ejection period) and the peripheral pulse (Obrist, *et al.*, 1979). In general, as pulse wave velocity increases, so does blood pressure.

Blood pressure biofeedback using any of these mechanisms has not been demonstrated to be any more effective than relaxation at six months, and in some cases, it has been demonstrated to be less effective than relaxation. However, as can be seen in Figure 1, two studies have reported significant decreases in blood pressure from posttreatment to three and four months. In the three-month follow-up study, Kristt and Engel (1975) taught patients to control their blood pressure outside the clinical setting. This generalization training may be the crucial variable in producing long-term change.

Summary. The studies thus far reported in the behavioral medicine literature suggest that behavioral interventions, particularly relaxation and related techniques, may be of value

in the areas we mentioned in the beginning of this section, that is, in patients (1) who are intolerant to medications and are poorly controlled on medication and (2) who have blood pressures at levels not customarily treated by physicians but who might benefit from reduced blood pressure levels. Behavioral techniques might also be useful in all patients as an adjunct to other therapies.

Cardiac Arrhythmias. The treatment of cardiac arrhythmias has been widely studied in behavioral research, although mostly with single-case and single-group outcome studies.

Ectopic Beats. Ectopic beats (called *premature ventricular contractions*, or *PVCs*) represent beats that originate outside the usual conduction system of the heart and interfere with it. PVCs are often harmless but may, especially if they occur frequently, indicate cardiopathology.

Behavioral techniques have been most successful with single ectopic beats. In an early study, Pickering and Miller (1977) trained a 35-year-old male who had PVCs for one year to increase his heart rate. The patient wore a cardiac monitor to give him feedback on his heart rate. After five months of practice, he was able to increase his heart rate by 20–40 beats per minute with or without feedback and was able to suppress his PVCs approximately 50% of the time. By the end of a second training period, which followed five months of practice at home, he was able to suppress his PVCs 100% of the time. (The clinical importance of this study is not clear.) A second patient was unable to maintain a normal sinus rhythm without feedback. In a larger study, Weiss and Engel (1971) studied eight patients. All eight subjects learned some degree of heart-rate control; five were able to control the frequency of PVCs in the laboratory, and four subjects showed decreased PVCs at the time of follow-up visits up to 21 months after training. Benson, Alexander, and Feldman (1975) taught 11 subjects the "relaxation response." A significant reduction in PVCs occurred in 8 of the 11 patients. The absolute decrease was slight (from 2.5 to 2.2 PVCs per minute), but the decrease in 3 of these patients was over 85%.

A series of single-case studies suggests that similar procedures may be useful in reducing the frequency and type of multiple ectopic beats. No controlled-outcome study with multiple PVCs has been reported.

Other Arrhythmias. Behavioral procedures have been used with a variety of other arrhythmias. Biofeedback to reduce heart rate, as well as relaxation and related procedures, has been demonstrated in single cases to reduce the frequency of paroxysmal atrial tachycardia, a condition in which the heart rate periodically accelerates to potentially dangerous levels (Engel & Bleecker, 1974); sinus tachycardia (Scott, Blanchard, Edmundson, & Young, 1973; Engel & Bleecker, 1974), a condition in which heart rates are consistently elevated; and Wolff-Parkinson-White syndrome (Bleecker & Engel, 1973a). In most cases, improvement has been demonstrated. Two clients with chronic atrial fibrillation were able to reduce their ventricular rate during training, but neither client showed any reduction in day-to-day variability (Bleecker & Engel, 1973b). Biofeedback and other psychological therapies have not been found effective in third-degree heart block (Engel & Bleecker, 1974).

Summary. It appears that heart-rate control results in the elimination or reduction of the frequency of PVCs in some patients. The training procedure that appears to be most effective is one that includes sessions in heart-rate deceleration, acceleration, or a combination. The relaxation response has been successfully used to reduce PVCs. Deceleration through biofeedback also appears useful in reducing heart rate in stress-related tachycardia. Behavior interventions seem to be most useful in treating arrhythmias that are not caused by arteriosclerosis; however, interventions that may affect the development of arteriosclerosis are obviously relevant to preventing arrhythmias.

Type A Behavior. The third area of major focus in behavioral approaches to cardiovascular diseases has been with so-called Type A behavior. *Type A behavior* is a term used by Friedman and Rosenman (1974) to characterize the behavior of many patients they were seeing in their clinical cardiology practice. Type A patients suffer from a chronic sense of time urgency, impose unrealistic and frequent deadlines, interrupt, and, in general,

appear aggressive and hostile (Friedman & Rosenman, 1974). Type A patients have demonstrated significantly more coronary morbidity and mortality than patients without these characteristics. Recent studies have also shown that Type As suffer more physiological arousal under stress and have more serious arteriosclerosis in their angiograms (Blumenthal *et al.*, 1978; Dembroski, MacDougall, Shields, Petitto, & Lushene, 1978). However, it is not clear exactly how Type A behavior leads to coronary artery disease. One intriguing suggestion has been made by Henry and Stephens (1977): like dominant mice that show continued sympathetic arousal and are prone to develop cardiovascular disease, Type As exhibit marked catecholamine excretion under stress, whereas subordinate mice exhibit a different physiological profile of stress. They suggest that Type A patients may be under continual sympathetic arousal.

It is not clear if all Type A patients are at risk to develop coronary artery disease or what the critical links may be in humans between the various components of Type A behavior and their physiological properties and cardiovascular illness.

Because of the suggested connection between Type A behavior and cardiovascular illness, interventions have been developed directed at changing the lifestyle of Type A individuals. The procedures that have been used include relaxation, stress management techniques, improvement in interpersonal techniques, and general modification of Type A behaviors (Suinn, 1974). For instance, with stress management techniques, Type A individuals are taught to leave or avoid stressful areas, to improve time management, to change scheduling so that stressful interviews are interspersed with nonstressful ones, to delegate tasks, to refuse to take on overwhelming tasks, to increase the amount of recreation, to learn to rely on others for emotional support, to reduce their rate of speech, eating, and movements, etc.

In one study, a procedure that utilizes these techniques was applied to two groups in a cardiac rehabilitation program (Suinn, 1974). Both groups received the same exercise prescription, physiological stress testing, dietary assistance, and smoking management, but only the stress management group received behavioral training. This group showed significant reductions in serum cholesterol compared with controls (2.6% mg compared with 15.0% mg). In another study, on a paper-and-pencil test (the Jenkins Activity Survey), patients with Type A behavior were taught relaxation techniques to control anxiety (Suinn & Bloom, 1978). The treated group showed trends toward reductions in blood pressure (mean systolic reduction was 14 mm Hg, not significant compared with controls). Several large-scale studies are now under way to determine the impact of these procedures in reducing morbidity and mortality from heart disease in Type A individuals.

Cardiovascular Risk Reduction. The fourth and perhaps major area where behavioral approaches have contributed to the treatment of cardiovascul problems is the provision of techniques to reduce cardiovascular risk factors (Enelow & Henderson, 1975). Large prospective studies have shown that cigarette smoking, weight, blood pressure, and diet are related to cardiovascular morbidity and mortality, and that reducing or eliminating these risks is associated with decreased morbidity and mortality (Blackburn, 1978). Other data suggest that exercise and perhaps stress are also related to cardiovascular risk (Paffenbarger, Hale, Brand, & Hyde, 1977). Thus, interventions directed at smoking cessation and weight reduction are directly related to cardiovascular risk reduction. The effectiveness of such interventions is addressed in another section of this book. Similarly, interventions that encourage salt intake reduction, change in diet from high cholesterol to low cholesterol, increases in fiber in the diet, and exercise are directly important in cardiovascular disease. In another section, we review behavioral approaches to nutrition and exercise.

Raynaud's Disease. Patients with Raynaud's disease suffer from pain in the hands and feet. This disorder is thought to be secondary to extreme vasoconstriction. Two types of biofeedback for peripheral blood flow have been used to treat the disorder: direct training in peripheral vasodilation feedback and hand-warming feedback. Shapiro and Schwartz (1972) reported the only cases in which blood volume feedback has been used. One patient given this feedback improved; a second failed to show improvement. On the other hand, hand-warming feedback proved relatively more successful. Jacobson, Hackett, Surman, and Silverberg (1973), Blanchard and Haynes (1975), and Sunderman and Delk (1978) have all reported success with one client. Taub (1977) reported success in two cases.

May and Weber (1976) reported four case studies of patients with Raynaud's disease and four with Raynaud's phenomenon, caused by scleroderma or lupus. The treatment consisted of sixteen 50-minute temperature-feedback sessions over eight weeks. Five normal controls were also studied. The patients with Raynaud's phenomenon showed the most consistent and most effective control. The subjects with severe symptoms performed better and achieved more symptom reduction than those with mild symptoms, an effect the authors attributed to increased motivation. They commented that "the success of the training depends more on the subject achieving mental contact with his fingers (perhaps easier for a Raynaud's subject since his disease is a sign of a connection, albeit a maladaptive one) and on the motivation of the subject . . . than it depends on the degree of physiological pathology present" (p. 50).

One study compared the hand-warming feedback plus autogenic phrases with autogenic therapy phrases alone (Surwit, Pilon, & Fenton, 1978). Fifteen subjects were randomized to the two treatments. In addition, half of the subjects in each group were trained primarily in the laboratory, while the other half received most of their training at home. The results indicated that the laboratory and the home treatment groups showed equal improvement in their ability to warm their hands and equally significant clinical improvement. However, there were no group differences between subjects receiving hand-warming feedback plus autogenic phrases or autogenic phrases alone. Both groups demonstrated significant gains. Because thermal imagery, suggestion, and self-instruction can lead to vasodilation, the specific usefulness of biofeedback for the disorder remains unproved (Conners, 1980).

Respiratory Disorders

Asthma. Behavioral treatment approaches to respiratory disorders have focused primarily on bronchial asthma. Asthma would seem to be a condition amenable to behavioral interventions because (1) asthma attacks seem to occur during times of emotional stress or are made worse by such stress; (2) bronchial spasms may, in some cases, represent a classically conditioned response; and (3) the management of the illness requires considerable effort on the part of the patient and the family. Studies have been directed at developing interventions appropriate for each of these areas.

Stress Reduction. Many studies using systematic desensitization and relaxation suggest that such procedures produce an immediate effect on improving airway functioning (Alexander, 1972; Alexander, Cropp, & Chai, 1979; Alexander, Micklich, & Hershkoff, 1972). Unfortunately, the extent of these changes has been less than 15%, relative to baseline. Changes not exceeding 30% are required before a therapy appears to produce relief (in most patients).

Anxiety or fears that may alter lung function directly (and remember that sympathetic activity usually results in bronchodilation) are very different from the anxiety or stress that *results* from asthma. Stimuli associated with asthma (e.g., tightness and wheezing) are presumed to have become classically conditioned to trigger fear and anxiety responses (Walton, 1969). Eckert, McHugh, Philander, and Blumenthal (1979) used a desensitization technique to produce anxiety conditioned to increasing expiratory resistance in nine patients. Treatment was significantly more effective in the patients who received desensitization than in those who received relaxation control.

Biofeedback. Biofeedback of respiratory rate and airflow has been used to increase these variables in asthmatics. Vachon and Rich (1976) and Fieldman (1976) used forced-oscillation feedback to increase the respiratory rate in asthmatics, but its clinical usefulness was not evaluated. Khan and his associates (Khan, 1977; Khan & Olson, 1977; Khan, Staerk, & Bonk, 1973, 1974) have undertaken a series of studies to determine the effects of increasing bronchodilation using biofeedback of airflow in asthmatic children. The subjects receive verbal praise from the experimenter contingent on specified increases in airflow. Khan and Olson (1977) found the technique to be effective in reducing the number of asthma attacks, the amount of medication used, and the number of emergency room visits, effects that were maintained at 8- to 10-month follow-up. However, another investigation did not confirm Khan's findings (Danker, Miklich, Prott, & Creer, 1975).

Illness and Management. The third respiratory-illness area where behavioral techniques have been demonstrated to be useful involves problems that result from having asthma and the constant struggle to cope with and adapt to it (Creer, 1978). Disease-related problems include poor medication compliance, maladaptive behaviors, untoward specific emotional reactions, or the development of symptoms (like a cough) that begin to occur autonomously from the asthma itself. There have been many case reports indicating the usefulness of behavioral procedures in reducing these problems. The studies have been focused on children, but the techniques could be used equally with adults.

For example, Rene and Creer (1976) used operant conditioning techniques to teach four asthmatic children to correctly use an intermittent-positive-pressure breathing device. The authors documented that the training procedure significantly reduced the amount of drug required during the subsequent treatments and, furthermore, that the procedure could be used by nurses.

Summary. Behavioral approaches are useful for at least three aspects of asthma. First, relaxation and desensitization and daily relaxation practice invariably lead to statistical improvement in airway function, although the extent of changes may not bring much relief to the patient. The role of biofeedback in improving airway function remains uncertain. Second, behavioral techniques may make important contributions to reducing the anxiety secondary to the patient's asthma. Third, behavioral treatments are useful in reducing behavioral excesses or deficits involved in the ongoing management of the patient's asthma.

Other Disorders. Behavioral medicine has also had an impact on some other aspects of respiratory illness. Since respiratory disease is a major side effect of smoking, behavioral interventions designed to reduce and eliminate smoking behavior have obvious importance to respiratory disease. These interventions are reviewed in another chapter of this handbook.

Gastrointestinal System

Behavioral researchers have paid surprisingly little attention to the treatment of gastrointestinal disorders (excluding obesity and anorexia as gastrointestinal disorders). Gastrointestinal problems caused by stress or anxiety constitute as much as 50% of the disorders seen in gastrointestinal practice, and we would assume that stress reduction interventions would be of some use. In fact, the most extensive work in this area has focused on the control of esophageal and rectal sphincter control and not on more common problems, like irritable bowel and peptic ulcer disease.

Nausea. Persistent nausea without medical cause has received some attention from behavioral researchers. Ingersoll and Curry (1977) used social and activity reinforcers to alter (1) the amount of time food was retained and (2) the type of fluid in the drink of a patient with a persistent amount of vomiting and nausea. The treatment lasted for five days, after which the patient was no longer vomiting. Also, she was not vomiting at one-year follow-up according to her self-report. Alford, Blanchard, and Buckley (1972) used contingent social contact and reduced the tension to eliminate vomiting in a 17-year-old female. There was no report of a recurrence seven months after treatment stopped. In another case, Tasto and Chesney (1977) used emotive imagery to decondition nausea in a 25-year-old engineer. The patient reported no symptoms at the one-year follow-up. These three individual cases suggest that behavioral techniques could be very useful with persistent nausea and vomiting, but they have not been applied to nausea secondary to medications, one of the most common causes of nausea.

Diarrhea and Irritable Bowel. While diarrhea and the irritable bowel syndrome are often caused by different problems, both relate to increased gastric motility and are discussed together here. Diarrhea is often a symptom of irritable bowel syndrome, although abdominal pain with alternating diarrhea and constipation may be the presenting complaint. Stress has been clearly demonstrated to increase gastric motility (Almy & Tulin, 1947). Of the two general behavioral approaches to the irritable bowel syndrome, one is to provide biofeedback to decrease colonic motility; the second is to desensitize or to use relaxation procedures, presumably to reduce the amount of the patient's stress or anxiety. Cohen and Reed (1968) used systematic desensitization to treat two patients with diarrhea, exacerbated when the patients were required to travel. Using freedom of activity and frequency of self-report outcome measures, the patients described modest gains, which remained at 6- and 12-month follow-up. Hedberg (1973) also used systematic desensitization to treat a patient with chronic diarrhea. His patient averaged 10 bowel movements a day. Bowel control was achieved by the eighth session and was maintained at two-month follow-up.

Biofeedback has been used in several different ways. Furman (1973) had patients listen to their bowel sounds monitored with an electronic stethoscope. The patients were taught to increase or decrease their peristaltic activity. The author reported that within five training sessions, all patients showed some degree of control over their intestinal motility and apparently experienced symptomatic improvement. Weinstock (1976), however, had no success with 12 patients trained in this method, although 9 of the 12 later improved using a combination of EMG biofeedback and relaxation. Similarly, Tarler-Benlolo and Love (1977) successfully treated a patient with long-standing spastic colon with the same combination of EMG biofeedback and relaxation.

Another approach to reducing these symptoms has been to provide direct feedback of rectosigmoid distension to patients with irritable bowel syndrome, by using the same techniques that have been developed for biofeedback treatment of fecal incontinence. In a typical system, three balloons are inserted rectally. The uppermost is lodged in the rectosigmoid space. The next balloon is positioned in the internal sphincter, and the third balloon is in the external sphincter. Subjects are instructed both to increase and to decrease distension in the rectosigmoid space and thus gain control over sphincter tone. The procedure was tried with 21 patients (with an average duration of symptoms of seven years) (Bueno-Miranda, Cerulli, & Schuster, 1976). Of the 21 patients, 14 were able to increase distension by 34% and decrease distension by an average of 29%. The same patients were able to continue such suppression eight weeks later. The effects on the functional bowel syndrome were not reported, but the authors have used this procedure with some patients with irritable bowel syndrome and claim some success.

Fecal Incontinence. Biofeedback techniques have been successfully developed for treating fecal incontinence. This has been accomplished with feedback provided by changes in sphincter pressure, also measured with balloons (Engel, Nikoomanesh, & Schuster, 1974). Thus, subjects are able to gain control of their sphincter tone. In one study, 40 patients (6 to 96 years old) were treated with this procedure. Of these patients, 28 responded well as evidenced by the disappearance of incontinence or by a decrease in frequency of incontinence of at least 90%.

Peptic Ulcer Disease. Peptic ulcer disease is one of the most common human ailments. Although peptic activity is the ultimate damaging agent responsible for mucosal ulceration, many other factors influence the development of ulcers. Studies have shown that stress is one factor that contributes to the development of peptic ulcer disease in some patients. In several interesting studies, it has been demonstrated that gastric acid secretion can be altered by means of feedback techniques. For instance, in an early study, Welgan (1974) continuously aspirated gastric secretions and measured the pH. pH feedback and instruction led to significant reductions in acid secretion.

Whitehead, Renault, and Goldiamond (1975) developed an ingenious technique to provide direct feedback of acid secretion. Subjects swallowed a plastic tube that contained a pH detection tube and two other tubes. One tube was used to inject sodium bicarbonate and another drove an electric relay, signaling that the pH had dropped to certain levels. When the pH dropped to this level, sodium bicarbonate was used as the independent measure of gastric acid secretion. Four subjects underwent a design involving baseline, followed by instructions to increase gastric secretion, and then instructions to decrease acid secretion. During the increase or decrease secretion periods, the subjects were given visual feedback of their gastric acid secretion as determined from the sodium bicarbonate intake. Two subjects were able both to increase and to decrease gastric acid secretion, one subject was able to increase only, and one subject showed no changes in either condition. The authors suggested that the latter subject had been conditioned to gastric emptying rather than pH change. These two studies offer exciting directions for the possibility of operant conditioning of gastric acid secretion.

Pain Syndromes

Pain is one of the most common human experiences: at any one time, 10% of the population may, for instance, suffer from headache. In this section, we review the behavioral approaches to three important pain problems: chronic pain, migraine headaches, and tension headaches.

Chronic Pain. A few patients with acute pain eventually develop chronic pain, defined as pain of at least six months' continuous duration, with no organic base to explain its origin. Often these patients suffer from polysurgery, polymedication, and polyaddiction. There has been much speculation as to how an acute pain can develop into a chronic pain. Fordyce (1976), a pioneer in the development of treatment approaches to chronic pain, assumes that some patients develop chronic pain as a result of being reinforced for pain behavior in their environments. He differentiates between respondent pain, which represents a classically conditioned response to a particular stimulus, and operant pain, which results from reinforced pain behavior. Fordyce's program is significant in providing a comprehensive treatment approach that has now been applied to thousands of patients in many different settings.

Fordyce begins his treatment approach with a complete evaluation of the patient. The evaluation is designed to identify the relationship between the patient's behavior and the environmental events or consequences resulting from this behavior. Fordyce analyzes the time pattern of the pain, the environmental events that increase or diminish the pain, the effect of tension and relaxation on the pain, and the changes in activity level as a result of the pain. Patients who seem amenable to a behavioral program are then accepted into an inpatient program. The goals of the program are to reduce pain behavior, to increase activity, to retrain the family to provide appropriate environmental contingencies, to reduce excessive health-care utilization, and to establish and maintain well behavior. Patients addicted or habituated to medication are slowly withdrawn by means of a pain cocktail containing the patient's baseline medications mixed with a color- and taste-masking vehicle. The cocktail is first administered as needed. Then the active ingredients are slowly faded, and the cocktail is finally terminated when the active ingredients reach zero. To increase activity, subjects are given a selection of easily monitored exercises relevant to posttreatment activities. Patients work to quotas determined by previously achieved levels of exercise and the symptoms that may occur from excessive exercise. Quotas and the success in achieving these quotas are graphed, and verbal praise is given for achieving quotas. Patients may also be given vocation and career counseling as appropriate to increase general levels of activity.

Several studies have reported the effects of inpatient programs modeled after Fordyce's. Unfortunately, the outcome measures have varied so widely between these programs (the methodology has been fairly inadequate, and no controls were employed in any study) that it is hard to determine the effects of these various programs (Anderson, Cole, Gullickson, Hudgens, & Roberts, 1979; Cairns, Thomas, Mooney, & Pace, 1976; Fordyce, Fowler, Lehmann, DeLateur, Sand, & Trieschmann, 1973; Newman, Seres, Yospe, & Garlington, 1978; Sternbach, 1974; Swanson, Floreen, & Swenson, 1976). In general, inpatient programs have led to significant pre- and posttreatment reductions in chronic pain complaint and medication use, as well as significant increases in activity. Follow-up results of six

months and longer have indicated that the increases in activity are maintained, that the disability claims have decreased, that employment has increased, and that the pain has usually decreased or increased slightly but has not returned to preadmission levels. Medication reduction is also maintained at follow-up. These studies are tantalizing but inconclusive. It is not clear, for instance, which components of the multicomponent programs that have evolved are necessary for treating patients or even if these programs could be successfully carried out in an outpatient setting.

Headache. Headaches account for much human suffering. At any one time, 10% of the adult population may be affected by headaches (Ogden, 1952). The two most common headache complaints are migraine and tension headaches. Although we discuss these two entities separately, the distinction between these two types of headaches is often unclear; in practice, patients often report symptoms compatible with both types of headache.

Migraine Headaches. Migraine headache is a vascular condition characterized by episodic and severe pain, usually occurring on one side of the head. Four behavioral treatments have been evaluated extensively: skin temperature biofeedback, cephalic vasomotor feedback, relaxation, and combinations (particularly of skin temperature and relaxation).

Skin Temperature Biofeedback. With skin temperature biofeedback, skin temperature is monitored at a peripheral site, such as an index finger, and the subjects receive continuous feedback of change in their finger temperature. The goal is to produce vasodilation at the local site and to redirect the blood flow from the cephalic beds, reducing blood volume in the temple arteries. The results of several studies have shown that skin temperature feedback generally leads to headache symptom reduction (Mullinix, Norton, Hack, & Fishman, 1978; Reading & Mohr, 1976; Sargent, Walters, & Green, 1973; Turin & Johnson, 1976; Wickramasekera, 1973b).

Other authors have combined hand warming with other procedures like psychotherapy (Adler & Adler, 1976), frontalis EMG (Medina, Diamond, & Franklin, 1976), and autogenic instructions (Mitch, McGrady, & Iannone, 1976).

Few studies have used control groups, but

a few clever strategies have been used to control for nonspecific factors. In one strategy, Turin and Johnson (1976) included an irrelevant feedback condition prior to the introduction of hand-warming feedback. The migraine clients first received training in reducing their hand temperature and were led to believe that *hand cooling* was an effective treatment. The hand-cooling condition proved ineffective in reducing symptoms, whereas the next phase of hand-warming feedback resulted in symptom reduction. This study provides some evidence that the effectiveness of hand-warming biofeedback is not totally the result of nonspecific factors.

A second strategy involved the use of false feedback (Mullinix *et al.*, 1978) and led to an opposite conclusion. Although the subjects in the group receiving true temperature feedback altered their skin temperatures significantly more than the false feedback group, both groups showed similar reductions in headache symptoms. These results suggest that nonspecific factors contribute to the success of hand-warming training. In a test of the basic assumption behind hand warming—that the procedure may reduce the flow to cephalic beds—Koppman, McDonald, and Kunzel (1974) found that feedback-influenced vasodilation of the temple artery was not correlated with digital blood-flow changes. Price and Tursky (1976) pointed out that skin temperature feedback may act to increase an overall state of relaxation and in this way may produce vasodilation in cephalic and digital sites together.

The relative effects of skin temperature biofeedback and relaxation were directly assessed in one controlled study (Blanchard, Theobald, Williamson, Silver, & Brown, 1978). The authors compared the effects of temperature biofeedback and progressive muscle relaxation to a waiting-list control group on multiple measures of migraine symptoms. The two treatment groups differed significantly from the waiting-list control group on all dependent measures except headache frequency, but there were no significant differences between the groups. Moreover, a one-year follow-up also showed no differences between the conditions (Blanchard & Ahles, 1979).

Cephalic Vasomotor Feedback. Cephalic vasomotor feedback (CVMF) has also been used to reduce migraine headaches. With the procedure, the patient is given visual or auditory feedback reflecting the momentary changes in blood volume pulse of the temporal artery. Feuerstein, Adams, and Beiman (1976) compared frontalis EMG feedback and CVMF in a single-case study of a mixed migraine–tension-headache client. CVMF was superior to EMG in the overall reduction of headache activity. In a well-controlled group-outcome study, Friar and Beatty (1976) gave feedback of the temporal artery to one group of migraine patients while a second group received feedback for peripheral vasoconstriction. Both groups showed criteria changes in vasoconstriction at the site of feedback. Cranial and peripheral vasomotor changes within the subject were uncorrelated. Statistically significant changes in headache activity were noted for the group receiving feedback for cranial vasoconstriction.

Relaxation. Relaxation has also been demonstrated to show some effectiveness in the treatment of migraine headaches. Two single-group uncontrolled-outcome studies indicate that about two-thirds of patients given a brief course of relaxation and related techniques improve (Hay & Madders, 1971; Warner & Lance, 1975), while about one-third improve from brief training in a passive meditation form of relaxation (Benson, Beary, & Carol, 1974a). Two controlled studies found that relaxation led to similar improvement as temperature biofeedback training combined with autogenic training and regular home practice at the three-month follow-up (Blanchard *et al.*, 1978) and posttreatment (Andreychuk & Skriver, 1975). Why CVMF (resulting in vasoconstriction) and relaxation (involving vasodilation) are both effective in reducing migraine frequency remains uncertain.

Other Approaches. Mitchell and Mitchell (1971) have reported on the use of a behavioral treatment package to reduce migraine headaches. In the first study, three students received a behavioral package including training in progressive relaxation, systematic desensitization, assertiveness training, and training in problem solving for daily living. Three other students only monitored headache activity. At the two-month follow-up, the treated subjects were significantly improved and the controls were unchanged. In the next study, the combined behavioral treatment ($n = 7$) was compared with relaxation alone ($n = 7$) and no treatment ($n = 3$). The combined behavioral treatment was superior to relaxation and to no treatment. In the next study, Mitchell and White (1977) gave 12 patients various parts of the treatment package. The total package, administered almost entirely from audiotapes and written instructions, resulted in significantly greater improvement than that found in a group receiving relaxation training and systematic desensitization. Of the patients treated with this package, 100% showed substantial improvement. These impressive results certainly bear repeating by other investigators and in other settings. Holroyd, Andrasik, and Westbrook (1977) compared EMG biofeedback with a cognitive therapy that focused on teaching clients more effective ways to cope with stress. The cognitive procedure was more effective than the biofeedback procedure, which was not more effective than the control—a finding inconsistent with most other studies.

Summary. In summary, skin temperature feedback and relaxation procedures are both effective in reducing the frequency and the intensity of migraine headache report. One procedure does not appear superior to the other. Cephalic vasomotor feedback may also be useful. Behavioral treatment packages have shown dramatic effectiveness in a few cases.

Tension Headaches. Headache pain is so common that 65% of nonclinical populations report periodic headache (Ogden, 1952). Tension headaches are typically assumed to be the result of sustained contraction of the facial, scalp, neck, or shoulder muscles. However, the available data do not support the assumption that changes in the level of muscular activity are the basis for the headaches (Epstein & Cinciripini, 1980; Phillips, 1977). This is important, of course, because EMG feedback is frequently used to treat tension headaches.

Biofeedback (EMG). The first treatment involving biofeedback and related procedures to treat tension headaches was reported by Budzynski, Stoyva, and Adler (1973). They illustrated that EMG changes could be influenced by analogue auditory stimuli and that the observed changes in muscle activity were a function of the relationship between contingent changes in the feedback signal. Three of five clients taught to reduce EMG levels reported

decreases in headaches. Wickramasekera (1973b) found similar results of biofeedback in a single-group outcome study. In a controlled-group outcome study, Budzynski, Stoyva, Adler & Mullaney (1973) compared the effects of analogue feedback plus self-instructed home relaxation to pseudobiofeedback plus relaxation instruction and to a no-treatment control group that received no relaxation. Both feedback groups had a decline in EMG activity, although during follow-up, the EMG activity was lower only for the biofeedback group. Headache frequency was significantly reduced for the biofeedback group and only slightly for the pseudobiofeedback group. That the controls were unchanged suggests that the biofeedback procedures and not the home relaxation instructions were the critical variable. Other authors have found significant reduction in headache activity with EMG feedback (Chesney & Shelton, 1976; Haynes, Griffin, Mooney, & Parise, 1975; Hutchings & Reinking, 1976; Peck & Kraft, 1977), although one study found no effect (Holroyd *et al.*, 1977). Epstein and Cinciripini (1980) reported on a single-case evaluation of the influence of biofeedback on EMG activity and headache pain using an A-B-A-B experimental control design. The authors showed that feedback had a controlling effect on EMG levels and the pain reports. Wickramasekera (1973a) and Kondo and Center (1977) used true and false feedback. In the latter study, during the false biofeedback condition, subjects were told that the feedback represented actual muscle tension. True but not false biofeedback led to reduction in headache intensity, although it is not certain that the subjects believed that the false biofeedback actually reflected reduced muscle tension.

Relaxation. Three single-group outcome studies (Fitchler & Zimmerman, 1973; Tasto & Hinkle, 1973; Warner & Lance, 1975) have shown substantial reductions in headache pain report. Cox, Freundlick, and Meyer (1975), Haynes *et al.* (1975), and Chesney and Shelton (1976) found that relaxation was superior to controls.

Comparison of Biofeedback and Relaxation. The three previously mentioned studies also compared relaxation with biofeedback. In all of these studies, relaxation was equal or superior to EMG biofeedback. One study has reported an advantage of biofeedback training over relaxation training (Hutchings & Reinking, 1976), although the authors used an amalgamation of several relaxation techniques for brief training periods. In a follow-up study, Hutchings and Reinking (1976) found that patients receiving EMG biofeedback, with or without relaxation training were significantly more improved (at one-month posttreatment) than those receiving relaxation training alone. By three months, those receiving the combined treatment were better than those in the other two conditions; at two months, six months, and one year, all differential treatment effects had vanished. Regular practice of relaxation was associated with significantly fewer headaches regardless of initial treatment.

Summary. Behavioral approaches have been extensively evaluated with three chronic pain problems. Behaviorally oriented inpatient units are effective in reducing much of the disability associated with chronic pain in some patients. Unfortunately, the methodology will have to be improved and long-term outcome studies will have to be undertaken before the specific usefulness of these packages has been demonstrated. Both relaxation and biofeedback (particularly of skin temperature) are useful in reducing the frequency and intensity of migraine headaches. Finally, relaxation appears to be the treatment of choice for reducing the frequency and the intensity of headaches due to chronic tension, although EMG biofeedback works equally well.

Other case reports have demonstrated the usefulness of a variety of behavioral approaches to other pain problems. For instance, relaxation was used to reduce the frequency of pain reported in patients with phantom limb pain (Sherman, Gall, & Gormly, 1979), a condition in which patients experience excruciating pain in a limb that has been amputated. EMG feedback has been demonstrated to reduce myofascial pain dysfunction symptom (Dohrmann & Laskin, 1978).

Central Nervous System

Hearing and Vision. Behavioral techniques have been used for some time in the assessment and modification of hearing and visual problems. As much of this work has occurred with children, it is not reviewed in this section. However, with adults, several applications of behavioral principles have been applied to myopic subjects and are of both theoretical interest and perhaps practical importance. Epstein, Collins, Hannay, and Looney (1978) used a fading-plus-reinforcement project to modify acuity in myopic subjects. The technique involved gradually increasing the distance at which the myopic subjects could discriminate visual stimuli, and contingent approval was provided for correct discriminations. The fading-plus-reinforcement treatment was compared with a matched no-treatment control group on a measure of visual acuity. Discrimination improvement was shown for the experimental subjects. In a second study (Epstein, Greenwald, Hennon, & Hiedorn, 1981), four replications of a multiple-baseline design across stimuli were used to evaluate changes in visual acuity. Three of the four subjects showed changes appropriate for the fading-plus-reinforcement procedures. One subject given acuity training to pass the medical portion of a job screening showed changes in both eyes from 20/40, 20/50, to 20/20, 20/25.

Seizures. Several studies have clearly shown that the frequency of seizures can be reduced by means of various behavioral techniques. Biofeedback has been studied most extensively, although other techniques have also been used.

Biofeedback. Three different frequencies of electrocortical activity have been studied in attempts to provide feedback to a patient. The most extensively studied electrocortical activity is the so-called sensorimotor rhythm, a 12–15 Hz rhythm over the sensorimotor cortex (SMR). Interest in using the rhythm derived from basic science work with cats. When cats were taught to remain motionless (Roth, Sterman, & Clemente, 1967), this rhythm became more apparent. Furthermore, it was found that increases in SMR rhythm could be operantly conditioned in cats, resulting in a greater resistance to drug-induced seizures. In an early experiment, Sterman and Friar (1972) provided SMR feedback to a 23-year-old female with a history of major motor seizures since age 16. The subject observed a series of lamps, which successively became lit as she increased her SMR activity. The subject was able to increase her SMR activity and experienced only one seizure during the next four months of training. Several other clients have also experienced reduction in seizures with SMR training (Finley, Smith, & Etherton, 1975; Sterman, 1973), although the procedure has not been consistently effective (Kaplan, 1975; Kuhlman & Allison, 1977; Lubar, 1975) and may require continued practice (Sterman, 1973). Other researchers have used mu rhythm or somatomotor rhythm with varying success with several clients (Kaplan, 1975) and alpha, again with varying success.

Deconditioning. Parrino (1971) reduced the frequency of grand mal seizures in a 36-year-old male. Before therapy, the base rate of seizures was approximately 58 per day. Because the patient reported that his seizures were triggered by anxiety-producing stimuli, he was started on a course of systematic desensitization. Over a treatment period of three months, his seizure frequency dropped to 10 per day. When the patient returned to work, he experienced an increase in seizures but applied a self-desensitization system. At five-month follow-up, all medications had been withdrawn and the patient was seizure-free. Similar procedures have been reported with a 12-year-old boy with petit mal and grand mal seizures (Ince, 1976), but cue-controlled relaxation was added. Wells, Turner, Bellack, and Hersen (1978) conducted a single-case analysis of cue-controlled relaxation in the treatment of a 22-year-old female with psychomotor seizures. After baseline, the rates of seizure and anxiety level decreased when treatment was provided and increased when treatment was removed.

Forster (1967) developed various procedures based on classical conditioning to treat the so-called reflex epilepsies. In a typical procedure, he presented the conditioned stimuli repeatedly until the conditioned response no longer occurred. For instance, with a 21-year-old woman who experienced stroboscopically induced seizures, he repeatedly presented stroboscopic illumination until no response occurred. The seizures were subsequently eliminated in response to a 22 cps stroboscopic frequency but did not generalize to values either lower or higher than 11 cps; extinction trials had to be initiated at all frequencies from 15 to 35 cps. Forster (1967) also used fading and other techniques to similarly reduce dys-

rhythmia and seizures precipitated by many other types of stimuli.

Other Techniques. In a very early study, Efron (1956) reported on the case of a 41-year-old woman who had suffered from grand mal attacks for over 26 years. He assumed that the seizure was the end response of a chain of responses that went from feelings of depersonalization, to "forced thinking," to olfactory hallucinating, to auditory hallucinating, to right-direction head movement, and finally to a grand mal seizure. He found that the inhalation of fumes from a vial of hydrogen sulfide prior to the olfactory hallucination prevented the seizure. The patient was seizure-free at 14-month follow-up. Zlutnick, Mayville, and Moffat (1975) also developed a procedure to break chains associated with the development of major and minor seizures in five children. Other procedures used to control seizures in adults have included covert and operant conditioning (Daniels, 1975) and contingency management (Flannery & Cautela, 1973; Richardson, 1972). This has been reviewed recently by Mostofsky and Balaschak (1977).

Memory. An interesting area of importance to aging individuals and perhaps crucial to the survival of some is the development of techniques to improve memory. Many of these techniques are behavioral. Successful use of memory improvement, especially through techniques that use paired-association memory tasks, have been reported for community-dwelling elderly people (Patten, 1972; Robertson-Tchabo, Nausman, & Arenberg, 1976; Rowe & Schnore, 1971) and the brain-injured (Benton & Spreen, 1964; Jones, 1974; Lewinsohn, Danaher, & Kikel, 1977). Systematic applications of these techniques, especially incorporating principles that would enhance the maintenance of procedures of learning in the laboratory, are now being undertaken.

Peripheral Nerve Damage. Biofeedback has been used in the rehabilitation of individuals with nerve damage secondary to a variety of causes. In an early study, Marinacci and Horande (1960) reported on seven cases in which EMG biofeedback helped reverse various neuromuscular dysfunctions. For example, using needle electrodes and auditory EMG feedback, one patient with a complete right facial paralysis of six years' duration was able to bring some previously dysfunctional motor units under voluntary control. After two sessions per week for six months, motor-unit EMG activity in some muscles increased from 400 mico V to 1500 mico V, and the patient experienced a 40% return of function in both the orbicularis and the frontalis muscles. Jankel (1978) used a baseline–treatment–baseline reversal design to demonstrate the specific usefulness of EMG feedback. The patient was asked to match EMG levels obtained from the paralyzed side of her face with EMG from her unaffected side of her face. She increased her EMG significantly during the intervention phase, an effect that carried over during the reversal. Other case examples have shown similar effects in patients with peripheral nerve damage (Booker, Rubow, & Coleman, 1969; Kukulka, Brown, & Basmajian, 1975).

Since biofeedback can be useful in improving conditions secondary to severe peripheral nerve damage, it is not surprising that similar findings have been demonstrated in patients with hemiplegia and paraplegia. In one large study, Brudny, Korein, Grynbaum, Friedmann, Weinstein, Sachs-Frankel, and Belandres (1976) used biofeedback with 39 patients with upper extremity hemiparesis who participated in an 8- to 12-week training period that required accomplishing progressively more demanding muscle tasks. At the end of the study, 27 of 39 patients exhibited greatly improved upper extremity function. At follow-up from two to three years later, 20 of the 39 patients maintained this greatly improved function.

Several controlled-group outcome studies have also been undertaken. Basmajian, Kukulka, Narayan, and Takebe (1975) compared the effects of traditional physical therapy with a combined treatment of traditional therapy and EMG. Twenty subjects with dorsiflexion paralysis (foot drop) were randomly assigned to the two treatment groups. Both groups increased ankle range of movement and strength, with the combined-treatment group showing average increases in both measures that were nearly twice as great as those of the physical-therapy-only group. The second controlled-group outcome study was reported by Mroczek, Halpern, and McHugh (1978). Nine patients with upper-extremity hemiplegia for at least one year were first trained with instruc-

tional procedures to contract or inhibit the biceps. Following baseline, the patients were randomly assigned to four weeks of biofeedback followed by four weeks of physical therapy or four weeks of physical therapy followed by four weeks of biofeedback. EMG and range of measurement (ROM) were measured during the treatment sessions. Pooled group analysis revealed no significant differences in either average EMG activity or active ROM between biofeedback and physical therapy.

Spasmodic Torticollis. Spasmodic torticollis is a dysfunction characterized by sustained constriction of muscles that rotate the head to one side. Several single-case studies and small-group designs have reported reduction in spasm with EMG feedback (Brudny, Grynbaum, & Korein, 1974a; Brudny et al., 1976; Cleeland, 1973). Brudny, Korein, Levidow, Grynbaum, Lieterman, and Friedman (1974) have reported on the effect of the procedure with 48 torticollis patients. Over follow-up periods ranging from three months to three years, 19 (40%) of the patients maintained improvement. Improvement included large reductions in EMG activity in the formerly hypertrophied sternocleidomastoid muscles, and many subjects could return their heads to a normal position. Other behavioral approaches, like negative practice (Agras & Marshall, 1965; Meares, 1973), have shown inconsistent and equivocal results.

Tics. Tics are frequent and troublesome twitches of involuntary muscles. In an early study, Yates (1958) instructed patients to repeat the unwanted response until it became effortful and tiresome, a procedure he called "mass practice." The procedure produced encouraging results, but its effects have not been consistent (Agras & Marshall, 1965; Nicassio, Liberman, Patterson, & Ramirez, 1972). Other procedures that have been used include brief seclusion to eliminate an obscene tic (Lahey, McNees, & McNees, 1973); time-out from pleasant music to reduce multiple tics (Barrett, 1962); self-monitoring and systematic desensitization (Thomas, Abrams, & Johnson, 1971); self-monitoring alone (Hutzell, Platzek, & Logue, 1974); and so-called habit reversal (Azrin & Nunn, 1973).

Sleep. In a recent review, Bootzin and Nicassio (1978) concluded that relaxation has been clearly demonstrated to result in moderate improvement among mild to severe cases of insomnia. Unfortunately, these studies were conducted without EEG records substantiating these effects. Two studies have, however, demonstrated that progressive relaxation produces changes in EEG sleep parameters (Borkovec & Weerts, 1976; Freedman & Papsdorf, 1976). Borkovec, Grayson, O'Brien, and Weerts (1979) evaluated the effects of relaxation on subtypes of insomnia—those with pseudoinsomnia, who show little evidence of sleep deficit according to EEG criteria, and those with real insomnia, who show clear sleep retardation and deficits as measured by the EEG. Twenty-nine insomniacs participated in the study and were assigned to three conditions: progressive relaxation, a condition with progressive relaxation instructions but no muscle-tension releasing, and a no-treatment control condition. The tension release and progressive muscle relaxation were more effective than the other two conditions on subjective sleep measures, regardless of insomnia subtype, and on objective sleep measures only for idiopathic insomniacs. Subjective improvement was maintained for all treatment groups at 12-month follow-up. This study demonstrates the importance of objective measures of sleep and the possible interactions that may exist between treatments and the etiology of the condition.

Thoresen, Coates, Zarcone, Kirmil-Gray, and Rosekind (1980) have described a self-management procedure to manage a variety of behaviors associated with insomnia. The program includes relaxation training, self-monitoring, self-hypnosis, cognitive restruction, and problem solving as necessary.

Other Disorders. Behavioral procedures have been used with other neurological problems. Successful applications of biofeedback have been reported to increase function in patients with hemifacial spasms, dystonia, dysphagia, and muscle atrophy (Brudny *et al.*, 1976); to increase the facial expressiveness of blind patients (Webb, 1977); and to decrease chronic eye blinking (Peck & Kraft, 1977; Roxanas, Thomas, & Rapp, 1978). Nonbiofeedback procedures have been useful in reducing tardive-dyskinesia movement in at least one case of tardive dyskinesia (Taylor, Zlutnick, & Hoehle, 1979).

Health Care Behavior

Epidemiological studies have clearly demonstrated that our lifestyle contributes to our illnesses. What we eat, how we handle stress, how we sleep, how much we exercise, and the quality of our air (severely compromised in smokers) are major factors in determining what diseases we develop. It is also clear that changes in some aspect of our lifestyle, like reducing our cholesterol intake or stopping smoking, lead to reduced morbidity and mortality. It is less clear who is responsible for effecting these changes: certainly the traditional health-care system has shown little interest in prevention in well populations, although this may have changed in recent years. (For instance, the National Center for Disease Control, previously concerned mostly with infectious disease, has now established national prevention goals in all areas of lifestyle.) The technology for implementing such changes lags behind the obvious importance of making such changes, and it is perhaps in this area more than in any other—affecting lifestyle change—that behavioral medicine will make its greatest contribution. The most extensive work in behavioral medicine, in fact, has been directed at changing eating and smoking behavior (the present status of this work is reviewed in other chapters). But there has also been extensive work in four other areas: nutrition, adherence to medication, exercise, and stress reduction.

Nutrition. Large prospective studies have shown that reductions in serum cholesterol are associated with lower morbidity and mortality, at least with hyperlipidemic males, and other evidence is overwhelming that diet contributes to heart disease. Other evidence has demonstrated that increased salt intake is associated with increased blood pressure and, conversely, that reduction in salt intake is associated with lowered blood pressure. There is less convincing but still suggestive evidence that diet may also be related to such problems as colon cancer. Certainly, the majority of Americans consume a diet that is considerably out of line with that recently recommended by the American Select Commission on Nutrition. It is surprising that so few studies have looked at behavioral approaches to diet. An early study was conducted by Meyer and Henderson (1974), who treated 36 subjects at an industrial site with behavior modification, including modeling and token reward, individual counseling, or a single-physician consultation. At 11 weeks posttreatment and at three-month follow-up, all three groups showed a statistically significant reduction in cholesterol and triglycerides. At a follow-up three months later, the behavioral group was significantly different in cholesterol from the other two groups.

This same approach was incorporated and expanded in the intensive instruction portion of the Stanford Three Community Study. Comparisons involved the effects of media plus intensive instruction and media alone with a control in effecting nutrition change as measured by serum chemistries. This study was accomplished in a longitudinal cohort in three California towns of about 14,000 (Farquhar, Maccoby, Wood, Alexander, Breitrose, Brown, Haskell, McAlister, Meyer, Nash, & Stern, 1977). Significant reductions occurred in plasma cholesterol after two years in the towns provided with the media campaign. There were no significant differences in the high-risk group between those given intensive instruction and those exposed to media only.

Foreyt, Scott, Mitchell, and Giotto (1979) have reported on the success of three types of diet intervention programs: diet booklet only, nutrition education, and behavioral intervention with nutrition education for reducing plasma cholesterol and triglycerides. The results from 183 subjects showed that at 6 months, the subjects who received the behavioral intervention with nutrition education had a significantly greater reduction in cholesterol than those in the other two conditions. Both nutrition education and behavioral intervention groups had small but statistically significant cholesterol and triglyceride reduction at 12 months.

Finally, Foxx and Rubinoff (1979) reported on the effects of reducing caffeine ingestion in three habitual coffee addicts. Caffeine increases plasma catecholamines and is, in general, associated with increased blood pressure. The treatment involved a gradual reduction in caffeine to 600 mg per day (fewer than five cups of brewed coffee). The subjects determined their baseline rate of caffeine use, subtracted 600 mg from this figure, and divided the difference by 4 to determine the goals of reduction for each phase. The coffee drinkers were required to self-monitor and plot their daily intake of caffeine. They received monetary prizes for not exceeding the treatment phase criteria and forfeited a portion of the treatment deposits when they did. Coffee reduction averaged 69% during the four weeks of treatment and 67% at 10-month follow-up. Similar procedures could be applied to a variety of nutritional practices.

Adherence to Medication (and Medical Advice). The importance of this area is illustrated by the fact that 33%–82% of patients do not follow or err in following regimens (Becker & Morman, 1975; Stewart & Cluff, 1972).

A behavioral analysis of adherence to medication and interventions to improve adherence has been a small but exciting part of the behavioral medicine literature, as we noted in the introduction. Although behavioral studies have shown the superiority of simple over complex regimens, the instructional component has not been carefully studied. Such variables as prompts have been shown to improve adherence. Counseling in adherence by paraprofessionals has also been shown to improve adherence. In a recent study, 60 poor adherers from lipid research clinics were randomly allocated to one of three groups: a multicomponent procedure, an attention-control group, and a usual-care group (Dunbar, 1977). The multicomponent package consisted of scheduled phone calls for social reinforcement and individual analysis of medication. The multicomponent package was more effective in bringing a significantly greater proportion of patients above a preestablished adherence criterion than either of the other treatments.

Exercise. There has been surprisingly little attention paid to improving exercise. Exercise behaviors comprise a large number of overt motoric responses that differ in topography, intensity, frequency, and duration and thus are ideal for behavioral measurement techniques. Several studies have attempted to increase exercise adherence. In one study, Epstein and Wing (1980) compared the effects of three contract groups, a lottery group, and a no-treatment control group to increase exercise in 37 female college students. The contract groups differed according to exercise intensity. Subjects in the contract group deposited $5 prior to the study and were refunded $1 per week, contingent on attendance at four of the five exercise sessions. Subjects in the lottery condition deposited $3 prior to the study and were able to earn a chance in the lottery by attending four of the five exercise sessions for a given week. An analysis of the attendance data showed that the mean number of sessions attended by the three contract groups and the lottery group was equivalent or superior to the attendance in the control group.

Wysocki, Hall, Iwata, and Riordan (1979) demonstrated that behavioral contracting can increase physical activity among college students. The authors used aerobic points as outcome measures, which had the advantage that inexperienced observers could be quickly trained to observe exercise behavior and to translate these observations into their aerobic point equivalents. At follow-up some 12 months later, seven of the eight subjects reported that they were earning more aerobic points per week than had been the case during baseline.

Self-Management and Cognitive Strategies. Lifestyle changes have been the focus of self-management studies. Although some proponents of self-management apply the term to the application of behavior therapy principles to oneself, the term has come to refer to a variety of processes, and it is often used synonymously with *self-control* and *self-regulation*. With self-control, the external constraints are inconspicuous. Mahoney and Arnkoff (1979) recently articulated some of the problems and ironies of self-control. For instance, they noted, ''We tend to attribute more self-control to the person who is just beginning a personal change . . . after ten years of abstinence, for example, an ex-smoker is not given as much credit when he or she turns down a cigarette'' (pp. 79–80). Furthermore, the term *self-control* seems to be used when the change is motivated by noble ideals, involves sacrifice, and is socially desirable.

A number of procedures have emerged from this literature that have been applied to medical problems. These procedures include: self-monitoring, used for instance to record the number of cigarettes smoked or bites eaten; and cueing strategies, which involve a variety

of stimulus control strategies like notes on a calendar reminding an individual who has been adhering to a diet change to record the cholesterol in his cupboards. Rehearsal is a strategy in which an individual practices a response in anticipation of a particular event (e.g., a patient learns an alternative response to her husband, which may reduce blood pressure rises during that condition). Self-punishment is a strategy in which an individual administers a punishment for a particular behavior (e.g., he obtains a slight shock when he removes a cigarette from a case). Self-reward is a strategy that provides the individual with a reward for a particular change. A related strategy is to incorporate these same principles into a cognitive strategy.

Although some studies have shown the effectiveness of self-management packages in reducing symptoms like migraine headache (Mitchell & White, 1977), Type A behavior (Suinn & Bloom, 1978), and insomnia (Thoresen *et al.,* 1980), their effectiveness has not been well established or evaluated, particularly as compared with other, simpler techniques.

Disability

Throughout the preceding two sections, we provided examples of the use of behavioral techniques to reduce the severity of a particular illness or symptom and to improve health-care behavior. But behavioral approaches are equally important in reducing the disability that results from a disease. From a behavioral standpoint, the procedures used to change the diet of a young person with minimal arteriosclerosis may be similar to those used to change the diet of a person with established arteriosclerosis, but most studies have focused on the prevention of disease rather than minimizing disability. From society's standpoint, the latter is critically important. The U.S. Department of Commerce estimates that as many as 30 million Americans suffer from some chronic disorder or disability. In this section, we focus on reducing the disabilities and improving the life of three types of disabled individuals: outpatients, inpatients, and shut-ins.

Outpatient Strategies. In the previous sections, we provided a few examples of behavioral approaches to minimizing the consequences of illness or to improving a patient's management of his/her illness. For instance, relaxation and desensitization may reduce the anxiety and fear conditioned to symptoms in patients with chronic asthma, and reinforcement with instructions facilitates the use of a respirator in chronic asthma patients.

An example of the use of behavioral techniques to facilitate the management of a patient's complex medical regimen to reduce disability was recently reported by Dapcich-Muria and Hovell (1979). They used a token reinforcement system to improve an elderly patient's adherence to a complex medical regimen. Using a multiple-baseline and reversal single-case design, the authors demonstrated that the reinforcement contingency was responsible for doubling walking, increasing orange juice consumption, and increasing pill taking.

Inpatient Management Strategies. The second area of treatment of chronic illnesses has been in the inpatient setting. We reviewed the results of Fordyce's inpatient treatment programs earlier. Other authors have described treatment programs designed to decrease patients' illness behavior and to increase their self-care. Wooley, Blackwell, and Winget (1978) reviewed the global outcomes of 300 patients treated on a "psychosomatic unit" employing a learning model of chronic illness behavior. The overall philosophy of the program requires independent action by the patient at each step of treatment in order to progress to the next. Before admission, patients must specify their goals in each of four areas: symptom management, social functioning, family interaction, and life plans. Current status, immediately accepted outcome, and ideal outcome in each are listed and given numerical values of 0–100. The treatment includes biofeedback, skill training, family therapy, and group sessions. In a series of studies, Wooley's group has shown that the program has altered the social contingencies supporting illness behavior, has reduced verbal complaint behavior, and has led to global improvement, maintained at one-year follow-up in the focus target areas for at least one subset of patients.

Shut-Ins. Programs have been developed to enhance the care of patients in institutional settings, like nursing homes, geriatric wards, or board-and-care facilities. For instance,

Baltes, Burgess, and Stewart (1978) have recently reported on techniques to measure self-care behaviors in a nursing home. Geiger and Johnson (1974) developed methods to measure and increase correct eating skills in elderly patients. The measurement procedures involved having observers watch each feeding response and record the type of action involved (scooping, cutting, drinking, etc.), the degree of independence, and any errors, such as spilling food or using the hands instead of the proper utensils. Other investigators have focused on methods of assessing and improving ambulation (McClannahan & Risley, 1974), reducing incontinence (McClannahan, 1973), and improving toileting in general (Pollock & Liberman, 1974; Risley, Spangler, & Edwards, 1978) and intellectual performance. The latter area is particularly exciting because it may be possible to improve intellectual performance in individuals with organic diseases.

A behavioral analysis of a patient's living environment may reveal obvious areas where simple changes may improve patients' functioning. For instance, Peterson, Knapp, Rosen, and Pither (1977) have demonstrated that furniture arrangement can affect the social interaction of geriatric residents in mental hospital wards. McClannahan and Risley (1974) improved social and leisure-time participation on the part of residents by creating a store in the lobby of a nursing home. In another study, they found that the level of leisure participation of severely disable nursing-home residents could increase significantly if they were provided with proper recreational equipment. The simple procedure of serving meals in large bowls (family style), as opposed to serving the food in individual plates, increased verbal interactions (Risley, Gottula, & Edwards, 1978).

Overview of Relaxation and Related Techniques and Biofeedback

Because of their extensive use in behavioral medicine, in this section we review the uses of biofeedback and relaxation.

Relaxation and Related Techniques

Relaxation-centered behavior therapy is an adjunct to systematic desensitization. Wolpe

(1958) shortened Jacobson's progressive muscle relaxation to provide an easy-to-learn procedure that presumably inhibited fear when paired with a fear-arousing situation. However, it became clear that relaxation was not necessary for systematic desensitization. Meanwhile, relaxation began to be used to treat a variety of problems in which anxiety or stress appeared to be the major factor. In fact, Jacobson (1938) had developed relaxation primarily to treat anxiety-related disorders. In a now classic paper, Benson, Beary and Carol (1974), building on work by Gellhorn (1970), observed that progressive muscle relaxation, hypnosis, many forms of meditation, and autogenic training shared several properties: the subject assumes a passive frame of mind in a relaxing position, repeats a simple phrase, and breathes in a deep, regular manner. They argued that this technique elicits the so-called relaxation response, which tends to reduce central-nervous-system sympathetic activity, which, in turn, reduces peripheral sympathetic activity. They noted that a variety of studies have demonstrated that these techniques elicit physiological changes, like decreased muscle tone, blood pressure, heart rate, and skin conductance, which are consistent with decreased sympathetic activity. Many of the treatment effects of relaxation are explained by this reduction in sympathetic activity, and there is even direct evidence of such changes (Davidson *et al.*, 1979). Because of the similarities among progressive relaxation, hypnotic relaxation instructions, autogenic training, many forms of meditation, and relaxation response technique, we classify them together as *relaxation and related techniques*.

Not all authors are convinced that relaxation induces a central trophotropic response. For instance, Henry and Stephens (1977) noted that the central response need not be hypothesized to explain the effects of relaxation. Sympathetic activity can be reduced simply by changing the level of input or response in midbrain regulatory centers. Furthermore, the findings of reduced sympathetic activity are not consistent across these procedures meant to induce the relaxation response (Lang, Dehof, Meurer, & Kaufmann, 1979). Some of the apparent effects of relaxation (like increased flow rates in asthmatics) are responses that are not under sympathetic control. Finally, it should be kept in mind that many forms of meditation, hypnotic procedures, and autogenic training induce increased, and not decreased, sympathetic activity (Corby, Roth, Zarcone, & Kopell, 1978). Nevertheless, it is clear that relaxation shares an illustrious history with procedures practiced in most cultures for all recorded history.

A variety of progressive-muscle-relaxation programs have been described in the literature, but the superiority of one over the other has not been demonstrated. Nor is it clear for how long, or under what circumstances, an individual should practice relaxation. In general, programs that use one session are less effective than longer ones. Taped sessions are usually as effective as live programs (but see Brauer, Horlick, Nelson, Farquhar, & Agras, 1979), and group sessions are as effective as individual sessions. Most clinicians have subjects practice at least five sessions and teach them how to generalize their relaxation to other settings. It is not clear for how long subjects should practice relaxation. Subjects who continue to practice seem to do better than those who stop, but the issue has never been empirically investigated in a long-term study.

In Table 2, we have listed the conditions in which relaxation has been demonstrated to be useful. To be classified as probably useful, relaxation in at least two controlled-group outcome studies must have demonstrated its superiority over control groups for at least three months (the paucity of carefully controlled outcome studies of six months or longer is shocking). Relaxation has been most extensively studied and demonstrated to be useful in treating patients with essential hypertension. It also appears to be useful to patients with migraine and tension headaches. The evidence also suggests that it is useful with sleep-onset insomnia. Relaxation may be useful in the other conditions listed in the table, although the studies are too few to justify any clear recommendations. Relaxation has been reported in single-case reports to be useful for literally hundreds of other problems, at least as an adjunct to different therapies. It does not appear to be useful in cases where structural disturbances have produced fixed abnormalities (e.g., in patients with conduction difficul-

Table 2. Summary of Usefulness of Relaxation

Probably useful	Possibly useful	Not useful
Essential hypertension	PVCs	Intrinsic conduction disturbance of heart
Migraine headaches	Paroxysmal atrial tachycardia	Muscle rehabilitation
Tension headaches	Asthma	
Sleep-onset insomnia	Nausea	
	Irritable bowel	
	Pain tolerance	
	Muscle spasm	

ties resulting from damage to the myocardium).

Biofeedback

One of the more extraordinary and exciting observations in recent times has been the systematic study of a person's ability to control her/his own physiology. Of course, voluntary control of physiological functions has been reported for centuries by religious mystics. But in recent times, the use of inexpensive technology has allowed the average person to achieve the same phenomenon. Shapiro and Surwit (1979) defined *biofeedback* as the "application of operant conditioning methods to the control of visceral, somatomotor, and central nervous system activities" (p. 45).

Uses of Biofeedback. Biofeedback can be conceptualized from three standpoints: (1) it provides an ideal method of enhancing unspecified (placebo) therapeutic effects; (2) it facilitates the relaxation response; and (3) it induces specific therapeutic effects.

Biofeedback as a Placebo. We have previously argued that unspecified therapeutic effects account for much of the success of many medical procedures. To say that biofeedback acts as a placebo is to say that for some people, it offers considerable help. From a clinical standpoint, biofeedback is appealing to many patients who might otherwise refuse to engage in some treatment of possible help to them. Biofeedback instrumentation—with flashing lights, noises, and other techniques to enhance a person's control of her/his physiology—may induce the same effect that Goldring (1956) elicited in his classic experiment on unspecified effects on hypertension. Goldring manufactured an elaborate electronic gun with flashing lights and complicated switches. He then aimed it at subjects and told them that it would reduce their blood pressures, as indeed it did (for as long as the subjects remained in the study). Stroebel and Glueck (1973) have even argued that biofeedback is the ultimate placebo in the sense that it "provides the patient with an effective means of preventing illness and/or potentially curing himself by helping him regulate the pace of his daily life-style . . . his habits etc." (p. 20). Also, the "word ultimate implies a self-individualized path with many different options where the person himself owns responsibility for achieving the goal of therapy" (p. 20).

Induction of the Relaxation Response. Another general use of biofeedback may be to elicit the relaxation response. Brener (1974), for instance, has shown that physiological functions are not entirely independent and that learned or instructed changes in one system may induce changes in others. Other authors have found that subjects are repeating words to themselves like "Heart rate still," a message similar to autogenic instructions when attempting to comply with feedback instructions to reduce blood pressure.

Specific Biofeedback Effects. Biofeedback may be a specific treatment for some disorders, when neither relaxation nor nonspecific factors result in significant changes. Single-case and group-outcome studies have shown the biofeedback is useful in treating fecal incontinence and encopresis (anal sphincter feedback) and for muscle retraining (EMG feedback), particularly for foot drop, torticollis, and stroke rehabilitation. In Table 3, we have listed the conditions in which biofeedback is probably useful.

Table 3. Summary of Usefulness of Biofeedback[a]

Probably useful	Possibly useful
Encophoresis, fecal incontinence (anal sphincter)	Blood pressure (Pulse Transit Time, actual BP)
Migraine headache (skin temperature)	PVCs (heart rate)
Tension headache (EMG)	Paroxysmal atrial tachycardia (heart rate)
Muscle retraining (EMG)	Sinus tachycardia (heart rate)
	Postural hypotension (actual BP)
	Wolff-Parkinson-White syndrome (heart rate)
	Asthma (respiratory flow rate)
	Irritable bowel (rectosigmoid pressure)
	Peptic ulcer disease (gastric pH)
	Raynaud's syndrome (skin temperature)
	Migraine headache (cephalic blood volume, EMG)
	Major motor seizures (SMR)
	Temporomandibular joint dysfunction (EMG)
	Torticollis (EMG)
	Back pain (EMG)

[a] The type of feedback is in parentheses.

Future Perspectives

The future of behavioral medicine is rosy. The interest of practitioners and researchers of behavior therapy and applied behavioral analysis in medical problems will greatly enhance our understanding of the relationship between health, disease, and behavior. In particular, a technology may be developed to improve self-care, to maintain health, and to minimize disability and discomfort from disease.

On a basic science level, we can anticipate that behavioral medicine researchers will continue to make important contributions to medical science. Medicine prides itself on the specificity of measurement, but rarely has behavior been included in this measurement. Such straightforward but critical behaviors, such as actual drug use in an experiment of the effects of a procedure on a class of behaviors, are rarely described in even the most sophisticated medical articles. As behavioral techniques are proved beneficial, it becomes important to determine the reasons for these effects, for instance, how relaxation may induce changes in blood pressure.

On a treatment level, more techniques will be developed and practiced. The success of the application of these techniques will be de-

termined as much by political and social factors—like how adequately behavioral medicine practitioners are reimbursed and how easily they become incorporated into the medical system—as by scientific ones. We can anticipate that some techniques, currently oversold, will lose credibility, if not in the eyes of the public, then certainly in the practice of traditional medical practitioners, who currently seem infatuated with behavioral medicine techniques. But it may occur that physicians, who are used to dramatic changes in physiological variables and are trained to think in clinical and not statistical terms, will become discouraged by the immediate and sometimes small impact of a particular behavioral intervention. And how behavioral techniques may achieve widespread use of their most promising effects—prevention and rehabilitation—is an even more complicated question.

We can expect that behavioral medicine techniques will play an even more important part in prevention and rehabilitation. Programmed techniques will be developed to facilitate the management of complex regimens and to minimize disability. The impetus for adopting such changes and the philosophy for incorporating these changes may have to come from social and political forces, since commitment to prevention has been minimal on the part of traditional medical practitioners. On a more optimistic note, prevention has been designated as a very important national health goal and one we must strive to achieve.

Summary

In the last 10 years, behavior therapy techniques and practices have moved from being applied to a few medical problems to becoming a major new discipline. Hypertension, arrhythmias, Type A behavior, and risk reduction have been the most extensively studied areas of cardiovascular problems in behavioral medicine. Relaxation has been demonstrated to be of benefit in reducing blood pressure in some patients with essential hypertension. However, the role of biofeedback is less clear. Both relaxation and biofeedback may help in reducing the frequency of some types of arrhythmias. Self-management strategies are being developed for changing Type A behavior; their usefulness has yet to be determined. Management of a patient's illness and reducing the anxiety and stress accompanying it are helpful in the case of asthma.

There has been less work done specifically on gastrointestinal system disorders. Various behavioral techniques have shown promise in reducing the complaint of nausea and symptoms of the irritable bowel syndrome and the reducing gastric acid in peptic ulcer disease. Carefully controlled trials are urgently needed in this area.

Impressive treatment gains have been made in reducing the severity and the extent of migraine and tension headache complaints. Inpatient programs have been developed for the treatment of chronic pain but have not, as yet, been extensively evaluated. Behavioral techniques have been applied to a variety of health care behaviors. A few studies have shown that instructions and simple behavior therapy programs improve nutrition, increase exercise, and increase adherence to medication. Self-management and cognitive strategies may offer particular promise in this area.

Biofeedback has been demonstrated to be effective in reducing fecal incontinence, migraine and tension headache, and muscle retraining. The evidence is less substantial but promising for many other conditions.

References

Adams, N., Ferguson, J., Stunkard, A. J., & Agras, S. The eating behavior of obese and nonobese women. *Behaviour Research and Therapy*, 1978, *16*, 225–232.

Adler, C., & Adler, S. Biofeedback-psychotherapy for the treatment of headaches: A five-year clinical follow-up. *Headache*, 1976, *16*, 189–191.

Agras, S., & Marshall, C. The application of negative practice to spasmodic torticollis. *American Journal of Psychiatry*, 1965, *122*, 579–582.

Alexander, A. B. Systematic relaxation and flow rates in asthmatic children: Relationship to emotional precipitants and anxiety. *Journal of Psychosomatic Research*, 1972, *16*, 405–410.

Alexander, A. B., Miklich, D. R., & Hershkoff, H. The immediate effects of systematic relaxation training on peak expiratory flow rates in asthmatic children. *Psychosomatic Medicine*, 1972, *34*, 388–394.

Alexander, A. B., Cropp, G. J. A., & Chai, H. Effects of relaxation training on pulmonary mechanics in children with asthma. *Journal of Applied Behavior Analysis*, 1979, *12*, 27–35.

Alexander, F., French, T. M., & Pollock, G. H. *Psychosomatic specificity*. Chicago: University of Chicago Press, 1968.

Alford, G. S., Blanchard, E. B., & Buckley, T. M. Treatment of hysterical vomiting by modification of social contingencies: A case study. *Journal of Behavior Therapy and Experimental Psychiatry*, 1972, *3*, 209–212.

Almy, T. P., & Tulin, M. Alterations in colonic function by men under stress: Experimental production of changes simulating the "irritable colon." *Gastroenterology*, 1947, *8*, 616–626.

Anderson, T. P., Cole, T. M., Gullickson, G., Hudgens, A., & Roberts, A. H. Behavior modification of chronic pain: A treatment program by a multidisciplinary team. *Journal of Clinical Orthopedics and Related Research*, 1977, *129*, 96–100.

Andreychuk, T., & Skriver, C. Hypnosis and biofeedback in the treatment of migraine headache. *International Journal of Clinical and Experimental Hypnosis*, 1975, *23*, 172–183.

Azrin, N., & Nunn, R. Habit reversal: A method of eliminating nervous habits and tics. *Behaviour Research and Therapy*, 1973, *11*, 619–628.

Baltes, M. M., Burgess, R. L., & Stewart, R. B. *Independence and dependence in nursing home residents: An operant ecological study*. Paper presented at the Nova Behavioral Conference on Aging, Port St. Lucie, Fla., 1978.

Barrett, B. Reduction in rate of multiple tics by free operant conditioning methods. *Journal of Nervous and Mental Disease*, 1962, *135*, 187–195.

Basmajian, J. V. *Muscles alive: Their functions revealed by electromyography* (3rd ed.). Baltimore: Williams & Wilkins, 1974.

Basmajian, J. V., Kukulka, C. G., Narayan, M. G., &

Takebe, K. Biofeedback treatment of footdrop after stroke compared with standard rehabilitation technique. Effects on voluntary control and strength. *Archives of Physical Medicine and Rehabilitation*, 1975, *56*, 231–236.

Becker, M. H., & Morman, L. A. Sociobehavioral determinants of compliance with health and medical care recommendations. *Medical Care*, 1975, *13*, 10–24.

Benson, H. *The relaxation response*. New York: William Morrow, 1975.

Benson, H., Beary, J. F., & Carol, M. P. The relaxation response. *Psychiatry*, 1974, *37*, 37.

Benson, H., Klemchuk, H. P., & Graham, J. R. The usefulness of the relaxation response in the therapy of headache. *Headache*, 1974, *14*, 14–52.

Benson, H., Alexander, S., & Feldman, C. L. Decreased premature ventricular contractions through use of the relaxation response in patients with stable ischaemic heart-disease. *Lancet*, 1975, *2*, 380–382.

Benton, A., & Spreen, O. Visual memory test performance in mentally deficient and brain damaged patients. *American Journal of Mental Deficiency*, 1964, *68*, 630–633.

Binger, C. *Revolutionary doctor: Benjamin Rush, 1746–1813*. New York: Norton, 1966.

Birk, L. *Biofeedback: Behavioral medicine*. New York: Grune & Stratton, 1973.

Blackburn, H. Diet and mass hyperlipidemia: Public health considerations. In R. Levy, B. Rifkind, B. Dennis, & N. Ernst (Eds.), *Nutrition and coronary heart disease*. New York: Raven Press, 1978.

Blanchard, E. B., & Ahles, T. A. Behavioral treatment of psychophysical disorders. *Behavior Modification*, 1979, *3*, 518–549.

Blanchard, E. B., & Haynes, M. R. Biofeedback treatment of a case of Raynaud's disease. *Journal of Behavior Therapy and Experimental Psychiatry*, 1975, *6*, 230–234.

Blanchard, E. B., Theobald, D., Williamson, D., Silver, B., & Brown, B. Temperature feedback in the treatment of migraine headaches. *Archives of General Psychiatry*, 1978, *35*, 581–588.

Bleecker, E. R., & Engel, B. T. Learned control of cardiac rate and cardiac conduction in the Wolff-Parkinson-White syndrome. *New England Journal of Medicine*, 1973, *288*, 560–562. (a)

Bleecker, E. R., & Engel, B. T. Learned control of ventricular rate in patients with atrial fibrillation. *Psychosomatic Medicine*, 1973, *35*, 161–170. (b)

Blumenthal, J. A., Williams, R. B., Wong, Y., Schanberg, S. M., & Thompson, L. W. Type A behavior pattern and coronary atherosclerosis. *Circulation*, 1978, *58*, 634–639.

Booker, H. B., Rubow, R. T., & Coleman, P. J. Simplified feedback in neuromuscular training: An automated approach using electromyographic signals. *Archives of Physical Medicine and Rehabilitation*, 1969, *50*, 621–625.

Bootzin, R. R., & Nicassio, P. M. Behavioral treatment for insomnia. In M. Hersen, R. M. Eisler, & P. M. Miller (Eds.), *Progress in behavior modification*, Vol. 6. New York: Academic Press, 1978.

Borkovec, T. D., & Weerts, T. C. Effects of progressive relaxation on sleep disturbance: An electroencephalic evaluation. *Psychosomatic Medicine*, 1976, *38*, 173–180.

Borkovec, T. D., Grayson, J. B., O'Brien, G. T., & Weerts, T. C. Relaxation treatment of pseudoinsomnia and idiopathic insomnia: An electroencephalographic evaluation. *Journal of Applied Behavior Analysis*, 1979, *12*, 37–54.

Brauer, A. P., Horlick, L., Nelson, E., Farquhar, J. W., & Agras, W. S. Relaxation therapy for essential hypertension: A Veterans Administration outpatient study. *Journal of Behavioral Medicine*, 1979, *2*, 21–29.

Brener, J. A general model of voluntary control applied to the phenomena of learned cardiovascular change. In P. A. Obrist, A. H. Black, J. Brener, & L. V. DiCara (Eds.), *Cardiovascular psychophysiology*. Chicago: Aldine, 1974.

Brudny, J., Grynbaum, B. B., & Korein, J. Spasmodic torticollis: Treatment by feedback display of the EMG. *Archives of Physical Medicine and Rehabilitation*, 1974, *55*, 403–408.

Brudny, J., Korein, J., Levidow, L., Grynbaum, B. B., Lieberman, A., & Friedman, L. W. Sensory feedback therapy as a modality of treatment in central nervous systems disorders of voluntary movement. *Neurology*, 1974, *24*, 925–932.

Brudny, J., Korein, J., Grynbaum, B. B., Friedman, L. W., Weinstein, S., Sachs-Frankel, G., & Belandres, P. V. EMG feedback therapy: Review of treatment of 114 patients. *Archives of Physical Medicine and Rehabilitation*, 1976, *57*, 55–61.

Budzynski, T., Stoyva, J., & Adler, C. Feedback-induced muscle relaxation: Application to tension headache. *Journal of Behavior Therapy and Experimental Psychiatry*, 1970, *1*, 205–211.

Budzynski, T. H., Stoyva, J. M., Adler, C. S., & Mullaney, D. EMG biofeedback and tension headache: A controlled-outcome study. *Psychosomatic Medicine*, 1973, *35*, 484–496.

Bueno-Miranda, F., Cerulli, M., & Schuster, M. M. Operant conditioning of colonic motility in irritable bowel syndrome (IBS). *Gastroenterology*, 1976, *70*, 867.

Cairns, D., Thomas, L., Mooney, V., & Pace, J. B. A comprehensive treatment approach to chronic low back pain. *Pain*, 1976, *2*, 301–308.

Chesney, M. A., & Shelton, J. L. A comparison of muscle relaxation and electromyogram biofeedback treatments for muscle contraction headache. *Journal of Behavior Therapy and Experimental Psychiatry*, 1976, *7*, 221–225.

Cleeland, C. S. Behavioral techniques in the modification of spasmodic torticollis. *Neurology*, 1973, *23*, 1241–1247.

Cohen, S. I., & Reed, J. L. The treatment of "nervous diarrhea" and other conditioned autonomic disorders by desensitization. *British Journal of Psychiatry*, 1968, *114*, 1275–1280.

Conners, C. K. Behavioral and psychophysiological aspects of Raynaud's disease. In J. M. Ferguson & C. B. Taylor (Eds.), *The comprehensive handbook of behavioral medicine*. Jamaica, N.Y.: SP Medical & Scientific Books, 1980.

Corby, J. C., Roth, W. T., Zarcone, V. P., Jr., & Kopell, B. S. Psychophysiological correlates of practice of Tantric Yoga meditation. *Archives of General Psychiatry*, 1978, *35*, 571–577.

Cox, D. J., Freundlick, A., & Meyer, R. G. Differential effectiveness of electromyograph feedback, verbal relaxation instructions, and medication placebo with tension headaches. *Journal of Consulting and Clinical Psychology*, 1975, *43*, 892–899.

Creer, T. L., Asthma: Psychological aspects and management. In E. Middleton, C. Reed, & E. Ellis (Eds.), *Allergy: Principles and practice.* St. Louis: Mosby, 1978.

Daniels, L. K. Treatment of grand mal epilepsy by covert and operant conditioning techniques. *Psychosomatics*, 1975, *16*, 65–67.

Danker, D. S., Miklich, D. R., Prott, C., & Creer, T. L. An unsuccessful attempt to instrumentally condition peak expiratory flow rates in asthmatic children. *Journal of Psychosomatic Research*, 1975, *19*, 209–215.

Dapcich-Miura, E., & Hovell, M. F. Contingency management of adherence to a complex medical regimen in an elderly heart patient. *Behavior Therapy*, 1979, *10*, 193–201.

Datey, L. K., Deshmukh, S. N., Dalvi, C. P., & Vinekar, S. L. "Shavasan": A yogic exercise in the management of hypertension. *Angiology*, 1969, *20*, 325–333.

Davidson, D. M., Winchester, M. A., Taylor, C. B., Alderman, E. A., & Ingels, N. B., Jr. Effects of relaxation therapy on cardiac performance and sympathetic activity in patients with organic heart disease. *Psychosomatic Medicine*, 1979, *41*, 303–309.

Dembroski, T. D., MacDougall, J. L., Shields, J. L., Petitto, J., & Lushene, R. Component of the Type A coronary-prone behavior pattern and cardiovascular responses to psychomotor performance challenge. *Journal of Behavioral Medicine*, 1978, *1*, 159–176.

Dohrmann, R. J., & Laskin, D. M. An evaluation of electromyographic biofeedback in the treatment of myofascial pain-dysfunction syndrome. *Journal of the American Dental Association*, 1978, *96*, 656–662.

Dunbar, J. *Adherence to medication: An intervention study for poor adherers.* Doctoral thesis, Stanford University, 1977.

Eckert, E., McHugh, R. B., Philander, D. A., & Blumenthal, M. N. Bronchial asthma: Improved lung function after behavior modification. *Psychosomatics*, 1979, *20*, 325–331.

Efron, R. The effect of olfactory stimuli in arresting uncinate fits. *Brain*, 1956, *79*, 267–277.

Efron, R. The conditioned inhibition of uncinate fits. *Brain*, 1957, *80*, 251–262.

Enelow, A. J., & Henderson, T. B. (Eds.), *Applying behavioral science to cardiovascular risk.* Dallas: American Heart Association, 1975.

Engel, B. T., & Bleecker, E. R. Application of operant conditioning techniques to the control of cardiac arrhythmias. In P. A. Obrist, A. H. Black, J. Brener, & L. V. DiCara (Eds.), *Cardiovascular psychophysiology.* Chicago: Aldine, 1974.

Engel, B. T., Nikoomanesh, P., & Schuster, M. M. Operant conditioning of rectosphincteric responses in the treatment of fecal incontinence. *New England Journal of Medicine*, 1974, *290*, 646–649.

Epstein, L. H., & Cinciripini, C. M. Behavioral control of tension headaches. In J. M. Ferguson & C. B. Taylor (Eds.), *The comprehensive handbook of behavioral medicine, Vol. 2.* Jamaica, N.Y.: SP Medical & Scientific Books, 1980.

Epstein, L. H., & Masek, B. J. Behavioral control of medicine compliance. *Journal of Applied Behavior Analysis*, 1978, *11*, 1–9.

Epstein, L. H., & Wing, R. Behavioral approaches to exercise habits and athletic performance. In J. M. Ferguson & C. B. Taylor (Eds.), *The comprehensive handbook of behavioral medicine.* Jamaica, N.Y.: SP Medical & Scientific Books, 1980.

Epstein, L. H., Doke, L. A., Sajwaj, T. E., Sorrell, S., & Rimmer, B. Generality and side effects of overcorrection. *Journal of Applied Behavior Analysis*, 1974, *7*, 385–390.

Epstein, L. H., Collins, F. L., Jr., Hannay, H. J., & Looney, R. L. Fading and feedback in the modification of visual acuity. *Journal of Behavioral Medicine*, 1978, *1*, 273–287.

Epstein, L. H., Greenwald, D. J., Hennon, D., & Hiedorn, B. The effects of monocular fading and feedback on vision changes in the trained and untrained eye. *Behavior Modification*, 1981, *5*, 171–186.

Farquhar, J. W., Maccoby, N. M., Wood, P. D., Alexander, J. K., Breitrose, H., Brown, B. W., Haskell, W. L., McAlister, A. L., Meyer, A. J., Nash, J. D., & Stern, M. P. Community education for cardiovascular health. *Lancet*, 1977, *1*, 1192–1195.

Ferster, C. B., Nurnberger, J. I., & Levitt, E. B. The control of eating. *Journal of Mathetics*, 1962, *1*, 87–109.

Feuerstein, M., Adams, H. E., & Beiman, I. Cephalic vasomotor and electromyographic feedback in the treatment of combined muscle contraction and migraine headaches in a geriatric case. *Headache*, 1976, *16*, 232–237.

Fieldman, C. M. The effect of biofeedback training on respiratory resistance of asthmatic children. *Psychosomatic Medicine*, 1976, *38*, 27–34.

Finley, W. W., Smith, H. A., & Etheron, M. D. Reduction of seizures and normalization of the EEG in a severe epileptic following sensorimotor biofeedback training: Preliminary study. *Biological Psychology*, 1975, *2*, 189–203.

Fitchler, H., & Zimmerman, R. R. Change in reported pain from tension headaches. *Perceptual and Motor Skills*, 1973, *36*, 712.

Flannery, R. B., Jr., and Cautela, J. R. Seizures: Controlling the uncontrollable. *Journal of Rehabilitation*, 1973, *39*, 34–36.

Fordyce, W. F. *Behavioral methods for chronic pain and illness.* St. Louis: Mosbey, 1976.

Fordyce, W., Fowler, R., Lehmann, J., DeLateur, B., Sand, B., & Trieschmann, R. Operant conditioning in the treatment of chronic pain. *Archives of Physical Medicine and Rehabilitation*, 1973, *54*, 399–408.

Foreyt, J., Scott, L. W., Mitchell, R. E., & Giotto, A. M. Plasma lipid changes in the normal population following behavioral treatment. *Journal of Consulting and Clinical Psychology*, 1979, *47*, 440–452.

Forster, F. M. Conditioning of cerebral dysrhythmia induced by pattern presentation and eye-closure. *Conditional Reflex*, 1967, *2*, 236–244.

Forster, F. M. *Reflex epilepsy, behavioral therapy and conditional reflexes.* Springfield, Ill.: Charles C Thomas, 1977.

Forster, F. M., Paulsen, W. A., & Baughman, F. A. Clinical therapeutic conditioning in reading epilepsy. *Neurology*, 1969, *19*, 717–723.

Foxx, R. M., & Rubinoff, A. Behavioral treatment of caffeinism: Reducing excessive coffee drinking. *Journal of Applied Behavior Analysis*, 1979, *12*, 315–324.

Freedman, R., & Papsdorf, J. D. Biofeedback and progressive relaxation treatment of sleep-onset insomnia: A controlled, all-night investigation. *Biofeedback and Self-Regulation*, 1976, *1*, 253–271.

French, A. P., Schmid, A. C., & Ingalls, E. Transcendental meditation, altered reality testing, and behavioral change: A case report. *Journal of Nervous and Mental Disease*, 1976, *161*, 55–59.

Friar, L. R., & Beatty, J. Migraine: Management by trained control of vasoconstriction. *Journal of Consulting and Clinical Psychology*, 1976, *44*, 46–53.

Friedman, M., & Rosenman, R. H. *Type A behavior and your heart.* New York: Knopf, 1974.

Furman, S. Intestinal biofeedback in functional diarrhea: A preliminary report. *Journal of Behavior Therapy and Experimental Psychiatry*, 1973, *4*, 317–321.

Geiger, O. G., & Johnson, L. A. Positive education for elderly persons: Correct eating through reinforcement. *The Gerontologist*, 1974, *14*, 432–436.

Goldring, W., Chasis, H., Schreiner, G. E., & Smith, H. W. Reassurance in the management of benign hypertensive disease. *Circulation*, 1956, *14*, 260–264.

Goodman, M. A., & Gilman, A. *The pharmacological basis of therapeutics* (3rd ed.). New York: Macmillan, 1966.

Goodwin, J. S., Goodwin, J. M., & Vogel, A. V. Knowledge and use of placebos by house officers and nurses. *Annals of Internal Medicine*, 1979, *91*, 106–110.

Hay, K. M., & Madders, J. Migraine treated by relaxation therapy. *Journal of the Royal College of General Practitioners*, 1971, *21*, 449–664.

Haynes, S. N., Griffin, R., Mooney, D., & Parise, M. Electromyographic biofeedback and relaxation instructions in the treatment of muscle contraction headaches. *Behavior Therapy*, 1975, *6*, 672–678.

Hedberg, A. G. The treatment of chronic diarrhea by systematic desensitization: A case report. *Journal of Behavior Therapy and Experimental Psychiatry*, 1973, *4*, 67–68.

Henry, J. P., & Stephens, P. M. The social environment and essential hypertension in mice: Possible role of the innervation of the adrenal cortex. In W. De Jong, A. P. Provost, & A. P. Shapiro (Eds.), *Hypertension and brain mechanisms: Progress in Brain Research*, 1977, *47*, 263–277.

Holroyd, K., Andrasik, F., & Westbrook, T. Cognitive control of tension headache. *Cognitive Therapy and Research*, 1977, *1*, 121–133.

Horan, J. J., Hackett, G., Nicholas, W. C., Linberg, S. E., Stone, C. I., & Lukaski, H. C. Rapid smoking: A cautionary note. *Journal of Consulting and Clinical Psychology*, 1977, *45*, 341–343.

Hutchings, D., & Reinking, R. Tension headaches: What form of therapy is most effective? *Biofeedback and Self-Regulation*, 1976, *1*, 183–190.

Hutzell, R., Platzek, D., & Logue, P. Control of Gilles de la Tourette's syndrome by self-monitoring. *Journal of Behavior Therapy and Experimental Psychiatry*, 1974, *5*, 71–76.

Hypertension Detection and Follow-Up Program Cooperative Group. Five-year findings of the hypertension detection and follow-up program. *Journal of the American Medical Association*, 1979, *242*, 2562–2577.

Illich, I. D. *Medical nemesis: The expropriation of health.* New York: Pantheon, 1976.

Ince, L. P. The use of relaxation training and a conditioned stimulus in the elimination of epileptic seizures in a child: A case study, *Journal of Behavior Therapy and Experimental Psychiatry*, 1976, *7*, 39–42.

Ingersoll, B. F., & Curry, F. Rapid treatment of persistence, vomiting in a 14-year-old female by shaping and time out. *Journal of Behavior Therapy and Experimental Psychiatry*, 1977, *8*, 305–307.

Jacob, R. G., Kraemer, H. C., & Agras, W. S. Relaxation therapy in the treatment of hypertension: A review. *Archives of General Psychiatry*, 1977, *34*, 1417–1427.

Jacobson, A. M., Hackett, T. P., Surman, O. S., & Silverberg, E. Raynaud phenomenon: Treatment with hypnotic and operant technique. *Journal of the American Medical Association*, 1973, *225*, 739–740.

Jacobson, E. *Progressive relaxation.* Chicago: University of Chicago Press, 1938.

Jankel, W. R. Bell palsy: Muscle reeducation by electromyographic feedback. *Archives of Physical Medicine and Rehabilitation*, 1978, *59*, 240–242.

Jones, M. K. Imagery as a mnemonic aid after left temporal lobectomy: Contrast between material-specific and generalized memory disorders. *Neuropsychologia*, 1974, *12*, 21–30.

Kaplan, B. J. Biofeedback in epileptics: Equivocal relationship of reinforced EEG frequency to seizure reduction. *Epilepsia*, 1975, *16*, 477–485.

Katz, R. C., & Zlutnick, S. (Eds.). *Behavior therapy and health care: Principles and applications.* New York: Pergamon, 1975.

Kentsmith, D., Strider, F., Copenhaver, J., & Jacques, D. Effects of biofeedback upon the suppression of migraine symptoms and plasma dopamine-B hydroxylase activity. *Headache*, 1976, *16*, 173–177.

Khan, A. V. Effectiveness of biofeedback and counterconditioning in the treatment of bronchial asthma. *Journal of Psychosomatic Research*, 1977, *21*, 97–104.

Khan, A. V., & Olson, D. L. Deconditioning of exercise-induced asthma. *Psychosomatic Medicine*, 1977, *39*, 382–392.

Khan, A. V., Staerk, M., & Bonk, C. Role of counterconditioning in the treatment of asthma. *Journal of Psychosomatic Research*, 1973, *17*, 389–394.

Khan, A. V., Staerk, M., & Bonk, C. Role of counterconditioning in the treatment of asthma. *Journal of Psychosomatic Research*, 1974, *18*, 89–93.

Kondo, C., & Canter, A. True and false electromyographic feedback: Effect on tension headache. *Journal of Abnormal Psychology*, 1977, *86*, 93–95.

Koppman, J. W., McDonald, R. D., & Kunzel, M. G. Voluntary regulation of temporal artery diameter in migraine patients. *Headache*, 1974, *14*, 133–138.

Kraemer, H. C., Jacob, R. G., Jeffery, R. W., & Agras, W. S. Empirical selection of matching factors in matched-pairs and matched-blocks small-sample research designs. *Behavior Therapy*, 1979, *10*, 615–628.

Kristt, D. A., & Engel, B. T. Learned control of blood

pressure in patients with high blood pressure. *Circulation*, 1975, *51*, 370–378.

Kuhlman, W. N., & Allison, T. EEG feedback training in the treatment of epilepsy: Some questions and answers. *Pavlovian Journal of Biological Science*, 1977, *12*, 112–122.

Kukulka, C. G., Brown, D. M., & Basmajian, J. V. A preliminary report on biofeedback training for early finger joint mobilization. *American Journal of Occupational Therapy*, 1975, *29*, 469–470.

Lahey, B., McNees, P., & McNees, M. Control of an obscene "verbal tic" through timeout in an elementary school classroom. *Journal of Applied Behavior Analysis*, 1973, *6*, 101–104.

Lang, R., Dehof, K., Meurer, K. A., & Kaufmann, W. Sympathetic activity and transcendental meditation. *Journal of Neural Transmission*, 1979, *44*, 117–135.

Lewinsohn, P. M., Danaher, B. G., & Kikel, S. Visual imagery as a mnemonic aid for brain-injured persons. *Journal of Consulting and Clinical Psychology*, 1977, *45*, 717–723.

Lichtenstein, E., & Glasgow, R. E. Rapid smoking: Side effects and safeguards. *Journal of Consulting and Clinical Psychology*, 1977, *45*, 815–821.

Lipowski, Z. J. Psychosomatic medicine in the seventies: An overview. *American Journal of Psychiatry*, 1977, *154*, 233–244.

Lipowski, Z. J., Lipsitt, D. R., & Whybrow, P. C. *Psychosomatic medicine*. New York: Oxford, 1977.

Lubar, J. F. Behavioral management of epilepsy through sensorimotor rhythm EEG biofeedback conditioning. *National Spokesman*, 1975, *8*, 6–7.

Mahoney, M. J., & Arnkoff, D. B. Self-management. In O. F. Pomerleau & J. P. Brady (Eds.), *Behavioral medicine: Theory and practice*. Baltimore: Williams & Wilkins, 1979.

Marholin, D., II, Touchette, P. E., & Malcolm, S. R. Withdrawal of chronic chlorpromazine medication: An experimental analysis. *Journal of Applied Behavior Analysis*, 1979, *12*, 159–172.

Marinacci, A. A., & Horande, M. Electromyogram in neuromuscular reeducation. *Bulletin of the Los Angeles Neurological Society*, 1960, *25*, 57–71.

May, D. S., & Weber, C. A. Temperature feedback training for symptom reduction in Raynaud's disease: A controlled study. *Proceedings of the 7th Annual Meeting of the Biofeedback Research Society*. 1976, p. 50.

McClannahan, L. E. Therapeutic and prosthetic living environments for nursing home residents. *The Gerontologist*, 1973, *13*, 424–429.

McClannahan, L. E., & Risley, T. R. Design of living environments for nursing home residents. *The Gerontologist*, 1974, *14*, 236–240.

Meares, R. Behavior therapy and spasmodic torticollis. *Archives of General Psychiatry*, 1973, *28*, 104–107.

Medina, J. L., Diamond, S., & Franklin, M. A. Biofeedback therapy for migraine. *Headache*, 1976, *16*, 115–118.

Meyer, A. J., & Henderson, J. B. Multiple risk factor reduction in the prevention of cardiovascular disease. *Preventive Medicine*, 1974, *3*, 225–236.

Mitch, P. S., McGrady, A., & Iannone, A. Autogenic feedback training in migraine: A treatment report. *Headache*, 1976, *15*, 267–270.

Mitchell, K. R., & Mitchell, D. W. Migraine: An explor-atory treatment application of programmed behavior therapy techniques. *Journal of Psychosomatic Research*, 1971, *15*, 137–157.

Mitchell, K. R., & White, R. G. Behavioral self-management: An application to the problem of migraine headaches. *Behavior Therapy*, 1977, *8*, 213–221.

Mostofsky, D. I., & Balaschak, B. A. Psychobiological control of seizures. *Psychological Bulletin*, 1977, *84*, 723–750.

Mroczek, N., Halpern, D., & McHugh, R. Electromyographic feedback and physical therapy for neuromuscular retraining in hemiplegia. *Archives of Physical Medicine and Rehabilitation*, 1978, *59*, 258–267.

Mullinix, J., Norton, B., Hack, S., & Fishman, M. Skin temperature biofeedback and migraine. *Headache*, 1978, *17*, 242–244.

Newman, R., Seres, J., Yospe, L., & Garlington, B. Multidisciplinary treatment of chronic pain: Long-term follow-up of low-back pain patients. *Pain*, 1978, *4*, 283–292.

Nicassio, F., Liberman, R. P., Patterson, R., & Ramirez, E. The treatment of tics by negative practice. *Journal of Behavior Therapy and Experimental Psychiatry*, 1972, *3*, 281–287.

Obrist, P. A., Light, K. C., McCubbin, J. A., Hutcheson, J. S., & Hoffer, J. L. Pulse transit time: Relationship to blood pressure and myocardial performance. *Psychophysiology*, 1979, *16*, 292–301.

Ogden, H. D. Headache studies. Statistical data. I: Procedure and sample distribution. *Journal of Allergy*, 1952, *23*, 58–75.

Paffenbarger, R. S., Hale, W. E., Brand, R. J., & Hyde, R. T. Work energy level, personal characteristics and fatal heart attack: A birth-cohort effect. *American Journal of Epidemiology*, 1977, *105*, 200–213.

Parrino, J. J. Reduction of seizures by desensitization. *Journal of Behavior Therapy and Experimental Psychiatry*, 1971, *2*, 215–218.

Patel, C. H. Yoga and biofeedback in the management of hypertension. *Lancet*, 1973, *2*, 1053–1055.

Patten, B. M. The ancient art of memory—Usefulness in treatment. *Archives of Neurology*, 1972, *26*, 25–31.

Peck, C. L., & Kraft, G. H. Electromyographic biofeedback for pain related to muscle tension: Study of tension headache, back, and jaw pain. *Archives of Surgery*, 1977, *112*, 889–895.

Peterson, R. G., Knapp, T. J., Rosen, J. C., & Pither, B. F. The effects of furniture arrangement. *Behavior Therapy*, 1977, *8*, 464–467.

Phillips, C. The modification of tension headache pain using EMG biofeedback. *Behaviour Research and Therapy*, 1977, *15*, 119–129.

Pickering, T. G., & Miller, N. E. Learned voluntary control of heart rate and rhythm in two subjects with premature ventricular contractions. *British Heart Journal*, 1977, *39*, 152–159.

Pollock, D. D., & Liberman, R. P. Behavior therapy of incontinence in demented inpatients. *The Gerontologist*, 1974, *14*, 488–491.

Price, K. P., & Tursky, B. Vascular reactivity of migraineurs and nonmigraineurs: A comparison of responses to self-control procedures. *Headache*, 1976, *16*, 210–217.

Raymond, M. J. The treatment of addiction by aversion conditioning with apomorphine. *Behaviour Research and Therapy*, 1964, *1*, 287–291.

Reading, C., & Mohr, P. D. Biofeedback control of migraine: A pilot study. *British Journal of Social and Clinical Psychology,* 1976, *15,* 429–433.

Rene, C., & Creer, T. L. The effects of training on the use of inhalation therapy equipment by children with asthma. *Journal of Applied Behavior Analysis,* 1976, *9,* 1–11.

Richardson, R. A. *Environmental contingencies in seizure disorders.* Paper presented at the Association for Advancement of Behavior Therapy, New York, Oct. 1972.

Risley, T. R., Gottula, P., & Edwards, K. A. *Social interaction during family and institutional style meal service in a nursing home dining room.* Paper presented at the Nova Behavioral Conference on Aging, Port St. Lucie, Fla., 1978.

Risley, T. R., Spangler, P. F., & Edwards, K. A. *Behavioral care of nonambulatory geriatric patients.* Paper presented at the Nova Behavioral Conference on Aging, Port St. Lucie, Fla., 1978.

Robertson-Tchabo, E. A., Nausman, C. P., & Arenberg, D. A trip that worked: A classical mnemonic for older learners. *Educational Gerontology,* 1976, *1,* 216–226.

Roth, S. R., Sterman, M. B., & Clemente, C. D. Comparison of EEG correlates of reinforcement, internal inhibition, and sleep. *Electroencephalography and Clinical Neurophysiology,* 1967, *23,* 509–520.

Rowe, E. C., & Schnore, M. N. Item concreteness and reported strategies in paired-associate learning as a function of age. *Journal of Gerontology,* 1971, *26,* 470–475.

Roxanas, M. R., Thomas, M. R., & Rapp, M. S. Biofeedback treatment of blepharospasm with spasmodic torticollis. *Canadian Medical Association Journal,* 1978, *119,* 48–49.

Sargent, J. D., Walters, E. E., & Green, E. D. Psychosomatic self-regulation of migraine headaches. In L. Birk (Ed.), *Biofeedback: Behavioral medicine.* New York: Grune & Stratton, 1973.

Scott, R. W., Blanchard, E. B., Edmundson, E. D., & Young, L. D. A shaping procedure for heart rate control in chronic tachycardia. *Perceptual and Motor Skills,* 1973, *37,* 327–338.

Shapiro, D., & Schwartz, G. E. Biofeedback and visceral learning: Clinical applications. *Seminars in Psychiatry,* 1972, *4,* 171–184.

Shapiro, D., & Surwit, R. S. Biofeedback. In O. F. Pomerleau & J. P. Brady (Eds.), *Behavioral medicine: Theory and practice.* Baltimore: Williams & Wilkins, 1979.

Shapiro, D., Mainardi, J. A., & Surwit, R. S. Biofeedback and self-regulation in essential hypertension. In G. E. Schwartz & J. Beatty (Eds.), *Biofeedback: Theory and research.* New York: Academic Press, 1977.

Sherman, R. A., Gall, N., & Gormly, J. Treatment of phantom limb pain with muscular relaxation training to disrupt the pain anxiety tension cycle. *Pain,* 1979, *6,* 47–55.

Smith, W. M. Epidemiology of hypertension. *Medical Clinics of North America,* 1977, *61,* 467–486. (a)

Smith, W. M. Treatment of mild hypertension: Results of a ten-year intervention trial. *Circulation Research,* 1977, *40* (Suppl. 1), 98–105. (b)

Sterman, M. B. Neurophysiological and clinical studies of sensorimotor EEG biofeedback training: Some ef-fects on epilepsy. In L. Birk (Ed.), *Biofeedback: Behavioral medicine.* New York: Grune & Stratton, 1973.

Sterman, M. B., & Friar, L. Suppression of seizures in an epileptic following sensorimotor EEG feedback training. *Electroencephalography and Clinical Neurophysiology,* 1972, *33,* 89–95.

Sternbach, R. A. *Pain patients: Traits and treatment.* New York: Academic Press, 1974.

Stewart, R. B., & Cluff, L. E. Commentary: A review of medication errors and compliance in ambulant patients. *Clinical and Pharmacological Therapy,* 1972, *13,* 463–468.

Stone, R. A., & DeLeo, J. Psychotherapeutic control of hypertension. *New England Journal of Medicine,* 1976, *294,* 80–84.

Stroebel, C. F., & Glueck, B. C. Biofeedback treatment in medicine and psychiatry: An ultimate placebo? In L. Birk (Ed.), *Biofeedback: Behavioral medicine.* New York: Grune & Stratton, 1973.

Suinn, R. M. Behavior therapy for cardiac patients. *Behavior Therapy,* 1974, *5,* 569–571.

Suinn, R. M., & Bloom, L. J. Anxiety management training for Pattern A behavior. *Journal of Behavioral Medicine,* 1978, *1,* 25–35.

Sunderman, R., & Delk, J. Treatment of Raynaud's disease with temperature biofeedback. *Southern Medical Journal,* 1978, *71,* 340–342.

Surwit, R., Pilon, R., & Fenton, C. Behavioral treatment of Raynaud's disease. *Journal of Behavioral Medicine,* 1978, *1,* 323–335.

Swanson, D., Floreen, A., & Swenson, W. Program for managing chronic pain. II: Short-term results. *Mayo Clinical Proceedings,* 1976, *51,* 409–411.

Swanson, D. W., Swenson, W. M., Huizenga, K. A., & Melson, S. J. Persistent nausea without organic cause. *Mayo Clinical Proceedings,* 1976, *51,* 257–262.

Tarler-Benlolo, L., & Love, W. A. *EMG-biofeedback treatment of spastic colon: A case report.* Presented at the meeting of the Biofeedback Society of America, Orlando, Fla., March 1977.

Tasto, D. K., & Chesney, M. A. The deconditioning of nausea and of crying by emotional imagery: A report of two cases. *Journal of Behavior Therapy and Experimental Psychiatry,* 1977, *8,* 139–142.

Tasto, D. L., & Hinkle, J. E. Muscle relaxation treatment for tension headaches. *Behaviour Research and Therapy,* 1973, *11,* 347–349.

Taub, E. Self-regulation of human tissue temperature. In G. Schwartz & J. Beatty (Eds.), *Biofeedback: Therapy and research.* New York: Academic Press, 1977.

Taylor, C. B. Behavioral approaches to essential hypertension. In J. M. Ferguson & C. B. Taylor (Eds.), *The comprehensive handbook of behavioral medicine,* Vol. 1. Jamaica, N.Y.: SP Medical & Scientific Books, 1980.

Taylor, C. B., Zlutnick, S. I., & Hoehle, W. The effects of behavioral procedures on tardive dyskinesias. *Behavior Therapy,* 1979, *10,* 37–45.

Thomas, E., Abrams, K., & Johnson, J. Self-monitoring and reciprocal inhibition in the modification of multiple tics of Gilles de la Tourette's syndrome. *Journal of Behavior Therapy and Experimental Psychiatry,* 1971, *2,* 159–171.

Thoresen, C. E., Coates, T. J., Zarcone, V. P., Kirmil-

Gray, K., & Rosekind, M. R. Treating the complaint of insomnia: Self-management perspectives. In J. M. Ferguson & C. B. Taylor (Eds.), *The comprehensive handbook of behavioral medicine,* Vol. 1. Jamaica, N.Y.: SP Medical & Scientific Books, 1980.

Turin, A., & Johnson, W. G. Biofeedback therapy for migraine headaches. *Archives of General Psychiatry,* 1976, *33,* 517–519.

U.S. Department of Commerce, U.S. Bureau of Census. *Statistical abstract of the United States, 1977.* Washington, D.C.: U.S. Government Printing Office, 1977.

U.S. Government Printing Office. *Dietary goals for the United States.* Washington, D.C.: U.S. Government Printing Office, 1978.

Vachon, L., & Rich, E. S. Visceral learning in asthma. *Psychosomatic Medicine,* 1976, *38,* 122–130.

Walton, D. The application of learning theory to the treatment of a case of bronchial asthma. In H. J. Eysenck (Ed.), *Behaviour therapy and the neuroses.* New York: Macmillan, 1969.

Warner, G., & Lance, J. W. Relaxation therapy in migraine and chronic tension headache. *Medical Journal of Australia,* 1975, *1,* 298–301.

Webb, N. C. The use of myoelectric feedback in teaching facial expression to the blind. *Biofeedback and Self-Regulation,* 1977, *2,* 147–160.

Weiner, H. M. *The psychobiology of human illness.* New York: Elsevier, 1977.

Weinstock, S. A. *The reestablishment of intestinal control in functional colitis.* Presented at the meeting of the Biofeedback Research Society, Colorado Springs, Feb. 1976.

Weiss, T., & Engel, B. T. Operant conditioning of heart rate in patients with premature ventricular contractions. *Psychosomatic Medicine,* 1971, *33,* 301–321.

Welgan, P. R. Learned control of gastric acid secretions in ulcer patients. *Psychosomatic Medicine,* 1974, *36,* 411–419.

Wells, K. C., Turner, S. M., Bellack, A. S., & Hersen, M. Effects of cue controlled relaxation on psychomotor seizures: An experimental analysis. *Behaviour Research and Therapy,* 1978, *16,* 51–53.

Whitehead, W. E., Renault, P. F., & Goldiamond, I. Modification of human gastric acid secretion with operant conditioning procedures. *Journal of Applied Behavior Analysis,* 1975, *8,* 147–156.

Wickramasekera, I. Application of verbal instructions and EMG feedback training to the management of tension headache: Preliminary observations. *Headache,* 1973, *13,* 74–76. (a)

Wickramasekera, I. Temperature feedback for the control of migraine. *Journal of Behavior Therapy and Experimental Psychiatry,* 1973, *4,* 343–345. (b)

Wolff, H. G., & Goodell, H. *Stress and disease* (2nd ed.). Springfield, Ill.: Charles C Thomas, 1968.

Wolpe, J. *Psychotherapy by reciprocal inhibition.* Stanford, Calif.: Stanford University Press, 1958.

Wooley, S. C., Blackwell, B., & Winget, C. A learning theory model of chronic illness behavior: Theory, treatment and research. *Psychosomatic Medicine,* 1978, *40,* 379–401.

Wysocki, T., Hall, G., Iwata, B., & Riordan, M. Behavioral management of exercise: Contracting for aerobic points. *Journal of Applied Behavior Analysis,* 1979, *12,* 55–64.

Yates, A. J. The application of learning theory to the treatment of tics. *Journal of Abnormal and Social Psychology,* 1958, *56,* 175–182.

Zlutnick, S., Mayville, W. J., & Moffat, S. Modification of seizure disorders: The interruption of behavioral chains. *Journal of Applied Behavior Analysis,* 1975, *8,* 1–12.

CHAPTER 17

Alcohol and Drug Problems

Mark B. Sobell, Linda C. Sobell, Seth Ersner-Hershfield, and Ted D. Nirenberg

Introduction

Alcohol and other drugs are an integral part of our society. In fact, the use of alcohol is pervasive in most societies and has been so for many centuries (Keller, 1976). While the use of various other drugs has had a similarly long history (Einstein, 1975; Ray, 1972), the variety and use of such substances has increased markedly during the present century, a growth commensurate with the science of pharmacology (Brecher and Consumer Report Editors, 1972). In most societies, a majority of persons at one time or another drink or use other drugs (e.g., medicinal compounds) without incurring major problems for themselves or society, but others use drugs in ways that produce negative consequences, both personal and social.

For the purposes of this chapter, *uses of alcohol or other drugs that result in adverse consequences for the user, for society, or both are referred to as alcohol and drug problems.*

While there have been numerous attempts to provide more circumscribed definitions of alcohol- and drug-related behavioral aberrations (e.g., American Psychiatric Association, 1968, 1980; Jellinek, 1960; Keller, 1960; National Council on Alcoholism, 1972; Seixas, Blume, Cloud, Lieber, & Simpson, 1976; World Health Organization, 1964), each of these definitions have their advantages and disadvantages. In this regard, the definition offered above captures the essence of most descriptions.

Typically, drugs are classed according to their pharmacological actions. However, legal definitions sometimes blur the distinctions (Kalant & Kalant, 1971). The basic classes of drugs of interest in this chapter include the depressants, the stimulants, and a set of drugs that have been referred to as *hallucinogens, psychedelics,* or *distorters of consciousness and perception* (Einstein, 1975; Kalant & Kalant, 1971). The use of nicotine and caffeine is not considered in this chapter.

Depressant drugs act on the central nervous system to decrease arousal; they include alcohol, narcotics (opiate and synthetic opiate compounds such as heroin, morphine, codeine, and methadone), barbiturates, tranquilizers, and a variety of other substances such as anesthetics and solvent vapors. Many of these drugs share the phenomena of toler-

Mark B. Sobell and Linda C. Sobell • Clinical Institute, Addiction Research Foundation and University of Toronto, Toronto, Ontario, Canada M5S 2S1.   Seth Ersner-Hershfield, • Newton Memorial Hospital, Newton, New Jersey 07860.   Ted D. Nirenberg • Sea Pines Behavioral Institute, Hilton Head Island, South Carolina 29928.

ance and physical dependence. Basically, *tolerance* means an apparent biological adaptation: as a person has repeated experiences with a tolerance-inducing drug, the person requires an increasing dose of the drug to achieve the same degree of subjective or objective effect (Kalant, LeBlanc, & Gibbins, 1971). As people become capable of sustaining higher and higher levels of the drug in their bloodstream, physical dependence may be initiated. *Physical dependence* is a state inferred from the appearance of withdrawal symptoms on cessation of drug use. In many ways, these withdrawal symptoms can be described as a time-limited relative hyperactivity of the central nervous system that may include psychomotor tremors, hallucinations, seizures, and similar symptoms. This state should be distinguished from what has sometimes been called *psychological dependence,* in which the individual manifests a strong desire to use the drug but exhibits no observable withdrawal symptoms if the drug is not taken.

Stimulant drugs act to increase central-nervous-system arousal and include the amphetamines, cocaine, caffeine, and other less-used substances. Although some stimulants have been demonstrated to induce tolerance, it is not yet clear whether they produce physical dependence (Ray, 1972). In any event, the central-nervous-system consequences of the cessation of stimulant use following chronic use are minor compared with those following withdrawal from depressants (Ray, 1972).

The *hallucinogens* include lysergic acid diethylamide (LSD), mescaline, psilocybin, cannabis (marijuana), and several other synthetic or natural compounds. The pharmacological mechanisms by which these drugs produce their effects are not yet well understood, but the effects of "bad trips" can be pervasively deleterious and include panic reactions, depersonalization, and psychosis (Kalant & Kalant, 1971). It is not known, however, whether these states are drug-induced or are simply due to predispositions that are triggered by the drug experience.

While there is an abundance of similarities and differences among various drugs in terms of their use, effects, and consequences, one commonality particularly germane to this chapter is that drug-taking behavior has repeatedly been shown to have respondent and operant learning components in both human and infrahuman organisms (e.g., Altman, Meyer, Mirin, McNamee, & McDougle, 1976; Cappell & Pliner, 1974; Krasnagor, 1978, 1979; Mello, 1972; Mello & Mendelson, 1971; Mello, Mendelson, Kuehnle, & Sellers, 1978; Mendelson, Kuehnle, Greenberg, & Mello, 1976; Nathan, Marlatt, & Løberg, 1978; Schuster & Johanson, 1973; Thompson & Schuster, 1968; Wikler, 1971). Respondent (classical) conditioning aspects have generally concerned conditioned withdrawal reactions (O'Brien, Testa, O'Brien, Brady, & Wells, 1977; Teasdale, 1973; Wikler, 1965) whereby individuals who have been physically dependent on drugs are postulated to experience conditioned aversive components of the withdrawal reaction (e.g., anxiety) when in the presence of drug cues. This state of conditioned withdrawal may be associated with subsequent drug-seeking to alleviate those symptoms. Numerous studies based on operant conditioning paradigms have demonstrated that drug use can be considered a discriminated operant: it occurs in certain contexts and can be modified by altering its antecedents and consequences. To date, the operant perspective, wherein drug use is conceptualized as being a function of particular antecedents and consequences, has yielded the most treatment applications.

This chapter presents a summary and evaluation of current behavioral treatment of both alcohol and other drug problems (hereafter referred to as *drug problems*) in the context of a historical perspective on traditional and behavioral treatment methods. The chapter concludes with a general discussion outlining possible future developments in this area.

Traditional and Behavioral Treatment Methods

For many years, few objective data were available regarding the nature of alcohol and drug problems. In the absence of scientific evidence, popular conceptions of the phenomena were based largely on phenomenological reports from alcohol and drug abusers and persons who had successfully dealt with those problems. In the alcohol field, these popular beliefs became reified, including such notions as that once an individual had been addicted to (physically dependent on) alcohol, readdiction would occur simply by consumption of a very small amount of alcohol (Pattison, Sobell, & Sobell, 1977). The advent of basic behavioral research in the 1960s marked the beginning of an era of rapid growth of knowledge about alcohol problems that has necessitated a pervasive reformulation of concepts about alcohol problems. For a review of the revolutionary changes now under way in conceptualizing alcohol problems, interested readers are referred to Pattison *et al.* (1977).

At the treatment level, traditional non-data-based notions have dominated among treatment approaches to alcohol problems. Most often, treatment has been conducted by paraprofessionals who frequently are associated with Alcoholics Anonymous. Tournier (1979) has recently argued that this influence is so pervasive that it constitutes an ideology rather than a treatment method. Consequently, treatment has usually focused on inpatient care for chronically physically dependent individuals, although such persons are a minority of those who have serious drinking problems (National Institute on Alcohol Abuse and Alcoholism, 1978). Traditional treatment methods, although poorly elucidated in the literature, have basically included inpatient detoxification and/or counseling, halfway houses, and attendance at Alcoholics Anonymous meetings. Therapeutic styles have emphasized supportive counseling and confrontation of the purported denial of the severity of drinking problems. While such methods may be appropriate in some cases, increasing attention has been given to a multivariate approach to treatment that postulates that the population of persons with alcohol problems is heterogeneous, as are the problems themselves, and that treatment services should be matched to individual case needs (Pattison *et al.,* 1977). This is an admirable long-term objective; however, little empirical information is currently available regarding what client–treatment matches are most effective.

Although aversive therapy based on Pavlovian conditioning (reviewed later in this chapter) was used to treat problem drinkers early in this century (Kantorovich, 1929; Voegtlin & Lemere, 1942), the development of sophisticated behavioral treatments is a recent occurrence. The modern use of behavioral treatment methods was foreshadowed by the pioneering work of Mendelson and his colleagues (Mendelson, 1964), who experimentally studied alcoholics given access to alcohol in a laboratory setting. These and similar early demonstrations of the operant modifiability of drinking behavior rapidly led to the plethora of alcohol-treatment research reviewed in this chapter.

Interestingly, the field of other drug problems has followed a similar development. The development of treatments for heroin addicts (again, the most seriously impaired and societally distressing members of a larger population of problem drug-users) occurred largely in the 1950s with the recognition of an increasing number of young heroin addicts in large urban areas (Jaffe, 1979). Popular conceptions of drug addiction abound, and in the 1960s paraprofessionals, largely recovered drug addicts, came to play a major role in the treatment of drug problems. The most notable paraprofessional program has been Synanon, an ex-addict–governed therapeutic community emphasizing strong confrontation and peer-group pressure as treatment facilitators.

A major breakthrough in the treatment of heroin addiction occurred in the 1960s when Dole and Nyswander (1965) reported the successful use of methadone as a heroin substitute. Methadone inhibits withdrawal symptoms in addicts, is an analgesic, is longer-acting than heroin, and can be administered orally. It can be used either for detoxification (by transferring the dependency to methadone and then gradually decreasing the dosage) or maintenance (basically as a substitute for heroin; it is thought to have less deleterious effects and, most importantly, is available by medical prescription). An advantage of methadone treatment is that it can be easily used on an outpatient basis. Again, applications of Pavlovian aversive conditioning were reported in the 1930s (Rubenstein, 1931), but basic demonstrations of the operant nature of heroin use have occurred only recently (see Krasnagor, 1978, 1979). As might be expected, in recent years there has been a remarkable increase in the publication of studies on the behavioral treatment of problem drug-users.

It is evident, then, that the development of behavioral treatments for both alcohol and drug problems has occurred relatively recently. Thus, this review constitutes an appraisal of present treatments and prospects for future developments.

Distinctions and Problems

Before considering the treatment research in detail, some basic comments about the nature of the literature need to be addressed. First, unimodal studies should be distinguished from multimodal studies. As we use the term, a *unimodal study* primarily examines the utility of one particular treatment procedure (e.g., skills training, aversive conditioning, or systematic desensitization). If appropriate comparison conditions are used, these studies have the advantage of unequivocally demonstrating the efficacy of a given technique. However, considering the complexity of human behavior, unimodal studies run the risk of concluding that a given technique is not helpful when in fact it may be effective when combined with other treatment strategies. Inferences made from unimodal studies, therefore, should be carefully limited to situations where the particular method is used in isolation. Multimodal studies typically are based on the rationale that an individual has a cluster of behavioral problems, all of which need to be addressed in order for treatment to be effective. Thus, multimodal studies examine the efficacy of a combination of treatment procedures, and the contributions of specific procedures usually cannot be evaluated. The expectation is that once an effective treatment package has been delineated, further research can determine the vital components.

Several methodological and conceptual problems pervade many behavioral alcohol and drug treatment studies. For instance, subject populations are sometimes so poorly described that comparisons between studies are impossible. For drug studies in particular, comparability among studies is further hampered by regional or ethnic differences in sample composition (Callahan & Rawson, 1980),

and generalizability to typical treatment populations is clouded by the use of atypical (e.g., highly motivated, college-educated) subjects in many research studies (Callner, 1975). Also, for pragmatic reasons, behavioral interventions have often been overlaid on established traditional treatment programs. This procedure, unfortunately, can lead to a confounding of the results. Additionally, many studies have lacked control or comparison groups, a factor that greatly complicates the task of drawing conclusions.

Other questions are raised by case reports or studies involving extremely small samples without appropriate single-subject designs (Hersen & Barlow, 1976). While this procedure occurs frequently in a newly developing area of clinical research, the resultant conclusions must clearly be tempered since individual differences as well as extraneous variables cannot be ruled out as alternative explanations of the findings (Campbell & Stanley, 1966). Additionally, very few alcohol studies and only a slightly greater proportion of drug studies have used females as subjects. Thus, this review relates primarily to male alcohol and drug abusers; extrapolations to females must be made cautiously.

Another factor confusing the interpretation of results is that many studies, especially drug treatment studies, use subjects who are coerced by the courts to participate in treatment. Moreover, sometimes both coerced and noncoerced subjects are used in a single study and are neither equalized among groups nor differentiated in the analysis of the results. Finally, a very serious problem is that very few of the studies reviewed report long-term follow-up results. Therefore, although many studies demonstrate a treatment impact, few provide evidence that treatment gains are maintained.

Behavioral Treatment of Alcohol and Drug Problems

Unimodal Methods

Aversive Conditioning: Alcohol Abusers. There are several procedural variations of aversive conditioning therapy (Cautela & Rosenstiel, 1975; Davidson, 1974; Elkins, 1975;

Rachman & Teasdale, 1969), but all basically involve the pairing of a noxious stimulus (electric shock, nausea or apnea-inducing substances, or imaginal aversive events) with drinking cues (e.g., visual, olfactory) or actual drinking. The intention is to produce a conditioned aversive response to drinking-related cues so that the individual will seek to escape from those cues rather than to drink. Despite several early reports (e.g., Blake, 1965; Vogler, Lunde, Johnson, & Martin, 1970) that electrical aversive conditioning was an effective intervention, some well-designed basic research studies have provided convincing evidence that the postulated conditioned aversive response to drinking cues does not develop (Hallam, Rachman, & Falkowski, 1972) and that drinking in a laboratory situation is not reduced following a series of aversive treatments (Miller, Hersen, Eisler, & Hemphill, 1973; Wilson, Leaf, & Nathan, 1975). Considering this evidence, as well as ethical constraints, electrical aversive conditioning does not seem a worthwhile avenue for further exploration.

Chemical aversive conditioning, using substances such as emetine or Anectine (the former elicits nausea, the latter respiratory paralysis) requires medical supervision. While early reports of success are plentiful (e.g., Lemere & Voegtlin, 1950; Raymond, 1964; Thimann, 1949; Voegtlin & Lemere, 1942), the results of later studies have provided conflicting evidence. Holzinger, Mortimer, and Van Dusen (1967) and Farrar, Powell, and Martin (1968) have reported unfavorable results, while Wiens, Montague, Manaugh, and English (1976) reported positive findings. In general, studies of chemical aversive conditioning have been poorly controlled and included aversive therapy as one of several treatment components. Rachman and Teasdale (1969) have discussed at length the theoretical problems of using nausea-inducing agents (the paradigm may constitute backward classical conditioning) as unconditioned stimuli. In terms of the temporal placement of the aversive event, respiratory arrest techniques are theoretically stronger than emetic methods, but ethical considerations would seem to weigh heavily against the use of such methods except as a last resort. A recent development in this area is the use

of taste aversion conditioning, conceptually premised on the notion of the biological preparedness of the organism to associate particular stimuli. This work stems largely from studies by Garcia (e.g., Garcia & Koelling, 1966) indicating that conditioned taste aversions can develop even with considerable (e.g., 24-hr) temporal separation of the unconditioned and conditioned stimuli if illness is the aversive event. A recent study by Baker (1980) has shown that taste aversion conditioning can produce physiologically verified conditioned aversions in alcoholics.

Imaginal aversive stimuli have been used in several studies, most usually in a covert sensitization paradigm (Cautela, 1966; reviewed by Cautela & Rosenstiel, 1975) where strong images of highly aversive events are paired with images of drinking. An advantage of this method is that the subjects can be instructed to self-administer the aversive association if they feel an urge to drink. Unfortunately, inadequate controls and follow-up, as well as the conjoint use of additional treatment procedures, make it impossible to determine the validity of this technique (Little & Curran, 1978). An interesting variation of covert sensitization has been reported as a case study by Smith and Gregory (1976). The subject was instructed to imagine that he had been responsible for a fatal automobile accident while driving drunk. Although the subject was reported abstinent at a six-month follow-up, it is impossible to determine whether the outcome was a result of the sensitization procedure.

Summary. Overall, although aversive methods may possibly have some short-term utility in preventing drinking while individuals participate in the treatment, evidence is mounting against their long-term effectiveness. Furthermore, on ethical grounds, it is difficult to justify the preference of aversive conditioning methods over other methods, such as the use of disulfiram (Antabuse), which causes an aversive reaction (disulfiram-ethanol reaction) only if the individual drinks. Moreover, even if conditioned aversions can be reliably produced, it seems likely that they will be found to be easily extinguishable.

Aversive Conditioning: Drug Abusers. Aversive methods have been extensively used in the treatment of drug abusers. This emphasis is possibly related to (1) Wikler's (1965) contention that drug cues can elicit conditioned withdrawal reactions; (2) the prevalent idea that the reinforcing effects of some drugs are very strong (Smith & Gay, 1972); or (3) the fact that drug abusers often participate in treatment only because of court coercion.

Chemical and Electrical Aversive Stimuli. Chemical aversive conditioning was one of the earliest behavioral methods used with drug abusers. Raymond (1964) reported treating a female methadone addict by aversion to apomorphine (an emetic). After eight days of treatment, the aversion sessions were discontinued as the subject became severely depressed and was then treated by electroconvulsive shock therapy. Aversive therapy was later reinstated, and the subject was reported as drug-free at a 30-month follow-up.

Based on Wikler's (1965) model of opiate addiction, Liberman (1968) reported two case studies (one male, one female) of narcotic addicts treated by apomorphine aversive conditioning. The subjects were both reported as highly motivated and were scheduled for 38 sessions over a five-week period. The female subject was reported as not readdicted at a one-year follow-up; the male subject, however, became distrustful after a placebo trial, terminated treatment, and relapsed.

Thompson and Rathod (1968) treated 10 hospitalized heroin addicts using Scoline, which produces respiratory paralysis. There were 6 other addicts, who were admitted before the aversive conditioning program began, who served as control subjects. Just before the onset of paralysis during aversive conditioning trials, the subjects were given accounts of the dangers of heroin use, including how death could occur by respiratory paralysis. Also, on five nights during the treatment, the subjects were supplied with a small amount of heroin and told to use it if they found it irresistible. No subject used the heroin during the treatment, and 8 of the 10 subjects were reported as drug-free at follow-up intervals varying from 3 to 30 weeks. The control subjects, although not randomly assigned, all relapsed following traditional treatment.

Electrical aversive stimuli have also been used in several studies. O'Brien, Raynes, and Patch (1972) reported two case studies in which heroin addicts were first taught relaxation skills and then treated by electrical aversive conditioning, with the conditioned stimuli being stories about the act of fixing (injecting heroin). Before and at various times throughout the conditioning series, the subjects were asked to use a 5-point scale to rate their desire to use heroin. One subject, a 30-year-old female, was subsequently treated by systematic desensitization for a fear that developed after she was forcibly restrained by a pusher and injected with narcotics while on a pass from the program. After 27 total conditioning sessions, she was discharged but returned as an outpatient for booster treatments. She was reported drug-free at a 14-month follow-up. The other subject, a 24-year-old male, was reported drug-free at a 6-month follow-up but refused booster sessions.

Spevak, Pihl, and Rowan (1973) reported three case studies of male adolescents who were amphetamine abusers and were treated by electrical aversive conditioning. Over the course of the treatment, the subjects' attitudes toward drug-ritual–related stimuli were assessed by use of a semantic differential, the subjects' self-reported urges to use drugs, and their reported use of drugs. Although both their drug thoughts and their use decreased over treatment, two of the three subjects relapsed during a seven-month follow-up period.

Electrical aversion was also employed by Lubetkin and Fishman (1974) in treating a 23-year-old male graduate student who used heroin from two to three times per week. Conditioned stimuli were produced by the subject's imagining various aspects of the drug use situation. Although the subject was reported drug free at an eight-month follow-up, the use of other therapy components (group therapy and marital counseling) makes it difficult to ascertain the influence of aversive conditioning.

Copemann (1976) treated 30 young, black, court-coerced heroin addicts using a combination of electrical aversive conditioning, behaviorally oriented group therapy, and relaxation training. Cessation of shock was contingent on the subjects' verbalizing socially appropriate behaviors. Follow-up assessment based on urinalysis, as well as interviews with the subjects and their collaterals, revealed that of those subjects who stayed in the treatment for six months, all remained drug-free for seven months, 20% relapsed during the eighth month of follow-up, and 80% remained drug-free from that time through a two-year follow-up. If it is taken into consideration that the subjects were coerced, it is likely that the outcome rate was superior to the rate that would have resulted from traditional treatment, although no control group was used.

Covert Aversive Stimuli. Several studies have investigated the use of covert conditioning methods with drug abusers (reviewed by Cautela & Rosensteil, 1975). Cautela and Rosenstiel (1975) described the advantages of covert methods as including (1) a low treatment-dropout rate; (2) no need for specialized equipment; and (3) applicability to self-control methods.

Early case studies of aversive conditioning using covert methods were reported by Kolvin (1967) and Anant (1968). Kolvin (1967) discussed a case in which aversive imagery was used with an adolescent who frequently sniffed gasoline vapors. Aversive imagery (fear of heights and falling) was used rather than other modes of therapy because the subject was of low intelligence (IQ = 63), and his drug abuse was very persistent and hazardous. Twenty conditioning sessions were conducted, and the subject was reported drug-free at a 13-month follow-up. Anant (1968) reported using covert sensitization to treat a 32-year-old female who was dependent on tranquilizers and alcohol. The subject was reported to be drug-free at a three-month follow-up.

Wisocki (1973) used covert techniques to treat a 26-year-old college graduate heroin addict. The methods included covert reinforcement of thoughts and behaviors antagonistic to heroin use, thought stopping of drug-related thoughts, and covert sensitization to create an aversion to heroin use. The treatment lasted 4 months, and the subject was reported drug-free at an 18-month follow-up. Steinfeld, Rautio, Rice, and Egan (1974) used group covert sensitization and a variety of other methods to treat eight federal prisoners who were drug addicts. Unfortunately, the outcome data were restricted to evidence of rearrest, which probably related only tangentially to drug use.

An interesting variation was added to the covert techniques by Maletzky (1974), who found that imaginal scenes were often not sufficiently vivid to induce a conditioned aversive reaction. He performed a controlled study using drug-abusing military personnel as subjects (10 subjects used primarily alcohol, 2 used cigarettes, and 8 used other drugs). The subjects were randomly assigned to either an experimental or a control group. In addition to covert sensitization, the experimental subjects also received individual therapy and Antabuse (if they abused alcohol). The sensitization procedure was aided by having the subjects sniff valeric acid, a harmless procedure that added vivid noxious olfactory cues. An extensive battery of outcome data revealed that at a six-month follow-up, both groups showed significant decreases in drug use, with 90% of the experimental and 50% of the control subjects reducing their drug use.

In one of the few studies consistent with Wikler's (1965) theory of conditioned withdrawal, Götestam and Melin (1974) treated four female intravenous amphetamine addicts using covert extinction. The subjects were told to imagine the injection situation and then to imagine that they got no "flash" from the injection and felt no drug effects whatsoever. About 200 extinction trials were conducted per subject. Three subjects were reported drug-free at a 9-month follow-up, while one relapsed 2½ months after treatment began.

Copemann (1977) presented three case studies of covert sensitization with polydrug-abusing young heroin addicts. Originally electrical aversive stimuli were to be used, but the subjects reported that they had trouble relaxing during conditioning sessions because they anticipated the shocks. Further problems ensued when covert methods were used, as the subjects reported that although the imagined scenes were initially aversive, their impact soon dissipated. Covert sensitization was then conducted under hypnosis, a procedure the author found to be effective. Two of the subjects were reported drug-free at 18- and 36-month follow-ups. The other subject was drug-free for 18 months and then relapsed.

Snowden (1978) used a technique he called "personality tailored covert sensitization" to treat 43 methadone maintenance patients who had been enrolled in a maintenance program for at least two months and had at least two weekly urinalyses positive for morphine over the seven weeks before treatment. The entire sample was maintained in the study by making methadone contingent on participation, and eventually by paying subjects for their participation. A 2 × 3 experimental design was utilized, blocking subjects by two levels of locus of control (a median split on internal–external control) and randomly assigning subjects within blocks to three treatment conditions: internal therapy orientation (stressing personal responsibility and willpower), external therapy orientation (stressing the therapist's responsibility and the avoidance of unmanageable situations), and control (relaxation training and empathic listening). Five treatment sessions were conducted over a maximum period of three weeks. The aversive situations involved imagining feelings of nausea, depression, and infestation with abscesses. Covert reinforcement was also used, emphasizing feeling satisfied and in good health after refusing drugs. Additionally, the subjects were given homework assignments, and their urine was monitored weekly for seven weeks. It was found that the subjects with matching locus-of-control and therapeutic orientations improved the most in terms of fewer dirty urines. Although this interaction was not probed statistically, it appeared to derive primarily from subjects in the internal–internal condition showing the greatest gain. The results were also compared with urinalysis data for 68 individuals who were not in the study but met its criteria. The number of subjects in the internal–internal experimental condition who had fewer post- than pretreatment dirty urines was significantly greater than the base rate of dirty urines for the comparison sample. When the number of subjects in each condition with no posttreatment dirty urines was compared with the comparison group base rate, the internal–internal, internal–external, and external–external groups all differed significantly from the comparison group. Of course, these comparisons must be interpreted cautiously, since the comparison subjects were not exposed to any extra treatment, nor was it clear that they would have volunteered for a research study.

Droppa (1978) reported disappointing findings using covert methods to treat four opiate addicts. In three cases, covert sensitization was found to produce no more than a tem-porary decrease in drug taking and urges, and in the other case, desensitization was not successful in reducing the subject's drug cravings.

Finally, Duehn (1978) used group covert sensitization to treat seven self-referred adolescents with a history of amphetamine, LSD, and marijuana use. The six subjects found for an 18-month follow-up reported no LSD use. These subjects' use of other drugs was not reported.

Other Aversive Methods. MacDonough (1976a,b) has reported using a confrontative "feedback" method with 131 alcohol and polydrug abusers (no heroin addicts) in a military inpatient program. The feedback sessions involved daily individual sessions in which the subjects were given an evaluation of their actions of the past day and rewards and punishments were administered. Comparisons were made with 220 presumably comparable hospitalized drug abusers who did not participate in the feedback program. Successful outcomes were classified as subjects who had at least eight consecutive weeks of clean urines, returned to their work assignment for at least 60 days, and were evaluated by their supervisors as performing their jobs effectively. Of the polydrug abusers in the feedback group, 12% satisfied the criteria, as compared with 4% of the control subjects. Although statistically significant, the overall outcome, as judged by the specified criteria, is hardly impressive. Among the alcohol abusers, 61% of the feedback subjects and 50% of the control subjects met the success criteria; this difference was not significant.

Lastly, Hirt and Greenfield (1979) evaluated the efficacy of implosive therapy in helping methadone maintenance patients complete detoxification. Twenty-four male heroin addicts who had participated in the outpatient methadone program for at least six months were randomly assigned to implosive therapy, eclectic counseling, or no treatment while their methadone dose was reduced. After six weeks of treatment, the results indicated that the methadone dose was significantly lower for the implosive therapy subjects than for the other subjects.

Summary. While studies using aversive methods in the treatment of drug problems have been plentiful, controlled experimental evaluations have been rare. The outcomes of the few available controlled studies have been mixed, and these methods are subject to the same liabilities as described for alcohol treatment studies. Perhaps the most promising approach in this area is that of Snowden (1978), who has sought to identify the subsets of drug abusers who might benefit most from aversive methods.

Anxiety Management: Alcohol Abusers. Since alcohol is a central-nervous-system depressant, excessive drinking has often been viewed as an anxiety-reducing behavior (Conger, 1956). Cappell and Herman (1972) have pointed out that although alcohol has tension-reducing properties, the evidence is equivocal regarding whether people drink to reduce anxiety. Although this question is still being debated in the literature (e.g., Hodgson, Stockwell, & Rankin, 1979), many alcohol abusers describe their drinking as a way of coping with stress (Marlatt, 1973; Ludwig, 1972). Based on this rationale, several studies have investigated whether training in alternative methods of inducing relaxation reduces the alcohol consumption of normal and problem drinkers.

Relaxation Training. Marlatt and Marques (1977) compared the effectiveness of progressive muscle-relaxation training, meditation, attention-placebo control, and no-treatment conditions on the drinking behavior of male normal drinkers. During a seven-week follow-up, the subjects in all but the no-treatment group reported a reduction in their alcohol consumption, and the subjects in the three treatment groups (including attention-placebo) reported significantly less drinking than the no-treatment subjects. Parker, Gilbert, and Thoreson (1978) similarly compared the effects of relaxation training, meditation training, and an attention-placebo procedure on inpatient alcoholics' anxiety (questionnaire and physiological measures). While all the subjects showed reduced state anxiety, the relaxation and meditation subjects also showed improvement in blood pressure readings as compared with the attention-placebo subjects. No drinking measures or follow-up data were reported.

Strickler, Bigelow, Wells, and Liebson (1977) examined the effects of relaxation training on alcoholics' frontal electromyographic (EMG) potentials using a between-subject controlled design. The subjects' EMG levels were recorded as they listened to a tape recording supposedly made by a problem drinker discussing his relapse into drinking. The relaxation-training subjects had significantly lower EMG levels than the control subjects during the stressful test situation. In a second study, Strickler, Tomaszenski, Maxwell, and Suib (1979) instructed subjects who were normal drinkers that they were about to perform a public speaking task. The subjects then listened to either a relaxation-training tape, a neutral tape, or a sensitization tape (describing aversive experiences in public speaking). Pre- and posttest *ad lib* drinking sessions revealed that the relaxation subjects drank significantly less than the other subjects in the posttest.

Systematic Desensitization. Except as part of multimodal treatment packages, systematic desensitization (Wolpe, 1969), incorporating relaxation training with gradual exposure to anxiety-provoking stimuli, has been used sparingly with alcohol abusers. Kraft (1969) and Kraft and Al-Issa (1967, 1968) have reported successful case studies where alcohol abusers were treated by systematic desensitization. Since appropriate single-subject designs were not employed by these investigators, it is impossible to evaluate the actual contribution of the technique to treatment outcomes. Lanyon, Primo, Terrell, and Wener (1972) investigated the effects of systematic desensitization combined with "interpersonal aversion" on alcoholics' posttreatment drinking. Although the authors reported that the experimentally treated subjects had better outcomes than the aversion treated subjects, several methodological problems in the gathering of the outcome data unfortunately preclude a clear interpretation of these findings.

Biofeedback. Steffen (1975) gave four alcoholic subjects EMG biofeedback training to reduce tension using a controlled within-subject design. The subjects showed reduced EMG levels and less self-reported disturbance during *ad lib* drinking periods following EMG training, compared with pretraining and placebo sessions. However, the number of drinks ordered by the subjects during the *ad lib* drinking sessions following biofeedback and placebo training did not differ significantly.

Some evidence suggests that alcoholics may

produce lower proportions of alpha waves (associated with relaxed states) than nonalcoholics (e.g., Davis, Gibbs, Davis, Jetter, & Trowbridge, 1941). Jones and Holmes (1976) attempted but failed to train alcoholics and matched control subjects to increase their alpha production during three training sessions. While Jones and Holmes urged caution in assuming that alpha training findings with college students readily generalize to other populations, Glaros (1977) has suggested that the lack of alpha-activity changes in the Jones and Holmes study may have occurred because the training conditions were so conducive to alpha production that there may have been little opportunity for alpha-activity change.

Watson, Herder, and Passini (1978) compared alpha training to an attention control condition in inpatient alcoholics. Alpha-trained subjects showed greater alpha activity and a reduction in state–trait anxiety scores over training. At an 18-month follow-up, the alpha-trained subjects still had lower anxiety scores but differed from control subjects on only 1 (length of time without drinking) of 13 drinking outcome measures.

Summary. While anxiety management techniques appear to have some promise as effective interventions, most studies have failed to investigate the long-term effects of these procedures on the drinking of alcohol abusers. Considering the great popularity of the belief that people drink to reduce stress, it is surprising that this area has not been more thoroughly researched. In view of the relatively positive results of laboratory and analogue studies, further controlled clinical trials of anxiety management methods seem warranted.

Anxiety Management: Drug Abusers. As in the treatment of alcohol problems, various anxiety-management procedures have also been evaluated with drug abusers.

Relaxation Training. In contrast to alcohol treatment research, few studies have used relaxation training in the treatment of drug abusers except as part of a systematic desensitization treatment. In a previously mentioned study, O'Brien *et al.* (1972) taught heroin addicts relaxation skills as an adjunct to the use of aversive conditioning. Dreilinger and Thayer (1974) presented a case report of the treatment

of a male adolescent LSD user whose parents had requested assistance in helping their son lessen the effects of a bad trip. Deep muscle relaxation was claimed to be helpful in this regard.

Systematic Desensitization. A variety of studies have examined the utility of systematic desensitization in treating drug problems. Kraft (1968) used systematic desensitization in treating a 20-year-old Drinamyl abuser who was experiencing paranoia as a toxic side effect of the drug. Sessions focused on diminishing social anxieties; relaxation was induced by hypnosis. The interval between the sessions was gradually increased from 1 to 14 days. At a nine-month follow-up, the subject was reported to be drug-free. In another case study reported by Kraft (1969), a 50-year-old female barbiturate addict who had a lumbar disk lesion was treated by electroconvulsive shock therapy just before receiving systematic desensitization as an outpatient. The desensitization, aided by intravenous Brevital, focused on the subject's fears of being independent. After 72 daily (on weekdays) sessions, the subject reported no further use of barbiturates.

The series of case reports by Spevak *et al.* (1973), which were discussed earlier, included a case in which systematic desensitization was used to treat a 17-year-old male who was suffering LSD flashbacks. Desensitization was used to treat acquired fears of flashback-related situations (e.g., music, crowds, darkness); 10 sessions occurred over a two-month period. Significant decreases in fear of these situations over the course of treatment were indicated by self-reports, fear-survey-schedule ratings, and decreases in heart rate. No recurrences of flashbacks were reported over a one-year follow-up.

Finally, Paynard and Wolf (1974) used systematic desensitization in treating an outpatient male heroin addict who was in methadone treatment. The subject was unassertive with females and also fearful of methadone detoxification. As desensitization for these fears was implemented, it was determined that the subject's supposed fear of the methadone withdrawal reaction was actually a fear of being without medication. In this regard, the authors reported that the subject's methadone dosage was decreased without his knowledge until he was detoxified. At a one-year follow-up, the subject was more confident in interpersonal relationships. Although no specific report was given on the subject's drug use, it presumably was absent.

Biofeedback Methods. Khatami, Mintz, and O'Brien (1977) conducted a pilot study investigating the utility of frontalis EMG biofeedback to reduce conditioned drug cravings and withdrawal symptoms in 20 male methadone-maintenance patients. The subjects, all of whom received regular methadone program services, were randomly assigned to either a biofeedback ($N = 13$) or control ($N = 7$) condition. Although both groups showed general improvements, the biofeedback subjects were significantly more improved than the control subjects on Hamilton Anxiety Scale ratings. In a further analysis, clearly confounded by a subject selection factor, Khatami *et al.* (1977) found that the seven biofeedback subjects who had missed less than three sessions differed significantly from the controls on the Hamilton Anxiety and Depression Scales, had more clean urinalyses, and were more likely to attain drug-free states.

Goldberg, Greenwood, and Taintor (1976, 1977) treated four methadone-maintenance patients using alpha biofeedback training. In addition to the value of this method in inducing relaxation, Goldberg *et al.* (1977) also speculated that equipment-laden biofeedback techniques might appeal to drug addicts, who often have negative attitudes toward counseling or therapy. It was further hypothesized that alpha biofeedback might be a good substitute for drug use in terms of producing a change in state of consciousness and enabling the subjects to learn to control a physiological component of their behavior. In addition to a decrease over treatment in the incidence of dirty urines, the subjects reported that the training helped them to cope better with anxieties. Brinkman (1978) also claimed that biofeedback was useful in reducing the anxiety of two highly motivated methadone-maintenance patients.

Summary. The single controlled investigation (Khatami *et al.*, 1977) of the use of anxiety management methods in the treatment of drug problems produced unimpressive findings and was compromised by inappropriate data analyses. Consequently, these methods are basically untested.

Skills Training: Alcohol Abusers. Based on a functional analysis of drinking behavior (Bandura, 1969; Miller, 1976; M. B. Sobell & L. C. Sobell, 1973a), several behavioral techniques have been used to train alcohol abusers in alternative ways of responding to drinking situations.

Drinking Skills Training. The realization that many alcohol abusers, particularly those who have not been physically dependent on alcohol, can achieve non-problem-drinking outcomes has slowly been accepted by scientists in the alcohol field (M. B. Sobell, 1978; M. B. Sobell & L. C. Sobell, 1982). This radical change in conceptions about the nature of alcohol problems has been accompanied by the investigation of methods designed to help alcohol abusers drink appropriately. This research has been complemented by a considerable amount of basic research investigating the drinking behavior of alcohol abusers and the situational antecedents of drinking. In an early study, Mills, Sobell, and Schaefer (1971) shaped the drinking behavior of 13 chronic alcoholic subjects using shock-avoidance conditioning procedures. Of these subjects, 9 completed all 14 training sessions; over the course of treatment, all showed shaping to criterion (consumption of three or less drinks during the sessions, the avoidance of ordering straight drinks, and sipping rather than gulping). Although this method was later incorporated into an effective multimodal treatment package, M. B. Sobell and L. C. Sobell (1978) concluded that avoidance contingencies are neither a necessary nor a desirable treatment component since instructions can achieve the same results.

In an instructive multiple-baseline study, Miller, Becker, Foy, and Wooten (1976) evaluated the effects of verbal instructions on the drinking behavior of three chronic alcoholics. They found that the modification of one component of the drinking response led to undesirable changes in the other components, suggesting that overall alcohol consumption may not change unless all the components of the drinking response are attended to simultaneously.

Blood-alcohol-level (BAL) discrimination

training is another aversive method used to shape appropriate drinking behavior in alcohol abusers (Lovibond & Caddy, 1970). In the Lovibond and Caddy studies (1970; Caddy & Lovibond, 1976), BAL discrimination training was used as part of a behavioral counseling treatment program. The subjects, outpatient problem drinkers, were instructed about the relationship between the alcohol consumed, the temporal parameters, and the BAL. They were then asked to participate in drinking sessions in which they were instructed to attend to the physical sensations produced by drinking, and they were administered electric shocks if their BALs exceeded a moderate level (.065%). Follow-up data showed the treatment package to be successful, although the contribution of BAL discrimination training cannot be isolated from the counseling components. Several recent investigations, attempting to elucidate the critical components of BAL discrimination training, have suggested that attendance to physical sensations (in the absence of instructions, verbal feedback, and reinforcement) is ineffective for both alcoholics (Briddell & Nathan, 1975) and normal drinkers (Maisto & Adesso, 1977). This finding has limited clinical relevance, however, since external cue training (educational instruction) tends to be effective.

In summary, the above studies offer preliminary evidence that education about drinking skills and the effects of drinking on the BAL may enable alcohol abusers to reduce their alcohol consumption or to maintain low BALs. This hypothesis is in need of further experimental test, since the use of alcohol education has been prolific in treatment and prevention programs.

Interpersonal Skills Training. Some evidence suggests that alcohol abusers have deficits in interpersonal skills (Miller & Eisler, 1977; O'Leary, O'Leary, & Donovan, 1976) or drink as a coping response to stressful interpersonal situations (Higgins & Marlatt, 1975; Miller, Hersen, Eisler, & Hilsman, 1974). Further, whether or not deficits exist, it is possible that enhancement of interpersonal skills may help an individual resist drinking cues. Studies investigating the utility of interpersonal skills training with alcohol abusers have largely examined the effects of as-

sertiveness training (Miller, 1976; Miller & Mastria, 1977).

Eisler, Hersen, and Miller (1974) reported a single-case study using assertiveness training with a male alcoholic who reported drinking heavily in response to stressful work situations. Videotapes of role-playing situations indicated that the subject made poor eye contact and exhibited general compliance with unreasonable requests in such situations. After several sessions of assertiveness training, the subject had improved his assertiveness skills within sessions. Unfortunately, the subject terminated treatment prematurely, and the effects of the training on his posttreatment drinking are unknown.

Using a pretest–posttest design, Hirsch, Von Rosenberg, Phelan, and Dudley (1978) demonstrated increased assertiveness in inpatient alcoholics as a result of assertiveness training. However, no assessment was made of the subjects' posttreatment drinking. In a more clinically relevant study, Foy, Miller, Eisler, and O'Toole (1976) trained two chronic alcoholics in methods of refusing drinks that were offered to them. Three-month follow-up data indicated improvement on all ratings of effective drink refusal, and the subjects reported that they had better control over their drinking.

In a well-controlled between-subjects design experiment, Chaney, O'Leary, and Marlatt (1978) evaluated the effectiveness of social skills training with inpatient alcoholics. Forty subjects were randomly assigned to either skills training, discussion, or no additional treatment (control). The skills training focused on assertiveness and problem solving and was conducted in eight 90-min sessions. The subjects in the discussion condition conversed about the same general situations used with the skills training subjects, but the group leadership was nondirective. On multiple and verified measures of outcome, at a 1 year follow-up the skills-training subjects were found to be superior to the discussion and no-additional-treatment groups in terms of fewer days drunk, less total alcohol consumption, and a shorter average length of drinking episodes.

Finally, Cohen, Appelt, Olbrich, and Watzl (1979) reported one of the few behavioral treatment studies using female subjects. The 60 subjects were treated in an abstinence-oriented 3-month inpatient program emphasizing a functional analysis of drinking, training in alternative coping behaviors, role playing, covert techniques, and *in vivo* applications (the subjects were all allowed four home visits while hospitalized). The outcome data for 13–29 months of follow-up indicated that 52% of the subjects were abstinent or had reduced their drinking. Unfortunately, no control group was used, so it is impossible to determine whether the reported outcomes differed from those that could be expected from other types of treatment.

Vocational Skills Training. Many problem drinkers have a poor employment history, making job seeking difficult even after they have successfully dealt with their drinking problems. Other problem drinkers, particularly outpatients, are employed while in treatment but are either in jeopardy of losing their jobs or report that work stresses contribute to their drinking. Foy, Massey, Dyer, Ross, and Wooten (1979) examined the effectiveness of assertiveness training with three employed problem drinkers who reported interpersonal difficulties at work. Although the subjects were reported to have increased their assertiveness at follow-up, no data were presented regarding their drinking behavior.

Vocational counseling was included by Miller, Stanford, and Hemphill (1974) as part of a multimodal inpatient treatment for alcoholics, followed by one year of outpatient treatment. The training included the preparation of job résumés, interview responses, and social skills that could be used to handle interactions with employers and co-workers. The trainees also negotiated a contract with their employers specifying that they would regularly take Antabuse. Miller (1976) reported that 62% of the subjects were either abstinent or drinking in a more controlled manner 8–24 months after treatment. Again, no control group was included in the design, so comparative judgments of the value of vocational counseling are not possible.

Summary. Skills training appears to be a promising area for future research. Unfortunately, thus far, only a few studies have used experimental designs. There is also a lack of sufficient evidence showing that alcohol abusers are deficient in interpersonal skills although, theoretically at least, drinking problems seem bound to produce impaired social relationships. Better documentation of the need for skills training would be helpful, since it is doubtful that all alcohol abusers have such deficiencies or that the problems they experience have a greater prevalence than in the general population.

Skills Training: Drug Abusers. Considering popular notions about the drug subculture and addicts' lifestyles, it is curious that few studies have focused on skills training as a treatment intervention for drug abusers. Reeder and Kunce (1976) used a "vicarious behavior induction" method in an experimental study of 22 black heroin addicts, some of whom were court-coerced. The subjects were randomly assigned to either a videolecture group, which viewed a taped lecture on coping behavior, or to a videomodel group, which watched a taped model successfully solve problems related to maintaining abstinence. Six-month outcome data, with success operationalized as employment or being enrolled in school, showed that the videomodel subjects had significantly better outcomes than the videolecture subjects (46% vs. 18%). For unknown reasons, no drug use data were reported. Also, the results may have been biased by the treatment staff, who became so enamored of the videomodel approach that it was made a standard part of the regular treatment program even before the follow-up data had been collected.

Callner and Ross (1978) performed a controlled study of assertiveness training in the treatment of eight inpatient drug abusers, including five heroin users, five Methedrine users, and one user of LSD (some subjects used more than one drug). In addition to their regular treatment, four of the subjects were randomly assigned to assertiveness training and received nine training sessions over three weeks. The results were measured pre- and posttraining by means of a specially designed assertion questionnaire, as well as by the subjects' rated performance in role-playing situations. Significant differences were found in role-played verbal behavior, but not in scale scores. No drug-use outcome data were reported.

Summary. Skills training with drug abusers would seem a very promising research area, in view of the interpersonal pressures often reported by drug abusers (e.g., resisting drug pushers and encountering situations in which drugs are being used). Yet, the few studies published in this area have failed to report drug-use outcome data.

Contingency Management: Alcohol Abusers. Contingency management involves arranging a person's environment so that positive consequences follow desired behaviors and either no consequences or negative consequences follow nondesired behaviors. A substantial amount of basic research supports the potential utility of such methods with alcohol abusers. One drawback of contingency management techniques is their usual dependence on persons other than the alcohol abuser to enforce the contingencies. Thus, such methods have most often been used in dealing with couples, in negotiating agreements with employers, and in dealing with persons who are court-coerced to enter treatment.

Miller, Hersen, Eisler, and Watts (1974) reported a case study using a single-subject design. The subject, being seen for outpatient alcoholism treatment, received monetary rewards if his BAL was zero when tested at randomly scheduled times in his home and at his place of work. The subject's drinking was much reduced during the contingent-reinforcement phases as compared with baseline and with the non-contingent-reinforcement phases of the study.

Miller (1975) reported an exemplary study in which he enlisted the cooperation of community agencies (e.g., the Salvation Army, various missions) serving a skid-row population. Twenty chronic alcoholics were randomly assigned to either a contingent-reinforcement or a non-contingent-reinforcement group, with agency services made contingent on relative sobriety for the contingent-reinforcement group. When the contingent-reinforcement subjects were observed to be grossly intoxicated or registered a BAL in excess of .10%, the provision of goods and services was suspended for five days. The data collected for two months prior to the initiation of the study and two months following its implemen-

tation revealed that the contingent-reinforcement subjects had decreased intoxication, had fewer arrests for public drunkenness, and spent a greater number of hours employed than the non-contingent-reinforcement subjects. Unfortunately, the community agencies chose not to continue the program following the conclusion of the study, indicating that demonstrations of treatment efficacy are only one variable influencing whether a given treatment will be implemented.

Liebson, Tommasello, and Bigelow (1978) arranged contingencies for methadone patients who also abused alcohol. The subjects were randomly assigned to either a reinforced disulfiram group, in which methadone was dispensed contingent on the ingestion of disulfiram (Antabuse), or to a control group, in which the subjects were advised to take disulfiram but received their methadone whether or not they used disulfiram. During the six-month treatment period, the reinforced disulfiram subjects drank on only 2% of all days, whereas the control subjects drank on 21% of all days, a statistically significant difference. The reinforced disulfiram subjects also spent less time using illicit drugs, spent more time employed, and had fewer arrests than the control subjects.

In a comprehensive contingency-management program they called "community-reinforcement," Hunt and Azrin (1973) attempted to increase the frequency of positive reinforcers in alcoholic subjects' daily living situations. Eight subjects were assigned to the community-reinforcement treatment, and eight to a control condition. The community-reinforcement program included vocational counseling, marital and family counseling, the creation of "synthetic" families (social support systems), participation in a social club designed to provide a setting for nondrinking socialization, and reinforcer-access counseling, whereby the counselor helped the subjects to obtain items to facilitate their access to jobs and friends. Participation in the program was contingent on sobriety. The control subjects received 25 one-hour didactic sessions of alcohol education and an introduction to Alcoholics Anonymous. At a six-month follow-up, the community-reinforcement subjects, compared with the control subjects, were found to have spent significantly less time unemployed, away from home, drinking, and institutionalized.

Azrin (1976) extended the community-reinforcement method by including the use of disulfiram to prevent impulsive drinking, a buddy system whereby a paraprofessional counselor provided the subjects with advice on practical problems, an "early-warning system" for identifying problems that might precipitate drinking, and a group treatment that reduced the amount of therapy time required of the therapists. As in the Hunt and Azrin (1973) study, 20 alcoholics were randomly assigned to either the community-reinforcement or a control condition. In this case, a two-year follow-up showed that the community-reinforcement subjects had spent significantly less time drinking, out of their homes, unemployed, and institutionalized than the control subjects.

Fredericksen and Miller (1976) have reported one of the few investigations of the effects of behavioral interventions on the treatment process. Alcoholic subjects in a behaviorally oriented treatment program were given points (exchangeable for goods) based on the frequency of their comments in group therapy. At different phases in the study, the point allotment was determined either by the subjects themselves or by the other members. These contingent phases were separated by noncontingent phases, during which the subjects routinely received a set amount of points. Unfortunately, the contingency was found to have no effect on verbal output.

Several studies using contingency contracting with alcohol abusers have explicitly specified the contingencies in a signed written agreement. In an early study, Miller, Hersen, and Eisler (1974) compared a variety of instructional procedures with written contracting in regulating the drinking behavior of inpatient alcoholics. It was found that conditions that included reinforcement contingencies were significantly more effective than simple instructions.

Vannicelli (1979) compared the efficacy of different contracting procedures with 100 alcoholic inpatients. The contracts specified the treatment plans and goals, as well as the consequences of noncompliance. Overall, it was found that the use of contracts provided no advantages. Ersner-Hershfield and Sobell (1979) compared four different contracting procedures (factorially crossing written and verbal contracts with written and verbal agreements) with no contracts in an attempt to reduce absences from outpatient treatment sessions by court-referred drinking drivers. The subjects in a no-contract control group were referred back to court for noncompliance (the specified consequence) more frequently than the subjects in the contract conditions.

Robichaud, Strickler, Bigelow, and Liebson (1979) studied 21 persons referred for monitored (observed-ingestion) disulfiram treatment by their employers. During the average 10.6 month treatment period, the subjects missed significantly fewer days from work (median = 1.7%) than during the two years prior to treatment (median = 9.8%) or during an average posttreatment period of 4.4 months (median = 6.7%). Although no control group was used, Robichaud *et al.* argued that the reversibility of the effect indicated that the contingencies involved in the monitored disulfiram program were the primary determinants of the subjects' behavior rather than the threat of employer action. However, the evidence supporting the reversibility of the treatment effects makes questionable the utility of these methods for achieving long-term objectives.

Bigelow, Strickler, Liebson, and Griffiths (1976) had outpatient alcohol abusers post a monetary deposit that was refunded if they took disulfiram daily for three months. A contracting procedure was used, and the subjects received only a partial refund if they failed to take their disulfiram daily. Although the subjects reported longer periods of abstinence than they had experienced during the preceding three years, the absence of a control condition prohibits an evaluation of the effectiveness of the refundable-deposit procedure.

Summary. Contingency management procedures have generally shown positive results in terms of treatment effectiveness. It has not been demonstrated, however, that the effects achieved by contingency management can be maintained once those contingencies are removed, and it is difficult to imagine situations in which contingencies could realistically be expected to last indefinitely. It is curious that little research has been reported on the transfer of contingency management effects to the natural environment (for example, see Azrin, 1976; Hunt & Azrin, 1973).

Contingency Management: Drug Abusers. Several published reports (Eriksson, Götestam, Melin, & Öst, 1975; Glicksman, Ottomanelli, & Cutler, 1971; Melin, Andersson, & Götestam, 1976; O'Brien, Raynes, & Patch, 1971; Pickens, 1979) have simply described various inpatient behavior-management systems similar in principle to token economies (Ayllon & Azrin, 1968). Others have indirectly addressed contingency management. For example, Copemann and Shaw (1976) did examine contingency management, defined by the subjects' being in treatment with court charges pending, on probation (having completed court proceedings), or voluntarily. It was found that individuals with pending criminal charges did better in treatment than probationers and volunteers.

Melin and Götestam (1973) used an inpatient contingency-management system for intravenous amphetamine addicts. The system was based on the Premack principle (Premack, 1959), in which high-frequency behaviors are used as reinforcers for lower-frequency behaviors. Sixteen subjects in the contingency management program were compared with patients who had been treated at the same facility prior to the institution of the contingency system. Because this procedure left numerous variables uncontrolled, the finding that significantly more of the contingency-management subjects (36%) were drug-free at a one-year follow-up than the control subjects (7%) must be considered cautiously.

Boudin (1972) reported a case study using contingency contracting with a black female graduate student who abused amphetamines. The contract required the subject to keep the therapist informed of her whereabouts, to cease using drugs, and to contact the therapist if she were exposed to a situation that might precipitate drug use. A joint bank account was established by the subject in the subject's and the therapist's names, and violations of the contractual obligations resulted in payments

being made to the Ku Klux Klan. The subject abused amphetamines only once during the three-month contract period and was reported to be drug-free at an eighteen-month follow-up.

Liebson, Bigelow, and Flamer (1973) described an innovative study using contingency management with six outpatient methadone-maintenance subjects who were also alcohol abusers. Initially, all of the subjects received mandatory disulfiram for a two-week period. Then, three of the subjects received their daily methadone only if they took disulfiram, whereas the other three subjects (noncontingent) were encouraged but not required to continue taking disulfiram. For two subjects in each group, the contingency conditions were reversed midway in the treatment (a crossover design). The results were reported for intervals ranging from 54 to 147 days. The dependent measures included urinalysis, breath tests for alcohol, and interviews with the subjects and their collaterals. It was found that when the disulfiram contingencies were in effect, the subjects engaged in significantly fewer drinking days.

Frederiksen, Jenkins, and Carr (1976) used contingency contracting with a 17-year-old polydrug abuser referred for outpatient family therapy by the juvenile authorities. The contracts dealt primarily with family matters; consequences were never directly contingent on drug use. At a one-year follow-up, all parties reported high ratings of satisfaction (as assessed by a Parent-Child Happiness Scale developed by the authors). Only 1 of 19 randomly scheduled in-field urine tests obtained during the follow-up period was positive for drugs, and that instance occurred during the second week of the contract.

Hall, Cooper, Burmaster, and Polk (1977) reported six case studies of contingency contracting with methadone maintenance subjects. The contracts they used involved a variety of incentives, such as home delivery of methadone, tickets to special events, and, for probationers, time off probation. Yen (1974) and Stitzer and Bigelow (1978) have found that methadone maintenance patients rate the privilege of taking their methadone home as a very powerful reinforcer. A 4-week baseline period was followed by contingent, noncontingent, contingent, and follow-up phases. During the second contingent phase, the amount of reinforcement was gradually decreased. The outcome was evaluated in terms of individualized goals, only some of which appeared to relate to drug use. The goals included morphine-free urines ($n = 1$), more days of arriving at work on time ($n = 1$), more days of arriving at the clinic on time ($n = 1$), and weight loss ($n = 3$). Overall, three subjects were considered successes, but the authors concluded that the outcomes appeared to be related to the contingencies in only two of the three cases.

Boudin and his colleagues (Boudin, 1980; Boudin & Valentine, 1973; Boudin, Valentine, Inghram, Brantley, Ruiz, Smith, Catlin, & Regan, 1977) conducted an exemplary, multifaceted contingency-management program known as the Drug Project. Primarily, the program served well-motivated, legally coerced opiate abusers. Typical subjects were young ($M = 22.7$ yrs), white (88.7%), male (62.9%), high-school–educated ($M = 12.2$ yrs) opiate abusers, although other drug abusers were included in the subject population. Contingency contracting was the primary mode of treatment, and the subjects had to satisfy stringent requirements for entry into the program. For instance, they had to provide evidence of their willingness to (1) self-record a variety of target behaviors (called "pinpoints," these were behaviors functionally related to drug use in each individual case); (2) make telephone contact with their therapist every three waking hours; and (3) agree to relinquish control of some possessions of great value (e.g., their paychecks) to the treatment program. The articles describing the Drug Project are very instructive with regard to the development of innovative, well-specified, and individualized contingency contracts. For instance, this was one of the first programs to utilize adverse consequences for contract violations defined in this case as financial contributions to organizations personally despised by the subjects (e.g., the Ku Klux Klan). Similarly, the therapists also agreed to contribute to a disliked organization if the subjects failed to meet an obligation (e.g., to attend a scheduled session). The program also incorporated sequential levels of contracting, including (1) managerial contracts, which were highly structured and related to program efficiency considerations

as well as to individual goals; (2) transitional contracts, which reduced the structure, focusing mainly on individual short-term goals; and (3) personal contracts, which were aimed at accomplishing long-term goals. Although various other methods (e.g., aversion therapy, marriage counseling, and behavioral rehearsal) were used infrequently, most of the interventions were accomplished by contracting. For this reason, it seems most appropriate to consider the Drug Project a contingency-management rather than a multimodal program.

One of the great strengths of the Drug Project was the abundance of data routinely gathered on each subject. For example, the subjects had to make periodic telephone calls to their therapist, provide regular urine samples, maintain daily logs, and attend treatment sessions on time. Individual pinpoints were even more elaborate. Such elaboration is exemplified in a case study reported by Boudin and Valentine (1973), in which a young female heroin addict with a partial college education maintained daily recordings of her drug thoughts, drug urges, blocks on urges, general frustrations, marijuana tokes, hashish tokes, thoughts about breaking the contract, karma balance (mental contentment), number of cigarettes smoked per day, number of Quaaludes taken per day, discomfort in social situations, sexual frustrations, sexual relations, and the number of times each day she was able to relax. By examining this plethora of data, the investigators were able to identify a convergence of conditions (drug thoughts, drug urges, increased frustrations, decreased karma balance, and increased thoughts about breaking the contract) that were predictive of drug use.

In the final report on the Drug Project (Boudin, 1980), outcome results were reported for 62 subjects. In order to enhance the chances of obtaining more complete data, the researchers paid the subjects five dollars per week throughout the follow-up period for providing urine samples and written evidence of work attendance or school participation. However, 34 of the 62 subjects left the geographical area of the program after treatment was completed, and validated data were collected for only some of these subjects. In addition to drug use data, treatment outcome data were presented by means of several innovative methods. For example, vocational behavior was quantified as a "full-time work equivalent" (basically, the ratio of the number of days actually worked to the number of days that the subject could have worked, if working full time), and school participation was quantified as a "full-time school equivalent." Furthermore, treatment effects were analyzed separately (1) immediate posttreatment effects (representing treatment gains) and (2) follow-up effects (representing the maintenance of treatment gains). The subjects with usable outcome data were classified as either program graduates ($n = 15$), self-terminators ($n = 17$) who had been in treatment 30 days or less, and other terminators ($n = 10$). More program graduates (80%) were included in the follow-up than subjects from any other group (18%–55%). For all but first-month self-terminators (typically uncoerced subjects who decreased their drug use only slightly), the overall results showed a significant decrease in drug use, an increase in work rates, and no change in school attendance. Only program graduates also showed a significant increase in school attendance. Importantly, disproportionately large numbers ($p < .05$) of program graduates were coerced, and a significantly greater number of self-terminators were uncoerced. When success was defined as no illegitimate drug use except marijuana, no felony convictions, and at least 50% time spent in work or school activities, 57.1% of the program graduates were judged to be successes. If one illegitimate drug use was allowed, the proportion of successes among program graduates increased to 71.0%. Unfortunately, the lack of a control or comparison group prohibits drawing conclusions about the relative efficacy of the program for this select population.

A within-subject (A-B-C-B-A) design was used by Beatty (1978) to investigate the effects of contingency contracting as a treatment for eight male heroin addicts participating in a halfway house program. Following a baseline phase, the subjects signed a written contract that did not specify contingencies (noncontingent phase). After this phase, a contract with contingencies was implemented, followed by additional noncontingent and baseline phases. The contingencies were found to be effective in producing program management behaviors (e.g., attending sessions, keeping logs), but ineffective in reducing drug use. Beatty (1978) speculated that the contracts may have been ineffective because of a lack of powerful reinforcers. Milby, Garrett, English, Fritschi, and Clarke (1978) also found mixed results using contingency contracts. Their 69 subjects were a group of methadone maintenance patients who were mixed in age and race and who had been enrolled in treatment for at least 90 days. The subjects were randomly assigned to either an immediate-contingency group or a delayed-contingency group. The group differed in that the subjects could earn methadone take-home privileges if they achieved seven consecutive clean weekly urines, were engaged full time in productive activity, and followed program rules. The dependent variables, assessed for two months before and after contracting was instituted, included (1) the frequency of dirty urines; (2) the number of weeks engaged in productive activity; and (3) the number of violations of program rules. Only the immediate-contingency group showed significant treatment effects, and only in terms of increased productivity. There was no overall difference in the number of clean urines obtained from the subjects, but the immediate-contingency subjects had a significantly greater number of consecutive clean urines. The authors noted that the lack of effects for the delayed-contingency group might have resulted from a ceiling effect, since 88.1% of this group's pretreatment urines were clean (as compared with 80.1% for the immediate-contingency group).

Stitzer, Bigelow, and Liebson (1979a,b) have reported two studies of the effects of contingency management on methadone maintenance patients. The first report (Stitzer *et al.*, 1979a) presented two uncontrolled studies. The first study was of six black patients on methadone maintenance who had positive urinalyses for drugs on at least 30% of twice-weekly screenings conducted over five weeks and who were exposed to contingency management during randomly selected weeks of their treatment. During the contingent period, the subjects who had clean urines obtained the privilege of taking home their methadone, of regulating (within limits) their own dose of methadone for a day, or of receiving $7.50

cash. Since this contingency was not effective, the reinforcers were enhanced in value to provide an increased incentive. Four of the six original subjects participated in the enhanced-incentive phase of the study, and three of the four showed a decrease in drug use. A "superincentive" set of contingencies ($30 per clean urine) was used for the one recalcitrant subject in this group for an additional period of three weeks, after which the subject was opiate-free for 8½ months. The second study (Stitzer et al., 1979b) involved five methadone patients who supplemented their drug use with benzodiazepines. The procedures used were similar to those in the earlier study (Stitzer et al., 1979a), but the design was better controlled in terms of introducing the contingent and noncontingent phases. Although taking home methadone was found to be a highly effective reinforcer, the subjects used several illicit drugs throughout their treatment, and no follow-up data were presented.

The utility of contingency management in outpatient heroin detoxification was examined by Hall, Bass, Hargreaves, and Loeb (1979). Forty-three subjects were assigned to either experimental ($n = 23$) or control ($n = 19$) conditions. Both the control and the experimental subjects could earn $1 daily for providing urine specimens, but the experimental subjects could also earn as much as an additional $49 if they completed detoxification and their urines were morphine- and barbiturate-free. In this case, no significant differences were found between the groups in terms of the proportion of the subjects completing detoxification or the number of clean urines.

The same article (Hall et al., 1979) also reported the use of similar contingencies with 81 outpatient methadone-detoxification subjects who were assigned to either an experimental group ($n = 40$) or a control group ($n = 41$). In addition to payment for drug-free urines, the experimental subjects received feedback about the results of their urine tests, were periodically reminded of the payment contingencies, and received brief supportive counseling. In this study, the subjects in the experimental group produced significantly more drug-free urine samples than the control subjects, the difference being about 20%. The experimental subjects also had a lower, but a not significantly different, premature termination rate than the control subjects. This study suggests that contingency management may be relatively effective in reducing the use of illicit drugs during methadone detoxification.

Summary. In general, contingency management methods have achieved only modest success with drug abusers. Not only are well-controlled outcome studies a rarity, but even the better controlled studies have usually investigated only limited, within-treatment effects (attending sessions, using fewer illicit drugs while detoxifying, etc.). It is disappointing that only the studies of Boudin and his colleagues (Boudin, 1980; Boudin & Valentine, 1973; Boudin et al., 1977) have used designs aimed at transferring control to the natural environment or have given much attention to the maintenance of treatment gains once formal treatment has been completed. Basically, contingency management methods have been found to have some value in terms of behavior management during treatment, but their efficacy in contributing to successful treatment outcomes is unknown.

Self-Management Procedures: Alcohol Abusers. Self-management strategies, in which individuals serve as the mediators of their own treatment, have great potential utility in that the generalization and the maintenance of the treatment effects are likely to be maximized. Of course, these techniques are likely to be useful only with motivated persons who are willing to assume the responsibility for regulating their own behavior.

One major component of self-management programs is the use of self-monitoring, wherein subjects are taught to attend to and monitor particular target behaviors. In one such study (L. C. Sobell & M. B. Sobell, 1973), outpatient alcohol abusers maintained alcohol intake logs, in which they recorded information regarding their drinking behavior, including the amount and the type of the beverage, the time of drinking, and the circumstances surrounding the event. When self-damaging drinking was reported (subjects were reinforced for reporting such drinking), it was made clear to the subjects, while analyzing the real and potential consequences of the drinking, that it was the reporting that was being reinforced and not the drinking. Sobell and

Sobell reported, anecdotally, that self-monitoring (1) encouraged subjects to be constantly aware of their drinking and to analyze their environment for situations that might lead to problem drinking; (2) encouraged within-treatment discussion of drinking episodes; and (3) facilitated early treatment intervention by identifying the onset of problem drinking.

Miller (1978) compared the effectiveness of self-control training, self-control training plus BAL discrimination training and aversive conditioning, and aversive conditioning alone. All these treatments had a goal of nonproblem drinking. The self-control strategies included the functional analysis of drinking, the learning of appropriate alternative behaviors for dealing with high-risk drinking situations, and several other methods described in detail by Miller and Muñoz (1976). At the end of treatment and at a 12-month follow-up, all treatment groups showed a significant reduction in drinking, although the group that received aversive conditioning alone showed the least change. However, since a self-help manual was given to a random sample of the subjects at the end of treatment and to all remaining subjects at a 3-month follow-up interview, and since a control group was not used, it is not possible to determine the relative efficacy of the various methods.

Miller (1977) also reported on two studies examining the utility of a self-help manual (Miller & Muñoz, 1976). Miller, Gribskov, and Mortell (1976) presented alcohol abusers with either a self-help manual and self-monitoring cards or the manual and the cards plus 10 sessions in which the subjects discussed methods of self-control with a therapist. Although both treatments were equally effective in reducing the subjects' drinking at a three-month follow-up, the failure to use control or comparison conditions precludes making clear inferences about treatment outcome. Miller, Pechacek, and Hamburg (1976) examined the utility of the self-help manual combined with weekly group-therapy meetings. Again, although no control group was used, the authors reported that the subjects and their significant others attested to a general improvement in the subjects' drinking at a three-month follow-up.

Using a multiple-baseline design, Murray and Hobbs (1977) investigated the effectiveness of a self-imposed time-out procedure with a married couple. The subjects recorded their daily alcohol consumption during all phases of the study. In various phases, the subjects administered time-out contingent on mixing drinks with more than 1 oz of beverage alcohol, consuming more than four drinks per day, or consuming any drink within less than 30 min. The time-out contingency was effective in reducing the target behaviors, and the subjects' total alcohol consumption was less during all phases of the treatment and at a short two-week follow-up than during baseline.

Summary. Self-management techniques with alcohol abusers appear promising but are in great need of controlled clinical evaluation. To the authors' knowledge, no studies have been reported investigating the efficacy of self-management techniques with drug abusers.

Behavioral Marital Therapy: Alcohol Abusers. Disrupted marital relations frequently result from drinking problems (Towle, 1974). Recently, several studies have investigated the behavioral treatment of married couples of whom at least one partner had a drinking problem.

Cheek, Franks, Laucius, and Burtle (1971) hypothesized that wives' reactions to their husbands' drinking behavior contributes to marital distress. In this study, 24 wives of alcohol abusers were scheduled to participate in group sessions that included desensitization to stressful situations, relaxation training, and training in reinforcing desirable behaviors. However, only 3 subjects completed 6 or more of the 10 scheduled sessions. The subjects reported that while the program helped them cope at home, it had no effect on their husbands' drinking. In contrast to this study, most marital therapy studies have involved the conjoint treatment of the partners.

Hedberg and Campbell (1974) compared behavioral family counseling, systematic desensitization, covert sensitization, and electric-shock aversive conditioning. At a six-month follow-up, a higher percentage of subjects in the groups receiving behavioral family counseling (74%) and systematic desensitization (67%) reported reaching their treatment goals, as compared with the covert-sensitization (40%) and the aversive-conditioning (10%) groups. However, since the subjects were not randomly assigned to the groups, and the outcome measures were global evaluations, these results are tenuous.

A comprehensive treatment program for a couple when the husband's drinking had resulted in serious consequences was reported by Miller and Hersen (1976). A thorough assessment conducted while the husband was an inpatient—including conjoint interviews, videotapes of the couple discussing problem and nonproblem areas of their marriage, and audiotapes of two mealtime discussions at home—was utilized in treatment planning. Various methods (e.g., assertiveness training, coaching, modeling, and videotape feedback) were used to help the couple learn to reinforce desired behaviors, to compromise, and to increase the frequency of certain nonverbal behaviors (e.g., eye contact and smiling). At the conclusion of the treatment, the couple reported that the husband had stopped drinking and that their relationship had improved. This outcome was verified by a videotaped interaction in the hospital prior to the husband's discharge, and the continued improved relations were corroborated by the couple's children at a nine-month follow-up. Similar case studies reporting successful outcomes can be found in the literature (Miller, 1972; Wilson & Rosen, 1975).

A study by McCrady, Paolino, Longabaugh, and Rossi (1977) compared three methods of behavioral marital therapy for couples where the husband abused alcohol: group treatment for the husbands only, group treatment for the couples, and group treatment for the couples combined with admission of the couple to an inpatient treatment program. The 33 couples, blocked on marital adjustment and drinking variables, were randomly assigned among the three conditions. Six-month follow-up revealed that alcohol consumption by the husbands in both groups that had received couples treatment decreased more than for husbands assigned to individual group therapy. There were no significant differences among the three groups on self-report measures of marital problems and other psychopathology.

Summary. The few marital therapy studies reported to date provide strong early evidence that both members of the couple should participate in therapy when one member has a drinking problem. Couples therapy would seem to be of obvious value when marital problems are clearly associated with the drinking problem, or when the treatment progress of one individual is obstructed by his or her spouse. However, couples therapy may be contraindicated or impossible when one member refuses to participate or has problems that would be better addressed without the other member's being present. Research should be done on the question of which individuals are most likely to fare significantly better if involved in couples therapy rather than individual or group therapy.

No studies on behavioral marital therapy with drug abusers have been reported, to our knowledge.

Maintenance of Treatment Gains: Alcohol Abusers. A separate issue from the gains made in treatment is whether those changes are maintained after treatment terminates. This question is especially important in the case of alcohol problems, because treated individuals typically show some incidence of renewed drinking problems, and few persons maintain a long-term pattern of either complete abstinence or nonproblem drinking (Polich, Armor, & Braiker, 1980). As mentioned earlier in this chapter, Marlatt (1973) and Ludwig (1972) examined the precipitants of relapse in alcoholics and found stressful events to be the predominant perceived cause of relapse. Litman, Eisler, Rawson, and Oppenheim (1979) investigated situations perceived by alcoholics as likely to precipitate relapse and found that persons who relapsed shortly after participating in the study had evaluated a greater number of situations as risk-laden. Finally, Sobell, Sobell, and Christelman (1972) and others have postulated that the unsubstantiated traditional dictum "One drink, one drunk" might serve as a self-fulfilling prophecy for some individuals should they ingest a small amount of alcohol.

Marlatt (1978) has hypothesized that many substance abusers may relapse as the result of a cognitive process that he has labeled the "abstinence violation effect." He postulated that when individuals have committed themselves to a course of action such as abstinence and then violate that commitment (i.e., by taking a drink), they may unnecessarily continue drinking because of the combined effects of cognitive dissonance and personal attribution. Traditional beliefs about the nature of alcoholism provide alcohol abusers with a convenient way of reducing the dissonance: the notion that they are diseased individuals. This way of thinking combined with the self-attribution of personal failure, might result in the individual's being unlikely to exert self-control and to resist further drinking. Marlatt has suggested treatment strategies that may be useful in preventing relapse exacerbation by the abstinence violation effect. The most notable strategy is the use of a "programmed relapse," in which the individual, while in treatment, experiences the effects of a single drink under the therapist's supervision. By planning reactions to a drinking episode and learning that further drinking is not inevitable, the impact of drinking or excessive drinking episodes might be minimized. Marlatt is currently investigating the value of such promising interventions. No studies have been reported on methods of helping drug abusers to deal with relapses.

Multimodal Methods

Treatment of Alcohol Abusers. Lazarus (1965), one of the foremost advocates of multimodal approaches, provided an early demonstration of multimodal treatment with an alcoholic. The treatment procedures in this case study included medical treatment, aversive therapy, relaxation training, systematic desensitization, and a hypnotic suggestion that the subject could drink in a controlled fashion but would experience abdominal upset if he drank to excess. At a 14-month follow-up, the subject was maintaining nonproblem drinking.

Sobell and Sobell (1973a,b, 1976, 1978) evaluated the effectiveness of a multimodal approach they called "individualized behavior therapy" (IBT) with inpatient chronic alcohol-abusers. In this study, 70 subjects were assigned to either a non-problem-drinking ($n = 40$) or an abstinence ($n = 30$) treatment goal, based on a research staff assessment. The subjects within each treatment-goal condition were then randomly assigned to either the IBT program in conjunction with the standard hospital treatment program or to the hospital treatment program alone (control treatment). The major components of the IBT program were (1) a videotaped self-confrontation of drunken behavior; (2) problem-solving training, including operationalizing problems, generating a set of possible alternative responses to drinking, evaluating alternatives for their short- and long-term potential consequences, and practicing selected alternatives; (3) assertiveness training, including training to resist social pressures to drink; (4) aversive contingencies for inappropriate drinking behaviors; and (5) access to alcohol during treatment sessions. An extensive battery of follow-up measures was used, and a follow-up was conducted at monthly intervals over two years. It was found that IBT-treated subjects with a goal of nonproblem drinking fared significantly better than their respective control subjects throughout the two years. The differences between the abstinence-goal groups were significant at the one-year follow-up interval (the IBT subjects had superior outcomes) but failed to retain significance over the second year of follow-up. A unique feature of this study is that a third-year outcome investigation, conducted by independent investigators, supported the two-year results (Caddy, Addington, & Perkins, 1978). Vogler, Compton, and Weissbach (1975) conducted a similar multimodal treatment study and reported similarly positive results.

The effectiveness of a multimodal, group-behavioral, treatment program for outpatient problem drinkers was compared with a traditional group-psychotherapy approach by Pomerleau, Pertschuk, Adkins, and Brady (1978). The behavioral treatment included (1) a functional analysis of the subject's drinking, using daily drinking records; (2) contingency management to shape reduced drinking; (3) behavior therapy for problems associated with drinking; (4) strengthening of nondrinking activities; and (5) efforts to facilitate the maintenance of treatment gains. The traditional program focused on (1) confrontation of denial regarding drinking; (2) social support for nondrinking; and (3) psychotherapy. The traditional program stressed a goal of abstinence, while the behavioral program emphasized moderate drinking unless medically contraindicated. The subjects in the behavioral program also paid a $300 deposit, which was returned to them contingent on their attending sessions (larger refunds were given for attending the later sessions in the treatment), keeping drinking records, having a zero BAL at treatment sessions, and being involved in nondrinking activities. A major finding of the study was that fewer subjects dropped out of the behavioral program (2 of 18) than of the traditional program (6 of 14). Most of those who dropped out of the traditional program did so shortly after the intense confrontation phase of the treatment. One-year follow-up showed that 72% of the behavioral treatment subjects were either abstinent (6%) or drinking below pretreatment levels (66%), as compared with 50% of the traditional treatment subjects (14% abstinent and 36% with reduced consumption). This difference, however, was not statistically significant (Pomerleau & Adkins, 1980).

In a recent study, Sanchez-Craig (1980) investigated the effect of a cognitive-behavior therapy program on the goals of either abstinence or nonproblem drinking. Seventy socially stable alcohol abusers, randomly assigned to each of these treatment goals, received cognitive-behavioral outpatient treatment, including self-monitoring, training in problem solving and cognitive coping, and several other minor treatment components. The preliminary findings revealed that the subjects randomly assigned to the abstinence goal drank significantly more per occasion during the first three weeks of treatment (when the subjects in both goal groups were expected to be abstinent) than subjects assigned to the non-problem-drinking goal. Additionally, while the subjects in each group were unaware that other subjects were being treated for different goals, the subjects assigned to the abstinence goal reported significantly more reservations about their goal assignment than the subjects assigned to the non-problem drinking goal.

Summary. To date, multimodal studies have provided highly positive evidence for the use of behavioral treatment with alcohol abusers, especially with nonabstinent goals. Future research can be expected to refine these methods in terms of delineating the elements essential for treatment success.

Treatment of Drug Abusers. It should be noted that several of the drug treatment stud-ies reviewed under the unimodal heading could be considered multimodal in design. Our decisions in classifying studies were determined primarily by the extent to which each study might contribute to a particular area of knowledge.

Coghlan, Gold, Dohrenwend, and Zimmerman (1973) described a program combining psychodynamic and behavioral principles in the residential treatment of adolescent drug abusers. Phase level and point systems were used, but no data were presented in support of the methods.

The use of behavior modification techniques as an adjunct in helping methadone maintenance patients restructure their lifestyle was investigated by Cheek, Tomarchio, Standen, and Albahary (1973). No comparison group was used, and the subjects were described as being motivated. The treatment program included relaxation training, systematic desensitization, behavioral rehearsal, and assertiveness training. The six-month outcome data, including measures of anxiety levels, the degree of assertiveness, and the nature of the subjects' self-images, were collected for 33 of the 43 subjects and were compared with the six-month outcome data for 20 individuals who had participated in the traditional methadone-maintenance program prior to the initiation of the study. The primary outcome criterion was a global assessment made by social workers familiar with the cases; each subject was subjectively classified by the social workers as either a success, marginally improved, or a failure. Although several significant changes in the dependent measures (e.g., assertiveness) were observed during the treatment, the six-month outcomes classified 58% of the behaviorally treated subjects as successes, as compared with 45% of the traditionally treated subjects; this difference was not significant.

Polakow (1975) reported a case study using multimodal methods with an unmotivated barbiturate addict on three years' probation for felony drug offenses and robbery. The treatment, conducted at weekly sessions for 15 months, combined covert sensitization with contingency contracting to accelerate prosocial behaviors. The subject received one week off her probation requirement for each session attended, and she received additional weeks off probation contingent on her involvement in verifiable nondrug activities. By the 37th week, the subject had ceased drug use, and by the 35th week, the number of nondrug activities in which she engaged weekly had risen from none to five. In a follow-up conducted 18 months after the treatment ended, the subject had maintained her drug-free status, had had no new arrests, and was gainfully employed.

Another case study was reported by Lesser (1967, 1976), who used multimodal methods with an exceptionally motivated young college student who was a narcotics user. The subject had formerly been a morphine addict, and was using narcotics two to three times per week when treatment began. The treatment methods included relaxation training, assertiveness training, and, following a relapse during treatment, electrical aversive conditioning. The subject experienced one more relapse to morphine use over the 4½ months of treatment, but he also reported not experiencing the expected effects of the drug, because of the aversive conditioning. Although this is a single-case study, one exemplary feature is that the author presented 10-year outcome data: the subject reported never having used narcotics after the treatment and claimed still to have a conditioned aversion to narcotics.

Abrahms (1979) reported a group study of cognitive behavior modification with inpatient methadone-maintenance patients. Eight subjects were randomly assigned to an experimental group and attended 10 weekly, two-hour group sessions that focused on anxiety management, methods for alleviating depression (e.g., reducing negative self-evaluations), and assertiveness training. Seven subjects were randomly assigned to a control condition: the same topics were discussed in weekly groups with nondirective leadership. A problem in interpreting this study's results is that two of the control subjects participated in the cognitive behavioral treatment after being in the control treatment. Data were presented for 10 weeks prior to treatment, 10 weeks during treatment, and 16 weeks following treatment. It was found that the behaviorally treated subjects reported lowered levels of anxiety, depression, and situational nonassertiveness. Although the tendency was nonsignificant, the behaviorally treated subjects tended to have fewer contaminated urines than the control subjects.

Lastly, Rawson and his colleagues (Rawson, Atkins, Glazer, & Callahan, 1977; Rawson, Glazer, Callahan, & Liberman, 1979) conducted a well-designed, controlled evaluation of the use of multimodal behavior therapy as an adjunct to Naltrexone in the treatment of predominantly (54%) Chicano heroin addicts. Naltrexone is a narcotic antagonist that inhibits the euphoric effects of heroin intoxication. The subjects were randomly assigned to one of three groups: Naltrexone only (N: $n = 55$), behavior therapy only (BT: $n = 71$), and Naltrexone with behavior therapy (N/BT: $n = 55$). The subjects given Naltrexone received the drug over a 10-month period in a gradually reduced dosage. The behavioral treatment package included contingency contracting, individualized behavior therapy as needed, and assistance in life management oriented toward helping the subjects to refuse heroin and to expand their interests and experiences in the "straight" world (e.g., job-finding skills). A well-developed battery of process and outcome measures was used to assess treatment effects.

In terms of process measures, it was found that a nonsignificantly greater number of subjects randomly assigned to the N and N/BT groups had attempted to enter the program (the subjects had to demonstrate their sincerity by meeting certain criteria). Overall, 44% of all those attempting entry into the program were unsuccessful. Importantly, the authors noted that the behavioral treatment seemed to evoke the least enthusiasm among the subjects. Only 15 of the 71 (21%) eligible BT subjects earned entry into treatment, and only 2 of those subjects (13%) completed as many as 24 weeks of treatment. In contrast, 41% of the group N subjects and 36% of the group N/BT subjects earned entry into treatment, and more than 60% of those group N and N/BT subjects who entered treatment stayed in treatment longer than 24 weeks. During the treatment, the subjects in groups N and N/BT also produced significantly fewer urines positive for opiates than the subjects in the BT group.

In this study, follow-up data were reported for 89.5% (51 of 57) of the treated subjects for a minimum period of one year. Although the difference was not significant, only 28% (4 of 14) of the BT subjects were opiate-free at follow-up, compared with 48% (10 of 21) of the subjects in group N and 50% (8 of 16) of those in group N/BT. In contrasting their negative findings with the positive results of Boudin (1980), the authors noted that subject differences may account for the differences in the efficacy of the behavioral methods. Boudin's subjects were mostly middle-class, nonminority, employed, and educated, whereas the subjects in Rawson *et al.*'s study were mostly minority, lower-class, and less-educated and had longer histories of heroin use.

Summary. The study by Rawson *et al.* (1977, 1979) is perhaps the best-controlled treatment evaluation study conducted to date on behavioral interventions for drug abusers. The results of that study, particularly considering the time and energy required for the behavioral treatment, are discouraging. That study, in particular, points out the critical need for well-controlled experimental investigations, rather than case studies or inadequately controlled designs. Since even this multifaceted, well-implemented study produced nonsignificant results, one cannot help but wonder whether studies of isolated treatment components with this population can generate useful treatment-outcome information.

Treatment Outcome Evaluation: Alcohol Abusers

An additional benefit of behavioral treatment studies of alcohol abusers is that they have fostered greatly improved methodological and measurement sophistication in treatment outcome evaluation. These contributions have been summarized by Sobell (L. C. Sobell, 1978) as including (1) more sensitive and quantifiable measures of drinking behavior (e.g., daily drinking dispositions) and other areas of life health functioning (e.g., number of days employed), as well as an improved quantification of outcome measures, resulting in a more sensitive evaluation of changes; (2) a delineation of the conditions under which alcohol abusers' self-reports can be expected to be valid; and (3) more effective methods of

tracking subjects (made necessary by the seeking of more precise data).

Treatment Outcome Evaluation: Drug Abusers

Some studies, particularly those by Boudin (1980) and Rawson *et al.* (1977, 1979) have demonstrated that well-operationalized process and outcome measures can be developed for use with this population. Unfortunately, such methods have been used sparingly.

The State of the Art

Investigations of the behavioral treatment of alcohol and drug problems have produced valuable knowledge. However, a fair appraisal also suggests that these studies, generally, have not achieved their full potential, especially in the drug field. Over the past decade, behavioral treatment methods have been increasingly recognized as making valuable contributions to the treatment of alcohol problems (National Institute on Alcohol Abuse and Alcoholism, 1971, 1974, 1978). This recognition has resulted, in large part, from relatively well-controlled demonstrations of multimodal treatment efficacy. While it might be premature to expect similar results in the area of drug treatment, the few well-controlled studies conducted to date have provided somewhat unimpressive results.

Two striking aspects of the existing literature are the general lack of controlled investigations and the relative paucity of studies attempting to evaluate the long-term efficacy of behavioral treatments. Perhaps the lack of well-designed clinical trials is related to the recency of most research in these areas. Whatever the reasons, it is clear that the time has passed when uncontrolled case studies and simple demonstrations of the within-treatment modifiability of alcohol- and drug-using behavior are likely to precipitate major practical research or clinical gains. Contingency management techniques are an excellent example of an area in which plentiful investigations have failed to give sufficient attention to the ultimate question of treatment research: Does the method of intervention produce lasting treatment gains? To achieve this objective, investigators must be concerned with the problem of creating circumstances within the individual and/or the natural environment that are conducive to the maintenance of the behavior changes achieved during treatment.

Another major inadequacy of much of the present research is that despite advances in the methodology of treatment outcome evaluation, it is impossible to demonstrate convincing treatment successes without adequate follow-up. Although both alcohol and drug treatment studies have been deficient in presenting adequate outcome data, at least some alcohol studies and a few drug studies have documented that long-term treatment-outcome data can be obtained. Nevertheless, when reporting outcomes, most studies in both areas have reported poorly validated findings for disturbingly short follow-up periods. An additional problem is that many studies have failed to measure the defining characteristic of the problems, that is, alcohol or drug use.

The fact that an abundance of studies has been published despite their disregard for evaluating the impact of treatment on the individual would also appear to indicate that the editorial standards for professional publications in these fields have been inordinately lax. Minimum follow-up intervals of five years for drug abusers (Vaillant, 1974) and eighteen months for alcohol abusers (Sobell & Sobell, 1978) have been suggested in the literature. While it would be unreasonable to insist that treatment research studies not be published unless fully adequate follow-up results are presented, it would be justifiable to require that articles include at least some specified follow-up length (e.g., six months) and a stated intention of providing further reports covering longer intervals.

It might also be profitable for investigators to take a more comprehensive overview of the treatment process, attending, for example, to the variables that affect entering and staying in treatment, as well as posttreatment factors that might influence outcomes. There have been few behavioral studies on the factors that influence treatment entry. Most studies addressing this topic are drug studies that report only the characteristics and numbers of individuals who refuse to enter treatment or who fail to satisfy the program entry criteria.

Much of the contingency management literature in the drug field, as well as some alcohol studies (e.g., Pomerleau & Adkins, 1980), have provided information about why persons continue in or drop out of treatment, but these findings have almost always been derived from retrospective analyses of dropouts rather than from prospective studies examining the ways of reducing premature terminations of treatment. In this regard, it would seem especially important to pay greater attention to enhancing positively reinforcing life circumstances for clients, with continued access to those reinforcers contingent on refraining from alcohol or drug abuse. Azrin (1976; Hunt & Azrin, 1973) has demonstrated the promise of such methods with alcohol abusers.

The influence of posttreatment factors on outcome has been relatively uninvestigated, although the complete and lasting achievement of an alcohol- or drug-free state after treatment has been shown to be a relatively rare phenomenon in both alcohol (Polich *et al.*, 1980) and drug (Vaillant, 1974) studies. Perhaps Marlatt's (1978, 1979) recent promising work on how alcohol and drug abusers deal with relapses signals forthcoming advances in this area. Another method of minimizing relapses might be to shape the termination of treatment by gradually increasing the interval between treatment sessions (Sobell & Sobell, 1978); this concept, however, has not yet been experimentally investigated.

Both alcohol and drug studies would also benefit from attending to the heterogeneity that exists among treatment populations. For example, based on actuarial data, it appears that alcohol abusers who have not been physically dependent on alcohol are more likely to achieve non-problem drinking outcomes than persons who have been addicted (L. C. Sobell, 1978). Goldberg *et al.* (1977) have suggested a possibly useful differentiation among drug abusers, that is, the separation of those who use drugs as an apparent coping response from those who seek a euphoric effect. Also, the variable of coercion has often been uncontrolled, particularly in studies of drug abuse, where coercion is quite prevalent. Perhaps a differentiation between cases where secondary gain is either clearly evident or nonevident would be useful, as has been suggested by Blanchard and Hersen (1976) in the case of hysterical neuroses. At the least, using grossly heterogeneous subject populations (e.g., different types of primary drugs of abuse, mixed sexes, widely different problem severities) would seem unfruitful unless a sufficient number of subjects are included so that retrospective correlational analyses can suggest whether the treatment was differentially effective for different types of subjects. Unfortunately, the use of samples large enough to allow such determinations has been infrequent.

Given our focus on the weaknesses, as well as the strengths, of the behavioral treatment studies of alcohol and drug problems, a reiteration of the achievements of this research is in order. First, compared with traditional treatments, the investigation of behavioral interventions for alcohol and drug problems is a recent occurrence. Second, despite their recency, these studies have already had a major impact on fields in which treatment has traditionally been viewed as very difficult and the target populations have been viewed as highly recalcitrant to change. Regardless whether these popular beliefs are valid, behavioral methods have made substantial and increasingly recognized contributions to the management and treatment of alcohol and drug abusers. Lastly, alcohol and drug use are clearly discrete and identifiable behaviors and, as such, are especially suitable to a functional analysis. Thus, while much work remains to be done, there are vast opportunities for future investigations.

Summary

With the exception of aversive conditioning methods, the applications of behavioral principles and technology to the treatment of alcohol and drug problems have largely occurred over the past 15 years. This chapter gives a critical review of the published literature on the behavioral treatment of alcohol and drug problems. While there have been some clear demonstrations of the efficacy of behavioral methods in the treatment of alcohol abusers, similarly strong support for the effectiveness of behavioral methods in treating drug abusers is lacking, mostly because few well-controlled studies have been conducted.

The most striking features of the literature are the relative paucity of controlled clinical trials, the lack of comparability among studies, and particularly the frequent lack of adequate long-term outcome reports. It is suggested that in the publication of such studies, editorial standards should require a clear description of the subject populations, the use of controlled designs, and the presentation of long-term treatment-outcome results. Finally, recent research focusing on methods of enhancing the maintenance of treatment gains (e.g., relapse prevention) seems to reveal a particularly promising area.

Despite the problems that pervade this literature, behavioral studies have made substantial and recognized contributions to the management and treatment of alcohol and drug abusers. These studies are also seen as having a potential for making future major contributions. These fields are in the midst of a maturation process, where simple case studies and demonstrations of the laboratory modifiability of alcohol- and drug-taking behavior no longer have substantial import unless they introduce novel innovations. More consistently high-quality and relevant investigations of the behavioral treatment of alcohol and drug problems can and should be guided by peer-review processes (e.g., for publication and grants).

References

Abrahms, J. L. A cognitive-behavioral versus nondirective group treatment program for opioid-addicted persons: An adjunct to methadone maintenance. *The International Journal of the Addictions*, 1979, *14*, 503–511.

Altman, J. L., Meyer, R. E., Mirin, S. M., McNamee, H. B., & McDougle, M. Opiate antagonists and the modification of heroin self-administration behavior in man: An experimental study. *The International Journal of the Addictions*, 1976, *11*, 485–499.

American Psychiatric Association. *Diagnostic and statistical manual of mental disorders* (2nd ed.). Washington, D.C.: American Psychiatric Association, 1968.

American Psychiatric Association. *Diagnostic and statistical manual of mental disorders* (3rd ed.). Washington, D.C.: American Psychiatric Association, 1980.

Anant, S. S. Treatment of alcoholics and drug addicts by verbal conditioning techniques. *The International Journal of the Addictions,* 1968, *3,* 381–388.

Ayllon, T., & Azrin, N. H. *The token economy.* New York: Appleton-Century-Crofts, 1968.

Azrin, N. H. Improvements in the community-reinforcement approach to alcoholism. *Behaviour Research and Therapy,* 1976, *14,* 339–348.

Baker, T. B. Personal communication. University of Wisconsin, Madison, 1980.

Bandura, A. *Principles of behavior modification.* New York: Holt, Rinehart & Winston, 1969.

Beatty, D. B. Contingency contracting with heroin addicts. *The International Journal of the Addictions,* 1978, *13,* 509–527.

Bigelow, G., Strickler, D., Liebson, I., & Griffiths, R. Maintaining disulfiram ingestion among outpatient alcoholics: A security-deposit contingency contracting procedure. *Behaviour Research and Therapy,* 1976, *14,* 378–381.

Blake, B. G. The application of behavior therapy to the treatment of alcoholism. *Behaviour Research and Therapy,* 1965, *3,* 75–85.

Blanchard, E. B., & Hersen, M. Behavioral treatment of hysterical neurosis: Symptom substitution and symptom return reconsidered. *Psychiatry,* 1976, *39,* 118–129.

Boudin, H. M. Contingency contracting as a therapeutic tool in the deceleration of amphetamine use. *Behavior Therapy,* 1972, *3,* 604–608.

Boudin, H. M. Contingency contracting with drug abusers in the natural environment: Treatment evaluation. In L. C. Sobell, M. B. Sobell, & E. Ward (Eds.), *Evaluating alcohol and drug abuse treatment effectiveness: Recent advances.* New York: Pergamon Press, 1980.

Boudin, H. M., & Valentine, V. E. Behavioral techniques as an alternative to methadone maintenance. Paper presented at the meeting of the Association for Advancement of Behavior Therapy, Miami, Fla. 1973.

Boudin, H. M., Valentine, V. E., Inghram, R. D., Brantley, J. M., Ruiz, M. R., Smith, G. G., Catlin, R. P., & Regan, E. J., Jr. Contingency contracting with drug abusers in the natural environment. *The International Journal of the Addictions,* 1977, *12,* 1–10.

Brecher, E. M., and Consumer Report Editors. *Licit and illicit drugs.* Boston: Little, Brown, 1972.

Briddell, D. W., & Nathan, P. E. Behavior assessment and modification with alcoholics: Current status and future trends. In M. Hersen, R. M. Eisler, & P. M. Miller (Eds.), *Progress in behavior modification.* New York: Academic Press, 1975.

Brinkman, D. N. Biofeedback application to drug addiction in the University of Colorado Drug Rehabilitation Program. *The International Journal of the Addictions,* 1978, *13,* 817–830.

Caddy, G. R., & Lovibond, S. H. Self-regulation and discriminated aversion conditioning in the modification of alcoholics' drinking behavior. *Behavior Therapy,* 1976, *7,* 223–230.

Caddy, G. R., Addington, H. J., Jr., & Perkins, D. Individualized behavior therapy for alcoholics: A third year independent double-blind follow-up. *Behaviour Research and Therapy,* 1978, *16,* 345–362.

Callahan, E. J., & Rawson, R. A. Behavioral assessment and treatment evaluation of narcotic addiction. In L. C.

Sobell, M. B. Sobell, & E. Ward (Eds.), *Evaluating alcohol and drug abuse treatment effectiveness: Recent advances.* New York: Pergamon Press, 1980.

Callner, D. A. Behavioral treatment approaches to drug abuse: A critical review of the research. *Psychological Bulletin,* 1975, *82,* 143–162.

Callner, D. A., & Ross, S. H. The assessment and training of assertive skills with drug addicts: A preliminary study. *The International Journal of the Addictions,* 1978, *13,* 227–239.

Campbell, D. T., & Stanley, J. C. *Experimental and quasi-experimental designs for research.* Chicago: Rand McNally, 1966.

Cappell, H., & Herman, C. P. Alcohol and tension reduction: A review. *Quarterly Journal of Studies on Alcohol,* 1972, *33,* 33–64.

Cappell, H., & Pliner, P. Cannibus intoxication: The role of pharmacological and psychological variables. In L. Miller (Ed.), *Marijuana: Effects on human behavior.* San Francisco: Academic Press, 1974, pp. 233–263.

Cautela, J. R. Treatment of compulsive behavior by covert sensitization. *Psychological Record,* 1966, *16,* 33–41.

Cautela, J. R., & Rosenstiel, A. K. The use of covert conditioning in the treatment of drug abuse. *The International Journal of the Addictions,* 1975, *10,* 277–303.

Chaney, E. F., O'Leary, M. R., & Marlatt, G. A. Skill training with alcoholics. *Journal of Consulting and Clinical Psychology,* 1978, *46,* 1092–1104.

Cheek, F. E., Franks, C. M., Laucius, J., & Burtle, V. Behavior modification training for wives of alcoholics. *Quarterly Journal of Studies on Alcohol,* 1971, *32,* 456–461.

Cheek, F. E., Tomarchio, T., Standen, J., & Albahary, R. S. Methadone plus—A behavior modification training program in self-control for addicts on methadone maintenance. *The International Journal of the Addictions,* 1973, *8,* 969–996.

Coghlan, A. J., Gold, S. R., Dohrenwend, E. F., & Zimmerman, R. S. A psychobehavioral residential drug abuse program: A new adventure in adolescent psychiatry. *The International Journal of the Addictions,* 1973, *8,* 767–777.

Cohen, R., Appelt, H., Olbrich, R., & Watzl, H. Alcoholic women treated by behaviorally oriented therapy: An 18-month follow-up study. *Drug and Alcohol Dependence,* 1979, *4,* 489–498.

Conger, J. J. Alcoholism: Theory, problems and challenge: II. Reinforcement theory and the dynamics of alcoholism. *Quarterly Journal of Studies on Alcohol,* 1956, *17,* 296–305.

Copemann, C. D. Drug addiction: II. An aversive counterconditioning technique for treatment. *Psychological Reports,* 1976, *38,* 1271–1281.

Copemann, C. D. Treatment of polydrug abuse by covert sensitization: Some contraindications. *The International Journal of the Addictions,* 1977, *12,* 17–23.

Copemann, C. D., & Shaw, P. L. Effects of contingent management of addicts expecting commitment to a community based treatment program. *British Journal of Addiction,* 1976, *71,* 187–191.

Davidson, W. S., II. Studies of aversive conditioning for alcoholics: A critical review of theory and research methodology. *Psychological Bulletin,* 1974, *81,* 571–581.

Davis, P., Gibbs, F., Davis, H., Jetter, W., & Trowbridge,

L. The effects of alcohol upon the electrocephalogram (brain waves). *Quarterly Journal of Studies on Alcohol*, 1941, *1*, 626–637.

Dole, V. P., & Nyswander, M. A medical treatment for diacetylmorphine (heroin) addiction. *Journal of the American Medical Association*, 1965, *193*, 80–84.

Dreilinger, C., & Thayer, L. C. Relaxation techniques in drug related crises: A case report. *Drug Forum*, 1974, *4*, 73–78.

Droppa, D. C. The application of covert conditioning procedures to the outpatient treatment of drug addicts: Four case studies. *The International Journal of the Addictions*, 1978, *13*, 657–673.

Duehn, W. D. Covert sensitization in group treatment of adolescent drug abusers. *The International Journal of the Addictions*, 1978, *13*, 485–491.

Einstein, S. *Beyond drugs*. New York: Pergamon Press, 1975.

Eisler, R. M., Hersen, M., & Miller, P. M. Shaping components of assertive behavior with instructions and feedback. *American Journal of Psychiatry*, 1974, *30*, 643–649.

Elkins, R. L. Aversion therapy for alcoholism: Chemical, electrical, or verbal imagery. *The International Journal of the Addictions*, 1975, *10*, 157–209.

Eriksson, J. H., Götestam, K. G., Melin, L., & Öst, L. A token economy treatment of drug addiction. *Behaviour Research and Therapy*, 1975, *13*, 113–125.

Ersner-Hershfield, S., & Sobell, L. C. Behavioral contracts with clients court referred for alcohol treatment. Paper presented at the 13th Annual Meeting of the Association for the Advancement of Behavior Therapy, San Francisco, Calif., December 1979.

Farrar, C. H., Powell, B. J., & Martin, L. K. Punishment of alcohol consumption by apneic paralysis. *Behaviour Research and Therapy*, 1968, *6*, 13–16.

Foy, D. W., Massey, F. H., Dyer, J. D., Ross, J. M., & Wooten, L. S. Social skills training to improve alcoholics' vocational interpersonal competency. *Journal of Counseling Psychology*, 1979, *26*, 128–132.

Foy, D. W., Miller, P. M., Eisler, R. M., & O'Toole, D. H. Social skills training to teach alcoholics to refuse drink effectively. *Journal of Alcohol Studies*, 1976, *37*, 1340–1345.

Frederiksen, L. W., & Miller, P. M. Peer-determined and self-determined reinforcement in group therapy with alcoholics. *Behaviour Research and Therapy*, 1976, *14*, 385–388.

Frederiksen, L. W., Jenkins, J. O., & Carr, C. R. Indirect modification of adolescent drug abuse using contingency contracting. *Journal of Behavior Therapy and Experimental Psychiatry*, 1976, *7*, 377–378.

Garcia, J., & Koelling, R. A. Relation of cue to consequence in avoidance learning. *Psychonomic Science*, 1966, *4*, 123–124.

Glaros, A. G. Comment on "Alcoholism, alpha production and biofeedback." *Journal of Consulting and Clinical Psychology*, 1977, *45*, 698–699.

Glicksman, M., Ottomanelli, G., & Cutler, R. The earn-your-way credit system: Use of a token economy in narcotic rehabilitation. *The International Journal of the Addictions*, 1971, *6*, 525–531.

Goldberg, R. J., Greenwood, J. C., & Taintor, Z. Alpha conditioning as an adjunct treatment for drug dependence: I. *The International Journal of the Addictions*, 1976, *11*, 1085–1089.

Goldberg, R. J., Greenwood, J. C., & Taintor, Z. Alpha conditioning as an adjunct treatment for drug dependence, II. *The International Journal of the Addictions*, 1977, *12*, 195–204.

Götestam, K. G., & Melin, L. Covert extinction of amphetamine addiction. *Behavior Therapy*, 1974, *5*, 90–92.

Hall, S. M., Cooper, J. L., Burmaster, S., & Polk, A. Contingency contracting as a therapeutic tool with methadone maintenance clients: Six single subject studies. *Behaviour Research and Therapy*, 1977, *15*, 438–441.

Hall, S. M., Bass, A., Hargreaves, W. A., & Loeb, P. Contingency management and information feedback in outpatient heroin detoxification. *Behavior Therapy*, 1979, *10*, 443–451.

Hallam, R., Rachman, S., & Falkowski, W. Subjective, attitudinal, and physiological effects of electrical aversion therapy. *Behaviour Research and Therapy*, 1972, *10*, 1–13.

Hedberg, A. G., & Campbell, L., III. A comparison of four behavioral treatments of alcoholism. *Journal of Behavior Therapy and Experimental Psychiatry*, 1974, *5*, 251–256.

Hersen, M., & Barlow, D. H. *Single case experimental designs: Strategies for studying behavior change*. New York: Pergamon Press, 1976.

Higgins, R. L., & Marlatt, G. A. Fear of interpersonal evaluations as a determinant of alcohol consumption in male social drinkers. *Journal of Abnormal Psychology*, 1975, *84*, 644–651.

Hirsch, S. M., Von Rosenberg, R., Phelan, C., & Dudley, H. K., Jr. Effectiveness of assertiveness training with alcoholics. *Journal of Studies on Alcohol*, 1978, *39*, 89–97.

Hirt, M., & Greenfield, H. Implosive therapy treatment of heroin addicts during methadone detoxification. *Journal of Consulting and Clinical Psychology*, 1979, *47*, 982–983.

Hodgson, R. J., Stockwell, T. R., & Rankin, H. J. Can alcohol reduce tension? *Behaviour Research and Therapy*, 1979, *17*, 459–466.

Holzinger, R., Mortimer, R., & Van Dusen, W. Aversion conditioning treatment of alcoholism. *American Journal of Psychiatry*, 1967, *124*, 246–247.

Hunt, G. M., & Azrin, N. H. A community-reinforcement approach to alcoholism. *Behaviour Research and Therapy*, 1973, *11*, 91–104.

Jaffe, J. H. The swinging pendulum: The treatment of drug users in America. In R. I. DuPont, A. Goldstein, & J. O'Donnell (Eds.), *Handbook on drug abuse*. Washington, D.C.: National Institute on Drug Abuse, 1979, pp. 3–16.

Jellinek, E. M. *The disease concept of alcoholism*. New Brunswick, N.J.: Hillhouse Press, 1960.

Jones, F. W., & Holmes, D. S. Alcoholism, alpha production and biofeedback. *Journal of Consulting and Clinical Psychology*, 1976, *44*, 224–228.

Kalant, H., & Kalant, O. J. *Drugs, society and personal choice*. Toronto: PaperJacks, Division of General Publishing Co., 1971.

Kalant, H., LeBlanc, A. E., & Gibbins, R. J. Tolerance to, and dependence on, ethanol. In Y. Israel & J. Mardones (Eds.), *Biological basis of alcoholism*. New York: Wiley, 1971, pp. 235–369.

Kantorovich, N. V. An attempt at association reflex therapy in alcoholism. *Nov. Refleksol. Fizl. Nervous Syst.*, 1929, *3*, 435–447.

Keller, M. Definition of alcoholism. *Quarterly Journal of Studies on Alcohol*, 1960, *21*, 125–134.

Keller, M. Problems with alcohol: An historical perspective. In W. J. Filstead, J. J. Rossi, & M. Keller (Eds.), *Alcohol and alcohol problems: New thinking and new directions*. Cambridge, Mass.: Ballanger, 1975, pp. 5–28.

Khatami, M., Mintz, J., & O'Brien, C. P. Biofeedback-mediated relaxation in narcotic addicts. *Behavior Therapy*, 1977, *8*, 968–969.

Kolvin, T. "Aversive imagery" treatment in adolescents. *Behaviour Research and Therapy*, 1967, *5*, 245–248.

Kraft, T. Successful treatment of a case of drinamyl addiction. *British Journal of Psychiatry*, 1968, *114*, 1363–1364.

Kraft, T. Successful treatment of a case of barbiturate addiction. *British Journal of Addiction*, 1969, *64*, 115–120.

Kraft, T., & Al-Issa, I. Alcoholism treated by desensitization: A case report. *Behaviour Research and Therapy*, 1967, *5*, 69–70.

Kraft, T., & Al-Issa, I. Desensitization and the treatment of alcohol addiction. *British Journal of Addiction*, 1968, *63*, 19–23.

Krasnagor, N. A. (Ed.), *Self-administration of abused substances: Methods for study*. NIDA Research Monograph 20. Washington, D.C.: National Institute on Drug Abuse, 1978.

Krasnagor, N. A. (Ed.). *Behavioral analysis and treatment of substance abuse*. NIDA Research Monograph 25. Washington D.C.: National Institute on Drug Abuse, 1979.

Lanyon, R. I., Primo, R. V., Terrell, F., & Wener, A. An aversion–desensitization treatment for alcoholism. *Journal of Consulting and Clinical Psychology*, 1972, *38*, 394–398.

Lazarus, A. A. Towards the understanding and effective treatment of alcoholism. *South African Medical Journal*, 1965, *39*, 736–741.

Lemere, F., & Voegtlin, W. L. An evaluation of the aversion treatment of alcoholism. *Quarterly Journal of Studies on Alcohol*, 1950, *11*, 199–204.

Lesser, E. Behavior therapy with a narcotics user: A case report. *Behaviour Research and Therapy*, 1967, *5*, 251–252.

Lesser, E. Behavior therapy with a narcotics user: A case report. Ten-year follow-up. *Behaviour Research and Therapy*, 1976, *14*, 381.

Liberman, R. Aversive conditioning of drug addicts: A pilot study. *Behaviour Research and Therapy*, 1968, *6*, 229–231.

Liebson, I., Bigelow, G., & Flamer, R. Alcoholism among methadone patients: A specific treatment method. *American Journal of Psychiatry*, 1973, *130*, 483–485.

Liebson, I. A., Tommasello, A., & Bigelow, G. E. A behavioral treatment of alcoholic methadone patients. *Annals of Internal Medicine*, 1978, *89*, 342–344.

Litman, G. K., Eisler, J. R., Rawson, N. S., & Oppenheim, A. M. Differences in relapse precipitants and coping behavior between alcohol relapsers and survivors. *Behaviour Research and Therapy*, 1979, *17*, 89–94.

Little, L. M., & Curran, J. P. Covert sensitization: A clinical procedure in need of some explanations. *Psychological Bulletin*, 1978, *85*, 513–531.

Lovibond, S. H., & Caddy, G. Discriminated aversive control in the moderation of alcoholics' drinking behavior. *Behavior Therapy*, 1970, *1*, 437–444.

Lubetkin, B. S., & Fishman, S. T. Electrical aversion therapy with a chronic heroin user. *Journal of Behavior Therapy and Experimental Psychiatry*, 1974, *5*, 193–195.

Ludwig, A. M. On and off the wagon. *Quarterly Journal of Studies on Alcohol*, 1972, *33*, 91–96.

MacDonough, T. S. Evaluation of the effectiveness of intensive confrontation in changing the behavior of drug and alcohol abusers. *Behavior Therapy*, 1976, *7*, 408–409. (a)

MacDonough, T. S. The relative effectiveness of a medical hospitalization program vs. a feedback-behavior modification program in treating alcohol and drug abusers. *The International Journal of the Addictions*, 1976, *11*, 269–282. (b)

Maisto, S. A., & Adesso, V. J. The effect of instructions and feedback on blood alcohol level discrimination in nonalcoholic drinkers. *Journal of Consulting and Clinical Psychology*, 1977, *45*, 625–636.

Maletzky, B. M. Assisted covert sensitization for drug abuse. *The International Journal of the Addictions*, 1974, *9*, 411–429.

Marlatt, G. A. A comparison of aversive conditioning procedures in the treatment of alcoholism. Paper presented at the meeting of the Western Psychological Association, Anaheim, Calif., April, 1973.

Marlatt, G. A. Alcohol, stress and cognitive control. In P. E. Nathan & G. A. Marlatt (Eds.), *Experimental and behavioral approaches to alcoholism*. New York: Plenum Press, 1978.

Marlatt, G. A. A cognitive-behavioral model of the relapse process. In N. A. Krasnegor (Ed.), *Behavioral analysis and treatment of substance abuse*. NIDA Reseach Monograph No. 25. Washington, D.C.: National Institute on Drug Abuse, 1979.

Marlatt, G. A., & Marques, J. K. Meditation, self-control and alcohol use. In R. B. Stuart (Ed.), *Behavioral self-management: Strategies, techniques and outcome*. New York: Bruner/Mazel, 1977.

McCrady, B. S., Paolino, T. J., Longabaugh, R. L., & Rossi, J. Effects on treatment outcome of joint admission and spouse involvement in treatment of hospitalized alcoholics. Unpublished manuscript. Cited in T. J. Paolino & B. S. McCrady, *The alcoholic marriage*. New York: Grune & Stratton, 1977.

Melin, L., Andersson, B. E., & Götestam, K. G. Contingency management in a methadone maintenance treatment program. *Addictive Behaviors*, 1976, *1*, 151–158.

Melin, G. L., & Götestam, K. G. A contingency management program on a drug-free unit for intravenous amphetamine addicts. *Journal of Behavior Therapy and Experimental Psychiatry*, 1973, *4*, 331–337.

Mello, N. K. Behavioral studies of alcoholism. In B. Kissin & H. Begleiter (Eds.), *The biology of alcoholism*, Vol. 2: *Physiology and behavior*. New York: Plenum Press, 1972.

Mello, N. K., & Mendelson, J. H. (Eds.), *Recent advances in studies of alcoholism: An interdisciplinary symposium.* Washington, D.C.: U.S. Government Printing Office, 1971.

Mello, N. K., Mendelson, J. H. Kuehnle, J. C., & Sellers, M. L. Human polydrug use: Marihuana and alcohol. *Journal of Pharmacology and Experimental Therapies,* 1978, *207,* 992–935.

Mendelson, J. H. (Ed.), Experimentally induced chronic intoxication and withdrawal in alcoholics. *Quarterly Journal of Studies on Alcohol,* 1964, Supplement No. 2.

Mendelson, J. H., Kuehnle, J. C., Greenberg, I., & Mello, N. K. Operant acquisition of marijuana in man. *Journal of Pharmacology and Experimental Therapeutics,* 1976, *198,* 42–53.

Milby, J. B., Garrett, C., English, C., Fritschi, O., & Clarke, C. Take-home methadone: Contingency effects on drug-seeking and productivity of narcotic addicts. *Addictive Behaviors,* 1978, *3,* 215–220.

Miller, P. M. The use of behavioral contracting in the treatment of alcoholism: A case report. *Behavior Therapy,* 1972, *3,* 593–596.

Miller, P. M. A behavioral intervention program for chronic public drunkenness offenders. *Archives of General Psychiatry,* 1975, *32,* 915–918.

Miller, P. M. *Behavioral treatment of alcoholism.* New York: Pergamon Press, 1976.

Miller, P. M., & Eisler. R. M. Assertive behavior of alcoholics: A descriptive analysis. *Behavior Therapy,* 1977, *8,* 146–149.

Miller, P. M., & Hersen, M. Modification of marital interactions patterns between an alcoholic and his wife. In J. D. Krumboltz & C. E. Thoresen (Eds.), *Counseling methods.* New York: Holt, Rinehart & Winston, 1976.

Miller, P. M., & Mastria, M. A. *Alternatives to alcohol abuse: A social learning model.* Champaign, Ill.: Research Press, 1977.

Miller, P. M., Hersen, M., Eisler, R. M., & Hemphill, D. P. Electrical aversion therapy with alcoholics: An analogue study. *Behaviour Research and Therapy,* 1973, *11,* 491–497.

Miller, P. M., Hersen, M., & Eisler, R. M. Relative effectiveness of instructions, agreements, and reinforcements in behavioral contracts with alcoholics. *Journal of Abnormal Psychology,* 1974, *83,* 548–553.

Miller, P. M., Hersen, M., Eisler, R. M., & Hilsman, G. Effects of social stress on operant drinking of alcoholics and social drinkers. *Behaviour Research and Therapy,* 1974, *12,* 67–72.

Miller, P. M., Hersen, M., Eisler, R. M., & Watts, J. G. Contingent reinforcement of lowered blood/alcohol levels in an outpatient chronic alcoholic. *Behaviour Research and Therapy,* 1974, *12,* 261–263.

Miller, P. M., Stanford, A. G., & Hemphill, D. P. A social-learning approach to alcoholism treatment. *Social Casework,* 1974, *55,* 279–284.

Miller, P. M., Becker, J. V., Foy, D. W., & Wooten, L. S. Instructional control of the components of alcoholic drinking behavior. *Behavior Therapy,* 1976, *7,* 472–480.

Miller, W. R. Behavioral self-control training in the treatment of problem drinkers. In R. B. Stuart (Ed.), *Behavioral self-management: Strategies, techniques, and outcome.* New York: Bruner/Mazel, 1977.

Miller, W. R. Behavioral treatment of problem drinkers: A comparative outcome study of three controlled drinking therapies. *Journal of Consulting and Clinical Psychology,* 1978, *46,* 74–86.

Miller, W. R., & Munõz, R. F. Control over drinking: A self-help manual. In *A guide to rational drinking: A self-help manual.* Englewood Cliffs, N.J.: Prentice-Hall, 1976.

Miller, W. R., Gribskov, C., & Mortell, R. The effectiveness of a self-control manual for problem drinkers with and without therapist contact. Unpublished manuscript, University of Oregon, 1976, cited in W. R. Miller. Behavioral self-control training in the treatment of problem drinkers. In R. B. Stuart (Ed.), *Behavioral self-management: Strategies, techniques and outcome.* New York: Bruner/Mazel, 1977.

Miller, W. R., Pechacek, T. F., & Hamburg, S. A minimal therapist-contact behavioral treatment for problem drinking. Unpublished manuscript. Palo Alto, Calif.: Veterans Administration Hospital, 1976. Cited in W. R. Miller. Behavioral self-control training in the treatment of problem drinkers. In R. B. Stuart (Ed.), *Behavioral self-management: Strategies, techniques and outcome.* New York: Bruner/Mazel, 1977.

Mills, K. C., Sobell, M. B., & Schaefer, H. H. Training social drinking as an alternative to abstinence for alcoholics. *Behavior Therapy,* 1971, *2,* 18–27.

Murray, R. G., & Hobbs, S. A. The use of self-imposed timeout procedure in the modification of excessive alcohol consumption. *Journal of Behavior Therapy and Experimental Psychiatry,* 1977, *8,* 377–380.

Nathan, P. E., Marlatt, G. A., & Løberg, *Alcoholism: New directions in behavioral research and treatment.* New York: Plenum Press, 1978.

National Council on Alcoholism. *Criteria for the diagnosis of alcoholism,* March, 1972.

National Institute on Alcohol Abuse and Alcoholism. *First report to the Congress.* Washington, D.C.: U.S. Government Printing Office, 1971.

National Institute on Alcohol Abuse and Alcoholism. *Second report to the Congress.* Washington, D.C.: U.S. Government Printing Office, 1974.

National Institute on Alcohol Abuse and Alcoholism. *Third report to the Congress.* Washington, D.C.: U.S. Government Printing Office, 1978.

O'Brien, C. P., Testa, T., O'Brien, T. J., Brady, J. P., & Wells, B. Conditioned narcotic withdrawal in humans. *Science,* 1977, *195,* 1000–1002.

O'Brien, J. S., Raynes, A. E., & Patch, V. D. An operant reinforcement system to improve ward behavior in inpatient drug addicts. *Journal of Behavior Therapy and Experimental Psychiatry,* 1971, *2,* 239–242.

O'Brien, J. S., Raynes, A. E., & Patch, V. D. Treatment of heroin addiction with aversion therapy, relaxation training and systematic desensitization. *Behaviour Research and Therapy,* 1972, *10,* 77–80.

O'Leary, D. E., O'Leary, M. R., & Donovan, D. M. Social skill acquisition and psychosocial development of alcoholics: A review. *Addictive Behaviors,* 1976, *1,* 111–120.

Parker, J. C., Gilbert, G. S., & Thoreson, R. W. Reduction

of autonomic arousal in alcoholics: A comparison of relaxation and mediation techniques. *Journal of Consulting and Clinical Psychology,* 1978, *46,* 879–886.

Pattison, E. M., Sobell, M. B., & Sobell, L. C. (Eds.). *Emerging concepts of alcohol dependence.* New York: Springer, 1977.

Paynard, C., & Wolf, K. The use of systematic desensitization in an outpatient drug treatment center. *Psychotherapy: Theory, Research and Practice,* 1974, *11,* 329–330.

Pickens, R. A behavioral program for treatment of drug dependence. In N. A. Krasnegor (Ed.), *Behavioral analysis and treatment of substance abuse.* NIDA Research Monograph No. 25. Washington, D.C.: National Institute on Drug Abuse, 1979.

Polakow, R. L. Covert sensitization treatment of a probationed barbiturate addict. *Journal of Behavior Therapy and Experimental Psychiatry,* 1975, *6,* 53–54.

Polich, J. M., Armor, D. J., & Braiker, H. B. *The course of alcoholism: Four years after treatment.* Santa Monica, Calif.: Rand Corporation, 1980.

Pomerleau, O., & Adkins, D. Evaluating behavioral and traditional treatment for problem drinkers. In L. C. Sobell, M. B. Sobell, & E. Ward (Eds.), *Evaluating alcohol and drug abuse treatment effectiveness: Recent advances.* New York: Pergamon Press, 1980.

Pomerleau, O., Pertschuk, M., Adkins, D., & Brady, J. P. A comparison of behavioral and traditional treatment for middle income problem drinkers. *Journal of Behavioral Medicine,* 1978, *1,* 187–200.

Premack, D. Toward empirical behavior laws: I. Positive reinforcement. *Psychological Review,* 1959, *66,* 219–233.

Rachman, S., & Teasdale, J. *Aversion therapy and behavior disorders.* Coral Gables: University of Miami Press, 1969.

Rawson, R. A., Atkins, F., Glazer, M., & Callahan, E. J. A comprehensive behavior therapy program for the outpatient treatment of heroin addiction. Paper presented at the National Drug Abuse Conference, 1977.

Rawson, R. A., Glazer, M., Callahan, E. J., & Liberman, R. P. Naltrexone and behavior therapy for heroin addiction. In N. A. Krasnegor (Ed.), *Behavioral analysis and treatment of substanse abuse.* NIDA Research Monograph No. 25. Washington, D.C.: National Institute on Drug Abuse, 1979.

Ray, O. S. *Drugs, society, and human behavior.* St. Louis: C. V. Mosby, 1972.

Raymond, M. The treatment of addiction by aversion conditioning with apomorphine. *Behaviour Research and Therapy,* 1964, *1,* 287–291.

Reeder, C. W., & Kunce, J. T. Modeling techniques, drug-abstinence behavior, and heroin addicts: A pilot study. *Journal of Counseling Psychology,* 1976, *23,* 560–562.

Robichaud, C., Strickler, D., Bigelow, G., & Liebson, I. Disulfiram maintenance employee alcoholism treatment: A three-phase evaluation. *Behaviour Research and Therapy,* 1979, *17,* 618–621.

Rubenstein, C. The treatment of morphine addiction in tuberculosis by Pavlov conditioning model. *American Review of Tuberculosis,* 1931, *24,* 682–685.

Sanchez-Craig, M. Random assignment to abstinence or controlled drinking in a cognitive-behavioral program: Short-term effects on drinking behavior. *Addictive Behaviors,* 1980, *5,* 35–40.

Schuster, C. R., & Johanson, C. E. Behavior analysis of opiate dependence. In S. Fisher & A. Freedman (Eds.), *Opiate addiction: Origins and treatment.* New York: Wiley, 1973.

Seixas, F., Blume, S., Cloud, L., Lieber, C. S., & Simpson, D. Definition of alcoholism (letter). *Annals of Internal Medicine,* 1976, *85,* 764.

Smith, D. E., & Gay, G. R. (Eds.). *"It's so good, don't even try it once": Heroin in perspective.* Englewood Cliffs, N.J.: Prentice-Hall, 1972.

Smith, R. E., & Gregory, P. B. Covert sensitization by induced anxiety in the treatment of an alcoholic. *Journal of Behavior Therapy and Experimental Psychiatry,* 1976, *7,* 31–33.

Snowden, L. R. Personality tailored covert sensitization of heroin abuse. *Addictive Behaviors,* 1978, *3,* 43–49.

Sobell, L. C. Alcohol treatment outcome evaluation: Contributions from behavioral research. In P. E. Nathan & G. E. Marlatt (Eds.), *Alcoholism: New directions in behavioral research and treatment.* New York: Plenum Press, 1978, pp. 255–269.

Sobell, L. C., & Sobell, M. B. A self-feedback technique to monitor drinking behavior in alcoholics. *Behaviour Research and Therapy,* 1973, *11,* 237–238.

Sobell, L. C., Sobell, M. B., & Christelman, W. C. The myth of "one drink." *Behaviour Research and Therapy,* 1972, *10,* 119–123.

Sobell, M. B. Alternatives to abstinence. Evidence, issues and some proposals. In P. E. Nathan & G. A. Marlatt (Eds.), *Experimental and behavioral approaches to alcoholism.* New York: Plenum Press, 1978.

Sobell, M. B., & Sobell, L. C. Alcoholics treated by individualized behavior therapy: One year treatment outcome. *Behaviour Research and Therapy,* 1973, *11,* 599–618. (a)

Sobell, M. B., & Sobell, L. C. Individualized behavior therapy for alcoholics. *Behavior Therapy,* 1973, *4,* 49–72. (b)

Sobell, M. B., & Sobell, L. C. Second year treatment outcome of alcoholics treated by individualized behavior therapy: Results. *Behaviour Research and Therapy,* 1976, *14,* 195–215.

Sobell, M. B., & Sobell, L. C. *Behavioral treatment of alcohol problems: Individualized therapy and controlled drinking.* New York: Plenum Press, 1978.

Sobell, M. B., & Sobell, L. C. Controlled drinking: A concept coming of age. In K. R. Blankstein & J. Polivy (Eds.), *Advances in the study of communication and affect,* Vol. 7: *Self-control and self-modification of emotional behavior.* New York: Plenum Press, 1982.

Spevak, M., Pihl, R., & Rowan, T. Behavior therapies in the treatment of drug abuse: Some case studies. *The Psychological Record,* 1973, *23,* 179–184.

Steffen, J. J. Electromyographically induced relaxation in the treatment of chronic alcohol abuse. *Journal of Consulting and Clinical Psychology,* 1975, *43,* 275.

Steinfeld, G. J., Rautio, F. A., Rice, A. H., & Egan, M. J. Group covert sensitization with narcotic addicts: Further comments. *The International Journal of the Addictions,* 1974, *9,* 447–464.

Stitzer, M., & Bigelow, G. Contingency management in a methadone maintenance program: Availability of reinforcers. *The International Journal of the Addictions,* 1978, *3,* 737–746.

Stitzer, M., Bigelow, G., & Liebson, I. Reducing benzodiazepine self-administration with contingent reinforcement. *Addictive Behaviors*, 1979, *4*, 245–252. (a)

Stitzer, M., Bigelow, G., & Liebson, I. Reinforcement of drug abstinence: A behavioral approach to drug abuse treatment. In N. A. Krasnegor (Ed.), *Behavioral analysis and treatment of substance abuse*. NIDA Research Monograph No. 25, Washington, D.C.: National Institute on Drug Abuse, 1979. (b)

Stickler, D., Bigelow, G., Wells, D., & Liebson, I. Effects of relaxation instructions on the electromyographic responses of abstinent alcoholics to drinking related stimuli. *Behaviour Research and Therapy*, 1977, *15*, 500–502.

Strickler, D. P., Thomaszenski, R., Maxwell, W. A., & Suib, M. The effects of relaxation instructions on drinking behavior in the presence of stress. *Behaviour Research and Therapy*, 1979, *17*, 45–51.

Teasdale, J. D. Conditioned abstinence in narcotic addicts. *The International Journal of the Addictions*, 1973, *8*, 273–292.

Thimann, J. Conditioned reflex treatment of alcoholism. *New England Journal of Medicine*, 1949, *241*, 368–370, 408–410.

Thompson, I. G., & Rathod, N. H. Aversion therapy for heroin dependence. *The Lancet*, 1968, *31*, 382–384.

Thompson, T., & Schuster, C. *Behavioral pharmacology*. Englewood Cliffs, N.J.: Prentice-Hall, 1968.

Tournier, R. E. Alcoholics Anonymous as treatment, Alcoholics Anonymous as ideology. *Journal of Studies on Alcohol*, 1979, *40*, 230–239.

Towle, L. H. Alcoholism treatment outcome in different populations. *Proceedings from the Fourth Annual Alcohol Conference of the NIAAA*, April 1974.

Vaillant, G. E. Outcome research in narcotic addiction: Problems and perspectives. *American Journal of Drug and Alcohol Abuse*, 1974, *1*, 25–36.

Vannicelli, M. Treatment contracts in an inpatient alcoholism treatment setting. *Journal of Studies on Alcohol*, 1979, *40*, 457–471.

Voegtlin, W. L., & Lemere, F. The treatment of alcohol addiction: A review of the literature. *Quarterly Journal of Studies on Alcohol*, 1942, *2*, 717–803.

Vogler, R. E., Lunde, S. E., Johnson, G. R., & Martin, P. L. Electrical aversion conditioning with chronic alcoholics. *Journal of Consulting and Clinical Psychology*, 1970, *34*, 302–307.

Vogler, R. E., Compton, J. V., & Weissbach, T. A. Integrated behavior change techniques for alcoholics. *Journal of Consulting and Clinical Psychology*, 1975, *43*, 233–243.

Watson, C. G., Herder, J., & Passini, F. T. Alpha biofeedback therapy in alcoholics: An 18-month follow-up. *Journal of Clinical Psychology*, 1978, *34*, 765–769.

Wiens, A. N., Montague, J-R., Manaugh, T. S., & English, C. J. Pharmacological aversive counterconditioning to alcohol in a private hospital: One year follow-up. *Journal of Studies on Alcohol*, 1976, *37*, 1320–1324.

Wikler, A. Conditioning factors in opiate addiction and relapse. In D. Wikler & G. Kassebaum (Eds.), *Narcotics*. New York: McGraw-Hill, 1965, pp. 85–100.

Wikler, A. Some implications of conditioning theory for problems of drug abuse. *Behavioral Science*, 1971, *16*, 92–97.

Wilson, G. T., & Rosen, R. Training controlled drinking in an alcoholic through a multi-faceted behavioral treatment program: A case study. In J. D. Krumboltz & C. E. Thoresen (Eds.), *Counseling methods*. New York: Holt, Rinehart & Winston, 1975.

Wilson, G. T., Leaf, R. C., & Nathan, P. E. Aversive control of excessive alcohol consumption by chronic alcoholics in laboratory setting. *Journal of Applied Behavior Analysis*, 1975, *8*, 13–26.

Wisocki, P. A. The successful treatment of a heroin addict by covert conditioning techniques. *Journal of Behavior Therapy and Experimental Psychiatry*, 1973, *4*, 55–61.

Wolpe, J. *The practice of behavior therapy*. New York: Pergamon Press, 1969.

World Health Organization. World Health Organization Expert Committee on Addiction-Producing Drugs. Geneva: WHO Technical Report Series No. 273, 1964.

Yen, S. Availability of activity reinforcers in a drug abuse clinic: A preliminary report. *Psychological Reports*, 1974, *34*, 1021–1022.

CHAPTER 18

Obesity

Albert J. Stunkard

Introduction

In 1967, a small paper on "Behavioral Control of Overeating" (Stuart) signaled, indeed provoked, the start of an explosion of interest in the use of behavior therapy for obesity. More than a hundred papers in the professional literature paced an unprecedented interest in behavior modification in lay publications. A concern with obesity swept departments of psychology throughout the country; the treatment of obesity became an increasingly common part of clinical programs, and obesity supplanted snake phobias as the largest single topic of research on treatment.

This interest in the use of behavior therapy for obesity has not been confined to the field of psychology. Obesity occupies a central position in the concerns of the burgeoning new field of behavioral medicine. Historically, behavioral control of obesity was one of the first medical concerns to be subjected to careful behavioral analysis. Currently, more people are receiving behavioral treatment for obesity than are receiving behavioral treatment for all other conditions combined. In the future, the path traveled in the development of behavioral approaches to obesity may well serve as a guide to the development of behavioral medicine.

This chapter updates and expands earlier reviews of the behavioral treatment of obesity (Abramson, 1973, 1977; Leon, 1976; Stuart, 1976; Stunkard, 1975; Stunkard & Mahoney, 1976; Wilson, 1980). It gives a short description of the standard elements of behavioral weight-control programs and reviews some key papers in the development of the field. The current empirical status of the behavioral treatment of obesity is then described, with emphasis on achievements in decreasing the rate of dropouts from treatment and of untoward side effects of treatment. The modest record in terms of weight loss and the maintenance of weight loss is noted, together with a short account of the beginning application of behavioral treatment to childhood obesity. Some assumptions about behavioral weight control are examined, together with the evidence that shows them to have been in error.

The search for improving treatment in the future is taking two forms, one clinical and one social. Promising measures for improving clinical approaches to obesity are combining behavioral treatments with special diets, increasing the use of exercise, and increasing the duration and the intensity of treatment. The social measures for improving the control of obesity consist of efforts to introduce behav-

Albert J. Stunkard • Department of Psychiatry, University of Pennsylvania, Philadelphia, Pennsylvania 19104.

ioral principles into large groups. The provision of low-cost interventions for large numbers of people by such means may compensate for the limited clinical efficacy of behavioral treatments for obesity. Self-help groups, worksite treatment, and geographical communities are promising possibilities for such interventions.

Description of a Behavioral Program

A detailed description of behavioral treatments for obesity is beyond the scope of this report, and the interested reader is referred to the extended descriptions by Mahoney and Mahoney (1976), Jordan, Levitz, and Kimbrell (1976), and Stuart (1978), as well as to the manuals by Ferguson (1975). Nevertheless, a brief description of some of the essential elements may be useful. Measures for increasing physical activity and providing nutrition education are important components, but we will focus here on five more explicitly behavioral measures designed to control food intake: (1) self-monitoring (a description of the behavior to be controlled); (2) control of the stimuli that precede eating; (3) development of techniques for controlling the act of eating; (4) reinforcement of the prescribed behaviors; and (5) cognitive restructuring. The first four have been elements of most behavioral programs; the fifth is increasingly utilized in these programs.

Self-Monitoring: Description of the Behavior to be Controlled

Patients are asked to keep careful records of the food that they eat. Each time they eat, they write down precisely what they ate, how much, at what time of day, where they were, who they were with, and how they felt. The immediate reaction of many patients to this time-consuming and inconvenient procedure is grumbling and complaints. Such reaction occurred far more frequently in the early days of these programs and may well have been due to the therapists' own uncertainty about the techniques. More recently, patients have responded more positively. Many come to the view that record keeping may be the single

most important part of the behavioral program. It vastly increases patients' awareness of their eating behavior. Despite their years of struggle with the problem, once patients begin to keep records, they are surprised at how much they eat and how varied are the circumstances in which they eat.

There is a surprising unanimity on the value of self-monitoring. It is true that some have found the effects rather weak (Mahoney, Moura, & Wade, 1973; Stollak, 1967) or of limited duration (Mahoney, 1974; Stuart & Davis, 1972). Others, however, report robust effects (Bellack, Rozensky, & Schwartz, 1974; Green, 1978; Romanczyk, 1974; Romanczyk, Tracey, Wilson, & Thorpe, 1973). The more specific the items monitored, the more effective the results. Not only is self-monitoring a key element in the process of behavior change, it is the mainstay of the behavioral assessment of obesity (Brownell, 1980).

Control of the Stimuli That Precede Eating

A behavioral analysis traditionally begins with a study of the events antecedent to the behavior to be controlled. Stimulus control of eating involves many kinds of measures that are traditional in weight-reduction programs. For example, every effort is made to limit the amount of high-calorie food kept in the house and to limit accessibility to food that must be kept in the house. For times when eating cannot be resisted, adequate amounts of low-calorie foods, such as celery and raw carrots, are kept readily available.

In addition, behavioral programs have introduced new and distinctive measures. For example, most patients report that their eating takes place in a wide variety of places and at many different times during the day. Some note that if they eat while watching television, it is not long before watching television makes them eat. It is as if the various times and places had become discriminative stimuli for eating. In an effort to decrease the number and the potency of discriminative stimuli that control their eating, patients are encouraged to confine all eating, including snacking, to one place. In order not to disrupt domestic routines, this place is very frequently the kitchen.

A parallel effort is made to develop new discriminative stimuli for eating and to increase their power. For example, patients are encouraged to use distinctive table settings (perhaps an unusual-colored place mat and napkin, along with special silver). No effort is made to decrease the amount of food the patients eat, but they are encouraged to use the distinctive table settings whenever they eat, even for a small between-meal snack. One middle-aged housewife, convinced of the importance of this measure, went so far as to take her distinctive table setting with her whenever she dined out. She was an early success.

Stimulus control has occupied a central position in most behavioral weight-control programs of the past decade, but its independent contribution to the efficacy of these programs is not known. Only two studies have attempted to assess this efficacy by comparing stimulus control alone with other treatment modalities, and they reached opposite conclusions. McReynolds, Lutz, Paulsen, and Kohrs (1976) reported that stimulus control alone was as effective as a treatment package that contained it, while Loro, Fisher, and Levenkron (1979) found stimulus control alone "to be a relatively ineffective weight-loss procedure." This latter study, it should be noted, involved weight losses of only 2.7 kg and 3.2 kg, even in the relatively more effective weight-loss procedures. Stimulus control appears sufficiently useful to continue as a major element in behavioral programs, despite the sparsity of controlled evidence for its independent efficacy. Its efficacy is likely to be considerably increased if it is used specifically for persons in whom pre-treatment behavioral assessment has revealed deficiencies in this area (Coates, 1977).

Development of Techniques for Controlling the Act of Eating

Specific techniques are utilized to help patients decrease their speed of eating, to become aware of all the components of the eating process, and to gain control over these components. The exercises include counting each mouthful of food eaten during a meal, each chew, or each swallow. Patients are encouraged to practice putting down their eating utensils after every third mouthful until that mouthful is chewed and swallowed. Then longer delays are introduced, starting with one minute toward the end of the meal, when it is more easily tolerated, and moving to more frequent delays, longer ones, and ones earlier in the meal.

Patients are encouraged to stop pairing their eating with such activities as reading the newspaper and watching television, and to make conscious efforts to make eating a pure experience. They are urged to do whatever they can to make meals a time of comfort and relaxation, particularly to avoid old arguments and new problems at the dinner table. They are encouraged to savor the food as they eat it, to make a conscious effort to become aware of it as they are chewing, and to enjoy the act of swallowing and the warmth and fullness in their stomachs. To the extent that they succeed in this endeavor, they eat less and enjoy it more.

Reinforcement of the Prescribed Behaviors

In addition to the informal and incidental rewards that patients receive from the behavioral program, a system of formal rewards is also used. Separating the reward schedules for changes in behavior and for weight loss is useful; rewards for changing behavior may be the more effective.

In order to decrease the time between the exercise of a specific behavior and the attendant reward, patients are awarded a certain number of points for each of the activities that they are learning: record keeping, counting chews and swallows, pausing during the meal, eating in one place, and so forth. Not only do patients receive a certain number of points for each activity, but they can earn extras, such as double the number of points, when they devise an alternative to eating in the face of strong temptation.

These points, which serve to provide immediate reinforcement of a behavior, are accumulated and converted into more tangible rewards, often in concert with the spouse. Popular rewards include a trip to the movies or relief from housekeeping chores. A more impersonal reward is the conversion of points into money, which patients bring to the next meeting and donate to the group. Surprisingly altruistic courses may be chosen. In an early program, one group donated its savings to the Salvation Army and another to a needy friend of one of the members.

The promptness of the reinforcement seems to be a key to success. One middle-aged housewife said, ''My husband was always offering to buy me a car if I lost 50 pounds. I used to work away at it and knock myself out and lost 30 pounds, which was a lot of weight, but what did it get me? I didn't get half a car. I got nothing. I've only lost eight pounds in this program so far, and he's done all sorts of good things for me.''

Cognitive Restructuring

In the quite recent past, behavior therapy has been enriched by an interest in cognitions and by the whole new field of cognitive-behavior modification. Concern with cognitions has received less attention in the treatment of obesity than have more traditional operant approaches, and there has been as yet only limited experimental evidence of the efficacy of cognitive strategies in the treatment of obesity. Nevertheless, these strategies have been attracting increasing attention, and several clinicians believe that they can make a useful contribution to an overall program of treatment for obesity.

A feature that has made cognitions palatable to the more behavioristic therapists is the recognition that the internal monologues that occupy so much of our time are readily accessible. Furthermore, they can be quantified and treated very much as any traditional operant in terms of reinforcement, extinction, and so forth. Mahoney and Mahoney (1976) have directed attention to the critical role that cognitions and private monologues may play in the maintenance and control of obesity. The first step in applying cognitive strategies to weight control is to help patients discover their most common negative monologues, or self-statements, and to estimate their frequency. Then, in the manner described by Beck (1976) and by Meichenbaum (1977), patients are taught arguments against these monologues. Since negative monologues tend to be ster-

eotyped and limited in number, it is usually not difficult to construct arguments against them. The patient is then helped to learn—and overlearn—these more appropriate self-statements so that they can use them almost automatically in response to the negative statements. Training in this kind of arguing with oneself seems to produce benefits in terms of improved morale, as has been shown quite convincingly in the case of depression, and probably also in more effective weight-reducing behaviors. Simply repeating the counterarguments over a period of time may help, even if the person does not completely believe them at the onset.

In their description of ''cleaning up the cognitive ecology,'' the Mahoneys (1976) described five kinds of negative self-statements. Examples from my own experience, together with the counterarguments, are:

Weight loss: ''It's taking so long to lose weight.'' A counterargument is, ''But I am losing it. And this time I'm going to learn how to keep it off.''

Ability to lose weight: ''I've never done it before. Why should I succeed this time?'' A counterargument is, ''There always has to be a first time. And this time I've got a good new program going for me.''

Goals: ''I've got to stop snacking!'' A counterargument is, ''That is an unrealistic goal. Just keep on trying to cut down the number of snacks.''

Food thoughts: ''I keep finding myself thinking how good chocolate tastes.'' A useful response is, ''Stop that! It's just frustrating you. Think of lying on the beach in the sun'' (or whatever activity the patient finds particularly enjoyable).

Excuses: ''Everyone in my family has a weight problem. It's in my genes.'' A counterargument is, ''That just makes it harder, not impossible. If I stick with this program I will succeed.''

Historical Perspective on Behavioral Weight Control

The history of behavioral control of obesity began in 1962, with a long theoretical paper by Ferster, Nurnberger, and Levitt. Although their therapeutic results were never published and are said to have been modest (Stunkard, 1975), this paper has informed and inspired a generation of workers in the field. As the first detailed operant analysis of a health-related behavior, it served as an important counterweight to the largely classical-conditioning character of behavior therapy that then dominated the field as a result of the achievements of systematic desensitization.

It was five years before the theory proposed by Ferster *et al.* (1962) was put into practice. But when it was applied, by Stuart in 1967, the results were so striking as to initiate a widespread interest in the behavioral control of obesity and a virtual explosion of research on the topic. The reason for the remarkable impact of this report is not hard to find: it described an effective treatment.

It has been, in the past, fairly easy to assess the effectiveness of any outpatient treatment for obesity because the results of traditional treatments have been so uniformly poor and the treatments so obviously ineffective. Only 25% of persons entering conventional outpatient treatment for obesity lose more than 9.1 kg, and only 5% lose more than 18.2 kg (Stunkard & McLaren-Hume, 1959).

Against this background, the report on "Behavioral Control of Overeating" (Stuart, 1967) stands out, for it describes the best results obtained to that time in the outpatient treatment of obesity and constitutes a landmark in our understanding of this disorder. Even the absence of a control group does not vitiate the significance of its findings. Figures 1 and 2 show that the 8 patients who remained in treatment out of an original 10 lost large amounts of weight: 3 lost more than 18.2 kg and 6 more than 13.6 kg.

Harris

Soon after Stuart's landmark program, the first controlled-outcome study of the behavior modification of obesity reported an average weight loss of 4.8 kg among moderately overweight women university students (Harris, 1969). The subjects in a no-treatment control group gained 1.6 kg, a significant difference ($p < .01$).

A no-treatment control group, such as that used by Harris, was acceptable in behavioral research in 1969. Yet it has serious disadvan-

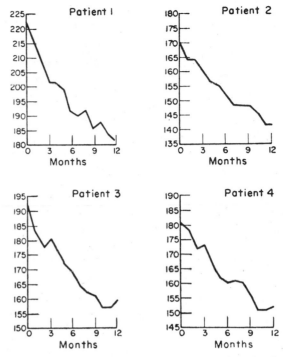

Figure 1. Weight profiles of four women undergoing behavior therapy for obesity. (From "Behavioral Control of Overeating" by R. B. Stuart, *Behaviour Research and Therapy*, 1967, *5*, 357–365, Fig. 1. Copyright 1967, Pergamon Press, Ltd. Reprinted by permission.)

tages, for refusing treatment to someone who has come seeking it is far from a neutral event. The resultant disappointment could well produce weight gains that would make the treatment condition appear to be more effective than it actually was. The problem calls for the use of a placebo control group to match the attention and interest received by the patients in the active treatment program. An ambitious study by Wollersheim (1970) provided precisely such controls and opened up new vistas in behavioral research.

Wollersheim

Wollersheim's factorial design contained four experimental conditions: behavioral treatment, "nonspecific therapy" based on traditional psychiatric methods, "social pressure" modeled on lay weight-control programs, and finally a no-treatment control group. Four therapists each treated one group of five patients in each of the three treatment

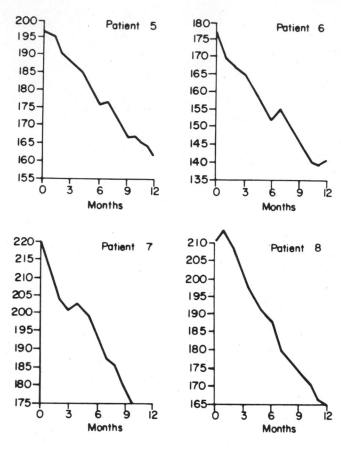

Figure 2. Weight profiles of four women undergoing behavior therapy for obesity. (From "Behavioral Control of Overeating" by R. B. Stuart, *Behaviour Research and Therapy*, 1967, 5, 357–365, Fig. 2. Copyright 1967 Pergamon Press, Ltd. Reprinted by permission.)

conditions for 10 sessions over a three-month period. Figure 3 shows that at the end of treatment, and at eight-week follow-up, the subjects in the behavioral ("focal") treatment condition had lost more weight than those in the no-treatment condition. In addition, they had lost significantly more weight than those in the two placebo control conditions, who had themselves lost significantly more weight than those in the no-treatment condition. The behavioral treatment clearly contributed something to the outcome over and above the usual effects of psychotherapy.

This contribution seemed to have resulted from the specific effects of the behavioral intervention, for not only did this condition produce greater weight loss, but it also produced major changes in self-reports of eating behaviors. Statistically significant differences between the "focal" therapy and the other three conditions were found in four of the six factors

assessed by the questionnaire: "emotional and uncontrolled eating," "eating in isolation," "eating as a reward," and "between-meal eating." Whatever caused the weight loss in the two placebo control conditions apparently did it without affecting these behaviors. The "focal" therapy apparently produced weight loss by means of its proposed rationale.

Wollersheim's study deserves careful attention because of the critical place it occupies in the history of behavioral weight control. For better or for worse, it has become a kind of prototype of research in this area. Its positive features are worthy of reemphasis (i.e., the introduction of nontrivial control groups, of multiple therapists, of large treatment populations [90 subjects], and of the assessment of the relationship between reports of behavior and weight loss). But the limitations of the study are also worth emphasis, for one of the striking facts of research in this field is that in the 12 years since the publication of Wollersheim's report, these limitations continue to afflict most of the research in this field. These limitations are:

1. The subjects of Wollersheim's study were mildly overweight college women. Most subsequent studies have been confined to the same type of population. Studies of clinically obese persons have been few and far between.
2. The treatment lasted no more than eight weeks. Again, such short treatment in a pioneering study is understandable. It is less understandable that 12 years later the average duration of a large series of studies of behavioral treatment of obesity was 10½ weeks.
3. The treatment was carried out by graduate students with little clinical experience. The use of clinically inexperienced therapists has been the usual practice in the studies of the past 12 years.
4. Weight losses in the behavioral condition (4.5 kg), although statistically significantly greater than those in the placebo

conditions, were modest and disappointing from the perspective of clinical utility. Such weight losses have been the rule in the 12 years since Wollersheim's paper.
5. Follow-up was confined to eight weeks. Only recently have longer follow-up studies been reported.

With the decline in the epidemic of snake phobias that swept American campuses during the 1960s, departments of psychology began a search for another condition that might lend itself as well to research on behavioral therapy. With recognition of the remarkable reliability, validity, and economy of weight change in pounds as a dependent variable, this search came to an end. The past 12 years have seen an unprecedented upsurge of research on obesity by behavior therapists. This research has consisted to a remarkable degree of studies very similar to that of Wollersheim. We will return to the implications of this development when we consider the current status of the behavioral control of obesity. In the meantime, we will consider a study that shows that it is possible to carry out meaningful studies

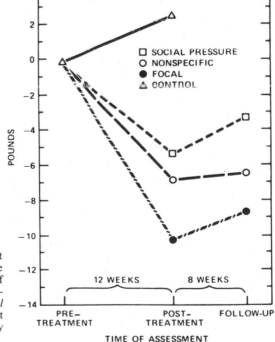

Figure 3. Mean weight loss of the focal (behavioral) treatment group, the two alternative treatment control groups, and the no-treatment control group. (From "The Effectiveness of Group Therapy Based upon Learning Principles in the Treatment of Overweight Women" by J. F. Wollersheim, *Journal of Abnormal Psychology*, 1970, *76*, 462–474, Fig. 2. Copyright 1970 by the American Psychological Association. Reprinted by permission.)

of clinically obese persons. This study was undertaken, in part, to approach a problem uncovered by Wollersheim's report: the problem of experimenter bias.

Penick *et al.*

Wollersheim's placebo treatments controlled for the patient's expectations of treatment. They could not, however, control for the therapist's. And therapist bias is not a trivial matter: a large measure of therapeutic effectiveness is that conveyed by the therapist's expectations. The development of the methodology of the double-blind experiment in psychopharmacology has shown how powerful this influence can be when dealing with drugs. It is surely more powerful in the more emotional case of the behavioral therapies. It is unlikely that research on behavior therapy will soon attain the economy and the elegance of the double-blind methodology of psychopharmacology. The control of bias will require methods tailored to the special needs and opportunities of behavioral research. Such methods were explored by Penick, Filion, Fox, and Stunkard (1971) in one of the few behavioral studies of clinically obese (78% overweight) persons.

The essence of Penick's study was to give up at the outset the notion that therapists could be unbiased in the use of the therapies that they favored—and disfavored. Instead, the therapists were selected on the basis of their commitment either to behavioral or to traditional treatment. Then, the outcome was biased against the behavioral approach by selecting therapists of vastly differing experience for the two conditions. For the behavioral treatment, the therapists were beginners; for the traditional treatment, they were experts. Penick, an internist experienced in the treatment of obesity, used all traditional treatment methods: diet, medication, nutritional education, exhortation, and his own highly developed personal skills. The behavioral treatment was administered by a psychologist with no previous clinical experience. Each treatment team began with the conviction that its method was superior and sought to prove it.

Two cohorts were treated in each condition during weekly group meetings of two hours for a period of three months. The weight losses for each subject are plotted in Figures 4 and 5, and they show that the subjects treated with behavior modification lost more weight than those treated by the full armamentarium of traditional therapy. In each cohort, the median

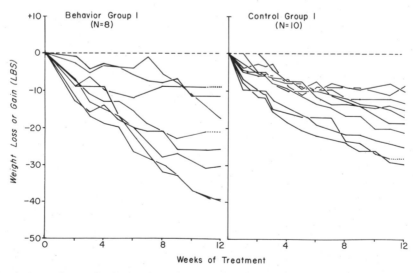

Figure 4. Weight changes of severely obese persons in two cohorts. Dotted lines represent interpolated data based on weights obtained during follow-up. (From "Behavior Modification in the Treatment of Obesity" by S. B. Penick *et al., Psychosomatic Medicine*, 1971, *33*, 49–55, Fig. 1. Copyright 1971 psychosomatic Medicine. Reprinted by permission.)

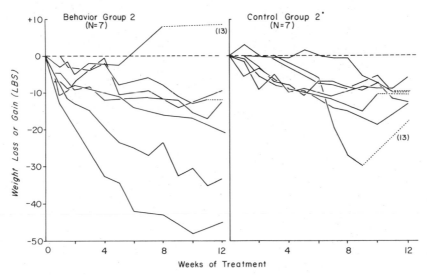

Figure 5. Second cohort of the study described in Figure 4. (From "Behavior Modification in the Treatment of Obesity" by S. B. Penick *et al.*, *Psychosomatic Medicine*, 1971, *33*, 49–55, Fig. 2. Copyright 1971 Psychosomatic Medicine. Reprinted by permission.)

weight loss for the behavior modification group was greater than that of the control group: 10.9 kg versus 8.2 kg for the first cohort; 5.9 kg versus 5.0 kg for the second.

The weight losses of the control group are comparable to those found in the medical literature: none lost 18.2 kg, and only 24% lost more than 9.1 kg. By contrast, 13% of the behavior modification group lost more than 18.2 kg, and 53% lost more than 9.1 kg. Although the differences between the experimental and the control groups for these weight losses did not reach statistical significance, that for weight losses of over 13.6 kg did ($p = .015$, by the Fisher exact probability test).

One further point should be noted. The variability in the weight losses of the behavior modification subjects was considerably greater than that of the patients treated by traditional methods ($F = 4.38$, $p < .005$). The five best performers were patients in the behavior modification condition as was the single least effective patient, the only patient who actually gained weight during the treatment. Greater variability in weight loss by behavioral patients has since been confirmed. Such greater variability has in other circumstances been associated with greater specificity of the treatment, and this explanation of the findings

seems reasonable. It would appear that for half of the patients, behavior modification seemed to offer something specific that resulted in greater weight loss than usual. For about another half, it seemed of considerably less value. By contrast, the results of traditional treatment seemed much more homogeneous, reflecting, perhaps, such nonspecific effects of therapy as attention, support, and encouragement.

Craighead *et al.*

A serious criticism that has been leveled against studies of behavior therapy is that the control treatments against which it has been compared have often not been credible. As a result, their often-demonstrated superiority to alternative treatments may not be as meaningful as it might be. The study by Penick *et al.* (1971) is one of the few to escape such criticism. Another is the study by Craighead, Stunkard, and O'Brien (1981), which has provided what is probably the strongest evidence for the efficacy of the behavior therapy of obesity that has yet been obtained.

Two major developments in the treatment of behavioral disorders of the last decade have been behavior therapy and pharmacotherapy.

Each has demonstrated its efficacy in the treatment of conditions as diverse as depression, phobias, anorexia nervosa, and obesity. Yet it is a paradox that behavior therapy and pharmacotherapy have developed in almost complete isolation from each other.

Nowhere has this isolation been more pronounced than in the field of obesity. In the 15 years since its introduction into the treatment of obesity, behavior therapy has been employed in more than 50 controlled clinical trials. The number of controlled clinical trials of medication for the treatment of obesity runs into several hundred. Yet, until recently, little was known about their relative merits.

The first three studies of behavioral and pharmacological treatments for obesity provided some preliminary information on this topic. Öst and Götestam (1976) reported that patients who received 16 weeks of behavior therapy lost more weight (9.4 kg) than did those who received 16 weeks of the appetite suppressant fenfluramine (5.8 kg). Two other studies compared, instead, behavioral treatments with and without medication and reported that adding medication increased the rate of weight loss. In the study by Brightwell and Naylor (1979), this increase was statistically significant; in that by Walker, Ballard and Gold (1977), it was not. Methodological problems left unanswered questions about all three studies.

Many of these questions were answered by an ambitious study of the relative merits of behavior therapy, pharmacological therapy, and their combination (Craighead et al., 1981). This study showed, for example, that medication produces greater weight losses than does behavior therapy, but that the latter treatment leads to far better maintenance of weight loss.

The study enrolled 145 persons with clinical obesity (60% overweight), who were treated for six months. Follow-up information was obtained one year after the end of the treatment on 98% of those who completed it. The three major treatments were (1) *behavior modification* in groups that used Ferguson's "Learning to Eat" manual (1975); (2) *medication* (fenfluramine) administered to patients who also met in groups to control for the effects of group contact in the behavior modification condition; and (3) a *combined treat-*

ment of behavior modification and medication, as administered in the previous two conditions. In addition, there was a doctor's-office medication condition and a no-treatment control condition. The doctor's-office medication condition was an effort to approximate the standard medical-office treatment of obesity, utilizing primarily medication and diet. Since several patients refused assignment to this condition, it was treated as a quasi control.

Figure 6 shows the results of this treatment and of the follow-up. The patients in the behavior modification condition lost 11.4 kg, perhaps the largest weight losses yet reported in a controlled clinical trial of this modality. The patients in the medication condition lost 14.5 kg. Adding the two treatments had no effect on weight loss: patients in the combined treatment condition lost 15.0 kg.

The results one year after the end of the treatment throw a completely different light on this picture. The patients in the behavior modification condition maintained their weight losses surprisingly well, regaining only 1.8 kg during the course of the year. Those in the group medication condition, not unexpectedly, regained 8.6 kg. The combined treatment group showed the most surprising, and disappointing, results. They regained no less than 9.5 kg during the course of the year, ending it at only 4.5 kg less than the weight at which they had started treatment!

The addition of medication can increase the rate of weight loss of persons receiving behavioral treatment for obesity. This benefit, however, is more than outweighed by what appears to be a deleterious effect of medication on the maintenance of weight loss. Over the long run behavior therapy clearly outperformed the most potent alternative treatment with which it has yet been compared. This most recent study provides grounds for optimism as to the future of behavioral treatment of obesity.

Current Empirical Status: What Behavior Therapy Can Do

The 15 years since the publication of Stuart's landmark study have been characterized by a vast amount of work on the behavioral treatment of obesity. It is now possible to look back

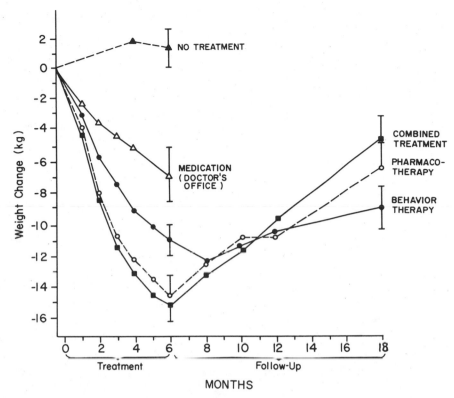

Figure 6. Weight losses among obese women in four treatment conditions and weight gain in a no-treatment control group. The patients in the doctor's-office treatment condition lost 6.8 kg. The three group treatments produced weight losses of 11.4 kg by behavior modification, 14.5 kg by medication, and 15.0 kg by combined treatment. At the one-year follow-up, the patients in the behavior modification condition had maintained weight loss, while those in the two medication conditions had regained much of the weight that they had lost. (From "Behavior Therapy and Pharmacotherapy of Obesity" by L. Craighead *et al.*, *Archives of General Psychiatry*, 1981, *38*, 763–768, Fig. 1. Copyright 1981 by the American Medical Association. Reprinted by permission.)

on these 15 years of activity and to sort out what has, and what has not, been accomplished, for the demonstration that behavior therapy is more effective than traditional therapy, although well established, tells us little about its effectiveness as a practical measure for the control of obesity. How effective is it?

Several factors make it difficult to get a clear picture of the clinical impact of behavioral treatments on obesity. As we noted in describing Wollersheim's prototypical study, treatment has been carried out largely by inexperienced therapists and has been restricted to short periods of time. Most of the subjects of the studies have been mildly overweight college women and far too many of the studies have been content with ascertaining the relative effectiveness of small differences in techniques. Changes of no more than marginal sta-

tistical significance have been accepted, without replication, as established findings. Until recently, only short term follow up data have been available. But some definitive findings have emerged from these efforts. A review of 21 of the better reports and of the results of the more-or-less routine clinical treatment of the first 125 patients on a well-established clinical service gives a basis for ascertaining the overall efficacy of behavioral treatments for obesity (Jeffery, Wing, & Stunkard, 1978).

1. The first important finding is that great progress has been made in decreasing the number of drop-outs from treatment. Whereas dropouts from traditional outpatient treatment have been as high as 25%–75% (Stunkard & McLaren-Hume, 1959), most behavioral programs report rates of 15% or less. A well-controlled clinical trial (Hagen, Foreyt, & Dur-

ham, 1976) has confirmed the widespread clinical impression that contingency contracting, or the earning back of deposits made by the patients at the beginning of treatment, is very effective in decreasing the number of dropouts. Other aspects of behavioral programs probably also play a part in this salutary development.

2. The second major advance has been in reducing the untoward side effects of weight reduction regimens, a problem that has plagued the routine medical-office treatment of obesity. As many as half of all obese patients undergoing this kind of treatment may suffer from such symptoms as anxiety, irritability, and depression (Stunkard & Rush, 1974). By contrast, untoward reactions to behavioral programs are uncommon, and half the patients feel better.

3. The most important measure of treatment efficacy is weight loss. Wing and Jeffery's (1979) review of the literature on the treatment of obesity during the decade preceding their article reveals that weight losses produced by behavior therapy do not differ greatly from those produced by other forms of treatment, and that none is particularly effective. Figure 7 shows that behavior therapy and pharmacotherapy contributed the largest number of studies. In each, the average weight loss was no more than 11.2 lb.

A more detailed analysis of behavioral programs was presented by Jeffery *et al.* (1978), who confined their review to 21 reports that met the basic criteria of adequacy for a research design. These criteria include basing the results on all the patients who started the treatment, excluding dropouts, and reporting weight losses in pounds rather than simply in percentages of excess weight. Table 1 shows that the weight losses in no more than half the programs exceeded 4.5 kg and that the weight losses in only 20% exceeded 6.8 kg. There are many reasons for these limitations: most of the programs were short-term, many involved patients who were only mildly overweight, and a large number were carried out by inexperienced therapists. But the fact remains: the results are modest and, from the perspective of clinical utility, disappointing. Furthermore, progress is hard to see; no report has even equaled the results of Stuart's original 1967 report.

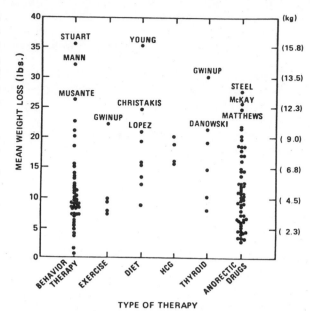

Figure 7. Distribution of weight losses for studies of outpatient therapy for obesity. (From "Outpatient Treatments of Obesity: A Comparison of Methodology and Clinical Results" by R. R. Wing and R. W. Jeffery, *International Journal of Obesity,* 1979, *3,* 261–279, Fig. 1. Copyright 1979 by International Journal of Obesity. Reprinted by permission.)

These results from the research literature are not dissimilar to those from a program with a primarily clinical focus. Jeffery *et al.* (1978) found a weight loss of no more than 5.0 kg among the first 125 patients in a behaviorally oriented obesity-treatment program.

4. There is great variability in weight changes during treatment, as first noted by Penick *et al.* (1971), and even greater variability following treatment. Wilson (1980) noted that such variability suggests either that the critical variables governing weight loss have not been identified or that current behavioral methods are appropriate only for persons with some still-undetermined characteristics.

5. Prediction of the outcome of behavioral treatments for obesity has not been very successful, and only a few relatively weak predictors have been discovered. This failing is particularly troubling in view of the marked variability in the outcome of treatment, for if we could predict outcome more accurately, we could make more effective use of scarce treatment resources and would spare many patients the time, effort, and discouragement

of still another experience of failure. Demographic and personality variables have been notably unsuccessful in predicting outcome in numerous published studies (Balch & Ross, 1975; Bellack, 1977; Jeffrey *et al.*, 1978; Stunkard & Mahoney, 1976) and in a far larger number of unpublished studies.

Reports from two behavioral programs described weak predictors. Bellack has noted that a pretreatment assessment of patients' performance on tasks related to the treatment program predicted weight loss during treatment (1977). Consistent with this finding, Jeffery *et al.* (1978) found that the extent of weight loss early in treatment presaged total weight loss. Weight loss during the first week correlated .4 with that during the next 20 weeks. This finding is particularly instructive since the patients' only assignment during the first week had been to monitor their eating behavior. Also, they had been explicitly asked not to make any changes in their eating habits until their usual patterns had been assessed.

Two biological variables have been found to predict weight loss. Percentage overweight consistently predicts outcome with a low level of statistical significance, heavier persons losing more weight than lighter ones. This finding is a very general one, applying not only to behavioral treatments (Murray, 1975) but also to nonbehavioral treatments such as patient self-help groups (Garb & Stunkard, 1974), intestinal bypass surgery (Mills & Stunkard, 1976), and diet (Genuth, Vertes, & Hazleton, 1978). Percentage overweight is closely related to another predictor reported by Krotkiewski, Garellick, Sjöström, Persson, Bjurö, & Sullivan (1980). An equation incorporating fat cell number, basal metabolic rate, and cephalic insulin secretion predicted 80% of the variance in weight loss in the obesity clinic at the University of Göteborg in Sweden.

6. Patients with onset of obesity early in life lose as much weight as those with onset in adult life (Jeffery *et al.*, 1978). This finding appears to be somewhat at variance with pre-

Table 1. Results of Behavioral Treatments for Obesity

Study	Number of patients	Initial weight (kg)	Mean weight loss (kg)[a]	Treatment length (weeks)
Abrahms & Allen (1974)	23	83.0	5.4	9
Hagen (1974)	18	69.5	6.8	10
Hall (1972)	10	78.6	1.5	4
Hall *et al.* (1974)	40	—	5.0	10
Hall *et al.* (1975)	25	89.8	6.8[b]	12
Hanson *et al.* (1976)	32	96.4	5.9[b]	10
Harris (1969)	7	77.8	3.1	10
Harris & Bruner (1971)	11	74.9	3.4	12
Harris & Bruner (1971)	6	65.3	.8	16
Harris & Hallbauer (1973)	27	75.2	3.6	12
Jeffrey (1974)	34	83.5	2.7	7
Levitz & Stunkard (1974)	73	82.2	1.9	12
Mahoney (1974)	9	—	3.4	8
McReynolds *et al.* (1976)	41	81.1	7.4	15
Penick *et al.* (1971)	15	114.1	10.1	12
Romanczyk (1974)	17	79.9	4.8	6
Romanczyk *et al.* (1973)	18	81.3	3.2	4
Romanczyk *et al.* (1973)	18	78.6	3.6	4
Stuart (1967)	8	83.4	17.2	52
Stuart (1971)	6	—	6.4	15
Wollersheim (1970)	18	70.0	4.7	12

[a] Amounts of mean weight loss are given for the most effective treatment combination only. The results from control groups and partial treatments are not included.
[b] Extrapolated from weight reduction indexes.

dictions based on expected fat cell size and number. There is no information on possible differences in the ability to *maintain* weight loss by juvenile-onset and by adult-onset obese persons.

7. Although behavioral techniques can be adapted for use by less skilled therapists, the skill of the therapist appears to have a modified effect on the outcome of therapy. Two studies have shown that the therapist's experience was positively related to weight loss (Levitz & Stunkard, 1974; Jeffery *et al.*, 1978).

8. Clinically significant weight losses achieved by behavioral treatment are not well maintained. A recent review by Stunkard and Penick (1979) permits a thorough assessment of the data from which this conclusion has been drawn. This review contains the first five-year follow-up of behavioral treatment for obesity, plus an analysis of nine other follow-up studies of at least one year in duration, essentially all of such studies yet conducted. The five-year follow-up was carried out on 28 of the 29 survivors of the study by Penick *et al.* (1971), described above. A new method of displaying and analyzing data was developed to prevent the misleading inferences that have at times been drawn from the use of grouped data. This method involved plotting weight loss at the end of treatment on the horizontal axis and plotting weight loss (from the beginning of treatment) to the end of follow-up on the vertical axis. The data points of patients who simply maintained the weight they lost during treatment thus fall along the main diagonal. Continuing weight loss is represented by data points above the main diagonal, weight gain by points below it. Changes in weight from the end of treatment to the the one- and five-year follow-ups are plotted in Figures 8 and 9, respectively.

For one year following treatment, most patients apparently continued to lose weight; during the next four years, they began to regain it. Figure 8 shows that one year after treatment, the majority of patients (17 of 28) in both the behavioral and the traditional treatment conditions weighed less than they had at the end of treatment. Five years after treatment, only a minority (7 of 26) weighed less.

The continuing weight loss at one year applied equally to the behavioral (8 of 13) and

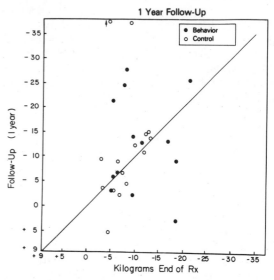

Figure 8. Weight changes from end of treatment to one-year follow-up. (From "Behavior Modification in the Treatment of Obesity: The Problem of Maintaining Weight Loss" by A. J. Stunkard and S. B. Penick, *Archives of General Psychiatry*, 1979, *36*, 801–806, Fig. 1. Copyright 1979 by the American Medical Association. Reprinted by permission.)

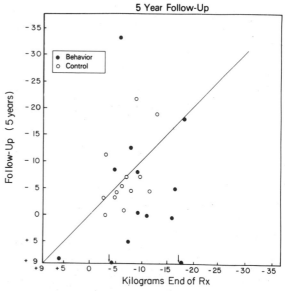

Figure 9. Weight changes from end of treatment to five-year follow-up. (From "Behavior Modification in the Treatment of Obesity: The Problem of Maintaining Weight Loss" by A. J. Stunkard and S. B. Penick, *Archives of General Psychiatry*, 1979, *36*, 801–806, Fig. 2. Copyright 1979 by the American Medical Association. Reprinted by permission.)

traditional (9 of 15) treatment groups. Similarly, the weight gain four years later was also characteristic of both groups. Only 3 of 12 behavioral and 4 of 13 traditional treatment patients weighed less than they had at the end of treatment. (One traditional-treatment patient was precisely at posttreatment weight: 7.3 kg below pretreatment weight.)

Figure 8 shows that even this summary is misleading, in that it overestimates the weight loss by behavior therapy patients at one year. Paradoxically, those who lost weight during treatment tended to regain it during follow-up, while those who failed to lose weight during treatment tended to lose during follow-up. The correlation coefficient (r) between weight change during treatment and during follow-up was $-.499$ ($p < .1$). Thus, of the seven patients who had lost more than 9.1 kg during treatment, four gained weight during the first year after treatment; the other three did no better than maintain their weight. By contrast, five of the six who lost less than 9.1 kg during treatment continued to lose afterward.

The results of this follow-up study were paralleled by those of nine other follow-up studies of patients who had lost smaller amounts of weight. An assessment of these nine studies includes a reanalysis of previously unpublished data from five studies: by Mahoney (1974), Ferstl, Jokusch, and Brengelmann (1975), Ashby and Wilson (1977), Kingsley and Wilson (1977), and Beneke, Paulsen, McReynolds, Lutz, and Kohrs (1978). The results of this assessment are summarized in Table 2.

Table 2 shows that clinically important weight losses, even those no greater than 6.4 kg, were not well maintained. The problem is accentuated by the rarity of such weight losses. Table 2 shows that only four of these studies reported median weight losses of more than 6.4 kg.

The major conclusion to be drawn from these results is that clinically important weight losses achieved by behavioral treatments are not well maintained. The study by Craighead et al. (1981) shows that such weight losses are better maintained than those achieved by pharmacotherapy. But the early hope that behavioral treatments might produce enduring changes in weight-related behaviors—and, as a consequence, long-term weight loss—has

not been fully realized. How are we to understand this failing?

Bandura (1978) has suggested that behavior change can be subdivided into three subprocesses of change: the induction of the new behavior, its generalization, and its maintenance. There is no reason to believe that the processes that induce a change in behavior are the same as those that generalize it, or that these processes necessarily bear any relationship to the maintenance of this behavioral change. Behavioral approaches to obesity have until now been devoted almost exclusively to the first two subprocesses: induction and generalization. The time is ripe for attention to the third: maintenance.

The maintenance of change has been a neglected area in the behavioral literature in general and has been almost ignored in the behavioral literature on obesity. Yet, the very nature of eating behavior makes it clear that the maintenance of changes in it presents unique and unusually difficult problems. The relief of phobias and obsessions restores people's freedom and enables them to participate in new and rewarding activities. Their new behavior is readily maintained by these rewards. In addictions, such as smoking and drinking, behavioral treatment not only helps patients to eliminate the rewarding substances from their lives but also helps them to enjoy the rewards of a drug-free existence.

But no one can avoid eating. In fact, in our society, three times each day, preceded by a bombardment of inducements to eat high-calorie foods and followed by the powerful biological reward of satiety, obese people are supposed to eat in moderation. The implication of this situation may be appreciated by considering the problem of an alcoholic asked to drink in moderation three times a day. Basic considerations of behavior modification would predict that changes in eating behavior produced by the contingencies of therapy would not survive their absence in the face of the presence of these powerful antagonistic contingencies. The institution of once-weekly meetings for three months is a pathetically small effort to pit against the powerful influence of a society that always, and a biology that often, continues to foster obesity.

When we turn to the few maintenance stra-

Table 2. Follow-Up Studies on Weight Loss

		Treatment			Follow-up			5-year	
		Mean % overweight	Duration week	Weight loss (kg) Mean	Duration (months)	Weight loss (kg) Mean		Duration (months)	Weight loss (kg) Mean
Stunkard & Penick (1979)	Behavioral	78	12	10.1	12	12.6		60	5.3
	Traditional	78	12	7.5	12	12.1		60	5.5
Öst & Göttestam (1976)	Behavioral	36	16	9.4	12	4.6			
	Medication	41	16	5.7	12	0.8			
	No-treatment	29	16	3.5	12	2.4			
McReynolds et al. (1976)	Stimulus control only	39	15	8.4	12	6.5			
	Behavioral	39	15	7.4	12	5.8			
Ferstl et al. (1975)	Behavioral	29	12	7.5	24	4.2			
Foreyt & Kennedy (1971)	Experimental	10	9	6.0	12	4.2			

Study	Condition					
Kingsley & Wilson (1977)	No booster, individual behavioral	49	8	5.6	12	0.0
	Group behavioral	39	8	4.9	12	6.6
	Social pressure	39	8	3.0	12	3.0
	Booster, individual behavioral	35	8	3.4	12	4.6
	Group behavioral	52	8	5.3	12	5.4
	Social pressure	48	8	3.4	12	4.6
Ashby & Wilson (1977)	First replication					
	Behavioral, booster	49	8	4.3	12	2.7
	Nonspecific, booster	64	8	4.6	12	3.4
	Control, no booster	56	8	5.4	12	2.5
	Second replication					
	Behavioral, booster	54	8	3.8	12	4.4
	Nonspecific, booster	53	8	3.4	12	4.7
	Control, no booster	64	8	3.6	12	5.5
Hall (1973)	Behavioral	24	10	3.8	24	4.7
Mahoney (1974)	Self-reward, habit	20	8	3.4	12	3.7
	Self-reward, weight	20	8	3.0	12	6.5
	Self-monitoring	20	8	3.7	12	2.8
	Control	20	8	4.1	12	3.5
Harris & Bruner (1971)	Behavioral	—	12	3.4	10	1.6

tegies that have proved effective in behavior therapy, we find that the unique characteristics of eating behavior present serious problems. For example, fading reinforcement contingencies is useful in the development of social and cognitive skills because other sources of reward—the natural benefits of the skills—take over the reinforcing functions. One might predict that such measures would be less effective in coping with the special problem of weight control. This is, in fact, the case. The ambitious assessment of "booster" sessions conducted in the study by Craighead *et al.* (1981) confirmed the ineffectiveness previously found by Kingsley and Wilson (1977) and Ashby and Wilson (1977).

The Special Case of Childhood Obesity

The treatment of obesity in children is important for two reasons: (1) obese children suffer from a number of physical and psychological problems: and (2) their obesity tends to persist into adult life (Brownell & Stunkard, 1980). The physical burdens imposed on children by their obesity are imperfectly documented, but they may be severe, and their severity increases with the magnitude of the obesity. These burdens are much the same as those of obese adults: carbohydrate intolerance, hyperinsulinism, hyperlipidemia, and hypertension. A larger percentage of obese children than of obese adults are afflicted with psychological problems arising from their obesity. These problems, as the obesity itself, tend to persist into adult life. Obese children are more prone to experiencing disturbed family interactions, the disapproval of their peers, academic discrimination, and an impaired self-image.

Obesity in young children is far less common than is obesity among adults. About 10% of young children are obese. The prevalence of obesity rises throughout adolescence and, in fact, well into middle age. Such rising prevalence is a result of continuing recruitment of persons into the obese population and no losses from it; few obese children or adolescents become lean adults. In fact, Stunkard

and Burt (1967) have calculated the odds against an obese child's becoming a thin adult as 4 to 1 before adolescence and as 28 to 1 if weight reduction has not occurred by the end of adolescence. Psychological problems similarly persist. Body-image disparagement occurs almost exclusively among persons who have been obese since childhood, as do the twin problems of bulimia and night eating (Grinker, Hirsch, & Levin, 1973; Stunkard & Mahoney, 1976). The successful treatment of obesity in childhood could yield great benefits, both physical and psychological. But success has eluded the treatment of obesity in children to as great an extent as it has eluded the treatment of obesity in adults. The discouraging results of traditional treatment approaches has provided a favorable climate for the introduction of new methods. Foremost among these methods has been behavior modification.

Most of the behavioral programs for children have concentrated on reducing food intake; increasing physical activity has played little or no part. Although this concentration on food intake rather than on exercise appears not to have been the result of deliberate choice, it was probably a wise one. At least four studies that used objective measures of physical activity failed to reveal significant differences between obese and nonobese children, and only one reported that obese children were less active (Brownell & Stunkard, 1980). Furthermore, a recent intensive study of energy intake and expenditure suggests that excessive food intake maintains childhood obesity. Waxman and Stunkard (1980) directly measured food intake and energy expenditure in four families during meals and at play in three different settings. The subjects were four obese boys and the controls were their nonobese brothers, who were less than two years younger or older. The oxygen consumption of the subjects at four levels of activity was measured in the laboratory to permit a calculation of energy expenditure from time-sampled measures of observed activity. The obese boys consumed far more calories than did their nonobese brothers and also *expended* somewhat more calories. These findings need to be confirmed with larger samples and with studies of girls, but the evidence of overeating by these obese boys is so striking that it justifies directing treatment at this problem.

Eight studies of the behavioral treatment of childhood obesity have been reported. The results warrant a cautious optimism; behavior therapy may well prove as effective in the treatment of obese children as it has been in the treatment of obese adults. Table 3 summarizes these results.

Two uncontrolled pilot studies had similar results. Rivinus, Drummond, and Combrinck-Graham (1976) and Gross, Wheeler, and Hess (1976) reported weight losses of 2.7 and 3.2 kg, respectively, during treatment programs of 10 weeks duration. Somewhat surprisingly, persisting effects were observed in both studies, two years after treatment in the study by Rivinus *et al.* and 12 weeks after treatment in that by Gross *et al.* Efforts to advance the understanding of behavioral treatments by the introduction of control groups were made by Wheeler and Hess (1976) and by Weiss (1977). As is the case with so many other behavioral studies, methodological refinement was probably premature in the face of essentially trivial weight losses. These weight losses were said to have been significantly greater in the behavioral condition.

Two studies have explored the effects of including parents in the treatment process. Kingsley and Shapiro (1977) found a trend in the predicted direction, although it did not reach statistical significance, perhaps because the sample size was small and the weight losses were small and variable. Brownell, Kelman, and Stunkard (submitted for publication, 1982), on the other hand, found that treating children and their mothers was significantly more effective than treating them alone. They further found that the method by which the mothers and children were involved in treatment affected outcome. The most effective combination was treating mothers and children in separate groups, which produced a weight loss of 8.4 kg, compared with a loss of 5.3 kg for mothers and children treated in the same groups and 3.3 kg for children treated alone. At one year follow-up the children in the mother-and-child-separately condition had maintained their weight loss, while children in the other two conditions had gained some weight.

One study has directed its primary attention to contingency contracting, a modality that has shown considerable promise in the treatment of behavior disorders in children. Children and their parents contract to receive rewards such as praise, privileges, and prizes or the return of deposits of toys and money in return for changes in behavior. Aragona, Cassady, and Drabman (1975) showed that the method was feasible, and that significant weight losses could be produced.

A study important for its theoretical as well as its practical results was carried out by Coates (1977) with two obese adolescent girls. The unique aspect of this study was the careful behavioral assessment conducted by nonparticipant observation in the subjects' homes before and during the treatment. This assessment revealed that one subject ate rapidly but was not exposed to high-calorie foods in her home environment; the second subject showed the opposite pattern. The emphasis of the treatment of the first subject was, accordingly, on eating behavior, of the second subject on stimulus control. This treatment resulted in weight losses of 9.5 and of 5.5 kg in 10 weeks. Furthermore, behavioral changes occurred only in the problem areas. This kind of intensive single-case study is much needed to further our understanding of the behavioral treatment of obesity and it has been all too rare.

The Problem of Faulty Assumptions

Behavioral therapy has not fully realized the bright hopes that were held out for it in the early days. A common response to such disappointment is to return to the basics and to review the assumptions on which the treatment was based. Precisely this course has been taken by two leading theorists in recent reviews of the status of the behavioral treatment of obesity (Mahoney, 1978; Wilson, 1980). Each found that many, if not most, of the assumptions (both explicit and implicit) on which the behavioral treatment of obesity was based were invalid. Mahoney has summarized six such assumptions (1978):

1. Obesity is a learning disorder, created by and amenable to principles of conditioning.

Table 3. Findings from Studies on Behavior Therapy for Obese Children and Adolescents

Study	Subjects	Experimental conditions	No. of subjects	Weight loss (kg) Initial weight	Weight loss (kg) End of treatment	Weight loss (kg) Follow-up	Percentage overweight Initial	Percentage overweight Change at end of treatment	Percentage overweight Change at follow-up	Comments
Rivinus et al. (1976)	7 girls, 3 boys; aged 8–13; low SES; black	1. Behavioral self-control	10	67.5	(10 weeks) −2.8	(2 yr) −3.0	71		−51	Weekly 2-hr group sessions with group supper.
Gross et al. (1976)	10 girls; aged 13–17; lower-middle-class black	1. Behavioral self-control	10	81.5	(10 weeks) −3.3	(12 weeks) −5.7	39.2	−4.7	−7.7	Group meetings for discussion of self-recording, calories, and social consequences of obesity.
Wheeler & Hess (1976)	48 children; aged 2–11; average age 7.1 years	1. Behavioral self-control	14	—	—	—	40.4	(8 months) −4.1		Individual treatments every 2 weeks for undisclosed period, then less frequent meetings; mother and child treated together.
		2. No-treatment control	14				38.9	+6.3		
		3. (Dropouts)	12				46.3	+3.0		
Weiss (1977)	11 boys, 36 girls; aged 9–18	1. Diet, no reward	9	73.1	(12 weeks) −0.3	(1 yr) +4.3	30.7	−3.2	+2.8	Weekly sessions of 10–15 min; parents not involved; 14 subjects dropped.
		2. Diet, self-reward	10	66.4	−1.2	+3.5	37.5	−5.2	−0.1	
		3. Stimulus control	12	80.1	−0.8	−0.1	47.2	−5.5	−10.5	
		4. Stimulus-control diet, self-reward	9	66.5	−1.3	+0.7	46.2	−6.9	−9.0	
		5. No-treatment control	7	73.0	+1.9	+8.2	52.1	+1.0	+7.4	

Study	Subjects	Groups	N	% Overweight	Change	Change	% OW	Change	Change	Comments
Kingsley & Shapiro (1977)	24 boys, 16 girls; aged 10–11; relatively affluent	1. Child only	10		(8 weeks) −1.5	(20 weeks) +1.1				Weekly group treatment, $30 deposit earned back for attendance.
		2. Mother only	8		−1.6	+1.2				
		3. Mother and child together	8		−1.6	−0.1				
		4. Waiting-list control	10		+0.9	—				
Brownell, Kelman, & Stunkard	30 girls, 9 boys; aged 12–16; mixed SES; mothers willing to participate	1. Mother and child together	15	80.5	(16 weeks) −5.3	(1 yr) +2.9	50	−7	−6	Weekly group meetings; $15 deposit from parents returned for attendance; child deposited $2 each week, returned for weight loss.
		2. Mother and child separately	14	83.6	−8.4	−7.7	60	−17	−21	
		3. Child alone	13	81.1	−3.3	+3.2	57	−7	−6	
Aragona et al. (1975)	15 girls; aged 5–10; overweight by report	1. Response cost	3	47.9	(12 weeks) −4.3	(31 weeks) +3.3				Weekly group meetings; parents deposited money on a sliding scale; 25% refunded for record keeping, 25% for attendance, 50% for weight loss.
		2. Response cost plus reinforcement	4	48.0	−5.1	−0.3				
		3. No-treatment control	5	45.1	+0.4	—				
Coates (1977)	3 girls; aged 16, 16 and 15	1. Treatment subject	1	130.0	(10 weeks) −9.5		128.4	−16.9		Individual treatment, twice-weekly meetings; 5 meetings in the home with entire family.
		2. Treatment subject	1	88.1	−5.2		71.4	−10.6		
		3. Control subject	1	98.0	+2.2		72.9	+4.0		

2. Obesity is a simple disorder resulting from excess caloric intake.
3. The obese individual is an overeater.
4. Obese persons are more sensitive to food stimuli than are nonobese individuals.
5. There are important differences in the "eating style" of obese and nonobese persons.
6. Training an obese person to behave like a nonobese one will result in weight loss. (p. 657)

"Obesity Is a Learning Disorder" and "Results from Excess Caloric Intake"

Let us consider the first two assumptions, that "obesity is a learning disorder" and that it is "a simple disorder resulting from excess caloric intake." The assumption that obesity results from excess caloric intake is, of course, true in the sense that excessive body fat has been stored during periods when caloric intake has exceeded caloric expenditure. It is, however, anything but a simple disorder, and principles of learning may have little or nothing to do with its origins. An admirable recent review by Wooley, Wooley, and Dyrenforth (1979) has detailed some of the poorly understood aspects of caloric balance that led them to conclude that metabolic and not behavioral functions account for much experimental and human obesity. Several investigators have contributed significantly to this conclusion. Bray (1976) has shown that dieting can produce a decrease in metabolic rate of over 20% in two weeks, as well as decreases as high as 30% soon afterward. Garrow (1974) has shown that metabolic rate falls more rapidly with each period of caloric restriction and that it returns to baseline more slowly with each such period. Hamilton (1969) showed the similar phenomenon of a progressive decrease in the number of calories needed to regain weight lost during each period of caloric restriction.

Keesey (1980) has provided strong support for the role of metabolic processes in obesity on the basis of the remarkable stability of body weight (body fat) in the face of marked variations in caloric intake. He suggested that the amount of body fat is normally set at different levels for different organisms, and he described profound metabolic adaptations that may occur, apparently to defend that "set point" in the face of changes in caloric intake. He concluded that viewing persons "as dif-

fering not in how they regulate body weight but rather in terms of the set point each is prepared to defend, we might better understand why most of us remain at essentially the same body weight without so much as trying while others remain obese no matter how hard they try to change" (p. 163). The recent work on fat cell anatomy by Krotkiewski and his colleagues (1980) has given added reason to credit the importance of metabolic factors in obesity. Clearly, obesity is neither a simple disorder nor one explainable solely in terms of learning theory.

"The Obese Individual Is an Overeater"

As Wooley *et al.* (1979) pointed out; "It is, of course, true that obese people overeat in the sense that their caloric intake is too great to keep them thin. But what is usually meant is that they eat abnormally large amounts of food relative to a lean population" (p. 5). Some massively obese persons on metabolic wards do have very large food intakes, but most studies of mild to moderately overweight persons have found no difference between their food intake and that of persons of normal weight. There are many such reports and little contradictory evidence. Twelve of 13 studies cited by Garrow (1974) found that obese persons ate no more than nonobese persons; the results of one study were equivocal. Seven other studies cited by Wooley also found no difference. Such unanimity is almost unprecedented; mild and moderately obese adults probably do not overeat.

"Obese Persons Are More Sensitive to Food Stimuli than Are Nonobese Individuals"

Schachter's externality theory proposed that "the eating behavior of the obese, under conditions of high cue or cognitive salience, is stimulus bound. A food-relevant cue, above a given level of prominence, appears more likely to trigger an eating response in an overweight than in a normal weight person. . . . The obese do not simply eat, they overeat once they are 'turned on' by potent stimuli" (Rodin, 1980, p. 228). Although Schachter's reports (1971) on externality theory were published after Stuart's original paper, the compatibility of this theory with the prescription of stimulus control was so great that it was promptly accorded a central position in the rationale of behavior therapy for obesity. Recent studies have failed to find evidence that overweight people are any more responsive to external cues than persons of normal weight, and externality theory has fallen from favor. Most people are responsive to some external food cues, and some people in all weight categories may be responsive to many of them (Leon, Roth, & Hewitt, 1977; Mahoney, 1974; Milich, 1975; Milich, Anderson, & Mills, 1976; Meyers, Stunkard, & Coll, 1980). Externality appears to be a valid psychological characteristic; the problem is that it is not peculiar to obesity. Rodin (1980) has recently reviewed the status of externality theory and concluded that "the internal versus external view is far too simple a description of, or explanation for, differences between obese and normal-weight individuals . . . the extreme separation of these factors is no longer conceptually useful or empirically supported" (p. 230).

"There Are Important Differences in the Eating Style of Obese and Nonobese Persons"

No one aspect of the behavior therapy for obesity has attracted more attention or been subjected to more intense investigation than the idea that obese persons show a distinctive "obese eating style." Originally proposed without empirical support by Ferster et al. (1962), the obese eating style was initially accepted as a valid behavioral description, as a cause of obesity, and as a target for therapeutic intervention. According to Ferster et al., the obese eating style consisted of the rapid intake of food by means of large bites at frequent intervals. A large part of behavioral weight-reduction programs was designed to slow the rate of eating by such devices as placing the food utensils on the plate after each bite and introducing short delays in the course of the meal.

A series of increasingly well-controlled studies has finally laid to rest the myth of the obese eating style (Adams, Ferguson, Stunkard, & Agras, 1978; Kissileff, Jordan, & Lev-

itz, 1978; Rosenthal & Marx, 1978; Stunkard & Kaplan, 1977; Stunkard, Coll, Lundquist, & Meyers, 1980). Obese people do not eat more rapidly than or differently from nonobese people. It is, of course, still possible that slowing eating behavior might help, even though obese people do not eat more rapidly than others. But even this possibility seems to have been ruled out by Rosenthal and Marx (1978). These authors showed that a behavioral treatment program did markedly slow the eating rate of obese subjects, but that successful subjects did not slow their rate any more than did unsuccessful subjects.

"Training an Obese Person to Eat like a Nonobese One Will Result in Weight Loss"

The relationship between behavior change and weight loss is one of the weakest links in the entire chain of the use of behavior therapy for obesity. We still do not know whether the weight lost in behavioral programs is a result of the specific behavioral changes prescribed by the programs (Brownell & Stunkard, 1978).

At first glance, this ignorance seems puzzling. Three early studies, including Wollersheim's (1970), reported significant correlations between weight loss and behavior change, as assessed by questionnaire (Hagen, 1974; Mahoney, 1974). But each of these studies relied on a single retrospective self-report by subjects whose answers may have been biased by their knowledge of the outcome of their treatment. Four more recent studies utilized concurrent measures of weight change and behavior change, as well as behavior change measures that were more comprehensive and presumably more valid than those of earlier studies. None supported the notion that weight change results from the prescribed behavior changes (Bellack, Rozensky, & Schwartz, 1974; Brownell, Heckerman, Westlake, Hayes & Monti, 1978; Jeffery, Wing, & Stunkard, 1978; Stalonas, Johnson, & Christ, 1978). There are at least two possible explanations for this failure to find a relationship between behavior change and weight change: (1) the accuracy of the self-monitoring of behaviors may have been low, or the measures may have failed to reflect the important behavioral change that did occur; and (2) the weight change may have been caused by factors other than those prescribed in the programs.

What are the implications of the discovery that the initial assumptions that guided behavior therapy for obesity were incorrect? The strongly empirical nature of behavior therapy and the self-examination already under way as a result of therapeutic disappointments mean that the behavioral treatment of obesity is not likely to be greatly shaken. As Wilson (1980) pointed out, "examples of demonstrably effective treatment techniques that have been derived from theories that were ultimately discredited are not hard to find in the psychotherapy and behavior therapy literature" (p. 327) or, indeed, in much of the medical literature. The search for new treatment measures will undoubtedly continue apace. A number of perspectives for the future are possible: some are clinical, some are social.

Future Perspectives: Clinical Measures

Fifteen years after its introduction there has been no improvement on the results of the first report of the behavioral control of obesity. This fact suggests that the limits of the effectiveness of current behavioral technologies may have been reached. Even a continuation of the plethora of small modifications in technique that have flooded the literature would appear unlikely to influence this unfortunate state of affairs. To go beyond the current limits may require new technologies or new combinations of behavioral techniques with other methods for the treatment of obesity. The most prominent such method is diet.

Combining Diet and Behavior Modification

During the past 15 years, behavioral treatments for obesity have developed in isolation from dietary treatments for obesity. This is a surprising fact, since this period has seen a remarkable degree of interest in both forms of treatment. The lists of best-selling books have consistently included ones on diets, and even serious efforts by the American Medical As-sociation have had little apparent effect on the sale of books prescribing clearly harmful diets (Van Itallie, 1978). The reason for this curious lack of communication between the dietary and the behavioral approaches may lie, at least in part, in the predilection of behavior therapists for dietary management by means of small, incremental changes. This approach appears far more likely to produce enduring changes in eating behavior than do traditional dietary approaches. Behavior therapists have rightly cautioned against the expectations aroused by "going on a diet." Anyone who "goes on a diet" must one day "come off the diet," and very often without having learned anything about how to maintain the weight losses achieved by this unusual behavior. Furthermore, most behavior therapists have treated patients who are only mildly overweight, for whom it is acceptable to lose 4.5–6.8 kg at a rate of .7 kg a week. Such weight losses, however, have a minimal effect on the health of clinically obese persons, and such rates of weight loss are often insufficient to maintain their interest in treatment. Weight losses produced by diets, on the other hand, have long obviated these problems.

A recent popular diet, the "protein-sparing modified fast," is a good example of the strengths of dietary management. This diet, to be distinguished from the "liquid protein diets" composed of hydrolyzed protein of poor biological quality, contains no more than 300–700 calories, usually of high-quality protein, sometimes mixed with small amounts of carbohydrate. Bistrian, Blackburn, Flatt, Sizer, Scrimshaw, and Sherman (1976) have shown that they could maintain nitrogen balance in outpatients engaging in a wide variety of occupations and lifestyles with a diet that contained no more than 1.4 g of protein per kilogram of lean body mass per day. Genuth *et al.* (1978) have treated the largest number of patients (1,200) with protein-sparing modified fasts, and they have reported excellent initial results. Thus, 75% of their patients lost more than 18.2 kg. The maintenance of these losses, however, was described as "a persistent and difficult therapeutic challenge."

The possibility of improving the maintenance of the large weight losses produced by the protein-sparing modified fast was explored by Lindner and Blackburn (1976). The protein-sparing modified fast was integrated into a weight reduction program that relied heavily on behavioral principles. Treatment took place according to two similar protocols at two clinics: 67 patients were treated in a private weight-reduction clinic, another 100 in a university medical center. The patients were mostly women who were an average age of 43 and were from 50% to 80% overweight.

The first phase of the program consisted of a period of evaluation, during which the patients continued their usual food intake, recorded it in a food diary, measured their physical activity with a pedometer, and were introduced to behavioral techniques in a classroom setting. The protein-sparing modified fast was introduced after the patients had made satisfactory progress in the first, behavioral, phase. The diet consisted of three meals a day containing from 270 to 700 calories, in the form of either protein hydrolyzate or protein (lean meat, fish, or fowl). Their intake was calculated to yield 1.4 g of protein per kilogram of lean body mass per day. Vitamin and mineral supplements were used.

The patients were seen as often as five times a week for the first two weeks of the program and then with a decreasing frequency, which reached once a week for most of the program. The treatment averaged 48 weeks in duration, and an effort was made to reduce patients to their desirable weight. The patients were encouraged to continue their normal activities and to increase them with the aid of feedback from the pedometer. When the patients reached a desirable weight, or if they were unable to continue weight loss, they began to first eat vegetables, then fruit, then an increasingly varied diet that restricted only refined carbohydrates. During this termination phase, the group sessions emphasized more detailed behavioral techniques, and an effort was made to shift the responsibility for treatment from staff management to self-management.

The weight losses were comparable to those reported by other programs that have utilized the protein-sparing modified fast. Half of the patients lost 18.2 kg, and over 80% lost 9.1 kg. The mean weight loss at one of the clinics was 20.5 kg. Lindner and Blackburn stated that the majority of the patients at this clinic maintained their weight loss. Clearly, the combination of diet and behavior therapy merits further exploration.

Exercise

Exercise is one of the most honored components of behavioral weight-reduction programs, but, like other worthy customs, it is one honored more in the breach than in the observance. The frequent exhortations to include exercise in these programs are usually ignored. It appears that exercise has general health benefits, but this review is confined to its influence on weight loss.

The interest in exercise as a part of weight reduction programs is based on only limited evidence from the behavioral literature. One study has recently shown that the weight loss produced by adding an exercise program to an eating-habits program was greater than that produced by either program alone (Dahlkoetter, Callahan, & Linton, 1979). Two other studies, however, found no effect: adding exercise to more traditional programs did not increase weight loss (Harris & Hallbauer, 1973; Stalonas et al., 1978). In each of these studies, it was reported that the maintenance of weight loss, at seven months and at one year, respectively, favored the programs that had included exercise. The statistical significance of this finding, however, was marginal: in the study by Stalonas et al., $p < .10$; in the study by Harris and Hallbauer, complicated by a substantial dropout rate, $p < .05$.

An important study by Gwinup (1975), the only one that assessed the effect of exercise alone, reported significant weight losses: a mean of 10.0 kg, with a range from 4.5 to 17.3 kg. This study provided a good idea of the problems of exercise in promoting weight reduction, for it took a year to achieve these results, during which time 68% of the patients (including all the men) dropped out of the program. Furthermore, the weight loss did not begin until walking (or its equivalent) exceeded 30 min a day, and the three patients with the greatest weight losses all exercised for 3 hr a day.

That it should be difficult to lose weight by exercise should not come as a surprise. It is true that obese people have often been reported to be less active than nonobese people, and three studies have actually measured these differences (Brownell, Stunkard, & Albaum, 1980; Chirico & Stunkard, 1960; Meyers, Stunkard, Coll, & Cooke, 1980). But the differences have been relatively small in terms of estimated caloric expenditure. The total physical activity of a group of obese women as measured by mechanical pedometers was the equivalent of 2.0 miles a day, that of matched nonobese women 4.9 miles a day. The comparable figures for men were 3.7 and 6.0 miles per day. Energy expenditure was not measured, but the greater body mass of the obese persons could well mean that they expended as many calories as the nonobese people in carrying out their lesser amounts of measured physical activity. Because of this greater mass, increasing their activity to the level of nonobese people would contribute to the caloric balance of obese persons.

Even if obese people did not expend less energy than nonobese people, increasing their physical activity to the level of that of nonobese people might help to control their obesity, at least in part because of their greater body mass and consequently greater energy expenditure. Chirico and Stunkard (1960) had found that the physical activity of obese women was less than that of nonobese women by the equivalent of 3 miles/day of walking. Increasing their activity by this amount would require them to perform an extra hour a day of physical activity, an amount shown by Gwinup (1975) to be sufficient to produce weight loss in his patients.

The mechanism whereby this weight loss occurs is unclear. The mean body weight of Gwinup's patients was 74.5 kg. It is estimated that a 75.0-kg woman walking 3 miles/hr expends 5.6 cal/min, compared with a resting expenditure of 1.3 cal/min. Gwinup's half-hour-a-day of walking would thus expend no more than an extra 129 cal. If physical activity helps to control obesity, it seems unlikely that it does so solely by its contribution to the calorie expenditure side of the energy balance ledger. It may, however, act via two other mechanisms.

Physical activity may influence obesity by influencing metabolic rates. Resting metabolism is responsible for a far larger percentage of total energy expenditure than is physical activity in all but the most active people. If, therefore, physical activity produces even small increases in metabolic rate, it could increase an energy expenditure out of all proportion to that produced by the activity itself. Although such a possibility cannot be excluded, it has never been demonstrated.

Physical activity may influence obesity by influencing food intake. Here, there is evidence in support of theory. Several years ago, Mayer (1967) demonstrated the paradoxical effect of physical activity on the food intake of sedentary rats. Although the food intake of normal rats of the Sprague-Dawley strain increased with increasing energy expenditures over a wide range of energy demands, the intake did not decrease proportionately when physical activity fell below a certain minimal value, and body weight increased. Alternatively, the food intake of sedentary rats decreased as they spent increasing amounts of time in an exercise wheel (up to 1 hr/day), and their body weight fell. At levels of activity of greater than 1 hr/day, their caloric intake equaled their caloric expenditure, and their body weight remained constant.

This important observation was not exploited for several years. Quite recently, however, the phenomenon of activity-induced decreases in food intake has been demonstrated in three quite different forms of experimental obesity. Two of these forms of experimental obesity were of hereditary origin: the Danforth yellow obese mouse studied by Stern, Dunn, and Johnson (1977) and the Zucker obese rat (Stern & Johnson, 1977). One form was environmentally determined: the dietary obese rat studied by Sclafani and Springer (1976). In each case, the effects of physical activity on food intake were greater than those observed in the nonobese Sprague-Dawley rats. The phenomenon is clearly more general than we had thought and is perhaps of special relevance to organisms with a tendency toward obesity.

Despite the potential importance of this phenomenon, little is known about its occurrence in humans. Only two studies using humans have specifically investigated it; both found evidence for it. Stunkard and Pestka (1962) studied obese and nonobese girls at home and at a summer camp. Pedometer measurements showed that the obese girls were just as active as the nonobese girls at both sites. They responded differently, however, to the great increase in physical activity at camp. The obese girls lost more weight. It appeared that under conditions of increased physical activity, they did not increase their food intake as much as did the nonobese girls. A study by Epstein, Masek, and Marshall (1978) found similar results on a short-term basis. Obese girls ate less when their recess preceded, rather than followed, lunch.

Clearly, there is a theoretical rationale for the incorporation of exercise into weight reduction programs. Equally clearly, we know little about how to do it, except that it is difficult. These circumstances would seem to invite behavioral investigations of this problem.

Couples Training

Interest has recently been aroused by explorations of the effect of including the spouses of patients with the patients as integral members of weight reduction programs. The rationale for such a practice is unexceptionable. What better means could there be of assisting in stimulus control and the control of eating, or of providing effective schedules of reinforcement, than training the patient's spouse in these modalities along with the patient? Furthermore, two studies had provided evidence that spousal support could help. Stuart and Davis (1972) reported that an analysis of mealtime interactions revealed that husbands may exert either a positive or a negative influence on their wives' efforts to lose weight. Mahoney and Mahoney (1976) noted a high correlation between indexes of "social support" within the family and weight loss during treatment.

The first controlled trial of couples training found support for its effectiveness: Brownell et al. (1978) found that patients treated with their spouses lost more weight than those treated alone and that the difference in weight loss had increased at a six-month follow-up. This promising approach has been vigorously explored in the past three years, with results that must be viewed as equivocal. Four relatively small-scale studies replicated the findings of Brownell et al. (Fremouw & Zitter, 1980; Israel & Saccone, 1979; Pearce, 1979; Rosenthal, Allen, & Winter, 1980). Four others, however, failed to replicate these findings (O'Neil, Currey, Hirsch, Riddle, Taylor, Malcolm, & Sexauer, 1979; Weisz & Bucher, 1980; Wilson & Brownell, 1978; Zitter & Fremouw, 1978). The largest and most recent study, of 124 obese men and women, found no effect of couples training (Brownell & Stunkard, 1981). The future of couples training in the treatment of obesity is now uncertain.

Increasing the Duration and Intensity of Treatment

Most behavioral treatment programs have been quite brief. The mean duration of treatment in the 21 studies reviewed in Table 1 was only 11.9 weeks, hardly time enough to produce clinically significant weight losses at the slow rates characteristic of these programs. Jeffery et al. (1978) reported that their review of the literature, not unexpectedly, found the longer the duration of treatment, the greater the weight loss. The largest weight losses reported in the behavioral literature all occurred after prolonged treatment; one year (Lindner & Blackburn, 1976; Stuart, 1967); six months (Craighead, Stunkard, & O'Brien, 1981).

Similarly, increasing the intensity of treatment may improve its results. Wilson (1980) has noted that "the usual practice of scheduling treatment sessions on a fixed, weekly basis is an arbitrary one that undoubtedly is based more on the convenience it affords the investigators than on any advantage it may offer the subjects" (p. 331). Larger weight losses have been associated with more frequent patient visits, especially at the outset of treatment (Lindner & Blackburn, 1976; Stuart, 1967), although Ferstl, Jokusch, and Brengelmann (1975) reported weight losses of 7.5 kg in a program that involved twice-weekly meetings throughout the treatment.

Therapist's Skill

The therapist's skill has rarely been considered in evaluating the results of behavioral treatment programs, and yet it must play some part in outcome. Levitz and Stunkard (1974) showed that treatment conducted by professional therapists produced greater weight loss than that conducted by peer counselors using the same treatment manual. Jefferv *et al.* (1978) showed that even small increases in the therapists' experience resulted in greater effectiveness. Most behavioral weight-control programs have been carried out by relatively inexperienced therapists. The use of more experienced and more skillful therapists could be expected to improve the results of treatment.

Social Skills Training

Social skills training has not been used in behavioral weight-reduction programs despite its apparent value in the treatment of similar problems, such as alcoholism. Wilson (1980) noted that "declining a cocktail when dining out with friends or acquaintances at a restaurant is no different from refusing dessert. The obese person has to have the assertive skills to be able to say 'no' without suffering feelings of guilt, shame or rejection" (p. 334).

Future Perspective on Clinical Measures: One Conclusion

We have suggested that the limits of the effectiveness of current behavioral technologies may have been reached. It is entirely possible that the measures described in the foregoing section can extend these limits and result in further progress. But relatively small incremental advances in the improvement of clinical practice ignore what may be the major contribution of behavioral technologies to the improvement of health care in general and of obesity in particular; that is, their applicability to large groups.

Future Perspectives: Social and Public-Health Measures

One of the most important implications of the study by Penick *et al.* (1971) was its promise of a wider applicability of the behavioral therapies, for it showed that behavior modification, conducted by a team with little clinical experience, was more effective in the treatment of obesity than was the best alternative program that could be devised by a highly skilled research team. In fact, the inexperienced therapists achieved a two-fold increase in weight loss over conventional measures. Lesser increases in effectiveness have brought about major changes in the management of other disorders. The question arises as to how these advances in behavioral weight control can be exploited more effectively. Can they be applied to populations larger than the clinical ones for which they were developed?

What we know about the social environment suggests that the answer is "yes," for the social environment exerts a powerful influence on obesity—and leanness. One single social variable—social class—has an influence on the prevalence of obesity greater than that of any known physical determinant. Studies by Moore, Stunkard, and Srole (1962) and by Goldblatt, Moore, and Stunkard (1965) have established that obesity is six times more prevalent among women of lower socioeconomic status than among women of upper socioeconomic status (see Figure 10).

A notable feature of these studies was that they permitted causal inferences about the influence of socioeconomic status. This was achieved by ascertaining not only the socioeconomic status of the respondents at the time of the study, but also that of their parents when the respondents were 8 years old. Although a person's obesity might influence his or her own social class, it could not have influenced his or her parents' social class. Therefore, associations between the social class of the respondents' parents and obesity can be viewed

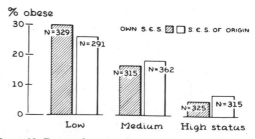

Figure 10. Decreasing prevalence of obesity with increase in socioeconomic status (SES) in women. (From "Social Factors in Obesity" by P. B. Goldblatt *et al., Journal of the American Medical Association,* 1965, *192,* 1039–1044, Fig. 1. Copyright 1979 by the American Medical Association. Reprinted by permission.)

as causal. These associations were almost as powerful as those between the respondents' own social class and obesity. For example, 7% of the offspring of upper-class parents were obese, compared with 5% of the *members* of the upper class; 26% of the offspring of lowerclass parents were obese, compared with 30% of *members* of the lower class.

Since this first report, studies in other parts of the world have confirmed the strong relationship between social factors and obesity; social factors must be regarded as being among the most important, if not as being *the* most important, influence on the prevalence of obesity (Stunkard, 1975).

There are many ways in which social factors influence people—and their eating and obesity. Food advertising plays an important part in the life of most Americans. Labor-saving devices have profoundly influenced our lifestyles during this century. But there is another, more personal, way in which the social environment influences us: through the communities of which we are a part.

The idea of community brings to mind, of course, the place where we live. But we are all part of a large number of different, and overlapping, communities. For *community* simply means "people with common interests or characteristics." Different communities involve us in different ways. Some of our communities have a profound influence on the way we live, on our lifestyles. Some are far better able to supply the cues and consequences of our behavior than is a therapist. And some of them are doing just that, in a systematic manner, to improve the health behaviors of their members.

At least three kinds of communities have undertaken such activities. They can be called the *community of the afflicted,* the *community at the work site,* and the *geographical community.* We will discuss representatives of each of these kinds of communities and their efforts to help their members control their obesity.

The Community of the Afflicted

In the early days of our nation, Alexis de Tocqueville described the proclivity of Americans to organize in informal groups to achieve ends that are the responsibility of government in other societies. Nowhere is this proclivity more impressively expressed than in the organization of patients to cope with their illnesses. Although the origins of the self-help movement can be traced to nineteenth-century England, and beyond, the pioneering American institution was Alcoholics Anonymous, and many of the current self-help groups have been modeled on it. The largest of these is TOPS (Take Off Pounds Sensibly), a 30-year-old organization that enrolls more than 300,000 members in 12,000 chapters in all parts of the country. The first, cross-sectional study of TOPS revealed that its membership was almost exclusively female, white, and middle-class (Stunkard, Levine, & Fox, 1970). The average member was a 42-year-old woman whose ideal weight was 54.1 kg and who entered TOPS weighing 81.8 kg, or 58% overweight. She stayed in Tops for 16½ months and lost 6.8 kg. A later, longitudinal study, however, showed that these early figures had overestimated the effectiveness of TOPS (Garb & Stunkard, 1974). By failing to take into account the high dropout rate, the earlier study had based its findings on those hardy individuals who had stayed in the organization and who had therefore lost the most weight.

TOPS's problem with high dropout rates and small weight losses was also an opportunity, for it made TOPS a promising vehicle for testing the possibility of introducing into large organizations programs that had initially been devised for clinical settings. Levitz and Stunkard (1974) carried out such a program with all 290 female members of 16 TOPS chapters situated in West Philadelphia and its adjacent suburbs.

Four treatment conditions, each containing four matched TOPS chapters, were employed for a total of 12 weeks. They were (1) behavior modification by psychiatrists; (2) behavior modification by (lay) TOPS chapter leaders who had received brief training in the procedures and who used the same manual as the psychiatrists; (3) nutritional education carried out by chapter leaders who had received an amount of training in nutrition comparable to that provided to the chapter leaders in behavior modification; and finally, (4) continuation of the standard TOPS program.

The most striking effects of the program were on the major problem of TOPS: the high attrition rate. As shown in Figure 11 the attrition rate in the two behavior-modification conditions was lower during treatment, and significantly lower one year later. At follow-up, 38% and 41% of subjects had dropped out of the two chapters that had received behavior modification, compared with 55% of those who had received nutritional education and 67% of those who had experienced the standard TOPS programs. These differences were highly significant.

Despite the bias against the results of behavior modification because of the differential attrition rates, behavior modification produced significantly greater weight loss than did the control conditions, both at the end of treatment and at the one-year follow-up.

This feasibility study showed that behavior modification could be introduced into large self-help groups and could improve their performance. TOPS, curiously, made no effort to capitalize on the program to which it had made such an important contribution, and the chief beneficiaries were TOPS' competitors, the commercial weight-reduction organizations. Stuart has constructed a detailed behavioral component for Weight Watchers Programs, which had traditionally been confined to inspirational lectures, nutritional education, and group pressure. It is estimated that 400,000 Americans are now exposed each week to behavioral measures for the control of obesity under these auspices. A study of the efficacy of the newly introduced behavioral program revealed that it improved performance (Stuart, 1977). Weight losses that had averaged 0.51 kg per week under the traditional program increased to 0.61 kg per week with the use of the behavioral program, and when only patients with the best attendance were considered, this difference rose from 0.51 to 0.59 kg per week for the traditional program, and from 0.61 to 0.73 kg per week for the combined program.

The major problem in commercial weight-reduction programs, as in TOPS, is the high attrition rate. A recent report by Volkmar, Stunkard, Woolston, and Bailey (1981) indicates that this problem is serious enough to suggest caution in the interpretation of data

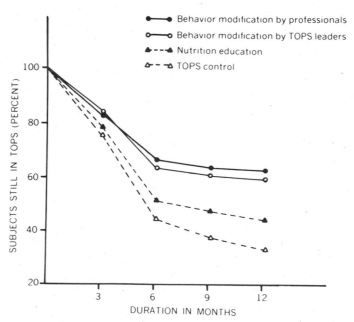

Figure 11. Attrition rate of TOPS subjects over a one-year period under four experimental conditions. (From "A Therapeutic Coalition for Obesity: Behavior Modification and Patient Self-Help" by L. Levitz and A. J. Stunkard, *American Journal of Psychiatry*, 1974, *131*, 423–427, Fig. 1. Copyright 1974 by the American Psychiatric Association. Reprinted by permission.)

based on the weight losses of persons who remain in these programs. Thus, a study of a well-known commercial weight-reduction program revealed that 50% of the participants had dropped out in 6 weeks and 70% in 12 weeks, and similar attrition rates have been reported in five other commercial weight-reduction programs in three countries.

The Community at the Work Site

A second kind of community is the community at work. Most people spend more time at work than at any other activity, and their relationships with their fellow workers are often among the most important of their lives. Only recently, however, have this time and these relationships been used in a planned way to achieve health benefits. A progressive union has shown the promise of such efforts.

The United Store Workers Union has demonstrated the feasibility of work site treatment for hypertension and, quite recently, for obesity. Hypertension, like obesity, is rarely cured, but it can be controlled. Most hypertensives, however, receive treatment that is inadequate to control their blood pressure. Thus, a survey of the members of the United Store Workers Union in New York City revealed that less than 50% of the hypertensives who had been receiving conventional treatment had achieved satisfactory results. By contrast, the innovative work-site program of Alderman and Schoenbaum (1975), conducted primarily by nurse practioners, achieved long-term control of blood pressure in over 80% of the participants and radically reduced the number of days of hospitalization for cardiovascular causes. Two of the key elements of this program were the scheduling of appointments by the union secretary and the positive reinforcement of hypertensives by their fellow workers for control of their blood pressure.

The success of the hypertension program and the development of behavioral treatments for obesity simple enough to be administered by people with no professional training led Stunkard and Brownell (1980) to undertake a work site program to control obesity in this same union. As in the earlier TOPS program, efforts were made to assess the feasibility of lay persons' (union members) carrying out be-

havioral weight-reduction programs. In addition, an effort was made to assess the relative merits of an innovative four-day-a-week treatment program proposed, significantly, by the union leadership. Fifty-two women, on the average 57% overweight, were randomly assigned to behavioral treatments with lay or professional leaders.

The study showed the feasibility of the work site treatment of obesity. It also showed some barriers to its success, particularly a high attrition rate. During the 16-week course of treatment, 56% of the subjects dropped out. Low attrition rates in the much simpler hypertension program had led us to expect low rates in the obesity program. Nevertheless, even these high rates compared favorably with those of self-help groups, even after their years of experience.

There were two other important findings. First, the attrition rates were no greater in the groups led by lay therapists than in groups led by a professional therapist. Second, the group receiving the innovative four-times-weekly treatment showed a lower attrition rate than the groups receiving the more conventional once-weekly treatments. A third key question could not be answered by the results of this study: whether the work site treatment is more effective than medical site treatment, when administered by the same person.

The weight losses of persons who completed the program were modest (3.6 kg per person), but they, too, compared favorably with the losses of members of self-help groups. There was no significant difference between the weight losses in the different conditions.

The results of this first study were sufficiently encouraging to merit further effort, now under way. It is clear that simply treating people at work is not sufficient to ensure their adherence or even their attendance; the use of the powerful rewards and sanctions of the work site are also necessary. Unions are not the only institutions sponsoring work-site treatment programs. Management also has this capability.

Health promotion rather than treatment of disease characterizes a program recently introduced by Johnson & Johnson, the medical supply company (K. Wilbur, personal communication). The goal of "Live for Life" is to encourage employees to follow lifestyles that will result in good health. The goal is being approached primarily by means of a series of courses carefully designed to help employees learn the behavioral skills necessary to lose weight, eat a nonatherogenic diet, stop smoking, increase exercise, and manage stress. The curricula for these courses have been designed by a group of outstanding behavior therapists, and each employee is encouraged to enroll in one of them. As in the Store Workers Union program, the leadership of these small groups is to be provided not by professionals but by employees. Special curricula for training the employees who will lead groups have also been devised by the same behavior therapists who have worked out the basic courses in health behavior change. By thus placing the burden of the program on the employees themselves, Johnson & Johnson expects to institutionalize the program so that it can be continued with minimal professional contribution.

The courses meet weekly near the employee's place of work—in at least one instance, in recreational facilities built for the employees by the company. The activities take place during the working day, and employees must arrange with their superiors for time necessary to participate. One might suppose that company sponsorship of the program would make these arrangements a simple matter. In fact, they may be no simpler than those of union members arranging time with their supervisors for the obesity program. Johnson & Johnson is a profit-making institution, and much as a supervisor may want to accommodate an employee's participation in "Live for Life," the supervisor still has deadlines to meet and quotas to fill.

A notable feature of "Live for Life" is the unusually thorough evaluation to which it is being subjected. A carefully controlled trial has been devised by expert epidemiological consultants. The size of Johnson & Johnson permits experimentation on a very broad scale. The outcome will be measured by differences between whole companies: those into which "Live for Life" has been introduced and those into which it has not. Careful baseline measures are being obtained on all persons enrolling in the program, and these measure-

ments are to be repeated in one and two years. These measures include a number of easily quantifiable health indexes that reflect the objectives of the different courses: body weight, percentage body fat, smoking habits, blood pressure, and serum cholesterol. Another important measure of outcome reflects the business ethos of the sponsor of the program. Careful cost–benefit analyses will compare the costs of the program with the expected benefits (in health indexes and in health-care costs) between companies that have introduced Johnson & Johnson's "Live for Life" and those that have not.

The Geographical Community

When we think of community, most of us think first of our geographical community, where we live and what we call home. It is in our geographical community that impersonal social forces and intimate personal forces have their major impact on us. The fact that obesity is six times more prevalent among lower-class women than among upper-class women suggests the power of the influences exerted on us in our geographical communities. Here would seem to be the place, *par excellence,* where favorable changes in health behavior can be taught, and learned. A whole new type of research enterprise, focusing on geographical communities, has begun to explore this possibility. Three such efforts have been begun, and the first signs are promising.

The Stanford Three-Community Study was an innovative broad-scale program for reducing coronary risk factors in two towns, each with populations of 14,000 (Farquhar, Maccoby, Wood, & Alexander, 1977). A rigorous evaluation compared the changes in risk factors in these towns with those in a control town of the same size and demographic characteristics.

The major intervention in this study was an intensive and sophisticated media campaign that each year contained 50 television and 100 radio spots, three hours of television and several hours of radio programming, newspaper columns, stories and advertisements in the local weekly newspapers, posters and billboards, printed matter sent via direct mail, and other materials. The dominant characteristic of the media campaign was its organization as a totally integrated information system based initially on data gathered from preliminary surveys and later on information collected during the course of the campaign. In one of the towns, the media campaign was supplemented by a face-to-face instruction program directed at two-thirds of the participants identified as being in the top quartile of risk of coronary heart disease.

Coronary heart disease was the primary target of the campaign, and control of obesity did not receive special emphasis. Nevertheless, this experiment was relevant to efforts to control obesity and, indeed, any condition that is based, at least in part, on lifestyle and personal habits. The results were most encouraging. By the end of the second year of the campaign, the risk of coronary disease had decreased by 17% in the treatment communities as measured by the Cornfield index of risk of coronary disease, whereas it had increased by 6% in the control community.

The Stanford program was carried out on such relatively small populations that no measurable impact on mortality and morbidity from heart disease had been expected. Indeed, none was found. Stanford is now undertaking a new five-city study with populations large enough to show changes in rates of heart disease.

A similar study in Finland has reported significant decreases in the rate of heart disease and, unexpectedly, of stroke. The North Karelia Project has been directed toward a population of 180,000, large enough to allow the hope that an effective intervention would be able to reduce the rate of heart disease (Puska, 1981). The major objectives were decreasing mortality and morbidity from cardiovascular disease, particularly in middle-aged men. To reach this major objective, two intermediate objectives were defined: (1) the reduction of the three coronary risk factors of smoking, elevated serum cholesterol, and high blood pressure, and (2) the detection, treatment, and rehabilitation of persons already suffering from heart disease. (Obesity was sufficiently infrequent so that it was not a target of the campaign.)

Great reliance was placed on the dissemination of health information, through the media, as in the Stanford Program, and also through a variety of community agencies. Although television was not available, extensive use was made of the radio in the form of interviews, lectures, short courses, question-and-answer sessions, and even a smoking-cessation course. The county newspapers were actively engaged in the project. An effort was made to publish something about the project every other day throughout its five years: news of the project, articles on risk factors, and practical suggestions for changing health behaviors. The close contact of project personnel with local reporters played a key part in the effectiveness of the media campaign. Posters and leaflets, prepared by the project and published by local printers, were used extensively. Joint campaigns with the county's school department were carried out, both for their effect on risk factor prevention by the pupils and for the effect of the messages that the pupils took home to their parents. The local heart associations played an active part in health education, sponsoring public meetings at which physicians spoke to community groups. A particularly effective agency was the important Finnish housewives' organization known as the Martha Associations. They carried a heavy burden of nutrition education.

The first step in implementation of the project was the formulation of a "community diagnosis." The typical features of the population were determined, as well as how its members saw the problems of cardiovascular disease and possible solutions. A general survey of the resources and the service structure of the community was carried out. Vigorous efforts were made to identify leaders, both the recognized leaders of labor, civic, and voluntary organizations and the equally important informal opinion leaders. Twelve hundred were identified.

The project's risk factor reduction paralleled that of the Stanford Program. But the goal of the North Karelia Project was not just reduction in risk factors. Stanford had already shown that risk factors could be reduced. The payoff was in "events": Did the program reduce mortality and morbidity? The answer was "yes."

The preliminary results revealed that the incidence of myocardial infarction decreased by 21% and that of stroke by 31% (Report of the WHO meeting, November, 1978). These reductions in incidence was paralleled by reductions in mortality. There was a 20% decline in mortality for both men and women when "all cardiovascular disease," which includes strokes, was considered. These first results give reason to hope that a program for a geographical community can measurably improve the health of that community.

This hope has inspired the most recent project to improve health in a geographical community: the Pennsylvania Community Health Intervention Project (Stunkard, 1979), which is taking place in Lycoming County, a region of 115,000 people, in north-central Pennsylvania. It is similar to the North Karelia Project in being a cooperative enterprise among different groups: the Department of Health of the Commonwealth of Pennsylvania, the University of Pennsylvania, Pennsylvania State University, and the Lycoming County community. A media program is a central part of the intervention effort. In addition, a Community Resource Inventory has identified more than 300 possible agencies, a number of which have already begun to work on the program.

The priorities for the reduction of risk factors are similar to those in the North Karelia Project. The three primary behavioral targets are smoking, hypertension, and dietary change. Two secondary behavioral goals are decreasing obesity and increasing exercise.

The Pennsylvania project is similar to the North Karelia Project in many ways. Its importance lies in determining whether this unique blend of governmental, academic, and community resources can be achieved in the United States. Both the Stanford programs were funded as research projects, at levels far higher than those of the Pennsylvania project. If they are able to determine whether community intervention can lower the rate of cardiovascular disease, they will have amply repaid this investment, but they will probably not have produced a model that can be put into practice on an economical scale in the rest of the country. The leaders of the Pennsylvania project hope to create just this kind of model, easily replicable through the nation.

Toward this end, a careful cost–effectiveness analysis is being conducted.

Summary

Behavioral treatments for obesity have become sufficiently standardized so that five elements are common to most programs: self-monitoring, stimulus control, techniques for controlling the act of eating, the reinforcement of prescribed behaviors, and cognitive restructuring. Most of these elements were present in five prototypical studies: that by Ferster *et al.* (1962), which proposed the ideas; that by Stuart (1967), which made the ideas work; that by Wollersheim (1970), which introduced careful experimental designs; that by Penick *et al.* (1971), which demonstrated the superiority of behavioral treatments to conventional medical management; and that by Craighead *et al.* (1981), which demonstrated their superiority to pharmacotherapy. These outcome studies and at least 50 others have made it possible for us to gain a clear idea of what behavioral treatment for obesity can, and cannot, do.

The two most important advances introduced by behavioral treatments for obesity have been markedly decreasing the number of dropouts from treatment and the number of untoward side effects of treatment. Dropouts and untoward symptoms had long been the biggest problems in the treatment of obesity; both are well controlled by behavioral measures. Weight losses, however, have been modest. A review of 21 reports revealed that the weight losses of only 20% of the subjects exceeded 6.8 kg. Problems of maintenance mirror those of treatment. Clinically important weight losses achieved by behavioral treatments for obesity are not well maintained. A very recent study shows that they are better maintained than are weight losses achieved by pharmacotherapy, but the early hope that behavioral treatments might produce enduring changes in weight-related behaviors, as well as long-term weight loss, has not been fully realized. The behavioral treatment of obese children is just beginning. Nine studies give grounds for cautious optimism.

Several factors seem to account for the disappointing progress in the behavioral treatment of obesity. Treatment has been carried out largely by inexperienced therapists over short periods of time. Most of the subjects of the studies have been mildly overweight college women, and far too many of these studies have been devoted to ascertaining the relative effectiveness of small differences in technique. In addition, several of the early assumptions of behavior therapists about obesity are apparently in error: that obesity is largely a learning disorder, that obese people "overeat" and are more sensitive to food stimuli than are nonobese people, that there is an "obese eating style," and that training an obese person to eat as a nonobese one does will result in weight loss.

Fifteen years after its introduction, there has been no improvement on the results of the first report of the behavioral control of obesity. It appears that the limits of current behavioral technologies have been reached and that even the continuing plethora of small modifications in technique that have flooded the literature appear unlikely to improve the situation. The search for significant improvement in treatment results is taking two forms: one clinical and one social.

One of the most promising approaches to improving the clinical management of obesity is combining behavioral measures with diet. Increasing the duration and the intensity of treatment should also improve the results of behavioral treatments. Exercise has rarely been actively pursued in weight reduction programs and might well be of value. But relatively small incremental advances in the improvement of clinical practice ignore what may be the major contribution of behavioral technologies to the improvement of health care in general and of obesity in particular: their applicability to large groups.

The introduction of behavioral technologies into large groups has been explored most thoroughly in the self-help groups, where they have been shown to improve the performance of both voluntary and profit-making organizations. A detailed behavioral program has been added to the largest commercial weight-reduction program (Weight Watchers), and it is estimated that 400,000 Americans are now exposed each week to behavioral measures for the control of obesity under these auspices.

Other institutions would appear to offer an opportunity for the large-scale introduction of behavioral technologies; early experience with work site intervention showed its feasibility and also the barriers to its success. The greatest promise of behavioral technologies in the health area may lie in their application to geographical communities, for in these communities, behavioral principles can be applied to several risk factors for cardiovascular disease at little greater cost than to one risk factor alone. The opportunity for changing the behavior of large numbers of people by low-cost interventions may go far toward compensating for the limited clinical efficacy of the behavioral treatment of obesity.

References

Abrahms, J. L., & Allen, G. J. Comparative effectiveness of situational programming, financial pay-offs, and group pressure in weight reduction. *Behavior Therapy,* 1974, *5,* 391–400.

Abramson, E. E. A review of behavioral approaches to weight control. *Behaviour Research and Therapy,* 1973, *11,* 547–556.

Abramson, E. E. Behavioral approaches to weight control: An updated review. *Behaviour Research and Therapy,* 1977, *15,* 355–363.

Adams, N., Ferguson, J., Stunkard, A. J., & Agras, W. S. The eating behavior of obese and nonobese women. *Behaviour Research and Therapy,* 1978, *16,* 225–232.

Alderman, M. H. & Schoenbaum, E. E. Detection and treatment of hypertension at the work site. *New England Journal of Medicine,* 1975, *293,* 65–68.

Aragona, J., Cassady, J., & Drabman, R. S. Treating overweight children through parental training and contingency contracting. *Journal of Applied Behavior Analysis,* 1975, *8,* 269–278.

Ashby, W. A., & Wilson, G. T. Behavior therapy for obesity: Booster sessions and long-term maintenance of weight loss. *Behaviour Research and Therapy,* 1977, *15,* 451–464.

Balch, P., & Ross, A. W. Predicting success in weight reduction as a function of locus of control: A unidimensional and multidimensional approach. *Journal of Consulting and Clinical Psychology,* 1975, *43,* 119.

Bandura, A. On paradigms and recycled ideologies. *Cognitive Therapy and Research,* 1978, *2,* 79–103.

Beck, A. T. *Cognitive therapy and the emotional disorders.* New York: International Universities Press, 1976.

Bellack, A. S. Behavioral treatment for obesity: Appraisal and recommendations. In M. Hersen, R. M. Eisler, & P. M. Miller (Eds.), *Progress in behavior modification,* Vol. 4. New York: Academic Press, 1977.

Bellack, A. S., Rozensky, R., & Schwartz, J. S. A comparison of two forms of self monitoring in a behavioral weight reduction program. *Behavior Therapy*, 1974, *5*, 523–530.

Benecke, W. M., Paulsen, B., McReynolds, W. T., Lutz, R., & Kohrs, M. B. Long-term results of two behavior modification weight loss programs using nutritionists as therapists. *Behaviour Research and Therapy*, 1978, *9*, 501–507.

Bistrian, B. R., Blackburn, G. L., Flatt, J. P., Sizer, J., Scrimshaw, N. S. & Sherman, M. Nitrogen metabolism and insulin requirements in obese diabetic adults on a protein sparing modified fast. *Diabetes*, 1976, *25*, 494–504.

Bray, G. A. *The obese patient*. Philadelphia: Saunders, 1976.

Brightwell, D. R., & Naylor, C. S. Effects of a combined behavioral and pharmacologic program on weight loss. *International Journal of Obesity*, 1979, *3*, 141–148.

Brownell, K. D. Assessment in the treatment of eating disorders. In D. H. Barlow (Ed.), *Behavioral assessment of adult disorders*. New York: Guilford, 1980.

Brownell, K. D., & Stunkard, A. J. Behavior therapy and behavior change: Uncertainties in programs for weight control. *Behaviour Research and Therapy*, 1978, *16*, 301.

Brownell, K. D., & Stunkard, A. J. Behavioral treatment for obese children and adults. In A. J. Stunkard (Ed.), *Obesity*. Philadelphia: Saunders, 1980.

Brownell, K. D., & Stunkard, A. J. Couples training, pharmacotherapy, and behavior therapy in the treatment of obesity. *Archives of General Psychiatry*, 1981, *38*, 1224–1229.

Brownell, K. D., Heckerman, C. L., Westlake, R. J., Hayes, S. C., & Monti, P. M. The effect of couples training and partner cooperativeness in the behavioral treatment of obesity. *Behaviour Research and Therapy*, 1978, *16*, 323–333.

Brownell, K. D., Stunkard, A. J., & Albaum, J. M. Evaluation and modification of activity patterns in the natural environment. *American Journal of Psychiatry*, 1980, *137*, 1540–1545.

Brownell, K. D., Kelman, J. H., & Stunkard, A. J. The treatment of obese children with and without their mothers: Changes in weight and blood pressure. Submitted for publication.

Chirico, A. M., & Stunkard, A. J. Physical activity and human obesity. *New England Journal of Medicine*, 1960, *263*, 935–940.

Coates, T. J. The efficacy of a multicomponent self-control program in modifying the eating habits and weight of three obese adolescents. Unpublished doctoral dissertation, Stanford University, 1977.

Craighead, L. W., Stunkard, A. J., & O'Brien, R. Behavior therapy and pharmacotherapy of obesity. *Archives of General Psychiatry*, 1981, *38*, 763–768.

Dahlkoetter, J., Callahan, E. J., & Linton, J. Obesity and the unbalanced energy equation: Exercise versus eating habit change. *Journal of Consulting and Clinical Psychology*, 1979, *47*, 898–905.

Epstein, L. H., Masek, B., & Marshall, W. Pre-lunch exercise and lunch-time caloric intake. *The Behavior Therapist*, 1978, *1*, 15.

Farquhar, J. W., Maccoby, N., Wood, P. D., & Alexander, J. Community education for cardiovascular health. *The Lancet*, June 4, 1977, 1192–1195.

Ferguson, J. M. *Learning to eat: Leaders manual and patients manual*. Palo Alto: Bull Publishing, 1975.

Ferster, C. B., Nurnberger, J. I., & Levitt, E. B. The control of eating. *Journal of Mathetics*, 1962, *1*, 87–109.

Ferstl, R., Jokusch, V., & Brengelmann, J. C. Die verhaltungstherapeutische Behandlung des Übergewichts. *International Journal of Health Education*, 1975, *18*, 3–20.

Foreyt, J. P., & Kennedy, W. A. Treatment of overweight by aversion therapy. *Behaviour Research and Therapy*, 1971, *9*, 29–34.

Fremouw, W. J., & Zitter, R. E. Individual and couple behavioral contracting for weight reduction and maintenance. *The Behavior Therapist*, 1980, *3*, 15–16.

Garb, J. R., & Stunkard, A. J. A further assessment of the effectiveness of TOPS in the control of obesity. *Archives of Internal Medicine*, 1974, *134*, 716–720.

Garrow, J. *Energy balance and obesity in man*. New York: Elsevier, 1974.

Genuth, S. M., Vertes, V., & Hazleton, I. Supplemented fasting in the treatment of obesity. In G. Bray (Ed.), *Recent advances in obesity research*, Vol. 2. London: Newman, 1978.

Goldblatt, P. B., Moore, M. E., & Stunkard, A. J. Social factors in obesity. *Journal of the American Medical Association*, 1965, *192*, 1039–1044.

Grinker, J., Hirsch, J., & Levin, B. The affective response of obese patients to weight reduction: A differentiation based on age at onset of obesity. *Psychosomatic Medicine*, 1973, *35*, 57–63.

Gross, I., Wheeler, M., & Hess, R. The treatment of obesity in adolescents using behavioral self-control. *Clinical Pediatrics*, 1976, *15*, 920–924.

Gwinup, G. Effect of exercise alone on the weight of obese women. *Archives of Internal Medicine*, 1975, *135*, 676–680.

Hagen, R. L. Group therapy vs. bibliotherapy in weight reduction. *Behavior Therapy*, 1974, *5*, 224–234.

Hagen, R. L., Foreyt, J. P., & Durham, T. W. The dropout problem: Reducing attrition in obesity research. *Behavior Therapy*, 1976, *7*, 463–471.

Hall, S. M. Self-control and therapist control in the behavioral treatment of overweight women. *Behaviour Research and Therapy*, 1972, *10*, 59–68.

Hall, S. M. Behavioral treatment of obesity: A two year follow-up. *Behaviour Research and Therapy*, 1973, *11*, 647–648.

Hall, S. M., Hall, R. G., Hanson, R. W., & Borden, B. L. Permanence of two self-managed treatments of overweight in university and community populations. *Journal of Consulting and Clinical Psychology*, 1974, *42*, 781–786.

Hall, S. M., Hall, R. G., Borden, B. L., & Hanson, R. W. Follow-up strategies in the treatment of overweight. *Behaviour Research and Therapy*, 1975, *13*, 167–172.

Hamilton, C. L. Problems of refeeding after starvation in the rat. *Annals of the New York Academy of Science*, 1969, *157*, 1004.

Hanson, R. W., Borden, B. L., Hall, S. M., & Hall, R. G. Use of programmed instruction in teaching self-management skills to overweight adults. *Behavior Therapy*, 1976, *7*, 366–373.

Harris, M. B. Self-directed program for weight control:

A pilot study. *Journal of Abnormal Psychology*, 1969, *74*, 263–270.

Harris, M. B., & Bruner, C. G. A comparison of self-control and a contract procedure for weight control. *Behaviour Research and Therapy*, 1971, *9*, 347–354.

Harris, M. B., & Hallbauer, E. S. Self-directed weight control through eating and exercise. *Behaviour Research and Therapy*, 1973, *11*, 523–529.

Israel, A. C., & Saccone, A. J. Follow-up effects of choice of mediator and target of reinforcement on weight loss. *Behavior Therapy*, 1979, *10*, 260–265.

Jeffery, R. W., Wing, R. R., & Stunkard, A. J. Behavioral treatment of obesity: The state of the art in 1976. *Behavior Therapy*, 1978, *9*, 189–199.

Jeffrey, D. B. A comparison of the effects of external control and self control on the modification and maintenance of weight. *Journal of Abnormal Psychology*, 1974, *83*, 404–410.

Jordan, H. A., Levitz, L. S., & Kimbrell, G. M. *Eating is okay*. New York: Rawson, 1976.

Keesey, R. E. The regulation of body weight: A set-point analysis. In A. J. Stunkard (Ed.), *Obesity*, Philadelphia: Saunders, 1980.

Kingsley, R. G., & Shapiro, J. A comparison of three behavioral programs for the control of obesity in children. *Behavior Therapy*, 1977, *8*, 30–36.

Kingsley, R. G., & Wilson, G. T. Behavior therapy for obesity: A comparative investigation of long-term efficacy. *Journal of Consulting and Clinical Psychology*, 1977, *4*, 288–298.

Kissileff, K. S., Jordan, H. H., & Levitz, L. S. Eating habits of obese and normal weight humans. *International Journal of Obesity*, 1978, *2*, 379.

Krotkiewski, M., Garellick, G., Sjöström, Persson, G., Bjurö, G. T., & Sullivan, L. Fat cell number, resting metabolic rate, mean heart rate and insulin elevation while seeing and smelling food as predictors of slimming. *Metabolism*, 1980, *19*, 1003–1012.

Leon, G. R. Current directions in the treatment of obesity. *Psychological Bulletin*, 1976, *83*, 557–578.

Leon, G. R., Roth, L., & Hewitt, M. I. Eating patterns, satiety, and self-control behavior of obese persons during weight reduction. *Obesity and Bariatric Medicine*, 1977, *6*, 172–181.

Levitz, L., & Stunkard, A. J. A therapeutic coalition for obesity: Behavior modification and patient self-help. *American Journal of Psychiatry*, 1974, *131*, 423–427.

Lindner, P. G., & Blackburn, G. L. Multidisciplinary approach to obesity utilizing fasting modified by protein-sparing therapy. *Obesity and Bariatric Medicine*, 1976, *5*, 198–216.

Loro, A. D., Fisher, E. B., & Levenkron, J. C. Comparison of established and innovative weight-reduction treatment procedures. *Journal of Applied Behavior Analysis*, 1979, *12*, 141–155.

Mahoney, M. J. Self-reward and self-monitoring techniques for weight control. *Behavior Therapy*, 1974, *5*, 48–57.

Mahoney, M. J. Behavior modification in the treatment of obesity. *Psychiatric Clinics of North America*, 1978, *1*, 651–660.

Mahoney, M. J., & Mahoney, K. *Permanent weight control*. New York: Norton, 1976.

Mahoney, M. J., Moura, N. G. M., & Wade, T. C. The relative efficacy of self-reward, self-punishment, and self-monitoring techniques for weight loss. *Journal of Consulting and Clinical Psychology*, 1973, *40*, 404–407.

Mayer, J., & Thomas, D. Regulation of food intake and obesity. *Science*, 1967, *156*, 328–337.

McReynolds, W. T., Lutz, R. N., Paulsen, B. K., & Kohrs, M. B. Weight loss resulting from two behavior modification procedures with nutritionists as therapists. *Behavior Therapy*, 1976, *7*, 283–291.

Meichenbaum, D. *Cognitive behavior modification*. New York: Plenum, 1977.

Meyers, A. W., Stunkard, A. J., & Coll, M. Food accessibility and food choice: A test of Schachter's externality hypothesis. *Archives of General Psychiatry*, 1980, *37*, 1133–1135.

Meyers, A. W., Stunkard, A. J., Coll, M., & Cooke, C. J. Stairs, escalators and obesity. *Behavior Modification*, 1980, *4*, 355–359.

Milich, R. S. A critical analysis of Schachter's theory of obesity. *Journal of Abnormal Psychology*, 1975, *84*, 586–588.

Milich, R. S., Anderson, J., & Mills, M. Effects of visual presentation of caloric values on food buying by normal and obese persons. *Perceptual and Motor Skills*, 1976, *42*, 155–162.

Mills, M. J., & Stunkard, A. J. Behavioral changes following surgery for obesity. *American Journal of Psychiatry*, 1976, *133*, 527–531.

Moore, M. E., Stunkard, A. J., & Srole, L. Obesity, social class and mental illness. *Journal of the American Medical Association*, 1962, *181*, 962–966.

Murray, D. C. Treatment of overweight: The relationship between initial weight and weight change during behavior therapy of overweight individuals. Analysis of data from previous studies. *Psychological Reports*, 1975, *37*, 243–248.

O'Neil, P. M., Currey, H. S., Hirsch, A. A., Riddle, F. E., Taylor, C. I., Malcolm, R. J., & Sexauer, J. D., Effects of sex of subject and spouse involvement on weight loss in a behavioral treatment program: A retrospective investigation. *Addictive Behaviors*, 1979, *4*, 167–178.

Öst, L. G., & Götestam, K. G. Behavioral and pharmacological treatments for obesity: An experimental comparison. *Addictive Behaviors*, 1976, *1*, 331–338.

Pearce, J. W. The role of spouse involvement in the behavioral treatment of obese women. Unpublished doctoral dissertation, University of Manitoba, 1979.

Penick, S. B., Filion, R., Fox, S., & Stunkard, A. J. Behavior modification in the treatment of obesity. *Psychosomatic Medicine*, 1971, *33*, 49–55.

Puska, P. The North Karelia Project: An example of health promotion in action. In L. Ng (Ed.), *The promotion of health: New trends and perspectives*. New York: Von Nostrand Reinhold, 1981, pp. 317–335.

Report of the WHO Meeting on comprehensive cardiovascular community control programmes, Edmonton, Alberta, Canada, 22–24, November 1978. Divison of Cardiovascular Disease, World Health Organization, Geneva, Switzerland.

Rivinus, T. M., Drummond, T., & Combrinck-Graham, L. A group-behavior treatment program for overweight children: The results of a pilot study. *Pediatric and Adolescent Endocrinology*, 1976, *1*, 212–218.

Rodin, J. The externality theory today. In A. J. Stunkard (Ed.), *Obesity*. Philadelphia: Saunders, 1980.

Romanczyk, R. G. Self-monitoring in the treatment of obesity: Parameters of reactivity. *Behavior Therapy*, 1974, *5*, 531–540.

Romanczyk, R. G., Tracey, D. A., Wilson, G. T., & Thorpe, G. L. Behavioral techniques in the treatment of obesity: A comparative analysis. *Behaviour Research and Therapy*, 1973, *11*, 629–640.

Rosenthal, B., Allen, G. J., & Winter, C. Husband involvement in the behavioral treatment of overweight women: Initial effects and long-term follow-up. *International Journal of Obesity*, 1980, *4*, 165–173.

Rosenthal, B. S., & Marx, R. D. Differences in eating patterns of successful and unsuccessful dieters, untreated overweight and normal weight individuals. *Addictive Behaviors*, 1978, *3*, 129–134.

Schachter, S. Some extraordinary facts about obese humans and rats. *American Psychologist*, 1971, *25*, 120–144.

Sclafani, A., & Springer, D. Dietary obesity in adult rats: Similarities to hypothalamic and human obesity syndromes. *Physiology and Behavior*, 1976, *17*, 461–471.

Stalonas, P. M., Johnson, W. G., & Christ, M. Behavior modification for obesity: The evaluation of exercise, contingency management and program adherence. *Journal of Consulting and Clinical Psychology*, 1978, *46*, 463–469.

Stern, J. S., & Johnson, P. R. Spontaneous activity and adipose cellularity in the genetically obese Zucker rat. *Metabolism*, 1977, *26*, 371–380.

Stern, J. S., Dunn, J. R., & Johnson, P. R. Effects of exercise on the development of obesity in the yellow obese mouse. Presented at the Second International Conference on Obesity, Washington, D.C., October 1977.

Stollack, G. E. Weight loss obtained under different experimental procedures. *Psychotherapy: Theory, Research and Practice*, 1967, *4*, 61–64.

Stuart, R. B. Behavioral control of overeating. *Behaviour Research and Therapy*, 1967, *5*, 357–365.

Stuart, R. B. A three-dimensional program for the treatment of obesity. *Behaviour Research and Therapy*, 1971, *9*, 177–186.

Stuart, R. B. Behavioral control of overeating: A status Report. G. A. Bray (Ed.), *Obesity in perspective*, Washington, D.C.: DHEW Publication No. (NIH, 75-708), 1976.

Stuart, R. B. Self-help group approach to self-management. In R. B. Stuart (Ed.), *Behavioral self-management*. New York: Brunner/Mazel, 1977.

Stuart, R. B. *Act thin, stay thin*. New York: Norton, 1978.

Stuart, R. B., & Davis, B. *Slim chance in a fat world: Behavioral control of obesity*. Champaign, Ill.: Research Press, 1972.

Stunkard, A. J. From explanation to action in psychosomatic medicine: The case of obesity. *Psychosomatic Medicine*, 1975, *37*, 195–236.

Stunkard, A. J. Statement on the Pennsylvania Community Health Intervention Project. *Congressional Record* 96-4: 32–45, March 21, 1979.

Stunkard, A. J., & Brownell, K. D. Work site treatment for obesity. *American Journal of Psychiatry*, 1980, *137*, 252–253.

Stunkard, A. J., & Burt, V. Obesity and the body image: II. Age at onset of disturbances in the body image. *American Journal of Psychiatry*, 1967, *123*, 1443–1447.

Stunkard, A. J., & Kaplan, D. Eating in public places: A review of reports of the direct observation of eating behavior. *International Journal of Obesity*, 1977, *1*, 89–101.

Stunkard, A. J., & Mahoney, M. J. Behavioral treatment of the eating disorders. In H. Leitenberg (Ed.), *Handbook of behavior modification and behavior therapy*. Englewood Cliffs, N.J.: Prentice-Hall, 1976.

Stunkard, A. J., & McLaren-Hume, M. The results of treatment of obesity: A review of the literature and report of a series. *Archives of Internal Medicine*, 1959, *103*, 79–85.

Stunkard, A. J., & Penick, S. B. Behavior modification in the treatment of obesity: The problem of maintaining weight loss. *Archives of General Psychiatry*, 1979, *36*, 801–806.

Stunkard, A. J., & Pestka, J. The physical activity of obese girls. *American Journal of Diseases of Children*, 1962, *103*, 812–817.

Stunkard, A. J., & Rush, A. J. Dieting and depression reexamined: A critical review of reports of untoward responses during weight reduction for obesity. *Annals of Internal Medicine*, 1974, *81*, 526–533.

Stunkard, A. J., Levine, H., & Fox, S. The management of obesity: Patient self-help and medical treatment. *Archives of Internal Medicine*, 1970, *125*, 1067–1072.

Stunkard, A. J., Coll, M., Lundquist, S., & Meyers, A. Obesity and eating style. *Archives of General Psychiatry*, 1980, *37*, 1127–1129.

Van Itallie, T. B. Liquid protein mayhem. *Journal of the American Medical Association*, 1978, *240*, 144–145.

Volkmar, F. R., Stunkard, A. J., Woolston, J., & Bailey, R. A. High attrition rates in commercial weight reduction programs. *Archives of Internal Medicine*, 1981, *141*, 426–428.

Walker, B. R., Ballard, I. M., & Gold, J. A. A multicentre study comparing Mazindol and placebo in obese patients. *Journal of Internal Medicine and Research*, 1977, *5*, 85–90.

Waxman, M., & Stunkard, A. J. Caloric intake and expenditure of obese boys. *Journal of Pediatrics*, 1980, *96*, 187–193.

Weiss, A. R. A behavioral approach to the treatment of adolescent obesity. *Behavior Therapy*, 1977, *8*, 720–726.

Weisz, G., & Bucher, B. Involving husbands in treatment of obesity—Effects on weight loss, depression and marital satisfaction, *Behavior Therapy*, 1980, *11*, 643–650.

Wheeler, M. E., & Hess, K. W. Treatment of juvenile obesity by successive approximation control of eating. *Journal of Behavior Therapy and Experimental Psychiatry*, 1976, *7*, 235–241.

Wilson, G. T. Behavior modification and the treatment of obesity. In A. J. Stunkard (Ed.), *Obesity*. Philadelphia: Saunders, 1980.

Wilson, G. T., & Brownell, K. D. Behavior therapy for obesity: Including family members in the treatment process. *Behavior Therapy*, 1978, *9*, 943–945.

Wing, R. R., & Jeffery, R. W. Outpatient treatments of obesity: A comparison of methodology and clinical results. *International Journal of Obesity,* 1979, *3,* 261–279.

Wollersheim, J. P. The effectiveness of group therapy based upon learning principles in the treatment of overweight women. *Journal of Abnormal Psychology,* 1970, *76,* 462–474.

Wooley, S. C., Wooley, O. W., & Dyrenforth, S. R. Theoretical, practical and social issues in behavioral treatments of obesity. *Journal of Applied Behavior Analysis,* 1979, *12,* 3–25.

Zitter, R. E., & Fremouw, R. E. Individual versus partner consequation for weight loss. *Behavior Therapy,* 1978, *9,* 808 813.

CHAPTER 19

Current Trends in the Modification of Cigarette Dependence

Edward Lichtenstein and Richard A. Brown

Introduction

Cigarette smoking is the largest preventable cause of death in the United States. Each year, there are 80,000 deaths from lung cancer, 22,000 deaths from other cancers, up to 225,000 deaths from cardiovascular disease, and more than 19,000 deaths from pulmonary disease, all causally related to cigarette smoking. A 30- to 35-year-old two-pack-a-day smoker has a mortality rate twice that of a nonsmoker. The annual cost of health damage resulting from smoking is estimated to be $27 billion in medical care, absenteeism, decreased work productivity, and accidents. Compared with nonsmokers, smokers compile 81 million excess days of lost work each year and 145 million excess days of disability. These facts, compiled by the U.S. Surgeon General (U.S. Department of Health, Education, and Welfare, 1979), but also applicable to most Western nations, provide powerful reasons for the development and delivery of effective and economical smoking-control programs.

There is evidence that the data on the health consequences of smoking have affected the attitude and motivation of current smokers. Survey data indicate that about half of current smokers want to quit and have tried to do so without success (Gallup Opinion Index, 1974). In another survey, fully 61% of current smokers reported making at least one serious attempt to quit, and it was estimated that 90% of current smokers have either made an effort to stop smoking or would do so were an easy method available (U.S. Public Health Service, 1976). Clearly, there is a market for an effective and economical smoking-cessation technology.

Because of the importance of this issue, there has been a marked increase in research on smoking and smoking cessation, as well as an explosion of review papers. More than 20 papers reviewing behavioral research on smoking control have been published (Bernstein, 1969; Bernstein & Glasgow, 1979; Bernstein & McAlister, 1976; Best & Bloch, 1979; Bradshaw, 1973; Glasgow & Bernstein, 1981;

Edward Lichtenstein and Richard A. Brown • Department of Psychology, University of Oregon, Eugene, Oregon 97403.

Hunt & Bespalec, 1974; Keutzer, Lichtenstein, & Mees, 1968; Lichtenstein & Brown, 1980; Lichtenstein & Danaher, 1976; Lichtenstein & Keutzer, 1971; McAlister, 1975; Pechacek, 1979; Pechacek & Danaher, 1979; Pechacek & McAlister, 1979; Raw, 1976; Schwartz, 1969, 1979; Schwartz & Rider, 1977, 1978; Thompson, 1978).

Given this extensive prior scholarship, we have chosen to emphasize significant trends in research since 1975 and the implications of this work for clinical work with smokers. In particular, our departure point is a previous review by Lichtenstein and Danaher (1976), which comprehensively reviewed smoking cessation work through the mid-1970s. We begin with a description of the natural history of smoking behavior and an analysis of why it is so dependency-producing. Recent developments in the continuing debate over the relative contribution of pharmacological and psychosocial variables in the maintenance and modification of smoking are reviewed. The assessment of smoking behavior, especially the data on physiological measurement, is then discussed. The bulk of the paper considers the literature on smoking cessation methods. Controlled smoking, alternative means of delivering services (e.g., media, self-help books, and the prevention of smoking) are also considered. The final sections discuss implications for research and clinical applications.

The Natural History of Cigarette Smoking

The complexity of cigarette smoking can be appreciated by considering its natural history. Table 1 depicts the four stages fo a smoker's career: initiation, maintenance, cessation, and resumption or relapse. In Table 1 are also listed the main factors thought to be involved in each of the stages. Some factors are more strongly supported by experimental or correlational data, others are more speculative. It can be seen that psychosocial factors are the determinants of starting to smoke. The pharmacological effects of nicotine however, are crucial in the continuation of smoking, along with learned psychosocial factors including cognitions. The decision to quit and success

in so doing are again largely a psychosocial matter. The resumption of smoking, or relapse, is a phenomenon about which we know relatively little, but it appears that withdrawal symptoms (Shiffman, 1979), stress, social pressure, and the abstinence violation effect (Marlatt & Gordon, 1980) are key factors. That different processes are involved at the different stages has important implications for intervention.

The Tenaciousness of Cigarette Smoking

It is very difficult to quit smoking, but just how difficult cannot be precisely stated. British data indicate that only one in four smokers succeeds in stopping permanently before the age of 60 (Lee, 1976). United States data indicate that the majority of smokers wish that they could quit and have tried unsuccessfully to do so (U.S. Public Health Service, 1976). More information is available on cessation rates for persons seeking help from smoking control programs. It is likely that program participants are the more "difficult" cases, since they have invariably failed in their unaided efforts to quit. Our review of the literature indicates that at six months or one year after treatment, the average participant in the average smoking-control program has a 15–20% chance of being abstinent. More successful programs report abstinence rates of 30–40%. Anything better than that is very good indeed.

It is the interaction of the pharmacological and the psychosocial factors noted in Column 2 of Table 1 that makes smoking so dependency-producing. Smoking delivers nicotine to the brain very quickly, in about seven seconds (Russell, 1976). Much convergent evidence indicates that nicotine is a powerful primary reinforcer (Russell, 1976). Many smokers, especially heavy smokers, appear to smoke in such a way as to regulate their dosage of nicotine (Schachter, 1977, 1978). While the data do not show that nicotine is the necessary and sufficient factor in accounting for smoking behavior, there is no doubt that it is a strong factor for many persons.

Smoking is possible in a wide variety of circumstances and settings. These numerous settings become discriminative for smoking and often later come to serve as learned reinforcers

Table 1. The Natural History of Smoking[a]

Starting→	Continuing→	Stopping→	Resuming
Availability	Nicotine	Health	Withdrawal symptoms
Curiosity	Immediate positive	Expense	Stress and frustration
Rebelliousness	consequences	Social pressure	Social pressure
Anticipation of adulthood	Signals (cues) in environs	Self-mastery	Alcohol consumption
Social confidence	Avoiding negative effects	Aesthetics	Abstinence violation
Modeling: peers, siblings, parents	(withdrawal)	Example to others	effect
Psychosocial	Physiological + Psychosocial	Psychosocial	Psychosocial + Physiological

[a] Adapted from Lichtenstein and Brown (1980).

for smoking An urge is subjectively experienced when these situations are encountered. Smoking then comes to be reinforced by the enjoyment of the oral, manual, and respiratory manipulations involved in the process of lighting, puffing, and handling cigarettes; by the pleasure and relaxation associated with using alcohol, finishing a good meal, or having a cup of coffee; and by the perceived diminution of unpleasant affective states of anxiety, tension, boredom, or fatigue. For some smokers, the combination of nicotine and psychosocial learning produces such a dependency that going without a cigarette is highly unpleasant. Smoking is then further reinforced by the reduction of withdrawal or anticipated withdrawal reactions. Learning of this sort makes it possible for the same smoker to reach for a cigarette when relaxed, bored, tense, upset, tired, or in need of a lift.

Another significant factor in the tenacity of the smoking habit is the sheer number of trials, or the amount of practice: 20 cigarettes a day adds up to about 7,300 cigarettes a year. Each trial—in fact, each puff—is an occasion for experiencing one or more of the rewards just noted. A fourth factor is the encouragement and modeling of smoking provided by the environment in the form of other smokers as well as cigarette advertising.

In sum, cigarette smoking is a highly practiced, overlearned behavior reinforced by both physiological events and a wide variety of psychosocial events. It is cued by a large array of environmental and internal stimuli and is socially and legally acceptable in most set-tings. No other substance can provide so many kinds of reinforcement, is so readily and cheaply available, and can be used in so many settings and situations. While there are numerous immediate positive consequences, the negative consequences are delayed and probabilistic.

This analysis of the complexity and tenacity of smoking provides a background for evaluating treatment effectiveness and also sets the stage for a review of recent research on the relative roles of nicotine and psychosocial variables in maintaining the smoking habit.

Pharmacological Influences on Smoking

There is growing evidence that pharmacological factors play a significant role in the process of cigarette dependence. While cigarette smoke contains a number of chemical compounds, it is generally believed that nicotine is the major reinforcing component in cigarette smoking (Jaffe & Kanzler, 1979; Jarvik, 1979a; Russell, 1976; Schachter, 1978). Russell (1974b, 1976) and Schachter (1978) have generally been the two major proponents of a nicotine-dependence model of cigarette smoking, and considerable research has been conducted in this area since Russell's (1974b) colorful and oft-quoted assertion that "there is little doubt that if it were not for the nicotine in tobacco smoke, people would be little more inclined to smoke than they are to blow bubbles or light sparklers" (p. 793).

Addiction or Dependence

Is tobacco smoking addicting or dependence-producing? Although the terms are often used interchangeably, their definitions are not well agreed upon, thus lending an element of confusion to this controversy. In conventional usage, the term *addiction* refers to a physiological process characterized by tolerance and withdrawal. Jarvik (1979b) defined tolerance as "a decreasing response to repeated administrations of the same dose of a drug, or . . . increasing doses in order to elicit the same response" (p. 150) and asserted that tolerance to tobacco products has been "clearly demonstrated" both in humans and in animals.

A tobacco withdrawal syndrom has been identified (Shiffman, 1979; Jaffe & Jarvik, 1978). Shiffman (1979) acknowledged that there is much individual variability in withdrawal but concluded that some consistent patterns emerge. Objective indicators of the withdrawal syndrome include changes in EEG and cardiovascular function, decrements in psychomotor performance, and weight gain. The major subjective symptoms are irritability, anxiety, inability to concentrate, disturbances of arousal (e.g., insomnia), and especially the intense craving for cigarettes that is nearly always reported. Shiffman observed that "although reports vary regarding the prevalence, severity and course of these symptoms, there is nevertheless sufficient consensus to justify the conclusion that a withdrawal syndrome occurs in habitual tobacco users" (p. 178). Thus, by most standard definitions, cigarette smoking qualifies as an addiction in that both tolerance and withdrawal have been demonstrated.

Shiffman noted that the duration of the withdrawal syndrome is quite variable and that "no definitive estimate is yet available" (p. 168). The degree of deprivation appears to be an important variable. Totally abstinent smokers show a marked decrease in withdrawal symptoms during the first week of abstinence and then level off or may even show increases in symptomatology (Shiffman & Jarvik, 1976). Partially abstinent smokers, on the other hand, do not show this early sharp decrease in withdrawal and seem to maintain withdrawal symptoms at close to their high initial levels (Coleman, Hughes, Epstein, & Ossip, 1979; Shiffman, 1979). The relative ineffectiveness of gradual withdrawal as a method of smoking cessation is probably related to this phenomenon.

Clinical experience indicates that withdrawal reactions, especially cravings, may occur intermittently for long periods post-abstinence but are typically associated with specific cues or situations. These are typically situations that have been discriminitive for smoking in the past but have not been encountered very recently. A short questionnaire has been developed to measure withdrawal reactions (Shiffman & Jarvik, 1976). While this instrument is not yet well validated, it can be useful both to investigators and to clinicians who might want to use the information to make adjustments or modifications in treatment programs.

The term *dependence,* on the other hand, is often used to refer to either a psychologically or a physiologically mediated state. However, as Russell (1978) noted, this is a false dichotomy, since the two are largely interrelated. He prefers to use the terms *dependence* and *addiction* interchangeably to apply to "a state in which the urge or need for something is so strong that the individual suffers or has great difficulty in going without it, and in extreme cases cannot stop doing it, or using it, when it is available" (p. 101). This definition tends to focus largely on the strength of the urge or need to indulge, and it is capable of incorporating physiological, psychological, and behavioral factors into the analysis. Dependence thereby becomes a matter of degree, with smokers falling along a continuum from more to less dependent, with the recognition that multiple factors contribute to the dependency. This conceptualization seems to us to be a more functional position regarding the addiction–dependency issue, and one that has greater utility for the clinical-empirical study of cigarette smoking as a multifaceted behavior.

Nicotine Regulation

Schachter (1977, 1978) has been a strong proponent of a model that suggests that smokers regulate (or titrate) their level of smoking to maintain a certain level of nicotine in the body. This "set-point" model is generally thought to imply the existence of a "nicostat" mechanism that monitors nicotine and regulates intake to keep nicotine at a constant level.

Supportive evidence comes from a series of studies by Schachter and his colleagues. Schachter (1977) found that smokers increased their smoking rate (heavy smokers by 25.3%; light smokers by 17.5%) when given cigarettes of lowered nicotine content, and he concluded that these increases served to keep smokers' nicotine at a roughly constant level. Schachter, Kozlowski, and Silverstein (1977) suggested an internal mechanism for the detection of bodily nicotine levels and the consequent regulation of smoking: the urinary secretion of nicotine. When the urine is acid, four or five times as much nicotine is excreted as when the urine is alkaline. These investigators hypothesized that increasing the acidity of the urine would increase smoking, relative to when urinary pH was unchanged or made more basic. When they manipulated urinary pH by administering acidifying or alkalizing agents as compared with placebo, smoking rates were altered in the hypothesized directions.

Subsequent studies in the series were intended to evaluate the possibility that the urinary pH excretion may serve as a mediating mechanism to account for much of the variation in smoking rate previously attributed to psychological factors—particularly stress. Party going was shown to increase smoking rate as well as to increase the acidity of the urine (Silverstein, Kozlowski, & Schachter, 1977). Similarly, stress was shown to lead to increased smoking and acidification of the urine across multiple settings (Schachter, Silverstein, Kozlowski, Herman, & Liebling, 1977). Finally, when stress and urinary pH were independently manipulated, smoking rate was shown to vary with urinary pH rather than with stress (Schachter, Silverstein, & Perlick, 1977), a finding leading to the conclusion that the "urinary pH mechanism is the crucial biochemical mediator of the stress-smoking relation" (p. 39).

While Schachter's work is frequently cited and identified with the nicotine titration hypothesis, it is only one of several approaches to this problem. Jaffe and Kanzler (1979) described various methodologies of nicotine titration studies as including those in which (1) nicotine is administered and the number of cigarettes smoked, the number of puffs taken, and/or the degree of satisfaction is assessed; (2) the nicotine content of the tobacco is altered and the resulting smoking patterns and/or plasma nicotine levels are measured; and (3) various drugs are administered that alter the pharmacological effects of nicotine or its disposition, and subsequent changes in smoking behavior and psychological effects of smoking are observed. While the majority of these studies suggested that some regulation of nicotine intake was taking place (e.g., Goldfarb, Gritz, Jarvik, & Stolerman, 1976; Herman, 1974; Jarvik, Glick, & Nakamura, 1970; Kozlowski, Jarvik, & Gritz, 1975; Lucchesi, Schuster, & Emley, 1967; Russell, Wilson, Patel, Cole, & Feyerabend, 1973; Schachter, 1977), only one study indicated precise regulation (Ashton & Watson, 1970), and several do not support the nicotine titration hypothesis (e.g., Forbes, Robinson, Hanley, & Colburn, 1976; Kumar, Cooke, Lader, & Russell, 1977).

Admittedly, these data are difficult to reconcile parsimoniously. Schachter (1979) has referred to the data in support of nicotine addiction–regulation as "flimsy," since only one study indicates precise regulation consistent with the set-point–nicostat conceptualization and since many smokers are "blatant exceptions," in that they are able to refrain from smoking at various times and in various situations despite their plasma-level nicotine. Indeed, many smokers maintain low levels of cigarette consumption on a long-standing basis. Schachter recognized the existence of these "nonaddicted" smokers as opposed to the majority of the "addicted" smokers, thus invoking an individual-differences explanation of the conflicting data. He believes that nonaddicted smokers who attempt to control their smoking will show less obvious manifestations of addiction (i.e., withdrawal effects). Thus, he asserted that the key to understanding nicotine addiction rests in the study of nonaddicted smokers and of the withdrawal syndrome.

Russell (1978) noted that self-regulation downward to avoid excessive nicotine intake may be more "sensitive and complete" then self-regulation upward to avoid reduced nicotine intake. Titration data indicating smokers' "need" for nicotine could plausibly be interpreted, according to Russell, as showing nicotine to be pharmacologically aversive rather than reinforcing, as is generally assumed. He also recognized the contributions of psychosocial motives to smoking, based on the results of a factor-analytic study (Russell, Peto, & Patel, 1974). Herman and Kozlowski (1979) attempted to reconcile the titration data by proposing a regulatory model of consumption, as opposed to the unitary set-point model. They suggested that smokers regulate nicotine intake within a boundary or range, so as to avoid the aversive excessive nicotine intake at the upper limit and withdrawal effects (also aversive) at the lower limit. They assumed that situational and cognitive factors affect self-regulation within these limits. This model accounts for the imprecision of nicotine titration, as well as allowing for the incorporation of psychosocial factors' affecting consumption. The incompleteness of the nicotine titration model has also been noted by other workers (Jaffe & Kanzler, 1979; Leventhal & Cleary, 1980; Pomerleau, 1979a).

Nevertheless, we can reasonbly conclude that "within limits, heavy smokers do attempt to regulate their plasma nicotine levels by adjusting the rate and amount of tobacco smoked" (Jaffe & Kanzler, 1979, p. 10). Pharmacological factors, therefore, play a significant role in cigarette dependence and should be considered in the development of effective smoking-control strategies. While these factors have heretofore been generally ignored in smoking control work, intervention strategies might deal with dependency in at least three different ways: (1) by helping smokers to lessen their physical reliance on cigarettes through procedures involving gradual weaning to lowered nicotine dosage; (2) by helping to reduce cigarette dependence by nicotine replacement via sources other than smoking; and (3) by providing strategies to help smokers cope with physical withdrawal reactions.

Since there is consensus that there are individual differences in nicotine dependency, the reliable measurement of these differences could have important clinical implications. Two promising developments are scales developed in England (Russell, *et al.*, 1974) and Sweden (Fagerström, 1978, 1980). In the Russell *et al.* study, nicotine dependence emerges as one of two second-order factors in a factor-analytic study. Fagerström's (1978) tolerance scale has been validated against behavioral and physiological (e.g., temperature change) criteria and has predicted response to a nicotine chewing-gum treatment (Fagerström, 1980).

Behavioral Influences on Smoking

Several essentially behavioral accounts of smoking have been offered (e.g., Eysenck, 1973; Hunt & Matarazzo, 1970; Mausner & Platt, 1971; Solomon & Corbit, 1973; Tomkins, 1966). These are efforts to construe smoking within the frameworks of broader psychological theories in the hope that this approach would have heuristic utility for research or clinical application. Several of these models were discussed by Lichtenstein and Danaher (1976), who commented, "While it is too soon to judge the eventual fruitfulness of these approaches, we are currently pessimistic about their clinical utility" (p. 82). We judge this pessimistic prediction to have been relatively accurate and further suggest that psychological models of smoking have had only a limited role in guiding research.

Tomkins's (1966) model relating smoking to affect management is possibly the most influential formulation. It was tested in two studies, both of which classified smokers on the basis of test scores and then observed their smoking behavior under experimentally controlled conditions (e.g., with or without deprivation; pleasant or tense situations). Leventhal and Avis (1976) found support for the pleasure–taste and habit dimensions but not for the addiction factor. Adesso and Glad (1978) found no support for any of the three dimensions studied: positive affect, negative affect, or social stimulation. While self-report questionnaires can reliably classify subjects along Tomkins's dimensions (Adesso & Glad, 1978; Kozlowski, 1979; Leventhal & Avis, 1976; Russell *et al.*

1974), the relationship of the classifications to smoking behavior or smoking cessation remains unclear.

Pomerleau (1979a) has provided a succinct summary of the social learning account of smoking and has also attempted to integrate social learning principles into a broader psychological model (Pomerleau, 1979b). The heuristic value of this formulation remains to be evaluated. The thrust of recent behavioral accounts of smoking, however, is heavily cognitive, paralleling developments in the broader domain of behavior therapy.

Cognitive-Behavioral Approaches

Bandura (1977) suggested that two types of expectations, efficacy and outcome, mediate behavior change. In relation to smoking, efficacy expectations refer to a person's belief or confidence that she or he can cope with formerly smoking-inducing situations without smoking. Outcome expectations reflect beliefs that quitting smoking will lead to certain benefits, such as improved physical health and longer life. Pechacek and Danaher (1979), in a cognitive-behavioral analysis of smoking, pointed out that efficacy and outcome expectancies can vary independently, yielding various combinations of the two within an individual at any given time. They equate one particular combination: high outcome expectations (valuing cessation highly) and low self-efficacy (doubting one's ability to quit successfully), with a learned helplessness pattern of responding. This combination may, in fact, affect many smokers who are aware of the health risks involved and would prefer to quit, yet who continue to smoke (Pechachek & Danaher, 1979).

While such behavior may seem irrational or self-destructive, Eiser and Sutton (1977) have suggested that it may be the result of a "subjectively rational decision," when one recognizes that the smoker's choice is not between smoking and quitting, but between smoking and *trying* to quit. Smoking may thus represent the more cautious alternative, when one considers the personal costs involved in failing to quit after a serious attempt to do so.

Marlatt (Marlatt, 1978; Marlatt & Gordon, 1980) has proposed a cognitive-behavioral model of the relapse process in addictive behavior that builds on self-efficacy theory. This model suggests that one's ability to cope with a high risk situation determines one's probability of success or failure in maintaining treatment gains. If someone who has recently quit smoking finds himself or herself in a high-risk situation (e.g., drinking beer with friends who are smoking) and executes an effective coping response (e.g., responding assertively in the face of social pressure to smoke), the result is an increase in self-efficacy and perceived control, and a decrease in the probability of relapse. On the other hand, the inability to make an effective coping response results in decreased self-efficacy and perceived control. Decreased self-efficacy, combined with positive expectations about the effects of smoking (e.g., "a cigarette would taste good right now"), heightens the probability of an initial abstinence violation or "slip."

If the person does slip and smoke a cigarette, Marlatt's model predicts that two consequences will combine to further increase the probability of a full-blown relapse: the initial reinforcing effect of smoking, and a negative cognitive-affective reaction to the slip, termed the *abstinence violation effect*. The abstinence violation effect consists of two components; (1) guilt or cognitive dissonance, as the smoking episode is discrepant with the person's new self-image as a nonsmoker and (2) a personal attribution that the slip was due to personal weakness or lack of willpower. Thus, increased positive expectancies for smoking combine with further decreases in self-efficacy and perceived control, to enhance the probability of a full-blown relapse. Treatment applications of this theory are reviewed in the maintenance section of this paper.

In our own laboratory, Condiotte and Lichtenstein (1981) demonstrated a strong correspondence between clients' self-reported efficacy expectations and the maintenance of treatment gains, lending support to Bandura's formulations. Furthermore, posttreatment efficacy self-ratings regarding potential smoking (relapse) situations were predictive of actual relapse situations (i.e., subjects were accurate predictors of their own relapse situations). Consistent with Marlatt's description of the abstinence violation effect, those subjects who had a complete relapse generally experienced mild to severe guilt reactions and reported decreases in self-efficacy following their first abstinence violation.

Bandura and Marlatt have provided integrative and complementary accounts of the mechanisms underlying treatment successes and failures in smoking cessation. Both models offer plausible and testable conceptualizations, which are likely to generate future research.

Other cognitive variables have been regarded as important to the study of smoking cessation. Kreitler, Shahar, and Kreitler (1976) applied to smoking a cognitive orientation theory that assumes that meanings and beliefs guide behavior. A cognitive orientation measure sampling four cognitive contents with regard to smoking (beliefs about norms, beliefs about goals, beliefs about self, and general beliefs) was found to be predictive of subsequent smoking reduction at posttreatment and short-term follow-up. Sjöberg and Johnson (1978) have argued for the importance of volition or will in the analysis of smoking. Specifically, they have argued that breakdowns of the will are due to "shortsighted and twisted reasoning" (i.e., cognitive distortions) resulting from mood pressure due to various stressors. Thus, rational arguments against smoking may be abandoned in the face of emotional stress. This type of process would appear to be implicated in Marlatt's abstinence violation effect. While Sjöberg and Johnson's approach was nonempirical, they reported that interview data from students attempting to quit smoking were consistent with the theory in 9 of 10 cases.

Environmental Determinants of Smoking

A standard part of nearly every behavioral smoking-control program is training in the self-management or stimulus control of smoking. Usually starting from self-monitoring data, smokers are trained to discriminate the cues or signals that elicit their smoking and later to use this information as a way of reducing, stopping, or coping with urges to smoke. Implicit in this approach is the notion that environmental stimuli are discriminative for smoking. There is, however, surprisingly little empirical

evidence that cigarette smoking is reinforced behavior or that it is under environmental discriminative control. Only recently has there been any systematic work on environmental determinants.

Casual observation, as well as clinical work with smokers, suggests that smoking is related to alcohol and coffee consumption. Experimental data confirm these relationships. The smoking behavior of detoxified alcoholics was observed in a residential laboratory setting under conditions of ethanol or placebo solution consumption. Ethanol consumption was found to increase smoking from 26% to 170% in the five subjects observed, and the ethanol effect was replicated 15 times in a within-subject design (Griffiths, Bigelow, & Liebson, 1976). It would be useful to study the covariation between alcohol consumption and smoking in normal, social drinkers in either laboratory or naturalistic settings. Retrospective interview data indicate that alcohol consumption is frequently associated with relapse (Lichtenstein, Antonuccio, & Rainwater, 1977).

College student smokers were found to increase their rates significantly when provided with coffee (Marshall, Epstein, & Green, 1980). In a second experiment, subjects receiving either caffeinated or decaffeinated coffee smoked more than subjects in a no-coffee or water-drinking control group (Marshall et al., 1980). In a subsequent study, smoking rates were higher whenever coffee was provided independent of whether sodium bicarbonate or ascorbic acid was added (Marshall, Green, Epstein, Rogers, & McCoy, 1980). The latter substances would affect urinary pH levels, which have been shown to affect smoking rate (Schachter, 1977). When coffee was pitted against nicotine—by means of preloading subjects or depriving them—preload affected cigarette smoking, but the coffee manipulation effect was not significant (Ossip & Epstein, 1981).

Everyday observation and clinical experience also point to the importance of another person's smoking as a variable driving the smoking habit. Exposure to other smokers in a small-group setting induced significantly more light smokers than heavy smokers to smoke (Glad & Adesso, 1976). Using a within-subjects design, Antonuccio and Lichtenstein

(1980) found that a high-smoking-rate model (a confederate) induced significantly more smoking compared with a low-smoking-rate model. The authors found no differences, however, between high- and low-rate smokers in susceptibility to the modeling effect. Nor did the modeling manipulation affect topographic variables such as puff rate or puff duration.

Miller, Frederiksen, and Hosford (1979) observed subjects smoking alone or while conversing with two research assistants who did not smoke. Smoking rates were not affected by the absence or presence of others, but the topography of low-rate smokers was significantly affected: light smokers took more frequent and longer puffs when smoking alone than while interacting socially. Heavy smokers were unaffected by the social conditions.

The comparison of heavy and light smokers in these studies relates to the issue of nicotine effects on smoking. The nicotine regulation hypothesis predicts that heavy smokers would be more under the control of internal or pharmacological cues, while light smokers would be more under the control of environmental stimuli. With the exception of the Antonuccio and Lichtenstein study, the data tend to support this hypothesis, as do data from Herman (1974), who found that only light smokers were affected by a saliency manipulation: variations in the illumination of cigarettes available in the room for smoking. The studies thus far reported are consistent with clinical observations that social interaction in general and the presence of other smokers in particular importantly affects smoking behavior.

Measurement of Smoking

In an earlier review, we observed that "With but few exceptions, all smoking control research has relied on self-reports for information about smoking rates" (Lichtenstein & Danaher, 1976, p. 85). It is encouraging to note that this state of affairs is no longer true. Much smoking modification research in the last five years has utilized informants or physiological measurements as ways of validating self-reports. Most service programs, however, continue to rely on self-report.

Abstinence and Rate Data

There are two widely used measures of smoking behavior: rate and abstinence. Rate data typically use days as the unit of time and are often expressed as a percentage of baseline smoking; abstinence is the number or percentage of subjects not smoking. It is important to recognize that the two indexes have different metric properties, which yield different implications for measurement in research and service settings (Lichtenstein & Danaher, 1976).

Abstinence is a nominal scale datum that requires less powerful, nonparametric statistical analyses and is less likely to yield statistical significance than are rate data, which can be analyzed with more powerful parametric procedures. Abstinence, therefore, is a less sensitive indicator of differential treatment effects, but it is a more inherently meaningful outcome in that it is the goal of most smokers who seek help. Most persons who substantially decrease but do not stop their smoking subsequently return to baseline levels. In evaluating the absolute effects or practical value of any smoking treatment, the proportion of subjects achieving and maintaining abstinence is a critical index.

Abstinence is also less susceptible to reactivity effects of self-monitoring (Kazdin, 1974) and to variations in the method of obtaining self-report data (Lichtenstein & Danaher, 1976). Self-monitoring has been shown to affect the rate of smoking, at least on a short term basis (Frederiksen, Epstein, & Kosevsky, 1974; McFall, 1970), but has rarely been shown to produce abstinence and intuitively would not be expected to do so. Since subjects can readily discriminate whether or not they are smoking at all, it matters little how self-report abstinence data are obtained or whether the mode of data collection changes from treatment to follow-up. Global retrospective reports, daily estimates, or cigarette-by-cigarette record keeping would all be expected to produce equivalent results.

The crucial concern about abstinence is the possibility that subjects might not be telling the truth. Abstinence can, however, be corroborated in ways not possible for rate data. The use of informants or observers who interact with the subject provides partial corroboration of whether he or she is smoking or not (Lichtenstein, Harris, Birchler, Wahl, & Schmahl, 1973; Schmahl, Lichtenstein, & Harris, 1972). That a subject might be smoking outside the informant's presence or be in collusion with the informant is still possible. Physiological measurement offers a more powerful and reliable way of corroborating reports of abstinence and may also yield some information about rate.

It appears that discrepancies between self-reported abstinence and physiological indicators is a function of the contingencies for abstinence. The largest discrepancy that we are aware of occurred in a study where there was a significant financial payoff for being abstinent and where the subjects were intentionally kept unaware of the purpose of the blood samples (Goeckner, 1979).

Rate data are attractive because they offer a more precise and sensitive dependent measure that can be subjected to powerful, parametric statistical procedures (Lichtenstein & Danaher, 1976; Pechacek, 1979). Rate data are affected by digit bias, the tendency to report in multiples of five or half-pack units (Pechacek, 1979), and by mode of procedure. Some kind of self-monitoring procedure is typically used to improve the quality of rate data, but self-monitoring produces reactivity effects and tends to underestimate the true smoking rate (Lichtenstein & Danaher, 1976; Pechacek, 1979). It is also difficult to verify rate data through informants or physiological measures.

Physiological Measurement

In the last five years, there have been important advances in the physiological measurement of smoking behavior. Three physiological measures have been developed, varying in intrusiveness, cost, and sensitivity: carbon monoxide; nicotine or its derivative, cotinine; and thiocyanate.

Carbon Monoxide (CO). Smoking involves the intake of carbon monoxide, which increases carboxyhemoglobin. Carboxyhemoglobin can be measured directly from blood samples and can also be reliably estimated in a much less intrusive way by analyzing the carbon monoxide content in breath samples

(Frederiksen, 1977; Pechacek, 1979). The apparatus for the reliable measurement of carbon monoxide is available for approximately $1,500, making it well within the reach of many research programs and service clinics.

Carbon monoxide provides reliable but crude measures of smoking behavior. There is usually some overlap between smokers and nonsmokers that has nothing to do with false reporting. A subject can be exposed to carbon monoxide in ways other than by smoking tobacco. Working in a smoky room, exposure to car exhaust fumes, or smoking marijuana all elevate carbon monoxide values. A second cause of overlap is the relatively short half-life of carbon monoxide, generally estimated at between two and five hours. If the subject has not smoked for several hours, the procedure does not detect much carbon monoxide. The short half-life permits verification of cessation during or immediately after treatment but greatly weakens the value of carbon monoxide in follow-up assessment. Carbon monoxide is also subject to diurnal fluctuations, so that measurements should be taken at a constant time of day, and it is also influenced by alcohol consumption.

The short half-life of carbon monoxide also makes it useful in demonstrating some immediate consequences of quitting. We concur with Frederiksen's (1977) suggestion that providing subjects with feedback on their reduced levels of carbon monoxide may be useful for treatment purposes.

Thiocyanate. The presence of small nontoxic amounts of cyanide in tobacco permits the detection of thiocyanate in either blood samples (Brockway, 1978; Goeckner, 1979) or saliva (Luepker, Pechacek, Murray, Johnson, Hurd, & Jacobs, in press; Prue, Martin, & Hume, 1980). Thiocyanate analysis has several attractive properties, including a long half-life (estimated to be 14 days) and a minimal possibility of exposure from other sources (there are only a few foods that can increase levels). Reliability has been found to be satisfactory (Luepker *et al.*, in press). Saliva samples can be easily obtained by having subjects hold a cotton dental roll between gums and cheek for a few minutes and then sealing the wet roll in a test tube. Samples can be frozen and shipped for analysis in a central laboratory facility. The long half-life of thiocyanate makes it ideally suited for follow-up assessment where stable abstinence is a key issue. Conversely, the long half-life limits its utility in assessing end-of-treatment abstinence. The combined use of both carbon monoxide and thiocyanate can provide an especially powerful test of abstinence (Pechacek, 1979). Procedural guidelines for thiocyanate analysis can be found in Prue *et al.* (1980) and Luepker *et al.* (in press).

Nicotine. Blood nicotine analysis offers a way of corroborating self-reported smoking, but it is intrusive and expensive. The detectability of nicotine in the urine provides a much less intrusive alternative. Urinary nicotine levels have been found to discriminate reliably between smokers and nonsmokers, and detection was possible up to 15 hours after smoking (Paxton & Bernacca, 1979).

The developing technology for the physiological detection of smoking, together with studies reporting discrepancies between physiological indicators and self-report, has important implications. It is no longer acceptable to rely on self-reported smoking rates, no matter how the self-monitoring is done. The use of significant others as informants is simple and unobtrusive, and it should be used routinely. The technology and economy of physiological corroboration have advanced to the point where one of the three indicators noted above is a necessary part of any serious evaluation of smoking cessation methods. The physiological indicators yield another potential bonus in that they probably increase the validity of self-report (Evans, Rozelle, Mittelmark, Hansen, Bane, & Havis, 1978).

Intervention Strategies

Our review of the literature departs from the standard approach in that we do not consider several specific methods (e.g., self-monitoring, stimulus control, and contingency contracting) in categorical fashion. The specific techniques are adequately reviewed elsewhere and, further, are rarely employed separately; instead, they are embedded in multicomponent packages. We begin with a more standard review of aversive methods since these remain the most frequently used strategy. Nicotine-focused strategies, both behavioral and pharmacological, and controlled-smoking strategies are then considered, followed by a brief section on tailoring. In keeping with its theoretical and practical importance noted above, we give heavy emphasis to maintenance strategies. Multicomponent programs are then discussed. The intervention section concludes with an overview of alternative service delivery methods.

A review of the smoking treatment literature requires both a relative and an absolute perspective. A relative perspective draws comparisons between behavioral treatment and attention-placebo, nonbehavioral or no-treatment control groups. An absolute perspective emphasizes the degree of cessation or reduction achieved. Since smoking has an "absolute zero" point—complete abstinence—it is possible to use this perspective (Lichtenstein & Danaher, 1976).

Aversion Strategies

Three major kinds of aversive stimuli have been used: electric shock, imaginal stimuli, and cigarette smoke itself. Lichtenstein and Danaher (1976) reviewed the relative procedural advantages of each, as well as surveying the empirical literature.

Electric Shock. We shall treat electrical aversion briefly because the literature consistently shows it to be ineffective in producing long-term smoking cessation, especially when paired with overt smoking behavior (e.g., Russell, Armstrong, & Patel, 1976). One exception to this generalization (Dericco, Brigham, & Garlington, 1977) has not withstood replication (Brigham, Jacobson-Brigham, & Garlington, 1980). In another apparent exception, Pope and Mount (1975) employed a portable shocking device, similar to that used by Azrin and Powell (1968), with 43 college student subjects, 39 of whom completed the lengthy study. One-year follow-up on 35 of these subjects revealed 27 to be nonsmoking and 6 to be smoking minimally, a striking result. However, there was no corroboration of self-report, nor did the design of the study provide information about what were the controlling variables. Electric shock also has limited practical utility, since it requires individual apparatus and/or administration.

Aversive stimuli can be paired with covert behavior such as urges or imaginal smoking situations. Berecz (1972, 1976, 1979) has persistently argued for the utility of pairing aversive stimuli with triggering cognitions and has found suggestive support for this approach, although with only a few subjects. In one report, self-administered shock helped three of six men achieve two-year posttreatment abstinence (Berecz, 1976). In another study (Berecz, 1979), five of seven males were abstinent at one-year follow-up using a similar paradigm but with a wrist rubber band as the self-administered punisher. In both of these studies, the aversion procedures were ineffective with female subjects.

Covert Sensitization. Imaginal aversion—more specifically, covert sensitization—is attractive because it is safe and portable, but it is also more difficult to quantify and control. The research literature on covert sensitization also continues to be equivocal at best. Covert sensitization has tended to produce more smoking reduction than control procedures, but the differences have not been statistically significant (Murphy, 1976; Primo, 1973). In other studies, covert sensitization has not been superior to an attention-placebo control (Madof, 1976), has yielded poorer results than rapid smoking (Barbarin, 1978), or has added nothing to the effects of a self-control package (Lowe, Fisher, Green, Kurtz, & Ashenburg, 1979). Process measures in two studies did not support a conditioning interpretation of covert sensitization (Murphy, 1977; Primo, 1973). More promising findings were reported by Severson, O'Neal, and Hynd (1977), who found that 5 of 10 subjects were abstinent at nine-month follow-up. However, their procedure included one session of rapid smoking as a means of increasing the salience or vividness of the covertly imagined punishing images. These recent findings seem consistent with earlier literature (Lichtenstein & Danaher, 1976) in failing to show any clinical effectiveness for the covert sensitization procedure.

Satiation. Cigarette smoke may be an appropriate aversive stimulus because aversion is more potent when the target behavior and the associated aversive stimuli exhibit topo-graphical similarities (Lublin, 1969; Wilson & Davison, 1969). The initial use of cigarette smoke was by means of a cumbersome apparatus that blew smoke into the subject's face (Franks, Fried, & Ashem, 1966; Lublin & Joslyn, 1968; Wilde, 1964). The smoke machine gave way to two more convenient procedures: rapid smoking and satiation. These are procedurally distinct procedures that are sometimes confused. Satiation is a take-home procedure wherein the subject doubles or triples the baseline smoking rate in the natural environment. It is very convenient but difficult to monitor or control. Rapid smoking is essentially a clinic or laboratory procedure wherein subjects smoke continually, inhaling every six to eight seconds, until tolerance is reached.

Following two encouraging reports on the effectiveness of satiation (Resnick, 1968a,b), there was a series of negative results (e.g., Sushinsky, 1972; Young, 1973). In most of the satiation studies, there was minimal treatment time or experimenter contact. More recent work with satiation has been in the context of more intensive, multicomponent programs. The research programs headed by Best (Best, Owen, & Trentadue, 1978) and Lando (1977) have found impressive outcomes using satiation in multicomponent programs. Delahunt and Curran (1976) obtained similarly positive results.

The convenience of satiation is a definite asset, but the potential risks or stressful effects are a practical liability. While the risks of rapid smoking have been extensively studied, there are surprisingly, no data on the risks of satiation. The screening and selection procedures recommended for rapid smoking (Lichtenstein & Glasgow, 1977) should also be applied to satiation.

Rapid Smoking. Rapid smoking continues to be the most widely researched aversion method. There are three distinguishable sets of studies spawned by rapid smoking: (1) a sizable outcome literature on the effectiveness of the procedure as the primary treatment or as part of a multicomponent program; (2) a lively literature concerning the physiological effects and health risks; and (3) a search for less risky alternative procedures that still involve the use of cigarette smoke.

Effectiveness of Rapid Smoking. A series of influential studies by Lichtenstein and his associates found abstinence rates of 50% or better at three- or six-month follow-up (Harris & Lichtenstein, 1971; Lichtenstein *et al.,* 1973; Schmahl *et al.,* 1972). Later work with rapid smoking was more equivocal. Danaher (1977b) reviewed 22 studies employing rapid smoking. Of the 14 studies Danaher found that permitted a comparison with placebo control or alternative treatment, rapid smoking was found to be more effective in producing long-term abstinence in 10, but in no case were these relative differnces statistically significant. In 11 comparison studies reporting smoking rate data, rapid smoking was superior in 8, and the difference reached statistical significance in 3 of the studies. While acknowledging that there was much variability in the findings, Danaher concluded that rapid smoking appeared to be the most effective single treatment option available.

Since Danaher's review, work on rapid smoking has continued at a moderate pace, slowed perhaps by developing concern about the physiological side effects and the necessity of implementing selection and screening procedures prior to treatment. A long-term follow-up (two to six years posttreatment) of subjects in the original series of rapid-smoking studies by Lichtenstein and his colleagues revealed a moderate degree of relapse. Of these subjects, 34% were now abstinent, down from more than 50% at three- or six-month follow-up (Lichtenstein & Rodrigues, 1977). There are no other long-term follow-up data with which to compare these results.

More recent rapid smoking studies have continued to show both positive results (e.g., Best *et al.,* 1978; Elliott & Denney, 1978; Hall, Sachs, & Hall, 1979) and rather weak findings (e.g., Gordon, 1978; Raw & Russell, 1980). The positive findings tend to outnumber the negative, but this imbalance could reflect publication contingencies that work against negative results.

The evaluation of rapid smoking is further complicated in that recent work tends to include it as part of a multicomponent package (e.g., Best *et al.,* 1978), and the contribution of rapid smoking *per se* is not always assessed (Tongas, 1979; Younggren & Parker, 1977). In fact, if satiation is included, some of the best outcomes reported have involved multicomponent programs that include cigarette smoke aversion (e.g., Best *et al.,* 1978; Lando, 1977; Lando & McCullough, 1978). Two problems with both satiation and rapid smoking are that either requires costly screening procedures and that persons with smoking-related illness—who most need treatment—are likely to be excluded. We conclude that rapid smoking is an effective procedure but that its use will be constrained by how researchers and service deliverers view the risk involved and the "costs" of the necessary screening procedures.

Side Effects of Rapid Smoking. Cigarette smoking increases the level of nicotine and carbon monoxide in the blood and thereby accelerates and stresses the cardiovascular system. Rapid smoking intensifies these effects. Since Hauser's (1974) conjectures about the risks of rapid smoking, a sizable literature has accumulated. The early work has been summarized by Lichtenstein and Glasgow (1977), who also offered recommendations for screening and selection.

It is clear that compared with regular smoking, rapid smoking produces significant increases in heart rate, carboxyhemoglobin, other blood gases, and blood nicotine levels (Hall *et al.,* 1979; Miller, Schilling, Logan, & Johnson, 1977; Russell, Raw, Taylor, Feyerabend, & Saloojee, 1978; Sachs, Hall, & Hall, 1978). The clinical and practical significance of these findings remains controversial in that contributors to the literature differ in their interpretation of the risks involved. One study suggested that rapid smoking might lead to nicotine poisoning (Horan, Linberg, & Hackett, 1977). A direct comparison of blood nicotine levels under regular and rapid-smoking conditions indicated that nicotine poisoning was highly unlikely (Russell *et al.,* 1978).

Cardiac complications remain the major concern with rapid smoking. Cardiovascular irregularities, as measured by EKG readings, have been reported in several studies (e.g., Horan, Hackett, Nicholas, Linberg, Stone, & Lukoski, 1977; Hall *et al.,* 1979), but these have not led to any signifigant clinical symptoms. Sachs, Hall, and Hall (1978) concluded that in healthy individuals, rapid smoking is safe and beneficial. However, in their experimental work (Hall *et al.*, 1979), they used such extensive and expensive screening procedures to determine "healthiness" that these would be out of the reach of most investigators. By contrast, the screening procedures suggested by Lichtenstein and Glasgow (1977) are less costly and less rigorous.

Lichtenstein and Glasgow (1977) estimated that rapid smoking had been used with approximately 35,000 individuals with no known serious consequences and relatively few reports of notable side effects. The number of persons exposed to the procedure has increased considerably since that report, and we are still unaware of any serious side effects from rapid smoking. We conclude that rapid smoking is safe for healthy young adults. Risk–benefit assessment is a trickier judgment to make since it depends in part on the availability and the effectiveness of nonaversive or less risky alternatives (Sachs, Hall, Pechacek, & Fitzgerald, 1979). Rapid smoking is probably best used in medical settings, where screening is more cheaply available and backup emergency care is also on hand.

Alternatives to Rapid Smoking. The use of cigarette smoke as an aversive stimulus remains appealing, in part because of theoretical conjecture (e.g., Wilson & Davidson, 1969) and in part because of the good results sometimes obtained with rapid smoking. Aversion is an attractive strategy for bringing about cessation in a relatively quick and efficient manner in multicomponent programs as well. Therefore, investigators have sought variations of rapid smoking that would avoid or minimize its riskiness, while retaining its therapeutic effectiveness. Three alternatives have been suggested.

The most frequently used alternative is regular-paced aversive smoking (Danaher, 1977a; Glasgow, 1978; Lichtenstein *et al.*, 1973), or focused smoking (Hackett & Horan, 1978), in which subjects smoke at a normal rate while instructed to concentrate closely on their negative sensations. This procedure was originally used as an attention-placebo control in the early work at Oregon, where it was effective in the short run, though not at follow-up (Lichtenstein *et al.*, 1973). Other studies from the Oregon program found no difference between rapid and regular-paced aversive smoking, although the absolute results were modest (Danaher, 1977a; Glasgow, 1978).

Hackett and Horan reported more promising results. Six-month follow-up abstinence rates of 40% and 56% were obtained in two, small studies. The authors aptly termed the procedure "focused smoking" (Hackett & Horan, 1978, 1979). The focused smoking procedure, however, was not effective with a sample of chronically ill subjects who had strong medical reasons to quit smoking (Henderson, Bachman, Barstow, Hall, & Jones, 1979).

It is not yet clear just how effective focused smoking is or whether its effects are primarily suggestion or placebo. In a comparison of subjective reactions to regular-paced and rapid smoking, it was found that rapid smoking produced much more aversion during the initial sessions, but by the end of the sixth session, the regular-paced procedure was eliciting just as much reported discomfort (Glasgow, Lichtenstein, Beaver, & O'Neill, 1981).

The original work on rapid smoking (Lublin & Joslyn, 1968; Schmahl *et al.*, 1972) employed both rapid smoking and the blowing of warm, smoky air in the subject's face. In a component analysis by Lichtenstein *et al.* (1973) these two procedures were found to be equivalently effective, and rapid smoking was then opted for because of its convenience. Theoretically, however, the smoke-blowing procedure alone should be much less risky since it would affect the eyes, the nose, and the throat but should involve less absorption of carbon monoxide and nicotine. Paradoxically, it was found that the smoke blowing produced cardiac arrhythmia in healthy young smokers (Pechacek, Danaher, Hall, Sachs, & Hall, 1979). Given this finding, together with the inconvenience of this procedure, a return to the smoke-blowing machine does not seem warranted.

The most recent alternative on the scene is termed *smoke holding*, wherein subjects simply hold smoke in their mouths for a specified period of time. The initial work indicates that this procedure produces minimum physiological stress and has led to a 33% abstinence rate at six-month follow-up (Kopel, Suckerman, & Baksht, 1979). In a study conducted in a

589

fee-paying, private-practice context, smoke holding and rapid smoking were equally effective. The six-month follow-up abstinence rates were 68% and 60%, respectively (Tori, 1978). The interpretation of these data is qualified by the fact that all the subjects received five weekly booster hypnotherapy sessions, and only self-reports of abstinence were obtained. Overall, the data do suggest that smoke holding warrants further exploration.

Nicotine Chewing Gum

Amidst the growing recognition of the addictive nature of cigarette smoking, two procedures have recently been developed that take nicotine effects into account: monitored nicotine fading is a behavioral procedure wherein subjects switch to cigarette brands with progressively lower nicotine content; nicotine chewing gum is a pharmacological approach.

It is reasoned that nicotine chewing gum can provide for smokers' "nicotine needs" while they are in the process of quitting. Once cessation has been achieved and maintained, withdrawal from the gum itself can be dealt with separately. Another assumption underlying this approach is that the consumption of tar and gaseous elements is the more noxious physiological consequence of cigarette smoking, and thus the continued intake of nicotine via the chewing gum is an acceptable intermediary strategy for achieving smoking withdrawal. To date, all of the work done with nicotine gum has been conducted in Europe, as the substance has been less tightly controlled abroad than in the United States.

An early double-blind study (Brantmark, Ohlin, & Westling, 1973) found that the active treatment group smoked significantly less (as measured in grams/day) than those in the placebo group, and that the active treatment subjects chewed significantly fewer pieces of gum. The two groups did not differ with regard to withdrawal symptoms. After one week, the subjects in both groups were offered nicotine chewing gum at varying strengths. From the one-week to the six-month follow-up, the number abstinent subjects increased (from 5 to 12) in the "initial-placebo" group, while abstinence in the "initial-nicotine" group remained

fairly constant (decreasing from 12 to 10), suggesting again an effect of the nicotine chewing gum. The side effects produced by the gum included local irritation in the mouth, heartburn, and hiccups.

In a well-designed study, Russell, Wilson, Feyerabend, and Cole (1976) compared the therapeutic efficacy of 2 mg nicotine chewing gum to placebo gum, using a double-blind, randomized, crossover design. Of the subjects in this study, 70% quit smoking during treatment, although only 23% remained abstinent after one year. During the initial period of unrestricted smoking, cigarette consumption was reduced more with the nicotine gum than with placebo (37% versus 31%), as was carboxyhemoglobin (COHb) level (25% versus 15%). When attempting to quit, the subjects further reduced cigarette consumption, although there were no longer any differences between the active groups and the placebo group. The average COHb levels, however, remained lower with the nicotine gum. The nicotine gum was reported to be more helpful and satisfying than the placebo gum, and only one subject chose the placebo gum for continued use. Twenty-two subjects experienced side effects with the nicotine gum, but seven of these complained of side effects with the placebo gum as well.

Puska, Björkquist, and Koskela (1979) conducted a double-blind comparison of 4 mg nicotine chewing gum and placebo gum, within the context of a three-week health-education-oriented smoking-cessation course in Finland. Of the 229 subjects who began the trial, 70% of the active group quit smoking during treatment, as compared with 54% of the placebo group. At six-month follow-up, the results still favored the active group (35% versus 28% abstinent), although the difference was no longer significant. Interestingly, analyses revealed that the subjects who used the nicotine gum for at least 10 days were no more successful than those who did not. Withdrawal symptoms did not differ between the active and the placebo groups, and, contrary to earlier studies, the authors reported that no major problems were experienced with the nicotine chewing gum.

An important question is whether the nicotine gum produces blood nicotine levels comparable to those produced by cigarette smoking. If the gum's action is pharmacological, somewhat comparable levels of nicotine intake would be required. In two studies, Russell and his associates (Russell, Feyerabend, & Cole, 1976; Russell, Sutton, Feyerabend, Cole, & Saloojee, 1977) found that 4-mg gum chewed hourly did produce blood nicotine levels comparable to those produced by smoking but that 2 mg did not. The side effects, however, appeared to be dose-related and were worse for the 4-mg gum. Despite these unpleasant effects, 17 of the 21 subjects reported experiencing some degree of satisfaction using the gum.

The Russell group has continued work with nicotine gum using the less aversive 2-mg dosage, with improved flavor, over longer time periods. In a clinical trial study, 26 (38%) of 69 heavy smokers were abstinent at one-year follow-up. This was a significantly better result than that of a comparison group (not a control group) that had received purely psychological treatment, including rapid smoking (Raw, Jarvis, Feyerabend, & Russell, 1980). Blood nicotine levels averaged half that of smoking values, and only two subjects became dependent on the gum. Importantly, only 13% of the subjects reported unpleasant side effects. Guidelines for the clinical use of nicotine chewing gum are presented by Russell, Raw, and Jarvis (1980).

Taken together, these few studies suggest a demonstrable but modest effect of nicotine chewing gum as an aid to smoking cessation. In all cases, the nicotine chewing gum produced lower cigarette consumption and greater abstinence than placebo gum or alternative treatments, both during treatment and at follow-up. In absolute terms, cessation rates produced with the nicotine gum were modest, but many of the subjects were heavy smokers.

The idea of using a nicotine chewing gum to assist in smoking cessation is an appealing one, and research in the area is undoubtedly in its infant stages, particularly if the gum becomes more accessible in the United States. The rationale for its use is a persuasive one that is likely to "join" the belief systems of the many smokers who feel that they are truly addicted to cigarettes. Furthermore, nicotine chewing gum offers a convenient cessation strategy that is highly cost-effective for both client and therapist. One problem with the use of the gum, to date, has been the occurrence of unwanted side effects. A variety of side effects have been reported by many subjects using both 2- and 4-mg gum. The reduction of side effects would represent a major accomplishment in the applicability of nicotine chewing gum.

Future research should explore the parameters of successful treatment in terms of optimal dosage level, therapeutic regimen, and interactions with smoker type. Preliminary evidence suggests that the gum may be more useful for heavy smokers (Brantmark *et al.*, 1973)—a promising lead for future research.

Nicotine Fading

Monitored nicotine fading is a procedure that provides for progressive reductions in nicotine intake and associated nicotine dependence, in an attempt to achieve either abstinence or, for those unwilling or unable to abstain, controlled smoking by maintaining consumption of a reduced-tar-and-nicotine cigarette brand (Foxx & Brown, 1979). After a baseline week of smoking their regular brand of cigarette, clients switch brands each week to ones containing 30%, 60%, and 90% less nicotine than their original brand. Concurrently, clients self-monitor nicotine and tar reductions and get feedback by calculating and plotting their estimated intake of nicotine and tar each day.

In an initial study using monitored nicotine fading, Foxx and Brown (1979) evaluated the procedure by comparing it with its two component procedures—nicotine fading alone and self-monitoring (of nicotine and tar intake) alone—and to an American Cancer Society stop-smoking program. Of the 10 nicotine-fading–self-monitoring clients studied, 4 were completely abstinent after 18 months, while the other 6 were smoking cigarettes lower in nicotine and tar content than their baseline brands. The nicotine-fading–self-monitoring group maintained nicotine and tar reductions from baseline 61% and 70%, respectively, after 18 months. The three control groups were less successful, though the differences were not significant.

In a second study, Beaver, Brown, and Lichtenstein (1981) tested the monitored nicotine-fading procedure both alone and in conjunction with an anxiety management procedure. Monitored nicotine fading produced less long-term abstinence than was found by Foxx and Brown (1979). Beaver *et al.* (1981) suggested that this result may have been due, in part, to the lack of group experience and the paraprofessional nature of the therapist in this study. However, the study does provide additional evidence that nonabstinent nicotine-fading subjects can control their smoking by continuing to smoke a lower-nicotine–lower-tar cigarette than their baseline brand. Of the 21 nonabstinent subjects, 18 accomplished this secondary goal in the Beaver *et al.* study. The mean nicotine reduction (from baseline) of their current brands at six-month follow-up was .6 mg.

Brown and Lichtenstein (1980) combined monitored nicotine fading with self-management and added a cognitive-behavioral relapse-prevention program designed to improve nonsmoking maintenance. A clinical trial evaluation of this multicomponent package yielded 45.8% abstinence (11 of 24) at six-month follow-up. Of the 13 nonabstainers, 9 maintained consumption of a low-nicotine–low-tar cigarette. Unfortunately, a subsequent controlled study (Brown, Lichtenstein, McIntyre, & Harrington-Kostur, 1982) resulted in lower abstinence rates (30% at three-month follow-up), although as in the previous nicotine-fading studies, nonabstainers achieved controlled, low-nicotine–low-tar smoking.

In a related study, Jaffe, Kanzler, Cohen, and Kaplan (1978) attempted to induce low-nicotine–low-tar smoking in women by providing economic incentives for purchasing cigarettes yielding progressively less nicotine and tar. While not significantly different from a group who purchased cigarettes at the same price regardless of brand, these smokers maintained significant reductions in tar and nicotine intake at six-month follow-up. While this procedure does not require smokers to change brands, the controlled smoking effect appears similar to that obtained with nicotine fading.

Although it may have limited impact on abstinence, the convenient, nonaversive features of nicotine fading–brand switching, together with its controlled smoking effects, suggest that it warrants further research.

Controlled Smoking

Brand reduction approaches such as monitored nicotine fading exemplify the broader domain of alternative approaches to cessation termed *controlled smoking*. Russell (1974a) first proposed the goal of controlled or moderate smoking in an article entitled, "Realistic Goals for Smoking and Health: A Case for Safer Smoking." The logic of the controlled smoking approach is that the traditional goal of abstinence for all smokers has not proved feasible, and thus we should consider "less hazardous" smoking as a more realistic alternative for some smokers. In addition to those who are unable to quit, there may be many who are unwilling to quit, but who would embrace the goals of less hazardous smoking.

Frederiksen (1977) noted three major components of the smoking habit that may be modified to achieve moderate smoking: rate, substance, and topography. Rate, the most familiar component, has traditionally been the primary concern of both smokers and smoking researchers. Substance, or what is smoked, is gaining recognition as an important component of the smoking habit. Consumer trends indicate that smokers are switching to lower-tar–lower-nicotine brands, while new treatment programs such as nicotine fading emphasize progressive substance reductions. Topography, or the way in which the substance is consumed, is perhaps the most complex and least well understood of the three. Until recently, topographical components such as depth of inhalation, puff frequency, puff duration, and amount of cigarette smoked were largely ignored.

Rate, substance, and topography combine to determine the amount of harmful elements ingested by the smoker. The assessment and alteration of these components become particularly important, given the mounting evidence that the health risks of smoking are dosage-related (Hammond, Garfinkel, Seidman, & Lew, 1976; Wynder, Mushinski, & Stellman, 1976).

Frederiksen and his colleagues have been most active in demonstrating that smoking topography can be reliably monitored, measured, and modified. Federiksen, Miller, and Peterson (1977) identified five topographical variables to be studied: interpuff intervals, cigarette duration, puff length, puff frequency, and percentage of tobacco burned. Using three subjects in varying multiple-baseline designs across topographical components, these investigators demonstrated that the above variables can be identified and reliably monitored. They found that topographical components were relatively stable across sessions and were responsive to experimental manipulation. Not surprisingly, their findings suggested the existence of functional interrelationships among the topographical components studied.

In a subsequent study, Frederiksen and Simon (1978a) employed a single-case design in which they demonstrated that smoking topography could be effectively modified by means of simple verbal instructions ("Take shorter puffs" or "Take six puffs or less on each cigarette") and frequent practice. These effects were maintained at one-week follow-up, where assessments took place outside the laboratory setting. Concurrently, reductions were demonstrated in carbon monoxide (CO) levels, CO boost (the difference between CO readings before and after a cigarette is smoked), and the percentage of tobacco burned. In an extension of this work, Frederiksen and Simon (1978b) studied three subjects using a multiple-baseline design across topographical components. These findings corroborated those of the earlier study in that verbal instructions were effective in modifying smoking topography. While the researchers did discover a tendency among smokers to compensate in topography during one phase of instruction (i.e., reductions in puff frequency resulted in increased puff duration), such changes appear to have been countered effectively by verbal instructions to the contrary (i.e., "Take shorter puffs"). The effects; were shown to generalize over time for two of the three subjects, while the other subject was shown to have increased his puff frequency over six-month follow-up. This finding may not be surprising, as no attempt was made to ensure the generalization or the maintenance of the treatment effects. CO levels were shown to be functionally re-

lated to smoking topography. An interesting finding of this study is that when the subjects reduced their smoking rate, they did not compensate by reversing these gains in other areas of smoking topography.

Martin and Frederiksen (1980) demonstrated that smokers could be reliably trained to estimate their own levels of carbon monoxide—one of the dangerous gases ingested during smoking that has been implicated as a risk factor in cardiovascular disease. The training procedure involved a prediction–feedback paradigm wherein subjects predicted their CO level and were provided with immediate feedback regarding their actual CO level. In a reversal design with three subjects, CO estimate accuracy was shown to be functionally related to feedback. Teaching smokers to track their CO levels accurately could serve as a useful adjunct to training in modifying smoking topography.

Taken together, these studies provide preliminary evidence that smoking topography can be reliably measured and modified and that one biochemical risk factor (CO) can be reliably estimated. The limitations of these studies include the restricted number and type of subjects assessed, as well as the fact that (with one exception) all the subjects were trained and assessed in a laboratory situation. The maintenance and generalization of these changes must also be addressed. However, the results of these clinical–developmental trials appear promising, and extension of this work to larger and more diverse populations is awaited.

A study by Mittelmark (1979) suggests that various combined approaches to controlled smoking are effective in reducing the health risks associated with smoking. There were over 2,000 subjects who were previously unwilling or unable to achieve smoking abstinence in an intensive multicomponent program. The subjects were encouraged to reduce their smoking dosage in one or more of the following ways: reducing the rate of cigarettes smoked, the rate of puffing, or the depth of inhalation; decreasing the proportion of the cigarette smoked; and switching gradually to lower-tar and lower-nicotine brands of cigarettes. As a group, these smokers showed improvement on a compilation of the self-reported degree of inhalation, the portion of the cigarette smoked, the average number of cigarettes smoked per day, and the tar and nicotine levels of the brand smoked. Although these measures were all self-reported and no control-group data were reported, it appears that the cigarette-dosage-reduction program did result in less hazardous overall levels of smoking.

Goals of Intervention: Abstinence or Controlled Smoking?

Monitored nicotine-fading and controlled-smoking strategies raise some important issues concerning the goals of smoking-control intervention. Given the relative lack of success achieved with current abstinence-oriented procedures and the 54 million Americans who continue to smoke cigarettes despite public health efforts to dissuade them (U.S. Department of Health, Education, and Welfare, 1979), less hazardous, low-tar–low-nicotine smoking has been proposed as a more realistic goal for many who do not wish to or are unable to quit (Foxx & Brown, 1979; Frederiksen, 1977; Gori & Lynch, 1978; Jaffe *et al.*, 1978; Russell, 1974a; Wynder *et al.*, 1976). However, both Schachter (1977, 1978) and Russell (1976, 1978) have argued strongly *against* low-nicotine–low-tar smoking, based on their extrapolations from the nicotine regulation literature.

Both Schachter and Russell have reasoned that since many individuals smoke so as to regulate or maintain nicotine intake at a constant level, smokers switching to cigarettes with lower nicotine yields inadvertently compensate by increasing their smoking rate or altering their smoking topography. These researchers have argued that the result of these attempts to titrate nicotine dosage would actually be an increased consumption of tar and noxious gaseous elements (e.g., carbon monoxide, hydrogen cyanide, and nitric oxide), and thus an increase rather than a decrease in the health risks associated with lower-nicotine–lower-tar smoking. These authors have suggested that the ideal cigarette (not currently available) would combine a low yield of tar and gases with medium to high nicotine yield, and thus, they warn against the notion of switching to current low-tar–low-nicotine brands.

While it is worthy of serious consideration, we believe that this argument is problematic because it is based largely on laboratory research on the role of nicotine in smoking, using subjects who are ostensibly unmotivated to control their smoking in a significant way. Furthermore, these studies have generally dealt with abrupt and substantial nicotine reductions, rather than gradual, progressive reductions such as those reflected in the nicotine-fading procedure and/or those self-administered by the smoking population at large. It has been suggested that this type of gradual weaning from nicotine may lead to a loss of tolerance (Jaffe *et al.*, 1978), which could gradually counteract the type of nicotine regulation effect reported in these laboratory studies. Russell (1976) has acknowledged that titration upward is less well documented then downward titration. Thus, we question the generalizability of nicotine regulation findings to the applied domain of low-tar–low-nicotine cigarette usage.

Results from field investigations of reductions to low-tar–low-nicotine cigarettes call into question the arguments of Schachter and Russell. These findings suggest that the majority of smokers switching to lower-tar–lower-nicotine brands increased neither their rate (Beaver *et al.*, 1981; Foxx & Brown, 1979; Jaffe, *et al.*, 1978; Prue, Krapfl, & Martin, 1981; Wynder & Stellman, 1979) nor their exposure to mouth level nicotine (Forbes *et al.*, 1976), carbon monoxide (Jaffe *et al.*, 1978; Prue *et al.*, 1981), or thiocyanate (Prue *et al.*, 1981). The Prue *et al.*, 1981 study is notable in that nine subjects undergoing a procedure similar to nicotine fading all showed reduced biochemical exposure (carbon monoxide and saliva thiocyanate) at posttreatment. Investigations of changes in smoking topography are needed.

Perhaps most critical to the question of smoking low-tar–low-nicotine cigarettes are epidemiological data that assess the associated health risk in terms of morbidity and mortality from smoking-related diseases. A 12-year longitudinal study of over 1 million men and women (Hammond, *et al.,* 1976) indicated that smokers of low-nicotine–low-tar cigarettes were less likely to die of lung cancer and coronary heart disease than smokers of high-nicotine–high-tar brands.

While more research in this area is clearly needed and undoubtedly will be forthcoming, "Persuading the smoker to wean himself to progressively less hazardous cigarettes . . . is an approach that has the potential to reduce the current epidemic of smoking-associated diseases to a considerably less serious public health problem " (Gori & Lynch, 1978, p. 1259). In our clinical work, we encourage participants to maintain their controlled smoking gains. We suggest that in so doing, they will reduce their risk somewhat, as well as making it easier to quit in the future. That abstinence is the best way to reduce risk still must be emphasized, lest the controlled-smoking rationale be used as an excuse to continue the habit.

Tailoring

A hallmark of the social learning approach to behavior change is tailoring strategies and tactics to coordinate with the specific nature of a client's problem. In principle then, different interventions might be appropriate for different kinds of smokers or different smoking patterns. Self-management strategies are consistent with this philosophy in that individuals are trained to track their smoking in order to become more aware of idiosyncratic discriminative stimuli and reinforcers and to develop personalized strategies and tactics based on this information. In effect, a functional analysis of a smoker's behavior is performed, and intervention is geared accordingly.

Tailoring treatment to match subjects' dispositional tendencies (traits) or behavioral characteristics is another approach. Best and his colleagues (Best, 1975; Best & Steffy, 1975) found significant interactions between internal as opposed to external locus of control (Rotter, 1966) and type of treatment. Internal subjects were more successful with satiation or rapid smoking, while external subjects did better with stimulus control procedures. The consistency of findings in these two studies

was suggestive, though surprising, since externally administered aversion was construed as an internally focused procedure, and stimulus control analysis, which involves active problem-solving by the subject, was considered an externally focused treatment. These findings have not, however, been pursued, and Best himself has modified his view and has concluded that dispositional traits are not a solid basis for tailoring (Best, 1978).

Eysenck (1973) and Ikard and Tomkins (1973) have also proposed tailoring, using different frameworks and different individual difference dimensions. Thus far, however, there is no empirical work attesting to the usefulness of these approaches in guiding the choice of treatment strategies.

Another venture in tailoring by trait has focused on smokers' level of trait anxiety. Pechacek (1977) reasoned that smokers high in trait anxiety would profit more from stress management procedures than low-anxiety smokers. Pechacek's data were supportive of this notion, but not strongly so. In our own laboratory, we were unable to replicate this effect. High-trait-anxiety subjects who received stress management procedures were the least successful at six-month follow-up (Beaver *et al.,* 1981). It is possible that the somewhat complex program used in this study confused, and perhaps made more anxious, the already highly anxious subjects.

A more straightforward approach to tailoring is based on the strength of the smoking habit, or the degree of dependency. There is both theoretical and some empirical support for the notion that heavy smokers (e.g., of two or more packs a day) are more nicotine-dependent, while light smokers are more under the control of external or social cues (e.g., Herman, 1974). If nicotine-dependent smokers could be reliably identified, their treatment might include components focused on nicotine withdrawal. Either nicotine-fading procedures, or nicotine chewing gum, if available, would be likely candidates. The reliable identification of nicotine-dependent smokers has not yet been accomplished. The number of cigarettes smoked is only one indicator; the nicotine content of the cigarettes and the puff frequency and volume are also important. The Tolerance Questionnaire (Fagerström, 1978) developed in Sweden has shown some validity and is one possible candidate. The questionnaire developed by Russell *et al.* (1974) also appears to be a promising and efficient instrument.

Maintenance

The maintenance of behavior change is a critical issue for any serious intervention effort. Treatment gains are of little value if not maintained over time and across settings. The issue of maintenance has been a particularly salient one in smoking cessation. While most treated smokers are able to quit initially, the majority of them resume smoking within a few months of termination (Hunt & Bespalec, 1974). Reviewers of the literature have been virtually unanimous in their call for increased attention to the issue of maintenance in smoking research. It is thus encouraging to report a noticeable increase in the number of studies focused on the maintenance of smoking cessation.

Are different processes involved in cessation and maintenance, and do they therefore require different intervention strategies? There is no definitive empirical answer to this question, although recent writings on smoking comes down on the side of there being different processes (Lichtenstein & Danaher, 1976; Marlatt & Gordon, 1980). Pomerleau, Adkins, and Pertschuk (1978) found that there were different predictors for end-of-treatment and for follow-up, lending a bit of empirical support to the assumption of differences.

Until recently, work on maintenance has been largely atheoretical, a trial-and-error search for procedures that might work. Lichtenstein (1979) identified three distinguishable but not mutually exclusive maintenance strategies: social support, coping skills, and cognitive restructuring. Central to the social support approach is the notion that the support and/or influence of a group or other can help the individual sustain the necessary motivation in order to maintain some standard of behavior, such as not smoking, not drinking, or not using certain drugs.

The coping skills approach, the social learning favorite, assumes that the individual lacks the needed knowledge and skills to become a permanent nonsmoker. What is required is training in dealing with the discomfort involved in depriving oneself of cigarettes, in developing substitute responses that would replace smoking, in learning to recognize and modify the cues (discriminative stimuli) antecedent to the smoking act, and in altering the consequences of smoking. Many of these strategies and tactics have been encompassed under the rubric of *self-control* (Thoresen & Mahoney, 1974) and have been applied to smoking reduction in a number of studies (cf. Lichtenstein & Danaher, 1976; Pechacek, 1979).

The cognitive restructuring approach to maintenance is the most difficult to define and the least well developed with respect to smoking. This approach assumes that some change must occur "within the head" in order for behavior change to endure. Such changes may involve attitudes, self-perceptions, or covert verbalization. The application of attribution theory (Kopel & Arkowitz, 1975) is one variation within the cognitive framework that has been applied to smoking (Kopel, 1975; Colletti & Kopel, 1979). Bandura's (1977) self-efficacy theory is another approach.

Social Support. In the area of addictive behaviors, social support has a long clinical history as exemplified by such programs as Alcoholics Anonymous, Synanon, and Weight Watchers. Until quite recently, systematic evaluation and implementation of social-support maintenance strategies with respect to smoking were almost nonexistent. Recent work with group meetings intended to provide nonspecifics such as encouragement, information, and moral support has been generally disappointing. Several studies have yielded negative results (Elliott & Denney, 1978; Gordon, 1978; Rodgers, 1977), with the two latter investigators noting that the approach was effective until its termination, which resulted in an increased relapse rate relative to comparison conditions. Gordon (1978) termed this a "backfire effect." Derden (1977) claimed support for the group support approach but provided no follow-up data beyond the maintenance intervention, nor did he demonstrate the statistical superiority of group support over comparison and control conditions. The one positive finding in this area (Powell & Mc-

Cann, 1981), combined a five-day, aversion-based cessation procedure with group support maintenance, yielding 76.5% abstinence at six-month follow-up. Unfortunately, this finding is obscured by its lack of statistical superiority over a group phone-contact (64.7% abstinence) and a no-contact control (88.2% abstinence) condition. Since the preabstinence program was intensive and aversive in nature and was conducted by a sole therapist in a large group ($N = 51$), several alternative explanations for these results suggest themselves. Nonetheless, this effort clearly merits an attempt at replication, in light of the absolute levels of complete abstinence.

Providing support for the maintenance of nonsmoking over the telephone is clearly a more cost-effective alternative to scheduled, in-person meetings. As mentioned above, telephone contact can be either with fellow program participants or with a therapist. Clients may be paired up and instructed or requested to call their designated partner in what is referred to as a *buddy system*. While this approach has been used fairly often—at least on an informal basis—during many smoking control programs, investigations of this procedure have been limited, yielding one positive (Janis & Hoffman, 1970) and one negative (Rodrigues & Lichtenstein, 1977) finding.

A variant of the buddy system, the telephone contact system, allows participants to call any and all of their fellow group members. Powell and McCann's (1981) innovative version of this procedure involves a rotating "contact leader" who is responsible for contacting each member twice during the week, recording certain particulars of the calls, and submitting the information to the therapist at the week's end. This procedure yielded a 64.7% abstinence rate at six-month follow-up; however, interpretation of the results is limited by the factors mentioned previously regarding this study. Nevertheless, the procedure is imaginative and warrants further research. Hamilton and Bornstein (1979) report some success using a buddy system along with several procedures designed to increase public commitment to remain abstinent. While the exact nature of the buddy system was not specified (i.e., partner- or group-oriented phone contact), the procedure yielded promising results, albeit with a small number of subjects.

Telephone support for the maintenance of nonsmoking may also be provided through regular phone contacts by the therapist. This basic approach has intuitive appeal and is highly cost-effective. Unfortunately, the results of such interventions have generally been negative (Danaher, 1977a; Kopel, 1975; Relinger, Bornstein, Bugge, Carmody, & Zohn, 1977), and in some instances, subjects have fared worse than if contacted less frequently (Schmahl *et al.*, 1972) or not at all (Best, Bass, & Owen, 1977).

The one positive finding in this area (Colletti & Kopel, 1979) was serendipitous in that weekly therapist phone contacts, conceived of as "a minimal, phone contact only, maintenance strategy control" (p. 615), surpassed the two experimental maintenance conditions. However, Colletti and Supnick (1980) were unable to fully replicate these results, as phone contact maintenance differed from no-maintenance control at six-month, but not at one-year follow-up. These investigators (Colletti, 1978; Colletti & Kopel, 1979) suggested that the procedure differed from its (less successful) predecessors in that the subjects were given support and encouragement regardless of how well they were doing, and that the subjects' contact with the program was gradually faded, as the subjects were required to phone their smoking rates into a clinic secretary following the therapist-phone-contact phase of the program. Thus, while therapist-administered telephone support has generally not served to enhance maintenance, further investigation of this version of the procedure may be warranted.

Finally, an innovative approach to telephone maintenance that demonstrated significant results compared with a control condition (at one-month follow-up) is the use of a recorded message service that provides a series of daily tips, encouragement, and reinforcement for nonsmoking (Dubren, 1977). Further work with this approach also appears to be warranted.

Several investigators have hypothesized that subsequent program involvement with new smoking clients may serve to enhance the maintenance of treatment gains. Colletti and Kopel (1979) employed subjects who had undergone a behavioral, nonaversive treatment to serve as either models or participant observers with groups of new treatment subjects. Both procedures attained marginal success and proved inferior to the phone contact "control" described above. Hamilton and Bornstein (1979) employed subjects as paraprofessional trainers (with new subjects), in combination with the "social support" procedures described previously. Their finding of 36% abstinence (4 of 11) at six-month follow-up compared favorably with that obtained with the preabstinence program either alone or in combination with social support and maintenance. The idea of converting former clients to paraprofessional trainers is plausible and should be further evaluated.

Coping Skills. In general, the approaches described above were intended to provide clients with an experience that would encourage, support, and help maintain their motivation to remain abstinent from smoking. These interventions could well be considered nonspecific in focus, in that they did not involve the appliction of a specifiable coping skill or cognitive approach in the service of maintenance.

Some investigators have developed multicomponent programs incorporating maintenance procedures and have evaluated the total treatment package, rather than the incremental effect of the maintenance components. Coping skills, or self-management training, have been the usual approach to maintenance in these studies. Several of these programs have yielded good results (Best *et al.*, 1977; Brengelmann & Sedlmayr, 1977; Chapman, Smith, & Layden, 1971; Harrup, Hansen, & Soghikian, 1979; Lando, 1977; Pomerleau *et al.*, 1978), although most have not. When combined with rapid smoking, self-management training was not found to have any incremental effect (Danaher, 1977a; Glasgow, 1978). Goeckner's (1979) study emphasized considerable coping-skills training, including visits to restaurants and taverns. Yet, the results were relatively weak: only 29% abstinence confirmed by physiological measures. It may be that development of knowledge about

maintenance–relapse processes is necessary if we are to learn which coping skills are needed for which clients.

Recently, Marlatt has proposed a cognitive-behavioral model of the relapse process (Marlatt, 1978; Marlatt & Gordon, 1980), which was described above. Marlatt and Gordon (1980) outlined some specific cognitive-behavioral treatment strategies to prevent relapse after the initial suppression of behavior.

Brown and Lichtenstein (1980) packaged some of these strategies into a relapse-prevention–maintenance program (described in Lichtenstein & Brown, 1980) for smokers, consisting of five components: identification of high-risk situations, coping rehearsal, avoidance of the abstinence violation effect, lifestyle balance, and self-rewards. A clinical trial evaluation of this program in combination with monitored nicotine fading and self-management training yielded 45.8% abstinence (11 of 21) at six-month follow-up. Unfortunately, a controlled study found relapse prevention not to be superior to a discussion-control group, and three-month follow-up abstinence rates were only 30% (Brown & Lichtenstein, 1980). Cooney and Kopel (1979) compared a controlled-relapse–maintenance approach (based on Marlatt's model) with an absolute abstinence approach. Controlled relapse involved educating subjects about the abstinence violation effect, and giving them an opportunity to cope with an abstinence violation by having them smoke one cigarette in the treatment setting. With the use only of subjects who were abstinent for 10 days, the results showed no difference in abstinence at six-month follow-up (55% for absolute abstinence vs. 50% for controlled relapse). Interestingly, controlled-relapse subjects showed significantly greater increases on self-rated cognitive-impact variables, such as self-efficacy and ability to cope successfully with a future abstinence violation, suggesting that these cognitive changes may not necessarily be related to more successful outcomes. While no conclusions are possible based on these initial evaluations, Marlatt's cognitive-behavioral model represents a promising development that will undoubtedly generate considerable research in the future.

Cognitive Approaches. Cognitive approaches to maintain are the least well developed. There have been efforts to employ the attribution theory notion that behavior change that is self-attributed is more durable than change attributed to external factors (Kopel & Arkowitz, 1975). Kopel (1975) found at-home, self-administered rapid smoking to be no more effective then the clinic version, and the self-administering subjects did not self-attribute treatment gains any more then those treated in the clinic. Recent work on attribution has yielded more promising results. Chambliss and Murray (1979) found that of subjects given a placebo smoking-reduction medication, those who were later told the truth about the placebo so that they could attribute their success to themselves were more successful than those who were told that their success was due to the drug. A significant interaction with locus of control was also demonstrated, with internals being more susceptible to the manipulation.

Nentwig (1978) compared four attributional conditions with groups receiving the same self-monitoring and stimulus control treatment. An internal approach stressed self-control and the subject's own effort; an external approach stressed participation and compliance with treatment; a neutral condition stressed both of the above; and a very external condition was the same as external, with the addition of a placebo "smoking-deterrent drug." Unexpectedly, the very external group showed the greatest smoking reductions at posttreatment. However, as predicted, the internal group was superior at six-month follow-up. The author concluded that while external "positive placebo effects" may prevail in the short run, internal attribution of the factors causing improvement promotes greater maintenance of behavior change.

Colletti and Kopel (1979) provided confirmatory evidence in this regard, as they reported a significant correlation between self-attributions of change and superior maintenance of treatment gains across differing maintenance approaches to smoking cessation. Finally, Hunt (1979) compared successful quitters (of at least six-months' duration) with recidivists on self-report measure and analogue tasks using an *ex post facto* design. He found that successful quitters were predisposed toward more positive self-evaluation, more self-reward, and less self-punishment than recidivists. These later findings suggest a cognitive mediating mechanism that may be related to both self-efficacy and self-attribution of change.

Bandura's self-efficacy theory also has treatment implications, but these have yet to be directly exploited. The instrument developed by Condiotte and Lichtenstein (1981) could be used to give subjects feedback about classes of situations where efficacy is low and to set the stage for training procedures to enhance efficacy. One study lends indirect support to self-efficacy theory. Blittner, Goldberg, and Merbaum (1978) found that subjects who were led to believe that they had strong willpower and great potential to control their behaviors were found to have significantly lower posttreatment and follow-up smoking rates then the stimulus-control-alone or wait-list control subjects. No direct assessment of changes in self-efficacy were made; however, increases in internal locus of control were demonstrated in the cognitive group.

Earlier, we reviewed work with rapid smoking that has aimed primarily at achieving abstinence. Rapid-smoking booster sessions have also been employed in an effort to promote maintained abstinence, an approach that falls outside our social-support, coping skills, cognitive schema. The results, however, have been consistently negative (Elliott & Denney, 1978; Gordon, 1978; Kopel, 1975; Relinger *et al.*, 1977). It may be that a more flexible, individualized scheduling of rapid-smoking booster sessions would serve to increase their effect, as Danaher (1977b) has suggested regarding the premaintenance-sessions-to-cessation procedure.

As yet, there are no empirically validated principles for enhancing maintenance; however, it is encouraging to see the new developments, both theoretical and empirical, that are taking shape in this area. Investigators evaluating maintenance procedures should be aware that methodological requirements may differ, as outcomes should necessarily be considered in terms of those subjects who were able to quit initially. Clearly, the ability of a procedure to promote maintained abstinence cannot be truly tested unless abstinence is first achieved. Thus, researchers could choose to evaluate maintenace strategies using only abstinent subjects or, minimally, could perform subanalyses using only initially abstinent subjects.

Multicomponent Treatment Programs

Most behavioral work on smoking now includes a variety of methods, even when a study is designed to evaluate the impact of one particular strategy. Self-control procedures such as self-monitoring, stimulus control, and the development of substitute behaviors for smoking are almost always included. Relaxation training (e.g., Danaher, 1977a; Glasgow, 1978), stress management (e.g., Pechacek, 1977), self-reward (e.g., Pomerleau & Pomerleau, 1977), or contingency contracting (e.g., Spring, Sipich, Trimble, & Goeckner, 1978) may also be used. Many multicomponent programs include a manual, a document that provides an overview of the behavioral perspective on smoking, gives instructions for the implementation of self-control techniques, and often permits homework assignments (Lichtenstein & Danaher, 1976; Glasgow & Rosen, 1978).

Different components are packaged together not because they have been effective when used individually but in the hope that combining procedures may yield a unique and stronger effect (Lichtenstein & Danaher, 1976). Given the complexity of smoking behavior and individual differences among smokers, multicomponent programs seem plausible since no single method is likely to work with all subjects. But studies that empirically evaluate the additive effects of combining treatment components yield mixed results. Much of this work has centered on the question of whether aversion (rapid smoking or satiation) plus some kind of self-management training is significantly better than just the aversion program alone. While some studies have shown an incremental effect with the use of self-management procedures (e.g., Elliott & Denney, 1978; Lando, 1977), other well-controlled investigations have not (e.g., Danaher, 1977a; Glasgow, 1978). Covert sensitization was found to add nothing to the effects of a self-control program (Lowe et al., 1979). Contingency contracting did add to the effectiveness of a self-control program at six-month follow-up, but the differences were not significant (Spring et al., 1978). Stress management training did not add to the effectiveness of a nicotine fading program and may even have detracted from it (Beaver et al., 1981).

As Franks and Wilson (1978) noted, "more is not always better" (p. 409). It is possible that some multicomponent programs confuse subjects because of their complexity. Intensive aversion procedures such as rapid smoking may lead participants to adopt a passive "do-it-to-me" set, which is incompatible with efforts to teach self-control problem-solving strategies. Or the data may simply reflect the operation of nonspecific effects that are sufficiently represented in the simpler treatments. The current data do not permit us to choose among these alternatives.

Multicomponent programs can be usefully divided into those that do or do not include an aversion component. The distinction is important in a practical sense because the use of aversion—especially the frequently used rapid-smoking or satiation techniques—requires costly screening procedures and the exclusion of some potential subjects.

Unfortunately, the more successful multicomponent programs tend to be ones that utilize aversion, especially rapid smoking or satiation (e.g., Best et al., 1978; Lando, 1977; Tongas, 1979). The work of Lando and his associates is especially noteworthy because they have found abstinence rates of 50% or better at six-month follow-up in several studies (Lando, 1977; Lando & McCullough, 1978; Lando, Shirley, Gregory, & McCullough, 1979). Lando's basic program consists of five daily (group) meetings in which satiation and/or rapid smoking are used to achieve abstinence. These five meetings are followed by seven maintenance sessions. The frequency of the maintenance sessions is gradually reduced. Lando's work suggests that an effective, replicable program has been developed. A manual describing the program is available (Lando, 1976).

A challenge for behavioral workers is the development of effective nonaversive methods. While there have been occasional good results with nonaversive programs (e.g., Pomerleau *et al.,* 1978; Brockway, Kleinmann, Edleson, & Gruenwald, 1977), the data are scattered and inconsistent. Multicomponent programs remain attractive because they can deal with the multiple factors maintaining smoking as well as with the considerable individual differences among smokers. But investigators and clinicians should be aware that more is not always better.

Alternative Service-Delivery Methods

Our focus thus far has been on the development and evaluation of smoking cessation methods for individuals or small groups. But in the real world, smoking cessation services are delivered in a variety of other ways. Physicians try to influence patients to stop smoking. Voluntary health organizations and churches operate smoking clinics. There have been communitywide efforts, especially involving television and other mass media. Several self-help books for smoking cessation have been published. Last, but far from least, there is much activity in the realm of the prevention of smoking. Behavioral workers have been active in all of the areas noted. The interventions themselves often have an eclectic character, but behavioral elements are frequently quite distinguishable. In this section, we summarize and evaluate recent work on these fronts, emphasizing work influenced by social learning principles.

Physician's Influence

Physicians frequently try to intervene with smoking, especially with patients who have smoking related illness. Since physicians are prestigious and see smokers when they are vulnerable and concerned about their health, the potential for change is considerable (Lichtenstein & Danaher, 1978). There is evidence that when patients experience an acute smoking-related illness such as a heart attack, the physician's influence on cessation can be substantial (Lichtenstein & Danaher, 1978). It has also been shown in England that after one year, simple advice and instruction had a

small, but statistically significant effect on the smoking cessation of randomly selected patients, compared to controls (Russell, Wilson, Taylor, & Baker, 1979). The potential cost-effectiveness of this approach is excellent. We suggest that the smoker's physician be enlisted to cooperate in whatever treatment program is being implemented. Many physicians would welcome consultation and materials that would improve their effectiveness in advising and instructing their clients. The National Cancer Institute has developed materials for use by physicians and has mounted a campaign to attain widespread usage (Bratic & Ellis, 1979). Lichtenstein and Danaher (1978) have summarized the evidence concerning physician intervention and have described several possible roles for the physician to play.

Consultant to Voluntary Health Organizations

The bulk of smoking service delivery is accomplished by voluntary health organizations, such as the American Lung Association and the American Cancer Society, and by institutions such as the Seventh Day Adventist Church, which sponsors the Five Day Plan. We have read descriptions of, observed, and even participated in a number of these programs. It is our impression that they embody a number of ideas and methods that are behavioral in nature, although the language or terminology is different. We see two major differences between them and behavioral treatment of smoking. One is that these programs do not implement behavioral principles *systematically,* especially in the sense of monitoring to ensure follow-through and compliance. For example, self-monitoring is included in nearly all these behavioral programs, but it rarely occurs in a systematic way. Second, the evaluation of outcome is often weak or nonexistent. We suggest that there are important roles for behavioral workers to play as consultants to or collaborators in such programs. It should be possible to "join" these programs in the sense of accepting their basic approach and terminology while seeking to build in more systematic, basic behavioral methods, as well as increased accountability.

Communitywide Approaches

Mass media technology permits the delivery of information and advice to entire communities. Various smoking-control programs have been disseminated by this means, ranging from a nationally televised series sponsored by the Office on Smoking and Health to local Five Day Plan programs carried out on camera.

The influence of behavioral principles, careful evaluation, and follow-up make the Stanford Heart Disease Prevention program noteworthy. Two California communities received an extensive two-year mass-media campaign aimed at reducing the risk of coronary heart disease, while a third community served as a control. Group behavioral counseling was offered to two-thirds of the high-risk subjects in one of the media communities. The combination of media campaign plus group behavioral counseling produced significant, long-term (three-year follow-up) cessation of smoking (Meyer, Nash, McAlister, Maccoby, & Farquhar, 1980). It should be emphasized that the media presentations alone did not appreciably reduce smoking. It has been hypothesized that media-disseminated information and advice should be supplemented by peer-group or professional support (McAlister, 1978).

Best (1979) reported the results of a media-delivered behavioral program comprised of six weekly half-hour programs assisted by a written self-help guide. At six-month follow-up, 17.6% of the 71.4% of subjects who responded were abstinent. As Best (1979) clearly acknowledged, these data are difficult to interpret in the absence of a control group or a corroboration of self-reported smoking rates. However, his report is a useful guide for those contemplating a media intervention.

Self-Help Books

Ideally, a self-help book should be based on demonstrably effective clinical procedures. Two behavioral self-help books essentially repackage treatment programs that have been evaluated in laboratory or clinical settings (Danaher & Lichtenstein, 1978a; Pomerleau & Pomerleau, 1977). These two books are based on extensive clinical research programs that have shown modest effectiveness. None of these programs, however, has been evaluated or validated in its self-help form. We know nothing of the helpfulness of these programs purchased over the counter. To the extent that one believes that this is a critical issue, such self-help programs are weak (Glasgow & Rosen, 1978). Given that self-help books are proliferating, there is a need for investigations of who buys them, to what degree the buyers follow their procedures, and with what effects.

Self-help books and client manuals can still be useful adjuncts to individual or group treatment and can reduce the amount of counselor time required. There is evidence that clinic clients working with a manual can do as well with minimal therapist contact as they do with regular therapist contact (Glasgow, 1978). Written materials presenting behavioral instructions have also been disseminated by mail, and the results from two studies are promising. One in Germany (Brengelmann & Sedlmayr, 1977) found that a behavioral program delivered by mail was as effective as a clinic program. A recent study in the United States also showed promising results (Jeffrey, Danaher, Killen, Kinnier, & Farquhar, in press). It must be emphasized that these programs involved the formal recruitment of motivated participants into a structured program. The results of such programs cannot be generalized to self-help books sold over the counter (Glasgow & Rosen, 1978).

Audiotapes are another potential adjunctive procedure (e.g., Danaher & Lichtenstein, 1978b). Audiotapes were used to present the rapid-smoking and focused-smoking procedures in a study that found 37.5% and 29% abstinence for the two conditions, respectively, at eight-month follow-up (Danaher et al., 1980). The actual contribution of the audiotapes to the program was not evaluated.

Prevention

Children and youth have been subjected to educational materials emphasizing the health and social consequences of using and/or abusing various substances, including tobacco. Such programs have consistently been found to be ineffective or weak in preventing smoking (Thompson, 1978). More recently, there have been systematic efforts to develop prevention programs based on a mix of social-psychological and social learning principles.

The work of Evans and his colleagues (Evans *et al.,* 1978) was based on the assumption that teenagers' experimentation with cigarettes is strongly influenced by social pressures from peers, the media, and family members. The influence processes described by Evans and other workers in prevention are very similar to the social learning mechanism of modeling and social reinforcement. Evans's group developed a series of four videotapes depicting social pressures and effective strategies for resisting them, thus attempting to innoculate students against expected pressures. Increasing knowledge of the *immediate* physiological effects was also a key part of the program. The program was systematically evaluated in seventh-grade classrooms. Sophisticated monitoring of smoking, including the use of a "bogus pipeline" and physiological measurement, revealed modest but significant differences at 10-week follow-up between experimental groups and a control group receiving only pre- and posttesting.

Programs at Stanford University and the University of Minnesota have modified and extended Evans's work but are based on similar assumptions concerning peer-group and media pressure and the importance of children's developing skills in analyzing and resisting such pressures. The Stanford program employs high-school peer leaders and more active role-playing of influence situations and possible ways to resist. Seventh-graders are again the target population. At one year follow-up, significant differences have been obtained between experimental and control schools (Gordon, Kearny, McAlister, Perry, Telch, & Killen, 1980).

The Minnesota program (Murray, Johnson, Luepker, Pechacek, & Jacobs, 1980) employed peer models via videotape and also incorporated commitment via videotaping students' declarations that they would not smoke. The curriculum that included social pressure training and commitment appeared to yield the best results.

Prevention has been accorded a high prior-ity by federal policymakers, and smoking is a particularly suitable target for prevention because it can be reliably and objectively measured. The behavioral analysis of the onset of smoking and of preventive strategies in youth has a rich potential.

Implications for Research and Practice

It is clear that there is much to be learned about the nature of smoking behavior and how to modify it. Fortunately, there is much work now under way, in both laboratory and field settings, that should deepen our understanding of cigarette smoking. Significant treatment breakthroughs will probably have to await advances in basic research.

This delay should not discourage the development and the evaluation of treatment strategies based on current theory and knowledge. Guidelines for the conduct of outcome research on cigarette smoking have been implied throughout this paper and have been set forth explicitly elsewhere (Bernstein & McAlister, 1976; *Guidelines . . . ,* 1974; Lichtenstein & Danaher, 1976; McFall, 1978). We will emphasize here some procedural necessities and will make some comments on outcome research strategy.

No serious, systematic outcome study should rely solely on self-reported smoking rates. Physiological measurement and the use of informants are mandatory, and the technology for achieving these is well within the reach of nearly every serious investigator. Follow-up is another critical issue, since the sharp post-treatment relapse phenomenon in smoking and other dependency disorders is well known (Hunt & Bespalec, 1974). A three-month follow-up is a minimal period, perhaps sufficient for graduate students facing master's or doctoral work deadlines. But published work should routinely report six-month or even one-year follow-ups.

A third issue is sample size. If a relatively small subject pool is distributed over treatment conditions in such a way that there are fewer than 15 subjects per cell, then it is unlikely that there will be statistically significant results. Smoking rate is a dependent variable with much within-group variability; in any condition, some will quit, and some will not. Whether one uses abstinence or rate as the dependent measure, a good-sized number of subjects is needed to detect significant effects. If subjects are scarce, it is probably wise to give the best possible treatment to all the subjects and to conduct an adequate assessment (including physiological measures) with reasonable follow-up. If the results seem promising in an absolute sense, then more systematic work can be undertaken either by the original investigator or by others. While it may seem heretical to advise against a control group, and students facing thesis committees may be unable to follow our advice, the proposed strategy is more likely to advance our knowledge of smoking cessation methods then controlled studies with inadequate numbers of subjects.

The use of single-subject designs should also be given serious consideration. These designs are particularly useful when subjects are scarce, when the investigator is developing treatment strategies, or when a fine-grained analysis of specified variables is sought. Frederiksen (1976) has provided a useful discussion of the use of single-subject designs in studies of smoking behavior.

The importance of pilot work or prior clinical experience with smokers before a comparative outcome study is undertaken cannot be overemphasized. Elsewhere, we have noted the social contingencies that lead to armchair analyses followed by controlled studies with ineffective treatments (Lichtenstein, 1971, 1979). Smokers do not seek treatment in mental health settings, so most behavioral workers have not had clinical experience with them prior to mounting a research design. Hopefully, this situation will improve as smoking receives more attention, and smokers may then profit from both the clinical *and* the research skills of behavioral workers.

Implications for Clinical Work

The empirical literature does not, unfortunately, produce clear prescriptions for clinicians who must work with dependent smokers. Nevertheless, some workers have attempted to provide guidelines for clinical work with smokers based on the available data (e.g., Danaher & Lichtenstein, 1978a; Lichtenstein & Brown, 1980; Pomerleau & Pomerleau, 1977), which reflect the current advances, modest though they may be. Here, we summarize some of the important themes, borrowing most heavily from Lichtenstein and Brown (1980).

Given its tenacious, multidetermined nature, cigarette smoking behavior is unlikely to bend to a single treatment strategy. Thus, multicomponent programs are desirable. It is useful to construe the treatment of smoking as comprised of three stages: preparing to quit; quitting; and maintenance.

There are three tasks to accomplish during the preparation phase. First, the participants' motivation and commitment to the program should be reviewed and strengthened. A money deposit, with return contingent on attendance and program follow-through, is strongly recommended. Second, there should be a period of self-monitoring, both to establish baseline smoking levels and to help the participants learn more about the nature of their own particular smoking pattern. Third, a target quit date should be set and agreed to. Our clinical experience suggests that the quit data should be set down the road far enough to permit the learning of maintenance skills.

Quitting is a critical stage but should not be emphasized to such an extent that maintenace is forgotten or neglected. Cold-turkey quitting seems to be more effective than gradual reduction, although some prior reduction—perhaps to about 50% of baseline—may be useful. Quitting may be accomplished in a variety of ways that vary in intensity and response cost. We recommend four major approaches: contracting with self or others; self-management training; aversion strategies; and nicotine fading. These approaches have been discussed above and are described in procedural detail elsewhere (Danaher & Lichtenstein, 1978a; Lichtenstein & Brown, 1980; Pomerleau & Pomerleau, 1977). Aversive techniques do appear to be effective, but they are more costly because they require cumbersome screening and informed-consent procedures, as well as posing more risk. Contracting for a target quit date is the simplest quitting procedure; self-management and nicotine fading are nonrisky but require more training time.

The literature concerning maintenance is even more ambiguous and less helpful than that regarding quitting. Much of the literature seeks out relationships between demographic or smoking-history variables and relapse (e.g., Eisinger, 1971; Graham & Gibson, 1971). Even when significant differences emerge, they are not helpful in selecting treatment strategies. The finding that early compliance with the program is related to success, however, seems useful (Pomerleau *et al.*, 1978). The data do suggest that mere extended contact or booster sessions do not help. It is more difficult to say what does. The provision of social support, through buddy systems or supportive social networks, may be helpful, though there is limited evidence. While readers of this review will have noted that we are intrigued by cognitive relapse-prevention strategies, it must be acknowledged that so far, evidence of their success is lacking. The relationship between posttreatment self-efficacy ratings and maintenance of nonsmoking may have useful clinical implications. Efficacy ratings can help identify situations or classes of situations that require attention from program and participants. The clinical utility of this approach, however, remains to be demonstrated.

Like the other substance-abuse problems, cigarette smoking is critically important to health yet difficult to change. Perhaps because smoking is easier to assess then many behavioral problems, we know more about treatment outcomes and so must be cautious in what we can offer clients. While there is a great need for more research, we should not be deterred from implementing our available knowledge. Behavioral approaches still appear to be the most useful, and certainly the most accountable, approach now available for the modification of cigarette smoking.

References

Adesso, V. J., & Glad, W. R. A behavioral test of a smoking typology. *Addictive Behaviors*, 1978, *3*, 35–38.

Antonuccio, D. O., & Lichtenstein, E. Peer modeling influences on smoking behavior of heavy and light smokers. *Addictive Behaviors*, 1980, *5*, 299–306.

Ashton, H., & Watson, D. W. Puffing frequency and nicotine intake in cigarette smokers. *British Medical Journal*, 1970, *3*, 679–681.

Azrin, N. H., & Powell, J. Behavioral engineering: The reduction of smoking behavior by a conditioning apparatus and procedure. *Journal of Applied Behavior Analysis*, 1968, *1*, 193–200.

Bandura, A. Self-efficacy: Toward a unifying theory of behavioral change. *Psychological Review*, 1977, *84*, 191–215.

Barbarin, O. A. Comparison of symbolic and overt aversion in the self-control of smoking. *Journal of Consulting and Clinical Psychology*, 1978, *46*, 1569–1571.

Beaver, C., Brown, R. A., & Lichtenstein, E. Effects of monitored nicotine fading and anxiety management training on smoking reduction. *Addictive Behaviors*, 1981, *6*, 301–305.

Berecz, J. M. Modification of smoking behaviors through self-administered punishment of imagined behavior: A new approach to aversion therapy. *Journal of Consulting and Clinical Psychology*, 1972, *38*, 244–250.

Berecz, J. M. Treatment of smoking with cognitive conditioning therapy: A self-administered aversion technique. *Behavior Therapy*, 1976, *7*, 641–648.

Berecz, J. M. The reduction of cigarette smoking through self-administered wrist band aversion therapy. *Behavior Therapy*, 1979 *10*, 669–675.

Bernstein, D. A. The modification of smoking behavior: An evaluative review. *Psychological Bulletin*, 1969, *71*, 418–440.

Bernstein, D. A., & Glasgow, R. E. The modification of smoking behavior. In O. F. Pomerleau & J. P. Brady (Eds.), *Behavioral medicine: Theory and practice*. Baltimore: Williams & Wilkins, 1979.

Bernstein, D. A., & McAlister, A. L. The modification of smoking behavior: Progress and problems. *Addictive Behaviors*, 1976, *1*, 89–102.

Best, J. A. Tailoring smoking withdrawal procedures to personality and motivational differences. *Journal of Consulting and Clinical Psychology*, 1975, *43*, 1–8.

Best, J. A. Targeting and self-selection of smoking modification methods. In J. L. Schwartz (Ed.), *Progress in smoking cessation: Proceedings of International Conference on Smoking Cessation*. New York: American Cancer Society, 1978.

Best, J. A. Mass media, self-management, and smoking modification. In P. O. Davidson (Ed.), *Changing health lifestyles*. New York: Brunner/Mazel, 1979.

Best, J. A., & Bloch, M. Compliance in the control of cigarette smoking. In R. B. Haynes, D. W. Taylor, & D. L. Sackett (Eds.), *Compliance in health care*. Baltimore: Johns Hopkins University Press, 1979.

Best, J. A., & Steffy, R. A. Smoking modification procedures for internal and external locus of control clients. *Canadian Journal of Behavioral Science*, 1975, *7*, 155–165.

Best, J. A., Bass, F., & Owen, L. E. Mode of service delivery in a smoking cessation program for public health. *Canadian Journal of Public Health*, 1977, *68*, 469–473.

Best, J. A., Owen, L. E., & Trentadue, L. Comparison of satiation and rapid smoking in self-managed smoking cessation. *Addictive Behaviors*, 1978, *3*, 71–78.

Blittner, M., Goldberg, J., & Merbaum, M. Cognitive self control factors in the reduction of smoking behavior. *Behavior Therapy*, 1978, *9*, 553–561.

Bradshaw, P. W. The problem of cigarette smoking and its control. *The International Journal of the Addictions*, 1973, *2*, 353–371.

Brantmark, B., Ohlin, P., & Westling, H. Nicotine-containing chewing gum as an anti-smoking aid. *Psychopharmacologia*, 1973, *31*, 191–200.

Bratic, E., & Ellis, B. H. *An approach to utilizing the physician to help smokers quit.* Paper presented at the Fourth World Conference on Smoking and Health, Stockholm, 1979.

Brengelmann, J. C., & Sedlmayer, E. Experiments in the reduction of smoking behavior. In J. Steinfeld, W. Griffiths, K. Ball, & R. M. Taylor (Eds.), *Health consequences, education, cessation activities and governmental action*, Vol. 2. Proceedings of the Third World Conference on Smoking and Health, New York, 1975. DHEW Publication No. (NIH 77-1413), 1977, pp. 533–543.

Brigham, T. A., Jacobson-Brigham, J., & Garlington, W. K. The punishment of smoking: A field test and failure to replicate. Unpublished manuscript, Washington State University, Pullman, Wash., 1980.

Brockway, B. S. Chemical validation of self-reported smoking rates. *Behavior Therapy*, 1978, *9*, 685–686.

Brockway, B. S., Kleinmann, G., Edleson, J., & Gruenewald, K. Non-aversive procedures and their effects on cigarette smoking: A clinical group study. *Addictive Behaviors*, 1977, *2*, 121–128.

Brown, R. A., & Lichtenstein, E. *Effects of a cognitive-behavioral relapse prevention program for smokers.* Paper presented at 88th Annual Convention of the American Psychological Association, Montreal, 1980.

Brown, R. A., Lichtenstein, E., McIntyre, K., & Harrington-Kostur, J. *Effects of nicotine fading and cognitive relapse prevention in smoking treatment.* Manuscript in preparation, 1982.

Chambliss, C., & Murray, E. J. Cognitive procedures for smoking reduction: Symptom attribution versus efficacy attribution. *Cognitive Therapy and Research*, 1979, *3*, 91–95.

Chapman, R. F., Smith, J. W., & Layden, T. A. Elimination of cigarette smoking by punishment and self-management training. *Behaviour Research and Therapy*, 1971, *9*, 255–264.

Coleman, D., Hughes, J. R., Epstein, L. H., & Ossip, D. J. *Withdrawal symptoms during gradual reduction of cigarette smoking.* Paper presented at the Meeting of the Society of Behavioral Medicine, San Francisco, 1979.

Colletti, G. The relative efficacy of participant modeling, participant observer, and self-monitoring procedures as maintenance strategies following a positive behaviorally based treatment for smoking reduction. *Dissertation Abstracts International*, 1978, *38*(11-B), 5561, (University Microfilms No. 7805068.)

Colletti, G., & Kopel, S. A. Maintaining behavior change: An investigation of three maintenance strategies and the relationship of self-attribution to the long-term reduction of cigarette smoking. *Journal of Consulting and Clinical Psychology*, 1979, *47*, 614–617.

Colletti, G., & Supnick, J. A. *Continued therapist contact as a maintenance strategy for smoking reduction.* Unpublished manuscript, State University of New York at Binghamton, 1980.

Condiotte, M. M., & Lichtenstein, E. Self-efficacy and relapse in smoking cessation programs. *Journal of Consulting and Clinical Psychology*, 1981, *49*, 648–658.

Cooney, N. L., & Kopel, S. A. *A preliminary investigation of controlled relapse: A social learning approach to preventing smoking recidivism.* Paper presented at the 13th Annual Convention of the Association for Advancement of Behavior Therapy, San Francisco, December 1979.

Danaher, B. G. Rapid smoking and self-control in the modification of smoking behavior. *Journal of Consulting and Clinical Psychology*, 1977, *45*, 1068–1075. (a)

Danaher, B. G. Research on rapid smoking: Interim summary and recommendations. *Addictive Behaviors*, 1977, *2*, 151–166. (b)

Danaher, B. G., & Lichtenstein, E. *Become an ex-smoker: A comprehensive program for permanent smoking control.* Englewood Cliffs, N.J.: Prentice-Hall, 1978. (a)

Danaher, B. G., & Lichtenstein, E. *Comprehensive smoking cessation program.* New York: BMA Audio Cassettes, 1978. (b)

Danaher, B. G., Jeffrey, R. W., Zimmerman, R., & Nelson, E. Aversive smoking using printed instructions and audiotape adjuncts. *Addictive Behaviors*, 1980, *5*, 353–358.

Delahunt, J., & Curran, J. P. Effectiveness of negative practice and self-control techniques in the reduction of smoking behavior. *Journal of Consulting and Clinical Psychology*, 1976, *44*, 1002–1007.

Derden, R. H. The effectiveness of follow-up strategies in smoking cessation. *Dissertation Abstracts International*, 1977, *38*(5-B), 2359–2360. (University Microfilms No. 77-23, 582.)

Dericco, A., Brigham, T. A., & Garlington, W. K. Development and evaluation of treatment paradigms for the suppression of smoking behavior. *Journal of Applied Behavior Analysis*, 1977, *10*, 173–181.

Dubren, R. Self-reinforcement by recorded telephone messages to maintain nonsmoking behavior. *Journal of Consulting and Clinical Psychology*, 1977, *45*, 358–360.

Eiser, J. R., & Sutton, S. R. Smoking as a subjectively rational choice. *Addictive Behaviors*, 1977, *2*, 129–134.

Eisinger, R. A. Psychosocial predictors of smoking recidivism. *Journal of Health and Social Behavior*, 1971, *12*, 355–362.

Elliott, C. H., & Denney, D. R. A multi-component treatment approach to smoking reduction. *Journal of Consulting and Clinical Psychology*, 1978, *46*, 1330–1339.

Evans, R. I., Rozelle, R. M., Mittelmark, M. B., Hansen, W. B., Bane, A. L., & Havis, J. Deterring the onset of smoking in children: Coping with peer pressure, media pressure, and parent modeling. *Journal of Applied Social Psychology*, 1978, *8*, 126–135.

Eysenck, H. J. Personality and the maintenance of the smoking habit. In W. L. Dunn Jr. (Ed.), *Smoking behavior: Motives and incentives.* Washington D.C.: Winston & Sons, 1973.

Fagerström, K-O. Measuring degree of physical dependence to tobacco smoking with reference to individualization of treatment. *Addictive Behaviors*, 1978, *3*, 235–241.

Fagerström, K-O. *Smoking cessation with behavior therapy and nicorette.* Paper presented at the 14th Annual Convention of the Association for Advancement of Behavior Therapy, New York, November 1980.

Forbes, W. F., Robinson, J. C., Hanley, J. A., & Colburn, H. N. Studies on the nicotine exposure of individual smokers: I. Changes in mouth-level exposure to nicotine on switching to lower nicotine cigarettes. *The International Journal of the Addictions*, 1976, *11*, 933–950.

Foxx, R. M., & Brown, R. A. Nicotine fading and self-monitoring for cigarette abstinence or controlled smoking. *Journal of Applied Behavior Analysis*, 1979, *12*, 111–125.

Franks, C. M., & Wilson, G. T. *Annual review of behavior therapy: Theory and practice*, Vol. 6, New York: Brunner/Mazel, 1978.

Franks, C. M., Fried, R., & Ashem, B. An improved apparatus for the aversive conditioning of cigarette smokers. *Behaviour Research and Therapy*, 1966, *4*, 301–308.

Frederiksen, L. W. Single-case designs in the modification of smoking. *Addictive Behaviors*, 1976, *1*, 311–319.

Frederiksen, L. W. *"But I don't want to quit smoking": Alternatives to abstinence.* Paper presented at the meeting of the Association for Advancement of Behavior Therapy, Atlanta, 1977.

Frederiksen, L. W., & Simon, S. J. Modification of smoking topography: A preliminary analysis. *Behavior Therapy*, 1978, *9*, 146–949. (a)

Frederiksen, L. W., & Simon, S. J. Modifying how people smoke: Instructional control and generalization. *Journal of Applied Behavior Analysis*, 1978, *11*, 431–432. (b)

Frederiksen, L. W., Epstein, L. H., & Kosevsky, B. P. *Reliability and controlling effects of three procedures for self-monitoring smoking.* Unpublished manuscript, V.A. Hospital, Jackson, Miss., 1974.

Frederiksen, L. W., Miller, P. M., & Peterson, G. L. Topographical components of smoking behavior. *Addictive Behaviors*, 1977, *2*, 55–61.

Gallup Opinion Index. Public puffs on after ten years of warnings. *Gallup Opinion Index* (Report No. 108), 1974, 20–21.

Glad, W. R., & Adesso, V. J. The relative importance of socially-induced tension and behavioral contagion for smoking behavior. *Journal of Abnormal Psychology*, 1976, *85*, 119–121.

Glasgow, R. E. Effects of a self-control manual, rapid smoking, and amount of therapist contact on smoking reduction. *Journal of Consulting and Clinical Psychology*, 1978, *46*, 1439–1447.

Glasgow, R. E., & Bernstein, D. A. Behavioral treatment of smoking behavior. In C. K. Prokop & L. A. Bradley (Eds.), *Medical psychology: A new perspective.* New York: Academic Press, 1981.

Glasgow, R. E., & Rosen, G. M. Behavioral bibliotherapy: A review of self-help behavior therapy manuals. *Psychological Bulletin*, 1978, *85*, 1–23.

Glasgow, R. E., Lichtenstein, E., Beaver, C., & O'Neill, H. K. Subjective reactions to rapid and normal paced aversive smoking. *Addictive Behaviors*, 1981, *6*, 53–59.

Goeckner, D. J. A multifaceted approach to smoking modification: Training in alternate response strategies. *Dissertation Abstracts International*, 1979, *40*(1-B), 450. (University Microfilms No. 7915354.)

Goldfarb, T. L., Gritz, E. R., Jarvik, M. E., & Stolerman, I. P. Reactions to cigarettes as a function of nicotine and "tar." *Clinical Pharmacology and Therapeutics*, 1976, *19*, 767–772.

Gordon, J. R. The use of rapid smoking and group support to induce and maintain abstinence from cigarette smoking. *Dissertation Abstracts International*, 1978, *39*(5-A), 2831. (University Microfilms No. 7820725.)

Gordon, N., Kearny, S., McAlister, A., Perry, C., Telch, M., & Killen, J. *Harvard-Stanford project: Focus on the peer leadership approach to smoking prevention.* Paper presented at the 88th Annual Convention of the American Psychological Association, Montreal, September 1980.

Gori, G. B., & Lynch, C. J. Toward less hazardous cigarettes: Current advances. *Journal of the American Medical Association*, 1978, *240*, 1255–1259.

Graham, S., & Gibson, R. W. Cessation of patterned behavior: Withdrawal from smoking. *Society Science and Medicine*, 1971, *5*, 319–337.

Griffiths, R. R., Bigelow, G. E., & Liebson, I. Facilitation of human tobacco self-administration by ethanol: A behavior analysis. *Journal of the Experimental Analysis of Behavior*, 1976, *25*, 279–292.

Guidelines for Research on the Effectiveness of Smoking Cessation Programs: A Committee Report. National Interagency Council on Smoking and Health. Chicago: American Dental Association, 1974.

Hackett, G., & Horan, J. J. Focused smoking: An unequivocably safe alternative to rapid smoking. *Journal of Drug Education*, 1978, *8*, 261–265.

Hackett, G., & Horan, J. J. Partial component analysis of a comprehensive smoking program. *Addictive Behaviors*, 1979, *4*, 259–262.

Hall, R. G., Sachs, D. P. L., & Hall, S. M. Medical risk and therapeutic effectiveness of rapid smoking. *Behavior Therapy*, 1979, *10*, 249–259.

Hamilton, S. B., & Bornstein, P. H. Broad-spectrum behavioral approach to smoking cessation: Effects of social support and paraprofessional training on the maintenance of treatment effects. *Journal of Consulting and Clinical Psychology*, 1979, *47*, 598–600.

Hammond, E. C., Garfinkel, L., Seidman, H., & Lew, E. A. "Tar" and nicotine content of cigarette smoke in relation to death rates. *Environmental Research*, 1976, *12*, 263–274.

Harris, D. E., & Lichtenstein, E. *Contribution of nonspecific social variables to a successful behavioral treatment of smoking.* Paper presented at the Meeting of the Western Psychological Association, San Francisco, April 1971.

Harrup, T., Hansen, B. A., & Soghikian, K. Clinical methods in smoking cessation: Description and evaluation of a stop smoking clinic. *American Journal of Public Health*, 1979, *69*, 1226–1331.

Hauser, R. Rapid smoking as a technique of behavior modification: Caution in selection of subjects. *Journal of Consulting and Clinical Psychology*, 1974, *42*, 625.

Henderson, J. B., Bachman, J., Barstow, R., Hall, S. M.,

& Jones, R. T. *Smoking cessation in the chronically ill: An exploratory study.* Paper presented at the 13th Annual Convention of the Association for Advancement of Behavior Therapy, San Francisco, December 1979.

Herman, C. P. External and internal cues as determinants of the smoking behavior of light and heavy smokers. *Journal of Personality and Social Psychology, 1974, 30,* 664–672.

Herman, C. P., & Kozlowski, L. T. Indulgence, excess, and restraint: Perspectives on consummatory behavior in everyday life. *Journal of Drug Issues, 1979, 9,* 185–196.

Horan, J. J., Hackett, G., Nicholas, W. C., Linberg, S. E., Stone, C. I., & Lukoski, H. C. Rapid smoking: A cautionary note. *Journal of Consulting and Clinical Psychology, 1977, 45,* 341–343.

Horan, J. J., Linberg, S. E., & Hackett, G. Nicotine poisoning and rapid smoking. *Journal of Consulting and Clinical Psychology, 1977, 45,* 344–347.

Hunt, P. T. A study of three cognitive-behavioral indices of self control in smoking cessation. *Dissertation Abstracts International, 1979, 40*(5-B), 2368. (University Microfilms No. 7924910.)

Hunt, W. A., & Bespalec, D. A. An evaluation of current methods of modifying smoking behavior. *Journal of Clinical Psychology, 1974, 30,* 431–438.

Hunt, W. A., & Matarazzo, J. D. Habit mechanisms in smoking. In W. A. Hunt (Ed.), *Learning mechanisms in smoking.* Chicago: Aldine, 1970.

Ikard, F. F., & Tomkins, S. S. The experience of affect as a determinant of smoking behavior: A series of validity studies. *Journal of Abnormal Psychology, 1973, 81,* 172–181.

Jaffe, J. H., & Jarvik, M. E. Tobacco use and tobacco use disorder. In M. A. Lipton, A. DiMascio, & K. F. Killam (Eds.), *Psychopharmacology: A generation of progress.* New York: Raven Press, 1978.

Jaffe, J. H., & Kanzler, M. Smoking as an addictive disorder. In N. A. Krasnegor (Ed.), *Cigarette smoking as a dependence process* (NIDA Research Monograph 23, DHEW Publication Number (ADM) 79-800). Washington D.C.: U.S. Government Printing Office, 1979.

Jaffe, J. H., Kanzler, M., Cohen, M., & Kaplan, T. Inducing low tar-nicotine cigarette smoking in women. *British Journal of Addiction, 1978, 73,* 271–281.

Janis, I. L., & Hoffman, D. Facilitating effects of daily contact between partners who make a decision to cut down on smoking. *Journal of Personality and Social Psychology, 1970, 17,* 25–35.

Jarvik, M. E. Biological influences on cigarette smoking. In N. A. Krasnegor (Ed.), *The behavioral aspects of smoking* (NIDA Research Monograph 26, DHEW Publication No. (ADM) 79-882). Washington D.C.: U.S. Government Printing Office, 1979. (a)

Jarvik, M. E. Tolerance to the effects of tobacco. In N. A. Krasnegor (Ed.), *Cigarette smoking as a dependence process* (NIDA Research Monograph 23, DHEW Publication No. (ADM) 79-800). Washington D.C.: U.S. Government Printing Office, 1979 (b)

Jarvik, M. E., Glick, S. D., & Nakamura, R. K. Inhibition of cigarette smoking by orally administered nicotine. *Clinical Pharmacology and Therapeutics, 1970, 11,* 574–576.

Jeffrey, R. W., Danaher, B. G., Killen, J., Kinnier, R., & Farquhar, J. D. Self-administered programs for health behavior change: Smoking cessation and weight reduction by mail. *Addictive Behaviors,* in press.

Kazdin, A. E. Self-monitoring and behavior change. In M. J. Mahoney & C. E. Thoresen (Eds.), *Self control: Power to the person.* Monterey, Calif.: Brooks/Cole, 1974.

Keutzer, C. S., Lichtenstein, E., & Mees, H. L. Modification of smoking behavior: A review. *Psychological Bulletin, 1968, 70,* 520–533.

Kopel, S. A. The effects of self-control, booster sessions, and cognitive factors on the maintenance of smoking reduction. *Dissertation Abstracts International, 1975, 35,* 4182B–4183B. (University Microfilms No. 75-3895.)

Kopel, S. A., & Arkowitz, H. The role of attribution and self-perception in behavior change: Implications for behavior therapy. *Genetic Psychology Monographs, 1975, 92,* 175–212.

Kopel, S. A., Suckerman, K. R., & Baksht, A. *Smoke holding: An evaluation of physiological effects and treatment efficacy of a new nonhazardous aversive smoking procedure.* Paper presented at the 13th Annual Meeting of the Association for Advancement of Behavior Therapy, San Francisco, December 1979.

Kozlowski, L. T. *The role of nicotine in the maintained use of cigarettes.* Paper presented at the Technical Review on Cigarette Smoking as an Addiction, National Institute on Drug Abuse, Rockville, Md., August 1979.

Kozlowski, L. T., Jarvik, M. E., & Gritz, E. R. Nicotine regulation and cigarette smoking. *Clinical Pharmacology and Therapeutics, 1975, 17,* 93–97.

Kreitler, S., Shahar, A., & Kreitler, H. Cognitive orientation, type of smoker and behavior therapy of smoking. *British Journal of Medical Psychology, 1976, 49,* 167–175.

Kumar, R., Cooke, E. C., Lader, M. H., & Russell, M. A. H. Is nicotine important in tobacco-smoking? *Clinical Pharmacology and Therapeutics, 1977, 21,* 520–529.

Lando, H. A. Manual for a broad-spectrum behavioral approach to cigarette smoking. *Catalog of Selected Documents in Psychology, 1976, 6,* 113–114.

Lando, H. A. Successful treatment of smokers with a broad-spectrum behavioral approach. *Journal of Consulting and Clinical Psychology, 1977, 45,* 361–366.

Lando, H. A., & McCullough, J. A. Clinical application of a broad-spectrum behavioral approach to chronic smokers. *Journal of Consulting and Clinical Psychology, 1978, 46,* 1583–1585.

Lando, H. A., Shirley, R. J., Gregory, V. R., & McCullough, J. A. *Broad-spectrum treatment in eliminating smoking: Preparation, aversion, and maintenance.* Paper presented at the Annual Meeting of the American Psychological Association, New York, September 1979.

Lee, P. N. (Ed.). Statistics of smoking in the United Kingdom. *Research Paper 1* (7th ed.). London: Tobacco Research Council, 1976.

Leventhal, H., & Avis, N. Pleasure, addiction, and habit: Factors in verbal report or factors in smoking behavior? *Journal of Abnormal Psychology, 1976, 85,* 478–488.

Leventhal, H., & Cleary, P. D. The smoking problem: A review of the research and theory in behavioral risk modification. *Psychological Bulletin, 1980, 88,* 370–405.

Lichtenstein, E. Modification of smoking behavior: Good

designs—ineffective treatments. *Journal of Consulting and Clinical Psychology,* 1971, *36,* 163–166.

Lichtenstein, E. Future needs and direction in smoking cessation. In J. L. Schwartz (Ed.), *Progress in smoking cessation: Proceedings of international conference on smoking cessation.* New York: American Cancer Society, 1978.

Lichtenstein, E. Social learning, smoking, and substance abuse. In N. A. Krasnegor (Ed.), *Behavioral analysis and treatment of substance abuse* (NIDA Research Monograph 25, DHEW Publication No. (ADM) 79-839). U.S. Government Printing Office, 1979, pp. 114–127.

Lichtenstein, E., & Brown, R. A. Smoking cessation methods: Review and recommendations. In W. R. Miller (Ed.), *The addictive behaviors: Treatment of alcoholism, drug abuse, smoking, and obesity.* Oxford: Pergamon Press, 1980.

Lichtenstein, E., & Danaher, B. G. Modification of smoking behavior: A critical analysis of theory, research and practice. In M. Hersen, R. M. Eisler, & P. M. Miller (Eds.), *Progress in behavior modification.* New York: Academic Press, 1976.

Lichtenstein, E., & Danaher, B. G. What can the physician do to assist the patient to stop smoking? In R. E. Brashear & M. L. Rhodes (Eds.), *Chronic obstructive lung disease: Clinical treatment and management.* St. Louis: C. V. Mosby, 1978.

Lichtenstein, E., & Glasgow, R. E. Rapid smoking: Side effects and safeguards. *Journal of Consulting and Clinical Psychology,* 1977, *45,* 815–821.

Lichtenstein, E., & Keutzer, C. S. Modification of smoking behavior: A later look. In R. D. Rubin, H. Fensterheim, A. A. Lazarus, & C. M. Franks (Eds.), *Advances in behavior therapy.* New York: Academic Press, 1971.

Lichtenstein, E., & Rodrigues, M-R. P. Long-term effects of rapid smoking treatment for dependent cigarette smokers. *Addictive Behaviors,* 1977, *2,* 109–112.

Lichtenstein, E., Harris, D. E., Birchler, G. R., Wahl, J. M., & Schmahl, D. P. Comparison of rapid smoking, warm, smoky air, and attention placebo in the modification of smoking behavior. *Journal of Consulting and Clinical Psychology,* 1973, *40,* 92–98.

Lichtenstein, E., Antonuccio, D. O., & Rainwater, G. *Unkicking the habit: The resumption of cigarette smoking.* Paper presented at the Annual Meeting of the Western Psychological Association, Seattle, April 1977.

Lowe, M. R., Fisher, E. B., Green, L., Kurtz, S., & Ashenberg, Z. *Self-control with and without covert sensitization in smoking cessation.* Paper presented at the 87th Annual Convention of the American Psychological Association, New York, September 1979.

Lublin, I. Principles governing the choice of unconditioned stimuli in aversive conditioning. In R. D. Rubin & C. M. Franks (Eds.), *Advances in behavior therapy, 1968.* New York: Academic Press, 1969.

Lublin, I., & Joslyn, L. *Aversive conditioning of cigarette addiction.* Paper presented at the Meeting of the Western Psychological Association, Los Angeles, September 1968.

Lucchesi, B. R., Schuster, C. R., & Emley, G. S. The role of nicotine as a determinant of cigarette smoking in man with observations of certain cardiovascular ef-

fects associated with the tobacco alkaloid. *Clinical Pharmacology and Therapeutics,* 1967, *8,* 789–796.

Luepker, R. V., Pechacek, T. F., Murray, D. M., Johnson, C. A., Hurd, P., & Jacobs, D. R. Saliva thiocyanate: A chemical indicator of cigarette smoking in adolescents. *American Journal of Public Health,* in press.

Madof, F. The effect of certain learning variables, applied in imagination, on the modification of smoking behavior. *Dissertation Abstracts International,* 1976, *36*(12-B), 6360. (University Microfilms No. 76-12,015.)

Marlatt, G. A. Craving for alcohol, loss of control, and relapse: A cognitive-behavioral analysis. In P. E. Nathan, G. A. Marlatt, & T. Loberg (Eds.), *Alcoholism: New directions in behavioral research and treatment.* New York: Plenum Press, 1978.

Marlatt, G. A., & Gordon, J. R. Determinants of relapse: Implications for the maintenance of behavior change. In P. O. Davidson & S. M. Davidson (Eds.), *Behavioral medicine: Changing health lifestyles.* New York: Brunner/Mazel, 1980.

Marshall, W. R., Epstein, L. H., & Green, S. B. Coffee drinking and cigarette smoking: I. Coffee, caffeine and cigarette smoking behavior. *Addictive Behaviors,* 1980, *5,* 389–394.

Marshall, W. R., Green, S. B., Epstein, L. H., Rogers, C. M., & McCoy, J. F. Coffee drinking and cigarette smoking: II. Coffee, urinary pH and cigarette smoking behavior. *Addictive Behaviors,* 1980, *5,* 395–400.

Martin, J. E., & Frederiksen, L. W. Self-training of carbon monoxide levels by smokers. *Behavior Therapy,* 1980, *11,* 577–587.

Mausner, B., & Platt, E. S. *Smoking: A behavioral analysis.* New York: Pergamon, 1971.

McAlister, A. Helping people quit smoking: Current progress. In A. Enelow & J. Henderson (Eds.), *Applying behavioral science to cardiovascular disease.* New York: American Heart Association, 1975.

McAlister, A. L. Mass communication of cessation counseling: Combining television and self-help groups. In J. L. Schwartz (Ed.), *Progress in smoking cessation: Proceedings of international conference on smoking cessation.* New York: American Cancer Society, 1978.

McFall, R. M. Effects of self-monitoring on normal smoking behavior. *Journal of Consulting and Clinical Psychology,* 1970, *35,* 135–142.

McFall, R. M. Smoking-cessation research. *Journal of Consulting and Clinical Psychology,* 1978, *46,* 703–712.

Meyer, A. J., Nash, J. D., McAlister, A. L., Maccoby, N., & Farquhar, J. W. Skills training in a cardiovascular health education campaign. *Journal of Consulting and Clinical Psychology,* 1980, *48,* 129–142.

Miller, L. C., Schilling, H. F., Logan, D. L., & Johnson, R. L. Potential hazards of rapid smoking as aversion therapy. *New England Journal of Medicine,* 1977, *297,* 590–592.

Miller, P. M., Frederiksen, L. W., & Hosford, R. L. Social interaction and smoking topography in heavy and light smokers. *Addictive Behaviors,* 1979, *4,* 147–153.

Mittelmark, M. B. *Cigarette dosage reduction in the multiple risk factor intervention trial.* Paper presented at the 87th Annual Convention of the American Psychological Association, New York, September 1979.

Murphy, W. D. The contribution of relaxation and relief

to covert sensitization in the treatment of smoking. *Dissertation Abstracts International,* 1977, *37*(8-B), 4157. (University Microfilms No. 77-3487.)

Murray, D., Johnson, C. A., Luepker, R., Pechacek, T. F., & Jacobs, D. *Minnesota smoking prevention program.* Paper presented at the 88th Annual Convention of the American Psychological Association, Montreal, September 1980.

Nentwig, C. G. Attribution of cause and long-term effects of the modification of smoking behavior. *Behavioral Analysis and Modification,* 1978, *2*, 285–295.

Ossip, D. J., & Epstein, L. H. Relative effects of nicotine and coffee on cigarette smoking. *Addictive Behaviors,* 1981, *6*, 35–40.

Paxton, R., & Bernacca, G. Urinary nicotine concentration as a function of time since last cigarette: Implications for detecting faking in smoking clinics. *Behavior Therapy,* 1979, *10*, 523–528.

Pechacek, T. F. An evaluation of cessation and maintenance strategies in the modification of smoking behavior. *Dissertation Abstracts International,* 1977, *38*(5-B), 2380. (University Microfilms No. 77-23,013.)

Pechacek, T. F. Modification of smoking behavior. In *Smoking and health: A report of the surgeon general.* (DHEW Publication No. (PHS) 79-50066.) Washington D.C.: U.S. Government Printing Office, 1979.

Pechacek, T. F., & Danaher, B. G. How and why people quit smoking: A cognitive-behavioral analysis. In P. C. Kendall & S. D. Hollon (Eds.), *Cognitive-behavioral interventions: Theory, research, and procedures.* New York: Academic Press, 1979.

Pechacek, T. F., & McAlister, A. Strategies for the modification of smoking behavior: Treatment and prevention. In J. Ferguson & C. B. Taylor (Eds.), *A comprehensive handbook of behavioral medicine.* New York: Spectrum Publications, 1979.

Pechacek, T. F., Danaher, B. G., Hall, R. G., Sachs, D. P. L., & Hall, S. M. *Evaluation of cardiopulmonary effects in response to the warm, smoky air procedure.* Paper presented at the 13th Annual Convention of the Association for Advancement of Behavior Therapy, San Francisco, December 1979.

Pomerleau, O. F. Behavioral factors in the establishment, maintenance, and cessation of smoking. In N. A. Krasnegor (Ed.), *The behavioral aspects of smoking* (NIDA Research Monograph 26, DHEW Publication No. (ADM) 79-882). Washington D.C.: U.S. Government Printing Office, 1979, pp. 46–67. (a)

Pomerleau, O. F. Why people smoke: Current psychobiological models. In P. Davidson (Ed.), *Behavioral medicine: Changing health lifestyles.* New York: Brunner/Mazel, 1979. (b)

Pomerleau, O. F., & Pomerleau, C. S. *Break the smoking habit: A behavioral program for giving up cigarettes.* Champaign, Ill.: Research Press, 1977.

Pomerleau, O. F., Adkins, D., & Pertschuk, M. Predictors of outcome and recidivism in smoking cessation treatment. *Addictive Behaviors,* 1978, *3*, 65–70.

Pope, J. W., & Mount, G. R. The control of cigarette smoking through the application of a portable electronic device designed to dispense an aversive stimulus in relation to subject's smoking frequency. *Behavioral Engineering,* 1975, *2*, 52–56.

Powell, D. R., & McCann, B. S. The effect of multiple treatment and multiple maintenance procedures on smoking cessation. *Preventive Medicine,* 1981, *10*, 94–104.

Primo, R. V. Covert avoidance learning: A refined covert sensitization method for the modification of smoking behavior. *Dissertation Abstracts International,* 1973, *33*(8-B), 3958–3959. (University Microfilms No. 73-4992.)

Prue, D. M., Martin, J. E., & Hume, A. S. A critical evaluation of thiocyanate as a biochemical index of smoking exposure. *Behavior Therapy,* 1980, *11*, 368–379.

Prue, D. M., Krapfl, J. E., & Martin, J. E. Brand fading: The effects of gradual changes to low tar and nicotine cigarettes on smoking rate, carbon monoxide, and thiocyanate levels. *Behavior therapy,* 1981, *12*, 400–416.

Puska, P., Björkqvist, S., & Koskela, K. Nicotine-containing chewing gum in smoking cessation: A double blind trial with half year follow-up. *Addictive Behaviors,* 1979, *4*, 141–146.

Raw, M. Persuading people to stop smoking. *Behaviour Research and Therapy,* 1976, *14*, 97–101.

Raw, M., & Russell, M. A. H. Rapid smoking, cue exposure and support in the modification of smoking. *Behaviour Research and Therapy,* 1980, *18*, 363–372.

Raw, M., Jarvis, M. J., Feyerabend, C., & Russell, M. A. H. Comparison of nicotine chewing-gum and psychological treatments for dependent smokers. *British Medical Journal,* 1980, *1*, 481–484.

Relinger, H., Bornstein, P. H., Bugge, I. D., Carmody, T. P., & Zohn, C. J. Utilization of adverse rapid smoking in groups: Efficacy of treatment and maintenance procedures. *Journal of Consulting and Clinical Psychology,* 1977, *45*, 245–249.

Resnick, J. H. The control of smoking by stimulus satiation. *Behaviour Research and Therapy,* 1968, *6*, 113–114. (a)

Resnick, J. H. Effects of stimulus satiation on the overlearned maladaptive response of cigarette smoking. *Journal of Consulting and Clinical Psychology,* 1968, *32*, 501–505. (b)

Rodgers, M. P. The effect of social support on the modification of smoking behavior. *Dissertation Abstracts International,* 1977, *38*(3-B), 1448. (University Microfilms No. 77-18,105.)

Rodrigues, M-R. P., & Lichtenstein, E. *Dyadic interaction for the control of smoking.* Unpublished manuscript, University of Oregon, Eugene, Ore., 1977.

Rotter, J. B. Generalized expectancies for internal versus external control of reinforcement. *Psychological monographs,* 1966, *80* (Whole No. 609).

Russell, M. A. H. Realistic goals for smoking and health: A case for safer smoking. *The Lancet,* 1974, *1*, 254–258. (a)

Russell, M. A. H. The smoking habit and its classification. *The Practitioner,* 1974, *212*, 791–800. (b)

Russell, M. A. H. Tobacco smoking and nicotine dependence. In R. J. Gibbons, Y. Israel, H. Kalent, R. E. Popham, W. Schmidt, & R. G. Smart (Eds.), *Research advances in alcohol and drug problems,* Vol. 3. New York: Wiley, 1976.

Russell, M. A. H. Smoking addiction: Some implications for cessation. In J. L. Schwartz (Ed.), *Progress in smok-*

ing cessation: Proceedings of International Conference on Smoking Cessation. New York: American Cancer Society, 1978.

Russell, M. A. H., Wilson, C., Patel, U. A., Cole, P. V., & Feyerabend, C. Comparison of effect on tobacco consumption and carbon monoxide absorption of changing to high and low nicotine cigarettes. *British Medical Journal*, 1973, *4*, 512–516.

Russell, M. A. H., Peto, J., & Patel, U. A. The classification of smoking by factorial structure of motives. *The Journal of the Royal Statistical Society*, 1974, *137*, 313–346.

Russell, M. A. H., Armstrong, E., & Patel, U. A. The role of temporal contiguity in electric aversion therapy for cigarette smoking: Analysis of behavior changes. *Behaviour Research and Therapy*, 1976, *14*, 103–123.

Russell, M. A. H., Feyerabend, C., & Cole, P. V. Plasma nicotine levels after cigarette smoking and chewing nicotine gum. *British Medical Journal*, 1976, *1*, 1043–1046.

Russell, M. A. H., Wilson, C., Feyerabend, C., & Cole, P. V. Effect of nicotine chewing gum on smoking behaviour and as an aid to cigarette withdrawal. *British Medical Journal*, 1976, *2*, 391–393.

Russell, M. A. H., Sutton, S. R., Feyerabend, C., Cole, P. V., & Saloojee, Y. Nicotine chewing gum as a substitute for smoking. *British Medical Journal*, 1977, *1*, 1060–1063.

Russell, M. A. H., Raw, M., Taylor, C., Feyerabend, C., & Saloojee, Y. Blood nicotine and carboxyhemoglobin levels after rapid-smoking aversion therapy. *Journal of Consulting and Clinical Psychology*, 1978, *46*, 1423–1431.

Russell, M. A. H., Wilson, C., Taylor, C., & Baker, C. D. Effect of general practitioners' advice against smoking. *British Medical Journal*, 1979, *2*, 231–235.

Russell, M. A. H., Raw, M., & Jarvis, M. J. Clinical use of nicotine chewing-gum. *British Medical Journal*, 1980, *2*, 1599–1602.

Sachs, D. P. L., Hall, R. G., & Hall, S. M. Effects of rapid smoking: Physiologic evaluation of a smoking-cessation therapy. *Annals of Internal Medicine*, 1978, *88*, 639–641.

Sachs, D. P. L., Hall, R. G., Pechacek, T. F., & Fitzgerald, J. Clarification of risk-benefit issues in rapid smoking. *Journal of Consulting and Clinical Psychology*, 1979, *47*, 1053–1060.

Schachter, S. Nicotine regulation in heavy and light smokers. *Journal of Experimental Psychology: General*, 1977, *106*, 5–12.

Schachter, S. Pharmacological and psychological determinants of smoking. *Annals of Internal Medicine*, 1978, *88*, 104–114.

Schachter, S. Regulation, withdrawal, and nicotine addiction. In N. A. Krasnegor (Ed.), *Cigarette smoking as a dependence process* (NIDA Research Monograph 23, DHEW Publication No. (ADM) 79-800). Washington D.C.: U.S. Government Printing Office, 1979.

Schachter, S., Kozlowski, L. T., & Silverstein, B. Effects of urinary pH on cigarette smoking. *Journal of Experimental Psychology: General*, 1977, *106*, 13–19.

Schachter, S., Silverstein, B., Kozlowski, L. T., Herman, C. P., & Liebling, B. Effects of stress on cigarette smoking and urinary pH. *Journal of Experimental Psychology: General*, 1977, *106*, 24–30.

Schachter, S., Silverstein, B., & Perlick, D. Psychological and pharmacological explanations of smoking under stress. *Journal of Experimental Psychology: General*, 1977, *106*, 31–40.

Schmahl, D. P., Lichtenstein, E., & Harris, D. E. Successful treatment of habitual smokers with warm, smoky air and rapid smoking. *Journal of Consulting and Clinical Psychology*, 1972, *38*, 103–111.

Schwartz, J. L. A critical review and evaluation of smoking control methods. *Public Health Reports*, 1969, *84*, 489–506.

Schwartz, J. L. Review and evaluation of methods of smoking cessation, 1969–1977. *Public Health Reports*, 1979, *94*, 558–563.

Schwartz, J. L., & Rider, G. Smoking cessation methods in the United States and Canada: 1969–1974. In J. Steinfeld, W. Griffiths, K. Ball, & R. M. Taylor (Eds.), *Health consequences, education, cessation activities and governmental action*, Vol. 2. Proceedings of the Third World Conference on Smoking and Health, New York, 1975. (DHEW Publication No. (NIH) 77-1413), 1977.

Schwartz, J. L., & Rider, G. *Review and evaluation of smoking control methods: The United States and Canada, 1969–1977.* Atlanta: Center for Disease Control, 1978.

Severson, H. H., O'Neal, M., & Hynd, G. W. *Cognitive coping strategies and aversive counterconditioning in the modification of smoking behavior.* Paper presented at the meeting of the Western Psychological Association, Seattle, April 1977.

Shiffman, S. M. The tobacco withdrawal syndrome. In N. A. Krasnegor (Ed.), *Cigarette smoking as a dependence process* (NIDA Research Monograph 23, DHEW Publication No. (ADM) 79-800). Washington D.C.: U.S. Government Printing Office, 1979.

Shiffman, S. M., & Jarvik, M. E. Smoking withdrawal symptoms in two weeks of abstinence. *Psychopharmacology*, 1976, *50*, 35–39.

Silverstein, B., Kozlowski, L. T., & Schachter, S. Social life, cigarette smoking, and urinary pH. *Journal of Experimental Psychology: General*, 1977, *106*, 20–23.

Sjöberg, L., & Johnson, T. Trying to give up smoking: A study of volitional breakdowns. *Addictive Behaviors*, 1978, *3*, 149–164.

Solomon, R. L., & Corbit, J. D. An opponent-process theory of motivation: II. Cigarette addiction. *Journal of Abnormal Psychology*, 1973, *81*, 158–171.

Spring, F. L., Sipich, J. F., Trimble, R. W., & Goeckner, D. J. Effects of contingency and noncontingency contracts in the context of a self-control-oriented smoking modification program. *Behavior Therapy*, 1978, *9*, 967–968.

Sushinsky, L. W. Expectation of future treatment, stimulus satiation, and smoking. *Journal of Consulting and Clinical Psychology*, 1972, *39*, 343.

Thompson, E. L. Smoking education programs, 1960–1976. *American Journal of Public Health*, 1978, *68*, 250–257.

Thoresen, C. E., & Mahoney, M. J. *Behavioral self-control.* New York: Holt, Rinehart & Winston, 1974.

Tomkins, S. S. Psychological model for smoking behavior. *American Journal of Public Health*, 1966, *12*, 17–20.

Tongas, P. N. The Kaiser-Permanente smoking control

program: Its purpose and implications for an HMO. *Professional Psychology,* 1979, *10,* 409–418.

Tori, C. D. A smoking satiation procedure with reduced medical risk. *Journal of Clinical Psychology,* 1978, *34,* 574–577.

U.S. Department of Health, Education, and Welfare. *Smoking and health: A report of the surgeon general.* (DHEW Publication No. (PHS) 79-50066.) Washington D.C.: U.S. Government Printing Office, 1979.

U.S. Public Health Service. *Adult use of tobacco, 1975.* Atlanta: Center for Disease Control, 1976.

Wilde, G. J. S. Behavior therapy for addicted smokers. *Behaviour Research and Therapy,* 1964, *2,* 107–110.

Wilson, G. T., & Davison, G. C. Aversion techniques in behavior therapy: Some theoretical and metatheoretical considerations. *Journal of Consulting and Clinical Psychology,* 1969, *33,* 327–329.

Wynder, E. L., & Stellman, S. D. Impact of long-term filter cigarette usage on lung and larynx cancer risk: A case-control study. *Journal of National Cancer Institution,* 1979, *62,* 471–477.

Wynder, E. L., Mushinsky, M., & Stellman, S. The epidemiology of the less harmful cigarette. In E. L. Wynder, G. B. Gori, & D. Hoffman (Eds.), *Proceedings of the Third World Conference on Smoking and Health, Vol. 1: Modifying the risk for the smoker.* (DHEW Publication No. (NIH) 76-1221.) Washington D.C.: U.S. Government Printing Office, 1976.

Young, F. D. *The modification of cigarette smoking by oversatiation and covert behavior rehearsal.* Unpublished doctoral dissertation, University of Windsor, Canada, 1973.

Younggren, J. N., & Parker, R. A. The smoking control clinic: A behavioral approach to quitting smoking. *Professional Psychology,* 1977, *8,* 81–87.

CHAPTER 20

Crime and Delinquency

John D. Burchard and Theodore W. Lane

Overview

Until recently most research relating to the use of behavior-modification programs with criminals and delinquents has focused on the short-term effect of contingency management procedures (Braukmann & Fixsen, 1975; Burchard & Harig, 1976; Davidson & Seidman, 1974). The results have been very impressive. Given the tight control of relevant reinforcement, as well as punishment contingencies and behavioral targets that are defined in specific and observable terms, significant change in the behavior of delinquents and criminals has generally been achieved. This result has been demonstrated in institutional as well as community-based settings, and it applies to the elimination of undesirable, antisocial behavior as well as the development of incompatible, prosocial behavior and academic and vocational skills.

John D. Burchard and Theodore W. Lane • Department of Psychology, University of Vermont, Burlington, Vermont 05401. John D. Burchard is currently on extended leave from the University of Vermont and is serving as Commissioner of the Department of Social and Rehabilitation Services for the State of Vermont. Theodore W. Lane is also serving as Director of the ONTOP Program, a regional, community-based educational program for adjudicated adolescents administered through the Burlington Public School System.

The primary purpose of this review is to look at the long-term effects of the behavior-modification approach with respect to both the youth who participate in those programs and the justice and social service systems within which they are administered. In both cases, the primary issue is one of generalization: To what extent do these programs influence the rate at which the offender returns to criminal or delinquent behavior, and to what extent have the programs changed the traditional ways in which we handle people who do or might engage in criminal or delinquent behavior?

On the surface, the long-term impact of behavior-modification programs on both the client and the system has been discouraging. Consider the following:

1. In an excellent book on the social learning approach to criminal behavior, Nietzel (1979) reviewed a total of six prison token-economies (Walter Reed Hospital in Washington, D.C.; Draper Correctional Center in Alabama; Special Treatment and Rehabilitative Program, also referred to as START, in Missouri; Contingency Management Program in Virginia; Patuxent Institution in Maryland; and Junction City Treatment Center in Ohio). There are no meaningful outcome data associated with any of the six programs, and only one of the programs (Draper Correctional Cen-

ter) continues to function in a similar manner today.

2. In 1976, Burchard and Harig reviewed three institutional behavior-modification programs for delinquents (Intensive Training Program in Butner, North Carolina; National Training School for Boys in Washington, D.C.; and Karl Holton School in California). Only one program (Holton) was associated with any meaningful outcome data (which were positive in comparison with baseline institutional recidivism rates). However, none of those programs are operating now in the manner described in that review.

3. The only controlled, experimental outcome study (e.g., random assignment) of an institutional behavior-modification program for juveniles involved the Karl Holton School program. The results indicated that there was no difference between it and a transactional analysis program; both led to a 12-month recidivism rate of 32% (Jesness, 1975a).

4. According to the *preliminary* results of a controlled comparison of 27 behavior-modification-group home programs (e.g., the teaching-family model) and 25 comparison-group homes, there has been no difference in the reduction of postprogram offense rates, although the teaching-family program was one-third less expensive (Jones, 1978).

5. In a controlled experimental comparison of a nonresidential, community-based behavior-modification program with a no-treatment control group, it was determined that juveniles with previous records did better than their controls. However, juveniles without a previous record did worse than their corresponding controls (Fo & O'Donnell, 1975).

To conclude, however, that the behavior-modification approach has been a failure or that it should be abandoned in favor of some other approach would be unwarranted for several reasons. First, it is important to recognize that the baseline with respect to the empirical verification of the success of any rehabilitation programs for delinquents and criminals is equally discouraging. Lipton, Martinson, and Wilks (1975) conducted a thorough search of the corrections literature between 1945 and 1967, looking for any studies whose designs and methodologies yielded interpretable findings. They employed fairly rigorous criteria,

in which a study had to (1) be an evaluation of a treatment method, (2) employ an independent measure of improvement, and (3) utilize a control group, and they identified 231 studies. Because of the many differences in subjects, outcome measures, and treatment procedures, as well as the few attempts to replicate findings, the picture was far from definitive. Nevertheless, the authors concluded that with a few isolated exceptions, the rehabilitation efforts that had been evaluated to that point had no appreciable effect on the rate at which the offender returned to crime (i.e., recidivism). Other reviews of evaluative treatment studies (Bailey, 1966; Robinson & Smith, 1971; Romig, 1978) are equally pessimistic: There has been very little evidence to support any program's claim to superior rehabilitative efficacy.

The second major reason that a dismantling of behavior-modification programs would be premature is that the purpose of program evaluation should be to provide information relevant to program improvement, not program elimination. This is particularly true for the social learning model, in which behavioral data are required to determine whether or not a particular intervention is effective. Given negative results, intervention procedures are systematically changed in an effort to obtain a more positive outcome. Although this process has been used more with quasi-experimental, single-subject designs, the benefits also apply to controlled-outcome studies. If postprogram recidivism rates are not acceptable, or if a comparison program appears more effective, program revision in the context of further evaluation is necessary. For example, the Youth Center Research Project referred to above (Jesness, 1975a) provided data indicating that behavior-modification programs may be more effective for some youth, while the transactional analysis programs may be more effective for others. The author's suggestion that a combination of the two programs may be the most productive direction to take warrants further consideration.

Third, a final argument in defense of a behavioral approach is that the lack of impressive outcome data is forcing behaviorists to become more innovative and to explore new intervention strategies. As will be seen, the primary problem in existing behavioral programs lies more in the areas of maintenance and generalization than in the absence of any direct effect. Recent developments in self-government, self-control, cognitive behavior modification, and prevention programs suggest promising areas of benefit, although empirical verification is still lacking.

Institutional Behavior-Modification Programs

The development of behavior-modification programs in institutional settings for criminals and delinquents began in the mid-1960s and expanded to the point where it is now estimated that in almost every state, there is some variation of a token-economy system within an institutional setting. Initially, the development of these programs was accompanied by an enthusiasm that was based on the following assumptions:

1. Delinquent and criminal behavior is a function of one's social learning history; in other words, delinquent and criminal behavior has been shaped and maintained through reinforcement and punishment contingencies in one's past and present environments.

2. Given appropriate reinforcement and punishment contingencies, individuals who engage in delinquent and criminal behavior can learn socially adaptive behaviors as well as learning not to engage in antisocial behavior.

3. An institutional or correctional setting is especially suitable for the modification of delinquent and criminal behavior because it is a physically contained environment and the reinforcement and punishment contingencies can be regulated with laboratorylike precision.

4. By regulating the reinforcement and punishment contingencies in accordance with social learning principles, socially adaptive behavior can be strengthened and antisocial behavior can be weakened.

5. The behavioral change that occurs in an institutional setting will generalize to the natural environment, especially if there is a gradual transition from artificial to natural contingencies.

The first two assumptions, that delinquent and criminal behavior is learned and that individuals who engage in delinquent and criminal behavior can learn not to engage in such behavior, are basic to the social learning approach and relate to all areas of behavior modification. Although simplistic and too general to be disproved, little evidence has been accumulated that is contrary to such a position. While there are some data suggesting that there *may* be physiological and biological characteristics that influence the learning of social and antisocial behavior, the direct link between biological impairment and criminal behavior has yet to be established (Shah & Roth, 1974). Clearly, from a social learning standpoint, the most promising direction involves the development of an optimal environment for teaching the criminal or delinquent offenders how to gratify their needs in socially acceptable ways. The extent to which that environment should involve contingent punishment, contingent reinforcement, psychotherapy, counseling, etc., however, is still at issue. The latter three assumptions refer to the implementation of behavior-modification procedures within an institutional setting, the direct behavioral effect of those behavior-modification procedures, and the generalization of those effects to the natural environment.

The Implementation of Behavior-Modification Procedures

From a social learning standpoint, the implementation of behavior-modification procedures within an institutional environment was met with considerable enthusiasm because of the apparent ease of regulating reinforcement and punishment contingencies. According to the prevailing logic, if the critical component for habilitation was the control of the antecedents and the consequences of behavior, this could be accomplished more easily in an institutional environment (where the people who control the relevant stimulus events are trained professionals) rather than in the natural environment (where the relevant contingencies occur in a multitude of settings and are controlled by a wide variety of people, many of whom are themselves conditioned to prompt, reinforce, and punish the wrong behavior).

It is now clear that some of the initial optimism that was associated with the implementation of behavior-modification programs in institutional settings is no longer justified. While there are ample data to document successful behavioral change given the systematic manipulations of reinforcement and punishment contingencies, the appropriate manipulation of those contingencies has often been difficult, if not impossible, to achieve, and even where it has been achieved, there is little evidence that the corresponding behavioral change has generalized beyond the artificial or unnatural environment of the institution.

With respect to the implementation of behavior-modification programs in institutional settings, significant problems have been encountered in two general areas. The first is a general resistance to change, on the part of both the administrators and the staff or guards who interact directly with the inmates or residents. The second problem relates to a bad reputation, a problem not very dissimilar to that of the bully on the block who occasionally exercises poor judgment and employs excessive aversive techniques to get his or her way.

With respect to the first problem (resistance to change), behavior-modification advocates who do not recognize that much of their time will be spent trying to change the behavior of the staff and the decisions and policy of administrators are in for a rude awakening. A good example of this resistance occurred at the Connecticut School for Boys (Dean & Reppucci, 1974). In 1970, a much-publicized crisis involving a shooting incident by one of the residents and a subsequent allegation of brutality by various staff members provided the impetus for changing the school from a custody-oriented to a rehabilitation-oriented institution. The primary objective of a newly hired superintendent and a team of professional consultants from a nearby university was to establish a 24-hour-a-day rehabilitation program based on a token-economy system. in which points would serve as a medium of exchange for the purchase of all the goods and privileges available to the boys at the school.

A major effort was made on the part of the superintendent and his consultants to incor-porate the work-for-pay program that existed at the school into the overall token-economy point system, and to orient the program less toward manual labor and more toward teaching useful skills. Although this change would appear to have had rather strong administrative support, it could not be implemented. In this case, the resistance came from a state department commissioner who felt that it would be politically impossible to obtain legislative approval for such a change; a business office that could not become involved in exchanging points for money; and some on-line supervisory staff who felt that they were responsible for seeing that work was accomplished and that teaching skills would impair effectiveness and might even be dangerous. Similar kinds of resistance are apt to be encountered in trying to revise institutional policy so that (1) inmates or residents can learn to make decisions on their own (when to go to bed or get up, whether to go to school or to a job, etc.); (2) inmates or residents have opportunities to learn relevant, noninstitutional skills (trips to town, relationships with girls and women, increased interaction with families and relatives); and (3) there is access to back up reinforcers in addition to the privileges normally encountered in a custodial type of program. These and other obstacles that can interfere with the success of behavior-modification programs are discussed in an excellent review article by Reppucci and Saunders (1974).

The resistance to the implementation of behavior-modification programs is not restricted to administrators and institutional policy. Staff members are frequently resistant to changes that involve increased data collection and record keeping as well as to efforts to encourage them to utilize more positive reinforcement and less punishment. For example, in one program at the Draper Correctional Center (Kennedy, 1976; McKee, Smith, Wood, & Milan, 1975), the guards went through an extensive behavioral training program that emphasized the use of positive reinforcement procedures. However, when required to make use of what they had learned in the individual practicum part of the program, almost all of the guards used negative reinforcement, punishment, or time-out rather than positive reinforcement.

According to the authors, the training program did not counteract the guards' social learning experiences, which had taught them that the most effective behavior-management system in prison is to grant reinforcers on a noncontingent basis and then to control behavior through their removal (Kennedy, 1976).

A second illustration of this problem is provided by Bassett and Blanchard (1977). In October 1973, a token-economy program was initiated for the inmates of the Shelby County Penal Farm. By the end of the first three months, it appeared that the token-economy system, involving primarily the administration of points for the completion of relevant target behaviors, was functioning successfully. At that point, the project director went on a four-month leave of absence, eliminating the direct, on-site supervision of the behavior-management program. On his return, a retrospective analysis of the data revealed that in the absence of the direct on-site supervision, there was an increase in the use of punishment (response cost), in terms of both the number of categories of behavior for which it was administered and the frequency of its use. A corresponding decrease in the use of punishment on the return of the project director indicated that an important part of the stimulus control for the staff's behavior was the presence of the project director. Whether or not the project director functioned as a positive reinforcer or a negative reinforcer is unclear. What is clear is that in the absence of the director, the staff reverted to a more habitual way of responding to the inmates. Obviously, the issues related to the maintenance of modified staff and inmate behavior are very similar, and further research is needed if we are to learn how to achieve more positive results in both areas.

Because of the tendency to report and publish success rather than failure, it is impossible to document the number of institutional behavior-modification programs that have succumbed to the vigorous resistance to institutional change. No doubt this number is considerable. The problem has been best illustrated by Burton Blatt in his book *Exodus from Pandemonium* (1970). Almost all of the concerns regarding the evils of institutionalization expressed by Dorothy Dix to the Massachusetts Legislature in 1866 were the same

as those expressed by Blatt to the same legislature 100 years later. Clearly, the task of changing institutional programs and policies is not to be taken for granted, and it may be more appropriate for behavior modifiers to focus on institutional procedures and policies as the data base, rather than the behavior of the inmates or residents. Social learning theory and applied behavior analysis clearly have the technology to create significant change at the systems level.

The second obstacle to the implementation of behavior-modification programs in institutional settings has been a poor reputation. It is ironic that the therapeutic orientation that has so vociferously attacked the use of labels (e.g., *delinquent, hyperkinetic, incorrigible,* and *unmanageable*) is itself the victim of negative labeling (e.g., *inhumane, punitive, rigid, regressive,* and *dehumanizing*). Part of the problem relates to the use of behavioral techniques to achieve submission to custodial-like objectives. An example is the now-inoperative Special Treatment Rehabilitation Training Program (START) developed in 1972 at the Medical Center for Federal Prisoners in Springfield, Missouri. The program incorporated a token-economy system to deal with hard-to-manage prisoners in the federal prison system. For the most part, the program relied on the use of negative reinforcement to shape institutional compliance. Inmates began the program on a nonprivileged, segregation status. By engaging in such behaviors as cleaning designated areas without bickering and performing industry assignments without controversy (Federal Bureau of Prisons, 1972; Kennedy, 1976), they could earn back access to local newspapers and magazines, personal property, commissary items, and additional recreational time (Nietzel, 1979). Noncompliance or the occurrence of antisocial, disruptive behavior resulted in the loss of status and/or good time (Nietzel, 1979).

In the midst of legal and professional criticism, the program was closed in 1974. Although the government announced that the program was closed for economic reasons (Warren, 1974), the termination was more likely a response to increasing concern over (1) an involuntary admissions policy; (2) an excessive reliance on aversive control to achieve institutional compliance and submission; and (3) the absence of any substantial program to teach anger or impulse control, problem solving, decision making, or any other skills related to helping inmates develop competence and coping with the complex pressures of noninstitutional life (Azrin, 1974; Cohen, 1974; DeRisi, 1974).

Unfortunately, the failure of programs like START lends credence to the belief that behavior-modification programs are rigid, aversive, and unmanageable, and that they attempt only to produce submissive inmates. However, before making such a generalization, two points need to be considered. First, it seems somewhat shortsighted to close down a program for being too aversive and then to replace it with a more standard correctional program that relies even more on aversive control (Nietzel, 1979). Second, while it is possible to label the START program as a behavior-modification program, it was probably not much more so than the standard correctional program that exists today. Certainly, there is nothing inherent in the technology of behavior modification that says that program recipients should be enrolled on an involuntary basis, and there is very little evidence that the most effective way to teach new coping skills is through aversive control.

The negative labeling that is associated with behavior-modification programs was further exemplified by a contingency management program (CMT) that was funded by the Law Enforcement Assistance Association and was developed in Virginia (Johnson & Geller, 1973; Nietzel, 1979). Even at its inception, this particular token-economy program involved more skill-development components than existed at START, and participation in the program was voluntary. Also, following a site visit in 1974 by representatives of the funding agency, educational opportunities were expanded, and there was a marked reduction in the contingency that emphasized institutional compliance behavior and personal appearance (Nietzel, 1979). Nevertheless, the program was discontinued shortly thereafter, partly because of inaccurate and inflammatory labeling on the part of its critics (Geller, Johnson, Hamlin, & Kennedy, 1977).

Direct Behavioral Effects

The most positive aspect of the implementation of behavior-modification programs in institutional studies is their direct, short-term effects on behavior. When there is an opportunity to regulate environmental contingencies in accordance with social learning principles, successful behavioral change has usually been achieved. In a review of the research literature on behavior modification and juvenile delinquency, Davidson and Seidman (1974) cited 33 studies between 1964 and 1973. Of these studies, 60% (20) were conducted in an institutional as opposed to a community-based setting. The focuses of the 20 institutional studies were fairly equally distributed across three general target areas: educational behavior, program behavior (e.g., rule compliance), and delinquent behavior (e.g., disruptive behavior). For the most part, the purpose of each study was to demonstrate a functional relationship between a contingency-management procedure and a subsequent change in behavior. The subjects were used as their own control in all of the studies, and only two studies also included separate control groups (Cohen & Filipczak, 1971; Pavlott, 1971). As Davidson and Seidman pointed out, there are methodological weaknesses in many of the studies. Only 9 of the 20 studies contained adequate baselines, only 5 involved the systematic manipulation of treatment variables, and in only 1 setting were data obtained by unbiased data collectors. Nevertheless, in every study, a substantial change in behavior seemed to be associated with a corresponding change in a reinforcement and/or a punishment contingency.

Several additional demonstrations of such functional relationships have taken place in the past five years. At the Junction City Treatment Center (JCTC) in Ohio, McNamara and Andrasik (1977) conducted a series of quasi-experimental evaluations of different components of a behavioral program for 50 male felons between 18 and 35 years of age. The program was arranged so that the inmates could progress through a multiple-step privilege system on the basis of weekly performances related to maintenance behavior (e.g., dressing properly, cleaning one's living area, etc.), self-improvement behavior (e.g., participation in education, employment, activity therapy, and counseling programs), and inappropriate behavior (e.g., rule infractions, physical and verbal aggression). In an effort to evaluate a portion of the program, an A-B-C design was utilized in which Condition A (4 weeks) was an unobtrusive baseline, Condition B (7 weeks) was an obtrusive baseline with feedback to the inmates regarding their performance, and Condition C (4 weeks) consisted of a contingency in which progress through the tier system was determined by satisfactory performance of the three types of behavior. The results demonstrated a significant improvement in all three types of behavior during Condition B (i.e., feedback on performance only), to the point where there was little room for improvement in the maintenance and self-improvement categories. During Condition C, where progress was contingent on performance, the improvements in maintenance and self-improvement were maintained, and there was some additional decline in inappropriate behavior. Although the design was basically an A-B design, the data suggest that feedback alone resulted in significant improvement in inmate behavior. What is less clear is why the contingency phase was implemented (particularly for the maintenance of self-improvement behavior) when there was little room for any additional positive change in behavior. Maintaining control with the obtrusive feedback condition would seem to be preferable to the performance contingency for two reasons: *first*, feedback alone is a more natural consequence for such behaviors as cleaning one's living area and participating in educational programs, and *second*, the reinforcement associated with the feedback is more intrinsic than the reinforcement associated with the more external regulation of privileges. For both of these reasons, the feedback condition would seem to promote greater generalization than the contingency procedures introduced in Condition C.

Another study focusing on contingency management procedures was conducted at the Draper Correctional Center in Elmore, Alabama (Milan & McKee, 1976). In a 14-month

sequential analysis of the relationship between various point contingencies and various maintenance behaviors it was found that contingent reinforcement was associated with performance levels that exceeded 85%, whereas performance levels fluctuated between 65% and 75% during baseline and noncontingent point conditions. The fact that baseline performance after 14 months of intervention was very similar to the original baseline performance, however, suggests that the duration of contingent reinforcement alone is not sufficient to establish maintenance of the target behavior.

At an adult prison farm, Bassett, Blanchard, and Koshland (1975) replicated a television-news-quiz effect that was demonstrated by Tyler and Brown (1968) with juveniles. There were approximately 70% correct responses to news quizzes when reinforcement was contingent, as compared with 40% correct responses during a noncontingent reinforcement condition. The authors concluded that inmates watched and comprehended more TV when relatively strong reinforcement was provided for doing so. In a second part of the study, Bassett and his colleagues found that the inmates responded to opportunities to participate in a remedial education program in the same fashion. When the contingent point reinforcement was doubled, attendance went from 20% to 45%. Following a second baseline, during which attendance returned to a 20% level, a second bonus-points condition produced an attendance level of approximately 90% for a period of 3.5 months. The effect of the bonus reinforcement was very durable, although it is doubtful that attendance would have remained at such a high level on a subsequent return to baseline.

In terms of the number of subjects involved, one of the most convincing demonstrations of the effects of contingent reinforcement in an institutional-correctional setting was provided by Hobbs and Holt (1976). The subjects were 125 adjudicated 12- to 15-year-old boys residing at the Alabama Boys Industrial School. Focusing on social behaviors, following rules and instructions, completing chores, and avoiding antisocial behaviors, the authors utilized a multiple-baseline design across three different cottages (a fourth cottage was a control cottage) to evaluate the effect of a token-economy program. In this particular program, paper money served as tokens that could be exchanged for commissary items, off-campus trips, passes home, and final release from the institution. In general, the results demonstrated the power of the token-economy system: Each time contingencies were applied to a different cottage, there was a marked improvement in the specific target behaviors of the boys in that cottage.

In summary, it is clear that contingency-management systems are effective in modifying the behavior of delinquents and criminals within institutional settings. There is also convincing evidence that such programs are more effective than the traditional "correctional" methods of behavior management in producing short-term, direct effects. Although there are fewer data on cost-effectiveness, it appears that most of the differential benefit of the behavior-modification approach could be achieved without a significant increase in cost. If so, institutional administrators should consider implementing positive behavioral programs, since the results are likely to be better than or at least equal to those of the more traditional methods of behavior management.

Generalization to the Natural Environment

Given extensive evidence that indicates that behavior-modification programs can improve the behavior of delinquents and criminals within institutional settings, it is important to ask whether the positive effects will generalize to improved functioning back in the community. In attempting to answer this question in the past, the biggest problem has been the dearth of good, evaluative outcome studies. While this situation still exists, the few studies that have been conducted are not very promising.

The results of the programmed-learning–token-economy program that Cohen and his associates administered at the National Training School in Washington, D.C., suggested less recidivism at the end of the one- and two-year follow-up periods, but equal recidivism at the end of the third year (Cohen &

Filipczak, 1971). However, it should be noted that there were significant problems with respect to the adequacy of the control groups (Burchard & Harig, 1976).

At the Draper Correctional Center in Alabama, 29 participants in the cell-block token-economy program and 113 other prisoners in three control groups were followed up for an average of 18 postrelease months (Jenkins, Witherspoon, DeVine, DeZalera, Muller, Barton, & McKee, 1974). At the follow-up, 28% of the token-economy group had committed a criminal offense, compared with 47% in the occupational training group, 32% in the state-trade-school group, and 37% in the group who had been in the regular Draper program. Unfortunately, the subjects in the experimental and the control groups were neither matched nor randomly assigned; thus, the comparability of the groups is placed in question (Milan & McKee, 1974).

In the 1970s, the California Youth Authority conducted two outcome studies analyzing the effects of contingency-contracting and token-economy programs in institutional settings. In the first study, follow-up data on 452 youths who participated in a contingency-contracting program in one institution were compared with 329 youths of comparable age at another institution in which the program was more traditional (Ferdun, Webb, Lockard, & Mahan, 1972). The results showed a 50% decrease in the base rate of parole violations for the "experimental" institution. However, the recidivism rate was almost 10% higher than that for the "control" institution. Once again, the youths were not randomly assigned to the two institutions, and the only variable on which they were matched was age.

In a second, more methodologically sophisticated, outcome study at the California Youth Authority (Jesness, 1975a), youths were randomly assigned to either a behavior-modification or a transactional analysis program. While there were some problems relating to the administration of the study (Burchard & Harig, 1976), the fact that there was random assignment and that follow-up data were obtained on the 453 transactional-analysis-program youths and the 398 behavior-modification-program youths makes this study one of the best institutional outcome-studies of a behavior modification program to date. Nevertheless, the results are somewhat discouraging. At 12 months after parole release, 32% of both groups had been returned to an institution, and at 24 months, the failure rates in both groups had increased to 48%. As for the magnitude of the recidivism rate, some encouragement can be obtained from a comparison with somewhat higher 12-month rates for those same institutions one and two years prior to the study (40–49% range) and with the 12-month rates for two seemingly comparable institutions during the same time period as the study (42%). However, the rates are still unacceptably high and call for a continued search for more effective institutional programs and for the development of more effective alternatives to institutionalization.

The final outcome study involved a comparison of 25 juvenile females who went through a token-economy–contingency-management program with 25 matched control subjects (Ross & McKay, 1976). The results of a 12-month follow-up indicated significantly higher recidivism rates and increased negative reports for the girls who went through the behavior-modification program.

Considering the vast number of institutional programs that have adopted behavior-modification techniques in an effort to rehabilitate the delinquent and/or the criminal offender, it is somewhat astonishing that there are only a handful of studies that contain any kind of follow-up data. One could argue that because of methodological flaws and/or inept program administration, the five studies cited above represent a biased picture of the present state of this field. If so, the onus is on the behavior-modification advocate to demonstrate that the long-term outcome of institutional behavior-modification programs is in fact better than "incarceration-as-usual." Until that happens, the conclusion has to be that behavior-modification programs can be used to effect change in institutional behavior (and are very defensible on that basis) but that the positive results do not generalize to improved functioning back in the community.

If behavior-modification techniques produce better behavior in the institution but not nec-

essarily better behavior in the community, it is important to ask what additional changes might be made to maintain the effect on the individual when he or she returns home. The biggest obstacle to achieving lower recidivism rates appears to be the heavy emphasis on external control. Institutions, by their very nature, impose changes in behavior that in many cases are necessary and justified (e.g., in terms of the protection of self or of other inmates). However, forced behavioral change is not compatible with learning self-control, and for that reason, many individuals whose behavior is not dangerous to themselves or others are being removed from institutions.

In many ways, behavior-modification programs also force a change in behavior. Decisions are made by the staff as to which behaviors will result in powerful reinforcement. In one way or another, the inmate is typically told, "Here are lots of things you can do, and these are the positive things that will happen if you do them." Both the target behaviors (goals) and the contingencies are externally developed and controlled. An alternative might be to set up a system to shape decision making, problem solving, and self-control. Instead of imposing a token-economy system on the individual, individuals can be taught to develop their own day-to-day objectives, and they can be provided with opportunities to reinforce their own behavior. While this more cognitive form of behavior management is primarily used in the community (Kendall & Hollon, 1979), it also has potential for behavior-management programs within institutional settings.

There are two compelling explanations for the dearth of outcome studies pertaining to the effectiveness of institutional behavior-modification programs. One is the difficulty of obtaining adequate comparison groups. Thus far, there has been little headway in convincing judges, prosecutors, social service personnel, and institution administrators of the merits of random assignment. The second is that many of the advocates of behavioral technology have gravitated toward the development and evaluation of community-based alternatives to institutionalization. Given what data there are, this would seem to be a logical transition. The remainder of this chapter focuses on the effectiveness of some of those efforts.

Community-Based, Residential Behavior-Modification Programs

With the trend toward deinstitutionalization, particularly for juvenile delinquents, there has been a significant increase in the development of community-based residential programs. For the most part, this change has been reflected in an increased number of foster homes and group homes, although there has also been some additional use of boarding homes and apartments as well as an increased tendency to leave youth in their own homes.

Although it cannot always be documented by hard data, behavior-modification procedures have played a significant role in this development. With respect to foster home programs, for example, while there are no studies that compare the effectiveness of foster parents who use behavior-modification techniques with those who do not, there are an increasing number of foster-parent training programs that incorporate a variety of behavioral techniques into their curriculum (Guerney, 1976; Ryan, 1978).

During the past five years, the Vermont Foster Parent Training Program has developed and evaluated a curriculum for training foster-parent trainers (i.e., foster parents who are qualified to teach other foster parents). The curriculum for the 16-week training program focuses on three general types of skills: communication skills, behavior-management skills, and conflict-resolution skills. At present, there are 21 qualified trainers located in different geographical regions of the state who offer the course on a periodic basis. While there are some data that suggest that foster parent trainers do acquire new skills and that paraprofessional foster-parent trainers are as effective in teaching the course as professional staff from the university, there are no data to indicate whether foster parents who go through the training program are any more or less effective with their foster children than foster parents who do not. Likewise, there are no data that compare the effectiveness of foster parents who utilize behavioral techniques with that of

group home programs that also employ behavioral procedures. This lack is especially unfortunate from the standpoint of cost-effectiveness, since most group homes are much more expensive than foster homes.

In terms of evaluation data, the picture regarding the effectiveness of behaviorally oriented group homes is not nearly as bleak. The most familiar behavior-modification program at the group home level is the teaching-family program. Starting with Achievement Place in the late 1960s, the teaching-family program has now expanded to more than 200 group homes located in more than 20 states throughout the country. In 1977, a national teaching-family association was established, which now coordinates the operation of teaching-family training sites located in at least 5 different states.

Given the data-based approach that is basic to the teaching-family model, more than 60 studies have been published that relate primarily to the process variables of the program. While most of this review focuses on two more recent outcome-studies of the teaching-family model, a brief review of some of the direct effects of the program is presented first.

In terms of process research, the results are consistent with the results of the contingency-management procedures employed in institutional settings: a wide variety of behaviors have been modified by means of the systematic manipulation of strong reinforcement and punishment contingencies. A major difference from the institutional studies is that the target behaviors seem to relate more to community survival, and the behavioral change is achieved in a less controlled environment. Some of the specific behaviors that have been modified in teaching-family programs include classroom behaviors (Bailey, Wolf, & Phillips, 1970; Kirigin, Phillips, Timbers, Fixsen, & Wolf, 1975); interview skills (Braukmann, Maloney, Fixsen, Phillips, & Wolf, 1974); negotiation skills (Kifer, Lewis, Green, & Phillips, 1974); communication skills (Bailey, Timbers, Phillips, & Wolf, 1971; Maloney, Harper, Braukmann, Fixsen, Phillips, & Wolf, 1976); vocational skills (Ayala, Minkin, Phillips, Fixsen, & Wolf, 1973); and more effective skills to employ with encounters with police (Werner, Minkin, Minkin, Fixsen, Phillips, & Wolf,

1975). Also, several useful papers have been published about staff training (Maloney, Phillips, Fixsen, & Wolf, 1975) and the certification of teaching parents (Braukmann, Fixsen, Kirigin, Phillips, Phillips, & Wolf, 1975). One of the more recent developments in this regard has been an effort to train staff in the specific social behaviors that are preferred by the residents (Willner, Braukmann, Kirigin, Fixsen, Phillips, & Wolf, 1977). This approach would seem to be a refreshing reversal from traditional residential programs, where almost all of the emphasis is on changing the residents' behavior in the direction preferred by the staff, and could have a significant payoff in terms of resident motivation and overall program effectiveness.

In addition to the process studies conducted within the teaching-family program, attempts have been made to replicate some of the procedural effects in other community-based, residential programs. For example, at Welcome House in Santa Paula, California, contingent points enhanced table-setting behavior and meal promptness, while contingent-point fines reduced conversational interruptions (Liberman, Ferris, Salgado, & Salgado, 1975). In the few instances where the findings were not replicated, the discrepancies were attributed to minor differences in the values, expectancies, and training of the teaching parents. Also, at the Crisis Care Center in Danville, Illinois, there were multiple demonstrations of the direct effects of a contingency-management system similar to that employed at Achievement Place (Davidson & Wolfred, 1977; Emshoff, Redd, & Davidson, 1974).

With respect to outcome studies of the teaching-family model, two preliminary sources of data are now available: one generated by the staff and advocates of the teaching-family program and one by an independent research corporation that specializes in program evaluations. In addition, one outcome study of a program similar to the teaching-family program will be discussed here.

In a recent article entitled "Achievement Place: A Preliminary Outcome Evaluation" (Kirigin, Wolf, Braukmann, Fixsen, & Phillips, 1979), data are presented that compare 26 youths who have been in Achievement Place with 37 "seemingly comparable" youth who have not. The comparison is broken down into two subgroups. The first subgroup involved a comparison of 18 Achievement Place youths with 19 Boys School (institutional) youths. The Boys School youths were selected by asking the probation officer to review youths who had been sent to the Boys School over the preceding three years and to select those who in the opinion of the probation officer would have been eligible for Achievement Place. Whether or not the Boys School youths would actually have gone to Achievement Place is uncertain, just as it is uncertain whether the Achievement Place youths would have gone to Boys School had that particular program not existed. Nevertheless, in terms of the subsequent return to an institution, the results favored the Achievement Place youths. The institutionalization rate for the Achievement Place youths during the first follow-up year (17%) and the second follow-up year (22%) is approximately one-half the rate for the Boys School youth for each follow-up year (42% and 47%, respectively).

Even greater differences were obtained in a preliminary comparison of a second set of subgroups. In this case, the selection of the two groups was random. Because there were more referrals than Achievement Place could accommodate, each youth who was admitted (by random selection) could subsequently be compared with one or two youths who were not selected. By using this selection procedure, random groups of 8 Achievement Place youths and 18 control-group youths were established. Thus far, the two-year rate of post-selection institutionalization for the Achievement Place group (12% and 12%, respectively) has been much smaller than that for the non-Achievement Place youths (44% and 56%, respectively).

These data should be treated with caution, however, since the Boys School youths were older than the Achievement Place youths (14.5 vs. 13.2 years of age) and had had more police and court contacts (3.89 vs. 2.89) and less school attendance (44% vs. 72%) during the previous year. Also, by the time both groups of youths averaged age 15.8, the mean number of police and court contacts per year was 1.7 for the Achievement Place group and 1.5 for the Boys School group. Nevertheless, a two-year recidivism rate of 12% is encouraging, especially if, as reported, the daily cost of Achievement Place is $15, compared with a cost of $44 a day for the Boys School (Kirigin *et al.*, 1979).

The second outcome evaluation of the teaching-family program represents an interest on the part of the National Institute of Mental Health (Center for Studies in Crime and Delinquency) in evaluating programs through third-party, independent resources. In this case, the NIMH is funding an intensive five-year outcome study conducted by the Evaluation Research Group (ERG) in Eugene, Oregon (Howard, 1979; Jones, 1978, 1979; Jones & Weinrott, 1977; Weinrott, 1979). This longitudinal study, which is near completion, involves a comparison of 27 teaching-family group homes with 25 non-teaching-family "comparison" group homes. The 52 group homes (located in 10 different states) are community-based, residential programs for troubled youth of both sexes, ranging in age between 12 and 16. Approximately one-half the youth who reside in these group homes have been adjudicated delinquent by local juvenile courts. Where possible, the comparison homes were chosen because they were likely alternative community placements for the teaching-family youths, had the teaching-family programs not been in existence. A suitable comparison could not always be achieved, however, since in at least four instances, the experimental and control group homes are not located in the same state.

In March 1979, when the ERG was 4 months into a 12-month data analysis and dissemination period, *preliminary* findings were presented (Jones, 1979). Based on a sample of slightly more than 300 youth in each type of group home, the findings were as follows:

1. About 60% of the youth in both teaching-family and non-teaching-family samples had completed their programs, a percentage suggesting that the internal failure rate for these community-based programs is around 40%.

2. The grade-point averages of the youth tended to stabilize during the program year in the teaching-family sample, whereas they tended to show a continuing decline in the non-teaching-family sample.

3. There was a reduction in offense rates from preprogram to postprogram periods:

67.5% for the teaching-family youth and 62% for the non-teaching-family youth. These recidivism findings were based on coded juvenile-court and social-agency records.

4. There appears to have been less use of postprogram services by teaching-family youth than by non-teaching-family youth, including youth-training schools, institutions, parole and probation services, and various forms of therapy. These findings were based on self-report data.

5. Community consumers tended to rate the teaching-family programs more favorably than they rated the non-teaching-family programs on the dimensions of effectiveness and cooperation, as well as other aspects of program operations.

6. In terms of annual costs per youth, the teaching-family programs cost about one-third less than the non-teaching-family programs.

Based on these preliminary data, the ERG made the following summary statement:

Placed in the perspective of several decades of evaluation of social and correctional programs, these findings seem to be favorable for the Teaching Family model. Many evaluation studies show no difference on any characteristics of an innovative program versus existing or competitive programs. Subsequent analysis probably will support these first findings, so that when our final report is written, the bottom line will be, in effect, that the Teaching Family model costs less, is liked better, and gets the same level of change in youth's behavior as other community-based programs. (Jones, 1979)

In interpreting the preliminary results of this study, it is important to determine any differences that exist between the two samples of group homes. Through an impressive array of data-collection instruments, the ERG has compiled a wealth of information about the programs and their operations, the staff who conduct the programs, the community environments in which they are located, and the characteristics of the youth served by the programs. With respect to the youth, the ERG has concluded that their analyses thus far have shown a very close similarity between the two samples, so that comparisons on various programmatic and outcome measures would seem to be fair and scientifically defensible (Jones, 1979). Data have been presented on the first 503 youths (269 teaching-family and 234 comparison youths), for whom there were no significant differences in age of entry (approximately 14 years), age of termination (approximately 15 years), socioeconomic status of the family, race, functional literacy, or previous offenses. The only significant difference was a 37% proportion of females in the teaching-family sample as compared with a 27% proportion of females in the comparison group homes. This sex difference was controlled in the preliminary findings listed above.

With respect to program differences, the ERG has concluded that the only significant differences between the two samples of group homes are those that would be expected to differentiate a teaching-family and a non-teaching-family type of program. For example, in teaching-family group homes there are many more staff contacts with community agencies, particularly school systems. In addition, the teaching-family program shows a greater emphasis on behavioral, scholastic, and community-oriented objectives and a greater use of the token economy and the teaching interaction, but not a greater use of counseling in community-relations activities. The teaching parents are also reported to have a higher level of staff professionalism, experience and training, and satisfaction with program responsibility than non-teaching-family staff. However, in reviewing the data presented by the ERG, it would appear that a few other differences should be pointed out for consideration. For example, it appears that the teaching-family group homes involve less outside job training and less use of volunteers than the comparison group homes. In addition, it appears that the difference between teaching-family and non-teaching family group homes may not be as large as expected in some of the more critical program characteristics. For example, the program staff assigned ranks to various treatment approaches. The behavioral or token-economy approach was ranked first by 80% of the teaching-family program staff. In contrast, 53% of the comparison-group home staff ranked a behavioral or token approach first (Jones & Weinrott, 1977). It is not clear why 20% of the teaching-family programs do not give a behavioral interpretation to their program. Further, these data suggest that there is a strong behavioral component in at least half the comparison group home programs. While the primary purpose of the ERG's study is to compare the teaching-family

model with whatever other group homes there are, it is important in reviewing the literature on the effects of behavior-modification programs to know that half of those other group homes may at least *describe* their programs as being governed by a behavioral or token-economy approach.

Given the large number of data on the teaching-family model, the ERG is conducting several other studies to determine what other process variables within the teaching-family program might be associated with outcome results. For example, the correlation between changes in grade-point average and the amount of school-related treatment activity is .50. This is an expected linkage between a process-and-outcome variable, since the teaching-family program places so much emphasis on school performance. A second, less expected linkage is a correlation of .45 between "therapeutic activity" in the teaching-family program and a subsequent reduction in official offense rates (Jones, 1979).

Although the ERG outcome evaluation of the teaching-family group homes is not complete, the ERG and the NIMH (and the 52 group homes involved in the study) should be commended for this particular study. While program administrators can and have provided important process information on the direct effects of their procedures, outcome data have been more difficult to accumulate, largely because of the relatively small numbers of residents who receive the services of a particular group home and the limited funds that have been available to collect relevant follow-up data. Hopefully, additional independent third-party outcome studies will be conducted in the near future. A final report on the results of the ERG evaluation of the teaching-family program is expected to appear in book form in 1982.

Overall, the outcome data reviewed thus far in terms of the teaching-family model are moderately positive: the Achievement Place data indicate that the program may be more effective than the traditional institutional program, and the independent evaluation suggests that it is as effective as other community-based group-home programs, and less expensive. However, an outcome evaluation of a residential program that incorporates many components of the teaching-family program was less optimistic. The program is the Crisis Care Center in Danville, Illinois, which was established in 1970 as a short-term residential treatment program for predelinquent or behavior-problem youth between the ages of 7 and 17 (Davidson & Wolfred, 1977).

The Crisis Care Center included a token economy (e.g., a point system) overlaid with a progressive-level system similar to that of Achievement Place (Phillips, 1968). In terms of target behaviors, primary emphasis was placed on problem-solving skills (D'Zurilla & Goldfried, 1971), appropriate social skills (Lazarus, 1971), daily school performance (Bailey *et al.*, 1970), leading group discussions (Fixsen, Phillips, & Wolf, 1973), and participating in discharge plans. For the purposes of study, 42 youths who went through the program were compared with 42 youths selected from the records of the Illinois Department of Children and Family Services Office in a nearby city of comparable demographic characteristics. The control and the experimental subjects were matched on an individual basis in terms of sex, age within six months, grade in school, major presenting problem, and date of contact with state or juvenile authorities within one year.

On preprogram measures, the control group had slightly better school attendance and tended to be in foster homes more often than the experimental subjects. There were no significant differences between the two groups in terms of grades, juvenile contacts, criminal contacts, placement changes, institutional placements, or family placements. In the nine-month follow-up data, there were no changes in the desired directions. In fact, the Crisis Care Program apparently facilitated the very changes it had been designed to prevent: The control subjects displayed a significantly higher rate of school attendance, while the experimental subjects were significantly higher in terms of juvenile contacts, criminal contacts, and institutional placements. Also, in terms of pre–post comparisons for just the experimental subjects, the only significant change was an increase in institutional placements.

Certainly, the results of this study should be alarming to those who advocate behaviorally oriented, residential programs in the community. However, in terms of responding to this alarm, it is necessary to replicate this type of study, preferably in a variety of different settings. Because the authors could not achieve random assignment, they chose to carefully match subjects from two separate (but similar) communities across six relevant variables. They then compared the two groups on eight preprogram measures. This procedure is sound, and the authors should be commended for what they did. However, the assumption that the two groups were, in fact, comparable is not as justifiable as it would have been with the use of random assignment. Therefore, a need for replication still exists. In addition, it is not clear what happened to the control subjects between the pre- and postmeasures. For each experimental subject, there was a change of residence as he or she was placed in the Crisis Care Center. For the control subjects to be comparable to the experimental subjects, they, too, should have been placed in some other residence. If there was a change of placement for the control subjects, it is not known what it was. If there was not, it is difficult to argue that the level of adjustment was the same for both groups at the start of the study.

While the outcome studies described above have not provided definitive information, they have provided the clearest picture to date. The preliminary conclusion would seem to be that community-based, residential behavior-modification programs are (1) probably more effective than institutional programs for most troubled youths; (2) probably as effective as and less expensive than other community-based group-home programs; and (3) possibly less effective than other community-based, non-group-home residential alternatives. Obviously, these conclusions demand further substantiation.

Community-Based, Nonresidential Behavior-Modification Programs

Family Behavior-Modification Programs

In an impressive series of studies, Alexander, Parsons, and their associates have documented the development, application, and evaluation of an intervention technology for modifying the behavior of families with delinquent adolescents, designated as "Short-Term Behavioral Systems Therapy" (Alexander, 1973; Alexander & Parsons, 1973; Alexander, Barton, Schiavo, & Parsons, 1976; Klein, Alexander, & Parsons, 1977; Parsons & Alexander, 1973). The research program was predicated on four sequential steps: identification of process, modification of process, impact, and long-range effect (Klein *et al.*, 1977). Given the importance of this body of research, both in terms of apparent effectiveness and in terms of the research approach, some time is given here to its review.

From previous research that analyzed interaction patterns among families with and without delinquent adolescents (e.g., Alexander, 1973), Parsons and Alexander (1973) and Alexander and Parsons (1973) generated an intervention program designed to modify the interaction patterns of families with delinquent adolescents so as to approximate the patterns demonstrated by families without delinquent adolescents. While the objective of treatment was to replace maladaptive family interaction with contingency contracting, the emphasis was clearly placed on the communication and negotiation processes involved in establishing a contingency contract. Thus, therapists modeled, prompted, and reinforced the clear communication of substance and feelings, the clear presentation of demands and alternatives, and negotiations. In addition to focusing initially on relatively nonthreatening issues, the therapists differentiated rules from requests, trained families in skills related to social reinforcement and solution-oriented communication (i.e., making positive interruptions related to clarification, increasing topic or personal information, and providing positive feedback to other family members), and explicitly stated the meaning and purposes of positive interruptions and how they would reinforce these interruptions (i.e., by verbal and nonverbal praise). In addition to the above intervention procedures, the treatment included bibliotherapy for some families (e.g., a behavior modification manual), while token economy programs were sometimes used in families with younger adolescents (Alexander & Barton, 1976). Thus, it appears that the therapists played an active and supportive role in guiding the *process* of family interaction, in addition to focusing on the specific behavioral targets identified for modification via contingency contracting.

In an initial report (Parsons & Alexander, 1973), 40 families were randomly assigned to one of four experimental conditions after the arrest or detention of the targeted adolescent. The families were referred by the Salt Lake County Juvenile Court for one or more of several behavioral offenses on the part of their 13- to 16-year-old adolescents. The offenses were largely noncriminal, including running away, being ungovernable, and being truant. The families were predominantly upper-lower-class and middle-class, Protestant (Mormon), and relatively intact (Patterson & Fleischman, 1979). On the average, the treatment involved a total of eight hours' time.

Four interaction measures were used to assess activity levels (silence, frequency, and duration of simultaneous speech) and verbal reciprocity (equality of speech) within the families. No significant differences were found between the pretested groups on these measures before intervention. The results indicated that the behavioral treatment groups were significantly different from the two control groups at posttest, however. These differences were all in the direction hypothesized, indicating that the treatment manipulation produced positive changes in the interaction patterns of the families. Specifically, the treatment families became less silent, talked more equally, and experienced an increase in both the frequency and the duration of simultaneous speech. The control families did not improve on any of the four interaction measures. It is unclear whether the raters were naive to the experimental conditions, however, and no data were provided regarding reliability for these measures.

In a subsequent report (Alexander & Parsons, 1973), additional families were randomly assigned to the experimental and the client-centered conditions, and additional comparison groups were added. Specifically, 46 families randomly assigned to the behavioral family condition were compared with 19 families randomly assigned to a client-centered family-group program, 11 families randomly assigned to a psychodynamic family condition, and 10 families randomly assigned to a no-treatment control group. No significant preintervention differences were found among these groups in terms of age, socioeconomic status, distribution of sex, prior recidivism rates, or pretest scores on three interaction measures; thus, the randomization procedure was effective. Two additional groups were utilized for the sake of comparisons: a *post hoc* selected treatment control group ($n = 46$), whose juvenile-member referral dates and offenses approximated those of the other groups, and a group of 2,800 cases providing a baseline recidivism rate for the entire county. The adolescents ranged in age from 13 to 16 and had been arrested or detained at the juvenile court for a behavioral offense.

Recidivism was assessed at a 6- to 18-month interval following the termination of the treatment programs. Although the authors pointed out that the follow-up periods were comparable across the groups, no data were provided and no statistical analyses were performed in this regard. *Recidivism* was defined as referral to the juvenile court for a behavioral offense as recorded in the court records. The results indicated recidivism rates of 50% for the randomly assigned no-treatment controls, 48% for the *post hoc* no-treatment controls, 51% for the entire county, 47% for the client-centered group, and 73% for the psychodynamic family-treatment group. In contrast, the short-term family behavioral group demonstrated a recidivism rate of 26%. The differences between the groups were significant. It is unclear, however, why a baseline-to-follow-up comparison was not made. The differences between the groups in terms of criminal offenses were not significant, although the behavioral group still demonstrated the lowest rate (i.e., 17% versus a range of 21–27% for the other groups). In an additional analysis of these data, the nonrecidivism cases demonstrated significantly lower talk-time variance (e.g., more equality) and silence, as well as significantly more positive interruptions than the recidivism cases, indicating a relationship between family interaction and recidivism.

In an interesting and important subsequent study, Alexander *et al.* (1976) assessed therapist variables as these relate to outcome in the context of the systems-behavioral approach with families of delinquents. In the study, 21 therapists were used in providing treatment to 21 families similar to those seen in the Alexander and Parsons (1973) study (e.g., families with adolescent "status" offenders: runaway, ungovernable, truancy, and curfew problems). Following a 10-week training program, the therapists were rated on eight 5-point scales prior to direct treatment. On the basis of the initial correlational analyses between therapist variables and outcome, these process variables were collapsed into two global mean scores for each therapist: (1) "relationship" skills, which included the therapist's characteristics of affect–behavior integration, warmth, and humor; and (2) "structuring" skills, which included the dimensions of directiveness and self-confidence. These global mean scores were entered as independent variables against the dependent variable of outcome in multiple-regression analyses. Poor versus good outcome was assessed in terms of a 4-point scale tied to remaining in versus dropping out of treatment (e.g., completion of therapy program): (1) terminators after first session ($n = 4$ families); (2) attended several sessions but terminated against advice ($n = 5$ families); (3) completed treatment with positive changes in communication but without ability to solve problems spontaneously, without assistance ($n = 5$ families); and (4) termination jointly agreed on ($n = 7$ families).

The results indicated that the relationship and structuring scores accounted jointly for 59.65% of the variance in outcome. Since each therapist was responsible for providing treatment to only one family, the therapists could be divided between good-outcome therapists (3's and 4's) and poor-outcome therapists (1's and 2's). Significant differences were found between good-outcome therapists and poor-outcome therapists in terms of both relationship skills and structuring skills, with good-outcome therapists demonstrating greater ability in both areas. The authors also reported an interesting finding relating therapy outcome (in terms of therapy completion on the same 4-point scale) with recidivism. Recidivism included referral to juvenile court or a community mental-health center 12 to 15 months following intervention. The results indicated recidivism rates of 60% and 50%, respectively, for the poor-outcome conditions 1 and 2. In contrast, 0% recidivism was demonstrated by both good-outcome conditions, suggesting a relationship between therapy attrition and recidivism.

These results indicated an overall recidivism rate for these families of 24%, which was very similar to the previously reported recidivism rate of 26% (Alexander & Parsons, 1973). In addition, Alexander and Barton (1976) reported an overall recidivism rate of 27% for a replication sample of 45 families treated during 1972–1973 that had characteristics similar to those of the families reported above. It is unclear when the follow-up data were collected for this sample, however, although the follow-up was assessed as soon as three months postintervention for at least some families.

The most recent report (Klein *et al.*, 1977) was a 2½- to 3½-year follow-up of families treated in the Alexander and Parsons (1973) study. Rather than tracking the treated adolescents, however, the authors assessed recidivism in the siblings of these delinquents. Klein *et al.* (1977) stated, "Since the goal of treatment is to modify the family system along communication and reciprocity variables to create a more efficient problem-solving unit, the program would be expected to assist the family in dealing more effectively with subsequent developmental changes in younger siblings (p. 472)." Thus, this analysis involved an assessment of the intervention's impact in terms of "primary prevention."

The results indicated sibling recidivism rates of 40% for the randomly assigned no-treatment control group, 59% for the client-centered group, and 63% for the eclectic-dynamic group. In contrast, a sibling-recidivism rate of 20% was demonstrated for the short-term behavioral family system group. A chi-square analysis indicated that these differences were significant. Thus, the intervention program produced an incidence of sibling delinquency one-third to one-half lower than the sibling delinquency rates in the other comparison groups. Unfortunately, no breakdown was given in terms of status offenses versus criminal offenses. As in previous studies, posttest family-process measures were compared for families with sibling recidivism and families with no sibling recidivism (independent of treatment condition), with a finding of signif-

icant differences in the frequency of interruptions for clarification and feedback, as well as the duration of positive interruptions. No significant differences were found in equality of talk time or silence. Thus, it appears that changes in family interaction are related to sibling recidivism.

While these results appear positive, no information was provided concerning preintervention offense rates, the age of the siblings during the intervention or the follow-up, the number of siblings per family, the percentage of families with siblings across conditions, or the number of parents residing in the home. If the siblings in the behavioral group were younger than the siblings in the comparison groups, for instance, the results would be biased in favor of the behavioral group. A similar problem would arise with respect to the various preintervention offense rates across groups. Finally, it is unfortunate that the recidivism rates for the original experimental and comparison groups at three-year follow-up were not also provided, given Patterson's (1979) observation that positive one-year follow-up findings often tend to disappear by two years postintervention.

Overall, this series of studies is impressive and seems to suggest the following conclusions:

1. There are specific family interaction patterns that distinguish families with delinquent youth from families without delinquent adolescents.

2. Short-term behavioral intervention with families that include an adolescent exhibiting primarily status offenses can produce relevant changes in family interaction across family members.

3. Changes in family interaction are related to reduced recidivism rates (primarily for noncriminal offenses) in comparison with alternative treatments, or no treatment, for periods of up to 18 months.

4. Relationship and structuring skills demonstrated by therapists are positively related to treatment outcome (i.e., nonattrition). Further, positive treatment outcome is related to reduced recidivism, suggesting a relationship between therapists' skills and recidivism.

5. While long-term effectiveness has not been demonstrated for treated adolescents

(e.g., over two years' follow-up), there does seem to be an indication that siblings of treated youth demonstrate lower recidivism than siblings in families receiving either alternative treatments or no treatment at three-year follow-up.

6. Whether these results can be generalized to (1) families with more clearly "delinquent" adolescents, (2) families with lower incomes, or (3) families that are more disorganized remains to be demonstrated. In this regard, according to Barton (personal communication, 1980), 43 families with "hard-core" delinquents (e.g., murderers and rapists) have received treatment and have demonstrated a recidivism rate of 32–35%, compared with a base rate of 70–75% in Utah. Thus, although these data are preliminary, there is some indication that the treatment program should not be limited to families with adolescents exhibiting primarily status offenses.

In contrast to the positive results found by Alexander, Parsons, and their associates, Weathers and Liberman (1975), using a similar treatment program, reported essentially negative results with a group of 28 families with delinquents. The families included male and female probationers who were between 14 and 17 years of age and had multiple offenses. The intervention consisted of the development of contingency contracts and interpersonal communication as well as negotiation skills training. There were three intervention sessions, lasting an average total time of 5.6 hours.

The effectiveness of the treatment was impossible to evaluate because of a dropout rate of 79%: 43% of the families dropped out before the initial home visit (not part of intervention proper), an additional 29% dropped out after the initial home visit but before treatment, and a final 7% dropped out during intervention. Thus, out of an initial sample of 28 families, only 6 completed treatment.

There were two differences between the Weathers and Liberman (1975) and Alexander and Parsons (1973) studies that may account for the different outcomes. First, there were more single-parent, low-income, dysfunctional families in the Weathers and Liberman study, which may account for the high dropout rate (cf. Wahler, Berland, & Coe, 1979). Second, Weathers and Liberman subjects were

multiple offenders, whereas largely first offenders were treated in the Alexander and Parsons study. The higher (and possibly more serious) rate of offenses displayed by the Weathers and Liberman delinquents (pretreatment) may account for the differential follow-up across studies in terms of recidivism.

Barnard, Gant, Kuehn, Jones, and Christophersen (1980) presented findings relating to the use of an intensive home-based behavioral treatment program with the families of juvenile probationers. Court-referred youths and their families who consented to receive treatment were randomly assigned to the Family Training Program (FTP; $n = 37$) or treatment consisting of traditional court services ($n = 35$). On the average, these youths had committed about three offenses during the year prior to intervention. Of the youths in each group, 54% had been adjudicated: 19% of the FTP youths were adjudicated delinquent (versus 14% of the comparison youths) and 35% were adjudicated as "status" offenders (versus 40% of the controls). None of the youths in either group had previously been placed on probation. The mean age in each group was 14.5 years, consisting of 73% males in the FTP group and 74% males in the comparison group. In general, the two groups did not vary in terms of the demographic information assessed.

The FTP treatment involved the whole family, was home-based, and relied heavily on a home accounting and motivation system that consisted of youths' earning points for appropriate behavior and losing points for inappropriate behavior. In addition to the point system, the following intervention procedures were utilized: (1) behavioral rehearsal and practicing of behaviors that the parents, youths, or therapists identified as important; (2) family conferences; (3) negotiation skills training; (4) home consequences for in-school problem behavior; and (5) a gradual phasing out of the treatment. The average length of the treatment was seven months and involved about 51 contacts, for an average total treatment duration of 57 hours (in contrast, the average comparison treatment consisted of 16 contacts for a total treatment duration of 12 hours over a period of seven months).

Adjudicated youths in the comparison group

generally received probation services, which varied across probation officers but tended to include probation plans (e.g., "limits" in terms of curfew, association with other probationers, school attendance, and violation of city and state ordinances), theme writing, restitution, and counseling. Some nonadjudicated youths, on the other hand, were given recommendations to receive services provided by the community (e.g., psychological evaluations and counseling). It is unclear, however, whether or how many of these youths actually received treatment.

The outcome measures included reported offenses before, during, and one year following treatment; the seriousness of reported offenses; readjudication during treatment and at one- and two-year follow-up; detention rates; and long-term residential placement rates. The outcome in terms of reported offenses was assessed for 28 youths in each group, as data were not accessible for all the youths. Reported offenses were collected from juvenile court records and were defined as "any acts of misbehavior committed by a youth which were brought to the attention of the court." The results indicated that the FTP youths demonstrated significantly greater reductions in the rate of reported offenses than control the youths from preintervention to follow-up (i.e., 89% total reduction in offense rate versus 34% total reduction in offense rate). No significant differences were found between groups in terms of offense seriousness (average ratings of about 2 for each group, where 1's are status offenses and 4's are hard-core offenses).

The results were not as positive in terms of the other outcome measures, however. Although almost twice as many controls were readjudicated as FTP youths, this difference was not statistically significant. In addition, the controls were more frequently readjudicated for more than one offense at the time of their readjudication and were more frequently readjudicated as "delinquent" than FTP subjects. Unfortunately, these data were not analyzed statistically. No differences were found between the groups in terms of subsequent detention or out-of-home placement.

The results appear mixed in terms of the differential effectiveness of the two treatment conditions. In terms of reported offenses, the results seem relatively clear and suggest a more potent effect on the part of the FTP treatment program. There is also some support for the FTP treatment in terms of readjudication. No differences were found in terms of subsequent detentions or out-of-home placements—a finding that seems to bring into question the meaning and/or the relevance of the "reported offense" data. Furthermore, given the lack of differences between the groups on these measures, it is unclear whether or how the youths gained any benefit as a function of their lowered reported offense rates. Finally, whereas the FTP treatment cost approximately $1,115 per youth, the probation services provided by the juvenile court cost only $350 per youth. Thus, until further follow-up data are available, it is important to question the benefit of the FTP treatment program relative to the probation services typically provided by the juvenile court, given the substantial difference in cost, the greater intrusiveness of the FTP treatment, the fact that probation services were provided only for adjudicated youths (whereas both adjudicated and nonadjudicated youths received FTP treatment), and the less-than-substantial differences in terms of recidivism across the measures of readjudication, detention, and out-of-home placement.

Patterson and his associates (Oregon Social Learning Project) have studied and/or treated over 100 families with "out-of-control" children between 3 and 12 years of age. Since this body of research has been extensively reviewed recently (see Burchard & Harig, 1976; O'Donnell, 1977; Patterson, 1979; Patterson & Fleischman, 1979), it will only be summarized here. As described in their treatment manual (Patterson, Reid, Jones, & Conger, 1975), the goal of treatment involved the reduction of reciprocally coercive behavior among all family members. This treatment included a focus on family interaction (e.g., communication skills and negotiation skills) and effective behavior-management skills.

The assessment techniques included an extensive behavioral observation system (Reid, 1978), which utilized trained observers and involved in-home observations, as well as parent ratings. The evaluation of the treatment included process as well as outcome measures.

In terms of process, significant changes in family interaction were found in the following areas: (1) reductions in sibling coercive behavior; (2) reductions in the mother's coercive behavior; (3) reductions in the proportions of positive consequences provided by parents for coercive child behaviors; (4) reductions in the proportions of aversive consequences provided by mothers for prosocial child behavior; and (5) reductions in the proportions of aversive consequences provided by mothers for coercive child behaviors (Patterson & Fleischman, 1979). Various positive changes have also been demonstrated in parents' perceptions of their children, their families, and themselves (Patterson & Fleischman, 1979). Thus, as in the studies by Alexander, Parsons, and their associates, changes in the family process in the expected direction have been documented (via direct behavioral observation, in addition to self-report measures). Outcome evaluations have demonstrated reductions in the aversive behavior of targeted children in terms of behavioral observations as well as parental ratings for up to 12 months. These changes were statistically significant, and the reduced rates of deviant behavior at follow-up were generally within the range demonstrated by nonproblem children (Patterson & Fleischman, 1979).

Moore, Chamberlain, and Mukai (1979) reported an interesting follow-up study of 46 children previously treated at the Oregon Social Learning Project. Three groups of children were compared: (1) 21 children seen two to nine years earlier for problems of aggression in the home; (2) 25 children seen previously for stealing problems; and (3) 14 children constituting a normative sample. The mean age of the children at intake was 8, 11.1, and 8.9 years, respectively, for aggressive, stealing, and normative groups. The mean age at follow-up was 16.4, 15.8, and 16.3, respectively. Thus, the mean number of years to follow-up was 7.6, 4.1, and 7.3, respectively. The follow-up assessment consisted of subsequent juvenile-court contacts (although both status and non-status offenses were collected, only non-status, or criminal, offenses were used in the analyses).

Subsequent to the intervention, 84% of the stealers, 24% of the aggressive group, and 21% of the normative group had court contacts involving criminal offenses. Since the children in these groups sometimes displayed both aggressive and stealing behaviors, a subsequent analysis was computed comparing recidivism across children with both stealing and aggression ($n = 14$), children with stealing alone ($n = 13$), children with aggression alone ($n = 13$), and children with neither stealing nor aggression ($n = 15$). In this case, the recidivism rates were 79%, 85%, 15%, and 25%, respectively. Thus, compared with children who had records of stealing (with or without aggression) and who demonstrated a recidivism rate of 77%, children with aggression alone displayed a rate of 13%, and the normative group acquired a rate of 21%. Interestingly, 42% of the children in the stealing group had had court contacts before the intervention, compared with 0% in the aggressive group and 7% in the normative group. If we look only at children with no prior court contacts (i.e., preintervention), 56% of the stealers, 13% of the aggressives, and 15% of the normative group demonstrated subsequent court contacts. Further, the mean number of offenses per year during follow-up given one offense was 1.2 for children in the stealer group, .54 for children referred due to aggression, and .31 for the normative group. Fifty-two percent of the stealers had four or more offenses. Finally, the stealers' average age at first offense was 10 years, versus 14.5 and 14 years, respectively, for the aggressives and normatives.

These results are meaningful in a number of ways. First, aggressive children were no more likely to engage in subsequent delinquent behavior than nonaggressive children; therefore, either the treatment was successful in terms of delinquency prevention or aggressive children are not at risk for subsequent delinquency. Second, children who engage in parent-identified stealing run a high risk of juvenile court contact, and once court contact has been made, they run a high risk of further, multiple contacts. In this sample of stealers, 92% of the first offenders committed an additional offense. Of these, 91% committed a third offense, and 80% of third offenders committed a fourth offense. Thus, parent-identified stealing may serve as a useful assessment for early delinquency-prevention attempts. On the other hand, these results indicate that the family intervention utilized with this group of children was largely ineffective, and they bring into question the extent to which parent identification and/or subsequent treatment could be a catalyst of the problem through negative labeling. In addition to further research aimed at developing effective treatment techniques for children who steal, it would be worthwhile to replicate the Moore *et al.* (1979) study, given the striking results and the small sample size utilized.

It was suggested earlier that families of one-parent households and/or lower incomes were at risk for treatment dropout and/or treatment ineffectiveness (e.g., Wahler *et al.*, 1979; Weathers & Liberman, 1975). In an interesting study, Fleischman (1979) assessed the impact of "parenting salaries" (i.e., parents were paid one dollar per day contingent on compliance with treatment tasks) on treatment cooperation and attrition. The subjects included 18 families with aggressive children between the ages of 3 and 12 (mean = 6.7 years) treated by the Family Center, the clinical adjunct of the Oregon Social Learning Center. The treatment was similar to that outlined in Patterson *et al.* (1975).

The results indicated that for the low-income and/or single-parent families, those who received a salary were cooperative 85% of the treatment days, whereas those receiving no salary were cooperative 50% of the time. For the middle-income, two-parent families the ratings were 94% and 90%, respectively. Statistical analysis indicated a significant interaction (in addition to a significant main effect for salaries), suggesting that salaries made a difference for low-income and/or single-parent families. In addition to cooperation, significant results were reported in terms of treatment attrition among low-income and/or single-parent families: Whereas nonsalaried families dropped out of treatment prematurely in the rate of 100% (*n* = 4 families), none of the salaried low-income and/or single-parent families dropped out of treatment (*n* = 4). Again, the differences between middle-income, two-parent families were not significant in this regard.

This study adds support to previous studies that found significant rates of attrition among nonintact, low-income families. Of significance, however, is the finding that the provision of a parenting salary (average cost of $77 per family) significantly reduced attrition, from 100% to 0%. While the sample size was small in this study, the magnitude of the effects seems to offset this problem to some extent. Whether these results can be replicated with families that include older delinquent adolescents remains to be demonstrated.

In summary, these studies seem to suggest the following:

1. There is relatively clear evidence that behavioral intervention can successfully effect positive changes in family interaction and that at least in families with younger aggressive children, these positive changes are maintained for up to one year postintervention.

2. It appears that positive changes in family interaction are related to (a) significant reductions in aversive child behavior; (b) significant reductions in postintervention offense rates on the part of adolescents referred for "soft" and "moderate" delinquency; and (c) reduced sibling recidivism in terms of reported offenses. Preliminary evidence also suggests reduced offense rates on the part of adolescents referred for "hard" delinquency.

3. Family behavioral intervention appears to be more effective than client-centered family treatment, psychodynamic family treatment, traditional probation services, and no treatment in bringing about significant reductions in postintervention offense rates.

4. When the follow-up of behavioral intervention has been assessed by means of measures other than subsequent offense rates, however, the results have not been as positive. Thus, no differences between groups have yet been found in terms of subsequent criminal offenses, readjudications, detentions, or out-of-home placements.

5. The lack of differences in terms of subsequent criminal offenses, out-of-home placements, etc., seems to bring into question the meaning and/or the significance of the positive effects noted above in terms of subsequent offense rates. At the very least, these results indicate that multiple measures of outcome are needed in future evaluations of behavioral interventions with families of delinquent adolescents. Further, these measures should

include "positive" indicators, such as employment rates and income levels, as well as "negative" indicators, such as criminal offense rates and out-of-home placements. While it is unclear at the present time what benefits, if any, stem from reduced offense rates, for example, it may be that reduced offense rates are associated with enhanced employability or some other positive outcome.

School Behavior-Modification Programs

One of the most extensive school-based programs reported in the literature, Preparation through Responsive Educational Programs (PREP), has served over 600 troubled students within the Maryland public school system under the direction of James Filipczak (Filipczak, Friedman, & Reese, 1979). After a two-year pilot program performed within a laboratory setting (the program served 30 students), Filipczak and his colleagues were able to move the federally funded program into three different schools, representing a suburban, a rural, and an urban setting, for a five-year period. Students were recommended for the program by school staff on the basis of strong evidence of academic and/or social problems: failing grades, disciplinary referrals, absenteeism, tardiness, suspensions, poor performance on standardized tests, and contacts with the police or other agencies that serve troubled youth (Filipczak, Friedman, & Reese, 1979). Students voluntarily enrolled in the PREP program for one year during their seventh-, eighth-, or ninth-grade school year.

The PREP program can be divided into two components: (1) for students, academic training in reading, English, and mathematics; social or interpersonal skills training that facilitated immediate and generalizable social skills for in- and out-of-school problems; and family skills training that promoted increased parental involvement in school activities in addition to family management programs in the home; and (2) training for teachers and other staff that helped them conduct all phases of the programs (the model dictated that regular public-school teachers run the classes). In addition to the 2 hours of academics and 45 minutes of interpersonal skills training each day, the students were generally enrolled in four other classes within the regular non-PREP school program. Most academic learning was managed in a self-instructional medium, although some specific topics or objectives were organized for small-group instruction. Small- and large-group instructional processes were utilized during the interpersonal skills classes. Additionally, the PREP classes were run on a behavioral system, and contracts were often used in relation to performance in the non-PREP classes. Thus, in addition to praise, ratings, and grades given by their teachers, the students earned tangible rewards (such as leisure-time coke breaks) and/or activity rewards (such as movies, field trips, or game time). For a more detailed description of the overall program operations, see Filipczak, Friedman, and Reese (1979). For a detailed description of the social–interpersonal-skills component, see Filipczak, Archer, and Friedman (1980). An interesting account of some of the implementation difficulties that PREP encountered, especially in terms of political issues (e.g., negative press reports) and research issues (e.g., professional, parental, teacher, and student controls exerted over PREP's operation), is given in Filipczak and Friedman (1978).

The evaluation system used was very extensive and complex, allowing for process, component, outcome, and follow-up assessments. For a more comprehensive understanding of the research design, several different studies must be analyzed (e.g., Filipczak & Friedman, 1978; Filipczak, Archer, Neale, & Winett, 1979; Filipczak, Friedman, & Reese, 1979; Filipczak et al., 1980; Friedman, Filipczak, & Fiordaliso, 1977; Reese & Filipczak, 1980). The most helpful single report in this regard is Filipczak, Archer et al. (1979). To enhance the following analyses of the data, a review of the research design is presented first.

PREP was provided in a suburban junior high school during the first two years of the program (seventh- and eighth-graders):

Suburban Year 1 (1971–1972):
    1. PREP: total program ($n = 30$), versus
    2. No-treatment control group ($n = 30$)
Suburban Year 2 (1972–1973):
    1. PREP: total program ($n = 16$), versus
    2. PREP: academic only ($n = 16$), versus

3. PREP: social only ($n = 16$), versus
4. PREP: family only ($n = 16$), versus
5. No-treatment control group ($n = 16$)

Beginning during the third program year, PREP operated in a rural junior high school over a three-year period (seventh- and eighth-graders):

Rural Year 3 (1973–1974):
   1. PREP: academic only ($n = 39$), versus
   2. PREP: social and family only ($n = 39$)
Rural Year 4 (1974–1975):
   1. PREP: academic only ($n = 39$), versus
   2. PREP: social and family only ($n = 36$), versus
   3. No-treatment control group ($n = 37$)
Rural Year 5 (1975–1976):
   1. Factor 1: academic versus no academic ($n = 48$)
   2. Factor 2: social versus no social ($n = 48$)

Beginning during the fourth program year, PREP was also provided in an urban junior high school over a two-year period (seventh-, eighth-, and ninth-graders):

Urban Year 4 (1974–1975):
   1. PREP: total program ($n = 47$), versus
   2. No-treatment control group ($n = 36$)
Urban Year 5 (1975–1976):
   1. PREP: total program ($n = 60$), versus
   2. No-treatment control group ($n = 60$)

Before reviewing the published results, it should be pointed out that the data are difficult to analyze. It is not always clear what precise measures were used, which of the subjects in any given year were included in the analyses, which of the groups were compared (especially problematical during years including component analyses such as Suburban Year 2), whether or when random assignment was utilized, whether the groups varied significantly on relevant measures initially, and which specific statistical analyses were used. Raw data were seldom reported (e.g., test scores, attendance rate, and number of suspensions) at preintervention or at postintervention. Finally, and of particular importance, contradictions across reports were noticed

(e.g., attendance measures for Suburban Year 2 and Rural Year 3: Filipczak, Archer *et al.*, 1979, versus Filipczak, Friedman, & Reese, 1979).

With the above problems in mind, an attempt will be made to review the published findings. It should be noted at the outset that the conclusions of this review are less positive than those provided by Filipczak and his colleagues, partly because of the exclusion of differences reported at the .10 level, many of which favored PREP (whereas Filipczak and his colleagues at times included these marginal differences in their analyses). Our review of the findings includes direct results, one-year follow-up data, and four-year follow-up data.

In terms of direct outcome, assessment included standardized test scores, grades (PREP classes and non-PREP classes), negative in-school behavior, and attendance. Significant differences were obtained on 21 out of 48 measures, all of which were in favor of the PREP groups (Filipczak, Friedman, & Reese, 1979). However, the results clearly favored PREP students in only two site/years (i.e., Suburban Year 1 and Rural Year 4), with less clear support for the PREP academic component during Rural Year 3. It is possible that the positive results found during Rural Year 4 were partially a function of the students' longer period of involvement in the PREP program (i.e., two years rather than one year).

Class grades were also used as outcome measures. Friedman *et al.* (1977) reported changes in mean grade-point average from prior year to program year for PREP academic groups versus comparison groups for Years 1 through 4. Reese and Filipczak (1980) reported similar results for Urban Year 5. In terms of grades in non-PREP classes, these analyses generally parallel the results obtained on achievement tests. More specifically, the results clearly favored PREP students in only two site/years (i.e., Suburban Year 1 and Rural Year 4). While grade changes were also reported in PREP classes and all classes combined (Filipczak, Archer *et al.*, 1979; Filipczak, Friedman, & Reese, 1979), the strength of these measures is questionable, given the opportunity for bias on the part of the PREP teachers. In general, however, the results for the PREP classes were consistently positive for the suburban and rural sites, and mixed for the urban site.

The positive results obtained in non-PREP class grades, although limited, appear to be a function of the academic component of the PREP program. Although Filipczak *et al.* (1980) reported findings that they suggested support the social component in terms of enhancing students' grades in the non-PREP classes, their interpretation is questionable. Out of six comparisons involving students participating in the social component during the years involving "clearly interpretable designs," only three were significant in favor of the social component. However, except for two of these six comparisons (i.e., during Rural Year 3), it is unclear who the social component group was being compared with. In addition, one of these significant differences was obtained during Rural Year 4, which consisted of students who had participated in the academic component of PREP the previous year. The other two significant differences, which were obtained during Rural Year 3, appear to be at odds with the results reported by Friedman *et al.* (1977), which tended to support the academic component rather than the social component in this regard.

Nonacademic measures of outcome have also been reported (Filipczak, Friedman, & Reese, 1979; Filipczak *et al.*, 1980). PREP students demonstrated significantly greater attendance than comparison groups in four out of seven site/years. It is interesting that in three of these successful site/years the PREP program included a component specifically designed to increase student attendance, while no specific programming was included during other years. Negative or antisocial student behavior was measured in various ways across six different site/years (e.g., suspensions, disciplinary referrals, and teacher ratings). Differences between groups were significant and in favor of PREP students on only 11 out of 33 measures. These significant differences were spread across different site/years, however, so that the results did not clearly favor PREP during any single site/year. The social skills component apparently did not enhance students' performance in this regard (Filipczak *et al.*, 1980).

These initial outcome data seem to suggest the following:

1. PREP has demonstrated limited to moderate success in terms of increasing students' academic achievement as measured by standardized tests and class grades.
2. The academic component of the PREP program appears to be a critical element, whereas the importance of the social skills and family components remains to be demonstrated.
3. PREP does not appear to effect change in terms of students' in-school negative behavior.

A follow-up of one and four years for the Suburban Year 1 (1971–1972) PREP program has been reported by Wodarski, Filipczak, McCombs, Koustenis, and Rusilko (1979). Sixty students were randomly assigned either to the total PREP program or to a no-treatment control group (subsequent to being matched on criterion measures such as grades, school attendance, in-school behavioral problems, and test scores). Each group included 30% girls and 30% nonwhites and consisted equally of seventh- and eighth-graders. These students participated in PREP for one year.

This particular follow-up is especially relevant for a number of reasons. First, the students were matched and randomly assigned to conditions during this site/year; the treatment condition included all of the components in PREP's overall program; and the direct outcome data suggest that this was probably the most successful year in PREP's history. Thus, the probability of finding significant and positive long-term effects seemed high for this particular site/year relative to other site/years.

At the one-year follow-up, the PREP students were found to have fewer suspensions, fewer disciplinary referrals, better school attendance, and better overall grade-point averages for English and math classes than the controls (Wodarski *et al.*, 1979). It is unclear whether these differences were statistically significant, however.

The four-year follow-up was reported for 40 of the original sample of 60 students (21 PREP and 19 control). These students were in their junior and senior years of high school at the time of follow-up (21 juniors and 19 seniors) and had a mean age of 17.8 years. Since not all of the original sample participated in the follow-up, the baseline data available to the authors were used in the following comparisons: experimental follow-up students versus experimental dropout students, control follow-up versus control dropout, experimental follow-up versus control follow-up, and experimental dropout versus control dropout. Out of 64 comparisons, only 4 were significant, and all of these were between control follow-up subjects and control dropout subjects, suggesting that the follow-up sample was comparable to the original sample. It is unclear why the authors limited the follow-up assessment to these 40 students, however, since they apparently located 90% of the original sample (Wodarski *et al.*, 1979).

Unfortunately, data based on official school and court records were not provided. Rather, various self-report measures were utilized. Parents also filled out an inventory in which about 20% of the items were comparable to items contained within the students' inventory. The interitem reliability agreement was .75, which tends to support the accuracy of the information obtained. Comparisons were made with *t* tests on 119 variables from among four general areas: access to socially acceptable roles (31 variables), reinforcing relationships (25 variables), increased incentives for prosocial behavior (30 variables), and decreased juvenile problem behavior (33 variables). Of these 119 comparisons, only 10 significant differences were found, of which 6 are relevant (4 of these were related to students' satisfaction with PREP staff and program). Of these, 3 favored the PREP sample and 3 favored the control sample. In making 119 comparisons, 6 significant differences would be expected by chance (as the authors pointed out). Thus, in addition to finding a school dropout rate of 33% for both groups (apparently), no significant differences were found between the groups four years after treatment.

Preliminary follow-up reports of the Suburban Year 2 program and both urban site/years seem to parallel the follow-up data reviewed above in relation to Suburban Year 1 (Filipczak, Archer *et al.*, 1979). A "representative" subsample of 34 students (43%)

from the Suburban Year 2 program was assessed at four years postintervention. Those students in the PREP academic component performed significantly better than other PREP groups and controls in terms of reading comprehension at follow-up (no differences were found among follow-up groups for the treatment year scores). Suburban Years 1 and 2 were combined in a four-year follow-up of school year completions. None of the experimental groups for either year completed more years in school than the controls. In fact, the controls performed marginally better overall in this regard. In other comparisons for the most part, the Suburban Year 2 students performed no better than the controls. The students who had participated during Urban Years 4 and 5 were assessed at two-year follow-up on the SAT reading subtest. No differences were found between the subsamples of experimental and control students for preintervention to follow-up comparisons. Other comparisons relative to the Urban Years await data analyses.

Finally, it may be of some interest to report one follow-up measure of the students who participated in the initial laboratory PREP program, since court records were provided for these students (in contrast to all subsequent students). The results indicated that for this group of approximately 30 students, arrests and detentions declined significantly during the program, were maintained at this low level for a year after the program, but returned to the preprogram level by the four-year follow-up (Filipczak, Archer *et al.*, 1979). Unfortunately, these data are somewhat ambiguous because of the lack of a comparison group.

These analyses seem to suggest the following in relation to the PREP program:

1. Although PREP was able to effect limited to moderate changes in the academic behavior of the youth it served, these benefits appear largely to have disappeared within four years.
2. There was little, if any, evidence of long-term change in nonacademic areas (including delinquency) as measured by self-report, parent report, and official court records.
3. There was no difference in subsequent

dropout rate between PREP students and non-PREP students.

4. The relevance of the academic benefits is questionable, given the lack of maintenance of these effects and what appears to have been a high subsequent dropout rate and a lack of effect in terms of subsequent delinquency.

Overall, the PREP program was impressive, given the large number of subjects studied, the variety of settings in which the program was implemented, the successful use of regular schoolteachers in the implementation of the program, the extensive research design, and the long-term follow-up reported. Unfortunately, however, the results do not tend to support the efficacy of the program. Thus, on the basis of these data, the utility of school-based delinquency-prevention programs (at least at the junior-high-school level) is called into question.

Heaton, Safer, Allen, Spinnato, and Prumo (1976) reported the results of a contingency-management program established in a junior high school for eighth-graders. The 14 students were selected by the assistant principal on the basis of serious discipline problems during the previous year. Specifically, students who had received two or more suspensions for reasons other than smoking (or one suspension plus multiple disciplinary referrals) were selected for inclusion. These 14 students were compared with 32 similar students from two other junior high schools.

The students in the treatment group received a special class program in the morning, which included academic instruction (individualized) in English, social studies, math, and science. During these morning sessions, the students received points for appropriate academic behavior (e.g., starting, maintaining, and completing assigned work) and appropriate social behavior. The academic and behavioral goals were largely derived from weekly contracts negotiated by the individual student and his or her teacher for that subject. The points earned during the morning session were exchangeable for various reinforcers during the afternoon session: access to the "reinforcement room" (which contained games

such as pool, table tennis, cards, and checkers, in addition to soft drinks and candy); participation in a weekly auction for materials donated by local businesses (e.g., movie and dance tickets); admission to special classes held in the school during the afternoon (such as art, music, gym, and shop); and early dismissal from school with parental consent (which was the most popular reinforcer). The students received a "disturbing and disruptive behavior slip" when they engaged in serious misconduct in the school. If two slips were received during one class period, the students were dismissed from the program, sent home, and required to participate in a parent conference before reentry into school. In addition to the above components, meetings were held periodically with the parents in order to provide feedback on student performance in school and to develop home-based reinforcement systems to support appropriate school behaviors and academic accomplishment (home reinforcers were negotiated in a family conference). The 32 students included in the control group remained in their regular school classes. The authors reported that these students were "identified" to school personnel as being highly vulnerable, with a high potential for school dropout, low academic achievement, and continued deviant behavior. All customary mental-health services remained available to these students.

The results indicated significant differences in favor of the treatment students in terms of leaving school (7.1% versus 43.8%), absenteeism (26.3% versus 41.6%), discipline referrals, and suspensions. Significant differences were also obtained on the reading section of the WRAT, although no differences between groups were demonstrated on the spelling or arithmetic sections of the WRAT.

While these results appear positive, a number of problems make the data difficult to interpret. The control group consisted of students attending different schools from the treatment subjects, raising the question of whether the differences obtained were a function of the treatment or a function of the particular school setting. It is unclear why the authors identified the control students to school personnel in such a negative fashion. It seems possible that this procedure resulted in negative outcomes for the control subjects, raising the question of whether the differences obtained were a function of positive treatment effects for the experimental group or a function of negative "treatment" effects for the control subjects. While the preintervention differences between treatment and control subjects were not statistically significant, the control subjects tended to have more suspensions, more office visits, and more absences than the treatment subjects during the prior year. Finally, no follow-up data were reported.

Stuart and his associates have reported a number of studies that have involved the use of behavioral contracts with predelinquent youth in school settings (Stuart & Tripodi, 1973; Stuart, Jayaratne, & Tripodi, 1976; Stuart, Tripodi, Jayaratne, & Camburn, 1976). Stuart and Tripodi (1973) compared the results of treatment prescribed to terminate in 15 days ($n = 26$), 45 days ($n = 27$), or 90 days ($n = 26$). In addition, the results of these treatment programs were compared to those of a *post hoc* untreated control group consisting of subjects whose parents declined an initial interview with the project staff ($n = 15$). The students, who were in junior high school, were referred for service relating to the control of severe social disruption in school, and 16% demonstrated preintervention court contacts. The treatment included the development of behavioral contracts followed by the initiation of procedures for modifying communicational behavior, facilitating adherence to contracts, and coordinating the school-related efforts of parents and teachers.

In general, the results indicated no differences between the treatment groups, indicating that the length of the treatment was not related to its outcome. Although significant differences were found in favor of the treatment students (in relation to control students) for attendance and grades in school, no differences were found between groups in terms of tardiness or court contacts. These results have to be interpreted with caution, however, because of the nature of the control group (i.e., treatment refusals). In this regard, however, it is interesting that no differences were found between these groups in terms of subsequent court contacts, again raising the question whether in-school delinquency-prevention programs in the junior high school relate to subsequent reduced delinquency.

Subsequently, Stuart and his associates provided behavioral intervention for 87 predelinquents in the context of the Family and School Consultation Project, a federally funded program (Stuart, Jayaratne, & Tripodi, 1976; Stuart, Tripodi *et al.*, 1976). The students were referred for the services by school personnel from grades 6 through 10. Across both studies, 56% of the students' families were one-parent households, 49% had incomes of less than $9,000, and approximately 61% of the families included four or more children. The students generally had no previous court contacts. The intervention consisted of approximately 15 hours devoted entirely to the use of behavioral contracting (i.e., no focus on family interaction or communication skills). Contracts were established between the student and the teacher as well as between the student and the family, and specified privileges that could be earned by meeting specific responsibilities. Bonuses were provided for unusually positive achievements, and sanctions were applied for lapses in contract compliance. The family contracts tended to involve home-based consequences for school behavior initially, while subsequent targets involved home behavior.

The experimental subjects were compared with randomly assigned controls on various parent- and teacher-report measures as well as on school grades, school attendance, and subsequent court contacts. Across the studies, only 9 out of the 18 measures of parent and teacher ratings were statistically significant, all favoring the treatment group. No differences were found in grades, attendance, or court contacts. Thus, these data suggest that the treatment was, to a large extent, unsuccessful.

These school-based programs had certain characteristics in common: (1) all provided services primarily to junior-high-school students; (2) all tended to involve delinquency *prevention*; (3) all attempted to enhance the students' academic achievement; (4) all attempted to decrease the extent to which the students engaged in negative in-school behavior; and (5) all included some type of family-intervention component. The results taken as a whole seem to suggest the following:

1. There is limited to moderate evidence of the ability of these programs to effect short-term changes in academic performance, in-school negative behavior, and problem home behavior.
2. There is little, if any, evidence of a long-term maintenance of these effects (e.g., two to four years in terms of academic achievement, negative in-school behavior, or problem home behavior).
3. There is no indication that these programs enhance the probability that the students who participate in them will remain in school longer than the students who do not participate in them.
4. There is little, if any, indication that these programs reduce the probability of subsequent court contacts (e.g., delinquent behavior) for the students who participate in them.
5. Given the above conclusions, one has to question the cost-effectiveness of these school-based delinquency-prevention programs. If the goal of these programs is to reduce crime and/or school attrition, it has to be concluded that the goal has not yet been met.

Employment-Related Behavior-Modification Programs

Mills and Walter (1979) provided a "behavioral-employment" intervention program for 53 delinquent youths aged 14–17 years. These youths were referred to the program by juvenile court probation or intake caseworkers and were described as the court's most serious offenders, with from one to eight prior convictions (mean = 3.85) including a significant number of felony offenses (e.g., arson, armed robbery, and rape). Of the 76 referred delinquents, 23 were assigned to a control group in a nonrandom fashion (e.g., because jobs were unavailable). Although data were presented that allowed the two groups to be compared in terms of demographic characteristics, preintervention offense rates were not reported sep-

arately for each group, and no statistical analyses were performed. While it appears that the subjects were similar in age, other variables suggest dissimilarity (e.g., sex distribution, SES status, and job history).

The intervention consisted of (1) the recruitment and behavioral training of local employers; (2) the establishment of contingency contracts between the delinquents and the experimenter; (3) the shaping of the delinquents in proemployment behaviors; and (4) the placement of the delinquents on jobs (Mills & Walter, 1979). The intervention took place in three phases, beginning with more intensive contact and work with both the youth and the employers and, over time, fading out experimenter support. The job training included modeling and role playing of job interviews, weekly feedback via checklists of job-appropriate behaviors, points and verbal reinforcement, weekly employer feedback, and contingency contracting. Attendance at weekly and biweekly counseling sessions was tied to receiving paychecks (i.e., the subjects were not paid until the following week whenever a session was missed). In addition, program failure resulted in a return to full court jurisdiction and possible institutionalization.

The results indicated that 90.6% of the experimental subjects had no further arrests and were not institutionalized at a follow-up of approximately one year, while only 30.4% of the control subjects had no further arrests and only 47.8% avoided institutionalization. In addition, 85.7% of the experimental subjects who were initially in school were still in school at follow-up, versus only 33.3% of the controls. Finally, 100% of the experimental subjects obtained jobs, and 34% were still on jobs at follow-up (mean tenure of 13.6 weeks), whereas only 39% of the control subjects obtained jobs and 0% were still on jobs at follow-up (mean tenure of 2.7 weeks).

Unfortunately, the subjects were not randomly assigned to the conditions, and it appears that there were a number of differences between the groups at preintervention. In addition, the follow-up analyses did not control for these preintervention differences. It is also unclear whether the follow-up assessment was performed at equal intervals across groups. Nevertheless, the results are striking and clearly merit replication, especially considering the severity of subjects' offenses prior to intervention.

The value of an employment-related emphasis in treatment programs for delinquents is given further support by the 15-year follow-up results reported by Shore and Massimo (1979). Although the authors did not describe their treatment program as "behavioral," the intervention was clearly skills-oriented, and the therapist took a very active role in assisting the youth in becoming more proficient in the area of employment. Twenty adolescent males, aged 15 to 17, who had been suspended from school (or had dropped out of school) and had a history of antisocial behavior (e.g., repeated truancy, long-standing problems in school adjustment and performance, overt aggression toward peers and authority, and a reputation familiar to attendance officers, courts, or police) were randomly assigned to the experimental conditions, which included a treatment program and a no-treatment control group.

The treatment program included the following components (Massimo & Shore, 1963; Shore & Massimo, 1979):

1. Crisis intervention (i.e., intervention was initiated when the subjects were expelled from school or dropped out for reasons of their own).
2. Noncompulsory participation (the youth were responsible for making all decisions).
3. Flexibility of technique and service (e.g., the therapist spoke with or saw the youth at any time of the day or night and as often as 8–10 times a week).
4. Preemployment counseling focusing on job readiness.
5. Job placement based on the youth's interests, abilities, and goals.
6. Employment counseling focusing on interpersonal problems.
7. Remedial education programs initially related to work performance.

Unfortunately, the subjects were not matched on any variables prior to their random assignment to the experimental conditions. Given the small number of subjects involved in the study, matching subjects would seem to have been important to ensure the absence of preintervention differences on relevant variables (e.g., prior offense rates). Additionally, the preintervention offense rates were not reported, so that it was impossible to compare the groups in this regard. Nevertheless, preintervention differences were not found between the groups on the basis of age, IQ, or socioeconomic status, so that some support is given to the conclusion that the randomization procedure was effective.

Results have been reported at postintervention, 2½-year follow-up, 5-year follow-up, 10-year follow-up, and 15-year follow-up (Massimo & Shore, 1963; Shore & Massimo, 1966, 1969, 1973, 1979). In academic achievement, the experimental subjects improved significantly more than the control subjects in reading, vocabulary, arithmetic fundamentals, and arithmetic problems at postintervention and 2½-year follow-up, as measured by the Metropolitan Achievement Tests. In terms of recidivism, at postintervention 30% of the experimental subjects were on probation, 10% had a hearing pending, and 0% were institutionalized, whereas 60% of the control subjects were on probation, 40% had hearings pending, and 20% were institutionalized. Thus, 30% of the experimental group were on probation and/or had a hearing pending versus a rate of 70% for the control group. Over the 15 years since the intervention, 30% of the experimental subjects were arrested at least once for nontraffic violations, whereas 90% of the controls were arrested at least once. Additionally, 10% of the experimental subjects served at least one prison term compared with 60% of the controls. Finally, whereas one subject (10%) in the experimental group was hospitalized at least once for psychiatric reasons, no control subjects were hospitalized.

In terms of job histories, 100% of the experimental subjects held at least one job during the 10-month intervention period, and 70% were still on jobs at postintervention. In contrast, 70% of the control subjects held at least one job during the 10-month period, and 50% were still on jobs at postintervention. Of those subjects who had held at least one job during intervention, 20% of the experimental subjects were fired at least once in contrast to 50% of the control subjects. Over the 15 years subsequent to intervention, 70% of the experimental subjects had successful and progressing employment over the full 15-year period, and an additional 10% had successful employment for the first 10 years. In contrast, of the nine control subjects who were followed over the full 15-year period (one subject was unemployed at the 2½-year follow-up but then moved and could not be found), only 44% had successful, progressing employment. Finally, 70% of the control subjects were married at some time, of which 71% were subsequently divorced, whereas 80% of the experimental subjects were married, of which 25% were subsequently divorced.

Unfortunately, the authors did not report any statistical analyses of these data. Nevertheless, the results appeared to be quite impressive and remained essentially stable over 15 years. Together with the Mills and Walter (1979) study, these data suggest that interventions that stress job placement and provide training in relevant job-related skills (e.g., academic, interpersonal, and problem-solving) are quite powerful in terms of reducing subsequent criminal behavior and in terms of enhancing subsequent employability. In this regard, Glaser (1979) reviewed the literature assessing the relationship between youth unemployment and delinquency or crime and concluded, "To combat youth crime is largely futile unless an effort is also made to assure legitimate employment for youths." Clearly, however, the outcome studies described above have not provided definitive information, and therefore, further empirical investigations of employment-related treatment programs are necessary.

Probation Behavior-Modification Programs

The Cooperative Behavior Demonstration Project involved an extensive effort by Carl Jesness and his research colleagues at the California Youth Authority to train and evaluate probation officers in the use of contingency-contracting procedures (Jesness, 1975b). The project, which lasted three years, involved 90 probation officers and 412 youths. The youths ranged in age from 8 to 22 (mean age of 15.1), were 52% white, 30% black, 13% Mexican-

American, and 5% of other ethnic groups; 72% of the youths were placed on probation for criminal offenses (e.g., robbery, theft, and assault) and 28% for "status" offenses (e.g., running away, truancy, and incorrigibility). The project involved a triadic implementation model whereby the project staff first trained 33 supervisory personnel, who were in turn responsible for training 90 field officers from 16 probation units located in eight adjacent counties. Each probation officer received 40 hours of basic classroom training and an average of 22 hours of consultation in contingency contracting from the staff during the project.

In general, the outcome of the project was as follows:

1. Among the 412 project probationers, 1,248 behavioral problems were identified and targeted for change. Contingency contracts were written on 269 (22%) of those behaviors. By the end of the project, 59% of the problem behaviors involving contingency contracts were in remission, and 43% of the problem behaviors not involving contingency contracts were remitted. Although this is a significant difference in favor of contingency contracting, its importance is reduced by at least two potential sources of bias: First, it is quite possible that the behaviors that did result in contracts were less difficult to modify than the behaviors that did not, and second, the determination of remission was a judgment made by the probation officer rather than by an independent, blind observer.

2. In terms of six-month recidivism rates (i.e., illegal behavior recorded in the probation office files), there was no statistically significant difference between the project probationers who were involved in contingency contracting (14% violators) and the project probationers who were not (20% violators).

3. There was a significant relationship between a probation officer's expressed regard for a client and the client's six-month recidivism rate. The project probationers for whom officers expressed above-average positive regard had lower recidivism rates (11% violators) than the project probationers whose officers expressed below-average regard for them (33% violators).

4. There was no significant difference in the six-month recidivism rates of the first 194 ex-

perimental subjects and a control group of probationers who were not part of the project (both 18% violators).

While this study does provide some support for contingency contracting, especially when used by probation officers who have a high positive regard for their clients, two major problems make this interpretation very tentative: the extent to which the experimental group actually received contingency contracting and the adequacy of the control group that did not receive contingency contracting. The first problem showed up in the lack of maintenance and generalization of the effects of the training program. Although 91% of the supervisors and 77% of the field oficers achieved 100% of the 22 training objectives relating to the understanding of the principles and procedures of contingency management and the implementation of those procedures with a specific case, only 33% of the probation officers who went through the classroom training program subsequently wrote one or more contracts that met the project's standards. Because of the lack of transfer of classroom information to field skills, it appears that more emphasis should be given to on-the-job training. On the other hand, in those situations where changes in the performance of field skills is dependent on classroom instruction, it is important to monitor the performance of field skills closely to see if, in fact, such change is occurring.

The second problem concerns the experimental design and the absence of any data to support the assumption that the experimental and the control groups were similar prior to the contingency-contracting intervention. No data are presented that would enable the reader to make any comparisons between the experimental and the control groups. Whether the only difference between the two groups was that some of the probationers in the experimental group received contingency contracting is questionable.

Fitzgerald (1974) reported the results of a study in which contingency contracts were developed with 20 male juvenile probationers from ages 14 to 17 (mean age of 15.3). These youths were randomly selected from a pool of 86 males who were first offenders. Subsequently, the subjects were randomly assigned to one of four groups: (1) a control group; (2) a contingency group involving a reduction in time on probation for work done (the subjects had fines to pay by court order; (3) a contingency group involving increased participation in recreational activities for work done, and (4) a contingency group involving both time off probation and recreational activities for work done. The recreational activities primarily involved attending various sports events. The work activities ranged from yard work to the repair and repainting of the neighborhood counseling houses used by the Salt Lake City Juvenile Court. The subjects earned $1.50 for each hour of work performed, and this money was credited to their accounts at the court toward paying off their fines (no money actually changed hands).

The results indicated a significant difference among groups in terms of the total number of hours worked. Specifically, the groups that had contingency contracts including recreational activities as reinforcers (Groups 3 and 4) worked significantly more hours than either of the other two groups. In addition, the time-off probation group worked significantly more hours than the control group. The maximum amount of time that the youths were able to work was limited to 214 hours. The total amount of time worked across groups was 6.75 hours, 50.5 hours, 127.75 hours, and 187.5 hours, respectively, for the control group, the time-off group, the activity group, and the time-off-plus-activity group.

While these results do not provide information about whether the increase in work output resulted in other positive outcomes (e.g., reduced recidivism), they do suggest that time off probation is not a potent reinforcer (probably because of the extended delay in actual payoff) and that positive reinforcement in the guise of a behavioral contract can be successfully utilized by probation officers to effect changes in probationers' behavior.

Burkhart, Behles, and Stumphauzer (1976) trained nine probation officers in the use of behavior modification during a six-week training program. These nine subjects were compared with nine untrained probation officers in terms of their knowledge of behavioral principles, their attitudes toward behavior modification, and their competence in the use of behavioral methods. The training course included sections on the general principles of behavior therapy, behavioral assessment, techniques of intervention, and generalization to the natural environment. The sessions involved a combination of didactic presentations (first hour) and application (second hour) involving experiential activities, discussion of cases, modeled interviewing, group problem-solving, and homework assignments.

Three types of measures were used in evaluating the training program: (1) a paper-and-pencil, multiple-choice test that assessed general, fundamental knowledge of behavioral principles; (2) a 7-point semantic differential scale that measured attitudes toward behavior modification across the characteristics of sincerity, effectiveness, naturalness, superficiality, warmth, cruelty, speed of treatment, and lasting effects; and (3) a behavioral measure that involved the scoring of the probation officers' behavior analysis and intervention plans established during a 30-minute interview with a client (a confederate who had been trained to role-play a probationer) according to a 35-item checklist. No significant differences were found between the groups on the first two measures (i.e., knowledge of behavioral principles and attitudes toward behavior therapy) either before or after intervention. On the third measure (i.e., behavioral competency), however, the experimental subjects were rated significantly higher than the control subjects (i.e., 45.44 versus 16.88).

Thus, both groups of probation officers scored relatively high (at both pretest and posttest) on their attitudes toward behavior therapy and their knowledge of behavioral principles, whereas only those probation officers who participated in the training program were able to demonstrate competency in the implementation of behavioral techniques. These results seem to support the importance of that part of the training program that involved the application of behavioral principles (e.g., experiential activities, discussion of cases, modeled interviewing, group problem-solving, and homework, which required the officers to develop a behavioral intervention plan for one of their clients) and to point out that knowledge of behavioral principles and a positive attitude about their use do not automatically result in competency in their use.

Six months after the training was completed, interviews conducted with the nine probation officers who had participated in the program (Stumphauzer, Candelora, & Venema, 1976) indicated that seven of the nine trainees were utilizing the behavioral skills in their work (because of job reassignment, the other two officers apparently had less opportunity for application); eight of the nine trainees had applied some aspect of the training with either their families or themselves; and all nine trainees suggested that greater use of the procedures would have occurred if support and assistance had been provided from within the department. In this regard, the officers suggested changes in the training program or the department that would enhance the application of behavioral procedures: (1) reduced case loads; (2) the training of supervisory staff; (3) an adaption of the existing forms and procedures to accommodate the behavioral approach; and (4) continued consultation with the trainers on actual cases. Unfortunately, the study did not indicate whether the use of these methods resulted in greater behavioral change on the part of the probationers.

The studies reviewed above seem to suggest the following about the use of behavioral technology by probation officers:

1. Positive regard is a necessary ingredient in effective contingency contracting.

2. Given a probation officer who has high positive regard for her or his client, contingency contracting appears to facilitate a desirable modification of most specific target behaviors, and it will probably reduce the likelihood of recidivism.

3. Most probation officers do not acquire the necessary skills of contingency contracting through conventional classroom instruction, nor do most probation officers maintain the appropriate use of this procedure without ongoing support and/or supervision.

While these conclusions are based on a limited number of studies containing methodological weaknesses, they do suggest promise, and they clearly support further investigation.

Mediated Behavior-Modification Programs

Employing a triadic model, Tharp and Wetzel (1969) developed a system in which a small number of consultants supervised a larger number of natural mediators (parents, peers, relatives, teachers, employers, etc.), who, in turn, administered contingency contracts with a still larger number of youths. The project was beneficial in demonstrating:

1. That there is a cadre of potential contract mediators within each youth's natural environment who can be taught the basic skills of contingency contracting,
2. That there was a noticeable change in 88% of the 135 target behaviors of the first youths who were referred to the program.
3. That by six months following the termination of the intervention, 35% of the total group of 77 youths had been arrested for juvenile status or criminal offenses.

Because of the lack of a control group, the relative effectiveness of the Tharp and Wetzel model could not be determined. In the early 1970s, however, a similar program, referred to as the *buddy system*, was developed in Hawaii (Fo & O'Donnell, 1974). The primary ways in which the buddy system differed from the Tharp and Wetzel program were that (1) indigenous nonprofessionals were recruited through advertisements and trained in contingency-management procedures in order to function as "buddies" or mediators in the place of natural mediators; (2) the youths who were referred to the program ranged in age from 11 to 17 instead of 6 to 17; and (3) the subjects were randomly assigned to one of the following four intervention conditions for a period of six weeks: (a) a warm and positive relationship plus $10 monthly allotment to be spent on the youth in a noncontingent manner; (b) social approval *contingent* on the performance of a desired behavior plus a $10 monthly allotment to be spent on the youth in a noncontingent manner; (c) social and material reinforcement ($10 allotment) *contingent* on the performance of a desired behavior, and (d) a control group who were not invited to participate in the project.

While the "buddies" focused on assorted behavioral problems, the three different intervention conditions were evaluated in terms of their effects on truancy rates. Although the small sample size (five to seven per group)

precludes any strong conclusions, the results provide additional support for the effects of contingency management in a community setting. Given a baseline of 50% school attendance for all four groups, the truancy rates dropped to approximately 20% in the two response-contingent conditions while remaining unchanged in the relationship and control conditions. Then, during a subsequent condition in which the subjects in the relationship group were administered contingent social and material reinforcement, the truancy rates for those subjects dropped to 25%. In addition to the differential reduction of truancy rates, the authors presented data to demonstrate that for six additional youths with other problem behaviors (e.g., fighting, not doing chores, staying out too late, and not doing homework assignments), the social and material reinforcement was also effective.

The lack of outcome data on the effectiveness of the buddy system was rectified in a subsequent study conducted by Fo and O'Donnell (1975). Although delinquent behaviors were not targeted directly for intervention in the buddy system, the implicit assumption was that such acts would be modified by targeting the problem behaviors mentioned above. In a test of this assumption, 264 youths were assigned to the adult "buddies" and were compared with 178 youths who were also referred to the program but were randomly assigned to a no-treatment control group. The two groups were similar in terms of major offenses (auto thefts, burglary, and assault) prior to when the experimental group began the buddy system. The results suggested that whether participation in the buddy system reduced the commitment of major delinquent acts depended on the previous record of the subject. For youths who had committed major offenses during the year prior to the study, significantly fewer buddy-system participants committed a major offense during the project year than the no-treatment controls (37.5% vs. 64%). In contrast, however, for youths with no record of major offenses in the preceding year, approximately one out of six experimental subjects committed a major offense during the project year. This rate is significantly higher than the rate of the control subjects (15.7% vs. 7.2%). On the basis of these data, the authors concluded that the buddy system was most effective for youth already identified as delinquent, and they speculated that the negative effects on the less delinquent youths was a function of modeling by other, more delinquent youths. The authors also suggested, appropriately, that preventive efforts and early identification of potential youthful offenders may do more harm than good.

In the most recent report, O'Donnell, Lydgate, and Fo (1979) presented follow-up data on 335 youths (206 males and 129 females) who had participated in the buddy system and 218 youths (151 males and 67 females) who had not (on the basis of random assignment). These youths included all youngsters who had participated in the buddy system during its three-year history (1970–1973) and therefore included some youths not included in the Fo and O'Donnell (1975) report. Of the 335 experimental youth, 255 had participated in the buddy system for one year, 73 for two years, and 7 for all three years. Additionally, 50 of these experimental subjects (15%) had committed at least one major offense during the year prior to intervention, and 23 of the control subjects (11%) had committed major offenses prior to intervention.

Arrest records were analyzed and provided information on the offenses of each youth one year prior to participation, during participation, and two years after the initial year of participation in the buddy system. The dependent variable was the number of youth arrested for at least one offense in the three-year period, which included their initial year of participation plus the next two years. Only major offenses were included in the data analyses (e.g., murder, rape, and burglary). The results indicated that (1) the experimental subjects with prior offenses demonstrated a significantly lower arrest rate than the control subjects with prior offenses (56.0% vs. 78.3%); (2) the experimental subjects without prior offenses demonstrated a significantly greater arrest rate than the control subjects without prior offenses (22.5% vs. 16.4%); and (3) the experimental subjects without prior offenses who participated in the buddy system for more than one year demonstrated a significantly greater arrest rate than the experimental subjects without prior offenses who participated for only one year (34.4% vs. 18.8%).

Thus, the results of this follow-up assessment tend to correspond with the results reported by Fo and O'Donnell (1975) for the second project year: The buddy system is most effective with those youths who have been arrested for major offenses in the preceding year. While this is an important conclusion, the arrest rate for these youths was still unacceptably high (i.e., 62.2% for the males and 38.5% for the females), especially as these arrest rates include only major offenses. Also supporting previous conclusions, these follow-up data indicate that the buddy system is detrimental to youths without prior arrest records for major offenses. The authors pointed out that the effectiveness of preventive intervention is unlikely, given the low base rate of arrests demonstrated by the control condition youths. In other words, these base rates indicate that a preventive program must be more than 80% effective with males and 90% effective with females in order to be successful (i.e., compared with no intervention at all). These data also suggest that increasing a program's intensity and/or duration, given the absence of positive results, is probably not a sound procedure and may enhance the likelihood of negative outcomes.

There have been few efforts to evaluate community-based behavior-modification programs that involve primarily hard-core delinquent youth. During a two-year period ending in August of 1971, Davidson and Robinson (1975) developed and evaluated such a program (Kentfields Rehabilitation Program) for 125 chronic male delinquents who were being considered for a long-term institutional placement. On the average, the participating youths were 16 years old, were functioning at the 5.3 grade level, had been on probation 2.6 years, and had committed an average of 2.95 offenses per year during that time (i.e., while on probation). Of these youths, 80% lived in the inner city (Grand Rapids, Michigan), and approximately 60% were nonwhites. The most common offenses were larceny, breaking and entering, and auto theft.

For three hours each weekday morning, the subjects engaged in various work projects run by a nonprofessional undergraduate student. Three additional hours each afternoon were spent on individualized programmed instruction, the production of plays, and the writing of newspaper articles. This portion of the program was conducted by a teacher's aide who had completed less than one full year of college. Group sessions were held two afternoons per week following the educational component and focused on the youth's positive accomplishments, personal problems, and status in the group, suggestions for change and on open discussions. These group sessions were run by upper-level program participants on an alternating basis. The program utilized a contingency point system focusing on the areas of work performance, academic performance, and appropriate verbalizations in group sessions. Participants in the program moved through three hierarchical levels before graduating. On the average, it took nine weeks to complete the program.

Reversal designs were utilized to demonstrate the short-term effectiveness of the point-system contingencies. As for the long-term effects of the program, follow-up data are presented on 117 subjects: 95 graduates of the program and 22 nongraduates. Eighteen months after the graduates had completed the Kentfields program, 29% were in school, 35% were employed, and 17% were in correctional institutions. For the nongraduates, 0% were in school, 9% were employed, and 53% were in correctional institutions. Also reported is a postprogram arrest rate of .46 per year for the 95 graduates. While this is a significant reduction from the average preprogram arrest rate of 2.95 for all of the subjects, it is difficult to interpret since the two rates do not involve the same youths. Unfortunately, the authors did not disclose the pre- and postprogram arrest rates of just those graduates who did not go to the institution ($n = 79$). Without such data, it is difficult to determine whether going through the program was correlated with a reduction in arrest rates. Nevertheless, this study offers several very positive contributions. First, if it is true that these youths were headed for institutional settings, the cost differential was significant. At the time of follow-up, 28 youths had been sent to the institution and 89 had not. The authors estimated the average cost of institutionalized treatment as $8,000 per youth (for a 10-month average stay). Had the remaining 89 youths gone to the

institution, the cost would have been $712,000. The total cost of the Kentfields program was $30,000. Second, the program did modify the behaviors and attitudes of the people who controlled its maintenance; as a result, the program was continued with local financial support. The authors reported that many of the original local governmental officials who were skeptics became the program's most ardent advocates and recommended similar approaches in other areas. Much of this change was probably a function of the reduction in arrest rates, the resulting reduced costs, and the innovative community projects that were conducted in the process of developing prosocial skills. These results also appear to give further support to (1) the practice of using nonprofessional mediators in program implementation; (2) the utility of work-related interventions; and (3) the adequacy and effectiveness of relatively brief treatment programs.

Summary of Community-Based, Nonresidential Programs

If we take these community-based, nonresidential intervention studies as a whole, the following conclusions seem to be suggested:

1. Possibly the most salient observation involves the differential effectiveness of these programs as a function of subject population. These programs appear generally useful with prior offenders, whereas preventive efforts have consistently proved ineffective and/or detrimental in terms of recidivism. The most promising direction of preventive efforts, however, appears to be family behavioral intervention.

2. High positive regard, affect–behavior integration, self-confidence, etc., on the part of the service providers (e.g., therapists and probation officers) appear to be necessary but not sufficient to effect positive change in youthful offenders.

3. It appears that short-term intervention (i.e., eight or nine weeks) and the use of nonprofessional mediators do not detract from the positive outcome of intervention and are thus cost-effective procedures.

4. In terms of content, the following emphases appear useful: (a) family interaction (e.g., communication skills and negotiation

skills); (b) job skills; (c) job placement; and (d) academic skills functionally related to employment and/or graduation (i.e., diploma or equivalency). While cognitive-behavioral intervention procedures appear promising, they currently lack empirical support via evaluative outcome studies (cf. Kendall & Hollon, 1979).

Summary

The primary focus of this review has been the long-term effectiveness of behavior-modification programs in reducing the frequency of delinquent or criminal behavior. On the basis of this review, the effectiveness of these programs depends largely on the setting in which they are applied, the specific behaviors that are being modified, and the characteristics of both the service providers and the clients. Although there are too few outcome studies to warrant any detailed analysis of the interactions among these variables, the preliminary data that are available do permit some interesting speculations.

Within institutional settings, there is little evidence of rehabilitative superiority. Behavior-modification techniques have been shown to be very effective in the direct modification of maintenance and educational types of behaviors, but there is no good empirical evidence that either is related to recidivism. While it is possible to argue that the effect is there and would be confirmed given a good, sound methodological study, it is doubtful that the major problem is one of evaluation. It is also possible that the modification of maintenance and/or educational behavior is a necessary condition but that it is not sufficient to bring about rehabilitation without a good transition program and more corresponding modifications of the natural environment. While both of these explanations could account for the lack of empirical support for existing institutional behavior-modification programs for delinquents or criminals, behaviorists should also consider a change in the target behaviors they are attempting to modify. In addition to the teaching of maintenance and educational behaviors, more emphasis should be placed on teaching inmates and residents to plan, problem-solve, and make decisions relevant to the

community-based environment they will eventually live in. Granted the inmate cannot be given the degrees of freedom that exists in a group home; nevertheless, he or she can be taught how to plan day-to-day objectives, how to solve problems and how to modify solutions when the intended behavior or situation does not occur.

With respect to residential, community-based programs, the outlook is somewhat more positive, particularly in terms of the quality of the data that are beginning to emerge. Three controlled-outcome studies on the teaching-family group home were reviewed, one involving a matched comparison with youths from another location; the second involving a random assignment to the teaching-family program; and the third consisting of a comprehensive comparison of 27 teaching-family group homes with 25 non-teaching-family group homes located in 10 different states. Although the last two studies are incomplete and the data are very limited, the preliminary findings suggest that the teaching-family group home is more effective than an institutional program, as effective as but less expensive than a non-teaching-family group home, but possibly less effective than other community-based alternatives. Hopefully, more definitive conclusions will be reached in the near future when the last two ongoing studies are completed.

The picture with respect to nonresidential, community-based programs is one of differential effectiveness. One of the more promising programs appears to be family intervention. However, it seems clear that this approach will be most effective if the families are relatively intact, the target youths are in early as opposed to late adolescence, and there is considerable emphasis on the training of communication and negotiation skills. While this approach would exclude the older adolescent from less intact families, it would appear that the treatment of choice for that individual would be a short-term contingency-contracting program with mediators who focus on employment-related targets, particularly if the youth is not a first offender.

Finally, there are a few areas of caution with respect to nonresidential, community-based programs. First, there are few data to support behaviorally oriented, alternative school programs unless the youths are older, experienced offenders and there is a strong job-training and placement component in the program. Younger adolescents would seem to need less emphasis on special school programs and more emphasis on behavioral, family interventions. Second, with first offenders of any age, the emphasis should be on supporting and reestablishing ties within the normalized settings (family, school, and employment) before placing the youth in any special contingency-contracting program that increases his or her contact with other offenders.

Finally it should be noted that while the behavioral approach offers a specific technology that can be used effectively with delinquents and criminals, it is most effective when used with service providers (e.g., probation officers, guards, mediators, therapists, and counselors) who have a high degree of positive regard for their clients and can establish a relationship with each client in which they themselves function as positive reinforcers.

References

Alexander, J. F. Defensive and supportive communications in normal and deviant families. *Journal of Consulting and Clinical Psychology*, 1973, *40*, 223–231.

Alexander, J. F., & Barton, C. Short-term behavioral systems therapy with delinquent families. In D. H. Olsen (Ed.), *Treating relationships*. Lake Mills, Iowa: Graphic Publishing Company, 1976.

Alexander, J. F., & Parsons, B. V. Short-term behavioral intervention with delinquent families: Impact on family process and recidivism. *Journal of Abnormal Psychology*, 1973, *81*, 219–225.

Alexander, J. F., Barton, C., Schiavo, R. S., & Parsons, B. V. Systems-behavioral intervention with families of delinquents: Therapist characteristics, family behavior, and outcome. *Journal of Consulting and Clinical Psychology*, 1976, *44*, 656–664.

Ayala, H. E., Minkin, N., Phillips, E. L., Fixsen, D. L., & Wolf, M. M. Achievement Place: *The training and analysis of vocational behaviors*. Paper presented at the meeting of the American Psychological Association, 1973.

Azrin, N. H. *Responses to questions asked of the panel of experts*. In the United States District Court for the Western District of Missouri, Southern Division, 1974. Available from National Prison Project, Washington, D.C.

Bailey, J. S., Wolf, M. M., & Phillips, E. L. Home-based reinforcement and the modification of pre-delinquents' classroom behavior. *Journal of Applied Behavior Analysis*, 1970, *3*, 223–233.

Bailey, J. S., Timbers, G. D., Phillips, E. L., & Wolf, M. M. Modification of articulation errors of pre-delinquents by their peers. *Journal of Applied Behavior Analysis*, 1971, *4*, 265–281.

Bailey, W. W. Correctional outcome: An evaluation of 100 reports. *Journal of Criminal Law, Criminology, and Police Science*, 1966, *57*, 153–160.

Barnard, J. D., Gant, B. L., Kuehn, F. E., Jones, H. H., & Christophersen, E. R. Home-based treatment of the juvenile probationer. Submitted for publication, 1980.

Bassett, J. E., & Blanchard, E. B. The effect of the absence of close supervision on the use of response cost in a prison token economy. *Journal of Applied Behavior Analysis*, 1977, *10*, 375–379.

Bassett, J. E., Blanchard, E. B., & Koshland, E. Applied behavior analysis in a penal setting: Targeting "free world" behaviors. *Behavior Therapy*, 1975, *6*, 639–648.

Blatt, B. *Exodus from pandemonium*. Boston: Allyn & Bacon, 1970.

Braukmann, C. J., & Fixsen, D. L. Behavior modification with delinquents. In M. Hersen, R. M. Eisler, & P. M. Miller (Eds.), *Progress in behavior modification*, Vol. 1. New York: Academic Press, 1975.

Braukmann, C. J., Maloney, D. M., Fixsen, D. L., Phillips, E. L., & Wolf, M. M. An analysis of a selection interview training package for predelinquents at Achievement Place. *Criminal Justice and Behavior*, 1974, *1*, 30–42.

Braukmann, C. J., Fixsen, D. L., Kirigin, K. A., Phillips, E. A., Phillips, E. L., & Wolf, M. M. Achievement Place: The training and certification of teaching-parents. In W. S. Wood (Ed.), *Issues in evaluating behavior modification*. Champaign, Ill.: Research Press, 1975.

Burchard, J. D., & Harig, P. T. Behavior modification and juvenile delinquency. In H. Leitenberg (Ed.), *Handbook of behavior modification and behavior therapy*. Englewood Cliffs, N.J.: Prentice-Hall, 1976.

Burkhart, B. R., Behles, M. W., & Stumphauzer, J. S. Training juvenile probation officers in behavior modification: Knowledge, attitude change, or behavioral competence? *Behavior Therapy*, 1976, *7*, 47–53.

Cohen, H. L. *Responses to questions asked of the panel of experts*. In the United States District Court for the Western District of Missouri, Southern Division, 1974. Available from National Prison Project, Washington, D.C.

Cohen, H. L., & Filipczak, J. A. *A new learning environment*. San Francisco: Jossey-Bass, 1971.

Davidson, W. S., & Robinson, M. J. Community psychology and behavior modification: A community-based program for the prevention of delinquency. *Journal of Corrective Psychiatry and Behavior Therapy*, 1975, *21*, 1–12.

Davidson, W. S., & Seidman, E. Studies of behavior modification and juvenile delinquency: A review, methodological critique, and social perspective. *Psychological Bulletin*, 1974, *81*, 998–1011.

Davidson, W. S., & Wolfred, T. R. Evaluation of a community-based behavior modification program for prevention of delinquency: The failure of success. *Community Mental Health Journal*, 1977, *13*, 296–306.

Dean, C. W., & Reppucci, N. D. Juvenile correctional institutions. In D. Glaser (Ed.), *Handbook of criminology*. Chicago: Rand McNally, 1974.

DeRisi, W. J. *Responses to questions asked to the panel of experts.* In the United States District Court for the Western District of Missouri, Southern Division, 1974. Available from National Prison Project, Washington, D.C.

D'Zurilla, T. J., & Goldfried, N. R. Problem solving and behavior modification. *The Journal of Abnormal Psychology,* 1971, *78,* 107–126.

Emshoff, J., Redd, W., & Davidson, W. S. *Generalization training and the transfer of treatment effects.* Paper presented at American Psychological Association Convention, New Orleans, 1974.

Federal Bureau of Prisons. *START-revised programs.* Washington, D.C.: Federal Bureau of Prisons, 1972.

Ferdun, G. S., Webb, M. P., Lockard, H. R., & Mahan, J. *Compensatory Education 1971–1972.* Sacramento: California Youth Authority, 1972.

Filipczak, J., & Friedman, R. M. Some controls on applied research in a public secondary school: Project PREP. In A. C. Catania & T. A. Brigham (Eds.), *Handbook of applied behavior analysis: Social and instructional processes.* New York: Irvington Publishers, 1978.

Filipczak, J., Archer, M. B., Neale, M. S., & Winett, R. A. Issues in multivariate assessment of a large-scale behavioral program. *Journal of Applied Behavior Analysis,* 1979, *12,* 593–613.

Filipczak, J., Friedman, R. M., & Reese, S. C. PREP: Educational programming to prevent juvenile problems. In J. S. Stumphauzer (Ed.), *Progress in behavior therapy with delinquents.* Springfield, Ill.: Charles C Thomas, 1979.

Filipczak, J., Archer, M. B., & Friedman, R. M. In-school social skills training: Use with disruptive adolescents. *Behavior Modification,* 1980, *4,* 243–264.

Fitzgerald, T. J. Contingency contracting with juvenile offenders. *Criminology,* 1974, *12,* 241–248.

Fixsen, D. L., Phillips, E. L., & Wolf, M. M. Achievement Place: Experiments in self-government with predelinquents. *Journal of Applied Behavior Analysis,* 1973, *6,* 31–47.

Fleischman, M. J. Using parenting salaries to control attrition and cooperation in therapy. *Behavior Therapy,* 1979, *10,* 111–116.

Fo, W. S. O., & O'Donnell, C. R. The Buddy System: Relationship and contingency conditions in a community intervention program for youth and nonprofessionals as behavior change agents. *Journal of Consulting and Clinical Psychology,* 1974, *42,* 163–169.

Fo, W. S. O., & O'Donnell, C. R. The Buddy System: Effect of community intervention on delinquent offenses. *Behavior Therapy,* 1975, *6,* 522–524.

Friedman, R. M., Filipczak, J., & Fiordaliso, R. Within-school generalization of the Preparation through Responsive Educational Programs (PREP) academic project. *Behavior Therapy,* 1977, *8,* 986–995.

Geller, E. S., Johnson, D. F., Hamlin, P. H., & Kennedy, T. D. Behavior modification in a prison: Issues, problems, and compromises. *Criminal Justice and Behavior,* 1977, *4,* 11–43.

Glaser, D. Economic and sociocultural variables affecting rates of youth unemployment, delinquency, and crime. *Youth and Society,* 1979, *11,* 53–82.

Guerney, L. F. A program for training agency personnel as foster parent trainers. *Child Welfare,* 1976, *25,* 652–660.

Heaton, R. C., Safer, D. J., Allen, R. P., Spinnato, N. C., & Prumo, F. M. A motivational environment for behaviorally deviant junior high school students. *Journal of Abnormal Child Psychology,* 1976, *4,* 263–275.

Hobbs, T. R., & Holt, N. M. The effects of token reinforcement on the behavior of delinquents in cottage settings. *Journal of Applied Behavior Analysis,* 1976, *9,* 189–198.

Howard, J. R. *Consumer evaluations of teaching family group homes for delinquents.* Paper presented at the meeting of American Psychological Association, New York, 1979.

Jenkins, W. O., Witherspoon, A. D., DeVine, M. D., DeZalera, E. K., Muller, J. B., Barton, M. C., & McKee, J. M. *The post-prison analysis of criminal behavior and longitudinal follow-up evaluation of institutional treatment.* Montgomery, Ala.: Rehabilitation Research Foundation, 1974.

Jesness, C. F. Comparative effectiveness of behavior modification and transactional analysis programs for delinquents. *Journal of Consulting and Clinical Psychology,* 1975, *43,* 758–799. (a)

Jesness, C. F. *The Cooperative Behavior Demonstration Project: Submitted as the final report to the office of criminal justice planning.* Sacramento: California Youth Authority, 1975. (b)

Johnson, D. F., & Geller, E. S. *Operation manual: Contingency management program.* Blacksburg: Virginia Polytechnic Institute and State University, 1973.

Jones, R. R. *First findings from the national evaluation of the teaching family model.* Paper presented at the meeting of the National Teaching Family Association, Boys Town, Neb. October 25–27, 1978.

Jones, R. R. *Therapeutic effects of the teaching family group home model.* Paper read at the meeting of American Psychological Association, New York, September 1979.

Jones, R. R., & Weinrott, N. R. *Comparability between pre-existing samples of the community-based programs for delinquent youth.* Paper presented at the meeting of the Western Psychological Association, Seattle, April 1977.

Kendall, P. C., & Hollon, S. D. (Eds.). *Cognitive-behavioral interventions: Theory, research, and procedures.* New York: Academic Press, 1979.

Kennedy, R. E. Behavior modification in prisons. In W. E. Craighead, A. E. Kazdin, & M. J. Mahoney (Eds.), *Behavior modification: Principles, issues and application.* Boston: Houghton-Mifflin, 1976.

Kifer, R. E., Lewis, M. A., Green, D. R., & Phillips, E. L. Training pre-delinquent youths and their parents to negotiate conflict situations. *Journal of Applied Behavior Analysis,* 1974, *7,* 357–364.

Kirigin, K. A., Phillips, E. L., Timbers, G. D., Fixsen, D. L., & Wolf, M. M. Achievement Place: The modification of academic behavior problems of youths in a group home setting. In B. C. Etzel, J. M. LeBlanc, & D. M. Baer (Eds.), *New developments in behavioral research: Theory, method and application.* Hillsdale, N.J.: Lawrence Erlbaum, 1975.

Kirigin, K. A., Wolf, M. M., Braukmann, C. J., Fixsen,

D. L., & Phillips, E. L. Achievement Place: A preliminary outcome evaluation. In J. S. Stumphauzer (Ed.), *Progress in behavior therapy with delinquents*. Springfield, Ill.: Charles C Thomas, 1979.

Klein, N. C., Alexander, J. F., & Parsons, B. V. Impact of family systems intervention on recidivism and sibling delinquency: A model of primary prevention and program evaluation. *Journal of Consulting and Clinical Psychology*, 1977, *45*, 469–474.

Lazarus, A. *Behavior therapy and beyond*. New York: McGraw-Hill, 1971.

Liberman, R. P., Ferris, C., Salgado, P., & Salgado, J. Replication of the Achievement Place model in California. *Journal of Applied Behavior Analysis*, 1975, *8*, 287–299.

Lipton, D., Martinson, R., & Wilks, J. *The effectiveness of correctional treatment: A survey of treatment evaluation studies*. New York: Praeger, 1975.

Maloney, D. M., Phillips, E. L., Fixsen, D. L., & Wolf, M. M. Training techniques for staff in group homes for juvenile offenders: An analysis. *Criminal Justice and Behavior*, 1975, *2*, 195–216.

Maloney, D. M., Harper, T. M., Braukmann, C. J., Fixsen, D. L., Phillips, E. L., & Wolf, M. M. Teaching conversation skills to predelinquent girls. *Journal of Applied Behavior Analysis*, 1976, *9*, 371.

Massimo, J. L., & Shore, M. F. The effectiveness of a comprehensive, vocationally oriented psychotherapeutic program for adolescent delinquent boys. *American Journal of Orthopsychiatry*, 1963, *33*, 634–642.

McKee, J. M., Smith, R. R., Wood, L. F., & Milan, M. A. Selecting and implementing an intervention approach that employs correctional officers as behavior change agents. In M. A. Bernal (Ed.), *Training in behavior modification*. Belmont, Calif.: Brooks-Cole, 1975.

McNamara, J. R., & Andrasik, S. Systematic program change: Its effects on resident behavior in a forensic psychiatry institution. *Journal of Behavior Therapy and Experimental Psychiatry*, 1977, *8*, 19–23.

Milan, M. A., & McKee, J. M. Behavior modification: Principles and applications in corrections. In D. Glaser (Ed.), *Handbook of criminology*. Chicago: Rand McNally, 1974.

Milan, M. A., & McKee, J. M. The cellblock token economy: Token reinforcement procedures in a maximum security correctional institution for adult male felons. *Journal of Applied Behavior Analysis*, 1976, *9*, 254–275.

Mills, C. M., & Walter, T. L. Reducing juvenile delinquency: A behavioral-employment intervention. In J. S. Stumphauzer (Ed.), *Progress in behavior therapy with delinquents*. Springfield, Ill.: Charles C Thomas, 1979.

Moore, D. R., Chamberlain, P., & Mukai, L. H. Children at risk for delinquency: A follow-up comparison of aggressive children and children who steal. *Journal of Abnormal Child Psychology*, 1979, *7*, 345–355.

Nietzel, N. T. *Crime and its modification: A social learning perspective*. New York: Pergamon Press, 1979.

O'Donnell, C. R. Behavior modification in community settings. In M. Hersen, R. Eisler, & P. Miller (Eds.), *Progress in behavior modification*, Vol. 4. New York: Academic Press, 1977.

O'Donnell, C. R., Lydgate, T., & Fo, W. S. O. The buddy

system: Review and follow-up. *Child Behavior Therapy*, 1979, *1*, 161–169.

Parsons, B. V., & Alexander, J. F. Short-term family intervention: A therapy outcome study. *Journal of Consulting and Clinical Psychology*, 1973, *41*, 195–201.

Patterson, G. R. Treatment for children with conduct problems: A review of outcome studies. In S. Feshback & A. Fraczek (Eds.), *Aggression and behavior change: Biological and social processes*. New York: Praeger, 1979.

Patterson, G. R., & Fleischman, M. J. Maintenance of treatment effects: Some considerations concerning family systems and follow-up data. *Behavior Therapy*, 1979, *10*, 168–185.

Patterson, G. R., Reid, J. B., Jones, R. R., & Conger, R. E. *A social learning approach to family intervention: I. Families with aggressive children*. Eugene, Ore.: Castalia Press, 1975.

Pavlott, J. Effects of reinforcement procedures on negative behaviors in delinquent girls. Unpublished doctoral dissertation, University of Pittsburgh, 1971.

Phillips, E. L. Achievement Place: Token economy reinforcement procedures in a home style rehabilitation setting for pre-delinquent boys. *Journal of Applied Behavior Analysis*, 1968, *1*, 213–223.

Reese, S. C., & Filipczak, J. Assessment of skill generalization: Measurement across setting, behavior, and time in an educational setting. *Behavior Modification*, 1980, *4*, 209–224.

Reid, J. B. (Ed.). *A social learning approach to family intervention: II. Observations in home settings*. Eugene, Ore.: Castalia Press, 1978.

Reppucci, N. D., & Saunders, J. T. Social psychology of behavior modification: Problems of implementation in natural settings. *American Psychologist*, 1974, *29*, 649–660.

Robinson, J., & Smith, G. The effectiveness of correctional programs. *Crime and Delinquency*, 1971, *17*, 67–80.

Romig, D. A. *Justice for our children: An examination of juvenile delinquent rehabilitation programs*. Lexington, Mass.: Heath, 1978.

Ross, R. R., & McKay, H. B. A study of institutional treatment programs. *International Journal of Offender Therapy and Comparative Criminology*, 1976, *20*, 165–173.

Ryan, P. *Training foster parents to serve dependent children* (DHEW Publication No., ADM, 78-591). Washington, D.C.: U.S. Government Printing Office, 1978.

Shah, S. A., & Roth, L. H. Biological and psychophysiological factors in criminality. In D. Glaser (Ed.), *Handbook of criminology*. Chicago: Rand McNally, 1974.

Shore, M. F., & Massimo, J. L. Comprehensive vocationally oriented psychotherapy for adolescent delinquent boys: A follow-up study. *American Journal of Orthopsychiatry*, 1966, *36*, 609–616.

Shore, M. F., & Massimo, J. L. Five years later: A follow-up study of comprehensive vocationally oriented psychotherapy. *American Journal of Orthopsychiatry*, 1969, *39*, 769–773.

Shore, M. F., & Massimo, J. L. After ten years: A follow-up study of comprehensive vocationally oriented psychotherapy. *American Journal of Orthopsychiatry*, 1973, *43*, 128–132.

Shore, M. F., & Massimo, J. L. Fifteen years after treatment: A follow-up study of comprehensive vocationally-oriented psychotherapy. *American Journal of Orthopsychiatry*, 1979, *49*, 240–245.

Stuart, R. B., & Tripodi, T. Experimental evaluation of three time-constrained behavioral treatments for predelinquents and delinquents. In R. D. Rubin, J. P. Brady, & J. D. Henderson (Eds.), *Advances in behavior therapy*, Vol. 4. New York: Academic Press, 1973.

Stuart, R. B., Jayaratne, S., & Tripodi, T. Changing adolescent deviant behavior through reprogramming the behavior of parents and teachers: An experimental evaluation. *Canadian Journal of Behavioral Science*, 1976, *8*, 132–144.

Stuart, R. B., Tripodi, T., Jayaratne, S., & Camburn, D. An experiment in social engineering in serving the families of predelinquents. *Journal of Abnormal Child Psychology*, 1976, *4*, 243–261.

Stumphauzer, J. S., Candelora, K., & Venema, H. B. A follow-up of probation officers trained in behavior modification. *Behavior Therapy*, 1976, *7*, 713–715.

Tharp, R. G., & Wetzel, R. J. *Behavior modification in the natural environment*. New York: Academic Press, 1969.

Tyler, V. O., & Brown, G. D. Token reinforcement of academic performance with institutionalized delinquent boys. *Journal of Educational Psychology*, 1968, *59*, 164–168.

Wahler, R. G., Berland, R. M., & Coe, T. D. Generalization processes in child behavior change. In B. B. Lahey & A. E. Kazdin (Eds.), *Advances in clinical child psychology*, Vol. 2. New York: Plenum Press, 1979.

Warren, J. Potpourri. *APA Monitor*, 1974, *5*, 3.

Weathers, L., & Liberman, R. P. Contingency contracting with families of delinquent adolescents. *Behavior Therapy*, 1975, *6*, 356–366.

Weinrott, N. R. *Assessing the cost effectiveness of the teaching family programs*. Paper presented at the meeting of the American Psychological Association, New York, 1979.

Werner, J. S., Minkin, N., Minkin, B. L., Fixsen, D. L., Phillips, E. L., & Wolf, M. M. Intervention package: An analysis to prepare juvenile delinquents for encounters with police officers. *Criminal Justice and Behavior*, 1975, *2*, 55–83.

Willner, A. G., Braukmann, C. J., Kirigin, K. A., Fixsen, D. L., Phillips, E. L., & Wolf, M. M. The training and validation of youth-preferred social behaviors of child-care workers. *Journal of Applied Behavior Analysis*, 1977, *10*, 219–230.

Wodarski, J. S., Filipczak, J., McCombs, D., Koustenis, G., & Rusilko, S. Follow-up on behavioral intervention with troublesome adolescents. *Journal of Behavior Therapy and Experimental Psychiatry*, 1979, *10*, 181–188.

CHAPTER 21

Sexual Dysfunctions and Their Treatment

CURRENT STATUS

Jerry M. Friedman, Stephen J. Weiler,
Joseph LoPiccolo, and Douglas R. Hogan

Introduction

If we broadly define sexual dysfunctions as physiological, cognitive-affective, or behavioral problems that prevent an individual from engaging in or enjoying satisfactory sexual activity, intercourse, or orgasm, then we can be sure that sexual dysfunctions have been around as long as sex has. Only recently, however, has a discipline been developed that attempts to describe, assess, and treat sexual dysfunctions in an integrated and scientific manner.

In this chapter, we review the antecedents of sex therapy and its development into a discipline. We then consider its expansion and differentiation in several areas. These areas include classification systems, assessment and treatment procedures, and the treatment of individuals previously not considered suitable for sex therapy. Also, we consider the special professional and ethical issues of this new discipline.

Sex Therapy: The Roots

Interventions for problems of sexual functioning date back to earliest recorded history. At the beginning of the twentieth century, Freud's influence led to a view of sexual dysfunctions as manifestations of psychopathology, treatable, if at all, only by the lengthy and costly procedures based on a psychoanalytic model of therapy. Traditional analytic psychotherapy viewed sexual dysfunction as the result of deep-seated personality conflicts generated early in individual psychosocial development. More specifically, sexual dysfunction was viewed as a failure to resolve the Oedipal complex (Freud, 1905/1962). For example, erectile failure was seen as unconscious guilt or

Jerry M. Friedman, Stephen J. Weiler, Joseph LoPiccolo, and Douglas R. Hogan • Sex Therapy Center, Department of Psychiatry and Behavioral Science, Health Sciences Center, State University of New York at Stony Brook, Stony Brook, Long Island, New York 11794. Preparation of this chapter was supported, in part, by a grant from the National Institute of Mental Health, Department of Health and Human Services.

as castration anxiety. Dynamically, the guilt was thought to be the result of the failure to differentiate forbidden incestuous sex-with-mother from sex-with-other-women. Castration anxiety was thought to be due to the unconscious fear that the father would punish the subject for engaging in sex with a woman (mother). Similarly, orgasmic dysfunction in women was conceptualized as reflecting a failure to resolve penis envy, or as a failure to transfer sexual excitability from the clitoris to the vagina. Thus, the major etiological factor in producing sexual dysfunction was the early parent–child interaction around the instinctual Oedipal complex. The treatment involved the reenactment of the Oedipal situation or other unresolved conflicts in the transference relationship with the therapist, thus completing in a healthy way those developmental tasks that were not completed in childhood. Since sexual conflict was seen in psychodynamic theory as the cause of almost all psychopathology, the application of psychodynamic therapy to sexual dysfunction did not require any special adaptation (O'Connor & Stern, 1972), and treatment was essentially the same as for other problems.

Criticisms of analytic theory with regard to sexuality are too numerous to detail here. At a theoretical level, analytic theory was, of course, developed at a period when knowledge of the basic physiology of sexual response was virtually nonexistent. Thus, a number of Freud's theories about the nature of sexuality have since become insupportable in the light of advances in our biological knowledge. An obvious example of analytic theoretical speculation, since contradicted by empirical research, is the famous distinction between clitoral and vaginal orgasm. The data of Kinsey, Pomeroy, Martin, and Gebhard (1953), and Masters and Johnson's (1966) physiological data have made this distinction dubious, at best.

Another difficulty with analytic theory is the inflexibility of viewing unconscious conflict as the only underlying cause of sexual problems, and the resolution of these conflicts as the only cure (Kaplan & Kohl, 1972). If one recognizes that many cases of sexual dysfunction may be caused simply by a lack of knowledge and experience, then the nondirective, passive role of the analyst may not be best suited to helping

to alleviate the problem. Focusing on a woman's childhood for months or years is not likely to help her have orgasms with her partner if the major problem is that neither of them knows where her clitoris is and the role it plays in female orgasm.

It is at the level of therapeutic effectiveness that inflexibly applied analytic therapy is most vulnerable to criticism. In the few empirical studies that have been done, it is apparent that analytic psychotherapy simply does not work very well with sexual problems (Cooper, 1971; Hogan, 1978; LoPiccolo & Hogan, 1979: Reynolds, 1977; Wright, Perreault, & Mathieu, 1977). Even those who do claim effectiveness admit that the length of time required for successful analysis is prohibitive (Bergler, 1951).

In the late 1950s and early 1960s, a new approach to the treatment of sexual dysfunction was developed based on learning theory. The focus of behavior therapy was on the immediate causes of the dysfunction, treated in short-term target-directed therapy. Unlike psychoanalytic treatment, which attempted to reconstruct the personality, behavior therapy aimed directly at the relief of the sexual symptom. Wolpe (1958) made a major contribution by conceptualizing sexual dysfunction as being conditioned anxiety responses to the sexual situation and therefore treatable by systematic desensitization to the anxiety-producing stimulus. In systematic desensitization, a hierarchy of anxiety-producing situations is developed, and the person being desensitized is exposed to these items imaginally, or *in vivo*, while using progressive relaxation techniques, hypnorelaxation, or drug-induced relaxation. The procedure is continued through the hierarchy until relaxation is possible in the situation producing the most anxiety. There is a substantial literature on the effectiveness of this technique in the treatment of sexual dysfunction in both men and women (Dengrove, 1973; D. Friedman, 1968; Laughren & Kass, 1975; Obler, 1973). However, as in the analytic literature, these are mostly case studies with little controlled research (Hogan, 1978; Wright, 1977).

Assertiveness training has also been used as a component in the behavioral treatment of sexual dysfunction (Dengrove, 1967; Lazarus, 1965; Wolpe & Lazarus, 1966). Behavioral rehearsal and modeling are used to improve communication skills, to provide practice in social interaction, and thereby to reduce anxiety.

A number of cognitive-attentional techniques have been developed to treat sexual dysfunction. Thought stopping has been used to stop obsession about performance (Garfield, McBrearty, & Dichter, 1969), and attention has been directed to physical sensation instead of performance (Ellis, 1962; Lazarus, 1968). Ellis's rational-emotive therapy includes skill training and education, as well as anxiety reduction, by restructuring irrational thoughts about the catastrophic nature of sexual dysfunction, and replacing these irrational thoughts with rational ones (Ellis, 1962, 1971).

Another quasi-behavioral technique described for the treatment of premature ejaculation was introduced by Semans (1956). The technique consists basically of repeated pauses in stimulation of the penis immediately before the point of ejaculation, and it was described by Semans as 100% effective. This technique and its variations have remained a major part of the treatment of this dysfunction. Behavioral interventions had only a minor impact on prevailing therapeutic practice. The main objection by the predominantly psychodynamic therapeutic community was that viewing symptom relief as cure would produce symptom substitution and patient relapse (Reynolds, 1977).

In addition to the techniques and interventions discussed above, a wide variety of "commonsense" procedures and remedies have been attempted, some of which have been incorporated into subsequent therapy programs. Suggestions have included the wearing of several condoms and thinking distracting thoughts for overcoming premature ejaculation; drinking alcohol as an antianxiety agent; and having an affair with a more sexy partner as treatment for erectile failure. The most common advice for women with orgasmic dysfunction has been to forget about lack of interest or to fake orgasm (J. LoPiccolo & Hogan, 1979). Such advice most likely reflects the previous lack of concern about female enjoyment of sexual activity.

Medical and surgical treatments were also being used long before the development of sex therapy as a discipline. For instance, surgical therapies for erectile failure involving both implants and vascular procedures date back into the 1930s. Hormonal treatment was first attempted by the transplantation of gonadal tissue as early as 1919 (Gee, 1975). However, medical treatment has been hampered in the past by the lack of knowledge of the physiology of human sexual response and by the inability to differentially diagnose sexual dysfunction along the psychological-physiological dimension. For example, one treatment for erectile failure has been the automatic administration of testosterone, even to men who have been shown to have normal endogenous plasma-testosterone levels. Such administration has been demonstrated more recently to have no effect beyond placebo effect on erections (Benkert, Witt, Adam, & Leitz, 1978). Another treatment, for vaginismus, has been surgical enlargement of the vaginal opening, even though vaginismus is a spastic contraction of the vaginal musculature and is not caused by a small opening.

Thus, by the end of the 1960s, the prevailing treatment for sexual dysfunction was psychoanalytically oriented psychotherapy, and the prognosis for treatment was poor. Behavioral interventions seemed to be more successful but had only a minor impact on prevailing therapeutic practice. Both psychoanalytic and behavior therapists worked primarily with individuals in the treatment of their sexual dysfunctions, and little or no work had been done with couples (Kaplan, 1979). Medical interventions were quite minimal because of the belief that the vast majority of sexual dysfunctions were due to psychological causes and because physicians had little to offer in the way of effective medical treatment. All of this was soon to change with the introduction of Masters and Johnson's sex therapy program in 1970.

Sex Therapy: The Development of a Discipline

Masters and Johnson

The publication of Masters and Johnson's *Human Sexual Inadequacy* (1970) has had a tremendous impact on the treatment of sexual dysfunction. Their approach involves brief, time-limited, directive counseling of the couple aimed at symptom removal rather than attaining insight, uncovering repressions, or resolving unconscious conflict. The program of brief, direct therapy consists of a group of procedures designed to deal with the immediate causes of dysfunction, which Masters and Johnson view as performance anxiety, lack of information, difficulties with sexual communication, and the taking on of the spectator role during sexual activity.

Masters and Johnson operationally described several sexual dysfunctions that they treated in their program. The male disorder, *premature ejaculation*, was defined as the inability to control the ejaculatory process during intravaginal containment for a time sufficient to satisfy the female partner at least 50% of the time. *Ejaculatory incompetence* was diagnosed when there was an inability by the male to ejaculate intravaginally. It was considered the "reverse" of premature ejaculation (Masters & Johnson, 1970). *Primary impotence* was defined as an inability throughout the male's lifetime to attain and/or to maintain an erection of sufficient quality to have successful intercourse. Masters and Johnson used the term *secondary impotence* to refer to the same symptom when it occurred after some history of successful erection.

Several female dysfunctions were also described and treated. The diagnosis of *primary orgasmic dysfunction* was given to a woman who reported an inability to attain orgasm throughout her lifetime. *Situational orgasmic dysfunction* was diagnosed if a woman had some history of orgasm, but was no longer able to reach orgasm or was able to do so only in some situations. *Vaginismus* was defined as a psychophysiological syndrome in which involuntary spastic contraction of the vaginal and/or pelvic musculature made vaginal penetration impossible. The term *dyspareunia* was used to refer to intercourse that was painful from any cause in either females or males.

In the Masters and Johnson program there are some common treatment elements for all dysfunctions. Therapy is always done with a couple, who are treated by a co-therapy team consisting of a male and a female therapist. The couple rather than the individual are con-sidered mutually responsible for the dysfunction and its cure. The program itself consists of 15 daily sessions. The couples come to the treatment center for a period of two weeks, taking a "vacation" from their usual environment. The program begins with an extensive history, followed by a round-table discussion, with the therapists offering some possible explanation of the etiology of the problem. A graded series of sexual tasks is then introduced as homework, along with a ban on sexual intercourse. This ban theoretically serves to reduce the anxiety of having to "perform." The emphasis is on discovering and communicating new sensual experiences. The initial exercises, known as "sensate focus," have the triple purpose of removing performance anxiety by creating a no-demand experience; eliminating the spectator role by encouraging the couple to tune into their own sexual experiences and feelings; and increasing sexual communication of what feels good to each individual.

At first, stimulation of breasts and genitals are proscribed. Gradually, breast and genital stimulation is added to the sensual body massage, and eventually intercourse is introduced. In addition, during therapy, there is a focus on education and counseling to help eliminate sexual myths and to work on verbal and nonverbal communication. The use of a male–female co-therapy team facilitates the modeling of sex roles and appropriate communication. Although no credit is given to Wolpe (1958), one can clearly conceptualize the gradual advance from sensate focus to intercourse as a form of *in vivo* systematic desensitization (Laughren & Kass, 1975; Wright, 1977). In their treatment of premature ejaculation, Masters and Johnson borrow from the pause technique introduced by Semans (1956). They use a modification of this technique. Instead of pausing, pressure is applied to the coronal ridge of the penis until the desire to ejaculate has passed. Masters and Johnson took these training techniques; added sex education, skills training, communication, and a recognition of the key role of the interactive system in sexual functioning; and put all this together into one comprehensive package. Their data on the program's effectiveness have led to a widespread acceptance of these techniques, and many clinics based on the Masters and Johnson model have emerged worldwide.

Criticisms and Modifications

In addition to the tremendous positive response to the Masters and Johnson sex-therapy program, their work has also prompted some criticisms. This criticism has led to modifications by other clinicians to remedy some of the perceived shortcomings of Masters and Johnson's program. One criticism is that their population was very nonrepresentative of the dysfunctional population. Couples, in order to be accepted into their program, had to be relatively free of marital problems and individual behavior problems (Caird & Wincze, 1977). In addition, those entering their program had to be sufficiently motivated and wealthy enough to pay the large fee for a two-week treatment program, and to take time away from work to reside in St. Louis for the duration of treatment.

Lobitz and LoPiccolo (1972) have presented several modifications of the Masters and Johnson program. These include seeing patients once a week while they remain in their usual environment, allowing couples to make changes within their lifestyle and, therefore, reducing the problem of lack of generalization; keeping daily record forms on sexual assignments, thus providing detailed data on sexual activity and patient reaction; and using a penalty deposit to provide an incentive to do the assignments and to complete the therapy. These authors have also suggested the use of role playing, modeling and therapist self-disclosure, and an orgasmic reconditioning program to help condition arousal to the partner. In the treatment of premature ejaculation, they proposed learning the squeeze and/or pause through individual masturbation before involving the female partner. Additionally, in what has become a widely used procedure, they introduced a nine-step treatment program, beginning with masturbation, for the treatment of primary inorgasmic women.

The criticism that Masters and Johnson's success rate was due to their extreme selectivity in choosing couples has gained some credence from the work of other therapists who have treated a less select group (Kaplan & Kohl, 1972; Lansky & Davenport, 1975). However, while the overall success rate may be somewhat lower, their sex therapy procedures do seem to be generally applicable to a wide range of couples.

Another criticism leveled at Masters and Johnson concerns the issue of sex therapy's focusing only on the sexual "symptom" and not on any underlying psychopathology. Without dealing with such psychodynamic factors, it is argued, some other symptom will be substituted for the sexual problem if it is directly eliminated. Kaplan pointed out that most couples do respond to a treatment that addresses their sexual symptoms, and that the analytic predictions that symptom substitution would take place has by and large not occurred. However, she stated that when the symptom *is* associated with deep intrapsychic conflict in one of the individuals, and when it serves as a protection and a defense, more extensive treatment may be necessary (Kaplan & Kohl, 1972). With the publication of *The New Sex Therapy* (1974), Kaplan made a major contribution to the integration of brief sex therapy and psychodynamic psychotherapy. Indeed, within the overall field of psychotherapy, sex therapy is a pioneer in such integration. Kaplan pragmatically contended that the current sexual behaviors of the couple should be focused on until strong resistance emerges. At this point, it may be necessary to interrupt the couple therapy for brief insight therapy with the individual. Although there are few data to support the adjunct use of psychodynamic techniques, we have found it to be extremely useful clinically, particularly with complex cases in which skill deficits and conditioned anxiety are not paramount factors.

Direct Treatment Principles

In varying degrees, the following principles are used by most clinicians who follow the brief, direct treatment approach, with variations dependent partly on the clinician's theoretical viewpoint and partly on the needs, history, and specific dysfunctions of the particular couple.

Mutual Responsibility. The couple, not the individual, are considered mutually responsible for the maintenance of the dysfunction (if not the cause) and, therefore, for its cure. Care is usually taken to make a distinction between "responsibility" and "blame." Regardless of the cause of the dysfunction, both partners are responsible for future change and the solution of their problems.

Eliminating Performance Anxiety. As previously mentioned, the key to successful therapy is seen as freeing the dysfunctional couple from anxiety about their sexual performance. They are told to stop "keeping score" and to stop being goal-oriented for erection, orgasm, or ejaculation, or any particular result. Instead, they are asked to focus on enjoying the process. Banning intercourse and giving them "permission" to engage in other sexual activities aid in this therapy process. Formal desensitization may be indicated where anxiety is severe.

Education. Many people suffering from sexual dysfunction are ignorant of both basic sexual physiology and effective sexual techniques. In direct therapy, therefore, there is an emphasis on accurate knowledge of the sexual response cycle as well as the general principles of effective sexual techniques. This knowledge is provided through verbal discussion, appropriate reading materials, and educational films. With the recent avalanche of sex information in the popular media, this particular component has become less salient for some of the couples who enter formal sex therapy.

Attitude Change. In spite of the so-called sexual revolution, and the more positive attitudes about male and female sexuality that have resulted, many negative attitudes toward sexuality remain among those individuals presenting for sex therapy. Thus, the therapist may have to induce attitude change directly by assigning reading material that comments positively on sexuality, arranging consultations with sympathetic clergy, recommending lectures and workshops on sexuality and sexual values, and using the therapeutic relationship itself through encouragement and self-disclosure.

Increasing Communication. Inhibitions about discussing sex openly frequently make it impossible for dysfunctional couples to communicate clearly their sexual likes and dislikes to each other. Direct therapy encour-ages sexual experimentation and open and effective communication about technique and response. Such experimentation and communication can be facilitated by having couples read explicit erotic literature, share their fantasies with each other, see and then discuss sexually explicit movies, guide their partner's hands during sexual activity, and give each other direct verbal and nonverbal feedback during sex.

Prescribing Changes in Behavior. The direct treatment of sexual dysfunction is characterized by the prescription of specific sexual behaviors to be performed by the couple in privacy. Often, this directiveness can also be used to encourage couples to change destructive lifestyles that may be contributing to the sexual dysfunction.

The actual program of sexual assignments varies among therapeutic settings, but it is usually characterized by the use of graded sexual assignments, progressing from nongenital and nonbreast pleasuring to sexual intercourse. There are also some assignments specific to the various dysfunctions. Following is a brief review of specific approaches to the various dysfunctions.

Premature Ejaculation. In assignments, the couple is encouraged to focus on the penis and feelings of pleasure. Whether the pause technique (Semans, 1956) or the squeeze technique (Masters & Johnson, 1970) is used, the male learns to experience a massive amount of stimulation without ejaculation, thereby having an opportunity to gain ejaculatory control. The number of pauses or squeezes required to sustain stimulation and delay ejaculation rapidly decreases over successive occasions with these procedures, and the male soon gains the capacity for penile stimulation of greater duration without any pauses or squeezes at all. As more control is gained through manual stimulation, vaginal containment without thrusting is reintroduced, and finally unrestricted intercourse.

Erectile Failure. The graded sexual assignments that are the cornerstone of the direct treatment method are particularly well suited to this dysfunction. As the couple's repertoire of sexual activities progresses from nonsexual massage to include genitals and breasts, the woman is instructed to stop stimulation of the penis should an erection occur. Only when the penis is flaccid should stimulation be resumed. This procedure, which has been called the "teasing technique" (Masters & Johnson, 1970), convinces the couple that if an erection is lost, it can be regained. Next, penile insertion into the vagina is allowed, but only with the female physically pushing the male's flaccid penis into her vagina while she sits astride his body. Again, the couple is told, "This procedure works best with a flaccid penis. Please try not to have an erection." Once the male has been unable to avoid an erection during vaginal containment, slow pelvic thrusting by each partner and finally vigorous intercourse and coital ejaculation can be prescribed.

Ejaculatory Incompetence. In treating ejaculatory incompetence, the couple is instructed in the technique of providing massive amounts of stimulation of the male's penis, and eventually introducing vaginal containment only at the point of orgasm for the male. Once this has been achieved, and the male has ejaculated intravaginally, the timing of the penetration can be slowly moved back.

Orgasmic Dysfunction. Lobitz and LoPiccolo (1972) described a nine-step program for primary inorgasmic women. The first step involves visual examination of the genitals by the woman using a mirror. In Steps 2 and 3, she tactually explores her genitals to locate pleasure-sensitive areas. In Steps 4 and 5, she learns to stimulate these areas intensely while using erotic fantasies or explicit literature and photos. She is also taught to recognize and label any physiological responses that she may have as sexual pleasure rather than as anxiety or tension. If orgasm does not occur, a vibrator is introduced as Step 6. Steps 7 through 9 involve skill training for her partner. He observes his partner's masturbation, learns to bring her to orgasm in this way, and finally pairs it with coitus. The use of masturbation is based on the Kinsey *et al.* (1953) finding that for the average woman, the probability of orgasm through masturbation is greater than through coitus. Other elements of the treatment of inorgasmic women involve the disinhibition of arousal and teaching behaviors that may trigger the orgasm response. Some or all of the above may also be used with secondary inorgasmic women (what Masters and Johnson

called "situational orgasmic dysfunction"), although such women may respond more readily to a combination of sex and marital therapy (Snyder, LoPiccolo, & LoPiccolo, 1975).

Vaginismus. With vaginismus, in cases where medical pathology has been ruled out or corrected, a graduated series of dilators is usually used to enable the woman to learn to tolerate vaginal intromission. The dilation program may be carried out by a gynecologist in the office or by the woman or her husband at home, and it can be most effective when used within the context of a sex therapy program as outlined above.

Summary

The last decade has seen tremendous changes in the field of sex therapy. Behavior therapy and social learning theory have contributed most of the effective techniques that now comprise sex therapy (Hogan, 1978; J. LoPiccolo, 1977). Despite the domination of the sex therapy field by behavior therapy, other therapy approaches have been useful adjunct techniques. Cognitive therapy (Ellis, 1962, 1971), general systems therapy (von Bertalanffy, 1968; Kaplan, 1974), communication therapy (Watzlawick, Beavin, & Jackson, 1967), humanistic-existential therapy (Lobitz, LoPiccolo, Lobitz, & Brockway, 1976), psychodynamic theory (Kaplan, 1974, 1979), and Gestalt therapy have contributed conceptualizations and techniques that appear to be helpful at the clinical level. Because of increased public demand, sex therapy programs around the country and the world have proliferated. Similarly, there has been a tremendous increase in research in this important area of human functioning, and therapists from many different orientations have come together and worked toward the further expansion and differentiation of this field.

Sex Therapy: Expansion and Differentiation

As the field of sex therapy has continued to develop, researchers and therapists have turned their attention to expanding outward in new directions as well as looking inward to further differentiate and process the knowledge already gained. In the following sections, we consider some of the current issues in this expansion and differentiation in the field of sex therapy.

Diagnostic Terminology and Classification

Until recently, there has been a lack of consensus and precision in the terminology and classification of sexual dysfunctions. As outcome research in sex therapy has developed and expanded, classification has gone from the extremely oversimplified categories of impotence and frigidity to complex classification systems. With the development of these systems, problems of overlapping definitions and lack of consensus among research and clinical settings have become more salient.

Problems of Terminology and Classification. The terminology used to describe sexual dysfunctions has a history of inconsistency and imprecision. In some instances, the same term has been used to describe very different dysfunctions, while in others, different terms have been used to describe the same dysfunction. An example of the former is the term *impotence. Impotence* has been used to describe any male sexual dysfunction, including low sexual interest, difficulty with erection, dysfunctions of orgasm, failure to satisfy one's partner, and even problems of fertility. Likewise, the term *frigidity* has been used to describe any sexual dysfunction of the female, including difficulties of interest, arousal, or orgasm, and even painful intercourse.

Attempts to define particular sexual dysfunctions with more precision have also presented some difficulties. There has been more than one term used to describe almost every dysfunction. To further complicate things, these terms are often used interchangeably, although they may have somewhat different operational definitions.

Masters and Johnson (1970) defined *primary impotence* as the inability to achieve and/or maintain erections sufficient to accomplish successful coitus. They defined *secondary impotence* as an inability to achieve or maintain erections during at least 25% of coital attempts. To receive this diagnosis, the client must have a history of at least one successful coital attempt with erection. According to this definition, men who successfully achieve and maintain erections during 75% of their coital experiences would still be labeled as impotent.

Kaplan (1974) and others have made a strong argument for the elimination of the term *impotence*, partially because it is not very descriptive, and partially because it may imply pejorative personality attributes. Kaplan (1979), however, continued to use the term *impotence* to describe males with difficulty in attaining or maintaining erection. Other terms in use that are somewhat more descriptive include *erectile failure* and *erectile dysfunction*. The current psychiatric diagnostic term for this dysfunction is "inhibited sexual excitement" (American Psychiatric Association, 1980), which is somewhat less descriptive than any definition that incorporates the term *erection*. This terminology remains somewhat imprecise in that it makes no distinction between difficulties in achieving an erection and difficulties in maintaining an erection. It also supplies no information about the presence or absence of subjective arousal in individuals with erectile difficulties. Indeed, the terminology is actually somewhat misleading, in that it implies that these men do not subjectively experience excitement, while the majority of men with erectile failure *do* feel subjective excitement.

Premature ejaculation is perhaps the most difficult of the male dysfunctions to define precisely, although the term itself has been most consistently used in all descriptions of sexual dysfunction. One of the major difficulties with an acceptable definition of this term is deciding what is meant by the word *premature. Premature* is inherently a relative term. When the dysfunction is defined in terms of the partner's responsivity, then it is possible for a male with a one-hour latency to be labeled a premature ejaculator if his partner does not achieve an orgasm within this time (Masters & Johnson 1970). When *premature* is defined strictly in terms of latency to orgasm, then the problem is to decide what length of time or what other measure provides the cutoff between functional and dysfunctional orgasm. Kaplan (1974) attempted to avoid these problems by suggesting that the crucial aspect of prematurity is the absence of voluntary control over the ejaculatory reflex. The current psychiatric diagnostic term incorporates this idea by defining premature ejaculation as "ejaculation . . . before the individual wishes it, because of recurrent and persistent absence of reasonable and voluntary control of ejaculation and orgasm during sexual activity" (American Psychiatric Association, 1980). While this definition has the advantage of being more independent of partner response and time variables, the concept of *reasonable control* is still relative and is left open to a therapist's interpretation. Thus, there is still a problem of imprecision and the probable unreliability in this definition as well. Indeed, it is questionable whether the orgasm reflex is subject to "voluntary" control at all.

Another orgasmic dysfunction in males is difficulty in achieving orgasm. *Ejaculatory incompetence, retarded ejaculation,* and *delayed ejaculation* are terms that have been used to describe this dysfunction. This dysfunction should not be confused with *retrograde ejaculation,* which almost always implies a medical problem involving the loss of the ejaculate into the bladder.

The female dysfunctions have also been variously labeled with imprecise terms. Masters and Johnson (1970) rejected the term *frigidity* as "poor slang" and defined a woman with *primary orgasmic dysfunction* as one who has never had an orgasm by any method. A woman with *situational orgasmic dysfunction* is someone who has experienced at least one orgasm, regardless of how it was induced. Kaplan (1974) has similar definitions of this female dysfunction but substitutes the term *secondary orgasmic dysfunction* for Masters and Johnson's term *situational orgasmic dysfunction.* Masters and Johnson (1970) described only two other female dysfunctions: *dyspareunia* (painful intercourse) and *vaginismus* (a spastic contraction of the vaginal muscle, making penetration difficult or impossible). These definitions have been used rather consistently to describe these dysfunctions by other writers as well. Kaplan (1974) also described the dysfunction of "general sexual dysfunction (frigidity)," which is defined as the absence of erotic pleasure from sexual stimulation and an absence of sexual feelings. On a physiological level, this dysfunction is expressed by a lack of genital vasocongestion in response to sexual stimulation, but again, as with erectile failure, the relationship between subjective experience and physiological measures of arousal is highly variable.

In an attempt to add more precision to the definitions of sexual dysfunction, Masters and Johnson (1970) and Kaplan (1974, 1979) and others have added modifiers to the dysfunction labels mentioned above. For example, the *primary/secondary* modifier is an attempt to describe a dysfunction along an "always/never" dimension. The use of modifiers, while very helpful descriptively, has added to the difficulties of inconsistent terminology. For example, if a women has had an orgasm by some means other than coitus, she would not be described as having a primary inorgasmic dysfunction by either Masters and Johnson or Kaplan. However, if a man has had an erection in situations other than coitus, his dysfunction would still be labeled primary impotence by Masters and Johnson because he had never had an erection during coitus.

These problems of terminology and consequently of classification of sexual dysfunction reflect major inconsistencies associated with three underlying factors: (1) the concept of *sexual dysfunction* is not value-free, and values vary over time and across individuals; (2) systems of classification vary according to the purposes for which they are constructed, and thus, differing systems reflect the needs of those who construct them; and (3) all of the current systems of classifications are typological, and typologies have severe inherent limitations.

The Problem of Values. It is clear that in classifying sexual dysfunctions consensus needs to begin with the term *sexual dysfunction* itself. Masters and Johnson described in clearcut operational terms the particular problems that they believed constituted sexual dysfunction, although they never actually defined the term *per se.* Their operational definitions were in all cases descriptions of interferences in the physiological aspects of sexual expressions occurring within a sexual relationship (Masters & Johnson, 1970). Kaplan (1974) defined *sexual dysfunctions* as "impairments of physical components of the sex response." In practice, the meaning of the term *sexual dysfunction* has changed over time, so that classes of people who would not have been diagnosed as dysfunctional years ago might be considered dysfunctional now, and other classes of formerly dysfunctional people might no longer be considered dysfunctional. For example, neither Masters and Johnson (1970) nor Kaplan (1974) described a male dysfunction involving lack of sexual desire, but more recently, Kaplan has included a classification for male and female "hypoactive sexual desire" (Kaplan, 1977, 1979). Women who were unable to reach orgasm during coitus were considered dysfunctional by Masters and Johnson (1970) but were considered normal by Kaplan (1974).

The problem of values in the classification of sexual dysfunctions stems from an assumption that "sexual dysfunction" must be discretely distinct from "normal sexual function." *Normal functioning*, however, can be defined objectively only in a statistical sense and, in many instances, must depend on the sexual attitudes, values, and behaviors of a particular society, historical period, or researcher. Thus, to a large extent, society's view of female sexual functioniong determines whether the lack of orgasm during intercourse is normal and healthy or dysfunctional. Likewise, labeling "low" sexual desire as dysfunctional depends on such factors as the frequency of sexual intercourse in a society, the society's belief about what constitutes normal and abnormal frequency, and the individual investigator's beliefs and values (J. LoPiccolo & Heiman, 1978; Strupp & Hadley, 1977).

Inconsistencies in the definition of sexual dysfunctions are compounded by the rapidity with which change in sexual beliefs and attitudes has been occurring, particularly in the latter half of this century, and by the lack of a widely accepted, consistent view in our society at any time of what constitutes healthy or unhealthy, normal or abnormal sexual functioning (J. LoPiccolo & Heiman, 1978). The fact that the terms *normal sexual functioning* and *sexual dysfunction* are value-laden does not imply that they are invalid concepts. However, it does point up the difficulties in using highly relative concepts that will continue to change over time.

The Problem of Differing Purposes. A second major problem in establishing a widely acceptable and useful classification system for sexual dysfunction has been the differing purposes for which these systems have been developed. Investigators in the area of psychiatric nosology (Kanfer & Saslow, 1969; Spitzer, Sheehy, & Endicott, 1977; Spitzer & Wilson, 1975) have listed a number of possible purposes: (1) communication between researchers and clinicians in the area; (2) understanding of the dysfunction in terms of etiology, maintaining variables, and process of pathology; (3) prediction of behavior in various situations, or prognosis with or without treatment; and (4) selection of appropriate treatment.

The difficulty comes not so much from differences of purpose *per se* but from lack of discussion and communication of these purposes. This lack has led to confusion among individuals who are attempting to integrate similar-sounding but differently purposed terms and even whole systems. An obvious but difficult-to-implement solution to this problem is for all investigators to discuss their concept of a classification system and the purposes with which they have determined and operationally defined them.

The Problem of Typologies. Another major problem in currently existing classifications systems is that they are based on a system of typology, which divides dysfunctions into discrete types. Bandura (1968) and Hempel (1965) have pointed out several inherent shortcomings in such typologies. First, the problems with which individuals present are often distributed along various continua and may not fit neatly into discrete classes, no matter how specifically these are defined. The more discrete the typological class, the more the incidence of borderline cases that are difficult to classify.

Second, if typologies are broad, the cases within each category may resemble one another only remotely. For example, the category of situational orgasmic dysfunction in women can include women who experience orgasm with masturbation only, with vibrator only, or by any means except intercourse. It may include those who can experience orgasm with one partner but not with another or those who did experience orgasm in the past through intercourse but now do not. Also, as broad as this category is, there still may be difficulty differentiating borderline cases at one end from primary orgasmic dysfunction and at the other end from cases of nondysfunction. Thus, a typological classification that includes only situational orgasmic dysfunction leaves out much important information that might be specifically useful to an understanding of etiology, prognosis, and treatment choice.

Third, a typological classification may limit diagnostic choices unrealistically because an individual may have several dysfunctions simultaneously. For example, Cooper (1968) reported on a series of cases of male dysfunction in which individuals reported low sex desire, erectile failure, and premature ejaculation. All of Masters and Johnson's (1970) vaginismus cases also reported orgasmic dysfunction. Another difficulty with typological systems is that they allow for inclusion in or exclusion from a category, but not for quantification. In addition, the ability to describe an interaction among sexual dysfunctions is limited, as well as an interaction of sexual dysfunction with marital, psychological, or physiological systems.

More recently, multiaxial systems have been considered and developed. Such systems allow for diagnosis or classification along several dimensions for the same individual. A mosaic, or pattern, can emerge that presents a detailed description of an individual's personal and interactive functioning.

Classification Systems. Masters and Johnson (1970) were the first to break down the various dysfunctions into descriptive categories. They included in their list of sexual dysfunctions premature ejaculation, impotence (primary and secondary), ejaculatory incompetence, orgasmic dysfunction (primary and situational), vaginismus, and painful intercourse. They did not attempt to describe this list as a classification system, nor did they indicate any underlying organizational principles.

In 1974, Kaplan introduced a classification system that did attempt to organize and classify the dysfunctions according to a biphasic description of the sexual response cycle that allowed parallel diagnoses for males and females. The dysfunctions were divided into difficulties in the excitement phase and difficulties in the orgasmic phase.

The excitement phase dysfunctions included "erectile dysfunction" in males and "general sexual dysfunction" in females. The orgasm phase dysfunctions included premature and retarded ejaculation in men and orgasmic dysfunction in women. In addition to these dysfunctions, Kaplan also described another female dysfunction, vaginismus.

Kaplan further subdivided these dysfunctions along a temporal (primary–secondary) and a situational (absolute–situational) dimension. A *primary* dysfunction is one that has always existed in the individual, while *secondary* denotes at least one successful experience in the past. An *absolute* dysfunction is present under all circumstances (all partners and self-stimulation) while a *situational* dysfunction is present in only some circumstances (Kaplan, 1974).

Later, Kaplan expanded and refined her classification system (Kaplan, 1979). Dysfunction of an additional phase of sexual response, the desire phase, was described. The male and female diagnoses of hypoactive sexual desire and inhibition of sexual desire were added to her classification system. Excitement-phase and orgasmic-phase dysfunctions remained the same, and sexual phobias were added to vaginismus as dysfunctions related to sexual anxiety and amenable to sex therapy. The term *inhibited sexual desire* was defined as "persistent and pervasive inhibition of sexual desire not exclusively caused by other organic and psychiatric disorders." *Hypoactive sexual desire* was used when the etiology of this same disorder was undetermined.

The recently adopted *Diagnostic and Statistical Manual of Mental Disorders*, Third Edition (American Psychiatric Association, 1980) includes a slightly modified version of Kaplan's classification system in its section "Psychosexual Disorders." In this classification system an attempt is made to classify dysfunctions defined as "inhibition in the appetitive, or psychophysiological changes that characterize the complete sexual response cycle." The diagnoses used in this system include inhibited sexual desire, inhibited sexual excitement (which includes erectile failure in males and failure to obtain or maintain the lubrication–swelling response of sexual excitement in females), inhibited female orgasm, inhibited male orgasm, premature ejaculation, functional dyspareunia, functional vaginismus, and atypical psychosexual dysfunction, a broad category for "psychosexual dysfunctions that cannot be classified as a specific psychosexual dysfunction" (American Psychiatric Association, 1980). Although the Kaplan and the APA systems are the most comprehensive of those currently in use, they share some of the shortcomings mentioned above because most of the diagnoses are very broad and contain a large variety of unspecified subtypes.

Sharpe, Kurlansky, and O'Connor (1976) presented a multiaxial classification system with five diagnostic categories: disturbances of the physiological sexual response cycle, disturbances of the perceptual component of the sexual response cycle, disturbances of subjective satisfaction in the sexual response cycle, distress concerning sexual functioning associated with false beliefs or lack of sexual knowledge, and sociosexual distress. This system has several advantages in that it is based on objective behavior and a model of normal physiological functioning; it describes behavior and does not postulate disease entities or reactions; and it presents a framework of analogous dysfunctions in males and females. Before this system could be widely adopted, the emergence of problems of sexual desire as an important component of sexual dysfunction left it outmoded.

Recently, a multiaxial diagnostic system that may be clinically useful was developed at the Sex Therapy Center at Stony Brook, for use in its continuing research studies (Schover, Friedman, Weiler, Heiman, & LoPiccolo, in press). It uses six axes to record diagnostic and descriptive information for each partner in a sexually dysfunctional relationship. The categories include desire phase, arousal phase, orgasm phase, coital pain, satisfaction with current frequency of sex, and qualifying information. Within each category, there is a list of specifically described problems, of which only one may be selected (except for "qualifying information," which allows four). For example, in the arousal phase category, both physiological and subjective descriptions are provided. A distinction is made among failure to achieve erection, failure to maintain erection, and failure both to achieve and to maintain erection.

Similar fine-grained distinctions are made in other categories as well. Each individual in the relationship may be given a separate diagnosis in each of the categories, as applicable. Each diagnosis is modified by a set of three modifiers: the first specifies whether the problem is lifelong, the second specifies whether the problem is situational or "global" (whether it occurs in all situations where the behavior is attempted); and the third specifies if it is a presenting problem or only determined by the therapist. This classification system attempts to describe sexual dysfunction behaviorally not only in accordance with the sexual response cycle but in terms of subjective experience. The qualifying information category allows the recording of data on past or present behaviors, experiences, or diagnoses that may be related in some instances to sexual dysfunction. For example, experiences of incest are recorded, since recent clinical reports suggest that incest may be an important correlate of adult sexual dysfunction (Renshaw, 1977). This classification system is intended to be descriptive and is not intended to imply a particular etiology.

Clearly, sex therapy classification has advanced considerably since all dysfunctions were described by one or two terms. While classification systems may be of greater concern to researchers than to clinicians, the process of developing such systems provides important input that benefits clinicians and those seeking therapy as well.

Advances in Assessment

As new developments and understanding of sexual dysfunctions and treatments have evolved, so has the assessment and evaluative process evolved. Often, advances in assessment and advances in treatment are linked in a stepwise manner, so that newly developed effective treatments lead to refinements in assessment, which lead to new developments in treatment, and so on. However, assessment of sexual dysfunction produces some special difficulties. First, both social stigma and personal embarrassment often create impediments to the truthful and complete gathering of the data useful in assessment. Also, the complex nature of sexual functioning requires that the assessors have a broad range of knowledge about the psychological, physiological, and interpersonal aspects of sexual functioning. The contributions of physiological and psychological factors to the cause and maintenance of sexual dysfunction are extremely complex and difficult to assess.

Assessment Techniques. The basic components of the assessment of sexual dysfunction have remained unchanged from the time Masters and Johnson (1970) described their techniques. Interviews for the gathering of basic descriptive information and history, appropriate psychometric testing, and medical evaluation have always been an integral part of most approaches to sexual dysfunction. However, within these broad components, specific techniques and approaches have undergone significant modification and development in the recent past. In addition, significant advances have been made in the synthesis of assessment data into an holistic understanding of sexual problems.

Interview. Interview techniques are always a part of sex therapy programs (Hartman and Fithian, 1972; Kaplan, 1974; Masters and Johnson, 1970). However, the amount and type of information gathered seem to be variable according to the therapist's orientation. Behaviorally oriented therapists and therapists with psychodynamic, marital, or family therapy orientations tend to get information according to their own perspectives. Medical practitioners gather medically pertinent information and often disregard all but the most superficial psychological information. When such discipline-oriented interviews are conducted, significant information may be overlooked or ignored. Recently, there has been more emphasis on a more comprehensive, structured, or semistructured interview format.

The primary goal of the initial assessment interview is to determine if sex therapy is appropriate for a couple. Lobitz and Lobitz (1978) presented several areas of inquiry to follow in making this determination. These include (1) demographic information about both individuals, including occupation, previous marriages, and length of present relationship; (2) a description of the sexual difficulty, including the couple's hypotheses about its etiology and what attempts they have made to resolve the difficulty themselves; (3) a description of their current sex life, including coital and noncoital activities, difficulties with erection and ejaculation in the male, and the female's orgasmic functioning, subjective arousal, and desire; (4) a psychosexual history of each partner, focusing on past and present psychological difficulties, as well as the sexual messages each individual has learned; (5) each partner's opinion of the quality of their relationship; (6) their individual and joint motivations for treatment; and (7) their medical history and physical status.

It is frequently possible to collect a good deal of the above information through paper-and-pencil assessment devices or inventories. When this is the case, more time in the initial session can be spent in focusing on those areas that are more difficult to assess, such as the quality of the couple's relationship. Clinical information can also be gleaned from observing the couple's interaction, the manner in which information is related, and other nonverbal communication. The interview may also provide important information about the degree of individual psychopathology that may be present in either partner, as well as each partner's motivation for treatment.

Once a couple has been accepted for treatment, a detailed sex history interview is usually conducted. Such an interview allows the therapist to acquire sufficiently detailed information to enable him or her to formulate the case in terms of those factors that may contribute to the etiology or the maintenance of the dysfunction and to develop an intervention strategy. A good example of a relatively complete, yet brief, sex history interview is provided by L. LoPiccolo and Heiman (1978). In addition to information gathering, history interviews may serve a rapport-building function by demonstrating the therapist's interest, and they may help allay anxiety by providing a conceptual framework for the problem.

Psychometric Testing. Psychometric instruments specifically designed for the assessment of sexual functioning have only recently been developed. Previously, other projective and empirical psychometric tests were the only devices available to be used in the assessment of sexual complaints. However, these instruments rely on inferred rather than direct material. In the past decade, serious efforts have been made to develop psychometrics that directly measure human sexual functioning.

Direct questionnaires that call for direct responses about the occurrence of sexual behaviors and sexual dysfunctions were the first form of paper-and-pencil tests developed. Early attempts lacked appropriate statistical analysis for reliability and validity (e.g., El-Senoussi, 1964), and some early nonempirically based questionnaires have been shown to be invalid for the measurement of sexual dysfunction (Beutler, Karacan, Anch, Salis, Scott, & Williams, 1975).

Three paper-and-pencil inventories that have been developed for the assessment of sexual dysfunction among heterosexuals have in common more elegant statistical characteristics. The Sexual Arousal Inventory (Hoon, Hoon, & Wincze, 1976) is specific to females and is a measure of the arousal a woman experiences in response to various sexual activities. The Derogatis Sexual Function Inventory (Derogatis, 1976) is intended to measure individual sexual functioning on a nine-dimensional basis. The Sexual Interaction Inventory (J. LoPiccolo & Steeger, 1974) attempts to describe a couple's sexual relationship in terms of the frequency and the enjoyment of specific sexual activities as well as the communication between the sexual partners about these activities. It results in 11 subscales from which much information about the sexual functioning of a couple can be gathered, primarily at a behavioral level.

All of these instruments have been statistically validated, but none provides symptom-specific descriptions of particular sexual dysfunctions, nor do they clarify etiology. They are intended to provide guidelines for treatment by identifying arousal deficits, problem behaviors, and possible underlying issues that may be important in sexual functioning. One problem is that such inventories are direct and unambiguous in their questions about sexual dysfunctioning and, therefore, very susceptible to social desirability, defensiveness, and simple falsification by the respondent (Jemail & LoPiccolo, in press).

Many other psychometric tests have been developed that may also be useful in sex therapy. Attitudinal tests and instruments that are intended to measure sexual guilt, anxiety, fear, pleasure, orientation, compatability, experience, and arousability have all been developed in the last decade. An excellent review of all of these tests has appeared in a special issue of the *Journal of Sex and Marital Therapy* (1979, Volume 5, Number 3).

Medical and Physiological Assessment. A variety of medical and physiological advances have been made that have greatly increased the capability of discerning the physical components of sexual dysfunction. These include refinements and modifications of the traditional physical examination, special applications of other medical diagnostic procedures, applications of genital plethysmography, and various biochemical laboratory studies.

Some specific diagnostic procedures that are usually not a part of routine physical examinations have been identified as particularly important for use with those complaining of sexual dysfunction. These include an elicitation of the five different spinal reflexes pertinent to the genital and pelvic area (Lundberg, 1977) and careful assessment of the sensory aspect of the genitals, including elicitation of vibration sense. Examination of the vascular system has been receiving increased emphasis for men presenting with erectile failure. Such an examination includes the detection of penile pulses and penile blood-pressure measurement (Abelson, 1975; Gaskell, 1971). For complaints of painful intercourse, vaginismus or inorgasmia in women, examination of the vaginal introitus for such previously overlooked pathology as hymenal remnants has been suggested (Abarbanel, 1978).

Several specialized medical diagnostic procedures have been developed for the assessment of any underlying pathology that may affect sexual response. The importance of the vascular system in sexual response has led to a number of developments for the assessment of genital and pelvic vascularity. A particularly useful and noninvasive procedure for the assessment of erectile failure is the measurement of penile blood pressure by a device that allows such measurement in small-caliber arteries (Abelson, 1975; Gaskell, 1971). Even more refined, but invasive, radiographic techniques have also been developed for visualization of the vascular system. These include angiographic examinations of penile and pelvic arteries (Michal & Pospichal, 1978) and cavernosograms (Fitzpatrick & Cooper, 1975). In addition, neurological techniques, such as electromyograms of the bulbocavernosus muscle reflex (Ertekin & Reel, 1976), have been recently applied to the assessment of erectile failure.

Genital plethysmography, the measurement of genital changes due to vasocongestion, has been applied in various ways to aid in the assessment of sexual dysfunction in both men and women. The most commonly used device for men has been the penile strain gauge, which measures changes in the circumference of the penis with tumescence (Rosen & Keefe, 1978). Other forms of plethysmography, particularly applicable to females, measure blood flow change by differences in reflected light using light-emitting diodes and sensors (Sintchak & Geer, 1975).

One application of penile plethysmography has been the measurement of erections occurring during sleep for the assessment of erectile failure. Periods of nocturnal penile tumescence (NPT) associated with periods of rapid-eye-movement (REM) sleep occur consistently in physiologically intact males several times per night over the life span (Karacan, Williams, Thornby, & Salis, 1975). Knowledge of these expected periods of tumescence has led to the development of a new diagnostic procedure (Karacan, 1978). In this procedure, the occurrence of normal nighttime erections in men complaining of erectile dysfunction is taken as evidence of the physiological intactness of the erectile system, and as an indication that the dysfunction is most likely to be of a psychogenic origin. While this technique is being accepted as an extremely useful tool in the assessment of this complex problem, there are some problems associated with its use, including its expense, if conducted in a clinical sleep laboratory, and its

reliability and validity, if conducted at home. Although total lack of erection during normal sleep clearly suggests organic etiology, there remains some question of interpretation if some erection occurs with an abnormal pattern (e.g., short duration or incomplete erection).

Another area in which the assessment of sexual functioning has been refined is in the evaluation of the hormonal status of those with sexual dysfunctions. Recent studies suggest the importance of the measurements of testosterone, follicle-stimulating hormone, luteinizing hormone, prolactin, and thyroid hormone (Spark, White, & Connolly, 1980). In addition to the simple circulating levels of these hormones, their variations and complex interactions may also be important in their effects. For instance, testosterone function may vary according to its protein binding, its tissue receptivity, or its interaction with other hormones, such as prolactin or estrogen. To date, most studies of hormonal function have centered on male sexuality and male sexual dysfunction. One can expect that as further refinements occur, the hormonal impact on female sexuality and dysfunctions will also receive increasing attention.

Multidimensional Assessment. When referrals are made from medical sources to psychologically oriented therapists, it is usually assumed that complete medical evaluation has occurred. Similarly, medically oriented practitioners may assume that adequate psychological assessment has occurred when referral has been made to them. Neither of these may be true, and lack of communication can further compromise adequate evaluation. For instance, referrals from a urologist to a sex therapist for the treatment of erectile failure would seem to require no further medical evaluation. However, in our experience, even routine evaluation is not guaranteed from such a source, and the more refined and newly developed techniques to aid in differential diagnosis usually have not been performed. It is clear that a careful assessment of sexual complaints must include physiological, psychological, and behavioral components. It is only in this way that the most appropriate interventions can be planned. Positive physical or medical findings do not rule out sex therapy as an intervention, but they may have an enormous impact on the goals of such therapy. For example, acceptance of physical limitations and the expansion of the sex behavior repertoire may be beneficial goals for someone with irreversible organic erectile failure.

All of the preceding advances and specific techniques of assessment have created the ability to make clearer and more highly sophisticated differentiations of the various etiologies and factors in sexual dysfunction than were previously possible. However, none of these strategies alone offers an adequate assessment scheme for the comprehensive understanding of sexual dysfunction. Clearly, sexual dysfunction is related to a number of historical, behavioral, personal, relationship, and physiological factors. An evaluation of each of these factors seems to be needed for an adequate assessment of sexual dysfunction. It is also important to recognize that psychological and physiological causes and maintainers of sexual dysfunction may not be mutually exclusive. In some cases, the presence of both physiological and psychological factors may be necessary to produce sexual dysfunction. For example, physiological problems may make the attainment of an erection more difficult and thus may increase susceptibility to psychologically mediated inhibition. It must also be kept in mind that the original cause and the current maintaining cause of sexual dysfunction may be different.

We suggest that the integration of the following multidimensional components is necessary for the comprehensive assessment of sexual dysfunction.

1. *History*. A comprehensive history should include information about the sexual development of each partner, as well as the history of their sexual interaction, their sexual dysfunction, and the impact of the dysfunction on their relationship.

2. *Current behavior*. The therapist should have a thorough understanding of the actual sexual behaviors in which the couple is currently engaging. This would include sexual approaches, sexual communication, length and kind of foreplay, types of activity resulting in orgasm, and current sexual experiences outside the relationship, including masturbation,

other partners, and other sexually related activities.

3. *Attitudinal and cognitive factors*. It is important to explore the attitudes, cognitions, and beliefs regarding sexuality that each partner brings to the relationship.

4. *Psychodynamic and intrapsychic defenses*. Assessment should include an evaluation of the likely resistances and defense mechanisms that each partner brings to the relationship and to the therapy.

5. *Interpersonal systems*. It is important to explore the role of the sexual dysfunction in the couple's broader emotional relationship. For example, one would wish to know if the dysfunction serves a functional purpose, such as the avoidance of intimacy or an attempt to gain control.

6. *Psychiatric status*. Each individual's psychiatric status should be assessed in terms of thought disorder, affective disorder, and serious characterological disorder. Individual psychopathology may influence the individual's sexual functioning, the couple's interaction, and the outcome of therapy.

7. *Biological factors*. A thorough assessment of the many biological factors that may interfere with sexual functioning should be conducted, as discussed above.

New Populations

The couples originally accepted for treatment by Masters and Johnson (1970), and by other similar programs that followed, had very circumscribed problems, primarily involving psychologically mediated difficulties in the physiological expression of the sexual response. Those with individual psychopathology and severe marital distress were systematically screened out of these programs, as were individuals with medically complicated histories. As the field of sex therapy has continued to expand, there has been a greater focus on treating all of these problems. One reason is that cases of "pure" sexual dysfunction without such auxiliary problems are becoming increasingly rare, as many people with less complex problems are taking advantage of self-help books and the information available in the public press to help themselves. Another change is the increasing number of clinical cases presenting with complaints of low desire or aversion to sex.

Problems of Desire. As already noted, in the past, problems of sexual desire were not differentiated from other sexual complaints. Now that this differentiation is being made, it has become clear to therapists and researchers that this area of sexual difficulty is extremely difficult to treat by the currently available methods. A major difficulty in addressing the issue of low desire is operationally defining the term. The question of what constitutes a low rate of sexual desire is difficult to answer. It remains unclear whether desire difficulties represent some sort of physiological or psychological pathology or whether they represent end points on a continuum of normal sexual interest along which individuals are widely distributed.

Recently, some data were reported on the incidence of problems of desire and aversion to sex in a normal population (Frank, Anderson, & Rubenstein, 1978). Analysis of the data from a sample of 100 predominantly white, nonclinical couples showed a surprisingly high incidence of problems and difficulties relating to low sexual desire: 50% of the men and 70% of the women reported experiencing sexual "difficulties," which included such feelings as "inability to relax," "disinterest in sex," feeling "turned off," or being "repulsed by sex." There are certain limitations, however, to this and similar studies. Frequency of intercourse, for example, was the only sexual behavior measured. No data were gathered on the incidence of masturbation or other sexual activities that might reflect the presence of some level of sexual desire. Also measures of the desired (as opposed to actually occurring) frequency of intercourse as well as other sexual behaviors are lacking. However, these data clearly indicate that the incidence of lack of interest in and distaste for sex in a nonclinical population may be higher than has previously been assumed.

One of the major difficulties with operationally defining and assessing problems of sexual desire is that there seem to be many differences among the clinical cases that present with this complaint. In some cases, the individuals may have little or no spontaneously occurring desire for sexual activity with their partner or spouse but experience pleasure at those times when they do engage in sex with their partner. These cases are especially puzzling, in that if sex is pleasurable and stress-free, behavioral principles would predict a desire for further sexual experiences. In other cases, low desire is associated with other sexual dysfunctions. One can hypothesize that the other dysfunctions are due to lack of desire, that the lack of desire is the result of the other dysfunctions, or that both are due to still other factors. Some individuals may experience extreme anxiety in sexual situations and, as a result of this sexual phobia, avoid sex with their partner. Others are not aware of experiencing anxiety but feel that sex is not particularly rewarding for them. Still others avoid sex with such intense negative affect or repulsion that for them, it is clearly an aversive stimulus. The presence of such differences makes it likely that low sexual desire is not a discrete dysfunction but can be thought of as various syndromes, all of which involve the common manifestation of low desire.

In an attempt to address this problem of definition, Kaplan (1977, 1979) has applied the concepts of primary-secondary and global-situational (discussed above) for classifying cases of low sexual desire. Thus, in primary low sexual desire, there has been a total lack of sexual desire throughout the individual's life. In secondary low desire, the desire was present at some point in the individual's life but then disappeared. In situational low desire, the individual experiences desire in particular situations while not in others; and in global low desire, a current lack of desire occurs regardless of situational variables.

These distinctions would seem to have important implications for the development of an effective treatment program. It seems reasonable to assume that the etiology of the various forms of low desire that Kaplan has identified may differ, as may the psychological components involved in the maintenance of these problems. Kaplan (1979) has also attempted to differentiate those cases for which a psychological etiology is assumed (termed "inhibited sexual desire") from those cases for which the etiology is unclear (termed "hypoactive sexual desire").

A review of 39 recently completed cases at the Sex Therapy Center, Stony Brook, showed that 27 (69%) of the cases included a complaint of low sexual desire. This high incidence is similar to that reported by other sex therapy centers (Kaplan, 1979) and is most interesting, since low desire was not even identified as a sexual problem by Masters and Johnson (1970) or by Kaplan in her earlier work (1974). This apparent increased incidence may be a reflection of therapists' recent recognition of these difficulties, or an actual change in those who present for therapy. With more sophisticated terminology, classification, and assessment, it is possible for therapists to differentiate this problem without its being obscured by the presence of another, more easily identified, dysfunction. Also, a review of previous treatment failures has led to an increased recognition of this syndrome (Kaplan, 1979). Alternatively, actual increases in the number of people with problems of desire seeking sex therapy may be due to changes in cultural values regarding sexuality. For instance, sexual functioning is currently valued in our culture, and individuals with low sexual desire may be under increasing pressure to enter therapy. Certainly, it is the case that males presenting with low sexual desire, in the absence of any other dysfunction, were virtually unknown even four years ago, and the increase in this complaint may be a reflection of the changing sex roles in our society.

The etiological basis of low sexual desire is still relegated to theoretical speculation and clinical impression. Anxiety has been implicated as having a role in the etiology of almost all other sexual dysfunctions, but its role in the etiology of low sexual desire is more ambiguous. It is possible that an avoidance of anxiety associated with sex may account for low desire in some people, or that anxiety may produce a physiological state capable of interfering with desire. However, it is also clear that there are many cases to which this paradigm does not apply. Rather, some men and women with low desire find sex arousing and enjoyable but infrequently or never initiate it of their own volition. For these individuals,

sex does not seem particularly important. They would never seek therapy if it were not for the distress of their partners. Often, such individuals respond to questions about how they feel about their lack of desire with statements such as, "It really wouldn't bother me if I never had sex again," or as one man said, "I'd be more upset about missing a meal." It is possible that these individuals are out of touch with their true feelings and that other means such as psychophysiological measurements would reveal the presence of anxiety. However, this possibility remains to be demonstrated.

Psychological conditions other than anxiety that may contribute to low sexual desire include stress response syndromes, depression, and cognitive mislabeling. Stress response syndromes, although physiologically similar in effect to specific sexual anxieties, are due to other environmental stress and may produce a physiological state capable of inhibiting sexual desire. Depression has long been associated with decreased interest in sexual activity. Cognitions can have a profound effect on what is perceived as sexually arousing and ultimately on the subjective experience of pleasure.

In addition to psychological factors, there possibly are physiological explanations for many cases of low sexual desire. It is known that significantly low testosterone leads to low desire, and that administration of testosterone to women leads to increased desire. Subtle variations in testosterone production, circulation, and tissue receptivity may influence sexual desire. In addition, there is evidence of the involvement of other hormones in the determination of sexual interest and behavior. These hormones include the gonadotropic hormones (the follicle-stimulating hormones and luteinizing hormones) and prolactin. Also of recent interest is the relationship between higher centers of the central nervous system, the hypothalamus, and the pituitary gland.

Another influence on sexual desire may be the ingestion of chemical substances. Drugs may affect neurotransmitter function in the central nervous system. This possibility is based on a hypothesis of "sex centers" in the brain (Kaplan, 1979).

Thus, while research into the etiology and

the description of low sexual desire is in the developmental stage, it is clear that there exists a population of individuals with desire dysfunction, for whom it is necessary to develop effective treatments.

At the other end of the spectrum, hypersexual desire has rarely been considered a sexual dysfunction among sex therapists and is rarely a presenting problem. In the past, hypersexuality in women was frequently labeled a sexual disorder (nymphomania) subject to psychiatric treatment. It was rarely considered a problem in males except if associated with deviant sexual behavior and/or such psychotic states as mania. As with low sexual desire, it becomes difficult to stipulate exactly what is meant by *hypersexuality*. Problems of frequency, low or high, are of concern to sex therapists only when a couple shows a significant discrepancy in the desired frequency of sex. Additional information about people with high rates of sexual activity may be important to an overall understanding of sexual functioning, and researchers are continuing to show interest in this area.

Psychopathological Disorders. In the past, those with severe psychopathology have been routinely screened from sex therapy (Kockett, Dittmar, & Nusselt, 1975; Lobitz & J. LoPiccolo, 1972; Obler, 1973). Masters and Johnson (1970) excluded from therapy anyone presumed to have major psychopathology, which they defined as psychosis. Pinderhughes, Grace, and Reyna (1972) reported that recovery from psychiatric disorders might be hindered by sexual activity. However, recently, there has been a greater tendency among sex therapists to accept for therapy those with major psychopathology, even those potentially psychotic, provided that they are under appropriate treatment and compensation (Kaplan, 1974). In treating such individuals, it is important to understand how the disorder and its treatments may affect sexuality and how sex therapy may impact on the disorder.

In the psychiatric literature, there have long been references to problems of sexuality associated with various psychiatric disorders. For instance, depression has been associated with low libido, erectile failure, and inorgasmia (Winokur, 1963; Woodruff, Murphy, & Herjonic, 1967). Problems with hypersexuality

and inappropriate sexual behaviors are common in such psychotic states as mania and some forms of schizophrenia. Also, among males suffering from schizophrenia, problems of erectile failure and ejaculatory disturbances are not uncommon, although these may be due to medication. Social isolation and difficulties in interpersonal communication may also contribute to significant problems in sexual functioning among individuals with psychotic disorders, even when these are in remission. Other nonpsychotic disorders have also been thought to severely complicate the treatment of sexual dysfunction. These include conversion and major personality disorders such as passive-aggressive personality, obsessive-compulsive personality, asthenic and cyclothymic personalities, and antisocial personalities (Kolodny, Masters, & Johnson, 1979).

Recently, sex therapists have been treating sexual dysfunctions within these groups. The treatment of hospitalized psychotic patients has shown some initially promising results (Lobitz, personal communication, 1978). Likewise, the treatment of couples one member of which is a schizophrenic has been described (Renshaw, 1977).

Marital Dysfunctions. In the past, sex therapists have routinely attempted to assess and screen couples with severe marital or relationship problems from sex therapy (Lobitz & Lobitz, 1978). It has been pointed out that difficulties with intimacy, including severe hostility, would make the successful completion of such assignments as sensate focus nearly impossible (Sager, 1974, 1976). More recently, couples with more severe marital discord have been presenting for sex therapy (Sager, 1976), and sex therapists with some marital therapy training are more willing to accept them. Marital and sex therapists are finding it much less useful to distinguish between sexual and relationship problems, because it is not always possible to segregate these areas of distress in people's lives.

While it is undoubtedly true that many couples exhibiting extreme anger and hostility toward each other may not be willing to engage in intimate sexual activities, it is also true that any skill deficits in communication and negotiation that may contribute to their marital distress can also have a profound effect on their sexual interaction. Frequently, it becomes impossible, in the presence of sexual dysfunction, to determine if the dysfunction is responsible for the marital distress or the marital distress is responsible for the dysfunction. Issues over and above those of sexual function that may need to be addressed include ways of showing caring and love, sex roles and role expectations within the relationship, the effect of children on the relationship, jealousy about outside interests or friends, and different needs for intimacy, dependence–independence, affection, conversation, and companionship. All these topics and more may need to become grist for the therapeutic mill, along with the sexual interaction. Just as marital therapists cannot ignore the sexual area in their treatment, sex therapists cannot ignore the other relationship issues. While there clearly is considerable overlap between marital and sex therapies, it is surprising that there is little discussion in the literature regarding the integration of these two subspecialties. It is clear that this division must change as the problems presented by couples in therapy continue to require an integrative approach to treatment.

The Medically Ill and the Handicapped. The sexual needs and problems of the medically ill and the handicapped have rarely been considered in the past. This lack of attention may have been due partly to societal attitudes that denied sexual feelings and behaviors to all but the young and physically attractive, and partly to the fact that many physicians, like others, have found it uncomfortable to discuss sexuality. Hellerstein and Friedman (1970) stated, "During their training [physicians] learn something about sexual anatomy and about conception, pregnancy, and birth. Few are given any conception of the physiology of normal coitus and orgasm, or the psychopathology of sex." This statement is probably less true today.

With the addition of courses in human sexual behavior to many medical school curricula, the attitudes of physicians and society alike have begun to change. These changes reflect an increasing awareness of the needs of the handicapped; advances in medicine that have made it possible for the handicapped and the medically ill to lead longer, more normal lives;

and a general societal desensitization to and acceptance of sexual issues. Society has begun to recognize that one's sexuality does not disappear because of injury and illness, and that sexuality is a birthright of all people.

Self-help groups and patients' organizations have helped raise the consciousness of patients and health providers alike to an awareness of sexual issues. Heart clubs, mastectomy clubs, amputee clubs, spinal cord groups, multiple sclerosis societies, and other such groups provide an opportunity for people to share their common concerns and to seek solutions to their common problems. Because sexual health is now more often viewed as an appropriate concern, professionals are being called on to help patients to integrate the emotional and social aspects of sexuality with their particular physical limitations. The recent interest in sex for the ill and the handicapped has resulted in increased research and publication in this area. A new journal[1] devoted entirely to sexuality and disability is available, as are several excellent books (Comfort, 1978; Kolodny et al., 1979; Sha'ked, 1978).

When considering the effects of illness or disability on sexual functioniong, it is helpful to consider several groups: There are those with clear-cut physical handicaps that directly interfere with usual sexual functioning. In this category are likely to be the spinal-cord–injured, those with irreversible neuropathy, some amputees, those who have neurological disabilities such as multiple sclerosis, and some of those who have suffered from cerebrovascular accident. There is also a group whose handicaps result in psychological reactions that may interfere with sexual function, such as mastectomy patients, ostomy patients, some cancer patients, some of those who have had a myocardial infarction, some patients with renal disease, and, in general, those for whom illness or disability has created body–image problems. While this breakdown provides a conceptual framework, both physical and psychological factors can influence sexual functioning in both groups. Another group consists

---

[1] *Sexuality and Disability*, New York, Human Sciences Press.

of those for whom sexual activity exacerbates current illness or disability. These would include arthritis patients, those suffering from pectoral angina or congestive heart failure, and patients with emphysema or other cardiopulmonary difficulties. There are also those whose sexual functioning may be affected by sensory limitations (the blind and the deaf) and others with cognitive limitations (the retarded or the brain-damaged).

Some of the basic principles of the direct treatment approach to sexual dysfunction make it particularly well-suited for counseling the handicapped or the medically ill patient. The emphasis on education to help people understand their sexual functioning and capabilities, the emphasis on exploring other forms of sexual expression besides sexual intercourse, and the deemphasis on genital sex as a necessary component to all sexual pleasure—all contribute to the kind of program that is necessary for those who have to make some adjustments in their sexual behavior. Also, conjoint therapy allows the needs and concerns of the partner of the ill or handicapped patient to be expressed and considered, something that has not traditionally been the concern of the medical profession.

Sexual problems in the ill or the handicapped, while often the result of the illness or the handicap itself, may also occur for some of the same reasons that these problems occur in the physically healthy. For example, performance anxiety, ineffective communication, lack of information, and distressed marital relationships may be directly responsible for sexual difficulty among the disabled as well as among those without disability. The problem facing sex therapists in ascertaining the relative contribution of physical and psychological factors to sexual dysfunction is particularly salient when dealing with the handicapped or the medically ill. Particularly when the illness or the disability may interfere directly with sexual functioning, it is easy to attribute all sexual problems to physical limitations, whereas in most cases the dysfunction or dissatisfaction is actually due to a combination of physical and psychological factors. Sex therapy for the handicapped and the medically ill entails a broader multidimensional assessment, edu-cation, and practical suggestions on the mechanical aspects of sexual activity, as well as the usual components of traditional sex therapy. Therapists working in this area should have, in addition to knowledge and expertise in sex therapy, a thorough understanding of the disorders of sexual response that are due to the specific pathophysiologies of the patients they may treat. They also need an understanding of the course, the prognosis, and the treatment of these pathophysiologies and the likely associated psychological responses.

Other Populations. There are several other populations of patients who are receiving increased attention from sex therapists. These include the aged, those with alternative sexual lifestyles, and those who label themselves dysfunctional because of culturally induced expectations.

Older couples have been treated as sex therapy patients since Masters and Johnson (1970) introduced their program. However, it has been commonly believed by the elderly and sex therapists alike that sexual activity gradually declines with age. This belief has been reinforced by research data from several sociological studies (Kinsey, Pomeroy, & Martin, 1948; Kinsey et al., 1953; Pfeiffer, Verwoerdt, & Wang, 1968). A more recent study (George & Weiler, 1981) suggests the stability of sexual functioning late into life and postulates that the previous findings of decline were based on inaccurate interpretations of cross-sectional data. Thus, many sexually dysfunctional elderly individuals may not be dysfunctional because of the physiological changes of aging per se, but possibly because of their reaction to minor physiological changes, to medication, and to their socially induced expectation of sexual involution. With increased societal awareness of the needs of the elderly, and their assertiveness in demanding attention to these needs, the services that can be provided by sex therapists are increasingly being requested by this segment of the population.

Individuals and couples with a homosexual orientation are likewise seeking services for sexual dysfunction. As therapists are more accepting of homosexual couples, and as they make it clear that they are willing to treat their sexual dysfunction, rather than trying to change their sexual orientation, homosexual couples have felt more confident in seeking sex therapy. McWhirter and Mattison (1980) have successfully treated many such couples using standard sex therapy techniques.

Some sex therapists (Masters & Johnson, 1979) have treated patients with a homosexual orientation by brief sex therapy techniques, with the intention of reorienting them toward a heterosexual object choice. Significant controversy exists over the appropriateness of offering such therapy (Davison, 1976). Questions also exist as to the efficacy of such treatment procedures, and the data reported by Masters and Johnson (1979) indicate a considerably higher success rate than other research would suggest is possible.

Sex therapists have also been seeing increasing numbers of people whose sexual complaints are primarily derived from personal comparison with culturally induced expectations and the acceptance of newly created sexual myths. Examples of such problems are males or females who accept, from the popular press, notions of high levels of sexual activity as the norm. Magazines such as *Playboy, Penthouse,* and many women's magazines help to create an idea that frequent sexual activity, frequent orgasms, and constant desire are the minimal norm for all individuals. Often, those who cannot meet these standards feel inadequate, label themselves or their partners as dysfunctional, and present for sex therapy. "Women's liberation" and "men's liberation" seem to have had the effect of challenging and changing the traditional sex roles. To the extent that such changes produce misunderstanding or fear, significant anxiety can result, which may interfere with sexual functioning. While much of the open discussion about sexual function and changing sex roles in the popular press has been beneficial for large segments of the population, for some it may be responsible for an unrealistic expectation about or the disruption of sexual functioning.

New Treatment Procedures

With the growth of sex therapy, and the changing clinical populations, there has been an increased focus on treatment variation and innovation as well. We examine here some of the issues in the treatment of low sexual desire and review some of the variations and innovations in the treatment of other dysfunctions.

Problems of Desire. With the increasing number of cases of low sexual desire presenting to sex therapy centers around the country, there has been increased attention paid to treatment procedures for this problem. As previously discussed, there seem to be many differences among the clinical cases that present with low sexual desire as a problem. While brief sex therapy seems to be effective in the treatment of excitement– and orgasm–phase dysfunctions, it is less effective with desire–phase dysfunctions (Kaplan, 1979). Therefore, in treating other sexual dysfunctions, it is especially important to identify this negative prognostic factor.

The treatment of desire–phase disorders is obviously dependent on those factors found to be most significant in the etiology of a particular case. In instances where aversion becomes severe, treatment techniques for phobias seem most appropriate, that is, behavioral treatment of the specific phobia and/or medication to decrease anxiety and panic attacks. Biological factors may also have etiological significance and require biological intervention. The use of androgens for women with low sexual desire (Carney, Bancroft, & Mathews, 1978) or for hypogonadal males is an example. Very often the causes of low desire are more psychologically remote and the dynamics more complex. In such cases, a lengthier, more flexible, more insight-oriented sex therapy may be necessary (Kaplan, 1979).

In general, a comprehensive program needs to be formulated that focuses on those dimensions that are most relevant. Treatment may incorporate any or all of the following elements and interventions (L. LoPiccolo, 1980):

1. Hormonal therapy
2. Treatment for poor health
3. Treatment for specific dysfunctions, if present
4. Anxiety reduction
5. Treatment of depression
6. Increasing sensory awareness (accurate labeling of sensations or responses)
7. Improving the relationship

8. Enhancing sexual experiences (by educational and sexual communication training)
9. Facilitation of erotic responses
10. Resolution of intrapsychic conflicts (fears of intimacy, fears of the opposite sex, fears of loss of control)
11. Dynamic exploration of historical influences

While these interventions are not unique to cases of low sexual desire, there may be a need to focus on some of them with a greater emphasis. Applying a standard, uniform treatment to all cases of low desire has not been effective. Individualizing therapy to the particular case shows promise of increasing therapeutic effectiveness.

Physically Focused Treatment Innovations. In the past several years, some physically focused treatments have been suggested that seem to show promise. It is difficult to differentiate placebo from actual effects in some of these procedures because appropriate double-blind studies have rarely been done. However, some of these procedures may offer significant benefit when combined with sex therapy or counseling.

Pharmacotherapy, including hormonal treatments, have been found helpful in the treatment of some sexual dysfunctions. The use of antidepressant medications for mildly to moderately depressed individuals with sexual dysfunction, especially low sexual desire, seems helpful. However, the possibility of the contribution to sexual problems by the anticholinergic effects of most of these agents must be considered. Treatment with antianxiety agents in cases of erectile failure or orgasmic dysfunction related to severe anxiety has been described as effective when used in conjunction with behavior therapy (Brady, 1966; Friedman, 1968; Kraft, 1969a,b). There is some suggestion in recent animal experimentation literature that dopamine facilitates sexual arousal and function, and that serotonin has an opposite effect (Gessa & Tagliamonte, 1974). This finding is supported by clinical reports of increased sexual drive produced by agents such as L-dopa, parachlorophenylalanine (PCPA), and apomorphine (Jarvik & Brecher, 1977). However, the possible thera-

peutic use of such substances must await further research.

Hormonal treatments of sexual dysfunction are helpful in some situations, the most obvious of which is when there is a documented endocrine disorder. Hyperprolactinemia, hyperthyroidism, and hypogonadism are all disorders that can be treated pharmacologically, in some instances with associated improvement in sexual dysfunction. The exogenous administration of testosterone has generally not been found to be useful in the treatment of erectile failure in men with normal endogenous plasma–testosterone levels (Jarvik & Brecher, 1977). However, there are a few double-blind studies that suggest that androgens may have some role in treatment. Two double-blind, crossover studies of Afrodex, a testosterone-containing compound, have suggested some effectiveness in the treatment of "impotence" (Roberts & Sloboda, 1974). There is also evidence, as already mentioned, that exogenous testosterone administration may have beneficial effects on sexually unresponsive women (Carney et al., 1978), although in some instances the responses occur only when the doses are high enough to cause undesirable virilizing side effects (Kennedy, 1973). Treatment with a luteinizing hormone-releasing hormone (LHRH) has been described as having a statistically significant "therapeutic effect" in a single clinical study (Benkert, 1975).

The history of surgical interventions for sexual dysfunctions goes back at least to the beginning of this century (Gee, 1975). Recently, there have been newly suggested surgical interventions for erectile failure. Vascular surgery for problems of erection has become more effective, with improved diagnostic procedures guiding patient selection, and improved surgical procedures leading to more definitive corrective surgery. The vascular surgeries for the treatment of erectile failure include arterial surgery to improve arterial-pelvic blood flow (Britt, Kemmerer, & Robison, 1971; May, DeWeese, & Rob, 1969) and the surgical treatment of abnormal venous outflow with a technique performed under local anesthetic (Wagner & Ebbenhøj, 1978).

In instances of erectile failure due to untreatable medical conditions, implantations of penile prostheses have become more common in the past decade. These procedures fall into two categories, depending on the type of prosthesis used. The simpler surgical technique involves the implantation of a silicone prosthesis, which results in a permanent tumescent state (Small, Carrion, & Gordon, 1975). Another technique, of a more complicated nature, involves the implantation of an inflatable penile prosthesis that allows for a change in penile state analagous to tumescence and detumescence (Scott, Bradley, & Timm, 1973). Both techniques seem to result in reasonably satisfactory erectile states. Although there have been a few studies on surgical complications, there has been almost no research on the psychological impact of this surgery and its resultant effects on the sexual relationship (Sotile, 1979). However, the use of sex therapy and sex counseling with recipients of penile prostheses and their sexual partners has already been suggested (Bullard, Mann, Caplan, & Stoklosa, 1978; Divita & Olsson, 1975).

A few surgical procedures have been suggested for treating female dysfunction. One such procedure involves narrowing the vaginal opening, tucking the clitoris and labia into the introitus, and cutting the pubococcygeal muscle to displace the vagina so that penile thrusting can be in a plane that leads to penile-clitoral contact and presumably to orgasm (Burt & Burt, 1965). Another procedure is circumcision of the clitoral hood, or a freeing of adhesions between the clitoral hood and the shaft (Barbach, 1975). The lack of proof of the effectiveness of these procedures and the issue of possible subsequent complications raise significant questions about their appropriateness.

A form of physical therapy or isometric exercise has been found to be a useful adjunct in the treatment of orgasmic dysfunction in females. Originally, these vaginal muscle exercises were developed by Kegel (1952) for the treatment of urinary stress incontinence, but it was soon discovered that a serendipitous side effect of strengthening the pubococcygeal musculature was the occurrence of orgasm in some previously inorgasmic women. Thus, Kegel exercises are now often incorporated into the treatment programs for female dysfunction (Kline-Graber & Graber, 1975).

Any of the above interventions are most effective within the context of a comprehensive sex therapy program, since the difficulties they treat must be considered within the psychological system of the individual and the interpersonal system of the relationship.

Other Treatment Modalities. One of the cornerstone features of the Masters and Johnson treatment program is the use of the dual sex-therapy team. They believe that each partner in the couple needs a same-sexed "interpreter" to understand and present her or his point of view. Also they believe that when only one therapist is present, the opposite-sexed spouse will feel "ganged-up on" (Masters & Johnson, 1970). Partly because of limited therapeutic resources and partly because of the high cost of a dual therapy team, many therapy centers have started using a single therapist to do sex therapy. There are now some largely anecdotal reports that seem to indicate an equally successful outcome with single therapists (Franks & Wilson, 1974; Hogan, 1978; Kaplan, 1974; Laughren & Kass, 1975; Mathews, Bancroft, Whitehead, Hackman, Julier, Gath, & Shaw, 1976). Our center at Stony Brook has recently completed a relatively rigorous test of single as opposed to dual sex cotherapy. With 90 cases randomly assigned to a male therapist, a female therapist, or a dual-sex co-therapy team, outcome and follow-up data were taken on a variety of assessment instruments. The results of extensive data analysis supports the previously mentioned clinical impression that co-therapists are no more effective than a single therapist.

Another step in the direction of cutting down expense and therapist time has been the use of bibliotherapy with minimal therapist contact. This approach has been shown to be effective in the treatment of premature ejaculation (Mikulas & Lowe, 1974; Zeiss, 1977) and a mixed group of dysfunctions (Mathews et al., 1976). A study of minimal therapist contact for primary orgasmic dysfunction has been run at the Sex Therapy Center at Stony Brook. Couples are seen for four sessions, four weeks apart. They continue to do weekly homework assignments and have their therapy supplemented by books and films. Although the results are still being analyzed, this study seems to indicate effectiveness equal to a 15-session treatment. The reports to date are mostly case studies, and more controlled research is needed in this area. Minimal therapist contact is probably most useful for the simpler sexual dysfunctions (i.e., primary orgasmic dysfunction and premature ejaculation), where clear-cut instructional programs are available (Kaplan, Kohl, Pomeroy, Offit, & Hugon, 1974).

Since Masters and Johnson (1970) helped shift the unit of therapeutic intervention for sexual dysfunction from the individual to the couple, singles have, for the most part, been excluded from this new sex therapy or have been treated with a surrogate partner. Recently, there has been an increased interest in treating sexual dysfunction in individuals without partners with group therapy. As a treatment modality, group therapy has proved successful in the treatment of orgasmic dysfunction (Barbach, 1974; McGovern, Kirkpatrick, & LoPiccolo, 1974), male dysfunctions (Kaplan et al., 1974; Zeiss, Christensen, & Levine, 1978; Zilbergeld, 1975), and a heterogeneous group (Leiblum, Rosen, & Pierce, 1976). The group modality is particularly valuable for single individuals in that it provides an environment of mutual support and encouragement. It also provides the opportunity for skill training and sexual communication training by role playing, modeling, and group discussion. Although group therapy has not often been utilized with couples, it may have some of the same advantages as with individuals. In addition, the cost-effectiveness of group therapy is greater than that of co-therapy or therapy with an individual therapist.

Biofeedback is another promising treatment modality coming out of the laboratory study of human behavior. Research on the correlation between subjective measures of sexual arousal and physiological measures of genital response show evidence of both independence and concordance. Geer, Morokoff, and Greenwood (1974) found nonsignificant or inconsistent correlations between self-reported and genital measures of sexual arousal in women. Wincze, Hoon, and Hoon (1976) had similar findings. However, Henson, Rubin, Henson, and Williams (1977) found significant positive correlations between genital vasocongestion and subjectively measured sexual arousal. Heiman (1977) found high correlations between genital pulse amplitude and genital

blood volume for males in response to erotic tapes, with subjective response significantly correlated with pulse amplitude. Wilson and Lawson (1976) found that with increasing dosages of alcohol, women reported more arousal, while their vaginal response showed less arousal. These studies suggest that the mind and the body do not always correspond in sexual arousal. Physical arousal may be mislabeled or overlooked because of competing emotions, such as anxiety, or because of a general lack of experience in labeling these responses. Biofeedback may be clinically useful in helping people to recognize the physiological aspects of arousal, to label them, and by doing so, to increase arousal through the completion of a psychological feedback system. Theoretically, this approach would be more helpful to women, since men have a visual form of biofeedback, namely, the penis. Although there is not a convincing body of evidence to date that biofeedback is of great value as a therapeutic intervention (Heiman & Hatch, 1980), it remains a promising area of research and application because of the psychophysiological nature of human sexual function and dysfunction.

In summary, then, the field of sex therapy has seen rapid growth and expansion over the last few years. This expansion has included new therapy programs, application to a broader range of clinical populations, and increased accuracy of diagnosis. With these positive changes, however, have come some negative developments, involving ethics, fees, and the exploitation of patients.

Ethical Issues: Trick or Treatment?

Changing cultural attitudes about sex and the development of new psychotherapeutic techniques have combined to create a high public demand for sex therapy. As a combined result of this demand, a lack of action by the professional psychotherapy disciplines, and the inadequate laws regulating psychotherapeutic practice, a major problem has arisen regarding the competence of some of those people who call themselves sex therapists. Currently, there is virtually no legal or professional protection for the consumer seeking such therapy. As a result of this lack of regulation, a number of centers have sprung up, claiming to be sex therapy centers. Some of these operations are run by people with no professional training at all, while others have a staff of mental health professionals whose only exposure to sex therapy training has been attendance at a workshop or two.

It is remarkable that in the United States, the average cost range for 15 hours of outpatient psychotherapy with a private-practice psychologist or psychiatrist is between $300 and $750, yet the average cost range for 15 hours (the usual duration) of sex therapy from one of the many new sex therapy centers is between $2,500 and $4,000. While there is an obvious reason for higher fees when two therapists see a given couple—a male–female cotherapy team is common in sex-therapy practice—a fee level that is 5–10 higher cannot be justified on any rational grounds.

Sex therapists, as discussed above, often have less formal training and experience than psychotherapists. The sex therapy consumer is not paying for longer training or expensive equipment, which are the usual reasons for the higher fees of specialty practitioners. Regarding the necessity for higher fees to pay two therapists, as previously discussed, recent research indicates that therapy with a single therapist may be just as effective.

As a third ethical concern, there is a growing tendency for sex therapy to include some form of sexual or quasi-sexual contact with the patient and therapist. Such procedures include nudity, massage, the use of hot tubs, and "sexological" exams, in which the therapist uses sexual stimulation to "demonstrate and evaluate" sexual responsivity. None of these procedures has a firm theoretical or empirical base to support its effectiveness, and the potential for abuse is obvious.

The most direct form of sexual contact is, of course, for the therapist—or a surrogate partner provided by the therapist—actually to go through the therapy program with the individual in therapy. Masters and Johnson started this approach, using carefully screened and trained surrogates under close supervision, in cases where a man lacked a sexual partner. They discontinued this approach, partly because of legal problems and partly because they noticed a selective tendency for their surrogates to become emotionally involved with wealthy men in therapy.

Today, there is an International Professional Surrogates Association, which makes surrogates available to therapists who would like to use them. While the use of surrogates has been described as "thinly veiled prostitution," the use of a surrogate is at least a seemingly logical approach (although not the only approach, as the surrogate advocates claim) for the dysfunctional individual who does not have a sexual partner. Again, there is an obvious problem: while the advocates of surrogate therapy claim high success, data on whether any newfound ability to function generalizes from the surrogate to another sexual partner are almost totally nonexistent. In the absence of such data, the practice of providing surrogates to married men with wives who are unwilling to enter therapy with their husbands is at best questionable, even if we ignore the other issues involved in such cases. Perhaps more disturbingly, there is a current trend for these surrogates to move toward becoming independent therapists and to operate without any professional consultation or supervision.

In all procedures involving nudity, touching, and sexual activity between patient and therapist, even the most charitable observer must question the therapist's motives for using such procedures. Is there a theoretical rationale or actual data to support the utility of such risky procedures? Is the enjoyment and gratification of the therapist, rather than the welfare of the person in treatment, a major factor in the decision to use such procedures? The issue of exploitation of the patient is an enormous one, yet one that is simply denied by the advocates of this approach. Because of the obvious risk of the exploitation, sex between therapists and those in treatment is considered unethical by all professional psychotherapy disciplines.

Summary

In this chapter, we have reviewed the development of sex therapy from a collection of informal techniques to a discipline with an extensive clinical literature, an increasingly sophisticated assessment procedure, and emerging status as a separate subspecialty field. What still remains to be developed, however, is a more complete empirical base for the discipline. As noted in a recent review (Lo-Piccolo, 1978), much of the literature in this field suffers from basic methodological errors, and major questions regarding diagnosis, treatment techniques, and the characteristics of patients have yet to be adequately researched. It is our hope that another review, written some years from now, will be able to survey a large collection of methodologically sound, clinically relevant, empirical literature.

References

Abarbanel, A. R. Diagnosis and treatment of coital discomfort. In J. LoPiccolo & L. LoPiccolo (Eds.), *Handbook of sex therapy*. New York: Plenum Press, 1978.

Abelson, D. Diagnostic value of the penile pulse and blood pressure: A doppler study of impotence in diabetics. *Journal of Urology*, 1975, *113*, 636.

American Psychiatric Association. *Diagnostic and Statistical Manual of Mental Disorders* (3rd ed.). Washington, D.C.: Author, 1980.

Bandura, A. A social learning interpretation of psychological dysfunctions. In P. London & D. Rosenhan (Eds.), *Foundation of abnormal psychology*. New York: Holt, Rinehart, & Winston, 1968.

Barbach, L. G. Group treatment of preorgasmic women. *Journal of Sex and Marital Therapy*, 1974, *1*, 139–145.

Barbach, L. G. *For yourself: The fulfillment of female sexuality*. New York: Doubleday, 1975.

Benkert, O. Clinical studies on the effects of neurohormones on sexual behavior. In M. Sandler & G. L. Gessa (Eds.), *Sexual behavior: Pharmacology and biochemistry*. New York: Raven Press, 1975.

Benkert, O., Witt, W., Adam, W., & Leitz, A. Effects of testosterone decanoate on sexual potency and the hypothalamic-pituitary-gonadal axis of impotent males. *Archives of Sexual Behavior*, 1978, *8*, 471–479.

Bergler, E. *Neurotic counterfeit-sex*. New York: Grune & Stratton, 1951.

Beutler, L., Karacan, I., Anch, A., Salis, P., Scott, F., & Williams, R. MMPI and MIT discriminators of biogenic and psychogenic impotence. *Journal of Consulting and Clinical Psychology*, 1975, *43*, 899–903.

Brady, J. P. Brevital-relaxation treatment of frigidity. *Behaviour Research and Therapy*, 1966, *4*, 71–77.

Britt, D. B., Kemmerer, W. T., & Robison, J. R. Penile blood flow determination by mercury strain gauge plethysmography. *Investigative Urology*, 1971, *8*, 673–677.

Bullard, D. G., Mann, J., Caplan, H., & Stoklosa, J. M. Sex counseling and the penile prosthesis. *Sexuality and Disability*, 1978, *1*, 184–189.

Burt, J. E., & Burt, J. C. *The surgery of love*. New York: Carlton, 1975.

Caird, W., & Wincze, J. P. *Sex therapy: A behavioral approach*. New York: Harper & Row, 1977.

Carney, A., Bancroft, J., & Mathews, A. A combination of hormonal and psychological treatment for female sexual unresponsiveness: A comparative study. *British Journal of Psychiatry*, 1978, *132*, 339–346.

Comfort, A. (Ed.). *Sexual consequences of disability*. Philadelphia: Stickley, 1978.

Cooper, A. J. A factual study of male potency disorders. *British Journal of Psychiatry*, 1968, *114*, 719–731.

Cooper, A. J. Treatments of male potency disorders: The present status. *Psychosomatics*, 1971, *12*, 335–344.

Davison, G. C. Homosexuality: The ethical challenge. *Journal of Consulting and Clinical Psychology*, 1976, *44*, 157–162.

Dengrove, E. Behavior therapy of the sexual disorders. *Journal of Sex Research*, 1967, *3*, 49–61.

Dengrove, E. The uses of hypnosis in behavior therapy. *International Journal of Clinical and Experimental Hypnosis*, 1973, *21*, 13–17.

Derogatis, L. R. Psychological assessment of sexual disorders. In J. Meyer (Ed.), *Clinical management of sexual disorders*. Baltimore, Md.: Williams & Wilkins, 1976.

Divita, E. C., & Olsson, P. A. The use of sex therapy in a patient with a penile prosthesis. *Journal of Sex and Marital Therapy*, 1975, *1*, 305–311.

Ellis, A. *Reason and emotion in psychotherapy*. New York: Lyle Stuart, 1962.

Ellis, A. Rational-emotive treatment of impotence, frigidity and other sexual problems. *Professional Psychology*, 1971, *2*, 346–349.

El-Senoussi, A. *The male impotence test*. Los Angeles, Calif.: Western Psychological Services, 1964.

Ertekin, C., & Reel, F. Bulbacavernosa reflex in normal men and in patients with neurogenic bladder and/or impotence. *Journal of Neurological Sciences*, 1976, *28*, 1–15.

Fitzpatrick, T. J., & Cooper, J. F. A cavernosogram study on the valvular competence of the human deep dorsal vein. *The Journal of Urology*, 1975, *113*, 479–499.

Frank, E., Anderson, C., & Rubenstein, D. Frequency of sexual dysfunction in normal couples. *New England Journal of Medicine*, 1978, *299*, 111–115.

Franks, C. M., & Wilson, G. T. (Eds.). *Annual review of behavior therapy: Theory and practice*. New York: Brunner/Mazel, 1974.

Freud, S. *Three essays on the theory of female sexuality*. New York: Avon, 1962. (Originally published, 1905.)

Friedman, D. The treatment of impotence by Brevital relaxation therapy. *Behaviour Research and Therapy*, 1968, *6*, 257–261.

Garfield, Z. H., McBrearty, J. E., & Dicter, M. A case of impotence successfully treated with desensitization combined with in-vivo operant training and thought substitution. In R. D. Rubin & C. M. Franks (Eds.), *Advances in behavior therapy*. New York: Academic Press, 1969.

Gaskell, P. The importance of penile blood pressure in cases of impotence. *Canadian Medical Association Journal*, 1971, *105*, 1047–1052.

Gee, W. F. A history of surgical treatment of impotence. *Urology*, 1975, *5*, 401–405.

Geer, J. H., Morokoff, P. J., & Greenwood, P. Sexual arousal in women: The development of a measurement device for vaginal blood volume. *Archives of Sexual Behavior*, 1974, *3*, 559–564.

George, L. K., & Weiler, S. J. Sexuality in middle and late life: The effects of age, education, and gender. *Archives of General Psychiatry*, 1981, *38*, 919–923.

Gessa, G. L., & Tagliamonte, A. Possible role of brain serotonin and dopamine in controlling male sexual behavior. In E. Costa, G. L. Gessa, & M. Sandler (Eds.), *Advances in Biochemical Psychopharmacology*, 1974, *11*, 217–228.

Hartman, W. E., & Fithian, M. A. *Treatment of sexual dysfunction*. Long Beach, Calif. Center for Marital and Sexual Studies, 1972.

Heiman, J. Issues in the use of psychophysiology to assess female sexual dysfunction. *Journal of Sex and Marital Therapy*, 1976, *2*, 197–204.

Heiman, J. A psychophysiological exploration of sexual arousal patterns in females and males. *Psychophysiology*, 1977, *14*, 266–274.

Heiman, J., & Hatch, J. Conceptual and therapeutic contribution of psychophysiology to sexual dysfunction. In S. Haynes & L. Gannon (Eds.), *Psychosomatic disorders: A psychophysiological approach to etiology and treatment*. New York: Gardner Press, 1980.

Hellerstein, H., & Friedman, E. J. Sexual activity and the postcoronary patient. *Archives of Internal Medicine*, 1970, *125*, 987.

Hempel, C. G. Fundamentals of taxonomy. In C. G. Hempel, *Aspects of scientific explanations and other essays in the philosophy of science*. New York: Free Press, 1965.

Henson, D., Rubin, H., Henson, C., & Williams, J. Temperature change of the labia minora as an objective measure of human female eroticism. *Journal of Behavior Therapy and Experimental Psychiatry*, 1977, *8*, 401–410.

Hogan, D. R. The effectiveness of sex therapy: A review of the literature. In J. LoPiccolo & L. LoPiccolo (Eds.), *Handbook of Sex Therapy*. New York: Plenum Press, 1978.

Hoon, E. F., Hoon, P. W., & Wincze, J. The SAI: An inventory for the measurement of female sexual arousal. *Archives of Sexual Behavior*, 1976, *5*, 208–215.

Jarvik, M. E., & Brecher, E. M. Drugs and sex: Inhibition and enhancement effects. In J. Money & H. Musaph (Eds.), *Handbook of sexology*. New York: Elsevier-North Holland, 1977.

Jemail, J. A., & LoPiccolo, J. A sexual and a marriage defensiveness scale for each sex. *American Journal of Family Therapy*, in press.

Kanfer, F. H., & Saslow, G. Behavioral diagnosis. In C. M. Franks (Ed.), *Behavior therapy: Appraisal and status*. New York: McGraw Hill, 1969.

Kaplan, H. S. *The new sex therapy*. New York: Brunner/Mazel, 1974.

Kaplan, H. S. Hypoactive sexual desire. *Journal of Sex and Marital Therapy*, 1977, *3*, 3–9.

Kaplan, H. S. *Disorders of sexual desire*. New York: Brunner/Mazel, 1979.

Kaplan, H. S., & Kohl, K. Adverse reactions to rapid treatment of sexual problems. *Psychosomatics*, 1972, *13*, 3–5.

Kaplan, H. S., Kohl, R. N., Pomeroy, W. B., Offit, A. K., & Hugon, B. Group treatment of premature ejaculation. *Archives of Sexual Behavior*, 1974, *3*, 443–452.

Karacan, I. Advances in the psychophysiological evaluation of male erectile impotence. In L. LoPiccolo & J. LoPiccolo (Eds.), *Handbook of sex therapy*. New York: Plenum Press, 1978.

Karacan, I., Williams, R. I., Thornby, J. I., & Salis, M. A. Sleep related tumescence as a function of age. *American Journal of Psychiatry*, 1975, *132*, 932–937.

Kegel, A. H. Sexual function of the pubococcygeus muscle. *Western Journal of Obstetrics and Gynecology*, 1952, *60*, 521.

Kennedy, B. J. Effect of massive doses of sex hormones on libido. *Medical Aspects of Human Sexuality*, 1973, *7*, 67–80.

Kinsey, A. C., Pomeroy, W. B., & Martin, C. W. *Sexual behavior in the human male*. Philadelphia: W. B. Saunders, 1948.

Kinsey, A. C., Pomeroy, W. B., Martin, C. W., & Gebhard, P. H. *Sexual behavior in the human female*. Philadelphia: W. B. Saunders, 1953.

Kline-Graber, G., & Graber, B. *Woman's orgasm*. New York: Bobbs-Merrill, 1975.

Kockett, G., Dittmar, F., & Nusselt, L. Systematic desensitization of erectile impotence: A controlled study. *Archives of Sexual Behavior*, 1975, *4*, 493–500.

Kolodny, R. C., Masters, W. H., & Johnson, V. E. *Textbook of sexual medicine*. Boston: Little Brown, 1979.

Kraft, T. Behavior therapy and target symptoms. *Journal of Clinical Psychology*, 1969, *25*, 105–109. (a)

Kraft, T. Desensitization and the treatment of sexual disorders. *Journal of Sex Research*, 1969, *5*, 130–134. (b)

Lansky, M., & Davenport, A. Difficulties in brief conjoint treatment of sexual dysfunction. *American Journal of Psychiatry*, 1975, *132*, 177–179.

Laughren, T. P., & Kass, D. J. Desensitization of sexual dysfunction: The present status. In A. S. Gurman & D. G. Rice (Eds.), *Couples in conflict: New directions in marital therapy*. New York: John Ahrenson, 1975.

Lazarus, A. A. The treatment of a sexually inadequate man. In L. Ullman & L. Krasner (Eds.), *Case studies in behavior modification*. New York: Holt, Rinehart & Winston, 1965.

Lazarus, A. A. Behavior therapy in groups. In G. M. Gazda (Ed.), *Basic approaches to group psychotherapy and group counselling*. Springfield, Ill.: Charles C Thomas, 1968.

Leiblum, S. R., Rosen, R. C., & Pierce, D. Group treatment format: Mixed sexual dysfunctions. *Archives of Sexual Behavior*, 1976, *5*, 313–322.

Lobitz, W. C. Personal communication, 1978.

Lobitz, W. C., & Lobitz, G. K. Clinical assessment in the treatment of sexual dysfunction. In J. LoPiccolo & L. LoPiccolo (Eds.), *Handbook of Sex Therapy*. New York: Plenum Press, 1978.

Lobitz, W. C., & LoPiccolo, J. New methods in the behavioral treatment of sexual dysfunction. *Journal of Behavior Therapy and Experimental Psychiatry*, 1972, *3*, 265–271.

Lobitz, W. C., LoPiccolo, J., Lobitz, G., & Brockway, J. A closer look at "simplistic" behavior therapy for sexual dysfunction: Two case studies. In H. J. Eysenck (Ed.), *Case studies in behavior therapy*. London, England: Routledge & Kegan Paul, 1976.

LoPiccolo, J. Direct treatment of sexual dysfunction in the couple. In J. Money & H. Musoff (Eds.), *Handbook of sexology*. New York: Elsevier/North Holland, 1977.

LoPiccolo, J. Methodological issues in research and treatment of sexual dysfunction. Chapter in R. Green & J. Winer (Eds.), *Methodological issues in sex research*. Washington, D.C.: U.S. Government Printing Office, 1978.

LoPiccolo, J., & Heiman, J. The role of cultural values in the prevention and treatment of sexual problems. In C. B. Qualls, J. P. Wincze, & D. H. Barlow (Eds.), *The prevention of sexual disorders: Issues and approaches*. New York: Plenum Press, 1978.

LoPiccolo, J., & Hogan, D. Multidimensional behavioral treatment of sexual dysfunction. In O. Pomerlieu & J. P. Brady (Eds.), *Behavioral medicine*. Baltimore: Williams & Wilkins, 1979.

LoPiccolo, J., & Steger, J. C. The sexual interaction inventory: A new instrument for assessment of sexual dysfunction. *Archives of Sexual Behavior*, 1974, *3*, 585–595.

LoPiccolo, L. Low sexual desire. In S. Leiblum & L. Pervin (Eds.), *Principles and practices of sex therapy*. New York: Guildford Press, 1980.

LoPiccolo, L., & Heiman, J. Sexual assessment and history interview. In J. LoPiccolo & L. LoPiccolo (Eds.), *Handbook of sex therapy*. New York: Plenum Press, 1978.

Lundberg, P. O. Sexual dysfunction in patients with neurological disorders. In R. Gemme & C. C. Wheeler (Eds.), *Progress in sexology*. New York: Plenum Press, 1977.

Masters, W. H., & Johnson, V. E. *Human sexual response*. Boston: Little, Brown, 1966.

Masters, W. H., & Johnson, V. E. *Human sexual inadequacy*. Boston: Little, Brown, 1970.

Masters, W. H., & Johnson, V. E. *Homosexuality in perspective*. Boston: Little, Brown, 1979.

Mathews, A., Bancroft, J., Whitehead, A., Hackman, A., Julier, D., Gath, D., & Shaw, P. The behavioral treatment of sexual inadequacy: A comparative study. *Behaviour Research and Therapy*, 1976, *14*, 427–436.

May, A., DeWeese, J., & Rob, C. Changes in sexual function following operation on the abdominal aorta. *Surgery*, 1969, *65*, 41–47.

McGovern, K., Kirkpatrick, C., & LoPiccolo, J. A behavioral group treatment program for sexually dysfunctional couples. *Journal of Marriage and Family Counseling*, October 1974, 397–404.

McWhirter, D., & Mattison, A. Treatment of sexual dysfunction in homosexual male couples. In S. Leiblum & L. Pervin (Eds.), *Principles and Practice of Sex Therapy*. New York: Guilford Press, 1980.

Michal, V., & Pospichal, J. Phalloarteriography in the diagnosis of erectile impotence. *World Journal of Surgery*, 1978, *2*, 239–248.

Mikulas, W. L., & Lowe, J. C. *Self-control of premature ejaculation*. Paper presented at Rocky Mountain Psychological Association, Denver, Colo., 1974.

Obler, M. Systematic desensitization in sexual disorders. *Journal of Behavior Therapy and Experimental Psychiatry*, 1973, *4*, 93–101.

O'Conner, J. F., & Stern, L. Results of treatment in functional sexual disorders. *New York State Journal of Medicine*, 1972, *72*, 15.

Pfeiffer, E., Verwoerdt, A., & Wang, H. S. The sexual behavior in aged men and women: I. Observations on 254 community volunteers. *Archives of General Psychiatry*, 1968, *19*, 753–758.

Pinderhughes, C. A., Grace, E. B., & Reyna, L. J. Psychiatric disorders and sexual functioning. *American Journal of Psychiatry*, 1972, *128*, 1276–1283.

Renshaw, D. *Healing the incest wound*. Paper presented at the meeting of the American Association of Sex Educators, Counsellors and Therapists, Washington, D.C., March 1977.

Reynolds, B. S. Psychological treatment models and outcome results for erectile dysfunction: A critical review. *Psychological Bulletin*, 1977, *84*, 1218–1238.

Roberts, C. D., & Sloboda, W. Afrodex vs. placebo in the treatment of male impotence: Statistical analysis of two double-blind crossover studies. *Current Therapeutic Research*, 1974, *16*, 96–99.

Rosen, R. C., & Keefe, F. J. The measurement of human penile tumescence. *Psychophysiology*, 1978, *15*, 366–376.

Sager, C. J. Sexual dysfunctions and marital discord. In H. S. Kaplan, *The new sex therapy*. New York: Brunner/Mazel, 1974.

Sager, C. J. The role of sex therapy in marital therapy. *American Journal of Psychiatry*, 1976, *133*, 555–559.

Schover, L., Friedman, J. M., Weiler, S. J., Heiman, J., & LoPiccolo, J. A multiaxial descriptive system for the sexual dysfunctions. *Archives of General Psychiatry*, in press.

Scott, F. B., Bradley, W. E., & Timm, G. W. Management of erectile impotence. *Urology*, 1973, *2*, 80–82.

Semans, J. H. Premature ejaculation: A new approach. *Southern Medical Journal*, 1956, *49*, 353–357.

Sha'ked, A. *Human sexuality in physical and mental illness and disability: An annotated bibliography*. Bloomington: Indiana University, 1978.

Sharpe, L., Kurlansky, J. B., & O'Conner, J. F. A preliminary classification of human sexual disorders. *Journal of Sex and Marital Therapy*, 1976, *2*, 106–114.

Sintchak, G., & Geer, J. H. A vaginal plethysmography system. *Psychophysiology*, 1975, *12*, 113–115.

Small, M. P., Carrion, H. M., & Gordon, J. A. Small-Carrion penile prosthesis. *Urology*, 1975, *5*, 479–486.

Snyder, A., LoPiccolo, L., & LoPiccolo, J. Secondary orgasmic dysfunction: II. A case study. *Archives of Sexual Behavior*, 1975, *4*, 277–283.

Sotile, W. M. The penile prosthesis: A review. *Journal of Sex and Marital Therapy*, 1979, *5*, 90–102.

Spark, R. F., White, R. A., & Connolly, M. S. Impotence is not always psychogenic. *Journal of American Medical Association*, 1980, *243*, 750–755.

Spitzer, R. L., & Wilson, P. T. Nosology and the official psychiatric nomenclature. In A. M. Freedman, H. I. Kaplan, & B. J. Sadoch (Eds.), *Comprehensive textbook of psychiatry*, Vol. 2. Baltimore: Williams & Wilkins, 1975.

Spitzer, R. L., Sheehy, M., & Endicott, J. DSM-III: Guiding principles. In V. M. Rakoff, H. C. Stancer, & H. B. Kedward (Eds.), *Psychiatric diagnosis*. New York: Brunner/Mazel, 1977.

Strupp, H. H., & Hadley, S. W. A tripartite model of mental health and therapeutic outcomes. *American Psychologist*, 1977, *32*, 191–196.

von Bertalanffy, L. *General systems theory: Foundations, developments, applications*. New York: Braziller, 1968.

Wagner, G., & Ebbenhøj, J. *Erectile dysfunction caused by abnormal outflow from the corpus cavernosum*. Paper presented at Third International Congress of Medical Sexology, Rome, Italy, 1978.

Watzlawick, P., Beavin, J., & Jackson, D. *Pragmatics of human communication*. New York: Norton, 1967.

Wilson, G. T., & Lawson, D. M. Effects of alcohol on sexual arousal in women. *Journal of Abnormal Psychology*, 1976, *85*, 489–497.

Wincze, J., Hoon, E., & Hoon, P. Physiological responsivity of normal and sexually dysfunctional women during erotic stimulus exposure. *Journal of Psychosomatic Research*, 1976, *20*, 445–451.

Winokur, G. Sexual behavior: Its relationship to certain affects and psychiatric diseases. In G. Winokur (Ed.), *Determinants of human sexual behavior*. Springfield, Ill.: Charles C Thomas, 1963.

Wolpe, J. *Psychotherapy by reciprocal inhibition*. Stanford, Calif.: Stanford University Press, 1958.

Wolpe, J., & Lazarus, A. A. *Behavior therapy techniques*. New York: Pergamon Press, 1966.

Woodruff, R. A., Murphy, G. E., & Herjonic, M. The natural history of affective disorders: I. Symptoms of 72 patients at the time of index hospital admission. *Journal of Psychiatric Research*, 1967, *5*, 255–263.

Wright, S., Perreault, R., & Mathieu, M. Treatment of sexual dysfunction: A review. *Archives of General Psychiatry*, 1977, *34*, 881–890.

Zeiss, R. A. Self-directed treatment for premature ejaculation: Preliminary case reports. *Journal of Behavior Therapy and Experimental Psychiatry*, 1977, *8*, 87–91.

Zeiss, R., Christensen, A., & Levine, A. Treatment for premature ejaculation through male only groups. *Journal of Sex and Marital Therapy*, 1978, *4*, 139–143.

Zilbergeld, B. Group treatment of sexual dysfunction in men without partners. *Journal of Sex and Marital Therapy*, 1975, *3*, 443–452.

CHAPTER 22

Sexual Deviation

Nathaniel McConaghy

Introduction: Assessment and Treatment of Arousal and Orgasm Anomalies

Until the last three decades, deviations from the sexual behaviors of the majority of the population have been noted mainly in relation to the nature of the stimuli producing sexual arousal and the activities used to achieve orgasm. With the development of operations enabling the morphology of the external genitalia to be changed from male to female or vice versa, considerable attention was given to transsexualism, the rare condition of those people whose major anomaly appears to be a desire to live as a member of the sex morphologically opposite to their own. It was concluded that transsexuals had a disorder of sexual identity (Worden & Marsh, 1955).

More recently, with the increased interest in the behavior of humans and animals in relation to their sex, significance has been attached to sex-dimorphic behaviors, nonsexual behaviors that are shown significantly more commonly by members of one rather than the other sex of a species. In some circumstances, opposite sex-dimorphic behavior in humans is regarded as requiring treatment.

Homosexuality

People with a homosexual component experience sexual arousal in response to persons of the same sex. When the term *homosexual* is used in this review, without qualification, it refers to such people. The majority of homosexuals in this sense are predominantly heterosexual. Initial investigations of homosexuality were mainly of overt behavior. The development of techniques for measuring the physiological aspects of human sexual arousal has shifted the emphasis to the investigation of subjects' sexual feelings, presumably because these, rather than overt behavior, relate more meaningfully to measures of physiological arousal.

Physiological Measures of Sexual Arousal and Orientation

Freund (1963) initiated the use of plethysmograph measures of penile volume to diagnose the predominance of homo- or heteroerotic interest in the male. He was able to classify correctly all of 65 relatively exclusive heterosexuals and 48 of 58 relatively exclusive homosexuals from their penile volume responses to 13-sec exposures of colored pictures of nude men, women, and children.

McConaghy (1967) described a simpler ap-

Nathaniel McConaghy • School of Psychiatry, University of New South Wales, Sydney, Australia.

paratus for measuring penile volume responses and a relatively brief standardized procedure for presenting the sexually arousing material. Subjects' responses were recorded while they viewed a movie film of landscapes into which were inserted, at minute intervals, ten 10-sec segments of pictures of nude women alternating with ten 10-sec pictures of nude men. Each subject's 10 responses to the pictures of women were compared with his 10 responses to the pictures of men, by means of the Mann-Whitney U-test. A U-score of 77 or more indicated that the subject's responses to pictures of women were significantly greater ($p = .05$, two-tailed) than his responses to men. Of 60 volunteer male students, 54 (90%) obtained U-scores of 77 and above (Barr & McConaghy, 1971). A U-score of 23 or less indicated that the subject's responses to pictures of men were significantly greater than

his responses to women. None of the students obtained scores in this range. Of 24 male transsexuals who reported predominant or exclusive homosexuality, 21 obtained U-scores of 23 or less (Barr, 1973). The mean scores of these and other groups of subjects with sexual anomalies are given in Table 1.

Bancroft, Jones, and Pullan (1966) reported the use of a strain gauge to measure what they termed penile erection, which they identified with the response Freund had measured with a volume plethysmograph. The strain gauge used by Bancroft *et al.* (1966) was fitted around the shaft of the penis. It measured changes in penile circumference, not penile volume. The responses measured by Freund occurred to a 13-sec exposure to an erotic stimulus. Bancroft *et al.* (1966) stated that with their instrument, most responses occurred within 5-min and that usually some mental im-

Table 1. U-Scores of Heterosexual and Anomalous Groups

Study	Subjects	U-scores Mean	U-scores Range
McConaghy (1967)	11 exclusively heterosexual	95	67–100 (9, > 95)
Barr & McConaghy (1971)	60 university students	90	SD 16.3 (0, ⩽ 23; 54, ⩾ 77)
McConaghy (1975)	18 heterosexual deviants	91	(0, ⩽ 50; 13, > 77)
Buhrich & McConaghy (1977b)	19 nuclear transvestities	80	50–98.5 (0, < 50; 12, ⩾ 77)
	13 marginal transvestities	66	31–100 (1, < 50; 3, ⩾ 77)
Buhrich & McConaghy (1978a)	5 fetishistic transsexuals	48	4–79 (2, < 50; 1, ⩾ 77)
	21 nuclear transsexuals	13	0–42.5 (17, ⩽ 23)
McConaghy (1978)	20 married homosexuals, history hetero intercourse with other than wife	42	0–93.5 (8, ⩽ 23; 3, 24–50; 3, ⩾ 77)
	58 single homosexuals, history hetero intercourse	35	0–99.5 31 (25, ⩽ 23; 18, 24–50; 4, ⩾ 77)
	79 single homosexuals, no history hetero intercourse	28	0–92.5 (41, ⩽ 23; 24, 24–50; 4, ⩾ 77)
	24 married homosexuals, no history hetero intercourse with other than wife	19	0–62 (17, ⩽ 23; 4, 24–50; 0, ⩾ 77)
Barr (1973)	44 homosexuals	32	SD 31.9
	24 transsexuals	16	SD 27 (21, ⩽ 23)

agery was required to produce them. These facts indicate that the two responses being measured differed considerably.

Bancroft (1971) reported a validation study of the strain gauge as a measure of sexual interest. Thirty homosexuals were shown five pictures of men and five of women, each for 120 sec, and were asked to produce an erotic fantasy in association with each picture. In only 14 of 30 homosexuals was there a significant correlation between erectile response and the individual's subjective rating of his sexual interest in the series of slides. It would appear from this study and from those of Freund and McConaghy that the physiological measure of an *individual* subject's sexual orientation derived from penile circumference responses as determined by the strain gauge is much less valid than that obtained by penile volume plethysmography.

Paradoxical Penile-Circumference Changes

McConaghy (1974) compared a volumetric and penile circumference measure to assess the penile changes in subjects who watched 10-sec segments of moving pictures of men and women. Some subjects showed circumference and volume changes that were reasonably similar; others showed responses that were mirror images. The volumetric responses were more consistent with the subjects' stated sexual orientation. To determine the significance of the responses that were mirror images, the subjects who showed such responses to the 10-sec film segments were shown a series of erotic slides with the aim of causing them to have an erection. The volume measure showed a gradual increase from within a few seconds of the onset of the first slide. The circumference measure showed a decrease until almost 2 min later, when an increase occurred (McConaghy, 1977). This finding suggests that in these subjects, sexual arousal was accompanied by a penile volume increase but an initial circumference decrease. McConaghy (1974) pointed out that the disparate measures of the two instruments could be explained if sexual arousal caused the penis to increase in length at a rate faster than its blood supply

increased. Thus, the penis would show an initial volume increase but a concomitant decrease in circumference.

A penile-circumference strain gauge would appear to be a completely satisfactory instrument for detecting complete or almost complete erection. For the assessment of sexual orientation and of minor degrees of sexual arousal in men, penile volume plethysmography is, on present evidence, significantly superior.

A vaginal photoplethysmograph has been introduced to measure sexual arousal in women (Sintchack & Geer, 1975), but its use in assessing sexual orientation has so far not been reported.

Incidence of Homosexuality

The finding of Kinsey, Pomeroy, and Martin (1948) that 37% of white males interviewed in the United States had had at least one experience of homosexual arousal to orgasm has become widely accepted as indicative of the prevalence of such experiences, at least in males in the Western world. Of the women interviewed in a later study (Kinsey, Pomeroy, Martin, & Gebhard, 1953), 20% reported specific homosexual contacts, and 14% reported homosexual arousal to orgasm. The majority of men and women who reported these homosexual experiences had had a much greater number of heterosexual experiences. These figures suggest that a degree of bisexuality is relatively common. No survey of the incidence of bisexual feelings in a sample of the normal population appears to have been conducted.

Approximately one-half of 196 medical students (138 men and 58 women) reported that they were aware of some homosexual attraction, though only 15% of the women and 8% of the men regarded these feelings as being as strong as or stronger than their heterosexual feelings (McConaghy, Armstrong, Birrell, & Buhrich, 1979). Medical students who reported homosexual feelings also reported opposite sex-dimorphic behaviors (see Table 2). Homosexuals in several studies have reported similar opposite sex-dimorphic behaviors. The presence of the association in the students'

Table 2. Spearman Correlations of Present Homosexual Feeling with Sex-Dimorphic Items and Other Variables in Medical Students

	Statistical significance of difference of item in men and women	Men	Women
Until age 7: preferred to play with boys	< .001	.15[a]	− .15
Until age 7: disliked outdoor games	NS[b]	.25	.13
Until age 7: disliked rough-and-tumble games	< .001	.18	.18
Until age 8–13: disliked outdoor sports	= .01	.29	.03
Until age 8–13: disliked contact sports	< .005	.17	.03
Until age 14–18: disliked outdoor sports	< .001	.19	.03
Until age 14–18: disliked contact sports	< .001	.21	− .02
As a child, degree liked to spend time with father	< .05	− .11	− .34
Until age 13: extent involved fighting	NS	− .17	− .01
Age 8–15: tried to look neat and tidy	< .01	.12	− .37
Until age 10: avoided being hurt	< .05	.16	− .06
Degree enjoys music now	< .05	.19	− .04
Degree prefers classical music now	< .001	.27	.24
Until puberty: poor relationship with father	NS	− .04	.22
Until age 16: "crushes" on older person of same sex	NS	.20	.18
Until age 15: degree of homosexual component	NS	.59	.47
Age 6–12: wish to be of opposite sex	< .001	.13	.29
Since age 12: wish to be of opposite sex	< .001	.18	.24
At present: degree feels has mental component of opposite sex	NS	.32	.25
At present: degree feels has behavior traits of opposite sex	< .01	.32	.24
At present: feels has effeminate or butch traits	NS	.35	.34
At present: feels uncertain identity with same sex	NS	.16	.21
At present: strength of identity with opposite sex	NS	.28	.46
Eysenck N Score		.02	.04
Father's age		− .11	.16
Mother's age		− .08	.18

[a] Items underlined are statistically significant ($p < .05$).
[b] NS = not significant.

reports indicated that the reports were valid. It would seem that some degree of bisexual interest as well as behavior is relatively common.

Etiology of Homosexuality

Psychodynamic Theories. Though a variety of views have been expressed by the psychodynamically oriented as to the etiology of homosexuality, these have usually been based on clinical impression. Bieber (1962) provided research data in support of his theory derived from a comparison of 106 male homosexuals and 100 male controls.

Bieber reported that the mothers of homosexuals tended to establish a close-binding, often explicitly seductive, relationship with their sons, producing sexual overstimulation and intense guilt and anxiety about heterosexual behavior, thus promoting compulsive homosexual activity. The fathers of homosexuals were detached, hostile, and rejecting, so that they did not act as male models to protect their sons from demasculinization. Bieber reported that in comparison with controls, in childhood significantly more homosexuals were fearful of physical injury, avoided fights, played predominantly with girls, and avoided participating in competitive sports. That is to say, they showed the characteristic features of the effeminate-boy syndrome. Bieber attributed this behavior to maternal overprotection. Bene (1965a,b) advanced evidence that in both male and female homosexuals, poor relationships with their fathers were more common than undue attachments to their mothers.

Correlations do not necessarily imply causal relations. The evidence now appears convincing that during childhood, male homosexuals are likely to show the effeminacy syndrome and female homosexuals are likely to show tomboyism and greater aggression, which could lead to paternal rejection rather than result from it.

Learning Theories. McGuire, Carlisle, and Young (1965) believed that an initial deviant sexual experience supplied the basis for subsequent fantasies accompanying masturbation, thus increasing the stimulus value of the deviant form of sexual expression and extinguishing normal sexual stimuli through lack of reinforcement. Barlow (1973) pointed out that a number of psychoanalytical and behavior theorists have considered heterosexual fear and avoidance the major determinants of homosexuality. These theories would account for exclusive homosexuality but would require considerable modification to explain the fact that the majority of people with a homosexual component appear to be predominantly heterosexual, as well as the association of homosexuality with opposite sex-dimorphic behavior in childhood.

Biological Theories. Heston and Shields (1968) determined the presence of homosexuality in the male twins on the register of twins admitted to the Maudsley Hospital, London, from 1948 to 1966. Concordance was between 40% and 60% for monozygotic and 14% for dizygotic twins. These figures suggest that genetic factors play a significant role in the etiology of homosexuality.

Hormonal factors have been commonly regarded as contributing to homosexuality. However, no systematic differences have been shown in testosterone or gonadotropin levels between male homosexuals and controls or between homosexuals with different Kinsey ratings (Meyer-Bahlburg, 1977). About a third of the lesbian and transsexual women studied had elevated androgen levels (Meyer-Bahlburg, 1979).

A more plausible biological theory of the etiology of homosexual feelings, is based on the finding that opposite sex-dimorphic behavior and some features of opposite sexual behavior are produced in many mammals if they are exposed while *in utero* (or in some species, shortly after birth) to reduce effective testosterone levels, in the case of males, or increased testosterone levels, in the case of females (Reinisch, 1974).

One of the most definitive forms of sex-dimorphic behavior found in many primates as well as in humans is the increased initiation of and persistence in rough-and-tumble play shown by the male as compared with the female infant (Hutt, 1972). This behavior is under prenatal hormonal influence. The female offspring of pregnant rhesus monkeys injected with male hormone showed in infancy levels of rough-and-tumble play approaching those of males (Reinisch, 1974). Rough-and-tumble play is of particular interest in relation to theories of the etiology of homosexuality, as avoidance of games and sports tends to characterize the childhood of male homosexuals, whereas female homosexuals report a high incidence of "tomboyish" behavior. Evidence that tomboyish behavior in girls is in part under prenatal hormonal control has been provided (Ehrhardt & Baker, 1974).

The most economical theory that unifies these data is that sexual orientation and its associated opposite sex-dimorphic behavior are determined *in utero* by the sex hormonal balance operating at the critical period of brain development for these feelings or behaviors. The hormone balance is determined in part by genetic factors and in part by environmental factors. An example of the latter has been put forward in relation to monozygotic twins discordant for homosexuality. In all cases reported, the homosexual, in comparison with the heterosexual, male twin showed female sex-dimorphic behavior in early childhood. It was suggested that such factors as the transfusion syndrome acting *in utero* resulted in a level of stress on the homosexual twin greater than that acting on the heterosexual twin, thus differentially altering their intrinsic production of sex hormones (McConaghy & Blaszczynski, 1980; Zuger, 1976).

This etiological theory is of considerable significance in relation the treatment of homosexuality. If hormonal factors acting at a critical period of brain development are responsible for an individual's balance of heterosexual and homosexual feelings, it is unlikely that this balance can later be altered by psychological treatment, whether of a dynamic or a behavioral nature. In this case, treatment would be aimed at helping people achieve their aims in relation to how they wish to express their feelings behaviorally, rather than at altering their feelings.

Homosexual Adjusment and Lifestyles

Hooker (1957) published data that, as she pointed out, questioned the then-current psychiatric and psychological opinion that homosexual behavior was a symptom of severe emotional disorder.

She believed that that clinical opinion concerning homosexuality was based on experience with homosexuals seeking help or found in mental hospitals or prisons. To obtain a sample of overt homosexuals who could have an average adjustment, she investigated 30 relatively exclusive homosexuals from among members of the Mattachine Society and their friends. They were matched for age, education, and IQ with exclusively heterosexual men from community organizations. Relying mainly on projective tests, Hooker cautiously concluded that homosexuality may represent a severe form of maladjustment to society in the sexual sector of behavior, but this need not mean that the homosexual is severely maladjusted in other sectors of his behavior.

Subsequently, a number of studies have compared groups of nonpatient homosexuals with heterosexuals matched on various variables, by the use of clinical impression or a variety of tests to judge the subjects' adjustment.

In many studies of female homosexuals, no significant differences in personality adjustment were found in comparison with hetero-

sexual controls (Hopkins, 1969; Wilson & Greene, 1971). Male homosexuals were generally more psychiatrically disturbed than heterosexual controls on some measures, reporting higher levels of tension, depression, or suicidal behavior; obtaining higher neuroticism scores; or being more likely to seek psychiatric treatment (Bell & Weinberg, 1978; Saghir & Robins, 1973).

Homosexuals in these studies cannot be considered representative of all homosexuals in the community. Indeed, they cannot be considered representative of a particular subgroup, as different exclusion criteria were employed in different studies. Hooker (1957) excluded subjects with a history of considerable disturbance or of heterosexual experience. Saghir and Robins excluded subjects who were nonwhite or who had been hospitalized for psychiatric reasons, but not if they had had heterosexual experience. Of their male homosexuals, 59% gave a history of a heterosexual romantic attachment; 60%, of sexual arousal in heterosexual physical contact; 48% of heterosexual intercourse (10% currently); and 53% of a sustained heterosexual relationship. Comparable incidence of these behaviors in the female homosexuals were 49%, 70%, 79%, (9%); and 44% respectively.

Clearly, such research studies cannot be used to determine whether homosexuality has a specific association with personality disorder or emotional maladjustment. Nevertheless, the fact that a significant percentage of homosexuals in these studies showed no evidence of either has doubtless been a crucial determinant of the view held currently by many psychiatrists and psychologists that homosexuality is not necessarily associated with significant personality or social maladjustment.

The most consistent finding of studies investigating the sexual lifestyles of heterosexuals and homosexuals is that homosexual males have sexual relationships with a much greater number of partners, and that the relationships of male and female homosexuals with one partner are significantly briefer than those of heterosexuals (Saghir & Robins, 1973; Schaefer, 1977). Regular, casual infidelity was characteristic of the majority of homosexual males who reported prolonged homosexual relationships. Humphreys (1970) provided evidence that a percentage of heterosexually married men who would be unlikely to acknowledge their homosexuality sought male partners in public lavatories.

Given the marked divergence of aspects of the male homosexual's experience from the stereotypically idealized heterosexual love relationship with which he is constantly socially confronted, it is understandable that he experiences shame and guilt commonly and for a much longer period of his life than does the female homosexual (Saghir & Robins, 1973). This factor, combined with the much stronger social and legal sanctions against male as opposed to female homosexuality, may explain why the subjects seeking treatment for problems related to inability to accept their homosexuality are almost invariably male.

Treatment in Homosexuality

About two decades ago, a number of workers reported that it was possible, with treatment, to change homosexuals into heterosexuals (Bieber, 1962; Freund, 1960; Woodward, 1956). The interest in reorienting homosexuals to heterosexuality persisted throughout the 1960s. But with the rise of homosexual liberation movements and the greater acceptance by many therapists of homosexuality as an acceptable alternative lifestyle, interest in this particular goal of treatment diminished. At the same time, new goals developed as it became clearer what treatments could accomplish and as homosexuals continued to present for help with the difficulties that they encountered in maintaining or changing particular patterns of behavior that might be homosexual, heterosexual, or bisexual.

Behavioral Treatment Aimed at Reorienting Homosexuals. Freund (1960) treated 67 male subjects with 24 daily administrations of an emetic mixture of emetine and apomorphine, and while its effects lasted, the subjects were shown slides of clothed and nude men. Subsequently, the subjects were given 10 mg of testosterone propionate and 7 hr later were shown films of nude or seminude women. Following this treatment, 10 patients (15%) made a heterosexual adaptation lasting weeks or months and 12 (18%), made such an adaptation

lasting several years. Freund decided that the treatment acted by altering the patients' motivations or cognitions, but subsequent workers who used aversive therapy in homosexuality believed that it acted by conditioning. They mainly used electric shock delivered according to a variety of conditioning paradigms. In the earlier studies, it was suggested that an occasional patient showed some degree of aversive response to homosexual stimuli following treatment (Thorpe, Schmidt, & Castell, 1963). However, in later studies with larger patient numbers, there was no report of this response, though following the treatment, the patients reduced or ceased homosexual behavior (Schmidt, Castell, & Brown, 1965; Solyom & Miller, 1965). The latter workers stated that the change following the treatment related to the fact that the patients found their homosexual desires easier to control.

Despite the lack of conditioned aversion responses in patients showing a therapeutic response to aversive therapy, workers continued to believe it acted by conditoning. On the basis of this belief, MacCulloch and Feldman (1967) developed an elaborate form of anticipatory avoidance conditioning, in which the patients could on some occasions avoid shock by an immediate response of rejecting a slide of a nude male; on other occasions, could avoid shock only by making this response after a delay; and on other occasions, could not avoid shock at all. Forty-one male and two female homosexual patients recieved from 5 to 38 sessions of treatment, each lasting 20–25 min, during which time the slide of a person of the same sex was presented on about 24 occasions. The treatment was continued until either a change of interest occurred or it became clear that no change was likely. At the 12-months follow-up the major response reported was, in 20 subjects, a loss of homosexual interest and, in 6, a marked reduction of such interest. No aversive responses to homosexual stimuli were reported.

Aversive Therapies Do Not Act by Conditioning. It was not until 1969 that the significance of this absence of conditioned responses following aversive therapy was stressed. Bancroft (1969), reporting the treatment of 10 male homosexuals with aversive electric shock, pointed out that when evidence of conditioned anxiety did appear following aversive therapy, it was usually short-lived. He thought that the effects of the therapy would be understood not in terms of conditioning and learning but in terms of changing attitudes. McConaghy (1969) treated male homosexuals with electrical aversion-relief or apomorphine aversive therapy. He commented; "The conditioned response to a stimulus reinforced with a painful electric shock to the hand is limb withdrawal and anxiety; to a stimulus reinforced with apomorphine is nausea. In the present investigation, patients after treatment did not report such responses to phrases associated with homosexuality or to photographs of attractive males" (p. 729).

Further evidence that aversive therapy does not act by conditioning was provided by a series of controlled studies (Feldman & MacCulloch, 1971; McConaghy, 1970; McConaghy & Barr, 1973, McConaghy, Proctor, & Barr, 1972), which demonstrated that despite the conditioning paradigm used, the results of therapy were similar. The strength and the resistance to extinction of a conditioned response are determined by many variables, including the strength of the conditioned and unconditioned stimuli, the sensory modalities in which they are administered, the number of administrations, and the time interval between administrations (Pavlov, 1927). If aversive therapies were administered according to conditioning procedures that varied markedly on these variables, the resulting conditioned responses would vary markedly in strength and resistance to extinction. If the therapeutic response were dependent on conditioning, it should vary similarly.

In a study by McConaghy, (1969, 1970), 40 homosexual males were randomly assigned, 20 to receive aversion relief and 20 to receive apomorphine aversion. With aversion relief, the "conditioned stimuli" were phrases evocative of homosexual feelings. The "unconditioned stimuli" were unpleasant levels of electric shock to the fingertips. A total of 1,050 pairings of phrase and shock were presented to each patient in 15 sessions of treatment over five days. With apomorphine aversion, the "conditioned stimuli" were photographic slides of nude males, and the "unconditioned stim-

uli" were injections of apomorphine, 28 pairings of slides and apomorphine were administered to each patient in 28 sessions of treatment over five days. Both treatments produced equivalent responses. At one-year follow-up, about half the patients treated with either treatment reported a reduction of homosexual and an increase of heterosexual feelings. About a quarter ceased and a quarter reduced the frequency of homosexual behavior. A quarter increased the frequency of heterosexual intercourse, although only one commenced heterosexual intercourse without having experienced it prior to the treatment.

Feldman and MacCulloch (1971) randomly allocated 28 male and 2 female homosexuals to three groups, 2 to receive aversive therapies and 1 to receive psychotherapy. With the two aversive therapies, unpleasant levels of shock followed the presentation of slides of nudes of the same sex. One therapy utilized a simple classical-conditioning paradigm, the other the elaborate anticipatory-avoidance procedure developed by Feldman and MacCulloch with the expectation that it would be particularly effective as a conditioning technique. In their study, it proved no more effective than simple classical conditioning.

McConaghy *et al.* (1972) compared anticipatory avoidance with apomorphine aversion in the treatment of a further 40 male homosexuals. Again, there was no difference in outcome between treatments in terms of the number of subjects reporting a reduction in homosexual or an increase in heterosexual feelings and behavior. The results in these respects were similar to those found in the previous study by McConaghy (1969, 1970).

In view of the similar therapeutic response to these different "conditioning" techniques, it would appear that aversive therapies in homosexuality do not act by conditioning.

Do Aversive Therapies Convert Homosexuals into Heterosexuals? Freund (1960) reported that following treatment, 33% of male homosexuals showed a shift to heterosexual behavior, 18% maintaining this shift for many years. At the same time, Freund believed that there was no change in the degree of erotic attraction that these men experienced toward men and women. That is to say, behaviorally they became more heterosexual—in some cases, exclusively so—but their sexual interest in men as specific objects of attraction remained unchanged. Freund attributed the fact that some treated subjects reduced or ceased homosexual relations to their having learned to have heterosexual intercourse without a specific erotic attraction to women, so that their need for homosexual relations was reduced.

This conclusion about the effects of aversive therapy appears to be at variance with the results reported by subsequent workers. Solyom and Miller (1965) reported that following a form of aversion relief, patients found their homosexual desires easier to control, though they did not necessarily show sexual interest in women. This finding is compatible with the reviewer's experience (McConaghy, 1970; 1975).

Birk, Huddleston, Miller, and Cohler (1971) randomly allocated 8 of 16 male homosexuals to avoidance conditioning, the other 8 receiving a control treatment. Following treatment, five of the patients receiving avoidance conditioning reported the absence or a marked diminution of homosexual urges, feelings, and behavior. None of the patients receiving the control procedure reported this response. There was no consistent tendency for measures of heterosexual behavior to increase more in the group treated with avoidance, nor was there a significant difference in the Kinsey ratings of the two groups of subjects following treatment.

McConaghy (1970) provided evidence that there was no increase in subjects' heterosexual arousal as measured by penile plethysmography following aversive therapy. In view of this failure, an attempt was made to produce such arousal by positive conditioning (McConaghy, 1975). In this study, 31 homosexual males were randomly allocated to receive positive or aversive classical conditioning. With positive conditioning, the patients were shown slides of women for 10 sec followed also for 10 sec by sexually arousing slides of men or of couples in heterosexual physical relations. The patients' penile volume responses were recorded throughout both procedures. No penile response conditioning occurred to the slides of females in the positive conditioning procedure, though unconditioned penile-volume increases to the sexually arousing slides persisted throughout the treatment.

Following the treatment, significantly more subjects who received the aversive treatment, as compared with positive conditioning, reported a reduction in homosexual feelings and behavior. It was concluded that in contrast to positive conditioning, the aversive procedure produced a specific reduction of homosexual feelings and behavior. Small but statistically significant decrements in penile volume increases to pictures of men and in volume decreases to pictures of women followed both procedures. If these penile volume changes were a specific effect of the treatment related to reduction of homosexual feelings and behavior, they should have been greater following the aversive, as compared with the positive conditioning, procedure in this study, since the treatment response was significantly greater following the aversive procedure. As the penile changes following the aversive and positive conditioning procedures were comparable, it was concluded that they were nonspecific and unrelated to the treatment effect.

Hence, the degree to which homosexual subjects were sexually aroused by films of the male body as compared to the female body (as measured by penile plethysmography) was the same whether the subjects were treated by an effective aversive therapy or an ineffective placebo therapy, which cannot have altered their sexual orientation. Penile plethysmography, as used in these studies, remained a valid measure of sexual orientation following aversive therapy in that it differentiated treated homosexual subjects from treated heterosexual subjects with other sexual anomalies, such as exhibitionism or voyeurism (McConaghy, 1975). Hence, it can be concluded that aversive therapy does not change that aspect of subjects' sexual orientation that is determined by the degree of their genital arousal to the male and the female body.

Is Compulsive Sexuality Largely Independent of Primary Sexual Drive? Following aversive therapy for homosexuality, all studies have reported a diminution in homosexual feelings and behavior in a significant number of patients treated, many of whom did not increase heterosexual behavior. That these changes occurred without alteration in genital arousal to the male and female body shape is compatible with the hypothesis that aversive therapy does not reduce sexual behavior by weakening the primary sexual drive that originally motivated the behavior. It inhibits the state of heightened arousal produced when a habitual act is not completed. It was suggested (McConaghy, 1980) that a neurophysiological behavior-completion mechanism is established in the nervous system when an act becomes habitual, and that it is this behavior completion mechanism that assumes responsibility for motivating the completion of the habitual act, rather than the primary drive that originally motivated the act. If the act is interrupted prior to completion, the behavior completion mechanism activates the arousal system. The resulting high arousal is experienced by the subject as tension or anxiety and is sufficiently aversive to encourage him or her to complete the act, even if he or she does not wish to do so.

In the case of the male homosexual subject who wishes not to cruise a beat, when he is in the neighborhood of one he has cruised many times previously, the stimulus of his physical surroundings will lead to activation of a behavior completion mechanism. The subject will experience tension and excitement, which will tend to encourage him to cruise the beat against his will. This tension will be the harder to resist, as it is mixed with the pleasurable anticipatory components of the excitement he has previously experienced with sexual gratification while cruising the beat.

Bergin (1969) advanced a theory related to this concept of a behavior completion mechanism based on observations of a homosexual male. He thought that there seemed to be a spiraling sequence of stimuli and reactions, which, as they mounted in intensity, became impossible to control. He described the phenomenon as an impulse–response chain, analogous to stimulus–response chains in learning.

On the basis of this analysis, Bergin treated the patient with a self-regulation technique. The patient was instructed to pay close attention to enviromental situations and to personal reactions that might set off the undesired chain of events. Techniques for interrupting responses to stimuli early in the chains were practiced in imagination by the patient in treatment sessions. These included immediately switching to unrelated thoughts or activities, such as reading or walking. Eventually, the patient became totally unresponsive to the stimuli that had previously initiated the chains.

Aversive therapy acts not by reducing primary homosexual drive, but by reducing the arousal produced by failure to complete habitual sexual acts. This hypothesis accounts for the otherwise discrepant findings that aversive therapy, in comparison with placebo treatment, does not alter the patients' penile arousal to pictures of males, yet significantly reduces their urges to carry out homosexual behavior. It also accounts for the otherwise surprising evidence that systematic desensitization seems at least as effective as aversive therapy in increasing the ability of homosexuals to control their sexual behavior, without necessarily increasing heterosexual behavior.

Desensitization in Homosexuality. Bancroft (1970) compared systematic desensitization with aversive therapy, allocating 15 male patients to receive each therapy, and reported the response of the 23 subjects who completed treatment. Both therapies were administered in 30 sessions of one hour's duration, usually twice a week. The aversive therapy used was the contingent procedure introduced by Bancroft (1969). The patients received unpleasant levels of electric shock to the arm when they showed a penile diameter increase of about .3 mm to pictures of men or to homosexual fantasies. The selection of this criterion seems open to criticism, as Bancroft (1971) reported data indicating that increases in penile diameter of less than .4 mm have little validity as measures of subjects' sexual interest.

The desensitization procedure employed in Bancroft's study was based on Wolpe's method (1958). The aim was to reduce the patient's postulated fear of heterosexual approach behavior culminating in intercourse. Significant reduction in homosexual behavior followed treatment in both groups, but there was virtually no difference between the response of the group treated with the aversive procedure and that treated with desensitization. A nonsignificant increase in heterosexual behavior occurred in both groups.

Systematic desensitization was used in this study to reduce anxiety about heterosexual behavior. However, the significant change following both this treatment and the aversive procedure was not an increase in heterosexual behavior, but a decrease in homosexual behavior.

James (1978) randomly allocated 40 male homosexuals, 20 to receive anticipatory avoidance therapy and 20 to receive desensitization and erotic arousal. All 40 patients were given, in addition, a form of social skills training. Improvement at two years following treatment was rated on a scale combining reduction in homosexual drive and outlets and ability to form heterosexual relationships. The patients showed a significantly better response to desensitization and arousal than to anticipatory avoidance.

Masters and Johnson (1979), in an uncontrolled study using a male and a female therapist, treated 54 male and 13 female homosexuals seeking reorientation to heterosexuality. All patients were required to have a partner of the opposite sex to be accepted for treatment. Treatment consisted of counseling and desensitization, with sensate focusing to heterosexual situations. Masters and Johnson concluded that both the male and the female patients lost to follow-up would have responded as well as did those with whom contact was maintained, a very dubious assumption. It would mean that at the five-year follow-up, 67% of the men and 60% of the women responded to treatment. It is not clear whether Masters and Johnson thought that patients reoriented to heterosexuality showed a complete absence of homosexual feeling.

James (1978) reported that 5 of 20 patients treated with desensitization and erotic arousal claimed complete absence of homosexual fantasies, interest, and behavior. Only 1 of 20 patients treated with anticipatory avoidance claimed this degree of response. MacCulloch and Feldman (1967) reported that 20 of 43 patients treated with anticipatory avoidance claimed no homosexual practice or fantasy. In terms of loss of homosexual feeling, James's results, even with desensitization and erotic arousal, appear inferior to those of Mac-

Culloch and Feldman with anticipatory avoidance. James was not alone in her failure to replicate MacCulloch and Feldman's (1967) finding that one-third to one-half of treated patients reported loss of homosexual feelings. Birk *et al.* (1971) found that only 1 of 8, McConaghy *et al.* (1972) none of 20, and McConaghy and Barr (1973) 1 of 15 patients reported this response to anticipatory avoidance. The conclusion of James, that the patients' report of very good results in her study and those of MacCulloch and Feldman were not attributable to the specific effects of treatment but to the therapists' enthusiasm, seems possibly correct.

The failure of Feldman and MacCulloch, James, and Masters and Johnson to use a physiological measure of sexual orientation to assess patients' response to treatment is unfortunate, as their results were better than those obtained with behavior therapies (including anticipatory avoidance and systematic desensitization) by other workers in the treatment of a series of homosexual subjects (Bancroft, 1969; Birk *et al.* 1971; Freund, 1960; McConaghy, 1969; McConaghy & Barr, 1973; McConaghy *et al.*, 1972). It would be of the greatest importance to know whether a reasonable percentage of patients reporting the loss of all homosexual feeling in the studies of Feldman and MacCulloch and of James showed penile volume responses equivalent to those of the majority of "normal" male volunteers.

Reduction in homosexual urges has invariably been reported following aversive therapy. The studies of Bancroft (1970) and James (1978) suggest that the nonaversive technique of desensitization (with or without erotic arousal) results in a subjective awareness of reduction in homosexual interest at least equivalent to that following aversive therapy. It does not seem that such reduction is secondary to a reduction in the fear of heterosexuality.

An alternative explanation of how desensitization could reduce homosexual feelings and behavior to the same extent as does aversive therapy is based on the theory advanced in relation to the mode of action of aversive therapy. This theory postulates that the compulsive drive to carry out homosexual behavior is due to heightened arousal. A behavior completion mechanism is activated when subjects are exposed to stimuli that preceded homosexual behavior in the past. While the subjects fail to continue homosexual behavior to completion, the behavior completion mechanism leads to their experiencing a state of somewhat aversive arousal mixed with pleasurable anticipation. Systematic desensitization involves the patients in regular sessions of relaxation to reduce arousal, with the expectation that their general level of arousal will be lowered. This reaction would result in homosexual patients being less aroused when they fail to complete homosexual behavior, so that the drive to carry out that behavior is reduced following treatment. If this theory is correct, both aversive therapy and systematic desensitization reduce compulsive homosexual drive by diminishing the associated level of arousal. Aversive therapy does so by exerting an inhibitory effect on the arousal system, and systematic desensitization does so by the experience of a series of episodes of relaxation.

Covert Sensitization: Combined Aversive Therapy and Imaginal Desensitization. Cautela (1967) treated three male homosexuals with covert sensitization. Each patient, while relaxed, visualized being in a room with an attractive nude man. The patient visualized approaching the man, noticing he was covered in scabs and gave off a terrible stench, becoming nauseated, and vomiting over his surroundings. The patient then visualized turning away and starting to feel better. Two of the three homosexuals treated ceased homosexual behavior. The third, who was not overtly homosexual, experienced a great reduction in homosexual fantasies.

Barlow, Agras, Leitenberg, Callahan, and Moore (1972) used a single-subject design to compare covert sensitization with relaxation and the visualization of deviant images only, in the treatment of four homosexuals. Their total reliance on the patients' penile-circumference changes to pictures of males as a measure of response was unfortunate, as the majority of the penile changes were small and did not approach full erection. The lack of validity of such circumference changes as measures of sexual arousal was previously pointed out. Barlow and his colleagues commented that the patients reported reduction in homosexual

urges during treatment with relaxation and visualizing deviant images only, but the authors discounted this improvement as being discrepant with the objective penile-circumference measures.

McConaghy, Armstrong, and Blaszczynski (1981) randomly allocated 20 homosexual men, 10 to aversive therapy, and 10 to covert sensitization. The aversive therapy was the classical conditioning paradigm used in earlier studies (McConaghy & Barr, 1973); covert sensitization was administered as Cautela (1967) described. Both treatments were administered in 14 sessions over five days. The patients' responses, both at one-month and one-year follow-up, were similar to those following aversive therapy in the studies of McConaghy and his colleagues.

The technique of covert sensitization consists of imaginal desensitization with the addition of aversive imagery. Barlow *et al.* (1972) concluded that this addition resulted in an increased therapeutic effect over that of imaginal desensitization alone, but their evidence was based on the patients' penile-circumference responses, not changes in their feelings or behavior.

Increasing Heterosexuality in Homosexuals. Thorpe *et al.* (1963) introduced a technique, later termed *orgasmic reconditioning*, aimed at increasing heterosexual arousal in a homosexual. Thorpe and his colleagues initially instructed the patient to masturbate and to report when orgasm was being reached. He was then shown a picture of an attractive, scantily dressed woman until he reported he had ejaculated. His masturbatory fantasy remained entirely homosexual, and sessions of aversive therapy were alternated with the reconditioning procedure. Following treatment, although the patient had "occasional homosexual patterns of behavior" (presumably homosexual relations), he commenced masturbating to female pictures and fantasies.

Conrad and Wincze (1976) evaluated orgasmic reconditioning in the treatment of four homosexuals, using a single-subject design. The authors attached importance to the failure of the patients' reported improvement, their penile circumference measures, and their written records of sexual feelings to change in relation to the periods of withdrawal and reintroduction of active treatment. They implied that the patients may have reported changes they did not feel and that both the orgasmic reconditioning and the aversive treatments were unsuccessful. The failure of a relationship to emerge between the treatment effects and the cessation and reintroduction of treatment does not indicate that real treatment effects did not occur. It does indicate that if such effects occurred, they persisted despite the withdrawal of treatment, an eventuality that should delight rather than disappoint therapists.

The use of single-subject designs to evaluate therapeutic results largely reflects adherence to the nonbiological operant-learning-theory model of the mode of action of behavior therapies. With this model, continued reinforcement is required for the effects of therapies to persist. That is to say, this model ignores the possibility that stimulus patterns or treatments could modify the activity of central nervous processes in a manner that would persist for long periods of time following the cessation of the stimulus patterns. Such a permanent modification of nervous system activity was demonstrated repeatedly by Pavlov (1927) and is a basic principle of classical conditioning theory. If such permanent modification is accepted as occurring, the failure of a therapeutic effect to disappear when the therapeutic contingency is removed does not necessarily reflect the failure of the treatment. Clinicians preferentially seek treatments the effects of which persist when the treatment is ceased. Yet it is precisely such treatments that would be judged ineffective if evaluated by the single-subject design as commonly used. The study by Conrad and Wincze (1976) would seem to be best regarded as an uncontrolled study in which three patients reported increased heterosexual and decreased homosexual feelings with orgasmic reconditioning and a fourth did not but subsequently showed this response to aversive therapy.

Barlow, Agras, Abel, Blanchard, and Young (1975) provided feedback to three patients of the amount of their penile circumference increases to slides of women. Barlow and his colleagues used a single-subject design and reported that erectile response following the use of feedback did not weaken on withdrawal of feedback. They concluded that feedback was not responsible for the observed gains. This conclusion cannot be accepted, as feedback may have produced a persistent change not dependent on continued treatment. The study, like that of Conrad and Wincze (1976), is equivalent to an uncontrolled clinical trial reporting positive findings.

Herman, Barlow, and Agras (1974b), using a single-subject design, concluded that homosexual subjects showed increased penile circumference responses to pictures of women when repeatedly exposed to a 10-min movie of a nude, seductive woman assuming various sexual poses. Because of the failure to introduce and withdraw the treatment according to a predefined schedule, it cannot be accepted that the treatment did produce the response. This study must also be regarded as an uncontrolled report of positive findings.

The presentation of heterosexual and homosexual stimuli in temporal association in a variety of paradigms has been used in several studies with the aim of increasing heterosexual arousal in male homosexuals. Barlow and Agras (1973) reported the treatment of three patients with a fading procedure. Each patient was treated in a single-subject design. A control procedure, expected to be ineffective, was introduced between the initial and the final stages of the fading treatment. In the fading procedure, the slide of a male to which the patient showed a large penile response was projected for him to view. The illumination of the slide was decreased, and that of a slide of a female was increased, contingent on the patient's attaining 75% of a full erection as measured by penile circumference change. The procedure lasted 2 min and was repeated six times in a treatment session. The degree of generalization of the patient's response was tested the morning following treatment sessions. Penile circumference changes were measured while he viewed three slides of men and three of women, each for 2 min.

This study is, in the reviewer's opinion, a further example of the undue freedom provided by the single-subject design. A large number of observations were made on each subject. Some, possibly by chance, conformed to prediction; they were regarded as supporting the hypothesis. Others did not conform to the prediction. In view of the modifications in procedure introduced when expected penile circumference changes failed to take place during the control procedures, the reviewer is unconvinced that this study demonstrated that the penile changes were under the control of the contingency that was varied. An important observation reported in the study was that homosexuals can develop penile circumference increases up to 80% of full erection to pictures of women and be unaware of any heterosexual urges or fantasies.

McGrady (1973) reported the treatment of a homosexual by forward fading. This was the reverse of the treatment procedure used by Barlow and Agras (1973). McGrady showed the patient a female image, which was faded into a male image over 5 min. Meanwhile, the patient's penile circumference changes were monitored. One week following the completion of treatment, the patient showed a full erection to slides of nude females. However, when shown 10 slides of males and females, he reported no increased arousal to those of females and slightly more to those of males, compared with his response prior to treatment. The patient engaged in no overt heterosexual activity and had two homosexual experiences during treatment. He reported several heterosexual fantasies, most accompanying masturbation.

This study conforms with those of Barlow and Agras (1973) and Herman et al. (1974b) in demonstrating that homosexual subjects can show marked penile circumference increases to pictures of women following their repeatedly viewing such pictures, with or without the pictures being temporally associated with pictures of men. It also demonstrates that penile increases occurring in these conditions may not be associated with the development of sexual attraction to the female body shape.

Herman, Barlow, and Agras (1974a) reported the treatment of three homosexuals by a classical conditioning procedure. The patients were shown pictures of women for 1 min, followed by pictures of men or a film with homosexual content. Only the first of the three patients responded to the classical conditioning procedure without its being repeatedly modified on a *post hoc* basis. The third patient

failed to respond even to repeated modifications. Hence, only the first patient's responses tested the unmodified procedure, and only the strongly committed could conclude that his responses demonstrated that the control conditions isolated the critical variable.

The lack of relationship between the changes in the outcome measures and the introduction and cessation of the contingency varied seems no less in this study than in those of Conrad and Wincze (1976) and Barlow et al. (1975). It indicates the degree of arbitrariness allowed by single subject designs. The authors of some studies decided that the contingency varied was not responsible for the outcome, while the authors of the other studies decided that it was. A further problem with these single-subject studies is that such a large number of data are provided concerning the response of each subject that the reader, faced with the daunting task of examining them in detail, is likely to accept the authors' conclusion, whether it is positive or negative.

In this reviewer's opinion, all the single-subject studies discussed neither establish nor refute the possibility that the contingencies varied in them were responsible for the outcomes. They can be considered no more than uncontrolled reports of positive responses.

McConaghy (1975) compared a classical conditioning technique aimed at increasing heterosexual arousal, with aversive therapy. It was concluded that the conditioning procedure had no specific effect. Techniques for increasing heterosexual arousal in homosexuals have mainly concentrated on encouraging subjects to be either relaxed or sexually aroused in the presence of heterosexual stimuli. Relaxation would remove fears of heterosexuality, allowing the subjects' postulated inherent heterosexual feelings to express themselves. Sexual arousal in the presence of heterosexual stimuli would lead, by conditioning, to the subjects experiencing sexual arousal to heterosexual stimuli. If either procedure were effective, homosexuals who have had extensive experience of heterosexual intercourse should have become more heterosexual in orientation than those who lack such experience. This was not the case in 181 male subjects who sought behavioral treatment for homosexuality, when penile volume responses were used as a measure of sexual orientation (McConaghy, 1978). However, a number of these subjects who showed minimal evidence of heterosexual arousal on this measure had maintained a heterosexual marital relationship, on the average for over seven years. Also, they wished to continue to do so and therefore sought help to reduce their homosexual behavior. Many of these subjects felt that they had a very satisfying relationship with their wives, with whom they frequently reported they were in love. Many reported that they were sexually aroused by fantasies of their wives, though they felt no sexual attraction to other women, a fact suggesting that sexual arousal can be conditioned to a member of the nonpreferred sex but does not generalize to other members of that sex. Of the homosexuals investigated by Saghir and Robins (1973), 53% of the males and 44% of the females gave a history of a sustained heterosexual relationship. It is thus apparent that many homosexuals, including those males who show minimal evidence of heterosexuality as measured by penile volume responses, are able to establish and maintain a heterosexual relationship without treatment.

Male homosexuals who seek treatment to establish a heterosexual relationship usually do so because they lack social skills or are afraid that their female partner will immediately expect them to be active sexually. In addition, they fear that they will be impotent. Often they believe that this impotence will reveal that they are homosexual. Training in social and dating skills, as well as assertiveness, may be helpful, but in this reviewer's experience, often does not lead to these patients' finding a female partner. This finding is consistent with the findings of James (1978): Male homosexuals received, in addition to anticipatory avoidance, social skills training, sex education, and training in dating behavior and the interpretation of females' nonverbal communication. Their response to treatment was not as good in terms of reduction in homosexual outlets and ability to develop heterosexual relationships as was the response of subjects to anticipatory avoidance only, in a previous study (James, Orwin, & Turner, 1977). Of the

20 patients in James's study who received this training, as well as anticipatory avoidance, 2 at most had experienced successful heterosexual intercourse at two-year follow-up.

This reviewer has obtained better results by the referral of motivated patients to a surrogate, who can help these patients to obtain both dating and relationship skills and, by desensitization to sexual situations, confidence that they can perform successfully in heterosexual relationships.

Women homosexuals rarely seek treatment to establish heterosexual relationships, one reason presumably being that they do not need to be sexually aroused to perform sexually to the apparent satisfaction of their male partners. About 80% of the homosexual women in the studies of Saghir and Robins (1973) and of Bell and Weinberg (1978) had experienced heterosexual intercourse. Homosexual women who seek treatment to improve heterosexual functioning most commonly do so because they experience aversion, anxiety, or lack of pleasure in intercourse. They are usually treated with desensitization—in reality, if they have a male partner, or in imagination, if they have not. These treatments have not been evaluated in controlled studies.

Clinical Considerations Regarding the Reorientation of Homosexuals. Patients who seek treatment to make a more heterosexual adjustment while in a crisis situation, such as a depression following the breakup of a homosexual relationship, should be treated for their emotional disturbance. Any decision about treatment in relation to their sexual orientation should be postponed until they have returned to their normal emotional state. Equally, patients who are ambivalent about altering their sexual adjustment will usually accept, without opposition, counseling to help resolve this ambivalence without reaching any immediate decision about ultimate treatment aims.

This reviewer's practice is to inform homosexuals seeking to make a more heterosexual adjustment that there is no treatment that will alter their basic sexual orientation. There are treatments to help them reduce aspects of their homosexual behavior and to increase aspects of their heterosexual behavior. Following the former treatment they are still likely to feel the same initial physical attraction to the same-sexed people whom they encounter, though, if in the past they remained preoccupied with fantasies following a strong attraction, these are likely to disappear. The main effect of treatment will be enable them to stop sexual behaviors, such as cruising, if before treatment they wished to stop these behaviors but found themselves driven to complete them. Equally, there is no treatment to increase their physical feelings of sexual attraction to members of the opposite sex. If they have wished to attempt heterosexual intercourse but have avoided it for fear of failure, they can be helped to overcome this fear and to determine to what extent they would be able to obtain satisfaction in a heterosexual relationship.

As the present evidence indicates that all treatments aimed at reducing compulsive drive in both sexual and nonsexual behaviors are equally effective, the one that seems least likely to reduce the patient's self-esteem would seem to be the treatment of choice. In this reviewer's experience, this treatment is imaginal desensitization. Most patients find that it is easiest to have the treatment administered over one week. Patients receive three sessions of treatment a day for five days, each session lasting about 20 min. In the initial session, they are briefly trained in physical relaxation, by requesting them to tense and relax muscle groups. After about 5 min, they are asked to signal when they feel relaxed. Presumably the expectation that they should be relaxed is sufficiently great that they almost invariably signal that they are. They are then asked to visualize being in a situation where they would carry out the behavior they are trying to control and to signal when they are visualizing this and feel relaxed. They then visualize losing interest in completing the behavior, and leaving the situation before doing so, signaling when they are visualizing this and remaining relaxed. The same three or four such situations are presented in each treatment session. No attempt is made to establish a hierarchy in presenting these scenes.

At one-month follow-up, about 70% of patients report a significant reduction in the compulsive drive to carry out the behavior. A mi-

nority of those who do not report this response and wish to have a second course of therapy show a similar response to an alternative treatment, such as aversive therapy. But usually this response is transient. However, those patients who do report an initial definite response but relapse after some months or years usually show a more permanent response to a repetition of the original treatment.

Male patients who wish to establish a heterosexual relationship but are inhibited by anxiety are best treated by referral to a female surrogate, who can train them in dating and communication skills as well as desensitizing them to sexual intimacy culminating in intercourse. If a surrogate is not available, training in the skills necessary for the patient to form an emotional relationship with a woman can be attempted. The patient having sexual difficulties with a woman partner can be counseled in the technique for desensitization to sexual involvement. As previously discussed, male patients without a female partner rarely seem to obtain sufficient ability to establish a relationship with a woman in which they can become desensitized to sexual situations. The difficulty for which female patients seek help is rarely in establishing a relationship but is usually in being unable to enjoy heterosexual intercourse because of anxiety. If they have a male partner, they can be counseled in the technique of desensitization to situations of increasing physical intimacy. But if they are temporarily without a partner, they commonly respond to desensitization in imagination.

Improvement of Homosexual Functioning. Patients who have accepted their homosexuality may seek treatment for difficulties with particular sexual behaviors. Little has been published concerning the treatment of this group of patients. The largest series was reported by Masters and Johnson (1979). It consisted of 56 male and 25 female couples, of whom 57 men and 27 women were identified as having sexual dysfunction. The men all suffered primary or secondary impotence, and 4 had sexual aversion in addition. All the woman were anorgasmic, and 6 also had sexual aversion. Treatment was by counseling and desensitization to situations of increasing sexual intimacy. All but 4 of the 57 impotent males and 2 of the anorgasmic women responded to treatment. At five-year follow-up, 2 men and 1 woman had relapsed, and 3 men and 1 woman were not available for assessment.

Exhibitionism

Exhibitionism as a sexual deviation occurs exclusively in men. These men obtain a high level of excitement by exposing their penis to a woman, usually a stranger, in a public place. Exhibitionism is one of the commoner deviations leading to criminal convictions in European cultures (Rooth, 1973). Recidivism tends to be greater with exhibitionism than with other sexual offenses (Murphy, Abel, & Becker, 1980).

Etiology

The exhibitionist, as depicted in the clinical literature, is a passive, shy, dependent, and inhibited individual who lacks "male assertiveness," has difficulty expressing anger, and may be inadequate in heterosocial and heterosexual skills or may have various sexual dysfunctions (Langevin, Paitich, Ramsay, Anderson, Kamrad, Pope, Geller, Pearl, & Newman, 1979). Langevin *et al.* tested various etiological theories advanced in the literature by comparing exhibitionists presenting at a forensic institute with normals solicited by press advertisement. These workers concluded that the dating and heterosexual experience of exhibitionists were within normal range and suggested that exhibitionism may be basically a nonsexual act, pointing out that almost half their subjects exposed without apparent genital gratification.

The concept that exhibitionism is a nonsexual act is compatible with the theory that compulsive sexual behaviors for which subjects seek treatment may have been established under the influence of a sexual drive but were subsequently maintained by behavior completion mechanisms.

Kolarsky and Madlafousek (1972) reported that 15 male sexual deviants, of whom 9 were exhibitionists, showed no inhibition of penile sexual arousal when viewing moving pictures of women engaged in nonerotic movements, whereas control normals showed inhibition.

These authors suggested that such deviations were based on a dissociation of courtship from orgastic behavior, so that lack of courtship prevented normal males but not deviants from being sexually aroused. The mean age of the normals was 21 years, and of the deviants, 28 years, a factor that could be of importance, as sexual attitudes may change with increased experience.

Treatment

The range of treatments advocated in exhibitionism is virtually the same as that advocated in homosexuality. Successful responses to desensitization (Bond & Hutchison, 1960) and electric-shock aversive therapy (Evans, 1969) have been reported in uncontrolled studies. Shame aversion therapy (Serber, 1972) seems particularly applicable to exhibitionists. The patient is observed by a selected audience while he carries out his deviant behavior. Wickramasekera (1976) treated 16 exhibitionists with two 40-min videotaped sessions of intensive self-disclosure, self-exploration, and confrontation, and 20 min of exposure by the patient to five mental-health professionals. At the close of the exposure sessions, the patient was frequently reported to be in tears, trembling, weak, and nauseous. Follow-up ranged from three months to seven years. No relapse was detected. In view of the traumatic nature of the treatment, a controlled comparison with a treatment without this feature, such as imaginal desensitization, would seem advisable before it could be recommended.

Wardlaw and Miller (1978) reported a much less traumatic variant of shame aversion. Patients were instructed to "exhibit" hourly while they counted to 10, in situations where they did not place themselves at risk, mainly their own homes or secluded areas at work. No return of exhibitionistic behavior was reported by three subjects over the following three years.

The lack of validity of penile circumference changes in assessing the response to treatment of 16 exhibitionists was observed by Murphy *et al.* (1980). Deviant and nondeviant stimuli were presented with videotapes, slides, and free fantasy. During four baseline sessions without treatment, there was a marked decline in erectile responses to deviant images, which continued if the baseline periods were extended. The authors commented that the changes during treatment could not be attributed to the specific intervention when the dependent variable was decreasing prior to the introduction of treatment, and they suggested that the exhibitionists were suppressing their erection to deviant stimuli.

Relaxation, electric aversive therapy, and self-regulation were compared by Rooth and Marks (1973) in the treatment of 12 exhibitionists. Each subject received all three treatments in one or the other of the six possible combinations after observation for one week in the hospital without treatment, during which time baseline measures of exposure activity were obtained. Each of the three different treatments was administered for one week over the next three weeks. The patients spent the intervening weekends at home and during the week had to leave the hospital to go into situations where they would be tempted to expose themselves. This procedure was meant to enable the patient's response to each treatment to be assessed. Measures of response, including semantic differential scales and linear rating scales, were devised to reflect changes in exhibitionistic attitudes, urges, acts, and other problems.

When the scores on the various measures of subjective response before and after each treatment were examined, there was a significant improvement on four measures following aversion, on two following self-regulation, and on none following relaxation. In this reviewer's experience, patients are rarely able to assess their response to treatment while in the unusual environment of the hospital and its surroundings and need at least a few weeks out of the hospital before they can determine their response. It is possible that the changes in the various measures used by Rooth and Marks to assess patient improvement reflected the patients' expectancy of improvement with each treatment. The authors reported that there was definite therapist bias against relaxation therapy.

This reviewer's practice, which has not been evaluated in controlled studies, is to treat exhibitionists initially with imaginal desensiti-

zation in three half-hour sessions daily for five days. Subjects are briefly trained to relax and then to visualize situations where they are stimulated to expose themselves but do not do so. Over half the subjects significantly reduce the frequency of exposure, and about a quarter cease the behavior. About 10% of those who show a good response relapse but respond to further treatment. The use of drug therapy should be considered in those who show insufficient response to behavioral treatments to avoid probable conviction. Patients who have difficulties relating to women, but not sexual dysfunctions, are given, in addition, training in assertiveness and dating skills. This training has usually not proved very helpful in altering behavior. Those who have difficulties in relating to women as well as sexual dysfunctions are referred to a surrogate if they lack a partner and are financially able to afford this therapy.

Pedophilia

Pedophilia is sexual activity of a postpubertal person with a prepubertal person. As such activity is criminal in societies of European origin, it usually comes to the attention of students of sexual behavior only when the offender is charged. Pedophilia is considerably more common than the number of convictions indicates. Lukianowicz (1972) reported 26 cases of father–daughter incest occurring in 650 unselected female patients. Only two of the fathers were charged with incest.

In the cases of incestuous pedophilia reported by Lukianowicz, it is implied that sexual relations took the form of coitus. Nedoma, Mellan, and Pondelickova (1971) investigated 100 men in Czechoslovakia convicted of sexual offenses with children less than 15 years of age. They concluded that the subjects could be divided into three groups. One group consisted of those who had sexual relations with boys; 30% of this group also had relations with immature girls. Almost all of those who had relations exclusively with girls could be divided either into a group who had relations only with girls younger than 12 years or into a group who had relations only with girls above that age. The sexual activity in the last group mainly took the form of coitus. In the former two groups, coitus was rare, and the contacts were mainly limited to manual stimulation of the child, oral-genital contacts being uncommon in all three groups. Forcible aggressive action occurred in 2 of the 100 cases.

Etiology

Quinsey, Chaplin, and Carrigan (1979) investigated the penile circumference responses of molesters of female children to 30-sec exposures of males and females of various age categories. Incestuous subjects, particularly those with daughters or step daughters as victims, showed minimal penile responses to children, whereas the pedophiles who chose unrelated victims showed the greatest response, though less than that to adult women.

Freund, Langevin, Wescom, and Zajac (1975) determined the penile volume responses of heterosexuals and homosexuals in relation to pedophilia. Homosexuals attracted to adult males showed no arousal to children. Homosexuals attracted to children and responsible for most homosexual pedophilic offenses showed no arousal to adult males. Nondeviant adult males showed some arousal to female children, and a percentage of heterosexual pedophilic offenses were carried out by men who were not truly pedophilic in their sexual preference (Freund, McKnight, Langevin, & Cibiri, 1972).

Groth and Birnbaum (1978) investigated 175 men convicted of sexual assaults against children. The findings also indicated that there is a group who are attracted to and seek out male or female children or both, and who are not attracted to adults. Also, there is a group of predominantly or exclusively heterosexual men attracted to adults who at times have sexual relationships with children, mainly of the female sex, whom they know socially.

Of the categories of institutionalized sexual offenders against children whom they studied, Gebhard, Gagnon, Pomeroy, and Christenson (1965) concluded that a "man who is preoccupied with sex, who is often at home with the children during periods of unemployment (also the wife is frequently away working), and who drinks heavily, is a man ripe for an incest offence" (p. 229).

Treatment

Treatments of pedophilia are similar to those used for the other sexual deviations. VanDeventer and Laws (1978) reported the response to orgasmic reconditioning of two pedophiles, using as a major measure of outcome penile circumference responses to slides of males and females of various ages. Studies by Quinsey and Bergersen (1976, 1980), the latter study cited in Murphy et al. (1980), established that a number of normal subjects could fake their penile circumference responses to appear pedophilic. The one subject reported by VanDeventer and Laws to be successfully treated could have faked his response in the opposite direction.

This reviewer's practice in helping pedophiles who show evidence of a definite sexual attraction to children is to use techniques similar to those used with exhibitionists. In addition, patients who wish and are more likely to function successfully with appropriately aged male partners are reoriented in this direction, by means of the relevant techniques previously summarized. The sexual relationship of the incestuous pedophile with his wife is often inadequate, and counseling and the use of behavioral techniques both for this problem and for the emotional consequences of his pedophilia are advisable.

Voyeurism

Peepers are "adult males who, for their own sexual gratification looked into some private domicile . . . with the hope of seeing females nude or partially nude, the observation being without the consent of the females concerned" (Gebhard et al., 1965, p. 358). The rarer forms of voyeurism discussed by Smith (1976), in his excellent review, rarely lead to arrest or the seeking of treatment.

Etiology

There is no evidence that penile plethysmography responses to nude bodies are greater in voyeurs than in normals. Peepers, like exhibitionists, though not shy when they come for treatment, commonly report that as adolescents they were very shy in relating to and dating girls. Some also report that at that age, they accidentally witnessed a girl undressing and became very sexually aroused. Subsequently, they sought opportunities to see girls undress. Peeping behavior could thus develop a compulsive quality independent of the sexual drive. Peepers customarily progress to having normal sexual relations while continuing peeping.

The 56 peepers confined to institutions who were studied by Gebhard *et al.* (1965) were described as a "mixed group including the sociosexually underdeveloped, mental deficients, situational cases, drunks, and still other varieties" (p. 378). They also were described as a relatively inhibited, or least inactive, group, blossoming out in later life.

Treatment

There appear to be no significant innovative or controlled evaluative studies in the literature concerning the treatment of voyeurism. A delightful incongruity was noted by Smith (1976). Jackson (1969) treated a peeper by instructing him to masturbate while looking at the centerfold of *Playboy*. Gaupp, Stern, and Ratlieff (1971) treated a patient whose problems were voyeurism and masturbating to the *Playboy* centerfold. This was not the same man treated by Jackson, commented Smith (1976).

It is this reviewer's practice to treat peepers similarly to exhibitionists.

Fetishism, Bondage, and Sadomasochism

Festishists are sexually aroused by some part or deformity of the human body of the preferred sex (other than secondary sexual characteristics) or by some inanimate object. Fetishists are almost invariably male. The more common parts of the body that arouse fetishists are the hair, the feet, and the hands, and the more common objects are female underclothes, shoes, gloves, and diapers. The fetishist may wish his partner to stand on him in bare feet or in shoes, indicating the presence of a degree of *sadomasochism*, the anomaly in which sexual arousal is produced by the infliction of pain, subjugation, or humiliation by another person on the subject (masochism) or by the subject on another person (sadism). When corsets are the fetish, the subjects may put them on very tightly, achieving heightened arousal by constricting their bodies, suggesting the presence of some degree of the anomaly termed *bondage*.

With bondage, the subject achieves sexual arousal by being physically restrained or by restraining a partner. Fantasies or pictures of bound and gagged people also tend to arouse the subject.

As it is difficult at times to determine the actual nature of the activity or object that arouses the sexual deviant, the technique described by Abel, Blanchard, Barlow, and Mavissakalian (1975) may prove of value. In an initial trial, the patient's penile circumference changes were recorded while he described an erotic experience. The components of the subject's description that caused accelerating or decelerating penile responses were noted. In subsequent trials, a fantasy was described that contained the verbal cues regarded as producing, and those regarded as not producing, arousal. Thus, the initial impressions could be confirmed.

Spengler (1977) investigated sadomasochistic behavior by sending questionnaires to individuals who advertised for partners and to members of sadomasochistic clubs. He commented that there were very few women in the clubs and that there were no advertisements from women other than prostitutes, who may not have been sadomasochists. Responses were received from 245 men, of whom 30% were exclusively heterosexual, 31% bisexual, and 38% homosexual.

There appear to be few data concerning the incidence of fetishism, sadomasochism, or bondage. In the study of McConaghy *et al.* (1979), 28 of 138 male and 1 of 58 female medical students reported that they had used clothes of the opposite sex to arouse themselves sexually.

Etiology

Rachman (1966) demonstrated that penile circumference changes could be produced to a picture of women's boots if it was regularly followed by a picture of a nude woman. Rachman suggested this could be an experimental model of fetishism. This conditioning theory of the etiology of fetishism does not account for the fact that in most subjects, the interest in the fetish initially did not seem to have a sexual component and preceded the onset of puberty by several years.

An association has been repeatedly reported between fetishism and epilepsy originating in the temporal lobe (Epstein, 1961). It has not been substantiated in larger series of patients (Kolarsky, Freund, Machek, & Polak, 1967; Shukla, Srivastava, & Katiyar, 1979).

Treatment

Marks and Gelder (1967) treated two fetishists and three transvestites by administering electric shocks to the patients' arms or legs while they carried out their deviant behavior in fantasy and in reality. These authors were impressed that all subjects reported increasing difficulty in imagining deviant images during the course of aversive therapy and that the latency of obtaining these images increased regularly. They thought that it would be difficult for subjects to fake such latency curves. However, this reviewer has seen a similar increase in latency to fantasied images in patients treated with imaginal desensitization when no aversive stimuli were employed. Such latency curves could be the result of satiation.

It is this reviewer's practice to treat subjects with fetishism, bondage, and sadomasochism similarly to exhibitionists. Adolescent fetishists who used female underclothes in masturbatory practices usually show a good initial response to imaginal desensitization or to aversive therapy, used previously by this reviewer. However, in his experience, they have required follow-up over several years as they frequently relapsed, showing the same or new deviant behavior, such as exposure or, in one case, fire setting. Relapses usually responded well to further courses of treatment.

Rape

The traditional concept of rape as enforced coitus that the victim physically resists is under sustained attack by women's movements in favor of a much broader concept (Chappell, 1976).

Etiology

Studies of etiology have been confined to convicted rapists. Rada, Laws, and Kellner (1976) investigated the plasma testosterone levels of convicted rapists compared with those of child molesters and normals. There was no difference in the means or the range. The group of rapists judged most violent had significantly higher levels than did other rapists, child molesters, and normals. Abel, Barlow, Blanchard, and Guild (1977) and Barbaree, Marshall, and Lanthier (1979) both reported that convicted rapists showed mean penile-circumference responses to 2-min audiotape descriptions of sexual intercourse carried out by threat or force, equivalent to their responses to descriptions of mutually consenting intercourse. Nonrapists showed significantly less penile response to descriptions of rape than to those of consenting intercourse. Abel *et al.* (1977) also reported that the rapists in their study showed a mean penile response of 26% of full erection to descriptions of an assault on a woman without any sexual behavior. These findings suggest that at least in some rapists, physical assault on a woman is sexually arousing.

Convicted rapists in the study of Gebhard *et al.* (1965) were commonly antisocial men with an extensive nonsexual criminal history who were accustomed to take what they wanted with little concern for others; or feckless individuals who tended to have a marked double standard where women were concerned, regarding many as morally lax and therefore freely available for intercourse. Both tended to have a high sexual drive. Rada (1975) reported that convicted rapists commonly had a history of moderate to heavy drinking and had been drinking at the time of the offense.

Treatment

Abel, Blanchard, and Becker (1976) reviewed the psychological treatments of rapists: pastoral counseling, milieu and group therapy, psychotherapy, and behavior modification techniques. The behavioral approaches included training in heterosocial and heterosexual skills, directed masturbation, fading (to increase normal heterosexual intercourse), electric-shock aversive therapy, and covert sensitization to reduce deviant sexual feelings. Only the behavioral techniques have been systematically evaluated. These have been investigated in single-subject designs, which as employed in these studies do not, in this reviewer's opinion, control for the effects of suggestion and expectancy.

Miscellaneous Sexual Anomalies

A number of anomalies of sexual arousal exist for which treatment is seldom sought or which are rare, so there is little research information available concerning them. These include frotteurism, in which the subject rubs his genitals against the clothed body of a stranger, usually in crowded situations; sexual asphyxia, in which the subject partially smothers or strangles himself, sometimes producing presumably accidental death; sexual assaults, in which the subject touches, grasps, or pinches the body of a stranger, usually the breasts or buttocks, or attempts to put his hand up her skirt to touch her genitals; and obscene telephoning. If treatment is sought for these conditions because they have become compulsive, they should respond, as do the other deviations, to the treatments previously described.

Physical Treatment of Criminal Deviants

Sexual deviants who repeatedly commit a criminal sexual offense are often imprisoned for long periods. This practice has led some workers to try to help these subjects to control their sexual impulses with techniques that produce more profound or irreversible changes in functioning than the behavioral treatments already discussed. This approach would seem acceptable if the techniques have been shown in controlled studies to be more effective than less potentially harmful ones, and if these less harmful treatments have been tried unsuccessfully. This is not usually the case.

The most reversible of the physical treatments would appear to be the use of chemicals to reduce sexual drive. These include major tranquilizers, in particular, thioridazine; female sex hormones, usually diethylstilbestrol or medroxyprogesterone; and a male hormone antagonist, cyproterone. No controlled comparison of the effects of these chemicals with behavioral techniques appears to have been made.

This reviewer has found some of these drugs useful in patients who were at risk for prolonged imprisonment, as their compulsive sexual drive remained insufficiently controlled after repeated courses of behavior therapy, including imaginal desensitization and an aversive technique. Thioridazine is tried initially, but if it is ineffective or produces drowsiness, medroxyprogesterone is usually effective and rarely leads to troublesome side-effects.

Castration continues to be used in Europe for sex offenders. Heim and Hursch (1979) reviewed studies following up castrates. Recidivism rates were significantly lowered following castration. As the authors pointed out, the only comparisons made were with subjects who refused castration and who could therefore not be regarded as equivalent to those who accepted it, apparently at times as a condition for release from imprisonment.

Dieckmann and Hassler (1975) treated six recidivist sexual deviants by unilateral destruction of specific nuclei in the hypothalamus. The rationale for the procedure was that centers maintaining the deviant behavior were destroyed. Evidence has been advanced that compulsive sexual behavior can be controlled without reducing the underlying sexual drive as measured by penile volume plethysmography. It is most unfortunate that the proponents of surgery have not used this technique to determine whether reduction in sexual arousal to deviant erotic stimuli does follow the operation. Ethically, a controlled comparison with an effective behavioral technique would appear to be of the greatest urgency.

Assessment and Treatment of Sexual or Gender Identity Disorders

The fact that a number of people regularly dress in the clothes of the opposite sex (crossdress) provides striking evidence of the existence of anomalies of sexual identity. Further, such evidence appeared when a sex conversion operation was developed. A substantial number of men presented to medical practitioners at that time in an emotionally distressed state, often threatening self-castration or suicide unless they received this operation (Worden & Marsh, 1955). Polarization of opinion among involved professionals was marked as to whether or not the operation should be carried out.

The proponents of the operation emphasized the uniqueness of the condition of those who sought it (Benjamin, 1954; Hamburger, Sturup, & Dahl-Iversen, 1953). They were considered victims of a genetic constitution that resulted in their being women in men's bodies. Their femininity was apparent from early childhood. Their not being able to live as women caused them to suffer severe mental stress and could result in neurotic conflict. They often disliked their sexual organs. Their sexual life was largely cerebral and nongenital. Though attracted to normal men, they were disgusted by homosexual relationships. These authors appeared to believe that the personalities of such subjects were those of essentially normal women, though under severe stress because of their condition. They also believed that all attempts at treatment of the condition had failed and concluded that these subjects could achieve a reasonably contented existence only through surgery. Benjamin introduced the now-accepted term *transsexualism* to distinguish the condition of these subjects from *transvestism*, the term used until that time to include all forms of crossdressing.

The opponents of the operation saw transsexualism as a neurotic condition, largely or entirely psychological in origin. Rather than being normal women, transsexuals had an emotionally shallow, immature, and distorted concept of what women are like, socially, sexually, anatomically, and emotionally. Their reported lack of interest in sexual contacts was an expression of a neurotic aversion. To accept that they were women in men's bodies was to accept their own formulation. Histories of their past lives were not accurate, as they unconsciously reconstructed their memories. Surgery would still leave them neurotic individuals (Ostow, 1953; Worden & Marsh, 1955).

Transsexualism

The definition of transsexualism as a state of persistent opposite-sexual identity associated with a desire for physical sexual conversion would not be acceptable to all professionals treating subjects with this condition. Many attempt to define transsexualism in relation not to the condition of the subjects who seek the operation but to the condition of those considered suitable for it. As there is widespread disagreement concerning the characteristics of suitable candidates, no generally accepted definition has been advanced.

Stoller (1973) wished to restrict the diagnosis of male transsexualism to subjects who were feminine, not effeminate; who at no stage in early childhood showed masculine behavior; who were incapable of sexual relations with the opposite sex; and who had never shown fetishistic sexual arousal induced by female clothes.

Randell (1971) commented on 73 transsexuals whom he analyzed in depth that 48% had been married at some time and that it was surprising how many were well-developed males. Person and Ovesey (1974) interviewed 20 male transsexuals having sex-conversion therapy: 14 showed no evidence of feminine behavior in childhood; 5 had crossdressed with fetishistic arousal.

Barr (1973) investigated the sexual orientation, as measured by penile plethysmography, of 24 transsexuals (19 of whom were taking estrogen) and of 44 subjects who were seeking treatment for homosexual impulses. The transsexuals obtained U-scores indicative of a significantly more homosexual orientation than did the homosexuals (see Table 1).

Buhrich and McConaghy (1978b) investigated 30 male subjects requesting sex-conversion operations. Of these subjects, 5 gave a history of fetishistic arousal to crossdressing. They were significantly older, having a mean age of 40 years, compared with the other subjects, whose mean age was 26 years. The fetishistic group also differed significantly from the remainder in that they had had greater experience of heterosexual intercourse and in that more had married. Their sexual orientation, as measured by penile plethysmography, was significantly more heterosexual (Table 1). In view of the significant differences in the two groups, it was suggested that the syndromes they showed were clinically discrete, and could be termed *fetishistic transsexualism* and *nuclear transsexualism*.

Hoenig and Kenna (1974) attempted to calculate the prevalence of transsexualism from the number of transsexuals presenting to the Manchester University Department of Psychiatry. They concluded that there was one transsexual in 34,000 males and in 108,000 females. They pointed out that their figures were similar to those calculated for Sweden by Walinder: 1 in 37,000 for males and in 103,000 for females.

Etiology. The polarized views of early theorists concerning the biological or psychological etiology of transsexualism were unsupported by evidence. Stoller (1971) thought that transsexualism was produced by mothers who encouraged their sons to be feminine while the fathers remained withdrawn. No data were produced to support this theory apart from clinical impression.

Buhrich and McConaghy (1978a) compared the parental relationships in childhood of 29 male homosexuals, 34 male transvestites, 29 male transsexuals, and 30 male controls. The finding of most significance was the lack of differences between the reported parental relationships of the subjects with the three anomalies, suggesting that such relationships have no specific role in the etiology of the conditions in males.

Imperato-McGinley, Peterson, Gautier, and Sturla (1979) described 18 males who, because of an enzyme deficiency, were born with female-appearing genitalia and were raised as girls. At puberty, under the influence of the associated increase in testosterone, all developed a masculine build and a phallus capable of erection. Of these subjects, 17 adopted a male sexual identity and 16 a male sexual role. The authors concluded that the effect of testosterone predominated over the effect of being reared as a girl.

Pomeroy (1967) considered transsexualism a defense against homosexuality in subjects whose strict religious or moral code made it very difficult for them to accept their condition. It now appears to be established that homosexuality is associated with some degree of opposite-sex preference, identity, role, and dimorphic behavior. There must therefore exist a group of exclusively homosexually oriented subjects with very strong opposite-sex preference, identity, role, and dimorphic behavior. For such homosexuals, the acceptance of a transsexual solution would seem to have many advantages and few disadvantages.

Treatment. The view of earlier workers (Benjamin, 1954; Hamburger *et al.*, 1953) that no treatment is effective in transsexualism has become generally accepted, and the sex-conversion operation is commonly considered the only solution. Meyer and Reter (1979) reviewed the major follow-up studies of this operation, all of which were uncontrolled. Most patients were satisfied that they had had the operation, though in some, psychiatric disturbance and gross dyssocial behavior resulted. Surgical complications were not infrequent.

Meyer and Reter compared 11 men and 4 women who had received a sex-conversion operation at their clinic with 28 men and 7 women who had not, as they failed to complete the qualifying period of living and working in the desired role while taking opposite-sex hormones for one year. These authors concluded that sex-conversion surgery conferred no objective advantage in terms of social rehabilitation, although it remained subjectively satisfying to those who had rigorously pursued a trial period and had undergone the operation.

Barlow, Reynolds, and Agras (1973) reported the first change in sexual identity of a male transsexual following behavioral therapy. The patient was a 17-year-old boy who was considered too young for sex conversion, which he requested, and he accepted treatment aimed at changing his sexual identity. Direct modification of female sexual-specific patterns of sitting, walking, and standing was commenced by modeling and videotape feedback, with verbal praise when these patterns changed in the masculine direction. A positive conditioning procedure, electric aversive therapy, and covert sensitization then successfully increased heterosexual and reduced homosexual arousal, according to this patient's subjective report and penile circumference responses. Barlow, Abel, and Blanchard (1979) reported that at 6½ years following treatment, the patient believed that he was completely sexually reoriented to masculinity. He had not had heterosexual intercourse. It is particularly unfortunate that penile circumference rather than penile volume measures were employed in this study to determine sexual orientation, in view of the low validity of the former technique.

Barlow *et al.* (1979) reported in addition the response of two other transsexuals to similar treatment. The first adopted a masculine gender identity all the time, and the second when he wished. Treatment to alter the homosexual orientation of the first subject failed, and the second wished to remain homosexual.

The treatment of these patients was evaluated with single-subject designs, which do not exclude the possibility that the results were due to expectancy of change, rather than to the specific effects of the prolonged and varied treatments. In view of the finding of Meyer and Reter (1979) that a number of their subjects failed to complete the qualifying period for sex conversion, it is possible that the three patients treated by Barlow *et al.* would have modified their behavior in a more masculine direction without treatment. The same considerations apply to reports of transsexuals who have abandoned the desire for sex conversion with psychotherapy (Kirkpatrick & Friedmann, 1976). Barlow, Abel, and Blanchard (1977) described a reversal of sexual identity in a transsexual occurring in two hours with exorcism, demonstrating the importance of suggestion and expectancy in this reversal. The authors pointed out that all the components of masculine motor behavior were seemingly acquired in a matter of hours.

The fact that the techniques for curing transsexualism may not have acted specifically does not reduce the importance of these reports that such a cure is possible. There is urgent need for an evaluation of the alternatives to the present management of subjects requesting sex conversion, which tolerates or even encourages almost immediate trial of the effects of opposite-sex hormones, with the possible effect of confirming the subject in his or her transsexual identification.

Transvestism

Transvestism is characterised by periodic crossdressing, associated in adolescence with sexual arousal but becoming more prolonged and less sexually arousing with increasing age.

While crossdressed, the subject wishes to appear in public and be accepted as a woman in role but not in sexual behavior. Thirty-five members of a club for transvestites were studied by Buhrich and McConaghy (1977b). They were predominantly heterosexual. Of these subjects, 12 said they desired a sex-conversion operation. These 12 were significantly more likely than the rest, to feel like a woman when dressed as a man, or when crossdressed, and to fantasy living permanently as a woman. With penile plethysmography, they obtained U-scores indicative of a more homosexual orientation (Table 1). In regard to all the significant differences found, these transvestites seeking sex conversion resembled transsexuals more than did the remaining group of transvestites, indicating that their condition was an intermediate one. It was suggested that they be termed *marginal transvestites* and that those not seeking sex conversion be termed *nuclear transvestites*.

Hence, there appear to be two groups intermediate between transsexuals and transvestites: (1) fetishistic transsexuals, who identify themselves as transsexuals by seeking sex conversion, and (2) marginal transvestites, who though desiring sex conversion do not seek it and may identify themselves as transvestites by joining a club for transvestites.

With increasing age, over a quarter of the transvestites studied by Buhrich and McConaghy (1977a) no longer experienced sexual arousal to wearing women's clothes. Buhrich (1978) questioned them concerning their motivation for crossdressing both in adolescence and currently. Almost half considered sexual arousal a primary response in adolescence, but only 12% considered it currently of significance. Most reported a feeling of being comfortable, relaxed, and at ease, with relief from stress, tension, and masculine responsibility. Feelings of being sensual, elegant, and beautiful were the major primary sensations sought.

There seem to be few data concerning the incidence of transvestism. In the study of McConaghy *et al.* (1979), 15 of 138 male but none of 58 female medical students reported that they had obtained sexual arousal from dressing in the external clothes or the underclothes of the opposite sex. One had done this on seven occasions and the others no more than three. It seems likely, therefore, that consistent transvestite behavior would be shown by less than 1% of the male population. Female transvestism, if it exists at all, would seem to be very rare.

Etiology. An association has been reported in the literature between the presence of an XXY genetic constitution, Klinefelter's syndrome, and transvestism (Money & Pollitt, 1964). It was suggested that the XXY genotype may produce a disposition to defective psychosexual differentiation and that transvestism not associated with Klinefelter's syndrome might result from other such genotypes, interacting with unknown social and/or physical environmental factors.

The fact that some fetishistic transsexuals marry and only in middle age seek sex conversion indicates that with waning sexual interest in these bisexual subjects, their anomalous sexual identity becomes dominant. This finding suggests that biological and/or social factors can produce anomalies of both sexual orientation and sexual identity, which are to some extent independent. Markedly homosexual individuals with strong opposite-sex identity may attempt to resolve their adjustment difficulties when adolescent by seeking sex conversion and defining themselves as transsexual. Markedly heterosexual individuals with strong opposite sexual identity become nuclear transvestites. Intermediate degrees would produce fetishisitic transsexuals and marginal transvestites.

Treatment. Morgenstern, Pearce, and Rees (1965) treated 13 transvestites with apomorphine aversive therapy, in which nausea and vomiting were associated with crossdressing behavior. Follow-up, at from eight months to four years, revealed that 7 had ceased to crossdress, though 2 of these stated that when under stress, they experienced strong urges to do so. The other 6 showed a reduction in the frequency of crossdressing but relapsed in relation to stressful events. A similar rate of response of transvestites to electric aversive therapy was reported by Marks, Gelder, and Bancroft (1970).

Rosen and Rehm (1977) reported the relapse after some years of two transvestites who had at short-term follow-up appeared to have successfully responded to electric aversive therapy and training to increase male behavior.

This reviewer has also found relapse to be frequent in transvestites who showed a good initial response to imaginal desensitization or aversive therapy. Before such treatment is begun, the alternative option that the patient accept his transvestism should be explored. Clubs established by transvestites provide members with mutual support and the opportunity to crossdress in public. Female partners and children also use the organization to meet and obtain information and support.

Assessment and Treatment of Sex-Dimorphic Behavior

Clinicians have for many years identified the presence in male children of opposite sex-dimorphic behavior. These behavioral patterns characteristic of females were associated with current or subsequent homosexual behavior (Bender & Paster, 1941). Bakwin and Bakwin (1953) regarded boys as homosexual who early in life crossdressed at every opportunity, experimented with cosmetics, and postured like girls. Zuger (1978) followed into adulthood 16 boys who showed symptoms of feminine behavior from early childhood: 1 was heterosexual, 1 was probably heterosexual, 8 were homosexual, 2 were probably homosexual, 1 was transsexual, 1 was transvestite, and in 2, the outcome was uncertain. Money and Russo (1979) followed-up 5 of 11 effeminate boys. When they were over 20 years of age, all 5 reported that they were predominantly homosexual, although 1 was in the process of establishing a continued relationship with a woman. Few data are available on the outcome of "tomboyism," or masculine behavior in girls (Green, 1979).

At one time, clinicians appeared to believe that effeminate behavior in boys was a categorical condition, shown in complete form by a small number and not at all by the vast majority. Evidence suggests that effeminacy is on a continuum, as is tomboyism. Kagan and Moss (1962) investigated the presence of masculine and feminine interests in anatomically normal children. Interest in athletics, mechanical objects, and competitive activities was considered masculine. Gardening, music, cooking, and noncompetitive activities were considered feminine. Failure to adopt traditional masculine interests in boys, but not in girls, was associated with avoidance of heterosexual erotic behavior in adulthood.

The widespread impression that in childhood, significantly more male homosexuals in comparison with heterosexuals were fearful of physical injury, avoided fights, played predominantly with girls, and avoided participation in competitive sports has been substantiated in retrospective studies (Bieber, 1962; Evans, 1969; Holemon & Winokur, 1965; Saghir & Robins, 1973). Saghir and Robins were among the few who investigated childhood sex-dimorphic behavior in female as well as male homosexuals. Over two-thirds reported tomboyish behavior in childhood or adolescence as compared with 16% of the female heterosexual controls.

The study by McConaghy *et al.* (1979) appears to be the first in which the subjects reporting homosexual feelings and those reporting heterosexual feelings were drawn from and could be considered representative of a normal subgroup of the population (in this case, medical students). Male students who reported an awareness of homosexual feelings also reported the opposite sex-dimorphic behaviors in childhood shown by effeminate boys. The female students with homosexual feelings showed less evidence of tomboyism. The study was replicated with medical students in the subsequent year. The results are reported in Table 2.

The findings of these studies indicate that opposite sex-dimorphic behavior in childhood is not only shown by a small group of effeminate boys and tomboyish girls but occurs to a variable extent in members of a normal population. The extent correlates with the ratio of homosexual to heterosexual feelings experienced by the subject.

Etiology

Green and Money (1961) regarded gender role (the amount of same and opposite sex-dimorphic behavior shown by a person) as being learned in the first few years of life. On the basis of clinical impression, they argued that lack of forceful paternal dominance, greater concern by the mother about the son's behavioral anomalies, and the relatively fragile build of many of the boys are important factors in the etiology of effeminacy. Stoller (1970) believed that the preschool effeminate boy's parents found his femininity most endearing and encouraged it. Zuger (1966) thought that the closeness of effeminate boys with their mother was secondary to their femininity, rather than responsible for it. The theory that sex-dimorphic behavior in childhood and the related degree of homosexual and heterosexual orientation in adulthood are produced by the balance of sex hormones to which the individual was exposed at a critical period in uterine development was previously discussed.

Treatment

Bakwin and Bakwin (1953) recommended in the management of effeminate boys that the dominating mother be curbed, the passive father be encouraged to be actively involved with his child, and the child be encouraged in the behavior characteristics of his sex. Coercion, teasing, and shaming were to be avoided. The child's confusions about sex were to be clarified. These aims have characterized subsequent treatment regimes (Green & Money, 1961). Greenson (1966) reported the treatment of an effeminate boy who crossdressed, in which the therapist acted as a male role model, taught the boy to swim, and reinforced masculine behavior and interests in the games they played together. Bentler (1968), adopting a social learning theory of etiology, employed a similar treatment. Green, Newman, and Stoller (1972) reported the reduction of opposite sex-dimorphic behavior in five effeminate boys, who they decided were pretranssexual. The treatment was similar to that suggested by Bakwin and Bakwin in regard to changing the attitude of the parents. In addition, the need for a male therapist was stressed, both to provide a role model and to replace the physically or psychologically absent father. Myrick (1970) reported the successful treatment of an effeminate boy by two female teachers who were advised by a counselor. There was no involvement of the parents.

Rekers and Lovaas (1974) reported a single-subject study of a 5-year-old effeminate boy. During the treatment sessions, he played at a therapy table on which were different boys' and girls' toys. The mother was trained, by means of earphones, to reinforce masculine play by smiles and compliments and to ignore feminine play by reading a book.

The authors concluded that there was no doubt that the treatment intervention was responsible for the change. In this reviewer's opinion, the present and other similar single-subject design studies (Rekers, Willis, Yates, Rosen, & Low, 1977) do not exclude the possibility that the same changes would have occurred outside the treatment situation either spontaneously, in response to the parents' attitude changes consequent to their decision that the patient's behavior warranted treatment, or in response to the increase in the social intolerance of opposite sex-dimorphic behavior that the subject experienced as he grew older.

Bakwin (1960) reported the disappearance of crossgender preference, crossdressing, and opposite sex-dimorphic behavior within two years in a boy of 5 years and in three years in a girl of 11 years. Apparently no treatment was given, though presumably Bakwin recommended to the parents that they reinforce same sex- and discourage opposite sex-dimorphic behavior. This advice was given to the parents of effeminate boys. Zuger (1966) had previously commented at follow-up that "telltale symptoms of effeminacy were suppressed as a confirmed orientation toward homosexuality was taking place" (p. 1101). The five effeminate boys followed up by Money and Russo (1979) received what was termed a minimal form of treatment. Crossgender preference disappeared in all subjects, and crossdressing in all but one, who crossdressed for costume parties.

It would appear that sex-dimorphic behavior has a strong tendency to regress with age, though it is likely that specific treatment would accelerate this process, presumably to the advantage of the effeminate boy. Comparison trials of treatments with control procedures and long-term follow-up are clearly indicated. No treatment has apparently been given to tomboyish girls.

Summary and Conclusions

The scientific investigation of sexual deviation should have been greatly advanced by the development of objective measures of sexual arousal to normal and deviant stimuli. Unfortunately, with male subjects, most workers have utilized either penile volume or penile circumference measures and have considered the results equivalent. In fact, unlike small penile-volume responses, small penile-circumference responses have limited validity as measures of arousal and can be grossly misleading.

Homosexuality (sexual arousal in response to subjects of the same sex) is the commonest deviation from the major response pattern of the majority of human subjects. As a minor response pattern, it is probably experienced by about half such subjects in their pubertal years and by about a third in adulthood. Subjects of both sexes who report awareness of some degree of homosexual feelings also report that they showed opposite sex-dimorphic behavior when they were children. Generally, they had poor emotional relationships with their fathers. Opposite sex-dimorphic behavior in childhood is shown by girls who were exposed to excessive male hormones *in utero*. The most economical theory of the etiology of the homosexual–heterosexual balance of an individual is that it is produced by the ratio of male to female sex hormones to which the individual was exposed *in utero* when his or her nervous system was at a critical stage of development. The ratio of sex hormones *in utero* is determined genetically and by stresses acting on the developing fetus. If this theory is correct, it is unlikely that it will be possible to alter the homosexual–heterosexual balance of an individual by treatment in later life.

The initial behavioral treatments of homosexuality associated aversive stimuli with stimuli producing homosexual arousal, with the expectation that aversion to such stimuli would be produced by conditioning. Aversion was rarely reported. However, the subjects stated that after treatment, they could, if they wished, much more easily control their urges to carry out homosexual behavior. Aversive treatments administered in a variety of conditioning paradigms produced equivalent degrees of reduction of homosexual urges but did not specifically increase heterosexual behavior nor alter homosexual or heterosexual arousal as measured by penile volume plethysmography. It was suggested that aversive treatments acted by reducing the sense of tension or general arousal produced by behavior completion mechanisms in the central nervous system. These mechanisms were activated when subjects did not complete behaviors when exposed to stimuli that had preceded the completion of such behaviors in the past. Systematic desensitization and covert sensitization produced a therapeutic response in homosexuals similar to that produced by aversive therapy. With systematic desensitization and covert sensitization, homosexual stimuli are imagined by the subject while he remains relaxed. The reduction in arousal caused by relaxation results in the lowered strength of the homosexual urges produced by behavior completion mechanisms. There is no convincing evidence that sexual arousal to the body shape of women can be produced in male homosexuals by such techniques as showing them pictures of nude women in association with pictures of nude men or by exposing them to heterosexual stimuli when they are relaxed. However, homosexual men can learn to produce a marked increases in penile circumference responses to pictures of women if these are regularly shown for 30 sec or more. Homosexuals who are anxious about being impotent in heterosexual relations respond to the treatment used for impotence in heterosexuals.

As all behavioral treatments appear equally successful in reducing the strength of homosexual urges experienced as compulsive, it is suggested that imaginal desensitization should be used initially, since it is the least threatening to the patient's self-esteem. No controlled studies of behavioral treatments for improving homosexual functioning have been carried out. Sexual dysfunctions in homosexual relations are treated similarly to dysfunctions in heterosexual relations.

Exhibitionism (exposure of the penis to a strange woman) is the commonest deviation leading to criminal conviction in most European cultures. It appears to commence in shy adolescents and possibly is maintained by behavior completion mechanisms in adulthood. Penile circumference responses to deviant fantasy do not persist in exhibitionists and hence cannot be used to assess responses to treatment. Good results have been reported in uncontrolled studies with shame aversion (when the subject was requested to expose himself to a selected audience) and with repeated exposure in private. In the absence of evidence from controlled studies, it seems most reasonable to attempt initially to reduce this and other compulsive deviant urges with imaginal desensitization.

Pedophilia (sexual activity with children) occurs almost exclusively in men. It appears to be associated with a specific attraction to children in almost all homosexual pedophiles, who are rarely attracted to adult men. Heterosexual pedophiles are commonly attracted to adult women; many may have no stronger attraction to female children than normal heterosexuals have. Antisocial tendencies and fortuitous circumstances play a role in determining its occurrence. Normal subjects can fake their penile circumference responses to pictures of children and adults so as to appear to be pedophilic.

Peeping at women undressing or nude appears, like exhibitionism, to commence in shy adolescents and to be maintained by behavior completion mechanisms. Fetishism (sexual arousal produced by some part of the human body or by an object) is not infrequently associated with sadomasochism (sexual arousal produced by the infliction of pain) and bondage (sexual arousal produced by binding a person).

Rape (an enforced sexual act) is carried out by some subjects who show significantly greater penile circumference increases than do controls to descriptions of sexual and nonsexual assaults on women and men. Antisocial tendencies and the drinking of alcohol also play a role.

Sexual deviants who fail to respond to behavioral treatments and risk imprisonment report that their compulsive sexual urges are reduced by the major tranquilizers or by sex hormones. Castration and the destruction of hypothalamic nuclei in the brain continue to be used in Europe in such patients, though there is no evidence from controlled studies that these treatments are more effective than the behavioral or chemical therapies.

Sexual deviations of gender identity are characterized by the subjects' crossdressing. Transsexuals crossdress because they feel a sense of identity with and wish to live as members of the opposite sex. They seek to have their bodies converted into those of the opposite sex by hormones and surgery. Most transsexuals are exclusively or almost exclusively homosexual. It has been argued that transsexualism is irreversible and that the only form of treatment is bodily conversion by hormones and surgery. However, reports are appearing more frequently of patients' abandoning a transsexual identification with psychotherapy or behavior therapy.

Transvestism probably occurs only in males. Transvestites experience sexual arousal to crossdressing at puberty, though commonly they have crossdressed in childhood. In adulthood, sexual arousal to crossdressing, if it persists, usually becomes unimportant as a motivating factor. Transvestites experience some identification as a woman when crossdressed. Commonly, they want to be publicly accepted as women, at least periodically. Those who are exclusively heterosexual want to live as men most of the time. The stronger the homosexual component in the others, the more likely it is that as they approach middle age, they will seek sex conversion by hormones and surgery, so defining themselves as fetishistic transsexuals. Aversive therapy using electric shock has been the main behavioral treatment reported for transvestism. Long-term follow-up with further courses of treatment is advisable, as relapse following a good initial response appears not to be infrequent. Many transvestites accept their anomalous behavior, and clubs exist in most of the larger cities in Western societies to facilitate this acceptance.

The common belief that the presence of opposite sex-dimorphic behavior (effeminacy) in boys is associated with the later development of homosexuality has been validated in a series of prospective and retrospective studies. There appears to be a similar but weaker relationship in regard to the equivalent behavior (tomboyism) in girls. Effeminacy and tomboyism appear to regress spontaneously in most subjects. It has been treated in boys with both psychotherapy and behavior therapy aimed at reinforcing same sex- and discouraging opposite sex-dimorphic behavior. No studies have used comparison groups, but in those using single-subject designs, sex-dimorphic behavior in the treatment situation has been shown to be to some extent under the control of the contingencies manipulated.

The major impression obtained from reviewing the literature on the reduction of sexually deviant urges is that there is no shortage of relatively effective therapies, some using aversive stimuli, some producing emotional disturbance, and some being physically destructive to the subject treated. Important questions remain to challenge future research. Are the effects of these treatments specific? When two or more treatments exist for a condition, which is the more effective? Do elaborate treatments of long duration produce better long-term effects than brief, simple treatments? What are the characteristics of the patients who fail to respond to a treatment? What is the best alternative treatment for subjects who fail to respond? Controlled studies, both initial and replicatory, in which one treatment is compared with another or with a control procedure of equal expectancy value must be greatly expanded in number if these questions are to be answered in the present decade.

References

Abel, G. G., Blanchard, E. B., Barlow, D. H., & Mavissakalian, M. Identifying specific erotic cues in sexual deviations by audiotaped descriptions. *Journal of Applied Behavior Analysis*, 1975, *8*, 247–260.

Abel, G. G., Blanchard, E. B., & Becker, J. V. Psychological treatment of rapists. In M. J. Walker & S. L. Brodskey (Eds.), *Sexual assault*. Lexington: D. C. Heath, 1976.

Abel, G. G., Barlow, D. H., Blanchard, E. B., & Guild, D. The components of rapists' sexual arousal. *Archives of General Psychiatry*, 1977, *34*, 895–903.

Bakwin, H. Transvestism in children. *Journal of Pediatrics*, 1960, *56*, 294–298.

Bakwin, H., & Bakwin, R. M. Homosexual behavior in children. *Journal of Pediatrics*, 1953, *43*, 108–111.

Bancroft, J. Aversion therapy of homosexuality. *British Journal of Psychiatry*, 1969, *115*, 1417–1431.

Bancroft, J. A comparative study of aversion and desensitization in the treatment of homosexuality. In L. E. Burns & J. L. Worsley (Eds.), *Behavior therapy in the 1970s.* Bristol: John Wright and Sons, 1970.

Bancroft, J. Application of psychophysiological measures to the assessment and modification of sexual behaviour. *Behaviour Research and Therapy,* 1971, *9,* 119–130.

Bancroft, J., Jones, H. C., & Pullan, B. P. A simple transducer for measuring penile erections with comments on its use in the treatment of sexual disorders. *Behaviour Research and Therapy,* 1966, *4,* 239–241.

Barbaree, H. E., Marshall, W. L., & Lanthier, R. D. Deviant sexual arousal in rapists. *Behaviour Research and Therapy,* 1979, *17,* 215–222.

Barlow, D. H. Increasing heterosexual responsiveness in the treatment of sexual deviation: A review of the clinical and experimental evidence. *Behavior Therapy,* 1973, *4,* 655–671.

Barlow, D. H., & Agras, W. S. Fading to increase heterosexual responsiveness in homosexuals. *Journal of Applied Behavior Analysis,* 1973, *6,* 355–366.

Barlow, D. H., Agras, W. S., Leitenberg, H., Callahan, E. J., & Moore, R. C. The contribution of therapeutic instruction to covert sensitization. *Behaviour Research and Therapy,* 1972, *10,* 411–415.

Barlow, D. H., Reynolds, E. J., & Agras, W. S. Gender identity change in a transsexual. *Archives of General Psychiatry,* 1973, *28,* 560–576.

Barlow, D. H., Agras, W. S., Abel, G. G., Blanchard, E. B., & Young, L. D. Biofeedback and reinforcement to increase heterosexual arousal in homosexuals. *Behaviour Research and Therapy,* 1975, *13,* 45–50.

Barlow, D. H., Abel, G. G., & Blanchard, E. B. Gender identity change in a transsexual: An exorcism. *Archives of Sexual Behavior,* 1977, *6,* 387–395.

Barlow, D. H., Abel, G. G., & Blanchard, E. B. Gender identity change in transsexuals. *Archives of General Psychiatry,* 1979, *36,* 1001–1007.

Barr, R. F. Responses to erotic stimuli of transsexual and homosexual males. *British Journal of Psychiatry,* 1973, *123,* 579–585.

Barr, R. F., & McConaghy, N. Penile volume responses to appetitive and aversive stimuli in relation to sexual orientation and conditioning performance. *British Journal of Psychiatry,* 1971, *119,* 377–383.

Bell, A. P., & Weinberg, M. S. *Homosexualities: A study of diversity among men and women.* Artarmon: Macmillan, 1978.

Bender, L., & Paster, S. Homosexual trends in children. *American Journal of Orthopsychiatry,* 1941, *11,* 730–743.

Bene, E. On the genesis of female homosexuality. *British Journal of Psychiatry,* 1965, *111,* 815–821. (a)

Bene, E. On the genesis of male homosexuality: An attempt to clarify the role of the parents. *British Journal of Psychiatry,* 1965, *111,* 803–813. (b)

Benjamin, H. Transsexualism and transvestism as psychosomatic and somatopsychic syndromes. *American Journal of Psychotherapy,* 1954, *8,* 219–230.

Bentler, P. M. A note on the treatment of adolescent sex problems. *Journal of Child Psychology and Psychiatry,* 1968, *9,* 125–129.

Bergin, A. E. A self-regulation technique for impulse control disorders. *Psychotherapy: Theory, research and practice,* 1969, *6,* 113–118.

Bieber, I. *Homosexuality.* New York: Basic Books, 1962.

Birk, L., Huddleston, W., Miller, E., & Cohler, B. Avoidance conditioning for homosexuality. *Archives of General Psychiatry,* 1971, *25,* 314–323.

Bond, I. C., & Hutchison, H. C. Application of reciprocal inhibition therapy to exhibitionism. *Journal of the Canadian Medical Association,* 1960, *83,* 23–25.

Buhrich, N. Motivation for cross-dressing in heterosexual transvestism. *Acta Psychiatrica Scandanavica,* 1978, *57,* 145–152.

Buhrich, N., & McConaghy, N. The clinical syndrome of femmiphilic transvestism. *Archives of Sexual Behavior,* 1977, *6,* 397–412. (a)

Buhrich, N., & McConaghy, N. The discrete syndromes of transvestism and transsexualism. *Archives of Sexual Behavior,* 1977, *6,* 483–495. (b)

Buhrich, N., & McConaghy, N. Parental relationships during childhood in homosexuality, transvestism and transsexualism. *Australian and New Zealand Journal of Psychiatry,* 1978, *12,* 103–108. (a)

Buhrich, N., & McConaghy, N. Two clinically discrete syndromes of transsexualism. *British Journal of Psychiatry,* 1978, *133,* 73–76. (b)

Cautela, J. R. Covert sensitization. *Psychological Reports,* 1967, *20,* 459–468.

Chappell, D. Forcible rape and the criminal justice system: surveying present practices and projecting future trends. In M. J. Walker & S. L. Brodsky (Eds.), *Sexual assault.* Lexington: D. C. Heath, 1976.

Conrad, S. R., & Wincze, J. P. Orgasmic reconditioning: A controlled study of its effects upon the sexual arousal and behavior of adult male homosexuals. *Behavior Therapy,* 1976, *7,* 155–166.

Dieckmann, G., & Hassler, R. Unilateral hypothalamotomy in sexual delinquents. *Confinia Neurologica,* 1975, *37,* 177–186.

Ehrhardt, A. A., & Baker, S. W. Fetal androgens, human central nervous system differentiation, and behavior sex differences. In R. C. Friedman & R. M. (Eds.), *Sex differences in behavior.* New York: Wiley, 1974.

Epstein, A. W. Relationship of fetishism and transvestism to brain and particularly to temporal lobe dysfunction. *Journal of Nervous and Mental Disease,* 1961, *133,* 247–253.

Evans, R. B. Childhood parental relationships of homosexual men. *Journal of Consulting and Clinical Psychology,* 1969, *33,* 129–135.

Feldman, M. P., & MacCulloch, M. J. *Homosexual behavior: Therapy and assessment.* Oxford: Pergamon, 1971.

Freund, K. Some problems in the treatment of homosexuality. In H. J. Eysenck (Ed.), *Behavior therapy and the neuroses.* London: Pergamon Press, 1960.

Freund, K. A laboratory method of diagnosing predominance of homo- or heteroerotic interest in the male. *Behaviour Research and Therapy,* 1963, *1,* 85–93.

Freund, K., McKnight, C. K., Langevin, R., & Cibiri, S. The female child as a surrogate object. *Archives of Sexual Behavior,* 1972, *2,* 119–133.

Freund, K., Langevin, R., Wescom, T., & Zajac, Y. Heterosexual interest in homosexual males. *Archives of Sexual Behavior,* 1975, *4,* 509–518.

Gaupp, L. A., Stern, R. M., & Ratlieff, R. G. The use of

aversion-relief procedures in the treatment of a case of voyeurism. *Behavior Therapy*, 1971, *2*, 585–588.

Gebhard, P. H., Gagnon, J. H., Pomeroy, W. B., & Christenson, C. V. *Sex offenders: An analysis of types.* London: Heinemann, 1965.

Green, R. Childhood cross-gender behavior and subsequent sexual preference. *American Journal of Psychiatry*, 1979, *136*, 106–108.

Green, R., & Money, J. Effeminacy on prepubertal boys. *Pediatrics*, 1961, *27*, 286–291.

Green, R., Newman, L. E., & Stoller, R. J. Treatment of boyhood "transsexualism." *Archives of General Psychiatry*, 1972, *26*, 213–217.

Greenson, R. R. A transvestite boy and a hypothesis. *International Journal of Psycho-analysis*, 1966, *47*, 396–403.

Groth, A. N., & Birnbaum, H. J. Adult sexual orientation and attraction to underage persons. *Archives of Sexual Behavior*, 1978, *7*, 175–181.

Hamburger, C., Sturup, G. K., & Dahl-Iversen, E. Transvestism. *Journal of the American Medical Association*, 1953, *152*, 391–396.

Heim, N., & Hursch, C. J. Castration for sex offenders: treatment or punishment? A review and critique of recent European literature. *Archives of Sexual Behavior*, 1979, *8*, 281–304.

Herman, S. H., Barlow, D. H., & Agras, W. S. An experimental analysis of classical conditioning as a method of increasing heterosexual arousal in homosexuals. *Behavior Therapy*, 1974, *5*, 33–47. (a)

Herman, S. H., Barlow, D. H., & Agras, W. S. An experimental analysis of exposure to "elicit" heterosexual stimuli as an effective variable in changing arousal patterns in homosexuals. *Behavior Research and Therapy*, 1974, *12*, 315–345. (b)

Heston, L. L., & Shields, J. Homosexuality in twins. *Archives of General Psychiatry*, 1968, *18*, 149–160.

Hoenig, J., & Kenna, J. C. The prevalence of transsexualism in England and Wales. *British Journal of Psychiatry*, 1974, *124*, 181–190.

Holemon, R. E., & Winokur, G. Effeminate homosexuality: a disease of childhood. *American Journal of Orthopsychiatry*, 1965, *35*, 48–56.

Hooker, E. The adjustment of the male overt homosexual. *Journal of Projective Techniques*, 1957, *21*, 1–31.

Hopkins, J. H. The lesbian personality. *British Journal of Psychiatry*, 1969, *115*, 1433–1436.

Humphreys, L. *Tearoom trade.* Chicago: Aldine Publishing, 1970.

Hutt, C. *Males and females.* Harmondsworth: Penguin Books, 1972.

Imperato-McGinley, J., Peterson, R. E., Gautier, T., & Sturla, E. Androgens and the evolution of male-gender identity among male pseudohermaphrodites with 5 alpha-reductase deficiency. *New England Journal of Medicine*, 1979, *300*, 1233–1237.

Jackson, B. T. A case of voyeurism treated by counterconditioning. *Behaviour Research and Therapy*, 1969, *7*, 133–134.

James, S. Treatment of homosexuality: II. Superiority of desensitization arousal as compared with anticipatory avoidance conditioning: results of a controlled trial. *Behavior Therapy*, 1978, *9*, 28–36.

James, S., Orwin, A., & Turner, R. K. Treatment of ho-

mosexuality: I. Analysis of failure following a trial of anticipatory avoidance conditioning and the development of an alternative treatment system. *Behavior Therapy*, 1977, *8*, 840–848.

Kagan, J., & Moss, H. A. *Birth to maturity.* New York: Wiley, 1962.

Kinsey, A. C., Pomeroy, W. B., & Martin, C. E. *Sexual behavior in the human male.* Philadelphia: W. B. Saunders, 1948.

Kinsley, A. C., Pomeroy, W. B., Martin, C. E., & Gebhard, P. H. *Sexual behavior in the human female.* Philadelphia: W. B. Saunders, 1953.

Kirkpatrick, M., & Friedmann, C. T. H. Treatment of requests for sex-change surgery with psychotherapy. *American Journal of Psychiatry*, 1976, *133*, 1194–1196.

Kolarsky, A., & Madlafousek, J. Female behavior and sexual arousal in heterosexual male deviant offenders. *Journal of Nervous and Mental Disease*, 1972, *155*, 110–118.

Kolarsky, A., Freund, K., Machek, J., & Polak, O. Male sexual deviation. *Archives of General Psychiatry*, 1967, *17*, 735–743.

Langevin, R., Paitich, D., Ramsay, G., Anderson, C., Kamrad, J., Pope, S., Geller, G., Pearl, L., & Newman, S. Experimental studies of the etiology of genital exhibitionism. *Archives of Sexual Behavior*, 1979, *8*, 307–331.

Lukianowicz, N., Incest: I. Paternal Incest; II. Other types of incest. *British Journal of Psychiatry*, 1972, *120*, 301–313.

MacCulloch, M. J., & Feldman, M. P. Aversion therapy in the management of 43 homosexuals. *British Medical Journal*, 1967, *2*, 594–597.

Marks, I. M., & Gelder, M. G. Transvestism and fetishism: Clinical and psychological changes during faradic aversion. *British Journal of Psychiatry*, 1967, *113*, 711–729.

Marks, I. M., Gelder, M., & Bancroft, J. Sexual deviants two years after electric aversion. *British Journal of Psychiatry*, 1970, *117*, 173–185.

Masters, W. H., & Johnson, V. E. *Homosexuality in perspective.* Boston: Little, Brown, 1979.

McConaghy, N. Penile volume change to moving pictures of male and female nudes in heterosexual and homosexual males. *Behaviour Research and Therapy*, 1967, *5*, 43–48.

McConaghy, N. Subjective and penile plethysmograph responses following aversion-relief and apomorphine therapy for homosexual impulses. *British Journal of Psychiatry*, 1969, *145*, 723–730.

McConaghy, N. Subjective and penile plethysmograph responses to aversion therapy for homosexuality: A follow-up study. *British Journal of Psychiatry*, 1970, *117*, 555–560.

McConaghy, N. Measurements of change in penile dimensions. *Archives of Sexual Behavior*, 1974, *3*, 381–388.

McConaghy, N. Aversive and positive conditioning treatments of homosexuality. *Behavior Research and Therapy*, 1975, *13*, 309–319.

McConaghy, N. Behavioral treatment in homosexuality. In M. Hersen, R. M. Eisler, & P. M. Miller (Eds.). *Progress in behavior modification*, Vol. 5. New York: Academic Press, 1977.

McConaghy, N. Heterosexual experience, marital status

and orientation of homosexual males. *Archives of Sexual Behavior*, 1978, *7*, 575–581.

McConaghy, N. Behavior completion mechanisms rather than primary drives maintain behavioral patterns. *Activitas Nervosa Superior (Praha)*, 1980, *22*, 138–151.

McConaghy, N., & Barr, R. F. Classical, avoidance and backward conditioning treatments of homosexuality. *British Journal of Psychiatry*, 1973, *122*, 151–162.

McConaghy, N., & Blaszczynski, A. A pair of monozygotic twins discordant for homosexuality: Sex dimorphic behavior and penile volume responses. *Archives of Sexual Behavior*, 1980, *9*, 121–131.

McConaghy, N., Proctor, D., & Barr, R. Subjective and penile plethsmorgraphy responses to aversion therapy for homosexuality: A partial replication. *Archives of Sexual Behavior*, 1972, *2*, 65–78.

McConaghy, N., Armstrong, M. S., Birrell, P. C., & Buhrich, N. The incidence of bisexual feelings and opposite sex behavior in medical students. *Journal of Nervous and Mental Disease*, 1979, *167*, 685–688.

McConaghy, N., Armstrong, M. S., & Blaszczynski, A. Controlled comparison of aversive therapy and covert sensitization in compulsive homosexuality. *Behaviour Research and Therapy*, 1981, *19*, 425–434.

McGrady, R. E. A forward-fading technique for increasing heterosexual responsiveness in male homosexuals. *Journal of Behavior Therapy and Experimental Psychiatry*, 1973, *4*, 257–261.

McGuire, R. J., Carlisle, J. M., & Young, B. G. Sexual deviations as conditioned behavior: A hypothesis. *Behaviour Research and Therapy*, 1965, *2*, 185–190.

Meyer, J. K., & Reter, D. J. Sex reassignment. *Archives of General Psychiatry*, 1979, *36*, 1010–1015.

Meyer-Bahlburg, H. F. L. Sex hormones and male homosexuality in comparative perspective. *Archives of Sexual Behavior*, 1977, *6*, 297–325.

Meyer-Bahlburg, H. F. L. Sex hormones and female homosexuality. A critical examination. *Archives of Sexual Behavior*, 1979, *8*, 101–119.

Money, J., & Pollitt, E. Cytogenic and psychosexual ambiguity. *Archives of General Psychology*, 1964, *11*, 589–595.

Money, J., & Russo, A. J. Homosexual outcome of discordant gender identity/role in childhood: Longitudinal follow-up. *Journal of Pediatric Psychology*, 1979, *4*, 29–41.

Morgenstern, F. S., Pearce, J. F., & Rees, W. L. Predicting the outcome of behavior therapy by psychological tests. *Behavior Research and Therapy*, 1965, *2*, 191–200.

Murphy, W. D., Abel, G. G., & Becker, J. V. Research in exhibitionism. In D. J. Cox, R. J. Daitzman. (Eds.), *Exhibitionism: Description, assessment and treatment*. New York: Garland Publishing, 1980.

Myrick, R. O. The counselor consultant and the effeminate boy. *Personnel and Guidance Journal*, 1970, *48*, 355–361.

Nedoma, K., Mellan, J., & Pondelickova, J. Sexual behavior and its development in pedophilic men. *Archives of Sexual Behavior*, 1971, *1*, 267–271.

Ostow, M. Transvestism (letter). *Journal of the American Medical Association*, 1953, *152*, 1553.

Pavlov, I. P. *Conditioned reflexes* (C. V. Anrep, Tr. and Ed.). Oxford: University Press, 1927.

Person, E. S., & Ovesey, L. The psychodynamics of male transsexualism. In R. C. Friedman & R. M. Richart (Eds.), *Sex differences in behavior*. New York: Wiley, 1974.

Pomeroy, W. B. A report on the sexual histories of twenty-five transsexuals. *Transactions of the New York Academy of Sciences*, 1967, *29*, 444–447.

Quinsey, V. L., & Bergersen, S. G. Instructional control of penile circumference in assessment of sexual preference. *Behavior Therapy*, 1976, *7*, 489–493.

Quinsey, V. L., Chaplin, T. C., & Carrigan, W. F. Sexual preferences among incestuous and nonincestuous child molestors. *Behavior Therapy*, 1979, *10*, 562–565.

Rachman, S. Sexual fetishism: An experimental analogue. *Psychological Record*, 1966, *16*, 293–296.

Rada, R. T. Alcoholism and forcible rape. *American Journal of Psychiatry*, 1975, *132*, 444–446.

Rada, R. T., Laws, D. R., & Kellner, R. Plasma testosterone levels in the rapist. *Psychosomatic Medicine*, 1976, *38*, 257–268.

Randell, J. B. Indications for sex reassignment surgery. *Archives of Sexual Behavior*, 1971, *1*, 153–161.

Reinisch, J. Fetal hormones, the brain, and human sex differences: A heuristic, integrative review of the recent literature. *Archives of Sexual Behavior*, 1974, *3*, 51–90.

Rekers, G. A., & Lovaas, O. I. Behavioral treatment of deviant sex-role behavior in a male child. *Journal of Applied Behavior Analysis*, 1974, *7*, 173–190.

Rekers, G. A., Willis, T. J., Yates, C. E., Rosen, A. C., & Low, B. P. Assessment of childhood gender behavior change. *Journal of Child Psychology and Psychiatry*, 1977, *7*, 51–57.

Rooth, F. G. Exhibitionism outside Europe and America. *Archives of Sexual Behavior*, 1973, *2*, 351–363.

Rooth, F. G., & Marks, I. M. Persistent exhibitionism: short-term response to aversion, self-regulation and relaxation treatments. *Archives of Sexual Behavior*, 1973, *3*, 227–248.

Rosen, A. C., & Rehm, L. P. Long term follow-up in two cases of transvestism treated with aversion therapy. *Journal of Behavior Therapy and Experimental Psychiatry*, 1977, *8*, 295–300.

Saghir, M. T., & Robins, E. *Male and female homosexuality: A comprehensive investigation*. Baltimore: William & Wilkins, 1973.

Schaefer, S. Sociosexual behavior in male and female homosexuals: a study in sex differences. *Archives of Sexual Behavior*, 1977, *6*, 355–364.

Schmidt, E., Castell, D., & Brown, P. A. A retrospective study of 42 cases of behaviour therapy. *Behaviour Research and Therapy*, 1965, *3*, 9–19.

Serber, M. Shame aversion therapy with and without heterosexual retraining. In R. D. Rubin (Ed.), *Advances in behavior therapy*. News York: Academic Press, 1972.

Shukla, G. D., Srivastava, O. N., & Katiyar, B. C. Sexual disturbances in temporal lobe epilepsy: A controlled study. *British Journal of Psychiatry*, 1979, *134*, 288–292.

Sintchack, G., & Geer, J. H. A vaginal photoplethysmograph system. *Psychophysiology*, 1975, *12*, 113–115.

Smith, R. S. Voyeurism: A review of the literature. *Archives of Sexual Behavior*, 1976, *5*, 585–608.

Solyom, L., & Miller, S. A differential conditioning procedure as the initial phase of behaviour therapy of homosexuality. *Behaviour Research and Therapy*, 1965, *3*, 147–160.

Spengler, A. Manifest sadomasochism of males: Results of an empirical study. *Archives of Sexual Behavior*, 1977, *6*, 441–456.

Stoller, R. J. Psychotherapy of extremely feminine boys. *International Journal of Psychiatry*, 1970, *9*, 278–282.

Stoller, R. J. The term "transvestism." *Archives of General Psychiatry*, 1971, *24*, 230–237.

Stoller, R. J. Male transsexualism: uneasiness. *American Journal of Psychiatry*, 1973, *130*, 536–539.

Thorpe, J. G., Schmidt, E., & Castell, D. A comparison of positive and negative (aversive) conditioning in the treatment of homosexuality. *Behavior Research and Therapy*, 1963, *1*, 357–362.

Wardlaw, G. R., & Miller, P. J. Controlled exposure technique in the elimination of exhibitionism. *Journal of Behavior Therapy and Experimental Psychiatry*, 1978, *9*, 27–32.

Wickramasekera, I. Aversive behavior rehearsal for sex-ual exhibitionism. *Behavior Therapy*, 1976, *7*, 167–176.

Wilson, M. L., & Greene, R. L. Personality characteristics of female homosexuals. *Psychological Reports*, 1971, *28*, 407–412.

Wolpe, J. *Psychotherapy by reciprocal inhibition.* Stanford, Calif.: Stanford University Press, 1958.

Woodward, M. The diagnosis and treatment of homosexual offenders. *British Journal of Delinquency*, 1956, *9*, 44–59.

Worden, F. G., & Marsh, J. T. Psychological factors in men seeking sex transformation. *Journal of the American Medical Association*, 1955, *157*, 1292–1298.

Zuger, B. Effeminate behavior present in boys from early childhood. *Journal of Pediatrics*, 1966, *69*, 1098–1107.

Zuger, B. Monozygotic twins discordant for homosexuality: report of a pair and significance of the phenomenon. *Comprehensive Psychiatry*, 1976, *17*, 661–669.

Zuger, B. Effeminate behavior present in boys from childhood: Ten additional years of follow-up. *Comprehensive Psychiatry*, 1978, *19*, 363–369.

CHAPTER 23

Interpersonal Dysfunction

Alan S. Bellack and Randall L. Morrison

Introduction

It is a well-known truism that humans are "social animals." Social interactions are the hub of our existence, mediating work, leisure, the securing of food and shelter, and reproduction. The absence of quality interactions can have devastating consequences, ranging from retardation and autism in early infancy to the profound pattern of "institutionalization" found in many long-term residents of psychiatric hospitals. Consequently, it should not be surprising that social behavior has been a subject of great interest throughout history. Philosophers, theologians, and literary figures have long speculated on how and why people interact. More recently, social behavior has become a subject of scientific scrutiny. Social psychologists, linguists, sociologists, and anthropologists, among others, have devoted enormous energy to describing and understanding the rules, the content, and the structure of social encounters.

The relationship of social behavior to mental health and psychopathology was first highlighted by the personality theories of Carl Jung, Alfred Adler, and Harry Stack Sullivan. Their emphasis, naturally, was on the role of enduring, underlying traits, dispositions, and needs, which were thought to govern the form and quantity of interactions. Generally, the personality models made the tacit assumption that all people had the capability to interact effectively. Faulty interaction patterns were thought to result from problems in the personality structure (e.g., repressed hostility and anxiety). Hence, interpersonal difficulties were not viewed as problems in and of themselves. A strikingly different perspective was provided by the pioneering work of Zigler, Phillips, and their colleagues (Zigler & Levine, 1973; Zigler & Phillips, 1960, 1961, 1962). First, they emphasized the concept of *social competence*: the notion that effective social functioning depends on a set of abilities, which some people lack. Second, their work suggested that poor social functioning (i.e., low competence) could *lead to* psychopathology, rather than always resulting from it. While it is impossible to draw a direct connection from Zigler and Phillips to later behavioral work, their writings appear to have played an important role (cf. Bellack & Hersen, 1977a; Hersen & Bellack, 1976).

The primary stimulus for the behavioral interest in social functioning was the work of Wolpe and Lazarus (Wolpe, 1958; Wolpe &

Alan S. Bellack • Medical College of Pennsylvania at EPPI, 2900 Henry Avenue, Philadelphia, Pennsylvania 19129. Randall L. Morrison • Clinical Psychology Center, University of Pittsburgh, Pittsburgh, Pennsylvania 15260.

Lazarus, 1966). They highlighted the importance of assertiveness in a variety of "neurotic" problems, and they pioneered the use of assertiveness training to overcome social inhibitions and fears. Their early clinical work was followed up in the early 1970s by Michel Hersen, Richard Eisler, Richard McFall, and Arnold Goldstein, among others, who promulgated the *skills model* and developed empirically based training programs for alleviating skill deficits. In the ensuing years, behavioral interest in the area has mushroomed to staggering proportions. At least six behaviorally oriented books have been published on the topic in the last two years. Just about every recent issue of the *Journal of Consulting and Clinical Psychology*, as well as most behavioral journals, has at least one article on the behavioral assessment or treatment of interpersonal problems. Social-skills-training procedures have been applied or recommended for a wide variety of dysfunctions, including schizophrenia (Bellack, Hersen, & Turner, 1976); social isolation in children (Whitehill, Hersen, & Bellack, 1980); alcoholism (Miller & Eisler, 1977); depression (Bellack, Hersen, & Himmelhoch, 1981); hyperaggressivity (Fredericksen, Jenkins, Foy, & Eisler, 1976); sexual deviation (Barlow, Abel, Blanchard, Bristow, & Young, 1977); marital conflict (Birchler, 1979); drug addiction (Van Hasselt, Hersen, & Milliones, 1978); juvenile delinquency (Ollendick & Hersen, 1979); wife abuse (Rosenbaum & O'Leary, 1981); hysterical neurosis (Bellack & Hersen, 1978); heterosocial failure and shyness (Galassi & Galassi, 1979); and assertiveness deficits in women (Linehan & Egan, 1979). Either as a primary treatment or as a component of a treatment package, social skills training seems to have become a standard part of outpatient behavioral interventions. It is also widely accepted by society at large. Assertion training has become part of the "pop therapy" culture; assertion groups abound, and self-help books on the topic are big sellers. Interpersonal skills training is now a frequent curriculum component in elementary schools. Finally, skills training is one of the few psychosocial therapies generally recognized as effective with schizophrenics (Mosher & Keith, 1980).

Given the volume and diversity of material on this topic, it would be impossible to cover the literature in detail. Consequently, we present here an overview, highlighting the major issues. The interested reader is referred to the more specific review articles and book chapters that are cited throughout this chapter. We first consider just what the term *social skill* means: how it is defined and what elements comprise social skill. We also briefly examine how social skill develops and how it relates to psychopathology. Next, we discuss the assessment of social skill; this has been a problematic area. We describe the primary strategies that have been employed and highlight problems and limitations. The third major section deals with social-skill-training procedures. We describe the major strategies that are employed and give an overview of the literature on a number of behavioral dysfunctions, including depression, schizophrenia, dating skills, aggression, alcoholism, and unassertiveness. Finally, we briefly review some of the major problems confronting the field and consider research needs and future trends.

Nature of Social Skill

Definition

From a general perspective, everyone has a sense of what is meant by the term *social skill*, and there often is good agreement among friends and colleagues as to which acquaintances are unskilled. However, there has been remarkable difficulty in producing an acceptable definition of the term. Argyris (1965) referred to *social skill* as consisting of those behaviors that contributed to a person's effectiveness as part of a larger group of individuals. Weiss (1968) defined it in terms of communication, understanding, interest, and rapport between the speaker and the listener. According to Trower, Bryant, and Argyle (1978), "A person can be regarded as socially inadequate if he is unable to affect the behaviour and feelings of others in the way that he intends and society accepts. Such a person will appear annoying, unforthcoming, uninteresting, cold, destructive, bad-tempered, isolated or inept, and will generally be unrewarding to others" (p. 2). Libet and Lewinsohn (1973) defined *social skill* as "the complex ability both to emit behaviors which are positively or negatively reinforced and not to emit behaviors which are punished or extinguished by others'' (p. 304). Hersen and Bellack (1977) defined social skill as ''an individual's ability to express both positive and negative feelings in the interpersonal context without suffering consequent loss of social reinforcement. Such skill is demonstrated in a large variety of interpersonal contexts . . . and involve[s] the coordinated delivery of appropriate verbal and nonverbal responses. In addition, the socially skilled individual is attuned to the realities of the situation and is aware when he/she is likely to be reinforced for his/her efforts'' (p. 512).

Each of these definitions is effective in conveying a sense of what *social skill* connotes, but none is entirely satisfactory. The definitions tend to be too limited, omitting critical features. For example, the Trower *et al.* definition emphasizes society's response to the person and fails to specify what constitutes a skills repertoire. The other definitions are too inclusive, being so broad as to be functionally meaningless. Curran (1979) has explicated this point and highlighted one of the difficulties in arriving at an acceptable definition, using the Libet and Lewinsohn (1973) definition as an example: ''If a boxer ducks when an opponent throws him an overhand right, then the boxer is minimizing the strength of punishment from others, but is that an example of social skill? Why, on the other hand, do we not consider ducking as a social skill but regard eye contact as a component of social skill?'' (p. 321). Moreover, in some social contexts, physical violence is an acceptable response to conflict and thus might well be considered a social skill.

As indicated above, while no one definition has proved acceptable, there is general agreement on what the concept entails. First, the explicit use of the term *skills* signifies that interpersonal behavior consists of a set of learned performance abilities. The personality models presumed a more-or-less inherent capability to perform effectively. In contrast, the behavioral model emphasizes: (1) that response capability must be acquired, and (2) that it consists of an identifiable set of specific abilities, such as voice intonation and the use of social reinforcers (see below). The quality and the quantity of social behavior depend (to a great extent) on the individual's learned repertoire of social behaviors. By implication, some individuals have deficient learning histories, resulting in limited or faulty repertoires. They are defined as having *social skill deficits*. In keeping with a behavioral orientation, these deficits are presumed to be definable, measurable, and subject to remediation via education, practice, and reinforcement.

There are no definitive data on precisely how and when social skills are learned, but childhood is undoubtedly a critical period. For example, Kagan and Moss (1962) reported that ''passive withdrawal from stressful situations, dependency on the family, ease of anger arousal, involvement in intellectual mastery, social interaction anxiety, sex-role identification, and pattern of sexual behavior in adulthood were each related to reasonably analogous behavior dispositions during the early school years'' (p. 266). Case history reviews have demonstrated that the childhood years of adult schizophrenics were marked by interpersonal difficulties (cf. Roff & Knight, 1978). It has also been found that specific social-skill deficiencies could be identified in withdrawn and aggressive children as early as the third grade (Van Hasselt, Hersen, Whitehill, & Bellack, 1979).

> The most likely explanation for this early learning of social behavior is offered by social learning theory (cf. Bandura, 1977; Sherman & Farina, 1974). The most critical factor appears to be modeling. Children observe their parents interacting with them as well as with others, and model parental style. Both verbal behavior (e.g., conversational topics, expression of emotion and use of ''I'' statements, question asking and information giving), and non-verbal behavior (e.g., smiles, voice intonation, interpersonal distance) can be learned in this manner. Direct tuition (i.e., instruction) is another important vehicle for learning. Statements such as: ''Say you're sorry,'' ''We don't talk with food in our mouths,'' ''Don't talk to your brother that way,'' and ''Wash your hands before dinner,'' all shape social behavior. Finally, social responses can be directly reinforced or punished. For example, apologizing might be praised, question asking might be reinforced by interest and approval, and appropriate play behavior with friends might be encouraged and rewarded. Anecdotal evidence suggests that chronic patients typically have maladaptive family histories, which provides convergent validity for a social learning explanation of their social skill deficits. There are also some empirical data which demonstrate a high correlation between the social adequacy of adults and their parents (e.g., Sherman & Farina, 1974). (Bellack & Hersen, 1978, pp. 171–172)

Of course, the onus for faulty social functioning in adulthood (or encomiums for high skill) does not lay entirely with parents. Peers are important role models and sources of reinforcement, especially during adolescence. Social mores and customs, fads and styles of dress, and language all change during a person's lifetime; hence, one must continually learn in order to remain socially skilled. In this regard, skills can also be lost through disuse, as after lengthy periods of social isolation. Social performance can also be inhibited or disrupted by affective and cognitive disturbance (e.g., anxiety and depression).

A second generally accepted aspect of social skill is that "socially skilled behavior is situationally specific. Few, if any, aspects of interpersonal behavior are universally or invariably appropriate (or inappropriate). Both cultural and situational factors determine social norms. For example, in American society physical contact is sanctioned within families and between females, but not between males. Direct expression of anger is more acceptable within families and when directed toward an employee than with strangers or toward an employer" (Bellack & Hersen, 1978, p. 172). The acceptable form of eye contact, interpersonal (spatial) distance, voice intonation, posture, etc., vary according to sex, age, status, degree of familiarity, and the culture background of the interpersonal partner, as well as with the context of the interaction. The appropriateness of specific responses even varies at different stages of the same interaction:

The socially skilled individual must know when, where, and in what form different behaviors are sanctioned. Thus, social skill involves the ability to perceive and analyze subtle cues that define the situation, as well as the presence of a repertoire of appropriate responses.

The *third* asepct [of social skills] involves the maximization of reinforcement. Marriage, friendship, sexual gratification, employment, service (e.g., in stores, restaurants, etc.), and personal rights are all powerful sources of reinforcement which hinge on social skills. The unskilled individual is apt to fail in most or all or these spheres, and consequently experience anxiety, frustration, and isolation; all of which can (do!) result in psychopathology. Social skills are, thus, vehicles for receiving reinforcement and, indirectly, avoiding or reducing other dysfunctional behavior. (Bellack & Hersen, 1978, p. 172)

Social skillfulness must be appraised with regard to a functional criterion: How well can the person meet his or her own needs?

Components of Social Skill

Social skill is a broad construct that incorporates a variety of interpersonal response dimensions, such as assertiveness, friendliness, warmth, conversational facility, and empathy. While these lower-level constructs are somewhat more specific, they are not objectively defined and have defied objective measurement. Consequently, there has been an effort to break them down further by identifying the specific response parameters of which they are comprised. That is, what precise behaviors constitute friendliness or assertiveness? Unfortunately, this has been a most difficult task, and there is no specific blueprint for each (or any!) of the broad dimensions. However, there is agreement about which response elements generally tend to be most important (cf. Harper, Wiens, & Matarazzo, 1978; Trower *et al.*, 1978). As shown in Table 1, they can be divided into three categories: expressive elements, receptive elements, and interactive balance.

Expressive elements consist of those response parameters that communicate information to the interpersonal partner. The most important of these elements is speech content: what the person says. By far, this element transmits the most information and is the central factor in social skill. However important

Table 1. Components of Social Skills

A. Expressive elements
  1. Speech content
  2. Paralinguistic elements
    a. Voice volume
    b. Pace
    c. Pitch
    d. Tone
  3. Nonverbal behavior
    a. Proxemics
    b. Kinesics
    c. Gaze (eye control)
    d. Facial expression
B. Receptive elements (social perception)
  1. Attention
  2. Decoding
  3. "Social intelligence"
C. Interactive balance
  1. Response timing
  2. Turn taking

speech content is, it carries only part of the information that the listener receives. The way something is said and the associated bodily activity play a vital role in communication. They generally qualify speech content and can sometimes change the meaning of a message entirely.

Paralinguistic elements consist of the nonverbal aspects of speech that determine *how* something is said. Table 1 lists representative examples. *Voice volume* refers to how loud the person speaks. *Pace* refers to how rapidly the person speaks, as well as the use of pauses, phrasing, and latency. Pitch and tone are important features of voice quality. In general, the paralinguistic aspects of speech play a vital role in communicating affect and nuance. For example, the word *no* can be stated to reflect hostility, polite disagreement or refusal, a question (e.g., "Are you sure?"), nonhostile authoritativeness, or reluctant refusal and ambivalence, as a function of the manner in which the word is uttered. Humor, sarcasm, joy, despondency, anger, and anxiety can all be transmitted by voice characteristics, even when the speech content presents an alternative meaning.

Nonverbal behavior is bodily movement and posture. The major elements are listed in Table 1. Proxemics is "the manner in which individuals use physical space in their interactions with others and how physical space influences behavior" (Harper *et al.*, 1978, p. 246). The most important proxemic factor is interpersonal distance, which is bound by precise rules that vary across cultures, age groups, and sexes. The term *kinesics* subsumes a wide variety of body movements, including hand and arm gestures, head nods, and posture. Some movements, such as trembling hands, tense posture, and bouncing legs, are communicative even without speech. Others, such as head nods and illustrative hand gestures, provide emphasis to speech. Frequently referred to as *eye contact*, gaze involves how a person looks and what the person looks at, as well as eye-to-eye contact: "The main function of gaze is the perception of non-verbal signals from others; in addition, the amount and type of gaze communicates interpersonal attitudes. Gaze is closely coordinated with speech, and serves to add emphasis, provide feedback and attention, and manage speaking turns" (Trower *et al.*, 1978, p. 12). Facial expression also plays an important role in giving emphasis to and/or qualifying speech content. Moreover, it is thought to be the most important single factor in the communication of affect (Harper *et al.*, 1978).

The behavioral literature on both assessment of social skill and skills training has placed almost exclusive emphasis on observable response dimensions like those described above: "But, motor response skill is only one of the factors affecting performance in interpersonal interactions. . . . Subjects must also know when and where to emit the various responses in their repertoires. The most polished assertion response will not be functional if the individual does not know when he/she has been treated unfairly, or when assertion is likely to be appropriate" (Bellack, 1979b, p. 171). This aspect of social skill, which involves a set of receptive features, is typically referred to as *social perception* (Morrison & Bellack, 1981). Specifically, the individual must first attend to the cues provided by the interpersonal partner; these include all of the expressive elements described above. The information so received must then be effectively decoded. This is a cognitive event that is probably beyond the scope of work on social skill. Both of these processes require extensive knowledge about cultural mores and the significance of a tremendous number of expressive cues and response patterns in diverse settings. This factor is generally called *social intelligence*. Little is known about how receptive skills develop, how they may be assessed, or how they may be modified. Considering how vital they are to the smooth and effective use of response skills, this is an important area for future research.

We should point out that there is some controversy about whether social perception and cognitive processes should be considered a part of "social skill." This issue is cogently raised by Curran (1979):

However, I am troubled by the expansion of the construct when we are still far from a definition of social skill with respect to motoric behaviors. If we do not restrain ourselves and put some limits on the construct of social skill, it will expand to include all human behavior, and social skills training will soon come to mean any process which is capable of producing changes in human behavior. . . . My bias, at this time, is to limit the construct . . . to motoric behavior. We should measure cognitive processes because these processes are important with respect to both theory and treatment. However, let us agree not to call these cognitive processes components of social skill. (p. 323)

The final aspect of social skill is interactive balance. This is not a specific response; it is a general parameter related to the flow of social encounters. Interpersonal behavior is not static. It is *interactive*, and effective performance requires a delicate give-and-take, or meshing. The absolute quantity, rate, or intensity of responses is often less important than their timing: when they are emitted in relation to the partner's behavior. For example, Fischetti, Curran, and Wessberg (1977) found no difference in the number of social reinforcers supplied to a female partner by heterosocially anxious and nonanxious males, but the two groups differed substantially in the *timing* of reinforcing responses. In the same context, Duncan and Fiske (1977) reported that when two people converse, smooth transitions from one speaker to the other depend on the proper placement of up to six discrete "turn-taking cues." Moreover, several of these cues involve *change* in a response rather than the simple emission of a particular behavior (e.g., initiating or breaking off eye contact, altering voice pitch or pace). When conversants do not use these signals and match their behavior to one another, the conversation is marred by interruptions, simultaneous talking, and long pauses.

Associated Factors

The discussion to this point seemingly implies that the quality of interpersonal performance depends entirely on the individual's skill repertoire (including expressive, receptive, and interactive elements). The repertoire does play a vital role and determines the outer limit of performance quality, but a number of other factors also have a major impact on how much and how well one interacts. Some of the primary influences are presented in Table 2.

The history of reinforcement (or punishment) for various interpersonal responses can determine the types of social situations the individual will enter and the specific behaviors

Table 2. Factors Affecting Social Behavior

1. Reinforcement history
2. Cognitive factors
   a. Goals
   b. Expectancies
   c. Values
   d. Etc.
3. Affect
   a. Anxiety
   b. Depression
   c. Anger
   d. Etc.
4. Psychopathology
   a. Thought disorder
   b. Alcohol–drug addiction
   c. Etc.

he or she will perform. For example, a woman might have all the skills required to be assertive with her husband but not use them because previous attempts have been unreinforced or punished. Cognitive factors play a related role. Social situations are likely to be avoided and behaviors are likely to be inhibited if they are thought to be socially inappropriate, immoral, unfair, or likely to lead to unpleasant consequences (Eisler, Frederiksen, & Peterson, 1978). Thus, Fiedler and Beach (1978) found that whether people act assertively is a function of the consequences they anticipate for such behavior. Anecdotal clinical data suggest that many clients are reluctant to express complaints and to stand up for their rights, as they associate such assertiveness with hostility and aggression. Shyness in college males is often more a function of inaccurate self-evaluation and expectations of rejection than of heterosocial skill deficits (Arkowitz, 1977; Galassi & Galassi, 1979).

Another factor that can have a dramatic impact on interpersonal behavior is affect. Anxiety and anger can disrupt the smooth performance of well-learned routines, causing stuttering, trembling, rapid speech, poverty of speech content, etc. (Bellack, 1980). High levels of emotional arousal can interfere with the receptive and cognitive processes required for effective performance. Of course, social anxiety can also lead to the avoidance of social situations. Depression is associated with reduced behavioral output, loss of the desire and energy to pursue relationships, and a variety of responses that elicit aversive reactions from others (Coyne, 1976; Hammen & Peters, 1978; Howes & Hokanson, 1979).

The final factor presented in Table 2 is psychopathology. We use this term in a generic manner to represent major syndromes or patterns of behavioral dysfunction (e.g., schizophrenia and alcoholism). Some of the specific symptoms associated with such syndromes can have a dramatic impact on social behavior. For example, the thought disorder and the behavioral disorganization associated with schizophrenia obviously prevent smooth social performance. Alcohol and heroin have a general debilitative affect, as well as disrupting ongoing behavior. The gross mood swings produced by manic-depressive disorder similarly produce anomalous behavior. Not only can these disturbances interfere with the use of social skills in the repertoire, but they can cause the erosion and the loss of skills.

The previous discussion indicates that negative affect and psychopathology can lead to poor social performance. This is only one of the ways in which these factors can interface with social skill. As is discussed further below, social skills deficits have been implicated in the genesis of a number of disorders, including depression (Bellack, Hersen, & Himmelhoch, 1980; Libet & Lewinsohn, 1973); alcoholism (Miller & Eisler, 1977); and hysterical neurosis (Blanchard & Hersen, 1976). The general model for this line of causation is that skill deficits lead to interpersonal failure and/or inability to achieve goals. In turn, this results in stress, negative affect, and the development of maladaptive behavior patterns to meet goals. A third pattern of interaction involves multiple determinism, in which skills deficits lead to disturbances in conjunction with some other factor. For example, skills deficits might lead to clinical depression only in conjunction with adverse life events, such as the loss of a significant other. Unassertiveness might contribute to alcoholism only in individuals who have a biochemical susceptibility. This ''necessary but not sufficient'' pattern is probably the most common, although there are no specific data in its support.

Assessment of Social Skill

In keeping with the behavioral emphasis on assessment, there is a voluminous literature on the assessment of social skill. Several review articles and book chapters have appeared on this topic in the past few years (Arkowitz, 1977, 1981; Bellack, 1979a,b; Curran & Mariotto, 1981; Eisler, 1976; Hersen & Bellack, 1977). The reader is referred to these sources for a detailed account of the literature. In this section, we describe the primary strategies that have been employed and identify some of the problems confronting the field.

Interviewing

The clinical interview is probably the most widespread strategy employed. The patient is the best and sometimes the only source of information about his or her interpersonal experience and associated thoughts, affect, etc. The interview provides the most convenient and the most broad based strategy for securing this information. In addition to a description of current functioning, the interview also provides two other types of information: the interpersonal history and informal observational data. Historical information can provide important clues about the development of the current problem, whether the client ever performed effectively, etc. This information can be valuable in treatment planning (e.g., Is the interpersonal problem a by-product of other difficulties, or does it predate and underlie them?). The interview also affords the clinician an opportunity to observe the client interacting; it is, after all, an interpersonal encounter. The situation is unusual and some client behavior might be specific to it, but numerous important clues can be garnered: personal hygiene and grooming, use of social amenities, ability to perceive and respond to social cues, ease of establishing rapport, etc.

Unfortunately, interviewing is a highly inexact science, and there are few empirical data documenting its reliability and validity (Bellack & Hersen, 1977; Morganstern & Tevein, 1981). Patient reports are subject to the same bias, distortion, and faulty recollection associated with any self-report (cf. Bellack & Hersen, 1977). The interviewer is an imperfect observer and is another potential source of error. On the other hand, no objective assessment strategy has proved to be as sensitive in detecting the subtleties of performance quality as the subjective ratings of human observers (Curran, 1979). Hence, the standardization and the empirical evaluation of interview procedures is a high priority for future research.

Self-Monitoring

Self-monitoring (SM) has become one of the most widely used behavioral assessment procedures, yet it has been only a peripheral tool for the assessment of social skills. The only empirical literature which has regularly employed SM is research on heterosocial skills. . . . Subjects have frequently been asked to keep dating logs, recording information ranging from simple dating frequency to extensive self-evaluations of specific aspects of performance (Arkowitz, 1977). In addition to monitoring behavior, subjects have also been asked to rate subjective distress or anxiety and to note discriminative stimuli and environmental consequences to their behavior. Similar forms of SM would seem to be applicable for assessing other social skills as well, although anecdotal clinical reports outnumber research examples of this application. (Bellack, 1979a, p. 85)

The advantages and disadvantages of SM have been well-documented (Kazdin, 1974b; Nelson, 1977). It generally is more objective, reliable, and valid than other types of self-report data, but it is subject to reactivity and inconsistency. With regard to the recording of interpersonal behavior, SM has the special advantage of providing semiobjective data on behaviors that are not otherwise open to direct observation (e.g., intimate interactions, infrequent encounters and conflicts). Conversely, it is unlikely that people can accurately observe and evaluate molecular aspects of their performance (e.g., voice quality, gaze). It is difficult for trained observers to rate these responses from videotapes, let alone for subjects to recognize their fleeting occurrence during an interaction. Also, subjects often are unaware when they have misperceived a partner's behavior or have failed to identify the context of a situation correctly. Thus, SM is primarily useful for logging events, securing subject evaluations of performance, and developing a general picture of motor behavior categories (e.g., the general content of a conversation, the expression of praise).

Self-Report Inventories

Self-report scales and inventories comprise the most widely employed assessment strategy. In fact, almost every outcome study includes several overlapping scales measuring the central skill (e.g., assertiveness), as well as other scales that measure presumably related attributes (e.g., social anxiety). While such overkill guarantees breadth of coverage, it does not guarantee criterion validity, that is, an accurate picture of the subject's skill level and *in vivo* behavior.

Until recently, researchers in this area seemed to prefer to develop their own self-report instruments rather than to evaluate psychometrically and utilize existing devices. This "build-a-better-mousetrap" approach has produced a plethora of related instruments, but it has not provided a sound, consistently used battery. The existing instruments vary in reliability, validity, factorial structure, and item format. Several have been carefully constructed according to sound psychometric practice, but even the most sophisticated require further testing before they can be confidently recommended. In addition, even the best instruments are probably more useful for screening and gross categorization than for the precise evaluation of a specific subject's strengths and weaknesses. As stated above in regard to SM, subjects generally cannot report on much of their interpersonal behavior. In addition, the use of summative scores on these devices (e.g., adding up item scores to yield an overall score) masks the situational variability of performance. Thus, while self-report scales can be a valuable component of a comprehensive assessment package, they cannot be substituted for behavioral observation.

Behavioral Observation

One of the tenets of behavioral assessment is that direct observation is the most valid and desirable strategy. It should not be surprising that this approach has been widely employed in work on social skill. Three general strategies have been employed: observation in the natural environment, staged naturalistic interactions, and role-play enactments.

Observation in the Natural Environment. This is the most desirable strategy, but it has been extremely difficult to employ. Most interpersonal behaviors of interest (e.g., dating and assertion) occur in private circumstances and/or are infrequent and unpredictable. Hence, they are not readily accessible to the researcher or the clinician. The cost of sending observers into the community is another limiting factor. Given these difficulties, there are few examples of *in vivo* observation in the literature. King, Liberman, Roberts, and Bryan (1977) had chronic patients engage in a series of preplanned assertion situations with community residents. An observer escorted the patient to the setting and stood nearby during the interaction. Arkowitz and his colleagues have arranged dates for college students with heterosocial skill deficits and secured retrospective ratings from the dating partners (Christensen & Arkowitz, 1974; Royce & Arkowitz, 1976). The most systematic work on *in vivo* observation has been employed in research on family interaction (cf. Jacob, 1976; Patterson, 1974; Weiss & Margolin, 1977). Both live observers and automated tape recording systems have been stationed in the home. Observation is generally limited to circumscribed periods of high interaction, such as the dinner hour. This work has not generally been considered part of the social skill literature, but the focus on communication patterns makes it clearly relevant. The techniques employed (and their advantages and disadvantages) can be directly translated to work on social skill *per se*.

The *in vivo* observation strategies that have been employed have two primary limitations. First are the potential effects of reactivity (cf. Johnson & Bolstad, 1973). The presence of live observers would undoubtedly distort subject behavior in intimate situations and those associated with high affect arousal or socially undesirable behavior (e.g., wife abuse and intoxication). There is also the likelihood of reactivity on the part of the interpersonal partner, who is not a subject or a client. Thus, one is likely to observe the subject on his or her "best behavior" rather than exhibiting typical behavior. (Of course, this behavior does reflect some of the skills in the person's repertoire.) A second factor is restricted access to important situations. As previously stated, intimate interactions and infrequent events are generally not available for observation. *In vivo*

observation is most useful with "captive" populations, such as psychiatric inpatients or school-age children, and with highly public behaviors, such as play and casual conversation. Problems of reactivity and access are both limited in these contexts.

Staged Naturalistic Interactions. In response to the expense and the limited access of *in vivo* observation, many researchers have attempted to stage important interactions in the laboratory or clinic. Several different formats have been employed. Bellack, Hersen, and Lamparski (1979) surreptitiously observed male undergraduates interacting with a female confederate, who was introduced as another subject. The procedure was designed to assess the subject's ability to initiate a conversation with a potential dating partner. Arkowitz, Lichtenstein, McGovern, and Hines (1975) also used female confederates to assess dating skills. They avoided the use of deception by informing the subjects that the female partner was a research assistant. In one situation, the subjects were told to interact with the woman *as if* they had just met. In a second task, they engaged in a mock telephone conversation and responded as if they were trying to arrange a date with the confederate.

A third variation of this general strategy involves the use of so-called critical incidents. These are brief interchanges in which the subject is presented with a situation calling for an assertive response. For example, subjects have been deliberately shortchanged after participating in a study, pressured by confederates acting as magazine salespeople, asked to perform unreasonable favors, and denied earned privileges. In each case, the subject's skill in resisting social pressure or unfair treatment was assessed.

It is difficult to evaluate the utility and validity of these procedures on the basis of the existing literature. Most of the particular scenarios have been developed on an ad hoc basis in the context of specific research projects. They have each typically been orchestrated in an idiosyncratic fashion, according to face validity. In addition to content variations (e.g., waiting room versus prospective date), they also vary along a number of other potentially important dimensions. Durations have been arbitrarily varied from three minutes to 10 minutes, although behavior may well change at different points in the interaction. Confederates have been instructed to respond in a warm or neutral manner, to make comments after silences ranging from

5 seconds to 60 seconds, and to make only specified comments or to be more spontaneous. The effects of these variations are unknown, and warrant empirical evaluation. (Bellack, 1979b, p. 163)

A few conclusions can be drawn. The critical incident procedures generally tend to have anomalous stimulus elements and generally are not highly valid. The "act-as-if" format yields different results than interactions that employ deception. Subjects tend to perform better in the "as-if" context, but they report that the surreptitious format elicits more representative behavior (Higgins, Alonso, & Pendleton, 1979; Wessberg, Mariotto, Conger, Conger, & Farrell, 1979). There are also data to suggest that responses vary considerably when subjects are retested (Mungas & Walters, 1979). More general conclusions about reliability, validity, and format must await future research.

Role-Play Enactments. Role playing has been the most frequently employed strategy for assessing social skill. The basic procedure entails three steps: (1) an interpersonal scenario is described to the subject; (2) an experimental confederate, portraying someone in the scenario, delivers a prompt line; and (3) the subject responds to the confederate as if they were actually in the scenario. Numerous variations of this basic approach have been employed. Subjects have responded to audiotapes and videotapes as well as to live confederates. The interactions have been limited to one brief interchange or have been extended through varying numbers of retorts by the confederate. The number and content of the scenes have varied dramatically, as has the style of confederate behavior. Several features of role-play tests make them an attractive strategy. They are inexpensive and easy to employ, and the brief format makes it possible to present the subject with many different stimulus situations. Similarly, it is easy to construct a set of scenarios to fit each individual study or subject.

Unfortunately, the simplicity of constructing new items and the face validity of the procedure have proved to be disadvantages as well. There are widespread inconsistencies in format and content from study to study, making comparisons difficult. With few exceptions (cf. Freedman, Rosenthal, Donahoe, Schlundt,

& McFall, 1978; Perri & Richards, 1979), tests have been constructed solely on the basis of face validity and have uncertain psychometric adequacy. Moreover, many procedural variations that have been casually employed produce markedly different effects. There are substantial differences between brief and extended interactions, and between taped and live confederates (Galassi & Galassi, 1976). Subtle differences in scene content (e.g., the sex and the familiarity of the partner) produce dramatically different responses (Eisler, Hersen, Miller, & Blanchard, 1975; Hopkins, Krawitz, & Bellack, 1981). The effects of many other factors (e.g., the number of scenarios and the confederate's response style) are unknown but are probably meaningful as well.

Perhaps the greatest concern about role-play procedures pertains to the criterion validity of the entire strategy. That is, does performance on a role-play test correspond to the way subjects respond when actually confronted by the enacted situations? The answer to this question is a resounding *maybe not*! Primary support for the approach comes from studies in which "known groups" have been differentiated by role-play performance. For example, low-assertive psychiatric patients have performed more poorly than their high-assertive peers (Eisler *et al.*, 1975); low-frequency daters have been differentiated from high-frequency daters (Arkowitz *et al.*, 1975); and delinquent youths have been distinguished from nondelinquents (Freedman *et al.*, 1978). Numerous studies have also found that skill-deficient subjects who receive social skill training improve their performance on role-play tests more than similar subjects who do not receive such training. However, these data are not consistent, and they provide only convergent validational support.

Studies in which role-play behavior has been directly compared with performance in related criterion situations (Bellack, Hersen, & Lamparski, 1979; Bellack, Hersen, & Turner, 1978) or with identical situations *in vivo* (Bellack, Hersen, & Turner, 1979) have produced less positive results. The findings of these studies suggest that, at best, the traditional role-play procedure has modest validity. Furthermore, it appears to be differentially valid for males and females and for different specific behaviors. Much greater care is needed in the construction of role-play tests, and procedural modifications will be required if these devices are to prove useful.

The Focus of Assessment

The previous discussion pertains to *how* social skill can be assessed (e.g., self-report and role play). The question of *what* should be assessed is no less problematic. Two general strategies have been employed, singly or in combination: molecular and molar.

The molecular approach is closely tied to the behavioral model of social skill. Interpersonal behavior is broken down into specific component elements, such as the expressive features described above (e.g., eye contact and speech rate). These elements are then measured in a highly objective fashion (e.g., number of smiles and number of seconds of eye contact). Such measures are highly reliable and have good face validity. However, there are a number of serious problems with this approach. The most serious concern pertains to just how meaningful it is to measure such specific, static response characteristics. Social impact is determined not by the number of seconds of eye contact or by speech duration, but by a complex pattern of responses that occur in conjunction with the partner's behavior. Research suggests that the specific elements most commonly assessed do not account for much of the variance in response quality, either individually or when combined mathematically (cf. Romano & Bellack, 1980). Thus, the molecular measurement strategy might be yielding an elegant but trivial set of data. However, it must be emphasized that the behaviors commonly assessed have not been selected on an empirical basis. Only recently have researchers begun to analyze social skill systematically in an effort to determine precisely which response elements are critical (cf. Romano & Bellack, 1980; Royce & Weiss, 1975). The molecular approach might prove to be more useful when we learn more about what determines the impact of interpersonal behaviors and generate a socially validated assessment plan.

The molar approach to assessment eschews specific, objective ratings in favor of overall, subjective ratings. Judges employ Likert scales to rate overall skill, anxiety, assertiveness, etc. Their subjective impressions integrate the component response elements and provide a measure of how the subject impacts on others. These ratings tend to correspond better with meaningful external criteria, but they have somewhat lower reliability than molecular ratings. Their major disadvantage is that they fail to indicate what specifically the subject is doing well or poorly; hence, they do not provide information about which skills should be covered in training or which were improved in training. Nor do they specify whether the judges were focusing on the effectiveness or quality of the response (e.g., Did it get the job done?) or on their personal reaction to it (e.g., Do they like it, or would they respond in the same way?). Given that the purpose of assessment and training is ultimately tied to how the subjects affects others, qualitative ratings are vital. But it is important to break down such ratings and determine the cues that the judges use in making their judgments. Until problems with both the molar and the molecular approaches are resolved, the two procedures should be employed in conjunction with one another.

Two other issues pertaining to the focus of assessment also require brief comment. The first involves the assessment of receptive skills. As previously indicated, the importance of these elements has only recently been recognized; consequently, there are no acceptable instruments to assess them. This is a high priority for future work. The second issue concerns the role of social validation in the assessment process (cf. Kazdin, 1977). The primary criterion employed to identify targets for assessment and training and to evaluate outcome has been the researcher's own judgment about what is important and what is appropriate. It is now becoming apparent that much more attention must be paid to how the subject's environment evaluates his or her behavior. At one level, this can be accomplished by securing peer judgments about the importance and desirability of different behaviors. For example, several recent studies have investigated community reactions to different forms of assertion responses in order to determine the acceptability of various responses (Hollandsworth & Cooley, 1978; Hull & Schroeder, 1979). At another level, peers and significant others (e.g., spouses) are being asked to evaluate the subject's performance. Thus, the judgment of the researcher (the expert) is supplemented by the judgment of people with whom the subject will actually interact. While these measures have some distinct limitations (Kane & Lawler, 1978), they are an important addition to our "in-house" criteria.

Social Skills Training

Models of Social Skills Training

Interest in social skills training has increased dramatically as documentation regarding the relationship between social competence and behavioral disorder has accumulated in both the psychiatric and the psychological literature. As specific social deficits that are critical to diverse forms of maladaptive behavior have been identified, social-skills-training programs have been instituted to ameliorate these deficits. Currently, there are four major viewpoints regarding the etiology and the maintenance of social disability. These can be labeled the *skills deficit model*, the *conditioned-anxiety model*, the *cognitive-evaluative model*, and the *faulty-discrimination model*. Each of the four concepts has given rise to different social-skills-training protocols.

Skills Deficit Model. The great majority of the social-skills-training studies that have been reported in the literature have been based on the skills deficit model (Bellack & Hersen, 1978; Hersen & Bellack, 1976). According to this model, the individual who evidences poor social skills lacks certain specific motor responses from his or her behavioral repertoire and/or uses inappropriate responses. The individual may never have learned the appropriate behavior (at least, to sufficient strength for smooth application) or may have learned inappropriate behavior. Given this inadequate repertoire, the individual does not handle the demands of various interpersonal situations appropriately.

The most common training paradigm based on the skills deficit model is the response ac-

quisition approach. The treatment proceeds by training on each deficient response element (one at a time, in order of increasing difficulty) in a series of problem situations (sequentially, in order of increasing difficulty). The situation hierarchy must be determined for each patient. With regard to response elements, we have found it most effective to train the patient in conversational skills first, followed by perceptual skills and special problem areas. Within each of these areas, specific responses should be attacked in an order that maximizes the patient's success throughout the training (i.e., based on what the patient can most easily learn at each point). The strategy of focusing on the response elements one at a time and of ensuring continuous success throughout the treatment is especially important for patients with attentional difficulties (i.e., chronic schizophrenics). Training can be telescoped when the patient is less disturbed or when it has proceeded to a point where many responses are generalized across situations.

The training consists of five techniques: (1) instructions; (2) role play; (3) feedback and social reinforcement; (4) modeling; and (5) practice.

Instructions. The patient is first given specific instructions about the response at issue, including why and how it should be performed. For example, "If people are going to know you are serious, you must look at them when you speak. Try to look at my eyes or nose when you answer me."

Role Play. After instructions are given, the patient role-plays a scenario with the therapist or a role-model assistant. The format is analogous to the BAT-R, including a description of the situation and a prompt (or a series of prompts in an extended interaction).

Feedback and Social Reinforcement. Following the role play, the patient is given feedback about his or her performance. This feedback should be specific and should include positive social reinforcement for improved aspects of performance. Our clinical work suggests that social reinforcement, encouragement, and the frequent experience of some sucess play a vital role in maintaining the patient's interest and effort. An example of feedback is as follows: "You did much better that time. You told me that you wanted to go home in a clear manner, and you looked at me while you spoke. Let's try it again, and this time try to emphasize the word *no*. It will make your statement more convincing.'' This statement would be followed by further role-play.

Modeling. Some behaviors are relatively easy to learn (e.g., eye contact and response latency), and instructions, role play, and feedback will be sufficient. Similarly, higher functioning patients can master many of the responses with only these three techniques (cf. McFall & Twentyman, 1973; Rimm, Snyder, Depue, Haanstad, & Armstrong, 1976). However, more complex responses (e.g., most verbal content elements, intonation) and more regressed patients almost invariably require modeling (Edelstein & Eisler, 1976; Hersen, Eisler, Miller, Johnson, & Pinkston, 1973; Rimm *et al.*, 1976). Rather than simply instructing the patient in how to respond, the therapist or the role model actually performs (models) the appropriate response. The modeling display should focus on the particular response element at issue and should be prefaced and followed by a description of the relevant aspects of the display. The modeled response should also be based on the patient's previously role-played response. For example, ''That was better. This time let me try it. Listen to the way I make clear exactly what I want to do. 'I would like to help, but it's late, and I have to leave now.' See, I didn't simply say it was late, but I told him I had to leave right then.'' The patient would then be directed to role-play the response again. This sequence of instructions, role play, feedback and reinforcement, and modeling is repeated until the response is mastered. Training then shifts to the next response or, if the target situation has been mastered, to the next situation.

Practice. Regardless of how effectively the patient performs the requisite responses during the training sessions, there is little likelihood that her or his performance will generalize to the natural environment or be maintained in the absence of directed practice *in vivo*. The importance of practice is underscored by research in which success was achieved by practice alone (e.g., Christensen & Arkowitz, 1974; King *et al.*, 1977). Practice is encouraged both by giving general instruc-

tions to ''try things out'' and by giving specific homework assignments at the conclusion of each session (beginning after at least one response element has been mastered). The assignments should be relatively specific and should be geared to a level of difficulty and a situation that will maximize the probability of success (and reinforcement by the environment).

A second version of social skills training based on the skills deficit model is the use of covert modeling procedures in the assertion training protocol developed by Kazdin and his colleagues (Kazdin, 1974a, 1976; Hersen, Kazdin, Bellack, & Turner, 1979). Role-play scenarios again are used as the stimulus material, but they are rehearsed covertly (in imagination) rather than overtly. Each scene consists of three parts: (1) a description of the context and situation in which an assertive response is appropriate; (2) an imagined model who makes an assertive response (the model may be the individual undergoing assertion training); and (3) the favorable consequences that result from the model's response. During the training sessions, the subject is instructed to relax with his or her eyes closed and to imagine each scenario as it is presented by the therapist. Initially, the therapist presents the description of the situation. The subject signals by raising his or her index finger when he or she has a vivid image of the situation in mind. Next, the therapist presents the assertive response performed by the model for imagination by the subject. Finally, the therapist describes the positive consequences that are to be imagined by the subject. The training proceeds up a hierarchy of assertion scenarios as in the response acquisition approach. The covert modeling procedure is sometimes combined with behavior rehearsal. After covert imagery instructions, the subjects are asked to role-play the same situation. Homework assignments can be given for practicing the covert modeling procedure.

Conditioned-Anxiety Model. The conditioned-anxiety model assumes that the individual has the requisite skills in his or her repertoire but is inhibited from responding in a socially appropriate fashion because of conditioned-anxiety responses. Through aversive experiences or vicarious conditioning, previously neutral cues relating to social interactions have become associated with aversive stimuli. These conditioned reactions may develop regardless of the adequacy of the individual's repertoire of social skills.

Social dysfunction that results from conditioned anxiety may best be considered a form of anxiety disorder. As such, it is not included as a major focus of our discussion. According to the conditioned-anxiety model, the problem in social functioning can be eliminated only if the anxiety is extinguished, thereby permitting an opportunity for the expression of more appropriate behaviors. Anxiety reduction techniques, rather than social skills training, are treatments of choice (see Chapter 13 in this volume, by Emmelkamp).

Cognitive-Evaluative Model. The cognitive-evaluative model posits that the source of an individual's social inadequacy is faulty cognitive appraisal of social performance and the expectation of aversive consequences. Negative self-appraisals and negative self-statements are seen as mediating the social anxiety and/or the social avoidance of the interpersonally deficient individual. The social-skills-training procedures that follow from this model typically approximate the cognitive restructuring techniques outlined by Goldfried, Decenteceo, and Weinberg (1974). During training, the therapist provides instructions on how to restructure problem beliefs. The therapist also models a progression of thoughts to demonstrate the restructuring process. Third, the training sessions involve the practice of cognitive restructuring, using hierarchically presented imaginal situations during which the client searches for the rules and beliefs mediating his or her response and, if necessary, restructures the belief. Before each situation is practiced, the client is encouraged to verbalize one or more restructuring principles or adaptive beliefs that can guide the restructuring (self-instructions). After each practice sequence, the client self-evaluates and, if appropriate, self-reinforces the restructuring efforts. The therapist provides additional feedback, coaching, and response reinforcement. Also, homework is assigned involving *in vivo* practice of the cognitive restructuring procedures.

Faulty Discrimination Model. The faulty discrimination model assumes that the social disability is due to the individual's not knowing how to match specific social behaviors with specific social situations. Socially unskilled behavior may be the result of a failure on the part of the individual to discriminate adequately the situations in which a response already in the repertoire is likely to be effective. Therefore, the person may fail to respond or may respond inappropriately despite an adequate repertoire of interpersonal behaviors. This model suggests a therapy concerned with teaching the individual to discriminate which situations call for which behaviors.

Liberman, Wallace, and their colleagues (Wallace, 1978; Wallace, Nelson, Lukoff, Webster, Rappe, & Ferris, 1978) have developed such a package, which is intended to teach patients the "rules" or "language" of interpersonal interactions. As described by Wallace (1978), their program is an integrated assessment–treatment package for use with chronically relapsing schizophrenic patients. According to this program, social skills are considered problem-solving skills. Interpersonal communication is seen as the outcome of a three-part process. First, the individual has to correctly receive the "values" of all relevant situational parameters. These include the content of past and current messages, as well as the characteristics of the interpersonal partner, such as emotion, goals, and identity. Second, the individual must process the "values" of these parameters in order to generate potential responses, from which one is selected. The processing functions include the identification of one's own goals, the generation of response options, and the evaluation of the consequences of each option. Third, the individual must send the chosen response in a manner that will maximize the probability of attaining the goal that initially prompted the interpersonal communication. Sending involves numerous component behaviors, as specified in the skill deficit model.

The assessment–treatment package is implemented by means of a role-play format. After each situation is role-played with the patient, he or she is asked a series of questions designed to assess his or her knowledge of the receiving and processing variables. The questions used to assess accurate receiving might include (1) "Who spoke to you?" (2) "What was the main topic?'' (3) "What was ———— feeling?'' The questions used to assess correct processing might be (1) "What was your short-term goal?'' (2) "What was your long-term goal?'' (3) "If you did ———— what would ———— feel? What would ———— do? Would you get your short-term goal? Would you get your long-term goal?''

The questions serve as the assessment devices. Incorrect answers result in the application of training techniques designed to elicit the correct answers. Sending skills are evaluated during the role play and are trained by means of the typical response-acquisition procedures (e.g., modeling and feedback).

Social Skills Training with Schizophrenic Patients

Deficiencies in social skills are currently considered as central to the development and continuation of schizophrenia as its more noticeable aspects, such as thinking disturbances, delusional systems, gross mood anomalies, and idiosyncratic mannerisms and language (e.g., Goldsmith & McFall, 1975; Hersen & Bellack, 1976; Zigler & Phillips, 1961, 1962). Many schizophrenic patients are socially isolated. They often fail to become integrated into a natural social network that might assist them in coping with social demands (Gleser & Gottschalk, 1967; McClelland & Walt, 1968). The schizophrenic's family is often the only natural network of which he or she is a part. However, the interaction patterns of families of schizophrenics may actually serve to increase the probability of relapse (Brown, Birley, & Wing, 1972; Vaughn & Leff, 1976). Furthermore, the schizophrenic patient often lacks the requisite skills to deal with stressful interpersonal interactions.

There have been numerous investigations of social skills training with schizophrenic patients. Single-subject experimental case studies conducted by Hersen, Bellack, Eisler, and their colleagues (Bellack *et al.*, 1976; Edelstein & Eisler, 1976; Hersen & Bellack, 1976; Hersen, Turner, Edelstein, & Pinkston, 1975; Williams, Turner, Watts, Bellack, & Hersen, 1977) provide strong evidence of the clinical efficacy of social skills training with this population.

As an example, Hersen and Bellack (1976) convincingly demonstrated the controlling effects of social skills training on targeted behaviors with two chronic schizophrenics. In one case, the treatment consisted of instructions and feedback. In the second case, instructions, feedback, and modeling were used. The targeted behaviors (eye contact, speech duration, speech disruptions, smiles, requests for new behavior, and compliances) were treated sequentially and cumulatively in a multiple-baseline design. The BAT-R (Eisler *et al.*, 1975) was used as both the assessment and the training vehicle. The training was directed toward improving both positive and negative assertiveness. The training began after each patient's phenothiazines were regulated, with drug dosage maintained at a constant level in baseline, training, and follow-up. The results were positive for both patients. Specific target behaviors improved when the treatment was specifically directed toward them, and gradual gains in overall assertiveness were recorded by independent observers. Additionally, the treatment gains remained at two-, four-, six-, and eight-week follow-ups.

Bellack *et al.* (1976) reported positive results for two of three schizophrenic patients. Improvements on topographical behaviors (such as eye contact) generalized to novel scenes on the BAT-R and were maintained at an 8- to 10-week follow-up. However, appropriate requests for behavioral change did not generalize as well to novel situations as did the "simpler" topographical behaviors.

Single-case experimental designs by Liberman and his colleagues have provided further demonstrations of the effectiveness of social skills training, based on the completion of homework assignments. Using a multiple-baseline design across areas of homework assignments, Liberman, Lillie, Falloon, Vaughn, Harper, Leff, Hutchinson, Ryan, and Stoute (1978) evaluated the effects of training on three subjects. There were three areas of homework assignments: specified interactions with (1) members of the nursing staff; (2) with parents; and (3) with social and vocational contacts in the community. The training was conducted over a 10-week period. During Weeks 1 and

2, performance on all assigned tasks was assessed. Training was then introduced for interactions with the nursing staff during Weeks 3–6. The training was shifted to interactions with parents as well as nursing staff during Weeks 7–8. Finally, during Weeks 9 and 10, the training was focused on interactions with community agents, family, and nursing staff. The results indicated that the completion of homework assignments did not change until the training was applied to that specific area. Thus, the results suggest that the training was responsible for the increase in the rate of completed assignments. However, it should be noted that while demonstrating the controlling effects of social skills training, the results also suggest that little or no generalization of training occurred. That is, training that was focused on interactions that took place in one setting, or with certain individuals, did not affect the subjects' behavior in other settings, or with other individuals. The findings therefore indicate that although social skills training is an effective behavior-change technique for schizophrenic patients, particular attention should be directed toward ensuring that generalization of training to novel situations in the natural environment is attained.

A number of researchers have examined the effectiveness of social skills training for schizophrenics in a group context (Field & Test, 1975; Lomont, Gilner, Spector, & Skinner, 1969; Percell, Berwick, & Beigel, 1974; Williams *et al.*, 1977). These studies have reported improvements on a variety of self-report and behavioral measures ranging from significant decreases on the D and Pt scales of the MMPI (Lomont *et al.*, 1969) to significant increases in eye contact, speech duration, intonation, smiles, and physical gestures (Williams *et al.*, 1977).

There have been few well-controlled comparisons of the efficacy of social skills training and other modes of psychotherapy with schizophrenic patients. Goldsmith and McFall (1975) compared the effects of interpersonal skills training, a pseudotherapy control, and an assessment-only control. The interpersonal skills training resulted in significantly greater pre–post changes than the two controls.

The effectiveness of social skills training was compared with the effectiveness of a sen-sitivity-group training program by Monti, Curran, Corriveau, DeLancey, and Hagerman (1980). In this study, 46 psychiatric patients were randomly assigned to one of the treatments for 20 daily 1-hr training sessions. It should be noted that only 16 of the patients had been diagnosed as psychotic. The 30 remaining patients were "neurotics." Patients in the social-skills-training group improved significantly more on self-report questionnaires and a role-play assessment measure than did the patients in the sensitivity training group. With the exception of group mean scores on the Rathus Assertiveness Schedule (Rathus, 1973b), significant differences were maintained at a six-month follow-up.

An earlier study by Monti and his colleagues (Monti, Fink, Norman, Curran, Hayes, & Caldwell, 1979) compared the effectiveness of social skills training with that of a bibliotherapy program and a typical hospital-treatment control group. The subjects were 30 psychiatric patients (7 psychotics and 23 neurotics) who were randomly assigned to groups. The results indicated that the social-skills-training group improved significantly more on a role-play assessment of social skills than the hospital-treatment control group. This difference was maintained at a 10-month follow-up. The effects of social skills training generalized to novel scenes on the role-play test. Finally, the social skills group also evidenced superior performance on the Rathus Assertiveness Schedule. Other comparative outcome investigations have obtained similar findings (Lazarus, 1966; Marzillier, Lambert, & Kellett, 1976).

The limited number of well-controlled outcome studies precludes making broad generalizations about overall efficacy. The issue is further complicated by the difficulty encountered when trying to make comparisons across studies. There are often minor variations in both independent and dependent variables from one investigation to the next. Large group studies are frequently further complicated by heterogeneity with regard to diagnostic groupings. Several studies have included patients with a wide variety of diagnoses, including many who are not diagnosed as schizophrenic (e.g., Monti *et al.*, 1979, 1980). These qualifications notwithstanding, the foregoing single-case and group comparison studies do suggest that social skills training is useful in promoting improvements in the interpersonal functioning of schizophrenic patients. The results of these studies further suggest that the generalization of the effects of such training to the patient's natural environment is not automatic. Instead, it should be systematically programmed as a component of the training process. Research into the most effective means of promoting both generalization and durability of gains must be conducted. In our own research, we are analyzing the effects of guided *in vivo* practice and booster sessions to accomplish these ends. Other possibilities include the application of self-control techniques, although cognitive interventions of this sort may prove to be of greater utility with nonpsychotic populations.

Depression

Social skills training is one of five principal behavioral treatments of depression (Rehm & Kornblith, 1979). Its use is based on etiological conceptualizations that regard depression as resulting from a loss of reinforcers because of various interpersonal-skills deficits. According to Lewinsohn (1975), the depressed patient is under a schedule whereby response-contingent positive reinforcement is diminished. As a result of specific skill deficits, the depressed person is unable to obtain the kind of gratification needed from the environment. However, he or she does obtain attention for complaints of depression in the form of sympathetic social response, usually from family and friends. Thus, depressed behavior is inadvertently reinforced and maintained. However, this behavior is aversive to others, and it tends gradually to alienate people. This alienation often results in the depressed individual's being deserted and leads to further loss of reinforcement, further social isolation, and increased depression.

As noted by Hersen, Bellack, and Himmelhoch (1982), Lewinsohn's "notions suggest that depressed individuals will emit fewer behaviors, elicit more behaviors from others than they emit, interact with fewer numbers of individuals, emit fewer positive reactions to others' behaviors, and have longer action latencies than nondepressed individuals" (p.

162). A number of these hypotheses have been confirmed by Lewinsohn and his colleagues (Lewinsohn & Shaffer, 1971; Libet & Lewinsohn, 1973). In a recent study, Sanchez and Lewinsohn (1980) provided additional experimental data in support of Lewinsohn's theoretical stance. Specifically, they found a $-.50$ correlation between assertiveness and depression over a 12-week period in 12 depressed patients. Moreover, on those days when assertiveness was more evident, the level of depression was decreased. Quite interestingly, the "rate of emitted assertive behavior predicted subsequent (next day) level of depression at statistically significant levels, whereas level of depression did not reliably predict subsequent rate of emitted assertive behavior" (Sanchez & Lewinsohn, 1980, p. 119).

Lewinsohn's (1975) treatment for depression centers on having the patient (1) engage in pleasant activities and (2) improve his or her social skills. This is done in a three-month time-limited program, which first is concerned with establishing the diagnosis, the depth of the depression, and the potential for suicide. A functional analysis of depressed and other critical behaviors is then conducted. Behaviors that need to be increased or decreased are clearly identified and targeted for modification. At times, the depressed patient's behavior is evaluated in a group setting or in the presence of a family member.

Although Lewinsohn's theoretical approach to depression appears to be basically sound, the actual treatment package he uses is not as well developed as the model or the associated assessment strategy. Nonetheless, portions of Lewinsohn's skill-training package have received positive confirmation in outcome studies conducted by McLean, Ogston, and Grauer (1973) and by McLean and Hakstian (1979). However, it should be recognized that the social skills training in these studies comprised only a portion of the total behavioral strategy.

Preliminary support for the effectiveness of social skills training independent of other procedures has been provided in the form of several uncontrolled clinical studies (Wells, Hersen, Bellack, & Himmelhoch, 1979; Zeiss, Lewinsohn, & Munoz, 1979). The preliminary results of a large-scale, well-controlled outcome project offer further support (Bellack *et al.*, 1980). Four treatments for unipolar (nonpsychotic) depression were contrasted: amitriptyline, social skills training plus amitriptyline, social skills training plus placebo, and psychotherapy plus placebo. The subjects were 72 female outpatients. The four treatments, conducted by experienced clinicians, were each found to be effective; all produced statistically significant and clinically meaningful changes in symptomatology and social functioning. However, they were not all equivalent. There was a significant difference in premature terminations across groups, from a high of 55.6% for amitriptyline to a low of 15% for social skills plus placebo. There was also a substantial difference across conditions in the proportion of patients who were significantly improved. Social skills plus placebo was also the most effective treatment on this dimension. These data suggest that social skills training is an effective strategy for the treatment of depression. However, until we know more about its long-term impact, a more definitive evaluation must be reserved.

Alcoholism

Social skills deficits have frequently been implicated as a major problem in alcoholism. Alcoholics have been found to be especially lacking in the interpersonal skills necessary to handle conflict situations. For example, Miller, Hersen, Eisler, and Hilsman (1974) reported that alcoholics tend to increase their consumption subsequent to interpersonal stress. The results of a study by Miller and Eisler (1977) indicated that the amount that alcoholics consumed on a laboratory drinking task was inversely correlated with ratings of their assertiveness on a behavioral role-playing test. Despite these findings, there have been relatively few studies in which the effects of social skills training on alcoholics have been evaluated.

Eisler, Hersen, and Miller (1974) evaluated the effects of social skills training on a 34-year-old, twice-divorced male with a history of alcoholism. A pretreatment role-play assessment involving six interpersonal encounters revealed four deficit behaviors: eye contact, compliance, affect, and behavioral requests. In a multiple-baseline design across behaviors, training resulted in marked improvements in all targets on both trained and untrained items on a posttreatment role-play assessment. However, a postdischarge follow-up was disappointing in that the patient was eventually arrested for drunken driving and admitted to a state hospital for further treatment.

Foy, Miller, Eisler, and O'Toole (1976) used social-skills-training procedures to teach alcoholics to effectively refuse drinks offered to them by others. The patients were two chronic alcoholics with 15- and 25-year drinking histories. A multiple-baseline design across behaviors was used in each case to evaluate the effects of the training. Based on a behavioral analysis, the behaviors that were targeted for training were (1) requests for change; (2) offering of alternatives to drinking; (3) changing the subject of conversation; (4) duration of looking; and (5) affect. The training consisted of modeling and instructions conducted in nine sessions over a two-week period. The results indicated that both men had improved ratings on all target behaviors at posttreatment. These improvements were maintained at a three-month follow-up. However, although one patient was abstinent at that time, the other had resumed heavy drinking and required "booster" treatments.

Several controlled-group outcome studies have included social skills training as components in comprehensive treatment packages. Hedberg and Campbell (1974) randomly assigned 49 outpatient alcoholics to behavioral family counseling, systematic desensitization, covert sensitization, or faradic aversion. The behavioral family counseling incorporated assertiveness training with behavior rehearsal as a means of improving the quality of verbal interaction between the patients and their family members. The results indicated that this group had the highest percentage of subjects achieving their goal of either abstinence or controlled drinking at a six-month follow-up.

Sobell and Sobell (1973) assigned 70 male inpatient alcoholics to a treatment goal of either abstinence or controlled drinking. The subjects assigned to each treatment goal were then further subdivided into two therapy conditions: (1) "conventional" therapy, consisting of group meetings, AA meetings, chemotherapy, psychotherapy, and industrial therapy; or (2) "conventional" therapy plus behavior therapy (stimulus control training, faradic aversion, and behavioral rehearsal). The behavioral rehearsal component involved the practice of socially appropriate responses to the interpersonal situations that typically precipitated heavy drinking. The alcoholics who underwent the behavior therapy program functioned significantly better (defined in terms of drinking dispositions at six-week and six-month intervals) than the alcoholics who received only the conventional therapy. This finding held true regardless of the initial treatment goals.

A short-term skill-training intervention that taught male alcoholics to generate appropriate behaviors in problem situations was evaluated by Chaney, O'Leary, and Marlatt (1978). Forty inpatient alcoholics were assigned to a skill training group, a discussion group, or a no-additional-treatment control group. The skill training incorporated instruction, modeling, behavioral rehearsal, and coaching for both overt behavior and the cognitive process for generating the response (using D'Zurilla and Goldfried's, 1971, stepwise analysis of problem solving). A role-play measure indicated significant improvement at posttreatment for the training group as compared with the control groups. A one-year follow-up indicated that the skill training had decreased the duration and the severity of relapse episodes.

Thus, social skills training appears to hold considerable promise for the treatment of problem drinking. However, in several of the investigations, adequate maintenance was not obtained. It appears to be vital to include specific techniques for promoting maintenance. Finally, it should be noted that these conclusions are based on a relatively small number of controlled research investigations, several of which involved only one or two subjects. Additionally, in several of the investigations, social skills training was one component of a comprehensive behavioral treatment package. Therefore, further research is needed to isolate the specific effects of such training.

Aggression

There has been considerable theoretical and empirical support regarding the etiological role of interpersonal skills deficits in aggressive or violent behavior. Bandura (1973) and Toch (1969) have both concluded that many aggressive persons tend to be deficient in social skills. As a result, they have few options available in responding to stressful and/or aggression-eliciting situations. Aggression may be elicited or facilitated by arousal resulting from an inability to respond to interpersonal conflict in an effective (assertive) fashion.

Evidence suggests that both underassertiveness and aggression frequently occur among offenders and may be related to their antisocial behavior. Megargee (1966, 1971, 1973) reported a series of investigations concerned with the interpersonal skills repertoire of offenders convicted for violent aggressive acts. Both overcontrolled individuals (whose behavior would be predominantly unassertive) and undercontrolled individuals (whose behavior would be predominantly overassertive or aggressive) were found to be disproportionately represented in the offender group.

Anchor, Sandler, and Cherones (1977) compared men who had exhibited antisocial aggression with men from various control groups. One of the findings was that the aggressive subjects employed fewer outlets for self-disclosure—a behavior incorporated into most definitions of positive assertiveness (e.g., Eisler et al., 1975; Hersen & Bellack, 1977; Galassi, DeLeo, Galassi, & Bastien, 1974; Lange & Jakubowski, 1976). Jenkins, Witherspoon, DeVine, deValera, Muller, Barton, and McKee (1974) observed that the best predictors of recidivism in incarcerated violent offenders were (1) fear of the environment outside the prison and (2) failure to maintain steady employment. Those individuals not likely to be steadily employed had difficulty establishing and maintaining relationships with fellow employees and supervisors.

Finally, Kirchner, Kennedy, and Draguns (1979) compared groups of convicted offenders and demographically similar participants in a publicly supported vocational rehabilitation program. The results of a role-play assessment of interpersonal skills indicated significantly higher aggressiveness among the offenders. Conversely, there was a significantly higher level of rated assertion among the nonoffenders.

A number of single-case experimental analyses and group-outcome studies have appeared in the literature in the last several years in which skills-training approaches have been applied to patients evidencing aggressive and explosive behaviors (Eisler *et al.*, 1974; Elder, Edelstein, & Narick, 1979; Foy, Eisler, & Pinkston, 1975; Frederiksen & Eisler, 1977; Frederiksen *et al.*, 1976; King *et al.*, 1977; Matson & Stephens, 1978; Rimm, Hill, Brown, & Stuart, 1974; Turner, Hersen, & Bellack, 1978). Foy, Eisler, and Pinkston (1975) reported one of the first studies describing the effects of modeled assertion in a case of explosive rage. The patient was a 56-year-old, twice-married carpenter who frequently responded to "unreasonable demand from others" with verbal abuse and assaultiveness. Although he was separated at the time of the investigation, the patient's marriage had been characterized by strife and repeated incidents of wife battering. The training was intended to teach the patient to respond appropriately to difficult interpersonal situations encountered at work. A pretreatment role-play assessment involving seven work-related situations led to the identification of specific behavioral excesses, and deficits. The training consisted of modeling, instructions, behavioral rehearsal, and feedback. The training procedures resulted in a marked improvement in all the targeted behaviors. The patient continued to exhibit his new repertoire of responses to role-played situations over a six-month follow-up period. Furthermore, the patient reported that his work-related aggressiveness and interpersonal discord had considerably decreased.

Social skills training was used by Frederiksen *et al.* (1976) in the modification of abusive verbal outbursts by two adult psychiatric inpatients. The training was conducted in a role-play format. Improved responding generalized to novel (untrained) role-play scenes at posttreatment. The only behavior showing incomplete generalization was appropriate requests. Also, there was evidence that socially appropriate responding generalized to those situations on the hospital ward that had previously elicited abusive behaviors. However, no follow-up data were reported.

Matson and Stephens (1978) employed social skills training with four severely debilitated female patients who had spent the previous 3–11 years in a psychiatric hospital. The four had been characterized as "loud, uncooperative, hostile, and combative" (Matson & Stephens, 1978, p. 64). Social skills training was evaluated in a multiple-baseline design across behaviors and subjects. Generalization of improved social behavior to the ward setting was observed at posttreatment. Furthermore, the treatment gains were maintained at a three-month follow-up. Similarly, Elder *et al.* (1979) modified the aggressive behavior of four adolescent psychiatric patients using social skills training. Generalization of the treatment effects to behavior on the psychiatric ward was demonstrated. These four patients showed a significant reduction in the need for seclusion and the number of token economy fines. Moreover, at a three-month follow-up, three of the four patients had been discharged to the community and subsequently remained there for nine months.

Using a group-trained format, Rimm *et al.* (1974) evaluated the effects of social skills training on male subjects who reported a history of expressing anger in an inappropriate or antisocial manner. The subjects were randomly assigned to either group assertion training or a placebo control group. The subjects in the assertion-training group showed greater improvement on a role-play test of assertiveness than the subjects in the placebo group. However, no follow-up data were obtained.

The results of the foregoing investigations appear promising. However, very limited information has been obtained regarding the impact of these training programs on the subjects' behavior outside the hospital setting. While laboratory and hospital ward observations of subjects' behavior have provided support for the efficacy of social skills training, we know little about the effect of these training programs on behavior in other environments. Such data are needed before firm conclusions can be reached regarding the merit of social skills training in the treatment of aggressivity.

Minimal Dating

One of the major hypotheses regarding impairment in heterosocial functioning is that the difficulty results from an inadequate or inappropriate behavioral repertoire (e.g., Curran, 1977; Galassi & Galassi, 1979; Twentyman

& McFall, 1975). An individual may never have learned appropriate heterosocial behavior or may have learned inappropriate behavior. The performance of competent males in heterosocial interactions has been differentiated from that of incompetent males on a number of dimensions. These include global ratings of skill (Arkowitz et al., 1975; Borkovec, Stone, O'Brien, & Kaloupek, 1974); number of silences and amount of talk time (Twentyman, Boland, & McFall, 1978); quality of verbal content (Perri & Richards, 1979; Perri, Richards, & Goodrich, 1978); responses to positive female approach-cues (Curran, Little, & Gilbert, 1978); and response timing and placement (Fischetti et al., 1977). These findings have stimulated numerous studies on the use of social skills training to increase the frequency and the quality of heterosocial interactions. The majority have been conducted with male undergraduates who report low frequencies of dating.

Twentyman and McFall (1975) evaluated the effects of social skills training on shy males who reported dating less than once a month and who scored at least one standard deviation below the mean on the Survey of Heterosexual Interactions (SHI). The three-session training program consisted of covert and overt rehearsal, coaching, modeling, and homework. In comparison with a no-treatment control group, the experimental subjects showed some indication of reduced physiological response in a heterosocial performance situation, significant increases on the SHI, and less avoidance responding during a role-play test. In a variety of performance situations, neither self-ratings nor the judges' ratings of anxiety consistently differentiated between the two groups. Only one of two global ratings of skill differentiated the experimental group from the control subjects. Finally, the experimental subjects reported more frequent, and longer, interactions at posttest than did the subjects in the control group. The treatment gains were not maintained at a six-month follow-up. However, subject attrition may have obscured between-group differences on the follow-up data.

Kramer (1975) found social skills training to be as effective as practice dating or practice dating with cognitive restructuring. Male and female subjects in all three treatment conditions reported increased heterosocial interactions and decreased heterosocial anxiety in comparison with a waiting-list control group. McGovern, Arkowitz, and Gilmore (1975) reported data comparing social skills training with a discussion therapy condition and a waiting-list control. The subjects were male low-frequency daters. The social skills training appeared to be no better than the discussion condition on self-reports of the frequency of heterosocial interactions and anxiety and skill during those interactions. However, no follow-up data were reported. Furthermore, the criteria for inclusion in the study were lenient (i.e., three or less dates in the month preceding the study).

Similarly, a study by Melnick (1973) is confounded by the subject selection procedures that were utilized as well as by the lack of follow-up data. In this investigation, low-frequency daters were defined as dating less than two times per week. Comparisons were made among six treatment conditions: video modeling, participant modeling, participant modeling and video feedback, participant modeling plus video feedback and analogue reinforcement, a discussion control, and a no-treatment control. The subjects in the two video feedback conditions appeared to benefit the most on global ratings of anxiety and skill in post-treatment analogue interaction-assessments. However, no differences were reported for any of the groups on dating frequency. This latter finding is confounded by the fact that the subjects in the study were not dating at a very low frequency to begin with.

Curran and his colleagues (Curran, 1975; Curran & Gilbert, 1975; Curran, Gilbert, & Little, 1976) have conducted a series of comparative-outcome investigations that provide support for the effectiveness of heterosocial skills training while rectifying some of the methodological shortcomings of the previous studies. In the first of these studies (Curran, 1975), social skills training was compared with systematic desensitization, an attention placebo condition (relaxation training), and a waiting-list control. Male and female subjects were recruited through a newspaper advertisement. The subjects who scored in the upper third of the distribution on the Situation Questionnaire (Rehm & Marston, 1968) were randomly assigned across treatments. Both social skills training and systematic desensitization resulted in significant pre–post changes in behavioral ratings of anxiety and skill during a simulated heterosocial interaction. The results thus provide support for the effectiveness of both social skills training and systematic desensitization in the treatment of heterosocial disability. However, no data were obtained regarding either pre or posttreatment dating frequencies, and no follow-up data were reported.

In the second investigation (Curran & Gilbert, 1975), social skills training was again compared with systematic desensitization and a waiting-list control. The subjects were male and female introductory psychology students who scored in the upper third of the distribution on both the Situation Questionnaire and the interpersonal items of the Fear Survey Schedule (Wolpe & Lang, 1964). Over 50% of the subjects had not dated during the eight weeks prior to the investigation. Social skills training and systematic desensitization resulted in significant posttreatment decreases on self-report measures of skill and anxiety and on behavioral ratings of anxiety in the simulated interaction. The subjects in the social-skills-training group scored significantly higher on the behavioral ratings of heterosocial skill than the subjects in the waiting-list control. At a six-month follow-up, the subjects in the social skills group received significantly higher skill ratings than the subjects in either the systematic desensitization or the waiting-list conditions. The subjects in both treatment conditions showed significant increases in dating frequency during and after treatment. Thus, both treatments appeared to effect changes in the subjects' heterosocial anxiety and dating frequency. However, only social skills training resulted in increases in the rated skill level.

The third study (Curran et al., 1976) compared social skills training and sensitivity training for heterosocially anxious students. The subjects in the study had had a mean of 1.08 dates in the preceding two months. At posttreatment, the subjects in the skills training group rated themselves as significantly more skilled on a simulated heterosocial interaction than the subjects in either of the other groups. Trained observers rated the subjects from the skills-training group as more skilled and less anxious than subjects in the sensitivity group. Indeed, there was no improvement from pre- to posttreatment for the sensitivity group. Finally, there were significant within group changes in dating frequency only for the skills-training group. Thus, in this and the previous study, skills training resulted in significant changes in the subjects' behavior in both laboratory assessment procedures and an indirect measure of transfer of training.

Similar improvements were noted in an outcome study by MacDonald, Lindquist, Kramer, McGrath, and Rhyne (1975). Comparisons were made among social skills training, social skills training with homework assignments, and attention-placebo therapy condition, and a waiting-list control. There were two groups of six persons in each condition. The subjects were male undergraduates who had dated four or fewer times during the past 12 months. The results indicated that three of the four skills-training groups showed significant increases in ratings of dating-skill level on a role-played dating-interaction measure. None of the attention-placebo or waiting-list control groups improved significantly. No follow-up data were reported.

A study by Bander, Steinke, Allen, and Mosher (1975) compared social skills training, social skills training plus systematic desensitization, and sensitivity training. The subjects were recruited from a pool of volunteers from an introductory psychology class. They were selected on the basis of self-reports of dating behavior and anxiety. However, no data were provided as to their degree of anxiety or dating frequency. The social skills group was equivalent to the social skills plus systematic desensitization group on behavioral and self-report measures at posttreatment. Both social skills groups were superior to the sensitivity-training group on a behavioral measure. However, the results were confounded by the fact that the subjects were not assessed on the behavioral measure prior to treatment.

Finally, Glass, Gottman, and Shmurak (1976) studied the effects of social skills training in comparison with a cognitive self-statement approach, a combined skills-training–self-statement approach, and a waiting-list control in the treatment of shy males. The subjects were undergraduates who volunteered for a dating-skills-development program. The results at posttreatment and six-month follow-up indicated that all the treatment groups performed significantly better than the waiting-list control group on items from a role-play test on which they had received training. At posttreatment, both the skills-training and the combined treatment groups were significantly better on trained items than the self-statement group. The two groups that had received training in the modification of self-statements were the only groups to show improvement on the untrained items of the role-play test. This improvement was maintained at follow-up. The subjects' performance on a posttreatment phone-call task indicated that the self-statement modification group made more phone calls and were rated as more impressive than the other groups. Differences in the ratings of impressiveness were not maintained at follow-up. Finally, no significant between-group differences were observed at follow-up on a dating-frequency measure or on a measure of feelings of competency in dating situations. These findings suggest that while social skills training emphasizing behavior rehearsal may produce enhanced functioning in laboratory assessment procedures, the effects of training may fail to generalize to novel and/or more naturalistic measures of heterosocial competence. However, the findings are confounded by the fact that the only apparent qualification for inclusion in the study was a desire to participate in a dating-skills development program. Therefore, as with several other investigations in this area, it is questionable whether the subjects who participated in the study experienced marked heterosocial dysfunction.

It is difficult to derive firm conclusions regarding the overall utility of heterosocial skills training. Many of the investigations that have appeared in the literature have been marked by serious methodological shortcomings. There have been critical variations across studies with regard to the specific skills-training paradigms that have been utilized. Furhermore, the outcome measures have differed across the studies. Finally, the subjects recruited for the various investigations have differed greatly with regard to their degree of heterosexual dysfunction. Despite these issues, it does appear that heterosocial skills training can result in increased heterosocial competence as assessed by laboratory procedures. However, the effects of training have often failed to generalize to the natural environment. Future research is needed to develop and evaluate procedures that are intended to promote the transfer of training. The results of the studies by MacDonald *et al.* (1975) and Bander *et al.* (1975) suggest that homework assignments and/or cognitive training procedures may be useful in this regard. The durability of the effects of heterosocial skills training has yet to be adequately evaluated. In those studies where follow-up data have been reported, they have generally supported treatment effectiveness. However, follow-ups have frequently involved only self-report data gathered at disappointingly short intervals after the treatment was terminated. Further investigation is necessary before definitive conclusions regarding the maintenance of effects can be reached.

In closing this section, we should point out that our focus has been almost exclusively on the response acquisition approach. However, as we have suggested, the skills deficit hypothesis is only one of several models of social dysfunction. While considerable evidence exists to support the use of social skills training in the modification of minimal dating, there exists perhaps equally strong evidence supporting both the conditioned-anxiety and the cognitive-evaluative models of heterosocial failure. Positive results have been reported from the use of anxiety reduction strategies (e.g., Christensen, Arkowitz, & Anderson, 1975) and cognitive modification procedures (Glass *et al.*, 1976). Another factor may be the physical attractiveness of the individual (Arkowitz, 1977; Curran, 1977; Galassi & Galassi, 1979). Of course, these are not mutually exclusive factors. For example, a given individual may be heterosocially inadequate as a result of skills deficits, or anxiety, or both. Careful assessment of the *nature* of the interpersonal dysfunction (e.g., skills deficit or conditioned anxiety) is necessary in order to determine what treatment is appropriate. Presumably, the effective matching of the subject and the treatment will produce the best results.

Unassertiveness

Assertion training has become one of the most popular techniques in the armamentarium of the clinical behavior therapist. For example, assertion training for women has become increasingly common as a result of the women's movement (e.g., Linehan & Egan, 1979). College students are a second population who frequently avail themselves of assertion-training programs (e.g., Galassi, Galassi, & Litz, 1974; McFall & Marston, 1970; McFall & Lillesand, 1971; McFall & Twentyman, 1973; Rathus, 1972, 1973b). Many clinicians routinely administer assertion training as part of a comprehensive treatment program.

Numerous controlled-outcome evaluations of assertion training have been reported. McFall and Marston (1970) conducted a study involving college students who reported significant difficulty in behaving assertively. The results indicated that the subjects exposed to behavior rehearsal (either with or without performance feedback) evidenced significantly greater pre–post changes on behavioral, self-report, and physiological measures than the subjects given placebo therapy or no treatment. The transfer of training was assessed during a two-week follow-up assessment in which the subjects' responses to a telephone salesperson's repeated requests were audiotaped. The results of the phone-call follow-up followed the patterns seen on the laboratory measures, but the differences between the experimental and the control groups were generally not significant.

McFall and Lillesand (1971) assigned unassertive college students to one of three different groups: (1) behavior rehearsal with overt performance; (2) behavior rehearsal with covert performance; or (3) a no-treatment control group. The posttreatment assessment consisted of a role-play task including trained and untrained items, as well as a one-item extended-interaction test in which a prerecorded confederate made increasingly insistent requests following a subject's refusal. A follow-up measure assessed the subjects' refusal of a telephone salesperson's repeated requests.

The subjects in the two experimental groups showed the most pronounced pre–post changes on the outcome measures. The experimental subjects showed some generalization to similar refusal situations in which they had received no training, including the extended interaction. However, the effects of the training did not generalize to the telephone follow-up. In a third report, comprised of four separate experiments, McFall and Twentyman (1973) again observed poor transfer. The effects of the training did not generalize to follow-up assessments involving the subjects' refusal of requests by a telephone salesperson.

Young, Rimm, and Kennedy (1973) compared modeling and modeling plus verbal reinforcement. Both modeling groups were superior to two control conditions in response to trained situations. However, the modeling-only condition resulted in greater generalization to untrained situations. Although reinforcement did not appear to supplement the effectiveness of modeling, the reinforcement procedures were general and poorly specified. There were no differences between the treatment groups on the self-report measures.

Kazdin (1974a) conducted a study with volunteer subjects recruited from a university community. Participation in the project was based on performance on self-report measures and a behavioral role-playing test. In four treatment sessions, both covert modeling and covert modeling plus model reinforcement resulted in considerable improvement on the self-report and behavioral measures of assertive responding. Model and model-reinforcement subjects were more assertive on a set of generalization situations included in the role-playing test than either a no-modeling (imagined scenes with neither an assertive model nor favorable consequences) or a delay-treatment control group. The model-reinforcement group tended to show greater assertiveness at posttreatment and at a three-month follow-up, during which self-report data were collected. On a two-week follow-up phone-call assessment, in which the subjects were phoned and asked to do volunteer work, the four groups did not differ on the majority of behavioral ratings that were made.

In a second study, using similar subject recruitment and selection criteria, Kazdin (1976) evaluated the effects of multiple models (imagining a single model versus several models performing assertively) and of model reinforcement (imagining favorable consequences following model behavior versus no consequences). Again, a nonassertive-model control group that imagined assertion-relevant scenes was included in the design. The results after four treatment sessions indicated that covert modeling produced significant increases in assertive behavior as reflected on self-report and behavioral measures. Imagining several models responding assertively and favorable consequences following the model's performance enhanced the treatment effects. The effects of the treatment generalized to novel role-playing situations and were maintained at a four-month follow-up on self-report measures.

In an application of his covert-modeling assertion-training paradigm to psychiatric patients, Kazdin and his colleagues (Hersen *et al.*, 1979) compared five training conditions: (1) test–retest; (2) live modeling plus rehearsal; (3) live modeling without rehearsal; (4) covert modeling plus rehearsal; and (5) covert modeling without rehearsal. In this study, 50 psychiatric patients who scored 19 or below on the Wolpe-Lazarus Assertiveness Scale were randomly assigned across groups. Live modeling and covert modeling effected improvements in the assertive responding of the patients on a role-play test. The two treatments were not differentially effective. Generally, the addition of rehearsal to live or covert modeling failed to enhance the treatment. There was evidence of a transfer of treatment effects on generalization scenes of the role-play test.

Modeling, behavioral rehearsal, and modeling plus behavioral rehearsal conditions were compared by Friedman (1969). Undergraduate subjects in all three treatment conditions responded more assertively on a behavioral measure than subjects who received "nonassertive readings." The modeling plus rehearsal condition was superior to the other two treatments. There were no differences between groups on self-report measures.

A number of investigators have developed comprehensive training protocols for use with nonassertive undergraduates. Galassi *et al.* (1974) reported on the use of a systematic, short-term group assertion-training procedure comprising behavior rehearsal, videotaped modeling, videotape feedback, group feedback, trainer feedback, bibliotherapy, and homework assignments. A group of male and female college students were randomly assigned to either the assertion-training condition or an attention-control procedure. The subjects receiving assertion training were superior to the controls on a number of behavioral and self-report measures. The treatment gains were maintained at a one-year follow-up (Galassi, Kosta, & Galassi, 1975). Rathus (1972, 1973a) has conducted two studies investigating the efficacy of assertion training in groups with female college students. Although assertion training appeared superior to discussion or no-treatment control conditions in both studies, only self-report data were provided.

Several studies have been conducted to evaluate the effectiveness of treatment packages based on the cognitive-evaluative model of social skills deficits. As we have discussed, according to this model, maladaptive self-statements, beliefs, and expectations about assertive encounters are responsible for the individual's failure to respond effectively. Alden, Safran, and Weideman (1978) and Linehan, Goldfried, and Goldfried (1979) compared a cognitive-restructuring training procedure with a behavior rehearsal condition. With few exceptions, they observed no differences between the two treatments on behavioral measures of assertive responding and the subjects' reports of comfort in situations that required assertion. A study by Derry and Stone (1979) showed that a cognitive training procedure resulted in superior maintenance and generalization of assertive responses in comparison with a behavioral rehearsal condition. However, only two sessions of training were administered. Both the study by Linehan *et al.* (1979) and an earlier investigation by Wolfe and Fodor (1977) examined the combined effects of behavior rehearsal and cognitive restructuring. Although the findings suggest that the cognitive component may increase the effectiveness of behavior rehearsal, they are far from straightforward. In the study by Wolfe and Fodor, the combined training package was superior on self-reports of anxiety in situations requiring assertion, but not on behavioral outcome measures. However, the treatment consisted of only two sessions. Linehan *et al.* based their conclusion regarding the superiorty of the combined treatment on the comparison of each treatment with control conditions. They report that there were no significant differences between the two treatments themselves.

Other studies have examined the effects of variations in procedural aspects of assertion training. For example, Linehan, Walker, Bronheim, Haynes, and Yevzeroff (1979) found no significant differences between group and individual assertion training. Rakos and Schroeder (1979) reported the development and the empirical evaluation of a self-administered assertiveness-training program. The program resulted in superior performance on a role-play assessment in comparison with a procedurally parallel placebo program.

Overall, these data suggest that assertion-training techniques can effect durable improvements in assertive responding as assessed by self-report and laboratory behavioral measures. However, the effects of training have often failed to genealize to more naturalistic outcome measures, such as follow-up telephone-call assessment procedures. However, several methodological issues may be at least partly responsible for these failures to obtain generalization. The various studies that have relied on such naturalistic assessments have often involved analogue applications of assertion-training techniques. The treatments have often been of extremely short duration (e.g., Kazdin, 1974a) and have consisted of only one or two of the numerous techniques that have been identified as potentially important components of a comprehensive skills-training protocol (e.g., McFall & Lillesand, 1971; McFall & Marston, 1970; McFall & Twentyman, 1973). Second, the use of volunteer subjects (e.g., Kazdin, 1974a, 1976) may lead to outcomes that are not representative of those that would be obtained with clients or patients who actively seek help for assertiveness skill deficits. Certainly, the generalization of the effects of comprehensive assertion-training programs with persons who suffer clinically significant deficits warrants additional attention. Finally, the assessment

procedures themselves may not be valid indicators of *in vivo* performance.

Summary and Conclusions

In preparing our reference list, it was apparent that we reviewed an extensive literature. Yet in some respects we felt as if we had barely scratched the surface. There were many many studies that we did not cite. Some subareas, such as skills training for juvenile delinquency and sociometric assessment, were totally omitted or mentioned only in passing. As indicated at the beginning of this chapter, the area is simply too overwhelming to cover in a single review.

In a similar vein, it is difficult to make an overall appraisal of the area; it is too diverse and complex. Yet several points come up repeatedly. First, assessment is both a strength and a handicap. We have overcome our early naiveté and learned some hard lessons about the difficulty of appraising social skill. Many cherished beliefs and strategies have proved to be invalid. Others account for only a small portion of the variance. Yet, the baby must not be thrown out with the bathwater. Role play, staged interactions, and molecular analyses can all be useful. We simply must be aware of their limitations. Further research is needed to outline their utility clearly, as well as to develop new and better procedures.

A somewhat different problem must be faced in the area of skills training. We have also been overly enthusiastic about these techniques, but this overenthusiasm has not yet been widely recognized. Skills training clearly *works*, in the sense that it efficiently develops new behavioral skills in diverse populations. Yet, the clinical utility of the procedures is still uncertain in many respects. There are generalization and maintenance problems here, as there are in almost every other behavioral technique. We do not know how well and for how long people can transfer their newly learned response capabilities to their daily environments. Do they really use these responses on a day-to-day basis? No one knows. This is a vital area for research. Moreover, even if skills do transfer, do they make a significant impact on the person's life? In other words, are we teaching important responses? Does skills training make a difference?

The questions just raised lead to a final set of questions that pertain to the skills model. Earlier, we outlined several ways in which skills deficits can interface with psychopathology. Our training programs are based primarily on the notion that skills deficits are causal or maintaining factors. If not, such training may be a meaningless exercise. Yet, there are few solid data on this issue. We are operating mainly on the basis of a convincing model (otherwise known as "a wing and a prayer"!). This issue must be subjected to careful scrutiny. Skills training will clearly make no meaningful difference in the patient's life if skills deficits are not critical factors in the dysfunction.

References

Alden, L., Safran, J., & Weideman, R. A comparison of cognitive and skills training strategies in the treatment of unassertive clients. *Behavior Therapy*, 1978, *9*, 843–846.

Anchor, K. N., Sandler, H. M., & Cherones, J. H. Maladaptive antisocial aggressive behavior and outlets for intimacy. *Journal of Clinical Psychology*, 1977, *33*, 947–949.

Argyris, C. Explorations in interpersonal competence: I. *Journal of Applied Behavioral Science*, 1965, *1*, 58–83.

Arkowitz, H. Measurement and modification of minimal dating behavior. In M. Hersen, R. M. Eisler, & P. M. Miller (Eds.), *Progress in behavior modification*, Vol. 5. New York: Academic Press, 1977.

Arkowitz, H. The assessment of social skills. In M. Hersen & A. S. Bellack (Eds.), *Behavioral assessment: A practical handbook* (2nd ed). New York: Pergamon Press, 1981.

Arkowitz, H., Lichtenstein, E., McGovern, K., & Hines, P. The behavioral assessment of social competence in males. *Behavior Therapy*, 1975, *6*, 3–13.

Bander, K. W., Steinke, G. V., Allen, G. J., & Mosher, D. L. Evaluation of three dating-specific treatment approaches for heterosexual dating anxiety. *Journal of Consulting and Clinical Psychology*, 1975, *43*, 259–265.

Bandura, A. *Aggression: A social learning analysis*. Englewood Cliffs, N.J.: Prentice-Hall, 1973.

Bandura, A. *Social learning theory*. Englewood Cliffs, N.J.: Prentice-Hall, 1977.

Barlow, D. H., Abel, G. G., Blanchard, E. B., Bristow, A. R., & Young, L. D. A heterosocial skills behavior checklist for males. *Behavior Therapy*, 1977, *8*, 229–239.

Bellack, A. S. Behavioral assessment of social skills. In A. S. Bellack & M. Hersen (Eds.), *Research and practice in social skills training*. New York: Plenum Press, 1979. (a)

Bellack, A. S. A critical appraisal of strategies for assessing social skill. *Behavioral Assessment*, 1979, *1*, 157–176. (b)

Bellack, A. S. Anxiety and neurotic disorders. In A. E. Kazdin, A. S. Bellack, & M. Hersen (Eds.), *New perspectives in abnormal psychology*. New York: Oxford University Press, 1980.

Bellack, A. S., & Hersen, M. *Behavior modification: An introductory textbook*. New York: Oxford University Press, 1977. (a)

Bellack, A. S., & Hersen, M. The use of self-report inventories in behavioral assessment. In J. D. Cone & R. P. Hawkins (Eds.), *Behavioral assessment: New directions in clinical psychology*. New York: Brunner/Mazel, 1977. (b)

Bellack, A. S., & Hersen, M. Chronic psychiatric patients: Social skills training. In M. Hersen & A. S. Bellack (Eds.), *Behavior therapy in the psychiatric setting*. Baltimore: Williams & Wilkins, 1978.

Bellack, A. S., & Hersen, M. *Introduction to clinical psychology*. New York: Oxford University Press, 1979.

Bellack, A. S., Hersen, M., & Turner, S. M. Generalization effects of social skills training in chronic schizophrenics: An experimental analysis. *Behaviour Research and Therapy*, 1976, *14*, 391–398.

Bellack, A. S., Hersen, M., & Turner, S. M. Role play tests for assessing social skills: Are they valid? *Behavior Therapy*, 1978, *9*, 448–461.

Bellack, A. S., Hersen, M., & Lamparski, D. Role play tests for assessing social skills: Are they valid? Are they useful? *Journal of Consulting and Clinical Psychology*, 1979, *47*, 335–342.

Bellack, A. S., Hersen, M., & Turner, S. M. The relationship of role playing and knowledge of appropriate behavior to assertion in the natural environment. *Journal of Consulting and Clinical Psychology*, 1979, *47*, 670–678.

Bellack, A. S., Hersen, M., & Himmelhoch, J. M. Social skills training for depression: A treatment manual. *JSAS Catalog of Selected Documents in Psychology*, 1980, *10*, 92. (Ms. No. 2156.)

Bellack, A. S., Hersen, M., & Himmelhoch, J. M. Social skills training, pharmacotherapy, and psychotherapy for unipolar depression. *American Journal of Psychiatry*, 1981, *138*, 1562–1567.

Birchler, G. R. Communication skills in married couples. In A. S. Bellack & M. Hersen (Eds.), *Research and practice in social skills training*. New York: Plenum Press, 1979.

Blanchard, E. B., & Hersen, M. Behavioral treatment of hysterical neuroses: Symptom substitution and symptom return reconsidered. *Psychiatry*, 1976, *39*, 118–129.

Borkovec, T. D., Stone, N., O'Brien, G., & Kaloupek, D. Identification and measurement of a clinically relevant target behavior for analogue outcome research. *Behavior Therapy*, 1974, *5*, 503–513.

Brown, G. W., Birley, J. L. T., & Wing, J. K. Influence of family life on the course of schizophrenic disorders: A replication. *British Journal of Psychiatry*, 1972, *121*, 241–258.

Chaney, E. F., O'Leary, M. R., & Marlatt, G. A. Skill training with alcoholics. *Journal of Consulting and Clinical Psychology*, 1978, *46*, 1092–1104.

Christensen, A., & Arkowitz, H. Preliminary report on practice dating and feedback as treatment for college dating problems. *Journal of Counseling Psychology*, 1974, *21*, 92–95.

Christensen, A., Arkowitz, H., & Anderson, J. Practice dating as treatment for college dating inhibitions. *Behaviour Research and Therapy*, 1975, *13*, 321–331.

Coyne, J. C. Depression and the response of others. *Journal of Abnormal Psychology*, 1976, *85*, 186–193.

Curran, J. P. An evaluation of a skills training program and a systematic desensitization program in reducing dating anxiety. *Behaviour Research and Therapy*, 1975, *13*, 65–68.

Curran, J. P. Skills training as an approach to the treatment of heterosexual-social anxiety: A review. *Psychological Bulletin*, 1977, *84*, 140–157.

Curran, J. P. Social skills: Methodological issues and future directions. In A. S. Bellack & M. Hersen (Eds.), *Research and practice in social skills training*. New York: Plenum Press, 1979.

Curran, J. P., & Gilbert, F. S. A test of the relative effectiveness of a systematic desensitization program and an interpersonal skills training program with date anxious subjects. *Behavior Therapy*, 1975, *6*, 510–521.

Curran, J. P., & Mariotto, M. J. A conceptual structure for the assessment of social skills. In M. Hersen, R. M. Eisler, & P. M. Miller (Eds.), *Progress in behavior modification*, Vol. 10. New York: Academic Press, 1981.

Curran, J. P., Gilbert, F. S., & Little, L. M. A comparison between behavioral training and sensitivity training approaches to heterosexual dating anxiety. *Journal of Counseling Psychology*, 1976, *23*, 190–196.

Curran, J. P., Little, L. M., & Gilbert, F. S. Reactivity of males of differing heterosexual social anxiety to female approach and non-approach cue conditions. *Behavior Therapy*, 1978, *9*, 961.

Derry, P. A., & Stone, G. L. Effects of cognitive-adjunct treatments on assertiveness. *Cognitive Therapy and Research*, 1979, *3*, 213–221.

Duncan, S., Jr., & Fiske, D. *Face to face interaction: Research, methods, and theory*. New York: Lawrence Erlbaum, 1977.

D'Zurilla, T. J., & Goldfried, M. R. Problem-solving and behavior modification. *Journal of Abnormal Psychology*, 1971, *78*, 107–126.

Edelstein, B. A., & Eisle, R. M. Effects of modeling and modeling with instructions and feedback on the behavioral components of social skills of a schizophrenic. *Behavior Therapy*, 1976, *7*, 382–389.

Eisler, R. M. The behavioral assessment of social skills. In M. Hersen & A. S. Bellack (Eds.), *Behavioral assessment: A practical handbook*. New York: Pergamon Press, 1976.

Eisler, R. M., Hersen, M., & Miller, P. M. Shaping components of assertiveness with instructions and feedback. *American Journal of Psychiatry*, 1974, *131*, 1344–1347.

Eisler, R. M., Hersen, M., Miller, P. M., & Blanchard, E. B. Situational determinants of assertive behaviors. *Journal of Consulting and Clinical Psychology*, 1975, *43*, 330–340.

Eisler, R. M., Frederiksen, L. W., & Peterson, G. L. The relationship of cognitive variables to the expression of assertiveness. *Behavior Therapy*, 1978, *9*, 419–427.

Elder, J. P., Edelstein, B. A., & Narick, M. M. Social skills training in the modification of aggressive behavior of adolescent psychiatric patients. *Behavior Modification*, 1979, *3*, 161–178.

Fiedler, D., & Beach, L. R. On the decision to be assertive. *Journal of Consulting and Clinical Psychology*, 1978, *46*, 537–546.

Field, G. D., & Test, M. A. Group assertiveness training for severely disturbed patients. *Journal of Behavior Therapy and Experimental Psychiatry*, 1975, *6*, 129–134.

Fischetti, M., Curran, J. P., & Wessberg, H. W. Sense of timing: A skill deficit in heterosexual-socially anxious males. *Behavior Modification*, 1977, *1*, 179–195.

Foy, D. W., Eisler, R. M., & Pinkston, S. G. Modeled assertion in a case of explosive rage. *Journal of Behavior Therapy and Experimental Psychiatry*, 1975, *6*, 135–137.

Foy, D. W., Miller, P. M., Eisler, R. M., & O'Toole, D. H. Social skills training to teach alcoholics to refuse drinks effectively. *Journal of Studies on Alcohol*, 1976, *37*, 1340–1345.

Frederiksen, L. W., & Eisler, R. M. The control of explosive behavior: A skill-development approach. In D. Upper (ed.), *Perspectives in behaviour therapy*. Kalamazoo, Mich.: Behaviordelia, 1977.

Fredriksen, L. W., Jenkins, J. O., Foy, D. W., & Eisler, R. M. Social skills training in the modification of abusive verbal outbursts in adults. *Journal of Applied Behavior Analysis*, 1976, *9*, 117–125.

Freedman, B. J., Rosenthal, L., Donahoe, J. R., Schlundt, D. G., & McFall, R. M. A social-behavioral analysis of skill deficits in delinquent and nondelinquent adolescent boys. *Journal of Consulting and Clinical Psychology*, 1978, *46*, 1448–1462.

Friedman, P. H. The effects of modeling and roleplaying on assertive behavior. (Doctoral dissertation, University of Wisconsin, 1968). *Dissertation Abstracts International*, 1969, *29*, 4844B. (University Microfilms No. 69-912.)

Galassi, J. P., & Galassi, M. D. Modification of heterosocial skills deficits. In A. S. Bellack & M. Hersen (Eds.), *Research and practice in social skills training*. New York: Plenum Press, 1979.

Galassi, J. P., DeLeo, J. S., Galassi, M. D., & Bastien, S. The College Self-Expression Scale: A measure of assertiveness. *Behavior Therapy*, 1974, *5*, 165–171.

Galassi, J. P., Galassi, M. D., & Litz, M. C. Assertive training in groups using video-feedback. *Journal of Counseling Psychology*, 1974, *21*, 390–394.

Galassi, J. P., Kosta, M. P., & Galassi, M. D. Assertive training: A one-year follow-up. *Journal of Counseling Psychology*, 1975, *22*, 451–452.

Galassi, M. D., & Galassi, J. P. The effects of role playing variations on the assessment of assertive behavior. *Behavior Therapy*, 1976, *7*, 343–347.

Glass, C. R., Gottman, J. M., & Shmurak, S. H. Response-acquisition and cognitive self-statement modification approaches to dating-skills training. *Journal of Counseling Psychology*, 1976, *23*, 520–526.

Gleser, G. C., & Gottschalk, L. A. Personality characteristics of chronic schizophrenics in relationship to sex and current functioning. *Journal of Clinical Psychology*, 1967. *23*, 349–354.

Goldfried, M. R., Decenteceo, E. T., & Weinberg, L. Systemic rational restructuring as a self-control technique. *Behavior Therapy*, 1974, *5*, 247–254.

Goldsmith, J. B., & McFall, R. M. Development and evaluation of an interpersonal skill-training program for psychiatric patients. *Journal of Abnormal Psychology,* 1975, *84,* 51–58.

Hammen, C. L., & Peters, S. D. Interpersonal consequences of depression: Responses to men and women enacting a depressed role. *Journal of Abnormal Psychology,* 1978, *87,* 322–332.

Harper, R. G., Wiens, A. N., & Matarazzo, J. D. *Nonverbal communication: The state of the art.* New York: Wiley, 1978.

Hedberg, A. S., & Campbell, L. A. A comparison of four behavioral treatments of alcoholism. *Journal of Behavior Therapy and Experimental Psychiatry,* 1974, *5,* 251–256.

Hersen, M., & Bellack, A. S. Social skills training for chronic psychiatric patients: Rationale, research findings, and future directions. *Comprehensive Psychiatry,* 1976, *17,* 559–580.

Hersen, M., & Bellack, A. S. Assessment of social skills. In A. R. Ciminero, K. S. Calhoun, & H. E. Adams (Eds.), *Handbook for behavioral assessment.* New York: Wiley, 1977.

Hersen, M., Eisler, R. M., Miller, P. M., Johnson, M. B., & Pinkston, S. G. Effect of practive, instructions, and modeling on components of assertive behavior. *Behaviour Research and Therapy,* 1973, *11,* 443–451.

Hersen, M., Turner, S. M., Edelstein, B. A., & Pinkston, S. G. Effects of phenothiazines and social skills training in a withdrawn schizophrenic. *Journal of Clinical Psychology,* 1975, *34,* 588–594.

Hersen, M., Kazdin, A. E., Bellack, A. S., & Turner, S. M. Effects of live modeling, covert modeling, and rehearsal on assertiveness in psychiatric patients. *Behaviour Research and Therapy,* 1979, *17,* 369–377.

Hersen, M., Bellack, A. S., & Himmelhoch, J. M. Social skills training with unipolar depressed women. In J. P. Curran & P. M. Monti (Eds.), *Social skills training: A practical handbook for assessment and treatment.* New York: Guilford Press, 1982.

Higgins, R. L., Alonso, R. R., & Pendleton, M. G. The validity of role-play assessments of assertiveness. *Behavior Therapy,* 1979, *10,* 655–662.

Hollandsworth, J. G., Jr., & Cooley, M. L. Provoking anger and gaining compliance with assertive versus aggressive responses. *Behavior Therapy,* 1978, *9,* 640–646.

Hopkins, J., Krawitz, G., & Bellack, A. S. The effects of situational variations in role-play scenes on assertive behavior. *Journal of Behavior Assessment,* in press.

Howes, M. J., & Hokanson, J. E. Conversational and social responses to depressive interpersonal behavior. *Journal of Abnormal Psychology,* 1979, *88,* 625–634.

Hull, D. B., & Schroeder, H. E. Some interpersonal effects of assertion, nonassertion, and aggression. *Behavior Therapy,* 1970, *10,* 20–28.

Jacob, T. Assessment of marital dysfunction. In M. Hersen & A. S. Bellack (Eds.), *Behavioral assessment: A practical handbook.* New York: Pergamon Press, 1976.

Jenkins, W. O., Witherspoon, A. D., DeVine, M. D., deValera, E. K., Muller, J. B., Barton, M. C., & McKee, J. M. *The post-prison analysis of criminal behavior and longitudinal follow-up evaluation of institutional treatment.* Elmore, Ala.: Rehabilitation Research Foundation, 1974.

Johnson, S. M., & Bolstad, O. D. Methodological issues in naturalistic observation: Some problems and solutions for field research. In L. A. Hamerlynck, L. C. Handy, & E. J. Mash (Eds.), *Behavior change: Methodology, concepts, and practice.* Champaign, Ill.: Research Press, 1973.

Kagan, J., & Moss, H. A. *Birth to maturity: A study in psychological development.* New York: Wiley, 1962.

Kane, J. S., & Lawler, E. E., III. Methods of peer assessment. *Psychological Bulletin,* 1978, *85,* 555–586.

Kazdin, A. E. Effects of covert modeling and model reinforcement on assertive behavior. *Journal of Abnormal Psychology,* 1974, *83,* 240–252. (a)

Kazdin, A. E. Self-monitoring and behavior change. In M. J. Mahoney & C. E. Thoresen (Eds.), *Self-control: Power to the person.* Monterey, Calif.: Brooks/Cole, 1974. (b)

Kazdin, A. E. Effects of covert modeling, multiple models, and model reinforcement on assertive behavior. *Behavior Therapy,* 1976, *7,* 211–222.

Kazdin, A. E. Assessing the clinical or applied importance of behavior change through social validation. *Behavior Modification,* 1977, *4,* 427–452.

King, L. W., Liberman, R. P., Roberts, J., & Bryan, E. Personal effectiveness: A structured therapy for improving social and emotional skills. *European Journal of Behavioural Analysis and Modification,* 1977, *2,* 82–91.

Kirchner, E. P., Kennedy, R. E., & Draguns, J. G. Assertion and aggression in adult offenders. *Behavior Therapy,* 1979, *10,* 452–471.

Kramer, S. R. Effectiveness of behavior rehearsal and practice dating to increase heterosexual social interaction. (Doctoral dissertation, University of Texas, 1975.) *Dissertation Abstracts International,* 1975, *36,* 913B–914B. (University of Microfilms, No. 75-16, 693.)

Lange, A. J., & Jakubowski, P. *Responsible assertive behavior.* Champaign, Ill.: Research Press, 1976.

Lazarus, A. A. Behaviour rehearsal vs. non-directive therapy vs. advice in effecting behaviour change. *Behaviour Research and Therapy,* 1966, *4,* 209–212.

Lewinsohn, P. M. The behavioral study and treatment of depression. In M. Hersen, R. M. Eisler, & P. M. Miller (Eds.), *Progress in behavior modification,* Vol 1. New York: Academic Press, 1975.

Lewinsohn, P. M., & Shaffer, M. Use of home observations as an integral part of the treatment of depression: Preliminary report and case studies. *Journal of Consulting and Clinical Psychology,* 1971, *37,* 87–94.

Liberman, R. P., Lillie, F., Falloon, I., Vaughn, C., Harper, E., Leff, J., Hutchinson, W., Ryan, P., & Stoute, M. *Social skills training for schizophrenic patients and their families.* Unpublished manuscript, 1978.

Libet, J. M., & Lewinsohn, P. M. Concept of social skill with special reference to the behavior of depressed persons. *Journal of Consulting and Clinical Psychology,* 1973, *40,* 304–312.

Linehan, M. M., & Egan, K. J. Assertion training for women. In A. S. Bellack & M. Hersen (Eds.), *Research and practice in social skills training.* New York: Plenum Press, 1979.

Linehan, M. M., Goldfried, M. R., & Goldfried, A. P. Assertion therapy: Skill training or cognitive restructuring. *Behavior Therapy,* 1979, *10,* 372–388.

Linehan, M. M., Walker, R. O., Bronheim, S., Haynes, K. F., & Yevzeroff, H. Group versus individual assertion training. *Journal of Consulting and Clinical Psychology*, 1979, *47*, 1000–1002.

Lomont, J. F., Gilner, F. H., Spector, N. J., & Skinner, B. F. Group assertion training and group insight therapies. *Psychological Reports*, 1969, *23*, 463–470.

MacDonald, M. L., Lindquist, C. U., Kramer, J. A., McGrath, R. A., & Rhyne, L. D. Social skills training: Behavior rehearsal in groups and dating skills. *Journal of Counseling Psychology*, 1975, *22*, 224–230.

Marzillier, J. S., Lambert, C., & Kellett, J. A controlled evaluation of systematic desensitization and social skills for socially inadequate psychiatric patients. *Behaviour Research and Therapy*, 1976, *14*, 225–238.

Matson, J. L., & Stephens, R. M. Increasing appropriate behavior of explosive chronic psychiatric patients with a social-skills training package. *Behavior Modfication*, 1978, *2*, 61–76.

McClelland, D. C., & Walt, N. F. Sex role alienation in schizophrenia. *Journal of Abnormal Psychology*, 1968, *12*, 217–220.

McFall, R. M., & Lillesand, D. B. Behavior rehearsal with modeling and coaching in assertion training. *Journal of Abnormal Psychology*, 1971, *77*, 313–323.

McFall, R. M., & Marston, A. An experimental investigation of behavioral rehearsal in assertive training. *Journal of Abnormal Psychology*, 1970, *76*, 295–303.

McFall, R. M., & Twentyman, C. T. Four experiments on the relative contributions of rehearsal, modeling, and coaching to assertion training. *Journal of Abnormal Psychology*, 1973, *81*, 199–218.

McGovern, K. B., Arkowitz, H., & Gilmore, S. K. Evaluation of social skills training programs for college dating inhibitions. *Journal of Counseling Psychology*, 1975, *22*, 505–512.

McLean, P. D., & Hakstian, A. R. Clinical depression: Comparative efficacy of outpatient treatments. *Journal of Consulting and Clinical Psychology*, 1979, *47*, 818–836.

McLean, P. D., Ogston, K., & Grauer, L. A behavioral approach to the treatment of depression. *Journal of Behavior Therapy and Experimental Psychiatry*, 1973, *4*, 323–330.

Megargee, E. I. Undercontrolled and overcontrolled personality types in extreme antisocial aggression. *Psychological Monographs*, 1966, *80*, (Whole No. 611).

Megargee, E. I. The role of inhibition in the assessment and understanding of violence. In J. E. Singer (Ed.), *The control of aggression and violence: Cognitive and physiological factors*. New York: Academic Press, 1971.

Megargee, E. I. Recent research on overcontrolled and undercontrolled personality patterns among violent offenders. *Social Symposium*, 1973, *9*, 37–50.

Melnick, J. A. A comparison of replication techniques in the modification of minimal dating behavior. *Journal of Abnormal Psychology*, 1973, *81*, 51–59.

Miller, P. M., & Eisler, R. M. Assertive behavior of alcoholics: A descriptive analysis *Behavior Therapy*, 1977, *8*, 146–149.

Miller, P. M., Hersen, M., Eisler, R. M., & Hilsman, G. Effects of social stress on operant drinking of alcoholics and social drinkers. *Behaviour Research and Therapy*, 1974, *12*, 65–72.

Monti, P. M., Fink, E., Norman, W., Curran, J., Hayes, S., & Caldwell, A. Effect of social skills training groups and social skills bibliotherapy with psychiatric patients.

Journal of Consulting and Clinical Psychology, 1979, *47*, 189–191.

Monti, P. M., Curran, J. P., Corriveau, D. P., DeLancey, A. L., & Hagerman, S. M. Effects of social skills training groups and sensitivity training groups with psychiatric patients. *Journal of Consulting and Clinical Psychology*, 1980, *48*, 241–248.

Morganstern, K. P., & Tevein, H. E. Behavioral interviewing: The initial stages of assessment. In M. Hersen & A. S. Bellack (Eds.), *Behavioral assessment: A practical handbook* (2nd ed.). New York: Pergamon Press, 1981.

Morrison, R. L., & Bellack, A. S. The role of social perception in social skill. *Behavior Therapy*, 1981, *12*, 69–79.

Mosher, L. R., & Keith, S. J. Psychosocial treatment: Individual, group, family, and community support approaches. *Schizophrenia Bulletin*, 1980, *6*, 10–41.

Mungas, D. M., & Walters, H. A. Pretesting effects in the evaluation of social skills training. *Journal of Consulting and Clinical Psychology*, 1979, *47*, 216–218.

Nelson, R. O. Methodological issues in assessment via self-monitoring. In J. D. Cone & R. P. Hawkins (Eds.), *Behavioral assessment: New directions in clinical psychology*. New York: Brunner/Mazel, 1977.

Ollendick, T. H., & Hersen, M. Social skills training for juvenile delinquents. *Behaviour Research and Therapy*, 1979, *17*, 547–554.

Patterson, G. R. Interventions for boys with conduct problems.: Multiple settings, treatments and criteria. *Journal of Consulting and Clinical Psychology*, 1974, *42*, 471–481.

Percell, L. P., Berwick, P. T., & Beigel, A. The effects of assertive training on self-concept and anxiety. *Archives of General Psychiatry*, 1974, *31*, 502–504.

Perri, M. G., & Richards, C. S. Assessment of heterosocial skills in male college students: Empirical development of a behavioral role-playing test. *Behavior Modification*, 1979, *3*, 337–354.

Perri, M. G., Richards, C. S., & Goodrich, J. D. The heterosocial adequacy test (HAT): A behavioral role-playing test for the assessment of heterosocial skills in male college students. *JSAS Catalog of Selected Documents in Psychology*, 1978, *8*, 16 (MS. No. 1650).

Rakos, R. F., & Schroeder, H. E. Development and empirical evaluation of a self-administered assertiveness training program. *Journal of Consulting and Clinical Psychology*, 1979, *47*, 991–993.

Rathus, S. A. An experimental investigation of assertive training in a group setting. *Journal of Behavior Therapy and Experimental Psychiatry*, 1972, *3*, 81–86.

Rathus, S. A. Instigation of assertive behavior through videotape-mediated assertive models and directed practice. *Behaviour Research and Therapy*, 1973, *11*, 57–65. (a)

Rathus, S. A. A 30-item schedule for assessing assertive behavior. *Behavior Therapy*, 1973, *4*, 398–406. (b)

Rehm, L. P., & Kornblith, S. J. Behavior therapy for depression: A review of recent developments. In M. Hersen, R. M. Eisler, & P. M. Miller (Eds.), *Progress in behavior modification*, Vol. 7. New York: Academic Press, 1979.

Rehm, L. P., & Marston, A. R. Reduction of social anxiety through modification of self-reinforcement: An instigation therapy technique. *Journal of Consulting and Clinical Psychology*, 1968, *32*, 565–574.

Rimm, D. C., Hill, G. A., Brown, N. N., & Stuart, J. E. Group-assertive training in treatment of expression of inappropriate anger. *Psychological Reports*, 1974, *34*, 791–798.

Rimm, D. C., Snyder, J. J., Depue, R. A., Haanstad, M. J., & Armstrong, D. P. Assertive training versus rehearsal and the importance of making an assertive response. *Behaviour Research and Therapy*, 1976, *14*, 315–322.

Roff, J. D., & Knight, R. Young adult schizophrenics: Prediction of outcome and antecedent childhood factors. *Journal of Consulting and Clinical Psychology*, 1978, *46*, 947–952.

Romano, J. M., & Bellack, A. S. Social validation of a component model of assertive behavior. *Journal of Consulting and Clinical Psychology*, 1980, *48*, 478–490.

Rosenbaum, A., & O'Leary, K. D. Marital violence: Characteristics of abusive couples. *Journal of Consulting and Clinical Psychology*, 1981, *49*, 63–71.

Royce, W. S., & Arkowitz, H. *Multi-model evaluation of in vivo practice as treatment for social isolation.* Unpublished manuscript, University of Arizona, 1976.

Royce, W. S., & Weiss, R. L. Behavioral cues in the judgment of marital satisfaction: A linear regression analysis. *Journal of Consulting and Clinical Psychology*, 1975, *43*, 816–824.

Sanchez, V., & Lewinsohn, P. M. Assertive behavior and depression. *Journal of Consulting and Clinical Psychology*, 1980, *48*, 119–120.

Sherman, H., & Farina, A. Social adequacy of parents and children. *Journal of Abnormal Psychology*, 1974, *83*, 327–330.

Sobell, M. B., & Sobell, L. C. Individualized behavior therapy for alcoholics. *Behavior Therapy*, 1973, *4*, 49–72.

Toch, H. *Violent men.* Chicago: Aldine, 1969.

Trower, P., Bryant, B., & Argyle, M. *Social skills and mental health.* Pittsburgh: University of Pittsburgh Press, 1978.

Turner, S. M., Hersen, M., & Bellack, A. S. Social skills training to teach prosocial behavior in an organically impaired and retarded ambulatory patient. *Journal of Behavior Therapy and Experimental Psychiatry*, 1978, *9*, 253–258.

Twentyman, C. T., & McFall, R. M. Behavioral training of social skills in shy males. *Journal of Consulting and Clinical Psychology*, 1975, *43*, 384–395.

Twentyman, C. T., Boland, T., & McFall, R. M. *Five studies exploring the problem of heterosocial avoidance in college males.* Unpublished manuscript, 1978.

Van Hasselt, V. B., Hersen, M., & Milliones, J. Social skills training in alcoholics and drug addicts: A review. *Addictive Behaviors*, 1978, *3*, 221–233.

Van Hasselt, V. B., Hersen, M., Whitehill, M., & Bellack, A. S. Assessment and modification of social skills in children. *Behaviour Research and Therapy*, 1979, *17*, 413–438.

Vaughn, C. E., & Leff, J. P. The influence of family and social factors on the course of psychiatric illness: A comparison of schizophrenic and depressed neurotic patients. *British Journal of Psychiatry*, 1976, *129*, 125–137.

Wallace, C. J. *The assessment of interpersonal problem-solving skills with chronic schizophrenics.* Paper presented at the Annual Meeting of the American Psychological Association, New York, September 1978.

Wallace, C. J., Nelson, C., Lukoff, D., Webster, C., Rappe, S., & Ferris, C. *Cognitive skills training.* Paper presented at the Annual Meeting of the Association for Advancement of Behavior Therapy, Chicago, November 1978.

Weiss, R. L. Operant conditioning techniques in psychological assessment. In P. McReynolds (Ed.), *Advances in psychological assessment.* Palo Alto, Calif.: Science & Behavior, 1968.

Weiss, R. L., & Margolin, G. Marital conflict and accord. In A. R. Ciminero, K. S. Calhoun, & H. E. Adams (Eds.), *Handbook for behavioral assessment.* New York: Wiley, 1977.

Wells, K. C., Hersen, M., Bellack, A. S., & Himmelhoch, J. Social skills training in unipolar nonpsychotic depression. *American Journal of Psychiatry*, 1979, *136*, 1331–1332.

Wessberg, H. W., Mariotto, M. J., Conger, A. J., Conger, J. C., & Farrell, A. D. The ecological validity of role plays for assessing heterosocial anxiety and skill of male college students. *Journal of Consulting and Clinical Psychology*, 1979, *47*, 525–535.

Whitehill, M. B., Hersen, M., & Bellack, A. S. Conversation skills training for socially isolated children. *Behaviour Research and Therapy*, 1980, *18*, 217–225.

Williams, M. T., Turner, S. M., Watts, J. G., Bellack, A. S., & Hersen, M. Groups social skills training for chronic psychiatric patients. *European Journal of Behavioural Analysis and Modification*, 1977, *1*, 223–229.

Wolfe, J. L., & Fodor, I. G. A comparison of three approaches to modifying assertive behavior in women: Modeling-plus-behavior rehearsal, modeling-plus behavior rehearsal-plus-rational therapy, and consciousness-raising. *Behavior Therapy*, 1977, *8*, 567–574.

Wolpe, J. *Psychotherapy by reciprocal inhibition.* Stanford, Calif.: Stanford University Press, 1958.

Wolpe, J., & Lang, P. J. A fear survey schedule for use in behavior therapy. *Behaviour Research and Therapy*, 1964, *2*, 27–30.

Wolpe, J., & Lazarus, A. A. *Behavior therapy techniques.* New York: Pergamon Press, 1966.

Young, E. R., Rimm, D. C., & Kennedy, T. D. An experimental investigation of modeling and verbal reinforcement in the modification of assertive behavior. *Behaviour Research and Therapy*, 1973, *11*, 317–319.

Zeiss, A. M., Lewinsohn, P. M., & Muñoz, R. F. Nonspecific improvement effects in depression using interpersonal skills training, pleasant activity schedules, or cognitive training. *Journal of Consulting and Clinical Psychology*, 1979, *47*, 427–439.

Zigler, E., & Levine, J. Premorbid adjustment and paranoid-nonparanoid status in schizophrenia. *Journal of Abnormal Psychology*, 1973, *82*, 189–199.

Zigler, E., & Phillips, L. Social effectiveness and symptomatic behaviors. *Journal of Abnormal and Social Psychology*, 1960, *61*, 231–238.

Zigler, E., & Phillips, L. Social competence and outcome in psychiatric disorder. *Journal of Abnormal and Social Psychology*, 1961, *63*, 264–271.

Zigler, E., & Phillips, L. Social competence and the process-reactive distinction in psychopathology. *Journal of Abnormal and Social Psychology*, 1962, *65*, 215–222.

CHAPTER 24

Obsessional-Compulsive Disorders

S. J. Rachman

Introduction

It is pleasing to record that during the past 10 years significant advances have been made in dealing with obsessional-compulsive disorders. For the first time, psychologists are in possession of a treatment program—exposure and response prevention—that is demonstrably successful in reducing the difficulties of most obsessional patients. On average, the improvements are moderate to marked, but a significant minority of people are free of obsessional problems at the conclusion of their training program. This turn of events is doubly welcome. We are now in a position to provide useful help to people suffering from a distressing and disabling disorder, and the recent clinical research has also enabled us to close the gap between the early advances made in dealing with phobic disorders and our relative helplessness in dealing with a comparable type of neurosis.

These welcome developments are, however, clouded by increasing doubts about the desirability of continuing to conduct clinical research in the manner that has characterized the past 25 years. It is becoming evident that some of the central assumptions on which conventional outcome research is based are dubious. The most promising alternative is to adopt a properly psychological approach to these disorders and their modification (see Rachman & Philips, 1978; Rachman & Wilson, 1980).

Obsessional-compulsive disorders can be both distressing and disabling, sometimes to the point of destroying a person's life. Clinical examples of severe disorders are given by Jaspers (1963) and by Rachman and Hodgson (1980), among others. Although the problems that characterize these disorders are probably widespread in the general population, they become matters of clinical concern only when the intensity and/or the frequency of the problem becomes a matter of distress or disablement. In conventional terms, obsessional-compulsive disorders have a relatively low incidence. On present estimates, it seems likely that these disorders comprise roughly .5% of all neurotic outpatients, but a higher proportion of neurotic inpatients—in the region of

S. J. Rachman • Department of Psychology, University of British Columbia, Vancouver, British Columbia, V6T 1Y7, Canada. Much of the research described in the section "Current Status" of this chapter was supported by grants from the British Medical Research Council.

2% (see Black, 1974; Hare, Price, & Slater, 1971; Rachman & Hodgson, 1980). As these proportions indicate, obsessional disorders tend to be rather more serious than the general run of neurotic problems.

Since the introduction of the concept of obsessional-compulsive disorders well over 100 years ago, the definition of this type of problem has produced little controversy. As a result of recent research and clinical findings, it is now possible to clarify and review this and related concepts. Jaspers's (1963) definition is representative and comprehensive: "In a strict sense of the term, compulsive thoughts, impulses, etc., should be confined to anxieties or impulses which can be experienced by the individual as an incessant preoccupation, though he is convinced of the *groundlessness* of the anxiety, the *senselessness* of the impulse and the *impossibility* of the notion. Thus, the compulsive events, strictly speaking, are all such events the existence of which is strongly resisted by the individual in the first place, and the *content* of which appears to him as groundless, meaningless or relatively incomprehensible" (p. 134, original emphasis). Few substantial changes have been introduced into that definition, but we are now in a position to specify more closely the relevant phenomena and to say more about the content of the disorders, as well as the relations between different aspects of the problems experienced by the affected person.

An *obsession* is an intrusive, repetitive thought, image, or impulse that is unacceptable or unwanted and gives rise to subjective resistance. It generally produces distress and is characteristically difficult to remove or control. The affected person generally acknowledges the senselessness of the impulse or idea. The content of an obsession is repugnant, worrying, blasphemous, obscene, nonsensical, or all of these. The person might be repetitively troubled by the thought that he or she might have killed an old person, or by images of mutilated babies, or by doubts about whether he or she is moral or intensely evil, or about whether he or she might have a compulsive urge of genitalia exposure in public, or shout obscenities, and so on. In an analysis of 81 obsessional neurotics, Akhtar, Wig, Verma, Pershod, and Verma (1975) found that the con-

tent of obsessional material could be broken down into five categories, which are given here in descending order of frequency: dirt and contamination, aggression, orderliness of inanimate objects, sex, and religion. In support of Lewis's (1966) claim that the content of the obsession is of little use prognostically, Akhtar *et al.* found no relation between content and outcome.

Compulsions are repetitive, stereotyped acts. They may be wholly unacceptable, or more often partly acceptable, but are regarded by the person as being excessive or exaggerated. They are preceded or accompanied by a subjective sense of compulsion, and they generally provoke subjective resistance. They usually produce distress, and the person can acknowledge the senselessness of his or her activities, when judged in calmer moments. Although the activities are within the person's voluntary control, the urge to carry out the acts can be extremely powerful, and hence the person experiences a sense of diminished volition. The two most common types of compulsive activity, often referred to as compulsive rituals, are repetitive cleaning and checking. The classical example of the former type is a compulsive hand-washer, and a common example of the second type is the person who compulsively checks the security of appliances and of entrances to her or his home.

There is a close and probably a causal relationship between compulsive urges and compulsive acts, with the former producing the latter. Obsessions and compulsions are closely related, and in the study by Akhtar and his colleagues referred to earlier, it was found that 25% of the patients reported having obsessions that were not associated with overt acts. In a study of 150 obsessional inpatients, Welner, Reich, Robins, Fishman, and van Doren (1976) reported that 69% of the patients complained of both obsessions and compulsions, 25% had obsessions only, and a mere 6% had compulsions only.

One can describe a person as having an obsessional-compulsive disorder if his or her major complaint is the repeated occurrence of an obsession and/or compulsion, if there are accompanying behavioral signs of such experiences, and if the complaint and signs are associated with distress and some impairment of psychological functioning (socially, occupationally, sexually, etc.). The experience of subjective compulsion, the report of internal resistance, and the presence of insight are generally regarded as the three indicators of an obsessional-compulsive disorder. Outside of the obsessional problems, the affected person generally has what is described somewhat clumsily as an "intact personality." These working definitions of the major phenomena encountered in these disorders are not without their difficulties (see Rachman & Hodgson, 1980, for an extended analysis), but they will suffice for present purposes.

In summary form, the necessary and sufficient conditions for describing repetitive behavior as *compulsive* are an experienced sense of pressure to act and an attribution of this pressure to internal sources. The occurrence of resistance is a confirmatory feature but is neither necessary nor sufficient. The necessary and sufficient features for defining a repetitive thought, impulse, or image as obsessional are intrusiveness, internal attribution, unwantedness, and difficulty of control. The confirmatory indicators are resistance and an alien quality. An obsessional-compulsive disorder is one in which the person's major complaint is of distress caused by obsessions or compulsions. The overt indicators are repetitive, stereotyped behavior and a degree of psychological and social impairment associated with the complaints.

The so-called natural history of obsessional disorders has been described admirably by a number of contributors. In essence, these disorders emerge in early adulthood, are closely associated with affective disorders, often take a fluctuating course in the early stages, and have roughly a one-in-three chance of becoming chronic problems. Full accounts can be found in Black (1974), Goodwin, Guze, and Robins (1969), Kringlen (1965, 1970), Templer (1972), Rachman and Hodgson (1980), and Videbech (1975).

The study of these disorders is of considerable interest because in many ways, they are the purest example of abnormal behavior. People whose behavior is in most respects well within rational borders carry out repetitive acts that they recognize as being senseless. To a considerable extent, they are executing urges against their rational inclinations. For many patients, the relatively uncontrolled repetitive conduct of essentially irrational acts is the greatest source of distress. An improved understanding of these disorders is also desirable for humane reasons. Despite their relatively uncommon occurrence, these disorders can be extraordinarily distressing for the affected person, and often for large numbers of friends and relatives, who can rarely escape the adverse consequences of this distressing and disabling behavior. From a narrower point of view, an improved understanding and control of obsessional-compulsive disorders would constitute an important advance for practitioners of behavior therapy. A convincing demonstration of the ability to modify these otherwise intractable problems would give the clearest possible demonstration of the power of these methods to modify not only the minor fears of university students, often the subject of unwarranted devaluation (see Borkovec & Rachman, 1979) but also one of the most serious and unyielding neurotic disorders one can encounter.

Having defined the disorder and explained its significance, I devote the remainder of this chapter to an account of conventional treatment and of the progress of behavioral research into the nature and the modification of the disorders.

Historical Perspective

In order to appreciate the significance of the recent progress in developing behavioral methods for modifying obsessional-compulsive disorders, it is advisable to begin with a short account of the therapeutic alternatives. This account is then followed by a brief sketch of the historical development of the newer behavioral methods.

The pessimism that permeates the psychiatric literature on obsessions and compulsions is nowhere more evident than in discussions of the outcome of these disorders. Most writers simply discount the possibility that the outcome can be influenced by treatment. The outcome statistics are usually presented without reference to treatment, and instead, the evidence is discussed regardless of the type or the duration of the treatment provided, even though few patients fail to receive some form of treatment. There is so little confidence in conventional treatment that few writers take the trouble to distinguish between spontaneous remission rates and treatment remission rates! Similarly, most discussions of the prognosis of the disorder contain no mention of the possible influence of formal treatment (e.g., Kringlen, 1970; Lewis, 1966; Lo, 1967).

Grimshaw (1964) conducted a useful retrospective study of 100 obsessional patients, followed for a mean of five years. He found that roughly two-thirds were improved as far as their symptoms were concerned, and approximately 40% had shown "very considerable improvement." However, he noted that the "improvement could not be attributed to any definite form of treatment" (p. 1055). He noted that this conclusion was in agreement with the views of most other writers on the subject. In his review, as in those of others, it was found that the proportion of improved cases was not different in any of the major treatment groups. In fact, "the group receiving no specialist treatment fared the best of all, with about 70% having a satisfactory result" (p. 1055). In a wider review covering 13 studies, Goodwin *et al*. (1969) concluded that obsessional neurosis is a chronic illness for which there is no specific treatment. A later comprehensive review by Black (1974) ended with the conclusion that "no treatment has been shown to influence long-term outcome of obsessional illness . . . the influence of different therapies can be discounted" (p. 43).

Accurate information on the spontaneous remission rate for this type of disorder is not available, but Cawley (1974) succinctly summarized the position. Among patients with obsessional disorders that are severe enough to require their admission to a hospital, roughly one-quarter recover within five years. About one-half improve a good deal, and the remaining one-quarter are unchanged or worse. For patients whose problems are not sufficiently severe to require hospitalization, roughly two-thirds improve to some extent, while the remaining third perhaps show slight improvement or remain unchanged or worse. Further consideration of spontaneous remission rates in this and related disorders is given by Rach-

man and Wilson (1980). In view of the occurrence of spontaneous remissions, a fact of considerable importance to practicing clinicians and their patients, it is essential that the claims made on behalf of any form of treatment be evaluated against the naturally occurring remission rate.

In the use of medication for obsessional disorders, this type of controlled evaluation has rarely been carried out, and therefore, one has to regard with some caution the claims that have been made on behalf of various drugs. On present evidence, the only types of drugs worthy of some consideration as possible therapeutic agents in coping with obsessional disorders are the so-called antidepressants. Given the close association between depression and obsessional disorders (see Rachman & Hodgson, 1980), it is reasonable to expect that any successful antidepressant treatment, using drugs or other means, should be capable of producing useful changes in many cases. The antidepressant drug that has attracted most attention so far is clomipramine. This drug has achieved some popularity not only because of its satisfactorily demonstrated effects on depression, but also because it has been claimed that the drug has a specific therapeutic effect on obsessional complaints (e.g., Capstick, 1975; Fernandez & Lopez-Ibor, 1969, among others).

Although some of the claims made on behalf of clomipramine, particularly the clinical descriptions, were persuasive, the first evidence from a controlled trial was not published until 1979 (Rachman, Cobb, Grey, MacDonald, Mawson, Sartory, & Stern). The design and outcome of this randomized control trial carried out on 40 moderately to severely disabled obsessional patients, with its major emphasis on the effects of behavioral treatment, are described below. For the present, it is sufficient to remark that convincing evidence was obtained that clomipramine had a primary therapeutic effect on depression and a secondary effect on obsessional problems. Those obsessional patients who were not unduly troubled by depression prior to the administration of the drug showed few signs of any improvement in their obsessional problems as a consequence of taking clomipramine. On the other hand, there was good evidence that among those patients who were suffering from at least moderate levels of depression as well as obsessional problems, the successful use of the antidepressant drug was, on the whole, followed by a significant improvement in some of the obsessional difficulties.

Although some ambitious claims have been made on behalf of the therapeutic power of interpretive psychotherapy, Cawley (1974) concluded his review of the evidence by saying that "there is no evidence to support or refute the proposition that formal psychotherapy helps patients with obsessional disorders" (p. 288). His conclusion that these disorders are unlikely to be helped by formal psychotherapy appears to be shared by a majority of writers, excluding those, of course, who are proponents of the psychoanalytic method. A wide-ranging review of this subject is provided by Rachman (1971) and by Rachman and Wilson (1980).

For a period lasting approximately 15 years, psychosurgery was a commonly used form of treatment for obsessional problems, particularly those of a seemingly intractable character. Because of the seriousness of these operations, and because they are still in use albeit on a greatly reduced scale, a fuller examination of the evidence on this subject appears to be warranted (see also Rachman, 1980b). The belief that psychosurgery is an effective method of treating obsessional disorders rests on two main claims. In the first place, it is argued that psychosurgery is particularly suitable for treating such disorders, and second, it is claimed to be the only effective method of treating the most severe and intractable cases. If sustained, these claims would be of considerable importance, offering, as they do, some hope for those patients who, by definition, are beyond help by other methods.

Before examining the evidence on the effects of psychosurgery, it is useful to recall that these operations were initially introduced as a cure not for obsessions, but for schizophrenia. Predictably, the use of surgery was soon extended to a wide range of disorders, from depression to delinquency (see Rachman, 1980b). As the skepticism about the value of psychosurgery as a treatment for schizophrenia grew, a shift of emphasis occurred, and more and more obsessional patients received the operation. It need hardly be argued that the use of radical surgical procedures can be justified only on the grounds of demonstrable success in the absence of satisfactory alternatives.

The first reason for misgivings is that no serious attempt has ever been made to explain why psychosurgery *should* alleviate obsessional disorders. Even if we possessed acceptable empirical proof of its therapeutic value, we would remain in the dark about the causal processes involved. The earlier but now discredited claim that psychosurgery is an effective treatment for schizophrenia is doubly worrying. It reminds us of our credulity in therapeutic matters and also reminds us that the recommendation of surgery for obsessional disorders is secondhand and atheoretical. It is also worth bearing in mind that the use of surgery is based on and helps to perpetuate the dubious notion that all obsessional disorders are illnesses. There can be little doubt that the acceptance of the alternative view, that obsessional disorders are better construed as psychological problems (see Rachman & Hodgson, 1980), would reduce the likelihood of anyone's recommending a surgical solution.

An extensive review of the major reports on the effect of psychosurgery is given in Rachman (1980b) and the present account is confined to the most recent and major studies. Smith, Kilch, Cochrane, and Kljajic (1976) evaluated the effects of leukotomy on 43 patients, including 5 obsessional cases. Of these patients, 3 died, 3 developed adverse personality changes, and 1 had repeated seizures. At the six-month follow-up, 58% of the patients were said to be markedly improved, but the obsessional patients did slightly less well than the others. Among these patients, the improvement was only slight to moderate. The best results in this series appear to have been achieved by the depressed patients, a not-uncommon finding (see Rachman, 1980b). As the Smith study met few of the criteria generally regarded as being necessary for controlled studies, this partial evidence cannot be given much weight. The comparatively favorable reports by Sykes and Tredgold (1964) and by Strom-Olsen and Carlisle (1971) cannot be ignored, but as both these reports are retrospective, nonrandom, uncontrolled, and based on a partial sample of patients, firm conclusions cannot be reached. On the question of whether the operation is best reserved for the most intractable cases, the information that in the Strom-Olsen series, 4 of the 20 patients were operated on after a duration of illness of less than five years is a disturbing feature. The operation is not, in practice, reserved for chronic or intractable disorders.

Kelly, Richardson, Mitchell-Heggs, Greemy, Chen, and Hafner (1973) reported a favorable improvement rate of 90% for the 40 patients who were included in their prospective non-controlled study. Of the 40 patients, 17 had a diagnosis of obsessional neurosis. Although cured or much improved outcomes were reported for 7 of the 17 patients, by counting the 6 patients who fell into the center of the rating scale Kelly *et al.* were able to quote an improvement rate of 76% for the obsessional subsample. This optimistic picture, however, must be seen against the similar claim of a 66% improvement rate for most of their patients who were diagnosed as schizophrenic—a very unusual result. These almost entirely favorable results, observed six weeks after the operation, should be regarded with caution, as the study suffered from the defects of rater contamination, confounded treatments, absence of a control, and so on.

A follow-up report on this study was given by Mitchel-Heggs, Kelly, and Richardson (1976). Their impressive follow-up data should not obscure the original defects of the study. It should also be mentioned that the ages of the patients at the time of the operation ranged from 21 to 65 years. The lower limit confirms that the operation is not reserved for chronic cases. Furthermore, roughly 12% had had an illness duration of less than five years. Even if one sets aside the flaws in the design of the study, the reasons for the apparent improvement are unknown. The explanations that are offered, and all of these are tentative, suggest that the reduction in obsessional problems that might have occurred are, in any event, bound to be *secondary*. But if this is granted, then it must be demonstrated that the *primary* action, be it the relief of anxiety or the reduction of depression, cannot be achieved by easier and noninstrusive means. Even if the astonishing claim of an 80% success rate for the schizophrenic patients gives rise to considerable caution, their claims at least establish that psychosurgery might be worth investigation if a plausible rationale can be offered and if there is no alternative form of therapy available. In a broader view, however, it might be argued, as I do, that psychosurgery is a redundant and undesirable treatment and that there are, indeed, preferable alternatives.

Bridges, Goktepe, and Maratos (1973) carried out a retrospective follow-up study of 24 obsessional patients and 24 depressive patients who had undergone psychosurgery at least three years earlier. Although the information on the status of the patients was gathered in a direct and methodical manner, the absence of any preoperative information is a serious shortcoming. For what it is worth, however, the depressed patients in this retrospective survey did as well as, or slightly better than, the obsessional patients. This result serves to emphasize the point made earlier that whatever else it is, psychosurgery of this kind is not a *specific* remedy for obsessional neuroses. Furthermore, evidence of serious unwanted effects was uncovered in the Bridges survey (e.g., 5 of the 48 patients suffered fits after the operation; 10 of the 48 patients had to have more than one operation, etc.).

In regard to the common claim that psychosurgery is particularly effective for chronic intractable cases, the obsessional patients who did worst in this retrospective survey had an illness duration of 13 years, and those who did best had an illness duration of 9 years. Those patients who had the longest admissions to the hospital prior to the operation did worst of all. In a later and more extensive review, Goktepe, Young, and Bridges (1975) found a similar pattern among a larger sample of patients. As in most of these reports, the depressive patients appear to have done best. So even if the evidence were interpreted, with minimal caution, as showing that psychosurgery benefits a proportion of obsessional patients, it certainly cannot be concluded that this surgery is particularly suitable for managing this type of neurosis. Finally, both Cawley (1974) and Sternberg (1974) concluded that those patients who have a better prognosis without psychosurgery are precisely the ones who are said to respond well to the operation. In Ingram's (1961) summary: "Many of the factors said to favour the outcome of the operation are seen to be the same as those favouring spontaneous improvement" (p. 399).

To return to the opening question of this section, it must be concluded on present evidence that neither of the therapeutic claims made on behalf of psychosurgery is supportable. Psychosurgery is not particularly suitable for treating obsessional disorders, and it is not most effective for treating chronic or intractable cases. Proponents of psychosurgery justify its use on empirical grounds, but it turns out that this empirically based treatment has an inadequate empirical basis. In the present circumstances, there is little reason to recommend psychosurgery for obsessional disorders.

It should be borne in mind, however, that the resort to psychosurgery often was an act of desperation on the part of clinicians whose therapeutic efforts all too often proved to be powerless. With psychosurgery as the last, or all but last, procedure available to clinicians, it can be seen how very important it was, and is, to find acceptable alternatives. In fact, the looming threat of surgery for neurotic patients proved a vital spur to behavioral psychologists on a number of important occasions. There can be little doubt that as the power and range of behavioral and other psychological methods for dealing with obsessional-compulsive disorders increases, we shall see the last of psychosurgery as a method for dealing with these difficulties. There is a good deal to be said for reminding oneself, and others, that for a period of nearly 20 years, behavioral methods of treating obsessional-compulsive disorders were in active competition with psychosurgery.

Current Status

It is generally agreed that the first successes achieved by behavior therapists dealing with neuroses came in the modification of phobias. Wolpe's (1958) invaluable pioneering work has been consolidated by the addition of new information and the development of refined and novel techniques (see Rachman, 1978, for ex-

amples). Among these new techniques, flooding and participant modeling are among the most promising. Unfortunately, the early successes achieved in the treatment of phobias were not accompanied by progress in dealing with obsessional disorders. Until recently, therapists approached the treatment of obsessional disorders with realistic caution. Even when the traditional fear-reducing method of desensitization was successfully used, the treatment turned out to be laborious and time-consuming. The position prevailing at the end of the 1960s is summarized in a review by Meyer, Levy, and Schnurer (1974). They concluded that the success rates reported by behavior therapists dealing with obsessional problems were significantly lower than those achieved in working with other disorders. They collected clinical reports on the treatment of 61 obsessional patients, and the overall success rate was discouraging. Moreover, they noted that a surprisingly large number of treatment variations have been attempted, and this is seldom a good sign.

The medley of predominantly imaginal methods that were tried on obsessional-compulsive patients during the 1960s gradually gave way to *in vivo* methods of treatment, with modeling, exposure, and response prevention techniques taking places of major importance. By the early 1970s, a significant change had occurred, and now, participation in a program of behavioral treatment helped a majority of people suffering from obsessional-compulsive disorders to achieve substantial relief and benefits. This advance occurred as a result of a combination of several events and influences. In the first place, there was a shift in emphasis in treatment programs provided for phobic patients, from a reliance on imaginal presentations to *in vivo* exposures. This change in emphasis, in turn, was influenced by claims that implosion was capable of producing large and rapid clinical improvements. At approximately the same time, and for some common reasons, researchers began to show renewed interest in the therapeutic possibilities of flooding, defined concisely as relatively prolonged exposures to high-intensity stimulation. This interest was boosted by the methodical and helpful research carried out on animals by Baum (1970). He was able to demonstrate that the technique of response prevention is capable of reducing intense avoidance behavior in a relatively short time. Soon attempts were being made to reduce people's fears by exposing them to intense stimulation for prolonged periods while discouraging their attempts at escape.

Bandura's (1969) brilliant revival of the concept of imitation and his development of social learning theory (see Bandura, 1977) were soon followed by the appearance of therapeutic modeling procedures. Therapeutic modeling was one of the first methods ever to produce a result that exceeded the fear-reducing effects of desensitization (Bandura, Grusec, & Menlove, 1967). Like flooding, therapeutic modeling is almost always carried out *in vivo*.

Because of the now-evident similarities between phobias and certain types of obsessional-compulsive disorder, notably those predominantly involving cleaning rituals, it was inevitable that these new fear-reducing techniques would be recruited in a fresh attack on unyielding compulsions and obsessions. Therapists also drew valuable encouragement and advice from Meyer's (1966) extremely instructive account of his success in treating two seriously handicapped patients. He regarded the favorable outcome in these two cases as being the result of a successful attempt to modify the patients' expectations. He also laid emphasis on the need for the treatment to "be intensive" and "to have a strict control over the patient's behaviour" (p. 280). While engaged in research into the fear-reducing mechanisms involved in flooding and in Stampfl's implosion method, Hodgson and Rachman (1970) decided to test the value of these methods during the course of their protracted attempts to help three severely disabled obsessional-compulsive patients. The development of this work, with its disappointments and successes, is recounted by Rachman and Hodgson (1980). For present purposes, it is sufficient to say that we were encouraged in our belief that modeling exposure and response prevention might prove to be a sufficiently powerful combination to modify even such an unyielding disorder as obsessional-compulsive disturbances. As a result, a connected series of clinical trials was undertaken in collaboration with

G. Röper, I. Marks, G. Sartory, S. Grey, R. McDonald, and a number of other colleagues.

The first clinical study (Rachman, Hodgson, & Marks, 1971) was designed to test the therapeutic value of behavioral treatment compared with a relaxation control treatment, and the secondary aim was to make a preliminary comparison of the effects of a participant modeling treatment and a flooding procedure. The study was carried out on 10 moderately to severely disabled chronic patients who had been in serious difficulty for at least one year and had already received psychiatric treatment of one kind or another. In this first study, as in subsequent studies in this series, we included patients who displayed overt compulsive behavior; those who complained of obsessions unaccompanied by compulsions (a small minority) were investigated separately. The average duration of the clinical problem for our group of 10 patients was 10 years, and their mean age was 35.

The basic plan of the study, followed with some variations in the succeeding investigations, was as follows. After selection at an outpatient interview, arrangements were made for those selected to be admitted to the hospital. In the first week of their stay, detailed observations and measurements were taken. In the next three weeks, they were seen every weekday for approximately 45 min per session, during which they all received relaxation control treatment. Before entering the next three-week stage of the treatment, they were reassessed. Each patient was then allocated randomly to one of two behavioral treatments, either flooding or participant modeling. At the conclusion of this three-week period, they were reassessed again. Those who required further treatment at the end of the experimental period received it. Hence, the reassessments carried out after 3 months, 6 months, and 24 months do not give an indication of the effects of the control and experimental treatments unconfounded by further treatment. During the relaxation-control-treatment period and the behavioral treatment period, the patients were strongly encouraged to refrain from carrying out their compulsive activities (response prevention was instituted).

On all of the important comparisons, both

forms of behavioral treatment were more effective than the control treatment. With a few minor exceptions, the changes observed after flooding or modeling treatment could not be distinguished from each other. In a vain attempt to identify prognostic factors, we correlated 21 pretreatment variables with 5 outcome criteria, but no pointers emerged. Nevertheless, we were left with some clear impressions. Some patients failed to improve despite high motivation and adequate cooperation, while others appeared to benefit despite poor motivation and cooperation. Two patients who showed substantial improvement in the hospital but less satisfactory improvement at home drew our attention to the importance of incorporating some domiciliary treatment.

The absence of any differences between the effects of flooding and those of modeling presented interesting questions. The most obvious possibility was that both methods were acting through a common factor, one that might also have been present in the method used by Meyer (1966). In all three methods, the patients are exposed, in the therapist's presence, to situations that evoke discomfort, and they are then discouraged from undoing the consequences of this exposure.

As our first study showed that flooding and modeling were comparably effective, we then considered the possibility that in combination, they might achieve more than either would achieve separately. So the major aim of the second study was to determine whether the combined effects of the two methods might exceed their separate effects (Hodgson, Rachman, & Marks, 1972). For the second study, we selected five more patients drawn from the same general pool as the original group. The mean age of the second group was 32 years, and the duration of their problem was eight years on average. In brief, we found that the combined treatment method produced results that were slightly better than either treatment given separately, but the differences were not statistically significant. However, the second study was useful in providing a reassuring replication of the apparent power of behavioral treatment. It is worth mentioning at this point that the changes observed in the first two studies were in some instances of a dramatic magnitude. The decline in avoidance behavior and associated anxiety was steep, and there were satisfying changes observed in the form of improved adjustment at work and socially. Contrary to the fears expressed by some writers, there was little evidence of deterioration in family relationships after successful behavioral treatment. The failure rate recorded in these first 15 patients was roughly 1 out of 3.

In order to confirm the main effects, we then carried out another small replication of the second study, using five additional patients drawn from the same general pool (Rachman, Marks, & Hodgson, 1973). The results achieved with these five patients were consistent with those obtained in the first two studies, and the overall conclusion reached at this stage can be summarized in this way.

Of the 20 chronic patients treated in these first three studies, 13 responded very well to treatment, 1 responded moderately well, and 6 responded only slightly or not at all. The 15 patients who received three weeks of relaxation control treatment showed no changes on the measures of obsessional-compulsive behavior but did report some improvement in depression and anxiety. The changes observed after behavioral treatment were rapid and steep and were most evident in the behavioral tests, in subjective discomfort, and the clinical ratings.

At this stage, it seemed probable that the behavioral treatments were effective and clearly superior to relaxation control. The improvements were consistent across measures and between studies. Nevertheless, six patients had failed to benefit to any significant degree. Five of these were unable to comply with the instructions to refrain from engaging in rituals between sessions; that is, the response prevention component could not be carried out. The sixth patient cooperated fully yet failed for reasons that were not clear. At this stage, no differences between the two variants of behavioral treatment had emerged. The clinical impression was that participant modeling is more easily accepted by patients, but there was little reason to suppose that it would produce a superior outcome.

Our interest in the mechanisms responsible

for these therapeutic changes led us to examine the relative contribution made by the passive or symbolic aspects of the modeling treatment and the more active, participant aspects of treatment. The design of the fourth study in this series was dictated by this aim, but it followed the pattern of the earlier experiments. Ten patients drawn from the same general pool were selected for this study (Röper, Rachman, & Marks, 1975). Five of them started with three weeks of relaxation control treatment, while the other five had an initial period of three weeks comprising 15 daily sessions of passive modeling treatment, during which they were simply required to observe the therapist engaging in adaptive behavior in the presence of stimuli or conditions that would provoke discomfort or distress in the patients themselves (e.g., the therapist handled contaminated material and then refrained from cleaning away the effects of such contact). During the second three-week period, all 10 patients were given participant modeling treatment. Moderate declines in fear and avoidance were observed after passive modeling, and these changes were significantly greater than those observed after the relaxation control treatment had been provided. However, the reductions in fear and avoidance observed after the completion of the participant modeling treatment were considerably larger. It was concluded that although symbolic modeling was capable of engendering useful changes, it lacked the power of the participant modeling method. It is also worth mentioning that the overall results of this fourth study were entirely in keeping with those of the first three studies. That is to say, the range and extent of the therapeutic changes observed after treatment were reassuringly consistent.

The fifth and largest study in this series was conducted on 40 patients with chronic obsessional disorders drawn once more from the same general pool. In this experiment, the effects of behavioral treatment, consisting of exposure with participant modeling and self-imposed response prevention, were assessed with and without supplementary medication (Rachman, Cobb, Grey, McDonald, Mawson, Sartory, & Stern, 1979). The study was planned as a rigorous and extensive evaluation of the

method that, by now, had been developed, while at the same time investigating the value of an antidepressant drug clomipramine, which was said to be of particular value in treating obsessional disorders (e.g., Capstick, 1975).

The effects of the treatment were assessed on a range of behavioral and mood measures. As before, the behavioral treatment was followed by significant improvements on most behavioral measures. Interestingly, the administration of clomipramine was followed by significant improvements on most of the mood scales and on some behavioral measures. There were no significant interactions between these two experimental conditions. Subanalyses showed that the clomipramine had little direct effect on obsessional behavior; instead, the drug was followed by broad improvements, and although we obtained clear evidence of an antidepressant effect, there was little sign that it had a direct effect on the obsessional behavior itself. The results of the behavioral treatment were behavioral and specific (see Figures 1–4). The four figures illustrate the major results from the controlled trial carried out by Rachman *et al.* (1979). Each of the four groups underwent two conditions (drug vs. placebo, and behavioral treatment vs. relaxation control) in a 2 × 2 design. Between Occasions 1 and 2, they received drug or placebo, and between 2 and 3, relaxation or behavioral treatment was added. Between Oc-

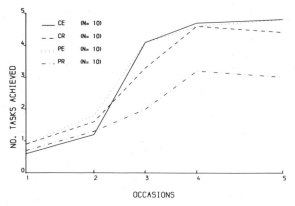

Figure 1. Mean performance measures on the behavioral avoidance test for each of the four groups of patients. The five measurement occasions refer to assessments at 0, 4, 7, 10, and 18 weeks, respectively. E = behavioral treatment; R = relaxation control treatment; P = placebo; and C = clomipramine.

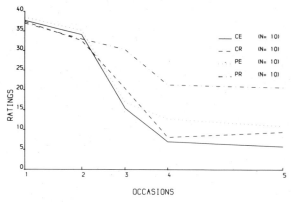

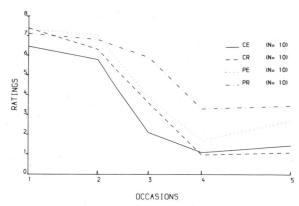

Figure 2. Mean subjective discomfort ratings recorded during the behavioral tests.

Figure 4. Mean scores on the Wakefield self-rated inventory of depression.

casions 3 and 4, all patients received behavioral treatment, and from Occasion 4 to Occasion 5, they all reverted to their original drug or placebo groups. The compulsive behavior changed as predicted and was seldom accompanied by alterations in other aspects of the person's problems. The absence of concomitant mood or other changes emphasizes the specificity of the changes observed to follow this form of treatment. Although moderately disappointing for clinicians, this outcome encourages the view that there is a direct connection between the treatment provided and the effects observed. The specificity of the observed effects discourages explanations that rest on the operation of nonspecific factors such as the influence of the relationship between therapist and patient.

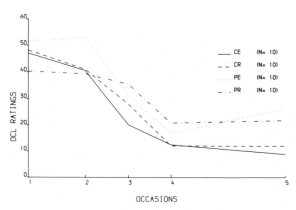

Figure 3. Mean ratings of compulsive activities (external blind assessor).

The results of these five studies indicate that behavioral treatment, coupled with instructions to refrain from carrying out compulsive rituals, is capable of bringing about significant therapeutic improvements in a relatively short period. These improvements are reassuringly stable (e.g., Marks, Hodgson, & Rachman, 1975) and are generally followed by all-round improvements. We obtained very little evidence of the emergence of new problems in the form of putative symptom substitutes or other manifestations.

Leaving aside the problem of those patients who refuse the treatment as offered, we have encountered two main reasons for failure. The first and most common is the inability or unwillingness of the patient to suspend or delay carrying out his or her rituals. The second type of failure arises from an inability to tolerate the distress of the treatment sessions and from the associated requirement that the patient refrain from neutralizing matters by carrying out his or her rituals after each session.

Independent Studies

As always, the evaluation of a comparatively new form of treatment rests mainly on independent confirmations. Before embarking on a comparative analysis of the findings reported from different laboratories and clinics, the general position can be anticipated by observing that the pattern is encouraging despite 1½ exceptions. Only 8 of the 17 reports deal with studies that incorporate at least a degree of experimental control, so a rigid division into controlled and noncontrolled series would be unwieldy. Naturally, one places a different interpretation on the two types of studies, but some of the noncontrolled studies contain important information (see reviews by Beech & Vaughan, 1978; Foa & Steketee, 1980; Meyer *et al.*, 1974).

So, for example, Meyer and his colleagues have presented the results obtained with their method of treatment in assisting 15 moderately to severely ill compulsive patients (Meyer *et al.*, 1974). Their method, developed from Meyer's pioneering work, bears many similarities to the one that we have been employing but involves continual supervision of the patient during the early stages of treatment, in order to ensure that all rituals will be prevented. The similarities between the methods used by the two groups of workers are greater than the differences, and this similarity perhaps explains why the results are broadly comparable, with Meyer and his colleagues (1974) enjoying a slight superiority in outcome. They summarized their results as follows: "With the exception of Case No. 9, every patient showed a marked diminution in compulsive behaviour, sometimes amounting to a total cessation of the rituals . . . it will be seen that at the end of treatment, out of 15 cases in the main group, 10 were either much improved or totally asymptomatic" (p. 251). The significance of this extraordinarily good therapeutic outcome will not be lost on anyone who has tried to help severely disabled obsessional patients to overcome their problems.

In a noncontrolled clinical study, Wonnenberger, Henkel, Arentewicz, and Hasse (1975) also achieved excellent, if narrow, therapeutic results, but with inadequate generalization. Their method of treatment bears a resemblance to the methods that Hodgson and Rachman and their colleagues have been using at the Maudsley Hospital, and that Meyer and his colleagues have been using at the Middlesex Hospital.

The exposure and response prevention procedure is now being widely investigated, and the most recent research reports have come from Emmelkamp and van Kraanen (1977), Emmelkamp, Helm, van Zanten, and Plochg (1980), Foa and Goldstein (1978), and Boersma, Den Hengst, Dekker, and Emmelkamp (1976). In the first of these studies, the results obtained with 14 patients who underwent gradual exposure are given in detail. The outcome was extremely encouraging, and the magnitude of the behavioral changes was summarized as no less than 74%. The stability of these improvements was confirmed at a three-month checkpoint. In their later report, Emmelkamp and his colleagues (1980) have more or less repeated this result with another 15 patients, observed for at least six months after treatment. Once more the results were extremely encouraging. Foa and Goldstein have provided important supporting evidence in the excellent results they obtained with their 21 patients. In certain respects, their results are superior even to those reported by Meyer and his colleagues at the Middlesex Hospital. The most striking feature of Foa and Goldstein's results is that "two-thirds of the patients became asymptomatic after treatment" (p. 173).

It is, of course, true that in none of these studies were control groups employed; nevertheless, the findings are impressive, as the changes were large, stable, and generalized. The major changes were observed within a remarkably short space of time, and this fact, while not excluding the operation of nonspecific factors, rules out at least some of the factors that are believed to contribute to the spontaneous remission rate in this and other neurotic disorders.

Boersma and his colleagues (1976) carried out a small, controlled trial and found that response prevention was a very effective method for modifying compulsions. In the clinical trial reported by Rabavilas, Boulougouris, and Stefanis (1976, 1979) significant clinical improvements were obtained in a group of 12 obsessional patients. The improvements were obtained on all of the main clinical measures of obsessional behavior, in anxiety, and in avoidance behavior. At the conclusion of comparatively brief period of experimental treatment, all but 2 patients showed moderate to major improvement.

Other reports, smaller in scope or in size, which nevertheless produced positive results, are shown in Table 1. We have now to turn to the 1½ exceptions. After studying Meyer's

Table 1. Effectiveness of Behavior Therapy for Obsessional-Compulsive Disorders

Authors	Sample size	Exposure and response prevention	Control group	Outcome (as described)	Follow-up
Studies without experimental controls					
Meyer et al. (1974)	15	Yes	—	10 asymptomatic or greatly improved	1–6 years
Wonnenberger et al. (1975)	6	Yes	—	5 significantly improved	2 months
Mills et al. (1973)	5	Yes	—	5 significantly improved	Unsystematic
Foa & Goldstein (1978)	21	Yes	—	14 asymptomatic, 4 improved, 3 failures	±6 months
Marks et al. (1976)	34	Plus supplements	—	Significant group results overall	Variable
Catts & McConaghy (1975)	6	Yes	—	All 6 improved	6 months
Heyse (1975)	24	Yes	—	7 failures, 10 much improved	1 month
Ramsey & Sikkel (1971)	4	Yes	—	3 significantly improved	Variable
Studies with experimental controls					
Rachman et al. (1971)	10	Yes	Own control[a] (relaxation)	6 much improved, 4 failures	2 years
Rachman et al. (1973)	10	Yes	Own control[a] (relaxation)	7 much improved, 2 failures	2 years
Röper et al. (1975)	10	Yes	Own control[a] (relaxation)	8 improved, 2 failures	6 months
Rachman et al. (1979)	40	± Clomipra-mine	Own control[a] (relaxation)	Significant behavioral improvements	1 year
Boersma et al. (1976)	13	Yes	Behavioral variants[b]	Average 75% improvement	3 months
Emmelkamp & Kraanen (1977)	14	Yes	Waiting list[c] and variants	Average 75% improvement	3 months
Emmelkamp et al. (1980)	15	Yes	With self-instruction	Large, broad improvements	6 months
Hackmann & McClean (1975)	10	Yes	Thought stopping[d]	Significant group changes	No
Rabavilas & Boulougouris (1976)	12	Yes	Behavioral variants[b]	6 much improved, 2 failures	No

[a] Relaxation control consisted of 15 sessions of training in therapeutic muscle relaxation.
[b] Behavioral variants consisted of exposure given in unconventional ways, such as in very brief presentation or purely in fantasy, or in the absence of a therapist.
[c] Waiting-list control consisted of a no-treatment waiting period.
[d] Thought stopping consisted of instruction in and practice of interrupting unwanted thinking.

methods in London, Heyse (1975) returned to Munich and treated 24 inpatients, but with far less success than his mentor: 7 remained unchanged, 7 were slightly improved, and 10 showed moderate improvements. This report is the least encouraging so far and cannot be ignored, especially as the reasons for the 7 failures are not known. Even though the results appear to be superior to those claimed by rival techniques, this report does recommend a sense of caution. The question of why Meyer's method on this occasion lost some of its effectiveness in transport across the Channel remains unanswered. The other slight exception is a small series reported by Ramsay and Sikkel (1971), and Ramsay (1976), who obtained mixed results.

On a slightly different subject, Stern, Lipsedge, and Marks (1973) obtained a poor clinical result in their study of the effects of thought stopping on obsessions. The results reported by Solyom, Zamanzadeh, Ledwidge, and Kenny (1971) are rather difficult to interpret, as their group of patients appear to have been more hetereogenous than the others and included an unusually large percentage of doubters and ruminators. (See Rachman & Hodgson, 1980, for a fuller analysis of the exceptions and the main results.)

With the exceptions mentioned, the information gathered in most studies is strikingly consistent. For example, in all of the studies incorporating control groups, the average improvement in the obsessional-compulsive behavior was steep and swift, commonly dropping from severe to slight or mild. Where the information has been gathered, admittedly in far too few instances, the changes appear to have been stable. Moreover, in the control studies that employed placebo conditions, therapeutic changes observed after behavioral treatment have always been significantly superior to those observed after the control condition, on most measures.

With the exception of the greater power of participant over symbolic modeling, surprisingly few differences between behavioral variations of treatment have been discovered. Naturally, this finding suggests that the factors responsible for the therapeutic changes are common to all methods; an even more prominent possibility arises from the fact that almost all of the treatment variations have been supplemented by response prevention procedures. If it can be shown that response prevention methods alone are capable of producing changes of the same magnitude as those already reported, then the theoretical analysis will, of course, be greatly simplified. This point of view was forcefully argued by Mills, Agras, Barlow, and Mills (1973) on the basis of their extremely interesting series of case studies. The case is not conclusive, however, and on the face of it, it seems improbable that response prevention alone has been responsible for the range of therapeutic improvements observed so far. At the same time, the work of Mills and the general trend of the results described above make it extremely likely that the response prevention component of the treatment has played an important if not exclusive part in the production of the therapeutic changes. Rachman and Hodgson (1980) have, in fact, argued that the contribution made by the response prevention component of the treatment can be expected to vary, depending on the particular nature of the problems presented by the patient. For example, they argue that response prevention is likely to be the crucial component responsible for modifying compulsive checking behavior, but that the exposure component is likely to be of particular value in treating cleaning compulsions. These and other problems of interpretation were dealt with at length by Rachman and Hodgson (1980).

Practical Considerations

As matters now stand, which method is to be preferred? The management of the difficult but unusual types of obsessional disorder known as *primary slowness* and *pure obsessions* require separate consideration and are discussed below. To begin with, it is best to concentrate on the most common of the obsessional disorders, namely, those characterized by repetitive compulsive activities. At present, the best combination method we have comprises the two elements of exposure and response prevention. Some patients benefit considerably from the supplementary use of participant modeling, and my strong impression is that when this variant is used in a gradual manner, it is not only effective but also more easily accepted by patients. It is advisable to carry out as much of the treatment on a domiciliary basis as is possible and appropriate. Often, the domiciliary part of the treatment has to be postponed until there is some clear signs that progress has been made in the contained but safe setting of a clinic.

The combination of exposure and response prevention is a powerful and reliable method for producing changes. As mentioned earlier, it seems improbable that response prevention will by itself achieve much success, except in those cases that are predominantly of the checking variety. The reason for having reservations about the value of response prevention acting alone is that unless the person is being exposed to the provoking stimulation, the prevention of compulsive responses is likely to be empty. Stated plainly, there has to be a response to prevent. It would be meaningless to ask compulsive hand-washers to refrain from washing their hands unless they are already in a contaminated state.

How important is the therapeutic contribution of exposure? It would appear that although exposure alone may be sufficient in some instances, a failure to institute response prevention procedures might well undermine the otherwise beneficial effects of exposure. In cases where there is a strong phobic element, repeated exposures can be expected to achieve a good deal, regardless of response prevention. In checking compulsions, however, failure to institute response prevention is likely to end in therapeutic failure.

Returning to the question of therapeutic failure, in addition to the two possible causes referred to earlier (refusal of treatment or inability to comply with the response prevention requirements), two recent observations made by Foa (1979) must be mentioned because of their potential importance. She has suggested that severely depressed patients may show little or no habituation, even during the treatment sessions themselves. Second, she perceptively noted a peculiar habituation pattern in two of her obsessional patients who had overvalued ideas. Although they showed signs of habituating to the provoking stimuli during treatment sessions, no lasting decrements occurred. At the start of the next session, their responses were once again strong. The suggestion implicit in both of these observations is that the presence of depression and/or overvalued ideas impedes the emotional processing of the relevant material (see Rachman, 1980b).

Returning to the less common forms of obsessional disorder, it has to be admitted that at present, we are inadequately prepared for dealing with primary obsessional slowness or pure obsessions. Until we are in possession of information gathered from properly conducted controlled trials, the following guidelines are offered in the hope that they might be of value to therapists.

Patients suffering from primary obsessional slowness appear to respond well to a program based on modeling and target-setting therapeutic instructions (see Rachman & Hodgson, 1980). Once an appropriate program incorporating a ladder of targets is constructed, the therapist provides modeling for the patient. Thereafter, the patient's progress is monitored in a way that enables both therapist and patient to overcome obstacles as they arise. These programs generally require a good deal of domiciliary practice.

Obsessions, pure but seldom simple, are a far more puzzling phenomenon than primary obsessional slowness, and at present, we have an insecure grasp of their nature (Rachman, 1978a, Steketee & Foa; 1982). In cases of pure obsessions, uncomplicated by overt compulsive acts, at present the best approach would appear to be habituation training carried out under relaxation and/or the evocation of the thoughts to therapeutic instruction. Where the obsessions are followed by internal or external neutralizing activities, these should be put under response prevention instructions. Further advice on this subject must await the outcome of current research programs.

Obsessions and Compulsions

It is impossible to work with obsessional patients for any length of time without becoming intrigued by the nature of the disorder. For example, the extraordinary persistence of unwanted, aversive, and self-defeating obsessions and compulsions is a major puzzle. From the therapeutic point of view, as well as from that of scientific interest, an improved understanding of this undue persistence would be invaluable. The most favored answer is that compulsive behavior persists because it reduces anxiety. As a result of a series of experiments (see Rachman & Hodgson, 1980, for a full account), we were able to conclude that the most common sequence of events is for the execution of the compulsive ritual to be followed by a decrease in anxiety or discomfort. However, we also obtained evidence of other sequences. In a minority of instances, the completion of the compulsive activity is followed by no change in anxiety or discomfort, or even, in some instances, by an increase in anxiety or discomfort. Obsessional cleaning rituals appear most often to follow the discomfort-reducing pattern, whereas obsessions often tend to follow the third pattern; that is, frequently, they are followed by an increase in discomfort. Allowing for the exceptions already mentioned, the results of five related experiments on the subject led us to conclude that when patients touch a contaminating object, they experience an increase in subjective discomfort. Second, when they complete an appropriate washing ritual after such contamination, they experience a reduction in subjective discomfort. Third, and contrary to prediction, we observed that the interruption of a cleaning ritual did not produce an *increase* in subjective discomfort. Most of these findings fit comfortably with the anxiety-reduction hypothesis. Nevertheless, some exceptions have been observed, and these present considerable theoretical problems (see Rachman & Hodgson, 1980). These and other experiments also led us to conclude that there is a significant overlap between phobic disorders and compulsive cleaning disorders. Checking compulsions are less similar to phobic disorders, and obsessions bear only very slight resemblance to phobic disorders.

Future Directions

In summary, a behavioral treatment that combines exposure and response prevention has been shown to be at least moderately effective in reducing obsessional-compulsive behavior. These improvements are stable and are seldom followed by the emergence of new problems. On the experimental side, it appears that most compulsive rituals are followed by a reduction in discomfort, and the exceptions are confined largely to checking rituals. The evidence gathered so far is for the most part consistent with an anxiety-reduction explanation. Although there is a good deal of common ground between various kinds of compulsions and obsessions, there is evidence that permits a division of compulsive rituals to two main categories: cleaning and checking.

Not for the first time, our ability to modify a behavior disorder has outstripped our understanding of its nature. In the coming years, we can look forward to an improvement and a refinement of our therapeutic procedures, to their extension to incorporate the rare but resistant variations of obsessional disorder, and to further efforts designed to improve our understanding of the mode of operation of the successful techniques. Although there is no shortage of explanations to account for the available information (see review by Rachman & Hodgson, 1980), at present we do not have sufficient information to enable us to reach safe conclusions about the mechanisms involved in the effective therapeutic procedures currently in use. While acknowledging the presence of a number of practical obstacles to unraveling the relative contribution of the various components of the treatment procedures, they are in principle easy to investigate by the familiar dismantling strategy that proved so successful in research on desensitization. Investigations of the nature and means of modifying obsessions, on the other hand, present theoretical and practical problems of considerable magnitude. As one of the most important contributors to our understanding of obsessions remarked in 1935: "It may well be that obsessional illness cannot be understood altogether without understanding the nature of man" (Lewis, 1936, p. 325). At the very least, a proper understanding of obsessions will certainly demand a greatly improved understanding of the nature of thinking and imagery, and that is a task that will undoubtedly occupy psychologists for many decades to come.

References

Akhtar, S., Wig, N. H., Verma, V. K., Pershod, D., & Verma, S. K. A phenomenological analysis of symptoms in obsessive-compulsive neuroses. *British Journal of Psychiatry*, 1975, *127*, 342–348.

Bandura, A. *The principles of behavior modification*. New York: Holt, Rinehart & Winston, 1969.

Bandura, A. *Social learning theory*. Englewood Cliffs, N.J.: Prentice-Hall, 1977.

Bandura, A., Grusec, J., & Menlove, F. Vicarious extinction of avoidance behavior. *Journal of Personality and Social Psychology*, 1967, *5*, 449–455.

Baum, M. Extinction of avoidance responding through response prevention (flooding). *Psychological Bulletin*, 1970, *74*, 276.

Beech, H. R. (Ed.). *Obsessional states*. London: Methuen, 1974.

Beech, H. R., & Vaughan, M. *Behavioural treatment of obsessional states*. New York: Wiley, 1978.

Black, A. The natural history of obsessional neurosis. In H. R. Beech (Ed.), *Obsessional states*. London: Methuen, 1974.

Boersma, K., Den Hengst, S., Dekker, J., & Emmelkamp, P. Exposure and response prevention: A comparison with obsessive-compulsive patients. *Behaviour Research and Therapy*, 1976, *14*, 19–24.

Borkovec, T., & Rachman, S. The utility of analogue research. *Behaviour Research and Therapy*, 1979, *17*, 253–262.

Bridges, P., Goktepe, E., & Maratos, J. A comparative review of patients with obsessional neurosis and with depression treated by psychosurgery. *British Journal of Psychiatry*, 1973, *123*, 663–674.

Capstick, N. Clomipramine in the treatment of true obsessional state—A report on four patients. *Psychosomatics*, 1975, *16*, 21–25.

Catts, S., & McConaghy, N. Ritual prevention in the treatment of obsessive-compulsive neurosis. *Australian and New Zealand Journal of Psychiatry*, 1975, *9*, 37–41.

Cawley, R. H. Psychotherapy and obsessional disorders. In H. R. Beech (Eds.), *Obsessional states*. London: Methuen, 1974.

Emmelkamp, P., & van Kraanen, J. Therapist-controlled exposure in vivo vs. self-controlled exposure in vivo: A comparison with obsessive-compulsive patients. *Behaviour Research and Therapy*, 1977, *15*, 491–496.

Emmelkamp, P., Helm, M., van Zanten, B., & Plochg, I. Treatment of obsessive-compulsive patients. *Behaviour Research and Therapy*, 1980, *18*, 61–66.

Fernandez, R., & Lopez-Ibor, R. Mono-clorimipramine in the treatment of psychiatric patients resistant to other therapies. *Acta Espana Neurologica*, 1969, *26*, 119–147.

Foa, E. B. Lecture at Maudsley Hospital, London, 1979.

Foa, E. B., & Goldstein, A. Continuous exposure and strict response prevention in the treatment of obsessive-compulsive neurosis. *Behaviour Therapy*, 1978, *17*, 169–176.

Foa, E. B., & Steketee, G. Obsessive-compulsives. In M. Hersen, R. M. Eisler, & P. Miller (Eds.), *Progress in Behavior Therapy, Vol. 8*. New York: Academic Press, 1980.

Goktepe, E., Young, L., & Bridges, P. A further review of the results of the results of stereotactic subcaudate tractotomy. *British Journal of Psychiatry*, 1975, *126*, 270–280.

Goodwin, D., Guze, S., & Robins, E. Follow-up studies in obsessional neurosis. *Archives of General Psychiatry*, 1969, *20*, 182–187.

Grimshaw, L. Obsessional disorder and neurological illness. *Journal of Neurology, Neurosurgery and Psychiatry*, 1964, *27*, 229–231.

Hackmann, A., & McClean, C. A comparison of flooding and thought-stopping treatment. *Behaviour Research and Therapy*, 1975, *13*, 263–269.

Heyse, H. Response prevention and modeling in the treatment of obsessive-compulsive neurosis. In J. Brengelmann (Ed.), *Progress in Behavior Therapy*. Berlin: Springer Verlag, 1975.

Hodgson, R. J., & Rachman, S. An experimental investigation of the implosion technique. *Behaviour Research and Therapy*, 1970, *8*, 21–27.

Hodgson, R., Rachman, S., & Marks, I. The treatment of chronic obsessive compulsive neurosis. *Behaviour Research and Therapy*, 1972, *10*, 181–189.

Ingram, I. M. Obsessional illness in mental hospital patients. *Journal of Mental Science*, 1961, *197*, 382–402.

Jaspers, K. *General psychopathology*. Chicago: University of Chicago, 1963.

Kelly, D., Richardson, A., Mitchell-Heggs, N., Greemy, J., Chen, D., & Hafner, R. Stereotactic limbic leucotomy. *British Journal of Psychiatry*, 1973, *123*, 141–148.

Kringlen, E. Obsessional neurotics: A long-term follow-up. *British Journal of Psychiatry*, 1965, *111*, 709–722.

Kringlen, E. Natural history of obsessional neurosis. *Seminars in Psychiatry*, 1970, *2*, 403–419.

Lewis, A. Problems of obsessional illness. *Proceedings of Royal Society of Medicine*, 1936, *29*, 325–336.

Lewis, A. Obsessional disorder. In R. Scott (Ed.), *Price's Textbook of the Practice of Medicine*, (10th ed.). London: Oxford University Press, 1966.

Lo, W. A follow-up study of obsessional neurotics in Hong Kong Chinese. *British Journal of Psychiatry*, 1967, *113*, 823–832.

Marks, I. M., Hodgson, R., & Rachman, S. Treatment of chronic obsessive-compulsive neurosis by in vivo exposure. *British Journal of Psychiatry*, 1975, *127*, 349–364.

Marks, I. M., Hallam, R., Connolly, J., & Philpott, R. *Nursing in behavioral psychotherapy*. London: Royal College of Nursing. 1976.

Meyer, V. Modification of expectations in cases with obsessional rituals. *Behaviour Research and Therapy*, 1966, *4*, 273–280.

Meyer, V., Levy, R., & Schnurer, A. The behavioral treatment of obsessive-compulsive disorder. In H. R. Beech (Ed.), *Obsessional states*. London: Methuen, 1974.

Mills, H., Agras, S., Barlow, D., & Mills, J. Compulsive rituals treated by response prevention. *Archives of General Psychiatry*, 1973, *28*, 524–529.

Mitchell-Heggs, N., Kelly, D., & Richardson, A. A stereotactic limbic leucotomy—A follow-up at 16 months. *British Journal of Psychiatry*, 1976, *128*, 226–240.

Rabavilas, A., & Boulougouris, J. Mood changes and flooding outcome in obsessive-compulsive patients.

Journal of Nervous and Mental Disorders, 1979, *167,* 495–499.

Rabavilas, A., Boulougouris, J., & Stefanis, C. Duration of flooding sessions in treatment of obsessive patients. *Behaviour Research and Therapy,* 1976, *14,* 349–356.

Rachman, S. *The effects of psychotherapy.* Oxford: Pergamon Press, 1971.

Rachman, S. *Fear and courage.* San Francisco: W. H. Freeman. 1978.

Rachman, S. Emotional processing. *Behaviour Research and Therapy,* 1980, *18,* 51–60. (a)

Rachman, S. Psychosurgical treatment of obsessional-compulsive disorders. In E. Valenstein (Ed.), *The psychosurgery debate.* San Francisco: W. H. Freeman. 1980. (b)

Rachman, S., & Hodgson, R. *Obsessions & compulsions.* Englewood Cliffs, N.J.:Prentice-Hall, 1980.

Rachman, S., & Philips, C. *Psychology and medicine.* Middlesex: Penguin Books, 1978.

Rachman, S., & Philips, C. *Psychology and behavioral medicine.* New York: Cambridge University Press, 1980.

Rachman, S., & Wilson, G. T. *The effects of psychological therapy.* Oxford: Pergamon, 1980.

Rachman, S., Hodgson, R., & Marks, I. The treatment of chronic obsessional neurosis. *Behaviour Research and Therapy,* 1971, *9,* 237–247.

Rachman, S., Marks, I., & Hodgson, R. The treatment of chronic obsessive-compulsive neurosis by modeling and flooding in vivo. *Behaviour Research and Therapy,* 1973, *11,* 463–471.

Rachman, S., Cobb, J., Gray, S., MacDonald, R., Mawson, D., Sartory, G., & Stern, R. The behavioural treatment of obsessional-compulsive disorders with and without clomipramine. *Behaviour Research and Therapy,* 1979, *17,* 467–478.

Ramsay, R. Behavioral approaches to obsessive-compulsive neurosis. In J. C. Boulougouris & A. D. Rabavilas (Eds.), *The treatment of phobic and obsessive-compulsive disorders.* Oxford: Pergamon, 1976.

Ramsay, R., & Sikkel, R. Behavior therapy and obsessive neurosis. *Proceedings of the European Conference on Behavior Therapy,* Munich, 1971.

Röper, G., Rachman, S., & Marks, I. Passive and participant modeling in exposure treatment of obsessive-compulsive neurotics. *Behaviour Research and Therapy,* 1975, *13,* 271–279.

Smith, S., Kiloh, L., Cochrane, N., & Kljajic, I. A prospective evaluation of open prefrontal leucotomy. *Medical Journal of Australia,* 1976, *1,* 731–735.

Solyom, L., Zamanzadeh, D., Ledwidge, B., & Kenny, F. Aversion relief treatment of obsessive neurosis. In R. Rubin (Ed.), *Advances in behavior therapy.* London: Academic Press, 1971.

Steketee, G., & Foa, E. B. Typology of obsessive-compulsive disorders. In I. Hand. (Eds.), *Obsessions and compulsions.* New York: Springer, 1982.

Stern, R. S., Lipsedge, M., & Marks, I. Obsessive Ruminations: A controlled trial of a thought-stopping technique. *Behaviour Research and Therapy,* 1973, *11,* 659–662.

Sternberg, M. Physical treatments in obsessional disorders. In H. R. Beech (Ed.), *Obsessional states.* London: Methuen, 1974.

Strom-Olsen, R., & Carlisle, S. Bi-frontal stereotactic trachotomy. *British Journal of Psychiatry,* 1971, *118,* 141–154.

Sykes, M., & Tredgold, R. Restricted orbital undercutting. *British Journal of Psychiatry,* 1964, *110,* 609–640.

Templer, D. I. The obsessive-compulsive neurosis: Review of research findings. *Comprehensive Psychiatry,* 1972, *13,* 375–383.

Videbech, T. The psychopathology of anancastic endogenous depression. *Acta Psychiatrica Scandinavica,* 1975, *52,* 336–373.

Welner, A., Reich, T., Robins, I., Fishman, R., & van Doren, T. Obsessive-compulsive neurosis. *Comprehensive Psychiatry,* 1976, *17,* 527–539.

Wolpe, J. *Psychotherapy by reciprocal inhibition.* Stanford, Calif.: Stanford University Press, 1958.

Wonnenberger, M., Henkel, D., Arentewicz, G., & Hasse, A. Studie zu einem Selbsthilfeprogram für zwangneurotische Patienten. *Zeitschrift für Klinische Psychologie,* 1975, *4,* 124–136.

CHAPTER 25

Marital Distress

Robert L. Weiss and Gary B. Wieder

Introduction and Overview

In clinical applications of behavioral technology, the individual typically has been defined as the target of concern. The rapid growth in interest in behavioral marital therapy (BMT)—from its dawning in the late 1960s—promised a technology for assessing and effecting changes in committed adult relationships such as marriage. Sometimes by default, but more recently by design, BMT has stressed the importance of the partners' mutual dependency in such relationships and how this mutuality is expressed in a myriad of daily transactions. However, the tendency throughout has been to rely on therapist-controlled response contingencies programmed individually for the partners. In discussing ways from a behavioral standpoint in which marital therapy is complex, Patterson, Weiss, and Hops (1976) observed, "Intervention with couples in severe conflict requires simultaneous changes in contingencies for both members of the dyad. . . . The clinician must be prepared to design and monitor *two programs simultaneously* usually in an atmosphere of tension and mistrust" (p. 243; italics added). Although early it was clear

that work with couples is made particularly difficult because of complexities inherent in "reciprocal determinism" (Bandura, 1977b), there was little direct effort to conceptualize the relationship *per se* as the target of intervention and change, in part, because (1) BMT maintained a commitment to reinforcement orthodoxy and (2) it was a hybrid undertaking, combining, as it did, operant, social exchange, and systems theory concepts. In any event, an additive view of relationships has prevailed, one that holds that the behaviors of the partners as individuals can be added together, with the sum representing the relationship.

A spirited debate on the conceptual nature of BMT focused on the related issue of whether BMT was based on a "simplistic form of Skinnerian reinforcement theory" (Gurman & Kniskern, 1978a; Jacobson & Weiss, 1978). The argument had been advanced that the learning theory model on which BMT was based had been all but abandoned by behaviorally inclined clinicians. The critics of BMT (most notably Gurman, 1978) have taken issue with its reliance on a performance-based technology; BMT had no soul! Indeed, it was argued that an emphasis on teaching external contingency control to intimates might actually prove deleterious to the relationship. BMT does not, the argument continues, recognize the role of self-esteem; relationship

Robert L. Weiss and Gary B. Wieder • Department of Psychology, Straub Hall, University of Oregon, Eugene, Oregon 97403.

transactions represent negotiations about self-worth, and these negotiations are not explicit and systematic but are based on dynamic forces understandable only from the broader perspective of personality theory. To oversimplify somewhat, BMT has been criticized for not having been sufficiently cognitive in its emphasis.

In a field (marriage research) not generally known for its methodological elegance or empirical productivity, BMT certainly has been conspicuous as a systematic, empirically based technology for distressed marriages. Yet, until quite recently, the conceptual basis and the outcome effectiveness of BMT have rested on a paucity of empirically controlled studies. Not uncharacteristically, the conceptual development of this area has outrun its empirical knowledge base within behavioral research, and the nonbehavioral theories have been criticized as being poorly developed (cf. Gottman, 1979; Gurman, 1978; Laws, 1971; Olson, 1970). We have, therefore, an area of considerable clinical significance that has been criticized for failing to capture the nature of intimate relationships, one said to be based on an outmoded theory of learning, and one in which the empirical support for the enterprise itself may be grossly overrated.

Perhaps, as is the case with marriage itself, the behavioral perspective on marriage and marital therapy is beset with conflict, spirited differences of opinion, and challenges to the adequacy of the concepts themselves. Yet, it is an area of enormous clinical and research interest. Also like marriage, it is not the fact of conflict or difference but *the form of attempts made to resolve the differences* that deserves our careful consideration. Behavioral conceptions of marriage (and more generally, committed adult intimacy) have been particularly helpful in narrowing the gap between a preoccupation with the individual's dynamics (traits, motives) on the one hand and broader contextual aspects of social reality (social adjustment, physical health status). BMT has always focused on the social skill capacity of partners; in a real sense, it has embraced a social competency model of human adjustment, concerned with how the transactions of persons bring about changes in the environment, which, in turn, influence the sta-

tus of the persons. Viewed in this way, the nonrational aspects of marriage (choice of partner, etc.) become less important relative to an understanding of the structure and the dynamics (the *form*) of the partners' ability to accomplish their ends within some broader social context. If we accept this social-psychological focus of BMT, it seems that an understanding of marriage will also facilitate our understanding of personal and social adjustment, and that marriage (the management of committed adult intimacy) may provide an axis for conceptualizing psychopathology more generally. Thus, rather than starting with particular individual manifestations of clinical significance (e.g., depression) and then looking for the relevance of marriage to the particular dysfunction, we might be better advised to look at the manifestation of any dysfunction as an expression of the current relationship. The focus is not so much on an individual manifesting depressive behaviors who happens to be married; it is on a relationship in which the form of coping also includes the expression and the management of depressive behaviors.

Behavioral interest in marriage and marital therapy, therefore, has ranged widely from the specifics of a microanalysis of facilitating and disruptive elements of communication exchanges (Gottman, 1979), to more macrolevel concerns, such as being able to predict parenting coping ability with a first child from marital variables measured prior to the birth of the first child (Vincent, Cook, & Messerly, 1980), or macrorelationships between physical health status and marital satisfaction (Weiss & Aved, 1978). In a related yet somewhat oversimplified way, we might argue that the deleterious effects of separation and divorce (Bloom, Asher, & White, 1978) found on health-related measures suggest that adult intimacy is central to the everyday functioning of these individuals. If disengagement produces fairly significant effects—even for relatively short periods of time—clearly we must comprehend the form of such intimacy.

Although the emphasis on social competency can be recorded as a major strength of the behavioral approaches to marriage and marital therapy, as we have briefly suggested above, many unresolved issues remain within this approach. We have alluded to the concern that cognitive variables have been underrepresented in BMT. As will be discussed in detail in later sections, BMT has been quite active in developing a model of marital satisfaction (e.g., Wills, Weiss, & Patterson, 1974). Specifically, how do partners utilize the events of their daily transactions in developing cognitions about marital bliss? Or, do preexisting cognitions determine whether events will be recorded as pleasant or not (Weiss & Margolin, 1977)? The interface between behaviors and cognitions is an important area of current concern.

On a more general level, it should be noted that a collection of techniques cannot pass for a theory of operations. There are numerous specific behavioral techniques available to marital therapists. Our concern, however, is with the system of rules that orchestrates the application of these techniques, *a theory of practice,* so to speak (cf. Weiss, 1980). The development of such a theory of practice is one of the goals of those interested in BMT.

Given the areas of conflict within and outside BMT, the relatively slow pace of theory development, and the limited empirical knowledge base for the technology, our aims for this chapter may be judged to be overly ambitious, if not downright premature. Our major objective is to impose a conceptual organization on the clinical research literature judged to be relevant to BMT. In this way, our presentation differs from the general and special purpose reviews of the BMT literature that have analyzed and reanalyzed a fairly circumscribed empirical body of studies (e.g., Geer & D'Zurilla, 1975; Gurman & Kniskern, 1978b; Jacobson, 1979; Jacobson & Martin, 1976; Patterson *et al.* 1976). We will use a somewhat expanded version of the BMT model described by Weiss (1978) as the Oregon Marital Studies Program (OMSP), a modular approach to intervention. This is basically a competency-based model dealing with relationship performances. We will review the literature relevant to the assumptions of BMT and to evidence about the outcome effectiveness of the various technological elements of BMT. The chapter is organized into a brief historical perspective on the concepts; a major section covering current empirical studies, which is the

heart of our review; sections on future perspectives; and a summary and conclusions.

Historical Perspective

In its relatively brief history, BMT has progressed through three more-or-less discernible phases. The first, an innovative demonstration stage, saw demonstrations and case studies presented by behaviorally oriented clinicians. Not uncommonly, the techniques described were applied to persons who happened to be married rather than to "relationships" (e.g., Goldiamond, 1965; Goldstein & Francis, 1969); the notable exceptions were the more clinically oriented applications by Lazarus (1968) and Liberman (1970). Goldiamond taught stimulus control procedures to a husband bothered by recurring thoughts about his wife's fidelity. Goldstein and Francis reported on the results of teaching wives (the husbands were not seen) operant principles so that they could modify specific behaviors of their husbands. These were important beginnings characterized by a monothematic approach to complex (relationship-relevant) behaviors, that is, the application of learning theory approaches and typically operant notions. (The reader is referred to Olson's 1970 review of the literature prior to 1970.)

The second phase in the developing BMT sophistication was characterized by dual broadening efforts: (1) behavioral technology—already used with families containing a problem child—was now applied to couples; and (2) initial attempts were made to integrate reinforcement and other models (notably from systems theory) with an obvious couples' focus. The work in the second phase showed a much more explicit concern with the mutual dependencies that characterize ongoing intimate relationships. Liberman's (1970) description of how reinforcement theory could be applied to families and couples was among the clearest statements of this position. The work of Patterson and his associates (Patterson & Reid, 1970) provided a richly descriptive model for behavioral sequences between and among family members based on operant reinforcement principles. In 1969, Richard Stuart published his "Operant Interpersonal Treatment for Marital Discord,'' the first attempt to integrate reinforcement, social-psychological, and "systems theory" approaches. Patterson and Reid (1970) had already included concepts from Thibaut and Kelley's (1959) social-exchange theory, in such notions as *reciprocity* and *coercion,* but it was Stuart who saw the potential for introducing communication theory ideas into the mix (e.g., the works of Jackson, 1965; Haley, 1963). Stuart's actual demonstration of the "operant interpersonal" approach utilized a form of *quid pro quo* contracting involving the use of token reinforcers to change problem behaviors. Problem behaviors (defined by each spouse individually) were made interdependent, so that the occurrence of a wife-desired behavior (e.g., husband provides wife conversation) resulted in tokens exchangeable for a husband-desired behavior (e.g., wife provides sex). How necessary the actual theoretical model was to these intervention techniques can be questioned, since a few years later Azrin, Naster, and Jones (1973) presented their model of "reciprocity counseling," based entirely on operant reinforcement techniques. Whereas Stuart's integrative approach clearly embraced *cognitive* (generally nonbehavioral) possibilities, Azrin *et al.* presented a straightforward, sequenced program for bringing spouse behaviors under direct contingency control.

During this same period, the late 1960s, the collaboration of Gerald R. Patterson (Oregon Research Institute), Robert L. Weiss, and Robert C. Ziller (both of the University of Oregon) gave rise to a program of clinical and social-psychological research on the common theme of "conflict in small groups." An Office of Naval Research contract was awarded to the three as principle investigators, and together with their graduate students (Gary Birchler, Hyman Hops, John Vincent, and Tom Wills), they planned studies around the theme of conflict, especially marital conflict. Patterson's work with the families of aggressive children, Weiss's interest in interpersonal accord and his involvement with clinical training, and Ziller's interest in conflict containment made the study of marital conflict a natural focus for the group. Much of the early clinical activity with couples was conducted at the Psychology Clinic of the University of Oregon in conjunc-

tion with clinical psychology students enrolled in the original "marriage practicum." Patterson and Hops (1972) published the first case seen in the original Oregon Program based on the techniques developed by the clinical research group during these early years. In 1973, Weiss, Hops, and Patterson published the first systematic account of the BMT model and the research that the group had been doing on marital distress. The time and the setting were somewhat unusual in the extent to which such a concentrated effort was focused on maritally related issues and the development of an assessment and intervention technology.

During this same period of the early and mid-1970s, the Oregon program provided an impetus for the important yet different contributions of Neil Jacobson (then a student at North Carolina) and John Gottman (a faculty member at Indiana). Jacobson (1977) undertook the herculean task of replicating the effects of the behavioral treatment package developed at Oregon, focusing on the efficacy of contingency contracting. Gottman and his students (Gottman, Notarius, Gonso, & Markman, 1976) published a treatment manual based on their own empirical work with couples, the heart of which utilized a modification of the original behavioral coding system (Marital Interactional Coding System) developed by the Oregon group.

In 1975, Stuart published an expanded version of his operant interpersonal approach, which more directly incorporated communication theory concepts and the modular approach to intervention described by Weiss *et al.* (1973).

The period from 1976 on marks what we have labeled the third phase of the development of BMT. In this phase, we see (1) direct attempts to broaden the behavioral conception of marriage interactions; (2) the utilization of techniques developed specifically for couples, and (3) a much more explicit inclusion of communication training, often derived from nonbehavioral points of view. In addition to the Gottman *et al.* (1976) manual just mentioned, Jacobson and Margolin (1979) have published a practitioner's guide that presents a detailed accounting of BMT technology stimulated by the "Oregon models." In 1975, Margolin *et al.* published a case study entitled "Contracts,

Cognition and Change: A Behavioral Approach to Marriage Therapy," a title that also signaled recent conceptual developments: the importance of including cognitive variables (in this instance attributional change) in BMT. Margolin's dissertation (Margolin & Weiss, 1978) also focused directly on the intimate relationship, again through the use of attributions about the partnership *per se*. In 1978, Weiss presented a much broader integrated model of BMT that explicitly incorporated systems theory concepts.

The development of behaviorally oriented assessment procedures (and outcome measures) was characteristic of the later phases of the development of BMT. (The role of assessment in BMT has been reviewed in depth by Weiss & Margolin, 1977; Jacobson, Elwood, & Dallas, 1981.) The approach characteristically has been multimodal, involving self-report, spouses' observations of themselves, and observations by trained others (coders). A number of self-report questionnaires have been developed in order to objectify specific aspects of intimate relationships derived from the BMT conception itself. The forerunner of the Areas of Change Questionnaire was the Willingness to Change Questionnaire (Weiss *et al.*, 1973, which sought to measure the degree to which partners admitted to wanting the other to change; specific behavioral situations were presented, and the partners indicated whether they desired more or less of that behavior (for example, "I want my partner to participate in financial decisions . . ." could be rated along a scale from "Very Much More" through "No Change" to "Very Much Less.") The Marital Status Inventory (MSI) was intended to provide an intensity measure of the number of steps each partner had taken toward divorce (Weiss & Cerreto, 1980). The "reinforcingness" of partner activities alone and together was assessed by the original Marital Activities Inventory, which now consists of 100 nonutilitarian activities ("We played a board game," "Watched a sunset," "Had a fancy dinner"), which partners check with regard to the frequency of engaging in each activity alone, with the partner, with others, etc. (cf. Weiss & Margolin, 1977).

Spouse observation was accomplished by having spouses track the pleasing and dis-pleasing events of their daily interactions by means of specially prepared forms and wrist counters (cf. Wills *et al.*, 1974). This pleases–displeases technique gave rise to many subsequent investigations, as we shall see in later sections. It was used initially as a means of helping couples to make discriminations in their behavioral environments and as an outcome measure (Weiss *et al.*, 1973).

The last of the assessment approaches to be mentioned in this brief historical review of the phases of BMT development is the venerable Marital Interaction Coding System (MICS). Although developed especially for research and clinical work with couples (Hops, Wills, Patterson, & Weiss, 1971), it was based largely on the earlier coding system developed by Patterson for coding parent–child interactions (Patterson, Ray, Shaw, & Cobb, 1969). A series of 30 behavior codes was used to describe the ongoing interaction of a couple as they discussed some problem germane to their relationship (or by means of a simulation procedure using the revealed-differences task). The interactions were videotaped for subsequent coding by pairs of coders. As already noted, Gottmann *et al.* (1976) both expanded and simplified the original MICS by means of their system (CISS, Couples Interaction Scoring System), which includes affect as well as content coding. (See Gottman, 1979 and Wieder & Weiss, 1980 for technical details about the generalizability of these systems.) The original MICS provided a detailed description of a couples' ongoing interaction and served as the basic measure of relationship status (cf. Birchler, Weiss, & Vincent, 1975; Vincent, Weiss, & Birchler, 1975).

Before concluding this section, it may be helpful to draw out some general historical developments relevant to BMT. The issues of importance to those who developed BMT were not often congruent with those found in the general sociological literature on marriage. (Gurman, 1978, made a similar observation when comparing BMT to other nonbehavioral points of view.) For example, BMT has shown little concern about issues of mate selection or relationship development. As Gottman (1979) has correctly observed, BMT has been influenced minimally by the sociological literature; concepts of power and dominance, for example, simply have not found their way into BMT formulations. Although "satisfaction" has been retained as a variable, treatment in the behavioral literature depends less on global measurement and more on describing behaviorally based correlates (Weiss & Margolin, 1977).

Finally, it is not surprising to learn that techniques often prompted conceptual elaboration in this area. In part, this reflects the paucity of assessment options in the very early days of BMT. After various behaviorally based procedures were developed, the instruments themselves often prompted new questions. For example, the advent of a behavioral coding system made possible the analysis of sequences of interactional behaviors. It was also the case that many of the original concepts about ongoing interactions led to the selection of assessment instruments, as we have already noted.

Conceptual Developments in BMT

Here, we review briefly aspects of the conceptual development of BMT by first considering the major assumptions and concepts. The Oregon Marital Studies Program (OMSP) model is presented as a preface to our review of the empirical literature.

Basic Assumptions and Concepts

For ease of presentation, we consider here three focal points in the organization of BMT concepts: the question of the *patterning* of interactional behaviors, notions about *beneficial exchanges,* and the role of *communication* training.

Throughout its history, BMT has been primarily a performance-based conception of adult intimacy emphasizing the conditions that seem to account for patterning in the daily exchanges of marital partners. This patterning was described in behavioral terms by the processes of *reciprocity* and *coercion* (Patterson & Reid, 1970). Earlier family interaction studies had shown parity in the exchange of positive behaviors between family members. Persons who provided positive consequences to others received these in turn at a comparable

rate when the data were summated over time; in this sense, stable reciprocal interactions were described. Coercion, on the other hand, is a process involving the strategic placement temporally of aversive stimulation at either of two points in an ongoing interaction, points that correspond to the functional definition of *punishment* and *negative reinforcement*: "It [aversive stimulus] can be delivered contingently following a certain response which is to be suppressed, or it can be presented prior to the behavior which is to be manipulated and then withdrawn only when the other person complies" (Patterson, Weiss, & Hopps, 1976, p. 244). In the first instance (punishment), the aversive stimulus (e.g., threats) suppresses ongoing behavior (e.g., nagging), whereas in the second (negative reinforcement), a response by the partner terminates the aversive stimulus (e.g., a threat as to what will occur if nagging does not stop!). Both partners are changed by these consequences; that is, they learn either to use aversive stimuli or to make compliant responses to terminate them. (Stuart, 1969, noted that coercion involves one person's attempt to gain positive outcomes through the use of negative behaviors, i.e., by leveraging benefits through low-cost investments.) When the punishment-negative reinforcement combination is repeated over time, a given couple displays a highly predictable (patterned) style of interaction that usually terminates in withdrawal or some other form of noncompletion of the task at hand (e.g., discussions that never end constructively). The reliance on aversive control techniques characterizes distressed relationships. The issue is not that the partners must deal with conflict (defined as a demand for immediate behavior change) but the continued use of aversive control as behavior change techniques.

A second tenet of BMT holds that distressed relationships are characterized by a critically low rate of exchange of positive reinforcements, suggesting a form of behavioral economics; spouses in unsatisfactory relationships fail to exchange benefits at a sufficiently high rate. There have been numerous problems associated with this assertion: Persons remain in relationships that, to outsiders, appear to be all cost and no benefit; is the rate of exchange too low or do the partners lack in reinforcingness? Reward and reinforcement often have been used interchangeably without independent demonstration that Stimulus X or Y was indeed a reinforcing stimulus. Couples effectively present stimuli to one another; they are, after all, effective punishers. Defining the reward value for a particular relationship obviously requires a topographical analysis of the classes of such behaviors. As Jacobson (1979) noted, the reinforcement hypothesis is not specific with regard to etiology, that is, whether the low rates of positive exchange cause marital distress or whether distress leads to low rates.

In their 1973 paper, Weiss *et al.* distinguished between the stimulus control and the contingency control of interactional behavior. A considerable therapeutic effort was devoted to teaching couples discriminations about their daily behaviors, for example, specific-pinpointing training. Contracting procedures were utilized to bring the targeted problem behaviors under contingency control (p. 324). BMT differed from other approaches (e.g., Guerney, 1977) in that communication training (if utilized at all) was used only as an adjunct to the real work of therapy, notably teaching contingency management skills (i.e., negotiation and contracting skills) to spouses in distressed relationships. In their original formulation, Weiss *et al.* (1973) placed communication skills training *last* in a series of in-depth options if spouses had difficulty defining pleasing and displeasing daily behavioral events. In fact, the entire structure of this modular approach was based on the idea that impediments (skill deficits) to contingency management techniques were to be successively eliminated. However, Stuart's (1975) broadened version of his operant interpersonal model placed considerably more emphasis on communication skills training, yet still within the basic modular structure proposed earlier.

The OMSP Behavioral-Systems Model

The behavioral systems approach (Weiss, 1978, 1980) integrates performance-based BMT concepts with general systems-theory concepts. Systems theory approaches to family interactions stress the interdependencies of the members by considering the organizational structure of transactions. For at least one prominent group representing the systems perspective (Haley, 1963; Watzlawick *et al.*, 1974), intimate relationships are rule-governed systems that require a language for describing the various manifestations of rule development and maintenance. Systems and behavioral perspectives both focus on the patterning of transactions. *Stimulus control* is a form of rule-controlled behavior (Weiss, 1978), whereas *reinforcing control* describes behavioral sequences organized on a response-contingency basis. Gottman (1979) made the distinction between reciprocity based on short-term versus long-term exchanges; the former refer to tit-for-tat reciprocity (1) at the level of an immediate return of a behavior in kind or (2) at the level of reciprocation in the sense of a particular response's being more probable given a prior stimulus provided by the other person. *Longer-term reciprocity* refers to noncontingency between stimulus and response sequences; Gottman has labeled this the "bank account" model of exchange. Not every reward, for example, must be immediately reciprocated; the partners can draw down their individual accounts before it is necessary to make another deposit (or reward). From this type of analysis, it was hypothesized that distressed couples operate largely on the basis of response-contingent (or reinforcing-control) types of exchanges, whereas nondistressed couples function under the bank account model, which is organized around stimulus control (rule control). This distinction between short- and long-term reciprocity should be found to hold especially for exchanges of aversive stimuli. Thus, it was suggested (Weiss, 1978) that distressed and nondistressed couples would differ in their reliance on *quid pro quo* exchanges and that aversive exchanges are governed by response contingencies.

The behavioral systems model also emphasized the give–get balance in marriage, suggesting that attempts to establish parity when the give–get balance is upset are themselves behavior change operations; that is, the partners engage in behaviors that are designed to increase the benefits received by the person who feels slighted. Thus, it becomes important in this model to assess all the classes of behavior change techniques used by the couple, that is, how they attempt to bring about change or solve their problems.

The criteria of a well-functioning intimate relationship were first described (Weiss, 1978) in terms of four areas of accomplishment, labeled "objectification," "support/understanding," "problem solving," and "behavior change." These were taken as four generic classes of competence, requisite to a functioning relationship. In the model proposed by Weiss (1978), these areas of accomplishment were further specified by defining 12 categories of marital interaction, or content areas, such as companionship, sex, and consideration. The result was a 4 × 12 matrix of cells that could be used to assess relationship strengths and weaknesses. The four areas of accomplishment defined generic skills, whereas the content areas focused on specific skills, such as objectification about sex and parenting. (The reader is referred to Weiss, 1978, and Weiss & Birchler, 1978, for a detailed explanation of the model.)

We have used the OMSP model as a means of organizing our review of the literature relevant to BMT. Each of the four accomplishments provides a major heading. One of the assessment and intervention tactics of BMT is to train couples to make reliable discriminations (objectifications) in their behavioral environments, that is, learning to pinpoint or otherwise label the elements in their transactions. (Contrast this approach with the tendency of couples to "explain" one another's motives by traitlike concepts.) *Objectification serves the functions of stimulus control.* Similarly, a relationship must provide affective and companionable benefits to the partners. Exchanges in intimate relationships are value-based and are related to self-esteem; being understood by one's partner has far more impact than being understood by an acquaintance. *Intimacy is based on shared understanding, closeness, and support.* We expect differences in skills relating to support–understanding accomplishments, so this becomes a point of interest in the BMT literature.

Both problem solving and behavior change represent goal-oriented functions in relationships. *Problem solving refers to those skills necessary for allocating resources and accomplishing ends.* Bringing behavior under stimulus control so that decisions can be made requires the ability to differentiate what may be needed (whether supportive or problem-solving behaviors) and the appropriateness of preplanning (e.g., agenda sessions) prior to launching into a problem-solving (negotiating) session. *Behavior change, on the other hand, refers to explicit, usually structured procedures that can be taught to couples in order to change the nature of their exchanges by positive rather than aversive control tactics.* Each module is introduced sequentially: objectification training precedes problem solving, etc. By overcoming relationship complaints through the use of the earlier modules, more involved procedures can be reserved for more intractable problems. For example, a couple may benefit greatly from the increased communication effectiveness of objectification training and may see each other as more understanding and willing to improve the relationship than ever before. This view will make it much easier for them to approach and to work on other more difficult problems.

In the following section, we organize our review of the empirical literature around the OMSP model, especially its major areas of accomplishment.

Finally, for each of the four accomplishment headings we consider outcome studies germane to that accomplishment. Thus, for example, we attempt to answer the question: What has been shown about the possible outcome effectiveness of objectification training? In this way, we cover both the clinical research pertaining to the accomplishment (and its possible targets) and the outcome literature pertaining to each.

Current Empirical Status

Our review of the empirical literature considers three targets for each of the four areas of accomplishment, that is, behaviors, cognitions, and situations. The review is organized into 12 subsections. For example, under "Objectification," the literature pertaining to the objectification of benefits, cognitions, and situations is considered. This same pattern is followed for each of the other three major accomplishment headings (i.e., "Support–Understanding," "Problem Solving," and "Behavior Change"). (It would not be feasible nor is there sufficient literature to warrant an organization based on the 12 interaction categories noted above, e.g., sex, companionship, etc.)

Objectification

From a behavioral perspective, the subjective satisfaction of married partners is thought to be determined at least in part by specific relationship events capable of objective evaluation. BMT often begins with an assessment of the behavioral components of marital satisfaction. In practice, this has meant that spouses were given training to identify behaviors and situations that seem to be associated with the enhancement or diminution of daily marital satisfaction. More recently, the cognitive components of marital satisfaction have become targets of research and clinical interest (Margolin & Weiss, 1978). In current behavioral treatments of marital discord, three targets are identified: (1) behaviors, (2) cognitions, and (3) situations. The modification of each is expected to enhance the satisfaction of spouses. BMT assumes a relationship between satisfaction and these targets, making it necessary to demonstrate that specific occurrences of behaviors, situations, and cognitions in everyday life account for a large proportion of the variance in daily marital satisfaction (DMS). The empirical research findings pertaining to each of the three targets as they relate to DMS is reviewed here. Since couples are often trained to make discriminations in their behavioral environments, we also review attempts to teach couples objectification skills. Most often these are presented early in treatment, and they are the least costly of the treatment procedures. Gains from such interventions can be compared with the techniques associated with more costly and more complex treatment options in the other three modalities, that is, support–understanding, problem solving, and behavior change. We turn next to a consideration of each of the targets.

Targets

Behavior. The typical research format here is to establish the proportion of variance in subjective ratings of daily marital satisfaction (DMS) accounted for by the specific behaviors emitted by the spouses. Studies in this area have used the Spouse Observation Checklist (SOC), or some variant thereof, as a means of assessing daily rates of behaviors that the spouses identify as either pleasing or displeasing events, defined subjectively. Each of the 400 items, expressed in behaviorally objective terms ("Spouse warmed my cold feet"), is scrutinized by the partners and rated as a please or a displease for that day. (Much of the research has presented the items pre-grouped into please or displease categories; in other cases, the items can be responded to idiosyncratically, thus allowing a "typical" please to be rated as a displease.) In addition to counts of such events, the partners also record their marital satisfaction for that day, typically by means of a 7- or 9-point Likert scale. Self-reported rates of pleases and displeases are then used to predict the DMS.

In the first of six studies in this area, Wills *et al.* (1974) instructed seven nondistressed couples to track instrumental and affectional pleases and displeases for a period of 14 days. In addition, daily ratings of marital satisfaction were made, as were ratings of satisfaction with nonmaritally related (outside) events.

Rates of pleasing and displeasing relationship events accounted for 25% of the variance in daily marital satisfaction ratings. Displeasing events accounted for almost twice as much of the explained variance as did pleasing events. Events occurring outside the relationship were not found to be significantly related to daily marital satisfaction.

Using a similar procedure, Barnett and Nietzel (1979) had distressed and nondistressed couples track pleasing and displeasing relationship events over 14 days, together with daily ratings of marital satisfaction. Significant correlations were found between DMS and rates of instrumental pleases ($r = .31$, $p <$

.05), displeases ($r = -.41$, $p < .05$), and affectional DMS displeases ($r = -.42$, $p < .05$); affectional pleases were not related to DMS ($r = -.05$, ns). Unfortunately, these analyses combined marital distress statuses and obscure differences between distressed and nondistressed groups.

Robinson and Price (1980) used a shortened version of the SOC to determine the relationship between global ratings of marital happiness and either affectional or instrumental pleases (displeases). Significant ($p < .05$) correlations were found between marital happiness and affectional pleases ($r = .51$) and instrumental displeases ($r = -.59$); neither affectional displeases nor instrumental pleases were significantly related to marital satisfaction. Correlations were based on the total sample of both maritally satisfied and maritally dissatisfied couples.

In a cross-sectional study of marital longevity (Paige, 1978), 121 couples, distributed equally among three marital life stages, tracked pleasing and displeasing events on seven consecutive days. Local ads recruited "couples in satisfying relationships seeking marital enrichment" who had been married (1) less than 6 years; (2) from 10 to 15 years, or (3) for more than 20 years. Daily rates of pleasing and displeasing events accounted for a total of 50%, 40%, and 31% of DMS variance, respectively, in the three longevity groups. The magnitude of the DMS-to-daily-behavior correlations was a decreasing function of length of marriage; daily behaviors were less predictive of DMS for those married longest. Categories of behavior predicted satisfaction differently for the groups as well: affectional and sexual behaviors were most highly predictive of DMS in the younger groups, whereas companionship and communication items were most highly predictive of DMS in the older group. These are interesting *patterns* of change, although the design was not longitudinal; the groups did not differ in their average level of satisfaction, but only in which categories of behavioral events correlated with DMS.

Self-reported rates of pleasing and displeasing behaviors have accounted for a significant proportion of the variance in DMS ratings as shown by the four studies just mentioned. Roughly from 25% to 50% of DMS variance

can be explained by spouse ratings of behaviors emitted by the partner.

Jacobson (1978) has noted two methodological problems in the conception of these determinants-of-marital-satisfaction studies that rely on self-report data of this type. Since both measures (of spouse behavior and satisfaction ratings) are made by the same person, there is a built-in correlational bias: on relatively high satisfaction days, spouses may record high DMS ratings and be inclined to evaluate daily events as more pleasant (or, at least, less displeasing). The same would be expected on days of relatively low DMS, *mutatis mutandis*. Jacobson noted that DMS ratings are made typically *after* recording pleasing and displeasing events; the satisfaction rating, like a response set, may have been induced by the prior recording activity itself. After checking many pleasing items, one would be more likely to rate satisfaction higher than after checking fewer pleasing or many more displeasing items. From Wills *et al.* (1974), we would suspect that satisfaction ratings would be most influenced by displeasing events. In any event, the argument holds that rating specific behavior items can be reactive on the rating of satisfaction.

As a means of separating these methodological intricacies from the best estimate of the relationship between satisfaction ratings (DMS) and the occurrence of daily relationship-related events, Jacobson, Waldron, and Moore (1980) investigated the empirical relationship between DMS and the frequency (not the subjective evaluation) of behavioral events. Both distressed and nondistressed couples rated their DMS *prior* to recording daily behavior. The status of an event as pleasing or displeasing was defined by its empirically demonstrated relationship to DMS. (Stimuli provided by one's partner that, in fact, alter the rate of some behavior are closer to the meaning of reinforcing stimuli than are terms like *pleasing* or *reward*.) Jacobson, Waldron, and Moore (1980) defined positively correlated events as pleases and negatively correlated events as displeases. For two separate samples of couples, empirically defined pleases and displeases accounted for between 21% and 34% of the DMS variance. Thus, despite what may be an improved methodology, approximately the same amount of satisfaction variance was accounted for by occurrences of daily behavioral events.[1]

Jacobson, Waldron, and Moore (1980) did find differences between distressed and nondistressed marital groups in the topography of behaviors related to DMS. Unlike the Wills, Weiss, and Patterson (1974) finding, positive events best predicted DMS ratings for nondistressed couples, whereas negative events were the best predictors of DMS for distressed couples.

When marital distress groups are analyzed separately, as in Jacobson *et al.*'s study, and when empirically defined positive and negative events are differentially related to DMS, the tracking strategy used by couples may differ according to their distress status. For example, Williams (1979) examined the behavioral diaries of couples who tracked the quality (positive, neutral, or negative) of time segments spent throughout the day with the partner and not specific behavior events, as in the preceding studies. For her satisfied couples, pleasant interactions were associated with *commissions of positive* behaviors (e.g., "Spouse kissed me"), whereas for dissatisfied couples, pleasant interactions were associated with *omissions of negative* behaviors ("Spouse did not argue with me"). Unpleasant interactions were defined differentially by satisfied and dissatisfied groups as well: for satisfied spouses, unpleasant interactions were characterized by omissions of positive behaviors ("Spouse did not say good-bye"), while for dissatisfied spouses it was the commissions of negative behaviors ("Spouse yelled at me"). We have in effect a 2 × 2 table of marital satisfaction status and omission–commission alternatives. The presence or absence of a positive or negative event has different significances depending on the status of relationship satisfaction.

Although Jacobson *et al.* (1980) did not ask

their couples to record these different response alternatives (omission vs. commission) we are tempted to suggest, following Williams's lead, that perhaps satisfied (i.e., nondistressed) couples will report relatively high marital satisfaction on days characterized by a high rate of positives, and relatively low satisfaction on days characterized by lower rates of positives. Conversely, distressed couples are more likely to report relatively higher DMS on days characterized by a low rate of negatives and relatively low DMS on days characterized by higher rates of displeases. These are only conjectures, data about which would help our understanding of objectification *per se.*

From these six methodologically distinct studies we are able nonetheless to trace some of the threads between daily marital satisfaction and emitted behaviors:

1. Each of the studies has presented evidence to support an empirical association between DMS and behaviors. Whether the behaviors are recorded as subjectively weighted pleasing–displeasing events or simply as having occurred, they account for approximately 25%–50% of the variance of DMS.

2. The specific behavioral components (topography) differ for levels of marital distress, with stage of marital life cycle (relationship longevity), and perhaps with sample characteristics; in general, marital satisfaction appears to be most highly related to positive events in nondistressed relationships, and to negative events in distressed relationships.

3. It has not yet been shown that events outside the relationship *per se* account for DMS variance; perhaps, the frequency of these events is not as crucial as how a given couple handles these external events.

4. Although daily behaviors do account for DMS variance, much of that variance remains unexplained to date. Both the reliability of spouse reporting and the representativeness of the SOC items constitute two methodologically based sources of "error," and must be considered here.

The *reliability* of spouse monitoring has been studied along a number of dimensions, for example, degree of prior training in tracking procedures, explicitness of criteria, target behaviors, and mode of tracking (whether *in*

---

[1] It is not more reasonable to assume unidirectional causality in these kinds of studies: satisfaction ratings may color how one sees events, but events checked as pleasing or displeasing may "add up to" a total satisfaction rating. A study by Volkin (1979) addressed the issue of rating bias, and the results supported the conclusion that rating pleasing events apparently has little reactivity effect on the satisfaction rating *per se.*

vivo or from videotapes). Each dimension selects a different reliability question and, accordingly, shifts the focus of investigation.

Jacobson *et al.* (1980) examined interspouse reliability using nondistressed and distressed couples who tracked *in vivo* shared daily activities (essentially, shared recreational and companionship items from the SOC). Interspouse agreement (*r*'s) was reported to be .75 (range: .68–.82) and .73 (range: .65–.82) for nondistressed and distressed couples, respectively. Christensen and King (1979), using a telephone survey of couples, reported significant correlations between husbands' and wives' recollections of events (during the past 24 hours) for arguments, social engagements, sexual intercourse, and total time spent together. In a different survey, Christensen and Nies (1980) asked spouses to record any of 179 SOC items that they remembered having occurred during the past 24-hour period. The overall agreement between spouses was 84% when agreements on both occurrences and nonoccurrences were scored (chance = 65%); when agreements were computed for occurrences only, the percentage dropped to 48% (range: 11%–66% for individual couples) (chance = 13%). Clearly, husband–wife agreements greatly exceeded chance expectations, but the obtained percentage-of-agreement figures nevertheless were lower than those typically required of observers.

Several studies have examined the reliability of spouses and trained outside observers (coders) in either laboratory or home settings. Birchler (1979) asked spouses to rate their own 5-min videotaped interactions on each of four MICS summary codes (problem solving, verbal positive, nonverbal positive, and verbal negative) and then compared these ratings with the frequencies reported by trained coders on the same taped interactions. Not only did husbands and wives show within-couple agreement, but 12 of 32 possible correlations for husbands and wives and trained coders ranged from .34 to .66 (all significant at less than a .05 level).

Robinson and Price (1980) compared agreements between spouses and trained observers for the frequency of positive behaviors emitted and received during interactions observed *in vivo*. Whereas spouses and trained observers agreed on the ratings of overall positiveness (*r*s ranged from .39 to .59), there was unsatisfactory agreement on the set of nine individual behaviors tracked (percentage of agreement ranged from .23 to .29).

Margolin (1976) examined the correlations between spouses' and trained observers' ratings of "communication positiveness" in a sample of distressed couples. In contrast to the procedures of Birchler (1979) and of Robinson and Price (1980), the spouses were not instructed about what constituted "communication positiveness"; of six possible correlations (*r*s ranged from .24 to .42), only one reached significance: husbands and trained observers agreed on their ratings of the wives' positiveness (*r* = .42, *p* < .05).

A number of conclusions about reliability can be drawn from these studies:

1. Agreements (interspouse and spouse-to-trained-observer) are highest when the spouses are trained in tracking procedures and/or are given explicit criteria to use in making their judgments. Studies by Jacobson *et al.* (1980), Robinson and Price (1980), and Birchler (1979) all meet these criteria and, despite diverse methodology, have reported the most encouraging findings supportive of reliability.

2. The reliability of spouse-monitored *in vivo* behavior appears to decrease as the monitoring criteria become more specific. The overall rates of positive or negative behavior can be estimated by husbands and wives somewhat accurately, but their estimates of more precisely defined behavioral events are considerably less reliable. These findings are consistent with those reported by Nelson (1977) on the reliability of *in vivo* behavioral monitoring. For example, it would appear that spouses could accurately estimate overall levels of negative behavior but not criticisms *per se*. (It is also possible, yet untested, that spouses react to certain behaviors and screen out subsequent inconsistent behaviors.)

3. When estimating the interspouse reliability of SOC tracking, it is necessary to base the computations on shared activities, as was done by Jacobson *et al.* (1980).

The *representativeness* of SOC items themselves is a second possible methodological weakness that could account for the unexplained variance in DMS ratings: perhaps the

400 SOC items do not adequately represent the universe of events occurring in daily relationship exchanges. Christensen and Nies (1980) addressed this issue directly. They obtained the endorsement frequency of each of 179 randomly selected SOC items used in their study. They found that most SOC items were endorsed by not more than 20% of their sample of 50 couples; they recommended that only the more frequently occurring items be included.

The findings of the Christensen and Nies study must be viewed cautiously: measures of endorsement frequency provide an index of item representativeness only in a nomothetic sense. Since only 44% of the original SOC items were included in their study, there is reason to question further how representative these items were for any given couple during their 24-hour reporting period. There can be little surprise that so many items were not endorsed by large numbers of couples; for example, "We watched a sunset" may be limited first by the environment and then by the particular couple's 24-hour period. It is questionable to assume (on an idiographic basis) that commonly occurring events (across couples) are the most important determinants of DMS. In most cases, we might argue, it is the infrequent event that more adequately accounts for satisfaction on a given day. Our aim is to create a checklist of events likely to have an impact on the subjective satisfaction of spouses. The nomothetic model employed by Christensen and Nies has not, in our view, adequately provided an assessment of the representativeness of the SOC items. At the very least, we would suggest examining within-couples representativeness, an examination that would, of course, necessitate samples from the same couples over 24-hour periods.

On balance, we view the case for the reliability of reporting as having been better documented than the case for the representativeness of the items. To date, the only experimental manipulation of daily behavioral events was reported by Wills *et al.* (1974), in an attempt to determine whether spouses were reporting events accurately. It will be recalled that these investigators instructed the husbands to double their affectional pleases for two days and then determined the corresponding increase in the wives' reported affectional pleases re-

ceived. This type of method remains to be used in broader-based studies, but it certainly suggests one approach to the reliability issue.

Next, we consider cognitions as targets of objectification and examine the relationships between cognitions and rate satisfaction.

Cognition. Initial attempts to investigate the relationship between marital satisfaction and cognitions were limited to case study observations. Patterson and Hops (1972) reported a case in which a husband and wife tracked "pleasant thoughts" about the spouse and found an inverse relationship between such thoughts and coded rates of aversive behavior in the home. Weiss and Margolin (1977) reported on a case in which there was a positive relationship between pleasant thoughts and the frequency of affectional events. Neither of these cases involving tracking addressed the issue of causality: Do cognitions lead to behavior changes, or vice versa?

Also in a correlational study, Weiss and Isaac (1976) sought the relative ability of either cognitive or behavioral "ratings" to account for marital satisfaction ratings. Parallel forms containing 84 SOC items, representing 12 cognitively defined relationship categories (e.g., affection, communication process, and consideration), were rated by 46 couples. Each couple rated both the cognitive categories as well as the individual behavioral items (presented in random order) for pleasantness during the past 24 hours. In addition, the couples made a global Likert scale rating of relationship satisfaction during that same 24-hour period. The behavioral items were then regrouped into their appropriate category (e.g., affection items and consideration items), so that for each of the 12 relationship categories, a derived behavioral rating score was obtained that corresponded to the cognitive label rating score. Predictions of marital satisfaction then could be made from either the behavior-category or the cognitive-category ratings. For this sample, 40% of DMS variance was accounted for by category label ratings, whereas 98% was accounted for by the behavioral ratings. Behavioral events better represented the partners' ratings of DMS than did the category ratings, which reflected cognitions (not events) during the past 24-hour period.

Epstein, Finnegan, and Bythell (1979) ex-

amined the relationship between irrational beliefs and perceptions of marital interactions
using college students who scored high or low
on Jones's (1968) Irrational Beliefs Test (IBT).
High-scoring subjects on the IBT reported observing significantly more conflict and disagreement between spouses shown in a videotaped role-play of an interview. The high-
scoring subjects seemed to have a much lower
threshold for what constituted "marital conflict" than those endorsing less extreme positions.

By far the best analysis of the causal relationship between cognitions and emitted pleasing–displeasing behaviors has been reported
by Vincent, Cook, and Messerly (1980). As
part of a larger ongoing project of prenatal
predictors of relationship strengths, these investigators reported on a sample of first-time
parent couples in their second postnatal month.
Using cross-panel techniques they found an
empirical relationship between increases in
the wives' DMS and subsequent increases in
reported pleases and decreases in reported
displeases. It appears that as marital satisfaction increased, behavioral events were perceived as more positive and less negative.
Thus, the perception of relationship events is
mediated by rated daily relationship satisfaction. Robinson and Price (1980) made a similar
observation for their distressed and nondistressed couples; the distressed couples did not
agree with the trained coders on what was perceived as pleasing. The use of cross-panel
techniques by Vincent *et al.* is an important
first step in pinning down the role of cognitive
set on the tracking of pleases and displeases.

The number of studies is limited, but a few
generalizations are possible at this time:

1. The cognitions that spouses hold of one
another are related to both the frequency and
the subjective evaluation of relationship events.
Favorable cognitions are associated with increased rates of pleasing and decreased rates
of displeasing behaviors.

2. Changes in the perception of behavioral
events (i.e., how these will be rated) are mediated by prior ratings of DMS. As satisfaction
decreases, events are perceived as less pleasing and more displeasing; satisfaction levels
set the parity of event value.

3. Behavioral events account for a greater
proportion of DMS than do ratings of popular
cognitive categories of interaction.

A more direct test of the links between cognitions and reported marital satisfaction requires our examining the effects of increased
or decreased marital satisfaction on the emitted rates of objectively defined pleases or displeases. By *objectively defined,* we mean
events that have been shown to be related to
DMS *and* whose topography can be identified
by outside coders. The question remains
whether some behavior has occurred (outside
rating) and, if it did, whether it also is rated
as positive. A cognitive filter could operate on
either or both levels: screening out an occurrence and/or devaluing an occurrence.

Situations. Given the emphasis in behavioral theory on the importance of situations in
the control of behavior, there have been surprisingly few attempts to investigate systematically the effects of situations on marital satisfaction. There is, of course, the classic case
study by Goldiamond (1965), which attempted
to bring the behavior of a spouse under stimulus control; as a means of dealing with obsessive thoughts of jealousy, the husband restricted his jealous thoughts to a time of day
in a specific location.

The literature on satisfaction at different
stages of the marital life cycle is germane,
since it is assumed that there are considerable
situational demands peculiar to each stage that
run independently of couple abilities. Thus,
studies have typically reported a decrease or
at least a leveling off in marital satisfaction
following the birth of the first child, followed
by a subsequent increase in marital satisfaction (e.g., Miller, 1976). These studies do not
isolate concurrent behavioral changes during
these periods.

Vincent, Friedman, Nugent, and Messerly
(1979) have provided some information about
behavioral changes that coincide with postnatal decreases in marital satisfaction. The
focus here was on changes in interactional
rather than trait (global satisfaction) terms.
These authors used the SOC and a newly developed 115-item Parent-Infant Observation
Checklist (PIOC), geared toward specific parenting behaviors (e.g., "Spouse played with

infant''), to examine behavioral exchanges between husbands and wives at 30 and 60 days following the birth of the first child; the spouses reported on behaviors that occurred during the previous 24-hour period.

Among the findings of interest to our consideration of situational factors in satisfaction were the following: (1) marital satisfaction for both husbands and wives tended to be lower at 60 days postnatally; (2) at 60 days, there was also evidence of increased reciprocity of both positive and negative SOC and positive PIOC behaviors, and decreased reciprocity of negative PIOC behaviors; and (3) at 60 days, SOC and PIOC behaviors accounted for a greater amount of satisfaction variance. Although the results were based on a limited sampling of behavior, the findings suggest that decreases in postnatal marital satisfaction are associated with changes in the behavioral exchanges of spouses, particularly with increased reciprocity and saliency of behavioral events. In effect, the situational demands of having a newborn baby increase the impact of the couple's specific skills and coping behaviors as determinants of marital satisfaction relative to global sentiment toward the spouse (cf. Weiss, 1978). The study is one of the first to provide empirical evidence that the predictive components of marital satisfaction change as a result of the situational demands of this marital life stage.

A laboratory approach to the role of situational factors in marital satisfaction is provided by Wieder and Weiss (1980). They examined the cross-situational specifity of couples' problem-solving behavior when both topics and occasions were varied. Fourteen distressed couples were videotaped in their attempt to resolve two different relationship problems on two occasions. An analysis-of-variance model was used to isolate proportions of variance in MICS coded behavior accounted for by couples and the interaction of the couples by situations (topics and occasions). Rates of positive behaviors appeared to be more situationally specific than negative behaviors; the latter remained consistent across situations. The finding of greater situational consistency of negative behaviors (as coded from couple interactions) is consistent with the

results reported by others (e.g., Birchler, 1979) and suggests that distressed couples have difficulty breaking their negative cycles despite differences in situations (e.g., topic and occasion). Positive behaviors do not reflect this traitlike consistency.

There is a lack of information on the possible influence of situations on behavior and marital satisfaction. A few studies have reported analyses of marital interactions where situations can be identified as a meaningful variable. These are the first steps in systematically identifying the role of situational factors; there is a critical need for assessing the topography of important relationship situations related to marital satisfaction. For example, Margolin (1979) has made a first attempt to develop an assessment instrument for identifying the situational variables (time of day, setting, etc.) associated with stressful transactions involving anger and anger control. This approach is consistent with our hope that others will isolate instances of stimulus control.

Summary. We have reviewed studies that help to identify the empirical association between subjective ratings of marital satisfaction and specific behaviors, cognitions, and situations, that is, the three targets of current BMT interventions. Research on the behavioral components of satisfaction has shown that daily behavioral events account for 25%–50% of the variance in DMS. We have suggested that the remaining proportions of variance might be attributed to methodological "error" (the reliability and representativeness of the measures) or the overriding cognitive sets of the spouses (e.g., attributions and selective attention) that decrease the subjective impact of behavior. Most likely, both explanations will prove to be correct. For example, it has been shown that generalized satisfaction with the relationship, as well as beliefs about marital conflict, affects the way in which behaviors are perceived. Literature on the marital life cycle has also demonstrated an empirical association between the birth of the first child and changes in marital satisfaction, reciprocity, and the impact of behavioral events. Of greatest interest to us, but least represented in the marital literature, are studies that identify (1) the causal relationship between behavior and cognition and (2) the relative importance of behavioral, attributional (cognitive interpretations of behavior), and purely cognitive (expectancies, sentiment) variables in the prediction of daily marital satisfaction.

Outcome. Several techniques have been used to help spouses objectify the relationship events presumed to be related to marital satisfaction. Three distinct procedures have been used to train couples in objectifying relationship events, although none are represented as being therapeutic *per se*: (1) the monitoring of daily behavior exchanges; (2) the use of videotape feedback; and (3) specific training in precise denotative statements, for example, pinpointing skills.

Monitoring daily behaviors generally has proved to be ineffective as a means of altering either marital satisfaction or the behaviors of distressed spouses. Jacobson (1979) reported results for six severely distressed couples who tracked SOC daily behaviors over two weeks of baseline and found no increase in SOC pleases, no decreases in SOC displeases, and no changes in daily satisfaction as a result of tracking. Volkin (1979), mentioned above, found no systematic effect of tracking on reported pleasing events or satisfaction ratings. After two weeks of tracking positive behaviors, Robinson and Price's (1980) nondistressed spouses reported some increase in marital satisfaction; none was reported by the distressed spouses. Neither group reported increases in the frequency of daily pleasing events (on a variant of the SOC).

The efficacy of videotape feedback, as a means of training couples to objectify helpful and unhelpful communication behaviors has been investigated with videotapes of couples and actors modeling successful and unsuccessful interactions. Birchler (1979) presented distressed and nondistressed couples with videotaped role-play examples of good and bad interactions and then assessed changes in the couples' ability to perceive positive and negative behaviors in their own videotaped interactions. Neither group increased their perceptual accuracy after being presented with videotaped models. The training lacked specific therapist feedback and coaching, components that when combined with videotape viewing may increase the efficacy of this kind

of treatment. Mayadas and Duehn (1977) compared the efficacy of two types of videotape feedback with verbal counseling alone (VC); couples were presented with videotapes modeling 19 desirable and undesirable interactions presented alone (VT) or with therapist instructions, feedback, and behavioral rehearsal (VF). All treatments ran for eight sessions. Audiotaped coding at pre- and postintervention of countercomplaining, vagueness, failure to acknowledge, dogmatic assertion, and history statements revealed significant changes in the VF group on all five behaviors, on three of five behaviors in the VT group, and on one of five behaviors in the VC group. However, since measures of marital satisfaction were not included and the behavioral measures have no demonstrated validity, the findings must be interpreted cautiously.

Several different strategies have been employed to modify directly the specificity and assertiveness of couples' denotative statements about their relationship. Carter and Thomas (1973) used their intervention device (SAM) to help spouses signal desired floor switches and give each other feedback on the specificity of their communication. Following treatment, increases were observed in both parity of talk time and communication specificity.

Flowers (1978) used a simulation game to help spouses objectify positive and negative problem-solving behaviors. After eight sessions with the game, significant improvements were reported in six targeted verbal behaviors (interruptions, threats, off-subject remarks, lengthy statements, difference in amount of time talked, and unusual rapidity). Despite pre-to-post reductions in verbal behaviors, spouses reported no differences in their perceptions of conflict outcome, a finding that undermines the validity of the dependent measures.

Finally, Epstein and his associates (Epstein, DeGiovanni, & Jayne-Lazarus, 1978; Epstein & Jackson, 1978) have examined the efficacy of assertion training for couples' groups, designed to increase the specificity of denotative relationship statements. In their first study (Epstein & Jackson, 1978), assertion training was compared with an insight interaction group and a no-treatment control. Eleven verbal behaviors were coded from audiotapes at pre- and posttreatment (e.g., assertive requests, attacks, support, and giving opinion). At posttreatment, the assertion group emitted significantly more assertive requests than either the insight or the control group, as well as significantly fewer attacks than the control group (the insight group fell between the other two groups). The two treatment groups decreased their rates of disagreements relative to the controls but did not differ from one another.

In a second study (Epstein *et al.*, 1978), a single, two-hour couples' assertiveness workshop was compared with a treatment that omitted the specific assertiveness treatment components. The assertiveness group, relative to the controls, significantly increased in rates of verbal assertion and significantly decreased in rates of verbal aggression. In addition, the assertion group, relative to the controls, showed greater increases in self-reported clarity of self and spouse talk and in positive interaction-by-self.

In both of Epstein's studies, assertiveness training proved effective in altering emitted rates of behavior thought to have implications for the marital happiness of couples. However, as yet, these behaviors have not been empirically related to marital satisfaction or effective problem-solving. Evidence would need to be provided that changes in assertive behavior significantly increase marital satisfaction before this treatment can be deemed efficacious as an intervention for marital problems.

To summarize this portion of the outcome literature, there is no conclusive evidence that either behavioral tracking, videotape feedback, or *in vivo* modifications of denotative relationship statements produce significant changes in either marital satisfaction or the verbal behaviors that are thought to have implications for the happiness of distressed couples. Studies reporting significant improvements on behavioral measures have suffered from their exclusive reliance on unvalidated instruments and analogue populations. At best, objectification skill training may be a necessary but not a sufficient component of marital treatment. Naturally, videotape feedback and assertion training are of considerable interest and can be incorporated credibly into

actual marital therapy: perhaps these have the greatest potential. Assertiveness-training applications to relationship problems are of particular significance (cf. Epstein, 1980), but investigation of the efficacy of these techniques has lacked sophisticated methodology and has failed to assess changes in clinically significant targeted behaviors. Furthermore, investigators have a responsibility to assess the credibility of their interventions, since this will necessarily have an impact on the efficacy of treatment.

Support–Understanding

In order to accomplish goals related to support–understanding, skills are needed for providing affection, companionship, and comforting—generally, expressions of affectional closeness that define the experience of intimacy. Two categories of skill are required: verbal and nonverbal communication skills (attending, reflecting, listening, and speaking skills) and skills for engineering situations themselves (being able to plan quality time). The effectiveness of "objectively" defined supportive skill behaviors—the marital enrichment literature contains many useful examples of skills taught to couples (e.g., Gurman & Kniskern, 1977)—depends in large measure on the spouses' ability to perceive these behaviors as subjectively supportive. Thus, it may not be sufficient merely to provide objectively defined supportive–understanding skills. In some instances, attributions are made to the "wrong" sources: a spouse's intention may be implicated, or the action is seen as being dictated by the therapist, or an otherwise pleasant behavior is attributed to chance. Spouses are less likely to make correct attributions to *situations*: attempts to accomplish supportive–understanding aims may be at odds with the setting itself and not attributable to the traits of the other. Clearly then, the subjective evaluation of such behaviors is critical to outcome, although this injunction to consider subjectivity is a behavioral anathema. In this section, we review the research germane to both the objective (behavioral and situational) and the subjective (cognitive) skill components necessary to the accomplishment of support–understanding. Outcomes of treatments intended as means of enhancing support–understanding are also critically evaluated.

Targets

Behavior. We have seen that the exchange of daily behaviors in part determines DMS; we now consider the role of supportive behaviors as predictors of DMS. By the nature of adult intimacy, it should not be surprising to find that, overall, the "appetitive" behaviors as a group (Weiss, 1978)—affection, consideration, companionship, and sex—show a substantial relationship to DMS. We consider first the correlational evidence.

In a cross-sectional analysis of DMS at various stages of the marital life cycle, Paige (1978) found classes of appetitive behaviors (affection, consideration, etc.) to be among the best predictors of DMS for basically nondistressed couples. (Correlations between appetitive category scores from the Spouse Observation Checklist and DMS ranged from .40 to .66, and all were highly significant.) Jacobson *et al.* (1980) found affectional and companionship SOC items to be among the three best predictors of DMS ratings for both distressed and nondistressed couples. In three studies where SOC affectional events were included along with a measure of DMS, either 26%, 39%, or 98% of DMS variance was accounted for by affectional item scores (i.e., Robinson & Price, 1980; Wills *et al.,* 1974; and Weiss & Isaac, 1976, respectively). Wills *et al.* (1974) reported a quasi-experimental manipulation of affectional events by surreptitiously instructing husbands to double their rate of providing wives daily affectional behaviors. Although the wives reported a significant increase in affectional behaviors received (+78%), it is interesting to note that they also reported receiving significantly more instrumental behaviors compared with premanipulation rates. In both instances, only the pleasurable (and not the displeasurable) behavioral events increased. Thus, while the husbands could discriminate pleasurable from displeasurable behaviors given, they did less well discriminating between affectional and instrumental events. The report did not include separate mention

of the DMS rating and the rate of affectional events on the experimental days.

The interactions between spouses from distressed and nondistressed relationships provide an opportunity to describe supportive skills capability based on an analysis of the topography of such communications. The majority of these studies (which involve baserate analyses of group differences) have found significant differences between marital satisfaction groups on rates of both aversive and supportive behaviors; as expected, distressed marriages show greater exchanges of aversively coded behaviors in interactions and, similarly, fewer exchanges of positively coded behaviors (Birchler, 1977, 1979; Vincent *et al.,* 1979). Earlier, Birchler, Weiss, and Vincent (1975) reported the same differential results for distressed and nondistressed samples during a problem-solving (but not a casual-conversation) sample of interaction: the issue of whether couples are dealing with high- or low-conflict material is also germane here.

The hypothesis that distressed couples may be deficient in supportive skills was not upheld in three other studies. Klier and Rothberg (1977) discriminated satisfied and dissatisfied couples in terms of aversive, but not supportive, behavioral exchanges. Robinson and Price (1980) found no differences between distressed and nondistressed couples in rates of positive MICS coded behaviors observed in home interactions. Haynes, Follingstad, and Sullivan (1979) coded the home interactions of distressed and nondistressed couples and consistently differentiated the groups on the basis of negative (aversive) codes; however, distressed couples also emitted significantly higher rates of some positive behaviors (eye contact, agreement) but not others (positive physical contact).

Interaction studies of couples' communication have become methodologically more sophisticated by the incorporation of finer distinctions between and among important behaviors and by the use of sequential probability analyses (serial dependencies such as in Markov chains). The work of Gottman and his associates (Gottman, 1979; Gottman, Markman, & Notarius, 1977) and Margolin and Wampold (1980) are particularly noteworthy examples of this advancement. Gottman separated the content (verbal) and the affect (nonverbal) components of supportive communication by means of his Couple Interaction Coding System (CISS), which is similar to the MICS but provides greater in-depth coding of affective behaviors. In terms of the content codes, distressed couples, relative to nondistressed couples, disagreed more than they agreed and were more likely to summarize self than partner (i.e., restated their own position rather than paraphrasing, etc.). In terms of the affect codes, distressed, relative to nondistressed, couples were more likely to communicate *both* positive- and negative-statement content with negative nonverbal affect. The latter was the most accurate predictor of marital distress, better, in fact, than the traditional agreement–disagreement ratio (Riskin & Faunce, 1972).

The analysis of stimulus–response chains in ongoing interactional samples provides a more complex analysis of the functional effects of "supportive" behaviors. The question asked here is whether the likelihood of a particular supportive or aversive response changes if one knows the quality of the preceding one, two, three . . . , *n*, responses. Whenever knowledge of some preceding response improves the prediction of a subsequent response beyond the expectation provided by base rates, important serial dependencies exist in the interactional sample. Typically, these approaches are useful in answering questions about reciprocity in marital exchanges, and Gottman has been influential in drawing attention to these kinds of data.

Margolin and Wampold (1980) have carried the search for topographical differences in the interactions of distressed and nondistressed couples one step further by attempting to differentiate these groups in terms of a sequential analysis of supportive and aversive coded behaviors. Both groups showed evidence of reciprocity of positive behaviors that extended into the first two of the three consecutive sequence lags analyzed; being nice begets a nice response in turn. Negative reciprocity characterizes distressed couples (being not nice begets a not-nice response in turn!), and being not-nice produces a short-term (lag 1) negative reactivity effect: an aversive response within a distressed couple's interaction reduces the

probability of a subsequent positive response below the level expected from base rates alone. Margolin and Wampold's results led them to conclude that distressed couples do not recover as quickly as nondistressed couples from the effects of discrete negative behaviors in the course of an interaction. Therapy should focus on the nature of the sequences of positive and negative behaviors, not simply the totals; reducing total negatives in therapy is not the same as dealing with the sequential control that negatives have over succeeding responses.

The studies of couples' interactions favor the conclusion that distressed couples display more aversive behaviors, but not necessarily less positive behaviors. Sequential analysis of stimulus–response chains (coded from interactions) establishes the functional effectiveness of aversive behaviors in distressed couples.

In the foregoing discussion, support behaviors were defined *a priori* according to the professional judgments of trained others. As noted before, the "impact" of a behavioral event requires the assessment of a spouse's perceptions. Although no empirical comparison has yet directly compared observations by trained coder(s) and spouse(s), two studies have differentiated distress status on the basis of cues used by nontrained judges as they observed sample interactions of couples. (In this sense, these studies provide a first step in establishing the external validity of the widely used "supportive" behavior codes.) Distressed and nondistressed couples' interactions can be discriminated by untrained judges, and the results indicate that the discrimination is made on the basis of aversive (negative) and not supportive (positive) behaviors. Royce and Weiss (1975) found that untrained judges' ratings of marital satisfaction (from observation of videotaped interactions) were significantly related to the number of objectively coded aversive behaviors ($r = -.41, p < .01$). Resick, Barr, Sweet, Kieffer, Ruby, and Spiegel (1981) found that aversive cues generated by judges (criticism, sarcasm, disagreement, and speech volume) successfully discriminated ($p < .001$) marital conflict and accord. Thus, untrained observers replicated the findings of trained coders to the extent of implicating aversive behaviors in discriminating distress status.

The unreliability of "supportive" behaviors in discriminating between distress statuses may be attributed to the fact that the topography of supportive behaviors is less important than the idosyncratic meanings attached to common behavioral acts. Noninferential coding systems cannot speak to this issue. It is also possible that we have not yet adequately sampled the universe of supportive behaviors, focusing as we have on problem-solving types of interactions. The interface between objectively defined and spouse-defined examples of supportive behaviors requires further work.

Cognition. When we consider the role of cognitions in supportive–understanding behaviors, the question arises whether there is a skill deficit or whether attitudinal factors override the effects of the sheer frequency of behavioral events. Partners may fail to identify instances of supportive behaviors because (1) the rates of such behaviors are too low; (2) the behaviors occur with nontrivial frequency but are not discriminated; or (3) the behaviors are discriminated but are judged to have little positive impact. Options (1) and (2) are commonly seen as skill deficits and can be treated as such. But option (3) provides a greater challenge, since it really describes two different states. Early in a relationship, there may be a positive sentiment override (Weiss, 1980), so that the partner is judged to be noncontingently positive; what he or she does is of lesser importance than the fact of his or her presence! In distressed relationships, the sentiment override may operate in a noncontingently negative manner; regardless of the "good" one does, it still reads negatively! In both cases, there is a separation between behavioral events and the subsequent judgment of the valence of the other person.

Gottman and his associates (Gottman, 1979; Gottman, Notarius, Markman, Bank, & Yoppi, 1976) have argued that a communication deficit can be said to exist only when there is perceptual incongruence, that is, when behaviors are intended by the sender in a way perceived to be different by the receiver. Thus, it is the incongruency between the sender's intent and the receiver's impact that defines a true communication (skill) deficit; a mes-

sage, for example, that was intended to be negative and was received as negative (had a negative impact) is *not* a communication fault.

In their attempts to gain precise control over these aspects of communication exchange, Gottman's group devised the "talk table," which made it possible for speaker and listener to rate the intent and the impact of single-sentence messages on a 5-point Likert scale (ranging from "Super Positive" to "Super Negative"). Not surprisingly, both the distressed and the nondistressed couples *intended* their messages to be positive (there were no group differences on this measure), although the distressed couples rated the *impact* of the messages they received as significantly less positive than their nondistressed counterparts.

In the absence of a detailed objective coding of the interaction, it is not possible to decide whether the perceptual deficit existed in the speaker, in the listener, or in both. A comparison of the rates of positive behaviors observed by spouses with those observed by trained coders was made in the Robinson and Price (1980) study. The spouses and the coders were trained to monitor six positive behaviors (agreement, positive physical contact, concern, humor, approval, smile–laugh) during a one-hour home interaction. Although distressed and nondistressed pairs did not differ in their actual rates of emitted and received positive behaviors, they differed in their perceptions of positive behavior rates: the distressed pairs underestimated the coded rates of emitted and received positive behaviors by 50%. The nondistressed pairs agreed more closely with the rates reported by the trained coders. Unfortunately, we still lack all the pieces to the puzzle posed by Gottman; neither the Gottman nor the Robinson–Price studies combined all the necessary comparisons in the same study so that we cannot settle the question of the nature of the deficit.

Studies by Birchler (1979) and Margolin (1976) suggest that spouse perceptions of supportiveness (and aversiveness) are not correlated significantly with objectively coded positive and negative behavioral rates, lending further support to the hypothesis that supportiveness is idiosyncratically defined and relatively independent of actual public behaviors. Retrospective ratings of interaction positiveness were not correlated significantly with frequencies of MICS positive or negative codes when the behavioral criteria for the ratings either were made explicit (i.e., by giving the couples global MICS category labels to rate; Birchler, 1979) or were left to each spouse to decide (Margolin, 1976).

The long-range utility of the impact ratings has been demonstrated in a longitudinal study of couples reported by Markman (1979). Couples' relationship satisfaction some 2½ years subsequent to initial assessment was predicted from their earlier behavioral impact ratings ($r = .67, p < .01$). Individuals who were relatively pleased with their partner's communication during the initial sessions reported higher relationship satisfaction (relative to displeased partners) 2½ years later.

The cognitive appraisal of spouse-related behaviors may be contained in what behavioral therapists refer to as *reinforcingness*; however, there have been few clear attempts to independently assess the reinforcing status of couple-related behaviors. The issue is whether positive sentiment is incremental with each occurrence of an objectively defined positive behavior (provided by the spouse), or whether there exists a cognitive filter that effectively sets the values for objective behaviors. We address this issue more fully in the final section of the chapter; our objective here is still to review the literature on each of the components of the larger model.

Situations. The situations that comprise day-to-day living provide a third potential source of relationship support and understanding. To what extent can environments be altered to produce increased supportive benefits?

Shared recreational activities provide one source of situationally based closeness. It has been shown that compared with unhappy couples, happy couples engage in more frequent shared activities. Birchler *et al.* (1975) used the Inventory of Rewarding Activities (IRA) and showed that nondistressed couples reported engaging in shared activities with the spouse and others for the previous 30 days to a significantly greater degree than did distressed couples. (The same findings have been replicated by Birchler and Webb, 1977; Birchler, 1979; and Barnett and Nietzel, 1979.)

The between-group comparisons of shared activities do not answer whether the sharing of rewarding activities increases daily marital satisfaction. Once again, distress status is important: Jacobson *et al.* (1980) found that the frequency of SOC-defined shared activities was positively correlated with DMS in happy ($r = .36, p < .05$) but not in unhappy ($r = .05$, ns) relationships. The effectiveness of what you do as a means of incrementing DMS depends on whom you are with! Williams (1979) showed that quality of time together was a function of distress status *and* whether children were present. Happy couples without children reported greater proportions of positive time together (70%) than did happy couples with children (65%), whereas distressed couples without children reported *lower* proportions of positive time together (66%) than distressed couples with children (73%). These results are merely suggestive of future hypotheses and certainly do not establish cause–effect relationships. (There is, of course, a sociological literature that suggests that reported marital satisfaction decreases during the child-rearing years, e.g., Miller, 1976.)

By changing the situational demands of laboratory tasks, it may be possible to manipulate experimentally the supportive behaviors in couple interactions. Vincent *et al.* (1979) sampled couple interactions on IMC tasks under instructions to act typical (baseline) and to act as the happiest (fake good) and unhappiest (fake bad) couple imaginable. Under faking conditions, both distressed and nondistressed couples significantly altered their verbal supportive behavior relative to baseline; under instructions to "fake good," the rates of supportive behavior increased, and the rates of aversive behavior decreased; under instructions to "fake bad," the rates of supportive behavior decreased, and the rates of aversive behavior increased. But across all the instructional conditions, the nondistressed couples were significantly more supportive, and significantly less aversive, than the distressed couples. Although both groups altered their supportive and aversive behavior under different conditions of situational demand, the nondistressed couples still appeared to be more skilled in expressing support for their spouses. Using somewhat different experimental procedures, Cohen and Christensen (1980) failed to replicate these findings. No differences were found in the verbal behaviors of distressed and nondistressed couples across the baseline and the modified-instruction conditions. In contrast to the Vincent *et al.* (1979) study, these couples discussed *real* relationship problems and were instructed to demonstrate good and bad interactions typical of *their* relationship (as opposed to mimicking happy and unhappy couples). Either of these procedural differences may have accounted for the discrepant findings.

The situational context of marital interactions influences the quality of dyadic exchanges: couples can increase or decrease their rate of support during simulated conflict tasks as a result of instructions, suggesting that relationship support may be controlled partially by situational variables. Children may affect the quality of marital relationships, particularly that of time together. Shared activities increase the daily satisfaction of satisfied, but not dissatisfied, couples. Cognitions about one's ability to cope with situations certainly figure in the total picture of situational control of behavior; that is, here again, cognitive appraisals may be a necessary factor for our assessment.

Summary. Integrating research findings on the behavioral, cognitive, and situational components of relationship support–understanding is difficult in the absence of studies designed to investigate the interfaces among these three variables. Certainly, the majority of empirical research has focused on behavioral supportive skills, but thus far, maritally distressed and nondistressed couples have been differentiated on the basis of aversive, not supportive, behaviors. The evidence supports only one side of the behavioral skills deficit model. Studies of the cognitive components of support have found that distressed spouses typically do not "see" the positive behaviors that are emitted (Robinson & Price, 1980) or the behaviors that are intended to be positive (Gottman, Notarius, Markman, Bank, & Yoppi, 1976). The most discriminating components of relationship support–understanding may prove to be the cognitions and attributions that are attached to objective behavioral events. Studies are needed that address the interface be-

tween cognitions and behavior. Finally, although some empirical association has been found between the quality of marital relationships and situational variables (shared activities, children, and demand characteristics), there have been few attempts to investigate the influence of situational control. Without question, the situational control of marital interaction remains a relatively unknown and rarely considered topic of empirical investigation.

Outcome. Most of the treatments designed specifically to increase couples' supportiveness have been based on three marital enrichment programs: Conjugal Relationship Enhancement (CRE), developed by Guerney (1977) and modeled after Rogerian client-centered techniques (cf. Rappaport, 1976); the Minnesota Couples Communication Program (MCCP), which focuses on couples' awareness of dyadic interactions (Miller, Nunnally, & Wackman, 1976); and empathetic skill training based on Carkhuff's model (cf. Turkewitz & O'Leary, 1979). These programs address supportiveness by teaching couples helpful communicative skills. An outcome study from the Oregon group aimed at increasing positive communications provides a more explicitly behavioral example of training couples to be supportive.

CRE. Rappaport (1976) evaluated the effectiveness of CRE in promoting behavioral and self-reported change. Twenty-one couples were assessed initially, following a two-month waiting period, and after treatment. No significant changes were observed during the waiting period, but at posttreatment, significant improvements were found on both behavioral observation (speaker's responsibility for feelings and listener's empathy) and self-report measures. The design did not rule out competing hypotheses, for example, nonspecifics, demand characteristics, and time.

In a controlled study of CRE, Ely, Guerney, and Stover (1973) compared moderately distressed couples treated with CRE to a waiting-list group who later received treatment. At posttreatment, the treated group evidenced significant improvement on behavioral observations (expressing feelings and clarifying feeling statements) and self-report measures. No differences were found in the waiting-list group during the 10-week waiting period, but similar changes were reported for this group after they received treatment.

Wieman (1973) compared CRE with a behavioral-exchange treatment and a waiting-list control group. Both treatment groups exhibited significant self-reported change compared with the waiting-list controls, and both treatments were equally effective in promoting change. Behavioral observations were not included in this study.

Although significant pre- to posttreatment changes have been reported on both behavioral observations and self-report measures of couples who have received CRE treatment, the investigations have been methodologically limited. Typically, couples are recruited from populations of relatively nondistressed couples. It is difficult to assess the clinical significance of the observed behavior change because the validity of the behavioral measures has not been established. The long-term benefits of CRE are essentially unknown because of the absence of follow-up results.

MCCP. Miller, Nunnally, and Wackman (1976) evaluated the efficacy of this treatment by comparing treated couples with waiting-list controls recruited from a university population and randomly assigned to treatment or no-treatment groups. Couples were assessed on two behavioral ratings of their interaction ("recall accuracy" and "work pattern communication"). MCCP couples exhibited significantly greater behavioral change at posttreatment than the no-treatment controls. The use of relatively unknown dependent measures, the failure to assess relationship satisfaction, and recruited (relatively nondistressed) couples limit the generality of these results.

In a comparative outcome study, Stein (1978) randomly assigned 24 moderately distressed couples to either MCCP training; to Blechman's Family Contract Game (FCG) (Blechman & Olson, 1976), designed to train couples in problem-solving and contracting skills; or to a behavioral self-monitoring minimal treatment. Multiple dependent measures were employed, including self-reported marital satisfaction, MICS supportive and aversive behaviors, and SOC daily exchanged pleases and displeases. At posttreatment, the couples

in the FCG condition emitted significantly higher rates of verbal and nonverbal support than both the MCCP and the minimal treatment couples. Analyses of pre- to posttreatment changes *within* couples revealed that the treatments had differential effects. Whereas the FCG increased the couples' overall rate of supportive behaviors, enhanced their marital satisfaction, and lowered their daily exchange of displeases, the MCCP *decreased* couples' rate of supportive behaviors, decreased their marital satisfaction, and lowered their daily exchange of displeases *and* pleases. In effect, MCCP-treated couples deteriorated.

These findings, if replicated by others outside the MCCP group, are noteworthy. They suggest that supportive communication training by itself can have deleterious effects on some distressed couples. It is often difficult to teach spouses to be supportive of one another when there are obvious and severe conflicts between them. Treatment programs that focus on problem-solving and contracting skill training (i.e., that provide strategies for coping with and resolving relationship conflicts) may be needed in meeting the needs of distressed couples and may be more efficacious in promoting positive relationship change than treatments that focus exclusively on increasing supportive behaviors.

Carkhuff Model. O'Leary and Turkewitz (1981) compared a communication training program based on Carkhuff's model of empathetic listening with behavioral therapy and a no-treatment control. Each of the 30 distressed couples was randomly assigned to conjoint treatment or to the no-treatment group. The dependent measures included self-reported marital satisfaction and positive feelings toward the spouse, as well as behavioral observations based on a coding system derived from the MICS and the CISS. At posttreatment, the couples in both treatment conditions reported significantly higher marital satisfaction than the no-treatment controls, but none of the three groups differed on the behavioral observation measures. However, a significant age × treatment interaction was found, suggesting that the younger couples benefited more from behavioral therapy, while the older couples benefited more from communication training. Behavioral marital therapy, which

uses problem-solving and contracting procedures to resolve conflicts and define relationship rules, may be more effective for newer
relationships, which have relatively undefined
relationship rules (e.g., who does the house-
work and who is responsible for structuring
shared activities), and less appropriate for
older relationships with well-established rules;
older couples may benefit more from skill
training in the supportive components of relationship interaction. If replicated, these findings would provide a basis for assigning couples to specific treatments known to be
differentially effective.

Oregon. Margolin and Weiss (1978) reported
a treatment technique useful for increasing the
rates of spouses' helpful behaviors. Twenty-
seven distressed couples were randomly assigned to a behavioral (BT), a behavioral-at-
tribution (BA), or a nonspecific control (NS)
group. The BA couples worked to increase
their rates of *mutually* defined helpful behaviors; the BT couples worked to increase their
rates of *individually* defined helpful behaviors;
and the NS couples engaged in the same assessment procedures but did not receive specific instructions to increase helpful behaviors.
The treatment groups engaged in conflict resolution negotiations and were rewarded (with
a chime) for instances of emitted helpful behaviors and "punished" (with a buzzer) for
failures to emit such behaviors; the NS couples enacted uninterrupted negotiations. The
treatment groups also worked to increase helpful behaviors in the home; the NS couples
merely tracked daily pleases and displeases.

At posttreatment, all three groups showed
significant reductions in negative behaviors
but did not differ from one another. Couples
in the BA treatment, relative to couples in the
BT and NS groups, showed significantly greater
improvements in MICS-coded supportive behaviors, SOC pleases, and marital satisfaction.
Treatment efficacy appeared to be enhanced
by the addition of the attribution treatment
component, which consisted of *mutually* targeting behaviors for change, in contrast to
treatments that typically required each spouse
individually to target behaviors for change. It
appears to be relatively easy to reduce negative behaviors, since the NS couples who en-

gaged in the assessment procedures also decreased their aversiveness.

In sum, the outcome studies on communication treatments designed to increase couple
support skills are not free of methodological
weaknesses. Studies focus primarily on recruited couples, have rarely employed externally validated measures and typically do not
control for nonspecific treatment effects; this
is especially true of the marital enrichment
treatment packages (CRE, MCCP, and Carkhuff). Of the five controlled-outcome studies,
only two included a nonspecific control group.
In one instance reviewed, the MCCP has been
shown to have deleterious effects on distressed couples (Stein, 1978) and communication training based on Carkhuff's model has
failed to promote significant behavioral change
in treated couples (O'Leary & Turkewitz,
1981). A nonspecific control group evidenced
reductions in negative behavior that were
comparable to those found in treated couples
(Margolin & Weiss, 1978). The addition of attributional components in otherwise strictly
behavioral treatments (Margolin & Weiss,
1978) represents a promising first step in providing an operationally defined and replicable
definition of a more cognitively based treatment component. The need is for more methodologically sound research (cf. O'Leary &
Turkewitz, 1978) on the efficacy of communication treatments and for further investigations of possible iatrogenic effects of these
types of therapy on distressed couples.

Problem Solving

Unlike other forms of communication training that focus on enhancing the awareness, the
understanding, and the supportive skills of
couples, problem-solving training emphasizes
productive outcomes: couples learn skills mutually to resolve relationship problems and to
allocate relationship resources. Problem solving (PS) and behavior change differ in aim: the
former pertains to resource management skills,
while the latter pertains to formal attempts at
behavior change. In this section, we first consider the specific behaviors, cognitions, and
situations that have been shown to facilitate
or to hinder the problem-solving process, after

which we critically examine the outcome literature on problem-solving–based treatments.

Targets

Behavior. The majority of studies on decision making in marriage have attempted to isolate the behaviors necessary to successful problem-solving by comparing the differences between distressed and nondistressed couples. Assertions about behaviors that facilitate or hinder the problem-solving process are based, for the most part, on the topography of problem-solving behaviors as described by current interaction coding systems (Gottman, 1979; Weiss & Margolin, 1977), but not on lawful associations established between specific behaviors and conflict resolution outcomes. Examples of behaviors defined by coding systems are proposing solutions to problems, compromising, and accepting responsibility (cf. Weiss *et al.*, 1973).

Although the behaviors selected for study may have limited ecological validity, studies of the attempts made by distressed and nondistressed couples to negotiate conflict resolution support the problem-solving skills-deficit model of relationship distress. Studies fall in two categories: (1) analyses of base-rate coded behaviors and (2) codes examined sequentially. Investigators have employed either simulated (analogue) conflict tasks or samples of real (idiosyncratic) conflict issues; Gottman (1979) distinguished between high- and low-conflict tasks.

Base-rate analyses of laboratory interactions have not discriminated between distressed and nondistressed couples consistently on the basis of their problem-solving competency with either simulated or real problems. One of four studies using simulated conflict tasks, as well as two of four studies using real conflict tasks, has failed to differentiate distressed and nondistressed couples' rate of problem-solving behavior. Turning first to studies of problem solving on simulated conflict tasks, Vincent *et al.* (1975) used the MICS to assess problem-solving behaviors on IMC (low) conflict tasks and found that distressed couples emitted significantly lower rates of positive (e.g., propose solutions or compro-

mise) problem-solving behavior and significantly higher rates of negative (e.g., deny responsibility or excuse) problem-solving behavior than nondistressed couples. Vincent *et al.* (1979) replicated these same findings. Birchler (1977), however, also used the IMC conflict tasks to assess the problem-solving skills of distressed and nondistressed couples but failed to discriminate between the two groups of couples in terms of MICS codes.

Rubin (cited in Gottman, 1979) analyzed problem-solving interactions on simulated conflict tasks (similar to IMC tasks) using the CISS. Spouses attempted to resolve biased conflicting vignettes on problem issues (e.g., sex and child rearing). On two of the three conflict tasks reported, the distressed couples emitted significantly more problem-solving statements than the nondistressed couples; on the third task, no differences were found between the distressed and the nondistressed couples.

Studies of marital problem-solving using discussions of real problems have similarly yielded equivocal results. None of the four studies cited here has successfully discriminated between distressed and nondistressed husbands, while only two have discriminated between distressed and nondistressed wives. Birchler (1977) used the MICS to assess rates of problem-solving behavior during discussions of real relationship problems and found significant differences between distressed and nondistressed wives; distressed wives emitted significantly fewer problem-solving statements than nondistressed wives. Birchler (1979) replicated these findings; once again, differences were found between distressed and nondistressed wives (but not husbands).

Two other studies of base rates using real conflicts have failed to demonstrate differences in problem-solving behaviors between distressed and nondistressed spouses. Gottman, Markman, and Notarius (1977) used the CISS to measure the rates of problem solution statements during real conflict tasks and found no differences between distressed and nondistressed couples. Similarly, Stein (1978) failed to find significant correlations between the problem-solving behaviors defined by the MICS and many "satisfaction measures," for example, scores on the Dyadic Adjustment Scale (Spanier, 1976), the Marital Happiness Scale (Azrin, Naster, & Jones, 1973), the Stuarts's (1972) Precounseling Inventory, and the SOC Satisfaction Rating. Unexpectedly, the rates of problem-solving behavior and the rates of daily SOC *displeasing* events received were significantly related ($r = .35$, $p < .01$). Spouses who experienced numerous displeasing events emitted relatively higher rates of problem-solving behavior when discussing their own conflicts. It would be unwise to offer explanations of this finding, given the magnitude of the correlation and the need for replication; however, couples in the earlier stages of conflict may make active attempts to problem-solve (the daily irritants), but after prolonged conflict, they may "give up" problem-solving tactics.[2]

Overall, base-rate analyses of couples' problem solving have failed to demonstrate unequivocally that distressed couples are less skilled in resolving marital conflicts than nondistressed couples. But since all of the dependent variables have been judged *a priori* to be positive or negative (i.e., not shown to be functionally related to successful or unsuccessful outcomes), it is still unclear whether the coding systems are assessing behaviors that actually facilitate the problem-solving process. Nor do gross base-rate analyses suggest possible treatment tactics beyond increasing overall rates of problem-solving behaviors.

By far, the most important studies of marital conflict resolution, both in terms of describing the differences between maritally distressed and satisfied couples and in terms of suggesting implications for treatment, are those based on sequential analyses of dyadic interactions. Rather than focusing on the total behavioral output of spouses, these studies assess the sequential patterns of behavior, a more transactional approach to the investigation of marital problem-solving.

Gottman and his associates (Gottman, 1979; Gottman *et al.*, 1977) have contributed a significant conceptualization of the marital decision-making process by their sequential analyses of couple interactions. Conflict negotiations were divided into equal thirds (based on the "thought unit" as a behavioral chunk) labeled *agenda building, problem exploration,* and the *negotiation phase* of problem-solving. Both satisfied and dissatisfied couples tended to express their feelings during the first, agenda-building, phase. However, satisfied couples tended to validate each other's feelings (feeling expression → agreement → feeling expression), whereas dissatisfied couples tended to cross-complain (feeling expression → feeling expression → feeling expression). During the next phase of problem solving (problem exploration), both groups of couples tended to disagree (disagree → disagree) reciprocally. In the final, negotiation phase, satisfied couples recovered from their exchange of disagreements and established contractual agreements (problem solution → agreement). This was not true of dissatisfied couples; they tended to propose countersolutions (problem solution → problem solution). We note in passing that Royce and Weiss (1975) also reported that nondistressed couples engaged in more problem solution → agreement sequential patterns than distressed couples in their study.

Thus, it appears that dissatisfied couples initially approach problem-solving situations with fewer supportive skills and subsequently demonstrate fewer problem-solving skills than satisfied couples, a finding that establishes empirically the need for support–understanding and problem-solving modalities as suggested by the Oregon model.

For the most part, the studies are flawed by methodological weaknesses. Both simulated and real conflict tasks have inherent methodological problems that may influence couple interactions. Simulated conflict tasks may not generalize to real-life conflict situations; the intensity of real-life conflict tasks obviously differs for distressed and nondistressed couples. Both the generalizability of laboratory conflict tasks to real conflict situations and the ways of defining the comparability of problem intensity across couples need to be estab-

---

[2] O'Leary and Turkewitz (1981) found differences between maritally younger and older couples with regard to differences in the effectiveness of contracting versus communication-based behavior-change tactics. Couples' methods of handling daily problems may change over time; frontal attacks (PS) early on and isolating tactics later on.

lished. The generalizability of behavioral observations across different coding systems must be established as new and revised coding systems are designed. Most importantly, criteria for evaluating the outcome of problem resolution, including measures of spouse-reported satisfaction with the outcome, are needed. Thus far, behavioral treatments have been based exclusively on conceptualizations of facilitative and nonfacilitative marital decision-making processes that lack empirically demonstrated functional validity. Skill training should be based on the empirical associations between behavior and outcome.

Cognition. The significance of cognitive variables in marital problem-solving has been suggested by both Weiss (1978) and Jacobson and Margolin (1979). Although empirical investigations have only recently appeared, there is a general belief that misattributions and misperceptions of a partner's intentions serve to hinder the problem-solving process. Additionally, the success of marital negotiations may depend on partners' self-efficacy of their problem-solving capabilities, as well as their expectation of a successful outcome (Weiss, 1980).

Peterson (1979) examined the feelings, beliefs, and expectations of spouses following significant daily interactions with their partner. Sixty-three couples recorded accounts of daily marital interactions (for a period of one week), which included a description of the situational context, the antecedent events, and behavioral exchanges that accompanied each interaction, together with the feelings and expectations that accompanied each interchange. Descriptive accounts of these events were then coded by trained judges on the dimensions of affect, construal, and expectation. Interjudge reliability for the three categories was a respectable 82%, 84%, and 86%, respectively.

The findings indicated differences between satisfied and dissatisfied couples on all three measures. After marital interaction, satisfied spouses were more likely to experience affectionate feelings, positive construals of their relationship, and expectations of compliance and cooperation on the part of their partners. Dissatisfied spouses, on the contrary, were more likely to experience aggressive feelings, negative construals of the relationship and expectations of noncompliance and withdrawal on the part of their mates.

Most pertinent to our discussion of problem solving are the reported differences between distressed and nondistressed spouses' expectations. Nondistressed spouses expected their partners to be compliant and cooperative, whereas distressed spouses expected their partners to be noncompliant or to withdraw from the scene of conflict. As suggested by Bandura's (1977a) model of self-efficacy and outcome expectations, as well as Weiss's (1980) applications of this model to marital relationships, the expectations that spouses hold about the potential success or failure of marital problem-solving are thought to regulate their actual behavior. Thus, we would expect spouses with positive expectancies to emit relatively more positive and relatively less negative behavior than spouses with negative expectancies.

The empirical association between generalized expectancies and interactional behavior was examined by Doherty and Ryder (1979) in a study that compared rates of assertive behavior with spouses' locus-of-control orientation (Rotter, 1966) and interpersonal trust (Rotter, 1967). Audiotapes of 86 newlywed couples attempting to resolve IMC-simulated conflicts were coded with the Marital and Family Interaction Coding System (Olson & Ryder, 1970). Assertive behavior was defined as an attempt either to stand one's ground or to influence the partner's opinion.

The findings indicated a locus-of-control main effect for husbands ("internals" were significantly more assertive than "externals") and a significant interaction effect for wives ("internal–low trust" wives were most assertive). Spouses who believed that they were in control of their own lives pursued the desired outcomes with more vigor than spouses who believed that their lives were governed by external circumstances. However, assertiveness in this study represented a tendency to be competitive and hence does not necessarily reflect a desirable response to marital conflict. Therefore, although "internals" may exhibit greater vigor in their efforts to win agreements, they may also experience greater marital conflict and have a poorer prognosis in treatment. As the marital treatment literature suggests (Jacobson & Margolin, 1979; Weiss, 1978), couples who attribute the primary responsibility for their marital problems to external circumstances may stand a greater chance of resolving disagreements by "joining forces" against a common enemy, whereas couples who attribute marital problems to their own or their partner's inherent traits assign blame to themselves or to the spouse; consequently, they face a greater struggle in resolving their problems.

The role of expectancies and attributions in marital problem-solving has only recently been subjected to empirical scrutiny, yet these cognitive factors have been held accountable for such phenomena as client resistance and behavioral treatment failures (cf. Weiss, 1979, 1980). Thus, they could be valuable as predictive measures of treatment outcome. To the extent that problem-solving negotiations are under the influence of cognitive variables such as expectancy, locus of control, and trust, behavioral skill training may fall short of addressing the critical factors that hold the success or the failure of problem solving in check.

Situation. As defined here, problem-solving training addresses the control of the situational variables (e.g., settings and use of agendas) that combine to bring spouses' behaviors under stimulus control. Relatively little work has been done with the influences of situations on problem solving *per se*. Studies that have addressed possible situational factors test for consistency of behaviors across situations (i.e., the state vs. trait distinction).

Vincent *et al.* (1975) were the first to examine the specificity of problem-solving behaviors (MICS), by using spouses from distressed and nondistressed marriages who were then recombined to form two *ad hoc* stranger dyads. This procedure provided samples of problem-solving (PS) behaviors for natural and *ad hoc* dyad pairings when the same persons were employed overall: "Not only were married subjects, in general, more negative to their spouses than to average strangers, *but the distressed subjects were most negative of all,"* (pp. 481–482; italics added). The nondistressed subjects were more variable, depending on the situation, whereas the distressed subjects seemed to carry their negative PS with them from situation to situation.

Whether PS behaviors are consistent across problem topics and occasions has been the focus of other investigations. The issue may be stated as follows: if PS is situationally specific (in the sense defined here), then the determinants within situations that control that form of behavior become important. Wieder and Weiss (1980) examined the consistency of the PS behaviors of 14 distressed couples attempting to resolve real conflicts across occasions and topics (prior to intervention). From ANOVAs of the MICS-coded PS behaviors, situational factors accounted for only 27% of the variance in PS, suggesting that, at least prior to intervention, married distressed couples are quite consistent in their PS behaviors; this finding is consistent with the earlier Vincent *et al.* (1975) finding.

The consistency of PS behaviors across settings was examined by Gottman (1979), using a between-subjects design that compared real conflict negotiations between two matched groups of couples who interacted in either the laboratory or their own home. Home interactions, relative to laboratory interactions, were significantly more negative (included greater negative reciprocity and cross-complaining and fewer feeling-validations and contractual agreements) and were significantly better discriminators of marital distress status. Laboratory situational variables (e.g., the demand characteristics, the unfamiliar setting, and the presence of outside observers) appeared to elicit more positive interactions than those found in the home samples. Further evidence of the influence of demand characteristics on PS behavior was provided by Vincent *et al.* (1979) in the study described above: they successfully manipulated the rates of PS behavior by instructing couples to act happy or distressed.

On the basis of the collective findings, PS interactions appear to be under the control of the partner, the setting, and the demands imposed by outside parties. At least one study has found that maritally distressed couples problem-solve in stereotypical and stable ways across situations. These findings suggest that the behaviors are under the control of cues provided by the partner and not the situation, and they raise the interesting, but unorthodox, question: Can distressed couples be taught problem-solving skills more efficiently in conjoint therapy with the married partner or in conjoint therapy with a stranger? Distressed partners may elicit from each other stereotypical and destructive patterns of behavior that are relatively resistant to behavioral treatment. Perhaps a temporary removal from the situational control of the relationship (i.e., the partner) would facilitate behavioral change.

Summary. The marital PS research has identified many of the behavioral and situational variables associated with what are thought to be facilitative and nonfacilitative decision-making processes. More recently, the role of cognitive variables such as outcome expectations, self-efficacy, and locus of control have been discussed and are being subjected to empirical investigation. Most of the research to date has utilized between-subjects designs that reveal differences between distressed and nondistressed couples but provide little information about the cues that contribute to relatively successful and unsuccessful interactions *within* marital relationships. Objective measures of outcome are now lacking. The development of PS outcome measures would help establish the association between specific behaviors and outcome; conceptualizations of marital relationships would no longer be based on inferences about what is facilitative behavior. Gottman's brilliant work has combined micro- and macroconceptualizations of problem solving that describe sequential processes during three distinct phases of negotiation; there appears to be great potential in sequential methods, both for describing the stylistic differences between distressed and satisfied couples in approaches to problem solving, and for suggesting treatments.

Outcome. Problem-solving training teaches couples to discuss their problems and to manipulate their environment in ways likely to enable them to attain mutually satisfying resolutions of relationship conflict (cf. Jacobson, 1978; Jacobson & Margolin, 1979). Specifically, treatment may involve any one of a number of modalities (e.g., behavioral rehearsal, videotape feedback, therapist instructions, or homework assignments) that are all designed to help couples define relationship problems, generate alternative solutions, and reach mutually satisfying outcomes. The focus is usually on communication skills, although other ingredients are often applied to help couples structure their problem-solving environment, for example, agenda sessions and administrative meetings (Weiss & Birchler, 1978).

Jacobson (1979) used a single-subject design to investigate the effects of problem-solving training on six severely distressed couples. All couples underwent two weeks of baseline assessment, followed by an instruction phase that encouraged them to increase their positive behaviors. There were no reported increases in positive behaviors as a result of either the baseline or the instructional phases. The couples were then taught problem-solving skills, with their own problems used as the content for discussion. The treatment involved modeling, coaching, behavioral rehearsal, and videotaped feedback. Data collected systematically from five of the six couples revealed that the PS training was responsible for promoting positive changes on self-reported and behavioral (MICS) measures in four of the five couples. A modified instruction phase increased the positive behaviors of the fifth couple. All the couples reported higher marital satisfaction posttreatment, fewer requests for relationship change, exhibited increased rates of positive and problem-solving behaviors, and decreased rates of negative behaviors. These gains were maintained at six-month follow-up.

Jacobson and Anderson (1980) compared the efficacy of problem-solving training using videotaped feedback (VF), behavioral rehearsal (BR), a combination treatment (VF and BR), and therapist instructions (I) as vehicles for training. A waiting-list (WL) control group was also included. The couples in all the treatments were taught to express appreciation of their partner, to pinpoint problems, to paraphrase, to generate potential solutions to relationship problems, and to adopt mutually satisfying resolutions. The treatments lasted for three sessions and were evaluated on the basis of videotaped interactions coded for positive problem-solving behaviors (MICS) and rated for overall problem-solving effectiveness. Only the combined (VF and BR) group improved significantly more than the WL group on both the observational and the global measures posttreatment. The combined treatment group also improved significantly more than the other three treatment groups on MICS problem-solving behaviors and significantly more than the VF and I groups on global ratings of problem-solving effectiveness. Thus, the combination of videotaped feedback and behavioral rehearsal proved to be more effective than either modality alone, therapist instructions, or waiting-list controls.

Cadogan (1973) compared alcoholic couples treated with communication skill training that emphasized feeling expressions (learning the impact of behavior and PS) with a no-treatment control group. Forty couples were randomly assigned to one of the two groups. Six months after hospital discharge, the abstinence rates for the treated and control groups were 45% and 10%, respectively. The groups did not differ on measures of marital satisfaction. The use of PS treatment for alcohol problems relative to untreated groups was successful in reducing the rate of relapse, but the absence of observational data makes it difficult to determine whether the reported improvements were due to changes in behavioral skills.

Peterson and Frederiksen (1976) provided a case illustration of a modular treatment approach designed to train couples in either PS or supportive skills. Two couples were first taught to discriminate the goal of their discussion (i.e., to express feelings or problem-solve) and then were taught skills appropriate to each situation. The training involved sequentially ordered components: (1) rationale and instructions; (2) a videotaped presentation of a couple modeling the specific skills; (3) behavioral rehearsal and videotaping; (4) videotape feedback, coaching, and behavioral rehearsal; and (5) instructions for home assignments. The two distressed couples revealed posttreatment improvements in the targeted behaviors and the percentage of negotiated agreements; one also reported increased marital satisfaction and satisfaction with conflict resolutions.

The model is noteworthy in several respects. Couples discriminate the goal of their discussions at the onset and apply skills appropriate to each type of interaction. The training is presented in a standardized format, allowing for easy replication and components analysis. Finally, multiple assessment measures—and in particular, measures of the percentage of negotiated agreements and satisfaction with conflict resolution—are included. The initial results of this treatment have been encouraging.

Margolin (personal communication, 1979) has developed a treatment approach for reducing spouse anger and abuse that combines cognitive restructuring and behavioral problem-solving components. Although the efficacy of this program has yet to be established, the preliminary data have been positive.

Two other treatment approaches to spouse anger have been suggested. Dayringer (1976) designed a treatment called *fair fighting,* in which couples use their anger constructively to solve relationship problems. But at least one study (Straus, 1974) suggests that fair fighting may actually increase the likelihood of physical violence. In Straus's investigation of domestic violence, it was found that as the intensity of verbal abuse increased, so did the likelihood of physical abuse. Thus, marital conflict might actually be exacerbated by the fair-fighting treatment. Proponents of behavioral therapy (most notably Stuart, 1975) have suggested that spouses place themselves in time-out (i.e., temporary separation) when there is any potential for verbal or physical fighting. Rosenblatt, Titus, and Cunningham (1977) suggested that couples who distance after a fight are less likely to express negative behavior (and hence be physically abusive) during conflictual interactions. Time-out procedures may be preferable to fair-fighting tactics.

Surprisingly, although behavioral theories of marital distress suggest that ongoing marital conflicts are the result of PS skill deficits, there have been relatively few outcome investigations of PS training *per se.* Surely, the fact that most behavioral treatments are presented in a package form that combines problem-solving skill training and contingency contracting makes separate outcome evaluations of each component impossible. Future controlled investigations are needed to evaluate the efficacy of problem-solving training and, more specifically, different treatment modalities (behavioral rehearsal, videotaped feedback, etc.).

Several interesting and potentially efficacious treatment packages have been suggested but await empirical validation. Most importantly, there is need for a continued use of multiple-outcome measures, and controls for nonspecific factors and for distressed client populations.

Behavior Change

The aim of behavior change is to provide couples with skills for effecting orderly changes in relationship behaviors, behaviors that are maintained by coercion techniques in distressed relationships. Within BMT, behavior change (as a separate competency) is coterminous with contracting. Behavior change contracts vary in their degree of structure; they range from informal "agreements" to highly structured "good faith contracts" that tend to orchestrate reward–penalty contingencies. Contracts are reasonably complex compared with other forms of BMT techniques. Behavior change contracts involve elements of both stimulus control and contingency control (Weiss, 1978). A couple may fail to reward themselves for executing a targeted behavior even though explicit rewards have been built into the contract structure. Instead, they may find it useful "just to know that we are both trying," which is an agreement (metacontract) entered into with the therapist; that is, therapy provides a structure that makes it possible for both persons to initiate changes independently of the particular payoff matrix already built into the change agreement.

Some of the complexity of contracting procedures (cf. Weiss *et al.*, 1974) can be reduced if we categorize behavior change contracts according to *quid pro quo* or "good-faith" principles. Contracts that make one set of behaviors contingent on behaviors emitted by the other partner are *quid pro quo* or *response-contingent* contracts. On the other hand, the so-called good-faith or parallel contractual structure relies on behavior–reward (penalty) contingencies, but not on response-controlled contingencies. Thus, in the parallel contract format, both partners agree to accelerate a targeted behavior (e.g., conversation and parenting behaviors), but here the targets are not made contingent on one another. The good-faith agreement requires that each will work on his or her targets, and for so doing, built-in rewards (penalties) are given for enacting (failing to enact) the targeted behavior at a specified rate.

Within BMT, only direct contingency control can be expected to be beneficial (i.e., to produce the desired behavior change). The good-faith contract is conceptually less likely to be effective. Outside the BMT framework, it can be argued that any form of response contingency is destined to foster reward devaluation (e.g., Gurman & Knudson, 1978; Gurman & Kniskern, 1978a). It has been argued that providing explicit rewards for behaviors in marriage is a form of control that mimics the very coercive control that distressed coupled display without benefit of therapy.

Clearly then, behavior change, as exemplified in contracting technology, is not without its controversial elements. In this section, we focus primarily on reciprocity, since for conceptual reasons, reciprocity describes a major way in which behaviors are patterned in relationships, and for clinical reasons, much of BMT technology is based on behavioral exchanges; differences in patterns of reciprocity are thought to describe distressed and nondistressed couples.

Targets

Behavior. Reciprocity of positive behaviors over long periods of time has been singled out as the most important descriptor of satisfying relationships (Gottman, 1979; Stuart, 1969). Happily married couples are thought to exchange positive behaviors at equitable rates over time. Wills *et al.* (1974) have provided empirical support for this hypothesis. In their study, nondistressed couples were perfectly rank-ordered on the basis of their long-term exchange of SOC pleasing behavior (mean daily pleases over 14 days); there were clear within-couple consistencies in positive exchanges over time. When studies employ both distressed and nondistressed samples, the groups cannot be differentiated on the basis of positive reciprocity alone. Birchler (1972) reported daily reciprocity (over 5 days) of SOC pleases for *both* distressed and nondistressed couples. Robinson and Price (1980) found that the daily rates of SOC pleases reported by husbands and wives in both distressed *and* nondistressed relationships were significantly correlated within groups. The hypothesis that positive reciprocity is a characteristic unique to happily married couples is not supported.

Findings have been consistent in support of the hypothesis that distressed couples reciprocate negative behaviors to a greater extent than nondistressed couples, even though for all couples, the tendency to reciprocate negatives is greater than it is for positives. This generalization is strengthened by the diversity of tasks and settings employed in the studies reported to date. Two studies sought reciprocity relationships using daily SOC behaviors. Margolin (1977) found greater overall reciprocity of negative behaviors (SOC-defined displeases) for distressed couples, as measured by the magnitude of correlations between husbands' and wives' reported displeases. Both Margolin (1977) and Jacobson, Waldron, and Moore (1980) reported the relationship between DMS and daily rates of SOC displeases to be higher for distressed couples than for nondistressed couples. Jacobson's group also reported a relationship between the level of distress and the impact of daily SOC displeases on DMS; the greater the marital distress, the greater the impact of displeases on DMS.

Reciprocity of negative behaviors, a characteristic of distressed relationships, has also been demonstrated in correlational studies involving laboratory tasks designed to elicit conflictual interactions. When reciprocity was defined more stringently by means of a sequential analysis of probability changes, Gottman *et al.* (1977) found a clear tendency for all couples immediately to reciprocate negative behaviors compared with positive behaviors. However, negative reciprocity was more likely and positive reciprocity more immediate for distressed couples. Margolin (1977) also reported that distressed couples tended to respond immediately to positive and negative behaviors. From the MICS coding of interactions, she found significant reciprocity of negative, positive, and problem-solving behaviors for her distressed-couple group. Distressed, compared with nondistressed, couples appeared to be more sensitive to immediate contingencies within their interactions. Billings (1979) used a very different coding methodology (based on Leary, 1957, and Raush, Barry, Heitel, & Swain, 1974) and also found that distressed couples (relative to nondistressed couples) showed greater negative reciprocity on analogue conflict-interaction tasks.

Margolin and Wampold (1980) examined positive and negative reciprocity, as well as *negative reactivity* (lower than base-rate probability of a positive response given a negative stimulus), in distressed and nondistressed couple interactions. Distressed couples at lag 1 reciprocated negative behavior to a greater degree and emitted positive responses to negative behavior to a lesser degree than their nondistressed counterparts. (Both groups evidenced comparable degrees of positive reciprocity.) At lags 2 and 3, no significant differences were found between distressed and nondistressed couples on any of the three measures. Apparently, distressed and nondistressed couples differ only in their immediate (lag 1) reactions.

In an experimental manipulation of dyadic interactions, Lochman and Allen (1979) increased the approval and disapproval behaviors of one member of a dating couple and then observed the impact of these behavioral changes on the other member. Eighty dating partners role-played typical conflict situations, which were recorded and later coded by the MICS. Whenever the elicitors became more disapproving (because of instructions), their partners significantly increased their own rate of verbal disapproval behavior (negative reciprocity), decreased their rate of verbal approval behavior, and reported significantly less satisfaction with the interaction relative to baseline. Whenever the elicitors became more approving (true of females only), the tendency to reciprocate was significant but weak; the partners significantly increased their rate of nonverbal approval and reported significantly higher satisfaction with the interaction relative to baseline. Most of the variance in satisfaction ratings (of the interaction itself) was accounted for by rates of *disapproval*, providing yet more evidence that negative behaviors have a greater immediate impact on satisfaction ratings than positive behaviors.

Collectively, the evidence suggests that behavioral exchange is more contingent within maritally dissatisfied than within satisfied couples. Distressed, relative to nondistressed, spouses are more sensitive to immediate fluctuations in behavior and more reciprocal in their negative exchanges. Although distressed and nondistressed couples do not seem to differ in their overall tendency to reciprocate positive behavior, distressed couples appear to reciprocate positive behaviors more immediately (i.e., at earlier lags) than nondistressed couples. If these findings can be interpreted as providing an empirical test of the theoretical underpinnings of contingency management procedures, then the results do not support the conceptual foundation of contracting. However, it does not follow that because response-contingent exchanges are more characteristic of distressed relationships, the teaching of contingent exchanges is also in appropriate for bringing couples' behavior under stimulus (rule) control. Contingency contracting as an intervention may be clinically efficacious even though the conceptual foundation of the intervention is wrong. Certainly, this possibility does not absolve us of the responsibility of understanding the process conceptually.

Cognition. If cognitions are to be the target of behavior change, the empirical basis for reciprocity is much more limited. In a parallel with the reciprocity of positively or negatively coded *behaviors*, we can ask whether reciprocity exists for *subjectively made ratings of behavioral transactions*. If an information analysis approach is used, the question becomes: Does the probability of the wife's rating some transaction positively (negatively) increase or stay the same if the husband has just rated some transaction positively (negatively)? Here, *reciprocity* means whether subjective ratings are constrained; in the preceding section, *reciprocity* meant constraints on (objectively coded) positive or negative behaviors. Presumably, the subjective rating would be tied to the behaviors exchanged, but this condition is not necessary for the analysis

under examination here. For example, subjective ratings may be influenced by communication channels not monitored by the particular coding system (either MICS or CISS).

Gottman, Markman, and Notarius (1976) compared positive and negative reciprocity using the subjective ratings of affective impact provided by distressed and nondistressed couples themselves. Spouses independently rated the impact of their partners' ongoing behavior during five very different conflict-interaction tasks, that is, tasks that are likely to induce conflict between the participants as they attempt to resolve the differences posited by the instructions. The analyses of conditional probabilities indicated that the groups (distressed versus nondistressed) could not be differentiated on the basis of either positive or negative reciprocity *of subjective ratings* of interaction behaviors; that is, there was no predictive improvement over base-rate expectations. A tendency for nondistressed wives to reciprocate positive ratings with positive ratings was not replicated in the second of the two reported studies. As with objectively coded interaction behaviors, Gottman *et al.* replicated the finding that nondistressed couples rate the impact of each other's behaviors significantly more positively than do distressed spouses; the findings of a significant difference in the ratings of negative impact were not replicated across the two studies, nor was it possible to differentiate the distress groups on ratings of intention; both groups *intended* their messages to have a positive impact.

One feature of the Gottman, Markman, and Notarius (1976) study should be noted: the talk-table procedure forces both groups of couples to adopt similar strategies for monitoring and evaluating the spouse's behaviors. *Each thought unit (behavioral chunk) is to be evaluated as it occurs*, which also parallels the natural tendency of distressed couples to track the value of responses (Jacobson, 1978; Weiss, 1978). Have the authors concealed real differences between the groups (natural tracking style and tendency to reciprocate immediately) by using a procedure that forces very immediate evaluation of small segments of the interaction? The reactivity of the procedure is unknown, yet any ongoing, subjectively based evaluation would have the same effect on nondistressed couples, that is, forcing a tit-for-tat reciprocity of value of behavior.

Situation. The tendency to reciprocate behavior has been compared across spouse and stranger dyads. Murstein, Cerreto, and MacDonald (1977), using attitude measures, found that *quid pro quo* exchange orientations were inversely related to marital satisfaction but positively related to friendship intensity. Reciprocity may be characteristic of less intimate relationships. In an examination of behavioral reciprocity within intimate and acquaintance dyads, Morton (1978) randomly assigned 24 married spouses and 24 opposite-sex stranger pairs to a spouse or stranger dyad; the former paired spouses with their marriage partners, while the latter paired opposite-sex strangers. Verbal and nonverbal behaviors during videotaped discussions of four topics were coded for descriptive (i.e., private or public fact) and evaluative (i.e., personal or impersonal feeling) intimacy. Reciprocity was assessed by comparing the behavioral rates of dyadic partners during three sequential time blocks in the interaction. (Reciprocity was operationally defined as rate equity, not contingency.) Overall, the spouses reciprocated intimacy less across the three segments than the strangers. Although both the spouses and the strangers tended to reciprocate intimacy at equitable rates early in their discussions, the spouses became less reciprocal over time, whereas the strangers maintained their initial level of reciprocity throughout their discussions.

The results imply that reciprocity of self-disclosure is more characteristic of acquaintanceships than of intimate relations. The interactions of opposite-sex strangers, in the author's words, were governed by "a cautious tit-for-tat reciprocity" (p. 79). On the other hand, married partners self-disclosed at less equitable rates; when intimate statements were made, they were not immediately reciprocated. This noncontingent positive exchange (i.e., the exchange that was found in married dyads but not in stranger dyads) is thought to be more characteristic of satisfied couples than of dissatisfied couples (Williams, 1979). It is hypothesized that as intimacy between partners increases, positive behavioral exchange becomes less contingent. Morton's (1978) findings support this hypothesis.

Summary. A consistent picture of behavioral exchange in marital relationships emerges from these studies. Overall, the interactions of distressed couples are more reciprocal, showing a greater tendency toward negative reciprocity, far more immediate reciprocity of positives, and greater reactivity to immediate events. Taken together, the findings support the hypothesis that behavioral exchanges in distressed relationships are controlled on a response-by-response basis, whereas behavioral exchanges in nondistressed relationships are controlled by relationship rules; we suspect that spouses hold a generalized expectancy that benefits will be distributed equitably over time, so that short-term inequities are less demonstrably important.

At the same time, these findings about behavior change strategies raise a conceptual dilemma. The use of contracting techniques endeavors to establish relationship rule control and the expectancy that contingencies will be applied fairly and consistently, while also increasing the likelihood that positive and negative behaviors will be reciprocated immediately. Accordingly, spouses are forced to become more responsive, rather than less responsive, to immediate contingencies. The paradox of behavior change strategies notwithstanding, the use of contracting to establish positive control may be necessary to offset the aversive control that seems to govern distressed relationships. Contracting, and its structured control, may be necessary before spouses can be expected to exchange relationship rewards noncontingently. Once positive contingencies are established, rewards may be applied noncontingently.

Outcome. Empirical outcome studies of *quid pro quo* (QPQ) and good faith (GF) contracting are reviewed separately.

Quid Pro Quo. Three early studies were reported but all lacked control groups. Weiss and Patterson (Weiss, Patterson, & Hops, 1973; Patterson, Hops, & Weiss, 1975) treated 10 distressed couples with a multifaceted behavioral treatment that included QPQ contracting. The spouses agreed to change their behavior contingent on changes in their partners' behavior, and violations of the contract resulted in applications of previously designated penalties. At posttreatment, 8 of the 10 couples demonstrated significant improvements in their communication skills as evidenced by a significant increase in MICS facilitative behavior and a significant decrease in MICS nonfacilitative behavior. Furthermore, the positive exchanges were more reciprocal, and the negative exchanges less reciprocal, at posttreatment than at baseline. SOC data on 6 of the 8 improved couples revealed significant increases in the pleasing behaviors of both the husbands and the wives, but significant decreases in the displeasing behaviors of the husbands only. However, at posttreatment, there was significantly greater reciprocity of displeasing behaviors. Thus, although significant improvements were observed in overall behavioral rates, the nature in which these behaviors were exchanged was more characteristic of distressed relationships at posttreatment than at baseline. Although the long-term implications of these findings are not now known, the efficacy of this treatment depends on one's interpretation of the data on the rate and the reciprocity of behavioral exchange.

Stuart (1969) initially used QPQ contracting with four couples whose husbands complained of infrequent sex and whose wives complained of infrequent conversation. Contracts were established that made sex contingent on a certain amount of conversation. At posttreatment, 24-week follow-up, and 48-week follow-up, increases in both frequency of conversation and sex were reported. No other dependent measures were employed.

Azrin *et al.* (1973) treated 12 couples with 3 weeks of catharsis counseling, designed as a nonspecific control, followed by reciprocity training, designed to establish equitable exchanges of relationship benefits. Of the 12 couples, 11 reported significantly greater improvements in marital satisfaction after reciprocity training than after catharsis counseling. The design did not control for a possible sequence effect, nor were any behavioral measures employed.

Venema (1975) compared QPQ contingency contracting, communication skill training, and a combination treatment that included both components. The couples, who were relatively

nondistressed, participated in a 7-week workshop. Only minimal pre- to posttreatment change was reported on a series of self-report measures; significantly greater improvement was found for the combination than for either of the other treatments.

Roberts (1975) randomly assigned nondistressed couples to either contracting training, a nonspecific control group, or a waiting list. Treatment was conducted over three one-hour sessions. Self-report measures indicated significant improvements for couples in the contracting treatment, relative to the waiting-list controls, and only a trend in favor of contracting over the nonspecific control group. Contracting did not produce significantly greater posttreatment improvements than the control condition.

Tsoi-Hoshmand (1976) compared a QPQ contracting group with a waiting-list group and a normal sample. The couples were solicited in different ways, were treated at different geographical locations, and were not randomly assigned to conditions. Three self-report measures indicated significant improvements for the contracting group relative to controls. A one- to four-month follow-up suggested that the treatment gains were maintained in 70% of the couples. The methodological problems in this study make an interpretation of the results difficult.

In a controlled study that included behavioral observations, Harrell and Guerney (1976) evaluated the efficacy of a behavioral treatment that emphasized problem-solving-skill training and contingent behavioral exchange, compared with a waiting-list control. The treatment was conducted in eight weekly two-hour sessions. Significantly greater improvements in problem-solving behavior, as measured by the MICS, were found in the treated group relative to the controls, but self-report measures of marital satisfaction failed to differentiate the groups at posttreatment. Thus, changes in the rate of facilitative behavior were not accompanied by increases in marital satisfaction. Although the reciprocity of behavioral exchange was not assessed, these findings could be interpreted to mean that contingency management training, in which couples are taught to reciprocate behaviors, does not significantly enhance the perceived quality of marital relationships. Thus, marital satisfaction may depend on the contingency of behavioral exchange as well as the rate of positive and negative exchange. These conclusions are, of course, speculative and would require an assessment of the reciprocity of behavioral exchange.

Outcome studies of QPQ contracting have suffered from methodological problems of inadequate controls, almost exclusive reliance on self-report measures, and failure to assess pre- to posttreatment changes in the reciprocity of behavioral exchange. Furthermore, since most of the treatments were multifaceted, the specific effects of QPQ contracting are difficult, if not impossible, to isolate. Of the seven outcome studies reviewed, four included only self-report measures, one included self-report and behavioral measures, and one included only behavioral measures. Interestingly enough, only two of the five studies that included self-report measures found significant improvements at posttreatment; another study (which included behavioral measures) found increases in negative reciprocity. It is possible that QPQ contracting is efficacious in improving rates of targeted behavior but not in significantly enhancing the quality of the marital relationship, as evidenced by the lack of improvement on self-report measures. Whether this is because QPQ establishes greater contingencies for positive and negative behavior remains to be seen.

Good Faith. Jacobson (1977) compared a behavioral treatment that included problem-solving and contingency management (GF) components with a waiting-list control. Couples were recruited from the community and randomly assigned to one of the conditions; all the couples fell within the distressed range. The treated couples received eight 1½-hour sessions from the investigator. On MICS positive and negative behavior, as well as marital satisfaction measures, the treated couples evidenced significantly greater improvements at posttreatment than the waiting-list controls. Within-group analyses corroborated these findings. The gains were maintained at a one-year follow-up.

Liberman, Levine, Wheeler, Sanders, and Wallace (1976) compared a behavioral treatment with problem-solving communication and GF contracting components with an interactional insight treatment that emphasized empathic communication. Mean Locke-Wallace scores for the behavioral and interactional groups increased from 75 to 93 and from 65 to 92, respectively, over baseline to a 6-month follow-up; between-group differences were not statistically significant. The behavioral group improved significantly more on MICS nonverbal positive and negative measures relative to the interactional group. Thus, the couples in the behavioral treatment group improved significantly more than the couples in the interaction insight group on behavioral, but not self-report, measures.

As mentioned earlier, Stein (1978) compared a contracting treatment with MCCP and a waiting-list control. Twenty-four distressed couples were randomly assigned to the groups. On behavioral (MICS and SOC) and self-report (Locke-Wallace) measures, the couples in the contracting group improved significantly more than the couples in either the communication training or the waiting-list control groups.

O'Leary and Turkewitz (1978) reported a controlled comparative outcome study of GF contracting, communication training, and waiting-list control. The couples in the behavioral group were trained to pinpoint and implement desired behavior change via GF contracts. In contrast with other studies, this appears to be the only study that did not confound communication and contracting treatments.

Several self-report measures revealed significant improvements in both the treatment groups relative to the controls, although no differences were found between the treatment groups. Behavioral observations of problem-solving interactions coded with a system derived from the MICS and the CISS failed to reveal differences between any of the three groups at posttreatment, but the contracting group would not be expected to exhibit behavioral improvement on problem-solving tasks because problem-solving skill training was not part of the GF treatment. On the other hand, the findings indicate that the supportive skill training was not more efficacious in producing behavioral changes on problem-solving tasks than the other treatments. (The changes appeared to be specific to the treatment that was offered.) An age × treatment effect was observed, however, with younger couples benefiting more from GF contracting and older couples benefiting more from supportive communication training. Establishing explicit relationship rule control (via GF contracts) promotes greater change in newer relationships than in older relationships, where the rules are likely to be well established.

Finally, in a well-controlled comparative study of GF and QPQ contracting methods, Jacobson (1978) randomly assigned 32 couples to one of two contracting groups (GF or QPQ), a nonspecific group that was perceived to be as credible as the actual treatment groups, or a waiting list. Both contracting groups included specific training in problem solving and contracting, differing only in the method of contracting employed. Both groups, GF and QPQ, relative to the controls, improved significantly on MICS and Locke-Wallace measures. All three treated groups (including the nonspecific controls) improved significantly more than the waiting-list controls on the Stuarts's (1972) Precounseling Inventory. However, no differences between GF and QPQ groups were found on either self-report or behavioral measures. The author concluded that there appeared to be no difference between the efficacy of GF and QPQ contracting methods and further recommended that QPQ methods be employed because they are easier to implement. Yet, these conclusions are premature in the absence of comparative outcome studies of GF and QPQ contracting that control for problem-solving components (although the study does suggest that GF and QPQ contracting methods are equally efficacious when combined with a problem-solving-skill training component).

Overall, the outcome studies of GF contracting have been accompanied by more sophisticated methodology, and greater success, than the outcome studies of QPQ contracting. Of the five GF outcome studies reviewed here, four indicated significant behavioral improvements from pre- to posttreatment; the fifth (which did not include a problem-solving treatment component) evidenced no behavioral improvement. All five studies also found significant increases in marital satisfaction from pre-

to posttreatment. The studies indicate that GF contracting can be used effectively to promote behavioral and self-report change in maritally distressed couples. The cost-effectiveness of these methods must be established by future investigations.

Future Perspectives

In this section, we consider briefly three categories of the BMT enterprise by suggesting some future directions. This is as much our own crystal-ball-gazing as it is our recommendations for the field itself.

Theory

BMT is destined to give greater importance to cognitive variables than it has thus far. Based on our review of the literature, it appears that behavioral events only imperfectly influence the cognitions that spouses hold about one another. Although partners in distressed relationships often benefit from training, we cannot conclude that these skills are *necessary* for marital satisfaction. The OMSP model has postulated, in broad outline, areas of relationship accomplishment in hopes of stimulating the thinking of relationships as competency-based transactions, so that the nature of intimate transactions can be operationalized more readily. If, as we suspect, the slippage between contingencies and sentiment is great, how might we approach the problem in order to account for more variance?

Behavioral models of marital adjustment might do well to include such cognitively based concepts as "efficacy expectations" (Bandura, 1977a). The reward value of adult behavior in ongoing intimate relationships is set by the beliefs and attitudes that the members hold. Weiss (1980) has attempted to spell out ways in which restructuring techniques can be included in BMT. Spouses hold theories of their relationship very dear, theories that "explain" all sorts of partner behaviors. The performance emphasis of BMT conceptions has focused attention on *outcome expectations*, that is, teaching couples about what responses lead to what outcomes. This approach does not consider efficacy expectation, whether a couple sees itself as capable of engaging in Performance A or B. The attributional processes that spouses engage in to explain one another's successes and failures are relatively unstudied in BMT. It would be useful to know how to weight such real-world factors as actual success in problem solving with the partner and the perceived benefits derived from the relationship in order to determine a comparison level for alternatives (CLA). (CLA, it will be recalled, sets the cost–benefit ratios in a relationship, since one is supposed to tolerate a current situation, in part, given available alternative options.)

If BMT and systems conceptions integrate further, it will be necessary to view marriages within a somewhat larger context, for example, support networks (Ridley & Avery, 1979). The quality of a given transaction may well depend on nonrelationship ambience, for example, success and failure in a job and with other social contacts. Consideration of psychopathology as well would be made easier from this broader perspective.

Methodology

The difficulties encountered in using spouses as subjects are considerable. The development of dependent measures has progressed to the point where it is now possible to raise questions about the psychometric properties of many of the assessment procedures (Weiss & Margolin, 1977; Jacobson *et al.,* 1981). The quasi-self-report technology of spouse observation (e.g., SOC data) continues to suffer from problems of interspouse agreement. The definition of an appropriate temporal behavioral unit is a major problem. We clearly need a technology for collecting discrete behavioral events that also allows us to detect statistically meaningful patterning of behavior. Currently, each discrete behavioral event is given equal weight, and spouse nonagreement about such small units reduces the reliability of observation. A means of clustering behaviors is needed in order to determine functional equivalences and then to establish agreement on functionally defined classes of behavior. It seems that for research purposes, at least, the focus on discrete acts is too fine-grained.

The reliability issue can also be defined

somewhat differently by focusing on the information-processing capability of the system itself. Given the highly affective and personally relevant nature of the information obtained from couples, it might be advisable to look at the perceptual and memory-distorting processes known to exist when persons are asked to recall affective information from memory. Current spouse-observation devices (e.g., SOC) rely on aided recall, since the items are presented to the subject. But as part of a new interest in attributional processes, it would be well to look at how spouses are influenced by recency and context factors.

Therapy

The biggest single need in BMT is a much clearer understanding of how to deal with couple noncompliance. The use of contingency deposits and continual shaping are often difficult for therapists to maintain with couples, in large part because such "resistances" appear to be part and parcel of the problem itself. Finding entry points into a highly patterned set of transactions is difficult on a level of just behavioral technology. Often the couple is unaware of beneficial exchange possibilities; that is, reward devaluation and erosion have occurred broadly. It may prove useful for BMT practitioners to learn techniques for rapidly destabilizing a distressed interaction pattern in ways similar to those suggested by strategic family therapists (e.g., Andolfi, 1979; Sluzki, 1978). Suggestions along these lines have already been made by behavioral therapists (Birchler & Spinks, 1980; Weiss, 1979, 1980).

Summary and Conclusions

The purpose of this chapter has been to review the development of marital and family distress from a behavioral perspective and to organize an empirical literature review around the model of behavioral marital therapy developed at Oregon by Weiss and his associates. Although the focus throughout has been largely on marital conflict and accord, the implications for family distress are there nonetheless.

During its early developmental phases, BMT

was characterized by its reliance on specific operant techniques applied to persons in intimate relationships. Later developments have seen the introduction of more complex theoretical notions and an integration with systems theory concepts.

The OMSP model is basically a competency-based approach to adult conflict and accord. Building on the concepts of social exchange, reciprocity, and coercion, the model postulates four generic areas of relationship accomplishment: objectification, support–understanding, problem solving, and behavior change. A couple requires skills for managing their relationship within these four areas. Within the OMSP model, 12 categories of interaction are defined (e.g., sex, consideration, and parenting) providing a 4 × 12 matrix of competency type by specific category of interaction. The 48 cells provide a map for assessing marital distress and a guide for directing intervention.

The empirical literature was reviewed to establish what is known from clinical research and outcome studies about the various facets of the OMSP model. Instead of attempting to document the 48 cells—not enough has been done in the area—we have defined three targets for each of the four generic competencies: behaviors, situations, and cognitions. The question asked was, For each of the four competencies, what has been shown when behaviors, situations, or cognitions are the target of interest?

In addition to the research relevant to the competency × target matrix, we also reviewed "outcome" studies germane to each of the four competencies, even though no single intervention strategy would qualify for status as a complete intervention package. Essentially, we have dissected the elements of BMT and sought evidence of the effectiveness of each.

Implications for Marital Satisfaction

Discrete behavioral events making up the texture of daily transactions account for 25%–50% of the variance in measured daily satisfaction. The direction of causality between events and satisfaction is not yet established. Initial evidence suggests that spouses' perception of behavioral events is mediated by their overall satisfaction with the marriage. A circular causality seems the best hypothesis at this time.

Supportive skills are important to marital happiness and have been shown to have important implications for the daily satisfaction of marital partners. Although communication supportiveness on laboratory tasks does not differentiate distressed from nondistressed couples, the *impact* of spouse communication segments has present and long-range predictive validity in determining relationship satisfaction.

Through the use of a sequential analysis of conflict resolution interactions, Gottman (1979) has delineated three stages of negotiation that support the OMSP hierarchical treatment structure: (1) agenda building—distressed couples use this for complaints, whereas nondistressed couples use it for validating feelings; (2) problem exploration—both distressed and nondistressed couples disagree during this phase; and (3) contractual—distressed couples continue to propose countersolutions, whereas nondistressed couples establish contractual agreements.

Of considerable theoretical importance is the finding that the behavioral exchanges of distressed relative to nondistressed couples are more reciprocal and show a greater tendency toward negative reciprocity and more immediate positive reciprocity—a greater reactivity, in general, to immediate events.

Implications for Treatment

There is no conclusive evidence that behavioral tracking, videotape feedback, or *in vivo* modifications of denotative relationship statements (all forms of objectification training) produce significant changes in marital satisfaction or in behaviors that have ecological validity.

The majority of studies germane to support–understanding objectives contain methodological weaknesses, for example, inadequate controls. But defining *mutual* relationship goals appears to be more facilitating as far as improving couples' skills goes than does defining individual goals.

There are perhaps more techniques available for training couples in problem-solving skills than in other areas. The evaluation of the efficacy of this particular treatment module has not been separated generally from contingency contracting. The treatment (PS) seems to work, although only a limited number of researchers have studied PS treatments alone. The cost-effectiveness of the separate ingredients has not been established.

The case for behavior change contracting suggests that it is an effective procedure (perhaps especially suited to younger couples). Although Jacobson found no difference between the *quid pro quo* and the good-faith contractual formats, his treatments were confounded with PS training as well. From the available literature, it would seem that good-faith contracting has been accompanied by greater increases of marital satisfaction and behavioral changes.

Our review has noted an increased interest in cognitive applications within BMT, and we see a useful place for these. Finally, the significance of intimate relationships in general life adjustment cannot be overemphasized, and much research is needed in this complex area.

References

Andolfi, M. *Family therapy.* New York: Plenum Press, 1979.

Azrin, N., Naster, B., & Jones, R. Reciprocity counseling: A rapid learning-based procedure for marital counseling. *Behaviour Research and Therapy*, 1973, *11*, 365–382.

Bandura, A. Self-efficacy: Toward a unifying theory of behavior change. *Psychological Review*, 1977, *84*, 191–215. (a)

Bandura, A. *Social learning theory.* Englewood Cliffs, N.J.: Prentice-Hall, 1977. (b)

Barnett, L. R., & Nietzel, M. T. Relationship of instrumental and affectional behavior and self-esteem to marital satisfaction in distressed and nondistressed couples. *Journal of Consulting and Clinical Psychology*, 1979, *47*, 946–957.

Billings, A. Conflict resolution in distressed and nondistressed married couples. *Journal of Consulting and Clinical Psychology*, 1979, *47*, 368–376.

Birchler, G. R. *Differential patterns of instrumental affiliative behavior as a function of degree of marital distress and level of intimacy.* Unpublished doctoral dissertation, University of Oregon, 1972.

Birchler, G. R. *A multimethod analysis of distressed and nondistressed marital interactions: A social learning approach.* Paper presented at the Western Psychological Association Meetings, Seattle, April 1977.

Birchler, G. R. *Perceptual biases of distressed and nondistressed marital partners concerning conflict resolution.* Paper presented at the Western Psychological Association Convention, San Diego, April 1979.

Birchler, G. R., & Spinks, S. H. Behavioral-systems marital and family therapy: Integration and clinical application. *American Journal of Family Therapy*, 1980, *8*, 6–28.

Birchler, G. R., & Webb, L. J. Discriminating interaction behaviors in happy and unhappy marriages. *Journal of Consulting and Clinical Psychology*, 1977, *45*, 494–495.

Birchler, G. R., Weiss, R. L., & Vincent, J. P. A multimethod analysis of social reinforcement exchange between maritally distressed and nondistressed spouse and stranger dyads. *Journal of Personality and Social Psychology*, 1975, *31*, 349–360.

Blechman, E. A., & Olson, D. H. L. Family contract game: Description and effectiveness. In D. H. L. Olson (Ed.), *Treating relationships.* Lake Mills, Iowa: Graphic Publishing, 1976.

Bloom, B. L., Asher, S. J., & White, S. W. Marital disruption as a stressor: A review and analysis. *Psychological Bulletin*, 1978, *85*, 867–894.

Cadogan, D. A. Marital group therapy in the treatment of alcoholism. *Quarterly Journal of Studies on Alcohol*, 1973, *34*, 1187–1194.

Carter, R. D., & Thomas, E. J. A case application of a signaling system (SAM) to the assessment and modification of selected problems of marital communication. *Behavior Therapy*, 1973, *4*, 629–645.

Christensen, A., & King, C. *Marital arguments, sexual intercourse and happiness ratings.* Paper presented at the Annual Meeting of the American Psychological Association, New York, September 1979.

Christensen, A., & Nies, D. C. The spouse observation checklist: Empirical analysis and critique. *The American Journal of Family Therapy*, 1980, *8*, 69–79.

Cohen, R. S., & Christensen, A. Further examination of demand characteristics in marital interaction. *Journal of Consulting and Clinical Psychology*, 1980, *48*, 121–123.

Dayringer, R. Fair-fight for change: A therapeutic use of aggressiveness in couples counseling. *Journal of Marriage and Family Counseling*, 1976, *2*, 115–130.

Doherty, W. J., & Ryder, R. G. Locus of control, interpersonal trust and assertive behavior among newlyweds. *Journal of Personality and Social Psychology*, 1979, *37*, 2212–2220.

Ely, A. L., Guerney, B. G., & Stover, L. Efficacy of the training phase of conjugal therapy. *Psychotherapy: Theory, Research and Practice*, 1973, *10*, 210–217.

Epstein, N. Assertiveness training in marital treatment. In G. P. Sholevar (Ed.), *Marriage is a family affair: A textbook of marriage and marital therapy.* New York: Spectrum, 1980.

Epstein, N., & Jackson, E. An outcome study of short-term communication training with married couples. *Journal of Consulting and Clinical Psychology*, 1978, *46*, 207–212.

Epstein, N., DeGiovanni, I. S., & Jayne-Lazarus, C. Assertion training for couples. *Journal of Behavior Therapy and Experimental Psychiatry*, 1978, *9*, 149–155.

Epstein, N., Finnegan, D., & Bythell, D. Irrational beliefs and perceptions of marital conflict. *Journal of Consulting and Clinical Psychology*, 1979, *47*, 608–610.

Flowers, J. V. A simulation game to systematically improve relationship communication. *Journal of Marriage and Family Counseling*, 1978, *4*, 51–57.

Geer, S. E., & D'Zurilla, T. J. A review of marital behavioral therapy. *Journal of Marriage and Family Counselling*, 1975, *1*, 299–316.

Goldiamond, I. Self-control procedures in personal behavior problems. *Psychological Reports*, 1965, *17*, 851–868.

Goldstein, J. K., & Francis, B. *Behavior modification of husbands by wives.* Paper presented at the National Council on Family Relations Annual Meeting, Washington, October 1969.

Gottman, J. M. *Marital interaction: Experimental investigations.* New York: Academic Press, 1979.

Gottman, J., Notarius, C., Gonso, J., & Markman, H. *A couple's guide to communication.* Champaign, Ill.: Research Press, 1976.

Gottman, J., Notarius, C., Markman, H., Bank, S., & Yoppi, B. Behavior exchange theory and marital decision making. *Journal of Personality and Social Psychology*, 1976, *34*, 14–23.

Gottman, J., Markman, H., & Notarius, C. The topography of marital conflict: A sequential analysis of verbal and nonverbal behavior. *Journal of Marriage and the Family*, 1977, *39*, 461–477.

Guerney, B. *Relationship enhancement.* San Francisco: Jossey-Bass, 1977.

Gurman, A. S. Contemporary marital therapies: A critique and comparative analysis of psychoanalytic behavioral and systems theory approaches. In T. J. Paolino, Jr., & B. S. McCrady (Eds.), *Marriage and marital therapy.* New York: Brunner/Mazel, 1978.

Gurman, A. S., & Kniskern, D. P. Enriching research on marital enrichment programs. *Family Coordinator*, 1977, *3*, 3–11.

Gurman, A. S., & Kniskern, D. P. Behavioral marriage therapy: II. Empirical perspective. *Family Process*, 1978, *17*, 139–148. (a)

Gurman, A. S., & Kniskern, D. P. Research on marital and family therapy: Progress, perspective and prospect. In S. L. Garfield & A. E. Bergin (Eds.), *Handbook of psychotherapy and behavior change: An empirical analysis* (2nd ed.). New York: Wiley, 1978. (b)

Gurman, A. S., & Knudson, R. M. Behavioral marriage therapy: I. A psychodynamic-systems analysis and critique. *Family Process*, 1978, *17*, 121–138.

Haley, J. *Strategies of psychotherapy.* New York: Grune & Stratton, 1963.

Harrell, J., & Guerney, Jr., B. G., Training married couples in conflict negotiation skills. In D. H. L. Olson (Ed.), *Treating relationships.* Lake Mills, Iowa: Graphic Publishing, 1976.

Haynes, S. N., Follingstad, D. R., & Sullivan, J. C. Assessment of marital satisfaction and interaction. *Journal of Consulting and Clinical Psychology*, 1979, *47*, 789–791.

Hops, H., Wills, T. A., Patterson, G. R., & Weiss, R. L. *The marital interaction coding system (MICS).* Unpublished manuscript. Department of Psychology, University of Oregon, 1971.

Jackson, D. D. Family rules: Marital quid pro quo. *Archives of General Psychiatry*, 1965, *12*, 589–594.

Jacobson, N. S. Problem solving and contingency contracting in the treatment of marital discord. *Journal of Consulting and Clinical Psychology*, 1977, *45*, 92–100.

Jacobson, N. S. Specific and nonspecific factors in the effectiveness of a behavioral approach to the treatment of marital discord. *Journal of Consulting and Clinical Psychology*, 1978, *46*, 442–452.

Jacobson, N. S. Behavioral treatments of marital discord: A critical appraisal. In M. Hersen, R. M. Eisler, & P. M. Miller (Eds.), *Progress in behavior modification.* New York: Academic Press, 1979.

Jacobson, N. S., & Anderson, E. A. The effects of behavior rehearsal and feedback on the acquisition of problem-solving skills in distressed and nondistressed couples. *Behaviour Research and Therapy*, 1980, *18*, 25–36.

Jacobson, N. S., & Margolin, G. *Marital therapy: Strategies based on social learning and behavior exchange principles.* New York: Brunner/Mazel, 1979.

Jacobson, N. S., & Martin, B. Behavioral marriage therapy: Current status. *Psychological Bulletin*, 1976, *83*, 540–566.

Jacobson, N. S., & Weiss, R. L. Behavioral Marriage Therapy: III. The contents of Gurman *et al.* may be hazardous to our health. *Family Process*, 1978, *17*, 149–163.

Jacobson, N. S., Waldron, H., & Moore, D. Toward a behavioral profile of marital distress. *Journal of Consulting and Clinical Psychology*, 1980, *48*, 696–703.

Jacobson, N. S., Elwood, R., & Dallas, M. The behavioral assessment of marital dysfunction. In D. H. Barlow (Ed.), *Behavioral assessment of adult disorders.* New York: Guilford Press, 1981.

Jones, R. G. *A factored measure of Ellis' irrational belief system with personality and maladjustment correlates.* Unpublished doctoral dissertation, Texas Technological College, 1968.

Klier, J. L., & Rothberg, M. *Characteristics of conflict resolution in couples.* Paper presented at the Annual Meeting of the Association for the Advancement of Behavior Therapy, Atlanta, December 1977.

Laws, J. L. A feminist review of marital adjustment literature: The rape of the locke. *Journal of Marriage and the Family*, 1971, *33*, 483–515.

Lazarus, A. A. Behavior therapy and marriage. *Journal of the American Society of Psychosomatic Dentistry and Medicine*, 1968, *15*, 49–56.

Leary, T. F. *Interpersonal diagnosis of personality.* New York: Ronald Press, 1957.

Liberman, R. Behavioral approaches to family and couple therapy. *American Journal of Orthopsychiatry*, 1970, *40*, 106–118.

Liberman, R. P., Levine, J., Wheeler, E., Sanders, N., & Wallace, C. J. Marital therapy in groups: A comparative evaluation of behavioral and interactional formats. *Acta Psychiatrica Scandinavica*, Supplementum 266, Munksgaard, Copenhagen, 1976.

Lochman, J. E., & Allen, G. Elicited effects of approval and disapproval: An examination of parameters having implications for counseling couples in conflict. *Journal of Consulting and Clinical Psychology*, 1979, *47*, 634–636.

Margolin, G. *A sequential analysis of dyadic communication.* Paper presented at the Association for the Advancement of Behavior Therapy, Atlanta, December 1977.

Margolin, G. Conjoint marital therapy to enhance anger management and reduce spouse abuse. *American Journal of Family Therapy*, 1979, *7*, 13–23.

Margolin, G. *A comparative evaluation of therapeutic components associated with behavioral marital treatments.* Unpublished doctoral dissertation, University of Oregon, 1976.

Margolin, G., Christensen, A., & Weiss, R. L. Contracts, cognition and change: A behavioral approach to marriage therapy. *The Counselling Psychologist*, 1975, *5*, 15–26.

Margolin, G., & Wampold, B. E. Sequential analysis of conflict and accord in distressed and nondistressed marital partners. *Journal of Consulting and Clinical Psychology*, 1981, *49*, 554–567.

Margolin, G., & Weiss, R. L. Communication training and assessment: A case of behavioral marital enrichment. *Behavior Therapy*, 1978, *9*, 508–520.

Margolin, G., & Weiss, R. L. Comparative evaluation of therapeutic components associated with behavioral marital treatments. *Journal of Consulting and Clinical Psychology*, 1978, *46*, 1476–1486.

Markman, H. J. The application of a behavioral model of marriage in predicting relationship satisfaction of couples planning marriage. *Journal of Consulting and Clinical Psychology*, 1979, *47*, 743–749.

Mayadas, N. S., & Duehn, W. D. Stimulus modeling (SM) videotape for marital counseling: method and application. *Journal of Marriage and Family Counseling*, 1977, *3*, 35–42.

Miller, B. C. A multivariate developmental model of marital satisfaction. *Journal of Marriage and the Family*, 1976, *38*, 643–657.

Morton, T. L. Intimacy and reciprocity of exchange: A comparison of spouses and strangers. *Journal of Personality and Social Psychology*, 1978, *36*, 72–81.

Murstein, B. I., Cerreto, M., & MacDonald, M. G. A theory and investigation of the effect of exchange-orientation on marriage and friendship. *Journal of Marriage and the Family*, 1977, *39*, 543–548.

Nelson, R. O. Methodological issues in assessment via self-monitoring. In J. D. Cone & R. P. Jawloms (Eds.), *Behavioral Assessment: New Directions in Clinical Psychology*. New York: Brunner/Mazel, 1977.

O'Leary, K. D., & Turkewitz, H. Marital therapy from a behavioral perspective. In T. J. Paolino & B. S. McCrady (Eds.), *Marriage and marital therapy: Psychoanalytic, behavioral and systems theory perspectives*. New York: Brunner/Mazel, 1978.

O'Leary, K. D., & Turkewitz, H. A comparative outcome study of behavioral marital therapy and communication therapy. *Journal of Marital and Family Therapy*, 1981, *7*, 159–169.

Olson, D. H. Marital and family therapy: Integrative review and critique. *Journal of Marriage and the Family*, 1970, *32*, 501–538.

Olson, D. H., & Ryder, R. G. Inventory of marital conflicts: An experimental interaction procedure. *Journal of Marriage and the Family*, 1970, *32*, 443–448.

Paige, R. V. *Behavioral correlates of marital satisfaction during three stages of the marital life cycle.* Unpublished doctoral dissertation, University of Oregon, 1978.

Patterson, G. R., & Hops, H. Coercion, a game for two: Intervention techniques for marital conflict. In R. E. Ulrich & P. Mountjoy (Eds.), *The experimental analysis of social behavior*. New York: Appleton-Century-Crofts, 1972.

Patterson, G. R., & Reid, J. B. Reciprocity and coercion: Two facets of social systems. In C. Neuringer & J. Michael (Eds.), *Behavior modification in clinical psychology*. New York: Appleton-Century-Crofts, 1970.

Patterson, G. R., Ray, R. S., Shaw, D. A., & Cobb, J. A. *Manual for coding of family interactions.* ASIS/NAPS, c/o Microfiche Publications, 305 E. 46th Street, New York, N.Y. 10017.

Patterson, G. R., Hops, H., & Weiss, R. L. Interpersonal skills training for couples in early stages of conflict. *Journal of Marriage and the Family*, 1975, *37*, 295–302.

Patterson, G. R., Weiss, R. L., & Hops, H. Training of marital skills: Some problems and concepts. In H. Leitenberg (Ed.), *Handbook of behavior modification and behavior therapy*. Englewood Cliffs, N.J.: Prentice-Hall, 1976.

Peterson, D. R. Assessing interpersonal relationships by means of interaction records. *Behavioral Assessment*, 1979, *1*, 221–226.

Peterson, G. L., & Frederiksen, L. W. *Developing behavioral competencies in distressed marital couples.* Paper presented at the 10th Annual Meeting of the Association for the Advancement of Behavior Therapy, New York, December 1976.

Rappaport, A. F. Conjugal relationship enhancement program. In D. H. L. Olson (Ed.), *Treating relationships*. Lake Mills, Iowa: Graphic Publishing, 1976.

Raush, H. L., Barry, W. A., Heitel, R. K., & Swain, M. A. *Communication, conflict and marriage*. San Francisco: Jossey-Bass, 1974.

Resick, R. A., Sweet, J. J., Kieffer, D. M., Barr, P. K., & Ruby, N. L. *Perceived and actual discriminators of conflict and accord in marital communication.* Paper presented at the Annual Meeting of the Association for the Advancement of Behavior Therapy, Atlanta, December 1979.

Ridley, C. A., & Avery, A. W. Social network influence on the dyadic relationship. In R. L. Burgess & T. L. Huston (Eds.), *Social exchange in developing relationships*. New York: Academic Press, 1979.

Riskin, J. M., & Faunce, E. E. *An evaluative review of family interaction research*. Family Process, 1972, *11*, 365–455.

Roberts, P. V. *The effects on marital satisfaction of brief training in behavioral exchange negotiation mediated by differentially experienced trainers.* (Doctoral Dissertation, Fuller Theological Seminary, 1974). *Dissertation Abstracts International*, 1975, *36*, 457B.

Robinson, E. A., & Price, M. G. Pleasurable behavior in marital interaction: An observational study. *Journal of Consulting and Clinical Psychology*, 1980, *48*, 117–118.

Rosenblatt, P. C., Titus, S. L., & Cunningham, M. R. *Perfection, disrespect, tension and apartness in marriage.* Unpublished manuscript, 1977.

Rotter, J. B. Generalized expectancies for internal versus external control of reinforcement. *Psychological Monographs*, 1966, *80* (1, Whole No. 609).

Rotter, J. B. A new scale for the measurement of interpersonal trust. *Journal of Personality*, 1967, *35*, 651–655.

Royce, W. S., & Weiss, R. L. Behavioral cues in the judgment of marital satisfaction: A linear regression analysis. *Journal of Consulting and Clinical Psychology*, 1975, *43*, 816–824.

Sluzki, C. E. Marital therapy from a systems perspective. In T. J. Paolino, Jr., & B. S. McCrady (Eds.), *Marriage and marital therapy*. New York: Brunner/Mazel, 1978.

Spanier, G. B. Measuring dyadic adjustment: New scales for assessing the quality of marriage and similar dyads. *Journal of Marriage and the Family*, 1976, *38*, 15–28.

Stein, S. J. Effects of communication training and contracting on distorted marital relationships. Unpublished dissertation, University of Ottawa, Canada, 1978.

Straus, M. A. Leveling, civility, and violence in the family. *Journal of Marriage and the Family*, 1974, *36*, 13–29.

Stuart, R. B. Operant interpersonal treatment for marital discord. *Journal of Consulting and Clinical Psychology*, 1969, *33*, 675–682.

Stuart, R. B. Behavioral remedies for marital ills: A guide to the use of operant-interpersonal techniques. In A. S. Gurman & D. G. Rice (Eds.), *Couples in conflict: New directions in marital therapy*. New York: Aronson, 1975.

Thibaut, J., & Kelley, H. H. *The social psychology of groups*. New York: Wiley, 1959.

Tsoi-Hoshmand, R. Marital therapy: An integrative behavioral-learning model. *Journal of Marriage and Family Counselling*, 1976, *2*, 179–191.

Venema, H. B. *Marriage enrichment: A comparison of the behavioral exchange negotiation and communication models*. Unpublished doctoral dissertation, Fuller Theological Seminary, 1975.

Vincent, J. P., Weiss, R. L., & Birchler, G. R. Dyadic problem solving behavior as a function of marital distress and spousal vs. stranger interactions. *Behavior Therapy*, 1975, *6*, 475–487.

Vincent, J. P., Friedman, L. C., Nugent, J., & Messerly, L. Demand characteristics in observations of marital interaction. *Journal of Consulting and Clinical Psychology*, 1979, *47*, 557–566.

Vincent, J. P., Cook, N. I., & Messerly, I. A social learning analysis of couples during the second post natal month. *The American Journal of Family Therapy*, 1980, *8*, 49–68.

Volkin, J. I. *A comparison of the effects of spouse-monitoring across aware and unaware conditions*. Unpublished master's thesis, University of Pittsburgh, 1979.

Watzlawick, P., Weakland, J., & Fisch, R. *Change: Principles of problem formation and problem resolution*. New York: Norton, 1974.

Weiss, R. L. The conceptualization of marriage and marriage disorders from a behavioral perspective. In T. J. Paolino & B. S. McCrady (Eds.), *Marriage and marital therapy: Psychoanalytic, behavioral, and systems theory perspectives*. New York: Brunner/Mazel, 1978.

Weiss, R. L. Resistance in behavioral marriage therapy. *American Journal of Family Therapy*, 1979, *7*, 3–6.

Weiss, R. L. Strategic behavioral marital therapy: Toward a model for assessment and intervention. In J. P. Vincent (Ed.), *Advances in family intervention, assessment and theory*. Greenwich: JAI Press, 1980.

Weiss, R. L., & Aved, B. M. Marital satisfaction and depression as predictors of physical health status. *Journal of Consulting and Clinical Psychology*, 1978, *46*, 1379–1384.

Weiss, R. L., & Birchler, G. R. Adults with marital dysfunction. In M. Hersen & A. S. Bellack (Eds.), *Behavior therapy in the psychiatric setting*. Baltimore: Williams & Wilkins, 1978.

Weiss, R. L., & Cerreto, M. C. The marital status inventory: Development of a measure of dissolution potential. *American Journal of Family Therapy*, 1980, *8*, 80–85.

Weiss, R. L., & Issac J. *Behavior versus cognitive measures as predictors of marital satisfaction*. Paper presented at the Western Psychological Association meeting, Los Angeles, April 1976.

Weiss, R. L., & Margolin, G. Marital conflict and accord. In A. R. Ciminero, K. S. Calhoun, & H. E. Adams (Eds.), *Handbook for behavioral assessment*. New York: Wiley, 1977.

Weiss, R. L., Hops, H., & Patterson, G. R. A framework for conceptualizing marital conflict, a technology for altering it, some data for evaluating it. In F. W. Clark & L. A. Hamerlynck (Eds.), *Critical issues in research and practice: Proceedings of the Fourth Banff International Conference on Behavior Modification*. Champaign, Ill.: Research Press, 1973.

Weiss, R. L., Birchler, G. R., & Vincent, J. P. Contractual models for negotiation training in marital dyads. *Journal of Marriage and the Family*, 1974, *36*, 321–330.

Wieder, G. B., & Weiss, R. L. Generalizability theory and the coding of marital interactions. *Journal of Consulting and Clinical Psychology*, 1980, *48*, 469–477.

Wieman, R. J. *Conjugal relationship modification and reciprocal reinforcement: A comparison of treatments for marital discord*. Unpublished doctoral dissertation, Pennsylvania State University, 1973.

Williams, A. M. The quantity and quality of marital interaction related to marital satisfaction: A behavioral analysis. *Journal of Applied Behavior Analysis*, 1979, *12*, 665–678.

Wills, T. A., Weiss, R. L., & Patterson, G. R. A behavioral analysis of the determinants of marital satisfaction. *Journal of Consulting and Clinical Psychology*, 1974, *42*, 802–811.

PART V

Intervention and Behavior Change

CHILD

CHAPTER 26

Habit Disorders

Richard I. Lanyon and Robert J. Goldsworthy

Introduction

The term *habit disorders* can be traced to the writings of Knight Dunlap (1932) and his book *Habits: Their Making and Unmaking*. As an experimental psychologist, Dunlap was interested in the nature of the learning process, and he believed that a wide variety of problem behaviors developed through learning processes and could therefore be unlearned. The specific therapeutic technique that he advocated, negative practice, is nowadays of little significance; however, his work is notable because it anticipated later developments in behavior modification (Kazdin, 1978).

Dunlap's work is also of interest because he attempted to grapple with the question of whether habit disorders should be considered an integral part of a neurosis or psychosis, or whether they should be regarded as existing independently and therefore as being treatable in their own right. He resolved this question by proposing a specific definition of a habit disorder as any learned behavior that is detrimental to the individual personally and that can be successfully treated through relearning procedures. Under this rubric, he offered a colorful list of behaviors that were potentially treatable, including rudeness and insolence, pathological cleanliness, polygamous excitability, and offensive table manners! However, the disorders that were most central to his conceptual approach (and that he believed were amenable to treatment through negative practice) were stuttering, tics and related movements, thumb sucking, nail biting, and "bad sexual habits or vices."

Over the years, the term has retained some of the meaning ascribed to it by Dunlap and tends to be most commonly associated with problems that involve some unwanted or involuntary bodily movement, such as tics, stuttering, and nail biting. In the present chapter, we use the term in a somewhat broader sense, and we orient it more toward children than toward adults. We have included a number of problem behaviors that are widely viewed as amenable to treatment through behavioral procedures but that do not fit comfortably into other categories in this handbook. Thus, certain disorders of eating and elimination are included, while sexual behaviors are excluded because they are covered elsewhere. As is true of problem behaviors in general, most of the behaviors covered in this chapter can be found in the repertoire of the majority of people at some time or other. They become problems that require treatment if the frequency is suf-

Richard I. Lanyon and Robert J. Goldsworthy • Department of Psychology, Arizona State University, Tempe, Arizona 85281.

ficiently different from the age norms as to draw attention to the person, or if it is sufficiently excessive to present personal or social difficulties. For example, the lack of bladder control is called *enuresis* only in persons whose peers have achieved bladder control, and dysfluent speech tends to be termed *stuttering* only when it presents an interpersonal problem.

A major criterion for the inclusion of a topic in this chapter was that it should represent a problem that is significant to children. For several such topics, however (e.g., stuttering), the majority of the treatment literature to date has been about adults. For some of these problems, it would appear that the difficulties may be less complex in childhood than in adulthood, so that childhood may be the time of choice for treatment. For some disorders that are reviewed, such as encopresis, the possibility of a physiological basis should be taken into account in designing treatment. In such cases, we have noted this fact but have not discussed it. We have omitted several interesting but rare disorders, such as uncontrollable sneezing, hiccups, or yawning, because of the virtual absence of literature.

The topics that we have selected for review are *stuttering, enuresis, encopresis, psychogenic vomiting and rumination, thumb-sucking, nail-biting, pica, tics and Tourette's syndrome, tantrums, and compulsive hair pulling* (*trichotillomania*). The organization of the topics within the chapter is arbitrary and is not intended to reflect a particular conceptual framework. Each section of the chapter discusses definitions of the disorder; identifies previous reviews; examines the behavioral treatment literature, with an emphasis on controlled studies where available; and evaluates the current state of the field.

Stuttering

Stuttering is easily recognizable as a problem, although a precise definition is difficult to formulate. Wingate's (1964) widely cited "standard definition" includes, in part, "Disruption in the fluency of verbal expression, which is characterized by involuntary, audible or silent, repetitions or prolongations in the utterance of short speech elements. . . . The disruptions occur frequently or are marked in character and are not readily controllable" (p. 488). The onset of stuttering occurs in childhood, with essentially no onsets after age 9 (Young, 1975). Prevalence figures vary, but the average is about .7% for both children and young adults. There is a vast literature on stuttering, dating back to Hippocrates, and technical writings appeared as early as 1583 (Rieber & Wollock, 1977). Although the literature contains a wide array of etiological theories, basic research, and suggestions for treatment, the nature of the disorder is still not understood, and the treatment procedures have not been proved to be effective. In particular, while initial improvements in fluency can be produced relatively easily, the transfer and the maintenance of the changes present major obstacles. In the past 20–30 years, there has been a substantial increase in the rate of research and theorizing, and this work has been summarized in texts on stuttering by Bloodstein (1969), Van Riper (1971, 1973), and Wingate (1976), among others. In addition, the *Journal of Fluency Disorders*, initiated in 1976, is devoted entirely to the topic of stuttering.

Behavioral approaches to the treatment of stuttering have always been popular, in part because stuttering severity has long been known to diminish under a variety of specific conditions, such as reading in chorus, rhythmic speech, singing, speaking when alone, talking to animals or infants, use of masking noise, use of delayed auditory feedback, and speech shadowing. Some of these conditions have been utilized as the basis for therapeutic programs, with varied results as reviewed below. Because of the development of behavior therapy, behavioral approaches to stuttering have rapidly increased in popularity over the past 15 years and now constitute the majority of therapeutic endeavors.

The present review follows the organization used by Ingham and Andrews (1973b) in reviewing this topic: rhythmic speech, speech shadowing, delayed auditory feedback and/or prolonged speech, use of masking noise, anxiety reduction, and reinforcement-based procedures. The first four categories involve the systematic application of procedures that are

815

associated with diminished stuttering, while the last three involve mainstream behavior-therapy techniques. Two additional categories reviewed here are the use of EMG biofeedback and direct voice production. Negative practice is omitted because it has been little explored (Ingham & Andrews, 1973b) and has generated essentially no literature in the past 20 years. Because of the large volume of writings on stuttering, some selectivity in reviewing is necessary.

Rhythmic Speech

This approach is based on the consistent observation that stuttering is significantly diminished when the stutterer speaks in a rhythmic manner, such as in time to a metronome, one syllable per beat. The usual therapeutic procedure involves having subjects initially count or read simple words in time to the metronome in the therapy or laboratory setting until they are comfortable with the procedure. There is then a gradual progression through speech tasks and situations of increasing difficulty, and at some point, the subject may be given a hearing-aid-style miniaturized metronome to wear so that the pattern can be generalized into everyday speaking situations.

Meyer and Comley (1969) and Meyer and Mair (1963) reported the use of an electronic metronome with a total of 48 subjects, beginning with a laboratory training situation and progressing to more difficult situations. Of these 48 subjects, 17 failed in the initial mastery of rhythmic speech, but the results were stated to be promising for the rest of the subjects. However, adequate quantitative results and follow-up data are not available. A more systematic study was reported by Brady (1968, 1971) in which 26 subjects followed the steps outlined above. Brady systematically increased the rate of the metronome in the therapy situation and paid special attention to increasing the steps of anxiety in developing the hierarchy of situations beyond the treatment setting. Improvement was reported for 90% of the subjects, and an overall disfluency reduction of 64% was reported at follow-up. However, no subject was completely fluent.

Andrews and his associates have also reported a series of studies on rhythmic or syl-lable-timed (ST) speech. Andrews and Harris (1964) treated 30 adults in an intensive 10-day course and demonstrated marked improvement, although some relapses occurred and the rate of speech remained unnatural. Brandon and Harris (1967) treated 28 further patients and reported that two-thirds achieved reductions in stuttering of 60% or more. Holgate and Andrews (1966) treated 10 adults with a combination of ST speech and psychotherapy and reported better results, possibly because of the milder initial severity of stuttering in these subjects. None of these studies reported results in sufficient detail to permit firm conclusions. Ingham, Andrews, and Winkler (1972) used ST speech in combination with one or more procedures: group therapy, increased stuttering, and a token system. A comparison of 10 subjects who received all four treatments with 10 who received all but ST therapy showed evidence of a unique contribution of ST therapy. No follow-up was reported, however.

Öst, Götestam, and Melin (1976) compared metronome-conditioned rhythmic speech with a speech-shadowing procedure and a waiting-list control. At a 14-month follow-up, the rhythmic speech group showed a greater reduction in stuttering than the other two groups but did not show an increase in speech rate. In the only study that specifically reported using children as subjects, Greenberg (1970) had 10 stutterers pace their spontaneous speech with a metronome, while another 10 were given no instructions regarding the metronome, which operated throughout. Both groups showed equivalent reductions in stuttering, suggesting that the metronome might act therapeutically as a distraction rather than as a pacing device. Stuttering returned to baseline levels when the metronome was removed. There have been additional reports on the use of rhythmic speech, but none have presented useful evaluative data.

Interest in rhythmic speech as a therapeutic approach to stuttering reached its peak in the 1960s. While some definite changes have been reported for some subjects, their quality of speech is not ideal, and they rarely achieve complete fluency. Also, the question of the permanence of the changes has not been adequately addressed.

Speech Shadowing

Like rhythmic speech, the use of shadowing as a therapeutic procedure became popular in the 1960s but has been little reported since that time. In shadowing, the stutterer generally reads aloud from the same material as another reader, and a fraction of a second behind. Stuttering generally decreases markedly under these conditions. As with rhythmic speech, the subject is usually moved through a hierarchy of situations in order of increasing difficulty. In the earliest study, Cherry and Sayers (1956) used shadowing, both in the office and at home, with 10 subjects ranging in age from 4 to 59 years. While 7 of these subjects reportedly improved, adequate data for evaluation were not presented. Kelham and McHale (1966) treated 38 subjects, many of them children, in group settings. Success was reported for about 74%, but no reliable data or follow-up performance were reported. Kondas (1967) also used shadowing for 19 child stutterers in combination with breathing exercises and a desensitization procedure. Anecdotal data for follow-up over 3–5 years showed close to 60% reported success. Öst et al. (1976) found that shadowing reliably produced an increased reading rate but no decrease in stuttering. Improvement in several individual case studies has also been reported.

The status of speech shadowing as a therapeutic procedure must be regarded as unproven, and interest in this procedure is minimal at the present time. Possible reasons for the lack of interest include the cumbersome nature of the procedures that would be needed for bringing about the transfer of speech changes to new situations, and the difficulty in designing a shadowing procedure that involves spontaneous speech.

Delayed Auditory Feedback

Lee (1951) was the first to report that stuttering-like speech can be induced in normals by having them hear their speech approximately .2 sec after speaking rather than instantaneously. Paradoxically, stutterers' speech fluency tends to increase under such feedback, and this artificial fluency effect has been employed as the first step in a shaping procedure

to make stuttered speech more normal. Adamczyk (1959) applied it to 15 child and adult stutterers and reported considerable improvement in 13 of them, although no supporting data were provided. Goldiamond (1965, 1967) extended the procedure, initially through attempts to use the withdrawal of delayed auditory feedback (DAF) as a contingency to decrease stuttering. The resulting pattern of speech was fluent but prolonged, and this pattern was then transferred to other speaking situations. Goldiamond (1967) also reported that the DAF procedures were apparently unnecessary to the development of the prolonged speech and its transfer. Positive results were reported for 48 stuttering children and adults but were not adequately documented.

Another program making use of DAF for the instatement or shaping of fluent speech was described by Webster (1970, 1971; Webster & Lubker, 1968). Webster employed continuous rather than response-contingent DAF and instructed subjects to use a slow speech rate and smooth transitions between sounds and words. While 100 stutterers were reportedly treated, with 70% success, the data were minimal and were presented on only 16 subjects. Webster (1977) later reported a somewhat similar therapeutic procedure but without the use of DAF. Ryan (1969, 1971; Ryan & Van Kirk, 1974) also initially used DAF to establish a fluent, prolonged speech pattern and subsequently omitted the DAF but retained the prolonged speech.

A major research program involving DAF was reported by Perkins and Curlee and their associates (Curlee & Perkins, 1969, 1973; Perkins, 1973a; Perkins, Rudas, Johnson, Michael, & Curlee, 1974). In their first study, 30 stutterers each spent 90 hr in treatment, first in a DAF-based shaping procedure to develop fluent speech, and then in a stepwise transfer to a variety of everyday speaking situations. A unique and laudable feature of this project was its emphasis on the assessment of fluency in situations outside the laboratory, in both "easy" and "difficult" situations. Of these 30 subjects, 30% showed a 95% reduction in syllables stuttered six months after the termination of the therapy. In a second study, some subjects who had been through the first 90-hr program were given additional treatment lasting anywhere from 1 to 90 hr and involving two additional procedures: breath stream management and training in prosody, or the normalization of overall speech pattern. These data are discussed below under the heading of "Direct Voice Production." Although this project provided a great deal of interesting clinical information, it is not possible to ascertain exactly what aspects of the procedure resulted in the sustained fluency that was developed by some subjects. Thus, the contribution of DAF is unknown.

Early findings raised the hope that DAF would provide a simple tool for the development of fluent speech in stutterers. Extensive clinical experience, however, led to the conclusion that the type of prolonged speech produced through DAF could be just as effectively produced by simple instructions, and that whatever therapeutic utility there was for such speech did not rely specifically on DAF. Thus, the use of DAF has diminished greatly from its original popularity, gained in the mid and late 1960s.

Masking Noise

The use of masking noise as a therapeutic procedure is based on the common finding that stuttering is greatly diminished when the stutterer cannot hear his or her own voice. This technique generated a small literature in the 1960s. As in the other fluency-inducing procedures, the subjects first use an auditory masking unit in the laboratory situation and then transfer the newly acquired skill in gradual steps to everyday speaking situations. There have been a number of case reports (Derazne, 1966; Gruber, 1971; MacCulloch, Eaton, & Long, 1970; Perkins & Curlee, 1969; Trotter & Lesch, 1967), but no lasting benefits have been documented.

Anxiety Reduction

Anxiety has traditionally been regarded as a central component of stuttering (see Bloodstein, 1969), both in psychodynamic formulations of the problem and in learning-based approaches in the Hullian tradition. Consistent with the view that anxiety causes, or at least mediates, stuttering, there have been a number of reports on the use of Wolpean systematic desensitization with stutterers, some reporting significant degrees of improvement and some not (e.g., Adams, 1972; Boucheau & Jeffry, 1973; Burgraff, 1974; Lanyon, 1969; Tyre, Stephen, Maisto, & Companik, 1973; Wolpe, 1961; Yonovitz, Shepard, & Garrett, 1977). Two extensive projects have also been conducted in this area. Gray and England (1969, 1972) treated 30 stutterers with extensive systematic desensitization (23 30-min sessions at increasing intervals over a one-year period). Data based on the 15 subjects who completed the program showed that while there was significant anxiety reduction and significant reduction in stuttering, there was no correspondence between anxiety reduction and stuttering reduction. Brutten and Shoemaker (1967) advanced a two-factor theory of stuttering and its treatment, based largely on anxiety. Stuttering was seen in the first instance as a classically conditioned negative emotional response, which the stutterer learns to avoid through a variety of secondary behaviors acquired through negative reinforcement. Although these authors described the theoretical and clinical aspects of their approach in considerable detail, only anecdotal data were reported on the outcome of its application (Brutten, 1969). In another study involving the assessment of the components of stuttering, Lanyon, Goldsworthy, and Lanyon (1978) showed that stuttering behavior and anxiety were relatively independent dimensions.

While it is clear that stutterers have a substantial amount of anxiety related to speaking, the one study investigating its causal contribution suggested that it is an effect of stuttering rather than a cause. A variety of other evidence (see Bloodstein, 1975; Lanyon, 1978) supports this view, namely, that the anxiety experienced by stutterers is a realistic outcome of the problem itself rather than a causal component. Thus, the contribution of systematic desensitization would be to reduce debilitating anxiety so that other interventions can be employed. An alternative view, as yet untested, is that stuttering behavior and anxiety are both effects of a more basic problem.

Reinforcement-Based Procedures

The use of reinforcement-based procedures has steadily increased in frequency in the treatment of stuttering since their introduction by Flanagan, Goldiamond, and Azrin (1958). Since these treatment programs have become more and more complex, it is difficult to separate components of the operant procedure from the overall treatment package. There has also been a substantial basic research literature on the effects on stuttering of a wide variety of contingent and noncontingent stimuli. An early review of this literature by Siegel (1970) showed that stuttering decreases as a result of just about any contingency, no matter whether positive, aversive, or neutral. While it was initially hoped that stuttering could be cured by simple operant manipulation (and indeed there are case studies illustrating such an approach), the mainstream of research and application in this area has tended to involve more and more complex programs utilizing reinforcement procedures at a number of different levels (Ingham, 1975).

Ryan (1969) suggested the application of an overall model that has become the accepted framework for operant approaches to the treatment of stuttering: the establishment of fluency, transfer, and maintenance. The establishment is carried out by any one of a number of shaping operations, such as DAF, syllable-timed speech, or prolonged speech, as previously described. The transfer phase involves the use of this new, fluent speech in situations of gradually increasing difficulty, with specific performance criteria to be reached in each situation before the subject passes on to the next. In the maintenance phase, the stutterer's dependence on therapy is gradually decreased in favor of self-management procedures. The amount of time required by each of these stages varies widely, but in general, an overall program may take a year or even more.

Applying this approach, Ryan (1977) treated five children ranging in age from 6 to 9 using verbal and social reinforcement. Each of the three stages was designed individually for each of the subjects to provide an optimal fit with their specific patterns of difficulty. Treatment times averaged 39 hr, and follow-up observations 15–23 months from the beginning of treatment showed fluent conversational speech for all five children. Ryan and Van Kirk (1974) used a similar program with 50 adult stutterers, requiring a mean of 20 therapy sessions. The establishment phase was structured into 27 specific steps, and the transfer phase involved nine different types of speaking situations and a total of 20–60 steps. Once again, reinforcement was verbal and social. Standardized speech samples collected in the therapy setting showed highly significant improvements overall, and at the time of writing, 30 clients had completed the transfer program and were on maintenance, requiring an average of one hour of therapy over a five-month period.

The work of Perkins, Curlee, and their associates, described above, can also be viewed as an operant program. In the first study, fluency was instated in 27 subjects through DAF-based prolonged speech over 90 hr of treatment, while in the second study, involving 17 subjects over 91–184 hr, additional procedures were included to facilitate the normal management of the breathstream, phrasing, and prosody, as well as fluency. The transfer and maintenance procedures, described in detail by Perkins (1973b), were similar for both groups. Of both groups, 70% achieved an 85% reduction in stuttering during treatment, which dropped to 30% (Study I) and 53 % (Study II) at six-month follow-up.

Another major treatment project based on the operant model was carried out by Ingham and Andrews and their colleagues (Ingham, 1975; Ingham & Andrews, 1973a), who developed an inpatient token-economy system. Four groups of 10 stutterers spent 21 days in a residential setting while a DAF procedure was instituted; subjects were reinforced with tokens for changing their speech according to the DAF procedure. Tokens could be exchanged for items such as cigarettes and meals. The transfer stage required the subjects to collect 1,000-word cassette tape recordings of their speech in four situations of increasing difficulty. Nine months after the treatment, 60% of the subjects were said to be "free of stutter," although a covert assessment after 15 months showed less impressive results. A comparison of DAF with syllable-timed speech to initiate fluency showed that the DAF procedure ultimately resulted in the more acceptable speech characteristics.

Shames and Egolf (1976) presented a book-length account of their operant approach to stuttering therapy. The book gives a sophisticated clinical description of many different ways in which operant procedures (reinforcement, extinction, shaping, punishment, etc.) can be applied to different aspects of stutterers' verbal output in order to bring it closer to stable fluency. Case studies are presented for both children and adults, reporting major speech improvements in therapy-related situations. However, the lack of systematic outcome data and follow-up precludes a quantitative evaluation of the program.

In addition to the programmatic reports described above, there is a continuing research literature on the application of reinforcement contingencies to different aspects of stuttering (e.g., Hegde & Brutten, 1977; Hutchinson & Norris, 1977; Lanyon & Barocas, 1975), which continues to verify aspects of this technology. One potentially promising contingency that has received little attention is time-out. Adams and Popelka (1971) showed it to be effective in increasing fluency in eight stutterers, while Martin and Haroldson (1979) demonstrated a greater effect for time-out than for the comparable use of DAF, masking noise, the word *wrong* contingent on stuttering, and a metronome.

The use of simple reinforcement-based procedures for altering unadaptive behaviors came to stuttering from mainstream behavior modification some 20–25 years ago. While this unitary approach proved unequal to the complexities of stuttering, it did contribute significantly to the area by establishing a framework (Ryan, 1969) within which nearly all therapeutic approaches to stuttering are now conceptualized, and by contributing a wealth of technology that is now utilized in more complex attempts to bring about the many types of behavior changes that are needed in treating this disorder. Thus, while the available outcome data are not yet convincing, the behavioral treatment of stuttering has become substantially more sophisticated as a result of the introduction of operant conceptualizations and technology. Biofeedback and voice production methods, covered in the following two sections, are also reinforcement-based and can perhaps be viewed as products of this increased sophistication.

Biofeedback

The application of biofeedback to the treatment of stuttering is a new area that is achieving considerable popularity. All of the work to date has involved electromyographic (EMG) feedback, based on the general hypothesis that stuttering is in part caused by, or is critically influenced by, excessive muscle tension (e.g., Lanyon, 1978). Using auditory or visual feedback and surface electrodes placed over the masseter muscles, the chin, or the laryngeal area, several studies have demonstrated significant reductions in stuttering in individual subjects under laboratory conditions (Cross, 1977; Guitar, 1975; Hanna, Wilfling, & McNeill, 1975; Lanyon, Barrington, & Newman, 1976; Moore, 1978). Evidence in several of the studies suggested that the changes were at least in part a function of the contingent nature of the feedback, and that some transfer occurred to other situations.

Lanyon (1977) trained stutterers to make accurate discriminations of their muscle tension and further developed the procedure to the point of spontaneous speech within the therapy setting without direct feedback. Four case studies extending the method were also reported (Lanyon, 1978), involving 26–56 sessions and home practice with a portable EMG biofeedback device. Hierarchies of transfer situations were employed as described in previous sections, and follow-up at 6–18 months showed sustained improvement.

Although some promising findings exist, there are insufficient data at the present time to determine either whether EMG biofeedback is effective as a treatment focus for stuttering or whether the active component in this procedure is actually muscle relaxation. Thus, further research is needed.

Direct Voice Production

Another new group of treatment procedures for stuttering involves direct attention to the process of phonation. The impetus for these procedures has come from divergent sources; for example, the somewhat fortuitous discovery that the prolonged speech produced by DAF was therapeutically useful independently of the DAF technique, Wingate's (1976) hypothesis that certain fluency-inducing conditions for stutterers have their effect by producing changes in vocalization, and a developing research interest in the electrophysiology of the larynx.

Perkins's (1973a,b) project, as reviewed above, included 17 clients for whom the emphasis was on the control of rate to facilitate management of the breathstream, phrasing, and prosody. These subjects reportedly did better than those not receiving the additional techniques. Azrin and Nunn (1974) treated 14 stutterers with their "habit reversal procedure," of which the major aspect was the regularization of breathing and pausing, in addition to a variety of other instructions. The subjects were given a single 2-hr training session, during which they were taught speaking activities that were incompatible with stuttering, most prominently a slowed and relaxed breathing procedure. An overall success rate of 99% fluency after four months was reported, although adequate data were not given. Azrin, Nunn, and Frantz (1979) treated 21 subjects with their regulated breathing method and compared them with 17 subjects treated by abbreviated systematic desensitization. These authors reported better than a 90% reduction in stuttering compared with minimal change after desensitization, although once again the data were inadequate.

R. Webster (1971, 1977) described an intensive three-week live-in procedure, the Hollins Precision Fluency Shaping Program, in which stutterers were retrained in physically forming sounds, syllables, words, and sentences. The subjects were first taught four foundation target behaviors, the use of which produced a slow-motion form of utterance that was gradually extended to continuous speech. D. Schwartz and L. Webster (1977a,b) criticized R. Webster's reports of high success rates as being based on unreliable data, and they conducted their own outcome study of these procedures, involving a less-intensive, three-month treatment period. Of their 29 subjects, 97% reportedly improved, and the 8 subjects for whom a 45-day follow-up was available showed sustained improvement.

There have been two further reports of therapy programs of this type. M. Schwartz (1976) described a procedure based primarily on teaching the subject to maintain appropriate airflow during speech. However, no data were reported. In Weiner's (1978) procedure, termed *vocal control therapy*, a comprehensive package of techniques was used, prominent among them being the maintenance of adequate airflow as a basis for relaxed, sustained phonation; voice quality training; and desensitization of anxiety. Posttherapy data showed greatly reduced stuttering, and a follow-up questionnaire completed by some subjects showed self-reports of sustained change.

Procedures involving the shaping of breathing behavior and other aspects of voice production have become popular in the past few years and have generated enthusiastic clinical reports of success. Since these procedures have been employed, for the most part, within the context of comprehensive programs involving other techniques, the specific contribution of the voice production procedures is not known. However, the fact that a number of therapy programs have independently converged on this procedure with reported success suggests that carefully controlled research to document its effectiveness should be given a high priority. It is cautioned that the procedures are quite complex and involve techniques that are not currently within the mainstream of behavior therapy. Thus, the formal training and the supervised practice of the therapist would seem to be a necessity.

Summary

Over the past 20 years, the treatment literature on stuttering has shown two apparent trends. One is the increasing emphasis on behavioral methods of treatment. The second, and more recent, trend is toward complex rather than simple treatment models for stuttering. Both of these trends are, of course, also evident in the psychological treatment literature taken as a whole, but they are particularly evident in the treatment of stuttering. The literature gives the impression that stuttering is considerably easier to treat in children than in adults, for whom it is a disorder of considerable complexity and pervasive influence. The most successful contemporary treatment programs tend to rely on the painstaking construction of normal speech patterns, beginning with relatively simple behaviors (such as prolonged utterances, highly relaxed utterances, or constant airflow) and progressing through sounds, syllables, words, phrases, and sentences. The second stage involves the transfer of the newly acquired skills to stimulus situations that are progressively different from the therapy office or laboratory, and the third involves maintenance, or stable self-regulation. The procedures for achieving the first of these three steps are reasonably well documented, and the procedures for enhancing transfer have also received considerable attention. However, the extent of the difficulties involved in maintenance are only now beginning to receive concentrated attention (e.g., Boberg, Howie, & Woods, 1979).

The assessment of stuttering severity is much more complex than it might appear (Andrews & Ingham, 1971; Bloodstein, 1969). Although measures of stuttering frequency and speech rates tend to be relatively stable within a given stimulus situation, they vary widely and unpredictably among different situations. Also, stutterers adapt readily to the therapy environment, so that they may be fluent there but disfluent elsewhere. Further, the measurement of stuttering is reactive, in that the overt presence of recording equipment usually diminishes the problem. Yet another assessment difficulty is that relapse is common, so that it is essential to obtain follow-up data in a manner that prevents methodological difficulties. Several of the comprehensive treatment programs involving the three steps of the operant model (e.g., Ingham & Andrews, 1973a; Perkins, 1973a) have utilized assessment procedures that meet these methodological requirements and have demonstrated some successful outcomes. The task for the future will be to ascertain the most effective ingredients of these programs and to utilize them in a manner that is much more economical of therapist time.

Enuresis

Enuresis is urinary incontinence in which psychogenic factors are considered the primary causative agents, as opposed to physiological or anatomical abnormalities (Campbell, 1970; Lund, 1963). Enuresis may occur during the day (diurnal) or the night (nocturnal) and has been differentiated according to the toileting history of the child. In primary enuresis, the child has never developed nocturnal micturitional control, while in secondary enuresis, continence has at one time been established, usually for six months, but relapse has occurred (Yates, 1970).

There is disagreement in the literature as to the lower age limit at which a child may be considered enuretic, with estimates ranging from 3 to 5 years (Doleys, 1978). However, incidence data reveal that there is no age at which bed-wetting ceases in normal children (Yates, 1970). Nocturnal incontinence is found to decrease sharply between the ages of 2 and 4, gradually tapering off into adulthood (Yates, 1970). Investigations have reported that approximately 15% of all 5-year-old children exhibit nocturnal enuresis (Bloomfield & Douglas, 1956; Pierce, 1975; Young, 1969), decreasing to approximately 2% at ages 12–14 (Oppel, Harper, & Rider, 1968). Approximately twice as many males as females exhibit enuresis (Cohen, 1975). While there is an extensive literature on enuresis in children, little has been written about adults, except for retarded persons.

Physiologically, micturition is known to be quite complex, involving the coordinated sequential execution of five simple reflexes (Yates, 1970). Yates has argued that cortical control must be established over this pattern of reflexes, requiring sensitivity to internal cues, inhibition of micturition, voluntary release of urine, and transfer of daytime inhibitory control to periods of sleep. The pairing of internal cues with external situational cues is also needed to allow anticipation of the need to void. However, other authors have emphasized social and emotional factors as playing as vital a role as physiological factors in establishing nocturnal continence (Atthowe, 1973; Azrin, Sneed, & Foxx, 1973, 1974).

The literature, as reviewed below, is consistent in indicating the superiority of behavioral approaches as opposed to medical or psychotherapeutic interventions (Atthowe, 1973; Doleys, 1978; Yates, 1970). Behavioral approaches have included the use of the urine alarm and related mechanical devices, other operant approaches, and retention control training. Because of space limitations, procedures and studies involving toilet training in the context of normal development or the development of the retarded are mentioned here only briefly.

Urine Alarm

The earliest successful behavioral procedure involved the urine alarm (Mowrer & Mowrer, 1938), which consists of a multilayered pad, on which the child sleeps. The passage of urine activates an alarm that awakens the child, who then turns off the device and completes urination in the appropriate receptacle. In some instances, the child is required to change the sheets, reset the alarm, and return to bed (O'Leary & Wilson, 1975). The basic procedure has been described in detail by Lovibond (1964). Theoretically, Mowrer and Mowrer (1938) originally proposed that the mechanism of treatment involved classical conditioning, although currently it is most commonly regarded as being operant in nature (Lovibond & Coote, 1970; Turner, Young, & Rachman, 1970). Since the introduction of the urine alarm, two other devices have been proposed, one essentially similar but involving two signals (Lovibond, 1964) and the other incorporated into training pants ("buzzer pants") for daytime use with younger children (Stegat, 1966; Van Wagenen & Murdock, 1966). However, the present review focuses exclusively on the urine alarm, which has generated a substantial amount of literature on general effectiveness, procedural variations, and comparisons with pharmacological or psychotherapeutic interventions.

Two relatively recent surveys have reviewed findings in regard to the urine alarm (Doleys, 1977; Yates, 1970), involving a total of 27 studies. In terms of general effectiveness, Yates reported a mean initial success rate of 78% (range 21–100), while Doleys, utilizing stricter methodological criteria for inclusion in his review, reported a mean success rate of 75% (range 0–90). Other reviewers have reported slightly higher success rates of 80–90% (Lovibond, 1964; Lovibond & Coote, 1970; Turner, 1973). Yates's review reported relapse rates of 4%–80%, with a further relapse rate of 0%–20 in those studies utilizing additional treatment following an initial relapse. Doleys

reported an overall mean relapse rate of 41% (range 12–79), with a mean retreatment relapse rate of 32%. Relapse rates appear to vary as a function of age, with one study reporting relapse rates ranging from 5% at age 7–8 to 50% at age 9–10 (Finley, Wansley, & Blenkarn, 1977). The length of treatment in Doleys's review ranged from 5 to 12 weeks, while Yates indicated only that treatment occurred over a relatively short period.

To summarize, the literature suggests a success rate of approximately 75% and a relapse rate of approximately 40% of those successfully treated. Retreatment is effective in some cases. These findings support the use of the urine alarm, but as noted by Doleys, the high relapse rate suggests the need for refinements in the procedure. The single most common reason for treatment failure appears to be lack of parental cooperation (Collins, 1973; Forsythe & Redmond, 1970; Fraser, 1972; McConaghy, 1969; Morgan & Young, 1972; Young, 1965). Werry and Cohrssen (1965) noted that higher rates of successful treatment are associated with close supervision by the parents, which, in turn, may be affected by proper instructions and supervision by the clinician. Apparatus failures have also been noted, most notably false alarms and lack of sensitivity to small amounts of urine (Doleys, 1978). Although "buzzer ulcers" have been a problem in the past (Borrie & Fenton, 1966), Meadow (1973) has provided guidelines for the construction and operation of devices to circumvent such difficulties.

A number of minor procedural variations in using the urine alarm have been reported. In general, it has been found that continuous and intermittent schedules are equally effective, with intermittent schedules tending to result in lower relapse rates (Abelew, 1972; Finley, Besserman, Bennett, Clapp, & Finley, 1973; Finley & Wansley, 1976; Finley et al. 1977; Taylor & Turner, 1975; Turner, Young, & Rachman, 1970). Most of these investigations have used a 70% intermittent variable-ratio reinforcement schedule, with one investigation (Taylor & Turner, 1975) suggesting that the use of a 50% schedule may result in a higher relapse rate.

In another procedural variation, Young and Morgan (1972) used an overlearning procedure, involving generalization of the conditioned response (inhibition of micturition) to a number of bladder pressures and volumes. Following seven dry nights using the standard urine alarm procedures, the children were required to drink 32 ounces of liquid one hour before bedtime. These authors reported a lower relapse rate (13% vs. 35%) for subjects who completed the overlearning treatment. In a related study, Taylor and Turner (1975) compared an overlearning group with continuous and 50% variable-ratio alarm groups and found that overlearning resulted in significantly lower relapse rates. Thus, it would appear that relapse rates can be reduced through the use of either an intermittent alarm schedule or an overlearning procedure.

A number of studies have compared the effectiveness of the urine alarm with either drugs alone or drugs in combination with the urine alarm. Although a number of different drugs have been tried (see Blackwell & Currah, 1973, for a review), the most promising have been the amphetamines and the tricyclic antidepressants (imipramine). However, when drugs are used alone, the success rates are not particularly high and there are numerous relapses. Further, studies involving the use of drugs in combination with the urine alarm indicate that the addition of pharmacological agents does not produce marked improvement over the urine alarm alone. For example, Young and Turner (1965) reported accelerated conditioning using either dexamphetamine sulphate (Dexedrine) or methylamphetamine hydrochloride (Methedrine) in conjunction with the urine alarm. However, the relapse rate of the Dexedrine group was significantly higher than that of the Methedrine group, which was comparable to that of a conditioning-alone group (Turner & Young, 1966). Doleys (1978) noted that the high relapse rates may be due to either the use of drugs or the accelerated conditioning, and data presented by Lovibond (1964) suggest the latter. Kennedy and Sloop (1968) failed to replicate the accelerated conditioning effect with normals but noted accelerated conditioning with retarded subjects. In a study involving imipramine, Philpott and Flasher (1970) concluded that it was more beneficial to add the drug after beginning treatment with the urine alarm rather than before. However, this study must be viewed with caution because of inadequate data. Doleys (1977)

has listed a number of problems in using drugs, such as behavioral side effects (irritability, loss of appetite, restlessness, behavioral disruptions, and headaches), poisoning due to overdose (Parkin & Fraser, 1972), difficulty with parental compliance (Ney, 1969), and higher relapse rates.

The effectiveness of the urine alarm has been compared with psychotherapy and a combination of advice and encouragement. These studies have generally favored the urine alarm. For example, Werry and Cohrssen (1965) found that the urine alarm was superior to both six to eight sessions of psychodynamically oriented therapy and an appropriate control, with no differences between the latter two groups. Dische (1971) treated 126 children with a program of advice and encouragement consisting of self-monitoring by the child, positive reinforcement by the therapist, and instructions to the parents to deal in a matter-of-fact manner with wetting episodes, avoiding punishment. If this procedure failed, the subjects were treated with the urine alarm. Advice and encouragement resulted in a 37% success rate and one relapse at follow-up, while the subsequent urine alarm treatment resulted in a 92% success rate and 30% relapse. Similar success rates for advice and encouragement were reported by Meadow (1970) and White (1968).

To summarize, the use of the urine alarm has been shown to be a moderately successful method of treating nocturnal enuresis, having an ultimate success rate of approximately 50% when relapses and retreatments are taken into account. The use of procedural variations such as intermittent reinforcement and overlearning may improve the success rates. The success rates appear to be higher than those of verbal treatment or drugs, and it is uncertain whether combinations of procedures improve on the success of the urine alarm used alone. One such complex combination—the procedure termed *dry-bed training*, to be discussed below—does possibly provide higher success rates.

Other Operant Approaches

A number of other procedures have been employed that emphasize the role of reinforcement and punishment contingencies, either alone or in combination. Tough, Hawkins, MacArthur, and Ravensway (1971) used punishment in combination with differential reinforcement in treating nocturnal urinary incontinence in an 8-year-old multiply handicapped boy and his brother. The punishment consisted of dipping the child in a tub of cold water immediately after each wetting episode. Total continence was reached in 22 and 16 nights, respectively. One subject remained continent, whereas the other relapsed, and retreatment was unsuccessful.

Three studies have used a wakening procedure in combination with reinforcement. Samaan (1972) had parents repeatedly awaken their 7-year-old child during the night, direct her to the bathroom, and reinforce voiding in the toilet. Awakening was then discontinued and the reinforcement schedule was made increasingly intermittent. Eventually, reinforcement was given only in the morning after a dry night. The treatment was successful, and a two-year follow-up indicated no relapse. Young (1964) reported improvement in 67% of 58 subjects who were awakened once each night at varying times. Creer and Davis (1975) woke their nine subjects three times each night during the first two weeks of treatment, twice during the second two weeks, and once during the final four weeks. At a four-week follow-up, four of the nine subjects had had two or fewer enuretic episodes, with some gains persisting at a one-year follow-up.

A comprehensive treatment package employing a variety of techniques administered in phases has been introduced by Azrin et al. (1973, 1974). The program, known as *dry-bed training*, involves an initial training session in which a urine alarm is installed and all behaviors involved in appropriate toileting are rehearsed. The first night inolves a complex series of procedures, including hourly wakening, behavior rehearsal, and overcorrection if bed-wetting occurs. On subsequent nights, the child is awakened prior to the parents' bedtime at progressively earlier times in conjunction with the continued use of the urine alarm. If bed-wetting occurs, the child engages in both cleanliness training (changing the sheets and night clothes) and positive practice (behavior rehearsal). If the child remains dry throughout the night, he or she is reinforced verbally.

After seven consecutive dry nights, the last phase of the program is initiated, involving removal of the urine alarm and continuation of previous contingencies.

Azrin et al. (1974) reported complete continence for all 24 subjects in this program within a four-week period. The relapse rate is difficult to assess, however, since the procedure required the reinstitution of the urine alarm following two enuretic episodes in a single week. In their earlier study, Azrin et al. (1973) reported similar results with a retardate population. In attempting to replicate these results, Doleys, Ciminero, Tollison, Williams, and Wells (1977) reported substantial decreases in the frequency of enuresis in all of their 11 subjects, with 6 remaining continent at a six-month follow-up. Ballard and Woodroffe (1977) investigated the dry-bed program with a slight modification and reported that all 14 of their subjects were successful over a median treatment period of 12 days. A six-month follow-up revealed two relapses. An attempt to use the procedure without the urine alarm for 10 children resulted in decreased enuresis, but none of the children became completely continent.

The results of studies utilizing operant methods in establishing nocturnal urinary continence appear promising, particularly in light of the substantial relapse rates associated with the use of the urine alarm alone. The dry-bed-training program (which includes the urine alarm) appears particularly promising, as it emphasizes the natural consequences associated with soiling and the establishment of appropriate toileting behaviors. However, these conclusions are only tentative, and well-controlled, between-group studies are needed.

Although the focus of this section is on enuresis, a brief mention should be made of the work of Foxx and Azrin on normal toilet training. Foxx and Azrin (1973) developed a complex program involving reinforcement, modeling, guided performance, and symbolic rehearsal of the benefits of appropriate toileting in establishing diurnal urinary continence. Modeling was employed by having the subject observe a doll engaging in appropriate toileting activities and receiving reinforcement. The subjects were encouraged to remain dry to please the significant others in their lives, including symbolic heroes such as Santa Claus. In a sample of 34 children, accidents were reduced from a baseline level of 6 per day to a posttreatment level of .2 per day. A four-month follow-up indicated that the treatment gains had been maintained. Approximately 30% of the sample achieved and maintained nocturnal continence, although the treatment was not implemented for this purpose.

Azrin and Foxx (1974) explained their program for the lay audience in the volume *Toilet Training in Less than a Day*. In an empirical test of this program, Butler (1976) found that 77% of 49 children were successfully toilet trained by parents as a result of reading the book in combination with three lectures and consultation either in class or over the phone. Similar results were reported by Matson (1975). Matson and Ollendick (1977) found that training was more effective for mothers who were supervised than for mothers who were not supervised. Negative emotional side effects in combination with treatment failure were reported in a small number of children in both Matson reports.

Retention Control Training

Operant procedures have also been employed in an attempt to increase functional bladder capacity, usually involving the reinforcement of the retention of urine for increasingly longer periods of time. This procedure, known as *retention control training,* is based on research sugesting that enuretic children have a smaller functional bladder capacity than nonenuretics (Hallman, 1950; Muellner, 1960a,b; Starfield, 1967; Troup & Hodgson, 1971; Zaleski, Gerrard, & Shokier, 1973). The treatment literature on this topic consists mainly of case studies.

Two aspects of retention control training have been studied: whether bladder capacity actually increases as a result of training, and whether continence can be established. Studies examining the first question have generally been positive (Doleys & Wells, 1975; Harris & Purohit, 1977; Starfield & Mellits, 1968). Miller (1973), using an A-B-A-B design, reported that the frequency of both diurnal and nocturnal voiding decreased during experimental but not during control periods, sug-

gesting increased bladder capacity. However, Doleys and Ciminero (1976) reported negative results.

Studies investigating reductions in the frequency of enuretic behavior following retention control training have yielded mixed results. Kimmel and Kimmel (1970) used reinforcement to increase liquid intake and gradually to increase the retention interval in small steps up to a limit of 30 min. Successful results were reported in all three subjects, with a 12-month follow-up showing no relapses. Stedman (1972) reported similar results after 12 weeks of treatment, but some subsequent relapses. Miller (1973) achieved positive results with two subjects after 14–16 weeks without using reinforcement, and follow-ups at four and seven months showed no relapse. On the other hand, a controlled study by Harris and Purohit (1977) failed to show increased nocturnal control. In replicating the Kimmel and Kimmel (1970) investigation, Paschalis, Kimmel, and Kimmel (1972) reported that only 14 of 35 children became dry, while Starfield and Mellits (1968) reported that only 6 of 53 children became continent after a six-month program. Rocklin and Tilker (1973) also failed to achieve significant results in a controlled study comparing retention control training with time-contingent and base-rate control groups. Doleys and Wells (1975) found that continence was not established until additional procedures were employed (awakening and toileting).

Taken as a whole, the use of retention control training in eliminating nocturnal enuresis has not received strong research or clinical support. Although the issue of bladder capacity in relation to other treatment techniques has not been directly investigated, Doleys, McWhorter, Williams, and Gentry (1977) found that successful treatment using the dry-bed method did not result in increased bladder capacity. Thus, it can be said only that this procedure may be appropriate for children who exhibit frequent urination and small functional bladder capacity.

Other Urinary Problems

There is a small literature on other problems involving urination, including urinary retention, excessive frequency of urination, and the establishment of continence in persons with related medical disorders.

Psychogenic urinary retention can occur in both children and adults, although the behavioral treatment literature on adults consists only of case studies. Barnard, Flesher, and Steinbook (1966) used assertiveness training and an electric shock procedure with a 27-year-old woman who had experienced urinary retention for 12 years. Electrical stimulation applied to the legs was hypothesized to cause paradoxical rebound of the parasympathetic discharge associated with urination. The treatment lasted approximately 4 months, and an 18-month follow-up showed no relapse. LaMontagne and Marks (1973) reported success using a procedure similar to flooding in two cases in which urinary retention occurred only in toilets outside the home. The subjects refrained from urinating until the urge was strong, then stayed at the toilet until micturition occurred. The toilet environment involved a hierarchy of cues associated with increasing amounts of anxiety.

Several case studies have reported the use of behavioral techniques in treating excessive frequency of urination (pollakiuria). Conceptualizing frequent urination as a response to strong fears, Taylor (1972) reported success with a 15-year-old girl using systematic desensitization, with hierarchy items consisting of those situations associated with anxiety and an urge to urinate. Millard (1966) reported success in a case of urinary incontinence in response to giggling in a 19-year-old female by the use of a portable shocking device. In another case study, Masur (1976) used a combination of retention control training, progressive relaxation, reinforcement of incompatible behaviors, and time-out. Treatment over five months reduced self-reported frequencies of urination from 15–20 times per day to 5 times per day. A four-year follow-up showed continued success. Poole and Yates (1975) reported successful results with a 24-year-old male utilizing a variation of retention control training. At a three-year follow-up, frequency was somewhat higher than at treatment termination, but the effects were essentially maintained (Poole & Yates, 1977).

Several case studies have involved the use

of behavioral programs to develop continence in individuals with various medical disorders. Butler (1976) described the use of the Azrin *et al.* (1973, 1974) procedure with a 4-year-old boy suffering from spina bifida meningomyelocele. Substantial improvement was noted, and changes were maintained at seven-month follow-up. Epstein and McCoy (1977) used a variation of the dry pants procedure (Foxx & Azrin, 1973) in establishing bladder and bowel control in a 3-year-old female following surgery for Hirschsprung's disease. Ince, Brucker, and Alba (1976) employed a classical conditioning procedure in establishing bladder control in two adult males with spinal cord lesions. Mild electrical stimulation of the thigh was paired with a stronger electrical stimulation of the abdomen, which previously had been demonstrated to elicit voiding. After conditioning, voiding could be initiated by electrical stimulation of the thigh.

Summary

The most common method of treating enuresis has been the use of the urine alarm, and a substantial amount of research has shown a moderate degree of success for this procedure. Success rates have reportedly been increased by using the urine alarm in combination with a variety of other reinforcement-based procedures, and the work of Azrin and his co-workers has been particularly innovative in this regard. Such procedures have been demonstrated to be preferable to the use of medication, psychotherapy, and retention control training. A small literature of case studies exists on the treatment of other urinary disorders, such as urinary retention and excessive frequency of urination. While successes have been reported for the use of behavioral procedures, insufficient data exist to draw any conclusions regarding the success rates or the preferred methods.

Encopresis

Encopresis refers to a number of disturbances in the regulation of bowel evacuation (Warson, Caldwell, Warinner, Kirk, & Jensen, 1954). While there is no consensus as to the age at which a child should be considered encopretic, nearly all normal children attain bowel control by 4 years of age (Bellmon, 1966; Stein & Susser, 1967), and this criterion seems to be the most widely accepted (Doleys, 1978). The incidence of encopresis appears to be somewhere around 3% (Levine, 1975; Shirley, 1938; Yates, 1970). and the ratio of males to females is approximately 6 to 1 (Levine, 1975).

Since constipation frequently accompanies incontinence, a distinction has been made with respect to the presence of fecal retention (e.g., Johnson & Van Bourgondien, 1977; O'Leary & Wilson, 1975; Yates, 1970). Two types of encopresis have been identified that involve fecal retention: Hirschsprung's disease, which is usually correctable by surgery, and "psychogenic megacolon" (Garrard & Richmond, 1952; Richmond, Eddy, & Garrard, 1954). Apart from Hirschsprung's disease, a number of other physical factors may be associated with encopresis, including an imperforate anus, spinal canal defects, or spinal cord inflammation due to injury or disease (O'Leary & Wilson, 1975). Physical complications may also be associated with psychogenic megacolon, since fecal buildup in the rectum may lead to habituation to rectal sensations and subsequent impaction. Because of the likelihood of physical factors, a physical examination is necessary prior to the initiation of treatment.

A discrimination has also been made between "continuous" encopresis, in which the child has never established bowel control, and "discontinuous" encopresis, in which control had been established at one time (Anthony, 1957). It has been speculated that continuous encopresis is associated with a lack of or laxness of toilet training, while the discontinuous type is associated with overly rigid and coercive toilet training (Anthony, 1957). Gavanski (1971) has differentiated encopretics as retentive (the child refuses to void in the appropriate receptacle because of anger or fear); nonretentive (appropriate toileting behavior was never learned); or falling into a mixed category, including constipation with leakage, irritable colon, incontinence due to distraction, or staining of clothing without soiling. However, the literature has not established the utility of these various classifications.

Although encopresis has not been as thoroughly studied as enuresis, there is a body of literature on behavioral approaches to its treatment, mostly case studies and mostly operant in nature. This work can be categorized into procedures involving positive contingencies, negative contingencies, or both of these factors in combination with other treatment techniques. Except for the studies of Azrin and Foxx, which are included here because of their seminal nature, work with retarded populations is not covered in this chapter. Bowel training in the context of normal childhood development is also excluded.

A number of case studies have reported positive results using positive reinforcement for defecation in the appropriate receptacle with no specific consequences for soiling. Neale (1963) treated four child inpatients by taking them to the toilet after each meal and at bedtime until defecation occurred, to a maximum of five minutes. Next, the subjects were required to self-initiate toileting behavior when necessary. The contingencies were repeatedly explained verbally, and reinforcement consisted of pennies, stars, candy, and peanuts given in association with praise. Laxatives were also used in two cases. Three subjects became continent with two to three months.

Bach and Moylan (1975) and Keehn (1965) also reported success using positive reinforcement for appropriate defecation. Young (1973) included laxatives and frequent potting of the child and reported success in 22 of 24 subjects, with follow-ups of 6–60 months indicating four relapses. Two studies (Balsom, 1973; Conger, 1970) reported success using differential parental attention. Successful outcomes were also reported in two studies in which reinforcement was contingent on fecal continence rather than on appropriate defecation (Ayllon, Simon, & Wildman, 1975; Pedrini & Pedrini, 1971). However, this procedure fails to teach appropriate toileting behaviors and may result in bowel retention (Doleys, 1978).

Two studies utilized punishment as the primary treatment procedure. Freinden and Van Handel (1970) successfully employed an aversive contingency over five months in which the child cleaned both himself and his clothes with cold water and strong soap following soiling. Edelman (1971) used a 30-min time-out period as the aversive contingency over 10 weeks and reported a decrease in soiling behavior from 6.3 to 3.7 times per week. When a negative reinforcer was added (avoidance of dishwashing), the mean further decreased to .93 times per week.

A number of studies have successfully used programs involving both positive reinforcement and punishment. In a case study by Barrett (1969), the reinforcement consisted of cookies and praise for appropriate defecation, while the punishment consisted of restraint to a chair for 30–40 min following incontinent behavior. Bowel retention developed but was treated with suppositories. Gelber and Meyer (1965) reported similar success with a 13-year-old inpatient using time off the ward as reinforcement and loss of time off the ward as punishment. Nilsson (1976) used a similar program, with the addition of an enema after soiling. Plachetta (1976) used reinforcement for both going to the toilet and defecating, in combination with having the child wash out his clothes if soiling occurred. Ashkenazi (1975) used potting following eating, positive reinforcement for appropriate elimination and nonsoiling, and suppositories if defecation did not occur. Within two months, 16 of the 18 subjects were successfully treated, with no relapses at a six-month follow-up.

Several investigators have developed comprehensive treatment programs. Wright (1973, 1975) and Wright and Walker (1976) employed positive reinforcement, mild punishment, potting, and cathartics. Reinforcement was contingent on appropriate defecation and continence for 24-hr periods, while soiling was followed by punishment in the form of extra chores or loss of privileges. Toileting behavior was shaped by attempting to induce defecation on arising, either through reinforcement or the use of cathartics (which were progressively withdrawn). Using this set of procedures, Wright (1973) reported success with all but one subject in a sample of approximately 36. In the later study, Wright (1975) successfully established continence in all 14 of his subjects, with a treatment duration ranging from 10 to 38 weeks. A six-month follow-up indicated one relapse. Christofferson and Rainey (1976) also used a comprehensive approach involving positive reinforcement, glycerin suppositories and

enemas, pants checks with appropriate consequences, and aversive contingencies consisting of the child's cleaning himself and washing out his soiled clothing. Laxatives were used only in the morning when necessary, ensuring a daily bowel movement to be reinforced. Continence was maintained in all three subjects at follow-up periods ranging from 2 to 10 months.

Azrin and Foxx (1971) and Foxx and Azrin (1973) developed a comprehensive program for bowel training in retarded children, consisting of reinforcement, full cleanliness training, and positive practice. Full cleanliness training involved having the child clean both his clothes and himself following a soiling incident. In positive practice, the child was required to engage in the entire chain of behaviors involved in appropriate toileting (Foxx & Azrin, 1973). A high degree of success was reported by these authors, and other investigators have also reported the successful use of programs based on their work. Doleys and Arnold (1975) and Doleys et al. (1977) utilized a procedure whereby pants were checked on a regular schedule, initially hourly and then with decreasing frequency. During pants checks, the child was praised for clean pants, placed on the toilet, urged to defecate, and reinforced for attempting to defecate. Accidents were followed by verbal displeasure from the parents, 40 min of clothes scrubbing, and a 10-minute bath in cool or cold water. Fecal incontinence was successfully treated in four subjects over 9–15 weeks with only one relapse. Butler (1975) successfully used a similar procedure with the addition of positive practice following each soiling incident. Freeman and Pribble (1974) also reported successful results in treating an institutionalized autistic child.

In a case involving physical factors, Kohlenberg (1973) used a biofeedback procedure in eliminating encopresis in a 13-year-old male with Hirschsprung's disease. Based on the hypothesis that the child's sphincter tone was inadequate, a device was constructed to allow the subject to monitor sphincter contractions visually. Sphincter contraction on a bulb placed in the rectum caused colored water to rise in an attached tube in view of the subject. The treatment was conducted in 15 one-hour sessions, in which the therapist checked the fluid level every 10 sec. Levels above an established criterion resulted in monetary reinforcement. Sphincter control was established, and a reduction in the frequency of soiling was reported.

Summary

Because of the likelihood that physical factors might be involved in encopresis, a physical examination is necessary before deciding to embark on behavioral or any other treatment procedures. The behavioral treatment literature consists mainly of case reports employing operant methodologies. Successful results have been reported in cases using positive reinforcement for appropriate defecation or punishment for soiling. Comprehensive programs employing both kinds of contingencies plus the judicious use of laxatives have been reported as leading to high success rates. As with enuresis, the comprehensive program designed by Azrin and Foxx is noteworthy. Overall, the literature, while not extensive, gives the impression that behavioral treatment procedures for functionally based encopresis are relatively successful. Little has been published on the behavioral treatment of encopresis where a definite physical problem is involved.

Vomiting and Rumination

Psychogenic vomiting, involving the regular regurgitation of food under conditions that appear to preclude physical causes, is a disorder of both children and adults. Ruminative vomiting, which is also assumed to be psychogenic in nature, is a disorder of infancy characterized by the regurgitation, chewing, and reswallowing of food (Richmond, Eddy, & Green, 1958). This behavior can have serious consequences, such as malnutrition, dehydration, weight loss, and lowered resistance to disease (Sajwaj, Libet, & Agras, 1974), and in some cases, it has resulted in death (Gaddini & Gaddini, 1959; Kanner, 1957). Behavioral formulations of vomiting and ruminative vomiting are supported by early studies demonstrating that vomiting can be conditioned (Collins &

Tatum, 1925; Kleitman & Crisler, 1927; Pavlov, 1927). Toister, Condron, Worley, and Arthur (1975) have speculated that early in a child's history of vomiting behavior, adults have inadvertently reinforced it with attention until it becomes sufficiently severe to warrant medical intervention. In their own study, these authors noted that hospital staff tended to minimize social contact with the child, and to limit attention to times of cleaning, such as after vomiting.

The nonbehavioral literature on ruminative vomiting has usually conceptualized this disorder as being due to a disturbed mother–child relationship (Richmond et al., 1958), and treatment has been directed toward the remediation of emotional impoverishment, primarily involving very high levels of attention, with an adult spending up to eight hours a day interacting with the child and engaging in behaviors such as holding, smiling, talking, and playing. A number of anecdotal case studies have reported both weight gains and reductions in ruminative behavior (Fullerton, 1963; Gaddini & Gaddini, 1959; Hollowell & Gardner, 1965; Menking, Wagnitz, Burton, Coddington, & Sotos, 1969; Richmond et al., 1958; Stein, Rausen, & Blau, 1959). Reported treatment periods have ranged from four to eight weeks.

The behavioral treatment literature also consists of case studies, some involving experimental control procedures. Because the treatment procedures tend to be similar for vomiting with and without rumination, both disorders are discussed together here.

The most commonly reported procedures have involved aversive contingencies. Shock has been employed with both infant and retarded populations, although its use has generally been limited to situations in which other treatments have failed, with some cases reporting the possibility of death. Shock is made contingent either on emesis itself (e.g., Toister et al., 1975; Wright & Thalassinos, 1973) or various muscle contractions that precede emesis (e.g., Lang & Melamed, 1969; Kohlenberg, 1970; White & Taylor, 1967).

A number of studies have used aversive contingencies with infants. Lang and Melamed (1969) used brief shock administered to the calf of a 9-month-old infant whose life was endangered by persistent vomiting and chronic rumination. Assessment was accomplished with an EMG recording device to detect reverse peristalsis. The behavior was diminished following the second treatment session, and complete cessation of vomiting was reported during the sixth treatment period. Some spontaneous recovery occurred, but it was eliminated by additional treatment sessions, and a one-month follow-up showed no further relapse. Using a similar procedure, Toister *et al.* (1975) reported the elimination of vomiting in 11 treatment sessions for a 7-month-old infant. Once again, some slight recurrence of vomiting following treatment was eliminated by further sessions. Cunningham and Linscheid (1976) reported the use of shock with a 9-month-old boy following the failure of numerous other techniques, including withdrawal of attention. Generalization training was provided by administering contingencies in a variety of settings, including situations in which the child was alone. A rapid decrease in frequency was noted on the first day of treatment, with a temporary increase in vomiting whenever the settings were changed.

Distasteful food substances have also been employed as aversive contingencies. Sajwaj *et al.* (1974) used lemon juice, which was squirted into the mouth of an infant for either regurgitation or behaviors preceding regurgitation. This contingency resulted in a reduction in vomiting frequency, while its removal initially brought about a return to baseline frequencies. The treatment spanned eight weeks, with a six-week follow-up showing two additional vomiting episodes, which were also consequated with lemon juice. Murray, Keele, and McCarver (1977) used the aversive contingency of placing the infant in its crib and putting Tabasco brand pepper sauce on the tongue. Vomiting frequency quickly diminished, and a four-month follow-up indicated no relapse. Bright and Whaley (1968) reported substantial reductions in but not the complete elimination of regurgitation and vomiting using Tabasco sauce. Shock subsequently eliminated both behaviors within three additional days.

Shock has also been commonly employed in work with mentally retarded children and adults. Luckey, Watson, and Musick (1968)

monitored a 6-year-old severely mentally retarded male over 12-hr time periods, administering shock contingent on vomiting behavior via a belt containing a radio-controlled shocking device. By the fifth day of treatment, the mean frequency of vomiting had decreased from 10.6 to less than 1 incident per day, with no significant recurrence in a 93-day follow-up period. Both White and Taylor (1967) and Kohlenberg (1970) reported marked reductions or elimination of vomiting behavior in severely retarded adolescents and one adult when shock was made contingent on cues preceding actual emesis. Watkins (1972) reported greatly reduced frequencies of vomiting following seven weeks of treatment in a 14-year-old male, with a three-month follow-up indicating no relapse.

Two investigations have reported the use of overcorrection as a mildly aversive procedure. Azrin and Wesolowski (1975) used overcorrection and positive practice with a 36-year-old profoundly retarded woman who was unresponsive to both a 30-min time-out contingency and relaxation training. The overcorrection consisted of cleaning up the vomit, while the positive practice involved engaging in behaviors that were appropriate for handling urges to vomit. Vomiting was eliminated following one week of treatment, and a one-year follow-up showed no relapse. Duker and Seys (1977) reported similar results with a 19-year-old profoundly retarded female using a more aversive overcorrection procedure, requiring the subject also to clean walls, windowsills, and part of the floor. Numerous reversals indicated that the reduction in the number of vomiting responses was a function of the treatment procedure.

Another aversive technique has been the use of induced vomiting, employed by Spergel (1975) in the case of a 10-year-old boy with organic and psychotic pathology. Five trials were held during a single session, in which a nurse digitally induced vomiting in the presence of the ward staff. A seven-month follow-up revealed no recurrence. Ingersoll and Curry (1977) reported a program consisting of social, monetary, or activity reinforcers contingent on retaining food, in combination with a time-out contingency for vomiting. Vomiting immediately ceased following the administration of the time-out contingency, with no recurrence at a one-year follow-up.

Case studies with nonretarded children and adults have generally reported the use of procedures other than aversion. Burgess (1969) reported a case in which an 18-year-old female would vomit on mornings following a date the previous evening. The treatment consisted of a procedure that is perhaps best conceptualized as desensitization. The subject was instructed to date on a daily basis, and the length of the dates was initially set at one hour and gradually increased. A one-year follow-up revealed only two vomiting episodes. Mogan and O'Brien (1972) used small sips of ginger ale administered every 15 min to inhibit vomiting responses in a 60-year-old woman whose vomiting behavior appeared following an acute myocardial infarction. Ginger ale was used because it produces a behavior involving forward peristaltic activity, which is incompatible with vomiting. The subject was also concomitantly treated for depression. The vomiting ceased after the first treatment day, and a five-month follow-up showed no relapse.

Two studies have examined the effectiveness of an extinction procedure. Wolf, Birnbrauer, Williams, and Lawler (1965) reported a successful outcome with a 9-year-old girl in a classroom setting by having the teacher ignore the behavior and continue the class. Similarly, Alford, Blanchard, and Buckley (1972) reported that the withdrawal of attention and social contact had a very strong effect on "hysterical" vomiting in a 17-year-old female. Vomiting episodes, which occurred before treatment at the rate of one very five minutes or less, disappeared following treatment. Some accidental reversals of the contingency reportedly reinstituted the response.

Saunders (1976) described the use of in vivo and imaginal systematic desensitization in the case of a 13-year-old boy whose vomiting appeared to be related to traveling or thoughts of traveling in cars or buses. The hierarchy items consisted of scenes related to traveling and experiencing the symptoms of motion sickness. Vomiting ceased completely quite early in the treatment sequence, and a 19-month follow-up indicated no relapse. Desen-

sitization has also been employed successfully in treating vomiting due to anxiety concerning dating situations (D'Zurilla, 1969) and athletic competition (Katahn, 1967).

Summary

A literature consisting entirely of case studies has reported considerable success in the treatment of psychogenic vomiting by behavioral procedures. A number of aversive contingencies have been reported to be effective. Shock has been used primarily with infant and retarded populations, while the use of distasteful substances has been used with infants. Other studies have described the use of induced vomiting and time-out in combination with reinforcement, while overcorrection has been reported to be effective with retarded adults. With normal children and adults, the procedures have tended not to involve aversion but have employed extinction and desensitization techniques. Many of the case studies have reported changes in behaviors other than the specified target behavior of emesis. Nearly every study has noted weight gains either during or subsequent to treatment, and studies involving infants and young children have tended to report increases in social behaviors, suggesting that the effects of behavioral interventions generalize beyond the target behavior alone.

Thumb-Sucking

Thumb-sucking is a relatively common behavior. Traisman and Traisman (1958) have reported an incidence of 46% in a child population from birth to 16 years of age. Thumb-sucking is considered socially undesirable (Knight & McKenzie, 1974; Ross & Levine, 1972) and is often associated with dental problems (Haryett, Hansen, Davidson, & Sandilands, 1967; Longstreth, 1968; Norton & Gellin, 1968). Estimates of the incidence of dental malocclusions among thumb-suckers range from 10% to 30%, as compared with a normal base rate of 7%–9% (Murray & Anderson, 1969; Traisman & Traisman, 1958).

A large variety of treatments have been prescribed, including cementing a stainless steel spurred bar to the upper molars (Haryett, Hansen, & Davidson, 1970), sucking natural-shaped bottle-feeding nipples (Picard, 1959), sucking from the breast or the bottle (Spock, 1968), wearing special mittens to constrain movements (Benjamin, 1967), and applying bitter-tasting chemicals to the thumb (Watson, 1969). Remedies have also been advanced for the related problem of weaning from pacifiers, such as gradually shortening the nipple (McReynolds, 1972). Obviously, this procedure would be difficult to adapt to thumb-sucking. A number of behavioral procedures have been applied to thumb-sucking, including differential reinforcement, overcorrection procedures, and a modified time-out procedure in which positive reinforcement is withdrawn contingent on thumb-sucking. The literature consists essentially of case studies, some of which have employed adequate single-case experimental designs.

Several studies have successfully used the withdrawal of reinforcement. In a well-known controlled study, Baer (1962) made the presentation of cartoons contingent on non-thumb-sucking behavior. With one 5-year-old male, contingent presentation was alternated with uninterrupted presentation, while with two additional boys, a similar procedure was followed in which one was yoked to the other. In all cases, thumb-sucking decreased when cartoon presentation was contingent on non-thumb-sucking and remained at baseline levels when the contingency was not in effect. Bishop and Stumphauzer (1973) used a similar approach with four children aged 3–5, but these authors varied whether or not the subjects received verbal information concerning the contingency. The contingent withdrawal of reinforcement resulted in a cessation of thumb-sucking, with greater generalization tending to occur for the informed subjects. Using a similar procedure, in which the parents administered treatment, Shirbroun (1973) reported clear generalization in three of six children. Ross (1975) also employed the parents as change agents and reported a reduced rate of thumb-sucking using a 5-min time-out from TV watching plus the use of a bitter substance.

A number of studies have used differential reinforcement. Knight and McKenzie (1974)

trained parents to make reading contingent on non-thumb-sucking behavior and reported success with three girls aged 3, 6, and 8, with numerous reversals verifying the effects of the contingencies. An anecdotal four-year follow-up indicated that the treatment gains had been maintained. However, the results were confounded by the fact that the mothers had also been instructed to use attention as a differential reinforcement for non-thumb-sucking behavior. Successful results using contingent reading were also reported by Kauffman and Scranton (1974).

Several studies have used differential reinforcement in classroom settings. In a study by Ross and Levine (1972), it was planned that all members of the class would receive a reinforcer (candy) if thumb-sucking by the 9-year-old male subject remained below a certain frequency. Institution of the contingency resulted in an immediate cessation of thumb-sucking behavior, while the removal of the contingency resulted in reinstatement of the behavior. Ross (1974b) reported the case of a 10-year-old male who was reinforced for gradually increasing periods of time without thumb-sucking, starting at 30 min. His classmates were reinforced for catching the subject in thumb-sucking behavior. Once again, the frequency decreased when the contingency was in effect but gradually reverted to baseline levels during follow-up. Skiba, Pettigrew, and Alden (1971) used the teacher's attention contingent on the incompatible behaviors of writing and hand folding to eliminate thumb-sucking behavior in three 8-year-old children. Reversal of the contingencies indicated that the thumb-sucking response was under stimulus control. Similar results in a kindergarten child were reported by Meacham and Wiesen (1969).

Two studies have described the use of differential reinforcement in other settings. Repp, Deitz, and Deitz (1976) reported reductions in thumb-sucking frequency in a 4-year-old mildly retarded female, who was reinforced with M&M's for each 1-min interval in which thumb-sucking did not occur. No generalization or follow-up data were reported. Kauffman and Scranton (1974) found similar results with a 2-year-old girl, with differential reinforcement facilitating generalization to other settings, in contrast to contingent reading, which did not. Differential reinforcement consisted of praise and a star to be placed on a star chart during a reading period.

Two investigations used overcorrection in combination with differential reinforcement. Freeman, Moss, Somerset, and Ritvo (1977) reported the complete elimination of thumb-sucking in a 2-year-old autistic child using an overcorrection procedure, which consisted of holding the child's hands by his side for 30 sec contingent on the thumb-sucking response. Suppression generalized to the ward, even though overcorrection was never applied in that setting, and a 14-month follow-up indicated that the treatment gains had been maintained. Doke and Epstein (1975) described three experiments in which overcorrection was successfully used with two 4-year-olds in a day-care program. Previous treatment, including time-out and differential reinforcement alone, had been found to be ineffective. The overcorrection consisted of brushing the child's teeth briskly for 2-min with an oral antiseptic (undiluted Listerine). Maintenance and generalization of the change were achieved by the use of verbal threats (e.g., that thumb-sucking would be followed by overcorrection).

Summary

A number of controlled case studies have reported success using behavioral procedures to reduce the frequency of thumb-sucking. The withdrawal of positive reinforcement has shown some degree of success, with maintenance requiring the use of verbal mediation. Differential reinforcement appears to be the most widely reported procedure and has shown successful results, as has the use of overcorrection. Although the literature has not dealt adequately with the questions of maintenance and generalization, some studies have offered ideas on how they may be achieved. The possibilities include using the mother as a discriminative stimulus or using verbal warnings or threats as mediators.

Nail-Biting

Nail-biting is a relatively common behavior in both children and adults, although the ma-

jority of the literature tends to involve adolescents and adults rather than children. There are very few data concerning prevalence; in a college student population, Coleman and McCalley (1948) reported a prevalence of 27%. Behavioral approaches to treatment have included self-monitoring, positive and negative contingencies, covert sensitization, habit reversal, and relaxation.

Two controlled investigations have used self-monitoring (SM) as a basic treatment ingredient in combination with other procedures. Dependent measures have involved SM of either actual biting or putting the fingers to the mouth, along with laboratory measures of nail length. McNamara (1973) compared SM of an incompatible response (finger tapping), finger tapping alone, SM of nail-biting, SM of resistance responses to nail-biting, SM of nail-biting with no effort to stop, and a no-treatment control. All groups, including the controls, displayed significantly longer nails. Harris and McReynolds (1977) investigated the effects of meaningful and nonmeaningful self-instructions that were either contingent or noncontingent on nailbiting. SM was used with all groups except the no-treatment control. All the treatments were superior to no treatment, and the contingent groups showed greater nail length at follow up. In a case study, Horan, Hoffman, and Macri (1974) reported successful results utilizing a combination of SM, self-punishment, and self-reinforcement.

A number of case studies have examined the use of aversive contingencies. Using contingent negative practice, Smith (1957) reported that 21 of 57 nail-biting subjects were "cured." Bucher (1968) reported success with 13 of 20 subjects using a portable shock device that was activated when a finger was placed either in the mouth or on the lips. Many relapses were noted, however. Smith (1978) reported some degree of success using the snap of a rubber band as a punisher. Ross (1974a) successfully used the contingency of financial contribution to a highly disliked organization for failure to increase nail length, while Stephen and Koenig (1970) reported that the return of a cash deposit on a variety of schedules did not influence gain in nail length.

Two controlled studies have examined the use of contingencies. Vargas and Adesso

(1976) compared an attention-placebo control procedure with two aversive contingencies (shock and negative practice) and with the continuous use of a bitter substance. In addition, half of each group engaged in SM. Nail growth increased in all groups but was greater for SM subjects. In a similar study comparing control groups with positive contingencies, negative contingencies, and a combination of the two, Davidson (1977) reported success for all treatment groups in comparison with a waiting-list control group. The four-month follow-up favored the groups utilizing positive contingencies. In a study investigating the role of awareness in reducing nail-biting, Adesso, Vargas, and Siddall (1979) compared SM plus positive contingencies, SM plus negative contingencies, nail measuring alone, and a minimal contact control. A four-month follow-up showed approximately equal gains for all groups. Thus, measurement alone produced as much change as any other procedure.

The use of covert sensitization has also been reported, involving images of extremely aversive events that are systematically paired with images of nail-biting. Two case studies (Daniels, 1974; Paquin, 1977) reported success after one and seven sessions respectively, including home practice, with continued abstinence at a 6- to 9-month follow-up. In a controlled study, Davidson and Denney (1976) compared a covert sensitization group with an information-control group, a combined covert sensitization and information group, and a waiting-list control group. Only the information group achieved longer nails as compared with the waiting-list control group, suggesting that the changes were due to nonspecific treatment factors.

Azrin and Nunn (1973) employed their treatment package, known as *habit reversal*, with four nail-biters, who were instructed to engage in fist or object clenching in response to either temptation or actual nail-biting. Awareness training, motivation training, and generalization training were also included. Nail-biting reportedly disappeared for all subjects after one session, and a subsequent relapse was successfully re-treated (Nunn & Azrin, 1976). Delparto, Alch, Bambausch, and Barclay (1977) also reported success using habit reversal with three subjects. In a somewhat similar procedure, Barrios (1977) conceptualized nail-biting as a response to anxiety and taught two subjects to substitute cue-controlled relaxation. A three-month follow-up indicated that the treatment gains had been maintained.

Summary

A variety of behavioral treatment techniques have been successfully employed to counteract nail-biting. However, controlled studies have shown that attention-placebo or other control procedures, such as self-monitoring with no specific effort to stop, are frequently as successful as specific treatment techniques. Results from a number of sources suggest that the most potent treatment factor may well be simple attention to the behavior. The literature also indicates that nail-biting behavior is often not eliminated completely, leading to the suggestion that multiple techniques should be considered.

Pica

Pica is the persistent ingestion of nonnutritive substances, including trash (Ausman, Ball, & Alexander, 1974), cloth, cigarette butts, and paper (Foxx & Martin, 1974); it is primarily a disorder of children, particularly retarded children. When the nonnutritive substance is feces, the problem is called *coprophagia*. The problem is most frequently observed in institutions for the retarded (Albin, 1977) and may have direct adverse consequences, such as blockages (Ausman *et al.*, 1974) and intestinal parasites (Foxx & Martin, 1975). It has also been associated with lead poisoning, which in turn has been related to anemia, failure to thrive, mental retardation, and encephalitis (Moncrieff, Koumides, Clayton, Patrick, Renwick, & Roberts, 1964).

Three studies have investigated the use of behavioral techniques in eliminating pica. Ausman *et al.* (1974) reported a case of a 14-year-old severely retarded boy whose scavenging behavior resulted in numerous intestinal blockages requiring surgery. Pica was assessed by "baiting" the environment with his favorite nonharmful, nondigestible objects, such as string, gum wrappers, and syringe needle covers. The treatment consisted of 15-

min time-out periods in which the subject was required to wear a special helmet that prevented him from placing objects in his mouth. Differential reinforcement of other behavior was also employed, and generalization was deliberately programmed. A nine-month follow-up showed a high degree of control over the problem behavior.

Foxx and Martin (1975) employed overcorrection procedures with four profoundly retarded subjects who were suffering from whipworms because of the ingestion of feces. Overcorrection was applied whenever there was any evidence of pica, and it involved spitting out the objects; brushing the teeth and gums; and washing the mouth, hands, and fingernails—and also the anal area, in the case of coprophagia. In addition, the subjects were required to disinfect the area where the trash had been eaten. The entire procedure required approximately 20 min, and a high degree of success was reported within only four days. A number of coincident positive behavioral changes were also reported, including vocalization and social smiling. The use of controlled single-case designs with two subjects showed overcorrection to be more effective than physical restraint.

Bucher, Reykdal, and Albin (1976) used 30-sec periods of contingent physical restraint to control pica in two 6-year-old profoundly retarded children. Pica was measured by means of objects deliberately placed on the floor. The behavior was suppressed when contingencies were applied, and complete elimination was reported when restraint followed the earliest detectable behavior in the sequence.

Summary

The successful treatment of individual cases of pica and coprophagia has been reported through the use of overcorrection, physical restraint, and time-out plus differential reinforcement. Because of the very small number of the uncontrolled nature of the studies, however, conclusions must be highly speculative. Bucher *et al.* (1976) noted that the generalization of the treatment is both difficult and time-consuming, while Albin (1977) noted that the practice of "baiting" the subject's environment for the purpose of quantitative as-

sessment artificially inflates the frequency of pica behavior and may lead to overly favorable conclusions about the ease of treating the problem. The lack of long-term follow-up data exacerbates this concern.

Tics and Tourette's Syndrome

Meige and Feindel (1907) have provided an often-cited illustrative definition of a tic, as follows:

A tic is a coordinated purposive act, provoked in the first instance by some external cause or by an idea; repetition leads to its becoming habitual, and finally to its involuntary reproduction without cause and for no purpose, at the same time as its form, intensity, and frequency are exaggerated; it thus assumes the character of a convulsive movement, inopportune and excessive; its execution is often preceded by an irresistible impulse, its suppression associated with malaise. The effect of distraction or of volitional effort is to diminish its activity; in sleep it disappears. It occurs in predisposed individuals who usually show other indications of mental instability.

A somewhat more precise definition has been provided by Storrow (1969), who defined a tic as "an intermittent but recurring muscle spasm limited to a single muscle group" (p. 174), which tends to occur concomitantly with feelings of anxiety and tension. In addition, tics may occur without awareness.

According to Yates (1970), ticklike behaviors can be associated with both organic and functional conditions. Organic conditions include "spasms, choreas, and cerebellar and cerebello-rubrospinal tremor" (p. 321), and appropriate medical intervention can often eliminate the tic. Yates has offered a summary of the differences between psychogenic and organically based tics along 14 dimensions. However, the implications for treatment are unclear, since behavioral interventions may be possible and even preferable in such cases (e.g., Barrett, 1962). Theories of the psychogenic etiology and maintenance of tics include the model advanced by Yates (1970) based on Hullian drive-reduction theory and Mowrer's (1950) two-factor learning theory. Such theories have received indirect support from the animal learning literature and from observations of humans, although they have not been unequivocally supported by treatment data.

There are two additional syndromes whose primary manifestations involve compulsive ticlike movements: spasmodic torticollis and Gilles de la Tourette's syndrome. Spasmodic torticollis involves the jerking of the head due to a contraction of the muscles of the neck, which may be either spasmodic or constant (Hersen & Eisler, 1973). Since torticollis appears to be basically a disorder of adults, it is not reviewed in this chapter. Tourette's syndrome, first described by Gilles de la Tourette (1885), is a more complex syndrome consisting of widespread tics, coprolalia, echolalia, and echokinesis (Yates, 1970). Tics associated with this syndrome generally involve the musculature of the face, the neck, and the extremities.

Tics

The literature on the behavioral treatment of tics consists entirely of individual case studies. A number of behavioral procedures have been employed, including massed practice, habit reversal, prolonged exposure, contingency-based techniques, and combinations of these approaches. Massed practice has been the most popular approach, in part because of Dunlap (1932) and later its conceptualization directly within Hullian learning theory. For example, in Yates's (1970) view, massed practice results in the development of reactive inhibition (fatigue), which ultimately compels the person to "rest." The subsequent dissipation of reactive inhibition is said to constitute a reinforcing state of affairs for the elimination of the tic.

Studies using massed practice have shown only partial support for this approach. Yates (1958) worked with a 25-year-old female psychiatric patient who exhibited a stomach-contraction breathing tic, a nasal tic, a coughing tic, and a bilateral eyeblink tic (blepharospasm). His "standard procedure" consisted of five 1-min practice periods separated by 1-min rest periods, performed twice each day. Subsequent variations showed that the greatest decrease in tic frequency was accomplished through prolonged massed-practice sessions (four 1-hr periods followed by rest periods of 3 weeks). Jones (1960) later worked on a stomach tic in the same subject. All tics

were reduced in frequency but were exacerbated by illness or social and vocational frustrations.

In other work using massed practice alone, Ernst (1960) utilized 19 five-minute sessions plus homework with an inspiratory tic in a 13-year-old girl and reported complete elimination. Nicassio, Liberman, Patterson, and Ramirez (1972) reported success over a 33-day period in a 22-year-old male suffering from a clonic neck jerk. Six 10-min practice sessions per day were employed for a total of 16 hr of massed practice. An 18-month follow-up indicated no relapse. Lazarus (1960) reported success after one month using Yates's (1958) "standard procedure" with each of three tics in an 18-year-old male. However, the same procedure was reportedly unsuccessful in dealing with a foot-tapping tic (Rafi, 1962). Nicassio et al. (1972) reported only moderate improvement in using massed practice over extended sessions to treat a 33-year-old male suffering from multiple clonic and tonic tics. A completely unsuccessful outcome was reported by Feldman and Werry (1966) in attempting to treat multiple head tics in a 13-year-old boy. In this case, treatment exacerbated the tics.

A number of studies have utilized massed practice in combination with other procedures. Walton (1961) used antianxiety medication plus massed practice with an 11-year-old boy who exhibited a number of rather severe tics, sufficient in intensity to shake a car or a bed. After 29 sessions, his ability to voluntarily reproduce the major tic was markedly reduced, and an 18-month follow-up revealed only "one slight facial tic." Rafi (1962) used relaxation training plus 25 two-hour massed-practice sessions in successfully diminishing a tic consisting of facial grimacing and convulsive head movements. Walton (1964) used massed practice in combination with the drug amylobarbitone in reducing a hiccup tic, a nasal expiration tic, and a head-shaking tic over 109 sessions. In treating an eye-blink tic in a 20-year-old male, Knepler and Sewall (1974) paired 80 min of massed practice with the use of aromatic ammonia in order to increase the aversiveness of the massed-practice procedure. Almost complete remission was reported at a six-month follow-up. Frederick

(1971) reported the complete elimination of an eyeblink tic using systematic desensitization followed by massed practice on a variety of schedules. The hierarchy items consisted of anxiety-arousing topics that were noted as intensifing eyeblinking. A nine-month follow-up showed no recurrence.

One study employed a simple anxiety-reduction procedure. LaMontagne (1978) used flooding in the treatment of a socially aversive, piglike grunting tic in a 30-year-old woman. The tic was pronounced in social situations, particularly when meeting new people or when there was a lull in the conversation. For flooding, the therapist and four students sat and stared at the patient for increasingly longer periods of time. The frequency of grunting diminished from more than five to less than one per minute, and the change was maintained after six months.

Operant procedures have also been used in the treatment of tics. In a single-case experimental study of a 30-year-old male with multiple tics that had not been amenable to pharmacological intervention, Barrett (1962) designed a special chair to monitor tic behavior and compared self-control instructions with the effects of contingent and noncontingent music or with noise. Noncontingent noise had no effect, while the other three treatments reduced tic frequency. No attempts at maintenance were reported. Schulman (1974) treated a 14-year-old boy who exhibited tics only in the presence of his mother, with tic intensity increasing during times of conflict. The mother was instructed to ignore the tics, and the result was two tic free days by the end of the fifth week of treatment. A two-month follow-up revealed that the mother was again attending to the tics, which had returned to a midtreatment level. Rafi (1962) reported the successful treatment of a foot-tapping tic in a subject who had been unresponsive to massed practice. The subject placed her foot on a special treadle so that the tapping activated a buzzer, which she was instructed to try to avoid. A significant decrease in frequency was reported after 70 one-hour sessions.

Two further studies employed combinations of treatment procedures. Azrin and Nunn (1973) used their treatment package of habit reversal in three subjects who experienced a variety of tics, including shoulder jerking, elbow flapping, head jerking, and head shaking. The habit reversal consisted of engaging in a response that was opposite to the movement of the tics (e.g., head jerking was replaced by neck tensing). Also included were self-monitoring, numerous techniques for increasing awareness, and generalization training. The virtual or complete elimination of all tics was reported in only two treatment sessions. Clark (1963) treated a 30-year-old woman with numerous difficulties, including sexual adjustment problems, agoraphobia, and a hysterical jaw spasm. The latter two difficulties appeared to be related and were treated with relaxation in conjunction with counterconditioning and *in vivo* procedures. A general improvement was reported, but no follow-up was conducted.

Gilles de la Tourette's Syndrome

According to Clark (1966), Tourette's syndrome is "characterized by an interesting developmental pattern of symptoms beginning in the so-called latency period of childhood with a variety of muscular tics, often appearing first in the face, head, or shoulders and progressing to the arms and eventually legs. Gradually and insidiously there begins to occur a kind of thoracic spasm which expels air with a grunting sound, and after a time, often about puberty, the grunt imperceptibly becomes less an animal noise and more clearly a significant word, usually an obscenity or swearword but often also a coprolalic neologism" (p. 771).

The etiology of Tourette's syndrome is unknown. Some investigators have documented organic abnormalities (e.g., Balthazar, 1957; Feild, Corbin, Goldstein, & Klass, 1966), while others have not (e.g., Corbett, Mathews, Connell, & Shapiro, 1969; Morphew & Sim, 1969). A number of functional theories have also been proposed (Ascher, 1948; Mahler, 1944, 1949; Morphew & Sim, 1969). Use of the drug haloperidol has been widely investigated, with mixed results ranging from almost immediate relief to lack of a discernible effect (Abuzzahab, 1970; Challas & Brauer, 1963; Connell, Corbett, Horne, & Mathews, 1967; Ford & Gottlieb, 1969; Healy, 1970; Lucas, 1967; Shapiro & Shapiro, 1968; Stevens &

Blachly, 1966). Behavioral approaches to the treatment of Tourette's have shown some promise and have involved massed practice, anxiety reduction, and operant procedures.

The only study to use massed practice alone was unsuccessful. In attempting to eliminate coprolalia (obscenity), Hollandsworth and Bausinger (1978) reported not only a marked increase in frequency but also improved articulation from a disguised bark to an unmistakable four-letter word. A number of massed-practice schedules were tried; in one session, a total of 4,395 responses were emitted with only a slight decrease in frequency. Social contingencies were hypothesized to be maintaining the behavior.

Three studies have used massed practice plus other procedures. Sand and Carlson (1973) reported that massed practice, contingency management, and self-monitoring all reduced the frequency of tics to some degree, with massed practice producing the greatest change. The drug haloperidol brought about a further marked reduction. Clark (1966), working with three adult subjects with whom pharmacological approaches had been ineffective, used massed practice of the obscene verbalization (coprolalia) until it was reduced to less than one emission per minute. A metronome and shock were also employed. In two 30-min practice sessions daily, coprolalia was successfully eliminated for two of the patients in 25 and 49 sessions. A four-year follow-up indicated continued success. Tophoff (1973) treated a 13-year-old male using massed practice, *in vivo* relaxation, assertiveness training, and extinction by the parents. A total of 14 massed-practice sessions were administered at a rate of 2 per week, and a four-month follow-up showed continued success.

Contingency-based approaches have also been employed. Stevens and Blachly (1966) reported limited success using contingent shock in a 13-year-old female who displayed violent jerks of the head, neck, and shoulders. Finger shocks contingent on muscle jerks successfully eliminated the tics, but removal of the shock resulted in a return to baseline levels. The subject also developed a new tic during treatment. The subsequent use of haloperidol reduced the frequency of the tics.

Doleys and Kurtz (1974) used a token re-inforcement system to increase the frequency of tic-free time intervals and socially appropriate behaviors (eye contact, conversation) in a 14-year-old boy. Generalization outside the treatment setting was also reinforced, and new behaviors were added, resulting in marked improvements both within and outside the treatment sessions. Of interest, control over behavior in natural settings was more easily obtained when the new behaviors were first introduced in the treatment setting. Miller (1970) successfully reduced "barking" frequency in a 5-year-old boy by administering a candy reinforcer for 1-min intervals of bark-free behavior. Since the parents were found to be inadvertently reinforcing certain behaviors, they were taught reinforcement techniques that subsequently reduced the behavior at home. Transfer to the school setting was also arranged, and the treatment gains were maintained at an 18-month follow-up.

Several studies have combined contingency-based approaches with other procedures. Rosen and Wegner (1973) reported success with a child through a procedure in which 30-sec time intervals without vocal or gross motor responses resulted in a signal (light) that indicated that a backup reinforcement had been earned. The treatment effects were augmented by the use of a relaxation training. In an effort to transfer the treatment gains to a classroom setting, the entire class was reinforced for nontic behavior by the subject. Tic behavior quickly diminished but returned to baseline levels during periods of nonreinforcement. This problem was alleviated through infrequent monitoring periods, which were not announced to the subject, although generalization to new settings was not found.

A final study (Thomas, Abrams, & Johnson, 1971) employed self-monitoring and reciprocal inhibition procedures for the tics of an 18-year-old male. Stimulus conditions associated with increased and decreased frequency of tics were identified through observations in numerous settings, both within and outside the therapy setting. Self-monitoring markedly and immediately reduced vocal tics. A newly emerged vocal tic and a neck tic were subsequently reduced in frequency through a combination of massed practice and self-monitoring. Haloperidol was also taken prior to and throughout most of the treatment period, however.

Summary

The behavioral literature on the treatment of tics, while perhaps more promising than that for other treatment methods, shows mixed results, and the virtual absence of controlled investigations dictates further caution in drawing conclusions. Although massed practice has often been employed, its exclusive use has usually not led to successful outcomes. However, cases that have employed massed practice in combination with other interventions have reported more positive results. The same conclusions apply to Tourette's syndrome, with the additional comment that the concurrent (and sometimes exclusive) use of drugs has often resulted in successful outcomes. In general, individual patients have responded to quite a wide variety of different behavior interventions, and most case studies reporting success have employed more than one type of intervention. Again, questions of generalization and maintenance have not been adequately addressed.

Tantrums

Tantrum behavior has received relatively little attention in the behavioral literature, and as yet has not been clearly defined. A common hypothesis is that tantrums are maintained by the consequences that they usually evoke (O'Leary & Wilson, 1975), and a limited number of studies have reported successful results by changing the contingencies that follow the behavior. Treatment has primarily involved the use of extinction and various aversive contingencies.

Three studies have used extinction to reduce tantrum behavior. In an early investigation, Williams (1959) described the case of a 21-month-old infant who, because of illness, had received a great deal of attention during his first 18 months of life. He had tantrums at bedtime, which usually resulted in the parents' waiting in the child's room until he fell asleep. For treatment, the parents simply left the room and closed the door as soon as the child was put to bed. The length of the tantrums rapidly decreased from 45 min on the first night to 0 min by the seventh. The behavior recurred when a different caretaker put the child to bed, but again, it extinguished over a second week. Kakkar (1972) presented similar results using a similar treatment paradigm designed to reduce tantrums in a 2-year-old girl on being taken to school.

Extinction has also been used with autistic children. Davison (1965) reported the successful use of extinction plus verbal explanations with a 9-year-old autistic boy. Martin, England, Kaprowy, Kilgour, and Pilek (1968) employed a combination of extinction and differential reinforcement of quiet behavior in a classroom setting, and they reported a low frequency of tantrums after nine sessions.

The most commonly used aversive contingency has been time-out. Wolf, Risley, and Mees (1964) treated a 3-year-old autistic boy who exhibited a variety of behavioral problems including tantrums, and whose overall verbal and behavioral functioning was at a very low level. The treatment consisted of time-out contingent on tantrum behavior until the tantrum ceased. The more severe aspects (e.g., head banging, hair pulling, and face scratching) were eliminated after two months, and the tantrums were markedly reduced after four months. A number of uncontrolled factors were present in this work, however. In a case study involving a 6-year-old boy, Wetzel, Baker, Roney, and Martin (1966) gave an initial warning, followed by social isolation until the tantrum had ceased for 3 min. Tantrums were reduced to near 0 frequency within 1 month. Similar results were reported by Jensen and Womack (1967) and by Schell and Adams (1968), who also included the use of extinction. However, Solnick, Rincover, and Peterson (1977) found that time-out increased tantrums in a 6-year-old autistic girl. This result appeared to be due in large part to high frequencies of self-stimulation during time-out. In a second study involving spitting and self-injurious behavior in a retarded adolescent, these authors reported that the effectiveness of time-out was in fact dependent on the reinforcing qualities of the time-in environment.

In the only controlled group study, Ames

(1977) used normal children aged 2–6 to compare time-out, time-out with contingent social isolation, time-out with differential reinforcement, differential reinforcement alone, and a waiting-list control. All treatment groups improved significantly on 7 of the 10 dependent variables. However, except for the time-out with differential reinforcement, groups differed from the waiting-list control only on the tantrum frequency measure. A nine-month follow-up showed stable improvement on 6 of the 7 measures.

Successful results utilizing time-out procedures have prompted some further developments in this technique. Harris, Hershfield, Kaffashan, and Romanczyk (1974) developed a folding, relatively portable time-out room consisting of a three-panel screen sold by Sears department store. This room has the advantage of limiting the child's space to such an extent that opportunities for self-stimulation are restricted, although the constant presence of an adult is required to hold the "door" closed. Murray (1976) described three modified time-out procedures for controlling tantrum behaviors in public places, including placing the child in a corner or a restroom, taking him or her to the car and waiting outside, or throwing a small coat or blanket over his or her head. Time-out is used until the child ceases exhibiting tantrum behavior, and a further short time period of quiet (3–5 min) might also be required before continuing normal activities.

In a study employing an aversive contingency, Conway and Bucher (1974) followed each tantrum of a profoundly retarded female by squirting shaving cream into her mouth, and they reported a marked reduction from 10–12 per day to 1–2 per week. The change was maintained at six-month follow-up. Carlson, Arnold, Becker, and Madsen (1968) used both punishment and positive reinforcement in controlling the tantrum behavior of an 8-year-old girl in a classroom setting. The punishment involved holding the girl in her chair, while reinforcement consisted of a class party contingent on four continuous halfdays without a tantrum. Attention from peers was minimized by placing the girl's chair in the back of the room and reinforcing classmates for not turning around when tantrum behavior occurred. A marked reduction in tantrum frequency was reported. In a final study, Martin and Iagulli (1974) eliminated middle-of-the-night tantrums in a blind retarded girl by extending her bedtime from 8:00 P.M. to 12:00 midnight and subsequently returning it to 8:00 P.M.

Summary

A limited number of investigations, all but one at the case study level, have suggested that behavioral procedures can be effective in reducing or eliminating tantrums. To date, behavioral research has focused mainly on the use of time-out, but it has also involved other aversive consequences, extinction, and positive reinforcement for tantrum-free behavior. It is somewhat surprising that only 3 of the 12 studies reviewed involved normal children as opposed to autistic or retarded children, particularly as tantrums are common in normal children at an early age, and there is a definite potential for inadvertent reinforcement of this behavior by parents. The literature in this area also highlights the highly speculative nature of conclusions from case studies, since the one controlled investigation found effects attributable to treatment on only 1 of 10 dependent measures.

Trichotillomania

Trichotillomania is the name given to the rare behavior of compulsively pulling out the hair, usually to the extent of creating bald areas on the head. The behavioral treatment literature consists entirely of case studies, which is not surprising in view of the rarity of the disorder. Although there is no evidence that the disorder is primarily one of childhood, the cases reported have involved children more frequently than adults. Reported treatment techniques have included self-monitoring, contingency management, covert sensitization, relaxation, and aversive conditioning.

Two cases have involved self-monitoring. Anthony (1978) treated a 9-year-old boy in a single session by self-monitoring in combination with social reinforcement for data collection, plus the wearing of a baseball cap. Hair pulling ceased after 6 days, while hair-pulling impulses ceased after 16 days. A six-month follow-up showed that success had been maintained. In treating a 22-year-old female who pulled out single hairs, Bayer (1972) used a combination of self-monitoring plus the mildly aversive procedure of submitting all the pulled hairs to the therapist. Frequency declined from a mean of 20.6 hairs pulled during baseline to 0 at 16 days.

Four studies have successfully employed contingency management, with follow-up periods ranging up to seven months. One involved positive reinforcement alone: Stabler and Warren (1974) reported an immediate reduction in hair pulling in a 14-year-old female through a behavioral contract. Backup reinforcers were also available on a weekly basis in the form of interaction with the therapist and refreshments during the therapy hour. The other three studies have involved aversive contingencies plus either positive contingencies or an instruction for adaptive behavior. MacNeil and Thomas (1976) instructed a 21-year-old woman to do 15 sit-ups whenever she pulled hair or attempted to pull hair, and also to substitute hair grooming for hair pulling. Follow-up showed the virtual elimination of both hair pulling and urges to pull hair. In treating an 8-year-old girl, Evans (1976) used 5-min time-out periods coupled with a token program (stars exchangeable for pennies) for time periods free of hair pulling. McLaughlin and Nay (1975) reported the use of coverants, involving a pleasant scene, and response costs in treating a 17-year-old female. After four weeks of treatment, the response costs were increased from merely recording the hair-pulling incident to also going to a mirror and examining the scalp. The total treatment time was 18 weeks. A related problem of eyelash plucking was only moderately affected by the above procedures.

Several other behavioral procedures have also been successful. Wolff (1977) reported the case of a 6-year-old boy whose head was shaved by a ward attendant prior to intervention by a psychologist. A one-year follow-up showed a full head of hair. Levine (1976) used five treatment sessions of covert sensitization with a 26-year-old male who had a 17-year history of hair pulling. A six-month follow-up indicated no relapse. Horne (1977) reported two cases in which a variety of techniques were employed. Of specific interest is that in one case, after a number of unsuccessful interventions, electric shock administered to the hands while the subject watched a videotape of herself hair pulling resulted in complete elimination of the behavior. However, some hair pulling continued to occur during periods of stress.

Summary

The literature on trichotillomania consists entirely of case studies, and no single procedure appears to be preferable over any other. There is a very wide range in the ease of successful treatment and in the likelihood of relapse. A number of authors have informally noted that decreases in hair-pulling frequency following treatment have been maintained by natural social reinforcers in the environment, particularly in the case of children. Comments have also been made on anecdotal self-reports of feeling "in control" following treatment. These observations suggest that individuals may often be unaware of their behavior because of the lack of immediate aversive consequences. Thus, the effectiveness of various behavioral techniques, including self-monitoring alone, could be due in part to the nonspecific therapeutic effects of focused attention and an increased awareness of engaging in an undesired behavior.

Comments

The general topic of research methods in behavioral treatment is addressed in detail in other sections of this handbook. However, some comments are in order regarding the specific disorders addressed in the present chapter. First, with the exception of the research on stuttering and enuresis, there is relatively little well-controlled outcome research. Since some of the disorders are quite rare, the research strategy of choice would in most cases be the single-case experimental design. Second, it would appear that the emphasis on simple operant conceptualizations that was predominant in the early literature may have tended to interfere with the willingness of re-searchers to apply other principles that are now commonplace in behavior therapy. For example, relatively little attention has been paid to stimulus factors, that is, the identifi-cation of cues that might be triggering the un-adaptive behavior and the teaching of alter-native, adaptive responses to these cues.

Two further points of concern with the lit-erature have to do with the process of report-ing rather than the studies themselves. First, the publication process tends to lead to a sit-uation in which the only case studies that are published are the successful ones. Thus, a lit-erature made up largely of case studies may give a seriously inflated view of treatment suc-cess rates. This difficulty underscores the im-portance of group studies, which, at a mini-mum, report the overall success rates of using a particular treatment method. The second point concerns the ambiguity in much of the literature about exactly what treatment was offered. Authors frequently describe their be-havioral intervention in structured terms but mention only incidentally that, for example, other family members were involved in the treatment process, or that drugs were also used, or that the patient was concurrently in group psychotherapy. Thus, the specific con-tribution of the behavioral intervention is often in doubt. Clearly, a high priority should be given to more adequate research designs, and creative solutions should be sought to the task of controlling for the contribution of other on-going factors that could influence the outcome of treatment.

In regard to the problem behaviors them-selves, what can be said about the current sta-tus of behavioral treatment for habit disorders and needs for future research? First, it should be clearly stated that no highly successful treatment procedure has yet been discovered for any of these disorders. On the other hand, it is also obvious that behavioral treatment is in many instances successful, as shown by fol-low-up data. The development of these suc-cessful treatment strategies has tended to be a trial-and-error process, however, and etiol-ogical theories have played a negligible role.

It is instructive to consider the two disorders on which the greatest amount of research has been done: stuttering and enuresis. For both

disorders, the early emphasis on applying some particular behavioral technique in iso-lation has now given way to a more sophisti-cated strategy: the construction of compre-hensive treatment packages that are based on a careful analysis of the disorder and that are applied as systematic and stepwise retraining programs with specific performance criteria to be met at each step before proceeding to the next. This is, of course, the same strategy that is evolving in the behavioral treatment of many other disorders, such as depression, sexual dysfunctions, and obesity. It requires the ex-istence of a substantial research base regard-ing the behavioral treatment of the disorder, and its appearance in the literature on a par-ticular disorder can perhaps be regarded as signifying the "coming of age" of the appli-cation of behavior therapy to that disorder.

The disorders reviewed in this chapter differ widely in complexity. Some, such as nail-bit-ing, appear to be simple enough so that the optimal treatment approach might indeed turn out to be based on a single technique, such as self-monitoring, perhaps with the addition of a simple contingency. One task for research clinicians of the future is to become more sen-sitive to the differing degrees of complexity of different disorders and to gear their research efforts accordingly. Mistakes are commonly made in judging complexity: for example, the mediocre state of the outcome data on the treatment of tics would seem to suggest that this is a rather more complex problem than has previously been recognized. The com-plexity question also appears to be applicable in comparing different instances of the same disorder. For example, one particular case of compulsive hair-pulling might involve many more problem behaviors or controlling varia-bles than another. The determination of the complexity of a disorder or an individual case is a topic that needs to be addressed in future research.

What advice can currently be offered to the individual behavioral clinician? With disorders such as stuttering or enuresis, it would seem that optimal success involves the application of a complex treatment package, and also that a considerable amount of supervised training is required in order to learn and utilize the package. Thus, individual clinicians should be cautious about taking on such cases without adequate training, unless there is clearly no available alternative. With disorders that are in general less complex, the empirical findings suggest approaches that are potentially fruitful. And frustrating though it may be, the clinician must recognize that for reasons not adequately formulated, what works with one patient might not work with the next. Thus, we again call for more research, not only to improve treatment success rates, but to gain a more adequate conceptual understanding of why a particular strategy is to be preferred in one instance but not in another.

References

Abelew, P. H. Intermittent schedules of reinforcement applied to the conditioning treatment of enuresis. (Doctoral dissertation, Hofstra University, 1971.) *DAI*, 1972, *33*, 2799B–2800B. (University Microfilms No. 72-31, 951.)

Abuzzahab, F. S. Some uses of haloperidol in the treatment of psychiatric conditions. *Psychosomatics*, 1970, *11*, 188–193.

Adamczyk, B. (Use of instruments for the production of artificial feedback in the treatment of stuttering). *Folia Phoniatrica*, 1959, *11*, 216–218.

Adams, M. R. The use of reciprocal inhibition procedures in the treatment of stuttering. *Journal of Communication Disorders*, 1972, *5*, 59–66.

Adams, M. R., & Popelka, G. The influence of "time-out" on stutterers and their dysfluency. *Behavior Therapy*, 1971, *2*, 334–339.

Adesso, V. J., Vargas, J. M., & Siddall, J. W. The role of awareness in reducing nail-biting behavior. *Behavior Therapy*, 1979, *10*, 148–154.

Albin, J. B. The treatment of pica (scavenging) behavior in the retarded: A critical analysis and implications for research. *Mental Retardation*, 1977, *15*, 14–17.

Alford, G. S., Blanchard, E. B., & Buckley, T. M. Treatment of hysterical vomiting by modification of social contingencies: A case study. *Journal of Behavior Therapy and Experimental Psychiatry*, 1972, *3*, 209–212.

Andrews, G., & Harris, M. *The syndrome of stuttering*. Clinics in Developmental Medicine, No. 17. London: Heinemann, 1964.

Andrews, G., & Ingham, R. J. Stuttering: Considerations in the evaluation of treatment. *British Journal of Disorders of Communication*, 1971, *6*, 129–138.

Anthony, E. J. An experimental approach to the psychopathology of childhood encopresis. *British Journal of Medical Psychology*, 1957, *30*, 146–175.

Anthony, W. Z. Brief intervention in a case of childhood trichotillomania by self-monitoring. *Journal of Behavior Therapy and Experimental Psychiatry*, 1978, *9*, 173–175.

Ascher, E. Psychodynamic considerations in Gilles de la Tourette's disease (maladie des tics). *American Journal of Psychiatry*, 1948, *105*, 267–276.

Ashkenazi, Z. The treatment of encopresis using a discriminative stimulus and positive reinforcement. *Journal of Behavior Therapy and Experimental Psychiatry*, 1975, *6*, 1551–1557.

Atthowe, J. M. Nocturnal enuresis and behavior therapy: A functional analysis. In R. B. Rubin, J. Henderson, H. Fensterheim, & L. P. Ullmann (Eds.), *Advances in behavior therapy*, Vol. 4. New York: Academic Press, 1973.

Ausman, J., Ball, T. S., & Alexander, D. Behavior therapy of pica with a profoundly retarded adolescent. *Mental Retardation*, 1974, *12*, 16–18.

Ayllon, T., Simon, S. J., & Wildman, R. W. Instructions and reinforcement in the elimination of encopresis: A case study. *Journal of Behavior Therapy and Experimental Psychiatry*, 1975, *6*, 235–238.

Azrin, N. H., & Foxx, R. M. A rapid method of toilet training the institutionalized retarded. *Journal of Applied Behavior Analysis*, 1971, *4*, 89–99.

Azrin, N. H., & Foxx, R. M. *Toilet training in less than a day*. New York: Simon & Schuster, 1974.

Azrin, N. H., & Nunn, R. G. Habit reversal: A method of eliminating nervous habits. *Behavior Research and Therapy*, 1973, *11*, 619–628.

Azrin, N. H., & Nunn, R. G. A rapid method of eliminating stuttering by a regulated breathing approach. *Behaviour Research and Therapy*, 1974, *12*, 279–286.

Azrin, N. H., & Wesolowski, M. D. Eliminating habitual vomiting in a retarded adult by positive practice and self-correction. *Journal of Behavior Therapy and Experimental Psychiatry*, 1975, *6*, 145–148.

Azrin, N. H., Sneed, T. J., & Foxx, R. M. Dry bed: A rapid method of eliminating bedwetting (enuresis) of the retarded. *Behaviour Research and Therapy*, 1973, *11*, 427–434.

Azrin, N. H., Sneed, T. J., & Foxx, R. M. Dry bed: Rapid elimination of childhood enuresis. *Behaviour Research and Therapy*, 1974, *12*, 147–156.

Azrin, N. H., Nunn, R. G., & Frantz, S. E. Comparison of regulated breathing versus abbreviated desensitization on reported stuttering episodes. *Journal of Speech and Hearing Disorders*, 1979, *44*, 331–339.

Bach, R., & Moylan, J. M. Parent-administered behavior therapy for inappropriate urination and encopresis: A case study. *Journal of Behavior Therapy and Experimental Psychiatry*, 1975, *6*, 239–241.

Baer, D. M. Laboratory control of thumbsucking by withdrawal and re-presentation of reinforcement. *Journal of the Experimental Analysis of Behavior*, 1962, *5*, 525–528.

Balsom, P. M. Case study: Encopresis: A case with symptom substitution? *Behavior Therapy*, 1973, *4*, 134–136.

Balthazar, K. Über das anatomische Substrat der generalisierten Tickrankheit. Entwicklungshemmung des corpus striatum. *Archiv für Psychiatrie und Neurenkrankheiten*, 1957, *195*, 531–549.

Barnard, G. W., Flesher, C. K., & Steinbook, R. M. The treatment of urinary retention by aversive stimulus cessation and assertive training. *Behavior Research and Therapy*, 1966, *4*, 232–236.

Barrett, B. H. Reduction in rate of multiple tics by free

operant conditioning methods. *Journal of Nervous and Mental Disease*, 1962, *135*, 187–195.

Barrett, B. H. Behavior modification in the home: Parents adapt laboratory-developed tactics to bowel-train a 5½ year old. *Psychotherapy: Theory, Research and Practice*, 1969, *6*, 172–176.

Barrios, B. A. Cue-controlled relaxation in reduction of chronic nervous habits. *Psychological Reports*, 1977, *41*, 703–706.

Bayer, C. A. Self-monitoring and mild aversion treatment of trichotillomania. *Journal of Behavior Therapy and Experimental Psychiatry*, 1972, *3*, 139–141.

Bellmon, M. Studies on encopresis. *Acta Pediatrica Scandinavia*, 1966, *170* (Suppl.).

Benjamin, L. S. The beginning of thumbsucking. *Child Development*, 1967, *38*, 1065–1088.

Bishop, B. R., & Stumphauzer, J. S. Behavior therapy of thumbsucking in children: A punishment (time-out) and generalization effect: What's a mother to do? *Psychological Reports*, 1973, *33*, 939–944.

Blackwell, B., & Currah, J. The pharmacology of nocturnal enuresis. In I. Kolvin, R. C. MacKeith, & S. R. Meadow (Eds.), *Bladder control and enuresis*. Philadelphia: Lippincott, 1973.

Bloodstein, O. *A handbook on stuttering*. Chicago: National Easter Seal Society for Children and Adults, 1969.

Bloodstein, O. Stuttering as tension and fragmentation. In J. Eisenson (Ed.), *Stuttering: A second symposium*. New York: Harper & Row, 1975.

Bloomfield, J. M., & Douglas, J. W. B. Bedwetting: Prevalence among children aged 4–7 years. *Lancet*, 1956, *1*, 850–852.

Boberg, E., Howie, P., & Woods, L. Maintenance of fluency: A review. *Journal of Fluency Disorders*, 1979, *4*, 93–116.

Bollard, R. J., & Woodroffe, P. The effect of parent administered Dry-Bed training on nocturnal enuresis in children. *Behaviour Research and Therapy*, 1977, *15*, 159–165.

Borrie, P., & Fenton, J. C. B. Buzzer ulcers. *British Medical Journal*, 1966, *2*, 151–152.

Boucheau, L. D., & Jeffry, C. D. Stuttering treated by desensitization. *Journal of Behavior Therapy and Experimental Psychiatry*, 1973, *4*, 209–212.

Brady, J. P. A behavioral approach to the treatment of stuttering. *American Journal of Psychiatry*, 1968, *125*, 843–848.

Brady, J. P. Metronome-conditioned retraining for stuttering. *Behavior Therapy*, 1971, *2*, 129–150.

Brandon, S., & Harris, M. Stammering—an experimental treatment programme using syllable-timed speech. *British Journal of Disorders of Communication*, 1967, *2*, 64–86.

Bright, G. O., & Whaley, D. L. Suppression of regurgitation and rumination with aversive events. *Michigan Mental Health Research Bulletin*, 1968, *11*, 17–20.

Brutten, G. Stuttering: Reflections on a two-factor approach to the modification of stuttering. In B. B. Gray & G. England (Eds.), *Stuttering and the conditioning therapies*. Monterey, Calif.: Monterey Institute for Speech and Hearing, 1969.

Brutten, G. J., & Shoemaker, D. J. *The modification of stuttering*. Englewood Cliffs, N.J.: Prentice-Hall, 1967.

Bucher, B. D. A portable shock-device with application to nailbiting. *Behavior Research and Therapy*, 1968, *6*, 389–392.

Bucher, B., Reykdal, B., & Albin, J. B. Brief physical restraint to control pica in retarded children. *Journal of Behavior Therapy and Experimental Psychiatry*, 1976, *2*, 137–140.

Burgess, E. P. Elimination of vomiting behavior. *Behaviour Research and Therapy*, 1969, *7*, 173–176.

Burgraff, R. L. The efficacy of systematic desensitization via imagery as a therapeutic device with stutterers. *British Journal of Disorders of Communication*, 1974, *9*, 134–139.

Butler, J. F. *The treatment of encopresis by over-correction*. Unpublished manuscript. Lackland Air Force Base, Texas, 1975.

Butler, J. F. Toilet training a child with spina bifida. *Journal of Behavior Therapy and Experimental Psychiatry*, 1976, *7*, 63–65.

Campbell, M. F. Neuromuscular uropathy. In M. F. Campbell & T. H. Harrison (Eds.), *Urology*, Vol. 2. Philadelphia: Saunders, 1970.

Carlson, C. S., Arnold, C. R., Becker, W. C., & Madsen, C. H. The elimination of tantrum behavior of a child in an elementary classroom. *Behaviour Research and Therapy*, 1968, *6*, 117–119.

Challas, G., & Brauer, W. Tourette's disease: Relief of symptoms with R1625. *American Journal of Psychiatry*, 1963, *120*, 283–284.

Cherry, C., & Sayers, B. M. Experiments upon the total inhibition of stammering by external control, and some clinical results. *Journal of Psychomatic Research*, 1956, *1*, 233–246.

Christofferson, E. R., & Rainey, S. K. Management of encopresis through a pediatric outpatient clinic. *Journal of Pediatric Psychology*, 1976, *4*, 38–41.

Clark, D. F. The treatment of hysterical spasm and agoraphobia by behavior therapy. *Behaviour Research and Therapy*, 1963, *1*, 245–250.

Clark, D. F. Behavior therapy of Gilles de la Tourette's syndrome. *British Journal of Psychiatry*, 1966, *112*, 771–778.

Cohen, M. W. Enuresis. In S. B. Friedman (Ed.), *The pediatric clinics of North America*. Philadelphia: Saunders, 1975.

Coleman, J. C., & McCalley, J. E. Nailbiting among college students. *Journal of Abnormal and Social Psychology*, 1948, *43*, 517–525.

Collins, K. H., & Tatum, A. A conditioned salivary reflex established by chronic morphine poisoning. *American Journal of Physiology*, 1925, *74*, 14–15.

Collins, R. W. Importance of the bladder-cue buzzer contingency in the conditioning treatment for enuresis. *Journal of Abnormal Psychology*, 1973, *82*, 299–308.

Conger, J. C. The treatment of encopresis by the management of social consequences. *Behavior Therapy*, 1970, *1*, 386–390.

Connell, P. H., Corbett, J. A., Horne, D. J., & Mathews, A. M. Drug treatment of adolescent tiqueurs—A double blind trial of diazepam and haloperidol. *British Journal of Psychiatry*, 1967, *113*, 375–381.

Conway, J. B., & Bucher, B. D. "Soap in the mouth" as

an aversive consequence. *Behavior Therapy*, 1974, *5*, 154–156.

Corbett, J. A., Mathews, A. M., Connell, P. H., & Shapiro, D. A. Tics and Gilles de la Tourette's syndrome: A follow-up study and critical review. *British Journal of Psychiatry*, 1969, *115*, 1229–1241.

Creer, T. L., & Davis, M. H. Using a staggered-awakening procedure with enuretic children in an institutional setting. *Journal of Behavior Therapy and Experimental Psychiatry*, 1975, *6*, 23–25.

Cross, D. E. Effects of false increasing, decreasing, and true electromyographic biofeedback on the frequency of stuttering. *Journal of Fluency Disorders*, 1977, *2*, 109–116.

Cunningham, C. E., & Linscheid, T. R. Elimination of chronic infant ruminating by electric shock. *Behavior Therapy*, 1976, *7*, 231–234.

Curlee, R. F., & Perkins, W. H. Conversational rate control therapy for stuttering. *Journal of Speech and Hearing Disorders*, 1969, *34*, 245–250.

Curlee, R. F., & Perkins, W. H. Effectiveness of a DAF conditioning program for adolescent and adult stutterers. *Behaviour Research and Therapy*, 1973, *11*, 395–401.

Daniels, L. K. Rapid extinction of nail biting by covert sensitization: A case study. *Journal of Behavior Therapy and Experimental Psychiatry*, 1974, *5*, 91–92.

Davidson, A. Positive and negative behavioral approaches used in the treatment of nail-biting: An analogue study. (Doctoral dissertation, University of Kansas, 1977.) *DAI*, 1978, *38*, 3387B (University Microfilm No. 77-28, 854.)

Davidson, A., & Denney, D. R. Covert sensitization and information in the reduction of nailbiting. *Behavior Therapy*, 1976, *1*, 512–518.

Davison, G. C. An intensive long-term social-learning treatment program with an accurately diagnosed autistic child. *Proceedings of the 73rd Annual Convention of the American Psychological Association*, 1965, 203–204. (Summary.)

Delparto, D. J., Alch, E., Bambausch, J., & Barclay, L. A. Treatment of fingernail biting by habit reversal. *Journal of Behavior Therapy and Experimental Psychiatry*, 1977, *8*, 319.

Derazne, J. Speech pathology in the USSR. In R. W. Rieber & R. S. Brubaker (Eds.), *Speech pathology*. Amsterdam: North Holland, 1966.

Dische, S. Management of enuresis. *British Medical Journal*, 1971, *2*, 33–36.

Doke, L. A., & Epstein, L. H. Oral overcorrection: Side effects and extended applications. *Journal of Experimental Child Psychology*, 1975, *20*, 496–511.

Doleys, D. M. Behavioral treatments for nocturnal enuresis in children: A review of the recent literature. *Psychological Bulletin*, 1977, *84*, 30–54.

Doleys, D. M. Assessment and treatment of enuresis and encopresis in children. In M. Hersen, R. M. Eisler, & P. M. Miller (Eds.), *Progress in behavior modification*, Vol. 6. New York: Academic Press, 1978.

Doleys, D. M., & Arnold, S. Treatment of childhood encopresis: Full cleanliness training. *Mental Retardation*, 1975, *13*, 14–16.

Doleys, D. M., & Ciminero, A. R. Childhood enuresis:

Considerations in treatment. *Journal of Pediatric Psychology*, 1976, *4*, 21–23.

Doleys, D. M., & Kurtz, P. S. A behavioral treatment program for the Gilles de la Tourette syndrome. *Psychological Reports*, 1974, *35*, 43–48.

Doleys, D. M., & Wells, K. C. Changes in functional bladder capacity and bed-wetting during and after retention control training: A case study. *Behavior Therapy*, 1975, *6*, 685–688.

Doleys, D. M., Ciminero, A. R., Tollison, J. W., Williams, C. L., & Wells, K. C. Dry bed training and retention control training: A comparison. *Behavior Therapy*, 1977, *8*, 541–548.

Doleys, D. M., McWhorter, A. Q., Williams, S. C., & Gentry, R. Encopresis: Its treatment and relation to nocturnal enuresis. *Behavior Therapy*, 1977, *8*, 105–110.

Duker, P. C., & Seys, D. M. Elimination of vomiting in a retarded female using restitutional overcorrection. *Behavior Therapy*, 1977, *8*, 255–257.

Dunlap, K. *Habits: Their making and unmaking*. New York: Liveright, 1932.

D'Zurilla, T. J. Reducing heterosexual anxiety. In J. D. Krumboltz & C. E. Thoreson (Eds.), *Behavioral counseling: Cases and techniques*. New York: Holt, Rinehart & Winston, 1969.

Edelman, R. F. Operant conditioning treatment of encopresis. *Journal of Behavior Therapy and Experimental Psychiatry*, 1971, *2*, 71–73.

Epstein, L. H., & McCoy, J. F. Bladder and bowel control in Hirschsprung's disease. *Journal of Behavior Therapy and Experimental Psychiatry*, 1977, *8*, 97–99.

Ernst, E. Personal communication to H. G. Jones. Cited in "Continuation of Yates' treatment of tics." In H. J. Eysenck (Eds.), *Behavior therapy and the neuroses*. London: Pergamon, 1960.

Evans, B. A case of trichotillomania in a child treated in a home token program. *Journal of Behavior Therapy and Experimental Psychiatry*, 1976, *7*, 197–198.

Feild, J. R., Corbin, K. B., Goldstein, N. P., & Klass, D. W. Gilles de la Tourette's syndrome. *Neurology*, 1966, *16*, 453–462.

Finley, W. W., Besserman, R. L., Bennett, L. F. Clapp, R. K., & Finley, P. M. The effect of continuous, intermittent and "placebo" reinforcement on the effectiveness of the conditioning treatment for enuresis nocturna. *Behavior Research and Therapy*, 1973, *11*, 289–297.

Finley, W. W., & Wansley, R. A. Use of intermittent reinforcement in a clinical-research program for the treatment of enuresis nocturna. *Journal of Pediatric Psychology*, 1976, *4*, 24–27.

Finley, W. W., Wansley, R. A., & Blenkarn, M. M. Conditioning treatment of enuresis using a 70% intermittent reinforcement schedule. *Behaviour Research and Therapy*, 1977, *15*, 419–427.

Flanagan, B., Goldiamond, I., & Azrin, N. H. Operant stuttering: The control of stuttering behavior through response-contingent consequences. *Journal of the Experimental Analysis of Behavior*, 1958, *1*, 173–177.

Ford, C. V., & Gottlieb, F. An objective evaluation of haloperidol in Gilles de la Tourette's Syndrome. *Diseases of the Nervous System*, 1969, *30*, 328–332.

Forsythe, W. I., & Redmond, A. Enuresis and the electric

alarm: Study of 200 cases. *British Medical Journal,* 1970, *1,* 211–213.

Foxx, R. M., & Azrin, N. H. *Toilet training the retarded.* Champaign, Ill.: Research Press, 1973.

Foxx, R. M., & Martin, E. D. Treatment of scavenging behavior (coprophagy and pica) by overcorrection. *Behaviour Research and Therapy,* 1975, *13,* 153–162.

Fraser, M. S. Nocturnal enuresis. *The Practitioner,* 1972, *208,* 203–211.

Frederick, C. J. Treatment of a tic by systematic desensitization and massed response evocation. *Journal of Behavior Therapy and Experimental Psychiatry,* 1971, *2,* 281–283.

Freeman, B. J., & Pribble, W. Elimination of inappropriate toileting by overcorrection. *Psychological Reports,* 1974, *35,* 802.

Freeman, B. J., Moss, D., Somerset, T., & Ritvo, E. R. Thumbsucking in an autistic child overcome by overcorrection. *Journal of Behavior Therapy and Experimental Psychiatry,* 1977, *8,* 211–212.

Freinden, W., & Van Handel, D. Elimination of soiling in an elementary school child through application of aversive technique. *Journal of School Psychology,* 1970, *8,* 267–269.

Fullerton, D. T. Infantile rumination: A case report. *Archives of General Psychiatry,* 1963, *9,* 593–600.

Gaddini, R., & Gaddini, E. Rumination in infancy. In C. Jessner & E. Pavenstadt (Eds.), *Dynamic psychopathology in childhood.* New York: Grune & Stratton, 1959.

Garrard, S. D., & Richmond, J. B. Psychogenic megacolon mainifested by fecal soiling. *Pediatrics,* 1952, *10,* 474–483.

Gavanski, M. Treatment of non-retentive secondary encopresis with imipramine and psychotherapy. *Canadian Medical Association Journal,* 1971, *104,* 46–48.

Gelber, H., & Meyer, V. Behavior therapy and encopresis: The complexities involved in treatment. *Behaviour Research and Therapy,* 1965, *2,* 227–231.

Goldiamond, I. Stuttering and fluency as manipulatable operant response classes. In L. Krasner & L. P. Ullmann (Eds.), *Research in behavior modification.* New York: Holt, Rinehart & Winston, 1965.

Goldiamond, I. *Supplementary statement to operant analysis and control of fluent and nonfluent verbal behavior.* Report to the U.S. Department of Health, Education, and Welfare, Application No. MH08876-03, 1967.

Gray, B. B., & England, G. Stuttering: The measurement of anxiety during reciprocal inhibition. In B. B. Gray & G. England (Eds.), *Stuttering and the conditioning therapies.* Monterey, Calif.: Monterey Institute for Speech and Hearing, 1969.

Gray, B. B., & England, G. Some effects of anxiety deconditioning upon stuttering frequency. *Journal of Speech and Hearing Research,* 1972, *2,* 114–121.

Greenberg, J. B. The effect of a metronome on the speech of young stutterers. *Behavior Therapy,* 1970, *1,* 240–244.

Gruber, L. The use of the portable voice masker in stuttering therapy. *Journal of Speech and Hearing Disorders,* 1971, *36,* 287–289.

Guitar, B. Reduction of stuttering frequency using analog electromyographic feedback. *Journal of Speech and Hearing Research,* 1975, *18,* 672–685.

Hallman, N. On the ability of enuretic children to hold urine. *Acta Paediatrica,* 1950, *39,* 87.

Hanna, R., Wilfling, F., & McNeill, B. A biofeedback treatment for stuttering. *Journal of Speech and Hearing Disorders,* 1975, *40,* 270–273.

Harris, C. S., & McReynolds, W. T. Semantic cues and response contingencies in self-instructional control. *Journal of Behavior Therapy and Experimental Psychiatry,* 1977, *8,* 15–17.

Harris, L. S., & Purohit, A. P. Bladder training and enuresis: A controlled trial. *Behaviour Research and Therapy,* 1977, *15,* 485–490.

Harris, S. L., Hershfield, R. E., Kaffashan, L. C., & Romanczyk, R. G. The portable time-out room. *Behavior Therapy,* 1974, *5,* 687–688.

Haryett, R. D., Hansen, F. C., Davidson, P. O., & Sandilands, M. L. Chronic thumbsucking: The psychological effects and the relative effectiveness of various methods of treatment. *American Journal of Orthodontics,* 1967, *53,* 569–585.

Haryett, R. D., Hansen, F. C., & Davidson, P. O. Chronic thumbsucking: A second report on treatment and its psychological effects. *American Journal of Orthodontics,* 1970, *57,* 164–177.

Healy, C. E. Gilles de la Tourette's syndrome (maladie des tics): Successful treatment with haloperidol. *American Journal of Diseases of Children,* 1970, *120,* 62–63.

Hegde, M. N., & Brutten, G. J. Reinforcing fluency in stutterers: An experimental study. *Journal of Fluency Disorders,* 1977, *2,* 315–318.

Hersen, M., & Eisler, R. M. Behavioral approaches to study and treatment of psychogenic tics. *Genetic Psychology Monographs,* 1973, *87,* 289–312.

Holgate, D., & Andrews, G. The use of syllable-timed speech and group psychotherapy in the treatment of adult stutterers. *Journal of the Australian College of Speech Therapists,* 1966, *16,* 36–40.

Hollandsworth, J. G., Jr., & Bausinger, L. Unsuccessful use of massed practice in the treatment of Gilles de la Tourette's syndrome. *Psychological Report,* 1978, *43,* 671–677.

Hollowell, J. R., & Gardner, L. I. Rumination and growth failure in male fraternal twins: Association with disturbed family environment. *Pediatrics,* 1965, *36,* 565–571.

Horan, J. J., Hoffman, A. M., & Macri, M. Self-control of chronic fingernail biting. *Journal of Behavior Therapy and Experimental Psychiatry,* 1974, *5,* 307–309.

Horne, D. J. de L. Behaviour therapy for trichotillomania. *Behaviour Research and Therapy,* 1977, *15,* 192–196.

Hutchinson, J. M., & Norris, G. M. The differential effect of three auditory stimuli on the frequency of stuttering behaviors. *Journal of Fluency Disorders,* 1977, *2,* 283–294.

Ince, L. P., Brucker, B. S., & Alba, A. Behavioral techniques applied to the care of patients with spinal cord injuries: With an annotated reference list. *Behavioral Engineering,* 1976, *3,* 87–95.

Ingersoll, B., & Curry, F. Rapid treatment of persistent vomiting in a 14-year-old female by shaping and time-out. *Journal of Behavior Therapy and Experimental Psychiatry,* 1977, *8,* 305–307.

Ingham, R. J. Operant methodology in stuttering therapy.

847

In J. Eisenson (Ed.), *Stuttering: A second symposium.* New York: Harper & Row, 1975.

Ingham, R. J., & Andrews, G. An analysis of a token economy in stuttering therapy. *Journal of Applied Behavior Analysis,* 1973, *6*, 219–229. (a)

Ingham, R. J., & Andrews, G. Behavior therapy and stuttering: A review. *Journal of Speech and Hearing Disorders,* 1973, *38*, 405–441. (b)

Ingham, R. J., Andrews, G., & Winkler, R. Stuttering: A comparative evaluation of the short-term effectiveness of four treatment techniques. *Journal of Communication Disorders,* 1972, *5*, 91–117.

Jensen, G. D., & Womack, M. G. Operant conditioning techniques applied in the treatment of an autistic child. *American Journal of Orthopsychiatry,* 1967, *37*, 30–34.

Johnson, J. H., & Van Bourgondien, M. E. Behavior therapy and encopresis: A selective review of the literature. *Journal of Clinical Child Psychology,* 1977, *6*, 15–19.

Jones, H. G. Continuation of Yates' treatment of a ticqueur. In H. J. Eysenck (Ed.), *Behavior therapy and the neuroses.* London: Pergamon, 1960.

Kakkar, S. B. Experimental extinction of tantrum behavior. *Indian Journal of Experimental Psychology,* 1972, *6*, 76–77.

Kanner, L. *Child psychiatry* (3rd ed.). Springfield, Ill.: Charles C Thomas, 1957.

Katahn, M. Systematic desensitization and counseling for anxiety in a college basketball player. *Journal of Special Education,* 1967, *1*, 309–314.

Kauffman, J. M., & Scranton, T. R. Parent control of thumbsucking in the home. *Child Study Journal,* 1974, *4*, 1–10.

Kazdin, A. E. *History of behavior modification.* Baltimore: University Park Press, 1978.

Keehn, J. D. Brief case report: Reinforcement therapy of incontinence. *Behavior Research and Therapy,* 1965, *2*, 239.

Kelham, R., & McHale, A. The application of learning theory to the treatment of stuttering. *British Journal of Disorders of Communication,* 1966, *1*, 114–118.

Kennedy, W. A., & Sloop, E. W. Methedrine as an adjunct to conditioning treatment of nocturnal enuresis in normal and institutionalized retarded subjects. *Psychological Reports,* 1968, *22*, 997–1000.

Kimmel, H. D., & Kimmel, E. C. An instrumental conditioning method for the treatment of enuresis. *Journal of Behavior Therapy and Experimental Psychiatry,* 1970, *1*, 121–123.

Kleitman, N., & Crisler, G. A. A quantitative study of the conditioned salivary reflex. *American Journal of Physiology,* 1927, *79*, 571–614.

Knepler, K. N., & Sewall, S. Negative practice paired with smelling salts in the treatment of a tic. *Journal of Behavior Therapy and Experimental Psychiatry,* 1974, *5*, 189–192.

Knight, M. F., & McKenzie, H. S. Elimination of bedtime thumbsucking in home settings through contingent reading. *Journal of Applied Behavior Analysis,* 1974, *7*, 33–38.

Kohlenberg, R. J. The punishment of persistent vomiting: A case study. *Journal of Applied Behavior Analysis,* 1970, *3*, 241–245.

Kohlenberg, R. J. Operant conditioning of human anal sphincter pressure. *Journal of Applied Behavior Analysis,* 1973, *6*, 201–208.

Kondas, O. The treatment of stammering in children by the shadowing method. *Behavior Research and Therapy,* 1967, *5*, 325–329.

LaMontagne, Y. Treatment of a tic by prolonged exposure. *Behavior Therapy,* 1978, *9*, 647–651.

LaMontagne, Y., & Marks, I. M. Psychogenic urinary retention: Treatment by prolonged exposure. *Behavior Therapy,* 1973, *4*, 581–585.

Lang, P. J., & Melamed, B. G. Case report: Avoidance conditioning therapy of an infant with chronic ruminative vomiting. *Journal of Abnormal Psychology,* 1969, *74*, 1–8.

Lanyon, R. I. Behavior change in stuttering through systematic desensitization. *Journal of Speech and Hearing Disorders,* 1969, *34*, 253–260.

Lanyon, R. I. Effect of biofeedback-based relaxation on stuttering during reading and spontaneous speech. *Journal of Consulting and Clinical Psychology,* 1977, *45*, 860–866.

Lanyon, R. I. Behavioral approaches to stuttering. In M. Hersen, R. M. Eisler, & P. M. Miller (Eds.), *Progress in behavior modification,* Vol. 6. New York: Academic Press, 1978.

Lanyon, R. I., & Barocas, V. S. Effects of contingent events on frequency of stuttering. *Journal of Consulting and Clinical Psychology,* 1975, *43*, 786–793.

Lanyon, R. I., Barrington, C. C., & Newman, A. C. Modification of stuttering through EMG biofeedback: A preliminary study. *Behavior Therapy,* 1976, *7*, 96–103.

Lanyon, R. I., Goldsworthy, R. J., & Lanyon, B. P. Dimensions of stuttering and relationship to psychopathology. *Journal of Fluency Disorders,* 1978, *3*, 103–113.

Lazarus, A. A. Objective psychotherapy in the treatment of dysphemia. *Journal of the South African Logopedic Society,* 1960, *6*, 8–10.

Lee, B. Artificial stutter. *Journal of Speech and Hearing Disorders,* 1951, *16*, 53–55.

Levine, B. A. Treatment of trichotillomania by covert sensitization. *Journal of Behavior Therapy and Experimental Psychiatry,* 1976, *7*, 75–76.

Levine, M. D. Children with encopresis: A descriptive analysis. *Pediatrics,* 1975, *56*, 412–416.

Longstreth, L. E. *Psychological development of the child.* New York: Ronald, 1968.

Lovibond, S. H. *Conditioning and enuresis.* Oxford, England: Pergamon, 1964.

Lovibond, S. H., & Coote, M. A. Enuresis. In C. G. Costello (Ed.), *Symptoms of psychopathology.* New York: Wiley, 1970.

Lucas, A. R. Gilles de la Tourette's disease in children: Treatment with haloperidol. *American Journal of Psychiatry,* 1967, *124*, 243–245.

Luckey, R., Watson, C., & Musick, J. Aversive conditioning as a means of inhibiting vomiting and rumination. *American Journal of Mental Deficiency,* 1968, *73*, 139–142.

Lund, C. J. Types of urinary incontinence. In C. J. Lund (Ed.), *Clinical obstetrics and gynecology.* New York: Harper, 1963.

MacCulloch, M. J., Eaton, R., & Long, E. The long term effect of auditory masking on young stutterers. *British Journal of Disorders of Communication*, 1970, *5*, 165–173.

MacNeil, J., & Thomas, M. R. Treatment of obsessive-compulsive hair pulling (trichotillomania) by behavioral and cognitive contingency manipulation. *Journal of Behavior Therapy and Experimental Psychiatry*, 1976, *7*, 391–392.

Mahler, M. S. Tics and impulsions in children: A study of motility. *Psychoanalytic Quarterly*, 1944, *17*, 430–444.

Mahler, M. S. A psychoanalytic evaluation of tic in psychopathology of children: Symptomatic and tic syndrome. In R. S. Eissler *et al.* (Eds.), *Psychoanalytic study of the child*, Vol. 5. New York: International Universities Press, 1949.

Martin, G. L., England, G., Kaprowy, E., Kilgour, K., & Pilek, V. Operant conditioning of kindergarten class behavior in autistic children. *Behaviour Research and Therapy*, 1968, *6*, 281–294.

Martin, J. A., & Iagulli, D. M. Elimination of middle-of-the-night tantrums in a blind, retarded child. *Behavior Therapy*, 1974, *5*, 420–422.

Martin, R., & Haroldson, S. K. Effects of five experimental treatments on stuttering. *Journal of Speech and Hearing Research*, 1979, *22*, 132–146.

Masur, F. T. Behavior therapy in a case of pollakiuria. *Journal of Behavior Therapy and Experimental Psychiatry*, 1976, *7*, 175–178.

Matson, J. L. Some practical considerations for using the Foxx and Azrin rapid method of toilet training. *Psychological Reports*, 1975, *37*, 350.

Matson, J. L., & Ollendick, T. H. Issues in toilet training normal children. *Behavior Therapy*, 1977, *8*, 549–553.

McConaghy, N. A controlled trial of imipramine, amphetamine, pad-and-bell conditioning and random wakening in the treatment of nocturnal enuresis. *Medical Journal of Australia*, 1969, *2*, 237–239.

McLaughlin, J. G., & Nay, W. R. Treatment of trichotillomania using positive coverants and response cost: A case report. *Behavior Therapy*, 1975, *6*, 87–91.

McReynolds, W. T. A procedure for the withdrawal of an infant oral pacifier. *Journal of Applied Behavior Analysis*, 1972, *5*, 65–66.

Meacham, M. S., & Wiesen, A. E. *Changing classroom behavior: A manual for precision teaching*. Scranton, Pa.: International Textbook, 1969.

Meadow, S. R. Buzzer ulcers. In I. Kolvin, R. C. Mackeith, & S. R. Meadow (Eds.), *Bladder control and enuresis*. Philadelphia: Lippincott, 1973.

Meadow, R. Childhood enuresis. *British Medical Journal*, 1970, *4*, 787–789.

Meige, H., & Feindel, E. *Tics and their treatment*. London: Appleton, 1907.

Menking, M., Wagnitz, J., Burton, J., Coddington, R. D., & Sotos, J. Rumination—A new fatal psychiatric disease of infancy. *The New England Journal of Medicine*, 1969, *281*, 802–804.

Meyer, V., & Comley, J. A preliminary report on the treatment of stammer by the use of rhythmic stimulation. In B. B. Gray & G. England (Eds.), *Stuttering and the conditioning therapies*. Monterey, Calif.: Monterey Institute for Speech and Hearing, 1969.

Meyer, V., & Mair, J. M. A new technique to control

stammering: A preliminary report. *Behaviour Research and Therapy*, 1963, *1*, 251–254.

Millard, D. W. A conditioning treatment for giggle micturition. *Behavior Research and Therapy*, 1966, *4*, 229–231.

Miller, A. L. Treatment of a child with Gilles de la Tourette's syndrome using behavior modification techniques. *Journal of Behavior Therapy and Experimental Psychiatry*, 1970, *1*, 319–321.

Miller, P. M. An experimental analysis of retention control training in the treatment of nocturnal enuresis in two institutionalized adolescents. *Behavior Therapy*, 1973, *4*, 288–294.

Mogan, J., & O'Brien, J. S. The counterconditioning of a vomiting habit by sips of ginger ale. *Journal of Behavior Therapy and Experimental Psychiatry*, 1972, *3*, 135–137.

Moncrieff, A. A., Koumides, O. P., Clayton, B. E., Patrick, A. D., Renwick, A. G. C., & Roberts, G. E. Lead poisoning in children. *Archives of Disease in Childhood*, 1964, *39*, 1–13.

Moore, W. H., Jr. Some effects of progressively lowering electromyographic levels with feedback procedures on the frequency of stuttered verbal behaviors. *Journal of Fluency Disorders*, 1978, *3*, 127–138.

Morgan, R. T. T., & Young, G. C. The treatment of enuresis: Merits of conditioning methods. *Community Medicine*, 1972, *128*, 119–121.

Morphew, J. A., & Sim, M. Gilles de la Tourette's syndrome—A clinical and psychopathological study. *British Journal of Medical Psychology*, 1969, *42*, 293–301.

Mowrer, O. H. *Learning theory and personality dynamics*. New York: Ronald, 1950.

Mowrer, O. H., & Mowrer, W. M. Enuresis: A method for its study and treatment. *American Journal of Orthopsychiatry*, 1938, *8*, 436–459.

Muellner, S. R. Development of urinary control in children. *Journal of the American Medical Association*, 1960, *172*, 1256–1261. (a)

Muellner, S. R. Development of urinary control in children: A new concept in cause, prevention and treatment of primary enuresis. *Journal of Urology*, 1960, *84*, 714–716 (b)

Murray, A. B., & Anderson, D. O. The association of incisor protrusion with digit sucking and allergic nasal itching. *Journal of Allergy*, 1969, *44*, 239–247.

Murray, M. E. Modified time-out procedures for controlling tantrum behaviors in public places. *Behavior Therapy*, 1976, *7*, 412–413.

Murray, M. E., Keele, D. K., & McCarver, J. W. Treatment of ruminations with behavioral techniques: A case report. *Behavior Therapy*, 1977, *8*, 999–1003.

Neale, D. H. Behavior therapy and encopresis in children. *Behaviour Research and Therapy*, 1963, *1*, 139–149.

Ney, P. G. Psychological and physiological aspects of drug treatment in older children. *Illinois Medical Journal*, 1969, *136*, 147.

Nicassio, F. J., Liberman, R. P., Patterson, R. L., & Ramirez, E. The treatment of tics by negative practice. *Journal of Behavior Therapy and Experimental Psychiatry*, 1972, *3*, 281–287.

Nilsson, D. E. Treatment of encopresis: A token economy. *Journal of Pediatric Psychology*, 1976, *1*, 42–46.

Norton, L. A., & Gellin, M. E. Management of digital sucking and tongue thrusting in children. *Dental Clinics of North America,* July 1968, 365.

Nunn, R. G., & Azrin, N. H. Eliminating nail-biting by the habit reversal procedure. *Behaviour Research and Therapy,* 1976, *14,* 65–67.

O'Leary, K. D., & Wilson, G. T. *Behavior therapy: Application and outcome.* Englewood Cliffs, N.J.: Prentice-Hall, 1975.

Oppel, W. C., Harper, P. A., & Rider, R. V. The age of obtaining bladder control. *Pediatrics,* 1968, *42,* 614–626.

Öst, L., Götestam, K. G., & Melin, L. A controlled study of two behavioral methods in the treatment of stuttering. *Behavior Therapy,* 1976, *5,* 587–592.

Paquin, M. J. The treatment of a nail-biting compulsion by covert sensitization in a poorly motivated client. *Journal of Behavior Therapy and Experimental Psychiatry,* 1977, *8,* 181–183.

Parkin, J. M., & Fraser, M. S. Poisoning as a complication of enuresis. *Developmental Medicine and Child Neurology,* 1972, *14,* 727–730.

Paschalis, A. P., Kimmel, H. D., & Kimmel, E. Further study of diurnal instrumental conditioning in the treatment of enuresis nocturna. *Journal of Behavior Therapy and Experimental Psychiatry,* 1972, *3,* 253–256.

Pavlov, I. P. *Conditioned reflexes: An investigation of the physiological activity of the cerebral cortex, Lecture III.* Oxford, England: Oxford University Press, 1927.

Pedrini, B. C., & Pedrini, D. T. Reinforcement procedures in the control of encopresis: A case study. *Psychological Reports,* 1971, *28,* 937–938.

Perkins, W. H. *Behavioral management of stuttering.* Final report, Social and Rehabilitation Service Research Grant No. 14-P-55281, 1973. (a)

Perkins, W. H. Replacement of stuttering with normal speech: II. Clinical procedures. *Journal of Speech and Hearing Disorders,* 1973, *38,* 295–303. (b)

Perkins, W. H., & Curlee, R. F. Clinical impressions of portable masking unit effects in stuttering. *Journal of Speech and Hearing Disorders,* 1969, *34,* 360–362.

Perkins, W. H., Rudas, J., Johnson, L., Michael, W. B., & Curlee, R. F. Replacement of stuttering with normal speech: III. Clinical effectiveness. *Journal of Speech and Hearing Disorders,* 1974, *39,* 417–428.

Philpott, M. G., & Flasher, M. C. The treatment of enuresis: Further clinical experience with imipramine. *British Journal of Clinical Practice,* 1970, *24,* 327–329.

Picard, P. J. Bottle feeding as preventive orthodontics. *Journal of the California State Dental Association,* April 1959, 35.

Pierce, C. M. Enuresis and encopresis. In A. M. Friedman, H. T. Kaplan, & B. J. Sadock (Eds.), *Comprehensive textbook of psychiatry, Vol. 2.* Baltimore: Williams & Wilkins, 1975.

Plachetta, K. E. Encopresis: A case study utilizing contracting, scheduling and self-charting. *Journal of Behavior Therapy and Experimental Psychiatry,* 1976, *7,* 195–196.

Poole, A. D., & Yates, A. J. The modification of excessive frequency of urination: A follow-up note. *Behavior Therapy,* 1977, *8,* 494–495.

Rafi, A. A. Learning theory and the treatment of tics. *Journal of Psychosomatic Research,* 1962, *6,* 71–76.

Repp, A. C., Deitz, S. M., & Deitz, D. E. Reducing inappropriate behaviors in classrooms and in individual sessions through DRO schedules of reinforcement. *Mental Retardation,* 1976, *14,* 11–15.

Richmond, J. B., Eddy, E. J., & Garrard, S. D. The syndrome of fecal soiling and megacolon. *American Journal of Orthopsychiatry,* 1954, *24,* 391–401.

Richmond, J. B., Eddy, E., & Green, M. Rumination: A psychosomatic syndrome of infancy. *Pediatrics,* 1958, *22,* 49–54.

Rieber, R. W., & Wollock, J. The historical roots of the theory and therapy of stuttering. In R. W. Rieber (Eds.), *The problem of stuttering: Theory and therapy.* New York: Elsevier, 1977.

Rocklin, H., & Tilker, H. Instrumental conditioning of nocturnal enuresis: A reappraisal of some previous findings. *Proceedings of the 81st Annual Convention of the American Psychological Association,* 1973, *8,* 915–916.

Rosen, M., & Wegner, C. A behavioral approach to Tourette's syndrome. *Journal of Consulting and Clinical Psychology,* 1973, *41,* 308–313.

Ross, J. A. The use of contingency contracting in controlling adult nailbiting. *Journal of Behavior Therapy and Experimental Psychiatry,* 1974, *5,* 105–106. (a)

Ross, J. A. Use of teacher and peers to control classroom thumbsucking. *Psychological Reports,* 1974, *34,* 327–330. (b)

Ross, J. A. Parents modify thumbsucking: A case study. *Journal of Behavior Therapy and Experimental Psychiatry,* 1975, *6,* 248–249.

Ross, J. A., & Levine, B. A. Control of thumbsucking in the classroom: Case study. *Perceptual and Motor Skills,* 1972, *34,* 584–586.

Ryan, B. P. *Operant technology applied to therapy with children who stutter.* Presented at the Annual Convention of the American Speech and Hearing Association, Chicago, November 1969.

Ryan, B. P. Operant procedures applied to stuttering therapy for children. *Journal of Speech and Hearing Disorders,* 1971, *36,* 264–280.

Ryan, B. P., & Van Kirk, B. The establishment, transfer, and maintenance of fluent speech in 50 stutterers using delayed auditory feedback and operant procedures. *Journal of Speech and Hearing Disorders,* 1974, *39,* 3–10.

Sajwaj, T., Libet, J., & Agras, S. Lemon-juice therapy: The control of life-threatening rumination in a six-month-old infant. *Journal of Applied Behavior Analysis,* 1974, *7,* 557–563.

Samaan, M. The control of nocturnal enuresis by operant conditioning. *Journal of Behavior Therapy and Experimental Psychiatry,* 1972, *3,* 103–105.

Sand, P. L., & Carlson, C. Failure to establish control of tics in the Gilles de la Tourette's syndrome with behavior therapy techniques. *British Journal of Psychiatry,* 1973, *122,* 665–670.

Saunders, D. G. A case of motion sickness treated by systematic desensitization and in vivo relaxation. *Journal of Behavior Therapy and Experimental Psychiatry,* 1976, *7,* 381–382.

Schell, R. E., & Adams, W. P. Training parents of a young child with profound behavior deficits to be teacher-therapists. *Journal of Special Education,* 1968, *2,* 439–454.

Schulman, M. Control of tics by maternal reinforcement. *Journal of Behavior Therapy and Experimental Psychiatry*, 1974, *5*, 95–96.

Schwartz, D., & Webster, L. M. A clinical adaptation of the Hollins Precision Fluency Shaping Program through de-intensification. *Journal of Fluency Disorders*, 1977, *2*, 3–10. (a)

Schwartz, D., & Webster, L. M. More on the efficacy of a protracted precision fluency shaping program. *Journal of Fluency Disorders*, 1977, *2*, 205–215. (b)

Schwartz, M. *Stuttering solved*. New York: McGraw-Hill, 1976.

Shames, G. H., & Egolf, D. B. *Operant conditioning and the management of stuttering*. Englewood Cliffs, N.J.: Prentice-Hall, 1976.

Shapiro, A. K., & Shapiro, E. Treatment of Gilles de la Tourette's syndrome with haloperidol. *British Journal of Psychiatry*, 1968, *114*, 345–350.

Shirbroun, D. D. *Generalization and maintenance of intervention effects across time and across settings for thumbsucking treatment in children*. (Doctoral dissertation, Fuller Theological Seminary Graduate School of Psychology, 1973). *DAI*, 1974, *34*, 5691B–5692B. (University Microfilms No. 73-31, 503.)

Shirley, H. Encopresis in children. *Journal of Pediatrics*, 1938, *12*, 367–380.

Siegel, G. M. Punishment, stuttering, and disfluency. *Journal of Speech and Hearing Research*, 1970, *13*, 677–714.

Skiba, E. A., Pettigrew, E., & Alden, S. E. A behavioral approach to the control of thumbsucking in the classroom. *Journal of Applied Behavior Analysis*, 1971, *4*, 121–125.

Smith, F. H. *Effects of a treatment for nail-biting*. (Doctoral dissertation, Brigham Young University, 1978.) *DAI*, 1978, *39*, 789A. (University Microfilms No. 78-13, 810.)

Smith, M. Effectiveness of symptomatic treatment of nail-biting in college students. *Psychological Newsletter*, 1957, *8*, 219–231.

Solnick, J. V., Rincover, A., & Peterson, C. R. Some determinants of the reinforcing and punishing effects of timeout. *Journal of Applied Behavior Analysis*, 1977, *10*, 415–424.

Spergel, S. M. Induced vomiting treatment of acute compulsive vomiting. *Journal of Behavior Therapy and Experimental Psychiatry*, 1975, *6*, 85–86.

Spock, B. *Baby and child care*. New York: Pocket Books, 1968.

Stabler, B., & Warren, A. B. Behavioral contracting in treating trichotillomania: Case note. *Psychological Reports*, 1974, *34*, 401–402.

Starfield, B. Functional bladder capacity in enuretic and nonenuretic children. *Journal of Pediatrics*, 1967, *70*, 777–782.

Starfield, B., & Mellits, E. D. Increase in functional bladder capacity and improvements in enuresis. *Journal of Pediatrics*, 1968, *72*, 483–487.

Stedman, J. M. An extension of the Kimmel treatment method for enuresis to an adolescent: A case report. *Journal of Behavior Therapy and Experimental Psychiatry*, 1972, *3*, 307–309.

Stegat, H. A theoretical learning method for the treatment of enuresis. In F. Merz (Ed.), *Bericht über den 25. Kongress der deutschen Gesellschaft für Psychologie*. Munich, Germany, 1966.

Stein, M. L., Rausen, A. R., & Blau, A. Psychotherapy of an infant with rumination. *Journal of the American Medical Association*, 1959, *171*, 2309–2312.

Stein, Z., & Susser, M. Nocturnal enuresis as a phenomenon of institutions. *Developmental Medicine and Child Neurology*, 1967, *9*, 692–706.

Stephen, L. S., & Koenig, K. L. Habit modification through threatened loss of money. *Behaviour Research and Therapy*, 1970, *8*, 211–212.

Stevens, J. R., & Blachly, P. H. Successful treatment of the maladie des tics. *American Journal of Disorders of Children*, 1966, *112*, 541–545.

Storrow, H. A. *Outline of clinical psychiatry*. New York: Appleton-Century-Crofts, 1969.

Taylor, D. V. Treatment of excessive frequency of urination by desensitization. *Journal of Behavior Therapy and Experimental Psychiatry*, 1972, *3*, 311–313.

Taylor, P. D., & Turner, R. K. A clinical trial of continuous, intermittent and overlearning "bell and pad" treatments for nocturnal enuresis. *Behaviour Research and Therapy*, 1975, *13*, 281–293.

Thomas, E. J., Abrams, K. S., & Johnson, J. B. Self-monitoring and reciprocal inhibition in the modification of multiple tics of Gilles de la Tourette's syndrome. *Journal of Behavior Therapy and Experimental Psychiatry*, 1971, *2*, 159–171.

Toister, R. P., Condron, C. J., Worley, L., & Arthur, D. Faradic therapy of chronic vomiting in infancy: A case study. *Journal of Behavior Therapy and Experimental Psychiatry*, 1975, *6*, 55–60.

Tophoff, M. Massed practice, relaxation, and assertion training in the treatment of Gilles de la Tourette's syndrome. *Journal of Behavior Therapy and Experimental Psychiatry*, 1973, *4*, 71–73.

Tough, J. H., Hawkins, R. P., MacArthur, M. M., & Ravensway, S. V. Modification of enuretic behavior by punishment: A new use for an old device. *Behavior Therapy*, 1971, *2*, 567–574.

Tourette, G. de la. Etude sur une affection nerveuse caractérisée par de l'incoordination motrice accompagnée d'écholalie et de coprolalie. *Archives of Neurology*, 1885, *9*, 19–42, 158–200.

Traisman, A. S., & Traisman, H. S. Thumb and finger sucking: A study of 2650 infants and children. *Journal of Pediatrics*, 1958, *52*, 566–572.

Trotter, W. D., & Lesch, M. M. Personal experiences with a stutter-aid. *Journal of Speech and Hearing Disorders*, 1967, *32*, 270–272.

Troup, C. W., & Hodgson, N. B. Nocturnal functional bladder capacity of enuretic children. *Pediatric Urology*, 1971, *105*, 129–132.

Turner, R. K. Conditioning treatment of nocturnal enuresis. In I. Kolvin, R. C. MacKeith, & S. R. Meadow (Eds.), *Bladder control and enuresis*. Philadelphia: Lippincott, 1973.

Turner, R. K., & Young, G. C. CNS stimulant drugs and conditioning treatment of nocturnal enuresis: A long-term follow-up study. *Behavior Research and Therapy*, 1966, *4*, 225–228.

Turner, R. K., Young, G. C., & Rachman, S. Treatment of nocturnal enuresis by conditioning techniques. *Behaviour Research and Therapy*, 1970, *8*, 367–381.

Tyre, T., Stephen, M., Maisto, A., & Companik, P. The use of systematic desensitization in the treatment of chronic stuttering behavior. *Journal of Speech and Hearing Disorders*, 1973, *38*, 514–519.

Van Riper, C. *The nature of stuttering*. Englewood Cliffs, N.J.: Prentice-Hall, 1971.

Van Riper, C. *The treatment of stuttering*. Englewood Cliffs, N.J.: Prentice-Hall, 1973.

Van Wagenen, R. K., & Murdock, E. E. A transistorized signal package for toilet training of infants. *Journal of Experimental Child Psychology*, 1966, *3*, 312–314.

Vargas, J. M., & Adesso, V. J. A comparison of aversion therapies for nailbiting behavior. *Behavior Therapy*, 1976, *1*, 322–329.

Walton, D. Experimental psychology and the treatment of a ticqueur. *Journal of Child Psychology and Psychiatry*, 1961, *2*, 148–155.

Walton, D. Massed practice and simultaneous reduction in drive level—Further evidence of the efficacy of this approach to the treatment of tics. In H. J. Eysenck (Ed.), *Experiments in behavior therapy*. London: Pergamon, 1964.

Warson, S. R., Caldwell, M. R., Warinner, A., Kirk, A. J., & Jensen, R. A. The dynamics of encopresis. *American Journal of Orthopsychiatry*, 1954, *24*, 402–415.

Watkins, J. T. Treatment of chronic vomiting and extreme emaciation by an aversive stimulus: Case study. *Psychological Reports*, 1972, *31*, 803–805.

Watson, D. H. Orthodontics and the growing child problems encountered in the primary dentition. *International Journal of Orthodontics*, 1969, *1*, 68–75.

Webster, R. L. Stuttering: A way to eliminate it and a way to explain it. In R. Ulrich, T. Stachnik, & J. Mabry (Eds.). *Control of human behavior*, Vol. 2. Glenview, Ill.: Scott, Foresman, 1970.

Webster, R. L. *Successive approximation to fluency: Operant response shaping procedures for use with stutterers*. Presented at the Seventeenth International Congress of Applied Psychology, Liège, Belgium, July 1971.

Webster, R. L. A few observations on the manipulation of speech response characteristics in stutterers. *Journal of Communication Disorders*, 1977, *10*, 73–76.

Webster, R. L., & Lubker, B. B. Interrelationships among fluency producing variables in stuttered speech. *Journal of Speech and Hearing Research*, 1968, *11*, 754–766.

Weiner, A. E. Vocal control therapy for stutterers: a trial program. *Journal of Fluency Disorders*, 1978, *3*, 115–126.

Werry, J. S., & Cohrssen, J. Enuresis: An etiologic and therapeutic study. *Journal of Pediatrics*, 1965, *67*, 423–431.

Wetzel, R. J., Baker, J., Roney, M., & Martin, M. Outpatient treatment of autistic behavior. *Behaviour Research and Therapy*, 1966, *4*, 169–177.

White, J. C., & Taylor, D. J. Noxious conditioning as a treatment for rumination. *Mental Retardation*, 1967, *5*, 30–33.

White, M. A thousand consecutive cases of enuresis: Results of treatment. *The Medical Officer*, 1968, *120*, 151–155.

Williams, C. D. The elimination of tantrum behavior by extinction procedures. *Journal of Abnormal and Social Psychology*, 1959, *59*, 269.

Wingate, M. E. A standard definition of stuttering. *Journal of Speech and Hearing Disorders*, 1964, *29*, 484–489.

Wingate, M. E. *Stuttering: Theory and treatment*. New York: Irvington, 1976.

Wolf, M. M., Risley, T., & Mees, J. Application of operant conditioning procedures to the behavior problems of an autistic child. *Behaviour Research and Therapy*, 1964, *1*, 305–312.

Wolf, M. M., Birnbrauer, J. S., Williams, T., & Lawler, J. A note on apparent extinction of the vomiting behavior of a retarded child. In L. P. Ullmann & L. Krasner (Eds.), *Case studies in behavior modification*. New York: Holt, Rinehart & Winston, 1965.

Wolff, R. Trichotillamania: Harriet's treatment. *Psychological Reports*, 1977, *40*, 50.

Wolpe, J. The systematic desensitization treatment of neuroses. *Journal of Nervous and Mental Disease*, 1961, *132*, 189–203.

Wright, L. Handling the encopretic child. *Professional Psychology*, 1973, *4*, 137–144.

Wright, L. Outcome of a standardized program for treating psychogenic encopresis. *Professional Psychology*, 1975, *6*, 453–456.

Wright, L., & Thalassinos, P. A. Success with electroshock in habitual vomiting: Report of two cases in young children. *Clinical Pediatrics*, 1973, *12*, 594–597.

Wright, L., & Walker, C. E. Behavioral treatment of encopresis. *Journal of Pediatric Psychology*, 1976, *4*, 35–37.

Yates, A. J. The application of learning theory to the treatment of tics. *Journal of Abnormal and Social Psychology*, 1958, *56*, 175–182.

Yates, A. J. Tics. In C. G. Costello (Ed.), *Symptoms of psychopathology*. New York: Wiley, 1970.

Yonovitz, A., Shepard, W. T., & Garrett, S. Hierarchical stimulation: Two case studies of stuttering modification using systematic desensitization. *Journal of Fluency Disorders*, 1977, *2*, 21–28.

Young, G. C. A "staggered-wakening" procedure in the treatment of enuresis. *Medical Officer*, 1964, *111*, 142–143.

Young, G. C. The aetiology of enuresis in terms of learning theory. *The Medical Officer*, 1965, *113*, 19–22.

Young, G. C. The problem of enuresis. *British Journal of Hospital Medicine*, 1969, *2*, 628–632.

Young, G. C. The treatment of childhood encopresis by conditioned gastroileal reflex training. *Behaviour Research and Therapy*, 1973, *11*, 499–503.

Young, G. C., & Morgan, R. T. T. Overlearning in the conditioning treatment of enuresis. *Behaviour Research and Therapy*, 1972, *10*, 419–420.

Young, G. C., & Turner, R. K. CNS stimulant drugs and conditioning of nocturnal enuresis. *Behaviour Research and Therapy*, 1965, *3*, 93–101.

Young, M. A. Onset, prevalence, and recovery from stuttering. *Journal of Speech and Hearing Disorders*, 1975, *40*, 49–58.

Zaleski, A., Gerrard, J. W., & Shokier, M. H. K. Nocturnal enuresis: The importance of a small bladder capacity. In I. Kolvin, R. C. MacKeith, & S. R. Meadow (Eds.), *Bladder control and enuresis*. Philadelphia: Lippincott, 1973.

CHAPTER 27

Retardation

John T. Neisworth and Ronald A. Madle

Defining retardation is a complicated task. The problems exhibited by individuals who have been labeled retarded can be extensive, affecting many areas of human functioning. In fact, one problem encountered in surveying behavior modification and therapy in the field of retardation is that *retardation* is a diagnostic term. As such, it identifies a category of people rather than a specific set of behaviors—the real domain of behavior modification. To align things appropriately, this chapter emphasizes, as have Bijou (1963) and Lindsley (1964), that behaviors, as opposed to individuals, are retarded. This perspective raises an issue about the term *mental retardation* when used by a behaviorist. Whatever is retarded when viewed from the standpoint of behaviorism is not "mentality." Some individuals in the field have advocated replacing the term *mental* with either *developmental* or *behavioral* (cf. Bijou, 1966). Neither of these alternatives appears to have met with widespread acceptance.

An alternative approach, as used in this chapter, is simply to use the term *retardation* to refer to a condition in which there is a generalized delay in a wide range of behavioral domains (Neisworth & Smith, 1974). While this type of definition allows individuals labeled with other traditional diagnoses, such as autism, to be included, it is highly consistent with many other contemporary definitions of mental retardation as well as the term *developmental disabilities* (Public Law 95.517, 1970), which is gradually becoming more dominant than the large number of traditional diagnostic labels for severe disorders that manifest themselves during the early part of the lifespan. Most current definitions outside the field of medicine emphasize the severity of the delays in various behavioral domains rather than the etiology of the delays.

Traditional Definitions of Mental Retardation

Although there have been a number of historically significant definitions of retardation, the most commonly accepted one today was developed by the American Association on Mental Deficiency (Grossman, 1977). This def-

John T. Neisworth • Department of Special Education, The Pennsylvania State University, University Park, Pennsylvania 16802. **Ronald A. Madle** • Director of Training and Evaluation, Laurelton Center, Laurelton, Pennsylvania 17835 and Division of Individual and Family Studies, The Pennsylvania State University, University Park, Pennsylvania 16802.   The contributions of the authors were equal with authorship order being arbitrarily selected.

inition indicates that *mental retardation* "refers to significantly subaverage intellectual functioning existing concurrently with deficits in adaptive behavior and manifested during the developmental period" (Grossman, 1977, p. 13). It should be noted that this definition refers to a delayed or deficient level of behavioral performance without reference to actual or presumed causes.

As far as intellectual performance is concerned, *significantly subaverage* is operationally defined as two or more standard deviations below the mean (IQ 69 or 70, depending on the test employed). While intellectual performance is still the most salient criterion used in identifying retardation, the concept of adaptive behavior has greatly changed the manner in which intervention is approached. In essence, adaptive behavior consists of the large set of behaviors that an individual must possess to "make it in society." These include behaviors typically grouped under behavioral domains such as self-care, motor ability, communication, socialization, and self-governance. Measures of these behaviors have not impacted significantly on practices in labeling individuals as retarded, since there are no simple cutoff points and scores for measures of adaptive behavior. These measures are usually put in the form of checklists enumerating the various significant capabilities. This measure, however, has significantly affected intervention practices. It has resulted in a sharper focus on changing adaptive behaviors rather than "mental" functioning. Therefore, most current approaches to intervening with the retarded more closely resemble behavioral approaches than they did a decade ago.

Given the great range and diversity of human functioning represented by the term *retardation*, individuals are typically classified into one of four levels of functioning. These levels are mild, moderate, severe, and profound retardation.

Mild retardation involves the least delay. The level of functioning differs little from that of other individuals of the same chronological age. Usually, the primary areas of delay are in academic and interpersonal skills. Most typically, people who display mild retardation are not even diagnosed or identified until they enter elementary school and begin having trouble academically. Once the person with mild retardation leaves school, he or she also is frequently able once again to "blend into" society and escape the "retarded" label that was acquired during school.

At the more impaired levels of functioning, individuals need some kinds of services throughout their lives. At the moderately retarded level, individuals show increased difficulty in doing tasks that are taken for granted by others. In addition to academic and interpersonal deficits, which are markedly more severe, the individual encounters difficulty with simple daily tasks, such as self-dressing, performing simple household chores, using money, and using leisure time effectively.

At the severely and profoundly retarded levels, the deficits become pronounced in all areas. Such simple tasks as toilet training, attending to people, and following instructions are learned only through systematic and intensive training. It is with this level that behavior modification will meet its greatest challenge in the near future. Legal mandates to provide education and training for the severely and profoundly retarded are now a fact. While behavioral techniques have been shown to be effective with these individuals in highly controlled settings, the task will now be to demonstrate that they can be effective in situations using parents, teachers, and other paraprofessionals as change agents.

Retardation is a problem of major social significance, as prevalence estimates range from 1% to as high as 11% or 12%, based on projections from the normal distribution of intelligence scores and from empirical studies. Dingman and Tarjan (1960) indicated that the actual prevalence may, in fact, be higher. Of course, the actual factors contributing to prevalence make this figure vary across geographic regions, sexes, ages, and so forth. For example, countries that are more tolerant of minor deviations from the norm, such as the Scandinavian countries, generally show a lower prevalence of retarded individuals, since their cutoff point for identifying this condition is lower than in many other countries. Whatever the criteria, however, retardation is a universal and significant social problem.

Behavioral Models of Retardation

Behavioral models of retardation have been discussed by a number of individuals (Bijou, 1963, 1966; Lindsley, 1964; Neisworth & Smith, 1973). Most current theoretical models are extensions of the model initially advanced by Bijou (1963). Basically, this analysis was derived from Skinner's (1953) objections to inferring personal traits from observed behavior and then, in turn, using the trait as an explanation of the behavior itself. Instead of viewing the cause of retardation as a theoretical construct such as mentality, or as a biological phenomenon such as impairment of the brain, Bijou suggested that retardation be conceived of as a *behavioral* deficiency generated by adverse reinforcement histories or as failures of stimulus-and-response functions. This form of functional analysis suggests a search into learning variables such as intermittent reinforcement and extinction, inadequate reinforcement history, severe punishment, and other factors such as extreme satiation and deprivation. A major advantage of this approach is that the variables suggested as causing regarded behaviors are all subject to objective definition and are all manipulable or potentially manipulable, a feature that is obviously desirable for empirical research and application. In addition, Bijou's theory requires not a special theory of retardation but an extension of the principles of operant learning theory to both the explanation and the modification of retarded behavior. Bijou's (1963) 4-point system of explaining the development and the maintenance of retarded behavior is described below.

Biological and Physiological Factors

While biological factors are included in this model of retardation, we will present it in such a way as to link them clearly to the development of behavior. This model specifies three specific ways in which biological apparatus can affect the development of behavior. First, essential response equipment may be impaired. A child is not able to perform tasks that require responses that are impossible to execute because the necessary biological structures are absent or deficient. The child is not able to perform the task regardless of the amount of stimulation or exposure or training provided. Other responses that serve the same function and that compensate for this impairment *may* be learned, however. An excellent example has been the development of nonspeech methods of communication for individuals who are unable to speak.

The second way in which biological factors may limit the development of behavioral repertoires is the restriction of the stimuli that ordinarily are available to human beings. The child who can see, hear, smell, and feel objects and events can have infinitely more experiences than the child whose sensory mechanisms are impaired. Many times, this type of restriction can also be compensated for by other people and events in the child's environment. Some approaches to this problem are evident in Lindsley's (1964) statement about retardation, to be discussed shortly.

The third way in which biological impairment might restrict developmental opportunities is related to the way the person appears to others. Physical attractiveness, in part, controls opportunities for learning. The ugly child or one with certain repelling characteristics is deprived of the usual positive social stimulation provided to the "cute," normal child (see Neisworth, Jones, & Smith, 1978, for an expansion of this topic).

Intermittent Reinforcement and Extinction

Bijou (1963) discussed several ways in which intermittent reinforcement and extinction may operate to delay progressive changes in behavior. First, it is possible that for some parents, it is reinforcing to see their child remain helpless, ineffective, and infantile. Under these circumstances, they are likely to reinforce dependent behavior and systematically extinguish, or even punish, independent behaviors. Research on parent–child interactions with their handicapped and nonhandicapped children have confirmed these speculations (Campbell, 1973). The second possibility is that intermittent reinforcement is too lean and actual extinction may operate to weaken the development of classes of behavior that depend on frequent and consistent parental reinforcement. These especially include the social and language behaviors so necessary to early development.

Inadequate Reinforcement History

When an environment is dull, routine, unvaried, and limited in range, interactions are also restricted. Conditions of this sort would most likely limit repertoires in self-care, emotional-social reactions, and preacademic and academic skills. This type of reinforcement history may be expected, since retarded children are frequently raised under conditions that are less than optimal. These include being raised in isolated communities, in institutions where the conditions for good family living are not present, and in families with disturbed or deficient parenting.

Severe Punishment

The last factor that would be likely to retard development is *severe* punishment. Consequences of this sort may operate in several ways. For example, if a child is punished by his or her parents for saying negative things about a younger sibling, he or she may react by eventually garbling words in such a fashion that they do not elicit punishment. Such a change prevents the punishment but certainly does not lead to adequate language growth. Second, there is a large body of evidence (Azrin & Holz, 1966) indicating that severe punishment stops ongoing behavior. If such punishment is mild, it may well be possible to reestablish the behavior, but, if the punishment is severe, it may have long-lasting suppressing effects that would be extremely resistive to change. In addition, these effects become very disruptive when either response or stimulus generalization occurs. In this case, not only are the punished behaviors suppressed, but related behaviors in similar settings are suppressed. Additionally, previously neutral stimuli, such as the situation in which the punishment occurred, may become aversive. The prepotent response becomes one of avoiding the punishing situation, in which many skills are learned normally, and constitutes negative reinforcement for avoiding potential learning situations.

While Bijou's (1963) analysis is now almost two decades old, it is nonetheless still current. Little systematic effort has been put into further developing an overall behavioral model of retardation or into systematically developing a comprehensive and coherent system of behavioral technology with the retarded that encompasses assessment, prescription, intervention, and evaluation.

The one possible extension of Bijou's theory occurred when Lindsley (1964) posited that *children* are not retarded, only their behavior in average environments is sometimes retarded. The primary emphasis of Lindsley's work was oriented to dealing with the biological conditions that Bijou discussed. His basic premise was that various forms of prostheses were available, including devices that could be carried about by an individual, training that could overcome behavioral handicaps, and the construction of prosthetic environments where the performance of the child would be more normal than in the average environment.

Probably the most influential aspect of Lindsley's work was his pointing out the fallacy of *similia similibus curantur,* or the "like-cures-like" doctrine. Lindsley pointed out that treatment need not be dictated by the alleged cause of a dysfunction. Even practitioners who do not accept a behavioral model of retarded development are likely to be able to employ behavioral procedures in modifying retarded development. Subsequent applied research on behavior modification with the retarded and a rapidly expanding literature clearly support either the adequacy of a behavioral model or at least the relevance of Lindsley's formulations.

Historical Perspectives on Treatment

In the more than 25 centuries that retardation has been recognized as a problem, there have been four major eras in approaches to the treatment of the retarded. During primitive times, the basic approach was survival. The retarded, like many other handicapped individuals, were simply not fit to exist and were allowed to die. As the fight for survival became less pressing, a somewhat humanitarian trend emerged. While not as frequently destroyed, the retarded were often ridiculed. Some became slaves; others were taken in by beggars and deliberately maimed so that they could solicit alms. Some of the more fortunate were taken in by wealthy families and kept as a source of amusement for family members and guests. Some were employed as court jesters or companions for the wealthy. While no longer eliminated, the retarded did not yet fare well.

During the Middle Ages, the religious movements brought increased humanitarianism. Retarded individuals were often taken in as wards of the church and cared for in monasteries and asylums. Of course, during the same era, there were some throwbacks to earlier times as, for example, when Martin Luther advocated throwing the retarded into the River Themes to perish, since he thought they were possessed by demons. The last era in the treatment of the retarded did not begin until around the seventeenth century and arose in the theories of John Locke (who was also a prominent figure in the development of behavioral approaches). Since Locke felt that the capabilities of human beings are primarily a function of the environment, this viewpoint brought a new optimism that the mentally retarded could be educated and trained rather than simply cared for.

The current era is one of treatment and training. Perhaps one of the earliest forms of treatment during this era was "moral treatment," in which it was felt that both the retarded and the mentally ill could be cured or at least improved through humane treatment. Unfortunately, the relative ineffectiveness of this approach to treatment, as well as the prevailing sociopolitical conditions (Sarason & Doris, 1969), resulted in a backlash and the establishment of the eugenics movement. The basic theme of this movement is that retardation is a genetic or biological problem that is not amenable to treatment. During this period, the retarded were segregated from society and in many cases sterilized to prevent the propagation of defective organisms. Even when this overall policy of segregation and sterilization

ended, the continued reliance on biological models resulted in the dominance of the medical profession in the care and treatment of the retarded. As is true in general, we appear to be recycling at this point and are now in an era close to moral treatment, that is, the philosophy of normalization. Once again, there are signs that this phase may be coming to a close and a backlash may be occurring. There is one primary difference between this point in the cycle and the late 1800s, when the last era of moral treatment ended: the presence of behavioral technology and its demonstrated effectiveness in training and habilitating the retarded.

Behavioral work with the mentally retarded began, for all practical purposes, with the work of Jean Itard, a physician and educator in the eighteenth century. It was Itard who, upon hearing the stories about a "wolf-child" found in the forests of France, decided to work with the child and attempt to train him to live in society. While Itard emphasized the sensory aspects of his techniques, it has become clear from an examination of the detailed records that he kept that many of the methods he used were in fact similar to those employed by current behavior modifiers. Given the lack of a coherent behavioral model in Itard's work, subsequent applications of his procedures were conducted by Maria Montessori, who again emphasized the sensory training aspects of his methodology. It was not until the middle of the twentieth century that behavioral techniques were once again applied to the training of the mentally retarded.

In an isolated report, Fuller (1949) demonstrated that the arm movement of a profoundly retarded adult could be brought under reinforcement control with the application of operant procedures. In 1963, Ellis produced a theoretical account of how the toilet training of the retarded might be accomplished through the systematic application of learning principles. Basic research in learning with the retarded began in earnest during the 1950s with the purpose of demonstrating that operant principles were applicable to the behavior and the learning of the mentally retarded. It was at this point that prominent behavioral researchers such as Sidney Bijou, Norman Ellis, Beatrice Barrett, Ogden Lindsley, Joseph

Spradlin, and Edward Zigler were prominent. They set the foundation for applied behavior analysis with the retarded. At this point began the vigorous work in applying and validating behavioral procedures to changing the practical behaviors of the retarded.

A survey of the current status of behavior modification and therapy with the retarded is presented in the next section. This survey of the literature is organized around three major areas. The first of these is the reporting of significant work related to *targets for change*, such as toileting, dressing, and social behaviors. Then we move on to the various *behavioral tactics* that have been applied with the retarded. Last, there is discussion of the overall *strategies* by which the behavioral tactics are applied.

Current Empirical Status and Developments

Targets for Change

Much of the early application of behavior modification with the retarded was to the development of such self-care behaviors as toilet training, dressing, grooming, and feeding among the severely and profoundly retarded individuals living in institutions. Operant techniques have been particularly well-suited to dealing with these groups because of the relatively little emphasis placed on the verbal skills of such clients.

Toilet Training. Toileting of the retarded has received a great deal of attention. One of the first theoretical analyses of applying behavior modification to the retarded was Ellis's (1963) analysis of how operant principles might be used in toilet training. Early applications of this suggested approach included work by Dayan (1964), Hundziak, Maurer, and Watson (1965), Minge and Ball (1967), Giles and Wolf (1966), and Watson (1968). Toilet training offers an excellent example of the progressive refinement of behavioral techniques.

Early work concentrated primarily on the use of positive reinforcement and punishment, and there was little application of other behavioral techniques. For example, Dayan (1964) had severely retarded children placed on the toilet every two hours. Reinforcement was then delivered for elimination during these periods of time. The only real refinement came about when Watson (1968) developed an automated toilet trainer, which administered reinforcement when the child eliminated into the toilet. The primary advantage of these methods over traditional toilet training was the addition of appropriate consequences for toileting behavior to the toileting schedule procedure that already existed in most institutions.

At this point, a significant increase in the effectiveness of toileting programs occurred when Azrin and Foxx (1971) recognized the need for multiple intensive procedures. In addition to using an apparatus to signal when toileting occurred and providing appropriate consequences, the Azrin–Foxx procedure included modeling, priming to increase urination frequency, food and social reinforcement for urinating correctly or staying dry, reprimands and time-out for soiling, and shaping self-initiation of toileting. While previous behavioral and nonbehavioral approaches to toilet training the retarded required months of training and statistical tests to demonstrate their effectiveness, Azrin and Foxx (1971) trained nine profoundly retarded adults in a median time of four days. The longest training time for these nine individuals was 12 days. Procedures were also included in the program to ensure the long-term maintenance of toileting behaviors. While other toilet training programs have been effective, studies have demonstrated that a combination of procedures, including at least reinforcement, the chaining and shaping of responses, prompting, and punishment, are necessary (Baumeister & Klosowski, 1965; Kimbrell, Luckey, Barbuto, & Love, 1967; Mahoney, Van Wagenen, & Meyerson, 1971; Van Wagenen, Meyerson, Kerr, & Mahoney, 1969). Little further progress has occurred in the area of toilet training. The Azrin–Foxx program has virtually become a standard against which other techniques are assessed. In spite of the effectiveness of the procedure as reported by Azrin and Foxx, some individuals (e.g., Birnbrauer, 1976) have questioned the effectiveness of the procedure, since no independent replications have been reported. In addition, it has been the experience of one of the authors of this chapter (Madle) that many attempts to apply the Azrin–Foxx method have been halfhearted and have used only those components that the individual practioners have felt were necessary. Unpublished work currently going on has indicated, however, that the consistent and precise application of the method has resulted in an effectiveness comparable with that of Azrin and Foxx. This work, however, has had to employ eight separate trainers working with each individual resident, somewhat decreasing the overall efficiency of the procedure.

While most work on toileting has emphasized skill development, other studies have dealt with related toileting problems. For example, Luiselli (1977) reported a case of toileting phobia in a 15-year-old retarded male who manifested an intense fear of urinating in a toilet. As a result, he wet his pants at a frequent rate. Through a combination of various response-contingent consequences and the gradual introduction of structured contingencies, a steady reduction in the frequency of wetting was noted. By the end of a follow-up phase, the individual was self-initiating toileting in an appropriate manner.

A second related area has been the reduction of enuretic behaviors. One of the most prominent methods of accomplishing this is the pad-and-buzzer technique, developed by Mowrer and Mowrer (1938). Sloop and Kennedy (1973) conducted a study on two groups of individuals to evaluate the effectiveness of this procedure. In this study, the subjects treated with the pad-and-buzzer method had significantly more success than the control group in meeting the criterion of 13 dry nights. Unfortunately, 4 of the 11 successful subjects relapsed within 36–72 days. In the long run, only one-third of the treated group remained dry. It would seem that this technique may benefit from the addition of supplemental techniques, much as the early toilet training was improved by Azrin and Foxx. A second method of dealing with enuresis has been developed by Kimmel and Kimmel (1970) and consists of simply prompting the child to report when he or she needs to urinate during the day and instructing him or her to wait, briefly at first and then for longer periods. A controlled study by Paschalis, Kimmel, and Kimmel (1972) showed impressive results.

Feeding. Another behavior receiving early attention in the literature was self-feeding. Like other self-care behaviors, this was frequently given high priority since the ability of retarded individuals to care for themselves drastically reduces the amount of individualized attention necessary to maintain the individual and allows greater amounts of time to be spent on active training to become more self-sufficient and competent in other areas. Gorton and Hollis (1965) described the steps used to shape feeding skills in a task analysis of the various steps involved in filling a spoon from a tray or dish and moving the spoon toward and into the mouth. The basic technique employed was backward chaining and manual guidance, and the individual's hand was guided in filling the utensil, bringing the spoon to the mouth, and releasing the subject's hand just prior to the spoon's going into the mouth. As progress occurred at each stage, the hand was released further and further from the mouth, until eventually, the child was able to fill the spoon and feed herself or himself. Repeated demonstrations of these techniques (Henriksen & Doughty, 1967; Barton, Guess, Garcia, & Baer, 1970; Martin, McDonald, & Omichinski, 1971; Zeiler & Jervey, 1968) showed that this technique could be effective. Again, the primary innovation during this period of time was simply the addition of aversive contingencies, such as food removal for inappropriate behavior occurring in the training situation. This contingency somewhat increased the efficacy of the procedure.

Azrin's group at Anna State Hospital (O'Brien, Bugle, & Azrin, 1972) once again developed a superior procedure by combining a number of behavioral tactics into a coherent package. Later, Azrin (Azrin & Armstrong, 1973; O'Brien & Azrin, 1972) further developed the technology of feeding programs for the adult institutionalized person by using "minimeals" served regularly throughout a nine-hour training period. This increase in the number of training sessions, combined with the procedures of continuous reinforcement, graduated guidance, mastery of each utensil separately, multiple trainers, correction of errors, and positive practice, resulted in the rapid acquisition of feeding skills in previously unmanageable adult retarded persons.

An independent replication by Stimbert, Minor, and McCoy (1977) demonstrated that all the individuals in their study achieved correct eating responses to nearly optimal levels, that incorrect eating responses were reduced to minimal levels, and that inappropriate or disruptive behaviors were virtually eliminated. In addition, follow-up data at intervals of up to one year indicated that the effects of the program were quite durable and justified the effort expended during the training period. Nelson, Cone, and Hanson (1975) compared two techniques for training correct utensil use in retarded children: modeling and physical guidance. This study demonstrated that physical guidance was effective while modeling only was not. While much of the work on mealtime behavior with the retarded has been conducted in one-to-one settings using staff trainers, Mercatoris, Hahn, and Craighead (1975) used higher-functioning retarded residents of an institution to train 30 residents of another living unit in appropriate mealtime behaviors.

Dressing. Normally, children learn to dress with no special training; moderately to profoundly retarded individuals are unlikely to learn even minimal dressing skills unless special training has been provided. Initial behavior-modification programs, such as Bensberg's (1965) early effort, offered hope that low-functioning retarded persons could be taught to dress themselves. The procedures that were developed appeared to be effective for higher-functioning individuals; however, there was little or no evidence of success with low-functioning persons. Minge and Ball (1967) trained six profoundly retarded girls for 30 hours and found some improvement in undressing but virtually no improvement in the development of dressing skills. In 1970, Horner provided dressing training to 83 severely and profoundly retarded persons and found that one-third did not benefit from the training. The other individuals required approximately 70 sessions to reach criterion. Ball, Seric, and Payne (1971) found only slight improvement in the dressing skills of retarded boys after 90 days of training. Watson (1972) estimated that with this procedure, 8–12 months would be required to teach the profoundly retarded to dress themselves.

Several reinforcement procedures for teaching dressing skills have been described in detail along with the overall rationale (Ball *et al.,* 1971; Bensberg, Colwell, & Cassell, 1965; Bensberg & Slominski, 1965; Horner, 1970; Minge & Ball, 1967; Watson, 1972). Virtually all of these procedures have the following common characteristics: food or praise as reinforcers; reinforcement given at the completion of the act of taking off or putting on a specific garment; instructions given to start each trial for a given garment; backward chaining for each garment, whereby the instructor puts on or takes off the garment, allowing the subject to do only the final portion; instruction provided on one article of clothing before proceeding to the next; and finally, fading of the instructions and reinforcers. Brief training sessions of about 15 minutes' duration were used over a period of many weeks or months.

The status of dressing training indicates that another procedure developed by Azrin, Schaeffer, and Wesolowski (1976) is currently the most effective procedure for teaching low-functioning individuals to dress themselves. In contrast to prior programs, this technique includes rather lengthy and intensive training sessions, a forward sequence of steps rather than backward training, graduated and intermittent manual guidance, continuous talking and praising, graduated-sized clothing, and an emphasis on reinforcers natural to the dressing process. In the process of validating their program, Azrin *et al.* (1977) were able to train seven out of seven profoundly retarded adults both to dress and to undress themselves in an average of 12 hours distributed over three or four training days.

Other Self-Care Behaviors. While toileting, feeding, and dressing have been the most common areas of interest in self-care, a number of other areas have been touched on. Token reinforcement has been employed to a significant degree. Girardeau and Spradlin (1964) used this method with severely and moderately retarded women. Tokens were delivered for a variety of self-care, grooming, and social behaviors, including making beds, washing hair, and being on time for activities. For a few children, individualized contingencies were used to develop persistence at a task, cooperative play, and academic skills. This program emphasized individual improvement in behaviors rather than the performance of a predetermined response. Marked gains were reported 4½ months after the inception of the program.

Hunt, Fitzhugh, and Fitzhugh (1968) used token reinforcement to improve the personal appearance of 12 retarded individuals. Initially, continuous reinforcement was given when the subjects met the criterion for personal appearance. Subsequently, reinforcement was given intermittently. The individuals improved under the reinforcement program and showed the highest gains under the intermittent reinforcement condition. When reinforcement was totally withdrawn, their personal appearance deteriorated.

Barry, Apolloni, and Cooke (1977) assessed the effects of a contingency-contracting procedure on the personal hygiene skills of three retarded adults. These skills included such areas as clean hair, combed hair, clean teeth, and the absence of an objectionable body odor. In a reversal design, Barry *et al.* (1977) demonstrated that low levels of baseline responding could be increased significantly by providing rewards through a contingency-contracting procedure.

Horner and Keilitz (1975) developed a comprehensive toothbrushing program that included task analysis and training procedures specific to each component of the task analysis. Eight mentally retarded adolescents in two groups received individual acquisition training that included scheduled opportunities for independent performances, verbal instruction, modeling, demonstration, and physical assistance. Four of the subjects received tokens plus social reinforcement, while the other four received social reinforcement alone. All eight subjects showed improved toothbrushing when compared with baseline. Six of the eight subjects correctly performed all toothbrushing steps in two of three consecutive sessions. While other researchers (e.g., Abramson & Wunderlich, 1972; Lattal, 1969) have reported on toothbrushing programs, the results of Horner and Keilitz (1975) appear to be the most effective to date.

Language and Communication. The dysfunctions of the retarded within the communication domain include a large variety of behaviors, such as basic language skills, receptive and productive language, conversational skills, and various speech and articulation problems. The initial problem encountered in communication skills is usually a rate problem. The individual must first be made to emit various verbal operants at a satisfactory rate. Later, the primary issue becomes one of stimulus control, that is, training the client to emit the proper response to an appropriate stimulus.

Increasing Verbalization Rates. In the case of very severe communication disorders, the first step in working with the client is to begin by teaching simple vocal imitation skills. This typically has been accomplished by prompting behaviors in response to a modeled behavior and then reinforcing the imitative response (e.g., Garcia, Baer, & Firestone, 1971; Sloane, Johnston, & Harris, 1968). Before using vocal responses as imitative stimuli, it has generally been necessary to begin with simple motor-response imitation (e.g., Baer, Peterson, & Sherman, 1967) to build the basic imitative skills needed for early language training. While in early training only those imitations that are reinforced are imitated, soon the client begins to imitate all modeled behaviors at a high rate—a phenomenon referred to as *generalized imitation.*

Establishing Stimulus Control of Verbalizations. Once the client is able to imitate vocal stimuli, the next task is to bring these verbalizations under the stimulus control of appropriate stimuli, such as objects and pictures. The usual procedure for training basic labeling skills has been to show the client a picture or an object and to ask, "What is this?" Through a combination of prompting and reinforcement procedures, the client learns to label objects correctly (e.g., Risley & Wolf, 1967), and the prompts and reinforcement are gradually faded.

After labeling has been established, the client is taught generative speech, whereby she or he can emit a large number of possible phrases and sentences without specific training for each one. This training is the logical extension of generalized imitation training. Generative speech is produced by training the individual to respond to a selected number of individual elements of a given response class in order to establish a larger use of that class. As an example, Lutzker and Sherman (1974) established the appropriate use of sentences involving plural and singular subject–verb agreement by providing training in selected subject–verb combinations. As an increasing number of these sentences were taught, the individuals also began to use correct subject–verb combinations that had never been taught. Various syntactic aspects of communication, such as the use of plurals, have been taught in this manner.

Training in the receptive portion of communication skills has typically included establishing generalized instruction-following responses, including pointing to pictures and following action instructions. For example, Striefel, Wetherby, and Karlan (1976) trained retarded children to respond correctly to various verb–noun instructions that were recombined into new combinations. As the training increased, the children increasingly became able to respond correctly to novel noun–verb combinations on the first trial. Baer and Guess (1971) were also able to train the correct receptive use of the comparative and the superlative forms of various adjectives, such as *big, bigger, biggest,* through similar procedures. In each of the above cases of language training, the primary task was to train the retarded person to respond to a given stimulus with the ''correct'' response—a problem in establishing appropriate stimulus control.

Numerous investigators have trained instruction-following skills in retarded children and adults (Kazdin & Erickson, 1975; Striefel & Wetherby, 1973; Zimmerman, Zimmerman, & Russell, 1969) through procedures similar to those for teaching imitation. A command or an instruction is given, and the response is prompted, usually through physical guidance. Once emitted, the response is then reinforced. Over time, the individual becomes able to respond to a large number of commands without specific training on each one. In fact, both generalized imitation and instruction following appear to be in the same response class. The only difference is that the first is an exact reproduction of behavior, while the second is a generation of the behavior based on a topographically dissimilar command.

While the majority of studies in the communication area have been concerned with narrowly defined parts of the communication process, Keilitz, Tucker, and Horner (1973)

concentrated on teaching three retarded males increased verbalization about current events. Each of the men individually viewed a videotape of a brief televised newscast and then received tokens for correct responses about the content of the materials. This training subsequently increased verbalizations about current events.

Speech. Other commonly encountered communication problems in the retarded individual include various dysfunctions in speech rather than in the language components of the process. One common problem has been voice volume. Some retarded individuals speak either too softly or too loudly. Jackson and Wallace (1974), for example, worked with a girl whose speech was barely audible. Through a microphone system in which the volume could be quantified, the girl received reinforcement for speech that exceeded a criterion. Her voice volume increased in the training sessions and eventually generalized to the classroom setting. Other topographical aspects of speech that have been worked with include articulation (Griffiths & Craighead, 1972; Murdock, Garcia, & Hardman, 1977); perseveration (Butz & Hasazi, 1973), echolalia (Palyo, Schuler, Cooke, & Apolloni, 1979); and dysfluencies (Kazdin, 1973).

Nonvocal Communication. Since many retarded individuals have structural abnormalities in their speech apparatus that limit normal speaking, a number of investigators have trained them to communicate either through sign language or a more recent technique: the communication board. Some investigators have used manual signs or gestures as aids in teaching a variety of language skills to normally hearing children (Bricker, 1972; Miller & Miller, 1973). A recent study by VanBiervliet (1977) demonstrated that six institutionalized retarded males were able to learn manual sign training to establish words and objects as functionally equivalent. The teaching of sign language to retarded children is still fraught with many difficulties, given the motor skills that are involved.

The use of communication boards has become much more widespread and is more easily taught. Reid and Hurlbut (1977) evaluated a training program for teaching communication skills to nonvocal retarded adults. Each of the four subjects was severely physically disabled and had never demonstrated functional speech. Each person was taught either to use a prosthetic head pointer or to point with the hand in using a communication board for expressive language. This study consisted of a series of three experiments. The first implemented coordination training, consisting of instructions, manual guidance, praise, feedback, and practice. Each person demonstrated a higher frequency of accurate pointing to the designated areas on the board during the coordination training than during baseline. In the second experiment, using identification training, instructions, praise, feedback, and practice, it was demonstrated that the subjects pointed more frequently to specific word–photograph combinations that corresponded to descriptive verbal labels after the introduction of identification training. Social validation was accomplished in the third experiment, which indicated that the communication board skills were functional in providing a method of expressing a choice of leisure activity to people who previously could not understand the subject's communication attempts. The acquired skills were maintained through a seven-week follow-up period.

Social Skills. Adequate social behavior is often cited as a major behavioral deficit of retarded persons, particularly those who are institutionalized. While the research in this area has been somewhat limited, Mayhew, Enyart, and Anderson (1978) indicated that three different basic strategies can be utilized in developing the social behavior of the retarded: (1) overall enrichment of the living environment; (2) direct training of specific cooperative tasks; and (3) direct training of specific response components of social behavior.

Enrichment programs are aimed at improving or at least maintaining the existing social-skill levels. Individuals in such programs generally engage in a higher frequency of informal and formal training situations in comparison with the regular ward routine and enjoy a more favorable staff-to-client ratio (Mitchell & Smeriglio, 1970). Most reports of this type have been anecdotal, although some research indicates that there may be drawbacks to enrichment programs. Harris, Veit, Allen, and Chinsky (1974) provided data suggesting that certain activities often reported as enriching, such as the improving of physical conditions and more favorable staff-to-client ratios, have only a minimal beneficial impact. In addition, a study by Wheeler and Wislocki (1977) demonstrated that peer conversation was differentially affected by the presence or absence of ward attendants. Interestingly, peer conversation decreased rather drastically when aides were present on the ward, certainly an undesirable condition. These authors also demonstrated, however, that the systematic removal of these aides and fading them back into the situation allowed high levels of social behavior to continue.

The second approach to social response development is the direct training of a few specific kinds of behaviors, such as ball rolling or block passing, that involve cooperation among a small number of individuals (Morris & Dolker, 1974; Samaras & Ball, 1975; Whitman, Mercurio, & Caponigri, 1970). While studies have generally shown that the development of these behaviors is not particularly difficult, an issue arises when the responses must be generalized to new settings and/or new individuals. An example of this type of approach is the study by Samaras and Ball (1975), in which seven dyads of retarded children and adults were placed in an environment where the cooperative operation of a task apparatus yielded reinforcement. During this period of time, cooperative behavior among the experimental subjects increased radically.

The third approach to training social responses involves direct training in specific response components, such as hand waving and playing with others (Stokes, Baer, & Jackson, 1974). An early attempt of this type (Hopkins, 1968) used candy and social reinforcement to develop smiling in two retarded boys. For both children, candy reinforcement was shown to control the frequency of smiling. After the initiation of a maintenance and generalization procedure, the children continued to show high rates of appropriate smiling on termination of the program. This approach has become more popular in recent years, especially with higher-functioning retarded persons, witness the development of structured learning therapy (Goldstein, 1973) and social-skills-training packages (Hersen & Bellack, 1976).

Perry and Cerreto (1977) reported on a prescriptive teaching approach that utilized modeling, role playing, and social reinforcement in a group to teach social skills to 10 retarded young adults. At the same time, 10 matched subjects were taught the same social skills in a discussion format, and 10 others received no treatment. The structured approach was considerably more effective in changing the social skills, both in a structured situation test that measured social interaction and in observation during the normal mealtime period. Matson and Stephens (1978) reported on the use of a social-skills-training package to increase the appropriate social behavior of explosive, chronic psychiatric patients, some of whom were mentally retarded. After targeting behaviors within each training session for individual subjects, the training involved instructions, modeling, role playing, and feedback. Using a multiple-baseline design, these authors demonstrated the effectiveness of this approach in strengthening the target behaviors. The trained skills also generalized to the ward setting, and the number of antisocial behaviors, such as arguing and fighting, was markedly reduced, indicating that many problem behaviors demonstrated by the retarded may, in fact, be due to their inability to emit appropriate social behaviors.

Whatever approach is taken, the problem of the generalization and maintenance of social behaviors continues to exist. The study by Mayhew *et al.* (1978) was designed to determine if the deficit in social behavior of retarded persons might be due in part to the failure of their environment to maintain that behavior. In a reversal design, a group of severely and profoundly retarded institutionalized adolescents were alternately ignored or given social reinforcement for appropriate social behaviors. Social behavior decreased during the nonreinforcement conditions and increased during reinforcement conditions. These data suggest that deficits in the social behavior of retarded persons may be due to the failure of their environment to maintain such behavior rather than to a lack of the skills needed.

Community and Vocational Preparation. The community and vocational preparation of the retarded has taken on increasing importance in recent years, largely because of the current emphasis on placing retarded individuals in the community rather than segregating them in specialized residential services (Wolfensberger, 1972). Both of these areas are typically considered developmental tasks during the adult portion of the life span. The American Association on Mental Deficiency (Grossman, 1977) has pointed out that living and working in the community are the primary adaptive behaviors developed during adulthood.

Community Preparation. While the literature on community preparation is somewhat sketchy, there are several studies indicating increased activity in this area. Iwata and his associates (Page, Iwata, & Neef, 1976; Neef, Iwata, & Page, 1978) conducted two studies on increasing the mobility of the retarded person in the community. In the first of these (Page *et al.,* 1976), five retarded males were taught basic pedestrian skills in a classroom setting. The training was conducted on a model built to simulate city traffic conditions. Each of the subjects was taught the specific skills involved in street crossing, including intersection recognition, pedestrian light skills, traffic light skills, and skills for two different stop-sign conditions. Before, during, and after the training, the subjects were tested on generalization probes on a classroom model and under actual city-traffic conditions. The results of the multiple-baseline design across both subjects and behaviors indicated that after receiving classroom training on the skills, each subject exhibited appropriate pedestrian skills under city traffic conditions. In addition, training in some skills appeared to facilitate performance skills not yet trained.

In the second study (Neef *et al.,* 1978), a classroom program was developed to teach bus-riding skills. Five retarded males were taught each component derived from a task analysis (locating, signaling, boarding, riding, and leaving a bus). The skills were taught sequentially by means of role playing, manipulating the actions of a doll on a simulated model, and responding to questions about slide sequences. Before, during, and after training, the subjects were tested on generalization both in the classroom and in the natural environment. The results indicated that up to 12 months after training, the subjects exhibited appropriate bus-riding skills on actual city buses. Interestingly, Neff *et al.* (1978) also trained two additional subjects *in vivo* on city buses. They found that both the classroom and the *in vivo* procedures were equally effective, but that the *in vivo* procedure was considerably more time-consuming and costly.

A second community-preparation area is clothing selection. This has traditionally been ignored, even though the importance of clothing to a handicapped person's lifestyle and acceptance has been emphasized for decades (Newton, 1976). Following this lead, Nutter and Reid (1978) taught clothing selection skills to five institutionalized retarded women. After observing women's apparel in a local community, a training program was developed using a puzzle simulation of a woman with alternative pieces of colored clothing. The color-coordination training was conducted using modeling, instruction, practice, praise, and feedback to teach popular selections of color combinations. The training was accompanied by large increases in the percentages of popular color selections in both the puzzle situation and actual clothing usage during generalization probes. These increases were maintained over seven 14-week follow-up periods. As in the earlier study on public transportation skills, Nutter and Reid (1978) concluded that the simulation approach resulted in considerable efficiency over an approach relying on the use of actual clothing.

Marholin, O'Toole, Touchette, Berger, and Doyle (1979) trained four retarded adult males to ride a bus to a specific destination, purchase an item, and order and pay for a meal. The training was conducted in the community and included graduated prompting, modeling, corrective feedback, social reinforcement, behavioral rehearsal, and occasional brief time-outs administered on a multiple-baseline across subjects. Correct performance increased during training and was transferred to a novel environment.

One additional community preparation area that is important is leisure-time behavior. The importance of appropriate leisure-time skills for the retarded individual should not be underemphasized. Many studies of the reasons for returning to an institutional setting have indicated that the most common reason is the inability to use discretionary leisure time appropriately. Rarely are persons returned because of their inability to work or to care for themselves adequately. Johnson and Bailey (1977) investigated the effect of the availability of materials, prizes for participation, and instruction on the leisure behavior of 14 retarded adults in a halfway house. A leisure program was conducted on weekday evenings, during which the residents could choose to participate in any of six activities offered: puzzles, card games, play, painting, weaving, and rug making. Instruction in weaving and rug making significantly increased the percentage of residents participating in these activities, and following instruction, prizes were not necessary to maintain high levels of participation. In contrast, prizes were more effective than the mere availability of materials in maintaining participation in the other activities. Interestingly, a point not raised by Johnson and Bailey (1977) is the choice of the six activities. A careful look at the six activities shows that weaving and rug making, which did not require prizes for maintenance, are more typical of adult discretionary activities, whereas the remaining items are more typically child-oriented, requiring special incentives to maintain participation.

Additional work in the area of community preparation includes problem solving and planning (Ross & Ross, 1973); making correct change (Lowe & Cuvo, 1976); cooking (Bellamy & Clark, 1977); housekeeping (Bauman & Iwata, 1977); using the telephone (Leff, 1974, 1975); and completing biographical information forms (Clark, Boyd, & Macrae, 1975).

Vocational Preparation. In 1973, Gold published a comprehensive and provocative review of the research in the vocational habilitation of the retarded. It would be difficult to improve on this review because of the brief time since then. Therefore, only some highlights of research on vocational habilitation are presented here.

Much of the vocational preparation of the retarded takes place in either a sheltered-workshop setting or in a specifically designed, task-analyzed program for teaching job skills. Some early studies are briefly reviewed here.

Zimmerman, Stuckey, Garlick, and Miller

(1969) used token reinforcement to increase the productivity of 16 multiply handicapped retarded individuals. After baseline rates were gathered on production, the subjects were trained in the use of tokens and could practice earning tokens without actually receiving them. Feedback was given by explaining how many tokens would have been earned. Eventually, the tokens were given for improvements in production. Practice alone was effective in increasing production over baseline; however, even greater improvements were seen when tokens were provided. The elimination of tokens at the end of the study resulted in a significant decrease in productivity.

Zimmerman, Overpeck, Eisenberg, and Garlick (1969) reported a different procedure, which resulted in long-lasting behavioral change after the contingencies were removed. In this case, an avoidance procedure was used in which the subjects worked at a table with other trainees. An individualized criterion was set for each person, and if his or her production goal was not met on a given day, the trainee had to work the next day isolated from the group. The avoidance procedure consistently improved performance, and when the contingency was finally withdrawn, the gains in production were maintained for up to two weeks and did not return to initial baseline levels. Most other studies in sheltered workshops (e.g., Brown & Pearce, 1970; Evans & Spradlin, 1966; Hunt & Zimmerman, 1969) have typically employed various incentive conditions to increase productivity and have found similar results.

Most of the work in teaching specific jobs to retarded individuals outside the sheltered-workshop setting has consisted of anecdotal case studies. Cuvo, Leaf, and Borakove (1978), however, described empirical research on teaching janitorial skills to the retarded. A task analysis of the janitorial skills required for cleaning a restroom was developed. A total of six subtasks, consisting of 181 component responses, was identified. The subjects were required to progress through a series of four prompt levels, ordered generally from more to less direct assistance, for 20 of the most difficult component steps. Another series of four prompts, ordered from less to more direct assistance, was used to teach the other 161

responses. The subjects progressed to the next, more-intense prompt level contingent on their failure to respond appropriately with less assistance. Six moderately retarded adolescents were trained in their public school. The results showed rapid response acquisition, skill generalization to a second restroom, and maintenance of the newly learned behaviors. Hopefully, future research in this area will employ as systematic and effective procedures as the Cuvo *et al.* (1978) study.

Academic Skills. Research with the mildly retarded has emphasized deceleration targets or, at best, the acquisition of prerequisite or "readiness" skills. This emphasis is apparently based on the presumption that a reduction of competing behaviors (such as out-of-seat behavior and impulsiveness) will automatically pave the way for academic improvement (Kazdin, 1978). Actually, the weight of evidence does not support such a presumption. A focus on prerequisite skills, such as paying attention and being in one's seat, does not result, *ipso facto,* in academic improvement (Ferritor, Buckholdt, Hamblin, & Smith, 1972). On the other hand, reinforcement for specified academic improvement does boost academic performance and prerequisite skills such as attentiveness and work-related conduct (e.g., Ayllon & Robert, 1974; Haubrich & Shores, 1976; Marholin, Steinman, McInnis, & Heads, 1975). With the movement toward specific academic targets, progress has been demonstrated among the mildly retarded in arithmetic, reading, writing, spelling, and vocabulary (Kazdin, 1978) and students who receive positive reinforcement in school generally show improvement in achievement test performance. Incidentally, it also appears that reinforcement provided *during* achievement testing also raises scores (Ayllon & Kelly, 1972; Edlund, 1972).

There are a number of curricula and programs emerging for use with mildly retarded students. Among the more successful appears to be the Ross and Ross (1972, 1974) program, which includes students with measured IQs of 40–80. The program is based on the assumption of a "central mediational process deficit." Regardless of the theoretical bases of learning problems, the program is basically behavioral, emphasizing active child involvement, explicit reinforcement, and observational learning. It appears to be successful in promoting academic progress in mildly retarded students. Thus, it appears that appropriate reinforcement procedures applied directly to academic behaviors can improve both academic learning and performance. The preoccupation with getting rid of competing behaviors before academic progress is attempted seems unwarranted.

Among the moderately and severely retarded, research itself has been retarded. Evidently, the continuing assumption has prevailed that academic progress is simply not possible by reason of constitutional deficit and/or that there are better things to teach the retarded. Kirk's (1972) assertion still seems to set the parameters of research attempts: "In general, trainable children do not learn to read from even first grade books. Some trainable children with special abilities can learn to read. Most who learn to read, however, are probably educable mentally retarded children" (p. 231).

Indeed, over the past several decades, the little research there has been aimed at teaching "the three R's" to moderately and severely retarded students has, for the most part, met with little or no success. Reynolds and Kiland (1953) provided an account of an unsuccessful program in academics, and Warren (1963) reported that a highly structured reading program failed to produce any significant results in children of IQ 50 or below. Tobias (1963) did offer some success in a program designed to teach telling time by five-minute intervals.

Because of past failures and the prevailing notion of "limited potential," most recent curricula for the moderately to severely retarded do not include academics. Of notable exception are several research efforts in reading during the 1970s. Brown, Fenrick, and Klemme (1971) taught basic sight vocabulary through reinforcement and modeling. Successful students then taught other students, although generalization outside the classroom was, alas, a problem. Emphasizing prerequisite word-recognition skills (discrimination, recall, sequencing, and association), Duffy and Sherman (1977) reported success in teaching functional reading to moderately retarded persons. The look–say approach of Sidman (1971;

Sidman & Cresson, 1973) also has yielded some success. Nevertheless, the picture is generally dim, and there is no pervasive use of materials or methods for teaching academics to moderately and severely retarded students. It appears that what we do know about learning principles has not become a part of the materials for teaching. The learning materials are, for the most part, haphazard and devoid of a systematic use of learning principles (Coleman, 1970). With the exceptions cited above, the picture has not changed substantially to the present.

Maladaptive Behaviors. Contrary to the opinion of many people, exhibiting retarded behavior does not rule out various forms of maladaptive behavior, such as hitting, biting, scratching, and fears. In fact, there is considerable evidence that the retarded may be more likely to encounter these problems because of their limited ability to cope with various forms of environmental stimulation (Robinson & Robinson, 1976). The fact that these same problems are frequently found among groups of individuals who have not been labeled retarded means that the substantial literature on the behavioral treatment of maladaptive behavior is equally applicable to a retarded population. However, specific modifications of techniques may be necessary to adjust for appropriate developmental levels. Given this state of affairs, we do not attempt here to review fully the available literature that could be used in treating maladaptive behaviors; rather, we highlight some specific studies and trends in this area of application to the retarded.

Self-Injurious and Self-Stimulatory Behaviors. Retarded persons, especially those who have been institutionalized, frequently engage in stereotypical acts and self-stimulatory behaviors that appear to have no functional value (Berkson & Davenport, 1962). While often viewed as unusual, stereotypical behaviors are shared by many populations, ranging from the retarded and the autistic to the so-called normal population. Most frequently, the problem in deviant populations is one not of rate but of form and intensity. Stereotypical behaviors can be relatively innocuous, such as hand waving and rocking, or they can be self-injurious, such as slapping, biting, and head banging.

Eliminating self-injurious and self-stimulatory behaviors has been the focus of a large literature on retardation. Work in this area is covered in detail in several excellent reviews (Baumeister & Forehand, 1973; Forehand & Baumeister, 1976; Frankel & Simmons, 1976). Some highlights are provided here, as well as some updating of these earlier reviews.

The most common approach to self-stimulatory and self-injurious behavior, at least in the early literature, has been punishment. Aversive events such as shock, lemon juice in the mouth, and ammonia vapors have been used frequently and with great effect; a major advantage has been their relatively rapid impact on the targeted behavior. Shock has effectively eliminated behaviors such as rocking, head banging, and face slapping in a number of studies (e.g., Baumeister & Forehand, 1972; Corte, Wolf, & Locke, 1971; Lovaas & Simmons, 1969; Tate & Baroff, 1966; Young & Wincze, 1974).

Baumeister and Baumeister (1978) successfully used contingent inhalation of aromatic ammonia to decrease extremely high rates of severely self-injurious behaviors in two severely retarded institutionalized children. Other aversive stimuli that have been used include hair pulling (Griffin, Locke, & Landers, 1975); slapping (Foxx & Azrin, 1973); a loud noise (Sajwaj & Hedges, 1971); and reprimands (Baumeister & Forehand, 1972). While shock and other severely aversive stimuli can be extremely effective in the suppression of these behaviors, a major problem is that in many settings such procedures are now prohibited, and even if they were not prohibited, many people find them reprehensible. In fact, a survey of psychologists in facilities for the mentally retarded has shown that they would be hesitant to employ aversive stimuli such as shock in the treatment of self-injurious and self-stimulatory behavior, even if such treatment were not prohibited (Wallace, Burger, Neal, van Brero, & Davis, 1976). In fact, it has been the experience of one of the authors (Madle) that electric shock equipment purchased nearly 10 years ago has not yet been used because other effective means of dealing with these behaviors do exist.

Another procedure that has been employed frequently in institutions for this type of behavior has been some form of physical restraint. Typically, in the past, these restraints were used purely as a control measure, and little attention was paid to making physical restraint into an effective behavior-change procedure. Several recent studies have indicated an increased attention to developing restraint as an effective procedure (Barkley & Zupnick, 1976; Bucher, Reykdal, & Albin, 1976; Favell, McGimsey, & Jones, 1978; Schroeder, Peterson, Solomon, & Artley, 1977). For example, Schroeder *et al.* (1977) investigated the effects of contingent restraint with and without EMG feedback on head-banging behavior. The contingent restraint decreased the head-banging behavior and, when it was combined with EMG feedback, was even more effective: little head banging occurred during periods of deep-muscle relaxation.

Favell *et al.* (1978) reaffirmed the need to analyze functionally the consequences being employed when they determined that for three profoundly retarded persons, physical restraint, which had been used to prevent self-injury, appeared to be functioning as a positive reinforcer. By rearranging the contingencies and requiring increasing periods without self-injurious behavior to gain access to physical restraint, Favell *et al.* (1978) were able to decrease self-injurious behavior drastically.

Several investigations using time-out procedures have shown that self-injurious behavior can be decreased through this means (Hamilton, Stephens, & Allen, 1967; Nunes, Murphy, & Ruprecht, 1977; Tate & Baroff, 1966; Wolf, Risley, & Mees, 1964). While time-out procedures have shown relatively rapid suppression of the behaviors, they typically required a detailed analysis of contingencies and may be severely impeded if the individual's environment includes few positive reinforcers. Nunes *et al.* (1977), however, demonstrated a procedure for using time-out by providing a vibratory stimulus to the subjects and then withdrawing it contingent on self-injurious behavior. This approach was effective in decreasing the behavior. An alternative approach to using stimulation was reported by Evans (1979), who demonstrated that increasing the overall level of stimulation in the environment successfully resulted in decreases in self-stimulatory behavior.

Extinction procedures have been moderately successful in decreasing self-injurious behavior (Bucher & Lovaas, 1968; Corte *et al.*, 1971; Lovaas & Simmons, 1969). The major problem with the use of extinction is determining exactly what the reinforcers are that maintain the self-injurious or self-stimulatory behavior. In many cases, this is virtually impossible.

Recently, the most commonly employed punishment procedure has been overcorrection and positive practice. Positive practice consists of requiring the individual to practice forms of acceptable behavior that are incompatible with the stereotyped or self-injurious acts, contingent on the occurrence of these acts. For example, Azrin, Kaplan, and Foxx (1973) reduced rocking and head weaving in severely and profoundly retarded adults using positive practice and reinforcement of incompatible behaviors. The combined practice and reinforcement procedures rapidly reduced self-stimulation to almost zero. Measel and Alfieri (1976) demonstrated similar effects of overcorrection and reinforcement for incompatible behavior on head-slapping and head-banging behaviors in two profoundly retarded boys. Additional research on the effectiveness of overcorrection and positive practice has been reported by DeCatanzaro and Baldwin (1978), Harris and Romanczyk (1976), Ollendick, Matson, and Martin (1978), and Kelly and Drabman (1977). The generalizability of the results obtained from overcorrection is still in question. Kelly and Drabman (1977) reported generalization across settings, while Coleman, Whitman, and Johnson (1979) indicated that there was no evidence of generalized changes in self-stimulatory behavior across teachers and settings when an overcorrection procedure had been used.

Various reinforcement techniques, such as differential reinforcement of other behavior (DRO), of incompatible behavior (DRI), and of low rates (DRL), have been employed for self-stimulatory and self-injurious behavior (Repp & Deitz, 1974; Tarpley & Schroeder, 1979; Repp, Deitz, & Speir, 1974). Differential

reinforcement procedures have generally been found to be effective when consistently applied. Typically, studies have shown that DRI, in which a specific incompatible response is reinforced, produces superior effects to DRL or DRO (e.g., Tarpley & Schroeder, 1979).

Disruptive and Aggressive Behavior. The elimination of disruptive and aggressive behaviors has also been a popular and frequently attended-to area. In essence, the methods used with these types of behaviors in nonretarded populations show similar results with the retarded. In a recent review, Harris and Ersner-Hershfield (1978) dealt with the available research on the behavioral suppression of severely disruptive behavior in both psychotic and retarded individuals, with special attention to the use of punishment. This section highlights some of the techniques and behaviors that have been used for treatment.

As with self-injurious and self-stimulatory behavior, electric shock has been used a number of times to reduce disruptive behavior, particularly during the 1960s. Electric shock has been used to modify such hazardous behaviors as stereotyped screaming (Hamilton & Standahl, 1969); chronic ruminative vomiting (Luckey, Watson, & Musick, 1968); and dangerous climbing (Risley, 1968). Other forms of direct punishment that have been used with disruptive and aggressive behaviors include physical restraint (O'Brien, Bugle, & Azrin, 1972); slapping (Marshall, 1966; Morrison, 1972); shaking (Stark, Meisel, & Wright, 1969); aversive tickling (Greene & Hoats, 1971); and unpleasant-tasting or -smelling liquids (Sajwaj, Libet, & Agras, 1974).

Overcorrection has been extremely effective in reducing a number of aggressive behaviors. These have included hitting, biting, and throwing objects (Foxx & Azrin, 1972; Matson & Stephens, 1977); recurrent vomiting (Duker & Seys, 1977); public disrobing (Foxx, 1976); and noncompliance (Doleys, Wells, Hobbs, Roberts, & Cartelli, 1976).

Generally, overcorrection has been shown to be more effective than several alternative modes of intervention. Overcorrection has been shown to be superior to simple correction (Azrin, & Wesolowski, 1974, 1975); contingent social isolation and physical restraint (Foxx,

1976); DRO (Foxx & Azrin, 1973); and verbal warnings with response-cost procedures (Azrin & Powers, 1975). Only Doleys *et al.* (1976) found overcorrection less effective than another procedure, verbal scolding.

Extinction has been found of relatively little use in the suppression of severely disruptive behaviors in the retarded. Occasionally, it has been effective. For example, Duker (1975) reported that ignoring the self-biting and other disruptive behaviors of a retarded boy led to a decline in biting, but not in head banging. Martin and Foxx (1973) also demonstrated the use of extinction to reduce the aggressive behavior of a retarded woman. Other studies have demonstrated no decrease in behavior when extinction procedures were initiated (Ross, Meichenbaum, & Humphrey, 1971; Sajwaj, Twardosz, & Burke, 1972; Wolf, Birnbrauer, Williams, & Lawler, 1965). The ineffectiveness of extinction in these cases may possibly be attributable to difficulty in identifying the reinforcers maintaining the behavior (this finding is not unlike that of the operant laboratory). Extinction frequently fails to weaken behavior in simple operant tasks in a retarded population (Cairns & Paris, 1971; Madle, 1976).

Generally, the contingent removal of reinforcement (as in time-out and response-cost procedures) has proved moderately effective in dealing with aggressive and disruptive behavior in the retarded. These procedures have been used effectively to reduce inappropriate eating (Barton *et al.,* Baer, 1970; O'Brien & Azrin, 1972); escape from living quarters (Husted, Hall, & Agin, 1971); obscene speech (Lahey, McNees, & McNees, 1973); crying (Stark *et al.,* 1969); and inappropriate attention-seeking (Wiesen & Watson, 1967).

DRO and DRI should be seen as the first choice of techniques for dealing with inappropriate behavior, since it does not rely on aversive procedures that raise ethical issues. DRO increased sitting behavior in a hyperactive boy (Twardosz & Sajwaj, 1972), improved a retarded child's interaction with other youngsters (Wiesen & Watson, 1967), and decreased ward disruption by four retarded people (Mulhern & Baumeister, 1969). Frankel, Moss, Schofield, and Simmons (1976) reported dramatic decreases in aggression and head banging through the differential reinforcement of other behavior, whereas two different time-out procedures had failed previously. Repp and his associates (Deitz, Repp, & Deitz, 1976; Repp & Deitz, 1974) reported the successful use of DRO for both aggressive behavior and inappropriate classroom behaviors.

Occasionally, other techniques have been used to deal with aggressive and disruptive behavior. Jackson, Johnson, Ackron, and Crowley (1975) used food satiation to decrease vomiting in profoundly retarded adults. One of the most recent approaches has been the application of structured learning and assertion training to retarded populations. Fleming (1976) reported the effectiveness of using structured learning to teach assertive behaviors to both passive and aggressive mentally retarded children. The results indicated that the children were able to learn the skills involved in the training, but the results did not transfer to real-life situations. On the other hand, Matson and Stephens (1978) reported on social skills training with four inpatients with mixed schizophrenic and retarded diagnoses. The training consisted of instructions, modeling, role playing, and feedback and was effective in developing assertive behaviors. In addition, the trained skills generalized to the ward, and arguing and fighting were reduced markedly, a reduction maintained over a three-month follow-up period.

Anxiety. Only a few studies have dealt with anxiety or fear in the retarded. Freeman, Roy, and Hemmick (1976) and Mansdorf (1976) reported using operant techniques such as extinction and token rewards in eliminating the behavioral fears of physical examinations and riding in a car, respectively. Reisinger (1972) reported the use of extinction, positive reinforcement, and response-cost to eliminate severe disabling anxiety-based crying in a retarded woman. Silvestri (1977) investigated the effectiveness of implosive therapy with emotionally disturbed retarded individuals. Following the treatment, the implosive therapy group showed significantly more improvement than a pseudotherapy group and a no-treatment control group, although these gains were considerably lessened at a follow-up measurement. Desensitization procedures were used to eliminate phobias in 20 midly retarded subjects (Peck, 1977). The greatest effectiveness was found with a contact desensitization procedure, which did not rely on symbolic imagery in the subjects.

Seizure Disorders. Several studies have been reported in which seizures have been effectively dealt with by means of behavioral procedures. Zlutnick, Mayville, and Moffat (1975) investigated the effects of interruption and differential reinforcement on seizures. Seizures were conceptualized as the last link in a behavioral chain. This strategy attempted to identify and modify behaviors that reliably preceded the seizure climax. The seizure frequency was reduced in four of five subjects, whereas the frequency of preseizure behavior was reduced in only three. Iwata and Lorentzson (1976) were able successfully to reduce long-standing seizurelike behavior in a 41-year-old retarded male using a program of increased daily activities, DRO, and time-out. By the end of the 10th week of treatment, a gradual fading procedure was begun, and the decrease in seizure activity was maintained. Wells, Turner, Bellack, and Hersen (1978) were able to decrease the seizure activity of a retarded female through the use of cue-controlled relaxation by teaching the individual to relax herself when a seizure was imminent.

Behavioral Tactics

Other sections of this handbook cover specific behavioral tactics and the factors that determine their effectiveness; here, we highlight specific observations about the use of these techniques with retarded populations. By far, the majority of work on retardation has been done by individuals adhering to an operant orientation. Operant techniques have been particularly useful in developing the specific skills needed to overcome the severe response deficits present in retardation. In addition, they are particularly useful in eliminating the high frequency of inappropriate or problem behavior seen in a retarded population.

Positive Reinforcement. Since the beginning of behavioral work with the retarded, the manipulation of positive and negative consequences has received the greatest attention of any technique. Following responses with consequences that strengthen behavior has overcome specific response deficits where behaviors are not performed and has also developed responses that are capable of competing with and eliminating undesirable behaviors. Since the early work by Fuller (1949) demonstrating the conditioning of the arm movement of a profoundly retarded adolescent using reinforcement, the introduction of positive consequences to increase varied behaviors has remained a highly popular and frequently used technique.

Food Reinforcement. Food and other consumables have effectively altered a variety of behaviors. The effects of food are often great because it is a primary reinforcer and does not require preparatory conditioning to be effective. In many cases, entire meals or portions of meals, cereal, cookies, ice cream, soft drinks, and other similar items have been used as reinforcement. Sometimes food has been a natural consequence of the task being taught, as in the case of teaching self-feeding. In this case, food in the mouth is the logical reinforcement for the proper use of the spoon. However, in other cases, food has been introduced into a situation that would normally not contain it, for example, when it is used as a reinforcement in a toilet-training program (Azrin & Foxx, 1971).

While food has frequently been a very effective consequence, several limitations have restricted its use. First of all, it is difficult to deliver food immediately after a response, since there is some manipulation involved in using it. In addition, it is difficult to carry quantities of food around so that it may be used as needed. While neither of these factors is very important when food is naturally present, they limit the use of food to reinforce other types of responses. Another reason that food is difficult to use except in a one-to-one training program is that different types of food are reinforcing to different individuals. It would be impossible to carry the relatively large variety needed in daily situations. A fourth factor is that, in other than natural situations, eating can actually interfere with conditioning by interrupting the behavioral response patterns. The last major factor, which has become increasingly important, is that individuals cannot be deprived of food to the extent necessary to make it an effective reinforcer. Such deprivation raises ethical issues that are difficult to deal with. Therefore, much of the use of food as a reinforcer is actually the use of food preference, which creates many of the above-noted problems.

Feedback Reinforcement. The use of feedback as a reinforcer with the retarded can often be effective, especially with the mildly retarded, although uses have been noted at the more severe levels of impairment. Feedback can be particularly important with retarded individuals, since they frequently have difficulty evaluating the appropriateness of their own behaviors (Robinson & Robinson, 1976). The potential of feedback as a reinforcer has been minimally explored with retarded populations. It has primarily been used in vocational settings (Jens & Shores, 1969).

The use of feedback had advantages since it is relatively easy to provide in written or verbal forms and need not interfere to any great extent with ongoing response chains. While feedback has been quite variable in its effectiveness with retarded individuals, this is certainly also true of its effects on nonretarded populations. Feedback procedures can probably be developed that will have more consistent effects on behavior. It is important that feedback be developed as a method of working with retarded individuals, since it is a necessary first step in the development of adequate behavioral self-control procedures (Thoreson & Mahoney, 1974).

Social Approval. Forms of social approval such as verbal praise, attention, and physical contact have been used effectively in working with retarded individuals. As an example, Reisinger (1972) increased smiling behavior in a retarded woman, who exhibited many depressive behaviors, by providing her with both tokens and social approval for smiling. After the intervention was complete, he found that social approval alone effectively maintained the target behavior. Numerous other applications of social reinforcement have been reported in studies using aides, parents, and teachers (Panda & Lynch, 1972).

The use of social approval as a consequence has numerous advantages, including ease of administration and immediacy of delivery to the individual or group. Satiation is also not commonly found when social reinforcement is employed. Perhaps one of the greatest advantages, however, is that social reinforcement is a "naturally occurring" form of reinforcement, so that behaviors developed through this means are more readily generalized. Since social approval is frequently initially not reinforcing to the individual, additional procedures must be undertaken to establish its reinforcement value. In fact, with retarded individuals, some unusual phenomenon may be present. For example, Madle (1976) found that low-functioning retarded individuals who had been institutionalized for significant periods of their life responded well to social reinforcement that was delivered with inappropriate affect. That is, social reinforcement delivered in a "flat" tone of voice actually resulted in greater behavior change than that delivered in an appropriately and positively intoned manner.

Tokens. When a reinforcement system is based on the delivery of tokens, it is referred to as a *token economy.* Such methods have been used extensively in the treatment, habilitation, and educational programming of the retarded (cf. Kazdin, 1977). One of the earliest publicized programs for institutionalized retarded persons provided tokens for a wide range of behaviors, such as making one's bed, dressing for meals, taking showers, cleaning, and attending assignments (Girardeau & Spradlin, 1964; Lent, 1968; Spradlin & Girardeau, 1966). In this program, a rather sophisticated token economy was set up with numerous backup reinforcers, such as food, clothes, cosmetics, and equipment rental. An overall evaluation of this program after several years indicated a rather significant degree of success in programming for a population that had previously been considered essentially unchangeable. After this demonstration, numerous other reports of token economies for the retarded (see Kazdin, 1977, for a more thorough review) were reported.

Several advantages accrue from the use of tokens over other types of reinforcers. One is that tokens are often more effective because they are typically backed up by a large number of potential reinforcers, and at any one time, a retarded individual is highly unlikely to be satiated with all the available backup reinforcers. It should be noted that this advantage applies only when there is indeed a wide array of backup reinforcers.

Tokens can also be used merely as a substitute for a primary reinforcer. In some cases, token reinforcers are used primarily as a convenience and are exchangeable only for consumable reinforcers, often of one type. In this case, the use of tokens has many of the same disadvantages as the use of the original backup reinforcer. In fact, there may be some decrement in the power of the backup reinforcer because of its delayed delivery.

A third advantage is that tokens can be provided without overly disrupting ongoing response sequences and therefore do not interfere with behaviors in progress.

One of the last and most important advantages is that token reinforcers can provide a common medium of exchange; therefore, they can be used for a large number of individuals for whom different backup reinforcers have been identified.

Perhaps the most outstanding disadvantage of the use of tokens is that they are highly artificial reinforcers and require systematic generalization programs for transferring the learned behaviors from the original token-based setting to the natural situation. Kazdin (1977) has also pointed out a number of practical obstacles particular to token programs, such as the stealing or hoarding of tokens, the loss of tokens, and the need to maintain an effective record-keeping system of token earning and exchange.

It would appear that token economies are, at present, somewhat underutilized in the field of retardation. While the early work in the field stimulated a great number of token economies, these programs were generally conducted with mild to moderate retardates. A scanning of the current literature on retardation shows very little use of tokens with the severely and profoundly retarded. Such a phenomenon is difficult to understand, given the apparent power of token economies. One of the most likely reasons is the failure to employ procedures for establishing neutral objects as tokens with this group of low-functioning people. It is possible, however, to establish token use with very low-functioning individuals, as evidenced by the early work on tokens (Baer & Sherman, 1964).

Another possible reason might be the criticism of the early token economies (Subcommittee on Constitutional Rights, 1974), which attacked their nonindividualized approach to a given client group. Unfortunately, these problems have contributed to the current under-utilization of this type of program.

Activity Reinforcers. The last major class of positive reinforcers used with the retarded is activity reinforcers. These reinforcers are generally implemented by allowing individuals access to highly preferred activities contingent on the completion of expected target behaviors. This ability of high-frequency, preferred activities to reinforce lower-frequency, non-preferred activities was initially described by Premack (1959) and is referred to as the *Premack principle.*

Preferred behaviors are often useful reinforcers since they are readily available in most settings. For example, engaging in recreational activities, going on field trips, and talking to friends at meals can be made contingent on the desired performances. Even being physically restrained (Favell, McGimsey, & Jones, 1978) has been shown to function as a reinforcer for other behaviors. One of the major limitations of Premack-type reinforcers is that they are frequently not available immediately on the emission of the target behavior and, if available, disrupt the ongoing response chain. Such limitations, however, are relatively easily overcome by using activity reinforcers as backups in a token-based reinforcement system.

Differential Reinforcement Procedures. Positive reinforcement can also be used to reduce the rates of undesirable behavior through procedures known as differential reinforcement of low rates (DRL), differential reinforcement of other behavior (DRO), and differential reinforcement of incompatible behavior (DRI).

In DRL, certain responses must be reduced but not necessarily eliminated, and the contingency is set up so that the reinforcement is received only when a low rate of behavior is exhibited. Deitz and Repp (1973) reported the successful use of DRL with a group of 10 moderately retarded children who engaged in frequent "talk-out" behavior (talking, singing, and humming). The contingency was set so that when the group made five or fewer talk-outs in 15 minutes, each member would receive two pieces of candy of their own choice. Talking-out behavior immediately declined to an average of 3.1 instances per session, from a baseline of 32.7.

In DRO, the procedure consists of reinforcing the omission or absence of a specified target behavior. Baer *et al.* (1967) reported a study in which they taught profoundly retarded children to imitate. First, the children were reinforced with food and praise for engaging in imitative behaviors; such behaviors increased substantially. In order to demonstrate that the reinforcing contingencies were responsible for the change, a DRO schedule was instituted. Reinforcement was then delivered after a period of time in which the imitative behavior was not emitted. Imitative behavior plunged rapidly under DRO. Repp and Deitz (1974) reported the successful combining of DRO with other procedures to reduce aggressive and self-injurious behavior in institutionalized retarded children.

The last method, DRI, consists of identifying a behavior that will compete with an undesirable behavior. Reinforcement is then provided for exhibiting the incompatible behavior, and there is a corresponding decrease in the undesirable one. An example was reported by Allen, Henke, Harris, Baer, and Reynolds (1967), who decreased hyperactivity in a preschooler. Moving from one activity to another at a high rate brought the child low reinforcement, but engaging in one activity for predetermined periods of time was socially reinforced. As a result, the hyperactive behavior was substantially reduced.

Negative Reinforcement. Negative reinforcement (i.e., the removal of an aversive event after a behavior, thus increasing the probability of that response) has been used infrequently in retardation. It has been difficult to justify ethically the use of aversive procedures when positive reinforcement programs can be effective (Repp & Dietz, 1978). Even so, several instances of negative reinforcement have been reported. Whaley and Tough (1970) increased a retarded child's use of toys through a negative reinforcement procedure. A toy truck was placed in front of the

child, and a buzzer and a shock were presented. When the boy's hands touched the truck, the buzzer and shock were eliminated. Eventually, both events were avoided if the boy continued to hold the truck, as well as other toys. The increase in this response was considered valuable since it was incompatible with the boy's high frequency of head banging. Negative reinforcement, however, need not utilize aversize events that cause physical discomfort. Greene and Hoats (1969) found that television distortion could be used as an aversive event to control the work behavior of a mildly retarded adult. In order to remove the distortion of the television picture, the individual had to maintain acceptably high rates of work production.

Punishment. Punishment is operationally defined as the presentation or withdrawal of an event after a behavior that decreases that behavior. If the decrease in response strength is accomplished through the presentation of an aversive event, it is typically called *punishment by application* (or *positive punishment*). If, on the other hand, a procedure is used in which a positive event is removed contingent on a response, the procedure goes by the designation of *punishment by removal* (or *negative punishment*).

Punishment by Application. Punishment by application is used less frequently than punishment by removal for several reasons. First, punishment by application has been shown frequently to produce highly undesirable emotional side effects. Second, and even more importantly, current ethical standards (Sajwaj, 1977) in the field of retardation have severely curtailed the use of aversive stimulation. While the use of a strong aversive event such as an electric shock has not been completely ruled out, it is limited to areas where a response is highly dangerous either to the retarded individual or to other people. Lovaas and Simmons (1969), for example, eliminated the self-destructive behavior of both retarded and autistic children by using electric shock contingent on self-destructive behavior. After a few sessions and a small number of shocks, the behavior was completely eliminated. The most common approach taken today is that highly aversive procedures can be employed only after properly applied, less aversive procedures have been demonstrated to be ineffective.

Milder forms of aversive events have been used with somewhat more frequency. These include noxious liquids, reprimands, threats and warnings, and disapproval. While these forms of punishment have been effective at times in removing undesirable behaviors, their effects are by no means as consistent as those of more powerful forms of punishment, such as electric shock.

Punishment by Removal. The two primary techniques of punishment by removal are response-cost and time-out from positive reinforcement. Time-out from reinforcement can be effective even when used with brief time-out periods. Nunes *et al.* (1977) found that the brief withdrawal of a vibratory stimulus was successful in suppressing the self-abusive behavior of profoundly retarded individuals. In this case, vibratory stimulation was used as a reinforcer and was withdrawn whenever the self-abusive behaviors occurred.

One of the major conditions of the effective use of time-out is that the environment from which the individual is removed must be more reinforcing than the time-out environment (Solnick, Rincover, & Peterson, 1977). Unfortunately, the settings for working with severely and profoundly retarded children are frequently extremely impoverished. Without additional enrichment, such circumstances will not lead to the effective use of time-out procedures. In the above example (Nunes *et al.*, 1977), a new reinforcer (vibratory stimulation) had to be added to the environment before an effective time-out contingency could be used. Another consideration in the use of time-out is that the operating reinforcer in the situation must be identified. Lucero, Frieman, Spoering, and Fehrenbacher (1976) compared the effects of food withdrawal, attention withdrawal, and combined food–attention withdrawal on the rate of self-injurious behavior of three profoundly retarded girls during mealtime. Both the withdrawal of food and the withdrawal of food and attention combined led to a marked reduction of self-injurious behavior. The withdrawal of attention alone, however, resulted in an increased rate of two sub-jects' self-injurious behavior and had little effect on the rate of self-injurious behavior of the third.

In more recent usage, two forms of time-out have been identified. The first of these is exclusionary time-out, in which the individual is actually removed from a reinforcing environment. The second is nonexclusionary time-out in which access to a reinforcer is denied, although the individual is not removed from the situation. Foxx and Shapiro (1978) explored the use of a time-out ribbon; the child wore a colored ribbon and received snacks and praise every few minutes for good behavior and for wearing the ribbon. When the time-out contingency was added, the child's ribbon was removed for any instance of misbehavior. The teacher's attention and participation activities ceased for three minutes or until the misbehavior stopped. Reinforcement continued at other times for appropriate behavior. The results indicated that the ribbon procedure is a viable form of time-out, provided the disruptive behaviors during the time-out can be tolerated within the setting or a backup procedure, such as exclusionary time-out, is available when needed.

The need to develop nonexclusionary procedures has been generated by frequent criticism of the misuse of time-out procedures. In many cases, children or adults who are displaying disruptive behavior are removed from a situation under a time-out contingency and left out of the environment for too long a period. In many cases, exclusionary time-out can cause staff members to operate a program on a passive-avoidance contingency, where they no longer need to respond to the disruption that the child displays. Under these conditions, time-out generally lasts too long. An alternative is an apparatus described by Neisworth and Madle (1976) which cast the staff's avoidance response into an active-avoidance paradigm: the period for which the child was to remain in time-out was predetermined and set on a timer; at the end of the interval, the door to the time-out room automatically opened and allowed the child to rejoin the others. If additional time-out was required, the staff actively had to avoid the reentry of the child by resetting the timer.

In response-cost, a positive reinforcer is taken away, or there is a penalty involving some work or effort after an undesired response. Typically, response-cost involves the loss of a privilege or a token. Response-cost has been applied in different forms with the retarded. As usually applied, response-cost is implemented by withdrawing tokens for performance. Kazdin (1971) reduced the bizarre statements of a 20-year-old adult in a sheltered-workshop setting by following frequent outbursts of irrational statements with the loss of reinforcers. A dramatic reduction in irrational verbalizations was maintained through a four-week follow-up period.

Overcorrection. A relatively new punishment procedure, called *overcorrection*, was developed by Foxx and Azrin (1972). It is particularly useful in situations in which extinction, positive reinforcement, response-cost, and time-out have little chance of succeeding. Overcorrection is a specific type of mild punishment designed to minimize the negative reactions caused by intense punishment. Essentially, there are two components in an overcorrection procedure. The first is to overcorrect the environmental effects of an inappropriate act, and the second is to require of the individual an intensive practice of overly correct forms of relevant behavior (Foxx & Azrin, 1973). The first component is referred to as *restitutional overcorrection*, and the second is called *positive practice*. An example of this procedure was reported by Azrin and Wesolowski (1974), in which they attempted to teach retarded clients not to steal one another's food. In the overcorrection procedure, the individuals were required not only to return the snacks that they stole (restitution) but also to practice the positive action of giving their own snacks to the victims (positive practice). Overcorrection has been particularly effective in toilet training (Azrin & Foxx, 1971) and the elimination of self-injurious and self-stimulatory behaviors (Foxx & Azrin, 1972, 1973).

Extinction. *Extinction* means withholding reinforcement for a response in order to decrease the frequency of that response. Often, this means no longer providing attention for inappropriate responses that have been inadvertently reinforced. Extinction has been found to be effective in reducing a wide variety of behaviors, especially when used in combination with other procedures. These behaviors include throwing glasses, disruptive classroom behavior, aggressive behavior, tantrums, and excessive classroom noise.

If extinction is used with maximum effectiveness, its results can be enduring. Unfortunately, the use of extinction in the natural setting is often difficult. It may be difficult to identify the reinforcers maintaining the behavior, and when the reinforcers have been identified, it may be difficult actually to remove them from the setting. An example of this problem was encountered by Neisworth, Madle, and Goeke (1975) when the contingent attention maintaining a preschooler's crying behavior on the mother's departure was difficult to remove from the setting. Student teachers in the classroom found it very difficult to ignore the crying of the 4-year-old and, in spite of well-intentioned contingencies, provided attention after a period of time. As an alternative, a fading procedure was used in which the mother was gradually faded out of the setting, with successful elimination of the behavior and little crying during the treatment phase. Another problem that has typically plagued attempts to use extinction procedures is the exhibition of the "extinction burst," in which the individual undergoing extinction displays higher rates of behavior immediately after the reinforcer has been removed. Often, this reaction is interpreted as a worsening of behavior, and the extinction contingency is removed too quickly. Extinction procedures often do require perseverance before any major success can be noted.

Other Behavioral Tactics. A number of other behavioral tactics, such as prompting, fading, modeling, behavioral rehearsal, systematic desensitization, implosion, assertion training, and self-control procedures have been used with the retarded.

Prompting and Fading. Prompting and fading have typically been employed in work with the retarded in combination with various reinforcement procedures. They have often, however, been ignored in critical settings where they could be effective. Most of the effective use of prompts has occurred in educational settings, particularly in teaching academic skills. One major application has been the use of prompting and fading in teaching sight vocabulary to retarded individuals (Dorry, 1976; Gamache & Madle, 1976; Walsh & Lamberts, 1979). Generally, in these situations, a word to be read is paired with a stimulus that already evokes the desired vocal response, such as a picture. While reinforcement is provided for saying the word in response to the picture, the picture is gradually, rather than abruptly, removed. The individual is able to "read" the word without the prompt by the end of the training sequence. There appears to be relatively little use of prompting and fading procedures outside the teaching of academic skills. In the earlier study by Neisworth *et al.* (1975) already mentioned, prompting and fading were systematically applied to eliminate a preschooler's crying. In another application by Petersen, Austin, and Lang (1979), prompts were used to increase the rate of social behavior of three severely and profoundly retarded adolescents.

Modeling. Modeling, which is also known as *observational learning* or *vicarious learning*, means developing behaviors by providing other individuals, or models, who perform the behavior. Modeling, a critical means by which individuals increase their behavioral repertoires, has been somewhat ignored in the area of retardation, especially with the severely and profoundly retarded. The importance of this technique was recognized early when Baer *et al.* (1967) developed a procedure for teaching profoundly retarded individuals to imitate. The successful development of the imitative response resulted in a substantial increase in the rate at which the individual could learn new motor and verbal behaviors. Modeling has been much used in teaching language skills to the retarded (Snyder, Lovitt, & Smith, 1975). In addition, modeling has been used in conjunction with a number of other techniques, such as positive reinforcement, to develop new behaviors, for example, telephone use (Stephan, Stephano, & Talkington, 1973).

Behavioral Rehearsal and Role Playing. Behavioral rehearsal and role playing involve practicing an overt behavior under simulated or real-life conditions. These approaches contrast with modeling, where learning is based primarily on observation rather than on active practice. The two procedures are often combined by having individuals rehearse an appropriate response under simulated conditions after it has been modeled.

An example of role playing was provided by Strain (1975), who increased the social play of severely retarded preschool children by having them act out storybook characters as the teacher read various stories. After story time, the children were observed in free play. Social play for all eight children increased during the free-play period.

Rehearsal and role playing are also used extensively in combination with other operant procedures. Overcorrection and positive practice include the rehearsal of behaviors that are incompatible with the responses to be suppressed. In these procedures, rehearsal is part of a much larger training package that utilizes prompts, reinforcing consequences, modeling, and other tactics. The primary advantage of rehearsal is that appropriate responses can be prompted with a high enough frequency to be reinforced and installed in an individual's repertoire.

Recent work in the area of retardation has been aimed toward the development of various social-skills-training packages for the retarded. Perry and Cerreto (1977) reported on a prescriptive teaching approach that used modeling, role playing, and social reinforcement to teach social skills to a group of 10 mentally retarded young adults. At the same time, 10 matched subjects were taught the same social skills in a discussion format, and another 10 controls received no treatment. The structured role-play training was significantly superior to either of the alternatives in producing appropriate social skills. Matson and Stephens (1978) used social skill training with four inpatients. Behaviors were targeted individually for each subject based on pretreatment observation. Instructions, modeling, role playing, and feedback were effective as shown with a multiple-baseline design. The trained skills generalized to the ward, resulting in markedly reduced arguing and fighting that was maintained during postcheckups three months following training.

Relaxation Training and Systematic Desensitization. While employed widely with a number of other dysfunctions, relaxation tech-

PART V • INTERVENTION AND BEHAVIOR CHANGE: CHILD

niques have received minimal use with the retarded (Harvey, 1979), in spite of Bijou's (1966) suggestion that the behavior of the retarded is frequently characterized by escape and avoidance patterns triggered by anxiety-related, specific, aversive environmental consequences.

Perhaps one of the earliest applications of densitization to the retarded was by Guralnick (1973). In this study, tension–release relaxation training, in conjunction with desensitization procedures, was used with a severely retarded male. Little data were presented, however, to support the utility of relaxation with this type of individual. Peck (1977) used densensitization procedures with 20 mildly retarded subjects who exhibited a fear of either heights or rats. She randomly assigned the subjects to contact densensitization, vicarious symbolic desensitization, systematic densensitization, placebo attention control, and no treatment. The subjects were provided with up to 15 sessions of treatment. Contact desensitization proved the most effective approach. Peck reported that the subjects in the systematic and vicarious densensitization groups were able to respond to relaxation instructions and generally to learn realxation without undue difficulty; they were also able to report on their feeling state and to discriminate between feelings of anxiety and relaxation.

Harvey, Karan, Bhargava, and Morehouse (1978) reported the use of relaxation training with a moderately retarded female exhibiting violent temper tantrums. The relaxation was used to reduce her overall anxiety level and to permit an ongoing, appropriate coping response for dealing with social and vocational stress. In addition, a cue-conditioning procedure was added after deep relaxation was achieved. The subject was finally able to eliminate the tantrums both at work and at home.

Wells *et al.* (1978) employed cue-controlled relaxation for psychomotor seizures in a 22-year-old borderline retarded female. The study suggested that cue-controlled relaxation contributed significantly to minimizing her psychomotor seizures. In addition, the treatment effects were maintained across a three-month follow-up period although little contact with the therapist occurred during this period.

Implosive Therapy. In the only available study of implosive therapy with the retarded, Silvestri (1977) randomly assigned 24 retarded subjects to one treatment and two control groups. The treatment group received 10 sessions of implosive therapy, while the control groups received either no treatment or 10 sessions of pseudotreatment discussions. While the subjects in the implosive therapy group showed significantly more improvement across all indexes than those in either of the other two groups, the superiority was considerably less at a follow-up.

Self-Control Techniques. Like relaxation training, self-control procedures have been subject to increasing experimentation with other dysfunctions yet have been virtually ignored in the field of retardation. Kurtz and Neisworth (1976) reported on a number of possible adaptations of self-control procedures for use with the retarded, and Mahoney and Mahoney (1976) indicated that such procedures were, in fact, effective if appropriately structured. While self-control procedures have been attempted with the retarded (e.g., Long & Williams, 1976), they have typically employed higher-functioning subjects who deviated little from normal levels.

Overall, it would appear that a great deal of work has been accomplished in the field of retardation by applying tactics consisting of positive and negative reinforcement and punishment. Other forms of behavioral treatment (e.g., relaxation training, self-control, and behavioral rehearsal) have received far less attention and need considerable expansion to determine their potential effectiveness with retarded persons.

Strategies for Applying Behavioral Tactics

In addition to the behavioral tactics discussed above, one must consider overall strategies in delivering behaviorally based services. Essentially, three models have been used in delivering behavioral services to the retarded: professionally administered individualized programs, group-based programs, and programs mediated by paraprofessionals and parents.

Professionally administered individual programs have been used widely in areas such as the teaching of imitative skills and have been successful in demonstrating the power of behavioral tactics; however, such a delivery model restricts the number of clients who can be helped. Professional time spent on a one-to-one basis limits both the scope and the efficiency of the behavioral intervention.

Essentially, two strategies can be employed to extend the delivery of behavioral programs. The first is the use of group-based programs. The most common of these group-based programs have been those employing token economies, such as the work of Lent (1968), and the classroom delivery of services in special education. Typically this strategy has been employed with mildly and moderately retarded individuals. The consensus once was that behavioral programs for the severely and profoundly retarded required intensive one-to-one program delivery. Recently, Storm and Willis (1978) and Favell, Favell, and Mc-Gimsey (1978) compared group and individualized training methods in teaching severely and profoundly retarded individuals. In both studies, small-group training was determined to be at least as effective as one-to-one training. In addition, other advantages (such as increased activity and socialization levels for the clients) suggested that group instruction may actually be a preferred method for teaching some skills to severely and profoundly retarded individuals.

While the use of small-group programs increases the number of clients that can be worked with by an individual, the other major alternative is to increase the number of individuals who are available to carry out behavioral programming for retarded persons. This strategy has been employed extensively through the use of parents and paraprofessionals for the application of behavioral tactics (Madle, 1975). The available literature strongly suggests that paraprofessionals and parents can effectively modify retarded behaviors, given adequate training and supervision (e.g., Greene, Willis, Levy, & Bailey, 1978). To be effective, however, programs must employ systematic monitoring, feedback, and incentives for the paraprofessional staff (Iwata, Bailey, Brown, Foshee, & Alpern, 1976; Repp & Deitz, 1979; Favell, Favell, Seals, & Risley 1978).

In addition to adequate monitoring and supervision, training must be provided for para-professionals and parents so that they can properly carry out the procedures being used. The available evidence indicates that to be effective, such training programs must themselves employ behavioral tactics in developing behavior modification skills. Generally, the programs that have been successful have employed structured training and such techniques as modeling, feedback, prompting, and fading (Gardner, 1973; Nay, 1975; Parsonson, Baer, & Baer, 1974). Overall the literature suggests that in the absence of such behaviorally based training programs, parents and paraprofessionals can acquire the necessary terms for discussing behavior modification tactics but cannot actually apply them (Gardner, 1972; Lindsley, 1966).

The increased emphasis on teaching parents to apply behavioral technology with their children has allowed for the possibility of an effective early intervention and preventive strategy. An excellent example is the recent work in teaching the parents of Down's syndrome infants (Hanson, 1977) to use behavioral tactics in developing skills in their retarded children. Research on such projects has demonstrated that Down's syndrome children, who frequently function at severely and profoundly low levels by school age, may be able to function in the mildly retarded range when their parents have been trained and supervised in the application of behavioral tactics.

Future Perspectives and Directions

Before examining the directions that behavior modification with the retarded may or should take, it is appropriate to examine the trends over the past several years. In Table 1, a comparison is made of the pre-1973 behavioral literature on the retarded and the literature that appeared from 1976 to 1978. Approximately 100 articles that appeared from 1976 to 1978 were coded on the following variables: the ages of the clients, their level of retardation, the tactics used, and the intervention setting. A similar coding was also done on the studies appearing in the mental retardation section of Kazdin and Craighead's (1973) review.

Table 1. Comparison of the Pre-1973 with the 1976–1978 Behavioral Literature on Selected Variables

Category	Value	Pre-1973[a] n	Pre-1973[a] %	1976–1978 n	1976–1978 %
Age	Birth–21	36	87.8	104	79.5
	Over 21	5	12.2	27	20.5
Level of retardation	Mild	9	19.2	44	32.4
	Moderate	14	29.8	34	25.0
	Severe/profound	24	51.0	58	42.6
Setting	Institutional	38	92.7	59	39.3
	Community	3	7.3	91	60.7
Tactics	Reinforcement	21	48.8	96	69.5
	Punishment	6	14.6	18	13.7
	Time-out	10	24.4	13	9.9
	Response-cost	4	9.8	7	5.3
	Overcorrection	0	0.0	11	8.4
	Extinction	2	4.9	4	3.1
	DRO–Alt R	1	2.4	7	5.3
	Prompting	11	26.8	43	32.8
	Fading	4	9.8	15	11.5

Note: The Year spans Pre-1973[a] and 1976–1978.

[a] Kazdin and Craighead (1973).

Several trends are evident in this comparison. The setting in which the intervention occurred has been gradually shifting from institutions to the home and the community. Somewhat surprisingly, the level of retardation being dealt with in the literature has not shifted from the mild to the severe and the profound as much as current legislation and regulations would suggest. Instead, there has been somewhat of an increase in studies reporting on the mildly retarded. The reason, however, becomes obvious when it is noted that the studies are taking place at an increasing rate in community agencies. That is, the mildly retarded person is being placed in the community and therefore is becoming used increasingly in behavioral research.

While there have been no major shifts in the techniques reported, there does appear to have been some reduction in the use of punishment techniques and a corresponding increase in the use of reinforcement. The one exception is the use of overcorrection, which was very new in 1973. Studies also seem currently to be beginning to increase their attention to antecedent variables, as in prompting. Unfortunately, much of the early behavioral research relied heavily on the consequation of behavior, which is effective in increasing or decreasing existing behaviors but has little effect on teaching the new behaviors that are so needed by the retarded.

In looking at an overall view of the literature, we can detect weaknesses or problems of both a conceptual (or philosophical) and a methodological nature. A critique from the conceptual or philosophical perspective concerns dealing with the scope, the appropriateness, and the social relevance of the literature. These, of course, shift with changing social values, legislation, and litigation.

Of primary concern to us was the seeming preoccupation with behavioral *reduction* or *elimination*. A majority of reported studies focused on the use of techniques for weakening or narrowing problem behaviors. This is not surprising since most agencies and facilities are concerned, first, with maintaining order, discipline, and nondisruption. This preoccupation is perhaps also evident in the general behavior-modification literature addressed to regular classroom use and even self-management. The reasons for such a preoccupation may be administrative convenience (and staff sanity!) as well as the alleged therapeutic position that constructive changes (i.e., behavior building) depends on the elimination of interfering responses. Whatever the reasons, we see a picture of devotion to behavior *management* in a custodial sense; behavior modification, then, becomes a substitute for chains and/or drugs. The immediate aim is to subdue, "civilize," or discipline the subject rather than to install or strengthen adaptive skills. This "zombie" model for the use of behavior modification does not constitute much in the way of progress in a conceptual or philosophical sense. Therapists, educators, and care givers must have more progressive goals for their clients than mere management. The production of persons who *do not* do this or that is certainly not in keeping with the more comprehensive social goals of normalization, mainstreaming, and civil rights.

A second need would appear to be increased attention to the development of generalized social skills in the same manner that programs have been developed to create generalized imitation and language skills. The behavioral literature in other areas of dysfunction has increasingly reported the use of structured social-skills training as a means of increasing the interpersonal and social capabilities of the clients. Much of the work in retardation, however, still concentrates on the development of discrete, individually trained social behaviors. Given that interpersonal and social skills are one of the major lacks in retarded persons that prevents their placement in the community, this would appear to be a priority need for future development.

Another consideration is the need for validated disseminable packages that can be used by parents and paraprofessionals. For behavior modification to realize its potential impact on the field, a series of carefully developed, valid programs that can be consistently applied by trained paraprofessional-level personnel is also needed (Azrin, 1977). Too much of the reported work in retardation still examines fundamental principles and isolated techniques that must be applied by individual practitioners.

The last apparent need is for the development of practical extensions of Bijou's (1966) behavioral model of retardation to assist practitioners in the systematic selection of appropriate techniques for dealing with specific target behaviors. It seems, at the present, that most applications of behavioral technology to the retarded have been derived from one of three sources: (1) the percolation of behavioral programs from other areas, as in systematic social skills training; (2) fads in behavioral technology, that is, "Here's a new technique that hasn't been tried with the retarded"; and (3) the trial-and-error approach, in which a practitioner tries various tactics until she or he finds one that works.

The need in the area of model development is to move practitioners back to the basics of the functional rather than the topographical analysis of problems. A functional analysis of behavior must consider both antecedent and consequent events, as well as measures of the appropriateness or the inappropriateness of behaviors. An initial concern is to determine if the overall *rate* of behavior shown by the individual is deficient or excessive. That is, certain behaviors, such as expressive language skills, can be absent or deficient. On the other hand, a behavior such as head banging or self-stimulation can be considered excessive, regardless of the situation in which it occurs. In addition to the rate of behavior, the *setting* in which it occurs must be considered. That is, the behavior itself may not be inappropriate, but its timing or place of occurrence may be the problem. For example, when teaching retarded persons to dress themselves, the behavior of dressing oneself may occur at an appropriate rate; however, the behavior may occur only in response to the verbal command "Dress yourself" or "Get dressed," rather than in response to the typical cues that prompt dressing. In this case, there is still a problem that requires behavioral intervention. The types of interventions selected are different, however, from those needed for dealing with rate problems. A second aspect of the prevailing stimulus conditions that may cause a problem is that a behavior may occur in response to the wrong cues. Again, the individual may undress at a typical frequency per day, but if the undressing occurs in public, a problem exists that is related to the antecedent conditions of the behavior.

The topographical classification of behavior may be more familiar to individuals working with the retarded, but it is not appropriate to a behavioral perspective of retardation. Problems such as inarticulate speech, bed wetting, fighting, rocking, tardiness, and failure to carry out duties are typically encountered among persons with retarded behavior. These terms, however, are not tied to a behavioral model, nor do they particularly suggest intervention strategies based on behavioral principles. The labeling of problem behaviors in terms of contingent variables does offer both theoretical and heuristic leverage in classifying and dealing with problems. Many times, the selection of an inappropriate behavioral tactic may occur without attention to the functional analytical considerations. In many cases, the tactic selected may, in fact, effectively modify the behavior. The problem, however, will be seen in the maintenance of the behavior. In order to develop an effective and systematic approach to the selection and application of behavioral tactics, a new practical model must be developed in which specific measures or guidelines can be used to assess the functional "cause" of the behavior and then to provide for the selection of appropriate tactics for dealing with the situation. The development and the validation of such a model may deal with the often-reported difficulty of generalizing the effects of behavioral programs across settings (Kazdin, 1978).

Summary

It seems clear that progress in our understanding of retardation and its treatment and the refinement of behavioral approaches is reciprocal. Trends in each influence the other. The recent shifts to natural settings and the use of paraprofessionals and parents are en- couraging. The preoccupation with "management" and the paucity of research on the programmatic use of developmental objectives to expand the retarded individual's repertoire are not so encouraging. The most pressing need appears to be for an inclusive behavioral model of retarded development that systematically delineates targets, settings, strategies, tactics, and evaluation procedures. As was mentioned, Bijou's (1966) model may provide the basis for a comprehensive and programmatic guide to behavioral interventions for remediation, therapy, and education in the personal development of our retarded citizens.

ACKNOWLEDGMENTS

The authors would like to acknowledge the assistance of the following students in reviewing the literature: Sue Devenney, Sharon Harrity, Chris Hanneman, Betsy Llewellyn, Audrey Matty, Art Pentz, Sue Reinhard, Patti Skelly, and Dave Snell.

References

Abramson, E. E., & Wunderlich, R. A. Dental hygiene training for retardates: An application of behavioral techniques. *Mental Retardation*, 1972, *10*, 6–8.

Allen, K. E., Henke, L. B., Harris, F. R., Baer, D. M., & Reynolds, N. J. Control of hyperactivity by social reinforcement of attending behavior. *Journal of Educational Psychology*, 1967, *58*, 231–237.

Ayllon, T., & Kelly, K. Effects of reinforcement on standardized test performance. *Journal of Applied Behavior Analysis*, 1972, *5*, 447–484.

Ayllon, T., & Robert, M. D. Eliminating discipline problems by strengthening academic performance. *Journal of Applied Behavior Analysis*, 1974, *7*, 71–76.

Azrin, N. H. A strategy for applied research: Learning based but outcome oriented. *American Psychologist*, 1977, *32*, 140–149.

Azrin, N. H., & Armstrong, P. M. The "mini-meal"—A method of teaching eating skills to the profoundly retarded. *Mental Retardation*, February 1973, *11*, 9–13.

Azrin, N. H., & Foxx, R. M. A rapid method of toilet training the institutionalized retarded. *Journal of Applied Behavior Analysis*, 1971, *4*, 89–99.

Azrin, N. H., & Holz, W. C. Punishment. In W. K. Honig (Ed.), *Operant behavior: Areas of research and application.* New York: Appleton-Century-Crofts, 1966.

Azrin, N. H., & Powers, M. A. Eliminating classroom disturbances of emotionally-disturbed children by positive practice procedures. *Behavior Therapy*, 1975, *6*, 525–534.

Azrin, N. H., & Wesolowski, M. D. Theft reversal: An

overcorrection procedure for eliminating stealing by retarded persons. *Journal of Applied Behavior Analysis,* 1974, *7,* 577–581.

Azrin, N. H., & Wesolowski, M. D. The use of positive practice to eliminate persistant floor sprawling by profoundly retarded persons. *Behavior Therapy,* 1975, *6,* 627–631.

Azrin, N. H., Kaplan, S. J., & Foxx, R. M. Autism reversal: Eliminating stereotyped self-stimulation of retarded individuals. *American Journal of Mental Deficiency,* 1973, *78,* 241–248.

Azrin, N. H., Schaeffer, R. M., & Wesolowski, D. A rapid method of teaching profoundly retarded persons to dress by a reinforcement-guidance method. *Mental Retardation,* 1976, *14,* 29–33.

Baer, D. M., & Guess, D. Receptive training of adjectival inflections in mental retardates. *Journal of Applied Behavior Analysis,* 1971, *4,* 129–139.

Baer, D. M., & Sherman, J. A. Reinforcement control of generalized imitation in young children. *Journal of Experimental Child Psychology,* 1964, *1,* 37–49.

Baer, D. M., Peterson, R. F., & Sherman, J. A. The development of imitation by reinforcing behavioral similarity to a model. *Journal of the Experimental Analysis of Behavior,* 1967, *10,* 405–416.

Ball, T. S., Seric, K., & Payne, L. E. Long-term retention of self-help skill training in the profoundly retarded. *American Journal of Mental Deficiency,* 1971, *76,* 378 382.

Barkley, R. A., & Zupnick, S. Reduction of stereotypic body contortions using physical restraint and DRO. *Journal of Behavior Therapy and Experimental Psychiatry,* 1976, *8,* 167–170.

Barry, K., Apolloni, T., & Cooke, T. P. Improving the personal hygiene of mildly retarded men in a community-based residential training program. *Corrective and Social Psychiatry and Journal of Behavior Technology Methods and Therapy,* 1977, *23,* 65–68.

Barton, E. S., Guess, D., Garcia, E., & Baer, D. M. Improvement of retardates' mealtime behaviors by timeout procedures using multiple baseline techniques. *Journal of Applied Behavior Analysis,* 1970, *3,* 77 84.

Bauman, K. E., & Iwata, B. A. Maintenance of independent housekeeping skills using scheduling plus self-recording procedures. *Behavior Therapy,* 1977, *8,* 554–560.

Baumeister, A., & Klosowski, R. An attempt to group toilet train severely retarded patients. *Mental Retardation,* December 1965, *3,* 24–26.

Baumeister, A. A., & Baumeister, A. A. Suppression of repetitive self-injurious behavior by contingent inhalation of aromatic ammonia. *Journal of Autism and Childhood Schizophrenia,* 1978, *8,* 71–77.

Baumeister, A. A., & Forehand, R. Effects of contingent shock and verbal command on body rocking of retardates. *Journal of Clinical Psychology,* 1972, *28,* 586–590.

Baumeister, A. A., & Forehand, R. Stereotyped acts. In N. R. Ellis (Ed.), *International review of research in mental retardation,* Vol. 6. New York: Academic Press, 1973.

Bellamy, A. T., & Clark, G. Picture recipe cards as an approach to teaching severely and profoundly retarded adults to cook. *Education and Training of the Mentally Retarded,* 1977, *12,* 69–73.

Bensberg, G. J. (Ed.). *Teaching the mentally retarded.* Atlanta: Southern Regional Education Board, 1965.

Bensberg, G. J., & Slominski, A. Helping the retarded learn self-care. In G. J. Bensberg (Ed.), *Teaching the mentally retarded: A handbook for ward personnel.* Atlanta: Southern Regional Education Board, 1965.

Bensberg, G. J., Colwell, C. N., & Cassel, R. H. Teaching the profoundly retarded self-help activities by behavior shaping techniques. *American Journal of Mental Deficiency,* 1965, *69,* 674–679.

Berkson, G., & Davenport, R. K. Stereotyped movements in mental defectives: I. Initial survey. *American Journal of Mental Deficiency,* 1962, *66,* 849–852.

Bijou, S. W. Theory and research in mental (developmental) retardation. *Psychological Record,* 1963, *13,* 95–110.

Bijou, S. W. A functional analysis of retarded development. In N. R. Ellis (Ed.), *International review of research in mental retardation.* New York: Academic Press, 1966.

Birnbrauer, J. S. Mental retardation. In H. Leitenberg (Ed.), *Handbook of behavior modification and behavior therapy.* Englewood Cliffs, N.J.: Prentice-Hall, 1976.

Bricker, D. D. Imitative sign training as a facilitator of word-object association with low-functioning children. *American Journal of Mental Deficiency,* 1972, *76,* 509–516.

Brown, L., & Pearce, F. Increasing the production rates of trainable retarded students in a public school simulated workshop. *Education and Training of the Mentally Retarded,* 1970, *5,* 15–22.

Brown, L., Fenrick, N., & Klemme, H. Trainable pupils learn to teach each other. *Teaching Exceptional Children,* 1971, *4,* 18–24.

Bucher, B., & Lovaas, O. I. Use of aversive stimulation in behavior modification. In M. R. Jones (Ed.), *Miami Symposium on the Prediction of Behavior, 1967: Aversive stimulation.* Coral Gables, Fla.: University of Miami Press, 1968.

Bucher, B., Reykdal, B., & Albin, J. Brief physical restraint to control Pica in retarded children. *Journal of Behavior Therapy and Experimental Psychiatry,* 1976, *7,* 137–140.

Butz, R. A., & Hasazi, J. E. The effects of reinforcement on perseverative speech in a mildly retarded boy. *Journal of Behavior Therapy and Experimental Psychiatry,* 1973, *4,* 167–170.

Cairns, R. B., & Paris, S. G. Informational determinants of social reinforcement effectiveness among retarded children. *American Journal of Mental Deficiency,* 1971, *76,* 362–369.

Campbell, S. B. Mother-child interaction in reflective, impulsive, and hyperactive children. *Developmental Psychology,* 1973, *8,* 341–349.

Clark, H. B., Boyd, S. B., & Macrae, J. W. A classroom program teaching disadvantaged youths to write biographic information. *Journal of Applied Behavior Analysis,* 1975, *8,* 67–75.

Coleman, E. B. Collecting a data base for reading technology. *Journal of Educational Psychology Monograph,* 1970, *61*(4, Pt. 2), 1–23.

Coleman, R. S., Whitman, T. L., & Johnson, M. R. Suppression of self-stimulatory behavior of a profoundly retarded boy across staff and settings: An assessment of situational generalization. *Behavior Therapy*, 1979, *10*, 266–280.

Corte, H. E., Wolf, M. M., & Locke, B. J. A comparison of procedures for eliminating self-injurious behavior of retarded adolescents. *Journal of Applied Behavior Analysis*, 1971, *4*, 201–213.

Cuvo, A. J., Leaf, R. B., & Borakove, L. S. Teaching janitorial skills to the mentally retarded: Acquisition, generalization, and maintenance. *Journal of Applied Behavior Analysis*, 1978, *11*, 345–355.

Dayan, M. Toilet training retarded children in a state residential institution. *Mental Retardation*, 1964, *2*, 116–117.

DeCatanzaro, D. A., & Baldwin, G. Effective treatment of self-injurious behavior through a forced arm exercise. *American Journal of Mental Deficiency*, 1978, *82*, 433–439.

Deitz, S. M., & Repp, A. C. Decreasing classroom misbehavior through the use of DRL schedules of reinforcement. *Journal of Applied Behavior Analysis*, 1973, *6*, 457–463.

Dietz, S. M., Repp, A. C., & Dietz, D. E. Reducing inappropriate classroom behavior of retarded students through three procedures of differential reinforcement. *Journal of Mental Deficiency Research*, 1976, *20*, 155–170.

Dingman, H. F., & Tarjan, G. Mental retardation and the normal distribution curve. *American Journal of Mental Deficiency*, 1960, *64*, 991–994.

Doleys, S. M., Wells, K. C., Hobbs, S. A., Roberts, M. W., & Cartelli, L. M. The effects of social punishment on noncompliance: A comparison with timeout and positive practice. *Journal of Applied Behavior Analysis*, 1976, *9*, 471–482.

Dorry, G. W. Attentional model for the effectiveness of fading in training reading-vocabulary with retarded persons. *American Journal of Mental Deficiency*, 1976, *81*, 271–279.

Duffy, G. G., & Sherman, G. B. *Systematic reading instruction* (2nd ed.). New York: Harper & Row, 1977.

Duker, P. C. Behaviour control of self-biting in a Lesch-Nyhan patient. *Journal of Mental Deficiency Research*, 1975, *19*, 11–19.

Duker, P. C., & Seys, D. M. Elimination of vomiting in a retarded female using restitutional overcorrection. *Behavior Therapy*, 1977, *8*, 255–257.

Edlund, C. V. The effect on the test behavior of children, as reflected in the IQ scores, when reinforced after each correct response. *Journal of Applied Behavior Analysis*, 1972, *5*, 317–319.

Ellis, N. R. Toilet training the severely defective patient: An S-R reinforcement analysis. *American Journal of Mental Deficiency*, 1963, *68*, 98–103.

Evans, G. W., & Spradlin, J. E. Incentives and instructions as controlling variables of productivity. *American Journal of Mental Deficiency*, 1966, *71*, 129–132.

Evans, R. G. The reduction of hyperactive behavior in three profoundly retarded adolescents through increased stimulation. *AAESPH Review*, 1979, *4*, 259–263.

Favell, J. E., Favell, J. E., & McGimsey, J. F. Relative effectiveness and efficiency of group vs. individual training of severely retarded persons. *American Journal of Mental Deficiency*, 1978, *83*, 104–109.

Favell, J. E., Favell, J. E., Seals, E., & Risley, T. R. *The evaluation-feedback system: Getting services to the people.* Unpublished manuscript, 1978.

Favell, J. E., McGimsey, J. F., & Jones, M. L. The use of physical restraint in the treatment of self-injury and as positive reinforcement. *Journal of Applied Behavior Analysis*, 1978, *11*, 225–241.

Ferritor, D. E., Buckholdt, D., Hamblin, R. L., & Smith, L. The non-effects of contingent reinforcement for attending behavior on work accomplished. *Journal of Applied Behavior Analysis*, 1972, *5*, 7–17.

Fleming, E. R. Training passive and aggressive educable mentally retarded children for assertive behaviors using three types of structured learning training. (Doctoral dissertation, Syracuse University.) *Dissertation Abstracts International*, 1976, *37A*, 235.

Forehand, R., & Baumeister, A. A. Deceleration of aberrant behavior among retarded individuals. In M. Hersen, R. M. Eisler, & P. M. Miller (Eds.), *Progress in behavior modification*. New York: Academic Press, 1976.

Foxx, R. M. The use of overcorrection to eliminate the public disrobing (stripping) of retarded women. *Behaviour Research and Therapy*, 1976, *14*, 53–67.

Foxx, R. M., & Azrin, N. H. Restitution: A method of eliminating aggressive-disruptive behavior of mentally retarded and brain damaged patients. *Behaviour Research and Therapy*, 1972, *10*, 15–27.

Foxx, R. M., & Azrin, N. H. The elimination of autistic self-stimulatory behavior by over-correction. *Journal of Applied Behavior Analysis*, 1973, *6*, 1–14.

Foxx, R. M., & Shapiro, S. T. The timeout ribbon: A nonexclusionary timeout procedure. *Journal of Applied Behavior Analysis*, 1978, *11*, 125–136.

Frankel, F., & Simmons, J. Q. Self-injurious behavior in schizophrenic and retarded children. *American Journal of Mental Deficiency*, 1976, *80*, 512–522.

Frankel, F., Moss, D., Schofield, S., & Simmons, J. Q. Case study: Use of differential reinforcement to suppress self-injurious and aggressive behavior. *Psychological Reports*, 1976, *39*, 843–849.

Freeman, B. J., Roy, R. R., & Hemmick, S. Extinction of a phobia of physical examination in a seven-year-old mentally retarded boy: A case study. *Behavior Research and Therapy*, 1976, *14*, 63–64.

Fuller, P. R. Operant conditioning of a vegetative human organism. *American Journal of Psychology*, 1949, *62*, 587–590.

Gamache, R. F., & Madle, R. A. Word discrimination in institutionalized mentally retarded adults utilizing a fading procedure. *Research and the Retarded*, 1976, *3*, 14–23.

Garcia, E., Baer, D. M., & Firestone, I. The development of generalized imitation within topographically determined boundaries. *Journal of Applied Behavior Analysis*, 1971, *4*, 101–112.

Gardner, J. M. Teaching behavior modification to nonprofessionals. *Journal of Applied Behavior Analysis*, 1972, *5*, 517–521.

Gardner, J. M. Training the trainers: A review of research on teaching behavior modification. In C. M. Franks & R. Rubin (Eds.), *Advances in behavior therapy: Proceedings, 1971*. New York: Academic Press, 1973.

Giles, D. K., & Wolf, M. M. Toilet training institutionalized, severe retardates: An application of operant behavior modification techniques. *American Journal of Mental Deficiency,* 1966, *70,* 766–780.

Girardeau, F. L., & Spradlin, J. E. Token rewards in a cottage program. *Mental Retardation,* 1964, *2,* 345–351.

Gold, M. W. Research on the vocational habilitation of the retarded: The present, the future. In N. R. Ellis (Ed.), *International review of research in mental retardation,* Vol. 6. New York: McGraw-Hill, 1973.

Goldstein, A. P. *Structured learning therapy: Toward a psychotherapy for the poor.* New York: Academic Press, 1973.

Gorton, C. E., & Hollis, J. H. Redesigning a cottage unit for better programming and research for the severely retarded. *Mental Retardation,* 1965, *3,* 16–21.

Greene, B. F., Willis, B. S., Levy, R., & Bailey, J. S. Measuring client gains from staff-implemented programs. *Journal of Applied Behavior Analysis,* 1978, *11,* 395–412.

Greene, R. J., & Hoats, D. L. Reinforcing capabilities of television distortion. *Journal of Applied Behavior Analysis,* 1969, *2,* 139–141.

Greene, R. J., & Hoats, D. L. Aversive tickling: A simple conditioning technique. *Behavior Therapy,* 1971, *2,* 389–393.

Griffin, J. C., Locke, B. J., & Landers, W. F. Manipulation of potential punishment parameters in the treatment of self-injury. *Journal of Applied Behavior Analysis,* 1975, *8,* 458.

Griffiths, H., & Craighead, W. E. Generalization in operant articulation therapy. *Journal of Speech and Hearing Disorders,* 1972, *37,* 485–494.

Grossman, W. J. (Ed.). *Manual on terminology and classification in mental retardation.* Washington, D.C.: American Association on Mental Deficiency, 1977.

Guralnick, M. J. Behavior therapy with an acrophobic mentally retarded young adult. *Journal of Behavior Therapy and Experimental Psychiatry,* 1973, *4,* 263–265.

Hamilton, J. W., & Standahl, J. Suppression of stereotyped screaming behavior in a 24 year old profoundly retarded girl. *Journal of Experimental Child Psychology,* 1969, *7,* 114–121.

Hamilton, J. W., Stephens, L. Y., & Allen, P. Controlling aggressive and destructive behavior in severely retarded institutionalized residents. *American Journal of Mental Deficiency,* 1967, *71,* 852–856.

Hanson, M. *Training your Down's syndrome infant: A guide for parents.* Eugene: University of Oregon Press, 1977.

Harris, J. M., Veit, S. W., Allen, A. J., & Chinsky, J. M. Aide-resident ratio and ward population density as mediators of social interaction. *American Journal of Mental Deficiency,* 1974, *79,* 320–326.

Harris, S. L., & Ersner-Hershfield, R. Behavioral suppression of seriously disruptive behavior in psychotic and retarded patients: A review of punishment and its alternatives. *Psychological Bulletin,* 1978, *85,* 1352–1375.

Harris, S. L., & Romanczyk, R. Treating self-injurious behavior of a retarded child by overcorrection. *Behavior Therapy,* 1976, *7,* 235–239.

Harvey, J. R. The potential of relaxation training for the mentally retarded. *Mental Retardation,* 1979, *17,* 71–76.

Harvey, J. R., Karan, O. C., Bhargava, D., & Morehouse, N. *Relaxation training and cognitively oriented behavioral procedures to reduce violent temper outbursts in a moderately retarded woman.* Unpublished manuscript, 1978.

Haubrich, P. A., & Shores, R. Attending behavior and academic performance of emotionally disturbed children. *Exceptional Children,* 1976, *42,* 337–338.

Henriksen, K., & Doughty, R. Decelerating undesirable mealtime behavior in a group of profoundly retarded boys. *American Journal of Mental Deficiency,* 1967, *72,* 40–44.

Hersen, M., & Bellack, A. S. Social skills training for chronic psychiatric patients: Rationale, research findings, and future directions. *Comprehensive Psychiatry,* 1976, *42,* 559–580.

Hopkins, B. L. Effects of candy and social reinforcement, instructions, and reinforcement schedule learning on the modification and maintenance of smiling. *Journal of Applied Behavior Analysis,* 1968, *1,* 121–129.

Horner, R. D. *Detailed progress report: Behavior modification program to develop self-help skills.* Final report. Wheat Ridge, Colo.: State Home and Training School, 1970.

Horner, R. D., & Keilitz, I. Training mentally retarded adolescents to brush their teeth. *Journal of Applied Behavior Analysis,* 1975, *8,* 301–309.

Hundziak, M., Maurer, R. A., & Watson, L. S., Jr. Operant conditioning in toilet training of severely mentally retarded boys. *American Journal of Mental Deficiency,* 1965, *70,* 120–124.

Hunt, J. G., & Zimmerman, J. Stimulating productivity in a simulated sheltered workshop setting. *American Journal of Mental Deficiency,* 1969, *74,* 43–49.

Hunt, J. G., Fitzhugh, L. C., & Fitzhugh, K. B. Teaching "exit-ward" patients appropriate personal appearance by using reinforcement techniques. *American Journal of Mental Deficiency,* 1968, *73,* 41–45.

Husted, J. R., Hall, P., & Agin, B. The effectiveness of time-out in reducing maladaptive behavior of autistic and retarded children. *Journal of Psychology,* 1971, *79,* 189–196.

Iwata, B. A., & Lorentzson, A. M. Operant control of seizure-like behavior in an institutionalized retarded adult. *Behavior Therapy,* 1976, *7,* 247–251.

Iwata, B. A., Bailey, J. S., Brown, K. M., Foshee, T. J., & Alpern, M. A performance-based lottery to improve residential care and training by institutional staff. *Journal of Applied Behavior Analysis,* 1976, *9,* 417–431.

Jackson, D. A., & Wallace, R. F. The modification and generalization of voice loudness in a fifteen-year-old retarded girl. *Journal of Applied Behavior Analysis,* 1974, *7,* 461–471.

Jackson, G. M., Johnson, C. R., Ackron, G. S., & Crowley, R. Food satiation as a procedure to decelerate vomiting. *American Journal of Mental Deficiency,* 1975, *80,* 223–227.

Jens, K. E., & Shores, R. E. Behavioral graphs as reinforcers for work behavior of mentally retarded adolescents. *Education and Training of the Mentally Retarded,* 1969, *4,* 21–28.

Johnson, M. S., & Bailey, J. S. The modification of leisure behavior in a half-way house for retarded women. *Journal of Applied Behavior Analysis,* 1977, *10,* 273–282.

Kazdin, A. E. Toward a client administered token reinforcement program. *Education and Training of the Mentally Retarded,* 1971, *6,* 52–55.

Kazdin, A. E. The effect of response cost and aversive stimulation in suppressing punished and nonpunished speech disfluencies. *Behavior Therapy,* 1973, *4,* 73–82.

Kazdin, A. E. *The token economy: A review and evaluation.* New York: Plenum Press, 1977.

Kazdin, A. E. Behavior modification in retardation. In J. T. Neisworth & R. M. Smith (Eds.), *Retardation: Issues, assessment, and intervention.* New York: McGraw-Hill, 1978.

Kazdin, A. E., & Craighead, W. E. Behavior modification in special education. In L. Mann & D. A. Sabatino (Eds.), *The first review of special education,* Vol. 2. Philadelphia: Buttonwood Farms, 1973.

Kazdin, A. E., & Erickson, L. M. Developing responsiveness to instructions in severely and profoundly retarded residents. *Journal of Behavior Therapy and Experimental Psychiatry,* 1975, *6,* 17–21.

Keilitz, I., Tucker, D. J., & Horner, R. D. Increasing mentally retarded adolescents' verbalizations about current events. *Journal of Applied Behavior Analysis,* 1973, *6,* 621–630.

Kelly, J. A., & Drabman, R. S. Generalizing response suppression of self-injurious behavior through an overcorrection punishment procedure: A case study. *Behavior Therapy,* 1977, *8,* 468–472.

Kimbrell, D. L., Luckey, R. E., Barbuto, P. F. P., & Love, J. G. Operation dry pants: An intensive habit-training program for severely and profoundly retarded. *Mental Retardation,* February 1967, *5,* 32–36.

Kimmel, H. D., & Kimmel, E. An instrumental conditioning method for the treatment of enuresis. *Journal of Behavior Therapy and Experimental Psychiatry,* 1970, *1,* 121–123.

Kirk, S. A. *Educating exceptional children* (2nd ed.). New York: Houghton-Mifflin, 1972.

Kurtz, P. D., & Neisworth, J. T. Self-control possibilities for exceptional children. *Exceptional Child,* 1976, *42,* 212–217.

Lahey, B. B., McNees, M. P., & McNees, M. C. Control of an obscene "verbal tic" through time-out in an elementary classroom. *Journal of Applied Behavior Analysis,* 1973, *6,* 101–104.

Lattal, K. A. Contingency management of toothbrushing in a summer camp for children. *Journal of Applied Behavior Analysis,* 1969, *2,* 195–198.

Leff, R. B. Teaching the TMR to dial the telephone. *Mental Retardation,* 1974, *12,* 12–13.

Leff, R. B. Teaching use of phone. *Mental Retardation,* 1975, *13,* 9–12.

Lent, J. R. Mimosa Cottage: Experiment in hope. *Psychology Today,* 1968, *2*(1), 50–58.

Lindsley, O. R. Direct measurement and prosthesis of retarded behavior. *Journal of Education,* 1964, *147,* 62–81.

Lindsley, O. R. An experiment with parents handling behavior in the home. *Johnstone Bulletin,* 1966, *9,* 27–36.

Long, J. D., & Williams, R. L. The utility of self-management procedure in modifying the classroom behaviors of mentally retarded adolescents. *Adolescence,* 1976, *11,* 29–38.

Lovaas, O. I., & Simmons, J. Q. Manipulation of self-destruction in three retarded children. *Journal of Applied Behavior Analysis,* 1969, *2,* 143–157.

Lowe, M. L., & Cuvo, A. J. Teaching coin summation to the mentally retarded. *Journal of Applied Behavior Analysis,* 1976, *9,* 483–489.

Lucero, W. J., Frieman, J., Spoering, K., & Fehrenbacher, J. Comparison of three procedures in reducing self-injurious behavior. *American Journal of Mental Deficiency,* 1976, *80,* 548–554.

Luckey, R. E., Watson, C. M., & Musick, J. K. Aversive conditioning as a means of inhibiting vomiting and rumination. *American Journal of Mental Deficiency,* 1968, *73,* 139–142.

Luiselli, J. K. Case report: An attendant-administered contingency management progamme for the treatment of a toileting phobia. *Journal of Mental Deficiency Research,* 1977, *21,* 283–288.

Lutzker, J. R., & Sherman, J. Producing generative sentence usage by imitation and reinforcement procedures. *Journal of Applied Behavior Analysis,* 1974, *7,* 447–460.

Madle, R. A. *Issues in research on paraprofessional training in behavior modification.* Paper presented at the Meeting of the Mideastern Region of the American Association on Mental Deficiency, Buckhill Falls, Pennsylvania, November 1975.

Madle, R. A. Intonation and instructions as factors in discrimination learning of institutionalized retarded adults. (Doctoral dissertation, The Pennsylvania State University.) *Dissertation Abstracts International,* 1976, *37A,* 189.

Mahoney, M. J., & Mahoney, K. Self-control techniques with the mentally retarded. *Exceptional Children,* 1976, *42,* 338–339.

Mahoney, K., Van Wagenen, R. K., & Meyerson, L. Toilet training of normal and retarded children. *Journal of Applied Behavior Analysis,* 1971, *4,* 173–182.

Mansdorf, I. J. Eliminating fear in a mentally retarded adult by behavioral hierarchies and operant techniques. *Journal of Behavior Therapy and Experimental Psychiatry,* 1976, *7,* 189–190.

Marholin, D., II, Steinman, W. M., McInnis, E. T., & Heads, T. B. The effect of a teacher's presence on the classroom behavior of conduct-problem children. *Journal of Abnormal Child Psychology,* 1975, *3,* 11–25.

Marholin, D., O'Toole, K., Touchette, P., Berger, P., & Doyle, D. "I'll have a Big Mac, large fries, large coke, and apple pie" . . . or teaching adaptive community skills. *Behavior Therapy,* 1979, *10,* 236–248.

Marshall, G. R. Toilet training of an autistic eight-year-old through conditioning therapy: A case report. *Behaviour Research and Therapy,* 1966, *4,* 242–245.

Martin, G. L., McDonald, S., & Omichinski, M. An operant analysis of response interactions during meals with severely retarded girls. *American Journal of Mental Deficiency,* 1971, *76,* 68–75.

Martin, P. L., & Foxx, R. M. Victim control of the aggression of an institutionalized retardate. *Journal of Behav-*

ior Therapy and Experimental Psychiatry, 1973, *4*, 161–165.

Matson, J., & Stephens, R. Overcorrection of aggressive behavior in a chronic psychiatric patient. *Behavior Modification*, 1977, *1*, 559–564.

Matson, J. L., & Stephens, R. M. Increasing appropriate behavior of explosive chronic psychiatric patients with a social-skills training package. *Behavior Modification*, 1978, *2*, 61–76.

Mayhew, G. L., Enyart, P., & Anderson, J. Social reinforcement and the naturally occuring social responses of severely and profoundly retarded adults. *American Journal of Mental Deficiency*, 1978, *83*, 164–170.

Measel, C. J., & Alfieri, P. A. Treatment of self-injurious behavior by a combination of reinforcement for incompatible behavior and overcorrection. *American Journal of Mental Deficiency*, 1976, *81*, 147–153.

Mercatoris, M., Hahn, L. G., & Craighead, W. E. Mentally retarded residents as paraprofessionals in modifying mealtime behavior. *Journal of Abnormal Psychology*, 1975, *84*, 299–302.

Miller, A., & Miller, E. E. Cognitive-developmental training with elevated boards and sign language. *Journal of Autism and Childhood Schizophrenia*, 1973, *3*, 65–85.

Minge, M. R., & Ball, T. S. Teaching of self-help skills to profoundly retarded patients. *American Journal of Mental Deficiency*, 1967, *71*, 864–868.

Mitchell, A. C., & Smeriglio, V. Growth in social competence in institutionalized mentally retarded children. *American Journal of Mental Deficiency*, 1970, *74*, 666–673.

Morris, R. J., & Dolker, M. Developing cooperative play in socially withdrawn retarded children. *Mental Retardation*, 1974, *12*, 24–27.

Morrison, D. Issues in the application of reinforcement theory in the treatment of a child's self-injurious behavior. *Psychotherapy: Theory, Research and Practice*, 1972, *9*, 40–45.

Mowrer, O. H., & Mowrer, W. M. Enuresis: A method for its study and treatment. *American Journal of Orthopsychiatry*, 1938, *8*, 436–459.

Mulhern, T., & Baumeister, A. A. An experimental attempt to reduce stereotypy by reinforcement procedures. *American Journal of Mental Deficiency*, 1969, *74*, 69–74.

Murdock, J. Y., Garcia, E. E., & Hardman, M. L. Generalizing articulation training with trainable mentally retarded subjects. *Journal of Applied Behavior Analysis*, 1977, *10*, 717–733.

Nay, W. R. A systematic comparison of instructional techniques for parents. *Behavior Therapy*, 1975, *6*, 14–21.

Neef, N. A., Iwata, B. A., & Page, T. J. Public transportation training: In vivo versus classroom instruction. *Journal of Applied Behavior Analysis*, 1978, *11*, 331–344.

Neisworth, J. T., & Madle, R. A. Time-out with staff accountability: A technical note. *Behavior Therapy*, 1976, *7*, 261–263.

Neisworth, J. T., & Smith, R. M. *Modifying retarded behavior*. Boston: Houghton Mifflin, 1973.

Neisworth, J. T., & Smith, R. M. Analysis and redefinition of "developmental disabilities." *Exceptional Children*, 1974, *40*, 345–347.

Neisworth, J. T., Madle, R. A., & Goeke, K. E. "Errorless" elimination of separation anxiety: A case study. *Journal of Behavior Therapy and Experimental Psychiatry*, 1975, *6*, 79–82.

Neisworth, J. T., Jones, R. T., & Smith, R. M. Body-behavior problems: A conceptualization. *Education and Training of the Mentally Retarded*, October 1978, *13*, 265–271.

Nelson, G. L., Cone, J. D., & Hanson, C. R. Training correct utensil use in retarded children: Modeling vs. physical guidance. *American Journal of Mental Deficiency*, 1975, *80*, 114–122.

Newton, A. Clothing: A positive part of the rehabilitation process. *Journal of Rehabilitation*, 1976, *42*, 18–22.

Nunes, D. L., Murphy, R. J., & Ruprecht, M. L. Reducing self-injurious behavior of severely retarded individuals through withdrawal of reinforcement procedures. *Behavior Modification*, 1977, *1*, 499–516.

Nutter, D., & Reid, D. H. Teaching retarded women a clothing selection skill using communicaty norms. *Journal of Applied Behavior Analysis*, 1978, *11*, 475–487.

O'Brien, F., & Azrin, N. H. Developing proper mealtime behaviors of the institutionalized retarded. *Journal of Applied Behavior Analysis*, 1972, *5*, 389–399.

O'Brien, F., Bugle, C., & Azrin, N. H. Training and maintaining a retarded child's proper eating. *Journal of Applied Behavior Analysis*, 1972, *5*, 67–72.

Ollendick, T. H., Matson, J. L., & Martin, J. E. Effectiveness of hand overcorrection for topographically similar and dissimilar self-stimulatory behavior. *Journal of Experimental Child Psychology*, 1978, *25*, 396–403.

Page, T. J., Iwata, B. A., & Neef, N. A. Teaching pedestrian skills to retarded persons: Generalization from the classroom to the natural environment. *Journal of Applied Behavior Analysis*, 1976, *9*, 433–444.

Palyo, W. J., Schuler, A. L., Cooke, T. P., & Apolloni, T. Modifying echolalic speech in preschool children: Training and generalization. *American Journal of Mental Deficiency*, 1979, *83*, 480–489.

Panda, K. C., & Lynch, W. W. Effects of social reinforcement on retarded children: A review and interpretation for classroom instruction. *Education and Training of the Mentally Retarded*, 1972, *7*, 115–123.

Parsonson, B. S., Baer, A. M., & Baer, D. M. The application of generalized correct social contingencies: An evaluation of a training program. *Journal of Applied Behavior Analysis*, 1974, *7*, 427–437.

Paschalis, A., Kimmel, H. D., & Kimmel, E. Further study of diurnal instrumental conditioning in the treatment of enuresis nocturna. *Journal of Behavior Therapy and Experimental Psychiatry*, 1972, *3*, 253–256.

Peck, C. L. Densensitization for the treatment of fear in the high level adult retardate. *Behavior Research and Therapy*, 1977, *18*, 137–148.

Perry, M. A., & Cerreto, M. C. Structured learning training of social skills for the retarded. *Mental Retardation*, 1977, *15*, 31–34.

Peterson, G. A., Austin, G. J., & Lang, R. P. Use of teacher prompts to increase social behavior: Generalization effects with severely and profoundly retarded adolescents. *American Journal of Mental Deficiency*, 1979, *84*, 82–86.

Premack, D. Toward empirical behavior laws: I. Positive reinforcement. *Psychological Review,* 1959, *66,* 219–233.

Public Law 91.517, 91st Congress, S.2846, October 30, 1970.

Reid, D. H., & Hurlbut, B. Teaching nonvocal communication skills to multihandicapped retarded adults. *Journal of Applied Behavior Analysis,* 1977, *10,* 591–603.

Reisinger, J. J. The treatment of "anxiety depression" via positive reinforcement and response cost. *Journal of Applied Behavior Analysis,* 1972, *5,* 125–130.

Repp, A. C., & Deitz, S. M. Reducing aggressive and self-injurious behavior of institutionalized retarded children through reinforcement of other behaviors. *Journal of Applied Behavior Analysis,* 1974, *7,* 313–325.

Repp, A. C., & Dietz, D. E. Ethical issues in reducing responding of institutionalized mentally retarded persons. *Mental Retardation,* 1978, *16,* 45–46.

Repp, A. C., & Dietz, D. Improving administrative-related staff behaviors at a state institution. *Mental Retardation,* 1979, *17,* 185–188.

Repp, A. C., Deitz, S. M., & Speir, N. C. Reducing stereotypic responding of retarded persons by the differential reinforcement of other behavior. *American Journal of Mental Deficiency,* 1974, *79,* 279–284.

Reynolds, M. C., & Kiland, J. R. *A study of public school children with severe mental retardation.* St. Paul, Minn.: State Department of Education, 1953.

Risley, T. R. The effects and side effects of punishing the autistic behaviors of a deviant child. *Journal of Applied Behavior Analysis,* 1968, *1,* 21–34.

Risley, T. R., & Wolf, M. M. Establishing functional speech in echolalic children. *Behaviour Research and Therapy,* 1967, *5,* 73–88.

Robinson, N. M., & Robinson, H. B. *The mentally retarded child: A psychological approach* (2nd ed.). New York: McGraw-Hill, 1976.

Ross, D. M., & Ross, S. A. The efficacy of listening training for educable mentally retarded children. *American Journal of Mental Deficiency,* 1972, *77,* 137–142.

Ross, D. M., & Ross, S. A. Cognitive training for the EMR child: Situational problem solving and planning. *American Journal of Mental Deficiency,* 1973, *78,* 20–26.

Ross, D. M., and Ross, S. A. *Pacemaker primary curriculum.* Belmont, Calif.: Fearon Publishers, 1974.

Ross, R. R., Meichenbaum, D. H., & Humphrey, C. Treatment of nocturnal head banging by behavior modification techniques: A case report. *Behaviour Research and Therapy,* 1971, *9,* 151–154.

Sajwaj, T. Issues and implications of establishing guidelines for the use of behavioral techniques. *Journal of Applied Behavior Analysis,* 1977, *10,* 531–540.

Sajwaj, T., & Hedges, D. "Side-effects" of a punishment procedure in an oppositional, retarded child. Paper presented at a meeting of the Western Psychological Association, San Francisco, April 1971.

Sajwaj, T., Twardosz, S., & Burke, M. Side effects of extinction procedures in a remedial preschool. *Journal of Applied Behavior Analysis,* 1972, *5,* 163–175.

Sajwaj, T., Libet, J., & Agras, S. Lemon-juice therapy: The control of life-threatening rumination in a six-month-old infant. *Journal of Applied Behavior Analysis,* 1974, *7,* 557–563.

Samaras, M. S., & Ball, T. S. Reinforcement of cooperation between profoundly retarded adults. *American Journal of Mental Deficiency,* 1975, *80,* 63–71.

Sarason, S. B., & Doris, J. *Psychological problems in mental deficiency.* New York: Harper & Row, 1969.

Schroeder, S. R., Peterson, C. R., Solomon, L. J., & Artley, J. J. EMG feedback and the contingent restraint of self-injurious behavior among the severely retarded: Two case illustrations. *Behavior Therapy,* 1977, *8,* 738–741.

Sidman, M. Reading and auditory-visual equivalences. *Journal of Speech and Hearing Research,* 1971, *14,* 5–13.

Sidman, M., & Cresson, O., Jr. Reading and cross modal transfer of stimulus equivalences in severe retardation. *American Journal of Mental Deficiency,* 1973, *77,* 515–523.

Silvestri, R. Implosive therapy treatment of emotionally disturbed retardates. *Journal of Consulting and Clinical Psychology,* 1977, *45,* 14–22.

Skinner, B. F. *Science and human behavior.* New York: Macmillan, 1953.

Sloane, H. N., Jr., Johnston, M. K., & Harris, F. R. Remedial procedures for teaching verbal behavior to speech deficient or defective young children. In H. N. Sloane, Jr., & B. D. MacAulay (Eds.), *Operant procedures in remedial speech and language training.* Boston: Houghton Mifflin, 1968.

Sloop, E. W., & Kennedy, W. A. Institutionalized retarded nocturnal enuretics treated by a conditioning technique. *American Journal of Mental Deficiency,* 1973, *77,* 717–721.

Snyder, L. K., Lovitt, T. C., & Smith, J. O. Language training for the severely retarded: Five years of behavior analysis research. *Exceptional Children,* 1975, *42*(1), 7–15.

Solnick, J. V., Rincover, A., & Peterson, C. R. Some determinants of the reinforcing and punishing effects of time-out. *Journal of Applied Behavior Analysis,* 1977, *10,* 415–424.

Spradlin, J. E., & Girardeau, F. L. The behavior of moderately and severely retarded persons. In N. Ellis (Ed.), *International review of research in mental retardation,* Vol. 1. New York: Academic Press, 1966.

Stark, J., Meisel, J., & Wright, T. S. Modifying maladaptive behavior in a non-verbal child. *British Journal of Disorders of Communication,* 1969, *4,* 67–72.

Stephan, C., Stephano, S., & Talkington, L. W. Use of modeling in survival social training with educable mentally retarded. *Training School Bulletin,* 1973, *70,* 63–68.

Stimbert, V. E., Minor, J. W., & McCoy, J. F. Intensive feeding training with retarded children. *Behavior Modification,* 1977, *1,* 517–530.

Stokes, T. F., Baer, D. M., & Jackson, R. L. Programming the generalization of a greeting response in four retarded children. *Journal of Applied Behavior Analysis,* 1974, *7,* 599–610.

Storm, R. M., & Willis, J. H. Small-group training as an alternative to individual programs for profoundly retarded persons. *American Journal of Mental Deficiency,* 1978, *83,* 283–288.

Strain, P. Increasing social play of severely retarded preschoolers with socio-dramatic activities. *Mental Retardation*, 1975, *13*, 7–9.

Striefel, S., & Wetherby, B. Instruction-following behavior of a retarded child and its controlling stimuli. *Journal of Applied Behavior Analysis*, 1973, *6*, 663–670.

Striefel, S., Wetherby, B., & Karlan, G. R. Establishing generalized verb-noun instruction-following skills in retarded children. *Journal of Experimental Child Psychology*, 1976, *22*, 247–260.

Subcommittee on Constitutional Rights. *Individual rights and the federal role in behavior modification*. Washington, D.C.: U.S. Government Printing Office, 1974.

Tarpley, H. D., & Schroeder, S. R. Comparison of DRO and DRI on rate of suppression of self-injurious behavior. *American Journal of Mental Deficiency*, 1979, *84*, 188–194.

Tate, B. G., & Baroff, G. S. Aversive control of self-injurious behavior in a psychotic boy. *Behaviour Research and Therapy*, 1966, *4*, 281–287.

Thoreson, C. E., & Mahoney, M. J. *Behavioral self-control*. New York: Holt, Rinehart & Winston, 1974.

Tobias, J. *Training for independent living: A three year report of occupation day center for mentally retarded adults*. New York: Association for Retarded Children, 1963, (Mimeographed.)

Twardosz, S., & Sajwaj, T. Multiple effects of a procedure to increase sitting in a hyperactive, retarded boy. *Journal of Applied Behavior Analysis*, 1972, *5*, 73–78.

VanBiervliet, A. Establishing words and objects as functionally equivalent through manual sign training. *American Journal of Mental Deficiency*, 1977, *82*, 178–186.

Van Wagenen, R. K., Meyerson, L., Kerr, N. J., & Mahoney, K. Field trials of a new procedure for toilet training. *Journal of Experimental Child Psychology*, 1969, *8*, 147–159.

Wallace, J., Burger, D., Neal, H. C., van Brero, M., & Davis, D. E. Aversive conditioning use in public facilities for the mentally retarded. *Mental Retardation*, 1976, *14*, 17–19.

Walsh, B. F., & Lamberts, F. Errorless discrimination and picture fading as techniques for teaching sight words to TMR students. *American Journal of Mental Deficiency*, 1979, *83*, 473–479.

Warren, S. A. Academic achievement of trainable pupils with five or more years of schooling. *Training School Bulletin*, 1963, *60*, 75–88.

Watson, L. S. Applications of behavior shaping-devices to training severely and profoundly retarded children in an institutional setting. *Mental Retardation*, 1968, *6*, 21–23.

Watson, L. S. *How to use behavior modification with mentally retarded and autistic children: Programs for administrators, teachers, parents, and nurses*. Libertyville, Ill.: Behavior Modification Technology, 1972.

Wells, K. C., Turner, J. M., Bellack, A. S., & Hersen,

M. Effects of cue-controlled relaxation on psychomotor seizures: An experimental analysis. *Behaviour Research and Therapy*, 1978, *16*, 51–53.

Whaley, D. L., & Tough, J. Treatment of a self-injuring mongoloid with shock-induced suppression and avoidance. In R. Ulrich, R. Stachnik, & J. Mabry (Eds.), *Control of human behavior*, Vol. 2. Glenview, Ill.: Scott, Foresman, 1970.

Wheeler, A. J., & Wislocki, E. B. Stimulus factors effecting peer conversation among institutionalized retarded women. *Journal of Applied Behavior Analysis*, 1977, *10*, 283–288.

Whitman, T. L., Mercurio, J. R., & Caponigri, V. Development of social responses in two severely retarded children. *Journal of Applied Behavior Analysis*, 1970, *3*, 133–138.

Wiesen, A. E., & Watson, E. Elimination of attention-seeking behavior in a retarded child. *American Journal of Mental Deficiency*, 1967, *72*, 50–52.

Wolf, M. M., Risley, T. R., & Mees, H. Application of operant conditioning procedures to the behaviour problems of an autistic child. *Behaviour Research and Therapy*, 1964, *1*, 305–312.

Wolf, M. M., Birnbrauer, J. S., Williams, T., & Lawler, J. A note on apparent extinction of the vomiting behavior of a retarded child. In L. Ullmann & L. Krasner (Eds.), *Case studies in behavior modification*. New York: Holt, Rinehart & Winston, 1965.

Wolfensberger, W. *Normalization: The principle of normalization in human services*. Toronto: National Institute on Mental Retardation, 1972.

Young, J. A., & Wincze, J. P. The effects of the reinforcement of compatible and incompatible alternative behaviors on the self-injurious and related behaviors of a profoundly retarded female adult. *Behavior Therapy*, 1974, *5*, 614–623.

Zieler, M. D., & Jervey, S. S. Development of behavior: Self-feeding. *Journal of Consulting and Clinical Psychology*, 1968, *32*, 164–168.

Zimmerman, J., Overpeck, C., Eisenberg, H., & Garlick, B. Operant conditioning in a sheltered workshop. *Rehabilitation Literature*, 1969, *30*, 326–334.

Zimmerman, J., Stuckey, T. E., Garlick, B. J., & Miller, M. Effects of token reinforcement on productivity in multiply handicapped clients in a sheltered workshop. *Rehabilitation Literature*, 1969, *30*, 34–41.

Zimmerman, E. H., Zimmerman, J., & Russell, D. Differential effects of token reinforcement on instruction-following behavior in retarded students instructed as a group. *Journal of Applied Behavior Analysis*, 1969, *2*, 101–118.

Zlutnick, S., Mayville, W. J., & Moffat, S. Modification of seizure disorders: The interruption of behavioral chains. *Journal of Applied Behavior Analysis*, 1975, *8*, 1–12.

CHAPTER 28

Autism

Laura Schreibman, Robert L. Koegel, Marjorie
H. Charlop, and Andrew L. Egel

Autism is a severe form of psychopathology
that is estimated to occur in about one of every
2,500 children and that is characterized, in
general, by extreme withdrawal and lack of
social behavior, severe language and attentional deficits, and the presence of bizarre,
repetitive behaviors (J. K. Wing, 1966). The
severity of the disorder typically causes great
turmoil in the family, affecting not only the
lives of the child and the parents, but the community as well. Autism is usually not diagnosed until the child is between 2 and 5 years
of age, and while there are currently many
theories relating to the etiology of the disorder,
there is no consistent evidence in support of
any one of them (Egel, Koegel, & Schreibman,

1980). Most professionals, however, do believe that autism is caused by organic factors,
and that the disorder is probably present from
birth. The severity of the disorder makes it
resistant to most forms of treatment intervention. Behavior-modification treatment procedures, however, have been quite successful,
probably because they do not depend heavily
on the child's verbal skills or the practitioner's
knowledge of the etiology of the disorder.

Overview

It is the purpose of this chapter to provide
the reader with a comprehensive discussion
of autism and behaviorally oriented treatment
programs. Any such discussion must begin
with a description of the syndrome of autism,
particularly because of its complexity and because the behavioral treatment of the disorder
so heavily emphasizes the treatment of the
particular behaviors that comprise the syndrome. In addition, a historical perspective is
presented to help elucidate the evolution of
the treatment approaches that have been applied to the disorder.

Following a description of the syndrome and
the historical perspective is a brief analysis of
the theoretical position offered by the behav-

Laura Schreibman • Psychology Department, Clare-
mont McKenna College, Claremont, California 91711.
Robert L. Koegel • Social Process Research
Institute, University of California, Santa Barbara, Cali-
fornia 93106. Marjorie H. Charlop • Division of
Behavioral Psychology, The Johns Hopkins University
School of Medicine, and the John F. Kennedy Institute,
707 North Broadway, Baltimore, Maryland 21205.
Andrew L. Egel • Department of Special Education,
University of Maryland, College Park, Maryland 20742.
Preparation of this chapter and portions of the research
reported therein, were supported by USPHS Research
Grants MH 28231 and MH 28210 from the National In-
stitute of Mental Health and by U.S. Office of Education
Research Grant G007802084 from the Bureau for the Ed-
ucation of the Handicapped.

ioral approach and how it differs from the more traditional, psychodynamic approach. Next is a discussion of specific treatment procedures directed at eliminating behavioral excesses in autism (e.g., disruptive behaviors, self-stimulation, and self-destructive behavior) and remediating behavioral deficiencies (e.g., stimulus functions, language, and stimulus overselectivity). This section also includes a discussion of new methods for increasing reinforcer effectiveness, as well as a discussion of different methods of structuring training trials. The following section presents a discussion of the expansion of the clinic-derived treatment procedures into additional treatment environments. These include the home (parent training), the classroom, and teaching homes.

Finally, we conclude with two new approaches to evaluating treatment effectiveness. One, social validation, seeks to ensure that the objective behaviors measured by behavior therapists are those behaviors that are subjectively meaningful and socially important. Second is a new and hopeful report on measured neurological changes in autistic children as a function of treatment.

Diagnosis

Leo Kanner first described the syndrome of autism in 1943. He called the disorder "early infantile autism" because the children tended to be aloof, withdrawn, and "autistic" from the beginning of life (Rimland, 1964). Kanner's description of autism was based on 11 cases with striking similarities. The 11 children were unable to relate to people and the environment normally. Kanner called their preference to be alone "extreme autistic aloneness" (Kanner, 1943). The majority of these children, while infants, didn't mold to their parent's body when picked up. Kanner (1943) pointed out that the children lacked appropriate speech, noting instances of echolalia as well as failure to use pronouns correctly. The children engaged in monotonous, repetitive movements and vocalizations; had an obsessive insistence on the preservation of sameness in the environment; and manifested surprisingly good rote memories (Eisenberg & Kanner, 1956; Kanner, 1943).

Kanner described autism as a syndrome, differing from other disorders, and characterized by the symptoms mentioned above. He later reduced these symptoms to two essential ones: (1) extreme aloneness and (2) preservation of sameness (Eisenberg & Kanner, 1956). Interestingly, this article omitted language abnormalities as an essential symptom, which Kanner had stressed in his earlier writings. Today, Rutter has delineated three general groups of symptoms. In addition to an age of onset before 3 years, Rutter proposed that the major symptoms of autism include (1) the manifestation of a profound and general failure to develop social relationships; (2) language abnormalities; and (3) ritualistic or compulsive behavior—the insistence on sameness (Rutter, 1978).

Social Behavior

The social behavior of an autistic child is profoundly impaired (Rimland, 1964; Rutter, 1978; L. Wing, 1976, 1978). Generally, autistic children do not interact with people and seem to prefer being alone. If they do interact, they tend to treat others more like objects than like people (Schreibman & Koegel, 1981). An autistic child, for example, may put his arms around his mother, not to give her a hug, but to reach behind her for a toy. As infants, autistic children lack attachment behavior and generally do not mold to their parent's body when held. They may remain stiff and rigid or may "go limp" when picked up. When older, they may seldom seek out their parents for comfort (Rutter 1978). In addition, autistic children typically lack eye-to-eye contact, making it rather difficult to gain their attention. And, as mentioned before, they are usually not interested in the attention of adults or of peers (Rutter, 1978; L. Wing, 1978).

Language

Autistic children generally do not use language to communicate (Ornitz & Ritvo, 1976; J. K. Wing, 1966; L. Wing 1976, 1978). Some autistic children are functionally mute, occasionally emitting only a few sounds. Others are echolalic and do not use words to communicate. Echolalic children repeat or "echo" words or phrases that they have just heard (immediate echolalia) or words that they have heard in the past (delayed echolalia) (Carr, Schreibman, & Lovaas, 1975; Schreibman & Carr, 1978). In immediate echolalia, for example, if the child were asked, "Jimmy, how old are you?" the child would not answer the question but might echo "Jimmy, how old are you?" In delayed echolalia, a child may recite the dialogue of a TV show viewed days before. The children typically do not appear to know the meaning of the words and phrases they echo.

For those who do use language to communicate, pronomial reversal is often present (Kanner, 1943; Rutter, 1978). The I–you pronomial reversal is most common. A child with this language abnormality might say, "*You* go play now" meaning "*I* want to play now." This phenomenon is thought of as being associated with echoing the pronouns others used when speaking to the child.

Ritualistic Behavior and the Insistence on Sameness

Rutter (1978) has delineated four common phenomena that fall into this category. First, autistic children often engage in limited and rigid play patterns. They may repeatedly line up toys or household goods, or they may collect many objects of a special shape or texture. Second, an autistic child may become so attached to a specific object that she or he must have it at all times. If the object is taken away, the child may vehemently protest. Third, many autistic children have unusual preoccupations with such things as numbers, geometric shapes, bus routes, and colors. Fourth, many autistic children display a marked resistance to changes in the environment. They often maintain rigid routines and are extremely distressed by even a small change in their environment. The child, for example, may become quite upset if furniture is rearranged, or if he or she is not greeted in exactly the same way.

Other Symptoms of Autism

Autistic children frequently *appear* to possess a *sensory deficit*. That is, they are generally unresponsive to external stimulation (Ornitz & Ritvo, 1976; Rimland, 1964; Schreibman & Koegel, 1981, 1982; J. K. Wing, 1966). At times, the child may appear to be quite normal and at other times may not respond at all. Because of this unresponsiveness, autistic children are often incorrectly suspected of being deaf or blind (Koegel & Schreibman, 1976; Ornitz & Ritvo, 1976; Rimland, 1964). It is not surprising that many parents have described their autistic child as "living in a world of his own" (Koegel & Schreibman, 1976).

Many autistic children engage in self-stimulatory behaviors (Egel, Koegel, & Schreibman, 1980; Ornitz & Ritvo, 1976; Rimland, 1964; L. Wing, 1978). These behaviors are stereotyped, repetitive movements, which seem to do nothing other than provide sensory input for the child. The most common self-stimulatory behavior involves the arms and hands (Ornitz & Ritvo, 1976). The child repeatedly waves or flaps the hands, usually in front of her or his eyes. Other self-stimulation involves the torso, such as rhythmic body rocking or swaying, repeatedly turning around in circles, quick darting movements, and body posturing. Toe walking, head rolling, and head banging are also frequently observed (Ornitz & Ritvo, 1976), while more subtle forms of self-stimulation, such as staring at lights and repeatedly rubbing the hands along a textured surface, also occur. When the children engage in such behaviors, they often appear much less responsive to the surrounding environment (Lovaas, Litrownik, & Mann, 1971; Ornitz & Ritvo, 1976; Schreibman & Koegel, 1982).

Related to self-stimulatory behavior is the autistic child's lack of appropriate play (Koegel, Firestone, Kramme, & Dunlap, 1974). Autistic children do not play with toys in the manner in which normal children do but usually manipulate them in a self-stimulatory manner. Instead of building a tower with blocks, for example, an autistic child might repetitively run his or her fingers around the edges of a block or wave it in front of his or her eyes. Typically, when given a car or truck to play with, an autistic child merely spins the wheels.

Autistic children may display inappropriate affect (Schreibman & Koegel, 1981; J. K.

Wing, 1966; L. Wing, 1976). Some children have tantrums or laugh hysterically for no apparent reason. Other children seldom display any emotions at all. Often, the affect is inappropriate for the situation. For example, autistic children may lack fear when they are in real danger, such as playing near the deep end of a swimming pool. Conversely, they may become terrified of something harmless, such as a specific toy or room (L. Wing, 1976).

In order to be diagnosed as autistic, the child should display a majority, but not necessarily all, of the behaviors described above. In addition to these major characteristics, autistic children tend to be healthy and attractive (Dunlap, Koegel, & Egel, 1979; Kanner, 1943; Rimland, 1964). Autistic children were initially thought to be quite intelligent (Eisenberg & Kanner, 1956; Kanner, 1943). Although normal or above-normal intelligence is not always thought of in association with autism today (Rutter, 1978; Schreibman & Koegel, 1981; 1982), many autistic children do show isolated areas of exceptional performance, especially in the areas of musical, mechanical, or mathematical skills (Applebaum, Egel, Koegel, & Imhoff, 1979; Rimland, 1978). This "autistic savant" behavior often accompanies below-age-level functioning in most, if not all, other areas.

Autism and Childhood Schizophrenia

The terms *autism* and *childhood schizophrenia* have often been used interchangeably because of the similarities in behavior of autistic and schizophrenic youngsters. There are, however, several differences between the two disorders. First, the age of onset differs: autism occurs much earlier in life (prior to 30 months), whereas childhood schizophrenia is usually diagnosed during puberty (Rutter, 1978). Schizophrenic children also tend to be more skilled in language and are more social than autistic children. The schizophrenic child may show irregular periods of recovery and regression, while the autistic child maintains a more stable level of functioning. Rimland (1964) has delineated other differences, for example, schizophrenic children's possessing abnormal EEG readings, being less healthy and less attractive, having poorer motor co-ordination, and maintaining a lower incidence of idiot savant performance than autistic children. In addition, schizophrenics tend to have delusions and hallucinations, which generally do not occur in autistic children (Rimland, 1964; Rutter, 1978). Although such differences between autistic and schizophrenic children do exist, they may be relatively unimportant with regard to behavioral treatment interventions. Since it is the behaviors of the children that are treated, there may be little advantage in differential diagnoses. Indeed, Davis and Cashdan (1963) argued that a differential diagnosis of behavioral disorders is justified only if such a differentiation also carries meaningful information about etiology, prognosis, or treatment.

Etiology and Past Treatment Approaches

Kanner, when discussing the etiology of autism, believed that the disorder was due to innate inabilities. He believed, however, that the innate nature of autism was confounded by emotionally cold, detached parents. Kanner noted that there was a coincidence of autistic children belonging to parents who tended to be intelligent, educated, and sophisticated, but who were also cold, preferred to be alone, and lived in an emotionally detached, mechanical manner (Eisenberg & Kanner, 1956; Kanner, 1943, 1949).

From 1943 until the 1960s, the psychogenic model of autism prevailed. Cold, "autistic-like" parents were thought (primarily by Bettelheim, 1967) to be causative agents in the development of autism in their children. The psychogenic approach implied that the child remained in a "disease state" of autism, caused by parental deficiencies in emotional responsiveness. In particular, inadequate mothering and the failure to form a normal mother–child bond during infancy were thought to be the crux of the disease (Bettelheim, 1967; O'Gorman, 1967). The behaviors of the child (the autistic symptoms discussed earlier) were said to be suggestive of the etiology of the disorder. That is, autistic behaviors expressed hostility and indifference to the parents (Bettelheim, 1967; Kugelmass, 1970). Since the mothers responded to their children with withdrawal, rejection, and hostility, the autistic behavior was the child's way of adapting to the cold, harsh environment (Bettelheim, 1967).

Such "adaptive" behaviors were the expression of the child's sickness and his or her means of coping with the environment. Thus, it was important to accept the child's behavior and to allow her or him to engage in autistic behaviors (Bettelheim, 1968). The treatment approaches concentrated on establishing environments in which the child no longer needed to express hostility toward his or her parents via autistic behaviors (Bettelheim, 1967; Kugelmass, 1970). According to this approach, the ego development of the child was encouraged in an environment that maintained a balanced combination of gratification and frustration. As the child's sense of self emerged, and his or her autistic barrier began to deteriorate, the therapist began to make small demands on the child (Kugelmass, 1970). The therapist provided the child with complete understanding and acceptance. The child eventually saw an environment that was not hostile, and her or his autistic behaviors decreased.

Although Bettelheim (1968) reported a high success rate from this type of treatment paradigm, he has been criticized for offering subjective case descriptions without supporting empirical evidence (e.g., Rimland, 1964; Rutter, 1971; Schopler & Reichler, 1971; J. K. Wing, 1968). In addition, researchers have failed to find a disproportionate incidence of emotionally cold parents with autistic offspring (Creak & Ini, 1960; Kolvin, 1971; Pitfield & Oppenheim, 1964). It has, in fact, been suggested that any pathological behavior on behalf of the parents may indeed be a reaction to rather than the cause of the child's disorder (Rimland, 1964; Rutter, 1978; Schopler & Reichler, 1971). It has also been suggested that institutionalization (often a treatment of choice for the disease model of autism) may worsen the child's condition (Lovaas, 1979). Recent literature stresses the importance of involving the family in the treatment of their child and, when possible, keeping the child out of institutions and in the home (Lovaas, Koegel, Simmons, & Long, 1973; Schopler, 1971; Schopler & Reichler, 1971; Schreibman & Koegel, 1975; Whittaker, 1975).

It was in light of these criticisms that other approaches, most importantly the behavioral model, became prominent in the study and treatment of autism.

Behavior Modification

Theoretical Perspective

The behavioral model differs greatly from the psychodynamic approach described above. Rather than postulating a specific etiology of autism (with the exception of Ferster, 1961), the behavioral approach views the disorder as a cluster of behaviors and has sought to promote specific changes in behavior that can be observed and measured directly. Behaviorists have suggested that child development consists primarily of the acquisition of behaviors and stimulus functions (Lovaas & Koegel, 1973; Lovaas & Newsom, 1976; Lovaas, Schreibman, & Koegel, 1974). Stimulus functions refer to those aspects of the environment that acquire "meanings" for the child, for example, the child's acquisition of secondary or conditioned reinforcers. Ferster (1961) has suggested that the failure of autistic children to develop normally results from a failure to be affected by conditioned reinforcers. Thus, behavior modification seeks to understand the behaviors of autistic children from an analysis of the variables that influence the acquisition of behavior and stimulus functions (Lovaas & Newsom, 1976; Lovaas et al., 1974; Schreibman & Koegel, 1981). From a behavioral perspective, one would attempt to increase the deficit behaviors by reinforcing their occurrence and to reduce the behavioral excesses either by systematically removing the reinforcers that may be maintaining those behaviors or by systematically applying aversive stimuli each time the behaviors occur. Similarly, one might attempt to treat autistic children by manipulating antecedents and consequences to make aspects of their environment more "meaningful" to them. These areas are covered in greater detail later in the chapter.

The work of Ferster and DeMyer (1962) is important in that it was the first empirical demonstration that the systematic manipulation of environmental contingencies could result in the acquisition of new behaviors in autistic children. Later studies (e.g., Wolf, Risley, & Mees, 1964; Wolf, Risley, Johnston, Harris, & Allen, 1967) confirmed and extended the findings of Ferster and DeMyer. These studies demonstrated that by arranging an extensive system of contingent rewards and punishments, the behavior of autistic children could be modified.

Treatment Procedures

Behavior modification has sought to develop procedures for changing individual behaviors based on an analysis of the variables that might influence them. An important aspect of a behavioral treatment program is its emphasis on the objective measurement of all phases of the program (Kozloff, 1974). Continuously measuring a behavior allows a therapist to assess whether or not the treatment is having any impact on the child's behavior.

A first step in developing a behavioral treatment program is to identify and to define operationally those behaviors that the therapist desires to change. Thus, the therapist will be able to make a precise discrimination of the correctness of a response and to determine the direction of treatment. Once the target behaviors have been operationally defined, the therapist should determine the antecedents and the consequences of the behaviors to be modified. Isolating these variables enables the therapist to manipulate them in order to facilitate the acquisition of appropriate behaviors and stimulus functions. For example, the type of instruction presented (antecedent event) may influence whether the child responds correctly. Schreibman and Koegel (1981) suggested that instructions that are long and complicated may contain a number of irrelevant stimuli that make it difficult for a child to discriminate the intent of the instruction. Such points are described below in extensive detail.

Eliminating Behavioral Excesses

Prior to teaching new skills, the therapist must reduce or eliminate any behaviors that significantly interfere with the acquisition of adaptive behaviors. The interfering behavior can usually be classified into three groups: (1) disruptive behaviors such as tantrums and aggression; (2) self-stimulatory behaviors; and (3) stimulus overselectivity.

Disruptive Behavior. One of the most difficult problems that a therapist must deal with is the disruptive behaviors of autistic children. The most salient of these are severe tantrums and self-injurious behavior. Extinction is an effective and frequently used procedure for reducing such undesirable behavior. Typically, in an extinction procedure, a therapist withholds a reinforcer (such as attention) contingent on a particular behavior. While extinction is an effective procedure, research has demonstrated several possible drawbacks to its use. First, there is usually a gradual reduction in the strength of the behavior, rather than a sharp, dramatic decrement (cf. Lovaas & Simmons, 1969). Second, there is usually an initial and temporary increase in the strength of the behavior. The therapist should be aware of, and anticipate, these events.

Punishment is also an effective treatment procedure for eliminating tantrums and aggressive behavior (Lichstein & Schreibman, 1976; Lovaas & Simmons, 1969; Tate & Baroff, 1966). A wide variety of effective punishment techniques are available, ranging from a mild "no" to physical punishment such as a quick slap on the leg or contingent electric shock. However, therapists may find the use of physical punishment too extreme for a particular behavior or inappropriate in certain situations. As a result, a variety of other punishment procedures have also been developed to control disruptive behavior.

One relatively mild, yet effective, procedure for dealing with outbursts is time-out. White, Nielsen, and Johnson (1972) have defined *time-out* as an "arrangement in which the occurrence of a response is followed by a period of time in which a variety of reinforcers are no longer available" (p. 111). Examples of the use of time-out include placing the child in a small, bare room for a specific period of time following the undesirable behavior, or having the therapist look away from the child, thus withdrawing attention. One of the earliest empirical demonstrations of the effectiveness of time-out was conducted by Wolf *et al.* (1964), who found that tantrums and self-injurious behavior in an autistic child could be reduced effectively by placing him or her alone in a room each time the behavior occurred. It is also, in these cases, desirable to positively reinforce incompatible nondeviant behavior in combination with time-out.

While time-out has been shown to be efficacious in reducing undesirable behavior, there are several important parameters to consider when implementing the procedure, one of which is the duration that a child should be placed in time-out. Time-out intervals ranging from 2 min (Bostow & Bailey, 1969) to 3 hr (Burchard & Tyler, 1965) have been used successfully. White *et al.* (1972) noted that a majority of investigators reported successful results using time-out durations in the range of 5–20 min. There is, however, no consensus on an "optimum" duration for time-out.

Solnick, Rincover, and Peterson (1977) suggested that there is no "standard" time-out procedure that will effectively reduce problem behavior. These researchers examined the possible punishing as well as reinforcing effects of time-out and found that in one case when time-out was employed to suppress tantrumous behavior, it had the opposite effect. That is, time-out resulted in a substantial increase in the frequency of tantrums. On further analysis, it was shown that the time-out period was used by the child to engage in self-stimulatory behavior.

The effectiveness of a time-out procedure also may be influenced by the nature of the "time-in" setting (Solnick *et al.,* 1977). Solnick *et al.* found that when the time-in setting was not highly reinforcing (i.e., was "impoverished"), time-out was ineffective. In a situation such as this, time-out may serve as a negative reinforcer in that the child's behavior removes her or him from an undesirable situation. However, when the time-in environment was highly reinforcing ("enriched"), the same time-out procedure was effective in reducing the undesirable behavior (Carr, Newsom, & Binkoff, 1976; Solnick *et al.,* 1977).

One final point to note about time-out is that in some cases, time-out may be costly in terms of available teaching time, since it requires the child to be removed from the teaching environment each time the inappropriate behavior occurs. As a result, an intermittent schedule of time-out may be a useful alternative (Clark,

Rowbury, Baer, & Baer, 1973). Clark *et al.* reported that time-out used as a consequence for every third or fourth occurrence of an inappropriate act was nearly as effective as a schedule in which time-out was applied for every occurrence of the disruptive behavior.

Foxx and Azrin (1972) reported on a method they called "overcorrection" for eliminating physically disruptive acts. The procedure proposed by Foxx and Azrin has two objectives: (1) to overcorrect the environmental effects of an inappropriate act; and (2) to require the disruptor to practice thoroughly overly correct forms of appropriate behavior. The first objective is achieved through the use of restitutional overcorrection. This procedure requires the disruptive individual to return the disturbed situation to a greatly improved state, thus providing an instructive situation in which the individual is required to assume personal responsibility for the disruptive act. For example, a child who smeared paint on a floor might be required to clean up the mess and then vacuum and wax the area. The second objective is achieved through positive practice overcorrection. In this procedure, the child who smeared the paint on the floor, rather than on an appropriate sheet of paper, might be required to paint appropriately on the paper several times. When no environmental disruption occurs, the restitutional overcorrection is not applicable and only the positive practice is used. The effectiveness of overcorrection as a procedure for eliminating aggressive disruptive behavior was clearly demonstrated by Foxx and Azrin (1972). They employed an overcorrection procedure to reduce aggressive behavior (e.g., physical assault, property damage, tantrums, and biting). The results showed that while time-out and social disapproval had all been ineffective in eliminating aggressive behaviors, overcorrection reduced the disruptive behaviors to a near-zero level within one to two weeks. Overcorrection thus appears to be a viable means of reducing aggressive behavior. In addition, the procedure (as described by its proponents) may minimize some of the negative properties of other punishment procedures; it may also educate the individual in appropriate behavior; and it appears to require relatively little staff training (Foxx & Azrin, 1972). Further research, however, appears necessary to substantiate these latter points. Axelrod, Brantner, and Meddock (1978), in a review of overcorrection research, noted that possible side effects have yet to be carefully examined, that the importance of maintaining topographical similarity between the response and its consequence is unclear, and that many parameters of maximally efficient administration of overcorrection (such as duration of consequence) are still unknown. These authors also pointed out that component analyses of the procedure may, in the future, serve to relate overcorrection more explicitly to punishment *per se*.

Self-Stimulatory Behavior. Self-stimulatory behavior is considered one of the most defining characteristics of autistic children. It is also one of the most formidable obstacles in educating these children. Lovaas, Litrownik, and Mann (1971) observed that responding to previously functional auditory cues was disrupted when a child was engaged in self-stimulatory behavior. They suggested that when a child is engaged in self-stimulation, she or he may not attend to more relevant stimuli. With this issue in mind, Koegel and Covert (1972) attempted to teach a discrimination task to three autistic children with high levels of self-stimulatory behavior. The results clearly established that self-stimulatory behavior interfered with the acquisition of the discrimination. However, when self-stimulation was suppressed, the children acquired the discrimination. This apparent inverse relationship between self-stimulation and the acquisition and performance of new, appropriate behaviors has been repeatedly demonstrated (Epstein, Doke, Sajwaj, Sorrell, & Rimmer, 1974; Foxx & Azrin, 1973a; Koegel *et al.*, 1974; Risley, 1968).

Therapeutic procedures utilized in attempts to suppress self-stimulation have varied, as have the results. One procedure involved reinforcing responses incompatible with self-stimulation. Mulhern and Baumeister (1969) reinforced two retarded children for sitting still in an attempt to reduce their self-stimulatory rocking behavior. They found that this procedure reduced the rocking behavior by about one-third. Others (e.g., Deitz & Repp, 1973; Herendeen, Jeffrey, & Graham, 1974) have also employed reinforcement to reduce self-

stimulatory behavior substantially. However, this procedure has not been successful in completely suppressing self-stimulatory behavior. Furthermore, others using this procedure (e.g., Foxx & Azrin, 1973a) have not obtained decreases in self-stimulatory behavior of the magnitude previously reported.

A second procedure that has been used effectively to reduce and eliminate self-stimulatory behavior employs punishment. The punishment has taken the form of contingent electric shock (Lovaas, Schaeffer, & Simmons, 1965; Risley, 1968), contingent slaps on the hand or the thigh (Bucher & Lovaas, 1968; Foxx & Azrin, 1973a; Koegel & Covert, 1972); and contingent restraint (Koegel *et al.*, 1974). Each of these studies has demonstrated that contingent physical punishment is a highly effective method for suppressing self-stimulation.

One "mild" punishment procedure that has been shown to be extremely effective in suppressing self-stimulation is overcorrection. Foxx & Azrin (1973a) compared several techniques used to suppress self-stimulation (including punishment by a slap and reinforcement for not engaging in self-stimulation) with positive practice overcorrection. Their results showed that the only procedure that eliminated self-stimulatory behavior was the positive-practice-overcorrection procedure. Furthermore, the results suggested that a verbal reprimand in conjunction with an occasional application of the overcorrection procedure was sufficient to maintain reduced levels of self-stimulation. Other investigators (Azrin, Kaplan, & Foxx, 1973; Epstein *et al.*, 1974; Harris & Wolchik, 1979; Herendeen *et al.*, 1974) have confirmed and extended the above findings. Thus, overcorrection appears to be a viable method for substantially reducing self-stimulatory behaviors. While positive practice overcorrection offers an effective alternative to intense physical punishment and the reinforcement of incompatible responses, its practicality in applied settings may be limited because of the demand on the therapist's time and energy.

Despite some successes by the above procedures in reducing self-stimulation, the "generalized, durable elimination of self-stimulatory behavior" has not yet been achieved

(Rincover & Koegel, 1977b). Recently, investigators have suggested that the difficulty in eliminating self-stimulation may be a function of its internal reinforcing properties. That is, self-stimulation may be conceptualized as operant behavior maintained by its sensory consequences (Rincover, Newsom, Lovaas, & Koegel, 1977). For example, a behavior such as finger flapping may be maintained by the resulting proprioceptive feedback. The conceptualization of self-stimulatory behavior as behavior maintained by the auditory, proprioceptive, or visual consequences has led to the development of a new procedure for eliminating self-stimulation. This procedure, sensory extinction, is based on the notion that self-stimulatory behavior should extinguish when the reinforcing (sensory) consequences are removed. Rincover (1978a) found that self-stimulation reliably extinguished when specific sensory consequences were removed and increased when those consequences were permitted. Since the sensory reinforcers maintaining the self-stimulation were distinct across children, different sensory extinction procedures were required for different self-stimulatory behaviors. For example, for one child, a blindfold was used to eliminate the visual feedback produced by twirling objects, while for another child, a carpeted area was used to mask the auditory feedback produced by plate spinning. The results of this procedure have far-ranging clinical implications. Rincover (1978a) suggested that the procedure requires very little staff training or child surveillance, has an immediate effect, and should require relatively little effort in programming the generalization and maintenance of treatment gains.

Stimulus Overselectivity. Characteristic of many autistic children is stimulus overselectivity, that is, the tendency to respond to only a very restricted portion of their environment (Lovaas, Schreibman, Koegel, & Rehm, 1971). Specifically, it appears that when autistic children are presented with a learning situation that requires responding to multiple cues within a complex stimulus, their behavior comes under the control of a very limited portion of those cues. In the first experimental demonstration of this problem, Lovaas et al. (1971) trained normal, retarded, and autistic children to make a response in the presence of a complex stimulus consisting of visual, auditory, and tactile cues. When the components of the stimulus complex were then presented individually, the authors found that the normal children responded equally to all three of the component cues, while the autistic children responded primarily to *one* of the component cues. In other words, each of the separate cues became equal in controlling the behavior of the normal children, but in marked contrast, the autistic child responded primarily in the presence of the auditory component (three children) or the visual component (two children) only. These investigators also demonstrated that this deficit was not a function of a specific sensory impairment, but a problem in responding to a component cue in the context of other cues. Since the original demonstrations by Lovaas *et al.*, this finding has been replicated in a two-cue situation (Lovaas & Schreibman, 1971); with all visual cues (Koegel & Wilhelm, 1973); and with cues presented auditorily (Reynolds, Newsom, & Lovaas, 1974). A comprehensive review of these and other studies related to stimulus overselectivity has been provided by Lovaas, Koegel, and Schreibman (1979).

The implications of these findings become apparent when one examines the number of situations encountered that require a response to multiple cues. Overselectivity has been discussed as a variable influencing language acquisition (Lovaas *et al.*, 1971; Reynolds *et al.*, 1974); social behavior (Schreibman & Lovaas, 1973), observational learning (Varni, Lovaas, Koegel, & Everett, 1979), prompting (Koegel & Rincover, 1976; Rincover, 1978b; Schreibman, 1975), and generalization (Rincover & Koegel, 1975).

The severity of overselectivity has led to research investigating treatment techniques for its elimination. In one study, Schover and Newsom (1976) attempted to teach autistic children to respond to multiple cues by overtraining an already learned discrimination. The results indicated that through overtraining, Schover and Newsom were able to increase the number of cues to which the children responded. Schreibman, Koegel, and Craig (1977), further investigating the overtraining procedure, found that overtraining *per se* (just exposure) did not increase the number of cues to which the child responded. Instead, they found that prolonged interspersing of the unreinforced probe trials with component cues among reinforced trials with the stimulus complex eliminated overselectivity (in 13 out of 16 autistic children who were initially overselective). Further, Koegel, Schreibman, Britten, and Laitinen (1979) provided evidence suggesting that the schedule of reinforcement affects overselectivity. Children trained on a variable ratio (VR):3 schedule showed less overselectivity on subsequent probe trials than children trained on a continuous reinforcement (CRF) schedule. This finding indicates that the reduced overselectivity found in previous studies with interspersed probe trials may have been due to the partial schedule produced by the interspersing of the probe and the training trials. In another attempt to reduce overselectivity, Koegel and Schreibman (1977) taught four autistic and four normal children a conditional discrimination requiring a response to multiple cross-modal (auditory and visual) cues. The results showed that the autistic children learned the discriminations, although they did not learn them with ease, nor in the same manner as normal children. The autistic children persistently tended to respond at a higher level to one of the component cues, and only after many (typically hundreds of) trials did they learn to respond on the basis of both cues. This result was, however, encouraging since they *did* learn to respond to multiple cues. Furthermore, in one case, when an autistic child was taught a series of successive conditional discriminations, the child eventually learned a generalized set to respond to new conditional discriminations on the basis of both component cues. The results of these studies suggest that the selective responding characteristic of many autistic children is a problem that is modifiable through the manipulation of environmental events.

Acquisition of New Behaviors and Stimulus Functions

The previous investigations have described a behavioral approach to reducing or eliminating behaviors that significantly interfere with the learning process. The manipulation of antecedent and consequent variables is also crucial in the teaching of new behaviors and stimulus functions. In a behavioral treatment program, the antecedent variables usually manipulated are the instructions (S^D) and the prompt stimuli. As previously suggested, the manner in which an instruction is given can influence whether a child learns a particular response. The therapist must make sure that the child is attending to the instruction and that the instruction serves as an easily discriminable cue for a particular response (Schreibman & Koegel, 1981).

The establishment of a stimulus as discriminative for a response (S^D) is one aspect of the acquisition of stimulus functions. In this case, the child learns to make a certain response when presented with a specific S^D and not to make the response when the S^D is absent. Carr *et al.* (1975) demonstrated how a particular antecedent event influenced immediate echolalia. They found that the children tended to echo only those questions and commands that had not previously been established as discriminative for a specific response. For example, a child might respond appropriately to the question, "What's your name?" but would echo a nonsense phrase such as "min dar snick." These authors suggested that those stimuli that were not discriminative for a response were meaningless to the children. The children tended to respond appropriately only to those stimuli that were meaningful. Lovaas and Newsom (1976) have also noted the importance of the acquisition of stimulus functions in the development of language. They pointed out that aspects of the child's environment must acquire discriminative properties (i.e., become functional) that serve to control verbal behavior. For example, one of the first steps in teaching language to autistic children is to establish the therapist's vocal instruction as meaningful for an imitative vocal response on the part of the child.

Often, the desired behavior is not evoked by the S^D alone. When this occurs, it may be necessary to manually guide or prompt the response. Prompts are typically extra cues that help guide the child to the correct response (Koegel & Rincover, 1976). For example, if the S^D "Touch red" does not evoke a correct response from the child, the therapist could manually guide the child's hand to the red stimulus while presenting the S^D. Prompting can be an extremely useful technique for establishing a response. However, it must be gradually *removed*, so that the control of the response is shifted from the prompt stimuli to the S^D. While this may seem to be a relatively simple procedure, many studies have shown that autistic children have a particularly difficult time shifting from prompt stimuli to training stimuli (e.g., Koegel & Rincover, 1976; Schreibman, 1975). This is not a surprising finding in light of what is known about stimulus overselectivity; most prompting procedures require the child to respond to multiple cues (prompt and training stimuli). Schreibman (1975) and Rincover (1978b) have attempted to remediate this problem by developing special treatment procedures for prompting and prompt fading. Schreibman used prompts that were contained within the training stimulus (within-stimulus prompt) and thus did not require the child to respond to multiple cues. She developed a method for allowing the autistic child to learn with prompts even while being overselective. In comparing the within-stimulus prompt with extra-stimulus prompts, Schreibman found that the children learned the discrimination only when the within-stimulus prompt was employed. The within-stimulus prompting procedure can be illustrated with the following example. In teaching a child to recognize the difference between a *p* and a *b*, a teacher might emphasize (through exaggeration) the orientation of the "stems" of the letters. The orientation of the stems is considered the relevant component of the discrimination, since the other components of the letters are redundant. The exaggerated component is then gradually faded until the child is discriminating between the appropriate-sized letters. Since the prompt is contained within the final stimulus, it requires the child to respond only on the basis of this stimulus and not other additional cues.

Rincover (1978b) has extended Schreibman's work by exaggerating and then fading a feature of one stimulus that is not a part of the other stimulus (i.e., a distinctive feature). In an *E* and *F* discrimination, for example, the bottom line of the *E* is the distinctive feature that would be emphasized. This procedure, a

special form of within-stimulus prompting, appears to be the most effective prompting procedure known for autistic children at this time.

There are two other procedures, besides prompting, that a behavior therapist can use to facilitate learning when the target response is not already in the child's repertoire. Both of these procedures involve breaking a complex behavior down into smaller steps, and the procedures are especially helpful when one is attempting to teach a complex response. In a *shaping* procedure, a therapist initially rewards the closest approximation to the appropriate response in the child's repertoire. Gradually, the therapist then requires the child to respond with closer and closer approximations until the complex response is made. The effectiveness of shaping as a treatment procedure was empirically demonstrated by Hewett (1965) and Lovaas (1969).

Complex behaviors can also be broken into a series of smaller component parts. Each component is taught individually until the child performs the complex response. While each component is taught individually, each step is dependent on the child's having learned the previous step. This procedure is referred to as *chaining*, since the individual responses can be viewed as links in a chain. Chaining is also a useful technique for teaching speech as well as a variety of self-help skills.

Increasing Reinforcer Effectiveness. Many researchers view the characteristic lack of motivation in autism as concerning the potency or desirability of available reinforcers (e.g., Ferster, 1961; Lovaas & Newsom, 1976). Most therapists working with autistic children rely on primary (e.g., food) and/or social (e.g., praise) reinforcers. A number of investigators (e.g., Ferster, 1961; Lovaas *et al.*, 1965; Lovaas & Newsom, 1976) have noted the difficulty involved in establishing meaningful social reinforcers for many autistic children. As a result, most therapists must depend on primary rewards such as food to motivate and maintain the children's behavior. Lovaas and Newsom (1976), however, pointed out that these primary rewards may become artificial for older children, since they exist only in limited settings such as treatment environments. The reliance on food rewards results in limited generalization, since other environments in which the child interacts may not provide primary rewards. Also, children may become satiated and as a result refuse to continue working. These issues can represent severe difficulties for a therapist attempting to teach and motivate autistic children.

Some investigators have attempted to help solve these difficulties by developing procedures for establishing functional secondary rewards and by investigating alternate forms of reinforcement. The acquisition of secondary reinforcers is seen as very important to overall development since events such as praise, hugs, smiles, approval, etc., appear to support so much behavior in normal individuals. While the autistic child's typical unresponsiveness to social stimuli makes those stimuli ineffective as reinforcers, two studies have succeeded in establishing social stimuli as reinforcers for autistic children. Using a negative reinforcement paradigm, Lovaas *et al.* (1965) set up a situation in which an appropriate response to a therapist's verbal command ("Come here") was required to terminate an aversive stimulus. The results demonstrated that schizophrenic children could be taught to respond to social stimuli. In another study, Lovaas, Freitag, Kinder, Rubenstein, Schaeffer, and Simmons (1966) established a social reward ("good") as a discriminative stimulus, thus making social stimuli reinforcing.

Other researchers have examined the problem of low motivation from a different perspective. In an investigation designed to assess globally autistic children's motivation (independent of the type of reinforcer), Koegel and Egel (1979) investigated the influence of correct task completion on motivation to respond to instructional activities. The results demonstrated that when the children worked at tasks on which they were typically incorrect, their overall attempts to respond to those tasks (i.e., their motivation) generally decreased. However, designing treatment procedures to maximize correct responding (and receipt of reinforcers) served to increase the children's motivation (overall attempts to respond) on those tasks.

Attempts have also been made to develop new reinforcers. As suggested previously, one can view self-stimulation as behavior being maintained by the sensory feedback it produces. This form of sensory stimulation may be inferred to be highly reinforcing, since autistic children characteristically spend hours engaged in such behavior (Rimland, 1964; Lovaas *et al.*, 1971). Rincover *et al.* (1977) investigated the reinforcing properties of sensory stimulation for autistic children. These investigators initially determined the preferred sensory stimuli for each child and then attempted to motivate the children to respond using the sensory stimuli as reinforcement. More specifically, brief presentations of the child's preferred sensory event (e.g., low-frequency strobe light, popular music) were presented contingent on correct responses. The results demonstrated that sensory stimulation, when used as reinforcement, produced high levels of responding that were relatively durable over time. The authors noted that the autistic children in this study never satiated in the general area of their preferred sensory stimulation. Although some satiation occurred on a specific sensory event (e.g., a particular song), a minor change in the sensory event led to a recovery of the high rate of responding. Rincover and Koegel (1977b) have pointed out that treatment gains might be enhanced if sensory reinforcers were used in therapy. This is especially true since (1) these types of reinforcers are relatively easy to identify and provide; and (2) their use may facilitate the generalization of treatment gains from the classroom to other situations, since sensory reinforcers are not necessarily limited to a particular setting.

Recently, we have begun to examine procedures for increasing the effectiveness of edible reinforcers so that satiation is prevented or considerably delayed. One variable that has been demonstrated to maintain behavior effectively is the presentation of novel stimuli (Berlyne, 1950, 1955, 1960; Cantor & Cantor, 1964a,b; Hutt, 1975; Young, 1969). This research has demonstrated that subjects are more "motivated" to respond to a novel, unfamiliar stimulus than they are to familiar stimuli. Fowler (1963, 1967, 1971) and others (Glanzer, 1953, 1958; Wilson, 1974) have argued that with continued exposure to a familiar stimulus, the subject would become satiated. Furthermore, satiation could be prevented by merely changing or varying the sensory stimulation.

Based on this literature, Egel (1979) designed a study to determine whether the rapid satiation typically found when using edible reinforcers could be reduced if the reinforcer was varied, rather than being held constant. Specifically, two major questions were addressed: (1) Would there be any differences in the total number of responses emitted when the reinforcer was held constant as opposed to being varied? and (2) Would there be any differences in response latencies for constant as opposed to varied reinforcer presentation?

To answer these questions, Egel randomly selected 10 children whose behavior was consistent with the diagnosis of autism. Each child was initially trained to press and release a bar and to consume the reinforcer that was delivered prior to making another response. Each child, following the pretraining period, participated in two experimental conditions. In the constant-reinforcer condition, the child was presented with the same reinforcer each time a response was made. The child was allowed to respond until satiation occurred (i.e., until the child emitted three or fewer responses for each of three consecutive minutes) or until 250 responses were completed. At this point, a second reinforcer was presented until one of the above criteria was met, at which time a third reinforcer was presented. The varied-reinforcer presentation condition was conducted in the same manner as described above except that for approximately every third response, the child received a different one of the three reinforcers used in the constant condition. In all conditions of this investigation, the reinforcers used for each child were chosen in advance from lists of edible reinforcers specific to each child. These lists were compiled by the experimenter and the classroom teacher of each child, and they included peanuts, raisins, and cookies.

A detailed analysis of the results clearly demonstrated that the children *satiated* more rapidly (i.e., emitted three or fewer responses for three consecutive minutes) when each of the reinforcers was individually presented (constant condition). Of the 10 children, 8 *never* did meet the satiation criterion when the reinforcer presentation was varied. Even when satiation did occur in the varied condition, the children emitted many more responses in that condition than for any of the individually presented reinforcers. In addition, the results showed that in every case, the children had shorter response latencies when the reinforcer presentation was varied.

The applied significance of these results lies in the identification of a relatively simple procedure for motivating autistic children. The data suggest that teachers and clinicians can sustain a relatively high level of motivation in autistic children merely by varying the presentation of previously functional, edible reinforcers. This finding seems particularly encouraging since the more motivated the children are to respond in a learning situation, the greater is the likelihood of obtaining significant improvements (Rincover & Koegel, 1977b).

Intertrial Interval and Learning. In addition to examining the influence of stimuli presented during a given teaching trial (S^Ds, prompts, reinforcers, etc.), several investigators have suggested the importance of manipulations made between trials, or during intertrial intervals (ITIs). For example, in a study by Koegel, Dunlap, and Dyer (1980), autistic children were taught social tasks under the same conditions existing in their regular treatment programs, except that the length of time between teaching trials was systematically manipulated. Within both multiple-baseline and repeated-reversal designs, two lengths of intertrial interval were employed: *short* intervals with the S^D for any given trial presented approximately one second following the reinforcer for the previous trial, versus *long* intervals with the S^D presented four or more seconds following the reinforcer for the previous trial. The results showed that (1) the short intertrial intervals always produced higher levels of correct responding than the long intervals; and (2) there were improving trends in performance and rapid acquisition with the short intertrial intervals, in contrast to minimal or no change with the long intervals. That is, the results showed that systematic manipulations of the ITI durations produced differential results in the percentage of correct responding of autistic children, and the superior intervals were those that were relatively short. This finding may not imply, however, that short intervals are always superior. Rather, we suspect that the major implications of these data are that (1) the length of the ITI is a functional variable; and (2) for these particular child–task combinations, the relatively short ITIs were superior.

The variables that may contribute to a more precise determination of optimal ITI durations are potentially numerous (ranging from possible variables suggested in the literature on massed vs. distributed practice, to research on ITIs directly). Among the most directly relevant variables that have been suggested in the literature are task characteristics (such as task complexity and acquisition versus maintenance) and child characteristics (such as age, memory span, attention, and level of off-task behavior) (e.g., Bourne & Bunderson, 1963; Croll, 1970; Holt & Shafer, 1973; Watson, 1967). Watson (1967), for example, has suggested that the memory span of very young children for discriminated operants may be very brief; thus, a brief ITI may help learning to occur.

The above statements regarding child variables seem particularly applicable to autistic children. For example, autistic children often display mental ages in the lower ranges and are very distractable. In addition, many authors (e.g., Hingtgen & Bryson, 1972) have suggested that short-term memory impairments may contribute to the poor performance of autistic children. Similarly, optimal ITI duration may be related to the extent of off-task (e.g., self-stimulatory) behavior produced by particular children. It is possible, with children known to display high rates of off-task behavior (i.e., most autistic children), that short ITIs may reduce the opportunity for such behaviors to occur and therefore might facilitate learning (cf. Koegel & Covert, 1972; Risley, 1968). Indeed, our incidental observations suggest that for at least some child–task combinations, shorter ITIs seem to produce a much lower level of self-stimulatory behavior.

In summary, it seems interesting to note that almost every variable discussed in the ITI duration literature is particularly applicable to the autistic population. Therefore, this seems like a very promising avenue of future research.

Treatment Environments

Parent Training

The importance of involving parents in the treatment of their autistic children became all too clear when Lovaas *et al.* (1973) reported the results of their follow-up investigation of autistic children in a behavior-modification program. These investigators reported on a group of children who were hospitalized and received behavior-modification treatment as inpatients. While the children received one year of intensive therapy, their parents were not involved in the treatment. All of these children made gains on pre- to posttreatment measures. After the treatment, the children then returned to their pretreatment environment, typically the home or a state hospital. When these children were again assessed at a one- or two-year follow-up, it was found that they had typically lost the gains they had made during treatment.

A subsequent group of children followed during this investigation were also given behavior-modification treatment for one year. However, in contrast to the first group of children, the second group was seen as outpatients, remaining in the home, and their parents were involved in the treatment. All of these children also made gains on pre- and posttreatment measures, and when they were reassessed at follow-up, it was found that they had either maintained their treatment gains or had continued to progress. Thus, the main point of this study is that it appears that if one desires the treatment to generalize, there is a better chance if the posttreatment environment continues the treatment contingencies. Parent training is an obvious means to this end.

Training the parents has several obvious advantages:

1. There is the increase in generalization of treatment effects over time mentioned above.

2. The treatment becomes more economical in that the parents can be trained with very little expense and then can provide continuous treatment for their children in a variety of settings.
3. The treatment becomes more available, since every child has a parent or a guardian responsible for her or his care. This parent or guardian can be trained, and even though the child may live in a geographical area devoid of special schools, treatment can be provided by the parent.
4. Parent training is relatively easy, since the principles of behavior modification are readily taught to nonprofessionals.

The issues of how best to train parents and the effectiveness of the training techniques have been addressed by many investigators (e.g., Barrett, 1969; Holland, 1969; Patterson, Shaw, & Ebner, 1969; Koegel, Glahn, & Nieminen, 1978; Koegel, Russo, & Rincover, 1977; Schreibman & Koegel, 1975; Wahler, 1969). Koegel *et al.* (1978) reported an investigation relating to the type of information that would be the most helpful to the parents of autistic children. First, these authors showed that without special training, adults are not effective teachers for autistic children. Second, they found that merely allowing an adult to observe a trained therapist working with a child was not effective, since the adults could then teach only the specific skills they had observed being taught. Thus, they did not acquire skills that would generalize to the teaching of other behavior. A third procedure did lead to successful generalized teaching skills. This involved training the adults in the procedural rules of behavior modification. These rules include (1) how to give instructions (S^Ds); (2) how to use prompts; (3) how to use shaping and chaining; and (4) how to deliver consequences. After training on these procedural rules, the adults could effectively teach a variety of new behaviors.

As for the effectiveness of parents as treatment providers, there is a great deal of evidence pointing to the success of parent-training programs (e.g., Berkowitz & Graziano, 1972; Johnson & Katz, 1973; Kozloff, 1973). Further research is needed on making the training more effective and more efficient as

well as on determining parent variables, such as motivation, rate of learning, and use of the trained skills after training is terminated.

Classroom Instruction

In the recent past, most autistic children were institutionalized before they reached the age of 12. One of the main reasons was that the schools simply could not cope with the severely disruptive behavior of the child and his or her profound learning problems. Thus, until recently, a large majority of autistic children were expelled from classrooms or were simply never admitted. As a result of legal issues and recent legislation, classrooms for all autistic children in the United States have been mandated by law. However, the presence of autism classrooms does not ensure the quality of these programs. Prerequisite is an analysis of the skills necessary for autistic children to be successful in a classroom situation and a technology for teaching these skills.

In order to develop an effective classroom program for autistic children, we know that two main skills must be established. One is to be able to learn in a large group. The other is to be able to work on an individualized task without constant teacher supervision (Koegel & Rincover, 1974; Rincover & Koegel, 1977a; Rincover, Koegel, & Russo, 1978).

One problem that immediately becomes apparent in a classroom setting is that behaviors acquired in a one-to-one situation often do not generalize to a larger group (Bijou, 1972; Koegel & Rincover, 1974; Peterson, Cox, & Bijou, 1971). Koegel and Rincover (1974) found that when eight autistic children were individually taught some basic classroom skills, the performance of these behaviors by any one child was greatly reduced when only one other child was introduced (i.e., in a group of two). In conjunction with these results, additional observations of these children in a classroom group of eight indicated that over a period of weeks, no new learning occurred. These investigators then developed a procedure for teaching autistic children to learn when in a large group.

The procedure developed (Koegel & Rincover, 1974) involved teaching the children in 1:1 training sessions in which the reinforcement schedule was thinned from CRF to fixed ratio (FR):2. Then, when each child performed two responses for only one reinforcer, two children were brought together with one teacher and two aides. The aides alternately reinforced one child on one trial and the other child on the next. When these children responded with no prompts on this schedule, the reinforcement schedule was thinned to FR:4. Then, two additional children (who had the same training) were brought together to form a group of four. These fading procedures continued until the children could perform in a group of eight. The investigators found that not only did the children perform the individually trained behaviors in a group but they also continued to learn new behaviors when instruction was presented by one teacher to the entire group.

In addition to learning in a group situation with one teacher, the individual differences in ability of the children often necessitate the incorporation of the essential features of individualized instruction into the group situation. Thus each child works on a specific task designed for his or her particular needs and at his or her own pace. In a second investigation, Rincover and Koegel (1977a) assessed the feasibility of teaching autistic children to work individually without constant teacher supervision. In order to work individually, the children were taught to work on long sequences of behavior after instruction by the teacher. To accomplish this, a shaping procedure was designed whereby a child was first required to make only one written response before teacher reinforcement. Then the response requirement was increased to two, then three, etc., until the child was completing an entire assigned task without continuous teacher supervision.

Thus, the work of Koegel and his colleagues has led to the design of classroom procedures that are specifically designed for the autistic child. These procedures greatly increase the chances of the child's learning in a classroom setting. However, it may be important to note that if such classrooms are effective, the children should eventually be able to progress into more normal classrooms. That is, if the classroom program is effective, the children should not remain autistic. Russo and Koegel (1977) have discussed this point in some detail and

have described methods for integrating autistic children into normal public-school classrooms. The results of that preliminary research have been extremely encouraging and suggest the importance of pursuing such research rather extensively.

Teaching Homes

While parent training has proved itself to be a form of treatment that can substantially improve the child's chances of remaining in the home and out of an institution, it is apparent that some autistic children cannot live in their own homes. The reasons for placing the child outside the home typically include (1) the child becomes a young adult and the parents become older and unable to take care of the child; (2) the child's behavior problems are so severe that untrained parents cannot cope with them; (3) the parents divorce or separate, and neither can care for the child; or (4) other factors such as the emotional stability of the parents, family illnesses, and the presence of many other children.

For whatever reason, many autistic children are placed in mental hospitals. There are several problems associated with institutionalization in mental hospitals. First, the children may acquire behaviors that are appropriate to the hospital environment but that will not help them function in the natural environment. Second, the hospital contingencies are typically so different from those of the natural environment's (e.g., the home's) contingencies that behavioral improvements are not likely to generalize from the hospital to the home. A third problem is the tremendous costs associated with building, staffing, and maintaining such institutions. Fourth, institutionalizing a child creates a distance between the child and her or his parents. Fifth, the reliance on three shifts of staff has produced numerous problems in trying to maintain continuity of treatment programming.

In response to the problems associated with the institutional treatment of autistic children, the concept of community-based "teaching homes" has been introduced (Lovaas, Glahn, Russo, Chock, Kohls, & Mills, in press; McClannahan, 1979). These homes are adapted from the Achievement Place model for treating delinquent youths developed by Montrose Wolf and his colleagues (cf. Phillips, Phillips, Fixsen, & Wolf, 1974; Wolf, Phillips, Fixsen, Braukmann, Kirigin, Wilner, & Schumaker, 1976). These homes are as much as possible like the child's natural home and are staffed with "teaching parents" specifically trained to work with autistic children. The homes provide a treatment environment that helps rectify some of the prominent problems of institutions. First, the behaviors that the children acquire are those behaviors associated with living in a home. These include self-help skills, cleaning up their rooms, preparing food, and table manners. In other words, rather than learning ward-appropriate behaviors, they learn home-appropriate behaviors. Second, the contingencies in the homes are made as natural as possible and as similar as possible to those likely to be encountered in the child's natural home. Third, this approach helps to maximize generalization for those children who are to return to their natural homes (or to foster-home placements in the community). Fourth, teaching homes are more cost-efficient than costly institutional environments (Lovaas et al., in press; Phillips et al., 1974). Fifth, since multiple shifts of staffing are not required, continuity of programming throughout the day is simplified.

The goal of the teaching-home model for providing treatment to autistic children is to help institutionalized autistic children learn skills that will increase the likelihood that they can leave the institution and go to a home environment. In addition, these homes may serve as an alternative placement for children who cannot live at home. Perhaps children can go to a teaching home for treatment first, followed by parent training, thus eliminating the necessity of institutional placement at all. The preliminary reports on this model are very encouraging, and we await more research on its effectiveness.

Critique of the Behavioral Approach

The behavioral treatment procedures have been successful in teaching autistic children a wide variety of adaptive behaviors, from self-care skills (e.g., Foxx & Azrin, 1973b; Marshall, 1966; Plummer, Baer, & LeBlanc, 1977) to reading (e.g., Hewett, 1964; Rosenbaum & Breiling, 1976). They have also been successful in reducing or eliminating those behaviors considered most deviant (e.g., Lovaas & Simmons, 1969; Rincover, 1978a). However, some aspects of the behavioral model have been criticized (e.g., Hemsley, Howlin, Berger, Hersov, Holbrook, Rutter, & Yule, 1978). A major criticism has been the failure of treatment gains to generalize from the clinic to other environments (e.g., home) (Baer, Wolf, & Risley, 1968; Birnbrauer, 1968; Kale, Kaye, Whelan, & Hopkins, 1968; Kazdin & Bootzin, 1972; Lovaas et al., 1973; Stokes & Baer, 1977; Stokes, Baer, & Jackson, 1974; Wahler, 1969; Walker & Buckley, 1972). Consequently, behavioral researchers have attempted to understand the variables that might influence generalization and to develop procedures for promoting generalization. One method of accomplishing this is to manipulate the number of relevant stimuli that control the behavior. Rincover and Koegel (1975) demonstrated that the failure of four autistic children to generalize a response learned in one setting to another setting was due to the acquisition of stimulus control by irrelevant stimuli that were not present in the extratherapy environment. In order to bring about the generalization of treatment gains to extratherapy settings, it was necessary to introduce into the extratherapy setting the stimuli that had come to control responding in the treatment environment.

It is interesting, however, to note that the above results did not hold true for all of the children in the study. Six children showed some transfer of treatment gains across settings without special intervention. These children had apparently learned to respond to a stimulus that was functional in both the therapy and the extratherapy settings. Rincover and Koegel suggested that in cases where the children do initially transfer (which may be more common than is apparent), it may be beneficial to emphasize methodologies for *maintaining* treatment gains in other settings rather than for producing transfer. Koegel and Rincover (1977) also designed a study to assess the possible differences between the variables affecting the transfer and the maintenance of treatment gains across settings. The authors initially recorded responding to a particular instruction (e.g., "Touch your nose") in both a therapy and an extratherapy setting. The results showed that while one child's responding failed to generalize to the extratherapy environment, the responding of two other children did generalize. However, further testing demonstrated that responding in the extratherapy setting was not maintained. These researchers suggested that the lack of response maintenance in the extratherapy setting may have been a result of the child's forming a discrimination between an environment in which contingent rewards were given and one in which few contingent rewards were provided.

In order to reduce the discriminability of the reinforcement schedules, Koegel and Rincover manipulated two variables: (1) the schedule of reinforcement in the treatment setting and (2) the presence of noncontingent reinforcement in the extratherapy environment. The results showed that extratherapy responding extinguished within a very few trials when a continuous reinforcement schedule (CRF) was employed in the treatment setting. As the schedule of reinforcement in the therapy setting was gradually thinned (from a CRF to FR:5), responding in the extratherapy environment was maintained over longer and longer periods of time. The presentations of noncontingent reinforcement (NCR) in the extratherapy setting had a similar effect on the durability of responding. Furthermore, the results showed that a thin schedule of reinforcement in the treatment environment in conjunction with the periodic use of noncontingent reinforcement in the extratherapy setting produced the greatest response maintenance.

Other procedures for promoting the generalization of treatment gains have been reported throughout the behavioral literature (cf. Stokes & Baer, 1977). Several procedures can be adapted quite easily for use in a treatment situation. Investigations have shown that multiple therapists can be employed to facilitate generalization from the original teacher to others in the child's environment (Lovaas & Simmons, 1969; Stokes et al., 1974). Additional research has also found that generalization is enhanced if instruction takes place in a number of settings beyond the original environment (e.g., Griffiths & Craighead, 1972; Lovaas & Simmons, 1969). Thus, the research has pointed out that in order to program generalization, it may be necessary to continue the training with other people in a variety of settings. As discussed above, parent training is a convenient method that incorporates both of these approaches (Kozloff, 1973; Schreibman & Koegel, 1975; L. Wing, 1972).

Investigations have also been conducted to determine if the generalization of treatment gains could be programmed from within the clinic. Most of these investigations have focused on the type of reinforcers used and the nature of the treatment setting. The problems encountered in using primary (food) rewards with autistic children have already been discussed: their use leads to rapid satiation and a lack of generalization because of the limited environment in which they are available. Thus, it is conceivable that generalization would be enhanced if reinforcers that were also present in the "natural" environment were used (Goetz, Schuler, & Sailor, 1979; Koegel & Williams, 1980; Stokes & Baer, 1977).

Rincover et al. (1977) have also suggested that the use of sensory reinforcers in the treatment or the classroom environment could significantly enhance the children's motivation to participate in learning tasks. The relationship between high levels of motivation within the treatment setting and the generalization of treatment gains was demonstrated by Turner (1978), who found that children who showed high levels of motivation (as measured by level of interest) in a language remediation program were more likely to generalize the use of target structures to a nonremediated environment.

Investigations have also been conducted to determine the parameters of response generalization. Lovaas et al. (1973), in discussing their results, noted that "the most significant disappointment was the failure to isolate a 'pivotal' response, or, as some might describe it, the failure to effect change in certain key intervening variables. This means that in the beginning, we searched for one behavior which, when altered, would produce a profound 'personality' change. We could not find it" (pp. 160–161). Rincover and Koegel (1977b) pointed out that what is needed is a technology of response generalization.

The search for this technology is reflected in the extensive research on generalized imitation. Baer and Sherman (1964) found that repeated social reinforcement for three imitative responses led to the imitation of a fourth response for which the children had never been reinforced. Manipulation of the contingencies demonstrated that it was the reinforcement of the initial imitative responses that maintained the fourth imitation. The authors suggested that the children had learned that behavioral similarity was discriminative for reinforcement. Therefore, these authors suggested that similarity should take on reinforcing as well as discriminative functions. This phenomenon has been especially important in teaching speech to autistic children. Lovaas, Berberich, Perloff, and Schaeffer (1966) found that as imitative speech training progressed, it became easier to evoke new, nonreinforced imitative vocalizations. Others have demonstrated that this type of generalization also occurs in the teaching of generative grammars (e.g., Baer & Guess, 1971; Guess, 1969; Guess, Sailor, Rutherford, & Baer, 1968; Schumaker & Sherman, 1970).

The procedures reviewed above exemplify a behavioral approach to a specific problem area. In this case, the research emphasis of the behavioral model has provided the beginnings of a technology for programming stimulus and response generalization.

A second criticism of the behavioral model is that the treatment relies heavily on a one-to-one therapist–child ratio (e.g., Callias, 1978). However, as we have already discussed, research has been completed that demonstrates that autistic children can learn in group situations (Hamblin, Buckholdt, Ferritor, Kozloff, & Blackwell, 1971; Koegel & Rincover, 1974; Rincover & Koegel, 1977a).

Finally, behaviorists have been criticized for their reliance on primary (food) reinforcers to develop appropriate behaviors. The problems associated with relying on primary rewards have already been discussed. However, recent research has sought to identify other types of functional rewards (Devany & Rincover, 1978; Rincover *et al.*, 1977; Rincover, Cook, Peoples, & Packard, 1979). In addition,

Rincover and Koegel (1977a) have suggested that combining the techniques developed by Lovaas *et al.* (1965; Lovaas, Freitag *et al.*, 1966) for conditioning social stimuli, and those developed for producing generalization and maintenance (Stokes & Baer, 1977), could lead to the generalized use of social reinforcement for the acquisition, generalization, and maintenance of behavior.

The strength of the behavioral model lies in its research-based treatment methodology. Unlike the results of other treatment approaches, which rely mainly on subjective impressions, the results of behavioral treatment programs can be directly measured. Compared with the other approaches, this emphasis has resulted in a number of advantages. First, it has led to an empirically based understanding of many of the variables that influence the behavior of autistic children. Second, the procedures have been clearly and operationally defined so that replication of the treatment procedures and the results is possible. Third, the procedures have been empirically demonstrated to be effective. Finally, the proponents of the behavioral model have succeeded in teaching autistic children a wide range of adaptive skills. Thus, at the present time, behavior modification appears to be the only model that has been empirically demonstrated to be effective.

New Approaches to Evaluating Treatment Effectiveness

Social Validation of Treatment Effectiveness

The behavior-modification treatment of autism has typically been considered successful if it can be shown that specific, objectively measured target behaviors change in a positive direction as a function of the treatment. For example, we typically measure treatment gains in terms of the percentage of occurrence changes in self-stimulation, psychotic speech, appropriate play, appropriate verbal behavior, etc. While we may be able to produce consistent and reliable changes in these objective behaviors, one can also ask just what these behavioral changes *mean* in terms of more global judgment of the child's progress. For example, are the objective measures of change such that the child is seen as more "normal looking," more "likable," less likely to be institutionalized, etc.? That is, can these objective measures be correlated with subjective judgments of change provided by naive observers? Obviously, any form of treatment that cannot produce changes that are not apparent to others cannot be said to be truly effective.

One study (Mills, Burke, Schreibman, & Koegel, 1979) sought to determine the relationship between objective, observational measures of pre–post treatment change in autistic children and the subjective impressions of change formed of those children by untrained, naive observers. First, undergraduate students were asked to view 5-min segments of videotapes showing autistic children interacting with their mothers in a room full of toys. The students were asked to write essays describing the children. A rating scale consisting of 19 Likert items was derived from these essays encompassing the areas of language, play, social interactions, and behaviors such as restlessness, wandering attention, and repetitive behaviors. Following the development of the scale, five more groups of undergraduates (the group size ranged from 25 to 40) were asked to view 5-min videotape segments of 14 autistic children taken before behavior-modification treatment and after six months of treatment (the pretreatment and the six-month progress tapes were presented in a randomized order) and to rate the children on the Likert-item rating scale. This scale provided a measure of the subjective impressions of the children.

For the objective measures, two trained observers scored the same segments of videotape for the percentage of occurrence of eight behaviors that are typically regarded as clinically important. These behaviors included self-stimulation, play, tantrums, appropriate language, psychotic language, social nonverbal behavior, and noncooperation.

When the judges' subjective ratings were correlated with the percentage of occurrence of the observed behaviors, we found a strong relationship between the two. That is, when looking at children who showed improvement on the behavioral measures from pre- to post-treatment, we saw a significant corresponding increase in the judges' subjective impressions. On these measures, these children were seen as significantly more skilled in language, more socially desirable, and more likable at posttreatment than at pretreatment. In contrast, children who showed very little or no gains in appropriate behavior on the objective measures were seen by the judges as unchanged or worse. In addition to this global result (that the judges could subjectively see the changes in the children's behavior), it was found that there were high correlations between our measured objective behaviors (e.g., "self-stimulation") and specific items on the subjective questionnaire (e.g., "Child engages in repetitive behavior"). These results lead us to believe that the objectively measured changes in the behavior of autistic children are apparent to naive judges and that the behaviors we focused on for our analyses are socially important.

Behavior Modification and Neurological Correlates of Treatment Gains

Accumulating evidence suggests either a primary or a secondary cortical dysfunction in the language-dominant hemisphere of autistic children (e.g., Blackstock, 1978; Hauser, DeLong, & Rosman, 1975; Hier, LeMay, & Rosenberger, 1979; Ornitz, 1974; Ornitz & Ritvo, 1976; Rutter & Bartak, 1971; Student & Sohmer, 1978). In our own laboratories, we have also begun a series of measurements that suggest cortical dysfunction in the central auditory nervous system (Miller, Koegel, & Mendel, 1979). In this study, central auditory function was assessed by means of a battery of tests, which included the Staggered Spondaic Word and Competing Environmental Sound Tests (Katz, 1976, 1977). All of the echolalic subjects whom we tested showed evidence of dysfunction of the central auditory nervous system in the language-dominant hemisphere, and this measure of dysfunction did not change on retesting for subjects who did not receive intensive behavior-modification treatment. However, subjects who did receive intensive behavior-modification treatment showed measurable improvement in central auditory function, which was consistent with behavior improvements shown over the course of treatment. We suspect that these results suggest the possibility of an interaction of neural plasticity and treatment. This interaction seems particularly likely in that the greatest improvement (a posttreatment measurement of near-normal neurological function) occurred only in those children who received intensive treatment at a very early age (prior to 5 years old). This research is still fairly preliminary. However, the results to date have been consistent for all the subjects tested, and we feel quite optimistic about this area for future research.

Conclusion

The above research shows that the treatment of autism within a learning framework has resulted in literally hundreds of measurable changes in the behavior of autistic children. Therefore, in the future, one might suspect that the treatment of autism may provide a relatively favorable prognosis. The results to date are extremely encouraging, and future research will undoubtedly lead to even further advances.

References

Applebaum, E., Egel, A. L., Koegel, R. L., & Imhoff, B. Measuring musical abilities of autistic children. *Journal of Autism and Developmental Disorders*, 1979, *9*, 279–285.

Axelrod, S., Brantner, J. P., & Meddock, T. D. Overcorrection: A review and critical analysis. *The Journal of Special Education*, 1978, *12*, 367–391.

Azrin, N. H., Kaplan, S. J., & Foxx, R. M. Autism reversal: Eliminating stereotyped self-stimulation of retarded individuals. *American Journal of Mental Deficiency*, 1973, *18*, 241–248.

Baer, D. M., & Guess, D. Receptive training of adjective inflections in mental retardates. *Journal of Applied Behavior Analysis*, 1971, *4*, 129–139.

Baer, D. M., & Sherman, J. Reinforcement control of generalized imitation in young children. *Journal of Experimental Child Psychology*, 1964, *1*, 37–39.

Baer, D. M., Wolf, M. M., & Risley, T. Some current dimensions of applied behavior analysis. *Journal of Applied Behavior Analysis*, 1968, *1*, 91–97.

Barrett, B. Behavior Modification in the home: Parents adapt laboratory-developed tactics to bowel-train a 5.5 year-old. *Psychotherapy: Theory, Research, Practice*, 1969, *6*, 172–176.

Berkowitz, B. P., & Graziano, A. M. Training parents as behavior therapists: A review. *Behaviour Research and Therapy*, 1972, *10*, 297–317.

Berlyne, D. E. Novelty and curiosity as determinants of exploratory behavior. *British Journal of Psychology*, 1950, *41*, 68–80.

Berlyne, D. E. The arousal and satiation of perceptual curiosity in the rat. *Journal of Comparative and Physiological Psychology*, 1955, *48*, 238–246.

Berlyne, D. E. *Conflict, arousal, and curiosity*. New York: McGraw-Hill, 1960.

Bettelheim, B. *The empty fortress*. New York: Free Press, 1967.

Bettelheim, B. Reply to G. G. Merritt's book review of "The empty fortress." *American Journal of Orthopsychiatry*, 1968, *38*, 930–933.

Bijou, S. W. The technology of teaching young handicapped children. In S. W. Bijou & E. Ribes-Inesta (Eds.), *Behavior Modification: Issues and extensions*. New York: Academic Press, 1972.

Birnbrauer, J. S. Generalization of punishment effects: A case study. *Journal of Applied Behavior Analysis*, 1968, *1*, 201–211.

Blackstock, E. Cerebral asymmetry and the development of early infantile autism. *Journal of Autism and Childhood Schizophrenia*, 1978, *8*, 339–353.

Bostow, D. E., & Bailey, J. B. Modification of severe disruptive and aggressive behavior using brief timeout and reinforcement procedures. *Journal of Applied Behavior Analysis*, 1969, *2*, 31–38.

Bourne, L. E., & Bunderson, C. V. Effects of delay of informative feedback and length of postfeedback interval on concept identification. *Journal of Experimental Psychology*, 1963, *65*, 1–5.

Burchard, J. D., & Tyler, V. O. The modification of delinquent behavior through operant conditioning. *Behaviour Research and Therapy*, 1965, *2*, 245–250.

Bucher, B., & Lovaas, O. I. Use of aversive stimulation in behavior modification. In M. R. Jones (Ed.), *Miami symposium on the prediction of behavior, 1967: Aversive stimulation*. Coral Gables, Fla.: University of Miami Press, 1968.

Calllas, M. Educational aims and methods. In M. Rutter & E. Schopler (Eds.), *Autism: Reappraisal of concepts and treatment*. New York: Plenum Press, 1978.

Cantor, J. H., & Cantor, G. N. Children's observing behavior as related to amount and recency of stimulus familiarization. *Journal of Experimental Child Psychology*, 1964, *1*, 241–247. (a)

Cantor, J. H., & Cantor, G. N. Observing behavior in children as a function of stimulus novelty. *Child Development*, 1964, *35*, 119–128. (b)

Carr, E. G., Schreibman, L., & Lovaas, O. I. Control of echolalic speech in psychotic children. *Journal of Abnormal Child Psychology*, 1975, *3*, 331–351.

Carr, E. G., Newsom, C. D., & Binkoff, J. A. Stimulus control of self-destructive behavior in a psychotic child. *Journal of Abnormal Child Psychology*, 1976, *4*, 139–153.

Clark, H. B., Rowbury, T., Baer, A. M., & Baer, D. M. Timeout as a punishing stimulus in continuous and intermittent schedules. *Journal of Applied Behavior Analysis*, 1973, *6*, 443–455.

Creak, M., & Ini, S. Families of psychotic children. *Journal of Child Psychology and Psychiatry*, 1960, *1*, 156.

Croll, W. L. Children's discrimination learning as a function of intertrial interval duration. *Psychonomic Science*, 1970, *18*, 321–322.

Davis, D. R., & Cashdan, A. Specific dyslexia. *British Journal of Educational Psychology*, 1963, *33*, 80–82.

Devany, J., & Rincover, A. *Experimental analysis of ethical issues: I. Using self-stimulation as a reinforcer in the treatment of developmentally delayed children.* Paper presented at the 12th annual meeting of the Association for Advancement of Behavior Therapy, Chicago, 1978.

Dietz, S. M., & Repp, A. L. Decreasing classroom misbehavior through the use of DRL schedules of reinforcement. *Journal of Applied Behavior Analysis*, 1973, *6*, 457–463.

Dunlap, G., Koegel, R. L., & Egel, A. L. Autistic children in school. *Exceptional Children*, 1979, *45*, 552–558.

Egel, A. L. *The effects of constant vs. varied reinforcer presentation on responding by autistic children.* Manuscript submitted for publication, 1979.

Egel, A. L., Koegel, R. L., & Schreibman, L. A review of educational treatment procedures for autistic children. In L. Mann & D. Sabatino (Eds.), *Fourth review of special education.* New York: Grune & Stratton, 1980.

Eisenberg, L., & Kanner, L. Early infantile autism: 1943–1955. *American Journal of Orthopsychiatry*, 1956, *26*, 55–65.

Epstein, L. H., Doke, L. A., Sajwaj, T. E., Sorrell, S., & Rimmer, B. Generality and side effects of overcorrection. *Journal of Applied Behavior Analysis*, 1974, *7*, 385–390.

Ferster, C. B. Positive reinforcement and behavioral deficits of autistic children. *Child Development*, 1961, *32*, 437–456.

Ferster, C. B., & DeMyer, M. A method for the experimental analysis of the behavior of autistic children. *American Journal of Orthopsychiatry*, 1962, *32*, 89–98.

Fowler, H. *Curiosity and exploratory behavior.* New York: Macmillan, 1963.

Fowler, H. Satiation and curiosity: Constructs for a drive and incentive-motivational theory of exploration. In K. W. Spence & J. T. Spence (Eds.), *The psychology of learning and motivation*, Vol. 1. New York: Academic Press, 1967.

Fowler, H. Implications of sensory reinforcement. In R. H. Glaser (Ed.), *The nature of reinforcement.* New York: Academic Press, 1971.

Foxx, R. M., & Azrin, N. H. Restitution: A method for eliminating aggressive disruptive behavior of retarded and brain damaged patients. *Behaviour Research and Therapy*, 1972, *10*, 15–27.

Foxx, R. M., & Azrin, N. H. The elimination of autistic self-stimulatory behavior by overcorrection. *Journal of Applied Behavior Analysis*, 1973, *6*, 1–14. (a)

Foxx, R. M., & Azrin, N. H. *Toilet training the retarded.* Champaign, Ill.: Research Press, 1973. (b)

Glanzer, M. Stimulus satiation: An explanation of spontaneous alternation and related phenomena. *Psychological Review*, 1953, *60*, 257–268.

Glanzer, M. Curiosity, exploratory drive, and stimulus satiation. *Psychological Bulletin*, 1958, *55*, 302–315.

Goetz, L., Schuler, A., & Sailor, W. Teaching functional speech to the severely handicapped: Current issues. *Journal of Autism and Developmental Disorders*, 1979, *9*, 325–343.

Griffiths, H., & Craighead, W. E. Generalization in operant speech therapy for misarticulation. *Journal of Speech and Hearing Disorders*, 1972, *37*, 457–468.

Guess, D. A functional analysis of receptive language and productive speech: Acquisition of the plural morpheme. *Journal of Applied Behavior Analysis*, 1969, *2*, 55–64.

Guess, D., Sailor, W., Rutherford, G., & Baer, D. An experimental analysis of linguistic development: The productive use of the plural morpheme. *Journal of Applied Behavior Analysis*, 1968, *1*, 292–307.

Hamblin, R. L., Buckholdt, D., Ferritor, D. E., Kozloff, M. A., & Blackwell, L. J. *The humanization process.* New York: Wiley, 1971.

Harris, S. L., & Wolchik, S. A. Suppression of self-stimulation: Three alternative strategies. *Journal of Applied Behavior Analysis*, 1979, *12*, 185–198.

Hauser, S., DeLong, G., & Rosman, N. Pneumographic findings in the infantile autism syndrome. *Brain*, 1975, *98*, 667–688.

Hemsley, R., Howlin, P., Berger, M., Hersov, L., Holbrook, D., Rutter, M., & Yule, W. Treating autistic children in a family context. In M. Rutter & E. Schopler (Eds.), *Autism: A reappraisal of concepts and treatment.* New York: Plenum Press, 1978.

Herendeen, D. L., Jeffrey, D. B., & Graham, M. C. *Reduction of self-stimulation in institutionalized children: Overcorrection and reinforcement for nonresponding.* Paper presented at the eighth annual meeting of the Association for Advancement of Behavior Therapy, Chicago, 1974.

Hewett, F. M. Teaching reading to an autistic boy through operant conditioning. *American Journal of Orthopsychiatry*, 1964, *34*, 613–618.

Hewett, F. M. Teaching speech to an autistic child through operant conditioning. *American Journal of Orthopsychiatry*, 1965, *35*, 927–936.

Hier, D., LeMay, M., & Rosenberger, P. Autism and unfavorable left-right asymmetries of the brain. *Journal of Autism and Developmental Disorders*, 1979, *9*, 153–159.

Hingtgen, J. W., & Bryson, C. Q. Research developments in the study of early childhood psychoses: Infantile autism, childhood schizophrenia, and related disorders. *Schizophrenia Bulletin*, 1972, *5*, 8–54.

Holland, C. Elimination by the parents of fire-setting behavior in a seven year old boy. *Behaviour Research and Therapy*, 1969, *7*, 135–137.

Holt, G. L., & Shafer, J. N. Function of intertrial interval in matching to sample. *Journal of the Experimental Analysis of Behavior*, 1973, *19*, 181–186.

Hutt, C. Degrees of novelty and their effects on children's attention and preference. *British Journal of Psychology*, 1975, *66*, 487–492.

Johnson, C. A., & Katz, R. C. Using parents as change agents for their children: A review. *Journal of Child Psychology and Psychiatry*, 1973, *14*, 181–200.

Kale, R. J., Kaye, J. H., Whelan, P. A., & Hopkins, B. L. The effects of reinforcement on the modification, maintenance and generalization of social responses of mental patients. *Journal of Applied Behavior Analysis*, 1968, *1*, 307–314.

Kanner, L. Autistic disturbances of affective contact. *The Nervous Child*, 1943, *3*, 217–250.

Kanner, L. Problems of nosology and psychodynamics of early infantile autism. *American Journal of Orthopsychiatry*, 1949, *19*, 416–426.

Katz, J. *The competing environmental sound test instructions*. St. Louis: Auditec, 1976.

Katz, J. The staggered spondaic word test. In R. Keith (Ed.), *Central auditory dysfunction*. New York: Grune & Stratton, 1977.

Kazdin, A. E., & Bootzin, R. R. The token economy: An evaluative review. *Journal of Applied Behavior Analysis*, 1972, *5*, 343–372.

Koegel, R. L., & Covert, A. The relationship of self-stimulation to learning in autistic children. *Journal of Applied Behavior Analysis*, 1972, *5*, 381–387.

Koegel, R. L., & Egel, A. L. Motivating autistic children. *Journal of Abnormal Psychology*, 1979, *88*, 418–426.

Koegel, R. L., & Rincover, A. Treatment of psychotic children in a classroom environment: I. Learning in a large group. *Journal of Applied Behavior Analysis*, 1974, *7*, 45–59.

Koegel, R. L., & Rincover, A. Some detrimental effects of using extra stimuli to guide learning in normal and autistic children. *Journal of Abnormal Child Psychology*, 1976, *4*, 59–71.

Koegel, R. L., & Rincover, A. Research on the difference between generalization and maintenance in extra-therapy responding. *Journal of Applied Behavior Analysis*, 1977, *10*, 1–12.

Koegel, R. L., & Schreibman, L. Identification of consistent responding to auditory stimuli by a functionally "deaf" autistic child. *Journal of Autism and Childhood Schizophrenia*, 1976, *6*, 147–156.

Koegel, R. L., & Schreibman, L. Teaching autistic children to respond to simultaneous multiple cues. *Journal of Experimental Child Psychology*, 1977, *24*, 299–311.

Koegel, R. L., & Wilhelm, H. Selective responding to the components of multiple visual cues by autistic children. *Journal of Experimental Child Psychology*, 1973, *15*, 442–453.

Koegel, R. L., & Williams, J. Direct vs. indirect response-reinforcer relationships in teaching autistic children. *Journal of Abnormal Child Psychology*, 1981, *4*, 537–547.

Koegel, R. L., Firestone, P. B., Kramme, K. W., & Dunlap, G. Increasing spontaneous play by suppressing self-stimulation in autistic children. *Journal of Applied Behavior Analysis*, 1974, *7*, 521–528.

Koegel, R. L., Russo, D. C., & Rincover, A. Assessing and training teachers in the generalized use of behavior modification with autistic children. *Journal of Applied Behavior Analysis*, 1977, *10*, 197–205.

Koegel, R. L., Glahn, T. J., & Nieminen, G. S. Generalization of parent-training results. *Journal of Applied Behavior Analysis*, 1978, *11*, 95–109.

Koegel, R. L., Schreibman, L., Britten, K., & Laitinen, R. The effect of schedule of reinforcement on stimulus overselectivity in autistic children. *Journal of Autism and Developmental Disorders*, 1979, *9*, 383–397.

Koegel, R. L., Dunlap, G., & Dyer, K. Intertrial interval duration and learning in autistic children. *Journal of Applied Behavior Analysis*, 1980, *13*, 91–99.

Kolvin, I. Psychosis in childhood: A comparative study. In M. Rutter (Ed.), *Infantile autism: Concepts, characteristics, and treatment*. London: Churchill-Livingstone, 1971.

Kozloff, M. *Reaching the autistic child*. Champaign, Ill.: Research Press, 1973.

Kozloff, M. *Educating children with learning and behavioral problems*. New York: Wiley, 1974.

Kugelmass, N. I. *The autistic child*. Springfield, Ill.: Charles C Thomas, 1970.

Lichstein, K. L., & Schreibman, L. Employing electric shock with autistic children: A review of the side effects. *Journal of Autism and Childhood Schizophrenia*, 1976, *6*, 163–174.

Lovaas, O. I. *Behavior modification: Teaching language to psychotic children*. New York: Appleton-Century-Crofts, 1969. (Film)

Lovaas, O. I. Contrasting illness and behavioral models for the treatment of autistic children: A historical perspective. *Journal of Autism and Developmental Disorders*, 1979, *9*, 315–323.

Lovaas, O. I., & Koegel, R. L. Behavior therapy with autistic children. In G. Thoresen (Ed.), *Seventy-second Yearbook of the National Society for the Study of Education: Behavior Modification, 1973*. Chicago: University of Chicago Press, 1973.

Lovaas, O. I., & Newsom, C. D. Behavior modification with psychotic children. In H. Leitenberg (Ed.), *Handbook of behavior modification and behavior therapy*. Englewood Cliffs, N.J.: Prentice-Hall, 1976.

Lovaas, O. I., & Schreibman, L. Stimulus overselectivity of autistic children in a two stimulus situation. *Behavior Research and Therapy*, 1971, *9*, 305–310.

Lovaas, O. I., & Simmons, J. Q. Manipulation of self-destruction in three retarded children. *Journal of Applied Behavior Analysis*, 1969, *2*, 143–157.

Lovaas, O. I., Schaeffer, B., & Simmons, J. Q. Building social behavior in autistic children by use of electric shock. *Journal of Experimental Research and Personality*, 1965, *1*, 99–109.

Lovaas, O. I., Berberich, J. P., Perloff, B. F., & Schaeffer, B. Acquisition of imitative speech in schizophrenic children. *Science*, 1966, *151*, 705–707.

Lovaas, O. I., Freitag, G., Kinder, M. I., Rubenstein, B. D., Schaeffer, B., & Simmons, J. Q. Establishment of social reinforcers in two schizophrenic children on the basis of food. *Journal of Experimental Child Psychology*, 1966, *4*, 109–125.

Lovaas, O. I., Koegel, R. L., Simmons, J. Q., & Long, J. S. Some generalization and follow-up measures on autistic children in behavior therapy. *Journal of Applied Behavior Analysis*, 1973, *6*, 131–166.

Lovaas, O. I., Schreibman, L., & Koegel, R. L. A behavior modification approach to the treatment of autistic children. *Journal of Autism and Childhood Schizophrenia*, 1974, *4*, 111–129.

Lovaas, O. I., Koegel, R. L., & Schreibman, L. Stimulus overselectivity and autism: A review of research. *Psychological Bulletin*, 1979, *86*, 1236–1254.

Lovaas, O. I., Litrownik, A., & Mann, R. Response latencies to auditory stimuli in autistic children engaged in self-stimulatory behavior. *Behaviour Research and Therapy*, 1979, *9*, 39–49.

Lovaas, O. I., Schreibman, L., Koegel, R. L., & Rehm, R. Selective responding by autistic children to multiple sensory input. *Journal of Abnormal Psychology*, 1979, *77*, 211–222.

Lovaas, O. I., Glahn, T. J., Russo, D. C., Chock, P. N., Kohls, S., & Mills, D. Teaching homes for autistic and retarded persons: I. Basic rationale. *Journal of Autism and Developmental Disorders*, in press.

Marshall, G. R. Toilet training of an autistic eight year old through operant conditioning therapy: A case report. *Behaviour Research and Therapy*, 1966, *4*, 242–245.

McClannahan, L. E., & Krantz, P. J. *Developing group homes for autistic and severe behavior problem children.* Paper presented at the Fifth Annual Convention of the Association for Behavior Analysis, Dearborn, 1979.

Miller, A., Koegel, R. L., & Mendel, M. *Central auditory nervous system dysfunction in echolalic autistic individuals.* Unpublished manuscript, University of California at Santa Barbara, 1979.

Mills, J., Burke, J., Schreibman, L., & Koegel, R. L. *The social validation of behavior therapy with autistic children.* Paper presented at the 13th Annual Convention of the Association for the Advancement of Behavior Therapy, San Francisco, 1979.

Mulhern, I., & Baumeister, A. A. An experimental attempt to reduce stereotype by reinforcement procedures. *American Journal of Mental Deficiency*, 1969, *74*, 69–74.

O'Gorman, G. *The nature of childhood autism.* London: Butterworths, 1967.

Ornitz, E. The modulation of sensory input and motor output in autistic children. *Journal of Autism and Childhood Schizophrenia*, 1974, *4*, 197–215.

Ornitz, E., & Ritvo, E. The syndrome of autism: A critical review. *The American Journal of Psychiatry*, 1976, *133*, 609–621.

Patterson, G. R., Shaw, D., & Ebner, M. Teachers, peers, and parents as agents of change in the classroom: Modifying deviant social behaviors in various classroom settings. (Benson, F. A. M., Ed.) *Monograph No. 1, 13–47*, University of Oregon, Eugene, Oregon, 1969.

Peterson, R. F., Cox, M. A., & Bijou, S. W. Training children to work productively in classroom groups. *Exceptional Children*, 1971, *37*, 491–500.

Phillips, E. L., Phillips, E. A., Fixsen, D. L., & Wolf, M. M. *The teaching family handbook.* Lawrence, Kansas: University Printing Service, 1974.

Pitfield, M., & Oppenheim, A. N. Child rearing attitudes of mothers of psychotic children. *Journal of Child Psychology and Psychiatry and Allied Disciplines*, 1964, *5*, 51–57.

Plummer, S., Baer, D. M., & LeBlanc, J. M. Functional considerations in the use of procedural time out and an effective alternative. *Journal of Applied Behavior Analysis*, 1977, *10*, 689–706.

Reynolds, B. S., Newsom, C. D., & Lovaas, O. I. Auditory overselectivity in autistic children. *Journal of Abnormal Child Psychology*, 1974, *2*, 253–263.

Rimland, B. *Infantile autism.* New York: Appleton-Century-Crofts, 1964.

Rimland, B. Inside the mind of an autistic savant. *Psychology Today*, 1978, *12*, 68–80.

Rincover, A. Sensory extinction: A procedure for eliminating self-stimulating behavior in autistic children. *Journal of Abnormal Child Psychology*, 1978, *6*, 299–310. (a)

Rincover, A. Variables affecting stimulus-fading and discriminative responding in psychotic children. *Journal of Abnormal Psychology*, 1978, *87*, 541–553. (b)

Rincover, A., Koegel, R. L. Setting generality and stimulus control in autistic children. *Journal of Applied Behavior Analysis*, 1975, *8*, 235–246.

Rincover, A., & Koegel, R. L. Classroom treatment of autistic children: II. Individualized instruction in a group. *Journal of Abnormal Child Psychology*, 1977, *5*, 113–126. (a)

Rincover, A., & Koegel, R. L. Research on the education of autistic children: Recent advances and future directions. In B. B. Lahey & A. E. Kazdin (Eds.), *Advances in clinical child psychology*, Vol. 1. New York: Plenum Press, 1977. (b)

Rincover, A., Newsom, C. D., Lovaas, O. I., & Koegel, R. L. Some motivational properties of sensory stimulation in psychotic children. *Journal of Experimental Child Psychology*, 1977, *24*, 312–323.

Rincover, A., Koegel, R. L., & Russo, D. C. Some recent behavioral research on the education of autistic children. *Education and Treatment of Children*, 1978, *1*, 31–45.

Rincover, A., Cook, R., Peoples, A., & Packard, D. Sensory extinction and sensory reinforcement principles for programming multiple adaptive behavior change. *Journal of Applied Behavior Analysis*, 1979, *12*, 221–233.

Risley, T. R. The effects and side effects of punishing the autistic behaviors of a deviant child. *Journal of Applied Behavior Analysis*, 1968, *1*, 21–34.

Rosenbaum, M. S., & Breiling, J. The development and functional control of reading comprehension behavior. *Journal of Applied Behavior Analysis*, 1976, *9*, 323–334.

Russo, D. C., & Koegel, R. L. A method for integrating an autistic child into a normal public-school classroom. *Journal of Applied Behavior Analysis*, 1977, *10*, 579–590.

Rutter, M. The description and classification of infantile autism. In D. W. Churchill, G. D. Alpern, & M. D. DeMyer (Eds.), *Infantile autism*. Springfield, Ill.: Charles C Thomas, 1971.

Rutter, M. Diagnosis and definition of childhood autism. *Journal of Autism and Childhood Schizophrenia*, 1978, *8*, 139–161.

Rutter, M., & Bartak, L. Causes of infantile autism: Some considerations from recent research. *Journal of Autism and Childhood Schizophrenia*, 1971, *1*, 20–32.

Schopler, E. Parents of psychotic children as scapegoats. *Journal of Contemporary Psychology*, 1971, *4*, 17–22.

Schopler, E., & Reichler, R. J. Developmental therapy by parents with their own autistic child. In M. Rutter (Ed.), *Infantile autism: Concepts characteristics, and treatment.* London: Churchill-Livingstone, 1971.

Schover, L. R., & Newsom, C. D. Overselectivity, developmental level and overtraining in autistic and normal children. *Journal of Abnormal Child Psychology,* 1976, *4,* 289–298.

Schreibman, L. Effects of within-stimulus and extra-stimulus prompting on discrimination learning in autistic children. *Journal of Applied Behavior Analysis,* 1975, *8,* 91–112.

Schreibman, L., & Carr, E. G. Elimination of echolalic responding to questions through the training of a generalized verbal response. *Journal of Applied Behavior Analysis,* 1978, *11,* 453–463.

Schreibman, L., & Koegel, R. L. Autism: A defeatable horror. *Psychology Today,* 1975, *8,* 61–67.

Schreibman, L., & Koegel, R. A guideline for planning behavior modification programs for autistic children. In S. Turner, K. Calhoun, & H. Adams (Eds.), *Handbook of clinical behavior therapy.* New York: Wiley, 1981.

Schreibman, L., & Koegel, R. L. Multiple cue responding in autistic children. In P. Karoly & J. Steffen (Eds.), *Advances in child behavior analysis and therapy.* Lexington, Mass.: D. C. Heath, 1982.

Schreibman, L., & Lovaas, O. I. Overselective response to social stimuli by autistic children. *Journal of Abnormal Child Psychology,* 1973, *1,* 152–168.

Schreibman, L., Koegel, R. L., & Craig, M. S. Reducing stimulus overselectivity in autistic children. *Journal of Abnormal Child Psychology,* 1977, *5,* 425–436.

Schumaker, J., & Sherman, J. A. Training generative verb usage by imitation and reinforcement procedures. *Journal of Applied Behavior Analysis,* 1970, *3,* 273–287.

Solnick, J. V., Rincover, A., & Peterson, C. R. Determinants of the reinforcing and punishing effects of time-out. *Journal of Applied Behavior Analysis,* 1977, *10,* 415–428.

Stokes, T. F., & Baer, D. M. An implicit technology of generalization. *Journal of Applied Behavior Analysis,* 1977, *10,* 349–368.

Stokes, T. F., & Baer, D. M., & Jackson, R. L. Programming the generalization of greeting responses in four retarded children. *Journal of Applied Behavior Analysis,* 1974, *7,* 599–610.

Student, M., & Sohmer, H. Evidence from auditory nerve and brainstem evoked responses for an organic brain lesion in children with autistic traits. *Journal of Autism and Childhood Schizophrenia,* 1978, *8,* 13–20.

Tate, B. G., & Baroff, G. S. Aversive control of self-injurious behavior in a psychotic boy. *Behaviour Research and Therapy,* 1966, *4,* 281–287.

Turner, B. L. *The effects of choice of stimulus materials on interest in the remediation process and the generalized case of language training.* Unpublished master's thesis, University of California at Santa Barbara, 1978.

Varni, J., Lovaas, O. I., Koegel, R. L., & Everett, N. L. An analysis of observational learning in autistic and

normal children. *Journal of Abnormal Child Psychology,* 1979, *7,* 31–43.

Wahler, R. G. Setting generality: Some specific and general effects of child behavior therapy. *Journal of Applied Behavior Analysis,* 1969, *2,* 239–246.

Walker, H. M., & Buckley, N. K. Programming generalization and maintenance of treatment effects across time and across settings. *Journal of Applied Behavior Analysis,* 1972, *5,* 209–224.

Watson, J. Memory and "contingency analysis" in infant learning. *Merrill-Palmer Quarterly,* 1967, *13,* 55–76.

White, G. D., Nielsen, G., & Johnson, S. M. Time-out duration and the suppression of deviant behavior in children. *Journal of Applied Behavior Analysis,* 1972, *5,* 111–120.

Whittaker, J. K. The ecology of child treatment: A developmental/educational approach to the therapeutic millieu. *Journal of Autism and Childhood Schizophrenia,* 1975, *5,* 223–237.

Wilson, M. M. Novelty as a reinforcer for position learning in children. *Journal of Experimental Child Psychology,* 1974, *18,* 51–61.

Wing, J. K. Diagnosis, epidemiology, aetiology. In J. K. Wing (Ed.), *Early childhood autism.* London: Pergamon Press, 1966.

Wing, J. K. Review of Bettelheim: "The empty fortress." *British Journal of Psychiatry,* 1968, *114,* 788–791.

Wing, L. *Autistic children: A guide for parents.* New York: Brunner/Mazel, 1972.

Wing, L. Diagnosis, clinical description, and prognosis. In L. Wing (Ed.), *Early childhood autism.* London: Pergamon Press, 1976.

Wing, L. Social, behavioral, and cognitive characteristics: An epidemiological approach. In M. Rutter & E. Schopler (Eds.), *Autism: A reappraisal of concepts and treatment.* New York: Plenum Press, 1978.

Wolf, M. M., Risley, T., & Mees, H. Application of operant conditioning procedures to the behaviour problems of an autistic child. *Behaviour Research and Therapy,* 1964, *1,* 305–312.

Wolf, M. M., Risley, T., Johnston, M., Harris, F., & Allen, E. Application of operant conditioning procedures to the behavior problems of an autistic child: A follow-up and extension. *Behaviour Research and Therapy,* 1967, *5,* 103–111.

Wolf, M. M., Phillips, E. L., Fixsen, D. L., Braukmann, C. J., Kirigin, K. A., Wilner, A. G., & Schumaker, J. Achievement Place: The teaching-family model. *Child Care Quarterly,* 1976, *5,* 92–103.

Young, S. *Visual attention in autistic and normal children: Effects of stimulus novelty, human attributes and complexity.* Unpublished doctoral dissertation, University of California at Los Angeles, 1969.

CHAPTER 29

The Modification of Child Behavior Problems in the Home

Beth Sulzer-Azaroff and Martin J. Pollack

Introduction

The problems created by children's troublesome behavior at home constitute one of the most serious sources of difficulty in our society. Children's problems may lead to dissatisfaction, to distress, or even to violence (Bell, 1979) among family members. Since its inception, the field of behavior modification has addressed children's home-based behavioral problems. Many problem areas have been addressed, from temper tantrums and other noxious social behaviors, to health-related behaviors, social skills, and many others. As the scope of the problems addressed broadens, new and effective treatment methods are being developed and research methodology is becoming more precise.

Over the years, one may begin to note the emergence of trends that characterize the field. There have been a number of specific problem areas that it has heavily emphasized. Other areas have either been overlooked, or perhaps effective treatment strategies have failed to be discovered. In the present chapter, it is our intention to (1) discuss the history of behavior modification with children at home; (2) elaborate on some of the more extensively addressed problem areas; (3) consider some of the trends that have characterized the development of the field and the underexplored areas of investigation; and (4) use a hopefully representative sample of reported findings to illustrate those points. Perhaps the general survey that we present will prompt refinements in methodology or new directions for research on the modification of children's problem behavior in the home.

The Historical Beginnings of Behavior Modification of Child Behavior Problems in the Home

The application of principles of operant and respondent conditioning to modify child behavior problems in the home goes back to the

Beth Sulzer-Azaroff • Department of Psychology, University of Massachusetts, Amherst, Massachusetts 01003. Martin J. Pollack • Department of Psychology, Mansfield Training School, Mansfield Depot, Connecticut 06251.

early years of the century. Kazdin (1978) has traced the development of the field from that time, citing early work in the conditioning of emotions (Jones, 1924) and other operant and respondent conditioning research with children. One important illustration is Mowrer's work on a conditioning treatment for enuresis: a pad with a buzzer that awakens the child at the onset of urination (Mowrer & Mowrer, 1938). In 1959, at a time when operant conditioning was beginning to be employed to treat adults (e.g., Ayllon & Michael, 1959), Williams (1959) conducted a now classic study. The parents of a child who exhibited severe temper tantrums at bedtime requested assistance. Noting that the tantrums accorded the child substantial attention, Williams counseled terminating the attention for that behavior. After consistently practicing the procedure, the tantrums did diminish substantially. A "natural reversal phase" was introduced when a concerned relative was a guest at the house. Her attention to the tantrums led to their rapid recovery. The noxious behavior again diminished when that attention was no longer forthcoming.

Perhaps one of the reasons that that particular case received so much notice was that it had several critical properties. First, the treatment approach was based on the operant conditioning principles of reinforcement and extinction. Second, data were recorded. Third, the natural reversal phase provided a source of experimental control, demonstrating that the behavior did appear to "turn on and off" as a function of the consequences.

In the early 1960s, Donald Baer and Sidney Bijou collaborated in developing some conceptual analyses of child development, from the perspective of operant and respondent conditioning (Bijou & Baer, 1961, 1965). Their colleagues and students also implemented various operant conditioning programs with children. Besides several school-based programs (e.g., Birnbrauer, Bijou, Wolf, & Kidder, 1965), a particularly fascinating case was undertaken with an autistic child (Wolf, Risley, & Mees, 1964). Although initially conducted in a hospital, the procedures were eventually transferred to the home. The child exhibited many of the extremely mala-daptive behaviors that frequently characterize children who are called autistic: a lack of functional language, high rates of tantrums, failure to follow directions, and other deviant behaviors. Wolf *et al.* demonstrated that shaping and other operant procedures were amenable to the clinical treatment of these extreme behavior problems.

Among some of the early applications of behavior modification in the home were several studies with children who exhibited either very disturbing or very objectionable behavior (Hawkins, Peterson, Schweid, & Bijou, 1966; Bernal, Duryee, Pruett, & Burns, 1968); isolation and noncompliance (Patterson, McNeal, Hawkins, & Phelps, 1967); and oppositional behavior (Wahler, 1969a). Hawkins *et al.*, (1966) argued for the value of the therapist's observing the child's problem behaviors and the interactions between child and parent in their natural surroundings in order to be able to make meaningful specific suggestions.

In the study conducted by Bernal *et al.* (1968), home observations and videotapes were used to identify the condition that appeared to maintain the child's problem behaviors. Modifying those conditions led to major reductions in the problems. Bernal continued this line of research, the next year publishing another study on the reduction of "brat" behaviors (Bernal, 1969) and reporting similar reductions in other noxious behaviors.

In the Patterson *et al.* study (1967), conditions in the home were reprogrammed through written and oral instructions and feedback based on clinic and home observations. This approach resulted in an increase in "warm" responding by a mother to her child and a reduction in the child's isolate behavior. In the study reported by Wahler (1969a), the parents were instructed and observed in the home. A combination of differential attention and time-out led to a reduction in the oppositional behavior of two children.

From those early beginnings, the field began to burgeon exponentially. So extensive is the collection of studies that it is no longer feasible to present a completely exhaustive review of the literature within the confines of a single chapter. We have elected instead to present summaries of a set of specific problem areas and then to discuss some of the critical aspects that characterize studies dealing with child behavior problems in the home.

Specific Problem Areas

The specific problem areas addressed by the field may be categorized in various ways. We have elected to start with individual problems (health, toileting problems, and nervous habits and fears) and then to move on to the more complex, family-related problems (noncompliance, sibling conflicts, and troublesome behavior while shopping). Next, we cover problems that involve the relations between home and school, such as the home-based management of school problems, attendance, and homework, followed by social isolation and elective mutism. Last, we focus on the positive: prosocial behaviors and social and conversational skills.

Health-Related Behavior of Children

The discipline of behavioral medicine has been evolving to such an extent that many medical schools and medical service facilities now incorporate behavior modification approaches within their assessment and therapy programs. Behavior modification methods are particularly relevant to the prevention and the treatment of the somatic disorders of children (Gentry, 1976).

Preventing and Treating. Parallel to its development in other disciplines, the modification of health-related behaviors initially tended to focus on those that were most serious and most resistant to treatment. Such serious conditions as chronic vomiting (Wolf, Birnbrauer, Williams, & Lawler, 1965); anorexia (Bachrach, Erwin, & Mohr, 1965); and excessive scratching to the point of inflicting tissue damage (Allen & Harris, 1966) were among the targets in studies reported initially. Since then, the kinds of behaviors that have been targeted for modification have broadened to include asthma (Neisworth & Moore, 1972); diet and nutrition (Fox & Roseen, 1977; Hebert-Jackson, & Risley, 1977; Tizard, 1977);

self-feeding and consuming nutritious table foods (Bernal, 1972); and other problems of food ingestion besides rumination and anorexia. Now, efforts are being made to treat children's obesity (Epstein, Masek, & Marshall, 1978; Aragona, Cassady, & Drabman, 1975) by working either with the children directly or with their parents.

Motivating compliance with prescribed regimens, such as special diets or the use of inhalation equipment by asthmatics (Renne & Creer, 1976), is another area of focus. Also, behaviors have been modified in order to prevent the development or the worsening of health problems; dental care (Horner & Keilitz, 1975) and cooperation with the dentist (Stokes & Kennedy, 1980); motor skill training (Hardiman, Goetz, Reuter, & LeBlanc, 1975); automobile safety (Christopherson, 1977); exercise such as swimming (McKenzie & Rushall, 1974); bathing a burn victim to prevent further complications (Weinstein, 1977); and foot care by a diabetic child (Lowe & Lutzker, 1979). Pain and complaints of pain are also being more effectively managed among children, as in studies by Miller and Kratochwill (1979) and Sank and Biglan (1974).

As is typical of the field, when behavior modification is applied to children's health behaviors, it tends to emphasize positive reinforcement heavily. Attention is often used as a reinforcer in conjunction with other procedures. It has been presented contingent on the absence of vomiting (Munford, 1979; Wright, Brown, & Andrews, 1978) or of complaints of abdominal pain (Miller & Kratochwill, 1979). Usually paired with praise, tokens or points exchangeable for backup rewards and privileges have been used to reduce scratching (Allen & Harris, 1966); to promote conforming to diet regimens (Fox & Roseen, 1977; Fox et al., 1977; Aragona et al., 1975); to reduce complaints of abdominal pain (Sank & Biglan, 1974); to reduce anorexia (Garfinkel, Kline, & Stancer, 1973); to improve nutrition (Epstein et al., 1978); and to promote dental cooperation (Stokes & Kennedy, 1980). Sometimes the backup reinforcers are contrived, selected solely for their powerful reinforcing quality, particularly when optimal compliance is of critical importance, while often reinforcers intrinsic to the situation are selected (e.g., Stokes & Kennedy, 1980).

Elements of stimulus control are incorporated within many of the procedures applied to modify children's health behaviors, as reinforcement is presented contingent on the response's occurring when paired with given antecedent stimuli. Rules and instructions are usually provided for nutritional and dieting regimens, as in the Aragona *et al.* (1975) study, in which parents were trained to treat their overweight children, and in that of Epstein *et al.* (1978), in which children were given reinforcement for selecting nutritious, low-calorie foods from among several offered. Often, too, complex tasks are analyzed for their subskills, and these are communicated to children, parents and/or care givers. For instance, Horner and Keilitz (1975) analyzed the task of tooth brushing, and Renne and Creer (1976) broke down the task of using inhalation therapy equipment into three specific subskills. Modeled prompts were provided by Stokes and Kennedy (1980), as they permitted clients to observe others behaving cooperatively in the dental situation. In many instances, the initial attempts to perform skills are fully guided or prompted. These prompts are then slowly faded. An illustration is Renne and Creer's (1976) manipulation of the patient's abdomen to guide the diaphragmatic breathing response. A program that effectively applied a complex combination of behavior procedures, feedback plus systematic desensitization or feedback plus cognitive restructuring, was conducted by Ollendick (1979) with a 16-year-old anorexic boy.

Issues. The moral and ethical justification of using negative reductive procedures, such as punishment, response cost, and time-out, is relatively less problematic when children's health is involved than it may be with less serious problems. Chronic rumination behavior is life-threatening, and the application of aversive stimuli contingent on the behavior or its precursors should meet with little opposition when less severe alternatives have a poor prospect of success. Among the noxious stimuli that have been applied in such cases have been electric shock (Lang & Melamed, 1969; Linscheid & Cunningham, 1977) and lemon juice (Becker, Turner & Sajwaj, 1978; Apolito

& Sulzer-Azaroff, 1981). Another form of punishment was used to interrupt the chain of behaviors that terminated in epileptic seizures (Zlutnick, Mayville, & Moffat, 1975). This consisted of a sharp "no" and grasping and shaking the child by the shoulder, contingent on the emission of the initiation of the chain. Response-cost in the form of loss of cash on deposit has been used to maintain parents' involvement in and implementation of weight reduction programs with their children (Aragona *et al.*, 1975), and time-out was used to reduce unwarranted complaints of pain (Miller & Kratochwill, 1979; Sank & Biglan, 1974). In most cases in which negative contingencies are arranged, either the program also provides for reinforcement of alternative behaviors, or reinforcement is intrinsic to improvement. Assuming they no longer earn reinforcement in the form of extensive attention, improvement in such distressing behaviors as seizures and vomiting is probably its own reward.

Other factors are particularly relevant to behavior modification and children's health. Often, initial interventions take place outside the home, which may limit transfer into the home (Wahler, 1969a). If anorexia is modified in the hospital (as in the program conducted by Garfinkel, Kline, & Stancer, 1973), it may reappear at home unless the procedures are transferred to that setting. One attempt to overcome that problem was described in a case by Azerrad and Stafford (1969), in which they trained the parents to implement their procedures. Recognizing the potential limitations of intervening outside the natural environment, Lowe and Lutzker (1979) left their offices to train their diabetic patient in her home, where she was expected to maintain the regimen. Their 10-week follow-up assessment supported the justifiability of that procedure.

Another problem is methodological. Often, problems are brought to the attention of the behavior modifier after they have become serious. Such methodological niceties as extended baselines, elaborate measures with demonstrated reliability, and within- or across-subject replications are luxuries that may not always prove feasible. Fortunately, some of these difficulties are not as serious as they might seem, since the medical field has developed many reliable and sophisticated instruments. Electromyograms, refined chemical analyses, and other methods have been utilized to assess changes in patients' behavior. For example, one of the measures used by Lowe and Lutzker (1979) to monitor their patient's compliance with her diet was the results of laboratory tests. When dependent measures are collected by objective, uninformed, analytically skilled technicians, potential confounds such as expectancy, bias, or observer drift are reasonably controlled in contrast to the direct collection of behavioral data by live observers.

As hospital costs rise and the trend continues toward maintaining children in the least restrictive environment possible, it is probable that the management of children's health behaviors will be based in the home more frequently. Improving technologies for training parents, as well as developing methods for promoting compliance and improvements in the precision of home-based data collection techniques, should permit increasingly effective methods for modifying children's health behaviors. It is probably not too farfetched to anticipate that medical-service-delivery organizations will increasingly seek the assistance of behavior modifiers to participate in the cooperative design, implementation, and evaluation of home-based programs for modifying children's health behaviors.

Toileting Problems

Soiling and wetting during the day or at night while asleep is a source of difficulty for children beyond the age of about 3 years and for their parents. Besides necessitating extra laundering chores, they cause embarrassment and may lead to social alienation. The behavioral treatment of these problems has a relatively long history, dating back to the invention of the bell-and-pad apparatus (Mowrer & Mowrer, 1938). Following a classical conditioning paradigm, a pad was devised that would set off an alarm bell (or buzzer) when urine came in contact with the pad. According to studies by Lovibond (1964) and Doleys (1977), the success rate has been found to range from 75% to 90%. Sacks and De Leon (1978) used the bell-and-pad method to successfully treat several emotionally disturbed children, although

the more severely disturbed children took longer to achieve a stable remission. Success with the apparatus has apparently been sufficient to establish the system as a standard method for treating nocturnal enuresis.

While the bell-and-pad system did make a major inroad toward the solution of bed wetting, problems remained. In addition to seeking further improvements in the treatment of nighttime enuresis, daytime enuresis and day and nighttime soiling required treatment. Also, a relapse rate of 40% (Lovibond, 1964; Doleys, 1977) suggested the need for methods that would produce more durable effects. Procedural and methodological questions also needed to be addressed: What components of the treatment procedures are critical for success? Who should conduct the interventions and how should those people be trained? Are outcome reports reliable? How can the reliability of reporting be improved? These are some of the questions that have been addressed by behavioral researchers within the recent past.

Procedures used to reduce incontinence have ranged from simple reinforcement for the successful use of the toilet or negative consequences for "accidents," to full cleanliness training. Among the reinforcers delivered contingent on successful toileting have been tokens exchangeable for weekend outings (Ayllon, Simon, & Wildman, 1975); money (Bach & Moylan, 1975), food and trinkets (Doley & Wells, 1975); and praise (Azrin, Sneed, & Foxx, 1974). Among the negative consequences that have been presented as a function of "accidents" have been overcorrection and positive practice (Crowley & Armstrong, 1977); full cleanliness training (Azrin et al., 1974; Doleys, McWhorter, Williams, & Gentry, 1977); and parental disapproval (Azrin et al., 1974; Doleys, McWhorter et al., 1977). In one study (Tough, Hawkins, McArthur & Ravensway, 1971), a brief cold bath was given as a consequence of a toileting accident. Other procedures have been tested recently. In a study by Azrin, Hontos, and Besalel-Azrin (1979), awareness training was used to heighten sensitivity to bladder sensations as one component of a program to eliminate enuresis. Discrimination training to establish stimulus control was successfully employed by using glycerine suppositories to stimulate bowel movements at times when parental supervision was possible (Ashkenazi, 1975). Behavioral rehearsal was found to be a helpful adjunct to a training program designed to teach parents and children to follow a prescribed set of procedures (Crowley & Armstrong, 1977). Several studies have included retention or bladder control training as an element of the program. Azrin et al. (1974) required positive practice and fluid intake before sleep and after periodic awakenings, in order to maximize the opportunities to practice appropriate urination. Once awake, the children were urged to retain urine for at least a few minutes, or until the next hourly awakening if possible, and were praised contingent on success. Doleys and Wells (1975) used a similar approach with a 42-month-old girl who received rewards for retaining her urine for gradually increasing intervals. Doleys, McWhorter et al. (1977) also supplemented their procedure with retention control training. In a more extensive application of retention control training, Harris and Purohit (1977) taught 18 children over five days, for 3 hr per day, to increase the duration of their retention intervals. Reinforcement was provided contingent on progressively longer intervals between drinking and urination and for releasing increasing volumes of urine at one time. The program was subsequently shifted to the home for maintenance by the parents.

Frequently, a variety of procedures are combined within a comprehensive package. The "dry-bed program" of Azrin et al. (1974), which has served as a model for many subsequent studies, has demonstrated its success repeatedly. Included in the package were: differential positive reinforcement, positive practice, cleanliness training, scheduled nighttime checks and awakenings, retention control training, and a urine alarm. The program maximized early success by using a trained therapist in the home for the first day of intensive training. Subsequent training was administered by the parents, who gradually faded out the urine alarm and the nightly awakenings as success was demonstrated. The program rapidly reduced rates of wetting for all children from a baseline median of seven per week to one per week during each of the first two weeks. Wettings were eliminated completely

by the fourth week. The 14-dry-night criterion was reached with an average of only two accidents per child. The maintenance of these effects was demonstrated over a six-month period in which no relapses occurred. These results compared favorably with the exclusive use of a standard urine-alarm procedure, which served as a control. In the latter group, only 2 of 13 children attained similar success. The Azrin et al. (1974) results have been replicated by Doleys, Ciminero, Tollison, Williams, and Wells (1977), and while the degree of effectiveness was less striking than that achieved by Azrin et al. (1974), the mean number of wetting accidents was reduced considerably.

The dry-bed procedure has been modified by Bollard and Woodroffe (1977). Parents, rather than trained therapists, conducted the program, and for one group, the alarm apparatus was not used. In a comparison of three groups, the authors found that the parents functioned effectively as trainers and achieved a reduction in wetting accidents from a baseline of seven per week to zero in 3 weeks, with the exception of a single child, for whom 13 weeks were required. Two children relapsed, but their rate of accidents did not return to the high baseline level, and both were retrained. The group not using the apparatus achieved only a partial reduction in the rate of accidental wetting, changing from a baseline average of seven to an average of three over a 6-week period. No children achieved a perfect record. The study showed that parents could function as effective trainers, perhaps because of their ability to respond quickly and consistently, particularly when cued by the activation of the alarm.

Daytime enuresis has been successfully treated through incentives for appropriate urination (e.g., money in a study by Bach and Moylan, 1975). Incentives may and can be aided by combining them with other procedures: regular pants checks that permit frequent reinforcement for dryness, and cleanliness training or overcorrection for accidents. Azrin and Foxx (1974) have developed an intensive multicomponent program leading to successful toilet training in a single day. Although these procedures include the use of a therapist in the home for the day, they lend themselves quite well to use by parents alone.

A study by Butler (1976) showed that presenting the Azrin and Foxx materials in three brief lectures was sufficient to enable parents to implement the procedures with a success comparable to that achieved with the therapists.

Studies have begun to investigate the function of various components of procedural packages. Azrin and Thienes (1978) compared results with a buzzer-and-pad alarm to those of the dry-bed procedure. The rates of accidental wetting dropped from an average of 90% during baseline to 76% for the group using the alarm alone, compared with 15% for the group that was given the dry-bed training program without the alarm. The superior results were replicated when the buzzer-and-pad control group was then provided the dry-bed program. Comparing the results of this dry-bed program with earlier results (Azrin et al., 1974), the authors concluded that the original dry-bed procedure, which included the alarm, was probably preferable, since the rates of reduction had been superior and had been achieved more quickly.

Another study (Catalina, 1976) compared success rates as a function of the people to whom the buzzer signal was directed: child only, parent only, both, or neither. (In the latter case, bed checks by the parents were scheduled.) The best results, a 90% reduction, were achieved with the two groups involving the parents. There was a 70% reduction when only the children were signaled, but just a 40% reduction for those not receiving any signal. Not only does this study underscore the importance of the alarm component in treating nocturnal enuresis, but it substantiates the findings of Azrin et al. (1974) in rejecting a classical conditioning explanation of the mechanism by which the alarm achieves its effectiveness. It seems more likely that an operant conditioning explanation is appropriate, the sound or being awakened by the parent functioning as an aversive consequence to beginning to urinate in bed, and also signaling that a continuation of the behavior is apt to result in negative consequences.

Does there have to be a one-to-one correspondence between wetting episodes and the sounding of the alarm? This question was addressed in a study by Finley, Wansley, and Blenkarn (1977). Rather than sounding every time, the buzzer was scheduled to sound 70% of the time. Under those conditions, 75 of 80 children achieved success within 14 nights. The one-year relapse rate was found to be 25%.

The degree of precision with which training strategies have been described in the literature has varied considerably. Additionally, it is often difficult to ascertain, from reading reports in this area, to what degree the instructions have been carried out. When such information is missing, the influence of the level of adherence to the program on the degree of success becomes an open question. Crowley and Armstrong (1977) conducted a study on three children with a lengthy history of encopresis. The report described the training methodology in precise detail. Additionally, weekly office visits by the clients and regular telephone contact served as a means of supplying additional information about the level of adherence and the results. Similarly, Azrin et al. (1979) have also used regular telephone contact in their attempt to attain more reliable data. These studies illustrate the kinds of efforts that are being made to overcome some of the deficiencies in reporting methods and outcomes within this problem area.

Many reports on this topic have consisted of case studies of the baseline (A)–treatment (B) variety. Unless the methodology is directly replicated across subjects, in a multiple-baseline fashion, the generality of findings must be questioned. Recently, however, instances of full experimental comparisons (e.g., Azrin & Thienes, 1978) are appearing more frequently in the literature. With such improvements in design strategies, confidence in the reliability of findings should continue to increase.

Also frequently absent from published reports on toilet training are data on convenience, preference, and other measures of consumer satisfaction. Such data would permit an assessment of the potential utilization of any given procedure. Preference for the dry-bed program was measured behaviorally in the Azrin and Thienes (1978) study by offering the parents of the children in the control group the option of having their children shift into the other group. The fact that 23 of the 29 subjects exercised the option served as evidence that the treatment was preferred. Verbal expressions of satisfaction with the dry-bed method provided additional supportive evidence.

The potential utilization rate may also depend on the side effects of a given course of treatment. Some studies have cited intitial resistance and aggression in response to the application of negative contingencies, such as cleanliness training and positive practice (Butler, 1976; Doleys, McWhorter, Williams, & Gentry, 1977) and to cold baths (Tough *et al.*, 1971). Other factors affecting the acceptability of a given method by consumers are frequently provided in reports: the number of days necessary to reach criterion; the amount of time required for training; the locus of training (at home or in the office); the necessity of professional or paraprofessional assistance; the costs of the services and the apparatus; and others.

In summary, although there are some areas of investigation remaining in this problem area, it is apparent that some very dramatic strides have been made. In a large number of instances, children with a variety of repertoires have been successfully taught appropriate toileting habits through the application of behaviorally based methods.

Nervous Habits and Fears

At various times, everyone engages in repetitive physical behaviors that have no discernible function: twiddling thumbs, pushing back hair, biting cuticles, and so on. It is only when those behaviors occur at a very high rate or so intensively that they are judged to be damaging or disfiguring or to impair personal or social functioning that they deserve to be identified as problem "nervous habits." Behavior modification approaches have been used to treat children for a variety of such habits: thumb sucking, tics, hair pulling or twirling, nail biting, stuttering, and others.

Children are also often fearful on appropriate occasions: when threatened or when coming in contact with objects or events that have, in their past experience, proved aversive. As with nervous habits, however, it is only when a fear is so severe that it interferes with normal functioning that it deserves to be called a problem. This may happen when a child reacts inordinately fearfully in a mildly threatening situation, such as attending school for the first time, or when the fear has no ground in reality. An example is a case reported by Waye (1979), in which a child was convinced that parts of her body were shrinking. Here we summarize some of the procedures that have been used to treat nervous habits and fears along with some special characteristics of those methods, and we discuss some of the issues that pertain specifically to this topic.

Treating Nervous Habits. Many standard behavior modification procedures have been used to treat children's nervous habits. These are generally combined into packages. Positive reinforcement, in the form of storytelling, token delivery, or simply attention contingent on intervals during which the behavior has been omitted, is one method that is frequently applied (Allen & Harris, 1966; Knight & McKenzie, 1974). Children have been given pennies (Lowitz & Suib, 1978) or food as reinforcers following intervals during which thumb sucking (Hughes, Hughes, & Dial, 1979) and scratching (Allen & Harris, 1966) were absent. Attention is systematically eliminated when it has been judged to have contributed to the maintenance of the nervous habit. This approach has been used to treat insomnia (Anderson, 1979) and multiple tics (Schulman, 1974). Another procedure has been labeled *vicarious learning*. The client observes as another child receives reinforcement for alternative acceptable behaviors. For example, Sanchez (1979) reported the case of a child who pulled her hair habitually. It was arranged that the mother would pay attention to a sibling's proper hair care, in the presence of the client.

Time-out is another procedure that has been used to reduce various nervous habits. Loss of free play time contingent on a tic response (Varni, Boyd, & Cataldo, 1978), loss of TV time for thumb sucking (Ross, 1975), and restriction to the child's room for hair pulling (Sanchez, 1979) are among the time-out procedures that have been successfully applied. Ross (1975) used access to TV as a contingency in a program that involved two sisters in an attempt to reduce their brother's thumb sucking. When the child was observed sucking his thumb, the TV was turned off for a period of time, thus both the child and his siblings were denied access to the TV. The siblings were also taught how to cue non-thumb-sucking.

Awareness training is a procedure that is reported to be an especially useful adjunct to modification programs designed to treat nervous habits (Azrin & Nunn, 1973). Awareness training consists of teaching clients to note when they are engaging in the habit. Various techniques have been used to teach clients to become more aware of their habitual responses: using a mirror to observe tic responses (Varni *et al.*, 1978); recording nail-biting and stuttering episodes (Azrin & Nunn, 1974, 1976); the therapist's demonstrating the behavior, such as barking and swearing by a child with Gilles de la Tourette's syndrome, and feedback to and rehearsal by the client (Hutzell, Platzek, & Logue, 1974). Lassen and Fluet (1978) reported using a glove during sleep to control thumb sucking. This probably assisted the child to be more aware of placing the thumb in her mouth. Vaseline was applied to a client's eyelids to draw attention to the fact that she was touching her lashes, and jangly bracelets and perfumed fingers cued awareness for arm and finger movements (McLaughlin & Nay, 1975). Naturally, the reduction in the rate of the response and increases in desirable alternatives must also be reinforced if the effect is to endure.

Relaxation training is another procedural component of many programs designed to treat nervous habits. The Azrin and Nunn habit-reversal program (1974, 1976) follows awareness training with training in relaxation. Sleep disturbances, such as insomnia (Anderson, 1979), have also been treated with relaxation training. In the latter study, although training was conducted in the therapist's office, the client was able to transfer its application to the home. Relaxation training may be facilitated by the use of audiotapes (Weil & Goldfried, 1973). The tape prompts may then be gradually faded by using a progression of shorter, more simplified tapes, eventually withdrawing them completely. Relaxation training was combined with covert reinforcement and response-cost procedures in treating a client's hair pulling in a study reported by McLaughlin and Nay (1975). For covert reinforcement, the client was instructed to fol-low successful efforts to avoid hair pulling by imagining the desirable outcomes that accompany having a full head of hair. For the response-cost, the client was instructed to interrupt her ongoing activities, inspect her scalp in the bathroom mirror, and log the behavior in detail.

Relaxation is also an integral part of the systematic desensitization procedure (Wolpe, 1974). In this procedure, the client learns to relax in the presence of a hierarchy of successively more anxiety-producing situations. In one report (Bornstein & Rychtarik, 1978), systematic desensitization was used to treat hair pulling. The hierarchy consisted of an arrangement of anxiety-producing situations associated with the habit.

Programs designed to reduce nervous habits may involve training the client directly in the clinic, as in the 2-hr intensive session used by Azrin and Nunn (1973, 1974), or the parents may be instructed to carry out specific procedures or may be trained to conduct a program either in the laboratory (Lowitz & Suib, 1978) or at home (Knight & McKenzie, 1974). Successful transfer may thus become an issue, as treatment shifts from the therapist to the patient or to the parents, or from one setting and time to another. The impressive results reported by Azrin and Nunn (e.g., 1974) and others are probably a function of directly training the client in a set of habit reversal skills that could readily be transferred outside the clinic. Alternatively, training parents directly in the home with provision for reliability of measurement as in Hughes *et al.* (1979) is another promising approach.

Issues. There are several methodological issues that are especially pertinent to the modification of nervous habits. One is that most of the reported studies have been conducted with only one subject. (Exceptions have included those of Azrin and Nunn; 1974, 1976, and Knight and McKenzie, 1974. In these studies, multiple replications added support to an otherwise limited A-B design.) Also, since many of the programs involve procedures to be implemented at home, assessing for reliability becomes difficult. In that regard, it is perhaps fortunate that many nervous habits leave their own records. For example, hair pulling may leave bald spots; thumb sucking, raw skin, and the results of nail biting are apparent. In fact, before-and-after photographs are used to validate procedural effectiveness in the Azrin and Nunn studies of nail biting. Such enduring outcomes may thus mitigate the problem of validity and reliability of recording.

Many of the procedures designed to treat nervous habits include features that must be managed by clients, such as self-recording, relaxation, and covert procedures. Therefore, the success of those programs often depends on the client's ability and willingness to follow instructions. The client's learning history in regard to self-management may thus prove very critical for success. Fortunately, motivation to follow through presents less of a hindrance in this as opposed to other problem areas, because the habit is often a source of embarrassment or stress to the client. Even young children have successfully followed through with monitoring and other self-control procedures (Azrin & Nunn, 1974; Varni *et al.*, 1978; Weil & Goldfried, 1973). But the very fact that self-management operations are often a major feature of programs for treating nervous habits also creates some confusion. It is difficult to identify exactly which features are functionally related to the change. For example, self-recording probably serves several functions: besides providing data on progress, it may heighten awareness and serve as a source of positive or negative feedback. These factors, in turn, may affect covert behaviors, which unless orally reported, remain obscure and inaccessible to functional analysis.

Treating Fears. Aside from school phobia, discussed below, childhood fears have been given relatively scant attention by researchers employing behavioral approaches. In a recent review of the literature, Graziano, DeGiovanni, and Garcia (1979) pointed out that research on childhood fears has almost exclusively involved mild to moderate fears as opposed to severe fears in which a significant disruption of daily routines is evident. In those studies in which fear reduction is the objective, three treatment approaches predominate: modeling (e.g., Bandura & Menlove, 1968), systematic desensitization plus contingency management packages (e.g., Mann, 1972), and cognitive or verbal-mediation approaches (e.g., Kanfer, Karoly, & Newman, 1975). In addition to being confined largely to fears that are not

debilitating, Graziano and his colleagues pointed out that the range of fears treated has been narrow. The bulk of the controlled studies, they found, have consisted of problems in medical and dental fears ($n = 9$), animal fears ($n = 7$), social interaction fears ($n = 5$), and fear of the dark ($n = 3$).

Of the major treatment approaches, modeling has provided by far the most extensive and consistently effective procedural option. The basic modeling paradigm consists of observation by the subject of a model approaching the feared stimuli, followed by attempts by the subject to approach the feared stimuli. Beneficial outcomes have been demonstrated by using live models (Bandura, Grusec, & Menlove, 1967) or symbolic models (e.g., via videotapes in Bandura & Menlove, 1968); by using single (Ritter, 1968) or multiple models (Bandura & Menlove, 1968); and by using modeling exclusively or in combination with a gradual active involvement with the models and the feared stimuli (Lewis, 1974; Murphy & Bootzin, 1973). Models have approached a single feared stimulus (Kornhaber & Schroeder, 1975) and multiple feared stimuli (Bandura & Menlove, 1968) introduced in a graduated sequence. Some evidence suggests that the similarity between the model and the subject may enhance fear reduction (Kornhaber & Schroeder, 1975). To be effective, symbolic modeling may require multiple trials, multiple models, and varied fear stimuli (see Bandura & Menlove, 1968), but symbolic modeling has important implications for prevention as well as treatment. Melamed and Siegel (1975) and Melamed, Yurchison, Fleece, Hutcherson, and Hawes (1978) used film models to reduce anxiety among children scheduled for surgical and dental procedures. Interestingly, it has been observed that models who themselves initially show fear when approaching the feared stimulus are more effective than models who exhibit no fear (see Meichenbaum, 1971; Rachman, 1972). Modeling has only infrequently been used to treat fears involving social stimuli. In one such study (O'Connor, 1969), nursery-school children exposed to social models successfully overcame their social withdrawal.

While Graziano *et al.*, (1979) suggested that desensitization and contingency management approaches have yet to demonstrate their effectiveness, there is some evidence that these approaches hold promise. In one study, a 4-year-old child had a fear of water. The treatment included *in vivo* modeling of the desensitization hierarchy by a paraprofessional and, later, the parent. As the child began to imitate, physical affection, praise, and edibles were provided contingently as he progressed through a 12-step hierarchy (Pomerantz, Peterson, Marholin, & Stern, 1977). The child reached the final step in the hierarchy by the eighth day of treatment.

In another study employing contingency management, Waye (1979) treated a child with a fear that her thumbs were shrinking by arranging for her parents to attend to her when she played appropriately. A cardboard tracing of the thumb was also presented in response to complaints of shrinking, to provide a realistic form of visual feedback and to dispel the fearful response.

Cognitive approaches are the least commonly reported in the treatment of children's fears. Recently, Graziano, Mooney, Huber, and Ignasiak (1979) described a verbal mediation technique combined with relaxation, self-monitoring, and the delivery of exchangeable tokens for "bravery." Children with severe fears of the dark were taught exercises in which they used self-directed statements of competence and courage. With some parental assistance in structuring times for the exercises, the children were able to reduce the frequency and the intensity of their fearful responses.

In summary, a variety of children's fears and nervous habits have been effectively modified. Treatment may be conducted directly by therapists, or the parents or the children themselves may, with therapeutic supervision, implement the package of procedures. Methodological problems include insufficient replications, the need for more reliable and valid measures, and the difficulty of separating the critical components of the program.

Noncompliance

Noncompliance is one of the behavior problems that parents cite most frequently (e.g., Karoly & Rosenthal, 1977; Patterson & Reid, 1973; Forehand, 1977). The child's response may consist of simply not performing the re-

quested behavior, doing it too slowly, stating a refusal to comply, promising to do it later but not following through on the commitment, engaging in a competing response, and others. Children might respond differentially to parental requests as a function of the way in which the request is given. For instance, a request posed in a tentative tone may occasion quite a different response than one stated firmly and decisively. Sometimes parents alter their requests, communicating conflicting messages, and the child is confused about which to follow. Parents may ask the impossible of their children at times. For instance, the child may not be capable of doing what is asked. There are apparently other conditions that evoke noncompliance as well.

Treatment Procedures. A consideration of the conditions that may control noncompliance is important if treatment strategies are to be planned. Suppose the requested behavior is part of the child's repertoire. Then, a modification of the consequences, such as reinforcing compliance and/or punishing noncompliance, or placing it on extinction, may be the most appropriate procedure. In a study by Schutte and Hopkins (1970), when the child followed instructions, attention by the teacher led to a major increase in instruction following. In a case reported by Fjellstedt and Sulzer-Azaroff (1973), the subject had been placed in a special class for emotionally disturbed children. Systematically decreasing latencies—the interval between the instructions and the response—led to a reinforcement with tokens. Improvement was sufficient to permit the child to return to a regular class. A case study reported by Wiltz and Gordon (1974) described a particularly difficult problem. A 9-year-old child was facing institutionalization for his extremely disturbing and often bizarre behaviors, among which was a very low rate of complying with parental instructions. Using an experimental residential apartment as the training site, the parents were successfully taught to combine points exchangeable for toys for compliance, and time-out for noncompliance or other inappropriate behaviors. A similar case reported by Ayllon, Garber, and Allison (1977) yielded comparable outcomes.

In some cases, low compliance rates are a function of particular antecedent conditions, such as the way in which the request is delivered. Then, the treatment of choice would be a modification in the manner of making the request. Many parent-training programs include portions that involve methods of effectively delivering instructions to children (e.g., Patterson, Cobb, & Ray, 1973). In one study (Peed, Roberts, & Forehand, 1977), positive treatment effects were observed in the home when the parents were instructed to give clear commands. They were also asked to avoid interrupting the children and to resist the temptation to carry out the requests themselves. In a study of four children who failed to reduce their oppositional behavior under a social-play-contracting contingency, Wahler and Fox (1980) altered the contract to a solitary-play-plus-time-out contingency, with dramatic improvement.

Forehand (1977) has extensively surveyed a series of outcome studies of behavioral treatments of noncompliance. The survey analyzed the results of studies conducted and assessed in the clinic, studies conducted in the clinic and assessed in both the clinic and the home, and those conducted and measured in the home. Studies in the laboratory have permitted the identification of some variables that control noncompliance. Among these are the consequences of responding, such as reinforcement for compliance or time-out for noncompliance (e.g., Forehand & King, 1974). But the generality of conclusions may be limited when findings have been isolated within the laboratory only. In contrast, in-home observations do permit an assessment of the transfer of treatment effects to the natural setting. Mixed results have been found when parents are trained in the clinic and assessment takes place in the home. Sometimes, as in Peed *et al.* (1977) and Reisinger and Ora (1977), generality into the home is demonstrated. In the latter case, parents were taught in a clinic setting to attend to their toddler's cooperative behavior and to withhold their attention when the child failed to follow instructions. The measures of change in the clinic resembled changes measured via live and taped observations. At other times, observations in the home show inconsistent transfer. An example is the study by Bizer, Sulzer-Azaroff, and Fredrickson (1978). Four pairs of children and their parents were taught to problem-solve by

using Blechman's (1974) family contract game. Noncompliance was one of the behaviors addressed. In some instances, measures from home observations closely matched those found in the laboratory. In others, there was no apparent match between laboratory and home problem-solving.

According to Forehand (1977), "Comparing across treatment and assessment settings, one would conclude that decreases in noncompliance in the home can best be affected by training parents in the home" (p. 141). His conclusion is supported by a set of research studies conducted by Wahler (1969b, 1975) and others. Patterson's (1976) research also supports that conclusion. Such studies have shown that when parents were trained in the home to modify their child's noncompliance, the changes tended to endure in that setting.

As in other problem areas, research on noncompliance has begun assessing collateral effects. In addition to examining transfer from the clinic to the home, several studies have examined the generality of effects from the training setting to the school or the application by parents across siblings. Wahler (1975) measured a child's noncompliance at home and in school. While the rate of noncompliance was reduced at home, a similar reduction did not take place in the school. In fact, at school, where it was not directly treated, it increased. An earlier study by Wahler (1969b) had shown that introducing treatment with the teacher subsequent to a home intervention did result in reducing noncompliance at school. Several experiments directly assessed the question of whether treatment would transfer from the treated to the untreated sibling (Arnold, Levine, & Patterson, 1975; Lavigueur, Peterson, Sheese, & Peterson, 1973; Humphreys, Forehand, McMahon, & Roberts, 1978). For example, Humphreys *et al.* (1978) arranged to have target children treated in the clinic, and both the parents' and the untreated siblings' behaviors were observed in the home. They found that the parents did transfer their newly acquired techniques to effectively handling the noncompliance of untreated siblings. Lavigueur *et al.* (1973) found similar results.

Issues. Any discussion of modifying children's noncompliance would be incomplete without some consideration of a prime philosophical issue: Is it ethically defensible to train compliance? Studies on obedience, such as those by Milgram (e.g., 1963), have raised some fundamental concern in that regard. (See Staub, 1978, Chapter 4, for an extensive discussion on this topic.) Training children to follow any and all instructions is indeed a questionable practice, which may have frightening results. Rather, children need to be taught to discriminate reasonable instructions from those that if followed would damage or harm themselves and others.

Within the field of behavior modification, targeting behaviors designed to teach children to be still, quiet, and docile has been questioned by Winett and Winkler (1972). Those authors have argued that the focus should be on behaviors that are to the advantage of the children themselves rather than to the teachers and other care givers. Certainly, there should be at least a reasonable balance between the two. Referring specifically to the control exerted by parents over their children's behavior, Peterson (1976) questioned whether parents might be overcontrolling their children. He dismissed arguments such as the natural reciprocity of control between children and parents by asserting that even though all members in a family may exert an influence on one another, the person in primary control is the one with the larger number of skills and responses, and thus with the broadest array of alternatives to bring to bear to the situation. Interpersonal power is based on the reinforcers, punishers, and other stimuli that one can manage over the behavior of the other. Overcontrol may exist when the distribution of contingency control is one-sided.

From the opposite perspective, one could provide a convincing argument for the importance of teaching children to comply with reasonable instructions. (In fact, the U.S. Supreme Court traditionally supports the family's ultimate right, if not responsibility, to manage their children.)

Few would argue with the need to require compliance with treatment regimens for such life-threatening behavior problems as anorexia or rumination, or with diets prescribed for children with kidney failure. A parent who failed to teach a child to follow the instruction to stop at a busy street corner or when reaching for poisonous or hazardous materials would surely be labeled negligent. Compliance with instructions to behave according to certain social mores permits children to attain reinforcement from the social setting as well as preventing their interference with others' attainment of reinforcement. There would probably be general agreement that compliance with instructions would be a justifiable goal for a child who refuses to stop running and screaming, throwing objects about, and generally interfering with the well-being of others.

When one begins to deal with behaviors in the gray area—for example, when it is unclear that compliance will further the well-being of the child or help avoid danger or disruption—the issue becomes more clouded. How important is it to teach a young man to rise when a woman enters a room? Is it essential that a child comply with instructions to button her coat or to turn in only perfect papers, or to sit with her hands folded, or to be quiet in class? Do the required behaviors reflect an unduly restrictive value system?

Also, other factors need to be considered: Is compliance being taught for the convenience of adults, and might it work eventually to the child's and the parents' disadvantage? A child who is never permitted to make decisions may remain continually dependent. How mature is the child? Is the child capable of entering into negotiation? Are the requisite negotiating and alternative skills part of the child's repertoire? Can they be taught? What are the "natural" baselines of child compliance under the given circumstances? Regarding the latter question, research data are providing a clearer picture of natural compliance rates and the factors that may influence them. Often these data are obtained from an analysis of preintervention baselines; at other times, they are discovered via naturalistic obervations in the clinic or the home. Forehand, King, and Yoder (1975) considered normative data in interpreting the results of a study in which they compared the compliance rates of clinical and nonclinical samples of children. They cited findings from their own research program (e.g., Forehand & King, 1974) and from the work of others (Johnson & Lobitz, 1974). Forehand *et al.* (1975) found that the rates of compliance by nonclinical children in the sample was about 62%, similar to that found by Johnson and Lobitz (1974). The clinical children's compliance rate of about 41% in Forehand *et al.* (1975) was similar to that found during the preintervention baseline phase of a treatment program for problem children in Forehand and King's study.

Forehand (1977) has summarized the current research on compliance norms, identifying those parameters that appear to control their rates: clinical versus nonclinical population, number and type of parental commands, consequences of noncompliance, other presenting problems, age, socioeconomic status, and sex. (Interestingly, in contrast with the other factors, there are no differences in rates of compliance between boys and girls, nor is there a difference when commands are delivered by the mother or by the father.)

Reference to normative information on compliance rates has been used to guide some designers of therapeutic interventions. Patterson (1976) and Eyberg and Johnson (1974) are among several who have utilized such information in analyzing their program outcomes. Forehand's (1977) citation of a range of rates of compliance to parental commands from 60% to 80% for nonclinical samples provides a rough basis for deciding if compliance rates are inadequate or excessive.

Peterson (1976) discussed several tactics for avoiding overcontrol by parents. Citing Hively and Duncan (1972), he endorsed their conviction that parents and children should mutually select the behaviors to be changed and that the child should be involved in recording and in negotiating motivational circumstances to bring about the change. Peterson also suggested that the setting conditions may be altered to avoid overcontrol: the physical environment might be altered, as in removing poisons from access. Natural consequences might be allowed to take over control, for example, letting the child learn to button her coat because she will get cold if she does not. Parents may be counseled against the use of overcontrol. Children may be taught techniques for managing the behavior of others and their own behavior. Children may set their own performance standards; administer their own reinforcers to themselves; operate self-government systems; and participate in self-re-

porting, evaluation, and recording. (See also the section on self-control elsewhere in this chapter.) Hopefully, such suggestions will be heeded by parents and those who provide them consultation.

Problems in Everyday Family Living

Often, no single behavior is the cause of family conflict. Rather, various behaviors combine to constitute a source of irritation among family members: whining, complaining, failing to perform assigned chores, or else doing them but not satisfactorily, dawdling, lateness, interrupting, demanding attention and unnecessary assistance, creating clutter, standing , climbing, kicking and screaming in the car, and so on. Such individual behaviors may not occur frequently enough to merit the designation "problem behavior," but combined, they can create difficulty within a family.

Some of these nuisance behaviors are targeted for change as components of other treatment programs (e.g., noncompliance; Forehand, 1977). Some of the irritating verbal behaviors, such as interrupting, are approached in some of the social (e.g., Bornstein, Bellack, & Hersen, 1977) or conversational skills programs (Lysaght & Burchard, 1975) discussed below. But an alternative method is to identify each of the behaviors in the cluster, define them operationally, and then manage contingencies to increase or decrease their rates.

The completion of household chores and the reduction of noxious social behaviors were targeted for change in a study by Christophersen, Arnold, Hill, and Quilitch (1972). Two different families were involved as subjects. In each case, specific behaviors were identified, and the parents collected baseline data on the rates of the behaviors. Occasionally, the experimenters made unannounced visits to the home to demonstrate the reliability of the measurement system. Using a multiple-baseline design, the authors demonstrated that the point system (a combination of points exchangeable for privileges and fines) effectively increased chore completion and decreased bickering, whining, and teasing. Christophersen (1977) found that not only standing and climbing but also kicking and screaming were dramatically reduced when young children were restrained in car seats.

Treating Sibling Conflict. Conflict among siblings has been reported as one of the more frequent behavior problems encountered in the home. Several procedures have been attempted to reduce that problem, including a combination of time-out for conflict and reinforcement for cooperative play (O'Leary, O'Leary, & Becker, 1967) and time-out alone (Allison & Allison, 1971).

Attempting to utilize positive rather than punitive contingencies, Leitenberg, Burchard, Burchard, Fuller, and Lysaght (1977) compared two positive reductive procedures: differential reinforcement of other behavior (DRO, also called *omission training*) and the reinforcement of alternative behaviors (Alt-R), in this case appropriate interactions.

The interventions were implemented in the homes of six families, and data were collected by the mothers and via direct or taped observations by the experimenters. In the DRO condition, the children were given pennies for not engaging in conflict during designated one-minute intervals. The Alt-R condition involved presenting a penny to each of the children who engaged in appropriate interactions during one-minute intervals. Both procedures were effective in suppressing conflict, while the Alt-R condition promoted higher rates of positive interactions than the DRO procedure. The DRO procedure, requiring simply the consequation of the elapsed time period in which conflict was absent, was simpler for the mothers to employ. Thus, that is the procedure they maintained following the formal intervention phases. Since DRO would permit children to attain reinforcers by isolating themselves from one another, parents probably should be guided to utilize the Alt-R procedure, at least intermittently, so that the siblings can acquire the skills required to interact appropriately with one another.

Treating Troublesome Behavior during Shopping. Shopping is another frequently cited source of family conflict. Children who are too young to remain at home alone must accompany their parents. Research into the specific nature of the difficulties encountered during family shopping expeditions has in-

cluded reviews of parenting texts, interviews with parents and store personnel, and direct observation. (See Barnard, Christophersen, & Wolf, 1977, and Clark, Greene, Macrae, McNees, Davis, & Risley, 1977, for summaries of that research.) The child behaviors that have been identified as particularly troublesome are running around the store and otherwise being out of the proximity of the parent, bumping into people and objects, touching merchandise, and distracting parents in various ways: asking questions not relevant to the activity, whining or asking for items, and other forms of aversive verbal behavior.

The two studies on shopping cited above (Barnard *et al.*, 1977, and Clark *et al.*, 1977) were directed toward the amelioration of troublesome child behaviors while shopping. Each showed that contingency management programs could lead to dramatic improvements in children's behavior. The focus of the Barnard *et al.* (1977) study was the child's proximity to the mother and the disturbance of products. Since all three subjects in the study had been functioning under token economies at home, the same procedures were then utilized in the supermarket. The mothers were instructed to present points to their sons at the rate of two to three per aisle traversed without any rule violations. Two points were to be deducted for each rule transgression. Verbal interactions between the mother and the child were tape-recorded so that their quality could be assessed, for example, whether what the mother said was positive, negative, or neutral. Findings monitored directly in the supermarket indicated that the procedures were strikingly effective, with the irritating behaviors almost completely eliminated. These improvements generally persisted over an extensive follow-up interval. Similarly, the quality of the mother's verbal interactions with the child became less negative and more positive or neutral. The evaluations by the consumers of the training package were very positive.

In a more extensive project (Clark *et al.*, 1977), a parent-advice package for family shopping trips was developed, distributed in written form, and validated. Specific rules on proximity, product disturbance, and the distraction of parents were communicated to the parents and three children in two "teaching families'' (foster-care family groupings for neglected dependent children). Using nickels as reinforcers, the parents were instructed during the first intervention to permit each child 50 cents for each shopping trip. Nickels were deducted from this amount for specific rule infractions. During that phase, the aversive child behaviors diminished substantially, but so did their positive social and educational comments. In the third phase, then, the parents were instructed to increase their rates of engaging in relevant social and educational conversation with the children, and the rates of the children's social and educational comments increased accordingly. Thus, the shopping activity became far less aversive and more reinforcing to both parents and children.

In the second phase, the written advice package was accompanied by quiz materials consisting of academic questions and multiple-choice questions about hypothetical family conversations. Also included was a shopping-list form that guided the parents to tally the nickels earned and lost and to use self-feedback checks. During this phase, the parents were directly guided by the experimenter to implement procedures according to the advice package. Initial trips were kept short: 15 min the first two times, 30 min the subsequent two. Interspersed within the first 15-min sessions were three 5-min feedback intervals in which the parents and the children checked on their adherence to the rules. Those self-check intervals were later extended to once each 10 min and ultimately to once at the end of the shopping event. The impressive improvement in the parents' implementation of the program and the children's behavior led to the last phase, an attempt to validate the revised written package as a completely independent program. The experimenter was involved only in collecting data and not in assisting in the intervention. Apparently, the written package was able to stand on its own, as the six families with which it was tested showed improvements comparable to those gained in the earlier phases. The package is currently available as a paperback book entitled *Shopping with Children* (1978)[1] and represents, along with

---

[1] Academic Therapy Publications, P.O. Box 899, San Raphael, Calif.

Azrin and Foxx's manual on toilet training (1974), one of the few extensively evaluated, specific parent-training packages available.

Home–School Relations

Events that occur in school may influence the child's behavior at home, while those at home may reflect on what the child does in school. Behavior modification has addressed some of the problems that fall within the realm of home–school relations. Examples are home-based systems of contingency management of school behaviors, methods for reducing absenteeism and for increasing the completion of homework, and the treatment of elective mutism. The first three problem areas are discussed here, while the last topic is discussed along with other social skills.

Managing School Behavior through Home-Based Contingencies. When behavior modification first began to be applied in schools, it was recognized that it would be sensible to involve parents in programs introduced to improve their children's school behavior (e.g., McKenzie, Clark, Wolf, Kothera, & Benson, 1968; Thorne, Tharp, & Wetzel, 1967). Parents control many of the important reinforcers in a young child's life and probably have the strongest investment in their child's development. Periodic progress reports have traditionally been used by schools. Thus, the progress reported could be modified and utilized as a relatively unobtrusive device. Reports have been completed by teachers daily (e.g., Bailey, Wolf, & Phillips, 1970); weekly (McKenzie, Clark, Wolf, Kothera, & Benson, 1968; Besalel-Azrin, Azrin, & Armstrong, 1977); or even following each class period (Thoresen, Thoresen, Klein, Wilbur, Becker-Haven, & Haven, 1977; Blackmore, Rich, Means, & Nally, 1976). These reports have permitted frequent reinforcement with minimal delay, two basic principles of effective reinforcement.

Barth (1979) and Atkeson and Forehand (1979) have recently presented detailed reviews of the operation of systems of home-based reinforcement of school behavior. Among the topics on which Barth has elaborated are the frequency of the report, the extent of differential feedback, parents' responses to the feedback, the use of the program by and its function for teachers, methods of enlisting parents' and teachers' involvement, types of home consequation, the use of home-based systems as an adjunct to school-based programs, the involvement of pupil personnel workers, and others. In general, parental involvement is attained via conferences (Karraker, 1972) or notes sent home (Lahey, Gendrich, Gendrich, Schnelle, Gant, & McNee, 1977). School reports are usually mailed or sent home with the child and are received by the parents, who are instructed to deliver prespecified consequences. The consequences are almost uniformly positive other than the simple withholding of unearned reinforcers. Typical home consequences are usually privileges, such as permission to go out on a date or to use the phone (Thorne *et al.*, 1967) or to go backpacking (Blackmore *et al.*, 1976), or material rewards such as allowances (McKenzie *et al.*, 1968).

Usually, the initial schedule of reporting is very frequent, for example, each day. As the targeted behaviors improve, the frequency of reporting is gradually faded, until it eventually begins to resemble the regular school system's reporting schedule, such as a six-week report-card interval. In some cases (e.g., Thoresen *et al.*, 1977), the students themselves gradually take over the responsibility of rating their own behavior. (Procedures for the fading of reinforcement in home reporting systems are detailed in a manual by Schumaker, Hovell, and Sherman, 1977. General procedures for promoting maintenance via the fading of reinforcement frequency are included in Sulzer Azaroff and Mayer, 1977, Unit 24.)

Home-based reinforcement systems have been used successfully to modify a variety of school behaviors, from truancy (Thorne *et al.*, 1967) and school phobia (MacDonald, Gallimore, & MacDonald, 1970) to disruption (Hawkins, Sluyter, & Smith, 1972; Ayllon, Garber, & Pisor, 1975); rule following (Besalel-Azrin *et al.*, 1977); aggression (O'Leary & Kent, 1974; Budd & Leibowitz, 1976); quality and completion of work in school (Schumaker *et al.*, 1977; McKenzie *et al.*, 1968) or at home (Dougherty & Dougherty, 1977); and many others. According to Atkeson and Forehand (1979), there have been methodological

flaws in many of the studies, particularly the omission of multiple outcome measures and follow-up data. Nevertheless, their evaluation of 21 studies of home-based reinforcement indicated that *all* reported that the system was effective.

Parents may participate in *school-based* reinforcement systems, as well as carrying out reinforcement procedures in the home. One way this might be accomplished is through their contribution of reinforcing materials or events. In an unpublished study, Whitley and Sulzer (1970) asked the parents to provide a reward for their son's school performance. The child earned gift certificates for bicycle parts for accomplishing specified criterion levels, until the whole bike was assembled. Parents may also provide reinforcing activities directly, as in the case of one of the present author's school programs (Sulzer, Hunt, Ashby Koniarski, & Krams, 1971). Parents brought and showed films, gave talks, presented musical activities in school, and accompanied the class on trips and outings, all of which activities served as backup reinforcers for tokens earned by the students for academic performance.

Mentioned in the reports of various behavior modification studies are incidents suggesting that the relationship between the school and the family has improved along with the targeted behavior. Communication presumably becomes more regular and attitudes more positive.

It stands to reason that if a program focuses on the improvement of positive, adaptive behaviors, such behaviors will be closely scrutinized by teachers and parents. Just the heightened awareness of the occurrence of those behaviors may thus serve to cue the parents and the teachers to deliver praise or to pay more attention when the behavior is observed. As with other effectively programmed reinforcement systems, parents, teachers, and, in particular, students should thus find their relationships becoming increasingly positive. Since punishment and extinction are reduced, their side effects, such as aggression and withdrawal, should lessen, along with rates of vandalism and truancy. (See Mayer & Butterworth, 1979.) Research on such strategies as home-based reinforcement systems (and systems that involve parents in school reinforcement activities) should include the gathering of evidence of any such collateral effects.

Failing to Attend School. Irregular attendance can become a problem. When a child refuses to attend school at all, the behavior pattern may be considered pathological and may be assigned the label *school phobia*. Regardless of the label, when children fail to attend school regularly, it is assumed that their learning suffers. The family is often inconvenienced and may be concerned about violation of compulsory attendance laws.

Several studies have dealt with school attendance (e.g., Ayllon, Smith, & Rogers, 1970; Copeland, Brown, Axelrod, & Hall, 1972; Hersen, 1970; Barber & Kagey, 1977). Often, the parents are involved. An illustrative example is the study by Copeland *et al.* (1972). The principal played an active role, calling the child's parents and praising them for their child's attendance. Increases in attendance rates resulted.

Sometimes, the process of traveling to school is the link in the chain that influences school attendance. Some children are reluctant to ride a school bus, and if other transportation is unavailable, obviously the child does not reach school. A case study reported by Luiselli (1978) described the treatment of an autistic child who exhibited severe emotional behavior when he was asked to board the school bus. The procedure followed was essentially "backward chaining." The first training step was initiated on the school bus, which was at the school and parked outside. With the mother on the bus and the therapist to assist, the child successfully boarded the bus, with no major emotional distress. Gradually, in small steps, the program moved backward. The child spent more and more time on the bus, with the mother and the therapist eventually fading out their presence.

Completing Homework. Another way that parents have been traditionally involved in their child's education has been in the supervision or tutoring of their child's homework. Several studies have addressed this problem. For instance, Broden, Beasley, and Hall (1978) showed how a child's spelling performance in school improved as a function of home tutoring by the mother. Hunt and Sulzer-Azaroff (1974) reported a study in which severely handicapped children were assigned, as a homework exercise, a prewriting activity that required parental supervision. Although all parents saw to it that the homework was attempted on some occasions, only when graphic feedback and notes acknowledging the parents' help were delivered regularly to the parents was the homework consistently returned to the teacher.

A third example (Pollack, Sulzer-Azaroff, & Williams, 1972) involved a predelinquent high-school boy who was progressing poorly. Completion of homework in two subjects, arithmetic and spelling (areas of particular difficulty), was targeted for modification. When the boy earned points exchangeable for on-the-job training in auto mechanics contingent on completing his homework, the rate increased as a function of the schedules of reinforcement employed.

Social Isolation

The time that severe social isolation becomes manifest is when the child is placed in a group situation, as in school or in a day-care setting. Rarely does the problem occur at home. As a result, the literature on that topic generally reports treatment within the out-of-the-home setting (e.g., Hart, Reynolds, Baer, Brawley, & Harris, 1968; O'Conner, 1969; Ragland, Kerr, & Strain, 1978; Strain, Shores, & Timm, 1977).

Treatment Procedures. Among the procedures that have been found to facilitate social interactions have been teacher attention (Hart *et al.*, 1968); approaches by confederate peers (Ragland *et al.*, 1978; Strain *et al.*, 1977); "symbolic modeling" in the form of a film in which social consequences are the result of interactions (O'Conner, 1969); and reinforcement of peers for interacting with the child (Kandel, Ayllon, & Rosenbaum, 1977).

Kandel *et al.* (1977) worked with a 4-year-old boy with a complexity of behavioral problems, including talking only to himself and to no one else. Fifteen children were selected as social stimuli, according to a "flooding paradigm," during which the other children received reinforcement for playing with the target child. There were dramatic and enduring changes. Self-talk decreased, and communication with others increased dramatically. A second case involved a 7-year-old autistic child. A similar flooding approach with seven children serving as social stimuli resulted in strong resistance by the subject and had to be terminated in favor of interaction with only two children. Interaction levels were shown to increase substantially from the baseline level of zero. In order to validate the criterion levels of interaction achieved with these children, the authors conducted naturalistic observations of "normal" children and demonstrated that the experimental subjects were within 10% of mean normal interaction levels. Collateral behaviors previously described as bizarre were noted to decrease as the interaction levels increased.

Elective Mutism

Occasionally, the literature has reported cases in which children communicate effectively and appropriately at home but fail to speak in school or sometimes anywhere outside the home (Reid, Hawkins, Keutzer, McNeal, Phelps, Reid, & Mees, 1967). The child is not mute, since normal speech is part of the repertoire, but exhibits mutism in school, where normal verbal behavior is critical for academic and social development. This pattern is called *elective* or *selective mutism*.[2]

Treatment Procedures. Generally, elective mutism is analyzed as a problem in stimulus control. Wulbert, Nyman, Snow, and Owen (1973), Richards and Hansen (1978), and Sanok and Streifel (1979) are among those who have assumed that there are some stimuli that occasion "normal" speaking and some that fail to occasion (or that "inhibit") it. Apparently, stimuli at home are discriminative for speaking; those at school exert the opposite influence. If that is the case, stimulus fading should solve the problem. The challenge is to identify those critical stimulus dimensions that control

both classes of behavior. The stimuli that evoke speaking are employed exclusively during the initial stages. Gradually, these are faded out, while those that previously occasioned nonresponding are faded in. Combined with the fading steps are strong reinforcing (and occasionally aversive) consequences for progress or lack of progress.

Emma, a 6-year-old girl, had not spoken in Sunday school or preschool for a period of 3 years. Wulbert *et al.* (1973) selected experimenters, presumably adults who were strangers to her, as the "stimuli" to be faded in as substitutes for those adults (initially the mother, later other adults) who reliably occasioned verbal responding. Following compliance with requests to perform motor and verbal tasks, Emma was given praise and candy. Later, time-out for noncompliance was added to the procedure. Fading was accomplished over approximately 25 steps, starting with the mother and Emma alone and ending with the experimenter and Emma alone. Although during the early stages of treatment, hundreds of trials were required for the verbal responses to occur in the presence of new experimenters, as treatment progressed fewer and fewer trials were required. Eventually, strangers began to occasion verbal responses just as Emma's mother had.

The success of the Wulbert *et al.* (1973) study probably encouraged others to attempt similar approaches. An illustrative case study, reported by Conrad, Delk, and Williams (1974), involved an 11-year-old American Indian girl who lived on a reservation. Since she had been observed to speak with her family and friends, cultural characteristics were one dimension included in the fading steps. Candy, grooming aids, and other material rewards were provided as a consequence of the girl's giving oral answers to flash card questions. An indigenous American Indian mental-health worker was faded into the situation on the initial day of training. As the training sessions progressed, the mother absented herself, and the teacher and classmates were faded in. The setting was also gradually changed: from the home, to the clinic, to, eventually, the classroom. A one-year follow-up indicated that the girl continued to answer questions in school but did not speak

---

[2] Since both these terms suggest "volition," preferable terms might be "discriminated" or "differential mutism," to reflect the control by discriminative stimuli.

spontaneously (probably because she had not received training in spontaneous speech).

Several stimulus-and-response dimensions were systematically varied in another case study, reported by Richards and Hansen (1978). The setting shifted from the home, to the school route, to the school playground, and ultimately to the classroom. The number of children progressed from none to: a close friend, a group, and finally the entire class. Response requirements involved stepwise increases in the volume and length of utterance: from a whisper to normal volume, from a single-word response ultimately to spontaneous speech. Perhaps it was the inclusion of several carefully programmed stimulus-and-response dimensions that accounted for the durability of the modified behavior over a 5-year follow-up period.

Several other studies have used similar approaches (e.g., Ayllon & Kelly, 1974; Sanok & Streifel, 1979). Ayllon and Kelly (1974) used shaping procedures to restore a retarded child's speech outside the classroom and later in the classroom, within a single four-hour session. The results were maintained over a one-year follow-up. Sanok and Streifel (1979) varied response requirements across five categories, shifted training settings, and introduced new adults into the training site. Their procedures included using pennies and praise as reinforcers for correct responses, plus response-cost (removal of pennies for inappropriate responding) and corrective feedback. Once the training criteria were achieved, praise and corrective feedback alone were substituted for the more contrived contingencies. A 10-month follow-up demonstrated the durability of the effect.

Bauermeister and Jemail (1975) reported the case of an electively mute child who had returned to Puerto Rico from the mainland United States. Response requirements were varied across two settings: homeroom and English class. Gold stars earned for meeting daily requirements were brought home. When he accumulated a sufficient number, he earned a bicycle.

In general, then, research has demonstrated that, as with other forms of language, children's oral communication may be modified or extended outside the home via operant techniques. The next section discusses social skills that enhance the amount of reinforcement that children receive.

Recruiting Reinforcement

When children use effective social skills, they are more likely to receive reinforcement from members of their social environment. There is an alternative method for attaining such reinforcers, that is, for the child to influence directly the behavior of the adults and the other children in his or her environment who control valuable sources of reinforcement. Contractual arrangements between children and parents often involve the parents' expression of satisfaction with the child's performance (Dardig & Heward, 1976). The child may identify the nature of the response to be required of the parent, just as the parent requires specific criteria in the child's behavior: "Whenever possible, let a child participate in choosing a reward. Let him know what is required to earn it, and discuss what you each consider reasonable. Participation will give children an added interest in and commitment to completing their part of the bargain. And that helps both of you" (Graubard, 1977, p. 19).

Such advice is frequently found in behavior modification texts for parents or other service personnel.

Treatment Procedures. Other than such general advice, it does not appear that children have been specifically involved in programs designed to teach them to recruit parental reinforcement at home. Again, studies conducted outside the home may have direct relevance. Several programs have involved teaching children to attain more reinforcement from adults. Graubard, Rosenberg, and Miller (1971) specifically taught schoolchildren methods for attaining reinforcement from their teachers. The methods resembled the types of interventions that teachers are instructed to use when attempting to reinforce their students' behaviors. Another method, suggested by the results of a study by Sherman and Cormier (1974), is to find the means to assist students to improve in their school performance. Sherman and Cormier found that when students' behavior became more appropriate, teachers began to increase their rates of praising.

One more alternative method for teaching children to enhance the reinforcement they receive is to teach them directly to cue praise from adults, as in a study by Seymour and Stokes (1976). Delinquent girls were directly instructed in methods for cuing praise from the staff of the institution in which they resided. The generality of that finding was tested by Stokes, Fowler, and Baer (1978), who replicated the procedures with preschool children. In a series of two experiments, they taught normal preschoolers to elicit praise for correct academic production. Then, several "deviant" children were taught to do the same. In the first experiment, the evidence showed that not only did the children learn how to elicit the praise effectively, but the praise, in turn, operated reciprocally to increase their rates of correct academic performance. The authors stressed the point that if such procedures are to be used, it is essential that the children learn accurately to assess their own performance and that they solicit praise only when deserving. Nor should they solicit it too often, as that might be a nuisance to teachers.

Positive Social Behavior

As we have noted in our historical recounting of the evolution of behavior modification applied to children's problems in the home, noxious or distressing social behaviors have tended to be frequently targeted for change. Frequently, reductive procedures, such as time-out (Forehand, 1977) or extinction (Williams, 1959), have been the primary method of treatment. Often the reductive procedures are paired with procedures designed to reinforce alternative behaviors, judged acceptable by parents and others (e.g., Patterson & Reid, 1973).

Another strategy is to focus on positive social behavior, either primarily or exclusively, and to operate under the assumption that positive and noxious social behaviors are incompatible with one another. Thus, as the former increase, the latter decrease. That such strategies may prove effective has been demonstrated in several instances (e.g., Sulzer *et al.*, 1971). Consider the problem of "selfishness."

Research has identified some of the critical variables that affect children's learning to help, share, and donate (see Staub, 1978), and some of these may be applied to modify a child's behavior.

Another advantage of focusing on the positive is that productive or prosocial behavior, such as helping, smiling, or complimenting, are usually reinforcing to others. Thus, increases in the rates of such behaviors may enrich the relationships between children and others in their lives.

As with other classes of behavior, prosocial behaviors have been shown to be modifiable through operant conditioning. Sharing and donating have been modified in laboratories (Azrin & Lindsley, 1956; Gelfand, Hartmann, Cromer, Smith, & Page, 1975; Hake & Vukelich, 1972; Hartmann, Gelfand, Smith, Paul, Cromer, Page, & Lebenta, 1976) and in the nursery-school settings (Rogers-Warren, & Baer, 1976; Serbin, Tonick, & Sternglanz, 1977); with schizophrenic children (Hingtgen, Sanders, & DeMyer, 1965); with hearing-impaired children (Barton & Ascione, 1979); and with severely retarded children (Whitman, Mercurio, & Caponigri, 1970). Retarded clients' rates of smiling were increased through social reinforcement (Hopkins, 1968). Children with social-emotional problems increased their rates of sharing, smiling, positive physical contact, and verbal complimenting when instructed via modeling, instructions, and verbal praise (Cooke & Apolloni, 1976).

Self-instruction has been used frequently to teach children to manage their social behaviors (see Karoly, 1977). As Karoly concluded, self-control training has been conducted mainly in the laboratory. This fact is also true of other forms of social skills training. In the research literature, one does not see studies in which social skills, as a general cluster, are taught directly in the home setting. Rather, there tends to be an emphasis on teaching general problem-solving strategies outside the home to parents alone (see for example, the survey by Berkowitz & Graziano, 1972) or to parents and children (Blechman, 1974; Robin, 1979). The assumption is that those skills should transfer back into the home (Bizer *et al.*, 1978; Blechman, Olsen, & Hellman, 1976; Robin, Kent, O'Leary, Foster, & Pritz, 1977). Also, although many texts written for parents do focus on the promotion of effective social skills, rarely are the outcomes of such training evaluated. (See Bernal and North, 1978, for a survey of parent training manuals, including information on evaluations.) Here, let us turn to summaries of two of the areas of social behavior that have been researched primarily outside the family but that do have particular relevance to children's behavioral problems at home: social and conversational skills.

Social Skills. Effective social-interactional skills must be acquired if a child is to develop satisfactorily. Children who suffer from social isolation, who are avoided or ignored or punished by peers, have a much poorer prognosis for future adjustment than children who are accepted and who interact freely and assert themselves positively (Kagan & Moss, 1962). Recognizing that fact, the field has leaned toward studying methods for promoting effective social interactions.

Treatment Procedures. Recently, Van Hasselt, Hersen, and Bellack (1979) prepared a review designed to evaluate the adequacy of strategies for assessing and modifying social skills. In particular, attention was given to evidence of the durability and the generality of effects.

Van Hasselt *et al.* surveyed definitions of social skills and found them to contain various components: the skills were situation-specific (i.e., were utilized under some conditions and not others), and they consisted of learned verbal responses; they would not harm others and would maximize reinforcement. Self-expression, agreeing with and praising others; assertiveness in the form of making requests, disagreeing with another's opinions, and denying unreasonable requests; communication; and interpersonal problem-solving—all were among the specific skills mentioned. Other important ingredients of social skills might include the ability to dispense positive reinforcers, to approach peers and respond positively when they approach, to discriminate and label emotions, to communicate accurately and effectively to others, to assume the perspective of another on perceptual tasks, and to consider simultaneously one's own and others' views. The assessment of social skills has been based

primarily on self-reports, sociometrics, and motoric responses.

According to Van Hasselt *et al.* (1979) research on social skills *training* has focused on individual case reports, single-case studies, and group comparisons. The latter approach has tended to emphasize modeling as an intervention strategy and has pointed to the importance of considering developmental variables in assessing and designing intervention programs, since the components of socially effective behavior at one age may be quite different from those at another. (We would also add the need to consider social-milieu group factors, socioeconomic status, and cultural characteristics as critical variables in designing intervention programs for individuals.) Single-case studies have proved particularly valuable in identifying effective stategies for promoting social skills. Besides focusing on individuals, they have attempted to select the training procedures and settings that most closely resemble natural conditions. Reports of effective social-skills training have cited the use not only of verbal instructions but of behavioral rehearsal, imitation of modeled behavior, reinforcement of appropriate modeling or approximations to increasingly more skilled responding, and feedback (e.g., Bornstein *et al.*, 1977; Goldstein, Sherman, Gershaw, Sprafkin, & Glick, 1978). To illustrate, Bornstein *et al.* (1977) used such techniques to teach hyperactive children to maintain eye contact while communicating, to speak at an adequate volume (or duration), and to make requests for new behavior. It is reported that training of this kind has produced results that have endured for several weeks. Some studies also have reported evidence of generalization into the natural setting.

Issues. It appears that social skills have begun to be adequately defined, assessed, and modified. There do, however, seem to be some issues that might well be addressed in this realm. Self-report and sociometrics are often used for assessment purposes. From our own perspective, such data should be supplementary to those obtained through direct observation, for although the results on one sociometric scale may serve as a good predictor of similar assessments in the future, they are not necessarily correlated with behavioral data assessed in the natural setting. Self-report measures are similarly limited.

It is likely that the most valid form of social skills assessment is that conducted in the natural setting, although as Van Hasselt *et al.* (1979) noted, even direct *in vivo* observation is fraught with difficulties. Naturalistic observational data may be biased by such conditions as expectancies and variables that affect the reliability of scoring, such as consensual drift, the complexity of the system, and knowledge that reliability is being assessed. We would add the critical issue of reactivity in cases where the observers' presence is not easily camouflaged. The validity of assessment through direct *in vivo* observation, however, can be improved by means of several tactics (attributed to Gottman, 1977): Observing all, not just target children (thus obscuring the influence of expectancies of change for just some); sequential time-sampling (which distributes observation intervals over a more representative time interval); and spot checks rather than scheduled checks for reliability.

Van Hasselt *et al.* (1979) also emphasize the need for techniques for promoting generalization from the training to the natural setting and for promoting (and assessing) the durability of trained skills. We would also add that other procedures may accomplish what social skills training is intended to accomplish. For instance, simple positive reinforcement may be the procedure of choice for children who have acquired the skills but may not be practicing them.

Progress is clearly being made in the realm of social skills assessment and training. Let us now turn to the recent research on training in conversational skills, which is particularly relevant to an analysis of social skills as they relate to child behavior problems in the home.

Conversational Skills: Treatment Procedures. Conversational skills are often taught as components of social-skills-training packages (e.g., Reese, 1979a). Specific skills such as attending without interrupting and reflecting the content of the speaker's conversation are stressed. For example, Arnold, Sturgis, and Forehand (1977) taught the mother of a 15-year-old retarded girl different categories of active conversational responses: encouraging, acknowledging, and questioning. Besides acquiring the general conversational skills, the girl increased her total rate of verbalizing.

At a much simpler level, behavioral programs have been designed to teach conversational skills to language-deficient children (e.g., Garcia, 1974). Presumably such procedures could readily be applied in the home with children deficient in conversational ability. Prompting, shaping, and reinforcement were used by Stokes, Baer, and Jackson (1974) to teach four retarded children to respond to others with a simple greeting, a hand wave. More importantly, they showed how to promote generalization across a large number of people by involving a second trainer. Luiselli, Colozzi, Donellon, Helfen, and Pemberton (1978) modeled the responses to be incorporated with a fairly complex verbal greeting exchange: "Hi," "Hi," "How are you today?" "I'm fine," and so on. Levels of complexity were shaped, and modeling prompts were faded as their moderately retarded, language-deficient subject began to acquire the appropriate response repertoire.

Conversational style becomes a different sort of a problem, though, when it is characterized not by insufficient skills but by qualities that interfere with positive social interactions. In that case, rather than simply teaching adaptive conversational skills, the task becomes one of teaching novel alternative behaviors, such as conflict resolution (Martin & Twentyman, 1976); negotiating skills (Kifer, Lewis, Green, & Phillips, 1974); or prosocial statements. This was the situation tackled by Sanson-Fisher, Seymour, Montgomery, & Stokes (1978). The subjects in their study were institutionalized delinquent girls who displayed very low rates of prosocial statements and of positive attention to statements made by peers and staff. The subjects were taught to say and to identify instances of prosocial comments and also to present positive attention to others. They were also shown how to record their own practice of those behaviors and were given tokens for meeting specific criteria. Although they did not learn to discriminate pro- and antisocial peer statements, they did substantially increase their rates of making prosocial comments and giving positive attention to others. Anecdotal reports indicated a simultaneous reduction in aggression and other negative social problems during the time that the self-recording phase was in effect.

In a similar study, conversations between a mother and a predelinquent 12-year-old boy were modified in a study by Lysacht and Burchard (1975). The youngster, who lived in a group home, was visited by his mother once a week. It was found that during baseline, the mother criticized twice as often as she praised and that she focused on inappropriate behaviors. Audiotapes of the conversations were used to provide the mother with feedback regarding her use of praise and criticism. During the treatment, her frequency of criticism diminished to zero. Alexander and Parsons (1973) compared several different family-intervention strategies to assess their impact on delinquent family process. The short-term behavioral treatment resulted in more equality among family members in talk time, silence, and interruptions. Also, recidivism rates were lower for that group.

Negative conversational interactions probably account for a substantial amount of difficulty experienced within families. Children may make negative, hostile, or antisocial remarks, thereby prompting negative reactions by parents and siblings. Extrapolating from the Sanson-Fisher *et al.* (1978) study, it should be possible to modify this form of behavior by teaching individual family members (1) to self-record accurately; (2) to discriminate their own and others' prosocial and other forms of positive and adaptive conversational content; and (3) to make such statements themselves. Contractual arrangements would be one way to increase both rates of recording and rates of the occurrence of the identified behaviors themselves.

Further Research on Positive Social Skills. Further research on techniques that parents can use to teach specific classes of prosocial behaviors would permit a heavier focus on preventing than on curing child behavior problems. The methods cited by Cooke and Apolloni (1976) and by Barton and Ascione (1979)—modeling, instructions, and contingent praise to teach specific social behaviors such as smil-

ing, sharing, and positive physical contact—should lend themselves readily to application in the home. There are probably several advantages to such an approach: Since the behaviors are discrete and specific, they should be easy for parents to demonstrate; they should be readily discriminable, so that the consequences may be presented at the appropriate time; and they should be readily quantified by parents. Generalization to the home should not be an issue, since that would be the base of training, and the behaviors should occasion not only programmed but also natural reinforcement. Instances of smiling, sharing, and positive physical contact would tend to stimulate in-kind responses from others, thereby introducing additional sources of reinforcement within the social environment.

Characteristics of Behavior Modification with Children in the Home

We have seen the breadth of children's home-based problem behaviors that have been addressed by the field of behavior modification. We have also had a chance to examine some of the behavioral approaches that have been applied to the treatment of those problems and to consider some issues that are specifically relevant to each area. Now, we turn to a discussion of the various issues that relate to the modification of children's behavior problems in the home in general. Included among them are the nature of the problems that have been addressed; behavioral assessment methods; the settings in which programs are conducted; the providers and targets of treatment; parent-training methods; self-management; the behavior modification procedures being applied; ethics and the law; and methodology.

The Nature of the Problem

As we have seen, the child behavior problems addressed by behavior modification have varied widely. Seriously disruptive behaviors such as noncompliance (Forehand, 1977), tantrums (Williams, 1959), oppositional responding (Wahler, 1969a), and aggression have received much attention, as have behaviors that are distressing or upsetting to family functioning. Relatively less attention has been devoted to the promotion of specific positive behaviors, such as assertiveness, creativity, helping and sharing, and honesty. However, outside the home, in laboratory and school settings, progressively more attention has been given to those areas.

The degree of *specificity* of the behavior targeted for change varies from case to case. Treatment may be directed toward changing a very discrete response, such as smiling (Hopkins, 1968) or reducing the initial link in a chain that terminates in a seizure (Zlutnick, Mayville, & Moffat, 1975); or more complex behaviors, such as a set of specific conversational skills (Sanson-Fisher *et al.*, 1978) or acceptable behavior while shopping (Barnard *et al.*, 1977), may be treated. Functional response classes (those behaviors that tend to covary as a function of the modification of any of the class members), such as imitative responding (Baer, Peterson, & Sherman, 1967), comprise yet another category in the specificity–generality dimension, while clusters of behaviors, often grouped together in common parlance, constitute an even more complex set: "Problem solving" (e.g., Blechman, 1974) is one such cluster. Other examples are "brat" (Bernal, 1969), "oppositional" (Wahler, 1969a), "noncompliant" (Forehand, 1977), "coercive" (Patterson, 1976), or "objectionable" (Hawkins *et al.*, 1966) behaviors, on the socially noxious side, and "nonassertiveness" (Bornstein *et al.*, 1977) on the side of social insufficiency. Each of those general terms actually consist of sets of discrete behaviors, such as failing to follow instructions, negating requests, and making derogatory comments. When research is conducted on such general behavioral categories, it is necessary to refine, operationalize, and specify precise measures for each component.

On the most comprehensive end of the continuum is child behavior in general, grouped into broad subcategories, such as those in need of increasing, decreasing, teaching, and so forth. Textbooks for providers of services to children and for parents, such as Sulzer-Azaroff and Mayer's (1977) and many in the group

reviewed by Bernal and North (1978), are intended to permit adults and children themselves to target the behaviors to be modified.

The desirability of involvement at one particular level of specificity appears to depend on a few factors. If transfer from one setting to another is of major concern, or if busy parents or teachers are to observe, record, and implement a program, it seems that very specific, clearly discrete behaviors are the most appropriate. (See Johnson, Bolstad, & Lobitz, 1976). Professionals, however, should be capable of analyzing and pinpointing the components of broad classes of behavior.

Assessing Behavior

In the early years of behavior modification, there was a definite trend away from the use of diagnostic instruments, other than direct observational recordings. The major emphasis was on improving and refining observational procedures (e.g., Reese, 1979b). Discovering critical contingency relationships was the prime objective of the field, since their discovery would permit management of the contingencies to set things right.

As the field has developed, however, other issues have emerged in relation to assessment. How does one decide whether a particular goal is reasonable for a particular child? What is the "normal" range of distribution of the behavior among children? Are the component or the prerequisite behaviors contained in the child's repertoire of behaviors? Will the environment support the projected change? The development of instruments that address such issues is on the increase.

One emphasis has been on observing "normal children" in natural settings, to permit an assessment of the appropriateness of the goals and the measurement of the behavior before, during, and following interventions. Examples are the work done by Twardosz, Schwartz, Fox, and Cunningham (1979), who developed and demonstrated the reliability and validity of a system designed to measure affectionate behavior, and by Peterson (1979), who used an interaction record to measure interpersonal relationships.

The development of observational forms and behavioral checklists has also been emphasized. These generally consist of a set of specific, clearly defined behaviors to be measured according to precisely specified criteria. Behavioral checklists are used by clients themselves, such as the Fear Survey Schedule (Scherer & Nakamura, 1968), or by trained observers conducting ecological assessments (Wahler, House, & Stambaugh, 1976).

As this area of focus in the field continues growing, one can anticipate a broader scope of application and methodological refinements. However, in contrast with more traditional child assessment, it can be predicted that behavioral assessment will focus on identifying "meaningful response units and the controlling variables for the purposes of understanding and altering behavior" (Nelson & Hayes, 1979, p. 13).

Settings

The programs described above have been located in various settings. Sometimes, training has taken place totally in the clinic, with the therapist initially treating the child and later shifting over the conduct of the therapy to the parent, as in the early phases of the Patterson *et al.* (1967) study. Frequently, the clinic or the community center has served as the training site. Sometimes, training conducted in the clinic has been shifted back to the home (e.g., Bernal, 1969), and frequently, treatment has taken place directly in the home throughout (e.g., Hawkins *et al.,* 1966).

The selection of settings for intervention and parent training has probably been based on convenience and practicality as much as on a consideration of empirical evidence for or against enduring effectiveness. For a trained therapist to expend considerable time traveling to homes, one would have to offer very convincing evidence of the superiority of that approach. Logic and informal observations of effective training in the home may not be as convincing as hard comparative data. Definitive studies that compare training and intervention sites remain to be conducted.

Providers and Targets of Treatment

Behavior modification programs are more frequently being incorporated within the child's natural social environment. We have seen how key individuals in the child's life have been trained to function as paraprofessional change agents: mothers (e.g., Shoemaker & Paulson, 1976), fathers (Rasbury, 1974), or both parents (e.g., Johnson & Lobitz, 1974); siblings (Steward & Steward, 1976), peers (Nelson, Worell, & Polsgrove, 1973), or even the children themselves (Benassi & Larson, 1976).

Sometimes the full family unit is treated (e.g., Alexander & Parsons, 1973), and individual members sometimes assume the role of change agents for specific purposes (e.g., Mealiea, 1976). This approach reflects the influence of the current focus on ecology (e.g., Rogers-Warren & Warren, 1977). The parent–child relationship is seen as reciprocal (Bell, 1979), or the family may be viewed as an "ecosystem." The Achievement Place teaching family (Phillips, Phillips, Fixsen, & Wolf, 1972) is a community-based group-home program for predelinquent youth. The program incorporates a sophisticated sequence of contingency arrangements for "family members." No single family member is the target of change. Rather, change is seen as a function of adjustments in the interaction among family members (e.g., Christophersen, Barnard, Ford, & Wolf, 1976). Studies of transfer and maintenance highlight the importance of incorporating support from within the natural setting (Conway & Bucher, 1976), especially if contrast effects are to be avoided (e.g., Wahler, 1969; Forehand *et al.,* 1975; Johnson, Bolstad, & Lobitz, 1976). Thus, depending on the nature of the problems of concern, the most responsible and effective strategy may be to direct treatment toward the total family as a functional ecosystem.

Instances in which full families are treated are becoming more frequent (e.g., Engeln, Knutson, Laughy, & Garlington, 1968; Mash, Hamerlynck, & Handy, 1976; Mash, Handy, & Hamerlynck, 1976). But usually such treatment incorporates training the parents, rather than all family members, to apply behavior modification procedures. In fact, very frequently, when children are to be treated at home, at least one parent, if not both parents, is given formal training, so that she or he may effectively conduct the modification program. Since there has been such a heavy emphasis on parent training, the next section is devoted to a summary of activities in that area.

Parent Training

Training should teach parents how their practices affect their children's behavior and how change may be supported: "the behavior modifier should focus efforts upon altering the social environment in which the child lives rather than directly with the deviant child. Within such a framework, alterations in the reinforcement schedules being used by the parents . . . would produce changes in the behavior of the child" (Patterson *et al.*, 1967, p. 181). Professional time can be saved by involving parents instead of professional change agents. Also, parents do have the ultimate responsibility for their (minor) children's behavior in our society. Most compelling, however, would be clear demonstrations that child behavior problems are better prevented or ameliorated when the parents are involved in the modification program.

Parents are becoming increasingly involved in programs with their children and probably will continue to be so. Thus, the challenge is to discover those variables that influence their effectiveness. Potentially critical variables have been identified in several review articles (Berkowitz & Graziano, 1972; Johnson & Katz, 1973; O'Dell, 1974; Reisenger, Ora, & Frangia, 1976), and by the editors and researchers in texts on the topic (e.g., Mash, Hamerlynck, & Handy, 1976; Mash, Handy, & Hamerlynck, 1976). Here, a sampling of some of the important variables is identified and discussed from the perspective of efficacy, practicality, and other considerations.

Complexity of Problems and Training. There has been a range in the level of the complexity of the problems targeted and in the procedures that parents have been trained to use. Examples of the very specific target behaviors are child behavior in a supermarket (Clark *et al.*, 1977) and proper use of the toilet (Azrin & Foxx, 1974). Somewhat more general are *sets* of behaviors, such as noncompliance (Forehand, 1977) or sibling conflict (Leitenberg *et al.*, 1977), and parents are taught specific strategies for treating them. For example, Resick, Forehand, and McWhorter (1976)

taught a mother to praise compliance or to use time-out for noncompliance. Patterson (e.g., Patterson & Reid, 1973) has developed a program to train parents to modify a broad range of "coercive" child behaviors by applying various reinforcing and punishing conditions. Still more general are the sorts of skills involved in family contracting (Blechman, 1974) or problem-solving communication training (Robin, 1979). Many textbooks written specifically for parents, such as some of those reviewed by Bernal and North (1978), or for any of a variety of managers of child behavior change (e.g., Sulzer-Azaroff & Mayer, 1977) teach general behavior-modification strategies almost in a cookbook fashion. Parents or other consumers of the books are expected to be able to apply a general model and then to select, implement, and evaluate the specific procedures appropriate to the problem at hand.

If a particular problem is the only one identified and tends to occur at a particular time and place, a specific set of instructions may be sufficient. But if parents are to be expected to practice effective behavioral skills across behaviors and conditions, it is probably preferable to instruct them in general as well as specific methods. This conclusion is supported on the basis of a study by Glogower and Sloop (1976), who compared those two treatment strategies among two small groups of mothers. They found that the group of mothers who were instructed in both general and specific procedures attained more stable and general change. Other relevant factors might be the history and background of the parents, particularly their ability to abstract and generalize; the amount of consultation they receive, and the number and type of examples that are supplied and that they are asked to generate themselves. These latter factors remain to be studied.

Where and with Whom Training Takes Place. Parents may receive their training individually or in groups; in a community setting, such as a clinic or school; or right at home. Sometimes the child or other family members are present; sometimes not. Where and with whom the training takes place may depend on the nature of the problem as well as on logistical and practical issues. It seems that target behaviors that are relatively independent of the setting are often treated outside the natural environment. For example, if the problem is in oral communication (Robin, 1979) or contracting (Blechman, 1974), it is probably readily transferable outside the training setting.

When the problem behavior has been firmly tied to conditions of the natural physical or social environment, home-based programs are often used. Bedtime tantrums (Williams, 1959), bed-wetting (Azrin & Thienes, 1978), completing chores (Phillips et al., 1972), and other behaviors depend in part on physical stimuli of the natural environment. The most concrete form of parent training would involve those objects—the bed, the cleaning implements, the items to be cleaned, and so on.

Whether other family members (particularly the child with the identified problem) are present seems to depend on the trainer's assumption about the parent's ability to transfer knowledge and skills into the family setting. Various programs have involved parents and their children, and sometimes other family members, directly in the training setting. The initial training may begin with the therapist and be gradually shifted over to the parent (Engeln et al., 1968), or it may involve parents throughout (Hawkins et al., 1966).

The decision about where training should take place and who should be present must rest on other factors as well. Cost factors, such as the time available to the trainer and the parent, commuting expenses, the comfort parents feel in receiving trainers in the home, and the physical facilities, may influence the value of a given program. Sometimes training may be conducted both in the clinic and in the home. Parents may be instructed intensively in the clinic, with a series of booster sessions to promote both generalization into the family constellation and long-term maintenance. Not all contacts need to be personal, either. Telephone calls (Holden & Sulzer-Azaroff, 1972) or notes (Hunt & Sulzer-Azaroff, 1974) may bridge the time gap between in-person communications. The issues of cost for parents and therapists have been discussed in detail by Kovitz (1976) and in various review articles (e.g., Johnson & Katz, 1973; O'Dell, 1974).

Problems Targeted for Change by Parents. A general review of the literature on parent training indicates that behavioral reduction is frequently the selected goal. Parents are trained in how to use time-out (Flanagan, Adams, & Forehand, 1979), response-cost (Miller, 1975), and other reductive procedures effectively. Often, but not always, training does involve techniques for increasing the rate of positive, constructive behaviors. Noncompliance may simply be punished, or noncompliance punished and compliance reinforced. In the latter case, a more acceptable behavior is being strengthened simultaneously with the reduction in the less acceptable one (Leitenberg, Burchard, Burchard, Fuller, & Lysaght, 1977).

An alternative approach would be to train parents to teach their children behaviors that are either incompatible with or that prevent the development of deviant behaviors in the first place. An example of the former is the general problem-solving communication approaches that Robin (1979), Weathers and Liberman (1975), and others have used. A step further is the strictly preventive method of teaching parents how to guide their children to avoid the development of problems. Presumably, if parents are trained to arrange the physical and the social environment to support their children's positive adaptive behaviors, there should be less need for therapeutic intervention.

Risley, Clark, and Cataldo (1976) have emphasized the importance of identifying critical problem areas in normal family life. Specific intervention packages may then be designed, tested, and disseminated (e.g., the family shopping package, by Risley et al., 1976, designed to promote not only compliance by the children but also important incidental learning).

Procedures Parents Are Trained to Use. The types of procedures that parents have been taught to use are mentioned throughout various sections of this chapter. When the problem is noxious, the parent is usually taught to use some form of reductive procedure: time-out (Flanagan et al., 1979); response-cost (Miller, 1975); punishment, such as a spanking (Bernal, 1969); or extinction (Engeln et al., 1968). Usually, those procedures are to be paired with the positive reinforcement of alternative behaviors. These might include attention (Wahler, 1969a); access to preferred activities (Hopkins, Schutte, &

Garton, 1971); money (Clark *et al.,* 1977); or other material rewards (Wiltz & Gordon, 1974). Training parents to use differential attention may backfire, however. Herbert, Pinkston, Hayden, Sajwaj, Pinkston, Cordua & Jackson (1973) found that when parents systematically withheld attention following their children's deviant behavior, those behaviors *increased.*

When the problem is a skill deficit, such as dressing, toileting, or following a health routine (such as using an inhalator), parents are taught to reinforce successive approximations and segments of the chain of responses. Many of the complex training packages also contain strategies for establishing effective stimulus control. For instance, parents are taught how to present instructions and, depending on the child's response, what consequences to deliver and when (Peed *et al.,* 1977).

Training manuals for parents often include the procedures cited above (e.g., Clark, 1975; Patterson, Reid, Jones, & Conger, 1975; Miller, 1975), as do textbooks designed for training professionals, paraprofessionals, and parents in the concepts (e.g., Sulzer-Azaroff & Mayer, 1977) and skills (e.g., Sulzer-Azaroff & Reese, 1982) of applying behavior analysis. Occasionally, a training manual is designed to teach one specific class of behaviors. An example is Markel and Greenbaum's (1979) *Parents Are to Be Seen and Heard,* a programmed text designed to teach parents to be assertive in the planning of their handicapped children's education.

It seems that if serious problem behaviors are to be prevented, there should be a wide dissemination of procedures for increasing positive behaviors. More parents will need to be taught how to use reinforcement effectively and how and when to reinforce differentially, when to withhold reinforcers, and how and when to apply reductive procedures. They would then be more apt to provide the conditions that enhance positive family interactions: cooperation, altruism, responsibility, creativity, and other socially desirable classes of behavior.

Procedures for Training Parents. The training of parents ranges from lectures and readings to more active involvement, such as observing models (e.g., Flanagan *et al.,* 1979; O'Dell, Mahoney, Horton, & Turner, 1979),

either in filmed form (O'Dell *et al.,* 1979) or with a live demonstration (Johnson & Brown, 1969). Parents may be encouraged to imitate the modeled behavior, rehearsing it repeatedly until a particular level of performance is met. Often, their children are also involved, and the parents are given immediate feedback via a bug-in-the-ear device (Green, Forehand, & McMahon, 1979) or a tone (Bernal, 1969). Videotapes are often used to provide specific feedback, permitting parents to analyze their own performance *vis-à-vis* their children (Bizer *et al.,* 1978). Sometimes simulated problem situations are presented so that the trainer can assess how effectively the parent solves the problem (Nay, 1975). In one case (O'Dell *et al.,* 1979), boys recruited by the trainers were rehearsed to exhibit problem and nonproblem behavior. Their behavior was used to test how effectively a group of parents had learned to apply time-out.

In general, it appears that those procedures that train skills in the home and that most closely resemble those to be ultimately applied are the most effective. For instance, Nay (1975) found that although all of the parents he trained acquired knowledge, it was only when written material and lectures were supplemented with a videotaped model or with role playing that the simulation test performance was superior. O'Dell *et al.* (1979) concluded that their training film enhanced performance, while Flanagan *et al.* (1979) found that in-home modeling procedures produced performance that was superior to that trained by lectures, written materials, and role playing outside the home.

Self-Management

Children are also being trained to manage their own behavior. The assumption (e.g., Brownell, Coletti, Ersner-Hershfield, & Wilson, 1977) is that their involvement should promote enduring change in the absence of externally imposed control. There are also the pragmatic advantages of saving the time and the effort of significant others in the child's life.

The topic of self-control among children has been studied most extensively in the laboratory (e.g., Weiner & Dubanowski, 1975) or in applied settings outside the home. (See Karoly, 1977; O'Leary & Dubey, 1979, and Rosenbaum & Drabman, 1979, for extensive reviews of the topic.) Those studies have yielded information on several facets of self-control: self-instruction, self-determined criteria, self-assessment, and self-reinforcement. In general, according to O'Leary and Dubey (1979), if children adhere to instructions to self-instruct, if they have a history of reinforcement for successful adherence, and if they are skilled in the required behavior, self-instruction can be very effective. Children may also be involved in setting the criteria for their successful performance. According to Brownell et al.'s (1977) finding, children achieved more by using stringent criteria than lenient ones. Children can be taught to assess their own behavior accurately. When they do so, the assessment may improve an already effective reward system. Children may reward their own behavior with as much effectiveness as when others deliver the rewards, and they may learn general or comprehensive procedures that can promote transfer across settings and maintained performance.

Examples of the use of self-control procedures by children are being seen increasingly in the literature. For example, various facets of self-control are integral to the "habit reversal" system developed by Azrin and his colleagues (e.g., Azrin & Nunn, 1974; Nunn & Azrin, 1976). Lowe and Lutzker (1979) taught their diabetic client to record the results of her own urine tests. In training conversational skills, Sanson-Fisher et al. (1978) taught their clients, delinquent girls, to assess and record the types of comments that they made. Further, Karoly (1977) has offered several useful suggestions for methods of teaching children self-control skills.

Parents are also being trained to make use of various self-control components to manage those of their own behaviors that may influence the behavior of their children (i.e., self-reinforcement; Brown, Gamboa, Birkimer, & Brown, 1976). Herbert and Baer (1972) trained parents to self-record their use of contingent attention with their children. In that instance, the self-recording alone was sufficient to promote more effective parenting skills.

Procedural Trends

Regardless of who manages the contingencies, some general procedural trends in the modification of children's behavior problems may be noted. (These are only briefly summarized here, as other sections in the chapter refer to procedures as well.) First, in treating children's behavior problems, rarely is one procedure implemented in its "pure" form. Rather, procedural "packages" (combinations of various procedures) tend to be used. Not only, for example, is good behavior while shopping reinforced, but prompting, conditioned reinforcement, and many other procedural features are incorporated into the program (Barnard et al., 1977). Relaxation training was combined with a number of other components in the habit reversal program of Azrin and Nunn (1973). In addition, one sees an increased reliance on procedures validated in the applied setting, trends away from contrived material rewards and painful punishers and toward managing antecedents to simple and complex behaviors.

As the field continues to develop, procedures are more apt to be selected on the basis of research evidence than on the basis of logic alone. The earliest behavior-modification procedures were based on principles derived from basic laboratory-based operant research (e.g., Williams, 1959). More recently, it has been increasingly possible to test procedures in the natural setting and, accordingly, to modify principles derived from that evaluation. For example, differential attention has been used effectively with a variety of child behaviors (e.g., Harris, Wolf, & Baer, 1964), but it may be limited to certain subject populations (Herbert et al., 1973).

There appears to be a trend away from the use of highly contrived material-reward systems. Perhaps this is a reaction to a series of studies based on the "overjustification theory." Data from laboratory studies indicated that some children may reduce their rates of engaging in a previously preferred activity following the termination of a phase in which they were given material rewards contingent on that behavior (e.g., Greene & Lepper, 1974). More recent research (e.g., Fisher, 1979; Ramey & Sulzer-Azaroff, 1977) suggests that the generality of those findings is probably limited. But as Fischer (1979) has demonstrated, it does seem that maintenance under extinction conditions is superior following minimal rather than very dense reinforcement conditions. Or perhaps the move away from contrived material rewards is a reaction to the legal restrictions placed on the withholding of material goods (*Wyatt* v. *Stickney, 1972*). At any rate, one is more apt to see preferred activities, social events, or more "natural" material rewards, such as allowances (Fredricksen, Jenkins, & Carr, 1976), used as reinforcers, rather than the more contrived material reward. Exceptions, of course, are made when the behavior must be modified rapidly, as in life-threatening situations (e.g., Magrab & Papadopoulou, 1977), or when the less contrived rewards are not sufficiently effective.

Another trend has been toward the increasing use of stimulus control procedures to modify children's behavior. Such antecedent conditions as rules (Stuart, 1971), self-instructions (Monahan & O'Leary, 1971), visual cues (Gold, 1972), and physical guidance (Striefel & Wetherby, 1973) are being paired with reinforcing consequences, as youngsters learn both simple response patterns and complex behaviors.

Sometimes antecedent cues are paired with shaping and chaining procedures, as young people begin to acquire the subskills identified via a task analysis. Unless the cues are intrinsic to the situation, they are usually gradually faded. An example is a study by Cronin and Cuvo (1979), in which retarded adolescents were taught mending skills. Each of the steps in their task analysis was prompted, if need be, according to a prompt sequence that involved progressively less assistance. The combination of task analyses, prompting, and the fading of prompts holds much promise for teaching children many complex skills that might serve to prevent the development of certain behavior problems altogether. A child might respond to his or her repeated failure to perform a particular skill by throwing a temper tantrum. This could be avoided by breaking the skill down into component tasks so that success is more likely (see Sulzer-Azaroff, Brewer, & Ford, 1978 for a manual designed to teach such instructional skills).

There appears to have been a gradual trend away from the use of punishers that induce pain. Spankings (Bernal, 1969) and electric shock (e.g., Linscheid & Cunningham, 1977) have tended to be replaced by the application of punishing stimuli that seem more benign, such as overcorrection (Foxx & Azrin, 1973); lemon juice (Apolito & Sulzer-Azaroff, 1981); a water mist (Dorsey, Iwata, Ong, & McSween, 1981); and requiring the child to engage in low-preference activities such as contingent running (Luce, Delquadri, & Hall, 1980). Although much attention has been paid to the ethical aspects of punishment by the behavior modification practitioners who have used painful stimuli (Lovaas & Simmons, 1969), it is probable that the experimenters themselves have been punished by the reactions of partially informed critics. Additionally, many constraints have been placed on the use of aversive procedures via agency and governmental policies (see, e.g., May, Risley, Twardosz, Friedman, Bijou, Wexler *et al.,* 1976). The issue of whether a very rapidly effective aversive procedure, such as electric shock, is or is not more humane than one that is less painful but slower to produce effective results remains unsettled. Nevertheless, any recommendation that physical forms of punishment be administered to modify children's behavior problems at home must be cautiously presented. Careful supervision must be provided, and procedures must be acceptable within current laws, policies, and ethical principles. (For a full discussion on this topic, see Carr & Lovaas, 1980).

Ethical and Legal Aspects

There has been a trend in all human service areas toward increasing concern about ethical and legal issues. The Education for All Handicapped Children Act (Public Law 94.142) epitomizes how these aspects have been incorporated within U.S. federal policy. The law includes a variety of provisions for ensuring due process and requires the specification of an individual educational plan to meet the child's special needs. Objective assessment and monitoring of progress toward meeting the goals of the educational program are also required. Children eligible to receive special services may also receive programs directed toward social and other problem areas that do not fall strictly under the heading of academic performance. Behavioral services would be among them (see Pollack & Sulzer-Azaroff, 1981). Thus, those behavior modification programs that are meeting the requirements of the law are conducted with parental approval, and the treatment setting is selected from the least restrictive alternative available for providing an appropriate program.

Integral to behavior modification is the recording of behavioral data. Thus, practitioners must meet the provisions of professional ethics codes related to both service and research (i.e., the *Ethical Principles in the Conduct of Research with Human Participants* by the American Psychological Association, 1973, and the American Psychological Association's *Ethical Standards of Psychologists,* 1979). Thus, the child's participation in the research should be voluntary, and informed consent should be obtained. (When children are too young or disabled to give their consent, a parent or an advocate often serves that function.) State, local, or agency laws and policies may also apply further constraints.

Although behavior modification with children has tended to adhere to legal and ethical requirements, it is only recently that such adherence has been cited or documented. Illustrative of such documentation is the following quote, taken from a study of recording methodology. Family interactions were taped at times known and times unknown to family members: "Three means of censorship were provided to protect the families' privacy. (1) The family could activate a censor switch located on the outside of the trunk to disconnect the receiver for 15 min. (b) The family could listen to and erase any part of the tapes before their coding by observers. (c) The family could listen to and erase any part of the tapes after their coding by observers. Confidentiality of all assessment materials was assured, and censorship was not discouraged" (Johnson *et al.,* 1976, p. 214).

Perhaps as a function of Public Law 94.142 and the trend toward maintaining children in their own homes rather than placing them in institutions, there has been an increasing focus on promoting developmental functioning. Par-

ent-training efforts have recently begun to include not only methods for getting rid of noxious behaviors but also methods for enhancing self-care (Bucher & Reaume, 1979) and other constructive activities for children. Efforts are also continually being made to discover optimal levels of stimulation to be applied to reduce undesirable behaviors. Examples are the trend toward using as brief a time-out period as may be effective (see Risley & Twardosz, 1974) or shorter positive-practice durations within the overcorrection procedure (Harris & Romanczyk, 1976).

Methodology

The methodological rigor with which child behavior problems in the home have been studied seems to vary considerably, particularly in the precision with which behavior has been observed and in the experimental designs of the studies. Many of the early studies relied, at least in part, on parental reporting. Later, along with the development of more precise observational technology (e.g., Bijou, Peterson, & Ault, 1968) within the behavior modification field in general, more precision could be seen in the study of the home-based problems of children. Observers began to receive more training, were kept as uninformed as possible about the interventions being used and the outcomes expected, and learned to avoid interacting with the families, and the *reliability* of their observational recording was estimated regularly. More recently, the *validity* of selected behavioral measures has begun to be assessed by referring to multiple sources, including interviews, case records, naturalistic observations, behavioral checklists, normative data, and standardized observations and tests (see, e.g., Johnson, Bolstad, & Lobitz, 1976.)

Another methodological problem that is particularly relevant here is reactivity to the measurement of behavior in the home. The behavior modification field has relied heavily on the use of live observers or in their stead, video or audio recorders. In a home, the presence of a noninteracting stranger is particularly obtrusive, and presumably, the observer's presence influences the data (Johnson & Bolstad, 1975). Audio recordings or radio transmitters (Johnson, Christensen, & Bellamy, 1976)—either activated by the parents, as in Bizer *et al.* (1978), or programmed by the experimenter to turn on at preset random times (Johnson, Christensen, & Bellamy, 1976)—have been used in attempts to minimize reactivity to observation. Another option is the involvement of family members in validating self-recording (Azrin & Nunn, 1973). Studies of the latter options suggest that reactivity can probably be reduced substantially. However, continued research on this problem is clearly needed.

The precision with which studies of child behavior problems in the home are experimentally designed also continues to vary. The range of designs covers individual and replicated case studies, reversal, within- and across-subject–multiple-baseline replications (according to the rules of single-subject research design), program reports, and group designs. In general, the studies that control for passage of time, variation of conditions from day to day, and other potentially confounding variables are those from which principles can most confidently be drawn.

There are situations in which the luxury of a highly sophisticated experimental design is not feasible. Occasionally, an infrequently observed condition requires modification (e.g., the modification of Gilles de la Tourette's syndrome might be difficult to replicate across subjects, as it is so rare a problem). Sometimes a behavior is so dangerous that sufficient baseline recording would not be feasible. A two-day unstable baseline prior to the treatment of a seriously debilitated infant for chronic rumination was judged in one case to be about as long as responsible ethics would permit (Lang & Melamed, 1969).

Future Perspectives

The field of behavior modification has demonstrated that parents, siblings, and other family members may take an active part in remediating children's problems. In many instances, the young clients themselves may effectively involve themselves in the treatment of their own problems. Success seems to depend on adequate training, supervision, consultation, monitoring, and follow-up. But much of the research on family and client involvement in the management of the treatment process has been conducted with select groups: people who have answered advertisements in the newspapers, people who have responded to cash incentives for participation, people who have sought assistance voluntarily, or people who have responded favorably to referrals for assistance. And so, the generality of research findings is of necessity limited.

It is very likely that many families who could profit from acquiring problem prevention and treatment skills are not being reached either as research subjects or as clients or trainees. Methods need to be devised to assist families to seek out services and to acquire the skills that will permit a more positive family life. Kazdin (1979) has discussed the problems of disseminating information about behavior modification to the public and of reaching those families that are most at risk. As more information about behavior modification is being included in the curriculum offerings of institutions of higher education, presumably more young adults will acquire knowledge of the model, and perhaps some skills, that they may apply later on with their own children. But again, such audiences are relatively restricted. One possible alternative is to turn to the social institution that does reach the large majority of potential parents: the secondary school. The high-school teaching of psychology is becoming increasingly prevalent. It should be possible to include content on effective parenting skills within, or in addition to, the general psychology course.

Regardless of how families are reached, simply teaching a chain of verbal behavior is insufficient. Active participation is essential. The literature on the training of clients, parents, family members, and professionals and paraprofessionals has demonstrated that behavior modification skills may be acquired by means of various innovative techniques: modeling and imitation of skilled demonstrators, behavior rehearsal–role playing, guided practice and other simulated practice, and practice *in vivo* under supervision and with appropriate feedback (e.g., Sulzer-Azaroff & Reese, 1982). Additionally, monitoring and feedback may be necessary if the acquired skills are to maintain and transfer. Research on the broad-scale dissemination of knowledge and skills and on training and management techniques for promoting the enduring practice of effective skills would contribute to the eventual improvement of family life.

In addition to efforts to promote the dissemination of information about effective preventive strategies, much remains to be accomplished in the realm of research. Within the sections on specific problem areas and on trends and issues, we have mentioned topics in need of further investigation. From the broad perspective, regardless of the problem area, some general research questions are especially timely.

What are the conditions that support the long-term maintenance of change in the behavior of parents and children? The assumptions about long-term maintenance need to be tested for extensive trial periods spanning several years. What conditions support the transfer of parental modification skills across different behaviors within the same child or across siblings or settings? What are the collateral effects of different child-management strategies *vis-à-vis* the child's behavior outside the home? Do some strategies promote positive spin-offs? Do others tend to produce antisocial reactions? Such questions call not only for effective training and supervision strategies but also for some fairly extensive ecological assessments.

There is a continuing need to seek procedural refinements that save funds and time, without sacrificing benefit. What strategies can be designed to allow power to be distributed fairly among family members? Studies in that realm should promote situations in which neither parents nor children wield excessive control over one another.

Then, there is the more traditional development of intervention strategies designed to resolve specific problems. Many family problems remain particularly difficult to treat: substance abuse, theft, and others that yield children rapid and powerful reinforcement, as well as neglect and physical abuse by their parents. Other family problems are just beginning to be recognized as being heavily influenced by environmental events: various health problems, activity level, affective "state," and others.

Undoubtedly, the scope of the problem areas addressed will continue to grow.

Finally, there is the whole area of how research findings might interface with public policy. Issues such as legal restrictions on the use of punishment, policies on the provision of behavioral services to children and families, school curricula, and others should increasingly reflect cognizance of research results in promoting policies to serve both individual children and the common good.

References

Alexander, J. F., & Parsons, B. V. Short-term behavioral intervention with delinquent families: Impact on family process and recidivism. *Journal of Abnormal Psychology*, 1973, *81*, 219–225.

Allen, K. E., & Harris, F. R. Elimination of a child's excessive scratching by training the mother in reinforcement procedures. *Behaviour Research and Therapy*, 1966, *4*, 79–84.

Allison, T. S., & Allison, S. L. Time-out from reinforcement: Effect on sibling aggression. *The Psychological Record*, 1971, *21*, 81–86.

American Psychological Association. *Ethical principles in the conduct of research with human participants*. Washington, D.C.: Author, 1973.

American Psychological Association. *Ethical standards of psychologists*. Washington, D.C.: Author, 1979.

Anderson, D. R. Treatment of insomnia in a 13 year old boy by relaxation training and reduction of parental attention. *Journal of Behavior Therapy and Experimental Psychiatry*, 1979, *10*, 263–265.

Apolito, P. M., & Sulzer-Azaroff, B. Lemon juice therapy: The control of chronic vomiting in a twelve year old profoundly retarded female. *Education and Treatment of Children*, 1981, *4*, 339–347.

Aragona, J., Cassady, J., & Drabman, R. S. Training overweight children through parental training and contingency contracting. *Journal of Applied Behavior Analysis*, 1975, *8*, 269–278.

Arnold, J. E., Levine, A. G., & Patterson, G. R. Changes in sibling behavior following family intervention. *Journal of Clinical and Consulting Psychology*, 1975, *43*, 683–688.

Arnold, S., Sturgis, E., & Forehand, R. Training a parent to teach communication skills: A case study. *Behavior Modification*, 1977, *1*, 259–276.

Ashkenazi, Z. The treatment of encopresis using a discriminitive stimulus and positive reinforcement. *Journal of Behavior Therapy and Experimental Psychiatry*, 1975, *6*(2), 155–157.

Atkeson, B. M., & Forehand, R. Home based reinforcement programs to modify classroom behavior: A review and methodological evaluation. *Psychological Bulletin*, 1979, *86*, 1298–1308.

Ayllon, T., & Kelly, K. Reinstating verbal behavior in a functionally mute retardate. *Professional Psychology*, 1974, *5*, 385–393.

Ayllon, T., & Michael, J. The psychiatric nurse as a behavioral engineer. *Journal of the Experimental Analysis of Behavior*, 1959, *2*, 323–334.

Ayllon, T., Smith, D., & Rogers, M. Behavior management of school phobia. *Journal of Behavior Therapy and Experimental Psychiatry*, 1970, *1*, 125–138.

Ayllon, T., Garber, S., & Pisor, K. The elimination of discipline problems through a combined school-home motivational system. *Behavior Therapy*, 1975, *6*, 616–626.

Ayllon, T., Simon, S. J., & Wildman, R. W. Instructions and reinforcement in the elimination of encopresis: A case study. *Journal of Behavior Therapy and Experimental Psychiatry*, 1975, *6*, 235–238.

Ayllon, T., Garber, S. W., & Allison, M. G. Behavioral treatment of childhood neurosis. *Psychiatry*, 1977, *40*, 315–322.

Azerrad, J., & Stafford, R. L. Restoration of eating behavior in anorexia nervosa through operant conditioning and environmental manipulation. *Behaviour Research and Therapy*, 1969, *7*, 165–171.

Azrin, N. H., & Foxx, R. M. *Toilet training in less than a day*. New York: Simon & Schuster, 1974.

Azrin, N. H., & Lindsley, O. R. The reinforcement of cooperation between children. *Journal of Abnormal and Social Psychology*, 1956, *52*, 100–102.

Azrin, N. H., & Nunn, R. G. Habit reversal: A method of eliminating nervous habits and tics. *Behaviour Research and Therapy*, 1973, *11*, 619–628.

Azrin, N. H., & Nunn, R. G. A rapid method of eliminating stuttering by a regulated breathing approach. *Behaviour Research and Therapy*, 1974, *12*, 279–286.

Azrin, N. H., & Nunn, R. G. Eliminating nail biting by the habit reversal procedure. *Behaviour Research and Therapy*, 1976, *14*, 65–67.

Azrin, N. H., & Thienes, P. M. Rapid elimination of enuresis by intensive learning without a conditioning apparatus. *Behavior Therapy*, 1978, *9*(3), 342–354.

Azrin, N. H., Sneed, T. J., & Foxx, R. M. Dry Bed: Rapid elimination of childhood enuresis. *Behaviour Research and Therapy*, 1974, *12*, 147–156.

Azrin, N. H., Hontos, P. T., & Besalel-Azrin, V. Elimination of enuresis without a conditioning apparatus: An extension by office instruction of the child and parents. *Behavior Therapy*, 1979, *10*, 14–19.

Bach, R., & Moylan, J. J. Parents administer behavior therapy for inappropriate urination and encopresis: A case study. *Journal of Behavior Therapy and Experimental Psychiatry*, 1975, *6*(13), 239–241.

Bachrach, H. J., Erwin, W. J., & Mohr, J. P. The control of eating behavior in an anorexic by operant conditioning techniques. In L. P. Ullmann & L. Krasner (Ed.), *Case studies in behavior modification*. New York: Holt, Rinehart & Winston, 1965.

Baer, D. M., Peterson, R. F., & Sherman, J. A. The development of imitation by reinforcing behavioral similarity to a model. *Journal of Experimental Analysis of Behavior*, 1967, *10*, 405–417.

Bailey, J. S., Wolf, M. M., Phillips, E. L. Home-based reinforcement and the modification of predelinquents' classroom behavior. *Journal of Applied Behavior Analysis*, 1970, *3*, 223–233.

Bandura, A., & Menlove, F. L. Factors determining vicarious extinction of avoidance behavior through symbolic modeling. *Journal of Personality and Social Psychology*, 1968, *8*, 99–108.

Bandura, A., Grusec, J. E., & Menlove, F. L. Vicarious extinction of avoidance behavior. *Journal of Personality and Social Psychology*, 1967, *5*, 16–23.

Barber, R. M., & Kagey, J. R. Modification of school attendance for an elementary population. *Journal of Applied Behavior Analysis*, 1977, *10*, 41–48.

Barnard, J. D., Christophersen, E. R., & Wolf, M. M. Teaching children appropriate shopping behavior through parent training in the supermarket setting. *Journal of Applied Behavior Analysis*, 1977, *1*, 45–59.

Barth, R. Home-based reinforcement of school behavior: A review and analysis. *Review of Educational Research*, 1979, *49*, 436–458.

Barton, E. J., & Ascione, E. R. Sharing in preschool children: Facilitation, stimulus generalization, response generalization, and maintenance. *Journal of Applied Behavior Analysis*, 1979, *12*, 417–430.

Bauermeister, J. J., & Jemail, J. A. Modification of "elective mutism" in the classroom setting: A case study. *Behavior Therapy*, 1975, 246–250.

Becker, J. V., Turner, S. M., & Sajwaj, T. E. Multiple behavioral effects of the use of lemon-juice with a ruminating toddler-age child. *Behavior Modification*, 1978, *1*, 267–278.

Bell, R. Q. Parent, child and reciprocal influences. *American Psychologist*, 1979, *34*, 821–826.

Benassi, V. A., & Larson, K. M. Modification of family interaction with the child as the behavior-change agent. In E. J. Mash, L. C. Handy, & L. A. Hamerlynck (Eds.), *Behavior modification and families*. New York: Brunner/Mazel, 1976.

Berkowitz, B. P., & Graziano, A. M. Training parents as behavior therapists. *Behaviour Research and Therapy*, 1972, *10*, 297–317.

Bernal, M. E. Behavioral feedback in the modification of brat behaviors. *The Journal of Nervous and Mental Disease*, 1969, *148*, 375–385.

Bernal, M. E. Behavioral treatment of a child's eating problem. *Journal of Behavior Therapy and Experimental Psychiatry*, 1972, *3*, 43–50.

Bernal, M. E., & North, J. A. A survey of parent training manuals. *Journal of Applied Behavior Analysis*, 1978, *11*, 533–544.

Bernal, M. E., Duryee, J. S., Pruett, H. L., & Burns, B. J. Behavior modification and the brat syndrome. *Journal of Consulting and Clinical Psychology*, 1968, *32*, 447–455.

Besalel-Azrin, V., Azrin, N. H., & Armstrong, P. M. The student-oriented classroom: A method of improving student conduct and satisfaction. *Behavior Therapy*, 1977, *8*, 193–204.

Bijou, S. W., & Baer, D. M. *Child development, Vol. 1: A systematic and empirical theory*. New York: Appleton-Century Crofts, 1961.

Bijou, S. W., & Baer, D. M. *Child development, Vol. II: Universal state of infancy*. New York: Appleton-Century Crofts, 1965.

Bijou, S. W., Peterson, R. F., & Ault, M. H. A method to integrate descriptive and experimental field studies at the level of data and empirical concepts. *Journal of Applied Behavior Analysis*, 1968, *1*, 175–191.

Birnbrauer, J. S., Bijou, S. W., Wolf, M. M., & Kidder, J. D. Programmed instruction in the classroom. In L. P. Ullmann & L. Krasner (Eds.), *Case studies in behavior modification*. New York: Holt, Rinehart & Winston, 1965.

Bizer, L. S., Sulzer-Azaroff, B., & Frederickson, R. H. *Parent child problem solving training—Generality from laboratory to home*. Paper presented at the annual meeting of the Association for the Advancement of Behavior Therapy; Chicago, December, 1978.

Blackmore, M., Rich, N., Means, Z., & Nally, M. Summer therapeutic environment program—STEP: A hospital alternative for children. In E. Mash, L. Hamerlynck, & L. Handy (Eds.), *Behavior Modification Approaches to Parenting*. New York: Brunner/Mazel, 1976.

Blechman, E. A. The family contract game: A tool to teach interpersonal problem solving. *Family Coordinator*, July 1974, 269–280.

Blechman, E. A., Olson, D. H. L., & Hellman, I. D. Stimulus control over family problem-solving behavior. *Behavior Therapy*, 1976, 7, 686–692.

Bollard, R. S., & Woodroffe, P. The effect of parent-administered dry-bed training on nocturnal enuresis in children. *Behaviour Research and Therapy*, 1977, 15(2), 159–166.

Bornstein, M. R., Bellack, A. S., & Hersen, M. Social-skills training for unassertive children: A multiple baseline analysis. *Journal of Applied Behavior Analysis*, 1977, 10, 183–195.

Bornstein, P. H., & Rychtarik, R. G. Multi-component behavioral treatment of trichotillomania: A case study. *Behaviour Research and Therapy*, 1978, 16, 217–220.

Broden, M., Beasley, A., & Hall, R. V. In-class spelling performance: Effects of home tutoring by a parent. *Behavior Modification*, 1978, 2, 511–530.

Brown, J. H., Gamboa, A. M., Birkimer, J., & Brown, R. Some possible effects of parent self-control training on parent-child interactions. In E. J. Mash, L. C. Handy, & L. A. Hamerlynck (Eds.), *Behavior modification approaches to parenting*. New York: Brunner/Mazel, 1976.

Brownell, K. D., Colletti, G., Ersner-Hershfield, R., Hershfield, S. M., & Wilson, G. T. Self-control in school children: Stringency and leniency in self-determined and externally imposed performance standards. *Behavior Therapy*, 1977, 8, 442–455.

Bucher, B., & Reaume, J. Generalization of reinforcement effects in a token program in the home. *Behavior Modification*, 1979, 3, 63–72.

Budd, K. S., & Liebowitz, J. M. *Programmed Activities for School Success (PASS): Modification of disruptive classroom behavior in young children through home-based contingencies*. Paper presented at the second annual convention of the Midwestern Association for Behavior Analysis, Chicago, May 1976.

Butler, J. F. The toilet training success of parents after reading *Toilet Training in Less Than a Day*. *Behavior Therapy*, 1976, 7, 185–191.

Carr, E. G., & Lovaas, O. I. Contingent electric shock as a treatment for severe behavior problems. In S. Axelrod & J. Apsche (Eds.), *Punishment: Its effects on human behavior*. Lawrence, Kans.: H. & H. Enterprises, 1980.

Catalina, D. *Enuresis: Parent mediated modification*. Paper presented at the Eastern Psychological Association Meeting, New York, 1976.

Christophersen, E. R. Children's behavior during automobile rides: Do car seats make a difference? *Pediatrics*, 1977, 60, 69–74.

Christophersen, E. R., Arnold, C. M., Hill, D. W., & Quilitch, H. R. The home point system: Token reinforcement procedures for application by parents of children with behavior problems. *Journal of Applied Behavior Analysis*, 1972, 5, 485–497.

Christophersen, E. R., Barnard, J. D., Ford, D., & Wolf, M. M. The family training program: Improving parent-child interaction patterns. In E. J. Mash, L. C. Handy, & L. A. Hamerlynck (Eds.), *Behavior modification approaches to parenting*. New York: Brunner/Mazel, 1976.

Clark, H. B., Greene, B. F., Macrae, J. W., McNees, M. P., Davis, J. L., & Risley, T. R. A parent advice package for family shopping trips: Development and evaluation. *Journal of Applied Behavior Analysis*, 1977, 10, 605–624.

Clark, M. L. *Responsive Parent Training Manual*, Box 4792, Overland Park, Kans., 1975.

Conrad, R. D., Delk, J. L., & Williams, C. Use of stimulus fading procedures in the treatment of situation specific mutism: A case study. *Behavior Therapy and Experimental Psychiatry*, 1974, 5, 99–100.

Conway, J. B., & Bucher, B. D. Transfer and maintenance of behavior change in children: A review and suggestions. In E. J. Mash, L. A. Hamerlynck, & L. C. Handy (Eds.), *Behavior modification and families*. New York: Brunner/Mazel, 1976.

Cooke, T. P., & Apolloni, T. Developing positive social-emotional behaviors: A study of training and generalization effects. *Journal of Applied Behavior Analysis*, 1976, 9, 65–78.

Copeland, R. E., Brown, R. E., Axelrod, S., & Hall, R. V. Effects of school principals praising parents for school attendance. *Educational Technology*, 1972, 12(7), 56–59.

Cronin, K. A., & Cuvo, A. J. Teaching mending skills to mentally retarded adolescents. *Journal of Applied Behavior Analysis*, 1979, 12, 401–406.

Crowley, C. P., & Armstrong, P. M. Positive practice, overcorrection and behavior rehearsal in the treatment of three cases of encopresis. *Journal of Behavior Therapy and Experimental Psychology*, 1977, 8(4), 411–416.

Dardig, J. C., & Heward, W. L. *Sign here: A contracting book for children and their parents*. Kalamazoo, Mich.: Behaviordelia, 1976.

Doleys, D. M. Behavioral treatments for nocturnal enuresis in children: A review of the recent literature. *Psychological Bulletin*, 1977, 84, 30–54.

Doleys, D. M., & Wells, K. C. Changes in functional bladder and bed-wetting during and after retention control training: A case study. *Behavior Therapy*, 1975, 6, 685–688.

Doleys, D. M., Ciminero, A. R., Tollison, J. W., Williams, S. C., & Wells, K. C. Dry-bed training and retention control training: A comparison. *Behavior Therapy*, 1977, 8, 541–548.

Doleys, D. M., McWhorter, A. Q., Williams, S. C., & Gentry, W. R. Encopresis: Its treatment and relation to nocturnal enuresis. *Behavior Therapy*, 1977, *8*, 77–82.

Dorsey, M. F., Iwata, B. A., Ong, P., & McSween, T. E. Treatment of self-injurious behavior using a water mist: Initial response suppression and generalization. *Journal of Applied Behavior Analysis*, 1980, *13*, 343–354.

Dougherty, E., & Dougherty, A. The daily report card: A simplified and flexible package for classroom behavior management. *Psychology in the Schools*, 1977, *14*, 191–195.

Engeln, R., Knutson, J., Laughy, L., & Garlington, W. Behaviour modification techniques applied to a family unit: A case study. *Journal of Child Psychology and Psychiatry*, 1968, *9*, 245–252.

Epstein, L. H., Masek, B. J., & Marshall, W. R. A nutritionally based school program for control of eating in obese children. *Behavior Therapy*, 1978, *9*, 766–788.

Eyberg, S., & Johnson, S. Multiple assessment of behavior modification with families: Effects of contingency contracting and order of treated problems. *Journal of Consulting and Clinical Psychology*, 1974, *42*, 594–606.

Finley, W. W., Wansley, R. A., & Blenkarn, M. M. Conditioning treatment of enuresis using a 70% intermittent reinforcement schedule. *Behaviour Research and Therapy*, 1977, *15*, 419–428.

Fisher, E. B. Overjustification effects in token economies. *Journal of Applied Behavior Analysis*, 1979, *12*, 407–415.

Fjellstedt, N., & Sulzer-Azaroff, B. Reducing the latency of a child responding to instructions by means of a token system. *Journal of Applied Behavior Analysis*, 1973, *6*, 125–130.

Flanagan, S., Adams, H. E., & Forehand, R. A comparison of four instructional techniques for teaching parents to use timeout. *Behavior Therapy*, 1979, *10*, 94–102.

Forehand, R. Child noncompliance to parental requests: Behavior analysis and treatment. In M. Hersen, R. M. Eisler, & P. M. Miller (Eds.), *Progress in behavior modification*. New York: Academic Press, 1977.

Forehand, R., & King, H. E. Pre-school children's noncompliance: Effects of short term behavior therapy. *Journal of Community Psychology*, 1974, *2*, 42–44.

Forehand, R., King, H. E., Peed, S., & Yoder, P. Mother-child interactions: Comparison of a non-compliant clinic group and a non-clinic group. *Behaviour Research and Therapy*, 1975, *13*, 79–84.

Fox, R. A., & Roseen, D. L. A parent administered token program for dietary regulation of phenylketonuria. *Journal of Behavior Therapy and Experimental Psychiatry*, 1977, *8*, 441–444.

Foxx, R. M., & Azrin, N. H. The elimination of autistic self-stimulatory behavior by overcorrection. *Journal of Applied Behavior Analysis*, 1973, *6*, 1–14.

Fredriksen, L. W., Jenkins, J. O., & Carr, C. R. Indirect modification of adolescent drug abuse using contingency contracting. *Journal of Behavior Therapy and Experimental Psychiatry*, 1976, *7*, 377–378.

Garcia, E. The training and generalization of a conversational speech form in nonverbal retardates. *Journal of Applied Behavior Analysis*, 1974, *7*, 137–149.

Garfinkel, P. E., Kline, S. H., & Stancer, H. C. Treatment of anorexia nervosa using operant conditioning techniques. *Journal of Nervous and Mental Disease*, 1973, *6*, 428–433.

Gelfand, D. M., Hartmann, D. P., Cromer, C. C., Smith, C. L., & Page, B. C. The effects of instructional prompts and praise on children's donating rates. *Child Development*, 1975, *40*, 980–983.

Gentry, W. D. Parents as modifiers of somatic disorders. In E. J. Mash, L. C. Handy, & L. A. Hamerlynck (Eds.), *Behavior modification approaches to parenting*. New York: Brunner/Mazel, 1976.

Glogower, F., & Sloop, E. W. Two strategies of group training of parents as effective behavior modifiers. *Behavior Therapy*, 1976, *7*, 177–184.

Gold, M. W. Stimulus factors in skill training of retarded adolescents on a complex assembly task: Acquisition, transfer, and retention. *American Journal of Mental Deficiency*, 1972, *76*, 517–526.

Goldstein, A. P., Sherman, B., Gershaw, N. J., Sprafkin, R. P., & Glick, B. Training aggressive adolescents in pro-social behavior. *Journal of Youth and Adolescence*, 1978, *7*, 73–92.

Gottman, J. M. Toward a definition of social isolation in children. *Child Development*, 1977, *48*, 513–517.

Graubard, P. S. *Positive parenthood: Solving parent-child conflicts through behavior modification.* New York: Bobbs-Merrill, 1977.

Graubard, P. S., Rosenberg, H., & Miller, M. B. Student applications of behavior modification to teachers and environment or ecological approaches to social deviancy. In E. A. Ramp & B. L. Hopkins (Eds.), *A new direction for education: Behavior analysis*. Lawrence: University of Kansas, 1971.

Graziano, A. M., DeGiovanni, I. S., & Garcia, K. A. Behavioral treatment of children's fears: A review. *Psychological Bulletin*, 1979, *86*, 804–830.

Graziano, A. M., Mooney, K. C., Huber, C., & Ignasiak, D. Self-instruction for children's fear reduction. *Journal of Behavior Therapy and Experimental Psychiatry*, 1979, *10*, 221–227.

Green, K. D., Forehand, R., & McMahon, R. J. Parental manipulation of compliance and non-compliance in normal and deviant children. *Behavior Modification*, 1979, *3*, 245–266.

Greene, D., & Lepper, M. R. Intrinsic motivation: How to turn play into work. *Psychology Today*, 1974, *8*, 49–54.

Hake, D. F., & Vukelich, R. A classification and review of cooperation procedures. *Journal of the Experimental Analysis of Behavior*, 1972, *18*, 333–343.

Hardiman, S. A., Goetz, E. M., Reuter, K. E., & LeBlanc, J. M. Primes, contingent attention, and training: Effects on a child's motor behavior. *Journal of Applied Behavior Analysis*, 1975, *8*, 399–409.

Harris, F. R., Wolf, M. M., & Baer, D. M. Effects of adult social reinforcement on child behavior. *Young Children*, 1964, *20*, 8–17.

Harris, L. S., & Purohit, A. P. Bladder training and enuresis: A controlled trial. *Behaviour Research and Therapy*, 1977, *15*, 485–490.

Harris, S. L., & Romanczyk, R. G. Treating self-injurious behavior of a retarded child by overcorrection. *Behavior Therapy*, 1976, *7*, 235–239.

Hart, B. M., Reynolds, N. J., Baer, D. M., Brawley, E. R., & Harris, F. R. Effect of contingent and non-contingent social reinforcement on the cooperative play of a preschool child. *Journal of Applied Behavior Analysis*, 1968, *1*, 73–76.

Hartmann, D. P., Gelfand, D. M., Smith, C. L., Paul, S. C., Cromer, C. C., Page, B. C., & Lebenta, D. V. Factors affecting the acquisition and elimination of children's donating behavior. *Journal of Experimental Child Psychology*, 1976, *21*, 328–338.

Hawkins, R. P., Peterson, R. F., Schweid, E., & Bijou, S. W. Behavior therapy in the home: Amelioration of problem parent-child relations with the parent in a therapeutic role. *Journal of Experimental Child Psychology*, 1966, *4*, 99–107.

Hawkins, R. P., Sluyter, D. J., & Smith, C. D. Modification of achievement by a simple technique involving parents and teachers. In M. B. Harris (Ed.), *Classroom uses of behavior modification*. Columbus, Ohio: Charles E. Merrill, 1972.

Herbert, E. W., & Baer, D. M. Training parents as behavior modifiers: Self-recording of contingent attention. *Journal of Applied Behavior Analysis*, 1972, *5*, 139–149.

Herbert, E. W., Pinkston, E. M., Hayden, M. L., Sajwaj, T. E., Pinkston, S., Cordua, G., & Jackson, C. Adverse effects of differential parental attention. *Journal of Applied Behavior Analysis*, 1973, *6*, 15–30.

Herbert-Jackson, E., and Risley, T. R. Behavioral nutrition: Consumption of foods of the future by toddlers. *Journal of Applied Behavior Analysis*, 1977, *10*, 407–414.

Hersen, M. Behavior modification approach to a school phobic case. *Journal of Clinical Psychology*, 1970, *26*, 128–132.

Hingtgen, J. N., Sanders, B. J., & DeMyer, M. K. Shaping cooperative responses in early childhood schizophrenics. In L. P. Ullmann and L. Krasner (Eds.), *Case studies in behavior modification*. New York: Holt, Rinehart & Winston, 1965.

Holden, B., & Sulzer-Azaroff, B. Schedules of follow-up and their effect upon the maintenance of a prescriptive teaching program. In G. Semb (Ed.), *Behavior analysis and education*. Lawrence: University of Kansas, Dept. of Human Development, 1972.

Hopkins, B. L. Effects of candy and social reinforcement, instructions, and reinforcement schedule learning on the modification and maintenance of smiling. *Journal of Applied Behavior Analysis*, 1968, *1*, 121–130.

Hopkins, B. L., Shutte, R. C., & Garton, K. L. The effects of access to a playroom on the rate and quality of printing and writing of first and second-grade students. *Journal of Applied Behavior Analysis*, 1971, *4*, 77–88.

Horner, R. D., & Keilitz, I. Training mentally retarded adolescents to brush their teeth. *Journal of Applied Behavior Analysis*, 1975, *8*, 301–309.

Hughes, H., Hughes, A., & Dial, H. Home-based treatment of thumbsucking: Omission training with edible reinforcers and a behavioral seal. *Behavior Modification*, 1979, *3*, 179–186.

Humphreys, L., Forehand, R., McMahon, R., & Roberts, M. Parent behavioral training to modify child noncompliance: Effects on untreated siblings. *Behavior Therapy and Experimental Psychiatry*, 1978, *9*, 235–238.

Hunt, S., & Sulzer-Azaroff, B. *Motivating parent participation in home training sessions with pre-trainable retardates*. Paper presented at the meeting of the American Psychological Association, New Orleans, September 1974.

Hutzell, R. R., Platzek, D., & Logue, P. E. Control of

symptoms of Gilles de la Tourette's syndrome by self-monitoring. *Journal of Behavior Therapy and Experimental Psychiatry*, 1974, *5*, 71–76.

Johnson, C. A., & Katz, R. C. Using parents as change agents for their children: A review. *Journal of Child Psychology and Psychiatry*, 1973, *14*, 181–200.

Johnson, S. A., & Brown, R. A. Producing behavior change in parents of disturbed children. *Journal of Child Psychology and Psychiatry*, 1969, *10*, 107–121.

Johnson, S. M., & Bolstad, O. D. Reactivity to home observation: A comparison of audio recorded behavior with observers present or absent. *Journal of Applied Behavior Analysis*, 1975, *8*, 181–185.

Johnson, S. M., & Lobitz, G. K. Parental manipulation of child behavior in home observations. *Journal of Applied Behavior Analysis*, 1974, *7*, 23–31.

Johnson, S. M., Bolstad, O. D., & Lobitz, G. K. Generalization and contrast phenomena in behavior modification with children. In E. J. Mash, L. A. Hamerlynck, & L. C. Handy (Eds.), *Behavior modification and families*. New York: Brunner/Mazel, 1976.

Johnson, S. M., Christensen, A., & Bellamy, G. T. Evaluation of family intervention through unobtrusive audio recordings: Experiences in "bugging" children. *Journal of Applied Behavior Analysis*, 1976, *9*, 213–219.

Jones, M. C. The elimination of children's fears. *Journal of Experimental Psychology*, 1924, *7*, 382–390.

Kagan, J., & Moss, H. A. *Birth to maturity*. New York: Wiley, 1962.

Kandel, H. J., Ayllon, T., & Rosenbaum, M. S. Flooding or systematic exposure to extreme social withdrawal in children. *Journal of Behavior Therapy and Experimental Psychiatry*, 1977, *8*, 75–81.

Kanfer, F. H., Karoly, P., & Newman, A. Reduction of children's fear of the dark by competence-related and situational threat-related verbal cues. *Journal of Consulting and Clinical Psychology*, 1975, *43*, 251–258.

Karoly, P. Behavioral self-management in children: Concepts, methods, issues and directions. In M. Hersen, R. M. Eisler, & P. M. Miller (Eds.), *Progress in behavior modification*, Vol. 5. New York: Academic Press, 1977.

Karoly, P., & Rosenthal, M. Training parents in behavior modification: Effects on perceptions of family interactions and deviant children. *Behavior Therapy*, 1977, *8*, 406–410.

Karraker, R. Increasing academic performance through home managed contingency programs. *Journal of School Psychology*, 1972, *10*, 173–179.

Kazdin, A. E. *History of behavior modification*. Experimental Foundation of Contemporary Research. Baltimore: University Park Press, 1978.

Kazdin, A. E. Advances in child behavior therapy. *American Psychologist*, 1979, *34*, 981–987.

Kifer, R. E., Lewis, M. A., Green, D. R., & Phillips, E. L. Training pre-delinquent youths and their parents to negotiate conflict situations. *Journal of Applied Behavior Analysis*, 1974, *7*, 257–364.

Knight, M. F., & McKenzie, H. S. Elimination of bedtime thumbsucking in home settings through contingent reading. *Journal of Applied Behavior Analysis*, 1974, *7*, 33–38.

Kornhaber, R. C., & Schroeder, H. E. Importance of

model similarity on the extinction of avoidance behavior in children. *Journal of Consulting and Clinical Psychology*, 1975, *43*, 601–607.

Kovitz, K. E. Comparing group and individual methods for training parents in child management techniques. In E. J. Mash, L. C. Handy, & L. A. Hamerlynck (Eds.), *Behavior modification approaches to parenting*. New York: Brunner/Mazel, 1976.

Lahey, B., Gendrich, J., Gendrich, S., Schnelle, L., Gant, D., & McNee, P. An evaluation of daily report cards with minimal teacher and parent contacts as an efficient method of classroom intervention. *Behavior Modification*, 1977, *3*, 381–394.

Lang, P. J., & Melamed, B. G. Case report: Avoidance conditioning therapy of an infant with chronic ruminative vomiting. *Journal of Abnormal Psychology*, 1969, *74*, 1–8.

Lassen, M. K., & Fluet, N. R. Elimination of nocturnal thumbsucking by glove wearing. *Journal of Behavior Therapy and Experimental Psychiatry*, 1978, *9*, 85.

Lavigueur, H., Peterson, R. F., Sheese, J. G., & Peterson, L. W. Behavioral treatment in the home: Effects on an untreated sibling and long term follow-up. *Behavior Therapy*, 1973, *4*, 431–441.

Leitenberg, H., Burchard, J. D., Burchard, S. N., Fuller, E. J., & Lysaght, T. V. Using positive reinforcement to suppress behavior: Some experimental comparisons with sibling conflict. *Behavior Therapy*, 1977, *8*, 168–182.

Lewis, S. A comparison of behavior therapy techniques in the reduction of fearful avoidance behavior. *Behavior Therapy*, 1974, *5*, 648–655.

Linscheid, T. R., & Cunningham, C. E. A controlled demonstration of the effectiveness of electric shock in the elimination of chronic infant rumination. *Journal of Applied Behavior Analysis*, 1977, *10*, 500.

Lovaas, O. I., & Simmons, J. Q. Manipulation of self-destruction in three retarded children. *Journal of Applied Behavior Analysis*, 1969, *2*, 143–157.

Lovibond, S. H. *Conditioning and enuresis*, Oxford, England: Pergamon Press, 1964.

Lowe, K., & Lutzker, J. F. Increasing compliance to a medical regimen with a juvenile diabetic. *Behavior Therapy*, 1979, *10*, 57–64.

Lowitz, G. H., & Suib, M. R. Generalized control of persistent thumbsucking by differential reinforcement of other behaviors. *Journal of Behavior Therapy and Experimental Psychiatry*, 1978, *9*, 343–346.

Luce, S., Delquadri, J., & Hall, R. V. Contingent exercise: A mild but powerful procedure for suppressing inappropriate verbal and aggressive behavior. *Journal of Applied Behavior Analysis*, 1980, *13*, 583–594.

Luiselli, J. K. Treatment of an autistic child's fear of riding a school bus through exposure and reinforcement. *Journal of Behavior Therapy and Experimental Psychiatry*, 1978, *9*, 169–172.

Luiselli, J. K., Colozzi, G., Donellon, S., Helfen, C. S., and Pemberton, B. W. Training and generalization of a greeting exchange with a mentally retarded, language deficient child. *Education and Treatment of Children*, 1978, *1*, 23–29.

Lysaght, T. V., & Burchard, J. D. The analysis and modification of a deviant parent-youth communication pattern. *Journal of Behavior Therapy and Experimental Psychology*, 1975, *6*, 339–342.

MacDonald, W., Gallimore, R., & MacDonald, G. Contingency counseling by school personnel: An economical model of intervention. *Journal of Applied Behavior Analysis*, 1970, *3*, 175–182.

Magrab, P. R., & Papadopoulou, Z. L. The effect of a token economy on dietary compliance for children on hemodialysis. *Journal of Applied Behavior Analysis*, 1977, *10*, 573–578.

Mann, R. A. The behavior-therapeutic use of contingency contracting to control an adult behavior problem: Weight control. *Journal of Applied Behavior Analysis*, 1972, *5*, 99–109.

Markel, G. P., & Greenbaum, J. *Parents are to be seen and heard: Assertiveness in educational planning for handicapped children*. San Luis Obispo, Calif.: Impact Publishers, 1979.

Martin, B., & Twentyman, C. Teaching conflict resolution skills to parents and children. In E. J. Mash, L. C. Handy, & L. A. Hamerlynck (Eds.), *Behavior modification approaches to parenting*. New York: Brunner/Mazel, 1976.

Mash, E. J., Hamerlynck, L. A., & Handy, L. C. *Behavior modification and families*. New York: Brunner/Mazel, 1976.

Mash, E. J., Handy, L. C., & Hamerlynck, L. A. *Behavior modification approaches to parenting*. New York: Brunner/Mazel, 1976.

May, J. G., Risley, T. R., Twardosz, S., Friedman, P., Bijou, S. W., Wexler, D., *et al. Guidelines for the use of behavioral procedures in state programs for retarded persons*. Arlington, Texas: National Association for Retarded Citizens, 1976.

Mayer, G. R., & Butterworth, T. W. A preventive approach to school violence and vandalism: An experimental study. *Personnel and Guidance Journal*, 1979, *57*, 436–441.

McKenzie, H., Clark, M., Wolf, M., Kothera, R., & Benson, C. Behavior modification of children with learning disabilities using grades as tokens and allowances as back-up reinforcers. *Exceptional Children*, 1968, *34*, 745–752.

McKenzie, T. L., & Rushall, B. S. Effects of self-recording on attendance and performance in a competitive swimming training environment. *Journal of Applied Behavior Analysis*, 1974, *7*, 199–206.

McLaughlin, J. G., & Nay, W. R. Treatment of trichotillomania using positive covarants and response cost: A case report. *Behavior Therapy*, 1975, *6*, 87–91.

Mealiea, W. L. Conjoint-behavior therapy: The modification of family constellations. In E. J. Mash, L. C. Handy, & L. A. Hamerlynck (Eds.), *Behavior modification approaches to parenting*. New York: Brunner/Mazel, 1976.

Meichenbaum, D. Examination of model characteristics in reducing avoidance behavior. *Journal of Personality and Social Psychology*, 1971, *17*, 298–307.

Melamed, B. G., & Siegel, L. J. Reduction of anxiety in children facing hospitalization and surgery by use of filmed modeling. *Journal of Consulting and Clinical Psychology*, 1975, *43*, 511–521.

Melamed, B. G., Yurchison, R., Fleece, E. D., Hutcherson, S., & Hawes, R. Effects of film modeling on the reduction of anxiety-related behaviors in individuals varying in level of previous experience in the stress situation. *Journal of Consulting and Clinical Psychology*, 1978, *46*, 1357–1367.

Milgram, S. The behavioral study of obedience. *Journal of Abnormal and Social Psychology*, 1963, *67*, 371–378.

Miller, A. J., & Kratochwill, T. R. Reduction of frequent stomach ache complaints by timeout. *Behavior Therapy*, 1979, *10*, 211–218.

Miller, W. H. *Systemic Parenting Training*. Champaign, Ill.: Research Press, 1975.

Monahan, J., & O'Leary, K. D. Effects of self-instruction on rule breaking behavior. *Psychological Reports*, 1971, *29*, 1059–1066.

Mowrer, O. H., & Mowrer, W. M. Enuresis: A method for its study and treatment. *American Journal of Orthopsychiatry*, 1938, *8*, 436–459.

Munford, P. Outpatient contingency management of operant monitoring. *Journal of Behavior Therapy and Experimental Psychiatry*, 1979, *10*, 135–137.

Murphy, C. M., & Bootzin, R. R. Active and passive participation in the contact desensitization of snake fear in children. *Behavior Therapy*, 1973, *4*, 203–211.

Nay, W. R. A systematic comparison of instructional techniques for parents. *Behavior Therapy*, 1975, *6*, 14–21.

Neisworth, J. T., & Moore, F. Operant treatment of asthmatic responding with the parent as therapist. *Behavior Therapy*, 1972, *3*, 95–99.

Nelson, C. M., Worell, J., & Polsgrove, L. Behaviorally disordered peers as contingency managers. *Behavior Therapy*, 1973, *4*, 270–276.

Nelson, R. O., & Hayes, S. C. Some current dimensions of behavioral assessment. *Behavioral Assessment*, 1979, *1*, 1–16.

Nunn, R. G., & Azrin, N. H. Elimination of nailbiting by the habit reversal procedure. *Behaviour Research and Therapy*, 1976, *14*, 65–67.

O'Connor, R. D. Modification of social withdrawal through symbolic modeling. *Journal of Applied Behavior Analysis*, 1969, *2*, 15–22.

O'Dell, S. Training parents in behavior modification. *Psychological Bulletin*, 1974, *81*, 418–433.

O'Dell, S. L., Mahoney, N. D., Horton, W. G., & Turner, P. E. Media assisted parent training: Alternative models. *Behavior Therapy*, 1979, *10*, 103–110.

O'Leary, K. D., & Kent, R. N. *A behavioral consultation program for parents and teachers of children with conduct problems*. Paper presented at the meeting of the American Psycho-pathological Association, Boston, December 1974.

O'Leary, K. D., O'Leary, S., & Becker, W. C. Modification of deviant sibling interaction patterns in the home. *Behaviour Research and Therapy*, 1967, *5*, 113–120.

O'Leary, S. G., & Dubey, D. R. Applications of self-control procedures by children: A review. *Journal of Applied Behavior Analysis*, 1979, *12*, 449–465.

Ollendick, T. H. Behavioral treatment of anorexia nervosa: A 5 year study. *Behavior Modification*, 1979, *3*, 124–135.

Patterson, G. R. The aggressive child: Victim and architect of a coersive system. In E. J. Mash, L. A. Hamerlynck, & L. C. Handy (Eds.), *Behavior modification*

and families. New York: Brunner/Mazel, 1976, pp. 267–316.

Patterson, G. R., & Reid, J. B. Intervention for families of aggressive boys: A replication study. *Behaviour Research and Therapy*, 1973, *11*, 383–394.

Patterson, G. R., McNeal, N., Hawkins, N., & Phelps, R. Reprogramming the social environment. *Journal of Child Psychology and Psychiatry*, 1967, *8*, 181–195.

Patterson, G. R., Cobb, J. A., & Ray, R. S. A social engineering technology for retraining the families of aggressive boys. In H. E. Adams & I. P. Unikel (Eds.), *Issues and trends in behavioral therapy*. Springfield, Ill.: Charles C Thomas, 1973.

Patterson, G. R., Reid, J. B., Jones, R. R., & Conger, R. E. *A social learning approach to family intervention*. Eugene, Ore.: Castalia Publishing, 1975.

Peed, S., Roberts, M. W., & Forehand, R. Evaluation of the effectiveness of a standardized parent training program in altering the interaction of mothers and their noncompliant children. *Behavior Modification*, 1977, *1*, 323–350.

Peterson, D. R. Assessing interpersonal relationships by means of interaction records. *Behavioral Assessment*, 1979, *1*, 221–236.

Peterson, R. F. Power, programming, and punishment: Could we be overcontrolling our children? In E. J. Mash, L. A. Hamerlynck, & L. C. Handy (Eds.), *Behavior modification and families*. New York: Brunner/Mazel, 1976, pp. 338–352.

Phillips, E. L., Phillips, E. M., Fixsen, D., & Wolf, M. M. *The teaching family handbook*. Lawrence: Department of Human Development, University of Kansas, 1972.

Pollack, M. J., & Sulzer-Azaroff, B. Protecting the educational rights of the handicapped child. In J. T. Hannah, H. B. Clark, & W. P. Christian (Eds.), *Preservation of client rights: A handbook for practitioners providing therapeutic, educational and rehabilitative services*. New York: Free Press, 1981.

Pollack, M. J., Sulzer-Azaroff, B., & Williams, R. The experimental analysis of a homeward educational program with a pre-delinquent juvenile. In G. Semb (Ed.), *Behavior analysis and education*. Lawrence: Department of Human Development, University of Kansas, 1972.

Pomerantz, P. B., Peterson, N. T., Marholin D., Stern, S. The *in vivo* elimination of a child's water phobia by a para-professional at home. *Journal of Behavior Therapy and Experimental Psychiatry*, 1977, *8*, 417–422.

Rachman, S. Clinical applications of observational learning, imitation and modeling. *Behaviour Research and Therapy*, 1972, *3*, 379–397.

Ragland, E. U., Kerr, M. M., & Strain, P. S. Behavior of withdrawn autistic children: Effects of peer social initiations. *Behavior Modification*, 1978, *2*, 565–578.

Ramey, G., & Sulzer-Azaroff, B. *Effects of extrinsic rewards on the subsequent choice behavior of academically delayed children*. Paper presented at the 1977 meeting of the American Educational Research Association, April 4–8, New York, N.Y.

Rasbury, W. C. Behavioral treatment of selective mutism: A case report. *Journal of Behavior Therapy and Experimental Psychiatry*, 1974, *5*, 103–104.

Reese, E. P. Interviewing for jobs or graduate programs.

South Hadley, Mass.: Mount Holyoke College, 1979. (a)

Reese, E. P. Observing, defining and recording. South Hadley, Mass.: Mount Holyoke College, 1979. (b)

Reid, J. B., Hawkins, N., Keutzer, C., McNeal, S. A., Phelps, R. E., Reid, K. M., and Mees, H. L. A marathon behavior modification, *Psychiatry*, 1967, *8*, 27–30.

Reisinger, J. J., & Ora, J. P. Parent-child and home interaction during toddler management training. *Behavior Therapy*, 1977, *8*, 771–786.

Reisinger, J. J., Ora, J. P., & Frangia, G. W. Parents as change agents for their children: A review. *Journal of Community Psychology*, 1976, *4*, 103–123.

Renne, C. M., & Creer, T. L. Training children with asthma to use inhalation therapy equipment. *Journal of Applied Behavior Analysis*, 1976, *9*, 1–12.

Resick, P. A., Forehand, R., & McWhorter, A. Q. The effect of parent treatment with one child on an untreated sibling. *Behavior Therapy*, 1976, *7*, 544–548.

Richards, C. S., & Hansen, M. K. A further demonstration of the efficacy of stimulus fading treatment of elective mutism. *Journal of Behavior Therapy and Experimental Psychiatry*, 1978, *9*, 57–60.

Risley, T. R., & Twardosz, S. *Suggested guidelines for the humane management of the behavior problems of the retarded.* Unpublished document, State of Florida, Department of Health and Rehabilitative Services, Division of Retardation, 1974.

Risley, T. R., Clark, H. B., & Cataldo, M. F. Behavioral technology for the normal middle-class family. In E. J. Mash, L. A. Hamerlynck, & L. C. Handy (Eds.), *Behavior modification and families.* New York: Brunner/Mazel, 1976.

Ritter, B. The group treatment of children's snake phobias using vicarious and contact desensitization procedures. *Behaviour Research and Therapy*, 1968, *6*, 1–6.

Robin, A. L. Problem-solving communication training: A behavioral approach to the treatment of parent-adolescent conflict. *American Journal of Family Therapy*, 1979, *7*, 69–82.

Robin, A. L., Kent, R., O'Leary, K. D., Foster, S., & Prinz, R. An approach to teaching parents and adolescents problem-solving communication skills: A preliminary report. *Behavior Therapy*, 1977, *8*, 639–643.

Rogers-Warren, A., & Baer, D. M. Correspondence between saying and doing: Teaching children to share and praise. *Journal of Applied Behavior Analysis*, 1976, *9*, 335–354.

Rogers-Warren, A., & Warren, S. F. (Eds.) *Ecological perspectives in behavior analysis.* Baltimore: University Park Press, 1977.

Rosenbaum, M. S., & Drabman, R. S. Self-control training in the classroom: A review and critique. *Journal of Applied Behavior Analysis*, 1979, *12*, 467–485.

Ross, J. Parents modify thumbsucking: A case study. *Journal of Behavior Therapy and Experimental Psychiatry*, 1975, *6*, 248–249.

Sacks, S., & De Leon, G. Training the disturbed enuretic. *Behaviour Research and Therapy*, 1978, *16*, 296–299.

Sanchez, V. Behavioral treatment of chronic hair pulling in a 2 year old. *Journal of Behavior Therapy and Experimental Psychiatry*, 1979, *10*, 241–245.

Sank, L. I., & Biglan, A. Operant treatment of a case of recurrent abdominal pain in a 10 year old boy. *Behavior Therapy*, 1974, *5*, 677–681.

Sanok, R. L., & Streifel, S. Elective mutism: Generalization of verbal responding across people and settings. *Behavior Therapy*, 1979, *10*, 357–371.

Sanson-Fisher, B., Seymour, F., Montgomery, W., & Stokes, T. Modifying delinquents' conversation using token reinforcement of self-recorded behavior. *Journal of Behavior Therapy and Experimental Psychiatry*, 1978, *9*, 163–168.

Scherer, M. W., & Nakamura, C. Y. A fear survey schedule for children: A factor analytic comparison with manifest anxiety. *Behaviour Research and Therapy*, 1968, *6*, 173–182.

Schulman, M. Control of tics by maternal reinforcement. *Journal of Behavior Therapy and Experimental Psychiatry*, 1974, *5*, 95–96.

Schumaker, J. B., Hovell, M. F., & Sherman, J. A. An analysis of daily report cards and parent managed privileges in the improvement of adolescents' classroom performance. *Journal of Applied Behavior Analysis*, 1977, *10*, 449–464.

Schutte, R. C., & Hopkins, B. L. The effects of teacher attention on following instructions in a kindergarten class. *Journal of Applied Behavior Analysis*, 1970, *3*, 117–122.

Serbin, L. A., Tonick, I. J., & Sternglanz, S. H. Shaping cooperative cross-sex play. *Child Development*, 1977, *48*, 924–929.

Seymour, F. W., & Stokes, T. F. Self-recording in training girls to increase work and evoke staff praise in an institution for offenders. *Journal of Applied Behavior Analysis*, 1976, *9*, 41–54.

Sherman, T. M., & Cormier, W. H. An investigation of the influence of student behavior on teacher behavior. *Journal of Applied Behavior Analysis*, 1974, *7*, 11–22.

Shoemaker, M. E., & Paulson, T. L. Group assertion training for mothers: A family intervention strategy. In E. J. Mash, L. C. Handy, & L. A. Hamerlynck (Eds.), *Behavior modification approaches to parenting.* New York: Brunner/Mazel, 1976.

Staub, E. *Positive social behavior and morality*, Vol. 1. New York: Academic Press, 1978.

Steward, M., & Steward, D. Parents and siblings as teachers. In E. J. Mash, L. C. Handy, & L. A. Hamerlynck (Eds.), *Behavior modification approaches to parenting.* New York: Brunner/Mazel, 1976.

Stokes, T. F., & Kennedy, S. H. Reducing child uncooperative behavior during dental treatment through modeling and reinforcement. *Journal of Applied Behavior Analysis*, 1980, *13*, 41–50.

Stokes, T. F., Baer, D. M., & Jackson, R. L. Programming the generalization of a greeting response in four retarded children. *Journal of Applied Behavior Analysis*, 1974, *7*, 599–610.

Stokes, T. F., Fowler, S. A., & Baer, D. M. Training preschool children to recruit natural communities of reinforcement. *Journal of Applied Behavior Analysis*, 1978, *11*, 285–303.

Strain, P. S., Shores, R. E., & Timm, M. A. Effects of peer social initiations on the behavior of withdrawn preschool children. *Journal of Applied Behavior Analysis*, 1977, *10*, 289–298.

Striefel, S., & Wetherby, B. Instruction-following behavior of a retarded child and its controlling stimuli. *Journal of Applied Behavior Analysis*, 1973, *6*, 663–670.

Stuart, R. B. Behavioral contracting within the families of delinquents. *Journal of Behavior Therapy and Experimental Psychiatry*, 1971, *2*, 1–11.

Sulzer, B., Hunt, S., Ashby, E., Koniarski, C., & Krams, M. Increasing rate and percentage correct in reading and spelling in a class of slow readers by means of a token system. In E. A. Ramp & B. L. Hopkins (Eds.), *New directions in education: Behavior analysis*. Lawrence: Department of Human Development (Follow Through Project), University of Kansas, 1971, pp. 5–28.

Sulzer-Azaroff, B., & Mayer, G. R. *Applying behavior analysis procedures with children and youth*. New York: Holt, Rinehart & Winston, 1977.

Sulzer-Azaroff, B., & Reese, E. P. *Applying behavior analysis: A program for developing professional competence*. New York: Holt, Rinehart & Winston, 1982.

Sulzer-Azaroff, B., Brewer, J., & Ford, L. *Making educational psychology work: Carrying concepts into action*. Santa Monica, Calif.: Goodyear Publishing, 1978.

Thoresen, K., Thoresen, C., Klein, S., Wilbur, C., Becker-Haven, J., & Haven, W. Learning house: Helping troubled children and their parents change themselves. In J. Stumphauzer (Ed.), *Progress in behavior therapy*, Vol. 2. Springfield, Ill.: Charles C Thomas, 1977.

Thorne, G. L., Tharp, R. G., & Wetzel, R. J. Behavior modification techniques: New tools for probation officers. *Federal Probation*, 1967, *31*, 21–27.

Tizard, J. Nutrition and human development. In B. C. Etzel, J. B. LeBlanc, & D. R. Baer (Eds.), *New developments in behavioral research*. Hillsdale, N.J.: Lawrence Erlbaum, 1977, pp. 111–118.

Tough, J. H., Hawkins, R. P., McArthur, M. M., & Ravensway, S. V. Modification of enuretic behavior by punishment: A new use for an old device. *Behavior Therapy*, 1971, *2*, 567–574.

Twardosz, S., Schwartz, S., Fox, J., & Cunningham, J. L. Development and evaluation of a system to measure affectionate behavior. *Behavioral Assessment*, 1979, *1*, 177–190.

Van Hasselt, V. B., Hersen, M., Whitehall, M. B., & Bellack, A. S. Social skill assessment and training for children: An evaluative review. *Behaviour Research and Therapy*, 1979, *17*, 413–438.

Varni, J. W., Boyd, E. F., & Cataldo, M. F. Self-monitoring, external reinforcement and timeout procedures in the control of high rate tic behaviors in a hyperactive child. *Journal of Behavior Therapy and Experimental Psychology*, 1978, *9*, 353–358.

Wahler, R. G. Oppositional children: A quest for parental reinforcement control. *Journal of Applied Behavior Analysis*, 1969, *2*, 159–170. (a)

Wahler, R. G. Setting generality: Some specific and general effects of child behavior therapy. *Journal of Applied Behavior Analysis*, 1969, *2*, 239–246. (b)

Wahler, R. G. Some structural aspects of deviant child behavior. *Journal of Applied Behavior Analysis*, 1975, *8*, 27–42.

Wahler, R. G., & Fox, J. J. Solitary toy play and time out: A family treatment package for children with ag-gressive and oppositional behavior. *Journal of Applied Behavior Analysis*, 1980, *13*, 23–39.

Wahler, R. G., House, A. E., & Stambaugh, E. E. *Ecological assessment of child problem behaviors*. Elmsford, N.Y.: Pergamon Press, 1976.

Waye, M. F. Behavioral treatment of a child displaying comic-book mediated fear of hand shrinking: A case study. *Journal of Pediatric Psychology*, 1979, *4*, 43–47.

Weathers, L., & Liberman, R. P. Contingency contracting with families of delinquent adolescents. *Behavior Therapy*, 1975, *6*, 356–366.

Weil, G., Goldfried, M. R. Treatment of insomnia in an eleven year old child through self-relaxation. *Behavior Therapy*, 1973, *4*, 282–284.

Weiner, H. R., & Dubanowski, R. A. Resistance to extinction as a function of self- or externally determined schedules of reinforcement. *Journal of Personality and Social Psychology*, 1975, *31*, 905–910.

Weinstein, D. J. Imagery and relaxation with a burn patient. *Behaviour Research and Therapy*, 1976, *14*, 481.

Whitley, A. D., & Sulzer, B. *Increasing reading response rate and accuracy through token reinforcement*. Unpublished paper. Southern Illinois University, Carbondale, 1970.

Whitman, T. L., Mercurio, J. R., & Caponigri, V. Development of social responses in two severely retarded children. *Journal of Applied Behavior Analysis*, 1970, *3*, 133–138.

Williams, C. D. The elimination of tantrum behavior by extinction procedures. *Journal of Abnormal and Social Psychology*, 1959, *59*, 269.

Wiltz, N. A., & Gordon, S. B. Parental modification of a child's behavior in an experimental residence. *Behavior Therapy and Experimental Psychiatry*, 1974, *5*, 107–109.

Winett, R. A., & Winkler, R. C. Current behavior modification in the classroom: Be still, be quiet, be docile. *Journal of Applied Behavior Analysis*, 1972, *5*, 499–504.

Wolf, M., Risley, T. R., & Mees, H. Application of operant conditioning procedures to the behaviour problems of an autistic child. *Behaviour Research and Therapy*, 1964, *1*, 305–312.

Wolf, M. M., Birnbrauer, J. S., Williams, T., & Lawler, J. A note on apparent extinction of the vomiting behavior of a retarded child. In L. P. Ullmann & L. Krasner (Eds.), *Case studies in behavior modification*. New York: Holt, Rinehart & Winston, 1965.

Wolpe, J. *The practice of behavior therapy*. Elmsford, N.Y.: Pergamon Press, 1974.

Wright, D. F., Brown, R. A., & Andrews, M. E. Remission of chronic ruminative vomiting through a reversal of social contingencies. *Behaviour Research and Therapy*, 1978, *16*, 134–136.

Wulbert, M., Nyman, B. A., Snow, D., & Owen, Y. The efficacy of stimulus fading and contingency management in the treatment of elective mutism: A case study. *Journal of Applied Behavior Analysis*, 1973, *6*, 435–442.

Wyatt v. *Stickney*, 344 F. Supp. 387 (M.D. Ala. 1972).

Zlutnick, S., Mayville, W. J., & Moffat, S. Modification of seizure disorders: The interruption of behavioral chains. *Journal of Applied Behavior Analysis*, 1975, *8*, 1–12.

CHAPTER 30

Behavior Analysis Procedures in Classroom Teaching

Ted R. Ruggles and Judith M. LeBlanc

Behavioral research conducted in classroom settings has analyzed behaviors contributing to the maintenance of order in the classrooms as well as behaviors involved in the actual learning of academic concepts. The procedures used to change these behaviors include those involving the manipulation of consequent stimuli and those involving the manipulation of antecedent stimuli. These delineations of procedures and behaviors provide essentially four general categories into which classroom behavioral research can be meaningfully divided: (1) research analyzing the effects of contingent relationships on the behaviors involved in maintaining order in the classroom; (2) research analyzing the effects of discriminative stimuli on behavior involved in maintaining order in the classroom; (3) research analyzing the effects of contingent relationships on the amount and correctness of work produced by the children in the classroom; and (4) research analyzing the effects of manipulating teachers' instructions and discriminative stimulus materials on children's learning academic concepts and skills.

Applied behavior-analysis research of the first type, involving the manipulation of consequent events in order to develop procedures to keep children orderly, working, and attentive in the classroom, is broad and varied. Some critics feel that this research supports questionable educational goals (Winnett & Winkler, 1972), that is, that its goal is keeping children quiet rather than enhancing their learning. It cannot be denied, however, that procedures are now available that can change the behaviors of problem children so that they may remain inside the classroom to learn rather than being sent outside the classroom to be disciplined. The breadth of the research included in this category is sufficient, in terms of populations, behaviors, settings, and procedures, to allow the production of entire books outlining procedures that teachers may use to maintain order (cf. O'Leary & O'Leary, 1972; Clark, Evans, & Hamerlynck, 1972; Hall, 1970; Kazdin, 1975).

Research of the second type, investigating the effects of antecedent stimuli on maintain-

Ted R. Ruggles and Judith M. LeBlanc • Department of Human Development, University of Kansas, Lawrence, Kansas 66045. Preparation of this manuscript and portions of the research described were supported by one or more of the following sources: The National Institute for Child Health and Human Development (HD 07066, HD 002528, 1-T32-HD-07173 and 1-T01-HD-00247) and the United States Department of Education, Bureau for the Education of the Handicapped (USOE 300-77-0308).

ing order in the classroom, is not nearly as common as that manipulating the consequences of this behavior. Studies of the relationship of behavior to environmental settings (Barker, 1968; Proshansky, Ittleson, & Rivlin, 1970) and findings reported within the generalization literature (Stokes & Baer, 1977) suggest that discriminative stimuli may be powerful determinants of the probability of certain behaviors. The few existing studies that are relevant to these considerations, in combination with studies still to emerge, may provide valuable information regarding how the physical arrangement of the classroom might best be programmed.

The third type of research, which seeks methods to increase the rate, accuracy, and performance of academic behavior in the classroom, is also not abundant but is becoming more so as researchers begin to attend to what children are actually learning in the classroom. This body of research indicates that it is the children who are experiencing difficulty learning who are frequently also those who create disturbances in the classroom. Thus, the emphasis in the research conducted in this category is on increasing the motivational level of children through reinforcement of productivity and correctness. Results from this type of research indicate that for some children, such procedures are quite adequate to increase and maintain productivity. For others, however, the procedures are not sufficient to increase academic learning. Thus, the fourth category of research includes those instances in which researchers have begun to analyze how and under what circumstances children can best learn.

In addition to analyzing how and under what conditions children learn, research involved in the fourth category seeks the best methods for teaching children who do not learn under ordinary circumstances. This research assumes that questions regarding motivation have been resolved and that therefore, something involved in the presentation of the stimulus materials and/or the instructions must be the factor limiting learning for the child having difficulty. Chronologically, this area of research closely parallels (but occurs about 10 years later in time) the development of the contingent relationships that are effective in

maintaining classroom order. That is, this research is being initially conducted with mentally handicapped and very young children, perhaps because the environment of these children is simpler and thus easier to operationally define, measure, and analyze. For example, it is easier to identify effective reinforcers for young and/or mentally handicapped children than for adolescents or adults. Similarly, concepts to be learned by young and/or handicapped children are simpler, and thus, techniques for teaching these children effectively can be more readily identified. As occurred in the sequential development of the application of contingent relationships, it is expected that techniques developed from research on instructional and stimulus control variables will ultimately be applied across various populations, handicaps, and ages.

Contingent Relationships and the Behavior Involved in the Maintenance of Classroom Order

The procedures effective in increasing desired classroom behavior (i.e., response-increment procedures) range from simple adult attention for desired behavior, through access to preferred activities, to many different types of token-reinforcement systems. Also varied are those procedures that have been demonstrated to effectively reduce undesired behavior in the classroom (i.e., response-decrement procedures). They include time-out, removal of tokens, reprimands, extinction, and differential reinforcement of low-rate behavior (DRL). Much of the classroom research analyzing the effectiveness of contingently applied procedures deals primarily with the maintenance of order in the classroom. Its focus of application has been primarily on sitting quietly and working in the classroom. Thus, the behaviors dealt with in this type of research may be, but are not necessarily, related to the academic performance of the children in the classroom. The research is, however, designed to develop a classroom atmosphere in which children's learning need not be disrupted by either their own behavior or that of others. Without the development of such procedures, it would be most difficult to begin to analyze the other factors that might be involved in children's academic learning in the classroom.

Response-Increment Procedures

Adult Attention as a Reinforcer. Prior to the use of behavior analysis in any classroom, operant principles were primarily implemented with infrahuman subjects, or occasionally with institutionalized populations (e.g., Ayllon & Michael, 1959; Ayllon & Haughton, 1962). The earliest applications of behavior analysis in the classroom seem to have evolved from concern for the social development of preschool children and depended on adult attention to manipulate children's social interaction. This preschool classroom research demonstrated that behavior analysis techniques could be successfully applied by classroom teachers to change specific undesirable behavior of children who usually were otherwise considered normal. Much of this early research involved procedures sometimes referred to as *praise-and-ignore* (i.e., reinforcement and extinction). Essentially, the overall amount of adult attention was usually not increased but was redistributed, so that most of the attention that a child received followed the occurrence of desired behaviors and little, if any, followed undesirable behavior. That is, desired behavior was reinforced and undesired behavior was ignored or extinguished.

Research involving praise-and-ignore procedures can be distinguished by whether the emphasis was on increasing desired behavior or decreasing undesired behavior. Some research was designed to increase a particular behavior through reinforcing that behavior and ignoring or extinguishing an incompatible class of behaviors. Other research using these procedures was designed to decrease a particular behavior through ignoring it when it occurred and reinforcing (with adult attention) incompatible or desired behaviors. (This procedure is a form of differential reinforcement of other behavior, i.e., DRO.)

An early study by Allen, Hart, Buell, Harris, and Wolf (1964) emphasized increasing the peer interaction of a preschool child through systematically presenting adult attention contingent on that behavior and ignoring attempted interaction with adults. In subsequent studies, this procedure was effective in increasing cooperative play (Hart, Reynolds, Baer, Brawley, & Harris, 1968); attending to play materials (Allen, Henke, Harris, Baer, & Reynolds, 1967), playing vigorously on playground equipment (Johnson, Kelley, Harris, & Wolf, 1966); and other social behaviors (Harris & Miksovic, 1972; Scott, Burton, & Yarrow, 1967). Hall and Broden (1967) also applied these procedures with brain-injured children in a special education setting to change their manipulation of materials, their physical activity, and their social interactions. Hart, Allen, Buell, Harris, and Wolf (1964) emphasized decreasing operant crying in two preschoolers by ignoring it when it occurred and reinforcing (with adult attention) those incompatible behaviors considered appropriate responses to minor injuries, arguments with peers, etc. Similar procedures have been used by Brown and Elliot (1965), by Allen, Turner, and Everett (1970), and by Hall, Panyan, Rabon, and Broden (1968). These latter studies also extended the application of praise-and-ignore to change the disruptive behavior of all children in a classroom.

Although adult attention was a functional reinforcer in the research thus far described, such may not always be the case. As a function of a child's history, adult attention may not acquire reinforcing properties, either because adults have not been sufficiently paired with more "basic" reinforcers (e.g., food and warmth) or because an adult's attention is consistently paired with aversive or neutral consequences and thus acquires punishing or neutral qualities. If children do not discriminate between adults, these pairings can affect the potency of the attention of all adults.

Tangible Reinforcement

Because adult attention is not always sufficiently powerful to produce behavior change, a number of studies have relied on the presentation of tangible reinforcers to increase the occurrence of specific social behaviors. Since tangible reinforcers are expensive to maintain for an extended period of time or with a large group of students, access to special activities

or free time has been frequently used as a behavioral consequence. Wasik (1970), for example, increased the amount of playtime children were allowed contingent on such
appropriate behaviors as sharing materials and
following directions. In addition, the amount
of playtime was *reduced* contingent on the
occurrence of inappropriate behaviors. Thus,
this procedure combined elements of both reinforcement and punishment. A similar combination was used by Dickinson (1968) for a
student in a regular classroom and by Osborne
(1969) in a classroom of deaf students.

The use of procedures employing tangible
reinforcement in classroom settings has been
greatly facilitated through the use of token reinforcement (see review by Kazdin, 1977). A
token, to the extent that it is associated with
the delivery of a desired event (a factor largely
determined by the success of the token exchange procedure), bridges the time between
behavior and reinforcement since it can be
delivered much more temporally approximate
to the behavior than can those reinforcers for
which it may be exchanged. In addition, the
token can signal the availability of a variety
of reinforcers, thus assuring the potency of the
reinforcement procedure across many subjects and/or across extended periods of time.
Finally, the delivery of token reinforcement
is not likely to disrupt ongoing sequences of
behavior in the same way as immediate access
to special activities or free play.

The earliest demonstration of procedures
roughly equivalent to present token systems
was accomplished with primates. For example, Wolfe (1936) taught chimpanzees to obtain
grapes by inserting tokens into a slot. The
chimps were then taught to obtain tokens by
pressing a lever and, finally, to obtain a specific number of tokens before an exchange was
possible. The conditioned reinforcing function
of tokens with primates has also been the focus
of research by Smith (1939) and by Kelleher
(1958).

An early investigation of the use of token
reinforcement to manipulate students' classroom behavior in a special education setting
was conducted by Birnbrauer and Lawler
(1964). Teachers conducted classes of 6–13
pupils, in which tokens, exchangeable for
candy and trinkets, were delivered for working

on tasks, entering the classroom quietly, hang-
ing up coats, and sitting at desks attentively.
These procedures improved the behavior of 37
of 41 students. However, the direct delivery
of candy and trinkets occurred in a portion of
the study, making a firm conclusion regarding
the effective elements of the token system impossible. Therefore, in a replication conducted
by Birnbrauer, Wolf, Kidder, and Tague (1965),
a reversal was conducted to compare performance when tokens were not presented with
performance when they were. Of the 15 subjects in the study, 10 evidenced decreases in
some aspects of academic productivity or increases in disruptive behavior when tokens
were not presented.

Tokens for Individuals. Tokens have frequently been used for individual children in
private sessions to teach behaviors that should
be exhibited in the classroom. Walker and
Buckley (1968) used a token system for increasing the proportion of time a 9-year-old
boy spent attending to assigned problems. The
subject in this experiment participated in treatment sessions conducted outside the regular
classroom. The subject earned points exchangeable for a model by meeting a criterion
for attending. After attending increased in the
experimental setting, the child returned to the
regular classroom, where intermittent reinforcement and a resulting increase in attending
in that setting occurred.

Patterson, Jones, Whittier, and Wright (1965)
extended the use of individually implemented
token systems to a hyperactive child in a special classroom. One of the primary aims of this
study was to demonstrate whether an increase
in attending would generalize across settings.
The subject wore an earphone during the training sessions from which a tone was heard contingent on the passage of 10 sec of "attention."
It was found that once conditioning in the experimental setting was complete, the subject
was more attentive in another (unmanipulated)
class period than a control child.

A unique method for individualizing a token
system to modify the social behavior of a single subject in a classroom setting was presented by Schwarz and Hawkins (1970). In this
procedure, a 12-year-old child's classroom
behavior was videotaped and later viewed by
the child and a therapist. The therapist gave

the child tokens (which were accumulated and exchanged for such items as jewelry and a dress) whenever the child's videotaped behavior met a predetermined criterion for reinforcement. This private, delayed-reinforcement procedure successfully decreased the target behaviors in the classroom setting and, in addition, resulted in behavioral changes during other periods of the day as well as in other, unmanipulated, behavior. Such procedures are especially useful in situations in which it is not possible (or advisable) to reinforce behavior at the actual time it occurs.

Token systems for individual children have also been used in the classroom, and in some cases, access to reinforcement for all members of the class has been dependent on the performance of the target child. In these procedures, referred to by Litlow and Pumroy (1975, p. 342)[1] as "dependent group-oriented contingencies," the target child earns rewards that are distributed across the classroom. Group systems are potentially quite powerful, since the probability is great that peer pressure for the target child to perform will occur. Although designing procedures to promote such pressure might be considered unethical, contingencies of this type no doubt will effect immediate and possibly more lasting behavioral change. In addition, these dependent group-oriented contingencies provide a vehicle for changing the behavior of one child without implementing a token system for all members of the class, an alternative that would be realistic if most of the class members did not demonstrate the types of behavioral problems that were addressed.

Patterson (1965) designed such a token system to decrease the disruptive behavior of a 9-year-old second-grade student who was "hyperactive" and "academically retarded" (p. 371). A light, placed on the child's desk, flashed whenever the child had not exhibited any disruptive behavior for a specific period of time. A counter next to the light counted the number of light flashes that had occurred during the observation period. Candy or pennies, in an amount indicated by the counter, were distributed to *all* members of the class at the end of each session. Patterson *et al.* (1965) reported using the same procedure to change essentially the same behavior. Other studies have utilized such procedures to modify off-task behavior (Coleman, 1970) and to change aspects of social behavior or academic productivity (Walker & Buckley, 1972).

Tokens with Groups. Token systems have often been used to change the behavior of whole groups of children in classroom settings. A common method for arranging the contingencies, referred to by Litlow and Pumroy (1975) as "independent group-oriented contingency systems," involves all members of a group's being simultaneously exposed to the same contingencies, with individual access to reinforcement determined by each child's performance. That is, if an individual child earns enough tokens, the backup reinforcement is forthcoming, and if not, the backup reinforcement is withheld.

Bushell, Wrobel, and Michaelis (1968) demonstrated the effectiveness of such independent group-oriented contingency systems in one of the earliest studies of token reinforcement used to modify the behavior of a group of children in a regular classroom. Attending and working by each of 12 preschool children was consequated independently of their classmates. It was demonstrated that a higher level of attending occurred when tokens, redeemable for access to a variety of special activities, were presented contingently rather than noncontingently.

In another examination of the effects of a token system on the behavior of a group of children, O'Leary, Becker, Evans, and Saudargas (1969) isolated the functions of classroom rules, structure, teacher praise, and tokens on the occurrence of disruptive behavior in the classroom. The subjects in this study were 7 members of a second-grade class of 21 economically disadvantaged children. The various contingencies examined were (1) no consequences for disruptive behavior; (2) daily explanations by the teacher of the rules for

---

[1] Litlow and Pumroy's brief review provides an excellent listing of group contingency studies not included in the present review. It should be noted that their classification includes not only those studies utilizing token procedures but also those using various other contingencies. We have utilized their classification in discussing token procedures with groups, since it provides a suitable framework within which to discuss these varied procedures.

classroom behavior; (3) rules plus structure or reorganization of the classroom schedule into 30-min periods in which specific activities occurred (spelling, reading, arithmetic, and science); (4) rules, structure, and praise for appropriate behavior and ignoring of inappropriate behavior; and (5) the previous conditions with the addition of tokens, exchangeable for a variety of small toys, for appropriate classroom behavior. For 6 of the 7 children, "rules, structure, praise, and ignore" did not appreciably lower disruptive behavior. The addition of the contingent delivery of tokens with the accompanying backup reinforcement, however, reduced disruptive behavior for 5 of the remaining subjects.

Independent group-oriented contingencies have been used in conjunction with tokens in a number of other classroom studies (Ayllon & Roberts, 1974; Bijou, Birnbrauer, Kidder, & Tague, 1966; Birnbrauer, Bijou, Wolf, & Kidder, 1965; Broden, Hall, Dunlap, & Clark, 1970; Drabman, 1973; Chadwick & Day, 1971; Drabman, Spitalnik, & O'Leary, 1973; Kuypers, Becker, & O'Leary, 1968; O'Leary & Becker, 1967). Independent group-oriented contingencies have been used for arranging access to activities (Homme, de Bacca, Devine, Steinhorst, & Rickert, 1963; Hopkins, Schutte, & Garton, 1971; Osborne, 1969; Wasik, 1970) and teacher attention (Hall, Panyan, Rabon, & Broden, 1968; Kazdin & Klock, 1973; Madsen, Becker, Thomas, Koser, & Plager, 1968; McAllister, Stachowiak, Baer, & Conderman, 1969).

Besides those systems in which access to reinforcement is based on the performance of selected individuals, Litlow and Pumroy (1975) described another category referred to as "interdependent group-oriented procedures," in which contingencies are specified in terms of group performance. In one of these procedures, the contingencies are specified in terms of the behavior of each student, but access to reinforcement is dependent on all children's meeting some behavioral criterion. Graubard (1969) used such a procedure to increase the appropriate behavior of a group of delinquent youths. In this study, points were given to each group member for appropriate conduct and academic output. The acquisition of backup reinforcement, however, was dependent on each group member's receiving a minimum number of points. Such procedures rely heavily on peer influence. In describing the study, Graubard reported that "subjects would spontaneously remind transgressors that inappropriate behavior affected them all" (p. 269). The reason for the paucity of research on such procedures is perhaps that in most cases, requiring the entire group to meet certain expectations simultaneously is not only unrealistic but perhaps not ethical.

In a second form of interdependent group-contingency arrangement, reward is dependent on the entire class's meeting some criterion without regard to the behavior of individual class members. Packard (1970) experimentally manipulated all members of a classroom as a unit by illuminating a red light mounted on the teacher's desk whenever *one or more* of the members of a classroom were attending. In comparison to no contingencies associated with the light illumination, access to play materials and privileges contingent on the class's reaching a criterion of attending resulted in increased attending. This research was replicated in kindergarten, third, fifth, and sixth grade. It is conceivable in this system that only one child could be attending for the entire class period and thus obtain reinforcement for all.

In addition to those procedures that base interdependent contingencies on the class as a whole, reinforcement has been based on the average, the highest, the lowest, or a randomly selected performance (Hamblin, Hathaway, & Wodarski, 1971; Drabman, Spitalnik, & Spitalnik, 1974). These procedures differ from the dependent group-oriented contingencies to the extent that the student, or students, on whose behavior the contingencies are based vary from day to day, and thus the criterion is not predictable prior to evaluation.

A variation on the use of the entire class as the group is to divide the class into smaller groups or "teams." Barrish, Saunders, and Wolf (1969) developed a "good-behavior game" for working with a group of 24 students, 7 of whom had been referred for problems such as being out of their seats, making noise, and other disruptive behaviors. The class was divided into two teams, and the number of "rule violations" for each team was recorded on the chalkboard. (Rules prohibited getting out of one's seat, talking without permission, making noise, sitting on desks, etc.). If one team got fewer marks than the other, or if both teams got fewer than 5 marks in a session, the team was allowed to participate in an extra 30-min free period, line up early, put stars by the team members' names on a chart, etc. In addition, if a team got fewer than 20 marks in a week, that team was allowed 4 min of extra recess time for a week.

Maloney and Hopkins (1973) extended the use of the good-behavior game to the manipulation of compositional variables with fourth-, fifth-, and sixth-grade children. They awarded points for the use of different adjectives, action verbs, etc. The members of the team who received the most points (or both teams, if they reached a predetermined point criterion) received candy and 5 min of extra recess. Harris and Sherman (1973) also utilized a version of the good-behavior game in fifth- and sixth-grade classrooms and analyzed the contributions of the various components of the procedure across a series of manipulations. Early dismissal from school, the criterion established for "winning" the game, and the division of the class into teams each seemed to contribute somewhat to the overall effectiveness of the procedure. Removal of any one component, however, did not drastically decrease the procedure's effectiveness. Other versions of the good-behavior game have been implemented by Medland and Stachnik (1972), Robertshaw and Hiebert (1973), and Wilson and Williams (1973).

The arrangement of contingencies based on the behavior of all or some portion of the children in a classroom represents a potentially substantial advance in the implementation of these procedures by classroom teachers. Further evidence supporting this contention is found in the fact that several comparisons of the relative effectiveness of group-oriented interdependent and group-oriented independent procedures suggest that the interdependent procedures are at least as effective as the independent procedures. Litlow and Pumroy (1975) reported that of 14 studies that have compared these two approaches, 7 have found no differences between the two (Axelrod, 1973; Drabman *et al.*, 1974; Grandy, Madsen & DeMersseman, 1973; Herman & Tramontana, 1971; Levin, 1971; Prentice, 1970; Turknett, 1971), and 6 have reported that interdependent procedures are more effective (Graubard, Lanier, Weisert, & Miller, 1970; Hamblin *et al.*, 1971; Jacobs, 1970; Long & Williams, 1973; McNamara, 1971; Witte, 1971).

Although powerful, the fact that group-contingency procedures are, to a large extent, based on the occurrence of social processes seems to demand that they be implemented with some degree of caution. O'Leary and Drabman (1971) have noted that problems may arise when particular children are unable to perform the required behavior, when such procedures result in undue pressure on individual children, or when one or more children subvert the program.

Token systems are efficient behavioral-change systems for teachers to use in classrooms. They provide an opportunity to make the delivery of reinforcement quite discriminable, and thus, behavior change is likely to occur more rapidly. In addition, the systems provide an opportunity for teachers to use a variety of reinforcers, which results in a greater potential for a reinforcer to be available for each child. There are, however, some drawbacks to token systems that must not be overlooked. The very discriminability that makes token systems immediately effective can also work to the ultimate detriment of the system. That is, once tokens are used with children, it is difficult, although not impossible, to "wean" them from the system. Such weaning is necessary, since the real world is not based on token systems.

As already indicated, the effectiveness of token systems lies somewhat in the opportunity to choose a reinforcer from among a variety of items. Thus, a teacher must either be extremely creative in development reinforcing items that are of low cost, or money must be available to purchase such items. A possible method for overcoming the cost problem lies in implementing a token system that has its backup basis in the home rather than in the classroom. Bailey, Wolf, and Phillips (1970) developed and successfully used such a procedure with predelinquent boys who lived in a special home with parents trained in behavior analysis skills. Schumaker, Hovell, and Sherman (1977) extended the use of such procedures to the natural parents of children who were experiencing difficulties in school.

Finally, token systems are more cumbersome and burdensome to use than teacher attention, grades, etc. Token systems require a much more elaborate "bookkeeping" system than more traditional classroom procedures. Even for token systems that are based in the home, it still remains for the teacher to assume the burden of the evaluation and bookkeeping system. Rather than assume the additional work involved, many busy teachers refuse to use the system until the disruptive behaviors of children reach totally unbearable levels.

Response-Decrement Procedures

There has been much public discussion regarding the use of punishment in school settings. Because of societal concerns and ethical issues, however, research involving the application of aversive stimuli in school settings is almost nonexistent. As Gardner (1969) remarked, punishment is often avoided "not on the basis of an objective evaluation of scientific data but on the basis of ethical, philosophical and sociopolitical considerations" (p. 88).

Among the popular arguments aimed at punishment is that all or many of the stimuli that accompany its occurrence may assume "conditioned punishing" qualities. Thus, it would follow that teachers who administer punishment, the classroom in which punishment is administered, and education in general may occasion avoidance of or escape from school by the child. Although there is no direct evidence to support or dispel this contention, examination of analogous positive reinforcement situations suggests that such generalization of effects probably does not occur as a matter of course.

A second argument against the use of punishment is that its effects are not considered long-lasting. This is not surprising, since positive reinforcement effects are similarly short-lived if the overall environmental arrangement of contingencies is not carefully programmed. Without careful planning, it is a rare bit of luck when a reinforcement procedure can be discontinued without a resulting reversal in behavior. It should, however, be possible to maintain the presence or absence of behavior through arranging the transfer of behavioral control from contrived punishing or reinforcing stimuli to stimuli that occur in the "natural community" (Stokes & Baer, 1977) of consequences.

While many generally held notions of punishment may not be empirically sound, there are reasons to avoid the use of such procedures whenever possible. Behavior analysts must respect, if not empirically agree with, societal restrictions on the use of punishment. Additionally, punishment is likely to be applied in situations in which desperation, anger, and lack of rational planning occur. Thus, it requires more careful planning and justification than does the use of positive reinforcement. Additionally, it should be remembered that response-decrement procedures should be used only in conjunction with response-increment procedures. Obviously, a reduction or elimination of an undesirable behavior does not ensure that more appropriate behavior will fill the behavioral void.

Not all punishment involves inflicting physical pain on the child (in fact, very few currently prescribed, applied procedures do). For example, MacMillan, Forness, and Trumbull (1973) noted that "teacher frowns, glances, reprimands, withdrawal of privileges" (p. 89) may be punishers. These authors suggested two points that should be considered in selecting a punishment procedure. First, the procedure should correspond to the "functional maturity of the child" (p. 89). If children operate at an extremely low developmental level, physically painful stimuli may be necessary, at least initially. If children develop normally and are socially adjusted, however, verbal reprimands may be sufficient. Second, a stimulus is punishing only if it results in a decrease in the behavior it consistently follows, or if the child avoids or chooses to get away from that stimulus.

In 1938, Skinner differentiated two types of punishment: first, the contingent presentation of an aversive event, and second, the contingent withholding or removal of a positive reinforcer. Since that time, much has been written regarding the operational definitions of punishment (cf. Azrin & Holz, 1966), and basic experimental punishment procedures continue to be divided into categories similar to those defined by Skinner. There is little research, however, involving the contingent application of aversive stimuli in applied settings. In fact, the response-decrement procedures most frequently used in applied settings involve both punishment and reinforcement, as well as other, less readily categorized, procedures. Thus, to divide *applied* response-decrement procedures into distinct punishment categories such as those found in the basic experimental literature is almost impossible.

One of the most frequently used response-decrement procedures in applied behavior analysis has been time-out from reinforcement or social isolation. Because of society's increasing resistance to the use of social isolation to decrease behavior, however, other, less aversive procedures have been developed. One of these, response-cost, is limited to those situations in which a token economy or a point system is in operation in the classroom. Other response-decrement procedures often used in classroom settings include reprimands, differential reinforcement of other (DRO) behavior, differential reinforcement of low-rate (DRL) behavior, paced instructions, and shifting a teacher's attention from a target child to another child contingent on an inappropriate aggressive behavior emitted by the target child.

Time-Out and Social Isolation. In describing the use of social isolation to decrease undesirable behavior, Wolf, Risley and Mees (1964) indicated that the procedure resembled Ferster and Appel's (1961) use of time-out from positive reinforcement as an aversive stimulus (Wolf *et al.*, 1964, p. 306). Subsequently, Drabman and Spitalnik (1973) attributed to them the popularization of the use of the term *time-out* to describe any situation in which a child is temporarily removed from ongoing activities as a consequence of some (undesired) behavior.

The term *time-out* implies that (1) the child is temporarily denied access to some positively reinforcing event, and (2) the denial is responsible for an observed decrease in behavior. Thus, for time-out to be effective, a reinforcing contingency to which the child can be temporarily denied access must be present in the environment. Also, as with all behavior-change procedures, there must be a demonstration that it is the denial and not some concurrently operating contingency that is responsible for the decrease in behavior. In many cases, time-out includes social isolation or other, possibly aversive, consequences. Changes in behavior that occur as a result of such ancillary procedures cannot usually be attributed solely to time-out. As Drabman and Spitalnik indicated, only when the reinforcing aspects of the environment have been directly manipulated is it possible to assess directly the individual contributions of time-out and social isolation.

Perhaps the largest difference between social isolation (also referred to as *room time-out*) and other time-out procedures is that social isolation involves removing the child from the classroom to an isolated area. Drabman and Spitalnik (1973), for example, placed institutionalized children in social isolation rooms for 10 min each time that disruptive behavior, aggression, and out-of-seat occurred. In a reversal design, the social isolation procedure was shown to be effective for reducing all three target behaviors in nearly all subjects. Clark, Rowbury, Baer, and Baer (1973) also used the removal of a mongoloid child from a preschool classroom to reduce severely disruptive behaviors. In addition to demonstrating the effectiveness of the procedure, it was indicated that "some schedules of intermittent punishment may be as effective as continuous punishment, at least in the case of the continued suppression of a response that has already been reduced to a low frequency" (p. 454).

Another type of time-out involves placing the child in a chair, apart from the ongoing activities in the classroom. LeBlanc, Busby, and Thomson (1973) used this chair time-out procedure to change the disruptive and aggressive behaviors of a preschool child. In this procedure, the child was placed on a chair, away from the center of activity, whenever a disruptive or aggressive behavior occurred. If the child refused to remain in the chair for the duration of the time-out period, a backup, (room time-out) was used for further isolation. The use of this backup room time-out appeared to strengthen the effectiveness of the chair time-out across the conditions of the experiment. That is, in the final manipulation of a three-component multiple-baseline design, the chair time-out alone was sufficient to eliminate the aggressive behavior, whereas in the prior two components, the room time-out was required on occasion to back up the chair time-out.

Another version of chair time-out was labeled "contingent observation" by Porterfield, Herbert-Jackson, and Risley (1976). The label *contingent observation* was used because when inappropriate behavior occurred, the children were told what they did wrong and what the appropriate alternative would be, and they were then separated from the group to *observe* the appropriate behavior of the other children. After indicating an understanding of what the appropriate behavior should be, a child was returned to participation in the group. In this chair time-out procedure, a backup room time-out was also used. This procedure was compared with a more traditional redirection of behavior and found to be more effective. However, it is not clear whether it was the contingent observation or the backup room time-out that made the contingent observation procedure more effective.

Chair time-out procedures remove the child from an activity that can still be observed, whereas social isolation procedures remove the child from all but the "memory" of the ongoing activity. Thus, in social isolation, it is doubtful, once isolation begins, that the procedure can accurately be labeled *time-out*. For very young and small children, chair time-out is probably as aversive and effective as room time-out, in that both remove the child from ongoing activities. Unlike the social isolation involved in room time-out, however, chair time-out does not seem to conflict with legal, ethical, and other societal points of view. For older and larger children, however, isolation may be the only effective treatment available because of the difficulties involved in keeping them seated.

Some time-out procedures do not involve the removal of the child from the setting in which reinforcement occurs; rather, they remove the opportunity to respond for reinforcement. Foxx and Shapiro (1978), for example, described a procedure in which each of five special-education students wore a ribbon indicating that the child was eligible to receive periodic teacher attention and to be allowed to participate in activities. If a child behaved inappropriately, the teacher removed the child's ribbon for 3 min. The procedure successfully reduced the occurrence of misbehavior without necessitating removal of the child from the setting.

In another procedure, Plummer, Baer, and LeBlanc (1977) removed materials, and the teacher turned away from the child to constitute a time-out for disruptive, aggressive and inappropriate behaviors that functionally retarded children emitted in response to the teacher's instructions in a one-to-one teaching situation. Although this time-out procedure was successful with many other children in the same teaching laboratory, it did not decrease the undesirable behaviors of these children. Plummer *et al.* indicated that removing the opportunity to obtain reinforcement might produce a negative rather than a positive reinforcement effect if other variables in the environment were aversive. That is, the children might be disruptive so that the teacher would remove the academic materials and the children would then not have to continue working. It was theorized that working on the tasks to obtain the available reinforcers was less reinforcing than it was to emit inappropriate behavior, which resulted in the removal of the sometimes difficult academic work. Thus, negative reinforcement may operate even though demonstrated positive reinforcers exist in the time-in environment, if the latter environment is relatively aversive in other ways.

Solnick, Rincover, and Peterson (1977) also used the removal of the reinforcers and the reinforcing agent as a time-out procedure. These procedures were ineffective for decreasing the tantrums of an autistic child and for decreasing the spitting and self-injurious behavior of a severely retarded child. With the autistic child, however, when the opportunity to engage in the self-stimulatory behaviors that occurred during time-out was made contingent on tantrums, the tantrums increased. In the case of the severely retarded child, enriching the time-in environment was sufficient to reduce spitting and self-injurious behavior; that is, when new toys and other interesting, stimulating objects were used rather than the typical activities, such as putting blocks in cans and sorting colors, the inappropriate behaviors decreased. It was concluded that the effectiveness of time-out is influenced by the nature of the behaviors that a child engages in while in time-out and by the characteristics of the time-in setting.

Paced Instructions. Plummer *et al.* (1977) worked with two subjects who often responded to instructions by emitting inappropriate behaviors. Consistent instruction was necessary, however, because the children would not engage in academic tasks without them. When time-out for inappropriate behaviors proved ineffective, a paced-instruction procedure was designed in which instructions were repeatedly given at 1-min intervals, regardless of the subject's behavior, until the subject complied. Since the subject was not allowed to escape from the instructions (through being timed out or by preventing instruction through disruption), compliance with instructions increased and inappropriate behavior decreased. The paced-instruction procedure used by Plummer *et al.* had an additional unexpected side effect. Teachers who had previously avoided instructing the children because they did not want disruptive behavior to occur were now willing to interact with the children. It was only at this point that academic learning could begin to occur.

Goldstein, Cooper, Ruggles, and LeBlanc (1980) implemented paced instructions at 10-sec intervals and increased rather than decreased a child's aggressive and destructive behaviors that accompanied the teacher's instruction. When paced reprimands for the occurrence of inappropriate behaviors were combined with paced instructions, there was an increase in task-related behavior and a decrease in inappropriate behavior. Possibly reprimands were a necessary addition to the paced-instruction procedure because the child was sophisticated enough to engage in self-reinforcing behavior. Apparently, the pacing procedures did not become aversive until paced reprimands were added. Only then did the child engage in task-related behavior to avoid the aversiveness of pacing.

Reprimands. Doleys, Wells, Hobbs, Roberts, and Cartelli (1976) examined the influence of loud verbal reprimands on noncompliance. In this study, conducted in a laboratory setting, developmentally handicapped children were reprimanded for not complying with instructions. The level of noncompliance during this condition was lower than in comparison conditions in which time-out and positive practice were used. Other researchers have variously demonstrated that reprimands from teachers may function as punishers or reinforcers for inappropriate behavior. This variability of results may stem from differences in style of reprimand presentation. O'Leary and Becker (1968) and O'Leary, Kaufman, Kass, and Drabman (1970) compared soft reprimands heard only by the children to whom they were directed with louder reprimands that could be heard by several other children in the class. The effects of soft versus loud reprimands on out-of-seat, talking out, off-task, aggression, etc., were analyzed by O'Leary *et al.* with 10 children (2 in each of five classes) who were selected on the basis of a high rate of such disruptive behaviors. In general, soft reprimands resulted in less disruptive behavior than loud reprimands.

Thomas, Becker, and Armstrong (1968) suggested that a teacher's disapproval may function as a reinforcer for maintaining the occurrence of inappropriate classroom behavior. The research by O'Leary *et al.* supports this contention; that is, disapproval heard only by the reprimanded student seemed to have less of a reinforcing value and more of a behaviorally depressing effect than loud reprimands that drew the attention of others to the child being reprimanded. It is also possible that the reinforcing effect is in the target subject's apparent control over the teacher in these situations. That is, when the teacher delivers loud reprimands, the target child's classmates may find it amusing that the teacher lost control of the target. If this is the case, then teachers who wish to use reprimands to change behavior should elect the quieter approach.

Response-Cost. Response-cost involves the contingent removal of an environmental stimulus that results in a decrease in the probability of the behavior on which the removal is contingent. Response-cost differs from extinction in that it generally involves the contingent removal of some object or activity that is assumed to function as a reinforcer, while extinction simply precludes the delivery of that reinforcer. Many token and point systems (previously described) have included re-sponse-cost components.

The effectiveness of response-cost proce-dures in changing human behavior was con-vincingly demonstrated in a series of basic experimental studies by Weiner (1962). This research alternated periods of positive rein-forcement with periods of response-cost. Most applied research incorporating response-cost does not utilize alternating periods; instead, it implements the response-cost contingency concurrently with reinforcement contingen-cies. It is not clear whether these procedural differences would seriously limit the effec-tiveness of response-cost. What is a definite limitation is that response-cost, of whichever type, cannot be implemented unless previ-ously earned reinforcers are present in the behavior change setting. In token systems, for example, the subject must always have some "reserve" tokens on which response-costs can be levied. In addition, the size and the frequency of response-cost must be sufficient to change behavior while allowing the subject access to reinforcement. This becomes ob-vious in token systems, since, in order to re-tain their reinforcing function, tokens must be regularly paired with existing (backup) rein-forcers.

In a number of cases, the effectiveness of response-cost has been compared with that of reward procedures for reducing inappropriate classroom behavior. The results of this re-search indicated that reward systems are equal to (Hundert, 1976; Iwata & Bailey, 1974; Kauf-man & O'Leary, 1972) or more effective than (McLaughlin & Malaby, 1972) response-cost procedures. These findings, in combination with the difficulties involved in maintaining the bookkeeping system (which are similar to those in maintaining token systems), may ac-count for the limited use of response-cost pro-cedures for changing classroom behavior.

Differential Reinforcement of Low-Rate Behavior. Procedures employing differential reinforcement of low rates of behavior (DRL) may be especially useful when the complete elimination of a behavior is not desirable or necessary, or when it is not reasonable to re-quire that a behavior not occur for some time before reinforcement can be delivered. Dietz and Repp (1973, 1974) utilized such proce-dures to lower the rate of verbalizations of students in special and regular classrooms. In one experiment, free play was contingent on maintaining a rate of talk-outs equal to or less than .06 per minute. Reinforcement was con-tingent on the occurrence of fewer than a spec-ified number of responses in a time period rather than the passage of a specific period of time with no responding. The results of this study suggested that the student's behavior was controlled by the parameters of the DRL schedule. In addition, the 1973 study demon-strated that the DRL rate limits could be grad-ually reduced until the behavior was elimi-nated. Thus, DRL could be a valuable response-elimination procedure in settings in which ab-rupt behavioral change might cause disrup-tions in other children's behavior and/or in the classroom routine.

Differential Reinforcement of Other Be-havior. Reynolds (1968) defined DRO as a pro-cedure in which reinforcement is delivered when a particular response has *not* occurred for a specified period of time. Thus, reinforce-ment can be delivered contingent on *any* be-havior, appropriate or inappropriate, that is occurring when the specified time period elapses. It was suggested by Uhl and Garcia (1969) that this type of DRO be referred to as "omission training" and that the term *DRO* be used only when reinforcement is delivered contingent on the occurrence of a *specific* other behavior or behaviors. Most applied re-search has implemented this latter type of DRO, primarily because it is difficult to im-plement the time-based DRO in applied set-tings and because it is frequently considered neither ethical nor functional to reinforce *any* behavior that occurs when a specified time period elapses. Time-based DRO has been used in one-to-one therapeutic settings in which the subjects have few responses in their repertoires other than the target responses, for example, self-stimulatory behavior (Corte, Wolf, & Locke, 1971), or in which there is only one other behavior that can be emitted and it is incompatible with the target response, for example, screaming (Bostow & Bailey, 1969). Research using DRO to change behav-ior in classroom situations is limited and, as with the research conducted by Twardosz and Sajwaj (1972), usually has not involved a time base. Their research indicated the usefulness of DRO to increase the amount of time a 4-year-old preschool child spent sitting in a chair. Increases in collateral behaviors, such as proximity to other children and use of toys, were also noted.

Differential reinforcement of other behavior is frequently used in classroom research as a reversal control procedure (Osborne, 1969; Peterson, Cox, & Bijou, 1971, Reynolds & Risley, 1968). Goetz, Holmberg, and LeBlanc (1975) compared the effectiveness of DRO and noncontingent reinforcement as reversal control procedures. DRO resulted in a faster, less variable, and more persuasive reversal of behavior than did noncontingent reinforcement. Even though DRO as a reversal control involves the ethically questionable procedure of reinforcing inappropriate behavior, it may be justified by the applied experimenter since it allows one to demonstrate experimental control quickly and to return to increasing desirable behavior.

Shifting the Teacher's Attention. While extinction has been a component of almost all procedures designed to modify classroom behaviors through reinforcement, its use in reducing aggression in classrooms has been uncommon. The most obvious reason for this fact is that it is not generally acceptable to allow a child's classmates to endure abuse while the gradual extinction of the behavior occurs. A procedure designed by Pinkston, Reese, LeBlanc, and Baer (1973) introduced a partial solution to this problem. In this study, aggressive behavior was followed by the teacher ignoring the aggressive child while attending to the child who had been attacked. This procedure reduced aggression without allowing further harm to come to the victim. In addition to extinction, the authors suggest that giving attention to the victim may have punished the aggressive act.

Summary

The breadth and scope of research analyzing the effects of contingent relationships on behavior involved in maintaining order in the classroom are currently sufficient to allow teachers to be knowledgeably advised regarding what to do with behavior-problem children. It should therefore no longer be acceptable for teachers to indicate that they cannot deal with problem children in the classroom. With the availability of the various teacher-attention and token-reinforcement systems, as well as response-cost, time-out, and other response-decrement procedures, it is possible to handle the majority of behavior problems that occur in most classroom settings. There is currently a need to impart the knowledge of behavior-analysis procedures to the practitioners in the field so that the use of these procedures can become more widespread. As this occurs, perhaps there will be more of an emphasis in classrooms on what and how we are teaching children rather than on how their behavior can be controlled so that the classroom can continue in operation.

The research emphasis in this area appears to be beginning to focus on refinements and combinations of the more general procedures used for many years, as evidenced in the research involving DRO, DRL, paced instructions, and the shifting of the teacher's attention from the target child to another child. Perhaps, in the future, this type of research will yield information regarding more efficient and less intrusive procedures that can be used in classroom settings to change inappropriate behavior.

Effects of Environmental Discriminative Stimuli on Behavior Involved in Maintaining Order in the Classroom

To the extent that a stimulus or a stimulus complex is consistently associated with a specific behavior and its consequences, it can control the future occurrence of similar responses. In applied behavior analysis, the control of behavior by discriminative stimuli has been most often considered in the context of the generalization of behavior across settings and/or experimenters or teachers. Researchers have frequently noted the failure to maintain or transfer behavior change across stimulus conditions (cf. Lovaas & Simmons, 1969; Meddock, Parsons, & Hill, 1971; Peterson & Whitehurst, 1971: Redd & Birnbrauer, 1969;

Tate & Baroff, 1966). This failure to transfer is often attributed to inconsistencies between controlling stimuli across settings (Marholin, Siegel, & Phillips, 1976; Marholin & Steinman, 1977). Failures to produce across-setting generalization demonstrate the power that discriminative stimuli can exert over the occurrence of a variety of behaviors.

Most applied behavioral research addressing the role of discriminative stimuli has emphasized procedures for facilitating the occurrence of a newly trained or manipulated behavior across settings. The direct manipulation of discriminative stimuli as a procedure for effecting behavior change occurs relatively infrequently in the literature. In fact, reviewers tend to dismiss this area of analysis by stating that there are few studies that have systematically manipulated antecedent conditions (Klein, 1979; O'Leary & O'Leary, 1976). Some researchers, however, have addressed issues that are either directly or indirectly related to developing an understanding of the role of discriminative stimulus variables in designing procedures to change classroom behavior. In general, research analyzing the role of discriminative stimuli in applied research can be categorized according to variables relating to the physical environment, to the behavior or presence of the teacher, and to the behavior or presence of a child's peers.

The Role of Physical Environment Characteristics as Discriminative Stimuli

The relationship between classroom characteristics and children's behavior has, at times, been examined in studies in which researchers have simply quantified the different behaviors that occurred in various stimulus settings. For example, parallel play in preschools most often occurs in the art and the play areas (Hartup, 1970), and social interaction seems to be controlled by dramatic play (Charlesworth & Hartup, 1967) and dolls (Shure, 1963). More direct analyses of the effects of the physical arrangement of the classroom on behavior have consisted of observing and recording behavior before and after some rearrangement of the physical environment. Using this tactic, Twardosz, Cataldo, and Ris-

ley (1974) demonstrated the effect of arranging an "open" classroom environment on the activities of infants and toddlers in a day-care setting, and Weinstein (1977) showed that the one-task behavior of second- and third-grade children was related to the location, the nature, and the quantity of classroom furniture.

In a study in which the manipulation of discriminative stimuli within the classroom was specifically designed to remediate social deficits, Mitaug and Wolfe (1976) increased the verbalizations of special-education pupils by presenting them with tasks that required the verbal response of peers before materials for completing the task could be received. Mitaug and Wolfe indicated that environmental restructuring becomes the procedure of choice for remediating behavior when the desired behaviors do not occur or occur too infrequently for reinforcement procedures to be optimally effective.

The Role of Teacher Verbalizations and Presence as Discriminative Stimuli

Just as aspects of the physical environment control the occurrence of behavior, aspects of teacher verbal behavior or even teacher presence can, depending on a child's history of reinforcement, function as stimuli that control behavior. For most children, compliance with instruction develops through experiencing instructions paired with consequences for responding or not responding. For these children, verbal instructions provide teachers with a means of evoking behavior that can, if desired, be strengthened through the concurrent application of consequent events.

In research designed to increase a child's involvement with large motor activities (Hardiman, Goetz, Reuter, & LeBlanc, 1975) and social interaction (Strain, Shores, & Kerr, 1976), a combination of teacher prompts and contingent attention was used. Hardiman *et al.* demonstrated that teacher prompts plus contingent attention were more effective than contingent attention alone in increasing the subject's involvement in motor activities. In describing their results, Hardiman *et al.* pointed out that during conditions using only attention, if the subject did not independently engage in an activity, there was no behavior to reinforce and thus behavioral change could not be effected. The manipulation of discriminative stimuli (instructions) to produce behaviors that could then be reinforced undoubtedly circumvented the arduous process of shaping successive approximations or simply waiting for a reinforceable instance of the behavior to occur.

In one study (Wulbert, Nyman, Snow, & Owen, 1973), manipulations of discriminative stimuli were used to teach a child to respond to verbal instructions given by many different people. Since the child responded only to verbalizations from her family members, the authors employed a fading procedure in which the child's mother initially administered the training items that required a verbal or motor response. Across trials, a stranger gradually entered the room, sat with mother and child, administered items simultaneously with the mother, and finally administered items to the child alone. After the child began to follow the stranger's instructions, the mother was gradually moved out of the room. Several other experimenters were subsequently faded into the setting in the same way. Finally, a similar stimulus-control procedure was implemented to move the child into the regular classroom, to establish verbal control by the classroom teacher, and to begin to produce interaction with classmates. While this procedure employed consequence manipulations (time-out and verbal reinforcement) in addition to the fading procedure, reinforcement alone would not have been effective, since the desired behavior never occurred and thus could not be reinforced.

Most young children have a reinforcement history that results in a certain amount of their behavior being controlled by an adult's presence. This is most evident in the differences found in children's behavior when the teacher is absent or present in the room. In one of the few studies to demonstrate such discriminative control, Marholin and Steinman (1977) showed that academic productivity and on-task behavior deteriorated less in the teacher's absence when reinforcement was contingent on academic productivity than when it was contingent on on-task behavior. These results seem to be attributable to the different amounts of discriminative control acquired by the teacher

in the two procedures. Since the teacher's presence was necessary for evaluation of the children's behavior in terms of the on-task contingency, there was a lack of powerful controlling stimuli in the teacher's absence. On the other hand, when the contingencies were placed on academic productivity, some portion of the functional discriminative stimulus complex (i.e., the academic materials themselves) remained present and functional even in the teacher's absence.

The Role of Peer Behavior as Discriminative Stimuli

It seems almost obvious that the behavior of students within the classroom may, like the physical environment and the teacher's behavior, acquire discriminative properties and affect the behavior of other students within the setting. Teachers often report, for example, that disruptive behavior by one or a few students in the classroom "sets off" disruption by others. The inverse, in which consequences directed to one or a few subjects in a group are accompanied by changes in the behavior of other children, is also common. Thus, it seems that the social process sometimes described as *observational learning* (see Whitehurst, 1978, for a review) may play an important role in the occurrence of some behavior within the classroom and could be important in the development of successful, economical classroom intervention strategies.

Whitehurst (1978) said that observational learning occurs when "the topography, functional outcome, and/or discriminative context of one organism's behavior controls a related characteristic of another's behavior" (p. 150). Thus, the meaning of observational learning is expanded from including only those instances in which the observer's behavior is topographically similar or identical to that of the model to include also those instances in which the behavior of the model and the observer is controlled by the same discriminative stimuli or context or the outcomes of those behaviors are functionally the same. Vicarious reinforcement, a process sometimes seen as separate from observational learning, is viewed by Whitehurst as one of a variety of contextual stimuli that determine which, if any, aspects of a model's behavior come to control the observer's behavior. Also included as contextual stimuli are the observer's past history with regard to reinforced imitation, verbal or other instructions, etc.

Perhaps the area of observational learning that has received the most attention by behavior analysts is vicarious consequences. Broden, Bruce, Mitchell, Carter, and Hall (1970), for example, reported that teacher attention delivered to one child for attending resulted in an increase in the attending of a child at an adjacent desk. The authors stated that the effects might be attributable to imitation, to the reinforcing aspects of the teacher's proximity, or to the possibility that increased attending by the target child resulted in fewer disruptions of the peer's study. Unfortunately, there were no controls that would dismiss such direct reinforcement (in the form of teacher proximity) as a cause for the increase in the child observer's behavior. Thus, any statement regarding the role of observation learning in this study is prohibited.

In a study conducted by Kazdin (1973), the target subjects of pairs of retarded children received adult praise for attending, and the attending of adjacent peers increased along with that of the target subjects. Of additional interest in this research was the fact that the observer subjects' behavior remained at the increased level even when the target subjects were praised for inappropriate behavior.

Several extensions of research on vicarious effects have been reported. Drabman and Lahey (1974), for example, reported that the behavior of the subject, a 10-year-old girl, as well as of her classmates, became less disruptive when feedback to the subject was given in the form of occasional teacher ratings. Strain *et al.* (1976) demonstrated that "spillover" effects were partially the function of the behavior and reinforcement history of peers and that such effects were greater when treatment was consistently applied to two children (as opposed to a single child). Finally, Kazdin, Silverman, and Sittler (1975) examined the use of prompts to enhance the effect of nonverbal approval on nontarget peers. It was reported that nonverbal reinforcement was sufficient to increase the target subject's attentive behavior, but vicarious effects were produced only when nonverbal plus verbal attention occurred or when the nonverbal approval was accompanied by a verbal prompt to classmates to look at the target subject when nonverbal approval occurred.

Summary

Relatively few researchers have directly investigated the manipulation of discriminative stimulus events to produce changes in the behaviors that allow children to function effectively in the classroom. Further study of this topic might shed light on the optimal arrangement of the physical environment for facilitating the emergence as well as the maintenance of desired behavior patterns. Such manipulations could be less costly in terms of time and money as well as simpler to implement in classroom settings than the procedures that are currently employed. In addition, a better understanding of the controlling relationships that exist between a child's behavior and that of the child's peers may allow the development of classroom maintenance procedures, based on observational learning, that could have broader effects across children.

Contingent Relationships and Attention, Rate, Accuracy, and Amount of Responding on Academic Tasks

The rationale for conducting applied behavior-analysis research that emphasizes the maintenance of classroom order is based on the assumption that children who engage in behaviors that are not obviously academically related disrupt their own learning process as well as that of their classmates. While most educators agree that some level of classroom decorum is necessary for learning to occur, the exact nature of the relationship between learning and classroom order has not been adequately demonstrated. The most outspoken criticism of applied behavior-analysis research that concentrates on decreasing disruptive behavior and on increasing on-task behavior was provided by Winett and Winkler (1972). They quoted Silberman's assessment (p. 10; Winett

& Winkler, p. 499) of public-school classrooms as "grim, joyless places" and suggested that behavior analysts (by developing the technology for accomplishing these goals) were "instruments of the *status quo*, unquestioning servants of a system of law and order to the apparent detriment of the educational process itself" (Winett & Winkler, p. 501). Winett and Winkler were also subject to criticism because they included only a limited and somewhat biased sample of behavior-analysis research in their survey (O'Leary, 1972). Their article, however, provoked a great deal of thought regarding the functional connection between disruptive or on-task behavior and academic productivity.

Not all researchers who investigated the development of academic productivity prior to the publication of the Winett and Winkler article were deserving of such criticism. In fact, a number of investigations had previously demonstrated the effectiveness of placing consequences directly on academic responding. For example, in some of this research, children were reinforced for work completion (Wolf, Giles, & Hall, 1968); correct responding on spelling tests (Lovitt, Guppy, & Blattner, 1969); the rate and accuracy of their printing (Hopkins *et al.*, 1971; Salzberg, Wheeler, Devar, & Hopkins, 1971); and the accuracy and/or the rate of various other academic tasks (Evans & Oswalt, 1968; Haring & Hauck, 1969; Lovitt & Curtiss, 1969; Tyler & Brown, 1968).

These early studies and some that followed approached the manipulation of academic productivity through reinforcing various aspects of academic production rate or accuracy. In addition, some of this research was designed to allow comparisons of the efficacy of targeting either or both of these variables as an alternative to or in combination with the reinforcement of on-task behavior.

Reinforcement of On-Task Behavior

In reviewing the literature dealing with on-task behavior, Klein (1979) included the research of O'Leary *et al.* (1969), Main and Munro (1977), Hall, Lund, and Jackson (1968), and Broden, Hall, and Mitts (1971). The behaviors targeted by O'Leary *et al.* and Main

and Munro included behaviors that the authors referred to as disruptive (wandering around the room, hitting, kicking, striking, clapping hands, stomping feet, etc.). Thus, so long as children were in their seats and quiet, they were not considered disruptive and were, according to Klein's distinction, on-task. The definitions used by Hall *et al.* and Broden *et al.*, on the other hand, specified that in order to be scored as on-task, children had to be facing the teacher, a peer, or the task material (depending on what activity was occurring at the time).

It might be argued that this latter type of definition requires that, to be scored as on-task, a child must be emitting behaviors that are likely to bring that child into contact with academic materials and teacher instruction, while such is not necessarily the case with the first type. At the same time, however, it is important to realize that in neither case should a consistent relationship between on-task behavior and academic productivity be expected; instances in which children meet the definitions for being on-task but fail to be academically productive (and vice versa) are common.

Included in research using reinforcement to increase on-task behavior are those studies demonstrating the effectiveness of verbal praise from teachers in normal (Hall, Lund, & Jackson, 1968; Main & Munro, 1977; Lobitz & Burns, 1977; Warner, Miller, & Cohen, 1977) as well as special (Broden *et al.*, 1970; Lewis & Strain, 1978) classrooms. In addition, at least one study (Darch & Thorpe, 1977) demonstrated that attention from the school principal increased on-task behavior when attention from the classroom teacher was not successful. Some critics feel that teacher praise directed to individual children may disrupt the work of nontarget children. In response, Kazdin and Klock (1973) developed a procedure involving nonverbal approval from the teacher (smiles and physical contact) that increased the attending of a group of moderately retarded children.

As would be expected, token-reinforcement systems have also been effectively administered to increase on-task behavior. Ascare and Axelrod (1973) demonstrated that tokens delivered for teacher ratings of on-task behavior increased that behavior. Alexander and Apfel (1976) further demonstrated that on-task behavior could be increased by changing the schedule of token delivery from once per hour to a variable- or fixed-interval of 3 min. Comparisons of the effects of token reinforcement with those of teacher attention (Broden *et al.,* 1970; Main & Munro, 1977) suggested that teacher attention combined with token delivery was more effective in increasing on-task behavior than teacher attention alone. Glynn, Thomas, and Shee (1973) demonstrated that the behavioral assessment of on-task behavior could be shifted from the teacher to the children, who engaged in self-assessment on which tokens were awarded. Thomas (1976) and Epstein and Goss (1978) have also shown self-assessment procedures in combination with token systems effectively maintain on-task behavior.

A combination of self-assessment and self-reinforcement was used by Bornstein and Quevillon (1976) to control on-task behavior. Broden *et al.* (1971) made a study of the effects of self-assessment and self-recording of on-task behavior paired with praise from a junior-high-school counselor in comparison with the same procedures *not* paired with praise. In both cases, on-task behavior increased, but the increase for the nonreinforced child was short-lived.

From this brief review, it is apparent that numerous procedures have effectively influenced that group of behaviors called *on-task*. Teacher attention can enhance the effectiveness of token procedures, and self-assessment procedures, especially in combination with token procedures, offer a powerful alternative to more time-consuming interventions controlled solely by the teacher. Conclusions regarding the literature involving the manipulation of on-task behavior are, of course, clouded by the controversy advanced by Winett and Winkler (1972). Perhaps their criticism can be aimed only at the research that does *not* require that children be actually engaged in task-related activities in order to be recorded as on-task. Put another way, a methodology currently exists to produce changes in academic behavior through direct intervention. Thus, manipulations of off-task or on-task behaviors that are not directly related to the academic requirements of the task do not represent the most efficient use of the techniques of behavior analysis.

Reinforcement of Rate of Academic Responding

On a few occasions, academic response rate alone has been measured and manipulated. Lovitt and Curtiss (1969), for example, compared the rate of completion of various academic tasks when the teacher determined the ratios of the amount of work to the points received, to the rate when the student determined this relationship. Performance on all tasks was better in the pupil-determined condition. In this study, however, no mention was made of whether the responses that the student made were correct or incorrect. The problem illustrated by this study is that procedures that measure and reinforce the rate of production without an accuracy criterion may functionally reinforce incorrect responses. Thus, most research involving the manipulation of rate have maintained some measure of work quality as well.

In a study by Lovitt and Esveldt (1970), for example, only the rate of *correct* responses was considered. Measures of error rate revealed that incorrect responding remained at a low level across experimental conditions. Saudargas, Madsen, and Scott (1977) compared the effects of two schedules of home reports indicating number of academic tasks completed and specified that only those assignments completed to a criterion of 85% accuracy were counted and reported as completed. In this study, the students completed a larger number of assignments when the home reports occurred on a variable as opposed to a fixed schedule.

Increases in the number of correct responses may not always reflect an increase in overall accuracy. Klein (1975) indicated that increases in the number of correct responses may reflect changes in the number of items attempted when the number of items assigned or attempted is variable. Brigham, Finfrock, Breunig, and Bushell (1972) had earlier demonstrated this possibility in a study that compared contingent with noncontingent tokens on accuracy on a handwriting task. In one condition of the study, accuracy did not increase when a contingency was placed on accurate responses. An analysis showed that a high rate of responding was sufficient to produce a number of tokens even though overall accuracy was low. The authors pointed out that children in this situation could increase the number of tokens received for accurate responses by increasing either accuracy or rate.

Reinforcement of Correct Academic Responding

Since the nature of the tasks used in the research just reported was generally such that the number of responses made within a given period of time could vary widely, rate was the primary variable of interest. When the number of responses is somewhat restricted by the nature of the task (e.g., completing a specified number of problems), the primary variable of interest becomes the proportion of a discrete number of responses that are correct. The academic tasks that have been manipulated by reinforcing correct responses include spelling (Evans & Oswalt, 1968; Foxx & Jones, 1978; Lovitt *et al.*, 1969); math (Johnson & Bailey, 1974; Harris & Sherman, 1974; Fink & Carnine, 1975; Evans & Oswalt, 1968); handwriting (Salzberg *et al.*, 1971; Trap, Milner-Davis, Joseph & Cooper, 1978); reading (Copeland, Brown, & Hall, 1974; Wolf *et al.*, 1968; Lahey & Drabman, 1974); social studies (Harris & Sherman, 1974); and retention of information from televised newscasts (Tyler & Brown, 1968).

The consequences that teachers have used to manipulate the proportion of correct responses have also been varied. In a number of studies, praise from teachers (Hasazi & Hasazi, 1972), peer tutors (Johnson & Bailey, 1974), or school principals (Copeland *et al.* 1974) has been shown to be effective in increasing the proportion of correct student responses. In addition, contingent free time (Salzberg *et al.*, 1971; Harris & Sherman, 1974; Lovitt *et al.*, 1969; Evans & OSwalt, 1968) has been a popular consequence for accurate responding.

A few studies have compared the effectiveness of various consequences. Some, for example, have suggested that a teacher's feedback regarding the correctness of responses is not, in itself, an effective consequence. Salzberg *et al.* (1971), for example, compared the effect of intermittent grading with that of intermittent grading plus contingent free time. The authors reported that intermittent feedback alone failed to produce increased accuracy, but when free time was made contingent on accuracy, accuracy increased. Fink and Carnine (1975) compared a condition in which the teacher provided feedback regarding the correctness of math problems with a condition that included feedback and having the children graph their performance. Again, the feedback condition was the less effective intervention. In one other study, Trap *et al.* (1978) compared feedback with a condition that included feedback, praise, and rewriting incorrectly printed words. In this comparison, feedback, praise, and rewriting seemed to be more effective. Even this combination, however, did not seem to be as effective as a condition that included praise, feedback, and rewriting plus the opportunity to win a "handwriting certificate." The results of the comparisons across conditions of this study must be considered tentative, however, since there was no experimental control for the order of treatments.

At least three studies have reported programs in which contingent tokens for correct responses have been compared with other procedures. Tyler and Brown (1968) compared a procedure in which tokens were awarded for correct answers on quizzes about newscast content with a procedure in which tokens were provided noncontingently. The authors reported that the contingent relationship was necessary for enhancing responding on the quizzes. Dalton, Rubino, and Hilsop (1973) compared the performance of two groups of Down's syndrome children who received either verbal praise or verbal praise plus tokens for correct responses on Distar Math and Language. The group who received tokens and praise showed achievement test gains in both language and math, while the group who received only verbal praise showed improvement only in language. A one-year follow-up showed that the token group maintained both gains, while the praise-only group lost the language gain shown on the earlier test. In another comparison, Lahey and Drabman (1974) compared token reinforcement with verbal reinforcement for the retention of sight words. Again, the token system proved to be more powerful.

Foxx and Jones (1978) compared procedures that included only weekly tests and combinations of weekly tests and positive practice procedures for incorrect responses. The combination of positive practice following pretest and weekly tests was the most effective. The use of positive practice, which operates primarily on the principle of negative reinforcement (avoidance), however, is ethically questionable in situations in which more positive procedures have been shown to be equally effective. In addition, the time and the teacher effort required to carry out the positive practice regimen would seem to be prohibitive in most applied settings.

The body of research that has demonstrated procedures through which correct responding may be increased is, for the most part, immediately applicable. Sufficient knowledge exists at this time so that we can make a number of observations and recommendations with respect to traditional educational practice. First, it seems safe to say that teacher feedback alone is not sufficient to increase correct responding. Therefore, it is unlikely that merely indicating that answers are correct or incorrect would have a consistent positive effect. There would seem to be some uncertainty with respect to the exact point at which teacher feedback may, if descriptive and positive, come to function as praise. Perhaps the obvious point is that when a great deal of teacher feedback centers on what the child has done incorrectly, its instructional role, in terms of what response should have been made, is minimal. Positive consequences, on the other hand, serve to inform the child immediately of the nature of the response that is, in that context, desired. Self-assessment and self-reinforcement also appear to serve such a positive function, in addition to having the potential of teaching children to be self-reliant.

Comparisons of Reinforcement of On-Task Behavior with Reinforcement of Productivity

Although research analyzing the various functions of reinforcement on on-task behavior, as well as on accuracy and rate, has added much to the development of techniques for increasing children's academic performance in the classroom, criticisms, such as those of Winett and Winkler (1972), have prompted questions regarding the most efficient and effective techniques to use in given situations. Perhaps the major empirical issue raised by Winett and Winkler was whether there is a relationship between on-task or disruptive behavior and academic productivity. A number of studies have addressed this issue by manipulating either on-task or academic productivity while measuring changes in both of these variables, or by systematically manipulating both variables.

In an early study by Birnbrauer, Wolf *et al.* (1965), the abrupt removal of token reinforcement for correct responses had no effect on the academic productivity or disruptiveness of 5 of 15 retarded subjects. For the remaining subjects, the manipulation resulted in decreased accuracy (6 subjects) or decreased accuracy and increased disruptive behavior (4 subjects). Following this study, other research has implemented reinforcement for academic productivity and measured the effects of this manipulation on on-task or disruptive behavior. Ayllon and Roberts (1974) delivered tokens for accuracy on reading workbook assignments and measured a decrease in off-task behavior such as out-of-seat and talking, while academic behaviors increased. Felixbrod and O'Leary (1973) compared the effectiveness of delivering tokens for correct math problems when the pupils determined the number of problems to be completed for each point in a point system with a yoked condition in which the children had no control over this relationship. Both procedures were equally effective in increasing academic productivity and in producing accompanying decreases in off-task behavior. Ballard and Glynn (1975) differentially reinforced various composition elements to produce changes in the composition of stories written by elementary-school children. This reinforcement, based on the children's self-assessment of their compositions, increased on-task as well as academic behavior.

Other research reporting concurrent decreases in off-task behavior with increases in academic performance has used reinforcement other than token systems. An adjusting ratio of teacher praise, used by Kirby and Shields

(1972), produced increases in the rate of the math problems completed and the proportion of time spent attending. Contingent free time or access to activities has also been demonstrated to result in similar concomitant changes in academic performance and time spent on-task (Aaron & Bostow, 1978; Morraco & Fasheh, 1978). In examining the effects of a package of procedures including timing, feedback, and the public posting of writing rate on writing rate and on-task behavior, Van Houten, Hill, and Parsons (175) reported that each contributed to the increases that resulted from the contingent application of the package.

Investigations manipulating accuracy and measuring on-task behavior suggest that reinforcing accuracy produces increases in accuracy as well as on-task behavior. Such research does not, however, indicate whether the reinforcement of attending results in increased attending as well as increased accuracy. Occasionally, researchers have arranged such consequences. For example, while comparing token reinforcement for compliance with classroom rules and token removal (response-cost) for rule violations, Iwata and Bailey (1974) found that each was equally effective in reducing rule violations but that neither affected the accuracy of the math problems worked during that period. This lack of effect may have been attributable to the fact that correct math problems were 80%–90% of the total completed throughout the study. To show further increases in accuracy would be difficult unless procedures were employed to remediate the errors that the students were producing. Conflicting with the no-effect conclusions drawn from the Iwata and Bailey research, a series of studies that reinforced on-task behavior resulted, although sometimes inconsistently, in increases in achievement test scores (Greenwood, Hops, & Walker, 1977; Hops & Cobb, 1973; Walker & Hops, 1976).

From the research that reinforced only academic accuracy, it appears that both accuracy and on-task behavior are increased, and from that reinforcing only on-task behavior, it appears that on-task behavior and achievement test scores are increased, but this has little effect on accuracy. These studies have manipulated only one or the other type of behavior and have simply observed the behavior that was not manipulated for concurrent changes. There has been, however, some research in which these concomitant changes have been compared through directing reinforcement first to either on-task behavior or accuracy and subsequently shifting the contingencies to the other behavior while recording both. McLaughlin and Malaby (1972), for example, first delivered tokens for the completion of a variety of academic tasks and then shifted the contingencies to reinforcement for being quiet. The shift resulted in some decrement in academic productivity. It is not possible to determine whether quiet behavior was similarly affected when academic productivity was reinforced, since there were no data presented on this variable. It was observed, however, that the productivity of a student who normally completed most assignments was much less affected by the shift in contingencies than was the productivity of a student who usually did not complete assignments.

Hay, Hay, and Nelson (1977) and Marholin and Steinman (1977) found that when on-task behavior was reinforced, only that behavior improved, but when contingencies were directed at academic productivity, increases in productivity and on-task behavior occurred. Marholin and Steinman also found that on-task behavior was much more affected by the teacher's presence than accuracy–rate measures. This finding suggests that the teacher acquired discriminative stimulus properties that controlled the occurrence of on-task behaviors when they were reinforced, but when academic productivity was reinforced, the academic materials apparently began to control the occurrence of the behaviors related to that productivity. Such findings have many implications for producing school environments in which academic learning could become reinforcing in itself. Ferritor, Buckholdt, Hamblin, and Smith (1972) produced findings somewhat contrary to those of Marholin and Steinman and of Hay *et al*. As expected, token reinforcement for attending decreased disruption but did not affect accuracy, but reinforcement for accuracy increased accuracy as well as disruption; a *decrease* in disruption had been expected. Only when reinforcement was contingent on both accuracy and attending did both behaviors increase. In discussing these results, the authors stated that "speculation of change in other than targeted behaviors may be misleading" (p. 16). They further stressed the importance of designing contingencies specifically for each target behavior.

Summary

The research that has compared the reinforcement of on-task behavior with the reinforcement of academic performance seems clearly to favor manipulations of rate or correctness as a means of increasing classroom productivity. Such procedures have been referred to as *parsimonious* (Broughton & Lahey, 1978) because they eliminate at least some off-task behavior while increasing the probability that the student's productive behavior will come under the control of the academic materials rather than the teacher's presence. The commonly advanced alternative—reinforcing on-task behavior—does not reliably result in concomitant increases in productivity and accuracy. Furthermore, this latter practice has come under some degree of ethical scrutiny in recent years.

Even with the application of the most ideal reinforcement procedures for academic productivity and accuracy and with off-task behavior held to reasonable levels in the learning environment, there will be children in the classroom who do not learn. Thus, it remains for educators not only to be mindful of optimal contingent relationships for producing academic productivity and accuracy but also to assess, under these optimal conditions, whether the children are progressing. If not, then alternative procedures, usually those involving the manipulation of discriminative stimuli in the curriculum, must be implemented.

Effects of Manipulating Discriminative Stimulus Materials and Teaching Procedure on Children's Learning of Academic Concepts and Skills

Although some reviewers have indicated the possible influence of antecedent events on children's academic behavior (e.g., LeBlanc, Etzel, & Domash, 1978), relatively few studies have examined the role of discriminative stimuli (such as teacher instructions or curriculum materials) in the learning process. The paucity of research in these areas continues, although teachers continually seek better teaching methods, especially for children experiencing difficulty in learning.

Etzel and LeBlanc (1979) pointed out that many children can learn irrespective of the nature of the curriculum materials or the instructions provided for them. For these children who learn easily, the major concern is that teaching be organized so that the skills are learned in some logical sequence, in which new components are introduced only when the necessary prerequisite skills have been acquired. Such sequencing allows learning to occur with optimal ease for both teacher and child. Task analyses, such as those which Resnick, Wang, and Kaplan (1973) presented for teaching mathematics to children, provide teachers with "an organized set of progressive learning objectives around which instructional programs of many types can be organized" (p. 700). The objective of such analyses is not to provide information regarding *how* each component should be taught but to indicate a sequence in which component skills can be taught. For children who do not experience problems in learning, such an approach would be appropriate and seems to follow what Etzel and LeBlanc (1979) referred to as the selection of the "simplest treatment alternative." In other words, in most cases, simply organizing the progression of task presentation into some logical sequence will result in children's acquiring the desired skills.

When children have difficulty learning in even well-organized instructional programs, an analysis of *how* teachers teach becomes critical. In such situations, intervention strategies are usually necessary. Perhaps the simplest of these derives from an analysis of the motivational system used in the teaching process. However, motivation through reinforcement may not always be sufficient, since some component of a to-be-learned skill must be emitted by the child for reinforcement to occur. If increased motivational levels do not enhance the learning process, according to the parsimonious "simplest treatment alternative" proposed by Etzel and LeBlanc, the next step is to analyze the effectiveness of the teacher's instructions and/or the method by which the curriculum materials are presented to the children. If altering the instructional mode does not effect learning in some children, it is proposed that arrangements of the stimulus materials themselves will be necessary to reduce errors and to allow learning to begin to occur.

Teacher Presentation of Materials and Instructions

Some children who are motivated, who are orienting to the task, and who possess the prerequisite skills for learning a new task still do not learn. In these situations, the learning environment must be analyzed for variables, such as instructions, feedback, sequence of task presentation, or other environmental stimuli, that may be impeding the learning process. In the last five years, some researchers have begun to analyze the learning environment from this viewpoint. Because of the paucity of research in this area, however, conclusions are, at best, limited.

Manipulations of Teacher Prompts and Instructions. Sometimes, it is possible to manipulate children's academic responding through the use of simple verbal prompts. Two studies, for example, have examined the relationship of question asking by teachers or students to other aspects of academic responding. When Broden, Copeland, Beasley, and Hall (1977) required teachers of junior-high special-education students to increase the number of questions they asked as well as the proportion of questions that required multiple-word answers, the students responded with answers of increased length. These authors also found that an increase in the proportion of complete sentence answers occurred when teachers instructed the children to answer in this fashion and ignored all nonsentence answers. Knapczyk and Livingston (1974) found that when teachers prompted question asking by educable mentally retarded students, the number of questions asked as well as the levels of reading comprehension and on-task behavior increased. Using a slightly different procedure, Lovitt and Curtiss (1968) demonstrated that a child's accuracy and rate of working mathematics problems could be en-

hanced by simply instructing the child to verbalize the problem before writing the answer. The authors stated that such memory aids may add a second stimulus dimension (oral recitation) to the learning process or may simply make the child more deliberate. A related but somewhat different explanation is that requiring the child to read the problem increased the probability that the child would attend to each part of that problem.

In another area of research, the content of teacher's verbal instructions has been shown to influence the academic learning of preschool children. Miller and LeBlanc (1973) compared instructions that merely stated what the children were to do in a visual discrimination task with instructions that added exemplar details to the basic statement. Thus, for example, the detailed instructions in one part of the experiment were: "This is the word 'dig.' You dig with a shovel. You dig in the sand. It's fun to dig. Point to 'dig' and say 'dig.'" The minimal instructions were merely: "This is the word 'dig.' Point to 'dig' and say 'dig.'" Discrimination acquisition between two three-letter words of similar configuration (e.g., *dig* and *dog*) occurred more rapidly with the minimal than with the detailed instructions.

Hass, Ruggles, and LeBlanc (1979) noted that the examples provided in the detailed instructions used by Miller and LeBlanc were not related to the critical (visual) differences between the two stimuli involved in the discrimination. To determine if this were essential to obtaining the differences that occurred, they compared the effects of minimal instructions (similar to those used by Miller and LeBlanc) with those of detailed instructions that focused the child's attention on the differences between the words that were most relevant to the discrimination. Thus, the detailed instructions were changed to "This is the word 'dig.' The word 'dig' has the letter 'i' in it. The letter 'i' looks like a shovel and you can dig with a shovel. Point to the 'i' in 'dig' and say 'dig.'" These criterion-related instructions were at least as effective, if not more so, than minimal instructions for enhancing discrimination acquisition. Further analyses also indicated that the discrimination acquisition effects of the non-criterion-related instructions originated by Miller and LeBlanc were enhanced when criterion-related detailed instructions were concurrently used to teach a separate discrimination. This research, which analyzed the differential effects of differing instructional content, demonstrates that manipulations as simple as changing the content of a teacher's instructions can substantially change the rate of discrimination acquisition.

Manipulation of Sequential Aspects of Task Presentations. Some research has indicated that the sequence in which stimulus materials are presented to individuals or groups of children may determine the efficacy of the teaching process. Neef, Iwata, and Page (1977), for example, studied acquisition in spelling and sight-reading tasks when previously learned items were interspersed with unknown items in comparison with that which occurred when only unknown items were presented. For six, individually trained, mentally retarded adolescents, acquisition and retention were enhanced for both tasks when known items were interspersed with unknown items. These differences could be partially due to the degree to which each of the procedures included consequences for attending to each stimulus presentation. That is, in the interspersed procedure, the intermittent appearance of a previously learned item on which the child could easily answer correctly may have reinforced the child for attending. Such would not be the case if only unknown items were presented.

Britten, Ruggles, and LeBlanc (1980) compared the effects of massed presentation of stimulus items to those that were intermixed. In a task involving the concurrent presentation of two visual stimuli, massed stimulus presentations involved requiring a response to one stimulus for 10 consecutive trials and then requiring a response to the other stimulus for another 10 trials. For the intermixed stimulus presentation, responses to the two different stimuli were randomly required. Although the preschool children generally performed better during recognition training with massed training, their performance on periodic probes of recognition and recall was better following intermixed training, possibly because the children could respond correctly on all but the initial trial in massed training by simply pointing to or saying the stimulus, which resulted

in reinforcement on the previous trial. Thus, the teacher's instructions were not required as a discriminative stimulus for making a particular choice. Intermixed training, on the other hand, did necessitate utilizing the teacher's instructions as a discriminative stimulus for choosing the correct stimulus or applying the proper label.

Other researchers examining the effects of the sequential presentation of stimuli on learning are Cuvo, Klevans, Borakove, Borakove, Van Landuyt, and Lutzker (1980) and Panyan and Hall (1978). Cuvo *et al.* compared the effects of massed, intermixed, and combined massed and intermixed stimulus presentations on the labeling of objects by college students, retarded children and adolescents, and normal preschool children. In massed (called *successive*) presentations, one stimulus was presented consecutively until the subject correctly responded 15 times. In intermixed (called *simultaneous* stimulus presentations, the five stimuli were put before the subject, who was required to label them in random order until the subject made 15 correct responses on each stimulus. The combined procedure involved aspects of both of the other procedures. Performance was better with the intermixed (or simultaneous) and combined procedures. Panyan and Hall compared concurrent training in which training on one task continued for 5 min, followed by 5 min of training on a second task and then a return to the first task, etc., with serial training in which one task was presented for an entire 15-min period. Concurrent training of tracing and vocal imitation by retarded students was as effective as serial training for acquisition, but concurrent training also produced more transfer to untrained items in generalization testing.

The research discussed to this point has shown that the sequence in which tasks are presented may determine the success with which children acquire discriminations. By strategically designing the sequence in which discriminations are trained, children who are trained in groups may not only acquire those discriminations that are directly taught to them but also those that are taught to others in the group or with which they have had little or no direct training. Sabbert, Holt, Nelson, Domash, and Etzel (1976a), for example, designed a near-errorless program to teach simple mathematics to preschool children. Although the program was originally designed, as are most errorless programs, to be presented to inividual children, Sabbert *et al.* analyzed the effects of presenting each of the steps in the program to different children, in a group. The 14-trial program was presented to groups of two, three, four, and five children, as well as to individual children. When the program was presented to five children, each child responded to only two or three trials from the entire program. Since the program was designed so that the information required to respond to each trial came from previous trials, the children were encouraged to attend to the training trials of the children who preceded them. Attending was also enhanced by randomly selecting the order in which the children were to answer. It was found that groups of two, three, four, and five children could be taught the mathematics concepts in the same number of total training trials as were required to teach one child individually, because the children were able to learn from the responses of the other children in the group.

The occurrence of learning without direct training has been demonstrated in several investigations. Sidman and Cresson (1973), for example, first trained individuals on the correspondence between a dictated word and a symbol and then on the correspondence between the same dictated word and its printed counterpart. Following this training, the subjects could match the picture to the printed word, a relationship on which the subject had received no direct training. Subsequent researchers have reported similar findings on variations of Sidman's original procedure (Barmeier, 1978, 1979; Gast, vanBiervliet, & Spradlin, 1979; Sidman, Cresson, & Willson-Morris, 1974; vanBiervliet, 1977).

A technique developed by Ruggles and LeBlanc (1979) combined the beneficial effects of learning through observation (as shown in the Sabbert *et al.* procedure) with a variation of Sidman and Cresson's procedure to teach discriminations to children in a group setting. In this study, two students in a preacademic group were trained to choose international agricultural symbols that corresponded to the teacher's instructions (e.g.,

point to the picture of the "cow"). Concurrently, the other two children were taught to choose the printed words that corresponded to the symbols taught to the first two children (e.g., point to the word "cow"). After training, a mediation test was conducted in which the children (in a match-to-sample format) were asked to match symbols to corresponding printed words. On the match-to-sample test, the children were able to use the information on which they were directly trained, in combination with the information learned through observing the other children's responses, to make the transfer response. A variation of the procedure by Ruggles and LeBlanc was subsequently used to increase the efficiency with which the academic concepts of *fruit* and *vegetable* could be trained to a group of preschool children (Fallows, Cooper, Etzel, LeBlanc, & Ruggles, 1980).

The mediated transfer research of Sidman and his colleagues demonstrated that through the proper arrangement of training, one untrained relationship would be learned when two were trained directly. The research by Ruggles and LeBlanc and by Fallows *et al.* demonstrated the practical implications of these findings for classroom teaching by showing that through the arrangement of training and a reliance on the occurrence of learning through observation, the acquisition of three or more relationships may occur when each group member is directly taught only one relationship.

Manipulation of the Temporal Parameters of Task Presentation or Responding. Some researchers have manipulated the temporal relationship between successive trial presentations, or between trial presentation and the child's response, to determine if timing influences learning. Busby and LeBlanc (1972), for example, compared a 4-sec time limit with no limit on a preschooler's responding for reinforcement on a picture bingo task. Response latencies during the time-limit conditions were, in general, shorter and less variable than those in the no-time-limit conditions. In a systematic replication of the Busby and LeBlanc research, Kramer, Ruggles, and LeBlanc (1979) found no consistent relationship between the time-limit condition and response latencies. Thus, exact conclusions regarding the effects of imposing time limits on responding in a discrete trial task are not clear.

Ayllon, Garber, and Pisor (1976) investigated the effect of a gradual reduction in the amount of time that educably retarded students were given to complete mathematics problems. During the first condition, the subjects were given 20 min to complete 20 problems. Following a condition in which the time allowed to complete the problems was abruptly decreased to 5 min, the time limit was gradually reduced, across four conditions, from 20 min to 5 min (20, 15, 10, and 5 min). The rate of correct problems per minute gradually increased from the abrupt imposition of the 5-min limit across the gradual reduction of the time limit to 5 min. While the results of the Ayllon *et al.* study are impressive, the possible influence of practice cannot be ignored. The same pool of math problems was apparently used throughout, and experimental controls in the form of control subjects or interspersed probes with the 5-min time limit were lacking.

Carnine (1976) has demonstrated that temporal manipulations involving the pace of teacher instructions influence responding. During a slow-rate condition, the teacher waited approximately 5 sec between each child's response and the presentation of the next trial. During the fast-rate condition, the teacher immediately proceeded to the next trial after a response from the child. For both experimental subjects (low-achieving first-graders), more correct responding and participation, as well as less off-task behavior, were evident in the fast-rate condition than in the slow-rate condition. Koegel, Dunlap, and Dyer (1980) also investigated the influence of the length of the intertrial interval on autistic children's learning on verbal-imitation, object-discrimination, object-labeling, and other tasks. Intertrial intervals of 1 sec produced a higher proportion of correct responding than intertrial intervals of 4 sec.

Research examining the pacing of stimulus presentations generally favors teaching sessions that move as quickly as possible. These findings counter more traditional notions that children must not be rushed but must be given as much time as possible to respond to academic materials. Empirically, it appears that extra time may not be necessary and, in fact,

may allow the development of behaviors that are incompatible with academic learning.

Temporal relationships between instructions and feedback have also been shown to influence learning. Touchette (1971), for example, trained three retarded subjects to select a red versus a white response key. On the first trial of the next phase of training, two forms were superimposed on the colored key, and the subject was reinforced for selecting the key with the form on the red background. On subsequent trials, the two forms were presented on the key, and the onset of the colored background was delayed. The length of the delay gradually increased across trials. Eventually, as the delay increased, the subjects began to select the correct form before the colored background was illuminated. Following Touchette's sample, Radgowski, Allen, Schilmoeller, Ruggles, and LeBlanc (1978) taught English-speaking preschool children to respond receptively and productively in French. In the early receptive training trials, the teacher gave an instruction in French and immediately modeled the response. Following the model, the child imitated the teacher's response. Across successive trials, the delay between the instruction and the model became progressively longer. As the delay increased, there came a point when most children began to respond with the correct answer before the model. Productive training was similar, except that the teacher demonstrated the motor response, then, following a delay, said the phrase. For most children, the delayed-cue procedure produced rapid learning with few or no errors.

Manipulating Curriculum Material Stimuli

Not all of the research related to teachers' presentation of curriculum materials and instructions has been conducted in applied settings (i.e., classrooms). The importance of such research to teachers who are faced with selecting the best procedures to use with children who have difficulty learning is, however, obvious. Such procedures as prompting children at strategic times, pacing the teaching, controlling the content of the instructions, setting time limits on responding, altering the sequences of task presentations, and arranging groups so that optimal learning can occur are a few among many potentially potent methods that teachers could use if research outcomes more clearly dictated when and how these procedures should be used. Even the most optimally arranged learning environments, however, are apparently not sufficient for some children to learn some tasks. Nevertheless, teachers are faced with the increasing demand from parents and government agencies that all children be educated. In response to such demands, researchers and teachers are becoming interested in errorless learning procedures and optimal arrangements of curriculum material stimuli.

Because of a particular theoretical bias in the experimental analysis of behavior, most early applied behavior-analysis researchers emphasized the reinforcement rather than the discriminative stimulus part of the three-term contingency $(S^d - R - S^{r+})$ on which operant psychology is based. For example, Skinner (1963) strongly cautioned against the use of instructional control procedures in learning experiments on the grounds that they circumvent and obscure the functional analysis of behavior. This theoretical bias was further supported by the immediacy of the need for the development of procedures that professionals could use to change the behaviors of persons who were not considered acceptable in society. The strength of reinforcement of such purposes cannot be denied. Applied researchers were attracted to reinforcement analyses because reinforcement is a powerful tool, and they provided immediate, dramatic results in both clinical and classroom settings. Thus, it was only after reinforcement procedures were well analyzed that a few researchers began to look at the behavioral effects that might emanate from manipulations of discriminative stimuli.

In classroom research, it is becoming obvious that educators need more information regarding what procedures they should use when children have difficulty learning. When reinforcement is functioning and learning is not occurring, only an analysis of discriminative stimulus functions can provide such information. In addition, if the precise rearrangement of instructions and material presentations does not result in learning for these children, then the visual and auditory stimuli directly involved in the learning process must be arranged so that they can learn. This requirement usually involves developing materials that will produce learning without errors. Materials designed to produce errorless learning involve discriminative stimulus manipulations that allow a child initially to make correct responses on a simple discrimination and to continue responding with few or no errors as the stimulus control is gradually transferred from the simple discrimination to a more complex one.

Errorless Learning. In the late 1950s and the early 1960s, some behavior-analysis researchers concentrated on programmed learning and automated self-instructional procedures (cf. Holland, 1960; Skinner, 1961). The emphasis in this research was learning with few or no errors and resulted in programmed texts designed primarily for higher education. The field of programmed instruction did not, however, reach down the educational ladder to public-school classroom research. Perhaps this was because the programmed instruction techniques were dependent on an already acquired reading ability, but in the first years of public school, reading is a central part of the curriculum rather than a tool of learning.

Information regarding the processes involved in visual errorless-discrimination learning was initially forthcoming from research with pigeons conducted by Terrace (1963a,b, 1966). Errorless learning was subsequently demonstrated with other infrahuman organisms, such as sea lions (Schusterman, 1967) and monkeys (Leith & Haude, 1969). During this period of the late 1960s, other researchers began to examine the feasibility and the implications of errorless learning in humans (cf. Bijou, 1968; Moore & Goldiamond, 1964; Sidman & Stoddard, 1966, 1968; Stoddard & Sidman, 1967; Touchette, 1969). This early research was conducted primarily with retardates in laboratory settings and on tasks involving simple discriminations. Only now, almost a decade later, are researchers beginning to focus on the implications of errorless-learning procedures for classroom teaching. Much of the support and the development of functional errorless-learning procedures that can be used by teachers are found in the work of Etzel and her colleagues (cf. Etzel & LeBlanc, 1979; Etzel, LeBlanc, Schilmoeller, & Stella, 1981). As indicated by Etzel and LeBlanc (1979), designing programs to teach children with few or no errors is a difficult task. However, they also indicated, "if simpler procedures are not effective for teaching difficult-to-teach children, then . . . the most complex procedure becomes the procedure of choice" (pp. 380–381).

Implications of Errorless-Learning Techniques for Classroom Teaching. Research involved in the development of errorless learning has, for the most part, been conducted in laboratory settings. One exception is the research conducted by Sabbert, Holt, Nelson Domash, and Etzel (1976a,b), which demonstrated that five children could learn as successfully as one in the same number of trials if errorless-learning procedures are used and if contingencies are arranged that require the children to observe the responses of the other children in the program. In another study using errorless-learning procedures in a classroom setting, Nelson, Holt, and Etzel (1976a,b) demonstrated that the prerequisite skills needed to learn math skills could be empirically determined (rather than being determined through guessing) while teaching small groups of children with procedures designed to preclude or reduce errors. Procedures were developed for identifying these skills and for teaching them (if necessary) before teaching more complex skills. The limited use of this new technology of stimulus-control procedures to solve applied educational problems historically parallels the limited applications of reinforcement procedures when operant psychology was moving from the laboratory into applied settings. That is, research was first conducted in infrahuman laboratories, interest was then sparked in human laboratory research, and finally research involving the application of procedures in applied settings was forthcoming. As occurred with the application of reinforcement procedures, it is expected that as the technology of applied stimulus-control procedures becomes better formulated, more direct applications of such procedures will be found in classroom settings.

There are essentially two methods for pro-ducing the errorless learning of visual discriminations: stimulus fading and stimulus shaping. These two methods are sometimes used in conjunction with the superimposition of one stimulus on the other, and the superimposed stimulus is either faded or shaped into the criterion stimulus involved in the discrimination being taught (Etzel & LeBlanc, 1979). Stimulus fading involves a gradual shift of discriminative control from a dominant stimulus element to a different, criterion stimulus. This shift is produced by fading along some physical dimension (e.g., intensity, size, or color) that changes the basis of the discrimination from one stimulus dimension to another one (which is usually more difficult for the learner). Stimulus shaping, attributed to Sidman and Stoddard (1966) by Etzel and LeBlanc (1979), involves a change in the topography (configuration) of the stimulus. That is, the initial stimulus on which a discrimination can be easily made (which does not resemble the ultimate stimulus) is topographically altered (changed in shape) until it resembles the stimulus on which the criterion (usually more difficult) discrimination is to be made.

Some research has indicated that fading is not always a successful learning procedure (cf. Cheney & Stein, 1974; Gollin & Savoy, 1968; Guralnick, 1975; Koegel & Rincover, 1976; Schwartz, Firestone, & Terry, 1971; Smith & Filler, 1975). Research conducted by Schilmoeller and Etzel (1977) and by Schilmoeller, Schilmoeller, Etzel, and LeBlanc (1979) indicates that these failures could be attributed to fading dimensions of the stimuli that were not related to the stimuli involved in the final criterion discrimination. That is, when the last discernable stimulus element that was being faded was removed, the subjects did not shift their discrimination from that stimulus element to the criterion stimulus. Doran and Holland (1979) demonstrated the importance of the criterion stimulus's controlling responding *before* the fading cue is completely removed.

The research of Schilmoeller and Etzel (1977) emphasized the need for manipulating only criterion-related stimuli and has obvious implications for the technology of developing curriculum materials for classroom use. Based on the assumption, introduced by Bijou (1968), that one should manipulate the part of a stimulus on which the ultimate or criterion discrimination will be made, Schilmoeller and Etzel developed a program that taught preschool children to discriminate between exceedingly complex stimuli with few or no errors. To demonstrate the importance of manipulating *only* those stimulus elements that are related to the criterion discrimination, the authors put a red square around the sample and the correct match on the initial trial of the successful program, and they gradually eliminated the red boxes across trials until the boxes were no longer visible at the end of the program. Thus, the red boxes (similar to those used in many children's workbooks) were used to cue the child to respond to the correct stimulus. The boxes apparently cued the child to attend only to the red boxes, however, and not to the stimuli that were gradually changing in the program that was demonstrated to be successful without the boxes. The children were unable to make the criterion discrimination when the red boxes were superimposed on the correct stimuli but were able to learn the discrimination with the same errorless-learning program when the red boxes were not used as cues.

Stimulus fading and stimulus shaping have been used to teach a variety of simple and complex concepts to preschool and elementary-school children. For example, the very difficult left–right relational abstraction has been programmed for retarded and preschool children (Bijou, 1968; Bybel & Etzel, 1973; Schreibman, 1975). Sidman and Stoddard (1966) developed a program for teaching a discrimination between a circle and an ellipse to retardates, and Powers, Cheney, and Agostino (1970) taught color discriminations to preschool children. A variety of simple and complex relational concepts, such as under, over, behind, top-left-back, and top-right-front, have been taught with few errors to preschool children by means of a three-dimensional house that they could manipulate (Dial & Etzel, (1972). Dixon, Spradlin, Girardeau, and Etzel (1974) taught severely retarded children an in-front discrimination using complex two-dimensional pictures with few or no errors, and this training generalized to other similar stimuli. Symmetrical and asymmetrical abstractions have and also been taught to young chil-

dren by Schwartz *et al.* (1971) and by Barrera and Schilmoeller (as reported by Etzel & LeBlanc, 1979). Conditional discriminations have been programmed for preschool children by Gollin (1965, 1966), by Gollin and Savoy (1968), and by Schilmoeller *et al.* (1979). One of the first applied stimulus-control programs to produce errorless learning was a shoe-tying program developed for retarded and developmentally delayed children (Cooper, LeBlanc, & Etzel, 1968). The oddity concept (i.e., indicating a stimulus that is different from an array of stimuli) was programmed by Etzel and Mintz (1970).

Along more academic lines, reading has been the target of several programs using errorless-learning techniques. For example, Corey and Shamow (1972) studied the effects of fading on reading acquisition; Guralnick (1975) examined the effects of fading on letter and form discriminations; Dorry and Zeaman (1975) compared fading and nonfading procedures while teaching a simple reading vocabulary to retarded children; Griffiths and Griffiths (1976), Egeland and Winer (1974), Karraker and Doke (1970), and Rincover (1978) established errorless-learning procedures to teach children letter discriminations; and Parr, Stella, and Etzel (reported in LeBlanc *et al.*, 1978) used stimulus shaping to teach children sight-word vocabularies with few errors.

Other academic concepts that have had errorless-learning procedures applied to them include simple addition (Sabbert *et al.*, 1976a,b); rote counting, number labeling, number writing, match-to-sample, and one-to-one correspondence (Nelson *et al.*, 1976a,b); addition, subtraction, and multiplication (Haupt, Van Kirk, & Terraciano, 1977); handwriting (Holt & Etzel, 1976); and the number of beats of musical notes (Stella & Etzel, 1977).

One reason that researchers may have begun to analyze the effects of errorless-learning procedures for purposes of application is that the autistic (Schreibman, 1975), the retarded, and other children experiencing learning problems often do not observe the cues that are relevant to making the discriminations being taught. Zeaman and House (1963) and Covill and Etzel (1976) both documented this fact with two very different groups of children. Stella and Etzel (1979a,b) indicated that this problem sometimes arises when children do not look at the stimulus materials. These authors developed a stimulus-shaping procedure to assess and to shape the children's attention so the opportunity to focus on the relevant stimulus dimension is at least available. Covill and Etzel (1976) further demonstrated that slow-learning children utilize inappropriate cues, such as the position of a stimulus, rather than the critical cues that allow discriminations to be made. Errorless-learning procedures, such as criterion-related fading, shaping, and the superimposition of stimuli, appear to help difficult-to-teach children to observe the relevant cues in learning. Thus, this technology can perhaps provide the avenue for behavior analysis to begin to deal with the problems of *educating* children rather than only modifying inappropriate behavior so as to maintain orderly behavior in the classroom.

Summary. There is a beginning technology of discriminative stimulus manipulations that appears to have implications for the use of behavior analysis not only to remediate behavioral problems but also to educate children. Etzel (1978) indicated that retarded and autistic children have waited for generations for scientists to find methods of teaching them. Perhaps the turning of scientific attention to the functions of discriminative stimuli and how they can best be manipulated to change and control behavior will provide these children with the learning programs they need. For years, classroom teachers have sought research outcomes that indicate what to do with children who experience learning difficulties. As more research is produced that analyzes the discriminations involved in the educational process, it is possible that some of the answers will come forth even before the beginning of the twenty-first century.

Summary

The most often heard complaints regarding public-school education are that there is no discipline in the classrooms and that the children are not learning anything other than how to misbehave. The current technology available for maintaining order in the classroom is vast and stems primarily from behavior-anal-

ysis research. However, there is sometimes a resistance to the application of behavior-analysis procedures in the classroom to maintain sufficient order for learning to occur. The rationale for such resistance is that children's creativity and openness should not be stifled in the name of education. It cannot be denied that creativity should be fostered in classrooms. Bedlam in classrooms is, however, frequently sufficient to preclude opportunities to foster such creativity. In this case, teachers should be encouraged to use reinforcement and even mild forms of punishment or response-decrement procedures to control the social climate of the classroom so that learning can occur and creativity can be enhanced. Research outcomes that indicate optimal procedures for controlling classroom behavior are currently sufficient for prescriptions to be developed for teachers to use when problems develop. It needs only to be done.

Once classroom order is maintained, teachers can then turn their attention to what and how much children are learning. The behavior-analysis technology for increasing children's motivation to learn and to produce at an acceptable rate is rapidly increasing. Currently, there are functional procedures that can be used for this purpose, and we, as a society, need only to begin to demand their implementation.

The available techniques that show teachers how to *teach* (in addition to how to discipline) are few. Such techniques would indicate how to arrange the learning environment so that all children can learn, starting from where they are and proceeding at a pace commensurate with their abilities. Research analyzing the effects of the manipulation of discriminative stimuli, such as teachers' instructions and curriculum materials, is beginning to provide information that is sorely needed by teachers who are faced with the education of all children, regardless of their learning ability. This research emanates primarily from the experimental laboratory, but it shows much promise in application for children who experience difficulty in learning.

When the behavior analysis technology of how to teach reaches the current level of sophistication of the technology of discipline and motivation, teachers will then be able to concentrate on the true issue of the profession, that is, teaching. There should, at that point, be few limitations on the learning progress that all children will be able to make. Then, education can become a pleasant affair rather than a laborious process for students, teachers, and parents alike.

References

Aaron, B. A., & Bostow, D. E. Indirect facilitation of on-task behavior produced by contingent free-time for academic productivity. *Journal of Applied Behavior Analysis*, 1978, *11*, 197.

Alexander, R. N., & Apfel, C. H. Altering schedules of reinforcement for improved classroom behavior. *Exceptional Children*, 1976, *43*, 97–99.

Allen, K. E., Hart, B. M., Buell, J. C., Harris, F. R., & Wolf, M. M. Effects of adult social reinforcement on isolate behavior of a nursery school child. *Child Development*, 1964, *35*, 511–518.

Allen, K. E., Henke, L. B., Harris, F. R., Baer, D. M., & Reynolds, N. J. Control of hyperactivity by social reinforcement of attending behavior. *Journal of Education Psychology*, 1967, *58*, 231–237.

Allen, K. E., Turner, K. D., & Everett, P. M. A behavior modification classroom for Head Start children with problem behaviors: Experiments 1–3. *Exceptional Children*, 1970, *37*, 119–127.

Ascare, D., & Axelrod, S. Use of a behavior modification procedure in four "open" classrooms. *Psychology in the Schoolds*, 1973, *10*, 249–252.

Axelrod, S. Comparison of individual and group contingencies in two special classes. *Behavior Therapy*, 1973, *4*, 83–90.

Ayllon, T., & Haughton, E. Control of the behavior of schizophrenic patients by food. *Journal of the Experimental Analysis of Behavior*, 1962, *5*, 343–352.

Ayllon, T., & Michael, J. The psychiatric nurse as a behavioral engineer. *Journal of the Experimental Analysis of Behavior*, 1959, *2*, 323–334.

Ayllon, T. A., & Roberts, M. D. Eliminating discipline problems by strengthening academic performance. *Journal of Applied Behavior Analysis*, 1974, *7*, 71–76.

Ayllon, T., Garber, S., & Pisor, K. Reducing time limits: A means to increase behavior of retardates. *Journal of Applied Behavior Analysis*, 1976, *9*, 247–252.

Azrin, N. H., & Holtz, W. C. Punishment. In W. K. Honig (Ed.), *Operant Behavior: Areas of Research and Application*. New York: Appleton-Century-Crofts, 1966.

Bailey, J. S., Wolf, M. M., & Phillips, E. L. Home-based reinforcement and the modification of pre-delinquents' classroom behavior. *Journal of Applied Behavior Analysis*, 1970, *3*, 223–233.

Ballard, K. D., & Glynn, T. Behavioral self-management in story writing with elementary school children. *Journal of Applied Behavior Analysis*, 1975, *8*, 387–398.

Barker, R. G. *Ecological psychology*. Stanford, Calif.: Stanford University Press, 1968.

Barmeier, A. A. *Mediated transfer in deaf reading instruction: A sign language model*. Paper presented at the meeting of the American Psychological Association, Toronto, August 1978.

Barmeier, A. A. *Mediated transfer in deaf reading instruction: A sign language model*. Paper presented at the meeting of the Association for Behavior Analysis, Dearborn, 1979.

Barrish, H. H., Saunders, M., & Wolf, M. M. Good behavior game: Effects of individual contingencies for group consequences on disruptive behavior in a classroom. *Journal of Applied Behavior Analysis*, 1969, *2*, 119–124.

Bijou, S. W. Studies in the experimental development of left-right concepts in retarded children using fading techniques. In Norman R. Ellis (Ed.), *International review of research in mental retardation*, Vol. 3. New York: Academic Press, 1968.

Bijou, S. W., Birnbrauer, J. S., Kidder, J. D., & Tague, C. E. Programmed instruction as an approach to the teaching of reading, writing and arithmetic to retarded children. *Psychological Record*, 1966, *16*, 505–522.

Birnbrauer, J. S., & Lawler, J. Token reinforcement for learning. *Mental Retardation*, October 1964, *2*, 275–279.

Birnbrauer, J. S., Bijou, S. W., Wolf, M. M., & Kidder, J. D. Programmed instruction in the classroom. In L. P. Ullmann & L. Krasner (Eds.), *Case studies in behavior modification*. New York: Holt, Rinehart & Winston, 1965, pp. 358–363.

Birnbrauer, J. S., Wolf, M. M., Kidder, J. D., & Tague, C. E. Classroom behavior of retarded pupils with token reinforcement. *Journal of Experimental Child Psychology*, 1965, *2*, 219–235.

Bornstein, P. H., & Quevillon, R. P. The effects of a self-instructional package on over-active preschool boys. *Journal of Applied Behavior Analysis*, 1976, *9*, 179–188.

Bostow, D. E., & Bailey, J. B. Modification of severe disruptive and aggressive behavior using brief timeout and reinforcement procedures. *Journal of Applied Behavior Analysis*, 1969, *2*, 31–38.

Brigham, T. A., Finfrock, S. R., Breunig, M. K., & Bushell, D. The use of programmed materials in the analysis of academic contingencies. *Journal of Applied Behavior Analysis*, 1972, *5*, 177–182.

Britten, K., Ruggles, T. R., & LeBlanc, J. M. *A comparison of massed and intermixed stimulus presentations*. Paper presented at the meeting of the Association for Behavior Analysis, Dearborn, 1980.

Broden, M., Bruce, C., Mitchell, M. A., Carter, V., & Hall, R. V. Effects of teacher attention on attending behavior of two boys at adjacent desks. *Journal of Applied Behavior Analysis*, 1970, *3*, 199–203.

Broden, M., Hall, R. V., Dunlap, A., & Clark, R. Effects of teacher attention and a token reinforcement system in a junior school special education class. *Exceptional Children*, 1970, *36*, 341–349.

Broden, M., Hall, R. V., & Mitts, B. The effect of self-recording on the classroom behavior of two eighth-grade students. *Journal of Applied Behavior Analysis*, 1971, *4*, 191–199.

Broden, M., Copeland, G., Beasley, A., & Hall, R. V. Altering student responses through changes in teacher verbal behavior. *Journal of Applied Behavior Analysis*, 1977, *10*, 479–488.

Broughton, S. F., & Lahey, B. B. Direct and collateral effects of positive reinforcement, response cost and mixed contingencies for academic performance. *Journal of School Psychology*, 1978, *16*, 126–136.

Brown, P., & Elliot, R. The control of aggression in a nursery school class. *Journal of Experimental Child Psychology*, 1965, *2*, 103–107.

Busby, K., & LeBlanc, J. M. *Response latency as a function of reinforcement and temporal contingencies.* Paper presented at the meeting of the American Psychological Association, Honolulu, 1972.

Bushell, D., Wrobel, P. A., & Michaelis, M. L. Applying "group" contingencies to the classroom study behavior of preschool children. *Journal of Applied Behavior Analysis*, 1968, *1*, 55–61.

Bybel, N. W., & Etzel, B. C. *A study of pretraining procedures for establishing cue relevance in the subsequent programming of a conceptual skill.* Paper presented to the Society for Research in Child Development, Philadelphia, March 1973.

Carnine, D. W. Effects of two teacher-presentation rates on off-task behavior, answering correctly, and participation. *Journal of Applied Behavior Analysis*, 1976, *9*, 199–206.

Chadwick, B. A., & Day, R. C. Systematic reinforcement: Academic performance of underachieving students. *Journal of Applied Behavior Analysis*, 1971, *4*, 311–320.

Charlesworth, R., & Hartup, W. W. Positive social reinforcement in the nursery school peer group. *Child Development*, 1967, *38*, 993–1002.

Cheney, T., & Stein, N. Fading procedures and oddity learning in kindergarten children. *Journal of Experimental Child Psychology*, 1974, *17*, 313–321.

Clark, F. W., Evans, D. R., & Hamerlynck, L. A. *Implementing behavioral programs for schools and clinics.* Proceedings of the Third Banff International Conference on Behavior Modification. Champaign, Ill.: Research Press, 1972.

Clark, H. B., Rowbury, T., Baer, A. M., & Baer, D. M. Timeout as a punishing stimulus in continuous and intermittent schedules. *Journal of Applied Behavior Analysis*, 1973, *6*, 443–456.

Coleman, R. A. Conditioning technique applicable to elementary school classrooms. *Journal of Applied Behavior Analysis*, 1970, *3*, 293–297.

Cooper, M. L., LeBlanc, J. M., & Etzel, B. C. *A shoe is to tie* (16mm color, 10-min film depicting a programmed sequence for teaching shoe-tying to preschool children). Available from Edna A. Hill Child Development Preschool Laboratory, Department of Human Development, University of Kansas, January 1968.

Copeland, R. E., Brown, R. E., & Hall, R. V. The effects of principal-implemented techniques on the behavior of pupils. *Journal of Applied Behavior Analysis*, 1974, *7*, 77–86.

Corey, J. R., & Shamow, J. The effects of fading on the acquisition and retention of oral reading. *Journal of Applied Behavior Analysis*, 1972, *5*, 311–315.

Corte, H. E., Wolf, M. M., & Locke, B. J. A comparison of procedures for eliminating self-injurious behavior of retarded adolescents. *Journal of Applied Behavior Analysis*, 1971, *4*, 201–214.

Covill, J. L., & Etzel, B. C. *Effects of errorless learning on problem-solving skills.* Presented at the 84th annual convention of the American Psychological Association, Washington, D.C., 1976.

Cuvo, A. J., Klevans, L., Borakove, S., Borakove, L. S., Van Landuyt, J., & Lutzker, J. R. A comparison of three strategies for teaching object names. *Journal of Applied Behavior Analysis*, 1980, *13*, 249–258.

Dalton, A. J., Rubino, C. A., & Hilsop, M. W. Some effects of token rewards on school achievement of children with Down's syndrome. *Journal of Applied Behavior Analysis*, 1973, *6*, 251–260.

Darch, C. B., & Thorpe, H. W. The principal game: A group consequence procedure to increase classroom on-task behavior. *Psychology in the Schools*, 1977, *14*, 341–347.

Dickinson, D. J. Changing behavior with behavioral techniques. *Journal of School Psychology*, 1968, *6*, 278–283.

Dietz, S. M., & Repp, A. C. Decreasing classroom misbehavior through the use of DRL schedules of reinforcement. *Journal of Applied Behavior Analysis*, 1973, *6*, 457–463.

Dietz, S. M., & Repp, A. C. Differentially reinforcing low rates of misbehavior with normal elementary school children. *Journal of Applied Behavior Analysis*, 1974, *7*, 622.

Dixon, L. S., Spradlin, J. E., Girrardeau, F. L., & Etzel, B. C. Facilitating the acquisition of an *in front* spatial discrimination. *ACTA Symbolica*, 1974, *5*, 1–21.

Doleys, D. M., Wells, K. C., Hobbs, S. A., Roberts, M. W., & Cartelli, L. M. The effects of social punishment on noncompliance: A comparison with timeout and positive practice. *Journal of Applied Behavior Analysis*, 1976, *9*, 471–482.

Doran, J., & Holland, J. G. Control by stimulus features during fading. *Journal of the Experimental Analysis of Behavior*, 1979, *31*, 177–187.

Dorry, G. W., & Zeaman, D. Teaching a simple reading vocabulary to retarded children: Effectiveness of fading and nonfading procedures. *American Journal of Mental Deficiency*, 1975, *79*, 711–716.

Drabman, R. S. Child- versus teacher-administered token programs in a psychiatric hospital school. *Journal of Abnormal Child Psychology*, 1973, *1*, 68–87.

Drabman, R. S., & Lahey, B. B. Feedback in classroom behavior modification: Effects on the target and her classmates. *Journal of Applied Behavior Analysis*, 1974, *7*, 591–598.

Drabman, R. S., & Spitalnik, R. Social isolation as a punishment procedure: A controlled study. *Journal of Experimental Child Psychology*, 1973, *16*, 236–249.

Drabman, R. S., Spitalnik, R., & O'Leary, K. D. Teaching self-control to disruptive children. *Journal of Abnormal Psychology*, 1973, *82*, 10–16.

Drabman, R., Spitalnik, R., & Spitalnik, K. Sociometric and disruptive behavior as a function of four types of token reinforcement programs. *Journal of Applied Behavior Analysis*, 1974, *7*, 93–101.

Egeland, B., & Winer, K. Teaching children to discriminate letters of the alphabet through errorless discrimination training. *Journal of Reading Behavior*, 1974, *2*, 191–194.

Epstein, R., & Goss, C. M. A self-control procedure for the maintenance of nondisruptive behavior in an elementary school child. *Behavior Therapy*, 1978, *9*, 109–117.

Etzel, B. C. *Errorless stimulus control in the modification of conceptual behavior.* Invited presentation, Midwest Association for Behavior Analysis, Chicago, 1978.

Etzel, B. C., & LeBlanc, J. M. The simplest treatment alternative: The law of parsimony applied to choosing appropriate instructional control and errorless-learning procedures for the difficult-to-teach child. *Journal of Autism and Developmental Disorders,* 1979, *9,* 361–382.

Etzel, B. C., & Mintz, M. S. *Stimulus control procedures to preclude or greatly decrease errors during the acquisition of the oddity abstraction with three- and four-year-old children.* Presented at the American Psychological Association, Miami, 1970.

Etzel, B. C., LeBlanc, J. M., Schilmoeller, K. J., & Stella, M. E. Stimulus control procedures in the education of young children. In S. W. Bijou & R. Ruez (Eds.), *Contributions of behavior modification to education.* Hillsdale, N.J.: Lawrence Erlbaum, 1981.

Evans, G., & Oswalt, G. Acceleration of academic progress through the manipulation of peer influence. *Behavior Research and Therapy,* 1968, *6,* 189–195.

Fallows, R. P., Cooper, A. V., Etzel, B. C., LeBlanc, J. M., & Ruggles, T. R. *The use of a stimulus equivalency paradigm, and observational learning in teaching concepts to preschool children.* Paper presented at the meeting of the American Psychological Association, Montreal, September 1980.

Felixbrod, J. J., & O'Leary, K. D. Effects of reinforcement on children's academic behavior as a function of self-determined and externally imposed contingencies. *Journal of Applied Behavior Analysis,* 1973, *6,* 241–250.

Ferritor, D. E., Buckholdt, D., Hamblin, R. L., & Smith, L. The noneffects of contingent reinforcement for attending behavior on work accomplished. *Journal of Applied Behavior Analysis,* 1972, *5,* 7–17.

Ferster, C., & Appel, J. Punishment of S responding in match to sample by timeout from positive reinforcement. *Journal of The Experimental Analysis of Behavior,* 1961, *4,* 45–46.

Fink, W. T., & Carnine, D. W. Control of arithmetic errors using informational feedback and graphing. *Journal of Applied Behavior Analysis,* 1975, *8,* 461

Foxx, R. M., & Jones, J. R. A remediation program for increasing the spelling achievement of elementary and junior high students. *Behavior Modification,* 1978, *2,* 211–230.

Foxx, R. M., & Shapiro, S. T. The timeout ribbon: A nonexclusionary timeout procedure. *Journal of Applied Behavior Analysis,* 1978, *11,* 125–136.

Gardner, W. I. Use of punishment with the severely retarded: A review. *American Journal of Mental Deficiency,* 1969, *74,* 86–103.

Gast, D. L., vanBiervliet, A., & Spradlin, J. E. Teaching number-word equivalences: A study of transfer. *American Journal of Mental Deficiency,* 1979, *83,* 524–527.

Glynn, E. L., Thomas, J. D., & Shee, S. M. Behavioral self-control of on-task behavior in an elementary classroom. *Journal of Applied Behavior Analysis,* 1973, *6,* 105–113.

Goetz, E. M., Holmberg, M. C., & LeBlanc, J. M. Differential reinforcement of other behavior and noncontingent reinforcement as control procedures during the modification of a preschooler's compliance. *Journal of Applied Behavior Analysis,* 1975, *8,* 77–82.

Goldstein, D. R., Cooper, A. Y., Ruggles, T. R., & LeBlanc, J. M. *The effects of paced instructions, reprimands and physical guidance on compliance.* Paper presented the annual meeting of the Association for Behavior Analysis, Dearborn, Michigan, June 1980.

Gollin, E. S. Factors affecting conditional discrimination in children. *Journal of Comparative and Physiological Psychology,* 1965, *40,* 422–427.

Gollin, E. S. Solution of conditional discrimination problems in young children. *Journal of Comparative and Physiological Psychology,* 1966, *62,* 454–456.

Gollin, E. S., & Savory, P. Fading procedures and conditional discrimination in children. *Journal of the Experimental Analysis of Behavior,* 1968, *11,* 443–451.

Grandy, G. S., Madsen, C. H., & DeMersseman, L. M. The effects of individual and interdependent contingencies on inappropriate classroom behavior. *Psychology in the Schools,* 1973, *10,* 488–493.

Graubard, P. S. Utilizing the group in teaching disturbed delinquents to learn. *Exceptional Children,* 1969, *36,* 267–272.

Graubard, P. S., Lanier, P., Weisert, H., & Miller, M. B. *An investigation into the use of indigenous grouping as the reinforcing agent in teaching maladjusted boys to read: Final report.* Yeshiva University, School of Education and Community Administration, June, 1970, Project No. 8-0174, Grant No. CEG-8-08174-4353, USOE Bureau of Education for the Handicapped.

Greenwood, C. R., Hops, H., & Walker, H. M. The program for academic survival skills (PASS): Effects on student behavior and achievement. *Journal of School Psychology,* 1977, *15,* 25–35.

Griffiths, K., & Griffiths, R. Errorless establishment of letter discrimination with a stimulus fading procedure in preschool children. *Perceptual and Motor Skills,* 1976, *42,* 387–396.

Gurulnick, J. J. Effects of distinctive feature training and instructional technique on letter and form discrimination. *American Journal of Mental Deficiency,* 1975, *80,* 202–207.

Hall, R. V., & Broden, M. Behavior changes in brain-injured children through social reinforcement. *Journal of Experimental Child Psychology,* 1967, *5,* 463–479.

Hall, R. V., Lund, D., & Jackson, D. Effects of teacher attention on study behavior. *Journal of Applied Behavior Analysis,* 1968, *1,* 1–12.

Hall, R. V., Panyan, M., Rabon, D., & Broden, M. Instructing beginning teachers in reinforcement procedures which improve classroom control. *Journal of Applied Behavior Analysis,* 1968, *1,* 315–322.

Hamblin, R. L., Hathaway, C., & Wodarski, J. S. Group contingencies, peer tutoring and accelerating academic achievement. In E. A. Ramp & B. L. Hopkins (Eds.), *A new direction for education: Behavior analysis,* Vol. 1. lawrence: University of Kansas, 1971.

Hardiman, S. A., Goetz, E. M., Reuter, K: E., & LeBlanc, J. M. Primes, contingent attention, and training: Effects on a child's motor behavior. *Journal of Applied Behavior Analysis,* 1975, *8,* 399–409.

Haring, N. G., & Hauck, M. A. Improved learning conditions in the establishment of reading skills with disabled readers. *Exceptional Children,* 1969, *35,* 341–352.

Harris, M. B., & Miksovic, R. S. Operant conditioning of social interaction in preschool children. In M. B.

Harris (Ed.), *Classroom uses of behavior modification.* Columbus, Ohio: Charles E. Merrill, 1972.

Harris, V. W., & Sherman, J. A. Use and analysis of the "good behavior game" to reduce disruptive classroom behavior. *Journal of Applied Behavior Analysis*, 1973, *6*, 405–418.

Harris, V. W., & Sherman, J. A. Homework assignments, consequences, and classroom performance in social studies and mathematics. *Journal of Applied Behavior Analysis*, 1974, *7*, 505–519.

Hart, B. M., Allen, K. E., Buell, J. S., Harris, F. R., & Wolf, M. M. Effects of social reinforcement on operant crying. *Journal of Experimental Child Psychology*, 1964, *1*, 145–153.

Hart, B. M., Reynolds, N. J., Baer, D. M., Brawley, F. R., & Harris, F. R. Effect of contingent and non-contingent social reinforcement on the cooperative play of a preschool child. *Journal of Applied Behavior Analysis*, 1968, *1*, 73–76.

Hartup, W. W. Peer interaction and social organization. In Paul H. Mussen (Ed.), *Carmichael's manual of child psychology.* New York: Wiley, 1970.

Hasazi, J. E., & Hasazi, S. E. Effects of teacher attention on digit-reversal behavior in an elementary school child. *Journal of Applied Behavior Analysis*, 1972, *5*, 157–162.

Hass, S. L., Ruggles, T. R., & LeBlanc, J. M. *Minimal vs. criterion-related detailed instructions.* Paper presented at the Biennial meeting of the Society of Research in Child Development, San Francisco, March 1979.

Haupt, E. J., Van Kirk, M. J., & Terraciano, T. An inexpensive fading procedure to decrease errors and increase retention of number facts. In E. Ramp & G. Semb (Eds.), *Behavior analysis: Areas of research and application.* Englewood Cliffs, N.J.: Prentice-Hall, 1977.

Hay, W. M., Hay, L., & Nelson, R. O. Direct and collateral changes in on-task and academic behavior resulting from on-task versus academic contingencies. *Behavior Therapy*, 1977, *8*, 431–441.

Herman, S. H., & Tramontana, J. Instructions and group versus individual reinforcement in modifying disruptive group behavior. *Journal of Applied Behavior Analysis*, 1971, *4*, 113–119.

Holland, J. G. Teaching machines: An application of principles from the laboratory. *Journal of the Experimental Analysis of Behavior*, 1960, *3*, 275–287.

Holt, W. J., & Etzel, B. C. *Cognitive by-products of motor training.* Paper presented at the meeting of the American Psychological Association, Washington, D.C., 1976.

Homme, L. E., deBacca, P., Devine, J. V., Steinhorst, R., & Rickert, E. J. Use of the Premack principle in controlling the behavior of school children. *Journal of the Experimental Analysis of Behavior*, 1963, *6*, 544.

Hopkins, B. L., Schutte, R. C., & Garton, K. L. The effects of access to a playroom on the rate and quality of printing and writing of first and second-grade students. *Journal of Applied Behavior Analysis*, 1971, *4*, 77–87.

Hops, H., & Cobb, J. A. Survival behaviors in the educational setting: Their implications for research and intervention. In L. A. Hamerlynck, L. C. Handy, & E. J. Mash (Eds.), *Behavior change: Methodology, concepts and practice.* Champaign, Ill.: Research Press, 1973.

Hundert, J. The effectiveness of reinforcement, response cost, and mixed programs on classroom behaviors. *Journal of Applied Behavior Analysis*, 1976, *9*, 107.

Iwata, B. A., & Bailey, J. S. Reward versus cost token systems: An analysis of the effects on students and teacher. *Journal of Applied Behavior Analysis*, 1974, *7*, 567–576.

Jacobs, J. F. *A comparison of group and individual rewards in teaching reading to slow learners: Final report.* University of Florida, College of Education, June 1970, Project No. 9-0257, Grant No. OEG-49-190257-0045 (010), USOE Bureau of Research.

Johnson, M. S., & Bailey, J. S. Cross-age tutoring: Fifth graders as arithmetic tutors for kindergarten children. *Journal of Applied Behavior Analysis*, 1974, *7*, 223–232.

Johnston, M. K., Kelley, C. S., Harris, F. R., & Wolf, M. M. An application of reinforcement principles to development of motor skills of a young child. *Child Development*, 1966, *37*, 379–387.

Karraker, J., & Doke, L. A. Errorless discrimination of alphabet letters: Effects of time and method of introducing competing stimuli. *The Journal of Experimental Education*, 1970, *38*, 4.

Kaufman, K. F., & O'Leary, K. D. Reward, cost, and self-evaluation procedures for disruptive adolescents in a psychiatric hospital school. *Journal of Applied Behavior Analysis*, 1972, *5*, 293–310.

Kazdin, A. E. The effect of vicarious reinforcement on attentive behavior in the classroom. *Journal of Applied Behavior Analysis*, 1973, *6*, 71–78.

Kazdin, A. E. *Behavior modification in applied settings.* Homewood, Ill.: Dorsey, 1975.

Kazdin, A. E. *The token economy: A review and evaluation.* New York: Plenum Press, 1977.

Kazdin, A. E., & Klock, J. The effect of nonverbal teacher approval on student attentive behavior. *Journal of Applied Behavior Analysis*, 1973, *6*, 643–654.

Kazdin, A. E., Silverman, N. A., & Sittler, J. L. The use of prompts to enhance vicarious effects of nonverbal approval. *Journal of Applied Behavior Analysis*, 1975, *8*, 279–286.

Kelleher, R. Fixed-ratio schedules of conditioned reinforcement with chimpanzees. *Journal of the Experimental Analysis of Behvior*, 1958, *3*, 281–289.

Kirby, F. D., & Shields, F. Modification of arithmetic response rate and attending behavior in a seventh-grade student. *Journal of Applied Behavior Analysis*, 1972, *5*, 79–84.

Klein, R. D. A brief research report on accuracy and academic performance. *Journal of Applied Behavior Analysis*, 1975, *8*, 121–122.

Klein, R. D. Modifying academic performance in the grade school classroom. In M. Hersen, R. M. Eisler, & P. M. Miller (Eds.), *Progress in behavior modification*, Vol. 8. New York: Academic Press, 1979.

Knapczyk, D., & Livingston, G. The effects of prompting question-asking upon on-task behavior and reading. *Journal of Applied Behavior Analysis*, 1974, *7*, 115–121.

Koegel, R. L., & Rincover, A. Some detrimental effects of using extra stimuli to guide learning in normal and autistic children. *Journal of Abnormal Child Psychology*, 1976, *4*, 59–71.

Koegel, R. L., Dunlap, G., & Dyer, K. Intertrial interval duration and learning in autistic children. *Journal of Applied Behavior Analysis*, 1980, *13*, 91–99.

Kramer, S., Ruggles, T. R., & LeBlanc, J. M. *The effects of imposing time limits on the responses of preschool children.* Paper presented at the meeting of the Association for the Advancement of Behavior Therapy, San Francisco, 1979.

Kuypers, D. S., Becker, W. C., & O'Leary, K. D. How to make a token system fail. *Exceptional Children*, October 1968, *11*, 101–109.

Lahey, B. B., & Drabman, R. S. Facilitation of the acquisition and retention of sight-word vocabulary through token reinforcement. *Journal of Applied Behavior Analysis*, 1974, *7*, 307–312.

LeBlanc, J. M., Busby, K. H., & Thomson, C. Functions of timeout for changing aggressive behavior of a preschool child. In R. E. Ulrich, T. S. Stachnik, & J. E. Mabry (Eds.), *Control of human behaior: In education*, Vol. 3. Glenview, Ill.: Scott, Foresman, 1973.

LeBlanc, J. M., Etzel, B. C., & Domash, M. A. A functional curriculum for early intervention. In K. E. Allen, V. A. Holm, & R. L. Schiefelbush (Eds.), *Early intervention—A team approach*. Baltimore: University Park Press, 1978.

Leith, N. J., & Haude, R. H. Errorless discrimination in monkeys. *Proceedings of 77th Annual Convention*. American Psychological Association, 1969, 799–800.

Levin, L. A comparison of individual and group contingencies with third and fourth-grade children. *Probe*, 1971, *1*, 101–107.

Lewis, B. L., & Strain, P. S. Effects of feedback, timing and motivational content on teachers' delivery of contingent social praise. *Psychology in the Schools*, 1978, *15*, 423–429.

Litlow, L., & Pumroy, D. K. A brief review of classroom group-oriented contingencies. *Journal of Applied Behavior Analysis*, 1975, *8*, 341–347.

Lobitz, W. C., & Burns, W. J. The "least intrusive intervention" strategy for behavior change procedures: The use of public and private feedback in school classrooms. *Psychology in the Schools*, 1977, *14*, 89–94.

Long, J. D., & Williams, R. L. The comparative effectiveness of group and individually contingent free time with innercity junior high school students. *Journal of Applied Behavior Analysis*, 1973, *6*, 465–474.

Lovaas, O. I., & Simmons, J. Q. Manipulation of self-destruction in three retarded children. *Journal of Applied Behavior Analysis*, 1969, *2*, 143–157.

Lovitt, T. C., & Curtiss, K. A. Effects of manipulating an antecedent event on mathematics response rate. *Journal of Applied Behavior Analysis*, 1968, *1*, 329–334.

Lovitt, T. C., & Curtiss, K. A. Academic response rate as a function of teacher- and self-imposed contingencies. *Journal of Applied Behavior Analysis*, 1969, *2*, 49–53.

Lovitt, T. C., & Esveldt, K. A. The relative effects on math performance of single versus multiple-ratio schedules: A case study. *Journal of Applied Behavior Analysis*, 1970, *3*, 261–270.

Lovitt, T. C., Guppy, T. E., & Blattner, J. E. The use of a free-time contingency with fourth-graders to increase spelling accuracy. *Behavior Research and Therapy*, 1969, *7*, 151–156.

MacMillan, D., Forness, S. R., & Trumball, B. M. The role of punishment in the classroom. *Exceptional Children*, 1973, *40*, 85–96.

Madsen, C. H., Becker, W. C., Thomas, D. R., Koser, L., & Plager, E. An analysis of the reinforcing function of "sit down" commands. In R. K. Parker (Ed.), *Readings in educational psychology*. Boston: Allyn & Bacon, 1968.

Main, G. C., & Munro, B. C. A token reinforcement program in a public Junior High School. *Journal of Applied Behavior Analysis*, 1977, *10*, 93–94.

Maloney, K. B., & Hopkins, B. L. The modification of sentence structure and its relationship to subjective judgments of creativity in writing. *Journal of Applied Behavior Analysis*, 1973, *6*, 425–434.

Marholin, D., & Steinman, W. M. Stimulus control in the classroom as a function of the behavior reinforced. *Journal of Applied Behavior Analysis*, 1977, *10*, 465–478.

Marholin, D., Siegel, L. J., & Phillips, D. Treatment and transfer: A search for empirical procedures. In M. Hersen, R. M. Eisler, & P. M. Miller (Eds.), *Progress in behavior modification*, Vol. 3. New York: Academic Press, 1976.

McAllister, L. W., Stachowiak, J. G., Baer, D. M., & Conderman, L. The application of operant conditioning techniques in a secondary school classroom. *Journal of Applied Behavior Analysis*, 1969, *2*, 277–285.

McLaughlin, T. F., & Malaby, J. Intrinsic reinforcers in a classroom token economy. *Journal of Applied Behavior Analysis*, 1972, *5*, 263–270.

McNamara, J. R. Behavioral intervention in the classroom: Changing students and training a teacher. *Adolescence*, 1971, *6*, 433–440.

Meddock, T. D., Parsons, J. A., & Hill, K. T. Effects of an adult's presence and praise on young children's performance. *Journal of Experimental Child Psychology*, 1971, *12*, 197–211.

Medland, M. B., & Stachnik, T. J. Good-Behavior Game: A replication and systematic analysis. *Journal of Applied Behavior Analysis*, 1972, *5*, 45–51.

Miller, R. M., & LeBlanc, J. M. *Experimental analysis of the effect of detailed and minimal instructions on the acquisition of preacademic skills.* Paper presented at the meeting of the American Psychological Association, Montreal, August 1973.

Mitaug, D. E., & Wolfe, M. S. Employing task arrangements and verbal contingencies to promote verbalizations between retarded children. *Journal of Applied Behavior Analysis*, 1976, *9*, 301–314.

Moore, R., & Goldiamond, I. Errorless establishment of visual discrimination using fading procedures. *Journal of the Experimental Analysis of Behavior*, 1964, *7*, 269–272.

Morraco, J. C., & Fasheh, V. Effects of contingency management on academic achievement and conduct of mentally retarded Arab students. *American Journal of Mental Deficiency*, 1978, *82*, 487–493.

Neef, N. A., Iwata, B. A., & Page, T. J. The effects of known-item interspersed on acquisition of spelling and sightreading words. *Journal of Applied Behavior Analysis*, 1977, *10*, 738.

Nelson, A. L., Holt, W. J., & Etzel, B. C. *A description of programs to teach beginning math skills.* Invited symposium on preparing atypical preschool children for future academic work. Presented at the Council for Exceptional Children, Chicago, 1976. (a)

Nelson, A. L., Holt, W. J., & Etzel, B. C. *Empirical analysis of essential skills in a complex task.* Presented at the American Psychological Association, Washington, D.C., 1976. (b)

O'Leary, K. D. Behavior modification in the classroom: A rejoinder to Winett and Winkler. *Journal of Applied Behavior Analysis,* 1972, *5,* 505–511.

O'Leary, K. D., & Becker, W. C. Behavior modification of an adjustment class: A token reinforcement program. *Exceptional Children,* 1967, *33,* 637–642.

O'Leary, K. D., & Becker, W. C. The effects of a teacher's reprimands on children's behavior. *Journal of School Psychology,* 1968, *7,* 8–11.

O'Leary, K. D., & Drabman, R. Token reinforcement programs in the classroom. *Psychological Bulletin,* 1971, *75,* 379–398.

O'Leary, K. D., & O'Leary, S. G. (Eds.) *Classroom management: The successful use of behavior modification.* New York: Pergamon Press, 1972.

O'Leary, S. G., & O'Leary, K. D. Behavior modification in the school. In H. Leitenberg (Ed.), *Handbook of behavior modification and behavior therapy.* New York: Prentice-Hall, 1976.

O'Leary, K. D., Becker, W. C., Evans, M. B., & Saudargas, R. A. A token reinforcement program in a public school: A replication and systematic analysis. *Journal of Applied Behavior Analysis,* 1969, *2,* 3–13.

O'Leary, K. D., Kauffman, K. F., Kass, R. E., & Drabman, R. S. The effects of loud and soft reprimands on the behavior of disruptive students. *Exceptional Children,* 1970, *37,* 145–155.

Osborne, J. G. Free time as a reinforcer in the management of classroom behavior. *Journal of Applied Behavior Analysis,* 1969, *2,* 113–118.

Packard, R. G. The control of "classroom attention": A group contingency for complex behavior. *Journal of Applied Behavior Analysis,* 1970, *3,* 13–28.

Panyan, M. C., & Hall, R. V. Effects of serial versus concurrent task sequencing on acquisition maintenance and generalization. *Journal of Applied Behavior Analysis,* 1978, *11,* 67–74.

Patterson, G. R. An application of conditioning techniques to the control of a hyperactive child. In L. P. Ullmann & L. Krasner (Eds.), *Case studies in behavior modification.* New York: Holt, Rinehart & Winston, 1965.

Patterson, G. R., Jones, R., Whittier, J., & Wright, M. A. A behavior modification technique for the hyperactive child. *Behavior Research and Therapy,* 1965, *2,* 217–226.

Peterson, R. F., & Whithurst, G. J. A variable influencing the performance of generalized imitation. *Journal of Applied Behavior Analysis,* 1971, *4,* 1–9.

Peterson, R. F., Cox, M. A., & Bijou, S. W. Training children to work productively in classroom groups. *Exceptional Children,* March 1971, *14,* 491–500.

Pinkston, E. M., Reese, N. M., LeBlanc, J. M., & Baer, D. M. Independent control of a preschool child's aggression and peer interaction by contingent teacher attention. *Journal of Applied Behavior Analysis,* 1973, *6,* 115–124.

Plummer, S., Baer, D. M., & LeBlanc, J. M. Functional

considerations in the use of procedural timeout and an effective alternative. *Journal of Applied Behavior Analysis,* 1977, *10,* 689–706.

Porterfield, J. K., Herbert-Jackson, E., & Risley, T. R. Contingent observation: An effective and acceptable procedure for reducing disruptive behavior of young children in a group setting. *Journal of Applied Behavior Analysis,* 1976, *9,* 55–64.

Powers, R. B., Cheney, C. D., & Agostino, N. R. Errorless training of a visual discrimination in preschool children. *The Psychological Record,* 1970, *20,* 45–50.

Prentice, B. S. *The effectiveness of group versus individual reinforcement for shaping attentive classroom behavior.* Unpublished doctoral dissertation, University of Arizona, 1970.

Proshansky, H. M., Ittleson, W. H., & Rivlin, L. G. (Eds.), *Environmental psychology.* New York: Holt, Rinehart & Winston, 1970.

Radgowski, T. A., Allen, K. E., Schilmoeller, G. L., Ruggles, T. R., & LeBlanc, J. M. *Delayed presentation of feedback in preschool group foreign language training.* Paper presented at the meeting of the American Psychological Association, Toronto, 1978.

Redd, W. H., & Birnbrauer, J. S. Adults as discriminative stimuli for different reinforcement contingencies with retarded children. *Journal of Experimental Child Psychology,* 1969, *7,* 440–447.

Resnick, L. B., Wang, M. C., & Kaplan, J. Task analysis in curriculum design: A hierarchically sequenced introductory mathematics curriculum. *Journal of Applied Behavior Analysis,* 1973, *6,* 679–709.

Reynolds, G. S. *A primer of operant conditioning.* Glenview, Ill.: Scott, Foresman, 1968.

Reynolds, N. J., & Risley, T. R. The role of social and material reinforcers in increasing talking of a disadvantaged preschool child. *Journal of Applied Behavior Analysis,* 1968, *1,* 253–262.

Rincover, A. Variables affecting stimulus fading and discriminative responding in psychotic children. *Journal of Abnormal Psychology,* 1978, *87,* 541–553.

Robertshaw, C. S., & Hiebert, H. D. The astronaut game: A group contingency applied to a first grade classroom. *School Applications of Learning Theory,* 1973, *6,* 28–33.

Ruggles, T. R., & LeBlanc, J. M. *Variables which affect the effectiveness of group training procedures designed for children with learning problems.* Paper presented at the 12th Annual Gatlinburg Conference on Research in Mental Retardation and Developmental Disabilities, Gulf Shores, Alabama, 1979.

Sabbert, J. K., Holt, W. J., Nelson, A. L., Domash, M. A., & Etzel, B. C. *Functional analysis of teaching different sizes of groups.* Presented at the American Psychological Association, Washington, D.C., 1976. (a)

Sabbert, J. K., Holt, W. J., Nelson, A. L., Domash, M. A., & Etzel, B. C. *Programming simple addition problems.* Invited symposium on preparing atypical preschool children for future academic work, Council on Exceptional Children, Chicago, 1976. (b)

Salzberg, B. H., Wheeler, A. J., Devar, L. T., & Hopkins, B. L. The effects of intermittent feedback and intermittent contingent access to play on printing of kindergarten children. *Journal of Applied Behavior Analysis,* 1971, *4,* 163–171.

Saudargas, R. W., Madsen, C. H., & Scott, J. W. Differential effects of fixed and variable-time feedback on production rates of elementary school children. *Journal of Applied Behavior Analysis*, 1977, *10*, 673.

Schilmoeller, K. J., & Etzel, B. C. An experimental analysis of criterion- and noncriterion-related cues in "errorless" stimulus control procedures. In B. C. Etzel, J. M. LeBlanc, & D. M. Baer (Eds.), *New developments in behavioral research: Theory, method and application. In honor of Sidney W. Bijou*. Hillsdale, N.J.: Lawrence Erlbaum, 1977.

Schilmoeller, G. L., Schilmoeller, K. J., Etzel, B. C., & LeBlanc, J. M. Conditional discrimination responding after errorless and trial-and-error training. *Journal of the Experimental Analysis of Behavior*, 1979, *31*, 405–420.

Schreibman, L. Effects of within-stimulus and extra-stimulus prompting on discrimination learning in autistic children. *Journal of Applied Behavior Analysis*, 1975, *8*, 91–112.

Schumaker, J. B., Hovell, M. F., & Sherman, J. A. An analysis of daily report cards and parent-managed privileges in the improvement of adolescents' classroom performance. *Journal of Applied Behavior Analysis*, 1977, *10*, 449–464.

Schusterman, R. J. Attention shift and errorless reversal learning by the California sea lion. *Science*, 1967, *156*, 833–835.

Schwartz, S. H., Firestone, I. J., & Terry, S. Fading techniques and concept learning in children. *Psychonomic Science*, 1971, *25*, 83–84.

Schwarz, M. L., & Hawkins, R. P. Application of delayed reinforcement procedures to the behavior of an elementary school child. *Journal of Applied Behavior Analysis*, 1970, *3*, 85–96.

Scott, P. M., Burton, R. V., & Yarrow, M. R. Social reinforcement under natural conditions. *Child Development*, 1967, *38*, 53–63.

Shure, M. B. Psychological ecology of a nursery school. *Child Development*, 1963, *34*, 979–992.

Sidman, M., & Cresson, O. Reading and cross-modal transfer of stimulus equivalences in severe retardation. *American Journal of Mental Deficiency*, 1973, *77*, 515–523.

Sidman, M., & Stoddard, L. T. Programming perception and learning for retarded children. In N. R. Ellis (Ed.), *International review of research in mental retardation*, Vol. 2. New York: Academic Press, 1966.

Sidman, M., & Stoddard, L. T. The effectiveness of fading in programming a simultaneous form discrimination for retarded children. *Journal of the Experimental Analysis of Behavior*, 1968, *10*, 3–15.

Sidman, M., Cresson, O., & Willson-Morris, M. Acquisition of matching to sample via mediated transfer. *Journal of the Experimental Analysis of Behavior*, 1974, *22*, 261–273.

Skinner, B. F. *The behavior of organisms*. New York: Appleton-Century, 1938.

Skinner, B. F. *Why we need teaching machines: Cumulative Record*. New York: Appleton-Century-Crofts, 1961.

Skinner, B. F. Operant behavior. *American Psychologist*, 1963, *18*, 503–515.

Smith, M. F. The establishment and extinction of the token reward habit in the cat. *Journal of General Psychology*, 1939, *20*, 475–486.

Smith, R. A., & Filler, J. W. Effects of a modified fading procedure on two-choice discrimination performance of toddler-age children. *Child Development*, 1975, *46*, 583–587.

Solnick, J. V., Rincover, A., & Peterson, C. R. Some determinants of the reinforcing and punishing effects of timeout. *Journal of Applied Behavior Analysis*, 1977, *10*, 415–424.

Stella, E. M., & Etzel, B. C. *The effects of daily criterion level probes on acquisition*. Presented at the American Psychological Association, San Francisco, 1977.

Stella, M. E., & Etzel, B. C. *A case for training eye orientations of difficult-to-educate children: Visual scanning differences between normal and retarded children*. Presented at the Association for Advancement of Behavior Therapy, San Francisco, 1979. (a)

Stella, M. E., & Etzel, B. C. *Manipulation of visual fixation on correct (S+) stimuli during acquisition*. Presented at the Society for Research in Child Development, San Francisco, 1979. (b)

Stoddard, L. T., & Sidman, M. The effects of errors on children's performance on a circle-ellipse discrimination. *Journal of the Experimental Analysis of Behavior*, 1967, *10*, 261–270.

Stokes, T. F., & Baer, D. M. An implicit technology of generalization. *Journal of Applied Behavior Analysis*, 1977, *10*, 349–368.

Strain, P. S., Shores, R. E., & Kerr, M. M. An experimental analysis of "spillover" effects on the social interaction of behaviorally handicapped preschool children. *Journal of Applied Behavior Analysis*, 1976, *9*, 31–40.

Tate, B. G., & Baroff, G. S. Aversive control of self-injurious behavior in a psychotic boy. *Behaviour Research and Therapy*, 1966, *4*, 281–287.

Terrace, H. S. Discrimination learning with and without "errors." *Journal of the Experimental Analysis of Behavior*, 1963, *6*, 1–27. (a)

Terrace, H. S. Errorless transfer of a discrimination across two continua. *Journal of the Experimental Analysis of Behavior*, 1963, *6*, 223–232. (b)

Terrace, H. S. Stimulus control. In W. K. Honig (Ed.), *Operant behavior: Areas of research and application*. New York: Meridith Corporation, 1966.

Thomas, J. D. Accuracy of self-assessment of on-task behavior by elementary school children. *Journal of Applied Behavior Analysis*, 1976, *9*, 209–210.

Touchette, P. E. The effects of graduated stimulus change on the acquisition of a simple discrimination in severely retarded boys. *Journal of the Experimental Analysis of Behavior*, 1969, *12*, 211–214.

Touchette, P. E. Transfer of stimulus control: Measuring the moment of transfer. *Journal of the Experimental Analysis of Behavior*, 1971, *15*, 347–354.

Trap, J. J., Milner-Davis, P., Joseph, S., & Cooper, J. O. The effects of feedback and consequences on transitional cursive letter formation. *Journal of Applied Behavior Analysis*, 1978, *14*, 381–394.

Turknett, R. L. *A study of the differential effects of individual versus group reward conditions on the creative productions of elementary school children*. Unpublished doctoral dissertation, University of Georgia, 1971.

Twardosz, S., & Sajwaj, T. Multiple effects of a procedure to increase sitting in a hyperactive retarded boy. *Journal of Applied Behavior Analysis*, 1972, *5*, 73–78.

Twardosz, S., Cataldo, M. F., & Risley, T. R. An open environment design for infant and toddler day care. *Journal of Applied Behavior Analysis*, 1974, *7*, 529–546.

Tyler, V., & Brown, G. Token reinforcement of academic performance with institutionalized delinquent boys. *Journal of Educational Psychology*, 1968, *59*, 164–168.

Uhl, C. N., & Garcia, E. E. Comparison of omission with extinction in response elimination in rats. *Journal of Comparative and Physiological Psychology*, 1969, *69*, 554–562.

vanBiervliet, A. Establishing words and objects as functionally equivalent through manual sign training. *American Journal of Mental Deficiency*, 1977, *82*, 178–186.

Van Houten, R., Hill, S., & Parsons, M. An analysis of a performance feedback system: The effects of timing and feedback, public posting, and praise upon academic performance and peer interaction. *Journal of Applied Behavior Analysis*, 1975, *8*, 449–457.

Walker, H. M., & Buckley, H. K. The use of positive reinforcement in conditioning attending behavior. *Journal of Applied Behavior Analysis*, 1968, *1*, 245–250.

Walker, H. M., & Buckley, N. K. Programming generalization and maintenance of treatment effects across time and across settings. *Journal of Applied Behavior Analysis*, 1972, *5*, 209–224.

Walker, H. M., & Hops, H. Increasing academic achievement by reinforcing direct academic performance and/or facilitative non-academic responses. *Journal of Educational Psychology*, 1976, *68*, 218–225.

Warner, S. P., Miller, F. D., & Cohen, M. W. Relative effectiveness of teacher attention and the "good behavior game" in modifying disruptive classroom behavior. *Journal of Applied Behavior Analysis*, 1977, *10*, 737.

Wasik, B. H. The application of Premack's generalization on reinforcement to the management of classroom be-havior. *Journal of Experimental Child Psychology*, 1970, *10*, 33–43.

Weiner, H. Some effects of response cost upon human operant behavior. *Journal of the Experimental Analysis of Behavior*, 1962, *5*, 201–208.

Weinstein, C. S. Modifying student behavior in an open classroom through changes in physical design. *American Educational Research Journal*, 1977, *14*, 249–262.

Whitehurst, G. J. Observational learning. In A. C. Catania & T. A. Brigham (Eds.), *Handbook of applied behavior analysis: Social and instructional processes*. New York: Irvington Publishers, 1978.

Wilson, S. H., & Williams, R. L. The effects of group contingencies on first garders' academic and social behaviors. *Journal of School Psychology*, 1973, *11*, 110–117.

Winett, R. A., & Winkler, R. C. Current behavior modification in the classroom. Be still, be quiet, be docile. *Journal of Applied Behavior Analysis*, 1972, *5*, 499–504.

Witte, P. H. *The effects of group reward structure on interracial acceptance, peer-tutoring, and academic performance*. Unpublished doctoral dissertation, Washington University, 1971.

Wolf, M. M., Risley, T. R., & Mees, H. L. Application of operant conditioning procedures to the behavior problems of an autistic child. *Behaviour Research and Therapy*, 1964, *1*, 305–312.

Wolf, M. M., Giles, D. K., & Hall, R. V. Experiments with token reinforcement in a remedial classroom. *Behaviour Research and Therapy*, 1968, *6*, 51–64.

Wolfe, J. B. Effectiveness of token rewards for chimpanzees. *Comparative Psychology Monograph*, 1936, *11* (5, Series No. 60).

Wulbert, M., Nyman, B. A., Snow, D., & Owen, Y. The efficacy of stimulus fading and contingency management in the treatment of elective mutism: A case study. *Journal of Applied Behavior Analysis*, 1973, *6*, 435–441.

Zeaman, D., & House, B. J. The role of attention in retardate discrimination learning. In N. R. Ellis (Ed.), *Handbook of mental deficiency: Psychological theory and research*. New York: McGraw-Hill, 1963.

CHAPTER 31

Treatment of Childhood Medical Disorders

Daniel M. Doleys and Jan Bruno

Introduction

This chapter contains a discussion of four medical problems found in children: seizures, asthma, obesity, and hyperactivity. Although there is no common etiological thread for these four disorders, they are linked by the following: (1) they are prevalent among children; (2) the first line of therapy is generally through the pediatrician; (3) each problem can affect the child academically, socially, and medically; and (4) one of the first lines of treatment is generally the use of some pharmacological agent.

The intention of this chapter is to provide a selective rather than an exhaustive review of various behavioral approaches that have been attempted with these four disorders. Examples of various procedures from the literature are provided to illustrate the application of a particular technique or approach. The intent is to provide the reader with an overview of the status of behavioral therapies in these various areas, rather than a detailed or in-depth analysis of any one technique or procedure.

Asthma

Introduction

Bronchial asthma is a reversible obstructive lung disorder that occurs in approximately 30 of every 1,000 persons in the United States (Department of Health, Education, and Welfare, 1973). Asthmatic attacks can be characterized by means of five categories of symptoms (Kinsman, Luparello, O'Banion, & Spector, 1973; Kinsman, Spector, Shucard, & Luparello, 1974). In decreasing frequency, these are bronchial constriction, fatigue, panic–fear, irritability, and hyperventilation–hypocapnia. To the patient, an asthma attack represents respiratory distress involving labored breathing, wheezing, tightness of the chest, anxiety, and coughing or gasping (Mathison, 1975). Physiologically, the asthmatic attack is characterized by a constriction of the

Daniel M. Doleys and Jan Bruno • Department of Psychology, University of Alabama Medical School, Birmingham, Alabama 35294. Preparation of this manuscript was supported in part by Project 910, U.S. Maternal and Child Health, H.S.M.S.A., Department of Health, Education and Welfare, as awarded to the Center for Developmental and Learning Disorders, University of Alabama in Birmingham School of Medicine, Birmingham, Alabama.

smooth muscles of the bronchioles, mucosal edema, and hypersecretion of viscus sputum, all resulting in increased airway resistance. The asthma attacks occur intermittently and vary in severity. Freedman and Pelletier (1970) suggested that asthma could be described as mild, persistent, or severe, and explosive. Eggleston (1976) employed a system of four categories, including sporadic attacks, continuous mild asthma, frequent episodes, and chronic or severe asthma. Asthma may be causally related to allergic hypersensitivity, psychological conflict, or some combination of the two (Blanchard & Aheles, 1970).

Behavioral treatments of asthma have generally adopted one of two approaches (Knapp & Wells, 1978). The first focuses on the asthmatic attacks themselves in an attempt to assess the antecedent stimulus conditions that come to be associated with the attacks. The second approach emphasizes an examination of reinforcing stimuli, which through operant conditioning, have come to maintain and/or exacerbate attacks.

Treatment

Relaxation and Systematic Desensitization. Relaxation training and systematic desensitization have been used with great regularity in the treatment of asthmatic patients. Such techniques can be applied to alter abnormal pulmonary functions in a direct or an indirect manner and to alter maladaptive emotional concomitants (Alexander, 1977; Phillip, Wilde, & Day, 1972). Through these procedures, it is suggested that the asthmatic's sensitivity and anxiety levels regarding asthmatic attacks and the stimuli that produced them can be lessened. Many of the studies in this area have used the peak expiratory flow rate (PEFR) as a measure of the maximum rate of airflow from the lungs during forced expiration. It is inversely correlated with the degree of airway constriction or obstruction. FEV_1 is the amount of forced air exhaled in one second. In order to be accurate, both measures require the cooperation of the asthmatic, who must attempt to produce maximum expiratory effect (Schaefer, Millman, & Levine, 1979).

Relaxation procedures have typically relied on the often-used tense–relax approach intro-

duced by Jacobson (1938). This may be accompanied by autogenic training (Schultz & Luthe, 1959). Alexander (1977) provided an excellent description of the application of these two procedures in relaxation with asthmatic children. In one of the earlier studies utilizing relaxation, Alexander, Miklich, and Hershkoff (1972) examined the effects of systematic relaxation on the PEFR of asthmatic children. Twenty-six children were divided equally according to demographic features and asthmatic severity. The subjects were then assigned to one of two groups. One group participated in three sessions of modified Jacobsonian systematic-relaxation training (tensing and relaxing hands, forearms, biceps, upper face, calves, and feet), while the second group was instructed to sit quietly during three sessions of equal duration. PEFR measures were obtained prior to and following each session. The results revealed a significant increase in PEFR over sessions for the relaxation group, while there was a nonsignificant decrease for the control subjects. Alexander (1972) replicated this procedure and confirmed the initial finding.

A variation of this relaxation training procedure was utilized by Sirota and Mahoney (1974), who utilized a portable timer that the subject set for various intervals and then relaxed on cue whenever it sounded. Other modifications included requiring the subject to briefly postpone the use of a bronchodilator by setting a timer for 3–4 min, during which time relaxation would be practiced, followed by the use of the bronchodilator if it was needed. Decreases in the inhalation of medication, the termination of corticosteroid therapy, a reduction of the use of an ephedrine bronchodilator, and the reduction or elimination of all asthmatic medications were noted.

Hock, Rodgers, Reddi, and Kennard (1978) compared relaxation training with assertion training involving role playing, the expression of positive and negative emotions, and the combination of these two procedures with asthmatic male adolescents. The treatment sessions occurred weekly for approximately one hour for seven to nine weeks. Relaxation was of the tense–relax type utilizing guided imagery. Pulmonary functions studies (FEV_1) and weekly attack-frequency measures were taken. The relaxation group and the relaxation and assertiveness training group showed significant decreases in the frequency of attacks and improved pulmonary function. The assertiveness-training-alone group and the untreated controls were unimproved. However, the frequency of attacks returned to pretreatment levels for each of the groups within four weeks after the end of the treatment, although pulmonary functions studies continued to be improved for those who received relaxation training alone or in combination with assertiveness training.

In summary, it would appear that relaxation is a potentially useful technique in reducing the frequency of asthmatic attacks and in promoting significant improvements in respiratory functions as measured by PEFR and FEV_1 (Alexander, 1972; Alexander *et al.,* 1972; Davis, Saunders, Creer, & Chai, 1973; Hock *et al.,* Scherr, Crawford, Sergent, & Scherr, 1975, 1978). The application of relaxation, however, may be limited to the older child and to the child who can concentrate for the length of training time needed and can follow the sequence of directions provided.

Once a relaxation response has been developed in the child, systematic desensitization can be added to the procedure. Under systematic desensitization, the child is exposed, usually imaginally, to a hierarchy of stimuli or situations generally known to be associated with asthmatic attacks. Moore (1965) compared relaxation, relaxation with suggestion, and relaxation with systematic desensitization. Systematic desensitization was found to be most effective in terms of improved PEFR, even though beneficial changes were noted for each of the three groups. Significant reductions in self-reported asthmatic attacks were also noted, but the differences were not statistically significant for the three groups.

Alexander (1977) described the use of *in vivo* as well as imaginal systematic desensitization. In the case of *in vivo* desensitization, a child who experienced anxiety any time she or he wheezed was first exposed to relaxation training. After this, the child was instructed to relax for a progressively longer period of time during wheezing, prior to the use of a nebulized bronchodilator.

Systematic desensitization appears to be somewhat more effective than relaxation training (Moore, 1965; Yorkston, McHugh, Brady, Serber, & Sergent, 1974). However, its application with younger children may be limited by the attentional capacities and imaginal abilities of the child. It is clear that more work is needed if we are to better evaluate the effective parameters of systematic desensitization, particularly in the *in vivo* type.

Biofeedback and Related Procedures. In some instances, relaxation has been facilitated by the use of EMG biofeedback (Davis *et al.,* 1973; Kotses, Glaus, Crawford, Edwards, & Scherr, 1976; Scherr *et al.,* 1975). Davis *et al.* (1973), for example, compared EMG feedback plus relaxation in one group to relaxation training alone in another; a control group was given reading materials and told to relax for a specific period of time. Frequency of asthmatic attacks and changes in PEFR were used as dependent measures. The outcome revealed that the EMG-biofeedback–assisted relaxation group produced the greatest positive change in the dependent measures. Relaxation training alone, however, was also noted to be effective. Interpretation of these data must be tempered by the fact that no differences were found for the severe steroid-dependent subjects and that the effects were not maintained at a one-week follow-up. In a similar study, Scherr *et al.* (1975) compared relaxation with EMG feedback to no treatment in a control group. The subjects were 44 children ranging in age from 6 to 15 years. The relaxation–EMG-feedback procedure was superior to no treatment on behavior ratings, changes in PEFR, reduction in number of asthmatic attacks, and reduction in medications.

Utilizing a slightly different approach, Khan and his associates (Khan, 1977; Khan & Olson, 1977; Khan, Staerk, & Bonk, 1974) employed operant shaping and counterconditioning in the treatment of asthmatics. Generally, asthmatic subjects were instructed to increase bronchodilation using a biofeedback apparatus that monitored airflow. A red light and praise were contingent on the subject's demonstrating an experimenter-specified FEV_1. Bronchial constriction was then experimentally induced, and the asthmatic attempted to overcome the constriction with the aid of the biofeedback apparatus. In one study (Khan,

1977), 80 asthmatic children (8–15 years old) were divided into "reacters" and "nonreacters" on the basis of whether they demonstrated significant bronchospasms after inhaling saline, which they were told contained allergens that would probably stimulate an attack. Half of each group then received treatment. Across the first eight, 50-min sessions, the treatment subjects were reinforced for gradually increasing their FEV_1. During the next 10 sessions, bronchial constriction was induced by any one of several procedures (saline vapors, tapes of wheezing children, etc.). The subjects were instructed to relax and to reduce airflow resistance when a bronchospasm was created. Isoproterenol (a bronchodilator) was given after 10 min to those who could not reduce resistance. The results showed a reduction in the frequency and the severity of attacks for the treated and the untreated "nonreacters" and for the treated "reacters." In another study, Kahn and Olson (1977) examined the effects of using inhaled isoproterenol on exercise-induced bronchial constriction (EIB). The subjects inhaled a mixture of .5 ml isoproterenol and 2.5 ml saline. The concentration of isoproterenol was reduced by .1 ml in each subsequent session for seven days. The mixture effectively prevented EIBs, even as the dose was gradually withdrawn and then eliminated. The effects were maintained at a three and six month follow-up.

Danker, Miklich, Pratt, and Creer (1975) replicated the Khan procedure in attempting to shape respiratory functions. In one study, none of the subjects showed evidence of increased PEFR. Three to five subjects in the second group showed significant increases in a comparison of baseline to treatment. However, when intersession data were analyzed, only one subject demonstrated a consistent increase following the beginning of treatment.

Feldman (1976) and Vachon and Rich (1976) employed total respiratory resistance (TRR) as a dependent measure. TRR is the total of several resistances involving the respiratory system, including upper and lower airway resistance and the viscous tissue resistance of the lung and the chest wall. Feldman (1976) selected four severe asthmatics whose conditions were considered primarily functional in nature. In a single-subject experimental design, the subjects were given a series of 30-min sessions in the biofeedback of inhaled isoproterenol. During biofeedback, the subjects were asked to synchronize their breathing rate with a signal heard over a set of earphones. A feedback signal in the form of a tone was provided to them based on the TRR levels. Pulmonary function studies were done before and after each session. Biofeedback was shown to be as effective as isoproterenol in reducing the TRR. Control subjects, who rested for 30 min, and normal subjects showed no significant changes in pulmonary functions.

Except for the study by Danker *et al.* (1975), there appears to be reason to believe that operant conditioning procedures can be effectively utilized to modify respiratory functioning. These procedures are somewhat confined by the necessity of employing instruments that may not be readily available.

Operant Conditioning Procedures. Several different operant-conditioning techniques have been used effectively in the management of maladaptive behavior patterns found in asthmatic children. Some studies have viewed asthmatic attacks as being induced and maintained by "secondary gains" and have focused on modifying the child's behavior and the consequences provided in the environment (Creer, 1970; Creer & Miklich, 1970; Creer, Weinberg, & Moulk, 1974; Gardner, 1968). Creer (1970), for example, modified the behavior of two asthmatic boys by manipulating the available reinforcers in a hospital setting. An A-B-A-B withdrawal design was used. Each subject had an extended history of repeated hospitalizations for asthmatic attacks. The children were attending a residential treatment center for severe asthmatics. During the first six weeks of the study, each subject was exposed to the usual hospital routine. Hospital admissions during the second six weeks resulted in exposure to the "time-out" condition: (1) each boy was placed alone in a room; (2) no visitors were allowed except medical or nursing personnel; (3) no visiting was allowed with other patients; (4) the child was allowed no TV or comic books, only schoolbooks; (5) the child could leave the room only to go to the bathroom with a nurse escort, and (6) all meals were eaten in the room alone. This treatment phase was followed by a 3-week return to baseline conditions and then another eight weeks of "time-out." The records showed a significant decrease in the frequency and duration of hospitalization during the time-out period for each of the subjects.

A similar approach was used by Creer *et al.* (1974) to reduce the frequency and the duration of the hospitalization in a 10-year-old male asthmatic. In this instance, time-out in the form of restriction of reinforcers was used, along with social reinforcement for improved school attendance and performance.

A variety of other procedures have been applied in studies utilizing one or two subjects. Gardner (1968) modified the disruptive and inappropriate behavior of a 6-year-old asthmatic by withdrawing attention contingent on the negative behavior and reinforcing appropriate behaviors, which were outlined to the child through instructions presented in stories. Creer and Miklich (1970) utilized videotape feedback in a self-modeling fashion to modify the inappropriate behaviors (temper tantrums, inappropriate social behavior, acting out) of a 10-year-old asthmatic child. Miklich (1973) reinforced quiet, relaxed sitting and then the calm acceptance of anxiety-provoking statements about asthma in a hyperactive 6-year-old boy to help reduce panic reactions to acute asthmatic attacks. Extinction has been used by Neisworth and Moore (1972) to reduce the frequency of excessive coughing displayed by a 7-year-old asthmatic child. Response cost has been applied (Creer & Yoches, 1971), as a means of increasing attending behaviors. Finally, Renna and Creer (1976) reported on the successful application of token reinforcement in the multiple-baseline design across four subjects (age 7–12 years) in teaching the proper use of inhalation therapy equipment.

Aversive conditioning procedures have been applied to control chronic coughing. Two studies (Alexander, 1977; Alexander, Chai, Creer, Miklich, Reane, & Cardoso, 1973) utilized an avoidance paradigm in which coughing had to be suppressed for gradually increasing periods of time in order for the subjects to avoid the onset of a brief electric shock to the forearm. In both cases, this approach was shown to be effective in suppressing coughing. In the latter study, a one-year follow-up supported the long-term maintenance of treatment effects.

Creer, Chai, and Hoffman (1977) used punishment to suppress coughing in a 14-year-old asthmatic boy. Unlike the avoidance paradigm, the punishment procedure resulted in the presentation of an uncomfortable electric shock (5 mA) to the forearm contingent on each cough. Quite dramatically, coughing was suppressed after only one application of the punishing stimulus. The effects were maintained at a 3-year follow-up, with no other maladaptive respiratory behaviors being demonstrated.

Convulsive Disorders

Introduction

Convulsive disorders occur in about 2% of the general population and are characterized by a variety of types of seizures. The most common types of seizures are grand mal, petit mal, and focal seizures of Jacksonian and psychomotor epilepsy. Seizures tend to be paroxysmal (sudden) events marked by a burst of cortical activity resulting from lesions or biochemical disruptions. Seizures are usually noticed as brief (1–2 min) interruptions in motor, sensory, cognitive, or conscious functions (Mostofsky & Iguchi, 1982). Whether "organic" in nature (i.e., associated with physical pathology) or "psychogenic," seizures can come under the control of environmental stimuli and can be evoked by stress and emotional factors (Schaefer *et al.*, 1979).

Treatment for seizure disorders consists primarily of medication. However, effective forms of treatment need to be developed for use when chemotherapy has not proved beneficial. Although increasing in number, the attempts to control or moderate seizure problems by any form of psychotherapy or behavior modification have been relatively infrequent (Mostofsky & Balaschak, 1977). An attempt is made here to review some of the behavioral treatment strategies that have been used. For convenience, the techniques have been categorized as (1) positive reinforcement, (2) aversive conditioning, (3) relaxation, (4) biofeedback, and (5) extinction (habituation). This system is similar to that used by Mostofsky and Balaschak (1977).

Treatment

Positive Reinforcement. Differential positive reinforcement involves the reinforcement of behavior other than, and preferably incompatible with, the target response, in this case seizures. Gardner (1967) utilized this strategy in the treatment of a 10-year-old girl who displayed "psychogenic" seizures. The child's parents were instructed to ignore their daughter's seizures and other inappropriate behavior. The parents were also instructed to utilize attention as a reinforcer whenever the child manifested appropriate behavior. Parent training was carried in over three weekly one-hour sessions. Ethical and practical considerations prevented the collection of adequate baseline data. However, within two weeks of discharge from the hospital and following the implementation of the treatment program, the frequency of seizure behavior dropped to zero, tantrum behavior increased in frequency to about three per week and then dropped, and the child's somatic complaints decreased and then increased to approximately one-half pretreatment level. Follow-up contact by phone every 2 weeks for 26 weeks revealed no resumption of seizure behavior.

Balaschak (1976) employed a contingency management program implemented by the teacher of an 11-year-old epileptic girl. A chart divided the school day into three periods, during which time the child received one check mark for each seizure-free time period. If the child accumulated a specified number of check marks by the end of the week, she received a reinforcer. The estimated baseline seizure rate was 60% of school days. For the 52 days during which the behavioral program was in effect, seizures were recorded on only 21% of the days. Following a lengthy absence due to illness, the teacher was unwilling to continue the program. During the remainder of the school year (40 days), the child had seizures on 62.5% of the days.

Zlutnick, Mayville, and Moffat (1975) described a case study wherein the seizures of a 17-year-old retarded female were decreased by the use of differential reinforcement for the cessation of preseizure behavior. Seizures were noted to be preceded by the girl's raising her arms. When the subject was observed raising her arms during treatment, her arms were placed at her side or in her lap. The subject was reinforced verbally and with candy if she kept them in that position for 5 sec. The use of an A-B-A-B withdrawal design revealed that there was a rapid decrease in daily seizure activity and that the decrease was a function of the treatment procedure. The effects were maintained through a 9-month follow-up.

Aversive Conditioning. Numerous aversive techniques, including punishment, escape–avoidance, and overcorrection, have been employed to reduce seizure behavior. Punishment reduces the rate of a target behavior as a function of the contingent presentation of an aversive stimulus. Wright (1973, 1976) used faradic stimulation as an aversive event to reduce seizure behavior in a 5-year old retarded boy and in a 14-year-old boy. The 5-year-old retarded child was observed to engage in self-induced seizures (Sherwood, 1962) at the rate of several hundred per day. He induced the seizures by waving his hand back and forth in front of his eyes and blinking while looking at a light. The treatment initially consisted of the application of .6 sec of 3 mA electric shock at approximately 60 V, contingent on hand waving. The shock was applied to the medial portion of the left midthigh. The treatment consisted of five 1-hr sessions over a three day period. Hand waving as a means of inducing seizures was totally eliminated, and a zero rate was maintained at a 7-month follow-up. Some five months after the initial treatment, the child was hospitalized for a second course of treatment as a result of self-inducing seizures by blinking. The same treatment protocol was utilized. The seizures were reduced from a base rate of 407 per hour to 36. At the month follow-up, seizures produced by blinking had increased over the frequency observed at the end of treatment but continued to be significantly less than pretreatment rates.

A similar procedure was used with the 14-year-old boy, who received mild electric shock contingent on his initiation of observable seizure-related behavior (Wright, 1976). The procedure was effective in reducing clinical and subclinical seizures. In both of these studies, punishment was attempted only after medically oriented treatments had been exhausted and with the approval of appropriate medical consultants.

Zlutnick *et al.* (1975) conceptualized seizures as the terminal behavior in a chain of events. Therefore, they reasoned that seizure frequency could be reduced by interrupting preseizure behaviors. Teachers and parents were trained to apply punishment contingent on observing preseizure behavior in four children (4–14 years old). Punishment included shouting "No" loudly and sharply, and grasping the child by the shoulders and shaking him or her vigorously. Three of the four children showed a significant, stable reduction in the frequency of seizures as a result of this procedure. Preseizure behavior, however, was reduced in only three of the four subjects, and two of the three responded to treatment.

Ounstead, Lee, and Hunt (1966) employed an escape–avoidance training paradigm to decrease seizures in an epileptic child. After determining that a 5-sec burst of photic stimulation was aversive to the child, it was programmed to occur contingent on spike-and-wave paroxysms in EEG activity. The aversive stimulus could be avoided if such EEG activity did not occur and was terminated as soon as it ceased. Caution must be used with this paradigm, as increased seizure activity and gastrointestinal disorders due to stress have been noted in epileptic monkeys during nontraining days when exposed to operant avoidance training (cf. Mostofsky & Iguchi, 1982).

Isolation, or time-out (Adams, Klinge, & Keiser, 1973), and overcorrection (Ashkenazi & Wisdom, 1957) have received some attention. Adams *et al.* (1973) used isolation from ward meetings, free periods, and eating with peers to reduce the self-injurious falling behavior of a 14-year-old mentally retarded female with a history of grand mal and petit mal seizures. Ashkenazi and Wisdom (1957) employed overcorrection to eliminate the preseizure head rolling and thus the frequency of seizures during treatment; these effects were not sustained in follow-up.

Relaxation. The role of anxiety in seizure activity has not been clearly delineated except for noting it to be very important. Mostofsky (1978) has proposed four mechanisms by which anxiety may provoke seizure activity: (1) direct physiochemical change; (2) indirect neurophysiological modulation; (3) psychophysiological modulation; and (4) schedule-induced effects.

Anxiety reduction via relaxation training, biofeedback, and systematic desensitization has been reported with adults (cf. Mostofsky & Balaschak, 1977), but little work appears to have been conducted with children. One case study by Ince (1976) did describe the utilization of relaxation training and desensitization in reducing seizures in a 12-year-old epileptic boy. The treatment initially involved the development of several hierarchies of anxiety-arousing situations and focused on the removal of anxiety that the child experienced concerning school. Complete relaxation was achieved within two treatment sessions. Relaxation was followed by 8 weeks of systematic desensitization. Twice during each session, following relaxation, the subject was instructed to slowly say "Relax" to himself 10 times, so as to associate the key word with bodily relaxation. He was also told to say the key word to himself repeatedly whenever he felt the onset of a seizure approaching. During baseline, the child was noted to have up to 10 grand mal and 26 petit mal seizures per week. By the end of the 17th week of treatment, the child experienced a seizure-free week. Both grand mal and petit mal seizures were reduced by the 30th session. These effects were maintained at a 6-month follow-up.

Biofeedback. Biofeedback involves instructing the subject to generate a certain bioelectrical pattern of waveform. Information is then fed back to the subject regarding his or her performance. Research into the use of biofeedback to reduce seizures was largely stimulated by the work of Sterman and his colleagues (Sterman & Friar, 1972; Sterman, 1973; cf. Mostofsky & Iguchi, 1982). These researchers focused their efforts on training animals to sensory motor rhythms (SMR), which consisted of 12–15 Hz activity. They discovered a marked decrease in susceptibility to monomethylhydrazine (MMN)-induced seizures in SMR-trained animals. Attempts to extend the findings to clinical work with humans were successful (Sterman & Friar, 1972; Sterman, McDonald, & Stone, 1974; Sterman, 1973). However, other studies (cf. Mostofsky & Iguchi, 1982; Mostofsky & Balaschak, 1977) produced mixed results and noted increased seizure activity when SMR biofeedback training was stopped.

As with many of the other procedures, relatively little work has been done with children using SMR biofeedback training. One such study, however, is reported by Finley, Smith, & Etherton (1975). The subject was a 13-year-old boy with a history of seizures dating from age 20. The training procedure employed was similar to that utilized by Sterman. The subject was reinforced with money for every 5 sec of uninterrupted SMR activity. The detection of a spike and/or a wave discharge was followed by the appearance of a red light. The subject attempted to turn out the red light and to keep it off as long as possible. The results showed that the boy's SMR activity increased from 10% to 65% as a function of biofeedback training. A concomitant reduction in seizures was noted.

Extinction (Habituation). The term *extinction procedures* in this instance relates to the repeated presentation of a stimulus or a stimulus condition known to evoke a seizure without the seizure's occurring. This usually involves one of two strategies. First, the seizure-provoking stimulus is introduced at subthreshold levels and is then gradually increased. Or second, the presence of the seizure-evoking stimulus is paired or associated with some non-seizure-evoking stimulus and then adjusted in its presence. An example of the second strategy would be the presentation of a non-seizure-evoking auditory stimulus whenever a seizure-evoking photic stimulus appeared. To the extent that the auditory stimulus sustained nonseizure responding, extinction regarding the photic seizure-producing stimulus could then occur. Forster (1969) has been a leader in developing these techniques for treating what have been referred as *reflex epilepsies*.

Attempts to use this procedure with children have been reported (Booker, Forster, & Klove, 1965; Forster, Ptacek, & Peterson, 1965; Forster, Booker, & Ansell, 1966). Auditory, visual, and combined auditory-visual stimuli have been used. Three or four children reported in the above studies showed a significant decrease in seizure frequency. The fourth child refused to wear the apparatus and thus did not complete the treatment. In one case (Forster, *et al.,* 1966), a 7-year-old girl known to have 20 minor seizures per day was exposed to 60 hr of extinction by means of stroboscopic stimulation produced by specially designed hearing-aid eyeglasses. While in treatment, the child averaged approximately one seizure per day, and four seizure-free days occurred in a 3-week period.

Forster *et al.* (1965) suggested that their approach was effective because the auditory clicking device served to elicit a nonseizure response, thus allowing extinction to seizure-producing stimuli. Alternatively, it has been suggested that the non-seizure-producing stimulus may well serve to divert the subject's attention from the seizure-producing stimulus (i.e., inattention). Therefore, any stimulation that leads to a competing response could effectively reduce seizure activity. Studies with adults using this competing-response paradigm seem to support this contention (cf. Mostofsky & Balaschak, 1977). Although most of the studies in this area have relied on exteroceptive stimuli, Forster (cited in Mostofsky & Balaschak, 1977) had indicated that seizures might be more broadly viewed "in a larger context of *communication disorders* in which the cognitive variables constitute a major contribution to both the generation and termination of seizures" (p. 737). This explanation would appear to open the door to the use of such stimuli as self-verbalizations as a means of controlling seizure frequency by diverting the subject's attention from seizure-provoking stimuli.

Childhood Obesity

Introduction

Childhood obesity is rapidly becoming a major health problem in the United States. Estimates of the percentage of children who are overweight varies with the criteria used but have ranged as high as 26% (Weiss, 1977). Perhaps equally surprising is an estimated increase from 12% to 20% in the incidence of obesity over the past 20 years (Mayer, 1973). There are many factors that contribute to or are associated with childhood obesity, including familiality (genetics), metabolic and endocrine factors, adipose hypercellularity, and environment. The predominating factor, if there is one, is likely to vary among children. It does appear that the longer a child stays obese, the more recalcitrant the condition becomes to treatment. Various estimates have noted a 70–80% likelihood that 9- to 12-year-old children who are obese will also be obese as adults (Abraham & Nordsieck, 1960; Lloyd, Wolf, & Whelen, 1961; Stunkard & Burt, 1967). Increased risk of diabetes, coronary artery disease, and hypertension have also been associated with childhood obesity (cf. Janzen, 1980). A separate but equally devastating effect is the trauma experienced by obese children through rejection, jokes, etc. (cf. Drabman, Jarvie, & Cordua y Cruz, 1982). These figures could support the need for a unified interdisciplinary and concentrated effort in the prevention and treatment of childhood obesity.

Treatment

Traditional Medical Approaches. Obese children have traditionally been exposed to one or more of the following treatments: (1) caloric restriction, (2) anorectic drugs, (3) physical exercise, (4) therapeutic starvation, (5) by-pass surgery, or (6) changes in habit patterns (Coates & Thoresen, 1978). Caloric restriction via nutritional counseling is perhaps the most time-honored approach. It usually takes the form of intermittent and few meetings with the child and/or the parent to review the nutritional guidelines and the imposing of a diet. The research data have shown this procedure, when used by itself, to fail repeatedly (cf. Coates & Thoresen, 1978; Drabman et al., 1982; Weiss, 1977). Anorectics, diuretics, and hormones have been used in the treatment of childhood obesity. Amphetamines were supposedly used to suppress appetite but were found to have little value above dietary restriction (Bray, 1972) and created a potential for habituation and abuse (Knittle, 1972; Grollman, 1975). Diuretics offer little but short-term reductions and may yield metabolic imbalances and nutritional deficiencies. Thyroid hormones may help some by increasing metabolic rate and caloric expenditure. However, the otherwise healthy child is at risk because of the demands placed on the body (Grollman, 1975; Rivlin, 1975).

Exercise has been shown to be effective in weight reduction (Moody, Wilmore, & Girandola, 1972; Keys, 1955). But the maintenance of exercise and the long-term benefits when it is not part of a treatment package have been discouraging. Little needs to be said about the potential problems of therapeutic fasting and the risks involved for disrupting normal growth and development. If conducted in a hospital setting under medical supervision, it *might* be useful in a small minority of cases. But it clearly cannot be said to be a viable option for the majority of overweight children. By-pass surgery, though often thought of as only for adults, is being witnessed with increased regularity in the child and adolescent populations. The results have been less than encouraging whether the surgery is of the gastric or the jejunoileal type, particularly in light of the risk factors (cf. Coates & Thoresen, 1978; Drabman et al., 1982).

Behavioral. Considering the magnitude of the problem and the amount of research on obese adults, there has been surprisingly little systematic research on the use of behavioral procedures in the treatment of childhood obesity. There have been some case studies (Dinoff, Richard, & Colwick, 1972; Foxx, 1972) and work with adolescents (Gross, Wheeler, & Hess, 1976; Weiss, 1977), which will not be detailed here. They have been reviewed elsewhere (Coates & Thoresen, 1978).

One of the earlier studies on children was conducted by Rivinus, Drummand, and Combrinck-Graham (1976). Ten children (8–13 years old), 35% or more overweight, were exposed to a treatment program consisting of self-monitoring, stimulus control, and reinforcement for desirable behaviors. A daily caloric intake was set, but nutritional education was minimal. Weekly sessions included eating dinner in a cafeteria setting where instructions were given regarding food selection and the parents modeled appropriate eating behaviors. Of the 10 subjects, 9 completed the 10-week treatment program and demonstrated an average weight loss of 6.1 lb. Weight decrease continued and reached 9.2 lb at a 20-week follow-up, but it averaged only 6.7 lb at a 120-week follow-up. Considering growth rate and the pretreatment rate of weight gain, as one must in treating children, these data appear very encouraging.

Other studies have also examined the effects of treatment "packages" (Aragona, Cassady, & Drabman, 1975; Epstein, Wing, Steranchak, Michelson, & Dickson, 1979; Kingsley & Shapiro, 1977; Wheeler & Hess, 1976). Aragona et al. (1975) were one of the first groups to employ parent training in the treatment of childhood obesity. The subjects were 15 overweight females 5–10 years of age assigned to either a response-cost-plus-reinforcement, a response-cost-only, or a no-treatment control group. Sessions occurred weekly for 12 weeks. The parents were instructed in exercise management, nutrition, and stimulus control procedures. They recorded their child's food intake, calories, and weight. Portions of refundable deposit were returned to the parents contingent on their attendance, their record keeping, and their child's meeting a specified weight-loss goal. In addition, the parents in the response-cost-plus-reinforcement group received instructions on how to engage their children in behavioral contracts targeting the relevant behaviors. The subjects in the response-cost-plus-reinforcement group lost an average of 11.3 lb (range 9.0–13.3), the response-cost-only group lost an average of 9.5 lb (range 2.3–13.7), and the no-treatment control subjects showed a gain of .9 lb (range −4.5–+4.5). The 31-week follow-up showed a return to baseline weight. The experimenters speculated that unprogrammed reinforcement of weight-loss-relevant behaviors by parents in the response-cost-only group probably accounted for the similarity in outcome of the two groups.

Wheeler and Hess (1976) compared the effects of individualized behavior therapy provided to mother–child (MC) pairs to no treatment for a control group. The treatment focused on instructions and the use of stimulus control, self-monitoring, and reinforcement procedures. Emphasis was placed on tailoring the treatment to fit the lifestyle of the family.

MC pairs were seen in 30-min sessions every other week, with the intersession interval increasing over time. The treatment time averaged 7.3 months. Of the original sample, 46% dropped out within the first four sessions. The treatment completers showed a decrease in percentage overweight of 4.1%, in comparison with a 3% and a 6% increase for dropout and treatment controls, respectively. Though statistically significant, these data can hardly be seen as clinically meaningful, as the subjects were an average of 40.4% overweight to begin with.

The modification of specific food-related behaviors has been demonstrated by Epstein and his colleagues (Epstein, Masek, & Marshall, 1978; Epstein, Parker, McCoy, & McGee, 1976). Epstein et al. (1976) showed that eating rates could be reduced effectively through instructions and positive reinforcement. Collateral behaviors incompatible with eating (i.e., talking, laughing, and moving about in a chair), though not targeted, decreased along with bite rate. Sip rate, however, was not affected throughout the study. Decreased bite rate was associated with a significant decrease in food consumption, but no weight loss was recorded. An analysis of food preference according to intake records kept by observers showed nonobese and obese children to differ only in that the nonobese consumed more bread and the obese showed a preference for more milk products.

In the second study, Epstein, Masek, and Marshall (1978) assessed the effects of increased premealtime activities on the amount consumed and the effects of instruction, praise, and token reinforcement on consumatory behavior in six obese children aged 5–6. Foods were grouped into three categories, red, yellow or green, according to their nutritional value and their caloric density. The colors corresponded to those of a traffic light, indicating that the child should not eat "reds," should eat some "yellows," and could eat all the "greens" he or she wanted. Food consumption was recorded during lunch and breakfast. Activity was increased through a 10-min period of prelunch structured play and exercise. When increased activity was introduced, a slight reduction in the consumption of "reds" and "yellows" was noted as compared with baseline. When prompts, praise, and token reinforcement were introduced for correct consummatory behavior, the intake of "reds" decreased to near zero, and there was a reduction in "yellows" and a significant increase in "greens." The treatment effects were replicated by means of a withdrawal design. The mean percentage overweight was decreased from 43.3% to 37.9% during the 7-month study, but it had increased to 52% at follow-up. The number of calories consumed during breakfast was reduced from 529 to 392, and from 487 to 380 during lunch.

Family Involvement. The importance of family involvement in the treatment of obesity was suggested by the work of Stuart and Davis (1972), Mahoney and Mahoney (1976), and Brownell, Heckerman, Westlake, Hayes, and Monti (1978) with adults. It has also been implicated by Aragona et al. (1975), Coates and Thoresen (1982), Wheeler and Hess (1976), and Gross et al. (1976). Kingsley and Shapiro (1977) have examined the effects of maternal participation on childhood obesity. Four groups were used: (1) a no-treatment control group (NT); (2) the child alone (C); (3) mother–child pairs (MC); and (4) mother only (M). The treatment consisted of exposure to a program like that of Stuart and Davis (1972), with nutritional education, self-monitoring of intake, caloric counting, and written instructions to parents on how to effectively employ positive reinforcement for their child's compliance. The treatment consisted of eight weekly sessions attended by the child only, the mother and the child, or the mother only. Each of the treatment groups lost more weight (1.6 kg) than the control group (.9 kg), but there were no differences between the treatment groups. However, the mothers in the M group showed a greater weight loss than the other mothers, and it was maintained. A 5-month follow-up of the children showed normal expected weight gains and no differences between the treatment groups. Although it would appear that parental presence does not make a difference, the authors did note resentment on the part of the mothers in the C group, who were excluded from treatment.

A second study examining family involvement was conducted by Epstein et al. (1979): 6 of 13 obese children and their mothers were assigned to a behavior modification group, and 7 mother–child pairs were assigned to a nutritional education group. Group therapy sessions occurred weekly for 7 weeks, with follow-up meetings monthly for 3 months. The mothers and their children were seen separately. Both the behavior modification and the nutrition education groups received instructions in diet and nutrition education. Calisthenics and a one- to two-mile walk occurred during each session. Each parent in both treatments participated in a contingency contract specifying the return of a refundable deposit contingent on fulfilling the requirements of this study. In addition, the behavior modification group was exposed to self-monitoring, training in social reinforcement, modeling, a sloweddown eating rate, and regular phone contact. Behavioral contracting for self-monitoring, not eating "red foods," and weight loss was also included for the behavior modification group. The data showed that the behavior modification group lost more weight, 7.2 lb (3.5 kg) versus 3.9 lb (1.8 kg), and showed a greater decrease in percentage overweight, 11.6% versus 5.1%. (Pretreatment percentage overweight was 69% for behavior modification group and 62% for the nutrition education group.) These differences were maintained at 3 months posttreatment. The authors noted a high correlation ($r = +.66$) between mother and child weight loss in the behavior modification group but not in the nutrition education group ($r = -.01$). They interpreted these data as suggesting the utility of changing eating and exercise habits at the family level.

Hyperactivity

Introduction

It is estimated that from 3% to 10% of schoolchildren demonstrate enough problem behaviors to be classified as hyperactive or hyperkinetic, and males are so diagnosed more often than females (Office of Child Development, 1971; Sleator, Von Neuman, & Sprague, 1974). Other labels that have been applied to hyperactive children include *maturational lag, hyperkinetic reaction, immaturity of the nervous system, minimal cerebral dysfunction, minimal brain damage,* and *minimal brain injury.* The later two names are fairly common but are incorrect, as most children with hyperactivity are not brain-damaged. The new DSM III offers yet another classification, as it describes attentional deficits with and without hyperactivity.

At one time, the hyperactive or hyperkinetic child was characterized as demonstrating a short attention span, restlessness, and overactivity. The definition, however, is misleading since there are many disorders of childhood that can encompass these problems. The term *minimal brain dysfunction* (Wender, 1971) has come into prominence. Others have looked at drug responsiveness as a means of defining hyperactivity, which carries with it its own sets of problems. Most recently, K. D. O'Leary (1980) suggested that the most "reasonable" approach is to regard hyperactivity as a set of behaviors, such as excessive restlessness and short attention span, that are qualitatively different from those of other children of the same sex and age. These behaviors should be confirmed by the use of measurement scales such as the Teacher's Rating Scale (TRS; Conners, 1969). In addition, O'Leary also suggested that one must be able to rule out chronic medical or neurological disease and severe behavioral disturbances as major contributing factors to the hyperactivity. Finally, it is suggested that it must be shown that hyperactive behaviors persist across time and situations. Safer (1982) described what he called "developmental hyperactivity." The essential features of this disorder are hyperactivity, which is usually associated with inattentiveness; a learning impediment or lag; misconduct; and immaturity.

Hyperactive children generally manifest their behavior throughout the elementary-school years. Their hyperactivity may begin to decrease from ages 13–15 years, but a relatively high level of restlessness frequently persists into young adulthood and adulthood. Even with decreasing symptomatology at puberty, the data suggest that hyperactive children have a lower chance of successful adjustment in adolescence and adulthood than nonhyperactive children (Mendelson, Johnson, & Stewart, 1971; Menkes, Rowe, & Menkes, 1967; Stewart, 1970). Historically, it is interesting to note that very little was written about the hyperactive child before about the last 20 years (K. D. O'Leary, 1980).

Treatment

Medication. Stimulant medication is one of the most common forms of treatment for the hyperactive child. Although first employed in the early 1900s, it has only been since the 1960s that its popularity has become evident. The percentage of children taking stimulant medication has risen steadily throughout the 1970s and was estimated at about 2.1% in 1977 (Safer, 1982). The most commonly prescribed stimulants are Ritalin (methylphenidate), Dexedrine (dextroamphetamine sulfate), and Cylert (pemoline). The popular media and the pharmaceutical advertisements have probably contributed heavily to the increased use of psychostimulants (K. D. O'Leary, 1980), which seems to be "outrunning" the rate with which research data are being produced.

In summarizing the use of stimulants, Safer (1982) noted that beneficial effects are achieved in over 70% of hyperactive children as compared to 10%–40% using placebos. In adequate doses, 35%–50% showed dramatic improvement, 30%–40% moderate improvement, and 15%–20% little or no change. Significant amounts of data exist showing that stimulant medications generally lead to increased attention, increased cooperativeness, and decreased disruptiveness in the classroom (cf. Cantwell & Carlson, 1978; Connors & Werry, 1979; Safer & Allen, 1976). The effect of stimulants on social behavior appears beneficial but remains under investigation. Questions have been raised about whether the observed effects are due to increased attention and decreased disruptiveness or are somehow mediated more directly by the medication (K. D. O'Leary, 1980). One study has found that children under stimulant medication initiated less social contact than when they were not medicated (Whalen, Henker, Collins, Finck, & Dotemoto, 1979).

Changes in school achievement also remain under scrutiny. Though positive changes have been reported by some (Bradley, 1937) they have not been found in most studies (cf. K. D. O'Leary, 1980). Consolidation of newly learned behavior does not appear to be facilitated (Rie & Rie, 1977), and there is some concern that learning under stimulant medication may be state-dependent, although it does not appear so under therapeutic doses (Aman & Sprague, 1974). One problem regarding this issue of increased academic performance has been the relative lack of long-term studies. Studies that are three to six months in length yield equivocal data with no consistent increases (Gittelman-Klein & Klein, 1976; Hoffman, Engelhardt, Margolis, Polizos, Waizer, & Rosenfeld, 1974). There is a strong likelihood that because of their improved attention and conduct under stimulant medication, the children only "appear" to be learning more.

S. G. O'Leary and Pelham (1978) have summarized the concerns over the use of medications as the sole treatment for hyperactivity. These concerns include the following: (1) there is no documentation of the long-term effect on academic achievement; (2) no long-term effect on disruptive social problems has not been demonstrated; (3) increases in heart rate and blood pressure, along with decreased rate of height and weight gains, although reversible, are present; (4) the medication may have deleterious long-term effects; and (5) because of the anorexic and sedative effects, medication is generally not administered in the late afternoon. For these reasons and because of some of the obvious beneficial effects of medication, greater attention is being given to a more in-depth examination of the interactions between the medications and the environment and the possibility of combining medication with behavioral therapies.

Whalen *et al.* (1979) focused on "social ecology," its effects on classroom behavior, and its interaction with medication. Though inattentiveness or "distractibility" is a major feature of the hyperactive child, it is clear that little is known about the environmental conditions that correlate with this problem (Doleys, 1976). Whalen *et al.* compared hyperactive boys on and off Ritalin with hyperactive boys on placebo, as well as comparison nonhyperactive boys in a "quasi-naturalistic setting." External stimulation (quiet versus noisy) and the type of tasks (self-paced versus other-paced) were manipulated. In general, these authors found that hyperactive boys on pla-

cebo tended to be much less attentive, more active, and more disruptive than their peers. Self-paced activities and high noise level both were shown to have detrimental effects on classroom behavior. A medication-by-situation interaction was observed. These data would appear to suggest that environmental conditions may (1) impact upon the child's behavior in a classroom and (2) could act synergistically or antagonistically with medication.

Behavioral Treatments

Positive Reinforcement. Hyperactive behavior has frequently been treated through the use of behavioral therapies (Gardner, 1970). One of the more common techniques has been the use of positive reinforcement with a token economy to strengthen incompatible behavior (Werry & Sprague, 1970). A number of studies carried out in the classroom have demonstrated the effectiveness of the use of these procedures in decreasing hyperactive behavior (Doubros & Daniels, 1966; Edelson & Sprague, 1974; Patterson, Jones, Whittier, & Wright, 1965), and increasing attending behavior (Allen, Henke, Harris, Baer, & Reynolds, 1967; Quay, Sprague, Werry, & McQueen, 1967; Walker & Buckley, 1968). Patterson *et al.* (1965) described a program in which token reinforcement was used to bring about significant increases in attention. Tokens were given after each 10 sec of uninterrupted attending. Doubros and Daniels (1966) used a token economy with six hyperactive mentally retarded children between the ages of 6 and 13. A checklist of hyperactive behaviors was constructed for each child. The children earned tokens for appropriate play during a 15-min play situation. A significant reduction of hyperactive behaviors was noted as a function of the treatment and continued through a 2-week follow-up. Edelson and Sprague (1974) instituted a token economy in a classroom that focused on the reinforcement of cooperative behavior. A substantial reduction in hyperactive behaviors and destructive acts along with a significant increase in attention level and class cooperation resulted. The removal of the token system was associated with the return of these behaviors to baseline levels.

Allen *et al.* (1967) focused on the time spent on a specific activity. Systematic programming of adult social reinforcement resulted in a decrease in the number of activity changes to 50% of preconditioning levels. Quay *et al.* (1967) examined procedures for modifying visual orientation in a group of five hyperactive children. The children were of normal intelligence and had been placed in a class for behavior problem students. The subjects were seated at desks in a semicircle around the teacher, with a small box containing a light mounted inside the box on the top of each desk. Each subject was observed for five 10-sec segments during each experimental session and was reinforced for attending on a variable ratio schedule. Reinforcement consisted of the light's flashing, followed by candy and/or social praise. Attending increased significantly under the candy-plus-social-reinforcement condition and decreased when the treatment was withdrawn. Similar effects were documented in studies by Krop (1971) and Mitchell and Crowell (1973), who used candy, praise, and contingent attention to increase attending behavior and to decrease "hyperactive" behavior. Such reinforcement procedures have also been effectively applied in groups (Schofield, Hedlund, & Worland, 1974; Pratt & Fischer, 1975).

Parents as Therapists. The importance of working with parents in counseling or guidance relationships has often been pointed out (Wender, 1971; Safer, 1982). Fraizer and Schnieder (1975) described a procedure carried out by parents to eliminate inappropriate hyperactive behavior during and following mealtime by employing a multiple-baseline procedure using contingent attention and time-out. The parents were trained to give positive attention to appropriate behavior and to ignore inappropriate behavior. Time-out was employed for inappropriate behaviors. The rate of inappropriate behavior decreased significantly and remained low for approximately 5 weeks thereafter. Furman and Feighner (1973) reported on the beneficial effects of videotape feedback in teaching parents operant techniques with their hyperactive children. The parents worked on specific target behaviors

and improvements in communication. Wiltz and Gordon (1974) worked with the parents of a 9-year-old hyperactive and aggressive boy. The family spent five consecutive days in an apartment-like setting with observational facilities. The training included instructional materials, prompting, modeling, and feedback. A follow-up by telephone revealed a significant reduction in noncompliance and destructive action.

Self-Regulation. Meichenbaum and Goodman (1971) suggested that impulsive or hyperactive children may be deficient or may have experienced inadequate training in controlling their motor behavior via self-commands. In their original study, these authors showed that children increased their response latency on a discrimination task after self-instructional training. However, the number of errors performed by the children did not decrease. Bornstein and Quevillon (1976) used a self-instructional package with three overactive preschool children 4 years old. The dependent variable was on-task behavior in the classroom. The treatment consisted of one massed self-instructional session that lasted for approximately 2 hr. During the training: (1) the experimenter modeled the task while talking out loud to himself or herself; (2) the subject performed the task while the experimenter instructed out loud; (3) the subject then performed the task, talking out loud to herself or himself while the experimenter whispered softly; (4) the subject performed the task, whispering softly, while the experimenter made lip movements but no sound; (5) the subject performed the task making lip movements without sound while the experimenter self-instructed covertly; and (6) the subject performed the task with covert self-instruction (Meichenbaum & Goodman, 1971; Bornstein & Quevillon, 1976). The content of the verbalizations that were modeled generally fell into one of four categories: (1) questions about the task; (2) answers to questions in the form of cognitive rehearsal ("Oh, that's right, I'm supposed to copy that picture"); (3) self-instructions that directed the task ("First, I draw this line, then I draw that line"); and (4) self-reinforcement ("How about that, I did it right!"). Significant and meaningful increases in the percentage of on-task behavior were noted immediately after self-instructional training. The treatment gains were maintained. The use of a multiple-baseline design across subjects helped to demonstrate that the effect was indeed a response to self-instructional training rather than to other extra-experimental factors.

A second study in this area was performed by Friedling and O'Leary (1979). These authors attempted to replicate the Bornstein and Quevillon (1976) results using older (7- to 8-year-old), nonmedicated hyperactive children. The dependent variable included on-task behavior in the classroom and performance on reading and arithmetic tasks when the difficulty was varied. The experimental group received self-instructional training in a 90-min session. A control group received the same amount of time with the experimenter but without training in providing self-instructions. This initial intervention did not prove effective in producing any significant changes. Therefore, it was replicated by providing the treatment group with two additional 40-min sessions on consecutive days. Again, the percentage of on-task and academic behavior did not change significantly. The authors then instituted a token economy wherein reinforcers were provided for on-task behavior. This manipulation did prove successful in significantly increasing the percentage of on-task behavior for both groups.

Although other researchers (K. D. O'Leary, 1968; Hartig & Kanfer (1973) have shown self-instructions to be effective in increasing the moral behavior of children, there appears to be some question about whether similar effects will be achieved in modifying the behavior of hyperactive children. It may be that there is an interaction between self-instructional treatment and the level of task performance (high versus low) and/or the complexity of the task (Friedling & S. G. O'Leary, 1979). That is, if the behavior already exists in the child's repertoire and can be easily performed by the child, then self-instructional procedures may be more effective than if the desired response is extremely complex and/or is relatively "weak."

Relaxation and Biofeedback. Because of the apparent cognitive and overt hyperactivity noted in children diagnosed as hyperactive, it was only natural that at some point consideration would be given to the use of relaxation techniques to help diminish this overt activity. One such study was conducted by Lupin, Braud, and Duer (1974). They presented relaxation instructions via a tape recorder to small groups of hyperactive children. Several physiological measures and behavioral ratings were taken before and after the treatment sessions. A group of children who were not exposed to the taped relaxation sessions were used as a control. The authors noted reduced forehead muscle tension, emotionality, and aggressiveness following the presentation of the tapes. Although not directly concerned about the reduction of hyperactive behavior in the classroom or at home, Putre, Loffio, Chorost, Marx, and Gilbert (1977) were interested in the relative effectiveness of a relaxation and control tape in producing a reduction in muscle tension. Twenty hyperactive boys ranging in age from 7 to 13 listened either to a relaxation tape utilizing the typical progressive relaxation instructions or to a control tape consisting of a story read from an adventure book. The tapes lasted approximately 15 min and were listened to on a daily basis for 2 weeks. Measurement of forehead muscle tension occurred periodically. The researchers reported no significant difference between the groups, and both showed a significant decrease in muscle tension (mean 34%).

Braud, Lupin, and Braud (1975) extended this work to the use of biofeedback technology. The subject was a 6.5-year-old hyperactive boy exposed to 11 sessions of frontalis electromyographic (EMG) biofeedback. The child was instructed to turn off the tone that signaled the presence of muscle tension. Muscle tension, as measured by the EMG, and overt activity decreased within and across sessions. The authors noted that the child was able to control his hyperactivity during a 7-month follow-up. Improvements were also noted on achievement tests, reports of self-confidence, and behavior at school and at home.

Combination Therapies. Although stimulant medication and behavior therapy have both been shown to be effective in treating various problems of the hyperactive child and some studies have found one to be better than the other, (Gittelman-Klein, Klein, Abikoff, Katz, Gloisten, & Kates, 1976), neither can be said to be the treatment of choice. Perhaps for this reason, increasing attention is being given to combined and more comprehensive therapies.

In one of the earlier studies, Christensen and Sprague (1973) studied two troups of six children. One group received behavior modification and a placebo, the other behavior modification and methylphenidate. Seat activity, as measured by a stabilimetric cushion, and performance on daily quizzes were examined. The behavior modification-plus-methylphenidate group showed lower rates of activity, but there was no different between the two groups in the number of correct answers on daily quizzes. In a study using mentally retarded, institutionalized "hyperactive" children, Christensen (1973) found significant improvement across a variety of academic and activity measures when behavior modification was applied. The effects did not appear to be enhanced by the addition of methylphenidate. Wolraich, Drummond, Salomon, O'Brien, and Sivage (1978) compared a combination (behavior therapy plus stimulant medication) treatment with behavior therapy alone. No difference was found between the two interventions. However, this may not have been an adequate test because of the short treatment duration (2 weeks) and a relatively low dose of methylphenidate (.3 mg/kg). In addition, these results are inconsistent with those of Gittelman-Klein et al. (1976), who, although finding medication to be more effective than behavior therapy over an 8-week treatment, did note that stimulant medications of considerably higher dosages enhanced the effects of behavior therapy.

S. G. O'Leary and Pelham (1978) looked at the utility of behavior therapy when applied after a stimulant medication was withdrawn. They found a significant increase in off-task and other maladaptive behavior when hyperactive children were taken off stimulant medication. The rebound was reduced to on-drug levels of behavior during a 4-month, 18-session (on the average) behavioral-intervention program involving parents and teachers. The authors noted that (1) there was individual variability in the subjects' responses to behavior therapy; (2) the treatment tended to be more effective in changing social behavior than in increasing attention skills; and (3) the changes noted in the classroom were highly correlated with the cooperation and commitment shown by individual teachers and principals. Although the therapy was effective in ameliorating the rebound effects observed following the withdrawal of the stimulant medication, the expense of such treatment in time and dollars, as well as the motivation required of the family, cannot be ignored in its evaluation.

In a recent paper, Pelham, Schnedler, Bologna, and Contreras (1980) used a 3-week medication probe period to evaluate the effects of combining stimulant medication with behavior therapy. The behavior therapy was ongoing and consisted of an average of 12 sessions across 5 months. The treatment included (1) weekly parent training sessions, with individual families focusing on the development and use of contingency management; (2) teacher training in behavioral approaches; and (3) child tutoring in self-instruction techniques. The dependent measures included classroom observations, teacher ratings, clinic observations, and parent ratings. In general, the results showed that behavior therapy was effective in reducing the target behaviors, but not maximally so. Increased on-task behavior and decreased parental punishment with some reinforcement were noted. Both medication and behavior therapy appeared to increase on-task behavior, but only behavior therapy was shown to increase the amount of work completed correctly. Behavior therapy was found to be as effective as low doses of methylphenidate, but not as effective as high doses. Medication seemed to have an incremental effect even after 13 weeks of behavior therapy. Even with the behavioral intervention, the subjects were not "normal" in their interpersonal relationships and social skills. On the basis of these data, the authors emphasized the potential of stimulant medications at therapeutic doses, as an adjunct to behavior therapy. They further emphasized that in both clinical and analogue research, the timing of the ratings should be carefully considered because the medication effects fluctuate during the day. The importance of the use of multiple dependent measures that cover a variety of behavioral domains was also pointed out, as was individual variation in reactions to medication and behavior therapy. In discussing multiple measures, they noted that low doses of psychostimulants appear to have their effect on cognitive abilities as reflected in on-task behavior, whereas higher doses seem to have a beneficial effect on interpersonal behavior and compliance of the type often found through teacher ratings.

References

Abraham, S., & Nordsieck, M. Relationship of excess weight in children and adults. *Public Health Reports,* 1960, *75,* 1516–1521.

Adams, K. M., Klinge, V., & Keiser, T. W. The extinction of a self-injurious behavior in an epileptic child. *Behaviour Research and Therapy,* 1973, *11,* 351–356.

Alexander, A. B. Systematic relaxation and flow rates in asthmatic children: Relationship to emotional participants and anxiety. *Journal of Psychosomatic Research,* 1972, *16,* 405–410.

Alexander, A. B. Behavioral methods in the clinical management of chronic asthma. In R. B. Williams & W. D. Gentry (Eds.), *Behavioral approaches to medical practice.* Cambridge: Ballinger, 1977.

Alexander, A. B., Miklich, D. R., & Hershoff, H. The immediate effects of systematic relaxation training on peak expiratory flow rates in asthmatic children. *Psychosomatic Medicine,* 1972, *38,* 388–394.

Alexander, A. B., Chai, H., Creer, T. L., Miklich, D. R., Reane, C. M., & Cardoso, R. R. deA. The elimination of chronic coughing by response suppression shaping. *Journal of Behavior Therapy and Experimental Psychiatry,* 1973, *4,* 75–80.

Allen, E. K., Henke, L. B., Harris, F. B., Baer, P. M., & Reynolds, N. J. Control of hyperactivity by social reinforcement of attending behaviors. *Journal of Educational Psychology,* 1967, *58,* 231–237.

Aman, M., & Sprague, R. L. The state-dependent effects of methylphenidate and dextroamphetamine. *Journal Nervous and Mental Diseases,* 1974, *158,* 268–279.

Aragona, J., Cassady, J., & Drabman, R. S. Treating overweight children through parental training and contingency contracting. *Journal of Applied Behavior Analysis,* 1975, *8,* 269–278.

Ashkenazi, Z., & Wisdom, S. *Elimination of head rolling in an epileptic retarded child.* Unpublished manuscript, Ministry of Health, Beer Sheba, Israel, 1957.

Balaschak, B. A. Teacher implemented behavior modification in a case of organically based epilepsy. *Journal of Consulting and Clinical Psychology,* 1976, *44,* 218–223.

Blanchard, E. B., & Ahles, T. A. Psychophysical disorders. *Behavior Modification,* 1979, *3,* 535–549.

Booker, H. E., Forster, F. M., & Klove, H. Extinction factor in startle (accusticomotor) seizures. *Neurology,* 1965, *15,* 1095–1103.

Bornstein, R., & Quevillon, R. The effects of a self-instructional package on overactive preschool boys. *Journal of Applied Behavior Analysis,* 1976, *9,* 179–188.

Bradley, C. The behavior of children receiving benzedrine. *American Journal of Psychiatry,* 1937, *94,* 579–585.

Braud, L. W., Lupin, M. N., & Braud, W. G. The use of electromyographic biofeedback in the control of hyperactivity. *Journal of Learning Disabilities,* 1975, *8,* 21–26.

Bray, G. A. Clinical management of the obese patient. *Postgraduate Medicine,* 1972, *51,* 125–130.

Brownell, K. D., Heckerman, C. L., Westlake, R. J., Hays, S. C., & Mont, P. M. The effect of couples training and partner cooperativeness in the behavioral treatment of obesity. *Behaviour Research and Therapy,* 1978, *16,* 323–333.

Cantwell, D. P., & Carlson, G. A. Stimulants. In J. S. Werry (Ed.), *Pediatric psychopharmacology: The use of behavior modifying drugs in children.* New York: Brunner/Mazel, 1978.

Christensen, D. *The combined effects of methylphenidate (Ritalin) and a classroom behavior modification program in reducing the hyperkinetic behavior of institutionalized mental retardes.* Unpublished doctoral dissertation, University of Illinois, 1973.

Christensen, D. E., & Sprague, R. L. Reduction of hyperactive behaviors by conditioning procedures alone and combined with methylphenidate (Ritalin). *Behaviour Research and Therapy,* 1973, *11,* 331–334.

Coates, T. J., & Thoresen, C. E. Treating obesity in children and adolescents: A review. *American Journal of Public Health,* 1978, *68,* 143–151.

Coates, T. J., & Thoresen, C. E. Treating obesity in children and adolescents: Is there any hope? In J. M. Ferguson, & C. B. Taylor (Eds.), *Advances in behavioral medicine.* Englewood Cliffs, N.J.: Spectrum, 1981.

Conners, C. K. A teacher rating scale for use in drug studies with children. *American Journal of Psychiatry,* 1969, *126,* 884–888.

Conners, C. K., & Werry, J. S. Pharmacotherapy of psychopathology in children. In H. C. Quay, & J. S. Werry (Eds.), *Psychopathological disorders of childhood* (2nd Ed.). New York: Wiley, 1979.

Creer, T. L. The use of time-out from positive reinforcement procedure with asthmatic children. *Journal of Psychosomatic Research,* 1970, *14,* 117–120.

Creer, T. L., & Miklich, D. R. The application of a self-modeling procedure to modify inappropriate behavior: a preliminary report. *Behaviour Research and Therapy,* 1970, *8,* 91–92.

Creer, T. L., & Yoches C. The modification of an inappropriate behavioral pattern in asthmatic children. *Journal of Chronic Diseases,* 1971, *24,* 507–513.

Creer, T. L., Weinberg, E., & Moulk, L. Managing a hospital behavior problem: Malingering. *Journal of Behavior Therapy and Experimental Psychiatry,* 1974, *5,* 259–262.

Creer, T. L., Chai, H., & Hoffman, A. A single application of an aversive stimulus to eliminate chronic cough. *Journal of Behavior Therapy and Experimental Psychiatry,* 1977, *8*(1), 107–109.

Danker, P. S., Miklich, D. R., Pratt, C., & Creer, T. L. An unsuccessful attempt to instrumentally condition peak experatory flow rates in asthmatic children. *Journal of Psychosomatic Research,* 1975, *19,* 209–213.

Davis, M. H., Saunders, D. F., Creer, T. L., & Chai, H.

Relaxation training facilitated by biofeedback apparatus as a supplemental treatment in bronchial asthma. *Journal of Psychosomatic Research*, 1973, *17*, 121–128.

Department of Health, Education, and Welfare. *Vital and Health Statistics, 1973, Prevalence of selected chronic respiratory conditions*. Washington, D.C.: USDHEW, Public Health Service, Series 10-No. 84, HRA-74-1511, September 1973, p. 17.

Dinoff, M., Richard, H. C., & Colwick, J. Weight reduction through succession contracts. *American Journal of Orthopsychiatry*, 1972, *42*, 110–113.

Doleys, D. M. Distractability and distracting stimuli: inconsistent and contradictory results. *Psychological Record*, 1976, *26*, 279–287.

Doubros, S. G., & Daniels, G. J. An experimental approach to the reduction of overactive behavior. *Behaviour Research and Therapy*, 1966, *4*, 251–258.

Drabman, R. S., Jarvie, G. J., & Cordua y Cruz, G. D. Childhood obesity: Assessment, etiology, risks and treatment. In D. M. Doleys & T. B. Vaughn (Eds.), *Assessment and treatment of developmental problems*. Englewood Cliffs, N.J.: Spectrum, 1982.

Edelson, R. I., & Sprague, R. L. Conditioning of activity level in a classroom with institutionalized retarded boys. *American Journal of Mental Deficiency*, 1974, *78*, 384–388.

Eggleston, P. A. Asthma in childhood. In H. F. Conn (Ed.), *Current therapy*. Philadelphia: Saunders, 1976.

Epstein, L. H., Parker, L., McCoy, J. F., & McGee, G. Descriptive analysis of eating regulation in obese and nonobese children. *Journal of Applied Behavior Analysis*, 1976, *9*, 407–415.

Epstein, L. H., Masek, B. J., & Marshall, W. R. A nutritionally basic school program for control of eating in obese children. *Behavior Therapy*, 1978, *9*, 766–778.

Epstein, L. H., Wing, R. R., Steranchuk, L., Michelson, J., & Dickson, B. *Comparison of family basic behavior modification and nutrition education for childhood obesity*. Paper presented at the AABT, San Francisco, December 1979.

Feldman, G. M. The effect of biofeedback training on respiratory resistance in asthmatic children. *Psychosomatic Medicine*, 1976, *38*, 27–34.

Finley, W. W., Smith, H. A., & Etherton, M. D. Reduction of seizures and normalization of the EEG in a severe epileptic following sensorimotor biofeedback training: A preliminary study. *Biological Psychology*, 1975, *2*, 189–203.

Forster, F. M. Conditioned reflexes and sensory-evoked epilepsy: The nature of the therapeutic process. *Conditioned Reflex*, 1969, *4*, 103–114.

Forster, F. M., Ptacek, L. J., & Peterson, W. G. Auditory clicks in extinction of stroboscopic-induced seizures. *Epilepsia*, 1965, *6*, 217–225.

Forster, F. M., Booker, H. E., & Ansell, S. Computer automation of the conditioning therapy of stroboscopic induced seizures. *Transactions of the American Neurological Association*, 1966, *91*, 232–233.

Foxx, R. M. Social reinforcement of weight reduction: A case report on an obese retarded adolescent. *Mental Retardation*, 1972, *10*(4), 21–23.

Fraizer, V. R., & Schneider, H. Parental management of inappropriate hyperactivity in a young retarded child.

Journal of Behavior Therapy and Experimental Psychiatry, 1975, *6*, 246–247.

Freedman, S. S., & Pelletier, G. A. Asthma in childhood: Treatment of 1070 cases. *Annals of Allergy*, 1970, *28*, 133–141.

Friedling, C., & O'Leary, S. G. Teaching self-instruction to hyperactive children: A replication. *Journal of Applied Behavior Analysis*, 1979, *12*, 211–219.

Furman, S., & Feighner, A. Video feedback in treating of hyperkinetic children: A preliminary report. *American Journal of Psychiatry*, 1973, *130*, 792–796.

Gardner, J. E. Behavior therapy treatment approach to a psychogenic seizure case. *Journal of Consulting Psychology*, 1967, *31*, 209–212.

Gardner, J. E. A blending of behavior therapy techniques in an approach to an asthmatic child. *Psychotherapy: Theory, Research and Practice*, 1968, *5*, 46–49.

Gardner, J. M. Behavior modification in mental retardation: A review of research and analysis of trends. In C. M. Franks & R. Rubin (Eds.), *Progress in behavior therapy*. New York: Academic Press, 1970.

Gittelman-Klein, R., & Klein, D. F. Methylphenidate effects in learning disabilities. *Archives of General Psychiatry*, 1976, *33*, 655–664.

Gittelman-Klein, R., Klein, D. F., Abikoff, H., Katz, S., Gloisten, A. C., & Kates, W. Relative efficacy of methylphenidate and behavior modification in hyperactive children: An item report. *Journal of Abnormal Child Psychology*, 1976, *4*, 361–379.

Grollman, A. Drug therapy of obesity in children. In P. J. Collipp (Ed.), *Childhood obesity*. Acton, Mass.: Publishing Science Group, 1975.

Gross, M. A., Wheeler, M., & Hess, K. The treatment of obesity in adolescents using behavioral self-control. *Clinical Pediatrics*, 1976, *15*, 920.

Hartig, M., & Kanfer, F. H. The role of verbal self-instruction in children's resistance to temptation. *Journal of Personality and Social Psychology*, 1973, *25*, 259–267.

Hock, R. A., Rodgers, C. H., Reddi, C., & Kennard, D. W. Medicopsychological interventions in male asthmatic children: An evaluation of physiological change. *Psychosomatic Medicine*, 1978, *40*, 210–215.

Hoffman, S., Engelhardt, D. M., Margolis, R. A., Polizos, P., Waizer, J., & Rosenfeld, T. Response to methylphenidate in low socioeconomic hyperactive children. *Archives of General Psychiatry*, 1974, *30*, 354–359.

Ince, L. P. The use of relaxation training and a conditioned stimulus in the elimination of epileptic seizures in a child: A case study. *Journal of Behavior Therapy and Experimental Psychiatry*. 1976, *7*, 39–42.

Jacobson, E. *Progressive relaxation*. Chicago: University of Chicago Press, 1938.

Janzen, G. S. Parental modeling and re-enforcement in the treatment of childhood obesity. Unpublished dissertation, University of Alabama, 1980.

Keys, A. Body composition and its change with age and diet. In E. S. Eppright, D. Swanson, & C. A. Iverson (Eds.), *Weight control*. Ames: Iowa State University Press, 1975.

Khan, A. V. Effectiveness of biofeedback and counter-conditioning in the treatment of bronchial asthma. *Journal of Psychosomatic Research*, 1977, *21*, 97–104.

Khan, A. V., & Olson, D. L. Deconditioning of exercise-induced asthma. *Psychosomatic Medicine*, 1977, *39*, 382–392.

Khan, A., Staerk, M., & Bonk, C. Role of counter-conditioning in the treatment of asthma. *Journal of Psychosomatic Research*, 1974, *18*, 89–92.

Kingsley, R. G., & Shapiro, J. A comparison of three behavioral programs for the control of obesity in children. *Behavior Therapy*, 1977, *8*, 30–36.

Kinsman, R. A., Luparello, T. O., O'Banion, K. O., & Spector, S. L. Multidimensional analysis of the subjective symptomology of asthma. *Psychosomatic Medicine*, 1973, *35*, 250–267.

Kinsman, R. A., O'Banion, K., Resnikoff, P., Laparello, T. J., & Sheldon, S. L. Subjective symptoms of acute asthma within a hetenogenous sample of asthmatics. *Journal of Allergy and Clinical Immunology*, 1973, *52*, 384–396.

Kinsman, R. A., Spector, S. L., Shucard, D. W., & Luparello, T. J. Observations on patterns of subjective symptomatology of acute asthma. *Psychosomatic Medicine*, 1974, *36*, 129–143.

Knapp, T. J., & Wells, L. A. Behavior therapy for asthma: A review. *Behaviour Research and Therapy*, 1978, *16*, 103–115.

Knittle, J. L. Obesity in children: A problem of adipose tissue development. *Journal of Pediatrics*, 1972, *81*, 1048–1059.

Kotses, H., Glaus, K. D., Crawford, P. L., Edwards, J. E., & Scherr, M. S. Operant reduction of frontalis EMG activity in the treatment of asthma in children. *Journal of Psychosomatic Research*, 1976, *20*, 453–459.

Krop, H. Modification of hyperactive behavior of a brain-damaged, emotionally disturbed child. *Training School Bulletin*, 1971, *68*, 49–54.

Lloyd, J. K., Wolf, O. H., & Whelen, W. S. Childhood obesity: A long-term study of height and weight. *British Medical Journal*, 1961, *2*, 145–148.

Lupin, M., Braud, W. G., & Duer, W. F. *Effects of relaxation upon hyperactivity using relaxation tapes for children and parents*. Paper presented at the 11th Annual Convention for Learning Disabilities, Houston, February 1974.

Mahoney, M. J., & Mahoney, K. Treatment of obesity: A clinical explanation. In B. J. Williams, S. Martin, & J. P. Foreyt (Eds.), *Obesity: Behavioral approaches to dietary management*. New York: Brunner/Mazel, 1976.

Mathison, D. A. Asthma. In H. F. Conn (Ed.), *Current therapy*. Philadelphia: Saunders, 1976.

Mayer, J. Fat babies grow into fat people. *Family Health*, 1973, *5*, 24–38.

Meichenbaum, D., & Goodman, J. Training impulsive children to talk to themselves: A means of developing self-control. *Journal of Abnormal Psychology*, 1971, *77*, 115–126.

Mendelson, W., Johnson, N., & Stewart, M. A. Hyperactive children as teenagers: A follow-up study. *Journal of Nervous and Mental Diseases*, 1971, *153*, 273–279.

Menkes, M. M., Rowe, J. S., & Menkes, J. H. A 25-year follow-up on the hyperkinetic child with minimal brain dysfunction. *Pediatrics*, 1967, *39*, 393–399.

Miklich, D. R. Operant conditioning procedures with systematic desensitization in a hyperkinetic asthmatic boy.

Journal of Behavior Therapy and Experimental Psychiatry, 1973, *4*, 177–182.

Mitchell, D. W., & Crowell, P. J. Modifying inappropriate behavior in an elementary art class. *Elementary School Guidance and Counseling*, 1973, *8*, 34–42.

Moody, D. L., Willmore, J. H., & Girandola, R. W. The effects of a jogging program on the body composition of normal and obese high school girls. *Medicine and Science in Sports*, 1972, *4*, 210–213.

Moore, N. Behavior therapy on bronchial asthma: A controlled study. *Journal of Psychosomatic Research*, 1965, *9*, 257–276.

Mostofsky, D. I. Epilepsy: Action for improving socialization and family support. In L. G. Perlman (Ed.), *The role of vocational and rehabilitation in the 1980's*. Washington, D.C.: National Rehabilitation Association, 1978.

Mostofsky, D. I., & Balaschak, B. A. Psychological control of seizures. *Psychological Bulletin*, 1977, *84*, 723–750.

Mostofsky, D. I., & Iguchi, M. Y. Behavior control of seizure disorders. In D. M. Doleys, R. L. Meredith, & A. R. Ciminero (Eds.), *Behavioral medicine: Assessment and treatment strategies*. New York: Plenum Press, 1982.

Neisworth, J. T., & Moore, F. Operant treatment of asthmatic responding with the parent as therapist. *Behavior Therapy*, 1972, *3*, 95–99.

Office of Child Development, Department of Health, Education, and Welfare. Report of the conference on the use of stimulant drugs in the treatment of behaviorally disturbed young school children. Washington, D.C.: U.S. Government Printing Office, 1971.

O'Leary, K. D. The effects of self-instruction on immoral behavior. *Journal of Experimental Child Psychology*, 1968, *6*, 297–301.

O'Leary, K. D. Pills and skills for hyperactive children. *Journal of Applied Behavior Analysis*, 1980, *13*, 191–204.

O'Leary, S. G., & Pelham, W. E. Behavior therapy and withdrawal of stimulant modification in hyperactive children. *Pediatrics*, 1978, *61*, 211–217.

Ounstead, C., Lee, D., & Hunt, S. J. Electroencephalographic and clinical changes in an epileptic child during repeated phobic stimulation. *Electroencephalography and Clinical Neurophysiology*, 1966, *21*, 388–391.

Patterson, G. R., Jones, R., Whittier, J., & Wright, M. A. A behavior modification program for the hyperactive child. *Behaviour Research Therapy*, 1965, *2*, 217–220.

Pelham, W. E., Schnedler, R. W., Bologna, N. C., & Contreras, J. A. Behavioral and stimulant treatment of hyperactive children: A therapy study with methylphenidate probes in a within subject design. *Journal Applied Behavior Analysis*, 1980, *13*, 221–236.

Phillip, R. L., Wilde, G. J. S., & Day, J. H. Suggestion and relaxation in asthmatics. *Journal of Psychosomatic Research*, 1972, *16*, 193–204.

Pratt, S. J., & Fischer, J. Behavior modification: Changing hyperactive behavior in a children's group. *Perspectives in Psychiatric Care*, 1975, *13*, 37–42.

Putre, W., Loffio, K., Chorost, S., Marx, V., & Gilbert, C. An effectiveness study of relaxation training tape with hyperactive children. *Behavior Therapy*, 1977, *8*, 355–359.

Quay, H., Sprague, R., Werry, J., & McQueen, M. Conditioning visual orientation of conduct problem in the classroom. *Journal of Experimental Child Psychology,* 1967, *5,* 512–517.

Renne, C. M., & Creer, T. L. Training children with asthma to use inhalation therapy equipment. *Journal of Applied Behavior Analysis,* 1976, *9,* 1–11.

Rie, E. D., & Rie, H. E. Recall, retention and Ritalin. *Journal of Consulting and Clinical Psychology,* 1977, *45,* 967–972.

Rivinus, T. M., Drummond, J., & Combrinck-Graham, L. A group behavioral treatment program for overweight children: Results of a pilot study. *Pediatric Adolescent Endocrinology,* 1976, *1,* 212.

Rivlin, R. S. The use of hormones in the treatment of obesity. In M. Winick (Ed.), *Childhood obesity.* New York: Wiley, 1975.

Safer, D. J. Hyperactive-attentional disorders. In D. M. Doleys & T. B. Vaughn (Eds.), *Assessment and treatment of developmental problems.* New York: Spectrum, 1982.

Safer, D. J., & Allen, R. P. *Hyperactive children: Diagnosis and management.* Baltimore: University Park Press, 1976.

Schaefer, C. E., Millman, H. L., & Levine, G. F. Therapies for psychosomatic disorders in children. San Francisco: Jossey-Bass, 1979.

Scherr, M. S., Crawford, P. L., Sergent, C. B., & Scherr, C. A. Effect of biofeedback techniques on chronic asthma in a summer camp environment. *Annals of Allergy,* 1975, *85,* 289–295.

Schofield, L. J., Hedlund, C., & Worland, J. Operant approaches to group therapy and effects on sociometric status. *Psychological Reports,* 1974, *35,* 83–90.

Schultz, J. H., & Luthe, W. *Autogenic training: A psychophysiologic approach in psychotherapy.* London: Grune & Stratton, 1959.

Sherwood, S. L. Self-induced epilepsy: A collection of self-induced epilepsy cases compared with some other photo-convulsive cases. *Archives of Neurology,* 1962, *6,* 63–77.

Sirota, A. D., & Mahoney, M. J. Relaxation on cue: The self-regulation of asthma. *Journal of Behavior Therapy and Experimental Psychiatry,* 1974, *5,* 65–66.

Sleator, E. K., Von Neuman, A., & Sprague, R. L. Hyperactive children. *Journal of the American Medical Association,* 1974, *229,* 316–317.

Sterman, M. B. Neurophysiologic and clinical studies of sensorimotor EEG biofeedback training: Some effect on epilepsy. *Seminars in Psychiatry,* 1973, *5,* 507–525.

Sterman, M. B., & Friar, L. Suppression of seizures in an epileptic following sensorimotor EEG feedback training. *Electroencephalography and Clinical Neurophysiology,* 1972, *33,* 89–95.

Sterman, M. B., McDonald, L. R., & Stone, R. K. Biofeedback training of the sensorimotor electro-ence-

phalogram rhythm in man: Effects on epilepsy. *Epilepsia,* 1974, *15,* 395–416.

Stewart, M. A. Hyperactive children. *Science American,* 1970, *222,* 94–98.

Stuart, R. B., & Davis, B. *Slim chance in a fat world: Behavioral control of obesity.* Champaign, Ill.: Research Press, 1972.

Stunkard, A. J., & Burt, V. Obesity and body image: II. Age of onset of disturbances in body image. *American Journal of Psychiatry,* 1967, *123,* 1443–1447.

Vachon, L., & Rich, E. S. Visceral learning in asthma. *Psychosomatic Medicine,* 1976, *38,* 122–130.

Walker, H. M., & Buckley, N. K. The use of positive reinforcement in conditioning attending behavior. *Journal of Applied Behavior Analysis,* 1968, *1,* 245–250.

Weiss, A. R. A behavioral approach to the treatment of adolescent obesity. *Behavior Therapy,* 1977, *8,* 720–726.

Wender, P. H. *Minimal brain dysfunction in children.* New York: Wiley-Interscience, 1971.

Wender, P. H. *The hyperactive child: A handbook for parents.* New York: Crown Publishers, 1973.

Werry, J. S., & Sprague, R. L. Hyperactivity. In C. G. Costello (Ed.), *Symptoms of psychopathology.* New York: Wiley, 1970.

Whalen, C. K., Henker, B., Collins, B. F., Finck, D., & Dotemoto, S. A social ecology of hyperactive boy: Medication by situation interactions. *Journal of Applied Behavior Analysis,* 1979, *12,* 65–81.

Wheeler, M. E., & Hess, K. W. Treatment of juvenile obesity by successive approximation control of eating. *Journal of Behavior Therapy and Experimental Psychiatry,* 1976, *7,* 235–241.

Wiltz, N. A., & Gordon, S. B. Parental modification of a child's behavior in an experimental residence. *Journal of Behavior Therapy Experimental Psychiatry,* 1974, *5,* 107–109.

Wolraich, M., Drummond, T., Salomon, M., O'Brien, M., & Sivage, G. Effects of methylphenidate alone and in combination with behavior modification procedures on the behavior and academic performance of hyperactive children. *Journal of Adolescent Child Psychology,* 1978, *6,* 149–161.

Wright, L. Aversive conditioning of self-induced seizures. *Behavior Therapy,* 1973, *4,* 712–713.

Wright, L. Psychology as a health profession. *Clinical Psychologist,* 1976, *29,* 16–19.

Yorkston, N. J., McHugh, R. B., Brady, R., Serber, M., & Sergent, H. G. S. Verbal desensitization in bronchial asthma. *Journal of Psychosomatic Research,* 1974, *18,* 371–376.

Zlutnick, S. I., Mayville, W. J., & Moffat, S. Modification of seizure disorders: The interruption of behavioral chains. *Journal of Applied Behavior Analysis,* 1975, *8,* 1–12.

Index

1017